Nancy Eve.

S0-DRA-001

January 1964

* conception of dynamics of lit in 20ᵗʰ cent.
  interpervatations

Amer Naturalism: Dreiser → Faulkner →
Hemingway → Farell → Salinger
wit & humor

THE

American Tradition
in Literature
REVISED

VOLUME 2

THE

AMERICAN TRADITION

IN LITERATURE

REVISED

VOLUME 1
Bradford to Lincoln

VOLUME 2
Whitman to the Present

THE

American Tradition in Literature

REVISED

Edited by

Sculley Bradley

PROFESSOR OF ENGLISH AND VICE-PROVOST
UNIVERSITY OF PENNSYLVANIA

Richmond Croom Beatty

LATE OF VANDERBILT UNIVERSITY

E. Hudson Long

PROFESSOR OF AMERICAN LITERATURE AND
CHAIRMAN OF THE ENGLISH DEPARTMENT
BAYLOR UNIVERSITY

VOLUME

2

Whitman to the Present

W · W · NORTON & COMPANY · INC · *New York*

Library of Congress Catalog Card No. 61-8916

Book design by John Woodlock

PRINTED IN THE UNITED STATES OF AMERICA
FOR THE PUBLISHERS BY W. P. C.

3 4 5 6 7 8 9

Contents

FRONTIERS OF FOLK LITERATURE AND HUMOR

Contents · xix

FICTION AS SOCIAL HISTORY

Preface

In compiling this work we have intended to provide a freshly considered collection of great American writings representing the range and power of our literature as a whole. Our effort has been to represent major authors in the fullness of their stature and variety. Besides the titans, we have included writers of lesser stature whose works endure; but no author was introduced primarily for the purpose of illustrating literary or social history. In the same way, works of popular literature and humor have been admitted as literature, not as social or cultural documents.

While we have made literary merit our final criterion for selection, we have attempted in our critical apparatus to emphasize the relations between the literary work and the general movements in American civilization and intellectual history. In the textual annotations, as in the introductory essays and biographical sketches, we have attempted to secure as much objectivity as possible, to suppress individualistic critical tendencies of our own in favor of the consensus of our professional peers, and to leave the reader free to pursue his own ideas and values without having to contend with ours. Yet we have annotated liberally, believing it our function as editors, while abstaining from the expression of personal prejudice or opinion, to elucidate any substantial obscurity that would handicap a reader lacking immediate access to the appropriate reference books.

During the present century the writings of Americans have become an important influence in the literature of the western world, and our second volume has considerably more than the usual representation of twentieth-century authors. But as early as the age of Jonathan Edwards and Franklin, and even more in that of Poe, Emerson, and Whitman, the voice of our young nation was heard far beyond the shores of our continent. In editing the present collection we have been fully aware of the increasing responsibilities involved in selecting from such a national inheritance the works that would best represent its nature and its values. In performing this task we have become indebted to the rapidly accumulating contributions of American scholars and critics, to whom we have acknowledged our precise obligations in our notes.

The study of American literature can be acceptably organized in several ways; we have therefore attempted to provide a certain flexibility in our sequence of authors and texts. In general we have followed a chronological order, but by a few slight departures we were also able to bring authors together under topical headings which represent the pronounced response of our literature, at one time or another, to regional influences, social forces, dominant ideas, historical events, or aesthetic values.

We have tried to avoid cutting a work. These volumes contain four complete novelettes, including Faulkner's *The Bear* (often reprinted in part). In the first volume, Melville's *Billy Budd* appears in a text which has been compared with manuscript sources and is here printed for the first time. The first volume also contains Emerson's *Nature* in its entirety. Obviously it was necessary to make selections from such lengthy works as Franklin's *Autobiography* and Thoreau's *Walden;* in all instances the omission of text has been indicated by three asterisks, and except where printed between square brackets titles are those of the original. Where possible, as in *Leaves of Grass,* we have preserved the original plan of the work.

Since masterpieces endure, many of our selections are, and should be, familiar; but wherever it seemed possible to make a fresh substitution without loss of values, we have done so. For example, besides the less usual selections previously named, we have included Jonathan Edwards' "The Nature of True Virtue," some of the poems of Thoreau, James's *Madame de Mauves*, some less familiar poems of Eliot, and Steinbeck's *The Red Pony*; and we have secured permission to exceed previous limitations upon the amount of material quoted, or the titles available for anthologies, from the works of Dreiser, Cather, and Hemingway.

We have gone to considerable lengths to provide in each case a faithful copy of the text which in our judgment is the best edition of the work. Like the text of *Billy Budd*, that of Emily Dickinson's poems represents a fresh comparison with the original manuscripts, since we were kindly given permission to follow the text newly established by Thomas H. Johnson in *The Poems of Emily Dickinson* (1955). Whether we use the first edition of a work, the last edition supervised by the author, or a later edited text, the source will be obvious in the bibliographical note or is given in a footnote. In editing the difficult texts of colonial writers we have been guided by the condition of the particular texts. Those, like Bradford's *Of Plymouth Plantation*, in which archaic spelling, punctuation, and abbreviations are a mechanical handicap for many readers, have been normalized in accordance with present practice. But the language has not been altered or "modernized," and the texts of colonial poets are untouched, and like most of the prose, clarified only by annotation. Where significant dates are established, they appear at the end of a selection; that of first publication in a volume or the author's standard collection at the right margin, preceded by the date of first serial publication; the date of composition at the left margin.

The essays introducing the four periods we deem significant are not intended to constitute a literary history. Most libraries have copies of one or more standard literary histories of the United States, and we have no thought to compete with them. Each essay is designed to introduce the literature we have collected for that period, and to present critical considerations not appropriate for treatment in the individual biographical headnotes.

It seems proper to acknowledge the responsibility of each collaborator. Mr. Bradley acted as general editor for the entire work, and wrote the introductory essays for each of the four historical periods. For the first volume Mr. Beatty prepared the texts, Mr. Bradley the headnotes and other critical apparatus. In the second volume, for the period from 1865 to 1914, Mr. Long edited and annotated the texts; the biographical essays for this period represent the collaboration of Mr. Long and Mr. Bradley. Mr. Bradley was responsible for the annotated texts and critical apparatus for the section on the twentieth-century revival after 1914.

We have received generous and expert advice from numerous friends and colleagues, to whom we here again extend our thanks. We must particularly acknowledge the assistance of Professor Robert E. Spiller, of the University of Pennsylvania, Professor Leon Howard, of the University of California, and Professor Robert H. Elias, of Cornell University. We are grateful for services rendered by the Vanderbilt University Library and the Baylor University Library. Especially we are indebted to the staff of the Rare Book Collection of the Library of the University of Pennsylvania, who put at our disposal an unusual collection of first editions and other basic texts represented in these volumes, and gave us expert assistance in the preparation of bibliographical data and footnotes. Dr. Esther Kaufman Jacobson and Mr. George P. Brockway of our publisher's staff, in editing this work, have given it the benefit of their unstinted energy and specialized knowledge of our field. Our indebtedness to various authors, publishers, literary agents, and copyright owners is acknowledged in the copyright notice.

The Edition of 1961

In preparing the second edition of *The American Tradition in Literature* the editors have benefited from their own experience and that of others who have made use of it. Both volumes have been significantly enriched by new selections. Recognizing the need for the critical study of some works of larger scope, we have added two complete full-length novels, each a masterpiece of its period: in Volume 1, Hawthorne's *The Scarlet Letter*; and in Volume 2, Mark Twain's *Adventures of Huckleberry Finn*. Our notes are intended to support the intrinsic criticism of these novels, and to provide an understanding of their place in the author's work as a whole. A number of the texts which appeared in the first edition of this anthology have been compared with recent scholarly editions, as in the case of Edward Taylor. In Volume 1 we have included new materials for Franklin; we have added Edwards' "Sinners in the Hands of an Angry God"; we have compiled a series of adventures representing the character of Natty Bumppo in Cooper's novels; we have also included Emerson's "Divinity School Address," new short stories by Poe and Hawthorne, a selection of Melville's poems, and his "Bartleby the Scrivener" to stand beside *Billy Budd*.

In Volume 2, besides the *Adventures of Huckleberry Finn*, we have completed Whitman's "Song of Myself"; we have included Howells' "Editha"; and we have increased the already large selection from Henry James by including "The Beast in the Jungle." We have introduced poems by Stephen Crane and an additional selection from Mencken's *Prejudices*. We have enriched the selections for several modern poets; we have introduced a selection of Marianne Moore's poetry and another new section of "mid-century poets," including Richard Eberhart, Muriel Rukeyser, Robert Lowell, and Richard Wilbur.

The headnotes for individual authors have been revised and corrected, and the results of recent research incorporated. Many footnotes, the general bibliography, and the author bibliographies have been amplified and brought up to date.

We applaud our publishers for being able to add 512 pages to the two volumes without appreciable increase in their bulkiness.

Again we are indebted for suggestions from a large group of persons, including our departmental colleagues, and to the staff of the Rare Book Collection of the University of Pennsylvania Library for indispensable assistance in reproducing the new literary texts and in preparing the new bibliographical materials.

S.B., R.C.B., E.H.L.

T H E

American Tradition
in Literature

REVISED

VOLUME **2**

The Emergence of Modern American Literature

The half century from the Civil War to the first World War was an epoch of dynamic change in American life, and of corresponding developments in literature. During this period the nation consolidated its continental domain, absorbed a host of immigrants, developed its potential as the most resourceful industrial powerhouse in the world, and moved toward a genuine hegemony in world affairs. The young nation finally put off its country ways and assumed the character of an urban civilization, while grappling, with uneven success, with the many responsibilities, political problems, and social disorders accompanying changes so fundamental and gigantic.

The conquered Southland, at the beginning of this era, was fully occupied with the problems of reconstruction and survival, but the industrial machine of the North, geared to a new high by the recent demands of the war, soon attained an unprecedented productive capacity. Immigrants thronged into the industrial centers, or joined the march of older Americans to the West, where the last frontiers gave way before the growth of railroads, the improvement of farm machinery, and expanding markets. Within a few years even the South, having survived military occupation, exploitation by carpetbaggers and scalawags, and political reprisals from Washington, had developed a new economy of small farmsteads and sharecroppers, with a newborn retail market at the crossroads and a revived urban prosperity responding to the mounting demand for staple crops. As a whole, the period immediately succeeding the Civil War was marked by the restless expansion of new lands and new wealth, by an increasing solidarity among the various sections of the country, by the discovery and exploitation of new natural resources, by the development of revolutionary inventions, new technologies, and new industries, by great accumulations of capital, and by a spirit of optimism and speculation so overwhelming that only the most serious gave attention to the burgeoning economic atrocities and delinquencies that are now associated with the period of Grant's presidency.

By the 1880's, however, the growing pains of rapid expansion, and the consequent social dislocations, were everywhere acutely evident. The agrarian interests, the still-feeble labor movement, and the underprivileged urban masses found common cause against the industrial giant and his financial overlords. Reform movements and labor unrest appeared in successive waves of protest, while financial crises, and the exposure of governmental and private schemes to exploit the economy, only accentuated the widening gap between the privileged or ruthless few and the great majority who did not seem to share proportionately in the prosperity of the world's richest nation. Confronted with the *laissez-faire* economics of the Gospel of Wealth, serious reform thinkers in the eighties and nineties viewed the existing order with increasing distaste and pessimism. Their concern was heightened by government acts of intervention and so-called financial "imperialism" overseas, of which the Spanish-American War of 1898 caused the most violent reactions among the liberals. By this time, however, the reform and labor movements, which had seemed so abortive only two decades earlier, had begun to consolidate and to exert strong political pressure, while new social and economic legislation improved the prospects of the average citizen. For more than a decade before the end of this period in 1914, the American scene was marked by relative domestic peace and orderly economic development, as though in preparation for the ordeals of world war which lay ahead.

FROM ROMANTICISM TO REALISM

American writers and thinkers, attempting to express the shifting tensions and complexities of these strenuous decades, moved steadily from romanticism toward increasingly realistic objectives and literary forms, and toward pragmatic, instrumental, or naturalistic interpretations of man and his destiny. The process was gradual, reflecting the periodic fluctuations in the history of American society. During this period, however, literature became a genuine instrument of evaluation and expression in American life; it found for the first time a vast and general audience representing the people as a whole; it ultimately produced a highly critical realistic movement whose characteristic works were quite clearly the product of a different world from that which, in the previous generation, had been represented by the romantic idealism of Cooper and Irving, Emerson, Hawthorne, and Longfellow.

In this process, the Civil War provided a dramatic point of cleavage. As Mark Twain shrewdly observed in writing *The Gilded Age:* "The eight years in America from 1860 to 1868 uprooted institutions that were centuries old, changed the politics of a people, transformed the social life of half the country, and wrought so profoundly upon the entire national character that the influence cannot be measured." For literature one measure of the change is to compare the popular and typical works of the five years before the war with those of the same period succeeding the struggle. The accepted tradition of our literature in the years from 1855 to 1861 was represented in the publication of Longfellow's *The Song of Hiawatha* and *The Courtship of Miles Standish,* Emerson's *English Traits* and *The Conduct of Life,* Simms's romances—*The Forayers* and *Eutaw*—Irving's *Life of Washington,* Hawthorne's *The Marble Faun,* Holmes's *Autocrat* papers, and Whittier's *Home Ballads.* By contrast, directly after the war, during the years from 1867 to 1872, the country heard for the first time the genuine voice of the new West, in such stories by Bret Harte as "The Luck of Roaring Camp"; in Mark Twain's earliest successes—*The Celebrated Jumping Frog of Calaveras County and Other Sketches, The Innocents Abroad,* and *Roughing It*; in John Hay's *Pike County Ballads* and Joaquin Miller's *Songs of the Sierras.* During the same years a new standard of reality in the portrayal of contemporary life was evident in such works as John W. De Forest's *Miss Ravenel's Conversion from Secession to Loyalty,* Thomas Bailey Aldrich's *The Story of a Bad Boy,* and Edward Eggleston's *The Hoosier Schoolmaster.* Above all, Henry James and William Dean Howells, who were destined to take their places beside Mark Twain as the great figures of the realistic movement, made their first important contributions: James in 1871, when he published "A Passionate Pilgrim" in a periodical, and Howells in his first novel, *Their Wedding Journey* (1872).

Yet the older voices were not stilled. Many romantic authors no longer living, such as Cooper, Irving, Poe, and Hawthorne, continued to grow in popularity; and new publications by such earlier writers as Emerson, Longfellow, Lowell, and Holmes continued to exert an influence. For two decades, beginning authors in this age of transition were caught between the ideals of the older world and those of a new age that was struggling to find its voice. It is no wonder that many young writers, especially among the pioneers of realism, were not able to be faithful to its demands. This was especially true of the early regionalists. Such writers as Harte, Cable, and Harris realistically depicted the daily and common actualities and dialects of their localities; they sought to identify characters with their surroundings, and sometimes achieved psychological penetration in this respect. In general, however, the regionalists exaggerated the picturesque, the charming, or the bizarre to create what came to be known as "local color"; and they all to some degree surrendered to the didactic impulse, and sentimentalized their characters in support of some predetermined moral judgment or ideal, as Bret Harte did in his picture of Poker Flat, with its outcasts and fallen women. In addition, the rise of realism was strenuously opposed by certain authors who, combining serious purpose with superior talents, regarded themselves as defenders of ideality, of aesthetic purity, or of certain fixed standards of propriety or morality. Even Howells, a vigorous defender of "decency" in literature, was criticized, because of his preference for the commonplace, as one who "copied life"—a familiar false charge—or built in paving blocks instead of Pentelican marble.

To be sure, the defenders of ideality found strenuous opponents. Even before the war, Whitman was attacking the code of chivalry, the wasted life of the sheltered female, and the unreality of the standards of fictional romance and Byronic poetry. He was soon assisted by younger authors, especially those of the western frontiers. Bret Harte's *Condensed Novels*, published in 1867, contained irresistible parodies of Dumas, Dickens, Cooper, and others; Mark Twain irreverently lampooned Scott for engendering the "Sir Walter Disease," and Cooper for his incredible Indians and his ignorance of the real frontier. Yet romanticism was not really vanquished at the popular level. The sentimental domestic novel continued to flourish, and the cheaper magazines, responding to a surge of newly won respectability among the middle class, still dripped with the didactic sentiment that had been established, principally by lady poets and novelists, before the war. Finally, the historical and regional romance, always widely read, reached new heights of popularity by the end of the century.

A comparatively few authors, with a more limited audience, became the pioneers of the literature now recognized as "modern" in spirit and in form. In the largest sense, this realistic modernity in a work of literature results from several factors: the author's insistence upon strict analytical observation of the subject, and his determination to portray it exactly; an increased awareness of psychological phenomena, which enlarges the writer's franchise and the reader's tolerance in the selection of materials that might once have been rejected as too commonplace or as actually sordid; and the full recognition of the writer's social function as the critic and interpreter of life. These factors, or a significant portion of them, were present in the best efforts of the memorable writers of the realistic movement in the nineteenth century, and taken as a whole, they may serve as a description, if not a definition, of the realistic impulse.

Three of the earliest poets to respond to the new spirit were actually rooted very deeply in the romantic idealism of the waning epoch, but because of particular gifts of character or fortune, Walt Whitman, Emily Dickinson, and Sidney Lanier each spoke with a new voice combining noble and enduring elements from both ages, the old and the new. Whitman, born the same year as Lowell, but slower in finding his subject, stood apart from the romantics even in 1855, when the first small edition of *Leaves of Grass* was an ugly duckling, while Longfellow's *Hiawatha* paddled approved down the mainstream of literature. Yet Whitman's vision of America was based on the idealism of the past—on the individualism of Jefferson and Tom Paine; on the intuitional faith of Emerson and on transcendental humanitarianism; on the reform movements and proletarian idealism that had accompanied the rise of the common man in the Age of Jackson. At the same time, Whitman produced a verse that was destined to revolutionize the form of modern poetry; his psychological realism, coupled with his interest in science, enabled him to transfigure "forbidden" subjects; and no later realist ever looked more sharply than he, or with more gusto, at the commonplace object or the lowly person. Emily Dickinson was a product of Amherst village, where colonial America lingered in puritan overtones. She inherited the tradition of the romantic nature poets; but her realism and psychological truth made her seem contemporary to a much later generation. Sidney Lanier, a Georgia regionalist bred in the old South, infused his nature poetry with the southern economics of corn and cotton, with incisive criticism of the growing abuses of the industrial and mercantile systems, and with a stirring sense of the complexities of individual responsibility.

REGIONALISM

Mark Twain, the earliest gigantic figure among the regionalists, was indebted, like Harte and Cable and other contemporaries, to progenitors among the humbler comic journalists. From the Age of Jackson onward, they had inundated the popular press with anecdotes and fiction drawn from sources deep in the common life of America. In this literature, most of it decidedly regional in character, the humorous anecdote mingled with white and Negro folklore, with frontier tall tales and hunting stories, and with folk song and balladry. The best of the regional literature, serious and comic, ultimately provided a better understanding of the United States as a whole. Whitman and Mark Twain both asserted that the great writer must "absorb" his country, but amid the swift changes of American life, the "great American novel" which critics had been demanding could not be written. However, as Eggleston remarked in 1892, looking back upon the regional movement, the great American novel appeared "in sections"—in the matured realism of Twain and Howells, in the novels of such lesser writers as Eggleston himself and De Forest, and in the stories of Cable and Harris, Aldrich, Mary E. Wilkins Freeman, Sarah Orne Jewett, Garland, and Crane. A movement that had begun in broad humor and in the wider horizons of the West and Southwest produced also, particularly among the women writers and the New Englanders, the accurate depiction of the domestic scene, the narrow life, the individual character, caught in some humble light that reminds the reader of the work of the *genre* painters of the Flemish school, at once highly individuated and intensely national. In fiction thus motivated, the increasing consciousness of the influence of environment on character and fate prepared the way for the growing spirit of naturalistic and sociological determinism.

THE GILDED AGE

This awareness of American social and economic life was characteristic of the later literature of the realistic movement. By 1870 the country had already begun to experience the abuses and dislocations that accompany a rapid change in the character of civilization, and by 1875 the public and private morality of the land had reached its lowest ebb, in the period called by Mark Twain "the Gilded Age," and by others "the Tragic Era" or "the Great Barbecue." Within a decade industrial production had tripled, and railroads spanning the continent had brought the shrinking frontiers into a national economy. The enlarged demand for labor had attracted immigrants in such numbers that there were nearly seven and a half million foreign born in a population of about forty million. The new Atlantic cable and the expansion of practicable telegraphic communications further augmented the great strides of American commerce and domestic trade. In the older cities, crowded with newcomers, fortunes were quickly made and lost amid a general atmosphere of speculation and chicanery, and the mansions of the new millionaires burgeoned in contrast with the poverty of the new slums. The endless drive to the West was now continued by a host of homesteading farmers and immigrants from north-

ern Europe; they suffered the privations and poverty of a new soil, but by 1880 they had brought into cultivation twenty million acres of virgin land and founded an agricultural economy which reached from the grain and cattle ranches of the Midwest to the orchards in the fertile valleys of the Pacific coast. In this West, with its limitless opportunities, its violent contrasts, and its seething mixture of old American settlers with immigrants from many lands, a social democracy developed that was new in the history of mankind.

However, the gap between the rich and the poor had actually widened in the industrial centers, and the vast numbers of workers, augmented by the hordes of underprivileged immigrants, began to form a working class in the European sense. Working conditions were still almost unregulated; a working day of from ten to twelve hours prevailed; and labor organizations were in the embryonic stage. Meanwhile, the operations of the "robber barons" of industry and finance, having gained their first real headway amid the scandals during Grant's administration, had risen to proportions justifying the unlovely epithets by which this age has been designated. Parrington, in *The Beginnings of Critical Realism in America*, says of the audacious leaders of the day that "they fought their way encased in rhinoceros hides" —the gamblers of Wall Street, the Drews, the Vanderbilts, Jim Fiske, Jay Gould, "blackguards for the most part, railway wreckers, cheaters and swindlers"; they were assisted by treasury-looting, vote-selling political bosses such as Tweed, Wood, and Cameron; they were supported by "professional keepers of the public morals" such as Comstock and Beecher; while the public in general seemed to take for granted the gaudy extravagance and "humbuggery" of an age in which Barnum was the predestined showman. A series of panics and depressions, beginning in 1873, increased the burdens and the discontent of the poor. A stouthearted believer in his country, Walt Whitman, excoriating his age with whiplash words in *Democratic Vistas* (1871), could only conclude that "the problem of the future of America is in certain respects as dark as it is vast."

This is not to assert that the realists at once devoted themselves primarily to the social and economic problem novel, although by 1890 many of them were doing so. The realists of the 1870's were sternly aware of the social problem, but their emphasis was on the character of the individual confronted by hardships or moral dilemmas. That the best of realism was not then a literature of reform is evident in the best work of the regionalists in general, and of Mark Twain, Howells, and Henry James, among the masters. For two decades Howells, who was chiefly distinguished for his novels of character, remained the spokesman of realism by virtue of his ability to communicate its spirit in fiction and essay, and to disseminate his *obiter dicta* from the editor's chair of the *Atlantic*, and later *Harper's Magazine*. Many other realists

imposed fewer restrictions as to propriety, and thus ranged over wider areas of life, but no other was more genuinely respected as an artist or more widely heard than Howells. Whether in his early comedies of manners, in his portrayals of the contrasts of international society, or in such novels concerning the business world as *The Rise of Silas Lapham* (1885), his emphasis was on character—until his declining years, after 1890, when his problem novels were written.

The greatest of the realists, Henry James, was the master of profundity and of a psychological subtlety more suited to the understanding of the present age than his own; his great novels are studies of character first of all, and the rise or ruin of his notable characters is predetermined at the very roots of existence or experience.

The work of the later American realists was both substantiated and strengthened by the new vogue of European realists, who had been disparaged by earlier readers on moral grounds—such Russians as Dostoevski, Turgenev, and Tolstoi, and the French naturalists, especially Zola, Flaubert, and Maupassant. The same sources may have strengthened the note of pessimistic determinism that steadily increased down into the nineties, when a full-fledged American naturalism developed. Mark Twain, however, came to this position independently. This gloomy attitude may be the necessary frame of reference for the great humorist; in the case of Twain, in any event, it dominated his genius. Even his earliest comic sketches are over-shadowed by the same specter of mankind's cruelty, greed, and stupidity that lurks in such later masterpieces as "The Man That Corrupted Hadleyburg" (1900) and *The Mysterious Stranger* (1916).

The social problems of the country grew in size with its in-dustrial and financial develop-ment, and it seemed that the American experiment, under-taken by Europeans to secure liberty, was doomed to produce for the masses only unrewarding poverty. During the later eighties the preoccupation of the national thought with social and eco-nomic problems was reflected in a swelling tide of literature. Con-servative economic ideas were championed by many, such as William Graham Sumner, who, in *What Social Classes Owe to Each Other* (1883), defended capitalism as the operation of a benign natural selection of those fit to survive. Andrew Carnegie's *Triumphant Democracy* (1886) sounded much the same note. Meanwhile the collectivists gained their widest audience in a long succession of utopian nov-els, of which Edward Bellamy's *Looking Backward* (1888) was the most influential. Howells, who by this time was a Christian socialist in theory, became the critic of economic society in *A Hazard of New Fortunes* (1890), the first of his economic novels, and in 1894 enriched the utopian movement by publishing *A Traveler from Altruria*. Actu-ally, in retrospect the social ad-vances of those years are seen to be considerable. They were the climax to a titanic economic de-velopment which had produced many social problems, but the gains were being consolidated, and were soon to be felt in per-manent improvements in the economic welfare of Americans in general. The Populist move-ment, begun in 1891, never won an election, but the members of that shifting coalition of farm-and labor-reform groups—chiefly sustained by the mounting de-mocracy of the West—under the leadership of Bryan saw most of their objectives enormously ad-vanced in little more than a dec-ade. Theodore Roosevelt, in lib-eral reforms from 1901 to 1909, curbed the monopolies and "the malefactors of great wealth," in-stituted a sound policy to con-serve the national resources for the people, and became the first president to make the welfare of "the little man" a powerful political issue. However, our literature had long before this developed, during the nineties, a naturalistic tendency which has survived well into the present troubled century.

SPIRITUAL UNREST

Strict naturalism in the Euro-pean sense did not at first flour-ish widely in this country, where it was understood that social remedies were available even if sometimes opposed or post-poned. After 1880, however, a growing spirit of skepticism, of spiritual unrest and disturbed religious faith, was reflected in the changing economic thought and morality of America and in the deterministic attitudes of in-tellectuals and writers. When Darwin published *The Origin of Species* in 1859 it was still pos-sible for Whitman to regard the book as an optimistic confirmation of the ancient belief in man's progress and gradual betterment. John Fiske, like lesser early popularizers of evolutionary science, expounded its theories in the light of theistic faith, and rejoiced that God was revealed in biology as in Scripture. However, it was soon evident that pessimistic determinism was inherent in the new biology, anthropology, and geology, as well as in the recent experiences of economic man. The theory that the human individual, as much as any creature of a lower order, is determined by accidents of heredity, environment, and natural selection, seemed to deprive him of that special place among the creatures of God that had been the comfort of his religion, and of that necessary exercise of individual responsibility which had been common to democratic idealism and the Christian ethic. Herbert Spencer's sociology utilized the biological theory of the survival of the fittest in support of competition as an agency which prevented "the artificial preservation of those least able to take care of themselves." Rugged individualists—*laissez-faire* economists such as Sumner or industrialists such as Carnegie —could take comfort, but many others watched the struggling industrial masses, still poverty-stricken amid plenty, and wondered whether these were really the ways of God.

The literary reactions were variously expressed by such thinkers as William James, Santayana, and Henry Adams, by poets like Moody, Lodge, and Robinson, by such social critics as Veblen and Steffens, and by the later realistic and naturalistic novelists, influenced, as they were, by the writings of the Russian and French naturalists. American philosophy, represented by William James, Santayana, and Dewey, tended toward instrumentalism and rationalism, in contrast with the intuitional idealism of the nineteenth century. If the thinkers of this period evaded outright pessimism, it was by some dualistic resolution of their systems of thought. From his researches in psychology, James drew his "radical empiricism" in *The Will to Believe* (1897)—a defense of the acceptance of metaphysical concepts on the evidence of faith alone. In *Pragmatism* (1907) he gave a name to his new philosophy, which asserts that the value of an idea is tested by its consequences in terms of satisfaction and behavior. John Dewey's instrumentalism was a projection of pragmatism in the evaluation of experience, education, and social instruments in an age of change. Santayana's complex and voluminous system cannot be recapitulated with any simplicity. Its dualism differentiates between the material universe—the reality that man can apprehend only through reason—and the "essences" of higher reality and supernal value in the "realms" of faith. Henry Adams suggested a correspondence between the science and the philosophy of the day in his dynamic theory of history. Accepting the Spencerian hypothesis that history is evolutionary, he sought its laws by analogy with the principle of thermodynamics that energy tends constantly to be dispersed from a center. In *Mont-Saint-Michel and Chartres* (1904) he depicted medieval Christianity as a "universe." By contrast, the contemporary world, depicted in *The Education of Henry Adams* (1907), was a "multiverse" whose symbol was the dynamo, dissipating its energies outward toward diverse poles, with consequent loss of emphasis on individual and social spiritual value.

NATURALISM

It was against this background of troubled thought that the first American naturalistic writers emerged in the 1890's, but they were by no means simply the product of philosophic thought. Artists first of all, and realists in their aims, they were in general impressed by the artistic success of European naturalists and by the resources of the empirical description of experience as a means for securing the realistic portrayal of life.

The typical American naturalists were generally concerned with concrete factors in character and environment. The short-lived and able Frank Norris, in such novels as *Moran of the Lady Letty* (1898) and *Mc-Teague* (1899), explored the personality with naturalistic fervor and only incidental social connotations; but in *The Octopus* (1901), his best-known work, he made a telling attack upon the ramified system of monopolistic financial and railroad power that for a time exploited and often ruined the farmers of the West. In *The Pit* (1903) he examined the drive for economic power in an analysis of the grain monopoly. Stephen Crane found vent for his naturalism in studies of the eastern slums, of the meanness of small-town life, and of the natural depravity of man. Hamlin Garland's conception of strict, delineative realism, which he called "veritism," was in fact naturalistic both in method and materials; his sketches in *Main-Travelled Roads* (1891) deal with characters whose choices are effectively canceled by circumstances or by the conditions of nature. Theodore Dreiser, who also belongs to this generation by date of birth, was the purest naturalist among American writers. Circumstances postponed the creation of *Sister Carrie* (1900), his first work, until he was nearly thirty; and the smothering of that book by unofficial censorship further delayed his active career as a novelist. Carrie Meeber conquers the nearly impossible conditions of poverty only by the animal law of survival, of which she takes advantage with intelligence, ruthlessness, and calm disregard of conventional moral restrictions.

Dreiser alone of these early naturalists and dissenters inherited the literary world after 1915, for which their generation had prepared the way. Garland in later years devoted himself for the most part to more popular forms of fiction. Norris and Crane both died at thirty. But younger authors continued the social dissent, the most important novelists among them being Upton Sinclair and Jack London, who both wrote with tempered naturalism. *The Jungle* (1906) grew out of Sinclair's investigation of the stockyards and packing industry, and brought results in the form of pure-food legislation; but its fictional interest is the story of Jurgis, the Slavic workman, trapped by the brutality, poverty, and disease in which he lives, until bereft of wife and family, brought to the brink of crime, he becomes a socialist agitator. Jack London, unlike Sinclair, remained throughout his career a naturalist and radical socialist. Typical are *The Call of the Wild* (1903), a study of the law of survival in the life of a wild dog; *The Sea-Wolf* (1904), in which the same motivations are transferred to the whaling Captain, Wolf Larsen, a ruthless superman; and *The Iron Heel* (1907), a novel of class warfare. In a sense the short-story formula that O. Henry employed to portray his children of chance—typically in *The Four Million* (1906)—is a satiric response to a naturalistic predisposition.

It is evident that there is no clear cleavage between the nineteenth and the twentieth century in American literature. Victorian acceptances and compromises, genteel survivals, lingered on until 1910 and beyond; but the modern temper which about 1915 produced the "twentieth-century renaissance" originated in the intellectual life of the previous century. The emerging modern American literature, which began with the optimistic voice of Whitman, closed the first decade of the twentieth century with social and economic protest. The one nation, strong and unified, which Lincoln had envisioned, had become an actuality. Urban industrialism posed still-imponderable questions of slum clearance, social welfare, and labor practices. The romantic idealism of 1865 had given way to the realism of Howells, to the psychological penetration of James, to the naturalism of Crane, Norris, and Dreiser. Yet our literature continued to reflect the survival in American life of those youthful virtues that remind us of what we have been and what we should ever strive to be.

Pioneers of a New Poetry

WALT WHITMAN
(1819–1892)

Walt Whitman is important to our literature first of all because he was a great poet. "When Lilacs Last in the Dooryard Bloom'd" or "Out of the Cradle Endlessly Rocking," or "Crossing Brooklyn Ferry"—to name only a few—would be masterpieces in any literature. Second, as an artist he had the kind of courage and vision upon which new epochs are founded. In 1855 he was the first voice of the revolution which after 1870 swept over European literature, and much later reached the United States.

That kind of genius which is uncommon sense made him know that the time had come for many barriers to fall—barriers to the welfare and the expression of the individual, which he valued above all else. Thus, in advance of the "new" psychology he insisted on the unity of the personality and the significant importance of all experience. He extolled the values of the common, the miracle of the mouse, the wholesome soundness of the calloused hand, the body's sweat. He attempted "to make illustrious" the "procreative urge of the universe," or of sex in man.

Whitman's free verse provided an example that slowly communicated itself to later poets who likewise sought to refresh their art. His use of rhythm as a fluid instrument of verse demonstrated a range of possibilities beyond that of conventional meter. He wrote symphonically, associating themes and melodies with great freedom and suggestiveness; he abandoned conventional and hackneyed poetic figures and drew his symbolism freshly from experience. He remains one of our most important poets because he announced and instructed a new age; but he is equally important as a defender of the central American idealism of the past. Spiritually he sprang from the tradition that Emerson represented—his was the transcendental or intuitional temperament that trusts the innate spiritual intimations of the individual and makes him responsible to them. On the plane of political thought he was also an apostle of individualism, and represented the nineteenth-century

16

projection of Jeffersonian idealism.

Walter Whitman was born on a farm on Long Island, then rural countryside, on May 31, 1819; his father was of British, his mother of Dutch, ancestry. Walter Whitman senior, a carpenter as well as a farmer, twice in Walt's youth tried his fortune at housebuilding in Brooklyn, at that time not quite a city in size. Thus the young poet experienced a vital cross section of American common life: about the island the farmers and fishermen, the sailors and clammers, and the hamlets in which they lived; the nascent urban community of Brooklyn, where a boy could still catch fish in a nearby pond; the great harbor with its ships, and across the water the spires of Manhattan, visited by means of the exciting ferryboats, and later to become for the poet always "my city." As a boy he had five years of common schooling in Brooklyn, then in 1830 began work as an office boy. But by natural instinct he turned to the printing offices. Until the early fifties he worked as a journalist, attaining a considerable position as editor of the Brooklyn *Eagle* (1846–1848). On the way up he was an apprentice on the Long Island *Patriot* (1832) and a journeyman printer in New York. Then, after teaching in various country schools on Long Island while contributing to local newspapers, he founded at Huntington his own weekly newspaper, the *Long Islander*, in 1838. In 1839 he was a compositor on the Long Island *Democrat*, and in 1840, at twenty-one, he stumped the Is-

land for Van Buren during the presidential campaign. During the next six years he was in New York, as newspaperman and as editor of the *Aurora*, the *Tatler*, and the New York *Democrat*. When he took over the *Eagle* in Brooklyn in 1846 he was seasoned in his profession, and he gained recognition in the New York area during his editorship. He resigned in 1848 because the backers of the paper, faced with the split in the Democratic party caused by the Mexican War, found it expedient to support compromise with the southern Democrats, while their editor was an unswerving free-soil Democrat. Probably for adventure's sake, Whitman then took the editorship of the New Orleans *Crescent*, traveling southward partly by Mississippi steamboat with his brother Jeff; he returned in six months to edit the Brooklyn *Freeman*.

But now he had in mind his great project. Shaken by the ominous shadows that gathered over the country as "the irrepressible conflict" took shape in the Mexican War, he had conceived of a book to interpret American democratic idealism as he had experienced it. It was to be a poem in a new form with which he had been experimenting since perhaps 1847. He gave up his newspaper work, and living with his parents in Brooklyn, worked as part-time carpenter while writing *Leaves of Grass*. The first edition went on sale in New York probably on July 4, 1855. It had been privately printed, as were all but two of the first seven editions. The frankness of *Leaves of Grass*, together with its revolutionary form, precluded the possibility of wide reception. It was simply about sixty years ahead of its time, and Whitman, realizing this, accepted the situation with equanimity, knowing "the amplitude of time." There was a dribble of orders for each successive edition, most of them sold from his home, wherever it then might be.

But it is a mistake to suppose that the author was neglected. Emerson wrote his famous message, "I greet you at the beginning of a great career," less than three weeks after Whitman sent him a copy. Within the year Thoreau and Bronson Alcott had ferreted out the author's dwelling in Brooklyn, and Emerson himself soon paid a visit. So through the years, leaders of thought saw the greatness of what he was doing. By 1868 the young John Burroughs had written a book on Whitman and William Michael Rossetti had responded to a growing interest among English intellectuals by publishing an English edition. During the 1870's Whitman's name began to be mentioned by German critics, and within another decade translations of his poems in German and French made him famous on the Continent. Still most Americans ignored his work, and he lived in poverty all his life.

From 1855 until 1862 he subsisted by literary hack work and journalism in Brooklyn, meanwhile enlarging his poems for the second edition of 1856 and the fundamental edition of 1860. There the poems began to fall into position as parts of a single "poem," as the author said. It was to represent life in terms of one life, which had to be seen through the poet's eyes, yet he would be reporting only what seemed true and important to everyone.

In 1862, his brother George was wounded, and Whitman went to the war front in Virginia. Finding his brother's condition not serious, he remained in Washington as a volunteer war nurse, visiting hospitals for a part of every day, and supporting himself by part-time work in the Army paymaster's office. This was the experience which led to the poems of *Drum-Taps* (1865). "When Lilacs Last in the Dooryard Bloom'd," written for the second issue of this book, after the assassination of Lincoln that April, provided a passionate climax for the theme of the entire volume in its veneration of the President, who represented for Whitman a shining example of democratic comradeship and love for man.

In 1865, Whitman was appointed clerk in the Bureau of Indian Affairs only to be discharged in six months by Secretary Harlan because of the unsavory reputation of his book. At once appointed to the attorney general's office he rather gained by the experience because his eloquent friend William Douglas O'Connor, in his fiery pamphlet *The Good Gray Poet* (1866), published a fine vindication of Whitman's work.

The poet held his position in Washington until 1874, and during that time published, two more editions of *Leaves of Grass*. In 1873, at fifty-four, he suffered a severe stroke of paralysis, and soon was an invalid at the home of his brother George in Camden, New Jersey. He never again recovered his full vitality, although he was well enough, on occasion, to give a public reading or lecture nearby, or to visit Burroughs, now an established naturalist, at his Hudson River farm. In 1879 he made his long-anticipated transcontinental journey, as far west as Nevada.

In 1881 *Leaves of Grass* found a publisher in Osgood and Company of Boston, but threatened action by Comstock's self-appointed censors caused the withdrawal of the edition. Whitman took the plates to Rees Welsh, later David McKay, in Philadelphia, where his works were published for many years thereafter. In 1882 he published his best prose essays as *Specimen Days and Collect*. For the first time his volumes had a considerable sale. He was able to buy his own little house, now famous, in Mickle Street, Camden, and in the last decade of his life it became a place of pilgrimage for many American and British visitors. Until his death in 1892 he was never far from the edge of poverty, but as he said, in his own time he had "really arrived."

The 1892 edition of *Leaves of Grass*, which he signed on his deathbed, is one of America's great books, and it has had world-wide influence.

Whitman's writings were collected as *The Complete Writings of Walt Whitman*, 10 vols., edited by R. M. Bucke and others, 1902, a limited edition long out of print. There are many editions of *Leaves of Grass*. A standard text is *Leaves of Grass*, inclusive edition, edited by Emory Holloway, 1924, 1954, with prefaces by Whitman and the variorum readings by O. L. Triggs from the *Complete Writings*. A new definitive edition of Whitman, general editors Sculley Bradley and Gay W. Allen, is in progress. Vols. I and II contain the correspondence of 1842–1867 and 1867–1875.

Gay W. Allen, *Walt Whitman Handbook*, 1946, is an indispensable aid, and includes excellent bibliographies. A penetrating study of Whitman is F. O. Matthiessen, "Whitman," in his *American Renaissance*, 1941, pp. 517–613. Henry S. Canby, *Walt Whitman, An American*, 1943, is a standard biography. Emory Holloway, *Whitman: An Interpretation in Narrative*, 1926, was the earliest modern authority. Frederik Schyberg, *Walt Whitman*, translated by Evie Allen, edited by Gay W. Allen, 1951, presents a thorough account of the growth and development of *Leaves of Grass* through its various editions. The most comprehensive biography is Gay W. Allen, *The Solitary Singer: A Critical Biography of Walt Whitman*, 1955. Biography and criticism are balanced in Roger Asselineau, *L'Evolution de Walt Whitman * * * *, 1954.

The following Whitman texts are from *Leaves of Grass*, Philadelphia, 1892, and *Complete Poems and Prose of Walt Whitman, 1855–1888*, Philadelphia, 1888.

From Preface to the 1855 Edition of Leaves of Grass[1]

America does not repel the past or what it has produced under its forms or amid other politics or the idea of castes or the old religions . . . accepts the lesson with calmness . . . is not so impa-

1. The preface to the first edition of *Leaves of Grass* (1855) was not reprinted in subsequent editions, but its ideas, even some of the expressions, were worked into a poem, "Many in One" (1856), which Whitman amplified and altered in successive editions until that of 1871, where it was entitled "By Blue Ontario's Shore." The poet's concept of individualism, his realization of the threat to the democratic individual in America, which reached a crisis with the Civil War, and the idea of universal brotherhood are embodied in this poem.

tient as has been supposed that the slough[2] still sticks to opinions and manners and literature while the life which served its requirements has passed into the new life of the new forms . . . perceives that the corpse is slowly borne from the eating and sleeping rooms of the house . . . perceives that it waits a little while in the door . . . that it was fittest for its days . . . that its action has descended to the stalwart and wellshaped heir who approaches . . . and that he shall be fittest for his days.

The Americans of all nations at any time upon the earth have probably the fullest poetical nature. The United States themselves are essentially the greatest poem. In the history of the earth hitherto the largest and most stirring appear tame and orderly to their ampler largeness and stir. Here at last is something in the doings of man that corresponds with the broadcast doings of the day and night. Here is not merely a nation but a teeming nation of nations. Here is action untied from strings necessarily blind to particulars and details magnificently moving in vast masses. Here is the hospitality which forever indicates heroes. . . . Here are the roughs and beards and space and ruggedness and nonchalance that the soul loves. Here the performance disdaining the trivial unapproached in the tremendous audacity of its crowds and groupings and the push of its perspective spreads with crampless and flowing breadth and showers its prolific and splendid extravagance. One sees it must indeed own the riches of the summer and winter, and need never be bankrupt while corn grows from the ground or the orchards drop apples or the bays contain fish or men beget children upon women.

Other states indicate themselves in their deputies . . . but the genius of the United States is not best or most in its executives or legislatures, nor in its ambassadors or authors or colleges or churches or parlors, nor even in its newspapers or inventors . . . but always most in the common people. Their manners speech dress friendships—the freshness and candor of their physiognomy—the picturesque looseness of their carriage . . . their deathless attachment to freedom—their aversion to anything indecorous or soft or mean—the practical acknowledgment of the citizens of one state by the citizens of all other states—the fierceness of their roused resentment—their curiosity and welcome of novelty—their self-esteem and wonderful sympathy—their susceptibility to a slight—the air they have of persons who never knew how it felt to stand in the presence of superiors—the fluency of their speech—their delight in music, the sure symptom of manly tenderness and native elegance of soul . . . their good temper and open-handedness—the terrible significance of their elections—the President's taking off his hat to them not

2. Dead tissue; also mire or muck.

they to him—these too are unrhymed poetry. It awaits the gigantic and generous treatment worthy of it. * * *

Of all nations the United States with veins full of poetical stuff most need poets and will doubtless have the greatest and use them the greatest. Their Presidents shall not be their common referee so much as their poets shall. Of all mankind the great poet is the equable man. Not in him but off from him things are grotesque or eccentric or fail of their sanity. Nothing out of its place is good and nothing in its place is bad. He bestows on every object or quality its fit proportions neither more nor less. He is the arbiter of the diverse and he is the key. He is the equalizer of his age and land . . . he supplies what wants supplying and checks what wants checking. If peace is the routine out of him speaks the spirit of peace, large, rich, thrifty, building vast and populous cities, encouraging agriculture and the arts and commerce—lighting the study of man, the soul, immortality—federal, state or municipal government, marriage, health, freetrade, intertravel by land and sea . . . nothing too close, nothing too far off . . . the stars not too far off. In war he is the most deadly force of the war. * * *

The greatest poet hardly knows pettiness or triviality. If he breathes into any thing that was before thought small it dilates with the grandeur and life of the universe. He is a seer . . . he is individual . . . he is complete in himself . . . the others are as good as he, only he sees it and they do not. He is not one of the chorus . . . he does not stop for any regulations . . . he is the president of regulation. What the eyesight does to the rest he does to the rest. Who knows the curious mystery of the eyesight? The other senses corroborate themselves, but this is removed from any proof but its own and foreruns the identities of the spiritual world. A single glance of it mocks all the investigations of man and all the instruments and books of the earth and all reasoning. What is marvelous? what is unlikely? what is impossible or baseless or vague? after you have once just opened the space of a peachpit and given audience to far and near and to the sunset and had all things enter with electric swiftness softly and duly without confusion or jostling or jam.

The land and sea, the animals, fishes and birds, the sky of heaven and the orbs, the forests mountains and rivers, are not small themes . . . but folks expect of the poet to indicate more than the beauty and dignity which always attach to dumb real objects . . . they expect him to indicate the path between reality and their souls. Men and women perceive the beauty well enough . . . probably as well as he. The passionate tenacity of hunters, woodmen, early risers, cultivators of gardens and orchards and fields, the love of healthy women for the manly form, seafaring persons, drivers of horses, the passion for light and the open air, all is an old varied sign of the unfailing perception of beauty and of a residence of the poetic in outdoor people. They can never be assisted by poets to perceive . . . some may but they never can. The poetic quality is not marshalled in rhyme or uniformity or abstract addresses to things nor in melancholy complaints or good precepts, but is the life of these and much else and is in the soul. The profit of rhyme is that it drops seeds of a sweeter and more luxuriant rhyme, and of uniformity that it conveys itself into its own roots in the ground out of sight. The rhyme and uniformity of perfect poems show the free growth of metrical laws and bud from them as unerringly and loosely as lilacs or roses on a bush, and take shapes as compact as the shapes of chestnuts and oranges and melons and pears, and shed the perfume impalpable to form. The fluency and ornaments of the finest poems or music or orations or recitations are not independent but dependent. All beauty comes from beautiful blood and a beautiful brain. If the greatnesses are in conjunction in a man or woman it is enough . . . the fact will prevail through the universe . . . but the gaggery and gilt of a million years will not prevail. Who troubles himself about his ornaments or fluency is lost. This is what you shall do: Love the earth and sun and the animals, despise riches, give alms to every one that asks, stand up for the stupid and crazy, devote your income and labor to others, hate tyrants, argue not concerning God, have patience and indulgence toward the people, take off your hat to nothing known or unknown or to any man or number of men, go freely with powerful uneducated persons and with the young and with the mothers of families, read these leaves in the open air every season of every year of your life, re-examine all you have been told at school or church or in any book, dismiss whatever insults your own soul, and your very flesh shall be a great poem and have the richest fluency not only in its words but in the silent lines of its lips and face and between the lashes of your eyes and in every motion and joint of your body. . . . The poet shall not spend his time in unneeded work. He shall know that the ground is always ready plowed and manured . . . others may not know it but he shall. He shall go directly to the creation. His trust shall master the trust of everything he touches . . . and shall master all attachment.

The known universe has one complete lover and that is the greatest poet. He consumes an eternal passion and is indifferent which chance happens and which possible contingency of fortune or misfortune and persuades daily and hourly his delicious pay. What balks or breaks others is fuel for his burning progress to contact and amorous joy. Other proportions of the reception of pleasure dwindle to nothing to his proportions. All expected from heaven or from the highest he is rapport[3] with in the sight of the daybreak or a scene of the winter-woods or the presence of children playing or with his arm round the neck of a man or woman. His love above all love has leisure and expanse . . . he leaves room ahead of himself. He is no irresolute or suspicious lover . . . he is sure . . . he scorns intervals. His experience and the showers and thrills are not for nothing. Nothing can jar him . . . suffering and darkness cannot—death and fear cannot. To him complaint and jealousy and envy are corpses buried and rotten in the earth . . . he saw them buried. The sea is not surer of the shore or the shore of the sea than he is of the fruition of his love and of all perfection and beauty. * * *

Without effort and without exposing in the least how it is done the greatest poet brings the spirit of any or all events and passions and scenes and persons some more and some less to bear on your individual character as you hear or read. To do this well is to compete with the laws that pursue and follow time. What is the purpose must surely be there and the clue of it must be there . . . and the faintest indication is the indication of the best and then becomes the clearest indication. Past and present and future are not disjoined but joined. The greatest poet forms the consistence of what is to be from what has been and is. He drags the dead out of their coffins and stands them again on their feet . . . he says to the past, Rise and walk before me that I may realize you. He learns the lesson . . . he places himself where the future becomes present. The greatest poet does not only dazzle his rays over character and scenes and passions . . . he finally ascends and finishes all . . . he exhibits the pinnacles that no man can tell what they are for or what is beyond . . . he glows a moment on the extremest verge. He is most wonderful in his last half-hidden smile or frown . . . by that flash of the moment of parting the one that sees it shall be encouraged or terrified afterwards for many years. The greatest poet does not moralize or make applications of morals . . . he knows the soul. The soul has that measureless pride which consists in never acknowledging any lessons but its own. But it has sympathy as measureless as its pride and the one balances the other and neither can stretch too far while it stretches in company with the other. The inmost secrets of art sleep with the twain. The greatest poet has lain close betwixt both and they are vital in his style and thoughts.

The art of art, the glory of expression and the sunshine of the light of letters is simplicity. Nothing is better than simplicity . . . nothing can make up for excess or for the lack of definiteness. To carry on the heave of impulse and pierce intellectual depths and give all

3. In harmonious relation; properly, *en rapport.*

subjects their articulations are powers neither common nor very uncommon. But to speak in literature with the perfect rectitude and insouciance of the movements of animals and the unimpeachableness of the sentiment of trees in the woods and grass by the roadside is the flawless triumph of art. If you have looked on him who has achieved it you have looked on one of the masters of the artists of all nations and times. You shall not contemplate the flight of the graygull over the bay or the mettlesome action of the blood horse or the tall leaning of sunflowers on their stalk or the appearance of the sun journeying through heaven or the appearance of the moon afterward with any more satisfaction than you shall contemplate him. The greatest poet has less a marked style and is more the channel of thoughts and things without increase or diminution, and is the free channel of himself. He swears to his art, I will not be meddlesome, I will not have in my writing any elegance or effect or originality to hang in the way between me and the rest like curtains. I will have nothing hang in the way, not the richest curtains. What I tell I tell for precisely what it is. Let who may exalt or startle or fascinate or sooth I will have purposes as health or heat or snow has and be as regardless of observation. What I experience or portray shall go from my composition without a shred of my composition. You shall stand by my side and look in the mirror with me. * * *

The poems distilled from other poems will probably pass away. The coward will surely pass away. The expectation of the vital and great can only be satisfied by the demeanor of the vital and great. The swarms of the polished deprecating and reflectors and the polite float off and leave no remembrance. America prepares with composure and goodwill for the visitors that have sent word. It is not intellect that is to be their warrant and welcome. The talented, the artist, the ingenious, the editor, the statesman, the erudite . . . they are not unappreciated . . . they fall in their place and do their work. The soul of the nation also does its work. No disguise can pass on it . . . no disguise can conceal from it. It rejects none, it permits all. Only toward as good as itself and toward the like of itself will it advance half-way. An individual is as superb as a nation when he has the qualities which make a superb nation. The soul of the largest and wealthiest and proudest nation may well go halfway to meet that of its poets. The signs are effectual. There is no fear of mistake. If the one is true the other is true. The proof of a poet is that his country absorbs him as affectionately as he has absorbed it.

1855

Song of Myself[4]

1

I celebrate myself, and sing myself,
And what I assume you shall assume,
For every atom belonging to me as good belongs to you.

I loafe and invite my soul,
I lean and loafe at my ease observing a spear of summer grass.   5

My tongue, every atom of my blood, form'd from this soil, this air,
Born here of parents born here from parents the same, and their
    parents the same,
I, now thirty-seven years old in perfect health begin,
Hoping to cease not till death.

Creeds and schools in abeyance,   10
Retiring back a while sufficed at what they are, but never forgotten,
I harbor for good or bad, I permit to speak at every hazard,
Nature without check with original energy.

2

Houses and rooms are full of perfumes, the shelves are crowded with
    perfumes,
I breathe the fragrance myself and know it and like it,   15
The distillation would intoxicate me also, but I shall not let it.

The atmosphere is not a perfume, it has no taste of the distillation,
    it is odorless,
It is for my mouth forever, I am in love with it,
I will go to the bank by the wood and become undisguised and
    naked,
I am mad for it to be in contact with me.   20

The smoke of my own breath,
Echoes, ripples, buzz'd whispers, love-root, silk-thread, crotch and
    vine,
My respiration and inspiration, the beating of my heart, the passing
    of blood and air through my lungs,
The sniff of green leaves and dry leaves, and of the shore and dark-
    color'd sea-rocks, and of hay in the barn,
The sound of the belch'd words of my voice loos'd to the eddies of
    the wind,   25
A few light kisses, a few embraces, a reaching around of arms,

4. This poem was untitled in the first
edition of *Leaves of Grass;* in the second edition it was called "Poem of Walt
Whitman, an American"; and finally,
in 1881–1882, it became "Song of Myself." The "I" or "myself" in the poem,
though sometimes personal, is more
often generic and cosmic.

The play of shine and shade on the trees as the supple boughs wag,
The delight alone or in the rush of the streets, or along the fields and
    hill-sides,
The feeling of health, the full-noon trill, the song of me rising from
    bed and meeting the sun.

Have you reckon'd a thousand acres much? have you reckon'd the
    earth much?
                                                          30
Have you practis'd so long to learn to read?
Have you felt so proud to get at the meaning of poems?

Stop this day and night with me and you shall possess the origin of
    all poems,
You shall possess the good of the earth and sun, (there are millions
    of suns left,)
You shall no longer take things at second or third hand, nor look
    through the eyes of the dead, nor feed on the spectres in
    books,
                                                          35
You shall not look through my eyes either, nor take things from me,
You shall listen to all sides and filter them from your self.

3

I have heard what the talkers were talking, the talk of the beginning
    and the end,
But I do not talk of the beginning or the end.

There was never any more inception than there is now,   40
Nor any more youth or age than there is now,
And will never be any more perfection than there is now,
Nor any more heaven or hell than there is now.

Urge and urge and urge,
Always the procreant urge of the world.   45
Out of the dimness opposite equals advance, always substance and
    increase, always sex,
Always a knit of identity, always distinction, always a breed of life.

To elaborate is no avail, learn'd and unlearn'd feel that it is so.

Sure as the most certain sure, plumb in the uprights, well entretied,
    braced in the beams,
Stout as a horse, affectionate, haughty, electrical,   50
I and this mystery here we stand.

Clear and sweet is my soul, and clear and sweet is all that is not my
    soul.

Lack one lacks both, and the unseen is proved by the seen,
Till that becomes unseen and receives proof in its turn.

Showing the best and dividing it from the worst age vexes age, 55
Knowing the perfect fitness and equanimity of things, while they
    discuss I am silent, and go bathe and admire myself.

Welcome is every organ and attribute of me, and of any man hearty
    and clean,
Not an inch nor a particle of an inch is vile, and none shall be less
    familiar than the rest.

I am satisfied—I see, dance, laugh, sing;
As the hugging and loving bed-fellow sleeps at my side through the
    night, and withdraws at the peep of the day with stealthy
    tread, 60
Leaving me baskets cover'd with white towels swelling the house
    with their plenty,
Shall I postpone my acceptation and realization and scream at my
    eyes,
That they turn from gazing after and down the road,
And forthwith cipher and show me to a cent,
Exactly the value of one and exactly the value of two, and which is
    ahead? 65

4

Trippers and askers surround me,
People I meet, the effect upon me of my early life or the ward and
    city I live in, or the nation,
The latest dates, discoveries, inventions, societies, authors old and
    new,
My dinner, dress, associates, looks, compliments, dues,
The real or fancied indifference of some man or woman I love, 70
The sickness of one of my folks or of myself, or ill-doing or loss or
    lack of money, or depressions or exaltations,
Battles, the horrors of fratricidal war, the fever of doubtful news, the
    fitful events;
These come to me days and nights and go from me again,
But they are not the Me myself.

Apart from the pulling and hauling stands what I am, 75
Stands amused, complacent, compassionating, idle, unitary,
Looks down, is erect, or bends an arm on an impalpable certain rest,
Looking with side-curved head curious what will come next,
Both in and out of the game and watching and wondering at it.

Backward I see in my own days where I sweated through fog with
    linguists and contenders, 80
I have no mockings or arguments, I witness and wait.

5

I believe in you my soul, the other I am must not abase itself to you,
And you must not be abased to the other.

Loafe with me on the grass, loose the stop from your throat,
Not words, not music or rhyme I want, not custom or lecture, not
    even the best, 85
Only the lull I like, the hum of your valvèd voice.

I mind how once we lay such a transparent summer morning,
How you settled your head athwart my hips and gently turn'd over
    upon me,
And parted the shirt from my bosom-bone, and plunged your tongue
    to my bare-stript heart,
And reach'd till you felt my beard, and reach'd till you held my
    feet. 90

Swiftly arose and spread around me the peace and knowledge that
    pass all the argument of the earth,
And I know that the hand of God is the promise of my own,
And I know that the spirit of God is the brother of my own,
And that all the men ever born are also my brothers, and the women
    my sisters and lovers,
And that a kelson of the creation is love, 95
And limitless are leaves stiff or drooping in the fields,
And brown ants in the little wells beneath them,
And mossy scabs of the worm fence, heap'd stones, elder, mullein
    and poke-weed.

6

A child said *What is the grass?* fetching it to me with full hands,
How could I answer the child? I do not know what it is any more
    than he. 100

I guess it must be the flag of my disposition, out of hopeful green
    stuff woven.

Or I guess it is the handkerchief of the Lord,
A scented gift and remembrancer designedly dropt,
Bearing the owner's name someway in the corners, that we may see
    and remark, and say *Whose?*

Or I guess the grass is itself a child, the produced babe of the vege-
    tation. 105

Or I guess it is a uniform hieroglyphic,
And it means, Sprouting alike in broad zones and narrow zones,
Growing among black folks as among white,

Kanuck, Tuckahoe, Congressman, Cuff,[5] I give them the same, I
   receive them the same.

And now it seems to me the beautiful uncut hair of graves.   110

Tenderly will I use you curling grass,
It may be you transpire from the breasts of young men,
It may be if I had known them I would have loved them,
It may be you are from old people, or from offspring taken soon out
   of their mothers' laps,
And here you are the mothers' laps.   115

This grass is very dark to be from the white heads of old mothers,
Darker than the colorless beards of old men,
Dark to come from under the faint red roofs of mouths.
O I perceive after all so many uttering tongues,
And I perceive they do not come from the roofs of mouths for
   nothing.   120

I wish I could translate the hints about the dead young men and
   women,
And the hints about old men and mothers, and the offspring taken
   soon out of their laps.

What do you think has become of the young and old men?
And what do you think has become of the women and children?

They are alive and well somewhere,   125
The smallest sprout shows there is really no death,
And if ever there was it led forward life, and does not wait at the
   end to arrest it,
And ceas'd the moment life appear'd.

All goes onward and outward, nothing collapses,
And to die is different from what any one supposed, and luckier.   130

7

Has any one supposed it lucky to be born?
I hasten to inform him or her it is just as lucky to die, and I know it.

I pass death with the dying and birth with the new-wash'd babe,
   and am not contain'd between my hat and boots,
And peruse manifold objects, no two alike and every one good,
The earth good and the stars good, and their adjuncts all good.   135

I am not an earth nor an adjunct of an earth,
I am the mate and companion of people, all just as immortal and
   fathomless as myself,
(They do not know how immortal, but I know.)

5. "Kanuck" denotes a French Canadian; "Tuckahoe," a Virginian who
lived on poor lands in the tidewater
region and ate tuckahoe, a fungus; and
"Cuff," a Negro.

Every kind for itself and its own, for me mine male and female,
For me those that have been boys and that love women,   140
For me the man that is proud and feels how it stings to be slighted,
For me the sweet-heart and the old maid, for me mothers and the
    mothers of mothers,
For me lips that have smiled, eyes that have shed tears,
For me children and the begetters of children.

Undrape! you are not guilty to me, nor stale nor discarded,   145
I see through the broadcloth and gingham whether or no,
And am around, tenacious, acquisitive, tireless, and cannot be
    shaken away.

8

The little one sleeps in its cradle,
I lift the gauze and look a long time, and silently brush away flies
    with my hand.

The youngster and the red-faced girl turn aside up the bushy
    hill,
I peeringly view them from the top.   150

The suicide sprawls on the bloody floor of the bedroom,
I witness the corpse with its dabbled hair, I note where the pistol has
    fallen.

The blab of the pave, tires of carts, sluff of boot-soles, talk of the
    promenaders,
The heavy omnibus, the driver with his interrogating thumb, the
    clank of the shod horses on the granite floor,   155
The snow-sleighs, clinking, shouted jokes, pelts of snow-balls,
The hurrahs for popular favorites, the fury of rous'd mobs,
The flap of the curtain'd litter, a sick man inside borne to the hos-
    pital,
The meeting of enemies, the sudden oath, the blows and fall,
The excited crowd, the policeman with his star quickly working his
    passage to the centre of the crowd,   160
The impassive stones that receive and return so many echoes,
What groans of over-fed or half-starv'd who fall sunstruck or in fits,
What exclamations of women taken suddenly who hurry home and
    give birth to babes,
What living and buried speech is always vibrating here, what howls
    restrain'd by decorum,
Arrests of criminals, slights, adulterous offers made, acceptances, re-
    jections with convex lips,   165
I mind them or the show or resonance of them—I come and I
    depart.

9

The big doors of the country barn stand open and ready,
The dried grass of the harvest-time loads the slow-drawn wagon,
The clear light plays on the brown gray and green intertinged,
The armfuls are pack'd to the sagging mow.   170

I am there, I help, I came stretch'd atop of the load,
I felt its soft jolts, one leg reclined on the other,
I jump from the cross-beams and seize the clover and timothy,
And roll head over heels and tangle my hair full of wisps.

10

Alone far in the wilds and mountains I hunt,   175
Wandering amazed at my own lightness and glee,
In the late afternoon choosing a safe spot to pass the night,
Kindling a fire and broiling the fresh-kill'd game,
Falling asleep on the gather'd leaves with my dog and gun by my
    side.

The Yankee clipper is under her sky-sails, she cuts the sparkle and
    scud,   180
My eyes settle the land, I bend at her prow or shout joyously from
    the deck.

The boatmen and clam-diggers arose early and stopt for me,
I tuck'd my trowser-ends in my boots and went and had a good time;
You should have been with us that day round the chowder-kettle.

I saw the marriage of the trapper in the open air in the far west, the
    bride was a red girl,   185
Her father and his friends sat near cross-legged and dumbly smok-
    ing, they had moccasins to their feet and large thick blankets
    hanging from their shoulders,
On a bank lounged the trapper, he was drest mostly in skins, his
    luxuriant beard and curls protected his neck, he held his bride
    by the hand,
She had long eyelashes, her head was bare, her coarse straight locks
    descended upon her voluptuous limbs and reach'd to her feet.

The runaway slave came to my house and stopt outside,
I heard his motions crackling the twigs of the woodpile,   190
Through the swung half-door of the kitchen I saw him limpsy and
    weak,
And went where he sat on a log and led him in and assured him,
And brought water and fill'd a tub for his sweated body and bruis'd
    feet,
And gave him a room that enter'd from my own, and gave him
    some coarse clean clothes,

And remember perfectly well his revolving eyes and his awkwardness,
And remember putting plasters on the galls of his neck and
    ankles;   196
He staid with me a week before he was recuperated and pass'd north,
I had him sit next to me at table, my fire-lock lean'd in the corner.

11

Twenty-eight young men bathe by the shore,
Twenty-eight young men and all so friendly;   200
Twenty-eight years of womanly life and all so lonesome.

She owns the fine house by the rise of the bank,
She hides handsome and richly drest aft the blinds of the window.

Which of the young men does she like the best?
Ah the homeliest of them is beautiful to her.   205

Where are you off to, lady? for I see you,
You splash in the water there, yet stay stock still in your room.

Dancing and laughing along the beach came the twenty-ninth
    bather,
The rest did not see her, but she saw them and loved them.

The beards of the young men glisten'd with wet, it ran from their
    long hair,   210
Little streams pass'd all over their bodies.

An unseen hand also pass'd over their bodies,
It descended tremblingly from their temples and ribs.

The young men float on their backs, their white bellies bulge to the
    sun, they do not ask who seizes fast to them,
They do not know who puffs and declines with pendant and bend-
    ing arch,   215
They do not think whom they souse with spray.

12

The butcher-boy puts off his killing-clothes, or sharpens his knife at
    the stall in the market,
I loiter enjoying his repartee and his shuffle[6] and break-down.

Blacksmiths with grimed and hairy chests environ the anvil,
Each has his main-sledge, they are all out, there is a great heat in the
    fire.   220

From the cinder-strew'd threshold I follow their movements,
The lithe sheer of their waists plays even with their massive arms,
Overhand the hammers swing, overhand so slow, overhand so sure,
They do not hasten, each man hits in his place.

6. A lazy dance, with sliding and tapping of the feet; a break-down is a rollicking,
noisy dance.

13

The negro holds firmly the reins of his four horses, the block swags
    underneath on its tied-over chain,   225
The negro that drives the long dray of the stone-yard, steady and tall
    he stands pois'd on one leg on the string-piece,
His blue shirt exposes his ample neck and breast and loosens over
    his hip-band,
His glance is calm and commanding, he tosses the slouch of his hat
    away from his forehead,
The sun falls on his crispy hair and mustache, falls on the black of
    his polish'd and perfect limbs.

I behold the picturesque giant and love him, and I do not stop
    there,   230
I go with the team also.

In me the caresser of life wherever moving, backward as well as for-
    ward sluing,
To niches aside and junior bending, not a person or object missing,
Absorbing all to myself and for this song.

Oxen that rattle the yoke and chain or halt in the leafy shade, what
    is that you express in your eyes?   235
It seems to me more than all the print I have read in my life.

My tread scares the wood-drake and wood-duck on my distant and
    day-long ramble,
They rise together, they slowly circle around.

I believe in those wing'd purposes,
And acknowledge red, yellow, white, playing within me,   240
And consider green and violet and the tufted crown intentional,
And do not call the tortoise unworthy because she is not something
    else,
And the jay in the woods never studied the gamut, yet trills pretty
    well to me,
And the look of the bay mare shames silliness out of me.

14

The wild gander leads his flock through the cool night,   245
Ya-honk he says, and sounds it down to me like an invitation,
The pert may suppose it meaningless, but I listening close,
Find its purpose and place up there toward the wintry sky.

The sharp-hoof'd moose of the north, the cat on the house-sill, the
    chickadee, the prairie-dog,
The litter of the grunting sow as they tug at her teats,   250
The brood of the turkey-hen and she with her half-spread wings,
I see in them and myself the same old law.

The press of my foot to the earth springs a hundred affections,
They scorn the best I can do to relate them.

I am enamour'd of growing out-doors,   255
Of men that live among cattle or taste of the ocean or woods,
Of the builders and steerers of ships and the wielders of axes and
    mauls, and the drivers of horses,
I can eat and sleep with them week in and week out.

What is commonest, cheapest, nearest, easiest, is Me,
Me going in for my chances, spending for vast returns,   260
Adorning myself to bestow myself on the first that will take me,
Not asking the sky to come down to my good will,
Scattering it freely forever.

15

The pure contralto sings in the organ loft,
The carpenter dresses his plank, the tongue of his foreplane whistles
    its wild ascending lisp,   265
The married and unmarried children ride home to their Thanksgiv-
    ing dinner,
The pilot seizes the king-pin, he heaves down with a strong arm,
The mate stands braced in the whale-boat, lance and harpoon are
    ready,
The duck-shooter walks by silent and cautious stretches,
The deacons are ordain'd with cross'd hands at the altar,   270
The spinning-girl retreats and advances to the hum of the big
    wheel,
The farmer stops by the bars as he walks on a First-day[7] loafe and
    looks at the oats and rye,
The lunatic is carried at last to the asylum a confirm'd case,
(He will never sleep any more as he did in the cot in his mother's
    bedroom;)
The jour printer[8] with gray head and gaunt jaws works at his
    case,   275
He turns his quid of tobacco while his eyes blurr with the manu-
    script;
The malform'd limbs are tied to the surgeon's table,
What is removed drops horribly in a pail;
The quadroon girl is sold at the auction-stand, the drunkard nods by
    the bar-room stove,
The machinist rolls up his sleeves, the policeman travels his beat, the
    gate-keeper marks who pass,   280

---

7. Quaker designation for Sunday.
8. Colloquial for journeyman printer,
i.e., one who has learned his trade but
is not yet a master printer. His "case"
is the box that holds his type.

The young fellow drives the express-wagon, (I love him, though I do
    not know him;)
The half-breed straps on his light boots to compete in the race,
The western turkey-shooting draws old and young, some lean on
    their rifles, some sit on logs,
Out from the crowd steps the marksman, takes his position, levels
    his piece;
The groups of newly-come immigrants cover the wharf or levee,   285
As the woolly-pates hoe in the sugar-field, the overseer views them
    from his saddle,
The bugle calls in the ball-room, the gentlemen run for their part-
    ners, the dancers bow to each other,
The youth lies awake in the cedar-roof'd garret and harks to the
    musical rain,
The Wolverine[9] sets traps on the creek that helps fill the Huron,
The squaw wrapt in her yellow-hemm'd cloth is offering moccasins
    and bead-bags for sale,   290
The connoisseur peers along the exhibition-gallery with half-shut
    eyes bent sideways,
As the deck-hands make fast the steamboat the plank is thrown for
    the shore-going passengers,
The young sister holds out the skein while the elder sister winds it
    off in a ball, and stops now and then for the knots,
The one-year wife is recovering and happy having a week ago borne
    her first child.
The clean-hair'd Yankee girl works with her sewing-machine or in
    the factory or mill,   295
The paving-man leans on his two-handed rammer, the reporter's
    lead flies swiftly over the note-book, the sign-painter is lettering
    with blue and gold,
The canal boy trots on the tow-path, the book-keeper counts at his
    desk, the shoemaker waxes his thread,
The conductor beats time for the band and all the performers follow
    him,
The child is baptized, the convert is making his first professions,
The regatta is spread on the bay, the race is begun, (how the white
    sails sparkle!)   300
The drover watching his drove sings out to them that would stray,
The pedler sweats with his pack on his back, (the purchaser higgling
    about the odd cent;)
The bride unrumples her white dress, the minute-hand of the clock
    moves slowly,
The opium-eater reclines with rigid head and just-open'd lips,

9. Native of Michigan.

The prostitute draggles her shawl, her bonnet bobs on her tipsy and
   pimpled neck,   305
The crowd laugh at her blackguard oaths, the men jeer and wink to
   each other,
(Miserable! I do not laugh at your oaths nor jeer you;)
The President holding a cabinet council is surrounded by the great
   Secretaries,
On the piazza walk three matrons stately and friendly with twined
   arms,
The crew of the fish-smack pack repeated layers of halibut in the
   hold,   310
The Missourian crosses the plains toting his wares and his cattle,
As the fare-collector goes through the train he gives notice by the
   jingling of loose change,
The floor-men are laying the floor, the tinners are tinning the roof,
   the masons are calling for mortar,
In single file each shouldering his hod pass onward the laborers;
Seasons pursuing each other the indescribable crowd is gather'd, it is
   the fourth of Seventh-month,[1] (what salutes of cannon and
   small arms!)   315
Seasons pursuing each other the plougher ploughs, the mower
   mows, and the winter-grain falls in the ground;
Off on the lakes the pike-fisher watches and waits by the hole in the
   frozen surface,
The stumps stand thick round the clearing, the squatter strikes deep
   with his axe,
Flatboatmen make fast towards dusk near the cotton-wood or pecan-
   trees,
Coon-seekers go through the regions of the Red river or through
   those drain'd by the Tennessee, or through those of the
   Arkansas,   320
Torches shine in the dark that hangs on the Chattahooche or Alta-
   mahaw,
Patriarchs sit at supper with sons and grandsons and great-grandsons
   around them,
In walls of adobie, in canvas tents, rest hunters and trappers after
   their day's sport,
The city sleeps and the country sleeps,
The living sleep for their time, the dead sleep for their time,   325
The old husband sleeps by his wife and the young husband sleeps by
   his wife;

---

1. Fourth of July. Such Quaker desig-
nations for months and days of the
week avoided the pagan implications
of the more usual names ("July," *e.g.,*
is derived from Caesar's first name,
Julius).

And these tend inward to me, and I tend outward to them,
And such as it is to be of these more or less I am,
And of these one and all I weave the song of myself.

16

I am of old and young, of the foolish as much as the wise,   330
Regardless of others, ever regardful of others,
Maternal as well as paternal, a child as well as a man,
Stuff'd with the stuff that is coarse and stuff'd with the stuff that is
     fine,
One of the Nation of many nations, the smallest the same and the
     largest the same,
A Southerner soon as a Northerner, a planter nonchalant and hos-
     pitable down by the Oconee I live,   335
A Yankee bound my own way ready for trade, my joints the limber-
     est joints on earth and the sternest joints on earth,
A Kentuckian walking the vale of the Elkhorn in my deer-skin
     leggings, a Louisianian or Georgian,
A boatman over lakes or bays or along coasts, a Hoosier, Badger,
     Buckeye;[2]
At home on Kanadian snow-shoes or up in the bush, or with fisher-
     men off Newfoundland,
At home in the fleet of ice-boats, sailing with the rest and tack-
     ing,   340
At home on the hills of Vermont or in the woods of Maine, or the
     Texan ranch,
Comrade of Californians, comrade of free North-Westerners, (lov-
     ing their big proportions,)
Comrade of raftsmen and coalmen, comrade of all who shake hands
     and welcome to drink and meat,
A learner with the simplest, a teacher of the thoughtfullest,
A novice beginning yet experient of myriads of seasons,   345
Of every hue and caste am I, of every rank and religion,
A farmer, mechanic, artist, gentleman, sailor, quaker,
Prisoner, fancy-man, rowdy, lawyer, physician, priest.

I resist any thing better than my own diversity,
Breathe the air but leave plenty after me,   350
And am not stuck up, and am in my place.

(The moth and the fish-eggs are in their place,
The bright suns I see and the dark suns I cannot see are in their
     place,

The palpable is in its place and the impalpable is in its place.)

2. Nicknames for people from Indiana, Wisconsin, and Ohio, respectively.

17

These are really the thoughts of all men in all ages and lands, they
    are not original with me,   355
If they are not yours as much as mine they are nothing, or next to
    nothing,
If they are not the riddle and the untying of the riddle they are
    nothing,
If they are not just as close as they are distant they are nothing.

This is the grass that grows wherever the land is and the water is,
This is the common air that bathes the globe.   360

18

With music strong I come, with my cornets and my drums,
I play not marches for accepted victors only, I play marches for
    conquer'd and slain persons.

Have you heard that it was good to gain the day?
I also say it is good to fall, battles are lost in the same spirit in which
    they are won.

I beat and pound for the dead,   365
I blow through my embouchures[3] my loudest and gayest for them.

Vivas to those who have fail'd!
And to those whose war-vessels sank in the sea!
And to those themselves who sank in the sea!
And to all generals that lost engagements, and all overcome heroes!
And the numberless unknown heroes equal to the greatest heroes
    known!   371

19

This is the meal equally set, this the meat for natural hunger,
It is for the wicked just the same as the righteous, I make appoint-
    ments with all,
I will not have a single person slighted or left away,
The kept-woman, sponger, thief, are hereby invited,   375
The heavy-lipp'd slave is invited, the venerealee is invited;
There shall be no difference between them and the rest.

This is the press of a bashful hand, this the float and odor of hair,
This the touch of my lips to yours, this the murmur of yearning,
This the far-off depth and height reflecting my own face,   380
This the thoughtful merge of myself, and the outlet again.

Do you guess I have some intricate purpose?
Well I have, for the Fourth-month showers have, and the mica on
    the side of a rock has.

3. Mouthpieces of musical instruments.

Do you take it I would astonish?
Does the daylight astonish? does the early redstart twittering
    through the woods?   385
Do I astonish more than they?

This hour I tell things in confidence,
I might not tell everybody, but I will tell you.

20

Who goes there? hankering, gross, mystical, nude;
How is it I extract strength from the beef I eat?   390

What is a man anyhow? what am I? what are you?

All I mark as my own you shall offset it with your own,
Else it were time lost listening to me.

I do not snivel that snivel the world over,
That months are vacuums and the ground but wallow and filth. 395

Whimpering and truckling fold with powders for invalids, conform-
    ity goes to the fourth-remov'd,
I wear my hat as I please indoors or out.

Why should I pray? why should I venerate and be ceremonious?

Having pried through the strata, analyzed to a hair, counsel'd with
    doctors and calculated close,
I find no sweeter fat than sticks to my own bones.   400

In all people I see myself, none more and not one a barley-corn less,
And the good or bad I say of myself I say of them.

I know I am solid and sound,
To me the converging objects of the universe perpetually flow,
All are written to me, and I must get what the writing means. 405

I know I am deathless,
I know this orbit of mine cannot be swept by a carpenter's compass,
I know I shall not pass like a child's carlacue cut with a burnt stick
    at night.

I know I am august,
I do not trouble my spirit to vindicate itself or be understood, 410
I see that the elementary laws never apologize,
(I reckon I behave no prouder than the level I plant my house by,
    after all.)

I exist as I am, that is enough,
If no other in the world be aware I sit content,
And if each and all be aware I sit content.   415

One world is aware and by far the largest to me, and that is myself,
And whether I come to my own to-day or in ten thousand or ten
    million years,
I can cheerfully take it now, or with equal cheerfulness I can wait.
My foothold is tenon'd and mortis'd in granite,[4]
I laugh at what you call dissolution,   420
And I know the amplitude of time.

21

I am the poet of the Body and I am the poet of the Soul,
The pleasures of heaven are with me and the pains of hell are with
    me,
The first I graft and increase upon myself, the latter I translate into
    a new tongue.

I am the poet of the woman the same as the man,   425
And I say it is as great to be a woman as to be a man,
And I say there is nothing greater than the mother of men.

I chant the chant of dilation or pride,
We have had ducking and deprecating about enough,
I show that size is only development.   430

Have you outstript the rest? are you the President?
It is a trifle, they will more than arrive there every one, and still pass
    on.

I am he that walks with the tender and growing night,
I call to the earth and sea half-held by the night.

Press close bare-bosom'd night—press close magnetic nourishing
    night!   435
Night of south winds—night of the large few stars!
Still nodding night—mad naked summer night.

Smile O voluptuous cool-breath'd earth!
Earth of the slumbering and liquid trees!
Earth of departed sunset—earth of the mountains misty-topt!   440
Earth of the vitreous pour of the full moon just tinged with blue!
Earth of shine and dark mottling the tide of the river!
Earth of the limpid gray of clouds brighter and clearer for my sake!
Far-swooping elbow'd earth—rich apple-blossom'd earth!
Smile, for your lover comes.   445

Prodigal, you have given me love—therefore I to you give love!
O unspeakable passionate love.

---

4. The tenon-and-mortise joint is noted for strength.

22

You sea! I resign myself to you also—I guess what you mean,
I behold from the beach your crooked inviting fingers,
I believe you refuse to go back without feeling of me,   450
We must have a turn together, I undress, hurry me out of sight of
    the land,
Cushion me soft, rock me in billowy drowse,
Dash me with amorous wet, I can repay you.

Sea of stretch'd ground-swells,
Sea breathing broad and convulsive breaths,   455
Sea of the brine of life and of unshovell'd yet always-ready graves,

Howler and scooper of storms, capricious and dainty sea,
I am integral with you, I too am of one phase and of all phases.

Partaker of influx and efflux I, extoller of hate and conciliation,
Extoller of amies and those that sleep in each others' arms.   460

I am he attesting sympathy,
(Shall I make my list of things in the house and skip the house that
    supports them?)

I am not the poet of goodness only, I do not decline to be the poet
    of wickedness also.

What blurt is this about virtue and about vice?
Evil propels me and reform of evil propels me, I stand indifferent,
My gait is no fault-finder's or rejecter's gait;   466
I moisten the roots of all that has grown.

Did you fear some scrofula out of the unflagging pregnancy?
Did you guess the celestial laws are yet to be work'd over and
    rectified?

I find one side a balance and the antipodal side a balance,   470
Soft doctrine as steady help as stable doctrine,
Thoughts and deeds of the present our rouse and early start.

This minute that comes to me over the past decillions,
There is no better than it and now.

What behaved well in the past or behaves well to-day is not such a
    wonder,   475
The wonder is always and always how there can be a mean man or
    an infidel.

23

Endless unfolding of words of ages!
And mine a word of the modern, the word En-Masse.

A word of the faith that never balks,
Here or henceforward it is all the same to me, I accept Time abso-
lutely.   480

It alone is without flaw, it alone rounds and completes all,
That mystic baffling wonder alone completes all.

I accept Reality and dare not question it,
Materialism first and last imbuing.

Hurrah for positive science! long live exact demonstration!   485
Fetch stonecrop[5] mixt with cedar and branches of lilac,
This is the lexicographer, this the chemist, this made a grammar of
the old cartouches,
These mariners put the ship through dangerous unknown seas,
This is the geologist, this works with the scalpel, and this is a mathe-
matician.

Gentlemen, to you the first honors always!   490
Your facts are useful, and yet they are not my dwelling,
I but enter by them to an area of my dwelling.

Less the reminders of properties told my words,
And more the reminders they of life untold, and of freedom and
extrication,
And make short account of neuters and geldings, and favor men and
women fully equipt.   495
And beat the gong of revolt, and stop with fugitives and them that
plot and conspire.

24

Walt Whitman, a kosmos,[6] of Manhattan the son,
Turbulent, fleshly, sensual, eating, drinking and breeding,
No sentimentalist, no stander above men and women or apart from
them,
No more modest than immodest.   500

Unscrew the locks from the doors!
Unscrew the doors themselves from their jambs!

Whoever degrades another degrades me,
And whatever is done or said returns at last to me.

Through me the afflatus surging and surging, through me the cur-
rent and index.   505

I speak the pass-word primeval, I give the sign of democracy,

5. A mosslike plant with yellow flowers, frequently found on rocks and walls.
6. German transcendental idealism, which influenced Whitman, stressed the relations between the individual micro-cosm and the universal macrocosm.

By God! I will accept nothing which all cannot have their counter-
    part of on the same terms.

Through me many long dumb voices,
Voices of the interminable generations of prisoners and slaves,
Voices of the diseas'd and despairing and of thieves and dwarfs,   510
Voices of cycles of preparation and accretion,
And of the threads that connect the stars, and of wombs and of the
    father-stuff,
And of the rights of them the others are down upon,
Of the deform'd, trivial, flat, foolish, despised,
Fog in the air, beetles rolling balls of dung.   515

Through me forbidden voices,
Voices of sexes and lusts, voices veil'd and I remove the veil,
Voices indecent by me clarified and transfigur'd.

I do not press my fingers across my mouth,
I keep as delicate around the bowels as around the head and heart,
Copulation is no more rank to me than death is.   521

I believe in the flesh and the appetites,
Seeing, hearing, feeling, are miracles, and each part and tag of me is
    a miracle.

Divine am I inside and out, and I make holy whatever I touch or
    am touch'd from,
The scent of these arm-pits aroma finer than prayer,   525
This head more than churches, bibles, and all the creeds.

If I worship one thing more than another it shall be the spread of
    my own body, or any part of it,
Translucent mould of me it shall be you!
Shaded ledges and rests it shall be you!
Firm masculine colter[7] it shall be you!   530
Whatever goes to the tilth[8] of me it shall be you!
You my rich blood! your milky stream pale strippings of my life!
Breast that presses against other breasts it shall be you!
My brain it shall be your occult convolutions!
Root of wash'd sweet-flag! timorous pond-snipe! nest of guarded
    duplicate eggs! it shall be you!   535
Mix'd tussled hay of head, beard, brawn, it shall be you!
Trickling sap of maple, fibre of manly wheat, it shall be you!
Suns so generous it shall be you!
Vapors lighting and shading my face it shall be you!

---

7. Sharp blade attached to a plow to cut the ground in advance of the plow-share.

8. Act of cultivation or tillage of the soil.

You sweaty brooks and dews it shall be you! 540
Winds whose soft-tickling genitals rub against me it shall be you!
Broad muscular fields, branches of live oak, loving lounger in my
    winding paths, it shall be you!
Hands I have taken, face I have kiss'd, mortal I have ever touch'd,
    it shall be you.

I dote on myself, there is that lot of me and all so luscious,
Each moment and whatever happens thrills me with joy, 545
I cannot tell how my ankles bend, nor whence the cause of my faint-
    est wish,
Nor the cause of the friendship I emit, nor the cause of the friend-
    ship I take again.

That I walk up my stoop, I pause to consider if it really be,
A morning-glory at my window satisfies me more than the meta-
    physics of books.

To behold the day-break! 550
The little light fades the immense and diaphanous shadows,
The air tastes good to my palate.

Hefts of the moving world at innocent gambols silently rising,
    freshly exuding,
Scooting obliquely high and low.

Something I cannot see puts upward libidinous prongs, 555
Seas of bright juice suffuse heaven.

The earth by the sky staid with, the daily close of their junction,
The heav'd challenge from the east that moment over my head,
The mocking taunt, See then whether you shall be master!

25

Dazzling and tremendous how quick the sun-rise would kill me, 560
If I could not now and always send sun-rise out of me.

We also ascend dazzling and tremendous as the sun,
We found our own O my soul in the calm and cool of the daybreak.

My voice goes after what my eyes cannot reach,
With the twirl of my tongue I encompass worlds and volumes of
    worlds. 565

Speech is the twin of my vision, it is unequal to measure itself,
It provokes me forever, it says sarcastically,
Walt you contain enough, why don't you let it out then?

Come now I will not be tantalized, you conceive too much of articu-
    lation,
Do you not know O speech how the buds beneath you are folded?

Waiting in gloom, protected by frost,   571
The dirt receding before my prophetical screams,
I underlying causes to balance them at last,
My knowledge my live parts, it keeping tally with the meaning of
    all things,
Happiness, (which whoever hears me let him or her set out in
    search of this day.)   575

My final merit I refuse you, I refuse putting from me what I really
    am,
Encompass worlds, but never try to encompass me,
I crowd your sleekest and best by simply looking toward you.

Writing and talk do not prove me,
I carry the plenum[9] of proof and every thing else in my face,   580
With the hush of my lips I wholly confound the skeptic.

                                        26
Now I will do nothing but listen,
To accrue what I hear into this song, to let sounds contribute
    toward it.

I hear bravuras of birds, bustle of growing wheat, gossip of flames,
    clack of sticks cooking my meals.
I hear the sound I love, the sound of the human voice,   585
I hear all sounds running together, combined, fused or following,
Sounds of the city and sounds out of the city, sounds of the day and
    night,
Talkative young ones to those that like them, the loud laugh of
    work-people at their meals,
The angry base of disjointed friendship, the faint tones of the sick,
The judge with hands tight to the desk, his pallid lips pronouncing
    a death-sentence,   590
The heave'e'yo of stevedores unlading ships by the wharves, the re-
    frain of the anchor-lifters,
The ring of alarm-bells, the cry of fire, the whirr of swift-streaking
    engines and hose-carts with premonitory tinkles and color'd
    lights,
The steam-whistle, the solid roll of the train of approaching cars,
The slow march play'd at the head of the association marching two
    and two,
(They go to guard some corpse, the flag-tops are draped with black
    muslin.)   595

I hear the violoncello, ('tis the young man's heart's complaint,)
I hear the key'd cornet, it glides quickly in through my ears,
It shakes mad-sweet pangs through my belly and breast.

9. Fullness.

I hear the chorus, it is a grand opera,
Ah this indeed is music—this suits me.   600

A tenor large and fresh as the creation fills me,
The orbic flex of his mouth is pouring and filling me full.

I hear the train'd soprano (what work with hers is this?)
The orchestra whirls me wider than Uranus[1] flies,
It wrenches such ardors from me I did not know I possess'd them,
It sails me, I dab with bare feet, they are lick'd by the indolent
    waves,   606
I am cut by bitter and angry hail, I lose my breath,
Steep'd amid honey'd morphine, my windpipe throttled in fakes[2] of
    death,
At length let up again to feel the puzzle of puzzles,
And that we call Being.   610

27

To be in any form, what is that?
(Round and round we go, all of us, and ever come back thither,)
If nothing lay more develop'd the quahaug[3] in its callous shell were
    enough.

Mine is no callous shell,
I have instant conductors all over me whether I pass or stop,   615
They seize every object and lead it harmlessly through me.

I merely stir, press, feel with my fingers, and am happy,
To touch my person to some one else's is about as much as I can
    stand.

28

Is this then a touch? quivering me to a new identity,
Flames and ether making a rush for my veins,   620
Treacherous tip of me reaching and crowding to help them,
My flesh and blood playing out lightning to strike what is hardly
    different from myself,
On all sides prurient provokers stiffening my limbs,
Straining the udder of my heart for its withheld drip,
Behaving licentious toward me, taking no denial,   625
Depriving me of my best as for a purpose,
Unbuttoning my clothes, holding me by the bare waist,
Deluding my confusion with the calm of the sunlight and pasture-
    fields,
Immodestly sliding the fellow-senses away,

---

1. The seventh major planet; in Greek mythology the personification of Heaven.

2. A nautical term for the windings of a coiled cable or hawser.
3. An edible Atlantic-coast clam.

They bribed to swap off with touch and go and graze at the edges
    of me,   630
No consideration, no regard for my draining strength or my anger,
Fetching the rest of the herd around to enjoy them a while,
Then all uniting to stand on a headland and worry me.
The sentries desert every other part of me,
They have left me helpless to a red marauder,   635
They all come to the headland to witness and assist against me.

I am given up by traitors,
I talk wildly, I have lost my wits, I and nobody else am the greatest
    traitor,
I went myself first to the headland, my own hands carried me
    there.

You villain touch! what are you doing? my breath is tight in its
    throat,   640
Unclench your floodgates, you are too much for me.

29

Blind loving wrestling touch, sheath'd hooded sharp-tooth'd touch!
Did it make you ache so, leaving me?

Parting track'd by arriving, perpetual payment of perpetual loan,
Rich showering rain, and recompense richer afterward.   645

Sprouts take and accumulate, stand by the curb prolific and vital,
Landscapes projected masculine, full-sized and golden.

30

All truths wait in all things,
They neither hasten their own delivery nor resist it,
They do not need the obstetric forceps of the surgeon,   650
The insignificant is as big to me as any,
(What is less or more than a touch?)

Logic and sermons never convince,
The damp of the night drives deeper into my soul.

(Only what proves itself to every man and woman is so,   655
Only what nobody denies is so.)

A minute and a drop of me settle my brain,
I believe the soggy clods shall become lovers and lamps,
And a compend of compends is the meat of a man or woman,
And a summit and flower there is the feeling they have for each
    other,   660
And they are to branch boundlessly out of that lesson until it be-
    comes omnific,
And until one and all shall delight us, and we them.

31

I believe a leaf of grass is no less than the journey-work of the stars,
And the pismire[4] is equally perfect, and a grain of sand, and the egg
of the wren,
And the tree-toad is a chef-d'œuvre for the highest,   665
And the running blackberry would adorn the parlors of heaven,
And the narrowest hinge in my hand puts to scorn all machinery,
And the cow crunching with depress'd head surpasses any statue,
And a mouse is miracle enough to stagger sextillions of infidels.

I find I incorporate gneiss, coal, long-threaded moss, fruits, grains,
esculent roots,   670
And am stucco'd with quadrupeds and birds all over,
And have distanced what is behind me for good reasons,
But call any thing back again when I desire it.

In vain the speeding or shyness,
In vain the plutonic rocks send their old heat against my approach,
In vain the mastodon retreats beneath its own powder'd bones,   676
In vain objects stand leagues off and assume manifold shapes,
In vain the ocean settling in hollows and the great monsters lying
low,
In vain the buzzard houses herself with the sky,
In vain the snake slides through the creepers and logs,   680
In vain the elk takes to the inner passes of the woods,
In vain the razor-bill'd auk sails far north to Labrador,
I follow quickly, I ascend to the nest in the fissure of the cliff.

32

I think I could turn and live with animals, they are so placid and
self-contain'd,
I stand and look at them long and long.   685

They do not sweat and whine about their condition,
They do not lie awake in the dark and weep for their sins,
They do not make me sick discussing their duty to God,
Not one is dissatisfied, not one is demented with the mania of
owning things,
Not one kneels to another, nor to his kind that lived thousands of
years ago,   690
Not one is respectable or unhappy over the whole earth.

So they show their relations to me and I accept them,
They bring me tokens of myself, they evince them plainly in their
possession.

4. An ant.

I wonder where they get those tokens,
Did I pass that way huge times ago and negligently drop them?   695

Myself moving forward then and now and forever,
Gathering and showing more always and with velocity,
Infinite and omnigenous, and the like of these among them,
Not too exclusive toward the reachers of my remembrancers,
Picking out here one that I love, and now go with him on brotherly
    terms.   700

A gigantic beauty of a stallion, fresh and responsive to my caresses,
Head high in the forehead, wide between the ears,
Limbs glossy and supple, tail dusting the ground,
Eyes full of sparkling wickedness, ears finely cut, flexibly moving.

His nostrils dilate as my heels embrace him,   705
His well-built limbs tremble with pleasure as we race around and
    return.
I but use you a minute, then I resign you, stallion,
Why do I need your paces when I myself out-gallop them?
Even as I stand or sit passing faster than you.

33

Space and Time! now I see it is true, what I guess'd at,   710
What I guess'd when I loaf'd on the grass,
What I guess'd while I lay alone in my bed,
And again as I walk'd the beach under the paling stars of the morn-
    ing.

My ties and ballasts leave me, my elbows rest in sea-gaps,
I skirt sierras, my palms cover continents,   715
I am afoot with my vision.

By the city's quadrangular houses—in log huts, camping with lum-
    bermen,
Along the ruts of the turnpike, along the dry gulch and rivulet bed,
Weeding my onion-patch or hoeing rows of carrots and parsnips,
    crossing savannas, trailing in forests,
Prospecting, gold-digging, girdling the trees of a new purchase,   720
Scorch'd ankle-deep by the hot sand, hauling my boat down the
    shallow river,
Where the panther walks to and fro on a limb overhead, where the
    buck turns furiously at the hunter,
Where the rattlesnake suns his flabby length on a rock, where the
    otter is feeding on fish,

Where the alligator in his tough pimples sleeps by the bayou,

Where the black bear is searching for roots or honey, where the
beaver pats the mud with his paddle-shaped tail;   725

Over the growing sugar, over the yellow-flower'd cotton plant, over
the rice in its low moist field,

Over the sharp-peak'd farmhouse, with its scallop'd scum and slender shoots from the gutters,

Over the western persimmon, over the long-leav'd corn, over the
delicate blue-flower flax,

Over the white and brown buckwheat, a hummer and buzzer there
with the rest,

Over the dusky green of the rye as it ripples and shades in the
breeze;   730

Scaling mountains, pulling myself cautiously up, holding on by low
scragged limbs,

Walking the path worn in the grass and beat through the leaves of
the brush,

Where the quail is whistling betwixt the woods and the wheat-lot,

Where the bat flies in the Seventh-month eve, where the great gold-
bug drops through the dark,

Where the brook puts out of the roots of the old tree and flows to
the meadow,   735

Where cattle stand and shake away flies with the tremulous shuddering of their hides,

Where the cheese-cloth hangs in the kitchen, where andirons strad-
dle the hearth-slab, where cobwebs fall in festoons from the
rafters;

Where trip-hammers crash, where the press is whirling its cylin-
ders,

Where the human heart beats with terrible throes under its ribs,

Where the pear-shaped balloon is floating aloft, (floating in it myself and looking composedly down,)   740

Where the life-car[5] is drawn on the slip-noose, where the heat
hatches pale-green eggs in the dented sand,

Where the she-whale swims with her calf and never forsakes it,

Where the steam-ship trails hind-ways its long pennant of smoke,

Where the fin of the shark cuts like a black chip out of the water,

Where the half-burn'd brig is riding on unknown currents,   745

Where shells grow to her slimy deck, where the dead are corrupting
below;

Where the dense-starr'd flag is borne at the head of the regiments,

Approaching Manhattan up by the long-stretching island,

Under Niagara, the cataract falling like a veil over my countenance,

---

5. Watertight vessel moved by ropes to rescue people from wrecked ships.

Upon a door-step, upon the horse-block of hard wood outside,   750
Upon the race-course, or enjoying picnics or jigs or a good game of
    base-ball,
At he-festivals, with blackguard jibes, ironical license, bull-dances,[6]
    drinking, laughter,
At the cider-mill tasting the sweets of the brown mash, sucking the
    juice through a straw,
At apple-peelings wanting kisses for all the red fruit I find,
At musters, beach-parties, friendly bees, huskings, house-raisings;
Where the mocking-bird sounds his delicious gurgles, cackles,
    screams, weeps,   756
Where the hay-rick stands in the barn-yard, where the dry-stalks are
    scatter'd, where the brood-cow waits in the hovel,
Where the bull advances to do his masculine work, where the stud
    to the mare, where the cock is treading the hen,
Where the heifers browse, where geese nip their food with short
    jerks,
Where sun-down shadows lengthen over the limitless and lonesome
    prairie,   760
Where herds of buffalo make a crawling spread of the square miles
    far and near,
Where the humming-bird shimmers, where the neck of the long-
    lived swan is curving and winding,
Where the laughing-gull scoots by the shore, where she laughs her
    near-human laugh,
Where bee-hives range on a gray bench in the garden half hid by
    the high weeds,
Where band-neck'd partridges roost in a ring on the ground with
    their heads out,   765
Where burial coaches enter the arch'd gates of a cemetery,
Where winter wolves bark amid wastes of snow and icicled trees,
Where the yellow-crown'd heron comes to the edge of the marsh at
    night and feeds upon small crabs,
Where the splash of swimmers and divers cools the warm noon,
Where the katy-did works her chromatic reed on the walnut-tree
    over the well,   770
Through patches of citrons and cucumbers with silver-wired leaves,
Through the salt-lick or orange glade, or under conical firs,
Through the gymnasium, through the curtain'd saloon, through the
    office or public hall;
Pleas'd with the native and pleas'd with the foreign, pleas'd with
    the new and old,
Pleas'd with the homely woman as well as the handsome,   775

6. Slang, derived from "buffalo dance," originally danced by Indians.

Pleas'd with the quakeress as she puts off her bonnet and talks
    melodiously,
Pleas'd with the tune of the choir of the whitewash'd church,
Pleas'd with the earnest words of the sweating Methodist preacher,
    impress'd seriously at the camp-meeting;
Looking in at the shop-windows of Broadway the whole forenoon,
    flatting the flesh of my nose on the thick plate glass,
Wandering the same afternoon with my face turn'd up to the
    clouds, or down a lane or along the beach,   780
My right and left arms round the sides of two friends, and I in the
    middle;
Coming home with the silent and dark-cheek'd bush-boy, (behind
    me he rides at the drape of the day,)
Far from the settlements studying the print of animals' feet, or the
    moccasin print,
By the cot in the hospital reaching lemonade to a feverish patient,
Nigh the coffin'd corpse when all is still, examining with a candle;
Voyaging to every port to dicker and adventure,   786
Hurrying with the modern crowd as eager and fickle as any,
Hot toward one I hate, ready in my madness to knife him,
Solitary at midnight in my back yard, my thoughts gone from me a
    long while,
Walking the old hills of Judæa with the beautiful gentle God by my
    side,   790
Speeding through space, speeding through heaven and the stars,
Speeding amid the seven satellites and the broad ring, and the
    diameter of eighty thousand miles,
Speeding with tail'd meteors, throwing fire-balls like the rest,
Carrying the crescent child that carries its own full mother in its
    belly,
Storming, enjoying, planning, loving, cautioning,   795
Backing and filling, appearing and disappearing,
I tread day and night such roads.

I visit the orchards of spheres and look at the product,
And look at quintillions ripen'd and look at quintillions green.

I fly those flights of a fluid and swallowing soul,   800
My course runs below the soundings of plummets.

I help myself to material and immaterial,
No guard can shut me off, no law prevent me.

I anchor my ship for a little while only,
My messengers continually cruise away or bring their returns to
    me.   805

I go hunting polar furs and the seal, leaping chasms with a pike-
pointed staff, clinging to topples of brittle and blue.

I ascend to the foretruck,
I take my place late at night in the crow's-nest,
We sail the arctic sea, it is plenty light enough,
Through the clear atmosphere I stretch around on the wonderful
beauty,   810
The enormous masses of ice pass me and I pass them, the scenery is
plain in all directions,
The white-topt mountains show in the distance, I fling out my
fancies toward them,
We are approaching some great battle-field in which we are soon to
be engaged,
We pass the colossal outposts of the encampment, we pass with still
feet and caution,
Or we are entering by the suburbs some vast and ruin'd city,   815
The blocks and fallen architecture more than all the living cities of
the globe.

I am a free companion, I bivouac by invading watchfires,
I turn the bridegroom out of bed and stay with the bride myself,
I tighten her all night to my thighs and lips.

My voice is the wife's voice, the screech by the rail of the stairs, 820
They fetch my man's body up dripping and drown'd.

I understand the large hearts of heroes,
The courage of present times and all times,
How the skipper saw the crowded and rudderless wreck of the
steamship, and Death chasing it up and down the storm,
How he knuckled tight and gave not back an inch, and was faithful
of days and faithful of nights,   825
And chalk'd in large letters on a board, *Be of good cheer, we will
not desert you;*
How he follow'd with them and tack'd with them three days and
would not give it up,
How he saved the drifting company at last,
How the lank loose-gown'd women look'd when boated from the
side of their prepared graves,
How the silent old-faced infants and the lifted sick, and the sharp-
lipp'd unshaved men;   830
All this I swallow, it tastes good, I like it well, it becomes mine,
I am the man, I suffer'd, I was there.
The disdain and calmness of martyrs,

The mother of old, condemn'd for a witch, burnt with dry wood,
    her children gazing on,
The hounded slave that flags in the race, leans by the fence, blow-
    ing, cover'd with sweat,   835
The twinges that sting like needles his legs and neck, the murderous
    buckshot and the bullets,
All these I feel or am.

I am the hounded slave, I wince at the bite of the dogs,
Hell and despair are upon me, crack and again crack the marksmen,
I clutch the rails of the fence, my gore dribs, thinn'd with the ooze
    of my skin,   840
I fall on the weeds and stones,
The riders spur their unwilling horses, haul close,
Taunt my dizzy ears and beat me violently over the head with
    whipstocks.

Agonies are one of my changes of garments.
I do not ask the wounded person how he feels, I myself become the
    wounded person,   845
My hurts turn livid upon me as I lean on a cane and observe.

I am the mash'd fireman with breast-bone broken,
Tumbling walls buried me in their debris,
Heat and smoke I inspired, I heard the yelling shouts of my
    comrades,
I heard the distant click of their picks and shovels,   850
They have clear'd the beams away, they tenderly lift me forth.

I lie in the night air in my red shirt, the pervading hush is for my
    sake,
Painless after all I lie exhausted but not so unhappy,
White and beautiful are the faces around me, the heads are bared of
    their fire-caps,
The kneeling crowd fades with the light of the torches.   855

Distant and dead resuscitate,
They show as the dial or move as the hands of me, I am the clock
    myself.

I am an old artillerist, I tell of my fort's bombardment,
I am there again.

Again the long roll of the drummers,   860
Again the attacking cannon, mortars,
Again to my listening ears the cannon responsive.

I take part, I see and hear the whole,
The cries, curses, roar, the plaudits for well-aim'd shots,
The ambulanza slowly passing trailing its red drip,   865
Workmen searching after damages, making indispensable repairs,
The fall of grenades through the rent roof, the fan-shaped explosion,
The whizz of limbs, heads, stone, wood, iron, high in the air.

Again gurgles the mouth of my dying general, he furiously waves
     with his hand,
He gasps through the clot *Mind not me—mind—the entrench-*
     ments.   870

34

Now I tell what I know in Texas in my early youth,
(I tell not the fall of Alamo,[7]
Not one escaped to tell the fall of Alamo,
The hundred and fifty are dumb yet at Alamo,)
'Tis the tale of the murder in cold blood of four hundred and
     twelve young men.[8]   875

Retreating they had form'd in a hollow square with their baggage
     for breastworks,
Nine hundred lives out of the surrounding enemy's, nine times their
     number, was the price they took in advance,
Their colonel was wounded and their ammunition gone,
They treated for an honorable capitulation, receiv'd writing and
     seal, gave up their arms and march'd back prisoners of war.

They were the glory of the race of rangers,   880
Matchless with horse, rifle, song, supper, courtship,
Large, turbulent, generous, handsome, proud, and affectionate,
Bearded, sunburnt, drest in the free costume of hunters,
Not a single one over thirty years of age.

The second First-day[9] morning they were brought out in squads and
     massacred, it was beautiful early summer,   885
The work commenced about five o'clock and was over by eight.

None obey'd the command to kneel,
Some made a mad and helpless rush, some stood stark and straight,
A few fell at once, shot in the temple or heart, the living and dead
     lay together,

7. A mission converted into a fort at San Antonio, where the Texas garrison of 180 was annihilated by four thousand Mexicans (March 6, 1836).
8. The massacre of Colonel James W. Fannin and his troops at Goliad on March 27, 1836. "Goliad" like "the Alamo" became a rallying cry for Texans in their fight for independence.
9. Quaker term for Sunday.

The maim'd and mangled dug in the dirt, the new-comers saw them
    there,   890
Some half-kill'd attempted to crawl away,
These were despatch'd with bayonets or batter'd with the blunts of
    muskets.
A youth not seventeen years old seiz'd his assassin till two more
    came to release him,
The three were all torn and cover'd with the boy's blood.

At eleven o'clock began the burning of the bodies;   895
That is the tale of the murder of the four hundred and twelve young
    men.

35

Would you hear of an old-time sea-fight?
Would you learn who won by the light of the moon and stars?
List to the yarn, as my grandmother's father the sailor told it to
    me.[1]

Our foe was no skulk in his ship I tell you, (said he,)   900
His was the surly English pluck, and there is no tougher or truer,
    and never was, and never will be;
Along the lower'd eve he came horribly raking us.

We closed with him, the yards entangled, the cannon touch'd,
My captain lash'd fast with his own hands.

We had receiv'd some eighteen pound shots under the water,   905
On our lower-gun-deck two large pieces had burst at the first fire,
    killing all around and blowing up overhead.

Fighting at sun-down, fighting at dark,
Ten o'clock at night, the full moon well up, our leaks on the gain,
    and five feet of water reported,
The master-at-arms loosing the prisoners confined in the after-hold
    to give them a chance for themselves.

The transit to and from the magazine is now stopt by the sen-
    tinels,   910
They see so many strange·faces they do not know whom to trust.

Our frigate takes fire,
The other asks if we demand quarter?
If our colors are struck and the fighting done?

1. The victory of John Paul Jones, commanding the *Bonhomme Richard*, over the British frigate *Serapis* in the North Sea during the American Revolution (September 23, 1779).

Now I laugh content, for I hear the voice of my little captain,   915
We have not struck, he composedly cries, *we have just begun our part of the fighting.*

Only three guns are in use,
One is directed by the captain himself against the enemy's main-mast,
Two well serv'd with grape and canister silence his musketry and clear his decks.

The tops alone second the fire of this little battery, especially the main-top,   920
They hold out bravely during the whole of the action.

Not a moment's cease,
The leaks gain fast on the pumps, the fire eats toward the powder-magazine.

One of the pumps has been shot away, it is generally thought we are sinking.

Serene stands the little captain,   925
He is not hurried, his voice is neither high nor low,
His eyes give more light to us than our battle-lanterns.

Toward twelve there in the beams of the moon they surrender to us.

36

Stretch'd and still lies the midnight,
Two great hulls motionless on the breast of the darkness,   930
Our vessel riddled and slowly sinking, preparations to pass to the one we have conquer'd,
The captain on the quarter-deck coldly giving his orders through a countenance white as a sheet,
Near by the corpse of the child that serv'd in the cabin,
The dead face of an old salt with long white hair and carefully curl'd whiskers,
The flames spite of all that can be done flickering aloft and below,
The husky voices of the two or three officers yet fit for duty,   936
Formless stacks of bodies and bodies by themselves, dabs of flesh upon the masts and spars,
Cut of cordage, dangle of rigging, slight shock of the soothe of waves,
Black and impassive guns, litter of powder-parcels, strong scent,
A few large stars overhead, silent and mournful shining,   940
Delicate sniffs of sea-breeze, smells of sedgy grass and fields by the

shore, death-messages given in charge to survivors,
The hiss of the surgeon's knife, the gnawing teeth of his saw,
Wheeze, cluck, swash of falling blood, short wild scream, and long,
    dull, tapering groan,
These so, these irretrievable.

37

You laggards there on guard! look to your arms!   945
In at the conquer'd doors they crowd! I am possess'd!
Embody all presences outlaw'd or suffering,
See myself in prison shaped like another man.
And feel the dull unintermitted pain.

For me the keepers of convicts shoulder their carbines and keep
    watch.   950
It is I let out in the morning and barr'd at night.

Not a mutineer walks handcuff'd to jail but I am handcuff'd to him
    and walk by his side,
(I am less the jolly one there, and more the silent one with sweat
    on my twitching lips.)

Not a youngster is taken for larceny but I go up too, and am tried
    and sentenced.

Not a cholera patient lies at the last gasp but I also lie at the last
    gasp,   955
My face is ash-color'd, my sinews gnarl, away from me people
    retreat.

Askers embody themselves in me and I am embodied in them,
I project my hat, sit shame-faced, and beg.

38

Enough! enough! enough!
Some how I have been stunn'd. Stand back!   960
Give me a little time beyond my cuff'd head, slumbers, dreams,
    gaping,
I discover myself on the verge of a usual mistake.

That I could forget the mockers and insults!
That I could forget the trickling tears and the blows of the bludg-
    eons and hammers!
That I could look with a separate look on my own crucifixion and
    bloody crowning!   965

I remember now,
I resume the overstaid fraction,
The grave of rock multiplies what has been confided to it, or to any
    graves,
Corpses rise, gashes heal, fastenings roll from me.

I troop forth replenish'd with supreme power, one of an average
    unending procession,   970
Inland and sea-coast we go, and pass all boundary lines,
Our swift ordinances on their way over the whole earth,
The blossoms we wear in our hats the growth of thousands of years.

Eleves,[2] I salute you! come forward!
Continue your annotations, continue your questionings.   975

39

The friendly and flowing savage, who is he?
Is he waiting for civilization, or past it and mastering it?

Is he some Southwesterner rais'd out-doors? is he Kanadian?
Is he from the Mississippi country? Iowa, Oregon, California?
The mountains? prairie-life, bush-life? or sailor from the sea?   980

Wherever he goes men and women accept and desire him,
They desire he should like them, touch them, speak to them, stay
    with them.

Behavior lawless as snow-flakes, words simple as grass, uncomb'd
    head, laughter, and naiveté,
Slow-stepping feet, common features, common modes and emana-
    tions,
They descend in new forms from the tips of his fingers,   985
They are wafted with the odor of his body or breath, they fly out of
    the glance of his eyes.

40

Flaunt of the sunshine I need not your bask—lie over!
You light surfaces only, I force surfaces and depths also.

Earth! you seem to look for something at my hands,
Say, old top-knot, what do you want?   990

Man or woman, I might tell how I like you, but cannot,
And might tell what it is in me and what it is in you, but cannot,
And might tell that pining I have, that pulse of my nights and days.

2. Pupils or disciples.

Behold, I do not give lectures or a little charity,
When I give I give myself.   995

You there, impotent, loose in the knees,
Open your scarf'd chops till I blow grit within you,
Spread your palms and lift the flaps of your pockets,
I am not to be denied, I compel, I have stores plenty and to spare,
And any thing I have I bestow.   1000

I do not ask who you are, that is not important to me,
You can do nothing and be nothing but what I will infold you.

To cotton-field drudge or cleaner of privies I lean,
On his right cheek I put the family kiss,
And in my soul I swear I never will deny him.   1005

On women fit for conception I start bigger and nimbler babes,
(This day I am jetting the stuff of far more arrogant republics.)

To any one dying, thither I speed and twist the knob of the door,
Turn the bed-clothes toward the foot of the bed,
Let the physician and the priest go home.   1010

I seize the descending man and raise him with resistless will,
O despairer, here is my neck,
By God, you shall not go down! hang your whole weight upon me.

I dilate you with tremendous breath, I buoy you up,
Every room of the house do I fill with an arm'd force,   1015
Lovers of me, bafflers of graves.

Sleep—I and they keep guard all night,
Not doubt, not disease shall dare to lay finger upon you,
I have embraced you, and henceforth possess you to myself,
And when you rise in the morning you will find what I tell you is
    so.   1020

41

I am he bringing help for the sick as they pant on their backs,
And for strong upright men I bring yet more needed help.

I heard what was said of the universe,
Heard it and heard it of several thousand years;
It is middling well as far as it goes—but is that all?   1025

Magnifying and applying come I,

Outbidding at the start the old cautious hucksters,[3]

Taking myself the exact dimensions of Jehovah,

Lithographing Kronos, Zeus his son, and Hercules his grandson,

Buying drafts of Osiris, Isis, Belus, Brahma, Buddha,   1030

In my portfolio placing Manito loose, Allah on a leaf, the crucifix engraved,

With Odin and the hideous-faced Mexitli and every idol and image,[4]

Taking them all for what they are worth and not a cent more,

Admitting they were alive and did the work of their days,

(They bore mites as for unfledg'd birds who have now to rise and fly and sing for themselves,)   1035

Accepting the rough deific sketches to fill out better in myself, bestowing them freely on each man and woman I see,

Discovering as much or more in a framer framing a house,

Putting higher claims for him there with his roll'd-up sleeves driving the mallet and chisel,

Not objecting to special revelations, considering a curl of smoke or a hair on the back of my hand just as curious as any revelation,

Lads ahold of fire-engines and hook-and-ladder ropes no less to me than the gods of the antique wars,   1040

Minding their voices peal through the crash of destruction,

Their brawny limbs passing safe over charr'd laths, their white foreheads whole and unhurt out of the flames;

By the mechanic's wife with her babe at her nipple interceding for every person born,

Three scythes at harvest whizzing in a row from three lusty angels with shirts bagg'd out at their waists,

The snag-tooth'd hostler with red hair redeeming sins past and to come,   1045

Selling all he possesses, traveling on foot to fee lawyers for his brother and sit by him while he is tried for forgery;

What was strewn in the amplest strewing the square rod about me, and not filling the square rod then,

The bull and the bug never worshipp'd half enough,

Dung and dirt more admirable than was dream'd,

The supernatural of no account, myself waiting my time to be one of the supremes,   1050

The day getting ready for me when I shall do as much good as the

3. Contemptuous term for broker or middleman.
4. Whitman hoped for a universal religion, embracing aspects of all faiths. In these lines he has listed deities from various religions and mythologies: Hebraic (Jehovah), Greek (Kronos, Zeus, Hercules), Egyptian (Osiris, Isis), Babylonian (Belus), Hindu (Brahma), Buddhist (Buddha), American Indian (Manito), Islamic (Allah), Norse (Odin), and Aztec (Mexitli).

best, and be as prodigious;
By my life-lumps! becoming already a creator,
Putting myself here and now to the ambush'd womb of the
shadows.

42

A call in the midst of the crowd,
My own voice, orotund sweeping and final.   1055

Come my children,
Come my boys and girls, my women, household and intimates,
Now the performer launches his nerve, he has pass'd his prelude on
the reeds within.

Easily written loose-finger'd chords—I feel the thrum of your climax
and close.

My head slues round on my neck,   1060
Music rolls, but not from the organ,
Folks are around me, but they are no household of mine.

Ever the hard unsunk ground,
Ever the eaters and drinkers, ever the upward and downward sun,
ever the air and the ceaseless tides,
Ever myself and my neighbors, refreshing, wicked, real,   1065
Ever the old inexplicable query, ever that thorn'd thumb, that
breath of itches and thirsts,
Ever the vexer's *hoot! hoot!* till we find where the sly one hides and
bring him forth,
Ever love, ever the sobbing liquid of life,
Ever the bandage under the chin, ever the trestles of death.

Here and there with dimes on the eyes walking,   1070
To feed the greed of the belly the brains liberally spooning,
Tickets buying, taking, selling, but in to the feast never once going,
Many sweating, ploughing, thrashing, and then the chaff for pay-
ment receiving,
A few idly owning, and they the wheat continually claiming.

This is the city and I am one of the citizens,   1075
Whatever interests the rest interests me, politics, wars, markets,
newspapers, schools,
The mayor and councils, banks, tariffs, steamships, factories, stocks,
stores, real estate and personal estate.

The little plentiful manikins skipping around in collars and tail'd
    coats,
I am aware who they are, (they are positively not worms or fleas,)
I acknowledge the duplicates of myself, the weakest and shallowest
    is deathless with me,   1080
What I do and say the same waits for them,
Every thought that flounders in me the same flounders in them.

I know perfectly well my own egotism,
Know my omnivorous lines and must not write any less,
And would fetch you whoever you are flush with myself.   1085

Not words of routine this song of mine,
But abruptly to question, to leap beyond yet nearer bring;
This printed and bound book—but the printer and the printing-
    office boy?
The well-taken photographs—but your wife or friend close and solid
    in your arms?
The black ship mail'd with iron, her mighty guns in her turrets—
    but the pluck of the captain and engineers?   1090
In the houses the dishes and fare and furniture—but the host and
    hostess, and the look out of their eyes?
The sky up there—yet here or next door, or across the way?
The saints and sages in history—but you yourself?
Sermons, creeds, theology—but the fathomless human brain,
And what is reason? and what is love? and what is life?   1095

43

I do not despise you priests, all time, the world over,
My faith is the greatest of faiths and the least of faiths,
Enclosing worship ancient and modern and all between ancient
    and modern,
Believing I shall come again upon the earth after five thousand
    years,
Waiting responses from oracles, honoring the gods, saluting the sun,
Making a fetish of the first rock or stump, powowing with sticks in
    the circle of obis,   1101
Helping the llama or brahmin as he trims the lamps of the idols,
Dancing yet through the streets in a phallic procession, rapt and
    austere in the woods a gymnosophist,
Drinking mead from the skull-cup, to Shastas and Vedas[5] admirant,
    minding the Koran,

5. Shastas (properly "shastras") are the books of instructions, the Vedas the most ancient sacred writings, of Hindu religion.

Walking the teokallis,[6] spotted with gore from the stone and knife,
    beating the serpent-skin drum,   1105
Accepting the Gospels, accepting him that was crucified, knowing
    assuredly that he is divine,
To the mass kneeling or the puritan's prayer rising, or sitting
    patiently in a pew,
Ranting and frothing in my insane crisis, or waiting dead-like till
    my spirit arouses me,
Looking forth on pavement and land, or outside of pavement and
    land,
Belonging to the winders of the circuit of circuits.   1110

One of that centripetal and centrifugal gang I turn and talk like a
    man leaving charges before a journey.

Down-hearted doubters dull and excluded,
Frivolous, sullen, moping, angry, affected, dishearten'd, atheistical,
I know every one of you, I know the sea of torment, doubt, despair
    and unbelief.

How the flukes splash!   1115
How they contort rapid as lightning, with spasms and spouts of
    blood!

Be at peace bloody flukes of doubters and sullen mopers,
I take my place among you as much as among any,
The past is the push of you, me, all, precisely the same,
And what is yet untried and afterward is for you, me, all precisely
    the same.   1120

I do not know what is untried and afterward,
But I know it will in its turn prove sufficient, and cannot fail.

Each who passes is consider'd, each who stops is consider'd, not a
    single one can it fail.

It cannot fail the young man who died and was buried,
Nor the young woman who died and was put by his side,   1125
Nor the little child that peep'd in at the door, and then drew back
    and was never seen again,
Nor the old man who has lived without purpose, and feels it with
    bitterness worse than gall,

6. Teocallis, ancient Aztec temples situated on terraced pyramids, up which the human sacrifices climbed to their doom.

Nor him in the poor house tubercled by rum and the bad disorder,
Nor the numberless slaughter'd and wreck'd, nor the brutish koboo[7]
    call'd the ordure of humanity,   1129
Nor the sacs merely floating with open mouths for food to slip in,
Nor any thing in the earth, or down in the oldest graves of the
    earth,
Nor any thing in the myriads of spheres, nor the myriads of
    myriads that inhabit them,
Nor the present, nor the least wisp that is known.

44

It is time to explain myself—let us stand up.

What is known I strip away,   1135
I launch all men and women forward with me into the Unknown.

The clock indicates the moment—but what does eternity indicate?

We have thus far exhausted trillions of winters and summers,
There are trillions ahead, and trillions ahead of them.

Births have brought us richness and variety,   1140
And other births will bring us richness and variety.

I do not call one greater and one smaller,
That which fills its period and place is equal to any.

Were mankind murderous or jealous upon you, my brother, my
    sister?
I am sorry for you, they are not murderous or jealous upon me,   1145
All has been gentle with me, I keep no account with lamentation,
(What have I to do with lamentation?)

I am an acme of things accomplish'd, and I an encloser of things to
    be.

My feet strike an apex of the apices of the stairs,
On every step bunches of ages, and larger bunches between the
    steps,   1150
All below duly travel'd, and still I mount and mount.

Rise after rise bow the phantoms behind me,
Afar down I see the huge first Nothing, I know I was even there,

7. Native of the Mariana Islands.

I waited unseen and always, and slept through the lethargic mist,
And took my time, and took no hurt from the fetid carbon.   1155

Long I was hugg'd close—long and long.

Immense have been the preparations for me,
Faithful and friendly the arms that have helped me.

Cycles ferried my cradle, rowing and rowing like cheerful boatmen,
For room to me stars kept aside in their own rings,   1160
They sent influences to look after what was to hold me.

Before I was born out of my mother generations guided me,
My embryo has never been torpid, nothing could overlay it.

For it the nebula cohered to an orb,
The long slow strata piled to rest it on,   1165
Vast vegetables gave it sustenance,
Monstrous sauroids transported it in their mouths and deposited it
    with care.[8]

All forces have been steadily employ'd to complete and delight me,
Now on this spot I stand with my robust soul.

45

O span of youth! ever-push'd elasticity.   1170
O manhood, balanced, florid and full.

My lovers suffocate me,
Crowding my lips, thick in the pores of my skin,
Jostling me through streets and public halls, coming naked to me at
    night,
Crying by day *Ahoy!* from the rocks of the river, swinging and chirp-
    ing over my head,   1175
Calling my name from flower-beds, vines, tangled underbrush,
Lighting on every moment of my life,
Bussing my body with soft balsamic busses,
Noiselessly passing handfuls out of their hearts and giving them to
    be mine.

Old age superbly rising! O welcome, ineffable grace of dying days!

8. *I.e.*, "Sauria"; mammoth reptiles, generally prehistoric. The idea that snakes carry their eggs in their mouths occurs in folklore.

Every condition promulges not only itself, it promulges what grows
    after and out of itself,   1181
And the dark hush promulges as much as any.

I open my scuttle at night and see the far-sprinkled systems,
And all I see multiplied as high as I can cipher edge but the rim of
    the farther systems.
Wider and wider they spread, expanding, always expanding,   1185
Outward and outward and forever outward.

My sun has his sun and round him obediently wheels,
He joins with his partners a group of superior circuit,
And greater sets follow, making specks of the greatest inside them.

There is no stoppage and never can be stoppage,   1190
If I, you, and the worlds, and all beneath or upon their surfaces,
    were this moment reduced back to a pallid float, it would not
    avail in the long run,
We should surely bring up again where we now stand,
And surely go as much farther, and then farther and farther.

A few quadrillions of eras, a few octillions of cubic leagues, do not ·
    hazard the span or make it impatient,
They are but parts, any thing is but a part.   1195

See ever so far, there is limitless space outside of that,
Count ever so much, there is limitless time around that.

My rendezvous is appointed, it is certain,
The Lord will be there and wait till I come on perfect terms,
The great Camerado, the lover true for whom I pine will be there.

46

I know I have the best of time and space, and was never measured
    and never will be measured.   1201

I tramp a perpetual journey, (come listen all!)
My signs are a rain-proof coat, good shoes, and a staff cut from the
    woods,
No friend of mine takes his ease in my chair,
I have no chair, no church, no philosophy,   1205
I lead no man to a dinner-table, library, exchange,
But each man and each woman of you I lead upon a knoll,
My left hand hooking you round the waist,
My right hand pointing to landscapes of continents and the public
    road.

Not I, not any one else can travel that road for you,   1210
You must travel it for yourself.

It is not far, it is within reach,
Perhaps you have been on it since you were born and did not know,
Perhaps it is everywhere on water and on land.

Shoulder your duds[9] dear son, and I will mine, and let us hasten
    forth,   1215
Wonderful cities and free nations we shall fetch as we go.

If you tire, give me both burdens, and rest the chuff of your hand
    on my hip,
And in due time you shall repay the same service to me,
For after we start we never lie by again.

This day before dawn I ascended a hill and look'd at the crowded
    heaven,   1220
And I said to my spirit *When we become the enfolders of those orbs,
    and the pleasure and knowledge of every thing in them, shall
    we be fill'd and satisfied then?*
And my spirit said *No, we but level that lift to pass and continue
    beyond.*

You are also asking me questions and I hear you,
I answer that I cannot answer, you must find out for yourself.

Sit a while dear son,   1225
Here are biscuits to eat and here is milk to drink,
But as soon as you sleep and renew yourself in sweet clothes, I kiss
    you with a good-by kiss and open the gate for your egress hence.

Long enough have you dream'd contemptible dreams,
Now I wash the gum from your eyes,
You must habit yourself to the dazzle of the light and of every mo-
    ment of your life.   1230

Long have you timidly waded holding a plank by the shore,
Now I will you to be a bold swimmer,
To jump off in the midst of the sea, rise again, nod to me, shout,
    and laughingly dash with your hair.

47

I am the teacher of athletes,
He that by me spreads a wider breast than my own proves the width
    of my own,   1235
He most honors my style who learns under it to destroy the teacher.

The boy I love, the same becomes a man not through derived power,
    but in his own right,
Wicked rather than virtuous out of conformity or fear,

9. A slang term for clothes.

Fond of his sweetheart, relishing well his steak,
Unrequited love or a slight cutting him worse than sharp steel cuts,
First-rate to ride, to fight, to hit the bull's eye, to sail a skiff, to sing
    a song or play on the banjo,   1241
Preferring scars and the beard and faces pitted with small-pox over
    all latherers,
And those well-tann'd to those that keep out of the sun.

I teach straying from me, yet who can stray from me?
I follow you whoever you are from the present hour,   1245
My words itch at your ears till you understand them.

I do not say these things for a dollar or to fill up the time while I
    wait for a boat,
(It is you talking just as much as myself, I act as the tongue of you,
Tied in your mouth, in mine it begins to be loosen'd.)

I swear I will never again mention love or death inside a house,   1250
And I swear I will never translate myself at all, only to him or her
    who privately stays with me in the open air.

If you would understand me go to the heights or water-shore,
The nearest gnat is an explanation, and a drop or motion of waves a
    key,
The maul, the oar, the hand-saw, second my words.

No shutter'd room or school can commune with me,   1255
But roughs and little children better than they.

The young mechanic is closest to me, he knows me well,
The woodman that takes his axe and jug with him shall take me
    with him all day,
The farm-boy ploughing in the field feels good at the sound of my
    voice,
In vessels that sail my words sail, I go with fishermen and seamen
    and love them.   1260

The soldier camp'd or upon the march is mine,
On the night ere the pending battle many seek me, and I do not fail
    them,
On that solemn night (it may be their last) those that know me seek
    me.

My face rubs to the hunter's face when he lies down alone in his
    blanket,
The driver thinking of me does not mind the jolt of his wagon,   1265
The young mother and old mother comprehend me,
The girl and the wife rest the needle a moment and forget where
    they are,
They and all would resume what I have told them.

48

I have said that the soul is not more than the body,
And I have said that the body is not more than the soul,   1270
And nothing, not God, is greater to one than one's self is,
And whoever walks a furlong without sympathy walks to his own
    funeral drest in his shroud,
And I or you pocketless of a dime may purchase the pick of the
    earth,
And to glance with an eye or show a bean in its pod confounds the
    learning of all times,
And there is no trade or employment but the young man following
    it may become a hero,   1275
And there is no object so soft but it makes a hub for the wheel'd
    universe,
And I say to any man or woman, Let your soul stand cool and com-
    posed before a million universes.

And I say to mankind, Be not curious about God,
For I who am curious about each am not curious about God,
(No array of terms can say how much I am at peace about God and
    about death.)   1280

I hear and behold God in every object, yet understand God not in
    the least,
Nor do I understand who there can be more wonderful than myself.

Why should I wish to see God better than this day?
I see something of God each hour of the twenty-four, and each
    moment then,
In the faces of men and women I see God, and in my own face in
    the glass,   1285
I find letters from God dropt in the street, and every one is sign'd by
    God's name,
And I leave them where they are, for I know that wheresoe'er I go
Others will punctually come for ever and ever.

49

And as to you Death, and you bitter hug of mortality, it is idle to
    try to alarm me.

To his work without flinching the accoucheur[1] comes,   1290
I see the elder-hand pressing receiving supporting,
I recline by the sills of the exquisite flexible doors,
And mark the outlet, and mark the relief and escape.

And as to you Corpse I think you are good manure, but that does
    not offend me,

---

1. Obstetrician, midwife.

I smell the white roses sweet-scented and growing.   1295
I reach to the leafy lips, I reach to the polish'd breasts of melons.

And as to you Life I reckon you are the leavings of many deaths,
(No doubt I have died myself ten thousand times before.)

I hear you whispering there O stars of heaven,
O suns—O grass of graves—O perpetual transfers and promotions,
If you do not say any thing how can I say any thing?   1301

Of the turbid pool that lies in the autumn forest,
Of the moon that descends the steeps of the soughing twilight,
Toss, sparkles of day and dusk—toss on the black stems that decay
     in the muck,
Toss to the moaning gibberish of the dry limbs.   1305

I ascend from the moon, I ascend from the night,
I perceive that the ghastly glimmer is noonday sunbeams reflected,
And debouch to the steady and central from the offspring great or
     small.

                              50
There is that in me—I do not know what it is—but I know it is in
     me.

Wrench'd and sweaty—calm and cool then my body becomes,   1310
I sleep—I sleep long.

I do not know it—it is without name—it is a word unsaid,
It is not in any dictionary, utterance, symbol.

Something it swings on more than the earth I swing on,
To it the creation is the friend whose embracing awakes me.   1315

Perhaps I might tell more. Outlines! I plead for my brothers and
     sisters.

Do you see O my brothers and sisters?
It is not chaos or death—it is form, union, plan—it is eternal life—
     it is Happiness.

                              51
The past and present wilt—I have fill'd them, emptied them,
And proceed to fill my next fold of the future.   1320

Listener up there! what have you to confide to me?
Look in my face while I snuff the sidle of evening,
(Talk honestly, no one else hears you, and I stay only a minute
     longer.)

Do I contradict myself?
Very well then I contradict myself,   1325
(I am large, I contain multitudes.)

I concentrate toward them that are nigh, I wait on the door-slab.

Who has done his day's work? who will soonest be through with his
 supper?
Who wishes to walk with me?

Will you speak before I am gone? will you prove already too late?

52

The spotted hawk swoops by and accuses me, he complains of my
 gab and my loitering. 1331

I too am not a bit tamed, I too am untranslatable,
I sound my barbaric yawp over the roofs of the world.

The last scud of day holds back for me,
It flings my likeness after the rest and true as any on the shadow'd
 wilds, 1335
It coaxes me to the vapor and the dusk.

I depart as air, I shake my white locks at the runaway sun,
I effuse my flesh in eddies, and drift it in lacy jags.

I bequeath myself to the dirt to grow from the grass I love,
If you want me again look for me under your boot-soles. 1340

You will hardly know who I am or what I mean,
But I shall be good health to you nevertheless,
And filter and fibre your blood.

Failing to fetch me at first keep encouraged,
Missing me one place search another, 1345
I stop somewhere waiting for you.

1855, 1881–1882

From CHILDREN OF ADAM
Out of the Rolling Ocean the Crowd

Out of the rolling ocean the crowd came a drop gently to me,
Whispering *I love you, before long I die,*
I have travel'd a long way merely to look on you to touch you,
For I could not die till I once look'd on you,
For I fear'd I might afterward lose you. 5

Now we have met, we have look'd, we are safe,
Return in peace to the ocean my love,
I too am part of that ocean my love, we are not so much separated,

Behold the great rondure, the cohesion of all, how perfect!
But as for me, for you, the irresistible sea is to separate us,   10
As for an hour carrying us diverse, yet cannot carry us diverse forever;
Be not impatient—a little space—know you I salute the air, the
     ocean and the land,
Every day at sundown for your dear sake my love.

                                                        1865, 1867

Once I Pass'd Through a Populous City

Once I pass'd through a populous city imprinting my brain for
     future use with its shows, architecture, customs, traditions,
Yet now of all that city I remember only a woman[1] I casually met
     there who detain'd me for love of me,
Day by day and night by night we were together—all else has long
     been forgotten by me,
I remember I say only that woman who passionately clung to me,
Again we wander, we love, we separate again,   5
Again she holds me by the hand, I must not go,
I see her close beside me with silent lips sad and tremulous.

                                                        1860, 1867

Facing West from California's Shores

Facing west from California's shores,
Inquiring, tireless, seeking what is yet unfound,
I, a child, very old, over waves, towards the house of maternity,[2] the
     land of migrations, look afar,
Look off the shores of my Western sea, the circle almost circled;
For starting westward from Hindustan, from the vales of Kashmere, 5
From Asia, from the north, from the God, the sage, and the hero,
From the south, from the flowery peninsulas and the spice islands,
Long having wander'd since, round the earth having wander'd,
Now I face home again, very pleas'd and joyous,
(But where is what I started for so long ago?   10
And why is it yet unfound?)

                                                        1860, 1867

As Adam Early in the Morning

As Adam early in the morning,
Walking forth from the bower refresh'd with sleep,
Behold me where I pass, hear my voice, approach,
Touch me, touch the palm of your hand to my body as I pass,
Be not afraid of my body.   5

                                                        1860, 1867

1. An early MS. of this poem shows "man" stricken out and "woman" substituted.

2. Asia interested Whitman as the supposed birthplace of the human race.

From CALAMUS[3]
For You O Democracy

Come, I will make the continent indissoluble,
I will make the most splendid race the sun ever shone upon,
I will make divine magnetic lands,
  With the love of comrades,
  With the life-long love of comrades.   5

I will plant companionship thick as trees along all the rivers of
  America, and along the shores of the great lakes, and all over
  the prairies,
I will make inseparable cities with their arms about each other's
  necks,
  By the love of comrades,
  By the manly love of comrades,

For you these from me, O Democracy, to serve you ma femme!   10
For you, for you I am trilling these songs.

              1860, 1881–1882

I Saw in Louisiana a Live-oak Growing

I saw in Louisiana a live-oak growing,
All alone stood it and the moss hung down from the branches,
Without any companion it grew there uttering joyous leaves of dark
  green,
And its look, rude, unbending, lusty, made me think of myself,
But I wonder'd how it could utter joyous leaves standing alone there
  without its friend near, for I knew I could not,   5
And I broke off a twig with a certain number of leaves upon it, and
  twined around it a little moss,
And brought it away, and I have placed it in sight in my room,
It is not needed to remind me as of my own dear friends,
(For I believe lately I think of little else than of them,)
Yet it remains to me a curious token, it makes me think of manly
  love;   10
For all that, and though the live-oak glistens there in Louisiana
  solitary in a wide flat space,
Uttering joyous leaves all its life without a friend a lover near,
I know very well I could not.

               1860, 1867

3. The "Calamus" poems first appeared in the third edition of *Leaves of Grass* (1860). The calamus, a species of water reed, sometimes appears in myth and literature, as it does here, as a symbol of male comradeship.

I Hear It Was Charged Against Me

I hear it was charged against me that I sought to destroy institutions,
But really I am neither for nor against institutions,
(What indeed have I in common with them? or what with the
    destruction of them?)
Only I will establish in the Mannahatta and in every city of these
    States inland and seaboard,
And in the fields and woods, and above every keel little or large that
    dents the water,   5
Without edifices or rules or trustees or any argument,
The institution of the dear love of comrades.

1860, 1867

Crossing Brooklyn Ferry[4]

1

Flood-tide below me! I see you face to face!
Clouds of the west—sun there half an hour high—I see you also
    face to face.

Crowds of men and women attired in the usual costumes, how
    curious you are to me!
On the ferry-boats the hundreds and hundreds that cross, returning
    home, are more curious to me than you suppose,
And you that shall cross from shore to shore years hence are more
    to me, and more in my meditations, than you might suppose. 5

2

The impalpable sustenance of me from all things at all hours of the
    day,
The simple, compact, well-join'd scheme, myself disintegrated, every
    one disintegrated yet part of the scheme,
The similitudes of the past and those of the future,
The glories strung like beads on my smallest sights and hearings,
    on the walk in the street and the passage over the river,
The current rushing so swiftly and swimming with me far away,   10
The others that are to follow me, the ties between me and them,
The certainty of others, the life, love, sight, hearing of others.

Others will enter the gates of the ferry and cross from shore to
    shore,
Others will watch the run of the flood-tide,
Others will see the shipping of Manhattan north and west, and the
    heights of Brooklyn to the south and east,   15
Others will see the islands large and small;

4. First called "Sun-Down Poem" in   (1856). This lyric was a favorite with
the second edition of *Leaves of Grass*   Thoreau.

Fifty years hence, others will see them as they cross, the sun half
an hour high,
A hundred years hence, or ever so many hundred years hence, others
will see them,
Will enjoy the sunset, the pouring-in of the flood-tide, the falling-
back to the sea of the ebb-tide.

3

It avails not, time nor place—distance avails not,   20
I am with you, you men and women of a generation, or ever so
many generations hence,
Just as you feel when you look on the river and sky, so I felt,
Just as any of you is one of a living crowd, I was one of a crowd,
Just as you are refresh'd by the gladness of the river and the bright
flow, I was refresh'd,
Just as you stand and lean on the rail, yet hurry with the swift cur-
rent, I stood yet was hurried,   25
Just as you look on the numberless masts of ships and the thick-
stemm'd pipes of steamboats, I look'd.

I too many and many a time cross'd the river of old,
Watched the Twelfth-month sea-gulls, saw them high in the air
floating with motionless wings, oscillating their bodies,
Saw how the glistening yellow lit up parts of their bodies and left
the rest in strong shadow,
Saw the slow-wheeling circles and the gradual edging toward the
south,   30
Saw the reflection of the summer sky in the water,
Had my eyes dazzled by the shimmering track of beams,
Look'd at the fine centrifugal spokes of light round the shape of
my head in the sunlit water,
Look'd on the haze on the hills southward and south-westward,
Look'd on the vapor as it flew in fleeces tinged with violet,   35
Look'd toward the lower bay to notice the vessels arriving,
Saw their approach, saw aboard those that were near me,
Saw the white sails of schooners and sloops, saw the ships at anchor,
The sailors at work in the rigging or out astride the spars,
The round masts, the swinging motion of the hulls, the slender
serpentine pennants,   40
The large and small steamers in motion, the pilots in their pilot-
houses,
The white wake left by the passage, the quick tremulous whirl of the
wheels,
The flags of all nations, the falling of them at sunset,
The scallop-edged waves in the twilight, the ladled cups, the frolic-
some crests and glistening,

The stretch afar growing dimmer and dimmer, the gray walls of the
    granite storehouses by the docks,   45
On the river the shadowy group, the big steam-tug closely flank'd on
    each side by the barges, the hay-boat, the belated lighter,
On the neighboring shore the fires from the foundry chimneys burn-
    ing high and glaringly into the night,
Casting their flicker of black contrasted with wild red and yellow
    light over the tops of houses, and down into the clefts of streets.

4

These and all else were to me the same as they are to you,
I loved well those cities, loved well the stately and rapid river,   50
The men and women I saw were all near to me,
Others the same—others who look back on me because I look'd
    forward to them,
(The time will come, though I stop here to-day and to-night.)

5

What is it then between us?
What is the count of the scores or hundreds of years between us? 55

Whatever it is, it avails not—distance avails not, and place avails
    not,
I too lived, Brooklyn of ample hills was mine,
I too walk'd the streets of Manhattan island, and bathed in the
    waters around it,
I too felt the curious abrupt questionings stir within me.
In the day among crowds of people sometimes they came upon
    me,   60
In my walks home late at night or as I lay in my bed they came upon
    me,
I too had been struck from the float forever held in solution,
I too had receiv'd identity by my body,
That I was I knew was of my body, and what I should be I knew I
    should be of my body.

6

It is not upon you alone the dark patches fall,   65
The dark threw its patches down upon me also,
The best I had done seem'd to me blank and suspicious,
My great thoughts as I supposed them, were they not in reality
    meagre?
Nor is it you alone who know what it is to be evil,
I am he who knew what it was to be evil,   70
I too knitted the old knot of contrariety,
Blabb'd, blush'd, resented, lied, stole, grudg'd,
Had guile, anger, lust, hot wishes I dared not speak,
Was wayward, vain, greedy, shallow, sly, cowardly, malignant,

The wolf, the snake, the hog, not wanting in me, 75
The cheating look, the frivolous word, the adulterous wish, not
    wanting,
Refusals, hates, postponements, meanness, laziness, none of these
    wanting,
Was one with the rest, the days and haps of the rest,
Was call'd by my nighest name by clear loud voices of young men
    as they saw me approaching or passing,
Felt their arms on my neck as I stood, or the negligent leaning of
    their flesh against me as I sat, 80
Saw many I loved in the street or ferry-boat or public assembly, yet
    never told them a word,
Lived the same life with the rest, the same old laughing, gnawing,
    sleeping,
Play'd the part that still looks back on the actor or actress,
The same old role, the role that is what we make it, as great as we
    like,
Or as small as we like, or both great and small. 85

7

Closer yet I approach you,
What thought you have of me now, I had as much of you—I laid
    in my stores in advance,
I consider'd long and seriously of you before you were born.

Who was to know what should come home to me?
Who knows but I am enjoying this? 90
Who knows, for all the distance, but I am as good as looking at
    you now, for all you cannot see me?

8

Ah, what can ever be more stately and admirable to me than mast-
    hemm'd Manhattan?
River and sunset and scallop-edg'd waves of flood-tide?
The sea-gulls oscillating their bodies, the hay-boat in the twilight,
    and the belated lighter?
What gods can exceed these that clasp me by the hand, and with
    voices I love call me promptly and loudly by my nighest name
    as I approach? 95

What is more subtle than this which ties me to the woman or man
    that looks in my face?
Which fuses me into you now, and pours my meaning into you?

We understand then do we not?
What I promis'd without mentioning it, have you not accepted?
What the study could not teach—what the preaching could not
    accomplish is accomplish'd, is it not? 100

9

Flow on, river! flow with the flood-tide, and ebb with the ebb-tide!
Frolic on, crested and scallop-edg'd waves!
Gorgeous clouds of the sunset! drench with your splendor me, or
    the men and women generations after me!
Cross from shore to shore, countless crowds of passengers!
Stand up, tall masts of Mannahatta![5] stand up, beautiful hills of
    Brooklyn!   105
Throb, baffled and curious brain! throw out questions and answers!
Suspend here and everywhere, eternal float of solution!
Gaze, loving and thirsting eyes, in the house or street or public
    assembly!
Sound out, voices of young men! loudly and musically call me by
    my nighest name!
Live, old life! play the part that looks back on the actor or actress! 110
Play the old role, the role that is great or small according as one
    makes it!
Consider, you who peruse me, whether I may not in unknown ways
    be looking upon you;
Be firm, rail over the river, to support those who lean idly, yet haste
    with the hasting current;
Fly on, sea-birds! fly sideways, or wheel in large circles high in the
    air;
Receive the summer sky, you water, and faithfully hold it till all
    downcast eyes have time to take it from you!   115
Diverge, fine spokes of light, from the shape of my head, or any
    one's head, in the sunlit water!
Come on, ships from the lower bay! pass up or down, white-sail'd
    schooners, sloops, lighters!
Flaunt away, flags of all nations! be duly lower'd at sunset!
Burn high your fires, foundry chimneys! cast black shadows at night-
    fall! cast red and yellow light over the tops of the houses!
Appearances, now or henceforth, indicate what you are,   120
You necessary film, continue to envelop the soul,
About my body for me, and your body for you, be hung our divinest
    aromas,
Thrive, cities—bring your freight, bring your shows, ample and
    sufficient rivers,
Expand, being than which none else is perhaps more spiritual,
Keep your places, objects than which none else is more lasting.   125

You have waited, you always wait, you dumb, beautiful ministers,
We receive you with free sense at last, and are insatiate hence-
    forward,

---

5. By using this name for Manhattan
Island, Whitman drew attention to its
Indian meaning—the dwelling of Man-
ito, the God. He also referred to Long
Island by its Indian name, Paumanok.

Not you any more shall be able to foil us, or withhold yourselves
    from us,
We use you, and do not cast you aside—we plant you permanently
    within us,
We fathom you not—we love you—there is perfection in you
    also,   130
You furnish your parts toward eternity,
Great or small, you furnish your parts toward the soul.

                          1856, 1881–1882

Song of the Redwood-Tree

1

A California song,
A prophecy and indirection, a thought impalpable to breathe as air,
A chorus of dryads, fading, departing, or hamadryads[6] departing,

A murmuring, fateful, giant voice, out of the earth and sky,
Voice of a mighty dying tree in the redwood forest dense.   5

Farewell my brethren,
Farewell O earth and sky, farewell ye neighboring waters,
My time has ended, my term has come.

Along the northern coast,
Just back from the rock-bound shore and the caves,   10
In the saline air from the sea in the Mendocino country,[7]
With the surge for base and accompaniment low and hoarse,
With crackling blows of axes sounding musically driven by strong
    arms,
Riven deep by the sharp tongues of the axes, there in the redwood
    forest dense,
I heard the mighty tree its death-chant chanting.   15

The choppers heard not, the camp shanties echoed not,
The quick-ear'd teamsters and chain and jack-screw men heard not,
As the wood-spirits came from their haunts of a thousand years to
    join the refrain,
But in my soul I plainly heard.

Murmuring out of its myriad leaves,   20
Down from its lofty top rising two hundred feet high,
Out of its stalwart trunk and limbs, out of its foot-thick bark,
That chant of the seasons and time, chant not of the past only but
    the future.

You untold life of me,
And all you venerable and innocent joys,   25

6. Wood nymphs.
7. A county in northwestern California on the Pacific Ocean; its ancient red-wood trees reach a height of two to three hundred feet.

Perennial hardy life of me with joys 'mid rain and many a summer
    sun,
And the white snows and night and the wild winds;
O the great patient rugged joys, my soul's strong joys unreck'd by
    man,
(For know I bear the soul befitting me, I too have consciousness,
    identity,
And all the rocks and mountains have, and all the earth,)   30
Joys of the life befitting me and brothers mine,
Our time, our term has come.

Nor yield we mournfully majestic brothers,
We who have grandly fill'd our time;
With Nature's calm content, with tacit huge delight,   35
We welcome what we wrought for through the past,
And leave the field for them.

For them predicted long,
For a superber race, they too to grandly fill their time,
For them we abdicate, in them ourselves ye forest kings!   40
In them these skies and airs, these mountain peaks, Shasta, Nevadas,
These huge precipitous cliffs, this amplitude, these valleys, far
    Yosemite,
To be in them absorb'd, assimilated.

Then to a loftier strain,
Still prouder, more ecstatic rose the chant,   **45**
As if the heirs, the deities of the West,
Joining with master-tongue bore part.

Not wan from Asia's fetiches,
Nor red from Europe's old dynastic slaughter-house,
(Area of murder-plots of thrones, with scent left yet of wars and
    scaffolds everywhere,)   50
But come from Nature's long and harmless throes, peacefully builded
    thence,
These virgin lands, lands of the Western shore,
To the new culminating man, to you, the empire new,
You promis'd long, we pledge, we dedicate.

You occult deep volitions,   55
You average spiritual manhood, purpose of all, pois'd on yourself,
    giving not taking law,
You womanhood divine, mistress and source of all, whence life and
    love and aught that comes from life and love,
You unseen moral essence of all the vast materials of America, (age
    upon age working in death the same as life,)

You that, sometimes known, oftener unknown, really shape and
  mould the New World, adjusting it to Time and Space,
You hidden national will lying in your abysms, conceal'd but ever
  alert,   60
You past and present purposes tenaciously pursued, may-be uncon-
  scious of yourselves,
Unswerv'd by all the passing errors, perturbations of the surface;
You vital, universal, deathless germs, beneath all creeds, arts, stat-
  utes, literatures,
Here build your homes for good, establish here, these areas entire,
  lands of the Western shore,
We pledge, we dedicate to you.   65

For man of you, your characteristic race,
Here may he hardy, sweet, gigantic grow, here tower proportionate
  to Nature,
Here climb the vast pure spaces unconfined, uncheck'd by wall or
  roof,
Here laugh with storm or sun, here joy, here patiently inure,
Here heed himself, unfold himself, (not others' formulas heed), here
  fill his time,   70
To duty fall, to aid, unreck'd at last,
To disappear, to serve.

Thus on the northern coast,
In the echo of teamsters' calls and the clinking chains, and the music
  of choppers' axes,
The falling trunk and limbs, the crash, the muffled shriek, the groan,
Such words combined from the redwood-tree, as of voices ecstatic,
  ancient and rustling,   76
The century-lasting, unseen dryads, singing, withdrawing,
All their recesses of forests and mountains leaving,
From the Cascade range to the Wasatch,[8] or Idaho far, or Utah,
To the deities of the modern henceforth yielding,   80
The chorus and indications, the vistas of coming humanity, the
  settlements, features all,
In the Mendocino woods I caught.

2

The flashing and golden pageant of California,
The sudden and gorgeous drama, the sunny and ample lands,
The long and varied stretch from Puget sound to Colorado south,   85
Lands bathed in sweeter, rarer, healthier air, valleys and mountain
  cliffs,

8. The Cascade Mountains, a northward continuation of the Sierra Nevada
range, run through Oregon and Washington; the Wasatch Mountains form
the backbone of the state of Utah.

The fields of Nature long prepared and fallow, the silent, cyclic
    chemistry,
The slow and steady ages plodding, the unoccupied surface ripen-
    ing, the rich ores forming beneath;
At last the New arriving, assuming, taking possession,
A swarming and busy race settling and organizing everywhere,   90
Ships coming in from the whole round world, and going out to the
    whole world,
To India and China and Australia and the thousand island para-
    dises of the Pacific,
Populous cities, the latest inventions, the steamers on the rivers, the
    railroads, with many a thrifty farm, with machinery,
And wool and wheat and the grape, and diggings of yellow gold.

3

But more in you than these, lands of the Western shore,   95
(These but the means, the implements, the standing-ground,)
I see in you, certain to come, the promise of thousands of years, till
    now deferr'd,
Promis'd to be fulfill'd, our common kind, the race.

The new society at last, proportionate to Nature,
In man of you, more than your mountain peaks or stalwart trees im-
    perial,   100
In woman more, far more, than all your gold or vines, or even vital
    air.

Fresh come, to a new world indeed, yet long prepared,
I see the genius of the modern, child of the real and ideal,
Clearing the ground for broad humanity, the true America, heir of
    the past so grand,
To build a grander future.   105

1874, 1881–1882

From Sea-Drift

Out of the Cradle Endlessly Rocking[9]

Out of the cradle endlessly rocking,
Out of the mocking-bird's throat, the musical shuttle,
Out of the Ninth-month[1] midnight,
Over the sterile sands and the fields beyond, where the child leaving
    his bed wander'd alone, bareheaded, barefoot,

9. "Out of the Cradle Endlessly Rocking" became the first poem in a section
entitled "Sea-Drift" in the 1881 edition
of *Leaves of Grass*. In the 1871 edition
this section was entitled "Sea-Shore
Memories." The sea provided inspiration for Whitman, who in these poems
hints at some of the major crises of his
life.
1. The Quaker designation for September may here also suggest the human
cycle of fertility and birth, in contrast
with "sterile sands" in the next line.

Down from the shower'd halo,   5
Up from the mystic play of shadows twining and twisting as if they
    were alive,
Out from the patches of briers and blackberries,
From the memories of the bird that chanted to me,
From your memories sad brother, from the fitful risings and fallings
    I heard,
From under that yellow half-moon late-risen and swollen as if with
    tears,   10
From those beginning notes of yearning and love there in the mist,
From the thousand responses of my heart never to cease,
From the myriad thence-arous'd words,
From the word stronger and more delicious than any,
From such as now they start the scene revisiting,   15
As a flock, twittering, rising, or overhead passing,
Borne hither, ere all eludes me, hurriedly,
A man, yet by these tears a little boy again,
Throwing myself on the sand, confronting the waves,
I, chanter of pains and joys, uniter of here and hereafter,   20
Taking all hints to use them, but swiftly leaping beyond them,
A reminiscence sing.

Once Paumanok,[2]
When the lilac-scent was in the air and Fifth-month grass was
    growing,
Up this seashore in some briers,   25
Two feather'd guests from Alabama, two together,
And their nest, and four light-green eggs spotted with brown,
And every day the he-bird to and fro near at hand,
And every day the she-bird crouch'd on her nest, silent, with bright
    eyes,
And every day I, a curious boy, never too close, never disturbing
    them,   30
Cautiously peering, absorbing, translating.

Shine! shine! shine!
Pour down your warmth, great sun!
While we bask, we two together.

Two together!   35
Winds blow south, or winds blow north,
Day come white, or night come black,
Home, or rivers and mountains from home,

2. Whitman liked the Indian name for Long Island; *cf.* the title "Starting from Paumanok" for a poem dealing with his origins and birthplace.

Singing all time, minding no time,
While we two keep together.[3]   40

Till of a sudden,
May-be kill'd, unknown to her mate,
One forenoon the she-bird crouch'd not on the nest,
Nor return'd that afternoon, nor the next,
Nor ever appear'd again.   45

And thenceforward all summer in the sound of the sea,
And at night under the full of the moon in calmer weather,
Over the hoarse surging of the sea,
Or flitting from brier to brier by day,
I saw, I heard at intervals the remaining one, the he-bird,   50
The solitary guest from Alabama.

Blow! blow! blow!
Blow up sea-winds along Paumanok's shore;
I wait and I wait till you blow my mate to me.

Yes, when the stars glisten'd,   55
All night long on the prong of a moss-scallop'd stake,
Down almost amid the slapping waves,
Sat the lone singer wonderful causing tears.

He call'd on his mate,
He pour'd forth the meanings which I of all men know.   60

Yes my brother I know,
The rest might not, but I have treasur'd every note,
For more than once dimly down to the beach gliding,
Silent, avoiding the moonbeams, blending myself with the shadows,
Recalling now the obscure shapes, the echoes, the sounds and sights
          after their sorts,   65
The white arms out in the breakers tirelessly tossing,
I, with bare feet, a child, the wind wafting my hair,
Listen'd long and long.

Listen'd to keep, to sing, now translating the notes,
Following you my brother.   70

Soothe! soothe! soothe!
Close on its wave soothes the wave behind,
And again another behind embracing and lapping, every one close,
But my love soothes not me, not me.

3. The mockingbird songs were altered for rhythmic verisimilitude in several editions subsequent to the magazine publication of 1859. Whitman, himself an ornithologist, had also the advice of his friend John Burroughs, the talented naturalist.

Low hangs the moon, it rose late,   75
It is lagging—O I think it is heavy with love, with love.

O madly the sea pushes upon the land,
With love, with love.

O night! do I not see my love fluttering out among the breakers?
What is that little black thing I see there in the white?   80

Loud! loud! loud!
Loud I call to you, my love!
High and clear I shoot my voice over the waves,
Surely you must know who is here, is here,
You must know who I am, my love.   85

Low-hanging moon!
What is that dusky spot in your brown yellow?
O it is the shape, the shape of my mate!
O moon do not keep her from me any longer.

Land! land! O land!   90
Whichever way I turn, O I think you could give me my mate back
*   again if you only would,*
For I am almost sure I see her dimly whichever way I look.

O rising stars!
Perhaps the one I want so much will rise, will rise with some of you.

O throat! O trembling throat!   95
Sound clearer through the atmosphere!
Pierce the woods, the earth,
Somewhere listening to catch you must be the one I want.

Shake out carols!
Solitary here, the night's carols!   100
Carols of lonesome love! death's carols!
Carols under that lagging, yellow, waning moon!
O under that moon where she droops almost down into the sea!
O reckless despairing carols.

But soft! sink low!   105
Soft! let me just murmur,
And do you wait a moment you husky-nois'd sea,
For somewhere I believe I heard my mate responding to me,
So faint, I must be still, be still to listen,
But not altogether still, for then she might not come immediately to
*   me.*   110

Hither my love!
Here I am! here!

With this just-sustain'd note I announce myself to you,
This gentle call is for you my love, for you.

Do not be decoy'd elsewhere,   115
That is the whistle of the wind, it is not my voice,
That is the fluttering, the fluttering of the spray,
Those are the shadows of leaves.

O darkness! O in vain!
O I am very sick and sorrowful.   120

O brown halo in the sky near the moon, drooping upon the sea!
O troubled reflection in the sea!
O throat! O throbbing heart!
And I singing uselessly, uselessly all the night.

O past! O happy life! O songs of joy!   125
In the air, in the woods, over fields,
Loved! loved! loved! loved! loved!
But my mate no more, no more with me!
We two together no more.

The aria sinking,   130
All else continuing, the stars shining,
The winds blowing, the notes of the bird continuous echoing,
With angry moans the fierce old mother incessantly moaning,
On the sands of Paumanok's shore gray and rustling,
The yellow half-moon enlarged, sagging down, drooping, the face of
    the sea almost touching,   135
The boy ecstatic, with his bare feet the waves, with his hair the at-
    mosphere dallying,
The love in the heart long pent, now loose, now at last tumultuously
    bursting,
The aria's[4] meaning, the ears, the soul, swiftly depositing,
The strange tears down the cheeks coursing,
The colloquy there, the trio, each uttering,   140
The undertone, the savage old mother incessantly crying,
To the boy's soul's questions sullenly timing, some drown'd secret
    hissing,
To the outsetting bard.

Demon or bird! (said the boy's soul,)
Is it indeed toward your mate you sing? or is it really to me?   145
For I, that was a child, my tongue's use sleeping, now I have heard
    you,
Now in a moment I know what I am for, I awake,

---

4. Robert Faner in *Whitman and the Opera* (1952) has shown Whitman's in-debtedness to opera forms in such poems as this.

And already a thousand singers, a thousand songs, clearer, louder and
    more sorrowful than yours,
A thousand warbling echoes have started to life within me, never
    to die.

O you singer solitary, singing by yourself, projecting me,   150
O solitary me listening, never more shall I cease perpetuating you,
Never more shall I escape, never more the reverberations,
Never more the cries of unsatisfied love be absent from me,
Never again leave me to be the peaceful child I was before what
    there in the night,
By the sea under the yellow and sagging moon,   155
The messenger there arous'd, the fire, the sweet hell within,
The unknown want, the destiny of me.

O give me the clew! (it lurks in the night here somewhere,)
O if I am to have so much, let me have more!

A word then, (for I will conquer it,)   160
The word final, superior to all,
Subtle, sent up—what is it?—I listen;
Are you whispering it, and have been all the time, you sea waves?
Is that it from your liquid rims and wet sands?

Whereto answering, the sea,   165
Delaying not, hurrying not,
Whisper'd me through the night, and very plainly before daybreak,
Lisp'd to me the low and delicious word death,
And again death, death, death, death,
Hissing melodious, neither like the bird nor like my arous'd child's
    heart,   170
But edging near as privately for me rustling at my feet,
Creeping thence steadily up to my ears and laving me softly all over,
Death, death, death, death, death.

Which I do not forget,
But fuse the song of my dusky demon and brother,   175
That he sang to me in the moonlight on Paumanok's gray beach,
With the thousand responsive songs at random,
My own songs awaked from that hour,
And with them the key, the word up from the waves,
The word of the sweetest song and all songs,   180
That strong and delicious word which, creeping to my feet,
(Or like some old crone rocking the cradle, swathed in sweet gar-
    ments, bending aside,)
The sea whisper'd me.

1859, 1881–1882

To the Man-of-War-Bird[5]

Thou who has slept all night upon the storm,
Waking renew'd on thy prodigous pinions,
(Burst the wild storm? above it thou ascended'st,
And rested on the sky, thy slave that cradled thee,)
Now a blue point, far, far in heaven floating,   5
As to the light emerging here on deck I watch thee,
(Myself a speck, a point on the world's floating vast.)

Far, far at sea,
After the night's fierce drifts have strewn the shore with wrecks,
With re-appearing day as now so happy and serene,   10
The rosy and elastic dawn, the flashing sun,
The limpid spread of air cerulean,
Thou also re-appearest.

Thou born to match the gale, (thou art all wings,)
To cope with heaven and earth and sea and hurricane,   15
Thou ship of air that never furl'st thy sails,
Days, even weeks untired and onward, through spaces, realms gyrating,
At dusk that look'st on Senegal,[6] at morn America,
That sport'st amid the lightning-flash and thunder-cloud,
In them, in thy experiences, had'st thou my soul,   20
What joys! what joys were thine![7]

1876, 1881–1882

From BY THE ROADSIDE
Gods

Lover divine and perfect Comrade,
Waiting content, invisible yet, but certain,
Be thou my God.

Thou, thou, the Ideal Man,
Fair, able, beautiful, content, and loving,   5
Complete in body and dilate in spirit,
Be thou my God.

O Death, (for Life has served its turn,)
Opener and usher to the heavenly mansion,
Be thou my God.   10

Aught, aught of mightiest, best I see, conceive, or know,
(To break the stagnant tie—thee, thee to free, O soul,)
Be thou my God.

5. This poem is based on a French poem by Jules Michelet; it was one of twenty new poems added in the seventh edition of *Leaves of Grass* (1881–1882).

6. Colony in French West Africa.
7. *Cf.* the last stanza of Shelley's "To a Skylark," a poem well known to Whitman.

All great ideas, the races' aspirations,
All heroisms, deeds of rapt enthusiasts,   15
Be ye my Gods.

Or Time and Space,
Or shape of Earth divine and wondrous,
Or some fair shape I viewing, worship,
Or lustrous orb of sun or star by night,   20
Be ye my Gods.

1870, 1881–1882

When I Heard the Learn'd Astronomer

When I heard the learn'd astronomer,
When the proofs, the figures, were ranged in columns before me,
When I was shown the charts and diagrams, to add, divide, and
    measure them,
When I sitting heard the astonomer where he lectured with much
    applause in the lecture-room,
How soon unaccountable I became tired and sick,   5
Till rising and gliding out I wander'd off by myself,
In the mystical moist night-air, and from time to time,
Look'd up in perfect silence at the stars.

1865, 1867

The Dalliance of the Eagles[8]

Skirting the river road, (my forenoon walk, my rest,)
Skyward in air a sudden muffled sound, the dalliance of the eagles,
The rushing amorous contact high in space together,
The clinching interlocking claws, a living, fierce, gyrating wheel,
Four beating wings, two beaks, a swirling mass tight grappling,   5
In tumbling turning clustering loops, straight downward falling,
Till o'er the river pois'd, the twain yet one, a moment's lull,
A motionless still balance in the air, then parting, talons loosing,
Upward again on slow-firm pinions slanting, their separate diverse
    flight,
She hers, he his, pursuing.   10

1880, 1881–1882

From Drum-Taps[9]

Beat! Beat! Drums!

Beat! beat! drums—blow! bugles! blow!
Through the windows—through doors—burst like a ruthless force,

8. This poem was written from an account furnished the poet by John Burroughs. It was included in the seventh
edition of *Leaves of Grass* (1881–
1882).
9. *Drum-Taps* (1865) contained fifty-
three poems, some of them written at
or near the battle front in Virginia.
These poems were later given a central
position in *Leaves of Grass*, as representing a crucial experience of democracy.

Into the solemn church, and scatter the congregation,
Into the school where the scholar is studying;
Leave not the bridegroom quiet—no happiness must he have now
    with his bride,   5
Nor the peaceful farmer any peace, ploughing his field or gathering
    his grain,
So fierce you whirr and pound you drums—so shrill you bugles blow.

Beat! beat! drums—blow! bugles! blow!
Over the traffic of cities—over the rumble of wheels in the streets;
Are beds prepared for sleepers at night in the houses? no sleepers
    must sleep in those beds,   10
No bargainers' bargains by day—no brokers or speculators—would
    they continue?
Would the talkers be talking? would the singer attempt to sing?
Would the lawyers rise in the court to state his case before the
    judge?
Then rattle quicker, heavier drums—you bugles wilder blow.

Beat! beat! drums!—blow! bugles! blow!   15
Make no parley—stop for no expostulation,
Mind not the timid—mind not the weeper or prayer,
Mind not the old man beseeching the young man,
Let not the child's voice be heard, nor the mother's entreaties,
Make even the trestles to shake the dead where they lie awaiting the
    hearses,   20
So strong you thump O terrible drums—so loud you bugles blow.

                              1865, 1867

Cavalry Crossing a Ford

A line in long array where they wind betwixt green islands,
They take a serpentine course, their arms flash in the sun—hark to
    the musical clank,
Behold the silvery river, in it the splashing horses loitering stop to
    drink,
Behold the brown-faced men, each group, each person a picture, the
    negligent rest on the saddles,
Some emerge on the opposite bank, others are just entering the
    ford—while,   5
Scarlet and blue and snowy white,
The guidon flags flutter gayly in the wind.

                              1865, 1871

Vigil Strange I Kept on the Field One Night

Vigil strange I kept on the field one night;
When you my son and my comrade dropt at my side that day,

One look I but gave which your dear eyes return'd with a look I shall
  never forget,
One touch of your hand to mine O boy, reach'd up as you lay on
  the ground,
Then onward I sped in the battle, the even-contested battle,   5
Till late in the night reliev'd to the place at last again I made my
  way,
Found you in death so cold dear comrade, found your body son of
  responding kisses, (never again on earth responding,)
Bared your face in the starlight, curious the scene, cool blew the
  moderate night-wind,
Long there and then in vigil I stood, dimly around me the battle-
  field spreading,
Vigil wondrous and vigil sweet there in the fragrant silent night,   10
But not a tear fell, not even a long-drawn sigh, long, long I gazed,
Then on the earth partially reclining sat by your side leaning my
  chin in my hands,
Passing sweet hours, immortal and mystic hours with you dearest
  comrade—not a tear, not a word,
Vigil of silence, love and death, vigil for you my son and my soldier,
As onward silently stars aloft, eastward new ones upward stole,   15
Vigil final for you brave boy, (I could not save you, swift was your
  death,
I faithfully loved you and cared for you living, I think we shall surely
  meet again,)
Till at latest lingering of the night, indeed just as the dawn appear'd,
My comrade I wrapt in his blanket, envelop'd well his form,
Folded the blanket well, tucking it carefully over head and carefully
  under feet,   20
And there and then and bathed by the rising sun, my son in his
  grave, in his rude-dug grave I deposited,
Ending my vigil strange with that, vigil of night and battle-field dim,
Vigil for boy of responding kisses, (never again on earth respond-
  ing,)
Vigil for comrade swiftly slain, vigil I never forget, how as day
  brighten'd,
I rose from the chill ground and folded my soldier well in his
  blanket,   25
And buried him where he fell.

1865, 1867

A Sight in Camp in the Daybreak Gray and Dim

A sight in camp in the daybreak gray and dim,
As from my tent I emerge so early sleepless,

As slow I walk in the cool fresh air the path near by the hospital
    tent,
Three forms I see on stretchers lying, brought out there untended
    lying,
Over each the blanket spread, ample brownish woolen blanket,   5
Gray and heavy blanket, folding, covering all.

Curious I halt and silent stand,
Then with light fingers I from the face of the nearest the first just
    lift the blanket;
Who are you elderly man so gaunt and grim, with well-gray'd hair,
    and flesh all sunken about the eyes?
Who are you my dear comrade?   10

Then to the second I step—and who are you my child and darling?
Who are you sweet boy with cheeks yet blooming?

Then to the third—a face nor child nor old, very calm, as of beauti-
    ful yellow-white ivory;
Young man I think I know you—I think this face is the face of the
    Christ himself,
Dead and divine and brother of all, and here again he lies.   15

1865, 1867

Look Down Fair Moon

Look down fair moon and bathe this scene,
Pour softly down night's nimbus floods on faces ghastly, swollen,
    purple,
On the dead on their backs with arms toss'd wide,
Pour down your unstinted nimbus sacred moon.

1865, 1867

Reconciliation

Word over all, beautiful as the sky,
Beautiful that war and all its deeds of carnage must in time be
    utterly lost,
That the hands of the sisters Death and Night incessantly softly
    wash again, and ever again, this soil'd world;
For my enemy is dead, a man divine as myself is dead,
I look where he lies white-faced and still in the coffin—I draw
    near,   5
Bend down and touch lightly with my lips the white face in the
    coffin.

1865–1866, 1881–1882

When Lilacs Last in the Dooryard Bloom'd[1]

1

When lilacs[2] last in the dooryard bloom'd,
And the great star early droop'd in the western sky in the night,
I mourn'd, and yet shall mourn with ever-returning spring.

Ever-returning spring, trinity sure to me you bring,
Lilac blooming perennial and drooping star in the west,   5
And thought of him I love.

2

O powerful western fallen star!
O shades of night—O moody, tearful night!
O great star disappear'd—O the black murk that hides the star!
O cruel hands that hold me powerless—O helpless soul of me!   10
O harsh surrounding cloud that will not free my soul.

3

In the dooryard fronting an old farm-house near the white-wash'd
    palings,
Stands the lilac-bush tall-growing with heart-shaped leaves of rich
    green,
With many a pointed blossom rising delicate, with the perfume
    strong I love,
With every leaf a miracle—and from this bush in the dooryard,   15
With delicate-color'd blossoms and heart-shaped leaves of rich green,
A sprig with its flower I break.

4

In the swamp in secluded recesses,
A shy and hidden bird is warbling a song.

Solitary the thrush,   20
The hermit withdrawn to himself, avoiding the settlements,
Sings by himself a song.

Song of the bleeding throat,
Death's outlet song of life, (for well dear brother I know,
If thou wast not granted to sing thou would'st surely die.)   25

5

Over the breast of the spring, the land, amid cities,
Amid lanes and through old woods, where lately the violets peep'd
    from the ground, spotting the gray debris,

1. "When Lilacs Last in the Dooryard
Bloom'd" is one of four elegies entitled
"Memories of President Lincoln," which
were added, after Lincoln's death, to
later issues of *Drum-Taps* (1865). It
is generally regarded as one of Whitman's greatest poems. The bard of
American democratic comradeship saw,
in the life and death of Lincoln, the
human symbol of his theme, and in the
Drum-Taps volumes, the keystone of
the arch of his *Leaves of Grass*.
2. The lilac, which may be Persian in
its origin, had, in Eastern symbolism, a
connection with manly love. Other symbols in this poem are the hermit thrush
and its song and the evening star. See
l. 205.

Amid the grass in the fields each side of the lanes, passing the end-
 less grass,
Passing the yellow-spear'd wheat, every grain from its shroud in the
 dark-brown fields uprisen,
Passing the apple-tree blows of white and pink in the orchards,   30
Carrying a corpse to where it shall rest in the grave,
Night and day journeys a coffin.

6

Coffin that passes through lanes and streets,[3]
Through day and night with the great cloud darkening the land,
With the pomp of the inloop'd flags with the cities draped in black,
With the show of the States themselves as of crape-veil'd women
 standing,   36
With processions long and winding and the flambeaus of the night,
With the countless torches lit, with the silent sea of faces and the
 unbared heads,
With the waiting depot, the arriving coffin, and the sombre faces,
With dirges through the night, with the thousand voices rising
 strong and solemn,   40
With all the mournful voices of the dirges pour'd around the coffin,
The dim-lit churches and the shuddering organs—where amid these
 you journey,
With the tolling tolling bells' perpetual clang,
Here, coffin that slowly passes,
I give you my sprig of lilac.   45

7

(Nor for you, for one alone,
Blossoms and branches green to coffins all I bring,
For fresh as the morning, thus would I chant a song for you O sane
 and sacred death.

All over bouquets of roses,
O death, I cover you over with roses and early lilies,   50
But mostly and now the lilac that blooms the first,
Copious I break, I break the sprigs from the bushes,
With loaded arms I come, pouring for you,
For you and the coffins all of you O death.)

8

O western orb sailing the heaven,   55
Now I know what you must have meant as a month since I walk'd,
As I walk'd in silence the transparent shadowy night,
As I saw you had something to tell as you bent to me night after
 night,

3. The funeral train of Abraham Lincoln passed, amid multitudes of mourners, through Maryland, Pennsylvania,
New Jersey, New York, Ohio, and Indiana, on its way to Springfield, Illinois,
where the martyred President was
buried.

As you droop'd from the sky low down as if to my side, (while the
other stars all look'd on,)
As we wander'd together the solemn night, (for something I know
not what kept me from sleep,) 60
As the night advanced, and I saw on the rim of the west how full
you were of woe,
As I stood on the rising ground in the breeze in the cool transparent
night,
As I watch'd where you pass'd and was lost in the netherward black
of the night,
As my soul in its trouble dissatisfied sank, as where you sad orb,
Concluded, dropt in the night, and was gone. 65

9

Sing on there in the swamp,
O singer bashful and tender, I hear your notes, I hear your call,
I hear, I come presently, I understand you,
But a moment I linger, for the lustrous star has detain'd me,
The star my departing comrade holds and detains me. 70

10

O how shall I warble myself for the dead one there I loved?
And how shall I deck my song for the large sweet soul that has
gone?
And what shall my perfume be for the grave of him I love?

Sea-winds blown from east and west,
Blown from the Eastern sea and blown from the Western sea, till
there on the prairies meeting, 75
These and with these and the breath of my chant,
I'll perfume the grave of him I love.

11

O what shall I hang on the chamber walls?
And what shall the pictures be that I hang on the walls,
To adorn the burial-house of him I love? 80

Pictures of growing spring and farms and homes,
With the Fourth-month eve at sundown, and the gray smoke lucid
and bright,
With floods of the yellow gold of the gorgeous, indolent, sinking
sun, burning, expanding the air,
With the fresh sweet herbage under foot, and the pale green leaves
of the trees prolific,
In the distance the flowing glaze, the breast of the river, with a
wind-dapple here and there, 85
With ranging hills on the banks, with many a line against the sky,
and shadows,
And the city at hand with dwellings so dense, and stacks of chimneys,

And all the scenes of life and the workshops, and the workmen
    homeward returning.

12

Lo, body and soul—this land,
My own Manhattan with spires, and the sparkling and hurrying
    tides, and the ships,   90
The varied and ample land, the South and the North in the light,
    Ohio's shores and flashing Missouri,
And ever the far-spreading prairies cover'd with grass and corn.

Lo, the most excellent sun so calm and haughty,
The violet and purple morn with just-felt breezes,
The gentle soft-born measureless light,   95
The miracle spreading bathing all, the fulfill'd noon,
The coming eve delicious, the welcome night and the stars,
Over my cities shining all, enveloping man and land.

13

Sing on, sing on you gray-brown bird,
Sing from the swamps, the recesses, pour your chant from the
    bushes,   100
Limitless out of the dusk, out of the cedars and pines.

Sing on dearest brother, warble your reedy song,
Loud human song, with voice of uttermost woe.

O liquid and free and tender!
O wild and loose to my soul—O wondrous singer!   105
You only I hear—yet the star holds me, (but will soon depart,)
Yet the lilac with mastering odor holds me.

14

Now while I sat in the day and look'd forth,
In the close of the day with its light and the fields of spring, and the
    farmers preparing their crops,
In the large unconscious scenery of my land with its lakes and for-
    ests,   110
In the heavenly aerial beauty, (after the perturb'd winds and the
    storms,)
Under the arching heavens of the afternoon swift passing, and the
    voices of children and women,
The many-moving sea-tides, and I saw the ships how they sail'd,
And the summer approaching with richness, and the fields all busy
    with labor,
And the infinite separate houses, how they all went on, each with its
    meals and minutia of daily usages,   115
And the streets how their throbbings throbb'd, and the cities pent—
    lo, then and there,

Falling upon them all and among them all, enveloping me with the
    rest,
Appear'd the cloud, appear'd the long black trail,
And I knew death, its thought, and the sacred knowledge of death.

Then with the knowledge of death as walking one side of me,   120
And the thought of death close-walking the other side of me,
And I in the middle as with companions, and as holding the hands
    of companions,
I fled forth to the hiding receiving night that talks not,
Down to the shores of the water, the path by the swamp in the dim-
    ness,
To the solemn shadowy cedars and ghostly pines so still.   125

And the singer so shy to the rest receiv'd me,
The gray-brown bird I know receiv'd us comrades three,
And he sang the carol of death, and a verse for him I love.

From deep secluded recesses,
From the fragrant cedars and the ghostly pines so still,   130
Came the carol of the bird.

And the charm of the carol rapt me,
As I held as if by their hands my comrades in the night,
And the voice of my spirit tallied the song of the bird.

Come lovely and soothing death,[4]   135
Undulate round the world, serenely arriving, arriving,
In the day, in the night, to all, to each,
Sooner or later delicate death.

Prais'd be the fathomless universe,
For life and joy, and for objects and knowledge curious,   140
And for love, sweet love—but praise! praise! praise!
For the sure-enwinding arms of cool-enfolding death.

Dark mother always gliding near with soft feet,
Have none chanted for thee a chant of fullest welcome?
Then I chant it for thee, I glorify thee above all,   145
I bring thee a song that when thou must indeed come, come unfal-
    teringly.

Approach strong deliveress,
When it is so, when thou hast taken them I joyously sing the dead,
Lost in the loving floating ocean of thee,
Laved in the flood of thy bliss O death.   150

4. Compare the song of the bird in this and the tree in "Song of the Redwood-
poem with the lyric songs of the bird in Tree."
"Out of the Cradle Endlessly Rocking"

From me to thee glad serenades,
Dances for thee I propose saluting thee, adornments and feastings
for thee,
And the sights of the open landscape and the high-spread sky are
fitting,
And life and the fields, and the huge and thoughtful night.

The night in silence under many a star,   155
The ocean shore and the husky whispering wave whose voice I know,
And the soul turning to thee O vast and well-veil'd death,
And the body gratefully nestling close to thee.

Over the tree-tops I float thee a song,
Over the rising and sinking waves, over the myriad fields and the
prairies wide,   160
Over the dense-pack'd cities all and the teeming wharves and ways,
I float this carol with joy, with joy to thee O death.

15

To the tally of my soul,
Loud and strong kept up the gray-brown bird,
With pure deliberate notes spreading filling the night.   165

Loud in the pines and cedars dim,
Clear in the freshness moist and the swamp-perfume,
And I with my comrades there in the night.

While my sight that was bound in my eyes unclosed,
As to long panoramas of visions.   170

And I saw askant the armies,
I saw as in noiseless dreams hundreds of battle-flags,
Borne through the smoke of the battles and pierc'd with missiles I
saw them,
And carried hither and yon through the smoke, and torn and bloody,
And at last but a few shreds left on the staffs, (and all in silence,)
And the staffs all splinter'd and broken.   176

I saw battle-corpses, myriads of them,
And the white skeletons of young men, I saw them,
I saw the debris and debris of all the slain soldiers of the war,
But I saw they were not as was thought,   180
They themselves were fully at rest, they suffer'd not,
The living remain'd and suffer'd, the mother suffer'd,
And the wife and the child and the musing comrade suffer'd,
And the armies that remain'd suffer'd.

16

Passing the visions, passing the night,   185
Passing, unloosing the hold of my comrades' hands,

Passing the song of the hermit bird and the tallying song of my soul,
Victorious song, death's outlet song, yet varying ever-altering song,
As low and wailing, yet clear the notes, rising and falling, flooding
  the night,
Sadly sinking and fainting, as warning and warning, and yet again
  bursting with joy,   190
Covering the earth and filling the spread of the heaven,
As that powerful psalm in the night I heard from recesses,
Passing, I leave thee lilac with heart-shaped leaves,
I leave thee there in the door-yard, blooming, returning with spring.

I cease from my song for thee,   195
From my gaze on thee in the west, fronting the west, communing
  with thee,
O comrade lustrous with silver face in the night.

Yet each to keep and all, retrievements out of the night,
The song, the wondrous chant of the gray-brown bird,
And the tallying chant, the echo arous'd in my soul,   200
With the lustrous and drooping star with the countenance full of
  woe,
With the holders holding my hand nearing the call of the bird,
Comrades mine and I in the midst, and their memory ever to keep,
  for the dead I loved so well,
For the sweetest, wisest soul of all my days and lands—and this for
  his dear sake,
Lilac and star and bird twined with the chant of my soul,   205
There in the fragrant pines and the cedars dusk and dim.

                                      1865, 1881–1882

From Autumn Rivulets[5]
There Was a Child Went Forth

There was a child went forth every day,
And the first object he look'd upon, that object he became,
And that object became part of him for the day or a certain part of
  the day,
Or for many years or stretching cycles of years.

The early lilacs became part of this child,   5
And grass and white and red morning-glories, and white and red
  clover, and the song of the phœbe-bird,
And the Third-month lambs and the sow's pink-faint litter, and the
  mare's foal and the cow's calf,

5. The title "Autumn Rivulets" does not refer in particular to the poet's later years, but in its imagery implies a "sea of time" to which the "wayward rivulets" of individual life flow. "Autumn Rivulets" as a group title first appeared in the seventh edition of *Leaves of Grass* (1881–1882).

And the noisy brood of the barnyard or by the mire of the pond-side,
And the fish suspending themselves so curiously below there, and
    the beautiful curious liquid,
And the water-plants with their graceful flat heads, all became part
    of him.   10

The field-sprouts of Fourth-month and Fifth-month became part of
    him,
Winter-grain sprouts and those of the light-yellow corn, and the
    esculent roots of the garden,
And the apple-trees cover'd with blossoms and the fruit afterward,
    and wood-berries, and the commonest weeds by the road,
And the old drunkard staggering home from the outhouse of the
    tavern whence he had lately risen,
And the schoolmistress that pass'd on her way to the school,   15
And the friendly boys that pass'd, and the quarrelsome boys,
And the tidy and fresh-cheek'd girls, and the barefoot negro boy
    and girl,
And all the changes of city and country wherever he went.

His own parents, he that had father'd him and she that had con-
    ceiv'd him in her womb and birth'd him,
They gave this child more of themselves than that,   20
They gave him afterward every day, they became part of him.

The mother at home quietly placing the dishes on the supper-table,
The mother with mild words, clean her cap and gown, a wholesome
    odor falling off her person and clothes as she walks by,
The father, strong, self-sufficient, manly, mean, anger'd, unjust,
The blow, the quick loud word, the tight bargain, the crafty lure,
The family usages, the language, the company, the furniture, the
    yearning and swelling heart,   26
Affection that will not be gainsay'd, the sense of what is real, the
    thought if after all it should prove unreal,
The doubts of day-time and the doubts of night-time, the curious
    whether and how,
Whether that which appears so is so, or is it all flashes and specks?
Men and women crowding fast in the streets, if they are not flashes
    and specks what are they?   30
The streets themselves and the façades of houses, and goods in the
    windows,
Vehicles, teams, the heavy-plank'd wharves, the huge crossing at the
    ferries,
The village on the highland seen from afar at sunset, the river be-
    tween,
Shadows, aureola and mist, the light falling on roofs and gables of
    white or brown two miles off,

The schooner near by sleepily dropping down the tide, the little
    boat slack-tow'd astern,   35
The hurrying tumbling waves, quick-broken crests, slapping,
The strata of color'd clouds, the long bar of maroon-tint away soli-
    tary by itself, the spread of purity it lies motionless in,
The horizon's edge, the flying sea-crow, the fragrance of salt marsh
    and shore mud,
These became part of that child who went forth every day, and who
    now goes, and will always go forth every day.

1855, 1871

This Compost[6]

1

Something startles me where I thought I was safest,
I withdraw from the still woods I loved,
I will not go now on the pastures to walk,
I will not strip the clothes from my body to meet my lover the sea,
I will not touch my flesh to the earth as to other flesh to renew
    me.   5

O how can it be that the ground itself does not sicken?
How can you be alive you growths of spring?
How can you furnish health you blood of herbs, roots, orchards,
    grain?
Are they not continually putting distemper'd corpses within you?
Is not every continent work'd over and over with sour dead?   10

Where have you disposed of their carcasses?
Those drunkards and gluttons of so many generations?
Where have you drawn off all the foul liquid and meat?
I do not see any of it upon you to-day, or perhaps I am deceiv'd,
I will run a furrow with my plough, I will press my spade through
    the sod and turn it up underneath,   15
I am sure I shall expose some of the foul meat.

2

Behold this compost! behold it well!
Perhaps every mite has once form'd part of a sick person—yet be-
    hold!
The grass of spring covers the prairies,
The bean bursts noiselessly through the mould in the garden,   20
The delicate spear of the onion pierces upward,
The apple-buds cluster together on the apple-branches,
The resurrection of the wheat appears with pale visage out of its
    graves,
The tinge awakes over the willow-tree and the mulberry-tree,

6. Rotted vegetable matter used for fertilizing land.

The he-birds carol mornings and evenings while the she-birds sit on
their nests,   25
The young of poultry break through the hatch'd eggs,
The new-born of animals appear, the calf is dropt from the cow, the
colt from the mare,
Out of its little hill faithfully rise the potato's dark green leaves,
Out of its hill rises the yellow maize-stalk, the lilacs bloom in the
dooryards,
The summer growth is innocent and disdainful above all those strata
of sour dead.   30

What chemistry!
That the winds are really not infectious,
That this is no cheat, this transparent green-wash of the sea which
is so amorous after me,
That it is safe to allow it to lick my naked body all over with its
tongues,
That it will not endanger me with the fevers that have deposited
themselves in it,   35
That all is clean forever and forever,
That the cool drink from the well tastes so good,
That blackberries are so flavorous and juicy,
That the fruits of the apple-orchard and the orange-orchard, that
melons, grapes, peaches, plums, will none of them poison me,
That when I recline on the grass I do not catch any disease,   40
Though probably every spear of grass rises out of what was once a
catching disease.

Now I am terrified at the Earth, it is that calm and patient,
It grows such sweet things out of such corruptions,
It turns harmless and stainless on its axis, with such endless suces-
sions of diseas'd corpses,
It distills such exquisite winds out of such infused fetor,   45
It renews with such unwitting looks its prodigal, annual, sumptuous
crops,
It gives such divine materials to men, and accepts such leavings from
them at last.

                                                                        1856, 1881–1882

To a Common Prostitute[7]

Be composed—be at ease with me—I am Walt Whitman, liberal
and lusty as Nature,
Not till the sun excludes you do I exclude you,

7. Whitman told William Sloane Ken-
nedy that this poem was inspired by
"the beautiful little idyl of the New
Testament concerning the woman taken
in adultery." *Cf*. John viii: 3–11.

Not till the waters refuse to glisten for you and the leaves to rustle
    for you, do my words refuse to glisten and rustle for you.

My girl I appoint with you an appointment, and I charge you that
    you make preparation to be worthy to meet me,
And I charge you that you be patient and perfect till I come.   5

Till then I salute you with a significant look that you do not forget
    me.

        1860

Passage to India[8]

1

Singing my days,
Singing the great achievements of the present,
Singing the strong light works of engineers,
Our modern wonders, (the antique ponderous Seven[9] outvied,)
In the Old World the east the Suez canal,   5
The New by its mighty railroad spann'd,
The seas inlaid with eloquent gentle wires;
Yet first to sound, and ever sound, the cry with thee O soul,
The Past! the Past! the Past!

The Past—the dark unfathom'd retrospect!   10
The teeming gulf—the sleepers and the shadows!
The past—the infinite greatness of the past!
For what is the present after all but a growth out of the past?
(As a projectile form'd, impell'd, passing a certain line, still keeps on,
So the present, utterly form'd, impell'd by the past.)   15

2

Passage O soul to India!
Eclaircise[1] the myths Asiatic, the primitive fables.

Not you alone proud truths of the world,
Nor you alone ye facts of modern science,
But myths and fables of eld, Asia's, Africa's fables,   20
The far-darting beams of the spirit, the unloos'd dreams,
The deep diving bibles and legends,

8. "Passage to India" was inspired by three great contemporary engineering feats: completion of the Suez Canal in 1869 (l.5); the linking of the East and the West by the meeting of the Central Pacific and Union Pacific railroads near Ogden, Utah on May 10, 1866 (l.6); and the successful completion of the Atlantic cable in 1866 (l.7). These great physical achievements, linking Europe, Asia, and America, impelled Whitman to affirm an increasing unity and spiritual progress for mankind.

9. The Seven Wonders of the World of ancient times were the Egyptian pyramids, the Mausoleum at Halicarnassus, the Temple of Artemis at Ephesus, the Hanging Gardens of Babylon, the Colossus of Rhodes, the statue of Zeus at Olympia, and the lighthouse at Alexandria.

1. From French *éclaircir*, "to clarify."

The daring plots of the poets, the elder religions;
O you temples fairer than lilies pour'd over by the rising sun!
O you fables spurning the known, eluding the hold of the known,
    mounting to heaven!   25
You lofty and dazzling towers, pinnacled, red as roses, burnish'd
    with gold!
Towers of fables immortal fashion'd from mortal dreams!
You too I welcome and fully the same as the rest!
You too with joy I sing.

Passage to India!   30
Lo, soul, seest thou not God's purpose from the first?
The earth to be spann'd, connected by network,
The races, neighbors, to marry and be given in marriage,
The oceans to be cross'd, the distant brought near,
The lands to be welded together.   35

A worship new I sing,
You captains, voyagers, explorers, yours,
You engineers, you architects, machinists, yours,
You, not for trade or transportation only,
But in God's name, and for thy sake O soul.   40

3

Passage to India!
Lo soul for thee of tableaus twain.
I see in one the Suez canal initiated, open'd,
I see the procession of steamships, the Empress Eugenie's leading
    the van,
I mark from on deck the strange landscape, the pure sky, the level
    sand in the distance,   45
I pass swiftly the picturesque groups, the workmen gather'd,
The gigantic dredging machines.

In one again, different, (yet thine, all thine, O soul, the same,)
I see over my own continent the Pacific railroad surmounting every
    barrier,[2]
I see continual trains of cars winding along the Platte carrying
    freight and passengers,   50
I hear the locomotives rushing and roaring, and the shrill steam-
    whistle,
I hear the echoes reverberate through the grandest scenery in the
    world,
I cross the Laramie plains, I note the rocks in grotesque shapes, the
    buttes,

2. In the next fifteen lines the poet indicates the route of the railroad by flashes of scenery from Omaha to San Francisco.

I see the plentiful larkspur and wild onions, the barren, colorless,
    sage-deserts,
I see in glimpses afar or towering immediately above me the great
    mountains, I see the Wind river and the Wahsatch moun-
    tains, 55
I see the Monument mountain and the Eagle's Nest, I pass the
    Promontory, I ascend the Nevadas,
I scan the noble Elk mountain and wind around its base,
I see the Humboldt range, I thread the valley and cross the river,
I see the clear waters of lake Tahoe, I see forests of majestic pines,
Or crossing the great desert, the alkaline plains, I behold enchanting
    mirages of waters and meadows, 60
Marking through these and after all, in duplicate slender lines,
Bridging the three or four thousand miles of land travel,
Tying the Eastern to the Western sea,
The road between Europe and Asia.

(Ah Genoese[3] thy dream! thy dream! 65
Centuries after thou art laid in thy grave,
The shore thou foundest verifies thy dream.)

4

Passage to India!
Struggles of many a captain, tales of many a sailor dead,
Over my mood stealing and spreading they come, 70
Like clouds and cloudlets in the unreach'd sky.

Along all history, down the slopes,
As a rivulet running, sinking now, and now again to the surface
    rising,
A ceaseless thought, a varied train—lo, soul, to thee, thy sight, they
    rise,
The plans, the voyages again, the expeditions; 75
Again Vasco de Gama[4] sails forth,
Again the knowledge gain'd, the mariner's compass,
Lands found and nations born, thou born America,
For purpose vast, man's long probation fill'd,
Thou rondure of the world at last accomplish'd. 80

5

O vast Rondure, swimming in space,
Cover'd all over with visible power and beauty,
Alternate light and day and the teeming spiritual darkness,
Unspeakable high processions of sun and moon and countless stars
    above,
Below, the manifold grass and waters, animals, mountains, trees, 85

3. Christopher Columbus.
4. Correctly *da Gama;* Portuguese navi-   gator, first European to sail around
    Africa to India (1497–1498).

With inscrutable purpose, some hidden prophetic intention,
Now first it seems my thought begins to span thee.

Down from the gardens of Asia descending radiating,
Adam and Eve appear, then their myriad progeny after them,
Wandering, yearning, curious, with restless explorations,   90
With questionings, baffled, formless, feverish, with never-happy
    hearts,
With that sad incessant refrain, *Wherefore unsatisfied soul?* and
    Whither O mocking life?

Ah who shall soothe these feverish children?
Who justify these restless explorations?
Who speak the secret of impassive earth?   95
Who bind it to us? what is this separate Nature so unnatural?
What is this earth to our affections? (unloving earth, without a
    throb to answer ours,
Cold earth, the place of graves.)

Yet soul be sure the first intent remains, and shall be carried out,   100
Perhaps even now the time has arrived.

After the seas are all cross'd, (as they seem already cross'd,)
After the great captains and engineers have accomplish'd their work,
After the noble inventors, after the scientists, the chemist, the
    geologist, ethnologist,
Finally shall come the poet worthy of that name,   105
The true son of God shall come singing his songs.

Then not your deeds only O voyagers, O scientists and inventors,
    shall be justified,
All these hearts as of fretted children shall be sooth'd,
All affection shall be fully responded to, the secret shall be told,
All these separations and gaps shall be taken up and hook'd and
    link'd together,   110
The whole earth, this cold, impassive, voiceless earth, shall be
    completely justified,
Trinitas divine shall be gloriously accomplish'd and compacted by
    the true son of God, the poet,
(He shall indeed pass the straits and conquer the mountains,
He shall double the cape of Good Hope to some purpose,)
Nature and Man shall be disjoin'd and diffused no more,   115
The true son of God shall absolutely fuse them.

6

Year at whose wide-flung door I sing!
Year of the purpose accomplish'd!
Year of the marriage of continents, climates and oceans!

(No mere doge of Venice now wedding the Adriatic,)[5]   120
I see O year in you the vast terraqueous globe given and giving all,
Europe to Asia, Africa join'd, and they to the New World,
The lands, geographies, dancing before you, holding a festival
    garland,
As brides and bridegrooms hand in hand.

Passage to India!   125
Cooling airs from Caucasus, far, soothing cradle of man,
The river Euphrates[6] flowing, the past lit up again.

Lo soul, the retrospect brought forward,
The old, most populous, wealthiest of earth's lands,
The streams of the Indus and the Ganges and their many afflu-
    ents,   130
(I my shores of America walking to-day behold, resuming all,)
The tale of Alexander[7] on his warlike marches suddenly dying,
On one side China and on the other Persia and Arabia,
To the south the great seas and the bay of Bengal,
The flowing literatures, tremendous epics, religions, castes,   135
Old occult Brahma interminably far back, the tender and junior
    Buddha,
Central and southern empires and all their belongings, possessors,
The wars of Tamerlane,[8] the reign of Aurungzebe,[9]
The traders, rulers, explorers, Moslems, Venetians, Byzantium, the
    Arabs, Portuguese,
The first traveler famous yet, Marco Polo,[1] Patouta, the Moor,[2] 140
Doubts to be solv'd, the map incognita, blanks to be fill'd,
The foot of man unstay'd, the hands never at rest,
Thyself O soul that will not brook a challenge.

The mediæval navigators rise before me,
The world of 1492, with its awaken'd enterprise,   145
Something swelling in humanity now like the sap of the earth in
    spring,
The sunset splendor of chivalry declining.

And who art thou sad shade?
Gigantic, visionary, thyself a visionary,
With majestic limbs and pious beaming eyes,   150

5. At the pinnacle of the power of Venice, the Doge annually performed a ceremonial wedding of the city to the sea by throwing a ring into the Adriatic.
6. The alleged cradle of the Western (Caucasian) races was the valley of the Euphrates.
7. Alexander the Great died during his **return from an invasion of** India (323 **B.C.).**

8. An Oriental warrior who conquered from the Persian Gulf to the Ganges during the fourteenth century.
9. One of the greatest of the Mogul emperors of Hindustan in the seventeenth century.
1. Venetian traveler (1254–1324) who penetrated into far Cathay.
2. Also, Batoutah (1303–1377); he traveled to Africa and Asia.

Spreading around with every look of thine a golden world,
Enhuing it with gorgeous hues.

As the chief histrion,[3]
Down to the footlights walks in some great scena,
Dominating the rest I see the Admiral[4] himself,   155
(History's type of courage, action, faith,)
Behold him sail from Palos[5] leading his little fleet,
His voyage behold, his return, his great fame,
His misfortunes, calumniators, behold him a prisoner, chain'd,
Behold his dejection, poverty, death.   160

(Curious in time I stand, noting the efforts of heroes,
Is the deferment long? bitter the slander, poverty, death?
Lies the seed unreck'd for centuries in the ground? lo, to God's due
      occasion,
Uprising in the night, it sprouts, blooms,
And fills the earth with use and beauty.)   165

7

Passage indeed O soul to primal thought,
Not lands and seas alone, thy own clear freshness,
The young maturity of brood and bloom,
To realms of budding bibles.

O soul, repressless, I with thee and thou with me,   170
Thy circumnavigation of the world begin,
Of man, the voyage of his mind's return.
To reason's early paradise,
Back, back to wisdom's birth, to innocent intuitions,
Again with fair creation.   175

8

O we can wait no longer,
We too take ship O soul,
Joyous we too launch out on trackless seas,
Fearless for unknown shores on waves of ecstasy to sail,
Amid the wafting winds, (thou pressing me to thee, I thee to me,
      O soul,)
Caroling free, singing our song of God,
Chanting our chant of pleasant exploration.

With laugh and many a kiss,
(Let others deprecate, let others weep for sin, remorse, humiliation,)
O soul thou pleasest me, I thee.   185

Ah more than any priest O soul we too believe in God,
But with the mystery of God we dare not dally.

3. Actor.
4. Columbus, "Admiral of the Ocean
Sea."

5. Spanish seaport from which Columbus sailed on August 3, 1492.

O soul thou pleasest me, I thee,
Sailing these seas or on the hills, or waking in the night,
Thoughts, silent thoughts, of Time and Space and Death, like waters
    flowing,   190
Bear me indeed as through the regions infinite,
Whose air I breathe, whose ripples hear, lave me all over,
Bathe me O God in thee, mounting to thee,
I and my soul to range in range of thee.

O Thou transcendent,   195
Nameless, the fibre and the breath,
Light of the light, shedding forth universes, thou centre of them,
Thou mightier centre of the true, the good, the loving,
Thou moral, spiritual fountain—affection's source—thou reservoir,
(O pensive soul of me—O thirst unsatisfied—waitest not there?   200
Waitest not haply for us somewhere there the Comrade perfect?)
Thou pulse—thou motive of the stars, suns, systems,
That, circling, move in order, safe, harmonious,
Athwart the shapeless vastnesses of space,
How should I think, how breathe a single breath, how speak, if out
    of myself,   205
I could not launch, to those, superior universes?

Swiftly I shrivel at the thought of God,
At Nature and its wonders, Time and Space and Death,
But that I, turning, call to thee O soul, thou actual Me,
And lo, thou gently masterest the orbs,   210
Thou matest Time, smilest content at Death,
And fillest, swellest full the vastnesses of Space.

Greater than stars or suns,
Bounding O soul thou journeyest forth;
What love than thine and ours could wider amplify?   215
What aspirations, wishes, outvie thine and ours O soul?
What dreams of the ideal? what plans of purity, perfection, strength,
What cheerful willingness for others' sake to give up all?
For others' sake to suffer all?

Reckoning ahead O soul, when thou, the time achiev'd,   220
The seas all cross'd, weather'd the capes, the voyage done,
Surrounded, copest, frontest God, yieldest, the aim attain'd,
As fill'd with friendship, love complete, the Elder Brother found,
The Younger melts in fondness in his arms.

9

Passage to more than India!   225
Are thy wings plumed indeed for such far flights?
O soul, voyagest thou indeed on voyages like those?

Disportest thou on waters such as those?
Soundest below the Sanscrit and the Vedas?[6]
Then have thy bent unleash'd.   230

Passage to you, your shores, ye aged fierce enigmas!
Passage to you, to mastership of you, ye strangling problems!
You, strew'd with the wrecks of skeletons, that, living, never reach'd
     you.

Passage to more than India!
O secret of the earth and sky!   235
Of you O waters of the sea! O winding creeks and rivers!
Of you O woods and fields! of you strong mountains of my land!
Of you O prairies! of you gray rocks!
O morning red! O clouds! O rain and snows!
O day and night, passage to you!   240

O sun and moon and all you stars! Sirius and Jupiter!
Passage to you!

Passage, immediate passage! the blood burns in my veins!
Away O soul! hoist instantly the anchor!
Cut the hawsers—haul out—shake out every sail!   245
Have we not stood here like trees in the ground long enough?
Have we not grovel'd here long enough, eating and drinking like
     mere brutes?
Have we not darken'd and dazed ourselves with books long enough?

Sail forth—steer for the deep waters only,
Reckless O soul, exploring, I with thee, and thou with me,   250
For we are bound where mariner has not yet dared to go,
And we will risk the ship, ourselves and all.

O my brave soul!
O farther farther sail!
O daring joy, but safe! are they not all the seas of God?   255
O farther, farther, farther sail!

                                                                              1871

Prayer of Columbus[7]

A batter'd, wreck'd old man,
Thrown on this savage shore, far, far from home,
Pent by the sea and dark rebellious brows, twelve dreary months,
Sore, stiff with many toils, sicken'd and nigh to death,

6. The ancient Hindu holy books, the Vedas, were written in Sanskrit.
7. "Prayer of Columbus" was written in 1874, when Whitman had little hope of recovering from his first severe stroke of paralysis. He often referred to his poems as a kind of exploration: *cf. Passage to India*.

I take my way along the island's edge,   5
Venting a heavy heart.

I am too full of woe!
Haply I may not live another day;
I cannot rest O God, I cannot eat or drink or sleep,
Till I put forth myself, my prayer, once more to Thee.   10
Breathe, bathe myself once more in Thee, commune with Thee,
Report myself once more to Thee.

Thou knowest my years entire, my life,
My long and crowded life of active work, not adoration merely;
Thou knowest the prayers and vigils of my youth,   15
Thou knowest my manhood's solemn and visionary meditations,
Thou knowest how before I commenced I devoted all to come to
    Thee,
Thou knowest I have in age ratified all those vows and strictly kept
    them,
Thou knowest I have not once lost nor faith nor ecstasy in Thee,
In shackles, prison'd, in disgrace, repining not,   20
Accepting all from Thee, as duly come from Thee.

All my emprises have been fill'd with Thee,
My speculations, plans, begun and carried on in thought of Thee,
Sailing the deep or journeying the land for Thee;
Intentions, purports, aspirations mine, leaving results to Thee.   25

O I am sure they really came from Thee,
The urge, the ardor, the unconquerable will,
The potent, felt, interior command, stronger than words,
A message from the Heavens whispering to me even in sleep,
These sped me on.   30

By me and these the work so far accomplish'd,
By me earth's elder cloy'd and stifled lands uncloy'd, unloos'd,
By me the hemispheres rounded and tied, the unknown to the
    known.

The end I know not, it is all in Thee,
O small or great I know not—haply what broad fields, what lands, 35
Haply the brutish measureless human undergrowth I know,
Transplanted there may rise to stature, knowledge worthy Thee,
Haply the swords I know may there indeed be turn'd to reaping-
    tools,
Haply the lifeless cross I know, Europe's dead cross, may bud and
    blossom there.

One effort more, my altar this bleak sand;   40
That Thou O God my life hast lighted,

With ray of light, steady, ineffable, vouchsafed of Thee,
Light rare untellable, lighting the very light,
Beyond all signs, descriptions, languages;
For that O God, be it my latest word, here on my knees,   45
Old, poor, and paralyzed, I thank Thee.

My terminus near,
The clouds already closing in upon me,
The voyage balk'd, the course disputed, lost,
I yield my ships to Thee.   50

My hands, my limbs grow nerveless,
My brain feels rack'd, bewilder'd,
Let the old timbers part, I will not part,
I will cling fast to Thee, O God, though the waves buffet me,
Thee, Thee at least I know.   55

Is it the prophet's thought I speak, or am I raving?
What do I know of life? what of myself?
I know not even my own work past or present,
Dim ever-shifting guesses of it spread before me,
Of newer better worlds, their mighty parturition,   60
Mocking, perplexing me.

And these things I see suddenly, what mean they?
As if some miracle, some hand divine unseal'd my eyes,
Shadowy vast shapes smile through the air and sky,
And on the distant waves sail countless ships,   65
And anthems in new tongues I hear saluting me.

1874, 1881–1882

From WHISPERS OF HEAVENLY DEATH
Darest Thou Now O Soul

Darest thou now O soul,
Walk out with me toward the unknown region,
Where neither ground is for the feet nor any path to follow?

No map there, nor guide,
Nor voice sounding, nor touch of human hand,   5
Nor face with blooming flesh, nor lips, nor eyes, are in that land.

I know it not O soul,
Nor dost thou, all is a blank before us,
All waits undream'd of in that region, that inaccessible land.

Till when the ties loosen,   10
All but the ties eternal, Time and Space,
Nor darkness, gravitation, sense, nor any bounds bounding us.

Then we burst forth, we float,
In Time and Space O soul, prepared for them,
Equal equipt at last, (O joy! O fruit of all!) them to fulfil O soul.   15

1871, 1881

Whispers of Heavenly Death[8]

Whispers of heavenly death murmur'd I hear,
Labial gossip of night, sibilant chorals,
Footsteps gently ascending, mystical breezes wafted soft and low,
Ripples of unseen rivers, tides of a current flowing, forever flowing,
(Or is it the plashing of tears? the measureless waters of human
    tears?)   5

I see, just see skyward, great cloud-masses,
Mournfully slowly they roll, silently swelling and mixing,
With at times a half-dimm'd sadden'd far-off star,
Appearing and disappearing.

(Some parturition rather, some solemn immortal birth;   10
On the frontiers to eyes impenetrable,
Some soul is passing over.)

1871

Chanting the Square Deific[9]

1

Chanting the square deific, out of the One advancing, out of the
    sides,
Out of the old and new, out of the square entirely divine,
Solid, four-sided, (all the sides needed,) from this side Jehovah am
    I,
Old Brahm I, and I Saturnius am;[1]
Not Time affects me—I am Time, old, modern as any,   5
Unpersuadable, relentless, executing righteous judgments,
As the Earth, the Father, the brown old Kronos,[2] with laws,
Aged beyond computation, yet ever new, ever with those mighty
    laws rolling,
Relentless I forgive no man—whoever sins dies—I will have that
    man's life;
Therefore let none expect mercy—have the seasons, gravitation, the
    appointed days, mercy? no more have I,   10

8. "Whispers of Heavenly Death" is
the title poem of a new section added
to *Leaves of Grass* in 1871.
9. In analyzing the religious experience
of mankind, Whitman follows trinitar-
ian orthodoxy in his references to God
the Father, or creator; God the Son, or
intercessor; and God the Holy Ghost,
or the intuitive revelation. But note
that in stanza 3 Whitman also places
Satan among the "deific" experiences.
1. Supreme gods of the Hebrew, Hindu,
and Roman religions.
2. The Greek god, more primitive than
Zeus, whose name, "Time," suggests an
origin before creation.

But as the seasons and gravitation, and as all the appointed days that
    forgive not,
I dispense from this side judgments inexorable without the least
    remorse.

2

Consolator most mild, the promis'd one advancing,
With gentle hand extended, the mightier God am I,
Foretold by prophets and poets in their most rapt prophecies and
    poems,   15
From this side, lo! the Lord Christ gazes—lo! Hermes[3]—I—lo! mine
    is Hercules'[4] face,
All sorrow, labor, suffering, I, tallying it, absorb in myself,
Many times have I been rejected, taunted, put in prison, and cruci-
    fied, and many times shall be again,
All the world have I given up for my dear brothers' and sisters' sake,
    for the soul's sake,
Wending my way through the homes of men, rich or poor, with
    the kiss of affection,   20
For I am affection, I am the cheer-bringing God, with hope and all
    enclosing charity,
With indulgent words as to children, with fresh and sane words,
    mine only,
Young and strong I pass knowing well I am destin'd myself to an
    early death;
But my charity has no death—my wisdom dies not, neither early
    nor late,
And my sweet love bequeath'd here and elsewhere never dies.   25

3

Aloof, dissatisfied, plotting revolt,
Comrade of criminals, brother of slaves,
Crafty, despised, a drudge, ignorant,
With sudra[5] face and worn brow, black, but in the depths of my
    heart, proud as any,
Lifted now and always against whoever scorning assumes to rule
    me,   30
Morose, full of guile, full of reminiscences, brooding, with many
    wiles,
(Though it was thought I was baffled and dispel'd, and my wiles
    done, but that will never be,)
Defiant, I, Satan, still live, still utter words, in new lands duly
    appearing, (and old ones also,)

---

3. Messenger for the gods on Olympus.
4. The most celebrated hero of classical
mythology, son of Zeus and a mortal
woman, worshiped for his many benefits
to mankind.
5. Among the Hindu castes of India,
the Sudra is the lowest, the caste of
the untouchables.

Permanent here from my side, warlike, equal with any, real as any,
Nor time nor change shall ever change me or my words.   35

4

Santa Spirita,[6] breather, life,
Beyond the light, lighter than light,
Beyond the flames of hell, joyous, leaping easily above hell,
Beyond Paradise, perfumed solely with mine own perfume,
Including all life on earth, touching, including God, including Saviour and Satan,   40
Ethereal, pervading all, (for without me what were all? what were God?)
Essence of forms, life of the real identities, permanent, positive, (namely the unseen,)
Life of the great round world, the sun and stars, and of man, I, the general soul,
Here the square finishing, the solid, I the most solid,
Breathe my breath also through these songs.   45

1865–1866, 1881–1882

A Noiseless Patient Spider

A noiseless patient spider,
I mark'd where on a little promontory it stood isolated,
Mark'd how to explore the vacant vast surrounding,
It launch'd forth filament, filament, filament, out of itself,
Ever unreeling them, ever tirelessly speeding them.   5

And you O my soul where you stand,
Surrounded, detached, in measureless oceans of space,
Ceaselessly musing, venturing, throwing, seeking the spheres to connect them,
Till the bridge you will need be form'd, till the ductile anchor hold,
Till the gossamer thread you fling catch somewhere, O my soul.   10

1862–1863   1871, 1881

From FROM NOON TO STARRY NIGHT[7]
To a Locomotive in Winter

Thee for my recitative,
Thee in the driving storm even as now, the snow, the winter-day declining,
Thee in thy panoply, thy measure'd dual throbbing and thy beat convulsive,
Thy black cylindric body, golden brass and silvery steel,
Thy ponderous side-bars, parallel and connecting rods, gyrating, shuttling at thy sides,   5

6. Holy Spirit. *Cf.* John xiv: 16–17.
7. Whitman first grouped a number of poems (some of them previously pub-lished) under the title "From Noon to Starry Night" in the seventh edition of *Leaves of Grass* (1881–1882).

Thy metrical, now swelling pant and roar, now tapering in the
    distance,
Thy great protruding head-light fix'd in front,
Thy long, pale, floating vapor-pennants, tinged with delicate purple,
The dense and murky clouds out-belching from thy smoke-stack,
Thy knitted frame, thy springs and valves, the tremulous twinkle of
    thy wheels,   10
Thy train of cars behind, obedient, merrily following,
Through gale or calm, now swift, now slack, yet steadily careering;
Type of the modern—emblem of motion and power—pulse of the
    continent,
For once come serve the Muse and merge in verse, even as here I
    see thee,
With storm and buffeting gusts of wind and falling snow,   15
By day thy warning ringing bell to sound its notes,
By night thy silent signal lamps to swing.

Fierce-throated beauty!
Roll through my chant with all thy lawless music, thy swinging
    lamps at night,
Thy madly-whistled laughter, echoing, rumbling like an earthquake,
    rousing all,   20
Law of thyself complete, thine own track firmly holding,
(No sweetness debonair of tearful harp or glib piano thine,)
Thy trills of shrieks by rocks and hills return'd,
Launch'd o'er the prairies wide, across the lakes,
To the free skies unpent and glad and strong.   25

                                  1876, 1881

By Broad Potomac's Shore

By broad Potomac's shore, again old tongue,
(Still uttering, still ejaculating, canst never cease this babble?)
Again old heart so gay, again to you, your sense, the full flush spring
    returning,
Again the freshness and the odors, again Virginia's summer sky,
    pellucid blue and silver,
Again the forenoon purple of the hills,   5
Again the deathless grass, so noiseless soft and green,
Again the blood-red roses blooming.

Perfume this book of mine O blood-red roses!
Lave subtly with your waters every line Potomac!
Give me of you O spring, before I close, to put between its pages! 10
O forenoon purple of the hills, before I close, of you!
O deathless grass, of you!

                                  1876, 1881

From SONGS OF PARTING[8]
Joy, Shipmate, Joy!

Joy, shipmate, joy!
(Pleas'd to my soul at death I cry,)
Our life is closed, our life begins,
The long, long anchorage we leave,
The ship is clear at last, she leaps!   5
She swiftly courses from the shore,
Joy, shipmate, joy!

1871

So Long![9]

To conclude, I announce what comes after me.

I remember I said before my leaves sprang at all,
I would raise my voice jocund and strong with reference to con-
    sumations.

When America does what was promis'd,
When through these States walk a hundred millions of superb
    persons,   5
When the rest part away for superb persons and contribute to them,
When breeds of the most perfect mothers denote America,
Then to me and mine our due fruition.

I have press'd through in my own right,
I have sung the body and the soul, war and peace have I sung, and
    the songs of life and death,   10
And the songs of birth, and shown that there are many births.

I have offer'd my style to every one, I have journey'd with confident
    step;
While my pleasure is yet at the full I whisper *So long!*
And take the young woman's hand and the young man's hand for
    the last time.

I announce natural persons to arise,   15
I announce justice triumphant,
I announce uncompromising liberty and equality,
I announce the justification of candor and the justification of pride.

I announce that the identity of these States is a single identity only,
I announce the Union more and more compact, indissoluble,   20

8. "Songs of Parting," which first appeared in the fourth edition of *Leaves
of Grass* (1867) as "Songs Before
Parting," was used to close the 1871
edition.
9. In an early form this poem appeared
in the third edition of *Leaves of Grass*

(1860). Thereafter the poet always
kept it at the end of the main body of
the book. Some poems concerning old
age were added as "annexes" in the
editions of 1888–1889 and 1891, but
they are not organically connected with
the major poetry of the *Leaves*.

I announce splendors and majesties to make all the previous politics
    of the earth insignificant.

I announce adhesiveness,[1] I say it shall be limitless, unloosen'd,
I say you shall yet find the friend you were looking for.

I announce a man or woman coming, perhaps you are the one, (*So
    long!*)   25
I announce the great individual, fluid as Nature, chaste, affectionate,
    compassionate, fully arm'd.

I announce a life that shall be copious, vehement, spiritual, bold,
I announce an end that shall lightly and joyfully meet its translation.

I announce myriads of youths, beautiful, gigantic, sweet-blooded,
I announce a race of splendid and savage old men.   30

O thicker and faster—(*So long!*)
O crowding too close upon me,
I foresee too much, it means more than I thought,
It appears to me I am dying.

Hasten throat and sound your last,   35
Salute me—salute the days once more. Peal the old cry once more.

Screaming electric, the atmosphere using,
At random glancing, each as I notice absorbing,
Swiftly on, but a little while alighting,
Curious envelop'd messages delivering,   40
Sparkles hot, seed ethereal down in the dirt dropping,
Myself unknowing, my commission obeying, to question it never
    daring,
To ages and ages yet the growth of the seed leaving,
To troops out of the war arising, they the task I have set promulging,
To women certain whispers of myself bequeathing, their affection
    me more clearly explaining,   45
To young men my problems offering—no dallier I—I the muscle of
    their brains **trying**,
So I pass, a little time vocal, visible, contrary,
Afterward a melodious echo, passionately bent for, (death making
    me really undying,)
The best of me then when no longer visible, for toward that I have
    been incessantly preparing.

What is there more, that I lag and pause and crouch extended with
    unshut mouth?   50
Is there a single final farewell?

1. Whitman borrowed "adhesiveness" pulse toward friendship or gregarious-
from phrenology as a term for the im- ness.

My songs cease, I abandon them,
From behind the screen where I hid I advance personally solely to
   you.

Camerado, this is no book,
Who touches this touches a man,   55
(Is it night? are we here together alone?)
It is I you hold and who holds you,
I spring from the pages into your arms—decease calls me forth.

O how your fingers drowse me,
Your breath falls around me like dew, your pulse lulls the tympans
   of my ears,   60
I feel immerged from head to foot,
Delicious, enough.

Enough O deed impromptu and secret,
Enough O gliding present—enough O summ'd-up past.

Dear friend whoever you are take this kiss,   65
I give it especially to you, do not forget me,
I feel like one who has done work for the day to retire awhile,
I receive now again of my many translations, from my avataras
   ascending, while others doubtless await me,
An unknown sphere more real than I dream'd, more direct, darts
   awakening rays about me, *So long!*
Remember my words, I may again return,   70
I love you, I depart from materials,
I am as one disembodied, triumphant, dead.

                                                              1860, 1881

From Democratic Vistas[2]
[American Democracy]

Political democracy, as it exists and practically works in America,
with all its threatening evils, supplies a training school for making
first-class men. It is life's gymnasium, not of good only, but of all.
We try often, though we fall back often. A brave delight, fit for
freedom's athletes, fills these arenas, and fully satisfies, out of the
action in them, irrespective of success. Whatever we do not attain,
we at any rate attain the experiences of the fight, the hardening of
the strong campaign, and throb with currents of attempt at least.
Time is ample. Let the victors come after us. Not for nothing does

2. After the ordeal of the Civil War,
Whitman wrote two essays analyzing
and criticizing the condition of democracy in the United States. "Democracy"
appeared in the *Galaxy*, December,

1867, and "Personalism" in the same
periodical in May, 1868. In 1871 the
two essays were consolidated in the
volume, *Democratic Vistas.*

evil play its part among us. Judging from the main portions of the history of the world, so far, justice is always in jeopardy, peace walks amid hourly pitfalls, and of slavery, misery, meanness, the craft of tyrants and the credulity of the populace, in some of the protean forms, no voice can at any time say, They are not. The clouds break a little, and the sun shines out—but soon and certain the lowering darkness falls again, as if to last forever. Yet is there an immortal courage and prophecy in every sane soul that cannot, must not, under any circumstances, capitulate. *Vive*, the attack—the perennial assault! *Vive*, the unpopular cause—the spirit that audaciously aims —the never-abandon'd efforts, pursued the same amid opposing proofs and precedents.

Once, before the war (alas! I dare not say how many times the mood has come!) I, too, was fill'd with doubt and gloom. A foreigner, an acute and good man, had impressively said to me, that day—putting in form, indeed, my own observations: "I have travel'd much in the United States, and watch'd their politicians, and listen'd to the speeches of the candidates, and read the journals, and gone into the public-houses, and heard the unguarded talk of men. And I have found your vaunted America honeycomb'd from top to toe with infidelism, even to itself and its own programme. I have mark'd the brazen hell-faces of secession and slavery gazing defiantly from all the windows and doorways. I have everywhere found, primarily, thieves and scalliwags arranging the nominations to offices, and sometimes filling the offices themselves. I have found the north just as full of bad stuff as the south. Of the holders of public office in the Nation or the States or their municipalities, I have found that not one in a hundred has been chosen by any spontaneous selection of the outsiders, the people, but all have been nominated and put through by little or large caucuses of the politicians, and have got in by corrupt rings and electioneering, not capacity or desert. I have noticed how the millions of sturdy farmers and mechanics are thus the helpless supple-jacks of comparatively few politicians. And I have noticed more and more, the alarming spectacle of parties usurping the government, and openly and shamelessly wielding it for party purposes."

Sad, serious, deep truths. Yet are there other, still deeper, amply confronting, dominating truths. Over those politicians and great and little rings, and over all their insolence and wiles, and over the powerfullest parties, looms a power, too sluggish maybe, but ever holding decisions and decrees in hand, ready, with stern process, to execute them as soon as plainly needed—and at times, indeed, summarily crushing to atoms the mightiest parties, even in the hour of their pride.

In saner hours far different are the amounts of these things from what, at first sight, they appear. Though it is no doubt important who is elected governor, mayor, or legislator (and full of dismay when incompetent or vile ones get elected, as they sometimes do), there are other, quieter contingencies, infinitely more important. Shams, etc., will always be the show, like ocean's scum; enough, if waters deep and clear make up the rest. Enough, that while the piled embroider'd shoddy gaud and fraud spreads to the superficial eye, the hidden warp and weft are genuine, and will wear forever. Enough, in short, that the race, the land which could raise such as the late rebellion, could also put it down.

The average man of a land at last only is important. He, in these States, remains immortal owner and boss, deriving good uses, somehow, out of any sort of servant in office, even the basest (certain universal requisites, and their settled regularity and protection, being first secured); a nation like ours, in a sort of geological formation state, trying continually new experiments, choosing new delegations, is not served by the best men only, but sometimes more by those that provoke it—by the combats they arouse. Thus national rage, fury, discussion, etc., better than content. Thus, also, the warning signals, invaluable for after times.

What is more dramatic than the spectacle we have seen repeated, and doubtless long shall see—the popular judgment taking the successful candidates on trial in the offices—standing off, as it were, and observing them and their doings for a while, and always giving, finally, the fit, exactly due reward? I think, after all, the sublimest part of political history, and its culmination, is currently issuing from the American people. I know nothing grander, better exercise, better digestion, more positive proof of the past, the triumphant result of faith in human-kind, than a well-contested American national election.

Then still the thought returns (like the thread-passage in overtures), giving the key and echo to these pages. When I pass to and fro, different latitudes, different seasons, beholding the crowds of the great cities, New York, Boston, Philadelphia, Cincinnati, Chicago, St. Louis, San Francisco, New Orleans, Baltimore—when I mix with these interminable swarms of alert, turbulent, good-natured, independent citizens, mechanics, clerks, young persons—at the idea of this mass of men, so fresh and free, so loving and so proud, a singular awe falls upon me. I feel, with dejection and amazement, that among our geniuses and talented writers or speakers, few or none have yet really spoken to this people, created a single image-making work for them, or absorb'd the central spirit and the idiosyncrasies which are theirs—and which, thus, in highest ranges, so far remain entirely uncelebrated, unexpress'd.

Dominion strong is the body's; dominion stronger is the mind's. What has fill'd, and fills today our intellect, our fancy, furnishing the standards therein, is yet foreign. The great poems, Shakspere included, are poisonous to the idea of the pride and dignity of the common people, the life-blood of democracy. The models of our literature, as we get it from other lands, ultramarine, have had their birth in courts, and bask'd and grown in castle sunshine; all smells of princes' favors. Of workers of a certain sort, we have, indeed, plenty, contributing after their kind; many elegant, many learn'd, all complacent. But touch'd by the national test, or tried by the standards of democratic personality, they wither to ashes. I say I have not seen a single writer, artist, lecturer, or what not, that has confronted the voiceless but ever erect and active, pervading, underlying will and typic aspiration of the land, in a spirit kindred to itself. Do you call those genteel little creatures American poets? Do you term that perpetual, pistareen, paste-pot work, American art, American drama, taste, verse? I think I hear, echoed as from some mountaintop afar in the west, the scornful laugh of the Genius of these States.

Democracy, in silence, biding its time, ponders its own ideals, not of literature and art only—not of men only, but of women. The idea of the women of America (extricated from this daze, this fossil and unhealthy air which hangs about the word *lady*) develop'd, raised to become the robust equals, workers, and, it may be, even practical and political deciders with the men—greater than man, we may admit, through their divine maternity, always their towering, emblematical attribute—but great, at any rate, as man, in all departments; or, rather, capable of being so, soon as they realize it, and can bring themselves to give up toys and fictions, and launch forth, as men do, amid real, independent, stormy life.

Then, as toward our thought's finalè (and, in that, over-arching the true scholar's lesson), we have to say there can be no complete or epical presentation of democracy in the aggregate, or anything like it, at this day, because its doctrines will only be effectually incarnated in any one branch, when, in all, their spirit is at the root and center. Far, far, indeed, stretch, in distance, our Vistas! How much is still to be disentangled, freed! How long it takes to make this American world see that it is, in itself, the final authority and reliance!

Did you, too, O friend, suppose democracy was only for elections, for politics, and for a party name? I say democracy is only of use there that it may pass on and come to its flower and fruits in manners, in the highest forms of interaction between men, and their beliefs—in religion, literature, colleges, and schools—democracy in all public and private life, and in the army and navy.[3] I have inti-

3. "The whole present system of the officering and personnel of the army and navy of these States, and the spirit and letter of their trebly-aristocratic rules and regulations, is a monstrous exotic, a nuisance and revolt, and belong here just as much as orders of nobility, or the Pope's council of cardinals. I say if the present theory of our army and navy is sensible and true, then the rest of America is an unmitigated fraud" [Whitman's note].

mated that, as a paramount scheme, it has yet few or no full realizers and believers. I do not see, either, that it owes any serious thanks to noted propagandists or champions, or has been essentially help'd, though often harm'd, by them. It has been and is carried on by all the moral forces, and by trade, finance, machinery, intercommunications, and, in fact, by all the developments of history, and can no more be stopp'd than the tides, or the earth in its orbit. Doubtless, also, it resides, crude and latent, well down in the hearts of the fair average of the American-born people, mainly in the agricultural regions. But it is not yet, there or anywhere, the fully receiv'd, the fervid, the absolute faith.

I submit, therefore, that the fruition of democracy, on aught like a grand scale, resides altogether in the future. As, under any profound and comprehensive view of the gorgeous-composite feudal world, we see in it, through the long ages and cycles of ages, the results of a deep, integral, human and divine principle, or fountain, from which issued laws, ecclesia, manners, institutes, costumes, personalities, poems (hitherto unequal'd), faithfully partaking of their source, and indeed only arising either to betoken it, or to furnish parts of that varied-flowing display, whose center was one and absolute—so, long ages hence, shall the due historian or critic make at least an equal retrospect, an equal history for the democratic principle. It too must be adorn'd, credited with its results—then, when it, with imperial power, through amplest time, has dominated mankind—has been the source and test of all the moral, æsthetic, social, political, and religious expressions and institutes of the civilized world—has begotten them in spirit and in form, and has carried them to its own unprecedented heights—has had (it is possible) monastics and ascetics, more numerous, more devout than the monks and priests of all previous creeds—has sway'd the ages with a breadth and rectitude tallying Nature's own—has fashion'd, systematized, and triumphantly finish'd and carried out, in its own interest, and with unparallel'd success, a new earth and a new man.

Thus we presume to write, as it were, upon things that exist not, and travel by maps yet unmade, and a blank. But the throes of birth are upon us; and we have something of this advantage in seasons of strong formations, doubts, suspense—for then the afflatus of such themes haply may fall upon us, more or less; and then, hot from surrounding war and revolution, our speech, though without polish'd coherence, and a failure by the standard called criticism, comes forth, real at least as the lightnings.

And maybe we, these days, have, too, our own reward—(for there are yet some, in all lands, worthy to be so encouraged). Though not for us the joy of entering at the last the conquered city—not ours the chance ever to see with our own eyes the peerless power and splendid *éclat* of the democratic principle, arriv'd at meridian, filling the world with effulgence and majesty far beyond those of past history's kings, or all dynastic sway—there is yet, to whoever is eligible among us, the prophetic vision, the joy of being toss'd in the brave turmoil of these times—the promulgation and the path, obedient, lowly reverent to the voice, the gesture of the god, or holy ghost, which others see not, hear not—with the proud consciousness that amid whatever clouds, seductions, or heart-wearying postponements, we have never deserted, never despair'd, never abandon'd the faith.

So much contributed, to be conn'd well, to help prepare and brace our edifice, our plann'd Idea—we still proceed to give it in another of its aspects—perhaps the main, the high façade of all. For to democracy, the leveler, the unyielding principle of the average, surely join'd another principle, equally unyielding, closely tracking the first, indispensable to it, opposite (as the sexes are opposite), and whose existence, confronting and ever modifying the other, often clashing, paradoxical, yet neither of highest avail without the other, plainly supplies to these grand cosmic politics of ours, and to the launch'd forth mortal dangers of republicanism, today, or any day, the counterpart and offset whereby Nature restrains the deadly original relentlessness of all her first-class laws. This second principle is individuality, the pride and centripetal isolation of a human being in himself—identity—personalism. Whatever the name, its acceptance and thorough infusions through the organizations of political commonalty now shooting Aurora-like about the world, are of utmost importance, as the principle itself is needed for very life's sake. It forms, in a sort, or is to form, the compensating balance-wheel of the successful working machinery of aggregate America.

And, if we think of it, what does civilization itself rest upon—and what object has it, what its religions, arts, schools, etc., but rich, luxuriant, varied personalism? To that, all bends; and it is because toward such result democracy alone, on anything like Nature's scale, breaks up the limitless fallows of human-kind, and plants the seed, and gives fair play, that its claims now precede the rest. The literature, songs, æsthetics, etc., of a country are of importance principally because they furnish the materials and suggestions of personality for the women and men of that country, and enforce them in a thousand effective ways.[4] As the topmost claim of a strong consolidating

4. "After the rest is satiated, all interest culminates in the field of persons, and never flags there. Accordingly in this field have the great poets and literatuses signally toiled. They too, in all ages, all lands, have been creators, fashioning, making types of men and women, as Adam and Eve are made in the divine fable. Behold, shaped, bred by orientalism, feudalism, through their long growth and culmination, and breeding back in return—(when shall we have an equal series, typical of democracy?)—behold, commencing in primal Asia (apparently formulated, in what beginning we know, in the gods of the mythologies, and coming down thence), a few samples out of the

of the nationality of these States is, that only by such powerful com-·
paction can the separate States secure that full and free swing within
their spheres, which is becoming to them, each after its kind, so
will individuality, and unimpeded branchings, flourish best under
imperial republican forms.

Assuming Democracy to be at present in its embryo condition,
and that the only large and satisfactory justification of it resides in
the future, mainly through the copious production of perfect characters among the people, and through the advent of a sane and
pervading religiousness, it is with regard to the atmosphere and
spaciousness fit for such characters, and of certain nutriment and
cartoon-draftings proper for them, and indicating them for New
World purposes, that I continue the present statement—an exploration, as of new ground, wherein, like other primitive surveyors, I
must do the best I can, leaving it to those who come after me to do
much better. (The service, in fact, if any, must be to break a sort of
first path or track, no matter how rude and ungeometrical.) * * *

There is, in sanest hours, a consciousness, a thought that rises,
independent, lifted out from all else, calm, like the stars, shining
eternal. This is the thought of identity—yours for you, whoever you
are, as mine for me. Miracle of miracles, beyond statement, most
spiritual and vaguest of earth's dreams, yet hardest basic fact, and
only entrance to all facts. In such devout hours, in the midst of the
significant wonders of heaven and earth (significant only because of
the Me in the center), creeds, conventions, fall away and become of
no account before this simple idea. Under the luminousness of real
vision, it alone takes possession, takes value. Like the shadowy dwarf
in the fable, once liberated and look'd upon, it expands over the
whole earth, and spreads to the roof of heaven.

The quality of BEING, in the object's self, according to its own
central idea and purpose, and of growing therefrom and thereto—
not criticism by other standards, and adjustments thereto—is the
lesson of Nature. True, the full man wisely gathers, culls, absorbs;
but if, engaged disproportionately in that, he slights or overlays the

countless product, bequeath'd to the
moderns, bequeath'd to America as
studies. For the men, Yudishtura,
Rama, Arjuna, Solomon, most of the
Old and New Testament characters;
Achilles, Ulysses, Theseus, Prometheus,
Hercules, Aeneas, Plutarch's heroes; the
Merlin of Celtic bards; the Cid, Arthur
and his knights, Siegfried and Hagen in
the Nibelungen; Roland and Oliver;
Roustam in the Shah-Nemah; and so
on to Milton's Satan, Cervantes' Don
Quixote, Shakspere's Hamlet, Richard
II, Lear, Marc Antony, etc., and the
modern Faust. These, I say, are models,
combined, adjusted to other standards
than America's, but of priceless value to
her and hers.

Among women, the goddesses of the
Egyptian, Indian, and Greek mythologies, certain Bible characters, especially the Holy Mother; Cleopatra,
Penelope; the portraits of Brunhelde
and Chriemhilde in the Nibelungen;
Oriana, Una, etc.; the modern Con-
suelo, Walter Scott's Jeanie and Effie
Deans, etc., etc. (Yet woman portrayed
or outlin'd at her best, or as perfect
human mother, does not hitherto, it
seems to me, fully appear in literature.)" [Whitman's note].

precious idiocrasy and special nativity and intention that he is, the man's self, the main thing, is a failure, however wide his general cultivation. Thus, in our times, refinement and delicatesse[5] are not only attended to sufficiently, but threaten to eat us up, like a cancer. Already, the democratic genius watches, ill-pleased, these tendencies. Provision for a little healthy rudeness, savage virtue, justification of what one has in one's self, whatever it is, is demanded. Negative qualities, even deficiencies, would be a relief. Singleness and normal simplicity and separation, amid this more and more complex, more and more artificialized state of society—how pensively we yearn for them! how we would welcome their return!

In some such direction, then—at any rate enough to preserve the balance—we feel called upon to throw what weight we can, not for absolute reasons, but current ones. To prune, gather, trim, conform, and ever cram and stuff, and be genteel and proper, is the pressure of our days. While aware that much can be said even in behalf of all this, we perceive that we have not now to consider the question of what is demanded to serve a half-starved and barbarous nation, or set of nations, but what is most applicable, most pertinent, for numerous congeries of conventional, over-corpulent societies, already becoming stifled and rotten with flatulent, infidelistic literature, and polite conformity and art. In addition to establish'd sciences, we suggest a science as it were of healthy average personalism, on original-universal grounds, the object of which should be to raise up and supply through the States a copious race of superb American men and women, cheerful, religious, ahead of any yet known.

America has yet morally and artistically originated nothing. She seems singularly unaware that the models of persons, books, manners, etc., appropriate for former conditions and for European lands, are but exiles and exotics here. No current of her life, as shown on the surfaces of what is authoritatively called her society, accepts or runs into social or æsthetic democracy; but all the currents set squarely against it. Never, in the Old World, was thoroughly upholster'd exterior appearance and show, mental and other, built entirely on the idea of caste, and on the sufficiency of mere outside acquisition—never were glibness, verbal intellect more the test, the emulation—more loftily elevated as head and sample—than they are on the surface of our republican States this day. The writers of a time hint the mottoes of its gods. The word of the modern, say these voices, in the word Culture.

We find ourselves abruptly in close quarters with the enemy. This word Culture, or what it has come to represent, involves, by contrast, our whole theme, and has been, indeed, the spur, urging us to en-

5. Borrowed from the French and used by Whitman to mean "fastidiousness to the point of squeamishness."

gagement. Certain questions arise. As now taught, accepted and carried out, are not the processes of culture rapidly creating a class of supercilious infidels, who believe in nothing? Shall a man lose himself in countless masses of adjustments, and be so shaped with reference to this, that, and the other, that the simply good and healthy and brave parts of him are reduced and clipp'd away, like the bordering of box in a garden? You can cultivate corn and roses and orchards—but who shall cultivate the mountain peaks, the ocean, and the tumbling gorgeousness of the clouds? Lastly—is the readily given reply that culture only seeks to help, systematize, and put in attitude, the elements of fertility and power, a conclusive reply?

I do not so much object to the name, or word, but I should certainly insist, for the purposes of these States, on a radical change of category, in the distribution of precedence. I should demand a programme of culture, drawn out, not for a single class alone, or for the parlors or lecture rooms, but with an eye to practical life, the west, the workingmen, the facts of farms and jackplanes and engineers, and of the broad range of the women also of the middle and working strata, and with reference to the perfect equality of women, and of a grand and powerful motherhood. I should demand of this programme or theory a scope generous enough to include the widest human area. It must have for its spinal meaning the formation of a typical personality of character, eligible to the uses of the high average of men—and *not* restricted by conditions ineligible to the masses. The best culture will always be that of the manly and courageous instincts, and loving perceptions, and of self-respect—aiming to form, over this continent, an idiocrasy of universalism, which, true child of America, will bring joy to its mother, returning to her in her own spirit, recruiting myriads of offspring, able, natural, perceptive, tolerant, devout believers in her, America, and with some definite instinct why and for what she has arisen, most vast, most formidable of historic births, and is, now and here, with wonderful step, journeying through Time.

The problem, as it seems to me, presented to the New World, is, under permanent law and order, and after preserving cohesion (ensemble-Individuality), at all hazards, to vitalize man's free play of special Personalism,[6] recognizing in it something that calls ever more to be consider'd, fed, and adopted as the sub-stratum for the best that belongs to us (government indeed is for it), including the new æsthetics of our future.

To formulate beyond this present vagueness—to help line and

6. It seems likely that Whitman first introduced the term "Personalism" to designate the fusion between the independent individual and the ideal democratic society. It was already an established term in German transcendentalism (in Schleiermacher's *Discourses,* not then translated). Bronson Alcott got it from Whitman; through the St. Louis transcendentalists it then passed into the general literature of American philosophy.

put before us the species, or a specimen of the species, of the democratic ethnology of the future, is a work toward which the genius of our land, with peculiar encouragement, invites her well-wishers. Already certain limnings, more or less grotesque, more or less fading and watery, have appear'd. We too (repressing doubts and qualms) will try our hand.

Attempting, then, however crudely, a basic model or portrait of personality for general use for the manliness of the State (and doubtless that is most useful which is most simple and comprehensive for all, and toned low enough), we should prepare the canvas well beforehand. Parentage must consider itself in advance. (Will the time hasten when fatherhood and motherhood shall become a science—and the noblest science?) To our model, a clear-blooded, strong-fibered physique is indispensable; the questions of food, drink, air, exercise assimilation, digestion, can never be intermitted. Out of these we descry a well-begotten selfhood—in youth, fresh, ardent, emotional, aspiring, full of adventure; at maturity, brave, perceptive, under control, neither too talkative nor too reticent, neither flippant nor somber; of the bodily figure, the movements easy, the complexion showing the best blood, somewhat flush'd, breast expanded, an erect attitude, a voice whose sound outvies music, eyes of calm and steady gaze, yet capable also of flashing—and a general presence that holds its own in the company of the highest. (For it is native personality, and that alone, that endows a man to stand before presidents or generals, or in any distinguished collection, with *aplomb*—and *not* culture, or any knowledge or intellect whatever.)

With regard to the mental-educational part of our model, enlargement of intellect, stores of cephalic knowledge, etc., the concentration thitherward of all the customs of our age, especially in America, is so overweening, and provides so fully for that part, that, important and necessary as it is, it really needs nothing from us here—except, indeed, a phrase of warning and restraint. Manners, costumes, too, though important, we need not dwell upon here. Like beauty, grace of motion, etc., they are results. Causes, original things, being attended to, the right manners unerringly follow. Much is said, among artists, of "the grand style," as if it were a thing by itself. When a man, artist or whoever, has health, pride, acuteness, noble aspirations, he has the motive-elements of the grandest style. The rest is but manipulation (yet that is no small matter).

Leaving still unspecified several sterling parts of any model fit for the future personality of America, I must not fail, again and ever, to pronounce myself on one, probably the least attended to in modern times—a hiatus, indeed, threatening its gloomiest consequences after us. I mean the simple, unsophisticated Conscience, the primary moral element. If I were asked to specify in what quarter lie the grounds of darkest dread, respecting the America of our hopes, I should have to point to this particular. I should demand the invariable application to individuality, this day and any day, of that old, ever-true plumb-rule of persons, eras, nations. Our triumphant modern civilizee,[7] with his all-schooling and his wondrous appliances, will still show himself but an amputation while this deficiency remains. Beyond (assuming a more hopeful tone), the vertebration of the manly and womanly personalism of our Western world, can only be, and is, indeed, to be (I hope), its all penetrating Religiousness.

The ripeness of Religion is doubtless to be looked for in this field of individuality, and is a result that no organization or church can ever achieve. As history is poorly retain'd by what the technists call history, and is not given out from their pages, except the learner has in himself the sense of the well-wrapt, never yet written, perhaps impossible to be written, history—so Religion, although casually arrested, and, after a fashion, preserv'd in the churches and creeds, does not depend at all upon them, but is a part of the identified soul, which, when greatest, knows not bibles in the old way, but in new ways—the identified soul, which can really confront Religion when it extricates itself entirely from the churches, and not before.

Personalism fuses this, and favors it. I should say, indeed, that only in the perfect uncontamination and solitariness of individuality may the spirituality of religion positively come forth at all. Only here, and on such terms, the meditation, the devout ecstasy, the soaring flight. Only here, communion with the mysteries, the eternal problems, whence? whither? Alone, and identity, and the mood—and the soul emerges, and all statements, churches, sermons, melt away like vapors. Alone, and silent thought and awe, and aspiration—and then the interior consciousness, like a hitherto unseen inscription, in magic ink, beams out its wondrous lines to the sense. Bibles may convey, and priests expound, but it is exclusively for the noiseless operation of one's isolated Self, to enter the pure ether of veneration, reach the divine levels, and commune with the unutterable.

To practically enter into politics is an important part of American personalism. To every young man, north and south, earnestly studying these things, I should here, as an offset to what I have said in former pages, now also say, that maybe to views of very large scope, after all, perhaps the political (perhaps the literary and sociological) America goes best about its development its own way—sometimes, to temporary sight, appalling enough. It is the fashion among dilettants and fops (perhaps I myself am not guiltless), to decry the

7. Whitman's coinage: one civilized to the point of weakness.

whole formulation of the active politics of America, as beyond redemption, and to be carefully kept away from. See you that you do
not fall into this error. America, it may be, is doing very well upon
the whole, notwithstanding these antics of the parties and their
leaders, these half-brain'd nominees, and many ignorant ballots, and
many elected failures and blatherers. It is the dillettants, and all who
shirk their duty, who are not doing well. As for you, I advise you to
enter more strongly yet into politics. I advise every young man to do
so. Always inform yourself; always do the best you can; always vote.
Disengage yourself from parties. They have been useful, and to some
extent remain so; but the floating, uncommitted electors, farmers,
clerks, mechanics, the masters of parties—watching aloof, inclining
victory this side or that side—such are the ones most needed, present and future. For America, if eligible at all to downfall and ruin,
is eligible within herself, not without; for I see clearly that the
combined foreign world could not beat her down. But these savage,
wolfish parties alarm me. Owning no law but their own will, more
and more combative, less and less tolerant of the idea of ensemble
and of equal brotherhood, the perfect equality of the States, the
ever-overarching American ideas, it behooves you to convey yourself
implicitly to no party, nor submit blindly to their dictators, but
steadily hold yourself judge and master over all of them.

1867–1868, 1871

SIDNEY LANIER

(1842–1881)

Sidney Lanier was born in
Macon, Georgia, on February 3,
1842, and he received his education at Oglethorpe University.
When the Civil War started,
Lanier enlisted as a Confederate
private, serving actively until
captured four months before the
end of the conflict. In the Federal prison at Point Lookout,
Maryland, he developed tuberculosis, and the remainder of his
life became a fight against poor
health and poverty. His first
published book was a novel,
Tiger-Lilies (1867), based upon
his experiences in the Civil War.

Though Lanier constantly devoted himself to poetry, it was
not until the publication of
"Corn" (1875) in *Lippincott's*
that he received recognition.
This poem and "The Sym-
phony" (1875), which followed,
were both timely in subject matter, the first touching on the
plight of penniless farmers, the
latter attacking the evils of commercialism. His cantata, *The
Centennial Meditation of Columbia, 1776–1876*, was performed at the opening of the
Centennial Exhibition in Philadelphia and was well received

when sung by a large chorus, but when published, without Dudley Buck's music, it was harshly criticized. In these works he was attempting a resolution between the rhythms of poetry and those of music, which he had studied all his life; but like Whitman he discovered that the majority of readers, accustomed to the established meters, were deaf to the new rhythms that he provided in such poems as "The Symphony" and "The Marshes of Glynn" (1878).

A volume of verse, *Poems* (1877), did not sell, and soon Lanier was forced into hack work to earn a living, made more difficult by ill health. A winter spent in San Antonio (1872) where he enjoyed the German choral societies, had been followed by his engagement in 1873 as flutist in the Peabody Orchestra in Baltimore. In 1878, still intent upon exploring the relations between poetry and music, he settled once more in Baltimore, where he again had the opportunity to serve as flutist in the Peabody Symphony Orchestra. There he added to his small earnings by lecturing on English literature and versification at the Johns Hopkins University in 1879. The same year he edited *The Boy's Froissart*, following it with his best-selling book, *The Boy's King Arthur* (1880). His lectures on versification, published as *The Science of English Verse* (1880), presented his thesis that poetry and music are governed by the same artistic laws. Though his study of prosody is no longer considered important, the book is nonetheless an interesting early

advocacy of fluid verse form. Lanier hoped it would bring him a professorship in the university, but critical reception was indifferent, and no professional advancement resulted. His final years were spent in gathering materials for his lectures and in writing some of his best poetry. He died when only forty years old, leaving a sufficient number of fine poems to suggest an even greater potentiality. Lanier's widow edited *Poems of Sidney Lanier* (1884), and some of his lectures at Johns Hopkins were later published as *The English Novel* (1883) and *Shakespeare and His Forerunners* (1902).

Though a southerner by tradition and chivalrous by nature, Lanier was never one to dwell on the dead past. In his social and economic criticism he was ahead of his times, and his dialect poems, with their mild humor, also give Lanier a place in the vanguard of regional realism.

A full critical edition of Lanier's writings is *The Centennial Edition of Sidney Lanier*, 10 vols., under the general editorship of Charles R. Anderson, 1945. Morgan Callaway, Jr., edited *Select Poems of Sidney Lanier*, 1895, with a scholarly introduction, notes, and bibliography. Henry W. Lanier edited *Selections from Sidney Lanier: Prose and Verse*, 1916; *Selected Poems of Sidney Lanier*, edited by Stark Young, 1947, contains some less accessible poems. *The Letters of Sidney Lanier, 1866–1881*, were edited by Henry Lanier, 1899.

There are three studies of Lanier's life and work: Edwin Mims, *Sidney Lanier*, 1905; Aubrey H. Starke, *Sidney Lanier: A Biographical and Critical Study*, 1933; and Lincoln Lorenz, *The Life of Sidney Lanier*, 1935. A good study of Lanier's versification is Gay W. Allen's "Sidney Lanier," in his *American Prosody*, 1935, pp. 277–306. The text for the following poems is based on the editions of 1877 and 1884.

The Symphony[1]

'O Trade! O Trade! would thou wert dead!
The Time needs heart—'tis tired of head:
We're all for love,' the violins said.
'Of what avail the rigorous tale[2]
Of bill for coin and box for bale?   5
Grant thee, O Trade! thine uttermost hope:
Level red gold with blue sky-slope,
And base it deep as devils grope:
When all's done, what hast thou won
Of the only sweet that's under the sun?   10
Ay, canst thou buy a single sigh
Of true love's least, least ecstasy?'
Then, with a bridegroom's heart-beats trembling,
All the mightier strings assembling
Ranged them on the violins' side   15
As when the bridegroom leads the bride,
And, heart in voice, together cried:
'Yea, what avail the endless tale
Of gain by cunning and plus by sale?
Look up the land, look down the land,   20
The poor, the poor, the poor, they stand
Wedged by the pressing of Trade's hand
Against an inward-opening door
That pressure tightens evermore:
They sigh a monstrous foul-air sigh   25
For the outside leagues of liberty,
Where Art, sweet lark, translates the sky
Into a heavenly melody.
"Each day, all day" (these poor folks say),
"In the same old year-long, drear-long way,   30
We weave in the mills and heave in the kilns,
We sieve mine-meshes under the hills,
And thieve much gold from the Devil's bank tills,
To relieve, O God, what manner of ills?—
The beasts, they hunger, and eat, and die;   35
And so do we, and the world's a sty;
Hush, fellow-swine: why nuzzle and cry?

1. "The Symphony" was written in Baltimore in March, 1875, and published in *Lippincott's* for June of that year; it was reprinted with revisions in *Poems* (1877) and with further revisions in *Poems of Sidney Lanier* (1884). Lanier's devotion to music, his strong belief that commercialism was destroying spiritual values, and his hope for a society based on harmony and love, are three persistent themes in all his writing. These lines offer a remarkable demonstration of his theory of the resemblances between music and poetry. See also the musical cadences of "The Marshes of Glynn."

2. A just count; a reckoning by number.

Swinehood hath no remedy
Say many men, and hasten by,
Clamping the nose and blinking the eye.   40
But who said once, in the lordly tone,
Man shall not live by bread alone
But all that cometh from the Throne?[3]
     Hath God said so?
     But Trade saith *No*:   45
And the kilns and the curt-tongued mills say *Go!*
There's plenty that can, if you can't: we know.
Move out, if you think you're underpaid.
The poor are prolific; we're not afraid;
"Trade is trade." '   50
Thereat this passionate protesting
Meekly changed, and softened till
It sank to sad requesting
And suggesting sadder still:
'And oh, if men might some time see   55
How piteous-false the poor decree
That trade no more than trade must be!
Does business mean, *Die, you—live, I?*
Then "Trade is trade" but sings a lie:
'Tis only war grown miserly.   60
If business is battle, name it so:
War-crimes less will shame it so,
And widows less will blame it so.
Alas, for the poor to have some part
In yon sweet living lands of Art,   65
Makes problem not for head, but heart.
Vainly might Plato's brain revolve it:
Plainly the heart of a child could solve it.'

And then, as when from words that seem but rude
We pass to silent pain that sits abrood   70
Back in our heart's great dark and solitude,
So sank the strings to gentle throbbing
Of long chords change-marked with sobbing—
Motherly sobbing, not distinctlier heard
Than half wing-openings of the sleeping bird,   75
Some dream of danger to her young hath stirred.
Then stirring and demurring ceased, and lo!
Every least ripple of the strings' song-flow
Died to a level with each level bow
And made a great chord tranquil-surfaced so,   80
As a brook beneath his curving bank doth go

3. *Cf.* Luke iv: 4.

To linger in the sacred dark and green
Where many boughs the still pool overlean
And many leaves make shadow with their sheen.
   But presently   85
A velvet flute-note fell down pleasantly
Upon the bosom of that harmony,
And sailed and sailed incessantly,
As if a petal from a wild-rose blown
Had fluttered down upon that pool of tone   90
And boatwise dropped o' the convex side
And floated down the glassy tide
And clarified and glorified
The solemn spaces where the shadows bide.
From the warm concave of that fluted note   95
Somewhat, half song, half odor, forth did float,
As if a rose might somehow be a throat:
'When Nature from her far-off glen
Flutes her soft messages to men,
     The flute can say them o'er again;   100
     Yea, Nature, singing sweet and lone,
Breathes through life's strident polyphone[4]
The flute-voice in the world of tone.
     Sweet friends,
     Man's love ascends   105
To finer and diviner ends
Than man's mere thought e'er comprehends,
For I, e'en I,
As here I lie,
A petal on a harmony,   110
Demand of Science whence and why
Man's tender pain, man's inward cry,
When he doth gaze on earth and sky?
I am not overbold:
     I hold   115
Full powers from Nature manifold.
I speak for each no-tonguèd tree
That, spring by spring, doth nobler be,
And dumbly and most wistfully
His mighty prayerful arms outspreads   120
Above men's oft-unheeding heads,
And his big blessing downward sheds.
I speak for all-shaped blooms and leaves,
Lichens on stones and moss on eaves,
Grasses and grains in ranks and sheaves;   125

4. A kind of lute. *Cf.* "polyphony," the multiplicity of sounds.

Broad-fronded ferns and keen-leaved canes,
And briery mazes bounding lanes,
And marsh-plants, thirsty-cupped for rains,
And milky stems and sugary veins;
For every long-armed woman-vine   130
That round a piteous tree doth twine;
For passionate odors, and divine
Pistils, and petals crystalline;
All purities of shady springs,
All shynesses of film-winged things   135
That fly from tree-trunks and bark-rings;
All modesties of mountain-fawns
That leap to covert from wild lawns,
And tremble if the day but dawns;
All sparklings of small beady eyes   140
Of birds, and sidelong glances wise
Wherewith the jay hints tragedies;
All piquancies of prickly burs,
And smoothnesses of downs and furs,
Of eiders[5] and of minivers;[6]   145
All limpid honeys that do lie
At stamen-bases, nor deny
The humming-birds' fine roguery,
Bee-thighs, nor any butterfly;
All gracious curves of slender wings,   150
Bark-mottlings, fibre-spiralings,
Fern-wavings and leaf-flickerings;
Each dial-marked leaf and flower-bell
Wherewith in every lonesome dell
Time to himself his hours doth tell;   155
All tree-sounds, rustlings of pine-cones,
Wind-sighings, doves' melodious moans,
And night's unearthly under-tones;
All placid lakes and waveless deeps,
All cool reposing mountain-steeps,   160
Vale-calms and tranquil lotos-sleeps;—
Yea, all fair forms, and sounds, and lights,
And warmths, and mysteries, and mights,
Of Nature's utmost depths and heights.
—These doth my timid tongue present,   165
Their mouthpiece and leal[7] instrument
And servant, all love-eloquent.
I heard, when *All for love* the violins cried:

5. Very soft feathers from the eider
duck, hence eider down.

6. A white fur valued highly for court
costumes in the Middle Ages.

7. Loyal.

So, Nature calls through all her system wide,
Give me thy love, O man, so long denied.   170
Much time is run, and man hath changed his ways,
Since Nature, in the antique fable-days,
Was hid from man's true love by proxy fays,
False fauns and rascal gods that stole her praise.
The nymphs, cold creatures of man's colder brain,   175
Chilled Nature's streams till man's warm heart was fain
Never to lave its love in them again.
Later, a sweet Voice *Love thy neighbor* said;[8]
Then first the bounds of neighborhood outspread
Beyond all confines of old ethnic dread.   180
Vainly the Jew might wag his covenant head:
All men are neighbors, so the sweet Voice said.
So, when man's arms had circled all man's race,
The liberal compass of his warm embrace
Stretched bigger yet in the dark bounds of space;   185
With hands a-grope he felt smooth Nature's grace,
Drew her to breast and kissed her sweetheart face:
Yea, man found neighbors in great hills and trees
And streams and clouds and suns and birds and bees,
And throbbed with neighbor-loves in loving these.   190
But oh, the poor! the poor! the poor!
That stand by the inward-opening door
Trade's hand doth tighten ever more,
And sigh their monstrous foul-air sigh
For the outside hills of liberty,   195
Where Nature spreads her wild blue sky
For Art to make into melody!
Thou Trade! thou king of the modern days!
    Change thy ways,
    Change thy ways;   200
Let the sweaty laborers file
    A little while,
    A little while,
Where Art and Nature sing and smile.
Trade! is thy heart all dead, all dead?   205
And hast thou nothing but a head?
I'm all for heart,' the flute-voice said,
And into sudden silence fled,
Like as a blush that while 'tis red
Dies to a still, still white instead.   210

    Thereto a thrilling calm succeeds,
Till presently the silence breeds

8. *Cf.* Matthew xxii: 39.

A little breeze among the reeds[9]
That seems to blow by sea-marsh weeds:
Then from the gentle stir and fret   215
Sings out the melting clarionet,
Like as a lady sings while yet
Her eyes with salty tears are wet.
'O Trade! O Trade!' the Lady said,
'I too will wish thee utterly dead   220
If all thy heart is in thy head.
For O my God! and O my God!
What shameful ways have women trod
At beckoning of Trade's golden rod!
Alas when sighs are traders' lies,   225
And heart's-ease eyes and violet eyes
    Are merchandise!
O purchased lips that kiss with pain!
O cheeks coin-spotted with smirch and stain!
O trafficked hearts that break in twain!   230
—And yet what wonder at my sisters' crime?
So hath Trade withered up Love's sinewy prime,
Men love not women as in olden time.
Ah, not in these cold merchantable days
Deem men their life an opal gray, where plays   235
The one red Sweet of gracious ladies'-praise.
Now, comes a suitor with sharp prying eye—
Says, *Here, you Lady, if you'll sell, I'll buy:*
Come, heart for heart—a trade? What! weeping? why?
Shame on such wooers' dapper mercery![1]   240
I would my lover kneeling at my feet
In humble manliness should cry, *O sweet!*
I know not if thy heart my heart will greet:
I ask not if thy love my love can meet:
Whate'er thy worshipful soft tongue shall say,   245
I'll kiss thine answer, be it yea or nay:
I do but know I love thee, and I pray
To be thy knight until my dying day.[2]
Woe him that cunning trades in hearts contrives!
Base love good women to base loving drives   250
If men loved larger, larger were our lives;
And wooed they nobler, won they nobler wives.'

---

9. Orchestral instruments with reeds for producing sound.
1. A mercer's wares; the mercer was a dealer in textiles.
2. In ll. 253–323, this idea is developed in the song of the Knight to the Lady, a reconstruction of a lyric form familiar in the medieval literature of chivalry. This remarkable lyric is in conformity with Lanier's social and artistic motivation as a writer, and with the southern tradition of which he was a creative spokesman.

There thrust the bold straightforward horn
To battle for that lady lorn,
With heartsome voice of mellow scorn, 255
Like any knight in knighthood's morn.
   'Now comfort thee,' said he,
      'Fair Lady.
For God shall right thy grievous wrong,
And man shall sing thee a true-love song, 260
Voiced in act his whole life long,
   Yea, all thy sweet life long,
      Fair Lady.
Where's he that craftily hath said,
The day of chivalry is dead? 265
I'll prove that lie upon his head,
   Or I will die instead,
      Fair Lady.
Is Honor gone into his grave?
Hath Faith become a caitiff knave, 270
And Selfhood turned into a slave
   To work in Mammon's cave,[3]
      Fair Lady?
Will Truth's long blade ne'er gleam again?
Hath Giant Trade in dungeons slain 275
All great contempts of mean-got gain
   And hates of inward stain,
      Fair Lady?
For aye shall name and fame be sold,
And place be hugged for the sake of gold, 280
And smirch-robed Justice feebly scold
   At Crime all money-bold,
      Fair Lady?
Shall self-wrapt husbands aye forget
Kiss-pardons for the daily fret 285
Wherewith sweet wifely eyes are wet—
   Blind to lips kiss-wise set—
      Fair Lady?
Shall lovers higgle, heart for heart,
Till wooing grows a trading mart 290
Where much for little, and all for part,
   Make love a cheapening art,
      Fair Lady?
Shall woman scorch for a single sin
That her betrayer may revel in, 295

3. Mammon personifies selfish devotion to riches. In Edmund Spenser's *Faërie Queene*, Book II, Canto vii, Sir Guyon (Temperance) visits Mammon's cave of worldly wealth but does not succumb to greed.

And she be burnt, and he but grin
   When that the flames begin,
      Fair Lady?
Shall ne'er prevail the woman's plea,
We maids would far, far whiter be   300
If that our eyes might sometimes see
   Men maids in purity,
      Fair Lady?
Shall Trade aye salve his conscience-aches
With jibes at Chivalry's old mistakes—   305
The wars that o'erhot knighthood makes
   For Christ's and ladies' sakes,
      Fair Lady?
Now by each knight that e'er hath prayed
To fight like a man and love like a maid,   310
Since Pembroke's[4] life, as Pembroke's blade,
   I' the scabbard, death, was laid,
      Fair Lady,
I dare avouch my faith is bright
That God doth right and God hath might.   315
Nor time hath changed His hair to white,
   Nor His dear love to spite,
      Fair Lady.
I doubt no doubts: I strive, and shrive my clay,
And fight my fight in the patient modern way   320
For true love and for thee—ah me! and pray
   To be thy knight until my dying day,
      Fair Lady.'
Made end that knightly horn, and spurred away
Into the thick of the melodious fray.   325

And then the hautboy[5] played and smiled,
And sang like any large-eyed child,
Cool-hearted and all undefiled.
   'Huge Trade!' he said,
'Would thou wouldst lift me on thy head   330
And run where'er my finger led!
Once said a Man—and wise was He—
Never shalt thou the heavens see,
Save as a little child thou be.'[6]
Then o'er sea-lashings of commingling tunes   335
The ancient wise bassoons,
   Like weird,

4. William Herbert, Third Earl of Pembroke, nephew of Sir Philip Sidney; the first folio of Shakespeare's plays was dedicated to him and his brother.

5. Oboe; a slender wood-wind instrument with a plaintive tone.
6. *Cf.* Matthew xix: 14, and Mark x: 15.

Gray-beard
Old harpers sitting on the high sea-dunes,
    Chanted runes:[7]   340
'Bright-waved gain, gray-waved loss,
The sea of all doth lash and toss,
One wave forward and one across:
But now 'twas trough, now 'tis crest,
And worst doth foam and flash to best,   345
    And curst to blest.

'Life! Life! thou sea-fugue,[8] writ from east to west,
    Love, Love alone can pore
    On thy dissolving score
    Of harsh half-phrasings,   350
       Blotted ere writ,
    And double erasings
       Of chords most fit.
Yea, Love, sole music-master blest,
May read thy weltering palimpsest.[9]   355
To follow Time's dying melodies through,
And never to lose the old in the new,
And ever to solve the discords true—
    Love alone can do.
And ever Love hears the poor-folks' crying,   360
And ever Love hears the women's sighing,
And ever sweet knighthood's death-defying,
And ever wise childhood's deep implying,
But never a trader's glozing and lying.

'And yet shall Love himself be heard,   365
Though long deferred, though long deferred:
O'er the modern waste a dove[1] hath whirred:
Music is Love in search of a word.'

                         1875, 1877

Evening Song[2]

Look off, dear Love, across the sallow sands,
    And mark yon meeting of the sun and sea,

7. Poems; originally runes were verses written in ancient characters used by the Norsemen.
8. A musical composition generally having several themes, enunciated in turn, and gradually reaching a marked climax at the end.
9. A parchment from which writing has been erased to make space for another text.
1. During the flood Noah sent the dove from the ark, seeking land. On the seventh day the dove returned with an olive leaf (Genesis viii: 8–11).
2. Written at West Chester, Pennsylvania, in the autumn of 1876, in response to a request from Dudley Buck for a song to be set to music. It was published in *Lippincott's* for January, 1877, and reprinted in *Poems of Sidney Lanier* (1884). It was also published with Buck's music as "Sunset."

How long they kiss in sight of all the lands.
    Ah! longer, longer, we.

Now in the sea's red vintage melts the sun,   5
    As Egypt's pearl[3] dissolved in rosy wine,
And Cleopatra night drinks all. 'Tis done,
    Love, lay thine hand in mine.

Come forth, sweet stars, and comfort heaven's heart;
    Glimmer, ye waves, round else unlighted sands.   10
O night! divorce our sun and sky apart
    Never our lips, our hands.

1876   1877, 1884

The Stirrup-Cup[4]

Death, thou 'rt a cordial old and rare:
Look how compounded, with what care!
Time got his wrinkles reaping thee
Sweet herbs from all antiquity.

David to thy distillage went,   5
Keats, and Gotama[5] excellent,
Omar Khayyám, and Chaucer bright,
And Shakspere for a king-delight.

Then, Time, let not a drop be spilt:
Hand me the cup whene'er thou wilt;   10
'Tis thy rich stirrup-cup to me;
I'll drink it down right smilingly.

1877, 1884

The Mocking Bird[6]

Superb and sole, upon a plumèd spray
That o'er the general leafage boldly grew,
He summ'd the woods in song; or typic drew

3. The second stanza alludes to the tradition that Cleopatra dissolved a pearl in her cup to toast Anthony's health.
4. Originally titled "Life's Stirrup-Cup." It was an old English custom, transplanted to parts of the South, to offer the guest a farewell drink as he mounted for departure. This poem gains some personal significance from the fact that it was written in January, 1877, just after the poet was ordered to Florida in the hope of recuperation from his deadly illness. It was first published in *Scribner's* for May, 1877, and reprinted with variations in *Poems of Sidney Lanier* (1884).
5. The Buddha (Sanskrit, "the enlightened one"), founder of Buddhism, was Gautama Siddhartha (563–483 B.C.).
6. Written during the spring of 1877, published in the *Galaxy* for August, 1877, and reprinted with alterations in *Poems of Sidney Lanier* (1884).

The watch of hungry hawks, the lone dismay
Of languid doves when long their lovers stray,   5
And all birds' passion-plays that sprinkle dew
At morn in brake or bosky avenue.
Whate'er birds did or dreamed, this bird could say.
Then down he shot, bounced airily along
The sward, twitched in a grasshopper, made song   10
Midflight, perched, prinked,[7] and to his art again.
Sweet Science, this large riddle read me plain:
How may the death of that dull insect be
The life of yon trim Shakspere on the tree?

1877, 1884

Song of the Chattahoochee[8]

Out of the hills of Habersham,
Down the valleys of Hall,[9]
I hurry amain to reach the plain,
Run the rapid and leap the fall,
Split at the rock and together again,   5
Accept my bed, or narrow or wide,
And flee from folly on every side
With a lover's pain to attain the plain
    Far from the hills of Habersham,
    Far from the valleys of Hall.   10

All down the hills of Habersham,
    All through the valleys of Hall,
The rushes cried *Abide, abide,*
The willful waterweeds held me thrall,
The laving laurel turned my tide,   15
The ferns and the fondling grass said *Stay,*
The dewberry dipped for to work delay,
And the little reeds sighed *Abide, abide,*
    Here in the hills of Habersham,
    Here in the valleys of Hall.   20

7. To primp or take special care of one's appearance.
8. The Chattahoochee is a small river in Lanier's native Georgia. The poet considered music and poetry to be a single and natural expression of his ideal theory of unity. He conceived of nature, society, and moral obligation as being unified by a single compulsion, as is the river, personified in its life-giving journey from its source to the great sea of eternity. This poem was published in the *Independent* for December 20, 1883, and reprinted with emendations in *Poems of Sidney Lanier* (1884).
9. Habersham is a county in the northeastern section of Georgia; Hall County is slightly to the southwest of it.

High o'er the hills of Habersham,
Veiling the valleys of Hall,
The hickory told me manifold
Fair tales of shade, the poplar tall
Wrought me her shadowy self to hold,   25
The chestnut, the oak, the walnut, the pine,
Overleaning, with flickering meaning and sign,
Said, *Pass not, so cold, these manifold*
Deep shades of the hills of Habersham,
These glades in the valleys of Hall.   30

And oft in the hills of Habersham,
And oft in the valleys of Hall,
The white quartz shone, and the smooth brook-stone
Did bar me of passage with friendly brawl,
And many a luminous jewel lone   35
—Crystals clear or a-cloud with mist,
Ruby, garnet and amethyst—
Made lures with the lights of streaming stone
In the clefts of the hills of Habersham,
In the beds of the valleys of Hall.   40

But oh, not the hills of Habersham,
And oh, not the valleys of Hall
Avail: I am fain for to water the plain.
Downward the voices of Duty call—
Downward, to toil and be mixed with the main,   45
The dry fields burn, and the mills are to turn,
And a myriad flowers mortally yearn,
And the lordly main from beyond the plain
Calls o'er the hills of Habersham,
Calls through the valleys of Hall.   50

1877   1883, 1884

The Marshes of Glynn[1]

Glooms of the live-oaks, beautiful-braided and woven
With intricate shades of the vines that myriad-cloven
Clamber the forks of the multiform boughs,—
Emerald twilights,—
Virginal shy lights,   5

1. Completed in July, 1878. Here again Lanier improvised orchestral effects, this time from phrases describing the appearance and the spiritual mood produced by the woods and marshes of the southern coast. The county of Glynn is located in the southeastern corner of Georgia on the Atlantic seacoast. This poem was published in *A Masque of Poets* (1878); it was reprinted with revisions as Section IV of "Hymns of the Marshes" in *Poems of Sidney Lanier* (1884).

Wrought of the leaves to allure to the whisper of vows,
When lovers pace timidly down through the green colonnades
Of the dim sweet woods, of the dear dark woods,
 Of the heavenly woods and glades,
That run to the radiant marginal sand-beach within   10
  The wide sea-marshes of Glynn;—

Beautiful glooms, soft dusks in the noon-day fire,—
Wildwood privacies, closets of lone desire,
Chamber from chamber parted with wavering arras of leaves,—
Cells for the passionate pleasure of prayer to the soul that grieves,
Pure with a sense of the passing of saints through the wood, 16
Cool for the dutiful weighing of ill with good;—

O braided dusks of the oak and woven shades of the vine,
While the riotous noon-day sun of the June-day long did shine
Ye held me fast in your heart and I held you fast in mine; 20
But now when the noon is no more, and riot is rest,
And the sun is a-wait at the ponderous gate of the West,
And the slant yellow beam down the wood-aisle doth seem
Like a lane into heaven that leads from a dream,—
Ay, now, when my soul all day hath drunken the soul of the oak, 25
And my heart is at ease from men, and the wearisome sound of the
  stroke
 Of the scythe of time and the trowel of trade is low,
 And belief overmasters doubt, and I know that I know,
 And my spirit is grown to a lordly great compass within,
That the length and the breadth and the sweep of the marshes of
  Glynn   30
Will work me no fear like the fear they have wrought me of yore
When length was fatigue, and when breadth was but bitterness sore,
And when terror and shrinking and dreary unnamable pain
Drew over me out of the merciless miles of the plain,—

Oh, now, unafraid, I am fain to face   35
 The vast sweet visage of space.
To the edge of the wood I am drawn, I am drawn,
Where the gray beach glimmering runs, as a belt of the dawn,
 For a mete and a mark
  To the forest-dark:—   40
     So:
Affable live-oak, leaning low,—
Thus—with your favor—soft, with a reverent hand,
(Not lightly touching your person, Lord of the land!)
Bending your beauty aside, with a step I stand 45
On the firm-packed sand,

Free
By a world of marsh that borders a world of sea.
  Sinuous southward and sinuous northward the shimmering band
Of the sand-beach fastens the fringe of the marsh to the folds of the
      land.   50
Inward and outward to northward and southward the beach-lines
      linger and curl
As a silver-wrought garment that clings to and follows the firm
      sweet limbs of a girl.
Vanishing, swerving, evermore curving again into sight,
Softly the sand-beach wavers away to a dim gray looping of light.
And what if behind me to westward the wall of the woods stands
      high?   55
The world lies east: how ample, the marsh and the sea and the sky!
A league and a league of marsh-grass, waist-high, broad in the
      blade,
Green, and all of a height, and unflecked with a light or a shade,
Stretch leisurely off, in a pleasant plain,
To the terminal blue of the main.   60

Oh, what is abroad in the marsh and the terminal sea?
  Somehow my soul seems suddenly free
From the weighing of fate and the sad discussion of sin,
By the length and the breadth and the sweep of the marshes of
      Glynn.

Ye marshes, how candid and simple and nothing-withholding and
      free   65
Ye publish yourselves to the sky and offer yourselves to the sea!
Tolerant plains, that suffer the sea and the rains and the sun,
Ye spread and span like the catholic[2] man who hath mightily won
God out of knowledge and good out of infinite pain
And sight out of blindness and purity out of a stain.   70

As the marsh-hen secretly builds on the watery sod,
Behold I will build me a nest on the greatness of God:
I will fly in the greatness of God as the marsh-hen flies
In the freedom that fills all the space 'twixt the marsh and the skies:
By so many roots as the marsh-grass sends in the sod   75
I will heartily lay me a-hold on the greatness of God:
Oh, like to the greatness of God is the greatness within
The range of the marshes, the liberal marshes of Glynn.

And the sea lends large, as the marsh: lo, out of his plenty the sea
Pours fast: full soon the time of the flood-tide must be: 80
Look how the grace of the sea doth go
2. Universal.

About and about through the intricate channels that flow
    Here and there,
               Everywhere,
Till his waters have flooded the uttermost creeks and the low-lying
    lanes,
And the marsh is meshed with a million veins,
That like as with rosy and silvery essences flow
   In the rose-and-silver evening glow.
          Farewell, my lord Sun!
The creeks overflow: a thousand rivulets run   90
'Twixt the roots of the sod; the blades of the marsh-grass stir;
Passeth a hurrying sound of wings that westward whirr;
Passeth, and all is still; and the currents cease to run;
And the sea and the marsh are one.

How still the plains of the waters be!   95
The tide is in his ecstasy.
The tide is at his highest height:
       And it is night.

And now from the Vast of the Lord will the waters of sleep
Roll in on the souls of men,   100
But who will reveal to our waking ken
The forms that swim and the shapes that creep
       Under the waters of sleep?
And I would I could know what swimmeth below when the tide
    comes in
On the length and the breadth of the marvellous marshes of
    Glynn.   105
              1878, 1884

Opposition[3]

    Of fret, of dark, of thorn, of chill,
      Complain no more; for these, O heart,
    Direct the random of the will
      As rhymes direct the rage of art.

    The lute's fixed fret, that runs athwart   5
      The strain and purpose of the string,
    For governance and nice consort
      Doth bar his wilful wavering.

3. Probably written in Baltimore during the spring of 1879, published in *Good Company* for January, 1880, and reprinted in *Poems of Sidney Lanier* (1884).

The dark hath many dear avails;
  The dark distils divinest dews;   10
The dark is rich with nightingales,
  With dreams, and with the heavenly Muse.

Bleeding with thorns of petty strife,
  I'll ease (as lovers do) my smart
With sonnets to my lady Life   15
  Writ red in issues from the heart.

What grace may lie within the chill
  Of favor frozen fast in scorn!
When Good's a-freeze, we call it Ill!
  This rosy Time is glacier-born.   20

Of fret, of dark, of thorn, of chill,
  Complain thou not, O heart; for these
Bank-in the current of the will
  To uses, arts, and charities.

1879   1880, 1884

EMILY DICKINSON
(1830–1886)

Emily Dickinson was born on December 10, 1830, in Amherst, Massachusetts, where her grandfather had been a leader in founding Amherst College. Her father, Edward Dickinson, a successful lawyer who became a member of Congress, served the college as a trustee, and was its treasurer for forty years. Though reported a stern and authoritarian moralist, he was perhaps no more patriarchal than other fathers of his time; but when he spoke, his timid wife "trembled, obeyed, and was silent." The conservative Amherst of that day, in which the church wielded the highest authority, was a small and rigid world, ideally constructed to provoke the rebelliousness latent in Emily Dickinson's spirit. Like her sister Lavinia, Emily never married; Austin, her lawyer brother, having surrendered to his father's opposition to his going west, opposed him by marrying Susan Gilbert, a "worldly" New Yorker, who became Emily's confidante. In her poems Emily Dickinson constructed her own world—of the garden and the beautiful Connecticut valley scenery; of the books, many of them forbidden, smuggled in by her brother; of her private and quite startling thoughts; for a time, of her few congenial friends at Amherst Academy. For less than a year (1847) she went over the hills to South Hadley Female Seminary (Mount Holyoke), but failing to respond to the academic severity of the famous Mary Lyon, she returned to Amherst, which she never again left, except for brief visits to Washington, Philadelphia, and Boston in the earlier years.

On her return from South Hadley, Emily may have fallen in love with young Ben Newton, who in 1848 was living with her family as her father's law apprentice. He was a brilliant freethinker, and introduced her to a new world of ideas; but he was too poor to marry, even if her father could conceivably have given approval. He died of tuberculosis five years later, having begun his practice in another town some distance away. In such poems as "My life closed twice before its close," however, Emily Dickinson acknowledges at least two persons in that complex and passionate world that her imagination created, perhaps to fill the void of not-having. According to the family tradition she met the Reverend Charles Wadsworth in Philadelphia in 1854, on one of her rare journeys, when she was on the way to visit her father, then in Washington for his term in Congress. Since Ben Newton had just died, and Emily was seeking spiritual assurance, it may have been Wadsworth who "tried to teach me immortality," as she wrote of someone not named, who afterward "left the land." Although married, Wadsworth continued to visit Emily in Amherst until 1862, when he accepted a call to California. The poet's family and friends as biographers supported the Amherst legend that Emily spent her middle years as a white-clad

recluse. However, new evidence continues to indicate that the poet's human associations were more continuous and varied than was before supposed, substantiating the passionate impulsiveness which animated her poetry as a whole. In her writing she was encouraged by her girlhood friend Helen Hunt Jackson, famous author of *Ramona*; and after 1862 by Thomas Wentworth Higginson, a literary friend of the family, who tried unsuccessfully to "improve" her unconventional style; she had the advice of Samuel Bowles, editor of the famous Springfield *Republican*, but probably no more than seven of her poems slipped into print during her lifetime. It was probably just as well. Readers of the twentieth century would understand her better, for it was their idiom that she spoke.

From 1884 until her death on May 16, 1886, Emily Dickinson was a semi-invalid, in a condition of mental decline. Three posthumous collections between 1890 and 1896 won her the reputation of a powerful eccentric; later collections of her poems, beginning in 1914, established her recognition as a major poet and her immediate influence upon those young writers who were then creating the radical poetry of the present century. By the instinct of the artist she had found her own way, in the 1860's, toward forms of expression which only became naturalized in the iconoclastic 1920's. Her style was simple yet passionate, and marked by economy and concentration. Like the later generation she discovered that the sharp, intense image is the poet's best instrument. She anticipated the modern enlargement of melody by assonance, dissonance, and "off-rhyme"; she discovered, as our contemporaries did, the utility of the ellipsis of thought and the verbal ambiguity. Her ideas were witty, rebellious, and original, yet she confined her materials to the world of her small village, her domestic circle, her garden, and a few good books. She possessed the most acute awareness of sensory experience and psychological actualities, and she expressed radical discoveries in these areas with frankness and force. Confronted with the question of how, in her narrow life, she came by these instruments and this knowledge, one can only conclude that it was by sheer genius. She remains incomparable because her originality sets her apart from all others, but her poems shed the unmistakable light of greatness.

Excepting seven poems that appeared in periodicals, Emily Dickinson's poetry was published posthumously. The definitive edition is *The Poems of Emily Dickinson*, edited by Thomas H. Johnson, 3 vols., 1955, which includes variant readings critically compared with all known manuscripts. With the kind permission of the Belknap Press of the Harvard University Press, the present edition follows Johnson's chronology and adopts his numbering of the poems; and the text used is that established by Johnson, except that capitalization and punctuation are regularized, as Johnson suggests Emily Dickinson would have expected had her poems been published in her lifetime. In the cases where the poet herself left variant readings of single words, the choice of previous editors is generally adopted.

Thomas H. Johnson has edited *Letters of Emily Dickinson*, 3 vols., 1958. For excellent accounts of Emily Dickinson's life see George F. Whicher, *This Was a Poet*, 1938; and Thomas H. Johnson, *Emily Dickinson: An Interpretive Biography*, 1955. Genevieve Taggard, *The Life and Mind of Emily Dickinson*, 1930, is a sound study.

Millicent T. Bingham, *Ancestors' Brocades*, 1945, gives intimate revelations of the Dickinson family. Good critical interpretations are Richard Chase, *Emily Dickinson*, American Men of Letters Series, 1951; Henry W. Wells, *Introduction to Emily Dickinson*, 1947; Charles R. Anderson, *Emily Dickinson's Poetry: Stairway to Surprise*, 1960; and Jay Leyda, *The Years and Hours of Emily Dickinson*, 1960.

J. 49

I never lost as much but twice,
And that was in the sod;
Twice have I stood a beggar
Before the door of God!

Angels, twice descending,   5
Reimbursed my store.
Burglar, banker, father,
I am poor once more!
1858?   1890

J. 67

Success is counted sweetest
By those who ne'er succeed.
To comprehend a nectar
Requires sorest need.

Not one of all the purple host   5
Who took the flag to-day
Can tell the definition,
So clear, of victory,

As he, defeated, dying,
On whose forbidden ear   10
The distant strains of triumph
Burst agonized and clear!
1859   1878, 1890

J. 76

Exultation is the going
Of an inland soul to sea,—

Past the houses, past the head-
  lands,
Into deep eternity!

Bred as we, among the mountains,   5
Can the sailor understand
The divine intoxication
Of the first league out from
  land?
1859?   1890

J. 130

These are the days when birds
  come back,
A very few, a bird or two,
To take a backward look.

These are the days when skies
  resume
The old, old sophistries of
  June,—   5
A blue and gold mistake.

Oh, fraud that cannot cheat the
  bee,
Almost thy plausibility
Induces my belief,

Till ranks of seeds their witness
  bear,   10
And softly through the altered
  air
Hurries a timid leaf!

Oh, sacrament of summer days,
Oh, last communion in the
  haze,
Permit a child to join,   15

Thy sacred emblems to partake,
Thy consecrated bread to take
And thine immortal wine!
1859?   1890

J. 148

All overgrown by cunning moss,
  All interspersed with weed,
The little cage of "Currer Bell,"[1]
  In quiet Haworth laid.

This bird, observing others,   5
  When frosts too sharp be-
    came,
Retire to other latitudes,
  Quietly did the same.

But differed in returning;
  Since Yorkshire hills are
    green,   10
Yet not in all the nests I meet
  Can nightingale be seen.

Gathered from any wanderings,
  Gethsemane[2] can tell
Through what transporting an-
  guish   15
  She reached the asphodel![3]

Soft falls the sounds of Eden
  Upon her puzzled ear;
Oh, what an afternoon for
  heaven,   19
  When Brontë entered there![4]
1859?   1896

J. 160

Just lost when I was saved!
Just felt the world go by!

1. Charlotte Brontë, British novelist
(1816–1855), wrote under the name of
"Currer Bell." She lived in Haworth,
Yorkshire (see next line).
2. A garden outside Jerusalem, where
Christ suffered agony before his betrayal and arrest (Matthew xxvi: 36).
3. In Greek mythology the flower of the
Elysian Fields, where the worthy dead
enjoy complete happiness.
4. "One may conjecture that ED intended a three-stanza poem but remained uncertain whether the version
she preferred should consist of the first
stanza plus the two stanzas preceding

Just girt me for the onset with
  eternity,
When breath blew back,
And on the other side   5
I heard recede the disappointed
  tide!

Therefore, as one returned, I
  feel,
Odd secrets of the line to tell!
Some sailor, skirting foreign
  shores,
Some pale reporter from the
  awful doors   10
Before the seal!

Next time, to stay!
Next time, the things to see
By ear unheard,
Unscrutinized by eye.   15

Next time, to tarry,
While the ages steal,—
Slow tramp the centuries,
And the cycles wheel.
1860?   1891

J. 162

My river runs to thee:
Blue sea, wilt welcome me?
My river waits reply.
Oh sea, look graciously!
I'll fetch thee brooks   5
From spotted nooks,—
Say, sea. Take me!
1860?   1890

J. 182

  If I shouldn't be alive
  When the robins come,

her division [after line 12] or the two
following" [Johnson's note].

Give the one in red cravat
A memorial crumb.

If I couldn't thank you,   5
Being fast asleep,
You will know I'm trying
With my granite lip!
1860?   1890

J. 214

I taste a liquor never brewed,
From tankards scooped in pearl;
Not all the vats upon the Rhine
Yield such an alcohol!

Inebriate of air am I,   5
And debauchee of dew,
Reeling, through endless summer
  days,
From inns of molten blue.

When   landlords   turn   the
  drunken bee
Out of the foxglove's door,   10
When butterflies renounce their
  drams,
I shall but drink the more!

Till seraphs swing their snowy
  hats,
And saints to windows run,
To see the little tippler   15
Leaning against the sun!
1860?   1861, 1890

J. 241

I like a look of agony,
Because I know it's true;
Men do not sham convulsion,
Nor simulate a throe.

The eyes glaze once, and that is
  death.   5

Impossible to feign
The beads upon the forehead
By homely anguish strung.
1861?   1890

J. 252

I can wade grief,
Whole pools of it,—
I'm used to that.
But the least push of joy
Breaks up my feet,   5
And I tip—drunken.
Let no pebble smile,
'T was the new liquor,—
That was all!

Power is only pain,   10
Stranded, through discipline,
Till weights will hang.
Give balm to giants,
And they'll wilt, like men.
Give Himmalch,⁵—   15
They'll carry him!
1861?   1891

J. 258

There's a certain slant of light,
Winter afternoons,
That oppresses, like the heft
Of cathedral tunes.

Heavenly hurt it gives us;   5
We can find no scar,
But internal difference
Where the meanings are.

None may teach it any:
'T is the seal, despair,—   10
An imperial affliction
Sent us of the air.

5. A personification of the Himalayas,
mountains in India, imagined as a god
in Hindu mythology.

When it comes, the landscape
    listens,
Shadows hold their breath;
When it goes, 'tis like the
    distance   15
On the look of death.
1861?   1890

J. 285

The robin's my criterion for tune
Because I grow where robins
    do—
But were I Cuckoo born
I'd swear by him—
The ode familiar rules the
    noon.   5
The Buttercup's my whim for
    bloom—
Because we're orchard-sprung—
But were I Britain-born
I'd daisies spurn—
None but the nut October fit   10
Because through dropping it
The seasons flit, I'm taught.
Without the snow's tableau
Winter were lie to me—
Because I see New Englandly.   15
The Queen discerns like me—
Provincially.
1861?   1929

J. 288

I'm nobody! Who are you?
Are you nobody, too?
Then there's a pair of us—don't
    tell!
They'd banish us, you know.

How dreary to be somebody!   5
How public, like a frog

To tell your name the livelong
    June
To an admiring bog!
1861?   1891

J. 303

The soul selects her own society,
Then shuts the door;
To her divine majority
Present no more.

Unmoved, she notes the chariots
    pausing   5
At her low gate;
Unmoved, an emperor be kneel-
    ing
Upon her mat.

I've known her from an ample
    nation
Choose one;   10
Then close the valves of her
    attention
Like stone.
1862?   1890

J. 318

I'll tell you how the sun rose,—
A ribbon at a time.
The steeples swam in amethyst,
The news like squirrels ran.
The hills untied their bonnets,   5
The bobolinks begun.
Then I said softly to myself,
"That must have been the sun!"
But how he set, I know not.
There seemed a purple stile   10
Which little yellow boys and
    girls
Were climbing all the while
Till when they reached the other
    side,

A dominie[6] in gray   14
Put gently up the evening bars,
And led the flock away.
1860?   1890

J. 322

There came a day at summer's
    full
Entirely for me;
I thought that such were for the
    saints,
Where resurrections be.

The sun, as common, went
    abroad,   5
The flowers, accustomed, blew,
As if no soul the solstice passed
That maketh all things new.

The time was scarce profaned
    by speech;
The symbol of a word   10
Was needless, as at sacrament
The wardrobe of our Lord.

Each was to each the sealed
    church,
Permitted to commune this
    time,
Lest we too awkward show   15
At supper of the Lamb.

The hours slid fast, as hours will,
Clutched tight by greedy hands;
So faces on two decks look back,
Bound to opposing lands.   20

And so, when all the time had
    leaked
Without external sound,
Each bound the other's crucifix,
We gave no other bond.

Sufficient troth that we shall
    rise—   25

6. A pastor or clergyman.

Deposed, at length, the grave—
To that new marriage, justified
Through Calvaries of Love!
1862   1890

J. 324

Some keep the Sabbath going to
    church;
I keep it staying at home,
With a bobolink for a chorister,
And an orchard for a dome.

Some keep the Sabbath in sur-
    plice;   5
I just wear my wings,
And instead of tolling the bell
    for church,
Our little sexton sings.

God preaches,—a noted clergy-
    man,—
And the sermon is never
    long;   10
So instead of getting to heaven
    at last,
I'm going all along!
1860?   1864, 1890

J. 328

A bird came down the walk:
He did not know I saw;
He bit an angle-worm in halves
And ate the fellow, raw.

And then he drank a dew   5
From a convenient grass,
And then hopped sidewise to
    the wall
To let a beetle pass.

He glanced with rapid eyes
That hurried all around—   10

They looked like frightened
    beads, I thought
He stirred his velvet head

Like one in danger; cautious,
I offered him a crumb,
And he unrolled his feathers   15
And rowed him softer home

Than oars divide the ocean,
Too silver for a seam,
Or butterflies, off banks of noon,
Leap, plashless, as they swim.   20
1862   1891

J. 333

The grass so little has to do,—
A sphere of simple green,
With only butterflies to brood,
And bees to entertain,

And stir all day to pretty
    tunes   5
The breezes fetch along,
And hold the sunshine in its lap
And bow to everything;

And thread the dews all night,
    like pearls,
And make itself so fine,—   10
A duchess were too common
For such a noticing.

And even when it dies, to pass
In odors so divine,
Like lowly spices lain to sleep,   15
Or spikenards perishing.

And then in sovereign barns to
    dwell,
And dream the days away,—
The grass so little has to do,
I wish I were a hay.   20
1862   1890

J. 341

After great pain a formal feeling comes—
The nerves sit ceremonious like
   tombs;
The stiff Heart questions—was
   it He that bore?
And yesterday—or centuries before?   4

The feet, mechanical, go round
A wooden way
Of ground, or air, or ought,[6]
Regardless grown,
A quartz contentment, like a
   stone.

This is the hour of lead   10
Remembered if outlived,
As freezing persons recollect the
   snow—
First chill, then stupor, then the
   letting go.
1862   1929

J. 401

What soft, cherubic creatures
   These gentlewomen are!
One would as soon assault a
   plush
   Or violate a star.

Such dimity convictions,   5
   A horror so refined
Of freckled human nature,
   Of Deity ashamed,—

It's such a common glory,
   A fisherman's degree!   10
Redemption, brittle lady,
   Be so, ashamed of thee.
1862?   1896
6. Nothing.

J. 435

Much madness is divinest sense
To a discerning eye;
Much sense the starkest mad-
   ness.
'T is the majority
In this, as all, prevail.   5
Assent, and you are sane;
Demur,—you're straightway dan-
   gerous,
And handled with a chain.
1862?   1890

J. 441

This is my letter to the world,
   That never wrote to me,—
The simple news that Nature
   told,
   With tender majesty.

Her message is committed   5
   To hands I cannot see,
For love of her, sweet country-
   men,
   Judge tenderly of me!
1862   1890

J. 449

I died for beauty, but was scarce
Adjusted in the tomb,
When one who died for truth
   was lain
In an adjoining room.

He questioned softly why I
   failed?   5
"For beauty," I replied.
"And I for truth—themself are
   one—
We brethren are," he said.

And so, as kinsmen met a night,
We   talked   between   the
    rooms,   10
Until the moss had reached our
    lips,
And covered up our names.
1862?   1890

J. 465

I heard a fly buzz when I died—
The stillness in the room
Was like the stillness in the air
Between the heaves of storm.

The eyes around had wrung
    them dry   5
And breaths were gathering firm
For that last onset when the
    King
Be witnessed in the room.

I willed my keepsakes, signed
    away
What portion of me be   10
Assignable—and then it was
There interposed a fly,

With blue, uncertain, stumbling
    buzz,
Between the light and me.
And then the windows failed,
    and then   15
I could not see to see.
1862?   1896

J. 478

I had no time to hate—
Because
The grave would hinder me,
And life was not so
Ample I   5
Could finish enmity.

Nor had I time to love—
But since
Some industry must be,
The little toil of love,   30
I thought,
Be large enough for me.
1862?   1890

J. 511

If you[7] were coming in the fall,
I'd brush the summer by
With half a smile and half a
    spurn,
As housewives do a fly.

If I could see you in a year,   5
I'd wind the months in balls,
And put them each in separate
    drawers,
For fear the numbers fuse.

If only centuries delayed,
I'd count them on my hand,   10
Subtracting   till   my   fingers
    dropped
Into Van Diemen's Land.[8]

If certain, when this life was out,
That yours and mine should be,
I'd toss it yonder like a rind, 15
And taste eternity.

But,   now,   uncertain   of   the
    length
Of this that is between,
It goads me, like the goblin bee,
That will not state its sting.   20
1862   1890

7. A   possible   reference   to   Charles
Wadsworth, who had moved to California.
8. Tasmania, an island off southeastern
Australia, was then being settled, and
was regarded as being extremely remote.

J. 526

To hear an oriole sing
May be a common thing,
Or only a divine.

It is not of the bird
Who sings the same, unheard,   5
As unto crowd.

The fashion of the ear
Attireth that it hear
In dun or fair.

So whether it be rune,   10
Or whether it be none,
Is of within;

The "tune is in the tree,"
The sceptic showeth me;
"No, sir! In thee!"   15
1862?   1891

J. 528

Mine, by the right of the white
     election!
Mine, by the royal seal!
Mine, by the sign in the scarlet
     prison,
Bars cannot conceal!

Mine, here in vision and in
     veto!   5
Mine, by the grave's repeal
Titled, confirmed—
Delirious charter!
Mine, long as Ages steal!
1862?   1890

J. 547

I've seen a dying eye
Run round and round a room

In search of something, as it
     seemed,
Then cloudier become;
And then, obscure with fog,   5
And then be soldered down
Without disclosing what it be,
'T were blessed to have seen.
1862?   1890

J. 556

The brain within its groove
Runs evenly and true;
But let a splinter swerve,
'T were easier for you

To put the waters back   5
When floods have slit the hills,
And scooped a turnpike for
     themselves,
And blotted out the mills!
1862?   1890

J. 579

I had been hungry all the years;
My noon had come, to dine;
I, trembling, drew the table near,
And touched the curious wine.

'T was this on tables I had
     seen,   5
When turning, hungry, home
I looked in windows, for the
     wealth
I could not hope for mine.

I did not know the ample bread,
'T was so unlike the crumb   10
The birds and I had often shared
In Nature's dining-room.

The plenty hurt me, 't was so
     new,—
Myself felt ill and odd,

As berry of a mountain bush   15
Transplanted to the road.

Nor was I hungry; so I found
That hunger was a way
Of persons outside windows,
The entering takes away.   20
1862?   1891

J. 581

I found the phrase to every
        thought
I ever had, but one;
And that defies me,
As a hand did try to chalk the
        sun.

To races nurtured in the
        dark;—   5
How would your own begin?
Can blaze be done in cochineal,⁹
Or noon in mazarin?¹
1862?   1891

J. 585

I like to see it lap the miles,
And lick the valleys up,
And stop to feed itself at tanks;
And then, prodigious, step

Around a pile of mountains,   5
And, supercilious, peer
In shanties by the sides of roads;
And then a quarry pare

To fit its sides
And crawl between   10
Complaining all the while
In horrid, hooting stanza;
Then chase itself down hill

And neigh like Boanerges;²
Then, punctual as a star,   15
Stop—docile   and   omnipo-
        tent—
At its own stable door.
1862?   1891

J. 636

The way I read a letter's this:
'T is first I lock the door,
And push it with my fingers
        next,
For transport it be sure.

And then I go the furthest off   5
To counteract a knock;
Then draw my little letter forth
And slowly pick the lock.

Then, glancing narrow at the
        wall,
And narrow at the floor,   10
For firm conviction of a mouse
Not exorcised before,

Peruse how infinite I am
To—no one that you know!
And sigh for lack of heaven,—
        but not   15
The heaven God bestow.
1862?   1891

J. 640

I cannot live with you,³
It would be life,
And life is over there
Behind the shelf

The sexton keeps the key to,   5
Putting up

9. A red dye.
1. Reddish-blue.

2. A surname meaning "sons of thunder," given by Christ to James and
John (Mark iii: 17).
3. The references to Christian ministry
associate this poem with Wadsworth.

Our life, his porcelain,
Like a cup

Discarded of the housewife,
Quaint or broke;   10
A newer Sèvres⁴ pleases,
Old ones crack.

I could not die with you,
For one must wait
To   shut   the   other's   gaze
        down,—   15
You could not.

And I, could I stand by
And see you freeze,
Without my right of frost,
Death's privilege?   20

Nor could I rise with you,
Because your face
Would put out Jesus',
That new grace

Glow plain and foreign   25
On my homesick eye,
Except that you, than he
Shone closer by.

They'd judge us—how?
For you served Heaven, you
        know,   30
Or sought to;
I could not,

Because you saturated sight,
And I had no more eyes
For sordid excellence   35
As Paradise.

And were you lost, I would be,
Though my name
Rang loudest
On the heavenly fame.   40

And were you saved,
And I condemned to be

Where you were not,
That self were hell to me.

So we must meet apart,   45
You there, I here,
With just the door ajar
That oceans are, and prayer,
And that white sustenance,
Despair.   50
1862?   1890

J. 650

Pain has an element of blank;
It cannot recollect
When it begun, or if there were
A day when it was not.

It has no future but itself,   5
Its infinite contain
Its past, enlightened to perceive
New periods of pain.
1862?   1890

J. 701

A thought went up my mind to-
        day
That I have had before,
But did not finish,—some way
        back,
I could not fix the year,

Nor where it went, nor why it
        came   5
The second time to me,
Nor definitely what it was,
Have I the art to say.

But somewhere in my soul, I
        know
I've met the thing before;   10
It just reminded me—'t was
        all—
And came my way no more.
1863?   1891

---

4. **A** fine porcelain made in the French
town of that name.

J. 712

Because I could not stop for
    Death,
He kindly stopped for me;
The carriage held but just our-
    selves
And Immortality.

We slowly drove, he knew no
    haste,   5
And I had put away
My labor, and my leisure too,
For his civility.

We passed the school, where
    children strove
At recess, in the ring;
We passed the fields of gazing
    grain,
We passed the setting sun.

Or rather, he passed us;
The dews grew quivering and
    chill,
For only gossamer my gown,   15
My tippet only tulle.

We paused before a house that
    seemed
A swelling of the ground;
The roof was scarcely visible,
The cornice in the ground.   20

Since then 'tis centuries, and yet
Feels shorter than the day
I first surmised the horses' heads
Were toward eternity.
1863?   1890

J. 732

She rose to his requirement,
    dropped
The playthings of her life

To take the honorable work
Of woman and of wife.

If aught she missed in her new
    day   5
Of amplitude, or awe,
Or first prospective, or the gold
In using wear away,

It lay unmentioned, as the sea
Develops pearl and weed,   10
But only to himself is known
The fathoms they abide.
1863?   1890

J. 816

A death-blow is a life-blow to
    some
Who, till they died, did not
    alive become;
Who, had they lived, had died,
    but when
They died, vitality begun.
1864?   1891

J. 823

Not what we did shall be the
    test
When act and will are done,
But what our Lord infers we
    would—
Had we diviner been.
1864?   1929

J. 986

A narrow fellow in the grass
Occasionally rides;
You may have met him? Did you
    not
His notice sudden is.

The grass divides as with a
  comb,   5
A spotted shaft is seen;
And then it closes at your feet
And opens further on.

He likes a boggy acre,
A floor too cool for corn,   10
Yet when a boy, and barefoot,
I more than once, at noon
Have passed, I thought, a whip-
  lash
Unbraiding in the sun,—
When, stooping to secure it,   15
It wrinkled, and was gone.

Several of nature's people
I know, and they know me;
I feel for them a transport
Of cordiality;   20

But never met this fellow,
Attended or alone,
Without a tighter breathing,
And zero at the bone.
1865   1866, 1891

J. 1052

I never saw a moor,
I never saw the sea;
Yet know I how the heather
  looks,
And what a billow be.

I never spoke with God,   5
Nor visited in heaven;
Yet certain am I of the spot
As if the checks were given.
1865?   1890

J. 1078

The bustle in a house
The morning after death

Is solemnest of industries
Enacted upon earth,—

The sweeping up the heart,   5
And putting love away
We shall not want to use again
Until eternity.
1866?   1890

J. 1082

Revolution is the pod
Systems rattle from
When the winds of Will are
  stirred.
Excellent is bloom,

But except its russet base,   5
Every summer be
The entomber of itself.
So of Liberty:

Left inactive on the stalk,
All its purple fled,   10
Revolution shakes it for
Test if it be dead.
1866?   1929

J. 1100

The last night that she lived,[5]
It was a common night,
Except the dying; this to us
Made nature different.

We noticed smallest things,—   5
Things overlooked before,
By this great light upon our
  minds
Italicized, as 't were.

5. "On Thursday, 3 May 1866, Laura
Dickey (Mrs. Frank W.) of Michigan,
youngest daughter of Mr. and Mrs. L.
M. Hills, died at her parents' home in
Amherst. The Hills land lay next to the
Dickinsons on the East" [Johnson's
note].

As we went out and in
Between her final room   10
And rooms where those to be
    alive
Tomorrow were, a blame

That others could exist
While she must finish quite,
A jealousy for her arose   15
So nearly infinite.

We waited while she passed;
It was a narrow time,
Too jostled were our souls to
    speak,
At length the notice came.   20

She mentioned, and forgot;
Then lightly as a reed
Bent to the water, shivered
    scarce,
Consented, and was dead.

And we, we placed the hair,   25
And drew the head erect;
And then an awful leisure was,
Our faith to regulate.
1866?   1890

J. 1176

We never know how high we are
    Till we are called to rise;
And then, if we are true to plan,
    Our statures touch the skies.

The heroism we recite   5
    Would be a daily thing,
Did not ourselves the cubits warp
    For fear to be a king.
1870?   1896

J. 1207

He preached upon "breadth" till
    it argued him narrow,—

The broad are too broad to de-
    fine;
And of "truth" until it pro-
    claimed him a liar,—
The truth never flaunted a sign.

Simplicity fled from this coun-
    terfeit presence   5
As gold the pyrites[6] would shun.
What confusion would cover
    the innocent Jesus
To meet so enabled a man!
1872   1891

J. 1263

There is no frigate like a book,
    To take us lands away,
Nor any coursers like a page
    Of prancing poetry.

This traverse may the poorest
    take   5
    Without oppress of toll;
How frugal is the chariot
    That bears a human soul!
1873?   1873, 1894

J. 1304

Not with a club the heart is
    broken,
    Nor with a stone;
A whip, so small you could not
    see it,
    I've known

To lash the magic creature   5
    Till it fell,
Yet that whip's name
    Too noble then to tell.

6. Iron pyrites, sometimes mistaken for
gold, and known as "fool's gold."

Magnanimous as bird
  By boy descried,   10
Singing unto the stone
  Of which it died.

Shame need not crouch
  In such an earth as ours—
Shame, stand erect,   15
  The universe is yours.
1874?   1896, 1947

J. 1332

Pink, small, and punctual,[7]
Aromatic, low,
Covert in April,
Candid in May,
Dear to the moss,   5
Known to the knoll,
Next to the robin
In every human soul.
Bold little beauty,
Bedecked with thee,   10
Nature forswears
Antiquity.
1875?   1890

J. 1463

A route of evanescence
With a revolving wheel;
A resonance of emerald,
A rush of cochineal;[8]
And every blossom on the bush   5
Adjusts its tumbled head,—
The mail from Tunis, probably,
An easy morning's ride.
1879?   1891

7. "(With the first Arbutus.)" [Dickinson's note].
8. A red dye.

J. 1465

Before you thought of spring,
Except as a surmise,
You see, God bless his sudden-
        ness,
A fellow in the skies
Of independent hues,   5
A little weather-worn,
Inspiriting habiliments
Of indigo and brown.
With specimens of song,
As if for you to choose,   10
Discretion in the interval,
With gay delays he goes
To some superior tree
Without a single leaf,
And shouts for joy to nobody   15
But his seraphic self!
1879   1891

J. 1510

How happy is the little stone
That rambles in the road alone,
And doesn't care about careers,
And exigencies never fears;
Whose   coat   of   elemental
        brown   5
A passing universe put on;
And independent as the sun,
Associates or glows alone,
Fulfilling absolute decree
In casual simplicity.[9]   10
1881?   1891

9. In a letter, probably to her sister-in-
law, Emily Dickinson adds beneath the
poem: "Heaven the Balm of a surly
Technicality!" In a letter to T. W. Higginson she adds the separate quatrain
(J. 1543): "Obtaining but our own extent / In   whatsoever   realm— / 'Twas
Christ's own personal expanse / That
bore him from the tomb." Johnson notes
that "the thought seems to be a reflection on the Calvinist orthodoxy that
only the 'saved' get into heaven."

J. 1540

As imperceptibly as grief
The summer lapsed away,—
Too imperceptible, at last,
To seem like perfidy.
A quietness distilled,   5
As twilight long begun,
Or Nature, spending with her-
  self
Sequestered afternoon.
The dusk drew earlier in,
The morning foreign shone,— 10
A courteous, yet harrowing grace,
As guest that would be gone.
And thus, without a wing,
Or service of a keel,
Our summer made her light
  escape   15
Into the beautiful.
1865, 1882   1891

J. 1587

He ate and drank the precious
  words,
His spirit grew robust;
He knew no more that he was
  poor,
Nor that his frame was dust.

He danced along the dingy
  days,   5
And this bequest of wings
Was but a book. What liberty
A loosened spirit brings!
1883?   1890

J. 1624

Apparently with no surprise
To any happy flower,
The frost beheads it at its play
In accidental power.
The blond assassin passes on,   5
The sun proceeds unmoved
To measure off another day
For an approving God.
1884?   1890

J. 1732

My life closed twice before its
  close;
It remains to see
If Immortality unveil
A third event to me,

So huge, so hopeless to conceive,   5
As these that twice befell.
Parting is all we know of
  heaven,
And all we need of hell.
?   1896

J. 1760

Elysium[1] is as far as to
The very nearest room,
If in that room a friend await
Felicity or doom.

What fortitude the soul con-
  tains,   5
That it can so endure
The accent of a coming foot,
The opening of a door!
1882?   1890

1. Paradise.

Frontiers of Folk Literature and Humor

NEGRO SONGS

It is likely that Negro spirituals, or religious lyrics, many of them magnificent in poetry and music, were originally inspired by camp meetings of southern white people, attended by Negro slaves before the Civil War; but the Negro infused into them his own racial idiom, mannerisms, and emotional experience. A race in slavery, yearning for freedom of spirit, mind, and body, found in Old Testament story its heroism and in the New Testament its hope. The spirituals that resulted are sometimes syncopated revival songs, but the best are the expression of profound and lyric exaltation.

Like all musical compositions these songs must be heard to be fully appreciated, and it is likely that no one else will ever again sing them as Negro singers of an earlier time were able to do. Another type of folk song also developed from slavery, the plantation melody of daily work, of gaiety, sorrow, or love. Gangs of slaves sang them in the cotton fields or along the levees; when slavery was abolished, labor gangs inherited this tradition. Many of the plantation songs, especially those of lively or humorous character, were popularized on the stage by white performers dressed as Negroes, in a form of entertainment known as the minstrel show, which remained an institution in the theater until well into the twentieth century. Another form of popular song, the blues, a lament, generally, of blighted love, came from the honky-tonks of such cities as St. Louis, Memphis, and New Orleans, and exerted an influence on the development of jazz music. Many of the American "city ballads," like "Frankie and Johnny," inherited the blues tradition, sometimes mingled with influences from the "poor white" of the cities.

A thorough, scholarly treatment of Negro lyrics is Newman I. White, *American Negro Folk-Songs*, 1928. A very good collection is John W. Work, *American Negro Songs and Spirituals*, 1940.

John Henry[1]

John Henry was a li'l baby, uh-huh,
He sat on his daddy's knee;
Said: "De Big Bend Tunnel on de C. & O. road
Gonna cause de death of me,
Lawd, Lawd, gonna cause de death of me."   5

Cap'n says to John Henry,
"Gonna bring me a steam drill 'round,
Gonna take dat steam drill out on de job,
Gonna whop dat steel on down,
Lawd, Lawd, gonna whop dat steel on down."   10

John Henry tol' his cap'n
Dat a man wuz a natural man,
An' befo' he'd let dat steam drill run him down,
He'd fall dead wid a hammer in his han',
He'd fall dead wid a hammer in his han'.   15

John Henry sez to his cap'n:
"Send me a twelve-poun' hammer aroun',
A twelve-poun' hammer wid a fo'-foot handle,
An' I beat yo' steam drill down,
An' I beat yo' steam drill down."   20

John Henry started on de right han',
De steam drill started on de lef'—
"Before I'd let dis steam drill beat me down,
I'd hammer my fool self to death,
Lawd, Lawd, I'd hammer my fool self to death."   25

Sun shine hot an' burnin',
Wer'n't no breeze a-tall,
Sweat ran down like water down a hill,
Dat day John Henry let his hammer fall,
Lawd, Lawd, dat day John Henry let his hammer fall.   30

White man tol' John Henry,
"Nigger, damn yo' soul,
You might beat dis steam an' drill of mine,
When de rocks in dis mountain turn to gol',   34
Lawd, Lawd, when de rocks in dis mountain turn to gol'."

John Henry hammered in de mountains,
An' his hammer was strikin' fire,

[1]. "John Henry" tells the story of a mythical strong man who worked on the Big Bend Tunnel of the Chesapeake and Ohio Railroad in West Virginia during the early 1870's. There are numerous versions.

He drove so hard till he broke his pore heart,
An' he lied down his hammer an' he died,
Lawd, Lawd, he lied down his hammer an' he died.   40

John Henry had a li'l baby,
Hel' him in de palm of his han'.
De las' words I heard de pore boy say:
"Son, yo're gonna be a steel-drivin' man,
Son, yo're gonna be a steel-drivin' man!"   45

John Henry had a pretty li'l 'ooman,
An' de dress she wo' was blue,
An' de las' words she said to him:
"John Henry, I've been true to you,
Lawd, Lawd, John Henry, I've been true to you."   50

John Henry had anothah 'ooman,
De dress she wo' wuz red.
De las' words I heard de pore gal say:
"I'm goin' w'eah mah man drapt daid,
I'm goin' w'eah mah man drapt daid!"   55

"Oh, who's gonna shoe yo' li'l feetses,
An' who's gonna glub yo' han's,
An' who's gonna kiss yo' rosy, rosy lips,
An' who's gonna be yo' man,
Lawd, Lawd, an' who's gonna be yo' man?"   60

Dey took John Henry to de graveyard,
An' dey buried him in de san',
An' every locomotive come roarin' by,
Says, "Dere lays a steel-drivin' man,
Lawd, Lawd, dere lays a steel-drivin' man."   65

Swing Low, Sweet Chariot

Swing low, sweet chariot,
Comin' for to carry me home;
Swing low, sweet chariot,
Comin' for to carry me home.
          (*Repeat as Refrain*)

I looked over Jordan and what did I see,   5
Comin' for to carry me home?
A band of angels comin' aftah me,
Comin' for to carry me home.
          (*Refrain*)

If you git there before I do,
Comin' for to carry me home,   10
Tell all my frien's I'm a-comin', too,
Comin' for to carry me home.
                    (*Refrain*)

The brightes' day that ever I saw,
Comin' for to carry me home,
When Jesus washed my sins away   15
Comin' for to carry me home.
                    (*Refrain*)

I'm sometimes up an' sometimes down,
Comin' for to carry me home,
But still my soul feel heavenly-boun',
Comin' for to carry me home.   20
                    (*Refrain*)

All God's Chillun Got Shoes[2]

You got shoes, I got shoes,
All God's chillun got shoes,
When I git to Heb'n goin' to put on my shoes
Goin' to walk all over God's Heb'n,
Heb'n, Heb'n, goin' to walk all over God's Heb'n.   5

I got a robe, you got a robe,
All God's chillun got a robe,
When I git to Heb'n goin' to put on my robe
Goin' to walk all over God's Heb'n,
Heb'n, Heb'n, goin' to walk all over God's Heb'n.   10

I got a crown, you got a crown,
All God's chillun got a crown,
When I git to Heb'n goin' to put on my crown
Goin' to walk all over God's Heb'n,
Heb'n, Heb'n, goin' to walk all over God's Heb'n.   15

I got a harp, you got a harp,
All God's chillun got a harp,
When I git to Heb'n goin' to play on my harp
Goin' to play all over God's Heb'n,
Heb'n, Heb'n, goin' to play all over God's Heb'n.   20

2. This great Negro spiritual, known equally for its poetic imagination and for its music, exists in a number of versions and recordings. In the present text, various sophistications and late interpolations have been excluded.

I got wings, you got wings,
All God's chillun got wings,
When I git to Heb'n goin' to put on my wings
Goin' to fly all over God's Heb'n,
Heb'n, Heb'n, goin' to fly all over God's Heb'n. 25

Go Down, Moses

When Israel was in Egypt's land,
    Let my people go!
Oppress'd so hard dey could not stand,
    Let my people go!

(*Refrain*)   Go down, Moses, 5
        Way down in Egypt's land.
    Tell ole Pha-roh,
        Let my people go!

Thus saith de Lawd, bold Moses said,
    Let my people go! 10
If not I'll smite your first-born dead,
    Let my people go!
        (*Refrain*)

No more shall dey in bondage toil,
    Let my people go!
Let dem come out wid Egypt's spoil, 15
    Let my people go!
        (*Refrain*)

Frankie and Johnny[3]

Frankie and Johnny were lovers, O lordy how they could love.
Swore to be true to each other, true as the stars above;
He was her man, but he done her wrong.

Frankie she was his woman, everybody knows.
She spent one hundred dollars for a suit of Johnny's clothes. 5
He was her man, but he done her wrong.

3. There are relatively few ballads of the city, but of these, "Frankie and Johnny" is the classic example—a true ballad of folk origin and oral dissemination. It probably originated in the middle of the nineteenth century, but it was the published version of 1912 that became popular through phonograph recordings. Known in the slums for nearly three quarters of a century, it then became current wherever people enjoyed jazz and popular songs. It is estimated that there are more than a hundred "Frankie" songs, and the variations of their words and music are legion. According to legend, the story deals with the murder of a Negro by his mistress in St. Louis sometime between 1840 and 1850, but of course it could have happened anywhere, in the tenderloin districts of many cities.

Frankie and Johnny went walking, Johnny in his bran' new suit,
"O good Lawd," says Frankie, "but don't my Johnny look cute?"
He was her man, but he done her wrong.

Frankie went down to Memphis; she went on the evening train. 10
She paid one hundred dollars for Johnny a watch and chain.
He was her man, but he done her wrong.

Frankie went down to the corner, to buy a glass of beer;
She says to the fat bartender, "Has my loving man been here?
He was my man, but he done me wrong." 15

"Ain't going to tell you no story, ain't going to tell you no lie,
I seen your man 'bout an hour ago with a girl named Alice Bly—
If he's your man, he's doing you wrong."

Frankie went back to the hotel, she didn't go there for fun,
Under her long red kimono she toted a forty-four gun. 20
He was her man, but he done her wrong.

Frankie went down to the hotel, looked in the window so high,
There was her lovin' Johnny a-lovin' up Alice Bly;
He was her man, but he done her wrong.

Frankie went down to the hotel, she rang that hotel bell, 25
"Stand back all of you floozies or I'll blow you all to hell,
I want my man, he's doin' me wrong."

Frankie threw back her kimono; took out the old forty-four;
Roota-toot-toot, three times she shot, right through that hotel door.
She shot her man, 'cause he done her wrong. 30

Johnny grabbed off his Stetson. "O good Lawd, Frankie, don't
    shoot."
But Frankie put her finger on the trigger, and the gun went roota-
    toot-toot.
He was her man, but she shot him down.

"Roll me over easy, roll me over slow,
Roll me over easy, boys, 'cause my wounds are hurting me so, 35
I was her man, but I done her wrong."

With the first shot Johnny staggered; with the second shot he fell;
When the third bullet hit him, there was a new man's face in hell.
He was her man, but he done her wrong.

Frankie heard a rumbling away down under the ground. 40
Maybe it was Johnny where she had shot him down.
He was her man, and she done him wrong.

"Oh, bring on your rubber-tired hearses, bring on your rubber-tired
 hacks,
They're takin' my Johnny to the buryin' groun' but they'll never
 bring him back.
He was my man, but he done me wrong."   45

The judge he said to the jury, "It's plain as plain can be.
This woman shot her man, so it's murder in the second degree.
He was her man, though he done her wrong."

Now it wasn't murder in the second degree, it wasn't murder in the
 third.
Frankie simply dropped her man, like a hunter drops a bird.   50
He was her man, but he done her wrong.

"Oh, put me in that dungeon. Oh, put me in that cell.
Put me where the northeast wind blows from the southeast corner
I shot my man 'cause he done me wrong."   [of hell.]

Frankie walked up to the scaffold, as calm as a girl could be,   55
She turned her eyes to heaven and said, "Good Lord, I'm coming to
 thee.
He was my man, and I done him wrong."

COWBOY BALLADS

It is natural that cowboy songs should follow the ballad tradition in form and style; for the cowboy generally hailed from the South, where the old English songs were sung. Yet in subject matters his songs were as fresh and new as the cattle domain itself, characteristically American, and like his profession unique in history.

Whether handed down orally or circulated in print the cowboy songs were sung around campfires and shouted on the roundups, and accompanied the lonely night herders. Like the West they were filled with the exploits of heroes, mischief-makers, and desperadoes; and like the traditional ballads they recounted love stories and adventure. The Montana cowboys and their songs varied from their Texas counterparts as much as the geography of their states; yet all had something in common—they were men of action, facing danger, and living in the open. These ballads of the West are among the most colorful parts of our folk literature.

A comprehensive collection of cowboy songs is John A. Lomax and Alan Lomax, *Cowboy Songs and Other Frontier Ballads*, 1910, revised 1938. A supplementary collection, still valuable, is John A. Lomax, *Songs of the Cattle Trail and Cow Camp*, 1919. The numerous variants in the printed texts of various editions, and in the recorded versions of these songs, are sometimes the result of late and sophisticated interpolations, which have been excluded from the present text.

The Old Chisholm Trail

Come along, boys, and listen to my tale,
I'll tell you of my troubles on the old Chisholm Trail.[1]

(*Refrain*)
   Coma ti yi youpy, youpy yea, youpy yea,
   Coma ti yi youpy, youpy yea.

I started up the trail October twenty-third,
I started up the trail with the 2-U herd.

Oh, a ten-dollar hoss and a forty-dollar saddle,
And I'm goin' to punchin' Texas cattle.

I woke up one morning on the old Chisholm Trail,
Rope in my hand and a cow by the tail.   10

I'm up in the mornin' afore daylight
And afore I sleep the moon shines bright.

Old Ben Bolt was a blamed good boss,
But he'd go to see the girls on a sore-backed hoss.

Old Ben Bolt was a fine old man   15
And you'd know there was whiskey wherever he'd land.

It's cloudy in the West, a-looking like rain,
And my damned old slicker's in the wagon again.

Crippled my hoss, I don't know how,
Ropin' at the horns of a 2-U cow.   20

We hit Caldwell and we hit her on the fly,
We bedded down the cattle on the hill close by.

No chaps, no slicker, and it's pouring down rain,
And I swear, by god, I'll never night-herd again.

Feet in the stirrups and seat in the saddle,   25
I hung and rattled with them long-horn cattle.

Last night I was on guard and the leader broke the ranks,
I hit my horse down the shoulders, and I spurred him in the flanks.

The wind commenced to blow, and the rain began to fall,
Hit looked, by grab, like we was goin' to lose 'em all.   30

1. The Chisholm Trail, leading from the Red River basin in southeastern Texas, through the Indian Territory into southern Kansas, was a principal route for the cattle herds bound for the government market, and later, to the railheads of the new transcontinental railroads.

Foot in the stirrup and hand on the horn,
Best damned cowboy ever was born.

We rounded 'em up and put 'em on the cars,
And that was the last of the old Two Bars.

Oh it's bacon and beans most every day,—   35
I'd as soon be a-eatin' prairie hay.

I'm on my best horse and I'm goin' at a run,
I'm the quickest shootin' cowboy that ever pulled a gun.

I went to the wagon to get my roll,
To come back to Texas, dad-burn my soul.   40

I went to the boss to draw my roll,
He had it figgered out I was nine dollars in the hole.

With my knees in the saddle and my seat in the sky,
I'll quit punching cows in the sweet by and by.

    Coma ti yi youpy, youpy yea, youpy yea,   45
    Coma ti yi youpy, youpy yea.

Git Along, Little Dogies

As I was a-walking one morning for pleasure,
I spied a cow-puncher a-riding along;
His hat was throwed back and his spurs were a-jinglin',
As he approached me a-singin' this song:

    (*Refrain*)
    Whoopee ti yi yo, git along, little dogies,[2]   5
    It's your misfortune and none of my own;
    Whoopee ti yi yo, git along, little dogies,
    For you know Wyoming will be your new home.

Early in the springtime we'll round up the dogies,
Slap on their brands, and bob off their tails;[3]
Round up our horses, load up the chuck wagon,[4]   10
Then throw those dogies upon the trail.

It's whooping and yelling and driving the dogies,
Oh, how I wish you would go on;

---

2. The term "dogie," or "dogy" (pronounced "doe-gy") was loosely used on the cattle trail, but specifically it referred to a young bull calf, separated from its mother in a herd destined to be gelded and fattened as beef steers.
3. The calves rounded up on the home range were gelded and identified by branding before being herded off to the cattle markets.

4. "Chuck" was cowboy slang for "food" (*cf.* "chow"); the "chuck wagon" was the commissary of the migrating cattle herders.

It's whooping and punching and go on, little dogies,   15
For you know Wyoming will be your new home.

Some of the boys goes up the trail for pleasure,
But that's where they git it most awfully wrong;
For you haven't any idea the trouble they give us
When we go driving them dogies along.   20

When the night comes on and we hold them on the bed-ground,
These little dogies that roll on so slow;
Roll up the herd and cut out the strays,
And roll the little dogies that never rolled before.

Your mother she was raised way down in Texas,   25
Where the jimson weed and sand burrs grow;
Now we'll fill you up on prickly pear and cholla
Till you are ready for the trail to Idaho.

Oh, you'll be soup for Uncle Sam's Injuns;[5]
"It's beef, heap beef," I hear them cry.   30
Git along, git along, git along, little dogies,
You're going to be beef steers by and by.

5. In early days, the government purchase of beef cattle for the Indian reservations provided a lively market for the ranchers.

COMIC JOURNALISM

The newspaper went west almost in advance of the pioneer, and clearly was often doing business before the church, the court, or the schoolhouse. Editors found the pioneer communities bubbling with an indigenous and racy humor which had produced a new form of oral anecdote. In their newspapers there was plenty of space, and they welcomed the oral anecdotes and comic stories that came to them from amateurs, often gifted—lawyers, doctors, and plain folk alike. In time the comic western story invaded the "sporting papers" of the East, and influenced the narrative realism of serious writers of fiction. Most importantly, it stimulated the work of such professional humorists as Josh Billings, John Phoenix, and Artemus Ward, who were among those whose contributions helped shape the early art of Mark Twain.

Fresh, boisterous, colorful, and strong, the literature of western humor was written for men who worked hard, lived roughly, and took their pleasures at the bar, around the poker table, or in the dance hall. It was filled with irreverence and crudities; Washoe miners roared approval when young Mark Twain described the gory details of scalping, throat slashing, and stabbing in his burlesque report of a "bloody massacre," and laughed delightedly at John Phoenix's description of a person's picking his nose. Physical discomfort was part of daily life, and so, unfortunately, were murder, violence, and drunkenness—all to be resolved by the amalgam of laughter. These westerners delighted in slang that was apt and accurate, in startling contrasts, outlandish hyperbole, and jolting anticlimax. It was a masculine world, where the weak were vanquished, and though strains of Victorian sentimentality paradoxically remained, the miners, gamblers, and gunmen enjoyed coarseness, noise, and commotion. The West was democratic, disliking pretense and snobbery, ridiculing frills and foppishness, giving its approval to strength, intelligence, and industry. The outrageous tall tale, with its fantastic exaggeration and solemn declarations of the utterly impossible, flourished in the West. Burlesque and extravagance won more attention than wit and satire in communities that were just being born.

JOSH BILLINGS

Henry Wheeler Shaw (1818–1885) was the popular crackerbox philosopher who wrote under the pseudonym of "Josh Billings." Born in Lanesboro, Massachusetts, he attended Lenox Academy and spent two years at Hamilton College. Not until he was forty-five did Shaw begin his career as a literary comedian by writing for small-town newspapers. When his comic writings were so widely copied that he found himself in demand as a

funny "philosopher," he moved to New York, making his home there permanently. Artemus Ward, already successful, arranged the publication of Shaw's first book, *Josh Billings, His Sayings* (1865). The *Farmer's Allminax*, begun in 1869, sold more than a hundred thousand copies nearly every year until Shaw ceased publishing it in 1880. His humor was so much in demand that he published eleven volumes and collections, including *Josh Billings on Ice* (1868), *Everybody's Friend* (1874), *Josh Billings' Trump Kards* (1877), *Old Probability* (1879), and *Josh Billings Struggling with Things* (1881). All were books of aphorisms and essays, marked by sharp common sense, expressed after the fashion of the day in queer spelling, unfortunate grammar, and outrageous puns. His *Complete Works* appeared in four volumes in 1888.

JOHN PHOENIX

George Horatio Derby (1823–1861) was born in Massachusetts. A West Point graduate who fought in the Mexican War, he experienced a varied career as military engineer, surveyor, and geologist before becoming a journalist. Derby's interest in geology took him west, where his ready wit and inclination to play practical jokes brought him a local reputation as a humorist. He began to write simply to entertain his friends and amuse himself, but his sketches, especially those written in California between 1849 and 1856, were reprinted by numerous newspapers and magazines. Derby took little interest in his writings beyond the fun they provided at the moment, but his friends insisted upon collecting a volume of scattered pieces written under the pseudonym of "John Phoenix," which they published as *Phoenixiana* (1856). Their enthusiasm was justified by its popular reception; *Phoenixiana; or, Sketches and Burlesques* was republished in New York in 1858, 1859, 1862, 1867, 1869, and 1903. A London edition was issued in 1856, and a two-volume edition including portions of Derby's notebooks was published in Chicago in 1897. After his death, friends collected *The Squibob Papers* (1865) written under the pseudonym of "Squibob," which Derby employed occasionally when not signing himself "John Phoenix."

ARTEMUS WARD

Charles Farrar Browne, (1834–1867), known on both sides of the Atlantic as "Artemus Ward," was born in Waterford, Maine. When Browne was fourteen, his father died; he became a printer's devil in Lancaster, New Hampshire, and then drifted from one New England paper to another. Soon he was trying to write, and moving to the Middle West he became editor of the Cleveland *Plain Dealer*, to which he contributed a series of "Artemus Ward's Sayings" relating the imaginary adventures of an itinerant showman. These letters, begun in 1858, won so large an audience

that he went to New York, there working on a comic magazine, *Vanity Fair*, and mingling with the Bohemians at Pfaff's restaurant. In 1861 he commenced lecturing, and during the next few years attracted large audiences wherever he went. His first publication, *Artemus Ward: His Book* (1862), sold widely, going through five American editions, two English, and one Canadian. Popular and successful, Browne was never spoiled, but generously aided other humorists through advice and influence with publishers. One of these was Mark Twain, whom he counseled, encouraged, and helped to publish an early story, "The Jumping Frog". A second volume, *Artemus Ward: His Travels* (1865), went through four editions. Additional sketches appeared in five later volumes. In 1866 he went to England, where he lectured to large, enthusiastic audiences and achieved popularity as a contributor to *Punch*. There he died of tuberculosis in 1867 at the age of thirty-three, while at the height of his fame. His works, first collected in 1869, reached their twelfth edition in 1910.

Constance M. Rourke, *American Humor: A Study of the National Character*, 1946, a historical and cultural study of the origins of our humorous literature and folklore, is useful for all categories of American humor. Selected bibliographies of the comic journalists and other humorous writers will be found in Walter Blair, *Native American Humor, 1800–1900*, 1937, together with selections and an introductory essay on the varieties of "humorous treatments of American character." Other standard references are Jennette R. Tandy, *Cracker-Box Philosophers in American Humor and Satire*, 1925; and Walter Blair, *Horse Sense in American Humor: From Benjamin Franklin to*

Ogden Nash, 1942, a critical anthology containing a bibliography.

The Complete Works of Josh Billings [Henry Wheeler Shaw] appeared in 1919, with previous publication in 4 vols., 1888. Selections are *Selections from the Writings of Josh Billings*, 1940; the *Farmer's Allminax*, 1870–1879, 1902; and *Uncle Sam's Uncle Josh*, 1953. The only full-length biography is Cyril Clemens, *Josh Billings: Yankee Humorist*, 1932.

There is no recent edition of John

Phoenix [George H. Derby]. John Kendrick Bangs wrote an introduction to *Phoenixiana*, 1903, which is useful, and the only full-length study is George Rippey Stewart, *John Phoenix, Esq. * * *, A Life of Captain George H. Derby, U.S.A.*, 1937.

A. J. Nock edited *Selected Works of Artemus Ward*, 1924. The most useful biography is Don C. Seitz, *Artemus Ward (Charles Farrar Browne): A Biography and Bibliography*, 1919.

JOSH BILLINGS: Essa on the Muel[1]

The muel iz haf hoss and haf Jackass, and then kums tu a full stop, natur diskovering her mistake.

Tha weigh more, akordin tu their heft, than enny other kreetur, except a crowbar.

Tha kant hear enny quicker, nor further than the hoss, yet their ears are big enuff for snow shoes.

You kan trust them with enny one whose life aint worth enny more than the muels. The only wa tu keep them in a paster, is tu turn them into a medder jineing, and let them jump out.

Tha are reddy for use, just as soon as they will du tu abuse.

Tha haint got enny friends, and will live on huckle berry brush, with an ocksional chanse at Kanada thistels.

Tha are a modern invenshun, i dont think the Bible deludes tu them at tall.

Tha sel for more money than enny other domestik animile. Yu kant tell their age by looking into their mouth, enny more than you kould a Mexican kannons. Tha never hav no dissease that a good club wont heal.

If tha ever die tha must kum rite tu life agin, for i never herd noboddy sa "ded muel."

Tha are like sum men, verry korrupt at harte; ive known them tu be good muels for 6 months, just tu git a good chanse to kick sumbody.

I never owned one, nor never mean to, unless thare is a United Staits law passed, requiring it.

The only reason why tha are pashunt, is bekause tha are ashamed ov themselfs.

I have seen eddikated muels in a sirkus.

Tha kould kick, and bite, tremenjis. I would not sa what I am forced tu sa again the muel, if his birth want an outrage, and man want tu blame for it.

1. Published in *Josh Billings, His Sayings* (1865).

Enny man who is willing tu drive a muel, ought to be exempt by law from running for the legislatur.

Tha are the strongest creeturs on earth, and heaviest akording tu their sise; I herd tell ov one who fell oph from the tow path, on the Eri kanawl, and sunk as soon as he touched bottom, but he kept rite on towing the boat tu the nex stashun, breathing thru his ears, which stuck out ov the water about 2 feet 6 inches; i didn't see this did, but an auctioneer told me ov it, and i never knew an auctioneer tu lie unless it was absolutely convenient.

1860, 1865

JOHN PHOENIX: Musical Review Extraordinary[1]

San Diego, July 10th, 1854.

As your valuable work is not supposed to be so entirely identified with San Franciscan interests,[2] as to be careless what takes place in other portions of this great *kedntry*,[3] and as it is received and read in San Diego with great interest (I have loaned my copy to over four different literary gentlemen, most of whom have read some of it), I have thought it not improbable that a few critical notices of the musical performances and the drama of this place might be acceptable to you, and interest your readers. I have been, moreover, encouraged to this task by the perusal of your interesting musical and theatrical critiques on San Francisco performers and performances; as I feel convinced that, if you devote so much space to them, you will not allow any little feeling of rivalry between the two great cities[4] to prevent your noticing ours, which, without the slightest feeling of prejudice, I must consider as infinitely superior. I propose this month to call your attention to the two great events in our theatrical and musical world—the appearance of the talented MISS PELICAN, and the production of Tarbox's celebrated "Ode Symphonie" of "The Plains."

The critiques on the former are from the columns of *The Vallecetos[5] Sentinel*, to which they were originally contributed by me, appearing on the respective dates of June 1st and June 31st.

1. Published in *Phoenixiana; or, Sketches and Burlesques* (1856). The present text is taken from this edition.
2. Derby often employed the tone of a newspaper correspondent in submitting his burlesque dispatches. This probably appeared in the San Diego *Herald*.
3. Apparently a burlesque pronunciation of "kentry" (country).
4. In the decade before the Civil War, San Francisco, Los Angeles, and San Diego all experienced booms; and when San Francisco emerged as the center of art, literature, and journalism, the rivalries among the cities became a stock joke.
5. Apparently a stage station between San Diego and El Centro.

From the Vallecetos Sentinel, June 1st.

MISS PELICAN.—Never during our dramatic experience, has a more exciting event occurred than the sudden bursting upon our theatrical firmament, full, blazing, unparalleled, of the bright, resplendent and particular star, whose honored name shines refulgent at the head of this article. Coming among us unheralded, almost unknown, without claptrap, in a wagon drawn by oxen across the plains, with no agent to get up a counterfeit enthusiasm in her favor, she appeared before us for the first time at the San Diego Lyceum, last evening, in the trying and difficult character of Ingomar,[6] or the Tame Savage. We are at a loss to describe our sensations, our admiration, at her magnificent, her superhuman efforts. We do not hesitate to say that she is by far the superior of any living actress; and, as we believe hers to be the perfection of acting, we cannot be wrong in the belief that no one hereafter will ever be found to approach her. Her conception of the character of Ingomar was perfection itself; her playful and ingenuous manner, her light girlish laughter, in the scene with Sir Peter, showed an appreciation of the savage character, which nothing but the most arduous study, the most elaborate training could produce; while her awful change to the stern, unyielding, uncompromising father in the tragic scene of Duncan's murder,[7] was indeed nature itself. Miss Pelican is about seventeen years of age, of miraculous beauty, and most thrilling voice. It is needless to say she dresses admirably, as in fact we have said all we can say when we called her most truthfully, perfection. Mr. John Boots took the part of Parthenia very creditably, etc., etc.

From the Vallecetos Sentinel, June 31st.

MISS PELICAN.—As this lady is about to leave us to commence an engagement on the San Francisco stage, we should regret exceedingly if any thing we have said about her, should send with her a *prestige* which might be found undeserved on trial. The fact is, Miss Pelican is a very ordinary actress; indeed, one of the most indifferent ones we ever happened to see. She came here from the Museum at Fort Laramie, and we praised her so injudiciously that she became completely spoiled. She has performed a round of characters during the last week, very miserably, though we are bound to confess that her performance of King Lear last evening, was superior to any thing of the kind we ever saw. Miss Pelican is about forty-three years of age, singularly plain in her personal appearance, awkward and embarrassed, with a cracked

---

6. *Ingomar the Barbarian* (*ca.* 1850) by Frederich Halm was a great stock-company favorite for half a century.

7. *Cf.* Shakespeare, *Macbeth*, Act II, Scene 2.

and squeaking voice, and really dresses quite outrageously. *She has much to learn—poor thing!*

I take it the above notices are rather ingenious. The fact is, I'm no judge of acting, and don't know how Miss Pelican will turn out. If well, why there's my notice of June the 1st; if ill, then June 31st comes in play, and, as there is but one copy of the *Sentinel* printed, it's an easy matter to destroy the incorrect one; *both can't be wrong*; so I've made a sure thing of it in any event. Here follows my musical critique, which I flatter myself is of rather superior order:

THE PLAINS. ODE SYMPHONIE PAR JABEZ TARBOX.—This glorious composition was produced at the San Diego Odeon, on the 31st of June, ult., for the first time in this or any other country, by a very full orchestra (the performance taking place immediately after supper), and a chorus composed of the entire "Sauer Kraut-Verein," the "Wee Gates Association,"[8] and choice selections from the "Gyascutus" and "Pikeharmonic" societies. The solos were rendered by Herr Tuden Links, the recitations by Herr Von Hyden Schnapps, both performers being assisted by Messrs. John Smith and Joseph Brown, who held their coats, fanned them, and furnished water during the more overpowering passages.

"The Plains" we consider the greatest musical achievement that has been presented to an enraptured public. Like Waterloo among battles; Napoleon among warriors; Niagara among falls, and Peck[9] among senators, this magnificent composition stands among Oratorios, Operas, Musical Melodramas and performances of Ethiopian Serenaders, peerless and unrivalled. *Il frappe toute chose parfaitement froid.*[1]

"It does not depend for its success" upon its plot, its theme, its school or its master, for it has very little if any of them, but upon its soul-subduing, all-absorbing, high-faluting effect upon the audience, every member of which it causes to experience the most singular and exquisite sensations. Its strains at times remind us of those of the old master of the steamer McKim, who never went to sea without being unpleasantly affected;—a straining after effect he used to term it. Blair[2] in his lecture on beauty, and Mills[3] in his treatise on logic (p. 31) have alluded to the feeling which might be produced in the human mind, by something of

8. Sauerkraut Club, and How Are You? [Wie geht's?] Association.
9. Elisha T. Peck, registered as a Whig, was state senator representing Butte and Plumas counties in California during 1854–55.
1. A burlesque translation into French of "It knocked them cold."

2. Probably Hugh Blair (1718–1800), Scottish divine whose published lectures on belles-lettres were greatly admired.
3. Apparently Derby means John Stuart Mill (1806–1873), the British philosopher.

this transcendentally sublime description, but it has remained for M. Tarbox, in the production of The Plains, to call this feeling forth.

The symphonie opens upon the wide and boundless plains, in longitude 115° W., latitude 35° 21′ 03″ N., and about sixty miles from the west bank of Pitt River. These data are beautifully and clearly expressed by a long (topographically) drawn note from an E flat clarinet. The sandy nature of the soil, sparsely dotted with bunches of cactus and artemisia, the extended view, flat and unbroken to the horizon, save by the rising smoke in the extreme verge, denoting the vicinity of a Pi Utah village, are represented by the bass drum. A few notes on the piccolo, calls the attention to a solitary antelope, picking up mescal beans in the foreground. The sun having an altitude of 36° 27′, blazes down upon the scene in indescribable majesty. "Gradually the sounds roll forth in a song" of rejoicing to the God of Day.

> "Of thy intensity
> And great immensity
> Now then we sing;
> Beholding in gratitude
> Thee in this latitude,
> Curious thing."

Which swells out into "Hey Jim along, Jim along Josey,"[4] then *decrescendo, mas o menos, poco pocita,*[5] dies away and dries up.

Suddenly we hear approaching a train from Pike County, consisting of seven families, with forty-six wagons, each drawn by thirteen oxen; each family consists of a man in butternut-colored clothing driving the oxen; a wife in butternut-colored clothing riding in the wagon, holding a butternut baby, and seventeen butternut children running promiscuously about the establishment; all are barefooted, dusty, and smell unpleasantly. (All these circumstances are expressed by pretty rapid fiddling for some minutes, winding up with a puff from the orpheclide[6] played by an intoxicated Teuton with an atrocious breath—it is impossible to misunderstand the description.) Now rises o'er the plains in mellifluous accents, the grand Pike County Chorus.[7]

> "Oh we'll soon be thar
> In the land of gold,

4. The refrain of a popular song.
5. The "gradually reducing force of loudness, more or less, little by little."
6. A wind instrument consisting of a conical metal tube bent double. It was replaced in American bands by the tuba.
7. Pike County characters were western emigrants, generally depicted as back-woodsmen with an exaggerated dialect, and Pike County was variously located in Missouri, Arkansas, or an adjacent state. Derby was the first to present the Pike as a specific character, though it remained for Bret Harte and John Hay to bring him before the general reading public.

> Through the forest old,
> O'er the mounting cold,
> With spirits bold—
> Oh, we come, we come,
> And we'll soon be thar.
>> Gee up Bolly! whoo, up, whoo haw!"

The train now encamp. The unpacking of the kettles and mess-pans, the unyoking of the oxen, the gathering about the various camp-fires, the frizzling of the pork, are so clearly expressed by the music, that the most untutored savage could readily comprehend it. Indeed, so vivid and lifelike was the representation, that a lady sitting near us, involuntarily exclaimed aloud, at a certain passage, *"Thar, that pork's burning!"* and it was truly interesting to watch the gratified expression of her face, when, by a few notes of the guitar, the pan was removed from the fire, and the blazing pork extinguished.

This is followed by the beautiful aria:—

> "O! marm, I want a pancake!"

Followed by that touching recitative:—

> "Shet up, or I will spank you!"

To which succeeds a grand *crescendo* movement, representing the flight of the child, with the pancake, the pursuit of the mother, and the final arrest and summary punishment of the former, represented by the rapid and successive strokes of the castanet.

The turning in for the night follows; and the deep and stertorous breathing of the encampment, is well given by the bassoon, while the sufferings and trials of an unhappy father with an unpleasant infant, are touchingly set forth by the *cornet à piston*.

Part Second—the night attack of the Pi Utahs; the fearful cries of the demoniac Indians; the shrieks of the females and children; the rapid and effective fire of the rifles; the stampede of the oxen; their recovery and the final repulse; the Pi Utahs being routed after a loss of thirty-six killed and wounded, while the Pikes lose but one scalp (from an old fellow who wore a wig, and lost it in the scuffle), are faithfully given, and excite the most intense interest in the minds of the hearers; the emotions of fear, admiration and delight, succeeding each other in their minds, with almost painful rapidity. Then follows the grand chorus:

> "Oh! we gin them fits,
> The Ingen Utahs.
> With our six-shooters—
> We gin 'em pertickuler fits."

After which, we have the charming recitative of Herr Tuden Links, to the infant, which is really one of the most charming gems in the performance:

> "Now, dern your skin, *can't* you be easy?"

Morning succeeds. The sun rises magnificently (octavo flute)— breakfast is eaten—in a rapid movement on three sharps; the oxen are caught and yoked up—with a small drum and triangle; the watches, purses, and other valuables of the conquered Pi Utahs, are stored away in a camp-kettle, to a small movement on the piccolo, and the train moves on, with the grand chorus:—

> "We'll soon be thar,
> Gee up Bolly! Whoo hup! whoo haw!"

The whole concludes with the grand hymn and chorus:—

> "When we die we'll go to Benton,
> Whup! Whoo, haw!
> The greatest man that e'er land saw,
> Gee!
> Who this little airth was sent on
> Whup! whoo, haw!
> To tell a 'hawk from a hand-saw!'
> Gee!"

The immense expense attending the production of this magnificent work; the length of time required to prepare the chorus; the incredible number of instruments destroyed at each rehearsal, have hitherto prevented M. Tarbox from placing it before the American public, and it has remained for San Diego to show herself superior to her sister cities of the Union, in musical taste and appreciation, and in high-souled liberality, by patronizing this immortal prodigy, and enabling its author to bring it forth in accordance with his wishes and its capabilities. We trust every citizen of San Diego and Vallecetos will listen to it ere it is withdrawn; and if there yet lingers in San Francisco one spark of musical fervor, or a remnant of taste for pure harmony, we can only say that the Southerner sails from that place once a fortnight and that the passage money is but forty-five dollars.

1854   1856

ARTEMUS WARD: One of Mr. Ward's Business
Letters[8]

To THE EDITOR OF THE——

Sir—I'm movin along—slowly along—down tords your place. I
want you should rite me a letter, sayin how is the show bizniss in
your place. My show at present consists of three moral Bares, a
Kangaroo (a amoozin little Raskal—t' would make you larf yerself
to deth to see the little cuss jump up and squeal) wax figgers of
G. Washington Gen. Tayler John Bunyan Capt. Kidd and Dr.
Webster in the act of killin Dr. Parkman,[9] besides several miscel-
lanyus moral wax statoots of celebrated piruts & murderers, &c.,
ekalled by few & exceld by none. Now Mr. Editor, scratch orf a few
lines sayin how is the show bizniss down to your place. I shall hav
my hanbills dun at your offiss. Depend upon it. I want you should
git my hanbills up in flamin stile. Also git up a tremenjus excite-
munt in yr. paper 'bowt my onparaleld Show. We must fetch the
public sumhow. We must wurk on their feelins. Cum the moral on
'em strong. If it's a temprance community tell 'em I sined the
pledge fifteen minits arter Ise born, but on the contery ef your
peple take their tods, say Mister Ward is as Jenial a feller as we
ever met, full of conwiviality, & the life an sole of the Soshul Bored.
Take, don't you? If you say anythin abowt my show say my snaiks
is as harmliss as the new born Babe. What a interestin study it is to
see a zewological animil like a snaik under perfeck subjecshun! My
kangaroo is the most larfable little cuss I ever saw. All for 15 cents.
I am anxyus to skewer your infloounce. I repeet in regard to them
hanbills that I shall git 'em struck orf up to your printin office.
My perliteral sentiments agree with yourn exactly. I know thay do,
becawz I never saw a man whoos didn't.

Respectively yures,
A. WARD.

P.S.—You scratch my back & Ile scratch your back.

1858   1862

---

8. Published in *Artemus Ward: His
Book* (1862). The present text is
based on the first edition.
9. Traveling wax museums presented
a conglomeration of statesmen, heroes,
outlaws, and murderers. Here we have
the first president of the United States;
the hero of the Mexican War, General
Zachary Taylor; John Bunyan, author
of *Pilgrim's Progress;* Captain William
Kidd, the notorious English pirate; and
the principals in the widely publicized
"Harvard Medical School Murder."

ARTEMUS WARD: Among the Free Lovers[1]

Some years ago I pitched my tent and onfurled my banner to the breeze, in Berlin Hites, Ohio. I had hearn that Berlin Hites was ockepied by a extensive seck called Free Lovers, who beleeved in affinertys and sich, goin back on their domestic ties without no hesitation whatsomever. They was likewise spirit rappers and high presher reformers on gineral principles. If I can improve these 'ere misgided peple by showin them my onparalleld show at the usual low price of admitants, methunk, I shall not hav lived in vane. But bitterly did I cuss the day I ever sot foot in the retchid place. I sot up my tent in a field near the Love Cure, as they called it, and bimeby the free lovers begun for to congregate around the door. A ornreer set I have never sawn. The men's faces was all covered with hare and they lookt half-starved to deth. They didn't wear no weskuts for the purpose (as they sed) of allowin the free air of hevun to blow onto their boozums. Their pockets was filled with tracks and pamplits and they was barefooted. They sed the Postles didn't wear boots, & why should they? That was their stile of argyment. The wimin was wuss than the men. They wore trowsis, short gownds, straw hats with green ribbins, and all carried bloo cotton umbrellers.

Presently a perfeckly orful lookin female presented herself at the door. Her gownd was skanderlusly short and her trowsis was shameful to behold.

She eyed me over very sharp, and then startin back she sed, in a wild voice:

"Ah, can it be?"

"Which?" sed I.

"Yes, 'tis troo, O 'tis troo!"

"15 cents, marm," I anserd.

She bust out a cryin & sed:

"An so I hav found you at larst—at larst, O at larst!"

"Yes," I anserd, "you have found me at larst, and you would hav found me at fust, if you had cum sooner."

She grabd me vilently by the coat collar, and brandishin her umbreller wildly round, exclaimed:

"Air you a man?"

Sez I, "I think I air, but if you doubt it, you can address Mrs. A. Ward, Baldinsville, Injianny, postage pade, & she will probly

1. "Some queer people, calling themselves 'Free Lovers,' and possessing very original ideas about life and morality, established themselves at Berlin Heights, in Ohio, a few years since. Public opinion was resistlessly against them, however, and the association was soon disbanded" [Browne's note]. There was a prevalence of cults during this period, and Browne is indulging in the popular sport of burlesquing them. This selection was printed in *Artemus Ward: His Book* (1862), and the present text follows the first edition.

giv you the desired informashun."

"Then thou ist what the cold world calls marrid?"

"Madam, I istest!"

The exsentric female then clutched me franticly by the arm and hollered:

"You air mine, O you air mine!"

"Scacely," I sed, endeverin to git loose from her. But she clung to me and sed:

"You air my Affinerty!"

"What upon arth is that?" I shouted.

"Dost thou not know?"

"No, I dostent!"

"Listen man, & I'll tell ye!" sed the strange female; "for years I hav yearned for thee. I knowd thou wast in the world, sumwhares, tho I didn't know whare. My hart sed he would cum and I took courage. He *has* cum—He's here—you air him—you air my Affinerty! O 'tis too mutch! too mutch!" and she sobbed agin.

"Yes," I anserd, "I think it is a darn site too mutch!"

"Hast thou not yearned for me?" she yelled, ringin her hands like a female play acter.

"Not a yearn!" I bellerd at the top of my voice, throwin her away from me.

The free lovers who was standin round obsarvin the scene commenst for to holler "shame!" "beast," etsettery, etsettery.

I was very mutch riled, and fortifyin myself with a spare tent stake, I addrest them as follers: "You pussylanermus critters, go away from me and take this retchid woman with you. I'm a law-abidin man, and beleeve in good, old-fashioned institutions. I am marrid & my orfsprings resemble me, if I am a showman! I think your Affinity bizniss is cussed noncents, besides bein outrajusly wicked. Why don't you behave desunt like other folks? Go to work and earn a honist livin and not stay round here in this lazy shiftless way, pizening the moral atmosphere with your pestifrous idees! You wimin folks go back to your lawful husbands if you've got any, and take orf them skanderlous gownds and trowsis, and dress respectful like other wimin. You men folks, cut orf them pirattercal whiskers, burn up them infurnel pamplits, put sum weskuts on, go to work choppin wood, splittin fence rales, or tillin the sile." I pored 4th my indignashun in this way till I got out of breth, when I stopt. I shant go to Berlin Hites agin, not if I live to be as old as Methooseler.

1862

The Triumph of Western Comic Realism

SAMUEL LANGHORNE CLEMENS
(1835–1910)

The pattern of the life of Samuel Langhorne Clemens, or "Mark Twain," for seventy-five years was the pattern of America— from frontier community to industrial urbanity, from river boats to railroads, from an aggressive, bumptious adolescence toward a troubled and powerful maturity. His intuitive and romantic response to that life was colored simultaneously by healthy skepticism, and a strong suspicion that the geography and citizens of America were not conforming to scriptural patterns of the Promised Land. This discrepancy between the American expectation and the disturbing reality, to which many writers have reacted with bitterness, or with gloomy acceptance and alarms, provoked Mark Twain to adopt the critical weapons of the humorist.

The inheritor of an indigenous tradition of humor compounded of Indian and Negro legend, New England wryness and dryness, and frontier extravagance, Mark Twain spent his early years in an ideal location for such influences to mold his life and his writing. Hannibal, Missouri, strategically placed on the banks of the Mississippi, in the period before the Civil War saw the commerce and travelers of a nation pass its wharfs and look westward from its streets. For a perceptive boy, such experiences were not to be forgotten, and later he preserved them in books that are world classics of the remembrance of a lost and happy time. His youth was typical of life in a fluid, diverse, yet morally exacting community in a chaotic period. His schooling was brief, and at eighteen he went to Philadelphia, New York, and Washington, doing itinerant newspaper work and sending his first travel letters to his brother Orion, who published them in his Muscatine *Journal*. He followed his brother to Keokuk, then moved on to Cincinnati, and from there embarked on an intended journey to South America, with the amusing results recounted in

Life on the Mississippi. Once he was on the river, his boyhood ambition to be a pilot returned, and discarding all thoughts of the Amazon, he persuaded Horace Bixby, a famous pilot, to school him in the intricate art of Mississippi navigation. After less than two years as a "cub," Twain received his pilot's license; the Civil War then put an end to piloting, but his nostalgic love of the river life was forever fixed in his pseudonym, "Mark Twain," the leadsman's cry meaning a two-fathom sounding, or "safe water."

The Civil War brought change and tension to the Clemens family who were, like so many, divided in their loyalty and allegiance. Orion Clemens, a strong Union man, campaigned for Lincoln and was appointed secretary of the Nevada Territory. Troubled by his brother's inclination toward the southern tradition of the family, Orion persuaded him, rather easily, to go west as his assistant, although he did not need one. In 1861 they traveled by stagecoach across the plains to Carson City, a journey described with hilarious half-truth and half-fiction in *Roughing It.* Neither the political job nor subsequent ventures in mining were profitable, and Twain began contributing letters, signed "Josh," to the Virginia City *Territorial Enterprise*, which led to his joining its staff in 1862. From that time he was to remain a writer, although he occasionally lectured and ventured into business on the side. The "Jumping Frog" story, now famous as "The Celebrated Jumping Frog of Calaveras County," published in the New York *Saturday Press* in 1865, brought him national attention; on the West Coast he was already well known as a journalistic associate of Bret Harte and Artemus Ward, remembered for his humorous sketches in various papers and for a successful reportorial trip to Hawaii. A commission from the *Alta California* to write a series of travel letters now enabled him for the first time to go to Europe.

Twain's excursion on the *Quaker City* to Europe and the Holy Land resulted in *The Innocents Abroad* (1869), a best seller, followed by an equally successful lecture tour. In 1870, he married Olivia Langdon and settled down as editor of the Buffalo *Express*, but he soon moved to Hartford. His first effort at a novel, *The Gilded Age* (1873), written in collaboration with Charles Dudley Warner, was a bitter yet amusing narrative of post-Civil War political and business corruption, and offers interesting parallels with *A Connecticut Yankee in King Arthur's Court* (1889), a comic critique of society in a fantastic vein. These books, with their quizzical and detached humor, suggest Twain's ability to view his age with qualified affection while satirizing the economic and spiritual disorders, the narrow insularity, of mid-nineteenth-century America. Yet that American provincialism, exploited for comic effect in *The Innocents Abroad* and in the later travel books, *A Tramp Abroad* (1880) and the classic *Life on the Mississippi* (1883), never overshadowed his love of the American land and its people. That love, intensified by childhood memories, evoked his two unquestioned masterpieces. *Tom Sawyer* (1876) and *Huckleberry Finn* (1885) combine recollections of Hannibal in Twain's youth, the spell of a great river, and the intangible quality of an art that relies on simplicity for its greatest effect. On one level, the nostalgic account of childhood, on another, the social and moral record and judgment of an epoch in American history, the two books have attained the position of classics in the world's literature. They were followed by lesser works, such as *The American Claimant* (1892), The £1,000,000 *Bank-Note* (1893), *The Tragedy of Pudd'nhead Wilson* (1894), *Personal Recollections of Joan of Arc* (1896), and *Following the Equator* (1897), the last of the travel volumes. *Tom Sawyer Abroad* (1894) and *Tom Sawyer, Detective* (1896) ended Twain's employment of Huck and Tom in fiction.

The tradition of American humor, from colonial folk myth and *Poor Richard's Almanack*, to the Yankee wit of Lowell's *Biglow Papers*, spreading through the national press from Josh Billings, John Phoenix, Artemus Ward, and unnumbered, forgotten local humorists, followed the pattern of any folk literature in its immediate and intuitive response to cultural and social patterns. Mark Twain is America's greatest humorist not only because of his unsurpassed mastery of that essential pattern, but because his humor served to point up errors in American life—its

gaucheries, pretenses, and political debilities—and at the same time expressed a faith in the American dream, optimistic and unquenchable.

The discrepancy between that dream and its questionable fulfillment, so obvious to the writers of the twentieth century, found expression also in Mark Twain's personal life. His literary successes and popularity in America and abroad were contrasted with emotional complexities, tragic losses, and business disappointments; his later writings evidence a skepticism saved from petulance by a great artist's sincerity. *The Man That Corrupted Hadleyburg* (1900), reprinted below, and *The Mysterious Stranger* (1916) are indictments of more than national cupidity and hypocrisy; they are troubled inquiries into the nature of man himself. And they appear to be at strange variance with such books as *Tom Sawyer* unless the reader recognizes in Twain the dichotomy of personality that William Dean Howells may have had in mind when he called him "the Lincoln of our literature."

There is no complete edition of Mark Twain now in print, though several have been published, such as a uniform trade edition, the limp-leather edition of the same, and the Mississippi Edition—all having the same pagination. The Author's National Edition, in 25 vols., 1907–1918, has not been reprinted. The rare, but definitive edition is *The Writings of Mark Twain*, 37 vols., edited by Albert Bigelow Paine, 1922–1925. A good one-volume collection is *The Portable Mark Twain*, edited by Bernard De Voto, 1946. *Huckleberry Finn, Tom Sawyer,* and *Life on the Mississippi* exist in several editions, and *A Connecticut Yankee, Roughing It,* and *Innocents Abroad* are readily available.

Mark Twain's Autobiography, edited

by Charles Neider, 1959, includes material not in the 1924 edition by Albert Bigelow Paine, nor in *Mark Twain in Eruption*, edited by Bernard De Voto, 1940. The authorized life by Albert Bigelow Paine, *Mark Twain, A Biography*, 3 vols., 1912, was reissued in 1935. This is supplemented by De-Lancey Ferguson, *Mark Twain, Man and Legend*, 1943; by Bernard De Voto, *Mark Twain's America*, 1932; and by Dixon Wecter's *Sam Clemens of Hannibal*, 1952, a valuable study of the first eighteen years of the novelist's life. Important collections of correspondence are *Mark Twain's Letters*, 2 vols., edited by Albert Bigelow Paine, 1917; *The Love Letters of Mark Twain*, edited by Dixon Wecter, 1949; and *Mark Twain–Howells Letters*, 2 vols., edited by Henry Nash Smith and William M. Gibson, 1960. The first collection of Twain's shorter fiction is *The Complete Short Stories*, edited by Charles Neider, 1957. A sound critical study is Edward Wagenknecht, *Mark Twain: The Man and His Work*, 1935. E. Hudson Long, *Mark Twain Handbook*, 1958, is useful. See also K. A. Lynn, *Mark Twain and Southwestern Humor*, 1959; W. Blair, *Mark Twain and Huck Finn*, 1960; R. B. Salomon, *Twain and the Image of History*, 1961; and A. E. Stone, Jr., *The Innocent Eye * * ***, 1961.

From Roughing It[1]
[*When the Buffalo Climbed a Tree*]

Next morning just before dawn, when about five hundred and fifty miles from St. Joseph,[2] our mud-wagon[3] broke down. We were to be delayed five or six hours, and therefore we took horses, by invitation, and joined a party who were just starting on a buffalo hunt. It was noble sport galloping over the plain in the dewy freshness of the morning, but our part of the hunt ended in disaster and disgrace, for a wounded buffalo bull chased the passenger Bemis nearly two miles, and then he forsook his horse and took to a lone tree. He was very sullen about the matter for some twenty-four hours, but at last he began to soften little by little, and finally he said:

"Well, it was not funny, and there was no sense in those gawks making themselves so facetious over it. I tell you I was angry in earnest for awhile. I should have shot that long gangly lubber they called Hank, if I could have done it without crippling six or seven other people—but of course I couldn't, the old 'Allen'[4]'s so confounded comprehensive. I wish those loafers had been up in the tree; they wouldn't have wanted to laugh so. If I had had a horse worth a cent—but no, the minute he saw that buffalo bull wheel on him and give a bellow, he raised straight up in the air and stood on his heels. The saddle began to slip, and I took him round the neck and laid close to him, and began to pray. Then he came down and stood up on the other end awhile, and the bull actually stopped

1. The sketches in *Roughing It* were based on Twain's memories, generously intermingled with elements of the tall tale, of his overland trip to Nevada in 1861 in company with his brother Orion, who had been appointed secretary of the Nevada Territory. Orion kept a journal which Mark drew on for certain facts. The present text of *Roughing It* is based on the first edition of 1872.
2. The Missouri gateway to the frontier, from which the overland stages started westward.
3. A less comfortable type of stagecoach, with open sides and simple benches.
4. A revolver named after its inventor, often called a "pepperbox" because it had six barrels.

pawing sand and bellowing to contemplate the inhuman spectacle. Then the bull made a pass at him and uttered a bellow that sounded perfectly frightful, it was so close to me, and that seemed to literally prostrate my horse's reason, and make a raving distracted maniac of him, and I wish I may die if he didn't stand on his head for a quarter of a minute and shed tears. He was absolutely out of his mind—he was, as sure as truth itself, and he really didn't know what he was doing. Then the bull came charging at us, and my horse dropped down on all fours and took a fresh start—and then for the next ten minutes he would actually throw one handspring after another so fast that the bull began to get unsettled, too, and didn't know where to start in—and so he stood there sneezing, and shoveling dust over his back, and bellowing every now and then, and thinking he had got a fifteen-hundred dollar circus horse for breakfast, certain. Well, I was first out on his neck—the horse's, not the bull's—and then underneath, and next on his rump, and sometimes head up, and sometimes heels—but I tell you it seemed solemn and awful to be ripping and tearing and carrying on so in the presence of death, as you might say. Pretty soon the bull made a snatch for us and brought away some of my horse's tail (I suppose, but do not know, being pretty busy at the time), but *something* made him hungry for solitude and suggested to him to get up and hunt for it. And then you ought to have seen that spider-legged old skeleton go! and you ought to have seen the bull cut out after him, too—head down, tongue out, tail up, bellowing like everything, and actually mowing down the weeds, and tearing up the earth, and boosting up the sand like a whirlwind! By George, it was a hot race! I and the saddle were back on the rump, and I had the bridle in my teeth and holding on to the pommel with both hands. First we left the dogs behind; then we passed a jackass rabbit;[5] then we overtook a cayote,[6] and were gaining on an antelope when the rotten girths let go and threw me about thirty yards off to the left, and as the saddle went down over the horse's rump he gave it a lift with his heels that sent it more than four hundred yards up in the air, I wish I may die in a minute if he didn't. I fell at the foot of the only solitary tree there was in nine counties adjacent (as any creature could see with the naked eye), and the next second I had hold of the bark with four sets of nails and my teeth, and the next second after that I was astraddle of the main limb and blaspheming my luck in a way that made my breath smell of brimstone. I *had* the bull, now, if he did not think of *one* thing. But that one thing I dreaded. I dreaded it very seriously. There was a possibility that the bull might not think of it, but there were

5. A large rabbit indigenous to the West, jokingly said to resemble a miniature donkey.

6. Twain's spelling for "coyote," a prairie wolf.

greater chances that he would. I made up my mind what I would
do in case he did. It was a little over forty feet to the ground from
where I sat. I cautiously unwound the lariat from the pommel of
my saddle—"

"Your *saddle?* Did you take your saddle up in the tree with you?"

"Take it up in the tree with me? Why, how you talk. Of course
I didn't. No man could do that. It *fell* in the tree when it came
down."

"Oh—exactly."

"Certainly. I unwound the lariat, and fastened one end of it to
the limb. It was the very best green raw-hide, and capable of sustaining tons. I made a slip-noose in the other end, and then hung
it down to see the length. It reached down twenty-two feet—half
way to the ground. I then loaded every barrel of the Allen with a
double charge. I felt satisfied. I said to myself, if he never thinks of
that one thing that I dread, all right—but if he does, all right anyhow—I am fixed for him. But don't you know that the very thing
a man dreads is the thing that always happens? Indeed it is so. I
watched the bull, now, with anxiety—anxiety which no one can
conceive of who has not been in such a situation and felt that at
any moment death might come. Presently a thought came into the
bull's eye. I knew it! said I—if my nerve fails now, I am lost. Sure
enough, it was just as I had dreaded, he started in to climb the
tree—"

"What, the bull?"

"Of course—who else?"

"But a bull can't climb a tree."

"He can't, can't he? Since you know so much about it, did you
ever see a bull try?"

"No! I never dreamt of such a thing."

"Well, then, what is the use of your talking that way, then? Because you never saw a thing done, is that any reason why it can't be
done?"

"Well, all right—go on. What did you do?"

"The bull started up, and got along well for about ten feet, then
slipped and slid back. I breathed easier. He tried it again—got up a
little higher—slipped again. But he came at it once more, and this
time he was careful. He got gradually higher and higher, and my
spirits went down more and more. Up he came—an inch at a time
—with his eyes hot, and his tongue hanging out. Higher and
higher—hitched his foot over the stump of a limb, and looked up, as
much as to say, 'You are my meat, friend.' Up again—higher and
higher, and getting more excited the closer he got. He was within
ten feet of me! I took a long breath,—and then said I, 'It is now
or never.' I had the coil of the lariat all ready; I paid it out slowly,

till it hung right over his head; all of a sudden I let go of the slack, and the slipnoose fell fairly round his neck! Quicker than lightning I out with the Allen and let him have it in the face. It was an awful roar, and must have scared the bull out of his senses. When the smoke cleared away, there he was, dangling in the air, twenty foot from the ground, and going out of one convulsion into another faster than you could count! I didn't stop to count, anyhow—I shinned down the tree and shot for home."

"Bemis, is all that true, just as you have stated it?"

"I wish I may rot in my tracks and die the death of a dog if it isn't."

"Well, we can't refuse to believe it, and we don't. But if there were some proofs—"

"Proofs! Did I bring back my lariat?"

"No."

"Did I bring back my horse?"

"No."

"Did you ever see the bull again?"

"No."

"Well, then, what more do you want? I never saw anybody as particular as you are about a little thing like that."

I made up my mind that if this man was not a liar he only missed it by the skin of his teeth.

1872

From Life on the Mississippi[7]

Frescoes from the Past[8]

Apparently the river was ready for business, now. But no; the distribution of a population along its banks was as calm and deliberate and time-devouring a process as the discovery and exploration had been.

Seventy years elapsed after the exploration before the river's borders had a white population worth considering; and nearly fifty more before the river had a commerce. Between La Salle's[9] opening

7. *Life on the Mississippi* (1883) is perhaps the finest literary treatment of a trade; it is also a poetic narrative in praise of the mighty Mississippi. The first half of the book—by far the better—is a nostalgic account of a boy's ambition to become a pilot and his experiences as a "cub" in the pilot house. The second half is a report of the author's recent journey on the river and of a visit to his old home. The Reverend Joseph Twichell, a lifelong friend, first suggested to Twain that his cub-pilot reminiscences would make wonderful reading matter, and inspired with the idea, he immediately began "Old Times on the Mississippi" (Chapters IV–XVII of *Life on the Mississippi*), which appeared in the *Atlantic Monthly* in 1875. These selections are reprinted from the first edition of the book.

8. This is Chapter III of *Life on the Mississippi,* and was first published in the book, not being a part of the earlier *Atlantic Monthly* series.

9. René Robert Cavelier de La Salle (1643–1687), the French explorer, de-

of the river and the time when it may be said to have become the vehicle of anything like a regular and active commerce, seven sovereigns had occupied the throne of England, America had become an independent nation, Louis XIV. and Louis XV. had rotted and died, the French monarchy had gone down in the red tempest of the Revolution, and Napoleon was a name that was beginning to be talked about. Truly, there were snails in those days.[1]

The river's earliest commerce was in great barges—keelboats, broadhorns.[2] They floated and sailed from the upper rivers to New Orleans, changed cargoes there, and were tediously warped and poled back by hand. A voyage down and back sometimes occupied nine months. In time this commerce increased until it gave employment to hordes of rough and hardy men; rude, uneducated, brave, suffering terrific hardships with sailor-like stoicism; heavy drinkers, coarse frolickers in moral sties like the Natchez-under-the-hill[3] of that day, heavy fighters, reckless fellows, every one, elephantinely jolly, foul-witted, profane, prodigal of their money, bankrupt at the end of the trip, fond of barbaric finery, prodigious braggarts; yet, in the main, honest, trustworthy, faithful to promises and duty, and often picturesquely magnanimous.

By and by the steamboat intruded. Then, for fifteen or twenty years, these men continued to run their keelboats down-stream, and the steamers did all of the up-stream business, the keelboatmen selling their boats in New Orleans, and returning home as deck-passengers in the steamers.

But after a while the steamboats so increased in number and in speed that they were able to absorb the entire commerce; and then keelboating died a permanent death. The keelboatman became a deckhand, or a mate, or a pilot on the steamer; and when steamer-berths were not open to him, he took a berth on a Pittsburg coal-flat, or on a pine raft constructed in the forests up toward the sources of the Mississippi.

In the heyday of the steamboating prosperity, the river from end to end was flaked with coal-fleets and timber-rafts, all managed by hand, and employing hosts of the rough characters whom I have been trying to describe. I remember the annual processions of mighty rafts that used to glide by Hannibal[4] when I was a boy—an acre or so of white, sweet-smelling boards in each raft, a crew of

scended the Mississippi River to its mouth and named the region Louisiana after the French king on April 9, 1682.
1. Literary references abound to the statement "There were giants in the earth in those days" (Genesis vi: 4).
2. The keelboat was a long, narrow craft, sharp at bow and stern, with a flat bottom; the broadhorn was an oblong flatboat, covered by an arched roof, with a long oar projecting from each side, giving it its name.
3. A place of prostitutes, gamblers, and gunmen situated at the base of the bluff below Natchez, Mississippi.
4. Hannibal, Missouri, the boyhood home of Mark Twain.

two dozen men or more, three or four wigwams scattered about the raft's vast level space for storm-quarters—and I remember the rude ways and the tremendous talk of their big crews, the ex-keelboatmen and their admiringly patterning successors; for we used to swim out a quarter or a third of a mile and get on these rafts and have a ride.

By way of illustrating keelboat talk and manners, and that now departed and hardly remembered raft life, I will throw in, in this place, a chapter from a book[5] which I have been working at, by fits and starts, during the past five or six years, and may possibly finish in the course of five or six more. The book is a story which details some passages in the life of an ignorant village boy, Huck Finn, son of the town drunkard of my time out West, there. He has run away from his persecuting father, and from a persecuting good widow who wishes to make a nice, truth-telling, respectable boy of him; and with him a slave of the widow's has also escaped. They have found a fragment of a lumber-raft (it is high water and dead summer-time), and are floating down the river by night, and hiding in the willows by day—bound for Cairo,[6] whence the negro will seek freedom in the heart of the free states. But, in a fog, they pass Cairo without knowing it. By and by they begin to suspect the truth, and Huck Finn is persuaded to end the dismal suspense by swimming down to a huge raft which they have seen in the distance ahead of them, creeping aboard under cover of the darkness, and gathering the needed information by eavesdropping:

But you know a young person can't wait very well when he is impatient to find a thing out. We talked it over, and by and by Jim said it was such a black night, now, that it wouldn't be no risk to swim down to the big raft and crawl aboard and listen—they would talk about Cairo, because they would be calculating to go ashore there for a spree, maybe; or anyway they would send boats ashore to buy whisky or fresh meat or something. Jim had a wonderful level head, for a nigger: he could most always start a good plan when you wanted one.

I stood up and shook my rags off and jumped into the river, and struck out for the raft's light. By and by, when I got down nearly to her, I eased up and went slow and cautious. But everything was all right—nobody at the sweeps. So I swum down along the raft till I was most abreast the camp-fire in the middle, then I crawled aboard and inched along and got in among some bundles of shingles on the weather side of the fire. There was thirteen men there—they was the watch on deck of course. And a mighty rough-looking lot, too. They had a jug, and tin cups, and they kept the jug moving. One man was singing—roaring, you may say; and it wasn't a nice song—for a parlor, anyway. He roared through his nose, and strung out the last word of every line very long. When he was done they all fetched a kind of Injun war-whoop, and then another was sung. It begun:

5. *Adventures of Huckleberry Finn* (1885). The passage is in smaller type, below; cf. also p. 327, note 8.

6. In the southern tip of Illinois, where the Mississippi is joined by the Ohio. (Pronounced "Kay-ro.")

"There was a woman in our towdn,
In our towdn did dwed'l [dwell],
She loved her husband dear-i-lee,
But another man twyste as wed'l.

"Singing too, riloo, riloo, riloo,
Ri-too, riloo, rilay - - - e,
She loved her husband dear-i-lee,
But another man twyste as wed'l."

And so on—fourteen verses. It was kind of poor, and when he was going to start on the next verse one of them said it was the tune the old cow died on; and another one said: "Oh, give us a rest!" And another one told him to take a walk. They made fun of him till he got mad and jumped up and begun to cuss the crowd, and said he could lam any thief in the lot.

They was all about to make a break for him, but the biggest man there jumped up and says:

"Set whar you are, gentlemen. Leave him to me; he's my meat."

Then he jumped up in the air three times, and cracked his heels together every time. He flung off a buckskin coat that was all hung with fringes, and says, "You lay thar tell the chawin-up's done"; and flung his hat down, which was all over ribbons, and says, "You lay thar tell his sufferin's is over."

Then he jumped up in the air and cracked his heels together again, and shouted out:

"Whoo-oop! I'm the old original iron-jawed, brass-mounted, copper-bellied corpse-maker from the wilds of Arkansaw! Look at me! I'm the man they call Sudden Death and General Desolation! Sired by a hurricane, dam'd by an earthquake, half-brother to the cholera, nearly related to the smallpox on the mother's side! Look at me! I take nineteen alligators and a bar'l of whisky for breakfast when I'm in robust health, and a bushel of rattlesnakes and a dead body when I'm ailing. I split the everlasting rocks with my glance, and I squench the thunder when I speak! Whoo-oop! Stand back and give me room according to my strength! Blood's my natural drink, and the wails of the dying is music to my ear. Cast your eye on me, gentlemen! and lay low and hold your breath, for I'm 'bout to turn myself loose!"[7]

All the time he was getting this off, he was shaking his head and looking fierce, and kind of swelling around in a little circle, tucking up his wristbands, and now and then straightening up and beating his breast with his fist, saying, "Look at me, gentlemen!" When he got through, he jumped up and cracked his heels together three times, and let off a roaring "Whoo-oop! I'm the bloodiest son of a wildcat that lives!"

Then the man that had started the row tilted his old slouch hat down over his right eye; then he bent stooping forward, with his back sagged and his south end sticking out far, and his fists a-shoving out and drawing in in front of him, and so went around in a little circle about three times, swelling himself up and breathing hard. Then he straightened, and jumped up and cracked his heels together three times before he lit again (that made them cheer), and he began to shout like this:

"Whoo-oop! bow your neck and spread, for the kingdom of sorrow's a-coming! Hold me down to the earth, for I feel my powers a-working! whoo-

7. This speech, the characters, and episode are in the tall-tale tradition of such backwoods heroes as Davy Crockett and Mike Fink, and illustrate the frontier brag, which echoed with whoops, boasting, and verbal thunder, and which reached its prime in the humor of the Old Southwest, 1830–1865.

oop! I'm a child of sin, *don't* let me get a start! Smoked glass, here, for all!
Don't attempt to look at me with the naked eye, gentlemen! When I'm
playful I use the meridians of longitude and parallels of latitude for a
seine, and drag the Atlantic Ocean for whales! I scratch my head with the
lightning and purr myself to sleep with the thunder! When I'm cold, I
bile the Gulf of Mexico and bathe in it; when I'm hot I fan myself with an
equinoctial storm; when I'm thirsty I reach up and suck a cloud dry like a
sponge; when I range the earth hungry, famine follows in my tracks! Whoo-
oop! Bow your neck and spread! I put my hand on the sun's face and make
it night in the earth; I bite a piece out of the moon and hurry the seasons;
I shake myself and crumble the mountains! Contemplate me through
leather—*don't* use the naked eye! I'm the man with a petrified heart and
biler-iron bowels! The massacre of isolated communities is the pastime of my
idle moments, the destruction of nationalities the serious business of my
life! The boundless vastness of the great American desert is my inclosed
property, and I bury my dead on my own premises!" He jumped up and
cracked his heels together three times before he lit (they cheered him
again), and as he come down he shouted out: "Whoo-oop! bow your neck
and spread, for the Pet Child of Calamity's a-coming!"

Then the other one went to swelling around and blowing again—the first
one—the one they called Bob; next, the Child of Calamity chipped in
again, bigger than ever; then they both got at it at the same time, swelling
round and round each other and punching their fists most into each other's
faces, and whooping and jawing like Injuns; then Bob called the Child
names, and the Child called him names back again; next, Bob called him a
heap rougher names, and the Child come back at him with the very worst
kind of language; next, Bob knocked the Child's hat off, and the Child
picked it up and kicked Bob's ribbony hat about six foot; Bob went and got
it and said never mind, this warn't going to be the last of this thing, because he was a man that never forgot and never forgive, and so the Child
better look out, for there was a time a-coming, just as sure as he was a
living man, that he would have to answer to him with the best blood
in his body. The Child said no man was willinger than he for that time
to come, and he would give Bob fair warning, *now*, never to cross his
path again, for he could never rest till he had waded in his blood, for
such was his nature, though he was sparing him now on account of his
family, if he had one.

Both of them was edging away in different directions, growling and
shaking their heads and going on about what they was going to do; but
a little black-whiskered chap skipped up and says:

"Come back here, you couple of chicken-livered cowards, and I'll thrash
the two of ye!"

And he done it, too. He snatched them, he jerked them this way and
that, he booted them around, he knocked them sprawling faster than they
could get up. Why, it warn't two minutes till they begged like dogs—and
how the other lot did yell and laugh and clap their hands all the way
through, and shout, "Sail in, Corpse-Maker!" "Hi! at him again, Child of
Calamity!" "Bully for you, little Davy!" Well, it was a perfect pow-wow
for a while. Bob and the Child had red noses and black eyes when they got
through. Little Davy made them own up that they was sneaks and cowards
and not fit to eat with a dog or drink with a nigger; then Bob and the Child
shook hands with each other, very solemn, and said they had always
respected each other and was willing to let bygones be bygones. So then
they washed their faces in the river; and just then there was a loud order
to stand by for a crossing, and some of them went forward to man the

sweeps there, and the rest went aft to handle the after sweeps.

I laid still and waited for fifteen minutes, and had a smoke out of a pipe that one of them left in reach; then the crossing was finished, and they stumped back and had a drink around and went to talking and singing again. Next they got out an old fiddle, and one played, and another patted juba, and the rest turned themselves loose on a regular old-fashioned keel-boat breakdown. They couldn't keep that up very long without getting winded, so by and by they settled around the jug again.

They sung "Jolly, Jolly Raftsman's the Life for Me," with a rousing chorus, and then they got to talking about differences betwixt hogs, and their different kind of habits; and next about women and their different ways; and next about the best ways to put out houses that was afire; and next about what ought to be done with the Injuns; and next about what a king had to do, and how much he got; and next about how to make cats fight; and next about what to do when a man has fits; and next about differences betwixt clear-water rivers and muddy-water ones. The man they called Ed said the muddy Mississippi water was wholesomer to drink than the clear water of the Ohio; he said if you let a pint of this yaller Mississippi water settle, you would have about a half to three-quarters of an inch of mud in the bottom, according to the stage of the river, and then it warn't no better than Ohio water—what you wanted to do was to keep it stirred up—and when the river was low, keep mud on hand to put in and thicken the water up the way it ought to be.

The Child of Calamity said that was so; he said there was nutritiousness in the mud, and a man that drunk Mississippi water could grow corn in his stomach if he wanted to. He says:

"You look at the graveyards; that tells the tale. Trees won't grow worth shucks in a Cincinnati graveyard, but in a Sent Louis graveyard they grow upwards of eight hundred foot high. It's all on account of the water the people drunk before they laid up. A Cincinnati corpse don't richen a soil any."

And they talked about how Ohio water didn't like to mix with Mississippi water. Ed said if you take the Mississippi on a rise when the Ohio is low, you'll find a wide band of clear water all the way down the east side of the Mississippi for a hundred mile or more, and the minute you get out a quarter of a mile from shore and pass the line, it is all thick and yaller the rest of the way across. Then they talked about how to keep tobacco from getting moldy, and from that they went into ghosts and told about a lot that other folks had seen; but Ed says:

"Why don't you tell something that you've seen yourselves? Now let me have a say. Five years ago I was on a raft as big as this, and right along here it was a bright moonshiny night, and I was on watch and boss of the stab-board oar forrard, and one of my pards was a man named Dick Allbright, and he come along to where I was sitting, forrard—gaping and stretching, he was—and stooped down on the edge of the raft and washed his face in the river, and come and set down by me and got out his pipe, and had just got it filled, when he looks up and says:

" 'Why looky-here,' he says, 'ain't that Buck Miller's place, over yander in the bend?'

" 'Yes,' says I, 'it is—why?' He laid his pipe down and leaned his head on his hand, and says:

" 'I thought we'd be furder down.' I says:

" 'I thought it, too, when I went off watch'—we was standing six hours on and six off—'but the boys told me,' I says, 'that the raft didn't seem to hardly move, for the last hour,' says I, 'though she's a-slipping along all right now,' says I. He give a kind of a groan, and says:

" 'I've seed a raft act so before, along here,' he says. ' 'pears to me the current has most quit above the head of this bend durin' the last two years,' he says.

"Well, he raised up two or three times, and looked away off and around on the water. That started me at it, too. A body is always doing what he sees somebody else doing, though there mayn't be no sense in it. Pretty soon I see a black something floating on the water away off to stabboard and quartering behind us. I see he was looking at it, too. I says:

" 'What's that?' He says, sort of pettish:

" ' 'Tain't nothing but an old empty bar'l.'

" 'An empty bar'l!' says I, 'why,' says I, 'a spy-glass is a fool to *your* eyes. How can you tell it's an empty bar'l?' He says:

" 'I don't know; I reckon it ain't a bar'l, but I thought it might be,' says he.

" 'Yes,' I says, 'so it might be, and it might be anything else too; a body can't tell nothing about it, such a distance as that,' I says.

"We hadn't nothing else to do, so we kept on watching it. By and by I says:

" 'Why, looky-here, Dick Allbright, that thing's a-gaining on us, I believe.'

"He never said nothing. The thing gained and gained, and I judged it must be a dog that was about tired out. Well, we swung down into the crossing, and the thing floated across the bright streak of the moonshine, and by George, it *was* a bar'l. Says I:

" 'Dick Allbright, what made you think that thing was a bar'l, when it was half a mile off?' says I. Says he:

" 'I don't know.' Says I:

" 'You tell me, Dick Allbright.' Says he:

" 'Well, I knowed it was a bar'l; I've seen it before; lots has seen it; they says it's a ha'nted bar'l.'

"I called the rest of the watch, and they come and stood there, and I told them what Dick said. It floated right along abreast, now, and didn't gain any more. It was about twenty foot off. Some was for having it aboard, but the rest didn't want to. Dick Allbright said rafts that had fooled with it had got bad luck by it. The captain of the watch said he didn't believe in it. He said he reckoned the bar'l gained on us because it was in a little better current than what we was. He said it would leave by and by.

"So then we went to talking about other things, and we had a song, and then a breakdown; and after that the captain of the watch called for another song; but it was clouding up now, and the bar'l stuck right thar in the same place, and the song didn't seem to have much warm-up to it, somehow, and so they didn't finish it, and there warn't any cheers, but it sort of dropped flat, and nobody said anything for a minute. Then everybody tried to talk at once, and one chap got off a joke, but it warn't no use, they didn't laugh, and even the chap that made the joke didn't laugh at it, which ain't usual. We all just settled down glum, and watched the bar'l, and was oneasy and oncomfortable. Well, sir, it shut down black and still, and then the wind began to moan around, and next the lightning began to play and the thunder to grumble. And pretty soon there was a regular storm, and in the middle of it a man that was running aft stumbled and fell and sprained his ankle so that he had to lay up. This made the boys shake their heads. And every time the lightning come, there was that bar'l, with the blue lights winking around it. We was always on the lookout for it. But by and by, toward dawn, she was gone. When the day come we couldn't see her anywhere, and we warn't sorry, either.

"But next night about half-past nine, when there was songs and high jinks going on, here she comes again, and took her old roost on the stabboard side. There warn't no more high jinks. Everybody got solemn; nobody talked; you couldn't get anybody to do anything but set around moody and look at the bar'l. It begun to cloud up again. When the watch changed, the off watch stayed up, 'stead of turning in. The storm ripped and roared around all night, and in the middle of it another man tripped and sprained his ankle, and had to knock off. The bar'l left toward day, and nobody see it go.

"Everybody was sober and down in the mouth all day. I don't mean the kind of sober that comes of leaving liquor alone—not that. They was quiet, but they all drunk more than usual—not together, but each man sidled off and took it private, by himself.

"After dark the off watch didn't turn in; nobody sung, nobody talked; the boys didn't scatter around, neither; they sort of huddled together, forrard; and for two hours they set there, perfectly still, looking steady in the one direction, and heaving a sigh once in a while. And then, here comes the bar'l again. She took up her old place. She stayed there all night; nobody turned in. The storm come on again, after midnight. It got awful dark; the rain poured down; hail, too; the thunder boomed and roared and bellowed; the wind blowed a hurricane; and the lightning spread over everything in big sheets of glare, and showed the whole raft as plain as day; and the river lashed up white as milk as far as you could see for miles, and there was that bar'l jiggering along, same as ever. The captain ordered the watch to man the after sweeps for a crossing, and nobody would go—no more sprained ankles for them, they said. They wouldn't even *walk* aft. Well, then, just then the sky split wide open, with a crash, and the lightning killed two men of the after watch, and crippled two more. Crippled them how, say you? Why, *sprained their ankles!*

"The bar'l left in the dark betwixt lightnings, toward dawn. Well, not a body eat a bite at breakfast that morning. After that the men loafed around, in twos and threes, and talked low together. But none of them herded with Dick Allbright. They all give him the cold shake. If he come around where any of the men was, they split up and sidled away. They wouldn't man the sweeps with him. The captain had all the skiffs hauled up on the raft, alongside of his wigwam, and wouldn't let the dead men be took ashore to be planted; he didn't believe a man that got ashore would come back; and he was right.

"After night come, you could see pretty plain that there was going to be trouble if that bar'l come again; there was such a muttering going on. A good many wanted to kill Dick Allbright, because he'd seen the bar'l on other trips, and that had an ugly look. Some wanted to put him ashore. Some said: 'Let's all go ashore in a pile, if the bar'l comes again.'

"This kind of whispers was still going on, the men being bunched together forrard watching for the bar'l, when lo and behold you! here she comes again. Down she comes, slow and steady, and settles into her old tracks. You could 'a' heard a pin drop. Then up comes the captain, and says:

"'Boys, don't be a pack of children and fools; I don't want this bar'l to be dogging us all the way to Orleans, and *you* don't: Well, then, how's the best way to stop it? Burn it up—that's the way. I'm going to fetch it aboard,' he says. And before anybody could say a word, in he went.

"He swum to it, and as he come pushing it to the raft, the men spread to one side. But the old man got it aboard and busted in the head, and there was a baby in it! Yes, sir; a stark-naked baby. It was Dick Allbright's baby; he owned up and said so.

" 'Yes,' he says, a-leaning over it, 'yes, it is my own lamented darling, my poor lost Charles William Allbright deceased,' says he—for he could curl his tongue around the bulliest words in the language when he was a mind to, and lay them before you without a jint started anywheres. Yes, he said, he used to live up at the head of this bend, and one night he choked his child, which was crying, not intending to kill it—which was prob'ly a lie—and then he was scared, and buried it in a bar'l, before his wife got home, and off he went, and struck the northern trail and went to rafting; and this was the third year that the bar'l had chased him. He said the bad luck always begun light, and lasted till four men was killed, and then the bar'l didn't come any more after that. He said if the men would stand it one more night—and was a-going on like that—but the men had got enough. They started to get out a boat to take him ashore and lynch him, but he grabbed the little child all of a sudden and jumped overboard with it, hugged up to his breast and shedding tears, and we never see him again in this life, poor old suffering soul, nor Charles William neither."

"*Who* was shedding tears?" says Bob; "was it Allbright or the baby?"

"Why, Allbright, of course; didn't I tell you the baby was dead? Been dead three years—how could it cry?"

"Well, never mind how it could cry—how could it *keep* all that time?" says Davy. "You answer me that."

"I don't know how it done it," says Ed. "It done it, though—that's all I know about it."

"Say—what did they do with the bar'l?" says the Child of Calamity.

"Why, they hove it overboard, and it sunk like a chunk of lead."

"Edward, did the child look like it was choked?" says one.

"Did it have its hair parted?" says another.

"What was the brand on that bar'l, Eddy?" says a fellow they called Bill.

"Have you got the papers for them statistics, Edmund?" says Jimmy.

"Say, Edwin, was you one of the men that was killed by the lightning?" says Davy.

"Him? Oh, no! he was both of 'em," says Bob. Then they all haw-hawed.

"Say, Edward, don't you reckon you'd better take a pill? You look bad—don't you feel pale?" says the Child of Calamity.

"Oh, come, now, Eddy," says Jimmy, "show up; you must 'a' kept part of that bar'l to prove the thing by. Show us the bung-hole—*do*—and we'll all believe you."

"Say, boys," says Bill, "less divide it up. Thar's thirteen of us. I can swaller a thirteenth of the yarn, if you can worry down the rest."

Ed got up mad and said they could all go to some place which he ripped out pretty savage, and then walked off aft, cussing to himself, and they yelling and jeering at him, and roaring and laughing so you could hear them a mile.

"Boys, we'll split a watermelon on that," says the Child of Calamity; and he came rummaging around in the dark amongst the shingle bundles where I was, and put his hand on me. I was warm and soft and naked; so he says "Ouch!" and jumped back.

"Fetch a lantern or a chunk of fire here, boys—there's a snake here as big as a cow!"

So they run there with a lantern, and crowded up and looked in on me.

"Come out of that, you beggar!" says one.

"Who are you?" says another.

"What are you after here? Speak up prompt, or overboard you go."

"Snake him out, boys. Snatch him out by the heels."

I began to beg, and crept out amongst them trembling. They looked me over, wondering, and the Child of Calamity says:

"A cussed thief! Lend a hand and less heave him overboard!"

"No," says Big Bob, "less get out the paint-pot and paint him a sky-blue all over from head to heel, and *then* heave him over."

"Good! that's it. Go for the paint, Jimmy."

When the paint come, and Bob took the brush and was just going to begin, the others laughing and rubbing their hands, I begun to cry, and that sort of worked on Davy, and he says:

" 'Vast there. He's nothing but a cub. I'll paint the man that teches him!"

So I looked around on them, and some of them grumbled and growled, and Bob put down the paint, and the others didn't take it up.

"Come here to the fire, and less see what you're up to here," says Davy. "Now set down there and give an account of yourself. How long have you been aboard here?"

"Not over a quarter of a minute, sir," says I.

"How did you get dry so quick?"

"I don't know, sir. I'm always that way, mostly."

"Oh, you are, are you? What's your name?"

I warn't going to tell my name. I didn't know what to say, so I just says: "Charles William Allbright, sir."

Then they roared—the whole crowd; and I was mighty glad I said that, because, maybe, laughing would get them in a better humor.

When they got done laughing, Davy says:

"It won't hardly do, Charles William. You couldn't have growed this much in five year, and you was a baby when you come out of the bar'l, you know, and dead at that. Come, now, tell a straight story, and nobody'll hurt you, if you ain't up to anything wrong. What *is* your name?"

"Aleck Hopkins, sir. Aleck James Hopkins."

"Well, Aleck, where did you come from, here?"

"From a trading-scow. She lays up the bend yonder. I was born on her. Pap has traded up and down here all his life; and he told me to swim off here, because when you went by he said he would like to get some of you to speak to a Mr. Jonas Turner, in Cairo, and tell him—"

"Oh, come!"

"Yes, sir, it's as true as the world. Pap he says—"

"Oh, your grandmother!"

They all laughed, and I tried again to talk, but they broke in on me and stopped me.

"Now, looky-here," says Davy; "you're scared, and so you talk wild. Honest, now, do you live in a scow, or is it a lie?"

"Yes, sir, in a trading-scow. She lays up at the head of the bend. But I warn't born in her. It's our first trip."

"Now you're talking! What did you come aboard here for? To steal?"

"No sir, I didn't. It was only to get a ride on the raft. All boys does that."

"Well, I know that. But what did you hide for?"

"Sometimes they drive the boys off."

"So they do. They might steal. Looky-here; if we let you off this time, will you keep out of these kind of scrapes hereafter?"

" 'Deed I will, boss. You try me."

"All right, then. You ain't but little ways from shore. Overboard with you, and don't you make a fool of yourself another time this way. Blast it, boy, some raftsmen would rawhide you till you were black and blue!"

I didn't wait to kiss good-by, but went overboard and broke for shore.

When Jim come along by and by, the big raft was away out of sight around the point. I swum out and got aboard, and was mighty glad to see home again.

The boy did not get the information he was after, but his adventure has furnished the glimpse of the departed raftsman and keelboatman which I desire to offer in this place.

I now come to a phase of the Mississippi River life of the flush times of steamboating, which seems to me to warrant full examination—the marvelous science of piloting, as displayed there. I believe there has been nothing like it elsewhere in the world.

The Boys' Ambition[8]

When I was a boy, there was but one permanent ambition among my comrades in our village[9] on the west bank of the Mississippi River. That was, to be a steamboatman. We had transient ambitions of other sorts, but they were only transient. When a circus came and went, it left us all burning to become clowns; the first negro minstrel show that ever came to our section left us all suffering to try that kind of life; now and then we had a hope that, if we lived and were good, God would permit us to be pirates. These ambitions faded out, each in its turn; but the ambition to be a steamboatman always remained.

Once a day a cheap, gaudy packet arrived upward from St. Louis, and another downward from Keokuk.[1] Before these events, the day was glorious with expectancy; after them, the day was a dead and empty thing. Not only the boys, but the whole village, felt this. After all these years I can picture that old time to myself now, just as it was then: the white town drowsing in the sunshine of a summer's morning; the streets empty, or pretty nearly so; one or two clerks sitting in front of the Water Street stores, with their splint-bottomed chairs tilted back against the walls, chins on breasts, hats slouched over their faces, asleep—with shingle-shavings enough around to show what broke them down; a sow and a litter of pigs loafing along the sidewalk, doing a good business in watermelon rinds and seeds; two or three lonely little freight piles scattered about the "levee"; a pile of "skids" on the slope of the stone-paved wharf, and the fragrant town drunkard asleep in the shadow of them; two or three wood flats at the head of the wharf, but nobody to listen to the peaceful lapping of the wavelets against them; the great Mississippi, the majestic, the magnificent Mississippi, rolling its mile-wide tide along, shining in the sun; the dense forest away on the other side; the "point" above the town, and the "point" be-

---

8. This is Chapter IV of *Life on the Mississippi*, and the first chapter of "Old Times on the Mississippi," published in the *Atlantic Monthly* in 1875.

9. "Hannibal, Missouri" [Twain's note].
1. In southeastern Iowa.

low, bounding the river-glimpse and turning it into a sort of sea, and withal a very still and brilliant and lonely one. Presently a film of dark smoke appears above one of those remote "points"; instantly a negro drayman, famous for his quick eye and prodigious voice, lifts up the cry, "S-t-e-a-m-boat a-comin'!" and the scene changes! The town drunkard stirs, the clerks wake up, a furious clatter of drays follows, every house and store pours out a human contribution, and all in a twinkling the dead town is alive and moving. Drays, carts, men, boys, all go hurrying from many quarters to a common center, the wharf. Assembled there, the people fasten their eyes upon the coming boat as upon a wonder they are seeing for the first time. And the boat *is* rather a handsome sight, too. She is long and sharp and trim and pretty; she has two tall, fancy-topped chimneys, with a gilded device of some kind swung between them; a fanciful pilot-house, all glass and "gingerbread," perched on top of the "texas" deck[2] behind them; the paddle-boxes are gorgeous with a picture or with gilded rays above the boat's name; the boiler-deck, the hurricane-deck, and the texas deck are fenced and ornamented with clean white railings; there is a flag gallantly flying from the jack-staff; the furnace doors are open and the fires glaring bravely; the upper decks are black with passengers; the captain stands by the big bell, calm, imposing, the envy of all; great volumes of the blackest smoke are rolling and tumbling out of the chimneys—a husbanded grandeur created with a bit of pitch-pine just before arriving at a town; the crew are grouped on the forecastle; the broad stage is run far out over the port bow, and an envied deck-hand stands picturesquely on the end of it with a coil of rope in his hand; the pent steam is screaming through the gauge-cocks; the captain lifts his hand, a bell rings, the wheels stop; then they turn back, churning the water to foam, and the steamer is at rest. Then such a scramble as there is to get aboard, and to get ashore, and to take in freight and to discharge freight, all at one and the same time; and such a yelling and cursing as the mates facilitate it all with! Ten minutes later the steamer is under way again, with no flag on the jack-staff and no black smoke issuing from the chimneys. After ten more minutes the town is dead again, and the town drunkard asleep by the skids once more.

My father was a justice of the peace, and I supposed he possessed the power of life and death over all men, and could hang anybody that offended him. This was distinction enough for me as a general thing; but the desire to be a steamboatman kept intruding, nevertheless. I first wanted to be a cabin-boy, so that I could come out with a white apron on and shake a table-cloth over the side,

2. The officers' quarters, largest on the boat, were called the "texas," and the deck just over them the "texas deck."

where all my old comrades could see me; later I thought I would rather be the deck-hand who stood on the end of the stage-plank with the coil of rope in his hand, because he was particularly conspicuous. But these were only day-dreams—they were too heavenly to be contemplated as real possibilities. By and by one of our boys went away. He was not heard of for a long time. At last he turned up as apprentice engineer or "striker" on a steamboat. This thing shook the bottom out of all my Sunday-school teachings. That boy had been notoriously worldly, and I just the reverse; yet he was exalted to this eminence, and I left in obscurity and misery. There was nothing generous about this fellow in his greatness. He would always manage to have a rusty bolt to scrub while his boat tarried at our town, and he would sit on the inside guard and scrub it, where we all could see him and envy him and loathe him. And whenever his boat was laid up he would come home and swell around the town in his blackest and greasiest clothes, so that nobody could help remembering that he was a steamboatman; and he used all sorts of steamboat technicalities in his talk, as if he were so used to them that he forgot common people could not understand them. He would speak of the "labboard" side of a horse in an easy, natural way that would make one wish he was dead. And he was always talking about "St. Looy" like an old citizen; he would refer casually to occasions when he was "coming down Fourth Street," or when he was "passing by the Planter's House," or when there was a fire and he took a turn on the brakes of "the old Big Missouri"; and then he would go on and lie about how many towns the size of ours were burned down there that day. Two or three of the boys had long been persons of consideration among us because they had been to St. Louis once and had a vague general knowledge of its wonders, but the day of their glory was over now. They lapsed into a humble silence, and learned to disappear when the ruthless "cub"-engineer approached. This fellow had money, too, and hair-oil. Also an ignorant silver watch and a showy brass watch-chain. He wore a leather belt and used no suspenders. If ever a youth was cordially admired and hated by his comrades, this one was. No girl could withstand his charms. He "cut out" every boy in the village. When his boat blew up at last, it diffused a tranquil contentment among us such as we had not known for months. But when he came home the next week, alive, renowned, and appeared in church all battered up and bandaged, a shining hero, stared at and wondered over by everybody, it seemed to us that the partiality of Providence for an undeserving reptile had reached a point where it was open to criticism.

This creature's career could produce but one result, and it speedily followed. Boy after boy managed to get on the river. The minister's son became an engineer. The doctor's and the post-master's sons became "mud clerks"; the wholesale liquor dealer's son became a barkeeper on a boat; four sons of the chief merchant, and two sons of the county judge, became pilots. Pilot was the grandest position of all. The pilot, even in those days of trivial wages, had a princely salary—from a hundred and fifty to two hundred and fifty dollars a month, and no board to pay. Two months of his wages would pay a preacher's salary for a year. Now some of us were left disconsolate. We could not get on the river—at least our parents would not let us.

So, by and by, I ran away. I said I would never come home again till I was a pilot and could come in glory. But somehow I could not manage it. I went meekly aboard a few of the boats that lay packed together like sardines at the long St. Louis wharf, and humbly inquired for the pilots, but got only a cold shoulder and short words from mates and clerks. I had to make the best of this sort of treatment for the time being, but I had comforting day-dreams of a future when I should be a great and honored pilot, with plenty of money, and could kill some of these mates and clerks and pay for them.

[A Mississippi Cub-Pilot][3]

Months afterward the hope within me struggled to a reluctant death, and I found myself without an ambition. But I was ashamed to go home. I was in Cincinnati, and I set to work to map out a new career. I had been reading about the recent exploration of the river Amazon by an expedition sent out by our government. It was said that the expedition, owing to difficulties, had not thoroughly explored a part of the country lying about the headwaters, some four thousand miles from the mouth of the river. It was only about fifteen hundred miles from Cincinnati to New Orleans, where I could doubtless get a ship. I had thirty dollars left; I would go and complete the exploration of the Amazon. This was all the thought I gave to the subject. I never was great in matters of detail. I packed my valise, and took passage on an ancient tub called the *Paul Jones*, for New Orleans. For the sum of sixteen dollars I had the scarred and tarnished splendors of "her" main saloon principally to myself, for she was not a creature to attract the eye of wiser travelers.

When we presently got under way and went poking down the broad Ohio, I became a new being, and the subject of my own admiration. I was a traveler! A word never had tasted so good in my mouth before. I had an exultant sense of being bound for mysterious lands and distant climes which I never have felt in so uplifting a degree since. I was in such a glorified condition that all ignoble

3. From *Life on the Mississippi*, Chapters V, VI, and VII.

feelings departed out of me, and I was able to look down and pity the untraveled with a compassion that had hardly a trace of contempt in it. Still, when we stopped at villages and wood-yards, I could not help lolling carelessly upon the railings of the boiler-deck to enjoy the envy of the country boys on the bank. If they did not seem to discover me, I presently sneezed to attract their attention, or moved to a position where they could not help seeing me. And as soon as I knew they saw me I gaped and stretched, and gave other signs of being mightily bored with traveling.

I kept my hat off all the time, and stayed where the wind and the sun could strike me, because I wanted to get the bronzed and weather-beaten look of an old traveler. Before the second day was half gone I experienced a joy which filled me with the purest gratitude; for I saw that the skin had begun to blister and peel off my face and neck. I wished that the boys and girls at home could see me now.

We reached Louisville in time—at least the neighborhood of it. We stuck hard and fast on the rocks in the middle of the river, and lay there four days. I was now beginning to feel a strong sense of being a part of the boat's family, a sort of infant son to the captain and younger brother to the officers. There is no estimating the pride I took in this grandeur, or the affection that began to swell and grow in me for those people. I could not know how the lordly steamboatman scorns that sort of presumption in a mere landsman. I particularly longed to acquire the least trifle of notice from the big stormy mate, and I was on the alert for an opportunity to do him a service to that end. It came at last. The riotous pow-wow of setting a spar was going on down on the forecastle, and I went down there and stood around in the way—or mostly skipping out of it—till the mate suddenly roared a general order for somebody to bring him a capstan bar. I sprang to his side and said: "Tell me where it is—I'll fetch it!"

If a rag-picker had offered to do a diplomatic service for the Emperor of Russia, the monarch could not have been more astounded than the mate was. He even stopped swearing. He stood and stared down at me. It took him ten seconds to scrape his disjointed remains together again. Then he said impressively: "Well, if this don't beat h——l!" and turned to his work with the air of a man who had been confronted with a problem too abstruse for solution.

I crept away, and courted solitude for the rest of the day. I did not go to dinner; I stayed away from supper until everybody else had finished. I did not feel so much like a member of the boat's family now as before. However, my spirits returned, in instalments, as we pursued our way down the river. I was sorry I hated the mate so, because it was not in (young) human nature not to admire him. He was huge and muscular, his face was bearded and whiskered all over; he had a red woman and a blue woman tattooed on his right arm—one on each side of a blue anchor with a red rope to it; and in the matter of profanity he was sublime. When he was getting out cargo at a landing, I was always where I could see and hear. He felt all the majesty of his great position, and made the world feel it, too. When he gave even the simplest order, he discharged it like a blast of lightning, and sent a long, reverberating peal of profanity thundering after it. I could not help contrasting the way in which the average landsman would give an order with the mate's way of doing it. If the landsman should wish the gang-plank moved a foot farther forward, he would probably say: "James, or William, one of you push that plank forward, please"; but put the mate in his place, and he would roar out: "Here, now, start that gang-plank for'ard! Lively, now! *What*'re you about! Snatch it! *snatch* it! There! there! Aft again! aft again! Don't you hear me? Dash it to dash! are you going to *sleep* over it! 'Vast heaving. 'Vast heaving, I tell you! Going to heave it clear astern? WHERE 're you going with that barrel! *for'ard* with it 'fore I make you swallow it, you dash-dash-dash-*dashed* split between a tired mud-turtle and a crippled hearse-horse!"

I wished I could talk like that. * * *

What with lying on the rocks four days at Louisville, and some other delays, the poor old *Paul Jones* fooled away about two weeks in making the voyage from Cincinnati to New Orleans. This gave me a chance to get acquainted with one of the pilots, and he taught me how to steer the boat, and thus made the fascination of river life more potent than ever for me.

It also gave me a chance to get acquainted with a youth who had taken deck passage—more's the pity; for he easily borrowed six dollars of me on a promise to return to the boat and pay it back to me the day after we should arrive. But he probably died or forgot, for he never came. It was doubtless the former, since he had said his parents were wealthy, and he only traveled deck passage because it was cooler.[4]

I soon discovered two things. One was that a vessel would not be likely to sail for the mouth of the Amazon under ten or twelve years; and the other was that the nine or ten dollars still left in my pocket would not suffice for so impossible an exploration as I had planned, even if I could afford to wait for a ship. Therefore it followed that I must contrive a new career. The *Paul Jones* was now bound for St. Louis. I planned a siege against my pilot, and at the end of three hard days he surrendered. He agreed to teach me the

4. " 'Deck' passage—*i.e.*, steerage passage" [Twain's note].

Mississippi River from New Orleans to St. Louis for five hundred dollars, payable out of the first wages I should receive after graduating. I entered upon the small enterprise of "learning" twelve or thirteen hundred miles of the great Mississippi River with the easy confidence of my time of life. If I had really known what I was about to require of my faculties, I should not have had the courage to begin. I supposed that all a pilot had to do was to keep his boat in the river, and I did not consider that that could be much of a trick, since it was so wide.

The boat backed out from New Orleans at four in the afternoon, and it was "our watch" until eight. Mr. Bixby, my chief, "straightened her up," plowed her along past the sterns of the other boats that lay at the Levee, and then said, "Here, take her; shave those steamships as close as you'd peel an apple." I took the wheel, and my heartbeat fluttered up into the hundreds; for it seemed to me that we were about to scrape the side off every ship in the line, we were so close. I held my breath and began to claw the boat away from the danger; and I had my own opinion of the pilot who had known no better than to get us into such peril, but I was too wise to express it. In half a minute I had a wide margin of safety intervening between the *Paul Jones* and the ships; and within ten seconds more I was set aside in disgrace, and Mr. Bixby was going into danger again and flaying me alive with abuse of my cowardice. I was stung, but I was obliged to admire the easy confidence with which my chief loafed from side to side of his wheel, and trimmed the ships so closely that disaster seemed ceaselessly imminent. When he had cooled a little he told me that the easy water was close ashore and the current outside, and therefore we must hug the bank, up-stream, to get the benefit of the former, and stay well out, down-stream, to take advantage of the latter. In my own mind I resolved to be a down-stream pilot and leave the up-streaming to people dead to prudence.

Now and then Mr. Bixby called my attention to certain things. Said he, "This is Six-Mile Point." I assented. It was pleasant enough information, but I could not see the bearing of it. I was not conscious that it was a matter of any interest to me. Another time he said, "This is Nine-Mile Point." Later he said, "This is Twelve-Mile Point." They were all about level with the water's edge; they all looked about alike to me; they were monotonously unpicturesque. I hoped Mr. Bixby would change the subject. But no; he would crowd up around a point, hugging the shore with affection, and then say: "The slack water ends here, abreast this bunch of China trees; now we cross over." So he crossed over. He gave me the wheel once or twice, but I had no luck. I either came near chipping off the edge of a sugar-plantation, or I yawed too far from shore, and so dropped back into disgrace again and got abused.

The watch was ended at last, and we took supper and went to bed. At midnight the glare of a lantern shone in my eyes, and the night watchman said:

"Come, turn out!"

And then he left. I could not understand this extraordinary procedure; so I presently gave up trying to, and dozed off to sleep. Pretty soon the watchman was back again, and this time he was gruff. I was annoyed. I said:

"What do you want to come bothering around here in the middle of the night for? Now, as like as not, I'll not get to sleep again tonight."

The watchman said:

"Well, if this ain't good, I'm blessed."

The "off-watch" was just turning in, and I heard some brutal laughter from them, and such remarks as "Hello, watchman! ain't the new cub turned out yet? He's delicate, likely. Give him some sugar in a rag, and send for the chambermaid to sing 'Rock-a-by Baby,' to him."

About this time Mr. Bixby appeared on the scene. Something like a minute later I was climbing the pilot-house steps with some of my clothes on and the rest in my arms. Mr. Bixby was close behind, commenting. Here was something fresh—this thing of getting up in the middle of the night to go to work. It was a detail in piloting that had never occurred to me at all. I knew that boats ran all night, but somehow I had never happened to reflect that somebody had to get up out of a warm bed to run them. I began to fear that piloting was not quite so romantic as I had imagined it was; there was something very real and worklike about this new phase of it.

It was a rather dingy night, although a fair number of stars were out. The big mate was at the wheel, and he had the old tub pointed at a star and was holding her straight up the middle of the river. The shores on either hand were not much more than half a mile apart, but they seemed wonderfully far away and ever so vague and indistinct. The mate said:

"We've got to land at Jones's plantation, sir."

The vengeful spirit in me exulted. I said to myself, "I wish you joy of your job, Mr. Bixby; you'll have a good time finding Mr. Jones's plantation such a night as this; and I hope you never *will* find it as long as you live."

Mr. Bixby said to the mate:

"Upper end of the plantation, or the lower?"

"Upper."

"I can't do it. The stumps there are out of water at this stage.

It's no great distance to the lower, and you'll have to get along with that."

"All right, sir. If Jones don't like it, he'll have to lump it, I reckon."

And then the mate left. My exultation began to cool and my wonder to come up. Here was a man who not only proposed to find this plantation on such a night, but to find either end of it you preferred. I dreadfully wanted to ask a question, but I was carrying about as many short answers as my cargo-room would admit of, so I held my peace. All I desired to ask Mr. Bixby was the simple question whether he was ass enough to really imagine he was going to find that plantation on a night when all plantations were exactly alike and all of the same color. But I held in. I used to have fine inspirations of prudence in those days.

Mr. Bixby made for the shore and soon was scraping it, just the same as if it had been daylight. And not only that, but singing:

"Father in heaven, the day is declining," etc.

It seemed to me that I had put my life in the keeping of a peculiarly reckless outcast. Presently he turned on me and said:

"What's the name of the first point above New Orleans?"

I was gratified to be able to answer promptly, and I did. I said I didn't know.

"Don't *know*?"

This manner jolted me. I was down at the foot again, in a moment. But I had to say just what I had said before.

"Well, you're a smart one!" said Mr. Bixby. "What's the name of the *next* point?"

Once more I didn't know.

"Well, this beats anything. Tell me the name of *any* point or place I told you."

I studied awhile and decided that I couldn't.

"Look here! What do you start out from, above Twelve-Mile Point, to cross over?"

"I—I—don't know."

"You—you—don't know?" mimicking my drawling manner of speech. "What *do* you know?"

"I—I—nothing, for certain."

"By the great Cæsar's ghost, I believe you! You're the stupidest dunderhead I ever saw or ever heard of, so help me Moses! The idea of *you* being a pilot—*you!* Why, you don't know enough to pilot a cow down a lane."

Oh, but his wrath was up! He was a nervous man, and he shuffled from one side of his wheel to the other as if the floor was hot. He would boil awhile to himself, and then overflow and scald me again.

"Look here! What do you suppose I told you the names of those points for?"

I tremblingly considered a moment, and then the devil of temptation provoked me to say:

"Well to—to—be entertaining, I thought."

This was a red rag to the bull. He raged and stormed so (he was crossing the river at the time) that I judged it made him blind, because he ran over the steering-oar of a trading-scow. Of course the traders sent up a volley of red-hot profanity. Never was a man so grateful as Mr. Bixby was; because he was brimful, and here were subjects who could *talk back*. He threw open a window, thrust his head out, and such an irruption followed as I never had heard before. The fainter and farther away the scowmen's curses drifted, the higher Mr. Bixby lifted his voice and the weightier his adjectives grew. When he closed the window he was empty. You could have drawn a seine through his system and not caught curses enough to disturb your mother with. Presently he said to me in the gentlest way:

"My boy, you must get a little memorandum-book; and every time I tell you a thing, put it down right away. There's only one way to be a pilot, and that is to get this entire river by heart. You have to know it just like A B C."

That was a dismal revelation to me; for my memory was never loaded with anything but blank cartridges. However, I did not feel discouraged long. I judged that it was best to make some allowances, for doubtless Mr. Bixby was "stretching." Presently he pulled a rope and struck a few strokes on the big bell. The stars were all gone now, and the night was as black as ink. I could hear the wheels churn along the bank, but I was not entirely certain that I could see the shore. The voice of the invisible watchman called up from the hurricane-deck:

"What's this, sir?"

"Jones's plantation."

I said to myself, "I wish I might venture to offer a small bet that it isn't." But I did not chirp. I only waited to see. Mr. Bixby handled the engine-bells, and in due time the boat's nose came to the land, a torch glowed from the forecastle, a man skipped ashore, a darky's voice on the bank said: "Gimme de k'yarpet-bag, Mass' Jones," and the next moment we were standing up the river again, all serene. I reflected deeply awhile, and then said—but not aloud—"Well, the finding of that plantation was the luckiest accident that ever happened; but it couldn't happen again in a hundred years." And I fully believed it *was* an accident, too.[5]

5. Several pages of expository matter have been omitted at this point. The young pilot has gained some confidence in the seven hundred miles of upstream navigation. At St. Louis, Mr. Bixby abandons the *Paul Jones* for "a

* * * The thing that was running in my mind was, "Now, if my ears hear aright, I have not only to get the names of all the towns and islands and bends, and so on, by heart, but I must even get up a warm personal acquaintanceship with every old snag and one-limbed cottonwood and obscure wood-pile that ornaments the banks of this river for twelve hundred miles; and more than that, I must actually know where these things are in the dark, unless these guests are gifted with eyes that can pierce through two miles of solid blackness. I wish the piloting business was in Jericho and I had never thought of it."

At dusk Mr. Bixby tapped the big bell three times (the signal to land), and the captain emerged from his drawing-room in the forward end of the "texas," and looked up inquiringly. Mr. Bixby said:

"We will lay up here all night, captain."

"Very well, sir."

That was all. The boat came to shore and was tied up for the night. It seemed to me a fine thing that the pilot could do as he pleased, without asking so grand a captain's permission. I took my supper and went immediately to bed, discouraged by my day's observations and experiences. My late voyage's note-booking was but a confusion of meaningless names. It had tangled me all up in a knot every time I had looked at in it the daytime. I now hoped for respite in sleep; but no, it reveled all through my head till sunrise again, a frantic and tireless nightmare.

Next morning I felt pretty rusty and low-spirited. We went booming along, taking a good many chances, for we were anxious to "get out of the river" (as getting out to Cairo was called) before night should overtake us. But Mr. Bixby's partner, the other pilot, presently grounded the boat, and we lost so much time getting her off that it was plain the darkness would overtake us a good long way above the mouth. This was a great misfortune, especially to certain of our visiting pilots, whose boats would have to wait for their return, no matter how long that might be. It sobered the pilot-house talk a good deal. Coming up-stream, pilots did not mind low water or any kind of darkness; nothing stopped them but fog. But downstream work was different; a boat was too nearly helpless, with a stiff current pushing behind her; so it was not customary to run downstream at night in low water.

There seemed to be one small hope, however: if we could get through the intricate and dangerous Hat Island crossing before night, we could venture the rest, for we would have plainer sailing and better water. But it would be insanity to attempt Hat Island at

big New Orleans boat * * * a grand affair," and takes his apprentice pilot with him. Now they are headed downstream, at a low and dangerous stage of the river, with several unemployed pilots who have come along just to watch the hazardous game.

night. So there was a deal of looking at watches all the rest of the day, and a constant ciphering upon the speed we were making; Hat Island was the eternal subject; sometimes hope was high and sometimes we were delayed in a bad crossing, and down it went again. For hours all hands lay under the burden of this suppressed excitement; it was even communicated to me, and I got to feeling so solicitous about Hat Island, and under such an awful pressure of responsibility, that I wished I might have five minutes on shore to draw a good, full, relieving breath, and start over again. We were standing no regular watches. Each of our pilots ran such portions of the river as he had run when coming up-stream, because of his greater familiarity with it; but both remained in the pilot-house constantly.

An hour before sunset Mr. Bixby took the wheel, and Mr. W. stepped aside. For the next thirty minutes every man held his watch in his hand and was restless, silent, and uneasy. At last somebody said, with a doomful sigh:

"Well, yonder's Hat Island—and we can't make it."

All the watches closed with a snap, everybody sighed and muttered something about its being "too bad, too bad—ah, if we could *only* have got here half an hour sooner!" and the place was thick with the atmosphere of disappointment. Some started to go out, but loitered, hearing no bell-tap to land. The sun dipped behind the horizon, the boat went on. Inquiring looks passed from one guest to another; and one who had his hand on the door-knob and had turned it, waited, then presently took away his hand and let the knob turn back again. We bore steadily down the bend. More looks were exchanged, and nods of surprised admiration—but no words. Insensibly the men drew together behind Mr. Bixby, as the sky darkened and one or two dim stars came out. The dead silence and sense of waiting became oppressive. Mr. Bixby pulled the cord, and two deep, mellow tones from the big bell floated off on the night. Then a pause, and one more note was struck. The watchman's voice followed, from the hurricane-deck:

"Labboard lead, there! Stabboard lead!"

The cries of the leadsmen began to rise out of the distance, and were gruffly repeated by the word-passers on the hurricane-deck.

"M-a-r-k three! M-a-r-k three! Quarter-less-three! Half twain! Quarter twain! M-a-r-k twain! Quarter-less—"

Mr. Bixby pulled two bell-ropes, and was answered by faint jinglings far below in the engine-room, and our speed slackened. The steam began to whistle through the gauge-cocks. The cries of the leadsmen went on—and it is a weird sound, always, in the night. Every pilot in the lot was watching now, with fixed eyes, and talking under his breath. Nobody was calm and easy but Mr. Bixby. He would put his wheel down and stand on a spoke, and as the steamer swung into her (to me) utterly invisible marks—for we seemed to be in the midst of a wide and gloomy sea—he would meet and fasten her there. Out of the murmur of half-audible talk, one caught a coherent sentence now and then—such as:

"There; she's over the first reef all right!"

After a pause, another subdued voice:

"Her stern's coming down just *exactly* right, by *George!*"

"Now she's in the marks; over she goes!"

Somebody else muttered:

"Oh, it was done beautiful—*beautiful!*"

Now the engines were stopped altogether, and we drifted with the current. Not that I could see the boat drift, for I could not, the stars being all gone by this time. This drifting was the dismalest work; it held one's heart still. Presently I discovered a blacker gloom than that which surrounded us. It was the head of the island. We were closing right down upon it. We entered its deeper shadow, and so imminent seemed the peril that I was likely to suffocate; and I had the strongest impulse to do *something*, anything, to save the vessel. But still Mr. Bixby stood by his wheel, silent, intent as a cat, and all the pilots stood shoulder to shoulder at his back.

"She'll not make it!" somebody whispered.

The water grew shoaler and shoaler, by the leadsman's cries, till it was down to:

"Eight-and-a-half! E-i-g-h-t feet! E-i-g-h-t feet! Seven-and—"

Mr. Bixby said warningly through his speaking-tube to the engineer:

"Stand by, now!"

"Ay, ay, sir!"

"Seven-and-a-half! Seven feet! Six-and—"

We touched bottom! Instantly Mr. Bixby set a lot of bells ringing, shouted through the tube, "*Now*, let her have it—every ounce you've got!" then to his partner, "Put her hard down! snatch her! snatch her!" The boat rasped and ground her way through the sand, hung upon the apex of disaster a single tremendous instant, and then over she went! And such a shout as went up at Mr. Bixby's back never loosened the roof of a pilot-house before!

There was no more trouble after that. Mr. Bixby was a hero that night; and it was some little time, too, before his exploit ceased to be talked about by river-men.

Fully to realize the marvelous precision required in laying the great steamer in her marks in that murky waste of water, one should know that not only must she pick her intricate way through snags and blind reefs, and then shave the head of the island so closely as to brush the overhanging foliage with her stern, but at one place she must pass almost within arm's reach of a sunken and invisible wreck that would snatch the hull timbers from under her if she should strike it, and destroy a quarter of a million dollars' worth of steamboat and cargo in five minutes, and maybe a hundred and fifty human lives into the bargain.

The last remark I heard that night was a compliment to Mr. Bixby, uttered in soliloquy and with unction by one of our guests. He said:

"By the Shadow of Death, but he's a lightning pilot!"

1874   1875, 1883

From Some Rambling Notes of an Idle Excursion[6]
[*Captain "Hurricane" Jones and the Prophets of Baal*]

There was a good deal of pleasant gossip about old Captain "Hurricane" Jones, of the Pacific Ocean—peace to his ashes! Two or three of us present had known him; I particularly well, for I had made four sea-voyages with him. He was a very remarkable man. He was born in a ship; he picked up what little education he had among his shipmates; he began life in the forecastle, and climbed grade by grade to the captaincy. More than fifty years of his sixty-five were spent at sea. He had sailed all oceans, seen all lands, and borrowed a tint from all climates. When a man has been fifty years at sea he necessarily knows nothing of men, nothing of the world but its surface, nothing of the world's thought, nothing of the world's learning but its A B C, and that blurred and distorted by the unfocused lenses of an untrained mind. Such a man is only a gray and bearded child. That is what old Hurricane Jones was—simply an innocent, lovable old infant. When his spirit was in repose he was as sweet and gentle as a girl; when his wrath was up he was a hurricane that made his nickname seem tamely descriptive. He was formidable in a fight, for he was of powerful build and dauntless courage. He was frescoed from head to heel with pictures and mottoes tattooed in red and blue India ink. I was with him one voyage when he got his last vacant space tattooed; this vacant space was around his left ankle. During three days he stumped about the ship with his ankle bare and swollen, and this legend gleaming red and angry out from a clouding of India ink: "Virtue is its own R'd." (There was a lack

6. "Some Rambling Notes of an Idle Excursion," was published in the *Atlantic* from October, 1877, through January, 1878, and then collected in *The Stolen White Elephant* (1882). Captain "Hurricane" Jones was based on Ned Wakeman, captain of the *America*, which took Mark Twain from San Francisco to the Isthmus in December, 1866. Captain Wakeman was a colorful personality—original, pious, resourceful, and full of roaring oaths. The Reverend Mr. Peters of the narrative was suggested by Twain's old friend the Reverend Joseph Twichell. The text is reprinted from the original edition of *The Stolen White Elephant*.

of room.) He was deeply and sincerely pious, and swore like a fish-woman. He considered swearing blameless, because sailors would not understand an order unillumined by it. He was a profound Biblical scholar—that is, he thought he was. He believed everything in the Bible, but he had his own methods of arriving at his beliefs. He was of the "advanced" school of thinkers, and applied natural laws to the interpretation of all miracles, somewhat on the plan of the people who make the six days of creation six geological epochs, and so forth. Without being aware of it, he was a rather severe satire on modern scientific religionists. Such a man as I have been describing is rabidly fond of disquisition and argument; one knows that without being told it.

One trip the captain had a clergyman on board, but did not know he was a clergyman, since the passenger-list did not betray the fact. He took a great liking to this Reverend Mr. Peters, and talked with him a great deal; told him yarns, gave him toothsome scraps of personal history, and wove a glittering streak of profanity through his garrulous fabric that was refreshing to a spirit weary of the dull neutralities of undecorated speech. One day the captain said, "Peters, do you ever read the Bible?"

"Well—yes."

"I judge it ain't often, by the way you say it. Now, you tackle it in dead earnest once, and you'll find it'll pay. Don't you get discouraged, but hang right on. First, you won't understand it; but by and by things will begin to clear up, and then you wouldn't lay it down to eat."

"Yes, I have heard that said."

"And it's so, too. There ain't a book that begins with it. It lays over 'm all, Peters. There's some pretty tough things in it—there ain't any getting around that—but you stick to them and think them out, and when once you get on the inside everything's plain as day."

"The miracles, too, captain?"

"Yes, sir! the miracles, too. Every one of them. Now, there's that business with the prophets of Baal; like enough that stumped you?"

"Well, I don't know but—"

"Own up now; it stumped you. Well, I don't wonder. You hadn't had any experience in raveling such things out, and naturally it was too many for you. Would you like to have me explain that thing to you, and show you how to get at the meat of these matters?"

"Indeed, I would, captain, if you don't mind."

Then the captain proceeded as follows: "I'll do it with pleasure. First, you see, I read and read, and thought and thought, till I got to understand what sort of people they were in the old Bible times, and then after that it was all clear and easy. Now this was the way

I put it up, concerning Isaac[7] and the prophets of Baal. There was some mighty sharp men among the public characters of that old ancient day, and Isaac was one of them. Isaac had his failings—plenty of them, too; it ain't for me to apologize for Isaac; he played it on the prophets of Baal, and like enough he was justifiable, considering the odds that was against him. No, all I say is, 'twa'n't any miracle, and that I'll show you so's't you can see it yourself.

"Well, times had been getting rougher and rougher for prophets —that is, prophets of Isaac's denomination. There was four hundred and fifty prophets of Baal in the community, and only one Presbyterian; that is, if Isaac *was* a Presbyterian, which I reckon he was, but it don't say. Naturally, the prophets of Baal took all the trade. Isaac was pretty low-spirited, I reckon, but he was a good deal of a man, and no doubt he went a-prophesying around, letting on to be doing a land-office business, but 'twa'n't any use; he couldn't run any opposition to amount to anything. By and by things got desperate with him; he sets his head to work and thinks it all out, and then what does he do? Why, he begins to throw out hints that the other parties are this and that and t'other—nothing very definite, maybe, but just kind of undermining their reputation in a quiet way. This made talk, of course, and finally got to the king. The king asked Isaac what he meant by his talk. Says Isaac, 'Oh, nothing particular; only, can they pray down fire from heaven on an altar? It ain't much, maybe, your majesty, only can they *do* it? That's the idea.' So the king was a good deal disturbed, and he went to the prophets of Baal, and they said, pretty airy, that if he had an altar ready, *they* were ready; and they intimated he better get it insured, too.

"So next morning all the children of Israel and their parents and other people gathered themselves together. Well, here was that great crowd of prophets of Baal packed together on one side, and Isaac walking up and down all alone on the other, putting up his job. When time was called, Isaac let on to be comfortable and indifferent; told the other team to take the first innings. So they went at it, the whole four hundred and fifty, praying around the altar, very hopeful, and doing their level best. They prayed an hour—two hours—three hours—and so on, plumb till noon. It wa'n't any use; they hadn't took a trick. Of course they felt kind of ashamed before all those people, and well they might. Now, what would a magnanimous man do? Keep still, wouldn't he? Of course. What did Isaac do? He graveled the prophets of Baal every way he could think of. Says he, 'You don't speak up loud enough; your god's asleep, like enough, or maybe he's taking a walk; you want to holler, you know' —or words to that effect; I don't recollect the exact language.[8]

7. "This is the captain's own mistake" [Twain's note]. *Cf.* I Kings, xviii: 17–40.

8. "And it came to pass at noon, that Elijah mocked them, and said, Cry aloud: for he *is* a god; either he is talk-

Mind, I don't apologize for Isaac; he had his faults.

"Well, the prophets of Baal prayed along the best they knew how all the afternoon, and never raised a spark. At last, about sundown, they were all tuckered out, and they owned up and quit.

"What does Isaac do now? He steps up and says to some friends of his there, 'Pour four barrels of water on the altar!' Everybody was astonished; for the other side had prayed at it dry, you know, and got whitewashed. They poured it on. Says he, 'Heave on four more barrels.' Then he says, 'Heave on four more.' Twelve barrels, you see, altogether. The water ran all over the altar, and all down the sides, and filled up a trench around it that would hold a couple of hogsheads—'measures,' it says; I reckon it means about a hogshead. Some of the people were going to put on their things and go, for they allowed he was crazy. They didn't know Isaac. Isaac knelt down and began to pray; he strung along, and strung along, about the heathen in distant lands, and about the sister churches, and about the state and the country at large, and about those that's in authority in the government, and all the usual program, you know, till everybody had got tired and gone to thinking about something else, and then, all of a sudden, when nobody was noticing, he outs with a match and rakes it on the under side of his leg, and *pff!* up the whole thing blazes like a house afire! Twelve barrels of *water? Petroleum*, sir, PETROLEUM! that's what it was!"

"Petroleum, captain?"

"Yes, sir, the country was full of it. Isaac knew all about that. You read the Bible. Don't you worry about the tough places. They ain't tough when you come to think them out and throw light on them. There ain't a thing in the Bible but what is true; all you want is to go prayerfully to work and cipher out how 'twas done."

1877–1878, 1882

The Man That Corrupted Hadleyburg[9]

I

It was many years ago. Hadleyburg was the most honest and upright town in all the region round about. It had kept that reputation unsmirched during three generations, and was prouder of it than of any other of its possessions. It was so proud of it, and so anxious to insure its perpetuation, that it began to teach the principles of honest dealing to its babies in the cradle, and made the like teach-

ing, or he is pursuing, or he is in a journey, or peradventure he sleepeth, and must be awaked" (I Kings xviii: 27).
9. This story was first published in *Harper's Magazine* for December, 1899, and then collected in *The Man That Corrupted Hadleyburg and Other Stories and Essays* (1900), which the present text follows.

ings the staple of their culture thenceforward through all the years devoted to their education. Also, throughout the formative years temptations were kept out of the way of the young people, so that their honesty could have every chance to harden and solidify, and become a part of their very bone. The neighboring towns were jealous of this honorable supremacy, and affected to sneer at Hadleyburg's pride in it and call it vanity; but all the same they were obliged to acknowledge that Hadleyburg was in reality an incorruptible town; and if pressed they would also acknowledge that the mere fact that a young man hailed from Hadleyburg was all the recommendation he needed when he went forth from his natal town to seek for responsible employment.

But at last, in the drift of time, Hadleyburg had the ill luck to offend a passing stranger—possibly without knowing it, certainly without caring, for Hadleyburg was sufficient unto itself, and cared not a rap for strangers or their opinions. Still, it would have been well to make an exception in this one's case, for he was a bitter man and revengeful. All through his wanderings during a whole year he kept his injury in mind, and gave all his leisure moments to trying to invent a compensating satisfaction for it. He contrived many plans, and all of them were good, but none of them was quite sweeping enough; the poorest of them would hurt a great many individuals, but what he wanted was a plan which would comprehend the entire town, and not let so much as one person escape unhurt. At last he had a fortunate idea, and when it fell into his brain it lit up his whole head with an evil joy. He began to form a plan at once, saying to himself, "That is the thing to do—I will corrupt the town."

Six months later he went to Hadleyburg, and arrived in a buggy at the house of the old cashier of the bank about ten at night. He got a sack out of the buggy, shouldered it, and staggered with it through the cottage yard, and knocked at the door. A woman's voice said "Come in," and he entered, and set his sack behind the stove in the parlor, saying politely to the old lady who sat reading the *Missionary Herald* by the lamp:

"Pray keep your seat, madam, I will not disturb you. There—now it is pretty well concealed; one would hardly know it was there. Can I see your husband a moment, madam?"

No, he was gone to Brixton, and might not return before morning.

"Very well, madam, it is no matter. I merely wanted to leave that sack in his care, to be delivered to the rightful owner when he shall be found. I am a stranger; he does not know me; I am merely passing through the town tonight to discharge a matter which has been long in my mind. My errand is now completed, and I go pleased and a little proud, and you will never see me again. There is a paper attached to the sack which will explain everything. Good-night, madam."

The old lady was afraid of the mysterious big stranger, and was glad to see him go. But her curiosity was roused, and she went straight to the sack and brought away the paper. It began as follows:

"TO BE PUBLISHED; *or, the right man sought out by private inquiry—either will answer. This sack contains gold coin weighing a hundred and sixty pounds four ounces—*"

"Mercy on us, and the door not locked!"

Mrs. Richards flew to it all in a tremble and locked it, then pulled down the window-shades and stood frightened, worried, and wondering if there was anything else she could do toward making herself and the money more safe. She listened awhile for burglars, then surrendered to curiosity and went back to the lamp and finished reading the paper:

"*I am a foreigner, and am presently going back to my own country, to remain there permanently. I am grateful to America for what I have received at her hands during my stay under her flag; and to one of her citizens—a citizen of Hadleyburg—I am especially grateful for a great kindness done me a year or two ago. Two great kindnesses; in fact. I will explain. I was a gambler. I say I WAS. I was a ruined gambler. I arrived in this village at night, hungry and without a penny. I asked for help—in the dark; I was ashamed to beg in the light. I begged of the right man. He gave me twenty dollars— that is to say, he gave me life, as I considered it. He also gave me fortune; for out of that money I have made myself rich at the gaming-table. And finally, a remark which he made to me has remained with me to this day, and has at last conquered me; and in conquering has saved the remnant of my morals; I shall gamble no more. Now I have no idea who that man was, but I want him found, and I want him to have this money, to give away, throw away or keep, as he pleases. It is merely my way of testifying my gratitude to him. If I could stay, I would find him myself; but no matter, he will be found. This is an honest town, an incorruptible town, and I know I can trust it without fear. This man can be identified by the remark which he made to me; I feel persuaded that he will remember it.*

"*And now my plan is this: If you prefer to conduct the inquiry privately, do so. Tell the contents of this present writing to any one who is likely to be the right man. If he shall answer, 'I am the man; the remark I made was so-and-so,' apply the test—to wit: open the sack, and in it you will find a sealed envelope containing that re-*"

mark. If the remark mentioned by the candidate tallies with it, give him the money, and ask no further questions, for he is certainly the right man.

"*But if you shall prefer a public inquiry, then publish this present writing in the local paper—with these instructions added, to wit: Thirty days from now, let the candidate appear at the town-hall at eight in the evening (Friday), and hand his remark, in a sealed envelope, to the Rev. Mr. Burgess (if he will be kind enough to act); and let Mr. Burgess there and then destroy the seals on the sack, open it, and see if the remark is correct; if correct, let the money be delivered, with my sincere gratitude, to my benefactor thus identified.*"

Mrs. Richards sat down, gently, quivering with excitement, and was soon lost in thinking—after this pattern: "What a strange thing it is! . . . And what a fortune for that kind man who set his bread afloat upon the waters! . . . If he had only been my husband that did it!—for we are so poor, so old and poor! . . ." Then, with a sigh—"But it was not my Edward; no, it was not he that gave the stranger twenty dollars. It is a pity too; I see it now. . . ." Then, with a shudder—"But it is *gambler's* money! the wages of sin: we couldn't take it; we couldn't touch it. I don't like to be near it; it seems a defilement." She moved to a farther chair. . . . "I wish Edward would come, and take it to the bank; a burglar might come at any moment; it is dreadful to be here all alone with it."

At eleven Mr. Richards arrived, and while his wife was saying, "I am *so* glad you've come!" he was saying, "I'm so tired—tired clear out; it is dreadful to be poor, and have to make these dismal journeys at my time of life. Always at the grind, grind, grind, on a salary—another man's slave, and he sitting at home in his slippers, rich and comfortable."

"I am so sorry for you, Edward, you know that; but be comforted; we have our livelihood; we have our good name—"

"Yes, Mary, and that is everything. Don't mind my talk—it's just a moment's irritation and doesn't mean anything. Kiss me—there, it's all gone now, and I am not complaining any more. What have you been getting? What's in the sack?"

Then his wife told him the great secret. It dazed him for a moment; then he said:

"It weighs a hundred and sixty pounds? Why, Mary, it's for-ty thou-sand dollars—think of it—a whole fortune! Not ten men in this village are worth that much. Give me the paper."

He skimmed through it and said:

"Isn't it an adventure! Why, it's a romance; it's like the impossible things one reads about in books, and never sees in life." He was well stirred up now; cheerful, even gleeful. He tapped his old wife on the cheek, and said, humorously, "Why, we're rich, Mary, rich; all we've got to do is to bury the money and burn the papers. If the gambler ever comes to inquire, we'll merely look coldly upon him and say: 'What is this nonsense you are talking? We have never heard of you and your sack of gold before;' and then he would look foolish, and——"

"And in the mean time, while you are running on with your jokes, the money is still here, and it is fast getting along toward burglar-time."

"True. Very well, what shall we do—make the inquiry private? No, not that: it would spoil the romance. The public method is better. Think what a noise it will make! And it will make all the other towns jealous; for no stranger would trust such a thing to any town but Hadleyburg, and they know it. It's a great card for us. I must get to the printing-office now, or I shall be too late."

"But stop—stop—don't leave me here alone with it, Edward!"

But he was gone. For only a little while, however. Not far from his own house he met the editor-proprietor of the paper, and gave him the document, and said, "Here is a good thing for you, Cox—put it in."

"It may be too late, Mr. Richards, but I'll see."

At home again he and his wife sat down to talk the charming mystery over; they were in no condition for sleep. The first question was, Who could the citizen have been who gave the stranger the twenty dollars? It seemed a simple one; both answered it in the same breath—

"Barclay Goodson."

"Yes," said Richards, "he could have done it, and it would have been like him, but there's not another in the town."

"Everybody will grant that, Edward—grant it privately, anyway. For six months, now, the village has been its own proper self once more—honest, narrow, self-righteous, and stingy."

"It is what he always called it, to the day of his death—said it right out publicly, too."

"Yes, and he was hated for it."

"Oh, of course; but he didn't care. I reckon he was the best-hated man among us, except the Reverend Burgess."

"Well, Burgess deserves it—he will never get another congregation here. Mean as the town is, it knows how to estimate *him*. Edward, doesn't it seem odd that the stranger should appoint Burgess to deliver the money?"

"Well, yes—it does. That is—that is—"

"Why so much that-*is*-ing? Would *you* select him?"

"Mary, maybe the stranger knows him better than this village does."

"Much *that* would help Burgess!"

The husband seemed perplexed for an answer; the wife kept a steady eye upon him, and waited. Finally Richards said, with the hesitancy of one who is making a statement which is likely to encounter doubt:

"Mary, Burgess is not a bad man."

His wife was certainly surprised.

"Nonsense!" she exclaimed.

"He is not a bad man. I know. The whole of his unpopularity had its foundation in that one thing—the thing that made so much noise."

"That 'one thing,' indeed! As if that 'one thing' wasn't enough, all by itself."

"Plenty. Plenty. Only he wasn't guilty of it."

"How you talk! Not guilty of it! Everybody knows he *was* guilty."

"Mary, I give you my word—he was innocent."

"I can't believe it, and I don't. How do you know?"

"It is a confession. I am ashamed, but I will make it. I was the only man who knew he was innocent. I could have saved him, and —and—well, you know how the town was wrought up—I hadn't the pluck to do it. It would have turned everybody against me. I felt mean, ever so mean; but I didn't dare; I hadn't the manliness to face that."

Mary looked troubled, and for a while was silent. Then she said, stammeringly:

"I—I don't think it would have done for you to—to—One mustn't—er—public opinion—one has to be so careful—so—" It was a difficult road, and she got mired; but after a little she got started again. "It was a great pity, but—Why, we couldn't afford it, Edward—we couldn't indeed. Oh, I wouldn't have had you do it for anything!"

"It would have lost us the good-will of so many people, Mary; and then—and then—"

"What troubles me now is, what *he* thinks of us, Edward."

"He? *He* doesn't suspect that I could have saved him."

"Oh," exclaimed the wife, in a tone of relief, "I am glad of that. As long as he doesn't know that you could have saved him, he—he —well, that makes it a great deal better. Why, I might have known he didn't know, because he is always trying to be friendly with us, as little encouragement as we give him. More than once people have twitted me with it. There's the Wilsons, and the Wilcoxes, and the Harknesses, they take a mean pleasure in saying, 'Your friend Burgess,' because they know it pesters me. I wish he wouldn't persist in liking us so; I can't think why he keeps it up."

"I can explain it. It's another confession. When the thing was new and hot, and the town made a plan to ride him on a rail, my conscience hurt me so that I couldn't stand it, and I went privately and gave him notice, and he got out of the town and staid out till it was safe to come back."

"Edward! If the town had found it out—"

"*Don't!* It scares me yet, to think of it. I repented of it the minute it was done; and I was even afraid to tell you, lest your face might betray it to somebody. I didn't sleep any that night, for worrying. But after a few days I saw that no one was going to suspect me, and after that I got to feeling glad I did it. And I feel glad yet, Mary—glad through and through."

"So do I, now, for it would have been a dreadful way to treat him. Yes, I'm glad; for really you did owe him that, you know. But, Edward, suppose it should come out yet, some day!"

"It won't."

"Why!"

"Because everybody thinks it was Goodson."

"Of course they would!"

"Certainly. And of course *he* didn't care. They persuaded poor old Sawlsberry to go and charge it on him, and he went blustering over there and did it. Goodson looked him over, like as if he was hunting for a place on him that he could despise the most, then he says, 'So you are the Committee of Inquiry, are you?' Sawlsberry said that was about what he was. 'Hm. Do they require particulars, or do you reckon a kind of a *general* answer will do?' 'If they require particulars, I will come back, Mr. Goodson; I will take the general answer first.' 'Very well, then, tell them to go to hell—I reckon that's general enough. And I'll give you some advice, Sawlsberry; when you come back for the particulars, fetch a basket to carry the relics of yourself home in.' "

"Just like Goodson; it's got all the marks. He had only vanity; he thought he could give advice better than any other person."

"It settled the business, and saved us, Mary. The subject was dropped."

"Bless you, I'm not doubting *that*."

Then they took up the gold-sack mystery again, with strong interest. Soon the conversation began to suffer breaks—interruptions caused by absorbed thinkings. The breaks grew more and more frequent. At last Richards lost himself wholly in thought. He sat long, gazing vacantly at the floor, and by-and-by he began to punctuate his thoughts with little nervous movements of his hands that seemed to indicate vexation. Meantime his wife too had relapsed into a thoughtful silence, and her movements were beginning to show a troubled discomfort. Finally Richards got up and strode aimlessly about the room, ploughing his hands through his hair, much as a somnambulist might do who was having a bad dream. Then he seemed to arrive at a definite purpose; and without a word he put on his hat and passed quickly out of the house. His wife sat brooding, with a drawn face, and did not seem to be aware that she was alone. Now and then she murmured, "Lead us not into t . . . but—but—we are so poor, so poor! . . . Lead us not into . . . Ah, who would be hurt by it?—and no one would ever know. . . . Lead us . . ." The voice died out in mumblings. After a little she glanced up and muttered in a half frightened, half-glad way—

"He is gone! But, oh dear, he may be too late—too late. . . . Maybe not—maybe there is still time." She rose and stood thinking, nervously clasping and unclasping her hands. A slight shudder shook her frame, and she said, out of a dry throat, "God forgive me—it's awful to think such things—but . . . Lord, how we are made—how strangely we are made!"

She turned the light low, and slipped stealthily over and kneeled down by the sack and felt of its ridgy sides with her hands, and fondled them lovingly; and there was a gloating light in her poor old eyes. She fell into fits of absence; and came half out of them at times to mutter, "If we had only waited!—oh, if we had only waited a little, and not been in such a hurry!"

Meantime Cox had gone home from his office and told his wife all about the strange thing that had happened, and they had talked it over eagerly, and guessed that the late Goodson was the only man in the town who could have helped a suffering stranger with so noble a sum as twenty dollars. Then there was a pause, and the two became thoughtful and silent. And by-and-by nervous and fidgety. At last the wife said, as if to herself:

"Nobody knows this secret but the Richardses . . . and us . . . nobody."

The husband came out of his thinkings with a slight start, and gazed wistfully at his wife, whose face was become very pale; then he hesitatingly rose, and glanced furtively at his hat, then at his wife —a sort of mute inquiry. Mrs. Cox swallowed once or twice, with her hand at her throat, then in place of speech she nodded her head. In a moment she was alone, and mumbling to herself.

And now Richards and Cox were hurrying through the deserted streets, from opposite directions. They met, panting, at the foot of the printing-office stairs; by the night-light there they read each other's face. Cox whispered:

"Nobody knows about this but us?"

The whispered answer was,

"Not a soul—on honor, not a soul!"

"If it isn't too late to—"

The men were starting up-stairs; at this moment they were over-taken by a boy, and Cox asked:

"Is that you, Johnny?"

"Yes, sir."

"You needn't ship the early mail—nor *any* mail; wait till I tell you."

"It's already gone, sir."

"*Gone?*" It had the sound of an unspeakable disappointment in it.

"Yes, sir. Time-table for Brixton and all the towns beyond changed to-day, sir—had to get the papers in twenty minutes earlier than common. I had to rush; if I had been two minutes later—"

The men turned and walked slowly away, not waiting to hear the rest. Neither of them spoke during ten minutes; then Cox said, in a vexed tone:

"What possessed you to be in such a hurry, *I* can't make out."

The answer was humble enough:

"I see it now, but somehow I never thought, you know, until it was too late. But the next time—"

"Next time be hanged! It won't come in a thousand years."

Then the friends separated without a good-night, and dragged themselves home with the gait of mortally stricken men. At their homes their wives sprang up with an eager "Well?"—then saw the answer with their eyes and sank down sorrowing, without waiting for it to come in words. In both houses a discussion followed of a heated sort—a new thing; there had been discussions before, but not heated ones, not ungentle ones. The discussions to-night were a sort of seeming plagiarisms of each other. Mrs. Richards said,

"If you had only waited, Edward—if you had only stopped to think; but no, you must run straight to the printing-office and spread it all over the world."

"It *said* publish it."

"That is nothing; it also said do it privately, if you liked. There, now—is that true, or not?"

"Why, yes—yes, it is true; but when I thought what a stir it would make, and what a compliment it was to Hadleyburg that a stranger should trust it so—"

"Oh, certainly, I know all that; but if you had only stopped to think, you would have seen that you *couldn't* find the right man, be-cause he is in his grave, and hasn't left chick nor child nor relation behind him; and as long as the money went to somebody that aw-fully needed it, and nobody would be hurt by it, and—and—"

She broke down, crying. Her husband tried to think of some com-forting thing to say, and presently came out with this:

"But after all, Mary, it must be for the best—it *must* be; we know that. And we must remember that it was so ordered—"

"Ordered! Oh, everything's *ordered*, when a person has to find some way out when he has been stupid. Just the same, it was *ordered* that the money should come to us in this special way, and it was you that must take it on yourself to go meddling with the designs of Providence—and who gave you the right? It was wicked, that is what it was—just blasphemous presumption, and no more becoming to a meek and humble professor of—"

"But, Mary, you know how we have been trained all our lives long, like the whole village, till it is absolutely second nature to us to stop not a single moment to think when there's an honest thing to be done—"

"Oh, I know it, I know it—it's been one everlasting training and training and training in honesty—honesty shielded, from the very cradle, against every possible temptation, and so it's *artificial* honesty, and weak as water when temptation comes, as we have seen this night. God knows I never had shade nor shadow of a doubt of my petrified and indestructible honesty until now—and now, under the very first big and real temptation, I—Edward, it is my belief that this town's honesty is as rotten as mine is; as rotten as yours is. It is a mean town, a hard, stingy town, and hasn't a virtue in the world but this honesty it is so celebrated for and so conceited about; and so help me, I do believe that if ever the day comes that its honesty falls under great temptation, its grand reputation will go to ruin like a house of cards. There, now, I've made confession, and I feel better; I am a humbug, and I've been one all my life, without knowing it. Let no man call me honest again—I will not have it."

"I—Well, Mary, I feel a good deal as you do; I certainly do. It seems strange, too, so strange. I never could have believed it—never."

A long silence followed; both were sunk in thought. At last the wife looked up and said:

"I know what you are thinking, Edward."

Richards had the embarrassed look of a person who is caught.

"I am ashamed to confess it, Mary, but—"

"It's no matter, Edward, I was thinking the same question myself."

"I hope so. State it."

"You were thinking, if a body could only guess out *what the remark was* that Goodson made to the stranger."

"It's perfectly true. I feel guilty and ashamed. And you?"

"I'm past it. Let us make a pallet here; we've got to stand watch till the bank vault opens in the morning and admits the sack. . . . Oh, dear, oh, dear—if we hadn't made the mistake!"

The pallet was made, and Mary said:

"The open sesame—what could it have been? I do wonder what that remark could have been? But come; we will get to bed now."

"And sleep?"

"No; think."

"Yes, think."

By this time the Coxes too had completed their spat and their reconciliation, and were turning in—to think, to think, and toss, and fret, and worry over what the remark could possibly have been which Goodson made to the stranded derelict: that golden remark; that remark worth forty thousand dollars, cash.

The reason that the village telegraph-office was open later than usual that night was this: The foreman of Cox's paper was the local representative of the Associated Press. One might say its honorary representative, for it wasn't four times a year that he could furnish thirty words that would be accepted. But this time it was different. His despatch stating what he had caught got an instant answer:

"Send the whole thing—all the details—twelve hundred words."

A colossal order! The foreman filled the bill; and he was the proudest man in the State. By breakfast-time the next morning the name of Hadleyburg the Incorruptible was on every lip in America, from Montreal to the Gulf, from the glaciers of Alaska to the orange-groves of Florida; and millions and millions of people were discussing the stranger and his money-sack, and wondering if the right man would be found, and hoping some more news about the matter would come soon—right away.

II

Hadleyburg village woke up world-celebrated—astonished—happy—vain. Vain beyond imagination. Its nineteen principal citizens and their wives went about shaking hands with each other, and beaming, and smiling, and congratulating, and saying *this* thing adds a new word to the dictionary—*Hadleyburg,* synonym for *incorruptible*—destined to live in dictionaries forever! And the minor and unimportant citizens and their wives went around acting in much the same way. Everybody ran to the bank to see the gold-sack; and before noon grieved and envious crowds began to flock in from Brixton and all the neighboring towns; and that afternoon and next day reporters began to arrive from everywhere to verify the sack and its history and write the whole thing up anew, and make dashing free-hand pictures of the sack and of Richards's house, and the bank, and the Presbyterian church, and the Baptist church, and the public square, and the town-hall where the test would be applied and the money delivered; and damnable portraits of the Richardses, and Pinkerton the banker, and Cox, and the foreman, and Reverend Burgess, and the postmaster—and even of Jack Halliday, who was the loafing, good-natured, no-account, irreverent fisherman, hunter, boys' friend, stray-dog's friend, typical "Sam Lawson"[1] of the town. The little mean, smirking, oily Pinkerton showed the sack to all comers, and rubbed his sleek palms together pleasantly, and enlarged upon the town's fine old reputation for honesty and upon this wonderful endorsement of it, and hoped and believed that the example would now spread far and wide over the American world, and be epoch-making in the matter of moral regeneration. And so on, and so on.

By the end of a week things had quieted down again; the wild intoxication of pride and joy had sobered to a soft, sweet, silent delight —a sort of deep, nameless, unutterable content. All faces bore a look of peaceful, holy happiness.

Then a change came. It was a gradual change: so gradual that its beginnings were hardly noticed; maybe were not noticed at all, except by Jack Halliday, who always noticed everything; and always made fun of it, too, no matter what it was. He began to throw out chaffing remarks about people not looking quite so happy as they did a day or two ago; and next he claimed that the new aspect was deepening to positive sadness; next, that it was taking on a sick look; and finally he said that everybody was become so moody, thoughtful, and absent-minded that he could rob the meanest man in town of a cent out of the bottom of his breeches pocket and not disturb his revery.

At this stage—or at about this stage—a saying like this was dropped at bedtime—with a sigh, usually—by the head of each of the nineteen principal households: "Ah, what *could* have been the remark that Goodson made!"

And straightway—with a shudder—came this, from the man's wife:

"Oh, *don't!* What horrible thing are you mulling in your mind? Put it away from you, for God's sake!"

But that question was wrung from those men again the next night —and got the same retort. But weaker.

And the third night the men uttered the question yet again— with anguish, and absently. This time—and the following night— the wives fidgeted feebly, and tried to say something. But didn't.

And the night after that they found their tongues and responded —longingly,

"Oh, if we *could* only guess!"

Halliday's comments grew daily more and more sparklingly disagreeable and disparaging. He went diligently about, laughing at the

1. A lazy, humorous Yankee character who appears in Harriet Beecher Stowe's *Oldtown Folks* (1869) and *Sam Lawson's Oldtown Fireside Stories* (1872).

town, individually and in mass. But his laugh was the only one left in the village: it fell upon a hollow and mournful vacancy and emptiness. Not even a smile was findable anywhere. Halliday carried a cigar-box around on a tripod, playing that it was a camera, and halted all passers and aimed the thing and said, "Ready!—now look pleasant, please," but not even this capital joke could surprise the dreary faces into any softening.

So three weeks passed—one week was left. It was Saturday evening—after supper. Instead of the aforetime Saturday-evening flutter and bustle and shopping and larking, the streets were empty and desolate. Richards and his old wife sat apart in their little parlor—miserable and thinking. This was become their evening habit now: the life-long habit which had preceded it, of reading, knitting, and contented chat, or receiving or paying neighborly calls, was dead and gone and forgotten, ages ago—two or three weeks ago; nobody talked now, nobody read, nobody visited—the whole village sat at home, sighing, worrying, silent. Trying to guess out that remark.

The postman left a letter. Richards glanced listlessly at the superscription and the post-mark—unfamiliar, both—and tossed the letter on the table and resumed his might-have-beens and his hopeless dull miseries where he had left them off. Two or three hours later his wife got wearily up and was going away to bed without a good-night—custom now—but she stopped near the letter and eyed it awhile with a dead interest, then broke it open, and began to skim it over. Richards, sitting there with his chair tilted back against the wall and his chin between his knees, heard something fall. It was his wife. He sprang to her side, but she cried out:

"Leave me alone, I am too happy. Read the letter—read it!"

He did. He devoured it, his brain reeling. The letter was from a distant State, and it said:

"*I am a stranger to you, but no matter: I have something to tell. I have just arrived home from Mexico, and learned about that episode. Of course you do not know who made that remark, but I know, and I am the only person living who does know. It was* GOODSON. *I knew him well, many years ago. I passed through your village that very night, and was his guest till the midnight train came along. I overheard him make that remark to the stranger in the dark—it was in Hale Alley. He and I talked of it the rest of the way home, and while smoking in his house. He mentioned many of your villagers in the course of his talk—most of them in a very uncomplimentary way, but two or three favorably: among these latter yourself. I say 'favorably'—nothing stronger. I remember his saying he did not actually* LIKE *any person in the town—not one; but that you—I* THINK *he said you—am almost sure, had done him a very*" great service once, possibly without knowing the full value of it, and he wished he had a fortune, he would leave it to you when he died, and a curse apiece for the rest of the citizens. Now, then, if it was you that did him that service, you are his legitimate heir, and entitled to the sack of gold. I know that I can trust to your honor and honesty, for in a citizen of Hadleyburg these virtues are an unfailing inheritance, and so I am going to reveal to you the remark, well satisfied that if you are not the right man you will seek and find the right one and see that poor Goodson's debt of gratitude for the service referred to is paid. This is the remark: 'YOU ARE FAR FROM BEING A BAD MAN: GO, AND REFORM.'

"HOWARD L. STEPHENSON"

"Oh, Edward, the money is ours, and I am so grateful, *oh*, so grateful—kiss me, dear, it's forever since we kissed—and we needed it so—the money—and now you are free of Pinkerton and his bank, and nobody's slave any more; it seems to me I could fly for joy."

It was a happy half-hour that the couple spent there on the settee caressing each other; it was the old days come again—days that had begun with their courtship and lasted without a break till the stranger brought the deadly money. By-and-by the wife said:

"Oh, Edward, how lucky it was you did him that grand service, poor Goodson! I never liked him, but I love him now. And it was fine and beautiful of you never to mention it or brag about it." Then, with a touch of reproach, "But you ought to have told *me*, Edward, you ought to have told your wife, you know."

"Well, I—er—well, Mary, you see——"

"Now stop hemming and hawing, and tell me about it, Edward. I always loved you, and now I'm proud of you. Everybody believes there was only one good generous soul in this village, and now it turns out that you—Edward, why don't you tell me?"

"Well—er—er— Why, Mary, I can't!"

"You *can't?* Why can't you?"

"You see, he—well, he—he made me promise I wouldn't."

The wife looked him over, and said, very slowly,

"Made—you—promise? Edward, what do you tell me that for?"

"Mary, do you think I would lie?"

She was troubled and silent for a moment, then she laid her hand within his and said:

"No . . . no. We have wandered far enough from our bearings— God spare us that! In all your life you have never uttered a lie. But now—now that the foundations of things seem to be crumbling from under us, we—we——" She lost her voice for a moment, then said, brokenly, "Lead us not into temptation. . . . I think you made the promise, Edward. Let it rest so. Let us keep away from that ground. Now—that is all gone by; let us be happy again; it is no time for clouds."

Edward found it something of an effort to comply, for his mind kept wandering—trying to remember what the service was that he had done Goodson.

The couple lay awake the most of the night, Mary happy and busy, Edward busy, but not so happy. Mary was planning what she would do with the money. Edward was trying to recall that service. At first his conscience was sore on account of the lie he had told Mary—if it was a lie. After much reflection—suppose it *was* a lie? What then? Was it such a great matter? Aren't we always *acting* lies? Then why not *tell* them? Look at Mary—look what she had done. While he was hurrying off on his honest errand, what was she doing? Lamenting because the papers hadn't been destroyed and the money kept! Is theft better than lying?

That point lost its sting—the lie dropped into the background and left comfort behind it. The next point came to the front: *had* he rendered that service? Well, here was Goodson's own evidence as reported in Stephenson's letter; there could be no better evidence than that—it was even *proof* that he had rendered it. Of course. So that point was settled. . . . No, not quite. He recalled with a wince that this unknown Mr. Stephenson was just a trifle unsure as to whether the performer of it was Richards or some other—and, oh dear, he had to put Richards on his honor! He must himself decide whither that money must go—and Mr. Stephenson was not doubting that if he was the wrong man he would go honorably and find the right one. Oh, it was odious to put a man in such a situation—ah, why couldn't Stephenson have left out that doubt! What did he want to intrude that for?

Further reflection. How did it happen that *Richards's* name remained in Stephenson's mind as indicating the right man, and not some other man's name? That looked good. Yes, that looked very good. In fact, it went on looking better and better, straight along —until by-and-by it grew into positive *proof*. And then Richards put the matter at once out of his mind, for he had a private instinct that a proof once established is better left so.

He was feeling reasonably comfortable now, but there was still one other detail that kept pushing itself on his notice: of course he had done that service—that was settled; but what *was* that service? He must recall it—he would not go to sleep till he had recalled it; it would make his peace of mind perfect. And so he thought and thought. He thought of a dozen things—possible services, even probable services—but none of them seemed adequate, none of them seemed large enough, none of them seemed worth the money— worth the fortune Goodson had wished he could leave in his will.

And besides, he couldn't remember having done them, anyway. Now, then—now, then—what *kind* of a service would it be that would make a man so inordinately grateful? Ah—the saving of his soul! That must be it. Yes, he could remember, now, how he once set himself the task of converting Goodson, and labored at it as much as—he was going to say three months; but upon closer examination it shrunk to a month, then to a week, then to a day, then to nothing. Yes, he remembered now, and with unwelcome vividness, that Goodson had told him to go to thunder and mind his own business—*he* wasn't hankering to follow Hadleyburg to heaven!

So that solution was a failure—he hadn't saved Goodson's soul. Richards was discouraged. Then after a little came another idea: had he saved Goodson's property? No, that wouldn't do—he hadn't any. His life? This is it! Of course. Why, he might have thought of it before. This time he was on the right track, sure. His imagination was hard at work in a minute, now.

Thereafter during a stretch of two exhausting hours he was busy saving Goodson's life. He saved it in all kinds of difficult and perilous ways. In every case he got it saved satisfactorily up to a certain point; then, just as he was beginning to get well persuaded that it had really happened, a troublesome detail would turn up which made the whole thing impossible. As in the matter of drowning, for instance. In that case he had swum out and tugged Goodson ashore in an unconscious state with a great crowd looking on and applauding, but when he had got it all thought out and was just beginning to remember all about it a whole swarm of disqualifying details arrived on the ground: the town would have known of it, it would glare like a limelight in his own memory instead of being an inconspicuous service which he had possibly rendered "without knowing its full value." And at this point he remembered that he couldn't swim, anyway.

Ah—*there* was a point which he had been overlooking from the start: it had to be a service which he had rendered "possibly without knowing the full value of it." Why, really, that ought to be an easy hunt—much easier than those others. And sure enough, by-and-by he found it. Goodson, years and years ago, came near marrying a very sweet and pretty girl, named Nancy Hewitt, but in some way or other the match had been broken off; the girl died, Goodson remained a bachelor, and by-and-by became a soured one and a frank despiser of the human species. Soon after the girl's death the village found out, or thought it had found out, that she carried a spoonful of negro blood in her veins. Richards worked at these details a good while, and in the end he thought he remembered things concerning them which must have gotten mislaid in his memory through long neglect. He seemed to dimly remember that it was *he* that found out about the negro blood; that it was he that told the village; that the village told Goodson where they got it; that he thus saved Goodson from marrying the tainted girl; that he had done him this great service "without knowing the full value of it," in fact without knowing that he *was* doing it; but that Goodson knew the value of it, and what a narrow escape he had had, and so went to his grave grateful to his benefactor and wishing he had a fortune to leave him. It was all clear and simple now, and the more he went over it the more luminous and certain it grew; and at last, when he nestled to sleep satisfied and happy, he remembered the whole thing just as if it had been yesterday. In fact, he dimly remembered Goodson's *telling* him his gratitude once. Meantime Mary had spent six thousand dollars on a new house for herself and a pair of slippers for her pastor, and then had fallen peacefully to rest.

That same Saturday evening the postman had delivered a letter to each of the other principal citizens—nineteen letters in all. No two of the envelopes were alike, and no two of the superscriptions were in the same hand, but the letters inside were just like each other in every detail but one. They were exact copies of the letter received by Richards—handwriting and all—and were all signed by Stephenson, but in place of Richards's name each receiver's own name appeared.

All night long eighteen principal citizens did what their caste-brother Richards was doing at the same time—they put in their energies trying to remember what notable service it was that they had unconsciously done Barclay Goodson. In no case was it a holiday job; still they succeeded.

And while they were at this work, which was difficult, their wives put in the night spending the money, which was easy. During that one night the nineteen wives spent an average of seven thousand dollars each out of the forty thousand in the sack—a hundred and thirty-three thousand altogether.

Next day there was a surprise for Jack Halliday. He noticed that the faces of the nineteen chief citizens and their wives bore that expression of peaceful and holy happiness again. He could not understand it, neither was he able to invent any remarks about it that could damage it or disturb it. And so it was his turn to be dissatisfied with life. His private guesses at the reasons for the happiness failed in all instances, upon examination. When he met Mrs. Wilcox and noticed the placid ecstasy in her face, he said to himself, "Her cat has had kittens"—and went and asked the cook; it was not so; the cook had detected the happiness, but did not know the cause. When Halliday found the duplicate ecstasy in the face of "Shadbelly" Billson (village nickname), he was sure some neighbor of Billson's had broken his leg, but inquiry showed that this had not happened. The subdued ecstasy in Gregory Yates's face could mean but one thing—he was a mother-in-law short; it was another mistake. "And Pinkerton—Pinkerton—he has collected ten cents that he thought he was going to lose." And so on, and so on. In some cases the guesses had to remain in doubt, in the others they proved distinct errors. In the end Halliday said to himself, "Anyway, it foots up that there's nineteen Hadleyburg families temporarily in heaven: I don't know how it happened; I only know Providence is off duty to-day."

An architect and builder from the next State had lately ventured to set up a small business in this unpromising village, and his sign had now been hanging out a week. Not a customer yet; he was a discouraged man, and sorry he had come. But his weather changed suddenly now. First one and then another chief citizen's wife said to him privately:

"Come to my house Monday week—but say nothing about it for the present. We think of building."

He got eleven invitations that day. That night he wrote his daughter and broke off her match with her student. He said she could marry a mile higher than that.

Pinkerton the banker and two or three other well-to-do men planned country-seats—but waited. That kind don't count their chickens until they are hatched.

The Wilsons devised a grand new thing—a fancy-dress ball. They made no actual promises, but told all their acquaintanceship in confidence that they were thinking the matter over and thought they should give it—"and if we do, you will be invited, of course." People were surprised, and said, one to another, "Why, they are crazy, those poor Wilsons, they can't afford it." Several among the nineteen said privately to their husbands, "It is a good idea, we will keep still till their cheap thing is over, then *we* will give one that will make it sick."

The days drifted along, and the bill of future squanderings rose higher and higher, wilder and wilder, more and more foolish and reckless. It began to look as if every member of the nineteen would not only spend his whole forty thousand dollars before receiving-day, but be actually in debt by the time he got the money. In some cases light-headed people did not stop with planning to spend, they really spent—on credit. They bought land, mortgages, farms, speculative stocks, fine clothes, horses, and various other things, paid down the bonus, and made themselves liable for the rest—at ten days. Presently the sober second thought came, and Halliday noticed that a ghastly anxiety was beginning to show up in a good many faces. Again he was puzzled, and didn't know what to make of it. "The Wilcox kittens aren't dead, for they weren't born; nobody's broken a leg; there's no shrinkage in mother-in-laws; *nothing* has happened—it is an insolvable mystery."

There was another puzzled man, too—the Rev. Mr. Burgess. For days, wherever he went, people seemed to follow him or to be watching out for him; and if he ever found himself in a retired spot, a member of the nineteen would be sure to appear, thrust an envelope privately into his hand, whisper "To be opened at the town-hall Friday evening," then vanish away like a guilty thing. He was expecting that there might be one claimant for the sack—doubtful, however, Goodson being dead—but it never occurred to him that all this crowd might be claimants. When the great Friday came at last, he found that he had nineteen envelopes.

III

The town-hall had never looked finer. The platform at the end of it was backed by a showy draping of flags; at intervals along the walls were festoons of flags; the gallery fronts were clothed in flags; the supporting columns were swathed in flags; all this was to impress the stranger, for he would be there in considerable force, and in a large degree he would be connected with the press. The house was full. The 412 fixed seats were occupied; also the 68 extra chairs which had been packed into the aisles; the steps of the platform were occupied; some distinguished strangers were given seats on the platform; at the horseshoe of tables which fenced the front and sides of the platform sat a strong force of special correspondents who had come from everywhere. It was the best-dressed house the town had ever produced. There were some tolerably expensive toilets there, and in several cases the ladies who wore them had the look of being unfamiliar with that kind of clothes. At least the town thought they had that look, but the notion could have arisen from the town's knowledge of the fact that these ladies had never inhabited such clothes before.

The gold-sack stood on a little table at the front of the platform where all the house could see it. The bulk of the house gazed at it with a burning interest, a mouth-watering interest, a wistful and pathetic interest; a minority of nineteen couples gazed at it tenderly, lovingly, proprietarily, and the male half of this minority kept saying over to themselves the moving little impromptu speeches of thankfulness for the audience's applause and congratulations which they were presently going to get up and deliver. Every now and then one of these got a piece of paper out of his vest pocket and privately glanced at it to refresh his memory.

Of course there was a buzz of conversation going on—there always is; but at last when the Rev. Mr. Burgess rose and laid his hand on the sack he could hear his microbes gnaw, the place was so still. He related the curious history of the sack, then went on to speak in warm terms of Hadleyburg's old and well-earned reputation for spotless honesty, and of the town's just pride in this reputation. He said that this reputation was a treasure of priceless value; that under Providence its value had now become inestimably enhanced, for the recent episode had spread this fame far and wide, and thus had focussed the eyes of the American world upon this village, and made its name for all time, as he hoped and believed, a synonym for commercial incorruptibility. [*Applause.*] "And who is to be the guardian of this noble treasure—the community as a whole? No! The responsibility is individual, not communal. From this day forth each and every one of you is in his own person its special guardian and individually responsible that no harm shall come to it. Do you —does each of you—accept this great trust? [*Tumultuous assent.*] Then all is well. Transmit it to your children and to your children's children. To-day your purity is beyond reproach—see to it that it shall remain so. To-day there is not a person in your community who could be beguiled to touch a penny not his own—see to it that you abide in this grace. ["*We will! we will!*"] This is not the place to make comparisons between ourselves and other communities—some of them ungracious toward us; they have their ways, we have ours; let us be content. [*Applause.*] I am done. Under my hand, my friends, rests a stranger's eloquent recognition of what we are: through him the world will always henceforth know what we are. We do not know who he is, but in your name I utter your gratitude, and ask you to raise your voices in endorsement."

The house rose in a body and made the walls quake with the thunders of its thankfulness for the space of a long minute. Then it sat down, and Mr. Burgess took an envelope out of his pocket. The house held its breath while he slit the envelope open and took from it a slip of paper. He read its contents—slowly and impressively— the audience listening with tranced attention to this magic document, each of whose words stood for an ingot of gold:

" '*The remark which I made to the distressed stranger was this:* "*You are very far from being a bad man; go, and reform.*" ' " Then he continued: "We shall know in a moment now whether the remark here quoted corresponds with the one concealed in the sack; and if that shall prove to be so—and it undoubtedly will—this sack of gold belongs to a fellow-citizen who will henceforth stand before the nation as the symbol of the special virtue which has made our town famous throughout the land—Mr. Billson!"

The house had gotten itself all ready to burst into a proper tornado of applause; but instead of doing it, it seemed stricken with a paralysis; there was a deep hush for a moment or two, then a wave of whispered murmurs swept the place—of about this tenor: "*Billson! oh, come, this is too thin!* Twenty dollars to a stranger—or *anybody*

—*Billson!* Tell it to the marines!" And now at this point the house caught its breath all of a sudden in a new access of astonishment, for it discovered that whereas in one part of the hall Deacon Billson was standing up with his head meekly bowed, in another part of it Lawyer Wilson was doing the same. There was a wondering silence now for a while. Everybody was puzzled, and nineteen couples were surprised and indignant.

Billson and Wilson turned and stared at each other. Billson asked, bitingly,

"Why do *you* rise, Mr. Wilson?"

"Because I have a right to. Perhaps you will be good enough to explain to the house why *you* rise?"

"With great pleasure. Because I wrote that paper."

"It is an impudent falsity! I wrote it myself."

It was Burgess's turn to be paralyzed. He stood looking vacantly at first one of the men and then the other, and did not seem to know what to do. The house was stupefied. Lawyer Wilson spoke up, now, and said,

"I ask the Chair to read the name signed to that paper."

That brought the Chair to itself, and it read out the name,

" 'John Wharton *Billson*.' "

"There!" shouted Billson, "what have you got to say for yourself, now? And what kind of apology are you going to make to me and to this insulted house for the imposture which you have attempted to play here?"

"No apologies are due, sir; and as for the rest of it, I publicly charge you with pilfering my note from Mr. Burgess and substituting a copy of it signed with your own name. There is no other way by which you could have gotten hold of the test-remark; I alone, of living men, possessed the secret of its wording."

There was likely to be a scandalous state of things if this went on; everybody noticed with distress that the short-hand scribes were scribbling like mad; many people were crying "Chair, Chair! Order! order!" Burgess rapped with his gavel, and said:

"Let us not forget the proprieties due. There has evidently been a mistake somewhere, but surely that is all. If Mr. Wilson gave me an envelope—and I remembered now that he did—I still have it."

He took one out of his pocket, opened it, glanced at it, looked surprised and worried, and stood silent a few moments. Then he waved his hand in a wandering and mechanical way, and made an effort or two to say something, then gave it up, despondently. Several voices cried out:

"Read it! read it! What is it?"

So he began in a dazed and sleep-walker fashion:

" ' *The remark which I made to the unhappy stranger was this:*

"*You are far from being a bad man.* [The house gazed at him, mar-velling.] *Go, and reform.*"' [*Murmurs:* "Amazing! what can this mean?"] This one," said the Chair, "is signed Thurlow G. Wilson."

"There!" cried Wilson, "I reckon that settles it! I knew perfectly well my note was purloined."

"Purloined!" retorted Billson. "I'll let you know that neither you nor any man of your kidney must venture to—"

The Chair. "Order, gentlemen, order! Take your seats, both of you, please."

They obeyed, shaking their heads and grumbling angrily. The house was profoundly puzzled; it did not know what to do with this curious emergency. Presently Thompson got up. Thompson was the hatter. He would have liked to be a Nineteener; but such was not for him; his stock of hats was not considerable enough for the position. He said:

"Mr. Chairman, if I may be permitted to make a suggestion, can both of these gentlemen be right? I put it to you, sir, can both have happened to say the very same words to the stranger? It seems to me—"

The tanner got up and interrupted him. The tanner was a dis-gruntled man; he believed himself entitled to be a Nineteener, but he couldn't get recognition. It made him a little unpleasant in his ways and speech. Said he:

"Sho, *that's* not the point! *That* could happen—twice in a hun-dred years—but not the other thing. *Neither* of them gave the twenty dollars!" [*A ripple of applause.*]

Billson. "I did!"

Wilson. "I did!"

Then each accused the other of pilfering.

The Chair. "Order! Sit down, if you please—both of you. Neither of the notes has been out of my possession at any moment."

A Voice. "Good—that settles *that!*"

The Tanner. "Mr. Chairman, one thing is now plain: one of these men has been eavesdropping under the other one's bed, and filching family secrets. If it is not unparliamentary to suggest it, I will remark that both are equal to it. [*The Chair.* "Order! order!"] I withdraw the remark, sir, and will confine myself to suggesting that *if* one of them has overheard the other reveal the test-remark to his wife, we shall catch him now."

A Voice. "How?"

The Tanner. "Easily. The two have not quoted the remark in exactly the same words. You would have noticed that, if there hadn't been a considerable stretch of time and an exciting quarrel inserted between the two readings."

A Voice. "Name the difference."

The Tanner. "The word *very* is in Billson's note, and not in the other."

Many Voices. "That's so—he's right."

The Tanner. "And so, if the Chair will examine the test-remark in the sack, we shall know which of these two frauds—[*The Chair.* "Order!"]—which of these two adventurers—[*The Chair.* "Order! order!"]—which of these two gentlemen—[*laughter and applause*] —is entitled to wear the belt as being the first dishonest blatherskite ever bred in this town—which he has dishonored, and which will be a sultry place for him from now out!" [*Vigorous applause.*]

Many Voices. "Open it!—open the sack!"

Mr. Burgess made a slit in the sack, slid his hand in and brought out an envelope. In it were a couple of folded notes. He said:

"One of these is marked, 'Not to be examined until all written communications which have been addressed to the Chair—if any— shall have been read.' The other is marked '*The Test.*' Allow me. It is worded—to wit:

" 'I do not require that the first half of the remark which was made to me by my benefactor shall be quoted with exactness, for it was not striking, and could be forgotten; but its closing fifteen words are quite striking, and I think easily rememberable; unless *these* shall be accurately reproduced, let the applicant be regarded as an imposter. My benefactor began by saying he seldom gave advice to any one, but that it always bore the hall-mark[2] of high value when he did give it. Then he said this—and it has never faded from my memory: "*You are far from being a bad man—*" ' "

Fifty Voices. "That settles it—the money's Wilson's! Wilson! Wilson! Speech! Speech!"

People jumped up and crowded around Wilson, wringing his hand and congratulating fervently—meantime the Chair was hammering with the gavel and shouting:

"Order, gentlemen! Order! Order! Let me finish reading, please." When quiet was restored, the reading was resumed—as follows:

" ' "*Go, and reform—or, mark my words—some day, for your sins, you will die and go to hell or Hadleyburg—*TRY AND MAKE IT THE FORMER." ' "

A ghastly silence followed. First an angry cloud began to settle darkly upon the faces of the citizenship; after a pause the cloud began to rise, and a tickled expression tried to take its place; tried so hard that it was only kept under with great and painful difficulty; the reporters, the Brixtonites, and other strangers bent their heads down and shielded their faces with their hands, and managed to hold in by main strength and heroic courtesy. At this most inop-

2. *I.e.*, the mark of truth, from the official mark of the Goldsmiths' Company in London, guaranteeing the purity of an object for sale at the Goldsmiths' Hall.

portune time burst upon the stillness the roar of a solitary voice—
Jack Halliday's:

"*That's* got the hall-mark on it!"

Then the house let go, strangers and all. Even Mr. Burgess's
gravity broke down presently, then the audience considered itself
officially absolved from all restraint, and it made the most of its
privilege. It was a good long laugh, and a tempestuously whole-
hearted one, but it ceased at last—long enough for Mr. Burgess to
try to resume, and for the people to get their eyes partially wiped;
then it broke out again; and afterward yet again; then at last Burgess
was able to get out these serious words:

"It is useless to try to disguise the fact—we find ourselves in the
presence of a matter of grave import. It involves the honor of your
town, it strikes at the town's good name. The difference of a single
word between the test-remarks offered by Mr. Wilson and Mr.
Billson was itself a serious thing, since it indicated that one or the
other of these gentlemen had committed a theft—"

The two men were sitting limp, nerveless, crushed; but at these
words both were electrified into movement, and started to get up—

"Sit down!" said the Chair, sharply, and they obeyed. "That, as
I have said, was a serious thing. And it was—but for only one of
them. But the matter has become graver; for the honor of *both* is
now in formidable peril. Shall I go even further, and say in inextricable peril? *Both* left out the crucial fifteen words." He paused.
During several moments he allowed the pervading stillness to
gather and deepen its impressive effects, then added: "There would
seem to be but one way whereby this could happen. I ask these
gentlemen—Was there *collusion?—agreement?*"

A low murmur sifted through the house; its import was, "He's
got them both."

Billson was not used to emergencies; he sat in a helpless collapse.
But Wilson was a lawyer. He struggled to his feet, pale and worried, and said:

"I ask the indulgence of the house while I explain this most
painful matter. I am sorry to say what I am about to say, since it
must inflict irreparable injury upon Mr. Billson, whom I have always esteemed and respected until now, and in whose invulner-
ability to temptation I entirely believed—as did you all. But for
the preservation of my own honor I must speak—and with frankness. I confess with shame—and I now beseech your pardon for it
—that I said to the ruined stranger all of the words contained in
the test-remark, including the disparaging fifteen. [*Sensation.*]
When the late publication was made I recalled them, and I resolved to claim the sack of coin, for by every right I was entitled
to it. Now I will ask you to consider this point, and weigh it well:

that stranger's gratitude to me that night knew no bounds; he said himself that he could find no words for it that were adequate, and that if he should ever be able he would repay me a thousandfold. Now, then, I ask you this: could I expect—could I believe—could I even remotely imagine—that, feeling as he did, he would do so ungrateful a thing as to add those quite unnecessary fifteen words to his test?—set a trap for me?—expose me as a slanderer of my own town before my own people assembled in a public hall? It was preposterous; it was impossible. His test would contain only the kindly opening clause of my remark. Of that I had no shadow of doubt. You would have thought as I did. You would not have expected a base betrayal from one whom you had befriended and against whom you had committed no offence. And so, with perfect confidence, perfect trust, I wrote on a piece of paper the opening words—ending with 'Go, and reform,'—and signed it. When I was about to put it in an envelope I was called into my back office, and without thinking I left the paper lying open on my desk." He stopped, turned his head slowly toward Billson, waited a moment, then added: "I ask you to note this: when I returned, a little later, Mr. Billson was retiring by my street door." (*Sensation.*)

In a moment Billson was on his feet and shouting:

"It's a lie! It's an infamous lie!"

The Chair. "Be seated, sir! Mr. Wilson has the floor."

Billson's friends pulled him into his seat and quieted him, and Wilson went on:

"Those are the simple facts. My note was now lying in a different place on the table from where I had left it. I noticed that, but attached no importance to it, thinking a draught had blown it there. That Mr. Billson would read a private paper was a thing which could not occur to me; he was an honorable man, and he would be above that. If you will allow me to say it, I think his extra word '*very*' stands explained; it is attributable to a defect of memory. I was the only man in the world who could furnish here any detail of the test-mark—by *honorable* means. I have finished."

There is nothing in the world like a persuasive speech to fuddle the mental apparatus and upset the convictions and debauch the emotions of an audience not practised in the tricks and delusions of oratory. Wilson sat down victorious. The house submerged him in tides of approving applause; friends swarmed to him and shook him by the hand and congratulated him, and Billson was shouted down and not allowed to say a word. The Chair hammered and hammered with its gavel, and kept shouting:

"But let us proceed, gentlemen, let us proceed!"

At last there was a measurable degree of quiet, and the hatter said:

"But what is there to proceed with, sir, but to deliver the money?"

Voices. "That's it! That's it! Come forward, Wilson!"

The Hatter. "I move three cheers for Mr. Wilson, Symbol of the special virtue which—"

The cheers burst forth before he could finish; and in the midst of them—and in the midst of the clamor of the gavel also—some enthusiasts mounted Wilson on a big friend's shoulder and were going to fetch him in triumph to the platform. The Chair's voice now rose above the noise—

"Order! To your places! You forget that there is still a document to be read." When quiet had been restored he took up the document, and was going to read it, but laid it down again, saying, "I forgot; this is not to be read until all written communications received by me have first been read." He took an envelope out of his pocket, removed its enclosure, glanced at it—seemed astonished —held it out and gazed at it—stared at it.

Twenty or thirty voices cried out:

"What is it? Read it! read it!"

And he did—slowly, and wondering:

" 'The remark which I made to the stranger—[*Voices.* "Hello! how's this?"]—was this: "You are far from being a bad man. [*Voices.* "Great Scott!"] Go, and reform." ' [*Voice.* "Oh, saw my leg off!"] Signed by Mr. Pinkerton the banker."

The pandemonium of delight which turned itself loose now was of a sort to make the judicious weep. Those whose withers were unwrung laughed till the tears ran down; the reporters, in throes of laughter, set down disordered pothooks which would never in the world be decipherable; and a sleeping dog jumped up, scared out of its wits, and barked itself crazy at the turmoil. All manner of cries were scattered through the din: "We're getting rich—*two* Symbols of Incorruptibility!—without counting Billson!" "*Three!*—count Shadbelly in—we can't have too many!" "All right—Billson's elected!" "Alas, poor Wilson—victim of *two* thieves!"

A Powerful Voice. "Silence! The Chair's fished up something more out of its pocket."

Voices. "Hurrah! Is it something fresh? Read it! read! read!"

The Chair [*reading*]. " 'The remark which I made,' etc. 'You are far from being a bad man. Go,' etc. Signed, 'Gregory Yates.' "

Tornado of Voices. "Four Symbols!" " 'Rah for Yates!" "Fish again!"

The house was in a roaring humor now, and ready to get all the the fun out of the occasion that might be in it. Several Nineteeners, looking pale and distressed, got up and began to work their way toward the aisles, but a score of shouts went up:

"The doors, the doors—close the doors; no Incorruptible shall leave this place! Sit down, everybody!"

The mandate was obeyed.

"Fish again! Read! read!"

The Chair fished again, and once more the familiar words began to fall from its lips—" 'You are far from being a bad man—' "

"Name! name! What's his name?"

" 'L. Ingoldsby Sargent.' "

"Five elected! Pile up the Symbols! Go on, go on!"

" 'You are far from being a bad—' "

"Name! name!"

" 'Nicholas Whitworth.' "

"Hooray! hooray! it's a symbolical day!"

Somebody wailed in, and began to sing this rhyme (leaving out "it's") to the lovely "Mikado" tune of "When a man's afraid, a beautiful maid—";[3] the audience joined in, with joy; then, just in time, somebody contributed another line—

"And don't you this forget———"

The house roared it out. A third line was at once furnished—

"Corruptibles far from Hadleyburg are———"

The house roared that one too. As the last note died, Jack Halliday's voice rose high and clear, freighted with a final line—

"But the Symbols are here, you bet!"

That was sung, with booming enthusiasm. Then the happy house started in at the beginning and sang the four lines through twice, with immense swing and dash, and finished up with a crashing three-times-three and a tiger for "Hadleyburg the Incorruptible and all Symbols of it which we shall find worthy to receive the hall-mark to-night."

Then the shoutings at the Chair began again, all over the place:

"Go on! go on! Read! read some more! Read all you've got!"

"That's it—go on! We are winning eternal celebrity!"

A dozen men got up now and began to protest. They said that this farce was the work of some abandoned joker, and was an insult to the whole community. Without a doubt these signatures were all forgeries—

"Sit down! sit down! Shut up! You are confessing. We'll find *your* names in the lot."

"Mr. Chairman, how many of those envelopes have you got?"

The Chair counted.

---

3. "When a man's afraid, / A beautiful maid / Is a cheering sight to see" (*The Mikado*, Act II).

"Together with those that have been already examined, there are nineteen."

A storm of derisive applause broke out.

"Perhaps they all contain the secret. I move that you open them all and read every signature that is attached to a note of that sort—and read also the first eight words of the note."

"Second the motion!"

It was put and carried—uproariously. Then poor old Richards got up, and his wife rose and stood at his side. Her head was bent down, so that none might see that she was crying. Her husband gave her his arm, and so supporting her, he began to speak in a quavering voice:

"My friends, you have known us two—Mary and me—all our lives, and I think you have liked us and respected us—"

The Chair interrupted him:

"Allow me. It is quite true—that which you are saying, Mr. Richards; this town *does* know you two; it *does* like you; it *does* respect you; more—it honors you and *loves* you—"

Halliday's voice rang out:

"That's the hall-marked truth, too! If the Chair is right, let the house speak up and say it. Rise! Now, then—hip! hip! hip!—all together!"

The house rose in mass, faced toward the old couple eagerly, filled the air with a snowstorm of waving handkerchiefs, and delivered the cheers with all its affectionate heart.

The Chair then continued:

"What I was going to say is this: We know your good heart, Mr. Richards, but this is not a time for the exercise of charity toward offenders. [Shouts of "Right! right!"] I see your generous purpose in your face, but I cannot allow you to plead for these men—"

"But I was going to—"

"Please take your seat, Mr. Richards. We must examine the rest of these notes—simple fairness to the men who have already been exposed requires this. As soon as that has been done—I give you my word for this—you shall be heard."

Many Voices. "Right!—the Chair is right—no interruption can be permitted at this stage! Go on!—the names! the names!—according to the terms of the motion!"

The old couple sat reluctantly down, and the husband whispered to the wife, "It is pitifully hard to have to wait; the shame will be greater than ever when they find we were only going to plead for *ourselves.*"

Straightway the jollity broke loose again with the reading of the names.

" 'You are far from being a bad man—' Signature, 'Robert J. Titmarsh.'

" 'You are far from being a bad man—' Signature, 'Eliphalet Weeks.'

" 'You are far from being a bad man—' Signature, 'Oscar B. Wilder.' "

At this point the house lit upon the idea of taking the eight words out of the Chairman's hands. He was not unthankful for that. Thenceforward he held up each note in its turn, and waited. The house droned out the eight words in a massed and measured and musical deep volume of sound (with a daringly close resemblance to a well-known church chant)—" 'You are f-a-r from being a b-a-a-a-d man.' " Then the Chair said, "Signature, 'Archibald Wilcox.' " And so on, and so on, name after name, and everybody had an increasingly and gloriously good time except the wretched Nineteen. Now and then, when a particularly shining name was called, the house made the Chair wait while it chanted the whole of the test-remark from the beginning to the closing words, "And go to hell or Hadleyburg—try and make it the for-or-m-e-r!" and in these special cases they added a grand and agonized and imposing "A-a-a-a-*men!*"

The list dwindled, dwindled, dwindled, poor old Richards keeping tally of the count, wincing when a name resembling his own was pronounced, and waiting in miserable suspense for the time to come when it would be his humiliating privilege to rise with Mary and finish his plea, which he was intending to word thus: ". . . for until now we have never done any wrong thing, but have gone our humble way unreproached. We are very poor, we are old, and have no chick nor child to help us; we were sorely tempted, and we fell. It was my purpose when I got up before to make confession and beg that my name might not be read out in this public place, for it seemed to us that we could not bear it; but I was prevented. It was just; it was our place to suffer with the rest. It has been hard for us. It is the first time we have ever heard our name fall from any one's lips—sullied. Be merciful—for the sake of the better days; make our shame as light to bear as in your charity you can." At this point in his revery Mary nudged him, perceiving that his mind was absent. The house was chanting. "You are f-a-r," etc.

"Be ready," Mary whispered. "Your name comes now; he has read eighteen."

The chant ended.

"Next! next! next!" came volleying from all over the house.

Burgess put his hand into his pocket. The old couple, trembling, began to rise, Burgess fumbled a moment, then said,

"I find I have read them all."

Faint with joy and surprise, the couple sank into their seats, and

Mary whispered:

"Oh, bless God, we are saved!—he has lost ours—I wouldn't give this for a hundred of those sacks!"

The house burst out with its "Mikado" travesty, and sang it three times with ever-increasing enthusiasm, rising to its feet when it reached for the third time the closing line—

"But the Symbols are here, you bet!"

and finishing up with cheers and a tiger for "Hadleyburg purity and our eighteen immortal representatives of it."

Then Wingate, the saddler, got up and proposed cheers "for the cleanest man in town, the one solitary important citizen in it who didn't try to steal that money—Edward Richards."

They were given with great and moving heartiness; then somebody proposed that Richards be elected sole Guardian and Symbol of the now Sacred Hadleyburg Tradition, with power and right to stand up and look the whole sarcastic world in the face.

Passed, by acclamation; then they sang the "Mikado" again, and ended it with,

"And there's *one* Symbol left, you bet!"

There was a pause; then—

A *Voice*. "Now, then, who's to get the sack?"

The Tanner (with bitter sarcasm). "That's easy. The money has to be divided among the eighteen Incorruptibles. They gave the suffering stranger twenty dollars apiece—and that remark—each in his turn—it took twenty-two minutes for the procession to move past. Staked the stranger—total contribution, $360. All they want is just the loan back—and interest—forty thousand dollars altogether."

Many voices [derisively]. "That's it! Divvy! divvy! Be kind to the poor—don't keep them waiting!"

The Chair. "Order! I now offer the stranger's remaining document. It says: 'If no claimant shall appear [*grand chorus of groans*], I desire that you open the sack and count out the money to the principal citizens of your town, they to take it in trust [*Cries of "Oh! Oh! Oh!"*], and use it in such ways as to them shall seem best for the propagation and preservation of your community's noble reputation for incorruptible honesty [*more cries*]—a reputation to which their names and their efforts will add a new and far-reaching lustre.' [*Enthusiastic outburst of sarcastic applause.*] That seems to be all. No—here is a postscript:

" 'P. S.—CITIZENS OF HADLEYBURG: There *is* no test-remark—nobody made one. [*Great sensation.*] There wasn't any pauper stranger, nor any twenty-dollar contribution, nor any accompanying benediction and compliment—these are all inventions. [*General buzz and hum of astonishment and delight.*] Allow me to tell my story—it will take but a word or two. I passed through your town at a certain time, and received a deep offense which I had not earned. Any other man would have been content to kill one or two of you and call it square, but to me that would have been a trivial revenge, and inadequate; for the dead do not *suffer*. Besides, I could not kill you all—and, anyway, made as I am, even that would not have satisfied me. I wanted to damage every man in the place, and every woman—and not in their bodies or in their estate, but in their vanity—the place where feeble and foolish people are most vulnerable. So I disguised myself and came back and studied you. You were easy game. You had an old and lofty reputation for honesty, and naturally you were proud of it—it was your treasure of treasures, the very apple of your eye. As soon as I found out that you carefully and vigilantly kept yourselves and your children *out of temptation*, I knew how to proceed. Why, you simple creatures, the weakest of all weak things is a virtue which has not been tested in the fire. I laid a plan, and gathered a list of names. My project was to corrupt Hadleyburg the incorruptible. My idea was to make liars and thieves of nearly half a hundred smirchless men and women who had never in their lives uttered a lie or stolen a penny. I was afraid of Goodson. He was neither born nor reared in Hadleyburg. I was afraid that if I started to operate my scheme by getting my letter laid before you, you would say to yourselves, "Goodson is the only man among us who would give away twenty dollars to a poor devil"—and then you might not bite at my bait. But Heaven took Goodson; then I knew I was safe, and I set my trap and baited it. It may be that I shall not catch all the men to whom I mailed the pretended test secret, but I shall catch the most of them, if I know Hadleyburg nature. [*Voices.* "Right—he got every last one of them."] I believe they will even steal ostensible *gamble*-money, rather than miss, poor, tempted, and mistrained fellows. I am hoping to eternally and everlastingly squelch your vanity and give Hadleyburg a new renown—one that will *stick*—and spread far. If I have succeeded, open the sack and summon the Committee on Propagation and Preservation of the Hadleyburg Reputation.' "

A *Cyclone of Voices*. "Open it! Open it! The Eighteen to the front! Committee on Propagation of the Tradition! Forward—the Incorruptibles!"

The Chair ripped the sack wide, and gathered up a handful of bright, broad, yellow coins, shook them together, then examined them—

"Friends, they are only gilded disks of lead!"

There was a crashing outbreak of delight over this news, and when the noise had subsided, the tanner called out:

"By right of apparent seniority in this business, Mr. Wilson is Chairman of the Committee on Propagation of the Tradition. I suggest that he step forward on behalf of his pals, and receive in trust the money."

A Hundred Voices. "Wilson! Wilson! Wilson! Speech! Speech!"

Wilson [*in a voice trembling with anger*]. "You will allow me to say, without apologies for my language, *damn* the money!"

A Voice. "Oh, and him a Baptist!"

A Voice. "Seventeen Symbols left! Step up, gentlemen, and assume your trust!"

There was a pause—no response.

The Saddler. "Mr. Chairman, we've got *one* clean man left, anyway, out of the late aristocracy; and he needs money, and deserves it. I move that you appoint Jack Halliday to get up there and auction off that sack of gilt twenty-dollar pieces, and give the result to the right man—the man whom Hadleyburg delights to honor—Edward Richards."

This was received with great enthusiasm, the dog taking a hand again; the saddler started the bids at a dollar, the Brixton folk and Barnum's representative fought hard for it, the people cheered every jump that the bids made, the excitement climbed moment by moment higher and higher, the bidders got on their mettle and grew steadily more and more daring, more and more determined, the jumps went from a dollar up to five, then to ten, then to twenty, then fifty, then to a hundred, then—

At the beginning of the auction Richards whispered in distress to his wife: "Oh, Mary, can we allow it? It—it—you see, it is an honor-reward, a testimonial to purity of character, and—and—can we allow it? Hadn't I better get up and—Oh, Mary, what ought we to do?—what do you think we—" [*Halliday's voice. "Fifteen I'm bid!—fifteen for the sack!—twenty!—ah, thanks!—thirty—thanks again! Thirty, thirty, thirty!—do I hear forty?—forty it is! Keep the ball rolling, gentlemen, keep it rolling!—fifty!—thanks, noble Roman!—going at fifty, fifty, fifty!—seventy!—ninety!—splendid!—a hundred!—pile it up, pile it up!—hundred and twenty—forty!—just in time!—hundred and fifty!—*two hundred!—superb!* Do I hear two h— thanks!—two hundred and fifty!——"*]

"It is another temptation, Edward—I'm all in a tremble—but, oh, we've escaped *one* temptation, and that ought to warn us, to—* [*"Six did I hear?—thanks!—six fifty, six f—*seven hundred!*"*] And yet, Edward, when you think—nobody susp—[*"Eight hundred dollars!—hurrah!—make it nine!—Mr. Parsons, did I hear you say—thanks!—nine!—this noble sack of virgin lead going at only nine hundred dollars, gilding and all—come! do I hear—a thousand!—*

gratefully yours!—did some one say eleven?—a sack which is going to be the most celebrated in the whole Uni——"] Oh, Edward" (*beginning to sob*), "we are *so* poor!—but—but—do as you think best—do as you think best."

Edward fell—that is, he sat still; sat with a conscience which was not satisfied, but which was overpowered by circumstances.

Meanwhile a stranger, who looked like an amateur detective gotten up as an impossible English earl, had been watching the evening's proceedings with manifest interest, and with a contented expression in his face; and he had been privately commenting to himself. He was now soliloquizing somewhat like this: "None of the Eighteen are bidding; that is not satisfactory; I must change that—the dramatic unities require it; they must buy the sack they tried to steal; they must pay a heavy price, too—some of them are rich. And another thing, when I make a mistake in Hadleyburg nature the man that puts that error upon me is entitled to a high honorarium, and some one must pay it. This poor old Richards has brought my judgment to shame; he is an honest man;—I don't understand it, but I acknowledge it. Yes, he saw my deuces—*and* with a straight flush, and by rights the pot is his. And it shall be a jackpot, too, if I can manage it. He disappointed me, but let that pass."

He was watching the bidding. At a thousand, the market broke; the prices tumbled swiftly. He waited—and still watched. One competitor dropped out; then another, and another. He put in a bid or two, now. When the bids had sunk to ten dollars, he added a five; some one raised him a three; he waited a moment, then flung in a fifty-dollar jump, and the sack was his—at $1,282. The house broke out in cheers—then stopped; for he was on his feet and had lifted his hand. He began to speak.

"I desire to say a word, and ask a favor. I am a speculator in rarities, and I have dealings with persons interested in numismatics all over the world. I can make a profit on this purchase, just as it stands; but there is a way, if I can get your approval, whereby I can make every one of these leaden twenty-dollar pieces worth its face in gold, and perhaps more. Grant me that approval, and I will give part of my gains to your Mr. Richards, whose invulnerable probity you have so justly and so cordially recognized to-night; his share shall be ten thousand dollars, and I will hand him the money to-morrow. [*Great applause from the house.* But the "invulnerable probity" made the Richardses blush prettily; however, it went for modesty, and did no harm.] If you will pass my proposition by a good majority—I would like a two-thirds vote—I will regard that as the town's consent, and that is all I ask. Rarities are always helped by any device which will rouse curiosity and compel remark. Now if I may have your permission to stamp upon the faces of each of these ostensible coins the names of the eighteen gentlemen who—"

Nine-tenths of the audience were on their feet in a moment—dog and all—and the proposition was carried with a whirlwind of approving applause and laughter.

They sat down, and all the Symbols except "Dr." Clay Harkness got up, violently protesting against the proposed outrage, and threatening to—

"I beg you not to threaten me," said the stranger, calmly. "I know my legal rights, and am not accustomed to being frightened at bluster." [*Applause.*] He sat down. "Dr." Harkness saw an opportunity here. He was one of the two very rich men of the place, and Pinkerton was the other. Harkness was proprietor of a mint; that is to say, a popular patent medicine. He was running for the Legislature on one ticket, and Pinkerton on the other. It was a close race and a hot one, and getting hotter every day. Both had strong appetites for money; each had bought a great tract of land, with a purpose; there was going to be a new railway, and each wanted to be in the Legislature and help locate the route to his own advantage; a single vote might make the decision, and with it two or three fortunes. The stake was large, and Harkness was a daring speculator. He was sitting close to the stranger. He leaned over while one or another of the other Symbols was entertaining the house with protests and appeals, and asked, in a whisper,

"What is your price for the sack?"

"Forty thousand dollars."

"I'll give you twenty."

"No."

"Twenty-five."

"No."

"Say thirty."

"The price is forty thousand dollars; not a penny less."

"All right, I'll give it. I will come to the hotel at ten in the morning. I don't want it known; will see you privately."

"Very good." Then the stranger got up and said to the house:

"I find it late. The speeches of these gentlemen are not without merit, not without interest, not without grace; yet if I may be excused I will take my leave. I thank you for the great favor which you have shown me in granting my petition. I ask the Chair to keep the sack for me until to-morrow, and to hand these three five-hundred-dollar notes to Mr. Richards." They were passed up to the Chair. "At nine I will call for the sack, and at eleven will deliver the rest of the ten thousand to Mr. Richards in person, at his home. Good-night."

Then he slipped out, and left the audience making a vast noise, which was composed of a mixture of cheers, the "Mikado" song, dog-disapproval, and the chant, "you are f-a-r from being a b-a-a-d man—a-a-a-a-men!"

IV

At home the Richardses had to endure congratulations and compliments until midnight. Then they were left to themselves. They looked a little sad, and they sat silent and thinking. Finally Mary sighed and said,

"Do you think we are to blame, Edward—*much* to blame?" and her eyes wandered to the accusing triplet of big bank-notes lying on the table, where the congratulators had been gloating over them and reverently fingering them. Edward did not answer at once; then he brought out a sigh and said, hesitatingly:

"We—we couldn't help it, Mary. It—well, it was ordered. *All* things are."

Mary glanced up and looked at him steadily, but he didn't return the look. Presently she said:

"I thought congratulations and praises always tasted good. But— it seems to me, now—Edward?"

"Well?"

"Are you going to stay in the bank?"

"N-no."

"Resign?"

"In the morning—by note."

"It does seem best."

Richards bowed his head in his hands and muttered:

"Before, I was not afraid to let oceans of people's money pour through my hands, but—Mary, I am so tired, so tired—"

"We will go to bed."

At nine in the morning the stranger called for the sack and took it to the hotel in a cab. At ten Harkness had a talk with him privately. The stranger asked for and got five checks on a metropolitan bank—drawn to "Bearer,"—four for $1,500 each, and one for $34,000. He put one of the former in his pocket-book, and the remainder, representing $38,500, he put in an envelope, and with these he added a note, which he wrote after Harkness was gone. At eleven he called at the Richards house and knocked. Mrs. Richards peeped through the shutters, then went and received the envelope, and the stanger disappeared without a word. She came back flushed and a little unsteady on her legs, and gasped out:

"I am sure I recognized him! Last night it seemed to me that maybe I had seen him somewhere before."

"He is the man that brought the sack here?"

"I am almost sure of it."

"Then he is the ostensible Stephenson too, and sold every important citizen in this town with his bogus secret. Now if he has sent checks instead of money, we are sold too, after we thought we had escaped. I was beginning to feel fairly comfortable once more, after my night's rest, but the look of that envelope makes me sick. It isn't fat enough; $8,500 in even the largest bank-notes makes more bulk than that."

"Edward, why do you object to checks?"

"Checks signed by Stephenson! I am resigned to take the $8,500 if it could come in bank-notes—for it does seem that it was so ordered, Mary—but I have never had much courage, and I have not the pluck to try to market a check signed with that disastrous name. It would be a trap. That man tried to catch me; we escaped some-how or other; and now he is trying a new way. If it is checks——"

"Oh, Edward, it is *too* bad!" and she held up the checks and began to cry.

"Put them in the fire! quick! we mustn't be tempted. It is a trick to make the world laugh at *us*, along with the rest, and—Give them to *me*, since you can't do it!" He snatched them and tried to hold his grip till he could get to the stove; but he was human, he was a cashier, and he stopped a moment to make sure of the signature. Then he came near to fainting.

"Fan me, Mary, fan me! They are the same as gold!"

"Oh, how lovely, Edward! Why?"

"Signed by Harkness. What can the mystery of that be, Mary?"

"Edward, do you think——"

"Look here—look at this! Fifteen—fifteen—fifteen—thirty-four. Thirty-eight thousand five hundred! Mary, the sack isn't worth twelve dollars, and Harkness—apparently—has paid about par for it."

"And does it all come to us, do you think—instead of the ten thousand?"

"Why, it looks like it. And the checks are made to 'Bearer,' too."

"Is that good, Edward? What is it for?"

"A hint to collect them at some distant bank, I reckon. Perhaps Harkness doesn't want the matter known. What is that—a note?"

"Yes. It was with the checks."

It was in the "Stephenson" handwriting, but there was no signa-ture. It said:

"I am a disappointed man. Your honesty is beyond the reach of temptation. I had a different idea about it, but I wronged you in that, and I beg pardon, and do it sincerely. I honor you—and that is sincere, too. This town is not worthy to kiss the hem of your garment. Dear sir, I made a square bet with myself that there were

nineteen debauchable men in your self-righteous community. I have lost. Take the whole pot, you are entitled to it."

Richards drew a deep sigh, and said:

"It seems written with fire—it burns so. Mary—I am miserable again."

"I, too. Ah, dear, I wish——"

"To think, Mary—he *believes* in me."

"Oh, don't, Edward—I can't bear it."

"If those beautiful words were deserved, Mary—and God knows I believed I deserved them once—I think I could give the forty thousand dollars for them. And I would put that paper away, as representing more than gold and jewels, and keep it always. But now—We could not live in the shadow of its accusing presence, Mary."

He put it in the fire.

A messenger arrived and delivered an envelope. Richards took from it a note and read it; it was from Burgess.

"You saved me, in a difficult time. I saved you last night. It was at cost of a lie, but I made the sacrifice freely, and out of grateful heart. None in this village knows so well as I know how brave and good and noble you are. At bottom you cannot respect me, knowing as you do of that matter of which I am accused, and by the general voice condemned; but I beg that you will at least believe that I am a grateful man; it will help me to bear my burden.

[*Signed*]   "BURGESS."

"Saved, once more. And on such terms!" He put the note in the fire. "I—I wish I were dead, Mary, I wish I were out of it all."

"Oh, these are bitter, bitter days, Edward. The stabs, through their very generosity, are so deep—and they come so fast!"

Three days before the election each of two thousand voters suddenly found himself in possession of a prized memento—one of the renowned bogus double-eagles. Around one of its faces was stamped these words: "THE REMARK I MADE TO THE POOR STRANGER WAS—" Around the other face was stamped these: "GO, AND REFORM. [SIGNED] PINKERTON." Thus the entire remaining refuse of the renowned joke was emptied upon a single head, and with calamitous effect. It revived the recent vast laugh and concentrated it upon Pinkerton; and Harkness's election was a walk-over.

Within twenty-four hours after the Richardses had received their checks their consciences were quieting down, discouraged; the old couple were learning to reconcile themselves to the sin which they had committed. But they were to learn, now, that a sin takes on new and real terrors when there seems a chance that it is going to be found out. This gives it a fresh and most substantial and important aspect. At church the morning sermon was of the usual pattern; it was the same old things said in the same old way; they had heard them a thousand times and found them innocuous, next to meaningless, and easy to sleep under; but now it was different: the sermon seemed to bristle with accusations; it seemed aimed straight and specially at people who were concealing deadly sins. After church they got away from the mob of congratulators as soon as they could, and hurried homeward, chilled to the bone at they did not know what—vague, shadowy, indefinite fears. And by chance they caught a glimpse of Mr. Burgess as he turned a corner. He paid no attention to their nod of recognition! He hadn't seen it; but they did not know that. What could his conduct mean? It might mean—it might mean—oh, a dozen dreadful things. Was it possible that he knew that Richards could have cleared him of guilt in that bygone time, and had been silently waiting for a chance to even up accounts? At home, in their distress they got to imagining that their servant might have been in the next room listening when Richards revealed the secret to his wife that he knew of Burgess's innocence; next, Richards began to imagine that he had heard the swish of a gown in there at that time; next, he was sure he *had* heard it. They would call Sarah in, on a pretext, and watch her face: if she had been betraying them to Mr. Burgess, it would show in her manner. They asked her some questions—questions which were so random and incoherent and seemingly purposeless that the girl felt sure that the old people's mind had been affected by their sudden good fortune; the sharp and watchful gaze which they bent upon her frightened her, and that completed the business. She blushed, she became nervous and confused, and to the old people these were plain signs of guilt—guilt of some fearful sort or other —without doubt she was a spy and a traitor. When they were alone again they began to piece many unrelated things together and get horrible results out of the combination. When things had got about to the worst, Richards was delivered of a sudden gasp, and his wife asked:

"Oh, what is it?—what is it?"

"The note—Burgess's note! Its language was sarcastic, I see it now." He quoted: " 'At bottom you cannot respect me, *knowing*, as you do, of *that matter* of which I am accused'—oh, it is perfectly plain, now, God help me! He knows that I know! You see the ingenuity of the phrasing. It was a trap—and like a fool, I walked into it. And Mary—?"

"Oh, it is dreadful—I know what your are going to say—he didn't return your transcript of the pretended test-remark."

"No—kept it to destroy us with. Mary, he has exposed us to some already. I know it—I know it well. I saw it in a dozen faces after church. Ah, he wouldn't answer our nod of recognition—*he* knew what he had been doing!"

In the night the doctor was called. The news went around in the morning that the old couple were rather seriously ill—prostrated by the exhausting excitement growing out of their great windfall, the congratulations, and the late hours, the doctor said. The town was sincerely distressed; for these old people were about all it had left to be proud of, now.

Two days later the news was worse. The old couple were delirious, and were doing strange things. By witness of the nurses, Richards had exhibited checks—for $8,500? No—for an amazing sum— $38,500! What could be the explanation of this gigantic piece of luck?

The following day the nurses had more news—and wonderful. They had concluded to hide the checks, lest harm come to them; but when they searched they were gone from under the patient's pillow—vanished away. The patient said:

"Let the pillow alone; what do you want?"

"We thought it best that the checks——"

"You will never see them again—they are destroyed. They came from Satan. I saw the hell-brand on them, and I knew they were sent to betray me to sin." Then he fell to gabbling strange and dreadful things which were not clearly understandable, and which the doctor admonished them to keep to themselves.

Richards was right; the checks were never seen again.

A nurse must have talked in her sleep, for within two days the forbidden gabblings were the property of the town; and they were of a surprising sort. They seemed to indicate that Richards had been a claimant for the sack himself, and that Burgess had concealed that fact and then maliciously betrayed it.

Burgess was taxed with this and stoutly denied it. And he said it was not fair to attach weight to the chatter of a sick old man who was out of his mind. Still, suspicion was in the air, and there was much talk.

After a day or two it was reported that Mrs. Richards's delirious deliveries were getting to be duplicates of her husband's. Suspicion flamed up into conviction, now, and the town's pride in the purity of its one undiscredited important citizen began to dim down and flicker toward extinction.

Six days passed, then came more news. The old couple were dying. Richards's mind cleared in his latest hour, and he sent for Burgess. Burgess said:

"Let the room be cleared. I think he wishes to say something in privacy."

"No!" said Richards; "I want witnesses. I want you all to hear my confession, so that I may die a man, and not a dog. I was clean —artificially—like the rest; and like the rest I fell when temptation came. I signed a lie, and claimed the miserable sack. Mr. Burgess remembered that I had done him a service, and in gratitude (and ignorance) he suppressed my claim and saved me. You know the thing that was charged against Burgess years ago. My testimony, and mine alone, could have cleared him, and I was a coward, and left him to suffer disgrace—"

"No—no—Mr. Richards, you—"

"My servant betrayed my secret to him—"

"No one has betrayed anything to me—"

—"and then he did a natural and justifiable thing, he repented of the saving kindness which he had done me, and he *exposed* me— as I deserved—"

"Never!—I make oath—"

"Out of my heart I forgive him."

Burgess's impassioned protestations fell upon deaf ears; the dying man passed away without knowing that once more he had done poor Burgess a wrong. The old wife died that night.

The last of the sacred Nineteen had fallen a prey to the fiendish sack; the town was stripped of the last rag of its ancient glory. Its mourning was not showy, but it was deep.

By act of the Legislature—upon prayer and petition—Hadleyburg was allowed to change its name to (never mind what—I will not give it away), and leave one word out of the motto that for many generations had graced the town's official seal.

It is an honest town once more, and the man will have to rise early that catches it napping again.

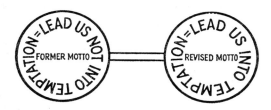

1899, 1900

Adventures of Huckleberry Finn[1]

(TOM SAWYER'S COMRADE)
SCENE: THE MISSISSIPPI
TIME: FORTY TO FIFTY YEARS AGO

NOTICE

Persons attempting to find a motive in this narrative will be prosecuted; persons attempting to find a moral in it will be banished; persons attempting to find a plot in it will be shot.

BY ORDER OF THE AUTHOR
PER G. G., CHIEF OF ORDNANCE.

EXPLANATORY

In this book a number of dialects are used, to wit: the Missouri negro dialect; the extremest form of the backwoods South-Western dialect; the ordinary "Pike-County" dialect; and four modified varieties of this last. The shadings have not been done in a hap-hazard fashion, or by guess-work; but pains-takingly, and with the trustworthy guidance and support of personal familiarity with these several forms of speech.

I make this explanation for the reason that without it many readers would suppose that all these characters were trying to talk alike and not succeeding.

THE AUTHOR

1. Several generations of Americans have read this, Mark Twain's masterpiece, with undiminished affection, because for each generation increasingly it has recaptured a lost world of childhood and an earlier reality of their country which it is valuable to keep in memory. But in the largest sense, "only adults will read it," as its author less aptly remarked of *Tom Sawyer*. On the adult level this is a complex work of art, sometimes approaching profundity in its psychological perceptions, its moral judgments, and its social criticism. It is precisely located in place and time; yet by its power and its truth it has attained universal recognition as a classic.

In structure, *Adventures of Huckleberry Finn* resembles the earliest and simplest form of the novel. In the novella known to Chaucer, just as in the earliest British novels shaped by Defoe or Fielding, the form was episodic; so was the frontier narrative that first influenced Mark Twain. In its most popular examples this literature always dealt with the roguish adventures of characters ranging from fantastic pranksters to genuine badmen.

This "picaresque" element was prominent in the burlesque romances, such as *Don Quixote* and *Gil Blas*, which inspired Mark Twain, in this book and elsewhere, in making his attack on the shams of romantic chivalry.

Huckleberry Finn was a literary creation from materials which were traditional in the sense that the humor, folkways, legends, and speech of a country are a common inheritance. Such characters as the duke, the king, Widow Douglas, and Colonels Grangerford and Sherburn, however much Twain individualized them, were recognizably derived from frontier legend and its literature. Mark Twain's accretions for this novel came first from his boyhood experience many years before, and second from a process not unusual in the literary shaping of traditional sources. He once said that he wrote on a plan of "spontaneous combustion" but in this case the spontaneity was only sporadically sustained. The book, like its legendary sources, had to grow up; the eight years' lapse between the beginning and the conclusion of this composition were necessary to let the book "make up its mind," as

Chapter I

You don't know about me, without you have read a book by
the name of "The Adventures of Tom Sawyer,"[2] but that ain't no
matter. That book was made by Mr. Mark Twain, and he told
the truth, mainly. There was things which he stretched, but mainly

Twain said. He began in 1876 what he
called then "another boy's book * * *
more to be at work than for anything
else," and he carried it through the
first sixteen chapters, when the raft
has missed the mouth of the Ohio and
gone below freedom-land. In two spurts
during 1879 and 1880 he added five
chapters, bringing the narrative through
the Grangerford feud and the Sherburn-
Boggs incident at Bricksville. He then
abandoned it. Huck somewhere remarks,
"Providence always did put the right
words in my mouth, if I left it alone";
and two years later, this happened to
the author as the result of a long summer visit among the old scenes on the
Mississippi. In a burst of inspiration
he finished the book in the next eighteen months.

His inspiration fulfilled again the exuberant demands of a literary genre long
neglected. Twain's novel is, as Fielding
called his early work, a "comic epic in
prose": comic, because it employs great
strokes of wit and humor—and the
scourge of laughter—to attack the evils
of mankind and the consequent sins of
society; epic, because its moving force,
the great River, is also a stream in time
and in history, bearing its raft of argonauts to various shores where lie the
relics, wrecks, and hopes of a civilization in transition. As his narrator,
Twain chose Huck; this was a clear
act of genius. Huck "had known and
suffered all" that was on the River,
and he could speak expertly, in the
speech of the author's boyhood Hannibal. In the speech of Huck Finn
Twain fashioned a new literary language in colloquial American, seen at
its best in the descriptions of the River,
where the cadences and vigor of the
spoken language are expressed by a
great artist with such authority that a
whole generation of realistic authors,
from Sherwood Anderson to Hemingway
and Faulkner, were influenced. As Eliot
remarked, "like Dryden and Swift," he
brought the language "up to date."

The River is a fundamental element
in the structure of this novel, but it is
also the central symbol to which other
symbolic elements are referred. "It's
lovely to live on a raft," says Huck,
and "sometimes we'd have that whole
river to ourselves for the longest time."
The literary discovery of the River,
which we owe to Mark Twain, made

it part of a continental myth somewhat
similar to those of the Ganges, the Nile,
and the Amazon, rivers which were also
gods. In this story the River accorded
with Huck's loneliness; and whether it
ravened the land or was at peace, it
was a clean and trustworthy reality for
Jim, a fugitive from slavery, and Huck,
fleeing from all the brutality of "civilization" epitomized in his father. The
Pokesvilles and Bricksvilles along the
shore were not all bad, nor were the
people, yet their pollution was always
sufficiently evident to make the return
to the raft a repeated experience of regeneration. Even though they were
driven by the storm beyond the mouth
of the Ohio, which was the gateway to
legal freedom for the slave, the River
and the raft still offered the best freedom of all. The intrusion of the king
and the duke upon this sanctuary, although it brought such evil as only the
community of man could foster, was
not disastrous, so long as they all
remained on the raft, where, as Huck
says, it is necessary "for everybody
to * * * feel right and kind toward
the others." This is the epitome of this
novel's social criticism. Whatever evil
appeared in society was the evil of men,
and Twain here used Huck to carry on
his relentless excoriation of "the
damned human race," and to condemn
stereotypes of right and wrong with
which the rulers of society justified
their own selfish interests. In this novel
the representative stereotype was slavery. Huck had to battle with his conscience continuously, because according
to the morality of society and church,
he should report as a runaway slave
this Jim whom he had come to love
as a brother. His final decision in Jim's
favor was concluded with his famous
reflection, "All right, then, I'll *go* to
hell!" Yet when Aunt Sally asked
whether the steamboat explosion hurt
anyone, he automatically responded,
"No'm. Killed a nigger."

The English edition of *Huckleberry
Finn* appeared on December 4, 1884,
some time before the first American
copies, dated 1885, were officially received for copyright. The present text
follows a photographic reproduction of
the first American edition, first issue,
1885, with the annotated correction of
typographical errors.

2. Published nine years earlier in 1876.

he told the truth. That is nothing. I never seen anybody but lied, one time or another, without it was Aunt Polly, or the widow, or maybe Mary. Aunt Polly—Tom's Aunt Polly, she is—and Mary, and the Widow Douglas, is all told about in that book—which is mostly a true book; with some stretchers, as I said before.

Now the way that the book winds up, is this: Tom and me found the money that the robbers hid in the cave, and it made us rich. We got six thousand dollars apiece—all gold. It was an awful sight of money when it was piled up. Well, Judge Thatcher, he took it and put it out at interest, and it fetched us a dollar a day apiece, all the year round—more than a body could tell what to do with. The Widow Douglas, she took me for her son, and allowed she would sivilize me; but it was rough living in the house all the time, considering how dismal regular and decent the widow was in all her ways; and so when I couldn't stand it no longer, I lit out. I got into my old rags, and my sugar-hogshead again, and was free and satisfied. But Tom Sawyer, he hunted me up and said he was going to start a band of robbers, and I might join if I would go back to the widow and be respectable. So I went back.

The widow she cried over me, and called me a poor lost lamb, and she called me a lot of other names, too, but she never meant no harm by it. She put me in them new clothes again, and I couldn't do nothing but sweat and sweat, and feel all cramped up. Well, then, the old thing commenced again. The widow rung a bell for supper, and you had to come to time. When you got to the table you couldn't go right to eating, but you had to wait for the widow to tuck down her head and grumble a little over the victuals, though there warn't really anything the matter with them. That is, nothing only everything was cooked by itself. In a barrel of odds and ends it is different; things get mixed up, and the juice kind of swaps around, and the things go better.

After supper she got out her book and learned me about Moses and the Bulrushers;[3] and I was in a sweat to find out all about him; but by-and-by she let it out that Moses had been dead a considerable long time; so then I didn't care no more about him; because I don't take stock in dead people.

Pretty soon I wanted to smoke, and asked the widow to let me. But she wouldn't. She said it was a mean practice and wasn't clean, and I must try to not do it any more. That is just the way with some people. They get down on a thing when they don't know nothing about it. Here she was a bothering about Moses, which was no kin to her, and no use to anybody, being gone, you see, yet finding a power of fault with me for doing a thing that had some

3. *Cf.* Exodus ii: 1–10.

good in it. And she took snuff too; of course that was all right, because she done it herself.

Her sister, Miss Watson, a tolerable slim old maid, with goggles
on, had just come to live with her, and took a set at me now, with
a spelling-book. She worked me middling hard for about an hour,
and then the widow made her ease up. I couldn't stood it much
longer. Then for an hour it was deadly dull, and I was fidgety. Miss
Watson would say, "Dont put your feet up there, Huckleberry;"
and "dont scrunch up like that, Huckleberry—set up straight;"
and pretty soon she would say, "Don't gap and stretch like that,
Huckleberry—why don't you try to behave?" Then she told me all
about the bad place, and I said I wished I was there. She got mad,
then, but I didn't mean no harm. All I wanted was to go somewheres; all I wanted was a change, I warn't particular. She said it
was wicked to say what I said; said she wouldn't say it for the whole
world; *she* was going to live so as to go to the good place. Well, I
couldn't see no advantage in going where she was going, so I made
up my mind I wouldn't try for it. But I never said so, because it
would only make trouble, and wouldn't do no good.

Now she had got a start, and she went on and told me all about
the good place. She said all a body would have to do there was
to go around all day long with a harp and sing, forever and ever.[4]
So I didn't think much of it. But I never said so. I asked her if
she reckoned Tom Sawyer would go there, and, she said, not by a
considerable sight. I was glad about that, because I wanted him
and me to be together.

Miss Watson she kept pecking at me, and it got tiresome and
lonesome. By-and-by they fetched the niggers[5] in and had prayers,
and then everybody was off to bed. I went up to my room with a
piece of candle and put it on the table. Then I set down in a chair
by the window and tried to think of something cheerful, but it
warn't no use. I felt so lonesome I most wished I was dead.[6] The
stars was shining, and the leaves rustled in the woods ever so
mournful; and I heard an owl, away off, who-whooing about somebody that was dead, and a whippowill and a dog crying about somebody that was going to die; and the wind was trying to whisper
something to me and I couldn't make out what it was, and so it
made the cold shivers run over me. Then away out in the woods

4. The traditional pearly-gate concept
of heaven was again ridiculed by Twain
in *Extract from Captain Stormfield's
Visit to Heaven* (1907).
5. In slave states, "nigger" was not
necessarily an abusive word, but merely
the ordinary colloquial term for a slave.
6. The essential loneliness of the individual, a recurrent theme in Twain's
work, is best symbolized in the boy,
Huck, confronted, as in the following
passage, by the vast wilderness of forests and waters. His superstitious
fancies, although common to all boyhood, are an emotional verification of
an American frontier experience.

I heard that kind of a sound that a ghost makes when it wants to tell about something that's on its mind and can't make itself understood, and so can't rest easy in its grave and has to go about that way every night grieving. I got so down-hearted and scared, I did wish I had some company. Pretty soon a spider went crawling up my shoulder, and I flipped it off and it lit in the candle; and before I could budge it was all shriveled up. I didn't need anybody to tell me that that was an awful bad sign and would fetch me some bad luck, so I was scared and most shook the clothes off of me. I got up and turned around in my tracks three times and crossed my breast every time; and then I tied up a little lock of my hair with a thread to keep witches away. But I hadn't no confidence. You do that when you've lost a horse-shoe that you've found, instead of nailing it up over the door, but I hadn't ever heard anybody say it was any way to keep off bad luck when you'd killed a spider.

I set down again, a shaking all over, and got out my pipe for a smoke; for the house was all as still as death, now, and so the widow wouldn't know. Well, after a long time I heard the clock away off in the town go boom—boom—boom—twelve licks—and all still again—stiller than ever. Pretty soon I heard a twig snap, down in the dark amongst the trees—something was a stirring. I set still and listened. Directly I could just barely hear a *"me-yow! me-yow!"* down there. That was good! Says I, *"me-yow! me-yow!"* as soft as I could, and then I put out the light and scrambled out of the window onto the shed. Then I slipped down to the ground and crawled in amongst the trees, and sure enough there was Tom Sawyer waiting for me.

Chapter II

We went tip-toeing along a path amongst the trees back towards the end of the widow's garden, stooping down so as the branches wouldn't scrape our heads. When we was passing by the kitchen I fell over a root and made a noise. We scrouched down and laid still. Miss Watson's big nigger, named Jim, was setting in the kitchen door; we could see him pretty clear, because there was a light behind him. He got up and stretched his neck out about a minute, listening. Then he says,

"Who dah?"

He listened some more; then he come tip-toeing down and stood right between us; we could a touched him, nearly. Well, likely it was minutes and minutes that there warn't a sound, and we all there so close together. There was a place on my ankle that got to itching; but I dasn't scratch it; and then my ear begun to itch; and next my back, right between my shoulders. Seemed like

I'd die if I couldn't scratch. Well, I've noticed that thing plenty of times since. If you are with the quality, or at a funeral, or trying to go to sleep when you ain't sleepy—if you are anywheres where it won't do for you to scratch, why you will itch all over in upwards of a thousand places. Pretty soon Jim says:

"Say—who is you? Whar is you? Dog my cats ef I didn' hear sumf'n. Well, I knows what I's gwyne to do. I's gwyne to set down here and listen tell I hears it agin."

So he set down on the ground betwixt me and Tom. He leaned his back up against a tree, and stretched his legs out till one of them most touched one of mine. My nose begun to itch. It itched till the tears come into my eyes. But I dasn't scratch. Then it begun to itch on the inside. Next I got to itching underneath. I didn't know how I was going to set still. This miserableness went on as much as six or seven minutes; but it seemed a sight longer than that. I was itching in eleven different places now. I reckoned I couldn't stand it more'n a minute longer, but I set my teeth hard and got ready to try. Just then Jim begun to breathe heavy; next he begun to snore—and then I was pretty soon comfortable again.

Tom he made a sign to me—kind of a little noise with his mouth—and we went creeping away on our hands and knees. When we was ten foot off, Tom whispered to me and wanted to tie Jim to the tree for fun; but I said no; he might wake and make a disturbance, and then they'd find out I warn't in. Then Tom said he hadn't got candles enough, and he would slip in the kitchen and get some more. I didn't want him to try. I said Jim might wake up and come. But Tom wanted to resk it; so we slid in there and got three candles, and Tom laid five cents on the table for pay. Then we got out, and I was in a sweat to get away; but nothing would do Tom but he must crawl to where Jim was, on his hands and knees, and play something on him. I waited, and it seemed a good while, everything was so still and lonesome.

As soon as Tom was back, we cut along the path, around the garden fence, and by-and-by fetched up on the steep top of the hill the other side of the house. Tom said he slipped Jim's hat off of his head and hung it on a limb right over him, and Jim stirred a little, but he didn't wake. Afterwards Jim said the witches bewitched him and put him in a trance, and rode him all over the State, and then set him under the trees again and hung his hat on a limb to show who done it. And next time Jim told it he said they rode him down to New Orleans; and after that, every time he told it he spread it more and more, till by-and-by he said they rode him all over the world, and tired him most to death, and his back was all over saddle-boils. Jim was monstrous proud about it, and he got so he wouldn't hardly notice the other niggers. Niggers would come miles to hear Jim tell about it, and he was more looked up to than any nigger in that country. Strange niggers would stand with their mouths open and look him all over, same as if he was a wonder. Niggers is always talking about witches in the dark by the kitchen fire; but whenever one was talking and letting on to know all about such things, Jim would happen in and say, "Hm! What you know 'bout witches?" and that nigger was corked up and had to take a back seat. Jim always kept that five-center piece around his neck with a string and said it was a charm the devil give to him with his own hands and told him he could cure anybody with it and fetch witches whenever he wanted to, just by saying something to it; but he never told what it was he said to it. Niggers would come from all around there and give Jim anything they had, just for a sight of that five-center piece; but they wouldn't touch it, because the devil had had his hands on it. Jim was most ruined, for a servant, because he got so stuck up on account of having seen the devil and been rode by witches.

Well, when Tom and me got to the edge of the hill-top, we looked away down into the village[7] and could see three or four lights twinkling, where there was sick folks, may be; and the stars over us was sparkling ever so fine; and down by the village was the river, a whole mile broad, and awful still and grand. We went down the hill and found Jo Harper, and Ben Rogers, and two or three more of the boys, hid in the old tanyard. So we unhitched a skiff and pulled down the river two mile and a half, to the big scar on the hillside, and went ashore.

We went to a clump of bushes, and Tom made everybody swear to keep the secret, and then showed them a hole in the hill, right in the thickest part of the bushes. Then we lit the candles and crawled in on our hands and knees. We went about two hundred yards, and then the cave opened up. Tom poked about amongst the passages and pretty soon ducked under a wall where you wouldn't a noticed that there was a hole. We went along a narrow place and got into a kind of room, all damp and sweaty and cold, and there we stopped. Tom says:

"Now we'll start this band of robbers and call it Tom Sawyer's Gang. Everybody that wants to join has got to take an oath, and write his name in blood."

Everybody was willing. So Tom got out a sheet of paper that he had wrote the oath on, and read it. It swore every boy to stick to the band, and never tell any of its secrets; and if anybody done anything to any boy in the band, whichever boy was ordered to kill

7. Hannibal, Missouri; other frontier river towns described in this book really portray various aspects of Hannibal.

that person and his family must do it, and he mustn't eat and he mustn't sleep till he had killed them and hacked a cross in their breasts, which was the sign of the band. And nobody that didn't belong to the band could use that mark, and if he did he must be sued; and if he done it again he must be killed. And if anybody that belonged to the band told the secrets, he must have his throat cut, and then have his carcass burnt up and the ashes scattered all around, and his name blotted off of the list with blood and never mentioned again by the gang, but have a curse put on it and be forgot, forever.

Everybody said it was a real beautiful oath, and asked Tom if he got it out of his own head. He said, some of it, but the rest was out of pirate books, and robber books, and every gang that was high-toned had it.[8]

Some thought it would be good to kill the *families* of boys that told the secrets. Tom said it was a good idea, so he took a pencil and wrote it in. Then Ben Rogers says:

"Here's Huck Finn, he hain't got no family—what you going to do 'bout him?"

"Well, hain't he got a father?" says Tom Sawyer.

"Yes, he's got a father, but you can't never find him, these days. He used to lay drunk with the hogs in the tanyard, but he hain't been seen in these parts for a year or more."

They talked it over, and they was going to rule me out, because they said every boy must have a family or somebody to kill, or else it wouldn't be fair and square for the others. Well, nobody could think of anything to do—everybody was stumped, and set still. I was most ready to cry; but all at once I thought of a way, and so I offered them Miss Watson—they could kill her. Everybody said:

"Oh, she'll do, she'll do. That's all right. Huck can come in."

Then they all stuck a pin in their fingers to get blood to sign with, and I made my mark on the paper.

"Now," says Ben Rogers, "what's the line of business of this Gang?"

"Nothing only robbery and murder," Tom said.

"But who are we going to rob? houses—or cattle—or—"

"Stuff! stealing cattle and such things ain't robbery, it's burglary," says Tom Sawyer. "We ain't burglars. That ain't no sort of style. We are highwaymen. We stop stages and carriages on the road, with masks on, and kill the people and take their watches and money."

"Must we always kill the people?"

8. Twain's comic portrayal of the boy's world of make-believe is consistent with his ridicule of romantic fiction and its writers.

"Oh, certainly. It's best. Some authorities think different, but mostly it's considered best to kill them. Except some that you bring to the cave here and keep them till they're ransomed."

"Ransomed? What's that?"

"I don't know. But that's what they do. I've seen it in books; and so of course that's what we've got to do."

"But how can we do it if we don't know what it is?"

"Why blame it all, we've *got* to do it. Don't I tell you it's in the books? Do you want to go to doing different from what's in the books, and get things all muddled up?"

"Oh, that's all very fine to *say*, Tom Sawyer, but how in the nation[9] are these fellows going to be ransomed if we don't know how to do it to them? that's the thing I want to get at. Now what do you *reckon* it is?"

"Well I don't know. But per'aps if we keep them till they're ransomed, it means that we keep them till they're dead."

"Now, that's something *like*. That'll answer. Why couldn't you said that before? We'll keep them till they're ransomed to death —and a bothersome lot they'll be, too, eating up everything and always trying to get loose."

"How you talk, Ben Rogers. How can they get loose when there's a guard over them, ready to shoot them down if they move a peg?"

"A guard. Well, that *is* good. So somebody's got to set up all night and never get any sleep, just so as to watch them. I think that's foolishness. Why can't a body take a club and ransom them as soon as they get here?"

"Because it ain't in the books so—that's why. Now Ben Rogers, do you want to do things regular, or don't you?—that's the idea. Don't you reckon that the people that made the books knows what's the correct thing to do? Do you reckon *you* can learn 'em anything? Not by a good deal. No, sir, we'll just go on and ransom them in the regular way."

"All right. I don't mind; but I say it's a fool way, anyhow. Say —do we kill the women, too?"

"Well, Ben Rogers, if I was as ignorant as you I wouldn't let on. Kill the women? No—nobody ever saw anything in the books like that. You fetch them to the cave, and you're always as polite as pie to them; and by-and-by they fall in love with you and never want to go home any more."

"Well, if that's the way, I'm agreed, but I don't take no stock in it. Mighty soon we'll have the cave so cluttered up with women, and fellows waiting to be ransomed, that there won't be no place for the robbers. But go ahead, I ain't got nothing to say."

9. Euphemism for "damnation."

Little Tommy Barnes was asleep, now, and when they waked him up he was scared, and cried, and said he wanted to go home to his ma, and didn't want to be a robber any more.

So they all made fun of him, and called him cry-baby, and that made him mad, and he said he would go straight and tell all the secrets. But Tom give him five cents to keep quiet, and said we would all go home and meet next week and rob somebody and kill some people.

Ben Rogers said he couldn't get out much, only Sundays, and so he wanted to begin next Sunday; but all the boys said it would be wicked to do it on Sunday, and that settled the thing. They agreed to get together and fix a day as soon as they could, and then we elected Tom Sawyer first captain and Jo Harper second captain of the Gang, and so started home.

I clumb up the shed and crept into my window just before day was breaking. My new clothes was all greased up and clayey, and I was dog-tired.

Chapter III

Well, I got a good going-over in the morning, from old Miss Watson, on account of my clothes; but the widow she didn't scold, but only cleaned off the grease and clay and looked so sorry that I thought I would behave a while if I could. Then Miss Watson she took me in the closet and prayed, but nothing come of it. She told me to pray every day, and whatever I asked for I would get it. But it warn't so. I tried it. Once I got a fish-line, but no hooks. It warn't any good to me without hooks. I tried for the hooks three or four times, but somehow I couldn't make it work. By-and-by, one day, I asked Miss Watson to try for me, but she said I was a fool. She never told me why, and I couldn't make it out no way.

I set down, one time, back in the woods, and had a long think about it. I says to myself, if a body can get anything they pray for, why don't Deacon Winn get back the money he lost on pork? Why can't the widow get back her silver snuff-box that was stole? Why can't Miss Watson fat up? No, says I to myself, there ain't nothing in it. I went and told the widow about it, and she said the thing a body could get by praying for it was "spiritual gifts." This was too many for me, but she told me what she meant—I must help other people, and do everything I could for other people, and look out for them all the time, and never think about myself. This was including Miss Watson, as I took it. I went out in the woods and turned it over in my mind a long time, but I couldn't see no advantage about it—except for the other people—so at last I reckoned I wouldn't worry about it any more, but just let it go.

Sometimes the widow would take me one side and talk about Providence in a way to make a boy's mouth water; but maybe next day Miss Watson would take hold and knock it all down again. I judged I could see that there was two Providences, and a poor chap would stand considerable show with the widow's Providence, but if Miss Watson's got him there warn't no help for him any more. I thought it all out, and reckoned I would belong to the widow's, if he wanted me, though I couldn't make out how he was agoing to be any better off then than what he was before, seeing I was so ignorant and so kind of low-down and ornery.[1]

Pap he hadn't been seen for more than a year, and that was comfortable for me; I didn't want to see him no more. He used to always whale me when he was sober and could get his hands on me; though I used to take to the woods most of the time when he was around. Well, about this time he was found in the river drowned, about twelve miles above town, so people said. They judged it was him, anyway; said this drowned man was just his size, and was ragged, and had uncommon long hair—which was all like pap— but they couldn't make nothing out of the face, because it had been in the water so long it warn't much like a face at all. They said he was floating on his back in the water. They took him and buried him on the bank. But I warn't comfortable long, because I happened to think of something. I knowed mighty well that a drownded man don't float on his back, but on his face. So I knowed, then, that this warn't pap, but a woman dressed up in a man's clothes. So I was uncomfortable again. I judged the old man would turn up again by-and-by, though I wished he wouldn't.

We played robber now and then about a month, and then I resigned. All the boys did. We hadn't robbed nobody, we hadn't killed any people, but only just pretended. We used to hop out of the woods and go charging down on hog-drovers and women in carts taking garden stuff to market, but we never hived any of them. Tom Sawyer called the hogs "ingots," and he called the turnips and stuff "julery" and we would go to the cave and pow-wow over what we had done and how many people we had killed and marked. But I couldn't see no profit in it. One time Tom sent a boy to run about town with a blazing stick, which he called a slogan (which was the sign for the Gang to get together), and then he said he had got secret news by his spies that the next day a whole parcel of Spanish merchants and rich A-rabs was going to camp in Cave Hollow with two hundred elephants, and six hundred camels, and over a thousand "sumter" mules, all loaded with di'monds, and they didn't have only a guard of four hundred sol-

1. Like Huck, the author pondered religious faith. Of the many instances in his writings, the massive example is *The Mysterious Stranger*. His comic criticism is largely of sentimentality and cant.

diers, and so we would lay in ambuscade, as he called it, and kill the lot and scoop the things. He said we must slick up our swords and guns, and get ready. He never could go after even a turnip-cart but he must have the swords and guns all scoured up for it; though they was only lath and broom-sticks, and you might scour at them till you rotted and then they warn't worth a mouthful of ashes more than what they was before. I didn't believe we could lick such a crowd of Spaniards and A-rabs, but I wanted to see the camels and elephants, so I was on hand next day, Saturday, in the ambuscade; and when we got the word, we rushed out of the woods and down the hill. But there warn't no Spaniards and A-rabs, and there warn't no camels nor no elephants. It warn't anything but a Sunday-school picnic, and only a primer-class at that. We busted it up, and chased the children up the hollow; but we never got anything but some doughnuts and jam, though Ben Rogers got a rag doll, and Jo Harper got a hymn-book and a tract; and then the teacher charged in and made us drop everything and cut. I didn't see no di'monds, and I told Tom Sawyer so. He said there was loads of them there, anyway; and he said there was A-rabs there, too, and elephants and things. I said, why couldn't we see them, then? He said if I warn't so ignorant, but had read a book called "Don Quixote," I would know without asking. He said it was all done by enchantment. He said there was hundreds of soldiers there, and elephants and treasure, and so on, but we had enemies which he called magicians, and they had turned the whole thing into an infant Sunday school, just for spite. I said, all right, then the thing for us to do was to go for the magicians. Tom Sawyer said I was a numskull.

"Why," says he, "a magician could call up a lot of genies, and they would hash you up like nothing before you could say Jack Robinson. They are as tall as a tree and as big around as a church."

"Well," I says, "s'pose we got some genies to help *us*—can't we lick the other crowd then?"

"How are you going to get them?"

"I don't know. How do *they* get them?"

"Why they rub an old tin lamp or an iron ring, and then the genies come tearing in, with the thunder and lightning a-ripping around and the smoke a-rolling, and everything they're told to do they up and do it. They don't think nothing of pulling a shot tower up by the roots, and belting a Sunday-school superintendent over the head with it—or any other man."[2]

2. The foregoing medley of events drawn from the ancient *Arabian Nights* (Aladdin's lamp) and Cervantes' seventeenth-century *Don Quixote* represents a cross-section of Tom's mind and Twain's memory of his childhood reading. More importantly, these make-believe adventures provide the background for the real experience of Huck and Jim in the escape down the river.

"Who makes them tear around so?"

"Why, whoever rubs the lamp or the ring. They belong to whoever rubs the lamp or the ring, and they've got to do whatever he says. If he tells them to build a palace forty miles long, out of di'monds, and fill it full of chewing gum, or whatever you want, and fetch an emperor's daughter from China for you to marry, they've got to do it—and they've got to do it before sun-up next morning, too. And more—they've got to waltz that palace around over the country wherever you want it, you understand."

"Well," says I, "I think they are a pack of fatheads for not keeping the palace themselves 'stead of fooling them away like that. And what's more—if I was one of them I would see a man in Jericho before I would drop my business and come to him for the rubbing of an old tin lamp."

"How you talk, Huck Finn. Why, you'd *have* to come when he rubbed it, whether you wanted to or not."

"What, and I as high as a tree and as big as a church? All right, then; I *would* come; but I lay I'd make that man climb the highest tree there was in the country."

"Shucks, it ain't no use to talk to you, Huck Finn. You don't seem to know anything, somehow—perfect sap-head."

I thought all this over for two or three days, and then I reckoned I would see if there was anything in it. I got an old tin lamp and an iron ring and went out in the woods and rubbed and rubbed till I sweat like an Injun, calculating to build a palace and sell it; but it warn't no use, none of the genies came. So then I judged that all that stuff was only just one of Tom Sawyer's lies. I reckoned he believed in the A-rabs and the elephants, but as for me I think different. It had all the marks of a Sunday school.[3]

Chapter IV

Well, three or four months run along, and it was well into the winter, now. I had been to school most all the time, and could spell, and read, and write just a little, and could say the multiplication table up to six times seven is thirty-five, and I don't reckon I could ever get any further than that if I was to live forever. I don't take no stock in mathematics, anyway.

At first I hated the school, but by-and-by I got so I could stand it. Whenever I got uncommon tired I played hookey, and the hiding I got next day done me good and cheered me up. So the longer I went to school the easier it got to be. I was getting sort of used to the widow's ways, too, and they warn't so raspy on me. Living in a

3. Huck identifies the fanciful elements of romance with the supernatural elements of religion.

house, and sleeping in a bed, pulled on me pretty tight, mostly, but before the cold weather I used to slide out and sleep in the woods, sometimes, and so that was a rest to me. I liked the old ways best, but I was getting so I liked the new ones, too, a little bit. The widow said I was coming along slow but sure, and doing very satisfactory. She said she warn't ashamed of me.

One morning I happened to turn over the salt-cellar at breakfast. I reached for some of it as quick as I could, to throw over my left shoulder and keep off the bad luck, but Miss Watson was in ahead of me, and crossed me off. She says, "Take your hands away, Huckleberry—what a mess you are always making." The widow put in a good word for me, but that warn't going to keep off the bad luck, I knowed that well enough. I started out, after breakfast, feeling worried and shaky, and wondering where it was going to fall on me, and what it was going to be. There is ways to keep off some kinds of bad luck, but this wasn't one of them kind; so I never tried to do anything, but just poked along low-spirited and on the watch-out.

I went down the front garden and clumb over the stile, where you go through the high board fence. There was an inch of new snow on the ground, and I seen somebody's tracks. They had come up from the quarry and stood around the stile a while, and then went on around the garden fence. It was funny they hadn't come in, after standing around so. I couldn't make it out. It was very curious, somehow. I was going to follow around, but I stooped down to look at the tracks first. I didn't notice anything at first, but next I did. There was a cross in the left boot-heel made with big nails, to keep off the devil.

I was up in a second and shinning down the hill. I looked over my shoulder every now and then, but I didn't see nobody. I was at Judge Thatcher's as quick as I could get there. He said:

"Why, my boy, you are all out of breath. Did you come for your interest?"

"No sir," I says; "is there some for me?"

"Oh, yes, a half-yearly is in, last night. Over a hundred and fifty dollars. Quite a fortune for you. You better let me invest it along with your six thousand, because if you take it you'll spend it."

"No sir," I says, "I don't want to spend it. I don't want it at all —nor the six thousand, nuther. I want you to take it; I want to give it to you—the six thousand and all."

He looked surprised. He couldn't seem to make it out. He says:

"Why, what can you mean, my boy?"

I says, "Don't you ask me no questions about it, please. You'll take it—won't you?"

He says:

"Well I'm puzzled. Is something the matter?"

"Please take it," says I, "and don't ask me nothing—then I won't have to tell no lies."

He studied a while, and then he says:

"Oho-o. I think I see. You want to *sell* all your property to me—not give it. That's the correct idea."

Then he wrote something on a paper and read it over, and says:

"There—you see it says 'for a consideration.' That means I have bought it of you and paid you for it. Here's a dollar for you. Now, you sign it."

So I signed it, and left.

Miss Watson's nigger, Jim, had a hair-ball as big as your fist, which had been took out of the fourth stomach of an ox, and he used to do magic with it.[4] He said there was a spirit inside of it, and it knowed everything. So I went to him that night and told him pap was here again, for I found his tracks in the snow. What I wanted to know, was, what he was going to do, and was he going to stay? Jim got out his hair-ball, and said something over it, and then he held it up and dropped it on the floor. It fell pretty solid, and only rolled about an inch. Jim tried it again, and then another time, and it acted just the same. Jim got down on his knees and put his ear against it and listened. But it warn't no use; he said it wouldn't talk. He said sometimes it wouldn't talk without money. I told him I had an old slick counterfeit quarter that warn't no good because the brass showed through the silver a little, and it wouldn't pass nohow, even if the brass didn't show, because it was so slick it felt greasy, and so that would tell on it every time. (I reckoned I wouldn't say nothing about the dollar I got from the judge.) I said it was pretty bad money, but maybe the hair-ball would take it, because maybe it wouldn't know the difference. Jim smelt it, and bit it, and rubbed it, and said he would manage so the hair-ball would think it was good. He said he would split open a raw Irish potato and stick the quarter in between and keep it there all night, and next morning you couldn't see no brass, and it wouldn't feel greasy no more, and so anybody in town would take it in a minute, let alone a hair-ball. Well, I knowed a potato would do that, before, but I had forgot it.

Jim put the quarter under the hair-ball and got down and listened again. This time he said the hair-ball was all right. He said it would tell my whole fortune if I wanted it to. I says, go on. So the hair-ball talked to Jim, and Jim told it to me. He says:

"Yo' ole father doan' know, yit, what he's a-gwyne to do. Some-

4. Visceral objects, like the hair-ball, have had ancient sooth-saying significance.

times he spec he'll go 'way, en den agin he spec he'll stay. De bes' way is to res' easy en let de ole man take his own way. Dey's two angels hoverin' roun' 'bout him. One uv 'em is white en shiny, en 'tother one is black. De white one gits him to go right, a little while, den de black one sail in en bust it all up. A body can't tell, yit, which one gwyne to fetch him at de las'. But you is all right. You gwyne to have considable trouble in yo' life, en considable joy. Sometimes you gwyne to git hurt, en sometimes you gwyne to git sick; but every time you's gwyne to git well agin. Dey's two gals flyin' 'bout you in yo' life. One uv 'em's light en 'tother one is dark. One is rich en 'tother is po'. You's gwyne to marry de po' one fust en de rich one by-en-by. You wants to keep 'way fum de water as much as you kin, en don't run no resk, 'kase it's down in de bills dat you's gwyne to git hung."

When I lit my candle and went up to my room that night, there set pap, his own self!

Chapter V

I had shut the door to. Then I turned around, and there he was. I used to be scared of him all the time, he tanned me so much. I reckoned I was scared now, too; but in a minute I see I was mistaken. That is, after the first jolt, as you may say, when my breath sort of hitched—he being so unexpected; but right away after, I see I warn't scared of him worth bothering about.

He was most fifty, and he looked it. His hair was long and tangled and greasy, and hung down, and you could see his eyes shining through like he was behind vines. It was all black, no gray; so was his long, mixed-up whiskers. There warn't no color in his face, where his face showed; it was white; not like another man's white, but a white to make a body sick, a white to make a body's flesh crawl—a tree-toad white, a fish-belly white. As for his clothes—just rags, that was all. He had one ankle resting on 'tother knee; the boot on that foot was busted, and two of his toes stuck through, and he worked them now and then. His hat was laying on the floor; an old black slouch with the top caved in, like a lid.

I stood a-looking at him; he set there a-looking at me, with his chair tilted back a little. I set the candle down. I noticed the window was up; so he had clumb in by the shed. He kept a-looking me all over. By-and-by he says:

"Starchy clothes—very. You think you're a good deal of a big-bug, *don't* you?"

"Maybe I am, maybe I ain't," I says.

"Don't you give me none o' your lip," says he. "You've put on considerble many frills since I been away. I'll take you down a peg before I get done with you. You're educated, too, they say; can read and write. You think you're better'n your father, now, don't you, because he can't? *I'll* take it out of you. Who told you you might meddle with such hifalut'n foolishness, hey?—who told you you could?"

"The widow. She told me."

"The widow, hey?—and who told the widow she could put in her shovel about a thing that ain't none of her business?"

"Nobody never told her."

"Well, I'll learn her how to meddle. And looky here—you drop that school, you hear? I'll learn people to bring up a boy to put on airs over his own father and let on to be better'n what *he* is. You lemme catch you fooling around that school again, you hear? Your mother couldn't read, and she couldn't write, nuther, before she died. None of the family couldn't, before *they* died. *I* can't; and here you're a-swelling yourself up like this. I ain't the man to stand it—you hear? Say—lemme hear you read."

I took up a book and begun something about General Washington and the wars. When I'd read about a half a minute, he fetched the book a whack with his hand and knocked it across the house. He says:

"It's so. You can do it. I had my doubts when you told me. Now looky here; you stop that putting on frills. I won't have it. I'll lay for you, my smarty; and if I catch you about that school I'll tan you good. First you know you'll get religion, too. I never see such a son."

He took up a little blue and yaller picture of some cows and a boy, and says:

"What's this?"

"It's something they give me for learning my lessons good."

He tore it up, and says—

"I'll give you something better—I'll give you a cowhide."

He set there a-mumbling and a-growling a minute, and then he says—

"*Ain't* you a sweet-scented dandy, though? A bed; and bedclothes; and a look'n-glass; and a piece of carpet on the floor—and your own father got to sleep with the hogs in the tanyard. I never see such a son. I bet I'll take some o' these frills out o' you before I'm done with you. Why there ain't no end to your airs—they say you're rich. Hey?—how's that?"

"They lie—that's how."

"Looky here—mind how you talk to me; I'm a-standing about all I can stand, now—so don't gimme no sass. I've been in town two days, and I hain't heard nothing but about you bein' rich. I heard about it away down the river, too. That's why I come. You git me that money to-morrow—I want it."

"I hain't got no money."

"It's a lie. Judge Thatcher's got it. You git it. I want it."

"I hain't got no money, I tell you. You ask Judge Thatcher; he'll tell you the same."

"All right. I'll ask him; and I'll make him pungle,[5] too, or I'll know the reason why. Say—how much you got in your pocket? I want it."

"I hain't got only a dollar, and I want that to—"

"It don't make no difference what you want it for—you just shell it out."

He took it and bit it to see if it was good, and then he said he was going down town to get some whisky; said he hadn't had a drink all day. When he had got out on the shed, he put his head in again, and cussed me for putting on frills and trying to be better than him; and when I reckoned he was gone, he come back and put his head in again, and told me to mind about that school, because he was going to lay for me and lick me if I didn't drop that.

Next day he was drunk, and he went to Judge Thatcher's and bullyragged him and tried to make him give up the money, but he couldn't, and then he swore he'd make the law force him.

The judge and the widow went to law to get the court to take me away from him and let one of them be my guardian; but it was a new judge that had just come, and he didn't know the old man; so he said courts mustn't interfere and separate families if they can help it; said he'd druther not take a child away from its father. So Judge Thatcher and the widow had to quit on the business.

That pleased the old man till he couldn't rest. He said he'd cowhide me till I was black and blue if I didn't raise some money for him. I borrowed three dollars from Judge Thatcher, and pap took it and got drunk and went a-blowing around and cussing and whooping and carrying on; and he kept it up all over town, with a tin pan, till most midight; then they jailed him, and next day they had him before court, and jailed him again for a week. But he said *he* was satisfied; said he was boss of his son, and he'd make it warm for *him*.

When he got out the new judge said he was agoing to make a man of him. So he took him to his own house, and dressed him up clean and nice, and had him to breakfast and dinner and supper with the family, and was just old pie to him, so to speak. And after supper he talked to him about temperance and such things till the old man cried, and said he'd been a fool, and fooled away his life;

5. Pay, or give up. Pap is claiming his legal right to his son's possessions. That is why, in Chapter IV, as soon as Huck saw his father's footprints he made a nominal transfer of his money to Judge Thatcher.

but now he was agoing to turn over a new leaf and be a man nobody wouldn't be ashamed of, and he hoped the judge would help
him and not look down on him. The judge said he could hug him
for them words; so *he* cried, and his wife she cried again; pap said
he'd been a man that had always been misunderstood before, and
the judge said he believed it. The old man said that what a man
wanted that was down, was sympathy; and the judge said it was so;
so they cried again. And when it was bedtime, the old man rose up
and held out his hand, and says:

"Look at it gentlemen, and ladies all; take ahold of it; shake it.
There's a hand that was the hand of a hog; but it ain't so no more;
it's the hand of a man that's started in on a new life, and 'll die
before he'll go back. You mark them words—don't forget I said
them. It's a clean hand now; shake it—don't be afeard."

So they shook it, one after the other, all around, and cried. The
judge's wife she kissed it. Then the old man he signed a pledge—
made his mark. The judge said it was the holiest time on record, or
something like that. Then they tucked the old man into a beautiful
room, which was the spare room, and in the night sometime he got
powerful thirsty and clumb out onto the porch-roof and slid down
a stanchion and traded his new coat for a jug of forty-rod,[6] and
clumb back again and had a good old time; and towards daylight he
crawled out again, drunk as a fiddler, and rolled off the porch and
broke his left arm in two places and was most froze to death when
somebody found him after sun-up. And when they come to look at
that spare room, they had to take soundings before they could navi-
gate it.

The judge he felt kind of sore. He said he reckoned a body could
reform the ole man with a shot-gun, maybe, but he didn't know no
other way.

Chapter VI

Well, pretty soon the old man was up and around again, and
then he went for Judge Thatcher in the courts to make him give up
that money, and he went for me, too, for not stopping school. He
catched me a couple of times and thrashed me, but I went to school
just the same, and dodged him or out-run him most of the time. I
didn't want to go to school much, before, but I reckoned I'd go now
to spite pap. That law trial was a slow business; appeared like they
warn't ever going to get started on it; so every now and then I'd
borrow two or three dollars off of the judge for him, to keep from
getting a cowhiding. Every time he got money he got drunk; and
every time he got drunk he raised Cain around town; and every time

6. **Whiskey** strong enough to knock a man forty rods.

he raised Cain he got jailed. He was just suited—this kind of thing was right in his line.

He got to hanging around the widow's too much, and so she told him at last, that if he didn't quit using around there she would make trouble for him. Well, *wasn't* he mad? He said he would show who was Huck Finn's boss. So he watched out for me one day in the spring, and catched me, and took me up the river about three mile, in a skiff, and crossed over to the Illinois shore where it was woody and there warn't no houses but an old log hut in a place where the timber was so thick you couldn't find it if you didn't know where it was.

He kept me with him all the time, and I never got a chance to run off. We lived in that old cabin, and he always locked the door and put the key under his head, nights. He had a gun which he had stole, I reckon, and we fished and hunted, and that was what we lived on. Every little while he locked me in and went down to the store, three miles, to the ferry, and traded fish and game for whisky and fetched it home and got drunk and had a good time, and licked me. The widow she found out where I was, by-and-by, and she sent a man over to try to get hold of me, but pap drove him off with the gun, and it warn't long after that till I was used to being where I was, and liked it, all but the cowhide part.

It was kind of lazy and jolly, laying off comfortable all day, smoking and fishing, and no books nor study. Two months or more run along, and my clothes got to be all rags and dirt, and I didn't see how I'd ever got to like it so well at the widow's, where you had to wash, and eat on a plate, and comb up, and go to bed and get up regular, and be forever bothering over a book and have old Miss Watson pecking at you all the time. I didn't want to go back no more. I had stopped cussing, because the widow didn't like it; but now I took to it again because pap hadn't no objections. It was pretty good times up in the woods there, take it all around.

But by-and-by pap got too handy with his hick'ry, and I couldn't stand it. I was all over welts. He got to going away so much, too, and locking me in. Once he locked me in and was gone three days. It was dreadful lonesome. I judged he had got drowned and I wasn't ever going to get out any more. I was scared. I made up my mind I would fix up some way to leave there. I had tried to get out of that cabin many a time, but I couldn't find no way. There warn't a window to it big enought for a dog to get through. I couldn't get up the chimbly, it was too narrow. The door was thick solid oak slabs. Pap was pretty careful not to leave a knife or anything in the cabin when he was away; I reckon I had hunted the place over as much as a hundred times; well, I was 'most all the time at it, because it was about the only way to put in the time. But this time

I found something at last; I found an old rusty wood-saw without any handle; it was laid in between a rafter and the clapboards of the roof. I greased it up and went to work. There was an old horse-blanket nailed against the logs at the far end of the cabin behind the table, to keep the wind from blowing through the chinks and putting the candle out. I got under the table and raised the blanket and went to work to saw a section of the big bottom log out, big enough to let me through. Well, it was a good long job, but I was getting towards the end of it when I heard pap's gun in the woods. I got rid of the signs of my work, and dropped the blanket and hid my saw, and pretty soon pap come in.

Pap warn't in a good humor—so he was his natural self. He said he was down to town, and everything was going wrong. His lawyer said he reckoned he would win his lawsuit and get the money, if they ever got started on the trial; but then there was ways to put it off a long time, and Judge Thatcher knowed how to do it. And he said people allowed there'd be another trial to get me away from him and give me to the widow for my guardian, and they guessed it would win, this time. This shook me up considerable, because I didn't want to go back to the widow's any more and be so cramped up and sivilized, as they called it. Then the old man got to cussing, and cussed everything and everybody he could think of, and then cussed them all over again to make sure he hadn't skipped any, and after that he polished off with a kind of a general cuss all round, including a considerable parcel of people which he didn't know the names of, and so called them what's-his-name, when he got to them, and went right along with his cussing.

He said he would like to see the widow get me. He said he would watch out, and if they tried to come any such game on him he knowed of a place six or seven mile off, to stow me in, where they might hunt till they dropped and they couldn't find me. That made me pretty uneasy again, but only for a minute; I reckoned I wouldn't stay on hand till he got that chance.[7]

The old man made me go to the skiff and fetch the things he had got. There was a fifty-pound sack of corn meal, and a side of bacon, ammunition, and a four-gallon jug of whisky, and an old book and two newspapers for wadding,[8] besides some tow.[9] I toted up a load, and went back and set down on the bow of the skiff to rest. I thought it all over, and I reckoned I would walk off with the gun and some lines, and take to the woods when I run away. I guessed I wouldn't stay in one place, but just tramp right across the country,

7. Preferring the freedom of the woods to the restrictions of town life, Huck does not make the final decision to escape until he has genuine fears for his own safety. This illustrates one factor of the concept of freedom which the novel defines.

8. Material employed in packing the load of the guns of the period.

9. Rope made from broken strands of flax or hemp.

mostly night times, and hunt and fish to keep alive, and so get so far away that the old man nor the widow couldn't ever find me any more. I judged I would saw out and leave that night if pap got drunk enough, and I reckoned he would. I got so full of it I didn't notice how long I was staying, till the old man hollered and asked me whether I was asleep or drownded.

I got the things all up to the cabin, and then it was about dark. While I was cooking supper the old man took a swig or two and got sort of warmed up, and went to ripping again. He had been drunk over in town, and laid in the gutter all night, and he was a sight to look at. A body would a thought he was Adam, he was just all mud. Whenever his liquor begun to work, he most always went for the govment. This time he says:

"Call this a govment! why, just look at it and see what it's like. Here's the law a-standing ready to take a man's son away from him —a man's own son, which he has had all the trouble and all the anxiety and all the expense of raising. Yes, just as that man has got that son raised at last, and ready to go to work and begin to do suthin' for *him* and give him a rest, the law up and goes for him. And they call *that* govment! That ain't all, nuther. The law backs that old Judge Thatcher up and helps him to keep me out o' my property. Here's what the law does. The law takes a man worth six thousand dollars and upards, and jams him into an old trap of a cabin like this, and lets him go round in clothes that ain't fitten for a hog. They call that govment! A man can't get his rights in a govment like this. Sometimes I've a mighty notion to just leave the country for good and all. Yes, and I *told* 'em so; I told old Thatcher so to his face. Lots of 'em heard me, and can tell what I said. Says I, for two cents I'd leave the blamed country and never come anear it agin. Them's the very words. I says, look at my hat—if you call it a hat—but the lid raises up and the rest of it goes down till it's below my chin, and then it ain't rightly a hat at all, but more like my head was shoved up through a jint o' stove-pipe. Look at it, says I—such a hat for me to wear—one of the wealthiest men in this town, if I could git my rights.

"Oh, yes, this is a wonderful govment, wonderful. Why, looky here. There was a free nigger there, from Ohio; a mulatter, most as white as a white man. He had the whitest shirt on you ever see, too, and the shiniest hat; and there ain't a man in that town that's got as fine clothes as what he had; and he had a gold watch and chain, and a silver-headed cane—the awfulest old gray-headed nabob in the State. And what do you think? they said he was a p'fessor in a college, and could talk all kinds of languages, and knowed every-thing. And that ain't the wust. They said he could *vote*, when he was at home. Well, that let me out. Thinks I, what is the country a-coming to? It was 'lection day, and I was just about to go and vote, myself, if I warn't too drunk to get there; but when they told me there was a State in this country where they'd let that nigger vote, I drawed out. I says I'll never vote again. Them's the very words I said; they all heard me; and the country may rot for all me —I'll never vote agin as long as I live. And to see the cool way of that nigger—why, he wouldn't a give me the road if I hadn't shoved him out o' the way. I says to the people, why ain't this nigger put up at auction and sold?—that's what I want to know. And what do you reckon they said? Why, they said he couldn't be sold till he'd been in the State six months, and he hadn't been there that long yet. There, now—that's a specimen. They call that a govment that can't sell a free nigger till he's been in the State six months. Here's a govment that calls itself a govment, and lets on to be a govment, and thinks it is a govment, and yet's got to set stock-still for six whole months before it can take ahold of a prowling, thieving, infernal, white-shirted free nigger, and—"[1]

Pap was agoing on so, he never noticed where his old limber legs was taking him to, so he went head over heels over the tub of salt pork, and barked both shins, and the rest of his speech was all the hottest kind of language—mostly hove at the nigger and the govment, though he give the tub some, too, all along, here and there. He hopped around the cabin considerable, first on one leg and then on the other, holding first one shin and then the other one, and at last he let out with his left foot all of a sudden and fetched the tub a rattling kick. But it warn't good judgment, because that was the boot that had a couple of his toes leaking out of the front end of it; so now he raised a howl that fairly made a body's hair raise, and down he went in the dirt, and rolled there, and held his toes; and the cussing he done then laid over anything he had ever done previous. He said so his own self, afterwards. He had heard old Sowberry Hagan in his best days, and he said it laid over him, too; but I reckon that was sort of piling it on, maybe.

After supper pap took the jug, and said he had enough whisky there for two drunks and one delirium tremens. That was always his word. I judged he would be blind drunk in about an hour, and then I would steal the key, or saw myself out, one or 'tother. He drank, and drank, and tumbled down on his blankets, by-and-by; but luck didn't run my way. He didn't go sound asleep, but was uneasy. He groaned, and moaned, and thrashed around this way and that, for a long time. At last I got so sleepy I couldn't keep my eyes open, all I could do, and so before I knowed what I was about I was sound asleep, and the candle burning.

1. According to Dixon Wecter, *Sam Clemens of Hannibal*, there were free Negroes in Hannibal in the 1840's.

I don't know how long I was asleep, but all of a sudden there was an awful scream and I was up. There was pap, looking wild and skipping around every which way and yelling about snakes. He said they was crawling up his legs; and then he would give a jump and scream, and say one had bit him on the cheek—but I couldn't see no snakes. He started and run round and round the cabin, hollering "take him off! take him off! he's biting me on the neck!" I never see a man look so wild in the eyes. Pretty soon he was all fagged out, and fell down panting; then he rolled over and over, wonderful fast, kicking things every which way, and striking and grabbing at the air with his hands, and screaming, and saying there was devils ahold of him. He wore out, by-and-by, and laid still a while, moaning. Then he laid stiller, and didn't make a sound. I could hear the owls and the wolves, away off in the woods, and it seemed terrible still. He was laying over by the corner. By-and-by he raised up, part way, and listened, with his head to one side. He says very low:

"Tramp—tramp—tramp; that's the dead; tramp—tramp—tramp; they're coming after me; but I won't go— Oh, they're here! don't touch me—don't! hands off—they're cold; let go— Oh, let a poor devil alone!"

Then he went down on all fours and crawled off begging them to let him alone, and he rolled himself up in his blanket and wallowed in under the old pine table, still a-begging; and then he went to crying. I could hear him through the blanket.

By-and-by he rolled out and jumped up on his feet looking wild, and he see me and went for me. He chased me round and round the place, with a clasp-knife, calling me the Angel of Death and saying he would kill me and then I couldn't come for him no more. I begged, and told him I was only Huck, but he laughed *such* a screechy laugh, and roared and cussed, and kept on chasing me up. Once when I turned short and dodged under his arm he made a grab and got me by the jacket between my shoulders, and I thought I was gone; but I slid out of the jacket quick as lightning, and saved myself. Pretty soon he was all tired out, and dropped down with his back against the door, and said he would rest a minute and then kill me. He put his knife under him, and said he would sleep and get strong, and then he would see who was who.

So he dozed off, pretty soon. By-and-by I got the old split-bottom[2] chair and clumb up, as easy as I could, not to make any noise, and got down the gun. I slipped the ramrod down it to make sure it was loaded, and then I laid it across the turnip barrel, pointing towards pap, and set down behind it to wait for him to stir. And how slow and still the time did drag along.

2. *I.e.,* splint-bottom.

Chapter VII

"Git up! what you 'bout!"

I opened my eyes and looked around, trying to make out where I was. It was after sun-up, and I had been sound asleep. Pap was standing over me, looking sour—and sick, too. He says—

"What you doin' with this gun?"

I judged he didn't know nothing about what he had been doing, so I says:

"Somebody tried to get in, so I was laying for him."

"Why didn't you roust me out?"

"Well I tried to, but I couldn't; I couldn't budge you."

"Well, all right. Don't stand there palavering all day, but out with you and see if there's a fish on the lines for breakfast. I'll be along in a minute."

He unlocked the door and I cleared out, up the river bank. I noticed some pieces of limbs and such things floating down, and a sprinkling of bark; so I knowed the river had begun to rise. I reckoned I would have great times, now, if I was over at the town. The June rise used to be always luck for me; because as soon as that rise begins, here comes cord-wood floating down, and pieces of log rafts —sometimes a dozen logs together; so all you have to do is to catch them and sell them to the wood yards and the sawmill.

I went along up the bank with one eye out for pap and 'tother one out for what the rise might fetch along. Well, all at once, here comes a canoe; just a beauty, too, about thirteen or fourteen foot long, riding high like a duck. I shot head first off the bank, like a frog, clothes and all on, and struck out for the canoe. I just expected there'd be somebody laying down in it, because people often done that to fool folks, and when a chap had pulled a skiff out most to it they'd raise up and laugh at him. But it warn't so this time. It was a drift-canoe, sure enough, and I clumb in and paddled her ashore. Thinks I, the old man will be glad when he sees this—she's worth ten dollars. But when I got to shore pap wasn't in sight yet, and as I was running her into a little creek like a gully, all hung over with vines and willows, I struck another idea; I judged I'd hide her good, and then, stead of taking to the woods when I run off, I'd go down the river about fifty mile and camp in one place for good, and not have such a rough time tramping on foot.

It was pretty close to the shanty, and I thought I heard the old man coming, all the time; but I got her hid; and then I out and looked around a bunch of willows, and there was the old man down the path apiece just drawing a bead on a bird with his gun. So he hadn't seen anything.

When he got along, I was hard at it taking up a "trot" line.[3] He abused me a little for being so slow, but I told him I fell in the river and that was what made me so long. I knowed he would see I was wet, and then he would be asking questions. We got five cat-fish off the lines and went home.

While we laid off, after breakfast, to sleep up, both of us being about wore out, I got to thinking that if I could fix up some way to keep pap and the widow from trying to follow me, it would be a certainer thing than trusting to luck to get far enough off before they missed me; you see, all kinds of things might happen. Well, I didn't see no way for a while, but by-and-by pap raised up a minute, to drink another barrel of water, and he says:

"Another time a man comes a-prowling round here, you roust me out, you hear? That man warn't here for no good. I'd a shot him. Next time, you roust me out, you hear?"

Then he dropped down and went to sleep again—but what he had been saying give me the very idea I wanted. I says to myself, I can fix it now so nobody won't think of following me.

About twelve o'clock we turned out and went along up the bank. The river was coming up pretty fast, and lots of drift-wood going by on the rise. By-and-by, along comes part of a log raft—nine logs fast together. We went out with the skiff and towed it ashore. Then we had dinner. Anybody but pap would a waited and seen the day through, so as to catch more stuff; but that warn't pap's style. Nine logs was enough for one time; he must shove right over to town and sell. So he locked me in and took the skiff and started off towing the raft about half-past three. I judged he wouldn't come back that night. I waited till I reckoned he had got a good start, then I out with my saw and went to work on that log again. Before he was 'tother side of the river I was out of the hole; him and his raft was just a speck on the water away off yonder.

I took the sack of corn meal and took it to where the canoe was hid, and shoved the vines and branches apart and put it in; then I done the same with the side of bacon; then the whisky jug; I took all the coffee and sugar there was, and all the ammunition; I took the wadding; I took the bucket and gourd, I took a dipper and a tin cup, and my own saw and two blankets, and the skillet and the coffee-pot. I took fish-lines and matches and other things—every-thing that was worth a cent. I cleaned out the place. I wanted an axe, but there wasn't any, only the one out at the wood pile, and I knowed why I was going to leave that. I fetched out the gun, and now I was done.

I had wore the ground a good deal, crawling out of the hole and

3. A line suspended across a stream holding at intervals single hooks hung by short lines.

dragging out so many things. So I fixed that as good as I could from the outside by scattering dust on the place, which covered up the smoothness and the sawdust. Then I fixed the piece of log back into its place, and put two rocks under it and one against it to hold it there,—for it was bent up at that place, and didn't quite touch ground. If you stood four or five foot away and didn't know it was sawed, you wouldn't ever notice it; and besides, this was the back of the cabin and it warn't likely anybody would go fooling around there.

It was all grass clear to the canoe; so I hadn't left a track. I followed around to see. I stood on the bank and looked out over the river. All safe. So I took the gun and went up a piece into the woods and was hunting around for some birds, when I see a wild pig; hogs soon went wild in them bottoms after they had got away from the prairie farms. I shot this fellow and took him into camp.

I took the axe and smashed in the door—I beat it and hacked it considerable, a-doing it. I fetched the pig in and took him back nearly to the table and hacked into his throat with the axe, and laid him down on the ground to bleed—I say ground, because it *was* ground—hard packed, and no boards. Well, next I took an old sack and put a lot of big rocks in it,—all I could drag—and I started it from the pig and dragged it to the door and through the woods down to the river and dumped it in, and down it sunk, out of sight. You could easy see that something had been dragged over the ground. I did wish Tom Sawyer was there, I knowed he would take an interest in this kind of business, and throw in the fancy touches. Nobody could spread himself like Tom Sawyer in such a thing as that.

Well, last I pulled out some of my hair, and bloodied the ax good, and stuck it on the back side, and slung the ax in the corner. Then I took up the pig and held him to my breast with my jacket (so he couldn't drip) till I got a good piece below the house and then dumped him into the river. Now I thought of something else. So I went and got the bag of meal and my old saw out of the canoe and fetched them to the house. I took the bag to where it used to stand, and ripped a hole in the bottom of it with the saw,[4] for there warn't no knives and forks on the place—pap done everything with his clasp-knife, about the cooking. Then I carried the sack about a hundred yards across the grass and through the willows east of the house, to a shallow lake that was five mile wide and full of rushes—and ducks too, you might say, in the season. There was a slough or a creek leading out of it on the other side, that went miles away, I don't know where, but it didn't go to the river. The meal sifted out and made a little track all the way to the lake. I dropped pap's whetstone there too, so as to look like it had been

4. Early issues of the first edition read "was."

done by accident. Then I tied up the rip in the meal sack with a string, so it wouldn't leak no more, and took it and my saw to the canoe again.

It was about dark, now; so I dropped the canoe down the river under some willows that hung over the bank, and waited for the moon to rise. I made fast to a willow; then I took a bite to eat, and by-and-by laid down in the canoe to smoke a pipe and lay out a plan. I says to myself, they'll follow the track of that sackful of rocks to the shore and then drag the river for me. And they'll follow that meal track to the lake and go browsing down the creek that leads out of it to find the robbers that killed me and took the things. They won't ever hunt the river for anything but my dead carcass. They'll soon get tired of that, and won't bother no more about me. All right; I can stop anywhere I want to. Jackson's Island[5] is good enough for me; I know that island pretty well, and nobody ever comes there. And then I can paddle over to town, nights, and slink around and pick up things I want. Jackson's Island's the place.

I was pretty tired, and the first thing I knowed, I was asleep. When I woke up I didn't know where I was, for a minute. I set up and looked around, a little scared. Then I remembered. The river looked miles and miles across. The moon was so bright I could a counted the drift logs that went a slipping along, black and still, hundred of yards out from shore. Everything was dead quiet, and it looked late, and *smelt* late. You know what I mean—I don't know the words to put it in.

I took a good gap and a stretch, and was just going to unhitch and start, when I heard a sound away over the water. I listened. Pretty soon I made it out. It was that dull kind of a regular sound that comes from oars working in rowlocks when it's a still night. I peeped out through the willow branches, and there it was—a skiff, away across the water. I couldn't tell how many was in it. It kept a-coming, and when it was abreast of me I see there warn't but one man in it. Thinks I, maybe it's pap, though I warn't expecting him. He dropped below me, with the current, and by-and-by he come a-swinging up shore in the easy water, and he went by so close I could a reached out the gun and touched him. Well, it *was* pap, sure enough—and sober, too, by the way he laid to his oars.

I didn't lose no time. The next minute I was a-spinning down stream soft but quick in the shade of the bank. I made two mile and a half, and then struck out a quarter of a mile or more towards the middle of the river, because pretty soon I would be passing the ferry landing and people might see me and hail me. I got out amongst the drift-wood and then laid down in the bottom of the

5. The island also famous in *Tom Sawyer;* actually Glasscock's Island, since eroded away by the Mississippi River.

canoe and let her float. I laid there and had a good rest and a smoke out of my pipe, looking away into the sky, not a cloud in it. The sky looks ever so deep when you lay down on your back in the moonshine; I never knowed it before. And how far a body can hear on the water such nights! I heard people talking at the ferry landing. I heard what they said, too, every word of it. One man said it was getting towards the long days and the short nights, now. 'Tother one said *this* warn't one of the short ones, he reckoned—and then they laughed, and he said it over again and they laughed again; then they waked up another fellow and told him, and laughed, but he didn't laugh; he ripped out something brisk and said let him alone. The first fellow said he 'lowed to tell it to his old woman—she would think it was pretty good; but he said that warn't nothing to some things he had said in his time. I heard one man say it was nearly three o'clock, and he hoped daylight wouldn't wait more than about a week longer. After that, the talk got further and further away, and I couldn't make out the words any more, but I could hear the mumble; and now and then a laugh, too, but it seemed a long ways off.

I was away below the ferry now. I rose up and there was Jackson's Island, about two mile and a half down stream, heavy-timbered and standing up out of the middle of the river, big and dark and solid, like a steamboat without any lights. There warn't any signs of the bar at the head—it was all under water, now.

It didn't take me long to get there. I shot past the head at a ripping rate, the current was so swift, and then I got into the dead water and landed on the side towards the Illinois shore. I run the canoe into a deep dent in the bank that I knowed about; I had to part the willow branches to get in; and when I made fast nobody could a seen the canoe from the outside.

I went up and set down on a log at the head of the island and looked out on the big river and the black driftwood, and away over to the town, three mile away, where there was three or four lights twinkling. A monstrous big lumber raft was about a mile up stream, coming along down, with a lantern in the middle of it. I watched it come creeping down, and when it was most abreast of where I stood I heard a man say, "Stern oars, there! heave her head to stabboard!" I heard that just as plain as if the man was by my side.

There was a little gray in the sky, now; so I stepped into the woods and laid down for a nap before breakfast.

Chapter VIII

The sun was up so high when I waked, that I judged it was after eight o'clock. I laid there in the grass and the cool shade, think-

ing about things and feeling rested and ruther comfortable and satisfied. I could see the sun out at one or two holes, but mostly it was
big trees all about, and gloomy in there amongst them. There was
freckled places on the ground where the light sifted down through
the leaves, and the freckled places swapped about a little, showing
there was a little breeze up there. A couple of squirrels set on a
limb and jabbered at me very friendly.

I was powerful lazy and comfortable—didn't want to get up and
cook breakfast. Well, I was dozing off again, when I thinks I hears
a deep sound of "boom!" away up the river. I rouses up and rests
on my elbow and listens; pretty soon I hears it again. I hopped up
and went and looked out at a hole in the leaves, and I see a bunch
of smoke laying on the water a long ways up—about abreast the
ferry. And there was the ferry-boat full of people, floating along
down. I knowed what was the matter, now. "Boom!" I see the white
smoke squirt out of the ferry-boat's side. You see, they was firing
cannon over the water, trying to make my carcass come to the top.

I was pretty hungry, but it warn't going to do for me to start a
fire, because they might see the smoke. So I set there and watched
the cannon-smoke and listened to the boom. The river was a mile
wide, there, and it always looks pretty on a summer morning—so I
was having a good enough time seeing them hunt for my remainders, if I only had a bite to eat. Well, then I happened to
think how they always put quicksilver in loaves of bread and float
them off because they always go right to the drownded carcass and
stop there. So says I, I'll keep a lookout, and if any of them's floating around after me, I'll give them a show. I changed to the Illinois
edge of the island to see what luck I could have, and I warn't disappointed. A big double loaf come along, and I most got it, with a
long stick, but my foot slipped and she floated out further. Of course
I was where the current set in the closest to the shore—I knowed
enough for that. But by-and-by along comes another one, and this
time I won. I took out the plug and shook out the little dab of
quicksilver, and set my teeth in. It was "baker's bread"—what the
quality eat—none of your low-down corn-pone.

I got a good place amongst the leaves, and set there on a log,
munching the bread and watching the ferry-boat, and very well
satisfied. And then something struck me. I says, now I reckon the
widow or the parson or somebody prayed that this bread would find
me, and here it has gone and done it. So there ain't no doubt but
there is something in that thing. That is, there's something in it
when a body like the widow or the parson prays, but it don't work
for me, and I reckon it don't work for only just the right kind.

I lit a pipe and had a good long smoke and went on watching.
The ferry-boat was floating with the current, and I allowed I'd

have a chance to see who was aboard when she come along, because she would come in close, where the bread did. When she'd got pretty well along down towards me, I put out my pipe and went to where I fished out the bread, and laid down behind a log on the bank in a little open place. Where the log forked I could peep through.

By-and-by she come along, and she drifted in so close that they could a run out a plank and walked ashore. Most everybody was on the boat. Pap, and Judge Thatcher, and Bessie Thatcher, and Jo Harper, and Tom Sawyer, and his old Aunt Polly, and Sid and Mary, and plenty more. Everybody was talking about the murder, but the captain broke in and says:

"Look sharp, now; the current sets in the closest here, and maybe he's washed ashore and got tangled amongst the brush at the water's edge. I hope so, anyway."

I didn't hope so. They all crowded up and leaned over the rails, nearly in my face, and kept still, watching with all their might. I could see them first-rate, but they couldn't see me. Then the captain sung out:

"Stand away!" and the cannon let off such a blast right before me that it made me deef with the noise and pretty near blind with the smoke, and I judged I was gone. If they'd a had some bullets in, I reckon they'd a got the corpse they was after. Well, I see I warn't hurt, thanks to goodness. The boat floated on and went out of sight around the shoulder of the island. I could hear the booming, now and then, further and further off, and by-and-by after an hour, I didn't hear it no more. The island was three mile long. I judged they had got to the foot, and was giving it up. But they didn't yet a while. They turned around the foot of the island and started up the channel on the Missouri side, under steam, and booming once in a while as they went. I crossed over to that side and watched them. When they got abreast the head of the island they quit shooting and dropped over to the Missouri shore and went home to the town.

I knowed I was all right now. Nobody else would come a-hunting after me. I got my traps out of the canoe and made me a nice camp in the thick woods. I made a kind of a tent out of my blankets to put my things under so the rain couldn't get at them. I catched a cat-fish and haggled him open with my saw, and towards sundown I started my camp fire and had supper. Then I set out a line to catch some fish for breakfast.

When it was dark I set by my camp fire smoking, and feeling pretty satisfied; but by-and-by it got sort of lonesome, and so I went and set on the bank and listened to the currents washing along, and counted the stars and drift-logs and rafts that come down, and then went to bed; there ain't no better way to put in time when you are lonesome; you can't stay so, you soon get over it.

And so for three days and nights. No difference—just the same thing. But the next day I went exploring around down through the island. I was boss of it; it all belonged to me, so to say, and I wanted to know all about it; but mainly I wanted to put in the time. I found plenty strawberries, ripe and prime; and green summer-grapes, and green razberries; and the green blackberries was just beginning to show. They would all come handy by-and-by, I judged.

Well, I went fooling along in the deep woods till I judged I warn't far from the foot of the island. I had my gun along, but I hadn't shot nothing; it was for protection; thought I would kill some game nigh home. About this time I mighty near stepped on a good sized snake, and it went sliding off through the grass and flowers, and I after it, trying to get a shot at it. I clipped along, and all of a sudden I bounded right on to the ashes of a camp fire that was still smoking.[6]

My heart jumped up amongst my lungs. I never waited for to look further, but uncocked my gun and went sneaking back on my tip-toes as fast as ever I could. Every now and then I stopped a second, amongst the thick leaves, and listened; but my breath come so hard I couldn't hear nothing else. I slunk along another piece further, then listened again; and so on, and so on; if I see a stump, I took it for a man; if I trod on a stick and broke it, it made me feel like a person had cut one of my breaths in two and I only got half, and the short half, too.

When I got to camp I warn't feeling very brash, there warn't much sand in my craw; but I says, this ain't no time to be fooling around. So I got all my traps into my canoe again so as to have them out of sight, and I put out the fire and scattered the ashes around to look like an old last year's camp, and then clumb a tree.

I reckon I was up in the tree two hours; but I didn't see nothing, I didn't hear nothing—I only *thought* I heard and seen as much as a thousand things. Well, I couldn't stay up there forever; so at last I got down, but I kept in the thick woods and on the lookout all the time. All I could get to eat was berries and what was left over from breakfast.

By the time it was night I was pretty hungry. So when it was good and dark, I slid out from shore before moonrise and paddled over to the Illinois bank—about a quarter of a mile. I went out in the woods and cooked a supper, and I had about made up my mind I would stay there all night, when I hear a *plunkety-plunk, plunkety-plunk*, and says to myself, horses coming; and next I hear people's

6. Huck's discovery of the ashes is a dramatic incident similar to Robinson Crusoe's discovery of the footprint on *his* island in Chapter XI of Daniel Defoe's novel.

voices. I got everything into the canoe as quick as I could, and then went creeping through the woods to see what I could find out. I hadn't got far when I hear a man say:

"We better camp here, if we can find a good place; the horses is about beat out. Let's look around."

I didn't wait, but shoved out and paddled away easy. I tied up in the old place, and reckoned I would sleep in the canoe.

I didn't sleep much. I couldn't, somehow, for thinking. And every time I waked up I thought somebody had me by the neck. So the sleep didn't do me no good. By-and-by I says to myself, I can't live this way; I'm agoing to find out who it is that's here on the island with me; I'll find it out or bust. Well, I felt better, right off.

So I took my paddle and slid out from shore just a step or two, and then let the canoe drop along down amongst the shadows. The moon was shining, and outside of the shadows it made it most as light as day. I poked along well onto an hour, everything still as rocks and sound asleep. Well by this time I was most down to the foot of the island. A little ripply, cool breeze begun to blow, and that was as good as saying the night was about done. I give her a turn with the paddle and brung her nose to shore; then I got my gun and slipped out and into the edge of the woods. I set down there on a log and looked out through the leaves. I see the moon go off watch and the darkness begin to blanket the river. But in a little while I see a pale streak over the tree-tops, and knowed the day was coming. So I took my gun and slipped off towards where I had run across that camp fire, stopping every minute or two to listen. But I hadn't no luck, somehow; I couldn't seem to find the place. But by-and-by, sure enough, I catched a glimpse of fire, away through the trees. I went for it, cautious and slow. By-and-by I was close enough to have a look, and there laid a man on the ground. It most give me the fan-tods. He had a blanket around his head, and his head was nearly in the fire. I set there behind a clump of bushes, in about six foot of him, and kept my eyes on him steady. It was getting gray daylight, now. Pretty soon he gapped, and stretched himself, and hove off the blanket, and it was Miss Watson's Jim! I bet I was glad to see him. I says:

"Hello, Jim!" and skipped out.

He bounced up and stared at me wild. Then he drops down on his knees, and puts his hands together and says:

"Doan' hurt me—don't! I hain't ever done no harm to a ghos'. I awluz liked dead people, en done all I could for 'em. You go en git in de river agin, whah you b'longs, en doan' do nuffn to Ole Jim, 'at 'uz awluz yo' fren'."

Well, I warn't long making him understand I warn't dead. I was ever so glad to see Jim. I warn't lonesome, now. I told him I warn't afraid of *him* telling the people where I was. I talked along, but he only set there and looked at me; never said nothing. Then I says:

"It's good daylight. Le's get breakfast. Make up your camp fire good."

"What's de use er makin' up de camp fire to cook strawbries en sich truck? But you got a gun, hain't you? Den we kin git sumfn better den strawbries."

"Strawberries and such truck," I says. "Is that what you live on?"

"I couldn' git nuffn else," he says.

"Why, how long you been on the island, Jim?"

"I come heah de night arter you's killed."

"What, all that time?"

"Yes-indeedy."

"And ain't you had nothing but that kind of rubbage to eat?"

"No, sah—nuffn else."

"Well, you must be most starved, ain't you?"

"I reck'n I could eat a hoss. I think I could. How long you ben on de islan'?"

"Since the night I got killed."

"No! W'y, what has you lived on? But you got a gun. Oh, yes, you got a gun. Dat's good. Now you kill sumfn en I'll make up de fire."

So we went over to where the canoe was, and while he built a fire in a grassy open place amongst the trees, I fetched meal and bacon and coffee, and coffee-pot and frying-pan, and sugar and tin cups, and the nigger was set back considerable, because he reckoned it was all done with witchcraft. I catched a good big cat-fish, too, and Jim cleaned him with his knife, and fried him.

When breakfast was ready, we lolled on the grass and eat it smoking hot. Jim laid it in with all his might, for he was most about starved. Then when we had got pretty well stuffed, we laid off and lazied.

By-and-by Jim says:

"But looky here, Huck, who wuz it dat 'uz killed in dat shanty, ef it warn't you?"

Then I told him the whole thing, and he said it was smart. He said Tom Sawyer couldn't get up no better plan than what I had. Then I says:

"How do you come to be here, Jim, and how'd you get here?"

He looked pretty uneasy, and didn't say nothing for a minute. Then he says:

"Maybe I better not tell."

"Why, Jim?"

"Well, dey's reasons. But you wouldn' tell on me ef I 'uz to tell you, would you, Huck?"

"Blamed if I would, Jim."

"Well, I b'lieve you, Huck. I—I *run off*."

"Jim!"

"But mind, you said you wouldn't tell—you know you said you wouldn't tell, Huck."

"Well, I did. I said I wouldn't, and I'll stick to it. Honest *injun* I will. People would call me a low down Abolitionist and despise me for keeping mum—but that don't make no difference. I ain't agoing to tell, and I ain't agoing back there anyways. So now, le's know all about it."

"Well, you see, it 'uz dis way. Ole Missus—dat's Miss Watson—she pecks on me all de time, en treats me pooty rough, but she awluz said she wouldn' sell me down to Orleans. But I noticed dey wuz a nigger trader roun' de place considable, lately, en I begin to git oneasy. Well, one night I creeps to de do', pooty late, en de do' warn't quite shet, en I hear ole missus tell de widder she gwyne to sell me down to Orleans, but she didn' want to, but she could git eight hund'd dollars for me, en it 'uz sich a big stack o' money she couldn' resis'. De widder she try to git her to say she wouldn' do it, but I never waited to hear de res'. I lit out mighty quick, I tell you.

"I tuck out en shin down de hill en 'spec to steal a skift 'long de sho' som'ers 'bove de town, but dey wuz people a-stirrin' yit, so I hid in de ole tumble-down cooper shop on de bank to wait for everybody to go 'way. Well, I wuz dah all night. Dey wuz somebody roun' all de time. 'Long 'bout six in de mawnin', skifts begin to go by, en 'bout eight er nine every skift dat went 'long wuz talkin' 'bout how yo' pap come over to de town en say you's killed. Dese las' skifts wuz full o' ladies en genlmen agoin' over for to see de place. Sometimes dey'd pull up at de sho' en take a res' b'fo' dey started acrost, so by de talk I got to know all 'bout de killin'. I 'uz powerful sorry you's killed, Huck, but I ain't no mo', now.

"I laid dah under de shavins all day. I 'uz hungry, but I warn't afeared; bekase I knowed ole missus en de widder wuz goin' to start to de camp-meetn' right arter breakfas' en be gone all day, en dey knows I goes off wid de cattle 'bout daylight, so dey wouldn' 'spec to see me roun' de place, en so dey wouldn' miss me tell arter dark in de evenin'. De yuther servants wouldn' miss me, kase dey'd shin out en take holiday, soon as de ole folks 'uz out'n de way.

"Well, when it come dark I tuck out up de river road, en went 'bout two mile er more to whah dey warn't no houses. I'd made up my mine 'bout what I's agwyne to do. You see ef I kep' on tryin' to git away afoot, de dogs 'ud track me; ef I stole a skift to cross over, dey'd miss dat skift, you see, en dey'd know 'bout whah I'd lan' on de yuther side en whah to pick up my track. So I says, a raff is what I's arter; it doan' *make* no track.

"I see a light a-comin' roun' de p'int, bymeby, so I wade' in en shove' a log ahead o' me, en swum more'n half-way acrost de river, en got in 'mongst de drift-wood, en kep' my head down low, en kinder swum agin de current tell de raff come along. Den I swum to de stern uv it, en tuck aholt. It clouded up en 'uz pooty dark for a little while. So I clumb up en laid down on de planks. De men 'uz all 'way yonder in de middle, whah de lantern wuz. De river wuz arisin' en dey wuz a good current; so I reck'n'd 'at by fo' in de mawnin' I'd be twenty-five mile down de river, en den I'd slip in, jis' b'fo' daylight, en swim asho' en take to de woods on de Illinoi side.[7]

"But I didn' have no luck. When we 'uz mos' down to de head er de islan', a man begin to come aft wid de lantern. I see it warn't no use fer to wait, so I slid overboad, en struck out fer de islan'. Well, I had a notion I could lan' mos' anywhers, but I couldn't— bank too bluff. I 'uz mos' to de foot er de islan' b'fo' I foun' a good place. I went into de woods en jedged I wouldn' fool wid raffs no mo' long as dey move de lantern roun' so. I had my pipe en a plug er dog-leg,[8] en some matches in my cap, en dey warn't wet, so I 'uz all right."

"And so you ain't had no meat nor bread to eat all this time? Why didn't you get mud-turkles?"

"How you gwyne to git'm? You can't slip up on um en grab um; en how's a body gwyne to hit um wid a rock? How could a body do it in de night? en I warn't gwyne to show myself on de bank in de daytime."

"Well, that's so. You've had to keep in the woods all the time, of course. Did you hear 'em shooting the cannon?"

"Oh, yes. I knowed dey was arter you. I see um go by heah; watched um thoo de bushes."

Some young birds come along, flying a yard or two at a time and lighting. Jim said it was a sign it was going to rain. He said it was a sign when young chickens flew that way, and so he reckoned it was the same way when young birds done it. I was going to catch some of them, but Jim wouldn't let me. He said it was death. He said his father laid mighty sick once, and some of them catched a bird, and his old granny said his father would die, and he did.

And Jim said you mustn't count the things you are going to cook for dinner, because that would bring bad luck. The same if you shook the table-cloth after sundown. And he said if a man owned

---

7. Illinois was legally free soil but was separated only by the Mississippi and Ohio Rivers from slave states. By state law, any Negro without freedom papers was subject to arrest and a system of indentured labor. Jim's most practical access to one of the northern states sympathetic to runaway slaves would be the Ohio River.

8. A cheap tobacco.

a bee-hive, and that man died, the bees must be told about it before sun-up next morning, or else the bees would all weaken down and quit work and die. Jim said bees wouldn't sting idiots; but I didn't believe that, because I had tried them lots of times myself, and they wouldn't sting me.

I had heard about some of these things before, but not all of them. Jim knowed all kinds of signs. He said he knowed most everything. I said it looked to me like all the signs was about bad luck, and so I asked him if there warn't any good-luck signs. He says:

"Mighty few—an' *dey* ain' no use to a body. What you want to know when good luck's a-comin' for? want to keep it off?" And he said: "Ef you's got hairy arms en a hairy breas', it's a sign dat you's agwyne to be rich. Well, dey's some use in a sign like dat, 'kase it's so fur ahead. You see, maybe you's got to be po' a long time fust, en so you might git discourage' en kill yo'sef 'f you didn' know by de sign dat you gwyne to be rich bymeby."

"Have you got hairy arms and a hairy breast, Jim?"

"What's de use to ax dat question? don' you see I has?"

"Well, are you rich?"

"No, but I ben rich wunst, and gwyne to be rich agin. Wunst I had foteen dollars, but I tuck to specalat'n', en got busted out."

"What did you speculate in, Jim?"

"Well, fust I tackled stock."

"What kind of stock?"

"Why, live stock. Cattle, you know. I put ten dollars in a cow. But I ain't gwyne to resk no mo' money in stock. De cow up 'n' died on my han's."

"So you lost the ten dollars."

"No, I didn' lose it all. I on'y los' 'bout nine of it. I sole de hide en taller for a dollar en ten cents."

"You had five dollars and ten cents left. Did you speculate any more?"

"Yes. You know dat one-laigged nigger dat b'longs to old Misto Bradish? well, he sot up a bank, en say anybody dat put in a dollar would git fo' dollars mo' at de en' er de year. Well, all de niggers went in, but dey didn' have much. I wuz de on'y one dat had much. So I stuck out for mo' dan fo' dollars, en I said 'f I didn' git it I'd start a bank myself. Well o' course dat nigger want' to keep me out er de business, bekase he say dey warn't business 'nough for two banks, so he say I could put in my five dollars en he pay me thirty-five at de en' er de year.

"So I done it. Den I reck'n'd I'd inves' de thirty-five dollars right off en keep things a-movin'. Dey wuz a nigger name' Bob, dat had ketched a wood-flat,[9] en his marster didn' know it; en I bought it off'n him en told him to take de thirty-five dollars when de en' er

9. A flat-bottomed boat for transporting timber.

de year come; but somebody stole de wood-flat dat night, en nex' day de one-laigged nigger say de bank 's busted. So dey didn' none uv us git no money."

"What did you do with the ten cents, Jim?"

"Well, I 'uz gwyne to spen' it, but I had a dream, en de dream tole me to give it to a nigger name' Balum—Balum's Ass[1] dey call him for short, he's one er dem chuckle-heads, you know. But he's lucky, dey say, en I see I warn't lucky. De dream say let Balum inves' de ten cents en he'd make a raise for me. Well, Balum he tuck de money, en when he wuz in church he hear de preacher say dat whoever give to de po' len' to de Lord, en boun' to git his money back a hund'd times. So Balum he tuck en give de ten cents to de po', en laid low to see what wuz gwyne to come of it."

"Well, what did come of it, Jim?"

"Nuffn' never come of it. I couldn' manage to k'leck dat money no way; en Balum he couldn'. I ain' gwyne to len' no mo' money 'dout I see de security. Boun' to git yo' money back a hund'd times, de preacher says! Ef I could git de ten *cents* back, I'd call it squah, en be glad er de chanst."

"Well, it's all right, anyway, Jim, long as you're going to be rich again some time or other."

"Yes—en I's rich now, come to look at it. I owns myself, en I's wuth eight hund'd dollars. I wisht I had de money, I wouldn' want no mo'."

Chapter IX

I wanted to go and look at a place right about the middle of the island, that I'd found when I was exploring; so we started, and soon got to it, because the island was only three miles long and a quarter of a mile wide.

This place was a tolerable long steep hill or ridge, about forty foot high. We had a rough time getting to the top, the sides was so steep and the bushes so thick. We tramped and clumb around all over it, and by-and-by found a good big cavern in the rock, most up to the top on the side towards Illinois. The cavern was as big as two or three rooms bunched together, and Jim could stand up straight in it. It was cool in there. Jim was for putting our traps in there, right away, but I said we didn't want to be climbing up and down there all the time.

Jim said if we had the canoe hid in a good place, and had all the traps in the cavern, we could rush there if anybody was to come to the island, and they would never find us without dogs. And besides, he said them little birds had said it was going to rain, and did I

1. The Biblical Balaam's ass, whose story is irrelevant here.

want the things to get wet?

So we went back and got the canoe and paddled up abreast the cavern, and lugged all the traps up there. Then we hunted up a place close by to hide the canoe in, amongst the thick willows. We took some fish off of the lines and set them again, and begun to get ready for dinner.

The door of the cavern was big enough to roll a hogshead in, and on one side of the door the floor stuck out a little bit and was flat and a good place to build a fire on. So we built it there and cooked dinner.

We spread the blankets inside for a carpet, and eat our dinner in there. We put all the other things handy at the back of the cavern. Pretty soon it darkened up and begun to thunder and lighten; so the birds was right about it. Directly it begun to rain, and it rained like all fury, too, and I never see the wind blow so. It was one of these regular summer storms. It would get so dark that it looked all blue-black outside, and lovely; and the rain would thrash along by so thick that the trees off a little ways looked dim and spider-webby; and here would come a blast of wind that would bend the trees down and turn up the pale underside of the leaves; and then a perfect ripper of a gust would follow along and set the branches to tossing their arms as if they was just wild; and next, when it was just about the bluest and blackest—*fst!* It was as bright as glory and you'd have a little glimpse of tree-tops a-plunging about, away off yonder in the storm, hundreds of yards further than you could see before; dark as sin again in a second, and now you'd hear the thunder let go with an awful crash and then go rumbling, grumbling, tumbling down the sky towards the under side of the world, like rolling empty barrels down stairs, where it's long stairs and they bounce a good deal, you know.

"Jim, this is nice," I says. "I wouldn't want to be nowhere else but here. Pass me along another hunk of fish and some hot corn-bread."

"Well, you wouldn't a ben here, 'f it hadn't a ben for Jim. You'd a ben down dah in de woods widout any dinner, en gittn' mos' drownded, too, dat you would, honey. Chickens knows when its gwyne to rain, en so do de birds, chile."

The river went on raising and raising for ten or twelve days, till at last it was over the banks. The water was three or four foot deep on the island in the low places and on the Illinois bottom. On that side it was a good many miles wide; but on the Missouri side it was the same old distance across—a half a mile—because the Missouri shore was just a wall of high bluffs.

Daytimes we paddled all over the island in the canoe. It was mighty cool and shady in the deep woods even if the sun was blazing

outside. We went winding in and out amongst the trees; and sometimes the vines hung so thick we had to back away and go some
other way. Well, on every old broken-down tree, you could see
rabbits, and snakes, and such things; and when the island had been
overflowed a day or two, they got so tame, on account of being
hungry, that you could paddle right up and put your hand on them
if you wanted to; but not the snakes and turtles—they would slide
off in the water. The ridge our cavern was in, was full of them. We
could a had pets enough if we'd wanted them.

One night we catched a little section of a lumber raft—nice pine
planks. It was twelve foot wide and about fifteen or sixteen foot
long, and the top stood above water six or seven inches, a solid level
floor. We could see saw-logs go by in the daylight, sometimes, but
we let them go; we didn't show ourselves in daylight.

Another night, when we was up at the head of the island, just
before daylight, here comes a frame house down, on the west side.
She was a two-story, and tilted over, considerable. We paddled out
and got aboard—clumb in at an up-stairs window. But it was too
dark to see yet, so we made the canoe fast and set in her to wait for
daylight.

The light begun to come before we got to the foot of the island.
Then we looked in at the window. We could make out a bed, and
a table, and two old chairs, and lots of things around about on the
floor; and there was clothes hanging against the wall. There was
something laying on the floor in the far corner that looked like a
man. So Jim says:

"Hello, you!"

But it didn't budge. So I hollered again, and then Jim says:

"De man ain't asleep—he's dead. You hold still—I'll go en see."

He went and bent down and looked, and says:

"It's a dead man. Yes, indeedy; naked, too. He's ben shot in de
back. I reck'n he's ben dead two er three days. Come in, Huck, but
doan' look at his face—it's too gashly."

I didn't look at him at all. Jim throwed some old rags over him,
but he needn't done it; I didn't want to see him. There was heaps
of old greasy cards scattered around over the floor, and old whisky
bottles, and a couple of masks made out of black cloth; and all over
the walls was the ignorantest kind of words and pictures, made with
charcoal. There was two old dirty calico dresses, and a sun-bonnet,
and some women's under-clothes, hanging against the wall, and
some men's clothing, too. We put the lot into the canoe; it might
come good. There was a boy's old speckled straw hat on the floor;
I took that too. And there was a bottle that had had milk in it; and
it had a rag stopper for a baby to suck. We would a took the bottle,
but it was broke. There was a seedy old chest, and an old hair trunk

with the hinges broke. They stood open, but there warn't nothing left in them that was any account. The way things was scattered about, we reckoned the people left in a hurry and warn't fixed so as to carry off most of their stuff.

We got an old tin lantern, and a butcher-knife without any handle, and a bran-new Barlow knife[2] worth two bits in any store, and a lot of tallow candles, and a tin candlestick, and a gourd, and a tin cup, and a ratty old bed-quilt off the bed, and a reticule with needles and pins and beeswax and buttons and thread and all such truck in it, and a hatchet and some nails, and a fish-line as thick as my little finger, with some monstrous hooks on it, and a roll of buckskin, and a leather dog-collar, and a horse-shoe, and some vials of medicine that didn't have no label on them; and just as we was leaving I found a tolerable good curry-comb, and Jim he found a ratty old fiddle-bow, and a wooden leg. The straps was broke off of it, but barring that, it was a good enough leg, though it was too long for me and not long enough for Jim, and we couldn't find the other one, though we hunted all around.

And so, take it all around, we made a good haul. When we was ready to shove off, we was a quarter of a mile below the island, and it was pretty broad day; so I made Jim lay down in the canoe and cover up with the quilt, because if he set up, people could tell he was a nigger a good ways off. I paddled over to the Illinois shore, and drifted down most a half a mile doing it. I crept up the dead water under the bank, and hadn't no accidents and didn't see nobody. We got home all safe.

Chapter X

After breakfast I wanted to talk about the dead man and guess out how he come to be killed, but Jim didn't want to. He said it would fetch bad luck; and besides, he said, he might come and ha'nt us; he said a man that warn't buried was more likely to go a-ha'nting around than one that was planted and comfortable. That sounded pretty reasonable, so I didn't say no more; but I couldn't keep from studying over it and wishing I knowed who shot the man, and what they done it for.

We rummaged the clothes we'd got, and found eight dollars in silver sewed up in the lining of an old blanket overcoat. Jim said he reckoned the people in that house stole the coat, because if they'd a knowed the money was there they wouldn't a left it. I said I reckoned they killed him, too; but Jim didn't want to talk about that. I says:

"Now you think it's bad luck; but what did you say when I

2. A one-bladed jackknife, named for the maker.

fetched in the snake-skin that I found on the top of the ridge day before yesterday? You said it was the worst bad luck in the world to touch a snake-skin with my hands. Well, here's your bad luck! We've raked in all this truck and eight dollars besides. I wish we could have some bad luck like this every day, Jim."

"Never you mind, honey, never you mind. Don't you git too peart. It's a-comin'. Mind I tell you, it's a-comin'.'"

It did come, too. It was a Tuesday that we had that talk. Well, after dinner Friday, we was laying around in the grass at the upper end of the ridge, and got out of tobacco. I went to the cavern to get some, and found a rattlesnake in there. I killed him, and curled him up on the foot of Jim's blanket, ever so natural, thinking there'd be some fun when Jim found him there. Well, by night I forgot all about the snake, and when Jim flung himself down on the blanket while I struck a light, the snake's mate was there, and bit him.

He jumped up yelling, and the first thing the light showed was the varmint curled up and ready for another spring. I laid him out in a second with a stick, and Jim grabbed pap's whisky jug and began to pour it down.

He was barefooted, and the snake bit him right on the heel. That all comes of my being such a fool as to not remember that wherever you leave a dead snake its mate always comes there and curls around it. Jim told me to chop off the snake's head and throw it away, and then skin the body and roast a piece of it. I done it, and he eat it and said it would help cure him. He made me take off the rattles and tie them around his wrist, too. He said that that would help. Then I slid out quiet and throwed the snakes clear away amongst the bushes; for I warn't going to let Jim find out it was all my fault, not if I could help it.

Jim sucked and sucked at the jug, and now and then he got out of his head and pitched around and yelled; but every time he come to himself he went to sucking at the jug again. His foot swelled up pretty big, and so did his leg; but by-and-by the drunk begun to come, and so I judged he was all right; but I'd druther been bit with a snake than pap's whisky.

Jim was laid up for four days and nights. Then the swelling was all gone and he was around again. I made up my mind I wouldn't ever take aholt of a snake-skin again with my hands, now that I see what had come of it. Jim said he reckoned I would believe him next time. And he said that handling a snake-skin was such awful bad luck that maybe we hadn't got to the end of it yet. He said he druther see the new moon over his left shoulder as much as a thousand times than take up a snake-skin in his hand. Well, I was getting to feel that way myself, though I've always reckoned that looking at the new moon over your left shoulder is one of the carelessest and foolishest things a body can do. Old Hank Bunker done it once, and bragged about it; and in less than two years he got drunk and fell off of the shot tower and spread himself out so that he was just a kind of layer, as you may say; and they slid him edgeways between two barn doors for a coffin, and buried him so, so they say, but I didn't see it. Pap told me. But anyway, it all come of looking at the moon that way, like a fool.

Well, the days went along, and the river went down between its banks again; and about the first thing we done was to bait one of the big hooks with a skinned rabbit and set it and catch a cat-fish that was as big as a man, being six foot two inches long, and weighed over two hundred pounds. We couldn't handle him, of course; he would a flung us into Illinois. We just set there and watched him rip and tear around till he drowned. We found a brass button in his stomach, and a round ball, and lots of rubbage. We split the ball open with the hatchet, and there was a spool in it. Jim said he'd had it there a long time, to coat it over so and make a ball of it. It was as big a fish as was ever catched in the Mississippi, I reckon. Jim said he hadn't ever seen a bigger one. He would a been worth a good deal over at the village. They peddle out such a fish as that by the pound in the market house there; everybody buys some of him; his meat's as white as snow and makes a good fry.

Next morning I said it was getting slow and dull, and I wanted to get a stirring up, some way. I said I reckoned I would slip over the river and find out what was going on. Jim liked that notion; but he said I must go in the dark and look sharp. Then he studied it over and said, couldn't I put on some of them old things and dress up like a girl? That was a good notion, too. So we shortened up one of the calico gowns and I turned up my trouser-legs to my knees and got into it. Jim hitched it behind with the hooks, and it was a fair fit. I put on the sun-bonnet and tied it under my chin, and then for a body to look in and see my face was like looking down a joint of stove-pipe. Jim said nobody would know me, even in the daytime, hardly. I practiced around all day to get the hang of the things, and by-and-by I could do pretty well in them, only Jim said I didn't walk like a girl; and he said I must quit pulling up my gown to get at my britches pocket. I took notice, and done better.

I started up the Illinois shore in the canoe just after dark.

I started across to the town from a little below the ferry landing, and the drift of the current fetched me in at the bottom of the town. I tied up and started along the bank. There was a light burning in a little shanty that hadn't been lived in for a long time, and I wondered who had took up quarters there. I slipped up and peeped in at the window. There was a woman about forty year old in there, knitting by a candle that was on a pine table. I didn't know her face; she was a stranger, for you couldn't start a face in that town that I didn't know. Now this was lucky, because I was weakening; I was getting afraid I had come; people might know my voice and find me out. But if this woman had been in such a little town two days she could tell me all I wanted to know; so I knocked at the door, and made up my mind I wouldn't forget I was a girl.

Chapter XI

"Come in," says the woman, and I did. She says:

"Take a cheer."

I done it. She looked me all over with her little shiny eyes, and says:

"What might your name be?"

"Sarah Williams."

"Where 'bouts do you live? In this neighborhood?"

"No'm. In Hookerville, seven mile below. I've walked all the way and I'm all tired out."

"Hungry, too, I reckon. I'll find you something."

"No'm, I ain't hungry. I was so hungry I had to stop two mile below here at a farm; so I ain't hungry no more. It's what makes me so late. My mother's down sick, and out of money and everything, and I come to tell my Uncle Abner Moore. He lives at the upper end of the town, she says. I hain't ever been here before. Do you know him?"

"No; but I don't know everybody yet. I haven't lived here quite two weeks. It's a considerable ways to the upper end of the town. You better stay here all night. Take off your bonnet."

"No," I says, "I'll rest a while, I reckon, and go on. I ain't afeard of the dark."

She said she wouldn't let me go by myself, but her husband would be in by-and-by, maybe in a hour and a half, and she'd send him along with me. Then she got to talking about her husband, and about her relations up the river, and her relations down the river, and about how much better off they used to was, and how they didn't know but they'd made a mistake coming to our town, instead of letting well alone—and so on and so on, till I was afeard I had made a mistake coming to her to find out what was going on in the town; but by-and-by she dropped onto pap and the murder, and then I was pretty willing to let her clatter right along. She told about me and Tom Sawyer finding the six thousand dollars (only she got it ten) and all about pap and what a hard lot he was, and what a hard lot I was, and at last she got down to where I was murdered. I says:

"Who done it? We've heard considerable about these goings on, down in Hookerville, but we don't know who 'twas that killed Huck Finn."

"Well, I reckon there's a right smart chance of people *here* that'd like to know who killed him. Some thinks old Finn done it himself."

"No—is that so?"

"Most everybody thought it at first. He'll never know how nigh he come to getting lynched. But before night they changed around and judged it was done by a runaway nigger named Jim."

"Why *he*—"

I stopped. I reckoned I better keep still. She run on, and never noticed I had put in at all.

"The nigger run off the very night Huck Finn was killed. So there's a reward out for him—three hundred dollars. And there's a reward out for old Finn too—two hundred dollars. You see, he come to town the morning after the murder, and told about it, and was out with 'em on the ferry-boat hunt, and right away after he up and left. Before night they wanted to lynch him, but he was gone, you see. Well, next day they found out the nigger was gone; they found out he hadn't ben seen sence ten o'clock the night the murder was done. So then they put it on him, you see, and while they was full of it, next day back comes old Finn and went boo-hooing to Judge Thatcher to get money to hunt for the nigger all over Illinois with. The judge give him some, and that evening he got drunk and was around till after midnight with a couple of mighty hard looking strangers, and then went off with them. Well, he hain't come back sence, and they ain't looking for him back till this thing blows over a little, for people thinks now that he killed his boy and fixed things so folks would think robbers done it, and then he'd get Huck's money without having to bother a long time with a lawsuit. People do say he warn't any too good to do it. Oh, he's sly, I reckon. If he don't come back for a year, he'll be all right. You can't prove anything on him, you know; everything will be quieted down then, and he'll walk into Huck's money as easy as nothing."

"Yes, I reckon so, 'm. I don't see nothing in the way of it. Has everybody quit thinking the nigger done it?"

"Oh, no, not everybody. A good many thinks he done it. But they'll get the nigger pretty soon, now, and maybe they can scare it out of him."

"Why, are they after him yet?"

"Well, you're innocent, ain't you! Does three hundred dollars lay round every day for people to pick up? Some folks thinks the nigger ain't far from here. I'm one of them—but I hain't talked it around. A few days ago I was talking with an old couple that lives next door in the log shanty, and they happened to say hardly anybody ever goes to that island over yonder that they call Jackson's Island. Don't anybody live there? says I. No, nobody, says they. I didn't say any more, but I done some thinking. I was pretty near certain I'd seen smoke over there, about the head of the island, a day or two before that, so I says to myself, like as not that nigger's hiding over there; anyway, says I, it's worth the trouble to give the place a hunt. I hain't seen any smoke sence, so I reckon maybe he's gone, if it was him; but husband's going over to see—him and another man. He was gone up the river; but he got back to-day and I told him as soon as he got here two hours ago."

I had got so uneasy I couldn't set still. I had to do something with my hands; so I took up a needle off of the table and went to threading it. My hands shook, and I was making a bad job of it. When the woman stopped talking, I looked up, and she was looking at me pretty curious, and smiling a little. I put down the needle and thread and let on to be interested—and I was, too—and says:

"Three hundred dollars is a power of money. I wish my mother could get it. Is your husband going over there to-night?"

"Oh, yes. He went up town with the man I was telling you of, to get a boat and see if they could borrow another gun. They'll go over after midnight."

"Couldn't they see better if they was to wait till daytime?"

"Yes. And couldn't the nigger see better, too? After midnight he'll likely be asleep, and they can slip around through the woods and hunt up his camp fire all the better for the dark, if he's got one."

"I didn't think of that."

The woman kept looking at me pretty curious, and I didn't feel a bit comfortable. Pretty soon she says:

"What did you say your name was, honey?"

"M—Mary Williams."

Somehow it didn't seem to me that I said it was Mary before, so I didn't look up; seemed to me I said it was Sarah; so I felt sort of cornered, and was afeard maybe I was looking it, too. I wished the woman would say something more; the longer she set still, the uneasier I was. But now she says:

"Honey, I thought you said it was Sarah when you first come in?"

"Oh, yes'm, I did. Sarah Mary Williams. Sarah's my first name. Some calls me Sarah, some calls me Mary."

"Oh, that's the way of it?"

"Yes'm."

I was feeling better, then, but I wished I was out of there, anyway. I couldn't look up yet.

Well, the woman fell to talking about how hard times was, and how poor they had to live, and how the rats was as free as if they owned the place, and so forth, and so on, and then I got easy again. She was right about the rats. You'd see one stick his nose out of a hole in the corner every little while. She said she had to have things handy to throw at them when she was alone, or they wouldn't give her no peace. She showed me a bar of lead, twisted up into a knot, and said she was a good shot with it generly, but she'd wrenched her arm a day or two ago, and didn't know whether she could throw true, now. But she watched for a chance, and directly she banged away at a rat, but she missed him wide, and said "Ouch!" it hurt her arm so. Then she told me to try for the next one. I wanted to be getting away before the old man got back, but of course I didn't let on. I got the thing, and the first rat that showed his nose I let drive, and if he'd a stayed where he was he'd a been a tolerable sick rat. She said that that was first-rate, and she reckoned I would hive the next one. She went and got the lump of lead and fetched it back and brought along a hank of yarn, which she wanted me to help her with. I held up my two hands and she put the hank over them and went on talking about her and her husband's matters. But she broke off to say:

"Keep your eye on the rats. You better have the lead in your lap, handy."

So she dropped the lump into my lap, just at that moment, and I clapped my legs together on it and she went on talking. But only about a minute. Then she took off the hank and looked me straight in the face, but very pleasant, and says:

"Come, now—what's your real name?"

"Wh-what, mum?"

"What's your real name? Is it Bill, or Tom, or Bob?—or what is it?"

I reckon I shook like a leaf, and I didn't know hardly what to do. But I says:

"Please to don't poke fun at a poor girl like me, mum. If I'm in the way, here, I'll——"

"No, you won't. Set down and stay where you are. I ain't going to hurt you, and I ain't going to tell on you, nuther. You just tell me your secret, and trust me. I'll keep it; and what's more, I'll help you. So'll my old man, if you want him to. You see, you're a run-away 'prentice—that's all. It ain't anything. There ain't any harm in it. You've been treated bad, and you made up your mind to cut. Bless you, child, I wouldn't tell on you. Tell me all about it, now

—that's a good boy."

So I said it wouldn't be no use to try to play it any longer, and I would just make a clean breast and tell her everything, but she mustn't go back on her promise. Then I told her my father and mother was dead, and the law had bound me out to a mean old farmer in the country thirty mile back from the river, and he treated me so bad I couldn't stand it no longer; he went away to be gone a couple of days, and so I took my chance and stole some of his daughter's old clothes, and cleared out, and I had been three nights coming the thirty miles; I traveled nights, and hid day-times and slept, and the bag of bread and meat I carried from home lasted me all the way and I had a plenty. I said I believed my uncle Abner Moore would take care of me, and so that was why I struck out for this town of Goshen."

"Goshen, child? This ain't Goshen. This is St. Petersburg.[3] Goshen's ten mile further up the river. Who told you this was Goshen?"

"Why, a man I met at day-break this morning, just as I was going to turn into the woods for my regular sleep. He told me when the roads forked I must take the right hand, and five mile would fetch me to Goshen."

"He was drunk I reckon. He told you just exactly wrong."

"Well, he did act like he was drunk, but it ain't no matter now. I got to be moving along. I'll fetch Goshen before day-light."

"Hold on a minute. I'll put you up a snack to eat. You might want it."

So she put me up a snack, and says:

"Say—when a cow's laying down, which end of her gets up first? Answer up prompt, now—don't stop to study over it. Which end gets up first?"

"The hind end, mum."

"Well, then, a horse?"

"The for'rard end, mum."

"Which side of a tree does the most moss grow on?"

"North side."

"If fifteen cows is browsing on a hillside, how many of them eats with their heads pointed the same direction?"

"The whole fifteen, mum."

"Well, I reckon you *have* lived in the country. I thought maybe you was trying to hocus me again. What's your real name, now?"

"George Peters, mum."

"Well, try to remember it, George. Don't forget and tell me it's Elexander before you go, and then get out by saying it's George-Elexander when I catch you. And don't go about women in that

3. Mark Twain's fictitious name for Hannibal.

old calico. You do a girl tolerable poor, but you might fool men, maybe. Bless you, child, when you set out to thread a needle, don't hold the thread still and fetch the needle up to it; hold the needle still and poke the thread at it—that's the way a woman most always does; but a man always does 'tother way. And when you throw at a rat or anything, hitch yourself up a tip-toe, and fetch your hand up over your head as awkward as you can, and miss your rat about six or seven foot. Throw stiff-armed from the shoulder, like there was a pivot there for it to turn on—like a girl; not from the wrist and elbow, with your arm out to one side, like a boy. And mind you, when a girl tries to catch anything in her lap, she throws her knees apart; she don't clap them together, the way you did when you catched the lump of lead. Why, I spotted you for a boy when you was threading the needle; and I contrived the other things just to make certain. Now trot along to your uncle, Sarah Mary Williams George Elexander Peters, and if you get into trouble you send word to Mrs. Judith Loftus, which is me, and I'll do what I can to get you out of it. Keep the river road, all the way, and next time you tramp, take shoes and socks with you. The river road's a rocky one, and your feet 'll be in a condition when you get to Goshen, I reckon."

I went up the bank about fifty yards, and then I doubled on my tracks and slipped back to where my canoe was, a good piece below the house. I jumped in and was off in a hurry. I went up stream far enough to make the head of the island, and then started across. I took off the sun-bonnet, for I didn't want no blinders on, then. When I was about the middle, I hear the clock begin to strike; so I stops and listens; the sound come faint over the water, but clear —eleven. When I struck the head of the island I never waited to blow, though I was most winded, but I shoved right into the timber where my old camp used to be, and started a good fire there on a high-and-dry spot.

Then I jumped in the canoe and dug out for our place a mile and a half below, as hard as I could go. I landed, and slopped through the timber and up the ridge and into the cavern. There Jim laid, sound asleep on the ground. I roused him out and says:

"Git up and hump yourself, Jim! There ain't a minute to lose. They're after us!"

Jim never asked no questions, he never said a word; but the way he worked for the next half an hour showed about how he was scared. By that time everything we had in the world was on our raft and she was ready to be shoved out from the willow cove where she was hid. We put out the camp fire at the cavern the first thing, and didn't show a candle outside after that.

I took the canoe out from shore a little piece and took a look, but if there was a boat around I couldn't see it, for stars and shadows ain't good to see by. Then we got out the raft and slipped along down in the shade, past the foot of the island dead still, never saying a word.

Chapter XII

Must a been close onto one o'clock when we got below the island at last, and the raft did seem to go mighty slow. If a boat was to come along, we was going to take to the canoe and break for the Illinois shore; and it was well a boat didn't come, for we hadn't ever thought to put the gun into the canoe, or a fishing-line or anything to eat. We was in ruther too much of a sweat to think of so many things. It warn't good judgment to put *everything* on the raft.

If the men went to the island, I just expect they found the camp fire I built, and watched it all night for Jim to come. Anyways, they stayed away from us, and if my building the fire never fooled them it warn't no fault of mine. I played it as low-down on them as I could.

When the first streak of day begun to show, we tied up to a tow-head in a big bend on the Illinois side, and hacked off cotton-wood branches with the hatchet and covered up the raft with them so she looked like there had been a cave-in in the bank there. A tow-head is a sand-bar that has cotton-woods on it as thick as harrow-teeth.

We had mountains on the Missouri shore and heavy timber on the Illinois side, and the channel was down the Missouri shore at that place, so we warn't afraid of anybody running across us. We laid there all day and watched the rafts and steamboats spin down the Missouri shore, and up-bound steamboats fight the big river in the middle. I told Jim all about the time I had jabbering with that woman; and Jim said she was a smart one, and if she was to start after us herself *she* wouldn't set down and watch a camp fire—no, sir, she'd fetch a dog. Well, then, I said, why couldn't she tell her husband to fetch a dog? Jim said he bet she did think of it by the time the men was ready to start, and he believed they must a gone up town to get a dog and so they lost all that time, or else we wouldn't be here on a tow-head sixteen or seventeen mile below the village—no, indeedy, we would be in that same old town again. So I said I didn't care what was the reason they didn't get us, as long as they didn't.

When it was beginning to come on dark, we poked our heads out of the cottonwood thicket and looked up, and down, and across; nothing in sight; so Jim took up some of the top planks of the raft and built a snug wigwam to get under in blazing weather and rainy, and to keep the things dry. Jim made a floor for the wigwam, and raised it a foot or more above the level of the raft, so now the blankets and all the traps was out of the reach of steamboat waves. Right in the middle of the wigwam we made a layer of dirt about five or six inches deep with a frame around it for to hold it to its place; this was to build a fire on in sloppy weather or chilly; the wigwam would keep it from being seen. We made an extra steering oar, too, because one of the others might get broke, on a snag or something. We fixed up a short forked stick to hang the old lantern on; because we must always light the lantern whenever we see a steamboat coming down stream, to keep from getting run over; but we wouldn't have to light it up for upstream boats unless we see we was in what they call a "crossing;" for the river was pretty high yet, very low banks being still a little under water; so up-bound boats didn't always run the channel, but hunted easy water.

This second night we run between seven and eight hours, with a current that was making over four mile an hour. We catched fish, and talked, and we took a swim now and then to keep off sleepiness. It was kind of solemn, drifting down the big still river, laying on our backs looking up at the stars, and we didn't ever feel like talking loud, and it warn't often that we laughed, only a little kind of a low chuckle. We had mighty good weather, as a general thing, and nothing ever happened to us at all, that night, nor the next, nor the next.

Every night we passed towns, some of them away up on black hillsides, nothing but just a shiny bed of lights, not a house could you see. The fifth night we passed St. Louis, and it was like the whole world lit up. In St. Petersburg they used to say there was twenty or thirty thousand people in St. Louis, but I never believed it till I see that wonderful spread of lights at two o'clock that still night. There warn't a sound there; everybody was asleep.

Every night, now, I used to slip ashore, towards ten o'clock, at some little village, and buy ten or fifteen cents' worth of meal or bacon or other stuff to eat; and sometimes I lifted a chicken that warn't roosting comfortable, and took him along. Pap always said, take a chicken when you get a chance, because if you don't want him yourself you can easy find somebody that does, and a good deed ain't ever forgot. I never see Pap when he didn't want the chicken himself, but that is what he used to say, anyway.

Mornings, before daylight, I slipped into corn fields and borrowed a watermelon, or a mushmelon, or a pumpkin, or some new corn, or things of that kind. Pap always said it warn't no harm to borrow things, if you was meaning to pay them back, sometime; but the widow said it warn't anything but a soft name for stealing, and no decent body would do it. Jim said he reckoned the widow was partly right and pap was partly right; so the best way would be for us to pick out two or three things from the list and say we wouldn't borrow them any more—then he reckoned it wouldn't be no harm to borrow the others. So we talked it over all one night, drifting along down the river, trying to make up our minds whether to drop the watermelons, or the cantelopes, or the mushmelons, or what. But towards daylight we got it all settled satisfactory, and concluded to drop crabapples and p'simmons. We warn't feeling just right, before that, but it was all comfortable now. I was glad the way it come out, too, because crabapples ain't ever good, and the p'simmons wouldn't be ripe for two or three months yet.

We shot a water-fowl, now and then, that got up too early in the morning or didn't go to bed early enough in the evening. Take it all around, we lived pretty high.

The fifth night below St. Louis we had a big storm after midnight, with a power of thunder and lightning, and the rain poured down in a solid sheet. We stayed in the wigwam and let the raft take care of itself. When the lightning glared out we could see a big straight river ahead, and high rocky bluffs on both sides. By-and-by says I, "Hel-*lo*, Jim, looky yonder!" It was a steamboat that had killed herself on a rock. We was drifting straight down for her. The lightning showed her very distinct. She was leaning over, with part of her upper deck above water, and you could see every little chimbly-guy clean and clear, and a chair by the big bell, with an old slouch hat hanging on the back of it when the flashes come.

Well, it being away in the night, and stormy, and all so mysterious-like, I felt just the way any other boy would a felt when I see that wreck laying there so mournful and lonesome in the middle of the river. I wanted to get aboard of her and slink around a little, and see what there was there. So I says:

"Le's land on her, Jim."

But Jim was dead against it, at first. He says:

"I doan' want to go fool'n 'long er no wrack. We's doin' blame' well, en we better let blame' well alone, as de good book says. Like as not dey's a watchman on dat wrack."

"Watchman your grandmother," I says; "there ain't nothing to watch but the texas and the pilot-house; and do you reckon anybody's going to resk his life for a texas[4] and a pilot-house such a night as this, when it's likely to break up and wash off down the river any minute?" Jim couldn't say nothing to that, so he didn't try. "And besides," I says, "we might borrow something worth having, out of the captain's stateroom. Seegars, *I* bet you—and cost

4. Officers' cabin (so called because it was the largest) on the upper deck of the steamboat, with the pilot house before or on top.

five cents apiece, solid cash. Steamboat captains is always rich, and get sixty dollars a month, and *they* don't care a cent what a thing costs, you know, long as they want it. Stick a candle in your pocket; I can't rest, Jim, till we give her a rummaging. Do you reckon Tom Sawyer would ever go by this thing? Not for pie, he wouldn't. He'd call it an adventure—that's what he'd call it; and he'd land on that wreck if it was his last act. And wouldn't he throw style into it?—wouldn't he spread himself, nor nothing? Why, you'd think it was Christopher C'lumbus discovering Kingdom-Come. I wish Tom Sawyer *was* here."

Jim he grumbled a little, but give in. He said we mustn't talk any more than we could help, and then talk mighty low. The lightning showed us the wreck again, just in time, and we fetched the starboard derrick, and made fast there.

The deck was high out, here. We went sneaking down the slope of it to labboard, in the dark, towards the texas, feeling our way slow with our feet, and spreading our hands out to fend off the guys,[5] for it was so dark we couldn't see no sign of them. Pretty soon we struck the forward end of the skylight, and clumb onto it; and the next step fetched us in front of the captain's door, which was open, and by Jimminy, away down through the texas-hall we see a light! and all in the same second we seem to hear low voices in yonder!

Jim whispered and said he was feeling powerful sick, and told me to come along. I says, all right; and was going to start for the raft; but just then I heard a voice wail out and say:

"Oh, please don't, boys; I swear I won't ever tell!"

Another voice said, pretty loud:

"It's a lie, Jim Turner. You've acted this way before. You always want more'n your share of the truck, and you've always got it, too, because you've swore 't if you didn't you'd tell. But this time you've said it jest one time too many. You're the meanest, treacherousest hound in this country."

By this time Jim was gone for the raft. I was just a-biling with curiosity; and I says to myself, Tom Sawyer wouldn't back out now, and so I won't either; I'm agoing to see what's going on here. So I dropped on my hands and knees, in the little passage, and crept aft in the dark, till there warn't but about one stateroom betwixt me and the cross-hall of the texas. Then, in there I see a man stretched on the floor and tied hand and foot, and two men standing over him, and one of them had a dim lantern in his hand, and the other one had a pistol. This one kept pointing the pistol at the man's head on the floor and saying—

"I'd *like* to! And I orter, too, a mean skunk!"

5. Ropes fastened aloft for hoisting or dropping cargo.

The man on the floor would shrivel up, and say: "Oh, please don't, Bill—I hain't ever goin' to tell."

And every time he said that, the man with the lantern would laugh, and say:

"'Deed you *ain't!* You never said no truer thing 'n that, you bet you." And once he said: "Hear him beg! and yit if we hadn't got the best of him and tied him, he'd a killed us both. And what *for?* Jist for noth'n. Jist because we stood on our *rights*—that's what for. But I lay you ain't agoin' to threaten nobody any more, Jim Turner. Put *up* that pistol, Bill."

Bill says:

"I don't want to, Jake Packard. I'm for killin' him—and didn't he kill old Hatfield jist the same way—and don't he deserve it?"

"But I don't *want* him killed, and I've got my reasons for it."

"Bless yo' heart for them words, Jake Packard! I'll never forgit you, long's I live!" says the man on the floor, sort of blubbering.

Packard didn't take no notice of that, but hung up his lantern on a nail, and started towards where I was, there in the dark, and motioned Bill to come. I crawfished[6] as fast as I could, about two yards, but the boat slanted so that I couldn't make very good time; so to keep from getting run over and catched I crawled into a stateroom on the upper side. The man come a-pawing along in the dark, and when Packard got to my stateroom, he says:

"Here—come in here."

And in he come, and Bill after him. But before they got in, I was up in the upper berth, cornered, and sorry I come. Then they stood there, with their hands on the ledge of the berth, and talked. I couldn't see them, but I could tell where they was, by the whisky they'd been having. I was glad I didn't drink whisky; but it wouldn't made much difference, anyway, because most of the time they couldn't a treed me because I didn't breathe. I was too scared. And besides, a body *couldn't* breathe, and hear such talk. They talked low and earnest. Bill wanted to kill Turner. He says:

"He's said he'll tell, and he will. If we was to give both our shares to him *now*, it wouldn't make no difference after the row, and the way we've served him. Shore's you're born, he'll turn State's evidence; now you hear *me*. I'm for putting him out of his troubles."

"So'm I," says Packard, very quiet.

"Blame it, I'd sorter begun to think you wasn't. Well, then, that's all right. Les' go and do it."

"Hold on a minute; I hain't had my say yit. You listen to me. Shooting's good, but there's quieter ways if the thing's *got* to be done. But what *I* say, is this; it ain't good sense to go court'n

6. Crawled backward.

around after a halter, if you can git at what you're up to in some
way that's jist as good and at the same time don't bring you into
no resks. Ain't that so?"

"You bet it is. But how you goin' to manage it this time?"

"Well, my idea is this: we'll rustle around and gether up whatever pickins we've overlooked in the staterooms, and shove for
shore and hide the truck. Then we'll wait. Now I say it ain't agoin'
to be more 'n two hours befo' this wrack breaks up and washes
off down the river. See? He'll be drownded, and won't have nobody
to blame for it but his own self. I reckon that's a considerable sight
better'n killin' of him. I'm unfavorable to killin' a man as long as
you can git around it; it ain't good sense, it ain't good morals. Ain't
I right?"

"Yes—I reck'n you are. But s'pose she *don't* break up and wash
off?"

"Well, we can wait the two hours, anyway, and see, can't we?"

"All right, then; come along."

So they started, and I lit out, all in a cold sweat, and scrambled
forward. It was dark as pitch there; but I said in a kind of a coarse
whisper, "Jim!" and he answered up, right at my elbow, with a
sort of a moan, and I says:

"Quick, Jim, it ain't no time for fooling around and moaning;
there's a gang of murderers in yonder, and if we don't hunt up
their boat and set her drifting down the river so these fellows can't
get away from the wreck, there's one of 'em going to be in a bad
fix. But if we find their boat we can put *all* of 'em in a bad fix—for
the Sheriff 'll get 'em. Quick—hurry! I'll hunt the labboard side,
you hunt the stabboard. You start at the raft, and—"

"Oh, my lordy, lordy! *Raf'*? Dey ain' no raf' no mo', she done
broke loose en gone!—'en here we is!"

Chapter XIII

Well, I catched my breath and most fainted. Shut up on a wreck
with such a gang as that! But it warn't no time to be sentiment-
ing. We'd got to find that boat, now—had to have it for ourselves.
So we went a-quaking and shaking down the stabboard side, and
slow work it was, too—seemed a week before we got to the stern.
No sign of a boat. Jim said he didn't believe he could go any further—so scared he hadn't hardly any strength left, he said. But I
said come on, if we get left on this wreck, we are in a fix, sure. So
on we prowled, again. We struck for the stern of the texas, and
found it, and then scrabbled along forwards on the skylight, hanging on from shutter to shutter, for the edge of the skylight was in
the water. When we got pretty close to the cross-hall door, there

was the skiff, sure enough! I could just barely see her. I felt ever so thankful. In another second I would a been aboard of her; but just then the door opened. One of the men stuck his head out, only about a couple of foot from me, and I thought I was gone; but he jerked it in again, and says:

"Heave that blame lantern out o' sight, Bill!"

He flung a bag of something into the boat, and then got in himself, and set down. It was Packard. Then Bill *he* come out and got in. Packard says, in a low voice:

"All ready—shove off!"

I couldn't hardly hang onto the shutters, I was so weak. But Bill says:

"Hold on—'d you go through him?"

"No. Didn't you?"

"No. So he's got his share o' the cash, yet."

"Well, then, come along—no use to take truck and leave money."

"Say—won't he suspicion what we're up to?"

"Maybe he won't. But we got to have it anyway. Come along."

So they got out and went in.

The door slammed to, because it was on the careened side; and in a half second I was in the boat, and Jim come a tumbling after me. I out with my knife and cut the rope, and away we went!

We didn't touch an oar, and we didn' speak nor whisper, nor hardly even breathe. We went gliding swift along, dead silent, past the tip of the paddle-box, and past the stern; then in a second or two more we was a hundred yards below the wreck, and the darkness soaked her up, every last sign of her, and we was safe, and knowed it.

When we was three or four hundred yards down stream, we see the lantern show like a little spark at the texas door, for a second, and we knowed by that that the rascals had missed their boat, and was beginning to understand that they was in just as much trouble, now, as Jim Turner was.

Then Jim manned the oars, and we took out after our raft. Now was the first time that I begun to worry about the men—I reckon I hadn't had time to before. I begun to think how dreadful it was, even for murderers, to be in such a fix. I says to myself, there ain't no telling but I might come to be a murderer myself, yet, and then how would *I* like it? So says I to Jim:

"The first light we see, we'll land a hundred yards below it or above it, in a place where it's a good hiding-place for you and the skiff, and then I'll go and fix up some kind of a yarn, and get somebody to go for that gang and get them out of their scrape, so they can be hung when their time comes."

But that idea was a failure; for pretty soon it begun to storm

again, and this time worse than ever. The rain poured down, and
never a light showed; everybody in bed, I reckon. We boomed
along down the river, watching for lights and watching for our raft.
After a long time the rain let up, but the clouds staid, and the
lightning kept whimpering, and by-and-by a flash showed us a
black thing ahead, floating, and we made for it.

It was the raft, and mighty glad was we to get aboard of it again.
We seen a light, now, away down to the right, on shore. So I said
I would go for it. The skiff was half full of plunder which that
gang had stole, there on the wreck. We hustled it onto the raft in a
pile, and I told Jim to float along down, and show a light when he
judged he had gone about two mile, and keep it burning till I
come; then I manned my oars and shoved for the light. As I got
down towards it, three or four more showed—up on a hillside. It
was a village. I closed in above the shore-light, and laid on my
oars and floated. As I went by, I see it was a lantern hanging on the
jackstaff of a double-hull ferry-boat. I skimmed around for the
watchman, a-wondering whereabouts he slept; and by-and-by I
found him roosting on the bitts,[7] forward, with his head down between his knees. I give his shoulder two or three little shoves, and
begun to cry.

He stirred up, in a kind of startlish way; but when he see it was
only me, he took a good gap and stretch, and then he says:

"Hello, what's up? Don't cry, bub. What's the trouble?"

I says:

"Pap, and mam, and sis, and—"

Then I broke down. He says:

"Oh, dang it, now, *don't* take on so, we all has to have our troubles and this'n 'll come out all right. What's the matter with 'em?"

"They're—they're—are you the watchman of the boat?"

"Yes," he says, kind of pretty-well-satisfied like. "I'm the captain and the owner, and the mate, and the pilot, and watchman, and
head deck-hand; and sometimes I'm the freight and passengers. I
ain't as rich as old Jim Hornback, and I can't be so blame' generous
and good to Tom, Dick and Harry as what he is, and slam around
money the way he does; but I've told him a many a time 't I
wouldn't trade places with him; for, says I, a sailor's life's the life
for me, and I'm derned if I'd live two mile out o' town, where there
ain't nothing ever goin' on, not for all his spondulicks and as much
more on top of it. Says I—"

I broke in and says:

"They're in an awful peck of trouble, and—"

"*Who* is?"

"Why, pap, and mam, and sis, and Miss Hooker; and if you'd

7. Timbers above the deck to which cables or hawsers can be fastened.

take your ferry-boat and go up there—"

"Up where? Where are they?"

"On the wreck."

"What wreck?"

"Why, there ain't but one."

"What, you don't mean the *Walter Scott?*"[8]

"Yes."

"Good land! what are they doin' *there*, for gracious sakes?"

"Well, they didn't go there a-purpose."

"I bet they didn't! Why, great goodness, there ain't no chance for 'em if they don't git off mighty quick! Why, how in the nation did they ever git into such a scrape?"

"Easy enough. Miss Hooker was a-visiting, up there to the town—"

"Yes, Booth's Landing—go on."

"She was a-visiting, there at Booth's Landing, and just in the edge of the evening she started over with her nigger woman in the horse-ferry, to stay all night at her friend's house, Miss What-you-may-call-her, I disremember her name, and they lost their steering-oar, and swung around and went a-floating down, stern-first, about two mile, and saddle-baggsed on the wreck, and the ferry man and the nigger woman and the horses was all lost, but Miss Hooker she made a grab and got aboard the wreck. Well, about an hour after dark, we come along down in our trading-scow, and it was so dark we didn't notice the wreck till we was right on it; and so *we* saddle-baggsed; but all of us was saved but Bill Whipple—and oh, he *was* the best cretur!—I most wish't it had been me, I do."

"My George! It's the beatenest thing I ever struck. And *then* what did you all do?"

"Well, we hollered and took on, but it's so wide there, we couldn't make nobody hear. So pap said somebody got to get ashore and get help somehow. I was the only one that could swim, so I made a dash for it, and Miss Hooker she said if I didn't strike help sooner, come here and hunt up her uncle, and he'd fix the thing. I made the land about a mile below, and been fooling along ever since, trying to get people to do something, but they said, 'What, in such a night and such a current? there ain't no sense in it; go for the steam-ferry.' Now if you'll go, and—"

"By Jackson, I'd *like* to, and blame it I don't know but I will; but who in the dingnation's agoin' to *pay* for it? Do you reckon your pap—"

"Why *that's* all right. Miss Hooker she told me, *particular*, that

8. Twain comically names the steam-boat for the English author of ro-mances which, in his estimation, also foundered.

her uncle Hornback—"

"Great guns! is *he* her uncle? Looky here, you break for that
light over yonder-way, and turn out west when you git there, and
about a quarter of a mile out you'll come to the tavern; tell 'em to
dart you out to Jim Hornback's and he'll foot the bill. And don't
you fool around any, because he'll want to know the news. Tell him
I'll have his niece all safe before he can get to town. Hump yourself, now; I'm agoing up around the corner here, to roust out my
engineer."

I struck for the light, but as soon as he turned the corner I went
back and got into my skiff and bailed her out and then pulled up
shore in the easy water about six hundred yards, and tucked myself
in among some woodboats; for I couldn't rest easy till I could see
the ferry-boat start. But take it all around, I was feeling ruther comfortable on accounts of taking all this trouble for that gang, for not
many would a done it. I wished the widow knowed about it. I
judged she would be proud of me for helping these rapscallions,
because rapscallions and dead beats is the kind the widow and good
people takes the most interest in.

Well, before long, here comes the wreck, dim and dusky, sliding
along down! A kind of cold shiver went through me, and then I
struck out for her. She was very deep, and I see in a minute there
warn't much chance for anybody being alive in her. I pulled all
around her and hollered a little, but there wasn't any answer; all
dead still. I felt a little bit heavy-hearted about the gang, but not
much, for I reckoned if they could stand it, I could.

Then here comes the ferry-boat; so I shoved for the middle of the
river on a long down-stream slant; and when I judged I was out of
eye-reach, I laid on my oars, and looked back and see her go and
smell around the wreck for Miss Hooker's remainders, because the
captain would know her uncle Hornback would want them; and
then pretty soon the ferry-boat give it up and went for shore, and
I laid into my work and went a-booming down the river.

It did seem a powerful long time before Jim's light showed up;
and when it did show, it looked like it was a thousand mile off. By
the time I got there the sky was beginning to get a little gray in
the east; so we struck for an island, and hid the raft, and sunk the
skiff, and turned in and slept like dead people.

Chapter XIV

By-and-by, when we got up, we turned over the truck the gang
had stole off of the wreck, and found boots, and blankets, and
clothes, and all sorts of other things, and a lot of books, and a
spyglass, and three boxes of seegars. We hadn't ever been this rich

before, in neither of our lives. The seegars was prime. We laid off all the afternoon in the woods talking, and me reading the books, and having a general good time. I told Jim all about what happened inside the wreck, and at the ferry-boat; and I said these kinds of things was adventures; but he said he didn't want no more adventures. He said that when I went in the texas and he crawled back to get on the raft and found her gone, he nearly died; because he judged it was all up with *him*, anyway it could be fixed; for if he didn't get saved he would get drownded; and if he did get saved, whoever saved him would send him back home so as to get the reward, and then Miss Watson would sell him South, sure. Well, he was right; he was most always right; he had an uncommon level head, for a nigger.

I read considerable to Jim about kings, and dukes, and earls, and such, and how gaudy they dressed, and how much style they put on, and called each other your majesty, and your grace, and your lordship, and so on, 'stead of mister; and Jim's eyes bugged out, and he was interested. He says:

"I didn' know dey was so many un um. I hain't hearn 'bout none un um, skasely, but ole King Sollermun, onless you counts dem kings dat's in a pack er k'yards. How much do a king git?"

"Get?" I says; "why, they get a thousand dollars a month if they want it; they can have just as much as they want; everything belongs to them."

"*Ain'* dat gay? En what they got to do, Huck?"

"*They* don't do nothing! Why how you talk. They just set around."

"No—is dat so?"

"Of course it is. They just set around. Except maybe when there 's a war; then they go to the war. But other times they just lazy around; or go hawking—just hawking and sp— Sh!—d' you hear a noise?"

We skipped out and looked; but it warn't nothing but the flutter of a steamboat's wheel, away down coming around the point; so we come back.

"Yes," says I, "and other times, when things is dull, they fuss with the parlyment; and if everybody don't go just so he whacks their heads off. But mostly they hang round the harem."

"Roun' de which?"

"Harem."

"What's de harem?"

"The place where he keep his wives. Don't you know about the harem? Solomon had one; he had about a million wives."

"Why, yes, dat's so; I—I'd done forgot it. A harem's a bo'd'n-house, I reck'n. Mos' likely dey has rackety times in de nussery. En

I reck'n de wives quarrels considable; en dat 'crease de racket. Yit dey say Sollermun de wises' man dat ever live'. I doan' take no stock in dat. Bekase why: would a wise man want to live in de mids' er sich a blimblammin' all de time? No—'deed he wouldn't. A wise man 'ud take en buil' a biler-factry; en den he could shet *down* de biler-factry when he want to res'."

"Well, but he *was* the wisest man, anyway; because the widow she told me so, her own self."

"I doan k'yer what de widder say, he *warn't* no wise man, nuther. He had some er de dad-fetchedes' ways I ever see. Does you know 'bout dat chile dat he 'uz gwyne to chop in two?"[9]

"Yes, the widow told me all about it."

"*Well*, den! Warn' dat de beatenes' notion in de worl'? You jes' take en look at it a minute. Dah's de stump, dah—dat's one er de women; heah's you—dat's de yuther one; I's Sollermun; en dish-yer dollar bill's de chile. Bofe un you claims it. What does I do? Does I shin aroun' mongs' de neighbors en fine out which un you de bill *do* b'long to, en han' it over to de right one, all safe en soun', de way dat anybody dat had any gumption would? No—I take en whack de bill in *two*, en give half un it to you, en de yuther half to de yuther woman. Dat's de way Sollermun was gwyne to do wid de chile. Now I want to ast you: what's de use er dat half a bill?—can't buy noth'n wid it. En what use is a half a chile? I would'n give a dern for a million un um."

"But hang it, Jim, you've clean missed the point—blame it, you've missed it a thousand mile."

"Who? Me? Go 'long. Doan' talk to *me* 'bout yo' pints. I reck'n I knows sense when I sees it; en dey ain' no sense in sich doin's as dat. De 'spute warn't 'bout a half a chile, de 'spute was 'bout a whole chile; en de man dat think he kin settle a 'spute 'bout a whole chile wid a half a chile, doan' know enough to come in out'n de rain. Doan' talk to me 'bout Sollermun, Huck, I knows him by de back."

"But I tell you you don't get the point."

"Blame de pint! I reck'n I knows what I knows. En mine you, de *real* pint is down furder—it's down deeper. It lays in de way Sollermun was raised. You take a man dat's got on'y one er two chillen; is dat man gwyne to be waseful o' chillen? No, he ain't; he can't 'ford it. *He* know how to value 'em. But you take a man dat's got 'bout five million chillen runnin' roun' de house, en it's diffunt. *He* as soon chop a chile in two as a cat. Dey's plenty mo'. A chile er two, mo' er less, warn't no consekens to Sollermun, dad fetch him!"

I never see such a nigger. If he got a notion in his head once,

9. *Cf.* I Kings iii: 16–27.

there warn't no getting it out again. He was the most down on Solomon of any nigger I ever see. So I went to talking about other kings, and let Solomon slide. I told about Louis Sixteenth that got his head cut off in France long time ago;[1] and about his little boy the dolphin,[2] that would a been a king, but they took and shut him up in jail, and some say he died there.

"Po' little chap."

"But some says he got out and got away, and come to America."

"Dat's good! But he'll be pooty lonesome—dey ain' no kings here, is dey, Huck?"

"No."

"Den he cain't git no situation. What he gwyne to do?"

"Well, I don't know. Some of them gets on the police, and some of them learns people how to talk French."

"Why, Huck, doan' de French people talk de same way we does?"

"No, Jim; you couldn't understand a word they said—not a single word."

"Well, now, I be ding-busted! How do dat come?"

"I don't know; but it's so. I got some of their jabber out of a book. Spose a man was to come to you and say *Polly-voo-franzy*— what would you think?"

"I wouldn' think nuff'n; I'd take en bust him over de head. Dat is, if he warn't white. I wouldn't 'low no nigger to call me dat."

"Shucks, it ain't calling you anything. It's only saying do you know how to talk French."

"Well, den, why couldn't he *say* it?"

"Why, he *is* a-saying it. That's a Frenchman's *way* of saying it."

"Well, it's a blame' ridicklous way, en I doan' want to hear no mo' 'bout it. Dey ain' no sense in it."

"Looky here, Jim; does a cat talk like we do?"

"No, a cat don't."

"Well, does a cow?"

"No, a cow don't, nuther."

"Does a cat talk like a cow, or a cow talk like a cat?"

"No, dey don't."

"It's natural and right for 'em to talk different from each other, ain't it?"

" 'Course."

"And ain't it natural and right for a cat and a cow to talk different from *us*?"

1. In the first edition, erroneously printed "age."
2. The Dauphin, Louis Charles (1785– 1795?) survived the execution of his father, Louis XVI, in 1793, and died in prison. Huck alludes to one of the persistent legends of his escape and survival. *Cf.* the bogus pedigree of the "king" (and of the "duke") in Chapter XIX.

"Why, mos' sholy it is."

"Well, then, why ain't it natural and right for a *Frenchman* to talk different from us? You answer me that."

"Is a cat a man, Huck?"

"No."

"Well, den, dey ain't no sense in a cat talkin' like a man. Is a cow a man?—er is a cow a cat?"

"No, she ain't either of them."

"Well, den, she ain' got no business to talk like either one er the yuther of 'em. Is a Frenchman a man?"

"Yes."

"*Well*, den! Dad blame it, why doan' he *talk* like a man? You answer me *dat!*"

I see it warn't no use wasting words—you can't learn a nigger to argue. So I quit.

Chapter XV

We judged that three nights more would fetch us to Cairo,[3] at the bottom of Illinois, where the Ohio River comes in, and that was what we was after. We would sell the raft and get on a steamboat and go way up the Ohio amongst the free States, and then be out of trouble.[4]

Well, the second night a fog begun to come on, and we made for a tow-head to tie to, for it wouldn't do to try to run in fog; but when I paddled ahead in the canoe, with the line, to make fast, there warn't anything but little saplings to tie to. I passed the line around one of them right on the edge of the cut bank, but there was a stiff current, and the raft come booming down so lively she tore it out by the roots and away she went. I see the fog closing down, and it made me so sick and scared I couldn't budge for most a half a minute it seemed to me—and then there warn't no raft in sight; you couldn't see twenty yards. I jumped into the canoe and run back to the stern and grabbed the paddle and set her back a stroke. But she didn't come. I was in such a hurry I hadn't untied her. I got up and tried to untie her, but I was so excited my hands shook so I couldn't hardly do anything with them.

As soon as I got started I took out after the raft, hot and heavy, right down the tow-head. That was all right as far as it went, but the tow-head warn't sixty yards long, and the minute I flew by the

3. Pronounced locally as "Kay-ro."
4. Critical debates have centered on why the author did not carry out this plan for Jim's freedom. Reports on the manuscript indicate that Twain laid the book aside near the end of Chapter XVI for probably two years. When he took up the story again, it appears that he was enamored of the idea of the freedom of the River itself, a kind of time stream, in whose current there would be the escape from the cruelty and hypocrisy abroad on the land. *Cf.* Chapter VIII, note 7, and title note.

foot of it I shot out into the solid white fog, and hadn't no more idea which way I was going than a dead man.

Thinks I, it won't do to paddle; first I know I'll run into the bank or a tow-head or something; I got to set still and float, and yet it's mighty fidgety business to have to hold your hands still at such a time. I whooped and listened. Away down there, somewheres, I hears a small whoop, and up comes my spirits. I went tearing after it, listening sharp to hear it again. The next time it come, I see I warn't heading for it but heading away to the right of it. And the next time, I was heading away to the left of it—and not gaining on it much, either, for I was flying around, this way and that and 'tother, but it was going straight ahead all the time.

I did wish the fool would think to beat a tin pan, and beat it all the time, but he never did, and it was the still places between the whoops that was making the trouble for me. Well, I fought along, and directly I hears the whoop *behind* me. I was tangled good, now. That was somebody else's whoop, or else I was turned around.

I throwed the paddle down. I heard the whoop again; it was behind me yet, but in a different place; it kept coming, and kept changing its place, and I kept answering, till by-and-by it was in front of me again and I knowed the current had swung the canoe's head down stream and I was all right, if that was Jim and not some other raftsman hollering. I couldn't tell nothing about voices in a fog, for nothing don't look natural nor sound natural in a fog.

The whooping went on, and in about a minute I come a booming down on a cut bank with smoky ghosts of big trees on it, and the current throwed me off to the left and shot by, amongst a lot of snags that fairly roared, the current was tearing by them so swift.

In another second or two it was solid white and still again. I set perfectly still, then, listening to my heart thump, and I reckon I didn't draw a breath while it thumped a hundred.

I just give up, then. I knowed what the matter was. That cut bank was an island, and Jim had gone down 'tother side of it. It warn't no tow-head, that you could float by in ten minutes. It had the big timber of a regular island; it might be five or six mile long and more than a half a mile wide.

I kept quiet, with my ears cocked, about fifteen minutes, I reckon. I was floating along, of course, four or five mile an hour; but you don't ever think of that. No, you *feel* like you are laying dead still on the water; and if a little glimpse of a snag slips by, you don't think to yourself how fast *you're* going, but you catch your breath and think, my! how that snag's tearing along. If you think it ain't dismal and lonesome out in a fog that way, by yourself, in the night, you try it once—you'll see.

Next, for about half an hour, I whoops now and then; at last I hears the answer a long ways off, and tries to follow it, but I couldn't do it, and directly I judged I'd got into a nest of tow-heads, for I had little dim glimpses of them on both sides of me, sometimes just a narrow channel between; and some that I couldn't see, I knowed was there, because I'd hear the wash of the current against the old dead brush and trash that hung over the banks. Well, I warn't long losing the whoops, down amongst the tow-heads; and I only tried to chase them a little while, anyway, because it was worse than chasing a Jack-o-lantern. You never knowed a sound dodge around so, and swap places so quick and so much.

I had to claw away from the bank pretty lively, four or five times, to keep from knocking the islands out of the river; and so I judged the raft must be butting into the bank every now and then, or else it would get further ahead and clear out of hearing—it was floating a little faster than what I was.

Well, I seemed to be in the open river again, by-and-by, but I couldn't hear no sign of a whoop nowheres. I reckoned Jim had fetched up on a snag, maybe, and it was all up with him. I was good and tired, so I laid down in the canoe and said I wouldn't bother no more. I didn't want to go to sleep, of course; but I was so sleepy I couldn't help it; so I thought I would take just one little cat-nap.

But I reckon it was more than a cat-nap, for when I waked up the stars was shining bright, the fog was all gone, and I was spinning down a big bend stern first. First I didn't know where I was; I thought I was dreaming; and when things begun to come back to me, they seemed to come up dim out of last week.

It was a monstrous big river here, with the tallest and the thickest kind of timber on both banks; just a solid wall, as well as I could see, by the stars. I looked away down stream, and seen a black speck on the water. I took out after it; but when I got to it it warn't nothing but a couple of saw-logs made fast together. Then I see another speck, and chased that; then another, and this time I was right. It was the raft.

When I got to it Jim was setting there with his head down between his knees, asleep, with his right arm hanging over the steering oar. The other oar was smashed off, and the raft was littered up with leaves and branches and dirt. So she'd had a rough time.

I made fast and laid down under Jim's nose on the raft, and begun to gap, and stretch my fists out against Jim, and says:

"Hello, Jim, have I been asleep? Why didn't you stir me up?"

"Goodness gracious, is dat you, Huck? En you ain' dead—you ain' drownded—you's back agin? It's too good for true, honey, it's too good for true. Lemme look at you, chile, lemme feel o' you. No,

you ain' dead! you's back agin, 'live en soun', jis de same ole Huck
—de same ole Huck, thanks to goodness!"

"What's the matter with you, Jim? You been a drinking?"

"Drinkin'? Has I ben a drinkin'? Has I had a chance to be a
drinkin'?"

"Well, then, what makes you talk so wild?"

"How does I talk wild?"

"*How?* why, hain't you been talking about my coming back, and
all that stuff, as if I'd been gone away?"

"Huck—Huck Finn, you look me in de eye; look me in de eye.
Hain't you ben gone away?"

"Gone away? Why, what in the nation do you mean? I hain't
been gone anywheres. Where would I go to?"

"Well, looky here, boss, dey's sumf'n wrong, dey is. Is I *me*, or
who *is* I? Is I heah, or whah *is* I? Now dat's what I wants to know?"

"Well, I think you're here, plain enough, but I think you're a
tangle-headed old fool, Jim."

"I is, is I? Well you answer me dis. Didn't you tote out de line
in de canoe, fer to make fas' to de tow-head?"

"No, I didn't. What tow-head? I hain't seen no tow-head."

"You hain't seen no tow-head? Looky here—didn't de line pull
loose en de raf' go a hummin' down de river, en leave you en de
canoe behine in de fog?"

"What fog?"

"Why *de* fog. De fog dat's ben aroun' all night. En didn't you
whoop, en didn't I whoop, tell we got mix' up in de islands en one
un us got los' en 'tother one was jis' as good as los', 'kase he didn'
know whah he wuz? En didn't I bust up agin a lot er dem islands
en have a turrible time en mos' git drownded? Now ain' dat so, boss
—ain't it so? You answer me dat."

"Well, this is too many for me, Jim. I hain't seen no fog, nor no
islands, nor no troubles, nor nothing. I been setting here talking
with you all night till you went to sleep about ten minutes ago, and
I reckon I done the same. You couldn't a got drunk in that time, so
of course you've been dreaming."

"Dad fetch it, how is I gwyne to dream all dat in ten minutes?"

"Well, hang it all, you did dream it, because there didn't any of
it happen."

"But Huck, it's all jis' as plain to me as—"

"It don't make no difference how plain it is, there ain't nothing
in it. I know, because I've been here all the time."

Jim didn't say nothing for about five minutes, but set there studying over it. Then he says:

"Well, den, I reck'n I did dream it, Huck; but dog my cats ef it
ain't de powerfullest dream I ever see. En I hain't ever had no

dream b'fo' dat's tired me like dis one."

"Oh, well, that's all right, because a dream does tire a body like everything, sometimes. But this one was a staving[5] dream—tell me all about it, Jim."

So Jim went to work and told me the whole thing right through, just as it happened, only he painted it up considerable. Then he said he must start in and " 'terpret" it, because it was sent for a warning. He said the first tow-head stood for a man that would try to do us some good, but the current was another man that would get us away from him. The whoops was warnings that would come to us every now and then, and if we didn't try hard to make out to understand them they'd just take us into bad luck, 'stead of keeping us out of it. The lot of tow-heads was troubles we was going to get into with quarrelsome people and all kinds of mean folks, but if we minded our business and didn't talk back and aggravate them, we would pull through and get out of the fog and into the big clear river, which was the free States, and wouldn't have no more trouble.

It had clouded up pretty dark just after I got onto the raft, but it was clearing up again, now.

"Oh, well, that's all interpreted well enough, as far as it goes, Jim," I says; "but what does *these* things stand for?"

It was the leaves and rubbish on the raft, and the smashed oar. You could see them first rate, now.

Jim looked at the trash, and then looked at me, and back at the trash again. He had got the dream fixed so strong in his head that he couldn't seem to shake it loose and get the facts back into its place again, right away. But when he did get the thing straightened around, he looked at me steady, without ever smiling, and says:

"What do dey stan' for? I's gwyne to tell you. When I got all wore out wid work, en wid de callin' for you, en went to sleep, my heart wuz mos' broke bekase you wuz los', en I didn' k'yer no mo' what become er me en de raf'. En when I wake up en fine you back agin', all safe en soun', de tears come en I could a got down on my knees en kiss' yo' foot I's so thankful. En all you wuz thinkin' 'bout wuz how you could make a fool uv ole Jim wid a lie. Dat truck dah is *trash*; en trash is what people is dat puts dirt on de head er dey fren's en makes 'em ashamed."

Then he got up slow, and walked to the wigwam, and went in there, without saying anything but that. But that was enough. It made me feel so mean I could almost kissed *his* foot to get him to take it back.

It was fifteen minutes before I could work myself up to go and humble myself to a nigger—but I done it, and I warn't ever sorry

5. Fine, splendid.

for it afterwards, neither. I didn't do him no more mean tricks, and I wouldn't done that one if I'd a knowed it would make him feel that way.[6]

Chapter XVI

We slept most all day, and started out at night, a little ways behind a monstrous long raft that was as long going by as a procession. She had four long sweeps[7] at each end, so we judged she carried as many as thirty men, likely. She had five big wigwams aboard, wide apart, and an open camp fire in the middle, and a tall flagpole at each end. There was a power of style about her. It *amounted* to something being a raftsman on such a craft as that.

We went drifting down into a big bend, and the night clouded up and got hot. The river was very wide, and was walled with solid timber on both sides; you couldn't see a break in it hardly ever, or a light. We talked about Cairo, and wondered whether we would know it when we got to it. I said likely we wouldn't, because I had heard say there warn't but about a dozen houses there, and if they didn't happen to have them lit up, how was we going to know we was passing a town? Jim said if the two big rivers joined together there, that would show. But I said maybe we might think we was passing the foot of an island and coming into the same old river again. That disturbed Jim—and me too. So the question was, what to do? I said, paddle ashore the first time a light showed, and tell them pap was behind, coming along with a trading-scow, and was a green hand at the business, and wanted to know how far it was to Cairo. Jim thought it was a good idea, so we took a smoke on it and waited.[8]

There warn't nothing to do, now, but to look out sharp for the town, and not pass it without seeing it. He said he'd be mighty sure to see it, because he'd be a free man the minute he seen it, but if he missed it he'd be in the slave country again and no more show for freedom. Every little while he jumps up and says:

"Dah she is!"

But it warn't. It was Jack-o-lanterns, or lightning-bugs; so he set down again, and went to watching, same as before. Jim said it made him all over trembly and feverish to be so close to freedom. Well, I can tell you it made me all over trembly and feverish, too, to hear

---

6. The simple nobility of Jim's speech needs no comment. But this episode is the author's first fully developed example of the revelation of man and nature that, often through Jim's agency, gave scope for the natural innocence of Huck, which otherwise might have been lost in the deep knowledge of evil which marked his boyhood.

7. A long oar used to propel or steer.
8. *Life on the Mississippi* (1883) incorporated Twain's serial articles and the "Raft Passage" (which followed immediately after this paragraph in the unfinished *Huck* MS.), a famous description of early river life; *q.v.*, p. 196 above.

him, because I begun to get it through my head that he *was* most free—and who was to blame for it? Why, *me*. I couldn't get that out of my conscience, no how nor no way. It got to troubling me so I couldn't rest; I couldn't stay still in one place. It hadn't ever come home to me before, what this thing was that I was doing. But now it did; and it staid with me, and scorched me more and more. I tried to make out to myself that *I* warn't to blame, because *I* didn't run Jim off from his rightful owner; but it warn't no use, conscience up and says, every time, "But you knowed he was running for his freedom, and you could a paddled ashore and told somebody." That was so—I couldn't get around that, noway. That was where it pinched. Conscience says to me, "What had poor Miss Watson done to you, that you could see her nigger go off right under your eyes and never say one single word? What did that poor old woman do to you, that you could treat her so mean? Why, she tried to learn you your book, she tried to learn you your manners, she tried to be good to you every way she knowed how. *That's* what she done."

I got to feeling so mean and so miserable I most wished I was dead. I fidgeted up and down the raft, abusing myself to myself, and Jim was fidgeting up and down past me. We neither of us could keep still. Every time he danced around and says, "Dah's Cairo!" it went through me like a shot, and I thought if it *was* Cairo I reckoned I would die of miserableness.[9]

Jim talked out loud all the time while I was talking to myself. He was saying how the first thing he would do when he got to a free State he would go to saving up money and never spend a single cent, and when he got enough he would buy his wife, which was owned on a farm close to where Miss Watson lived; and then they would both work to buy the two children, and if their master wouldn't sell them, they'd get an Ab'litionist to go and steal them.

It most froze me to hear such talk. He wouldn't ever dared to talk such talk in his life before. Just see what a difference it made in him the minute he judged he was about free. It was according to the old saying, "give a nigger an inch and he'll take an ell." Thinks I, this is what comes of my not thinking. Here was this nigger which I had as good as helped to run away, coming right out flat-footed and saying he would steal his children—children that belonged to a man I didn't even know; a man that hadn't ever done me no harm.

I was sorry to hear Jim say that, it was such a lowering of him. My conscience got to stirring me up hotter than ever, until at last

9. In the light of present attitudes toward slavery, one must remember that in the South, at the time of this story, slavery was supported by the social institutions of property and church. Huck was a boy caught between conflicting loyalties, and this conflict continues as a principal motivation throughout the book.

I says to it, "Let up on me—it ain't too late, yet—I'll paddle ashore at the first light, and tell." I felt easy, and happy, and light as a feather, right off. All my troubles was gone. I went to looking out sharp for a light, and sort of singing to myself. By-and-by one showed. Jim sings out:

"We's safe, Huck, we's safe! Jump up and crack yo' heels, dat's de good ole Cairo at las', I jis knows it!"

I says:

"I'll take the canoe and go see, Jim. It mightn't be, you know."

He jumped and got the canoe ready, and put his old coat in the bottom for me to set on, and give me the paddle; and as I shoved off, he says:

"Pooty soon I'll be a-shout'n for joy, en I'll say, it's all on accounts o' Huck; I's a free man, en I couldn't ever ben free ef it hadn' ben for Huck; Huck done it. Jim won't ever forgit you, Huck; you's de bes' fren' Jim's ever had; en you's de *only* fren' ole Jim's got now."

I was paddling off, all in a sweat to tell on him; but when he says this, it seemed to kind of take the tuck all out of me. I went along slow then, and I warn't right down certain whether I was glad I started or whether I warn't. When I was fifty yards off, Jim says:

"Dah you goes, de ole true Huck; de on'y white genlman dat ever kep' his promise to ole Jim."

Well, I just felt sick. But I says, I *got* to do it—I can't get *out* of it. Right then, along comes a skiff with two men in it, with guns, and they stopped and I stopped. One of them says:

"What's that, yonder?"

"A piece of a raft," I says.

"Do you belong on it?"

"Yes, sir."

"Any men on it?"

"Only one, sir."

"Well, there's five niggers run off to-night, up yonder above the head of the bend. Is your man white or black?"

I didn't answer up prompt. I tried to, but the words wouldn't come. I tried, for a second or two, to brace up and out with it, but I warn't man enough—hadn't the spunk of a rabbit. I see I was weakening; so I just give up trying, and up and says—

"He's white."

"I reckon we'll go and see for ourselves."

"I wish you would," says I, "because it's pap that's there, and maybe you'd help me tow the raft ashore where the light is. He's sick—and so is mam and Mary Ann."

"Oh, the devil! we're in a hurry, boy. But I s'pose we've got to. Come—buckle to your paddle, and let's get along."

I buckled to my paddle and they laid to their oars. When we had made a stroke or two, I says:

"Pap'll be mighty much obleeged to you, I can tell you. Everybody goes away when I want them to help me tow the raft ashore, and I can't do it by myself."

"Well, that's infernal mean. Odd, too. Say, boy, what's the matter with your father?"

"It's the—a—the—well, it ain't anything, much."

They stopped pulling. It warn't but a mighty little ways to the raft, now. One says:

"Boy, that's a lie. What *is* the matter with your pap? Answer up square, now, and it'll be the better for you."

"I will, sir, I will, honest—but don't leave us, please. It's the—the—gentlemen, if you'll only pull ahead, and let me heave you the head-line, you won't have to come a-near the raft—please do."

"Set her back, John, set her back!" says one. They backed water. "Keep away, boy—keep to looard. Confound it, I just expect the wind has blowed it to us. Your pap's got the small-pox, and you know it precious well. Why didn't you come out and say so? Do you want to spread it all over?"

"Well," says I, a-blubbering, "I've told everybody before, and then they just went away and left us."

"Poor devil, there's something in that. We are right down sorry for you, but we—well, hang it, we don't want the small-pox, you see. Look here, I'll tell you what to do. Don't you try to land by yourself, or you'll smash everything to pieces. You float along down about twenty miles and you'll come to a town on the left-hand side of the river. It will be long after sun-up, then, and when you ask for help, you tell them your folks are all down with chills and fever. Don't be a fool again, and let people guess what is the matter. Now we're trying to do you a kindness; so you just put twenty miles between us, that's a good boy. It wouldn't do any good to land yonder where the light is—it's only a wood-yard. Say—I reckon your father's poor, and I'm bound to say he's in pretty hard luck. Here —I'll put a twenty dollar gold piece on this board, and you get it when it floats by. I feel mighty mean to leave you, but my kingdom! it won't do to fool with small-pox, don't you see?"

"Hold on, Parker," says the other man, "here's a twenty to put on the board for me. Good-bye boy, you do as Mr. Parker told you, and you'll be all right."

"That's so, my boy—good-bye, good-bye. If you see any runaway niggers, you get help and nab them, and you can make some money by it."

"Good-bye, sir," says I, "I won't let no runaway niggers get by me if I can help it."

They went off, and I got aboard the raft, feeling bad and low, because I knowed very well I had done wrong, and I see it warn't no use for me to try to learn to do right; a body that don't get *started* right when he's little, ain't got no show—when the pinch comes there ain't nothing to back him up and keep him to his work, and so he gets beat. Then I thought a minute, and says to myself, hold on,—s'pose you'd a done right and give Jim up; would you felt better than what you do now? No, says I, I'd feel bad—I'd feel just the same way I do now. Well, then, says I, what's the use you learning to do right, when it's troublesome to do right and ain't no trouble to do wrong, and the wages is just the same? I was stuck. I couldn't answer that. So I reckoned I wouldn't bother no more about it, but after this always do whichever come handiest at the time.

I went into the wigwam; Jim warn't there. I looked all around; he warn't anywhere. I says:

"Jim!"

"Here I is, Huck. Is dey out o' sight yit? Don't talk loud."

He was in the river, under the stern oar, with just his nose out. I told him they was out of sight, so he come aboard. He says:

"I was a-listenin' to all de talk, en I slips into de river en was gwyne to shove for sho' if dey come aboard. Den I was gwyne to swim to de raf' agin when dey was gone. But lawsy, how you did fool 'em, Huck! Dat *wuz* de smartes' dodge! I tell you, chile, I 'speck it save' ole Jim—ole Jim ain't gwyne to forgit you for dat, honey."

Then we talked about the money. It was a pretty good raise, twenty dollars apiece. Jim said we could take deck passage on a steamboat now, and the money would last us as far as we wanted to go in the free States. He said twenty mile more warn't far for the raft to go, but he wished we was already there.

Towards daybreak we tied up, and Jim was mighty particular about hiding the raft good. Then he worked all day fixing things in bundles, and getting all ready to quit rafting.

That night about ten we hove in sight of the lights of a town away down in a left-hand bend.

I went off in the canoe, to ask about it. Pretty soon I found a man out in the river with a skiff, setting a trot-line. I ranged up and says:

"Mister, is that town Cairo?"

"Cairo? no. You must be a blame' fool."

"What town is it, mister?"

"If you want to know, go and find out. If you stay here botherin' around me for about a half a minute longer, you'll get something you won't want."

I paddled to the raft. Jim was awful disappointed, but I said never mind, Cairo would be the next place, I reckoned.

We passed another town before daylight, and I was going out again; but it was high ground, so I didn't go. No high ground about Cairo, Jim said. I had forgot it. We laid up for the day, on a towhead tolerable close to the left-hand bank. I begun to suspicion something. So did Jim. I says:

"Maybe we went by Cairo in the fog that night."

He says:

"Doan' less' talk about it, Huck. Po' niggers can't have no luck. I awluz 'spected dat rattle-snake skin warn't done wid it's work."

"I wish I'd never seen that snake-skin, Jim—I do wish I'd never laid eyes on it."

"It ain't yo' fault, Huck; you didn' know. Don't you blame yo'self 'bout it."

When it was daylight, here was the clear Ohio water in shore, sure enough, and outside was the old regular Muddy! So it was all up with Cairo.[1]

We talked it all over. It wouldn't do to take to the shore; we couldn't take the raft up the stream, of course. There warn't no way but to wait for dark, and start back in the canoe and take the chances. So we slept all day amongst the cotton-wood thicket, so as to be fresh for the work, and when we went back to the raft about dark the canoe was gone!

We didn't say a word for a good while. There warn't anything to say. We both knowed well enough it was some more work of the rattle-snake skin; so what was the use to talk about it? It would only look like we was finding fault, and that would be bound to fetch more bad luck—and keep on fetching it, too, till we knowed enough to keep still.

By-and-by we talked about what we better do, and found there warn't no way but just to go along down with the raft till we got a chance to buy a canoe to go back in. We warn't going to borrow it when there warn't anybody around, the way pap would do, for that might set people after us.

So we shoved out, after dark, on the raft.

Anybody that don't believe yet, that it's foolishness to handle a snake-skin, after all that that snake-skin done for us, will believe it now, if they read on and see what more it done for us.

The place to buy canoes is off of rafts laying up at shore. But we didn't see no rafts laying up; so we went along during three hours and more. Well, the night got gray, and ruther thick, which is the

1. Cairo lies at the confluence of the Ohio and Mississippi Rivers; hence they know they have passed the town in the fog when they see the clear water from the Ohio, still flowing along the east bank of the Mississippi, its waters not mingled with the Big Muddy. *Cf.* Chapter XV, note 4.

next meanest thing to fog. You can't tell the shape of the river, and you can't see no distance. It got to be very late and still, and then along comes a steamboat up the river. We lit the lantern, and judged she would see it. Up-stream boats didn't generly come close to us; they go out and follow the bars and hunt for easy water under the reefs; but nights like this they bull right up the channel against the whole river.

We could hear her pounding along, but we didn't see her good till she was close. She aimed right for us. Often they do that and try to see how close they can come without touching; sometimes the wheel bites off a sweep, and then the pilot sticks his head out and laughs, and thinks he's mighty smart. Well, here she comes, and we said she was going to try to shave us; but she didn't seem to be sheering off a bit. She was a big one, and she was coming in a hurry, too, looking like a black cloud with rows of glow-worms around it; but all of a sudden she bulged out, big and scary, with a long row of wide-open furnace doors shining like red-hot teeth, and her monstrous bows and guards hanging right over us. There was a yell at us, and a jingling of bells to stop the engines, a pow-wow of cussing, and whistling of steam—and as Jim went overboard on one side and I on the other, she come smashing straight through the raft.

I dived—and I aimed to find the bottom, too, for a thirty-foot wheel had got to go over me, and I wanted it to have plenty of room. I could always stay under water a minute; this time I reckon I staid under water a minute and a half. Then I bounced for the top in a hurry, for I was nearly busting. I popped out to my arm-pits and blowed the water out of my nose, and puffed a bit. Of course there was a booming current; and of course that boat started her engines again ten seconds after she stopped them, for they never cared much for raftsmen; so now she was churning along up the river, out of sight in the thick weather, though I could hear her.

I sung out for Jim about a dozen times, but I didn't get any answer; so I grabbed a plank that touched me while I was "treading water," and struck out for shore, shoving it ahead of me. But I made out to see that the drift of the current was towards the left-hand shore,[2] which meant that I was in a crossing; so I changed off and went that way.

It was one of these long, slanting, two-mile crossings; so I was a good long time in getting over. I made a safe landing, and clum up the bank. I couldn't see but a little ways, but I went poking along over rough ground for a quarter of a mile or more, and then I run across a big old-fashioned double log house before I noticed it. I was going to rush by and get away, but a log of dogs jumped

2. Kentucky, where the feud in the following chapters takes place.

out and went to howling and barking at me, and I knowed better than to move another peg.

Chapter XVII

About half a minute somebody spoke out of a window, without putting his head out, and says:

"Be done, boys! Who's there?"

I says:

"It's me."

"Who's me?"

"George Jackson, sir."

"What do you want?"

"I don't want nothing, sir. I only want to go along by, but the dogs won't let me."

"What are you prowling around here this time of night, for—hey?"

"I warn't prowling around, sir; I fell overboard off of the steamboat."

"Oh, you did, did you? Strike a light there, somebody. What did you say your name was?"

"George Jackson, sir. I'm only a boy."

"Look here; if you're telling the truth, you needn't be afraid—nobody'll hurt you. But don't try to budge; stand right where you are. Rouse out Bob and Tom, some of you, and fetch the guns. George Jackson, is there anybody with you?"

"No, sir, nobody."

I heard the people stirring around in the house, now, and see a light. The man sung out:

"Snatch that light away, Betsy, you old fool—ain't you got any sense? Put it on the floor behind the front door. Bob, if you and Tom are ready, take your places."

"All ready."

"Now, George Jackson, do you know the Shepherdsons?"

"No, sir—I never heard of them."

"Well, that may be so, and it mayn't. Now, all ready. Step forward, George Jackson. And mind, don't you hurry—come mighty slow. If there's anybody with you, let him keep back—if he shows himself he'll be shot. Come along, now. Come slow; push the door open, yourself—just enough to squeeze in, d' you hear?"

I didn't hurry, I couldn't if I'd a wanted to. I took one slow step at a time, and there warn't a sound, only I thought I could hear my heart. The dogs were as still as the humans, but they followed a little behind me. When I got to the three log door-steps, I heard them unlocking and unbarring and unbolting. I put my hand on the door and pushed it a little and a little more, till somebody said, "There, that's enough—put your head in." I done it, but I judged they would take it off.

The candle was on the floor, and there they all was, looking at me, and me at them, for about a quarter of a minute. Three big men with guns pointed at me, which made me wince, I tell you; the oldest, gray and about sixty, the other two thirty or more—all of them fine and handsome—and the sweetest old gray-headed lady, and back of her two young women which I couldn't see right well. The old gentleman says:

"There—I reckon it's all right. Come in."

As soon as I was in, the old gentleman he locked the door and barred it and bolted it, and told the young men to come in with their guns, and they all went in a big parlor that had a new rag carpet on the floor, and got together in a corner that was out of range of the front windows—there warn't none on the side. They held the candle, and took a good look at me, and all said, "Why *he* ain't a Shepherdson—no, there ain't any Shepherdson about him." Then the old man said he hoped I wouldn't mind being searched for arms, because he didn't mean no harm by it—it was only to make sure. So he didn't pry into my pockets, but only felt outside with his hands, and said it was all right. He told me to make myself easy and at home, and tell all about myself; but the old lady says:

"Why bless you, Saul, the poor thing's as wet as he can be; and don't you reckon it may be he's hungry?"

"True for you, Rachel—I forgot."

So the old lady says:

"Betsy" (this was a nigger woman), "you fly around and get him something to eat, as quick as you can, poor thing; and one of you girls go and wake up Buck and tell him— Oh, here he is himself. Buck, take this little stranger and get the wet clothes off from him and dress him up in some of yours that's dry."

Buck looked about as old as me—thirteen or fourteen or along there,[3] though he was a little bigger than me. He hadn't on anything but a shirt, and he was very frowsy-headed. He come in gaping and digging one fist into his eyes, and he was dragging a gun along with the other one. He says:

"Ain't they no Shepherdsons around?"

They said, no, 'twas a false alarm.

"Well," he says, "if they'd a ben some, I reckon I'd a got one."

They all laughed, and Bob says:

"Why, Buck, they might have scalped us all, you've been so slow in coming."

"Well, nobody come after me, and it ain't right. I'm always kep'

---

3. In a notebook Twain definitely said that Huck was a "boy of 14" (Walter   Blair, *Mark Twain and Huck Finn*, p. 143).

down; I don't get no show."

"Never mind, Buck, my boy," says the old man, "you'll have show enough, all in good time, don't you fret about that. Go 'long with you now, and do as your mother told you."

When we got up stairs to his room, he got me a coarse shirt and a roundabout[4] and pants of his, and I put them on. While I was at it he asked me what my name was, but before I could tell him, he started to telling me about a blue jay and a young rabbit he had catched in the woods day before yesterday, and he asked me where Moses was when the candle went out. I said I didn't know; I hadn't heard about it before, no way.

"Well, guess," he says.

"How'm I going to guess," says I, "when I never heard tell about it before?"

"But you can guess, can't you? It's just as easy."

"*Which* candle?" I says.

"Why, any candle," he says.

"I don't know where he was," says I; "where was he?"

"Why he was in the *dark!* That's where he was!"

"Well, if you knowed where he was, what did you ask me for?"

"Why, blame it, it's a riddle, don't you see? Say, how long are you going to stay here? You got to stay always. We can just have booming times—they don't have no school now. Do you own a dog? I've got a dog—and he'll go in the river and bring out chips that you throw in. Do you like to comb up, Sundays, and all that kind of foolishness? You bet I don't, but ma she makes me. Confound these ole britches, I reckon I'd better put 'em on, but I'd ruther not, it's so warm. Are you all ready? All right—come along, old hoss."

Cold corn-pone, cold corn-beef, butter and butter-milk—that is what they had for me down there, and there ain't nothing better that ever I've come across yet. Buck and his ma and all of them smoked cob pipes, except the nigger woman, which was gone, and the two young women. They all smoked and talked, and I eat and talked. The young women had quilts around them, and their hair down their backs. They all asked me questions, and I told them how pap and me and all the family was living on a little farm down at the bottom of Arkansaw, and my sister Mary Ann run off and got married and never was heard of no more, and Bill went to hunt them and he warn't heard of no more, and Tom and Mort died, and then there warn't nobody but just me and pap left, and he was just trimmed down to nothing, on account of his troubles; so when he died I took what there was left, because the farm didn't belong to us, and started up the river, deck passage, and fell overboard;

4. A short, close jacket.

and that was how I come to be here.[5] So they said I could have a
home there as long as I wanted it. Then it was most daylight, and
everybody went to bed, and I went to bed with Buck, and when I
waked up in the morning, drat it all, I had forgot what my name
was. So I laid there about an hour trying to think, and when Buck
waked up, I says:

"Can you spell, Buck?"

"Yes," he says.

"I bet you can't spell my name," says I.

"I bet you what you dare I can," says he.

"All right," says I, "go ahead."

"G-o-r-g-e J-a-x-o-n—there now," he says.

"Well," says I, "you done it, but I didn't think you could. It
ain't no slouch of a name to spell—right off without studying."

I set it down, private, because somebody might want *me* to spell
it, next, and so I wanted to be handy with it and rattle it off like
I was used to it.

It was a mighty nice family, and a mighty nice house, too. I
hadn't seen no house out in the country before that was so nice
and had so much style. It didn't have an iron latch on the front
door, nor a wooden one with a buckskin string, but a brass knob
to turn, the same as houses in a town. There warn't no bed in the
parlor, not a sign of a bed; but heaps of parlors in towns has beds in
them. There was a big fireplace that was bricked on the bottom,
and the bricks was kept clean and red by pouring water on them
and scrubbing them with another brick; sometimes they washed
them over with red waterpaint that they call Spanish-brown, same
as they do in town. They had big brass dog-irons that could hold up
a saw-log. There was a clock on the middle of the mantel-piece,
with a picture of a town painted on the bottom half of the glass
front, and a round place in the middle of it for the sun, and you
could see the pendulum swing behind it. It was beautiful to hear
that clock tick; and sometimes when one of these peddlars had been
along and scoured her up and got her in good shape, she would
start in and strike a hundred and fifty before she got tuckered out.
They wouldn't took any money for her.

Well, there was a big outlandish parrot on each side of the
clock, made out of something like chalk, and painted up gaudy. By
one of the parrots was a cat made of crockery, and a crockery dog by
the other; and when you pressed down on them they squeaked, but
didn't open their mouths nor look different nor interested. They
squeaked through underneath. There was a couple of big wild-

<hr/>

5. Huck's autobiographical inventions
are generally a commentary on the nature of his experience, compounded of
sudden crisis, disaster, and death.

Twain's use of these anecdotes is in
the great tradition of the comic criticism of life.

turkey-wing fans spread out behind those things. On a table in the middle of the room was a kind of lovely crockery basket that had apples and oranges and peaches and grapes piled up in it which was much redder and yellower and prettier than real ones is, but they warn't real because you could see where pieces had got chipped off and showed the white chalk or whatever it was, underneath.

This table had a cover made out of beautiful oil-cloth, with a red and blue spread-eagle painted on it, and a painted border all around. It come all the way from Philadelphia, they said. There was some books too, piled up perfectly exact, on each corner of the table. One was a big family Bible, full of pictures. One was "Pilgrim's Progress," about a man that left his family it didn't say why. I read considerable in it now and then. The statements was interesting, but tough. Another was "Friendship's Offering,"[6] full of beautiful stuff and poetry; but I didn't read the poetry. Another was Henry Clay's Speeches, and another was Dr. Gunn's Family Medicine, which told you all about what to do if a body was sick or dead. There was a Hymn Book, and a lot of other books. And there was nice split-bottom chairs, and perfectly sound, too—not bagged down in the middle and busted, like an old basket.

They had pictures hung on the walls—mainly Washingtons and Lafayettes, and battles, and Highland Marys, and one called "Signing the Declaration." There was some that they called crayons, which one of the daughters which was dead made her own self when she was only fifteen years old. They was different from any pictures I ever see before; blacker, mostly, than is common. One was a woman in a slim black dress, belted small under the armpits, with bulges like a cabbage in the middle of the sleeves, and a large black scoop-shovel bonnet with a black veil, and white slim ankles crossed about with black tape, and very wee black slippers, like a chisel, and she was leaning pensive on a tombstone on her right elbow, under a weeping willow, and her other hand hanging down her side holding a white handkerchief and a reticule, and underneath the picture it said "Shall I Never See Thee More Alas." Another one was a young lady with her hair all combed up straight to the top of her head, and knotted there in front of a comb like a chair-back, and she was crying into a handkerchief and had a dead bird laying on its back in her other hand with its heels up, and underneath the picture it said "I Shall Never Hear Thy Sweet Chirrup More Alas." There was one where a young lady was at a window looking up at the moon, and tears running down her cheeks; and she had an open letter in one hand with black sealing-

6. One of many successful annual collections of poetry and prose, designed as gift books.

wax showing on one edge of it, and she was mashing a locket with a chain to it against her mouth, and underneath the picture it said "And Art Thou Gone Yes Thou Art Gone Alas." These was all nice pictures, I reckon, but I didn't somehow seem to take to them, because if ever I was down a little, they always give me the fan-tods. Everybody was sorry she died, because she had laid out a lot more of these pictures to do, and a body could see by what she had done what they had lost. But I reckoned, that with her disposition, she was having a better time in the graveyard. She was at work on what they said was her greatest picture when she took sick, and every day and every night it was her prayer to be allowed to live till she got it done, but she never got the chance. It was a picture of a young woman in a long white gown, standing on the rail of a bridge all ready to jump off, with her hair all down her back, and looking up to the moon, with the tears running down her face, and she had two arms folded across her breast, and two arms stretched out in front, and two more reaching up towards the moon—and the idea was, to see which pair would look best and then scratch out all the other arms; but, as I was saying, she died before she got her mind made up, and now they kept this picture over the head of the bed in her room, and every time her birthday come they hung flowers on it. Other times it was hid with a little curtain. The young woman in the picture had a kind of a nice sweet face, but there was so many arms it made her look too spidery, seemed to me.

This young girl kept a scrap-book when she was alive, and used to paste obituaries and accidents and cases of patient suffering in it out of the *Presbyterian Observer*, and write poetry after them out of her own head. It was very good poetry. This is what she wrote about a boy by the name of Stephen Dowling Bots that fell down a well and was drownded:

ODE TO STEPHEN DOWLING BOTS, DEC'D.[7]

And did young Stephen sicken,
  And did young Stephen die?
And did the sad hearts thicken,
  And did the mourners cry?

No; such was not the fate of
  Young Stephen Dowling Bots;
Though sad hearts round him thickened,
  'Twas not from sickness' shots.

7. Twain's parody of the lugubrious popular poetry of the time, such as the saccharine and atrocious verse of "The Sweet Singer of Michigan" (Julia A. Moore, 1847–1920), which so delighted Mark Twain. He also gleefully encouraged the effusions of Bloodgood Cutter (1819–1906), the "poet lariat" on board the *Quaker City* excursion in *Innocents Abroad* (1869).

No whooping-cough did rack his frame,
Nor measles drear, with spots;
Not these impaired the sacred name
Of Stephen Dowling Bots.

Despised love struck not with woe
That head of curly knots,
Nor stomach troubles laid him low,
Young Stephen Dowling Bots.

O no. Then list with tearful eye,
Whilst I his fate do tell.
His soul did from this cold world fly,
By falling down a well.

They got him out and emptied him;
Alas it was too late;
His spirit was gone for to sport aloft
In the realms of the good and great.

If Emmeline Grangerford could make poetry like that before she was fourteen, there ain't no telling what she could a done by-and-by. Buck said she could rattle off poetry like nothing. She didn't ever have to stop to think. He said she would slap down a line, and if she couldn't find anything to rhyme with it she would just scratch it out and slap down another one, and go ahead. She warn't particular, she could write about anything you choose to give her to write about, just so it was sadful. Every time a man died, or a woman died, or a child died, she would be on hand with her "tribute" before he was cold. She called them tributes. The neighbors said it was the doctor first, then Emmeline, then the undertaker— the undertaker never got in ahead of Emmeline but once, and then she hung fire on a rhyme for the dead person's name, which was Whistler. She warn't ever the same, after that; she never complained, but she kind of pined away and did not live long. Poor thing, many's the time I made myself go up to the little room that used to be hers and get out her poor old scrapbook and read in it when her pictures had been aggravating me and I had soured on her a little. I liked all that family, dead ones and all, and warn't going to let anything come between us. Poor Emmeline made poetry about all the dead people when she was alive, and it didn't seem right that there warn't nobody to make some about her, now she was gone; so I tried to sweat out a verse or two myself, but I couldn't seem to make it go, somehow. They kept Emmeline's room trim and nice and all the things fixed in it just the way she liked to have them when she was alive, and nobody ever slept there. The old lady took care of the room herself, though there was plenty of niggers, and she sewed there a good deal and read her Bible there, mostly.

Well, as I was saying about the parlor, there was beautiful curtains on the windows: white, with pictures painted on them, of castles with vines all down the walls, and cattle coming down to drink. There was a little old piano, too, that had tin pans in it, I reckon, and nothing was ever so lovely as to hear the young ladies sing, "The Last Link is Broken" and play "The Battle of Prague" on it. The walls of all the rooms was plastered, and most had carpets on the floors, and the whole house was whitewashed on the outside.

It was a double house, and the big open place betwixt them was roofed and floored, and sometimes the table was set there in the middle of the day, and it was a cool, comfortable place. Nothing couldn't be better. And warn't the cooking good, and just bushels of it too!

Chapter XVIII

Col. Grangerford was a gentleman, you see. He was a gentleman all over; and so was his family. He was well born, as the saying is, and that's worth as much in a man as it is in a horse, so the Widow Douglas[8] said, and nobody ever denied that she was of the first aristocracy in our town; and pap he always said it, too, though he warn't no more quality than a mudcat,[9] himself. Col. Grangerford was very tall and very slim, and had a darkish-paly complexion, not a sign of red in it anywheres; he was clean-shaved every morning, all over his thin face, and he had the thinnest kind of lips, and the thinnest kind of nostrils, and a high nose, and heavy eyebrows, and the blackest kind of eyes, sunk so deep back that they seemed like they was looking out of caverns at you, as you may say. His forehead was high, and his hair was black and straight, and hung to his shoulders. His hands was long and thin, and every day of his life he put on a clean shirt and a full suit from head to foot made out of linen so white it hurt your eyes to look at it; and on Sundays he wore a blue tail-coat with brass buttons on it. He carried a mahogany cane with a silver head to it. There warn't no frivolishness about him, not a bit, and he warn't ever loud. He was as kind as he could be—you could feel that, you know, and so you had confidence. Sometimes he smiled, and it was good to see; but when he straightened himself up like a liberty-pole, and the lightning begun to flicker out from under his eyebrows you wanted to climb a tree first, and find out what the matter was afterwards. He didn't ever have to tell anybody to mind their manners—everybody was always good

8. Erroneously printed "Douglass" in 1885.   9. A less-esteemed variety of catfish.

mannered where he was. Everybody loved to have him around, too; he was sunshine most always—I mean he made it seem like good weather. When he turned into a cloud-bank it was awful dark for a half a minute and that was enough; there wouldn't nothing go wrong again for a week.

When him and the old lady come down in the morning, all the family got up out of their chairs and give them good-day, and didn't set down again till they had set down. Then Tom and Bob went to the sideboard where the decanters was, and mixed a glass of bitters and handed it to him, and he held it in his hand and waited till Tom's and Bob's was mixed, and then they bowed and said "Our duty to you, sir, and madam;" and *they* bowed the least bit in the world and said thank you, and so they drank, all three, and Bob and Tom poured a spoonful of water on the sugar and the mite of whisky or apple brandy in the bottom of their tumblers, and give it to me and Buck, and we drank to the old people too.

Bob was the oldest, and Tom next. Tall, beautiful men with very broad shoulders and brown faces, and long black hair and black eyes. They dressed in white linen from head to foot, like the old gentleman, and wore broad Panama hats.

Then there was Miss Charlotte, she was twenty-five, and tall and proud and grand, but as good as she could be, when she warn't stirred up; but when she was, she had a look that would make you wilt in your tracks, like her father. She was beautiful.

So was her sister, Miss Sophia, but it was a different kind. She was gentle and sweet, like a dove, and she was only twenty.

Each person had their own nigger to wait on them—Buck, too. My nigger had a monstrous easy time, because I warn't used to having anybody do anything for me, but Buck's was on the jump most of the time.

This was all there was of the family, now; but there used to be more—three sons; they got killed; and Emmeline that died.

The old gentleman owned a lot of farms, and over a hundred niggers. Sometimes a stack of people would come there, horseback, from ten or fifteen mile around, and stay five or six days, and have such junketings round about and on the river, and dances and picnics in the woods, day-times, and balls at the house, nights. These people was mostly kin-folks of the family. The men brought their guns with them. It was a handsome lot of quality, I tell you.

There was another clan of aristocracy around there—five or six families—mostly of the name of Shepherdson. They was as high-toned, and well born, and rich and grand, as the tribe of Grangerfords. The Shepherdsons and the Grangerfords used the same steamboat landing, which was about two mile above our house; so sometimes when I went up there with a lot of our folks I used to see a lot of the Shepherdsons there, on their fine horses.

One day Buck and me was away out in the woods, hunting, and heard a horse coming. We was crossing the road. Buck says:

"Quick! Jump for the woods!"

We done it, and then peeped down the woods through the leaves. Pretty soon a splendid young man came galloping down the road, setting his horse easy and looking like a soldier. He had his gun across his pommel. I had seen him before. It was young Harney Shepherdson. I heard Buck's gun go off at my ear, and Harney's hat tumbled off from his head. He grabbed his gun and rode straight to the place where we was hid. But we didn't wait. We started through the woods on a run. The woods warn't thick, so I looked over my shoulder, to dodge the bullet, and twice I seen Harney cover Buck with his gun; and then he rode away the way he come—to get his hat, I reckon, but I couldn't see. We never stopped running till we got home. The old gentleman's eyes blazed a minute—'twas pleasure, mainly, I judged—then his face sort of smoothed down, and he says, kind of gentle:

"I don't like that shooting from behind a bush. Why didn't you step into the road, my boy?"

"The Shepherdsons don't, father. They always take advantage."

Miss Charlotte she held her head up like a queen while Buck was telling his tale, and her nostrils spread and her eyes snapped. The two young men looked dark, but never said nothing. Miss Sophia she turned pale, but the color come back when she found the man warn't hurt.

Soon as I could get Buck down by the corn-cribs under the trees by ourselves, I says:

"Did you want to kill him, Buck?"

"Well, I bet I did."

"What did he do to you?"

"Him? He never done nothing to me."

"Well, then, what did you want to kill him for?"

"Why nothing—only it's on account of the feud."

"What's a feud?"

"Why, where was you raised? Don't you know what a feud is?"

"Never heard of it before—tell me about it."

"Well," says Buck, "a feud is this way. A man has a quarrel with another man, and kills him; then that other man's brother kills *him*; then the other brothers, on both sides, goes for one another; then the *cousins* chip in—and by-and-by everybody's killed off, and there ain't no more feud. But it's kind of slow, and takes a long time."

"Has this one been going on long, Buck?"

"Well I should *reckon!* it started thirty year ago, or som'ers along there. There was trouble 'bout something and then a lawsuit to settle it; and the suit went agin one of the men, and so he up and shot the man that won the suit—which he would naturally do, of course. Anybody would."

"What was the trouble about, Buck?—land?"

"I reckon maybe—I don't know."

"Well, who done the shooting?—was it a Grangerford or a Shepherdson?"

"Laws, how do *I* know? it was so long ago."

"Don't anybody know?"

"Oh, yes, pa knows, I reckon, and some of the other old folks; but they don't know, now, what the row was about in the first place."

"Has there been many killed, Buck?"

"Yes—right smart chance of funerals. But they don't always kill. Pa's got a few buck-shot in him; but he don't mind it 'cuz he don't weigh much anyway. Bob's been carved up some with a bowie, and Tom's been hurt once or twice."

"Has anybody been killed this year, Buck?"

"Yes, we got one and they got one. 'Bout three months ago, my cousin Bud, fourteen year old, was riding through the woods, on t'other side of the river, and didn't have no weapon with him, which was blame' foolishness, and in a lonesome place he hears a horse a-coming behind him, and sees old Baldy Shepherdson a-linkin' after him with his gun in his hand and his white hair a-flying in the wind; and 'stead of jumping off and taking to the brush, Bud 'lowed he could outrun him; so they had it, nip and tuck, for five mile or more, the old man a-gaining all the time; so at last Bud seen it warn't any use, so he stopped and faced around so as to have the bullet holes in front, you know, and the old man he rode up and shot him down. But he didn't git much chance to enjoy his luck, for inside of a week our folks laid *him* out."

"I reckon that old man was a coward, Buck."

"I reckon he *warn't* a coward. Not by a blame' sight. There ain't a coward amongst them Shepherdsons—not a one. And there ain't no cowards amongst the Grangerfords, either. Why, that old man kep' up his end in a fight one day, for a half an hour, against three Grangerfords, and come out winner. They was all a-horseback; he lit off of his horse and got behind a little wood-pile, and kep' his horse before him to stop the bullets; but the Grangerfords staid on their horses and capered around the old man, and peppered away at him, and he peppered away at them. Him and his horse both went home pretty leaky and crippled, but the Grangerfords had to be *fetched* home—and one of 'em was dead, and another died the next day. No, sir, if a body's out hunting for cowards, he

don't want to fool away any time amongst them Shepherdsons, becuz they don't breed any of that *kind*."

Next Sunday we all went to church, about three mile, everybody a-horseback. The men took their guns along, so did Buck, and
kept them between their knees or stood them handy against the
wall. The Shepherdsons done the same. It was pretty ornery preaching—all about brotherly love, and such-like tiresomeness; but everybody said it was a good sermon, and they all talked it over going
home, and had such a powerful lot to say about faith, and good
works, and free grace, and preforeordestination,[1] and I don't know
what all, that it did seem to me to be one of the roughest Sundays
I had run across yet.

About an hour after dinner everybody was dozing around, some
in their chairs and some in their rooms, and it got to be pretty
dull. Buck and a dog was stretched out on the grass in the sun,
sound asleep. I went up to our room, and judged I would take a nap
myself. I found that sweet Miss Sophia standing in her door,
which was next to ours, and she took me in her room and shut the
door very soft, and asked me if I liked her, and I said I did; and
she asked me if I would do something for her and not tell anybody, and I said I would. Then she said she'd forgot her Testament,
and left it in the seat at church, between two other books and
would I slip out quiet and go there and fetch it to her, and not
say nothing to nobody. I said I would. So I slid out and slipped
off up the road, and there warn't anybody at the church, except
maybe a hog or two, for there warn't any lock on the door, and
hogs likes a puncheon floor[2] in summer-time because it's cool. If
you notice, most folks don't go to church only when they've got to;
but a hog is different.

Says I to myself something's up—it ain't natural for a girl to be
in such a sweat about a Testament; so I give it a shake, and out
drops a little piece of paper with "*Half-past two*" wrote on it with
a pencil. I ransacked it, but couldn't find anything else. I couldn't
make anything out of that, so I put the paper in the book again,
and when I got home and up stairs, there was Miss Sophia in her
door waiting for me. She pulled me in and shut the door; then she
looked in the Testament till she found the paper, and as soon as she
read it she looked glad; and before a body could think, she grabbed
me and give me a squeeze, and said I was the best boy in the world,
and not to tell anybody. She was mighty red in the face, for a
minute, and her eyes lighted up and it made her powerful pretty.
I was a good deal astonished, but when I got my breath I asked

1. Following the frontier's comic pattern of "made-up" words, Huck confuses two cardinal doctrines of Pres-
byterianism: predestination and fore-
ordination.
2. Made of the first slabs cut from logs,
with the rounded sides downward.

her what the paper was about, and she asked me if I had read it, and I said no, and she asked me if I could read writing, and I told her "no, only coarse-hand,"[3] and then she said the paper warn't anything but a book-mark to keep her place, and I might go and play now.

I went off down to the river, studying over this thing, and pretty soon I noticed that my nigger was following along behind. When we was out of sight of the house, he looked back and around a second, and then comes a-running, and says:

"Mars Jawge, if you'll come down into de swamp, I'll show you a whole stack o' water-moccasins."

Thinks I, that's mighty curious; he said that yesterday. He oughter know a body don't love water-moccasins enough to go around hunting for them. What is he up to anyway? So I says—

"All right, trot ahead."

I followed a half a mile, then he struck out over the swamp and waded ankle deep as much as another half mile. We come to a little flat piece of land which was dry and very thick with trees and bushes and vines, and he says—

"You shove right in dah, jist a few steps, Mars Jawge, dah's whah dey is. I's seed 'm befo', I don't k'yer to see 'em no mo'."

Then he slopped right along and went away, and pretty soon the trees hid him. I poked into the place a-ways, and come to a little open patch as big as a bedroom, all hung around with vines, and found a man laying there asleep—and by jings it was my old Jim!

I waked him up, and I reckoned it was going to be a grand surprise to him to see me again, but it warn't. He nearly cried, he was so glad, but he warn't surprised. Said he swum along behind me, that night, and heard me yell every time, but dasn't answer, because he didn't want nobody to pick *him* up, and take him into slavery again. Says he—

"I got hurt a little, en couldn't swim fas', so I wuz a considable ways behine you, towards de las'; when you landed I reck'ned I could ketch up wid you on de lan' 'dout havin' to shout at you, but when I see dat house I begin to go slow. I 'uz off too fur to hear what dey say to you—I wuz 'fraid o' de dogs—but when it 'uz all quiet agin, I knowed you's in de house, so I struck out for de woods to wait for day. Early in de mawnin' some er de niggers come along, gwyne to de fields, en dey tuck me en showed me dis place, whah de dogs can't track me on accounts o' de water, en dey brings me truck to eat every night, en tells me how you's a gitt'n along."

"Why didn't you tell my Jack to fetch me here sooner, Jim?"

"Well, 'twarn't no use to 'sturb you, Huck, tell we could do

3. Printing.

sumfn—but we's all right, now. I ben a-buyin' pots en pans en vittles, as I got a chanst, en a patchin' up de raf', nights, when—"

"*What* raft, Jim?"

"Our ole raf'."

"You mean to say our old raft warn't smashed all to flinders?"

"No, she warn't. She was tore up a good deal—one en' of her
was—but dey warn't no great harm done, on'y our traps was mos'
all los'. Ef we hadn' dive' so deep en swum so fur under water, en
de night hadn' ben so dark, en we warn't so sk'yerd, en ben sich
punkin-heads, as de sayin' is, we'd a seed de raf'. But it's jis' as well
we didn't, 'kase now she's all fixed up agin mos' as good as new,
en we's got a new lot o' stuff, too, in de place o' what 'uz los'."

"Why, how did you get hold of the raft again, Jim—did you
catch her?"

"How I gwyne to ketch her, en I out in de woods? No, some er
de niggers foun' her ketched on a snag, along heah in de ben', en
dey hid her in a crick, 'mongst de willows, en dey wuz so much
jawin' 'bout which un 'um she b'long to de mos', dat I come to
heah 'bout it pooty soon, so I ups en settles de trouble by tellin'
'um she don't b'long to none uv um, but to you en me; en I ast
'm if dey gwyne to grab a young white genlman's propaty, en git a
hid'n for it? Den I gin 'm ten cents apiece, en dey 'uz mighty well
satisfied, en wisht some mo' raf's 'ud come along en make 'm rich
agin. Dey's mighty good to me, dese niggers is, en whatever I wants
'm to do fur me, I doan' have to ast 'm twice, honey. Dat Jack's a
good nigger, en pooty smart."

"Yes, he is. He ain't ever told me you was here; told me to come,
and he'd show me a lot of water-moccasins. If anything happens,
he ain't mixed up in it. He can say he never seen us together, and
it'll be the truth."

I don't want to talk much about the next day. I reckon I'll cut
it pretty short. I waked up about dawn, and was agoing to turn over
and go to sleep again, when I noticed how still it was—didn't seem
to be anybody stirring. That warn't usual. Next I noticed that
Buck was up and gone. Well, I gets up, a-wondering, and goes down
stairs—nobody around; everything as still as a mouse. Just the
same outside; thinks I, what does it mean? Down by the wood-pile
I comes across my Jack, and says:

"What's it all about?"

Says he:

"Don't you know, Mars Jawge?"

"No," says I, "I don't."

"Well, den, Miss Sophia's run off! 'deed she has. She run off in
de night, sometime—nobody don't know jis' when—run off to git
married to dat young Harney Shepherdson, you know—leastways,

so dey 'spec. De fambly foun' it out, 'bout half an hour ago—maybe a little mo'—en' I *tell* you dey warn't no time los'. Sich another hurryin' up guns en hosses *you* never see! De women folks has gone for to stir up de relations, en ole Mars Saul en de boys tuck dey guns en rode up de river road for to try to ketch dat young man en kill him 'fo' he kin git acrost de river wid Miss Sophia. I reck'n dey's gwyne to be mighty rough times."

"Buck went off 'thout waking me up."

"Well I reck'n he *did!* Dey warn't gwyne to mix you up in it. Mars Buck he loaded up his gun en 'lowed he's gwyne to fetch home a Shepherdson or bust. Well, dey'll be plenty un 'm dah, I reck'n, en you bet you he'll fetch one ef he gits a chanst."

I took up the river road as hard as I could put. By-and-by I begin to hear guns a good ways off. When I come in sight of the log store and the wood-pile where the steamboats lands, I worked along under the trees and brush till I got to a good place, and then I clumb up into the forks of a cotton-wood that was out of reach, and watched. There was a wood-rank four foot high, a little ways in front of the tree, and first I was going to hide behind that; but maybe it was luckier I didn't.

There was four or five men cavorting around on their horses in the open place before the log store, cussing and yelling, and trying to get at a couple of young chaps that was behind the wood-rank alongside of the steamboat landing—but they couldn't come it. Every time one of them showed himself on the riverside of the wood-pile he got shot at. The two boys was squatting back to back behind the pile, so they could watch both ways.

By-and-by the men stopped cavorting around and yelling. They started riding towards the store; then up gets one of the boys, draws a steady bead over the wood-rank, and drops one of them out of his saddle. All the men jumped off of their horses and grabbed the hurt one and started to carry him to the store; and that minute the two boys started on the run. They got half-way to the tree I was in before the men noticed. Then the men see them, and jumped on their horses and took out after them. They gained on the boys, but it didn't do no good, the boys had too good a start; they got to the wood-pile that was in front of my tree, and slipped in behind it, and so they had the bulge on the men again. One of the boys was Buck, and the other was a slim young chap about nineteen years old.

The men ripped around awhile, and then rode away. As soon as they was out of sight, I sung out to Buck and told him. He didn't know what to make of my voice coming out of the tree, at first. He was awful surprised. He told me to watch out sharp and let him know when the men come in sight again; said they was up to some devilment or other—wouldn't be gone long. I wished I was out of that tree, but I dasn't come down. Buck begun to cry and rip, and 'lowed that him and his cousin Joe (that was the other young chap) would make up for this day, yet. He said his father and his two brothers was killed, and two or three of the enemy. Said the Shepherdsons laid for them, in ambush. Buck said his father and brothers ought to waited for their relations—the Shepherdsons was too strong for them. I asked him what was become of young Harney and Miss Sophia. He said they'd got across the river and was safe. I was glad of that; but the way Buck did take on because he didn't manage to kill Harney that day he shot at him—I hain't ever heard anything like it.

All of a sudden, bang! bang! bang! goes three or four guns—the men had slipped around through the woods and come in from behind without their horses! The boys jumped for the river—both of them hurt—and as they swum down the current the men run along the bank shooting at them and singing out, "Kill them, kill them!" It made me so sick I most fell out of the tree. I ain't agoing to tell *all* that happened—it would make me sick again if I was to do that. I wished I hadn't ever come ashore that night, to see such things. I ain't ever going to get shut of them—lots of times I dream about them.

I staid in the tree till it begun to get dark, afraid to come down. Sometimes I heard guns away off in the woods; and twice I seen little gangs of men gallop past the logstore with guns; so I reckoned the trouble was still agoing on. I was mighty down-hearted; so I made up my mind I wouldn't ever go anear that house again, because I reckoned I was to blame, somehow. I judged that that piece of paper meant that Miss Sophia was to meet Harney somewheres at half-past two and run off; and I judged I ought to told her father about that paper and the curious way she acted, and then maybe he would a locked her up and this awful mess wouldn't ever happened.

When I got down out of the tree, I crept along down the river bank a piece, and found the two bodies laying in the edge of the water, and tugged at them till I got them ashore; then I covered up their faces, and got away as quick as I could. I cried a little when I was covering up Buck's face, for he was mighty good to me.

It was just dark, now. I never went near the house, but struck through the woods and made for the swamp. Jim warn't on his island, so I tramped off in a hurry for the crick, and crowded through the willows, red-hot to jump aboard and get out of that awful country—the raft was gone! My souls, but I was scared! I couldn't get my breath for most a minute. Then I raised a yell. A voice not twenty-five foot from me, says—

"Good lan'! is dat you, honey? Doan' make no noise."

It was Jim's voice—nothing ever sounded so good before. I run along the bank a piece and got aboard, and Jim he grabbed me and hugged me, he was so glad to see me. He says—

"Laws bless you, chile, I 'uz right down sho' you's dead agin. Jack's been heah, he say he reck'n you's ben shot, kase you didn' come home no mo'; so I's jes' dis minute a startin' de raf' down towards de mouf er de crick, so's to be all ready for to shove out en leave soon as Jack comes agin en tells me for certain you *is* dead. Lawsy, I's mighty glad to git you back agin, honey."

I says—

"All right—that's mighty good; they won't find me, and they'll think I've been killed, and floated down the river—there's something up there that'll help them to think so—so don't you lose no time, Jim, but just shove off for the big water as fast as ever you can."

I never felt easy till the raft was two mile below there and out in the middle of the Mississippi. Then we hung up our signal lantern, and judged that we was free and safe once more. I hadn't had a bite to eat since yesterday; so Jim he got out some corn-dodgers and buttermilk, and pork and cabbage, and greens—there ain't nothing in the world so good, when it's cooked right—and whilst I eat my supper we talked, and had a good time. I was powerful glad to get away from the feuds, and so was Jim to get away from the swamp. We said there warn't no home like a raft, after all. Other places do seem so cramped up and smothery, but a raft don't. You feel mighty free and easy and comfortable on a raft.[4]

Chapter XIX

Two or three days and nights went by; I reckon I might say they swum by, they slid along so quiet and smooth and lovely. Here is the way we put in the time. It was a monstrous big river down there—sometimes a mile and a half wide; we run nights, and laid up and hid day-times; soon as night was most gone, we stopped navigating and tied up—nearly always in the dead water under a tow-head; and then cut young cottonwoods and willows and hid the raft with them. Then we set out the lines. Next we slid into the river and had a swim, so as to freshen up and cool off; then we set down on the sandy bottom where the water was about knee deep, and watched the daylight come. Not a sound, anywheres—perfectly still—just like the whole world was asleep, only some-

4. The two chapters devoted to the Grangerford episode contrast the idyllic and picturesque description of the family and their home with the hideous and vainglorious inhumanity of the feud, which even Huck's experience has not prepared him to stomach. In addition, there is the subtle realization of Twain's continuous contrast of the River with the shore and simple nature with human nature, epitomized here in Huck's final comment.

times the bull-frogs a-cluttering, maybe. The first thing to see, looking away over the water, was a kind of dull line—that was the woods on t'other side—you couldn't make nothing else out; then a pale place in the sky; then more paleness, spreading around; then the river softened up, away off, and warn't black any more, but gray; you could see little dark spots drifting along, ever so far away —trading scows, and such things; and long black streaks—rafts; sometimes you could hear a sweep screaking; or jumbled up voices, it was so still, and sounds come so far; and by-and-by you could see a streak on the water which you know by the look of the streak that there's a snag there in a swift current which breaks on it and makes that streak look that way; and you see the mist curl up off of the water, and the east reddens up, and the river, and you make out a log cabin in the edge of the woods, away on the bank on t'other side of the river, being a wood-yard, likely, and piled by them cheats so you can throw a dog through it anywheres; then the nice breeze springs up, and comes fanning you from over there, so cool and fresh, and sweet to smell, on account of the woods and the flowers; but sometimes not that way, because they've left dead fish laying around, gars, and such, and they do get pretty rank; and next you've got the full day, and everything smiling in the sun, and the song-birds just going it!

A little smoke couldn't be noticed, now, so we would take some fish off of the lines, and cook up a hot breakfast. And afterwards we would watch the lonesomeness of the river, and kind of lazy along, and by-and-by lazy off to sleep. Wake up, by-and-by, and look to see what done it, and maybe see a steamboat coughing along up stream, so far off towards the other side you couldn't tell nothing about her only whether she was stern-wheel or side-wheel; then for about an hour there wouldn't be nothing to hear nor nothing to see—just solid lonesomeness. Next you'd see a raft sliding by, away off yonder, and maybe a galoot on it chopping, because they're almost always doing it on a raft; you'd see the ax flash, and come down—you don't hear nothing; you see that ax go up again, and by the time it's above the man's head, then you hear the *k'chunk!*—it had took all that time to come over the water. So we would put in the day, lazying around, listening to the stillness. Once there was a thick fog, and the rafts and things that went by was beating tin pans so the steamboats wouldn't run over them. A scow or a raft went by so close we could hear them talking and cussing and laughing—heard them plain; but we couldn't see no sign of them; it made you feel crawly, it was like spirits carrying on that way in the air. Jim said he believed it was spirits; but I says:

"No, spirits wouldn't say, 'dern the dern fog.' "

Soon as it was night, out we shoved; when we got her out to about the middle, we let her alone, and let her float wherever the current wanted her to; then we lit the pipes, and dangled our legs in the water and talked about all kinds of things—we was always naked, day and night, whenever the mosquitoes would let us—the new clothes Buck's folks made for me was too good to be comfortable, and besides I didn't go much on clothes, nohow.

Sometimes we'd have that whole river all to ourselves for the longest time. Yonder was the banks and the islands, across the water; and maybe a spark—which was a candle in a cabin window —and sometimes on the water you could see a spark or two—on a raft or a scow, you know; and maybe you could hear a fiddle or a song coming over from one of them crafts. It's lovely to live on a raft. We had the sky, up there, all speckled with stars, and we used to lay on our backs and look up at them, and discuss about whether they was made, or only just happened—Jim he allowed they was made, but I allowed they happened; I judged it would have took too long to *make* so many. Jim said the moon could a *laid* them; well, that looked kind of reasonable, so I didn't say nothing against it, because I've seen a frog lay most as many, so of course it could be done. We used to watch the stars that fell, too, and see them streak down. Jim allowed they'd got spoiled and was hove out of the nest.

Once or twice of a night we would see a steamboat slipping along in the dark, and now and then she would belch a whole world of sparks up out of her chimbleys, and they would rain down in the river and look awful pretty; then she would turn a corner and her lights would wink out and her pow-wow shut off and leave the river still again; and by-and-by her waves would get to us, a long time after she was gone, and joggle the raft a bit, and after that you wouldn't hear nothing for you couldn't tell how long, except maybe frogs or something.

After midnight the people on shore went to bed, and then for two or three hours the shore was black—no more sparks in the cabin windows. These sparks was our clock—the first one that showed again meant morning was coming, so we hunted a place to hide and tie up, right away.[5]

One morning about day-break, I found a canoe and crossed over a chute[6] to the main shore—it was only two hundred yards—and paddled about a mile up a crick amongst the cypress woods, to see if I couldn't get some berries. Just as I was passing a place where a kind of a cow-path crossed the crick, here comes a couple of men tearing up the path as tight as they could foot it. I thought I was a goner, for whenever anybody was after anybody I judged it was

5. In this, one of Twain's famous descriptive passages, the return to the raft and the River provides another experience of nature, an idyllic interlude between two revelations of man's inhumanity—tragic in the Grangerford feud and comic in the episodes to follow.
6. A narrow channel to the mainland, with swift-flowing water.

me—or maybe Jim. I was about to dig out from there in a hurry, but they was pretty close to me then, and sung out and begged me to save their lives—said they hadn't been doing nothing, and was being chased for it—said there was men and dogs a-coming. They wanted to jump right in, but I says—

"Don't you do it. I don't hear the dogs and horses yet; you've got time to crowd through the brush and get up the crick a little ways; then you take to the water and wade down to me and get in —that'll throw the dogs off the scent."

They done it, and soon as they was aboard I lit out for our tow-head, and in about five or ten minutes we heard the dogs and the men away off, shouting. We heard them come along towards the crick, but couldn't see them; they seemed to stop and fool around a while; then, as we got further and further away all the time, we couldn't hardly hear them at all; by the time we had left a mile of woods behind us and struck the river, everything was quiet, and we paddled over to the tow-head and hid in the cotton-woods and was safe.

One of these fellows was about seventy, or upwards, and had a bald head and very gray whiskers. He had an old battered-up slouch hat on, and a greasy blue woolen shirt, and ragged old blue jeans britches stuffed into his boot tops, and home-knit galluses—no, he only had one. He had an old long-tailed blue jeans coat with slick brass buttons, flung over his arm, and both of them had big fat ratty-looking carpet-bags.

The other fellow was about thirty and dressed about as ornery. After breakfast we all laid off and talked, and the first thing that come out was that these chaps didn't know one another.

"What got you into trouble?" says the baldhead to t'other chap.

"Well, I'd been selling an article to take the tartar off the teeth —and it does take it off, too, and generally the enamel along with it—but I staid about one night longer than I ought to, and was just in the act of sliding out when I ran across you on the trail this side of town, and you told me they were coming, and begged me to help you to get off. So I told you I was expecting trouble myself and would scatter out *with* you. That's the whole yarn—what's yourn?"

"Well, I'd ben a-runnin' a little temperance revival thar, 'bout a week, and was the pet of the women-folks, big and little, for I was makin' it mighty warm for the rummies, I *tell* you, and takin' as much as five or six dollars a night—ten cents a head, children and niggers free—and business a growin' all the time; when somehow or another a little report got around, last night, that I had a way of puttin' in my time with a private jug, on the sly. A nigger rousted me out this mornin', and told me the people was gatherin' on the quiet, with their dogs and horses, and they'd be along pretty soon and give me 'bout half an hour's start, and then run me down, if they could; and if they got me they'd tar and feather me and ride me on a rail, sure. I didn't wait for no breakfast—I warn't hungry."

"Old man," says the young one, "I reckon we might double-team it together; what do you think?"

"I ain't undisposed. What's your line—mainly?"

"Jour printer,[7] by trade; do a little in patent medicines; theatre-actor—tragedy, you know; take a turn at mesmerism and phrenology when there's a chance; teach singing-geography school for a change; sling a lecture, sometimes—oh, I do lots of things—most anything that comes handy, so it ain't work. What's your lay?"[8]

"I've done considerble in the doctoring way in my time. Layin' on o' hands is my best holt—for cancer, and paralysis, and sich things; and I k'n tell a fortune pretty good, when I've got somebody along to find out the facts for me. Preachin's my line, too; and workin' camp-meetin's; and missionaryin' around."

Nobody never said anything for a while; then the young man hove a sigh and says—

"Alas!"

"What 're you alassin' about?" says the baldhead.

"To think I should have lived to be leading such a life, and be degraded down into such company." And he begun to wipe the corner of his eye with a rag.

"Dern your skin, ain't the company good enough for you?" says the baldhead, pretty pert and uppish.

"Yes, it *is* good enough for me; it's as good as I deserve; for who fetched me so low, when I was so high? *I* did myself. I don't blame *you*, gentlemen—far from it; I don't blame anybody. I deserve it all. Let the cold world do its worst; one thing I know—there's a grave somewhere for me. The world may go on just as its always done, and take everything from me—loved ones, property, everything—but it can't take that. Some day I'll lie down in it and forget it all, and my poor broken heart will be at rest." He went on a-wiping.

"Drot your pore broken heart," says the baldhead; "what are you heaving your pore broken heart at *us* f'r? *We* hain't done nothing."

"No, I know you haven't. I ain't blaming you, gentlemen. I brought myself down—yes, I did it myself. It's right I should suffer—perfectly right—I don't make any moan."

"Brought you down from whar? Whar was you brought down from?"

"Ah, you would not believe me; the world never believes—let it pass—'tis no matter. The secret of my birth—"

"The secret of your birth? Do you mean to say—"

<hr/>

7. Journeyman printer: one who worked by the day, not yet a master printer.
8. The roving fraud was a stock comic character of frontier literature, but Twain turns his two specimens into real, fully drawn characters.

"Gentlemen," says the young man, very solemn, "I will reveal it to you, for I feel I may have confidence in you. By rights I am a duke!"

Jim's eyes bugged out when he heard that; and I reckon mine did, too. Then the baldhead says: "No! you can't mean it?"

"Yes. My great-grandfather, eldest son of the Duke of Bridgewater, fled to this country about the end of the last century, to breathe the pure air of freedom; married here, and died, leaving a son, his own father dying about the same time. The second son of the late duke seized the title and estates—the infant real duke was ignored. I am the lineal descendant of that infant—I am the rightful Duke of Bridgewater; and here am I, forlorn, torn from my high estate, hunted of men, despised by the cold world, ragged, worn, heart-broken, and degraded to the companionship of felons on a raft!"

Jim pitied him ever so much ,and so did I. We tried to comfort him, but he said it warn't much use, he couldn't be much comforted; said if we was a mind to acknowledge him, that would do him more good than most anything else; so we said we would, if he would tell us how. He said we ought to bow, when we spoke to him, and say "Your Grace," or "My Lord," or "Your Lordship"—and he wouldn't mind it if we called him plain "Bridgewater," which he said was a title, anyway, and not a name; and one of us ought to wait on him at dinner, and do any little thing for him he wanted done.

Well, that was all easy, so we done it. All through dinner Jim stood around and waited on him, and says, "Will yo' Grace have some o' dis, or some o' dat?" and so on, and a body could see it was mighty pleasing to him.

But the old man got pretty silent, by-and-by—didn't have much to say, and didn't look pretty comfortable over all that petting that was going on around that duke. He seemed to have something on his mind. So, along in the afternoon, he says:

"Looky here, Bilgewater," he says, "I'm nation sorry for you, but you ain't the only person that's had troubles like that."

"No?"

"No, you ain't. You ain't the only person that's ben snaked down wrongfully out'n a high place."

"Alas!"

"No, you ain't the only person that's had a secret of his birth." And by jings, *he* begins to cry.

"Hold! What do you mean?"

"Bilgewater, kin I trust you?" says the old man, still sort of sobbing.

"To the bitter death!" He took the old man by the hand and squeezed it, and says, "The secret of your being: speak!"

"Bilgewater, I am the late Dauphin!"

You bet you Jim and me stared, this time. Then the duke says: "You are what?"

"Yes, my friend, it is too true—your eyes is lookin' at this very moment on the pore disappeared Dauphin, Looy the Seventeen, son of Looy the Sixteen and Marry Antonette."

"You! At your age![9] No! You mean you're the late Charlemagne; you must be six or seven hundred years old, at the very least."

"Trouble has done it, Bilgewater, trouble has done it; trouble has brung these gray hairs and this premature balditude. Yes, gentlemen, you see before you, in blue jeans and misery, the wanderin', exiled, trampled-on and sufferin' rightful King of France."

Well, he cried and took on so, that me and Jim didn't know hardly what to do, we was so sorry—and so glad and proud we'd got him with us, too. So we set in, like we done before with the duke, and tried to comfort *him*. But he said it warn't no use, nothing but to be dead and done with it all could do him any good; though he said it often made him feel easier and better for a while if people treated him according to his rights, and got down on one knee to speak to him, and always called him "Your Majesty," and waited on him first at meals, and didn't set down in his presence till he asked them. So Jim and me set to majestying him, and doing this and that and t'other for him, and standing up till he told us we might set down. This done him heaps of good, and so he got cheerful and comfortable. But the duke kind of soured on him, and didn't look a bit satisfied with the way things was going; still, the king acted real friendly towards him, and said the duke's great-grandfather and all the other Dukes of Bilgewater was a good deal thought of by *his* father and was allowed to come to the palace considerable; but the duke staid huffy a good while, till by-and-by the king says:

"Like as not we got to be together a blamed long time, on this h-yer raft, Bilgewater, and so what's the use o' your bein' sour? It'll only make things oncomfortable. It ain't my fault I warn't born a duke, it ain't your fault you warn't born a king—so what's the use to worry? Make the best o' things the way you find 'em, says I—that's my motto. This ain't no bad thing that we've struck here—plenty grub and an easy life—come, give us your hand, Duke, and less all be friends."

The duke done it, and Jim and me was pretty glad to see it. It took away all the uncomfortableness, and we felt mighty good over it, because it would a been a miserable business to have any unfriendliness on the raft; for what you want, above all things, on a raft, is for everybody to be satisfied, and feel right and kind to-

9. *Cf.* Chapter XIV, note 2. Had the Dauphin lived, he would have been in his mid-fifties.

wards the others.

It didn't take me long to make up my mind that these liars warn't no kings nor dukes, at all, but just low-down humbugs and frauds. But I never said nothing, never let on; kept it to myself; it's the best way; then you don't have no quarrels, and don't get into no trouble. If they wanted us to call them kings and dukes, I hadn't no objections, 'long as it would keep peace in the family; and it warn't no use to tell Jim, so I didn't tell him. If I never learnt nothing else out of pap, I learnt that the best way to get along with his kind of people is to let them have their own way.

Chapter XX

They asked us considerable many questions; wanted to know what we covered up the raft that way for, and laid by in the day-time instead of running—was Jim a runaway nigger? Says I—

"Goodness sakes, would a runaway nigger run *south?*"

No, they allowed he wouldn't. I had to account for things some way, so I says:

"My folks was living in Pike County, in Missouri, where I was born, and they all died off but me and pa and by brother Ike. Pa, he 'lowed he'd break up and go down and live with Uncle Ben, who's got a little one-horse place on the river, forty-four mile below Orleans. Pa was pretty poor, and had some debts; so when he'd squared up there warn't nothing left but sixteen dollars and our nigger, Jim. That warn't enough to take us fourteen hundred mile, deck passage nor no other way. Well, when the river rose, pa had a streak of luck one day; he ketched this piece of raft; so we reckoned we'd go down to Orleans on it. Pa's luck didn't hold out; a steamboat run over the forrard corner of the raft, one night, and we all went overboard and dove under the wheel; Jim and me come up, all right, but pa was drunk, and Ike was only four years old, so they never come up no more. Well, for the next day or two we had considerable trouble, because people was always coming out in skiffs and trying to take Jim away from me, saying they believed he was a runaway nigger. We don't run day-times no more, now; nights they don't bother us."

The duke says—

"Leave me alone to cipher out a way so we can run in the day-time if we want to. I'll think the thing over—I'll invent a plan that'll fix it. We'll let it alone for to-day, because of course we don't want to go by that town yonder in daylight—it mightn't be healthy."

Towards night it begun to darken up and look like rain; the heat lightning was squirting around, low down in the sky, and the leaves was beginning to shiver—it was going to be pretty ugly, it was easy to see that. So the duke and the king went to overhauling our wigwam, to see what the beds was like. My bed was a straw tick—better than Jim's, which was a corn-shuck tick; there's always cobs around about in a shuck tick, and they poke into you and hurt; and when you roll over, the dry shucks sound like you was rolling over in a pile of dead leaves; it makes such a rustling that you wake up. Well, the duke allowed he would take my bed; but the king allowed he wouldn't. He says—

"I should a reckoned the difference in rank would a sejested to you that a corn-shuck bed warn't just fitten for me to sleep on. Your Grace'll take the shuck bed yourself."

Jim and me was in a sweat agin, for a minute, being afraid there was going to be some more trouble amongst them; so we was pretty glad when the duke says—

" 'Tis my fate to be always ground into the mire under the iron heel of oppression. Misfortune has broken my once haughty spirit; I yield, I submit; 'tis my fate. I am alone in the world—let me suffer; I can bear it."

We got away as soon as it was good and dark. The king told us to stand well out towards the middle of the river, and not show a light till we got a long ways below the town. We come in sight of the little bunch of lights by-and-by—that was the town, you know—and slid by, about a half a mile out, all right. When we was three-quarters of a mile below, we hoisted up our signal lantern; and about ten o'clock it come on to rain and blow and thunder and lighten like everything; so the king told us to both stay on watch till the weather got better; then him and the duke crawled into the wigwam and turned in for the night. It was my watch below, till twelve, but I wouldn't a turned in, anyway, if I'd had a bed; because a body don't see such a storm as that every day in the week, not by a long sight. My souls, how the wind did scream along! And every second or two there'd come a glare that lit up the white-caps for a half a mile around, and you'd see the islands looking dusty through the rain, and the trees thrashing around in the wind; then comes a *h-wack!*—bum! bum! bumble-umble-um-bum-bum-bum-bum—and the thunder would go rumbling and grumbling away, and quit—and then *rip* comes another flash and another sockdolager. The waves most washed me off the raft, sometimes, but I hadn't any clothes on, and didn't mind. We didn't have no trouble about snags; the lightning was glaring and flittering around so constant that we could see them plenty soon enough to throw her head this way or that and miss them.

I had the middle watch, you know, but I was pretty sleepy by that time, so Jim he said he would stand the first half of it for me; he was always mighty good, that way, Jim was. I crawled into the wigwam, but the king and the duke had their legs sprawled around so there warn't no show for me; so I laid outside—I didn't mind the rain, because it was warm, and the waves warn't running so high, now. About two they come up again, though, and Jim was going to call me, but he changed his mind because he reckoned they warn't high enough yet to do any harm; but he was mistaken about that, for pretty soon all of a sudden along comes a regular ripper, and washed me overboard. It most killed Jim a-laughing. He was the easiest nigger to laugh that ever was, anyway.

I took the watch, and Jim he laid down and snored away; and by-and-by the storm let up for good and all; and the first cabin-light that showed, I rousted him out and we slid the raft into hiding-quarters for the day.

The king got out an old ratty deck of cards, after breakfast, and him and the duke played seven-up a while, five cents a game. Then they got tired of it, and allowed they would "lay out a campaign," as they called it. The duke went down into his carpet-bag and fetched up a lot of little printed bills, and read them out loud. One bill said "The celebrated Dr. Armand de Montalban of Paris," would "lecture on the Science of Phrenology" at such and such a place, on the blank day of blank, at ten cents admission, and "furnish charts of character at twenty-five cents apiece." The duke said that was *him*. In another bill he was the "world renowned Shaksperean tragedian, Garrick the Younger,[1] of Drury Lane, London." In other bills he had a lot of other names and done other wonderful things, like finding water and gold with a "divining rod," "dissipating witch-spells," and so on. By-and-by he says—

"But the histrionic muse is the darling. Have you ever trod the boards, Royalty?"

"No," says the king.

"You shall, then, before you're three days older, Fallen Grandeur,"[2] says the duke. "The first good town we come to, we'll hire a hall and do the sword-fight in Richard III. and the balcony scene in Romeo and Juliet. How does that strike you?"

"I'm in, up to the hub, for anything that will pay, Bilgewater, but you see I don't know nothing about play-actn', and hain't ever seen much of it. I was too small when pap used to have 'em at the palace. Do you reckon you can learn me?"

"Easy!"

"All right. I'm jist a-freezn' for something fresh, anyway. Less commence, right away."

So the duke he told him all about who Romeo was, and who Juliet was, and said he was used to being Romeo, so the king could be Juliet.

1. *Cf.* the playbill and note 7 in Chapter **XXI** for the nonexistent David Garrick the *Younger*.
2. The frontiersman's dexterity in the coinage of ludicrous names as here in

"Bilgewater" and "Fallen Grandeur" persists as one of Twain's comic devices which assist him in individualizing these two characters.

"But if Juliet's such a young gal, Duke, my peeled head and my white whiskers is goin' to look oncommon odd on her, maybe."

"No, don't you worry—these country jakes won't ever think of that.[3] Besides, you know, you'll be in costume, and that makes all the difference in the world; Juliet's in a balcony, enjoying the moonlight before she goes to bed, and she's got on her night-gown and her ruffled night-cap. Here are the costumes for the parts."

He got out two or three curtain-calico suits, which he said was meedyevil armor for Richard III. and t'other chap, and a long white cotton night-shirt and a ruffled night-cap to match. The king was satisfied; so the duke got out his book and read the parts over in the most splendid spread-eagle way, prancing around and acting at the same time, to show how it had got to be done; then he give the book to the king and told him to get his part by heart.

There was a little one-horse town about three mile down the bend, and after dinner the duke said he had ciphered out his idea about how to run in daylight without it being dangersome for Jim; so he allowed he would go down to the town and fix that thing. The king allowed he would go too, and see if he couldn't strike something. We was out of coffee, so Jim said I better go along with them in the canoe and get some.

When we got there, there warn't nobody stirring; streets empty, and perfectly dead and still, like Sunday. We found a sick nigger sunning himself in a back yard, and he said everybody that warn't too young or too sick or too old, was gone to camp-meeting, about two mile back in the woods. The king got the directions, and allowed he'd go and work that camp-meeting for all it was worth,[4] and I might go, too.

The duke said what he was after was a printing office. We found it; a little bit of a concern, up over a carpenter shop—carpenters and printers all gone to the meeting, and no doors locked. It was a dirty, littered-up place, and had ink marks, and handbills with pictures of horses and runaway niggers on them, all over the walls. The duke shed his coat and said he was all right, now. So me and the king lit out for the camp-meeting.

We got there in about a half an hour, fairly dripping, for it was a most awful hot day. There was as much as a thousand people there, from twenty mile around. The woods was full of teams and wagons, hitched everywheres, feeding out of the wagon troughs and stomping to keep off the flies. There was sheds made out of

3. The king's appearance as Juliet would disturb the audience more because of his age than because of his sex; Wecter in *Sam Clemens of Hannibal*, p. 186, says that in that time and place no lady could appear on the stage, and feminine roles were carried by men or boys, as in seventeenth-century England.

4. A stock situation of frontier humor was the pious fraud who got away with the collection basket at a camp-meeting. The classic example of this is "The Captain Attends a Camp-Meeting," an episode in the life of the legendary Suggs collected by Johnson J. Hooper in his *Some Adventures of Captain Simon Suggs.*

poles and roofed over with branches, where they had lemonade and gingerbread to sell, and piles of watermelons and green corn and such-like truck.

The preaching was going on under the same kinds of sheds, only they was bigger and held crowds of people. The benches was made out of outside slabs of logs, with holes bored in the round side to drive sticks into for legs. They didn't have no backs. The preachers had high platforms to stand on, at one end of the sheds. The women had on sunbonnets; and some had linsey-woolsey frocks, some gingham ones, and a few of the young ones had on calico. Some of the young men was barefooted, and some of the children didn't have on any clothes but just a tow-linen shirt. Some of the old women was knitting, and some of the young folks was courting on the sly.

The first shed we come to, the preacher was lining out a hymn. He lined out two lines, everybody sung it, and it was kind of grand to hear it, there was so many of them and they done it in such a rousing way; then he lined out two more for them to sing—and so on. The people woke up more and more, and sung louder and louder; and towards the end, some begun to groan, and some begun to shout. Then the preacher begun to preach; and begun in earnest, too; and went weaving first to one side of the platform and then the other, and then a leaning down over the front of it, with his arms and his body going all the time, and shouting his words out with all his might; and every now and then he would hold up his Bible and spread it open, and kind of pass it around this way and that, shouting, "It's the brazen serpent in the wilderness! Look upon it and live!" And people would shout out, "Glory! —A-a-*men!*" And so he went on, and the people groaning and crying and saying amen:

"Oh, come to the mourners' bench! come, black with sin! (*amen!*) come, sick and sore! (*amen!*) come, lame and halt, and blind! (*amen!*) come, pore and needy, sunk in shame! (*a-a-men!*) come all that's worn, and soiled, and suffering!—come with a broken spirit! come with a contrite heart! come in your rags and sin and dirt! the waters that cleanse is free, the door of heaven stands open—oh, enter in and be at rest!" (*a-a-men! glory, glory hallelujah!*)

And so on. You couldn't make out what the preacher said, any more, on account of the shouting and crying. Folks got up, everywheres in the crowd, and worked their way, just by main strength, to the mourners' bench, with the tears running down their faces; and when all the mourners had got up there to the front benches in a crowd, they sung, and shouted, and flung themselves down on the straw, just crazy and wild.

Well, the first I knowed, the king got agoing; and you could hear him over everybody; and next he went a-charging up on to the platform and the preacher he begged him to speak to the people, and he done it. He told them he was a pirate—been a pirate for thirty years, out in the Indian Ocean, and his crew was thinned out considerable, last spring, in a fight, and he was home now, to take out some fresh men, and thanks to goodness he'd been robbed last night, and put ashore off of a steamboat without a cent, and he was glad of it, it was the blessedest thing that ever happened to him, because he was a changed man now, and happy for the first time in his life; and poor as he was, he was going to start right off and work his way back to the Indian Ocean and put in the rest of his life trying to turn the pirates into the true path; for he could do it better than anybody else, being acquainted with all the pirate crews in that ocean; and though it would take him a long time to get there, without money, he would get there anyway, and every time he convinced a pirate he would say to him, "Don't you thank me, don't you give me no credit, it all belongs to them dear people in Pokeville camp-meeting, natural brothers and benefactors of the race—and that dear preacher there, the truest friend a pirate ever had!"

And then he busted into tears, and so did everybody. Then somebody sings out, "Take up a collection for him, take up a collection!" Well, a half a dozen made a jump to do it, but somebody sings out, "Let *him* pass the hat around!" Then everybody said it, the preacher too.

So the king went all through the crowd with his hat, swabbing his eyes, and blessing the people and praising them and thanking them for being so good to the poor pirates away off there; and every little while the prettiest kind of girls, with the tears running down their cheeks, would up and ask him would he let them kiss him, for to remember him by; and he always done it; and some of them he hugged and kissed as many as five or six times—and he was invited to stay a week; and everybody wanted him to live in their houses, and said they'd think it was an honor; but he said as this was the last day of the camp-meeting he couldn't do no good, and besides he was in a sweat to get to the Indian Ocean right off and go to work on the pirates.

When we got back to the raft and he come to count up, he found he had collected eighty-seven dollars and seventy-five cents. And then he had fetched away a three-gallon jug of whisky, too, that he found under a wagon when we was starting home through the woods. The king said, take it all around, it laid over any day he'd ever put in in the missionarying line. He said it warn't no use talking, heathens don't amount to shucks, alongside of pirates, to work a campmeeting with.

The duke was thinking *he'd* been doing pretty well, till the king come to show up, but after that he didn't think so so much. He had set up and printed off two little jobs for farmers, in that printing office—horse bills—and took the money, four dollars. And he had got in ten dollars worth of advertisements for the paper, which he said he would put in for four dollars if they would pay in advance— so they done it. The price of the paper was two dollars a year, but he took in three subscriptions for half a dollar apiece on condition of them paying him in advance; they were going to pay in cord- wood and onions, as usual, but he said he had just bought the con- cern and knocked down the price as low as he could afford it, and was going to run it for cash. He set up a little piece of poetry, which he made, himself, out of his own head—three verses—kind of sweet and saddish—the name of it was, "Yes, crush, cold world, this breaking heart"—and he left that all set up and ready to print in the paper and didn't charge nothing for it. Well, he took in nine dollars and a half, and said he'd done a pretty square day's work for it.

Then he showed us another little job he'd printed and hadn't charged for, because it was for us. It had a picture of a runaway nigger, with a bundle on a stick, over his shoulder, and "$200 re- ward" under it. The reading was all about Jim, and just described him to a dot. It said he run away from St. Jacques' plantation, forty mile below New Orleans, last winter, and likely went north, and whoever would catch him and send him back, he could have the reward and expenses.

"Now," says the duke, "after to-night we can run in the daytime if we want to. Whenever we see anybody coming, we can tie Jim hand and foot with a rope, and lay him in the wigwam and show this handbill and say we captured him up the river, and were too poor to travel on a steamboat, so we got this little raft on credit from our friends and are going down to get the reward. Handcuffs and chains would look still better on Jim, but it wouldn't go well with the story of us being so poor. Too much like jewelry. Ropes are the correct thing—we must preserve the unities, as we say on the boards."

We all said the duke was pretty smart, and there couldn't be no trouble about running daytimes. We judged we could make miles enough that night to get out of the reach of the pow-wow we reck- oned the duke's work in the printing office was going to make in that little town—then we could boom right along, if we wanted to.

We laid low and kept still, and never shoved out till nearly ten o'clock; then we slid by, pretty wide away from the town, and didn't hoist our lantern till we was clear out of sight of it.

When Jim called me to take the watch at four in the morning, he says—

"Huck, does you reck'n we gwyne to run acrost any mo' kings on dis trip?"

"No," I says, "I reckon not."

"Well," says he, "dat's all right, den. I doan' mine one er two kings, but dat's enough. Dis one's powerful drunk, en de duke ain' much better."

I found Jim had been trying to get him to talk French, so he could hear what it was like; but he said he had been in this country so long, and had so much trouble, he'd forgot it.

Chapter XXI

It was after sun-up, now, but we went right on, and didn't tie up. The king and the duke turned out, by-and-by, looking pretty rusty; but after they'd jumped overboard and took a swim, it chippered them up a good deal. After breakfast the king he took a seat on a corner of the raft, and pulled off his boots and rolled up his britches, and let his legs dangle in the water, so as to be comfortable, and lit his pipe, and went to getting his Romeo and Juliet by heart. When he had got it pretty good, him and the duke begun to practice it together. The duke had to learn him over and over again, how to say every speech; and he made him sigh, and put his hand on his heart, and after while he said he done it pretty well; "only," he says, "you mustn't bellow out *Romeo!* that way, like a bull— you must say it soft, and sick, and languishy, so—R-o-o-meo! that is the idea; for Juliet's a dear sweet mere child of a girl, you know, and she don't bray like a jackass."

Well, next they got out a couple of long swords that the duke made out of oak laths, and begun to practice the sword-fight—the duke called himself Richard III.; and the way they laid on, and pranced around the raft was grand to see. But by-and-by the king tripped and fell overboard, and after that they took a rest, and had a talk about all kinds of adventures they'd had in other times along the river.

After dinner, the duke says:

"Well, Capet,[5] we'll want to make this a first-class show, you know, so I guess we'll add a little more to it. We want a little something to answer encores with, anyway."

"What's onkores, Bilgewater?"

The duke told him, and then says:

"I'll answer by doing the Highland fling or the sailor's hornpipe; and you—well, let me see—oh, I've got it—you can do Hamlet's soliloquy."

"Hamlet's which?"

5. In convicting Louis XVI the National Convention used his family name, Louis Capet. The duke may also be garbling Juliet's family name, Capulet.

"Hamlet's soliloquy, you know; the most celebrated thing in Shakespeare. Ah, it's sublime, sublime! Always fetches the house. I haven't got it in the book—I've only got one volume—but I reckon I can piece it out from memory. I'll just walk up and down a minute, and see if I can call it back from recollection's vaults."

So he went to marching up and down, thinking, and frowning horrible every now and then; then he would hoist up his eyebrows; next he would squeeze his hand on his forehead and stagger back and kind of moan; next he would sigh, and next he'd let on to drop a tear. It was beautiful to see him. By-and-by he got it. He told us to give attention. Then he strikes a most noble attitude, with one leg shoved forwards, and his arms stretched away up, and his head tilted back, looking up at the sky; and then he begins to rip and rave and grit his teeth; and after that, all through his speech he howled, and spread around, and swelled up his chest, and just knocked the spots out of any acting ever *I* see before. This is the speech—I learned it, easy enough, while he was learning it to the king:[6]

To be, or not to be; that is the bare bodkin
That makes calamity of so long life;
For who would fardels bear, till Birnam Wood do come to Dunsinane,
But that the fear of something after death
Murders the innocent sleep,
Great nature's second course,
And makes us rather sling the arrows of outrageous fortune
Than fly to others that we know not of.
There's the respect must give us pause:
Wake Duncan with thy knocking! I would thou couldst;
For who would bear the whips and scorns of time,
The oppressor's wrong, the proud man's contumely,
The law's delay, and the quietus which his pangs might take,
In the dead waste and middle of the night, when churchyards yawn
In customary suits of solemn black,
But that the undiscovered country from whose bourne no traveler returns,
Breathes forth contagion on the world,
And thus the native hue of resolution, like the poor cat i' the adage,
Is sicklied o'er with care,
And all the clouds that lowered o'er our housetops,
With this regard their currents turn awry,
And lose the name of action.
'Tis a consummation devoutly to be wished. But soft you, the fair

6. The duke's fractured Shakespeare, which is in the best impromptu frontier tradition, picks up and pieces together some of Shakespeare's most quotable lines.

Ophelia:
Ope not thy ponderous and marble jaws,
But get thee to a nunnery—go!

Well, the old man he liked that speech, and he mighty soon got it so he could do it first rate. It seemed like he was just born for it; and when he had his hand in and was excited, it was perfectly lovely the way he would rip and tear and rair up behind when he was getting it off.

The first chance we got, the duke he had some show bills printed; and after that, for two or three days as we floated along, the raft was a most uncommon lively place, for there warn't nothing but sword-fighting and rehearsing—as the duke called it—going on all the time. One morning, when we was pretty well down the State of Arkansaw, we come in sight of a little one-horse town in a big bend; so we tied up about three-quarters of a mile above it, in the mouth of a crick which was shut in like a tunnel by the cypress trees, and all of us but Jim took the canoe and went down there to see if there was any chance in that place for our show.

We struck it mighty lucky; there was going to be a circus there that afternoon, and the country people was already beginning to come in, in all kinds of old shackly wagons, and on horses. The circus would leave before night, so our show would have a pretty good chance. The duke he hired the court house, and we went around and stuck up our bills. They read like this:[7]

Shaksperean Revival! ! !
Wonderful Attraction!
For One Night Only!
The world renowned tragedians,
David Garrick the younger, of Drury Lane Theatre, London,
and
Edmund Kean the elder, of the Royal Haymarket Theatre, White-
chapel, Pudding Lane, Piccadilly, London, and the
Royal Continental Theatres, in their sublime
Shaksperean Spectacle entitled
The Balcony Scene
in
Romeo and Juliet! ! !
Romeo . . . . Mr. Garrick.
Juliet . . . . Mr. Kean.
Assisted by the whole strength of the company!
New costumes, new scenery, new appointments!
Also:
The thrilling, masterly, and blood-curdling
Broad-sword conflict

7. The duke blithely confuses three great English Shakespearian actors, David Garrick (1717–1779), Edmund Kean (the Elder; 1787?–1833), and Charles John Kean (the Younger; 1811?–1868), all of whom were prominent tragedians at Drury Lane Theatre in London. He carries forward this error in the poster for the "Royal Nonesuch" in Chapter XXII.

In Richard III.! ! !

Richard III .... Mr. Garrick.
Richmond .... Mr. Kean.

also:

(by special request,)
Hamlet's Immortal Soliloquy! !
By the Illustrious Kean!
Done by him 300 consecutive nights in Paris!
For One Night Only,
On account of imperative European engagements!
Admission 25 cents; children and servants, 10 cents.

Then we went loafing around the town.[8] The stores and houses was most all old shackly dried-up frame concerns that hadn't ever been painted; they was set up three or four foot above ground on stilts, so as to be out of reach of the water when the river was over-flowed. The houses had little gardens around them, but they didn't seem to raise hardly anything in them but jimpson weeds, and sun-flowers, and ash-piles, and old curled-up boots and shoes, and pieces of bottles, and rags, and played-out tin-ware. The fences was made of different kinds of boards, nailed on at different times; and they leaned every which-way, and had gates that didn't generly have but one hinge—a leather one. Some of the fences had been white-washed, some time or another, but the duke said it was in Clum-bus's time, like enough. There was generly hogs in the garden, and people driving them out.

All the stores was along one street. They had white-domestic awnings in front, and the country people hitched their horses to the awning-posts. There was empty dry-goods boxes under the awn-ings, and loafers roosting on them all day long, whittling them with their Barlow knives; and chawing tobacco, and gaping and yawning and stretching—a mighty ornery lot. They generly had on yellow straw hats most as wide as an umbrella, but didn't wear no coats nor waistcoats; they called one another Bill, and Buck, and Hank, and Joe, and Andy, and talked lazy and drawly, and used consider-able many cuss-words. There was as many as one loafer leaning up against every awning-post, and he most always had his hands in his britches pockets, except when he fetched them out to lend a chaw of tobacco or scratch. What a body was hearing amongst them, all the time was—

"Gimme a chaw 'v tobacker, Hank."

"Cain't—I hain't got but one chaw left. Ask Bill."

Maybe Bill he gives him a chaw; maybe he lies and says he ain't got none. Some of them kinds of loafers never has a cent in the world, nor a chaw of tobacco of their own. They get all their chaw-

---

8. The following is Twain's expression of contempt for the shiftless type of frontiersman and his unkempt town, showing another aspect of Hannibal, which Twain usually nostalgically de-scribed as idyllic.

ing by borrowing—they say to a fellow, "I wisht you'd len' me a chaw, Jack, I jist this minute give Ben Thompson the last chaw I had"—which is a lie, pretty much every time; it don't fool nobody but a stranger; but Jack ain't no stranger, so he says—

"*You* give him a chaw, did you? so did your sister's cat's grandmother. You pay me back the chaws you've awready borry'd off'n me, Lafe Buckner, then I'll loan you one or two ton of it, and won't charge you no back intrust, nuther."

"Well, I *did* pay you back some of it wunst."

"Yes, you did—'bout six chaws. You borry'd store tobacker and paid back nigger-head."

Store tobacco is flat black plug, but these fellows mostly chaws the natural leaf twisted. When they borrow a chaw, they don't generly cut it off with a knife, but they set the plug in between their teeth, and gnaw with their teeth and tug at the plug with their hands till they get it in two—then sometimes the one that owns the tobacco looks mournful at it when it's handed back, and says, sarcastic—

"Here, gimme the *chaw*, and you take the *plug*."

All the streets and lanes was just mud, they warn't nothing else *but* mud—mud as black as tar, and nigh about a foot deep in some places; and two or three inches deep in *all* the places. The hogs loafed and grunted around, everywheres. You'd see a muddy sow and a litter of pigs come lazying along the street and whollop herself down in the way, where folks had to walk around her, and she'd stretch out, and shut her eyes, and wave her ears, whilst the pigs was milking her, and look as happy as if she was on salary. And pretty soon you'd hear a loafer sing out, "Hi! *so* boy! sick him, Tige!" and away the sow would go, squealing most horrible, with a dog or two swinging to each ear, and three or four dozen more a-coming; and then you would see all the loafers get up and watch the thing out of sight, and laugh at the fun and look grateful for the noise. Then they'd settle back again till there was a dog-fight. There couldn't anything wake them up all over, and make them happy all over, like a dog-fight—unless it might be putting turpentine on a stray dog and setting fire to him, or tying a tin pan to his tail and see him run himself to death.

On the river front some of the houses was sticking out over the bank, and they was bowed and bent, and about ready to tumble in. The people had moved out of them. The bank was caved away under one corner of some others, and that corner was hanging over. People lived in them yet, but it was dangersome, because sometimes a strip of land as wide as a house caves in at a time. Sometimes a belt of land a quarter of a mile deep will start in and cave along and cave along till it all caves into the river in one summer. Such a town as that has to be always moving back, and back, and back, because the river's always gnawing at it.

The nearer it got to noon that day, the thicker and thicker was the wagons and horses in the streets, and more coming all the time. Families fetched their dinners with them, from the country, and eat them in the wagons. There was considerable whiskey drinking going on, and I seen three fights. By-and-by somebody sings out—

"Here comes old Boggs![9]—in from the country for his little old monthly drunk—here he comes, boys!"

All the loafers looked glad—I reckoned they was used to having fun out of Boggs. One of them says—

"Wonder who he's a gwyne to chaw up this time. If he'd a chawed up all the men he's ben a gwyne to chaw up in the last twenty year, he'd have considerble ruputation, now."

Another one says, "I wisht old Boggs'd threaten me, 'cuz then I'd know I warn't gwyne to die for a thousan' year."

Boggs comes a-tearing along on his horse, whooping and yelling like an Injun, and singing out—

"Cler the track, thar. I'm on the waw-path, and the price uv coffins is a gwyne to raise."

He was drunk, and weaving about in his saddle; he was over fifty year old, and had a very red face. Everybody yelled at him, and laughed at him, and sassed him, and he sassed back, and said he'd attend to them and lay them out in their regular turns, but he couldn't wait now, because he'd come to town to kill old Colonel Sherburn, and his motto was, "meat first, and spoon vittles to top off on."

He see me, and rode up and says—

"Whar'd you come f'm, boy? You prepared to die?"

Then he rode on. I was scared; but a man says—

"He don't mean nothing; he's always a carryin' on like that, when he's drunk. He's the best-naturedest old fool in Arkansaw—never hurt nobody, drunk nor sober."

Boggs rode up before the biggest store in town and bent his head down so he could see under the curtain of the awning, and yells—

"Come out here, Sherburn! Come out and meet the man you've swindled. You're the houn' I'm after, and I'm a gwyne to have you, too!"

And so he went on, calling Sherburn everything he could lay his tongue to, and the whole street packed with people listening and laughing and going on. By-and-by a proud-looking man about fifty-five—and he was a heap the best dressed man in that town, too—steps out of the store, and the crowd drops back on each side to let him come. He says to Boggs, mighty ca'm and slow—he says:

9. The following episode is based on an actual case in Hannibal, tried by Twain's father, Judge Clemens. *Cf.* Dixon Wecter, *Sam Clemens of Hannibal,* pp. 106–109.

"I'm tired of this; but I'll endure it till one o'clock. Till one o'clock, mind—no longer. If you open your mouth against me only once, after that time, you can't travel so far but I will find you."

Then he turns and goes in. The crowd looked mighty sober; nobody stirred, and there warn't no more laughing. Boggs rode off blackguarding Sherburn as loud as he could yell, all down the street; and pretty soon back he comes and stops before the store, still keeping it up. Some men crowded around him and tried to get him to shut up, but he wouldn't; they told him it would be one o'clock in about fifteen minutes, and so he *must* go home—he must go right away. But it didn't do no good. He cussed away, with all his might, and throwed his hat down in the mud and rode over it, and pretty soon away he went a-raging down the street again, with his gray hair a-flying. Everybody that could get a chance at him tried their best to coax him off of his horse so they could lock him up and get him sober; but it warn't no use—up the street he would tear again, and give Sherburn another cussing. By-and-by somebody says—

"Go for his daughter!—quick, go for his daughter; sometimes he'll listen to her. If anybody can persuade him, she can."

So somebody started on a run. I walked down street a ways, and stopped. In about five or ten minutes, here comes Boggs again—but not on his horse. He was a-reeling across the street towards me, bareheaded, with a friend on both sides of him aholt of his arms and hurrying him along. He was quiet, and looked uneasy; and he warn't hanging back any, but was doing some of the hurrying himself. Somebody sings out—

"Boggs!"

I looked over there to see who said it, and it was that Colonel Sherburn. He was standing perfectly still, in the street, and had a pistol raised in his right hand—not aiming it, but holding it out with the barrel tilted up towards the sky. The same second I see a young girl coming on the run, and two men with her. Boggs and the men turned round, to see who called him, and when they see the pistol the men jumped to one side, and the pistol barrel come down slow and steady to a level—both barrels cocked. Boggs throws up both of his hands, and says, "O Lord, don't shoot!" Bang! goes the first shot, and he staggers back clawing at the air—bang! goes the second one, and he tumbles backwards onto the ground, heavy and solid, with his arms spread out. That young girl screamed out, and comes rushing, and down she throws herself on her father, crying, and saying, "Oh, he's killed him, he's killed him!" The crowd closed up around them, and shouldered and jammed one another, with their necks stretched, trying to see, and people on the inside trying to shove them back, and shouting, "Back, back! give him air, give him air!"

Colonel Sherburn he tossed his pistol onto the ground, and turned around on his heels and walked off.

They took Boggs to a little drug store, the crowd pressing around, just the same, and the whole town following, and I rushed and got a good place at the window, where I was close to him and could see in. They laid him on the floor, and put one large Bible under his head, and opened another one and spread it on his breast—but they tore open his shirt first, and I seen where one of the bullets went in. He made about a dozen long gasps, his breast lifting the Bible up when he drawed in his breath, and letting it down again when he breathed it out—and after that he laid still; he was dead. Then they pulled his daughter away from him, screaming and crying, and took her off. She was about sixteen, and very sweet and gentle-looking, but awful pale and scared.

Well, pretty soon the whole town was there, squirming and scrouging and pushing and shoving to get at the window and have a look, but people that had the places wouldn't give them up, and folks behind them was saying all the time, "Say, now, you've looked enough, you fellows; 'taint right and 'taint fair, for you to stay thar all the time, and never give nobody a chance; other folks has their rights as well as you."

There was considerable jawing back, so I slid out, thinking maybe there was going to be trouble. The streets was full, and everybody was excited. Everybody that seen the shooting was telling how it happened, and there was a big crowd packed around each one of these fellows, stretching their necks and listening. One long lanky man, with long hair and a big white fur stove-pipe hat on the back of his head, and a crooked-handled cane, marked out the places on the ground where Boggs stood, and where Sherburn stood, and the people following him around from one place to t'other and watching everything he done, and bobbing their heads to show they understood, and stooping a little and resting their hands on their thighs to watch him mark the places on the ground with his cane; and then he stood up straight and stiff where Sherburn had stood, frowning and having his hat-brim down over his eyes, and sung out, "Boggs!" and then fetched his cane down slow to a level, and says "Bang!" staggered backwards, says "Bang!" again, and fell down flat on his back. The people that had seen the thing said he done it perfect; said it was just exactly the way it all happened. Then as much as a dozen people got out their bottles and treated him.

Well, by-and-by somebody said Sherburn ought to be lynched. In about a minute everybody was saying it; so away they went, mad and yelling, and snatching down every clothes-line they come to, to do the hanging with.

Chapter XXII

They swarmed up the street towards Sherburn's house, a-whooping and yelling and raging like Injuns, and everything had to clear the way or get run over and tromped to mush, and it was awful to see. Children was heeling it ahead of the mob, screaming and trying to get out of the way; and every window along the road was full of women's heads, and there was nigger boys in every tree, and bucks and wenches looking over every fence; and as soon as the mob would get nearly to them they would break and skaddle back out of reach. Lots of the women and girls was crying and taking on, scared most to death.

They swarmed up in front of Sherburn's palings as thick as they could jam together, and you couldn't hear yourself think for the noise. It was a little twenty-foot yard. Some sung out "Tear down the fence! tear down the fence!" Then there was a racket of ripping and tearing and smashing, and down she goes, and the front wall of the crowd begins to roll in like a wave.

Just then Sherburn steps out on to the roof of his little front porch, with a double-barrel gun in his hand, and takes his stand, perfectly ca'm and deliberate, not saying a word. The racket stopped, and the wave sucked back.

Sherburn never said a word—just stood there, looking down. The stillness was awful creepy and uncomfortable. Sherburn run his eye slow along the crowd; and wherever it struck, the people tried a little to outgaze him, but they couldn't; they dropped their eyes and looked sneaky. Then pretty soon Sherburn sort of laughed; not the pleasant kind, but the kind that makes you feel like when you are eating bread that's got sand in it.

Then he says, slow and scornful:

"The idea of *you* lynching anybody! It's amusing. The idea of you thinking you had pluck enough to lynch a *man!* Because you're brave enough to tar and feather poor friendless cast-out women that come along here, did that make you think you had grit enough to lay your hands on a *man?* Why, a *man's* safe in the hands of ten thousand of your kind—as long as it's day-time and you're not behind him.

"Do I know you? I know you clear through. I was born and raised in the South, and I've lived in the North; so I know the average all around. The average man's a coward. In the North he lets anybody walk over him that wants to, and goes home and prays for a humble spirit to bear it. In the South one man, all by himself, has stopped a stage full of men, in the day-time, and robbed the lot. Your newspapers call you a brave people so much that you think you *are* braver than any other people—whereas you're just *as* brave, and no braver. Why don't your juries hang murderers? Because they're afraid the man's friends will shoot them in the back, in the dark—and it's just what they *would* do.

"So they always acquit; and then a *man* goes in the night, with a hundred masked cowards at his back, and lynches the rascal. Your mistake is, that you didn't bring a man with you; that's one mistake, and the other is that you didn't come in the dark, and fetch your masks. You brought *part* of a man—Buck Harkness, there—and if you hadn't had him to start you, you'd a taken it out in blowing.

"You didn't want to come. The average man don't like trouble and danger. *You* don't like trouble and danger. But if only *half* a man—like Buck Harkness, there—shouts 'Lynch him, lynch him!' you're afraid to back down—afraid you'll be found out to be what you are—*cowards*—and so you raise a yell, and hang yourselves onto that half-a-man's coat tail, and come raging up here, swearing what big things you're going to do. The pitifulest thing out is a mob; that's what an army is—a mob; they don't fight with courage that's born in them, but with courage that's borrowed from their mass, and from their officers. But a mob without any *man* at the head of it, is *beneath* pitifulness. Now the thing for *you* to do, is to droop your tails and go home and crawl in a hole. If any real lynching's going to be done, it will be done in the dark, Southern fashion; and when they come they'll bring their masks, and fetch a *man* along. Now *leave*—and take your half-a-man with you"—tossing his gun up across his left arm and cocking it, when he says this.

The crowd washed back sudden, and then broke all apart and went tearing off every which way, and Buck Harkness he heeled it after them, looking tolerable cheap. I could a staid, if I'd a wanted to, but I didn't want to.

I went to the circus, and loafed around the back side till the watchman went by, and then dived in under the tent. I had my twenty-dollar gold piece and some other money, but I reckoned I better save it, because there ain't no telling how soon you are going to need it, away from home and amongst strangers, that way. You can't be too careful. I ain't opposed to spending money on circuses, when there ain't no other way, but there ain't no use in *wasting* it on them.

It was a real bully circus. It was the splendidest sight that ever was, when they all come riding in, two and two, a gentleman and lady, side by side, the men just in their drawers and under-shirts, and no shoes nor stirrups, and resting their hands on their thighs, easy and comfortable—there must a' been twenty of them—and every lady with a lovely complexion, and perfectly beautiful, and looking just like a gang of real sure-enough queens, and dressed in clothes that cost millions of dollars, and just littered with diamonds. It was a powerful fine sight; I never see anything so lovely. And then one by one they got up and stood, and went a-weaving around the ring so gentle and wavy and graceful, the men looking ever so tall and airy and straight, with their heads bobbing and skimming along, away up there under the tent-roof, and every lady's rose-leafy dress flapping soft and silky around her hips, and she looking like the most loveliest parasol.

And then faster and faster they went, all of them dancing, first one foot stuck out in the air and then the other, the horses leaning more and more, and the ring-master going round and round the centre-pole, cracking his whip and shouting "hi!—hi!" and the clown cracking jokes behind him; and by-and-by all hands dropped the reins, and every lady put her knuckles on her hips and every gentleman folded his arms, and then how the horses did lean over and hump themselves! And so, one after the other they all skipped off into the ring, and made the sweetest bow I ever see, and then scampered out, and everybody clapped their hands and went just about wild.

Well, all through the circus they done the most astonishing things; and all the time that clown carried on so it most killed the people. The ring-master couldn't ever say a word to him but he was back at him quick as a wink with the funniest things a body ever said; and how he ever *could* think of so many of them, and so sudden and so pat, was what I couldn't noway understand. Why, I couldn't a thought of them in a year. And by-and-by a drunk man tried to get into the ring—said he wanted to ride; said he could ride as well as anybody that ever was. They argued and tried to keep him out, but he wouldn't listen, and the whole show come to a standstill. Then the people begun to holler at him and make fun of him, and that made him mad, and he begun to rip and tear; so that stirred up the people, and a lot of men began to pile down off of the benches and swarm towards the ring, saying, "Knock him down! throw him out!" and one or two women begun to scream. So, then, the ring-master he made a little speech, and said he hoped there wouldn't be no disturbance, and if the man would promise he wouldn't make no more trouble, he would let him ride, if he thought he could stay on the horse. So everybody laughed and said all right, and the man got on. The minute he was on, the horse begun to rip and tear and jump and cavort around, with two circus men hanging onto his bridle trying to hold him, and the drunk man hanging onto his neck, and his heels flying in the air every jump, and the whole crowd of people standing up shouting and laughing till the tears rolled down. And at last, sure enough, all the circus men could do, the horse broke loose, and away he went like the very nation, round and round the ring, with that sot laying down on him and hanging to his neck, with first one leg hanging most to the ground on one side, and the t'other one on t'other side, and the people just crazy. It warn't funny to me, though; I was all of a tremble to see his danger. But pretty soon he struggled up astraddle and grabbed the bridle, a-reeling this way and that; and the next minute he sprung up and dropped the bridle and stood! and the horse agoing like a house afire too. He just stood up there, a-sailing around as easy and comfortable as if he warn't ever drunk in his life —and then he begun to pull off his clothes and sling them. He shed them so thick they kind of clogged up the air, and altogether he shed seventeen suits. And then, there he was, slim and handsome, and dressed the gaudiest and prettiest you ever saw, and he lit into that horse with his whip and made him fairly hum—and finally skipped off, and made his bow and danced off to the dressing-room, and everybody just a-howling with pleasure and astonishment.

Then the ring-master he see how he had been fooled, and he *was* the sickest ring-master you ever see, I reckon. Why, it was one of his own men! He had got up that joke all out of his own head, and never let on to nobody. Well, I felt sheepish enough, to be took in so, but I wouldn't a been in that ring-master's place, not for a thousand dollars. I don't know; there may be bullier circuses than what that one was, but I never struck them yet. Anyways it was plenty good enough for *me*; and wherever I run across it, it can have all of *my* custom, every time.

Well, that night we had *our* show; but there warn't only about twelve people there; just enough to pay expenses. And they laughed all the time, and that made the duke mad; and everybody left, anyway, before the show was over, but one boy which was asleep. So the duke said these Arkansaw lunkheads couldn't come up to Shakspeare; what they wanted was low comedy—and may be something ruther worse than low comedy, he reckoned. He said he could size their style. So next morning he got some big sheets of wrapping-paper and some black paint, and drawed off some handbills and stuck them up all over the village. The bills said:

AT THE COURT HOUSE!
FOR 3 NIGHTS ONLY!
The World-Renowned Tragedians
DAVID GARRICK THE YOUNGER
AND
EDMUND KEAN THE ELDER!
Of the London and Continental Theatres,
In their Thrilling Tragedy of
THE KING'S CAMELOPARD
OR
THE ROYAL NONESUCH!!!
Admission 50 cents.

Then at the bottom was the biggest line of all—which said:

LADIES AND CHILDREN NOT ADMITTED.

"There," says he, "if that line don't fetch them, I dont know Arkansaw!"

Chapter XXIII

Well, all day him and the king was hard at it, rigging up a stage, and a curtain, and a row of candles for footlights; and that night the house was jam full of men in no time. When the place couldn't hold no more, the duke he quit tending door and went around the back way and come onto the stage and stood up before the curtain, and made a little speech, and praised up this tragedy, and said it was the most thrillingest one that ever was; and so he went on a-bragging about the tragedy and about Edmund Kean the Elder, which was to play the main principal part in it; and at last when he'd got everybody's expectations up high enough, he rolled up the curtain, and the next minute the king come a-prancing out on all fours, naked; and he was painted all over, ring-streaked-and-striped, all sorts of colors, as splendid as a rainbow. And—but never mind the rest of his outfit, it was just wild, but it was awful funny. The people most killed themselves laughing; and when the king got done capering, and capered off behind the scenes, they roared and clapped and stormed and haw-hawed till he come back and done it over again; and after that, they made him do it another time. Well, it would a made a cow laugh to see the shines that old idiot cut.

Then the duke he lets the curtain down, and bows to the people, and says the great tragedy will be performed only two nights more, on accounts of pressing London engagements, where the seats is all sold aready for it in Drury Lane; and then he makes them another bow, and says if he has succeeded in pleasing them and instructing them, he will be deeply obleeged if they will mention it to their friends and get them to come and see it.

Twenty people sings out:

"What, is it over? Is that *all?*"[1]

The duke says yes. Then there was a fine time. Everybody sings out "sold," and rose up mad, and was agoing for that stage and them tragedians. But a big fine-looking man jumps up on a bench, and shouts:

"Hold on! Just a word, gentlemen." They stopped to listen. "We are sold—mighty badly sold. But we don't want to be the laughing-stock of this whole town, I reckon, and never hear the last of this thing as long as we live. *No.* What we want, is to go out of here quiet, and talk this show up, and sell the *rest* of the town! Then we'll all be in the same boat. Ain't that sensible?" ("You bet it is! —the jedge is right!" everybody sings out.) "All right, then—not a word about any sell. Go along home, and advise everybody to come and see the tragedy."

1. Reportedly based on an obscene tale that the raconteur Jim Gillis called to Twain's attention in the California days. The fraudulent dramatic performance was also prevalent in humorous frontier literature.

Next day you couldn't hear nothing around that town but how splendid that show was. House was jammed again, that night, and we sold this crowd the same way. When me and the king and the duke got home to the raft, we all had a supper; and by-and-by, about midnight, they made Jim and me back her out and float her down the middle of the river and fetch her in and hide her about two mile below town.

The third night the house was crammed again—and they warn't new-comers, this time, but people that was at the show the other two nights. I stood by the duke at the door, and I see that every man that went in had his pockets bulging, or something muffled up under his coat—and I see it warn't no perfumery neither, not by a long sight. I smelt sickly eggs by the barrel, and rotten cabbages, and such things; and if I know the signs of a dead cat being around, and I bet I do, there was sixty-four of them went in. I shoved in there for a minute, but it was too various for me, I couldn't stand it. Well, when the place couldn't hold no more people, the duke he give a fellow a quarter and told him to tend door for him a minute, and then he started around for the stage door, I after him; but the minute we turned the corner and was in the dark, he says:

"Walk fast, now, till you get away from the houses, and then shin for the raft like the dickens was after you!"

I done it, and he done the same. We struck the raft at the same time, and in less than two seconds we was gliding down stream, all dark and still, and edging towards the middle of the river, nobody saying a word. I reckoned the poor king was in for a gaudy time of it with the audience; but nothing of the sort; pretty soon he crawls out from under the wigwam, and says:

"Well, how'd the old thing pan out this time, Duke?"

He hadn't been up town at all.

We never showed a light till we was about ten mile below that village. Then we lit up and had a supper, and the king and the duke fairly laughed their bones loose over the way they'd served them people. The duke says:

"Greenhorns, flatheads! *I* knew the first house would keep mum and let the rest of the town get roped in; and I knew they'd lay for us the third night, and consider it was *their* turn now. Well, it *is* their turn, and I'd give something to know how much they'd take for it. I *would* just like to know how they're putting in their opportunity. They can turn it into a picnic, if they want to—they brought plenty provisions."

Them rapscallions took in four hundred and sixty-five dollars in that three nights. I never see money hauled in by the wagon-load like that, before.

By-and-by, when they was asleep and snoring, Jim says:

"Don't it 'sprise you, de way dem kings carries on, Huck?"

"No," I says, "it don't."

"Why don't it, Huck?"

"Well, it don't, because it's in the breed. I reckon they're all alike."

"But, Huck, dese kings o' ourn is regular rapscallions; dat's jist what dey is; dey's reglar rapscallions."

"Well, that's what I'm a-saying; all kings is mostly rapscallions, as fur as I can make out."

"Is dat so?"

"You read about them once—you'll see. Look at Henry the Eight; this'n 's a Sunday-School Superintendent to *him*. And look at Charles Second, and Louis Fourteen, and Louis Fifteen, and James Second, and Edward Second, and Richard Third, and forty more; besides all them Saxon heptarchies that used to rip around so in old times and raise Cain. My, you ought to seen old Henry the Eight when he was in bloom.[2] He *was* a blossom. He used to marry a new wife every day, and chop off her head next morning. And he would do it just as indifferent as if he was ordering up eggs. 'Fetch up Nell Gwynn,' he says. They fetch her up. Next morning, 'Chop off her head!' And they chop it off. 'Fetch up Jane Shore,' he says; and up she comes. Next morning 'Chop off her head'—and they chop it off. 'Ring up Fair Rosamun.' Fair Rosamun answers the bell. Next morning, 'Chop off her head.' And he made every one of them tell him a tale every night; and he kept that up till he had hogged a thousand and one tales that way, and then he put them all in a book, and called it Domesday Book—which was a good name and stated the case. You don't know kings, Jim, but I know them; and this old rip of ourn is one of the cleanest I've struck in history. Well, Henry he takes a notion he wants to get up some trouble with this country. How does he go at it—give notice? —give the country a show? No. All of a sudden he heaves all the tea in Boston Harbor overboard, and whacks out a declaration of independence, and dares them to come on. That was *his* style—he never give anybody a chance. He had suspicions of his father, the Duke of Wellington. Well, what did he do?—ask him to show up? No—drownded him in a butt of mamsey, like a cat. Spose people left money laying around where he was—what did he do? He collared it. Spose he contracted to do a thing; and you paid him, and didn't set down there and see that he done it—what did he do? He always done the other thing. Spose he opened his mouth—what then? If he didn't shut it up powerful quick, he'd lose a lie, every time. That's the kind of a bug Henry was; and if we'd a had him along 'stead of our kings, he'd a fooled that town a heap worse than ourn done. I don't say that ourn is lambs, because they ain't,

2. Huck's following description of Henry VIII (1509–1547) is a grand confusion of history with fiction (he confuses the historical *Domesday Book*

when you come right down to the cold facts; but they ain't nothing to *that* old ram, anyway. All I say is, kings is kings, and you got to make allowances. Take them all around, they're a mighty ornery lot. It's the way they're raised."

"But dis one do *smell* so like de nation, Huck."

"Well, they all do, Jim. We can't help the way a king smells; history don't tell no way."

"Now de duke, he's a tolerble likely man, in some ways."

"Yes, a duke's different. But not very different. This one's a middling hard lot, for a duke. When he's drunk, there ain't no near-sighted man could tell him from a king."

"Well, anyways, I doan' hanker for no mo' un um, Huck. Dese is all I kin stan'."

"It's the way I feel, too, Jim. But we've got them on our hands, and we got to remember what they are, and make allowances. Sometimes I wish we could hear of a country that's out of kings."

What was the use to tell Jim these warn't real kings and dukes? It wouldn't a done no good; and besides, it was just as I said; you couldn't tell them from the real kind.

I went to sleep, and Jim didn't call me when it was my turn. He often done that. When I waked up, just at day-break, he was setting there with his head down betwixt his knees, moaning and mourning to himself. I didn't take notice, nor let on. I knowed what it was about. He was thinking about his wife and his children, away up yonder, and he was low and homesick; because he hadn't ever been away from home before in his life; and I do believe he cared just as much for his people as white folks does for their'n. It don't seem natural, but I reckon it's so. He was often moaning and mourning that way, nights, when he judged I was asleep, and saying, "Po' little 'Lizabeth! po' little Johnny! its mighty hard; I spec' I ain't ever gwyne to see you no mo', no mo'!" He was a mighty good nigger, Jim was.

But this time I somehow got to talking to Jim about his wife and young ones; and by-and-by he says:

"What makes me feel so bad dis time, 'uz bekase I hear sumpn over yonder on de bank like a whack, er a slam, while ago, en it mine me er de time I treat my little 'Lizabeth so ornery. She warn't on'y 'bout fo' year ole, en she tuck de sk'yarlet-fever, en had a powful rough spell; but she got well, en one day she was a-stannin' aroun', en I says to her, I says:

" 'Shet de do'.'

with the fictional Scheherazade's *Arabian Nights*) and of persons, incidents, and even centuries that could have no connection with Henry's life or times. He makes sixteenth-century Henry VIII the son of the nineteenth-century Duke of Wellington, whom he confuses with the fifteenth-century Duke of Clarence (who was supposedly drowned in a butt of malmsey); he also has Henry VIII creating the eighteenth-century American Declaration of Independence; finally, Fair Rosamond was mistress to twelfth-century Henry II, Jane Shore to fifteenth-century Edward IV, Nell Gwyn to seventeenth-century Charles II.

"She never done it; jis' stood dah, kiner smilin' up at me. It make me mad; en I says again, mighty loud, I says:

" 'Doan' you hear me?—shet de do'!'

"She jis' stood de same way, kiner smilin' up. I was a-bilin'! I says:

" 'I lay I *make* you mine!'

"En wid dat I fetch' her a slap side de head dat sont her a-sprawlin'. Den I went into de yuther room, en 'uz gone 'bout ten minutes; en when I come back, dah was dat do' a-stannin' open *yit*, en dat chile stannin' mos' right in it, a-lookin' down and mournin', en de tears runnin' down. My, but I *wuz* mad, I was agwyne for de chile, but jis' den—it was a do' dat open innerds—jis' den, 'long come de wind en slam it to, behine de chile, ker-*blam!* —en my lan', de chile never move'! My breff mos' hop outer me; en I feel so—so—I doan' know *how* I feel. I crope out, all a-tremblin', en crope aroun' en open de do' easy en slow, en poke my head in behine de chile, sof' en still, en all uv a sudden, I says *pow!* jis' as loud as I could yell. *She never budge!* Oh, Huck, I bust out a-cryin' en grab her up in my arms, en say, 'Oh, de po' little thing! de Lord God Amighty fogive po' ole Jim, kaze he never gwyne to fogive hisself as long's he live!' Oh, she was plumb deef en dumb, Huck, plumb deef en dumb—en I'd ben a'treat'n her so!"

Chapter XXIV

Next day, towards night, we laid up under a little willow towhead out in the middle, where there was a village on each side of the river, and the duke and the king begun to lay out a plan for working them towns. Jim he spoke to the duke, and said he hoped it wouldn't take but a few hours, because it got mighty heavy and tiresome to him when he had to lay all day in the wigwam tied with the rope. You see, when we left him all alone we had to tie him, because if anybody happened on him all by himself and not tied, it wouldn't look much like he was a runaway nigger, you know. So the duke said it *was* kind of hard to have to lay roped all day, and he'd cipher out some way to get around it.

He was uncommon bright, the duke was, and he soon struck it. He dressed Jim up in King Lear's outfit—it was a long curtain-calico gown, and a white horse-hair wig and whiskers; and then he took his theatre-paint and painted Jim's face and hands and ears and neck all over a dead dull solid blue, like a man that's been drownded nine days. Blamed if he warn't the horriblest looking outrage I ever see. Then the duke took and wrote out a sign on a shingle so—

Sick Arab—but harmless when not out of his head.

And he nailed that shingle to a lath, and stood the lath up four or five foot in front of the wigwam. Jim was satisfied. He said it was a sight better than laying tied a couple of years every day and trembling all over every time there was a sound. The duke told him to make himself free and easy, and if anybody ever come meddling around, he must hop out of the wigwam, and carry on a little, and fetch a howl or two like a wild beast, and he reckoned they would light out and leave him alone. Which was sound enough judgment; but you take the average man, and he wouldn't wait for him to howl. Why, he didn't only look like he was dead, he looked considerable more than that.

These rapscallions wanted to try the Nonesuch again, because there was so much money in it, but they judged it wouldn't be safe, because maybe the news might a worked along down by this time. They couldn't hit no project that suited, exactly; so at last the duke said he reckoned he'd lay off and work his brains an hour or two and see if he couldn't put up something on the Arkansaw village; and the king he allowed he would drop over to t'other village, without any plan, but just trust in Providence to lead him the profitable way —meaning the devil, I reckon. We had all bought store clothes where we stopped last; and now the king put his'n on, and he told me to put mine on. I done it, of course. The king's duds was all black, and he did look real swell and starchy. I never knowed how clothes could change a body before. Why, before, he looked like the orneriest old rip that ever was; but now, when he'd take off his new white beaver and make a bow and do a smile, he looked that grand and good and pious that you'd say he had walked right out of the ark, and maybe was old Leviticus himself. Jim cleaned up the canoe, and I got my paddle ready. There was a big steamboat laying at the shore away up under the point, about three mile above town—been there a couple of hours, taking on freight. Says the king:

"Seein' how I'm dressed, I reckon maybe I better arrive down from St. Louis or Cincinnati, or some other big place. Go for the steamboat, Huckleberry; we'll come down to the village on her."

I didn't have to be ordered twice, to go and take a steamboat ride. I fetched the shore a half a mile above the village, and then went scooting along the bluff bank in the easy water. Pretty soon we come to a nice innocent-looking young country jake setting on a log swabbing the sweat off of his face, for it was powerful warm weather; and he had a couple of big carpet-bags by him.

"Run her nose in shore," says the king. I done it. "Wher' you bound for, young man?"

"For the steamboat; going to Orleans."

"Git aboard," says the king. "Hold on a minute, my servant 'll he'p you with them bags. Jump out and he'p the gentleman, Adolphus"—meaning me, I see.

I done so, and then we all three started on again. The young chap was mighty thankful; said it was tough work toting his baggage such weather. He asked the king where he was going, and the king told him he'd come down the river and landed at the other village this morning, and now he was going up a few mile to see an old friend on a farm up there. The young fellow says:

"When I first see you, I says to myself, 'It's Mr. Wilks, sure, and he come mighty near getting here in time.' But then I says again, 'No, I reckon it ain't him, or else he wouldn't be paddling up the river.' You *ain't* him, are you?"

"No, my name's Blodgett—Elexander Blodgett—*Reverend* Elexander Blodgett, I spose I must say, as I'm one o' the Lord's poor servants. But still I'm jist as able to be sorry for Mr. Wilks for not arriving in time, all the same, if he's missed anything by it—which I hope he hasn't."

"Well, he don't miss any property by it, because he'll get that all right; but he's missed seeing his brother Peter die—which he mayn't mind, nobody can tell as to that—but his brother would a give anything in this world to see *him* before he died; never talked about nothing else all these three weeks; hadn't seen him since they was boys together—and hadn't ever seen his brother William at all— that's the deef and dumb one—William ain't more than thirty or thirty-five. Peter and George was the only ones that come out here; George was the married brother; him and his wife both died last year. Harvey and William's the only ones that's left now; and, as I was saying, they haven't got here in time."

"Did anybody send 'em word?"

"Oh, yes; a month or two ago, when Peter was first took; because Peter said then that he sorter felt like he warn't going to get well this time. You see, he was pretty old, and George's g'yirls was too young to be much company for him, except Mary Jane the red-headed one; and so he was kinder lonesome after George and his wife died, and didn't seem to care much to live. He most desperately wanted to see Harvey—and William too, for that matter—because he was one of them kind that can't bear to make a will. He left a letter behind for Harvey, and said he'd told in it where his money was hid, and how he wanted the rest of the property divided up so George's g'yirls would be all right—for George didn't leave nothing. And that letter was all they could get him to put a pen to."

"Why do you reckon Harvey don't come? Wher' does he live?"

"Oh, he lives in England—Sheffield—preaches there—hasn't ever been in this country. He hasn't had any too much time—and besides he mightn't a got the letter at all, you know."

"Too bad, too bad he couldn't a lived to see his brothers, poor soul. You going to Orleans, you say?"

"Yes, but that ain't only a part of it. I'm going in a ship, next Wednesday, for Ryo Janeero, where my uncle lives."

"It's a pretty long journey. But it'll be lovely; I wisht I was agoing. Is Mary Jane the oldest? How old is the others?"

"Mary Jane's nineteen, Susan's fifteen, and Joanna's about fourteen—that's the one that gives herself to good works and has a hare-lip."

"Poor things! to be left alone in the cold world so."

"Well, they could be worse off. Old Peter had friends, and they ain't going to let them come to no harm. There's Hobson, the Babtis' preacher; and Deacon Lot Hovey, and Ben Rucker, and Abner Shackleford, and Levi Bell, the lawyer; and Dr. Robinson, and their wives, and the widow Bartley, and—well, there's a lot of them; but these are the ones that Peter was thickest with, and used to write about sometimes, when he wrote home; so Harvey'll know where to look for friends when he gets[3] here."

Well, the old man he went on asking questions till he just fairly emptied that young fellow. Blamed if he didn't inquire about everybody and everything in that blessed town, and all about all the Wilkses; and about Peter's business—which was a tanner; and about George's—which was a carpenter; and about Harvey's— which was a dissentering minister; and so on, and so on. Then he says:

"What did you want to walk all the way up to the steamboat for?"

"Because she's a big Orleans boat, and I was afeard she mightn't stop there. When they're deep they won't stop for a hail. A Cincinnati boat will, but this is a St. Louis one."

"Was Peter Wilks well off?"

"Oh, yes, pretty well off. He had houses and land, and it's reckoned he left three or four thousand in cash hid up som'ers."

"When did you say he died?"

"I didn't say, but it was last night."

"Funeral to-morrow, likely?"

"Yes, 'bout the middle of the day."

"Well, it's all terrible sad; but we've all got to go, one time or another. So what we want to do is to be prepared; then we're all right."

"Yes, sir, it's the best way. Ma used to always say that."

When we struck the boat, she was about done loading, and pretty soon she got off. The king never said nothing about going aboard, so I lost my ride, after all. When the boat was gone, the king made me paddle up another mile to a lonesome place, and then he got ashore, and says:

"Now hustle back, right off, and fetch the duke up here, and the new carpet-bags. And if he's gone over to t'other side, go over there and git him. And tell him to git himself up regardless. Shove along,

3. Erroneously printed "get's" in 1885.

now."

I see what *he* was up to; but I never said nothing, of course. When I got back with the duke, we hid the canoe and then they set down on a log, and the king told him everything, just like the young fellow had said it—every last word of it. And all the time he was a doing it, he tried to talk like an Englishman; and he done it pretty well too, for a slouch. I can't imitate him, and so I ain't agoing to try to; but he really done it pretty good. Then he says:

"How are you on the deef and dumb, Bilgewater?"

The duke said, leave him alone for that; said he had played a deef and dumb person on the histrionic boards. So then they waited for a steamboat.

About the middle of the afternoon a couple of little boats come along, but they didn't come from high enough up the river; but at last there was a big one, and they hailed her. She sent out her yawl, and we went aboard, and she was from Cincinnati; and when they found we only wanted to go four or five mile, they was booming mad, and give us a cussing, and said they wouldn't land us. But the king was ca'm. He says:

"If gentlemen kin afford to pay a dollar a mile apiece, to be took on and put off in a yawl, a steamboat kin afford to carry 'em, can't it?"

So they softened down and said it was all right; and when we got to the village, they yawled us ashore. About two dozen men flocked down, when they see the yawl a coming; and when the king says—

"Kin any of you gentlemen tell me wher' Mr. Peter Wilks lives?" they give a glance at one another, and nodded their heads, as much as to say, "What d' I tell you?" Then one of them says, kind of soft and gentle:

"I'm sorry, sir, but the best we can do is to tell you where he *did* live yesterday evening."

Sudden as winking, the ornery old cretur went all to smash, and fell up against the man, and put his chin on his shoulder, and cried down his back, and says:

"Alas, alas, our poor brother—gone, and we never got to see him; oh, it's too, *too* hard!"

Then he turns around, blubbering, and makes a lot of idiotic signs to the duke on his hands,[4] and blamed if *he* didn't drop a carpet-bag and bust out a-crying. If they warn't the beatenest lot, them two frauds, that ever I struck.

Well, the men gethered around, and sympathized with them, and said all sorts of kind things to them, and carried their carpet-bags up the hill for them, and let them lean on them and cry, and told the king all about his brother's last moments, and the king

4. Twain uses this deaf-and-dumb jape again in *Tom Sawyer, Detective* (1896).

he told it all over again on his hands to the duke, and both of them took on about that dead tanner like they'd lost the twelve disciples. Well, if ever I struck anything like it, I'm a nigger. It was enough to make a body ashamed of the human race.[5]

Chapter XXV

The news was all over town in two minutes, and you could see the people tearing down on the run, from every which way, some of them putting on their coats as they come. Pretty soon we was in the middle of a crowd, and the noise of the tramping was like a soldier-march. The windows and dooryards was full; and every minute somebody would say, over a fence:

"Is it *them?*"

And somebody trotting along with the gang would answer back and say,

"You bet it is."

When we got to the house, the street in front of it was packed, and the three girls was standing in the door. Mary Jane *was* red-headed, but that don't make no difference, she was most awful beautiful, and her face and her eyes was all lit up like glory, she was so glad her uncles was come. The king he spread his arms, and Mary Jane she jumped for them, and the hare-lip jumped for the duke, and there they *had* it! Everybody most, leastways women, cried for joy to see them meet again at last and have such good times.

Then the king he hunched the duke, private—I see him do it—and then he looked around and see the coffin, over in the corner on two chairs; so then, him and the duke, with a hand across each other's shoulder, and t'other hand to their eyes, walked slow and solemn over there, everybody dropping back to give them room, and all the talk and noise stopping, people saying "Sh!" and all the men taking their hats off and drooping their heads, so you could a heard a pin fall. And when they got there, they bent over and looked in the coffin, and took one sight, and then they bust out a crying so you could a heard them to Orleans, most; and then they put their arms around each other's necks, and hung their chins over each other's shoulders; and then for three minutes, or maybe four, I never see two men leak the way they done. And mind you, everybody was doing the same; and the place was that damp I never see anything like it. Then one of them got on one side of the coffin, and t'other on t'other side, and they kneeled down and rested their foreheads on the coffin, and let on to pray all to theirselves. Well,

5. In the Wilks episode the schemes of the king and the duke, hitherto at the level of Halloween frauds, for the first time sink to the depths of absolute immorality in the proposed exploitation of the grief-stricken family. Huck real- ized it was "enough to make a body ashamed of the human race" but did not expose them because he thought they knew that Jim was a runaway; see his conversation with Mary Jane, Chapter XXVIII.

when it come to that, it worked the crowd like you never see any-thing like it, and so everybody broke down and went to sobbing right out loud—the poor girls, too; and every woman, nearly, went up to the girls, without saying a word, and kissed them, solemn, on the forehead, and then put their hand on their head, and looked up towards the sky, with the tears running down, and then busted out and went off sobbing and swabbing, and give the next woman a show. I never see anything so disgusting.

Well, by-and-by the king he gets up and comes forward a little, and works himself up and slobbers out a speech, all full of tears and flapdoodle about its being a sore trial for him and his poor brother to lose the diseased, and to miss seeing diseased alive, after the long journey of four thousand mile, but its a trial that's sweet-ened and sanctified to us by this dear sympathy and these holy tears, and so he thanks them out of his heart and out of his brother's heart, because out of their mouths they can't, words being too weak and cold, and all that kind of rot and slush, till it was just sickening; and then he blubbers out a pious goody-goody Amen, and turns himself loose and goes to crying fit to bust.

And the minute the words was out of his mouth somebody over in the crowd struck up the doxolojer,[6] and everybody joined in with all their might, and it just warmed you up and made you feel as good as church letting out. Music *is* a good thing; and after all that soul-butter and hogwash, I never see it freshen up things so, and sound so honest and bully.

Then the king begins to work his jaw again, and says how him and his nieces would be glad if a few of the main principal friends of the family would take supper here with them this evening, and help set up with the ashes of the diseased; and says if his poor brother laying yonder could speak, he knows who he would name, for they was names that was very dear to him, and mentioned often in his letters; and so he will name the same, to-wit, as follows, vizz: —Rev. Mr. Hobson, and Deacon Lot Hovey, and Mr. Ben Rucker, and Abner Shackleford, and Levi Bell, and Dr. Robinson, and their wives, and the widow Bartley.

Rev. Hobson and Dr. Robinson was down to the end of the town, a-hunting together; that is, I mean the doctor was shipping a sick man to t'other world, and the preacher was pinting him right. Lawyer Bell was away up to Louisville on some business. But the rest was on hand, and so they all come and shook hands with the king and thanked him and talked to him; and then they shook hands with the duke, and didn't say nothing but just kept a-smiling and bobbing their heads like a passel of sapheads whilst he made all sorts of signs with his hands and said "Goo-goo—goo-goo-goo," all the time, like a baby that can't talk.

6. The Doxology.

So the king he blatted along, and managed to inquire about pretty much everybody and dog in town, by his name, and mentioned all sorts of little things that happened one time or another in the town, or to George's family, or to Peter; and he always let on that Peter wrote him the things, but that was a lie, he got every blessed one of them out of that young flathead that we canoed up to the steamboat.

Then Mary Jane she fetched the letter her father left behind, and the king he read it out loud and cried over it. It give the dwelling-house and three thousand dollars, gold, to the girls; and it give the tanyard (which was doing a good business), along with some other houses and land (worth about seven thousand), and three thousand dollars in gold to Harvey and William, and told where the six thousand cash was hid, down cellar. So these two frauds said they'd go and fetch it up, and have everything square and above-board; and told me to come with a candle. We shut the cellar door behind us, and when they found the bag they spilt it out on the floor, and it was a lovely sight, all them yallerboys. My, the way the king's eyes did shine! He slaps the duke on the shoulder, and says:

"Oh, *this* ain't bully, nor noth'n! Oh, no, I reckon not! Why, Biljy, it beats the Nonesuch, *don't* it!"

The duke allowed it did. They pawed the yaller-boys, and sifted them through their fingers and let them jingle down on the floor; and the king says:

"It ain't no use talkin'; bein' brothers to a rich dead man, and representatives of furrin heirs that's got left, is the line for you and me, Bilge. Thish-yer comes of trust'n to Providence. It's the best way, in the long run. I've tried 'em all, and ther' ain't no better way."

Most everybody would a been satisfied with the pile, and took it on trust; but no, they must count it. So they counts it, and it comes out four hundred and fifteen dollars short. Says the king:

"Dern him, I wonder what he done with that four hundred and fifteen dollars?"

They worried over that a while, and ransacked all around for it. Then the duke says:

"Well, he was a pretty sick man, and likely he made a mistake—I reckon that's the way of it. The best way's to let it go, and keep still about it. We can spare it."

"Oh, shucks, yes, we can *spare* it. I don't k'yer noth'n 'bout that—it's the *count* I'm thinkin' about. We want to be awful square and open and aboveboard, here, you know. We want to lug this h-yer money up stairs and count it before everybody—then ther' ain't noth'n suspicious. But when the dead man says ther's six thous'n dollars, you know, we don't want to—"

"Hold on," says the duke. "Less make up the deffisit"—and he begun to haul out yallerboys out of his pocket.

"It's a most amaz'n' good idea, duke—you *have* got a rattlin' clever head on you," says the king. "Blest if the old Nonesuch ain't a heppin' us out agin"—and *he* begun to haul out yallerjackets and stack them up.

It most busted them, but they made up the six thousand clean and clear.

"Say," says the duke, "I got another idea. Le's go up stairs and count this money, and then take and *give it to the girls*."

"Good land, duke, lemme hug you! It's the most dazzling idea 'at ever a man struck. You have cert'nly got the most astonishin' head I ever see. Oh, this is the boss dodge, ther' ain't no mistake 'bout it. Let 'em fetch along their suspicions now, if they want to— this'll lay 'em out."

When we got up stairs, everybody gethered around the table, and the king he counted it and stacked it up, three hundred dollars in a pile—twenty elegant little piles. Everybody looked hungry at it, and licked their chops. Then they raked it into the bag again, and I see the king begin to swell himself up for another speech. He says:

"Friends all, my poor brother that lays yonder, has done generous by them that's left behind in the vale of sorrers. He has done generous by these-yer poor little lambs that he loved and sheltered, and that's left fatherless and motherless. Yes, and we that knowed him, knows that he would a done *more* generous by 'em if he hadn't been afeard o' woundin' his dear William and me. Now, *wouldn't* he? Ther' ain't no question 'bout it, in *my* mind. Well, then— what kind o' brothers would it be, that 'd stand in his way at sech a time? And what kind o' uncles would it be that 'd rob—yes, *rob* —sech poor sweet lambs as these 'at he loved so, at sech a time? If I know William—and I *think* I do—he—well, I'll jest ask him." He turns around and begins to make a lot of signs to the duke with his hands; and the duke he looks at him stupid and leather-headed a while, then all of a sudden he seems to catch his meaning, and jumps for the king, goo-gooing with all his might for joy, and hugs him about fifteen times before he lets up. Then the king says, "I knowed it; I reckon *that* 'll convince anybody the way *he* feels about it. Here, Mary Jane, Susan, Joanner, take the money—take it *all*. It's the gift of him that lays yonder, cold but joyful."

Mary Jane she went for him, Susan and the hare-lip went for the duke, and then such another hugging and kissing I never see yet. And everybody crowded up with the tears in their eyes, and most shook the hands off of them frauds, saying all the time:

"You *dear* good souls!—how *lovely!*—how *could* you!"

Well, then, pretty soon all hands got to talking about the diseased again, and how good he was, and what a loss he was, and all that; and before long a big iron-jawed man worked himself in there from outside, and stood a listening and looking, and not saying anything; and nobody saying anything to him either, because the king was talking and they was all busy listening. The king was saying—in the middle of something he'd started in on—

"—they bein' partickler friends o' the diseased. That's why they're invited here this evenin'; but to-morrow we want *all* to come—everybody; for he respected everybody, he liked everybody, and so it's fitten that his funeral orgies sh'd be public."

And so he went a-mooning on and on, liking to hear himself talk, and every little while he fetched in his funeral orgies again, till the duke he couldn't stand it no more; so he writes on a little scrap of paper, "*obsequies*, you old fool," and folds it up and goes to goo-gooing and reaching it over people's heads to him. The king he reads it, and puts it in his pocket, and says:

"Poor William, afflicted as he is, his *heart's* aluz right. Asks me to invite everybody to come to the funeral—wants me to make 'em all welcome. But he needn't a worried—it was jest what I was at."

Then he weaves along again, perfectly ca'm, and goes to dropping in his funeral orgies again every now and then, just like he done before. And when he done it the third time, he says:

"I say orgies, not because it's the common term, because it ain't —obsequies bein' the common term—but because orgies is the right term. Obsequies ain't used in England no more, now—it's gone out. We say orgies now, in England. Orgies is better, because it means the thing you're after, more exact. It's a word that's made up out'n the Greek *orgo*, outside, open, abroad; and the Hebrew *jeesum*, to plant, cover up; hence in*ter*. So, you see, funeral orgies is an open er public funeral."

He was the *worst* I ever struck. Well, the iron-jawed man he laughed right in his face. Everybody was shocked. Everybody says, "Why *doctor!*" and Abner Shackleford says:

"Why, Robinson, hain't you heard the news? This is Harvey Wilks."

The king he smiled eager, and shoved out his flapper, and says: "*Is* it my poor brother's dear good friend and physician? I—"

"Keep your hands off of me!" says the doctor. "*You* talk like an Englishman—*don't* you? It's the worse imitation I ever heard. *You* Peter Wilks's brother. You're a fraud, that's what you are!"

Well, how they all took on! They crowded around the doctor, and tried to quiet him down, and tried to explain to him, and tell him how Harvey'd showed in forty ways that he *was* Harvey, and knowed everybody by name, and the names of the very dogs, and begged and *begged* him not to hurt Harvey's feelings and the poor girls' feelings, and all that; but it warn't no use, he stormed right along, and said any man that pretended to be an Englishman and couldn't imitate the lingo no better than what he did, was a fraud and a liar. The poor girls was hanging to the king and crying; and all of a sudden the doctor ups and turns on *them*. He says:

"I was your father's friend, and I'm your friend; and I warn you *as* a friend, and an honest one, that wants to protect you and keep you out of harm and trouble, to turn your backs on that scoundrel, and have nothing to do with him, the ignorant tramp, with his idiotic Greek and Hebrew as he calls it. He is the thinnest kind of an impostor—has come here with a lot of empty names and facts which he has picked up somewheres, and you take them for *proofs*, and are helped to fool yourselves by these foolish friends here, who ought to know better. Mary Jane Wilks, you know me for your friend, and for your unselfish friend, too. Now listen to me; turn this pitiful rascal out—I *beg* you to do it. Will you?"

Mary Jane straightened herself up, and my, but she was handsome! She says:

"*Here* is my answer." She hove up the bag of money and put it in the king's hands, and says, "Take this six thousand dollars, and invest it[7] for me and my sisters any way you want to, and don't give us no receipt for it."

Then she put her arm around the king on one side, and Susan and the hare-lip done the same on the other. Everybody clapped their hands and stomped on the floor like a perfect storm, whilst the king held up his head and smiled proud. The doctor says:

"All right, I wash *my* hands of the matter. But I warn you all that a time's coming when you're going to feel sick whenever you think of this day"—and away he went.

"All right, doctor," says the king, kinder mocking him, "we'll try and get 'em to send for you"—which made them all laugh, and they said it was a prime good hit.

Chapter XXVI

Well, when they was all gone, the king he asks Mary Jane how they was off for spare rooms, and she said she had one spare room, which would do for Uncle William, and she'd give her own room to Uncle Harvey, which was a little bigger, and she would turn into the room with her sisters and sleep on a cot; and up garret was a little cubby, with a pallet in it. The king said the cubby would do for his valley—meaning me.

So Mary Jane took us up, and she showed them their rooms, which was plain but nice. She said she'd have her frocks and a lot of other traps took out of her room if they was in Uncle Harvey's

7. "It" omitted in 1885.

way, but he said they warn't. The frocks was hung along the wall, and before them was a curtain made out of calico that hung down to the floor. There was an old hair trunk in one corner, and a guitar box in another, and all sorts of little knickknacks and jimcracks around, like girls brisken up a room with. The king said it was all the more homely and more pleasanter for these fixings, and so don't disturb them. The duke's room was pretty small, but plenty good enough, and so was my cubby.

That night they had a big supper, and all them men and women was there, and I stood behind the king and the duke's chairs and waited on them, and the niggers waited on the rest. Mary Jane she set at the head of the table, with Susan along side of her, and said how bad the biscuits was, and how mean the preserves was, and how ornery and tough the fried chickens was—and all that kind of rot, the way women always do for to force out compliments; and the people all knowed everything was tip-top, and said so—said "How *do* you get biscuits to brown so nice?" and "Where, for the land's sake *did* you get these amaz'n pickles?" and all that kind of humbug talky-talk, just the way people always does at a supper, you know.

And when it was all done, me and the hare-lip had supper in the kitchen off of the leavings, whilst the others was helping the niggers clean up the things. The hare-lip she got to pumping me about England, and blest if I didn't think the ice was getting mighty thin, sometimes. She says:

"Did you ever see the king?"

"Who? William Fourth? Well, I bet I have—he goes to our church." I knowed he was dead years ago, but I never let on. So when I says he goes to our church, she says:

"What—regular?"

"Yes—regular. His pew's right over opposite ourn—on 'tother side the pulpit."

"I thought he lived in London?"

"Well, he does. Where *would* he live?"

"But I thought *you* lived in Sheffield?"

I see I was up a stump. I had to let on to get choked with a chicken bone, so as to get time to think how to get down again. Then I says:

"I mean he goes to our church regular when he's in Sheffield. That's only in the summer-time, when he comes there to take the sea baths."

"Why, how you talk—Sheffield ain't on the sea."

"Well, who said it was?"

"Why, you did."

"I *didn't*, nuther."

"You did!"

"I didn't."

"You did."

"I never said nothing of the kind."

"Well, what *did* you say, then?"

"Said he come to take the sea *baths*—that's what I said."

"Well, then! how's he going to take the sea baths if it ain't on the sea?"

"Looky here," I says; "did you ever see any Congress water?"[8]

"Yes."

"Well, did you have to go to Congress to get it?"

"Why, no."

"Well, neither does William Fourth have to go to the sea to get a sea bath."

"How does he get it, then?"

"Gets it the way people down here gets Congress water—in barrels. There in the palace at Sheffield they've got furnaces, and he wants his water hot. They can't bile that amount of water away off there at the sea. They haven't got no conveniences for it."

"Oh, I see, now. You might a said that in the first place and saved time."

When she said that, I see I was out of the woods again, and so I was comfortable and glad. Next, she says:

"Do you go to church, too?"

"Yes—regular."

"Where do you set?"

"Why, in our pew."

"*Whose* pew?"

"Why, *ourn*—your Uncle Harvey's."

"His'n? What does *he* want with a pew?"

"Wants it to set in. What did you *reckon* he wanted with it?"

"Why, I thought he'd be in the pulpit."

Rot him, I forgot he was a preacher. I see I was up a stump again, so I played another chicken bone and got another think. Then I says:

"Blame it, do you suppose there ain't but one preacher to a church?"

"Why, what do they want with more?"

"What!—to preach before a king? I never see such a girl as you. They don't have no less than seventeen."

"Seventeen! My land! Why, I wouldn't set out such a string as that, not if I *never* got to glory. It must take 'em a week."

"Shucks, they don't *all* of 'em preach the same day—only *one* of 'em."

"Well, then, what does the rest of 'em do?"

"Oh, nothing much. Loll around, pass the plate—and one thing

8. Mineral water from the Congress Spring at Saratoga, New York.

or another. But mainly they don't do nothing."

"Well, then, what are they *for?*"

"Why, they're for *style.* Don't you know nothing?"

"Well, I don't *want* to know no such foolishness as that. How is servants treated in England? Do they treat 'em better 'n we treat our niggers?"

"*No!* A servant ain't nobody there. They treat them worse than dogs."

"Don't they give 'em holidays, the way we do, Christmas and New Year's week, and Fourth of July?"

"Oh, just listen! A body could tell *you* hain't ever been to England, by that. Why, Hare-l—why, Joanna, they never see a holiday from year's end to year's end; never go to the circus, nor theatre, nor nigger shows, nor nowheres."

"Nor church?"

"Nor church."

"But *you* always went to church."

Well, I was gone up again. I forgot I was the old man's servant. But next minute I whirled in on a kind of an explanation how a valley was different from a common servant, and *had* to go to church whether he wanted to or not, and set with the family, on account of it's being the law. But I didn't do it pretty good, and when I got done I see she warn't satisfied. She says:

"Honest injun, now, hain't you been telling me a lot of lies?"

"Honest injun," says I.

"None of it at all?"

"None of it at all. Not a lie in it," says I.

"Lay your hand on this book and say it."

I see it warn't nothing but a dictionary, so I laid my hand on it and said it. So then she looked a little better satisfied, and says:

"Well, then, I'll believe some of it; but I hope to gracious if I'll believe the rest."

"What is it you won't believe, Joe?" says Mary Jane, stepping in with Susan behind her. "It ain't right nor kind for you to talk so to him, and him a stranger and so far from his people. How would you like to be treated so?"

"That's always your way, Maim—always sailing in to help somebody before they're hurt. I hain't done nothing to him. He's told some stretchers, I reckon; and I said I wouldn't swallow it all; and that's every bit and grain I *did* say. I reckon he can stand a little think like that, can't he?"

"I don't care whether 'twas little or whether 'twas big, he's here in our house and a stranger, and it wasn't good of you to say it. If you was in his place, it would make you feel ashamed; and so you ought'nt to say a thing to another person that will make *them* feel ashamed."

"Why, Maim, he said—"

"It don't make no difference what he *said*—that ain't the thing. The thing is for you to treat him *kind*, and not be saying things to make him remember he ain't in his own country and amongst his own folks."

I says to myself, *this* is a girl that I'm letting that old reptle rob her of her money!

Then Susan *she* waltzed in; and if you'll believe me, she did give Hare-lip hark from the tomb!

Says I to myself, And this is *another* one that I'm letting him rob her of her money!

Then Mary Jane she took another inning, and went in sweet and lovely again—which was her way—but when she got done there warn't hardly anything left o' poor Hare-lip. So she hollered.

"All right, then," says the other girls, "you just ask his pardon."

She done it, too. And she done it beautiful. She done it so beautiful it was good to hear; and I wished I could tell her a thousand lies, so she could do it again.

I says to myself, this is *another* one that I'm letting him rob her of her money. And when she got through, they all jest laid theirselves out to make me feel at home and know I was amongst friends. I felt so ornery and low down and mean, that I says to myself, My mind's made up; I'll hive that money for them or bust.

So then I lit out—for bed, I said, meaning some time or another. When I got by myself, I went to thinking the thing over. I says to myself, shall I go to that doctor, private, and blow on these frauds? No—that won't do. He might tell who told him; then the king and the duke would make it warm for me. Shall I go, private, and tell Mary Jane? No—I dasn't do it. Her face would give them a hint, sure; they've got the money, and they'd slide right out and get away with it. If she was to fetch in help, I'd get mixed up in the business, before it was done with, I judge. No, there ain't no good way but one. I got to steal that money, somehow; and I got to steal it some way that they won't suspicion that I done it. They've got a good thing, here; and they ain't agoing to leave till they've played this family and this town for all they're worth, so I'll find a chance time enough. I'll steal it, and hide it; and by-and-by, when I'm away down the river, I'll write a letter and tell Mary Jane where it's hid. But I better hive it to-night, if I can, because the doctor maybe hasn't let up as much as he lets on he has; he might scare them out of here, yet.

So, thinks I, I'll go and search them rooms. Up stairs the hall was dark, but I found the duke's room, and started to paw around it with my hands; but I recollected it wouldn't be much like the king to let anybody else take care of that money but his own self; so then I went to his room and begun to paw around there. But I see I couldn't do nothing without a candle, and I dasn't light one, of course. So I judged I'd got to do the other thing—lay for them, and eavesdrop. About that time, I hears their footsteps coming, and was going to skip under the bed; I reached for it, but it wasn't where I thought it would be; but I touched the curtain that hid Mary Jane's frocks, so I jumped in behind that and snuggled in amongst the gowns, and stood there perfectly still.

They come in and shut the door; and the first thing the duke done was to get down and look under the bed. Then I was glad I hadn't found the bed when I wanted it. And yet, you know, it's kind of natural to hide under the bed when you are up to anything private. They sets down, then, and the king says:

"Well, what is it? and cut it middlin' short, because it's better for us to be down there a whoopin'-up the mournin', than up here givin' 'em a chance to talk us over."

"Well, this is it, Capet. I ain't easy; I ain't comfortable. That doctor lays on my mind. I wanted to know your plans. I've got a notion, and I think it's a sound one."

"What is it, duke?"

"That we better glide out of this, before three in the morning, and clip it down the river with what we've got. Specially, seeing we got it so easy—*given* back to us, flung at our heads, as you may say, when of course we allowed to have to steal it back. I'm for knocking off and lighting out."

That made me feel pretty bad. About an hour or two ago, it would a been a little different, but now it made me feel bad and disappointed. The king rips out and says:

"What! And not sell out the rest o' the property? March off like a passel o' fools and leave eight or nine thous'n' dollars' worth o' property layin' around jest sufferin' to be scooped in?—and all good salable stuff, too."

The duke he grumbled; said the bag of gold was enough, and he didn't want to go no deeper—didn't want to rob a lot of orphans of *everything* they had.

"Why, how you talk!" says the king. "We shan't rob 'em of nothing at all but jest this money. The people that *buys* the property is the suff'rers; because as soon's it's found out 'at we didn't own it—which won't be long after we've slid—the sale won't be valid, and it'll all go back to the estate. These-yer orphans 'll git their house back agin, and that's enough for *them;* they're young and spry, and k'n easy earn a livin'. *They* ain't agoing to suffer. Why, jest think—there's thous'n's and thous'n's that ain't nigh so well off. Bless you, *they* ain't got noth'n to complain of."

Well, the king he talked him blind; so at last he give in, and said all right, but said he believed it was blame foolishness to stay, and that doctor hanging over them. But the king says:

"Cuss the doctor! What do we k'yer for *him?* Hain't we got all the fools in town on our side? and ain't that a big enough majority in any town?"

So they got ready to go down stairs again. The duke says:

"I don't think we put that money in a good place."

That cheered me up. I'd begun to think I warn't going to get a hint of no kind to help me. The king says:

"Why?"

"Because Mary Jane 'll be in mourning from this out; and first you know the nigger that does up the rooms will get an order to box these duds up and put 'em away; and do you reckon a nigger can run across money and not borrow some of it?"

"Your head's level, agin, duke," says the king; and he come a fumbling under the curtain two or three foot from where I was. I stuck tight to the wall, and kept mighty still, though quivery; and I wondered what them fellows would say to me if they catched me; and I tried to think what I'd better do if they did catch me. But the king he got the bag before I could think more than about a half a thought, and he never suspicioned I was around. They took and shoved the bag through a rip in the straw tick that was under the feather bed, and crammed it in a foot or two amongst the straw and said it was all right, now, because a nigger only makes up the feather bed, and don't turn over the straw tick only about twice a year, and so it warn't in no danger of getting stole, now.

But I knowed better. I had it out of there before they was half-way down stairs. I groped along up to my cubby, and hid it there till I could get a chance to do better. I judged I better hide it outside of the house somewheres, because if they missed it they would give the house a good ransacking. I knowed that very well. Then I turned in, with my clothes all on; but I couldn't a gone to sleep, if I'd a wanted to, I was in such a sweat to get through with the business. By-and-by I heard the king and the duke come up; so I rolled off of my pallet and laid with my chin at the top of my ladder and waited to see if anything was going to happen. But nothing did.

So I held on till all the late sounds had quit and the early ones hadn't begun, yet; and then I slipped down the ladder.

Chapter XXVII

I crept to their doors and listened; they was snoring, so I tip-toed along, and got down stairs all right. There warn't a sound any-wheres. I peeped through a crack of the dining-room door, and see the men that was watching the corpse all sound asleep on their chairs. The door was open into the parlor, where the corpse was laying, and there was a candle in both rooms, I passed along, and the parlor door was open; but I see there warn't nobody in there but the remainders of Peter; so I shoved on by; but the front door was locked, and the key wasn't there. Just then I heard somebody coming down the stairs, back behind me. I run in the parlor, and took a swift look around, and the only place I see to hide the bag was in the coffin. The lid was shoved along about a foot, showing the dead man's face down in there, with a wet cloth over it, and his shroud on. I tucked the money-bag in under the lid, just down beyond where his hands was crossed, which made me creep, they was so cold, and then I run back across the room and in behind the door.

The person coming was Mary Jane. She went to the coffin, very soft, and kneeled down and looked in; then she put up her handkerchief and I see she begun to cry, though I couldn't hear her, and her back was to me. I slid out, and as I passed the dining-room I thought I'd make sure them watchers hadn't seen me; so I looked through the crack and everything was all right. They hadn't stirred.

I slipped up to bed, feeling ruther blue, on accounts of the thing playing out that way after I had took so much trouble and run so much resk about it. Says I, if it could stay where it is, all right; because when we get down the river a hundred mile or two, I could write back to Mary Jane, and she could dig him up again and get it; but that ain't the thing that's going to happen; the thing that's going to happen is, the money 'll be found when they come to screw on the lid. Then the king 'll get it again, and it 'll be a long day before he gives anybody another chance to smouch it from him. Of course I *wanted* to slide down and get it out of there, but I dasn't try it. Every minute it was getting earlier, now, and pretty soon some of them watchers would begin to stir, and I might get catched—catched with six thousand dollars in my hands that nobody hadn't hired me to take care of. I don't wish to be mixed up in no such business as that, I says to myself.

When I got down stairs in the morning, the parlor was shut up, and the watchers was gone. There warn't nobody around but the family and the widow Bartley and our tribe. I watched their faces to see if anything had been happening, but I couldn't tell.

Towards the middle of the day the undertaker come, with his man, and they set the coffin in the middle of the room on a couple of chairs, and then set all our chairs in rows, and borrowed more from the neighbors till the hall and the parlor and the dining-room was full. I see the coffin lid was the way it was before, but I dasn't go to look in under it, with folks around.

Then the people begun to flock in, and the beats and the girls took seats in the front row at the head of the coffin, and for a half an hour the people filed around slow, in single rank, and looked down at the dead man's face a minute, and some dropped in a tear, and it was all very still and solemn, only the girls and the beats holding handkerchiefs to their eyes and keeping their heads bent, and sobbing a little. There warn't no other sound but the scraping of the feet on the floor, and blowing noses—because people always blows them more at a funeral than they do at other places except church.

When the place was packed full, the undertaker he slid around in his black gloves with his softy soothering ways, putting on the last touches, and getting people and things all shipshape and comfortable, and making no more sound than a cat. He never spoke; he moved people around, he squeezed in late ones, he opened up passage-ways, and done it all with nods, and signs with his hands. Then he took his place over against the wall. He was the softest, glidingest, stealthiest man I ever see; and there warn't no more smile to him than there is to a ham.

They had borrowed a melodeum—a sick one; and when everything was ready, a young woman set down and worked it, and it was pretty skreeky and colicky, and everybody joined in and sung, and Peter was the only one that had a good thing, according to my notion. Then the Reverend Hobson opened up, slow and solemn, and begun to talk; and straight off the most outrageous row busted out in the cellar a body ever heard; it was only one dog, but he made a most powerful racket, and he kept it up, right along; the parson he had to stand there, over the coffin, and wait—you couldn't hear yourself think. It was right down awkward, and nobody didn't seem to know what to do. But pretty soon they see that long-legged undertaker make a sign to the preacher as much as to say, "Don't you worry—just depend on me." Then he stooped down and begun to glide along the wall, just his shoulders showing over the people's heads. So he glided along, and the pow-wow and racket getting more and more outrageous all the time; and at last, when he had gone around two sides of the room, he disappears down cellar. Then, in about two seconds we heard a whack, and the dog he finished up with a most amazing howl or two, and then everything was dead still, and the parson begun his solemn talk where he left off. In a minute or two here comes this undertaker's back and shoulders gliding along the wall again; and so he glided, and glided, around three sides of the room, and then rose up, and shaded his mouth with his hands, and stretched his neck out towards the preacher, over the people's heads, and says, in a kind of a coarse whisper, "*He had a rat!*" Then he drooped down and glided along the wall again to his place. You could see it was a great satisfaction to the people, because naturally they wanted to know. A little thing like that don't cost nothing, and it's just the little things that makes a man to be looked up to and liked. There warn't no more popular man in town than what that undertaker was.

Well, the funeral sermon was very good, but pison long and tiresome; and then the king he shoved in and got off some of his usual rubbage, and at last the job was through, and the undertaker begun to sneak up on the coffin with his screw-driver. I was in a sweat then, and watched him pretty keen. But he never meddled at all; just slid the lid along, as soft as mush, and screwed it down tight and fast. So there I was! I didn't know whether the money was in there, or not. So, says I, spose somebody has hogged that bag on the sly?—now how do *I* know whether to write to Mary Jane or not? 'Spose she dug him up and didn't find nothing— what would she think of me? Blame it, I says, I might get hunted up and jailed; I'd better lay low and keep dark, and not write at all; the thing's awful mixed, now; trying to better it, I've worsened it a hundred times, and I wish to goodness I'd just let it alone, dad fetch the whole business!

They buried him, and we come back home, and I went to watching faces again—I couldn't help it, and I couldn't rest easy. But nothing come of it; the faces didn't tell me nothing.

The king he visited around, in the evening, and sweetened every body up, and made himself ever so friendly; and he give out the idea that his congregation over in England would be in a sweat about him, so he must hurry and settle up the estate right away, and leave for home. He was very sorry he was so pushed, and so was everybody; they wished he could stay longer, but they said they could see it couldn't be done. And he said of course him and William would take the girls home with them; and that pleased everybody too, because then the girls would be well fixed, and amongst their own relations; and it pleased the girls, too—tickled them so they clean forgot they ever had a trouble in the world; and told him to sell out as quick as he wanted to, they would be ready. Them poor things was that glad and happy it made my heart ache to see them getting fooled and lied to so, but I didn't see no safe way for me to chip in and change the general tune.

Well, blamed if the king didn't bill the house and the niggers and all the property for auction straight off—sale two days after the funeral; but anybody could buy private beforehand if they wanted to.

So the next day after the funeral, along about noontime, the girls' joy got the first jolt; a couple of nigger traders come along, and the king sold them the niggers reasonable, for three-day drafts as they called it, and away they went, the two sons up the river to Memphis, and their mother down the river to Orleans. I thought them poor girls and them niggers would break their hearts for grief; they cried around each other, and took on so it most made me down sick to see it. The girls said they hadn't ever dreamed of seeing the family separated or sold away from the town. I can't ever get it out of my memory, the sight of them poor miserable girls and niggers hanging around each other's necks and crying; and I reckon I couldn't a stood it all but would a had to bust out and tell on our gang if I hadn't knowed the sale warn't no account and the niggers would be back home in a week or two.

The thing made a big stir in the town, too, and a good many come out flatfooted and said it was scandalous to separate the mother and the children that way. It injured the frauds some; but the old fool he bulled right along, spite of all the duke could say or do, and I tell you the duke was powerful uneasy.

Next day was auction day. About broad-day in the morning, the king and the duke come up in the garret and woke me up, and I see by their look that there was trouble. The king says:

"Was you in my room night before last?"

"No, your majesty"—which was the way I always called him when nobody but our gang warn't around.

"Was you in there yesterday er last night?"

"No, your majesty."

"Honor bright, now—no lies."

"Honor bright, your majesty, I'm telling you the truth. I hain't been anear your room since Miss Mary Jane took you and the duke and showed it to you."

The duke says:

"Have you seen anybody else go in there?"

"No, your grace, not as I remember, I believe."

"Stop and think."

I studied a while, and see my chance, then I says:

"Well, I see the niggers go in there several times."

Both of them give a little jump; and looked like they hadn't ever expected it, and then like they *had*. Then the duke says:

"What, *all* of them?"

"No—leastways not all at once. That is, I don't think I ever see them all come *out* at once but just one time."

"Hello—when was that?"

"It was the day we had the funeral. In the morning. It warn't early, because I overslept. I was just starting down the ladder, and I see them."

"Well, go on, go on—what did they do? How'd they act?"

"They didn't do nothing. And they didn't act anyway, much, as fur as I see. They tip-toed away; so I seen, easy enough, that they'd shoved in there to do up your majesty's room, or something, sposing you was up; and found you *warn't* up, and so they was hoping to slide out of the way of trouble without waking you up, if they hadn't already waked you up."

"Great guns, *this* is a go!" says the king; and both of them

looked pretty sick, and tolerable silly. They stood there a thinking
and scratching their heads, a minute, and then the duke he bust
into a kind of a little raspy chuckle, and says:

"It does beat all, how neat the niggers played their hand. They let
on to be *sorry* they was going out of this region! and I believed
they *was* sorry. And so did you, and so did everybody. Don't ever
tell *me* any more that a nigger ain't got any histrionic talent. Why,
the way they played that thing, it would fool *anybody*. In my
opinion there's a fortune in 'em. If I had capital and a theatre, I
wouldn't want a better lay out than that—and here we've gone
and sold 'em for a song. Yes, and ain't privileged to sing the song,
yet. Say, where *is* that song?—that draft."

"In the bank for to be collected. Where *would* it be?"

"Well, *that's* all right then, thank goodness."

Says I, kind of timid-like:

"Is something gone wrong?"

The king whirls on me and rips out:

"None o' your business! You keep your head shet, and mind y'r
own affairs—if you got any. Long as you're in this town, don't
you forget *that*, you hear?" Then he says to the duke, "We got to
jest swaller it, and say noth'n: mum's the word for *us*."

As they was starting down the ladder, the duke he chuckles again,
and says:

"Quick sales *and* small profits! It's a good business—yes."

The king snarls around on him and says,

"I was trying to do for the best, in sellin' 'm out so quick. If the
profits has turned out to be none, lackin' considable, and none to
carry, is it my fault any more'n it's yourn?"

"Well, *they'd* be in this house yet, and we *wouldn't* if I could a
got my advice listened to."

The king sassed back, as much as was safe for him, and then
swapped around and lit into *me* again. He give me down the banks
for not coming and *telling* him I see the niggers come out of his
room acting that way—said any fool would a *knowed* something was
up. And then waltzed in and cussed *himself* a while; and said it
all come of him not laying late and taking his natural rest that
morning, and he'd be blamed if he'd ever do it again. So they went
off a jawing; and I felt dreadful glad I'd worked it all off onto the
niggers and yet hadn't done the niggers no harm by it.

Chapter XXVIII

By-and-by it was getting-up time; so I come down the ladder
and started for down stairs, but as I come to the girls' room, the
door was open, and I see Mary Jane setting by her old hair trunk,
which was open and she'd been packing things in it—getting ready

to go to England. But she had stopped now, with a folded gown in her lap, and had her face in her hands, crying. I felt awful bad to see it; of course anybody would. I went in there, and says:

"Miss Mary Jane, you can't abear to see people in trouble, and *I* can't—most always. Tell me about it."

So she done it. And it was the niggers—I just expected it. She said the beautiful trip to England was most about spoiled for her; she didn't know *how* she was ever going to be happy there, knowing the mother and the children warn't ever going to see each other no more—and then busted out bitterer than ever, and flung up her hands, and says

"Oh, dear, dear, to think they ain't *ever* going to see each other any more!"

"But they *will*—and inside of two weeks—and I *know* it!" says I.

Laws it was out before I could think!—and before I could budge, she throws her arms around my neck, and told me to say it *again*, say it *again*, say it *again*!

I see I had spoke too sudden, and said too much, and was in a close place. I asked her to let me think a minute; and she set there, very impatient and excited, and handsome, but looking kind of happy and eased-up, like a person that's had a tooth pulled out. So I went to studying it out. I says to myself, I reckon a body that ups and tells the truth when he is in a tight place, is taking considerable many resks, though I ain't had no experience, and can't say for certain; but it looks so to me, anyway; and yet here's a case where I'm blest if it don't look to me like the truth is better, and actuly *safer*, than a lie. I must lay it by in my mind, and think it over some time or other, it's so kind of strange and unregular. I never see nothing like it. Well, I says to myself at last, I'm agoing to chance it; I'll up and tell the truth this time, though it does seem most like setting down on a kag of powder and touching it off just to see where you'll go to. Then I says:

"Miss Mary Jane, is there any place out of town a little ways, where you could go and stay three or four days?"

"Yes—Mr. Lothrop's. Why?"

"Never mind why, yet. If I'll tell you how I know the niggers will see each other again—inside of two weeks—here in this house—and *prove* how I know it—will you go to Mr. Lothrop's and stay four days?"

"Four days!" she says; "I'll stay a year!"

"All right," I says, "I don't want nothing more out of *you* than just your word—I druther have it than another man's kiss-the-Bible." She smiled, and reddened up very sweet, and I says, "If you don't mind it, I'll shut the door—and bolt it."

Then I come back and set down again, and says:

"Don't you holler. Just set still, and take it like a man. I got to tell the truth, and you want to brace up, Miss Mary, because it's a bad kind, and going to be hard to take, but there ain't no help for it. These uncles of yourn ain't no uncles at all—they're a couple[9] of frauds—regular dead-beats. There, now we're over the worst of it—you can stand the rest middling easy."

It jolted her up like everything, of course; but I was over the shoal water now, so I went right along, her eyes a blazing higher and higher all the time, and told her every blame thing, from where we first struck that young fool going up to the steamboat, clear through to where she flung herself onto the king's breast at the front door and he kissed her sixteen or seventeen times—and then up she jumps, with her face afire like sunset, and says:

"The brute! Come—don't waste a minute—not a *second*—we'll have them tarred and feathered, and flung in the river!"

Says I:

"Cert'nly. But do you mean, *before* you go to Mr. Lothrop's, or—"

"Oh," she says, "what am I *thinking* about!" she says, and set right down again. "Don't mind what I said—please don't—you *won't*, now, *will* you?" Laying her silky hand on mine in that kind of a way that I said I would die first. "I never thought, I was so stirred up," she says; "now go on, and I won't do so any more. You tell me what to do, and whatever you say, I'll do it."

"Well," I says, "it's a rough gang, them two frauds, and I'm fixed so I got to travel with them a while longer, whether I want to or not—I druther not tell you why—and if you was to blow on them this town would get me out of their claws, and I'd be all right, but there'd be another person that you don't know about who'd be in big trouble.[1] Well, we got to save *him*, hain't we? Of course. Well, then, we won't blow on them."

Saying them words put a good idea in my head. I see how maybe I could get me and Jim rid of the frauds; get them jailed here, and then leave. But I didn't want to run the raft in day-time, without anybody aboard to answer questions but me; so I didn't want the plan to begin working till pretty late to-night. I says:

"Miss Mary Jane, I'll tell you what we'll do—and you won't have to stay at Mr. Lothrop's so long, nuther. How fur is it?"

"A little short of four miles—right out in the country, back here."

"Well, that'll answer. Now you go along out there, and lay low till nine or half-past, to-night, and then get them to fetch you home again—tell them you've thought of something. If you get here before eleven, put a candle in this window, and if I don't turn up, wait *till* eleven, and *then* if I don't turn up it means I'm gone,

9. Erroneously printed "couples" in the first edition.

1. The Negro, Jim. *Cf.* the end of Chapter XXIV.

and out of the way, and safe. Then you come out and spread the news around, and get these beats jailed."

"Good," she says, "I'll do it."

"And if it just happens so that I don't get away, but get took up along with them, you must up and say I told you the whole thing beforehand, and you must stand by me all you can."

"Stand by you, indeed I will. They sha'n't touch a hair of your head!" she says, and I see her nostrils spread and her eyes snap when she said it, too.

"If I get away, I sha'n't be here," I says, "to prove these rapscallions ain't your uncles, and I couldn't do it if I *was* here. I could swear they was beats and bummers, that's all; though that's worth something. Well, there's others can do that better than what I can—and they're people that ain't going to be doubted as quick as I'd be. I'll tell you how to find them. Gimme a pencil and a piece of paper. There—'Royal Nonesuch, *Bricksville*.' Put it away, and don't lose it. When the court wants to find out something about these two, let them send up to Bricksville and say they've got the men that played the Royal Nonesuch, and ask for some witnesses—why, you'll have that entire town down here before you can hardly wink, Miss Mary. And they'll come a-biling, too."

I judged we had got everything fixed about right, now. So I says:

"Just let the auction go right along, and don't worry. Nobody don't have to pay for the things they buy till a whole day after the auction, on accounts of the short notice, and they ain't going out of this till they get that money—and the way we've fixed it the sale ain't going to count, and they ain't going to *get* no money. It's just like the way it was with the niggers—it warn't no sale, and the niggers will be back before long. Why, they can't collect the money for the *niggers*, yet—they're in the worst kind of a fix, Miss Mary."

"Well," she says, "I'll run down to breakfast now, and then I'll start straight for Mr. Lothrop's."

" 'Deed, *that* ain't the ticket, Miss Mary Jane," I says, "by no manner of means; go *before* breakfast."

"Why?"

"What did you reckon I wanted you to go at all for, Miss Mary?"

"Well, I never thought—and come to think, I don't know. What was it?"

"Why, it's because you ain't one of these leather-face people. I don't want no better book than[2] what your face is. A body can set down and read it off like coarse print. Do you reckon you can go and face your uncles, when they come to kiss you good-morning, and never—"

"There, there, don't! Yes, I'll go before breakfast—I'll be glad

2. Erroneously printed "that" in 1885.

to. And leave my sisters with them?"

"Yes—never mind about them. They've got to stand it yet a while. They might suspicion something if all of you was to go. I don't want you to see them, nor your sisters, nor nobody in this town—if a neighbor was to ask how is your uncles this morning, your face would tell something. No, you go right along, Miss Mary Jane, and I'll fix it with all of them. I'll tell Miss Susan to give your love to your uncles and say you've went away for a few hours for to get a little rest and change, or to see a friend, and you'll be back to-night or early in the morning."

"Gone to see a friend is all right, but I won't have my love given to them."

"Well, then, it sha'n't be." It was well enough to tell *her* so—no harm in it. It was only a little thing to do, and no trouble; and it's the little things that smoothes people's roads the most, down here below; it would make Mary Jane comfortable, and it wouldn't cost nothing. Then I says: "There's one more thing—that bag of money."

"Well, they've got that; and it makes me feel pretty silly to think *how* they got it."

"No, you're out, there. They hain't got it."

"Why, who's got it?"

"I wish I knowed, but I don't. I *had* it, because I stole it from them: and I stole it to give to you; and I know where I hid it, but I'm afraid it ain't there no more. I'm awful sorry, Miss Mary Jane, I'm just as sorry as I can be; but I done the best I could; I did, honest. I come nigh getting caught, and I had to shove it into the first place I come to, and run—and it warn't a good place."

"Oh, stop blaming yourself—it's too bad to do it, and I won't allow it—you couldn't help it; it wasn't you fault. Where did you hide it?"

I didn't want to set her to thinking about her troubles again; and I couldn't seem to get my mouth to tell her what would make her see that corpse laying in the coffin with that bag of money on his stomach. So for a minute I didn't say nothing—then I says:

"I'd ruther not *tell* you where I put it, Miss Mary Jane, if you don't mind letting me off; but I'll write it for you on a piece of paper, and you can read it along the road to Mr. Lothrop's, if you want to. Do you reckon that'll do?"

"Oh, yes."

So I wrote: "I put it in the coffin. It was in there when you was crying there, away in the night. I was behind the door, and I was mighty sorry for you, Miss Mary Jane."

It made my eyes water a little, to remember her crying there all by herself in the night, and them devils laying there right under her own roof, shaming her and robbing her; and when I folded it up and give it to her, I see the water come into her eyes, too; and she shook me by the hand, hard, and says:

"Good-bye—I'm going to do everything just as you've told me; and if I don't ever see you again, I sha'n't ever forget you, and I'll think of you a many and a many a time, and I'll *pray* for you, too!"—and she was gone.

Pray for me! I reckoned if she knowed me she'd take a job that was more nearer her size. But I bet she done it, just the same—she was just that kind. She had the grit to pray for Judus if she took the notion—there warn't no backdown to her, I judge. You may say what you want to, but in my opinion she had more sand in her than any girl I ever see; in my opinion she was just full of sand. It sounds like flattery, but it ain't no flattery. And when it comes to beauty—and goodness too—she lays over them all. I hain't ever seen her since that time that I see her go out of that door; no, I hain't ever seen her since, but I reckon I've thought of her a many and a many a million times, and of her saying she would pray for me; and if ever I'd a thought it would do any good for me to pray for *her*, blamed if I wouldn't a done it or bust.

Well, Mary Jane she lit out the back way, I reckon; because nobody see her go. When I struck Susan and the hare-lip, I says:

"What's the name of them people over on t'other side of the river that you all goes to see sometimes?"

They says:

"There's several; but it's the Proctors, mainly."

"That's the name," I says; "I most forgot it. Well, Miss Mary Jane she told me to tell you she's gone over there in a dreadful hurry—one of them's sick."

"Which one?"

"I don't know; leastways I kinder forget; but I think it's—"

"Sakes alive, I hope it ain't *Hanner*?"

"I'm sorry to say it," I says, "but Hanner's the very one."

"My goodness—and she so well only last week! Is she took bad?"

"It ain't no name for it. They set up with her all night, Miss Mary Jane said, and they don't think she'll last many hours."

"Only think of that, now! What's the matter with her!"

I couldn't think of anything reasonable, right off that way, so I says:

"Mumps."

"Mumps your granny! They don't set up with people that's got the mumps."

"They don't, don't they? You better bet they do with *these* mumps. These mumps is different. It's a new kind, Miss Mary Jane said."

"How's it a new kind?"

"Because it's mixed up with other things."

"What other things?"

"Well, measles, and whooping-cough, and erysiplas, and consumption, and yaller janders, and brain fever, and I don't know what all."

"My land! And they call it the *mumps?*"

"That's what Miss Mary Jane said."

"Well, what in the nation do they call it the *mumps* for?"

"Why, because it *is* the mumps. That's what it starts with."

"Well, ther' ain't no sense in it. A body might stump his toe, and take pison, and fall down the well, and break his neck, and bust his brains out, and somebody come along and ask what killed him, and some numskull up and say, 'Why, he stumped his *toe.*' Would ther' be any sense in that? *No.* And ther' ain't no sense in *this*, nuther. Is it ketching?"

"Is it *ketching?* Why, how you talk. Is a *harrow* catching?—in the dark? If you don't hitch onto one tooth, you're bound to on another, ain't you? And you can't get away with that tooth without fetching the whole harrow along, can you? Well, these kind of mumps is a kind of a harrow, as you may say—and it ain't no slouch of a harrow, nuther, you come to get it hitched on good."

"Well, it's awful, *I* think," says the hare-lip. "I'll go to Uncle Harvey and—"

"Oh, yes," I says, "I *would.* Of *course* I would. I wouldn't lose no time."

"Well, why wouldn't you?"

"Just look at it a minute, and maybe you can see. Hain't your uncles obleeged to get along home to England as fast as they can? And do you reckon they'd be mean enough to go off and leave you to go all that journey by yourselves? *You* know they'll wait for you. So fur, so good. Your uncle Harvey's a preacher, ain't he? Very well, then; is a *preacher* going to deceive a steamboat clerk? is he going to deceive a *ship clerk?*—so as to get them to let Miss Mary Jane go aboard? Now *you* know he ain't. What *will* he do, then? Why, he'll say, 'It's a great pity, but my church matters has got to get along the best way they can; for my niece has been exposed to the dreadful pluribus-unum mumps, and so it's my bounden duty to set down here and wait the three months it takes to show on her if she's got it.' But never mind, if you think it's best to tell your uncle Harvey—"

"Shucks, and stay fooling around here when we could all be having good times in England whilst we was waiting to find out whether Mary Jane's got it or not? Why, you talk like a muggins."

"Well, anyway, maybe you better tell some of the neighbors."

"Listen at that, now. You do beat all, for natural stupidness. Can't you *see* that *they'd* go and tell? Ther' ain't no way but just to not tell anybody at *all.*"

"Well, maybe you're right—yes, I judge you *are* right."

"But I reckon we ought to tell Uncle Harvey she's gone out a while, anyway, so he wont be uneasy about her?"

"Yes, Miss Mary Jane she wanted you to do that. She says, 'Tell them to give Uncle Harvey and William my love and a kiss, and say I've run over the river to see Mr.—Mr.—what *is* the name of that rich family your uncle Peter used to think so much of?—I mean the one that—"

"Why, you must mean the Apthorps, ain't it?"

"Of course; bother them kind of names, a body can't ever seem to remember them, half the time, somehow. Yes, she said, say she has run over for to ask the Apthorps to be sure and come to the auction and buy this house, because she allowed her uncle Peter would ruther they had it than anybody else; and she's going to stick to them till they say they'll come, and then, if she ain't too tired, she's coming home; and if she is, she'll be home in the morning anyway. She said, don't say nothing about the Proctors, but only about the Apthorps—which'll be perfectly true, because she *is* going there to speak about their buying the house; I know it, because she told me so, herself."

"All right," they said, and cleared out to lay for their uncles, and give them the love and the kisses, and tell them the message.

Everything was all right now. The girls wouldn't say nothing because they wanted to go to England; and the king and the duke would ruther Mary Jane was off working for the auction than around in reach of Doctor Robinson. I felt very good; I judged I had done it pretty neat—I reckoned Tom Sawyer couldn't a done it no neater himself. Of course he would a throwed more style into it, but I can't do that very handy, not being brung up to it.

Well, they held the auction in the public square, along towards the end of the afternoon, and it strung along, and strung along, and the old man he was on hand and looking his level piousest,[3] up there longside of the auctioneer, and chipping in a little Scripture, now and then, or a little goody-goody saying, of some kind, and the duke he was around goo-gooing for sympathy all he knowed how, and just spreading himself generly.

But by-and-by the thing dragged through, and everything was sold. Everything but a little old trifling lot in the graveyard. So they'd got to work *that* off—I never see such a giraft as the king was for wanting to swallow *everything*. Well, whilst they was at it, a steamboat landed, and in about two minutes up comes a crowd a whooping and yelling and laughing and carrying on, and singing out:

"*Here's* your opposition line! here's your two sets o' heirs to old Peter Wilks—and you pays your money and you takes your choice!"

3. In the first and many subsequent editions, this was printed as "pisonest," but the manuscript shows the correct reading.

Chapter XXIX

They was fetching a very nice looking old gentleman along, and a nice looking younger one, with his right arm in a sling. And my souls, how the people yelled, and laughed, and kept it up. But I didn't see no joke about it, and I judged it would strain the duke and the king some to see any. I reckoned they'd turn pale. But no, nary a pale did *they* turn. The duke he never let on he suspicioned what was up, but just went a goo-gooing around, happy and satisfied, like a jug that's googling out buttermilk; and as for the king, he just gazed and gazed down sorrowful on them newcomers like it give him the stomach-ache in his very heart to think there could be such frauds and rascals in the world. Oh, he done it admirable. Lots of the principal people gethered around the king, to let him see they was on his side. That old gentleman that had just come looked all puzzled to death. Pretty soon he begun to speak, and I see, straight off, he pronounced *like* an Englishman, not the king's way, though the king's *was* pretty good, for an imitation. I can't give the old gent's words, nor I can't imitate him; but he turned around to the crowd, and says, about like this:

"This is a surprise to me which I wasn't looking for; and I'll acknowledge, candid and frank, I ain't very well fixed to meet it and answer it; for my brother and me has had misfortunes, he's broke his arm, and our baggage got put off at a town above here, last night in the night by a mistake. I am Peter Wilks's brother Harvey, and this is his brother William, which can't hear nor speak—and can't even make signs to amount to much, now 't he's only got one hand to work them with. We are who we say we are; and in a day or two, when I get the baggage, I can prove it. But, up till then, I won't say nothing more, but go to the hotel and wait."

So him and the new dummy started off; and the king he laughs, and blethers out:

"Broke his arm—*very* likely *ain't* it?—and very convenient, too, for a fraud that's got to make signs, and hain't learnt how. Lost their baggage! That's *mighty* good!—and mighty ingenious—under the *circumstances!*"

So he laughed again; and so did everybody else, except three or four, or maybe half a dozen. One of these was that doctor; another one was a sharp looking gentleman, with a carpet-bag of the old-fashioned kind made out of carpet-stuff, that had just come off of the steamboat and was talking to him in a low voice, and glancing towards the king now and then and nodding their heads—it was Levi Bell, the lawyer that was gone up to Louisville; and another one was a big rough husky that come along and listened to all the old gentleman said, and was listening to the king now. And when the king got done, this husky up and says:

"Say, looky here; if you are Harvey Wilks, when'd you come to this town?"

"The day before the funeral, friend," says the king.

"But what time o' day?"

"In the evenin'—'bout an hour er two before sundown."

"*How'd* you come?"

"I come down on the *Susan Powell*, from Cincinnati."

"Well, then, how'd you come to be up at the Pint in the *mornin'* —in a canoe?"

"I warn't up at the Pint in the mornin'."

"It's a lie."

Several of them jumped for him and begged him not to talk that way to an old man and a preacher.

"Preacher be hanged, he's a fraud and a liar. He was up at the Pint that mornin'. I live up there, don't I? Well, I was up there, and he was up there. I *see* him there. He come in a canoe, along with Tim Collins and a boy."

The doctor he up and says:

"Would you know the boy again if you was to see him, Hines?"

"I reckon I would, but I don't know. Why, yonder he is, now. I know him perfectly easy."

It was me he pointed at. The doctor says:

"Neighbors, I don't know whether the new couple is frauds or not; but if *these* two ain't frauds, I am an idiot, that's all. I think it's our duty to see that they don't get away from here till we've looked into this thing. Come along, Hines; come along, the rest of you. We'll take these fellows to the tavern and affront them with t'other couple, and I reckon we'll find out *something* before we get through."

It was nuts for the crowd, though maybe not for the king's friends; so we all started. It was about sundown. The doctor he led me along by the hand, and was plenty kind enough, but he never let *go* my hand.

We all got in a big room in the hotel, and lit up some candles, and fetched in the new couple. First, the doctor says:

"I don't wish to be too hard on these two men, but I think they're frauds, and they may have complices that we don't know nothing about. If they have, won't the complices get away with that bag of gold Peter Wilks left? It ain't unlikely. If these men ain't frauds, they won't object to sending for that money and letting us keep it till they prove they're all right—ain't that so?"

Everybody agreed to that. So I judged they had our gang in a pretty tight place, right at the outstart. But the king he only looked sorrowful, and says:

"Gentlemen, I wish the money was there, for I ain't got no

disposition to throw anything in the way of a fair, open, out-and-out investigation o' this misable business; but alas, the money ain't there; you k'n send and see, if you want to."

"Where is it, then?"

"Well, when my niece give it to me to keep for her, I took and hid it inside o' the straw tick o' my bed, not wishin' to bank it for the few days we'd be here, and considerin' the bed a safe place, we not bein' used to niggers, and suppos'n' 'em honest, like servants in England. The niggers stole it the very next mornin' after I had went down stairs; and when I sold 'em, I hadn't missed the money yit, so they got clean away with it. My servant here k'n tell you 'bout it gentlemen."

The doctor and several said "Shucks!" and I see nobody didn't altogether believe him. One man asked me if I see the niggers steal it. I said no, but I see them sneaking out of the room and hustling away, and I never thought nothing, only I reckoned they was afraid they had waked up my master and was trying to get away before he made trouble with them. That was all they asked me. Then the doctor whirls on me and says:

"Are *you* English too?"

I says yes; and him and some others laughed, and said, "Stuff!"

Well, then they sailed in on the general investigation, and there we had it, up and down, hour in, hour out, and nobody never said a word about supper, nor ever seemed to think about it—and so they kept it up, and kept it up; and it *was* the worst mixed-up thing you ever see. They made the king tell his yarn, and they made the old gentleman tell his'n; and anybody but a lot of prejudiced chuckleheads would a *seen* that the old gentleman was spinning truth and t'other one lies. And by-and-by they had me up to tell what I knowed. The king he give me a left-handed look out of the corner of his eye, and so I knowed enough to talk on the right side. I begun to tell about Sheffield, and how we lived there, and all about the English Wilkses, and so on; but I didn't get pretty fur till the doctor begun to laugh; and Levi Bell, the lawyer, says:

"Set down, my boy, I wouldn't strain mself, if I was you. I reckon you ain't used to lying, it don't seem to come handy; what you want is practice. You do it pretty awkward."

I didn't care nothing for the compliment, but I was glad to be let off, anyway.

The doctor he started to say something, and turns and says:

"If you'd been in town at first, Levi Bell—"

The king broke in and reached out his hand, and says:

"Why, is this my poor dead brother's old friend that he's wrote so often about?"

The lawyer and him shook hands, and the lawyer smiled and

looked pleased, and they talked right along a while, and then got to one side and talked low; and at last the lawyer speaks up and says:

"That'll fix it. I'll take the order and send it, along with your brother's, and then they'll know it's all right."

So they got some paper and a pen, and the king he set down and twisted his head to one side, and chawed his tongue, and scrawled off something; and then they give the pen to the duke—and then for the first time, the duke looked sick. But he took the pen and wrote. So then the lawyer turns to the new old gentleman and says:

"You and your brother please write a line or two and sign your names."

The old gentleman wrote, but nobody couldn't read it. The lawyer looked powerful astonished, and says:

"Well, it beats *me*"—and snaked a lot of old letters out of his pocket, and examined them, and then examined the old man's writing, and then *them* again; and then says: "These old letters is from Harvey Wilks; and here's *these* two's handwritings, and anybody can see *they* didn't write them" (the king and the duke looked sold and foolish, I tell you, to see how the lawyer had took them in), "and here's *this* old gentleman's handwriting, and anybody can tell, easy enough, *he* didn't write them—fact is, the scratches he makes ain't properly *writing*, at all. Now here's some letters from—"

The new old gentleman says:

"If you please, let me explain. Nobody can read my hand but my brother there—so he copies for me. It's *his* hand you've got there, not mine."

"*Well!*" says the lawyer, "this *is* a state of things. I've got some of William's letters too; so if you'll get him to write a line or so we can com—"

"He *can't* write with his left hand," says the old gentleman. "If he could use his right hand, you would see that he wrote his own letters and mine too. Look at both, please—they're by the same hand."

The lawyer done it, and says:

"I believe it's so—and if it ain't so, there's a heap stronger resemblance than I'd noticed before, anyway. Well, well, well! I thought we was right on the track of a slution, but it's gone to grass, partly. But anyway, *one* thing is proved—*these* two ain't either of 'em Wilkses"—and he wagged his head towards the king and the duke.

Well, what do you think?—that muleheaded old fool wouldn't give in *then!* Indeed he wouldn't. Said it warn't no fair test. Said his brother William was the cussedest joker in the world, and hadn't *tried* to write—*he* see William was going to play one of his jokes the minute he put the pen to paper. And so he warmed up and went warbling and warbling right along, till he was actuly beginning to believe what he was saying, *himself*—but pretty soon the new old gentleman broke in, and says:

"I've thought of something. Is there anybody here that helped to lay out my br—helped to lay out the late Peter Wilks for burying?"

"Yes," says somebody, "me and Ab Turner done it. We're both here."

Then the old man turns towards the king, and says:

"Peraps this gentleman can tell me what was tatooed on his breast?"

Blamed if the king didn't have to brace up mighty quick, or he'd a squshed down like a bluff bank that the river has cut under, it took him so sudden—and mind you, it was a thing that was calculated to make most anybody sqush to get fetched such a solid one as that without any notice—because how was *he* going to know what was tatooed on the man? He whitened a little; he couldn't help it; and it was mighty still in there, and everybody bending a little forwards and gazing at him. Says I to myself, *Now* he'll throw up the sponge—there ain't no more use. Well, did he? A body can't hardly believe it, but he didn't. I reckon he thought he'd keep the thing up till he tired them people out, so they'd thin out, and him and the duke could break loose and get away. Anyway, he set there, and pretty soon he begun to smile, and says:

"Mf! It's a *very* tough question, *ain't* it! *Yes,* sir, I k'n tell you what's tatooed on his breast. It's jest a small, thin, blue arrow—that's what it is; and if you don't look clost, you can't see it. *Now* what do you say—hey?"

Well, *I* never see anything like that old blister for clean out-and-out cheek.

The new old gentleman turns brisk towards Ab Turner and his pard, and his eye lights up like he judged he'd got the king *this* time, and says:

"There—you've heard what he said! Was there any such mark on Peter Wilks's breast?"

Both of them spoke up and says:

"We didn't see no such mark."

"Good!" says the old gentleman. "Now, what you *did* see on his breast was a small dim P, and a B (which is an initial he dropped when he was young), and a W, with dashes between them, so: P—B—W"—and he marked them that way on a piece of paper. "Come—ain't that what you saw?"

Both of them spoke up again, and says:

"No, we *didn't*. We never seen any marks at all."

Well, everybody *was* in a state of mind, now; and they sings out:

"The whole *bilin'* of 'm 's frauds! Le's duck 'em! le's drown 'em! le's ride 'em on a rail!" and everybody was whooping at once, and there was a rattling pow-wow. But the lawyer he jumps on the table and yells, and says:

"Gentlemen—gentle*men*! Hear me just a word—just a *single* word—if you PLEASE! There's one way yet—let's go and dig up the corpse and look."

That took them.

"Hooray!" they all shouted, and was starting right off; but the lawyer and the doctor sung out:

"Hold on, hold on! Collar all these four men and the boy, and fetch *them* along, too!"

"We'll do it!" they all shouted: "and if we don't find them marks we'll lynch the whole gang!"

I *was* scared, now, I tell you. But there warn't no getting away, you know. They gripped us all, and marched us right along, straight for the graveyard, which was a mile and a half down the river, and the whole town at our heels, for we made noise enough, and it was only nine in the evening.

As we went by our house I wished I hadn't sent Mary Jane out of town; because now if I could tip her the wink, she'd light out and save me, and blow on our dead-beats.

Well, we swarmed along down the river road, just carrying on like wild-cats; and to make it more scary, the sky was darking up, and the lightning beginning to wink and flitter, and the wind to shiver amongst the leaves. This was the most awful trouble and most dangersome I ever was in; and I was kinder stunned; everything was going so different from what I had allowed for; stead of being fixed so I could take my own time, if I wanted to, and see all the fun, and have Mary Jane at my back to save me and set me free when the close-fit come, here was nothing in the world betwixt me and sudden death but just them tatoo-marks. If they didn't find them—

I couldn't bear to think about it; and yet, somehow, I couldn't think about nothing else. It got darker and darker, and it was a beautiful time to give the crowd the slip; but that big husky had me by the wrist—Hines—and a body might as well try to give Goliar[4] the slip. He dragged me right along, he was so excited; and I had to run to keep up.

When they got there they swarmed into the graveyard and washed over it like an overflow. And when they got to the grave, they found they had about a hundred times as many shovels as they wanted, but nobody hadn't thought to fetch a lantern. But they sailed into digging, anyway, by the flicker of the lightning,

4. Goliath.

and sent a man to the nearest house a half a mile off, to borrow one.

So they dug and dug, like everything; and it got awful dark, and the rain started, and the wind swished and swushed along, and the lightning come brisker and brisker, and the thunder boomed; but them people never took no notice of it, they was so full of this business; and one minute you could see everything and every face in that big crowd, and the shovelfuls of dirt sailing up out of the grave, and the next second the dark wiped it all out, and you couldn't see nothing at all.

At last they got out the coffin, and begun to unscrew the lid, and then such another crowding, and shouldering, and shoving as there was, to scrouge in and get a sight, you never see; and in the dark, that way, it was awful. Hines he hurt my wrist dreadful, pulling and tugging so, and I reckon he clean forgot I was in the world, he was so excited and panting.

All of a sudden the lightning let go a perfect sluice of white glare, and somebody sings out:

"By the living jingo, here's the bag of gold on his breast!"

Hines let out a whoop, like everybody else, and dropped my wrist and give a big surge to bust his way in and get a look, and the way I lit out and shinned for the road in the dark, there ain't nobody can tell.

I had the road all to myself, and I fairly flew—leastways I had it all to myself except the solid dark, and the now-and-then glares, and the buzzing of the rain, and the thrashing of the wind, and the splitting of the thunder; and sure as you are born I did clip it along!

When I struck the town, I see there warn't nobody out in the storm, so I never hunted for no back streets, but humped it straight through the main one; and when I begun to get towards our house I aimed my eye and set it. No light there; the house all dark— which made me feel sorry and disappointed, I didn't know why. But at last, just as I was sailing by, *flash* comes the light in Mary Jane's window! and my heart swelled up sudden, like to bust; and the same second the house and all was behind me in the dark, and wasn't ever going to be before me no more in this world. She *was* the best girl I ever see, and had the most sand.

The minute I was far enough above the town to see I could make the tow-head, I begun to look sharp for a boat to borrow; and the first time the lightning showed me one that wasn't chained, I snatched it and shoved. It was a canoe, and warn't fastened with nothing but a rope. The tow-head was a rattling big distance off, away out there in the middle of the river, but I didn't lose no time; and when I struck the raft at last, I was so fagged I would a just laid down to blow and gasp if I could afforded it. But I didn't. As I sprung aboard I sung out:

"Out with you Jim, and set her loose! Glory be to goodness, we're shut of them!"

Jim lit out, and was a coming for me with both arms spread, he was so full of joy; but when I glimpsed him in the lightning, my heart shot up in my mouth, and I went overboard backwards; for I forgot he was old King Lear and a drownded A-rab all in one, and it most scared the livers and lights out of me. But Jim fished me out, and was going to hug me and bless me, and so on, he was so glad I was back and we was shut of the king and the duke, but I says:

"Not now—have it for breakfast, have it for breakfast! Cut loose and let her slide!"

So, in two seconds, away we went, a sliding down the river, and it *did* seem so good to be free again and all by ourselves on the big river and nobody to bother us. I had to skip around a bit, and jump up and crack my heels a few times, I couldn't help it; but about the third crack, I noticed a sound that I knowed mighty well—and held my breath and listened and waited—and sure enough, when the next flash busted out over the water, here they come!—and just a laying to their oars and making their skiff hum! It was the king and the duke.

So I wilted right down onto the planks, then, and give up; and it was all I could do to keep from crying.

Chapter XXX

When they got aboard, the king went for me, and shook me by the collar, and says:

"Tryin' to give us the slip, was ye, you pup! Tired of our company—hey?"

I says:

"No, your majesty, we warn't—*please* don't, your majesty!"

"Quick, then, and tell us what *was* your idea, or I'll shake the insides out o' you!"

"Honest, I'll tell you everything, just as it happened, your majesty. The man that had aholt of me was very good to me, and kept saying he had a boy about as big as me that died last year, and he was sorry to see a boy in such a dangerous fix; and when they was all took by surprise by finding the gold, and made a rush for the coffin, he lets go of me and whispers, 'Heel it, now, or they'll hang ye, sure!' and I lit out. It didn't seem no good for *me* to stay—I couldn't do nothing, and I didn't want to be hung if I could get away. So I never stopped running till I found the canoe; and when I got here I told Jim to hurry, or they'd catch me and hang me yet, and said I was afeard you and the duke wasn't alive, now, and I was awful sorry, and so was Jim, and was awful glad when we see you coming, you may ask Jim if I didn't."

Jim said it was so; and the king told him to shut up, and said, "Oh, yes, it's *mighty* likely!" and shook me up again, and said he reckoned he'd drownd me. But the duke says:

"Leggo the boy, you old idiot! Would *you* a done any different? Did you inquire around for *him*, when you got loose? I don't remember it."

So the king let go of me, and begun to cuss that town and everybody in it. But the duke says:

"You better a blame sight give *yourself* a good cussing, for you're the one that's entitled to it most. You hain't done a thing, from the start, that had any sense in it, except coming out so cool and cheeky with that imaginary blue-arrow mark. That *was* bright —it was right down bully; and it was the thing that saved us. For if it hadn't been for that, they'd a jailed us till them Englishmen's baggage come—and then—the penitentiary, you bet! But that trick took 'em to the graveyard, and the gold done us a still bigger kindness; for if the excited fools hadn't let go all holts and made that rush to get a look, we'd a slept in our cravats to-night— cravats warranted to *wear*, too—longer than *we'd* need 'em."

They was still a minute—thinking—then the king says, kind of absent-minded like:

"Mf! And we reckoned the *niggers* stole it!"

That made me squirm!

"Yes," says the duke, kinder slow, and deliberate, and sarcastic, "*We* did."

After about a half a minute, the king drawls out:

"Leastways—*I* did."

The duke says, the same way:

"On the contrary—*I* did."

The king kind of ruffles up, and says:

"Looky here, Bilgewater, what'r you referrin' to?"

The duke says, pretty brisk:

"When it comes to that, maybe you'll let me ask, what was *you* referring to?"

"Shucks!" says the king, very sarcastic; "but *I* don't know— maybe you was asleep, and didn't know what you was about."

The duke bristles right up, now, and says:

"Oh, let *up* on this cussed nonsense—do you take me for a blame' fool? Don't you reckon *I* know who hid that money in that coffin?"

"*Yes*, sir! I know you *do* know—because you done it yourself!"

"It's a lie!"—and the duke went for him. The king sings out:

"Take y'r hands off!—leggo my throat!—I take it all back!"

The duke says:

"Well, you just own up, first, that you *did* hide that money there, intending to give me the slip one of these days, and come back and dig it up, and have it all to yourself."

"Wait jest a minute, duke—answer me this one question, honest and fair; if you didn't put the money there, say it, and I'll b'lieve you, and take back everything I said."

"You old scoundrel, I didn't, and you know I didn't. There, now!"

"Well, then, I b'lieve you. But answer me only jest this one more—now *don't* git mad; didn't you have it in your *mind* to hook the money and hide it?"

The duke never said nothing for a little bit; then he says:

"Well—I don't care if I *did*, I didn't *do* it, anyway. But you not only had it in mind to do it, but you *done* it."

"I wisht I may never die if I done it, duke, and that's honest. I won't say I warn't *goin'* to do it, because I *was*; but you—I mean somebody—got in ahead o' me."

"It's a lie! You done it, and you got to *say* you done it, or—"

The king begun to gurgle, and then he gasps out:

" 'Nough!—*I own up!*"

I was very glad to hear him say that, it made me feel much more easier than what I was feeling before. So the duke took his hands off, and says:

"If you ever deny it again, I'll drown you. It's *well* for you to set there and blubber like a baby—it's fitten for you, after the way you've acted. I never see such an old ostrich for wanting to gobble everything—and I a trusting you all the time, like you was my own father. You ought to been ashamed of yourself to stand by and hear it saddled onto a lot of poor niggers and you never say a word for 'em. It makes me feel ridiculous to think I was soft enough to *believe* that rubbage. Cuss you, I can see, now, why you was so anxious to make up the deffesit—you wanted to get what money I'd got out of the Nonesuch and one thing or another, and scoop it *all!*"

The king says, timid, and still a snuffling:

"Why, duke, it was you that said make up the deffersit, it warn't me."

"Dry up! I don't want to hear no more *out* of you!" says the duke. "And *now* you see what you *got* by it. They've got all their own money back, and all of *ourn* but a shekel or two, *besides*. G'long to bed—and don't you deffersit *me* no more deffersits, long 's *you* live!"

So the king sneaked into the wigwam, and took to his bottle for comfort; and before long the duke tackled *his* bottle; and so in about a half an hour they was as thick as thieves again, and the tighter they got, the lovinger they got; and went off a snoring in each other's arms. They both got powerful mellow, but I noticed the king didn't get mellow enough to forget to remember to not deny about hiding the money-bag again. That made me feel easy and satisfied. Of course when they got to snoring, we had a long gabble, and I told Jim everything.

Chapter XXXI

We dasn't stop again at any town, for days and days; kept right along down the river. We was down south in the warm weather, now, and a mighty long ways from home. We begun to come to trees with Spanish moss on them, hanging down from the limbs like long gray beards. It was the first I ever see it growing, and it made the woods look solemn and dismal. So now the frauds reckoned they was out of danger, and they begun to work the villages again.

First they done a lecture on temperance; but they didn't make enough for them both to get drunk on. Then in another village they started a dancing school; but they didn't know no more how to dance than a kangaroo does; so the first prance they made, the general public jumped in and pranced them out of town. Another time they tried a go at yellocution; but they didn't yellocute long till the audience got up and give them a solid good cussing and made them skip out. They tackled missionarying, and mesmerizering, and doctoring, and telling fortunes, and a little of everything; but they couldn't seem to have no luck. So at last they got just about dead broke, and laid around the raft, as she floated along, thinking, and thinking, and never saying nothing, by the half a day at a time, and dreadful blue and desperate.

And at last they took a change, and begun to lay their heads together in the wigwam and talk low and confidential two or three hours at a time. Jim and me got uneasy. We didn't like the look of it. We judged they was studying up some kind of worse deviltry than ever. We turned it over and over, and at last we made up our minds they was going to break into somebody's house or store, or was going into the counterfeit-money business, or something. So then we was pretty scared, and made up an agreement that we wouldn't have nothing in the world to do with such actions, and if we ever got the least show we would give them the cold shake, and clear out and leave them behind. Well, early one morning we hid the raft in a good safe place about two mile below a little bit of a shabby village, named Pikesville, and the king he went ashore, and told us all to stay hid whilst he went up to town and smelt around to see if anybody had got any wind of the Royal Nonesuch there yet. ("House to rob, you *mean*," says I to myself; "and when you get through robbing it you'll come back here and wonder what's become of me and Jim and the raft—and you'll have to take it out in wondering.") And he said if he warn't back by midday, the duke and me would know it was all right, and we was to come along.

So we staid where we was. The duke he fretted and sweated around, and was in a mighty sour way. He scolded us for everything, and we couldn't seem to do nothing right; he found fault with every little thing. Something was a-brewing, sure. I was good and glad when midday come and no king; we could have a change, anyway—and maybe a chance for *the* change, on top of it. So me and the duke went up to the village, and hunted around there for the king, and by-and-by we found him in the back room of a little low doggery,[5] very tight, and a lot of loafers bullyragging him for sport, and he a cussing and threatening with all his might, and so tight he couldn't walk, and couldn't do nothing to them. The duke he began to abuse him for an old fool, and the king begun to sass back; and the minute they was fairly at it, I lit out, and shook the reefs out of my hind legs, and spun down the river road like a deer—for I see our chance; and I made up my mind that it would be a long day before they ever see me and Jim again. I got down there all out of breath but loaded up with joy, and sung out—

"Set her loose, Jim, we're all right, now!"

But there warn't no answer, and nobody come out of the wigwam. Jim was gone! I set up a shout—and then another—and then another one; and run this way and that in the woods, whooping and screeching; but it warn't no use—old Jim was gone. Then I set down and cried; I couldn't help it. But I couldn't set still long. Pretty soon I went out on the road, trying to think what I better do, and I run across a boy walking, and asked him if he'd seen a strange nigger, dressed so and so, and he says:

"Yes."

"Whereabouts?" says I.

"Down to Silas Phelps's place, two mile below here. He's a runaway nigger, and they've got him. Was you looking for him?"

"You bet I ain't! I run across him in the woods about an hour or two ago, and he said if I hollered he'd cut my livers out—and told me to lay down and stay where I was; and I done it. Been there ever since; afeard to come out."

"Well," he says, "you needn't be afeard no more, becuz they've got him. He run off f'm down South, som'ers."

"It's a good job they got him."

"Well, I *reckon*! There's two hunderd dollars reward on him. It's like picking up money out'n the road."

"Yes, it is—and *I* could a had it if I'd been big enough; I see him *first*. Who nailed him?"

5. Groggery, or low-type saloon.

"It was an old fellow—a stranger—and he sold out his chance in him for forty dollars, becuz he's got to go up the river and can't wait. Think o' that, now! You bet I'd wait, if it was seven year."

"That's me, every time," says I. "But maybe his chance ain't worth no more than that, if he'll sell it so cheap. Maybe there's something ain't straight about it."

"But it *is*, though—straight as a string. I see the handbill myself. It tells all about him, to a dot—paints him like a picture, and tells the plantation he's frum, below Newr*leans*. No-siree-*bob*, they ain't no trouble 'bout *that* speculation, you bet you. Say, gimme a chaw tobacker, won't ye?"

I didn't have none, so he left. I went to the raft, and set down in the wigwam to think. But I couldn't come to nothing. I thought till I wore my head sore, but I couldn't see no way out of the trouble. After all this long journey, and after all we'd done for them scoundrels, here was it all come to nothing, everything all busted up and ruined, because they could have the heart to serve Jim such a trick as that, and make him a slave again all his life, and amongst strangers, too, for forty dirty dollars.

Once I said to myself it would be a thousand times better for Jim to be a slave at home where his family was, as long as he'd *got* to be a slave, and so I'd better write a letter to Tom Sawyer and tell him to tell Miss Watson where he was. But I soon give up that notion, for two things: she'd be mad and disgusted at his rascality and ungratefulness for leaving her, and so she'd sell him straight down the river again; and if she didn't, everybody naturally despises an ungrateful nigger, and they'd make Jim feel it all the time, and so he'd feel ornery and disgraced. And then think of *me!* It would get all around, that Huck Finn helped a nigger to get his freedom; and if I was to ever see anybody from that town again, I'd be ready to get down and lick his boots for shame. That's just the way: a person does a low-down thing, and then he don't want to take no consequences of it. Thinks as long as he can hide it, it ain't no disgrace. That was my fix exactly. The more I studied about this, the more my conscience went to grinding me, and the more wicked and low-down and ornery I got to feeling. And at last, when it hit me all of a sudden that here was the plain hand of Providence slapping me in the face and letting me know my wickedness was being watched all the time from up there in heaven, whilst I was stealing a poor old woman's nigger that hadn't ever done me no harm, and now was showing me there's One that's always on the lookout, and ain't agoing to allow no such miserable doings to go only just so fur and no further, I most dropped in my tracks I was so scared. Well, I tried the best I could to kinder soften it up somehow for myself, by saying I was brung up wicked, and so I warn't so much to blame; but something inside of me kept saying,

"There was the Sunday school, you could a gone to it; and if you'd a done it they'd a learnt you, there, that people that acts as I'd been acting about that nigger goes to everlasting fire."

It made me shiver. And I about made up my mind to pray; and see if I couldn't try to quit being the kind of a boy I was, and be better. So I kneeled down. But the words wouldn't come. Why wouldn't they? It warn't no use to try and hide it from Him. Nor from *me*, neither. I knowed very well why they wouldn't come. It was because my heart warn't right; it was because I warn't square; it[6] was because I was playing double. I was letting *on* to give up sin, but away inside of me I was holding on to the biggest one of all. I was trying to make my mouth *say* I would do the right thing and the clean thing, and go and write to that nigger's owner and tell where he was; but deep down in me I knowed it was a lie—and He knowed it. You can't pray a lie—I found that out.

So I was full of trouble, full as I could be; and didn't know what to do. At last I had an idea; and I says, I'll go and write the letter—and *then* see if I can pray. Why, it was astonishing, the way I felt as light as a feather, right straight off, and my troubles all gone. So I got a piece of paper and a pencil, all glad and excited, and set down and wrote:

Miss Watson your runaway nigger Jim is down here two mile below Pikesville and Mr. Phelps has got him and he will give him up for the reward if you send. HUCK FINN.

I felt good and all washed clean of sin for the first time I had ever felt so in my life, and I knowed I could pray now. But I didn't do it straight off, but laid the paper down and set there thinking—thinking how good it was all this happened so, and how near I come to being lost and going to hell. And went on thinking. And got to thinking over our trip down the river; and I see Jim before me, all the time, in the day, and in the night-time, sometimes moonlight, sometimes storms, and we a floating along, talking, and singing, and laughing. But somehow I couldn't seem to strike no places to harden me against him, but only the other kind. I'd see him standing my watch on top of his'n, stead of calling me, so I could go on sleeping; and see him how glad he was when I come back out of the fog; and when I come to him again in the swamp, up there where the feud was; and such-like times; and would always call me honey, and pet me, and do everything he could think of for me, and how good he always was; and at last I struck the time I saved him by telling the men we had small-pox aboard, and he was so grateful, and said I was the best friend old Jim ever had in the world, and the *only* one he's got now; and then

6. Erroneously printed "is" in 1885.

I happened to look around, and see that paper.

It was a close place. I took it up, and held it in my hand. I was a trembling, because I'd got to decide, forever, betwixt two things, and I knowed it. I studied a minute, sort of holding my breath, and then says to myself:

"All right, then, I'll *go* to hell"—and tore it up.

It was awful thoughts, and awful words, but they was said. And I let them stay said; and never thought no more about reforming. I shoved the whole thing out of my head; and said I would take up wickedness again, which was in my line, being brung up to it, and the other warn't. And for a starter, I would go to work and steal Jim out of slavery again; and if I could think up anything worse, I would do that, too; because as long as I was in, and in for good, I might as well go the whole hog.

Then I set to thinking over how to get at it, and turned over considerable many ways in my mind; and at last fixed up a plan that suited me. So then I took the bearings of a woody island that was down the river a piece, and as soon as it was fairly dark I crept out with my raft and went for it, and hid it there, and then turned in. I slept the night through, and got up before it was light, and had my breakfast, and put on my store clothes, and tied up some others and one thing or another in a bundle, and took the canoe and cleared for shore. I landed below where I judged was Phelps's place, and hid my bundle in the woods, and then filled up the canoe with water, and loaded rocks into her and sunk her where I could find her again when I wanted her, about a quarter of a mile below a little steam sawmill that was on the bank.

Then I struck up the road, and when I passed the mill I see a sign on it, "Phelps's Sawmill," and when I come to the farm-houses, two or three hundred yards further along, I kept my eyes peeled, but didn't see nobody around, though it was good daylight, now. But I didn't mind, because I didn't want to see nobody just yet—I only wanted to get the lay of the land. According to my plan, I was going to turn up there from the village, not from below. So I just took a look, and shoved along, straight for town. Well, the very first man I see, when I got there, was the duke. He was sticking up a bill for the Royal Nonesuch—three-night performance—like that other time. *They* had the check, them frauds! I was right on him, before I could shirk. He looked astonished, and says:

"Hel-*lo!* Where'd *you* come from?" Then he says, kind of glad and eager, "Where's the raft?—got her in a good place?"

I says:

"Why, that's just what I was agoing to ask your grace."

Then he didn't look so joyful—and says:

"What was your idea for asking *me?*" he says.

"Well," I says, "when I see the king in that doggery yesterday, I says to myself, we can't get him home for hours, till he's soberer; so I went a loafing around town to put in the time, and wait. A man up and offered me ten cents to help him pull a skiff over the river and back to fetch a sheep, and so I went along; but when we was dragging him to the boat, and the man left me aholt of the rope and went behind him to shove him along, he was too strong for me, and jerked loose and run, and we after him. We didn't have no dog, and so we had to chase him all over the country till we tired him out. We never got him till dark, then we fetched him over, and I started down for the raft. When I got there and see it was gone, I says to myself, 'they've got into trouble and had to leave; and they've took my nigger, which is the only nigger I've got in the world, and now I'm in a strange country, and ain't got no property no more, nor nothing, and no way to make my living;' so I set down and cried. I slept in the woods all night. But what *did* become of the raft then?—and Jim, poor Jim!"

"Blamed if *I* know—that is, what's become of the raft. That old fool had made a trade and got forty dollars, and when we found him in the doggery the loafers had matched half dollars with him and got every cent but what he'd spent for whisky; and when I got him home late last night and found the raft gone, we said, 'That little rascal has stole our raft and shook us, and run off down the river.'"

"I wouldn't shake my *nigger*, would I?—the only nigger I had in the world, and the only property."

"We never thought of that. Fact is, I reckon we'd come to consider him *our* nigger; yes, we did consider him so—goodness knows we had trouble enough for him. So when we see the raft was gone, and we flat broke, there warn't anything for it but to try the Royal Nonesuch another shake. And I've pegged along ever since, dry as a powderhorn. Where's that ten cents? Give it here."

I had considerable money, so I give him ten cents, but begged him to spend it for something to eat, and give me some, because it was all the money I had, and I hadn't had nothing to eat since yesterday. He never said nothing. The next minute he whirls on me and says:

"Do you reckon that nigger would blow on us? We'd skin him if he done that!"

"How can he blow? Hain't he run off?"

"No! That old fool sold him, and never divided with me, and the money's gone."

"*Sold* him?" I says, and begun to cry; "why, he was *my* nigger, and that was my money. Where is he?—I want my nigger."

"Well, you can't *get* your nigger, that's all—so dry up your blubbering. Looky here—do you think *you'd* venture to blow on us? Blamed if I think I'd trust you. Why, if you *was* to blow on us—"

He stopped, but I never see the duke look so ugly out of his eyes before. I went on a-whimpering, and says:

"I don't want to blow on nobody; and I ain't got no time to blow, nohow. I got to turn out and find my nigger."

He looked kinder bothered, and stood there with his bills fluttering on his arm, thinking, and wrinkling up his forehead. At last he says:

"I'll tell you something. We got to be here three days. If you'll promise you won't blow, and won't let the nigger blow, I'll tell you where to find him."

So I promised, and he says:

"A farmer by the name of Silas Ph——" and then he stopped. You see he started to tell me the truth; but when he stopped, that way, and begun to study and think again, I reckoned he was changing his mind. And so he was. He wouldn't trust me; he wanted to make sure of having me out of the way the whole three days. So pretty soon he says: "The man that bought him is named Abram Foster—Abram G. Foster—and he lives forty mile back here in the country, on the road to Lafayette."

"All right," I says, "I can walk it in three days. And I'll start this very afternoon."

"No you won't, you'll start *now*; and don't you lose any time about it, neither, nor do any gabbling by the way. Just keep a tight tongue in your head and move right along, and then you won't get into trouble with *us*, d'ye hear?"

That was the order I wanted, and that was the one I played for. I wanted to be left free to work my plans.

"So clear out," he says; "and you can tell Mr. Foster whatever you want to. Maybe you can get him to believe that Jim *is* your nigger—some idiots don't require documents—leastways I've heard there's such down South here. And when you tell him the handbill and the reward's bogus, maybe he'll believe you when you explain to him what the idea was for getting 'em out. Go 'long, now, and tell him anything you want to; but mind you don't work your jaw any *between* here and there."

So I left, and struck for the back country. I didn't look around, but I kinder felt like he was watching me. But I knowed I could tire him out at that. I went straight out in the country as much as a mile, before I stopped; then I doubled back through the woods towards Phelps's. I reckoned I better start in on my plan straight off, without fooling around, because I wanted to stop Jim's mouth till these fellows could get away. I didn't want no trouble with their kind. I'd seen all I wanted to of them, and wanted to get entirely shut of them.

Chapter XXXII

When I got there it was all still and Sunday-like, and hot and sunshiny—the hands was gone to the fields; and there was them kind of faint dronings of bugs and flies in the air that makes it seem so lonesome and like everybody's dead and gone; and if a breeze fans along and quivers the leaves, it makes you feel mournful, because you feel like it's spirits whispering—spirits that's been dead ever so many years—and you always think they're talking about *you*. As a general thing it makes a body wish *he* was dead, too, and done with it all.[7]

Phelps's was one of these little one-horse cotton plantations; and they all look alike.[8] A rail fence round a two-acre yard; a stile, made out of logs sawed off and up-ended, in steps, like barrels of a different length, to climb over the fence with, and for the women to stand on when they are going to jump onto a horse; some sickly grass-patches in the big yard, but mostly it was bare and smooth, like an old hat with the nap rubbed off; big double log house for the white folks—hewed logs, with the chinks stopped up with mud or mortar, and these mud-stripes been whitewashed some time or another; round-log kitchen, with a big broad, open but roofed passage joining it to the house; log smoke-house back of the kitchen; three little log nigger-cabins in a row t'other side the smokehouse; one little hut all by itself away down against the back fence, and some outbuildings down a piece the other side; ash-hopper, and big kettle to bile soap in, by the little hut; bench by the kitchen door, with bucket of water and a gourd; hound asleep there, in the sun; more hounds asleep, round about; about three shade-trees away off in a corner; some currant bushes and gooseberry bushes in one place by the fence; outside of the fence a garden and a water-melon patch; then the cotton fields begins; and after the fields, the woods.

I went around and clumb over the back stile by the ash-hopper, and started for the kitchen. When I got a little ways, I heard the dim hum of a spinning-wheel wailing along up and sinking along down again; and then I knowed for certain I wished I was dead—for that *is* the lonesomest sound in the whole world.

I went right along, not fixing up any particular plan, but just trusting to Providence to put the right words in my mouth when the time come; for I'd noticed that Providence always did put the right words in my mouth, if I left it alone.

When I got half-way, first one hound and then another got up

7. Almost the identical phrasing of this mood appears in the beginning paragraphs of *Tom Sawyer, Detective*, published eleven years later.
8. This plantation is much like the farm of Twain's uncle, John Quarles, near Hannibal. The Phelps place becomes the major locale and Aunt Sally and Uncle Silas important characters in *Tom Sawyer, Detective*, where Huck, again the narrator, and Tom become involved in a murder.

and went for me, and of course I stopped and faced them, and kept still. And such another pow-wow as they made! In a quarter of a minute I was a kind of a hub of a wheel, as you may say—spokes made out of dogs—circle of fifteen of them packed together around me, with their necks and noses stretched up towards me, a barking and howling; and more a coming; you could see them sailing over fences and around corners from everywheres.

A nigger woman come tearing out of the kitchen with a rolling-pin in her hand, singing out, "Begone! *you* Tige! you Spot! begone, sah!" and she fetched first one and then another of them a clip and sent him howling, and then the rest followed; and the next second, half of them come back, wagging their tails around me and making friends with me. There ain't no harm in a hound, nohow.

And behind the woman comes a little nigger girl and two little nigger boys, without anything on but tow-linen shirts, and they hung onto their mother's gown, and peeped out from behind her at me, bashful, the way they always do. And here comes the white woman running from the house, about forty-five or fifty year old, bare-headed, and her spinning-stick in her hand; and behind her comes her little white children, acting the same way the little niggers was doing. She was smiling all over so she could hardly stand—and says:

"It's *you*, at last!—*ain't* it?"

I out with a "Yes'm," before I thought.

She grabbed me and hugged me tight; and then gripped me by both hands and shook and shook; and the tears come in her eyes, and run down over; and she couldn't seem to hug and shake enough, and kept saying, "You don't look as much like your mother as I reckoned you would, but law sakes, I don't care for that, I'm *so* glad to see you! Dear, dear, it does seem like I could eat you up! Children, it's your cousin Tom!—tell him howdy."

But they ducked their heads, and put their fingers in their mouths, and hid behind her. So she run on:

"Lize, hurry up and get him a hot breakfast, right away—or did you get your breakfast on the boat?"

I said I had got it on the boat. So then she started for the house, leading me by the hand, and the children tagging after. When we got there, she set me down in a split-bottomed chair, and set herself down on a little low stool in front of me, holding both of my hands, and says:

"Now I can have a *good* look at you; and laws-a-me, I've been hungry for it a many and a many a time, all these long years, and it's come at last! We been expecting you a couple of days and more. What's kep' you?—boat get aground?"

"Yes'm—she—"

"Don't say yes'm—say Aunt Sally. Where'd she get aground?"

I didn't rightly know what to say, because I didn't know whether the boat would be coming up the river or down. But I go a good deal on instinct; and my instinct said she would be coming up— from down towards Orleans. That didn't[9] help me much, though; for I didn't know the names of bars down that way. I see I'd got to invent a bar, or forget the name of the one we got aground on—or— Now I struck an idea, and fetched it out:

"It warn't the grounding—that didn't keep us back but a little. We blowed out a cylinder-head."

"Good gracious! anybody hurt?"

"No'm. Killed a nigger."

"Well, it's lucky; because sometimes people do get hurt. Two years ago last Christmas, your uncle Silas was coming up from Newrleans on the old *Lally Rook*, and she blowed out a cylinder-head and crippled a man. And I think he died afterwards. He was a Babtist. Your uncle Silas knowed a family in Baton Rouge that knowed his people very well. Yes, I remember, now he *did* die. Mortification set in, and they had to amputate him. But it didn't save him. Yes, it was mortification—that was it. He turned blue all over, and died in the hope of a glorious resurrection. They say he was a sight to look at. Your uncle's been up to the town every day to fetch you. And he's gone again, not more'n an hour ago; he'll be back any minute, now. You must a met him on the road, didn't you?—oldish man, with a—"

"No, I didn't see nobody, Aunt Sally. The boat landed just at daylight, and I left my baggage on the wharf-boat and went looking around the town and out a piece in the country, to put in the time and not get here too soon; and so I come down the back way."

"Who'd you give the baggage to?"

"Nobody."

"Why, child, it'll be stole!"

"Not where *I* hid it I reckon it won't," I says.

"How'd you get your breakfast so early on the boat?"

It was kinder thin ice, but I says:

"The captain see me standing around, and told me I better have something to eat before I went ashore; so he took me in the texas to the officers' lunch, and give me all I wanted."

I was getting so uneasy I couldn't listen good. I had my mind on the children all the time; I wanted to get them out to one side, and pump them a little, and find out who I was. But I couldn't get no show, Mrs. Phelps kept it up and run on so. Pretty soon she made the cold chills streak all down my back, because she says:

"But here we're a running on this way, and you hain't told me a word about Sis, nor any of them. Now I'll rest my works a little, and you start up yourn; just tell me *everything*—tell me all about 'm all—every one of 'm; and how they are, and what they're doing,

9. Erroneously printed "did'nt" in 1885.

and what they told you to tell me; and every last thing you can think of."

Well, I see I was up a stump—and up it good. Providence had stood by me this fur, all right, but I was hard and tight aground, now. I see it warn't a bit of use to try to go ahead—I'd *got* to throw up my hand. So I says to myself, here's another place where I got to resk the truth. I opened my mouth to begin; but she grabbed me and hustled me in behind the bed, and says:

"Here he comes! stick your head down lower—there, that'll do; you can't be seen, now. Don't you let on you're here. I'll play a joke on him. Children, don't you say a word."

I see I was in a fix, now. But it warn't no use to worry; there warn't nothing to do but just hold still, and try and be ready to stand from under when the lightning struck.

I had just one little glimpse of the old gentleman when he come in, then the bed hid him. Mrs. Phelps she jumps for him and says:

"Has he come?"

"No," says her husband.

"Good-*ness* gracious!" she says, "what in the world *can* have become of him?"

"I can't imagine," says the old gentleman; "and I must say, it makes me dreadful uneasy."

"Uneasy!" she says, "I'm ready to go distracted! He *must* a come; and you've missed him along the road. I *know* it's so— something *tells* me so."

"Why Sally, I *couldn't* miss him along the road—*you* know that."

"But oh, dear, dear, what *will* Sis say! He must a come! You must a missed him. He—"

"Oh, don't distress me any more'n I'm already distressed. I don't know what in the world to make of it. I'm at my wit's end, and I don't mind acknowledging 't I'm right down scared. But there's no hope that he's come; for he *couldn't* come and me miss him. Sally, it's terrible—just terrible—something's happened to the boat, sure!"

"Why, Silas! Look yonder!—up the road!—ain't that somebody coming?"

He sprung to the window at the head of the bed, and that give Mrs. Phelps the chance she wanted. She stooped down quick, at the foot of the bed, and give me a pull, and out I come; and when he turned back from the window, there she stood, a-beaming and a-smiling like a house afire, and I standing pretty meek and sweaty alongside. The old gentleman stared, and says:

"Why, who's that?"

"Who do you reckon 't is?"

"I haint no idea. Who *is* it?"

"It's *Tom Sawyer!*"

By jings, I most slumped through the floor. But there warn't no time to swap knives; the old man grabbed me by the hand and shook, and kept on shaking; and all the time, how the woman did dance around and laugh and cry; and then how they both did fire off questions about Sid, and Mary, and the rest of the tribe.

But if they was joyful, it warn't nothing to what I was; for it was like being born again, I was so glad to find out who I was. Well, they froze to me for two hours; and at last when my chin was so tired it couldn't hardly go, any more, I had told them more about my family—I mean the Sawyer family—than ever happened to any six Sawyer families. And I explained all about how we blowed out a cylinder-head at the mouth of White River and it took us three days to fix it. Which was all right, and worked first rate; because *they* didn't know but what it would take three days to fix it. If I'd a called it a bolt-head it would a done just as well.

Now I was feeling pretty comfortable all down one side, and pretty uncomfortable all up the other. Being Tom Sawyer was easy and comfortable; and it stayed easy and comfortable till by-and-by I hear a steamboat coughing along down the river—then I says to myself, spose Tom Sawyer come down on that boat?—and spose he steps in here, any minute, and sings out my name before I can throw him a wink to keep quiet? Well, I couldn't *have* it that way—it wouldn't do at all. I must go up the road and waylay him. So I told the folks I reckoned I would go up to the town and fetch down my baggage. The old gentleman was for going along with me, but I said no, I could drive the horse myself, and I druther he wouldn't take no trouble about me.

Chapter XXXIII

So I started for town, in the wagon, and when I was half-way I see a wagon coming, and sure enough it was Tom Sawyer, and I stopped and waited till he come along. I says "Hold on!" and it stopped alongside, and his mouth opened up like a trunk, and staid so; and he swallowed two or three times like a person that's got a dry throat, and then says:

"I hain't ever done you no harm. You know that. So then, what you want to come back and ha'nt *me* for?"

I says:

"I hain't come back—I hain't been *gone.*"

When he heard my voice, it righted him up some, but he warn't quite satisfied yet. He says:

"Don't you play nothing on me, because I wouldn't on you. Honest injun, now, you ain't a ghost?"

"Honest injun, I ain't," I says.

"Well—I—I—well, that ought to settle it, of course; but I can't somehow seem to understand it, no way. Looky here, warn't you ever murdered *at all?*"

"No. I warn't ever murdered at all—I played it on them. You come in here and feel of me if you don't believe me."

So he done it; and it satisfied him; and he was that glad to see me again, he didn't know what to do. And he wanted to know all about it right off; because it was a grand adventure, and mysterious, and so it hit him where he lived. But I said, leave it alone till by-and-by; and told his driver to wait, and we drove off a little piece, and I told him the kind of a fix I was in, and what did he reckon we better do? He said, let him alone a minute, and don't disturb him. So he thought and thought, and pretty soon he says:

"It's all right, I've got it. Take my trunk in your wagon, and let on it's your'n; and you turn back and fool along slow, so as to get to the house about the time you ought to; and I'll go towards town a piece, and take a fresh start, and get there a quarter or a half an hour after you; and you needn't let on to know me, at first."

I says:

"All right; but wait a minute. There's one more thing—a thing that *nobody* don't know but me. And that is, there's a nigger here that I'm a-trying to steal out of slavery—and his name is *Jim*— old Miss Watson's Jim."

He says:

"What! Why Jim is—"

He stopped and went to studying. I says:

"*I* know what you'll say. You'll say it's dirty low-down business; but what if it is?—*I'm* low down; and I'm agoing to steal him, and I want you to keep mum and not let on. Will you?"

His eye lit up, and he says:

"I'll *help* you steal him!"

Well, I let go all holts then, like I was shot. It was the most astonishing speech I ever heard—and I'm bound to say Tom Sawyer fell, considerable, in my estimation. Only I couldn't believe it. Tom Sawyer a *nigger stealer!*[1]

"Oh, shucks," I says, "you're joking."

"I ain't joking, either."

"Well, then," I says, "joking or no joking, if you hear anything said about a runaway nigger, don't forget to remember that *you* don't know nothing about him, and *I* don't know nothing about him."

Then we took the trunk and put it in my wagon, and he drove off his way, and I drove mine. But of course I forgot all about

1. While Huck has reconciled *his* attitude toward freeing Jim, his recognition that Tom represents the "respectable" and law-abiding element of his community forces him to feel that Tom loses caste by entering into the plan for Jim's escape.

driving slow, on accounts of being glad and full of thinking; so I got home a heap too quick for that length of a trip. The old gentleman was at the door, and he says:

"Why, this is wonderful. Who ever would a thought it was in that mare to do it. I wish we'd a timed her. And she hain't sweated a hair—not a hair. It's wonderful. Why, I wouldn't take a hunderd dollars for that horse now; I wouldn't, honest; and yet I'd a sold her for fifteen before, and thought 'twas all she was worth."

That's all he said. He was the innocentest, best old soul I ever see. But it warn't surprising; because he warn't only just a farmer, he was a preacher, too, and had a little one-horse log church down back of the plantation, which he built it himself at his own expense, for a church and school-house, and never charged nothing for his preaching, and it was worth it, too. There was plenty other farmer-preachers like that, and done the same way, down South.

In about half an hour Tom's wagon drove up to the front stile, and Aunt Sally she see it through the window because it was only about fifty yards, and says:

"Why, there's somebody come! I wonder who 'tis? Why, I do believe it's a stranger. Jimmy" (that's one of the children), "run and tell Lize to put on another plate for dinner."

Everybody made a rush for the front door, because, of course, a stranger don't come *every* year, and so he lays over the yaller fever, for interest, when he does come. Tom was over the stile and starting for the house; the wagon was spinning up the road for the village, and we was all bunched in the front door. Tom had his store clothes on, and an audience—and that was always nuts for Tom Sawyer. In them circumstances it warn't no trouble to him to throw in an amount of style that was suitable. He warn't a boy to meeky along up that yard like a sheep; no, he come ca'm and important, like the ram. When he got afront of us, he lifts his hat ever so gracious and dainty, like it was the lid of a box that had butterflies asleep in it and he didn't want to disturb them, and says:

"Mr. Archibald Nichols, I presume?"

"No, my boy," says the old gentleman, "I'm sorry to say 't your driver has deceived you; Nichols's place is down a matter of three mile more. Come in, come in."

Tom he took a look back over his shoulder, and says, "Too late—he's out of sight."

"Yes, he's gone, my son, and you must come in and eat your dinner with us; and then we'll hitch up and take you down to Nichols's."

"Oh, I *can't* make you so much trouble; I couldn't think of it. I'll walk—I don't mind the distance."

"But we won't *let* you walk—it wouldn't be Southern hospitality to do it. Come right in."

"Oh, *do*," says Aunt Sally; "it ain't a bit of trouble to us, not a bit in the world. You *must* stay. It's a long, dusty three mile, and we *can't* let you walk. And besides, I've already told 'em to put on another plate, when I see you coming; so you mustn't disappoint us. Come right in, and make yourself at home."

So Tom he thanked them very hearty and handsome, and let himself be persuaded, and come in; and when he was in, he said he was a stranger from Hicksville, Ohio, and his name was William Thompson—and he made another bow.

Well, he run on, and on, and on, making up stuff about Hicksville and everybody in it he could invent, and I getting a little nervous, and wondering how this was going to help me out of my scrape; and at last, still talking along, he reached over and kissed Aunt Sally right on the mouth, and then settled back again in his chair, comfortable, and was going on talking; but she jumped up and wiped it off with the back of her hand, and says:

"You owdacious puppy!"

He looked kind of hurt, and says:

"I'm surprised at you, m'am."

"You're s'rp— Why, what do you reckon *I* am? I've a good notion to take and—say, what do you mean by kissing me?"

He looked kind of humble, and says:

"I didn't mean nothing, m'am. I didn't mean no harm. I—I— thought you'd like it."

"Why, you born fool!" She took up the spinning-stick, and it looked like it was all she could do to keep from giving him a crack with it. "What made you think I'd like it?"

"Well, I don't know. Only, they—they—told me you would."

"*They* told you I would. Whoever told you's *another* lunatic. I never heard the beat of it. Who's *they?*"

"Why—everybody. They all said so, m'am."

It was all she could do to hold in; and her eyes snapped, and her fingers worked like she wanted to scratch him; and she says:

"Who's 'everybody?' Out with their names—or ther'll be an idiot short."

He got up and looked distressed, and fumbled his hat, and says:

"I'm sorry, and I warn't expecting it. They told me to. They all told me to. They all said kiss her; and said she'll like it. They all said it—every one of them. But I'm sorry, m'am, and I won't do it no more—I won't, honest."

"You won't, won't you? Well, I sh'd *reckon* you won't!"

"No'm, I'm honest about it; I won't ever do it again. Till you ask me."

"Till I *ask* you! Well, I never see the beat of it in my born days! I lay you'll be the Methusalem-numskull of creation before ever *I* ask you—or the likes of you."

"Well," he says, "it does surprise me so. I can't make it out, somehow. They said you would, and I thought you would. But—" He stopped and looked around slow, like he wished he could run across a friendly eye, somewhere's; and fetched up on the old gentleman's, and says, "Didn't *you* think she'd like me to kiss her, sir?"

"Why, no, I—I—well, no, I b'lieve I didn't."

Then he looks on around, the same way, to me—and says:

"Tom, didn't *you* think Aunt Sally 'd open out her arms and say, 'Sid Sawyer—' "

"My land!" she says, breaking in and jumping for him, "you impudent young rascal, to fool a body so—" and was going to hug him, but he fended her off, and says:

"No, not till you've asked me, first."

So she didn't lose no time, but asked him; and hugged him and kissed him, over and over again, and then turned him over to the old man, and he took what was left. And after they got a little quiet again, she says:

"Why, dear me, I never see such a surprise. We warn't looking for *you*, at all, but only Tom. Sis never wrote to me about anybody coming but him."

"It's because it warn't *intended* for any of us to come but Tom," he says; "but I begged and begged, and at the last minute she let me come, too; so, coming down the river, me and Tom thought it would be a first-rate surprise for him to come here to the house first, and for me to by-and-by tag along and drop in and let on to be a stranger. But it was a mistake, Aunt Sally. This ain't no healthy place for a stranger to come."

"No—not impudent whelps, Sid. You ought to had your jaws boxed; I hain't been so put out since I don't know when. But I don't care, I don't mind the terms—I'd be willing to stand a thousand such jokes to have you here. Well, to think of that performance! I don't deny it, I was most putrified with astonishment when you give me that smack."

We had dinner out in that broad open passage betwixt the house and the kitchen; and there was things enough on that table for seven families—and all hot, too; none of your flabby tough meat that's laid in a cupboard in a damp cellar all night and tastes like a hunk of old cold cannibal in the morning. Uncle Silas he asked a pretty long blessing over it, but it was worth it; and it didn't cool it a bit, neither, the way I've seen them kind of interruptions do, lots of times.

There was a considerable good deal of talk, all the afternoon, and me and Tom was on the lookout all the time, but it warn't no use, they didn't happen to say nothing about any runaway nigger, and we was afraid to try to work up to it. But at supper, at night, one of the little boys says:

"Pa, mayn't Tom and Sid and me go to the show?"

"No," says the old man, "I reckon there ain't going to be any; and you couldn't go if there was; because the runaway nigger told Burton and me all about that scandalous show, and Burton said he would tell the people; so I reckon they've drove the owdacious loafers out of town before this time."

So there it was!—but *I* couldn't help it. Tom and me was to sleep in the same room and bed; so, being tired, we bid good-night and went up to bed, right after supper, and clumb out of the window and down the lightning-rod, and shoved for the town; for I didn't believe anybody was going to give the king and the duke a hint, and so, if I didn't hurry up and give them one they'd get into trouble sure.

On the road Tom he told me all about how it was reckoned I was murdered, and how pap disappeared, pretty soon, and didn't come back no more, and what a stir there was when Jim run away; and I told Tom all about our Royal Nonesuch rapscallions, and as much of the raft-voyage as I had time to; and as we struck into the town and up through the middle of it—it was as much as half-after eight, then—here comes a raging rush of people, with torches, and an awful whooping and yelling, and banging tin pans and blowing horns; and we jumped to one side to let them go by; and as they went by, I see they had the king and the duke astraddle of a rail—that is, I knowed it *was* the king and the duke, though they was all over tar and feathers, and didn't look like nothing in the world that was human—just looked like a couple of monstrous big soldier-plumes. Well, it made me sick to see it; and I was sorry for them poor pitiful rascals, it seemed like I couldn't ever feel any hardness against them any more in the world. It was a dreadful thing to see. Human beings *can* be awful cruel to one another.

We see we was too late—couldn't do no good. We asked some stragglers about it, and they said everybody went to the show looking very innocent; and laid low and kept dark till the poor old king was in the middle of his cavortings on the stage; then somebody give a signal, and the house rose up and went for them.

So we poked along back home, and I warn't feeling so brash as I was before, but kind of ornery, and humble, and to blame, somehow—though *I* hadn't done nothing. But that's always the way; it don't make no difference whether you do right or wrong, a person's conscience ain't got no sense, and just goes for him *anyway*. If I had a yaller dog that didn't know no more than a person's conscience does, I would pison him. It takes up more room than all the rest of a person's insides, and yet ain't no good, nohow. Tom Sawyer he says the same.

Chapter XXXIV

We stopped talking, and got to thinking. By-and-by Tom says:

"Looky here, Huck, what fools we are, to not think of it before! I bet I know where Jim is."

"No! Where?"

"In that hut down by the ash-hopper. Why, looky here. When we was at dinner, didn't you see a nigger man go in there with some vittles?"

"Yes."

"What did you think the vittles was for?"

"For a dog."

"So'd I. Well, it wasn't for a dog."

"Why?"

"Because part of it was watermelon."

"So it was—I noticed it. Well, it does beat all, that I never thought about a dog not eating watermelon. It shows how a body can see and don't see at the same time."

"Well, the nigger unlocked the padlock when he went in, and he locked it again when he come out. He fetched uncle a key, about the time we got up from table—same key, I bet. Watermelon shows man, lock shows prisoner; and it ain't likely there's two prisoners on such a little plantation, and where the people's all so kind and good. Jim's the prisoner. All right—I'm glad we found it out detective fashion; I wouldn't give shucks for any other way. Now you work your mind and study out a plan to steal Jim, and I will study out one, too; and we'll take the one we like the best."

What a head for just a boy to have! If I had Tom Sawyer's head, I wouldn't trade it off to be a duke, nor mate of a steamboat, nor clown in a circus, nor nothing I can think of. I went to thinking out a plan, but only just to be doing something; I knowed very well where the right plan was going to come from. Pretty soon, Tom says:

"Ready?"

"Yes," I says.

"All right—bring it out."

"My plan is this," I says. "We can easy find out if it's Jim in there. Then get up my canoe to-morrow night, and fetch my raft over from the island. Then the first dark night that comes, steal the key out of the old man's britches, after he goes to bed, and shove off down the river on the raft, with Jim, hiding daytimes and running nights, the way me and Jim used to do before. Wouldn't that plan work?"

"*Work?* Why cert'nly, it would work, like rats a fighting. But it's too blame' simple; there ain't nothing *to* it. What's the good of a plan that ain't no more trouble than that? It's as mild as goose-milk. Why, Huck, it wouldn't make no more talk than breaking into a soap factory."

I never said nothing, because I warn't expecting nothing different; but I knowed mighty well that whenever he got *his* plan ready it wouldn't have none of them objections to it.

And it didn't. He told me what it was, and I see in a minute it was worth fifteen of mine, for style, and would make Jim just as free a man as mine would, and maybe get us all killed besides. So I was satisfied, and said we would waltz in on it. I needn't tell what it was, here, because I knowed it wouldn't stay the way it was. I knowed he would be changing it around, every which way, as we went along, and heaving in new bullinesses wherever he got a chance. And that is what he done.

Well, one thing was dead sure; and that was, that Tom Sawyer was in earnest and was actuly going to help steal that nigger out of slavery. That was the thing that was too many for me. Here was a boy that was respectable, and well brung up; and had a character to lose; and folks at home that had characters; and he was bright and not leather-headed; and knowing and not ignorant; and not mean, but kind; and yet here he was, without any more pride, or rightness, or feeling, than to stoop to this business, and make himself a shame, and his family a shame, before everybody. I *couldn't* understand it, no way at all. It was outrageous, and I knowed I ought to just up and tell him so; and so be his true friend, and let him quit the thing right where he was, and save himself. And I *did* start to tell him; but he shut me up, and says:

"Don't you reckon I know what I'm about? Don't I generly know what I'm about?"

"Yes."

"Didn't I *say* I was going to help steal the nigger?"

"Yes."

"*Well* then."

That's all he said, and that's all I said. It warn't no use to say any more; because when he said he'd do a thing, he always done it. But *I* couldn't make out how he was willing to go into this thing; so I just let it go, and never bothered no more about it. If he was bound to have it so, *I* couldn't help it.

When we got home, the house was all dark and still; so we went on down to the hut by the ash-hopper, for to examine it. We went through the yard, so as to see what the hounds would do. They knowed us, and didn't make no more noise than country dogs is always doing when anything comes by in the night. When we got to the cabin, we took a look at the front and the two sides; and on the side I warn't acquainted with—which was the north side—we found a square window-hole, up tolerable high, with just one stout board nailed across it. I says:

"Here's the ticket. This hole's big enough for Jim to get through, if we wrench off the board."

Tom says:

"It's as simple as tit-tat-toe, three-in-a-row, and as easy as playing hooky. I should *hope* we can find a way that's a little more complicated than *that*, Huck Finn."

"Well then," I says, "how'll it do to saw him out, the way I done before I was murdered, that time?"

"That's more *like*," he says. "It's real mysterious, and troublesome, and good," he says; "but I bet we can find a way that's twice as long. There ain't no hurry; le's keep on looking around."

Betwixt the hut and the fence, on the back side, was a lean-to, that joined the hut at the eaves, and was made out of plank. It was as long as the hut, but narrow—only about six foot wide. The door to it was at the south end, and was padlocked. Tom he went to the soap kettle, and searched around and fetched back the iron thing they lift the lid with; so he took it and prized out one of the staples. The chain fell down, and we opened the door and went in, and shut it, and struck a match, and see the shed was only built against the cabin and hadn't no connection with it; and there warn't no floor to the shed, nor nothing in it but some old rusty played-out hoes, and spades, and picks, and a crippled plow. The match went out, and so did we, and shoved in the staple again, and the door was locked as good as ever. Tom was joyful. He says:

"Now we're all right. We'll *dig* him out. It'll take about a week!"

Then we started for the house, and I went in the back door—you only have to pull a buckskin latch-string, they don't fasten the doors—but that warn't romantical enough for Tom Sawyer: no way would do him but he must climb up the lightning-rod. But after he got up half-way about three times, and missed fire and fell every time, and the last time most busted his brains out, he thought he'd got to give it up; but after he was rested, he allowed he would give her one more turn for luck, and this time he made the trip.

In the morning we was up at break of day, and down to the nigger cabins to pet the dogs and make friends with the nigger that fed Jim—if it *was* Jim that was being fed. The niggers was just getting through breakfast and starting for the fields; and Jim's nigger was piling up a tin pan with bread and meat and things; and whilst the others was leaving, the key come from the house.

This nigger had a good-natured, chuckle-headed face, and his wool was all tied up in little bunches with thread. That was to keep witches off. He said the witches was pestering him awful, these nights, and making him see all kinds of strange things, and hear all kinds of strange words and noises, and he didn't believe he was ever witched so long, before, in his life. He got so worked up, and got to running[2] on so about his troubles, he forgot all about what he'd been agoing to do. So Tom says:

"What's the vittles for? Going to feed the dogs?"

The nigger kind of smiled around graduly over his face, like when you heave a brickbat in a mud puddle, and he says:

"Yes, Mars Sid, *a* dog. Cur'us dog, too. Does you want to go en look at 'im?"

"Yes."

I hunched Tom, and whispers:

"You going, right here in the day-break? *That* warn't the plan."

"No, it warn't—but it's the plan *now*."

So, drat him, we went along, but I didn't like it much. When we got in, we couldn't hardly see anything, it was so dark; but Jim was there, sure enough, and could see us; and he sings out:

"Why, *Huck!* En good *lan'!* ain' dat Misto Tom?"

I just knowed how it would be; I just expected it. *I* didn't know nothing to do; and if I had, I couldn't a done it; because that nigger busted in and says:

"Why, de gracious sakes! do he know you genlmen?"

We could see pretty well, now. Tom he looked at the nigger, steady and kind of wondering, and says:

"Does *who* know us?"

"Why, dish-yer runaway nigger."

"I don't reckon he does; but what put that into your head?"

"What *put* it dar? Didn' he jis' dis minute sing out like he knowed you?"

Tom says, in a puzzled-up kind of way:

"Well, that's mighty curious. *Who* sung out? *When* did he sing out. *What* did he sing out?" And turns to me, perfectly ca'm, and says, "Did *you* hear anybody sing out?"

Of course there warn't nothing to be said but the one thing; so I says:

"No; *I* ain't heard nobody say nothing."

Then he turns to Jim, and looks him over like he never see him before; and says:

"Did you sing out?"

"No, sah," says Jim; "*I* hain't said nothing, sah."

"Not a word?"

"No, sah, I hain't said a word."

"Did you ever see us before?"

"No, sah; not as *I* knows on."

---

2. Erroneously printed "runinng" in the first edition.

So Tom turns to the nigger, which was looking wild and distressed, and says, kind of severe:

"What do you reckon's the matter with you, anyway? What made you think somebody sung out?"

"Oh, it's de dad-blame' witches, sah, en I wisht I was dead, I do. Dey's awluz at it, sah, en dey do mos' kill me, dey sk'yers me so. Please to don't tell nobody 'bout it sah, er ole Mars Silas he'll scole me; 'kase he say dey *ain't* no witches. I jis' wish to goodness he was heah now—*den* what would he say! I jis' bet he couldn' fine no way to git aroun' it *dis* time. But it's awluz jis' so; people dat's *sot*, stays sot; dey won't look into nothn' en fine it out f'r deyselves, en when *you* fine it out en tell um 'bout it, dey doan' b'lieve you."

Tom give him a dime, and said we wouldn't tell nobody; and told him to buy some more thread to tie up his wool with; and then looks at Jim, and says:

"I wonder if Uncle Silas is going to hang this nigger. If I was to catch a nigger that was ungrateful enough to run away, *I* wouldn't give him up, I'd hang him." And whilst the nigger stepped to the door to look at the dime and bite it to see if it was good, he whispers to Jim, and says:

"Don't ever let on to know us. And if you hear any digging going on nights, it's us: we're going to set you free."

Jim only had time to grab us by the hand and squeeze it, then the nigger come back, and we said we'd come again some time if the nigger wanted us to; and he said he would, more particular if it was dark, because the witches went for him mostly in the dark, and it was good to have folks around then.

Chapter XXXV

It would be most an hour, yet, till breakfast, so we left, and struck down into the woods; because Tom said we got to have *some* light to see how to dig by, and a lantern makes too much, and might get us into trouble; what we must have was a lot of them rotten chunks that's called fox-fire[3] and just makes a soft kind of a glow when you lay them in a dark place. We fetched an armful and hid it in the weeds, and set down to rest, and Tom says, kind of dissatisfied:

"Blame it, this whole thing is just as easy and awkard as it can be. And so it makes it so rotten difficult to get up a difficult plan. There ain't no watchman to be drugged—now there *ought* to be a watchman. There ain't even a dog to give a sleeping-mixture to. And there's Jim chained by one leg, with a ten-foot chain, to the leg of his bed: why, all you got to do is to lift up the bedstead and

3. Phosphorescent glow from decaying wood.

slip off the chain. And Uncle Silas he trusts everybody; sends the key to the punkin-headed nigger, and don't send nobody to watch the nigger. Jim could a got out of that window hole before this, only there wouldn't be no use trying to travel with a ten-foot chain on his leg. Why, drat it, Huck, it's the stupidest arrangement I ever see. You got to invent *all* the difficulties. Well, we can't help it, we got to do the best we can with the materials we've got. Anyhow, there's one thing—there's more honor in getting him out through a lot of difficulties and dangers, where there warn't one of them furnished to you by the people who it was their duty to furnish them, and you had to contrive them all out of your own head. Now look at just that one thing of the lantern. When you come down to the cold facts, we simply got to *let on* that a lantern's resky. Why, we could work with a torchlight procession if we wanted to, *I* believe. Now, whilst I think of it, we got to hunt up something to make a saw out of, the first chance we get."

"What do we want of a saw?"

"What do we *want* of it? Hain't we got to saw the leg of Jim's bed off, so as to get the chain loose?"

"Why, you just said a body could lift up the bedstead and slip the chain off."

"Well, if that ain't just like you, Huck Finn. You *can* get up the infant-schooliest ways of going at a thing. Why, hain't you ever read any books at all?—Baron Trenck,[4] nor Casanova, nor Benvenuto Chelleeny, nor Henri IV., nor none of them heroes? Whoever heard of getting a prisoner loose in such an old-maidy way as that? No; the way all the best authorities does, is to saw the bed-leg in two, and leave it just so, and swallow the sawdust, so it can't be found, and put some dirt and grease around the sawed place so the very keenest seneskal can't see no sign of it's being sawed, and thinks the bed-leg is perfectly sound. Then, the night you're ready, fetch the leg a kick, down she goes; slip off your chain, and there you are. Nothing to do but hitch your rope-ladder to the battlements, shin down it, break your leg in the moat—because a rope-ladder is nineteen foot too short, you know—and there's your horses and your trusty vassles, and they scoop you up and fling you across a saddle and away you go, to your native Langudoc, or Navarre, or wherever it is. It's gaudy, Huck. I wish there was a moat to this cabin. If we get time, the night of the escape, we'll dig one."

I says:

"What do we want of a moat, when we're going to snake him out from under the cabin?"

4. ·All four of these—Baron Friedrich von Trenck, officer of Frederick the Great's staff; Benvenuto Cellini, the brilliant and politically-minded sculptor; Giacomo Girolamo Casanova, the famous Italian lover and adventurer; and King Henry IV of France—made daring attempted or successful escapes. "Langudoc," below, is Tom's pronunciation of Languedoc.

But he never heard me. He had forgot me and everything else. He had his chin in his hand, thinking. Pretty soon, he sighs, and shakes his head; then sighs again, and says:

"No, it wouldn't do—there ain't necessity enough for it."

"For what?" I says.

"Why, to saw Jim's leg off," he says.

"Good land!" I says, "why, there ain't *no* necessity for it. And what would you want to saw his leg off for, anyway?"

"Well, some of the best authorities has done it. They couldn't get the chain off, so they just cut their hand off, and shoved. And a leg would be better still. But we got to let that go. There ain't necessity enough in this case; and besides, Jim's a nigger and wouldn't understand the reasons for it, and how it's the custom in Europe; so we'll let it go. But there's one thing—he can have a rope-ladder; we can tear up our sheets and make him a rope-ladder easy enough. And we can send it to him in a pie; it's mostly done that way. And I've et worse pies."

"Why, Tom Sawyer, how you talk," I says; "Jim ain't got no use for a rope-ladder."

"He *has* got use for it. How *you* talk, you better say; you don't know nothing about it. He's *got* to have a rope ladder; they all do."

"What in the nation can he *do* with it?"

"*Do* with it? He can hide it in his bed, can't he? That's what they all do; and *he's* got to, too. Huck, you don't ever seem to want to do anything that's regular; you want to be starting something fresh all the time. Spose he *don't* do nothing with it? ain't it there in his bed, for a clew, after he's gone? and don't you reckon they'll want clews? Of course they will. And you wouldn't leave them any? That would be a *pretty* howdy-do, *wouldn't* it! I never heard of such a thing."

"Well," I says, "if it's in the regulations, and he's got to have it, all right, let him have it; because I don't wish to go back on no regulations; but there's one thing, Tom Sawyer—if we go to tearing up our sheets to make Jim a rope-ladder, we're going to get into trouble with Aunt Sally, just as sure as you're born. Now, the way I look at it, a hickry-bark ladder don't cost nothing, and don't waste nothing, and is just as good to load up a pie with, and hide in a straw tick, as any rag ladder you can start; and as for Jim, he ain't had no experience, and so *he* don't care what kind of a—"

"Oh, shucks, Huck Finn, if I was as ignorant as you, I'd keep still—that's what *I'd* do. Who ever heard of a state prisoner escaping by a hickry-bark ladder? Why, it's perfectly ridiculous."

"Well, all right, Tom, fix it your own way; but if you'll take my advice, you'll let me borrow a sheet off of the clothes-line."

He said that would do. And that give him another idea, and he says:

"Borrow a shirt, too."

"What do we want of a shirt, Tom?"

"Want it for Jim to keep a journal on."

"Journal your granny—*Jim* can't write."

"Spose he *can't* write—he can make marks on the shirt, can't he, if we make him a pen out of an old pewter spoon or a piece of an old iron barrel-hoop?"

"Why, Tom, we can pull a feather out of a goose and make him a better one; and quicker, too."

"*Prisoners* don't have geese running around the donjon-keep to pull pens out of, you muggins. They *always* make their pens out of the hardest, toughest, troublesomest piece of old brass candlestick or something like that they can get their hands on; and it takes them weeks and weeks, and months and months to file it out, too, because they've got to do it by rubbing it on the wall. *They* wouldn't use a goose-quill if they had it. It ain't regular."

"Well, then, what'll we make him the ink out of?"

"Many makes it out of iron-rust and tears; but that's the common sort and women; the best authorities uses their own blood. Jim can do that; and when he wants to send any little common ordinary mysterious message to let the world know where he's captivated, he can write it on the bottom of a tin plate with a fork and throw it out of the window. The Iron Mask[5] always done that, and it's a blame' good way, too."

"Jim ain't got no tin plates. They feed him in a pan."

"That aint' anything; we can get him some."

"Can't nobody *read* his plates."

"That ain't got nothing to *do* with it, Huck Finn. All *he's* got to do is to write on the plate and throw it out. You don't *have* to be able to read it. Why, half the time you can't read anything a prisoner writes on a tin plate, or anywhere else."

"Well, then, what's the sense in wasting the plates?"

"Why, blame it all, it ain't the *prisoner's* plates."

"But it's *somebody's* plates, ain't it?"

"Well, spos'n it is? What does the *prisoner* care whose—"

He broke off there, because we heard the breakfast-horn blowing. So we cleared out for the house.

Along during that morning I borrowed a sheet and a white shirt off of the clothes-line; and I found an old sack and put them in it, and we went down and got the fox-fire, and put that in too. I called it borrowing, because that was what pap always called it; but Tom said it warn't borrowing, it was stealing. He said we was representing prisoners; and prisoners don't care how they get a thing so they get it, and nobody don't blame them for it, either. It ain't no

5. Another source of Tom's romantic maunderings: the subject of Alexandre Dumas' novel *Vicomte de Bragelonne.* the mysterious masked prisoner who died unknown in the Bastille in 1703.

crime in a prisoner to steal the thing he needs to get away with, Tom said; it's his right; and so, as long as we was representing a prisoner, we had a perfect right to steal anything on this place we had the least use for, to get ourselves out of prison with. He said if we warn't prisoners it would be a very different thing, and nobody but a mean ornery person would steal when he warn't a prisoner. So we allowed we would steal everything there was that come handy. And yet he made a mighty fuss, one day, after that, when I stole a watermelon out of the nigger patch and eat it; and he made me go and give the niggers a dime, without telling them what it was for. Tom said that what he meant was, we could steal anything we *needed*. Well, I says, I needed the watermelon. But he said I didn't need it to get out of prison with, there's where the difference was. He said if I'd a wanted it to hide a knife in, and smuggle it to Jim to kill the seneskal with, it would a been all right. So I let it go at that, though I couldn't see no advantage in my representing a prisoner, if I got to set down and chaw over a lot of gold-leaf distinctions like that, every time I see a chance to hog a watermelon.

Well, as I was saying, we waited that morning till everybody was settled down to business, and nobody in sight around the yard; then Tom he carried the sack into the lean-to whilst I stood off a piece to keep watch. By-and-by he come out, and we went and set down on the wood-pile, to talk. He says:

"Everything's all right, now, except tools; and that's easy fixed."

"Tools?" I says.

"Yes."

"Tools for what?"

"Why, to dig with. We ain't agoing to *gnaw* him out, are we?"

"Ain't them old crippled picks and things in there good enough to dig a nigger out with?" I says.

He turns on me looking pitying enough to make a body cry, and says:

"Huck Finn, did you *ever* hear of a prisoner having picks and shovels, and all the modern conveniences in his wardrobe to dig himself out with? Now I want to ask you—if you got any reasonableness in you at all—what kind of a show would *that* give him to be a hero? Why, they might as well lend him the key, and done with it. Picks and shovels—why they wouldn't furnish 'em to a king."

"Well, then," I says, "if we don't want the picks and shovels, what do we want?"

"A couple of case-knives."

"To dig the foundations out from under that cabin with?"

"Yes."

"Confound it, it's foolish, Tom."

"It don't make no difference how foolish it is, it's the *right* way
—and it's the regular way. And there ain't no *other* way, that ever
I heard of, and I've read all the books that gives any information
about these things. They always dig out with a case-knife—and not
through dirt, mind you; generly it's through solid rock. And it takes
them weeks and weeks and weeks, and for ever and ever. Why, look
at one of them prisoners in the bottom dungeon of the Castle Deef,
in the harbor of Marseilles, that dug himself out that way; how
long was *he* at it, you reckon?"[6]

"I don't know."

"Well, guess."

"I don't know. A month and a half?"

"*Thirty-seven year*—and he come out in China. *That's* the kind.
I wish the bottom of *this* fortress was solid rock."

"*Jim* don't know nobody in China."

"What's *that* got to do with it? Neither did that other fellow.
But you're always a-wandering off on a side issue. Why can't you
stick to the main point?"

"All right—*I* don't care where he comes out, so he *comes* out;
and Jim don't, either, I reckon. But there's one thing, anyway—
Jim's too old to be dug out with a case-knife. He won't last."

"Yes he will *last*, too. You don't reckon it's going to take thirty-
seven years to dig out through a *dirt* foundation, do you?"

"How long will it take, Tom?"

"Well, we can't resk being as long as we ought to, because it
mayn't take very long for Uncle Silas to hear from down there by
New Orleans. He'll hear Jim ain't from there. Then his next move
will be to advertise Jim, or something like that. So we can't resk
being as long digging him out as we ought to. By rights I reckon
we ought to be a couple of years; but we can't. Things being so
uncertain, what I recommend is this: that we really dig right in,
as quick as we can; and after that, we can *let on*, to ourselves, that
we was at it thirty-seven years. Then we can snatch him out and rush
him away the first time there's an alarm. Yes, I reckon that'll be
the best way."

"Now, there's *sense* in that," I says. "Letting on don't cost nothing; letting on ain't no trouble; and if it's any object, I don't mind
letting on we was at it a hundred and fifty year. It wouldn't strain
me none, after I got my hand in. So I'll mosey along now, and
smouch a couple of case-knives."

"Smouch three," he says; "we want one to make a saw out of."

"Tom, if it ain't unregular and irreligious to sejest it," I says,
"there's an old rusty saw-blade around yonder sticking under the
weatherboarding behind the smoke-house."

6. The Dumas influence on Tom again—this time, the hero of *The Count of
Monte Cristo* at the Chateau d'If.

He looked kind of weary and discouraged-like, and says:

"It ain't no use to try to learn you nothing, Huck. Run along and smouch the knives—three of them." So I done it.

Chapter XXXVI

As soon as we reckoned everybody was asleep, that night, we went down the lightning-rod, and shut ourselves up in the lean-to, and got out our pile of fox-fire, and went to work. We cleared everything out of the way, about four or five foot along the middle of the bottom log. Tom said he was right behind Jim's bed now, and we'd dig in under it, and when we got through there couldn't nobody in the cabin ever know there was any hole there, because Jim's counterpin hung down most to the ground, and you'd have to raise it up and look under to see the hole. So we dug and dug, with the case-knives, till most midnight; and then we was dog-tired, and our hands was blistered, and yet you couldn't see we'd done anything, hardly. At last I says:

"This ain't no thirty-seven year job, this is a thirty-eight year job, Tom Sawyer."

He never said nothing. But he sighed, and pretty soon he stopped digging, and then for a good little while I knowed he was thinking. Then he says:

"It ain't no use, Huck, it ain't agoing to work. If we was prisoners it would, because then we'd have as many years as we wanted, and no hurry; and we wouldn't get but a few minutes to dig, every day, while they was changing watches, and so our hands wouldn't get blistered, and we could keep it up right along, year in and year out, and do it right, and the way it ought to be done. But *we* can't fool along, we got to rush; we ain't got no time to spare. If we was to put in another night this way, we'd have to knock off for a week to let our hands get well—couldn't touch a case-knife with them sooner."

"Well, then, what we going to do, Tom?"

"I'll tell you. It ain't right, and it ain't moral, and I wouldn't like it to get out—but there ain't only just the one way; we got to dig him out with the picks, and *let on* its's case-knives."

"*Now* you're *talking!*" I says; "your head gets leveler and leveler all the time, Tom Sawyer," I says. "Picks is the thing, moral or no moral; and as for me, I don't care shucks for the morality of it, nohow. When I start in to steal a nigger, or a watermelon, or a Sunday-school book, I ain't no ways particular how it's done so it's done. What I want is my nigger; or what I want is my watermelon; or what I want is my Sunday-school book; and if a pick's the handiest thing, that's the thing I'm agoing to dig that nigger or that watermelon or that Sunday-school book out with; and I don't give a dead rat what the authorities thinks about it nuther."

"Well," he says, "there's excuse for picks and letting-on in a case like this; if it warn't so, I wouldn't approve of it, nor I wouldn't stand by and see the rules broke—because right is right, and wrong is wrong, and a body ain't got no business doing wrong when he ain't ignorant and knows better. It might answer for *you* to dig Jim out with a pick, *without* any letting-on, because you don't know no better; but it wouldn't for me, because I do know better. Gimme a case-knife."

He had his own by him, but I handed him mine. He flung it down, and says:

"Gimme a *case-knife*."

I didn't know just what to do—but then I thought. I scratched around amongst the old tools, and got a pick-ax and give it to him, and he took it and went to work, and never said a word.

He was always just that particular. Full of principle.

So then I got a shovel, and then we picked and shoveled, turn about, and made the fur fly. We stuck to it about a half an hour, which was as long as we could stand up; but we had a good deal of a hole to show for it. When I got up stairs, I looked out at the window and see Tom doing his level best with the lightning-rod, but he couldn't come it, his hands was so sore. At last he says:

"It ain't no use, it can't be done. What you reckon I better do? Can't you think up no way?"

"Yes," I says, "but I reckon it ain't regular. Come up the stairs, and let on it's a lightning-rod."

So he done it.

Next day Tom stole a pewter spoon and a brass candlestick in the house, for to make some pens for Jim out of, and six tallow candles; and I hung around the nigger cabins, and laid for a chance, and stole three tin plates. Tom said it wasn't enough; but I said nobody wouldn't ever see the plates that Jim throwed out, because they'd fall in the dog-fennel and jimpson weeds under the window-hole—then we could tote them back and he could use them over again. So Tom was satisfied. Then he says:

"Now, the thing to study out is, how to get the things to Jim."

"Take them in through the hole," I says, "when we get it done."

He only just looked scornful, and said something about nobody ever heard of such an idiotic idea, and then he went to studying. By-and-by he said he had ciphered out two or three ways, but there warn't no need to decide on any of them yet. Said we'd got to post Jim first.

That night we went down the lightning-rod a little after ten, and took one of the candles along, and listened under the window-hole, and heard Jim snoring; so we pitched it in, and it didn't wake him. Then we whirled in with the pick and shovel, and in about two hours and a half the job was done. We crept in under Jim's bed and into the cabin, and pawed around and found the candle and lit it, and stood over Jim a while, and found him looking hearty and healthy, and then we woke him up gentle and gradual. He was so glad to see us he most cried; and called us honey, and all the pet names he could think of; and was for having us hunt up a cold chisel to cut the chain off of his leg with, right away, and clearing out without losing any time. But Tom he showed him how unregular it would be, and set down and told him all about our plans, and how we could alter them in a minute any time there was an alarm; and not to be the least afraid, because we would see he got away, *sure*. So Jim he said it was all right, and we set there and talked over old times a while, and then Tom asked a lot of questions, and when Jim told him Uncle Silas come in every day or two to pray with him, and Aunt Sally come in to see if he was comfortable and had plenty to eat, and both of them was kind as they could be, Tom says:

"*Now* I know how to fix it. We'll send you some things by them."

I said, "Don't do nothing of the kind; it's one of the most jackass ideas I ever struck;" but he never paid no attention to me; went right on. It was his way when he'd got his plans set.

So he told Jim how we'd have to smuggle in the rope-ladder pie, and other large things, by Nat, the nigger that fed him, and he must be on the lookout, and not be surprised, and not let Nat see him open them; and we would put small things in uncle's coat pockets and he must steal them out; and we would tie things to aunt's apron strings or put them in her apron pocket, if we got a chance; and told him what they would be and what they was for. And told him how to keep a journal on the shirt with his blood, and all that. He told him everything. Jim he couldn't see no sense in the most of it, but he allowed we was white folks and knowed better than him; so he was satisfied, and said he would do it all just as Tom said.

Jim had plenty corn-cob pipes and tobacco; so we had a right down good sociable time; then we crawled out through the hole, and so home to bed, with hands that looked like they'd been chawed. Tom was in high spirits. He said it was the best fun he ever had in his life, and the most intellectural; and said if he only could see his way to it we would keep it up all the rest of our lives and leave Jim to our children to get out; for he believed Jim would come to like it better and better the more he got used to it. He said that in that way it could be strung out to as much as eighty year, and would be the best time on record. And he said it would make us all celebrated that had a hand in it.

In the morning we went out to the wood-pile and chopped up the brass candlestick into handy sizes, and Tom put them and the pewter spoon in his pocket. Then we went to the nigger cabins, and while I got Nat's notice off, Tom shoved a piece of candlestick into the middle of a corn-pone that was in Jim's pan, and we went along with Nat to see how it would work, and it just worked noble; when Jim bit into it it most mashed all his teeth out; and there warn't ever anything could a worked better. Tom said so himself. Jim he never let on but what it was only just a piece of rock or something like that that's always getting into bread, you know; but after that he never bit into nothing but what he jabbed his fork into it in three or four places, first.

And whilst we was a standing there in the dimmish light, here comes a couple of the hounds bulging in, from under Jim's bed; and they kept on piling in till there was eleven of them, and there warn't hardly room in there to get your breath. By jings, we forgot to fasten that lean-to door. The nigger Nat he only just hollered "witches!" once, and keeled over onto the floor amongst the dogs, and begun to groan like he was dying. Tom jerked the door open and flung out a slab of Jim's meat, and the dogs went for it, and in two seconds he was out himself and back again and shut the door, and I knowed he'd fixed the other door too. Then he went to work on the nigger, coaxing him and petting him, and asking him if he'd been imagining he saw something again. He raised up, and blinked his eyes around, and says:

"Mars Sid, you'll say I's a fool, but if I didn't b'lieve I see most a million dogs, er devils, er some'n, I wisht I may die right heah in dese tracks. I did, mos' sholy. Mars Sid, I *felt* um—I *felt* um, sah; dey was all over me. Dad fetch it, I jis' wisht I could git my han's on one er dem witches jis' wunst—on'y jis' wunst—it's all I'd ast. But mos'ly I wisht dey'd lemme 'lone, I does."

Tom says:

"Well, I tell you what *I* think. What makes them come here just at this runaway nigger's breakfast-time? It's because they're hungry; that's the reason. You make them a witch pie; that's the thing for *you* to do."

"But my lan', Mars Sid, how's *I* gwyne to make 'm a witch pie? I doan' know how to make it. I hain't ever hearn er sich a thing b'fo.' "

"Well, then, I'll have to make it myself."

"Will you do it, honey?—will you? I'll wusshup de groun' und' yo' foot, I will!"

"All right, I'll do it, seeing it's you, and you've been good to us and showed us the runaway nigger. But you got to be mighty careful. When we come around, you turn your back; and then whatever we've put in the pan, don't you let on you see it at all. And don't you look, when Jim unloads the pan—something might happen, I don't know what. And above all, don't you *handle* the witch-things."

"*Hannel* 'm Mars Sid? What *is* you a talkin' 'bout? I wouldn' lay de weight er my finger on um, not f'r ten hund'd thous'n' billion dollars, I wouldn't."

Chapter XXXVII

That was all fixed. So then we went away and went to the rubbage-pile in the back yard where they keep the old boots, and rags, and pieces of bottles, and wore-out tin things, and all such truck, and scratched around and found an old tin washpan and stopped up the holes as well as we could, to bake the pie in, and took it down cellar and stole it full of flour, and started for breakfast and found a couple of shingle-nails that Tom said would be handy for a prisoner to scrabble his name and sorrows on the dungeon walls with, and dropped one of them in Aunt Sally's apron pocket which was hanging on a chair, and t'other we stuck in the band of Uncle Silas's hat, which was on the bureau, because we heard the children say their pa and ma was going to the runaway nigger's house this morning, and then went to breakfast, and Tom dropped the pewter spoon in Uncle Silas's coat pocket, and Aunt Sally wasn't come yet, so we had to wait a little while.

And when she come she was hot, and red, and cross, and couldn't hardly wait for the blessing; and then she went to sluicing out coffee with one hand and cracking the handiest child's head with her thimble with the other, and says:

"I've hunted high, and I've hunted low, and it does beat all, what *has* become of your other shirt."

My heart fell down amongst my lungs and livers and things, and a hard piece of corn-crust started down my throat after it and got met on the road with a cough and was shot across the table and took one of the children in the eye and curled him up like a fishing-worm, and let a cry out of him the size of a war-whoop, and Tom he turned kinder blue around the gills, and it all amounted to a considerable state of things for about a quarter of a minute or as much as that, and I would a sold out for half price if there was a bidder. But after that we was all right again—it was the sudden surprise of it that knocked us so kind of cold. Uncle Silas he says:

"It's most uncommon curious, I can't understand it. I know perfectly well I took it *off*, because——"

"Because you hain't got but one *on*. Just *listen* at the man! I know you took it off, and know it by a better way than your wool-gethering memory, too, because it was on the clo'es-line yester-day—I see it there myself. But it's gone—that's the long and the short of it, and you'll just have to change to a red flann'l one till

I can get time to make a new one. And it'll be the third I've made in two years; it just keeps a body on the jump to keep you in shirts; and whatever you do manage to *do* with 'm all, is more'n *I* can make out. A body'd think you *would* learn to take some sort of care of 'em, at your time of life."

"I know it, Sally, and I do try all I can. But it oughtn't to be altogether my fault, because you know I don't see them nor have nothing to do with them except when they're on me; and I don't believe I've ever lost one of them *off* of me."

"Well, it ain't *your* fault if you haven't, Silas—you'd a done it if you could, I reckon. And the shirt ain't all that's gone, nuther. Ther's a spoon gone; and *that* ain't all. There was ten, and now ther's only nine. The calf got the shirt I reckon, but the calf never took the spoon, *that's* certain."

"Why, what else is gone, Sally?"

"Ther's six *candles* gone—that's what. The rats could a got the candles, and I reckon they did; I wonder they don't walk off with the whole place, the way you're always going to stop their holes and don't do it; and if they warn't fools they'd sleep in your hair, Silas—*you'd* never find it out; but you can't lay the *spoon* on the rats, and that I *know.*"

"Well, Sally, I'm in fault, and I acknowledge it; I've been remiss; but I won't let to-morrow go by without stopping up them holes."

"Oh, I wouldn't hurry, next year'll do. Matilda Angelina Araminta *Phelps!*"

Whack comes the thimble, and the child snatches her claws out of the sugar-bowl without fooling around any. Just then, the nigger woman steps onto the passage, and says:

"Missus, dey's a sheet gone."

"A *sheet* gone! Well, for the land's sake!"

"I'll stop up them holes *to-day,*" says Uncle Silas, looking sorrowful.

"Oh, *do* shet up!—spose the rats took the *sheet? Where's* it gone, Lize?"

"Clah to goodness I hain't no notion, Miss Sally. She wuz on de clo's-line yistiddy, but she done gone; she ain' dah no mo', now."

"I reckon the world *is* coming to an end. I *never* see the beat of it, in all my born days. A shirt, and a sheet, and a spoon, and six can—"

"Missus," comes a young yaller wench, "dey's a brass cannelstick miss'n."

"Cler out from here, you hussy, er I'll take a skillet to ye!"

Well, she was just a biling. I begun to lay for a chance; I reckoned I would sneak out and go for the woods till the weather moderated. She kept a raging right along, running her insurrection all by herself, and everybody else mighty meek and quiet; and at last Uncle Silas, looking kind of foolish, fishes up that spoon out of his pocket. She stopped, with her mouth open and her hands up; and as for me, I wished I was in Jeruslem or somewheres. But not long; because she says:

"It's *just* as I expected. So you had it in your pocket all the time; and like as not you've got the other things there, too. How'd it get there?"

"I reely don't know, Sally," he says, kind of apologizing, "or you know I would tell. I was a-studying over my text in Acts Seventeen, before breakfast, and I reckon I put it in there, not noticing, meaning to put my Testament in, and it must be so, because my Testament ain't in, but I'll go and see, and if the Testament is where I had it, I'll know I didn't put it in, and that will show that I laid the Testament down and took up the spoon, and——"

"Oh, for the land's sake! Give a body a rest! Go 'long now, the whole kit and biling of ye; and don't come nigh me again till I've got back my peace of mind."

I'd a heard her, if she'd a said it to herself, let alone speaking it out; and I'd a got up and obeyed her, if I'd a been dead. As we was passing through the setting-room, the old man he took up his hat, and the shingle-nail fell out on the floor, and he just merely picked it up and laid it on the mantel-shelf, and never said nothing, and went out. Tom see him do it, and remembered about the spoon, and says:

"Well, it ain't no use to send things by *him* no more, he ain't reliable." Then he says: "But he done us a good turn with the spoon, anyway, without knowing it, and so we'll go and do him one without *him* knowing it—stop up his rat-holes."

There was a noble good lot of them, down cellar, and it took us a whole hour, but we done the job tight and good, and ship-shape. Then we heard steps on the stairs, and blowed out our light, and hid; and here comes the old man, with a candle in one hand and a bundle of stuff in t'other, looking as absent-minded as year before last. He went a mooning around, first to one rat-hole and then another, till he'd been to them all. Then he stood about five minutes, picking tallow-drip off of his candle and thinking. Then he turns off slow and dreamy towards the stairs, saying:

"Well, for the life of me I can't remember when I done it. I could show her now that I warn't to blame on account of the rats. But never mind—let it go. I reckon it wouldn't do no good."

And so he went on a mumbling up stairs, and then we left. He was a mighty nice old man. And always is.

Tom was a good deal bothered about what to do for a spoon, but he said we'd got to have it; so he took a think. When he had

ciphered it out, he told me how we was to do; then we went and
waited around the spoon-basket till we see Aunt Sally coming, and
then Tom went to counting the spoons and laying them out to
one side, and I slid one of them up my sleeve, and Tom says:

"Why, Aunt Sally, there ain't but nine spoons, *yet*."

She says:

"Go 'long to your play, and don't bother me. I know better, I
counted 'm myself."

"Well, I've counted them twice, Aunty, and *I* can't make but
nine."

She looked out of all patience, but of course she come to count
—anybody would.

"I declare to gracious ther' *ain't* but nine!" she says. "Why, what
in the world—plague *take* the things, I'll count 'm again."

So I slipped back the one I had, and when she got done counting, she says:

"Hang the troublesome rubbage, ther's *ten*, now!" and she
looked huffy and bothered both. But Tom says:

"Why, Aunty, *I* don't think there's ten."

"You numskull, didn't you see me *count* 'm?"

"I know, but—"

"Well, I'll count 'm *again*."

So I smouched one, and they come out nine same as the other
time. Well, she *was* in a tearing way—just a trembling all over, she
was so mad. But she counted and counted, till she got that addled
she'd start to count-in the *basket* for a spoon, sometimes; and so,
three times they come out right, and three times they come out
wrong. Then she grabbed up the basket and slammed it across the
house and knocked the cat galley-west; and she said cle'r out and
let her have some peace, and if we come bothering around her
again betwixt that and dinner, she'd skin us. So we had the odd
spoon; and dropped it in her apron pocket whilst she was a giving
us our sailing-orders, and Jim got it all right, along with her
shingle-nail, before noon. We was very well satisfied with this
business, and Tom allowed it was worth twice the trouble it took,
because he said *now* she couldn't ever count them spoons twice
alike again to save her life; and wouldn't believe she'd counted
them right, if she *did*; and said that after she'd about counted her
head off, for the next three days, he judged she'd give it up and
offer to kill anybody that wanted her to ever count them any
more.

So we put the sheet back on the line, that night, and stole one
out of her closet; and kept on putting it back and stealing it again,
for a couple of days, till she didn't know how many sheets she
had, any more, and said she didn't *care*, and warn't agoing to
bullyrag the rest of her soul out about it, and wouldn't count

them again not to save her life, she druther die first.

So we was all right now, as to the shirt and the sheet and the spoon and the candles, by the help of the calf and the rats and the mixed-up counting; and as to the candlestick, it warn't no consequence, it would blow over by-and-by.

But that pie was a job; we had no end of trouble with that pie. We fixed it up away down in the woods, and cooked it there; and we got it done at last, and very satisfactory, too; but not all in one day; and we had to use up three washpans full of flour, before we got through, and we got burnt pretty much all over, in places, and eyes put out with the smoke; because, you see, we didn't want nothing but a crust, and we couldn't prop it up right, and she would always cave in. But of course we thought of the right way at last; which was to cook the ladder, too, in the pie. So then we laid in with Jim, the second night, and tore up the sheet all in little strings, and twisted them together, and long before daylight we had a lovely rope, that you could a hung a person with. We let on it took nine months to make it.

And in the forenoon we took it down to the woods, but it wouldn't go in the pie. Being made of a whole sheet, that way, there was rope enough for forty pies, if we'd a wanted them, and plenty left over for soup, or sausage, or anything you choose. We could a had a whole dinner.

But we didn't need it. All we needed was just enough for the pie, and so we throwed the rest away. We didn't cook none of the pies in the washpan, afraid the solder would melt; but Uncle Silas he had a noble brass warming-pan which he thought considerable of, because it belonged to one of his ancestors with a long wooden handle that come over from England with William the Conqueror in the *Mayflower* or one of them early ships and was hid away up garret with a lot of other old pots and things that was valuable, not on acount of being any account because they warn't, but on account of them being relicts, you know, and we snaked her out, private, and took her down there, but she failed on the first pies, because we didn't know how, but she come up smiling on the last one. We took and lined her with dough, and set her in the coals, and loaded her up with rag-rope, and put on a dough roof, and shut down the lid, and put hot embers on top, and stood off five foot, with the long handle, cool and comfortable, and in fifteen minutes she turned out a pie that was a satisfaction to look at. But the person that et it would want to fetch a couple of kags of toothpicks along, for if that rope-ladder wouldn't cramp him down to business, I don't know nothing what I'm talking about, and lay him in enough stomach-ache to last him till next time, too.

Nat didn't look, when we put the witch-pie in Jim's pan; and

we put the three tin plates in the bottom of the pan under the
vittles; and so Jim got everything all right, and as soon as he was
by himself he busted into the pie and hid the rope-ladder inside
of his straw tick, and scratched some marks on a tin plate and
throwed it out of the window-hole.

Chapter XXXVIII

Making them pens was a distressid-tough job, and so was the
saw; and Jim allowed the inscription was going to be the toughest
of all. That's the one which the prisoner has to scrabble on the
wall. But we had to have it; Tom said we'd *got* to; there warn't no
case of a state prisoner not scrabbling his inscription to leave behind, and his coat of arms.

"Look at Lady Jane Grey," he says; "look at Gilford Dudley;
look at old Northumberland! Why, Huck, spose it *is* considerable
trouble?—what you going to do?—how you going to get around it?
Jim's *got* to do his inscription and coat of arms. They all do."

Jim says:

"Why, Mars Tom, I hain't got no coat o' arms; I hain't got
nuffn but dish-yer ole shirt, en you knows I got to keep de journal
on dat."

"Oh, you don't understand, Jim; a coat of arms is very different."

"Well," I says, "Jim's right, anyway, when he says he hain't got
no coat of arms, because he hain't."

"I reckon *I* knowed that," Tom says, "but you bet he'll have
one before he goes out of this—because he's going out *right*, and
there ain't going to be no flaws in his record."

So whilst me and Jim filed away at the pens on a brickbat apiece,
Jim a making his'n out of the brass and I making mine out of the
spoon, Tom set to work to think out the coat of arms. By-and-by
he said he'd struck so many good ones he didn't hardly know which
to take, but there was one which he reckoned he'd decide on. He
says:

"On the scutcheon we'll have a bend *or* in the dexter base, a
saltire *murrey* in the fess, with a dog, couchant, for common
charge, and under his foot a chain embattled, for slavery, with a
chevron *vert* in a chief engrailed, and three invected lines on a
field *azure*, with the nombril points rampant on a dancette in-
dented; crest, a runaway nigger, *sable*, with his bundle over his
shoulder on a bar sinister: and a couple of gules for supporters,
which is you and me; motto, *Maggiore fretta, minore atto*. Got it
out of a book—means, the more haste, the less speed."

"Geewhillikins," I says, "but what does the rest of it mean?"

"We ain't got no time to bother over that," he says, "we got
to dig in like all git-out."

"Well, anyway," I says, "what's *some* of it? What's a fess?"

"A fess—a fess is—*you* don't need to know what a fess is. I'll show him how to make it when he gets to it."

"Shucks, Tom," I says, "I think you might tell a person. What's a bar sinister?"

"Oh, *I* don't know. But he's got to have it. All the nobility does."

That was just his way. If it didn't suit him to explain a thing to you, he wouldn't do it. You might pump at him a week, it wouldn't make no difference.

He'd got all that coat of arms business fixed, so now he started in to finish up the rest of that part of the work, which was to plan out a mournful inscription—said Jim got to have one, like they all done. He made up a lot, and wrote them out on a paper, and read them off, so:

1. *Here a captive heart busted.*

2. *Here a poor prisoner, forsook by the world and friends, fretted out his sorrowful life.*

3. *Here a lonely heart broke, and a worn spirit went to its rest, after thirty-seven years of solitary captivity.*

4. *Here, homeless and friendless, after thirty-seven years of bitter captivity, perished a noble stranger, natural son of Louis XIV.*

Tom's voice trembled, whilst he was reading them, and he most broke down. When he got done, he couldn't no way make up his mind which one for Jim to scrabble onto the wall, they was all so good; but at last he allowed he would let him scrabble them all on. Jim said it would take him a year to scrabble such a lot of truck onto the logs with a nail, and he didn't know how to make letters, besides; but Tom said he would block them out for him, and then he wouldn't have nothing to do but just follow the lines. Then pretty soon he says:

"Come to think, the logs ain't agoing to do; they don't have log walls in a dungeon: we got to dig the inscriptions into a rock. We'll fetch a rock."

Jim said the rock was worse than the logs; he said it would take him such a pison long time to dig them into a rock, he wouldn't ever get out. But Tom said he would let me help him do it. Then he took a look to see how me and Jim was getting along with the pens. It was most pesky tedious hard work and slow, and didn't give my hands no show to get well of the sores, and we didn't seem to make no headway, hardly. So Tom says:

"I know how to fix it. We got to have a rock for the coat of arms and mournful inscriptions, and we can kill two birds with that same rock. There's a gaudy big grindstone down at the mill, and we'll smouch it, and carve the things on it, and file out the pens and the saw on it, too."

It warn't no slouch of an idea; and it warn't no slouch of a grindstone nuther; but we allowed we'd tackle it. It warn't quite midnight, yet, so we cleared out for the mill, leaving Jim at work. We smouched the grindstone, and set out to roll her home, but it was a most nation tough job. Sometimes, do what we could, we couldn't keep her from falling over, and she come mighty near mashing us, every time. Tom said she was going to get one of us, sure, before we got through. We got her half way; and then we was plumbed played out, and most drownded with sweat. We see it warn't no use, we got to go and fetch Jim. So he raised up his bed and slid the chain off of the bed-leg, and wrapt it round and round his neck, and we crawled out through our hole and down there, and Jim and me laid into that grindstone and walked her along like nothing;[7] and Tom superintended. He could out-superintend any boy I ever see. He knowed how to do everything.

Our hole was pretty big, but it warn't big enough to get the grindstone through; but Jim he took the pick and soon made it big enough. Then Tom marked out them things on it with the nail, and set Jim to work on them, with the nail for a chisel and an iron bolt from the rubbage in the lean-to for a hammer, and told him to work till the rest of his candle quit on him, and then he could go to bed, and hide the grindstone under his straw tick and sleep on it. Then we helped him fix his chain back on the bed-leg, and was ready for bed ourselves. But Tom thought of something, and says:

"You got any spiders in here, Jim?"

"No, sah, thanks to goodness I hain't, Mars Tom."

"All right, we'll get you some."

"But bless you, honey, I doan' *want* none. I's afeard un um. I jis' 's soon have rattlesnakes aroun'."

Tom thought a minute or two, and says:

"It's a good idea. And I reckon it's been done. It *must* a been done; it stands to reason. Yes, it's a prime good idea. Where could you keep it?"

"Keep what, Mars Tom?"

"Why, a rattlesnake."

"De goodness gracious alive, Mars Tom! Why, if dey was a rattlesnake to come in heah, I'd take en bust right out thoo dat log wall, I would, wid my head."

"Why, Jim, you wouldn't be afraid of it, after a little. You could

7. In these concluding chapters, the persistent horseplay may seem a cruelty toward Jim; yet here, as before, he participates in familiar antics with boys whom he trusts, although actually he could easily have escaped. The author, in this relaxed mood, employs the extravagance of comic statement and situation traditional with the frontier tall tale, but at the highest level of human understanding.

tame it.'"

"*Tame* it!"

"Yes—easy enough. Every animal is grateful for kindness and petting, and they wouldn't *think* of hurting a person that pets them. Any book will tell you that. You try—that's all I ask; just try for two or three days. Why, you can get him so, in a little while, that he'll love you; and sleep with you; and won't stay away from you a minute; and will let you wrap him round your neck and put his head in your mouth."

"*Please*, Mars Tom—*doan'* talk so! I can't *stan'* it! He'd *let* me shove his head in my mouf—fer a favor, hain't it? I lay he'd wait a pow'ful long time 'fo' I *ast* him. En mo' en dat, I doan' *want* him to sleep wid me."

"Jim, don't act so foolish. A prisoner's *got* to have some kind of a dumb pet, and if a rattlesnake hain't ever been tried, why, there's more glory to be gained in your being the first to ever try it than any other way you could ever think of to save your life."

"Why, Mars Tom, I doan' *want* no sich glory. Snake take 'n bite Jim's chin off, den *whah* is de glory? No, sah, I doan' want no sich doin's."

"Blame it, can't you *try*? I only *want* you to try—you needn't keep it up if it don't work."

"But de trouble all *done*, ef de snake bite me while I's a tryin' him. Mars Tom, I's willin' to tackle mos' anything 'at ain't onreasonable, but ef you en Huck fetches a rattlesnake in heah for me to tame, I's gwyne to *leave*, dat's *shore*."

"Well, then, let it go, let it go, if you're so bullheaded about it. We can get you some garter-snakes and you can tie some buttons on their tails, and let on they're rattlesnakes, and I reckon that'll have to do."

"I k'n stan' *dem*, Mars Tom, but blame' 'f I couldn' get along widout um, I tell you dat. I never knowed b'fo', 't was so much bother and trouble to be a prisoner."

"Well, it *always* is, when it's done right. You got any rats around here?"

"No, sah, I hain't seed none."

"Well, we'll get you some rats."

"Why, Mars Tom, I doan' *want* no rats. Dey's de dad-blamedest creturs to sturb a body, en rustle roun' over 'im, en bite his feet, when he's tryin' to sleep, I ever see. No, sah, gimme g'yartersnakes, 'f I's got to have 'm, but doan' gimme no rats, I ain' got no use f'r um, skasely."

"But Jim, you *got* to have 'em—they all do. So don't make no more fuss about it. Prisoners ain't ever without rats. There ain't no instance of it. And they train them, and pet them, and learn them tricks, and they get to be as sociables as flies. But you got to play music to them. You got anything to play music on?"

"I ain't got nuffn but a coase comb en a piece o' paper, en a juice-harp; but I reck'n dey wouldn' take no stock in a juice-harp."

"Yes they would. *They* don't care what kind of music 'tis. A jews-harp's plenty good enough for a rat. All animals likes music—in a prison they dote on it. Specially, painful music; and you can't get no other kind out of a jews-harp. It always interests them; they come out to see what's the matter with you. Yes, you're all right; you're fixed very well. You want to set on your bed, nights, before you go to sleep, and early in the mornings, and play your jews-harp; play The Last Link is Broken—that's the thing that'll scoop a rat, quicker'n anything else: and when you've played about two minutes, you'll see all the rats, and the snakes, and spiders, and things begin to feel worried about you, and come. And they'll just fairly swarm over you, and have a noble good time."

"Yes, *dey* will, I reck'n, Mars Tom, but what kine er time is *Jim* havin'? Blest if I kin see de pint. But I'll do it ef I got to. I reck'n I better keep de animals satisfied, en not have no trouble in de house."

Tom waited to think over, and see if there wasn't nothing else; and pretty soon he says:

"Oh—there's one thing I forgot. Could you raise a flower here, do you reckon?"

"I doan' know but maybe I could, Mars Tom; but it's tolable dark in heah, en I ain' got no use f'r no flower, nohow, en she'd be a pow'ful sight o' trouble."

"Well, you try it, anyway. Some other prisoners has done it."

"One er dem big cat-tail-lookin' mullen-stalks would grow in heah, Mars Tom, I reck'n, but she wouldn' be wuth half de trouble she'd coss."

"Don't you believe it. We'll fetch you a little one, and you plant it in the corner, over there, and raise it. And don't call it mullen, call it Pitchiola—that's its right name, when it's in a prison.[8] And you want to water it with your tears."

"Why, I got plenty spring water, Mars Tom."

"You don't *want* spring water; you want to water it with your tears. It's the way they always do."

"Why, Mars Tom, I lay I kin raise one er dem mullen-stalks twyste wid spring water whiles another man's a *start'n* one wid tears."

"That ain't the idea. You *got* to do it with tears."

"She'll die on my han's, Mars Tom, she sholy will; kase I doan' skasely ever cry."

So Tom was stumped. But he studied it over, and then said Jim would have to worry along the best he could with an onion. He

8. In J. X. Boniface's *Picciola* (1836) a plant sustains a noble prisoner.

promised he would go to the nigger cabins and drop one, private, in Jim's coffee-pot, in the morning. Jim said he would "jis' 's soon have tobacker in his coffee;" and found so much fault with it, and with the work and bother of raising the mullen, and jews-harping the rats, and petting and flattering up the snakes and spiders and things, on top of all the other work he had to do on pens, and inscriptions, and journals, and things, which made it more trouble and worry and responsibility to be a prisoner than anything he ever undertook, that Tom most lost all patience with him; and said he was just loadened down with more gaudier chances than a prisoner ever had in the world to make a name for himself, and yet he didn't know enough to appreciate them, and they was just about wasted on him. So Jim he was sorry, and said he wouldn't behave so no more, and then me and Tom shoved for bed.

Chapter XXXIX

In the morning we went up to the village and bought a wire rat trap and fetched it down, and unstopped the best rat hole, and in about an hour we had fifteen of the bulliest kind of ones; and then we took it and put it in a safe place under Aunt Sally's bed. But while we was gone for spiders, little Thomas Franklin Benjamin Jefferson Elexander Phelps found it there, and opened the door of it to see if the rats would come out, and they did; and Aunt Sally she come in, and when we got back she was a standing on top of the bed raising Cain, and the rats was doing what they could to keep off the dull times for her. So she took and dusted us both with the hickry, and we was as much as two hours catching another fifteen or sixteen, drat that meddlesome cub, and they warn't the likeliest, nuther, because the first haul was the pick of the flock. I never see a likelier lot of rats than what that first haul was.

We got a splendid stock of sorted spiders, and bugs, and frogs, and caterpillars, and one thing or another; and we like-to got a hornet's nest, but we didn't. The family was at home. We didn't give it right up, but staid with them as long as we could; because we allowed we'd tire them out or they'd got to tire us out, and they done it. Then we got allycumpain and rubbed on the places, and was pretty near all right again, but couldn't set down convenient. And so we went for the snakes, and grabbed a oouple of dozen garters and house-snakes, and put them in a bag, and put it in our room, and by that time it was supper time, and a rattling good honest day's work; and hungry?—oh, no, I reckon not! And there warn't a blessed snake up there, when we went back—we didn't half tie the sack, and they worked out, somehow, and left. But it didn't matter much, because they was still on the premises somewheres. So we judged we could get some of them again. No, there warn't no real scarcity of snakes about the house for a considerable spell. You'd see them dripping from the rafters and places, every now and then; and they generly landed in your plate, or down the back of your neck, and most of the time where you didn't want them. Well, they was handsome, and striped, and there warn't no harm in a million of them; but that never made no difference to Aunt Sally, she despised snakes, be the breed what they might, and she couldn't stand them no way you could fix it; and every time one of them flopped down on her, it didn't make no difference what she was doing, she would just lay that work down and light out. I never see such a woman. And you could hear her whoop to Jericho. You couldn't get her to take aholt of one of them with the tongs. And if she turned over and found one in bed, she would scramble out and lift a howl that you would think the house was afire. She disturbed the old man so, that he said he could most wish there hadn't ever been no snakes created. Why, after every last snake had been gone clear out of the house for as much as a week, Aunt Sally warn't over it yet; she warn't near over it; when she was setting thinking about something, you could touch her on the back of her neck with a feather and she would jump right out of her stockings. It was very curious. But Tom said all women was just so. He said they was made that way; for some reason or other.

We got a licking every time one of our snakes come in her way; and she allowed these lickings warn't nothing to what she would do if we ever loaded up the place again with them. I didn't mind the lickings, because they didn't amount to nothing; but I minded the trouble we had, to lay in another lot. But we got them laid in, and all the other things; and you never see a cabin as blithesome as Jim's was when they'd all swarm out for music and go for him. Jim didn't like the spiders, and the spiders didn't like Jim; and so they'd lay for him and make it mighty warm for him. And he said that between the rats, and the snakes, and the grindstone, there warn't no room in bed for him, skasely; and when there was, a body couldn't sleep, it was so lively, and it was always lively, he said, because *they* never all slept at one time, but took turn about, so when the snakes was asleep the rats was on deck, and when the rats turned in the snakes come on watch, so he always had one gang under him, in his way, and t'other gang having a circus over him, and if he got up to hunt a new place, the spiders would take a chance at him as he crossed over. He said if he ever got out, this time, he wouldn't ever be a prisoner again, not for a salary.

Well, by the end of three weeks, everything was in pretty good shape. The shirt was sent in early, in a pie, and every time a rat bit Jim he would get up and write a little in his journal whilst the ink was fresh; the pens was made, the inscriptions and so on was all carved on the grindstone; the bed-leg was sawed in two, and we had et up the sawdust, and it give us a most amazing stomach-ache. We reckoned we was all going to die, but didn't. It was the most undigestible sawdust I ever see; and Tom said the same. But as I was saying, we'd got all the work done, now, at last; and we was all pretty much fagged out, too, but mainly Jim. The old man had wrote a couple of times to the plantation below Orleans to come and get their runaway nigger, but hadn't got no answer, because there warn't no such plantation; so he allowed he would advertise Jim in the St. Louis and New Orleans papers; and when he mentioned the St. Louis ones, it give me the cold shivers, and I see we hadn't no time to lose. So Tom said, now for the nonnamous letters.

"What's them?" I says.

"Warnings to the people that something is up. Sometimes it's done one way, sometimes another. But there's always somebody spying around, that gives notice to the governor of the castle. When Louis XVI was going to light out of the Tooleries, a servant girl done it. It's a very good way, and so is the nonnamous letters. We'll use them both. And it's usual for the prisoner's mother to change clothes with him, and she stays in, and he slides out in her clothes. We'll do that too."

"But looky here, Tom, what do we want to *warn* anybody for, that something's up? Let them find it out for themselves—it's their lookout."

"Yes, I know; but you can't depend on them. It's the way they've acted from the very start—left us to do *everything*. They're so confiding and mullet-headed they don't take notice of nothing at all. So if we don't *give* them notice, there won't be nobody nor nothing to interfere with us, and so after all our hard work and trouble this escape 'll go off perfectly flat: won't amount to nothing—won't be nothing *to* it."

"Well, as for me, Tom, that's the way I'd like."

"Shucks," he says, and looked disgusted. So I says:

"But I ain't going to make no complaint. Anyway that suits you suits me. What you going to do about the servant-girl?"

"You'll be her. You slide in, in the middle of the night, and hook that yaller girl's frock."

"Why, Tom, that'll make trouble next morning; because of course she prob'bly hain't got any but that one."

"I know; but you don't want it but fifteen minutes, to carry the nonnamous letter and shove it under the front door."

"All right, then, I'll do it; but I could carry it just as handy in my own togs."

"You wouldn't look like a servant-girl *then*, would you?"

"No, but there won't be nobody to see what I look like, *any-*

way."

"That ain't got nothing to do with it. The thing for us to do, is just to do our *duty*, and not worry about whether anybody *sees* us do it or not. Hain't you got no principle at all?"

"All right, I ain't saying nothing; I'm the servant-girl. Who's Jim's mother?"

"I'm his mother. I'll hook a gown from Aunt Sally."

"Well, then, you'll have to stay in the cabin when me and Jim leaves."

"Not much. I'll stuff Jim's clothes full of straw and lay it on his bed to represent his mother in disguise, and Jim 'll take Aunt Sally's[9] gown off of me and wear it, and we'll all evade together. When a prisoner of style escapes, it's called an evasion. It's always called so when a king escapes, f'rinstance. And the same with a king's son; it don't make no difference whether he's a natural one or an unnatural one."

So Tom he wrote the nonamous letter, and I smouched the yaller wench's frock, that night, and put it on, and shoved it under the front door, the way Tom told me to. It said:

Beware. Trouble is brewing. Keep a sharp lookout.
UNKNOWN FRIEND.

Next night we stuck a picture which Tom drawed in blood, of a skull and crossbones, on the front door; and next night another one of a coffin, on the back door. I never see a family in such a sweat. They couldn't a been worse scared if the place had a been full of ghosts laying for them behind everything and under the beds and shivering through the air. If a door banged, Aunt Sally she jumped, and said "ouch!" if anything fell, she jumped and said "ouch!" if you happened to touch her, when she warn't noticing, she done the same; she couldn't face noway and be satisfied, because she allowed there was something behind her every time—so she was always a whirling around, sudden, and saying "ouch," and before she'd get two-thirds around, she'd whirl back again, and say it again; and she was afraid to go to bed, but she dasn't set up. So the thing was working very well, Tom said; he said he never see a thing work more satisfactory. He said it showed it was done right.

So he said, now for the grand bulge! So the very next morning at the streak of dawn we got another letter ready, and was wondering what we better do with it, because we heard them say at supper they was going to have a nigger on watch at both doors all night. Tom he went down the ligthning-rod to spy around; and the nigger at the back door was asleep, and he stuck it in the back of his neck and come back. This letter said:

9. The original edition and standard editions based on it erroneously read "the nigger woman's gown."

Don't betray me, I wish to be your friend. There is a desprate gang of cutthroats from over in the Ingean Territory[1] *going to steal your runaway nigger to-night, and they have been trying to scare you so as you will stay in the house and not bother them. I am one of the gang, but have got religgion and wish to quit it and lead a honest life again, and will betray the helish design. They will sneak down from northards, along the fence, at midnight exact, with a false key, and go in the nigger's cabin to get him. I am to be off a piece and blow a tin horn if I see any danger; but stead of that, I will* BA *like a sheep soon as they get in and not blow at all; then whilst they are getting his chains loose, you slip there and lock them in, and can kill them at your leasure. Don't do anything but just the way I am telling you, if you do they will suspicion something and raise whoopjamboreehoo. I do not wish any reward but to know I have done the right thing.*

UNKNOWN FRIEND.

Chapter XL

We was feeling pretty good, after breakfast, and took my canoe and went over the river a fishing, with a lunch, and had a good time, and took a look at the raft and found her all right, and got home late to supper, and found them in such a sweat and worry they didn't know which end they was standing on, and made us go right off to bed the minute we was done supper, and wouldn't tell us what the trouble was, and never let on a word about the new letter, but didn't need to, because we knowed as much about it as anybody did, and as soon as we was half up stairs and her back was turned, we slid for the cellar cubboard and loaded up a good lunch and took it up to our room and went to bed, and got up about half-past eleven, and Tom put on Aunt Sally's dress that he stole and was going to start with the lunch, but says:

"Where's the butter?"

"I laid out a hunk of it," I says, "on a piece of a corn-pone."

"Well, you *left* it laid out, then—it ain't here."

"We can get along without it," I says.

"We can get along *with* it, too," he says; "just you slide down cellar and fetch it. And then mosey right down the lightning-rod and come along. I'll go and stuff the straw into Jim's clothes to represent his mother in disguise, and be ready to *ba* like a sheep and shove soon as you get there."

So out he went, and down cellar went I. The hunk of butter, big as a person's fist, was where I had left it, so I took up the slab of corn-pone with it on, and blowed out my light, and started up

1. Oklahoma, the Indian federal land grant which became also a refuge for gunmen and lawbreakers.

stairs, very stealthy, and got up to the main floor all right, but here comes Aunt Sally with a candle, and I clapped the truck in my hat, and clapped my hat on my head, and the next second she see me; and she says:

"You been down cellar?"

"Yes'm."

"What you been doing down there?"

"Noth'n."

"*Noth'n!*"

"No'm."

"Well, then, what possessed you to go down there, this time of night?"

"I don't know'm."

"You don't *know?* Don't answer me that way, Tom, I want to know what you been *doing* down there?"

"I hain't been doing a single thing, Aunt Sally, I hope to gracious if I have."

I reckoned she'd let me go, now, and as a generl thing she would; but I spose there was so many strange things going on she was just in a sweat about every little thing that warn't yard-stick straight; so she says, very decided:

"You just march into that setting-room and stay there till I come. You been up to something you no business to, and I lay I'll find out what it is before *I'm* done with you."

So she went away as I opened the door and walked into the setting-room. My, but there was a crowd there! Fifteen farmers, and every one of them had a gun. I was most powerful sick, and slunk to a chair and set down. They was setting around, some of them talking a little, in a low voice, and all of them fidgety and uneasy, but trying to look like they warn't; but I knowed they was, because they was always taking off their hats, and putting them on, and scratching their heads, and changing their seats, and fumbling with their buttons. I warn't easy myself, but I didn't take my hat off, all the same.

I did wish Aunt Sally would come, and get done with me, and lick me, if she wanted to, and let me get away and tell Tom how we'd overdone this thing, and what a thundering hornet's nest we'd got ourselves into, so we could stop fooling around, straight off, and clear out with Jim before these rips got out of patience and come for us.

At last she come, and begun to ask me questions, but I *couldn't* answer them straight, I didn't know which end of me was up; because these men was in such a fidget now, that some was wanting to start right *now* and lay for them desperadoes, and saying it warn't but a few minutes to midnight; and others was trying to get them to hold on and wait for the sheep-signal; and here was aunty

pegging away at the questions, and me a shaking all over and ready
to sink down in my tracks I was that scared; and the place getting
hotter and hotter, and the butter beginning to melt and run down
my neck and behind my ears: and pretty soon, when one of them
says, "*I'm* for going and getting in the cabin *first*, and right *now*,
and catching them when they come," I most dropped; and a streak
of butter come a trickling down my forehead, and Aunt Sally she
see it, and turns white as a sheet, and says:

"For the land's sake what *is* the matter with the child!—he's got
the brain fever as shore as you're born, and they're oozing out!"

And everybody runs to see, and she snatches off my hat, and
out comes the bread, and what was left of the butter, and she
grabbed me, and hugged me, and says:

"Oh, what a turn you did give me! and how glad and grateful I
am it ain't no worse; for luck's against us, and it never rains but it
pours, and when I see that truck I thought we'd lost you, for I
knowed by the color and all, it was just like your brains would be
if— Dear, dear, whyd'nt you *tell* me that was what you'd been
down there for, I wouldn't a cared. Now cler out to bed, and don't
lemme see no more of you till morning!"

I was up stairs in a second, and down the lightning-rod in another one, and shinning through the dark for the lean-to. I
couldn't hardly get my words out, I was so anxious; but I told Tom
as quick as I could, we must jump for it, now, and not a minute
to lose—the house full of men, yonder, with guns!

His eyes just blazed; and he says:

"No!—is that so? *Ain't* it bully! Why, Huck, if it was to do over
again, I bet I could fetch two hundred! If we could put it off
till—"

"Hurry! *hurry!*" I says. "Where's Jim?"

"Right at your elbow; if you reach out your arm you can touch
him. He's dressed, and everything's ready. Now we'll slide out and
give the sheep-signal."

But then we heard the tramp of men, coming to the door, and
heard them begin to fumble with the padlock; and heard a man
say:

"I *told* you we'd be too soon; they haven't come—the door is
locked. Here, I'll lock some of you into the cabin and you lay for
'em in the dark and kill 'em when they come; and the rest scatter
around a piece, and listen if you can hear 'em coming."

So in they come, but couldn't see us in the dark, and most trod
on us whilst we was hustling to get under the bed. But we got
under all right, and out through the hole, swift but soft—Jim first,
me next, and Tom last, which was according to Tom's orders. Now
we was in the lean-to, and heard trampings close by outside. So
we crept to the door, and Tom stopped us there and put his eye

to the crack, but couldn't make out nothing, it was so dark; and whispered and said he would listen for the steps to get further, and when he nudged us Jim must glide out first, and him last. So he set his ear to the crack and listened, and listened, and listened, and the steps a scraping around, out there, all the time; and at last he nudged us, and we slid out, and stooped down, not breathing, and not makin the least noise, and slipped stealthy towards the fence, in Injun file, and got to it, all right, and me and Jim over it; but Tom's britches catched fast on a splinter on the top rail, and then he hear the steps coming, so he had to pull loose, which snapped the splinter and made a noise; and as he dropped in our tracks and started, somebody sings out:

"Who's that? Answer, or I'll shoot!"

But we didn't answer; we just unfurled our heels and shoved. Then there was a rush, and a *bang, bang, bang!* and the bullets fairly whizzed around us! We heard them sing out:

"Here they are! They've broke for the river! after 'em, boys! And turn loose the dogs!"

So here they come, full tilt. We could hear them, because they wore boots, and yelled, but we didn't wear no boots, and didn't yell. We was in the path to the mill; and when they got pretty close onto us, we dodged into the bush and let them go by, and then dropped in behind them. They'd had all the dogs shut up, so they wouldn't scare off the robbers; but by this time somebody had let them loose, and here they come, making pow-wow enough for a million; but they was our dogs; so we stopped in our tracks till they catched up; and when they see it warn't nobody but us, and no excitement to offer them, they only just said howdy, and tore right ahead towards the shouting and clattering; and then we up steam again and whizzed along after them till we was nearly to the mill, and then struck up through the bush to where my canoe was tied, and hopped in and pulled for dear life towards the middle of the river, but didn't make no more noise than we was obleeged to. Then we struck out, easy and comfortable, for the island where my raft was; and we could hear them yelling and barking at each other all up and down the bank, till we was so far away the sounds got dim and died out. And when we stepped onto the raft, I says:

"Now, old Jim, you're a free man *again*, and I bet you won't ever be a slave no more."

"En a mighty good job it wuz, too, Huck. It 'uz planned beautiful, en it 'uz *done* beautiful; en dey ain't *nobody* kin git up a plan dat's mo' mixed-up en splendid den what dat one wuz."

We was all as glad as we could be, but Tom was the gladdest of all, because he had a bullet in the calf of his leg.

When me and Jim heard that, we didn't feel so brash as what

we did before. It was hurting him considerble, and bleeding; so we laid him in the wigwam and tore up one of the duke's shirts for to bandage him, but he says:

"Gimme the rags, I can do it myself. Don't stop, now; don't fool around here, and the evasion booming along so handsome; man the sweeps, and set her loose! Boys, we done it elegant!—'deed we did. I wish *we'd* a had the handling of Louis XVI, there wouldn't a been no 'Son of Saint Louis, ascend to heaven!' wrote down in *his* biography: no, sir, we'd a whooped him over the *border*— that's what we'd a done with *him*—and done it just as slick as nothing at all, too. Man the sweeps—man the sweeps!"

But me and Jim was consulting—and thinking. And after we'd thought a minute, I says:

"Say it, Jim."

So he says:

"Well, den, dis is de way it look to me, Huck. Ef it wuz *him* dat 'uz bein' sot free, en one er de boys wuz to git shot, would he say, 'Go on en save me, nemmine 'bout a doctor f'r to save dis one? Is dat like Mars Tom Sawyer? Would he say dat? You *bet* he wouldn't! *Well*, den, is *Jim* gwyne to say it? No, sah—I doan' budge a step out'n dis place, 'dout a *doctor*; not if it's forty year!"

I knowed he was white inside, and I reckoned he'd say what he did say—so it was all right, now, and I told Tom I was agoing for a doctor. He raised considerble row about it, but me and Jim stuck to it and wouldn't budge; so he was for crawling out and setting the raft loose himself; but we wouldn't let him. Then he give us a piece of his mind—but it didn't do no good.

So when he see me getting the canoe ready, he says:

"Well, then, if you're bound to go, I'll tell you the way to do, when you get to the village. Shut the door, and blindfold the doctor tight and fast, and make him swear to be silent as the grave, and put a purse full of gold in his hand, and then take and lead him all around the back alleys and everywheres, in the dark, and then fetch him here in the canoe, in a roundabout way amongst the islands, and search him and take his chalk away from him, and don't give it back to him till you get him back to the village, or else he will chalk this raft so he can find it again. It's the way they all do."

So I said I would, and left, and Jim was to hide in the woods when he see the doctor coming, till he was gone again.

Chapter XLI

The doctor was an old man; a very nice, kind-looking old man, when I got him up. I told him me and my brother was over on Spanish Island hunting, yesterday afternoon, and camped on a piece of a raft we found, and about midnight he must a kicked his gun in his dreams, for it went off and shot him in the leg, and we wanted him to go over there and fix it and not say nothing about it, nor let anybody know, because we wanted to come home this evening, and surprise the folks.

"Who is your folks?" he says.

"The Phelpses, down yonder."

"Oh," he says. And after a minute, he says: "How'd you say he got shot?"

"He had a dream," I says, "and it shot him."

"Singular dream," he says.

So he lit up his lantern, and got his saddle-bags, and we started. But when he see the canoe, he didn't like the look of her—said she was big enough for one, but didn't look pretty safe for two. I says:

"Oh, you needn't be afeard, sir, she carried the three of us, easy enough."

"What three?"

"Why, me and Sid, and—and—and *the guns*; that's what I mean."

"Oh," he says.

But he put his foot on the gunnel, and rocked her; and shook his head, and said he reckoned he'd look around for a bigger one. But they was all locked and chained; so he took my canoe, and said for me to wait till he come back, or I could hunt around further, or maybe I better go down home and get them ready for the surprise, if I wanted to. But I said I didn't; so I told him just how to find the raft, and then he started.

I struck an idea, pretty soon. I says to myself, spos'n he can't fix that leg just in three shakes of a sheep's tail, as the saying is? spos'n it takes him three or four days? What are we going to do?—lay around there till he lets the cat out of the bag? No, sir, I know what *I'll* do. I'll wait, and when he comes back, if he says he's got to go any more, I'll get down there, too, if I swim; and we'll take and tie him, and keep him, and shove out down the river; and when Tom's done with him, we'll give him what it's worth, or all we got, and then let him get shore.

So then I crept into a lumber pile to get some sleep; and next time I waked up the sun was away up over my head! I shot out and went for the doctor's house, but they told me he'd gone away in the night, some time or other, and warn't back yet. Well, thinks I, that looks powerful bad for *Tom*, and I'll dig out for the island, right off. So away I shoved, and turned the corner, and nearly rammed my head into Uncle Silas's stomach! He says:

"Why, *Tom!* Where you been, all this time, you rascal?"

"*I* hain't been nowheres," I says, "only just hunting for the runaway nigger—me and Sid."

"Why, where ever did you go?" he says. "Your aunt's been mighty uneasy."

"She needn't," I says, "because we was all right. We followed the men and the dogs, but they out-run us, and we lost them; but we thought we heard them on the water, so we got a canoe and took out after them, and crossed over but couldn't find nothing of them; so we cruised along up-shore till we got kind of tired and beat out; and tied up the canoe and went to sleep, and never waked up till about an hour ago, then we paddled over here to hear the news, and Sid's at the post-office to see what he can hear, and I'm a branching out to get something to eat for us, and then we're going home."

So then we went to the post-office to get "Sid"; but just as I suspicioned, he warn't there; so the old man he got a letter out of the office, and we waited a while longer but Sid didn't come; so the old man said come along, let Sid foot it home, or canoe-it, when he got done fooling around—but we would ride. I couldn't get him to let me stay and wait for Sid; and he said there warn't no use in it, and I must come along, and let Aunt Sally see we was all right.

When we got home, Aunt Sally was that glad to see me she laughed and cried both, and hugged me, and give me one of them lickings of hern that don't amount to shucks, and said she'd serve Sid the same when he come.

And the place was plumb full of farmers and farmers' wives, to dinner; and such another clack a body never heard. Old Mrs. Hotchkiss was the worst; her tongue was agoing all the time. She says:

"Well, Sister Phelps, I've ransacked that-air cabin over an' I b'lieve the nigger was crazy. I says so to Sister Damrell—didn't I, Sister Damrell?—s'I, he's crazy, s'I—them's the very words I said. You all hearn me: he's crazy, s'I; everything shows it, s'I. Look at that-air grindstone, s'I; want to tell *me* 't any cretur 'ts in his right mind 's agoin' to scrabble all them crazy things onto a grindstone, s'I? Here sich 'n' sich a person busted his heart; 'n' here so 'n' so pegged along for thirty-seven year, 'n' all that—natcherl son o' Louis somebody, 'n' sich everlast'n rubbage. He's plumb crazy, s'I; it's what I says in the fust place, it's what I says in the middle, 'n' it's what I says last 'n' all the time—the nigger's crazy—crazy's Nebokoodneezer, s'I."

"An' look at that-air ladder made out'n rags, Sister Hotchkiss," says old Mrs. Damrell, "what in the name o' goodness *could* he ever want of—"

"The very words I was a-sayin' no longer ago th'n this minute to Sister Utterback, 'n' she'll tell you so herself. Sh-she, look at that-air rag ladder, sh-she; 'n' s'I, yes, *look* at it, s'I—what *could* he a wanted of it, s'I. Sh-she, Sister Hotchkiss, sh-she—"

"But how in the nation'd they ever *git* that grindstone *in* there, *any*way? 'n' who dug that-air *hole?* 'n' who—"

"My very *words*, Brer Penrod! I was a-sayin'—pass that-air sasser o' m'lasses, won't ye?—I was a-sayin' to Sister Dunlap, jist this minute, how *did* they git that grindstone in there, s'I. With-out *help*, mind you—'thout *help!* *Thar's* wher' 'tis. Don't tell *me*, s'I; there *wuz* help, s'I; 'n' ther' wuz a *plenty* help, too, s'I; ther's ben a *dozen* a-helpin' that nigger, 'n' I lay I'd skin every last nigger on this place, but *I'd* find out who done it, s'I; 'n' moreover, s'I—"

"A *dozen* says you!—*forty* couldn't a done everything that's been done. Look at them case-knife saws and things, how tedious they've been made; look at that bed-leg sawed off with 'em, a week's work for six men; look at that nigger made out'n straw on the bed; and look at—"

"You may *well* say it, Brer Hightower! It's jist as I was a-sayin' to Brer Phelps, his own self. S'e, what do *you* think of it, Sister Hotchkiss, s'e? think o' what, Brer Phelps, s'I? think o' that bed-leg sawed off that a way, s'e? *think* of it, s'I? I lay it never sawed *itself* off, s'I—somebody *sawed* it, s'I; that's my opinion, take it or leave it, it mayn't be no 'count, s'I, but sich as 't is, it's my opinion, s'I, 'n' if anybody k'n start a better one, s'I, let him *do* it, s'I, that's all. I says to Sister Dunlap, s'I—"

"Why, dog my cats, they must a ben a house-full o' niggers in there every night for four weeks, to a done all that work, Sister Phelps. Look at that shirt—every last inch of it kivered over with secret African writ'n done with blood! Must a ben a raft uv 'm at it right along, all the time, amost. Why, I'd give two dollars to have it read to me; 'n' as for the niggers that wrote it, I 'low I'd take 'n' lash 'm t'll—"

"People to *help* him, Brother Marples! Well, I reckon you'd *think* so, if you'd a been in this house for a while back. Why, they've stole everything they could lay their hands on—and we a watch-ing, all the time, mind you. They stole that shirt right off o' the line! and as for that sheet they made the rag ladder out of ther' ain't no telling how many times they *didn't* steal that; and flour, and candles, and candlesticks, and spoons, and the old warming-pan, and most a thousand things that I disremember, now, and my new calico dress; and me, and Silas, and my Sid and Tom on the constant watch day *and* night, as I was a telling you, and not a one of us could catch hide nor hair, nor sight nor sound of them; and here at the last minute, lo and behold you, they slides right in under our noses, and fools us, and not only fools *us* but the

Injun Territory robbers too, and actuly gets *away* with that nigger, safe and sound, and that with sixteen men and twenty-two dogs right on their very heels at that very time! I tell you, it just bangs anything I ever *heard* of. Why, *spirits* couldn't a done better, and been no smarter. And I reckon they must a *been* sperits—because, *you* know our dogs, and ther' ain't no better; well, them dogs never even got on the *track* of 'm, once! You explain *that* to me, if you can!—*any* of you!"

"Well, it does beat—"

"Laws alive, I never—"

"So help me, I wouldn't a be—"

"*House*-thieves as well as—"

"Goodnessgracioussakes, I'd a ben afeard to *live* in sich a—"

" 'Fraid to *live!*—why, I was that scared I dasn't[2] hardly go to bed, or get up, or lay down, or *set* down, Sister Ridgeway. Why, they'd steal the very—why, goodness sakes, you can guess what kind of a fluster *I* was in by the time midnight come, last night. I hope to gracious if I warn't afraid they'd steal some o' the family! I was just to that pass, I didn't have no reasoning faculties no more. It looks foolish enough, *now*, in the day-time; but I says to myself, there's my two poor boys asleep, 'way up stairs in that lonesome room, and I declare to goodness I was that uneasy 't I crep' up there and locked 'em in! I *did*. And anybody would. Because, you know, when you get scared, that way, and it keeps running on, and getting worse and worse, all the time, and your wits gets to addling, and you get to doing all sorts o' wild things, and by-and-by you think to yourself, spos'n *I* was a boy, and was away up there, and the door ain't locked, and you—" She stopped, looking kind of wondering, and then she turned her head around slow, and when her eye lit on me—I got up and took a walk.

Says I to myself, I can explain better how we come to not be in that room this morning, if I go out to one side and study over it a little. So I done it. But I dasn't go fur, or she'd a sent for me. And when it was late in the day, the people all went, and then I come in and told her the noise and shooting waked up me and "Sid," and the door was locked, and we wanted to see the fun, so we went down the lightning-rod, and both of us got hurt a little, and we didn't never want to try *that* no more. And then I went on and told her all what I told Uncle Silas before; and then she said she'd forgive us, and maybe it was all right enough anyway, and about what a body night expect of boys, for all boys was a pretty harum-scarum lot, as fur as she could see; and so, as long as no harm hadn't come of it, she judged she better put in her time being grateful we was alive and well and she had us still, stead of fretting

2. Erroneously printed "das'nt" in 1885.

over what was past and done. So then she kissed me, and patted me on the head, and dropped into a kind of a brown study; and pretty soon jumps up, and says:

"Why, lawsamercy, it's most night, and Sid not come yet! What *has* become of that boy?"

I see my chance; so I skips up and says:

"I'll run right up to town and get him," I says.

"No you won't," she says. "You'll stay right wher' you are; *one's* enough to be lost at a time. If he ain't here to supper, your uncle 'll go."

Well, he warn't there to supper; so right after supper uncle went.

He come back about ten, a little bit uneasy; hadn't run across Tom's track. Aunt Sally was a good *deal* uneasy; but Uncle Silas he said there warn't no occasion to be—boys will be boys, he said, and you'll see this one turn up in the morning, all sound and right. So she had to be satisfied. But she said she'd set up for him a while, anyway, and keep a light burning, so he could see it.

And then when I went up to bed she come up with me and fetched her candle, and tucked me in, and mothered me so good I felt mean, and like I couldn't look her in the face; and she set down on the bed and talked with me a long time, and said what a splendid boy Sid was, and didn't seem to want to ever stop talking about him; and kept asking me every now and then, if I reckoned he could a got lost, or hurt, or maybe drownded, and might be laying at this minute, somewheres, suffering or dead, and she not by him to help him, and so the tears would drip down, silent, and I would tell her that Sid was all right, and would be home in the morning, sure; and she would squeeze my hand, or maybe kiss me, and tell me to say it again, and keep on saying it, because it done her good, and she was in so much trouble. And when she was going away, she looked down in my eyes, so steady and gentle, and says:

"The door ain't going to be locked, Tom; and there's the window and the rod; but you'll be good, *won't* you? And you won't go? For *my* sake."

Laws knows I *wanted* to go, bad enough, to see about Tom, and was all intending to go; but after that, I wouldn't a went, not for kingdoms.

But she was on my mind, and Tom was on my mind; so I slept very restless. And twice I went down the rod, away in the night, and slipped around front, and see her setting there by her candle in the window with her eyes towards the road and the tears in them; and I wished I could do something for her, but I couldn't, only to swear that I wouldn't never do nothing to grieve her any more.

And the third time, I waked up at dawn, and slid down, and she was there yet, and her candle was most out, and her old gray head was resting on her hand, and she was asleep.

Chapter XLII

The old man was up town again, before breakfast, but couldn't get no track of Tom; and both of them set at the table, thinking, and not saying nothing, and looking mournful, and their coffee getting cold, and not eating anything. And by-and-by the old man says:

"Did I give you the letter?"

"What letter?"

"The one I got yesterday out of the post-office."

"No, you didn't give me no letter."

"Well, I must a forgot it."

So he rummaged his pockets, and then went off somewheres where he had laid it down, and fetched it, and give it to her. She says:

"Why, it's from St. Petersburg—it's from Sis."

I allowed another walk would do me good; but I couldn't stir. But before she could break it open, she dropped it and run—for she see something. And so did I. It was Tom Sawyer on a mattress; and that old doctor; and Jim, in *her* calico dress, with his hands tied behind him; and a lot of people. I hid the letter behind the first thing that come handy, and rushed. She flung herself at Tom, crying, and says:

"Oh, he's dead, he's dead, I know he's dead!"

And Tom he turned his head a little, and muttered something or other, which showed he warn't in his right mind; then she flung up her hands, and says:

"He's alive, thank God! And that's enough!" and she snatched a kiss of him, and flew for the house to get the bed ready, and scattering orders right and left at the niggers and everybody else, as fast as her tongue could go, every jump of the way.

I followed the men to see what they was going to do with Jim; and the old doctor and Uncle Silas followed after Tom into the house. The men was very huffy, and some of them wanted to hang Jim, for an example to all the other niggers around there, so they wouldn't be trying to run away, like Jim done, and making such a raft of trouble, and keeping a whole family scared most to death for days and nights. But the others said, don't do it, it wouldn't answer at all, he ain't our nigger, and his owner would turn up and make us pay for him, sure. So that cooled them down a little, because the people that's always the most anxious for to hang a nigger that hain't done just right, is always the very ones that ain't the most anxious to pay for him when they've got their satisfaction out of him.

They cussed Jim considerble, though, and give him a cuff or two, side the head, once in a while, but Jim never said nothing, and he never let on to know me, and they took him to the same cabin, and put his own clothes on him, and chained him again, and not to no bed-leg, this time, but to a big staple drove into the bottom log, and chained his hands, too, and both legs, and said he warn't to have nothing but bread and water to eat, after this, till his owner come or he was sold at auction, because he didn't come in a certain length of time, and filled up our hole, and said a couple of farmers with guns must stand watch around about the cabin every night, and a bull-dog tied to the door in the day-time; and about this time they was through with the job and was tapering off with a kind of generl good-bye cussing, and then the old doctor comes and takes a look, and says:

"Don't be no rougher on him than you're obleeged to, because he ain't a bad nigger. When I got to where I found the boy, I see I couldn't cut the bullet out without some help, and he warn't in no condition for me to leave, to go and get help; and he got a little worse and a little worse, and after a long time he went out of his head, and wouldn't let me come anigh him, any more, and said if I chalked his raft he'd kill me, and no end of wild foolishness like that, and I see I couldn't do anything at all with him; so I says, I got to have *help*, somehow; and the minute I says it, out crawls this nigger from somewheres, and says he'll help, and he done it, too, and done it very well. Of course I judged he must be a runaway nigger, and there I *was!* and there I had to stick, right straight along all the rest of the day, and all night. It was a fix, I tell you! I had a couple of patients with the chills, and of course I'd of liked to run up to town and see them, but I dasn't, because the nigger might get away, and then I'd be to blame; and yet never a skiff come close enough for me to hail. So there I had to stick, plumb till daylight this morning; and I never see a nigger that was a better nuss or faithfuller, and yet he was resking his freedom to do it, and was all tired out, too, and I see plain enough he'd been worked main hard, lately. I liked the nigger for that; I tell you, gentlemen, a nigger like that is worth a thousand dollars—and kind treatment, too. I had everything I needed, and the boy was doing as well there as he would a done at home— better, maybe, because it was so quiet; but there I *was*, with both of 'm on my hands; and there I had to stick, till about dawn this morning; then some men in a skiff come by, and as good luck would have it, the nigger was setting by the pallet with his head propped on his knees, sound asleep; so I motioned them in, quiet, and they slipped up on him and grabbed him and tied him before he knowed what he was about, and we never had no trouble. And the boy being in a kind of a flighty sleep, too, we muffled the oars and hitched the raft on, and towed her over very nice and quiet, and the nigger never made the least row nor said a word, from the start. He ain't no bad nigger, gentlemen; that's what I think about him."

Somebody says:

"Well, it sounds very good, doctor, I'm obleeged to say."

Then the others softened up a little, too, and I was mighty thankful to that old doctor for doing Jim that good turn; and I was glad it was according to my judgment of him, too; because I thought he had a good heart in him and was a good man, the first time I see him. Then they all agreed that Jim had acted very well, and was deserving to have some notice took of it, and reward. So every one of them promised, right out and hearty, that they wouldn't cuss him no more.

Then they come out and locked him up. I hoped they was going to say he could have one or two of the chains took off, because they was rotten heavy, or could have meat and greens with his bread and water, but they didn't think of it, and I reckoned it warn't best for me to mix in, but I judged I'd get the doctor's yarn to Aunt Sally, somehow or other, as soon as I'd got through the breakers that was laying just ahead of me. Explanations, I mean, of how I forgot to mention about Sid being shot, when I was telling how him and me put in that dratted night paddling around hunting the runaway nigger.

But I had plenty time. Aunt Sally she stuck to the sick-room all day and all night; and every time I see Uncle Silas mooning around, I dodged him.

Next morning I heard Tom was a good deal better, and they said Aunt Sally was gone to get a nap. So I slips to the sick-room, and if I found him awake I reckoned we could put up a yarn for the family that would wash. But he was sleeping, and sleeping very peaceful, too; and pale, not fire-faced the way he was when he come. So I set down and laid for him to wake. In about a half an hour, Aunt Sally comes gliding in, and there I was, up a stump again! She motioned me to be still, and set down by me, and begun to whisper, and said we could all be joyful now, because all the symptoms was first rate, and he'd been sleeping like that for ever so long, and looking better and peacefuller all the time, and ten to one he'd wake up in his right mind.

So we set there watching, and by-and-by he stirs a bit, and opened his eyes very natural, and takes a look, and says:

"Hello, why I'm at *home!* How's that? Where's the raft?"

"It's all right," I says.

"And *Jim?*"

"The same," I says, but couldn't say it pretty brash. But he never noticed, but says:

"Good! Splendid! *Now* we're all right and safe! Did you tell Aunty?"

I was going to say yes; but she chipped in and says:

"About what, Sid?"

"Why, about the way the whole thing was done."

"What whole thing?"

"Why, *the* whole thing. There ain't but one; how we set the runaway nigger free—me and Tom."

"Good land! Set the run— What *is* the child talking about! Dear, dear, out of his head again!"

"No, I ain't out of my HEAD; I know all what I'm talking about. We *did* set him free—me and Tom. We laid out to do it, and we *done* it. And we done it elegant, too." He'd got a start, and she never checked him up, just set and stared and stared, and let him clip along, and I see it warn't no use for *me* to put in. "Why, Aunty, it cost us a power of work—weeks of it—hours and hours, every night, whilst you was all asleep. And we had to steal candles, and the sheet, and the shirt, and your dress, and spoons, and tin plates, and case-knives, and the warming-pan, and the grindstone, and flour, and just no end of things, and you can't think what work it was to make the saws, and pens, and inscriptions, and one thing or another, and you can't think *half* the fun it was. And we had to make up the pictures of coffins and things, and nonnamous letters from the robbers, and get up and down the lightning-rod, and dig the hole into the cabin, and make the rope-ladder and send it in cooked up in a pie, and send in spoons and things to work with, in your apron pocket"—

"Mercy sakes!"

—"and load up the cabin with rats and snakes and so on, for company for Jim; and then you kept Tom here so long with the butter in his hat that you come near spiling the whole business, because the men come before we was out of the cabin, and we had to rush, and they heard us and let drive at us, and I got my share, and we dodged out of the path and let them go by, and when the dogs come they warn't interested in us, but went for the most noise, and we got our canoe, and made for the raft, and was all safe, and Jim was a free man, and we done it all by ourselves, and *wasn't* it bully, Aunty!"

"Well, I never heard the likes of it in all my born days! So it was *you*, you little rapscallions, that's been making all this trouble, and turn everybody's wits clean inside out and scared us all most to death. I've as good a notion as ever I had in my life, to take it out o' you this very minute. To think, here I've been, night after night, a—*you* just get well once, you young scamp, and I lay

I'll tan the Old Harry out o' both o' ye!"

But Tom, he *was* so proud and joyful, he just *couldn't* hold in, and his tongue just *went* it—she a-chipping in, and spitting fire all along, and both of them going it at once, like a cat-convention; and she says:

"*Well*, you get all the enjoyment you can out of it *now*, for mind I tell you if I catch you meddling with him again—"

"Meddling with *who*?" Tom says, dropping his smile and looking surprised.

"With *who*? Why, the runaway nigger, of course. Who'd you reckon?"

Tom looks at me very grave, and says:

"Tom, didn't you just tell me he was all right? Hasn't he got away?"

"*Him*?" says Aunt Sally; "the runaway nigger? 'Deed he hasn't. They've got him back, safe and sound, and he's in that cabin again, on bread and water, and loaded down with chains, till he's claimed or sold!"

Tom rose square up in bed, with his eye hot, and his nostrils opening and shutting like gills, and sings out to me:

"They hain't no *right* to shut him up! *Shove!*—and don't you lose a minute. Turn him loose! he ain't no slave; he's as free as any cretur that walks this earth!"

"What *does* the child mean?"

"I mean every word I *say*, Aunt Sally, and if somebody don't go, *I'll* go. I've knowed him all his life, and so has Tom, there. Old Miss Watson died two months ago, and she was ashamed she ever was going to sell him down the river, and *said* so; and she set him free in her will."

"Then what on earth did *you* want to set him free for, seeing he was already free?"

"Well, that *is* a question, I must say; and *just* like women! Why, I wanted the *adventure* of it; and I'd a waded neck-deep in blood to—goodness alive, Aunt Polly!"[3]

If she warn't standing right there, just inside the door, looking as sweet and contented as an angel half-full of pie, I wish I may never!

Aunt Sally jumped for her, and most hugged the head off of her, and cried over her, and I found a good enough place for me under the bed, for it was getting pretty sultry for *us*, seemed to me. And I peeped out, and in a little while Tom's Aunt Polly shook herself loose and stood there looking across at Tom over her spectacles—kind of grinding him into the earth, you know. And then she says:

"Yes, you *better* turn y'r head away—I would if I was you,

3. Aunt Polly, introduced in the first paragraph of the novel, is Tom's rela-tive and guardian, a major figure in *The Adventures of Tom Sawyer* (1876).

Tom."

"Oh, deary me!" says Aunt Sally; "*is* he changed so? Why, that ain't *Tom* it's Sid; Tom's—Tom's—why, where is Tom? He was here a minute ago."

"You mean where's Huck *Finn*—that's what you mean! I reckon I hain't raised such a scamp as my Tom all these years, not to know him when I *see* him. That *would* be a pretty howdy-do. Come out from under that bed, Huck Finn."

So I done it. But not feeling brash.

Aunt Sally she was one of the mixed-upest looking persons I ever see; except one, and that was Uncle Silas, when he come in, and they told it all to him. It kind of made him drunk, as you may say, and he didn't know nothing at all the rest of the day, and preached a prayer-meeting sermon that night that give him a rattling ruputation, because the oldest man in the world couldn't a understood it. So Tom's Aunt Polly, she told all about who I was, and what; and I had to up and tell how I was in such a tight place that when Mrs. Phelps took me for Tom Sawyer—she chipped in and says, "Oh, go on and call me Aunt Sally, I'm used to it, now, and 'tain't no need to change"—that when Aunt Sally took me for Tom Sawyer, I had to stand it—there warn't no other way, and I knowed he wouldn't mind, because it would be nuts for him, being a mystery, and he'd make an adventure out of it and be perfectly satisfied. And so it turned out, and he let on to be Sid, and made things as soft as he could for me.

And his Aunt Polly she said Tom was right about old Miss Watson setting Jim free in her will; and so, sure enough, Tom Sawyer had gone and took all that trouble and bother to set a free nigger free! and I couldn't ever understand, before, until that minute and that talk, how he *could* help a body set a nigger free, with his bringing-up.

Well, Aunt Polly she said that when Aunt Sally wrote to her that Tom and *Sid* had come, all right and safe, she says to herself:

"Look at that, now! I might have expected it, letting him go off that way without anybody to watch him. So now I got to go and trapse all the way down the river, eleven hundred mile, and find out what that creetur's up to, *this* time; as long as I couldn't seem to get any answer out of you about it."

"Why, I never heard nothing from you," says Aunt Sally.

"Well, I wonder! Why, I wrote to you twice, to ask you what you could mean by Sid being here."

"Well, I never got 'em, Sis."

Aunt Polly, she turns around slow and severe, and says:

"You, Tom!"

"Well—*what?*" he says, kind of pettish.

"Don't you what *me*, you impudent thing—hand out them

letters."

"What letters?"

"*Them* letters. I be bound, if I have to take aholt of you I'll—"

"They're in the trunk. There, now. And they're just the same as they was when I got them out of the office. I hain't looked into them, I hain't touched them. But I knowed they'd make trouble, and I thought if you warn't in no hurry, I'd—"

"Well, you *do* need skinning, there ain't no mistake about it. And I wrote another one to tell you I was coming; and I spose he—"

"No, it come yesterday; I hain't read it yet, but *it's* all right, I've got that one."

I wanted to offer to bet two dollars she hadn't, but I reckoned maybe it was just as safe to not to. So I never said nothing.

Chapter the Last

The first time I catched Tom, private, I asked him what was his idea, time of the evasion?—what it was he'd planned to do if the evasion worked all right and he managed to set a nigger free that was already free before? And he said, what he had planned in his head, from the start, if we got Jim out all safe, was for us to run him down the river, on the raft, and have adventures plumb to the mouth of the river, and then tell him about his being free, and take him back up home on a steamboat, in style, and pay him for his lost time, and write word ahead and get out all the niggers around, and have them waltz him into town with a torchlight procession and a brass band, and then he would be a hero, and so would we. But I reckened it was about as well the way it was.

We had Jim out of the chains in no time, and when Aunt Polly and Uncle Silas and Aunt Sally found out how good he helped the doctor nurse Tom, they made a heap of fuss over him, and fixed him up prime, and give him all he wanted to eat, and a good time, and nothing to do. And we had him up to the sickroom; and had a high talk; and Tom give Jim forty dollars for being prisoner for us so patient, and doing it up so good, and Jim was pleased most to death, and busted out, and says:

"*Dah*, now, Huck, what I tell you?—what I tell you up dah on Jackson islan'? I *tole* you I got a hairy breas', en what's de sign un it; en I *tole* you I ben rich wunst, en gwineter to be rich *agin*; en it's come true; en heah she *is*! *Dah*, now! doan' talk to *me*— signs is *signs*, mine I tell you; en I knowed jis' 's well 'at I 'uz gwineter be rich agin as I's a stannin' heah dis minute!"

And then Tom he talked along, and talked along, and says, le's all three slide out of here, one of these nights, and get an outfit, and go for howling adventures amongst the Injuns, over in the Territory, for a couple of weeks or two; and I says, all right, that suits me, but I aint got no money for to buy the outfit, and I reckon I couldn't get none from home, because it's likely pap's been back before now, and got it all away from Judge Thatcher and drunk it up.

"No he hain't," Tom says; "it's all there, yet—six thousand dollars and more; and your pap hain't ever been back since. Hadn't when I come away, anyhow."

Jim says, kind of solemn:

"He ain't a comin' back no mo', Huck."

I says:

"Why, Jim?"

"Nemmine why, Huck—but he ain't comin' back no mo'."

But I kept at him; so at last he says:

"Doan' you 'member de house dat was float'n down de river, en dey wuz a man in dah, kivered up, en I went in en unkivered him and didn' let you come in? Well, den, you k'n git yo' money when you wants it; kase dat wuz him."

Tom's most well, now, and got his bullet around his neck on a watch-guard for a watch, and is always seeing what time it is, and so there ain't nothing more to write about, and I am rotten glad of it, because if I'd a knowed what a trouble it was to make a book I wouldn't a tackled it and ain't[4] agoing to no more. But I reckon I got to light out for the Territory ahead of the rest, because Aunt Sally she's going to adopt me and sivilize me and I can't stand it. I been there before.

THE END. YOURS TRULY, HUCK FINN.

1876, 1879–80, 1883   1884, 1885

4. Erroneously printed "aint't" in 1885.

The Regional Realists

BRET HARTE

(1836–1902)

Through the dramatic, romantic, and humorous use of regional material from the gold camps of the Sierras, Bret Harte brought the heady smells of pines and campfires, the raucous sounds of Poker Flat and other ephemeral mining towns, and the hilarious contrast of westerner and eastern dude to the fascinated attention of the eastern states and England. He was born in Albany, New York. At the age of eighteen he accompanied his widowed mother to California, where he became a compositor on a small Humboldt County newspaper, the *Northern California*. Moving to San Francisco as typesetter on the *Golden Era*, he soon became its editor, and later was editor of the *Californian*. In 1864 he was appointed secretary to the California Mint, a sinecure leaving him free to write.

He published a volume of poems and a book of sketches in 1867 and then, as editor of the *Overland Monthly*—the *Atlantic Monthly* of the Pacific slope—he wrote a story which carried the name of Bret Harte across the continent, "The Luck of Roaring Camp" (August, 1868). Five months later came "The Outcasts of Poker Flat" (January, 1869), and then a humorous poem, "Plain Language from Truthful James" (September, 1870), each acclaimed on both seaboards. The poem, popularly called "The Heathen Chinee," was approvingly reprinted by American newspapers, and swept on to England. Abandoning California, refusing offers from Chicago, Harte chose Boston; there, feted by the Saturday Club, he became a contributing editor of the *Atlantic Monthly* with a stipend of ten thousand dollars for which he was to supply twelve selections.

Harte disappointed the editors of the *Atlantic* by his decline in effort and performance. Though popularity lingered through the appearance of several volumes of short stories, he could not repeat his first success. His ambition for worldly recognition caused him to seek an appointment in the diplomatic service. He served as United States consul at Crefeld, Germany, in 1878, and at Glasgow from 1880 to 1885. He collected his journalistic work into numerous books: *Tales of the Argonauts* (1875), *A Sappho of Green Springs* (1891), *Colonel Starbottle's Client* (1892), *A Protégée of Jack Hamlin's* (1894), *The Bell-Ringer of Angel's* (1894), *Mr. Jack Hamlin's Meditation* (1899), and *Condensed Novels* (1902). Harte also wrote several novels and novelettes, of which *M'liss: An Idyll of Red Mountain* (1873) and *Gabriel Conroy* (1876) continue to have some appeal. He tried his hand at the drama, collaborating with Mark Twain upon an unsuccessful play, *Ah Sin* (1877). The phenomenal success of his early work in England was largely responsible for his decision to remain there at the conclusion of his diplomatic service.

His work was often sentimental, melodramatic, and mawkish; yet in his best fiction and in his collected *Poems* (1871) he succeeded in catching the flavor of a time and place in American history whose like we shall never see again.

There are several collected editions of Bret Harte. Two of the best are *The Writings of Bret Harte*, 19 vols., 1896–1914; and *The Works of Bret Harte*, 25 vols., 1914. The best biography is George R. Stewart, Jr., *Bret Harte: Argonaut and Exile*, 1931. Good volumes of selections are *Tales of the Gold Rush*, with introduction by Oscar Lewis, 1944; and *Bret Harte: Representative Selections*, edited by Joseph B. Harrison, American Writers Series, 1941.

Important critical estimates are made by Fred Lewis Pattee, *The Development of the American Short Story*, 1923, pp. 220–244; and by Arthur H. Quinn, *American Fiction*, 1936, pp. 232–242.

Mrs. Judge Jenkins[1]

(BEING THE ONLY GENUINE SEQUEL TO "MAUD MULLER")

Maud Muller all that summer day
Raked the meadow sweet with hay;

Yet, looking down the distant lane,
She hoped the Judge would come again.

But when he came, with smile and bow,   5
Maud only blushed, and stammered, "Ha-ow?"

And spoke of her "pa," and wondered whether
He'd give consent they should wed together.

Old Muller burst in tears, and then
Begged that the Judge would lend him "ten";   10

For trade was dull, and wages low,
And the "craps," this year, were somewhat slow.

1. First published in the *San Francisco News Letter and California Advertiser* for January 19, 1867, then collected in *Poems* (1871), upon which the present text is based. In Whittier's poem "Maud Muller" (1854), the simple country maiden and the Judge are represented as cherishing a lifelong sorrow that their chance meeting did not result in their marriage.

And ere the languid summer died,
Sweet Maud became the Judge's bride.

But on the day that they were mated,   15
Maud's brother Bob was intoxicated;

And Maud's relations, twelve in all,
Were very drunk at the Judge's hall;

And when the summer came again,
The young bride bore him babies twain;   20

And the Judge was blest, but thought it strange
That bearing children made such a change;

For Maud grew broad and red and stout,
And the waist that his arm once clasped about

Was more than he now could span; and he   25
Sighed as he pondered, ruefully,

How that which in Maud was native grace
In Mrs. Jenkins was out of place;

And thought of the twins, and wished that they
Looked less like the men who raked the hay   30

On Muller's farm, and dreamed with pain,
Of the day he wandered down the lane.

And looking down that dreary track,
He half regretted that he came back;

For, had he waited, he might have wed   35
Some maiden fair and thoroughbred;

For there be women fair as she,
Whose verbs and nouns do more agree.

Alas for maiden! alas for judge!
And the sentimental,—that's one-half "fudge";   40

For Maud soon thought the Judge a bore,
With all his learning and all his lore;

And the Judge would have bartered Maud's
    fair face
For more refinement and social grace.

If, of all the words of tongue and pen,   45
The saddest are, "It might have been,"

More sad are these we daily see:
  "It is, but hadn't ought to be."[2]

1867, 1871

The Angelus[3]

(HEARD AT THE MISSION, DOLORES, 1868)

Bells of the Past, whose long-forgotten music
  Still fills the wide expanse,
Tingeing the sober twilight of the Present
  With color of romance!

I hear your call, and see the sun descending,   5
  On rock and wave and sand,
As down the coast the Mission voices, blending,
  Girdle the heathen land.

Within the circle of your incantation
  No blight nor mildew falls;   10
Nor fierce unrest, nor lust, nor low ambition
  Passes those airy walls.

Borne on the swell of your long waves receding,
  I touch the farther Past;
I see the dying glow of Spanish glory,   15
  The sunset dream and last!

Before me rise the dome-shaped Mission towers,
  The white Presidio;
The swart commander in his leathern jerkin,
  The priest in stole of snow.   20

Once more I see Portolá's[4] cross uplifting
  Above the setting sun;
And past the headland, northward, slowly drifting
  The freighted galleon.

O solemn bells! whose consecrated masses   25
  Recall the faith of old;
O tinkling bells! that lulled with twilight music
  The spiritual fold!

---

2. *Cf.* "For of all sad words of tongue
or pen, / The saddest are these: 'It
might have been!'" (Whittier's "Maud
Muller").
3. Bret Harte was inspired to write
"The Angelus" upon hearing the bells
of the old Spanish mission Dolores in
San Francisco. Originally published in
the *Overland Monthly* for October.
1868, it was collected in *Poems* (1871).
The text follows the 1871 edition.
4. Don Gaspar de Portolá, Spanish governor of Lower California, discovered
San Francisco Bay in 1769.

Your voices break and falter in the darkness,—
    Break, falter, and are still;   30
And veiled and mystic, like the Host descending,
    The sun sinks from the hill!

1868, 1871

The Society Upon the Stanislaus[5]

I reside at Table Mountain, and my name is Truthful James;
I am not up to small deceit or any sinful games;
And I'll tell in simple language what I know about the row
That broke up our Society[6] upon the Stanislow.[7]

But first I would remark, that it is not a proper plan   5
For any scientific gent to whale his fellow-man,
And, if a member don't agree with his peculiar whim,
To lay for that same member for to "put a head" on him.

Now nothing could be finer or more beautiful to see
Than the first six months' proceedings of that same Society,   10
Till Brown of Calaveras[8] brought a lot of fossil bones
That he found within a tunnel near the tenement of Jones.

Then Brown he read a paper, and he reconstructed there,
From those same bones, an animal that was extremely rare;
And Jones then asked the Chair for a suspension of the rules, 15
Till he could prove that those same bones was one of his lost mules.

Then Brown he smiled a bitter smile, and said he was at fault.
It seemed he had been trespassing on Jones's family vault;
He was a most sarcastic man, this quiet Mr. Brown,
And on several occasions he had cleaned out the town.   20

Now I hold it is not decent for a scientific gent
To say another is an ass,—at least, to all intent;
Nor should the individual who happens to be meant
Reply by heaving rocks at him, to any great extent.

Then Abner Dean of Angel's[9] raised a point of order, when   25
A chunk of old red sandstone took him in the abdomen,

5. First published in the *San Francisco News Letter * * **, in 1868, as "Proceedings of the Academy of Natural Sciences at Smith's Crossing, Tuolumne Country"; then collected in *Poems* (1871) as "The Society Upon the Stanislaus." The present text is based on the latter edition.
6. The persistent outbreak of literary and scientific societies in western mining towns and frontier outposts was a phenomenon frequently satirized at the time. Harte here burlesques the California Academy of Natural Science, San Francisco.
7. Stanislaus Peak in northeastern California.
8. Calaveras County, east of San Francisco. *Cf.* Harte's story "Brown of Calaveras" (1870), and Mark Twain's "The Celebrated Jumping Frog of Calaveras County."
9. Now Angels Camp, a mining town in northeastern California.

And he smiled a kind of sickly smile, and curled up on the floor,
And the subsequent proceedings interested him no more.

For, in less time than I write it, every member did engage
In a warfare with the remnants of a palæozoic age;   30
And the way they heaved those fossils in their anger was a sin,
Till the skull of an old mammoth caved the head of Thompson in.

And this is all I have to say of these improper games,
For I live at Table Mountain, and my name is Truthful James;
And I've told in simple language what I know about the row   35
That broke up our Society upon the Stanislow.

1868, 1871

"Crotalus"[1]

(RATTLESNAKE BAR, SIERRAS)

No life in earth, or air, or sky;
The sunbeams, broken silently,
On the bared rocks around me lie,—

Cold rocks with half-warmed lichens scarred,
And scales of moss; and scarce a yard   5
Away, one long strip, yellow-barred.

Lost in a cleft! 'T is but a stride
To reach it, thrust its roots aside,
And lift it on thy stick astride!

Yet stay! That moment is thy grace!   10
For round thee, thrilling air and space,
A chattering terror fills the place!

A sound as of dry bones that stir
In the Dead Valley! By yon fir
The locust stops its noonday whir!   15

The wild bird hears; smote with the sound,
As if by bullet brought to ground,
On broken wing, dips, wheeling round!

The hare, transfixed, with trembling lip,
Halts breathless, on pulsating hip,   20
And palsied tread, and heels that slip.

.   .   .   .

1. A rattlesnake. The poem first appeared in *Some Later Verses* (1898).

Enough old friend!—'t is thou. Forget
My heedless foot, nor longer fret
The peace with thy grim castanet!

I know thee! Yes! Thou mayst forego   25
That lifted crest; the measured blow
Beyond which thy pride scorns to go,

Or yet retract! For me no spell
Lights those slit orbs, where, some think, dwell
Machicolated[2] fires of hell!   30

I only know thee humble, bold,
Haughty, with miseries untold,
And the old Curse[3] that left thee cold,

And drove thee ever to the sun,
On blistering rocks; nor made thee shun   35
Our cabin's hearth when day was done,

And the spent ashes warmed thee best;
We knew thee,—silent, joyless guest
Of our rude ingle. E'en thy quest

Of the rare milk-bowl seemed to be   40
Naught but a brother's poverty,
And Spartan taste that kept thee free

From lust and rapine. Thou! whose fame
Searchest the grass with tongue of flame,
Making all creatures seem thy game;   45

When the whole woods before thee run,
Asked but—when all was said and done—
To lie, untrodden, in the sun!

1898

The Outcasts of Poker Flat[4]

As Mr. John Oakhurst, gambler, stepped into the main street of
Poker Flat on the morning of the 23d of November, 1850, he was
conscious of a change in its moral atmosphere since the preceding
night. Two or three men, conversing earnestly together, ceased as
he approached, and exchanged significant glances. There was a Sab-

2. Eyes like machicolations, projected openings through which missiles could be cast on an enemy beneath.
3. *Cf.* Genesis iii: 14.

4. First published in the *Overland Monthly* for January, 1869, and collected in *The Luck of Roaring Camp and Other Sketches* (1870), which the present text follows.

bath lull in the air, which, in a settlement unused to Sabbath influences, looked ominous.

Mr. Oakhurst's calm, handsome face betrayed small concern in these indications. Whether he was conscious of any predisposing cause, was another question. "I reckon they're after somebody," he reflected; "likely it's me." He returned to his pocket the handkerchief with which he had been whipping away the red dust of Poker Flat from his neat boots, and quietly discharged his mind of any further conjecture.

In point of fact, Poker Flat was "after somebody." It had lately suffered the loss of several thousand dollars, two valuable horses, and a prominent citizen. It was experiencing a spasm of virtuous reaction, quite as lawless and ungovernable as any of the acts that had provoked it. A secret committee[5] had determined to rid the town of all improper persons. This was done permanently in regard to two men who were then hanging from the boughs of a sycamore in the gulch, and temporarily in the banishment of certain other objectionable characters. I regret to say that some of these were ladies. It is but due to the sex, however, to state that their impropriety was professional, and it was only in such easily established standards of evil that Poker Flat ventured to sit in judgment.

Mr. Oakhurst was right in supposing that he was included in this category. A few of the committee had urged hanging him as a possible example, and a sure method of reimbursing themselves from his pockets of the sums he had won from them. "It's agin justice," said Jim Wheeler, "to let this yer young man from Roaring Camp —an entire stranger—carry away our money." But a crude sentiment of equity residing in the breasts of those who had been fortunate enough to win from Mr. Oakhurst overruled this narrower local prejudice.

Mr. Oakhurst received his sentence with philosophic calmness, none the less coolly that he was aware of the hesitation of his judges. He was too much of a gambler not to accept fate. With him life was at best an uncertain game, and he recognized the usual percentage in favor of the dealer.

A body of armed men accompanied the deported wickedness of Poker Flat to the outskirts of the settlement. Besides Mr. Oakhurst, who was known to be a coolly desperate man, and for whose intimidation the armed escort was intended, the expatriated party consisted of a young woman familiarly known as "The Duchess"; another, who had won the title of "Mother Shipton"; and "Uncle Billy," a suspected sluice-robber[6] and confirmed drunkard. The cavalcade provoked no comments from the spectators, nor was any word

5. Vigilance committees were often organized in the West for the protection of life and property.

6. In gold mining, the sluice was a trough or series of boxes through which gold was washed from gravel and sand.

uttered by the escort. Only when the gulch which marked the utter-most limit of Poker Flat was reached, the leader spoke briefly and to the point. The exiles were forbidden to return at the peril of their lives.

As the escort disappeared, their pent-up feelings found vent in a few hysterical tears from the Duchess, some bad language from Mother Shipton, and a Parthian[7] volley of expletives from Uncle Billy. The philosophic Oakhurst alone remained silent. He listened calmly to Mother Shipton's desire to cut somebody's heart out, to the repeated statements of the Duchess that she would die in the road, and to the alarming oaths that seemed to be bumped out of Uncle Billy as he rode forward. With the easy good humor charac-teristic of his class, he insisted upon exchanging his own riding-horse, "Five-Spot," for the sorry mule which the Duchess rode. But even this act did not draw the party into any closer sympathy. The young woman readjusted her somewhat draggled plumes with a feeble, faded coquetry; Mother Shipton eyed the possessor of "Five-Spot" with malevolence, and Uncle Billy included the whole party in one sweeping anathema.

The road to Sandy Bar—a camp that, not having as yet experi-enced the regenerating influences of Poker Flat, consequently seemed to offer some invitation to the emigrants—lay over a steep moun-tain range. It was distant a day's severe travel. In that advanced season, the party soon passed out of the moist, temperate regions of the foothills into the dry, cold, bracing air of the Sierras. The trail was narrow and difficult. At noon the Duchess, rolling out of her saddle upon the ground, declared her intention of going no farther, and the party halted.

The spot was singularly wild and impressive. A wooded amphi-theatre, surrounded on three sides by precipitous cliffs of naked granite, sloped gently toward the crest of another precipice that over-looked the valley. It was, undoubtedly, the most suitable spot for a camp, had camping been advisable. But Mr. Oakhurst knew that scarcely half the journey to Sandy Bar was accomplished, and the party were not equipped or provisioned for delay. This fact he pointed out to his companions curtly, with a philosophic com-mentary on the folly of "throwing up their hand before the game was played out." But they were furnished with liquor, which in this emergency stood them in place of food, fuel, rest, and prescience. In spite of his remonstrances, it was not long before they were more or less under its influence. Uncle Billy passed rapidly from a bellicose state into one of stupor, the Duchess became maudlin, and Mother Shipton snored. Mr. Oakhurst alone remained erect, leaning against

7. The Parthians, Asians of the first century B.C., would counterfeit wild flight from their enemies, and then wheel, catching them off guard with a quick volley.

a rock, calmly surveyed them.

Mr. Oakhurst did not drink. It interfered with a profession which required coolness, impassiveness, and presence of mind, and, in his own language, he "couldn't afford it." As he gazed at his recumbent fellow exiles, the loneliness begotten of his pariah trade, his habits of life, his very vices, for the first time seriously oppressed him. He bestirred himself in dusting his black clothes, washing his hands and face, and other acts characteristic of his studiously neat habits, and for a moment forgot his annoyance. The thought of deserting his weaker and more pitiable companions never perhaps occurred to him. Yet he could not help feeling the want of that excitement which, singularly enough, was most conducive to that calm equanimity for which he was notorious. He looked at the gloomy walls that rose a thousand feet sheer above the circling pines around him, at the sky ominously clouded, at the valley below, already deepening into shadow; and, doing so, suddenly he heard his own name called.

A horseman slowly ascended the trail. In the fresh, open face of the newcomer Mr. Oakhurst recognized Tom Simson, otherwise known as "The Innocent," of Sandy Bar. He had met him some months before over a "little game," and had, with perfect equanimity, won the entire fortune—amounting to some forty dollars—of that guileless youth. After the game was finished, Mr. Oakhurst drew the youthful speculator behind the door and thus addressed him: "Tommy, you're a good little man, but you can't gamble worth a cent. Don't try it over again." He then handed him his money back, pushed him gently from the room, and so made a devoted slave of Tom Simson.

There was a remembrance of this in his boyish and enthusiastic greeting of Mr. Oakhurst. He had started, he said, to go to Poker Flat to seek his fortune. "Alone?" No, not exactly alone; in fact (a giggle), he had run away with Piney Woods. Didn't Mr. Oakhurst remember Piney? She that used to wait on the table at the Temperance House? They had been engaged a long time, but old Jake Woods had objected, and so they had run away, and were going to Poker Flat to be married, and here they were. And they were tired out, and how lucky it was they had found a place to camp, and company. All this the Innocent delivered rapidly, while Piney, a stout, comely damsel of fifteen, emerged from behind the pine-tree, where she had been blushing unseen, and rode to the side of her lover.

Mr. Oakhurst seldom troubled himself with sentiment, still less with propriety; but he had a vague idea that the situation was not fortunate. He retained, however, his presence of mind sufficiently to kick Uncle Billy, who was about to say something, and Uncle Billy was sober enough to recognize in Mr. Oakhurst's kick a superior power that would not bear trifling. He then endeavored to dissuade Tom Simson from delaying further, but in vain. He even pointed out the fact that there was no provision, nor means of making a camp. But, unluckily, the Innocent met this objection by assuring the party that he was provided with an extra mule loaded with provisions, and by the discovery of a rude attempt at a log house near the trail. "Piney can stay with Mrs. Oakhurst," said the Innocent, pointing to the Duchess, "and I can shift for myself."

Nothing but Mr. Oakhurst's admonishing foot saved Uncle Billy from bursting into a roar of laughter. As it was, he felt compelled to retire up the cañon until he could recover his gravity. There he confided the joke to the tall pine-trees, with many slaps of his leg, contortions of his face, and the usual profanity. But when he returned to the party, he found them seated by a fire—for the air had grown strangely chill and the sky overcast—in apparently amicable conversation. Piney was actually talking in an impulsive girlish fashion to the Duchess, who was listening with an interest and animation she had not shown for many days. The Innocent was holding forth, apparently with equal effect, to Mr. Oakhurst and Mother Shipton, who was actually relaxing into amiability. "Is this yer a d——d picnic?" said Uncle Billy, with inward scorn, as he surveyed the sylvan group, the glancing firelight, and the tethered animals in the foreground. Suddenly an idea mingled with the alcoholic fumes that disturbed his brain. It was apparently of a jocular nature, for he felt impelled to slap his leg again and cram his fist into his mouth.

As the shadows crept slowly up the mountain, a slight breeze rocked the tops of the pine-trees and moaned through their long and gloomy aisles. The ruined cabin, patched and covered with pine bows, was set apart for the ladies. As the lovers parted, they unaffectedly exchanged a kiss, so honest and sincere that it might have been heard above the swaying pines. The frail Duchess and the malevolent Mother Shipton were probably too stunned to remark upon this last evidence of simplicity, and so turned without a word to the hut. The fire was replenished, the men lay down before the door, and in a few minutes were asleep.

Mr. Oakhurst was a light sleeper. Toward morning he awoke benumbed and cold. As he stirred the dying fire, the wind, which was now blowing strongly, brought to his cheek that which caused the blood to leave it,—snow!

He started to his feet with the intention of awakening the sleepers, for there was no time to lose. But turning to where Uncle Billy had been lying, he found him gone. A suspicion leaped to his brain. and a curse to his lips. He ran to the spot where the mules had been tethered—they were no longer there. The tracks were already rapidly disappearing in the snow.

The momentary excitement brought Mr. Oakhurst back to the fire with his usual calm. He did not waken the sleepers. The Innocent slumbered peacefully, with a smile on his good-humored, freckled face; the virgin Piney slept beside her frailer sisters as sweetly as though attended by celestial guardians; and Mr. Oakhurst, drawing his blanket over his shoulders, stroked his mustaches and waited for the dawn. It came slowly in a whirling mist of snowflakes that dazzled and confused the eye. What could be seen of the landscape appeared magically changed. He looked over the valley, and summed up the present and future in two words, "Snowed in!"

A careful inventory of the provisions, which, fortunately for the party, had been stored within the hut, and so escaped the felonious fingers of Uncle Billy, disclosed the fact that with care and prudence they might last ten days longer. "That is," said Mr. Oakhurst *sotto voce*[8] to the Innocent, "if you're willing to board us. If you ain't—and perhaps you'd better not—you can wait till Uncle Billy gets back with provisions." For some occult reason, Mr. Oakhurst could not bring himself to disclose Uncle Billy's rascality, and so offered the hypothesis that he had wandered from the camp and had accidentally stampeded the animals. He dropped a warning to the Duchess and Mother Shipton, who of course knew the facts of their associate's defection. "They'll find out the truth about us *all* when they find out anything," he added significantly, "and there's no good frightening them now."

Tom Simson not only put all his worldly store at the disposal of Mr. Oakhurst, but seemed to enjoy the prospect of their enforced seclusion. "We'll have a good camp for a week, and then the snow'll melt, and we'll all go back together." The cheerful gayety of the young man and Mr. Oakhurst's calm infected the others. The Innocent, with the aid of pine boughs, extemporized a thatch for the roofless cabin, and the Duchess directed Piney in the rearrangement of the interior with a taste and tact that opened the blue eyes of that provincial maiden to their fullest extent. "I reckon now you're used to fine things at Poker Flat," said Piney. The Duchess turned away sharply to conceal something that reddened her cheeks through their professional tint, and Mother Shipton requested Piney not to "chatter." But when Mr. Oakhurst returned from a weary search for the trail, he heard the sound of happy laughter echoed from the rocks. He stopped in some alarm, and his thoughts first naturally reverted to the whiskey, which he had prudently cachéd. "And yet it don't somehow sound like whiskey," said the gambler. It was not until he caught sight of the blazing fire through the still

8. In a low tone.

blinding storm, and the group around it, that he settled to the conviction that it was "square fun."

Whether Mr. Oakhurst had cachéd his cards with the whiskey as something debarred the free access of the community, I cannot say. It was certain that, in Mother Shipton's words, he "didn't say 'cards' once" during that evening. Haply the time was beguiled by an accordion, produced somewhat ostentatiously by Tom Simson from his pack. Notwithstanding some difficulties attending the manipulation of this instrument, Piney Woods managed to pluck several reluctant melodies from its keys, to an accompaniment by the Innocent on a pair of bone castanets. But the crowning festivity of the evening was reached in a rude camp-meeting hymn, which the lovers, joining hands, sang with great earnestness and vociferation. I fear that a certain defiant tone and Convenanter's[9] swing to its chorus, rather than any devotional quality, caused it speedily to infect the others, who at last joined in the refrain:

> "I'm proud to live in the service of the Lord,
> And I'm bound to die in His army."[1]

The pines rocked, the storm eddied and whirled above the miserable group, and the flames of their altar leaped heavenward, as if in token of the vow.

At midnight the storm abated, the rolling clouds parted, and the stars glittered keenly above the sleeping camp. Mr. Oakhurst, whose professional habits had enabled him to live on the smallest possible amount of sleep, in dividing the watch with Tom Simson somehow managed to take upon himself the greater part of that duty. He excused himself to the Innocent by saying that he had "often been a week without sleep." "Doing what?" asked Tom. "Poker!" replied Oakhurst sententiously. "When a man gets a streak of luck,—nigger-luck,[2]—he don't get tired. The luck gives in first. Luck," continued the gambler reflectively, "is a mighty queer thing. All you know about it for certain is that it's bound to change. And it's finding out when it's going to change that makes you. We've had a streak of bad luck since we left Poker Flat,—you come along, and slap you get into it, too. If you can hold your cards right along you're all right. For," added the gambler, with cheerful irrelevance—

> " 'I'm proud to live in the service of the Lord,
> And I'm bound to die in His army.' "

---

9. *I.e.*, the martial beat of the songs of the Scottish Covenanters, who militantly supported their claim for separation from the Church of England in the seventeenth century.
1. Refrain of an early American spiritual, "Service of the Lord."
2. Unexpected good luck.

The third day came, and the sun, looking through the white-cur-
tained valley, saw the outcasts divide their slowly decreasing store of
provisions for the morning meal. It was one of the peculiarities of
that mountain climate that its rays diffused a kindly warmth over
the wintry landscape, as if in regretful commiseration of the past.
But it revealed drift on drift of snow piled high around the hut,—a
hopeless, uncharted, trackless sea of white lying below the rocky
shores to which the castaways still clung. Through the marvelously
clear air the smoke of the pastoral village of Poker Flat rose miles
away. Mother Shipton saw it, and from a remote pinnacle of her
rocky fastness hurled in that direction a final malediction. It was her
last vituperative attempt, and perhaps for that reason was invested
with a certain degree of sublimity. It did her good, she privately informed the Duchess. "Just you go out there and cuss, and see." She
then set herself to the task of amusing "the child," as she and the
Duchess were pleased to call Piney. Piney was no chicken, but it
was a soothing and original theory of the pair thus to account for
the fact that she didn't swear and wasn't improper.

When night crept up again through the gorges, the reedy notes
of the accordion rose and fell in fitful spasms and long-drawn gasps
by the flickering campfire. But music failed to fill entirely the
aching void left by insufficient food, and a new diversion was proposed by Piney,—story-telling. Neither Mr. Oakhurst nor his female
companions caring to relate their personal experiences, this plan
would have failed too, but for the Innocent. Some months before
he had chanced upon a stray copy of Mr. Pope's ingenious translation of the Iliad. He now proposed to narrate the principal incidents of that poem—having thoroughly mastered the argument
and fairly forgotten the words—in the current vernacular of Sandy
Bar. And so for the rest of that night the Homeric demigods again
walked the earth. Trojan bully and wily Greek wrestled in the
winds, and the great pines in the cañon seemed to bow to the
wrath of the son of Peleus.[3] Mr. Oakhurst listened with quiet satisfaction. Most especially was he interested in the fate of "Ash-
heels,"[4] as the Innocent persisted in denominating the "swift-footed
Achilles."

So, with small food and much of Homer and the accordion, a
week passed over the heads of the outcasts. The sun again forsook
them, and again from leaden skies the snowflakes were sifted over
the land. Day by day closer around them drew the snowy circle,
until at last they looked from their prison over drifted walls of
dazzling white, that towered twenty feet above their heads. It became more and more difficult to replenish their fires, even from the

3. Achilles.
4. The mispronunciation is reinforced by the fact that Achilles could be wounded only in the heel.

fallen trees beside them, now half hidden in the drifts. And yet no one complained. The lovers turned from the dreary prospect and looked into each other's eyes, and were happy. Mr. Oakhurst settled himself coolly to the losing game before him. The Duchess, more cheerful than she had been, assumed the care of Piney. Only Mother Shipton—once the strongest of the party—seemed to sicken and fade. At midnight on the tenth day she called Oakhurst to her side. "I'm going," she said, in a voice of querulous weakness, "but don't say anything about it. Don't waken the kids. Take the bundle from under my head, and open it." Mr. Oakhurst did so. It contained Mother Shipton's rations for the last week, untouched. "Give 'em to the child," she said, pointing to the sleeping Piney. "You've starved yourself," said the gambler. "That's what they call it," said the woman querulously, as she lay down again, and, turning her face to the wall, passed quietly away.

The accordion and the bones were put aside that day, and Homer was forgotten. When the body of Mother Shipton had been committed to the snow, Mr. Oakhurst took the Innocent aside, and showed him a pair of snowshoes, which he had fashioned from the old pack-saddle. "There's one chance in a hundred to save her yet," he said, pointing to Piney; "but it's there," he added, pointing toward Poker Flat. "If you can reach there in two days she's safe." "And you?" asked Tom Simson. "I'll stay here," was the curt reply.

The lovers parted with a long embrace. "You are not going, too?" said the Duchess, as she saw Mr. Oakhurst apparently waiting to accompany him. "As far as the cañon," he replied. He turned suddenly and kissed the Duchess, leaving her pallid face aflame, and her trembling limbs rigid with amazement.

Night came, but not Mr. Oakhurst. It brought the storm again and the whirling snow. Then the Duchess, feeding the fire, found that some one had quietly piled beside the hut enough fuel to last a few days longer. The tears rose to her eyes, but she hid them from Piney.

The women slept but little. In the morning, looking into each other's faces, they read their fate. Neither spoke, but Piney, accepting the position of the stronger, drew near and placed her arm around the Duchess's waist. They kept this attitude for the rest of the day. That night the storm reached its greatest fury, and, rending asunder the protecting pines, invaded the very hut.

Toward morning they found themselves unable to feed the fire, which gradually died away. As the embers slowly blackened, the Duchess crept closer to Piney, and broke the silence of many hours: "Piney, can you pray?" "No, dear," said Piney simply. The Duchess, without knowing exactly why, felt relieved, and, putting her head upon Piney's shoulder, spoke no more. And so reclining, the younger and purer pillowing the head of her soiled sister upon her virgin breast, they fell asleep.

The wind lulled as if it feared to waken them. Feathery drifts of snow, shaken from the long pine boughs, flew like white-winged birds, and settled about them as they slept. The moon through the rifted clouds looked down upon what had been the camp. But all human stain, all trace of earthly travail, was hidden beneath the spotless mantle mercifully flung from above.

They slept all that day and the next, nor did they waken when voices and footsteps broke the silence of the camp. And when pitying fingers brushed the snow from their wan faces, you could scarcely have told, from the equal peace that dwelt upon them, which was she that had sinned. Even the law of Poker Flat recognized this, and turned away, leaving them still locked in each other's arms.

But at the head of the gulch, on one of the largest pinetrees, they found the deuce of clubs pinned to the bark with a bowie-knife. It bore the following, written in pencil in a firm hand:

†

BENEATH THIS TREE
LIES THE BODY
OF
JOHN OAKHURST,
WHO STRUCK A STREAK OF BAD LUCK
ON THE 23D OF NOVEMBER, 1850,
AND
HANDED IN HIS CHECKS
ON THE 7TH DECEMBER, 1850

↓

And pulseless and cold, with a Derringer[5] by his side and a bullet in his heart, though still calm as in life, beneath the snow lay he who was at once the strongest and yet the weakest of the outcasts of Poker Flat.

1869, 1870

5. A small pistol of large caliber, either single- or double-barreled.

GEORGE WASHINGTON CABLE
(1844–1925)

George Washington Cable, born in New Orleans of ancestry from Virginia on his father's side and from New England on his mother's, combined the grace of the Cavaliers with a strict

Puritan piety. After a short period of newspaper work in New Orleans, he held a position in the office of a cotton warehouse from 1865 until 1881. His leisure time was spent in observant rambles about the fascinating older, or Creole, quarters of New Orleans. His sketches and narratives, appearing from time to time in the New Orleans *Picayune*, began to attract attention, and *Scribner's Monthly* published " 'Sieur George" in October, 1873.

For six years he contributed to magazines before publishing his first collection, *Old Creole Days* (1879). Here are the old French quarter of New Orleans and ante-bellum Louisiana plantations, mellowed and heightened by a feeling for atmosphere and character that was learned from French masters of the short story. Strict realism in respect to dialect was combined with impressionistic treatment of background and character. Yet these stories are genuinely local in portraying the survival of the chivalric code, and the loyalty, devotion, and self-sacrifice prevailing in these families of ruined gentlemen and high-spirited women.

Among Cable's novels *The Grandissimes* (1880), in spite of its involved plot, is recognized as a pioneer among the fictional studies of the decadence resulting from slavery in the Old South. However, *Madame Delphine* (1881), a novelette, is Cable's masterpiece, a tragedy of miscegenation and mother love.

As with many of the local colorists, Cable's first stories were his best; and although he wrote novels and stories about the Civil War and the Reconstruction, he was most successful in dealing with an older Louisiana. In 1885 he moved to Northampton, Massachusetts, because of southern resentment at his outspoken liberalism, which he later expressed in such books as *The Silent South* (1885) and *The Negro Question* (1890).

There is no complete edition of Cable's work. A dependable biography is that by his daughter, Lucy L. C. Biklé, *George W. Cable: His Life and Letters*, 1928. Arlin Turner, *George W. Cable: A Biography*, 1956, is a thorough, scholarly treatment.

Belles Demoiselles Plantation[1]

The original grantee was Count——, assume the name to be De Charleu; the old Creoles[2] never forgive a public mention. He was the French king's commissary. One day, called to France to explain the lucky accident of the commissariat having burned down with his account-books inside, he left his wife, a Choctaw[3] Comptesse, behind.

1. First printed in *Scribner's Monthly* for April, 1874, this story was collected in *Old Creole Days* (1879), upon which the present text is based.
2. In Louisiana a person of French or French and Spanish ancestry.

3. A native American Indian of a peaceful tribe then living in a small area of Louisiana just north of Lake Pontchartrain; this was one of the first tribes with which the French made an alliance and traded.

Arrived at court, his excuses were accepted, and that tract granted him where afterwards stood Belles Demoiselles[4] Plantation. A man cannot remember every thing! In a fit of forgetfulness he married a French gentlewoman, rich and beautiful, and "brought her out."[5] However, "All's well that ends well;" a famine had been in the colony, and the Choctaw Comptesse had starved, leaving nought but a half-caste orphan family lurking on the edge of the settlement, bearing our French gentlewoman's own new name, and being mentioned in Monsieur's will.

And the new Comptesse—she tarried but a twelve-month, left Monsieur a lovely son, and departed, led out of this vain world by the swamp-fever.

From this son sprang the proud Creole family of De Charleu. It rose straight up, up, up, generation after generation, tall, branchless, slender, palm-like; and finally, in the time of which I am to tell, flowered with all the rare beauty of a century-plant, in Artemise, Innocente, Felicité, the twins Marie and Martha, Leontine and little Septima; the seven beautiful daughters for whom their home had been fitly named Belles Demoiselles.

The Count's grant had once been a long Pointe,[6] round which the Mississippi used to whirl, and seethe, and foam, that it was horrid to behold. Big whirlpools would open and wheel about in the savage eddies under the low bank, and close up again, and others open, and spin, and disappear. Great circles of muddy surface would boil up from hundreds of feet below, and gloss over, and seem to float away,—sink, come back again under water, and with only a soft hiss surge up again, and again drift off, and vanish. Every few minutes the loamy bank would tip down a great load of earth upon its besieger, and fall back a foot,—sometimes a yard,—and the writhing river would press after, until at last the Pointe was quite swallowed up, and the great river glided by in a majestic curve, and asked no more; the bank stood fast, the "caving" became a forgotten misfortune, and the diminished grant was a long, sweeping, willowy bend, rustling with miles of sugar-cane.

Coming up the Mississippi in the sailing craft of those early days, about the time one first could descry the white spires of the old St. Louis Cathedral,[7] you would be pretty sure to spy, just over to your right under the levee,[8] Belles Demoiselles Mansion, with its broad veranda and red painted cypress roof, peering over the embankment, like a bird in the nest, half hid by the avenue of willows which one of the departed De Charleus,—he that married a Marot,—had planted on the levee's crown.

4. French, meaning "beautiful young ladies."
5. *I.e.*, to colonial Louisiana.
6. Arrow-shaped cape.

7. St. Louis Cathedral, erected in 1794, stands on the site of the first church in New Orleans.
8. An embankment to prevent flooding.

The house stood unusually near the river, facing eastward, and standing four-square, with an immense veranda about its sides, and a flight of steps in front spreading broadly downward, as we open arms to a child. From the veranda nine miles of river were seen; and in their compass, near at hand, the shady garden full of rare and beautiful flowers; farther away broad fields of cane and rice, and the distant quarters of the slaves, and on the horizon everywhere a dark belt of cypress forest.

The master was old Colonel De Charleu,—Jean Albert Henri Joseph De Charleu-Marot, and "Colonel" by the grace of the first American governor.[9] Monsieur,—he would not speak to any one who called him "Colonel,"—was a hoary-headed patriarch. His step was firm, his form erect, his intellect strong and clear, his countenance classic, serene, dignified, commanding, his manners courtly, his voice musical,—fascinating. He had had his vices,—all his life; but had borne them, as his race do, with a serenity of conscience and a cleanness of mouth that left no outward blemish on the surface of the gentleman. He had gambled in Royal Street,[1] drank hard in Orleans Street,[2] run his adversary through in the duelling-ground at Slaughter-house Point,[3] and danced and quarrelled at the St. Philippe-street-theatre quadroon balls.[4] Even now, with all his courtesy and bounty, and a hospitality which seemed to be entertaining angels, he was bitter-proud and penurious, and deep down in his hard-finished heart loved nothing but himself, his name, and his motherless children. But these!—their ravishing beauty was all but excuse enough for the unbounded idolatry of their father. Against these seven goddesses he never rebelled. Had they even required him to defraud old De Carlos—

I can hardly say.

Old De Carlos was his extremely distant relative on the Choctaw side. With this single exception, the narrow thread-like line of descent from the Indian wife, diminished to a mere strand by injudicious alliances, and deaths in the gutters of old New Orleans, was extinct. The name, by Spanish contact, had become De Carlos; but this one surviving bearer of it was known to all, and known only, as Injin Charlie.

9. On March 26, 1806, Governor William C. C. Claiborne of the Mississippi Territory was appointed to administer the Territory of Orleans, acquired by the Louisiana Purchase.
1. Royal Street was lined with gambling houses from 1830 to 1860, the period when the steamboats brought wealth and the plantations flourished.
2. Orleans Street, named after the Regent, Duc d' Orleans, was the center of the original city and the main cross street.

3. Duels were prevalent; the old "Duelling Oaks," scene of a thousand encounters, are now enclosed in the City Park.
4. St. Philippe Theatre, once the fashionable rendezvous of the city, was the scene of the quadroon balls from 1810 to 1830. Quadroon girls—one-fourth Negro—were often chastely reared and trained in the social graces in hopes of finding a white "protector," since their Negro blood prohibited marriage with a white person, even if they were not slaves.

One thing I never knew a Creole to do. He will not utterly go back on the ties of blood, no matter what sort of knots those ties may be. For one reason, he is never ashamed of his or his father's sins; and for another,—he will tell you—he is "all heart!"

So the different heirs of the De Charleu estate had always strictly regarded the rights and interests of the De Carloses, especially their ownership of a block of dilapidated buildings in a part of the city, which had once been very poor property, but was beginning to be valuable. This block had much more than maintained the last De Carlos through a long and lazy lifetime, and, as his household consisted only of himself, and an aged and crippled negress, the inference was irresistible that he "had money." Old Charlie, though by *alias* an "Injin," was plainly a dark white man, about as old as Colonel De Charleu, sunk in the bliss of deep ignorance, shrewd, deaf, and, by repute at least, unmerciful.

The Colonel and he always conversed in English. This rare accomplishment, which the former had learned from his Scotch wife, —the latter from up-river traders,—they found an admirable medium of communication, answering, better than French could, a similar purpose to that of the stick which we fasten to the bit of one horse and breast-gear of another, whereby each keeps his distance. Once in a while, too, by way of jest, English found its way among the ladies of Belles Demoiselles, always signifying that their sire was about to have business with old Charlie.

Now a long-standing wish to buy out Charlie troubled the Colonel. He had no desire to oust him unfairly; he was proud of being always fair; yet he did long to engross the whole estate under one title. Out of his luxurious idleness he had conceived this desire, and thought little of so slight an obstacle as being already somewhat in debt to old Charlie for money borrowed, and for which Belles Demoiselles was, of course, good, ten times over. Lots, buildings, rents, all, might as well be his, he thought, to give, keep, or destroy. "Had he but the old man's heritage. Ah! he might bring that into existence which his *belles demoiselles* had been begging for, 'since many years;' a home,—and such a home,—in the gay city. Here he should tear down this row of cottages, and make his garden wall; there that long rope-walk[5] should give place to vine-covered arbors; the bakery yonder should make way for a costly conservatory; that wine warehouse should come down, and the mansion go up. It should be the finest in the State. Men should never pass it, but they should say—'the palace of the De Charleus; a family of grand descent, a people of elegance and bounty, a line as old as France, a fine old man, and seven daughters as beautiful as happy; whoever dare attempt to marry there must leave his own

5 **A** covered walk or room where ropes were manufactured.

name behind him!'

"The house should be of stones fitly set, brought down in ships from the land of 'les Yankees,' and it should have an airy belvedere,[6] with a gilded image tip-toeing and shining on its peak, and from it you should see, far across the gleaming folds of the river, the red roof of Belles Demoiselles, the country-seat. At the big stone gate there should be a porter's lodge, and it should be a privilege even to see the ground."

Truly they were a family fine enough, and fancy-free enough to have fine wishes, yet happy enough where they were, to have had no wish but to live there always.

To those, who, by whatever fortune, wandered into the garden of Belles Demoiselles some summer afternoon as the sky was reddening towards evening, it was lovely to see the family gathered out upon the tiled pavement at the foot of the broad front steps, gayly chatting and jesting, with that ripple of laughter that comes so pleasingly from a bevy of girls. The father would be found seated in their midst, the centre of attention and compliment, witness, arbiter, umpire, critic, by his beautiful children's unanimous appointment, but the single vassal, too, of seven absolute sovereigns.

Now they would draw their chairs near together in eager discussion of some new step in the dance, or the adjustment of some rich adornment. Now they would start about him with excited comments to see the eldest fix a bunch of violets in his button-hole. Now the twins would move down a walk after some unusual flower, and be greeted on their return with the high-pitched notes of delighted feminine surprise.

As evening came on they would draw more quietly about their paternal centre. Often their chairs were forsaken, and they grouped themselves on the lower steps, one above another, and surrendered themselves to the tender influences of the approaching night. At such an hour the passer on the river, already attracted by the dark figures of the broad-roofed mansion, and its woody garden standing against the glowing sunset, would hear the voices of the hidden group rise from the spot in the soft harmonies of an evening song; swelling clearer and clearer as the thrill of music warmed them into feeling, and presently joined by the deeper tones of the father's voice; then, as the daylight passed quite away, all would be still, and he would know that the beautiful home had gathered its nestlings under its wings.

And yet, for mere vagary, it pleased them not to be pleased.

"Arti!" called one sister to another in the broad hall, one morning,—mock amazement in her distended eyes,—"something is goin' to took place!"

6. An open, roofed gallery on the top story, built for a view of the scenery.

"*Comm-e-n-t?*"[7]—long-drawn perplexity.

"Papa is goin' to town!"

The news passed up stairs.

"Inno!"—one to another meeting in a doorway,—"something is goin' to took place!"

"*Qu'est-ce-que c'est!*"[8]—vain attempt at gruffness.

"Papa is goin' to town!"

The unusual tidings were true. It was afternoon of the same day that the Colonel tossed his horse's bridle to his groom, and stepped up to old Charlie, who was sitting on his bench under a China-tree, his head, as was his fashion, bound in a Madras handkerchief. The "old man" was plainly under the effect of spirits, and smiled a deferential salutation without trusting himself to his feet.

"Eh, well Charlie!"—the Colonel raised his voice to suit his kinsman's deafness,—"how is those times with my friend Charlie?"

"Eh?" said Charlie, distractedly.

"Is that goin' well with my friend Charlie?"

"In de house,—call her,"—making a pretence of rising.

"*Non, non!* I don't want,"—the speaker paused to breathe—"'ow is collection?"

"Oh!" said Charlie, "every day he make me more poorer!"

"What do you hask for it?" asked the planter indifferently, designating the house by a wave of his whip.

"Ask for w'at?" said Injin Charlie.

"De *house!* What you ask for it?"

"I don't believe," said Charlie.

"What you would *take* for it!" cried the planter.

"Wait for w'at?"

"What you would *take* for the whole block?"

"I don't want to sell him!"

"I'll give you *ten thousand dollah* for it."

"Ten t'ousand dollah for dis house? Oh, no, dat is no price. He is blame good old house,—dat old house." (Old Charlie and the Colonel never swore in presence of each other.) "Forty years dat old house didn't had to be paint! I easy can get fifty t'ousand dollah for dat old house."

"Fifty thousand picayunes;[9] yes," said the Colonel.

"She's a good house. Can make plenty money," pursued the deaf man.

"That's what make you so rich, eh, Charlie?"

"*Non,* I don't make nothing. Too blame clever, me, dat's de troub'. She's a good house,—make money fast like a steamboat,—make a barrel full in a week! Me, I lose money all de days. Too

7. What?
8. What is it?

9. A Spanish coin worth 6¼ cents, current in the Gulf States before the Civil War.

blame clever."

"Charlie!"

"Eh?"

"Tell me what you'll take."

"Make? I don't make *nothing*. Too blame clever."

"What will you *take*?"

"Oh! I got enough already,—half drunk now."

"What will you take for the 'ouse?"

"You want to buy her?"

"I don't know,"—(shrug),—"may*be*,—if you sell it cheap."

"She's a bully old house."

There was a long silence. By and by old Charlie commenced—

"Old Injin Charlie is a low-down dog."

"*C'est vrai, oui!*"[1] retorted the Colonel in an undertone.

"He's got Injin blood in him."

The Colonel nodded assent.

"But he's got some blame good blood, too, ain't it?"

The Colonel nodded impatiently.

"*Bien!*[2] Old Charlie's Injin blood says, 'sell de house, Charlie, you blame old fool!' *Mais*,[3] old Charlie's good blood says, 'Charlie! if you sell dat old house, Charlie, you low-down old dog, Charlie, what de Compte De Charleu make for you grace-gran'-muzzer, de dev' can eat you, Charlie, I don't care.' "

"But you'll sell it anyhow, won't you, old man?"

"No!" And the *no* rumbled off in muttered oaths like thunder out on the Gulf. The incensed old Colonel wheeled and started off.

"Curl!" (Colonel) said Charlie, standing up unsteadily.

The planter turned with an inquiring frown.

"I'll trade with you!" said Charlie.

The Colonel was tempted. " 'Ow'l you trade?" he asked.

"My house for yours!"

The old Colonel turned pale with anger. He walked very quickly back, and came close up to his kinsman.

"Charlie!" he said.

"Injin Charlie,"—with a tipsy nod.

But by this time self-control was returning. "Sell Belles Demoiselles to you?" he said in a high key, and then laughed "Ho, ho, ho!" and rode away.

A cloud, but not a dark one, overshadowed the spirits of Belles Demoiselles' plantation. The old master, whose beaming presence had always made him a shining Saturn, spinning and sparkling within the bright circle of his daughters, fell into musing fits, started

1. Yes, that's true!   3. But.
2. Right!

out of frowning reveries, walked often by himself, and heard business from his overseer fretfully.

No wonder. The daughters knew his closeness in trade, and attributed to it his failure to negotiate for the Old Charlie buildings, —so to call them. They began to depreciate Belles Demoiselles. If a north wind blew, it was too cold to ride. If a shower had fallen, it was too muddy to drive. In the morning the garden was wet. In the evening the grasshopper was a burden. *Ennui*[4] was turned into capital; every headache was interpreted a premonition of ague; and when the native exuberance of a flock of ladies without a want or a care burst out in laughter in the father's face, they spread their French eyes, rolled up their little hands, and with rigid wrists and mock vehemence vowed and vowed again that they only laughed at their misery, and should pine to death unless they could move to the sweet city. "Oh! the theatre! Oh! Orleans Street! Oh! the masquerade! the Place d'Armes! the ball!" and they would call upon Heaven with French irreverence, and fall into each other's arms, and whirl down the hall singing a waltz, end with a grand collision and fall, and, their eyes streaming merriment, lay the blame on the slippery floor, that would some day be the death of the whole seven.

Three times more the fond father, thus goaded, managed, by accident,—business accident,—to see old Charlie and increase his offer; but in vain. He finally went to him formally.

"Eh?" said the deaf and distant relative. "For what you want him, eh? Why you don't stay where you halways be 'appy? Dis is a blame old rat-hole,—good for old Injin Charlie,—da's all. Why you don't stay where you be halways 'appy? Why you don't buy somewheres else?"

"That's none of your business," snapped the planter. Truth was, his reasons were unsatisfactory even to himself.

A sullen silence followed. Then Charlie spoke:

"Well, now, look here; I sell you old Charlie's house."

"*Bien!*[5] and the whole block," said the Colonel.

"Hold on," said Charlie. "I sell you de 'ouse and de block. Den I go and git drunk, and go to sleep; de dev' comes along and says, 'Charlie! old Charlie, you blame low-down old dog, wake up! What you doin' here? Where's de 'ouse what Monsieur le Compte give your grace-gran-muzzer? Don't you see dat fine gentyman, De Charleu, done gone and tore him down and make him over new, you blame old fool, Charlie, you low-down old Injin dog!'"

"I'll give you forty thousand dollars," said the Colonel.

"For de 'ouse?"

"For all."

4. Boredom.   5. Here meaning "good!"

The deaf man shook his head.

"Forty-five!" said the Colonel.

"What a lie? For what you tell me 'What a lie?' I don't tell you no lie."

"*Non, non!* I give you *forty-five!*" shouted the Colonel.

Charlie shook his head again.

"Fifty!"

He shook it again.

The figures rose and rose to—

"Seventy-five!"

The answer was an invitation to go away and let the owner alone, as he was, in certain specified respects, the vilest of living creatures, and no company for a fine gentyman.

The "fine gentyman" longed to blaspheme,—but before old Charlie!—in the name of pride, how could he? He mounted and started away.

"Tell you what I'll make wid you," said Charlie.

The other, guessing aright, turned back without dismounting, smiling.

"How much Belles Demoiselles hoes me now?" asked the deaf one.

"One hundred and eighty thousand dollars," said the Colonel, firmly.

"Yass," said Charlie. "I don't want Belles Demoiselles."

The old Colonel's quiet laugh intimated it made no difference either way.

"But me," continued Charlie, "me,—I'm got le Compte De Charleu's blood in me, any'ow,—a litt' bit, any'ow, ain't it?"

The Colonel nodded that it was.

"*Bien!* If I go out of dis place and don't go to Belles Demoiselles, de peoples will say,—dey will say, 'Old Charlie he been all doze time tell a blame *lie!* He ain't no kin to his old grace-gran-muzzer, not a blame bit! He don't got nary drop of De Charleu blood to save his blame low-down old Injin soul! No, sare! What I want wid money, den? No, sare! My place for yours!"

He turned to go into the house, just too soon to see the Colonel make an ugly whisk at him with his riding-whip. Then the Colonel, too, moved off.

Two or three times over, as he ambled homeward, laughter broke through his annoyance, as he recalled old Charlie's family pride and the presumption of his offer. Yet each time he could but think better of—not the offer to swap, but the preposterous ancestral loyalty. It was so much better than he could have expected from his "low-down" relative, and not unlike his own whim withal—the proposition which went with it was forgiven.

This last defeat bore so harshly on the master of Belles Demoiselles, that the daughters, reading chagrin in his face, began to re-
pent. They loved their father as daughters can, and when they saw
their pretended dejection harassing him seriously they restrained
their complaints, displayed more than ordinary tenderness, and
heroically and ostentatiously concluded there was no place like
Belles Demoiselles. But the new mood touched him more than the
old, and only refined his discontent. Here was a man, rich without
the care of riches, free from any real trouble, happiness as native
to his house as perfume to his garden, deliberately, as it were with
premeditated malice, taking joy by the shoulder and bidding her be
gone to town, whither he might easily have followed, only that the
very same ancestral nonsense that kept Injin Charlie from selling
the old place for twice its value prevented him from choosing any
other spot for a city home.

But by and by the charm of nature and the merry hearts around
him prevailed; the fit of exalted sulks passed off, and after a while
the year flared up at Christmas, flickered, and went out.

New Year came and passed; the beautiful garden of Belles Demoiselles put on its spring attire; the seven fair sisters moved from
rose to rose; the cloud of discontent had warmed into invisible vapor
in the rich sunlight of family affection, and on the common memory the only scar of last year's wound was old Charlie's sheer im-
pertinence in crossing the caprice of the De Charleus. The cup of
gladness seemed to fill with the filling of the river.

How high that river was! Its tremendous current rolled and
tumbled and spun along, hustling the long funeral flotillas of drift,
—and how near shore it came! Men were out day and night, watching the levee. On windy nights even the old Colonel took part, and
grew light-hearted with occupation and excitement, as every minute
the river threw a white arm over the levee's top, as though it
would vault over. But all held fast, and, as the summer drifted in,
the water sunk down into its banks and looked quite incapable of
harm.

On a summer afternoon of uncommon mildness, old Colonel
Jean Albert Henri Joseph De Charleu-Marot, being in a mood for
revery, slipped the custody of his feminine rulers and sought the
crown of the levee, where it was his wont to promenade. Presently
he sat upon a stone bench,—a favorite seat. Before him lay his
broad-spread fields; near by, his lordly mansion; and being still,—
perhaps by female contact,—somewhat sentimental, he fell to
musing on his past. It was hardly worthy to be proud of. All its
morning was reddened with mad frolic, and far toward the meridian
it was marred with elegant rioting. Pride had kept him well-nigh
useless, and despised the honors won by valor; gaming had dimmed

prosperity; death had taken his heavenly wife; voluptuous ease had mortgaged his lands; and yet his house still stood, his sweet-smelling fields were still fruitful, his name was fame enough; and yonder and yonder, among the trees and flowers, like angels walking in Eden, were the seven goddesses of his only worship.

Just then a slight sound behind him brought him to his feet. He cast his eyes anxiously to the outer edge of the little strip of bank between the levee's base and the river. There was nothing visible. He paused, with his ear toward the water, his face full of frightened expectation. Ha! There came a single plashing sound, like some great beast slipping into the river, and little waves in a wide semi-circle came out from under the bank and spread over the water!

"My God!"

He plunged down the levee and bounded through the low weeds to the edge of the bank. It was sheer, and the water about four feet below. He did not stand quite on the edge, but fell upon his knees a couple of yards away, wringing his hands, moaning and weeping, and staring through his watery eyes at a fine, long crevice just discernible under the matted grass, and curving outward on either hand toward the river.

"My God!" he sobbed aloud; "my God!" and even while he called, his God answered: the tough Bermuda grass stretched and snapped, the crevice slowly became a gape, and softly, gradually, with no sound but the closing of the water at last, a ton or more of earth settled into the boiling eddy and disappeared.

At the same instant a pulse of the breeze brought from the garden behind, the joyous, thoughtless laughter of the fair mistresses of Belles Demoiselles.

The old Colonel sprang up and clambered over the levee. Then forcing himself to a more composed movement, he hastened into the house and ordered his horse.

"Tell my children to make merry while I am gone," he left word. "I shall be back to-night," and the horse's hoofs clattered down a by-road leading to the city.

"Charlie," said the planter, riding up to a window, from which the old man's nightcap was thrust out, "what you say, Charlie,—my house for yours, eh, Charlie—what you say?"

"Ello!" said Charlie; "from where you come from dis time of to-night?"

"I come from the Exchange[6] in St. Louis Street." (A small fraction of the truth.)

"What you want?" said matter-of-fact Charlie.

"I come to trade."

6. In New Orleans the saloons or "dram" shops were called "exchanges."

The low-down relative drew the worsted[7] off his ears. "Oh! yass," he said with an uncertain air.

"Well, old man Charlie, what you say: my house for yours,—like you said,—eh, Charlie?"

"I dunno," said Charlie; "it's nearly mine now. Why you don't stay dare youse'f?"

"*Because I don't want!*" said the Colonel savagely. "Is dat reason enough for you? You better take me in de notion, old man, I tell you,—yes!"

Charlie never winced; but how his answer delighted the Colonel! Quoth Charlie:

"I don't care—I take him!—*mais*, possession give right off."

"Not the whole plantation, Charlie; only"—

"I don't care," said Charlie; "we easy can fix dat. *Mais*, what for you don't want to keep him? I don't want him. You better keep him."

"Don't you try to make no fool of me, old man," cried the planter.

"Oh, no!" said the other. "Oh, no! but you make a fool of yourself, ain't it?"

The dumbfounded Colonel stared; Charlie went on:

"Yass! Belles Demoiselles is more wort' dan tree block like dis one. I pass by dare since two weeks. Oh, pritty Belles Demoiselles! De cane was wave in de wind, de garden smell like a bouquet, de white-cap was jump up and down on de river; seven *belles demoiselles* was ridin' on horses. 'Pritty, pritty, pritty!' says old Charlie. Ah! *Monsieur le père,* 'ow 'appy, 'appy, 'appy!"

"Yass!" he continued—the Colonel still staring—"le Compte De Charleu have two familie. One was low-down Choctaw, one was high up *noblesse*. He gave the low-down Choctaw dis old rat-hole; he give Belles Demoiselles to you gran-fozzer; and now you don't be *satisfait*. What I'll do wid Belles Demoiselles? She'll break me in two years, yass. And what you'll do wid old Charlie's house, eh? You'll tear her down and make you'se'f a blame old fool. I rather wouldn't trade!"

The planter caught a big breathful of anger, but Charlie went straight on:

"I rather wouldn't, *mais* I will do it for you;—just the same, like Monsieur le Compte would say, 'Charlie, you old fool, I want to shange houses wid you.'"

So long as the Colonel suspected irony he was angry, but as Charlie seemed, after all, to be certainly in earnest, he began to feel conscience-stricken. He was by no means a tender man, but his

7. A cloth made from long-stapled wool; here, "nightcap."

lately-discovered misfortune had unhinged him, and this strange, undeserved, disinterested family fealty on the part of Charlie touched his heart. And should he still try to lead him into the pitfall he had dug? He hesitated;—no, he would show him the place by broad daylight, and if he chose to overlook the "caving bank," it would be his own fault;—a trade's a trade.

"Come," said the planter, "come at my house to-night; to-morrow we look at the place before breakfast, and finish the trade."

"For what?" said Charlie.

"Oh, because I got to come in town in the morning."

"I don't want," said Charlie. "How I'm goin' to come dere?"

"I git you a horse at the liberty stable."

"Well—anyhow—I don't care—I'll go." And they went.

When they had ridden a long time, and were on the road darkened by hedges of Cherokee rose, the Colonel called behind him to the "low-down" scion:

"Keep the road, old man."

"Eh?"

"Keep the road."

"Oh, yes; all right; I keep my word; we don't goin' to play no tricks, eh?"

But the Colonel seemed not to hear. His ungenerous design was beginning to be hateful to him. Not only old Charlie's unprovoked goodness was prevailing; the eulogy on Belles Demoiselles had stirred the depths of an intense love for his beautiful home. True, if he held to it, the caving of the bank, at its present fearful speed, would let the house into the river within three months; but were it not better to lose it so, than sell his birthright? Again,—coming back to the first thought,—to betray his own blood! It was only Injin Charlie; but had not the De Charleu blood just spoken out in him? Unconsciously he groaned.

After a time they struck a path approaching the plantation in the rear, and a little after, passing from behind a clump of live-oaks, they came in sight of the villa. It looked so like a gem, shining through its dark grove, so like a great glow-worm in the dense foliage, so significant of luxury and gayety, that the poor master, from an overflowing heart, groaned again.

"What?" asked Charlie.

The Colonel only drew his rein, and, dismounting mechanically, contemplated the sight before him. The high, arched doors and windows were thrown wide to the summer air; from every opening the bright light of numerous candelabra darted out upon the sparkling foliage of magnolia and bay, and here and there in the spacious verandas a colored lantern swayed in the gentle breeze. A sound of revel fell on the ear, the music of harps; and across one window, brighter than the rest, flitted, once or twice, the shadows of dancers. But oh! the shadows flitting across the heart of the fair mansion's master!

"Old Charlie," said he, gazing fondly at his house, "You and me is both old, eh?"

"Yaas," said the stolid Charlie.

"And we has both been bad enough in our time, eh, Charlie?"

Charlie, surprised at the tender tone, repeated "Yaas."

"And you and me is mighty close?"

"Blame close, yaas."

"But you never know me to cheat, old man!"

"No,"—impassively.

"And do you think I would cheat you now?"

"I dunno," said Charlie. "I don't believe."

"Well, old man, old man,"—his voice began to quiver,—"I sha'n't cheat you now. My God!—old man, I tell you—you better not make the trade!"

"Because for what?" asked Charlie in plain anger; but both looked quickly toward the house! The Colonel tossed his hands wildly in the air, rushed forward a step or two, and giving one fearful scream of agony and fright, fell forward on his face in the path. Old Charlie stood transfixed with horror. Belles Demoiselles, the realm of maiden beauty, the home of merriment, the house of dancing, all in the tremor and glow of pleasure, suddenly sank, with one short, wild wail of terror—sunk, sunk, down, down, down, into the merciless, unfathomable flood of the Mississippi.

Twelve long months were midnight to the mind of the childless father; when they were only half gone, he took his bed; and every day, and every night, old Charlie, the "low-down," the "fool," watched him tenderly, tended him lovingly, for the sake of his name, his misfortunes, and his broken heart. No woman's step crossed the floor of the sick-chamber, whose western dormer-windows overpeered the dingy architecture of old Charlie's block; Charlie and a skilled physician, the one all interest, the other all gentleness, hope, and patience—these only entered by the door; but by the window came in a sweet-scented evergreen vine, transplanted from the caving bank of Belles Demoiselles. It caught the rays of sunset in its flowery net and let them softly in upon the sick man's bed; gathered the glancing beams of the moon at midnight, and often wakened the sleeper to look, with his mindless eyes, upon their pretty silvery fragments strewn upon the floor.

By and by there seemed—there was—a twinkling dawn of returning reason. Slowly, peacefully, with an increase unseen from day to day, the light of reason came into the eyes, and speech became coherent; but withal there came a failing of the wrecked body, and the doctor said that monsieur was both better and worse.

One evening, as Charlie sat by the vine-clad window with his fireless pipe in his hand, the old Colonel's eyes fell full upon his own, and rested there.

"Charl—," he said with an effort, and his delighted nurse hastened to the bedside and bowed his best ear. There was an unsuccessful effort or two, and then he whispered, smiling with sweet sadness,—

"We didn't trade."

The truth, in this case, was a secondary matter to Charlie; the main point was to give a pleasing answer. So he nodded his head decidedly, as who should say—"Oh yes, we did, it was a bonafide swap!" but when he saw the smile vanish, he tried the other expedient and shook his head with still more vigor, to signify that they had not so much as approached a bargain; and the smile returned.

Charlie wanted to see the vine recognized. He stepped backward to the window with a broad smile, shook the foliage, nodded and looked smart.

"I know," said the Colonel, with beaming eyes, "—many weeks."

The next day—

"Charl—"

The best ear went down.

"Send for a priest."

The priest came, and was alone with him a whole afternoon. When he left, the patient was very haggard and exhausted, but smiled and would not suffer the crucifix to be removed from his breast.

One more morning came. Just before dawn Charlie, lying on a pallet in the room, thought he was called, and came to the bedside.

"Old man," whispered the failing invalid, "is it caving yet?"

Charlie nodded.

"It won't pay you out."

"Oh, dat makes not'ing," said Charlie. Two big tears rolled down his brown face. "Dat makes not'in."

The Colonel whispered once more:

"*Mes belles demoiselles!* in paradise;—in the garden—I shall be with them at sunrise;" and so it was.

1874, 1879

JOEL CHANDLER HARRIS
(1848–1908)

Joel Chandler Harris made the only lasting literary record of those folk tales of American Indian and Negro origin in which the adventures of animals of the forest and field reflect the comedy of mankind. In the Uncle Remus tales he made the first dependable representation of the Negro dialects; and in his other works too, "Free Joe and the Rest of the World," for instance, he created a regional literature of impressive reality, depth, and permanence. Harris was born near Eatonton, Georgia, on December 9, 1848, to a mother whose husband had just deserted her. He had little formal schooling, but read extensively in Sir Thomas Browne, Addison and Steele, Shakespeare, the Bible, and especially Goldsmith. A printer in his youth, he graduated to a series of editorial positions, ultimately joining the Atlanta *Constitution*. He began to write poems and to reproduce the plantation stories learned from the Negroes, both for the *Constitution*, on which he ran a column, and as a contributor to the Savannah *Morning News*.

His first Uncle Remus story appeared in the *Constitution* in 1879. Harris soon collected a number of plantation legends, folk tales, Negro proverbs, a story of the war, and numerous "sayings"—all in the words of Uncle Remus—in *Uncle Remus: His Songs and His Sayings* (1881). The stories were genuine, and the character of Uncle Remus—one of the most memorable in American literature—lived for the reader as an embodiment of the entire plantation life. *Nights with Uncle Remus* (1883) introduced Daddy Jake and the dialect of the coastal rice plantations of South Carolina, which was more

difficult to understand. These two volumes represent Harris' best work in Negro characterization, dialect, and folklore; the first, containing the wonderful stories of the Tar Baby and the Briar Patch, has been translated into twenty-seven foreign languages. Brer Rabbit, who exhibits the tastes and thoughts of Uncle Remus himself, and Brer Bear, Brer Fox, Old Sis Cow, and the other animals, exhibit a wisdom learned in slavery; and they recall the animals of masters like Aesop and Chaucer. *Uncle Remus and His Friends* (1892), *Told by Uncle Remus* (1905), and the posthumous *Uncle Remus and the Little Boy* (1910) are further collections of the tales that Uncle Remus told the little boy, and through him, all children everywhere.

The success of Uncle Remus has obscured the achievement of Harris in his other books, such as *Free Joe and Other Georgian Sketches* (1887). Further collections of stories of the Negro, and of the life of the South in general, are *Balaam and His Master* (1891), *Tales of the Home Folks in Peace and War* (1898), and *The Chronicles of Aunt Minervy Ann* (1899). Among Harris' lesser works, two are still noteworthy: *On the Plantation* (1892), a novelette combining fiction and autobiography, and *Gabriel Tolliver* (1902), a novel, also based on events of his early life.

No standard edition of Harris' works has been published. There are many reprints of the favorite titles of the Uncle Remus series and the short stories. Miscellaneous writings were edited by Julia C. Harris, *Joel Chandler Harris: Editor and Essayist: Miscel-*

514 · *Joel Chandler Harris*

laneous Literary, Political, and Social Writings, 1931.

The standard biography is Julia C. Harris, *The Life and Letters of Joel Chandler Harris,* 1918. A study of Harris' early literary development is Robert L. Wiggins, *The Life of Joel Chandler Harris from Obscurity in Boyhood to Fame in Early Manhood,* 1918.

A readable life is Alvin F. Harlow, *Joel Chandler Harris (Uncle Remus): Plantation Storyteller,* 1941. A scholarly appraisal is Arthur H. Quinn, *American Fiction,* 1936, pp. 374–384. The best brief critique is Thomas H. English, "In Memory of Uncle Remus," *Southern Literary Messenger,* II (February, 1940), 77–83.

The Story of the Deluge and How It Came About.[1]

"One time," said Uncle Remus—adjusting his spectacles so as to be able to see how to thread a large darning-needle with which he was patching his coat—"one time, way back yander, 'fo' you wuz borned, honey, en 'fo' Mars John er Miss Sally wuz borned—way back yander 'fo' enny un us wuz borned, de anemils en de creeturs sorter 'leeshuneer[2] roun' 'mong deyselves, twel at las' dey 'greed fer ter have a 'sembly. In dem days," continued the old man, observing a look of incredulity on the little boy's face, "in dem days creeturs had lots mo' sense dan dey got now; let 'lone dat, dey had sense same like folks. Hit was tech and go wid um, too, mon, en w'en dey make up der mines w'at hatter be done, 'twant mo'n menshun'd 'fo' hit wuz done. Well, dey 'lected dat dey hatter hole er 'sembly fer ter sorter straighten out marters[3] en hear de complaints, en w'en de day come dey wuz on han'. De Lion, he wuz dar, kase he wuz de king, en he hatter be dar. De Rhynossyhoss, he wuz dar, en de Elephent, he wuz dar, en de Cammils, en de Cows, en plum down ter de Crawfishes, dey wuz dar. Dey wuz all dar. En w'en de Lion shuck his mane, en tuck his seat in de big cheer, den de sesshun begun fer ter commence."

"What did they do, Uncle Remus?" asked the little boy.

"I can't skacely call to mine 'zackly w'at dey did do, but dey spoke speeches, en hollered, en cusst, en flung der langwidge 'roun' des like w'en yo' daddy wuz gwineter run fer de legislater en got lef'. Howsomever, dey 'ranged der 'fairs, en splained der bizness. Bimeby,[4] w'ile dey wuz 'sputin' 'longer one er nudder,[5] de Elephent trompled on one er de Crawfishes. Co'se w'en dat creetur put his foot down, w'atsumever's under dar wuz boun' fer ter be squshed, en

1. "The Story of the Deluge and How It Came About," published in *Uncle Remus: His Songs and His Sayings* (1881), is one of the legends Harris collected from the Georgia Negroes. The stories of Uncle Remus were usually genuine folklore, tales which had been brought from Africa and, in most cases, modified in America through the influence of Indian legends and biblical stories. This story, and others told by Uncle Remus, contains social and political implications beyond the plantation world. The text is from the first edition.
2. Electioneered.
3. Matters.
4. By and by.
5. Disputing one with the other.

dey wa'n't nuff er dat Crawfish lef' fer ter tell dat he'd bin dar.

"Dis make de udder Crawfishes mighty mad, en dey sorter swarmed tergedder en draw'd up a kinder peramble wid some wharfo'es[6] in it, en read her out in de 'sembly. But, bless grashus! sech a racket wuz a gwine on dat nobody ain't hear it, 'ceppin may be de Mud Turkle en de Spring Lizzud, en dere enfloons[7] wuz pow'ful lackin'.

"Bimeby, w'iles de Nunicorn wuz 'sputin' wid de Lion, en w'ile de Hyener wuz a laughin' ter hisse'f, de Elephent squshed anudder one er de Crawfishes, en a little mo'n he'd er ruint de Mud Turkle. Den de Crawfishes, w'at dey wuz lef' un um, swarmed tergedder en draw'd up anudder peramble wid sum mo' wharfo'es; but dey might ez well er sung Ole Dan Tucker[8] ter a harrycane. De udder creeturs wuz too busy wid der fussin' fer ter 'spon'[9] unto de Crawfishes. So dar dey wuz, de Crawfishes, en dey didn't know w'at minnit wuz gwineter be de nex'; en dey kep' on gittin madder en madder en skeerder en skeerder, twel bimeby dey gun de wink ter de Mud Turkle en de Spring Lizzud, en den dey bo'd little holes in de groun' en went down outer sight."

"Who did, Uncle Remus?" asked the little boy.

"De Crawfishes, honey. Dey bo'd inter de groun'[1] en kep' on bo'in twel dey onloost de fountains er de earf; en de waters squirt out, en riz higher en higher twel de hills wuz kivvered, en de creeturs wuz all drownded; en all bekaze dey let on 'mong deyselves dat dey wuz bigger dan de Crawfishes."[2]

Then the old man blew the ashes from a smoking yam, and proceeded to remove the peeling.

"Where was the ark, Uncle Remus?" the little boy inquired presently.

"W'ich ark's dat?" asked the old man, in a tone of well-feigned curiosity.[3]

"Noah's ark," replied the child.

"Don't you pester wid ole man Noah, honey. I boun' he tuck keer er dat ark. Dat's w'at he wuz dar fer, en dat's w'at he done. Leas' ways, dat's w'at dey tells me. But don't you bodder longer dat ark, 'ceppin' your mammy fetches it up. Dey mout er bin two delooies, en den agin dey moutent. Ef dey wuz enny ark in dish yer w'at de

---

6. Wherefores.
7. Influence.
8. A popular song about an old man who got drunk, fell in the fire, and danced about wildly with a red-hot coal in his shoe.
9. Respond.
1. The crawfish normally takes refuge by boring into the bottoms of creeks or swamps.

2. Among the African nature myths that the Negroes brought to America was a story of the flood, which subsequently became confused with the Bible story.
3. The old narrator is sensitively attempting to avoid an embarrassing issue; he knows that Noah's ark did not figure in this African story, as it did in the Bible.

Crawfishes brung on, I ain't heern tell un it, en w'en dey ain't no
arks 'roun', I ain't got no time fer ter make um en put um in dar.
Hit's gittin' yo' bedtime, honey."

1881

Free Joe and the Rest of the World[4]

The name of Free Joe strikes humorously upon the ear of memory. It is impossible to say why, for he was the humblest, the
simplest, and the most serious of all God's living creatures, sadly
lacking in all those elements that suggest the humorous. It is certain, moreover, that in 1850 the sober-minded citizens of the little
Georgian village of Hillsborough were not inclined to take a humorous view of Free Joe, and neither his name nor his presence provoked a smile. He was a black atom, drifting hither and thither
without an owner, blown about by all the winds of circumstance,
and given over to shiftlessness.

The problems of one generation are the paradoxes of a succeeding
one, particularly if war, or some such incident, intervenes to clarify
the atmosphere and strengthen the understanding. Thus, in 1850,[5]
Free Joe represented not only a problem of large concern, but, in
the watchful eyes of Hillsborough, he was the embodiment of that
vague and mysterious danger that seemed to be forever lurking on
the outskirts of slavery, ready to sound a shrill and ghostly signal in
the impenetrable swamps, and steal forth under the midnight stars
to murder, rapine, and pillage—a danger always threatening, and
yet never assuming shape; intangible, and yet real; impossible, and
yet not improbable. Across the serene and smiling front of safety,
the pale outlines of the awful shadow of insurrection sometimes fell.
With this invisible panorama as a background, it was natural that
the figure of Free Joe, simple and humble as it was, should assume
undue proportions. Go where he would, do what he might, he could
not escape the finger of observation and the kindling eye of suspicion. His lightest words were noted, his slightest actions marked.

Under all the circumstances it was natural that his peculiar condition should reflect itself in his habits and manners. The slaves
laughed loudly day by day, but Free Joe rarely laughed. The slaves
sang at their work and danced at their frolics, but no one ever heard
Free Joe sing or saw him dance. There was something painfully

4. "Free Joe and the Rest of the
World" was published in *Free Joe and
Other Georgian Sketches* (1887). Harris
depicts the plight of a free Negro in
1850 and the tragedy of the individual
deprived of an accepted place within
the existing order. The text is taken
from the first edition.
5. The year 1850 was a time of great
tension over slavery, accentuated by the
Compromise of 1850; mob hysteria over
fugitive slaves occurred in the North,
while the South lived under the threat
of uprisings.

plaintive and appealing in his attitude, something touching in his anxiety to please. He was of the friendliest nature, and seemed to be delighted when he could amuse the little children who had made a playground of the public square. At times he would please them by making his little dog Dan perform all sorts of curious tricks, or he would tell them quaint stories of the beasts of the field and birds of the air; and frequently he was coaxed into relating the story of his own freedom. That story was brief, but tragical.

In the year of our Lord 1840, when a negro speculator of a sportive turn of mind reached the little village of Hillsborough on his way to the Mississippi region, with a caravan of likely negroes of both sexes, he found much to interest him. In that day and at that time there were a number of young men in the village who had not bound themselves over to repentance for the various misdeeds of the flesh. To these young men the negro speculator (Major Frampton was his name) proceeded to address himself. He was a Virginian, he declared; and, to prove the statement, he referred all the festively inclined young men of Hillsborough to a barrel of peach-brandy in one of his covered wagons. In the minds of these young men there was less doubt in regard to the age and quality of the brandy than there was in regard to the negro trader's birthplace. Major Frampton might or might not have been born in the Old Dominion—that was a matter for consideration and inquiry—but there could be no question as to the mellow pungency of the peach-brandy.

In his own estimation, Major Frampton was one of the most accomplished of men. He had summered at the Virginia Springs; he had been to Philadelphia, to Washington, to Richmond, to Lynchburg, and to Charleston, and had accumulated a great deal of experience which he found useful. Hillsborough was hid in the woods of Middle Georgia, and its general aspect of innocence impressed him. He looked on the young men who had shown their readiness to test his peach-brandy as overgrown country boys who needed to be introduced to some of the arts and sciences he had at his command. Thereupon the major pitched his tents, figuratively speaking, and became, for the time being, a part and parcel of the innocence that characterized Hillsborough. A wiser man would doubtless have made the same mistake.

The little village possessed advantages that seemed to be providentially arranged to fit the various enterprises that Major Frampton had in view. There was the auction block in front of the stuccoed court-house, if he desired to dispose of a few of his negroes; there was a quarter-track, laid out to his hand and in excellent order, if he chose to enjoy the pleasures of horse-racing; there were secluded pine thickets within easy reach, if he desired to indulge in the exciting pastime of cock-fighting; and variously lonely and unoccupied rooms in the second story of the tavern, if he cared to challenge the chances of dice or cards.

Major Frampton tried them all with varying luck, until he began his famous game of poker with Judge Alfred Wellington, a stately gentleman with a flowing white beard and mild blue eyes that gave him the appearance of a benevolent patriarch. The history of the game in which Major Frampton and Judge Alfred Wellington took part is something more than a tradition in Hillsborough, for there are still living three or four men who sat around the table and watched its progress. It is said that at various stages of the game Major Frampton would destroy the cards with which they were playing, and send for a new pack, but the result was always the same. The mild blue eyes of Judge Wellington, with few exceptions, continued to overlook "hands" that were invincible—a habit they had acquired during a long and arduous course of training from Sarotoga to New Orleans. Major Frampton lost his money, his horses, his wagons, and all his negroes but one, his body-servant. When his misfortune had reached this limit, the major adjourned the game. The sun was shining brightly, and all nature was cheerful. It is said that the major also seemed to be cheerful. However this may be, he visited the court-house, and executed the papers that gave his body-servant his freedom. This being done, Major Frampton sauntered into a convenient pine thicket, and blew out his brains.

The negro thus freed came to be known as Free Joe. Compelled, under the law, to choose a guardian, he chose Judge Wellington, chiefly because his wife Lucinda was among the negroes won from Major Frampton. For several years Free Joe had what may be called a jovial time. His wife Lucinda was well provided for, and he found it a comparatively easy matter to provide for himself; so that, taking all the circumstances into consideration, it is not matter for astonishment that he became somewhat shiftless.

When Judge Wellington died, Free Joe's troubles began. The judge's negroes, including Lucinda, went to his half-brother, a man named Calderwood, who was a hard master and a rough customer generally—a man of many eccentricities of mind and character. His neighbors had a habit of alluding to him as "Old Spite"; and the name seemed to fit him so completely that he was known far and near as "Spite" Calderwood. He probably enjoyed the distinction the name gave him, at any rate he never resented it, and it was not often that he missed an opportunity to show that he deserved it. Calderwood's place was two or three miles from the village of Hillsborough, and Free Joe visited his wife twice a week, Wednesday and Saturday nights.

One Sunday he was sitting in front of Lucinda's cabin, when Calderwood happened to pass that way.

"Howdy, marster?" said Free Joe, taking off his hat.

"Who are you?" exclaimed Calderwood abruptly, halting and staring at the negro.

"I'm name' Joe, marster. I'm Lucindy's ole man."

"Who do you belong to?"

"Marse John Evans is my gyardeen, marster."

"Big name—gyardeen. Show your pass."

Free Joe produced that document, and Calderwood read it aloud slowly, as if he found it difficult to get at the meaning:

"To whom it may concern: This is to certify that the boy Joe Frampton has my permission to visit his wife Lucinda."

This was dated at Hillsborough, and signed *"John W. Evans."*

Calderwood read it twice, and then looked at Free Joe, elevating his eyebrows, and showing his discolored teeth.

"Some mighty big words in that there. Evans owns this place, I reckon. When's he comin' down to take hold?"

Free Joe fumbled with his hat. He was badly frightened.

"Lucindy say she speck you wouldn't min' my comin', long ez I behave, marster."

Calderwood tore the pass in pieces and flung it away.

"Don't want no free niggers 'round here," he exclaimed. "There's the big road. It'll carry you to town. Don't let me catch you here no more. Now, mind what I tell you."

Free Joe presented a shabby spectacle as he moved off with his little dog Dan slinking at his heels. It should be said in behalf of Dan, however, that his bristles were up, and that he looked back and growled. It may be that the dog had the advantage of insignificance, but it is difficult to conceive how a dog bold enough to raise his bristles under Calderwood's very eyes could be as insignificant as Free Joe. But both the negro and his little dog seemed to give a new and more dismal aspect to forlornness as they turned into the road and went toward Hillsborough.

After this incident Free Joe appeared to have clearer ideas concerning his peculiar condition. He realized the fact that though he was free he was more helpless than any slave. Having no owner, every man was his master. He knew that he was the object of suspicion, and therefore all his slender resources (ah! how pitifully slender they were!) were devoted to winning, not kindness and appreciation, but toleration; all his efforts were in the direction of mitigating the circumstances that tended to make his condition so much worse than that of the negroes around him—negroes who had friends because they had masters.

So far as his own race was concerned, Free Joe was an exile. If the slaves secretly envied him his freedom (which is to be doubted, considering his miserable condition), they openly despised him, and lost no opportunity to treat him with contumely. Perhaps this was in some measure the result of the attitude which Free Joe chose to maintain toward them. No doubt his instinct taught him that to hold himself aloof from the slaves would be to invite from the whites the toleration which he coveted, and without which even his miserable condition would be rendered more miserable still.

His greatest trouble was the fact that he was not allowed to visit his wife; but he soon found a way out of his difficulty. After he had been ordered away from the Calderwood place, he was in the habit of wandering as far in that direction as prudence would permit. Near the Calderwood place, but not on Calderwood's land, lived an old man named Micajah Staley and his sister Becky Staley. These people were old and very poor. Old Micajah had a palsied arm and hand; but, in spite of this, he managed to earn a precarious living with his turning-lathe.

When he was a slave Free Joe would have scorned these representatives of a class known as poor white trash, but now he found them sympathetic and helpful in various ways. From the back door of their cabin he could hear the Calderwood negroes singing at night, and he sometimes fancied he could distinguish Lucinda's shrill treble rising above the other voices. A large poplar grew in the woods some distance from the Staley cabin, and at the foot of this tree Free Joe would sit for hours with his face turned toward Calderwood's. His little dog Dan would curl up in the leaves near by, and the two seemed to be as comfortable as possible.

One Saturday afternoon Free Joe, sitting at the foot of this friendly poplar, fell asleep. How long he slept, he could not tell; but when he awoke little Dan was licking his face, the moon was shining brightly, and Lucinda his wife stood before him laughing. The dog, seeing that Free Joe was asleep, had grown somewhat impatient, and he concluded to make an excursion to the Calderwood place on his own account. Lucinda was inclined to give the incident a twist in the direction of superstition.

"I 'uz settn' down front er de fireplace," she said, "cookin' me some meat, w'en all of a sudden I year[6] sumpin at de do'—scratch, scratch. I tuck'n tu'n de meat over, en make out I ain't year it. Bimeby it come dar 'gin—scratch, scratch. I up en open de do', I did, en, bless de Lord! dar wuz little Dan, en it look like ter me dat his ribs done grow terge'er. I gin 'im some bread, en den, w'en he start out, I tuck'n foller 'im, kaze,[7] I say ter myse'f, maybe my nigger man mought be some'rs 'roun'. Dat ar little dog got sense, mon."

Free Joe laughed and dropped his hand lightly on Dan's head. For a long time after that he had no difficulty in seeing his wife. He had only to sit by the poplar tree until little Dan could run and

6. Hear.   7. Because.

fetch her. But after a while the other negroes discovered that Lucinda was meeting Free Joe in the woods, and information of the fact soon reached Calderwood's ears. Calderwood was what is called a man of action. He said nothing; but one day he put Lucinda in his buggy, and carried her to Macon, sixty miles way. He carried her to Macon, and came back without her; and nobody in or around Hillsborough, or in that section, ever saw her again.

For many a night after that Free Joe sat in the woods and waited. Little Dan would run merrily off and be gone a long time, but he always came back without Lucinda. This happened over and over again. The "willis-whistlers"[8] would call and call, like fantom huntsmen wandering on a far-off shore; the screech-owl would shake and shiver in the depths of the woods; the night-hawks, sweeping by on noiseless wings, would snap their beaks as though they enjoyed the huge joke of which Free Joe and little Dan were the victims; and the whip-poor-wills would cry to each other through the gloom. Each night seemed to be lonelier than the preceding, but Free Joe's patience was proof against loneliness. There came a time, however, when little Dan refused to go after Lucinda. When Free Joe motioned him in the direction of the Calderwood place, he would simply move about uneasily and whine; then he would curl up in the leaves and make himself comfortable.

One night, instead of going to the poplar tree to wait for Lucinda, Free Joe went to the Staley cabin, and, in order to make his welcome good, as he expressed it, he carried with him an armful of fat-pine splinters. Miss Becky Staley had a great reputation in those parts as a fortune-teller, and the schoolgirls, as well as older people, often tested her powers in this direction, some in jest and some in earnest. Free Joe placed his humble offering of light-wood in the chimney corner, and then seated himself on the steps, dropping his hat on the ground outside.

"Miss Becky," he said presently, "whar in de name er gracious you reckon Lucindy is?"

"Well, the Lord he'p the nigger!" exclaimed Miss Becky, in a tone that seemed to reproduce, by some curious agreement of sight with sound, her general aspect of peakedness. "Well, the Lord he'p the nigger! hain't you been a-seein' her all this blessed time? She's over at old Spite Calderwood's, if she's anywheres, I reckon."

"No'm, dat I ain't, Miss Becky. I ain't seen Lucindy in now gwine on mighty nigh a mont'."

"Well, it hain't a-gwine to hurt you," said Miss Becky, somewhat sharply. "In my day an' time it wuz allers took to be a bad sign when niggers got to honeyin' 'roun' an' gwine on."

"Yessum," said Free Joe, cheerfully assenting to the proposition

8. Probably the willet, a shore bird with a loud, shrill whistle.

—"yessum, dat's so, but me an' my ole 'oman, we 'uz raise terge'er, en dey ain't bin many days w'en we 'uz' 'way fum one 'n'er like we is now."

"Maybe she's up an' took up wi' some un else," said Micajah Staley from the corner. "You know what the sayin' is: 'New master, new nigger.' "

"Dat's so, dat's de sayin', but tain't wid my ole 'oman like 'tis wid yuther niggers. Me en her wuz des natally raise up terge'er. Dey's lots likelier niggers dan w'at I is," said Free Joe, viewing his shabbiness with a critical eye, "but I knows Lucindy mos' good ez I does little Dan dar—dat I does."

There was no reply to this, and Free Joe continued:

"Miss Becky, I wish you please, ma'am, take en run yo' kyards[9] en see sump'n n'er 'bout Lucindy; kaze ef she sick, I'm gwine dar. Dey ken take en take me up en gimme a stroppin', but I'm gwine dar."

Miss Becky got her cards, but first she picked up a cup, in the bottom of which were some coffee-grounds. These she whirled slowly round and round, ending finally by turning the cup upside down on the hearth and allowing it to remain in that position.

"I'll turn the cup first," said Miss Becky, "and then I'll run the cards and see what they say."

As she shuffled the cards the fire on the hearth burned low, and in its fitful light the gray-haired, thin-featured woman seemed to deserve the weird reputation which rumor and gossip had given her. She shuffled the cards for some moments, gazing intently in the dying fire; then, throwing a piece of pine on the coals, she made three divisions of the pack, disposing them about in her lap. Then she took the first pile, ran the cards slowly through her fingers, and studied them carefully. To the first she added the second pile. The study of these was evidently not satisfactory. She said nothing, but frowned heavily; and the frown deepened as she added the rest of the cards until the entire fifty-two had passed in review before her. Though she frowned, she seemed to be deeply interested. Without changing the relative position of the cards, she ran them all over again. Then she threw a larger piece of pine on the fire, shuffled the cards afresh, divided them into three piles, and subjected them to the same careful and critical examination.

"I can't tell the day when I've seed the cards run this a-way," she said after a while. "What is an' what ain't, I'll never tell you; but I know what the cards sez."

"W'at does dey say, Miss Becky?" the negro inquired, in a tone the solemnity of which was heightened by its eagerness.

"They er runnin' quare. These here that I'm a-lookin' at," said

9. Cards.

Miss Becky, "they stan' for the past. Them there, they er the present; and the t'others, they er the future. Here's a bundle"— tapping the ace of clubs with her thumb—"an' here's a journey as plain as the nose on a man's face. Here's Lucinda—"

"Whar she, Miss Becky?"

"Here she is—the queen of spades."

Free Joe grinned. The idea seemed to please him immensely.

"Well, well, well!" he exclaimed. "Ef dat don't beat my time! De queen er spades! W'en Lucindy year dat hit'll tickle 'er, sho'!"

Miss Becky continued to run the cards back and forth through her fingers.

"Here's a bundle an' a journey, and here's Lucinda. An' here's ole Spite Calderwood."

She held the cards toward the negro and touched the king of clubs.

"De Lord he'p my soul!" exclaimed Free Joe with a chuckle. "De faver's[1] dar. Yesser, dat's him! W'at de matter 'long wid all un um, Miss Becky?"

The old woman added the second pile of cards to the first, and then the third, still running them through her fingers slowly and critically. By this time the piece of pine in the fireplace had wrapped itself in a mantle of flame, illuminating the cabin and throwing into strange relief the figure of Miss Becky as she sat studying the cards. She frowned ominously at the cards and mumbled a few words to herself. Then she dropped her hands in her lap and gazed once more into the fire. Her shadow danced and capered on the wall and floor behind her, as if, looking over her shoulder into the future, it could behold a rare spectacle. After a while she picked up the cup that had been turned on the hearth. The coffee grounds, shaken around, presented what seemed to be a most intricate map.

"Here's the journey," said Miss Becky, presently; "here's the big road, here's rivers to cross, here's the bundle to tote." She paused and sighed. "They hain't no names writ here, an' what it all means I'll never tell you. Cajy, I wish you'd be so good as to han' me my pipe."

"I hain't no hand wi' the kyards," said Cajy, as he handed the pipe, "but I reckon I can patch out your misinformation, Becky, bekaze the other day, whiles I was a-finishin' up Mizzers Perdue's rollin'-pin, I hearn a rattlin' in the road. I looked out, an' Spite Calderwood was a-drivin' by in his buggy, an' thar sot Lucinda by him. It'd in-about drapt out er my min'."

Free Joe sat on the door-sill and fumbled at his hat, flinging it from one hand to the other.

"You ain't see um gwine back, is you, Mars Cajy?" he asked after

1. Favor; *i.e.,* "resemblance."

a while.

"Ef they went back by this road," said Mr. Staley, with the aii of one who is accustomed to weigh well his words, "it must 'a' bin endurin' of the time whiles I was asleep, bekaze I hain't bin no furder from my shop than to yon bed."

"Well, sir!" exclaimed Free Joe in an awed tone, which Mr. Staley seemed to regard as a tribute to his extraordinary powers of statement.

"Ef it's my beliefs you want," continued the old man, "I'll pitch 'em at you fair and free. My beliefs is that Spite Calderwood is gone an' took Lucindy outen the county. Bless your heart and soul! when Spite Calderwood meets the Old Boy[2] in the road they'll be a turrible scuffle. You mark what I tell you."

Free Joe, still fumbling with his hat, rose and leaned against the door-facing. He seemed to be embarrassed. Presently he said:

"I speck I better be gittin' 'long. Nex' time I see Lucindy, I'm gwine tell 'er w'at Miss Becky say 'bout de queen er spades—dat I is. Ef dat don't tickle 'er, dey ain't no nigger 'oman never bin tickle'."

He paused a moment, as though waiting for some remark or comment, some confirmation of misfortune, or, at the very least, some endorsement of his suggestion that Lucinda would be greatly pleased to know that she had figured as the queen of spades; but neither Miss Becky nor her brother said anything.

"One minnit ridin' in the buggy 'longside er Mars Spite, en de nex' highfalutin' 'roun' playin' de queen er spades. Mon, deze yer nigger gals gittin' up in de pictur's; dey sholy is."

With a brief "Good night, Miss Becky, Mars Cajy," Free Joe went out into the darkness, followed by little Dan. He made his way to the poplar, where Lucinda had been in the habit of meeting him, and sat down. He sat there a long time; he sat there until little Dan, growing restless, trotted off in the direction of the Calderwood place. Dozing against the poplar, in the gray dawn of the morning, Free Joe heard Spite Calderwood's fox-hounds in full cry a mile away.

"Shoo!" he exclaimed, scratching his head, and laughing to himself, "dem ar dogs is des a-warmin' dat old fox up."

But it was Dan the hounds were after, and the little dog came back no more. Free Joe waited and waited, until he grew tired of waiting. He went back the next night and waited, and for many nights thereafter. His waiting was in vain, and yet he never regarded it as in vain. Careless and shabby as he was, Free Joe was thoughtful enough to have his theory. He was convinced that little Dan had found Lucinda, and that some night when the moon was shining

2. The Devil.

brightly through the trees, the dog would rouse him from his dreams as he sat sleeping at the foot of the poplar tree, and he would open his eyes and behold Lucinda standing over him, laughing merrily as of old; and then he thought what fun they would have about the queen of spades.

How many long nights Free Joe waited at the foot of the poplar tree for Lucinda and little Dan no one can ever know. He kept no account of them, and they were not recorded by Micajah Staley nor by Miss Becky. The season ran into summer and then into fall. One night he went to the Staley cabin, cut the two old people an armful of wood, and seated himself on the doorsteps, where he rested. He was always thankful—and proud, as it seemed—when Miss Becky gave him a cup of coffee, which she was sometimes thoughtful enough to do. He was especially thankful on this particular night.

"You er still layin' off for to strike up wi' Lucindy out thar in the woods, I reckon," said Micajah Staley, smiling grimly. The situation was not without its humorous aspects.

"Oh, dey er comin', Mars Cajy, dey er comin', sho," Free Joe replied. "I boun' I dey'll come; en w'en dey does come, I'll des take en fetch um yer, whar you kin see um wid you own eyes, you en Miss Becky."

"No," said Mr. Staley, with a quick and emphatic gesture of disapproval. "Don't! don't fetch 'em anywheres. Stay right wi' 'em as long as may be."

Free Joe chuckled, and slipped away into the night, while the two old people sat gazing in the fire. Finally Micajah spoke.

"Look at that nigger; look at 'im. He's pine-blank as happy now as a killdee by a mill-race. You can't faze 'em. I'd in-about give up my t'other hand ef I could stan' flat-footed, an' grin at trouble like that there nigger."

"Niggers is niggers," said Miss Becky, smiling grimly, "an' you can't rub it out; yit I lay I've seed a heap of white people lots meaner'n Free Joe. He grins—an' that's nigger—but I've ketched his under jaw a-tremblin' when Lucindy's name uz brung up. An' I tell you," she went on, bridling up a little, and speaking with almost fierce emphasis, "the Old Boy's done sharpened his claws for Spite Calderwood. You'll see it."

"Me, Rebecca?" said Mr. Staley, hugging his palsied arm; "me? I hope not."

"Well, you'll know it then," said Miss Becky, laughing heartily at her brother's look of alarm.

The next morning Micajah Staley had occasion to go into the woods after a piece of timber. He saw Free Joe sitting at the foot of the poplar, and the sight vexed him somewhat.

"Git up from there," he cried, "an' go an' arn your livin'. A mighty purty pass it's come to, when great big buck niggers can lie a-snorin' in the woods all day, when t'other folks is got to be up an' a-gwine.[3] Git up from there!"

Receiving no response, Mr. Staley went to Free Joe, and shook him by the shoulder; but the negro made no response. He was dead. His hat was off, his head was bent, and a smile was on his face. It was as if he had bowed and smiled when death stood before him, humble to the last. His clothes were ragged; his hands were rough and callous; his shoes were literally tied together with strings; he was shabby in the extreme. A passer-by, glancing at him, could have no idea that such a humble creature had been summoned as a witness before the Lord God of Hosts.

1887

3. Up and doing.

MARY E. WILKINS FREEMAN
(1852–1930)

Mary E. Wilkins Freeman came from a family rooted in Salem, Massachusetts. Her father, the first Wilkins to leave Salem, married into another old Massachusetts family at Randolph, where he lived before moving his family to a small village in Vermont. Mary Wilkins, born at Randolph, Massachusetts, in 1852, grew up handicapped by ill health. After her sister and mother died, she cared for her invalid father, living a lonely, secluded life in Vermont until his death. She then returned alone to the family home at Randolph and commenced writing short stories. She wrote to earn a living, for she was unable to teach or follow the other professions then open to women. She wrote about her own home, the Vermont villagers, and the people of the decaying old town of Randolph, simply setting forth what she saw in the light of her imagination.

Her first volume, *A Humble Romance and Other Stories* (1887), followed by *A New England Nun and Other Stories* (1891), established her high position in local-color fiction. Miss Wilkins selected the very humblest characters, imbuing them with qualities of individualism, fortitude, and courage that ennoble their unglamorous lives. The realism of her stories is intensified by her very strict use of the local speech. Especially with her women characters, who eclipse her men, she had a mastery of that psychological tension which occurs among humble people who struggle to maintain an older and admired tradition on the brink of social collapse. The almost hysterical repression in such individuals is a part of the social history of rural New England at that period. The persistent revolt of these characters had as its aim the preservation of their individualism, and it is emphasized by the author's tense but unadorned style. Typical is "A New England Nun," portraying a woman who values the independence of her spinsterhood in spite of the stereotyped pattern that demands marriage.

The success of Miss Wilkins' first two books brought her offers to write serials for women's magazines, which she accepted to the detriment of her art. In 1902 she married Dr. Charles M. Freeman, moving to Metuchen, New Jersey, where she spent the remainder of her life.

She was never again able wholly to regain the verity, the reality of dialect, and the simplicity of her early art, though *Edgewater People* (1918) contains distinguished work. She wrote several novels, but they do not equal her achievement in the short story, which was her natural medium.

There is no edition of Mrs. Freeman's works. Henry W. Lanier edited *The Best Stories of Mary E. Wilkins*, 1927. The first biography is Edward Foster's *Mary E. Wilkins Freeman*, 1956. Good historical evaluations are by Arthur H. Quinn, *American Fiction*, 1936, pp. 433–441; and by Fred Lewis Pattee, *A History of American Literature Since 1870*, 1915, pp. 235–240.

A Village Singer[1]

The trees were in full leaf, a heavy south wind was blowing, and there was a loud murmur among the new leaves. The people noticed it, for it was the first time that year that the trees had so murmured in the wind. The spring had come with a rush during the last few days.

The murmur of the trees sounded loud in the village church, where the people sat waiting for the service to begin. The windows were open; it was a very warm Sunday for May.

The church was already filled with this soft sylvan music—the tender harmony of the leaves and the south wind, and the sweet, desultory whistles of birds—when the choir arose and began to sing.

In the centre of the row of women singers stood Alma Way. All the people stared at her, and turned their ears critically. She was the new leading soprano. Candace Whitcomb, the old one, who had sung in the choir for forty years, had lately been given her dismissal. The audience considered that her voice had grown too cracked and uncertain on the upper notes. There had been much complaint, and after long deliberation the church-officers had made known their decision as mildly as possible to the old singer. She had sung for the last time the Sunday before, and Alma Way had been engaged to take her place. With the exception of the organist, the leading soprano was the only paid musician in the large choir. The salary was very modest, still the village people considered it large for

1. First published in *A New England Nun and Other Stories* (1891), from which the present text is reprinted.

a young woman. Alma was from the adjoining village of East Derby; she had quite a local reputation as a singer.

Now she fixed her large solemn blue eyes; her long, delicate face, which had been pretty, turned paler; the blue flowers on her bonnet trembled; her little thin gloved hands, clutching the singing-book, shook perceptibly; but she sang out bravely. That most formidable mountain-height of the world, self-distrust and timidity, arose before her, but her nerves were braced for its ascent. In the midst of the hymn she had a solo; her voice rang out piercingly sweet; the people nodded admiringly at each other; but suddenly there was a stir; all the faces turned toward the windows on the south side of the church. Above the din of the wind and the birds, above Alma Way's sweetly straining tones, arose another female voice, singing another hymn to another tune.

"It's her," the women whispered to each other; they were half aghast, half smiling.

Candace Whitcomb's cottage stood close to the south side of the church. She was playing on her parlor organ, and singing, to drown out the voice of her rival.

Alma caught her breath; she almost stopped; the hymn-book waved like a fan; then she went on. But the long husky drone of the parlor organ and the shrill clamor of the other voice seemed louder than anything else.

When the hymn was finished, Alma sat down. She felt faint; the woman next her slipped a peppermint into her hand. "It ain't worth minding," she whispered, vigorously. Alma tried to smile; down in the audience a young man was watching her with a kind of fierce pity.

In the last hymn Alma had another solo. Again the parlor organ droned above the carefully delicate accompaniment of the church organ, and again Candace Whitcomb's voice clamored forth in another tune.

After the benediction, the other singers pressed around Alma. She did not say much in return for their expressions of indignation and sympathy. She wiped her eyes furtively once or twice, and tried to smile. William Emmons, the choir leader, elderly, stout, and smooth-faced, stood over her, and raised his voice. He was the old musical dignitary of the village, the leader of the choral club and the singing-schools. "A most outrageous proceeding," he said. People had coupled his name with Candace Whitcomb's. The old bachelor tenor and old maiden soprano had been wont to walk together to her home next door after the Saturday night rehearsals, and they had sung duets to the parlor organ. People had watched sharply her old face, on which the blushes of youth sat pitifully, when William Emmons entered the singing-seats. They wondered if he would ever ask her to marry him.

And now he said further to Alma Way that Candace Whitcomb's voice had failed utterly of late, that she sang shockingly, and ought to have had sense enough to know it.

When Alma went down into the audience-room, in the midst of the chattering singers, who seemed to have descended, like birds, from song flights to chirps, the minister approached her. He had been waiting to speak to her. He was a steady-faced, fleshy old man, who had preached from that one pulpit over forty years. He told Alma, in his slow way, how much he regretted the annoyance to which she had been subjected, and intimated that he would endeavor to prevent a recurrence of it. "Miss Whitcomb—must be—reasoned with," said he; he had a slight hesitation of speech, not an impediment. It was as if his thoughts did not slide readily into his words, although both were present. He walked down the aisle with Alma, and bade her good-morning when he saw Wilson Ford waiting for her in the doorway. Everybody knew that Wilson Ford and Alma were lovers; they had been for the last ten years.

Alma colored softly, and made a little imperceptible motion with her head; her silk dress and the lace on her mantle fluttered, but she did not speak. Neither did Wilson, although they had not met before that day. They did not look at each other's faces—they seemed to see each other without that—and they walked along side by side.

They reached the gate before Candace Whitcomb's little house. Wilson looked past the front yard, full of pink and white spikes on flowering bushes, at the lace-curtained windows; a thin white profile, stiffly inclined, apparently over a book, was visible at one of them. Wilson gave his head a shake. He was a stout man, with features so strong that they overcame his flesh. "I'm going up home with you, Alma," said he; "and then—I'm just coming back, to give Aunt Candace one blowing up."

"Oh, don't, Wilson."

"Yes, I shall. If you want to stand this kind of a thing you may; I sha'n't."

"There's no need of your talking to her. Mr. Pollard's going to."

"Did he say he was?"

"Yes. I think he's going in before the afternoon meeting, from what he said."

"Well, there's one thing about it, if she does that thing again this afternoon, I'll go in there and break that old organ up into kindling-wood." Wilson set his mouth hard, and shook his head again.

Alma gave little side glances up at him, her tone was deprecatory, but her face was full of soft smiles. "I suppose she does feel dreadfully about it," said she. "I can't help feeling kind of guilty, taking her place."

"I don't see how you're to blame. It's outrageous, her acting so."

"The choir gave her a photograph album last week, didn't they?"

"Yes. They went there last Thursday night, and gave her an album and a surprise-party. She ought to behave herself."

"Well, she's sung there so long, I suppose it must be dreadful hard for her to give it up."

Other people going home from church were very near Wilson and Alma. She spoke softly that they might not hear; he did not lower his voice in the least. Presently Alma stopped before a gate.

"What are you stopping here for?" asked Wilson.

"Minnie Lansing wanted me to come and stay with her this noon."

"You're going home with me."

"I'm afraid I'll put your mother out."

"Put mother out! I told her you were coming, this morning. She's got all ready for you. Come along; don't stand here."

He did not tell Alma of the pugnacious spirit with which his mother had received the announcement of her coming, and how she had stayed at home to prepare the dinner, and make a parade of her hard work and her injury.

Wilson's mother was the reason why he did not marry Alma. He would not take his wife home to live with her, and was unable to support separate establishments. Alma was willing enough to be married and put up with Wilson's mother, but she did not complain of his decision. Her delicate blond features grew sharper, and her blue eyes more hollow. She had had a certain fine prettiness, but now she was losing it, and beginning to look old, and there was a prim, angular, old maiden carriage about her narrow shoulders.

Wilson never noticed it, and never thought of Alma as not possessed of eternal youth, or capable of losing or regretting it.

"Come along. Alma," said he; and she followed meekly after him down the street.

Soon after they passed Candace Whitcomb's house, the minister went up the front walk and rang the bell. The pale profile at the window had never stirred as he opened the gate and came up the walk. However, the door was promptly opened, in response to his ring. "Good-morning, Miss Whitcomb," said the minister.

"*Good*-morning." Candace gave a sweeping toss of her head as she spoke. There was a fierce upward curl to her thin nostrils and her lips, as if she scented an adversary. Her black eyes had two tiny cold sparks of fury in them, like an enraged bird's. She did not ask the minister to enter, but he stepped lumberingly into the entry, and she retreated rather than led the way into her little parlor. He settled into the great rocking-chair and wiped his face. Candace sat down again in her old place by the window. She was a tall woman, but very slender and full of pliable motions, like a blade of grass.

"It's a—very pleasant day," said the minister.

Candace made no reply. She sat still, with her head drooping. The wind stirred the looped lace-curtains; a tall rose-tree outside the window waved; soft shadows floated through the room. Candace's parlor organ stood in front of an open window that faced the church; on the corner was a pitcher with a bunch of white lilacs. The whole room was scented with them. Presently the minister looked over at them and sniffed pleasantly.

"You have—some beautiful—lilacs there."

Candace did not speak. Every line of her slender figure looked flexible, but it was a flexibility more resistant than rigor.

The minister looked at her. He filled up the great rocking-chair; his arms in his shiny black coat-sleeves rested squarely and comfortably upon the hair-cloth arms of the chair.

"Well, Miss Whitcomb, I suppose I—may as well come to—the point. There was—a little—matter I wished to speak to you about. I don't suppose you were—at least I can't suppose you were—aware of it, but—this morning, during the singing by the choir, you played and—sung a little too—loud. That is, with—the windows open. It —disturbed us—a little. I hope you won't feel hurt—my dear Miss Candace, but I knew you would rather I would speak of it, for I knew—you would be more disturbed than anybody else at the idea of such a thing."

Candace did not raise her eyes; she looked as if his words might sway her through the window. "I ain't disturbed at it," said she. "I did it on purpose; I meant to."

The minister looked at her.

"You needn't look at me. I know jest what I'm about. I sung the way I did on purpose, an' I'm goin' to do it again, an' I'd like to see you stop me. I guess I've got a right to set down to my own organ, an' sing a psalm tune on a Sabbath day, 'f I want to; an' there ain't no amount of talkin' an' palaverin' a-goin' to stop me. See there!" Candace swung aside her skirts a little. "Look at that!"

The minister looked. Candace's feet were resting on a large red-plush photograph album.

"Makes a nice footstool, don't it?" said she.

The minister looked at the album, then at her; there was a slowly gathering alarm in his face; he began to think she was losing her reason.

Candace had her eyes full upon him now, and her head up. She laughed, and her laugh was almost a snarl. "Yes; I thought it would make a beautiful footstool," said she. "I've been wantin' one for sometime." Her tone was full of vicious irony.

"Why, Miss—" began the minister; but she interrupted him:

"I know what you're a-goin' to say, Mr. Pollard, an' now I'm goin' to have my say; I'm a-goin' to speak. I want to know what you think of folks that pretend to be Christians treatin' anybody the way they've treated me. Here I've sung in those singin'-seats forty year. I 'ain't never missed a Sunday, except when I've been sick, an' I've gone an' sung a good many times when I'd better been in bed, an' now I'm turned out without a word of warnin'. My voice is jest as good as ever 'twas; there can't anybody say it ain't. It wa'n't ever quite so high-pitched as that Way girl's, mebbe; but she flats the whole durin' time. My voice is as good an' high to-day as it was twenty year ago; an' if it wa'n't, I'd like to know where the Christianity comes in. I'd like to know if it wouldn't be more to the credit of folks in a church to keep an old singer an' an old minister, if they didn't sing an' hold forth quite so smart as they used to, ruther than turn 'em off an' hurt their feelin's. I guess it would be full as much to the glory of God. S'pose the singin' an' the preachin' wa'n't quite so good, what difference would it make? Salvation don't hang on anybody's hittin' a high note, that I ever heard of. Folks are gettin' as high-steppin' an' fussy in a meetin'-house as they are in a tavern, nowadays. S'pose they should turn you off, Mr. Pollard, come an' give you a photograph album, an' tell you to clear out, how'd you like it? I ain't findin' any fault with your preachin'; it was always good enough to suit me; but it don't stand to reason folks'll be as took up with your sermons as when you was a young man. You can't expect it. S'pose they should turn you out in your old age, an' call in some young bob squirt, how'd you feel? There's William Emmons, too; he's three years older'n I am, if he does lead the choir an' run all the singin' in town. If my voice has gi'en out, it stan's to reason his has. It ain't, though. William Emmons sings jest as well as he ever did. Why don't they turn him out the way they have me, an' give him a photograph album? I dun know but it would be a good idea to send everybody, as soon as they get a little old an' gone by, an' young folks begin to push, onto some desert island, an' give 'em each a photograph album. Then they can sit down an' look at pictures the rest of their days. Mebbe government'll take it up.

"There they come here last week Thursday, all the choir, jest about eight o'clock in the evenin', an' pretended they'd come to give me a nice little surprise. Surprise! h'm! Brought cake an' oranges, an' was jest as nice as they could be, an' I was real tickled. I never had a surprise-party before in my life. Jenny Carr she played, an' they wanted me to sing alone, an' I never suspected a thing. I've been mad ever since to think what a fool I was, an' how they must have laughed in their sleeves.

"When they'd gone I found this photograph album on the table, all done up as nice as you please, an' directed to Miss Candace Whitcomb from her many friends, an' I opened it, an' there was the letter inside givin' me notice to quit.

"If they'd gone about it any decent way, told me right out honest that they'd got tired of me, an' wanted Alma Way to sing instead of me, I wouldn't minded so much; I should have been hurt 'nough, for I'd felt as if some that had pretended to be my friends wa'n't; but it wouldn't have been as bad as this. They said in the letter that they'd always set great value on my services, an' it wa'n't from any lack of appreciation that they turned me off, but they thought the duty was gettin' a little too arduous for me. H'm! I hadn't complained. If they'd turned me right out fair an' square, showed me the door, an' said, 'Here, you get out,' but to go an' spill molasses, as it were, all over the threshold, tryin' to make me think it's all nice an' sweet—

"I'd sent that photograph album back quick's I could pack it, but I didn't know who started it, so I've used it for a footstool. It's all it's good for, 'cordin' to my way of thinkin'. An' I ain't been particular to get the dust off my shoes before I used it neither."

Mr. Pollard, the minister, sat staring. He did not look at Candace; his eyes were fastened upon a point straight ahead. He had a look of helpless solidity, like a block of granite. This country minister, with his steady, even temperament, treading with heavy precision his one track for over forty years, having nothing new in his life except the new sameness of the seasons, and desiring nothing new, was incapable of understanding a woman like this, who had lived as quietly as he, and all the time held within herself the elements of revolution. He could not account for such violence, such extremes, except in a loss of reason. He had a conviction that Candace was getting beyond herself. He himself was not a typical New-Englander; the national elements of character were not pronounced in him. He was aghast and bewildered at this outbreak, which was tropical, and more than tropical, for a New England nature has a floodgate, and the power which it releases is an accumulation. Candace Whitcomb had been a quiet woman, so delicately resolute that the quality had been scarcely noticed in her, and her ambition had been unsuspected. Now the resolution and the ambition appeared raging over her whole self.

She began to talk again. "I've made up my mind that I'm goin' to sing Sundays the way I did this mornin', an' I don't care what folks say," said she. "I've made up my mind that I'm goin' to take matters into my own hands. I'm goin' to let folks see that I ain't trod down quite flat, that there's a little rise left in me. I ain't goin' to give up beat yet a while; an' I'd like to see anybody stop me. If I ain't got a right to play a psalm tune on my organ an' sing, I'd like to know. If you don't like it, you can move the meetin'-house."

Candace had had an inborn reverence for clergymen. She had always treated Mr. Pollard with the utmost deference. Indeed, her manner toward all men had been marked by a certain delicate stiffness and dignity. Now she was talking to the old minister with the homely freedom with which she might have addressed a female gossip over the back fence. He could not say much in return. He did not feel competent to make headway against any such tide of passion; all he could do was to let it beat against him. He made a few expostulations, which increased Candace's vehemence; he expressed his regret over the whole affair, and suggested that they should kneel and ask the guidance of the Lord in the matter, that she might be led to see it all in a different light.

Candace refused flatly. "I don't see any use prayin' about it," said she. "I don't think the Lord's got much to do with it, anyhow."

It was almost time for the afternoon service when the minister left. He had missed his comfortable noontide rest, through this encounter with his revolutionary parishioner. After the minister had gone, Candace sat by the window and waited. The bell rang, and she watched the people file past. When her nephew Wilson Ford with Alma appeared, she grunted to herself. "She's thin as a rail," said she; "guess there won't be much left of her by the time Wilson gets her. Little soft-spoken nippin' thing, she wouldn't make him no kind of a wife, anyway. Guess it's jest as well."

When the bell had stopped tolling, and all the people entered the church, Candace went over to her organ and seated herself. She arranged a singing-book before her, and sat still, waiting. Her thin, colorless neck and temples were full of beating pulses; her black eyes were bright and eager; she leaned stiffly over toward the music-rack, to hear better. When the church organ sounded out she straightened herself; her long skinny fingers pressed her own organ-keys with nervous energy. She worked the pedals with all her strength; all her slender body was in motion. When the first notes of Alma's solo began, Candace sang. She had really possessed a fine voice, and it was wonderful how little she had lost it. Straining her throat with jealous fury, her notes were still for the main part true. Her voice filled the whole room; she sang with wonderful fire and expression. That, at least, mild little Alma Way could never emulate. She was full of steadfastness and unquestioning constancy, but there were in her no smouldering fires of ambition and resolution. Music was not to her what it had been to her older rival. To this obscure woman, kept relentlessly by circumstances in a narrow track, singing in the village choir had been as much as Italy was to Napoleon—and now on her island of exile she was still showing fight.

After the church service was done, Candace left the organ and went over to her old chair by the window. Her knees felt weak, and shook under her. She sat down, and leaned back her head. There were red spots on her cheeks. Pretty soon she heard a quick slam of her gate, and an impetuous tread on the gravel-walk. She looked up, and there was her nephew Wilson Ford hurrying up to the door. She cringed a little, then she settled herself more firmly in her chair.

Wilson came into the room with a rush. He left the door open, and the wind slammed it to after him.

"Aunt Candace, where are you?" he called out, in a loud voice.

She made no reply. He looked around fiercely, and his eyes seemed to pounce upon her.

"Look here, Aunt Candace," said he, "are you crazy?" Candace said nothing. "Aunt Candace!" She did not seem to see him. "If you don't answer me," said Wilson, "I'll just go over there and pitch that old organ out of the window!"

"Wilson Ford!" said Candace, in a voice that was almost a scream.

"Well, what say! What have you got to say for yourself, acting the way you have? I tell you what 'tis, Aunt Candace, I won't stand it."

"I'd like to see you help yourself."

"I will help myself. I'll pitch that old organ out of the window, and then I'll board up the window on that side of your house. Then we'll see."

"It ain't your house, and it won't never be."

"Who said it was my house? You're my aunt, and I've got a little lookout for the credit of the family. Aunt Candace, what are you doing this way for?"

"It don't make no odds what I'm doin' so for. I ain't bound to give my reasons to a young fellar like you, if you do act so mighty toppin'. But I'll tell you one thing, Wilson Ford, after the way you've spoke to-day, you sha'n't never have one cent of my money, an' you can't never marry that Way girl if you don't have it. You can't never take her home to live with your mother, an' this house would have been mighty nice an' convenient for you some day. Now you won't get it. I'm goin' to make another will. I'd made one, if you did but know it. Now you won't get a cent of my money, you nor your mother neither. An' I ain't goin' to live a dreadful while longer, neither. Now I wish you'd go home; I want to lay down. I'm 'bout sick."

Wilson could not get another word from his aunt. His indignation had not in the least cooled. Her threat of disinheriting him did not cow him at all; he had too much rough independence, and indeed his aunt Candace's house had always been too much of an air-castle for him to contemplate seriously. Wilson, with his burly frame and his headlong common-sense, could have little to do with air-castles, had he been hard enough to build them over graves. Still, he had not admitted that he never could marry Alma. All his hopes were based upon a rise in his own fortunes, not by some sudden convulsion, but by his own long and steady labor. Some time, he thought, he should have saved enough for the two homes.

He went out of his aunt's house still storming. She arose after the door had shut behind him, and got out into the kitchen. She thought that she would start a fire and make a cup of tea. She had not eaten anything all day. She put some kindling-wood into the stove and touched a match to it; then she went back to the sitting-room, and settled down again into the chair by the window. The fire in the kitchen-stove roared, and the light wood was soon burned out. She thought no more about it. She had not put on the tea-kettle. Her head ached, and once in a while she shivered. She sat at the window while the afternoon waned and the dusk came on. At seven o'clock the meeting bell rang again, and the people flocked by. This time she did not stir. She had shut her parlor organ. She did not need to out-sing her rival this evening; there was only con-gregational singing at the Sunday-night prayer-meeting.

She sat still until it was nearly time for meeting to be done; her head ached harder and harder, and she shivered more. Finally she arose. "Guess I'll go to bed," she muttered. She went about the house, bent over and shaking, to lock the doors. She stood a minute in the back door, looking over the fields to the woods. There was a red light over there. "The woods are on fire," said Candace. She watched with a dull interest the flames roll up, withering and destroying the tender green spring foliage. The air was full of smoke, although the fire was half a mile away.

Candace locked the door and went in. The trees with their delicate garlands of new leaves, with the new nests of song birds, might fall, she was in the roar of an intenser fire; the growths of all her springs and the delicate wontedness of her whole life were going down in it. Candace went to bed in her little room off the parlor, but she could not sleep. She lay awake all night. In the morning she crawled to the door and hailed a little boy who was passing. She bade him go for the doctor as quickly as he could, then to Mrs. Ford's, and ask her to come over. She held on to the door while she was talking. The boy stood staring wonderingly at her. The spring wind fanned her face. She had drawn on a dress skirt and put her shawl over her shoulders, and her gray hair was blowing over her red cheeks.

She shut the door and went back to her bed. She never arose from it again. The doctor and Mrs. Ford came and looked after her, and she lived a week. Nobody but herself thought until the very last that she would die; the doctor called her illness merely a light run of fever; she had her senses fully.

But Candace gave up at the first. "It's my last sickness," she said to Mrs. Ford that morning when she first entered; and Mrs. Ford had laughed at the notion; but the sick woman held to it. She did not seem to suffer much physical pain; she only grew weaker and weaker, but she was distressed mentally. She did not talk much, but her eyes followed everybody with an agonized expression.

On Wednesday William Emmons came to inquire for her. Candace heard him out in the parlor. She tried to raise herself on one elbow that she might listen better to his voice.

"William Emmons come in to ask how you was," Mrs. Ford said, after he was gone.

"I—heard him," replied Candace. Presently she spoke again. "Nancy," said she, "where's that photograph album?"

"On the table," replied her sister, hesitatingly.

"Mebbe—you'd better—brush it up a little."

"Well."

Sunday morning Candace wished that the minister should be asked to come in at the noon intermission. She had refused to see him before. He came and prayed with her, and she asked his forgiveness for the way she had spoken the Sunday before. "I—hadn't ought to—spoke so," said she. "I was—dreadful wrought up."

"Perhaps it was your sickness coming on," said the minister, soothingly.

Candace shook her head. "No—it wa'n't. I hope the Lord will—forgive me."

After the minister had gone, Candace still appeared unhappy. Her pitiful eyes followed her sister everywhere with the mechanical persistency of a portrait.

"What is it you want, Candace?" Mrs. Ford said at last. She had nursed her sister faithfully, but once in a while her impatience showed itself.

"Nancy!"

"What say?"

"I wish—you'd go out when—meetin's done, an'—head off Alma an' Wilson, an'—ask 'em to come in. I feel as if—I'd like to —hear her sing."

Mrs. Ford stared. "Well," said she.

The meeting was now in session. The windows were all open, for it was another warm Sunday. Candace lay listening to the music when it began, and a look of peace came over her face. Her sister had smoothed her hair back, and put on a clean cap. The white curtain in the bedroom window waved in the wind like a white sail. Candace almost felt as if she were better, but the thought of death seemed easy.

Mrs. Ford at the parlor window watched for the meeting to be out. When the people appeared, she ran down the walk and waited for Alma and Wilson. When they came she told them what Candace wanted, and they all went in together.

"Here's Alma an' Wilson, Candace," said Mrs. Ford, leading them to the bedroom door.

Candace smiled. "Come in," she said, feebly. And Alma and Wilson entered and stood beside the bed. Candace continued to look at them, the smile straining her lips.

"Wilson!"

"What is it, Aunt Candace?"

"I ain't altered that—will. You an' Alma can—come here an' —live—when I'm—gone. Your mother won't mind livin' alone. Alma can have—all—my things."

"Don't, Aunt Candace." Tears were running over Wilson's cheeks, and Alma's delicate face was all of a quiver.

"I thought—maybe—Alma'd be willin' to—sing for me," said Candace.

"What do you want me to sing?" Alma asked, in a trembling voice.

" 'Jesus, lover of my soul.' "

Alma, standing there beside Wilson, began to sing. At first she could hardly control her voice, then she sang sweetly and clearly.

Candace lay and listened. Her face had a holy and radiant expression. When Alma stopped singing it did not disappear, but she looked up and spoke, and it was like a secondary glimpse of the old shape of a forest tree through the smoke and flame of the transfiguring fire the instant before it falls. "You flatted a little on —soul," said Candace.

1891

Masters of Critical Realism

WILLIAM DEAN HOWELLS
(1837–1920)

At the height of his career, about 1890, Howells was firmly established in serious literary opinion as the foremost man of letters of his generation in America. Today both Mark Twain and Henry James are considered greater authors than Howells. Yet his best writing is marked by truth and power; he is large both in the scope of his themes and in the volume of his output. Perhaps ten of his novels have held their appeal, and three— *A Modern Instance, The Rise of Silas Lapham,* and *Indian Summer*—are familiar classics of American fiction. He revitalized the realism of the day and opposed the prevalent sentimentality and idealization. As a critic he enthusiastically supported such younger radicals as Hamlin Garland and Stephen Crane, Frank Norris and the "questionable" dramatic realist, James A. Herne. He helped to establish the literary respectability in the East of that wild son of Missouri, Mark Twain. His criticism exerted a strong influence on his age. In his plays as in his fiction he advanced the comic criticism of society, and broadened it to

include the international contrast of manners. He wrote a number of notable books of travel, and his autobiographical sketches are distinguished.

From boyhood William Dean Howells smelled of printer's ink and manifested the instincts of the journalist. He was born on March 1, 1837, at Martin's Ferry, Ohio. His father, a country printer and newspaper publisher of roving disposition and literary inclinations, moved when the boy was three to Hamilton, twenty miles from Cincinnati, where he edited the Whig paper. There, by the age of nine, young Howells was setting type in his father's shop and listening to his Swedenborgian mysticism and literary idealism. His formal schooling was negligible, but he read unceasingly, and his natural gifts were such that at twenty-nine he became the assistant editor of the *Atlantic Monthly;* in his forties he was offered, and declined, professorships at Johns Hopkins and Harvard. In *A Boy's Town* (1890), Howells recorded his early adventures. When the boy was twelve his father bought an ill-fated news-

539

paper at Dayton; the next year they moved to the Little Miami River, where they experienced the primitive life described in *My Year in a Log Cabin* (1893). After several moves with the family paper, Howells struck out at nineteen as a newspaperman in Cincinnati and in Columbus, where he became editor of the *Ohio State Journal*; meanwhile his mammoth appetite for books led him deep into the literature reflected in *My Literary Passions* (1895). With a fellow journalist, John J. Piatt, he composed *Poems of Two Friends* (1860); the same year his biography of the Republican presidential candidate, Lincoln, provided him with funds for his long-awaited literary pilgrimage to the East, where he met Lowell, Holmes, Emerson, Hawthorne, and Whitman, as recounted in *Literary Friends and Acquaintance* (1900).

The Lincoln biography also won the young journalist an appointment as consul to Venice (1861–1865), and provided four years of relative leisure. He gathered material for such early travel books as *Venetian Life* (1866) and *Italian Journeys* (1867), and for the Italian scenes of three of his minor novels. In 1865 he returned to Boston to join the editorial staff of the *Nation*. Within the year he was assistant editor of the *Atlantic Monthly*, whose first editor, James Russell Lowell, had nine years earlier launched it with the distinction that Howells later maintained as editor, between 1871 and 1881. During this busy decade Howells

published six novels; his seventh, *A Modern Instance* (1882), although it is imperfect in construction, represents the first perfection of his characteristic quality. In portraying the disintegration of Bartley Hubbard's career and marriage, Howells for the first time fully demonstrated a realism that was primarily concerned, not with praise or blame, but with observing in human destinies the natural consequences of character.

Leaving the *Atlantic*, Howells spent four years abroad (1881–1885) in travel and study, and in 1885 published his best-known work, *The Rise of Silas Lapham*. In this novel of Boston life Howells contrasts the Corys of Beacon Hill with the Laphams, whose enterprising development of a paint factory on their Vermont farm has led to the founding of a Boston industry and a new fortune. Silas Lapham, who comes to terms with himself at the cost of his fortune, is a character not soon forgotten.

After 1886 Howells was closely associated with *Harper's Magazine*. In his column, "The Editor's Study," appeared much of his criticism of fiction, collected in 1891 as *Criticism and Fiction*. After 1900 he was the familiar essayist of "The Easy Chair," in which his *obiter dicta* became widely familiar. During this New York period he was captivated by Tolstoi, whose Christian socialism motivated several of his novels, of which *A Hazard of New Fortunes* (1890) and *A Traveler from Altruria* (1894), a utopian novel, are the best known. Among his novels of manners of this period, his masterpiece is *Indian Summer* (1886), a story of the second blooming of love in middle life. Charming, witty, and mature, it represents his best use of the Italian scene.

The close student of the period may take issue with Howells' contention that "the smiling aspects" of American life were the most prevalent and the most typical, and that American life was such that the novelist could confine himself to what would not offend the innocence of a young girl, and should therefore do so. But Howells perceptively explored the areas to which he limited himself, and within those limits his characters and their dialogue frequently attain a high degree of subtlety. In the psychological study of character and in his fascination with the dark or profound recesses of the human consciousness he acknowledged the inspiration of Hawthorne. The results in his writing, however, are independent of Hawthorne in both method and motivation. The best of his fiction stems from his analysis of character in social situations, from his abiding sense of the responsibility that people have for each other, and from his deft and witty revelation of the motives of men and women. Yet this high ability was increasingly diluted by his fictional propaganda for social and economic

improvement. In addition he wrote too much, and sometimes for an immediate public—more than thirty novels or novelettes, several volumes of short stories, and thirty-one dramas (chiefly one-act social comedies), as well as the sketches and travels. The best of his fiction, that dealing with character, like much of his autobiographical writing, continues to appeal with the freshness and power that belong to a master of literature.

There is no collected edition of Howells. Many editions of *The Rise of Silas Lapham* exist, and *Indian Summer* and *A Hazard of New Fortunes* have been reprinted. Henry Steele Commager edited *Selected Writings of William Dean Howells*, 1950, containing *The Rise of Silas Lapham, A Modern Instance, A Boy's Town*, and *My Mark Twain*. W. J. Meserve edited *Complete Plays of W. D. Howells*, 1960. O. W. Firkins wrote a critical biography, *William Dean Howells: A Study*, 1924. Mildred Howells edited *Life in Letters of William Dean Howells*, 2 vols., 1928. An indispensable study is the introduction by Clara and Rudolph Kirk to *William Dean Howells: Representative Selections*, American Writers Series, 1950. A large-scale critical study is Everett Carter, *Howells and the Age of Realism*, 1954. Edwin H. Cady, *The Road to Realism*, 1956, and *The Realist at War*, 1958, comprise studies of 1837–1885 and 1885–1920. Recent evaluations are Van Wyck Brooks, *Howells: His Life and Work*, 1959; R. L. Hough, *Quiet Rebel*, 1959; and George N. Bennett, *William Dean Howells: The Development of a Novelist, 1959*. See K. E. Eble, ed., *Howells: A Century of Criticism*, 1962. Howells' autobiographical reminiscences will be found in *A Boy's Town*, 1890; *My Year in a Log Cabin*, 1893; *My Literary Passions*, 1895; *Impressions and Experiences*, 1896; *Literary Friends and Acquaintance*, 1900; and *Years of My Youth*, 1916.

From Criticism and Fiction
[*The Smiling Aspects of Life*][1]

It is the difference of the American novelist's ideals from those of the English novelist that gives him his advantage, and seems to promise him the future. The love of the passionate and the heroic, as the Englishman has it, is such a crude and unwholesome thing, so deaf and blind to all the most delicate and important facts of art and life, so insensible to the subtle values in either that its presence or absence makes the whole difference, and enables one who is not obsessed by it to thank Heaven that he is not as that other man is.

There can be little question that many refinements of thought and spirit which every American is sensible of in the fiction of this continent, are necessarily lost upon our good kin beyond seas, whose thumb-fingered apprehension requires something gross and palpable for its assurance of reality. This is not their fault, and I am not sure that it is wholly their misfortune: they are made so as not to miss what they do not find, and they are simply content without those subleties of life and character which it gives us so keen a pleasure to have noted in literature. If they perceive them at all it is as something vague and diaphanous, something that filmily wavers before their sense and teases them, much as the beings of an invisible world might mock one of our material frame by intimations of their presence. It is with reason, therefore, on the part of an Englishman, that Mr. Henley[2] complains of our fiction as a shadow-land, though we find more and more in it the faithful report of our life, its motives and emotions, and all the comparatively etherealized passions and ideals that influence it.

In fact, the American who chooses to enjoy his birthright to the full, lives in a world wholly different from the Englishman's, and speaks (too often through his nose) another language: he breathes a rarefied and nimble air full of shining possibilities and radiant promises which the fog-and-soot-clogged lungs of those less-favored islanders struggle in vain to fill themselves with. But he ought to be modest in his advantage, and patient with the coughing and sputtering of his cousin who complains of finding himself in an exhausted receiver on plunging into one of our novels. To be quite just to the poor fellow, I have had some such experience as that myself in the atmosphere of some of our more attenuated romances.

Yet every now and then I read a book with perfect comfort and much exhilaration, whose scenes the average Englishman would gasp in. Nothing happens; that is, nobody murders or debauches

---

1. This selection was first printed in *Harper's* in slightly different form, the final part appearing in September, 1886, and the first in October, 1890. It was incorporated into Chapter XXI of *Criticism and Fiction* (1891), which the present text follows.
2. William Ernest Henley (1849–1903), English poet, critic, and editor.

anybody else; there is no arson or pillage of any sort; there is not a ghost, or a ravening beast, or a hair-breadth escape, or a shipwreck, or a monster of self-sacrifice, or a lady five thousand years old in the whole course of the story; "no promenade, no band of music, nossing!" as Mr. Du Maurier's[3] Frenchman said of the meet for a fox-hunt. Yet it is all alive with the keenest interest for those who enjoy the study of individual traits and general conditions as they make themselves known to American experience.

These conditions have been so favorable hitherto (though they are becoming always less so) that they easily account for the optimistic faith of our novel which Mr. Hughes[4] notices. It used to be one of the disadvantages of the practice of romance in America, which Hawthorne more or less whimsically lamented, that there were so few shadows and inequalities in our broad level of prosperity; and it is one of the reflections suggested by Dostoïevsky's[5] novel, The Crime and the Punishment, that whoever struck a note so profoundly tragic in American fiction would do a false and mistaken thing—as false and as mistaken in its way as dealing in American fiction with certain nudities which the Latin peoples seem to find edifying. Whatever their deserts, very few American novelists have been led out to be shot, or finally exiled to the rigors of a winter at Duluth;[6] and in a land where journeymen carpenters and plumbers strike for four dollars a day the sum of hunger and cold is comparatively small, and the wrong from class to class has been almost inappreciable, though all this is changing for the worse. Our novelists, therefore, concern themselves with the more smiling aspects of life, which are the more American, and seek the universal in the individual rather than the social interests. It is worth while, even at the risk of being called commonplace, to be true to our well-to-do actualities; the very passions themselves seem to be softened and modified by conditions which formerly at least could not be said to wrong any one, to cramp endeavor, or to cross lawful desire. Sin and suffering and shame there must always be in the world, I suppose, but I believe that in this new world of ours it is still mainly from one to another one, and oftener still from one to one's self. We have death too in America, and a great deal of disagreeable and painful disease, which the multiplicity of our patent medicines does not seem to cure; but this is tragedy that comes in the very nature of things, and is not peculiarly American, as the large, cheerful average of health and success and happy life is. It will not do to boast, but it is well to be true to the facts, and to see that, apart from

3. George du Maurier (1834–1896), English author born in Paris, best known as the author of the popular novel *Trilby* (1894).
4. An English journalist, E. Hughes, who had commented on the differences between English and American novels.

5. Fëdor Dostoevski (1821–1881), great Russian novelist whose work Howells helped introduce to American readers.
6. Dostoevski himself was exiled to the Siberian mines.

these purely mortal troubles, the race here has enjoyed conditions in which most of the ills that have darkened its annals might be averted by honest work and unselfish behavior.

1886–1890, 1891

[Decency Is True to Life][7]

The fact [is] generally lost sight of by those who censure the Anglo-Saxon novel for its prudishness, that it is really not such a prude after all; and that if it is sometimes apparently anxious to avoid those experiences of life not spoken of before young people, this may be an appearance only. Sometimes a novel which has this shuffling air, this effect of truckling to propriety, might defend itself, if it could speak for itself, by saying that such experiences happened not to come within its scheme, and that, so far from maiming or mutilating itself in ignoring them, it was all the more faithfully representative of the tone of modern life in dealing with love that was chaste, and with passion so honest that it could be openly spoken of before the tenderest society bud at dinner. It might say that the guilty intrigue, the betrayal, the extreme flirtation even, was the exceptional thing in life, and unless the scheme of the story necessarily involved it, that it would be bad art to lug it in, and as bad taste as to introduce such topics in a mixed company. It could say very justly that the novel in our civilization now always addresses a mixed company, and that the vast majority of the company are ladies, and that very many, if not most, of these ladies are young girls. If the novel were written for men and for married women alone, as in continental Europe, it might be altogether different. But the simple fact is that it is not written for them alone among us, and it is a question of writing, under cover of our universal acceptance, things for young girls to read which you would be put out-of-doors for saying to them, or of frankly giving notice of your intention, and so cutting yourself off from the pleasure—and it is a very high and sweet one—of appealing to these vivid, responsive intelligences, which are none the less brilliant and admirable because they are innocent.

One day a novelist who liked, after the manner of other men, to repine at his hard fate, complained to his friend, a critic, that he was tired of the restriction he had put upon himself in this regard; for it is a mistake, as can be readily shown, to suppose that others impose it. "See how free those French fellows are!" he rebelled. "Shall we always be shut up to our tradition of decency?"

"Do you think it's much worse than being shut up to their tradition of indecency?" said his friend. * * *

7. This passage is taken from an essay in *Harper's* for June, 1889, which later became Chapter XXIV of *Criticism and* *Fiction* (1891), the source of the present text.

But I do not mean to imply that his case covers the whole ground. So far as it goes, though, it ought to stop the mouths of those who complain that fiction is enslaved to propriety among us. It appears that of a certain kind of impropriety it is free to give us all it will, and more. But this is not what serious men and women writing fiction mean when they rebel against the limitations of their art in our civilization. They have no desire to deal with nakedness, as painters and sculptors freely do in the worship of beauty; or with certain facts of life, as the stage does, in the service of sensation. But they ask why, when the conventions of the plastic and histrionic arts liberate their followers to the portrayal of almost any phase of the physical or of the emotional nature, an American novelist may not write a story on the lines of *Anna Karenina* or *Madame Bovary*.[8] They wish to touch one of the most serious and sorrowful problems of life in the spirit of Tolstoy and Flaubert, and they ask why they may not. At one time, they remind us, the Anglo-Saxon novelist did deal with such problems—De Foe in his spirit, Richardson in his, Goldsmith in his.[9] At what moment did our fiction lose this privilege? In what fatal hour did the Young Girl arise and seal the lips of Fiction, with a touch of her finger, to some of the most vital interests of life?

Whether I wished to oppose them in their aspirations for greater freedom, or whether I wished to encourage them, I should begin to answer them by saying that the Young Girl has never done anything of the kind. The manners of the novel have been improving with those of its readers; that is all. Gentlemen no longer swear or fall drunk under the table, or abduct young ladies and shut them up in lonely country-houses, or so habitually set about the ruin of their neighbors' wives, as they once did. Generally, people now call a spade an agricultural implement; they have not grown decent without having also grown a little squeamish, but they have grown comparatively decent; there is no doubt about that. They require of a novelist whom they respect unquestionable proof of his seriousness, if he proposes to deal with certain phases of life; they require a sort of scientific decorum. He can no longer expect to be received on the ground of entertainment only; he assumes a higher function, something like that of a physician or a priest, and they expect him to be bound by laws as sacred as those of such professions; they hold him solemnly pledged not to betray them or abuse their confidence. If he will accept the conditions, they give him their confidence, and

8. Flaubert's *Madame Bovary* details the sordid plight of a weak woman lost in desolate love affairs; Tolstoi's *Anna Karenina* traces the tragedy of an illicit love which leads to death.
9. Daniel Defoe (1660–1731) treated illicit passion in *Moll Flanders* and *Roxana;* Samuel Richardson (1689–1761) wrote *Clarissa Harlowe,* in which the heroine dies of shame; and Oliver Goldsmith (1728–1774) dealt with seduction and desertion in *The Vicar of Wakefield.*

he may then treat to his greater honor, and not at all to his disadvantage, of such experiences, such relations of men and women as George Eliot treats in *Adam Bede*, in *Daniel Deronda*, in *Romola*, in almost all her books; such as Hawthorne treats in *The Scarlet Letter*; such as Dickens treats in *David Copperfield*; such as Thackeray treats in *Pendennis*, and glances at in every one of his fictions; such as most of the masters of English fiction have at some time treated more or less openly. It is quite false or quite mistaken to suppose that our novels have left untouched these most important realities of life. They have only not made them their stock in trade; they have kept a true perspective in regard to them; they have relegated them in their pictures of life to the space and place they occupy in life itself, as we know it in England and America. They have kept a correct proportion, knowing perfectly well that unless the novel is to be a map, with everything scrupulously laid down in it, a faithful record of life in far the greater extent could be made to the exclusion of guilty love and all its circumstances and consequences.

I justify them in this view not only because I hate what is cheap and meretricious, and hold in peculiar loathing the cant of the critics who require "passion" as something in itself admirable and desirable in a novel, but because I prize fidelity in the historian of feeling and character. Most of these critics who demand "passion" would seem to have no conception of any passion but one. Yet there are several other passions: the passion of grief, the passion of avarice, the passion of pity, the passion of ambition, the passion of hate, the passion of envy, the passion of devotion, the passion of friendship; and all these have a greater part in the drama of life than the passion of love, and infinitely greater than the passion of guilty love. Wittingly or unwittingly, English fiction and American fiction have recognized this truth, not fully, not in the measure it merits, but in greater degree than most other fiction.

1889, 1891

From Literary Friends and Acquaintance
[*My First Visit to New England*][1]

VII

* * * When I actually found myself in Boston, there were perhaps industries which it would have been well for me to celebrate, but I either made believe there were none, or else I honestly forgot all about them. In either case I released myself altogether to the literary and historical associations of the place. I need not say that I gave myself first to the first, and it rather surprised me to find that the literary associations of Boston referred so largely to Cambridge. I did not know much about Cambridge, except that it was the seat of the university where Lowell was, and Longfellow had been, professor;[2] and somehow I had not realized it as the home of these poets. That was rather stupid of me, but it is best to own the truth, and afterward I came to know the place so well that I may safely confess my earlier ignorance.

I had stopped in Boston at the Tremont House, which was still one of the first hostelries of the country, and I must have inquired my way to Cambridge there; but I was sceptical of the direction the Cambridge horse-car took when I found it, and I hinted to the driver my anxieties as to why he should be starting east when I had been told that Cambridge was west of Boston. He reassured me in the laconic and sarcastic manner of his kind, and we really reached Cambridge by the route he had taken.

The beautiful elms that shaded a great part of the way massed themselves in the "groves of academe"[3] at the Square, and showed pleasant glimpses of "Old Harvard's scholar factories red,"[4] then far fewer than now. It must have been in vacation, for I met no one as I wandered through the college yard, trying to make up my mind as to how I should learn where Lowell lived; for it was he whom I had come to find. He had not only taken the poems I sent him, but he had printed two of them in a single number of the *Atlantic*, and had even written me a little note about them, which I wore next my heart in my breast pocket till I almost wore it out; and so I thought I might fitly report myself to him. * * *

X

As it fell out, I lived without farther difficulty to the day and hour of the dinner Lowell made for me; and I really think, looking at myself impersonally, and remembering the sort of young fellow I was, that it would have been a great pity if I had not. The dinner was at the old-fashioned Boston hour of two, and the table was laid for four people in some little upper room at Parker's,[5] which I was never afterwards able to make sure of. Lowell was already there when I came, and he presented me, to my inexpressible delight and surprise, to Dr. Holmes, who was there with him.

2. Longfellow was Smith Professor of Modern Languages at Harvard from 1836 until 1855, when Lowell succeeded him, remaining until 1872.
3. *Cf.* Horace, *Epistles*, II, Book 2, l. 45: "*Atque inter silvas Academi quaerere verum.*" [And among the groves of Academe to seek the truth.] Horace refers to the "Academy" of Plato, in a grove sacred to the hero Academus.
4. *Cf.* James Russell Lowell, "An Invitation: To J.F.H."
5. The Parker House, a hotel in Boston, has long been famous.

Holmes was in the most brilliant hour of that wonderful second youth which his fame flowered into long after the world thought he had completed the cycle of his literary life. He had already received full recognition as a poet of delicate wit, nimble humor, airy imagination, and exquisite grace, when the Autocrat papers[6] advanced his name indefinitely beyond the bounds which most immortals would have found range enough. The marvel of his invention was still fresh in the minds of men, and time had not dulled in any measure the sense of its novelty. His readers all fondly identified him with his work; and I fully expected to find myself in the Autocrat's presence when I met Dr. Holmes. But the fascination was none the less for that reason; and the winning smile, the wise and humorous glance, the whole genial manner was as important to me as if I had foreboded something altogether different. I found him physically of the Napoleonic height[7] which spiritually overtops the Alps, and I could look into his face without that unpleasant effort which giants of inferior mind so often cost the man of five feet four.

A little while after, Fields[8] came in, and then our number and my pleasure were complete.

Nothing else so richly satisfactory, indeed, as the whole affair could have happened to a like youth at such a point in his career; and when I sat down with Doctor Holmes and Mr. Fields, on Lowell's right, I felt through and through the dramatic perfection of the event. The kindly Autocrat recognized some such quality of it in terms which were not the less precious and gracious for their humorous excess. I have no reason to think that he had yet read any of my poor verses, or had me otherwise than wholly on trust from Lowell; but he leaned over towards his host, and said, with a laughing look at me, "Well, James, this is something like the apostolic succession; this is the laying on of hands." I took his sweet and caressing irony as he meant it; but the charm of it went to my head long before any drop of wine, together with the charm of hearing him and Lowell calling each other James and Wendell, and of finding them still cordially boys together.

I would gladly have glimmered before those great lights in the talk that followed, if I could have thought of anything brilliant to say, but I could not, and so I let them shine without a ray of reflected splendor from me. It was such talk as I had, of course, never heard before, and it is not saying enough to say that I have never heard such talk since except from these two men. It was as light and

---

6. *The Autocrat of the Breakfast-Table* (1858).
7. The French emperor Napoleon was of very small stature, but magnetic personality.

8. James T. Fields (1817–1881), publisher, essayist, and poet, succeeded Lowell as editor of the *Atlantic Monthly* (1861–1870).

kind as it was deep and true, and it ranged over a hundred things, with a perpetual sparkle of Doctor Holmes's wit, and the constant glow of Lowell's incandescent sense. From time to time Fields came in with one of his delightful stories (sketches of character they were, which he sometimes did not mind caricaturing), or with some criticism of the literary situation from his stand-point of both lover and publisher of books. I heard fames that I had accepted as proofs of power treated as factitious, and witnessed a frankness concerning authorship, far and near, that I had not dreamed of authors using. When Doctor Holmes understood that I wrote for the *Saturday Press*,[9] which was running amuck among some Bostonian immortalities of the day, he seemed willing that I should know they were not thought so very undying in Boston, and that I should not take the notion of a Mutual Admiration Society too seriously, or accept the New York bohemian view of Boston as true. For the most part the talk did not address itself to me, but became an exchange of thoughts and fancies between himself and Lowell. They touched, I remember, on certain matters of technique, and the doctor confessed that he had a prejudice against some words that he could not overcome; for instance, he said, nothing could induce him to use *'neath* for *beneath*, no exigency of versification or stress of rhyme. Lowell contended that he would use any word that carried his meaning; and I think he did this to the hurt of some of his earlier things. He was then probably in the revolt against too much literature in literature, which every one is destined sooner or later to share; there was a certain roughness, very like crudeness, which he indulged before his thought and phrase mellowed to one music in his later work. I tacitly agreed rather with the doctor, though I did not swerve from my allegiance to Lowell, and if I had spoken I should have sided with him: I would have given that or any other proof of my devotion. Fields casually mentioned that he thought "The Dandelion" was the most popularly liked of Lowell's briefer poems, and I made haste to say that I thought so too, though I did not really think anything about it; and then I was sorry, for I could see that the poet did not like it, quite; and I felt that I was duly punished for my dishonesty.

Hawthorne was named among other authors, probably by Fields, whose house had just published his "Marble Faun,"[1] and who had recently come home on the same steamer with him. Doctor Holmes asked if I had met Hawthorne yet, and when I confessed that I had hardly yet even hoped for such a thing, he smiled his winning smile, and said: "Ah, well! I don't know that you will ever feel you have

9. A New York weekly, edited by Henry Clapp, which lasted only eight years; Whitman was a contributor, and one of its last issues contained Twain's "Jumping Frog."

1. A romance set in Rome, published in 1860.

really met him. He is like a dim room with a little taper of personality burning on the corner of the mantel."

They all spoke of Hawthorne, and with the same affection, but
the same sense of something mystical and remote in him; and
every word was priceless to me. But these masters of the craft I was
'prentice to probably could not have said anything that I should not
have found wise and well, and I am sure now I should have been the
loser if the talk had shunned any of the phases of human nature
which it touched. It is best to find that all men are of the same
make, and that there are certain universal things which interest them
as much as the supernal things, and amuse them even more. There
was a saying of Lowell's which he was fond of repeating at the
menace of any form of the transcendental, and he liked to warn
himself and others with his homely, "Remember the dinner-bell."
What I recall of the whole effect of a time so happy for me is that
in all that was said, however high, however fine, we were never
out of hearing of the dinner-bell; and perhaps this is the best effect
I can leave with the reader. It was the first dinner served in courses
that I had sat down to, and I felt that this service gave it a romantic
importance which the older fashion of the West still wanted. Even
at Governor Chase's[2] table in Columbus the Governor carved; I
knew of the dinner *à la Russe*,[3] as it was then called, only from
books; and it was a sort of literary flavor that I tasted in the successive dishes. When it came to the black coffee, and then to the
petits verres[4] of cognac, with lumps of sugar set fire to atop, it was
something that so far transcended my home-kept experience that it
began to seem altogether visionary.

Neither Fields nor Doctor Holmes smoked, and I had to confess
that I did not; but Lowell smoked enough for all three, and the
spark of his cigar began to show in the waning light before we rose
from the table. The time that never had, nor can ever have, its
fellow for me, had to come to an end, as all times must, and when
I shook hands with Lowell in parting, he overwhelmed me by saying
that if I thought of going to Concord[5] he would send me a letter to
Hawthorne. I was not to see Lowell again during my stay in Boston;
but Doctor Holmes asked me to tea for the next evening, and Fields
said I must come to breakfast with him in the morning.

XIV

I wonder if there is a stage that still runs between Lowell and
Concord, past meadow walls, and under the caressing boughs of
way-side elms, and through the bird-haunted gloom of woodland
roads, in the freshness of the summer morning? By a blessed chance

2. Salmon Portland Chase (1808–1873)
was the first Republican governor of
Ohio, from 1855 to 1859.
3. In the Russian manner, *i.e.*, in
courses served from other tables.
4. Small brandy glasses.
5. Concord, Massachusetts, home of
Hawthorne, Emerson, and Thoreau.

I found that there was such a stage in 1860, and I took it from my hotel, instead of going back to Boston and up to Concord as I must have had to do by train. The journey gave me the intimacy of the New England country as I could have had it in no other fashion, and for the first time I saw it in all the summer sweetness which I have often steeped my soul in since. The meadows were newly mown, and the air was fragrant with the grass, stretching in long windrows among the brown bowlders, or capped with canvas in the little haycocks it had been gathered into the day before. I was fresh from the affluent farms of the Western Reserve, and this care of the grass touched me with a rude pity, which I also bestowed on the meagre fields of corn and wheat; but still the land was lovelier than any I had ever seen, with its old farmhouses, and brambled gray stone walls, its stony hillsides, its staggering orchards, its wooded tops, and its thick-brackened valleys. From West to East the difference was as great as I afterwards found it from America to Europe, and my impression of something quaint and strange was no keener when I saw Old England the next year than when I saw New England now. I had imagined the landscape bare of trees, and I was astonished to find it almost as full of them as at home, though they all looked very little, as they well might to eyes used to the primeval forests of Ohio. The road ran through them from time to time, and took their coolness on its smooth hard reaches, and then issued again in the glisten of the open fields. * * *

XV

* * * I wasted that whole evening and the next morning in fond delaying, and it was not until after the indifferent dinner I got at the tavern where I stopped, that I found courage to go and present Lowell's letter to Hawthorne. I would almost have forgone meeting the weird genius only to have kept that letter, for it said certain infinitely precious things of me with such a sweetness, such a grace as Lowell alone could give his praise. Years afterwards, when Hawthorne was dead, I met Mrs. Hawthorne, and told her of the pang I had in parting with it, and she sent it me, doubly enriched by Hawthorne's keeping. But now if I were to see him at all I must give up my letter, and I carried it in my hand to the door of the cottage he called The Wayside. It was never otherwise than a very modest place, but the modesty was greater then than to-day, and there was already some preliminary carpentry at one end of the cottage, which I saw was to result in an addition to it. I recall pleasant fields across the road before it; behind rose a hill wooded with low pines, such as is made in *Septimius Felton*[6] the scene of the involuntary duel between Septimius and the young British offi-

---

6. *Septimius Felton* (1872) is a ro- of life, a story which involves the
mance of a scientist seeking an elixir legend of a bloody footstep.

cer. I have a sense of the woods coming quite down to the house, but if this was so I do not know what to do with a grassy slope which seems to have stretched part way up the hill. As I approached, I looked for the tower which the author was fabled to climb into at sight of the coming guest, and pull the ladder up after him; and I wondered whether he would fly before me in that sort, or imagine some easier means of escaping me.

The door was opened to my ring by a tall handsome boy whom I suppose to have been Mr. Julian Hawthorne;[7] and the next moment I found myself in the presence of the romancer, who entered from some room beyond. He advanced carrying his head with a heavy forward droop, and with a pace for which I decided that the word would be *pondering.* It was the pace of a bulky man of fifty, and his head was that beautiful head we all know from the many pictures of it. But Hawthorne's *look* was different from that of any picture of him that I have seen. It was sombre and brooding, as the look of such a poet should have been; it was the look of a man who had dealt faithfully and therefore sorrowfully with that problem of evil which forever attracted, forever evaded Hawthorne. It was by no means troubled; it was full of a dark repose. Others who knew him better and saw him oftener were familiar with other aspects, and I remember that one night at Longfellow's table, when one of the guests happened to speak of the photograph of Hawthorne which hung in a corner of the room, Lowell said, after a glance at it, "Yes, it's good; but it hasn't his fine *accipitral*[8] look."

In the face that confronted me, however, there was nothing of keen alertness; but only a sort of quiet, patient intelligence, for which I seek the right word in vain. It was a very regular face, with beautiful eyes; the mustache, still entirely dark, was dense over the fine mouth. Hawthorne was dressed in black, and he had a certain effect which I remember, of seeming to have on a black cravat with no visible collar. He was such a man that if I had ignorantly met him anywhere I should have instantly felt him to be a personage.

I must have given him the letter myself, for I have no recollection of parting with it before, but I only remember his offering me his hand, and making me shyly and tentatively welcome. After a few moments of the demoralization which followed his hospitable attempts in me, he asked if I would not like to go up on his hill with him and sit there, where he smoked in the afternoon. He offered me a cigar, and when I said that I did not smoke, he lighted it for himself, and we climbed the hill together. At the top, where there was an outlook in the pines over the Concord meadows, we found a log, and he invited me to a place on it beside him, and at intervals of a minute or so he talked while he smoked. Heaven preserved me from

7. Hawthorne's son (1846–1934), who later wrote about his father and also produced some popular fiction.
8. Like a hawk.

the folly of trying to tell him how much his books had been to me, and though we got on rapidly at no time, I think we got on better for this interposition. He asked me about Lowell, I dare say, for I told him of my joy in meeting him and Doctor Holmes, and this seemed greatly to interest him. Perhaps because he was so lately from Europe, where our great men are always seen through the wrong end of the telescope, he appeared surprised at my devotion, and asked me whether I cared as much for meeting them as I should care for meeting the famous English authors. I professed that I cared much more, though whether this was true, I now have my doubts, and I think Hawthorne doubted it at the time. But he said nothing in comment, and went on to speak generally of Europe and America. He was curious about the West, which he seemed to fancy much more purely American, and said he would like to see some part of the country on which the shadow (or, if I must be precise, the damned shadow) of Europe had not fallen. I told him I thought the West must finally be characterized by the Germans, whom we had in great numbers, and, purely from my zeal for German poetry, I tried to allege some proofs of their present influence, though I could think of none outside of politics, which I thought they affected wholesomely. I knew Hawthorne was a Democrat, and I felt it well to touch politics lightly, but he had no more to say about the fateful election then pending than Holmes or Lowell had.

With the abrupt transition of his talk throughout, he began somehow to speak of women, and said he had never seen a woman whom he thought quite beautiful. In the same way he spoke of the New England temperament, and suggested that the apparent coldness in it was also real, and that the suppression of emotion for generations would extinguish it at last. Then he questioned me as to my knowledge of Concord, and whether I had seen any of the notable people. I answered that I had met no one but himself, as yet, but I very much wished to see Emerson and Thoreau. I did not think it needful to say that I wished to see Thoreau quite as much because he had suffered in the cause of John Brown[9] as because he had written the books which had taken me; and when he said that Thoreau prided himself on coming nearer the heart of a pine-tree than any other human being, I could say honestly enough that I would rather come near the heart of a man. This visibly pleased him, and I saw that it did not displease him, when he asked whether I was not going to see his next neighbor Mr. Alcott,[1] and I confessed that I had never heard of him. That surprised as well as pleased him; he remarked, with whatever intention, that there was nothing like recognition to make a man modest; and he entered into some account of the philosopher, whom I suppose I need not be much

9. The abolitionist who raided Harpers Ferry, Virginia, in 1859 with the intention of freeing slaves by force.

1. Bronson Alcott (1799–1888), one of the founders of transcendentalism.

ashamed of not knowing then, since his influence was of the immediate sort that makes a man important to his townsmen while he is
still strange to his countrymen.

Hawthorne descanted a little upon the landscape, and said certain of the pleasant fields below us belonged to him; but he preferred
his hill-top, and if he could have his way those arable fields should
be grown up to pines too. He smoked fitfully, and slowly, and in
the hour that we spent together, his whiffs were of the desultory and
unfinal character of his words. When we went down, he asked me
into his house again, and would have me stay to tea, for which we
found the table laid. But there was a great deal of silence in it all,
and at times, in spite of his shadowy kindness, I felt my spirits sink.
After tea, he showed me a bookcase, where there were a few books
toppling about on the half-filled shelves, and said, coldly, "This
is my library." I knew that men were his books, and though I myself
cared for books so much, I found it fit and fine that he should care
so little, or seem to care so little. Some of his own romances were
among the volumes on these shelves, and when I put my finger on
the *Blithedale Romance* and said that I preferred that to the
others, his face lighted up, and he said that he believed the Germans
liked that best too.

Upon the whole we parted such good friends that when I offered
to take leave he asked me how long I was to be in Concord, and
not only bade me come to see him again, but said he would give
me a card to Emerson, if I liked. I answered, of course, that I should
like it beyond all things; and he wrote on the back of his card something which I found, when I got away, to be, "I find this young
man worthy." The quaintness, the little stiffness of it, if one pleases
to call it so, was amusing to one who was not without his sense of
humor, but the kindness filled me to the throat with joy. In fact,
I entirely liked Hawthorne. He had been as cordial as so shy a man
could show himself; and I perceived, with the repose that nothing
else can give, the entire sincerity of his soul. * * *

1894, 1900

Editha[1]

The air was thick with the war feeling, like the electricity of a
storm which has not yet burst. Editha sat looking out into the hot
spring afternoon, with her lips parted, and panting with the in-

---

1. "Editha," like Howells' most successful novels, combines a human situation
with a concrete social or moral problem
—in this case the problem of war—and
he supports his social purpose without
sacrificing the reality of his characters.
The war in the story resembles the brief
Spanish-American engagement of 1898.
"Editha" was first published in
Harper's Monthly Magazine in January,
1905, collected in *Between the Dark
and the Daylight* (1907).

tensity of the question whether she could let him go. She had decided that she could not let him stay, when she saw him at the end of the still leafless avenue, making slowly up toward the house, with his head down, and his figure relaxed. She ran impatiently out on the veranda, to the edge of the steps, and imperatively demanded greater haste of him with her will before she called aloud to him, "George!"

He had quickened his pace in mystical response to her mystical urgence, before he could have heard her; now he looked up and answered "Well?"

"Oh, how united we are!" she exulted, and then she swooped down the steps to him. "What is it?" she cried.

"It's war," he said, and he pulled her up to him, and kissed her.

She kissed him back intensely, but irrelevantly, as to their passion, and uttered from deep in her throat, "How glorious!"

"It's war," he repeated, without consenting to her sense of it; and she did not know just what to think at first. She never knew what to think of him; that made his mystery, his charm. All through their courtship, which was contemporaneous with the growth of the war feeling, she had been puzzled by his want of seriousness about it. He seemed to despise it even more than he abhorred it. She could have understood his abhorring any sort of bloodshed; that would have been a survival of his old life when he thought he would be a minister, and before he changed and took up the law. But making light of a cause so high and noble seemed to show a want of earnestness at the core of his being. Not but that she felt herself able to cope with a congenital defect of that sort, and make his love for her save him from himself. Now perhaps the miracle was already wrought in him. In the presence of the tremendous fact that he announced, all triviality seemed to have gone out of him; she began to feel that. He sank down on the top step, and wiped his forehead with his handkerchief, while she poured out upon him her question of the origin and authenticity of his news.

All the while, in her duplex emotioning, she was aware that now at the very beginning she must put a guard upon herself against urging him, by any word or act, to take the part that her whole soul willed him to take, for the completion of her ideal of him. He was very nearly perfect as he was, and he must be allowed to perfect himself. But he was peculiar, and he might very well be reasoned out of his peculiarity. Before her reasoning went her emotioning: her nature pulling upon his nature, her womanhood upon his manhood, without her knowing the means she was using to the end she was willing. She had always supposed that the man who won her would have done something to win her; she did not know what, but something. George Gearson had simply asked her for her love, on the way home from a concert, and she gave her love to him, without, as it were, thinking. But now, it flashed upon her, if he could do something worthy to *have* won her—be a hero, *her* hero—it would be even better than if he had done it before asking her; it would be grander. Besides, she had believed in the war from the beginning.

"But don't you see, dearest," she said, "that it wouldn't have come to this, if it hadn't been in the order of Providence? And I call any war glorious that is for the liberation of people who have been struggling for years against the cruelest oppression. Don't you think so too?"

"I suppose so," he returned, languidly. "But war! Is it glorious to break the peace of the world?"

"That ignoble peace! It was no peace at all, with that crime and shame at our very gates." She was conscious of parroting the current phrases of the newspapers, but it was no time to pick and choose her words. She must sacrifice anything to the high ideal she had for him, and after a good deal of rapid argument she ended with the climax: "But now it doesn't matter about the how or why. Since the war has come, all that is gone. There are no two sides, any more. There is nothing now but our country."

He sat with his eyes closed and his head leant back against the veranda, and he said with a vague smile, as if musing aloud, "Our country—right or wrong."

"Yes, right or wrong!" she returned fervidly. "I'll go and get you some lemonade." She rose rustling, and whisked away; when she came back with two tall glasses of clouded liquid, on a tray, and the ice clucking in them, he still sat as she had left him, and she said as if there had been no interruption: "But there is no question of wrong in this case. I call it a sacred war. A war for liberty, and humanity, if ever there was one. And I know you will see it just as I do, yet."

He took half the lemonade at a gulp, and he answered as he set the glass down: "I know you always have the highest idea. When I differ from you, I ought to doubt myself."

A generous sob rose in Editha's throat for the humility of a man, so very nearly perfect, who was willing to put himself below her.

Besides, she felt, more subliminally, that he was never so near slipping through her fingers as when he took that meek way.

"You shall not say that! Only, for once I happen to be right." She seized his hand in her two hands, and poured her soul from her eyes into his. "Don't you think so?" she entreated him.

He released his hand and drank the rest of his lemonade, and she added, "Have mine, too," but he shook his head in answering,

"I've no business to think so, unless I act so, too."

Her heart stopped a beat before it pulsed on with leaps that she felt in her neck. She had noticed that strange thing in men; they seemed to feel bound to do what they believed, and not think a thing was finished when they said it, as girls did. She knew what was in his mind, but she pretended not, and she said, "Oh, I am not sure," and then faltered.

He went on as if to himself without apparently heeding her, "There's only one way of proving one's faith in a thing like this."

She could not say that she understood, but she did understand.

He went on again. "If I believed—if I felt as you do about this war—Do you wish me to feel as you do?"

Now she was really not sure; so she said, "George, I don't know what you mean."

He seemed to muse away from her as before. "There is a sort of fascination in it. I suppose that at the bottom of his heart every man would like at times to have his courage tested; to see how he would act."

"How can you talk in that ghastly way?"

"It *is* rather morbid. Still, that's what it comes to, unless you're swept away by ambition, or driven by conviction. I haven't the conviction or the ambition, and the other thing is what it comes to with me. I ought to have been a preacher, after all; then I couldn't have asked it of myself, as I must, now I'm a lawyer. And you believe it's a holy war, Editha?" he suddenly addressed her. "Or, I know you do! But you wish me to believe so, too?"

She hardly knew whether he was mocking or not, in the ironical way he always had with her plainer mind. But the only thing was to be outspoken with him.

"George, I wish you to believe whatever you think is true, at any and every cost. If I've tried to talk you into anything, I take it all back."

"Oh, I know that, Editha. I know how sincere you are, and how—I wish I had your undoubting spirit! I'll think it over; I'd like to believe as you do. But I don't, now; I don't, indeed. It isn't this war alone; though this seems peculiarly wanton and needless; but it's every war—so stupid; it makes me sick. Why shouldn't this thing have been settled reasonably?"

"Because," she said, very throatily again, "God meant it to be war."

"You think it was God? Yes, I suppose that is what people will say."

"Do you suppose it would have been war if God hadn't meant it?"

"I don't know. Sometimes it seems as if God had put this world into men's keeping to work it as they pleased."

"Now, George, that is blasphemy."

"Well, I won't blaspheme. I'll try to believe in your pocket Providence," he said, and then he rose to go.

"Why don't you stay to dinner?" Dinner at Balcom's Works was at one o'clock.

"I'll come back to supper, if you'll let me. Perhaps I shall bring you a convert."

"Well, you may come back, on that condition."

"All right. If I don't come, you'll understand."

He went away without kissing her, and she felt it a suspension of their engagement. It all interested her intensely; she was undergoing a tremendous experience, and she was being equal to it. While she stood looking after him, her mother came out through one of the long windows, on to the veranda, with a catlike softness and vagueness.

"Why didn't he stay to dinner?"

"Because—because—war has been declared," Editha pronounced, without turning.

Her mother said, "Oh, my!" and then said nothing more until she had sat down in one of the large Shaker chairs, and rocked herself for some time. Then she closed whatever tacit passage of thought there had been in her mind with the spoken words, "Well, I hope *he* won't go."

"And I hope he *will*," the girl said, and confronted her mother with a stormy exultation that would have frightened any creature less unimpressionable than a cat.

Her mother rocked herself again for an interval of cogitation. What she arrived at in speech was, "Well, I guess you've done a wicked thing, Editha Balcom."

The girl said, as she passed indoors through the same window her mother had come out by, "I haven't done anything—yet."

In her room, she put together all her letters and gifts from Gearson, down to the withered petals of the first flower he had offered, with that timidity of his veiled in that irony of his. In the heart of the packet she enshrined her engagement ring which she had restored to the pretty box he had brought it her in. Then she sat down, if not calmly yet strongly, and wrote:

"George: I understood—when you left me. But I think we had better emphasize your meaning that if we cannot be one in everything we had better be one in nothing. So I am sending these things for your keeping till you have made up your mind.

"I shall always love you, and therefore I shall never marry any one else. But the man I marry must love his country first of all, and be able to say to me,

'I could not love thee, dear, so much,
Loved I not honor more.'

"There is no honor above America with me. In this great hour there is no other honor.

"Your heart will make my words clear to you. I have never expected to say so much, but it has come upon me that I must say the utmost.

Editha."

She thought she had worded her letter well, worded it in a way that could not be bettered; all had been implied and nothing expressed.

She had it ready to send with the packet she had tied with red, white, and blue ribbon, when it occurred to her that she was not just to him, that she was not giving him a fair chance. He had said he would go and think it over, and she was not waiting. She was pushing, threatening, compelling. That was not a woman's part. She must leave him free, free, free. She could not accept for her country or herself a forced sacrifice.

In writing her letter she had satisfied the impulse from which it sprang; she could well afford to wait till he had thought it over. She put the packet and the letter by, and rested serene in the consciousness of having done what was laid upon her by her love itself to do, and yet used patience, mercy, justice.

She had her reward. Gearson did not come to tea, but she had given him till morning, when, late at night there came up from the village the sound of a fife and drum with a tumult of voices, in shouting, singing, and laughing. The noise drew nearer and nearer; it reached the street end of the avenue; there it silenced itself, and one voice, the voice she knew best, rose over the silence. It fell; the air was filled with cheers; the fife and drum struck up, with the shouting, singing, and laughing again, but now retreating; and a single figure came hurrying up the avenue.

She ran down to meet her lover and clung to him. He was very gay, and he put his arm round her with a boisterous laugh. "Well, you must call me Captain, now; or Cap, if you prefer; that's what the boys call me. Yes, we've had a meeting at the town hall, and everybody has volunteered; and they selected me for captain, and I'm going to the war, the big war, the glorious war, the holy war ordained by the pocket Providence that blesses butchery. Come along; let's tell the whole family about it. Call them from their downy beds, father, mother, Aunt Hitty, and all the folks!"

But when they mounted the veranda steps he did not wait for a larger audience; he poured the story out upon Editha alone.

"There was a lot of speaking, and then some of the fools set up a shout for me. It was all going one way, and I thought it would be a good joke to sprinkle a little cold water on them. But you can't do that with a crowd that adores you. The first thing I knew I was sprinkling hell-fire on them. 'Cry havoc, and let slip the dogs of war.' That was the style. Now that it had come to the fight, there were no two parties; there was one country, and the thing was to fight the fight to a finish as quick as possible. I suggested volunteering then and there, and I wrote my name first of all on the roster. Then they elected me—that's all. I wish I had some ice-water!"

She left him walking up and down the veranda, while she ran for the ice-pitcher and a goblet, and when she came back he was still walking up and down, shouting the story he had told her to her father and mother, who had come out more sketchily dressed than they commonly were by day. He drank goblet after goblet of the ice-water without noticing who was giving it, and kept on talking, and laughing through his talk wildly. "It's astonishing," he said, "how well the worse reason looks when you try to make it appear the better. Why, I believe I was the first convert to the war in that crowd to-night! I never thought I should like to kill a man; but now, I shouldn't care; and the smokeless powder lets you see the man drop that you kill. It's all for the country! What a thing it is to have a country that *can't* be wrong, but if it is, is right anyway!"

Editha had a great, vital thought, an inspiration. She set down the ice-pitcher on the veranda floor, and ran up-stairs and got the letter she had written him. When at last he noisily bade her father and mother, "Well, good night. I forgot I woke you up; I sha'n't want any sleep myself," she followed him down the avenue to the gate. There, after the whirling words that seemed to fly away from her thoughts and refuse to serve them, she made a last effort to solemnize the moment that seemed so crazy, and pressed the letter she had written upon him.

"What's this?" he said, "Want me to mail it?"

"No, no. It's for you. I wrote it after you went this morning. Keep it—keep it—and read it sometime—" She thought, and then her inspiration came: "Read it if ever you doubt what you've done, or fear that I regret your having done it. Read it after you've started."

They strained each other in embraces that seemed as ineffective as their words, and he kissed her face with quick, hot breaths that were so unlike him, that made her feel as if she had lost her old lover and found a stranger in his place. The stranger said, "What a gorgeous flower you are, with your red hair, and your blue eyes that look black now, and your face with the color painted out by the white moonshine! Let me hold you under my chin, to see whether I love blood, you tiger-lily!" Then he laughed Gearson's laugh, and released her, scared and giddy. Within her wilfulness she had been frightened by a sense of subtler force in him, and mystically mastered as she had never been before.

She ran all the way back to the house, and mounted the steps panting. Her mother and father were talking of the great affair. Her mother said: "Wa'n't Mr. Gearson in rather of an excited state of mind? Didn't you think he acted curious?"

"Well, not for a man who'd just been elected captain and had to set 'em up for the whole of Company A," her father chuckled back.

"What in the world do you mean, Mr. Balcom? Oh! There's Editha!" She offered to follow the girl indoors.

"Don't come, mother!" Editha called, vanishing.

Mrs. Balcom remained to reproach her husband. "I don't see much of anything to laugh at."

"Well, it's catching. Caught it from Gearson. I guess it won't be much of a war, and I guess Gearson don't think so, either. The other fellows will back down as soon as they see we mean it. I wouldn't lose any sleep over it. I'm going back to bed, myself."

Gearson came again next afternoon, looking pale, and rather sick, but quite himself even to his languid irony. "I guess I'd better tell you, Editha, that I consecrated myself to your god of battles last night by pouring too many libations to him down my own throat. But I'm all right, now. One has to carry off the excitement, somehow."

"Promise me," she commanded, "that you'll never touch it again!"

"What! Not let the cannikin clink? Not let the soldier drink? Well, I promise."

"You don't belong to yourself now; you don't even belong to *me*. You belong to your country, and you have a sacred charge to keep yourself strong and well for your country's sake. I have been thinking, thinking all night and all day long."

"You look as if you had been crying a little, too," he said with his queer smile.

"That's all past. I've been thinking, and worshipping *you*. Don't you suppose I know all that you've been through, to come to this? I've followed you every step from your old theories and opinions."

"Well, you've had a long row to hoe."

"And I know you've done this from the highest motives—"

"Oh, there won't be much pettifogging to do till this cruel war is—"

"And you haven't simply done it for my sake. I couldn't respect you if you had."

"Well, then we'll say I haven't. A man that hasn't got his own respect intact wants the respect of all the other people he can corner. But we won't go into that. I'm in for the thing now, and we've got to face our future. My idea is that this isn't going to be a very protracted struggle; we shall just scare the enemy to death before it comes to a fight at all. But we must provide for contingencies, Editha. If anything happens to me—"

"Oh, George!" She clung to him sobbing.

"I don't want you to feel foolishly bound to my memory. I should hate that, wherever I happened to be."

"I am yours, for time and eternity—time and eternity." She liked the words; they satisfied her famine for phrases.

"Well, say eternity; that's all right; but time's another thing; and I'm talking about time. But there is something! My mother! If anything happens—"

She winced, and he laughed. "You're not the bold soldier-girl of yesterday!" Then he sobered. "If anything happens, I want you to help my mother out. She won't like my doing this thing. She brought me up to think war a fool thing as well as a bad thing. My father was in the civil war; all through it; lost his arm in it." She thrilled with the sense of the arm round her; what if that should be lost? He laughed as if divining her: "Oh, it doesn't run in the family, as far as I know!" Then he added, gravely, "He came home with misgivings about war, and they grew on him. I guess he and mother agreed between them that I was to be brought up in his final mind about it; but that was before my time. I only knew him from my mother's report of him and his opinions; I don't know whether they were hers first; but they were hers last. This will be a blow to her. I shall have to write and tell her—"

He stopped, and she asked, "Would you like me to write too, George?"

"I don't believe that would do. No, I'll do the writing. She'll understand a little if I say that I thought the way to minimize it was to make war on the largest possible scale at once—that I felt I must have been helping on the war somehow if I hadn't helped keep it from coming, and I knew I hadn't; when it came, I had no right to stay out of it."

Whether his sophistries satisfied him or not, they satisfied her. She clung to his breast, and whispered, with closed eyes and quivering lips, "Yes, yes, yes!"

"But if anything should happen, you might go to her, and see what you could do for her. You know? It's rather far off; she can't leave her chair—"

"Oh, I'll go, if it's the ends of the earth! But nothing will happen! Nothing *can!* I—"

She felt herself lifted with his rising, and Gearson was saying, with his arm still around her, to her father: "Well, we're off at once, Mr. Balcom. We're to be formally accepted at the capital, and then bunched up with the rest somehow, and sent into camp somewhere, and got to the front as soon as possible. We all want to be in the van, of course; we're the first company to report to the Governor. I came to tell Editha, but I hadn't got round to it."

She saw him again for a moment at the capital, in the station, just before the train started southward with his regiment. He looked well, in his uniform, and very soldierly, but somehow girlish, too, with his clean-shaven face and slim figure. The manly eyes and the strong voice satisfied her, and his preoccupation with some unexpected details of duty flattered her. Other girls were weeping and bemoaning themselves, but she felt a sort of noble distinction in the abstraction, the almost unconsciousness, with which they parted. Only at the last moment he said, "Don't forget my mother. It mayn't be such a walkover as I supposed," and he laughed at the notion.

He waved his hand to her, as the train moved off—she knew it among a score of hands that were waved to other girls from the platform of the car, for it held a letter which she knew was hers. Then he went inside the car to read it, doubtless, and she did not see him again. But she felt safe for him through the strength of what she called her love. What she called her God, always speaking the name in a deep voice and with the implication of a mutual understanding, would watch over him and keep him and bring him back to her. If with an empty sleeve, then he should have three arms instead of two, for both of hers should be his for life. She did not see, though, why she should always be thinking of the arm his father had lost.

There were not many letters from him, but they were such as she could have wished, and she put her whole strength into making hers such as she imagined he could have wished, glorifying and supporting him. She wrote to his mother glorifying him as their hero, but the brief answer she got was merely to the effect that Mrs. Gearson was not well enough to write herself, and thanking her for her letter by the hand of some one who called herself "Yrs truly, Mrs. W. J. Andrews."

Editha determined not to be hurt, but to write again quite as if the answer had been all she expected. But before it seemed as if she could have written, there came news of the first skirmish, and in the list of the killed which was telegraphed as a trifling loss on our side, was Gearson's name. There was a frantic time of trying to make out that it might be, must be, some other Gearson; but the name, and the company and the regiment, and the State were too definitely given.

Then there was a lapse into depths out of which it seemed as if she never could rise again; then a lift into clouds far above all grief, black clouds, that blotted out the sun, but where she soared with him, with George, George! She had the fever that she expected of herself, but she did not die in it; she was not even delirious, and it did not last long. When she was well enough to leave her bed, her one thought was of George's mother, of his strangely worded wish that she should go to her and see what she could do for her. In the exultation of the duty laid upon her—it buoyed her up instead of burdening her—she rapidly recovered.

Her father went with her on the long railroad journey from northern New York to western Iowa; he had business out at Davenport, and he said he could just as well go then as any other time; and he went with her to the little country town where George's mother lived in a little house on the edge of illimitable corn-fields, under trees pushed to a top of the rolling prairie. George's father had settled there after the civil war, as so many other old soldiers had done; but they were Eastern people, and Editha fancied touches of the East in the June rose overhanging the front door, and the garden with early summer flowers stretching from the gate of the paling fence.

It was very low inside the house, and so dim, with the closed blinds, that they could scarcely see one another: Editha tall and black in her crapes which filled the air with the smell of their dyes; her father standing decorously apart with his hat on his forearm, as at funerals; a woman rested in a deep armchair, and the woman who had let the strangers in stood behind the chair.

The seated woman turned her head round and up, and asked the women behind her chair, "Who did you say?"

Editha, if she had done what she expected of herself, would have gone down on her knees at the feet of the seated figure and said, "I am George's Editha," for answer.

But instead of her own voice she heard that other woman's voice, saying, "Well, I don't know as I *did* get the name just right. I guess I'll have to make a little more light in here," and she went and pushed two of the shutters ajar.

Then Editha's father said in his public will-now-address-a-few-remarks tone, "My name is Balcom, ma'am; Junius H. Balcom, of Balcom's Works, New York; my daughter—"

"Oh!" The seated woman broke in, with a powerful voice, the voice that always surprised Editha from Gearson's slender frame. "Let me see you! Stand round where the light can strike on your face," and Editha dumbly obeyed. "So, you're Editha Balcom," she sighed.

"Yes," Editha said, more like a culprit than a comforter.

"What did you come for?" Mrs. Gearson asked.

Editha's face quivered, and her knees shook. "I came—because —because George—" She could go no farther.

"Yes," the mother said, "he told me he had asked you to come if he got killed. You didn't expect that, I suppose, when you sent him."

"I would rather have died myself than done it!" Editha said with more truth in her deep voice than she ordinarily found in it. "I tried to leave him free—"

"Yes, that letter of yours, that came back with his other things, left him free."

Editha saw now where George's irony came from.

"It was not to be read before—unless—until—I told him so," she faltered.

"Of course, he wouldn't read a letter of yours, under the circumstances, till he thought you wanted him to. Been sick?" the woman abruptly demanded.

"Very sick," Editha said, with self-pity.

"Daughter's life," her father interposed, "was almost despaired of, at one time."

Mrs. Gearson gave him no heed. "I suppose you would have been glad to die, such a brave person as you! I don't believe *he* was glad to die. He was always a timid boy, that way; he was afraid of a good many things; but if he was afraid he did what he made up his mind to. I suppose he made up his mind to go, but I knew what it cost him, by what it cost me when I heard of it. I had been through *one* war before. When you sent him you didn't expect he would get killed."

The voice seemed to compassionate Editha, and it was time. "No," she huskily murmured.

"No, girls don't; women don't, when they give their men up to their country. They think they'll come marching back, somehow, just as gay as they went, or if it's an empty sleeve, or even an empty pantaloon, it's all the more glory, and they're so much the prouder of them, poor things."

The tears began to run down Editha's face; she had not wept till then; but it was now such a relief to be understood that the tears came.

"No, you didn't expect him to get killed," Mrs. Gearson repeated in a voice which was startlingly like George's again. "You just expected him to kill some one else, some of those foreigners, that weren't there because they had any say about it, but because they had to be there, poor wretches—conscripts, or whatever they call 'em. You thought it would be all right for my George, your George, to kill the sons of those miserable mothers and the husbands of those girls that you would never see the faces of." The woman lifted her powerful voice in a psalmlike note. "I thank my God he didn't live to do it! I thank my God they killed him first, and that he ain't livin' with their blood on his hands!" She dropped her eyes which she had raised with her voice, and glared at Editha. "What you got that black on for?" She lifted herself by her powerful arms so high that her helpless body seemed to hang limp its full length. "Take it off, take it off, before I tear it from your back!"

The lady who was passing the summer near Balcom's Works was sketching Editha's beauty, which lent itself wonderfully to the effects of a colorist. It had come to that confidence which is rather apt to grow between artist and sitter, and Editha had told her everything.

"To think of your having such a tragedy in your life!" the lady said. She added: "I suppose there are people who feel that way about war. But when you consider the good this war has done— how much it has done for the country! I can't understand such people, for my part. And when you had come all the way out there to console her—got up out of a sick bed! Well!"

"I think," Editha said, magnanimously, "she wasn't quite in her right mind; and so did papa."

"Yes," the lady said, looking at Editha's lips in nature and then at her lips in art, and giving an empirical touch to them in the picture. "But how dreadful of her! How perfectly—excuse me— how *vulgar!*"

A light broke upon Editha in the darkness which she felt had been without a gleam of brightness for weeks and months. The mystery that had bewildered her was solved by the word; and from that moment she rose from grovelling in shame and self-pity, and began to live again in the ideal.

1905, 1907

HENRY JAMES
(1843–1916)

Born in New York City on April 15, 1843, the brother of the philosopher-scientist William James, Henry James was influenced by the patrician attitudes of his father, who combined an interest in philosophy and theology with full enjoyment of the cultural life of his own city and of the world. The James children were privately tutored in New York, and received special schooling abroad between 1855 and 1860, when the family lived in London, Switzerland, France, and Germany—everywhere at a level of intense intellectual activity. Henry James studied painting briefly; but at the age of nineteen was admitted to Harvard Law School. Two years later he had plunged into authorship, and he won his way into the best literary magazines. Two long trips abroad are reflected in his *Atlantic* story "A Passionate Pilgrim" (1871), motivated by the cultural attraction and repulsion between England and America. The year before, Mary Temple, James's beloved cousin, had died; by 1876 he was settled in London, and thereafter made his home in England. In 1915, impatient at America's aloofness from World War I, he became a British citizen.

In 1875 he published his first collection of stories, *A Passionate Pilgrim and Other Tales,* and the *Atlantic* serialized his first novel of consequence, *Roderick Hudson,* in which a talented young American sculptor is transplanted to Florence for study, only to be crushed and destroyed by the artifice and materialistic cynicism of international society. These works established the theme and the techniques of his first period. Spending much time in Paris, he came to know Flaubert and Turgenev. The French and Russian realists and naturalists influenced his style, which became increasingly "chiseled," in Flaubert's sense. He accepted also the naturalists' concept of the novelist as the clinical researcher into life, but did not follow their unselective zeal to report everything observed; he admitted a measure of determinism, but rejected the pessimistic extreme according to which human character becomes the waif of chance.

Among other fine works, *The American* appeared in 1877, *Daisy Miller* in 1879, *The Portrait of a Lady,* his greatest novel of this period, in 1881, and *The Princess Casamassima* in 1886. In the first, a young American, having won a fortune in manufacturing and speculation, seeks abroad the development of cultural satisfactions. In this he succeeds, but he is wretchedly defeated in a genuine love affair by the rigid conventions and ingrained evil of French Bourbon aristocracy. Equally striking in its contrasts of social values is the story of Daisy, a hoydenish, healthy, and wholly lovable American girl of small-town wealth who in Florence runs afoul of the European codes of the cloistered woman. Isabel Archer, the "Lady" of the third novel, another American girl, triumphs over the rigidities of both British and Italian society and survives the bad marriage into which she has been tricked by a cynical fortune hunter and his worldly mistress, to arrive at a kind of austere selfhood and mastery of the Paris social world. In *The Princess Casamassima* James resumes the adventures of the pathetic heroine of *Roderick Hudson* and the cynical society she represents, but he also for once turns his mirror in the opposite direction, catching the social issues inherent in the lives of London's lower orders and the ominous premonitory specter of a social revolution.

From *The Tragic Muse* (1890) to the end of his career in fiction more than fifteen years later, James developed an increasingly complex style, marked by meaningful ambiguities and ellipses in the dialogue together with convoluted and modifier-ridden exposition. Thus the functions of prose rhythm were enlarged as by no other author in English fiction before Joyce. At the same time, the psychological motivations of his characters became more intense and more frequently abnormal, while the social situations possessed increasing subtlety. The earliest of the principal novels of this so-called "major phase" was *The Spoils of Poynton* (1897), in which the possession of a house and its *objets d'art* corrupts certain members of a family and their associates, and produces spiritual ruin and psychological disorder. *What Maisie Knew* (1897) uses the innocence of a little girl as the center of revelation for the idle and destructive amours of her divorced parents, with whom she lives alternately. *The Turn of the Screw* (1898) is superficially a story of the supernatural, involving two children and their governess in an ancient British country house, but fundamentally it studies the pathological effects of an evil influence from the past upon the innocence of the children. *The Awkward Age* (1899) follows the emotional life of Nanda Brookenham from the innocence of girlhood seclusion into her mother's sophisticated and selfish social world, through the period of matrimonial barter into a kind of detached acceptance. *The Wings of the Dove* (1902) studies the betrayal of the lovely Milly Theale by the cynical and fortune-hunting adultery carried on between her betrothed and her best friend, and her innocent revenge on their amorality. *The Ambassadors* (1903) is a brilliant and sardonic account of a succession of emissaries who attempt to persuade an American heir to leave Paris to take charge of his profitable business interests in Massachusetts, only to have the ambassadors themselves converted or diverted by Paris. In *The Golden Bowl* (1904) the admirable Maggie Verver is confronted with a continuing liaison between her husband and her father's young wife —her former friend. Her love and tact, together with her father's sensitive maturity, saves them all.

The short stories and the

novelettes of James are not minor works except in their length. In general they follow the patterns that have been suggested above for the novels. The critical writings of James, even excluding the penetrating essays with which he prefaced the New York Edition of the novels, would have given him a position as a major critic if he had not made his reputation as a novelist. His several dramas were not acceptable to the stage, in contrast with some of his novels recently staged with success: *Washington Square* (as *The Heiress*, 1948), *The Turn of the Screw* (as *The Innocents*, 1952), and *The Portrait of a Lady* (1954).

In his effort, through the international novel, to find a kind of cultural unity in western civilization, and in his turning to the older centers rather than to the newer soil of America, Henry James expressed a yearning which, although not confined to American authors, was certainly expressed dramatically by American expatriation during the years from his own generation to that of Eliot.

James's belief that prose was as subject as poetry to intensification and to investment with symbolic value has been profoundly influential on the generations since his death. He was a pioneer in utilizing psychological devices which communicated the more intense realization of character and situation. By transferring what he called "central consciousness" to the awakening mind of an innocent child, or to the confessional pages of a diary, for example, he implicated the reader in the analytic process and in the story itself, foreshadowing such psychological instruments as stream of consciousness.

Among the authors he influenced were Lawrence, Joyce, Conrad, Edith Wharton, Virginia Woolf, Willa Cather, and Eliot. In contrast with the European naturalists whose tutelage he acknowledged, he rebelled against the materialistic interpretation of human destiny, and struggled with the problem of undeniable evil as desperately as Hawthorne, whom, among earlier Americans, he most admired. He offset his portrayals of the evil tendencies of life toward greed, treachery, and pathological dualism by the constant representation of innocence, lofty choices, and moral idealism. His experience of life may seem limited and specialized, but he employed it for great and far-reaching ends.

The best edition of James's works, containing his last revised texts and valuable prefaces, is *The Novels and Tales of Henry James*, 26 vols., 1907–1917, known as the New York Edition. There is also a good English edition, *The Novels and Stories of Henry James*, 35 vols., 1921–1923. Philip Rahv edited *The Great Short Novels of Henry James*, 1944; Clifton Fadiman edited *The Short Stories of Henry James*, 1945; and F. O. Matthiessen edited *The American Novels and Stories of Henry James*, 1947. Other recent compilations are *The American Scene*, 1946; *Stories of Writers and Artists*, edited, with an introduction, by F. O. Matthiessen, 1944; *The Scenic Art*, edited by Allan Wade, 1948; and *The Ghostly Tales of Henry James*, with an introduction by Leon Edel, 1948. Leon Edel also edited *The Complete Plays of Henry James*, 1949. Percy Lubbock selected and edited *Letters of Henry James*, 2 vols., 1920. Also important is *The Selected Letters of Henry James*, edited by Leon Edel, 1955. R. P. Blackmur edited *The Art of the Novel: Critical Prefaces*, 1934. *The Notebooks of Henry James*, 1947, was edited by F. O. Matthiessen and K. B. Murdock.

Important are F. W. Dupee's *Henry James*, revised, 1956, and his edition of the *Autobiography*, 1956. A complete biography is Pelham Edgar, *Henry James: Man and Author*, 1927. Leon Edel is preparing a comprehensive biography, of which *Henry James 1843–* *1870: The Untried Years*, 1953, has appeared. Other important volumes are J. W. Beach, *The Method of Henry James*, revised, 1954; and F. O. Matthiessen, *Henry James, The Major Phase*, 1944. Leon Edel and Dan H. Laurence compiled *A Bibliography of Henry James*, 1957.

Madame de Mauves[1]

I

The view from the terrace at Saint-Germain-en-Laye[2] is immense and famous. Paris lies spread before you in dusky vastness, domed and fortified, glittering here and there through her light vapors, and girdled with her silver Seine. Behind you is a park of stately symmetry, and behind that a forest, where you may lounge through turfy avenues and light-checkered glades, and quite forget that you are within half an hour of the boulevards. One afternoon, however, in mid-spring, some five years ago, a young man seated on the terrace had chosen not to forget this. His eyes were fixed in idle wistfulness on the mighty human hive before him. He was fond of rural things, and he had come to Saint-Germain a week before to meet the spring half-way; but though he could boast of a six months' acquaintance with the great city, he never looked at it from his present standpoint without a feeling of painfully unsatisfied curiosity. There were moments when it seemed to him that not to be

1. "'Madame de Mauves' * * * is of the small group of my productions yielding to present research no dimmest responsive ghost of a traceable origin. These remarks have constituted to excess perhaps the record of what may have put this, that and the other treated idea into my head; but I am quite unable to say what, in the summer of 1873, may have put 'Madame de Mauves.' Save for a single pleasant image, and for the fact that, dispatched to New York, the tale appeared, early in the following year, in 'The Galaxy,' a periodical to which I find, with this, twenty other remembrances gratefully attached, not a glimmer of attendant reference survives. I recall the tolerably wide court of an old inn at Bad-Homburg in the Taunus hills—a dejected and forlorn little place (its *seconde jeunesse* not yet in sight) during the years immediately following the Franco-Prussian war, which had overturned, with that of Baden-Baden, its altar, the well-appointed worship of the great goddess Chance—a homely enclosure on the ground-level of which I occupied a dampish, dusky, unsunned room, cool, however, to the relief of the fevered muse, during some very hot weather. The place was so dark that I could see my way to and from my inkstand, I remember, but by keeping the door to the court open—thanks to which also the muse, witness of many mild domestic incidents, was distracted and beguiled. In this retreat I was visited by the gentle Euphemia; I sat in crepuscular comfort pouring forth again, and, no doubt, artfully editing, the confidences with which she honoured me. She again, after her fashion, was what I might have called experimentally international; she muffled her charming head in the lightest, finest, vaguest tissue of romance and put twenty questions by" [James's introduction]. "Madame de Mauves" was first published serially in *The Galaxy* from February to March, 1874, and collected in *A Passionate Pilgrim and Other Tales* (1875), which the present text follows.
2. The terrace, or promenade, of St. Germain, a suburb of Paris, extends for a mile and commands a beautiful view of Paris, the Seine, and the countryside.

there just then was to miss some thrilling chapter of experience. And yet his winter's experience had been rather fruitless, and he had closed the book almost with a yawn. Though not in the least a cynic, he was what one may call a disappointed observer; and he never chose the right-hand road without beginning to suspect after an hour's wayfaring that the left would have been the interesting one. He now had a dozen minds to go to Paris for the evening, to dine at the Café Brébant, and to repair afterwards to the Gymnase[3] and listen to the latest exposition of the duties of the injured husband. He would probably have risen to execute this project, if he had not observed a little girl who, wandering along the terrace, had suddenly stopped short and begun to gaze at him with round-eyed frankness. For a moment he was simply amused, for the child's face denoted helpless wonderment; the next he was agreeably surprised. "Why, this is my friend Maggie," he said; "I see you have not forgotten me."

Maggie, after a short parley, was induced to seal her remembrance with a kiss. Invited then to explain her appearance at Saint-Germain, she embarked on a recital in which the general, according to the infantine method, was so fatally sacrificed to the particular, that Longmore looked about him for a superior source of information. He found it in Maggie's mamma, who was seated with another lady at the opposite end of the terrace; so, taking the child by the hand, he led her back to her companions.

Maggie's mamma was a young American lady as you would immediately have perceived, with a pretty and friendly face and an expensive spring toilet. She greeted Longmore with surprised cordiality, mentioned his name to her friend, and bade him bring a chair and sit with them. The other lady, who, though equally young and perhaps even prettier, was dressed more soberly, remained silent, stroking the hair of the little girl, whom she had drawn against her knee. She had never heard of Longmore, but she now perceived that her companion had crossed the ocean with him, had met him afterwards in travelling, and (having left her husband in Wall Street) was indebted to him for various small services.

Maggie's mamma turned from time to time and smiled at her friend with an air of invitation; the latter smiled back, and continued gracefully to say nothing.

For ten minutes Longmore felt a revival of interest in his interlocutors; then (as riddles are more amusing than commonplaces) it gave way to curiosity about her friend. His eyes wondered; her volubility was less suggestive than the latter's silence.

The stranger was perhaps not obviously a beauty nor obviously

3. A famous theater in Paris, at that time featuring domestic-problem plays.

an American, but essentially both, on a closer scrutiny. She was slight and fair, and, though naturally pale, delicately flushed, apparently with recent excitement. What chiefly struck Longmore in her face was the union of a pair of beautifully gentle, almost languid gray eyes, with a mouth peculiarly expressive and firm. Her forehead was a trifle more expansive than belongs to classic types, and her thick brown hair was dressed out of the fashion, which was just then very ugly. Her throat and bust were slender, but all the more in harmony with certain rapid, charming movements of the head, which she had a way of throwing back every now and then, with an air of attention and a sidelong glance from her dovelike eyes. She seemed at once alert and indifferent, contemplative and restless; and Longmore very soon discovered that if she was not a brilliant beauty, she was at least an extremely interesting one. This very impression made him magnanimous. He perceived that he had interrupted a confidential conversation, and he judged it discreet to withdraw, having first learned from Maggie's mamma —Mrs. Draper—that she was to take the six-o'clock train back to Paris. He promised to meet her at the station.

He kept his appointment, and Mrs. Draper arrived betimes, accompanied by her friend. The latter, however, made her farewells at the door and drove away again, giving Longmore time only to raise his hat. "Who is she?" he asked with visible ardor, as he brought Mrs. Draper her tickets.

"Come and see me to-morrow at the Hôtel de l'Empire," she answered, "and I will tell you all about her." The force of this offer in making him punctual at the Hôtel de l'Empire Longmore doubtless never exactly measured; and it was perhaps well that he did not, for he found his friend, who was on the point of leaving Paris, so distracted by procrastinating milliners and perjured lingères that she had no wits left for disinterested narrative. "You must find Saint-Germain dreadfully dull," she said, as he was going. "Why won't you come with me to London?"

"Introduce me to Madame de Mauves," he answered, "and Saint-Germain will satisfy me." All he had learned was the lady's name and residence.

"Ah! she, poor woman, will not make Saint-Germain cheerful for you. She's very unhappy."

Longmore's further inquiries were arrested by the arrival of a young lady with a bandbox; but he went away with the promise of a note of introduction, to be immediately despatched to him at Saint-Germain.

He waited a week, but the note never came; and he declared that it was not for Mrs. Draper to complain of her milliner's treachery. He lounged on the terrace and walked in the forest, studied suburban street life, and made a languid attempt to investigate the records of the court of the exiled Stuarts;[4] but he spent most of his time in wondering where Madame de Mauves lived, and whether she never walked on the terrace. Sometimes, he finally discovered; for one afternoon toward dusk he perceived her leaning against the parapet, alone. In his momentary hesitation to approach her, it seemed to him that there was almost a shade of trepidation; but his curiosity was not diminished by the consciousness of this result of a quarter of an hour's acquaintance. She immediately recognized him on his drawing near, with the manner of a person unaccustomed to encounter a confusing variety of faces. Her dress, her expression, were the same as before; her charm was there, like that of sweet music on a second hearing. She soon made conversation easy by asking him for news of Mrs. Draper. Longmore told her that he was daily expecting news, and, after a pause, mentioned the promised note of introduction.

"It seems less necessary now," he said—"for me, at least. But for you—I should have liked you to know the flattering things Mrs. Draper would probably have said about me."

"If it arrives at last," she answered, "you must come and see me and bring it. If it doesn't, you must come without it."

Then, as she continued to linger in spite of the thickening twilight, she explained that she was waiting for her husband, who was to arrive in the train from Paris, and who often passed along the terrace on his way home. Longmore well remembered that Mrs. Draper had pronounced her unhappy, and he found it convenient to suppose that this same husband made her so. Edified by his six months in Paris—"What else is possible," he asked himself, "for a sweet American girl who marries an unclean Frenchman?"

But this tender expectancy of her lord's return undermined his hypothesis, and it received a further check from the gentle eagerness with which she turned and greeted an approaching figure. Longmore beheld in the fading light a stoutish gentleman, on the fair side of forty, in a high light hat, whose countenance, indistinct against the sky, was adorned by a fantastically pointed mustache. M. de Mauves saluted his wife with punctilious gallantry, and having bowed to Longmore, asked her several questions in French. Before taking his proffered arm to walk to their carriage, which was in waiting at the terrace gate, she introduced our hero as a friend of Mrs. Draper, and a fellow-countryman, whom she hoped to see at home. M. de Mauves responded briefly, but civilly, in very fair English, and led his wife away.

Longmore watched him as he went, twisting his picturesque

4. King James II of England (1633–1701) was exiled. His son, "the Old Pretender," and his heirs never gave up the Stuart family's claims to the English throne.

mustache, with a feeling of irritation which he certainly would have been at a loss to account for. The only conceivable cause was the light which M. de Mauves's good English cast upon his own bad French. For reasons involved apparently in the very structure of his being, Longmore found himself unable to speak the language tolerably. He admired and enjoyed it, but the very genius of awkwardness controlled his phraseology. But he reflected with satisfaction that Madame de Mauves and he had a common idiom, and his vexation was effectually dispelled by his finding on his table that evening a letter from Mrs. Draper. It enclosed a short, formal missive to Madame de Mauves, but the epistle itself was copious and confidential. She had deferred writing till she reached London, where for a week, of course, she had found other amusements.

"I think it is these distracting Englishwomen," she wrote, "with their green barege[5] gowns and their white-stitched boots, who have reminded me in self-defense of my graceful friend at Saint-Germain and my promise to introduce you to her. I believe I **told** you that she was unhappy, and I wondered afterwards whether I had not been guilty of a breach of confidence. But you would have found it out for yourself, and besides, she told me no secrets. She declared she was the happiest creature in the world, and then, poor thing, she burst into tears, and I prayed to be delivered from such happiness. It's the miserable story of an American girl, born to be neither a slave nor a toy, marrying a profligate Frenchman, who believes that a woman must be one or the other. The silliest American woman is too good for the best foreigner, and the poorest of us have moral needs a Frenchman can't appreciate. She was romantic and wilful, and thought Americans were vulgar. Matrimonial felicity perhaps *is* vulgar; but I think nowadays she wishes she were a little less elegant. M. de Mauves cared, of course, for nothing but her money, which he's spending royally on his *menus plaisirs*.[6] I hope you appreciate the compliment I pay you when I recommend you to go and console an unhappy wife. I have never given a man such a proof of esteem, and if you were to disappoint me I should renounce the world. Prove to Madame de Mauves that an American friend may mingle admiration and respect better than a French husband. She avoids society and lives quite alone, seeing no one but a horrible French sister-in-law. Do let me hear that you have drawn some of the sadness from that desperate smile of hers. Make her smile with a good conscience."

These zealous admonitions left Longmore slightly disturbed. He found himself on the edge of a domestic tragedy from which he

---

5. A gauzelike fabric for dresses and veils. 6. Little private pleasures.

instinctively recoiled. To call upon Madame de Mauves with his present knowledge seemed a sort of fishing in troubled waters. He was a modest man, and yet he asked himself whether the effect of his attentions might not be to add to her tribulation. A flattering sense of unwonted opportunity, however, made him, with the lapse of time, more confident,—possibly more reckless. It seemed a very inspiring idea to draw the sadness from his fair country-woman's smile, and at least he hoped to persuade her that there was such a thing as an agreeable American. He immediately called upon her.

II

She had been placed for her education, fourteen years before, in a Parisian convent, by a widowed mamma, fonder of Homburg[7] and Nice[8] than of letting out tucks in the frocks of a vigorously growing daughter. Here, besides various elegant accomplishments,—the art of wearing a train, of composing a bouquet, of presenting a cup of tea,—she acquired a certain turn of the imagination which might have passed for a sign of precocious worldliness. She dreamed of marrying a title,—not for the pleasure of hearing herself called Mme. la Vicomtesse (for which it seemed to her that she should never greatly care), but because she had a romantic belief that the best birth is the guaranty of an ideal delicacy of feeling. Romances are rarely shaped in such perfect good faith, and Euphemia's excuse was in the radical purity of her imagination. She was profoundly incorruptible, and she cherished this pernicious conceit as if it had been a dogma revealed by a white-winged angel. Even after experience had given her a hundred rude hints, she found it easier to believe in fables, when they had a certain nobleness of meaning, than in well-attested but sordid facts. She believed that a gentleman with a long pedigree must be of necessity a very fine fellow, and that the consciousness of a picturesque family tradition imparts an exquisite tone to the character. *Noblesse oblige*,[9] she thought, as regards yourself, and insures, as regards your wife. She had never spoken to a nobleman in her life, and these convictions were but a matter of transcendent theory. They were the fruit, in part, of the perusal of various ultramontane[1] works of fiction—the only ones admitted to the convent library—in which the hero was always a legitimist vicomte who fought duels by the dozen, but went twice a month to confession; and in part of the perfumed gossip of her companions, many of them *filles de haut lieu*,[2] who in the convent garden, after Sundays at home, depicted their brothers and cousins

7. Bad Homburg, a watering place near Frankfurt am Main.
8. A French resort on the Riviera, famous as a theatrical, artistic, and social center.

9. Rank has its obligations.
1. Supporting the Roman Catholic belief in papal supremacy, then associated with an Italian aristocracy.
2. Girls of high birth.

as Prince Charmings and young Paladins.[3] Euphemia listened and said nothing; she shrouded her visions of matrimony under a coronet in religious mystery. She was not of that type of young lady who is easily induced to declare that her husband must be six feet high and a little near-sighted, part his hair in the middle, and have amber lights in his beard. To her companions she seemed to have a very pallid fancy; and even the fact that she was a sprig of the trans-atlantic democracy never sufficiently explained her apathy on social questions. She had a mental image of that son of the Crusaders who was to suffer her to adore him, but like many an artist who has produced a masterpiece of idealization, she shrank from exposing it to public criticism. It was the portrait of a gentleman rather ugly than handsome, and rather poor than rich. But his ugliness was to be nobly expressive, and his poverty delicately proud. Euphemia had a fortune of her own, which, at the proper time, after fixing on her in eloquent silence those fine eyes which were to soften the feudal severity of his visage, he was to accept with a world of stifled protestations. One condition alone she was to make,—that his blood should be of the very finest strain. On this she would stake her happiness.

It so chanced that circumstances were to give convincing color to this primitive logic.

Though little of a talker, Euphemia was an ardent listener, and there were moments when she fairly hung upon the lips of Mademoiselle Marie de Mauves. Her intimacy with this chosen schoolmate was, like most intimacies, based on their points of dif-ference. Mademoiselle de Mauves was very positive, very shrewd, very ironical, very French,—everything that Euphemia felt herself unpardonable in not being. During her Sundays *en ville*[4] she had examined the world and judged it, and she imparted her impres-sions to our attentive heroine with an agreeable mixture of enthu-siasm and scepticism. She was moreover a handsome and well-grown person, on whom Euphemia's ribbons and trinkets had a trick of looking better than on their slender proprietress. She had, finally, the supreme merit of being a rigorous example of the virtue of exalted birth, having, as she did, ancestors honorably mentioned by Joinville[5] and Commines,[6] and a stately grandmother with a hooked nose, who came up with her after the holidays from a veritable *castel* in Auvergne. It seemed to Euphemia that these attributes made her friend more at home in the world than if she had been the daughter of even the most prosperous grocer. A certain

3. Knights.
4. In town.
5. Jean de Joinville (1224?–1317) was the first French historian of modern Europe.

6. Philippe de Commines (1445?–1509?), after 1472 became the intimate adviser and biographer of the French king Louis XI.

aristocratic impudence Mademoiselle de Mauves abundantly possessed, and her raids among her friend's finery were quite in the
spirit of her baronial ancestors in the twelfth century,—a spirit
which Euphemia considered but a large way of understanding
friendship,—a freedom from small deference to the world's opinions
which would sooner or later justify itself in acts of surprising magnanimity. Mademoiselle de Mauves perhaps enjoyed but slightly
that easy attitude toward society which Euphemia envied her. She
proved herself later in life such an accomplished schemer that her
sense of having further heights to scale must have awakened early.
Our heroine's ribbons and trinkets had much to do with the other's
sisterly patronage, and her appealing pliancy of character even
more; but the concluding motive of Marie's writing to her grand-
mamma to invite Euphemia for a three weeks' holiday to the *castel*
in Auvergne, involved altogether superior considerations. Mademoiselle de Mauves was indeed at this time seventeen years of age,
and presumably capable of general views; and Euphemia, who was
hardly less, was a very well-grown subject for experiment, besides
being pretty enough almost to pre-assure success. It is a proof of
the sincerity of Euphemia's aspirations that the *castel* was not a
shock to her faith. It was neither a cheerful nor a luxurious abode,
but the young girl found it as delightful as a play. It had battered
towers and an empty moat, a rusty drawbridge and a court paved
with crooked, grass-grown slabs, over which the antique coach-
wheels of the old lady with the hooked nose seemed to awaken the
echoes of the seventeenth century. Euphemia was not frightened
out of her dream; she had the pleasure of seeing it assume the
consistency of a flattering presentiment. She had a taste for old
servants, old anecdotes, old furniture, faded household colors, and
sweetly stale odors,—musty treasures in which the Château de
Mauves abounded. She made a dozen sketches in water-colors, after
her conventual pattern; but sentimentally, as one may say, she was
forever sketching with a freer hand.

Old Madame de Mauves had nothing severe but her nose, and
she seemed to Euphemia, as indeed she was, a graciously venerable
relic of a historic order of things. She took a great fancy to the
young American, who was ready to sit all day at her feet and listen
to anecdotes of the *bon temps*[7] and quotations from the family
chronicles. Madame de Mauves was a very honest old woman, and
uttered her thoughts with antique plainness. One day, after pushing
back Euphemia's shining locks and blinking at her with some
tenderness from under her spectacles, she declared, with an energetic shake of the head, that she didn't know what to make of her.
And in answer to the young girl's startled blush,—"I should like to

7. The good old days.

advise you," she said, "but you seem to me so all of a piece that I
am afraid that if I advise you, I shall spoil you. It's easy to see that
you're not one of us. I don't know whether you're better, but you
seem to me to listen to the murmur of your own young spirit, rather
than to the voice from behind the confessional or to the whisper of
opportunity. Young girls, in my day, when they were stupid, were
very docile, but when they were clever, were very sly. You're clever
enough, I imagine, and yet if I guessed all your secrets at this
moment, is there one I should have to frown at? I can tell you a
wickeder one than any you have discovered for yourself. If you
expect to live in France, and you want to be happy, don't listen too
hard to that little voice I just spoke of,—the voice that is neither the
curé's[8] nor the world's. You'll fancy it saying things that it won't help
your case to hear. They'll make you sad, and when you're sad you'll
grow plain, and when you're plain you'll grow bitter, and when
you're bitter you'll be very disagreeable. I was brought up to think
that a woman's first duty was to please, and the happiest women
I've known have been the ones who performed this duty faithfully.
As you're not a Catholic, I suppose you can't be a dévote;[9] and if
you don't take life as a fifty years' mass, the only way to take it is as
a game of skill. Listen: not to lose, you must,—I don't say cheat;
but don't be too sure your neighbor won't, and don't be shocked out
of your self-possession if he does. Don't lose, my dear; I beseech you,
don't lose. Be neither suspicious nor credulous; but if you find your
neighbor peeping, don't cry out, but very politely wait your own
chance. I've had my *revanche*[1] more than once in my day, but I'm
not sure that the sweetest I could take against life as a whole would
be to have your blessed innocence profit by my experience."

This was rather awful advice, but Euphemia understood it too
little to be either edified or frightened. She sat listening to it very
much as she would have listened to the speeches of an old lady in
a comedy, whose diction should picturesquely correspond to the
pattern of her mantilla[2] and the fashion of her headdress. Her indifference was doubly dangerous, for Madame de Mauves spoke at
the prompting of coming events, and her words were the result of a
somewhat troubled conscience,—a conscience which told her at
once that Euphemia was too tender a victim to be sacrificed to an
ambition, and that the prosperity of her house was too precious a
heritage to be sacrificed to a scruple. The prosperity in question had
suffered repeated and grievous breaches, and the house of De
Mauves had been pervaded by the cold comfort of an establishment
in which people were obliged to balance dinner-table allusions to
feudal ancestors against the absence of side dishes; a state of things

8. Parish priest.
9. A devoutly religious person.

1. Revenge.
2. A light cape, usually of silk or lace.

the more regrettable as the family was now mainly represented by a gentleman whose appetite was large, and who justly maintained that its historic glories were not established by underfed heroes.

Three days after Euphemia's arrival, Richard de Mauves came down from Paris to pay his respects to his grandmother, and treated our heroine to her first encounter with a gentilhomme[3] in the flesh. On coming in he kissed his grandmother's hand, with a smile which caused her to draw it away with dignity, and set Euphemia, who was standing by, wondering what had happened between them. Her unanswered wonder was but the beginning of a life of bitter perplexity, but the reader is free to know that the smile of M. de Mauves was a reply to a certain postscript affixed by the old lady to a letter promptly addressed to him by her granddaughter, after Euphemia had been admitted to justify the latter's promises. Mademoiselle de Mauves brought her letter to her grandmother for approval, but obtained no more than was expressed in a frigid nod. The old lady watched her with a sombre glance as she proceeded to seal the letter, and suddenly bade her open it again and bring her a pen.

"Your sister's flatteries are all nonsense," she wrote; "the young lady is far too good for you, *mauvais sujet*.[4] If you have a conscience you'll not come and take possession of an angel of innocence."

The young girl, who had read these lines, made up a little face as she redirected the letter; but she laid down her pen with a confident nod, which might have seemed to mean that, to the best of her belief, her brother had not a conscience.

"If you meant what you said," the young man whispered to his grandmother on the first opportunity, "it would have been simpler not to let her send the letter!"

It was perhaps because she was wounded by this cynical insinuation, that Madame de Mauves remained in her own apartment during a greater part of Euphemia's stay, so that the latter's angelic innocence was left entirely to the Baron's mercy. It suffered no worse mischance, however, than to be prompted to intenser communion with itself. M. de Mauves was the hero of the young girl's romance made real, and so completely accordant with this creature of her imagination, that she felt afraid of him, very much as she would have been of a supernatural apparition. He was thirty-five years old,—young enough to suggest possibilities of ardent activity, and old enough to have formed opinions which a simple woman might deem it an intellectual privilege to listen to. He was perhaps a trifle handsomer than Euphemia's rather grim, Quixotic ideal, but a very few days reconciled her to his good looks, as they would have reconciled her to his ugliness. He was quiet, grave, and eminently

3. A gentleman of the upper classes.   4. Rascal (jokingly).

distinguished. He spoke little, but his speeches, without being sen-
tentious, had a certain nobleness of tone which caused them to
re-echo in the young girl's ears at the end of the day. He paid her
very little direct attention, but his chance words—if he only asked
her if she objected to his cigarette—were accompanied by a smile of
extraordinary kindness.

It happened that shortly after his arrival, riding an unruly horse,
which Euphemia with shy admiration had watched him mount in
the castle yard, he was thrown with a violence which, without disparaging his skill, made him for a fortnight an interesting invalid,
lounging in the library with a bandaged knee. To beguile his con-
finement, Euphemia was repeatedly induced to sing to him, which
she did with a little natural tremor in her voice, which might have
passed for an exquisite refinement of art. He never overwhelmed
her with compliments, but he listened with unwandering attention,
remembered all her melodies, and sat humming them to himself.
While his imprisonment lasted, indeed, he passed hours in her
company, and made her feel not unlike some unfriended artist who
has suddenly gained the opportunity to devote a fortnight to the
study of a great model. Euphemia studied with noiseless diligence
what she supposed to be the "character" of M. de Mauves, and the
more she looked the more fine lights and shades she seemed to
behold in this masterpiece of nature. M. de Mauves's character
indeed, whether from a sense of being generously scrutinized, or
for reasons which bid graceful defiance to analysis, had never been
so amiable; it seemed really to reflect the purity of Euphemia's
interpretation of it. There had been nothing especially to admire
in the state of mind in which he left Paris,—a hard determination
to marry a young girl whose charms might or might not justify his
sister's account of them, but who was mistress, at the worst, of a
couple of hundred thousand francs a year. He had not counted out
sentiment; if she pleased him, so much the better; but he had left
a meagre margin for it, and he would hardly have admitted that so
excellent a match could be improved by it. He was a placid sceptic,
and it was a singular fate for a man who believed in nothing to be
so tenderly believed in. What his original faith had been he could
hardly have told you; for as he came back to his childhood's home
to mend his fortunes by pretending to fall in love, he was a thoroughly perverted creature, and overlaid with more corruptions than
a summer day's questioning of his conscience would have released
him from. Ten years' pursuit of pleasure, which a bureau full of
unpaid bills was all he had to show for, had pretty well stifled the
natural lad, whose violent will and generous temper might have
been shaped by other circumstances to a result which a romantic
imagination might fairly accept as a late-blooming flower of heredi-

tary honor. The Baron's violence had been subdued, and he had learned to be irreproachably polite; but he had lost the edge of his generosity, and his politeness, which in the long run society paid for, was hardly more than a form of luxurious egotism, like his fondness for cambric handkerchiefs, lavender gloves, and other fopperies by which shopkeepers remained out of pocket. In after years he was terribly polite to his wife. He had formed himself, as the phrase was, and the form prescribed to him by the society into which his birth and his tastes introduced him was marked by some peculiar features. That which mainly concerns us is its classification of the fairer half of humanity as objects not essentially different— say from the light gloves one soils in an evening and throws away. To do M. de Mauves justice, he had in the course of time encountered such plentiful evidence of this pliant, glove-like quality in the feminine character, that idealism naturally seemed to him a losing game.

Euphemia, as he lay on his sofa, seemed by no means a refutation; she simply reminded him that very young women are generally innocent, and that this, on the whole, was the most charming stage of their development. Her innocence inspired him with profound respect, and it seemed to him that if he shortly became her husband it would be exposed to a danger the less. Old Madame de Mauves, who flattered herself that in this whole matter she was being laudably rigid, might have learned a lesson from his gallant consideration. For a fortnight the Baron was almost a blushing boy again. He watched from behind the "Figaro,"[5] and admired, and held his tongue. He was not in the least disposed toward a flirtation; he had no desire to trouble the waters he proposed to transfuse into the golden cup of matrimony. Sometimes a word, a look, a movement of Euphemia's, gave him the oddest sense of being, or of seeming at least, almost bashful; for she had a way of not dropping her eyes, according to the mysterious virginal mechanism, of not fluttering out of the room when she found him there alone, of treating him rather as a benignant than as a pernicious influence,—a radiant frankness of demeanor, in fine, in spite of an evident natural reserve, which it seemed equally graceless not to make the subject of a compliment and indelicate not to take for granted. In this way there was wrought in the Baron's mind a vague, unwonted resonance of soft impressions, as we may call it, which indicated the transmutation of "sentiment" from a contingency into a fact. His imagination enjoyed it; he was very fond of music, and this reminded him of some of the best he had ever heard. In spite of the bore of being laid up with a lame knee, he was in a better humor than he had known for months; he lay smoking cigarettes and listening to the nightingales, with the comfortable smile of one of his country neighbors whose big ox should have taken the prize at a fair. Every now and then, with an impatient suspicion of the resemblance, he declared that he was pitifully *bête;*[6] but he was under a charm which braved even the supreme penalty of seeming ridiculous. One morning he had half an hour's tête-à-tête[7] with his grandmother's confessor, a soft-voiced old abbé, whom, for reasons of her own, Madame de Mauves had suddenly summoned, and had left waiting in the drawing-room while she rearranged her curls. His reverence, going up to the old lady, assured her that M. le Baron was in a most edifying state of mind, and a promising subject for the operation of grace. This was a pious interpretation of the Baron's momentary good-humor. He had always lazily wondered what priests were good for, and he now remembered, with a sense of especial obligation to the abbé, that they were excellent for marrying people.

A day or two after this he left off his bandages, and tried to walk. He made his way into the garden and hobbled successfully along one of the alleys; but in the midst of his progress he was seized with a spasm of pain which forced him to stop and call for help. In an instant Euphemia came tripping along the path and offered him her arm with the frankest solicitude.

"Not to the house," he said, taking it; "farther on, to the bosquet."[8] This choice was prompted by her having immediately confessed that she had seen him leave the house, had feared an accident, and had followed him on tiptoe.

"Why didn't you join me?" he had asked, giving her a look in which admiration was no longer disguised, and yet felt itself half at the mercy of her replying that a *jeune fille*[9] should not be seen following a gentleman. But it drew a breath which filled its lungs for a long time afterward, when she replied simply that if she had overtaken him he might have accepted her arm out of politeness, whereas she wished to have the pleasure of seeing him walk alone.

The bosquet was covered with an odorous tangle of blossoming vines, and a nightingale overhead was shaking out love-notes with a profuseness which made the Baron consider his own conduct the perfection of propriety.

"In America," he said, "I have always heard that when a man wishes to marry a young girl, he offers himself simply, face to face, without any ceremony,—without parents, and uncles, and cousins sitting round in a circle."

"Why, I believe so," said Euphemia, staring, and too surprised to be alarmed.

6. Stupid.
7. Private conversation.

8. A growth of shrubbery.
9. Young girl.

"Very well, then," said the Baron, "suppose our bosquet here to be American. I offer you my hand, à l'Américaine. It will make me intensely happy to have you accept it."

Whether Euphemia's acceptance was in the American manner is more than I can say; I incline to think that for fluttering, grateful, trustful, softly-amazed young hearts, there is only one manner all over the world.

That evening, in the little turret chamber which it was her happiness to inhabit, she wrote a dutiful letter to her mamma, and had just sealed it when she was sent for by Madame de Mauves. She found this ancient lady seated in her boudoir, in a lavender satin gown, with all her candles lighted, as if to celebrate her grandson's betrothal. "Are you very happy?" Madame de Mauves demanded, making Euphemia sit down before her.

"I'm almost afraid to say so," said the young girl, "lest I should wake myself up."

"May you never wake up, *belle enfant*,"[1] said the old lady, solemnly. "This is the first marriage ever made in our family in this way,—by a Baron de Mauves proposing to a young girl in an arbor, like Jeannot and Jeannette.[2] It has not been our way of doing things, and people may say it wants frankness. My grandson tells me he considers it the perfection of frankness. Very good. I'm a very old woman, and if your differences should ever be as frank as your agreement, I shouldn't like to see them. But I should be sorry to die and think you were going to be unhappy. You can't be, beyond a certain point; because, though in this world the Lord sometimes makes light of our expectations, he never altogether ignores our deserts. But you're very young and innocent, and easy to deceive. There never was a man in the world—among the saints themselves —as good as you believe the Baron. But he's a *galant homme*[3] and a gentleman, and I've been talking to him tonight. To you I want to say this,—that you're to forget the worldly rubbish I talked the other day about frivolous women being happy. It's not the kind of happiness that would suit you. Whatever befalls you, promise me this: to be yourself. The Baron de Mauves will be none the worse for it. Yourself, understand, in spite of everything,—bad precepts and bad examples, bad usage even. Be persistently and patiently yourself, and a De Mauves will do you justice!"

Euphemia remembered this speech in after years, and more than once, wearily closing her eyes, she seemed to see the old woman sitting upright in her faded finery and smiling grimly, like one of the Fates who sees the wheel of fortune turning up her favorite event. But at the moment it seemed to her simply to have the

1. Beautiful child.
2. Like any ordinary boy and girl.
3. A gallant man, attentive to ladies.

proper gravity of the occasion; this was the way, she supposed, in which lucky young girls were addressed on their engagement by wise old women of quality.

At her convent, to which she immediately returned, she found a letter from her mother, which shocked her far more than the remarks of Madame de Mauves. Who were these people, Mrs. Cleve demanded, who had presumed to talk to her daughter of marriage without asking her leave? Questionable gentlefolk, plainly; the best French people never did such things. Euphemia would return straightway to her convent, shut herself up, and await her own arrival.

It took Mrs. Cleve three weeks to travel from Nice to Paris, and during this time the young girl had no communication with her lover beyond accepting a bouquet of violets, marked with his initials and left by a female friend. "I've not brought you up with such devoted care," she declared to her daughter at their first interview, "to marry a penniless Frenchman. I will take you straight home, and you will please to forget M. de Mauves."

Mrs. Cleve received that evening at her hotel a visit from the Baron which mitigated her wrath, but failed to modify her decision. He had very good manners, but she was sure he had horrible morals; and Mrs. Cleve, who had been a very good-natured censor on her own account, felt a genuine spiritual need to sacrifice her daughter to propriety. She belonged to that large class of Americans who make light of America in familiar discourse, but are startled back into a sense of moral responsibility when they find Europeans taking them at their word. "I know the type, my dear," she said to her daughter with a sagacious nod. "He'll not beat you; sometimes you'll wish he would."

Euphemia remained solemnly silent; for the only answer she felt capable of making her mother was that her mind was too small a measure of things, and that the Baron's "type" was one which it took some mystical illumination to appreciate. A person who confounded him with the common throng of her watering-place acquaintance was not a person to argue with. It seemed to Euphemia that she had no cause to plead; her cause was in the Lord's hands and her lover's.

M. de Mauves had been irritated and mortified by Mrs. Cleve's opposition, and hardly knew how to handle an adversary who failed to perceive that a De Mauves of necessity gave more than he received. But he had obtained information on his return to Paris which exalted the uses of humility. Euphemia's fortune, wonderful to say, was greater than its fame, and in view of such a prize, even a De Mauves could afford to take a snubbing.

The young man's tact, his deference, his urbane insistence, won a concession from Mrs. Cleve. The engagement was to be suspended and her daughter was to return home, be brought out and receive the homage she was entitled to, and which would but too surely take a form dangerous to the Baron's suit. They were to exchange neither letters, nor mementos, nor messages; but if at the end of two years Euphemia had refused offers enough to attest the permanence of her attachment, he should receive an invitation to address her again.

This decision was promulgated in the presence of the parties interested. The Baron bore himself gallantly, and looked at the young girl, expecting some tender protestation. But she only looked at him silently in return, neither weeping, nor smiling, nor putting out her hand. On this they separated; but as the Baron walked away, he declared to himself that, in spite of the confounded two years, he was a very happy fellow,—to have a fiancée who, to several millions of francs, added such strangely beautiful eyes.

How many offers Euphemia refused but scantily concerns us,— and how the Baron wore his two years away. He found that he needed pastimes, and, as pastimes were expensive, he added heavily to the list of debts to be cancelled by Euphemia's millions. Sometimes, in the thick of what he had once called pleasure with a keener conviction than now, he put to himself the case of their failing him after all; and then he remembered that last mute assurance of her eyes, and drew a long breath of such confidence as he felt in nothing else in the world save his own punctuality in an affair of honor.

At last, one morning, he took the express to Havre with a letter of Mrs. Cleve's in his pocket, and ten days later made his bow to mother and daughter in New York. His stay was brief, and he was apparently unable to bring himself to view what Euphemia's uncle, Mr. Butterworth, who gave her away at the altar, called our great experiment in democratic self-government in a serious light. He smiled at everything, and seemed to regard the New World as a colossal *plaisanterie*.[4] It is true that a perpetual smile was the most natural expression of countenance for a man about to marry Euphemia Cleve.

III

Longmore's first visit seemed to open to him so large an opportunity for tranquil enjoyment, that he very soon paid a second, and, at the end of a fortnight, had spent a great many hours in the little drawing-room which Madame de Mauves rarely quitted except to drive or walk in the forest. She lived in an old-fashioned pavilion, between a high-walled court and an excessively artificial garden, beyond whose enclosure you saw a long line of tree-tops. Longmore

4. Something amusing.

liked the garden, and in the mild afternoons used to move his chair through the open window to the little terrace which overlooked it, while his hostess sat just within. After a while she came out and wandered through the narrow alleys and beside the thin-spouting fountain, and last introduced him to a little gate in the garden wall, opening upon a lane which led into the forest. Hitherward, more than once, she wandered with him, bareheaded and meaning to go but twenty rods, but always strolling good-naturedly farther, and often taking a generous walk. They discovered a vast deal to talk about, and to the pleasure of finding the hours tread inaudibly away, Longmore was able to add the satisfaction of suspecting that he was a "resource" for Madame de Mauves. He had made her acquaintance with the sense, not altogether comfortable, that she was a woman with a painful secret, and that seeking her acquaintance would be like visiting at a house where there was an invalid who could bear no noise. But he very soon perceived that her sorrow, since sorrow it was, was not an aggressive one; that it was not fond of attitudes and ceremonies, and that her earnest wish was to forget it. He felt that even if Mrs. Draper had not told him she was unhappy, he would have guessed it; and yet he could hardly have pointed to his evidence. It was chiefly negative,—she never alluded to her husband. Beyond this it seemed to him simply that her whole being was pitched on a lower key than harmonious Nature meant; she was like a powerful singer who had lost her high notes. She never drooped nor sighed nor looked unutterable things; she indulged in no dusky sarcasms against fate; she had, in short, none of the coquetry of unhappiness. But Longmore was sure that her gentle gayety was the result of strenuous effort, and that she was trying to interest herself in his thoughts to escape from her own. If she had wished to irritate his curiosity and lead him to take her confidence by storm, nothing could have served her purpose better than this ingenuous reserve. He declared to himself that there was a rare magnanimity in such ardent self-effacement, and that but one woman in ten thousand was capable of merging an intensely personal grief in thankless outward contemplation. Madame de Mauves, he instinctively felt, was not sweeping the horizon for a compensation or a consoler; she had suffered a personal deception which had disgusted her with persons. She was not striving to balance her sorrow with some strongly flavored joy; for the present, she was trying to live with it, peaceably, reputably, and without scandal,—turning the key on it occasionally, as you would on a companion liable to attacks of insanity. Longmore was a man of fine senses and of an active imagination, whose leading-strings had never been slipped. He began to regard his hostess as a figure haunted by a shadow which was somehow her intenser, more authentic self. This hovering mystery came to have for him an extraordinary charm. Her delicate beauty acquired to his eye the serious cast of certain blank-browed Greek statues, and sometimes, when his imagination, more than his ear, detected a vague tremor in the tone in which she attempted to make a friendly question seem to have behind it none of the hollow resonance of absent-mindedness, his marvelling eyes gave her an answer more eloquent, though much less to the point, than the one she demanded.

She gave him indeed much to wonder about, and, in his ignorance, he formed a dozen experimental theories upon the history of her marriage. She had married for love and staked her whole soul on it; of that he was convinced. She had not married a Frenchman to be near Paris and her base of supplies of millinery; he was sure she had seen conjugal happiness in a light of which her present life, with its conveniences for shopping and its moral aridity, was the absolute negation. But by what extraordinary process of the heart—through what mysterious intermission of that moral instinct which may keep pace with the heart, even when that organ is making unprecedented time—had she fixed her affections on an arrogantly frivolous Frenchman? Longmore needed no telling; he knew M. de Mauves was frivolous; it was stamped on his eyes, his nose, his mouth, his carriage. For French women Longmore had but a scanty kindness, or at least (what with him was very much the same thing) but a scanty gallantry; they all seemed to belong to the type of a certain fine lady to whom he had ventured to present a letter of introduction, and whom, directly after his first visit to her, he had set down in his note-book as "metallic." Why should Madame de Mauves have chosen a French woman's lot,—she whose character had a perfume which doesn't belong to even the brightest metals? He asked her one day frankly if it had cost her nothing to transplant herself,—if she was not oppressed with a sense of irreconcilable difference from "all these people." She was silent awhile, and he fancied that she was hesitating as to whether she should resent so unceremonious an allusion to her husband. He almost wished she would; it would seem a proof that her deep reserve of sorrow had a limit.

"I almost grew up here," she said at last, "and it was here for me that those dreams of the future took shape that we all have when we cease to be very young. As matters stand, one may be very American and yet arrange it with one's conscience to live in Europe. My imagination perhaps—I had a little when I was younger—helped me to think I should find happiness here. And after all, for a woman, what does it signify? This is not America, perhaps, about me, but it's quite as little France. France is out there, beyond the garden, in the town, in the forest; but here, close about me, in my room and"—she paused a moment—"in my mind, it's a nameless country of my own. It's not her country," she added, "that makes a woman happy or unhappy."

Madame Clairin, Euphemia's sister-in-law, might have been supposed to have undertaken the graceful task of making Longmore ashamed of his uncivil jottings about her sex and nation. Mademoiselle de Mauves, bringing example to the confirmation of precept, had made a remunerative match and sacrificed her name to the millions of a prosperous and aspiring wholesale druggist,—a gentleman liberal enough to consider his fortune a moderate price for being towed into circles unpervaded by pharmaceutic odors. His system, possibly, was sound, but his own application of it was unfortunate. M. Clairin's head was turned by his good luck. Having secured an aristocratic wife, he adopted an aristocratic vice and began to gamble at the Bourse.[5] In an evil hour he lost heavily and staked heavily to recover himself. But he overtook his loss only by a greater one. Then he let everything go,—his wits, his courage, his probity,—everything that had made him what his ridiculous marriage had so promptly unmade. He walked up the Rue Vivienne one day with his hands in his empty pockets, and stood for half an hour staring confusedly up and down the glittering boulevard. People brushed against him, and half a dozen carriages almost ran over him, until at last a policeman, who had been watching him for some time, took him by the arm and led him gently away. He looked at the man's cocked hat and sword with tears in his eyes; he hoped he was going to interpret to him the wrath of Heaven,— to execute the penalty of his dead-weight of self-abhorrence. But the sergent de ville only stationed him in the embrasure of a door, out of harm's way, and walked away to supervise a financial contest between an old lady and a cabman. Poor M. Clairin had only been married a year, but he had had time to measure the lofty spirit of a De Mauves. When night had fallen, he repaired to the house of a friend and asked for a night's lodging; and as his friend, who was simply his old head book-keeper and lived in a small way, was put to some trouble to accommodate him,—"You must excuse me," Clairin said, "but I can't go home. I'm afraid of my wife!" Toward morning he blew his brains out. His widow turned the remnants of his property to better account than could have been expected, and wore the very handsomest mourning. It was for this latter reason, perhaps, that she was obliged to retrench at other points and accept a temporary home under her brother's roof.

Fortune had played Madame Clairin a terrible trick, but had found an adversary and not a victim. Though quite without beauty, she had always had what is called the grand air, and her air from this time forward was grander than ever. As she trailed about in

5. The Paris stock exchange.

her sable furbelows, tossing back her well-dressed head, and holding up her vigilant eye-glass, she seemed to be sweeping the whole field of society and asking herself where she should pluck her revenge. Suddenly she espied it, ready made to her hand, in poor Longmore's wealth and amiability. American dollars and American complaisance had made her brother's fortune; why shouldn't they make hers? She overestimated Longmore's wealth and misinterpreted his amiability; for she was sure that a man could not be so contented without being rich, nor so unassuming without being weak. He encountered her advances with a formal politeness which covered a great deal of unflattering discomposure. She made him feel acutely uncomfortable; and though he was at a loss to conceive how he could be an object of interest to a shrewd Parisienne, he had an indefinable sense of being enclosed in a magnetic circle, like the victim of an incantation. If Madame Clairin could have fathomed his Puritanic soul, she would have laid by her wand and her book and admitted that he was an impossible subject. She gave him a kind of moral chill, and he never mentally alluded to her save as that dreadful woman,—that terrible woman. He did justice to her grand air, but for his pleasure he preferred the small air of Madame de Mauves; and he never made her his bow, after standing frigidly passive for five minutes to one of her gracious overtures to intimacy, without feeling a peculiar desire to ramble away into the forest, fling himself down on the warm grass, and, staring up at the blue sky, forget that there were any women in nature who didn't please like the swaying tree-tops. One day, on his arrival, she met him in the court and told him that her sister-in-law was shut up with a headache, and that his visit must be for her. He followed her into the drawing-room with the best grace at his command, and sat twirling his hat for half an hour. Suddenly he understood her; the caressing cadence of her voice was a distinct invitation to solicit the incomparable honor of her hand. He blushed to the roots of his hair and jumped up with uncontrollable alacrity; then, dropping a glance at Madame Clairin, who sat watching him with hard eyes over the edge of her smile, as it were, perceived on her brow a flash of unforgiving wrath. It was not becoming, but his eyes lingered a moment, for it seemed to illuminate her character. What he saw there frightened him, and he felt himself murmuring, "Poor Madame de Mauves!" His departure was abrupt, and this time he really went into the forest and lay down on the grass.

After this he admired Madame de Mauves more than ever; she seemed a brighter figure, dogged by a darker shadow. At the end of a month he received a letter from a friend with whom he had arranged a tour through the Low Countries, reminding him of his promise to meet him promptly at Brussels. It was only after his answer was posted that he fully measured the zeal with which he had declared that the journey must either be deferred or abandoned,—that he could not possibly leave Saint-Germain. He took a walk in the forest, and asked himself if this was irrevocably true. If it was, surely his duty was to march straight home and pack his trunk. Poor Webster, who, he knew, had counted ardently on this excursion, was an excellent fellow; six weeks ago he would have gone through fire and water to join Webster. It had never been in his books to throw overboard a friend whom he had loved for ten years for a married woman whom for six weeks he had—admired. It was certainly beyond question that he was lingering at Saint-Germain because this admirable married woman was there; but in the midst of all this admiration what had become of prudence? This was the conduct of a man prepared to fall utterly in love. If she was as unhappy as he believed, the love of such a man would help her very little more than his indifference; if she was less so, she needed no help and could dispense with his friendly offices. He was sure, moreover, that if she knew he was staying on her account, she would be extremely annoyed. But this very feeling had much to do with making it hard to go; her displeasure would only enhance the gentle stoicism which touched him to the heart. At moments, indeed, he assured himself that to linger was simply impertinent; it was indelicate to make a daily study of such a shrinking grief. But inclination answered that some day her self-support would fail, and he had a vision of this admirable creature calling vainly for help. He would be her friend, to any length; it was unworthy of both of them to think about consequences. But he was a friend who carried about with him a muttering resentment that he had not known her five years earlier, and a brooding hostility to those who had anticipated him. It seemed one of fortune's most mocking strokes, that she should be surrounded by persons whose only merit was that they threw the charm of her character into radiant relief.

Longmore's growing irritation made it more and more difficult for him to see any other merit than this in the Baron de Mauves. And yet, disinterestedly, it would have been hard to give a name to the portentous vices which such an estimate implied, and there were times when our hero was almost persuaded against his finer judgment that he was really the most considerate of husbands, and that his wife liked melancholy for melancholy's sake. His manners were perfect, his urbanity was unbounded, and he seemed never to address her but, sentimentally speaking, hat in hand. His tone to Longmore (as the latter was perfectly aware) was that of a man of the world to a man not quite of the world; but what it lacked in deference it made up in easy friendliness. "I can't thank you enough for having overcome my wife's shyness," he more than once declared. "If we left her to do as she pleased, she would bury herself alive. Come often, and bring some one else. She'll have nothing to do with my friends, but perhaps she'll accept yours."

The Baron made these speeches with a remorseless placidity very amazing to our hero, who had an innocent belief that a man's head may point out to him the shortcomings of his heart and make him ashamed of them. He could not fancy him capable both of neglecting his wife and taking an almost humorous view of her suffering. Longmore had, at any rate, an exasperating sense that the Baron thought rather less of his wife than more, for that very same fine difference of nature which so deeply stirred his own sympathies. He was rarely present during Longmore's visits, and made a daily journey to Paris, where he had "business," as he once mentioned,—not in the least with a tone of apology. When he appeared, it was late in the evening, and with an imperturbable air of being on the best of terms with every one and everything, which was peculiarly annoying if you happened to have a tacit quarrel with him. If he was a good fellow, he was surely a good fellow spoiled. Something he had, however, which Longmore vaguely envied—a kind of superb positiveness—a manner rounded and polished by the traditions of centuries—an amenity exercised for his own sake and not his neighbors'—which seemed the result of something better than a good conscience—of a vigorous and unscrupulous temperament. The Baron was plainly not a moral man, and poor Longmore, who was, would have been glad to learn the secret of his luxurious serenity. What was it that enabled him, without being a monster with visibly cloven feet, exhaling brimstone, to misprize so cruelly a lovely wife, and to walk about the world with a smile under his mustache? It was the essential grossness of his imagination, which had nevertheless helped him to turn so many neat compliments. He could be very polite, and he could doubtless be supremely impertinent; but he was as unable to draw a moral inference of the finer strain, as a school-boy who has been playing truant for a week to solve a problem in algebra. It was ten to one he didn't know his wife was unhappy; he and his brilliant sister had doubtless agreed to consider their companion a Puritanical little person, of meagre aspirations and slender accomplishments, contented with looking at Paris from the terrace, and, as an especial treat, having a countryman very much like herself to supply her with homely transatlantic gossip. M. de Mauves was tired of his companion: he relished a higher flavor in female society. She was too modest, too simple, too delicate; she had too few arts, too little coquetry, too much charity. M. de Mauves, some day, lighting a cigar, had probably decided she was stupid. It was the same sort of taste, Longmore moralized, as the taste for Gérôme[6] in painting and for M. Gustave Flaubert[7] in literature. The Baron was a pagan and his wife was a Christian, and between them, accordingly, was a gulf. He was by race and instinct a *grand seigneur*.[8] Longmore had often heard of this distinguished social type, and was properly grateful for an opportunity to examine it closely. It had certainly a picturesque boldness of outline, but it was fed from spiritual sources so remote from those of which he felt the living gush in his own soul, that he found himself gazing at it, in irreconcilable antipathy, across a dim historic mist. "I'm a modern *bourgeois*,"[9] he said, "and not perhaps so good a judge of how far a pretty woman's tongue may go at supper without prejudice to her reputation. But I've not met one of the sweetest of women without recognizing her and discovering that a certain sort of character offers better entertainment than Thérésa's[1] songs, sung by a dissipated duchess. Wit for wit, I think mine carries me further." It was easy indeed to perceive that, as became a *grand seigneur*, M. de Mauves had a stock of rigid notions. He would not especially have desired, perhaps, that his wife should compete in amateur operettas with the duchesses in question, chiefly of recent origin; but he held that a gentleman may take his amusement where he finds it, that he is quite at liberty not to find it at home; and that the wife of a De Mauves who should hang her head and have red eyes, and allow herself to make any other response to officious condolence than that her husband's amusements were his own affair, would have forfeited every claim to having her fingertips bowed over and kissed. And yet in spite of these sound principles, Longmore fancied that the Baron was more irritated than gratified by his wife's irreproachable reserve. Did it dimly occur to him that it was self-control and not self-effacement? She was a model to all the inferior matrons of his line, past and to come, and an occasional "scene" from her at a convenient moment would have something reassuring,—would attest her stupidity a trifle more forcibly than her inscrutable tranquillity.

Longmore would have given much to know the principle of her submissiveness, and he tried more than once, but with rather awkward timidity, to sound the mystery. She seemed to him to have been long resisting the force of cruel evidence, and, though she had succumbed to it at last, to have denied herself the right to

6. Jean Léon Gérôme (1824–1904), French painter and sculptor whose large historical canvas "The Age of Augustus and the Birth of Christ" was purchased by the state.
7. French novelist (1821–1880), whose *Madame Bovary* depicts the desolate love affairs of a weak, romantic woman in a dull, provincial town.
8. A great nobleman.
9. Middle-class person.
1. Emma Valadon (1837–1913), a French singer called Thérésa, popular in café concerts and variety theaters for her originality and vitality.

complain, because if faith was gone her heroic generosity remained. He believed even that she was capable of reproaching herself with having expected too much, and of trying to persuade herself out of her bitterness by saying that her hopes had been illusions and that this was simply—life. "I hate tragedy," she once said to him; "I have a really pusillanimous dread of moral suffering. I believe that—without base concessions—there is always some way of escaping from it. I had almost rather never smile all my life than have a single violent explosion of grief." She lived evidently in nervous apprehension of being fatally convinced,—of seeing to the end of her deception. Longmore, when he thought of this, felt an immense longing to offer her something of which she could be as sure as of the sun in heaven.

IV

His friend Webster lost no time in accusing him of the basest infidelity, and asking him what he found at Saint-Germain to prefer to Van Eyck and Memling, Rubens and Rembrandt. A day or two after the receipt of Webster's letter, he took a walk with Madame de Mauves in the forest. They sat down on a fallen log, and she began to arrange into a bouquet the anemones and violets she had gathered. "I have a letter," he said at last, "from a friend whom I some time ago promised to join at Brussels. The time has come,—it has passed. It finds me terribly unwilling to leave Saint-Germain."

She looked up with the candid interest which she always displayed in his affairs, but with no disposition, apparently, to make a personal application of his words. "Saint-Germain is pleasant enough," she said; "but are you doing yourself justice? Won't you regret in future days that instead of travelling and seeing cities and monuments and museums and improving your mind, you sat here—for instance—on a log, pulling my flowers to pieces?"

"What I shall regret in future days," he answered after some hesitation, "is that I should have sat here and not spoken the truth on the matter. I am fond of museums and monuments and of improving my mind, and I'm particularly fond of my friend Webster. But I can't bring myself to leave Saint-Germain without asking you a question. You must forgive me if it's unfortunate, and be assured that curiosity was never more respectful. Are you really as unhappy as I imagine you to be?"

She had evidently not expected his question, and she greeted it with a startled blush. "If I strike you as unhappy," she said, "I have been a poorer friend to you than I wished to be."

"I, perhaps, have been a better friend of yours than you have supposed. I've admired your reserve, your courage, your studied gayety. But I have felt the existence of something beneath them that was more *you*—more you as I wished to know you—than they were; something that I have believed to be a constant sorrow."

She listened with great gravity, but without an air of offence, and he felt that while he had been timorously calculating the last consequences of friendship, she had placidly accepted them. "You surprise me," she said slowly, and her blush still lingered. "But to refuse to answer you would confirm an impression which is evidently already too strong. An unhappiness that one can sit comfortably talking about, is an unhappiness with distinct limitations. If I were examined before a board of commissioners for investigating the felicity of mankind, I'm sure I should be pronounced a very fortunate woman."

There was something delightfully gentle to him in her tone, and its softness seemed to deepen as she continued: "But let me add, with all gratitude for your sympathy, that it's my own affair altogether. It needn't disturb you, Mr. Longmore, for I have often found myself in your company a very contented person."

"You're a wonderful woman," he said, "and I admire you as I never have admired any one. You're wiser than anything I, for one, can say to you; and what I ask of you is not to let me advise or console you, but simply thank you for letting me know you." He had intended no such outburst as this, but his voice rang loud, and he felt a kind of unfamiliar joy as he uttered it.

She shook her head with some impatience. "Let us be friends,— as I supposed we were going to be,—without protestations and fine words. To have you making bows to my wisdom,—that would be real wretchedness. I can dispense with your admiration better than the Flemish painters can,—better than Van Eyck and Rubens, in spite of all their worshippers. Go join your friend,—see everything, enjoy everything, learn everything, and write me an excellent letter, brimming over with your impressions. I'm extremely fond of the Dutch painters," she added with a slight faltering of the voice, which Longmore had noticed once before, and which he had interpreted as the sudden weariness of a spirit self-condemned to play a part.

"I don't believe you care about the Dutch painters at all," he said with an unhesitating laugh. "But I shall certainly write you a letter."

She rose and turned homeward, thoughtfully rearranging her flowers as she walked. Little was said; Longmore was asking himself, with a tremor in the unspoken words, whether all this meant simply that he was in love. He looked at the rooks wheeling against the golden-hued sky, between the tree-tops, but not at his companion, whose personal presence seemed lost in the felicity she had created. Madame de Mauves was silent and grave, because she was painfully disappointed. A sentimental friendship she had not desired; her scheme had been to pass with Longmore as a placid creature with a good deal of leisure which she was disposed to devote to profitable conversation of an impersonal sort. She liked him extremely, and felt that there was something in him to which, when she made up her girlish mind that a needy French baron was the ripest fruit of time, she had done very scanty justice. They went through the little gate in the garden wall and approached the house. On the terrace Madame Clairin was entertaining a friend,—a little elderly gentleman with a white mustache, and an order in his button-hole. Madame de Mauves chose to pass round the house into the court; whereupon her sister-in-law, greeting Longmore with a commanding nod, lifted her eye-glass and stared at them as they went by. Longmore heard the little old gentleman uttering some old-fashioned epigram about "la vieille galanterie Française,"[2] and then, by a sudden impulse, he looked at Madame de Mauves and wondered what she was doing in such a world. She stopped before the house, without asking him to come in. "I hope," she said, "you'll consider my advice, and waste no more time at Saint-Germain."

For an instant there rose to his lips some faded compliment about his time not being wasted, but it expired before the simple sincerity of her look. She stood there as gently serious as the angel of disinterestedness, and Longmore felt as if he should insult her by treating her words as a bait for flattery. "I shall start in a day or two," he answered, "but I won't promise you not to come back."

"I hope not," she said simply. "I expect to be here a long time."

"I shall come and say good by," he rejoined; on which she nodded with a smile, and went in.

He turned away, and walked slowly homeward by the terrace. It seemed to him that to leave her thus, for a gain on which she herself insisted, was to know her better and admire her more. But he was in a vague ferment of feeling which her evasion of his question half an hour before had done more to deepen than to allay. Suddenly, on the terrace, he encountered M. de Mauves, who was leaning against the parapet finishing a cigar. The Baron, who, he fancied, had an air of peculiar affability, offered him his fair, plump hand. Longmore stopped; he felt a sudden angry desire to cry out to him that he had the loveliest wife in the world; that he ought to be ashamed of himself not to know it; and that for all his shrewdness he had never looked into the depths of her eyes. The Baron, we know, considered that he had; but there was something in Euphemia's eyes now that was not there five years before. They talked for a while about various things, and M. de Mauves gave a humorous account of his visit to America. His tone was not sooth-

2. Traditional French gallantry.

ing to Longmore's excited sensibilities. He seemed to consider the country a gigantic joke, and his urbanity only went so far as to admit that it was not a bad one. Longmore was not, by habit, an aggressive apologist for our institutions; but the Baron's narrative confirmed his worst impressions of French superficiality. He had understood nothing, he had felt nothing, he had learned nothing; and our hero, glancing askance at his aristocratic profile, declared that if the chief merit of a long pedigree was to leave one so vaingloriously stupid, he thanked his stars that the Longmores had emerged from obscurity in the present century, in the person of an enterprising lumber merchant. M. de Mauves dwelt of course on that prime oddity of ours,—the liberty allowed to young girls; and related the history of his researches into the "opportunities" it presented to French noblemen,—researches in which, during a fortnight's stay, he seemed to have spent many agreeable hours. "I am bound to admit," he said, "that in every case I was disarmed by the extreme candor of the young lady, and that they took care of themselves to better purpose than I have seen some mammas in France take care of them." Longmore greeted this handsome concession with the grimmest of smiles, and damned his impertinent patronage.

Mentioning at last that he was about to leave Saint-Germain, he was surprised, without exactly being flattered, by the Baron's quickened attention. "I'm very sorry," the latter cried. "I hoped we had you for the summer." Longmore murmured something civil, and wondered why M. de Mauves should care whether he stayed or went. "You were a diversion to Madame de Mauves," the Baron added. "I assure you I mentally blessed your visits."

"They were a great pleasure to me," Longmore said gravely. "Some day I expect to come back."

"Pray do," and the Baron laid his hand urgently on his arm. "You see I have confidence in you!" Longmore was silent for a moment, and the Baron puffed his cigar reflectively and watched the smoke. "Madame de Mauves," he said at last, "is a rather singular person."

Longmore shifted his position, and wondered whether he was going to "explain" Madame de Mauves.

"Being as you are her fellow-countryman," the Baron went on "I don't mind speaking frankly. She's just a little morbid,—the most charming woman in the world, as you see, but a little fanciful, —a little *exaltée*.[3] Now you see she has taken this extraordinary fancy for solitude. I can't get her to go anywhere,—to see any one. When my friends present themselves she's polite, but she's freezing. She doesn't do herself justice, and I expect every day to hear two or three of them say to me, 'Your wife's *jolie à croquer*:[4] what a pity

3. Overexcitable.   4. "Pretty enough to eat."

she hasn't a little *esprit*.'[5] You must have found out that she has really a great deal. But to tell the whole truth, what she needs is to forget herself. She sits alone for hours poring over her English books and looking at life through that terrible brown fog which they always seem to me to fling over the world. I doubt if your English authors," the Baron continued, with a serenity which Longmore afterwards characterized as sublime, "are very sound reading for young married women. I don't pretend to know much about them; but I remember that, not long after our marriage, Madame de Mauves undertook to read me one day a certain Wordsworth,—a poet highly esteemed, it appears, *chez vous*.[6] It seemed to me that she took me by the nape of the neck and forced my head for half an hour over a basin of *soupe aux choux*,[7] and that one ought to ventilate the drawing-room before any one called. But I suppose you know him,—*ce génie là*.[8] I think my wife never forgave me, and that it was a real shock to her to find she had married a man who had very much the same taste in literature as in cookery. But you're a man of general culture," said the Baron, turning to Longmore and fixing his eyes on the seal on his watch-guard. "You can talk about everything, and I'm sure you like Alfred de Musset[9] as well as Wordsworth. Talk to her about everything, Alfred de Musset included. Bah! I forgot you're going. Come back then as soon as possible and talk about your travels. If Madame de Mauves too would travel for a couple of months, it would do her good. It would enlarge her horizon,"—and M. de Mauves made a series of short nervous jerks with his stick in the air,—"it would wake up her imagination. She's too rigid, you know,—it would show her that one may bend a trifle without breaking." He paused a moment and gave two or three vigorous puffs. Then turning to his companion again, with a little nod and a confidential smile:—"I hope you admire my candor. I wouldn't say all this to one of *us*."

Evening was coming on, and the lingering light seemed to float in the air in faintly golden motes. Longmore stood gazing at these luminous particles; he could almost have fancied them a swarm of humming insects, murmuring as a refrain, "She has a great deal of *esprit*,—she has a great deal of *esprit*." "Yes, she has a great deal," he said mechanically, turning to the Baron. M. de Mauves glanced at him sharply, as if to ask what the deuce he was talking about. "She has a great deal of intelligence," said Longmore, deliberately, "a great deal of beauty, a great many virtues."

M. de Mauves busied himself for a moment in lighting another cigar, and when he had finished, with a return of his confidential

5. Wit, understanding.
6. Among you.
7. Cabbage soup.
8. That type of person.

9. French poet, dramatist, and story writer (1810–1857), whose works have none of the didactic element present in those of Wordsworth.

smile, "I suspect you of thinking," he said, "that I don't do my wife justice. Take care,—take care, young man; that's a dangerous assumption. In general, a man always does his wife justice. More than justice," cried the Baron with a laugh,—"that we keep for the wives of other men!"

Longmore afterwards remembered it in favor of the Baron's grace of address that he had not measured at this moment the dusky abyss over which it hovered. But a sort of deepening subterranean echo lingered on his spiritual ear. For the present his keenest sensation was a desire to get away and cry aloud that M. de Mauves was an arrogant fool. He bade him an abrupt good-night, which must serve also, he said, as good by.

"Decidedly, then, you go?" said M. de Mauves, almost peremptorily.

"Decidedly."

"Of course you'll come and say good by to Madame de Mauves." His tone implied that the omission would be most uncivil; but there seemed to Longmore something so ludicrous in his taking a lesson in consideration from M. de Mauves, that he burst into a laugh. The Baron frowned, like a man for whom it was a new and most unpleasant sensation to be perplexed. "You're a queer fellow," he murmured, as Longmore turned away, not foreseeing that he would think him a very queer fellow indeed before he had done with him. Longmore sat down to dinner at his hotel with his usual good intentions; but as he was lifting his first glass of wine to his lips, he suddenly fell to musing and set down his wine untasted. His revery lasted long, and when he emerged from it, his fish was cold; but this mattered little, for his appetite was gone. That evening he packed his trunk with a kind of indignant energy. This was so effective that the operation was accomplished before bedtime, and as he was not in the least sleepy, he devoted the interval to writing two letters; one was a short note to Madame de Mauves, which he intrusted to a servant, to be delivered the next morning. He had found it best, he said, to leave Saint-Germain immediately, but he expected to be back in Paris in the early autumn. The other letter was the result of his having remembered a day or two before that he had not yet complied with Mrs. Draper's injunction to give her an account of his impressions of her friend. The present occasion seemed propitious, and he wrote half a dozen pages. His tone, however, was grave, and Mrs. Draper, on receiving them, was slightly disappointed—she would have preferred a stronger flavor of rhapsody. But what chiefly concerns us is the concluding sentences.

"The only time she ever spoke to me of her marriage," he wrote, "she intimated that it had been a perfect love-match. With all abatements, I suppose most marriages are; but in her case this would

mean more, I think, than in that of most women; for her love was
an absolute idealization. She believed her husband was a hero of
rose-colored romance, and he turns out to be not even a hero of
very sad-colored reality. For some time now she has been sounding
her mistake, but I don't believe she has touched the bottom of it
yet. She strikes me as a person who is begging off from full knowledge,—who has struck a truce with painful truth, and is trying
awhile the experiment of living with closed eyes. In the dark she
tries to see again the gilding on her idol. Illusion of course is illusion, and one must always pay for it; but there is something truly
tragical in seeing an earthly penalty levied on such divine folly as
this. As for M. de Mauves, he's a Frenchman to his fingers' ends;
and I confess I should dislike him for this if he were a much better
man. He can't forgive his wife for having married him too sentimentally and loved him too well; for in some uncorrupted corner of
his being he feels, I suppose, that as she saw him, so he ought to
have been. It's a perpetual vexation to him that a little American
bourgeoise should have fancied him a finer fellow than he is, or
than he at all wants to be. He hasn't a glimmering of real acquaintance with his wife; he can't understand the stream of passion flowing so clear and still. To tell the truth, I hardly can myself; but when
I see the spectacle I can admire it furiously. M. de Mauves, at any
rate, would like to have the comfort of feeling that his wife was as
corruptible as himself; and you'll hardly believe me when I tell you
that he goes about intimating to gentlemen whom he deems worthy
of the knowledge, that it would be a convenience to him to have
them make love to her."

V

On reaching Paris, Longmore straightway purchased a Murray's[1]
"Belgium," to help himself to believe that he would start on the
morrow for Brussels; but when the morrow came, it occurred to
him that, by way of preparation, he ought to acquaint himself more
intimately with the Flemish painters in the Louvre. This took a
whole morning, but it did little to hasten his departure. He had
abruptly left Saint-Germain, because it seemed to him that respect
for Madame de Mauves demanded that he should allow her husband no reason to suppose that he had understood him; but now
that he had satisfied this immediate need of delicacy, he found himself thinking more and more ardently of Euphemia. It was a poor
expression of ardor to be lingering irresolutely on the deserted boulevards, but he detested the idea of leaving Saint-Germain five hundred miles behind him. He felt very foolish, nevertheless, and
wandered about nervously, promising himself to take the next train;

---

1. John Murray (1808–1892), an English publisher of a series of guidebooks for
travelers on the Continent.

but a dozen trains started, and Longmore was still in Paris. This sentimental tumult was more than he had bargained for, and, as he looked in the shop windows, he wondered whether it was a "passion." He had never been fond of the word, and had grown up with a kind of horror of what it represented. He had hoped that when he fell in love, he should do it with an excellent conscience, with no greater agitation than a mild general glow of satisfaction. But here was a sentiment compounded of pity and anger, as well as admiration, and bristling with scruples and doubts. He had come abroad to enjoy the Flemish painters and all others; but what fair-tressed saint of Van Eyck or Memling was so appealing a figure as Madame de Mauves? His restless steps carried him at last out of the long villa-bordered avenue which leads to the Bois de Boulogne.[2]

Summer had fairly begun, and the drive beside the lake was empty, but there were various loungers on the benches and chairs, and the great café had an air of animation. Longmore's walk had given him an appetite, and he went into the establishment and demanded a dinner, remarking for the hundredth time, as he observed the smart little tables disposed in the open air, how much better they ordered this matter in France.

"Will monsieur dine in the garden, or in the salon?" asked the waiter. Longmore chose the garden; and observing that a great vine of June roses was trained over the wall of the house, placed himself at a table near by, where the best of dinners was served him on the whitest of linen, in the most shining of porcelain. It so happened that his table was near a window, and that as he sat he could look into a corner of the salon. So it was that his attention rested on a lady seated just within the window, which was open, face to face apparently to a companion who was concealed by the curtain. She was a very pretty woman, and Longmore looked at her as often as was consistent with good manners. After a while he even began to wonder who she was, and to suspect that she was one of those ladies whom it is no breach of good manners to look at as often as you like. Longmore, too, if he had been so disposed, would have been the more free to give her all his attention, that her own was fixed upon the person opposite to her. She was what the French call a *belle brune*,[3] and though our hero, who had rather a conservative taste in such matters, had no great relish for her bold outlines and even bolder coloring, he could not help admiring her expression of basking contentment.

She was evidently very happy, and her happiness gave her an air of innocence. The talk of her friend, whoever he was, abundantly suited her humor, for she sat listening to him with a broad, lazy

2. A fashionable Paris park.   3. Beautiful brunette.

smile, and interrupted him occasionally, while she crunched her bon-
bons, with a murmured response, presumably as broad, which
seemed to deepen his eloquence. She drank a great deal of champagne and ate an immense number of strawberries, and was plainly
altogether a person with an impartial relish for strawberries, champagne, and what she would have called *bêtises*.[4]

They had half finished dinner when Longmore sat down, and he
was still in his place when they rose. She had hung her bonnet on a
nail above her chair, and her companion passed round the table to
take it down for her. As he did so, she bent her head to look at a
wine stain on her dress, and in the movement exposed the greater
part of the back of a very handsome neck. The gentleman observed
it, and observed also, apparently, that the room beyond them was
empty; that he stood within eyeshot of Longmore he failed to observe. He stooped suddenly and imprinted a gallant kiss on the fair
expanse. Longmore then recognized M. de Mauves. The recipient
of this vigorous tribute put on her bonnet, using his flushed smile as
a mirror, and in a moment they passed through the garden, on their
way to their carriage.

Then, for the first time, M. de Mauves perceived Longmore. He
measured with a rapid glance the young man's relation to the open
window, and checked himself in the impulse to stop and speak to
him. He contented himself with bowing with great gravity as he
opened the gate for his companion.

That evening Longmore made a railway journey, but not to Brussels. He had effectually ceased to care about Brussels; the only thing
he now cared about was Madame de Mauves. The atmosphere of his
mind had had a sudden clearing up; pity and anger were still
throbbing there, but they had space to rage at their pleasure, for
doubts and scruples had abruptly departed. It was little, he felt,
that he could interpose between her resignation and the unsparing
harshness of her position; but that little, if it involved the sacrifice
of everything that bound him to the tranquil past it seemed to him
that he could offer her with a rapture which at last made reflection
a woefully halting substitute for faith. Nothing in his tranquil past
had given such a zest to consciousness as the sense of tending with
all his being to a single aim which bore him company on his journey
to Saint-Germain. How to justify his return, how to explain his
ardor, troubled him little. He was not sure, even, that he wished to
be understood; he wished only to feel that it was by no fault of his
that Madame de Mauves was alone with the ugliness of fate. He was
conscious of no distinct desire to "make love" to her; if he could
have uttered the essence of his longing, he would have said that he
wished her to remember that in a world colored gray to her vision

4. Frivolities.

by disappointment, there was one vividly honest man. She might certainly have remembered it, however, without his coming back to remind her; and it is not to be denied that, as he packed his valise that evening, he wished immensely to hear the sound of her voice.

He waited the next day till his usual hour of calling,—the late afternoon; but he learned at the door that Madame de Mauves was not at home. The servant offered the information that she was walking in the forest. Longmore went through the garden and out of the little door into the lane, and, after half an hour's vain exploration, saw her coming toward him at the end of a green by-path. As he appeared, she stopped for a moment, as if to turn aside; then recognizing him, she slowly advanced, and he was soon shaking hands with her.

"Nothing has happened," she said, looking at him fixedly. "You're not ill?"

"Nothing, except that when I got to Paris I found how fond I had grown of Saint-Germain."

She neither smiled nor looked flattered; it seemed indeed to Longmore that she was annoyed. But he was uncertain, for he immediately perceived that in his absence the whole character of her face had altered. It told him that something momentous had happened. It was no longer self-contained melancholy that he read in her eyes, but grief and agitation which had lately struggled with that passionate love of peace of which she had spoken to him, and forced it to know that deep experience is never peaceful. She was pale, and she had evidently been shedding tears. He felt his heart beating hard; he seemed now to know her secrets. She continued to look at him with a contracted brow, as if his return had given her a sense of responsibility too great to be disguised by a commonplace welcome. For some moments, as he turned and walked beside her, neither spoke; then abruptly,—"Tell me truly, Mr. Longmore," she said, "why you have come back."

He turned and looked at her with an air which startled her into a certainty of what she had feared. "Because I've learned the real answer to the question I asked you the other day. You're not happy, —you're too good to be happy on the terms offered you. Madame de Mauves," he went on with a gesture which protested against a gesture of her own, "I can't be happy if you're not. I don't care for anything so long as I see such a depth of unconquerable sadness in your eyes. I found during three dreary days in Paris that the thing in the world I most care for is this daily privilege of seeing you. I know it's absolutely brutal to tell you I admire you; it's an insult to you to treat you as if you had complained to me or appealed to me. But such a friendship as I waked up to there"—and he tossed his head toward the distant city—"is a potent force, I assure you; and when forces are compressed they explode. But if you had told me every trouble in your heart, it would have mattered little; I couldn't say more than I must say now,—that if that in life from which you've hoped most has given you least, *my* devoted respect will refuse no service and betray no trust."

She had begun to make marks in the earth with the point of her parasol; but she stopped and listened to him in perfect immobility. Rather, her immobility was not perfect; for when he stopped speaking a faint flush had stolen into her cheek. It told Longmore that she was moved, and his first perceiving it was the happiest instant of his life. She raised her eyes at last, and looked at him with what at first seemed a pleading dread of excessive emotion.

"Thank you—thank you! she said, calmly enough; but the next moment her own emotion overcame her calmness, and she burst into tears. Her tears vanished as quickly as they came, but they did Longmore a world of good. He had always felt indefinably afraid of her; her being had somehow seemed fed by a deeper faith and a stronger will than his own; but her half-dozen smothered sobs showed him the bottom of her heart, and assured him that she was weak enough to be grateful.

"Excuse me," she said; "I'm too nervous to listen to you. I believe I could have faced an enemy to-day, but I can't endure a friend."

"You're killing yourself with stoicism,—that's my belief," he cried. "Listen to a friend for his own sake, if not for yours. I have never ventured to offer you an atom of compassion, and you can't accuse yourself of an abuse of charity."

She looked about her with a kind of weary confusion which promised a reluctant attention. But suddenly perceiving by the wayside the fallen log on which they had rested a few evenings before, she went and sat down on it in impatient resignation, and looked at Longmore, as he stood silent, watching her, with a glance which seemed to urge that, if she was charitable now, he must be very wise.

"Something came to my knowledge yesterday," he said as he sat down beside her, "which gave me a supreme sense of your moral isolation. You are truth itself, and there is no truth about you. You believe in purity and duty and dignity, and you live in a world in which they are daily belied. I sometimes ask myself with a kind of rage how you ever came into such a world,—and why the perversity of fate never let me know you before."

"I like my 'world' no better than you do, and it was not for its own sake I came into it. But what particular group of people is worth pinning one's faith upon? I confess it sometimes seems to me that men and women are very poor creatures. I suppose I'm romantic. I have a most unfortunate taste for poetic fitness. Life is hard prose, which one must learn to read contentedly. I believe I once thought that all the prose was in America, which was very foolish. What I thought, what I believed, what I expected, when I was an ignorant girl, fatally addicted to falling in love with my own theories, is more than I can begin to tell you now. Sometimes, when I remember certain impulses, certain illusions of those days, they take away my breath, and I wonder my bedazzled visions didn't lead me into troubles greater than any I have now to lament. I had a conviction which you would probably smile at if I were to attempt to express it to you. It was a singular form for passionate faith to take, but it had all of the sweetness and the ardor of passionate faith. It led me to take a great step, and it lies behind me now in the distance like a shadow melting slowly in the light of experience. It has faded, but it has not vanished. Some feelings, I am sure, die only with ourselves; some illusions are as much the condition of our life as our heart-beats. They say that life itself is an illusion,—that this world is a shadow of which the reality is yet to come. Life is all of a piece, then, and there is no shame in being miserably human. As for my 'isolation,' it doesn't greatly matter; it's the fault, in part, of my obstinacy. There have been times when I have been frantically distressed, and, to tell you the truth, wretchedly homesick, because my maid—a jewel of a maid—lied to me with every second breath. There have been moments when I have wished I was the daughter of a poor New England minister, living in a little white house under a couple of elms, and doing all the housework."

She had begun to speak slowly, with an air of effort; but she went on quickly, as if talking were a relief. "My marriage introduced me to people and things which seemed to me at first very strange and then very horrible, and then, to tell the truth, very contemptible. At first I expended a great deal of sorrow and dismay and pity on it all; but there soon came a time when I began to wonder whether it was worth one's tears. If I could tell you the eternal friendships I've seen broken, the inconsolable woes consoled, the jealousies and vanities leading off the dance, you would agree with me that tempers like yours and mine can understand neither such losses nor such compensations. A year ago, while I was in the country, a friend of mine was in despair at the infidelity of her husband; she wrote me a most tragical letter, and on my return to Paris I went immediately to see her. A week had elapsed, and, as I had seen stranger things, I thought she might have recovered her spirits. Not at all; she was still in despair,—but at what? At the conduct, the abandoned, shameless conduct of Mme. de T. You'll imagine, of course, that Mme. de T. was the lady whom my friend's husband preferred to his wife. Far from it; he had never seen her. Who, then, was Mme. de T.? Mme de T. was cruelly devoted to M. de V. And who was M. de V.? M. de V.—in two words, my friend was cultivating two jealousies at once. I hardly know what I said to her; something, at any rate, that she found unpardonable, for she quite gave me up. Shortly afterward my husband proposed we should cease to live in Paris, and I gladly assented, for I believe I was falling into a state of mind that made me a detestable companion. I should have preferred to go quite into the country, into Auvergne, where my husband has a place. But to him Paris, in some degree, is necessary, and Saint-Germain has been a sort of compromise."

"A sort of compromise!" Longmore repeated. "That's your whole life."

"It's the life of many people, of most people of quiet tastes, and it is certainly better than acute distress. One is at loss theoretically to defend a compromise; but if I found a poor creature clinging to one from day to day, I should think it poor friendship to make him lose his hold." Madame de Mauves had no sooner uttered these words than she smiled faintly, as if to mitigate their personal application.

"Heaven forbid," said Longmore, "that one should do that unless one has something better to offer. And yet I am haunted by a vision of a life in which you should have found no compromises, for they are a perversion of natures that tend only to goodness and rectitude. As I see it, you should have found happiness serene, profound, complete; a *femme de chambre*[5] not a jewel perhaps, but warranted to tell but one fib a day; a society possibly rather provincial, but (in spite of your poor opinion of mankind) a good deal of solid virtue; jealousies and vanities very tame, and no particular iniquities and adulteries. A husband," he added after a moment,—"a husband of your own faith and race and spiritual substance, who would have loved you well."

She rose to her feet, shaking her head. "You are very kind to go to the expense of visions for me. Visions are vain things; we must make the best of the reality."

"And yet," said Longmore, provoked by what seemed the very wantonness of her patience, "the reality, if I'm not mistaken, has very recently taken a shape that keenly tests your philosophy."

She seemed on the point of replying that his sympathy was too zealous; but a couple of impatient tears in his eyes proved that it was founded on a devotion to which it was impossible not to defer. "Philosophy?" she said. "I have none. Thank Heaven!" she cried, with vehemence, "I have none. I believe, Mr. Longmore," she added in a moment, "that I have nothing on earth but a conscience,—it's a good time to tell you so,—nothing but a dogged,

5. Personal maidservant.

clinging, inexpugnable conscience. Does that prove me to be indeed of your faith and race, and have you one for which you can say as much? I don't say it in vanity, for I believe that if my conscience will prevent me from doing anything very base, it will effectually prevent me from doing anything very fine."

"I am delighted to hear it," cried Longmore. "We are made for each other. It's very certain I too shall never do anything fine. And yet I have fancied that in my case this inexpugnable organ you so eloquently describe might be blinded and gagged awhile, in a fine cause, if not turned out of doors. In yours," he went on with the same appealing irony, "is it absolutely invincible?"

But her fancy made no concession to his sarcasm. "Don't laugh at your conscience," she answered gravely; "that's the only blasphemy I know."

She had hardly spoken when she turned suddenly at an unexpected sound, and at the same moment Longmore heard a footstep in an adjacent by-path which crossed their own at a short distance from where they stood.

"It's M. de Mauves," said Euphemia directly, and moved slowly forward. Longmore, wondering how she knew it, had overtaken her by the time her husband advanced into sight. A solitary walk in the forest was a pastime to which M. de Mauves was not addicted, but he seemed on this occasion to have resorted to it with some equanimity. He was smoking a fragrant cigar, and his thumb was thrust into the armhole of his waistcoat, with an air of contemplative serenity. He stopped short with surprise on seeing his wife and her companion, and Longmore considered his surprise impertinent. He glanced rapidly from one to the other, fixed Longmore's eye sharply for a single instant, and then lifted his hat with formal politeness.

"I was not aware," he said, turning to Madame de Mauves, "that I might congratulate you on the return of monsieur."

"You should have known it," she answered gravely, "if I had expected Mr. Longmore's return."

She had become very pale, and Longmore felt that this was a first meeting after a stormy parting. "My return was unexpected to myself," he said. "I came last evening."

M. de Mauves smiled with extreme urbanity. "It's needless for me to welcome you. Madame de Mauves knows the duties of hospitality." And with another bow he continued his walk.

Madame de Mauves and her companion returned slowly home, with few words, but, on Longmore's part at least, many thoughts. The Baron's appearance had given him an angry chill: it was a dusky cloud reabsorbing the light which had begun to shine between himself and his companion.

He watched Euphemia narrowly as they went, and wondered what she had last had to suffer. Her husband's presence had checked her frankness, but nothing indicated that she had accepted the insulting meaning of his words. Matters were evidently at a crisis between them, and Longmore wondered vainly what it was on Euphemia's part that prevented an absolute rupture. What did she suspect?—how much did she know? To what was she resigned?—how much had she forgiven? How, above all, did she reconcile with knowledge, or with suspicion, that ineradicable tenderness of which she had just now all but assured him? "She has loved him once," Longmore said with a sinking of the heart, "and with her to love once is to commit one's being forever. Her husband thinks her too rigid! What would a poet call it?"

He relapsed with a kind of aching impotence into the sense of her being somehow beyond him, unattainable, immeasurable by his own fretful spirit. Suddenly he gave three passionate switches in the air with his cane, which made Madame de Mauves look round. She could hardly have guessed that they meant that where ambition was so vain, it was an innocent compensation to plunge into worship.

Madame de Mauves found in her drawing-room the little elderly Frenchman, M. de Chalumeau, whom Longmore had observed a few days before on the terrace. On this occasion, too, Madame Clairin was entertaining him, but as his sister-in-law came in she surrendered her post and addressed herself to our hero. Longmore, at thirty, was still an ingenuous youth, and there was something in this lady's large coquetry which had the power of making him blush. He was surprised at finding he had not absolutely forfeited her favor by his deportment at their last interview, and a suspicion of her meaning to approach him on another line completed his uneasiness.

"So you've returned from Brussels," she said, "by way of the forest."

"I've not been to Brussels. I returned yesterday from Paris by the only way,—by the train."

Madame Clairin stared and laughed. "I've never known a young man to be so fond of Saint-Germain. They generally declare it's horribly dull."

"That's not very polite to you," said Longmore, who was vexed at his blushes, and determined not to be abashed.

"Ah, what am I?" demanded Madame Clairin, swinging open her fan. "I'm the dullest thing here. They've not had your success with my sister-in-law."

"It would have been very easy to have it. Madame de Mauves is kindness itself."

"To her own countrymen!"

Longmore remained silent; he hated the talk. Madame Clairin looked at him a moment, and then turned her head and surveyed Euphemia, to whom M. de Chalumeau was serving up another epigram, which she was receiving with a slight droop of the head and her eyes absently wandering through the window. "Don't pretend to tell me," she murmured suddenly, "that you're not in love with that pretty woman."

"*Allons donc!*"[6] cried Longmore, in the best French he had ever uttered. He rose the next minute, and took a hasty farewell.

VI

He allowed several days to pass without going back; it seemed delicate not to appear to regard his friend's frankness during their last interview as a general invitation. This cost him a great effort, for hopeless passions are not the most deferential; and he had, moreover, a constant fear, that if, as he believed, the hour of supreme "explanations" had come, the magic of her magnanimity might convert M. de Mauves. Vicious men, it was abundantly recorded, had been so converted as to be acceptable to God, and the something divine in Euphemia's temper would sanctify any means she should choose to employ. Her means, he kept repeating, were no business of his, and the essence of his admiration ought to be to respect her freedom; but he felt as if he should turn away into a world out of which most of the joy had departed, if her freedom, after all, should spare him only a murmured "Thank you."

When he called again he found to his vexation that he was to run the gantlet of Madame Clairin's officious hospitality. It was one of the first mornings of perfect summer, and the drawing-room, through the open windows, was flooded with a sweet confusion of odors and bird-notes which filled him with the hope that Madame de Mauves would come out and spend half the day in the forest. But Madame Clairin, with her hair not yet dressed, emerged like a brassy discord in a maze of melody.

At the same moment the servant returned with Euphemia's regrets; she was indisposed and unable to see Mr. Longmore. The young man knew that he looked disappointed, and that Madame Clairin was observing him, and this consciousness impelled her to give him a glance of almost aggressive frigidity. This was apparently what she desired. She wished to throw him off his balance, and, if he was not mistaken, she had the means.

"Put down your hat, Mr. Longmore," she said, "and be polite for once. You were not at all polite the other day when I asked you that friendly question about the state of your heart."

"I have no heart—to talk about," said Longmore, uncompromisingly.

6. Come now!

"As well say you've none at all. I advise you to cultivate a little eloquence; you may have use for it. That was not an idle question of mine; I don't ask idle questions. For a couple of months now that you've been coming and going among us, it seems to me that you have had very few to answer of any sort."

"I have certainly been very well treated," said Longmore.

Madame Clairin was silent a moment, and then—"Have you never felt disposed to ask any?" she demanded.

Her look, her tone, were so charged with roundabout meanings that it seemed to Longmore as if even to understand her would savor of dishonest complicity. "What is it you have to tell me?" he asked, frowning and blushing.

Madame Clairin flushed. It is rather hard, when you come bearing yourself very much as the sibyl[7] when she came to the Roman king, to be treated as something worse than a vulgar gossip. "I might tell you, Mr. Longmore," she said, "that you have as bad a *ton*[8] as any young man I ever met. Where have you lived,—what are your ideas? I wish to call your attention to a fact which it takes some delicacy to touch upon. You have noticed, I supposed, that my sister-in-law is not the happiest woman in the world."

Longmore assented with a gesture.

Madame Clairin looked slightly disappointed at his want of enthusiasm. Nevertheless—"You have formed, I suppose," she continued, "your conjectures on the causes of her—dissatisfaction."

"Conjecture has been superfluous. I have seen the causes—or at least a specimen of them—with my own eyes."

"I know perfectly what you mean. My brother, in a single word, is in love with another woman. I don't judge him; I don't judge my sister-in-law. I permit myself to say that in her position I would have managed otherwise. I would have kept my husband's affection, or I would have frankly done without it, before this. But my sister is an odd compound; I don't profess to understand her. Therefore it is, in a measure, that I appeal to you, her fellow-countryman. Of course you'll be surprised at my way of looking at the matter, and I admit that it's a way in use only among people whose family traditions compel them to take a superior view of things." Madame Clairin paused, and Longmore wondered where her family traditions were going to lead her.

"Listen," she went on. "There has never been a De Mauves who has not given his wife the right to be jealous. We know our history for ages back, and the fact is established. It's a shame if you like,

---

7. The sibyls were inspired women of antiquity who were reputed to possess powers of prophecy; one of them visited Tarquin II, an early king of Rome, who purchased her wisdom for guidance in time of national calamity.

8. Manner, deportment.

but it's something to have a shame with such a pedigree. The De Mauves are real Frenchmen, and their wives—I may say it—have been worthy of them. You may see all their portraits in our Château de Mauves; every one of them an 'injured' beauty, but not one of them hanging her head. Not one of them had the bad taste to be jealous, and yet not one in a dozen was guilty of an escapade,—not one of them was talked about. There's good sense for you! How they managed—go and look at the dusky, faded canvases and pastels, and ask. They were femmes d'esprit. When they had a headache, they put on a little rouge and came to supper as usual; and when they had a heart-ache, they put a little rouge on their hearts. These are fine traditions, and it doesn't seem to me fair that a little American bourgeoise should come in and interrupt them, and should hang her photograph, with her obstinate little *air penché*,⁹ in the gallery of our shrewd fine ladies. A De Mauves must be a De Mauves. When she married my brother, I don't suppose she took him for a member of a *societé de bonnes œuvres*.¹ I don't say we're right; who is right? But we're as history has made us, and if any one is to change, it had better be Madame de Mauves herself." Again Madame Clairin paused and opened and closed her fan. "Let her conform!" she said, with amazing audacity.

Longmore's reply was ambiguous; he simply said, "Ah!"

Madame Clairin's pious retrospect had apparently imparted an honest zeal to her indignation. "For a long time," she continued, "my sister has been taking the attitude of an injured woman, affecting a disgust with the world, and shutting herself up to read the 'Imitation.'² I've never remarked on her conduct, but I've quite lost patience with it. When a woman with her prettiness lets her husband wander, she deserves her fate. I don't wish you to agree with me—on the contrary; but I call such a woman a goose. She must have bored him to death. What has passed between them for many months needn't concern us; what provocation my sister has had—monstrous, if you wish—what ennui my brother has suffered. It's enough that a week ago, just after you had ostensibly gone to Brussels, something happened to produce an explosion. She found a letter in his pocket—a photograph—a trinket—*que sais-je?*³ At any rate, the scene was terrible. I didn't listen at the keyhole, and I don't know what was said; but I have reason to believe that my brother was called to account as I fancy none of his ancestors have ever been,—even by injured sweethearts."

Longmore had leaned forward in silent attention with his elbows on his knees, and instinctively he dropped his face into his hands. "Ah, poor woman!" he groaned.

9. Downcast look.
1. A charitable or welfare organization.

2. *The Imitation of Christ* by Thomas à Kempis (1380–1471).
3. I don't know what.

"Voilà!"[4] said Madame Clairin. "You pity her."

"Pity her?" cried Longmore, looking up with ardent eyes and forgetting the spirit of Madame Clairin's narrative in the miserable facts. "Don't you?"

"A little. But I'm not acting sentimentally; I'm acting politically. I wish to arrange things,—to see my brother free to do as he chooses, —to see Euphemia contented. Do you understand me?"

"Very well, I think. You're the most immoral person I've lately had the privilege of conversing with."

Madame Clairin shrugged her shoulders. "Possibly. When was there a great politician who was not immoral?"

"Nay," said Longmore in the same tone. "You're too superficial to be a great politician. You don't begin to know anything about Madame de Mauves."

Madame Clairin inclined her head to one side, eyed Longmore sharply, mused a moment, and then smiled with an excellent imitation of intelligent compassion. "It's not in my interest to contradict you."

"It would be in your interest to learn, Madame Clairin," the young man went on with unceremonious candor, "what honest men most admire in a woman,—and to recognize it when you see it."

Longmore certainly did injustice to her talents for diplomacy, for she covered her natural annoyance at this sally with a pretty piece of irony. "So you *are* in love!" she quietly exclaimed.

Longmore was silent awhile. "I wonder if you would understand me," he said at last, "if I were to tell you that I have for Madame de Mauves the most devoted friendship?"

"You underrate my intelligence. But in that case you ought to exert your influence to put an end to these painful domestic scenes."

"Do you suppose," cried Longmore, "that she talks to me about her domestic scenes?"

Madame Clairin stared. "Then your friendship isn't returned?" And as Longmore turned away, shaking his head,—"Now, at least," she added, "she will have something to tell you. I happen to know the upshot of my brother's last interview with his wife." Longmore rose to his feet as a sort of protest against the indelicacy of the position into which he was being forced; but all that made him tender made him curious, and she caught in his averted eyes an expression which prompted her to strike her blow. "My brother is monstrously in love with a certain person in Paris; of course he ought not to be; but he wouldn't be a De Mauves if he were not. It was this unsanctified passion that spoke. 'Listen, madam,' he cried at last: 'let us live like people who understand life! It's unpleasant to be forced to say such things outright, but you have a way of bringing one down

4. There!

to the rudiments. I'm faithless, I'm heartless, I'm brutal, I'm everything horrible,—it's understood. Take your revenge, console yourself; you're too pretty a woman to have anything to complain of.
Here's a handsome young man sighing himself into a consumption
for you. Listen to the poor fellow, and you'll find that virtue is
none the less becoming for being good-natured. You'll see that it's
not after all such a doleful world, and that there is even an advantage
in having the most impudent of husbands.'" Madame Clairin
paused; Longmore had turned very pale. "You may believe it," she
said; "the speech took place in my presence; things were done in
order. And now, Mr. Longmore,"—this with a smile which he was
too troubled at the moment to appreciate, but which he remembered later with a kind of awe,—"we count upon you!"

"He said this to her, face to face, as you say it to me now?" Longmore asked slowly, after a silence.

"Word for word, and with the greatest politeness."

"And Madame de Mauves—what did she say?"

Madame Clairin smiled again. "To such a speech as that a woman
says—nothing. She had been sitting with a piece of needlework,
and I think she had not seen her husband since their quarrel the
day before. He came in with the gravity of an ambassador, and I'm
sure that when he made his *demande en mariage*[5] his manner was
not more respectful. He only wanted white gloves!" said Madame
Clairin. "Euphemia sat silent a few moments drawing her stitches,
and then without a word, without a glance, she walked out of the
room. It was just what she should have done!"

"Yes," Longmore repeated, "it was just what she should have
done."

"And I, left alone with my brother, do you know what I said?"
Longmore shook his head. "*Mauvais sujet!*" he suggested.

"'You've done me the honor,' I said, 'to take this step in my
presence. I don't pretend to qualify it. You know what you're
about, and it's your own affair. But you may confide in my discretion.' Do you think he has had reason to complain of it?" She
received no answer; Longmore was slowly turning away and passing
his gloves mechanically round the band of his hat. "I hope," she
cried, "you're not going to start for Brussels!"

Plainly, Longmore was deeply disturbed, and Madame Clairin
might flatter herself on the success of her plea for old-fashioned
manners. And yet there was something that left her more puzzled
than satisfied in the reflective tone with which he answered, "No, I
shall remain here for the present." The processes of his mind seemed
provokingly subterranean, and she would have fancied for a moment
that he was linked with her sister in some monstrous conspiracy of

5. Marriage proposal.

asceticism.

"Come this evening," she boldly resumed. "The rest will take care of itself. Meanwhile I shall take the liberty of telling my sister-in-law that I have repeated—in short, that I have put you *au fait*."[6]

Longmore started and colored, and she hardly knew whether he was going to assent or demur. "Tell her what you please. Nothing you can tell her will affect her conduct."

"Voyons![7] Do you mean to tell me that a woman, young, pretty, sentimental, neglected—insulted, if you will—? I see you don't believe it. Believe simply in your own opportunity! But for heaven's sake, if it's to lead anywhere, don't come back with that *visage de croquemort*.[8] You look as if you were going to bury your heart,— not to offer it to a pretty woman. You're much better when you smile. Come, do yourself justice."

"Yes," he said, "I must do myself justice." And abruptly, with a bow, he took his departure.

VII

He felt, when he found himself unobserved, in the open air, that he must plunge into violent action, walk fast and far, and defer the opportunity for thought. He strode away into the forest, swinging his cane, throwing back his head, gazing away into the verdurous vistas, and following the road without a purpose. He felt immensely excited, but he could hardly have said whether his emotion was a pain or a joy. It was joyous as all increase of freedom is joyous; something seemed to have been knocked down across his path; his destiny appeared to have rounded a cape and brought him into sight of an open sea. But his freedom resolved itself somehow into the need of despising all mankind, with a single exception; and the fact of Madame de Mauves inhabiting a planet contaminated by the presence of this baser multitude kept his elation from seeming a pledge of ideal bliss.

But she was there, and circumstance now forced them to be intimate. She had ceased to have what men call a secret for him, and this fact itself brought with it a sort of rapture. He had no prevision that he should "profit," in the vulgar sense, by the extraordinary position into which they had been thrown; it might be but a cruel trick of destiny to make hope a harsher mockery and renunciation a keener suffering. But above all this rose the conviction that she could do nothing that would not deepen his admiration.

It was this feeling that circumstance—unlovely as it was in itself —was to force the beauty of her character into more perfect relief,

6. In [possession of] the facts.   8. Undertaker's face.
7. See here!

that made him stride along as if he were celebrating a kind of spiritual festival. He rambled at random for a couple of hours, and found at last that he had left the forest behind him and had wandered into an unfamiliar region. It was a perfectly rural scene, and the still summer day gave it a charm for which its meagre elements but half accounted.

Longmore thought he had never seen anything so characteristically French; all the French novels seemed to have described it, all the French landscapists to have painted it. The fields and trees were of a cool metallic green; the grass looked as if it might stain your trousers, and the foliage your hands. The clear light had a sort of mild grayness; the sunbeams were of silver rather than gold. A great red-roofed, high-stacked farm-house, with whitewashed walls and a straggling yard, surveyed the high road, on one side, from behind a transparent curtain of poplars. A narrow stream, half choked with emerald rushes and edged with gray aspens, occupied the opposite quarter. The meadows rolled and sloped away gently to the low horizon, which was barely concealed by the continuous line of clipped and marshaled trees. The prospect was not rich, but it had a frank homeliness which touched the young man's fancy. It was full of light atmosphere and diffused sunshine, and if it was prosaic, it was soothing.

Longmore was disposed to walk further, and he advanced along the road beneath the poplars. In twenty minutes he came to a village which straggled away to the right, among orchards and *potagers*.[9] On the left, at a stone's throw from the road, stood a little pink-faced inn, which reminded him that he had not breakfasted, having left home with a prevision of hospitality from Madame de Mauves. In the inn he found a brick-tiled parlor and a hostess in sabots[1] and a white cap, whom, over the omelette she speedily served him,— borrowing license from the bottle of sound red wine which accompanied it,—he assured that she was a true artist. To reward his compliment, she invited him to smoke his cigar in her little garden behind the house.

Here he found a *tonnelle*[2] and a view of ripening crops, stretching down to the stream. The *tonnelle* was rather close, and he preferred to lounge on a bench against the pink wall, in the sun, which was not too hot. Here, as he rested and gazed and mused, he fell into a train of thought which, in an indefinable fashion, was a soft influence from the scene about him. His heart, which had been beating fast for the past three hours, gradually checked its pulses and left him looking at life with a rather more level gaze. The homely tavern sounds coming out through the open windows, the sunny stillness

9. Kitchen gardens.   2. Arbor.
1. Wooden shoes.

of the fields and crops, which covered so much vigorous natural life, suggested very little that was transcendental, had very little to say about renunciation,—nothing at all about spiritual zeal. They seemed to utter a message from plain ripe nature, to express the unperverted reality of things, to say that the common lot is not brilliantly amusing, and that the part of wisdom is to grasp frankly at experience, lest you miss it altogether. What reason there was for his falling a-wondering after this whether a deeply wounded heart might be soothed and healed by such a scene, it would be difficult to explain; certain it is that, as he sat there, he had a waking dream of an unhappy woman strolling by the slow-flowing stream before him, and pulling down the blossoming boughs in the orchards. He mused and mused, and at last found himself feeling angry that he could not somehow think worse of Madame de Mauves,—or at any rate think otherwise. He could fairly claim that in a sentimental way he asked very little of life,—he made modest demands on passion; why then should his only passion be born to ill-fortune? why should his first—his last—glimpse of positive happiness be so indissolubly linked with renunciation?

It is perhaps because, like many spirits of the same stock, he had in his composition a lurking principle of asceticism to whose authority he had ever paid an unquestioning respect, that he now felt all the vehemence of rebellion. To renounce—to renounce again—to renounce forever—was this all that youth and longing and resolve were meant for? Was experience to be muffled and mutilated, like an indecent picture? Was a man to sit and deliberately condemn his future to be the blank memory of a regret, rather than the long reverberation of a joy? Sacrifice? The word was a trap for minds muddled by fear, an ignoble refuge of weakness. To insist now seemed not to dare, but simply to be, to live on possible terms.

His hostess came out to hang a cloth to dry on the hedge, and, though her guest was sitting quietly enough, she seemed to see in his kindled eyes a flattering testimony to the quality of her wine.

As she turned back into the house, she was met by a young man whom Longmore observed in spite of his preoccupation. He was evidently a member of that jovial fraternity of artists whose very shabbiness has an affinity with the element of picturesqueness and unexpectedness in life which provokes a great deal of unformulated envy among people foredoomed to be respectable.

Longmore was struck first with his looking like a very clever man, and then with his looking like a very happy one. The combination, as it was expressed in his face, might have arrested the attention of even a less cynical philosopher. He had a slouched hat and a blond beard, a light easel under one arm, and an unfinished sketch in oils under the other.

He stopped and stood talking for some moments to the landlady with a peculiarly good-humored smile. They were discussing the possibilities of dinner; the hostess enumerated some very savory ones, and he nodded briskly, assenting to everything. It couldn't be, Longmore thought, that he found such soft contentment in the prospect of lamb chops and spinach and a *tarte à la crême*.[3] When the dinner had been ordered, he turned up his sketch, and the good woman fell a-wondering and looking off at the spot by the stream-side where he had made it.

Was it his work, Longmore wondered, that made him so happy? Was a strong talent the best thing in the world? The landlady went back to her kitchen, and the young painter stood as if he were waiting for something, beside the gate which opened upon the path across the fields. Longmore sat brooding and asking himself whether it was better to cultivate an art than to cultivate a passion. Before he had answered the question the painter had grown tired of waiting. He picked up a pebble, tossed it lightly into an upper window, and called, "Claudine!"

Claudine appeared; Longmore heard her at the window, bidding the young man to have patience. "But I'm losing my light," he said; "I must have my shadows in the same place as yesterday."

"Go without me, then," Claudine answered. "I will join you in ten minutes." Her voice was fresh and young; it seemed to say to Longmore that she was as happy as her companion.

"Don't forget the Chénier,"[4] cried the young man; and turning away, he passed out of the gate and followed the path across the fields until he disappeared among the trees by the side of the stream. Who was Claudine? Longmore vaguely wondered; and was she as pretty as her voice? Before long he had a chance to satisfy himself; she came out of the house with her hat and parasol, prepared to follow her companion. She had on a pink muslin dress and a little white hat, and she was as pretty as a Frenchwoman needs to be to be pleasing. She had a clear brown skin and a bright dark eye, and a step which seemed to keep time to some slow music, heard only by herself. Her hands were encumbered with various articles which she seemed to intend to carry with her. In one arm she held her parasol and a large roll of needlework, and in the other a shawl and a heavy white umbrella, such as painters use for sketching. Meanwhile she was trying to thrust into her pocket a paper-covered volume which Longmore saw to be the Poems of André Chénier; but in the effort she dropped the large umbrella, and uttered a half-smiling exclamation of disgust. Longmore stepped forward with a bow and picked up the umbrella, and as she, protesting her grati-

---

3. Tart with cream.

4. André Chénier (1762–1794), French poet of the early romantic movement.

tude, put out her hand to take it, it seemed to him that she was
unbecomingly overburdened.

"You have too much to carry," he said; "you must let me help
you."

"You're very good, monsieur," she answered. "My husband always forgets something. He can do nothing without his umbrella.
He is *d'une étourderie*[5]—"

"You must allow me to carry the umbrella," Longmore said. "It's
too heavy for a lady."

She assented, after many compliments to his politeness; and he
walked by her side into the meadow. She went lightly and rapidly,
picking her steps and glancing forward to catch a glimpse of her
husband. She was graceful, she was charming, she had an air of
decision and yet of sweetness, and it seemed to Longmore that a
young artist would work none the worse for having her seated at his
side, reading Chénier's iambics. They were newly married, he
supposed, and evidently their path of life had none of the mocking
crookedness of some others. They asked little; but what need one ask
more than such quiet summer days, with the creature one loves, by
a shady stream, with art and books and a wide, unshadowed horizon?
To spend such a morning, to stroll back to dinner in the red-tiled
parlor of the inn, to ramble away again as the sun got low,—all this
was a vision of bliss which floated before him, only to torture him
with a sense of the impossible. All Frenchwomen are not coquettes,
he remarked, as he kept pace with his companion. She uttered a
word now and then, for politeness' sake, but she never looked at
him, and seemed not in the least to care that he was a well-favored
young man. She cared for nothing but the young artist in the shabby
coat and the slouched hat, and for discovering where he had set up
his easel.

This was soon done. He was encamped under the trees, close to
the stream, and, in the diffused green shade of the little wood,
seemed to be in no immediate need of his umbrella. He received a
vivacious rebuke, however, for forgetting it, and was informed of
what he owed to Longmore's complaisance. He was duly grateful;
he thanked our hero warmly, and offered him a seat on the grass.
But Longmore felt like a marplot, and lingered only long enough
to glance at the young man's sketch, and to see it was a very clever
rendering of the silvery stream and the vivid green rushes. The
young wife had spread her shawl on the grass at the base of a tree,
and meant to seat herself when Longmore had gone, and murmur
Chénier's verses to the music of the gurgling river. Longmore looked
awhile from one to the other, barely stifled a sigh, bade them good
morning, and took his departure.

5. Absent-minded.

He knew neither where to go nor what to do; he seemed afloat on the sea of ineffectual longing. He strolled slowly back to the inn, and in the doorway met the landlady coming back from the butcher's with the lamb chops for the dinner of her lodgers.

"Monsieur has made the acquaintance of the *dame* of our young painter," she said with a broad smile,—a smile too broad for malicious meanings. "Monsieur has perhaps seen the young man's picture. It appears that he has a great deal of talent."

"His picture was very pretty," said Longmore, "but his *dame* was prettier still."

"She's a very nice little woman; but I pity her all the more."

"I don't see why she's to be pitied," said Longmore; "they seem a very happy couple."

The landlady gave a knowing nod.

"Don't trust to it, monsieur! Those artists,—*ça n'a pas de principes!*[6] From one day to another he can plant her there![7] I know them, *allez*. I've had them here very often; one year with one, another year with another."

Longmore was puzzled for a moment. Then, "You mean she's not his wife?" he asked.

She shrugged her shoulders. "What shall I tell you? They are not *des hommes sérieux*,[8] those gentlemen! They don't engage themselves for an eternity. It's none of my business, and I've no wish to speak ill of madame. She's a very nice little woman, and she loves her *jeune homme*[9] to distraction."

"Who is she?" asked Longmore. "What do you know about her?"

"Nothing for certain; but it's my belief that she's better than he. I've even gone so far as to believe that she's a lady,—a true lady,— and that she has given up a great many things for him. I do the best I can for them, but I don't believe she's been obliged all her life to content herself with a dinner of two courses." And she turned over her lamb chops tenderly, as if to say that though a good cook could imagine better things, yet if you could have but one course, lamb chops had much in their favor. "I shall cook them with bread crumbs. Voilà les femmes, monsieur!"[1]

Longmore turned away with the feeling that women were indeed a measureless mystery, and that it was hard to say whether there was greater beauty in their strength or in their weakness. He walked back to Saint-Germain, more slowly than he had come, with less philosophic resignation to any event, and more of the urgent egotism of the passion which philosophers call the supremely selfish one. Every now and then the episode of the happy young painter and the charming woman who had given up a great many things

6. They lack principles.
7. Drop her there (literally translated from the French, *la planter là*).
8. Men of good principles.
9. Young man.
1. That's women, sir!

for him rose vividly in his mind, and seemed to mock his moral unrest like some obtrusive vision of unattainable bliss.

The landlady's gossip cast no shadow on its brightness; her voice seemed that of the vulgar chorus of the uninitiated, which stands always ready with its gross prose rendering of the inspired passages in human action. Was it possible a man could take *that* from a woman,—take all that lent lightness to that other woman's footstep and intensity to her glance,—and not give her the absolute certainty of a devotion as unalterable as the process of the sun? Was it possible that such a rapturous union had the seeds of trouble,—that the charm of such a perfect accord could be broken by anything but death? Longmore felt an immense desire to cry out a thousand times "No!" for it seemed to him at last that he was somehow spiritually the same as the young painter, and that the latter's companion had the soul of Euphemia de Mauves.

The heat of the sun, as he walked along, became oppressive, and when he re-entered the forest he turned aside into the deepest shade he could find, and stretched himself on the mossy ground at the foot of a great beech. He lay for a while staring up into the verdurous dusk overhead, and trying to conceive Madame de Mauves hastening toward some quiet stream-side where he waited, as he had seen that trusting creature do an hour before. It would be hard to say how well he succeeded; but the effort soothed him rather than excited him, and as he had had a good deal both of moral and physical fatigue, he sank at last into a quiet sleep.

While he slept he had a strange, vivid dream. He seemed to be in a wood, very much like the one on which his eyes had lately closed; but the wood was divided by the murmuring stream he had left an hour before. He was walking up and down, he thought, restlessly and in intense expectation of some momentous event. Suddenly, at a distance, through the trees, he saw the gleam of a woman's dress, and hurried forward to meet her. As he advanced he recognized her, but he saw at the same time that she was on the opposite bank of the river. She seemed at first not to notice him, but when they were opposite each other she stopped and looked at him very gravely and pityingly. She made him no motion that he should cross the stream, but he wished greatly to stand by her side. He knew the water was deep, and it seemed to him that he knew that he should have to plunge, and that he feared that when he rose to the surface she would have disappeared. Nevertheless, he was going to plunge, when a boat turned into the current from above and came swiftly toward them, guided by an oarsman, who was sitting so that they could not see his face. He brought the boat to the bank where Longmore stood; the latter stepped in, and with a few strokes they touched the opposite shore. Longmore got out, and, though he was sure he had crossed the stream, Madame de Mauves was not there. He turned with a kind of agony and saw that now she was on the other bank,—the one he had left. She gave him a grave, silent glance, and walked away up the stream. The boat and the boatman resumed their course, but after going a short distance they stopped, and the boatman turned back and looked at the still divided couple. Then Longmore recognized him,—just as he had recognized him a few days before at the café in the Bois de Boulogne.

VIII

He must have slept some time after he ceased dreaming, for he had no immediate memory of his dream. It came back to him later, after he had roused himself and had walked nearly home. No great ingenuity was needed to make it seem a rather striking allegory, and it haunted and oppressed him for the rest of the day. He took refuge, however, in his quickened conviction that the only sound policy in life is to grasp unsparingly at happiness; and it seemed no more than one of the vigorous measures dictated by such a policy, to re-turn that evening to Madame de Mauves. And yet when he had decided to do so, and had carefully dressed himself, he felt an irresistible nervous tremor which made it easier to linger at his open window, wondering, with a strange mixture of dread and desire, whether Madame Clairin had told her sister-in-law that she had told him. . . . His presence now might be simply a gratuitous cause of suffering; and yet his absence might seem to imply that it was in the power of circumstances to make them ashamed to meet each other's eyes. He sat a long time with his head in his hands, lost in a painful confusion of hopes and questionings. He felt at moments as if he could throttle Madame Clairin, and yet he could not help asking himself whether it was not possible that she might have done him a service. It was late when he left the hotel, and as he entered the gate of the other house his heart was beating so that he was sure his voice would show it.

The servant ushered him into the drawing-room, which was empty, with the lamp burning low. But the long windows were open, and their light curtains swaying in a soft, warm wind, and Longmore stepped out upon the terrace. There he found Madame de Mauves alone, slowly pacing up and down. She was dressed in white, very simply, and her hair was arranged, not as she usually wore it, but in a single loose coil, like that of a person unprepared for company.

She stopped when she saw Longmore, seemed slightly startled, uttered an exclamation, and stood waiting for him to speak. He looked at her, tried to say something, but found no words. He knew it was awkward, it was offensive, to stand silent, gazing; but he could not say what was suitable, and he dared not say what he wished.

Her face was indistinct in the dim light, but he could see that her eyes were fixed on him, and he wondered what they expressed. Did they warn him, did they plead or did they confess to a sense of provocation? For an instant his head swam; he felt as if it would make all things clear to stride forward and fold her in his arms. But a moment later he was still standing looking at her; he had not moved; he knew that she had spoken, but he had not understood her.

"You were here this morning," she continued, and now, slowly, the meaning of her words came to him. "I had a bad headache and had to shut myself up." She spoke in her usual voice.

Longmore mastered his agitation and answered her without betraying himself: "I hope you are better now."

"Yes, thank you, I'm better—much better."

He was silent a moment, and she moved away to a chair and seated herself. After a pause he followed her and stood before her, leaning against the balustrade of the terrace. "I hoped you might have been able to come out for the morning into the forest. I went alone; it was a lovely day, and I took a long walk."

"It was a lovely day," she said absently, and sat with her eyes lowered, slowly opening and closing her fan. Longmore, as he watched her, felt more and more sure that her sister-in-law had seen her since her interview with him; that her attitude toward him was changed. It was this same something that chilled the ardor with which he had come, or at least converted the dozen passionate speeches which kept rising to his lips into a kind of reverential silence. No, certainly, he could not clasp her to his arms now, any more than some early worshipper could have clasped the marble statue in his temple. But Longmore's statue spoke at last, with a full human voice, and even with a shade of human hesitation. She looked up, and it seemed to him that her eyes shone through the dusk.

"I'm very glad you came this evening," she said. "I have a particular reason for being glad. I half expected you, and yet I thought it possible you might not come."

"As I have been feeling all day," Longmore answered, "it was impossible I should not come. I have spent the day in thinking of you."

She made no immediate reply, but continued to open and close her fan thoughtfully. At last,—"I have something to say to you," she said abruptly. "I want you to know to a certainty that I have a very high opinion of you." Longmore started and shifted his position. To what was she coming? But he said nothing, and she went on.

"I take a great interest in you; there's no reason why I should not say it,—I have a great friendship for you."

He began to laugh; he hardly knew why, unless that this seemed the very mockery of coldness. But she continued without heeding him.

"You know, I suppose, that a great disappointment always implies a great confidence—a great hope?"

"I have hoped," he said, "hoped strongly; but doubtless never rationally enough to have a right to bemoan my disappointment."

"You do yourself injustice. I have such confidence in your reason, that I should be greatly disappointed if I were to find it wanting."

"I really almost believe that you are amusing yourself at my expense," cried Longmore. "My reason? Reason is a mere word! The only reality in the world is *feeling!*"

She rose to her feet and looked at him gravely. His eyes by this time were accustomed to the imperfect light, and he could see that her look was reproachful, and yet that it was beseechingly kind. She shook her head impatiently, and laid her fan upon his arm with a strong pressure.

"If that were so, it would be a weary world. I know your feeling, however, nearly enough. You needn't try to express it. It's enough that it gives me the right to ask a favor of you,—to make an urgent, a solemn request."

"Make it; I listen."

"*Don't disappoint me.* If you don't understand me now, you will to-morrow, or very soon. When I said just now that I had a very high opinion of you, I meant it very seriously. It was not a vain compliment. I believe that there is no appeal one may make to your generosity which can remain long unanswered. If this were to happen,—if I were to find you selfish where I thought you generous, narrow where I thought you large,"—and she spoke slowly, with her voice lingering with emphasis on each of these words,—"vulgar where I thought you rare,—I should think worse of human nature. I should suffer,—I should suffer keenly. I should say to myself in the dull days of the future, 'There was one man who might have done so and so; and he, too, failed.' But this shall not be. You have made too good an impression on me not to make the very best. If you wish to please me forever, there's a way."

She was standing close to him, with her dress touching him, her eyes fixed on his. As she went on her manner grew strangely intense, and she had the singular appearance of a woman preaching reason with a kind of passion. Longmore was confused, dazzled, almost bewildered. The intention of her words was all remonstrance, refusal, dismissal; but her presence there, so close, so urgent, so personal, seemed a distracting contradiction of it. She had never been so lovely. In her white dress, with her pale face and deeply lighted eyes, she seemed the very spirit of the summer night. When she had ceased speaking, she drew a long breath; Longmore felt it on his cheek, and it stirred in his whole being a sudden, rapturous conjecture. Were her words in their soft severity a mere delusive spell, meant to throw into relief her almost ghostly beauty, and was this the only truth, the only reality, the only law?

He closed his eyes and felt that she was watching him, not without pain and perplexity herself. He looked at her again, met her own eyes, and saw a tear in each of them. Then this last suggestion of his desire seemed to die away with a stifled murmur, and her beauty, more and more radiant in the darkness, rose before him as a symbol of something vague which was yet more beautiful than itself.

"I may understand you to-morrow," he said, "but I don't understand you now."

"And yet I took counsel with myself to-day and asked myself how I had best speak to you. On one side, I might have refused to see you at all." Longmore made a violent movement, and she added: "In that case I should have written to you. I might see you, I thought, and simply say to you that there were excellent reasons why we should part, and that I begged this visit should be your last. This I inclined to do; what made me decide otherwise was—simply friendship! I said to myself that I should be glad to remember in future days, not that I had dismissed you, but that you had gone away out of the fulness of your own wisdom."

"The fulness—the fulness!" cried Longmore.

"I'm prepared, if necessary," Madame de Mauves continued after a pause, "to fall back upon my strict right. But, as I said before, I shall be greatly disappointed, if I am obliged to."

"When I hear you say that," Longmore answered, "I feel so angry, so horribly irritated, that I wonder it is not easy to leave you without more words."

"If you should go away in anger, this idea of mine about our parting would be but half realized. No, I don't want to think of you as angry; I don't want even to think of you as making a serious sacrifice. I want to think of you as—"

"As a creature who never has existed,—who never can exist! A creature who knew you without loving you,—who left you without regretting you!"

She turned impatiently away and walked to the other end of the terrace. When she came back, he saw that her impatience had become a cold sternness. She stood before him again, looking at him from head to foot, in deep reproachfulness, almost in scorn. Beneath her glance he felt a kind of shame. He colored; she observed it and withheld something she was about to say. She turned away again, walked to the other end of the terrace, and stood there looking away into the garden. It seemed to him that she had guessed he understood her, and slowly—slowly—half as the fruit of his vague self-reproach,—he did understand her. She was giving him a chance to do gallantly what it seemed unworthy of both of them he should do meanly.

She liked him, she must have liked him greatly, to wish so to spare him, to go to the trouble of conceiving an ideal of conduct for him. With this sense of her friendship,—her strong friendship she had just called it,—Longmore's soul rose with a new flight, and suddenly felt itself breathing a clearer air. The words ceased to seem a mere bribe to his ardor; they were charged with ardor themselves; they were a present happiness. He moved rapidly toward her with a feeling that this was something he might immediately enjoy.

They were separated by two thirds of the length of the terrace, and he had to pass the drawing-room window. As he did so he started with an exclamation. Madame Clairin stood posted there, watching him. Conscious, apparently, that she might be suspected of eavesdropping, she stepped forward with a smile and looked from Longmore to his hostess.

"Such a tête-à-tête as that," she said, "one owes no apology for interrupting. One ought to come in for good manners."

Madame de Mauves turned round, but she answered nothing. She looked straight at Longmore, and her eyes had extraordinary eloquence. He was not exactly sure, indeed, what she meant them to say; but they seemed to say plainly something of this kind: "Call it what you will, what you have to urge upon me is the thing which this woman can best conceive. What I ask of you is something she can't!" They seemed, somehow, to beg him to suffer her to be herself, and to intimate that that self was as little as possible like Madame Clairin. He felt an immense answering desire not to do anything which would seem natural to this lady. He had laid his hat and cane on the parapet of the terrace. He took them up, offered his hand to Madame de Mauves with a simple good night, bowed silently to Madame Clairin, and departed.

IX

He went home and without lighting his candle flung himself on his bed. But he got no sleep till morning; he lay hour after hour tossing, thinking, wondering; his mind had never been so active. It seemed to him that Euphemia had laid on him in those last moments an inspiring commission, and that she had expressed herself almost as largely as if she had listened assentingly to an assurance of his love. It was neither easy nor delightful thoroughly to understand her; but little by little her perfect meaning sank into his mind and soothed it with a sense of opportunity, which somehow stifled his sense of loss. For, to begin with, she meant that she could love him in no degree nor contingency, in no imaginable future. This was absolute; he felt that he could alter it no more than he could transpose the constellations he lay gazing at through his open window. He wondered what it was, in the background of her life, that she grasped so closely: a sense of duty, unquenchable to the end? a love that no offence could trample out? "Good heavens!" he thought, "is the world so rich in the purest pearls of passion, that such tenderness as that can be wasted forever,—poured away without a sigh into bottomless darkness?" Had she, in spite of the detestable present, some precious memory which contained the germ of a shrinking hope? Was she prepared to submit to everything and yet to believe? Was it strength, was it weakness, was it a vulgar fear, was it conviction, conscience, constancy?

Longmore sank back with a sigh and an oppressive feeling that it was vain to guess at such a woman's motives. He only felt that those of Madame de Mauves were buried deep in her soul, and that they must be of some fine temper, not of a base one. He had a dim, overwhelming sense of a sort of invulnerable constancy being the supreme law of her character,—a constancy which still found a foothold among crumbling ruins. "She has loved once," he said to himself as he rose and wandered to his window; "that's forever. Yes, yes,—if she loved again she would be *common*." He stood for a long time looking out into the starlit silence of the town and the forest, and thinking of what life would have been if *his* constancy had met hers unpledged. But life was this, now, and he must live. It was living keenly to stand there with a petition from such a woman to revolve. He was not to disappoint her, he was to justify a conception which it had beguiled her weariness to shape. Longmore's imagination swelled; he threw back his head and seemed to be looking for Madame de Mauves's conception among the blinking, mocking stars. But it came to him rather on the mild night-wind, as it wandered in over the house-tops which covered the rest of so many heavy human hearts. What she asked he felt that she was asking, not for her own sake (she feared nothing, she needed nothing), but for that of his own happiness and his own character. He must assent to destiny. Why else was he young and strong, intelligent and resolute? He must not give it to her to reproach him with thinking that she had a moment's attention for his love,—to plead, to argue, to break off in bitterness; he must see everything from above, her indifference and his own ardor; he must prove his strength, he must do the handsome thing; he must decide that the handsome thing was to submit to the inevitable, to be supremely delicate, to spare her all pain, to stifle his passion, to ask no compensation, to depart without delay and try to believe that wisdom is its own reward. All this, neither more nor less, it was a matter of friendship with Madame de Mauves to expect of him. And what should he gain by it? He should have pleased her! . . . He flung himself on his bed again, fell asleep at last, and slept till morning.

Before noon the next day he had made up his mind that he would leave Saint-Germain at once. It seemed easier to leave without seeing her, and yet if he might ask a grain of "compensation," it would be five minutes face to face with her. He passed a restless day. Wherever he went he seemed to see her standing before him in the dusky halo of evening, and looking at him with an air of still negation more intoxicating than the most passionate self-surrender. He must certainly go, and yet it was hideously hard. He compromised and went to Paris to spend the rest of the day. He strolled along the boulevards and looked at the shops, sat awhile in the Tuileries gardens[2] and looked at the shabby unfortunates for whom this only was nature and summer; but simply felt, as a result of it all, that it was a very dusty, dreary, lonely world into which Madame de Mauves was turning him away.

In a sombre mood he made his way back to the boulevards and sat down at a table on the great plain of hot asphalt, before a café. Night came on, the lamps were lighted, the tables near him found occupants, and Paris began to wear that peculiar evening look of hers which seems to say, in the flare of windows and theatre doors, and the muffled rumble of swift-rolling carriages, that this is no world for you unless you have your pockets lined and your scruples drugged. Longmore, however, had neither scruples nor desires; he looked at the swarming city for the first time with an easy sense of repaying its indifference. Before long a carriage drove up to the pavement directly in front of him, and remained standing for several minutes without its occupant getting out. It was one of those neat, plain coupés,[3] drawn by a single powerful horse, in which one is apt to imagine a pale, handsome woman, buried among silk cushions, and yawning as she sees the gas-lamps glittering in the gutters. At last the door opened and out stepped M. de Mauves. He stopped and leaned on the window for some time, talking in an excited manner to a person within. At last he gave a nod and the carriage rolled away. He stood swinging his cane and looking up and down the boulevard, with the air of a man fumbling, as one may say, with the loose change of time. He turned toward the café and was apparently, for want of anything better worth his attention,

2. An elaborate park laid out in the reign of Louis XIV, once the site of the royal palace which was burned in 1871 by the Commune.

3. The coupé was a closed, four-wheeled carriage with one seat for two persons inside, and an outside seat for the driver.

about to seat himself at one of the tables, when he perceived Long-more. He wavered an instant, and then, without a change in his nonchalant gait, strolled toward him with a bow and a vague smile.

It was the first time they had met since their encounter in the forest after Longmore's false start for Brussels. Madame Clairin's revelations, as we may call them, had not made the Baron especially present to his mind; he had another office for his emotions than disgust. But as M. de Mauves came toward him he felt deep in his heart that he abhorred him. He noticed, however, for the first time, a shadow upon the Baron's cool placidity, and his delight at finding that somewhere at last the shoe pinched *him*, mingled with his impulse to be as exasperatingly impenetrable as possible, enabled him to return the other's greeting with all his own self-possession.

M. de Mauves sat down, and the two men looked at each other across the table, exchanging formal greetings which did little to make their mutual scrutiny seem gracious. Longmore had no reason to suppose that the Baron knew of his sister's revelations. He was sure that M. de Mauves cared very little about his opinions, and yet he had a sense that there was that in his eyes which would have made the Baron change color if keener suspicion had helped him to read it. M. de Mauves did not change color, but he looked at Longmore with a half-defiant intentness, which betrayed at once an irritating memory of the episode in the Bois de Boulogne, and such vigilant curiosity as was natural to a gentleman who had in-trusted his "honor" to another gentleman's magnanimity,—or to his artlessness. It would appear that Longmore seemed to the Baron to possess these virtues in rather scantier measure than a few days before; for the cloud deepened on his face, and he turned away and frowned as he lighted a cigar.

The person in the coupé, Longmore thought, whether or not the same person as the heroine of the episode of the Bois de Boulogne, was not a source of unalloyed delight. Longmore had dark blue eyes, of admirable lucidity,—truth-telling eyes which had in his childhood always made his harshest taskmasters smile at his nursery fibs. An observer watching the two men, and knowing something of their relations, would certainly have said that what he saw in those eyes must not a little have puzzled and tormented M. de Mauves. They judged him, they mocked him, they eluded him, they threatened him, they triumphed over him, they treated him as no pair of eyes had ever treated him. The Baron's scheme had been to make no one happy but himself, and here was Longmore already, if looks were to be trusted, primed for an enterprise more inspiring than the finest of his own achievements. Was this candid young barbarian but a *faux bonhomme*[4] after all? He had puzzled the

4. One who deceives.

Baron before, and this was once too often.

M. de Mauves hated to seem preoccupied, and he took up the evening paper to help himself to look indifferent. As he glanced over it he uttered some cold commonplace on the political situation, which gave Longmore an easy opportunity of replying by an ironical sally which made him seem for the moment aggressively at his ease. And yet our hero was far from being master of the situation. The Baron's ill-humor did him good, so far as it pointed to a want of harmony with the lady in the coupé; but it disturbed him sorely as he began to suspect that it possibly meant jealousy of himself. It passed through his mind that jealousy is a passion with a double face, and that in some of its moods it bears a plausible likeness to affection. It recurred to him painfully that the Baron might grow ashamed of his political compact with his wife, and he felt that it would be far more tolerable in the future to think of his continued turpitude than of his repentance. The two men sat for half an hour exchanging stinted small-talk, the Baron feeling a nervous need of playing the spy, and Longmore indulging a ferocious relish of his discomfort. These rigid courtesies were interrupted however by the arrival of a friend of M. de Mauves;—a tall, pale, consumptive-looking dandy, who filled the air with the odor of heliotrope. He looked up and down the boulevard wearily, examined the Baron's toilet from head to foot, then surveyed his own in the same fashion, and at last announced languidly that the Duchess was in town! M. de Mauves must come with him to call; she had abused him dreadfully a couple of evenings before,—a sure sign she wanted to see him.

"I depend upon you," said M. de Mauves's friend with an infantine drawl, "to put her *entrain*."[5]

M. de Mauves resisted, and protested that he was *d'une humeur massacrante;*[6] but at last he allowed himself to be drawn to his feet, and stood looking awkwardly—awkwardly for M. de Mauves—at Longmore. "You'll excuse me," he said dryly; "you, too, probably, have occupation for the evening?"

"None but to catch my train," Longmore answered, looking at his watch.

"Ah, you go back to Saint-Germain?"

"In half an hour."

M. de Mauves seemed on the point of disengaging himself from his companion's arm, which was locked in his own; but on the latter uttering some persuasive murmur, he lifted his hat stiffly and turned away.

Longmore packed his trunk the next day with dogged heroism and wandered off to the terrace, to try and beguile the restlessness

5. In good spirits.   6. In a terribly bad humor.

with which he waited for evening; for he wished to see Madame de Mauves for the last time at the hour of long shadows and pale pink-reflected lights, as he had almost always seen her. Destiny, however, took no account of this humble plea for poetic justice; it was his fortune to meet her on the terrace sitting under a tree, alone. It was an hour when the place was almost empty; the day was warm, but as he took his place beside her a light breeze stirred the leafy edges on the broad circle of shadow in which she sat. She looked at him with candid anxiety, and he immediately told her that he should leave Saint-Germain that evening,—that he must bid her farewell. Her eye expanded and brightened for a moment as he spoke; but she said nothing and turned her glance away toward distant Paris, as it lay twinkling and flashing through its hot exhalations. "I have a request to make of you!" he added. "That you think of me as a man who has felt much and claimed little."

She drew a long breath, which almost suggested pain. "I can't think of you as unhappy. It's impossible. You have a life to lead, you have duties, talents, and interests. I shall hear of your career. And then," she continued after a pause and with the deepest seriousness, "one can't be unhappy through having a better opinion of a friend, instead of a worse."

For a moment he failed to understand her. "Do you mean that there can be varying degrees in my opinion of you?"

She rose and pushed away her chair. "I mean," she said quickly, "that it's better to have done nothing in bitterness,—nothing in passion." And she began to walk.

Longmore followed her, without answering. But he took off his hat and with his pocket-handkerchief wiped his forehead. "Where shall you go? what shall you do?" he asked at last, abruptly.

"Do? I shall do as I've always done,—except perhaps that I shall go for a while to Auvergne."

"I shall go to America. I have done with Europe for the present."

She glanced at him as he walked beside her after he had spoken these words, and then bent her eyes for a long time on the ground. At last, seeing that she was going far, she stopped and put out her hand. "Good by," she said; "may you have all the happiness you deserve!"

He took her hand and looked at her, but something was passing in him that made it impossible to return her hand's light pressure. Something of infinite value was floating past him, and he had taken an oath not to raise a finger to stop it. It was borne by the strong current of the world's great life and not of his own small one. Madame de Mauves disengaged her hand, gathered her shawl, and smiled at him almost as you would do at a child you should wish to encourage. Several moments later he was still standing watching her receding figure. When it had disappeared, he shook himself, walked rapidly back to his hotel, and without waiting for the evening train paid his bill and departed.

Later in the day M. de Mauves came into his wife's drawing-room, where she sat waiting to be summoned to dinner. He was dressed with a scrupulous freshness which seemed to indicate an intention of dining out. He walked up and down for some moments in silence, then rang the bell for a servant, and went out into the hall to meet him. He ordered the carriage to take him to the station, paused a moment with his hand on the knob of the door, dismissed the servant angrily as the latter lingered observing him, re-entered the drawing-room, resumed his restless walk, and at last stepped abruptly before his wife, who had taken up a book. "May I ask the favor," he said with evident effort, in spite of a forced smile of easy courtesy, "of having a question answered?"

"It's a favor I never refused," Madame de Mauves replied.

"Very true. Do you expect this evening a visit from Mr. Longmore?"

"Mr. Longmore," said his wife, "has left Saint-Germain." M. de Mauves started and his smile expired. "Mr. Longmore," his wife continued, "has gone to America."

M. de Mauves stared a moment, flushed deeply, and turned away. Then recovering himself,—"Had anything happened?" he asked. "Had he a sudden call?"

But his question received no answer. At the same moment the servant threw open the door and announced dinner; Madame Clairin rustled in, rubbing her white hands, Madame de Mauves passed silently into the dining-room, and he stood frowning and wondering. Before long he went out upon the terrace and continued his uneasy walk. At the end of a quarter of an hour the servant came to inform him that the carriage was at the door. "Send it away," he said curtly. "I shall not use it." When the ladies had half finished dinner he went in and joined them, with a formal apology to his wife for his tardiness.

The dishes were brought back, but he hardly tasted them; on the other hand, he drank a great deal of wine. There was little talk; what there was, was supplied by Madame Clairin. Twice she saw her brother's eyes fixed on her own, over his wineglass, with a piercing, questioning glance. She replied by an elevation of the eyebrows, which did the office of a shrug of the shoulders. M. de Mauves was left alone to finish his wine; he sat over it for more than an hour, and let the darkness gather about him. At last the servant came in with a letter and lighted a candle. The letter was a telegram, which M. de Mauves, when he had read it, burnt at the candle. After five minutes' meditation, he wrote a message on the back of a visiting-card and gave it to the servant to carry to the office. The man knew quite as much as his master suspected about the lady to whom the telegram was addressed; but its contents puzzled him; they consisted of the single word, *"Impossible."* As the evening passed without her brother reappearing in the drawing-room, Madame Clairin came to him where he sat, by his solitary candle. He took no notice of her presence for some time; but he was the one person to whom she allowed this license. At last, speaking in a peremptory tone, "The American has gone home at an hour's notice," he said. "What does it mean?"

Madame Clairin now gave free play to the shrug she had been obliged to suppress at the table. "It means that I have a sister-in-law whom I haven't the honor to understand."

He said nothing more, and silently allowed her to depart, as if it had been her duty to provide him with an explanation and he was disgusted with her levity. When she had gone, he went into the garden and walked up and down, smoking. He saw his wife sitting alone on the terrace, but remained below strolling along the narrow paths. He remained a long time. It became late and Madame de Mauves disappeared. Toward midnight he dropped upon a bench, tired, with a kind of angry sigh. It was sinking into his mind that he, too, did not understand Madame Clairin's sister-in-law.

Longmore was obliged to wait a week in London for a ship. It was very hot, and he went out for a day to Richmond.[7] In the garden of the hotel at which he dined he met his friend Mrs. Draper, who was staying there. She made eager inquiry about Madame de Mauves, but Longmore at first, as they sat looking out at the famous view of the Thames, parried her questions and confined himself to small-talk. At last she said she was afraid he had something to conceal; whereupon, after a pause, he asked her if she remembered recommending him, in the letter she sent to him at Saint-Germain, to draw the sadness from her friend's smile. "The last I saw of her was her smile," said he,—"when I bade her good by."

"I remember urging you to 'console' her," Mrs. Draper answered, "and I wondered afterwards whether—a model of discretion as you are—I hadn't given you rather foolish advice."

"She has her consolation in herself," he said; "she needs none that any one else can offer her. That's for troubles for which—be it more, be it less—our own folly has to answer. Madame de Mauves has not a grain of folly left."

"Ah, don't say that!" murmured Mrs. Draper. "Just a little folly

---

7. Visited by tourists for its fine deer park and the magnificent view of the Thames.

is very graceful."

Longmore rose to go, with a quick nervous movement. "Don't talk of grace," he said, "till you have measured her reason."

For two years after his return to America he heard nothing of Madame de Mauves. That he thought of her intently, constantly, I need hardly say: most people wondered why such a clever young man should not "devote" himself to something; but to himself he seemed absorbingly occupied. He never wrote to her; he believed that she preferred it. At last he heard that Mrs. Draper had come home, and he immediately called on her. "Of course," she said after the first greetings, "you are dying for news of Madame de Mauves. Prepare yourself for something strange. I heard from her two or three times during the year after your return. She left Saint-Germain and went to live in the country, on some old prop-erty of her husband's. She wrote me very kind little notes, but I felt somehow that—in spite of what you said about 'consolation'—they were the notes of a very sad woman. The only advice I could have given her was to leave her wretch of a husband and come back to her own land and her own people. But this I didn't feel free to do, and yet it made me so miserable not to be able to help her that I preferred to let our correspondence die a natural death. I had no news of her for a year. Last summer, however, I met at Vichy[8] a clever young Frenchman whom I accidentally learned to be a friend of Euphemia's lovely sister-in-law, Madame Clairin. I lost no time in asking him what he knew about Madame de Mauves, —a countrywoman of mine and an old friend. 'I congratulate you on possessing her friendship,' he answered. 'That's the charming little woman who killed her husband.' You may imagine that I promptly asked for an explanation, and he proceeded to relate to me what he called the whole story. M. de Mauves had *fait quelques folies*,[9] which his wife had taken absurdly to heart. He had repented and asked her forgiveness, which she had inexorably refused. She was very pretty, and severity, apparently, suited her style; for whether or no her husband had been in love with her before, he fell madly in love with her now. He was the proudest man in France, but he had begged her on his knees to be readmitted to favor. All in vain! She was stone, she was ice, she was outraged virtue. People noticed a great change in him: he gave up society, ceased to care for anything, looked shockingly. One fine day they learned that he had blown out his brains. My friend had the story of course from Madame Clairin."

Longmore was strongly moved, and his first impulse after he had recovered his composure was to return immediately to Europe. But

8. Resort city in central France, known for its mineral water.   9. Done some foolish things.

several years have passed, and he still lingers at home. The truth is, that in the midst of all the ardent tenderness of his memory of Madame de Mauves, he has become conscious of a singular feeling,— a feeling for which awe would be hardly too strong a name.

1874, 1875

The Real Thing[1]

I

When the porter's wife, who used to answer the house-bell, announced "A gentleman and a lady, sir," I had, as I often had in those days—the wish being father to the thought—an immediate vision of sitters. Sitters my visitors in this case proved to be; but not in the sense I should have preferred. There was nothing at first however to indicate that they mightn't have come for a portrait. The gentleman, a man of fifty, very high and very straight, with a moustache slightly grizzled and a dark grey walking-coat admirably fitted, both of which I noted professionally—I don't mean as a barber or yet as a tailor—would have struck me as a celebrity if celebrities often were striking. It was a truth of which I had for some time been conscious that a figure with a good deal of frontage was, as one might say, almost never a public institution. A glance at the lady helped to remind me of this paradoxical law: she also looked too distinguished to be a "personality." Moreover one would scarcely come across two variations together.

Neither of the pair immediately spoke—they only prolonged the preliminary gaze suggesting that each wished to give the other a

1. "* * * my much-loved friend George du Maurier had spoken to me of a call from a strange and striking couple desirous to propose themselves as artist's models for his weekly 'social' illustrations to 'Punch,' and the acceptance of whose services would have entailed the dismissal of an undistinguished but highly expert pair, also husband and wife, who had come to him from far back on the irregular day and whom, thanks to a happy, and to that extent lucrative, appearance of 'type' on the part of each, he had reproduced, to the best effect, in a thousand drawing-room attitudes and combinations. Exceedingly modest members of society, they earned their bread by looking and, with the aid of supplied toggery, dressing, greater favourites of fortune in that life; or, otherwise expressed, by skilfully feigning a virtue not in the least native to them. Here meanwhile were their so handsome proposed, so anxious, so almost haggard competitors, originally, by every sign, of the best condition and estate, but overtaken by reverse even while conforming impeccably to the standard of superficial 'smartness' and pleading with well-bred ease and the right light tone, not to say with feverish gaiety, that (as in the interest of art itself) *they* at least shouldn't have to 'make believe.' The question thus thrown up by the two friendly critics of the rather lurid little passage was of whether their not having to make believe *would* in fact serve them, and above all serve their interpreter as well as the borrowed graces of the comparatively sordid professionals who had had, for dear life, to *know how* (which was to have learnt how) to do something. The question, I recall, struck me as exquisite, and out of a momentary fond consideration of it 'The Real Thing' sprang at a bound" [James's introduction]. *The Real Thing and Other Tales* appeared in 1893. The present text is based on the New York Edition (Vol. XVIII, 1909).

chance. They were visibly shy; they stood there letting me take them in—which, as I afterwards perceived, was the most practical thing they could have done. In this way their embarrassment served their cause. I had seen people painfully reluctant to mention that they desired anything so gross as to be represented on canvas; but the scruples of my new friends appeared almost insurmountable. Yet the gentleman might have said "I should like a portrait of my wife," and the lady might have said "I should like a portrait of my husband." Perhaps they weren't husband and wife—this naturally would make the matter more delicate. Perhaps they wished to be done together—in which case they ought to have brought a third person to break the news.

"We come from Mr. Rivet," the lady finally said with a dim smile that had the effect of a moist sponge passed over a "sunk" piece of painting, as well as of a vague allusion to vanished beauty. She was as tall and straight, in her degree, as her companion, and with ten years less to carry. She looked as sad as a woman could look whose face was not charged with expression; that is, her tinted oval mask showed waste as an exposed surface shows friction. The hand of time had played over her freely, but to an effect of elimination. She was slim and stiff, and so well-dressed, in dark blue cloth, with lappets and pockets and buttons, that it was clear she employed the same tailor as her husband. The couple had an indefinable air of prosperous thrift—they evidently got a good deal of luxury for their money. If I was to be one of their luxuries it would behove me to consider my terms.

"Ah, Claude Rivet recommended me?" I echoed; and I added that it was very kind of him, though I could reflect that, as he only painted landscape, this wasn't a sacrifice.

The lady looked very hard at the gentleman, and the gentleman looked round the room. Then staring at the floor a moment and stroking his moustache, he rested his pleasant eyes on me with the remark: "He said you were the right one."

"I try to be, when people want to sit."

"Yes, we should like to," said the lady anxiously.

"Do you mean together?"

My visitors exchanged a glance. "If you could do anything with *me* I suppose it would be double," the gentleman stammered.

"Oh yes, there's naturally a higher charge for two figures than for one."

"We should like to make it pay," the husband confessed.

"That's very good of you," I returned, appreciating so unwonted a sympathy—for I supposed he meant pay the artist.

A sense of strangeness seemed to dawn on the lady. "We mean for the illustrations—Mr. Rivet said you might put one in."

"Put in—an illustration?" I was equally confused.

"Sketch her off, you know," said the gentleman, colouring.

It was only then that I understood the service Claude Rivet had rendered me; he had told them how I worked in black-and-white, for magazines, for storybooks, for sketches of contemporary life, and consequently had copious employment for models. These things were true, but it was not less true—I may confess it now; whether because the aspiration was to lead to everything or to nothing I leave the reader to guess—that I couldn't get the honours, to say nothing of the emoluments, of a great painter of portraits out of my head. My "illustrations" were my pot-boilers; I looked to a different branch of art—far and away the most interesting it had always seemed to me—to perpetuate my fame. There was no shame in looking to it also to make my fortune; but that fortune was by so much further from being made from the moment my visitors wished to be "done" for nothing. I was disappointed; for in the pictorial sense I had immediately *seen* them. I had seized their type—I had already settled what I would do with it. Something that wouldn't absolutely have pleased them, I afterwards reflected.

"Ah you're—you're—a—?" I began as soon as I had mastered my surprise. I couldn't bring out the dingy word "models": it seemed so little to fit the case.

"We haven't had much practice," said the lady.

"We've got to *do* something, and we've thought that an artist in your line might perhaps make something of us," her husband threw off. He further mentioned that they didn't know many artists and that they had gone first, on the off-chance—he painted views of course, but sometimes put in figures; perhaps I remembered—to Mr. Rivet, whom they had met a few years before at a place in Norfolk where he was sketching.

"We used to sketch a little ourselves," the lady hinted.

"It's very awkward, but we absolutely *must* do something," her husband went on.

"Of course we're not so *very* young," she admitted with a wan smile.

With the remark that I might as well know something more about them the husband had handed me a card extracted from a neat new pocket-book—their appurtenances were all of the freshest—and inscribed with the words "Major Monarch." Impressive as these words were they didn't carry my knowledge much further; but my visitor presently added: "I've left the army and we've had the misfortune to lose our money. In fact our means are dreadfully small."

"It's awfully trying—a regular strain," said Mrs. Monarch.

They evidently wished to be discreet—to take care not to swagger because they were gentlefolk. I felt them willing to recognise this as something of a drawback, at the same time that I guessed at an underlying sense—their consolation in adversity—that they *had* their points. They certainly had; but these advantages struck me as preponderantly social; such for instance as would help to make a drawing-room look well. However, a drawing-room was always, or ought to be, a picture.

In consequence of his wife's allusion to their age Major Monarch observed: "Naturally it's more for the figure that we thought of going in. We can still hold ourselves up." On the instant I saw that the figure was indeed their strong point. His "naturally" didn't sound vain, but it lighted up the question. "*She* has the best one," he continued, nodding at his wife with a pleasant after-dinner absence of circumlocution. I could only reply, as if we were in fact sitting over our wine, that this didn't prevent his own from being very good; which led him in turn to make answer: "We thought that if you ever have to do people like us we might be something like it. *She* particularly—for a lady in a book, you know."

I was so amused by them that, to get more of it, I did my best to take their point of view; and though it was an embarrassment to find myself appraising physically, as if they were animals on hire or useful blacks, a pair whom I should have expected to meet only in one of the relations in which criticism is tacit, I looked at Mrs. Monarch judicially enough to be able to exclaim after a moment with conviction: "Oh yes, a lady in a book!" She was singularly like a bad illustration.

"We'll stand up, if you like," said the Major; and he raised himself before me with a really grand air.

I could take his measure at a glance—he was six feet two and a perfect gentleman. It would have paid any club in process of formation and in want of a stamp to engage him at a salary to stand in the principal window. What struck me at once was that in coming to me they had rather missed their vocation; they could surely have been turned to better account for advertising purposes. I couldn't of course see the thing in detail, but I could see them make somebody's fortune—I don't mean their own. There was something in them for a waistcoat-maker, an hotel-keeper or a soap-vendor. I could imagine "We always use it" pinned on their bosoms with the greatest effect; I had a vision of the brilliancy with which they would launch a table d'hôte.

Mrs. Monarch sat still, not from pride but from shyness, and presently her husband said to her: "Get up, my dear, and show how smart you are." She obeyed, but she had no need to get up to show it. She walked to the end of the studio and then came back blushing, her fluttered eyes on the partner of her appeal. I was

reminded of an incident I had accidentally had a glimpse of in Paris
—being with a friend there, a dramatist about to produce a play,
when an actress came to him to ask to be entrusted with a part. She
went through her paces before him, walked up and down as Mrs.
Monarch was doing. Mrs. Monarch did it quite as well, but I
abstained from applauding. It was very odd to see such people
apply for such poor pay. She looked as if she had ten thousand a
year. Her husband had used the word that described her: she was
in the London current jargon essentially and typically "smart." Her
figure was, in the same order of ideas, conspicuously and irreproachably "good." For a woman of her age her waist was surprisingly
small; her elbow moreover had the orthodox crook. She held her
head at the conventional angle, but why did she come to *me?* She
ought to have tried on jackets at a big shop. I feared my visitors
were not only destitute but "artistic"—which would be a great
complication. When she sat down again I thanked her, observing
that what a draughtsman most valued in his model was the faculty
of keeping quiet.

"Oh *she* can keep quiet," said Major Monarch. Then he added
jocosely: "I've always kept her quiet."

"I'm not a nasty fidget, am I?" It was going to wring tears from
me, I felt, the way she hid her head, ostrich-like, in the other broad
bosom.

The owner of this expanse addressed his answer to me. "Perhaps
it isn't out of place to mention—because we ought to be quite
business-like, oughtn't we?—that when I married her she was
known as the Beautiful Statue."

"Oh dear!" said Mrs. Monarch ruefully.

"Of course I should want a certain amount of expression," I
rejoined.

"Of *course!*"—and I had never heard such unanimity.

"And then I suppose you know that you'll get awfully tired."

"Oh we *never* get tired!" they eagerly cried.

"Have you had any kind of practice?"

They hesitated—they looked at each other. "We've been photographed—*immensely*," said Mrs. Monarch.

"She means the fellows have asked us themselves," added the
Major.

"I see—because you're so good-looking."

"I don't know what they thought, but they were always after us."

"We always got our photographs for nothing," smiled Mrs.
Monarch.

"We might have brought some, my dear," her husband remarked.

"I'm not sure we have any left. We've given quantities away,"
she explained to me.

"With our autographs and that sort of thing," said the Major.

"Are they to be got in the shops?" I enquired as a harmless pleasantry.

"Oh yes, *hers*—they used to be."

"Not now," said Mrs. Monarch with her eyes on the floor.

II

I could fancy the "sort of thing" they put on the presentation copies of their photographs, and I was sure they wrote a beautiful hand. It was odd how quickly I was sure of everything that concerned them. If they were now so poor as to have to earn shillings and pence they could never have had much of a margin. Their good looks had been their capital, and they had good-humouredly made the most of the career that this resource marked out for them. It was in their faces, the blankness, the deep intellectual repose of the twenty years of country-house visiting that had given them pleasant intonations. I could see the sunny drawing-rooms, sprinkled with periodicals she didn't read, in which Mrs. Monarch had continuously sat; I could see the wet shrubberies in which she had walked, equipped to admiration for either exercise. I could see the rich covers the Major had helped to shoot and the wonderful garments in which, late at night, he repaired to the smoking-room to talk about them. I could imagine their leggings and waterproofs, their knowing tweeds and rugs, their rolls of sticks and cases of tackle and neat umbrellas; and I could evoke the exact appearance of their servants and the compact variety of their luggage on the platforms of country stations.

They gave small tips, but they were liked; they didn't do anything themselves, but they were welcome. They looked so well everywhere; they gratified the general relish for stature, complexion and "form." They knew it without fatuity or vulgarity, and they respected themselves in consequence. They weren't superficial; they were thorough and kept themselves up—it had been their line. People with such a taste for activity had to have some line. I could feel how even in a dull house they could have been counted on for the joy of life. At present something had happened—it didn't matter what, their little income had grown less, it had grown least—and they had to do something for pocket-money. Their friends could like them, I made out, without liking to support them. There was something about them that represented credit—their clothes, their manners, their type; but if credit is a large empty pocket in which an occasional chink reverberates, the chink at least must be audible. What they wanted of me was to help to make it so. Fortunately they had no children—I soon divined that. They would also perhaps wish our relations to be kept secret: this was why it was "for the figure"—the reproduction of the face would betray them.

I liked them—I felt, quite as their friends must have done—they were so simple; and I had no objection to them if they would suit. But somehow with all their perfections I didn't easily believe in them. After all they were amateurs, and the ruling passion of my life was the detestation of the amateur. Combined with this was another perversity—an innate preference for the represented subject over the real one: the defect of the real one was so apt to be a lack of representation. I like things that appeared; then one was sure. Whether they *were* or not was a subordinate and almost always a profitless question. There were other considerations, the first of which was that I already had two or three recruits in use, notably a young person with big feet, in alpaca, from Kilburn, who for a couple of years had come to me regularly for my illustrations and with whom I was still—perhaps ignobly—satisfied. I frankly explained to my visitors how the case stood, but they had taken more precautions than I supposed. They had reasoned out their opportunity, for Claude Rivet had told them of the projected *édition de luxe* of one of the writers of our day—the rarest of the novelists—who, long neglected by the multitudinous vulgar and dearly prized by the attentive (need I mention Philip Vincent?) had had the happy fortune of seeing, late in life, the dawn and then the full light of a higher criticism; an estimate in which on the part of the public there was something really of expiation. The edition preparing, planned by a publisher of taste, was practically an act of high reparation; the wood-cuts with which it was to be enriched were the homage of English art to one of the most independent representatives of English letters. Major and Mrs. Monarch confessed to me they had hoped I might be able to work *them* into my branch of the enterprise. They knew I was to do the first of the books, "Rutland Ramsay," but I had to make clear to them that my participation in the rest of the affair—this first book was to be a test—must depend on the satisfaction I should give. If this should be limited my employers would drop me with scarce common forms. It was therefore a crisis for me, and naturally I was making special preparations, looking about for new people, should they be necessary, and securing the best types. I admitted however that I should like to settle down to two or three good models who would do for everything.

"Should we have often to—a—put on special clothes?" Mrs. Monarch timidly demanded.

"Dear yes—that's half the business."

"And should we be expected to supply our own costumes?"

"Oh no; I've got a lot of things. A painter's models put on—or put off—anything he likes."

"And you mean—a—the same?"

"The same?"

Mrs. Monarch looked at her husband again.

"Oh she was just wondering," he explained, "if the costumes are in *general* use." I had to confess that they were, and I mentioned further that some of them—I had a lot of genuine greasy last-century things—had served their time, a hundred years ago, on living world-stained men and women; on figures not perhaps so far removed, in that vanished world, from *their* type, the Monarchs', *quoi!* of a breeched and bewigged age. "We'll put on anything that *fits*," said the Major.

"Oh I arrange that—they fit in the pictures."

"I'm afraid I should do better for the modern books. I'd come as you like," said Mrs. Monarch.

"She has got a lot of clothes at home: they might do for contemporary life," her husband continued.

"Oh I can fancy scenes in which you'd be quite natural." And indeed I could see the slipshod rearrangements of stale properties—the stories I tried to produce pictures for without the exasperation of reading them—whose sandy tracts the good lady might help to people. But I had to return to the fact that for this sort of work—the daily mechanical grind—I was already equipped: the people I was working with were fully adequate.

"We only thought we might be more like *some* characters," said Mrs. Monarch mildly, getting up.

Her husband also rose; he stood looking at me with a dim wistfulness that was touching in so fine a man. "Wouldn't it be rather a pull sometimes to have—a—to have—?" He hung fire; he wanted me to help him by phrasing what he meant. But I couldn't—I didn't know. So he brought it out awkwardly: "The *real* thing; a gentleman, you know, or a lady." I was quite ready to give a general assent—I admitted that there was a great deal in that. This encouraged Major Monarch to say, following up his appeal with an unacted gulp: "It's awfully hard—we've tried everything." The gulp was communicative; it proved too much for his wife. Before I knew it Mrs. Monarch had dropped again upon a divan and burst into tears. Her husband sat down beside her, holding one of her hands; whereupon she quickly dried her eyes with the other, while I felt embarrassed as she looked up at me. "There isn't a confounded job I haven't applied for—waited for—prayed for. You can fancy we'd be pretty bad first. Secretaryships and that sort of thing? You might as well ask for a peerage. I'd be *anything*—I'm strong; a messenger or a coalheaver. I'd put on a gold-laced cap and open carriage-doors in front of the haberdasher's; I'd hang about a station to carry portmanteaux; I'd be a postman. But they won't *look* at you; there are thousands as good as yourself already on the ground.

Gentlemen, poor beggars, who've drunk their wine, who've kept their hunters!"

I was as reassuring as I knew how to be, and my visitors were presently on their feet again while, for the experiment, we agreed on an hour. We were discussing it when the door opened and Miss Churm came in with a wet umbrella. Miss Churm had to take the omnibus to Maida Vale and then walk half a mile. She looked a trifle blowsy and slightly splashed. I scarcely ever saw her come in without thinking afresh how odd it was that, being so little in herself, she should yet be so much in others. She was a meagre little Miss Churm, but was such an ample heroine of romance. She was only a freckled cockney,[2] but she could represent everything, from a fine lady to a shepherdess; she had the faculty as she might have had a fine voice or long hair. She couldn't spell and she loved beer, but she had two or three "points," and practice, and a knack, and mother-wit, and a whimsical sensibility, and a love of the theatre, and seven sisters, and not an ounce of respect, especially for the *h*. The first thing my visitors saw was that her umbrella was wet, and in their spotless perfection they visibly winced at it. The rain had come on since their arrival.

"I'm all in a soak; there *was* a mess of people in the 'bus. I wish you lived near a stytion," said Miss Churm. I requested her to get ready as quickly as possible, and she passed into the room in which she always changed her dress. But before going out she asked me what she was to get into this time.

"It's the Russian princess, don't you know?" I answered; "the one with the 'golden eyes,' in black velvet, for the long thing in the *Cheapside*."

"Golden eyes? I *say!*" cried Miss Churm, while my companions watched her with intensity as she withdrew. She always arranged herself, when she was late, before I could turn round; and I kept my visitors a little on purpose, so that they might get an idea, from seeing her, what would be expected of themselves. I mentioned that she was quite my notion of an excellent model—she was really very clever.

"Do you think she looks like a Russian princess?" Major Monarch asked with lurking alarm.

"When I make her, yes."

"Oh if you have to *make* her—!" he reasoned, not without point.

"That's the most you can ask. There are so many who are not makeable."

"Well now, *here's* a lady"—and with a persuasive smile he passed his arm into his wife's—"who's already made!"

2. A native of London's East End slums.

"Oh I'm not a Russian princess," Mrs. Monarch protested a little coldly. I could see she had known some and didn't like them. There at once was a complication of a kind I never had to fear with Miss Churm.

This young lady came back in black velvet—the gown was rather rusty and very low on her lean shoulders—and with a Japanese fan in her red hands. I reminded her that in the scene I was doing she had to look over some one's head. "I forget whose it is; but it doesn't matter. Just look over a head."

"I'd rather look over a stove," said Miss Churm; and she took her station near the fire. She fell into position, settled herself into a tall attitude, gave a certain backward inclination to her head and a certain forward droop to her fan, and looked, at least to my prejudiced sense, distinguished and charming, foreign and dangerous. We left her looking so while I went downstairs with Major and Mrs. Monarch.

"I believe I could come about as near it as that," said Mrs. Monarch.

"Oh you think she's shabby, but you must allow for the alchemy of art."

However, they went off with an evident increase of comfort founded on their demonstrable advantage in being the real thing. I could fancy them shuddering over Miss Churm. She was very droll about them when I went back, for I told her what they wanted.

"Well, if *she* can sit I'll tyke to book-keeping," said my model.

"She's very ladylike," I replied as an innocent form of aggravation.

"So much the worse for *you*. That means she can't turn round."

"She'll do for the fashionable novels."

"Oh yes, she'll *do* for them!" my model humorously declared. "Ain't they bad enough without her?" I had often sociably denounced them to Miss Churm.

III

It was for the elucidation of a mystery in one of these works that I first tried Mrs. Monarch. Her husband came with her, to be useful if necessary—it was sufficiently clear that as a general thing he would prefer to come with her. At first I wondered if this were for "propriety's" sake—if he were going to be jealous and meddling. The idea was too tiresome, and if it had been confirmed it would speedily have brought our acquaintance to a close. But I soon saw there was nothing in it and that if he accompanied Mrs. Monarch it was—in addition to the chance of being wanted—simply because he had nothing else to do. When they were separate his occupation was gone and they never *had* been separate. I judged rightly that in their awkward situation their close union was their main comfort and that this union had no weak spot. It was a real marriage, an encouragement to the hesitating, a nut for pessimists to crack. Their address was humble—I remember afterwards thinking it had been the only thing about them that was really professional— and I could fancy the lamentable lodgings in which the Major would have been left alone. He could sit there more or less grimly with his wife—he couldn't sit there anyhow without her.

He had too much tact to try and make himself agreeable when he couldn't be useful; so when I was too absorbed in my work to talk he simply sat and waited. But I liked to hear him talk—it made my work, when not interrupting it, less mechanical, less special. To listen to him was to combine the excitement of going out with the economy of staying at home. There was only one hindrance—that I seemed not to know any of the people this brilliant couple had known. I think he wondered extremely, during the term of our intercourse, whom the deuce I *did* know. He hadn't a stray sixpence of an idea to fumble for, so we didn't spin it very fine; we confined ourselves to questions of leather and even of liquor—saddlers and breeches-makers and how to get excellent claret cheap—and matters like "good trains" and the habits of small game. His lore on these last subjects was astonishing—he managed to interweave the station-master with the ornithologist. When he couldn't talk about greater things he could talk cheerfully about smaller, and since I couldn't accompany him into reminiscences of the fashionable world he could lower the conversation without a visible effort to my level.

So earnest a desire to please was touching in a man who could so easily have knocked one down. He looked after the fire and had an opinion on the draught of the stove without my asking him, and I could see that he thought many of my arrangements not half knowing. I remember telling him that if I were only rich I'd offer him a salary to come and teach me how to live. Sometimes he gave a random sigh of which the essence might have been: "Give me even such a bare old barrack as *this*, and I'd do something with it!" When I wanted to use him he came alone; which was an illustration of the superior courage of women. His wife could bear her solitary second floor, and she was in general more discreet; showing by various small reserves that she was alive to the propriety of keeping our relations markedly professional—not letting them slide into sociability. She wished it to remain clear that she and the Major were employed, not cultivated, and if she approved of me as a superior, who could be kept in his place, she never thought me quite good enough for an equal.

She sat with great intensity, giving the whole of her mind to it, and was capable of remaining for an hour almost as motionless as before a photographer's lens. I could see she had been photographed often, but somehow the very habit that made her good for that purpose unfitted her for mine. At first I was extremely pleased with her ladylike air, and it was a satisfaction, on coming to follow her lines, to see how good they were and how far they could lead the pencil. But after a little skirmishing I began to find her too insurmountably stiff; do what I would with it my drawing looked like a photograph or a copy of a photograph. Her figure had no variety of expression—she herself had no sense of variety. You may say that this was my business and was only a question of placing her. Yet I placed her in every conceivable position and she managed to obliterate their differences. She was always a lady certainly, and into the bargain was always the same lady. She was the real thing, but always the same thing. There were moments when I rather writhed under the serenity of her confidence that she *was* the real thing. All her dealings with me and all her husband's were an implication that this was lucky for *me*. Meanwhile I found myself trying to invent types that approached her own, instead of making her own transform itself—in the clever way that was not impossible for instance to poor Miss Churm. Arrange as I would and take the precautions I would, she always came out, in my pictures, too tall—landing me in the dilemma of having represented a fascinating woman as seven feet high, which (out of respect perhaps to my own very much scantier inches) was far from my idea of such a personage.

The case was worse with the Major—nothing I could do would keep *him* down, so that he became useful only for the representation of brawny giants. I adored variety and range, I cherished human accidents, the illustrative note; I wanted to characterise closely, and the thing in the world I most hated was the danger of being ridden by a type. I had quarrelled with some of my friends about it: I had parted company with them for maintaining that one *had* to be, and that if the type was beautiful—witness Raphael and Leonardo—the servitude was only a gain. I was neither Leonardo nor Raphael—I might only be a presumptuous young modern searcher; but I held that everything was to be sacrificed sooner than character. When they claimed that the obsessional form could easily *be* character I retorted, perhaps superficially, "Whose?" It couldn't be everybody's —it might end in being nobody's.

After I had drawn Mrs. Monarch a dozen times I felt surer even than before that the value of such a model as Miss Churm resided precisely in the fact that she had no positive stamp, combined of course with the other fact that what she did have was a curious and inexplicable talent for imitation. Her usual appearance was like a curtain which she could draw up at request for a capital performance. This performance was simply suggestive; but it was a word to the wise—it was vivid and pretty. Sometimes even I thought it, though she was plain herself, too insipidly pretty; I made it a reproach to her that the figures drawn from her were monotonously (*bêtement*,[3] as we used to say) graceful. Nothing made her more angry; it was so much her pride to feel she could sit for characters that had nothing in common with each other. She would accuse me at such moments of taking away her "reputytion."

It suffered a certain shrinkage, this queer quantity, from the repeated visits of my new friends. Miss Churm was greatly in demand, never in want of employment, so I had no scruple in putting her off occasionally, to try them more at my ease. It was certainly amusing at first to do the real thing—it was amusing to do Major Monarch's trousers. They *were* the real thing, even if he did come out colossal. It was amusing to do his wife's back hair—it was so mathematically neat—and the particular "smart" tension of her tight stays. She lent herself especially to positions in which the face was somewhat averted or blurred; she abounded in ladylike back views and *profils perdus*.[4] When she stood erect she took naturally one of the attitudes in which court-painters represent queens and princesses; so that I found myself wondering whether, to draw out this accomplishment, I couldn't get the editor of the *Cheapside* to publish a really royal romance, "A Tale of Buckingham Palace." Sometimes however the real thing and the make-believe came into contact; by which I mean that Miss Churm, keeping an appointment or coming to make one on days when I had much work in hand, encountered her invidious rivals. The encounter was not on their part, for they noticed her no more than if she had been the housemaid; not from intentional loftiness, but simply because as yet, professionally, they didn't know how to fraternise, as I could imagine they would have liked—or at least that the Major would. They couldn't talk about the omnibus—they always walked; and they didn't know what else to try—she wasn't interested in good trains or cheap claret. Besides, they must have felt—in the air—that she was amused at them, secretly derisive of their ever knowing how. She wasn't a person to conceal the limits of her faith if she had had a chance to show them. On the other hand Mrs. Monarch didn't think her tidy; for why else did she take pains to say to me—it was going out of the way, for Mrs. Monarch—that she didn't like dirty women?

One day when my young lady happened to be present with my other sitters—she even dropped in, when it was convenient, for a chat—I asked her to be so good as to lend a hand in getting tea, a

3. Foolishly.   4. Half-rear views "losing" most of the profile.

service with which she was familiar and which was one of a class that, living as I did in a small way, with slender domestic resources, I often appealed to my models to render. They liked to lay hands on my property, to break the sitting, and sometimes the china—it made them feel Bohemian. The next time I saw Miss Churm after this incident she surprised me greatly by making a scene about it— she accused me of having wished to humiliate her. She hadn't resented the outrage at the time, but had seemed obliging and amused, enjoying the comedy of asking Mrs. Monarch, who sat vague and silent, whether she would have cream and sugar, and putting an exaggerated simper into the question. She had tried intonations—as if she too wished to pass for the real thing—till I was afraid my other visitors would take offence.

Oh, they were determined not to do this, and their touching patience was the measure of their great need. They would sit by the hour, uncomplaining, till I was ready to use them; they would come back on the chance of being wanted and would walk away cheerfully if it failed. I used to go to the door with them to see in what magnificent order they retreated. I tried to find other employment for them—I introduced them to several artists. But they didn't "take," for reasons I could appreciate, and I became rather anxiously aware that after such disappointments they fell back upon me with a heavier weight. They did me the honour to think me most *their* form. They weren't romantic enough for the painters, and in those days there were few serious workers in black-and-white. Besides, they had an eye to the great job I had mentioned to them—they had secretly set their hearts on supplying the right essence for my pictorial vindication of our fine novelist. They knew that for this undertaking I should want no costume-effects, none of the frippery of past ages—that it was a case in which everything would be contemporary and satirical and presumably genteel. If I could work them into it their future would be assured, for the labour would of course be long and the occupation steady.

One day Mrs. Monarch came without her husband—she explained his absence by his having had to go to the City. While she sat there in her usual relaxed majesty there came at the door a knock which I immediately recognised as the subdued appeal of a model out of work. It was followed by the entrance of a young man whom I at once saw to be a foreigner and who proved in fact an Italian acquainted with no English word but my name, which he uttered in a way that made it seem to include all others. I hadn't then visited his country, nor was I proficient in his tongue; but as he was not so meanly constituted—what Italian is?—as to depend only on that member for expression he conveyed to me, in familiar but graceful mimicry, that he was in search of exactly the employment in which the lady before me was engaged. I was not struck with him at first, and while I continued to draw I dropped few signs of interest or encouragement. He stood his ground however—not importunely, but with a dumb dog-like fidelity in his eyes that amounted to innocent impudence, the manner of a devoted servant—he might have been in the house for years—unjustly suspected. Suddenly it struck me that this very attitude and expression made a picture; whereupon I told him to sit down and wait till I should be free. There was another picture in the way he obeyed me, and I observed as I worked that there were others still in the way he looked wonderingly, with his head thrown back, about the high studio. He might have been crossing himself in Saint Peter's. Before I finished I said to myself "The fellow's a bankrupt orange-monger, but a treasure."

When Mrs. Monarch withdrew he passed across the room like a flash to open the door for her, standing there with the rapt pure gaze of the young Dante spellbound by the young Beatrice. As I never insisted, in such situations, on the blankness of the British domestic, I reflected that he had the making of a servant—and I needed one, but couldn't pay him to be only that—as well as of a model; in short I resolved to adopt my bright adventurer if he would agree to officiate in the double capacity. He jumped at my offer, and in the event my rashness—for I had really known nothing about him—wasn't brought home to me. He proved a sympathetic though a desultory ministrant, and had in a wonderful degree the *sentiment de la pose*.[5] It was uncultivated, instinctive, a part of the happy instinct that had guided him to my door and helped him to spell out my name on the card nailed to it. He had had no other introduction to me than a guess, from the shape of my high north window, seen outside, that my place was a studio and that as a studio it would contain an artist. He had wandered to England in search of fortune, like other itinerants, and had embarked, with a partner and a small green hand-cart, on the sale of penny ices. The ices had melted away and the partner had dissolved in their train. My young man wore tight yellow trousers with reddish stripes and his name was Oronte. He was sallow but fair, and when I put him into some old clothes of my own he looked like an Englishman. He was as good as Miss Churm, who could look, when requested, like an Italian.

IV

I thought Mrs. Monarch's face slightly convulsed when, on her coming back with her husband, she found Oronte installed. It was strange to have to recognise in a scrap of a lazzarone a competitor to her magnificent Major. It was she who scented danger first, for

---

5. Instinct for correct posing.

the Major was anecdotically unconscious. But Oronte gave us tea,
with a hundred eager confusions—he had never been concerned
in so queer a process—and I think she thought better of me for having at last an "establishment." They saw a couple of drawings that I
had made of the establishment, and Mrs. Monarch hinted that it
never would have struck her he had sat for them. "Now the drawings
you make from *us*, they look exactly like us," she reminded me,
smiling in triumph; and I recognised that this was indeed just their
defect. When I drew the Monarchs I couldn't anyhow get away
from them—get into the character I wanted to represent; and I
hadn't the least desire my model should be discoverable in my
picture. Miss Churm never was, and Mrs. Monarch thought I
hid her, very properly, because she was vulgar; whereas if she was
lost it was only as the dead who go to heaven are lost—in the gain
of an angel the more.

By this time I had got a certain start with "Rutland Ramsey,"
the first novel in the great projected series; that is I had produced
a dozen drawings, several with the help of the Major and his wife,
and I had sent them in for approval. My understanding with the
publishers, as I have already hinted, had been that I was to be
left to do my work, in this particular case, as I liked, with the
whole book committed to me; but my connexion with the rest
of the series was only contingent. There were moments when,
frankly, it *was* a comfort to have the real thing under one's hand;
for there were characters in "Rutland Ramsay" that were very
much like it. There were people presumably as erect as the Major
and women of as good a fashion as Mrs. Monarch. There was a
great deal of country-house life—treated, it is true, in a fine fanciful ironical generalised way—and there was a considerable implication of knickerbockers and kilts. There were certain things I
had to settle at the outset; such things for instance as the exact
appearance of the hero and the particular bloom and figure of the
heroine. The author of course gave me a lead, but there was a
margin for interpretation. I took the Monarchs into my confidence, I told them frankly what I was about, I mentioned my
embarrassments and alternatives. "Oh take *him!*" Mrs. Monarch
murmured sweetly, looking at her husband; and "What could you
want better than my wife?" the Major enquired with the comfortable candour that now prevailed between us.

I wasn't obliged to answer these remarks—I was only obliged
to place my sitters. I wasn't easy in mind, and I postponed a little
timidly perhaps the solving of my question. The book was a large
canvas, the other figures were numerous, and I worked off at first
some of the episodes in which the hero and the heroine were not
concerned. When once I had set *them* up I should have to stick

to them—I couldn't make my young man seven feet high in one place and five feet nine in another. I inclined on the whole to the latter measurement, though the Major more than once reminded me that *he* looked about as young as any one. It was indeed quite possible to arrange him, for the figure, so that it would have been difficult to detect his age. After the spontaneous Oronte had been with me a month, and after I had given him to understand several times over that his native exuberance would presently constitute an insurmountable barrier to our further intercourse, I waked to a sense of his heroic capacity. He was only five feet seven, but the remaining inches were latent. I tried him almost secretly at first, for I was really rather afraid of the judgment my other models would pass on such a choice. If they regarded Miss Churm as little better than a snare what would they think of the representation by a person so little the real thing as an Italian street-vendor of a protagonist formed by a public school?

If I went a little in fear of them it wasn't because they bullied me, because they had got an oppressive foothold, but because in their really pathetic **d**ecorum and mysteriously permanent new-ness they counted on me so intensely. I was therefore very glad when Jack Hawley came home: he was always of such good coun-sel. He painted badly himself, but there was no one like him for putting his finger on the place. He had been absent from England for a year; he had been somewhere—I don't remember where—to get a fresh eye. I was in a good deal of dread of any such organ, but we were old friends; he had been away for months and a sense of emptiness was creeping into my life. I hadn't dodged a missile for a year.

He came back with a fresh eye, but with the same old black velvet blouse, and the first evening he spent in my studio we smoked cigarettes till the small hours. He had done no work him-self, he had only got the eye; so the field was clear for the pro-duction of my little things. He wanted to see what I had produced for the *Cheapside*, but he was disappointed in the exhibition. That at least seemed the meaning of two or three comprehensive groans which, as he lounged on my big divan, his leg folded under him, looking at my latest drawings, issued from his lips with the smoke of the cigarette.

"What's the matter with you?" I asked.

"What's the matter with *you?*"

"Nothing save that I'm mystified."

"You are indeed. You're quite off the hinge. What's the mean-ing of this new fad?" And he tossed me, with visible irreverence, a drawing in which I happened to have depicted both my elegant models. I asked if he didn't think it good, and he replied that it struck him as execrable, given the sort of thing I had always represented myself to him as wishing to arrive at; but I let that pass—I was so anxious to see exactly what he meant. The two figures in the picture looked colossal, but I supposed this was *not* what he meant, inasmuch as, for aught he knew to the contrary, I might have been trying for some such effect. I maintained that I was working exactly in the same way as when he last had done me the honour to tell me I might do something some day. "Well, there's a screw loose somewhere," he answered; "wait a bit and I'll discover it." I depended upon him to do so: where else was the fresh eye? But he produced at last nothing more luminous than "I don't know—I don't like your types." This was lame for a critic who had never consented to discuss with me anything but the question of execution, the direction of strokes and the mystery of values.

"In the drawings you've been looking at I think my types are very handsome."

"Oh they won't do!"

"I've been working with new models."

"I see you have. *They* won't do."

"Are you very sure of that?"

"Absolutely—they're stupid."

"You mean *I* am—for I ought to get round that."

"You *can't*—with such people. Who are they?"

I told him, so far as was necessary, and he concluded heartlessly: "*Ce sont des gens qu'il faut mettre à la porte.*"[6]

"You've never seen them; they're awfully good"—I flew to their defence.

"Not seen them? Why all this recent work of yours drops to pieces with them. It's all I want to see of them."

"No one else has said anything against it—the *Cheapside* people are pleased."

"Every one else is an ass, and the *Cheapside* people the biggest asses of all. Come, don't pretend at this time of day to have pretty illusions about the public, especially about publishers and editors. It's not for *such* animals you work—it's for those who know, *color che sanno*;[7] so keep straight for *me* if you can't keep straight for yourself. There was a certain sort of thing you used to try for—and a very good thing it was. But this twaddle isn't *in* it." When I talked with Hawley later about "Rutland Ramsay" and its possible successors he declared that I must get back into my boat again or I should go to the bottom. His voice in short was the voice of warning.

I noted the warning, but I didn't turn my friends out of doors.

---

6. They are the kind of people one should get rid of.
7. Dante's reference to Aristotle: "*Vidi il Maestro di color che sanno*" ["I saw the master of those who know"], *Inferno*, iv, 131.

They bored me a good deal; but the very fact that they bored me
admonished me not to sacrifice them—if there was anything to be
done with them—simply to irritation. As I look back at this phase
they seem to me to have pervaded my life not a little. I have a
vision of them as most of the time in my studio, seated against
the wall on an old velvet bench to be out of the way, and resembling the while a pair of patient courtiers in a royal ante-chamber.
I'm convinced that during the coldest weeks of the winter they
held their ground because it saved them fire. Their newness was
losing its gloss, and it was impossible not to feel them objects of
charity. Whenever Miss Churm arrived they went away, and after
I was fairly launched in "Rutland Ramsay" Miss Churm arrived
pretty often. They managed to express to me tacitly that they
supposed I wanted her for the low life of the book, and I let them
suppose it, since they had attempted to study the work—it was
lying about the studio—without discovering that it dealt only
with the highest circles. They had dipped into the most brilliant
of our novelists without deciphering many passages. I still took
an hour from them, now and again, in spite of Jack Hawley's warning: it would be time enough to dismiss them, if dismissal should
be necessary, when the rigour of the season was over. Hawley had
made their acquaintance—he had met them at my fireside—and
thought them a ridiculous pair. Learning that he was a painter
they tried to approach him, to show him too that they were the
real thing; but he looked at them, across the big room, as if they
were miles away: they were a compendium of everything he most
objected to in the social system of his country. Such people as
that, all convention and patent-leather, with ejaculations that
stopped conversation, had no business in a studio. A studio was
a place to learn to see, and how could you see through a pair of
feather-beds?

The main inconvenience I suffered at their hands was that at
first I was shy of letting it break upon them that my artful little
servant had begun to sit to me for "Rutland Ramsay." They knew
I had been odd enough—they were prepared by this time to allow
oddity to artists—to pick a foreign vagabond out of the streets
when I might have had a person with whiskers and credentials;
but it was some time before they learned how high I rated his
accomplishments. They found him in an attitude more than once,
but they never doubted I was doing him as an organ-grinder. There
were several things they never guessed, and one of them was that
for a striking scene in the novel, in which a footman briefly figured,
it occurred to me to make use of Major Monarch as the menial.
I kept putting this off, I didn't like to ask him to don the livery—
besides the difficulty of finding a livery to fit him. At last, one day

late in the winter, when I was at work on the despised Oronte, who caught one's idea on the wing, and was in the glow of feeling myself go very straight, they came in, the Major and his wife, with their society laugh about nothing (there was less and less to laugh at); came in like country-callers—they always reminded me of that— who have walked across the park after church and are presently persuaded to stay to luncheon. Luncheon was over, but they could stay to tea—I knew they wanted it. The fit was on me, however, and I couldn't let my ardour cool and my work wait, with the fading daylight, while my model prepared it. So I asked Mrs. Monarch if she would mind laying it out—a request which for an instant brought all the blood to her face. Her eyes were on her husband's for a second, and some mute telegraphy passed between them. Their folly was over the next instant; his cheerful shrewdness put an end to it. So far from pitying their wounded pride, I must add, I was moved to give it as complete a lesson as I could. They bustled about together and got out the cups and saucers and made the kettle boil. I know they felt as if they were waiting on my servant, and when the tea was prepared I said: "He'll have a cup, please—he's tired." Mrs. Monarch brought him one where he stood, and he took it from her as if he had been a gentleman at a party squeezing a crush-hat with an elbow.

Then it came over me that she had made a great effort for me— made it with a kind of nobleness—and that I owed her a compensation. Each time I saw her after this I wondered what the compensation could be. I couldn't go on doing the wrong thing to oblige them. Oh it *was* the wrong thing, the stamp of the work for which they sat—Hawley was not the only person to say it now. I sent in a large number of the drawings I had made for "Rutland Ramsay," and I received a warning that was more to the point than Hawley's. The artistic adviser of the house for which I was working was of opinion that many of my illustrations were not what had been looked for. Most of these illustrations were the subjects in which the Monarchs had figured. Without going into the question of what *had* been looked for, I had to face the fact that at this rate I shouldn't get the other books to do. I hurled myself in despair on Miss Churm—I put her through all her paces. I not only adopted Oronte publicly as my hero, but one morning when the Major looked in to see if I didn't require him to finish a *Cheapside* figure for which he had begun to sit the week before, I told him I had changed my mind—I'd do the drawing from my man. At this my visitor turned pale and stood looking at me. "Is *he* your idea of an English gentleman?" he asked.

I was disappointed, I was nervous, I wanted to get on with my work; so I replied with irritation: "Oh my dear Major—I can't be ruined for *you!*"

It was a horrid speech, but he stood another moment—after which, without a word, he quitted the studio. I drew a long breath, for I said to myself that I shouldn't see him again. I hadn't told him definitely that I was in danger of having my work rejected, but I was vexed at his not having felt the catastrophe in the air, read with me the moral of our fruitless collaboration, the lesson that in the deceptive atmosphere of art even the highest respectability may fail of being plastic.

I didn't owe my friends money, but I did see them again. They reappeared together three days later, and, given all the other facts, there was something tragic in that one. It was a clear proof they could find nothing else in life to do. They had threshed the matter out in a dismal conference—they had digested the bad news that they were not in for the series. If they weren't useful to me even for the *Cheapside* their function seemed difficult to determine, and I could only judge at first that they had come, forgivingly, decorously, to take a last leave. This made me rejoice in secret that I had little leisure for a scene; for I had placed both my other models in position together and I was pegging away at a drawing from which I hoped to derive glory. It had been suggested by the passage in which Rutland Ramsay, drawing up a chair to Artemisia's piano-stool, says extraordinary things to her while she ostensibly fingers out a difficult piece of music. I had done Miss Churm at the piano before—it was an attitude in which she knew how to take on an absolutely poetic grace. I wished the two figures to "compose" together with intensity, and my little Italian had entered perfectly into my conception. The pair were vividly before me, the piano had been pulled out; it was a charming show of blended youth and murmured love, which I had only to catch and keep. My visitors stood and looked at it, and I was friendly to them over my shoulder.

They made no response, but I was used to silent company and went on with my work, only a little disconcerted—even though exhilarated by the sense that *this* was at least the ideal thing— at not having got rid of them after all. Presently I heard Mrs. Monarch's sweet voice beside or rather above me: "I wish her hair were a little better done." I looked up and she was staring with a strange fixedness at Miss Churm, whose back was turned to her. "Do you mind my just touching it?" she went on—a question which made me spring up for an instant as with the instinctive fear that she might do the young lady a harm. But she quieted me with a glance I shall never forget—I confess I should like to have been able to paint *that*—and went for a moment to my model. She spoke to her softly, laying a hand on her shoulder and bending over her; and as the girl, understanding, gratefully assented, she disposed her rough curls, with a few quick passes, in such a way as to make Miss Churm's head twice as charming. It was one of the most heroic personal services I've ever seen rendered. Then Mrs. Monarch turned away with a low sigh and, looking about her as if for something to do, stooped to the floor with a noble humility and picked up a dirty rag that had dropped out of my paint-box.

The Major meanwhile had also been looking for something to do, and, wandering to the other end of the studio, saw before him my breakfast-things neglected, unremoved. "I say, can't I be useful *here?*" he called out to me with an irrepressible quaver. I assented with a laugh that I fear was awkward, and for the next ten minutes, while I worked, I heard the light clatter of china and the tinkle of spoons and glass. Mrs. Monarch assisted her husband—they washed up my crockery, they put it away. They wandered off into my little scullery, and I afterwards found that they had cleaned my knives and that my slender stock of plate had an unprecedented surface. When it came over me, the latent eloquence of what they were doing, I confess that my drawing was blurred for a moment—the picture swam. They had accepted their failure, but they couldn't accept their fate. They had bowed their heads in bewilderment to the perverse and cruel law in virtue of which the real thing could be so much less precious than the unreal; but they didn't want to starve. If my servants were my models, then my models might be my servants. They would reverse the parts—the others would sit for the ladies and gentlemen and *they* would do the work. They would still be in the studio—it was an intense dumb appeal to me not to turn them out. "Take us on," they wanted to say—"we'll do *anything.*"

My pencil dropped from my hand; my sitting was spoiled and I got rid of my sitters, who were also evidently rather mystified and awestruck. Then, alone with the Major and his wife I had a most uncomfortable moment. He put their prayer into a single sentence: "I say, you know—just let *us* do for you, can't you?" I couldn't—it was dreadful to see them emptying my slops; but I pretended I could, to oblige them, for about a week. Then I gave them a sum of money to go away, and I never saw them again. I obtained the remaining books, but my friend Hawley repeats that Major and Mrs. Monarch did me a permanent harm, got me into false ways. If it be true I'm content to have paid the price—for the memory.

1893

The Art of Fiction[8]

I should not have affixed so comprehensive a title to these few remarks, necessarily wanting in any completeness upon a subject the full consideration of which would carry us far, did I not seem to discover a pretext for my temerity in the interesting pamphlet lately published under this name by Mr. Walter Besant.[9] Mr. Besant's lecture at the Royal Institution—the original form of his pamphlet—appears to indicate that many persons are interested in the art of fiction, and are not indifferent to such remarks, as those who practice it may attempt to make about it. I am therefore anxious not to lose the benefit of this favorable association, and to edge in a few words under cover of the attention which Mr. Besant is sure to have excited. There is something very encouraging in his having put into form certain of his ideas on the mystery of storytelling.

It is a proof of life and curiosity—curiosity on the part of the brotherhood of novelists as well as on the part of their readers. Only a short time ago it might have been supposed that the English novel was not what the French call *discutable*.[1] It had no air of having a theory, a conviction, a consciousness of itself behind it—of being the expression of an artistic faith, the result of choice and comparison. I do not say it was necessarily the worse for that: it would take much more courage than I possess to intimate that the form of the novel as Dickens and Thackeray (for instance) saw it had any taint of incompleteness. It was, however, *naïf* (if I may help myself out with another French word); and evidently if it be destined to suffer in any way for having lost its *naïveté* it has now an idea of making sure of the corresponding advantages. During the period I have alluded to there was a comfortable, good-humored feeling abroad that a novel is a novel, as a pudding is a pudding, and that our only business with it could be to swallow it. But within a year or two, for some reason or other, there have been signs of returning animation—the era of discussion would appear to have been to a certain extent opened. Art lives upon discussion, upon experiment, upon curiosity, upon variety of attempt, upon the exchange of views and the comparison of standpoints; and there is a presumption that those times when no one has anything particular to say about it, and has no reason to give for practice or preference, though they may be times of honor, are not times of development—are times, possibly even, a little of dullness. The successful application of any art is a delightful spectacle, but the theory too is interesting; and

---

8. Originally published in *Longman's Magazine* for September, 1884; included in *Partial Portraits* (1888), the source of the present text.

9. English novelist and critic (1836–1901).

1. Debatable.

though there is a great deal of the latter without the former I suspect there has never been a genuine success that has not had a latent core of conviction. Discussion, suggestion, formulation, these things are fertilizing when they are frank and sincere. Mr. Besant has set an excellent example in saying what he thinks, for his part, about the way in which fiction should be written, as well as about the way in which it should be published; for his view of the "art," carried on into an appendix, covers that too. Other laborers in the same field will doubtless take up the argument, they will give it the light of their experience, and the effect will surely be to make our interest in the novel a little more what it had for some time threatened to fail to be—a serious, active, inquiring interest, under protection of which this delightful study may, in moments of confidence, venture to say a little more what it thinks of itself.

It must take itself seriously for the public to take it so. The old superstition about fiction being "wicked" has doubtless died out in England; but the spirit of it lingers in a certain oblique regard directed toward any story which does not more or less admit that it is only a joke. Even the most jocular novel feels in some degree the weight of the proscription that was formerly directed against literary levity: the jocularity does not always succeed in passing for orthodoxy. It is still expected, though perhaps people are ashamed to say it, that a production which is after all only a "make-believe" (for what else is a "story"?) shall be in some degree apologetic— shall renounce the pretension of attempting really to represent life. This, of course, any sensible, wide-awake story declines to do, for it quickly perceives that the tolerance granted to it on such a condition is only an attempt to stifle it disguised in the form of generosity. The old evangelical hostility to the novel, which was as explicit as it was narrow, and which regarded it as little less favorable to our immortal part than a stage play, was in reality far less insulting. The only reason for the existence of a novel is that it does attempt to represent life. When it relinquishes this attempt, the same attempt that we see on the canvas of the painter, it will have arrived at a very strange pass. It is not expected of the picture that it will make itself humble in order to be forgiven; and the analogy between the art of the painter and the art of the novelist is, so far as I am able to see, complete. Their inspiration is the same, their process (allowing for the different quality of the vehicle) is the same, their success is the same. They may learn from each other, they may explain and sustain each other. Their cause is the same, and the honor of one is the honor of another. The Mahometans think a picture an unholy thing, but it is a long time since any Christian did, and it is therefore the more odd that in the Christian mind the traces (dissimulated though they may be) of a suspicion of the sister art should linger to this day. The only effectual way to lay it to rest is to emphasize the analogy to which I just alluded—to insist on the fact that as the picture is reality, so the novel is history. That is the only general description (which does it justice) that we may give of the novel. But history also is allowed to represent life; it is not, any more than painting, expected to apologize. The subject matter of fiction is stored up likewise in documents and records, and if it will not give itself away, as they say in California, it must speak with assurance, with the tone of the historian. Certain accomplished novelists have a habit of giving themselves away which must often bring tears to the eyes of people who take their fiction seriously. I was lately struck, in reading over many pages of Anthony Trollope,[2] with his want of discretion in this particular. In a digression, a parenthesis or an aside, he concedes to the reader that he and this trusting friend are only "making believe." He admits that the events he narrates have not really happened, and that he can give his narrative any turn the reader may like best. Such a betrayal of a sacred office seems to me, I confess, a terrible crime; it is what I mean by the attitude of apology, and it shocks me every whit as much in Trollope as it would have shocked me in Gibbon or Macaulay.[3] It implies that the novelist is less occupied in looking for the truth (the truth, of course I mean, that he assumes, the premises that we must grant him, whatever they may be) than the historian, and in doing so it deprives him at a stroke of all his standing room. To represent and illustrate the past, the actions of men, is the task of either writer, and the only difference that I can see is, in proportion as he succeeds, to the honor of the novelist, consisting as it does in his having more difficulty in collecting his evidence, which is so far from being purely literary. It seems to me to give him a great character, the fact that he has at once so much in common with the philosopher and the painter; this double analogy is a magnificent heritage.

It is of all this evidently that Mr. Besant is full when he insists upon the fact that fiction is one of the *fine* arts, deserving in its turn of all the honors and emoluments that have hitherto been reserved for the successful profession of music, poetry, painting, architecture. It is impossible to insist too much on so important a truth, and the place that Mr. Besant demands for the work of the novelist may be represented, a trifle less abstractly, by saying that he demands not only that it shall be reputed artistic, but that it shall be reputed very artistic indeed. It is excellent that he should have struck this note, for his doing so indicates that there was need of it, that his proposition may be to many people a novelty. One rubs one's eyes at the thought; but the rest of Mr. Besant's

2. English novelist (1815–1882).   3. English historians.

essay confirms the revelation. I suspect in truth that it would be possible to confirm it still further, and that one would not be far wrong in saying that in addition to the people to whom it has never occurred that a novel ought to be artistic, there are a great many others who, if this principle were urged upon them, would be filled with an indefinable mistrust. They would find it difficult to explain their repugnance, but it would operate strongly to put them on their guard. "Art," in our Protestant communities, where so many things have got so strangely twisted about, is supposed in certain circles to have some vaguely injurious effect upon those who make it an important consideration, who let it weigh in the balance. It is assumed to be opposed in some mysterious manner to morality, to amusement, to instruction. When it is embodied in the work of the painter (the sculptor is another affair!) you know what it is: it stands there before you, in the honesty of pink and green and a gilt frame; you can see the worst of it at a glance, and you can be on your *guard*. But when it is introduced into literature it becomes more insidious—there is danger of its hurting you before you know it. Literature should be either instructive or amusing, and there is in many minds an impression that these artistic preoccupations, the search for form, contribute to neither end, interfere indeed with both. They are too frivolous to be edifying, and too serious to be diverting; and they are moreover priggish and paradoxical and superfluous. That, I think, represents the manner in which the latent thought of many people who read novels as an exercise in skipping would explain itself if it were to become articulate. They would argue, of course, that a novel ought to be "good," but they would interpret this term in a fashion of their own, which indeed would vary considerably from one critic to another. One would say that being good means representing virtuous and aspiring characters, placed in prominent positions; another would say that it depends on a "happy ending," on a distribution at the last of prizes, pensions, husbands, wives, babies, millions, appended paragraphs, and cheerful remarks. Another still would say that it means being full of incident and movement, so that we shall wish to jump ahead, to see who was the mysterious stranger, and if the stolen will was ever found, and shall not be distracted from this pleasure by any tiresome analysis or "description." But they would all agree that the "artistic" idea would spoil some of their fun. One would hold it accountable for all the description, another would see it revealed in the absence of sympathy. Its hostility to a happy ending would be evident, and it might even in some cases render any ending at all impossible. The "ending" of a novel is, for many persons, like that of a good dinner, a course of dessert and ices, and the artist in fiction is regarded as a sort of meddlesome doctor who forbids agreeable aftertastes. It is therefore true that this conception of Mr. Besant's of the novel as a superior form encounters not only a negative but a positive indifference. It matters little that as a work of art it should really be as little or as much of its essence to supply happy endings, sympathetic characters, and an objective tone, as if it were a work of mechanics: the association of ideas, however incongruous, might easily be too much for it if an eloquent voice were not sometimes raised to call attention to the fact that it is at once as free and as serious a branch of literature as any other.

Certainly this might sometimes be doubted in presence of the enormous number of works of fiction that appeal to the credulity of our generation, for it might easily seem that there could be no great character in a commodity so quickly and easily produced. It must be admitted that good novels are much compromised by bad ones, and that the field at large suffers discredit from overcrowding. I think, however, that this injury is only superficial, and that the superabundance of written fiction proves nothing against the principle itself. It has been vulgarized, like all other kinds of literature, like everything else today, and it has proved more than some kinds accessible to vulgarization. But there is as much difference as there ever was between a good novel and a bad one: the bad is swept with all the daubed canvases and spoiled marble into some unvisited limbo, or infinite rubbish yard beneath the back windows of the world, and the good subsists and emits its light and stimulates our desire for perfection. As I shall take the liberty of making but a single criticism of Mr. Besant, whose tone is so full of the love of his art, I may as well have done with it at once. He seems to me to mistake in attempting to say so definitely beforehand what sort of an affair the good novel will be. To indicate the danger of such an error as that has been the purpose of these few pages; to suggest that certain traditions on the subject, applied *a priori*, have already had much to answer for, and that the good health of an art which undertakes so immediately to reproduce life must demand that it be perfectly free. It lives upon exercise, and the very meaning of exercise is freedom. The only obligation to which in advance we may hold a novel, without incurring the accusation of being arbitrary, is that it be interesting. That general responsibility rests upon it, but it is the only one I can think of. The ways in which it is at liberty to accomplish this result (of interesting us) strike me as innumerable, and such as can only suffer from being marked out or fenced in by prescription. They are as various as the temperament of man, and they are successful in proportion as they reveal a particular mind, different from others. A novel is in its broadest definition a personal, a direct impression of life: that, to begin with, constitutes its value, which is greater or less according to the intensity of the impression. But there will be no intensity at all, and therefore no value, unless there is freedom to feel and say. The tracing of a line to be followed, of a tone to be taken, of a form to be filled out, is a limitation of that freedom and a suppression of the very thing that we are most curious about. The form, it seems to me, is to be appreciated after the fact: then the author's choice has been made, his standard has been indicated; then we can follow lines and directions and compare tones and resemblances. Then in a word we can enjoy one of the most charming of pleasures, we can estimate quality, we can apply the test of execution. The execution belongs to the author alone; it is what is most personal to him, and we measure him by that. The advantage, the luxury, as well as the torment and responsibility of the novelist, is that there is no limit to what he may attempt as an executant—no limit to his possible experiments, efforts, discoveries, successes. Here it is especially that he works, step by step, like his brother of the brush, of whom we may always say that he has painted his picture in a manner best known to himself. His manner is his secret, not necessarily a jealous one. He cannot disclose it as a general thing if he would; he would be at a loss to teach it to others. I say this with a due recollection of having insisted on the community of method of the artist who paints a picture and the artist who writes a novel. The painter *is* able to teach the rudiments of his practice, and it is possible, from the study of good work (granted the aptitude), both to learn how to paint and to learn how to write. Yet it remains true, without injury to the *rapprochement*,[4] that the literary artist would be obliged to say to his pupil much more than the other, "Ah, well, you must do it as you can!" It is a question of degree, a matter of delicacy. If there are exact sciences, there are also exact arts, and the grammar of painting is so much more definite that it makes the difference.

I ought to add, however, that if Mr. Besant says at the beginning of his essay that the "laws of fiction may be laid down and taught with as much precision and exactness as the laws of harmony, perspective, and proportion," he mitigates what might appear to be an extravagance by applying his remark to "general" laws, and by expressing most of these rules in a manner with which it would certainly be unaccommodating to disagree. That the novelist must write from his experience, that his "characters must be real and such as might be met with in actual life"; that "a young lady brought up in a quiet country village should avoid descriptions of garrison life," and "a writer whose friends and personal experiences belong to the lower middle class should carefully avoid introducing his characters into society"; that one should enter one's notes in a common-place

4. Analogy.

book; that one's figures should be clear in outline; that making them clear by some trick of speech or of carriage is a bad method, and "describing them at length" is a worse one; that English fiction should have a "conscious moral purpose"; that "it is almost impossible to estimate too highly the value of careful workmanship—that is, of style"; that "the most important point of all is the story," that "the story is everything": these are principles with most of which it is surely impossible not to sympathize. That remark about the lower middle-class writer and his knowing his place is perhaps rather chilling; but for the rest I should find it difficult to dissent from any one of these recommendations. At the same time, I should find it difficult positively to assent to them, with the exception, perhaps, of the injunction as to entering one's notes in a commonplace book. They scarcely seem to me to have the quality that Mr. Besant attributes to the rules of the novelist—the "precision and exactness" of "the laws of harmony, perspective, and proportion." They are suggestive, they are even inspiring, but they are not exact, though they are doubtless as much so as the case admits of: which is a proof of that liberty of interpretation for which I just contended. For the value of these different injunctions—so beautiful and so vague—is wholly in the meaning one attaches to them. The characters, the situation, which strike one as real will be those that touch and interest one most, but the measure of reality is very difficult to fix. The reality of Don Quixote or of Mr. Micawber[5] is a very delicate shade; it is a reality so colored by the author's vision that, vivid as it may be, one would hesitate to propose it as a model: one would expose one's self to some very embarrassing questions on the part of a pupil. It goes without saying that you will not write a good novel unless you possess the sense of reality; but it will be difficult to give you a recipe for calling that sense into being. Humanity is immense, and reality has a myriad forms; the most one can affirm is that some of the flowers of fiction have the odor of it, and others have not; as for telling you in advance how your nosegay should be composed, that is another affair. It is equally excellent and inconclusive to say that one must write from experience; to our suppositious aspirant such a declaration might savor of mockery. What kind of experience is intended, and where does it begin and end? Experience is never limited, and it is never complete; it is an immense sensibility, a kind of huge spiderweb of the finest silken threads suspended in the chamber of consciousness, and catching every air-borne particle in its tissue. It is the very atmosphere of the mind; and when the mind is imaginative—much more when it happens to be that of a man of genius—it takes to itself the faintest hints of life, it converts the very pulses of the air into revelations. The young lady living in a

5. Character in Dickens' *David Copperfield*.

village has only to be a damsel upon whom nothing is lost to make it quite unfair (as it seems to me) to declare to her that she shall have nothing to say about the military. Greater miracles have been seen than that, imagination assisting, she should speak the truth about some of these gentlemen. I remember an English novelist, a woman of genius, telling me that she was much commended for the impression she had managed to give in one of her tales of the nature and way of life of the French Protestant youth. She had been asked where she learned so much about this recondite being, she had been congratulated on her peculiar opportunities. These opportunities consisted in her having once, in Paris, as she ascended a staircase, passed an open door where, in the household of a *pasteur*,[6] some of the young Protestants were seated at table round a finished meal. The glimpse made a picture; it lasted only a moment, but that moment was experience. She had got her direct personal impression, and she turned out her type. She knew what youth was, and what Protestantism; she also had the advantage of having seen what it was to be French, so that she converted these ideas into a concrete image and produced a reality. Above all, however, she was blessed with the faculty which when you give it an inch takes an ell,[7] and which for the artist is a much greater source of strength than any accident of residence or of place in the social scale. The power to guess the unseen from the seen, to trace the implication of things, to judge the whole piece by the pattern, the condition of feeling life in general so completely that you are well on your way to knowing any particular corner of it—this cluster of gifts may almost be said to constitute experience, and they occur in country and in town, and in the most differing stages of education. If experience consists of impressions, it may be said that impressions *are* experience, just as (have we not seen it?) they are the very air we breathe. Therefore, if I should certainly say to a novice, "Write from experience and experience only," I should feel that this was rather a tantalizing monition if I were not careful immediately to add, "Try to be one of the people on whom nothing is lost!"

I am far from intending by this to minimize the importance of exactness—of truth of detail. One can speak best from one's own taste, and I may therefore venture to say that the air of reality (solidity of specification) seems to me to be the supreme virtue of a novel—the merit on which all its other merits (including that conscious moral purpose of which Mr. Besant speaks) helplessly and submissively depend. If it be not there, they are all as nothing, and if these be there, they owe their effect to the success with which the author has produced the illusion of life. The cultivation of this success,

6. Pastor.

7. A unit of measure of cloth, usually forty-five inches.

the study of this exquisite process, form, to my taste, the beginning and the end of the art of the novelist. They are his inspiration, his despair, his reward, his torment, his delight. It is here in very truth that he competes with life; it is here that he competes with his brother the painter in *his* attempt to render the look of things, the look that conveys their meaning, to catch the color, the relief, the expression, the surface, the substance of the human spectacle. It is in regard to this that Mr. Besant is well inspired when he bids him take notes. He cannot possibly take too many, he cannot possibly take enough. All life solicits him, and to "render" the simplest surface, to produce the most momentary illusion, is a very complicated business. His case would be easier, and the rule would be more exact, if Mr. Besant had been able to tell him what notes to take. But this, I fear, he can never learn in any manual; it is the business of his life. He has to take a great many in order to select a few, he has to work them up as he can, and even the guides and philosophers who might have most to say to him must leave him alone when it comes to the application of precepts, as we leave the painter in communion with his palette. That his characters "must be clear in outline," as Mr. Besant says—he feels that down to his boots; but how he shall make them so is a secret between his good angel and himself. It would be absurdly simple if he could be taught that a great deal of "description" would make them so, or that on the contrary the absence of description and the cultivation of dialogue, or the absence of dialogue and the multiplication of "incident," would rescue him from his difficulties. Nothing, for instance, is more possible than that he be of a turn of mind for which this odd, literal opposition of description and dialogue, incident and description, has little meaning and light. People often talk of these things as if they had a kind of internecine distinctness, instead of melting into each other at every breath, and being intimately associated parts of one general effort of expression. I cannot imagine composition existing in a series of blocks, nor conceive, in any novel worth discussing at all, of a passage of description that is not in its intention narrative, a passage of dialogue that is not in its intention descriptive, a touch of truth of any sort that does not partake of the nature of incident, or an incident that derives its interest from any other source than the general and only source of the success of a work of art—that of being illustrative. A novel is a living thing, all one and continuous, like any other organism, and in proportion as it lives will it be found, I think, that in each of the parts there is something of each of the other parts. The critic who over the close texture of a finished work shall pretend to trace a geography of items will mark some frontiers as artificial, I fear, as any that have been known to history. There is an old-fashioned distinction between the novel of character and the novel of incident which must have cost many a smile to the intending fabulist who was keen about his work. It appears to me as little to the point as the equally celebrated distinction between the novel and the romance—to answer as little to any reality. There are bad novels and good novels, as there are bad pictures and good pictures; but that is the only distinction in which I see any meaning, and I can as little imagine speaking of a novel of character as I can imagine speaking of a picture of character. When one says picture one says of character, when one says novel one says of incident, and the terms may be transposed at will. What is character but the determination of incident? What is incident but the illustration of character? What is either a picture or a novel that is *not* of character? What else do we seek in it and find in it? It is an incident for a woman to stand up with her hand resting on a table and look out at you in a certain way; or if it be not an incident I think it will be hard to say what it is. At the same time it is an expression of character. If you say you don't see it (character in *that—allons donc!*[8]), this is exactly what the artist who has reasons of his own for thinking he *does* see it undertakes to show you. When a young man makes up his mind that he has not faith enough after all to enter the church as he intended, that is an incident, though you may not hurry to the end of the chapter to see whether perhaps he doesn't change once more. I do not say that these are extraordinary or startling incidents. I do not pretend to estimate the degree of interest proceeding from them, for this will depend upon the skill of the painter. It sounds almost puerile to say that some incidents are intrinsically much more important than others, and I need not take this precaution after having professed my sympathy for the major ones in remarking that the only classification of the novel that I can understand is into that which has life and that which has it not.

The novel and the romance, the novel of incident and that of character—these clumsy separations appear to me to have been made by critics and readers for their own convenience, and to help them out of some of their occasional queer predicaments, but to have little reality or interest for the producer, from whose point of view it is of course that we are attempting to consider the art of fiction. The case is the same with another shadowy category which Mr. Besant apparently is disposed to set up—that of the "modern English novel"; unless indeed it be that in this matter he has fallen into an accidental confusion of standpoints. It is not quite clear whether he intends the remarks in which he alludes to it to be didactic or historical. It is as difficult to suppose a person intending to write a modern English as to suppose him writing an ancient

8. Come now!

English novel: that is a label which begs the question. One writes the novel, one paints the picture, of one's language and of one's time, and calling it modern English will not, alas! make the difficult task any easier. No more, unfortunately, will calling this or that work of one's fellow artist a romance—unless it be, of course, simply for the pleasantness of the thing, as for instance when Hawthorne gave this heading to his story of *Blithedale*.[9] The French, who have brought the theory of fiction to remarkable completeness, have but one name for the novel, and have not attempted smaller things in it, that I can see, for that. I can think of no obligation to which the "romancer" would not be held equally with the novelist; the standard of execution is equally high for each. Of course it is of execution that we are talking—that being the only point of a novel that is open to contention. This is perhaps too often lost sight of, only to produce interminable confusions and cross purposes. We must grant the artist his subject, his idea, his *donnée*:[1] our criticism is applied only to what he makes of it. Naturally I do not mean that we are bound to like it or find it interesting: in case we do not, our course is perfectly simple—to let it alone. We may believe that of a certain idea even the most sincere novelist can make nothing at all, and the event may perfectly justify our belief; but the failure will have been a failure to execute, and it is in the execution that the fatal weakness is recorded. If we pretend to respect the artist at all, we must allow him his freedom of choice, in the face, in particular cases, of innumerable presumptions that the choice will not fructify. Art derives a considerable part of its beneficial exercise from flying in the face of presumptions, and some of the most interesting experiments of which it is capable are hidden in the bosom of common things. Gustave Flaubert has written a story[2] about the devotion of a servant girl to a parrot, and the production, highly finished as it is, cannot on the whole be called a success. We are perfectly free to find it flat, but I think it might have been interesting; and I, for my part, am extremely glad he should have written it; it is a contribution to our knowledge of what can be done—or what cannot. Ivan Turgénieff has written a tale[3] about a deaf and dumb serf and a lap dog, and the thing is touching, loving, a little masterpiece. He struck the note of life where Gustave Flaubert missed it— he flew in the face of a presumption and achieved a victory.

Nothing, of course, will ever take the place of the good old fashion of "liking" a work of art or not liking it: the most improved criticism will not abolish that primitive, that ultimate test. I mention this to guard myself from the accusation of intimating that the idea, the subject, of a novel or a picture, does not matter. It mat-

9. *The Blithedale Romance.*
1. Given starting point.

2. "A Simple Heart."
3. "Mumu."

ters, to my sense, in the highest degree, and if I might put up a prayer it would be that artists should select none but the richest. Some, as I have already hastened to admit, are much more remunerative than others, and it would be a world happily arranged in which persons intending to treat them should be exempt from confusions and mistakes. This fortunate condition will arrive only, I fear, on the same day that critics become purged from error. Meanwhile, I repeat, we do not judge the artist with fairness unless we say to him, "Oh, I grant you your starting point, because if I did not I should seem to prescribe to you, and heaven forbid I should take that responsibility. If I pretend to tell you what you must not take, you will call upon me to tell you then what you must take; in which case I shall be prettily caught. Moreover, it isn't till I have accepted your data that I can begin to measure you. I have the standard, the pitch; I have no right to tamper with your flute and then criticize your music. Of course I may not care for your idea at all; I may think it silly, or stale, or unclean; in which case I wash my hands of you altogether. I may content myself with believing that you will not have succeeded in being interesting, but I shall, of course, not attempt to demonstrate it, and you will be as indifferent to me as I am to you. I needn't remind you that there are all sorts of tastes: who can know it better? Some people, for excellent reasons, don't like to read about carpenters; others, for reasons even better, don't like to read about courtesans. Many object to Americans. Others (I believe they are mainly editors and publishers) won't look at Italians. Some readers don't like quiet subjects; others don't like bustling ones. Some enjoy a complete illusion, others the consciousness of large concessions. They choose their novels accordingly, and if they don't care about your idea they won't, *a fortiori*,[4] care about your treatment."

So that it comes back very quickly, as I have said, to the liking: in spite of M. Zola,[5] who reasons less powerfully than he represents, and who will not reconcile himself to this absoluteness of taste, thinking that there are certain things that people ought to like, and that they can be made to like. I am quite at a loss to imagine anything (at any rate in this matter of fiction) that people *ought* to like or to dislike. Selection will be sure to take care of itself, for it has a constant motive behind it. That motive is simply experience. As people feel life, so they will feel the art that is most closely related to it. This closeness of relation is what we should never forget in talking of the effort of the novel. Many people speak of it as a factitious, artificial form, a product of ingenuity, the business of which is to alter and arrange the things that surround us, to translate

4. All the more.
5. Émile Zola (1840–1902), novelist and author of *Le roman expérimental*, which explains his theories of fiction.

them into conventional, traditional molds. This, however, is a view of the matter which carries us but a very short way, condemns the art to an eternal repetition of a few familiar *clichés*, cuts short its development, and leads us straight up to a dead wall. Catching the very note and trick, the strange irregular rhythm of life, that is the attempt whose strenuous force keeps Fiction upon her feet. In proportion as in what she offers us we see life *without* rearrangement do we feel that we are touching the truth; in proportion as we see it *with* rearrangement do we feel that we are being put off with a substitute, a compromise and convention. It is not uncommon to hear an extraordinary assurance of remark in regard to this matter of rearranging, which is often spoken of as if it were the last word of art. Mr. Besant seems to me in danger of falling into the great error with his rather unguarded talk about "selection." Art is essentially selection, but it is a selection whose main care is to be typical, to be inclusive. For many people art means rose-colored window-panes, and selection means picking a bouquet for Mrs. Grundy.[6] They will tell you glibly that artistic considerations have nothing to do with the disagreeable, with the ugly; they will rattle off shallow commonplaces about the province of art and the limits of art till you are moved to some wonder in return as to the province and the limits of ignorance. It appears to me that no one can ever have made a seriously artistic attempt without becoming conscious of an immense increase—a kind of revelation—of freedom. One perceives in that case—by the light of a heavenly ray—that the province of art is all life, all feeling, all observation, all vision. As Mr. Besant so justly intimates, it is all experience. That is a sufficient answer to those who maintain that it must not touch the sad things of life, who stick into its divine unconscious bosom little prohibitory inscriptions on the end of sticks, such as we see in public gardens— "It is forbidden to walk on the grass; it is forbidden to touch the flowers; it is not allowed to introduce dogs or to remain after dark; it is requested to keep to the right." The young aspirant in the line of fiction whom we continue to imagine will do nothing without taste, for in that case his freedom would be of little use to him; but the first advantage of his taste will be to reveal to him the absurdity of the little sticks and tickets. If he have taste, I must add, of course he will have ingenuity, and my disrespectful reference to that quality just now was not meant to imply that it is useless in fiction. But it is only a secondary aid; the first is a capacity for receiving straight impressions.

Mr. Besant has some remarks on the question of "the story" which I shall not attempt to criticize, though they seem to me to contain

6. The stock personification of prudery. *Cf.* Thomas Morton's *Speed the Plough* (1798), a comedy in which Mrs. Grundy is a character.

a singular ambiguity, because I do not think I understand them. I cannot see what is meant by talking as if there were a part of a novel which is the story and part of it which for mystical reasons is not—unless indeed the distinction be made in a sense in which it is difficult to suppose that anyone should attempt to convey anything. "The story," if it represents anything, represents the subject, the idea, the *donnée* of the novel; and there is surely no "school"—Mr. Besant speaks of a school—which urges that a novel should be all treatment and no subject. There must assuredly be something to treat; every school is intimately conscious of that. This sense of the story being the idea, the starting point, of the novel, is the only one that I see in which it can be spoken of as something different from its organic whole; and since in proportion as the work is successful the idea permeates and penetrates it, informs and animates it, so that every word and every punctuation point contribute directly to the expression, in that proportion do we lose our sense of the story being a blade which may be drawn more or less out of its sheath. The story and the novel, the idea and the form, are the needle and thread, and I never heard of a guild of tailors who recommended the use of thread without the needle, or the needle without the thread. Mr. Besant is not the only critic who may be observed to have spoken as if there were certain things in life which constitute stories, and certain others which do not. I find the same odd implications in an entertaining article in the *Pall Mall Gazette,* devoted, as it happens, to Mr. Besant's lecture. "The story is the thing!" says this graceful writer, as if with a tone of opposition to some other idea. I should think it was, as every painter who, as the time for "sending in" his picture looms in the distance, finds himself still in quest of a subject—as every belated artist not fixed about his theme will heartily agree. There are some subjects which speak to us and others which do not, but he would be a clever man who should undertake to give a rule—an index expurgatorius[7]—by which the story and the no-story should be known apart. It is impossible (to me at least) to imagine any such rule which shall not be altogether arbitrary. The writer in the *Pall Mall* opposes the delightful (as I suppose) novel of *Margot la Balafrée*[8] to certain tales in which "Bostonian nymphs" appear to have "rejected English dukes for psychological reasons." I am not acquainted with the romance just designated, and can scarcely forgive the *Pall Mall* critic for not mentioning the name of the author, but the title appears to refer to a lady who may have received a scar[9] in some heroic adventure. I am inconsolable at not being acquainted with this episode, but am utterly at a loss to see why it is a story when the rejection (or

7. The allusion is to the Catholic "Index" of forbidden books.
8. A novel, published in 1884, by Fortuné Du Boisgobey.
9. *Balafrée* means "lady with a scar."

acceptance) of a duke is not, and why a reason, psychological or other, is not a subject when a cicatrix[1] is. They are all particles of the multitudinous life with which the novel deals, and surely no dogma which pretends to make it lawful to touch the one and unlawful to touch the other will stand for a moment on its feet. It is the special picture that must stand or fall, according as it seem to possess truth or to lack it. Mr. Besant does not, to my sense, light up the subject by intimating that a story must, under penalty of not being a story, consist of "adventures." Why of adventures more than of green spectacles?[2] He mentions a category of impossible things, and among them he places "fiction without adventure." Why without adventure, more than without matrimony, or celibacy, or parturition, or cholera, or hydropathy,[3] or Jansenism?[4] This seems to me to bring the novel back to the hapless little role of being an artificial, ingenious thing—bring it down from its large, free character of an immense and exquisite correspondence with life. And what *is* adventure, when it comes to that, and by what sign is the listening pupil to recognize it? It is an adventure—an immense one—for me to write this little article; and for a Bostonian nymph to reject an English duke is an adventure only less stirring, I should say, than for an English duke to be rejected by a Bostonian nymph. I see dramas within dramas in that, and innumerable points of view. A psychological reason is, to my imagination, an object adorably pictorial; to catch the tint of its complexion—I feel as if that idea might inspire one to Titianesque[5] efforts. There are few things more exciting to me, in short, than a psychological reason, and yet, I protest, the novel seems to me the most magnificent form of art. I have just been reading, at the same time, the delightful story of *Treasure Island,* by Mr. Robert Louis Stevenson and, in a manner less consecutive, the last tale from M. Edmond de Goncourt, which is entitled *Chérie.* One of these works treats of murders, mysteries, islands of dreadful renown, hairbreadth escapes, miraculous coincidences, and buried doubloons. The other treats of a little French girl who lived in a fine house in Paris, and died of wounded sensibility because no one would marry her. I call *Treasure Island* delightful because it appears to me to have succeeded wonderfully in what it attempts; and I venture to bestow no epithet upon *Chérie,* which strikes me as having failed deplorably in what it attempts—that is, in tracing the development of the moral consciousness of a child. But one of these productions strikes me as exactly as much of a novel as the other, and as having a "story" quite as much. The moral

1. Scar.
2. *Cf.* Oliver Goldsmith, *The Vicar of Wakefield.*
3. Water therapy.
4. Heretical doctrines of Cornelius Jansen (1585–1638), Catholic bishop of Ypres.
5. The allusion is to the sixteenth-century Venetian painter.

consciousness of a child is as much a part of life as the islands of the Spanish Main, and the one sort of geography seems to me to have those "surprises" of which Mr. Besant speaks quite as much as the other. For myself (since it comes back in the last resort, as I say, to the preference of the individual), the picture of the child's experience has the advantage that I can at successive steps (an immense luxury, near to the "sensual pleasure" of which Mr. Besant's critic in the *Pall Mall* speaks) say Yes or No, as it may be, to what the artist puts before me. I have been a child in fact, but I have been on a quest for a buried treasure only in supposition, and it is a simple accident that with M. de Goncourt I should have for the most part to say No. With George Eliot, when she painted[6] that country with a far other intelligence, I always said Yes.

The most interesting part of Mr. Besant's lecture is unfortunately the briefest passage—his very cursory allusion to the "conscious moral purpose" of the novel. Here again it is not very clear whether he be recording a fact or laying down a principle; it is a great pity that in the latter case he should not have developed his idea. This branch of the subject is of immense importance, and Mr. Besant's few words point to considerations of the widest reach, not to be lightly disposed of. He will have treated the art of fiction but superficially who is not prepared to go every inch of the way that these considerations will carry him. It is for this reason that at the beginning of these remarks I was careful to notify the reader that my reflections on so large a theme have no pretension to be exhaustive. Like Mr. Besant, I have left the question of the morality of the novel till the last, and at the last I find I have used up my space. It is a question surrounded with difficulties, as witness the very first that meets us, in the form of a definite question, on the threshold. Vagueness, in such a discussion, is fatal, and what is the meaning of your morality and your conscious moral purpose? Will you not define your terms and explain how (a novel being a picture) a picture can be either moral or immoral? You wish to paint a moral picture or carve a moral statue: will you not tell us how you would set about it? We are discussing the Art of Fiction; questions of art are questions (in the widest sense) of execution; questions of morality are quite another affair, and will you not let us see how it is that you find it so easy to mix them up? These things are so clear to Mr. Besant that he has deduced from them a law which he sees embodied in English fiction, and which is "a truly admirable thing and a great cause for congratulation." It is a great cause for congratulation indeed when such thorny problems become as smooth as silk. I may add that in so far as Mr. Besant perceives that in point of fact English fiction has addressed itself prepon-

6. *Cf. Silas Marner.*

derantly to these delicate questions he will appear to many people to have made a vain discovery. They will have been positively struck, on the contrary, with the moral timidity of the usual English novelist; with his (or with her) aversion to face the difficulties with which on every side the treatment of reality bristles. He is apt to be extremely shy (whereas the picture that Mr. Besant draws is a picture of boldness), and the sign of his work, for the most part, is a cautious silence on certain subjects. In the English novel (by which of course I mean the American as well), more than in any other, there is a traditional difference between that which people know and that which they agree to admit that they know, that which they see and that which they speak of, that which they feel to be a part of life and that which they allow to enter into literature. There is the great difference, in short, between what they talk of in conversation and what they talk of in print. The essence of moral energy is to survey the whole field, and I should directly reverse Mr. Besant's remark and say not that the English novel has a purpose, but that it has a diffidence. To what degree a purpose in a work of art is a source of corruption I shall not attempt to inquire; the one that seems to me least dangerous is the purpose of making a perfect work. As for our novel, I may say lastly on this score that as we find it in England today it strikes me as addressed in a large degree to "young people," and that this in itself constitutes a presumption that it will be rather shy. There are certain things which it is generally agreed not to discuss, not even to mention, before young people. That is very well, but the absence of discussion is not a symptom of the moral passion. The purpose of the English novel— "a truly admirable thing, and a great cause for congratulation"— strikes me therefore as rather negative.

There is one point at which the moral sense and the artistic sense lie very near together; that is in the light of the very obvious truth that the deepest quality of a work of art will always be the quality of the mind of the producer. In proportion as that intelligence is fine will the novel, the picture, the statue partake of the substance of beauty and truth. To be constituted of such elements is, to my vision, to have purpose enough. No good novel will ever proceed from a superficial mind; that seems to me an axiom which, for the artist in fiction, will cover all needful moral ground: if the youthful aspirant take it to heart it will illuminate for him many of the mysteries of "purpose." There are many other useful things that might be said to him, but I have come to the end of my article, and can only touch them as I pass. The critic in the *Pall Mall Gazette*, whom I have already quoted, draws attention to the danger, in speaking of the art of fiction, of generalizing. The danger that he has in mind is rather, I imagine, that of particularizing, for there are some comprehensive remarks which, in addition to those embodied in Mr. Besant's suggestive lecture, might without fear of misleading him be addressed to the ingenuous student. I should remind him first of the magnificence of the form that is open to him, which offers to sight so few restrictions and such innumerable opportunities. The other arts, in comparison, appear confined and hampered; the various conditions under which they are exercised are so rigid and definite. But the only condition that I can think of attaching to the composition of the novel is, as I have already said, that it be sincere. This freedom is a splendid privilege, and the first lesson of the young novelist is to learn to be worthy of it. "Enjoy it as it deserves," I should say to him; "take possession of it, explore it to its utmost extent, publish it, rejoice in it. All life belongs to you, and do not listen either to those who would shut you up into corners of it and tell you that it is only here and there that art inhabits, or to those who would persuade you that this heavenly messenger wings her way outside of life altogether, breathing a superfine air, and turning away her head from the truth of things. There is no impression of life, no manner of seeing it and feeling it, to which the plan of the novelist may not offer a place; you have only to remember that talents so dissimilar as those of Alexandre Dumas and Jane Austen, Charles Dickens and Gustave Flaubert have worked in this field with equal glory. Do not think too much about optimism and pessimism; try and catch the color of life itself. In France today we see a prodigious effort (that of Emile Zola,[7] to whose solid and serious work no explorer of the capacity of the novel can allude without respect), we see an extraordinary effort vitiated by a spirit of pessimism on a narrow basis. M. Zola is magnificent, but he strikes an English reader as ignorant; he has an air of working in the dark; if he had as much light as energy, his results would be of the highest value. As for the aberrations of a shallow optimism, the ground (of English fiction especially) is strewn with their brittle particles as with broken glass. If you must indulge in conclusions, let them have the taste of a wide knowledge. Remember that your first duty is to be as complete as possible—to make as perfect a work. Be generous and delicate and pursue the prize."

1884, 1888

7. *Cf.* James's study of Zola in *Notes on Novelists* (1914), pp. 26–64.

The Beast in the Jungle[1]

I

What determined the speech that startled him in the course of their encounter scarcely matters, being probably but some words spoken by himself quite without intention—spoke as they lingered and slowly moved together after their renewal of acquaintance. He had been conveyed by friends an hour or two before to the house at which she was staying; the party of visitors at the other house, of whom he was one, and thanks to whom it was his theory, as always, that he was lost in the crowd, had been invited over to luncheon. There had been after luncheon much dispersal, all in the interest of the original motive, a view of Weatherend itself[2] and the fine things, intrinsic features, pictures, heirlooms, treasures of all the arts, that made the place almost famous; and the great rooms were so numerous that guests could wander at their will, hang back from the principal group and in cases where they took such matters with the last seriousness give themselves up to mysterious appreciations and measurements. There were

1. Among the selections in this volume, "The Beast in the Jungle" represents the vintage James, with the highest complexity of symbolism and, at the same time, the greatest clarity of motivation. He wrote the story in 1901, immediately after completing *The Ambassadors*—to James' mind his most finished product—and it would seem that this story owes much to that novel for its motivation. Like Strether in *The Ambassadors*, John Marcher spends his life in the shadow of the more vivid experiences of others. Both lives are tragic because the means of escape lie at hand, ready for the grasping. By comparison, the force of this story is heightened because Marcher's predicament is recognized by only one individual, May Bartram, and she alone could have saved him.

In his preface to the story published in the New York Edition of his collected works, James describes his "poor gentleman" as having "the conviction, lodged in his brain, part and parcel of his imagination from far back, that experience would be marked for him, and whether for good or for ill, by some rare distinction, some incalculable violence or unprecedented stroke. * * * Therefore as each item of experience comes, with its possibilities, into view, he can but dismiss it under this sterilising habit of the failure to find it good enough and thence to appropriate it. * * * He is afraid to recognise what he incidentally misses, since what his

high belief amounts to is not that he shall have felt and vibrated less than any one else, but that he shall have felt and vibrated more; which no acknowledgment of the minor loss must conflict with." This fear James symbolizes as the threatened leap of the beast.

So Marcher moves on through his detached life, the jungle of his own egoism and fear of experience. In "The Art of Fiction" James defines experience as being never limited and never complete—"it is an immense sensibility." His fatal lack in this capacity prevents Marcher from comprehending his long awaited "rare and strange" fate to be simply that nothing will ever happen to him, that he is to be a man without being human. The figurative beast strikes when Marcher discovers, too late, that the springs of life were in May Bartram's more acute and suffering sensibility.

The story was first published in a volume of stories, *The Better Sort* (1903), but the author placed it in a collection of his tales of the "quasi-supernatural" in the volume entitled *The Altar of the Dead* in the New York Edition (1907–1917).

2. As Leon Edel points out in his introduction to *Henry James Selected Fiction*, the author sets the tone early in the story by the uncomplicated symbolism of Weatherend's name, "suggesting temporal changes and the seasons," and the suggestive comparison in the names of May and Marcher.

persons to be observed, singly or in couples, bending toward objects in out-of-the-way corners with their hands on their knees and their heads nodding quite as with the emphasis of an excited sense of smell. When they were two they either mingled their sounds of ecstasy or melted into silences of even deeper import, so that there were aspects of the occasion that gave it for Marcher much the air of the "look round," previous to a sale highly advertised, that excites or quenches, as may be, the dream of acquisition. The dream of acquisition at Weatherend would have had to be wild indeed, and John Marcher found himself, among such suggestions, disconcerted almost equally by the presence of those who knew too much and by that of those who knew nothing. The great rooms caused so much poetry and history to press upon him that he needed some straying apart to feel in a proper relation with them, though this impulse was not, as happened, like the gloating of some of his companions, to be compared to the movements of a dog sniffing a cupboard. It had an issue promptly enough in a direction that was not to have been calculated.

It led, briefly, in the course of the October afternoon, to his closer meeting with May Bartram, whose face, a reminder, yet not quite a remembrance, as they sat much separated at a very long table, had begun merely by troubling him rather pleasantly. It affected him as the sequel of something of which he had lost the beginning. He knew it, and for the time quite welcomed it, as a continuation, but didn't know what it continued, which was an interest or an amusement the greater as he was also somehow aware—yet without a direct sign from her—that the young woman herself hadn't lost the thread. She hadn't lost it, but she wouldn't give it back to him, he saw, without some putting forth of his hand for it; and he not only saw that, but saw several things more, things odd enough in the light of the fact that at the moment some accident of grouping brought them face to face he was still merely fumbling with the idea that any contact between them in the past would have had no importance. If it had had no importance he scarcely knew why his actual impression of her should so seem to have so much; the answer to which, however, was that in such a life as they all appeared to be leading for the moment one could but take things as they came. He was satisfied, without in the least being able to say why, that this young lady might roughly have ranked in the house as a poor relation; satisfied also that she was not there on a brief visit, but was more or less a part of the establishment—almost a working, a remunerated part. Didn't she enjoy at periods a protection that she paid for by helping, among other services, to show the place and explain it, deal with the tiresome people, answer questions about the dates of the building, the

styles of the furniture, the authorship of the pictures, the favour-
ite haunts of the ghost? It wasn't that she looked as if you could
have given her shillings—it was impossible to look less so. Yet
when she finally drifted toward him, distinctly handsome, though
ever so much older—older than when he had seen her before—
it might have been as an effect of her guessing that he had, within
the couple of hours, devoted more imagination to her than to all
the others put together, and had thereby penetrated to a kind of
truth that the others were too stupid for. She *was* there on harder
terms than any one; she was there as a consequence of things suffered, one way and another, in the interval of years; and she remembered him very much as she was remembered—only a good
deal better.

By the time they at last thus came to speech they were alone
in one of the rooms—remarkable for a fine portrait over the
chimney-place—out of which their friends had passed, and the
charm of it was that even before they had spoken they had practically arranged with each other to stay behind for talk. The charm,
happily, was in other things too—partly in there being scarce a
spot at Weatherend without something to stay behind for. It was
in the way the autumn day looked into the high windows as it
waned; the way the red light, breaking at the close from under a
low sombre sky, reached out in a long shaft and played over old
wainscots, old tapestry, old gold, old colour. It was most of all perhaps in the way she came to him as if, since she had been turned
on to deal with the simpler sort, he might, should he choose to
keep the whole thing down, just take her mild attention for a part
of her general business. As soon as he heard her voice, however,
the gap was filled up and the missing link supplied; the slight
irony he divined in her attitude lost its advantage. He almost
jumped at it to get there before her. "I met you years and years
ago in Rome. I remember all about it." She confessed to disappointment—she had been so sure he didn't; and to prove how well
he did he began to pour forth the particular recollections that
popped up as he called for them. Her face and her voice, all at
his service now, worked the miracle—the impression operating
like the torch of a lamplighter who touches into flame, one by one,
a long row of gas-jets. Marcher flattered himself the illumination
was brilliant, yet he was really still more pleased on her showing
him, with amusement, that in his haste to make everything right
he had got most things rather wrong. It hadn't been at Rome—it
had been at Naples; and it hadn't been eight years before—it had
been more nearly ten. She hadn't been, either, with her uncle and
aunt, but with her mother and her brother; in addition to which
it was not with the Pembles *he* had been, but with the Boyers,

coming down in their company from Rome—a point on which she insisted, a little to his confusion, and as to which she had her evidence in hand. The Boyers she had known, but didn't know the Pembles, though she had heard of them, and it was the people he was with who had made them acquainted. The incident of the thunderstorm that had raged round them with such violence as to drive them for refuge into an excavation—this incident had not occurred at the Palace of the Cæsars, but at Pompeii, on an occasion when they had been present there at an important find.

He accepted her amendments, he enjoyed her corrections, though the moral of them was, she pointed out, that he *really* didn't remember the least thing about her;[3] and he only felt it as a drawback that when all was made strictly historic there didn't appear much of anything left. They lingered together still, she neglecting her office—for from the moment he was so clever she had no proper right to him—and both neglecting the house, just waiting as to see if a memory or two more wouldn't again breathe on them. It hadn't taken them many minutes, after all, to put down on the table, like the cards of a pack, those that constituted their respective hands; only what came out was that the pack was unfortunately not perfect—that the past, invoked, invited, encouraged, could give them, naturally, no more than it had. It had made them anciently meet—her at twenty, him at twenty-five; but nothing was so strange, they seemed to say to each other, as that, while so occupied, it hadn't done a little more for them. They looked at each other as with the feeling of an occasion missed; the present would have been so much better if the other, in the far distance, in the foreign land, hadn't been so stupidly meagre. There weren't apparently, all counted, more than a dozen little old things that had succeeded in coming to pass between them; trivialities of youth, simplicities of freshness, stupidities of ignorance, small possible germs, but too deeply buried—too deeply (didn't it seem?) to sprout after so many years. Marcher could only feel he ought to have rendered her some service—saved her from a capsized boat in the Bay or at least recovered her dressing-bag, filched from her cab in the streets of Naples by a lazzarone with a stiletto. Or it would have been nice if he could have been taken with fever all alone at his hotel, and she could have come to look after him, to write to his people, to drive him out in convalescence. *Then* they would be in possession of the something or other that their actual show seemed to lack. It yet somehow presented itself, this show, as too good to be spoiled; so that they were reduced for a few minutes more to wondering a

---

3. A portent of their different degrees of awareness of life; the difference becomes more evident as their relationship grows.

little helplessly why—since they seemed to know a certain number of the same people—their reunion had been so long averted. They didn't use that name for it, but their delay from minute to minute to join the others was a kind of confession that they didn't quite want it to be a failure. Their attempted supposition of reasons for their not having met but showed how little they knew of each other. There came in fact a moment when Marcher felt a positive pang. It was vain to pretend she was an old friend, for all the communities were wanting, in spite of which it was as an old friend that he saw she would have suited him. He had new ones enough—was surrounded with them for instance on the stage of the other house; as a new one he probably wouldn't have so much as noticed her. He would have liked to invent something, get her to make-believe with him that some passage of a romantic or critical kind *had* originally occurred. He was really almost reaching out in imagination—as against time—for something that would do, and saying to himself that if it didn't come this sketch of a fresh start would show for quite awkwardly bungled. They would separate, and now for no second or no third chance. They would have tried and not succeeded. Then it was, just at the turn, as he afterwards made it out to himself, that, everything else failing, she herself decided to take up the case and, as it were, save the situation. He felt as soon as she spoke that she had been consciously keeping back what she said and hoping to get on without it; a scruple in her that immensely touched him when, by the end of three or four minutes more, he was able to measure it. What she brought out, at any rate, quite cleared the air and supplied the link—the link it was so odd he should frivolously have managed to lose.

"You know you told me something I've never forgotten and that again and again has made me think of you since; it was that tremendously hot day when we went to Sorrento, across the bay, for the breeze. What I allude to was what you said to me, on the way back, as we sat under the awning of the boat enjoying the cool. Have you forgotten?"

He had forgotten and was even more surprised than ashamed. But the great thing was that he saw in this no vulgar reminder of any "sweet" speech. The vanity of women had long memories, but she was making no claim on him of a compliment or a mistake. With another woman, a totally different one, he might have feared the recall possibly even of some imbecile "offer." So, in having to say that he had indeed forgotten, he was conscious rather of a loss than of a gain; he already saw an interest in the matter of her mention. "I try to think—but I give it up. Yet I remember the Sorrento day."

"I'm not very sure you do," May Bartram after a moment said; "and I'm not very sure I ought to want you to. It's dreadful to bring a person back at any time to what he was ten years before. If you've lived away from it," she smiled, "so much the better."

"Ah if *you* haven't why should I?" he asked.

"Lived away, you mean, from what I myself was?"

"From what *I* was. I was of course an ass," Marcher went on; "but I would rather know from you just the sort of ass I was than —from the moment you have something in your mind—not know anything."

Still, however, she hesitated. "But if you've completely ceased to be that sort—?"

"Why I can then all the more bear to know. Besides, perhaps I haven't."

"Perhaps. Yet if you haven't," she added, "I should suppose you'd remember. Not indeed that *I* in the least connect with my impression the invidious name you use. If I had only thought you foolish," she explained, "the thing I speak of wouldn't so have remained with me. It was about yourself." She waited as if it might come to him; but as, only meeting her eyes in wonder, he gave no sign, she burnt her ships. "Has it ever happened?"

Then it was that, while he continued to stare, a light broke for him and the blood slowly came to his face, which began to burn with recognition. "Do you mean I told you—?" But he faltered, lest what came to him shouldn't be right, lest he should only give himself away.

"It was something about yourself that it was natural one shouldn't forget—that is if one remembered you at all. That's why I ask you," she smiled, "if the thing you then spoke of has ever come to pass?"

Oh then he saw, but he was lost in wonder and found himself embarrassed. This, he also saw, made her sorry for him, as if her allusion had been a mistake. It took him but a moment, however, to feel it hadn't been, much as it had been a surprise. After the first little shock of it her knowledge on the contrary began, even if rather strangely, to taste sweet to him. She was the only other person in the world then who would have it, and she had had it all these years, while the fact of his having so breathed his secret had unaccountably faded from him. No wonder they couldn't have met as if nothing had happened. "I judge," he finally said, "that I know what you mean. Only I had strangely enough lost any sense of having taken you so far into my confidence."

"Is it because you've taken so many others as well?"

"I've taken nobody. Not a creature since then."

"So that I'm the only person who knows?"

"The only person in the world."

"Well," she quickly replied, "I myself have never spoken. I've never, never repeated of you what you told me." She looked at him so that he perfectly believed her. Their eyes met over it in such a way that he was without a doubt. "And I never will."

She spoke with an earnestness that, as if almost excessive, put him at ease about her possible derision. Somehow the whole question was a new luxury to him—that is from the moment she was in possession. If she didn't take the sarcastic view she clearly took the sympathetic, and that was what he had had, in all the long time, from no one whomsoever. What he felt was that he couldn't at present have begun to tell her, and yet could profit perhaps exquisitely by the accident of having done so of old. "Please don't then. We're just right as it is."

"Oh I am," she laughed, "if you are!" To which she added: "Then you do still feel in the same way?"

It was impossible he shouldn't take to himself that she was really interested, though it all kept coming as perfect surprise. He had thought of himself so long as abominably alone, and lo he wasn't alone a bit. He hadn't been, it appeared, for an hour—since those moments on the Sorrento boat. It was *she* who had been, he seemed to see as he looked at her—she who had been made so by the graceless fact of his lapse of fidelity. To tell her what he had told her—what had it been but to ask something of her? something that she had given, in her charity, without his having, by a remembrance, by a return of the spirit, failing another encounter, so much as thanked her. What he had asked of her had been simply at first not to laugh at him. She had beautifully not done so for ten years, and she was not doing so now. So he had endless gratitude to make up. Only for that he must see just how he had figured to her. "What, exactly, was the account I gave—?"

"Of the way you did feel? Well, it was very simple. You said you had had from your earliest time, as the deepest thing within you, the sense of being kept for something rare and strange, possibly prodigious and terrible, that was sooner or later to happen to you, that you had in your bones the foreboding and the conviction of, and that would perhaps overwhelm you."

"Do you call that very simple?" John Marcher asked.

She thought a moment. "It was perhaps because I seemed, as you spoke, to understand it."

"You do understand it?" he eagerly asked.

Again she kept her kind eyes on him. "You still have the belief?"

"Oh!" he exclaimed helplessly. There was too much to say.

"Whatever it's to be," she clearly made out, "it hasn't yet come."

He shook his head in complete surrender now. "It hasn't yet come. Only, you know, it isn't anything I'm to *do*, to achieve in the world, to be distinguished or admired for. I'm not such an ass as *that*. It would be much better, no doubt, if I were."

"It's to be something you're merely to suffer?"

"Well, say to wait for—to have to meet, to face, to see suddenly break out in my life; possibly destroying all further consciousness, possibly annihilating me; possibly, on the other hand, only altering everything, striking at the root of all my world and leaving me to the consequences, however they shape themselves."

She took this in, but the light in her eyes continued for him not to be that of mockery. "Isn't what you describe perhaps but the expectation—or at any rate the sense of danger, familiar to so many people—of falling in love?"

John Marcher wondered. "Did you ask me that before?"

"No—I wasn't so free-and-easy then. But it's what strikes me now."

"Of course," he said after a moment, "it strikes you. Of course it strikes *me*. Of course what's in store for me may be no more than that. The only thing is," he went on, "that I think if it had been that I should by this time know."

"Do you mean because you've *been* in love?" And then as he but looked at her in silence: "You've been in love, and it hasn't meant such a cataclysm, hasn't proved the great affair?"

"Here I am, you see. It hasn't been overwhelming."

"Then it hasn't been love," said May Bartram.[4]

"Well, I at least thought it was. I took it for that—I've taken it till now. It was agreeable, it was delightful, it was miserable," he explained. "But it wasn't strange. It wasn't what *my* affair's to be."

"You want something all to yourself—something that nobody else knows or *has* known?"

"It isn't a question of what I 'want'—God knows I don't want anything. It's only a question of the apprehension that haunts me—that I live with day by day."

He said this so lucidly and consistently that he could see it further impose itself. If she hadn't been interested before she'd have been interested now. "Is it a sense of coming violence?"

Evidently now too again he liked to talk of it. "I don't think of it as—when it does come—necessarily violent. I only think of it as natural and as of course above all unmistakeable. I think of

4. May's comment, relating both to Marcher's experiences in general and to his failure in participation, even in love, lights up the entire situation but leaves Marcher in the shadow.

it simply as *the* thing. *The* thing will of itself appear natural."

"Then how will it appear strange?"

Marcher bethought himself. "It won't—to *me*."

"To whom then?"

"Well," he replied, smiling at last, "say to you."

"Oh then I'm to be present?"

"Why you *are* present—since you know."

"I see." She turned it over. "But I mean at the catastrophe."

At this, for a minute, their lightness gave way to their gravity; it was as if the long look they exchanged held them together. "It will only depend on yourself—if you'll watch with me."

"Are you afraid?" she asked.

"Don't leave me *now*," he went on.

"Are you afraid?" she repeated.

"Do you think me simply out of my mind?" he pursued instead of answering. "Do I merely strike you as a harmless lunatic?"

"No," said May Bartram. "I understand you. I believe you."

"You mean you feel how my obsession—poor old thing!—may correspond to some possible reality?"

"To some possible reality."

"Then you *will* watch with me?"

She hesitated, then for the third time put her question. "Are you afraid?"

"Did I tell you I was—at Naples?"

"No, you said nothing about it."

"Then I don't know. And I should *like* to know," said John Marcher. "You'll tell me yourself whether you think so. If you'll watch with me you'll see."

"Very good then." They had been moving by this time across the room, and at the door, before passing out, they paused as for the full wind-up of their understanding. "I'll watch with you," said May Bartram.

II

The fact that she "knew"—knew and yet neither chaffed him nor betrayed him—had in a short time begun to constitute between them a goodly bond, which became more marked when, within the year that followed their afternoon at Weatherend, the opportunities for meeting multiplied. The event that thus promoted these occasions was the death of the ancient lady her great-aunt, under whose wing, since losing her mother, she had to such an extent found shelter, and who, though but the widowed mother of the new successor to the property, had succeeded—thanks to a high tone and a high temper—in not forfeiting the supreme position at the great house. The deposition of this personage arrived but with her death, which, followed by many changes, made in particular a difference for the young woman in whom Marcher's expert attention had recognised from the first a dependent with a pride that might ache though it didn't bristle. Nothing for a long time had made him easier than the thought that the aching must have been much soothed by Miss Bartram's now finding herself able to set up a small home in London. She had acquired property, to an amount that made that luxury just possible, under her aunt's extremely complicated will, and when the whole matter began to be straightened out, which indeed took time, she let him know that the happy issue was at last in view.[5] He had seen her again before that day, both because she had more than once accompanied the ancient lady to town and because he had paid another visit to the friends who so conveniently made of Weatherend one of the charms of their own hospitality. These friends had taken him back there; he had achieved there again with Miss Bartram some quiet detachment; and he had in London succeeded in persuading her to more than one brief absence from her aunt. They went together, on these latter occasions, to the National Gallery and the South Kensington Museum, where, among vivid reminders, they talked of Italy at large—not now attempting to recover, as at first, the taste of their youth and their ignorance. That recovery, the first day at Weatherend, had served its purpose well, had given them quite enough; so that they were, to Marcher's sense, no longer hovering about the headwaters of their stream, but had felt their boat pushed sharply off and down the current.

They were literally afloat together; for our gentleman this was marked, quite as marked as that the fortunate cause of it was just the buried treasure of her knowledge. He had with his own hands dug up this little hoard, brought to light—that is to within reach of the dim day constituted by their discretions and privacies—the object of value the hiding-place of which he had, after putting it into the ground himself, so strangely, so long forgotten. The rare luck of his having again just stumbled on the spot made him indifferent to any other question; he would doubtless have devoted more time to the odd accident of his lapse of memory if he hadn't been moved to devote so much to the sweetness, the comfort, as he felt, for the future, that this accident itself had helped to keep fresh. It had never entered into his plan that any one should "know," and mainly for the reason that it wasn't in him to tell any one. That would have been impossible, for nothing but the amusement of a cold world would have waited on it. Since, however, a mysterious fate had opened his mouth betimes, in spite of him, he would count that a compensation and profit by it to the

---

5. James' persistent preference for the financial independence of his characters did not result from any contempt of an earned salary, but from his wish to have characters "free" for the interplay of situation and response.

utmost. That the right person *should* know tempered the asperity of his secret more even than his shyness had permitted him to imagine; and May Bartram was clearly right, because—well, because there she was. Her knowledge simply settled it; he would have been sure enough by this time had she been wrong. There was that in his situation, no doubt, that disposed him too much to see her as a mere confidant, taking all her light for him from the fact—the fact only—of her interest in his predicament; from her mercy, sympathy, seriousness, her consent not to regard him as the funniest of the funny. Aware, in fine, that her price for him was just in her giving him this constant sense of his being admirably spared, he was careful to remember that she had also a life of her own, with things that might happen to *her*, things that in friendship one should likewise take account of. Something fairly remarkable came to pass with him, for that matter, in this connexion—something represented by a certain passage of his consciousness, in the suddenest way, from one extreme to the other.

He had thought himself, so long as nobody knew, the most disinterested person in the world, carrying his concentrated burden, his perpetual suspense, ever so quietly, holding his tongue about it, giving others no glimpse of it nor of its effect upon his life, asking of them no allowance and only making on his side all those that were asked. He hadn't disturbed people with the queerness of their having to know a haunted man, though he had had moments of rather special temptation on hearing them say they were forsooth "unsettled." If they were as unsettled as he was—he who had never been settled for an hour in his life—they would know what it meant. Yet it wasn't, all the same, for him to make them, and he listened to them civilly enough. This was why he had such good—though possibly such rather colourless—manners; this was why, above all, he could regard himself, in a greedy world, as decently—as in fact perhaps even a little sublimely—unselfish. Our point is accordingly that he valued this character quite sufficiently to measure his present danger of letting it lapse, against which he promised himself to be much on his guard. He was quite ready, none the less, to be selfish just a little, since surely no more charming occasion for it had come to him. "Just a little," in a word, was just as much as Miss Bartram, taking one day with another, would let him. He never would be in the least coercive, and would keep well before him the lines on which consideration for her—the very highest—ought to proceed. He would thoroughly establish the heads under which her affairs, her requirements, her peculiarities—he went so far as to give them the latitude of that name—would come into their intercourse. All this naturally was a sign of how much he took the intercourse itself for granted. There was nothing more to be done about *that*. It simply existed; had sprung into being with her first penetrating question to him in the autumn light there at Weatherend. The real form it should have taken on the basis that stood out large was the form of their marrying. But the devil in this was that the very basis itself put marrying out of the question. His conviction, his apprehension, his obsession, in short, wasn't a privilege he could invite a woman to share; and that consequence of it was precisely what was the matter with him. Something or other lay in wait for him, amid the twists and the turns of the months and the years, like a crouching beast in the jungle. It signified little whether the crouching beast were destined to slay him or to be slain. The definite point was the inevitable spring of the creature; and the definite lesson from that was that a man of feeling didn't cause himself to be accompanied by a lady on a tiger-hunt. Such was the image under which he had ended by figuring his life.

They had at first, none the less, in the scattered hours spent together, made no allusion to that view of it; which was a sign he was handsomely alert to give that he didn't expect, that he in fact didn't care, always to be talking about it. Such a feature in one's outlook was really like a hump on one's back. The difference it made every minute of the day existed quite independently of discussion. One discussed of course *like* a hunchback, for there was always, if nothing else, the hunchback face. That remained, and she was watching him; but people watched best, as a general thing, in silence, so that such would be predominantly the manner of their vigil. Yet he didn't want, at the same time, to be tense and solemn; tense and solemn was what he imagined he too much showed for with other people. The thing to be, with the one person who knew, was easy and natural—to make the reference rather than be seeming to avoid it, to avoid it rather than be seeming to make it, and to keep it, in any case, familiar, facetious even, rather than pedantic and portentous. Some such consideration as the latter was doubtless in his mind for instance when he wrote pleasantly to Miss Bartram that perhaps the great thing he had so long felt as in the lap of the gods was no more than this circumstance, which touched him so nearly, of her acquiring a house in London. It was the first allusion they had yet again made, needing any other hitherto so little; but when she replied, after having given him the news, that she was by no means satisfied with such a trifle as the climax to so special a suspense, she almost set him wondering if she hadn't even a larger conception of singularity for him than he had for himself. He was at all events destined to become aware little by little, as time went by, that she was all the while looking at his life, judging it, measuring it, in the light of the thing she knew, which grew to be at last, with the consecration of the years, never mentioned between them save as "the real truth" about him. That had always been his own form of reference to it, but she adopted the form so quietly that, looking back at the end of a period, he knew there was no moment at which it was traceable that she had, as he might say, got inside his idea, or exchanged the attitude of beautifully indulging for that of still more beautifully believing him.

It was always open to him to accuse her of seeing him but as the most harmless of maniacs, and this, in the long run—since it covered so much ground—was his easiest description of their friendship. He had a screw loose for her, but she liked him in spite of it and was practically, against the rest of the world, his kind wise keeper, unremunerated but fairly amused and, in the absence of other near ties, not disreputably occupied. The rest of the world of course thought him queer, but she, she only, knew how, and above all why, queer; which was precisely what enabled her to dispose the concealing veil in the right folds. She took his gaiety from him—since it had to pass with them for gaiety—as she took everything else; but she certainly so far justified by her unerring touch his finer sense of the degree to which he had ended by convincing her. *She* at least never spoke of the secret of his life except as "the real truth about you," and she had in fact a wonderful way of making it seem, as such, the secret of her own life too. That was in fine how he so constantly felt her as allowing for him; he couldn't on the whole call it anything else. He allowed for himself, but she, exactly, allowed still more; partly because, better placed for a sight of the matter, she traced his unhappy perversion through reaches of its course into which he could scarce follow it. He knew how he felt, but, besides knowing that, she knew how he *looked* as well; he knew each of the things of importance he was insidiously kept from doing, but she could add up the amount they made, understand how much, with a lighter weight on his spirit, he might have done, and thereby establish how, clever as he was, he fell short. Above all she was in the secret of the difference between the forms he went through—those of his little office under Government, those of caring for his modest patrimony, for his library, for his garden in the country, for the people in London whose invitations he accepted and repaid—and the detachment that reigned beneath them and that made of all behaviour, all that could in the least be called behaviour, a long act of dissimulation. What it had come to was that he wore a mask painted with the social simper, out of the eye-holes of which there looked eyes of an expression not in the least matching the other features. This the stupid world, even after years, had never more than half-discovered. It was only May Bartram who had, and she achieved, by an art indescribable, the feat of at once—or perhaps it was only alternately—meeting the eyes from in front and mingling her own vision, as from over his shoulder, with their peep through the apertures.

So while they grew older together she did watch with him, and so she let this association give shape and colour to her own existence. Beneath *her* forms as well detachment had learned to sit, and behaviour had become for her, in the social sense, a false account of herself. There was but one account of her that would have been true all the while and that she could give straight to nobody, least of all to John Marcher. Her whole attitude was a virtual statement, but the perception of that only seemed called to take its place for him as one of the many things necessarily crowded out of his consciousness. If she had moreover, like himself, to make sacrifices to their real truth, it was to be granted that her compensation might have affected her as more prompt and more natural. They had long periods, in this London time, during which, when they were together, a stranger might have listened to them without in the least pricking up his ears; on the other hand the real truth was equally liable at any moment to rise to the surface, and the auditor would then have wondered indeed what they were talking about. They had from an early hour made up their mind that society was, luckily, unintelligent, and the margin allowed them by this had fairly become one of their commonplaces. Yet there were still moments when the situation turned almost fresh—usually under the effect of some expression drawn from herself. Her expressions doubtless repeated themselves, but her intervals were generous. "What saves us, you know, is that we answer so completely to so usual an appearance: that of the man and woman whose friendship has become such a daily habit—or almost—as to be at last indispensable." That for instance was a remark she had frequently enough had occasion to make, though she had given it at different times different developments. What we are especially concerned with is the turn it happened to take from her one afternoon when he had come to see her in honour of her birthday. This anniversary had fallen on a Sunday, at a season of thick fog and general outward gloom; but he had brought her his customary offering, having known her now long enough to have established a hundred small traditions. It was one of his proofs to himself, the present he made her on her birthday, that he hadn't sunk into real selfishness.[6] It was mostly nothing more than a small trinket, but it was always fine of its kind, and he was

---

6. James makes use of smaller incidents to reveal Marcher's gift for deluding himself, on which the principal issue of the story depends.

regularly careful to pay for it more than he thought he could afford. "Our habit saves you at least, don't you see? because it makes you, after all, for the vulgar, indistinguishable from other men. What's the most inveterate mark of men in general? Why the capacity to spend endless time with dull women—to spend it I won't say without being bored, but without minding that they are, without being driven off at a tangent by it; which comes to the same thing. I'm your dull woman, a part of the daily bread for which you pray at church. That covers your tracks more than anything."

"And what covers yours?" asked Marcher, whom his dull woman could most to this extent amuse. "I see of course what you mean by your saving me, in this way and that, so far as other people are concerned—I've seen it all along. Only what is it that saves *you?* I often think, you know, of that."

She looked as if she sometimes thought of that too, but rather in a different way. "Where other people, you mean, are concerned?"

"Well, you're really so in with me, you know—as a sort of result of my being so in with yourself. I mean of my having such an immense regard for you, being so tremendously mindful of all you've done for me. I sometimes ask myself if it's quite fair. Fair I mean to have so involved and—since one may say it—interested you. I almost feel as if you hadn't really had time to do anything else."

"Anything else but be interested?" she asked. "Ah what else does one ever want to be? If I've been 'watching' with you, as we long ago agreed I was to do, watching's always in itself an absorption."

"Oh certainly," John Marcher said, "if you hadn't had your curiosity—! Only doesn't it sometimes come to you as time goes on that your curiosity isn't being particularly repaid?"

May Bartram had a pause. "Do you ask that, by any chance, because you feel at all that yours isn't? I mean because you have to wait so long."

Oh he understood what she meant! "For the thing to happen that never does happen? For the beast to jump out? No, I'm just where I was about it. It isn't a matter as to which I can *choose*, I can decide for a change. It isn't one as to which there *can* be a change. It's in the lap of the gods. One's in the hands of one's law —there one is. As to the form the law will take, the way it will operate, that's its own affair."

"Yes," Miss Bartram replied; "of course one's fate's coming, of course it *has* come in its own form and its own way, all the while. Only, you know, the form and the way in your case were to have been—well, something so exceptional and, as one may say, so particularly *your* own."

Something in this made him look at her with suspicion. "You say 'were to *have* been,' as if in your heart you had begun to doubt."

"Oh!" she vaguely protested.

"As if you believe," he went on, "that nothing will now take place."

She shook her head slowly but rather inscrutably. "You're far from my thought."

He continued to look at her. "What then is the matter with you?"

"Well," she said after another wait, "the matter with me is simply that I'm more sure than ever my curiosity, as you call it, will be but too well repaid."

They were frankly grave now; he had got up from his seat, had turned once more about the little drawing-room to which, year after year, he brought his inevitable topic; in which he had, as he might have said, tasted their intimate community with every sauce, where every object was as familiar to him as the things of his own house and the very carpets were worn with his fitful walk very much as the desks in old counting-houses are worn by the elbows of generations of clerks. The generations of his nervous moods had been at work there, and the place was the written history of his whole middle life. Under the impression of what his friend had just said he knew himself, for some reason, more aware of these things; which made him, after a moment, stop again before her. "Is it possibly that you've grown afraid?"

"Afraid?" He thought, as she repeated the word, that his question had made her, a little, change colour; so that, lest he should have touched on a truth, he explained very kindly: "You remember that that was what you asked *me* long ago—that first day at Weatherend."

"Oh yes, and you told me you didn't know—that I was to see for myself. We've said little about it since, even in so long a time."

"Precisely," Marcher interposed—"quite as if it were too delicate a matter for us to make free with. Quite as if we might find, on pressure, that I *am* afraid. For then," he said, "we shouldn't, should we? quite know what to do."

She had for the time no answer to this question. "There have been days when I thought you were. Only, of course," she added, "there have been days when we have thought almost anything."

"Everything. Oh!" Marcher softly groaned as with a gasp, half-spent, at the face, more uncovered just then than it had been for a long while, of the imagination always with them. It had always had its incalculable moments of glaring out, quite as with the very eyes of the very Beast, and, used as he was to them, they could still draw from him the tribute of a sigh that rose from the depths of his being. All they had thought, first and last, rolled over him; the past seemed to have been reduced to mere barren speculation. This in fact was what the place had just struck him as so full of—the simplification of everything but the state of suspense. That remained only by seeming to hang in the void surrounding it. Even his original fear, if fear it had been, had lost itself in the desert. "I judge, however," he continued, "that you see I'm not afraid now."

"What I see, as I make it out, is that you've achieved something almost unprecedented in the way of getting used to danger. Living with it so long and so closely you've lost your sense of it; you know it's there, but you're indifferent, and you cease even, as of old, to have to whistle in the dark. Considering what the danger is," May Bartram wound up, "I'm bound to say I don't think your attitude could well be surpassed."

John Marcher faintly smiled. "It's heroic?"

"Certainly—call it that."

It was what he would have liked indeed to call it. "I *am* then a man of courage?"

"That's what you were to show me."

He still, however, wondered. "But doesn't the man of courage know what he's afraid of—or *not* afraid of? I don't know *that*, you see. I don't focus it. I can't name it. I only know I'm exposed."

"Yes, but exposed—how shall I say?—so directly. So intimately. That's surely enough."

"Enough to make you feel then—as what we may call the end and the upshot of our watch—that I'm not afraid?"

"You're not afraid. But it isn't," she said, "the end of our watch. That is it isn't the end of yours. You've everything still to see."

"Then why haven't *you?*" he asked. He had had, all along, today, the sense of her keeping something back, and he still had it. As this was his first impression of that it quite made a date. The case was the more marked as she didn't at first answer; which in turn made him go on. "You know something I don't." Then his voice, for that of a man of courage trembled a little. "You know what's to happen." Her silence, with the face she showed, was almost a confession—it made him sure. "You know, and you're afraid to tell me. It's so bad that you're afraid I'll find out."

All this might be true, for she did look as if, unexpectedly to her, he had crossed some mystic line that she had secretly drawn round her. Yet she might, after all, not have worried; and the real climax was that he himself, at all events, needn't. "You'll never find out."[7]

---

7. From this point, their relationship undergoes a subtle change. Marcher is aware that May knows the root of his predicament, while she, by her admission of this knowledge, may assume in his eyes a superiority incompatible with his thinking of their marriage.

III

It was all to have made, none the less, as I have said, a date; which came out in the fact that again and again, even after long intervals, other things that passed between them wore in relation to this hour but the character of recalls and results. Its immediate effect had been indeed rather to lighten insistence—almost to provoke a reaction; as if their topic had dropped by its own weight and as if moreover, for that matter, Marcher had been visited by one of his occasional warnings against egotism. He had kept up, he felt, and very decently on the whole, his consciousness of the importance of not being selfish, and it was true that he had never sinned in that direction without promptly enough trying to press the scales the other way. He often repaired his fault, the season permitting, by inviting his friend to accompany him to the opera; and it not infrequently thus happened that, to show he didn't wish her to have but one sort of food for her mind, he was the cause of her appearing there with him a dozen nights in the month. It even happened that, seeing her home at such times, he occasionally went in with her to finish, as he called it, the evening, and, the better to make his point, sat down to the frugal but always careful little supper that awaited his pleasure. His point was made, he thought, by his not eternally insisting with her on himself; made for instance, at such hours, when it befell that, her piano at hand and each of them familiar with it, they went over passages of the opera together. It chanced to be on one of these occasions, however, that he reminded her of her not having answered a certain question he had put to her during the talk that had taken place between them on her last birthday. "What is it that saves *you?*" —saved her, he meant, from that appearance of variation from the usual human type. If he had practically escaped remark, as she pretended, by doing, in the most important particular, what most men do—find the answer to life in patching up an alliance of a sort with a woman no better than himself—how had she escaped it, and how could the alliance, such as it was, since they must suppose it had been more or less noticed, have failed to make her rather positively talked about?

"I never said," May Bartram replied, "that it hadn't made me a good deal talked about."

"Ah well then you're not 'saved.'"

"It hasn't been a question for me. If you've had your woman I've had," she said, "my man."

"And you mean that makes you all right?"

Oh it was always as if there were so much to say! "I don't know why it shouldn't make me—humanly, which is what we're speaking of—as right as it makes you."

"I see," Marcher returned. " 'Humanly,' no doubt, as showing that you're living for something. Not, that is, just for me and my secret."

May Bartram smiled. "I don't pretend it exactly shows that I'm not living for you. It's my intimacy with you that's in question."

He laughed as he saw what she meant. "Yes, but since, as you say, I'm only, so far as people make out, ordinary, you're— aren't you?—no more than ordinary either. You help me to pass for a man like another. So if I *am*, as I understand you, you're not compromised. Is that it?"

She had another of her waits, but she spoke clearly enough. "That's it. It's all that concerns me—to help you to pass for a man like another."

He was careful to acknowledge the remark handsomely. "How kind, how beautiful, you are to me! How shall I ever repay you?"

She had her last grave pause, as if there might be a choice of ways. But she chose. "By going on as you are."

It was into this going on as he was that they relapsed, and really for so long a time that the day inevitably came for a further sounding of their depths. These depths, constantly bridged over by a structure firm enough in spite of its lightness and of its occasional oscillation in the somewhat vertiginous air, invited on occasion, in the interest of their nerves, a dropping of the plummet and a measurement of the abyss. A difference had been made moreover, once for all, by the fact that she had all the while not appeared to feel the need of rebutting his charge of an idea within her that she didn't dare to express—a charge uttered just before one of the fullest of their later discussions ended. It had come up for him then that she "knew" something and that what she knew was bad—too bad to tell him. When he had spoken of it as visibly so bad that she was afraid he might find it out, her reply had left the matter too equivocal to be let alone and yet, for Marcher's special sensibility, almost too formidable again to touch. He circled about it at a distance that alternately narrowed and widened and that still wasn't much affected by the consciousness in him that there was nothing she could "know," after all, any better than he did. She had no source of knowledge he hadn't equally—except of course that she might have finer nerves. That was what women had where they were interested; they made out things, where people were concerned, that the people often couldn't have made out for themselves. Their nerves, their sensibility, their imagination, were conductors and revealers, and the beauty of May Bartram was in particular that she had given herself so to his case. He felt in these days what, oddly enough, he had never felt before, the growth of a dread of losing her by some catastrophe—some catastrophe that yet wouldn't at all be *the* catastrophe: partly because she had almost of a sudden begun to strike him as more useful to him than ever yet, and partly by reason of an appearance of uncertainty in her health, coincident and equally new. It was characteristic of the inner detachment he had hitherto so successfully cultivated and to which our whole account of him is a reference, it was characteristic that his complications, such as they were, had never yet seemed so as at this crisis to thicken about him, even to the point of making him ask himself if he were, by any chance, of a truth, within sight or sound, within touch or reach, within the immediate jurisdiction, of the thing that waited.

When the day came, as come it had to, that his friend confessed to him her fear of a deep disorder in her blood, he felt somehow the shadow of a change and the chill of a shock. He immediately began to imagine aggravations and disasters, and above all to think of her peril as the direct menace for himself of personal privation. This indeed gave him one of those partial recoveries of equanimity that were agreeable to him—it showed him that what was still first in his mind was the loss she herself might suffer. "What if she should have to die before knowing, before seeing—?" It would have been brutal, in the early stages of her trouble, to put that question to her; but it had immediately sounded for him to his own concern, and the possibility was what most made him sorry for her. If she did "know," moreover, in the sense of her having had some—what should he think?—mystical irresistible light, this would make the matter not better, but worse, inasmuch as her original adoption of his own curiosity had quite become the basis of her life. She had been living to see what would *be* to be seen, and it would quite lacerate her to have to give up before the accomplishment of the vision. These reflexions, as I say, quickened his generosity; yet, make them as he might, he saw himself, with the lapse of the period, more and more disconcerted. It lapsed for him with a strange steady sweep, and the oddest oddity was that it gave him, independently of the threat of much inconvenience, almost the only positive surprise his career, if career it could be called, had yet offered him. She kept the house as she had never done; he had to go to her to see her—she could meet him nowhere now, though there was scarce a corner of their loved old London in which she hadn't in the past, at one time or another, done so; and he found her always seated by her fire in the deep old-fashioned chair she was less and less able to leave. He had been struck one day, after an absence exceeding his usual measure, with her suddenly looking much older to him than he had ever thought of her being; then he recognised that the suddenness was all on his side—he had just simply and suddenly noticed. She looked older because inevitably, after so many years, she *was* old, or almost; which was of course true in still greater measure of her companion. If she was old, or almost, John Marcher assuredly was, and yet it was her showing of the lesson, not his own, that brought the truth home to him.[8] His surprises began here; when once they had begun they multiplied; they came rather with a rush: it was as if, in the oddest way in the world, they had all been kept back, sown in a thick cluster, for the late afternoon of life, the time at which for people in general the unexpected has died out.

One of them was that he should have caught himself—for he *had* so done—*really* wondering if the great accident would take form now as nothing more than his being condemned to see this charming woman, this admirable friend, pass away from him. He had never so unreservedly qualified her as while confronted in thought with such a possibility; in spite of which there was small doubt for him that as an answer to his long riddle the mere effacement of even so fine a feature of his situation would be an abject anti-climax. It would represent, as connected with his past attitude, a drop of dignity under the shadow of which his existence could only become the most grotesque of failures. He had been far from holding it a failure—long as he had waited for the appearance that was to make it a success. He had waited for quite another thing, not for such a thing as that. The breath of his good faith came short, however, as he recognised how long he had waited, or how long at least his companion had. That she, at all events, might be recorded as having waited in vain—this affected him sharply, and all the more because of his at first having done little more than amuse himself with the idea. It grew more grave as the gravity of her condition grew, and the state of mind it produced in him, which he himself ended by watching as if it had been some definite disfigurement of his outer person, may pass for another of his surprises. This conjoined itself still with another, the really stupefying consciousness of a question that he would have allowed to shape itself had he dared. What did everything mean—what, that is, did *she* mean, she and her vain waiting and her probable death and the soundless admonition of it all—unless that, at this time of day, it was simply, it was overwhelmingly too late? He had never at any stage of his queer consciousness admitted the whisper of such a correction; he had never till within these last few months been so false to his conviction as not to hold that what was to come to him had time, whether *he* struck himself as having it or not. That at

---

8. Marcher's sudden recognition of May's aging, in connection with her obviously serious illness, shatters his unawareness of his own age. The shock induces the notion that his encounter with destiny is to be, not spectacular, but too late.

last, at last, he certainly hadn't it, to speak of, or had it but in the scantiest measure—such, soon enough, as things went with him, became the inference with which his old obsession had to reckon: and this it was not helped to do by the more and more confirmed appearance that the great vagueness casting the long shadow in which he had lived had, to attest itself, almost no margin left. Since it was in Time that he was to have met his fate, so it was in Time that his fate was to have acted; and as he waked up to the sense of no longer being young, which was exactly the sense of being stale, just as that, in turn, was the sense of being weak, he waked up to another matter beside. It all hung together; they were subject, he and the great vagueness, to an equal and indivisible law. When the possibilities themselves had accordingly turned stale, when the secret of the gods had grown faint, had perhaps even quite evaporated, that, and that only, was failure. It wouldn't have been failure to be bankrupt, dishonoured, pilloried, hanged; it was failure not to be anything.[9] And so, in the dark valley into which his path had taken its unlooked-for twist, he wondered not a little as he groped. He didn't care what awful crash might overtake him, with what ignominy or what monstrosity he might yet be associated—since he wasn't after all too utterly old to suffer—if it would only be decently proportionate to the posture he had kept, all his life, in the threatened presence of it. He had but one desire left—that he shouldn't have been "sold."

IV

Then it was that, one afternoon, while the spring of the year was young and new she met all in her own way his frankest betrayal of these alarms. He had gone in late to see her, but evening hadn't settled and she was presented to him in that long fresh light of waning April days which affects us often with a sadness sharper than the greyest hours of autumn. The week had been warm, the spring was supposed to have begun early, and May Bartram sat, for the first time in the year, without a fire; a fact that, to Marcher's sense, gave the scene of which she formed part a smooth and ultimate look, an air of knowing, in its immaculate order and cold meaningless cheer, that it would never see a fire again. Her own aspect—he could scarce have said why—intensified this note. Almost as white as wax, with the marks and signs in her face as numerous and as fine as if they had been etched by a needle, with soft white draperies relieved by a faded green scarf on the delicate tone of which the years had further refined, she was the picture of a serene and exquisite but impenetrable sphinx, whose head, or indeed all

9. By his own failure to give love, and his consequent incapacity to receive it, Marcher invites the first stirring of the beast. The lair is time itself, a jungle to Marcher because he has wastefully stumbled through it.

whose person, might have been powdered with silver. She was a sphinx, yet with her white petals and green fronds she might have been a lily too—only an artificial lily, wonderfully imitated and constantly kept, without dust or stain, though not exempt from a slight droop and a complexity of faint creases, under some clear glass bell. The perfection of household care, of high polish and finish, always reigned in her rooms, but they now looked most as if everything had been wound up, tucked in, put away, so that she might sit with folded hands and with nothing more to do. She was "out of it," to Marcher's vision; her work was over; she communicated with him as across some gulf or from some island of rest that she had already reached, and it made him feel strangely abandoned. Was it—or rather wasn't it—that if for so long she had been watching with him the answer to their question must have swum into her ken and taken on its name, so that her occupation was verily gone? He had as much as charged her with this in saying to her, many months before, that she even then knew something she was keeping from him. It was a point he had never since ventured to press, vaguely fearing as he did that it might become a difference, perhaps a disagreement, between them. He had in this later time turned nervous, which was what he in all the other years had never been; and the oddity was that his nervousness should have waited till he had begun to doubt, should have held off so long as he was sure. There was something, it seemed to him, that the wrong word would bring down on his head, something that would so at least ease off his tension. But he wanted not to speak the wrong word; that would make everything ugly. He wanted the knowledge he lacked to drop on him, if drop it could, by its own august weight. If she was to forsake him it was surely for her to take leave. This was why he didn't directly ask her again what she knew; but it was also why, approaching the matter from another side, he said to her in the course of his visit: "What do you regard as the very worst that at this time of day *can* happen to me?"

He had asked her that in the past often enough; they had, with the odd irregular rhythm of their intensities and avoidances, exchanged ideas about it and then had seen the ideas washed away by cool intervals, washed like figures traced in sea-sand. It had ever been the mark of their talk that the oldest allusions in it required but a little dismissal and reaction to come out again, sounding for the hour as new. She could thus at present meet his enquiry quite freshly and patiently. "Oh yes, I've repeatedly thought, only it always seemed to me of old that I couldn't quite make up my mind. I thought of dreadful things, between which it was difficult to choose; and so must you have done."

"Rather! I feel now as if I had scarce done anything else. I appear to myself to have spent my life in thinking of nothing *but* dreadful things. A great many of them I've at different times named to you, but there were others I couldn't name."

"They were too, too dreadful?"

"Too, too dreadful—some of them."

She looked at him a minute, and there came to him as he met it an inconsequent sense that her eyes, when one got their full clearness, were still as beautiful as they had been in youth, only beautiful with a strange cold light—a light that somehow was a part of the effect, if it wasn't rather a part of the cause, of the pale hard sweetness of the season and the hour. "And yet," she said at last, "there are horrors we've mentioned."

It deepened the strangeness to see her, as such a figure in such a picture, talk of "horrors," but she was to do in a few minutes something stranger yet—though even of this he was to take the full measure but afterwards—and the note of it already trembled. It was, for the matter of that, one of the signs that her eyes were having again the high flicker of their prime. He had to admit, however, what she said. "Oh yes, there were times when we did go far." He caught himself in the act of speaking as if it all were over. Well, he wished it were; and the consummation depended for him clearly more and more on his friend.

But she had now a soft smile. "Oh far—!"

It was oddly ironic. "Do you mean you're prepared to go further?"

She was frail and ancient and charming as she continued to look at him, yet it was rather as if she had lost the thread. "Do you consider that we went far?"

"Why I thought it the point you were just making—that we *had* looked most things in the face."

"Including each other?" She still smiled. "But you're quite right. We've had together great imaginations, often great fears; but some of them have been unspoken."

"Then the worst—we haven't faced that. I *could* face it, I believe, if I knew what you think it. I feel," he explained, "as if I had lost my power to conceive such things." And he wondered if he looked as blank as he sounded. "It's spent."

"Then why do you assume," she asked, "that mine isn't?"

"Because you've given me signs to the contrary. It isn't a question for you of conceiving, imagining, comparing. It isn't a question now of choosing." At last he came out with it. "You know something I don't. You've shown me that before."

These last words had affected her, he made out in a moment, exceedingly, and she spoke with firmness. "I've shown you, my dear, nothing."

He shook his head. "You can't hide it."

"Oh, oh!" May Bartram sounded over what she couldn't hide. It was almost a smothered groan.

"You admitted it months ago, when I spoke of it to you as of something you were afraid I should find out. Your answer was that I couldn't, that I wouldn't, and I don't pretend I have. But you had something therefore in mind, and I now see how it must have been, how it still is, the possibility that, of all possibilities, has settled itself for you as the worst. This," he went on, "is why I appeal to you. I'm only afraid of ignorance to-day—I'm not afraid of knowledge." And then as for a while she said nothing: "What makes me sure is that I see in your face and feel here, in this air and amid these appearances, that you're out of it. You've done. You've had your experience. You leave me to my fate."

Well, she listened, motionless and white in her chair, as on a decision to be made, so that her manner was fairly an avowal, though still, with a small fine inner stiffness, an imperfect surrender. "It *would* be the worst," she finally let herself say. "I mean the thing I've never said."

It hushed him a moment. "More monstrous than all the monstrosities we've named?"

"More monstrous. Isn't that what you sufficiently express," she asked, "in calling it the worst?"

Marcher thought. "Assuredly—if you mean, as I do, something that includes all the loss and all the shame that are thinkable."

"It would if it *should* happen," said May Bartram. "What we're speaking of, remember, is only my idea."

"It's your belief," Marcher returned. "That's enough for me. I feel your beliefs are right. Therefore if, having this one, you give me no more light on it, you abandon me."

"No, no!" she repeated. "I'm with you—don't you see?—still." And as to make it more vivid to him she rose from her chair—a movement she seldom risked in these days—and showed herself, all draped and all soft, in her fairness and slimness. "I haven't forsaken you."

It was really, in its effort against weakness, a generous assurance, and had the success of the impulse not, happily, been great, it would have touched him to pain more than to pleasure. But the cold charm in her eyes had spread, as she hovered before him, to all the rest of her person, so that it was for the minute almost a recovery of youth. He couldn't pity her for that; he could only take her as she showed—as capable even yet of helping him. It was as if, at the same time, her light might at any instant go out; wherefore he must make the most of it. There passed before him with intensity the three or four things he wanted most to know; but the question that came of itself to his lips really covered the others. "Then tell me if I shall consciously suffer."

She promptly shook her head. "Never!"

It confirmed the authority he imputed to her, and it produced on him an extraordinary effect. "Well, what's better than that? Do you call that the worst?"

"You think nothing is better?" she asked.

She seemed to mean something so special that he again sharply wondered, though still with the dawn of a prospect of relief. "Why not, if one doesn't *know*?" After which, as their eyes, over his question, met in a silence, the dawn deepened and something to his purpose came prodigiously out of her very face. His own, as he took it in, suddenly flushed to the forehead, and he gasped with the force of a perception to which, on the instant, everything fitted. The sound of his gasp filled the air; then he became articulate. "I see—if I don't suffer!"

In her own look, however, was doubt. "You see what?"

"Why what you mean—what you've always meant."

She again shook her head. "What I mean isn't what I've always meant. It's different."

"It's something new?"

She hung back from it a little. "Something new. It's not what you think. I see what you think."

His divination drew breath then; only her correction might be wrong. "It isn't that I *am* a blockhead?" he asked between faintness and grimness. "It isn't that it's all a mistake?"

"A mistake?" she pityingly echoed. *That* possibility, for her, he saw, would be monstrous; and if she guaranteed him the immunity from pain it would accordingly not be what she had in mind. "Oh no," she declared; "it's nothing of that sort. You've been right."

Yet he couldn't help asking himself if she weren't, thus pressed, speaking but to save him. It seemed to him he should be most in a hole if its history should prove all a platitude. "Are you telling me the truth, so that I shan't have been a bigger idiot than I can bear to know? I *haven't* lived with a vain imagination, in the most besotted illusion? I haven't waited but to see the door shut in my face?"

She shook her head again. "However the case stands *that* isn't the truth. Whatever the reality, it *is* a reality. The door isn't shut. The door's open," said May Bartram.

"Then something's to come?"

She waited once again, always with her cold sweet eyes on him. "It's never too late." She had, with her gliding step, diminished the distance between them, and she stood nearer to him, close to him, a minute, as if still charged with the unspoken. Her movement might have been for some finer emphasis of what she was at once hesitating and deciding to say. He had been standing by the chimney-piece, fireless and sparely adorned, a small perfect old French clock and two morsels of rosy Dresden constituting all its furniture; and her hand grasped the shelf while she kept him waiting, grasped it a little as for support and encouragement. She only kept him waiting, however; that is he only waited. It had become suddenly, from her movement and attitude, beautiful and vivid to him that she had something more to give him; her wasted face delicately shone with it—it glittered almost as with the white lustre of silver in her expression. She was right, incontestably, for what he saw in her face was the truth, and strangely, without consequence, while their talk of it as dreadful was still in the air, she appeared to present it as inordinately soft. This, prompting bewilderment, made him but gape the more gratefully for her revelation, so that they continued for some minutes silent, her face shining at him, her contact imponderably pressing, and his stare all kind but all expectant. The end, none the less, was that what he had expected failed to come to him. Something else took place instead, which seemed to consist at first in the mere closing of her eyes. She gave way at the same instant to a slow fine shudder, and though he remained staring—though he stared in fact but the harder—turned off and regained her chair. It was the end of what she had geen intending, but it left him thinking only of that.

"Well, you don't say—?"

She had touched in her passage a bell near the chimney and had sunk back strangely pale. "I'm afraid I'm too ill."

"Too ill to tell me?" It sprang up sharp to him, and almost to his lips, the fear she might die without giving him light. He checked himself in time from so expressing his question, but she answered as if she had heard the words.

"Don't you know—now?"

" 'Now'—?" She had spoken as if some difference had been made within the moment. But her maid, quickly obedient to her bell, was already with them. "I know nothing." And he was afterwards to say to himself that he must have spoken with odious impatience, such an impatience as to show that, supremely disconcerted, he washed his hands of the whole question.

"Oh!" said May Bartram.

"Are you in pain?" he asked as the woman went to her.

"No," said May Bartram.

Her maid, who had put an arm round her as if to take her to her room, fixed on him eyes that appealingly contradicted her; in spite of which, however, he showed once more his mystification. "What then has happened?"

She was once more, with her companion's help, on her feet, and, feeling withdrawal imposed on him, he had blankly found his hat and gloves and had reached the door. Yet he waited for her answer. "What *was* to," she said.

V

He came back the next day, but she was then unable to see him, and as it was literally the first time this had occurred in the long stretch of their acquaintance he turned away, defeated and sore, almost angry—or feeling at least that such a break in their custom was really the beginning of the end—and wandered alone with his thoughts, especially with the one he was least able to keep down. She was dying and he would lose her; she was dying and his life would end. He stopped in the Park, into which he had passed, and stared before him at his recurrent doubt. Away from her the doubt pressed again; in her presence he had believed her, but as he felt his forlornness he threw himself into the explanation that, nearest at hand, had most of a miserable warmth for him and least of a cold torment. She had deceived him to save him—to put him off with something in which he should be able to rest. What could the thing that was to happen to him be, after all, but just this thing that had begun to happen? Her dying, her death, his consequent solitude—*that* was what he had figured as the Beast in the Jungle, that was what had been in the lap of the gods. He had had her word for it as he left her—what else on earth could she have meant? It wasn't a thing of a monstrous order; not a fate rare and distinguished; not a stroke of fortune that overwhelmed and immortalised; it had only the stamp of the common doom. But poor Marcher at this hour judged the common doom sufficient. It would serve his turn, and even as the consummation of infinite waiting he would bend his pride to accept it. He sat down on a bench in the twilight. He hadn't been a fool. Something had *been*, as she had said, to come. Before he rose indeed it had quite struck him that the final fact really matched with the long avenue through which he had had to reach it. As sharing his suspense and as giving herself all, giving her life, to bring it to an end, she had come with him every step of the way. He had lived by her aid, and to leave her behind would be cruelly, damnably to miss her. What could be more overwhelming than that?

Well, he was to know within the week, for though she kept him a while at bay, left him restless and wretched during a series of days on each of which he asked about her only again to have to turn away, she ended his trial by receiving him where she had always received him. Yet she had been brought out at some hazard into the presence of so many of the things that were, consciously, vainly, half their past, and there was scant service left in the gentleness of her mere desire, all too visible, to check his obsession and wind up his long trouble. That was clearly what she wanted, the one thing more for her own peace while she could still put out her hand. He was so affected by her state that, once seated by her chair, he was moved to let everything go; it was she herself therefore who brought him back, took up again, before she dismissed him, her last word of the other time. She showed how she wished to leave their business in order. "I'm not sure you understood. You've nothing to wait for more. It *has* come."

Oh how he looked at her! "Really?"

"Really."

"The thing that, as you said, *was* to?"

"The thing that we began in our youth to watch for."

Face to face with her once more he believed her; it was a claim to which he had so abjectly little to oppose. "You mean that it has come as a positive definite occurrence, with a name and a date?"

"Positive. Definite. I don't know about the 'name,' but oh with a date!"

He found himself again too helplessly at sea. "But come in the night—come and passed me by?"

May Bartram had her strange faint smile. "Oh no, it hasn't passed you by!"

"But if I haven't been aware of it and it hasn't touched me—?"

"Ah your not being aware of it"—and she seemed to hesitate an instant to deal with this—"your not being aware of it is the strangeness *in* the strangeness. It's the wonder *of* the wonder." She spoke as with the softness almost of a sick child, yet now at last, at the end of all, with the perfect straightness of a sibyl. She visibly knew that she knew, and the effect on him was of something co-ordinate, in its high character, with the law that had ruled him. It was the true voice of the law; so on her lips would the law itself have sounded. "It *has* touched you," she went on. "It has done its office. It has made you all its own."

"So utterly without my knowing it?"

"So utterly without your knowing it." His hand, as he leaned to her, was on the arm of her chair, and, dimly smiling always now, she placed her own on it. "It's enough if *I* know it."

"Oh!" he confusedly breathed, as she herself of late so often had done.

"What I long ago said is true. You'll never know now, and I think you ought to be content. You've *had* it," said May Bartram.

"But had what?"

"Why what was to have marked you out. The proof of your law. It has acted. I'm too glad," she then bravely added, "to have been able to see what it's *not*."

He continued to attach his eyes to her, and with the sense that it was all beyond him, and that *she* was too, he would still have sharply challenged her hadn't he so felt it an abuse of her weakness to do more than take devoutly what she gave him, take it hushed as to a revelation. If he did speak, it was out of the foreknowledge of his loneliness to come. "If you're glad of what it's 'not' it might then have been worse?"

She turned her eyes away, she looked straight before her; with which after a moment: "Well, you know our fears."

He wondered. "It's something then we never feared?"

On this slowly she turned to him. "Did we ever dream, with all our dreams, that we should sit and talk of it thus?"

He tried for a little to make out that they had; but it was as if their dreams, numberless enough, were in solution in some thick cold mist through which thought lost itself. "It might have been that we couldn't talk?"

"Well"—she did her best for him—"not from this side. This, you see," she said, "is the *other* side."

"I think," poor Marcher returned, "that all sides are the same to me." Then, however, as she gently shook her head in correction: "We mightn't, as it were, have got across—?"

"To where we are—no. We're *here*"—she made her weak emphasis.

"And much good does it do us!" was her friend's frank comment.

"It does us the good it can. It does us the good that *it* isn't here. It's past. It's behind," said May Bartram. "Before—" but her voice dropped.

He had got up, not to tire her, but it was hard to combat his yearning. She after all told him nothing but that his light had failed—which he knew well enough without her. "Before—?" he blankly echoed.

"Before, you see, it was always to *come*. That kept it present."

"Oh I don't care what comes now! Besides," Marcher added, "it seems to me I liked it better present, as you say, than I can like it absent with *your* absence."

"Oh mine!"—and her pale hands made light of it.

"With the absence of everything." He had a dreadful sense of standing there before her for—so far as anything but this proved, this bottomless drop was concerned—the last time of their life. It rested on him with a weight he felt he could scarce bear, and this weight it apparently was that still pressed out what remained in him of speakable protest. "I believe you; but I can't begin to pretend I understand. *Nothing*, for me, is past; nothing *will* pass till I pass myself, which I pray my stars may be as soon as possible. Say, however," he added, "that I've eaten my cake, as you contend, to the last crumb—how can the thing I've never felt at all be the thing I was marked out to feel?"

She met him perhaps less directly, but she met him unperturbed. "You take your 'feelings' for granted. You were to suffer your fate. That was not necessarily to know it."

"How in the world—when what is such knowledge but suffering?"

She looked up at him a while in silence. "No—you don't understand."

"I suffer," said John Marcher.

"Don't, don't!"

"How can I help at least *that?*"

"*Don't!*" May Bartram repeated.

She spoke it in a tone so special, in spite of her weakness, that he stared an instant—stared as if some light, hitherto hidden, had shimmered across his vision. Darkness again closed over it, but the gleam had already become for him an idea. "Because I haven't the right—?"

"Don't *know*—when you needn't," she mercifully urged. "You needn't—for we shouldn't."

"Shouldn't?" If he could but know what she meant!

"No—it's too much."

"Too much?" he still asked but, with a mystification that was the next moment of a sudden to give way. Her words, if they meant something, affected him in this light—the light also of her wasted face—as meaning *all*, and the sense of what knowledge had been for herself came over him with a rush which broke through into a question. "Is it of that then you're dying?"

She but watched him, gravely at first, as to see, with this, where he was, and she might have seen something or feared something that moved her sympathy. "I would live for you still—if I could." Her eyes closed for a little, as if, withdrawn into herself, she were for a last time trying. "But I can't!" she said as she raised them again to take leave of him.

She couldn't indeed, as but too promptly and sharply appeared, and he had no vision of her after this that was anything but darkness and doom. They had parted for ever in that strange talk; access to her chamber of pain, rigidly guarded, was almost wholly forbidden him; he was feeling now moreover, in the face of doctors, nurses, the two or three relatives attracted doubtless by the presumption of what she had to "leave," how few were the rights, as they were called in such cases, that he had to put forward, and how odd it might even seem that their intimacy shouldn't have given him more of them. The stupidest fourth cousin had more, even though she had been nothing in such a person's life. She had been a feature of features in *his*, for what else was it to have been so indispensable? Strange beyond saying were the ways of existence, baffling for him the anomaly of his lack, as he felt it to be, of producible claim. A woman might have been, as it were, everything to him, and it might yet present him in no connexion that any one seemed held to recognise. If this was the case in these closing weeks it was the case more sharply on the occasion of the last offices rendered, in the great grey London cemetery, to what had been mortal, to what had been precious, in his friend. The concourse at her grave was not numerous, but he saw himself treated as scarce more nearly concerned with it than if there had been a thousand others. He was in short from this moment face to face with the fact that he was to profit extraordinarily little by the interest May Bartram had taken in him. He couldn't quite have said what he expected, but he hadn't surely expected this approach to a double privation. Not only had her interest failed him, but he seemed to feel himself unattended—and for a reason he couldn't seize—by the distinction, the dignity, the propriety, if nothing else, of the man markedly bereaved. It was as if in the view of society he had not *been* markedly bereaved, as if there still failed some sign or proof of it, and as if none the less his character could never be affirmed nor the deficiency ever made up. There were moments as the weeks went by when he would have liked, by some almost aggressive act, to take his stand on the intimacy of his loss, in order that it *might* be questioned and his retort, to the relief of his spirit, so recorded; but the moments of an irritation more helpless followed fast on these, the moments during which, turning things over with a good conscience but with a bare horizon, he found himself wondering if he oughtn't to have begun, so to speak, further back.

He found himself wondering indeed at many things, and this last speculation had others to keep it company. What could he have done, after all, in her lifetime, without giving them both, as it were, away? He couldn't have made known she was watching him, for that would have published the superstition of the Beast. This was what closed his mouth now—now that the Jungle had been threshed to vacancy and that the Beast had stolen away. It sounded too foolish and too flat; the difference for him in this particular, the extinction in his life of the element of suspense, was such as in fact to surprise him. He could scarce have said what the effect resembled; the abrupt cessation, the positive prohibition, of music perhaps, more than anything else, in some place all adjusted and all accustomed to sonority and to attention. If he could at any rate have conceived lifting the veil from his image at some moment of the past (what had he done, after all, if not lift it to *her?*) so to do this to-day, to talk to people at large of the Jungle cleared and confide to them that he now felt it as safe, would have been not only to see them listen as to a goodwife's tale, but really to hear himself tell one. What it presently came to in truth was that poor Marcher waded through his beaten grass, where no life stirred, where no breath sounded, where no evil eye seemed to gleam from a possible lair, very much as if vaguely looking for the Beast, and still more as if acutely missing it. He walked about in an existence that had grown strangely more spacious and, stopping fitfully in places where the undergrowth of life struck him as closer, asked himself yearningly, wondered secretly and sorely, if it would have lurked here or there. It would have at all events *sprung*; what was at least complete was his belief in the truth itself of the assurance given him. The change from his old sense to his new was absolute and final: what was to happen *had* so absolutely and finally happened that he was as little able to know a fear for his future as to know a hope; so absent in short was any question of anything still to come. He was to live entirely with the other question, that of his unidentified past, that of his having to see his fortune impenetrably muffled and masked.

The torment of this vision became then his occupation; he couldn't perhaps have consented to live but for the possibility of guessing. She had told him, his friend, not to guess; she had forbidden him, so far as he might, to know, and she had even in a sort denied the power in him to learn: which were so many things, precisely, to deprive him of rest. It wasn't that he wanted, he argued for fairness, that anything past and done should repeat itself; it was only that he shouldn't, as an anticlimax, have been taken sleeping so sound as not to be able to win back by an effort of thought the lost stuff of consciousness. He declared to himself at moments that he would either win it back or have done with consciousness for ever; he made this idea his one motive in fine, made it so much his passion that none other, to compare with it, seemed ever to have touched him. The lost stuff of consciousness became thus for him as a strayed or stolen child to an unappeasable father; he hunted it up and down very much as if he were knocking at doors and enquiring of the police. This was the spirit in which, inevitably, he set himself to travel; he started on a journey that was to be as long as he could make it; it danced before him that, as the other side of the globe couldn't possibly have less to say to him, it might, by a possibility of suggestion, have more. Before he quitted London, however, he made a pilgrimage to May Bartram's grave, took his way to it through the endless avenues of the grim suburban metropolis, sought it out in the wilderness of tombs, and, though he had come but for the renewal of the act of farewell, found himself, when he had at last stood by it, beguiled into long intensities. He stood for an hour, powerless to turn away and yet powerless to penetrate the darkness of death; fixing with his eyes her inscribed name and date, beating his forehead against the fact of the secret they kept, drawing his breath, while he waited, as if some sense would in pity of him rise from the stones. He kneeled on the stones, however, in vain; they kept what they concealed; and if the face of the tomb did become a face for him it was because her two names became a pair of eyes that didn't know him. He gave them a last long look, but no palest light broke.

VI

He stayed away, after this, for a year; he visited the depths of Asia, spending himself on scenes of romantic interest, of superlative sanctity; but what was present to him everywhere was that for a man who had known what *he* had known the world was vulgar and vain. The state of mind in which he had lived for so many years shone out to him, in reflexion, as a light that coloured and refined, a light beside which the glow of the East was garish cheap and thin. The terrible truth was that he had lost—with everything else—a distinction as well; the things he saw couldn't help being common when he had become common to look at them. He was simply now one of them himself—he was in the dust, without a peg for the sense of difference; and there were hours when, before the temples of gods and the sepulchres of kings, his spirit turned for nobleness of association to the barely discriminated slab in the London suburb. That had become for him, and more intensely with time and distance, his one witness of a past glory. It was all that was left to him for proof or pride, yet the past glories of Pharaohs were nothing to him as he thought of it. Small wonder then that he came back to it on the morrow of his return. He was drawn there this time as irresistibly as the other, yet with a confidence, almost, that was doubtless the effect of the many months that had elapsed. He had lived, in spite of himself, into his change of feeling, and in wandering over the earth had wandered, as might be said, from the circumference to the centre of his desert. He had settled to his safety and accepted perforce his extinction; figuring to himself, with some colour, in the likeness of certain little old men he remembered to have seen, of whom, all meagre and wizened as they might look, it was related that they had in their time fought twenty duels or been loved by ten princesses. They indeed had been wondrous for others while he was but wondrous for himself; which, however, was exactly the cause of his haste to renew the wonder by getting back, as he might put it, into his own presence. That had quickened his steps and checked his delay. If his visit was prompt it was because he had been separated so long from the part of himself that alone he now valued.

It's accordingly not false to say that he reached his goal with a certain elation and stood there again with a certain assurance. The creature beneath the sod *knew* of his rare experience, so that, strangely now, the place had lost for him its mere blankness of expression. It met him in mildness—not, as before, in mockery; it wore for him the air of conscious greeting that we find, after absence, in things that have closely belonged to us and which seem to confess of themselves to the connexion. The plot of ground, the graven tablet, the tended flowers affected him so as belonging to him that he resembled for the hour a contented landlord reviewing a piece of property. Whatever had happened—well, had happened. He had not come back this time with the vanity of that question, his former worrying "what, *what?*" now practically so spent. Yet he would none the less never again so cut himself off from the spot; he would come back to it every month, for if he did nothing else by its aid he at least held up his head. It thus grew for him, in the oddest way, a positive resource; he carried out his idea of periodical returns, which took their place at last among the most inveterate of his habits. What it all amounted to, oddly enough, was that in his finally so simplified world this garden of death gave him the few square feet of earth on which he could still most live. It was as if, being nothing anywhere else for any one, nothing even for himself, he were just everything here, and if not a crowd of witnesses or indeed for any witness but John Marcher, then by clear right of the register that he could scan like an open page. The open page was the tomb of his friend, and *there* were the facts of the past, there the truth of his life, there the backward reaches in which he could lose himself. He did this from time to time with such effect that he seemed to wander through the old years with his hand in the arm of a companion who was, in the most extraordinary manner, his other, his younger self; and to wander, which was more extraordinary yet, round and round a third presence—not wandering she, but stationary, still, whose eyes, turning with his revolution, never ceased to follow him, and whose seat was his point, so to speak, of orientation. Thus in short he settled to live—feeding all on the sense that he once *had* lived, and dependent on it not alone for a support but for an identity.

It sufficed him in its way for months and the year elapsed; it would doubtless even have carried him further but for an accident, superficially slight, which moved him, quite in another direction, with a force beyond any of his impressions of Egypt or of India. It was a thing of the merest chance—the turn, as he afterwards felt, of a hair, though he was indeed to live to believe that if light hadn't come to him in this particular fashion it would still have come in another. He was to live to believe this, I say, though he was not to live, I may not less definitely mention, to do much else. We allow him at any rate the benefit of the conviction, struggling up for him at the end, that, whatever might have happened or not happened, he would have come round of himself to the light. The incident of an autumn day had put the match to the train laid from of old by his misery. With the light before him he knew that even of late his ache had only been smothered. It was strangely drugged, but it throbbed; at the touch it began to bleed. And the touch, in the event, was the face of a fellow mortal. This face, one grey afternoon when the leaves were thick in the alleys, looked into Marcher's own, at the cemetery, with an expression like the cut of a blade. He felt it, that is, so deep down that he winced at the steady thrust. The person who so mutely assaulted him was a figure he had noticed, on reaching his own goal, absorbed by a grave a short distance away, a grave apparently fresh, so that the emotion of the visitor would probably match it for frankness. This fact alone forbade further attention, though during the time he stayed he remained vaguely conscious of his neighbour, a middle-aged man apparently, in mourning, whose bowed back, among the clustered monuments and mortuary yews, was constantly presented. Marcher's theory that these were elements in contact with which he himself revived, had suffered, on this occasion, it may be granted, a marked, an excessive check. The autumn day was dire for him as none had recently been, and he rested with a heaviness he had not yet known on the low stone table that bore May Bartram's name. He rested without power to move, as if some spring in him, some spell vouchsafed, had suddenly been broken for ever. If he could have done that moment as he wanted he would simply have stretched himself on the slab that was ready to take him, treating it as a place prepared to receive his last sleep. What in all the wide world had he now to keep awake for? He stared before him with the question, and it was then that, as one of the cemetery walks passed near him, he caught the shock of the face.

His neighbour at the other grave had withdrawn, as he himself, with force enough in him, would have done by now, and was advancing along the path on his way to one of the gates. This brought him close, and his pace was slow, so that—and all the more as there was a kind of hunger in his look—the two men were for a minute directly confronted. Marcher knew him at once for one of the deeply stricken—a perception so sharp that nothing else in the picture comparatively lived, neither his dress, his age, nor his presumable character and class; nothing lived but the deep ravage of the features he showed. He *showed* them—that was the point; he was moved, as he passed, by some impulse that was either a signal for sympathy or, more possibly, a challenge to an opposed sorrow. He might already have been aware of our friend, might at some previous hour have noticed in him the smooth habit of the scene, with which the state of his own senses so scantly consorted, and might thereby have been stirred as by an overt discord. What Marcher was at all events conscious of was in the first place that the image of scarred passion presented to him was conscious too—of something that profaned the air; and in the second that, roused, startled, shocked, he was yet the next moment looking after it, as it went, with envy. The most extraordinary thing that had happened to him—though he had given that name to other matters as well—took place, after his immediate vague stare, as a consequence of this impression. The stranger passed, but the raw glare of his grief remained, making our friend wonder in pity what wrong, what wound it expressed, what injury not to be healed. What had the man *had*, to make him by the loss of it so bleed and yet live?

Something—and this reached him with a pang—that *he*, John Marcher, hadn't; the proof of which was precisely John Marcher's arid end. No passion had ever touched him, for this was what passion meant; he had survived and maundered and pined, but where had been *his* deep ravage? The extraordinary thing we speak of was the sudden rush of the result of this question. The sight that had just met his eyes named to him, as in letters of quick flame, something he had utterly, insanely missed, and what he had missed made these things a train of fire, made them mark themselves in an anguish of inward throbs. He had seen *outside* of his life, not learned it within, the way a woman was mourned when she had been loved for herself: such was the force of his conviction of the meaning of the stranger's face, which still flared for him as a smoky torch. It hadn't come to him, the knowledge, on the wings of experience; it had brushed him, jostled him, upset him, with the disrespect of chance, the insolence of accident. Now that the illumination had begun, however, it blazed to the zenith, and what he presently stood there gazing at was the sounded void of his life. He gazed, he drew breath, in pain; he turned in his dismay, and, turning, he had before him in sharper incision than ever the open page of his story. The name on the table smote him as the passage of his neighbour had done, and what it said to him, full in the face, was that *she* was what he had missed. This was the awful thought, the answer to all the past, the vision at the dread clearness of which he grew as cold as the stone beneath him. Everything fell together, confessed, explained, overwhelmed; leaving him most of all stupefied at the blindness he had cherished. The fate he had been marked for he had met with a vengeance—he had emptied the cup to the lees; he had been the man of his time, *the* man, to whom nothing on earth was to have happened. That was the rare stroke—that was his visitation. So he saw it, as we say, in pale horror, while the pieces fitted and fitted. So *she* had seen it while he didn't, and so she served at this hour to drive the truth home. It was the truth, vivid and monstrous, that all the while he had waited the wait was itself his portion. This the companion of his vigil had at a given moment made out, and she had then offered him the chance to baffle his doom. One's doom, however, was never baffled, and on the day she told him his own had come down she had seen him but stupidly stare at the escape she offered him.

The escape would have been to love her; then, *then* he would have lived. *She* had lived—who could say now with what passion?—since she had loved him for himself; whereas he had never thought of her (ah how it hugely glared at him!) but in the chill of his egotism and the light of her use. Her spoken words came back to him—the chain stretched and stretched. The Beast had lurked indeed, and the Beast, at its hour, had sprung;[1] it had sprung in that twilight of the cold April when, pale, ill, wasted, but all beautiful, and perhaps even then recoverable, she had risen from her chair to stand before him and let him imaginably guess. It had sprung as he didn't guess; it had sprung as she hopelessly turned from him, and the mark, by the time he left her, had fallen where it *was* to fall. He had justified his fear and achieved his fate; he had failed, with the last exactitude, of all he was to fail of; and a moan now rose to his lips as he remembered she had prayed he mightn't know. This horror of waking—*this* was knowledge, knowledge under the breath of which the very tears in his eyes seemed to freeze. Through them, none the less, he tried to fix it and hold it; he kept it there before him so that he might feel the pain. That at least, belated and bitter, had something of the taste of life. But the bitterness suddenly sickened him, and it was as if, horribly, he saw, in the truth, in the cruelty of his image, what had been appointed and done. He saw the Jungle of his life and saw the lurking Beast; then, while he looked, perceived it, as by a stir of the air, rise, huge and hideous, for the leap that was to

1. "She had loved him. With his base safety and shrinkage he never knew. *That* was what might have happened, and what *has* happened is that it didn't" (From a passage in James' notebooks on "The Beast in the Jungle").

settle him. His eyes darkened—it was close; and, instinctively turning, in his hallucination, to avoid it, he flung himself, face down, on the tomb.

1901   1903

The Literature of Ideas

HENRY ADAMS
(1838–1918)

From childhood Henry Adams bore the responsibility of living up to the greatness of his forebears. During the summers he was usually sent from Boston—where he was born on February 16, 1838—to nearby Quincy, where his grandfather, John Quincy Adams, still wielded the national influence and authority that duly follows a former president of the United States. Nearby in Quincy stood the home of John Adams, his great-grandfather. In Quincy young Adams could see famous visiting persons and hear scraps of conversation, often of international import. At home in Boston it was much the same, for his father, Charles Francis Adams, was already taking his independent place in the world as a man of power, preparing himself for national service as a member of Congress, and later, during the Civil War, as minister to England, where his brilliant diplomacy was a factor in the success of the northern cause.

Later, in *The Education of Henry Adams* (1907), the author adopted the attitude of one whose education had been useless for dealing with the rapidly changing pattern of his age, but he had the best that Boston could offer—the well-stored libraries of his father and grandfather, and private instruction there, followed by Harvard University and the study of law at the University of Berlin. Travel on the Continent proved more attractive than German scholarship to the young man; he sought first-hand knowledge of music and art and the majestic cathedrals. Adams then settled in Washington as secretary to his father, recently elected to Congress, and when Charles Francis Adams became minister to England a short time later, he took his son with him, still as secretary. From London young Adams became a lively contributor to Boston and New York newspapers and to the *North American Review*, disturbing conservatives with an energetic debunking of historical legends—such as that of Pocahontas and Captain John Smith—and upsetting fundamentalists with his insistence on the importance of evolution in the history of civilization.

sociology

On his return to Washington in 1868, Adams found himself completely at odds with Reconstruction politics and with the Gilded Age in general; after writing a number of critical articles he accepted an appointment at Harvard, where he taught history (1870–1877). His courses reflected his growing interest in the Middle Ages, which later bore fruit in his writing, but he also kept in touch with the present as editor of the *North American Review*. His "dynamic theory of history" as a science began to take shape, but it was not until later that he found what was for him the answer in the laws of physical science.

In 1872 Adams married Marian Hooper, the attractive daughter of a prominent Boston physician, and heiress to a fortune; after a year in Europe they returned to Harvard, where he taught until 1877. He next settled in Washington, apparently fascinated again by history in the making, becoming as he said, "stable-companion to statesmen," among whom William Evarts and John Hay were his intimates. His interest in important associates of Thomas Jefferson produced his collection of *The Writings of Albert Gallatin* (1879) and a biography of Gallatin the same year. His anonymous novel, *Democracy* (1880), a satire upon corruption in national government and social life, was followed by a biography, *John Randolph* (1882). Many of Adams' own critical ideas appear in his novel *Esther* (1884), in which his wife probably served as model for the heroine; the significance of this

is heightened by the suicide of Mrs. Adams in 1885, a crushing tragedy from which he never fully recovered. He first sought escape in a long journey through the Orient, then resumed his monumental undertaking, not completed until 1891, *The History of the United States during the Administrations of Jefferson and Madison,* in nine volumes. Thereafter Adams continued his writing through restless wanderings; *Historical Essays* (1891) and *Memoirs of Marau Taaroa, Last Queen of Tahiti* (1893) resulted from travel and research. More and more he saw history in terms of energy and force; he sought analogues in the physical sciences and consulted the scientists who were his friends. As he later explained in *The Education of Henry Adams*, and especially in the chapter entitled "The Dynamo and the Virgin," the scientific exhibits at the expositions in Chicago in 1893, and at Paris in 1900, were a concrete revelation of what he sought to know. The huge electro-dynamos became a symbol of the dawning age, in which "the human race may commit suicide by blowing up the world," as he prophetically foresaw in the *Education*. He now began to regard human thought, and hence the currents of history, as energetic forces, comparable to those physical energies described by the laws of thermodynamics, responding to similar laws of attraction and repulsion, acceleration, and dissipation. The significance of his theory for historians he succinctly expressed in "A Letter to American Teachers of History" (1910), reprinted by his brother, Brooks Adams, in *The Degradation of the Democratic Dogma* (1919).

The earliest literary fruit of Adams' theory was a masterpiece, *Mont-Saint-Michel and Chartres* (1904), which he called "A study of thirteenth-century unity," by contrast with his own age to be revealed in the *Education*—"A study of twentieth-century multiplicity." The power of the earlier age was the spiritual unity of philosophy, art, and vision that built the cathedrals, symbols of the Virgin; his own age presented no unity save the still-unsolved enigma of the atom. Never popular, Henry Adams was a sound scholar and a sincere artist, one whose message may be reconsidered today in the light of events not foreseen by his contemporaries.

There is no collected edition of Henry Adams. His most important works are *Democracy: An American Novel*, 1880, reprinted 1952; *Esther: A Novel*, 1884, reprinted with an introduction by Rob-ert E. Spiller, 1938; *History of the United States of America during the Administration of Thomas Jefferson* 1884–1885, and *History of the United States of America during the Administration of James Madison*, 1888–1889, both privately printed, published in 9 vols., 1889–1891, reprinted in 4 vols., with an introduction by Henry S. Commager, 1930, and condensed by Herbert Agar as *The Formative Years*, 1947; *Mont-Saint-Michel and Chartres*, 1904, reprinted 1936; *The Education of Henry Adams: An Autobiography*, privately printed 1907, published 1918, reprinted frequently; *The Degradation of the Democratic Dogma*, 1919, reprinted 1949; *Travels in Tahiti*; edited by Robert E. Spiller, 1947. Worthington C. Ford edited *A Cycle of Adams Letters, 1861–1865*, 2 vols., 1920, *Letters of Henry Adams, 1858–1891*, 1930, and *Letters of Henry Adams, 1892–1918*, 1938; Harold D. Cater edited *Henry Adams and His Friends: A Collection of His Unpublished Letters*, 1947. Newton Arvin edited *The Selected Letters of Henry Adams*, 1951.

Biographies are James Truslow Adams, *Henry Adams*, 1933; Ernest Samuels, *The Young Henry Adams*, 1948, and *Henry Adams: The Middle Years, 1877–1891*, 1958; Robert A. Hume, *Runaway Star: An Appreciation of Henry Adams*, 1951; Elizabeth Stevenson, *Henry Adams, A Biography*, 1955; and J. C. Levenson, *The Mind and Art of Henry Adams*, 1957.

American Ideals[1]

Nearly every foreign traveller who visited the United States during these early years, carried away an impression sober if not sad. A thousand miles of desolate and dreary forest, broken here and there by settlements; along the sea-coast a few flourishing towns devoted to commerce; no arts, a provincial literature, a cancerous disease of negro slavery, and differences of political theory fortified within geographical lines,—what could be hoped for such a country except to repeat the story of violence and brutality which the world already knew by heart, until repetition for thousands of years had wearied and sickened mankind? Ages must probably pass before

1. From the *History of the United States of America during the Administration of Thomas Jefferson* (1884–1885), Vol. I, Chapter 6. As relevant for the present as for the age of Jeffer-son, this masterly analysis of the American mind explores a continuing enigma of certain contradictions in the American character.

the interior could be thoroughly settled; even Jefferson, usually a sanguine man, talked of a thousand years with acquiescence, and in his first Inaugural Address, at a time when the Mississippi River formed the Western boundary, spoke of the country as having "room enough for our descendants to the hundredth and thousandth generation." No prudent person dared to act on the certainty that when settled, one government could comprehend the whole; and when the day of separation should arrive, and America should have her Prussia, Austria, and Italy, as she already had her England, France, and Spain, what else could follow but a return to the old conditions of local jealousies, wars, and corruption which had made a slaughter-house of Europe?

The mass of Americans were sanguine and self-confident, partly by temperament, but partly also by reason of ignorance; for they knew little of the difficulties which surrounded a complex society. The Duc de Liancourt,[2] like many critics, was struck by this trait. Among other instances, he met with one in the person of a Pennsylvania miller, Thomas Lea, "a sound American patriot, persuading himself that nothing good is done, and that no one has any brains, except in America; that the wit, the imagination, the genius of Europe are already in decrepitude;" and the duke added: "This error is to be found in almost all Americans,—legislators, administrators, as well as millers, and is less innocent there." In the year 1796 the House of Representatives debated whether to insert in the Reply to the President's Speech a passing remark that the nation was "the freest and most enlightened in the world,"—a nation as yet in swaddling-clothes, which had neither literature, arts, sciences, nor history; nor even enough nationality to be sure that it was a nation. The moment was peculiarly ill-chosen for such a claim, because Europe was on the verge of an outburst of genius. Goethe and Schiller, Mozart and Haydn, Kant and Fichte, Cavendish and Herschel[3] were making way for Walter Scott, Wordsworth, and Shelley, Heine and Balzac, Beethoven and Hegel, Oersted and Cuvier, great physicists, biologists, geologists, chemists, mathematicians, metaphysicians, and historians by the score. Turner was painting his earliest landscapes, and Watt completing his latest steam-engine; Napoleon was taking command of the French armies, and Nelson of the English fleets; investigators, reformers, scholars, and philosophers swarmed, and the influence of enlightenment, even amid universal war, was working with an energy such as the world had never before conceived. The idea that Europe was in her

2. François de La Rochefoucauld-Liancourt (1747–1827), a liberal French peer and philanthropist, who wrote *Travels Through the United States of America* (1799).

3. The paired names represent the distinction of the waning generation in literature, music, philosophy, and science, respectively.

decrepitude proved only ignorance and want of enlightenment, if not of freedom, on the part of Americans, who could only excuse their error by pleading that notwithstanding these objections, in matters which for the moment most concerned themselves Europe was a full century behind America. If they were right in thinking that the next necessity of human progress was to lift the average man upon an intellectual and social level with the most favored, they stood at least three generations nearer than Europe to their common goal. The destinies of the United States were certainly staked, without reserve or escape, on the soundness of this doubtful and even improbable principle, ignoring or overthrowing the institutions of church, aristocracy, family, army, and political intervention, which long experience had shown to be needed for the safety of society. Europe might be right in thinking that without such safeguards society must come to an end; but even Europeans must concede that there was a chance, if no greater than one in a thousand, that America might, at least for a time, succeed. If this stake of temporal and eternal welfare stood on the winning card; if man actually should become more virtuous and enlightened, by mere process of growth, without church or paternal authority; if the average human being could accustom himself to reason with the logical processes of Descartes and Newton![4]—what then?

Then, no one could deny that the United States would win a stake such as defied mathematics. With all the advantages of science and capital, Europe must be slower than America to reach the common goal. American society might be both sober and sad, but except for negro slavery it was sound and healthy in every part. Stripped for the hardest work, every muscle firm and elastic, every ounce of brain ready for use, and not a trace of superfluous flesh on his nervous and supple body, the American stood in the world a new order of man. From Maine to Florida, society was in this respect the same, and was so organized as to use its human forces with more economy than could be approached by any society of the world elsewhere. Not only were artificial barriers carefully removed, but every influence that could appeal to ordinary ambition was applied. No brain or appetite active enough to be conscious of stimulants could fail to answer the intense incentive. Few human beings, however sluggish, could long resist the temptation to acquire power; and the elements of power were to be had in America almost for the asking. Reversing the old-world system, the American stimulant increased in energy as it reached the lowest and most ignorant class, dragging and whirling them upward as in the blast of a furnace. The penniless and homeless Scotch or Irish immigrant was caught and consumed by it; for every stroke of the axe and the hoe made

4. René Descartes (1596–1650), French philosopher and mathematician; Sir Isaac Newton (1642–1727), British scientist and philosopher who formulated the laws of gravity and motion.

him a capitalist, and made gentlemen of his children. Wealth was the strongest agent for moving the mass of mankind; but political power was hardly less tempting to the more intelligent and better-educated swarms of American-born citizens, and the instinct of activity, once created, seemed heritable and permanent in the race.

Compared with this lithe young figure, Europe was actually in decrepitude. Mere class distinctions, the *patois* or dialect of the peasantry, the fixity of residence, the local costumes and habits marking a history that lost itself in the renewal of identical generations, raised from birth barriers which paralyzed half the population. Upon this mass of inert matter rested the Church and the State, holding down activity of thought. Endless wars withdrew many hundred thousand men from production, and changed them into agents of waste; huge debts, the evidence of past wars and bad government, created interests to support the system and fix its burdens on the laboring class; courts, with habits of extravagance that shamed common-sense, helped to consume private economics. All this might have been borne; but behind this stood aristocracies, sucking their nourishment from industry, producing nothing themselves, employing little or no active capital or intelligent labor, but pressing on the energies and ambition of society with the weight of an incubus. Picturesque and entertaining as these social anomalies were, they were better fitted for the theatre or for a museum of historical costumes than for an active workshop preparing to compete with such machinery as America would soon command. From an economical point of view, they were as incongruous as would have been the appearance of a mediæval knight in helmet and armor, with battle-axe and shield, to run the machinery of Arkwright's[5] cotton-mill; but besides their bad economy they also tended to prevent the rest of society from gaining a knowledge of its own capacities. In Europe, the conservative habit of mind was fortified behind power. During nearly a century Voltaire[6] himself— the friend of kings, the wit and poet, historian and philosopher of his age—had carried on, in daily terror, in exile and excommunication, a protest against an intellectual despotism contemptible even to its own supporters. Hardly was Voltaire dead, when Priestley,[7] as great a man if not so great a wit, trying to do for England what Voltaire tried to do for France, was mobbed by the people of Birmingham and driven to America. Where Voltaire and Priestley failed, common men could not struggle; the weight of society stifled their thought. In America the balance between conservative and

5. Sir Richard Arkwright (1732–1792), English inventor of the yarn spinning frame.
6. François Marie Arouet Voltaire (1694–1778), French philosopher and skeptic.
7. Joseph Priestley (1733–1804), English chemist and educator who was mobbed for his support of the French Revolution.

liberal forces was close; but in Europe conservatism held the physical power of government. In Boston a young Buckminster[8] might
be checked for a time by his father's prayers or commands in entering the path that led toward freer thought; but youth beckoned
him on, and every reward that society could offer was dangled before his eyes. In London or Paris, Rome, Madrid, or Vienna, he
must have sacrificed the worldly prospects of his life.

Granting that the American people were about to risk their
future on a new experiment, they naturally wished to throw aside
all burdens of which they could rid themselves. Believing that in
the long run interest, not violence, would rule the world, and that
the United States must depend for safety and success on the interests they could create, they were tempted to look upon war and
preparations for war as the worst of blunders; for they were sure
that every dollar capitalized in industry was a means of overthrowing their enemies more effective than a thousand dollars
spent on frigates or standing armies. The success of the American
system was, from this point of view, a question of economy. If they
could relieve themselves from debts, taxes, armies, and government interference with industry, they must succeed in outstripping
Europe in economy of production; and Americans were even then
partly aware that if their machine were not so weakened by these
economics as to break down in the working, it must of necessity
break down every rival. If their theory was sound, when the day of
competition should arrive, Europe might choose between American
and Chinese institutions, but there would be no middle path; she
might become a confederated democracy, or a wreck.

Whether these ideas were sound or weak, they seemed self-
evident to those Northern democrats who, like Albert Gallatin,[9]
were comparatively free from slave-owning theories, and understood
the practical forces of society. If Gallatin wished to reduce the
interference of government to a minimum, and cut down ex-
penditures to nothing, he aimed not so much at saving money as at
using it with the most certain effect. The revolution of 1800[1] was
in his eyes chiefly political, because it was social; but as a revolution
of society, he and his friends hoped to make it the most radical that
had occurred since the downfall of the Roman empire. Their ideas
were not yet cleared by experience, and were confused by many
contradictory prejudices, but wanted neither breadth nor shrewdness.

Many apparent inconsistencies grew from this undeveloped form

8. Joseph Stevens Buckminster (1784–
1812), Boston Unitarian clergyman.
9. Albert Gallatin (1761–1849),
Thomas Jefferson's secretary of the
treasury, the subject of a three-volume

study by Adams in 1879.
1. The election of Jefferson marked the
end of Federalist power and the rise
of the new Democratic-Republican
party.

of American thought, and gave rise to great confusion in the different estimates of American character that were made both at home and abroad.

That Americans should not be liked was natural; but that they should not be understood was more significant by far. After the downfall of the French republic they had no right to expect a kind word from Europe, and during the next twenty years they rarely received one. The liberal movement of Europe was cowed, and no one dared express democratic sympathies until the Napoleonic tempest had passed. With this attitude Americans had no right to find fault, for Europe cared less to injure them than to protect herself. Nevertheless, observant readers could not but feel surprised that none of the numerous Europeans who then wrote or spoke about America seemed to study the subject seriously. The ordinary traveller was apt to be little more reflective than a bee or an ant, but some of these critics possessed powers far from ordinary; yet Talleyrand[2] alone showed that had he but seen America a few years later than he did, he might have suggested some sufficient reason for apparent contradictions that perplexed him in the national character. The other travellers—great and small, from the Duc de Liancourt to Basil Hall,[3] a long and suggestive list—were equally perplexed. They agreed in observing the contradictions, but all, including Talleyrand, saw only sordid motives. Talleyrand expressed extreme astonishment at the apathy of Americans in the face of religious sectarians; but he explained it by assuming that the American ardor of the moment was absorbed in money-making. The explanation was evidently insufficient, for the Americans were capable of feeling and showing excitement, even to their great pecuniary injury, as they frequently proved; but in the foreigner's range of observation, love of money was the most conspicuous and most common trait of American character. "There is, perhaps, no civilized country in the world," wrote Félix de Beaujour,[4] soon after 1800, "where there is less generosity in the souls, and in the heads fewer of those illusions which make the charm or the consolation of life. Man here weighs everything, calculates everything, and sacrifices everything to his interest." An Englishman named Fearon,[5] in 1818, expressed the same idea with more distinctness: "'In going to America, I would say generally, the emigrant must expect to find, not an economical or cleanly people; not a social or

2. Charles Maurice de Talleyrand-Périgord (1754–1838), French statesman noted for his craftiness; his attempt to extort a bribe from the American commission sent by President Adams to Paris in 1797 caused such warlike reactions that the surprised French Directory undertook conciliation.

3. Basil Hall (1788–1844), British naval officer, author of *Travels in North America* (1829).
4. French diplomat (1765–1836), author of *A Survey of the United States to the Beginning of the 19th Century* (1814).
5. James Fearon, English author of *Sketches of America* (1818).

generous people; not a people of enlarged ideas; not a people of liberal opinions, or toward whom you can express your thoughts free as air; not a people friendly to the advocates of liberty in Europe; not a people who understand liberty from investigation and principle; not a people who comprehend the meaning of the words 'honor' and 'generosity.' " Such quotations might be multiplied almost without limit. Rapacity was the accepted explanation of American peculiarities; yet every traveller was troubled by inconsistencies that required explanations of a different kind. "It is not in order to hoard that the Americans are rapacious," observed Liancourt as early as 1796. The extravagance, or what economical Europeans thought extravagance, with which American women were allowed and encouraged to spend money, was as notorious in 1790 as a century later; the recklessness with which Americans often risked their money, and the liberality with which they used it, were marked even then, in comparison with the ordinary European habit. Europeans saw such contradictions, but made no attempt to reconcile them. No foreigner of that day—neither poet, painter, nor philosopher—could detect in American life anything higher than vulgarity; for it was something beyond the range of their experience, which education and culture had not framed a formula to express. Moore[6] came to Washington, and found there no loftier inspiration than any Federalist rhymester of Dennie's[7] school.

> "Take Christians, Mohawks, democrats and all,
> From the rude wigwam to the Congress hall,—
> From man the savage, whether slaved or free,
> To man the civilized, less tame than he:
> 'T is one dull chaos, one unfertile strife
> Betwixt half-polished and half-barbarous life;
> Where every ill the ancient world can brew
> Is mixed with every grossness of the new;
> Where all corrupts, though little can entice,
> And nothing's known of luxury but vice."[8]

Moore's two small volumes of Epistles, printed in 1807, contained much more so-called poetry of the same tone,—poetry more polished and less respectable than that of Barlow and Dwight;[9] while, as though to prove that the Old World knew what grossness was, he embalmed in his lines the slanders which the Scotch libeller Callender[1] invented against Jefferson:—

6. Thomas Moore (1779–1852), Irish poet.
7. Joseph Dennie (1768–1812), conservative New England editor, essayist, and poet, opposed to Jefferson and Gallatin.
8. "Epistle VIII. To the Honorable W. R. Spencer, from Buffalo, upon Lake Erie," in Thomas Moore's *Epistles, Odes, and Other Poems* (1807).
9. Joel Barlow (1754–1812) and Timothy Dwight (1752–1817), poets notable among the Connecticut Wits; Dwight, a prominent clergyman, became president of Yale.
1. James Thomson Callender (1758–

"The weary statesman for repose hath fled
From halls of council to his negro's shed;
Where, blest, he woos some black Aspasia's grace,
And dreams of freedom in his slave's embrace."

To leave no doubt of his meaning, he explained in a footnote that his allusion was to the President of the United States; and yet even Moore, trifler and butterfly as he was, must have seen, if he would, that between the morals of politics and society in America and those then prevailing in Europe, there was no room for comparison, —there was room only for contrast.

Moore was but an echo of fashionable England in his day. He seldom affected moral sublimity; and had he in his wanderings met a race of embodied angels, he would have sung of them or to them in the slightly erotic notes which were so well received in the society he loved to frequent and flatter. His remarks upon American character betrayed more temper than truth; but even in this respect he expressed only the common feeling of Europeans, which was echoed by the Federalist society of the United States. Englishmen especially indulged in unbounded invective against the sordid character of American society, and in shaping their national policy on this contempt they carried their theory into practice with so much energy as to produce its own refutation. To their astonishment and anger, a day came when the Americans, in defiance of self-interest and in contradiction of all the qualities ascribed to them, insisted on declaring war; and readers of this narrative will be surprised at the cry of incredulity, not unmixed with terror, with which Englishmen started to their feet when they woke from their delusion on seeing what they had been taught to call the meteor flag of England, which had burned terrific at Copenhagen and Trafalgar, suddenly waver and fall on the bloody deck of the "Guerriere."[2] Fearon and Beaujour, with a score of other contemporary critics, could see neither generosity, economy, honor, nor ideas of any kind in the American breast; yet the obstinate repetition of these denials itself betrayed a lurking fear of the social forces whose strength they were candid enough to record. What was it that, as they complained, turned the European peasant into a new man within half an hour after landing at New York? Englishmen were never at a loss to understand the poetry of more prosaic emotions. Neither they nor any of their kindred failed in later times to feel the "large excitement" of the country boy, whose "spirit leaped within him to be gone before him," when the lights of London first flared in the distance; yet none seemed ever to feel the larger excite-

1803), a Scotchman by birth, attacked Jefferson when he failed to secure appointment as postmaster of Richmond.

2. The British frigate *Guerrière* was defeated by the American *Constitution* ("Old Ironsides") in the War of 1812.

ment of the American immigrant. Among the Englishmen who criticized the United States was one greater than Moore,—one who thought himself at home only in the stern beauty of a moral presence. Of all poets, living or dead, Wordsworth felt most keenly what he called the still, sad music of humanity; yet the highest conception he could create of America was not more poetical than that of any Cumberland beggar he might have met in his morning walk:—

> "Long-wished-for sight, the Western World appeared;
> And when the ship was moored, I leaped ashore
> Indignantly,—resolved to be a man,
> Who, having o'er the past no power, would live
> No longer in subjection to the past,
> With abject mind—from a tyrannic lord
> Inviting penance, fruitlessly endured.
> So, like a fugitive whose feet have cleared
> Some boundary which his followers may not cross
> In prosecution of their deadly chase,
> Respiring, I looked round. How bright the sun,
> The breeze how soft! Can anything produced
> In the Old World compare, thought I, for power
> And majesty, with this tremendous stream
> Sprung from the desert? And behold a city
> Fresh, youthful, and aspiring! . . .
>   Sooth to say,
> On nearer view, a motley spectacle
> Appeared, of high pretensions—unreproved
> But by the obstreperous voice of higher still;
> Big passions strutting on a petty stage,
> Which a detached spectator may regard
> Not unamused. But ridicule demands
> Quick change of objects; and to laugh alone,
> . . . in the very centre of the crowd
> To keep the secret of a poignant scorn,
>   . . . is least fit
> For the gross spirit of mankind."[3]

Thus Wordsworth, although then at his prime, indulging in what sounded like a boast that he alone had felt the sense sublime of something interfused, whose dwelling is the light of setting suns, and the round ocean, and the living air, and the blue sky, and in the mind of man,—even he, whose moods the heavy and the weary weight of all this unintelligible world was lightened by his deeper sympathies with nature and the soul, could do no better, when he

3. *The Excursion*, Book III, ll. 870–911.

stood in the face of American democracy, than "keep the secret of a poignant scorn."

Possibly the view of Wordsworth and Moore, of Weld,[4] Dennie, and Dickens was right. The American democrat possessed little art of expression, and did not watch his own emotions with a view of uttering them either in prose or verse; he never told more of himself than the world might have assumed without listening to him. Only with diffidence could history attribute to such a class of men a wider range of thought or feeling than they themselves cared to proclaim. Yet the difficulty of denying or even ignoring the wider range was still greater, for no one questioned the force or the scope of an emotion which caused the poorest peasant in Europe to see what was invisible to poet and philosopher,—the dim outline of a mountain-summit across the ocean, rising high above the mist and mud of American democracy. As though to call attention to some such difficulty, European and American critics, while affirming that Americans were a race without illusions or enlarged ideas, declared in the same breath that Jefferson was a visionary whose theories would cause the heavens to fall upon them. Year after year, with endless iteration, in every accent of contempt, rage, and despair, they repeated this charge against Jefferson. Every foreigner and Federalist agreed that he was a man of illusions, dangerous to society and unbounded in power of evil; but if this view of his character was right, the same visionary qualities seemed also to be a national trait, for every one admitted that Jefferson's opinions, in one form or another, were shared by a majority of the American people.

Illustrations might be carried much further, and might be drawn from every social class and from every period in national history. Of all presidents, Abraham Lincoln has been considered the most typical representative of American society, chiefly because his mind, with all its practical qualities, also inclined, in certain directions, to idealism. Lincoln was born in 1809, the moment when American character stood in lowest esteem. Ralph Waldo Emerson, a more distinct idealist, was born in 1803. William Ellery Channing,[5] another idealist, was born in 1780. Men like John Fitch, Oliver Evans, Robert Fulton, Joel Barlow, John Stevens, and Eli Whitney[6] were all classed among visionaries. The whole society of Quakers belonged in the same category. The records of the popular religious

---

4. Isaac Weld, author of *Travels through the States of North America, and the Provinces of Upper and Lower Canada during 1795, 1796, and 1797* (1799).
5. William Ellery Channing, the elder (1780–1842), Christian Socialist, transcendentalist, and Unitarian minister.
6. These "visionaries" all made fundamental contributions to American

practical leadership: Fitch (1743–98) and Fulton (1765–1815)—the steamboat; Evans (1755–1819) and Stevens (1749–1838)—the steam engine and railroad; Whitney (1765–1825)—the cotton gin; and Barlow, a poet—practical support to Paine's concept of natural rights, fundamental to American democracy.

sects abounded in examples of idealism and illusion to such an extent that the masses seemed hardly to find comfort or hope in any authority, however old or well established. In religion as in politics, Americans seemed to require a system which gave play to their imagination and their hopes.

Some misunderstanding must always take place when the observer is at cross-purposes with the society he describes. Wordsworth might have convinced himself by a moment's thought that no country could act on the imagination as America acted upon the instincts of the ignorant and poor, without some quality that deserved better treatment than poignant scorn; but perhaps this was only one among innumerable cases in which the unconscious poet breathed an atmosphere which the self-conscious poet could not penetrate. With equal reason he might have taken the opposite view,—that the hard, practical, money-getting American democrat, who had neither generosity nor honor nor imagination, and who inhabited cold shades where fancy sickened and where genius died, was in truth living in a world of dream, and acting a drama more instinct with poetry than all the avatars of the East, walking in gardens of emerald and rubies, in ambition already ruling the world and guiding Nature with a kinder and wiser hand than had ever yet been felt in human history. From this point his critics never approached him,—they stopped at a stone's throw; and at the moment when they declared that the man's mind had no illusions, they added that he was a knave or a lunatic. Even on his practical and sordid side, the American might easily have been represented as a victim to illusion. If the Englishman had lived as the American speculator did,—in the future,—the hyperbole of enthusiasm would have seemed less monstrous. "Look at my wealth!" cried the American to his foreign visitor. "See these solid mountains of salt and iron, of lead, copper, silver, and gold! See these magnificent cities scattered broadcast to the Pacific! See my cornfields rustling and waving in the summer breeze from ocean to ocean, so far that the sun itself is not high enough to mark where the distant mountains bound my golden seas! Look at this continent of mine, fairest of created worlds, as she lies turning up to the sun's never-failing caress her broad and exuberant breasts, overflowing with milk for her hundred million children! See how she glows with youth, health, and love!" Perhaps it was not altogether unnatural that the foreigner, on being asked to see what needed centuries to produce, should have looked about him with bewilderment and indignation. "Gold! cities! cornfields! continents! Nothing of the sort! I see nothing but tremendous wastes, where sickly men and women are dying of home-sickness or are scalped by savages! mountain-ranges a thousand miles long, with no means of getting to them, and nothing in them when you get there! swamps and forests choked with their own rotten ruins! nor hope of better for a thousand years! Your story is a fraud, and you are a liar and swindler!"

Met in this spirit, the American, half perplexed and half defiant, retaliated by calling his antagonist a fool, and by mimicking his heavy tricks of manner. For himself he cared little, but his dream was his whole existence. The men who denounced him admitted that they left him in his forest-swamp quaking with fever, but clinging in the delirium of death to the illusions of his dazzled brain. No class of men could be required to support their convictions with a steadier faith, or pay more devotedly with their persons for the mistakes of their judgment. Whether imagination or greed led them to describe more than actually existed, they still saw no more than any inventor or discoverer must have seen in order to give him the energy of success. They said to the rich as to the poor, "Come and share our limitless riches! Come and help us bring to light these unimaginable stores of wealth and power!" The poor came, and from them were seldom heard complaints of deception or delusion. Within a moment, by the mere contact of a moral atmosphere, they saw the gold and jewels, the summer cornfields and the glowing continent. The rich for a long time stood aloof,—they were timid and narrow-minded; but this was not all,—between them and the American democrat was a gulf.

The charge that Americans were too fond of money to win the confidence of Europeans was a curious inconsistency; yet this was a common belief. If the American deluded himself and led others to their death by baseless speculations; if he buried those he loved in a gloomy forest where they quaked and died while he persisted in seeing there a splendid, healthy, and well-built city,—no one could deny that he sacrificed wife and child to his greed for gain, that the dollar was his god, and a sordid avarice his demon. Yet had this been the whole truth, no European capitalist would have hesitated to make money out of his grave; for, avarice against avarice, no more sordid or meaner type existed in America than could be shown on every 'Change in Europe. With much more reason Americans might have suspected that in America Englishmen found everywhere a silent influence, which they found nowhere in Europe, and which had nothing to do with avarice or with the dollar, but, on the contrary, seemed likely at any moment to sacrifice the dollar in a cause and for an object so illusory that most Englishmen could not endure to hear it discussed. European travellers who passed through America noticed that everywhere, in the White House at Washington and in log-cabins beyond the Alleghanies, except for a few Federalists, every American, from Jefferson and Gallatin down to the poorest squatter, seemed to nourish an idea that he was doing what he could to overthrow the tyranny which the past had fastened on the human mind. Nothing was easier than to laugh at the ludicrous expressions of this simple-minded conviction, or to cry out against its coarseness, or grow angry with its prejudices; to see its nobler side, to feel the beatings of a heart underneath the sordid surface of a gross humanity, was not so easy. Europeans seemed seldom or never conscious that the sentiment could possess a noble side, but found only matter for complaint in the remark that every American democrat believed himself to be working for the overthrow of tyranny, aristocracy, hereditary privilege, and priesthood, wherever they existed. Even where the American did not openly proclaim this conviction in words, he carried so dense an atmosphere of the sentiment with him in his daily life as to give respectable Europeans an uneasy sense of remoteness.

Of all historical problems, the nature of a national character is the most difficult and the most important. Readers will be troubled, at almost every chapter of the coming narrative, by the want of some formula to explain what share the popular imagination bore in the system pursued by government. The acts of the American people during the administrations of Jefferson and Madison were judged at the time by no other test. According as bystanders believed American character to be hard, sordid, and free from illusion, they were severe and even harsh in judgment. This rule guided the governments of England and France. Federalists in the United States, knowing more of the circumstances, often attributed to the democratic instinct a visionary quality which they regarded as sentimentality, and charged with many bad consequences. If their view was correct, history could occupy itself to no better purpose than in ascertaining the nature and force of the quality which was charged with results so serious; but nothing was more elusive than the spirit of American democracy. Jefferson, the literary representative of the class, spoke chiefly for Virginians, and dreaded so greatly his own reputation as a visionary that he seldom or never uttered his whole thought. Gallatin and Madison were still more cautious. The press in no country could give shape to a mental condition so shadowy. The people themselves, although millions in number, could not have expressed their finer instincts had they tried, and might not have recognized them if expressed by others.

In the early days of colonization, every new settlement represented an idea and proclaimed a mission. Virginia was founded by a great, liberal movement aiming at the spread of English liberty and empire. The Pilgrims of Plymouth, the Puritans of Boston, the Quakers of Pennsylvania, all avowed a moral purpose, and began by making institutions that consciously reflected a moral idea. No such character belonged to the colonization of 1800. From Lake Erie to

Florida, in long, unbroken line, pioneers were at work, cutting into the forests with the energy of so many beavers, and with no more express moral purpose than the beavers they drove away. The civilization they carried with them was rarely illumined by an idea; they sought room for no new truth, and aimed neither at creating, like the Puritans, a government of saints, nor, like the Quakers, one of love and peace; they left such experiments behind them, and wrestled only with the hardest problems of frontier life. No wonder that foreign observers, and even the educated, well-to-do Americans of the sea-coast, could seldom see anything to admire in the ignorance and brutality of frontiersmen, and should declare that virtue and wisdom no longer guided the United States! What they saw was not encouraging. To a new society, ignorant and semi-barbarous, a mass of demagogues insisted on applying every stimulant that could inflame its worst appetites, while at the same instant taking away every influence that had hitherto helped to restrain its passions. Greed for wealth, lust for power, yearning for the blank void of savage freedom such as Indians and wolves delighted in,—these were the fires that flamed under the caldron of American society, in which, as conservatives believed, the old, well-proven, conservative crust of religion, government, family, and even common respect for age, education, and experience was rapidly melting away, and was indeed already broken into fragments, swept about by the seething mass of scum ever rising in greater quantities to the surface.

Against this Federalist and conservative view of democratic tendencies, democrats protested in a thousand forms, but never in any mode of expression which satisfied them all, or explained their whole character. Probably Jefferson came nearest to the mark, for he represented the hopes of science as well as the prejudices of Virginia; but Jefferson's writings may be searched from beginning to end without revealing the whole measure of the man, far less of the movement. Here and there in his letters a suggestion was thrown out, as though by chance, revealing larger hopes,—as in 1815, at a moment of despondency, he wrote: "I fear from the experience of the last twenty-five years that morals do not of necessity advance hand in hand with the sciences."[7] In 1800, in the flush of triumph, he believed that his task in the world was to establish a democratic republic, with the sciences for an intellectual field, and physical and moral advancement keeping pace with their advance. Without an excessive introduction of more recent ideas, he might be imagined to define democratic progress, in the somewhat affected precision of his French philosophy: "Progress is either physical or intellectual. If we can bring it about that men are on the average an inch taller

7. *The Writings of Thomas Jefferson,* edited by H. A. Washington, 1853–1854, Vol. VI, p. 480.

in the next generation than in this; if they are an inch larger round the chest; if their brain is an ounce or two heavier, and their life a year or two longer,—that is progress. If fifty years hence the average man shall invariably argue from two ascertained premises where he now jumps to a conclusion from a single supposed revelation,—that is progress! I expect it to be made here, under our democratic stimulants, on a great scale, until every man is potentially an athlete in body and an Aristotle in mind." To this doctrine the New Englander[8] replied, "What will you do for moral progress?" Every possible answer to this question opened a chasm. No doubt Jefferson held the faith that men would improve morally with their physical and intellectual growth; but he had no idea of any moral improvement other than that which came by nature. He could not tolerate a priesthood, a state church, or revealed religion. Conservatives, who could tolerate no society without such pillars of order, were, from their point of view, right in answering, "Give us rather the worst despotism of Europe,—there our souls at least may have a chance of salvation!" To their minds vice and virtue were not relative, but fixed terms. The Church was a divine institution. How could a ship hope to reach port when the crew threw overboard sails, spars, and compass, unshipped their rudder, and all the long day thought only of eating and drinking. Nay, even should the new experiment succeed in a worldly sense, what was a man profited if he gained the whole world, and lost his own soul?[9] The Lord God was a jealous God, and visited the sins of the parents upon the children;[1] but what worse sin could be conceived than for a whole nation to join their chief in chanting the strange hymn with which Jefferson, a new false prophet, was deceiving and betraying his people: "It does me no injury for my neighbor to say there are twenty Gods or no God!"[2]

On this ground conservatism took its stand, as it had hitherto done with success in every similar emergency in the world's history, and fixing its eyes on moral standards of its own, refused to deal with the subject as further open to argument. The two parties stood facing opposite ways, and could see no common ground of contact.

Yet even then one part of the American social system was proving itself to be rich in results. The average American was more intelligent than the average European, and was becoming every year still more active-minded as the new movement of society caught him up and swept him through a life of more varied experiences. On all sides the national mind responded to its stimulants. Deficient

---

8. John Adams (1735–1826), second president of the United States; Adams and Jefferson conducted an extensive correspondence until their deaths on the same day, July 4, 1826.

9. *Cf.* Matthew xvi: 26.
1. *Cf.* Exodus xx: 5.
2. Query XVII, in *Notes on the State of Virginia* (1784–1785).

as the American was in the machinery of higher instruction; remote, poor; unable by any exertion to acquire the training, the capital, or even the elementary textbooks he needed for a fair development of his natural powers,—his native energy and ambition already responded to the spur applied to them. Some of his triumphs were famous throughout the world; for Benjamin Franklin had raised high the reputation of American printers, and the actual President of the United States, who signed with Franklin the treaty of peace with Great Britain, was the son of a small farmer, and had himself kept a school in his youth. In both these cases social recognition followed success; but the later triumphs of the American mind were becoming more and more popular. John Fitch was not only one of the poorest, but one of the least-educated Yankees who ever made a name; he could never spell with tolerable correctness, and his life ended as it began,—in the lowest social obscurity. Eli Whitney was better educated than Fitch, but had neither wealth, social influence, nor patron to back his ingenuity. In the year 1800 Eli Terry,[3] another Connecticut Yankee of the same class, took into his employ two young men to help him make wooden clocks, and this was the capital on which the greatest clock-manufactory in the world began its operations. In 1797 Asa Whittemore,[4] a Massachusetts Yankee, invented a machine to make cards for carding wool, which "operated as if it had a soul," and became the foundation for a hundred subsequent patents. In 1790 Jacob Perkins,[5] of Newburyport, invented a machine capable of cutting and turning out two hundred thousand nails a day; and then invented a process for transferring engraving from a very small steel cylinder to copper, which revolutionized cotton-printing. The British traveller Weld, passing through Wilmington, stopped, as Liancourt had done before him, to see the great flour-mills on the Brandywine. "The improvements," he said, "which have been made in the machinery of the flour-mills in America are very great. The chief of these consist in a new application of the screw, and the introduction of what are called elevators, the idea of which was evidently borrowed from the chain-pump." This was the invention of Oliver Evans, a native of Delaware, whose parents were in very humble life, but who was himself, in spite of every disadvantage, an inventive genius of the first order. Robert Fulton, who in 1800 was in Paris with Joel Barlow, sprang from the same source in Pennsylvania. John Stevens, a native of New York, belonged to a more favored class, but followed the same impulses. All these men were the outcome of typical American society, and all their inventions transmuted the democratic instinct

3. Inventor and pioneer clock manufacturer of Connecticut (1772–1852).
4. An English-born inventor and gunsmith who settled in Massachusetts (1759–1828).
5. A Massachusetts goldsmith who became a mint designer and currency engraver (1766–1849).

into a practical and tangible shape. Who would undertake to say that there was a limit to the fecundity of this teeming source? Who that saw only the narrow, practical, money-getting nature of these devices could venture to assert that as they wrought their end and raised the standard of millions, they would not also raise the creative power of those millions to a higher plane? If the priests and barons who set their names to Magna Charta had been told that in a few centuries every swine-herd and cobbler's apprentice would write and read with an ease such as few kings could then command, and reason with better logic than any university could then practise, the priest and baron would have been more incredulous than any man who was told in 1800 that within another five centuries the ploughboy would go a-field whistling a sonata of Beethoven, and figure out in quaternions[6] the relation of his furrows. The American democrat knew so little of art that among his popular illusions he could not then nourish artistic ambition; but leaders like Jefferson, Gallatin, and Barlow might without extravagance count upon a coming time when diffused ease and education should bring the masses into familiar contact with higher forms of human achievement, and their vast creative power, turned toward a nobler culture, might rise to the level of that democratic genius which found expression in the Parthenon; might revel in the delights of a new Buonarotti[7] and a richer Titian;[8] might create for five hundred million people the America of thought and art which alone could satisfy their omnivorous ambition.

Whether the illusions, so often affirmed and so often denied to the American people, took such forms or not, there were in effect the problems that lay before American society: Could it transmute its social power into the higher forms of thought? Could it provide for the moral and intellectual needs of mankind? Could it take permanent political shape? Could it give new life to religion and art? Could it create and maintain in the mass of mankind those habits of mind which had hitherto belonged to men of science alone? Could it physically develop the convolutions of the human brain? Could it produce, or was it compatible with, the differentiation of a higher variety of the human race? Nothing less than this was necessary for its complete success.

1884

6. Advanced mathematics, involving four geometrical elements.

7. Michelangelo (1475–1564), Italian sculptor, painter, architect, and poet.
8. Venetian painter (1477–1576).

The Dynamo and the Virgin[9]

Until the Great Exposition of 1900[1] closed its doors in November, Adams haunted it, aching to absorb knowledge, and helpless to find it. He would have liked to know how much of it could have been grasped by the best-informed man in the world. While he was thus meditating chaos, Langley[2] came by, and showed it to him. At Langley's behest, the Exhibition dropped its superfluous rags and stripped itself to the skin, for Langley knew what to study, and why, and how; while Adams might as well have stood outside in the night, staring at the Milky Way. Yet Langley said nothing new, and taught nothing that one might not have learned from Lord Bacon,[3] three hundred years before; but though one should have known the *Advancement of Science*[4] as well as one knew the *Comedy of Errors*, the literary knowledge counted for nothing until some teacher should show how to apply it. Bacon took a vast deal of trouble in teaching King James I and his subjects, American or other, towards the year 1620,[5] that true science was the development or economy of forces; yet an elderly American in 1900 knew neither the formula nor the forces; or even so much as to say to himself that his historical business in the Exposition concerned only the economies or developments of force since 1893, when he began the study at Chicago.[6]

Nothing in education is so astonishing as the amount of ignorance it accumulates in the form of inert facts. Adams had looked at most of the accumulations of art in the storehouses called Art Museums; yet he did not know how to look at the art exhibits of 1900. He had studied Karl Marx and his doctrines of history[7] with profound attention, yet he could not apply them at Paris. Langley, with the ease of a great master of experiment, threw out of the field every exhibit that did not reveal a new application of force, and naturally threw out, to begin with, almost the whole art exhibit. Equally, he ignored almost the whole industrial exhibit. He led his pupil directly to the forces. His chief interest was in new motors to

9. Chapter 25 of *The Education of Henry Adams*, written after Adams had seen the dynamos at the Paris Exposition of 1900. Like Eugene O'Neill, who later treated a similar theme dramatically in *Dynamo*, Adams saw physical power replacing the spiritual idealism symbolized for the Middle Ages in the power of the Virgin. Hence the chapter is one expression of the author's "dynamic theory of history," which attempts to explain history as the power of ideas functioning as force, controlled by laws analogous to the physical laws of thermodynamics.
1. Held in Paris.
2. Samuel Pierpont Langley (1834–1906), American physicist, who made important investigations in aeronautics and in the exploration of the solar spectrum.
3. Francis Bacon (1561–1626), British statesman and philosopher, a pioneer of modern inductive science.
4. Adams has in mind Bacon's *The Advancement of Learning* (1605).
5. Date of Bacon's *Novum Organum*.
6. The Columbian Exposition at Chicago (1893), where large technological exhibits were displayed.
7. Karl Marx (1818–1883), German economist who promulgated doctrines basic to modern Communism. *Das Kapital* is his classic expression of socialist economics and "doctrines of history" based on materialistic forces.

make his airship feasible, and he taught Adams the astonishing complexities of the Daimler[8] motor, and of the automobile, which, since 1893, had become a nightmare at a hundred kilometres an hour, almost as destructive as the electric tram which was only ten years older; and threatening to become as terrible as the locomotive steam-engine itself, which was almost exactly Adams's own age.

Then he showed his scholar the great hall of dynamos, and explained how little he knew about electricity or force of any kind, even of his own special sun, which spouted heat in inconceivable volume, but which, as far as he knew, might spout less or more, at any time, for all the certainty he felt in it. To him, the dynamo itself was but an ingenious channel for conveying somewhere the heat latent in a few tons of poor coal hidden in a dirty engine-house carefully kept out of sight; but to Adams the dynamo became a symbol of infinity. As he grew accustomed to the great gallery of machines, he began to feel the forty-foot dynamos as a moral force, much as the early Christians felt the Cross. The planet itself seemed less impressive, in its old-fashioned, deliberate, annual or daily revolution, than this huge wheel, revolving within arm's-length at some vertiginous speed, and barely murmuring—scarcely humming an audible warning to stand a hair's-breadth further for respect of power—while it would not wake the baby lying close against its frame. Before the end, one began to pray to it; inherited instinct taught the natural expression of man before silent and infinite force. Among the thousand symbols of ultimate energy, the dynamo was not so human as some, but it was the most expressive.

Yet the dynamo, next to the steam-engine, was the most familiar of exhibits. For Adams's objects its value lay chiefly in its occult mechanism. Between the dynamo in the gallery of machines and the engine-house outside, the break of continuity amounted to abysmal fracture for a historian's objects. No more relation could he discover between the steam and the electric current than between the Cross and the cathedral. The forces were interchangeable if not reversible, but he could see only an absolute fiat in electricity as in faith. Langley could not help him. Indeed, Langley seemed to be worried by the same trouble, for he constantly repeated that the new forces were anarchical, and especially that he was not responsible for the new rays, that were little short of parricidal in their wicked spirit towards science. His own rays, with which he had doubled the solar spectrum, were altogether harmless and beneficent; but Radium denied its God[9]—or what was to Langley the same thing, denied the truths of his Science. The force was wholly new.

A historian who asked only to learn enough to be as futile as

8. Gottlieb Daimler (1834–1900), German inventor of a high-speed internal-combustion engine.

9. Research in radium, with its "rays," was the first source of knowledge of the disintegration of atoms.

Langley or Kelvin,[1] made rapid progress under this teaching, and mixed himself up in the tangle of ideas until he achieved a sort of Paradise of ignorance vastly consoling to his fatigued senses. He wrapped himself in vibrations and rays which were new, and he would have hugged Marconi[2] and Branly[3] had he met them, as he hugged the dynamo; while he lost his arithmetic in trying to figure out the equation between the discoveries and the economies of force. The economies, like the discoveries, were absolute, super-sensual, occult; incapable of expression in horse-power. What mathematical equivalent could he suggest as the value of a Branly coherer? Frozen air, or the electric furnace, had some scale of measurement, no doubt, if somebody could invent a thermometer adequate to the purpose; but X-rays had played no part whatever in man's consciousness, and the atom itself had figured only as a fiction of thought. In these seven years man had translated himself into a new universe which had no common scale of measurement with the old. He had entered a supersensual world, in which he could measure nothing except by chance collisions of movements imperceptible to his senses, perhaps even imperceptible to his instruments, but perceptible to each other, and so to some known ray at the end of the scale. Langley seemed prepared for anything, even for an indeterminable number of universes interfused—physics stark mad in metaphysics.

Historians undertake to arrange sequences,—called stories, or histories—assuming in silence a relation of cause and effect. These assumptions, hidden in the depths of dusty libraries, have been astounding, but commonly unconscious and childlike; so much so, that if any captious critic were to drag them to light, historians would probably reply, with one voice, that they had never supposed themselves required to know what they were talking about. Adams, for one, had toiled in vain to find out what he meant. He had even published a dozen volumes of American history for no other purpose than to satisfy himself whether, by the severest process of stating, with the least possible comment, such facts as seemed sure, in such order as seemed rigorously consequent, he could fix for a familiar moment a necessary sequence of human movement. The result had satisfied him as little as at Harvard College. Where he saw sequence, other men saw something quite different, and no one saw the same unit of measure. He cared little about his experiments and less about his statesmen, who seemed to him quite as ignorant as himself and, as a rule, no more honest; but he insisted on a relation

1. William Thomson, Lord Kelvin (1824–1907), British physicist who made important contributions to electrodynamics and transatlantic telegraphy.

2. Marchese Guglielmo Marconi (1874–1937), Italian inventor of the wireless telegraph.
3. Edouard Branly (1846–1940), French inventor of the first practical detector for wireless waves.

of sequence, and if he could not reach it by one method, he would try as many methods as science knew. Satisfied that the sequence of men led to nothing and that the sequence of their society could lead no further, while the mere sequence of time was artificial, and the sequence of thought was chaos, he turned at last to the sequence of force; and thus it happened that, after ten years' pursuit, he found himself lying in the Gallery of Machines at the Great Exposition of 1900, his historical neck broken by the sudden irruption of forces totally new.

Since no one else showed much concern, an elderly person without other cares had no need to betray alarm. The year 1900 was not the first to upset schoolmasters. Copernicus and Galileo[4] had broken many professorial necks about 1600; Columbus had stood the world on its head towards 1500; but the nearest approach to the revolution of 1900 was that of 310, when Constantine[5] set up the Cross. The rays that Langley disowned, as well as those which he fathered, were occult, supersensual, irrational; they were a revelation of mysterious energy like that of the Cross; they were what, in terms of mediæval science, were called immediate modes of the divine substance.

The historian was thus reduced to his last resources. Clearly if he was bound to reduce all these forces to a common value, this common value could have no measure but that of their attraction on his own mind. He must treat them as they had been felt; as convertible, reversible, interchangeable attractions on thought. He made up his mind to venture it; he would risk translating rays into faith. Such a reversible process would vastly amuse a chemist, but the chemist could not deny that he, or some of his fellow physicists, could feel the force of both. When Adams was a boy in Boston, the best chemist in the place had probably never heard of Venus except by way of scandal, or of the Virgin except as idolatry; neither had he heard of dynamos or automobiles or radium; yet his mind was ready to feel the force of all, though the rays were unborn and the women were dead.

Here opened another totally new education, which promised to be by far the most hazardous of all. The knife-edge along which he must crawl, like Sir Lancelot in the twelfth century,[6] divided two kingdoms of force which had nothing in common but attraction. They were as different as a magnet is from gravitation, supposing

4. Copernicus (1473–1543), Polish astronomer who promulgated the theory that the earth rotates in an orbit around the sun; Galileo (1564–1642), Italian astronomer and physicist, reaffirmed the Copernican system, although required to recant by the Inquisition.

5. According to legend, the Roman emperor Constantine (280?–337) saw a vision of the Cross, bearing the words, "In this sign conquer," and proclaimed Christianity throughout the Roman world.

6. Thus Lancelot freed Guinevere imprisoned in a castle, in Chrétien de Troyes' *Chevalier de la Charratte.*

one knew what a magnet was, or gravitation, or love. The force of the Virgin was still felt at Lourdes,[7] and seemed to be as potent as X-rays; but in America neither Venus nor Virgin ever had value as force—at most as sentiment. No American had ever been truly afraid of either.

This problem in dynamics gravely perplexed an American historian. The Woman had once been supreme; in France she still seemed potent, not merely as a sentiment, but as a force. Why was she unknown in America? For evidently America was ashamed of her, and she was ashamed herself, otherwise they would not have strewn fig-leaves so profusely all over her. When she was a true force, she was ignorant of fig-leaves, but the monthly-magazine-made American female had not a feature that would have been recognized by Adam. The trait was notorious, and often humorous, but any one brought up among Puritans knew that sex was sin. In any previous age, sex was strength. Neither art nor beauty was needed. Every one, even among Puritans, knew that neither Diana of the Ephesians nor any of the Oriental goddesses was worshipped for her beauty. She was goddess because of her force; she was the animated dynamo; she was reproduction—the greatest and most mysterious of all energies; all she needed was to be fecund. Singularly enough, not one of Adams's many schools of education had ever drawn his attention to the opening lines of Lucretius, though they were perhaps the finest in all Latin Literature, where the poet invoked Venus exactly as Dante invoked the Virgin:—

> 'Quæ quoniam rerum naturam *sola* gubernas.'[8]

The Venus of Epicurean philosophy survived in the Virgin of the Schools:

> 'Donna, sei tanto grande, e tanto vali,
> Che qual vuol grazia, e a te non ricorre,
> Sua disianza vuol volar senz' ali.'[9]

All this was to American thought as though it had never existed. The true American knew something of the facts, but nothing of the feelings; he read the letter, but he never felt the law. Before this historical chasm, a mind like that of Adams felt itself helpless; he turned from the Virgin to the Dynamo as though he were a Branly coherer. On one side, at the Louvre and at Chartres, as he knew by

7. A French town at the foot of the Pyrenees, visited by pilgrims for its spring of healing waters, where a peasant girl, Bernadette Soubirous, had a vision of the Virgin Mary.
8. "Thou, since thou alone dost govern the nature of things" (*De Rerum Natura*, Book I, 21, by Lucretius, 95–51?

B.C., Roman poet and Epicurean philosopher).
9. "Lady, thou art so great in all things / That he who wishes grace, and seeks not thee, / Would have his wish fly upwards without wings" (Dante, *Paradiso*, xxxiii, 13–15).

the record of work actually done and still before his eyes, was the highest energy ever known to man, the creator of four-fifths of his noblest art, exercising vastly more attraction over the human mind than all the steam-engines and dynamos ever dreamed of; and yet this energy was unknown to the American mind. An American Virgin would never dare command; an American Venus would never dare exist.

The question, which to any plain American of the nineteenth century seemed as remote as it did to Adams, drew him almost violently to study, once it was posed; and on this point Langleys were as useless as though they were Herbert Spencers[1] or dynamos. The idea survived only as art. There one turned as naturally as though the artist were himself a woman. Adams began to ponder, asking himself whether he knew of any American artist who had ever insisted on the power of sex, as every classic had always done; but he could think only of Walt Whitman; Bret Harte, as far as the magazines would let him venture; and one or two painters, for the flesh-tones. All the rest had used sex for sentiment, never for force; to them, Eve was a tender flower, and Herodias[2] an unfeminine horror. American art, like the American language and American education, was as far as possible sexless. Society regarded this victory over sex as its greatest triumph, and the historian readily admitted it, since the moral issue, for the moment, did not concern one who was studying the relations of unmoral force. He cared nothing for the sex of the dynamo until he could measure its energy.

Vaguely seeking a clue, he wandered through the art exhibit, and, in his stroll, stopped almost every day before Saint-Gaudens's General Sherman,[3] which had been given the central post of honor. Saint-Gaudens himself was in Paris, putting on the work his usual interminable last touches, and listening to the usual contradictory suggestions of brother sculptors. Of all the American artists who gave to American art whatever life it breathed in the seventies, Saint-Gaudens was perhaps the most sympathetic, but certainly the most inarticulate. General Grant or Don Cameron[4] had scarcely less instinct of rhetoric than he. All the others—the Hunts, Richardson, John La Farge, Stanford White[5]—were exuberant; only

1. Herbert Spencer (1820–1903), English thinker, welcomed Darwinism and coined the phrase "survival of the fittest."
2. Lustful wife of King Herod, responsible for the death of John the Baptist. *Cf.* Mark vi: 17–28.
3. Augustus Saint-Gaudens (1848–1907), Irish-born American sculptor; he created the memorial in Rock Creek Cemetery, Washington, D. C., which Henry Adams erected to his wife. The Sherman statue on the Fifth Avenue

Plaza in New York commemorates General William T. Sherman of Civil War fame.
4. James Donald Cameron (1833–1918), secretary of war in Grant's cabinet.
5. William Morris Hunt (1824–1879), Vermont painter, and his brother Richard Morris Hunt (1828–1895), architect; Henry Hobson Richardson (1838–1886), New York architect; John La Farge (1835–1910), New York artist and author, who accompanied Adams

Saint-Gaudens could never discuss or dilate on an emotion, or suggest artistic arguments for giving to his work the forms that he felt. He never laid down the law, or affected the despot, or became brutalized like Whistler[6] by the brutalities of his world. He required no incense; he was no egoist; his simplicity of thought was excessive; he could not imitate, or give any form but his own to the creations of his hand. No one felt more strongly than he the strength of other men, but the idea that they could affect him never stirred an image in his mind.

This summer his health was poor and his spirits were low. For such a temper, Adams was not the best companion, since his own gaiety was not *folle;* but he risked going now and then to the studio on Mont Parnasse to draw him out for a stroll in the Bois de Boulogne, or dinner as pleased his moods, and in return Saint-Gaudens sometimes let Adams go about in his company.

Once Saint-Gaudens took him down to Amiens, with a party of Frenchmen, to see the cathedral. Not until they found themselves actually studying the sculpture of the western portal, did it dawn on Adams's mind that, for his purposes, Saint-Gaudens on that spot had more interest to him than the cathedral itself. Great men before great monuments express great truths, provided they are not taken too solemnly. Adams never tired of quoting the supreme phrase of his idol Gibbon,[7] before the Gothic cathedrals: "I darted a contemptuous look on the stately monuments of superstition." Even in the footnotes of his history, Gibbon had never inserted a bit of humor more human than this, and one would have paid largely for a photograph of the fat little historian, on the background of Notre Dame of Amiens, trying to persuade his readers—perhaps himself—that he was darting a contemptuous look on the stately monument, for which he felt in fact the respect which every man of his vast study and active mind always feels before objects worthy of it; but besides the humor, one felt also the relation. Gibbon ignored the Virgin, because in 1789 religious monuments were out of fashion. In 1900 his remark sounded fresh and simple as the green fields to ears that had heard a hundred years of other remarks, mostly no more fresh and certainly less simple. Without malice, one might find it more instructive than a whole lecture of Ruskin.[8] One sees what one brings, and at that moment Gibbon brought the French Revolution. Ruskin brought reaction against the Revolution. Saint-Gaudens had passed beyond all. He liked the stately monu-

to the South Seas in 1886; Stanford White (1853–1906), New York architect.

6. James Abbott McNeill Whistler (1834–1903), American portrait and landscape painter.

7. Edward Gibbon (1737–1794), English historian, author of *The History of the Decline and Fall of the Roman Empire.*

8. John Ruskin (1819–1900), English author who wrote on architecture and painting.

ments much more than he liked Gibbon or Ruskin; he loved their dignity; their unity; their scale; their lines; their lights and shadows; their decorative sculpture; but he was even less conscious than they of the force that created it all—the Virgin, the Woman—by whose genius "the stately monuments of superstition" were built, through which she was expressed. He would have seen more meaning in Isis[9] with the cow's horns, at Edfoo,[1] who expressed the same thought. The art remained, but the energy was lost even upon the artist.

Yet in mind and person Saint-Gaudens was a survival of the 1500; he bore the stamp of the Renaissance, and should have carried an image of the Virgin round his neck, or stuck in his hat, like Louis XI.[2] In mere time he was a lost soul that had strayed by chance into the twentieth century, and forgotten where it came from. He writhed and cursed at his ignorance, much as Adams did at his own, but in the opposite sense. Saint-Gaudens was a child of Benvenuto Cellini,[3] smothered in an American cradle. Adams was a quintessence of Boston, devoured by curiosity to think like Benvenuto. Saint-Gauden's art was starved from birth, and Adams's instinct was blighted from babyhood. Each had but half of a nature, and when they came together before the Virgin of Amiens they ought both to have felt in her the force that made them one; but it was not so. To Adams she became more than ever a channel of force; to Saint-Gaudens she remained as before a channel of taste.

For a symbol of power, Saint-Gaudens instinctively preferred the horse, as was plain in his horse and Victory of the Sherman monument. Doubtless Sherman also felt it so. The attitude was so American that, for at least forty years, Adams had never realized that any other could be in sound taste. How many years had he taken to admit a notion of what Michaelangelo and Rubens[4] were driving at? He could not say; but he knew that only since 1895 had he begun to feel the Virgin or Venus as force, and not everywhere even so. At Chartres—perhaps at Lourdes—possibly at Cnidos if one could still find there the divinely naked Aphrodite of Praxiteles[5]—but otherwise one must look for force to the goddesses of Indian mythology. The idea died out long ago in the German and English stock. Saint-Gaudens at Amiens was hardly less sensitive to the force of the female energy than Matthew Arnold at the Grand Chartreuse.[6] Neither of them felt goddesses as power—only as reflected emotion,

9. Egyptian nature goddess.
1. Edfu, city on the upper Nile.
2. French king (1423–1483), who prayed fervently and resorted to astrologers and physicians for guidance during his final years.
3. Florentine goldsmith and sculptor (1500–1571); his *Autobiography* celebrates a sexual dynamism.
4. Peter Paul Rubens (1577–1640), great painter of the Flemish school.

5. Greek sculptor (fourth century B.C.), whose statue of Aphrodite was placed in the temple at Cnidos in Asia Minor.
6. English Victorian poet (1822–1888), who wrote of La Grande Chartreuse, the chief home of the Carthusian order until 1903. There Arnold felt himself, "Wandering between two worlds, one dead,/ The other powerless to be born" ("Stanzas from the Grande Chartreuse," 1855).

human expression, beauty, purity, taste, scarcely even as sympathy. They felt a railway train as power; yet they, and all other artists, constantly complained that the power embodied in a railway train could never be embodied in art. All the steam in the world could not, like the Virgin, build Chartres.

Yet in mechanics, whatever the mechanicians might think, both energies acted as interchangeable forces on man, and by action on man all known force may be measured. Indeed, few men of science measured force in any other way. After once admitting that a straight line was the shortest distance between two points, no serious mathematician cared to deny anything that suited his convenience, and rejected no symbol, unproved or unproveable, that helped him to accomplish work. The symbol was force, as a compass-needle or a triangle was force, as the mechanist might prove by losing it, and nothing could be gained by ignoring their value. Symbol or energy, the Virgin had acted as the greatest force the Western world ever felt, and had drawn man's activities to herself more strongly than any other power, natural or super-natural, had ever done; the historian's business was to follow the track of the energy; to find where it came from and where it went to; its complex source and shifting channels; its values, equivalents, conversions. It could scarcely be more complex than radium; it could hardly be deflected, diverted, polarized, absorbed more perplexingly than other radiant matter. Adams knew nothing about any of them, but as a mathematical problem of influence on human progress, though all were occult, all reacted on his mind, and he rather inclined to think the Virgin easiest to handle.

The pursuit turned out to be long and tortuous, leading at last into the vast forests of scholastic science. From Zeno to Descartes, hand in hand with Thomas Aquinas, Montaigne, and Pascal,[7] one stumbled as stupidly as though one were still a German student of 1860. Only with the instinct of despair could one force one's self into this old thicket of ignorance after having been repulsed at a score of entrances more promising and more popular. Thus far, no path had led anywhere, unless perhaps to an exceedingly modest living. Forty-five years of study had proved to be quite futile for the pursuit of power; one controlled no more force in 1900 than in 1850, although the amount of force controlled by society had enormously increased. The secret of education still hid itself somewhere behind ignorance, and one fumbled over it as feebly as ever. In such labyrinths, the staff is a force almost more necessary than

7. Zeno of Elea (fifth century B.C.), Greek philosopher whose paradoxes stimulated dialectics; René Descartes (1596–1650), French philosopher and mathematician, father of modern philosophy; St. Thomas Aquinas (1225?– 1274), Italian philosopher and theologian; Michel de Montaigne (1533– 1592), French essayist and liberal thinker; Blaise Pascal (1623–1662) French mathematician, physicist, and moralist.

the legs; the pen becomes a sort of blind-man's dog, to keep him from falling into the gutters. The pen works for itself, and acts like a hand, modelling the plastic material over and over again to the form that suits it best. The form is never arbitrary, but is a sort of growth like crystallization, as any artist knows too well; for often the pencil or pen runs into side-paths and shapelessness, loses its relations, stops or is bogged. Then it has to return on its trail, and recover, if it can, its line of force. The result of a year's work depends more on what is struck out than on what is left in; on the sequence of the main lines of thought, than on their play or variety. Compelled once more to lean heavily on this support, Adams covered more thousands of pages with figures as formal as though they were algebra, laboriously striking out, altering, burning, experimenting, until the year had expired, the Exposition had long been closed, and winter drawing to its end before he sailed from Cherbourg, on January 19, 1901 for home.

1907

WILLIAM JAMES
(1842–1910)

William James, the brother of the novelist Henry James, was born in New York City on January 11, 1842. Educated in European schools and by tutors in New York he acquired a cosmopolitan outlook, yet retained his American roots. From his father, Henry James senior, a learned Swedenborgian, he early derived a mystical and religious idealism, which later scientific study led him to harmonize with physical facts. During 1860 William James seriously studied painting, but a stronger interest in science took him to the Lawrence Scientific School at Harvard, then to the Harvard Medical School, which he left in 1865 to join Louis Agassiz in a zoological expedition bound for the Amazon. James returned in 1866 and re-entered Harvard Medical School for a year, spent a year abroad, then received his M.D. at Harvard in 1869. Bad health, aggravated by nervousness, prevented active practice of medicine and handicapped his efforts in the laboratory. As a result, James suffered pathologically, from doubts and pessimism until, in 1870, a reading of Charles Renouvier's *Rational Psychology* strengthened his belief in the possibility of moral freedom, in the validity of human experience, and in immortality. With his own personal intellectual problem solved, James shook off his semi-invalidism in 1872 to accept an instructorship in physiology at Harvard, and within ten years he became the pioneer of a new psychology. In 1878 James married Alice Gibbens, of Cambridge, Massachusetts, who inspired him to creative thinking such as he had never before accomplished. In his *Principles of Psychology* (1890) is evident the empirical bias which reappeared in his philosophy of pragmatism. During the 1880's he had traveled much abroad, and been interested in experiments in extra-sensory perception, then called "psychical research." His confidence that these apparently occult manifestations were susceptible of empirical investigation had a recognizable influence on his religious speculations, as his writings make evident. Influenced by Darwin and Spencer, James sought to apply evolutionary theories to the mind of the individual, regarded as an organism adjusting to its environment; he acknowledged biological forces as tending to determine the life of man, but maintained that they left uncanceled a measure of freedom of moral choice.

His interest now shifted to philosophy. While publishing numerous papers and lecturing on philosophical subjects he entered actively into public affairs, opposing the growing Pacific imperialism emphasized by the Spanish-American War. *The Will to Believe and Other Essays in Popular Philosophy* (1897) asserts the validity of belief beyond the mere facts of proof. Other books of this period are *Human Immortality* (1898), *Talks to Teachers on Psychology* (1899), and *The Varieties of Religious Experience* (1902). James defended belief in immortality and stressed the practical values of religion in terms

of conduct. Never in conflict with either theology or science, *The Varieties of Religious Experience*, like most of James's writing, was so simple and informal that it enjoyed a wide range of popular influence. The book was based on his lectures as Gifford Lecturer on Natural Religion at the University of Edinburgh (1901–1902) after he had spent nearly two years in Europe in recovery of his health.

In 1902 James was again appointed as lecturer at Harvard University, and he devoted himself for five years to teaching philosophy and formalizing his own ideas. These, embodied in his lectures at the Lowell Institute (1906) and Columbia (1907), appeared in 1907 as *Pragmatism: A New Name for Some Old Ways of Thinking.* He sought to demonstrate that the value of any idea, concept, or choice is tested by its practical consequences in terms of human satisfaction or behavior. This relativism is traditional in the American experience, although James excluded its cynical and popular debasement, which asserts that whatever works best is therefore good or true. Extensions of his ideas may be found in *The Meaning of Truth, A Sequel to 'Pragmatism'* (1909). He died the next year. After James's death, H. M. Kallen prepared for publication *Some Problems of Philosophy* (1911), left as an unfinished manuscript, and William James's son, Henry, edited *Memories and Studies* (1911). His *Essays in Radical Empiricism* were collected in 1912, and a volume of *Collected Essays and Reviews* appeared in

1920. The philosophy of James was fundamentally optimistic, and predicated on faith in human progress. As translated by John Dewey's "instrumentalism" on the plane of social reconstruction, it supported the conviction that experience is the highest social reality, that knowledge is functional, and that the human environment is subject to control by social intelligence. Since these ideas have dominated American education for nearly half a century, James has been our most

influential philosopher, although critics hesitate to call him a great one.

There is no collected edition of William James. *The Varieties of Religious Experience* has been reprinted, 1936; and selections from his works are collected in *The Philosophy of William James: Drawn from His Own Works*, with an introduction by Horace M. Kallen, 1925. *The Letters of William James*, 2 vols., 1920, were edited by his son. An authoritative life is Ralph Barton Perry, *The Thought and Character of William James*, 2 vols., 1935. Lloyd Morris, *William James: The Message of a Modern Mind*, 1951, furnishes an insight into James's message for the present.

The Will to Believe[1]

In the recently published Life by Leslie Stephen[2] of his brother, Fitz-James,[3] there is an account of a school to which the latter went when he was a boy. The teacher, a certain Mr. Guest, used to converse with his pupils in this wise: "Gurney, what is the difference between justification[4] and sanctification?[5]—Stephen, prove the omnipotence of God!" etc. In the midst of our Harvard freethinking and indifference we are prone to imagine that here at your good old orthodox College conversation continues to be somewhat upon this order; and to show you that we at Harvard have not lost all interest in these vital subjects, I have brought with me tonight something like a sermon on justification by faith to read to you—I mean an essay in justification *of* faith, a defence of our right to adopt a believing attitude in religious matters, in spite of the fact that our merely logical intellect may not have been coerced. "The Will to Believe," accordingly, is the title of my paper.

I have long defended to my own students the lawfulness of voluntarily adopted faith; but as soon as they have got well imbued with the logical spirit, they have as a rule refused to admit my contention to be lawful philosophically, even though in point of fact they were personally all the time chock-full of some faith or other themselves. I am all the while, however, so profoundly convinced that my own

1. Originally an address to the Philosophical Clubs of Yale and Brown universities, and subsequently published in the *New World* for June, 1896. It was collected as the first of ten essays in *The Will to Believe and Other Essays in Popular Philosophy* (1897), the source of the present text.
2. Sir Leslie Stephen (1832–1904),

English man of letters and agnostic philosopher.
3. James Fitz-James Stephen (1829–1894), English jurist and essayist.
4. The belief that man is freed from the guilt of sin by the act of God.
5. The doctrine that men are purified and exalted to the love of righteousness through the redemption of Christ.

position is correct, that your invitation has seemed to me a good occasion to make my statements more clear. Perhaps your minds will be more open than those with which I have hitherto had to deal. I will be as little technical as I can, though I must begin by setting up some technical distinctions that will help us in the end.

I

Let us give the name of *hypothesis* to anything that may be proposed to our belief; and just as the electricians speak of live and dead wires, let us speak of any hypothesis as either *live* or *dead*. A live hypothesis is one which appeals as a real possibility to him to whom it is proposed. If I ask you to believe in the Mahdi,[6] the notion makes no electric connection with your nature—it refuses to scintillate with any credibility at all. As an hypothesis it is completely dead. To an Arab, however (even if he be not one of the Mahdi's followers), the hypothesis is among the mind's possibilities: it is alive. This shows that deadness and liveness in an hypothesis are not intrinsic properties, but relations to the individual thinker. They are measured by his willingness to act. The maximum of liveness in an hypothesis means willingness to act irrevocably. Practically, that means belief; but there is some believing tendency wherever there is willingness to act at all.

Next, let us call the decision between two hypotheses an *option*. Options may be of several kinds. They may be—1, *living* or *dead*; 2, *forced* or *avoidable*; 3, *momentous* or *trivial*; and for our purposes we may call an option a *genuine* option when it is of the forced, living, and momentous kind.

1. A living option is one in which both hypotheses are live ones. If I say to you: "Be a theosophist[7] or be a Mohammedan," it is probably a dead option, because for you neither hypothesis is likely to be alive. But if I say: "Be an agnostic[8] or be a Christian," it is otherwise: trained as you are, each hypothesis makes some appeal, however small, to your belief.

2. Next, if I say to you: "Choose between going out with your umbrella or without it," I do not offer you a genuine option, for it is not forced. You can easily avoid it by not going out at all. Similarly, if I say, "Either love me or hate me," "Either call my theory true or call it false," your option is avoidable. You may remain indifferent to me, neither loving nor hating, and you may decline to offer any judgment as to my theory. But if I say, "Either

---

6. A spiritual and temporal leader expected by the Moslems; *i.e.*, a messiah. In referring to a particular Mahdi, James recalls the defeat and death, in 1885, of the British soldier and administrator Charles George Gordon, at the siege of Khartoum in the Sudan by the forces of Mohammed Ahmed, a proclaimed Mahdi.

7. A believer in pantheistic evolution and the doctrine of reincarnation.

8. One who denies the possibility of any positive knowledge of God.

accept this truth or go without it," I put on you a forced option, for there is no standing place outside of the alternative. Every dilemma based on a complete logical disjunction, with no possibility of not choosing, is an option of this forced kind.

3. Finally, if I were Dr. Nansen[9] and proposed to you to join my North Pole expedition, your option would be momentous; for this would probably be your only similar opportunity, and your choice now would either exclude you from the North Pole sort of immortality altogether or put at least the chance of it into your hands. He who refuses to embrace a unique opportunity loses the prize as surely as if he tried and failed. *Per contra,*[1] the option is trivial when the opportunity is not unique, when the stake is insignificant, or when the decision is reversible if it later prove unwise. Such trivial options abound in the scientific life. A chemist finds an hypothesis live enough to spend a year in its verification; he believes in it to that extent. But if his experiments prove inconclusive either way, he is quit for his loss of time, no vital harm being done.

It will facilitate our discussion if we keep all these distinctions well in mind.

II

The next matter to consider is the actual psychology of human opinion. When we look at certain facts, it seems as if our passional and volitional nature lay at the root of all our convictions. When we look at others, it seems as if they could do nothing when the intellect had once said its say. Let us take the latter facts up first.

Does it not seem preposterous on the very face of it to talk of our opinions being modifiable at will? Can our will either help or hinder our intellect in its perceptions of truth? Can we, by just willing it, believe that Abraham Lincoln's existence is a myth, and that the portraits of him in *McClure's Magazine* are all of some one else? Can we, by any effort of our will, or by any strength of wish that it were true, believe ourselves well and about when we are roaring with rheumatism in bed, or feel certain that the sum of the two one-dollar bills in our pocket must be a hundred dollars? We can *say* any of these things, but we are absolutely impotent to believe them; and of just such things is the whole fabric of the truths that we do believe in made up—matters of fact, immediate or remote, as Hume[2] said, and relations between ideas, which are either there or not there for us if we see them so, and which if not there cannot be put there by any action of our own.

In Pascal's[3] *Thoughts* there is a celebrated passage known in liter-

9. Fridtjof Nansen (1861–1930), Norwegian polar explorer, was currently newsworthy because of his polar expedition of 1893–1897.
1. On the other hand.
2. David Hume (1711–1776), English philosopher, who wrote *Dialogues Concerning Natural Religion* (1779).
3. Blaise Pascal (1623–1662), French physicist and moralist, best known for his *Penseés* (*Thoughts*), from which James paraphrases the "wager."

ature as Pascal's wager. In it he tries to force us into Christianity by reasoning as if our concern with truth resembled our concern with the stakes in a game of chance. Translated freely his words are these: You must either believe or not believe that God is— which will you do? Your human reason cannot say. A game is going on between you and the nature of things which at the day of judgment will bring out either heads or tails. Weigh what your gains and your losses would be if you should stake all you have on heads, or God's existence: if you win in such case, you gain eternal beatitude; if you lose, you lose nothing at all. If there were an infinity of chances, and only one for God in this wager, still you ought to stake your all on God; for though you surely risk a finite loss by this procedure, any finite loss is reasonable, even a certain one is reasonable, if there is but the possibility of infinite gain. Go, then, and take holy water, and have masses said; belief will come and stupefy your scruples—*Cela vous fera croire et vous abêtira.*[4] Why should you not? At bottom, what have you to lose?

You probably feel that when religious faith expresses itself thus, in the language of the gaming-table, it is put to its last trumps. Surely Pascal's own personal belief in masses and holy water had far other springs; and this celebrated page of his is but an argument for others, a last desperate snatch at a weapon against the hardness of the unbelieving heart. We feel that a faith in masses and holy water adopted wilfully after such a mechanical calculation would lack the inner soul of faith's reality; and if we were ourselves in the place of the Deity, we should probably take particular pleasure in cutting off believers of this pattern from their infinite reward. It is evident that unless there be some pre-existing tendency to believe in masses and holy water, the option offered to the will by Pascal is not a living option. Certainly no Turk ever took to masses and holy water on its account; and even to us Protestants these means of salvation seem such foregone impossibilities that Pascal's logic, invoked for them specifically, leaves us unmoved. As well might the Mahdi write to us, saying, "I am the Expected One whom God has created in his effulgence. You shall be infinitely happy if you confess me; otherwise you shall be cut off from the light of the sun. Weigh, then, your infinite gain if I am genuine against your finite sacrifice if I am not!" His logic would be that of Pascal; but he would vainly use it on us, for the hypothesis he offers us is dead. No tendency to act on it exists in us to any degree.

The talk of believing by our volition seems, then, from one point of view, simply silly. From another point of view it is worse than silly, it is vile. When one turns to the magnificent edifice of the physical sciences, and sees how it was reared; what thousands of

[4] That will make you believe and humble yourself.

disinterested moral lives of men lie buried in its mere foundations; what patience and postponement, what choking down of preference, what submission to the icy laws of outer fact are wrought into its very stones and mortar; how absolutely impersonal it stands in its vast augustness—then how besotted and contemptible seems every little sentimentalist who comes blowing his voluntary smoke-wreaths, and pretending to decide things from out of his private dream! Can we wonder if those bred in the rugged and manly school of science should feel like spewing such subjectivism out of their mouths? The whole system of loyalties which grow up in the schools of science go dead against its toleration; so that it is only natural that those who have caught the scientific fever should pass over to the opposite extreme, and write sometimes as if the incorruptibly truthful intellect ought positively to prefer bitterness and unacceptableness to the heart in its cup.

> It fortifies my soul to know
> That though I perish, Truth is so—

sings Clough,[5] while Huxley[6] exclaims: "My only consolation lies in the reflection that, however bad our posterity may become, so far as they hold by the plain rule of not pretending to believe what they have no reason to believe, because it may be to their advantage so to pretend [the word 'pretend' is surely here redundant], they will not have reached the lowest depth of immorality." And that delicious *enfant terrible* Clifford[7] writes: "Belief is desecrated when given to unproved and unquestioned statements for the solace and private pleasure of the believer. . . . Whoso would deserve well of his fellows in this matter will guard the purity of his belief with a very fanaticism of jealous care, lest at any time it should rest on an unworthy object, and catch a stain which can never be wiped away. . . . If [a] belief has been accepted on insufficient evidence [even though the belief be true, as Clifford on the same page explains] the pleasure is a stolen one. . . . It is sinful because it is stolen in defiance of our duty to mankind. That duty is to guard ourselves from such beliefs as from a pestilence which may shortly master our own body and then spread to the rest of the town. . . . It is wrong always, everywhere, and for every one, to believe anything upon insufficient evidence."

5. Arthur Hugh Clough (1819–1861), English poet. His poem "With Whom Is No Variableness, Neither Shadow of Turning" begins with these lines. See the volume *Ambarvalia* (1849).
6. Thomas Henry Huxley (1825–1895), biologist, principal English advocate of Darwin's theories.
7. William Kingdon Clifford (1845–1879), English mathematician and philosopher, who died at thirty-four after developing revolutionary theories of the material basis of consciousness and morality.

III

All this strikes one as healthy, even when expressed, as by Clifford, with somewhat too much of robustious pathos in the voice. Free will and simple wishing do seem, in the matter of our credences, to be only fifth wheels to the coach. Yet if any one should thereupon assume that intellectual insight is what remains after wish and will and sentimental preference have taken wing, or that pure reason is what then settles our opinions, he would fly quite as directly in the teeth of the facts.

It is only our already dead hypotheses that our willing nature is unable to bring to life again. But what has made them dead for us is for the most part a previous action of our willing nature of an antagonistic kind. When I say "willing nature," I do not mean only such deliberate volitions as may have set up habits of belief that we cannot now escape from—I mean all such factors of belief as fear and hope, prejudice and passion, imitation and partisanship, the circumpressure of our caste and set. As a matter of fact we find ourselves believing, we hardly know how or why. Mr. Balfour[8] gives the name of "authority" to all those influences, born of the intellectual climate, that makes hypotheses possible or impossible for us, alive or dead. Here in this room, we all of us believe in molecules and the conservation of energy, in democracy and necessary progress, in Protestant Christianity and the duty of fighting for "the doctrine of the immortal Monroe,"[9] all for no reasons worthy of the name. We see into these matters with no more inner clearness, and probably with much less, than any disbeliever in them might possess. His unconventionality would probably have some grounds to show for its conclusions; but for us, not insight, but the *prestige* of the opinions, is what makes the spark shoot from them and light up our sleeping magazines of faith. Our reason is quite satisfied, in nine hundred and ninety-nine cases out of every thousand of us, if it can find a few arguments that will do to recite in case our credulity is criticized by some one else. Our faith is faith in some one else's faith, and in the greatest matters this is most the case. Our belief in truth itself, for instance, that there is a truth, and that our minds and it are made for each other—what is it but a passionate affirmation of desire, in which our social system backs us up? We want to have a truth; we want to believe that our experiments and studies and discussions must put us in a continually better and better position towards it; and on this line we agree to fight out our

8. Arthur James Balfour (1848–1930), British statesman, essayist, and skeptic.
9. President James Monroe (1758–1831) in 1823 promulgated the so-called Monroe Doctrine, declaring that Euro-pean intrusion into the domestic affairs of nations in the Americas would constitute "a manifestation * * * unfriendly * * * toward the United States."

thinking lives. But if a Pyrrhonistic[1] sceptic asks us *how we know* all this, can our logic find a reply? No! certainly it cannot. It is just one volition against another—we willing to go in for life upon a trust or assumption which he, for his part, does not care to make.[2]

As a rule we disbelieve all facts and theories for which we have no use. Clifford's cosmic emotions find no use for Christian feelings. Huxley belabors the bishops because there is no use for sacerdotalism[3] in his scheme of life. Newman,[4] on the contrary, goes over to Romanism, and finds all sorts of reasons good for staying there, because a priestly system is for him an organic need and delight. Why do so few "scientists" even look at the evidence for telepathy, so called? Because they think, as a leading biologist, now dead, once said to me, that even if such a thing were true, scientists ought to band together to keep it suppressed and concealed. It would undo the uniformity of Nature and all sorts of other things without which scientists cannot carry on their pursuits. But if this very man had been shown something which as a scientist he might *do* with telepathy, he might not only have examined the evidence, but even have found it good enough. This very law which the logicians would impose upon us—if I may give the name of logicians to those who would rule out our willing nature here—is based on nothing but their own natural wish to exclude all elements for which they, in their professional quality of logicians can find no use.

Evidently, then, our non-intellectual nature does influence our convictions. There are passional tendencies and volitions which run before and others which come after belief, and it is only the latter that are too late for the fair; and they are not too late when the previous passional work has been already in their own direction. Pascal's argument, instead of being powerless, then seems a regular clincher, and is the last stroke needed to make our faith in masses and holy water complete. The state of things is evidently far from simple; and pure insight and logic, whatever they might do ideally, are not the only things that really do produce our creeds.

IV

Our next duty, having recognized this mixed-up state of affairs, is to ask whether it be simply reprehensible and pathological, or whether, on the contrary, we must treat it as a normal element in making up our minds. The thesis I defend is, briefly stated, this: *Our passional nature not only lawfully may, but must, decide an option between propositions, whenever it is a genuine option that*

1. The Greek skeptic Pyrrho (365?–275? B.C.) believed that knowledge could not be established with certainty.
2. "Compare the admirable page 310 in S. H. Hodgson's *Time and Space,* London, 1865" [James's note].
3. Belief in a divinely authorized priesthood.
4. John Henry, Cardinal Newman (1801–1890), Anglican theologian, embraced Roman Catholicism in 1845.

cannot by its nature be decided on intellectual grounds; for to say, under such circumstances, "Do not decide, but leave the question open," is itself a passional decision—just like deciding yes or no— and is attended with the same risk of losing the truth. The thesis thus abstractly expressed will, I trust, soon become quite clear. But I must first indulge in a bit more of preliminary work.

V

It will be observed that for the purposes of this discussion we are on "dogmatic" ground—ground, I mean, which leaves systematic philosophical scepticism altogether out of account. The postulate that there is truth, and that it is the destiny of our minds to attain it, we are deliberately resolving to make, though the sceptic will not make it. We part company with him, therefore, absolutely, at this point. But the faith that truth exists, and that our minds can find it, may be held in two ways. We may talk of the *empiricist* way and of the *absolutist* way of believing in truth. The absolutists in this matter say that we not only can attain to knowing truth, but we can *know when* we have attained to knowing it; while the empiricists think that although we may attain it, we cannot infallibly know when. To *know* is one thing, and to know for certain *that* we know is another. One may hold to the first being possible without the second; hence the empiricists and the absolutists, although neither of them is a sceptic in the usual philosophic sense of the term, show very different degrees of dogmatism in their lives.

If we look at the history of opinions, we see that the empiricist tendency has largely prevailed in science, while in philosophy the absolutist tendency has had everything its own way. The characteristic sort of happiness, indeed, which philosophies yield has mainly consisted in the conviction felt by each successive school or system that by it bottom-certitude had been attained. "Other philosophies are collections of opinions, mostly false; *my* philosophy gives standing-ground forever"—who does not recognize in this the key-note of every system worthy of the name? A system, to be a system at all, must come as a *closed* system, reversible in this or that detail, perchance, but in its essential features never!

Scholastic[5] orthodoxy, to which one must always go when one wishes to find perfectly clear statement, has beautifully elaborated this absolutist conviction in a doctrine which it calls that of "objective evidence." If, for example, I am unable to doubt that I now exist before you, that two is less than three, or that if all men are mortal then I am mortal too, it is because these things illumine my intellect irresistibly. The final ground of this objective evidence

---

5. The Church Fathers founded their orthodox Scholastic philosophy on formal logic supported by authority.

possessed by certain propositions is the *adæquatio intellectûs nostri cum rê*.[6] The certitude it brings involves an *aptitudinem ad extorquendum certum assensum*[7] on the part of the truth envisaged, and on the side of the subject a *quietem in cognitione*,[8] when once the object is mentally received, that leaves no possibility of doubt behind; and in the whole transaction nothing operates but the *entitas ipsa*[9] of the object and the *entitas ipsa* of the mind. We slouchy modern thinkers dislike to talk in Latin,—indeed, we dislike to talk in set terms at all; but at bottom our own state of mind is very much like this whenever we uncritically abandon ourselves: You believe in objective evidence, and I do. Of some things we feel that we are certain: we know, and we know that we do know. There is something that gives a click inside of us, a bell that strikes twelve, when the hands of our mental clock have swept the dial and meet over the meridian hour. The greatest empiricists among us are only empiricists on reflection: when left to their instincts, they dogmatize like infallible popes.[1] When the Cliffords tell us how sinful it is to be Christians on such "insufficient evidence," insufficiency is really the last thing they have in mind. For them the evidence is absolutely sufficient, only it makes the other way. They believe so completely in an anti-Christian order of the universe that there is no living option: Christianity is a dead hypothesis from the start.

VI

But now, since we are all such absolutists by instinct, what in our quality of students of philosophy ought we to do about the fact? Shall we espouse and indorse it? Or shall we treat it as a weakness of our nature from which we must free ourselves, if we can?

I sincerely believe that the latter course is the only one we can follow as reflective men. Objective evidence and certitude are doubtless very fine ideals to play with, but where on this moonlit and dream-visited planet are they found? I am, therefore, myself a complete empiricist so far as my theory of human knowledge goes. I live, to be sure, by the practical faith that we must go on experiencing and thinking over our experience, for only thus can our opinions grow more true; but to hold any one of them—I absolutely do not care which—as if it never could be reinterpretable or corrigible, I believe to be a tremendously mistaken attitude, and I think that the whole history of philosophy will bear me out. There is but one indefectibly certain truth, and that is the truth that Pyrrhonistic scepticism itself leaves standing—the truth that the present phenomenon of consciousness exists. That, however, is the

6. The balancing of our mind with the fact.
7. An aptitude for compelling a definite agreement.
8. An assurance in the knowledge.

9. The entity itself.
1. The doctrine of the divine assurance of infallibility in official utterances of the pope was incorporated into Roman Catholic dogma in 1870.

bare starting-point of knowledge, the mere admission of a stuff to be philosophized about. The various philosophies are but so many attempts at expressing what this stuff really is. And if we repair to our libraries what disagreement do we discover! Where is a certainly true answer found? Apart from abstract propositions of comparison (such as two and two are the same as four), propositions which tell us nothing by themselves about concrete reality, we find no proposition ever regarded by any one as evidently certain that has not either been called a falsehood, or at least had its truth sincerely questioned by some one else. The transcending of the axioms of geometry, not in play but in earnest, by certain of our contemporaries (as Zöllner and Charles H. Hinton[2]), and the rejection of the whole Aristotelian logic by the Hegelians,[3] are striking instances in point.

No concrete test of what is really true has ever been agreed upon. Some make the criterion external to the moment of perception, putting it either in revelation, the *consensus gentium*,[4] the instincts of the heart, or the systematized experience of the race. Others make the perceptive moment its own test—Descartes,[5] for instance, with his clear and distinct ideas guaranteed by the veracity of God; Reid[6] with his "common-sense"; and Kant[7] with his forms of synthetic judgment *a priori*. The inconceivability of the opposite; the capacity to be verified by sense; the possession of complete organic unity or self-relation, realized when a thing is its own other—are standards which, in turn, have been used. The much lauded objective evidence is never triumphantly there; it is a mere aspiration or *Grenzbegriff*,[8] marking the infinitely remote ideal of our thinking life. To claim that certain truths now possess it, is simply to say that when you think them true and they *are* true, then their evidence is objective, otherwise it is not. But practically one's conviction that the evidence one goes by is of the real objective brand, is only one more subjective opinion added to the lot. For what a contradictory array of opinions have objective evidence and absolute certitude been claimed! The world is rational through and through—its existence is an ultimate brute fact; there is a personal God—a personal God is inconceivable; there is an extra-mental physical world immediately known—the mind can only know its own ideas;

2. Johann Karl Friedrich Zöllner (1834–1882), German astronomer and physicist, and Charles H. Hinton (1853–1907), British mathematician and author of *What Is the Fourth Dimension* (1883); both contributed to the broadening concepts of geometry.
3. The followers of the German philosopher Georg Wilhelm Friedrich Hegel (1770–1831).
4. Consent of the nations; *i.e.,* "universal opinion," "the agreement of everybody."
5. The French philosopher and mathematician René Descartes (1596–1650) sought mathematical certitude for belief. See his *Discours de la Méthode* (1637).
6. Thomas Reid (1710–1796), leader of the Scottish school of philosophy, which sought to combat skepticism by "common sense" concepts of matter and intuition.
7. Immanuel Kant (1724–1804), German philosopher.
8. Frontier of comprehension.

a moral imperative exists—obligation is only the resultant of desires; a permanent spiritual principle is in every one—there are only shifting states of mind; there is an endless chain of causes—there is an absolute first cause; an eternal necessity—a freedom; a purpose—no purpose; a primal One—a primal Many; a universal continuity—an essential discontinuity in things; an infinity—no infinity. There is this—there is that; there is indeed nothing which some one has not thought absolutely true, while his neighbor deemed it absolutely false; and not an absolutist among them seems ever to have considered that the trouble may all the time be essential, and that the intellect, even with truth directly in its grasp, may have no infallible signal for knowing whether it be truth or no. When, indeed, one remembers that the most striking practical application to life of the doctrine of objective certitude has been the conscientious labors of the Holy Office of the Inquisition, one feels less tempted than ever to lend the doctrine a respectful ear.

But please observe, now, that when as empiricists we give up the doctrine of objective certitude, we do not thereby give up the quest or hope of truth itself. We still pin our faith on its existence, and still believe that we gain an ever better position towards it by systematically continuing to roll up experiences and think. Our great difference from the scholastic lies in the way we face. The strength of his system lies in the principles, the origin, the *terminus a quo*[9] of his thought; for us the strength is in the outcome, the upshot, the *terminus ad quem*.[1] Not where it comes from but what it leads to is to decide. It matters not to an empiricist from what quarter an hypothesis may come to him: he may have acquired it by fair means or by foul; passion may have whispered or accident suggested it; but if the total drift of thinking continues to confirm it, that is what he means by its being true.

VII

One more point, small but important, and our preliminaries are done. There are two ways of looking at our duty in the matter of opinion—ways entirely different, and yet ways about whose difference the theory of knowledge seems hitherto to have shown very little concern. *We must know the truth*; and *we must avoid error*—these are our first and great commandments as would-be knowers; but they are not two ways of stating an identical commandment, they are two separable laws. Although it may indeed happen that when we believe the truth A, we escape as an incidental consequence from believing the falsehood B, it hardly ever happens that by merely disbelieving B we necessarily believe A. We may in escaping B fall into believing other falsehoods, C or D, just as bad as B; or

---

9. The terminal from which; *i.e.*, "the starting point."

1. The terminal to which; *i.e.*, "the destination."

we may escape **B** by not believing anything at all, not even **A**.

Believe truth! Shun error!—these, we see, are two materially different laws; and by choosing between them we may end by coloring differently our whole intellectual life. We may regard the chase for truth as paramount, and the avoidance of error as secondary; or we may, on the other hand, treat the avoidance of error as more imperative, and let truth take its chance. Clifford, in the instructive passage which I have quoted, exhorts us to the latter course. Believe nothing, he tells us, keep your mind in suspense forever, rather than by closing it on insufficient evidence incur the awful risk of believing lies. You, on the other hand, may think that the risk of being in error is a very small matter when compared with the blessings of real knowledge, and be ready to be duped many times in your investigation rather than postpone indefinitely the chance of guessing true. I myself find it impossible to go with Clifford. We must remember that these feelings of our duty about either truth or error are in any case only expressions of our passional life. Biologically considered, our minds are as ready to grind out falsehood as veracity, and he who says, "Better go without belief forever than believe a lie!" merely shows his own preponderant private horror of becoming a dupe. He may be critical of many of his desires and fears, but this fear he slavishly obeys. He cannot imagine any one questioning its binding force. For my own part, I have also a horror of being duped; but I can believe that worse things than being duped may happen to a man in this world: so Clifford's exhortation has to my ears a thoroughly fantastic sound. It is like a general informing his soldiers that it is better to keep out of battle forever than to risk a single wound. Not so are victories either over enemies or over nature gained. Our errors are surely not such awfully solemn things. In a world where we are so certain to incur them in spite of all our caution, a certain lightness of heart seems healthier than this excessive nervousness on their behalf. At any rate, it seems the fittest thing for the empiricist philosopher.

VIII

And now, after all this introduction, let us go straight at our question. I have said, and now repeat it, that not only as a matter of fact do we find our passional nature influencing us in our opinions, but that there are some options between opinions in which this influence must be regarded both as an inevitable and as a lawful determinant of our choice.

I fear here that some of you my hearers will begin to scent danger, and lend an inhospitable ear. Two first steps of passion you have indeed had to admit as necessary—we must think so as to avoid dupery, and we must think so as to gain truth; but the surest path to those ideal consummations, you will probably consider, is from now onwards to take no further passional step.

Well, of course, I agree as far as the facts will allow. Wherever the option between losing truth and gaining it is not momentous, we can throw the chance of *gaining truth* away, and at any rate save ourselves from any chance of *believing falsehood*, by not making up our minds at all till objective evidence has come. In scientific questions, this is almost always the case; and even in human affairs in general, the need of acting is seldom so urgent that a false belief to act on is better than no belief at all. Law courts, indeed, have to decide on the best evidence attainable for the moment, because a judge's duty is to make law as well as to ascertain it, and (as a learned judge once said to me) few cases are worth spending much time over: the great thing is to have them decided on *any* acceptable principle, and got out of the way. But in our dealings with objective nature we obviously are recorders, not makers, of the truth; and decisions for the mere sake of deciding promptly and getting on to the next business would be wholly out of place. Throughout the breadth of physical nature facts are what they are quite independently of us, and seldom is there any such hurry about them that the risks of being duped by believing a premature theory need be faced. The questions here are always trivial options, the hypotheses are hardly living (at any rate not living for us spectators), the choice between believing truth or falsehood is seldom forced. The attitude of sceptical balance is therefore the absolutely wise one if we would escape mistakes. What difference, indeed, does it make to most of us whether we have or have not a theory of the Röntgen[2] rays, whether we believe or not in mind-stuff, or have a conviction about the causality of conscious states? It makes no difference. Such options are not forced on us. On every account it is better not to make them, but still keep weighing reasons *pro et contra*[3] with an indifferent hand.

I speak, of course, here of the purely judging mind. For purposes of discovery such indifference is to be less highly recommended, and science would be far less advanced than she is if the passionate desires of individuals to get their own faith confirmed had been kept out of the game. See for example the sagacity which Spencer and Weismann[4] now display. On the other hand, if you want an absolute duffer in an investigation, you must, after all, take the man who has no interest whatever in its results: he is the warranted incapable, the positive fool. The most useful investigator, because

2. Wilhelm Konrad Röntgen (1845–1923) discovered X-rays—sometimes called Röntgen rays—the year before James gave this address.
3. For and against.
4. Herbert Spencer (1820–1903), Eng- lish philosopher, based his sociological theories on certain evolutionary hypotheses of Darwin; August Weismann (1834–1914), a German biologist, proposed the germ-plasm theory of heredity.

the most sensitive observer, is always he whose eager interest in one side of the question is balanced by an equally keen nervousness lest he become deceived.[5] Science has organized this nervousness into a regular *technique,* her so-called method of verification; and she has fallen so deeply in love with the method that one may even say she has ceased to care for truth by itself at all. It is only truth as technically verified that interests her. The truth of truths might come in merely affirmative form, and she would decline to touch it. Such truth as that, she might repeat with Clifford, would be stolen in defiance of her duty to mankind. Human passions, however, are stronger than technical rules. "*Le cœur a ses raisons,*" as Pascal says, "*que la raison ne connaît pas*";[6] and however indifferent to all but the bare rules of the game the umpire, the abstract intellect, may be, the concrete players who furnish him the materials to judge are usually, each one of them, in love with some pet "live hypothesis" of his own. Let us agree, however, that wherever there is no forced option, the dispassionately judicial intellect with no pet hypothesis, saving us, as it does, from dupery at any rate, ought to be our ideal.

The question next arises: Are there not somewhere forced options in our speculative questions, and can we (as men who may be interested at least as much in positively gaining truth as in merely escaping dupery) always wait with impunity till the coercive evidence shall have arrived? It seems *a priori* improbable that the truth should be so nicely adjusted to our needs and powers as that. In the great boarding-house of nature, the cakes and the butter and the syrup seldom come out so even and leave the plates so clean. Indeed, we should view them with scientific suspicion if they did.

IX

Moral questions immediately present themselves as questions whose solution cannot wait for sensible proof. A moral question is a question not of what sensibly exists, but of what is good, or would be good if it did exist. Science can tell us what exists; but to compare the *worths,* both of what exists and of what does not exist, we must consult not science, but what Pascal calls our heart. Science herself consults her heart when she lays it down that the infinite ascertainment of fact and correction of false belief are the supreme goods for man. Challenge the statement, and science can only repeat it oracularly, or else prove it by showing that such ascertainment and correction bring man all sorts of other goods which man's heart in turn declares. The question of having moral beliefs at all

5. "Compare Wilfrid Ward's Essay, 'The Wish to Believe,' in his *Witnesses to the Unseen,* Macmillan & Co., 1893" [James's note].

6. "The heart has its reasons which reason does not know"—a familiar quotation from Pascal's *Pensées.*

or not having them is decided by our will. Are our moral preferences true or false, or are they only odd biological phenomena, making things good or bad for *us*, but in themselves indifferent? How can your pure intellect decide? If your heart does not *want* a world of moral reality, your head will assuredly never make you believe in one. Mephistophelian scepticism,[7] indeed, will satisfy the head's play-instincts much better than any rigorous idealism can. Some men (even at the student age) are so naturally cool-hearted that the moralistic hypothesis never has for them any pungent life, and in their supercilious presence the hot young moralist always feels strangely ill at ease. The appearance of knowingness is on their side, of *naïveté* and gullibility on his. Yet, in the inarticulate heart of him, he clings to it that he is not a dupe, and that there is a realm in which (as Emerson says) all their wit and intellectual superiority is no better than the cunning of a fox. Moral scepticism can no more be refuted or proved by logic than intellectual scepticism can. When we stick to it that there *is* truth (be it of either kind), we do so with our whole nature, and resolve to stand or fall by the results. The sceptic with his whole nature adopts the doubting attitude; but which of us is the wiser, Omniscience only knows.

Turn now from these wide questions of good to a certain class of questions of fact, questions concerning personal relations, states of mind between one man and another. *Do you like me or not?*—for example. Whether you do or not depends, in countless instances, on whether I meet you half-way, am willing to assume that you must like me, and show you trust and expectation. The previous faith on my part in your liking's existence is in such cases what makes your liking come. But if I stand aloof, and refuse to budge an inch until I have objective evidence, until you shall have done something apt, as the absolutists say, *ad extorquendum assensum meum*,[8] ten to one your liking never comes. How many women's hearts are vanquished by the mere sanguine insistence of some man that they *must* love him! he will not consent to the hypothesis that they cannot. The desire for a certain kind of truth here brings about that special truth's existence; and so it is in innumerable cases of other sorts. Who gains promotions, boons, appointments, but the man in whose life they are seen to play the part of live hypotheses, who discounts them, sacrifices other things for their sake before they have come, and takes risks for them in advance? His faith acts on the powers above him as a claim, and creates its own verification.

A social organism of any sort whatever, large or small, is what it is because each member proceeds to his own duty with a trust that

7. A reference to Goethe's *Faust*, in which Mephistopheles appears as the spirit of perpetual denial of life.
8. Calculated to elicit my agreement.

the other members will simultaneously do theirs. Wherever a desired result is achieved by the co-operation of many independent persons, its existence as a fact is a pure consequence of the precursive faith in one another of those immediately concerned. A government, an army, a commercial system, a ship, a college, an athletic team, all exist on this condition, without which not only is nothing achieved, but nothing is even attempted. A whole train of passengers (individually brave enough) will be looted by a few highwaymen, simply because the latter can count on one another, while each passenger fears that if he makes a movement of resistance, he will be shot before any one else backs him up. If we believed that the whole car-full would rise at once with us, we should each severally rise, and train-robbing would never even be attempted. There are, then, cases where a fact cannot come at all unless a preliminary faith exists in its coming. *And where faith in a fact can help create the fact,* that would be an insane logic which should say that faith running ahead of scientific evidence is the "lowest kind of immorality" into which a thinking being can fall. Yet such is the logic by which our scientific absolutists pretend to regulate our lives!

X

In truths dependent on our personal action, then, faith based on desire is certainly a lawful and possibly an indispensable thing.

But now, it will be said, these are all childish human cases, and have nothing to do with great cosmical matters, like the question of religious faith. Let us then pass on to that. Religions differ so much in their accidents that in discussing the religious question we must make it very generic and broad. What then do we now mean by the religious hypothesis? Science says things are; morality says some things are better than other things; and religion says essentially two things.

First, she says that the best things are the more eternal things, the overlapping things, the things in the universe that throw the last stone, so to speak, and say the final word. "Perfection is eternal" —this phrase of Charles Secrétan[9] seems a good way of putting this first affirmation of religion, an affirmation which obviously cannot yet be verified scientifically at all.

The second affirmation of religion is that we are better off even now if we believe her first affirmation to be true.

Now, let us consider what the logical elements of this situation are *in case the religious hypothesis in both its branches be really true.* (Of course, we must admit that possibility at the outset. If we

9. A French religious philosopher (1815–1895) who tried to form a completely rational method of belief.

are to discuss the question at all, it must involve a living option. If for any of you religion be a hypothesis that cannot, by any living possibility, be true, then you need go no farther. I speak to the "saving remnant" alone.) So proceeding, we see, first, that religion offers itself as a *momentous* option. We are supposed to gain, even now, by our belief, and to lose by our non-belief, a certain vital good. Secondly, religion is a *forced* option, so far as that good goes. We cannot escape the issue by remaining sceptical and waiting for more light, because, although we do avoid error in that way *if religion be untrue*, we lose the good, *if it be true*, just as certainly as if we positively chose to disbelieve. It is as if a man should hesitate indefinitely to ask a certain woman to marry him because he was not perfectly sure that she would prove an angel after he brought her home. Would he not cut himself off from that particular angel-possibility as decisively as if he went and married some one else? Scepticism, then, is not avoidance of option; it is option of a certain particular kind of risk. *Better risk loss of truth than chance of error*—that is your faith-vetoer's exact position. He is actively playing his stake as much as the believer is; he is backing the field against the religious hypothesis, just as the believer is backing the religious hypothesis against the field. To preach scepticism to us as a duty until "sufficient evidence" for religion be found, is tantamount therefore to telling us, when in presence of religious hypothesis, that to yield to our fear of its being error is wiser and better than to yield to our hope that it may be true. It is not intellect against all passions, then; it is only intellect with one passion laying down its law. And by what, forsooth, is the supreme wisdom of this passion warranted? Dupery for dupery, what proof is there that dupery through hope is so much worse than dupery through fear? I, for one, can see no proof; and I simply refuse obedience to the scientist's command to imitate his kind of option, in a case where my own stake is important enough to give me the right to choose my own form of risk. If religion be true and the evidence for it be still insufficient, I do not wish, by putting your extinguisher upon my nature (which feels to me as if it had after all some business in this matter), to forfeit my sole chance in life of getting upon the winning side—that chance depending, of course, on my willingness to run the risk of acting as if my passional need of taking the world religiously might be prophetic and right.

All this is on the supposition that it really may be prophetic and right, and that, even to us who are discussing the matter, religion is a live hypothesis which may be true. Now, to most of us religion comes in a still further way that makes a veto on our active faith even more illogical. The more perfect and more eternal aspect of the universe is represented in our religions as having personal form.

The universe is no longer a mere *It* to us, but a *Thou*, if we are religious; and any relation that may be possible from person to person might be possible here. For instance, although in one sense we are passive portions of the universe, in another we show a curious autonomy, as if we were small active centres on our own account. We feel, too, as if the appeal of religion to us were made to our own active good-will, as if evidence might be forever withheld from us unless we met the hypothesis half-way. To take a trivial illustration: just as a man who in a company of gentlemen made no advances, asked a warrant for every concession, and believed no one's word without proof, would cut himself off by such churlishness from all the social rewards that a more trusting spirit would earn —so here, one who should shut himself up in snarling logicality and try to make the gods extort his recognition willy-nilly, or not get it at all, might cut himself off forever from his only opportunity of making the gods' acquaintance. This feeling, forced on us we know not whence, that by obstinately believing that there are gods (although not to do so would be so easy both for our logic and our life) we are doing the universe the deepest service we can, seems part of the living essence of the religious hypothesis. If the hypothesis *were* true in all its parts, including this one, then pure intellectualism, with its veto on our making willing advances, would be an absurdity; and some participation of our sympathetic nature would be logically required. I, therefore, for one, cannot see my way to accepting the agnostic rules for truth-seeking, or wilfully agree to keep my willing nature out of the game. I cannot do so for this plain reason, that *a rule of thinking which would absolutely prevent me from acknowledging certain kinds of truth if those kinds of truth were really there, would be an irrational rule.* That for me is the long and short of the formal logic of the situation, no matter what the kinds of truth might materially be.

I confess I do not see how this logic can be escaped. But sad experience makes me fear that some of you may still shrink from radically saying with me, *in abstracto*, that we have the right to believe at our own risk any hypothesis that is live enough to tempt our will. I suspect, however, that if this is so, it is because you have got away from the abstract logical point of view altogether, and are thinking (perhaps without realizing it) of some particular religious hypothesis which for you is dead. The freedom to "believe what we will" you apply to the case of some patent superstition; and the faith you think of is the faith defined by the schoolboy when he said, "Faith is when you believe something that you know ain't true." I can only repeat that this is misapprehension. *In concreto*, the freedom to believe can only cover living options which the intellect of the individual cannot by itself resolve; and living options never seem absurdities to him who has them to consider. When I look at the religious question as it really puts itself to concrete men, and when I think of all the possibilities which both practically and theoretically it involves, then this command that we shall put a stopper on our heart, instincts, and courage, and *wait*—acting of course meanwhile more or less as if religion were *not* true[1]—till doomsday, or till such time as our intellect and senses working together may have raked in evidence enough—this command, I say, seems to me the queerest idol ever manufactured in the philosophic cave.[2] Were we scholastic absolutists, there might be more excuse. If we had an infallible intellect with its objective certitudes, we might feel ourselves disloyal to such a perfect organ of knowledge in not trusting to it exclusively, in not waiting for its releasing word. But if we are empiricists, if we believe that no bell in us tolls to let us know for certain when truth is in our grasp, then it seems a piece of idle fantasticality to preach so solemnly our duty of waiting for the bell. Indeed we *may* wait if we will—I hope you do not think that I am denying that—but if we do so, we do so at our peril as much as if we believed. In either case we *act*, taking our life in our hands. No one of us ought to issue vetoes to the other, nor should we bandy words of abuse. We ought, on the contrary, delicately and profoundly to respect one another's mental freedom: then only shall we bring about the intellectual republic; then only shall we have that spirit of inner tolerance without which all our outer tolerance is soulless, and which is empiricism's glory; then only shall we live and let live, in speculative as well as in practical things.

I began by a reference to Fitz-James Stephen; let me end by a quotation from him. "What do you think of yourself? What do you think of the world? . . . These are questions with which all must deal as it seems good to them. They are riddles of the Sphinx, and in some way or other we must deal with them. . . . In all important transactions of life we have to take a leap in the dark. . . . If we decide to leave the riddles unanswered, that is a choice; if we waver in our answer, that, too, is a choice: but whatever choice we make, we make it at our peril. If a man chooses to turn his back

1. "Since belief is measured by action, he who forbids us to believe religion to be true, necessarily also forbids us to act as we should if we did believe it to be true. The whole defence of religious faith hinges upon action. If the action required or inspired by the religious hypothesis is in no way different from that dictated by the naturalistic hypothesis, then religious faith is a pure superfluity, better pruned away, and controversy about its legitimacy is a piece of idle trifling, unworthy of serious minds. I myself believe, of course, that the religious hypothesis gives to the world an expression which specifically determines our reactions, and makes them in a large part unlike what they might be on a purely naturalistic scheme of belief" [James's note]. 2. *Cf.* Francis Bacon, *Novum Organum*, Aphorisms, 39, 42, and 53–58. "The Idols of the Cave," says Bacon, "are the idols of the individual man," whose judgment may be misled by his inheritance, environment, and education.

altogether on God and the future, no one can prevent him; no one can show beyond reasonable doubt that he is mistaken. If a man thinks otherwise and acts as he thinks, I do not see that any one can prove that *he* is mistaken. Each must act as he thinks best; and if he is wrong, so much the worse for him. We stand on a mountain pass in the midst of whirling snow and blinding mist, through which we get glimpses now and then of paths which may be deceptive. If we stand still we shall be frozen to death. If we take the wrong road we shall be dashed to pieces. We do not certainly know whether there is any right one. What must we do? 'Be strong and of a good courage.' Act for the best, hope for the best, and take what comes. . . . If death ends all, we cannot meet death better."[3]

1896, 1897

3. *"Liberty, Equality, Fraternity,* p. 353, 2d edition. London, 1874" [James's note].

WILLIAM VAUGHN MOODY
(1869–1910)

Moody's birth in 1869 coincided with that of Edwin Arlington Robinson and Edgar Lee Masters. Only one or two years their junior were Stephen Crane and Theodore Dreiser. Together with the older Hamlin Garland, these may be regarded as the literary generation which first broke the established pattern of the nineteenth century. They were a transitional generation, and the public mind was not yet ready to receive them. Crane died at twenty-nine and Moody at forty-one, but even those who lived experienced the postponement of recognition until after 1910. Moody might later have stood beside his friend Robinson in the poetry of the twentieth century; yet even with his maturity unfulfilled, he holds a permanent place in our literature because from the beginning his poetry was genuine, original, and representative of the problems of the age.

Born in Spencer, Indiana, the son of a steamboat pilot, he was of New England stock, and represents the cultural flux from East to West that characterized his age. The early death of his father threw family responsibilities upon him, and he helped support the family while intermittently attending school. But he was genuinely precocious, eager for books, especially literature, and filled with the "back-trailing" yearning for the East that then manifested itself in the life of the West, and in the adventures of such authors as Twain, Howells, Garland, and Dreiser. When at nineteen he came to New York State to teach in a college-preparatory school, he had already taught for three winters in the high school at Spencer. On a scholarship and borrowed funds he entered Harvard at twenty, finished the course brilliantly in three years, and was permitted to spend the fourth as a traveling tutor for two boys who visited Greece and the eastern Mediterranean area. In Moody were equally blended the Puritan orthodoxy of his American ancestors and the pagan spirit of Greek beauty; in addition he was deeply concerned with the social and philosophical issues of his age.

Returning from the Mediterranean countries by way of Switzerland and Germany, he received his A.B. from Harvard in 1893, and continued in graduate study. He became an instructor in English in 1894, and the next year accepted a call to join the new and vital English department at the University of Chicago. There he established himself in his profession, published studies of English authors, especially Milton, and wrote, with Robert Morss Lovett, an excellent history of English literature. He published a notable edition of Milton's poems, and also edited a volume of Homer and classroom selections of Scott and De Quincey. Meanwhile his poems were appearing in periodicals, representing a sensibility strongly divergent from that prevailing in the period. Although he was an exquisite lyrist, the critical spirit was also very active in his work, whether directed at social problems, as in "Gloucester Moors," or at the contemporary perplexity evoked by new scientific concepts, as in "The Menagerie"; or expressed through a new critical symbolism, which became prevalent

only much later, as in "Thammuz." The utilization of myth and anthropology in that poem and others foreshadowed the complex poems of a period that had not yet dawned. On another level he was a brilliant satirist of public affairs, as shown in such poems as "Ode in Time of Hesitation" and "On a Soldier Fallen in the Philippines."

In 1900 his philosophical speculation culminated in a poetic drama, *The Masque of Judgment*; in 1901 he published his first collection of *Poems*; in 1903 he ventured to support himself by his pen alone, actuated by the compulsions of new inspiration and by the encouragement of a few friends— Robinson and Percy MacKaye, Josephine Preston Peabody, and others of their New York circle, with whom he spent holidays whenever he could be free to visit the new literary capital which was forming in Greenwich Village. The remainder of his brief career was spent in the successful creation of two plays, *A Sabine Woman* (1906, revised as *The Great Divide* 1909) and *The Faith Healer* (1909); in the revision of his lyrics; and in the development of his *Masque of Judgment* into a trilogy. In this poetic drama, as in his popular prose plays, Moody attacked the ancient concept of a God of Wrath, and the puritanical belief in man's original depravity, which, as he believed, resulted in a burden of guilt wholly inconsistent with the modern personality and knowledge; he substituted the authority of nature as the source of man's moral sense and his

knowledge of God, finding his
arguments both in Greek literary
thought and in modern science
and speculation. Very soon after
his marriage, long postponed for
economic reasons, he died suddenly in 1910.

John M. Manly edited *The Poems
and Plays of William Vaughn Moody*,
1912; Daniel G. Mason edited *Some
Letters of William Vaughn Moody*,
1913. A good edition of Moody's best
poems is *Selected Poems of William*

Vaughn Moody, edited by Robert Morss
Lovett, 1931.

A good general study of Moody as
poet and dramatist is David D. Henry,
William Vaughn Moody: A Study,
1934. The fullest treatment of Moody
as a dramatist is Arthur H. Quinn, *A
History of the American Drama from
the Civil War to the Present Day*,
revised edition, 1936, Vol. II, pp. 1–26.
See also Sculley Bradley, "The Emergence of the Modern Drama," in *Literary History of the United States*,
edited by Robert E. Spiller, Willard
Thorp, Thomas H. Johnson, and Henry
Seidel Canby, 1948, Vol. II, pp. 1013–
1015.

Gloucester Moors[1]

A mile behind is Gloucester town
Where the fishing fleets put in,
A mile ahead the land dips down
And the woods and farms begin.
Here, where the moors stretch free   5
In the high blue afternoon,
Are the marching sun and talking sea,
And the racing winds that wheel and flee
On the flying heels of June.

Jill-o'er-the-ground is purple blue,   10
Blue is the quaker-maid,
The wild geranium holds its dew
Long in the boulder's shade.
Wax-red hangs the cup
From the huckleberry boughs,   15
In barberry bells the grey moths sup
Or where the choke-cherry lifts high up
Sweet bowls for their carouse.

Over the shelf of the sandy cove
Beach-peas blossom late.   20
By copse and cliff the swallows rove
Each calling to his mate.
Seaward the sea-gulls go,
And the land-birds all are here;

1. According to Robert Morss Lovett,
the poet's friend (*Selected Poems of
William Vaughn Moody*, p. 206), this
poem had its inception during the
summer of 1900, when Moody spent a
vacation on Cape Ann, Massachusetts.
He was fresh, as he said, from "the
heart of the debtor's country," Chi-

cago, where he had been teaching. This
is the best known of the poems reflecting his literary connection with
social protest and the reform movement. It was published in *Scribner's*
for December, 1900, and collected in
Poems (1901), which the present text
follows.

That green-gold flash was a vireo,   25
And yonder flame where the marsh-flags grow
Was a scarlet tanager.

This earth is not the steadfast place
We landsmen build upon;
From deep to deep she varies pace,   30
And while she comes is gone.
Beneath my feet I feel
Her smooth bulk heave and dip;
With velvet plunge and soft upreel
She swings and steadies to her keel   35
Like a gallant, gallant ship.

These summer clouds she sets for sail,
The sun is her masthead light,
She tows the moon like a pinnace[2] frail
Where her phosphor wake churns bright.   40
Now hid, now looming clear,
On the face of the dangerous blue
The star fleets tack and wheel and veer,
But on, but on does the old earth steer
As if her port she knew.   45

God, dear God! Does she know her port,
Though she goes so far about?
Or blind astray, does she make her sport
To brazen and chance it out?
I watched when her captains passed: 50
She were better captainless.
Men in the cabin, before the mast,
But some were reckless and some aghast,
And some sat gorged at mess.

By her battened hatch I leaned and caught   55
Sounds from the noisome hold,—
Cursing and sighing of souls distraught
And cries too sad to be told.
Then I strove to go down and see;
But they said, "Thou art not of us!"   60
I turned to those on the deck with me
And cried, "Give help!" But they said, "Let be:
Our ship sails faster thus."

Jill-o'-er-the-ground is purple blue,
Blue is the quaker-maid,   65

---

2. Small boat, accessory to a larger vessel, often towed behind.

The alder-clump where the brook comes through
Breeds cresses in its shade.
To be out of the moiling street
With its swelter and its sin!
Who has given to me this sweet,   70
And given my brother dust to eat?
And when will his wage come in?

Scattering wide or blown in ranks,
Yellow and white and brown,
Boats and boats from the fishing banks   75
Come home to Gloucester town.
There is cash to purse and spend,
There are wives to be embraced,
Hearts to borrow and hearts to lend,
And hearts to take and keep to the end,—   80
O little sails, make haste!

But thou, vast outbound ship of souls,
What harbor town for thee?
What shapes, when thy arriving tolls,
Shall crowd the banks to see?   85
Shall all the happy shipmates then
Stand singing brotherly?
Or shall a haggard ruthless few
Warp[3] her over and bring her to,
While the many broken souls of men   90
Fester down in the slaver's pen,
And nothing to say or do?

1900, 1901

The Menagerie[4]

Thank God my brain is not inclined to cut
Such capers every day! I'm just about
Mellow, but then—There goes the tent-flap shut.
Rain's in the wind. I thought so: every snout
Was twitching when the keeper turned me out.   5

3. To move a vessel by hauling on a line attached to a buoy or some other fixed object.
4. Moody resisted the pessimistic determinism of his generation, which reflected the materialistic interpretation of Darwinian evolution, both in smaller poems and on the larger scale of the dramas *The Great Divide* and *The Faith Healer*. In his poetic trilogy, *The Masque of Judgment,* he extended his attack to include the older Christian fundamentalist orthodoxy with its deterministic dogma of original sin. "The Menagerie" first appeared in *Poems* (1901), from which the present text is taken.

That screaming parrot makes my blood run cold.
Gabriel's trump![5] the big bull elephant
Squeals 'Rain!' to the parched herd. The monkeys scold,
And jabber that it's rain water they want.
(It makes me sick to see a monkey pant.)   10

I'll foot it home, to try and make believe
I'm sober. After this I stick to beer,
And drop the circus when the sane folks leave.
A man's a fool to look at things too near:
They look back, and begin to cut up queer.   15

Beasts do, at any rate; especially
Wild devils caged. They have the coolest way
Of being something else than what you see:
You pass a sleek young zebra nosing hay,
A nylghau[6] looking bored and distingué,—   20

And think you've seen a donkey and a bird.
Not on your life! Just glance back, if you dare.
The zebra chews, the nylghau hasn't stirred;
But something's happened, Heaven knows what or where
To freeze your scalp and pompadour your hair.   25

I'm not precisely an æolian lute[7]
Hung in the wandering winds of sentiment,
But drown me if the ugliest, meanest brute
Grunting and fretting in that sultry tent
Didn't just floor me with embarrassment!   30

'Twas like a thunder-clap from out the clear,—
One minute they were circus beasts, some grand,
Some ugly, some amusing, and some queer:
Rival attractions to the hobo band,
The flying jenny,[8] and the peanut stand.   35

Next minute they were old hearth-mates of mine!
Lost people, eyeing me with such a stare!
Patient, satiric, devilish, divine;
A gaze of hopeless envy, squalid care,
Hatred, and thwarted love, and dim despair.   40

Within my blood my ancient kindred spoke,—
Grotesque and monstrous voices, heard afar

5. The trumpet of the last resurrection
(Isaiah xxvii: 13). Gabriel, an arch-
angel, usually a herald or divine messenger, became associated with this trumpet in the Jewish and Christian traditions.

6. The large Indian antelope.
7. Usually, "aeolian harp"; a stringed
musical instrument producing tones
when the wind blows across it.
8. A small merry-go-round.

Down ocean caves when behemoth[1] awoke,
Or through fern forests roared the plesiosaur[2]
Locked with the giant-bat in ghastly war.   45

And suddenly, as in a flash of light,
I saw great Nature working out her plan;
Through all her shapes from mastodon to mite
Forever groping, testing, passing on
To find at last the shape and soul of Man.   50

Till in the fullness of accomplished time,
Comes brother Forepaugh,[3] upon business bent,
Tracks her through frozen and through torrid clime,
And shows us, neatly labeled in a tent,
The stages of her huge experiment;   55

Blabbing aloud her shy and reticent hours;
Dragging to light her blinking, slothful moods;
Publishing fretful seasons when her powers
Worked wild and sullen in her solitudes,
Or when her mordant laughter shook the woods.   60

Here, round about me, were her vagrant births;
Sick dreams she had, fierce projects she essayed;
Her qualms, her fiery prides, her crazy mirths;
The troublings of her spirit as she strayed,
Cringed, gloated, mocked, was lordly, was afraid,   65

On that long road she went to seek mankind;
Here were the darkling coverts that she beat
To find the Hider she was sent to find;
Here the distracted footprints of her feet
Whereby her soul's Desire she came to greet.   70

But why should they, her botch-work, turn about
And stare disdain at me, her finished job?
Why was the place one vast suspended shout
Of laughter? Why did all the daylight throb
With soundless guffaw and dumb-stricken sob?   75

Helpless I stood among those awful cages;
The beasts were walking loose, and I was bagged!
I, I, last product of the toiling ages,
Goal of heroic feet that never lagged,—
A little man in trousers, slightly jagged.[4]   80

1. See Job xl: 15, where the behemoth is represented as a sort of colossal hippopotamus.
2. The plesiosaurus was a marine reptile of the age of dinosaurs, having a very long neck, small head, and limbs developed as paddles for swimming.
3. Adam Forepaugh was proprietor of a traveling circus and menagerie, popular in the nineties.
4. A slang expression then current for "intoxicated."

Deliver me from such another jury!
The Judgment Day will be a picnic to't.
Their satire was more dreadful than their fury,
And worst of all was just a kind of brute
Disgust, and giving up, and sinking mute.   85

Survival of the fittest, adaptation,
And all their other evolution terms,
Seem to omit one small consideration,
To wit, that tumblebugs and angleworms
Have souls: there's soul in everything that squirms.   90

And souls are restless, plagued, impatient things,
All dream and unaccountable desire;
Crawling, but pestered with the thought of wings;
Spreading through every inch of earth's old mire
Mystical hanker after something higher.   95

Wishes *are* horses, as I understand.
I guess a wistful polyp that has strokes
Of feeling faint to gallivant on land
Will come to be a scandal to his folks;
Legs he will sprout, in spite of threats and jokes.   100

And at the core of every life that crawls,
Or runs or flies or swims or vegetates—
Churning the mammoth's heart-blood, in the galls
Of shark and tiger planting gorgeous hates,
Lighting the love of eagles for their mates;   105

Yes, in the dim brain of the jellied fish
That is and is not living—moved and stirred
From the beginning a mysterious wish,
A vision, a command, a fatal Word:
The name of Man was uttered, and they heard.   110

Upward along the æons of old war
They sought him: wing and shank-bone, claw and bill
Were fashioned and rejected; wide and far
They roamed the twilight jungles of their will;
But still they sought him, and desired him still.   115

Man they desired, but mind you, Perfect Man,
The radiant and the loving, yet to be!
I hardly wonder, when they came to scan
The upshot of their strenuosity,
They gazed with mixed emotions upon *me.*   120

Well, my advice to you is, Face the creatures,
Or spot them sideways with your weather eye,
Just to keep tab on their expansive features;
It isn't pleasant when you're stepping high
To catch a giraffe smiling on the sly.   125

If nature made you graceful, don't get gay
Back-to before the hippopotamus;
If meek and godly, find some place to play
Besides right where three mad hyenas fuss:
You may hear language that we won't discuss.   130

If you're a sweet thing in a flower-bed hat,
Or her best fellow with your tie tucked in,
Don't squander love's bright springtime girding at
An old chimpanzee with an Irish chin:
There may be hidden meaning in his grin.   135

1901

Thammuz[5]

Daughters, daughters, do ye grieve?
Crimson dark the freshes flow!
Were ye violent at eve?
Crimson stains where the rushes grow!
What is this that I must know?   5

Mourners by the dark red waters,
Met ye Thammuz at his play?
Was your mood upon you, daughters?
Had ye drunken? O how grey
Looks your hair in the rising day!   10

Mourners, mourn not overmuch
That ye slew your lovely one.
Such ye are; and be ye such!
Lift your heads; the waters run
Ruby bright in the climbing sun.   15

5. Thammuz was a Babylonian god of fertility, corresponding to the Greek Adonis. According to one ancient ritual Thammuz was killed and given water burial by the women in the autumn, and rose again in the spring. Moody may also have in mind the Greek myth of Orpheus, the singer slain by love-crazed nymphs. In editing the works of Milton (Cambridge Edition, p. 395) Moody noted that "when the river Adonis becomes reddened by the mud [in] the spring torrents, it was believed [that] the flowing afresh of Thammuz's wounds caused the change of color." The poem concerns one of Moody's central themes, more extensively developed in *The Death of Eve* and "I Am the Woman." This poem was first published in *Scribner's* for October, 1906, and was collected in Manly's edition of *The Poems and Plays of William Vaughn Moody* (1912), which the present text follows.

Raven hair and hair of gold,
Look who bendeth over you!
This is not the shepherd old;
This is Thammuz, whom ye slew,
Radiant Thammuz, risen anew! 20

1906, 1912

Realism and Naturalism:
The Turn of the Century

"Character of Fate?" (handwritten)

EDITH WHARTON
(1862–1937)

In some of her best novels Mrs. Wharton satirized the same society as Henry James, but this fact does not diminish her independence. She frequently acknowledged her admiration for her older friend and fellow New Yorker, whose writing had given her encouragement and inspiration. As a whole, her work has a range different from his, and when she employed the Jamesian materials, as in *The House of Mirth, The Age of Innocence,* and *Old New York,* her point of view was significantly different. James dealt principally with the international contrast of character and custom, while Edith Wharton's interests were centered upon the changing society of New York City during her own lifetime. She viewed this genteel and formalized society with a woman's eye, and primarily as a satirist, and she was much more interested than James in the dynamics of the society itself. Temperamentally she was closest to James in her stories of the supernatural, often involving psychological morbidity; beyond this type her short stories show a wide and independent range of interest. Finally, she shows no relation to James in her early success with the historical novel and in her impressive studies of decadent rural life in *Summer* and *Ethan Frome,* the latter a masterpiece of its *genre.*

Born in 1862 near Washington Square, Edith Newbold Jones belonged to a family of wealth and distinction rooted in colonial times. She was educated privately at home and abroad, acquiring an early command of foreign languages and an easy familiarity with England and with continental social life. Her first writings were poems, published anonymously in the *Atlantic Monthly* in 1880. At twenty-three she married Edward Wharton of Boston. They lived at first in New York City, then successively in Newport, Rhode Island, and Lenox, Massachusetts, with frequent visits to Europe. In 1907 she settled

771

rigid stratification of N.Y. elite (handwritten)

permanently in France. Her ethical sense, poetic sensibility, and ironic compression were evident in her first collection of short stories, *The Greater Inclination* (1899). Her interest in eighteenth-century Italian life provided background for her first long novel, *The Valley of Decision* (1902), a study of the defeat of a liberal Italian nobleman by the apathy of the people whom he attempts to liberate from their aristocratic masters. *The Descent of Man* (1904) contains some of her most notable early short stories. In *The House of Mirth* (1905), her first enduring masterwork, the tragic power of formalized society to wreck lives is grimly studied. Lily Bart, a convincing and engaging character, has been prepared by her upbringing to marry well, but the bankruptcy and death of her father restricts her choice of suitors to the rich but undesirable, and to Seldon, a poor lawyer who has always loved her. She cannot finally bring herself to make a marriage of mere financial convenience, but fearing that she has now lost even Seldon, she dies of an overdose of sedative.

During her years of residence at Lenox, and on summer holidays, Mrs. Wharton had developed an interest in another pattern of social decay, then found in the country towns and upland valleys of Massachusetts. This produced one masterpiece, *Ethan Frome* (1911), and other good books, together with a number of stories. *The Fruit of the Tree* (1907), of more than passing interest, deals with the tragedy of a young industrialist

whose materialistic absorption in the "Works" loses him the love of his wife and of another to whom his weakness is tragedy. *Summer* (1917), a study of small-town degeneracy, is a work of stark power.

By this time, Edith Wharton had made three more collections of her remarkable short stories. *The Hermit and the Wild Woman and Other Stories* (1908) and *Xingu and Other Stories* (1916) are in varied moods of disenchantment, critical realism, satire, and comedy. *Tales of Men and Ghosts* (1910) contains some of her best stories of the supernatural. During the war years in France she gave much of her energy to the organization of relief activities on a national scale; her work was later recognized by the award of high honors from the French government. Her propaganda for the Allied cause is best represented in *Fighting France* (1915) and *The Marne* (1918), a war novel.

After the war, Edith Wharton returned to the material of her old New York. *The Age of Innocence* (1920), her greatest novel, was awarded the Pulitzer Prize and has remained a landmark in American fiction. In this novel she expertly reconstructed the social clan system of the 1870's, presided over by a small matriarchy of powerful dowagers, with allowances for male promiscuity and feminine flirtation, but only ostracism for those violating the code of stereotyped taboos and loyalties.

The four novelettes published together as *Old New York* in 1924 completed Edith Wharton's most important work. *False Dawn*, the first, depicts the New York scene in the 1840's. The second, *The Old Maid*, subtitled "The 'Fifties," in 1935 won the Pulitzer Prize in its adaptation by Zoë Akins for stage performance. It is a delicate study of the cousins, Charlotte and Delia, who represent the opposites of sacrificial and selfish love for the same man, now dead. *The Spark*, representing the 1860's, is a remarkable story of Walt Whitman's influence on a chance acquaintance; *New Year's Day*, representing "The 'Seventies," is a study of the unconventional life of an attractive but insecure woman. In *Hudson River Bracketed* (1929) Mrs. Wharton contrasted the traditional and settled institutions of the East with the new culture of the Middle West; the main character was

carried over into a sequel, *The Gods Arrive* (1932). Among Edith Wharton's many volumes of nonfiction. A *Backward Glance* (1934) remains one of the most charming and informative of modern autobiographies; and *The Writing of Fiction* (1925) not only illuminates her own work, but also provides a good critical approach to the problems of others of her literary generation.

There is no collected edition of Edith Wharton. Arthur H. Quinn has edited *An Edith Wharton Treasury*, 1950, containing *The Age of Innocence, The Old Maid,* and several short stories. Wayne Andrews has edited *Best Short Stories of Edith Wharton*, 1958.

The most recent biography of Mrs. Wharton is Percy Lubbock, *Portrait of Edith Wharton*, 1947. Earlier studies still useful are K. F. Gerould, *Edith Wharton: A Critical Study*, 1922; and R. M. Lovett, *Edith Wharton*, 1925. Blake Nevius, *Edith Wharton: A Study of Her Fiction*, 1953, is a full-length treatment.

After Holbein[1]

I

Anson Warley had had his moments of being a rather remarkable man; but they were only intermittent; they recurred at ever-lengthening intervals; and between times he was a small poor creature, chattering with cold inside, in spite of his agreeable and even distinguished exterior.

He had always been perfectly aware of these two sides of himself (which, even in the privacy of his own mind, he contemptuously refused to dub a dual personality); and as the rather remarkable man could take fairly good care of himself, most of Warley's attention was devoted to ministering to the poor wretch who took longer and longer turns at bearing his name, and was

1. "After Holbein" was first published in the *Saturday Evening Post* for May 5, 1928, and was collected in *Certain People* (1930). Hans Holbein (1497–1543), German painter, in 1536 became court painter to King Henry VIII of England. He is famous for the exquisite and precise characterization of his por-

traits, especially those of the highborn. Mrs. Wharton was no doubt familiar with the case of Mrs. Astor, who, for a year or more before her death in 1908, like Mrs. Jaspar of this story quite out of her mind, continued in regal splendor to hold receptions for imaginary guests long dead.

more and more insistent in accepting the invitations which New York, for over thirty years, had tirelessly poured out on him. It was in the interest of this lonely fidgety unemployed self that Warley, in his younger days, had frequented the gaudiest restaurants and the most glittering Palace Hotels of two hemispheres, subscribed to the most advanced literary and artistic reviews, bought the pictures of the young painters who were being the most vehemently discussed, missed few of the showiest first nights in New York, London or Paris, sought the company of the men and women—especially the women—most conspicuous in fashion, scandal, or any other form of social notoriety, and thus tried to warm the shivering soul within him at all the passing bonfires of success.

The original Anson Warley had begun by staying at home in his little flat, with his books and his thoughts, when the other poor creature went forth; but gradually—he hardly knew when or how—he had slipped into the way of going too, till finally he made the bitter discovery that he and the creature had become one, except on the increasingly rare occasions when, detaching himself from all casual contingencies, he mounted to the lofty water-shed which fed the sources of his scorn. The view from there was vast and glorious, the air was icy but exhilarating; but soon he began to find the place too lonely, and too difficult to get to, especially as the lesser Anson not only refused to go up with him but began to sneer, at first ever so faintly, then with increasing insolence, at this affectation of a taste for the heights.

"What's the use of scrambling up there, anyhow? I could understand it if you brought down anything worth while—a poem or a picture of your own. But just climbing and staring: what does it lead to? Fellows with the creative gift have got to have their occasional Sinaïs;[2] I can see that. But for a mere looker-on like you, isn't that sort of thing rather a pose? You talk awfully well—brilliantly, even (oh, my dear fellow, no false modesty between you and *me*, please!) But who the devil is there to listen to you, up there among the glaciers? And sometimes, when you come down, I notice that you're rather—well, heavy and tongue-tied. Look out, or they'll stop asking us to dine! And sitting at home every evening—brr! Look here, by the way; if you've got nothing better for tonight, come along with me to Chrissy Torrance's—or the Bob Briggses'—or Princess Kate's; anywhere where there's lots of racket and sparkle, places that people go to in Rollses, and that are smart and hot and overcrowded, and you have to pay a lot—in one way or another—to get in."

Once and again, it is true, Warley still dodged his double and

---

2. During the exodus of the Hebrews from Egypt, Moses met God on Mount Sinai, and received the Law and the Commandments (Exodus xix–xx).

slipped off on a tour to remote uncomfortable places, where there were churches or pictures to be seen, or shut himself up at home for a good bout of reading, or just, in sheer disgust at his companion's platitude, spent an evening with people who were doing or thinking real things. This happened seldomer than of old, however, and more clandestinely; so that at last he used to sneak away to spend two or three days with an archæologically-minded friend, or an evening with a quiet scholar, as furtively as if he were stealing to a lover's tryst; which, as lovers' trysts were now always kept in the limelight, was after all a fair exchange. But he always felt rather apologetic to the other Warley about these escapades—and, if the truth were known, rather bored and restless before they were over. And in the back of his mind there lurked an increasing dread of missing something hot and noisy and overcrowded when he went off to one of his mountain-tops. "After all, that high-brow business has been awfully overdone—now hasn't it?" the little Warley would insinuate, rummaging for his pearl studs, and consulting his flat evening watch as nervously as if it were a railway time-table. "If only we haven't missed something really jolly by all this backing and filling . . ."

"Oh, you poor creature, you! Always afraid of being left out, aren't you? Well—just for once, to humour you, and because I happen to be feeling rather stale myself. But only to think of a sane man's wanting to go to places just because they're hot and smart and overcrowded!" And off they would dash together. . .

II

All that was long ago. It was years now since there had been two distinct Anson Warleys. The lesser one had made away with the other, done him softly to death without shedding of blood; and only a few people suspected (and they no longer cared) that the pale white-haired man, with the small slim figure, the ironic smile and the perfect evening clothes, whom New York still indefatigably invited, was nothing less than a murderer.

Anson Warley—Anson Warley! No party was complete without Anson Warley. He no longer went abroad now; too stiff in the joints; and there had been two or three slight attacks of dizziness. . . Nothing to speak of, nothing to think of, even; but somehow one dug one's self into one's comfortable quarters, and felt less and less like moving out of them, except to motor down to Long Island for week ends, or to Newport for a few visits in summer. A trip to the Hot Springs, to get rid of the stiffness, had not helped much, and the ageing Anson Warley (who really, otherwise, felt as young as ever) had developed a growing dislike for the promiscuities of hotel life and the monotony of hotel food.

Yes; he was growing more fastidious as he grew older. A good sign, he thought. Fastidious not only about food and comfort but about people also. It was still a privilege, a distinction, to have him to dine. His old friends were faithful, and the new people fought for him, and often failed to get him; to do so they had to offer very special inducements in the way of *cuisine*, conversation or beauty. Young beauty; yes, that would do it. He did like to sit and watch a lovely face, and call laughter into lovely eyes. But no dull dinners for *him*, not even if they fed you off gold. As to that he was as firm as the other Warley, the distant aloof one with whom he had—er, well, parted company, oh, quite amicably, a good many years ago. . .

On the whole, since that parting, life had been much easier and pleasanter; and by the time the little Warley was sixty-three he found himself looking forward with equanimity to an eternity of New York dinners.

Oh, but only at the right houses—always at the right houses; that was understood! The right people—the right setting—the right wines . . . He smiled a little over his perennial enjoyment of them; said "Nonsense, Filmore," to his devoted tiresome manservant, who was beginning to hint that really, every night, sir, and sometimes a dance afterward, was too much, especially when you kept at it for months on end; and Dr. ——

"Oh, damn your doctors!" Warley snapped. He was seldom ill-tempered; he knew it was foolish and upsetting to lose one's self-control. But Filmore began to be a nuisance, nagging him, preaching at him. As if he himself wasn't the best judge. . .

Besides, he chose his company. He'd stay at home any time rather than risk a boring evening. Damned rot, what Filmore had said about his going out every night. Not like poor old Mrs. Jaspar, for instance. . . He smiled self-approvingly as he evoked her tottering image. "That's the kind of fool Filmore takes me for," he chuckled, his good-humour restored by an analogy that was so much to his advantage.

Poor old Evelina Jaspar! In his youth, and even in his prime, she had been New York's chief entertainer—"leading hostess", the newspapers called her. Her big house in Fifth Avenue had been an entertaining machine. She had lived, breathed, invested and reinvested her millions, to no other end. At first her pretext had been that she had to marry her daughters and amuse her sons; but when sons and daughters had married and left her she had seemed hardly aware of it; she had just gone on entertaining. Hundreds, no, thousands of dinners (on gold plate, of course, and with orchids, and all the delicacies that were out of season), had been served in that vast pompous dining-room, which one had only to close one's eyes to transform into a railway buffet for millionaires, at a big junction, before the investion of restaurant trains. . .

Warley closed his eyes, and did so picture it. He lost himself in amused computation of the annual number of guests, of saddles of mutton, of legs of lamb, of terrapin, canvas-backs, magnums of champagne and pyramids of hot-house fruit that must have passed through that room in the last forty years.

And even now, he thought—hadn't one of old Evelina's nieces told him the other day, half bantering, half shivering at the avowal, that the poor old lady, who was gently dying of softening of the brain, still imagined herself to be New York's leading hostess, still sent out invitations (which of course were never delivered), still ordered terrapin, champagne and orchids, and still came down every evening to her great shrouded drawing-rooms, with her tiara askew on her purple wig, to receive a stream of imaginary guests?

Rubbish, of course—a macabre pleasantry of the extravagant Nelly Pierce, who had always had her joke at Aunt Evelina's expense. . . But Warley could not help smiling at the thought that those dull monotonous dinners were still going on in their hostess's clouded imagination. Poor old Evelina, he thought! In a way she was right. There was really no reason why that kind of standardized entertaining should ever cease; a performance so undiscriminating, so undifferentiated, that one could almost imagine, in the hostess's tired brain, all the dinners she had ever given merging into one Gargantuan[3] pyramid of food and drink, with the same faces, perpetually the same faces, gathered stolidly about the same gold plate.

Thank heaven, Anson Warley had never conceived of social values in terms of mass and volume. It was years since he had dined at Mrs. Jaspar's. He even felt that he was not above reproach in that respect. Two or three times, in the past, he had accepted her invitations (always sent out weeks ahead), and then chucked her at the eleventh hour for something more amusing. Finally, to avoid such risks, he had made it a rule always to refuse her dinners. He had even—he remembered—been rather funny about it once, when someone had told him that Mrs. Jaspar couldn't understand . . . was a little hurt . . . said it couldn't be true that he always had another engagement the nights she asked him. . . "*True?* Is the truth what she wants? All right! Then the next time I get a 'Mrs. Jaspar requests the pleasure' I'll answer it with a 'Mr. Warley declines the boredom.' Think she'll understand that, eh?" And the phrase became a catchword in his little set that winter. " 'Mr. Warley declines the boredom'—good, good, *good!*" "Dear Anson, I do hope you won't decline the boredom of coming to lunch next

3. Of gigantic size, like Gargantua, hero of the romance *Gargantua* (1535), by François Rabelais (1494?–1553).

Sunday to meet the new Hindu Yoghi"—or the new saxophone soloist, or that genius of a mulatto boy who plays negro spirituals on a toothbrush; and so on and so on. He only hoped poor old Evelina never heard of it. . .

"Certainly I shall *not* stay at home tonight—why, what's wrong with me?" he snapped, swinging round on Filmore.

The valet's long face grew longer. His way of answering such questions was always to pull out his face; it was his only means of putting any expression into it. He turned away into the bedroom, and Warley sat alone by his library fire. . . Now what did the man see that was wrong with him, he wondered? He had felt a little confusion that morning, when he was doing his daily sprint around the Park (his exercise was reduced to that!); but it had been only a passing flurry, of which Filmore could of course know nothing. And as soon as it was over his mind had seemed more lucid, his eye keener, than ever; as sometimes (he reflected) the electric light in his library lamps would blaze up too brightly after a break in the current, and he would say to himself, wincing a little at the sudden glare on the page he was reading: "That means that it'll go out again in a minute."

Yes; his mind, at that moment, had been quite piercingly clear and perceptive; his eye had passed with a renovating glitter over every detail of the daily scene. He stood still for a minute under the leafless trees of the Mall,[4] and looking about him with the sudden insight of age, understood that he had reached the time of life when Alps and cathedrals become as transient as flowers.

Everything was fleeting, fleeting . . . yes, that was what had given him the vertigo. The doctors, poor fools, called it the stomach, or high blood-pressure; but it was only the dizzy plunge of the sands in the hour-glass, the everlasting plunge that emptied one of heart and bowels, like the drop of an elevator from the top floor of a sky-scraper.

Certainly, after that moment of revelation, he had felt a little more tired than usual for the rest of the day; the light had flagged in his mind as it sometimes did in his lamps. At Chrissy Torrance's, where he had lunched, they had accused him of being silent, his hostess had said that he looked pale; but he had retorted with a joke, and thrown himself into the talk with a feverish loquacity. It was the only thing to do; for he could not tell all these people at the lunch table that very morning he had arrived at the turn in the path from which mountains look as transient as flowers—and that one after another they would all arrive there too.

4. A promenade in Central Park, New York.

He leaned his head back and closed his eyes, but not in sleep. He did not feel sleepy, but keyed up and alert. In the next room he heard Filmore reluctantly, protestingly, laying out his evening clothes. . . He had no fear about the dinner tonight; a quiet intimate little affair at an old friend's house. Just two or three congenial men, and Elfmann, the pianist (who would probably play), and that lovely Elfrida Flight. The fact that people asked him to dine to meet Elfrida Flight seemed to prove pretty conclusively that he was still in the running! He chuckled softly at Filmore's pessimism, and thought: "Well, after all, I suppose no man seems young to his valet.[5] . . Time to dress very soon," he thought; and luxuriously postponed getting up out of his chair. . .

III

"She's worse than usual tonight," said the day nurse, laying down the evening paper as her colleague joined her. "Absolutely determined to have her jewels out."

The night nurse, fresh from a long sleep and an afternoon at the movies with a gentleman friend, threw down her fancy bag, tossed off her hat and rumpled up her hair before old Mrs. Jaspar's tall toilet mirror. "Oh, I'll settle that—don't you worry," she said brightly.

"Don't you fret her, though, Miss Cress," said the other, getting wearily out of her chair. "We're very well off here, take it as a whole, and I don't want her pressure rushed up for nothing."

Miss Cress, still looking at herself in the glass, smiled reassuringly at Miss Dunn's pale reflection behind her. She and Miss Dunn got on very well together, and knew on which side their bread was buttered. But at the end of the day Miss Dunn was always fagged out and fearing the worst. The patient wasn't as hard to handle as all that. Just let her ring for her old maid, old Lavinia, and say: "My sapphire velvet tonight, with the diamond stars"—and Lavinia would know exactly how to manage her.

Miss Dunn had put on her hat and coat, and crammed her knitting, and the newspaper, into her bag, which, unlike Miss Cress's, was capacious and shabby; but she still loitered undecided on the threshold. "I could stay with you till ten as easy as not. . ." She looked almost reluctantly about the big high-studded dressing-room (everything in the house was high-studded), with its rich dusky carpet and curtains, and its monumental dressing-table draped with lace and laden with gold-backed brushes and combs, gold-stoppered toilet-bottles, and all the charming paraphernalia of beauty at her glass. Old Lavinia even renewed every morning the

5. *Cf.* "No man is a hero to his valet," attributed, in the *Lettres* (xii) of Mlle. Aïssé (1694?–1733), to Mme. Cornuel (1605–1694); later a traditional saying.

roses and carnations in the slim crystal vases between the powder boxes and the nail polishers. Since the family had shut down the hot-houses at the uninhabited country place on the Hudson, Miss Cress suspected that old Lavinia bought these flowers out of her own pocket.

"Cold out tonight?" queried Miss Dunn from the door.

"Fierce. . . Reg'lar blizzard at the corners. Say, shall I lend you my fur scarf?" Miss Cress, pleased with the memory of her afternoon (they'd be engaged soon, she thought), and with the drowsy prospect of an evening in a deep arm-chair near the warm gleam of the dressing-room fire, was disposed to kindliness toward that poor thin Dunn girl, who supported her mother, and her brother's idiot twins. And she wanted Miss Dunn to notice her new fur.

"My! Isn't it too lovely? No, not for worlds, thank you. . ." Her hand on the door-knob, Miss Dunn repeated: "Don't you cross her now," and was gone.

Lavinia's bell rang furiously, twice; then the door between the dressing-room and Mrs. Jaspar's bedroom opened, and Mrs. Jaspar herself emerged.

"Lavinia!" she called, in a high irritated voice; then, seeing the nurse, who had slipped into her print dress and starched cap, she added in a lower tone: "Oh, Miss Lemoine, good evening." Her first nurse, it appeared, had been called Miss Lemoine; and she gave the same name to all the others, quite unaware that there had been any changes in the staff.

"I heard talking, and carriages driving up. Have people begun to arrive?" she asked nervously. "Where is Lavinia? I still have my jewels to put on."

She stood before the nurse, the same petrifying apparition which always, at this hour, struck Miss Cress to silence. Mrs. Jaspar was tall; she had been broad; and her bones remained impressive though the flesh had withered on them. Lavinia had encased her, as usual, in her low-necked purple velvet dress, nipped in at the waist in the old-fashioned way, expanding in voluminous folds about the hips and flowing in a long train over the darker velvet of the carpet. Mrs. Jaspar's swollen feet could no longer be pushed into the high-heeled satin slippers which went with the dress; but her skirts were so long and spreading that, by taking short steps, she managed (so Lavinia daily assured her) entirely to conceal the broad round tips of her black orthopædic shoes.

"Your jewels, Mrs. Jaspar? Why, you've got them on," said Miss Cress brightly.

Mrs. Jaspar turned her porphyry[6]-tinted face to Miss Cress, and

6. A rock consisting of feldspar crystals imbedded in a red or purplish mass.

looked at her with a glassy incredulous gaze. Her eyes, Miss Cress thought, were the worst. . . She lifted one old hand, veined and knobbed as a raised map, to her elaborate purple-black wig, groped among the puffs and curls and undulations (queer, Miss Cress thought, that it never occurred to her to look into the glass), and after an interval affirmed: "You must be mistaken, my dear. Don't you think you ought to have your eyes examined?"

The door opened again, and a very old woman, so old as to make Mrs. Jaspar appear almost young, hobbled in with sidelong steps. "Excuse me, madam. I was downstairs when the bell rang."

Lavinia had probably always been small and slight; now, beside her towering mistress, she looked a mere feather, a straw. Everything about her had dried, contracted, been volatilized into nothingness, except her watchful gray eyes, in which intelligence and comprehension burned like two fixed stars. "Do excuse me, madam," she repeated.

Mrs. Jaspar looked at her despairingly. "I hear carriages driving up. And Miss Lemoine says I have my jewels on; and I know I haven't."

"With that lovely necklace!" Miss Cress ejaculated.

Mrs. Jaspar's twisted hand rose again, this time to her denuded shoulders, which were as stark and barren as the rock from which the hand might have been broken. She felt and felt, and tears rose in her eyes. . .

"Why do you lie to me?" she burst out passionately.

Lavinia softly intervened. "Miss Lemoine meant, how lovely you'll be when you get the necklace on, madam."

"Diamonds, diamonds," said Mrs. Jaspar with an awful smile.

"Of course, madam."

Mrs. Jaspar sat down at the dressing-table, and Lavinia, with eager random hands, began to adjust the *point de Venise*[7] about her mistress's shoulders, and to repair the havoc wrought in the purple-black wig by its wearer's gropings for her tiara.

"Now you do look lovely, madam," she sighed.

Mrs. Jaspar was on her feet again, stiff but incredibly active. ("Like a cat she is," Miss Cress used to relate.) "I do hear carriages—or is it an automobile? The Magraws, I know, have one of those new-fangled automobiles. And now I hear the front door opening. Quick, Lavinia! My fan, my gloves, my handkerchief . . . how often have I got to tell you? I used to have a *perfect* maid—"

Lavinia's eyes brimmed. "That was me, madam," she said, bending to straighten out the folds of the long purple velvet train. ("To watch the two of 'em," Miss Cress used to tell a circle of appreciative friends, "is a lot better than any circus.")

7. A Venetian lace.

Mrs. Jaspar paid no attention. She twitched the train out of Lavinia's vacillating hold, swept to the door, and then paused there as if stopped by a jerk of her constricted muscles. "Oh, but my diamonds—you cruel woman, you! You're letting me go down without my diamonds!" Her ruined face puckered up in a grimace like a new-born baby's, and she began to sob despairingly. "Every-body. . . Every . . . body's . . . against me . . ." she wept in her powerless misery.

Lavinia helped herself to her feet and tottered across the floor. It was almost more than she could bear to see her mistress in distress. "Madam, madam—if you'll just wait till they're got out of the safe," she entreated.

The woman she saw before her, the woman she was entreating and consoling, was not the old petrified Mrs. Jaspar with porphyry face and wig awry whom Miss Cress stood watching with a smile, but a young proud creature, commanding and splendid in her Paris gown of amber *moiré*,[8] who, years ago, had burst into just such furious sobs because, as she was sweeping down to receive her guests, the doctor had told her that little Grace, with whom she had been playing all the afternoon, had a diphtheritic throat, and no one must be allowed to enter. "Everybody's against me, every-body . . ." she had sobbed in her fury; and the young Lavinia, stricken by such Olympian anger, had stood speechless, longing to comfort her, and secretly indignant with little Grace and the doctor. . .

"If you'll just wait, madam, while I go down and ask Munson to open the safe. There's no one come yet, I do assure you. . ."

Munson was the old butler, the only person who knew the combination of the safe in Mrs. Jaspar's bedroom. Lavinia had once known it too, but now she was no longer able to remember it. The worst of it was that she feared lest Munson, who had been spending the day in the Bronx, might not have returned. Munson was growing old too, and he did sometimes forget about these dinner-parties of Mrs. Jaspar's, and then the stupid footman, George, had to announce the names; and you couldn't be sure that Mrs. Jaspar wouldn't notice Munson's absence, and be excited and angry. These dinner-party nights were killing old Lavinia, and she did so want to keep alive; she wanted to live long enough to wait on Mrs. Jaspar to the last.

She disappeared, and Miss Cress poked up the fire, and per-suaded Mrs. Jaspar to sit down in an armchair and "tell her who was coming". It always amused Mrs. Jaspar to say over the long list of her guests' names, and generally she remembered them fairly well, for they were always the same—the last people, Lavinia and

8. A silk fabric with a watered appearance.

Munson said, who had dined at the house, on the very night before her stroke. With recovered complacency she began, counting over one after another on her ring-laden fingers: "The Italian Ambassador, the Bishop, Mr. and Mrs. Torrington Bligh, Mr. and Mrs. Fred Amesworth, Mr and Mrs. Mitchell Magraw, Mr. and Mrs. Torrington Bligh . . ." ("You've said them before," Miss Cress interpolated, getting out her fancy knitting—a necktie for her friend—and beginning to count the stitches.) And Mrs. Jaspar, distressed and bewildered by the interruption, had to repeat over and over: "Torrington Bligh, Torrington Bligh," till the connection was re-established, and she went on again swimmingly with "Mr. and Mrs. Fred Amesworth, Mr. and Mrs. Mitchell Magraw, Miss Laura Ladew, Mr. Harold Ladew, Mr. and Mrs. Benjamin Bronx, Mr. and Mrs. Torrington Bl—no, I mean, Mr. Anson Warley. Yes, Mr. Anson Warley; that's it," she ended complacently.

Miss Cress smiled and interrupted her counting. "No, that's *not* it."

"What do you mean, my dear—not it?"

"Mr. Anson Warley. He's not coming."

Mrs. Jaspar's jaw fell, and she stared at the nurse's coldly smiling face. "Not coming?"

"No. He's not coming. He's not on the list." (That old list! As if Miss Cress didn't know it by heart! Everybody in the house did, except the booby, George, who heard it reeled off every other night by Munson, and who was always stumbling over the names, and having to refer to the written paper.)

"Not on the list?" Mrs. Jaspar gasped.

Miss Cress shook her pretty head.

Signs of uneasiness gathered on Mrs. Jaspar's face and her lip began to tremble. It always amused Miss Cress to give her these little jolts, though she knew Miss Dunn and the doctors didn't approve of her doing so. She knew also that it was against her own interests, and she did try to bear in mind Miss Dunn's oft-repeated admonition about not sending up the patient's blood pressure; but when she was in high spirits, as she was tonight (they would certainly be engaged), it was irresistible to get a rise out of the old lady. And she thought it funny, this new figure unexpectedly appearing among those timeworn guests. ("I wonder what the rest of 'em 'll say to him," she giggled inwardly.)

"No; he's not on the list." Mrs. Jaspar, after pondering deeply, announced the fact with an air of recovered composure.

"That's what I told you," snapped Miss Cress.

"He's not on the list; but he promised me to come. I saw him yesterday," continued Mrs. Jaspar, mysteriously.

"You *saw* him—where?"

She considered. "Last night, at the Fred Amesworths' dance."

"Ah," said Miss Cress, with a little shiver; for she knew that Mrs. Amesworth was dead, and she was the intimate friend of the trained nurse who was keeping alive, by dint of *piqûres* and high frequency,[9] the inarticulate and inanimate Mr. Amesworth. "It's funny," she remarked to Mrs. Jaspar, "that you'd never invited Mr. Warley before."

"No, I hadn't; not for a long time. I believe he felt I'd neglected him; for he came up to me last night, and said he was so sorry he hadn't been able to call. It seems he's been ill, poor fellow. Not as young as he was! So of course I invited him. He was very much gratified."

Mrs. Jaspar smiled at the remembrance of her little triumph; but Miss Cress's attention had wandered, as it always did when the patient became docile and reasonable. She thought: "Where's old Lavinia? I bet she can't find Munson." And she got up and crossed the floor to look into Mrs. Jaspar's bedroom, where the safe was.

There an astonishing sight met her. Munson, as she had expected, was nowhere visible; but Lavinia, on her knees before the safe, was in the act of opening it herself, her twitching hand slowly moving about the mysterious dial.

"Why, I thought you'd forgotten the combination!" Miss Cress exclaimed.

Lavinia turned a startled face over her shoulder. "So I had, Miss. But I've managed to remember it, thank God. I *had* to, you see, because Munson's forgot to come home."

"Oh," said the nurse incredulously. ("Old fox," she thought, "I wonder why she always pretended she'd forgotten it.") For Miss Cress did not know that the age of miracles is not yet past.

Joyous, trembling, her cheeks wet with grateful tears, the little old woman was on her feet again, clutching to her breast the diamond stars, the necklace of *solitaires*, the tiara, the earrings. One by one she spread them out on the velvet-lined tray in which they always used to be carried from the safe to the dressing-room; then, with rambling fingers, she managed to lock the safe again, and put the keys in the drawer where they belonged, while Miss Cress continued to stare at her in amazement. "I don't believe the old witch is as shaky as she makes out," was her reflection as Lavinia passed her, bearing the jewels to the dressing-room where Mrs. Jaspar, lost in pleasant memories, was still computing: "The Italian Ambassador, the Bishop, the Torrington Blighs, the Mitchell Magraws, the Fred Amesworths. . ."

Mrs. Jaspar was allowed to go down to the drawing-room alone

9. Injections and a form of electric therapy then in fashion.

on dinner-party evenings because it would have mortified her too much to receive her guests with a maid or a nurse at her elbow; but Miss Cress and Lavinia always leaned over the stair-rail to watch her descent, and make sure it was accomplished in safety.

"She do look lovely yet, when all her diamonds is on," Lavinia sighed, her purblind eyes bedewed with memories, as the bedizened wig and purple velvet disappeared at the last bend of the stairs. Miss Cress, with a shrug, turned back to the fire and picked up her knitting, while Lavinia set about the slow ritual of tidying up her mistress's room. From below they heard the sound of George's stentorian monologue: "Mr. and Mrs. Torrington Bligh, Mr. and Mrs. Mitchell Magraw . . . Mr. Ladew, Miss Laura Ladew. . ."

IV

Anson Warley, who had always prided himself on his equable temper, was conscious of being on edge that evening. But it was an irritability which did not frighten him (in spite of what those doctors always said about the importance of keeping calm) because he knew it was due merely to the unusual lucidity of his mind. He was in fact feeling uncommonly well, his brain clear and all his perceptions so alert that he could positively hear the thoughts passing through his man-servant's mind on the other side of the door, as Filmore grudgingly laid out the evening clothes.

Smiling at the man's obstinacy, he thought: "I shall have to tell them tonight that Filmore thinks I'm no longer fit to go into society." It was always pleasant to hear the incredulous laugh with which his younger friends received any allusion to his supposed senility. "What, *you?* Well, that's a good one!" And he thought it was, himself.

And then, the moment he was in his bedroom, dressing, the sight of Filmore made him lose his temper again. "No; *not* those studs, confound it. The black onyx ones—haven't I told you a hundred times? Lost them, I suppose? Sent them to the wash again in a soiled shirt? That it?" He laughed nervously, and sitting down before his dressing-table began to brush back his hair with short angry strokes.

"Above all," he shouted out suddenly, "don't stand there staring at me as if you were watching to see exactly at what minute to telephone for the undertaker!"

"The under—? Oh, sir!" gasped Filmore.

"The—the—damn it, are you *deaf* too? Who said undertaker? I said *taxi*; can't you hear what I say?"

"You want me to call a taxi, sir?"

"No; I don't. I've already told you so. I'm going to walk." Warley straightened his tie, rose and held out his arms toward his dress-coat.

"It's bitter cold, sir; better let me call a taxi all the same."

Warley gave a short laugh. "Out with it, now! What you'd really like to suggest is that I should telephone to say I can't dine out. You'd scramble me some eggs instead, eh?"

"I wish you would stay in, sir. There's eggs in the house."

"My overcoat," snapped Warley.

"Or else let me call a taxi; now do, sir."

Warley slipped his arms into his overcoat, tapped his chest to see if his watch (the thin evening watch) and his note-case were in their proper pockets, turned back to put a dash of lavender on his handkerchief, and walked with stiff quick steps toward the front door of his flat.

Filmore, abashed, preceded him to ring for the lift; and then, as it quivered upward through the long shaft, said again: "It's a bitter cold night, sir; and you've had a good deal of exercise today."

Warley levelled a contemptuous glance at him. "Daresay that's why I'm feeling so fit," he retorted as he entered the lift.

It *was* bitter cold; the icy air hit him in the chest when he stepped out of the overheated building, and he halted on the doorstep and took a long breath. "Filmore's missed his vocation; ought to be nurse to a paralytic," he thought. "He'd love to have to wheel me about in a chair."

After the first shock of the biting air he began to find it exhilarating, and walked along at a good pace, dragging one leg ever so little after the other. (The *masseur* had promised him that he'd soon be rid of that stiffness.) Yes—decidedly a fellow like himself ought to have a younger valet; a more cheerful one, anyhow. He felt like a young'un himself this evening; as he turned into Fifth Avenue he rather wished he could meet some one he knew, some man who'd say afterward at his club: "Warley? Why, I saw him sprinting up Fifth Avenue the other night like a two-year-old; that night it was four or five below. . ." He needed a good counter-irritant for Filmore's gloom. "Always have young people about you," he thought as he walked along; and at the words his mind turned to Elfrida Flight, next to whom he would soon be sitting in a warm pleasantly lit dining-room—*where?*

It came as abruptly as that: the gap in his memory. He pulled up at it as if his advance had been checked by a chasm in the pavement at his feet. Where the dickens was he going to dine? And with whom was he going to dine? God! But things didn't happen in that way; a sound strong man didn't suddenly have to stop in the middle of the street and ask himself where he was going to dine. . .

"Perfect in mind, body and understanding." The old legal phrase bobbed up inconsequently into his thoughts. Less than minutes ago he had answered in every particular to that description; what was he now? He put his hand to his forehead, which was bursting; then he lifted his hat and let the cold air blow for a while on his overheated temples. It was queer, how hot he'd got, walking. Fact was, he'd been sprinting along at a damned good pace. In future he must try to remember not to hurry. . . Hang it—one more thing to remember! . . . Well, but what was all the fuss about? Of course, as people got older their memories were subject to these momentary lapses; he'd noticed it often enough among his contemporaries. And, brisk and alert though he still was, it wouldn't do to imagine himself totally exempt from human ills. . .

Where was it he was dining? Why, somewhere farther up Fifth Avenue; he was perfectly sure of that. With that lovely . . . that lovely. . . No; better not make any effort for the moment. Just keep calm, and stroll slowly along. When he came to the right street corner of course he'd spot it; and then everything would be perfectly clear again. He walked on, more deliberately, trying to empty his mind of all thoughts. "Above all," he said to himself, "don't worry."

He tried to beguile his nervousness by thinking of amusing things. "Decline the boredom—" He thought he might get off that joke tonight. "Mrs. Jaspar requests the pleasure—Mr. Warley declines the boredom." Not so bad, really; and he had an idea he'd never told it to the people . . . what in hell *was* their name? . . . the people he was on his way to dine with. . . *Mrs. Jaspar requests the pleasure.* Poor old Mrs. Jaspar; again it occurred to him that he hadn't always been very civil to her in old times. When everybody's running after a fellow it's pardonable now and then to chuck a boring dinner at the last minute; but all the same, as one grew older one understood better how an unintentional slight of that sort might cause offense, cause even pain. And he hated to cause people pain. . . He thought perhaps he'd better call on Mrs. Jaspar some afternoon. She'd be surprised! Or ring her up, poor old girl, and propose himself, just informally, for dinner. One dull evening wouldn't kill him—and how pleased she'd be! Yes—he thought decidedly. . . When he got to be her age, he could imagine how much he'd like it if somebody still in the running should ring him up unexpectedly and say—

He stopped, and looked up, slowly, wonderingly, at the wide illuminated façade of the house he was approaching. Queer coincidence—it was the Jaspar house. And all lit up; for a dinner evidently. And that was queerer yet; almost uncanny; for here he was, in front of the door, as the clock struck a quarter past eight; and of course—he remembered it quite clearly now—it was just here, it was with Mrs. Jaspar, that he was dining. . . Those little lapses

of memory never lasted more than a second or two. How right he'd
been not to let himself worry. He pressed his hand on the door-bell.

"God," he thought, as the double doors swung open, "but it's
good to get in out of the cold."

V

In that hushed sonorous house the sound of the door-bell was
as loud to the two women upstairs as if it had been rung in the
next room.

Miss Cress raised her head in surprise, and Lavinia dropped Mrs.
Jaspar's other false set (the more comfortable one) with a clatter
on the marble wash-stand. She stumbled across the dressing-room,
and hastened out to the landing. With Munson absent, there was
no knowing how George might muddle things. . .

Miss Cress joined her. "Who is it?" she whispered excitedly.
Below, they heard the sound of a hat and a walking stick being laid
down on the big marble-topped table in the hall, and then George's
stentorian drone: "Mr. Anson Warley."

"It is—it *is!* I can see him—a gentleman in evening clothes,"
Miss Cress whispered, hanging over the stair-rail.

"Good gracious—mercy me! And Munson not here! Oh, whatever, whatever shall we do?" Lavinia was trembling so violently that
she had to clutch the stair-rail to prevent herself from falling. Miss
Cress thought, with her cold lucidity: "She's a good deal sicker
than the old woman."

"What shall we do, Miss Cress? That fool of a George—he's
showing him in! Who could have thought it?" Miss Cress knew the
images that were whirling through Lavinia's brain: the vision of
Mrs. Jaspar's having another stroke at the sight of this mysterious
intruder, of Mr. Anson Warley's seeing her there, in her impotence
and her abasement, of the family's being summoned, and rushing in
to exclaim, to question, to be horrified and furious—and all because
poor old Munson's memory was going, like his mistress's, like
Lavinia's, and because he had forgotten that it was one of the
dinner nights. Oh, misery! . . . The tears were running down
Lavinia's cheeks, and Miss Cress knew she was thinking: "If the
daughters send him off—and they will—where's he going to, old
and deaf as he is, and all his people dead? Oh, if only he can hold
on till she dies, and get his pension. . ."

Lavinia recovered herself with one of her supreme efforts. "Miss
Cress, we must go down at once, at once! Something dreadful's
going to happen. . ." She began to totter toward the little velvet-
lined lift in the corner of the landing.

Miss Cress took pity on her. "Come along," she said. "But nothing dreadful's going to happen. You'll see."

"Oh, thank you, Miss Cress. But the shock—the awful shock

to her—of seeing that strange gentleman walk in."

"Not a bit of it." Miss Cress laughed as she stepped into the lift. "He's not a stranger. She's expecting him."

"Expecting him? Expecting Mr. Warley?"

"Sure she is. She told me so just now. She says she invited him yesterday."

"But, Miss Cress, what are you thinking of? Invite him—how? When you know she can't write nor telephone?"

"Well, she says she saw him; she saw him last night at a dance."

"Oh, God," murmured Lavinia, covering her eyes with her hands.

"At a dance at the Fred Amesworths'—that's what she said," Miss Cress pursued, feeling the same little shiver run down her back as when Mrs. Jaspar had made the statement to her.

"The Amesworths—oh, not the Amesworths?" Lavinia echoed, shivering too. She dropped her hands from her face, and followed Miss Cress out of the lift. Her expression had become less anguished, and the nurse wondered why. In reality, she was thinking, in a sort of dreary beatitude: "But if she's suddenly got as much worse as this, she'll go before me, after all, my poor lady, and I'll be able to see to it that she's properly laid out and dressed, and nobody but Lavinia's hands'll touch her."

"You'll see—if she was expecting him, as she says, it won't give her a shock, anyhow. Only, how did *he* know?" Miss Cress whispered, with an acuter renewal of her shiver. She followed Lavinia with muffled steps down the passage to the pantry, and from there the two women stole into the dining-room, and placed themselves noiselessly at its farther end, behind the tall Coromandel screen[1] through the cracks of which they could peep into the empty room.

The long table was set, as Mrs. Jaspar always insisted that it should be on these occasions; but old Munson not having returned, the gold plate (which his mistress also insisted on) had not been got out, and all down the table, as Lavinia saw with horror, George had laid the coarse blue and white plates from the servants' hall. The electric wall-lights were on, and the candles lit in the branching Sèvres[2] candelabra—so much at least had been done. But the flowers in the great central dish of Rose Dubarry porcelain, and in the smaller dishes which accompanied it—the flowers, oh shame, had been forgotten! They were no longer real flowers; the family had long since suppressed that expense; and no wonder, for Mrs. Jaspar always insisted on orchids. But Grace, the youngest daughter, who was the kindest, had hit on the clever device of arranging three beautiful clusters of artificial orchids and maidenhair, which had only to be lifted from their shelf in the pantry and set in the

1. A kind of Chinese lacquered folding screen.

2. A costly porcelain manufactured at Sèvres, France.

dishes—only, of course, that imbecile footman had forgotten, or had not known where to find them. And, oh, horror, realizing his oversight too late, no doubt, to appeal to Lavinia, he had taken some old newspapers and bunched them up into something that he probably thought resembled a bouquet, and crammed one into each of the priceless Rose Dubarry dishes.

Lavinia clutched at Miss Cress's arm. "Oh, look—look what he's done; I shall die of the shame of it. . . Oh, Miss, hadn't we better slip around to the drawing-room and try to coax my poor lady upstairs again, afore she ever notices?"

Miss Cress, peering through the crack of the screen, could hardly suppress a giggle. For at that moment the double doors of the dining-room were thrown open, and George, shuffling about in a baggy livery inherited from a long-departed predecessor of more commanding build, bawled out in his loud sing-song: "Dinner is served, madam."

"Oh, it's too late," moaned Lavinia. Miss Cress signed to her to keep silent, and the two watchers glued their eyes to their respective cracks of the screen.

What they saw, far off down the vista of empty drawing-rooms, and after an interval during which (as Lavinia knew) the imaginary guests were supposed to file in and take their seats, was the entrance, at the end of the ghostly cortège, of a very old woman, still tall and towering, on the arm of a man somewhat smaller than herself, with a fixed smile on a darkly pink face, and a slim erect figure clad in perfect evening clothes, who advanced with short measured steps, profiting (Miss Cress noticed) by the support of the arm he was supposed to sustain. "Well—I never!" was the nurse's inward comment.

The couple continued to advance, with rigid smiles and eyes staring straight ahead. Neither turned to the other, neither spoke. All their attention was concentrated on the immense, the almost unachievable effort of reaching that point, half way down the long dinner table, opposite the big Dubarry dish, where George was drawing back a gilt armchair for Mrs. Jaspar. At last they reached it, and Mrs. Jaspar seated herself, and waved a stony hand to Mr. Warley. "On my right." He gave a little bow, like the bend of a jointed doll, and with infinite precaution let himself down into his chair. Beads of perspiration were standing on his forehead, and Miss Cress saw him draw out his handkerchief and wipe them stealthily away. He then turned his head somewhat stiffly toward his hostess.

"Beautiful flowers," he said, with great precision and perfect gravity, waving his hand toward the bunched-up newspaper in the bowl of Sèvres.

Mrs. Jaspar received the tribute with complacency. "So glad . . .

orchids . . . From High Lawn . . . every morning," she simpered.

"Mar-vellous," Mr. Warley completed.

"I always say to the Bishop. . ." Mrs. Jaspar continued.

"Ha—of course," Mr. Warley warmly assented.

"Not that I don't think. . ."

"Ha—rather!"

George had reappeared from the pantry with a blue crockery dish of mashed potatoes. This he handed in turn to one after another of the imaginary guests, and finally presented to Mrs. Jaspar and her right-hand neighbour.

They both helped themselves cautiously, and Mrs. Jaspar addressed an arch smile to Mr. Warley. " 'Nother month—no more oysters."

"Ha—no more!"

George, with a bottle of Apollinaris[3] wrapped in a napkin, was saying to each guest in turn: "Perrier-Jouet, 'ninety-five." (He had picked that up, thought Miss Cress, from hearing old Munson repeat it so often.)

"Hang it—well, then just a sip," murmured Mr. Warley.

"Old times," bantered Mrs. Jaspar; and the two turned to each other and bowed their heads and touched glasses.

"I often tell Mrs. Amesworth. . ." Mrs. Jaspar continued, bending to an imaginary presence across the table.

"Ha—*ha!*" Mr. Warley approved.

George reappeared and slowly encircled the table with a dish of spinach. After the spinach the Apollinaris also went the round again, announced successively as Château Lafite, 'seventy-four, and "the old Newbold Madeira". Each time that George approached his glass, Mr. Warley made a feint of lifting a defensive hand, and then smiled and yielded. "Might as well—hanged for a sheep. . ." he remarked gaily; and Mrs. Jaspar giggled.

Finally a dish of Malaga grapes and apples was handed. Mrs. Jaspar, now growing perceptibly languid, and nodding with more and more effort at Mr. Warley's pleasantries, transferred a bunch of grapes to her plate, but nibbled only two or three. "Tired," she said suddenly, in a whimper like a child's; and she rose, lifting herself up by the arms of her chair, and leaning over to catch the eye of an invisible lady, presumably Mrs. Amesworth, seated opposite to her. Mr. Warley was on his feet too, supporting himself by resting one hand on the table in a jaunty attitude. Mrs. Jaspar waved to him to be reseated. "Join us—after cigars," she smilingly ordained; and with a great and concentrated effort he bowed to her as she passed toward the double doors which George was throwing open. Slowly, majestically, the purple velvet train disappeared down

3. A charged mineral water, here served in lieu of wine.

the long enfilade of illuminated rooms, and the last door closed behind her.

"Well, I do believe she's enjoyed it!" chuckled Miss Cress, taking Lavinia by the arm to help her back to the hall. Lavinia, for weeping, could not answer.

VI

Anson Warley found himself in the hall again, getting into his fur-lined overcoat. He remembered suddenly thinking that the rooms had been intensely over-heated, and that all the other guests had talked very loud and laughed inordinately. "Very good talk though, I must say," he had to acknowledge.

In the hall, as he got his arms into his coat (rather a job, too, after that Perrier-Jouet) he remembered saying to somebody (perhaps it was to the old butler): "Slipping off early—going on; 'nother engagement," and thinking to himself the while that when he got out into the fresh air again he would certainly remember where the other engagement was. He smiled a little while the servant, who seemed a clumsy fellow, fumbled with the fastening of the door. "And Filmore, who thought I wasn't even well enough to dine out! Damned ass! What would he say if he knew I was going on?"

The door opened, and with an immense sense of exhilaration Mr. Warley issued forth from the house and drew in a first deep breath of night air. He heard the door closed and bolted behind him, and continued to stand motionless on the step, expanding his chest, and drinking in the icy draught.

" 'Spose it's about the last house where they give you 'ninety-five Perrier-Jouet," he thought; and then: "Never heard better talk either. . ."

He smiled again with satisfaction at the memory of the wine and the wit. Then he took a step forward, to where a moment before the pavement had been—and where now there was nothing.

1928, 1930

O. HENRY

(1862–1910)

William Sidney Porter, or "O. Henry," was born in Greensboro, North Carolina, on September 11, 1862. He attended a school taught by his aunt, then clerked in his uncle's drugstore. In 1882 friends took him to Texas, where the young man absorbed the colorful, robust life of a ranch managed by "Red" Hall, famous Texas Ranger captain. Within two years he left the range for Austin, where he worked in the General Land Office, and later as a teller in the First National Bank. About the time of his marriage to Athol Estes in 1887 he began to write humorous sketches for newspapers, and in 1894 he started a burlesque weekly, *The Rolling Stone*, with the subtitle "Out for the Moss." When this journalistic venture failed financially he moved to Houston as daily columnist and occasional cartoonist for the *Post*.

In 1896 he was indicted for embezzlement of bank funds, a charge of which many bankers were technically guilty under the lax system then prevailing in Texas. With the aid of friends he fled to Honduras, stopping briefly in New Orleans, where, working on newspapers, he felt the spell of the old French quarter. He reached Honduras safely and might have remained there, absorbing the exotic beauty of its scenery and mingling with a fantastic colony of exiles, but news of his wife's fatal illness brought him back to Austin. The authorities permitted him to remain free until after her death; his sentence was the lightest possible. As a federal prisoner in the penitentiary at Columbus, Ohio, he turned to writing, needing money for the support of his little daughter, who was living with her grandparents. When he emerged three years and three months later from a sentence shortened by good behavior, W. S. Porter had become O. Henry.

In 1902 he arrived in New York—his "Little Old Bagdad on the Subway"—to begin a career as brief and brilliant as the burst of a comet. From December, 1903, to January, 1906, he produced a story a week for the New York *World*, while contributing to other Sunday supplements and to the syndicated magazines. His first book, *Cabbages and Kings* (1904) presents exiles, beachcombers, and soldiers of fortune against magnificently described Latin-American backgrounds. *The Four Million* (1906)—his finest book—reveals the lives of those who make up the multitude of New York, in their daily routines and searchings for romance and adventure. *The Trimmed Lamp* (1907), another volume of New York stories, like *The Four Million* explored metropolitan life. With *Heart of the West* (1907) the youthful observations of Will Porter in Texas were made into a collection of stories which J. Frank Dobie, in *Finding Literature on the Texas Plains*, describes as "true to the people and range of the old days as well as fascinating to readers of any day." Then in rapid succession appeared *The Voice of the City* (1908), *The Gentle Grafter* (1908), *Roads of Destiny* (1909), *Options* (1909), *Strictly Business* (1910), and *Whirligigs* (1910).

After O. Henry's death in 1910, his popularity continued with three more collected volumes: *Sixes and Sevens* (1911), *Rolling Stones* (1912), and *Waifs and Strays* (1917). Later seven fugitive stories and poems, entitled *O. Henryana* (1920), and his correspondence with Mabel Wagnalls, *Letters to Lithopolis* (1922), were published. His early work on the Houston *Post* was collected by Florence Stratton in *Postscripts* (1923), to which Mary S. Harrell added a supplement, *O. Henry Encore* (1939).

O. Henry exerted a pronounced influence on the development of the American short story, and he has had many imitators. His greatest faults are an overuse of trite slang, occasional buffoonery, and the frequent employment of coincidence, which makes even some of his better plots seem contrived. Yet it should be noted that his view of life, like his art, stressed the force of circumstances; indeed, his central theme, reflecting the hurly-burly of contemporary American life and its tempo, is the effect of coincidence on character, expressed in humor grim or ironic. At his best O. Henry produced vignettes, especially of Texas and New York, which are valuable social documents as well as artistic narratives.

All of O. Henry's stories are available in *The Complete Works of O. Henry,* 1 vol., 1927, reissued in 1937 with an introduction by William Lyon Phelps, and in 2 vols., 1953 with an introduction by Harry Hansen.

The authorized life is *O. Henry Biography,* 1916, by C. Alphonso Smith, and more recent studies are E. Hudson Long, *O. Henry: The Man and His Work,* 1949, and Gerald Langford, *Alias O. Henry,* 1957. There are critical evaluations by Fred Lewis Pattee, "O. Henry and the Handbooks," *The Development of the American Short Story,* 1923; and by Arthur H. Quinn, "The Journalists," *American Fiction,* 1936. An excellent appraisal is Van Wyck Brooks, "New York: O. Henry," *The Confident Years, 1885–1915,* 1952.

An Unfinished Story[1]

We no longer groan and heap ashes upon our heads when the flames of Tophet[2] are mentioned. For, even the preachers have begun to tell us that God is radium, or ether or some scientific compound, and that the worst we wicked ones may expect is a chemical reaction. This is a pleasing hypothesis; but there lingers yet some of the old, goodly terror of orthodoxy.

There are but two subjects upon which one may discourse with a free imagination, and without the possibility of being controverted. You may talk of your dreams; and you may tell what you heard a parrot say. Both Morpheus[3] and the bird are incompetent witnesses; and your listener dare not attack your recital. The baseless fabric of a vision, then, shall furnish my theme—chosen with apologies and regrets instead of the more limited field of pretty Polly's small talk.

I had a dream that was so far removed from the higher criticism that it had to do with the ancient, respectable, and lamented bar-of-judgment theory.

Gabriel[4] had played his trump; and those of us who could not

1. First published in *McClure's* for August, 1905, and collected in *The Four Million* (1906), which is the source of the present text.
2. Hell.
3. In Greek mythology, the god of dreams.
4. Gabriel, the angel trumpeter of resurrection day.

follow suit were arraigned for examination. I noticed at one side a gathering of professional bondsmen in solemn black and collars that buttoned behind; but it seemed there was some trouble about their real estate titles; and they did not appear to be getting any of us out.

A fly cop[5]—an angel policeman—flew over to me and took me by the left wing. Near at hand was a group of very prosperous-looking spirits arraigned for judgment.

"Do you belong with that bunch?" the policeman asked.

"Who are they?" was my answer.

"Why," said he, "they are——"

But this irrelevant stuff is taking up space that the story should occupy.

Dulcie worked in a department store. She sold Hamburg edging, or stuffed peppers, or automobiles, or other little trinkets such as they keep in department stores. Of what she earned, Dulcie received six dollars per week. The remainder was credited to her and debited to somebody else's account in the ledger kept by G—— Oh, primal energy, you say, Reverend Doctor—— Well, then, in the Ledger of Primal Energy.

During her first year in the store, Dulcie was paid five dollars per week. It would be instructive to know how she lived on that amount. Don't care? Very well; probably you are interested in larger amounts. Six dollars is a larger amount. I will tell you how she lived on six dollars per week.

One afternoon at six, when Dulcie was sticking her hat pin within an eighth of an inch of her *medulla oblongata*,[6] she said to her chum, Sadie—the girl that waits on you with her left side:

"Say, Sade, I made a date for dinner this evening with Piggy."

"You never did!" exclaimed Sadie, admiringly. "Well, ain't you the lucky one? Piggy's an awful swell; and he always takes a girl to swell places. He took Blanche up to the Hoffman House[7] one evening, where they have swell music, and you see a lot of swells. You'll have a swell time, Dulce."

Dulcie hurried homeward. Her eyes were shining, and her cheeks showed the delicate pink of life's—real life's—approaching dawn. It was Friday; and she had fifty cents left of her last week's wages.

The streets were filled with the rush-hour floods of people. The electric lights of Broadway were glowing—calling moths from miles, from leagues, from hundreds of leagues out of darkness around to come in and attend the singeing school. Men in accurate clothes, with faces like those carved on cherry stones by the old salts in

5. Slang for a policeman who is well posted and understands his business, generally a plain-clothes officer.
6. Lower part of the brain, continuous with the spinal cord.
7. An expensive hotel of that day, located on Broadway between Twenty-fourth and Twenty-fifth streets.

sailors' homes, turned and stared at Dulcie as she sped, unheeding, past them. Manhattan, the night-blooming cereus, was beginning to unfold its dead-white, heavy-odored petals.

Dulcie stopped in a store where goods were cheap and bought an imitation lace collar with her fifty cents. That money was to have been spent otherwise—fifteen cents for supper, ten cents for breakfast, ten cents for lunch. Another dime was to be added to her small store of savings; and five cents was to be squandered for licorice drops—the kind that made your cheek look like the toothache, and last as long. The licorice was an extravagance—almost a carouse—but what is life without pleasures?

Dulcie lived in a furnished room. There is this difference between a furnished room and a boarding-house. In a furnished room, other people do not know it when you go hungry.

Dulcie went up to her room—the third-floor-back in a West Side brownstone-front. She lit the gas. Scientists tell us that the diamond is the hardest substance known. Their mistake. Landladies know of a compound beside which the diamond is as putty. They pack it in the tips of gas-burners; and one may stand on a chair and dig at it in vain until one's fingers are pink and bruised. A hairpin will not remove it; therefore let us call it immovable.

So Dulcie lit the gas. In its one-fourth-candle-power glow we will observe the room.

Couch-bed, dresser, table, washstand, chair—of this much the landlady was guilty. The rest was Dulcie's. On the dresser were her treasures—a gilt china vase presented to her by Sadie, a calendar issued by a pickle works, a book of the divination of dreams, some rice powder[8] in a glass dish, and a cluster of artificial cherries tied with a pink ribbon.

Against the wrinkly mirror stood pictures of General Kitchener,[9] William Muldoon,[1] the Duchess of Marlborough, and Benvenuto Cellini. Against one wall was a plaster of Paris plaque of an O'Callahan in a Roman helmet. Near it was a violent oleograph[2] of a lemon-colored child assaulting an inflammatory butterfly. This was Dulcie's final judgment in art; but it had never been upset. Her rest had never been disturbed by whispers of stolen copes; no critic had elevated his eyebrows at her infantile entomologist.

Piggy was to call for her at seven. While she swiftly makes ready, let us discreetly face the other way and gossip.

For the room, Dulcie paid two dollars per week. On week-days

8. Face power made from pulverized rice.
9. Horatio Herbert Kitchener (1850–1916) became a popular hero, especially by leading the British forces in the capture of Khartoum, in the Egyptian Sudan (1898).

1. William Muldoon (1845–1933), famous athletic director and physical culturist, who introduced the boxer John L. Sullivan to the New York sporting public in 1881.
2. A print imitative of an oil painting.

her breakfast cost ten cents; she made coffee and cooked an egg over the gaslight while she was dressing. On Sunday mornings she feasted royally on veal chops and pineapple fritters at "Billy's" restaurant, at a cost of twenty-five cents—and tipped the waitress ten cents. New York presents so many temptations for one to run into extravagance. She had her lunches in the department-store restaurant at a cost of sixty cents for the week; dinners were $1.05. The evening papers—show me a New Yorker going without his daily paper! —came to six cents; and two Sunday papers—one for the personal column and the other to read—were ten cents. The total amounts to $4.76. Now, one has to buy clothes, and—

I give it up. I hear of wonderful bargains in fabrics, and of miracles performed with needle and thread; but I am in doubt. I hold my pen poised in vain when I would add to Dulcie's life some of those joys that belong to woman by virtue of all the unwritten, sacred, natural, inactive ordinances of the equity of heaven. Twice she had been to Coney Island and had ridden the hobby-horses. 'Tis a weary thing to count your pleasures by summers instead of by hours.

Piggy needs but a word. When the girls named him, an undeserving stigma was cast upon the noble family of swine. The words-of-three-letters lesson in the old blue spelling book begins with Piggy's biography. He was fat; he had the soul of a rat, the habits of a bat, and the magnanimity of a cat. . . . He wore expensive clothes; and was a connoisseur in starvation. He could look at a shop-girl and tell you to an hour how long it had been since she had eaten anything more nourishing than marshmallows and tea. He hung about the shopping districts, and prowled around in department stores with his invitations to dinner. Men who escort dogs upon the streets at the end of a string look down upon him. He is a type; I can dwell upon him no longer; my pen is not the kind intended for him; I am no carpenter.

At ten minutes to seven Dulcie was ready. She looked at herself in the wrinkly mirror. The reflection was satisfactory. The dark blue dress, fitting without a wrinkle, the hat with its jaunty black feather, the but-slightly-soiled gloves—all representing self-denial, even of food itself—were vastly becoming.

Dulcie forgot everything else for a moment except that she was beautiful, and that life was about to lift a corner of its mysterious veil for her to observe its wonders. No gentleman had ever asked her out before. Now she was going for a brief moment into the glitter and exalted show.

The girls said that Piggy was a "spender." There would be a grand dinner, and music, and splendidly dressed ladies to look at and things to eat that strangely twisted the girls' jaws when they tried to tell about them. No doubt she would be asked out again.

There was a blue pongee suit in a window that she knew—by saving twenty cents a week instead of ten in—let's see—— Oh, it would run into years! But there was a second-hand store in Seventh Avenue where——

Somebody knocked at the door. Dulcie opened it. The landlady stood there with a spurious smile, sniffing for cooking by stolen gas.

"A gentleman's downstairs to see you," she said. "Name is Mr. Wiggins."

By such epithet was Piggy known to unfortunate ones who had to take him seriously.

Dulcie turned to the dresser to get her handkerchief; and then she stopped still, and bit her underlip hard. While looking in her mirror she had seen fairyland and herself, a princess, just awakening from a long slumber. She had forgotten one that was watching her with sad, beautiful, stern eyes—the only one there was to approve or condemn what she did. Straight and slender and tall, with a look of sorrowful reproach on his handsome, melancholy face, General Kitchener fixed his wonderful eyes on her out of his gilt photograph frame on the dresser.

Dulcie turned like an automatic doll to the landlady.

"Tell him I can't go," she said, dully. "Tell him I'm sick, or something. Tell him I'm not going out."

After the door was closed and locked, Dulcie fell upon her bed, crushing her black tip, and cried for ten minutes. General Kitchener was her only friend. He was Dulcie's ideal of a gallant knight. He looked as if he might have a secret sorrow, and his wonderful moustache was a dream, and she was a little afraid of that stern yet tender look in his eyes. She used to have little fancies that he would call at the house sometime, and ask for her, with his sword clanking against his high boots. Once, when a boy was rattling a piece of chain against a lamp post she had opened the window and looked out. But there was no use. She knew that General Kitchener was away over in Japan, leading his army against the savage Turks; and he would never step out of his gilt frame for her. Yet one look from him had vanquished Piggy that night. Yes, for that night.

When her cry was over Dulcie got up and took off her best dress, and put on her old blue kimono. She wanted no dinner. She sang two verses of "Sammy."[3] Then she became intensely interested in a little red speck on the side of her nose. And after that was attended to, she drew up a chair to the rickety table, and told her fortune with an old deck of cards.

"The horrid, impudent thing!" she said aloud. "And I never gave him a word or a look to make him think it!"

---

3. A popular song from the musical comedy *The Wizard of Oz* (1903).

At nine o'clock Dulcie took a tin box of crackers and a little pot of raspberry jam out of her trunk and had a feast. She offered General Kitchener some jam on a cracker; but he only looked at her as the sphinx would have looked at a butterfly—if there are butterflies in the desert.

"Don't eat it if you don't want to," said Dulcie. "And don't put on so many airs and scold so with your eyes. I wonder if you'd be so superior and snippy if you had to live on six dollars a week."

It was not a good sign for Dulcie to be rude to General Kitchener. And then she turned Benvenuto Cellini face downward with a severe gesture. But that was not inexcusable; for she had always thought he was Henry VIII, and she did not approve of him.

At half-past nine Dulcie took a last look at the pictures on the dresser, turned out the light and skipped into bed. It's an awful thing to go to bed with a good-night look at General Kitchener, William Muldoon, the Duchess of Marlborough, and Benvenuto Cellini.

This story doesn't really get anywhere at all. The rest of it comes later—sometime when Piggy asks Dulcie again to dine with him, and she is feeling lonelier than usual, and General Kitchener happens to be looking the other way; and then——

As I said before, I dreamed that I was standing near a crowd of prosperous-looking angels, and a policeman took me by the wing and asked if I belonged with them.

"Who are they?" I asked.

"Why," said he, "they are the men who hired working-girls, and paid 'em five or six dollars a week to live on. Are you one of the bunch?"

"Not on your immortality," said I. "I'm only a fellow that set fire to an orphan asylum, and murdered a blind man for his pennies."

1905, 1906

HAMLIN GARLAND

(1860–1940)

Hannibal Hamlin Garland was born in Wisconsin and reared on a succession of pioneer farms in Iowa and South Dakota. An interest in literature turned him toward Boston, where after hard study and near starvation, he se-cured a teaching position at the Boston School of Oratory. Like many another young realist, Garland came under the influence and inspiration of Howells. After saving for two years, he was able in 1887 to revisit his old home at Osage, Iowa, and his father's home at Ordway, South Dakota; there Garland saw the lonely toil and hardships of the farmer's lot from a new perspective. Brooding and resentful at the waste of life that his family had experienced, Garland began to write immediately after his return to Boston. A second visit in 1889, during which his mother suffered a paralytic stroke resulting from her toil on their treeless farm, deepened his anger. His response may be found in the stories about the hardships of farmers of the Middle Border (the region of Minnesota, Wisconsin, Nebraska, and the Dakotas), six of which were published as *Main-Travelled Roads* (1891), five others being added to later editions. All are realistic protests against the abuses, the toil, and the poverty of the Middle Border frontier in the early days. Garland wanted to record the drudgery and the heroic endurance of that life as it really existed. His stories rank high as regional fiction, yet Garland had no interest in local color or picturesqueness; it was genuineness that he valued.

Often the propagandist in Garland overcame the artist, but even when wrathful, his stories are still dramatic. Through his work there runs a thread of romantic optimism; the most desperate situations are sometimes happily resolved. *Main-Travelled Roads* is unified by Garland's concept that "like the main-travelled road of life [this book] is traversed by many classes of people, but the poor and the weary predominate." Two other collections were made of his stories during these years—

Prairie Folks (1893) and *Wayside Courtships* (1897), both later edited to form *Other Main-Travelled Roads* (1910). These thirty stories of his early period, written with a crusading spirit and ethical force, constitute his best fiction. Among these "The Return of a Private" depicts the solitary homecoming of a Union veteran to resume "his daily running fight with nature and against the injustice of his fellow-men"; "Under the Lion's Paw" reveals the bitter plight of an honest, industrious farmer in the grasp of an unscrupulous landlord; "Up the Coolly" dramatically portrays the resentment of a farmer against his brother who has succeeded in the city; and "Among the Corn Rows" is a timeless comedy of love.

Garland believed he could crusade better through the novel than through the short story. *Jason Edwards: An Average Man* (1892) was written to help explain the single-tax theories of Henry George; the account of the rise of the Grange, the Farmers' Alliance, and the Populist party makes *A Spoil of Office* (1892) interesting to the historian, but the novel is little more than campaign material; *A Member of the Third House* (1892) exposes the power of the railroads over legislation. Much better is *A Little Norsk* (1892), the story of a Norwegian orphan girl reared on a bleak, dreary farm, and of her tragic marriage. *Rose of Dutcher's Coolly* (1895) depicts a girl's revolt against the monotony of farm life and her courageous struggles to secure a college education and professional security in Chicago. As his work became more popular, Garland's output declined in quality; he was unable to write of other localities with the same art that he had commanded in portraying the Middle West. *The Captain of the Gray-Horse Troop* (1902), his first financial success, was followed by *Hesper* (1903) and *Cavanagh, Forest Ranger* (1910).

A Son of the Middle Border (1917) an autobiography written in mellow retrospect, dramatizes the roving spirit of the pioneer farmer, and tells the story of his boyhood and youth in the Dakotas, California, and Chicago up to 1893. A sequel dealing with his marriage and literary career in Chicago, *A Daughter of the Middle Border* (1921), includes the frontier story of his wife's family. This volume, carrying the adventures of his family down to the first World War, was greatly praised and won the Pulitzer Prize. Garland now decided to investigate and record the beginnings of pioneering in his family. *Trail-Makers of the Middle Border* (1926) is partly fictional, but it incorporates an account of the westward journeys of his father from Maine to Wisconsin before 1865, the year in which the narrative of *A Son of the Middle*

Border, begins. In 1928 he completed the series with *Back-Trailers from the Middle Border,* which recounts the return to the East of various members of his semifictitious family, representing a typical reaction among families of the first frontiers.

These four volumes are of genuine literary merit and historical value, but other volumes of Garland's later years are either gossipy memoirs, potboilers, or topical works on spiritualism and the like. He remains in literary memory for the enduring value of the early stories of *Main-Travelled Roads,* in which he almost unwittingly contributed to early American naturalism, and for the "Middle Border" series, in which the history of a family of plain people is given historical and human significance.

There is no collected edition of Hamlin Garland now available, and his individual volumes have not been kept in print. The eleven-volume Border Edition, 1895–1910, has been long out of print. Jean Holloway, *Hamlin Garland: A Biography,* 1960, is a detailed account. Good studies of his work have been made by Arthur H. Quinn, *American Fiction,* 1936, pp. 454–459; and by Clarence Gohdes, in *The Literature of the American People,* by Arthur H. Quinn and others, 1951, pp. 648–651. Walter Fuller Taylor treats the economic aspects of Garland's fiction in *The Economic Novel in America,* 1942, pp. 148–183.

The Return of a Private[1]

I

The nearer the train drew toward La Crosse,[2] the soberer the little group of "vets" became. On the long way from New Orleans they

1. First published in the *Arena* for December, 1890, and included in *Main-Travelled Roads* (1891). The text is taken from the 1891 edition.

2. A city in western Wisconsin, Garland's native state, which he knew from childhood experiences on its frontier.

had beguiled tedium with jokes and friendly chaff; or with planning with elaborate detail what they were going to do now, after the war. A long journey, slowly, irregularly, yet persistently pushing northward. When they entered on Wisconsin territory they gave a cheer, and another when they reached Madison, but after that they sank into a dumb expectancy. Comrades dropped off at one or two points beyond, until there were only four or five left who were bound for La Crosse County.

Three of them were gaunt and brown, the fourth was gaunt and pale, with signs of fever and ague upon him. One had a great scar down his temple, one limped, and they all had unnaturally large, bright eyes, showing emaciation. There were no bands greeting them at the station, no banks of gayly-dressed ladies waving handkerchiefs and shouting "Bravo!" as they came in on the caboose of a freight train into the towns that had cheered and blared at them on their way to war. As they looked out or stepped upon the platform for a moment, as the train stood at the station, the loafers looked at them indifferently. Their blue coats, dusty and grimy, were too familiar now to excite notice, much less a friendly word. They were the last of the army to return, and the loafers were surfeited with such sights.

The train jogged forward so slowly that it seemed likely to be midnight before they should reach La Crosse. The little squad grumbled and swore, but it was no use; the train would not hurry, and, as a matter of fact, it was nearly two o'clock when the engine whistled "down brakes."

All of the group were farmers, living in districts several miles out of the town, and all were poor.

"Now, boys," said Private Smith, he of the fever and ague, "we are landed in La Crosse in the night. We've got to stay somewhere till mornin'. Now I ain't got no two dollars to waste on a hotel. I've got a wife and children, so I'm goin' to roost on a bench and take the cost of a bed out of my hide."

"Same here," put in one of the other men. "Hide 'll grow on again, dollars 'll come hard. It's goin' to be mighty hot skirmishin' to find a dollar these days."

"Don't think they'll be a deputation of citizens waitin' to 'scort us to a hotel, eh?" said another. His sarcasm was too obvious to require an answer.

Smith went on: "Then at daybreak we'll start for home—at least, I will."

"Well, I'll be dummed if I'll take two dollars out o' *my* hide," one of the younger men said. "I'm goin' to a hotel, ef I don't never lay up a cent."

"That'll do f'r you," said Smith; "but if you had a wife an' three young uns dependin' on yeh—"

"Which I ain't, thank the Lord! and don't intend havin' while the court knows itself."

The station was deserted, chill, and dark, as they came into it at exactly a quarter to two in the morning. Lit by the oil lamps that flared a dull red light over the dingy benches, the waiting-room was not an inviting place. The younger man went off to look up a hotel, while the rest remained and prepared to camp down on the floor and benches. Smith was attended to tenderly by the other men, who spread their blankets on the bench for him, and, by robbing themselves, made quite a comfortable bed, though the narrowness of the bench made his sleeping precarious.

It was chill, though August, and the two men, sitting with bowed heads, grew stiff with cold and weariness, and were forced to rise now and again and walk about to warm their stiffened limbs. It did not occur to them, probably, to contrast their coming home with their going forth, or with the coming home of the generals, colonels, or even captains—but to Private Smith, at any rate, there came a sickness at heart almost deadly as he lay there on his hard bed and went over his situation.

In the deep of the night, lying on a board in the town where he had enlisted three years ago, all elation and enthusiasm gone out of him, he faced the fact that with the joy of home-coming was already mingled the bitter juice of care. He saw himself sick, worn out, taking up the work on his half-cleared farm, the inevitable mortgage standing ready with open jaw to swallow half his earnings. He had given three years of his life for a mere pittance of pay, and now!—

Morning dawned at last, slowly, with a pale yellow dome of light rising silently above the bluffs, which stand like some huge storm-devastated castle, just east of the city. Out to the left the great river swept on its massive yet silent way to the south. Bluejays called across the river from hillside to hillside through the clear, beautiful air, and hawks began to skim the tops of the hills. The older men were astir early, but Private Smith had fallen at last into a sleep, and they went out without waking him. He lay on his knapsack, his gaunt face turned toward the ceiling, his hands clasped on his breast, with a curious pathetic effect of weakness and appeal.

An engine switching near woke him at last, and he slowly sat up and stared about. He looked out of the window and saw that the sun was lightening the hills across the river. He rose and brushed his hair as well as he could, folded his blankets up, and went out to find his companions. They stood gazing silently at the river and at the hills.

"Looks natcher'l, don't it?" they said, as he came out.

"That's what it does," he replied. "An' it looks good. D'yeh see that peak?" He pointed at a beautiful symmetrical peak, rising like a slightly truncated cone, so high that it seemed the very highest of them all. It was lighted by the morning sun till it glowed like a beacon, and a light scarf of gray morning fog was rolling up its shadowed side.

"My farm's just beyond that. Now, if I can only ketch a ride, we'll be home by dinner-time."

"I'm talkin' about breakfast," said one of the others.

"I guess it's one more meal o' hardtack f'r me," said Smith.

They foraged around, and finally found a restaurant with a sleepy old German behind the counter, and procured some coffee, which they drank to wash down their hardtack.

"Time'll come," said Smith, holding up a piece by the corner, "when this'll be a curiosity."

"I hope to God it will! I bet I've chawed hardtack enough to shingle every house in the coolly.[3] I've chawed it when my lampers was down, and when they wasn't. I've took it dry, soaked, and mashed. I've had it wormy, musty, sour, and blue mouldy. I've had it in little bits and big bits; 'fore coffee an' after coffee. I'm ready f'r a change. I'd like t' git holt jest about now o' some of the hot biscuits my wife c'n make when she lays herself out f'r company."

"Well, if you set there gablin', you'll never *see* yer wife."

"Come on," said Private Smith. "Wait a moment, boys; less take suthin'. It's on me." He led them to the rusty tin dipper which hung on a nail beside the wooden water-pail, and they grinned and drank. Then shouldering their blankets and muskets, which they were "takin' home to the boys," they struck out on their last march.

"They called that coffee Jayvy,"[4] grumbled one of them, "but it never went by the road where government Jayvy resides. I reckon I know coffee from peas."

They kept together on the road along the turnpike, and up the winding road by the river, which they followed for some miles. The river was very lovely, curving down along its sandy beds, pausing now and then under broad basswood trees, or running in dark, swift, silent currents under tangles of wild grape-vines, and drooping alders, and haw trees. At one of these lovely spots the three vets sat down on the thick green sward to rest, "on Smith's account." The leaves of the trees were as fresh and green as in June, the jays called cheery greetings to them, and kingfishers darted to and fro with swooping, noiseless flight.

"I tell yeh, boys, this knocks the swamps of Loueesiana into kingdom come."

3. Properly "coulee" or "coulée," a deep   4. Java.
gulch, usually dry, with sloping sides.

"You bet. All they c'n raise down there is snakes, niggers, and p'rticler hell."

"An' fightin' men," put in the older man.

"An' fightin' men. If I had a good hook an' line I'd sneak a pick'rel out o' that pond. Say, remember that time I shot that alligator—"

"I guess we'd better be crawlin' along," interrupted Smith, rising and shouldering his knapsack, with considerable effort, which he tried to hide.

"Say, Smith, lemme give you a lift on that."

"I guess I c'n manage," said Smith, grimly.

"Course. But, yo' see, I may not have a chance right off to pay yeh back for the times you've carried my gun and hull caboodle.[5] Say, now, gimme that gun, anyway."

"All right, if yeh feel like it, Jim," Smith replied, and they trudged along doggedly in the sun, which was getting higher and hotter each half-mile.

"Ain't it queer there ain't no teams comin' along," said Smith after a long silence.

"Well, no, seein 's it's Sunday."

"By jinks, that's a fact. It *is* Sunday. I'll git home in time f'r dinner, sure!" he exulted. "She don't hev dinner usially till about *one* on Sundays." And he fell into a muse, in which he smiled.

"Well, I'll git home jest about six o'clock, jest about when the boys are milkin' the cows," said old Jim Cranby. "I'll step into the barn, an' then I'll say: 'He*ah!* why ain't this milkin' done before this time o' day?" An' then won't they yell!" he added, slapping his thigh in great glee.

Smith went on. "I'll jest go up the path. Old Rover 'll come down the road to meet me. He won't bark; he'll know me, an' he'll come down waggin' his tail an' showin' his teeth. That's his way of laughin'. An' so I'll walk up to the kitchen door, an' I'll say, '*Dinner* f'r a hungry man!' An' then she'll jump up, an'—"

He couldn't go on. His voice choked at the thought of it. Saunders, the third man, hardly uttered a word. He walked silently behind the others. He had lost his wife the first year he was in the army. She died of pneumonia caught in the autumn rains, while working in the fields in his place.

They plodded along till at last they came to a parting of the ways. To the right the road continued up the main valley; to the left it went over the main ridge.

"Well, boys," began Smith, as they grounded their muskets and looked away up the valley, "here's where we shake hands. We've marched together a good many miles, an' now I s'pose we're done."

5. The whole lot or pack.

"Yes, I don't think we'll do any more of it f'r a while. I don't want to, I know."

"I hope I'll see yeh once in a while, boys, to talk over old times."

"Of course," said Saunders, whose voice trembled a little, too. "It ain't *exactly* like dyin'." They all found it hard to look at each other.

"But we'd ought'r go home with you," said Cranby. "You'll never climb that ridge with all them things on yer back."

"Oh, I'm all right! Don't worry about me. Every step takes me nearer home, yeh see. Well, good-by, boys."

They shook hands. "Good-by. Good luck!"

"Same to you. Lemme know how you find things at home."

"Good-by."

"Good-by."

He turned once before they passed out of sight, and waved his cap, and they did the same, and all yelled. Then all marched away with their long, steady, loping, veteran step. The solitary climber in blue walked on for a time, with his mind filled with the kindness of his comrades, and musing upon the many wonderful days they had had together in camp and field.

He thought of his chum, Billy Tripp. Poor Billy! A "minie" ball[6] fell into his breast one day, fell wailing like a cat, and tore a great ragged hole in his heart. He looked forward to a sad scene with Billy's mother and sweetheart. They would want to know all about it. He tried to recall all that Billy had said, and the particulars of it, but there was little to remember, just that wild wailing sound high in the air, a dull slap, a short, quick, expulsive groan, and the boy lay with his face in the dirt in the ploughed field they were marching across.

That was all. But all the scenes he had since been through had not dimmed the horror, the terror of that moment, when his boy comrade fell, with only a breath between a laugh and a death-groan. Poor handsome Billy! Worth millions of dollars was his young life.

These sombre recollections gave way at length to more cheerful feelings as he began to approach his home coulé. The fields and houses grew familiar, and in one or two he was greeted by people seated in the doorway. But he was in no mood to talk, and pushed on steadily, though he stopped and accepted a drink of milk once at the well-side of a neighbor.

The sun was getting hot on that slope, and his step grew slower, in spite of his iron resolution. He sat down several times to rest. Slowly he crawled up the rough, reddish-brown road, which wound along the hillside, under great trees, through dense groves of jack

---

6. A conical bullet with a hollow base which expanded when it was fired, named after its French inventor, C. E. Minié (1814–1879).

oaks, with tree-tops far below him on his left hand, and the hills far above him on his right. He crawled along like some minute, wingless variety of fly.

He ate some hardtack, sauced with wild berries, when he reached the summit of the ridge, and sat there for some time, looking down into his home coulé.

Sombre, pathetic figure! His wide, round gray eyes gazing down into the beautiful valley, seeing and not seeing, the splendid cloud-shadows sweeping over the western hills and across the green and yellow wheat far below. His head drooped forward on his palm, his shoulders took on a tired stoop, his cheek-bones showed painfully. An observer might have said, "He is looking down upon his own grave."

II

Sunday comes in a Western wheat-harvest with such sweet and sudden relaxation to man and beast that it would be holy for that reason, if for no other, and Sundays are usually fair in harvest-time. As one goes out into the field in the hot morning sunshine, with no sound abroad save the crickets and the indescribably pleasant, silken rustling of the ripened grain, the reaper and the very sheaves in the stubble seem to be resting, dreaming.

Around the house, in the shade of the trees, the men sit, smoking, dozing, or reading the papers, while the women, never resting, move about at the housework. The men eat on Sundays about the same as on other days, and breakfast is no sooner over and out of the way than dinner begins.

But at the Smith farm there were no men dozing or reading. Mrs. Smith was alone with her three children, Mary, nine, Tommy, six, and little Ted, just past four. Her farm, rented to a neighbor, lay at the head of a coule or narrow gulley, made at some far-off post-glacial period by the vast and angry floods of water which gullied these tremendous furrows in the level prairie—furrows so deep that undisturbed portions of the original level rose like hills on either side,—rose to quite considerable mountains.

The chickens wakened her as usual that Sabbath morning from dreams of her absent husband, from whom she had not heard for weeks. The shadows drifted over the hills, down the slopes, across the wheat, and up the opposite wall in leisurely way, as if, being Sunday, they could take it easy also. The fowls clustered about the housewife as she went out into the yard. Fuzzy little chickens swarmed out from the coops where their clucking and perpetually disgruntled mothers tramped about, petulantly thrusting their heads through the spaces between the slats.

A cow called in a deep, musical bass, and a calf answered from a little pen near by, and a pig scurried guiltily out of the cabbages. Seeing all this, seeing the pig in the cabbages, the tangle of grass in the garden, the broken fence which she had mended again and again— the little woman, hardly more than a girl, sat down and cried. The bright Sabbath morning was only a mockery without him!

A few years ago they had bought this farm, paying part, mortgaging the rest in the usual way. Edward Smith was a man of terrible energy. He worked "nights and Sundays," as the saying goes, to clear the farm of its brush and of its insatiate mortgage! In the midst of his herculean struggle came the call for volunteers, and with the grim and unselfish devotion to his country which made the Eagle Brigade able to "whip its weight in wild-cats," he threw down his scythe and grub-axe, turned his cattle loose, and became a blue-coated cog in a vast machine for killing men, and not thistles. While the millionaire sent his money to England for safekeeping, this man, with his girl-wife and three babies, left them on a mortgaged farm, and went away to fight for an idea. It was foolish, but it was sublime for all that.

That was three years before, and the young wife, sitting on the well-curb on this bright Sabbath harvest morning, was righteously rebellious. It seemed to her that she had borne her share of the country's sorrow. Two brothers had been killed, the renter in whose hands her husband had left the farm had proved a villain, one year the farm had been without crops, and now the over-ripe grain was waiting the tardy hand of the neighbor who had rented it, and who was cutting his own grain first.

About six weeks before, she had received a letter saying, "We'll be discharged in a little while." But no other word had come from him. She had seen by the papers that his army was being discharged, and from day to day other soldiers slowly percolated in blue streams back into the State and county, but still *her* hero did not return.

Each week she had told the children that he was coming, and she had watched the road so long that it had become unconscious, and as she stood at the well, or by the kitchen door, her eyes were fixed unthinkingly on the road that wound down the coulé.

Nothing wears on the human soul like waiting. If the stranded mariner, searching the sun-bright seas, could once give up hope of a ship, that horrible grinding on his brain would cease. It was this waiting, hoping, on the edge of despair, that gave Emma Smith no rest.

Neighbors said, with kind intentions, "He's sick, maybe, an' can't start north just yet. He'll come along one o' these days."

"Why don't he write?" was her question, which silenced them all. This Sunday morning it seemed to her as if she could not stand it longer. The house seemed intolerably lonely. So she dressed the little ones in their best calico dresses and home-made jackets, and closing up the house, set off down the coule to old Mother Gray's.

"Old Widder Gray" lived at the "mouth of the coolly." She was a widow woman with a large family of stalwart boys and laughing girls. She was the visible incarnation of hospitality and optimistic poverty. With Western open-heartedness she fed every mouth that asked food of her, and worked herself to death as cheerfully as her girls danced in the neighborhood harvest dances.

She waddled down the path to meet Mrs. Smith with a broad smile on her face.

"Oh, you little dears! Come right to your granny. Gimme a kiss! Come right in, Mis' Smith. How are yeh, anyway? Nice mornin', ain't it? Come in an' set down. Everything's in a clutter, but that won't scare you any."

She led the way into the best room, a sunny, square room, carpeted with a faded and patched rag carpet, and papered with white-and-green-striped wall-paper, where a few faded effigies of dead members of the family hung in variously-sized oval walnut frames. The house resounded with singing, laughter, whistling, tramping of heavy boots, and riotous scufflings. Half-grown boys came to the door and crooked their fingers at the children, who ran out, and were soon heard in the midst of the fun.

"Don't s'pose you've heard from Ed?" Mrs. Smith shook her head. "He'll turn up some day, when you ain't lookin' for 'm." The good old soul had said that so many times that poor Mrs. Smith derived no comfort from it any longer.

"Liz heard from Al the other day. He's comin' some day this week. Anyhow, they expect him."

"Did he say anything of—"

"No, he didn't," Mrs. Gray admitted. "But then it was only a short letter, anyhow. Al ain't much for writin', anyhow.—But come out and see my new cheese. I tell yeh, I don't believe I ever had better luck in my life. If Ed should come, I want you should take him up a piece of this cheese."

It was beyond human nature to resist the influence of that noisy, hearty, loving household, and in the midst of the singing and laughing the wife forgot her anxiety, for the time at least, and laughed and sang with the rest.

About eleven o'clock a wagon-load more drove up to the door, and Bill Gray, the widow's oldest son, and his whole family, from Sand Lake Coulé, piled out amid a good-natured uproar. Every one talked at once, except Bill, who sat in the wagon with his wrists on his knees, a straw in his mouth, and an amused twinkle in his blue eyes.

"Ain't heard nothin' o' Ed, I s'pose?" he asked in a kind of bellow. Mrs. Smith shook her head. Bill, with a delicacy very striking in such a great giant, rolled his quid in his mouth, and said:

"Didn't know but you had. I heard two or three of the Sand Lake boys are comin'. Left New Orleenes some time this week. Didn't write nothin' about Ed, but no news is good news in such cases, mother always says."

"Well, go put out yer team," said Mrs. Gray, "an' go 'n bring me in some taters, an', Sim, you go see if you c'n find some corn. Sadie, you put on the water to bile. Come now, hustle yer boots, all o' yeh. If I feed this yer crowd, we've got to have some raw materials. If y' think I'm goin' to feed yeh on pie—you're jest mightily mistaken."

The children went off into the fields, the girls put dinner on to boil, and then went to change their dresses and fix their hair. "Somebody might come," they said.

"Land sakes, *I hope* not! I don't know where in time I'd set 'em, 'less they'd eat at the second table," Mrs. Gray laughed, in pre tended dismay.

The two older boys, who had served their time in the army, lay out on the grass before the house, and whittled and talked desultorily about the war and the crops, and planned buying a threshing-machine. The older girls and Mrs. Smith helped enlarge the table and put on the dishes, talking all the time in that cheery, incoherent and meaningful way a group of such women have,—a conversation to be taken for its spirit rather than for its letter, though Mrs. Gray at last got the ear of them all and dissertated at length on girls.

"Girls in love ain't no use in the whole blessed week," she said. "Sundays they're a-lookin' down the road, expectin' he'll *come.* Sunday afternoons they can't think o' nothin' else, 'cause he's *here.* Monday mornin's they're sleepy and kind o' dreamy and slimpsy, and good f'r nothin' on Tuesday and Wednesday. Thursday they git absent-minded, an' begin to look off towards Sunday agin, an' mope aroun' and let the dishwater git cold, right under their noses. Friday they break dishes, an go off in the best room an' snivel, an' look out o' the winder. Saturdays they have queer spurts o' workin' like all p'ssessed, an' spurts o' frizzin' their hair. An' Sunday they begin it all over agin."

The girls giggled and blushed all through this tirade from their mother, their broad faces and powerful frames anything but suggestive of lackadaisical sentiment. But Mrs. Smith said:

"Now, Mrs. Gray, I hadn't ought to stay to dinner. You've got—"

"Now you set right down! If any of them girls' beaus comes, they'll have to take what's left, that's all. They ain't s'posed to have much appetite, nohow. No, you're goin' to stay if they starve, an' they ain't no danger o' that."

At one o'clock the long table was piled with boiled potatoes, cords of boiled corn on the cob, squash and pumpkin pies, hot biscuit, sweet pickles, bread and butter, and honey. Then one of the girls took down a conch-shell from a nail, and going to the door, blew a long, fine, free blast, that showed there was no weakness of lungs in her ample chest.

Then the children came out of the forest of corn, out of the creek, out of the loft of the barn, and out of the garden.

"They come to their feed f'r all the world jest like the pigs when y' holler 'poo—ee!' See 'em scoot!" laughed Mrs. Gray, every wrinkle on her face shining with delight.

The men shut up their jack-knives, and surrounded the horse-trough to souse their faces in the cold, hard water, and in a few moments the table was filled with a merry crowd, and a row of wistful-eyed youngsters circled the kitchen wall, where they stood first on one leg and then on the other, in impatient hunger.

"Now pitch in, Mrs. Smith," said Mrs. Gray, presiding over the table. "You know these men critters. They'll eat every grain of it, if yeh give 'em a chance. I swan, they're made o' India-rubber, their stomachs is, I know it."

"Haf to eat to work," said Bill, gnawing a cob with a swift, circular motion that rivalled a corn-sheller in results.

"More like workin' to eat," put in one of the girls, with a giggle. "More eat 'n' work with you."

"*You* needn't say anything, Net. Any one that'll eat seven ears—"

"I didn't, no such thing. You piled your cobs on my plate."

"That'll do to tell Ed Varney. It won't go down here where we know yeh."

"Good land! Eat all yeh want! They's plenty more in the fiel's, but I can't afford to give you young uns tea. The tea is for us women-folks, and 'specially f'r Mis' Smith an' Bill's wife. We're agoin' to tell fortunes by it."

One by one the men filled up and shoved back, and one by one the children slipped into their places, and by two o'clock the women alone remained around the debris-covered table, sipping their tea and telling fortunes.

As they got well down to the grounds in the cup, they shook them with a circular motion in the hand, and then turned them bottom-side up quickly in the saucer, then twirled them three or four times one way, and three or four times the other, during a breathless pause. Then Mrs. Gray lifted the cup, and, gazing into it with profound gravity, pronounced the impending fate.

It must be admitted that, to a critical observer, she had abundant preparation for hitting close to the mark, as when she told the girls that "somebody was comin'." "It's a man," she went on gravely. "He is cross-eyed—"

"Oh, you hush!" cried Nettie.

"He has red hair, and is death on b'iled corn and hot biscuit."

The others shrieked with delight.

"But he's goin' to get the mitten, that red-headed feller is, for I see another feller comin' up behind him."

"Oh, lemme see, lemme see!" cried Nettie.

"Keep off," said the priestess, with a lofty gesture. "His hair is black. He don't eat so much, and he works more."

The girls exploded in a shriek of laughter, and pounded their sister on the back.

At last came Mrs. Smith's turn, and she was trembling with excitement as Mrs. Gray again composed her jolly face to what she considered a proper solemnity of expression.

"Somebody is comin' to *you*," she said, after a long pause. "He's got a musket on his back. He's a soldier. He's almost here. See?"

She pointed at two little tea-stems, which really formed a faint suggestion of a man with a musket on his back. He had climbed nearly to the edge of the cup. Mrs. Smith grew pale with excitement. She trembled so she could hardly hold the cup in her hand as she gazed into it.

"It's Ed," cried the old woman. "He's on the way home. Heavens an' earth! There he is now!" She turned and waved her hand out toward the road. They rushed to the door and looked where she pointed.

A man in a blue coat, with a musket on his back, was toiling slowly up the hill on the sun-bright, dusty road, toiling slowly, with bent head half hidden by a heavy knapsack. So tired it seemed that walking was indeed a process of falling. So eager to get home he would not stop, would not look aside, but plodded on, amid the cries of the locusts, the welcome of the crickets, and the rustle of the yellow wheat. Getting back to God's country, and his wife and babies!

Laughing, crying, trying to call him and the children at the same time, the little wife, almost hysterical, snatched her hat and ran out into the yard. But the soldier had disappeared over the hill into the hollow beyond, and, by the time she had found the children, he was too far away for her voice to reach him. And, besides, she was not sure it was her husband, for he had not turned his head at their shouts. This seemed so strange. Why didn't he stop to rest at his old neighbor's house? Tortured by hope and doubt, she hurried up the coulé as fast as she could push the baby wagon, the blue-coated figure just ahead pushing steadily, silently forward up the coulé.

When the excited, panting little group came in sight of the gate they saw the blue-coated figure standing, leaning upon the rough rail fence, his chin on his palms, gazing at the empty house. His knapsack, canteen, blankets, and musket lay upon the dusty grass at his feet.

He was like a man lost in a dream. His wide, hungry eyes devoured the scene. The rough lawn, the little unpainted house, the field of clear yellow wheat behind it, down across which streamed the sun, now almost ready to touch the high hill to the west, the crickets crying merrily, a cat on the fence near by, dreaming, unmindful of the stranger in blue—

How peaceful it all was. O God! How far removed from all camps, hospitals, battle lines. A little cabin in a Wisconsin coulé, but it was majestic in its peace. How did he ever leave it for those years of tramping, thirsting, killing?

Trembling, weak with emotion, her eyes on the silent figure, Mrs. Smith hurried up to the fence. Her feet made no noise in the dust and grass, and they were close upon him before he knew of them. The oldest boy ran a little ahead. He will never forget that figure, that face. It will always remain as something epic, that return of the private. He fixed his eyes on the pale face covered with a ragged beard.

"Who *are* you, sir?" asked the wife, or, rather, started to ask, for he turned, stood a moment, and then cried:

"Emma!"

"Edward!"

The children stood in a curious row to see their mother kiss this bearded, strange man, the elder girl sobbing sympathetically with her mother. Illness had left the soldier partly deaf, and this added to the strangeness of his manner.

But the youngest child stood away, even after the girl had recognized her father and kissed him. The man turned then to the baby, and said in a curiously unpaternal tone:

"Come here, my little man; don't you know me?" But the baby backed away under the fence and stood peering at him critically.

"My little man!" What meaning in those words! This baby seemed like some other woman's child, and not the infant he had left in his wife's arms. The war had come between him and his baby—he was only a strange man to him, with big eyes; a soldier, with mother hanging to his arm, and talking in a loud voice.

"And this is Tom," the private said, drawing the oldest boy to him. "*He'll* come and see me. *He* knows his poor old pap when he comes home from the war."

The mother heard the pain and reproach in his voice and hastened to apologize.

"You've changed so, Ed. He can't know yeh. This is papa, Teddy; come and kiss him—Tom and Mary do. Come, won't you?" But Teddy still peered through the fence with solemn eyes, well out of reach. He resembled a half-wild kitten that hesitates, studying the tones of one's voice.

"I'll fix him," said the soldier, and sat down to undo his knapsack, out of which he drew three enormous and very red apples. After giving one to each of the older children he said:

"*Now* I guess he'll come. Eh, my little man? Now come see your pap."

Teddy crept slowly under the fence, assisted by the over-zealous Tommy, and a moment later was kicking and squalling in his father's arms. Then they entered the house, into the sitting-room, poor, bare, art-forsaken little room, too, with its rag carpet, its square clock, and its two or three chromos and pictures from *Harper's Weekly* pinned about.

"Emma, I'm all tired out," said Private Smith, as he flung himself down on the carpet as he used to do, while his wife brought a pillow to put under his head, and the children stood about munching their apples.

"Tommy, you run and get me a pan of chips, and Mary, you get the tea-kettle on, and I'll go and make some biscuit."

And the soldier talked. Question after question he poured forth about the crops, the cattle, the renter, the neighbors. He slipped his heavy government brogan shoes off his poor, tired, blistered feet, and lay out with utter, sweet relaxation. He was a free man again, no longer a soldier under command. At supper he stopped once, listened and smiled. "That's old Spot. I know her voice. I s'pose that's her calf out there in the pen. I can't milk her to-night, though. I'm too tired. But I tell you, I'd like a drink o' her milk. What's become of old Rove?"

"He died last winter. Poisoned, I guess." There was a moment of sadness for them all. It was some time before the husband spoke again, in a voice that trembled a little.

"Poor old feller! He'd 'a' known me a half a mile away. I expected him to come down the hill to meet me. It 'ud 'a' been more like comin' home if I could 'a' seen him comin' down the road an' waggin' his tail, an' laughin' that way he has. I tell yeh, it kind o' took hold o' me to see the blinds down an' the house shut up."

"But, yeh see, we—we expected you'd write again 'fore you started. And then we thought we'd see you if you *did* come," she hastened to explain.

"Well, I ain't worth a cent on writin'. Besides, it's just as well yeh didn't know when I was comin'. I tell you, it sounds good to hear them chickens out there, an' turkeys an' the crickets. Do you

know they don't have just the same kind o' crickets down south?
Who's Sam hired t' help cut yer grain?"

"The Ramsey boys."

"Looks like a good crop; but I'm afraid I won't do much gettin'
it cut. This cussed fever an' ague has got me down pretty low. I
don't know when I'll get rid of it. I'll bet I've took twenty-five
pounds of quinine if I've taken a bit. Gimme another biscuit. I tell
yeh, they taste good, Emma. I ain't had anything like it— Say, if
you'd 'a' hear'd me braggin' to th' boys about your butter 'n' biscuits
I'll bet your ears 'ud 'a' burnt."

The private's wife colored with pleasure. "Oh, you're always
a-braggin' about your things. Everybody makes good butter."

"Yes; old lady Snyder, for instance."

"Oh, well, she ain't to be mentioned. She's Dutch."

"Or old Mis' Snively. One more cup o' tea, Mary. That's my
girl! I'm feeling better already. I just b'lieve the matter with me is,
I'm *starved*."

This was a delicious hour, one long to be remembered. They were
like lovers again. But their tenderness, like that of a typical American family, found utterance in tones, rather than in words. He was
praising her when praising her biscuit, and she knew it. They grew
soberer when he showed where he had been struck, one ball burning
the back of his hand, one cutting away a lock of hair from his temple, and one passing through the calf of his leg. The wife shuddered
to think how near she had come to being a soldier's widow. Her
waiting no longer seemed hard. This sweet, glorious hour effaced
it all.

Then they rose, and all went out into the garden and down to the
barn. He stood beside her while she milked old Spot. They began to
plan fields and crops for next year.

His farm was weedy and encumbered, a rascally renter had run
away with his machinery (departing between two days), his children
needed clothing, the years were coming upon him, he was sick and
emaciated, but his heroic soul did not quail. With the same courage
with which he had faced his Southern march he entered upon a still
more hazardous future.

Oh, that mystic hour! The pale man with big eyes standing there
by the well, with his young wife by his side. The vast moon swinging
above the eastern peaks, the cattle winding down the pasture slopes
with jangling bells, the crickets singing, the stars blooming out
sweet and far and serene; the katydids rhythmetically calling, the
little turkeys crying querulously, as they settled to roost in the poplar
tree near the open gate. The voices at the well drop lower, the little
ones nestle in their father's arms at last, and Teddy falls asleep there.

The common soldier of the American volunteer army had returned. His war with the South was over, and his fight, his daily running fight with nature and against the injustice of his fellow-men, was begun again.

1890, 1891

STEPHEN CRANE

(1871–1900)

Among the *avant-garde* writers of the 1890's, Crane was most clearly the herald of the twentieth-century revolution in literature. Had he written *Maggie: A Girl of the Streets* (1893) or *The Red Badge of Courage* (1895) twenty-five years later, he would still have been as much a pioneer as Sherwood Anderson then was. Even more than Garland, Norris, Dreiser, or Robinson—his contemporaries—he made a clean break with the past in his selection of material, his craftsmanship, and his point of view. It was his nature to be experimental. At twenty he wrote *Maggie*, our first completely naturalistic novel. By the age of twenty-four he had produced, in his earliest short stories and his masterpiece, *The Red Badge of Courage*, the first examples of modern American impressionism. That year, in his collected poems, he was the first to respond to the radical genius of Emily Dickinson, and the result was a volume of imagist impressionism twenty years in advance of the official imagists. He was in every respect phenomenal. At twenty-two, a failure in newspaper reporting, he was living from hand to mouth and borrowing money to have *Maggie* printed; at twenty-four he was the author of a classic that was then, and still is, a best seller; at twenty-five he was a star feature writer for a great syndicate; and before he reached his twenty-ninth birthday he was dead, leaving writings that filled twelve volumes in a collected edition.

The fourteenth and youngest child of a Methodist minister, Stephen Crane was born on November 1, 1871, in Newark, New Jersey. During his first ten years the family lived in Jersey City, Bloomington, and Paterson, New Jersey and finally in Port Jervis, New York, giving him the experience of small-city and small-town life which he utilized in his *Whilomville Stories*. In 1880 his father died, and after several removals the family settled in 1882 at Asbury Park, a New Jersey resort town. There an older brother, Townley Crane, ran a news-reporting agency, and gave Stephen Crane his first newspaper experience, as a reporter of vacation news. He attended school at nearby Pennington Academy and later at the Hudson River Institute, a military academy at Claverock, New York. His abilities were then chiefly observable on the baseball diamond, and his apprenticeship on small-town sand lots and at preparatory school led, in college, to brief athletic distinction. After a term each at Lafayette and at Syracuse (1890–1891) he brought his college days to an end, and relieved his family of a financial burden that they could not sustain.

Crane was apparently a born writer, and he turned to newspaper work as the natural and expedient means to earn a living. While in college he had sold sketches to the Detroit *Free Press* and during the summers he had written news for his brother. However, in the three years from 1892 until the publication of *The Red Badge of Courage* he experienced professional difficulty and economic hardship. He was simply not adapted to doing the factual reporting of routine assignments then required of the cub newsman. While still in college, during "two days before Christmas," 1891, he had written the first draft of *Maggie*, but newspaper reporting was something else. Editors were not impressed by news stories in which sense impressions and atmospheric touches triumphed over factual detail. He was reduced to hack writing "on space," placing feature stories individually wherever he could, principally in the New York *Tribune*. In this free-lance experience he came to know the mean streets and the poverty-ridden slums of New York and the adjacent New Jersey cities; indeed, himself very poor, he lived for several years in such places. He had not found a pub-

lisher for *Maggie*, now rewritten, and in 1893 he borrowed seven hundred dollars from his brother and paid for a private printing. In yellow paper wrappers, under the pseudonym of "Johnston Smith" it appeared that year as *Maggie: A Girl of the Streets*, and it did not sell. But it was noticed by Hamlin Garland, who became the friend of the younger man, helped him to find markets for his sketches, and called the attention of Howells to the serial publication of *The Red Badge of Courage* in 1894. *Maggie* was regularly published in 1896. Crane's professional worries were over, for his high abilities as a feature writer and special correspondent needed only initial recognition to secure him a position in journalism.

Crane's first two novels, and the short stories that he was already writing, were faithful to an expressed creed which, if it came more directly from good journalism than from close study of the European naturalists, produced much the same results in practice. He was convinced that if a story is transcribed in its actuality, as it appeared to occur in life, it will convey its own emotional weight without sentimental heightening, moralizing, or even interpretive comment. This view coincided with what he knew of the objective method by which the French naturalists achieved a correspondence between their style and their materials; and he was initially in agreement with the naturalistic belief that the destiny of human beings, like the biological fate of other creatures, is so much determined by factors beyond the control of individual will or choice that ethical judgment or moral comment by the author is irrelevant or impertinent. His example, however, found little response until the next century, when Dreiser and Sherwood Anderson, Hemingway, Dos Passos, and many others were illustrating the same viewpoint.

Maggie is not a great book, but its terrifying picture of brutality and degradation in the New York slums was unique for its time. *The Red Badge of Courage* employs the same technique to show the actualities of war, in this case, the Battle of Chancellorsville. Written by a man who had had no battle experience but whose imagination quickly absorbed the tales of Civil War veterans and the dramatic reality of Matthew Brady's photographs of combat, the story has continued to convince veterans of two world wars. First appearing in the Philadelphia *Press* in 1894, the following year, with the help of Howells, it was published in book form and was immediately successful. Crane's subsequent experience reporting the Spanish-American and Graeco-Turkish wars for American and British newspapers resulted in such fine volumes as *The Little Regiment* (1896), *The Open Boat and other Tales of Adventure* (1898), and *Wounds in the Rain: War Stories* (1900). His tour of the West and Mexico in 1895 resulted in such famous western stories as "The Blue Hotel" and "The Bride Comes to Yellow Sky." His other major volumes include *George's Mother* (1896), *The Monster and Other Stories* (1899), *Whilomville Stories* (1900)— the last two being collections of short stories—and his poems: *The Black Riders and Other Lines* (1895), and *War is Kind* (1899).

Threatened with tuberculosis, he settled for a time in England, where he became the friend of Conrad, James, Barrie, Wells, and others, but his ill health demanded further seclusion and he went to Germany, where he died at Badenweiler on June 5, 1900.

The standard editions—*The Works of Stephen Crane*, 12 vols., 1925–1927, and *The Collected Poems of Stephen Crane*, 1930, both edited by Wilson Follett— are now out of print. Robert W. Stallman has edited *Stephen Crane: An Omnibus*, 1952. *The Sullivan County Sketches of Stephen Crane* was edited by Melvin Schoberlin, 1949, and *Stephen Crane Letters*, 1960, were edited by R. W. Stallman and Lillian Gilkes. Biographies are Thomas Beer, *Stephen Crane: A Study in American Letters*, 1923, and John Berryman, *Stephen Crane*, 1950. E. H. Cady edited C. K. Linson's reminiscences, *My Stephen Crane*, 1958. Daniel G. Hoffman gives a critical evaluation in *The Poetry of Stephen Crane*, 1957. A. W. Williams and Vincent Starrett edited *Stephen Crane: A Bibliography*, 1948.

A God in Wrath[1]

A god in wrath
Was beating a man;
He cuffed him loudly
With thunderous blows
That rang and rolled over the earth.   5
All people came running.
The man screamed and struggled,
And bit madly at the feet of the god.
The people cried,
"Ah, what a wicked man!"   10
And—
"Ah, what a redoubtable god!"

1895

Once I Saw Mountains Angry

Once I saw mountains angry,
And ranged in battle-front.
Against them stood a little man;
Ay, he was no bigger than my finger.
I laughed, and spoke to one near me,   5
"Will he prevail?"
"Surely," replied this other;
"His grandfathers beat them many times."
Then did I see much virtue in grandfathers—
At least, for the little man   10
Who stood against the mountains.

1895

A Man Saw a Ball of Gold in the Sky

A man saw a ball of gold in the sky;
He climbed for it,
And eventually he achieved it—
It was clay.

---

1. This poem, together with the three that follow, appeared in Crane's first book of verse, *The Black Riders and Other Lines* (1895). Since Crane did not give titles to any of his poems, the titles here have been added by the present editors.

Now this is the strange part: 5
When the man went to the earth
And looked again,
Lo, there was the ball of gold.
Now this is the strange part:
It was a ball of gold.   10
Ay, by the heavens, it was a ball of gold.

1895

God Lay Dead in Heaven

God lay dead in heaven;
Angels sang the hymn of the end;
Purple winds went moaning,
Their wings drip-dripping
With blood   5
That fell upon the earth.
It, groaning thing,
Turned black and sank.
Then from the far caverns
Of dead sins   10
Came monsters, livid with desire.
They fought,
Wrangled over the world,
A morsel.
But of all sadness this was sad—   15
A woman's arms tried to shield
The head of a sleeping man
From the jaws of the final beast.

1895

Do Not Weep, Maiden, For War Is Kind[2]

Do not weep, maiden, for war is kind.
Because your lover threw wild hands toward the sky
And the affrighted steed ran on alone,
Do not weep.
War is kind.   5

2. This poem and the three following ones were collected in *War Is Kind* (1899). The titles have been added by the present editors.

Hoarse, booming drums of the regiment,
Little souls who thirst for fight,
These men were born to drill and die.
The unexplained glory flies above them,
Great is the battle-god, great, and his kingdom—   10
A field where a thousand corpses lie.

Do not weep, babe, for war is kind.
Because your father tumbled in the yellow trenches,
Raged at his breast, gulped and died,
Do not weep.   15
War is kind.

Swift blazing flag of the regiment,
Eagle with crest of red and gold,
These men were born to drill and die.
Point for them the virtue of slaughter,   20
Make plain to them the excellence of killing
And a field where a thousand corpses lie.

Mother whose heart hung humble as a button
On the bright splendid shroud of your son,
Do not weep.   25
War is kind.

1895   1896, 1899

The Wayfarer

The wayfarer,
Perceiving the pathway to truth,
Was struck with astonishment.
It was thickly grown with weeds.
"Ha," he said,   5
"I see that none has passed here
In a long time."
Later he saw that each weed
Was a singular knife.
"Well," he mumbled at last,   10
"Doubtless there are other roads."

1899

A Man Said to the Universe

A man said to the universe:
"Sir, I exist!"
"However," replied the universe,
"The fact has not created in me
A sense of obligation."   5

1899

The Trees in the Garden Rained Flowers

The trees in the garden rained flowers.
Children ran there joyously.
They gathered the flowers
Each to himself.
Now there were some   5
Who gathered great heaps—
Having opportunity and skill—
Until, behold, only chance blossoms
Remained for the feeble.
Then a little spindling tutor   10
Ran importantly to the father, crying:
"Pray, come hither!
See this unjust thing in your garden!"
But when the father had surveyed,
He admonished the tutor: 15
"Not so, small sage!
This thing is just.
For, look you,
Are not they who possess the flowers
Stronger, bolder, shrewder   20
Than they who have none?
Why should the strong—
The beautiful strong—
Why should they not have the flowers?"
Upon reflection, the tutor bowed to the ground, 25
"My lord," he said,
"The stars are displaced
By this towering wisdom."

1899

The Blue Hotel[1]

I

The Palace Hotel at Fort Romper was painted a light blue, a shade that is on the legs of a kind of heron, causing the bird to declare its position against any background. The Palace Hotel, then, was always screaming and howling in a way that made the dazzling winter landscape of Nebraska seem only a gray swampish hush. It stood alone on the prairie, and when the snow was falling the town two hundred yards away was not visible. But when the traveller alighted at the railway station he was obliged to pass the Palace Hotel before he could come upon the company of low clapboard houses which composed Fort Romper, and it was not to be thought that any traveller could pass the Palace Hotel without looking at it. Pat Scully, the proprietor, had proved himself a master of strategy when he chose his paints. It is true that on clear days, when the great transcontinental expresses, long lines of swaying Pullmans, swept through Fort Romper, passengers were overcome at the sight, and the cult that knows the brown-reds and the subdivisions of the dark greens of the East expressed shame, pity, horror, in a laugh. But to the citizens of this prairie town and to the people who would naturally stop there, Pat Scully had performed a feat. With this opulence and splendor, these creeds, classes, egotisms, that streamed through Romper on the rails day after day, they had no color in common.

As if the display delights of such a blue hotel were not sufficiently enticing, it was Scully's habit to go every morning and evening to meet the leisurely trains that stopped at Romper and work his seductions upon any man that he might see wavering, gripsack in hand.

One morning, when a snow-crusted engine dragged its long string of freight cars and its one passenger coach to the station, Scully performed the marvel of catching three men. One was a shaky and quick-eyed Swede, with a great shining cheap valise; one was a tall bronzed cowboy, who was on his way to a ranch near the Dakota line; one was a little silent man from the East, who didn't look it, and didn't announce it. Scully practically made them prisoners. He was so nimble and merry and kindly that each probably felt it would be the height of brutality to try to escape. They trudged off over the creaking board sidewalks in the wake of the eager little Irishman. He wore a heavy fur cap squeezed tightly down on his head. It caused his two red ears to stick out stiffly, as if they were

1. First published in *Collier's Weekly* for November 26, 1898, and December 3, 1898, and then collected in *The Mon-* *ster and Other Stories* (1899), and included in *Stephen Crane: an Omnibus,* edited by Robert Stallman.

made of tin.

At last, Scully, elaborately, with boisterous hospitality, conducted them through the portals of the blue hotel. The room which they entered was small. It seemed to be merely a proper temple for an enormous stove, which, in the center, was humming with godlike violence. At various points on its surface the iron had become luminous and glowed yellow from the heat. Beside the stove Scully's son Johnnie was playing High-Five[2] with an old farmer who had whiskers both gray and sandy. They were quarrelling. Frequently the old farmer turned his face toward a box of sawdust—colored brown from tobacco juice—that was behind the stove, and spat with an air of great impatience and irritation. With a loud flourish of words Scully destroyed the game of cards, and bustled his son up-stairs with part of the baggage of the new guests. He himself conducted them to three basins of the coldest water in the world. The cowboy and the Easterner burnished themselves fiery red with this water, until it seemed to be some kind of metal polish. The Swede, however, merely dipped his fingers gingerly and with trepidation. It was notable that throughout this series of small ceremonies the three travellers were made to feel that Scully was very benevolent. He was conferring great favors upon them. He handed the towel from one to another with an air of philanthropic impulse.

Afterward they went to the first room, and, sitting about the stove, listened to Scully's officious clamor at his daughters, who were preparing the midday meal. They reflected in the silence of experienced men who tread carefully amid new people. Nevertheless, the old farmer, stationary, invincible in his chair near the warmest part of the stove, turned his face from the sawdust-box frequently and addressed a glowing commonplace to the strangers. Usually he was answered in short but adequate sentences by either the cowboy or the Easterner. The Swede said nothing. He seemed to be occupied in making furtive estimates of each man in the room. One might have thought that he had the sense of silly suspicion which comes to guilt. He resembled a badly frightened man.

Later, at dinner, he spoke a little, addressing his conversation entirely to Scully. He volunteered that he had come from New York, where for ten years he had worked as a tailor. These facts seemed to strike Scully as fascinating, and afterward he volunteered that he had lived at Romper for fourteen years. The Swede asked about the crops and the price of labor. He seemed barely to listen to Scully's extended replies. His eyes continued to rove from man to man.

Finally, with a laugh and a wink, he said that some of these

---

2. A card game popular in the nineties throughout the country, called "cinch" or "double pedro" in the far West.

Western communities were very dangerous; and after his statement he straightened his legs under the table, tilted his head, and laughed again, loudly. It was plain that the demonstration had no meaning to the others. They looked at him wondering and in silence.

II

As the men trooped heavily back into the front room, the two little windows presented views of a turmoiling sea of snow. The huge arms of the wind were making attempts—mighty, circular, futile—to embrace the flakes as they sped. A gate-post like a still man with a blanched face stood aghast amid this profligate fury. In a hearty voice Scully announced the presence of a blizzard. The guests of the blue hotel, lighting their pipes assented with grunts of lazy masculine contentment. No island of the sea could be exempt in the degree of this little room with its humming stove. Johnnie, son of Scully, in a tone which defined his opinion of his ability as a card-player, challenged the old farmer of both gray and sandy whiskers to a game of High-Five. The farmer agreed with a contemptuous and bitter scoff. They sat close to the stove, and squared their knees under a wide board. The cowboy and the Easterner watched the game with interest. The Swede remained near the window, aloof, but with a countenance that showed signs of an inexplicable excitement.

The play of Johnnie and the gray-beard was suddenly ended by another quarrel. The old man arose while casting a look of heated scorn at his adversary. He slowly buttoned his coat, and then stalked with fabulous dignity from the room. In the discreet silence of all the other men the Swede laughed. His laughter rang somehow childish. Men by this time had begun to look at him askance, as if they wished to inquire what ailed him.

A new game was formed jocosely. The cowboy volunteered to become the partner of Johnnie, and they all then turned to ask the Swede to throw in his lot with the little Easterner. He asked some questions about the game, and, learning that it wore many names, and that he had played it when it was under an alias, he accepted the invitation. He strode toward the men nervously, as if he expected to be assaulted. Finally, seated, he gazed from face to face and laughed shrilly. This laugh was so strange that the Easterner looked up quickly, the cowboy sat intent and with his mouth open, and Johnnie paused, holding the cards with still fingers.

Afterward there was a short silence. Then Johnnie said, "Well, let's get at it. Come on now!" They pulled their chairs forward until their knees were bunched under the board. They began to play, and their interest in the game caused the others to forget the manner of the Swede.

The cowboy was a board-whacker. Each time that he held superior cards he whanged them, one by one, with exceeding force, down upon the improvised table, and took the tricks with a glowing air of prowess and pride that sent thrills of indignation into the hearts of his opponents. A game with a board-whacker in it is sure to become intense. The countenances of the Easterner and the Swede were miserable whenever the cowboy thundered down his aces and kings, while Johnnie, his eyes gleaming with joy, chuckled and chuckled.

Because of the absorbing play none considered the strange ways of the Swede. They paid strict heed to the game. Finally, during a lull caused by a new deal, the Swede suddenly addressed Johnnie: "I suppose there have been a good many men killed in this room." The jaws of the others dropped and they looked at him.

"What in hell are you talking about?" said Johnnie.

The Swede laughed again his blatant laugh, full of a kind of false courage and defiance. "Oh, you know what I mean all right," he answered.

"I'm a liar if I do!" Johnnie protested. The card was halted, and the men stared at the Swede. Johnnie evidently felt that as the son of the proprietor he should make a direct inquiry. "Now, what might you be drivin' at, mister?" he asked. The Swede winked at him. It was a wink full of cunning. His fingers shook on the edge of the board. "Oh, maybe you think I have been to nowheres. Maybe you think I'm a tenderfoot?"

"I don't know nothin' about you," answered Johnnie, "and I don't give a damn where you've been. All I got to say is that I don't know what you're driving at. There hain't never been nobody killed in this room."

The cowboy, who had been steadily gazing at the Swede, then spoke: "What's wrong with you, mister?"

Apparently it seemed to the Swede that he was formidably menaced. He shivered and turned white near the corners of his mouth. He sent an appealing glance in the direction of the little Easterner. During these moments he did not forget to wear his air of advanced pot-valor.[3] "They say they don't know what I mean," he remarked mockingly to the Easterner.

The latter answered after prolonged and cautious reflection. "I don't understand you," he said, impassively.

The Swede made a movement then which announced that he thought he had encountered treachery from the only quarter where he had expected sympathy, if not help. "Oh, I see you are all against me. I see—"

The cowboy was in a state of deep stupefaction. "Say," he cried, as he tumbled the deck violently down upon the board, "say, what

3. "Pot-valiant" meant "brave only when drunk."

are you gittin' at, hey?"

The Swede sprang up with the celerity of a man escaping from a snake on the floor. "I don't want to fight!" he shouted. "I don't want to fight!"

The cowboy stretched his long legs indolently and deliberately. His hands were in his pockets. He spat into the sawdust-box. "Well, who the hell thought you did?" he inquired.

The Swede backed rapidly toward a corner of the room. His hands were out protectingly in front of his chest, but he was making an obvious struggle to control his fright. "Gentlemen," he quavered, "I suppose I am going to be killed before I can leave this house! I suppose I am going to be killed before I can leave this house!" In his eyes was the dying-swan look. Through the windows could be seen the snow turning blue in the shadow of dusk. The wind tore at the house, and some loose thing beat regularly against the clapboards like a spirit tapping.

A door opened, and Scully himself entered. He paused in surprise as he noted the tragic attitude of the Swede. Then he said, "What's the matter here?"

The Swede answered him swiftly and eagerly: "These men are going to kill me."

"Kill you!" ejaculated Scully. "Kill you! What are you talkin'?"

The Swede made the gesture of a martyr.

Scully wheeled sternly upon his son. "What is this, Johnnie?"

The lad had grown sullen. "Damned if I know," he answered. "I can't make no sense to it." He began to shuffle the cards, fluttering them together with an angry snap. "He says a good many men have been killed in this room, or something like that. And he says he's goin' to be killed here too. I don't know what ails him. He's crazy, I shouldn't wonder."

Scully then looked for explanation to the cowboy, but the cowboy simply shrugged his shoulders.

"Kill you?" said Scully again to the Swede. "Kill you? Man, you're off your nut."

"Oh, I know," burst out the Swede. "I know what will happen. Yes, I'm crazy—yes. Yes, of course, I'm crazy—yes. But I know one thing—" There was a sort of sweat of misery and terror upon his face. "I know I won't get out of here alive."

The cowboy drew a deep breath, as if his mind was passing into the last stages of dissolution. "Well, I'm doggoned," he whispered to himself.

Scully wheeled suddenly and faced his son. "You've been troublin' this man!"

Johnnie's voice was loud with its burden of grievance. "Why, good Gawd, I ain't done nothin' to 'im."

The Swede broke in. "Gentlemen, do not disturb yourselves. I will leave this house. I will go away, because"—he accused them dramatically with his glance—"because I do not want to be killed."

Scully was furious with his son. "Will you tell me what is the matter, you young divil? What's the matter, anyhow? Speak out!"

"Blame it!" cried Johnnie in despair, "don't I tell you I don't know? He—he says we want to kill him, and that's all I know. I can't tell what ails him."

The Swede continued to repeat: "Never mind, Mr. Scully; never mind. I will leave this house. I will go away, because I do not wish to be killed. Yes, of course, I am crazy—yes. But I know one thing! I will go away. I will leave this house. Never mind, Mr. Scully; never mind. I will go away."

"You will not go 'way," said Scully. "You will not go 'way until I hear the reason of this business. If anybody has troubled you I will take care of him. This is my house. You are under my roof, and I will not allow any peaceable man to be troubled here." He cast a terrible eye upon Johnnie, the cowboy, and the Easterner.

"Never mind, Mr. Scully; never mind. I will go away. I do not wish to be killed." The Swede moved toward the door which opened upon the stairs. It was evidently his intention to go at once for his baggage.

"No, no," shouted Scully peremptorily; but the white-faced man slid by him and disappeared. "Now," said Scully severely, "what does this mane?"

Johnnie and the cowboy cried together: "Why, we didn't do nothin' to 'im!"

Sully's eyes were cold. "No," he said, "you didn't?"

Johnnie swore a deep oath. "Why, this is the wildest loon I ever see. We didn't do nothin' at all. We were jest sittin' here playin' cards, and he—"

The father suddenly spoke to the Easterner. "Mr. Blanc," he asked, "what has these boys been doin'?"

The Easterner reflected again. "I didn't see anything wrong at all," he said at last, slowly.

Scully began to howl. "But what does it mane?" He stared ferociously at his son. "I have a mind to lather you for this, my boy."

Johnnie was frantic. "Well, what have I done?" he bawled at his father.

III

"I think you are tongue-tied," said Scully finally to his son, the cowboy, and the Easterner; and at the end of this scornful sentence he left the room.

Upstairs the Swede was swiftly fastening the straps of his great valise. Once his back happened to be half turned toward the door, and, hearing a noise there, he wheeled and sprang up, uttering a loud cry. Scully's wrinkled visage showed grimly in the light of the small lamp he carried. This yellow effulgence, streaming upward, colored only his prominent features, and left his eyes, for instance, in mysterious shadow. He resembled a murderer.

"Man! man!" he exclaimed, "have you gone daffy?"

"Oh, no! Oh, no!" rejoined the other. "There are people in this world who know pretty nearly as much as you do—understand?"

For a moment they stood gazing at each other. Upon the Swede's deathly pale cheeks were two spots brightly crimson and sharply edged, as if they had been carefully painted. Scully placed the light on the table and sat himself on the edge of the bed. He spoke ruminatively. "By cracky, I never heard of such a thing in my life. It's a complete muddle. I can't, for the soul of me, think how you ever got this idea into your head." Presently he lifted his eyes and asked: "And did you sure think they were going to kill you?"

The Swede scanned the old man as if he wished to see into his mind. "I did," he said at last. He obviously suspected that this answer might precipitate an outbreak. As he pulled on a strap his whole arm shook, the elbow wavering like a bit of paper.

Scully banged his hand impressively on the footboard of the bed. "Why, man, we're goin' to have a line of ilictric street-cars in this town next spring."

" 'A line of electric street-cars,' " repeated the Swede, stupidly.

"And," said Scully, "there's a new railroad goin' to be built down from Broken Arm to here. Not to mintion the four churches and the smashin' big brick schoolhouse. Then there's the big factory, too. Why, in two years Romper'll be a met-tro-*pol*-is."

Having finished the preparation of his baggage, the Swede straightened himself. "Mr. Scully," he said, with sudden hardihood, "how much do I owe you?"

"You don't owe me anythin'," said the old man, angrily.

"Yes, I do," retorted the Swede. He took seventy-five cents from his pocket and tendered it to Scully; but the latter snapped his fingers in disdainful refusal. However, it happened that they both stood gazing in a strange fashion at three silver pieces on the Swede's open palm.

"I'll not take your money," said Scully at last. "Not after what's been goin' on here." Then a plan seemed to strike him. "Here," he cried, picking up his lamp and moving toward the door. "Here! Come with me a minute."

"No," said the Swede, in overwhelming alarm.

"Yes," urged the old man. "Come on! I want you to come and

see a picter—just across the hall—in my room."

The Swede must have concluded that his hour was come. His jaw dropped and his teeth showed like a dead man's. He ultimately followed Scully across the corridor, but he had the step of one hung in chains.

Scully flashed the light high on the wall of his own chamber. There was revealed a ridiculous photograph of a little girl. She was leaning against a balustrade of gorgeous decoration, and the formidable bang to her hair was prominent. The figure was as graceful as an upright sled-stake, and, withal, it was of the hue of lead. "There," said Scully, tenderly, "that's the picter of my little girl that died. Her name was Carrie. She had the purtiest hair you ever saw! I was that fond of her, she—"

Turning then, he saw that the Swede was not contemplating the picture at all, but, instead, was keeping keen watch on the gloom in the rear.

"Look, man!" cried Scully, heartily. "That's the picter of my little gal that died. Her name was Carrie. And then here's the picter of my oldest boy. Michael. He's a lawyer in Lincoln, an' doin' well. I gave that boy a grand eddication, and I'm glad for it now. He's a fine boy. Look at 'im now. Ain't he bold as blazes, him there in Lincoln, an honored an' respicted gintleman! An honored and respicted gintleman," concluded Scully with a flourish. And, so saying, he smote the Swede jovially on the back.

The Swede faintly smiled.

"Now," said the old man, "there's only one more thing." He dropped suddenly to the floor and thrust his head beneath the bed. The Swede could hear his muffled voice. "I'd keep it under me piller if it wasn't for that boy Johnnie. Then there's the old woman— Where is it now? I never put it twice in the same place. Ah, now come out with you!"

Presently he backed clumsily from under the bed, dragging with him an old coat rolled into a bundle. "I've fetched him," he muttered. Kneeling on the floor, he unrolled the coat and extracted from its heart a large yellow-brown whiskey-bottle.

His first manœuvre was to hold the bottle up to the light. Reassured, apparently, that nobody had been tampering with it, he thrust it with a generous movement toward the Swede.

The weak-kneed Swede was about to eagerly clutch this element of strength, but he suddenly jerked his hand away and cast a look of horror upon Scully.

"Drink," said the old man affectionately. He had risen to his feet, and now stood facing the Swede.

There was a silence. Then again Scully said: "Drink!"

The Swede laughed wildly. He grabbed the bottle, put it to his mouth; and as his lips curled absurdly around the opening and his throat worked, he kept his glance, burning with hatred, upon the old man's face.

IV

After the departure of Scully the three men, with the card-board still upon their knees, preserved for a long time an astounded silence. Then Johnnie said: "That's the doddangedest Swede I ever see."

"He ain't no Swede," said the cowboy, scornfully.

"Well, what is he then?" cried Johnnie. "What is he then?"

"It's my opinion," replied the cowboy deliberately, "he's some kind of a Dutchman." It was a venerable custom of the country to entitle as Swedes all light-haired men who spoke with a heavy tongue. In consequence the idea of the cowboy was not without its daring. "Yes, sir," he repeated. "It's my opinion this feller is some kind of a Dutchman."

"Well, he says he's a Swede, anyhow," muttered Johnnie, sulkily. He turned to the Easterner: "What do you think, Mr. Blanc?"

"Oh, I don't know," replied the Easterner.

"Well, what do you think makes him act that way?" asked the cowboy.

"Why, he's frightened." The Easterner knocked his pipe against a rim of the stove. "He's clear frightened out of his boots."

"What at?" cried Johnnie and the cowboy together.

The Easterner reflected over his answer.

"What at?" cried the others again.

"Oh, I don't know, but it seems to me this man has been reading dime novels, and he thinks he's right out in the middle of it—the shootin' and stabbin' and all."

"But," said the cowboy, deeply scandalized, "this ain't Wyoming, ner none of them places. This is Nebrasker."

"Yes," added Johnnie, "an' why don't he wait till he gits *out West?*"

The travelled Easterner laughed. "It isn't different there even— not in these days. But he thinks he's right in the middle of hell."

Johnnie and the cowboy mused long.

"It's awful funny," remarked Johnnie at last.

"Yes," said the cowboy. "This is a queer game. I hope we don't git snowed in, because then we'd have to stand this here man bein' around with us all the time. That wouldn't be no good."

"I wish pop would throw him out," said Johnnie.

Presently they heard a loud stamping on the stairs, accompanied by ringing jokes in the voice of old Scully, and laughter, evidently from the Swede. The men around the stove stared vacantly at each other. "Gosh!" said the cowboy. The door flew open, and old Scully, flushed and anecdotal, came into the room. He was jabbering at the Swede, who followed him, laughing bravely. It was the entry of two roisterers from a banquet hall.

"Come now," said Scully sharply to the three seated men, "move up and give us a chance at the stove." The cowboy and the Easterner obediently sidled their chairs to make room for the newcomers. Johnnie, however, simply arranged himself in a more indolent attitude, and then remained motionless.

"Come! Git over, there," said Scully.

"Plenty of room on the other side of the stove," said Johnnie.

"Do you think we want to sit in the draught?" roared the father.

But the Swede here interposed with a grandeur of confidence. "No, no. Let the boy sit where he likes," he cried in a bullying voice to the father.

"All right! All right!" said Scully, deferentially. The cowboy and the Easterner exchanged glances of wonder.

The five chairs were formed in a crescent about one side of the stove. The Swede began to talk; he talked arrogantly, profanely, angrily. Johnnie, the cowboy, and the Easterner maintained a morose silence, while old Scully appeared to be receptive and eager, breaking in constantly with sympathetic ejaculations.

Finally the Swede announced that he was thirsty. He moved in his chair, and said that he would go for a drink of water.

"I'll git it for you," cried Scully at once.

"No," said the Swede, contemptuously. "I'll get it for myself." He arose and stalked with the air of an owner off into the executive parts of the hotel.

As soon as the Swede was out of hearing Scully sprang to his feet and whispered intensely to the others: "Up-stairs he thought I was tryin' to poison 'im."

"Say," said Johnnie, "this makes me sick. Why don't you throw 'im out in the snow?"

"Why, he's all right now," declared Scully. "It was only that he was from the East, and he thought this was a tough place. That's all. He's all right now."

The cowboy looked with admiration upon the Easterner. "You were straight," he said. "You were on to that there Dutchman."

"Well," said Johnnie to his father, "he may be all right now, but I don't see it. Other time he was scared, but now he's too fresh."

Scully's speech was always a combination of Irish brogue and idiom, Western twang and idiom, and scraps of curiously formal diction taken from the story-books and newspapers. He now hurled a strange mass of language at the head of his son. "What do I keep? What do I keep? What do I keep?" he demanded, in a voice of thunder. He slapped his knee impressively, to indicate that he himself was going to make reply, and that all should heed. "I keep a hotel," he shouted. "A hotel, do you mind? A guest under my roof has sacred privileges. He is to be intimidated by none. Not one word shall he hear that would prijudice him in favor of goin' away. I'll not have it. There's no place in this here town where they can say they iver took in a guest of mine because he was afraid to stay here." He wheeled suddenly upon the cowboy and the Easterner. "Am I right?"

"Yes, Mr. Scully," said the cowboy, "I think you're right."

"Yes, Mr. Scully," said the Easterner, "I think you're right."

V

At six-o'clock supper, the Swede fizzed like a fire-wheel. He sometimes seemed on the point of bursting into riotous song, and in all his madness he was encouraged by old Scully. The Easterner was encased in reserve; the cowboy sat in wide-mouthed amazement, forgetting to eat, while Johnnie wrathily demolished great plates of food. The daughters of the house, when they were obliged to replenish the biscuits, approached as warily as Indians, and, having succeeded in their purpose, fled with ill-concealed trepidation. The Swede domineered the whole feast, and he gave it the appearance of a cruel bacchanal. He seemed to have grown suddenly taller, he gazed, brutally disdainful, into every face. His voice rang through the room. Once when he jabbed out harpoon-fashion with his fork to pinion a biscuit, the weapon nearly impaled the hand of the Easterner, which had been stretched quietly out for the same biscuit.

After supper, as the men filed toward the other room, the Swede smote Scully ruthlessly on the shoulder. "Well, old boy, that was a good, square meal." Johnnie looked hopefully at his father; he knew that shoulder was tender from an old fall; and, indeed, it appeared for a moment as if Scully was going to flame out over the matter, but in the end he smiled a sickly smile and remained silent. The others understood from his manner that he was admitting his responsibility for the Swede's new view-point.

Johnnie, however, addressed his parent in an aside. "Why don't you license somebody to kick you downstairs?" Scully scowled darkly by way of reply.

When they were gathered about the stove, the Swede insisted on another game of High-Five. Scully gently deprecated the plan at first, but the Swede turned a wolfish glare upon him. The old man subsided, and the Swede canvassed the others. In his tone there was always a great threat. The cowboy and the Easterner both remarked indifferently that they would play. Scully said that he would presently have to go to meet the 6.58 train, and so the Swede turned menacingly upon Johnnie. For a moment their glances crossed like blades, and then Johnnie smiled and said, "Yes, I'll play."

They formed a square, with the little board on their knees. The Easterner and the Swede were again partners. As the play went on, it was noticeable that the cowboy was not board-whacking as usual. Meanwhile, Scully, near the lamp, had put on his spectacles and, with an appearance curiously like an old priest, was reading a newspaper. In time he went out to meet the 6.58 train, and, despite his precautions, a gust of polar wind whirled into the room as he opened the door. Besides scattering the cards, it chilled the players to the marrow. The Swede cursed frightfully. When Scully returned, his entrance disturbed a cosy and friendly scene. The Swede again cursed. But presently they were once more intent, their heads bent forward and their hands moving swiftly. The Swede had adopted the fashion of board-whacking.

Scully took up his paper and for a long time remained immersed in matters which were extraordinarily remote from him. The lamp burned badly, and once he stopped to adjust the wick. The newspaper, as he turned from page to page, rustled with a slow and comfortable sound. Then suddenly he heard three terrible words: "You are cheatin'!"

Such scenes often prove that there can be little of dramatic import in environment. Any room can present a tragic front; any room can be comic. This little den was now hideous as a torture-chamber. The new faces of the men themselves had changed it upon the instant. The Swede held a huge fist in front of Johnnie's face, while the latter looked steadily over it into the blazing orbs of his accuser. The Easterner had grown pallid; the cowboy's jaw had dropped in that expression of bovine amazement which was one of his important mannerisms. After the three words, the first sound in the room was made by Scully's paper as it floated forgotten to his feet. His spectacles had also fallen from his nose, but by a clutch he had saved them in air. His hand, grasping the spectacles, now remained poised awkwardly and near his shoulder. He stared at the card-players.

Probably the silence was while a second elapsed. Then, if the floor had been suddenly twitched out from under the men they could not have moved quicker. The five had projected themselves headlong toward a common point. It happened that Johnnie, in rising to hurl himself upon the Swede, had stumbled slightly because of his curiously instinctive care for the cards and the board. The loss of the moment allowed time for the arrival of Scully, and also allowed the cowboy time to give the Swede a great push which sent him staggering back. The men found tongue together, and hoarse shouts of rage, appeal, or fear burst from every throat. The cowboy pushed and jostled feverishly at the Swede, and the Easterner and Scully clung wildly to Johnnie; but through the smoky air, above the swaying bodies of the peace-compellers, the eyes of the two warriors ever sought each other in glances of challenge that were at once hot and steely.

Of course the board had been overturned, and now the whole company of cards was scattered over the floor, where the boots of the men trampled the fat and painted kings and queens as they gazed with their silly eyes at the war that was waging above them.

Scully's voice was dominating the yells. "Stop now! Stop, I say! Stop, now—"

Johnnie, as he struggled to burst through the rank formed by Scully and the Easterner, was crying, "Well, he says I cheated! He says I cheated! I won't allow no man to say I cheated! If he says I cheated, he's a —— ——!"

The cowboy was telling the Swede, "Quit, now! Quit, d'ye hear—"

The screams of the Swede never ceased: "He did cheat! I saw him! I saw him—"

As for the Easterner, he was importuning in a voice that was not heeded: "Wait a moment, can't you? Oh, wait a moment. What's the good of a fight over a game of cards? Wait a moment—"

In this tumult no complete sentences were clear. "Cheat"—"Quit"—"He says"—these fragments pierced the uproar and rang out sharply. It was remarkable that, whereas Scully undoubtedly made the most noise, he was the least heard of any of the riotous band.

Then suddenly there was a great cessation. It was as if each man had paused for breath; and although the room was still lighted with the anger of men, it could be seen that there was no danger of immediate conflict, and at once Johnnie, shouldering his way forward, almost succeeded in confronting the Swede. "What did you say I cheated for? What did you say I cheated for? I don't cheat, and I won't let no man say I do!"

The Swede said, "I saw you! I saw you!"

"Well," cried Johnnie, "I'll fight any man what says I cheat!"

"No, you won't," said the cowboy. "Not here."

"Ah, be still, can't you?" said Scully, coming between them.

The quiet was sufficient to allow the Easterner's voice to be heard. He was repeating, "Oh, wait a moment, can't you? What's the good of a fight over a game of cards? Wait a moment!"

Johnnie, his red face appearing above his father's shoulder, hailed the Swede again. "Did you say I cheated?"

The Swede showed his teeth. "Yes."

"Then," said Johnnie, "we must fight."

"Yes, fight," roared the Swede. He was like a demoniac. "Yes, fight! I'll show you what kind of a man I am! I'll show you who you want to fight! Maybe you think I can't fight! Maybe you think I can't! I'll show you, you skin, you card-sharp! Yes, you cheated! You cheated! You cheated!"

"Well, let's go at it, then, mister," said Johnnie, coolly.

The cowboy's brow was beaded with sweat from his efforts in intercepting all sorts of raids. He turned in despair to Scully. "What are you goin' to do now?"

A change had come over the Celtic visage of the old man. He now seemed all eagerness; his eyes glowed.

"We'll let them fight," he answered, stalwartly. "I can't put up with it any longer. I've stood this damned Swede till I'm sick. We'll let them fight."

VI

The men prepared to go out-of-doors. The Easterner was so nervous that he had great difficulty in getting his arms into the sleeves of his new leather coat. As the cowboy drew his fur cap down over his ears his hands trembled. In fact, Johnnie and old Scully were the only ones who displayed no agitation. These preliminaries were conducted without words.

Scully threw open the door. "Well, come on," he said. Instantly a terrific wind caused the flame of the lamp to struggle at its wick, while a puff of black smoke sprang from the chimney-top. The stove was in mid-current of the blast, and its voice swelled to equal the roar of the storm. Some of the scarred and bedabbled cards were caught up from the floor and dashed helplessly against the farther wall. The men lowered their heads and plunged into the tempest as into a sea.

No snow was falling, but great whirls and clouds of flakes, swept up from the ground by the frantic winds, were streaming southward with the speed of bullets. The covered land was blue with the sheen of an unearthly satin, and there was no other hue save where, at the low, black railway station—which seemed incredibly distant—one light gleamed like a tiny jewel. As the men floundered into a thigh-deep drift, it was known that the Swede was bawling out something. Scully went to him, put a hand on his shoulder, and projected an ear. "What's that you say?" he shouted.

"I say," bawled the Swede again, "I won't stand much show against this gang. I know you'll all pitch on me."

Scully smote him reproachfully on the arm. "Tut, man!" he yelled. The wind tore the words from Scully's lips and scattered them far alee.

"You are all a gang of—" boomed the Swede, but the storm also seized the remainder of this sentence.

Immediately turning their backs upon the wind, the men had

swung around a corner to the sheltered side of the hotel. It was the function of the little house to preserve here, amid this great devastation of snow, an irregular V-shape of heavily encrusted grass, which crackled beneath the feet. One could imagine the great drifts piled against the windward side. When the party reached the comparative peace of this spot it was found that the Swede was still bellowing.

"Oh, I know what kind of a thing this is! I know you'll all pitch on me. I can't lick you all!"

Scully turned upon him panther-fashion. "You'll not have to whip all of us. You'll have to whip my son Johnnie. An' the man what troubles you durin' that time will have me to dale with."

The arrangements were swiftly made. The two men faced each other, obedient to the harsh commands of Scully, whose face, in the subtly luminous gloom, could be seen set in the austere impersonal lines that are pictured on the countenances of the Roman veterans. The Easterner's teeth were chattering, and he was hopping up and down like a mechanical toy. The cowboy stood rock-like.

The contestants had not stripped off any clothing. Each was in his ordinary attire. Their fists were up, and they eyed each other in a calm that had the elements of leonine cruelty in it.

During this pause, the Easterner's mind, like a film, took lasting impressions of three men—the iron-nerved master of the ceremony; the Swede, pale, motionless, terrible; and Johnnie, serene yet ferocious, brutish yet heroic. The entire prelude had in it a tragedy greater than the tragedy of action, and this aspect was accentuated by the long, mellow cry of the blizzard, as it sped the tumbling and wailing flakes into the black abyss of the south.

"Now!" said Scully.

The two combatants leaped forward and crashed together like bullocks. There was heard the cushioned sound of blows, and of a curse squeezing out from between the tight teeth of one.

As for the spectators, the Easterner's pent-up breath exploded from him with a pop of relief, absolute relief from the tension of the preliminaries. The cowboy bounded into the air with a yowl. Scully was immovable as from supreme amazement and fear at the fury of the fight which he himself had permitted and arranged.

For a time the encounter in the darkness was such a perplexity of flying arms that it presented no more detail than would a swiftly revolving wheel. Occasionally a face, as if illumined by a flash of light, would shine out, ghastly and marked with pink spots. A moment later, the men might have been known as shadows, if it were not for the involuntary utterance of oaths that came from them in whispers.

Suddenly a holocaust of warlike desire caught the cowboy, and he bolted forward with the speed of a broncho. "Go it, Johnnie! go it! Kill him! Kill him!"

Scully confronted him. "Kape back," he said; and by his glance the cowboy could tell that this man was Johnnie's father.

To the Easterner there was a monotony of unchangeable fighting that was an abomination. This confused mingling was eternal to his sense, which was concentrated in a longing for the end, the priceless end. Once the fighters lurched near him, and as he scrambled hastily backward he heard them breathe like men on the rack.

"Kill him, Johnnie! Kill him! Kill him! Kill him!" The cowboy's face was contorted like one of those agony masks in museums.

"Keep still," said Scully, icily.

Then there was a sudden loud grunt, incomplete, cut short, and Johnnie's body swung away from the Swede and fell with sickening heaviness to the grass. The cowboy was barely in time to prevent the mad Swede from flinging himself upon his prone adversary. "No, you don't," said the cowboy, interposing an arm. "Wait a second."

Scully was at his son's side. "Johnnie! Johnnie, me boy!" His voice had a quality of melancholy tenderness. "Johnnie! Can you go on with it?" He looked anxiously down into the bloody, pulpy face of his son.

There was a moment of silence, and then Johnnie answered in his ordinary voice, "Yes, I—it—yes."

Assisted by his father he struggled to his feet. "Wait a bit now till you git your wind," said the old man.

A few paces away the cowboy was lecturing the Swede. "No, you don't! Wait a second!"

The Easterner was plucking at Scully's sleeve. "Oh, this is enough," he pleaded. "This is enough! Let it go as it stands. This is enough!"

"Bill," said Scully, "git out of the road." The cowboy stepped aside. "Now." The combatants were actuated by a new caution as they advanced toward collision. They glared at each other, and then the Swede aimed a lightning blow that carried with it his entire weight. Johnnie was evidently half stupid from weakness, but he miraculously dodged, and his fist sent the over-balanced Swede sprawling.

The cowboy, Scully, and the Easterner burst into a cheer that was like a chorus of triumphant soldiery, but before its conclusion the Swede had scuffled agilely to his feet and come in berserk abandon at his foe. There was another perplexity of flying arms, and Johnnie's body again swung away and fell, even as a bundle might fall from a roof. The Swede instantly staggered to a little wind-waved tree and leaned upon it, breathing like an engine, while his savage and flame-lit eyes roamed from face to face as the men bent over Johnnie. There was a splendor of isolation in his situation at this time which the Easterner felt once when, lifting his eyes from the man on the ground, he beheld that mysterious and lonely figure, waiting.

"Are you any good yet, Johnnie?" asked Scully in a broken voice.

The son gasped and opened his eyes languidly. After a moment he answered, "No—I ain't—any good—any—more." Then, from shame and bodily ill, he began to weep, the tears furrowing down through the blood-stains on his face. "He was too—too—too heavy for me."

Scully straightened and addressed the waiting figure. "Stranger," he said, evenly, "it's all up with our side." Then his voice changed into that vibrant huskiness which is commonly the tone of the most simple and deadly announcements. "Johnnie is whipped."

Without reply, the victor moved off on the route to the front door of the hotel.

The cowboy was formulating new and unspellable blasphemies. The Easterner was startled to find that they were out in a wind that seemed to come direct from the shadowed arctic floes. He heard again the wail of the snow as it was flung to its grave in the south. He knew now that all this time the cold had been sinking into him deeper and deeper, and he wondered that he had not perished. He felt indifferent to the condition of the vanquished man.

"Johnnie, can you walk?" asked Scully.

"Did I hurt—hurt him any?" asked the son.

"Can you walk, boy? Can you walk?"

Johnnie's voice was suddenly strong. There was a robust impatience in it. "I asked you whether I hurt him any!"

"Yes, yes, Johnnie," answered the cowboy, consolingly; "he's hurt a good deal."

They raised him from the ground, and as soon as he was on his feet he went tottering off, rebuffing all attempts at assistance. When the party rounded the corner they were fairly blinded by the pelting of the snow. It burned their faces like fire. The cowboy carried Johnnie through the drift to the door. As they entered, some cards again rose from the floor and beat against the wall.

The Easterner rushed to the stove. He was so profoundly chilled that he almost dared to embrace the glowing iron. The Swede was not in the room. Johnnie sank into a chair and, folding his arms on his knees, buried his face in them. Scully, warming one foot and then the other at a rim of the stove, muttered to himself with Celtic mournfulness. The cowboy had removed his fur cap, and with a dazed and rueful air he was running one hand through his tousled locks. From overhead they could hear the creaking of boards, as the Swede tramped here and there in his room.

The sad quiet was broken by the sudden flinging open of a door that led toward the kitchen. It was instantly followed by an inrush of women. They precipitated themselves upon Johnnie amid a chorus of lamentation. Before they carried their prey off to the kitchen, there to be bathed and harangued with that mixture of sympathy and abuse which is a feat of their sex, the mother straightened herself and fixed old Scully with an eye of stern reproach. "Shame be upon you, Patrick Scully!" she cried. "Your own son, too. Shame be upon you!"

"There, now! Be quiet, now!" said the old man, weakly.

"Shame be upon you, Patrick Scully!" The girls, rallying to this slogan, sniffed disdainfully in the direction of those trembling accomplices, the cowboy and the Easterner. Presently they bore Johnnie away, and left the three men to dismal reflection.

VII

"I'd like to fight this here Dutchman myself," said the cowboy, breaking a long silence.

Scully wagged his head sadly. "No, that wouldn't do. It wouldn't be right. It wouldn't be right."

"Well, why wouldn't it?" argued the cowboy. "I don't see no harm in it."

"No," answered Scully, with mournful heroism. "It wouldn't be right. It was Johnnie's fight, and now we mustn't whip the man just because he whipped Johnnie."

"Yes, that's true enough," said the cowboy; "but—he better not get fresh with me, because I couldn't stand no more of it."

"You'll not say a word to him," commanded Scully, and even then they heard the tread of the Swede on the stairs. His entrance was made theatric. He swept the door back with a bang and swaggered to the middle of the room. No one looked at him. "Well," he cried, insolently, at Scully, "I s'pose you'll tell me now how much I owe you?"

The old man remained stolid. "You don't owe me nothin'."

"Huh!" said the Swede, "huh! Don't owe 'im nothin'."

The cowboy addressed the Swede. "Stranger, I don't see how you come to be so gay around here."

Old Scully was instantly alert. "Stop!" he shouted, holding his hand forth, fingers upward. "Bill, you shut up!"

The cowboy spat carelessly into the sawdust-box. "I didn't say a word, did I?" he asked.

"Mr. Scully," called the Swede, "how much do I owe you?" It

was seen that he was attired for departure, and that he had his valise
in his hand.

"You don't owe me nothin'," repeated Scully in the same imperturbable way.

"Huh!" said the Swede. "I guess you're right. I guess if it was
any way at all, you'd owe me somethin'. That's what I guess." He
turned to the cowboy. " 'Kill him! Kill him! Kill him!' " he
mimicked, and then guffawed victoriously. " 'Kill him!' " He was
convulsed with ironical humor.

But he might have been jeering the dead. The three men were
immovable and silent, staring with glassy eyes at the stove.

The Swede opened the door and passed into the storm, giving
one derisive glance backward at the still group.

As soon as the door was closed, Scully and the cowboy leaped to
their feet and began to curse. They trampled to and fro, waving
their arms and smashing into the air with their fists. "Oh, but that
was a hard minute!" wailed Scully. "That was a hard minute! Him
there leerin' and scoffin'! One bang at his nose was worth forty
dollars to me that minute! How did you stand it, Bill?"

"How did I stand it?" cried the cowboy in a quivering voice.
"How did I stand it? Oh!"

The old man burst into sudden brogue. "I'd loike to take that
Swade," he wailed, "and hould 'im down on a shtone flure and bate
'im to a jelly wid a shtick!"

The cowboy groaned in sympathy. "I'd like to git him by the
neck and ha-ammer him"—he brought his hand down on a chair
with a noise like a pistol-shot—"hammer that there Dutchman
until he couldn't tell himself from a dead coyote!"

"I'd bate 'im until he—"

"I'd show *him* some things—"

And then together they raised a yearning, fanatic cry—"Oh-o-oh!
if we only could—"

"Yes!"

"Yes!"

"And then I'd—"

"O-o-oh!"

VIII

The Swede, tightly gripping his valise, tacked across the face of
the storm as if he carried sails. He was following a line of little
naked, gasping trees which, he knew, must mark the way of the
road. His face, fresh from the pounding of Johnnie's fists, felt more
pleasure than pain in the wind and the driving snow. A number of
square shapes loomed upon him finally, and he knew them as the
houses of the main body of the town. He found a street and made

travel along it, leaning heavily upon the wind whenever, at a corner, a terrific blast caught him.

He might have been in a deserted village. We picture the world as thick with conquering and elate humanity, but here, with the bugles of the tempest pealing, it was hard to imagine a peopled earth. One viewed the existence of man then as a marvel, and conceded a glamor of wonder to these lice which were caused to cling to a whirling, fire-smitten, ice-locked, disease-stricken, space-lost bulb. The conceit of man was explained by this storm to be the very engine of life. One was a coxcomb not to die in it. However, the Swede found a saloon.

In front of it an indomitable red light was burning, and the snowflakes were made blood-color as they flew through the circumscribed territory of the lamp's shining. The Swede pushed open the door of the saloon and entered. A sanded expanse was before him, and at the end of it four men sat about a table drinking. Down one side of the room extended a radiant bar, and its guardian was leaning upon his elbows listening to the talk of the men at the table. The Swede dropped his valise upon the floor and, smiling fraternally upon the barkeeper, said, "Gimme some whiskey, will you?" The man placed a bottle, a whiskey-glass, and a glass of ice-thick water upon the bar. The Swede poured himself an abnormal portion of whiskey and drank it in three gulps. "Pretty bad night," remarked the bartender, indifferently. He was making the pretension of blindness which is usually a distinction of his class; but it could have been seen that he was furtively studying the half-erased blood-stains on the face of the Swede. "Bad night," he said again.

"Oh, it's good enough for me," replied the Swede, hardily, as he poured himself some more whiskey. The barkeeper took his coin and manœuvred it through its reception by the high nickelled cash-machine. A bell rang; a card labelled "20 cts." had appeared.

"No," continued the Swede, "this isn't too bad weather. It's good enough for me."

"So?" murmured the barkeeper, languidly.

The copious drams made the Swede's eyes swim, and he breathed a trifle heavier. "Yes, I like this weather. I like it. It suits me." It was apparently his design to impart a deep significance to these words.

"So?" murmured the bartender again. He turned to gaze dreamily at the scroll-like birds and bird-like scrolls which had been drawn with soap upon the mirrors in back of the bar.

"Well, I guess I'll take another drink," said the Swede, presently. "Have something?"

"No, thanks; I'm not drinkin'," answered the bartender. Afterward he asked, "How did you hurt your face?"

The Swede immediately began to boast loudly. "Why, in a fight. I thumped the soul out of a man down here at Scully's hotel."

The interest of the four men at the table was at last aroused.

"Who was it?" said one.

"Johnnie Scully," blustered the Swede. "Son of the man what runs it. He will be pretty near dead for some weeks, I can tell you. I made a nice thing of him, I did. He couldn't get up. They carried him in the house. Have a drink?"

Instantly the men in some subtle way encased themselves in reserve. "No, thanks," said one. The group was of curious formation. Two were prominent local business men; one was the district attorney; and one was a professional gambler of the kind known as "square." But a scrutiny of the group would not have enabled an observer to pick the gambler from the men of more reputable pursuits. He was, in fact, a man so delicate in manner, when among people of fair class, and so judicious in his choice of victims, that in the strictly masculine part of the town's life he had come to be explicitly trusted and admired. People called him a thoroughbred. The fear and contempt with which his craft was regarded were undoubtedly the reason why his quiet dignity shone conspicuous above the quiet dignity of men who might be merely hatters, billiard-markers, or grocery-clerks. Beyond an occasional unwary traveller who came by rail, this gambler was supposed to prey solely upon reckless and senile farmers, who, when flush with good crops, drove into town in all the pride and confidence of an absolutely invulnerable stupidity. Hearing at times in circuitous fashion of the despoilment of such a farmer, the important men of Romper invariably laughed in contempt of the victim, and if they thought of the wolf at all, it was with a kind of pride at the knowledge that he would never dare think of attacking their wisdom and courage. Besides, it was popular that this gambler had a real wife and two real children in a neat cottage in a suburb, where he led an exemplary home life; and when any one even suggested a discrepancy in his character, the crowd immediately vociferated descriptions of this virtuous family circle. Then men who led exemplary home lives, and men who did not lead exemplary home lives, all subsided in a bunch, remarking that there was nothing more to be said.

However, when a restriction was placed upon him—as, for instance, when a strong clique of members of the new Pollywog Club refused to permit him, even as a spectator, to appear in the rooms of the organization—the candor and gentleness with which he accepted the judgment disarmed many of his foes and made his friends more desperately partisan. He invariably distinguished between himself and a respectable Romper man so quickly and frankly that his manner actually appeared to be a continual broadcast compliment.

And one must not forget to declare the fundamental fact of his entire position in Romper. It is irrefutable that in all affairs outside his business, in all matters that occur eternally and commonly between man and man, this thieving card-player was so generous, so just, so moral, that, in a contest, he could have put to flight the consciences of nine tenths of the citizens of Romper.

And so it happened that he was seated in this saloon with the two prominent local merchants and the district attorney.

The Swede continued to drink raw whiskey, meanwhile babbling at the barkeeper and trying to induce him to indulge in potations. "Come on. Have a drink. Come on. What—no? Well, have a little one, then. By gawd, I've whipped a man to-night, and I want to celebrate. I whipped him good, too. Gentlemen," the Swede cried to the men at the table, "have a drink?"

"Ssh!" said the barkeeper.

The group at the table, although furtively attentive, had been pretending to be deep in talk, but now a man lifted his eyes toward the Swede and said, shortly, "Thanks. We don't want any more."

At this reply the Swede ruffled out his chest like a rooster. "Well," he exploded, "it seems I can't get anybody to drink with me in this town. Seems so, don't it? Well!"

"Ssh!" said the barkeeper.

"Say," snarled the Swede, "don't you try to shut me up. I won't have it. I'm a gentleman, and I want people to drink with me. And I want 'em to drink with me now. *Now*—do you understand?" He rapped the bar with his knuckles.

Years of experience had calloused the bartender. He merely grew sulky. "I hear you," he answered.

"Well," cried the Swede, "listen hard then. See those men over there? Well, they're going to drink with me, and don't you forget it. Now you watch."

"Hi!" yelled the barkeeper, "this won't do!"

"Why won't it?" demanded the Swede. He stalked over to the table, and by chance laid his hand upon the shoulder of the gambler. "How about this?" he asked wrathfully. "I asked you to drink with me."

The gambler simply twisted his head and spoke over his shoulder. "My friend, I don't know you."

"Oh, hell!" answered the Swede, "come and have a drink."

"Now, my boy," advised the gambler, kindly, "take your hand off my shoulder and go 'way and mind your own business." He was a little, slim man, and it seemed strange to hear him use this tone of heroic patronage to the burly Swede. The other men at the table said nothing.

"What! You won't drink with me, you little dude? I'll make you, then! I'll make you!" The Swede had grasped the gambler frenziedly at the throat, and was dragging him from his chair. The other men sprang up. The barkeeper dashed around the corner of his bar. There was a great tumult, and then was seen a long blade in the hand of the gambler. It shot forward, and a human body, this citadel of virtue, wisdom, power, was pierced as easily as if it had been a melon. The Swede fell with a cry of supreme astonishment.

The prominent merchants and the district attorney must have at once tumbled out of the place backward. The bartender found himself hanging limply to the arm of a chair and gazing into the eyes of a murderer.

"Henry," said the latter, as he wiped his knife on one of the towels that hung beneath the bar rail, "you tell 'em where to find me. I'll be home, waiting for 'em." Then he vanished. A moment afterward the barkeeper was in the street dinning through the storm for help and, moreover, companionship.

The corpse of the Swede, alone in the saloon, had its eyes fixed upon a dreadful legend that dwelt atop of the cash-machine: "This registers the amount of your purchase."

IX

Months later, the cowboy was frying pork over the stove of a little ranch near the Dakota line, when there was a quick thud of hoofs outside, and presently the Easterner entered with the letters and the papers.

"Well," said the Easterner at once, "the chap that killed the Swede has got three years. Wasn't much, was it?"

"He has? Three years?" The cowboy poised his pan of pork, while he ruminated upon the news. "Three years. That ain't much."

"No. It was a light sentence," replied the Easterner as he unbuckled his spurs. "Seems there was a good deal of sympathy for him in Romper."

"If the bartender had been any good," observed the cowboy, thoughtfully, "he would have gone in and cracked that there Dutchman on the head with a bottle in the beginnin' of it and stopped all this here murderin'."

"Yes, a thousand things might have happened," said the Easterner, tartly.

The cowboy returned his pan of pork to the fire, but his philosophy continued. "It's funny, ain't it? If he hadn't said Johnnie was cheatin' he'd be alive this minute. He was an awful fool. Game played for fun, too. Not for money. I believe he was crazy."

"I feel sorry for that gambler," said the Easterner.

"Oh, so do I," said the cowboy. "He don't deserve none of it for killin' who he did."

"The Swede might not have been killed if everything had been square."

"Might not have been killed?" exclaimed the cowboy. "Everythin' square? Why, when he said that Johnnie was cheatin' and acted like such a jackass? And then in the saloon he fairly walked up to git hurt?" With these arguments the cowboy browbeat the Easterner and reduced him to rage.

"You're a fool!" cried the Easterner, viciously. "You're a bigger jackass than the Swede by a million majority. Now let me tell you one thing. Let me tell you something. Listen! Johnnie *was* cheating!"

" 'Johnnie,' " said the cowboy, blankly. There was a minute of silence, and then he said, robustly, "Why, no. The game was only for fun."

"Fun or not," said the Easterner, "Johnnie was cheating. I saw him. I know it. I saw him. And I refused to stand up and be a man. I let the Swede fight it out alone. And you—you were simply puffing around the place and wanting to fight. And then old Scully himself! We are all in it! This poor gambler isn't even a noun. He is kind of an adverb. Every sin is the result of a collaboration. We, five of us, have collaborated in the murder of this Swede. Usually there are from a dozen to forty women really involved in every murder, but in this case it seems to be only five men—you, I, Johnnie, old Scully; and that fool of an unfortunate gambler came merely as a culmination, the apex of a human movement, and gets all the punishment."

The cowboy, injured and rebellious, cried out blindly into this fog of mysterious theory: "Well, I didn't do anythin', did I?"

individual apprehension of forces vs. 1898, 1899
spiritual statement.

THEODORE DREISER *entrepreneur*

pessimistic deter (1871–1945)

Often termed the pioneer of naturalism in American letters, Theodore Dreiser equally deserves a place in our literature for his vigorous attack on the genteel tradition and his long and active interest in American social problems. His naturalism, different from Stephen Crane's, was based on a mechanistic concept of life; yet the reader of his novels becomes increasingly aware of a strong element of spiritual query verging on mysticism, of an undertone of naïve romanticism that makes his works notably unlike those of Zola. These contrasting ele-

Philosophical forerunners {
George Santana - materialistic naturalism
William James - pragmatism
Henry Adams - scientific historian
dynamic th. of hist - forces
}

Naturalistic Thought in transistion

ments are present in all his fiction, from *Sister Carrie* (1900) to *The Bulwark* (1946).

Exceptionally responsive to environment, Dreiser found more than the usual stimulus for his writing in the disparity between the rich and the poor, the cultured sophisticate and the provincial, and the powerful and the weak members of society. The shattering effect of nineteenth-century science on traditional religious and social patterns, the emergence of new power groups, and the development of new theories in economics and political science vitally affected his writing.

One of several children of German immigrant parents, Dreiser was born in Terre Haute, Indiana, and his early years were a series of exposures to poverty, emotional instability, and religious bigotry in the home, and of frequent moves dictated by financial necessity. By the time he entered Indiana University, which he attended for one year, the young man was understandably in a state of bewilderment and rebellion that made him eager for independence and financial success. The newspaper world offered an avenue of escape that led from the St. Louis *Globe-Democrat* to Chicago and Pittsburgh. He learned the profession of journalism by which he later earned a living from several magazines, notably the Butterick publications and the brilliant, satirical *American Spectator* (1932–1937), in association with such younger stars as G. J. Nathan, Ernest Boyd, Cabell, O'Neill, and Sherwood Anderson.

It is difficult for a mid-century reader of *Sister Carrie* to understand why the book should have been withdrawn from publication in 1900. Certainly this was not the first discussion of immorality and spiritual decay in literature. The difference—and the furor—resulted from the fact that Dreiser dared write what people had often observed but did not wish to admit explicitly: that men and women do not always suffer in this life for transgressions of the social and moral code. The same circumstances that leave Carrie apparently untouched send Hurstwood to destruction; later Lester Kane in *Jennie Gerhardt* escapes, while Jennie suffers from their relationship.

This apparent helplessness in the face of inscrutable laws of fate and nature is the most obvious characteristic of Dreiser's fiction, but the years that followed the publication of *Jennie Gerhardt* in 1911 saw the development of other aspects of his philosophy as well. In the Cowperwood trilogy—*The Financier* (1912), *The Titan* (1914), and the posthumously published *The Stoic* (1947)—all based on the life of Charles T. Yerkes, he explored the emotional and social ambitions of one of America's most startling financial buccaneers, not only because he was obeying his newspaperman's instinct for a good story, but also because he was fascinated by the ruthless tactics of a man who had few illusions and deliberately set out to conquer life with the weapons of cleverness, dishonesty, and ambition. The autobio-

indivd. life dominated by force — but all lives are dominated by sex graphical volumes, *A Book About Myself* (1922) and *Dawn* (1931), reveal the author's early confusions, his struggles to find a successful pattern for life, and his groping for an explanation of the disparity between man's desires and his ultimate accomplishment. *The "Genius"* (1915), an account of an artist's life, is useful for its thinly disguised autobiographical descriptions of Dreiser's efforts to gain a literary foothold in New York.

In 1925 he published his best-known volume, *An American Tragedy*, an impressive work which became for a generation of Americans a synonym for literary naturalism. Dreiser utilized an actual murder as the basis of an exhaustive portrayal of a young man's tragic attempt to make a place for himself in a world whose demands he was incapable of meeting. The resolution—showing that Clyde Griffiths' crime was the result of environmental factors over which his weak nature had little control, and that society, with its aggressive materialism, was at the bar of judgment along with the criminal—was a powerful fictional appraisal of fundamental modern dilemmas.

While charges of verboseness

and lack of integration of characters can be made against Dreiser, these defects result from his photographic realism. His insistence that the writer, as clinician of the forces of nature, must report life as he sees it, and therefore must have freedom to do so, has had an immeasurable influence on younger writers and an even greater though less tangible impact on American life.

Dreiser's works, in addition to the novels mentioned above, include the accounts of his travels in the United States and Russia, *A Traveller at Forty*, 1913; *A Hoosier Holiday*, 1916; and *Dreiser Looks at Russia*, 1928. His plays were collected in *Plays of the Natural and the Supernatural*, 1916; and *The Hand of the Potter*, 1918. His short stories appeared in *Free and Other Stories*, 1918; and *Chains*, 1927. *Twelve Men*, 1919, is a series of sketches of friends and acquaintances; and *A Gallery of Women*, 1929, is a semifictional account of the personalities of various women. *Hey Rub-a-Dub-Dub*, 1920, is a series of philosphical essays. His poems appeared as *Moods, Cadenced and Declaimed*, 1926. Other less important volumes are *The Color of a Great City*, 1923; *My City*, 1929; *The Aspirant*, 1929; *Epitaph*, 1929; *Fine Furniture*, 1930; and *Tragic America*, 1931.

Critical biographies are Robert H. Elias, *Theodore Dreiser: Apostle of Nature*, 1949, and F. O. Matthiessen, *Theodore Dreiser*, 1951. Of biographical interest is Helen Dreiser, *My Life with Dreiser*, 1951. Robert H. Elias has edited *Letters of Theodore Dreiser*, 3 vols., 1959.

The Old Neighborhood[1]

He came to it across the new bridge, from the south where the greater city lay—the older portion—and where he had left his car, and paused at the nearer bridgehead to look at it—the eddying

[1]. "The Old Neighborhood" first appeared in *Metropolitan Magazine* for December, 1918, and was first collected in *Chains: Lesser Novels and Stories* (1927), the source of the present text.

water of the river below, the new docks and piers built on either side since he had left, twenty years before; the once grassy slopes on the farther shore, now almost completely covered with factories, although he could see too, among them, even now, traces of the old, out-of-the-way suburb which he and Marie had known. Chadds Bridge, now an integral part of the greater city, connected by car lines and through streets, was then such a simple, unpretentious affair, a little suburban village just on the edge of this stream and beyond the last straggling northward streets of the great city below, where the car lines stopped and from which one had to walk on foot across this bridge in order to take advantage of the rural quiet and the cheaper—much cheaper—rents, so all-important to him then.

Then he was so poor—he and Marie—a mere stripling of a mechanic and inventor, a student of aeronautics, electricity, engineering, and what not, but newly married and without a dollar, and no clear conception of how his future was to eventuate, whereas now—but somehow he did not want to think of now. Now he was so very rich, comparatively speaking, older, wiser, such a forceful person commercially and in every other way, whereas then he was so lean and pathetic and worried and wistful—a mere uncertain stripling, as he saw himself now, with ideas and ambitions and dreams which were quite out of accord with his immediate prospects or opportunities. It was all right to say, as some one had— Emerson, he believed—"hitch your wagon to a star."[2] But some people hitched, or tried to, before they were ready. They neglected some of the slower moving vehicles about them, and so did not get on at all—or did not seem to, for the time being.

And that had been his error. He was growing at the time, of course, but he was so restless, so dissatisfied with himself, so unhappy. All the world was apparently tinkling and laughing by, eating, drinking, dancing, growing richer, happier, every minute; whereas he—he and Marie, and the two babies which came a little later—seemed to make no progress at all. None. They were out of it, alone, hidden away in this little semi-rural realm, and it was all so disturbing when elsewhere was so much—to him, at least, if not to her—of all that was worth while—wealth, power, gayety, repute. How intensely, savagely almost, he had craved all of those things in those days, and how far off they still were at that time!

Marie was not like him, soft, clinging little thing that she was, inefficient in most big ways, and yet dear and helpful enough in all little ones—oh, so very much so.

---

2. From Ralph Waldo Emerson's essay "Civilization" in *Society and Solitude* (1870).

When first he met her in Philadelphia, and later when he brought her over to New York, it seemed as though he could not possibly have made a better engagement for himself. Marie was so sweet, so gentle, with her waxy white pallor, delicately tinted cheeks, soft blackish brown eyes that sought his so gently always, as if seeming to ask, "And what can I do for my dearie now? What can he teach me to do for him?" She was never his equal, mentally or spiritually—that was the dreadful discovery he had made a few months after the first infatuation had worn off, after the ivory of her forehead, the lambent sweetness of her eyes, her tresses, and her delicately rounded figure, had ceased to befuddle his more poetical brain. But how delightful she seemed then in her shabby little clothes and her shabbier little home—all the more so because her delicate white blossom of a face was such a contrast to the drear surroundings in which it shone. Her father was no more than a mechanic, she a little store clerk in the great Rand[3] department store in Philadelphia when he met her, he nothing more than an experimental assistant with the Culver Electric Company, with no technical training of any kind, and only dreams of a technical course at some time or other. The beginnings of his career were so very vague.

His parents were poor too, and he had had to begin to earn his own living, or share, at fourteen. And at twenty-four he had contracted this foolish marriage when he was just beginning to dream of bigger things, to see how they were done, what steps were necessary, what studies, what cogitations and hard, grinding sacrifices even, before one finally achieved anything, especially in the electrical world. The facts which had begun to rise and take color and classify themselves in his mind had all then to develop under the most advantageous conditions thereafter. His salary did not rise at once by any means, just because he was beginning to think of bigger things. He was a no better practical assistant in a laboratory or the equipment department of the several concerns for which he worked, because in his brain were already seething dim outlines of possible improvements in connection with arms, the turbine gun, electro-magnetic distance control, and the rotary excavator. He had ideas, but also as he realized at the time he would have to study privately and long in order to make them real; and his studies at night and Sundays and holidays in the libraries and everywhere else, made him no more helpful, if as much so, in his practical, everyday corporation labors. In fact, for a long time when their finances were at the lowest ebb and the two children had appeared, and they all needed clothes and diversion, and his salary had not been raised, it seemed as though he were actually less valuable to everybody.

3. There was no such store.

But in the meantime Marie had worked for and with him, dear little thing, and although she had seemed so wonderful at first, patient, enduring, thoughtful, later because of their poverty and so many other things which hampered and seemed to interfere with his work, he had wearied of her a little. Over in Philadelphia, where he had accompanied her home of an evening and had watched her help her mother, saw her set the table, wash the dishes, straighten up the house after dinner, and then if it were pleasant go for a walk with him, she seemed ideal, just the wife for him, indeed. Later as he sensed the world, its hardness, its innate selfishness, the necessity for push, courage, unwillingness to be a slave and a drudge, these earlier qualities and charms were the very things that militated against her in his mind. Poor little Marie!

But in other ways his mind was not always on his work, either. Sometimes it was on his dreams of bigger things. Sometimes it was on his silly blindness in wanting to get married so soon, in being betrayed by the sweet innocence and beauty of Marie into saddling himself with this burden when he was scarcely prepared, as he saw after he was married, to work out his own life on a sensible, economic basis. A thought which he had encountered somewhere in some book of philosophy or other (he was always reading in those days) had haunted him—"He that hath wife and children hath given hostages to fortune"[4]—and that painful thought seemed to grow with each succeeding day. Why had he been so foolish, why so very foolish, as to get married when he was so unsuitably young! That was a thing the folly of which irritated him all the time.

Not that Marie was not all she should be—far from it!—nor the two little boys (both boys, think of that!), intensely precious to him at first. No, that was not it, but this, that whatever the values and the charms of these (and they were wonderful at first), he personally was not prepared to bear or enjoy them as yet. He was too young, too restless, too nebulous, too inventively dreamful. He did not, as he had so often thought since, know what he wanted—only, when they began to have such a very hard time, he knew he did not want that. Why, after the first year of their marriage, when Peter was born, and because of better trade conditions in the electrical world, they had moved over here (he was making only twenty-two dollars a week at the time), everything had seemed to go wrong. Indeed, nothing ever seemed to go right any more after that, not one thing.

First it was Marie's illness after Peter's birth, which kept him on tenterhooks and took all he could rake and scrape and save to pay the doctor's bill, and stole half her beauty, if not more. She always

4. Sir Francis Bacon, "Of Marriage and Single Life," *Essays or Counsels, Civil and Moral* (1625).

looked a little pinched and weak after that. (And he had charged that up to her, too!) Then it was some ailment which affected Peter for months and which proved to be undernourishment, due to a defect in Marie's condition even after she had seemingly recovered. Then, two years later, it was the birth of Frank, due to another error, of course, he being not intended in Marie's frail state; and then his own difficulties with the manager of the insulating department of the International Electric, due to his own nervous state, his worries, his consciousness of error in the manipulation of his own career—and Marie's. Life was slipping away, as he saw it then and he kept thinking he was growing older, was not getting on as he had thought he should, was not achieving his technical education; he was saddled with a family which would prevent him from ever getting on. Here, in this neighborhood, all this had occurred—this quiet, run-down realm, so greatly changed since he had seen it last. Yes, it had all happened here.

But how peaceful it was to-day, although changed. How the water ran under this bridge now, as then, eddying out to sea. And how this late October afternoon reminded him of that other October afternoon when they had first walked up here—warm, pleasant, colorful. Would he ever forget that afternoon? He had thought he was going to do so much better—was praying that he would, and they had done so much worse. He, personally, had grown so restless and dissatisfied with himself and her and life. And things seemed to be almost as bad as they could be, drifting indefinitely on to nothing. Indeed, life seemed to gather as a storm and break. He was discharged from the International Electric, due supposedly to his taking home for a night a battery for an experiment he was making but in reality because of the opposition of his superior, based on the latter's contempt for his constantly (possibly) depressed and dissatisfied air, his brooding mien, and some minor inattentions due to the state of his mind at the time.

Then, quite as swiftly (out of black plotting or evil thoughts of his own, perhaps), Peter had died of pneumonia. And three days later Frank. There were two funerals, two dreary, one-carriage affairs —he remembered that so well!—for they had no money; and his pawned watch, five dollars from Marie's mother, and seven chemical and electrical works sold to an old book man had provided the cash advance required by the undertaker! Then, spiritually, something seemed to break within him. He could not see this world, this immediate life in which he was involved, as having any significance in it for himself or any one after that. He could not stand it any more, the weariness, the boredom, the dissatisfaction with himself, the failure of himself, the sickening chain of disasters which had befallen this earlier adventure. And so—

But that was why he was here to-day, after all these years—
twenty-four, to be exact—with his interest in this old region so
keen, if so sad. Why, there—there!—was a flock of pigeons, just
like those of old Abijah Hargot's, flying around the sky now, as
then. And a curl of smoke creeping up from Tanzer's blacksmith
shop, or the one that had succeeded it, just one block from this
bridge. How well he remembered old Tanzer and his forge, his
swelling muscles and sooty face! He had always nodded in such a
friendly way as he passed and talked of the pest of flies and heat in
summer. That was why he was pausing on this bridge to-day, just
to see once more, to feel, standing in the pleasant afternoon sun of
this October day and gazing across the swirling waters below at
the new coal-pockets, the enlarged lamp works of the George C.
Woodruff Company, once a mere shed hidden away at a corner of
this nearest street and rented out here no doubt because it was cheap
and Woodruff was just beginning—just as he did twenty-four years
before. Time had sped by so swiftly. One's ideals and ideas changed
so. Twenty years ago he would have given so much to be what he
was now—rich and fairly powerful—and now—now— The beauty
of this old neighborhood, to-day, even.

The buff school which crowned the rise beyond, and the broad
asphalt of Edgewood Avenue leading up to the old five-story flat
building—the only one out here, and a failure financially—in which
he and Marie had had their miserable little apartment—here it
was, still to be seen. Yes, it and so many other things were all
here; that group of great oaks before old Hargot's door; the little
red—if now rusted—weather-vane over his carriage house; the tall
romantic tower of St. George's Episcopal Church—so far to the west
over the river, and the spars and masts of vessels that still docked
here for a while. But dark memories they generated, too, along with
a certain idyllic sweetness, which had seemed to envelop the whole
at first. For though it had had sweetness and peace at first, how
much that had been bitter and spiritually destroying had occurred
here, too.

How well he recalled, for instance, the day he and Marie had
wandered up here, almost hand in hand, across this very bridge and
up Edgewood Avenue, nearly twenty-four years before! They had
been so happy at first, dreaming their little dream of a wonderful
future for them—and now—well, his secret agency had brought
him all there was to know of her and her mother and her little
world after he had left. They had suffered so much, apparently, and
all on account of him. But somehow he did not want to think of
that now. It was not for that he had come to-day, but to see, to
dream over the older, the better, the first days.

He crossed over, following the old road which had then been a cobble wagon trail, and turned into Edgewood Avenue which led up past the line of semi-country homes which he used to dread so much, homes which because of their superior prosperity, wide lawns, flowers and walks, made the life which he and Marie were compelled to lead here seem so lean and meagre by contrast. Why, yes, here was the very residence of Gatewood, the dentist, so prosperous then and with an office downtown; and that of Dr. Newton, whom he had called in when Peter and Frank were taken ill that last time; and Temple, the druggist, and Stoutmeyer, the grocer—both of whom he had left owing money; and Dr. Newton, too, for that matter—although all had subsequently been paid. Not a sign of the names of either Gatewood or Newton on their windows or gates now; not a trace of Temple's drug store. But here was Stoutmeyer's grocery just the same. And Buchspiel, the butcher. (Could he still be alive, by any chance—was that his stout, aged figure within?) And Ortman, the baker—not a sign of change there. And over the way the then village school, now Public School No. 261, as he could see. And across from it, beyond, the slim little, almost accidental (for this region) five-story apartment house—built because of an error in judgment, of course, when they thought the city was going to grow out this way—a thing of grayish-white brick. On the fifth floor of this, in the rear, he and Marie had at last found a tiny apartment of three rooms and bath, cheap enough for them to occupy in the growing city and still pay their way. What memories the mere sight of the building evoked! Where were all the people now who used to bustle about here of a summer evening when he and Marie were here, boys and girls, grown men and women of the neighborhood? It had all been so pleasant at first, Marie up there preparing dinner and he coming home promptly at seven and sometimes whistling as he came! He was not always unhappy, even here.

Yes, all was exactly as it had been in the old days in regard to this building and this school, even—as he lived!—a "For Rent" sign in that very same apartment, four flights up, as it had been that warm October day when they had first come up here seeking.

But what a change in himself—stouter, so much older, gray now. And Marie—dying a few years after in this very region without his ever seeing her again or she him—and she had written him such pathetic letters. She had been broken, no doubt, spiritually and in every other way when he left her,—no pointless vanity in that, alas —it was too sad to involve vanity. Yes, he had done that. Would it ever be forgiven him? Would his error of ambition and self-dissatisfaction be seen anywhere in any kindly light—on earth or in heaven? He had suffered so from remorse in regard to it of late. Indeed, now that he was rich and so successful the thought of it had begun to torture him. Some time since—five years ago—he had thought to make amends, but then—well, then he had found that she wasn't any more. Poor little Marie!

But these walls, so strong and enduring (stone had this advantage over human flesh!), were quite as he had left them, quite as they were the day he and Marie had first come here—hopeful, cheerful, although later so depressed, the two of them. (And he had charged her spiritually with it all, or nearly so—its fatalities and gloom, as though she could have avoided them!)

The ruthlessness of it!

The sheer brutality!

The ignorance!

If she could but see him now, his great shops and factories, his hundreds of employés, his present wife and children, his great new home—and still know how he felt about her! If he could only call her back and tell her, apologize, explain, make some amends! But no; life did not work that way. Doors opened and doors closed. It had no consideration for eleventh-hour repentances. As though they mattered to life, or anything else! He could tell her something now, of course, explain the psychology, let her know how pathetically depressed and weary he had felt then. But would she understand, care, forgive? She had been so fond of him, done so much for him in her small, sweet way. And yet, if she only knew, he could scarcely have helped doing as he did then, so harried and depressed and eager for advancement had he been, self-convinced of his own error and failure before ever his life had a good start. If she could only see how little all his later triumphs mattered now, how much he would be glad to do for her now! if only—only—he could. Well, he must quit these thoughts. They did not help at all, nor his coming out here and feeling this way!

But life was so automatic and unconsciously cruel at times. One's disposition drove one so, shutting and bolting doors behind one, driving one on and on like a harried steer up a narrow runway to one's fate. He could have been happy right here with Marie and the children—as much so as he had ever been since. Or, if he had only taken Marie along, once the little ones were gone—they might have been happy enough together. They might have been! But no, no; something in him at that time would not let him. Really, he was a victim of his own grim impulses, dreams, passions, mad and illogical as that might seem. He was crazy for success, wild with a desire for a superior, contemptuous position in the world. People were so, at times. He had been. He had had to do as he did, so horribly would he have suffered mentally if he had not, all the theories of the moralists to the contrary notwithstanding. The notions of one's youth were not necessarily those of age, and that was why he was here to-day in this very gloomy and contrite mood.

He went around the corner now to the side entrance of the old apartment house, and paused. For there, down the street, almost—not quite—as he had left it, was the residence of the quondam old Abijah Hargot, he of the pigeons,—iron manufacturer and Presbyterian, who even in his day was living there in spite of the fact that the truly princely residence suburbs had long since moved much farther out and he was being entirely surrounded by an element of cheaper life which could not have been exactly pleasant to him. In those days he and Marie had heard of the hardwood floors, the great chandeliers, the rugs and pictures of the house that had once faced a wide sward leading down to the river's edge itself. But look at it now! A lumber-yard between it and the river! And some sort of a small shop or factory on this end of the lawn! And in his day, Abijah had kept a pet Jersey cow nibbling the grass under the trees and fantailed pigeons on the slate roof of his barn, at the corner where now was this small factory, and at the back of his house an immense patch of golden glow just outside the conservatory facing the east, and also two pagodas down near the river. But all gone! all gone, or nearly so. Just the house and a part of the lawn. And occupied now by whom? In the old days he had never dared dream, or scarcely so, that some day, years later—when he would be much older and sadder, really, and haunted by the ghosts of these very things—he would be able to return here and know that he had far more imposing toys than old Hargot had ever dreamed of, as rich as he was.

Toys!

Toys!

Yes, they were toys, for one played with them a little while, as with so many things, and then laid them aside forever.

Toys!

Toys!

But then, as he had since come to know, old Hargot had not been without his troubles, in spite of all his money. For, as rumor had it then, his oldest son, Lucien, his pride, in those days, a slim, artistic type of boy, had turned out a drunkard, gambler, night-life lover; had run with women, become afflicted with all sorts of ills, and after his father had cut him off and driven him out (refusing to permit him even to visit the home), had hung about here, so the neighbors had said, and stolen in to see his mother, especially on dark or rainy nights, in order to get aid from her. And, like all mothers, she had aided him secretly, or so they said, in spite of her fear of her husband. Mothers were like that—his mother, too. Neighbors testified that they had seen her whispering to him in the shade of the trees of the lawn or around the corner in the next street —a sad, brooding, care-worn woman, always in black or dark blue.

Yes, life held its disappointments for every one, of course, even old Abijah and himself.

He went on to the door and paused, wondering whether to go up or not, for the atmosphere of this building and this neighborhood was very, very sad now, very redolent of old, sweet, dead and half-forgotten things. The river there, running so freshly at the foot of the street; the school where the children used to play and shout, while he worked on certain idle days when there was no work at the factory; the little church up the street to which so many commonplace adherents used to make their way on Sunday; the shabby cabin of the plumber farther up this same street, who used to go tearing off every Saturday and Sunday in a rattle-trap car which he had bought second-hand and which squeaked and groaned, for all the expert repairing he had been able to do upon it.

The color, the humor, the sunshine of those old first days, in spite of their poverty!

He hesitated as to whether to ring the bell or no—just as he and Marie had, twenty-odd years before. She was so gay then, so hopeful, so all-unconscious of the rough fate that was in store for her here. . . . How would it be inside? Would Marie's little gas stove still be near the window in the combined kitchen, dining-room and laundry—almost general living-room—which that one room was? Would the thin single gas jet still be hanging from the ceiling over their small dining-room table (or the ghost of it) where so often after their meals, to save heat in the other room—because there was no heat in the alleged radiator, and their oil stove cost money—he had sat and read or worked on plans of some of the things he hoped to perfect—and had since, years since, but long after he had left her and this place? How sad! He had never had one touch of luck or opportunity with her here,—not one. Yet, if only she could, and without pain because of it, know how brilliantly he had finished some of them, how profitably they had resulted for him if not her.

But he scarcely looked like one who would be wanting to see so small an apartment, he now felt, tall and robust and prosperous as he was. Still might he not be thinking of buying this place? Or renting quarters for a servant or a relative? Who should know? What difference did it make? Why should he care?

He rang the bell, thinking of the small, stupid, unfriendly and self-defensive woman who, twenty or more years before, had come up from the basement below, wiping her hands on a gingham apron and staring at them querulously. How well he remembered her—and how unfriendly she had always remained in spite of their efforts to be friendly, because they had no tips to give her. She could not be here any longer, of course; no, this one coming was unlike her in everything except stupidity and grossness. But they were alike in that, well enough. This one was heavy, beefy. She would make almost two of the other one.

"The rooms," he had almost said "apartment," "on the top floor —may I see them?"

"Dey are only t'ree an' bat'—fourteen by der mont'."

"Yes, I know," he now added almost sadly. So they had not raised the rent in all this time, although the city had grown so. Evidently this region had become worse, not better. "I'll look at them, if you please, just the same," he went on, feeling that the dull face before him was wondering why he should be looking at them at all.

"Vait; I getcha der key. You can go up py yerself."

He might have known that she would never climb any four flights save under compulsion.

She returned presently, and he made his way upward, remembering how the fat husband of the former janitress had climbed up promptly every night at ten, if you please, putting out the wee lights of gas on the return trip (all but a thin flame on the second floor: orders from the landlord, of course), and exclaiming as he did so, at each landing, "Ach Gott, I go me up py der secon' floor ant make me der lights out. Ach Gott, I go me py der t'ird floor ant make me der lights out. Ach Gott, I go me py der fourt' floor ant make me der lights out," and so on until he reached the fifth, where they lived. How often he had listened to him, puffing and moaning as he came!

Yes, the yellowish-brown paper that they had abhorred then, or one nearly as bad, covered all these hall walls to-day. The stairs squeaked, just as they had then. The hall gas jets were just as small and surmounted by shabby little pink imitation glass candles—to give the place an air, no doubt! He and Marie would never have taken this place at all if it had depended on the hall, or if the views from its little windows had not been so fine. In the old days he had trudged up these steps many a night, winter and summer, listening, as he came, for sounds of Marie in the kitchen, for the prattle of the two children after they were with them, for the glow of a friendly light (always shining at six in winter) under the door and through the keyhole. His light! His door! In those early dark winter days, when he was working so far downtown and coming home this way regularly, Marie, at the sound of his key in the lock, would always come running, her heavy black hair done in a neat braid about her brow, her trim little figure buttoned gracefully into a house-dress of her own making. And she always had a smile and a "Hello, dearie; back again?" no matter how bad things were with them, how lean the little larder or the family purse. Poor little

Marie!

It all came back to him now as he trudged up the stairs and neared the door. God!

And here was the very door, unchanged—yellow, painted to imitate the natural grain of oak, but the job having turned out a dismal failure as he had noted years before. And the very lock the same! Could he believe? Scarcely any doubt of it. For here was that other old hole, stuffed with putty and painted over, which he and Marie had noted as being the scar of some other kind of a lock or knob that had preceded this one. And still stuffed with paper! Marie had thought burglars (!) might make their way in via that, and he had laughed to think what they would steal if they should. Poor little Marie!

But now, now—well, here he was all alone, twenty-four years later, Marie and Peter and Frank gone this long time, and he the master of so many men and so much power and so much important property. What was life, anyhow? What was it?

Ghosts! Ghosts!

Were there ghosts?

Did spirits sometimes return and live and dream over old, sad scenes such as this? Could Marie? Would she? Did she?

Oh, Marie! . . . Marie! Poor little weak, storm-beaten, life-beaten soul. And he the storm, really.

Well, here was the inside now, and things were not a bit different from what they had been in his and her day, when they had both been so poor. No, just the same. The floor a little more nail-marked, perhaps, especially in the kitchen here, where no doubt family after family had tacked down oil-cloth in place of other pieces taken up—theirs, for instance. And here in the parlor—save the mark!—the paper as violent as it had ever been! Such paper—red, with great bowls of pinkish flowers arranged in orderly rows! But then they were paying so little rent that it was ridiculous for them to suggest that they wanted anything changed. The landlord would not have changed it anyhow.

And here on the west wall, between the two windows, overlooking Abijah Hargot's home and the river and the creeping city beyond, was where he had hung a wretched little picture, a print of an etching of a waterscape which he had admired so much in those days and had bought somewhere second-hand for a dollar—a house on an inlet near the sea, such a house as he would have liked to have occupied, or thought he would—then. Ah, these windows! The northernmost one had always been preferred by him and her because of the sweep of view west and north. And how often he had stood looking at a soft, or bleak, or reddening, sunset over the river; or, of an early night in winter, at the lights on the water below. And the outpost apartments and homes of the great city beyond. Life had looked very dark then, indeed. At times, looking, he had been very sad. He was like some brooding Hamlet of an inventor as he stood there then gazing at the sweet little river, the twinkling stars in a steely black sky overhead; or, in the fall when it was still light, some cold red island of a cloud in the sky over the river and the city, and wondering what was to become of him—what was in store for him! The fallacy of such memories as these! Their futility!

But things had dragged and dragged—here! In spite of the fact that his mind was full of inventions, inventions, inventions, and methods of applying them in some general way which would earn him money, place, fame—as they subsequently did—the strange mysteries of ionic or electronic action, for instance, of motion, of attraction and polarity, of wave lengths and tensile strengths and adhesions in metals, woods and materials of all kinds—his apparent error in putting himself in a position where failure might come to him had so preyed on his mind here, that he could do nothing. He could only dream, and do common, ordinary day labor—skeleton wiring and insulating, for instance, electrical mapping, and the like. Again, later, but while still here, since he had been reading, reading, reading after marriage, and working and thinking, life had gone off into a kind of welter of conflicting and yet organized and plainly directed powers which was confusing to him, which was not to be explained by anything man could think of and which no inventor had as yet fully used, however great he was—Edison, Kelvin, or Bell. Everything as he knew then and hoped to make use of in some way was alive, everything full of force, even so-called dead or decaying things. Life was force, that strange, seemingly (at times) intelligent thing, and there was apparently nothing but force—everywhere—amazing, perfect, indestructible. (He had thought of all that here in this little room and on the roof overhead where he made some of his experiments, watching old Hargot's pigeons flying about the sky, the sound of their wings coming so close at times that they were like a whisper of the waves of the sea, dreams in themselves.)

But the little boundaries of so-called health and decay, strength and weakness, as well as all alleged *fixity* or changelessness of things, —how he had brooded on all that, at that time. And how all thought of fixity in anything had disappeared as a ridiculous illusion intended, maybe, by something to fool man into the belief that his world here, his physical and mental state, was real and enduring, a greater thing than anything else in the universe, when so plainly it was not. But not himself. A mere shadow—an illusion—nothing. On this little roof, here, sitting alone at night or by day in pleasant weather or gray, Saturdays and Sundays when it was warm and because they had no money and no particular place to go, and looking at the stars or the lights of the city or the sun shining on the waters of the little river below,—he had thought of all this. It had all come to him, the evanescence of everything, its slippery, protean changefulness. Everything was alive, and everything was nothing, in so far as its seeming reality was concerned. And yet everything was everything but still capable of being undermined, changed, improved, or come at in some hitherto undreamed-of way —even by so humble a creature as himself, an inventor—and used as chained force, if only one knew how. And that was why he had become a great inventor since—because he had thought so—had chained force and used it—even he. He had become conscious of anterior as well as ulterior forces and immensities and fathomless wells of wisdom and energy, and had enslaved a minute portion of them, that was all. But not here! Oh, no. Later!

The sad part of it, as he thought of it now, was that poor little Marie could not have understood a thing of all he was thinking, even if he had explained and explained, as he never attempted to do. Life was all a mystery to Marie—deep, dark, strange—as it was to him, only he was seeking and she was not. Sufficient to her to be near him, loving him in her simple, dumb way, not seeking to understand. Even then he had realized that and begun to condemn her for it in his mind, to feel that she was no real aid and could never be—just a mother-girl, a housewife, a social fixture, a cook, destined to be shoved back if ever he were really successful; and that was sad even then, however obviously true.

But to her, apparently, he was so much more than just a mere man—a god, really, a dream, a beau, a most wonderful person, dreaming strange dreams and thinking strange thoughts which would lead him heaven knows where; how high or how strange, though, she could never guess, nor even he then. And for that very reason—her blind, non-understanding adoration—she had bored him then, horribly at times. All that he could think of then, as he looked at her at times—after the first year or two or three, when the novelty of her physical beauty and charm had worn off and the children had come, and cares and worries due to his non-success were upon them—was that she was an honest, faithful, patient, adoring little drudge, but no more, and that was all she would ever be. Think of that! That was the way life was—the way it rewarded love! He had not begun to dislike her—no, that was not it—but it was because, as the philosopher had said, that in and through her and the babies he had given hostages to fortune, and that she was not exactly the type of woman who could further him as fast as he wished—that he had begun to weary of her. And that was practically the whole base of his objection to her,—not anything she did.

Yes, yes—it was that, *that*, that had begun to plague him as though he had consciously fastened a ball and chain on one foot and now never any more could walk quickly or well or be really free. Instead of being able to think on his inventions he was constantly being compelled to think on how he would make a living for her and them, or find ten more dollars, or get a new dress for Marie and shoes for the children! Or how increase his salary. That was the great and enduring problem all the time, and over and over here. Although healthy, vigorous and savagely ambitious, at that time, it was precisely because he was those things that he had rebelled so and had desired to be free. He was too strong and fretful as he could see now to endure so mean a life. It was that that had made him savage, curt, remote, indifferent so much of the time in these later days—here— And to her. And when she could not help it at all—poor little thing—did not know how to help it and had never asked him to marry her! Life had tinkled so in his ears then. It had called and called. And essentially, in his own eyes then, he was as much of a failure as a husband as he was at his work, and that was killing him. His mind had been too steadily depressed by his mistake in getting married, in having children so soon, as well as by his growing knowledge of what he might be fitted to do if only he had a chance to go off to a big technical school somewhere and work his way through alone and so get a new and better position somewhere else—to have a change of scene. For once, as he knew then, and with all his ideas, he was technically fitted for his work, with new light and experience in his mind, what wonders might he not accomplish! Sitting in this little room, or working or dreaming upstairs in the air, how often he had thought of all that!

But no; nothing happened for ever so long here. Days and weeks and months, and even years went by without perceptible change. Nature seemed to take a vicious delight in torturing him, then, in so far as his dreams were concerned, his hopes. Hard times came to America, blasting ones—a year and a half of panic really—in which every one hung on to his pathetic little place, and even he was afraid to relinquish the meagre one he had, let alone ask for more pay. At the same time his dreams, the passing of his youth, this unconscionable burden of a family, tortured him more and more. Marie did not seem to mind anything much, so long as she was with him. She suffered, of course, but more for him than for herself, for his unrest, and his dissatisfaction, which she feared. Would he ever leave her? Was he becoming unhappy with her? Her eyes so often asked what her lips feared to frame.

Once they had seventy dollars saved toward some inventive work of his. But then little Peter fell from the top of the washtub, where he had climbed for some reason, and broke his arm. Before it was healed and all the bills paid, the seventy was gone. Another time Marie's mother was dying, or so she thought, and she had to go back home and help her father and brother in their loneliness. Again, it was brother George who, broke, arrived from Philadelphia and lived with them a while because he had no place else to go. Also once he thought to better himself by leaving the International Electric, and joining the Winston Castro Generator Company. But when he had left the first, the manager of the second, to whom he had applied and by whom he had been engaged, was discharged ("let out," as he phrased it), and the succeeding man did not want him. So for three long months he had been without anything, and, like Job, finally, he had been ready to curse God and die.[5]

And then—right here in these rooms it was—he had rebelled, spiritually, as he now recalled, and had said to himself that he could not stand this any longer, that he was ruining his life, and that however much it might torture Marie—ruin her even—he must leave and do something to better his state. Yes quite definitely, once and for all, then, he had wished that he had not married Marie, that they had never been so foolish as to have children, that Marie was not dependent on him any more, that he was free to go, be, do, all the things he felt that he could go do, be—no matter where, so long as he went and was free. Yes, he had wished that in a violent, rebellious, prayerful way, and then—

Of all the winters of his life, the one that followed that was the blackest and bleakest, that last one with Marie. It seemed to bring absolutely nothing to either him or her or the children save disaster. Twenty-five dollars was all he had ever been able to make, apparently, while he was with her. The children were growing and constantly requiring more; Marie needed many things, and was skimping along on God knows what. Once she had made herself some corset slips and other things out of his cast-off underwear—bad as that was! And then once, when he was crossing Chadds Bridge, just below here, and had paused to meditate and dream, a new hat—his very best, needless to say, for he had worn his old one until it was quite gone—had blown off into the water, a swift wind and some bundles he was compelled to carry home aiding, and had been swiftly carried out by the tide. So much had he been harried in those days by one thing and another that at first he had not even raged, although he was accustomed so to do. Instead then he had just shut his teeth and trudged on in the biting wind, in danger of taking cold and dying of something or other—as he had

5. It was the wife of Job who said, "Dost thou still retain thine integrity? Curse God, and die" (Job ii: 9).

thought at the time—only then he had said to himself that he did not really mind now. What difference did it make to himself or anybody whether he died or not? Did anybody care really, God or anybody else, what became of him? Supposing he did it? What of it? Could it be any worse than this? To hell with life itself, and its Maker,—this brutal buffeting of winds and cold and harrying hungers and jealousies and fears and brutalities, arranged to drive and make miserable these crawling, beggarly creatures—men! Why, what had he ever had of God or any creative force so far? What had God ever done for him or his life, or his wife and children?

So he had defiantly raged.

And then life—or God, or what you will—had seemed to strike at last. It was as if some Jinnee[6] of humane or inhuman power had said, "Very well, then, since you are so dissatisfied and unhappy, so unworthy of all this (perhaps) that I have given you, you shall have your will, your dreams. You have prayed to be free. Even so—this thing that you see here now shall pass away. You have sinned against love and faith in your thoughts. You shall be free! Look! Behold! You shall be! Your dreams shall come true!"

And then, at once, as if in answer to this command of the Jinnee, as though, for instance, it had waved its hand, the final storm began which blew everything quite away. Fate struck. It was as if black angels had entered and stationed themselves at his doors and windows, armed with the swords of destruction, of death. Harpies and furies beset his path and perched on his roof. One night—it was a month before Peter and Frank died, only three days before they contracted their final illness—he was crossing this same bridge below here and was speculating, as usual, as to his life and his future, when suddenly, in spite of the wind and cold and some dust flying from a coal barge below, his eye was attracted by two lights which seemed to come dancing down the hill from the direction of his apartment and passed out over the river. They rose to cross over the bridge in front of him and disappeared on the other side. They came so close they seemed almost to brush his face, and yet he could not quite accept them as real. There was something too eerie about them. From the moment he first laid eyes on them in the distance they seemed strange. They came so easily, gracefully, and went so. From the first moment he saw them there below Teget-miller's paint shop, he wondered about them. What were they? What could they mean? They were so bluish clear, like faint, grey stars, so pale and watery. Suddenly it was as if something whispered to him, "Behold! These are the souls of your children. They are going—never to return! See! Your prayers are being answered!"

And then it was that, struck with a kind of horror and numb

6. In Moslem belief a supernatural being subject to magic control.

despair, he had hurried home, quite prepared to ask Marie if the two boys were dead or if anything had happened to them. But, finding them up and playing as usual he had tried to put away all thought of this fact as a delusion, to say nothing. But the lights haunted him. They would not stay out of his mind. Would his boys really die? Yet the first and the second day went without change. But on the third both boys took sick, and he knew his dread was well founded.

For on the instant, Marie was thrown into a deep, almost inexplicable, depression, from which there was no arousing her, although she attempted to conceal it from him by waiting on and worrying over them. They had to put the children in the one little bedroom (theirs), while they used an extension cot in the "parlor," previously occupied by the children. Young Dr. Newton, the one physician of repute in the neighborhood, was called in, and old Mrs. Wetzel, the German woman in front, who, being old and lonely and very fond of Marie, had volunteered her services. And so they had weathered along, God only knows how. Marie prepared the meals—or nearly all of them—as best she could. He had gone to work each day, half in a dream, wondering what the end was to be.

And then one night, as he and Marie were lying on the cot pretending to sleep, he felt her crying. And taking her in his arms he had tried to unwish all the dark things he had wished, only apparently then it was too late. Something told him it was. It was as though in some dark mansion somewhere—some supernal court or hall of light or darkness—his prayer had been registered and answered, a decision made, and that that decision could not now be unmade. No. Into this shabby little room where they lay and where she was crying had come a final black emissary, scaled, knightly, with immense arms and wings and a glittering sword, all black, and would not leave until all this should go before him. Perhaps he had been a little deranged in his mind at the time, but so it had seemed.

And then, just a few weeks after he had seen the lights and a few days after Marie had cried so, Peter had died—poor weak little thing that he was—and, three days later, Frank. Those terrible hours! For by then he was feeling so strange and sad and mystical about it all that he could neither eat nor sleep nor weep nor work nor think. He had gone about, as indeed had Marie, in a kind of stupor of misery and despair. True, as he now told himself—and then too, really,—he had not loved the children with all the devotion he should have or he would never have had the thoughts he had had—or so he had reasoned afterward. Yet then as now he suffered because of the love he should have given them, *and had not—*

and now could not any more, save in memory. He recalled how both boys looked in those last sad days, their pinched little faces and small weak hands! Marie was crushed, and yet dearer for the time being than ever before. But the two children, once gone, had seemed the victims of his own dark thoughts as though his own angry, resentful wishes had slain them. And so, for the time, his mood changed. He wished, if he could, that he might undo it all, go on as before with Marie, have other children to replace these lost ones in her affection—but no. It was apparently not to be, not ever any more.

For, once they were gone, the cords which had held him and Marie together were weaker, not stronger—almost broken, really. For the charm which Marie had originally had for him had mostly been merged in the vivacity and vitality and interest of these two prattling curly-headed boys. Despite the financial burden, the irritation and drain they had been at times, they had also proved a binding chain, a touch of sweetness in the relationship, a hope for the future, a balance which had kept even this uneven scale. With them present he had felt that however black the situation it must endure because of them, their growing interests; with them gone, it was rather plain that some modification of their old state was possible—just how, for the moment, he scarcely dared think or wish. It might be that he could go away and study for awhile now. There was no need of his staying here. The neighborhood was too redolent now of the miseries they had endured. Alone somewhere else, perhaps, he could collect his thoughts, think out a new program. If he went away he might eventually succeed in doing better by Marie. She could return to her parents in Philadelphia for a little while and wait for him, working there at something as she had before until he was ready to send for her. The heavy load of debts could wait until he was better able to pay them. In the meantime, also, he could work and whatever he made over and above his absolute necessities might go to her—or to clearing off these debts.

So he had reasoned.

But it had not worked out so of course. No. In the broken mood in which Marie then was it was not so easy. Plainly, since he had run across her that April day in Philadelphia when he was wiring for the great dry goods store, her whole life had become identified with his, although his had not become merged with hers. No. She was, and would be, as he could so plainly see, then, nothing without him, whereas he—he— Well, it had long since been plain that he would be better off without her—materially, anyhow. But what would she do if he stayed away a long time—or never came back? What become? Had he thought of that then? Yes, he had. He had even thought that once away he might not feel like renewing this situation which had proved so disastrous. And Marie had seemed to sense that, too. She was so sad. True he had not thought of all these things in any bold outright fashion then. Rather they were as sly, evasive shadows skulking in the remote recesses of his brain, things which scarcely dared show their faces to the light, although later, once safely away—they had come forth boldly enough. Only at that time, and later—even now, he could not help feeling that however much Marie might have lacked originally, or then, the fault for their might was his,—that if he himself had not been so dull in the first instance all these black things would not have happened to him or to her. But could she go on without him? Would she? he had asked himself then. And answered that it would be better for him to leave and build himself up in a different world, and then return and help her later. So he fretted and reasoned.

But time had solved all that, too. In spite of the fact that he could not help picturing her back there alone with her parents in Philadelphia, their poor little cottage in Leigh Street in which she and her parents had lived—not a cottage either, but a minute little brick pigeon-hole in one of those long lines of red, treeless, smoky barracks flanking the great mills of what was known as the Reffington District, where her father worked—he had gone. He had asked himself what would she be doing there? What thinking, all alone without him—the babies dead? But he had gone.

He recalled so well the day he left her—she to go to Philadelphia, he to Boston, presumably—the tears, the depression, the unbelievable sadness in her soul and his. Did she suspect? Did she foreknow? She was so gentle, even then, so trustful, so sad. "You will come back to me, dearie, won't you, soon?" she had said, and so sadly. "We will be happy yet, won't we?" she had asked between sobs. And he had promised. Oh yes; he had done much promising in his life, before and since. That was one of the darkest things in his nature, his power of promising.

But had he kept that?

However much in after months and years he told himself that he wanted to, that he must, that it was only fair, decent, right, still he had not gone back. No. Other things had come up with the passing of the days, weeks, months, years, other forces, other interests. Some plan, person, desire had always intervened, interfered, warned, counseled, delayed. Were there such counselors? There had been times during the first year when he had written her and sent her a little money—money he had needed badly enough himself. Later there was that long period in which he felt that she must be getting along well enough, being with her parents and at work, and he had not written. A second woman had already appeared on the scene by then as a friend. And then—

The months and years since then in which he had not done so! After his college course—which he took up after he left Marie, working his way—he had left Boston and gone to K—— to begin a career as an assistant plant manager and a developer of ideas of his own, selling the rights to such things as he invented to the great company with which he was connected. And then it was that by degrees the idea of a complete independence and a much greater life had occurred to him. He found himself so strong, so interesting to others. Why not be free, once and for all? Why not grow greater? Why not go forward and work out all the things about which he had dreamed? The thing from which he had extricated himself was too confining, too narrow. It would not do to return. The old shell could not now contain him. Despite her tenderness, Marie was not significant enough. So— He had already seen so much that he could do, be, new faces, a new world, women of a higher social level.

But even so, the pathetic little letters which still followed from time to time—not addressed to him in his new world (she did not know where he was), but to him in the old one—saying how dearly she loved him, how she still awaited his return, that she knew he was having a hard time, that she prayed always, and that all would come out right yet, that they would be able to be together yet!— she was working, saving, praying for him! True, he had the excuse that for the first four years he had not really made anything much, but still he might have done something for her,—might he not have?—gone back, persuaded her to let him go, made her comfortable, brought her somewhat nearer him even? Instead he had feared, feared, reasoned, argued.

Yes, the then devil of his nature, his ambition, had held him completely. He was seeing too clearly the wonder of what he might be, and soon, what he was already becoming. Everything as he argued then and saw now would have had to be pushed aside for Marie, whereas what he really desired was that his great career, his greater days, his fame, the thing he was sure to be now—should push everything aside. And so— Perhaps he had become sharper, colder, harder, than he had ever been, quite ready to sacrifice everything and everybody, or nearly, until he should be the great success he meant to be. But long before this he might have done so much. And he had not—had not until very recently decided to revisit this older, sweeter world.

But in the meantime, as he had long since learned, how the tragedy of her life had been completed. All at once in those earlier years all letters had ceased, and time slipping by—ten years really— he had begun to grow curious. Writing back to a neighbor of hers in Philadelphia in a disguised hand and on nameless paper, he had learned that nearly two years before her father had died and that she and her mother and brother had moved away, the writer could not say where. Then, five years later, when he was becoming truly prosperous, he had learned, through a detective agency, that she and her mother and her ne'er-do-well brother had moved back into this very neighborhood—this old neighborhood of his and hers!—or, rather, a little farther out near the graveyard where their two boys were buried. The simplicity of her! The untutored homing instinct!

But once here, according to what he had learned recently, she and her mother had not prospered at all. They had occupied the most minute of apartments farther out, and had finally been compelled to work in a laundry in their efforts to get along—and he was already so well-to-do, wealthy, really! Indeed three years before his detectives had arrived, her mother had died, and two years after that, she herself, of pneumonia, as had their children. Was it a message from her that had made him worry at that time? Was that why, only six months since, although married and rich and with two daughters by this later marriage, he had not been able to rest until he had found this out, returned here now to see? Did ghosts still stalk the world?

Yes, to-day he had come back here, but only to realize once and for all now how futile this errand was, how cruel he had been, how dreary her latter days must have been in this poor, out-of-the-way corner where once, for a while at least, she had been happy—he and she.

"Been happy!"

"By God," he suddenly exclaimed, a passion of self-reproach and memory overcoming him, "I can't stand this! It was not right, not fair. I should not have waited so long. I should have acted long, long since. The cruelty—the evil! There is something cruel and evil in it all, in all wealth, all ambition, in love of fame—too cruel. I must get out! I must think no more—see no more."

And hurrying to the door and down the squeaking stairs, he walked swiftly back to the costly car that was waiting for him a few blocks below the bridge—that car which was so representative of the realm of so-called power and success of which he was now the master—that realm which, for so long, had taken its meaningless lustre from all that had here preceded it—the misery, the loneliness, the shadow, the despair. And in it he was whirled swiftly and gloomily away.

1918, 1927

The Twentieth Century: Literary Renaissance and Social Challenge

Recent generations of writers have been concerned possibly more than ever before with immediate problems, both spiritual and social; and these problems have assumed world dimensions in consequence of mammoth and historic changes in society. The American literature of this age has been one of urgency and power. If it has reflected the violence and the upheavals of the century, it has also been humanized and enriched by restless and imaginative curiosity, by spiritual hunger, and by the search for understanding and wisdom. It has commanded a vast audience far beyond our shores and has become in fact a world literature, exerting an influence comparable to that of American material progress during the same period.

Twentieth-century spiritual unrest and skepticism were deeply rooted in nineteenth-century thought. The great English Victorians, from Matthew Arnold to Thomas Hardy, contributed to its growth, while in the United States it was transmitted to the twentieth century by such writers as William James, Santayana, Henry Adams, Garland, Dreiser, Moody, and Robinson. Similarly, the spirit of economic and social revolt can be traced without interruption from the later works of Twain and Howells to those of Sherwood Anderson, Sandburg, and Lewis. Twentieth-century realism and naturalism, as well as new experiments in literary form, continued to draw inspiration from such nineteenth-century masters as Dostoevski and Turgenev, Balzac, Zola, Flaubert, and the French symbolists; and from such transitional European writers as Hardy and George Moore, Ibsen and Shaw, Gide, Yeats, and Synge. Romanticism became a mere genteel survival; Poe and Melville

Nature of Climate of Ideas 1885 – 1915
1. rapid advance of sci thought (force)
2. conclusions regarding nature of man
3. ran to optimism

John Fisk - diest

were more highly esteemed than Irving or Longfellow; Whitman, largely neglected by Americans during his life, exerted a powerful influence; Emily Dickinson, posthumously published in 1890, became a living force after 1914; and Henry James, an exotic to his American contemporaries, entered the midstream of twentieth-century literature, influencing authors as widely different as Edith Wharton and T. S. Eliot.

TWENTIETH-CENTURY RENAISSANCE

By 1920, directly after the first World War, it was evident that a new age of literary expression was already well advanced. The volume of American literary activity, the large number of new authors—critics, poets, novelists, and playwrights —the high level of their powers, the originality, daring, and general success of many new forms of expression, and the absorbed response of a reading public larger and more critical than ever before, produced a new national literature at least as brilliant as the regional flowering of New England nearly a century earlier. The widely used phrase "twentieth-century renaissance" seems scarcely too pretentious to describe what was occurring.

Actually, however, the nature of this twentieth-century renaissance, and its dominant expression, had already been established during the second decade of the century; the temporary absorption of the country in the World War from 1917 to 1919 barely interrupted the tide of new literature, although it provided fresh themes and focused

even more sharply the spiritual problems and disillusionments of this critical generation of writers. If the war is regarded as a point of intellectual intensification and broadening experience, there may be some usefulness in the historical identification of the years before the war as a "little renaissance," distinguishing them from the full tide of accomplishment after 1920, when writers already established shared with younger newcomers in the expression of the mingled malaise, desire for social experiment, and tempered hope of the postwar generation. However, the years from about 1910 to V-E Day in 1945, ending World War II, may be viewed as a single literary period, punctuated and modified by World War I; by the financial crash of 1929 and the ensuing depression; by the "New Deal" recovery after 1933; and by World War II. The dominant character of this literature is its intensity and the almost scientific candor of its explorations into the spiritual nature of man and the value of his society and institutions, in an age of clashing ideologies during which American life, and established concepts of human faith, had to be reconstructed or defended.

By 1910 the nature of the new age was suggested in recent works of such writers as Henry James, William James, Henry Adams, Moody, Robinson, Gertrude Stein, Norris, London, Upton Sinclair, and Steffens. In 1911 Dreiser published *Jennie Gerhardt*, his first novel since 1900. In rapid succession appeared *The Financier* (1912),

Naturalism = i.e. an accepted fact of determinism i.e. aspects of personality and power of accomplishment were determined.

The Titan (1914), and *The "Genius"* (1915), establishing him as the great realist of his generation, and giving encouragement to the nascent naturalism of younger authors. In 1911 Edith Wharton temporarily abandoned the tradition of Henry James, producing in *Ethan Frome* a small naturalistic masterpiece of immediate influence. Ellen Glasgow in the same year published *The Miller of Old Church*, her first realistic novel of the soil.

It was also in 1911 that Ezra Pound, who had published his first *Personae* in 1909 in London, joined forces with T. E. Hulme, a young British thinker, in giving direction to the youthful group of American and British poets in London who soon were known as the imagists. They inaugurated the "new poetry" movement, published aesthetic manifestoes, attracted such American poets as "H.D.," William Carlos Williams, and Amy Lowell, and collected their poems in imagist anthologies. Their poems stimulated the development of free verse and other experimental forms. They contributed to the success of *Poetry: A Magazine of Verse*, founded in Chicago in 1912, which was destined to become an important vehicle for the astonishing flood of new and vital poetry. During this period Robinson reached the height of his poetic power with *The Man Against the Sky* (1916) and *Merlin* (1917). Frost published his first volume in 1913; by 1923, when his fourth volume appeared, the world had seen the bulk of his best-known poems.

A midwestern balladist, Vachel Lindsay, won a meteoric fame in three volumes between 1913 and 1917. The vital poetic criticism of midwestern life began with Masters' *Spoon River Anthology* in 1915; but even more impressive was the poetry of Sandburg who, in three volumes between 1916 and 1920, explored the lives of his midwestern commoners in a powerful free verse at once coarse and tender. Edna St. Vincent Millay published her first spectacular book of poems in 1917; T. S. Eliot, in two volumes published by 1920, appeared at once in his mature character, unique and powerful.

In this period a vigorous criticism was fostered by such writers as More, Babbitt, Huneker, Spingarn, Van Wyck Brooks, and Mencken. The latter had begun his crusade before 1910, and he reached the height of his satirical effectiveness as editor of the *American Mercury* after 1924. Essentially a conservative individualist, he waged unceasing war on the mass mind, excoriating alike the cultural imbecilities of *hoi polloi*, the sterile conventionality of the middle-class mind, the venality of political leaders, and the deference of high society toward Europe. He was a liberator: he directed his eloquent wrath against prohibitionists and puritans, against well-paid guardians of other people's morals, against the defenders of official "decency." He championed such "immoral" authors as Dreiser, Cabell, and Sherwood Anderson.

Cabell and Anderson were only two of many new experimentalists in fiction who had commanded attention before 1920. In a number of novels, of which *Jurgen* (1919) was best known, Cabell daringly infused medieval romance with somewhat too obvious sexual symbolism. The same year, in *Winesburg, Ohio*, Sherwood Anderson first exerted his influence as a pessimistic social critic and the subtle master of intense psychological motivations. Upton Sinclair, who had begun his attack on industrial capitalism in *The Jungle* (1906), was now publishing such books as *King Coal* (1917) and *The Brass Check* (1919). Ernest Poole, in *The Harbor* (1915), studied the degradation of the dock workers; Winston Churchill gained popular following with such liberal ethical novels as *The Inside of the Cup* (1913) and *A Far Country* (1915). Willa Cather, who was to make a great contribution to both symbolic fiction and regional realism, produced in *O Pioneers!* (1913), her first novel of the Nebraska frontier and the new immigrant Americans who enriched it with their lives. She returned to this theme in *My Ántonia* (1918), but meanwhile she had combined it, in *The Song of the Lark* (1915), with her discovery of the desert civilization of the Southwest, on which she later based her masterpiece, *Death Comes for the Archbishop* (1927).

Thus, by the time the Treaty of Versailles ended World War I, many of the powerful authors of this century had already created a new literature of enduring merit, characterized by aesthetic originality and rebellion, by the determination to shatter conventional taboos in their expression of physical and psychological actuality, by a mystical hunger for spiritual enlightenment which attracted them toward symbolic or primitivistic expression, and by a growing sense of responsibility for their fellow human beings, expressed in the directness of their attack upon the contemporary social order. Theirs was not the merely sentimental concern for the individual in society that had actuated humanitarian social critics a century earlier. Their target was the total society and its fundamental institutions; they were dedicated to the task of confirming the dignity and value of man in the face of complex new forces and ideas that threatened to dehumanize him. Authors in the generations younger than Dreiser, who had published many of his important works by 1915, have not adhered so rigorously to the formula of the naturalist Zola, yet our literature has continued to be preoccupied with the question of the extent of man's opportunity, as compared with that of other animals, to escape the determination of his fate by blind laws of heredity, environment, and survival. Characteristic influences of naturalism are apparent in the "hard-boiled" style of Hemingway's early work and that of many successors; naturalism is mingled with primitivism in the novels of Steinbeck and Faulkner, and with primitivistic and Freudian elements in Jeffers, Caldwell, and O'Neill; it is reflected in the presentation of the strict relations between environment and fate illustrated by the *Studs Lonigan* trilogy (1932–1935) of Farrell, and in the Marxist criticism of history best exemplified by Dos Passos in *U.S.A.* (1930–1936). Indeed, the events of the first World War and its aftermath only strengthened the growing belief that history is a mechanism responding to the obdurate dynamics of force and mass, rather than to the collective good will of men or to inspired leadership.

WORLD WAR I

To the authors of the 1920's, the architects of the second phase of our twentieth-century literature, the stupendous totality and horror of a world war was an inescapable demonstration of this mechanistic theory of history and human life. The human personality was dwarfed as much by the dehumanizing magnitude of modern events as by the obdurate tendency of natural laws to deny mankind a special destiny. The diminishment of individual identity has been intensified ever since by the depersonalizing bigness of industry and national affairs, the astronomical growth of populations in a mass civilization, the tendency of scientific knowledge to outrun humane controls, and the continued success of individual corruption and national aggression under the very shadow of recurrent and total warfare.

This crisis of mankind, and its consequent anxieties and tensions, has remained a dominant motivation of our literature to the very present, but the authors who faced the world of the 1920's had a more im-

mediate cause of disillusionment. Since the armistice of November 11, 1918, they had witnessed the tragic failure of the Versailles Treaty and the League of Nations—after a war which liberals and writers, as well as the American masses, had supported as a crusade to "end war," to "make the world safe for democracy," and to effect "a lasting peace founded on honor and justice." Wilson's Fourteen Points in 1918 sincerely represented this idealism, yet the European statesmen who accepted his preliminary conditions for a peace conference had already made secret agreements to promote French and British imperialism, and to perpetuate the explosive dangers in European life. The isolationist fears and selfish provinciality which obstructed President Wilson's idealism at home contributed to the success of his diplomatic enemies abroad, and although many historians now view these events in a different perspective, the important fact for literary history is the vast disillusionment of American liberals and writers, which coincided with the national extravagances, corruptions, and social decadence of the so-called Jazz Age, during the 1920's.

The earliest literary manifestations of this age recorded the revolt of youth, but the large body of writings attesting the condition of "flaming youth" or the delinquency of the "flapper" has left for posterity only the wit and daring of Edna Millay's earlier poems, and the first novels of F. Scott Fitzgerald, who remains the historian of this generation of young sophisticates. However, it would be a mistake to ignore their revolt, for to some degree it expressed the same attitudes that Mencken was displaying, and in the same disguise of meaningful badinage and uproar it revealed the spiritual perturbations which the greatest of our authors soon embodied in more enduring works. Youth was repelled by the reactionary sham and hypocrisy on every hand; by the "Red scares," witch-hunting, and prohibition fostered by the one-hundred-per-cent patriots and the new "puritans." This generation of "flaming" youth was actually a-fire with social revolt. However disorderly its noisy mixture of Byronism, Bohemianism, and gaiety, its object was the destruction of unhealthy psychological taboos; if it uncritically championed both Cabell's somewhat shallow *Jurgen* (1919) and Joyce's great *Ulysses* (1922), its object was to defeat the unfair censorship of both volumes.

The general disenchantment of serious writers after the war was only increased by the shocking prevalence of corruption and irresponsibility both in government and in private enterprise. In the years that followed, the European economies were crushed, while the United States became the economic capital of the world. But amid soaring prices, production, and profits, there was a brooding discontent among labor. The notorious scandals of the Harding administration (1920–1923) recalled the Gilded Age, while organized crime, thriving on the violation of the unpopular prohibition

laws and the venality of officials, produced an era of violence, terror, and moral delinquency. In spite of the conservative policies of Coolidge (1923–1929) the tide of inflation and expansion swept on until 1929, when the country plunged into the depths of its greatest financial depression.

Yet this decade, from 1919 to 1929, produced the greatest body of our twentieth-century literature. In general the new authors of the period responded, in various ways, to the social and moral confusions that have been described. Expatriation was an early symptom of their restlessness. Such authors as Pound, Eliot, MacLeish, Hemingway, and Edmund Wilson, thronging in the literary "colonies" of London or Paris, or in Italy or elsewhere, were not "a lost generation" as Gertrude Stein in Paris asserted, for they ultimately promoted the absorption of reinvigorating European influences into contemporary American writing. The war itself provided a vital subject for many new authors. It inspired the first novel of Dos Passos, but he did not win attention until 1921, when he published a second war novel, *Three Soldiers*. Eliot was already well known when he published *The Waste Land* (1922), but it established his greatness and dramatically advanced the pessimistic conclusion that the war was a final evidence of the collapse of Western civilization beneath the weight of materialism. Hemingway drew directly upon the spiritual consequences of the war in his early masterpieces,

In Our Time (1924), *The Sun Also Rises* (1926), and A *Farewell to Arms* (1929), contrasting the hard and wounded gallantry of individuals with the soft decadence of society. In the flourishing new theater, *What Price Glory* (1924), a tough and naturalistic transcript of the war, gave Maxwell Anderson (co-author with Laurence Stallings) his earliest success. Faulkner's first major work was a war novel, *Soldiers' Pay*, in 1926.

Other authors, responding to a variety of influences, gained prominence in other areas of literary revolt. Lewis, in *Main Street* (1920) and *Babbitt* (1922), appeared as the satirist of the patterned dullness of bourgeois success and the small-town mentality, while in 1925 Dreiser, in *An American Tragedy*, and Dos Passos, in *Manhattan Transfer*, pursued the theme of materialism in novels both naturalistic and tragic. During 1925 also, audiences were seeing, in George Kelly's tragedy of *Craig's Wife*, the ruin of a marriage by materialism, and Fitzgerald, in his masterpiece, *The Great Gatsby*, showed its consequences in terms of the fabulous high living, wild speculation, and organized criminality of the period.

The psychological probing of the spiritual personality, still continued by such earlier authors as Sherwood Anderson, Robinson, and Willa Cather, was augmented by the work of powerful new recruits. One was the brilliant Eugene O'Neill, who between 1919 and 1922 founded a new theater of spiritual symbolism, with such plays as *Anna Christie, Beyond the Horizon, The Emperor Jones,* and *The Hairy Ape.* Freudian conclusions appeared in the poems of Jeffers, beginning with *Tamar* (1924) and *Roan Stallion* (1925), and in the later novels of Faulkner, beginning with *The Sound and the Fury* (1929).

In the same year the powerful young voice of Thomas Wolfe was heard in *Look Homeward, Angel*, the first of the succession of novels in which he reflected the search of a spiritually homeless younger generation for a sense of unity with a world apparently so vast, complex, and impersonal. Wolfe's vitality and natural optimism were in contrast with the mood then possessing Archibald MacLeish, who embodied the darkness of youth in such poems as *The Hamlet of A. MacLeish* (1928).

POETRY AND DRAMA

One of the most noteworthy phenomena of this literary revival was the opulence, power, and popularity of poetry and drama, forms which had been relatively dormant for a longer period than fiction. The imagist and free-verse movements lost their momentum during the war, but such poets as Eliot, Jeffers, and MacLeish, in postwar works that have already been mentioned, gave new directions and new strength to American poetry.

In general our poetry in this century, until the time of the second World War, became increasingly subtle in its symbolism, more reliant upon allusions to earlier literary works or to suggestions of mythological meaning, and more inclined toward intellectual depth or brilliance rather than sheerly lyrical appeal. The imagists and Pound had found inspiration in the French symbolists, the classics, the troubadour poets, the Italian Renaissance, and even ancient Chinese and Japanese forms of verse. The erudition of Eliot emphasized, besides these sources, the inspiration of philosophy, religious thought, Eastern mysticism, and anthropological lore. Eliot and others rediscovered not only the Elizabethan poets and dramatists but also the English metaphysical poets of the Jacobean period, of whom John Donne was the most powerful exemplar.

The intense and often violent metaphysical image heightened the intellectual tension and symbolic range of poetry, making it more difficult, but also more capable as an instrument for representing by abstraction the emotional significance of ideas. Metaphysical tendencies characterized the poetry of MacLeish, Stevens, Williams, Marianne Moore, Cummings, Crane, and the Nashville "Fugitives," principally Ransom and Tate.

Much poetry of great interest or noble loftiness has resulted from this symbolist movement, although the tendency of critics to give this intellectual expression their sole attention has resulted in the apparent if not actual critical disparagement of great poets of other and simpler schools of expression, and in the gradual diminishment of the appeal of poetry to a wide audience.

American drama between the two wars became for the first time a widely recognized instrument of national expression, involving the intellectual and emotional life, as well as the urban and national problems, of the United States. During the first two decades of the century our theater, while flourishing, had relied principally on the long-established conventions of the drama. Slowly, however, it responded to the experimental, symbolic, and critical drama from abroad; to the influence of such dramatists as Ibsen, Strindberg, Hauptmann, Shaw, Galsworthy, and Maeterlinck, and to the sophisticated Viennese and French comedy and the French drama of social revolt.

Popular interest in the theater was quickened by the visits of companies from the experimental "art" theaters abroad, such as the Abbey Theatre of Dublin; and soon the little-theater movement was represented in the United States by many urban professional groups and by community or regional companies. O'Neill, as the earliest liberator, was the leading experimentalist of the Provincetown group in 1916. By 1925, he had achieved the dominant stature which he retained during the following decade. Each of his plays was a new experiment in form, but his emphasis was always on the psychological analysis and symbolic representation of character. A bit later Maxwell Anderson attained a position second only to that of O'Neill. His many dramas included social comedies, character problem plays and dramas of social protest, tragedies in classical form, and experiments in the poetic drama. The little theaters developed such regional writers as Paul Green and Lynn Riggs; while the metropolitan theater brought to prominence scores of brilliant new authors and actors and sent an abundance of new plays touring the country in spite of mounting costs and the competition of the motion pictures.

Social and domestic comedy and the character problem play attained especial brilliance in the hands of Rachel Crothers, Barry, Kelly, Kaufman, Connelly, Wilder, Sidney Howard, Behrman, and Sherwood. In the area of social protest and propaganda the name of Elmer Rice was perhaps most prominent, although such others as Odets and Kingsley are well remembered. The element of social protest was also strong in the work of O'Neill, Maxwell Anderson, Barry, Kaufman, and others.

The energies of the theater noticeably waned during World War II, and since then the combination of high production costs and the competition of mass vehicles of entertainment has prevented recovery, but the recent work of a few writers such as Tennessee Williams, Arthur Miller, and William Inge attests the continuing life of the theater.

PRIMITIVISM

In connection with all forms of literature in the present century, the presence in certain authors of Freudian or primitivistic tendencies has been noted. The artist might follow Freud, who emphasized sexual inhibition as the source of fixations and complexes resulting in neurotic behavior, or he might follow the school of Jung or of another; in any case, if his techniques involved the artistic analysis of psychological motivation, he was here provided with an instrument which he could employ in support of a naturalistic or deterministic interpretation of life. Also, Freudian techniques authorized the use of materials which had been taboo, a use dramatically illustrated by Joyce's *Ulysses*, which reveals the aberrant and violent images present in the stream of consciousness of the central character. O'Neill, Faulkner, and Jeffers are only the three most successful of the many American authors who have employed the analysis of the subconscious for characterization.

Similarly, primitivism, often supported by the premises of Freudian psychology, assumes that basic truths of human behavior are best observed where conditions are least inhibited by refinements or sophistication. The combination of the primitive with the picturesque provides the simple charm of balladry and other folk arts. However, violence is also primitive, and so is the untrammeled manifestation of sex, as these appear in works of London and Frank Norris, Faulkner, Hemingway, Steinbeck, and Jeffers; and it is assumed that refined persons can learn of humanity by observing the inhabitants of Tobacco Road or God's Little Acre. The range of both Freudian and primitivistic analysis is enormous.

The era of the 1920's ended with the Great Depression, following the financial crash of 1929. Paralleling the rise of Hitler and Mussolini abroad, the depression period brought economic distress, ideological unrest, and a general reappraisal of American values. Many writers discovered the depths of their loyalty to traditional American idealism. MacLeish published *New Found Land* (1930) and *Conquistador* (1932), and gave himself for a decade to the writing of democratic propaganda; as the clouds of a second war became ominous, he rallied his fellow authors to recognize "a time to speak" in defense of American ideals. Stephen Vincent Benét wrote *John Brown's Body* (1928); he reaffirmed his American loyalties in *Western Star* (1943); and he composed poems celebrating his early heroes, such as Jefferson and Audubon. Sandburg, who had begun his career with collectivist sympathies, now wrote lovingly of *The People, Yes* (1936) and turned to the completion of his mammoth study of Lincoln.

While many other writers had faith in the remedial processes of American democracy, a great many were impatient. The utopian promise of Marxism and various forms of state collectivism was reflected by such authors as Floyd Dell, Max Eastman, Ezra Pound, Granville Hicks, John Dos Passos, and Richard Wright. Many liberals, such as Dos Passos and Hemingway, were drawn temporarily to the left by sympathy for the loyalists in the Spanish civil

war in 1936. The best writing of Dos Passos is to be found in the books of his Marxist period—from *Manhattan Transfer* (1925) through the novels of the U.S.A. trilogy (1930–1936). Few such writers continued to maintain the Marxist position as it became clear that collectivism inevitably produced dictatorship, totalitarian suppression of the individual, and the inhuman excesses characterizing modern international aggression.

The political and social ideologies of writers have become increasingly influential in this century because democracy has been successful in producing literacy and social fluidity such as have never before been seen on a mammoth scale. By 1950 some twenty per cent of American youth entered college, as compared with two per cent in Great Britain. The remarkable growth of mass media of communication vastly increased the range of the writer's influence, and while such earlier authors as Fitzgerald were harmed by the temptation to write in accordance with the formula of a popular magazine, others have been able without compromise to find readers in the expanding audience for serious literature which has made possible, for example, the publication in 1952 of Hemingway's *The Old Man and the Sea* in a magazine committed to mass appeal. The circulation of books between 1925 and 1950 greatly increased, and the book clubs alone, during the prosperity of the 1940's, averaged an annual sale of a hundred million copies. With the growth of reprint publishing and the broadening potentialities of radio and television, the total opportunities for literature greatly exceed anything previously imagined, and the writer has become increasingly, in this period, a genuine instrument of the whole society.

The half century just concluded must go down in history as the most complex in the annals of modern mankind, and one of the most swiftly kaleidoscopic in its movements. Ideas and events have been mutually interactive. However the political events of this age may be viewed, the almost miraculous simultaneous appearance, about 1920, of a large number of greatly gifted writers in America produced an illustrious literary epoch. It is the individual power and accomplishments of the greatest of these writers that we have attempted to emphasize in the selections and notes that follow.

Scientific
Determinism:
Optimism — progress inherent
pessimism — no assumption that
Change ≡ progress (improvement)
but an adaptation to environment

American Revaluations

EDWIN ARLINGTON ROBINSON

Among the eight or ten most gifted of his country's poets, Edwin Arlington Robinson is also notable for the scale and versatility of his work, surpassing in this respect any contemporary except Yeats. Yet it is not easy to recall a poem, large or small, that does not illustrate his painstaking zeal for perfection even in the last detail of structure or phrasing. His perfectionism is not mere fussiness, but an intrinsic discipline of form and meaning. Robinson is truly philosophical, profound in thought and expression, and given to probing the subtlest areas of human psychology. He neither expected nor gained a large audience, yet today he towers, with Robert Frost and Eliot for company, above all other American poets since Whitman.

Robinson was descended through his mother from Anne Bradstreet, New England's first colonial poet. He was born at Head Tide, Maine, on December 22, 1869. His father, aged fifty, had just then retired from business, and the family at once moved twelve miles down the Kennebec, to Gardiner, the "Tilbury Town" of his poems.

The presumed unhappiness of Robinson's boyhood has been exaggerated, but it is true that he had more than the usual handicaps to overcome. Late-born into his family, he was made conscious, as he grew up, of the example of his materially successful brothers in a community where such success was taken for granted. After graduation from high school he spent four difficult years in apparent idleness while reading extensively and laboring steadily at his verse, which editors as steadily declined to publish.

At the age of twenty-two he entered Harvard University, and he remained for two years as a special student, principally of philosophy, literature, and languages. The death of his father in 1893 caused his withdrawal, and inaugurated a period of mental depression. A chronic abscess of his ear for several years kept him in pain, and he feared he would lose his mind. The family inheritance was greatly reduced by the panic of 1893.

Both his brothers, who had begun so brilliantly, proved unstable and then died within a few years, while his mother went into a long and harrowing illness. Just before his mother's death, the serious love affair of his youth was terminated in sorrow. Thereafter he shyly avoided such entanglements; in any case not until he was fifty could he have married on his income as a poet.

His mother's death relieved him of family responsibility. In 1896 he settled in New York, and unable to find a publisher, he had *The Torrent and the Night Before* printed at his own expense. The February, 1897, *Bookman* observed that his verse had the "true fire," but that "the world is not beautiful to him, but a prison house." Robinson's letter of reply, in the March number, contained a now-famous appraisal of his view of life. "The world is not a 'prison house,'" he said, "but a kind of spiritual kindergarten where millions of bewildered infants are trying to spell 'God' with the wrong blocks." The next year he included most of these poems in his second volume, *The Children of the Night* (1897), again defraying the costs of publication. These volumes ushered into the world such "bewildered infants," now famous, as Aaron Stark, with "eyes like little dollars," and Richard Cory, for whom a bullet was medicine, and Luke Havergal, caught in the web of fate.

After a year in New York he accepted an appointment at Harvard as office secretary to the president, but proved wholly unfit for such routine. Back in New York, while not gregarious, he was far from being such a recluse as is often imagined. According to Fullerton Waldo, he loved the bustling life of the streets as "Charles Lamb loved the tidal fullness along the Strand." For years he lived in Greenwich Village, in the then Bohemian area near Washington Square. There he had as intimates such writers and staunch friends as Josephine Preston Peabody and William Vaughn Moody, whom he had known at Harvard, and E. C. Stedman, Percy Mackaye, Hermann Hagedorn, Ridgely Torrence, and Daniel Gregory Mason, the composer, who taught music at Columbia. When *Captain Craig* finally secured a publisher in 1902, the poet was for a time spared the knowledge that it had been subsidized, secretly, by Gardiner friends. The revelation of this, together with the small sale of the volume, increased his desperation during 1903–1904, when he worked as a subway-construction inspector. Creative work under these circumstances was nearly impossible.

In March of 1905, he received his first check in ten years for writing accepted by a magazine, and within a week there arrived a letter from the President of the United States. Kermit Roosevelt, whose master at Groton was a Gardiner friend of the poet's, had sent his father a copy of *The Children of the Night*, which the President had much admired. Now, learning of the poet's plight, he had him appointed to a clerkship in the United States

Custom House at New York. The salary was small, but Robinson had once again the time and energy for poetry. By the end of Roosevelt's term he had prepared the volume *The Town Down the River* (1910), and the President's influence had secured its publication by Scribner's.

Although it is reported that for years this notable poet depended in part upon the unobtrusive benefactions of his admirers, he was never again forced to waste his limited strength to obtain mere subsistence. A studio was provided for him in New York. After 1911 he spent many summers at the MacDowell Colony at Peterborough, New Hampshire, a retreat for artists, established in memory of Edward MacDowell. There, through succeeding summers, he completed the longer works of his second period.

In the Arthurian poems, each the size of a separate volume, Robinson developed a highly individualized blank verse, lofty in character yet modern in its speech rhythms, equally adaptable for sustained narrative, dialogue, and dramatic effects, and for the poet's characteristic discussion of ideas. His wit, unsurpassed among modern writers, is nowhere seen to better advantage than in his long narratives. It is not dependent upon what is comic in the ordinary sense, but springs from the recognition of essential incongruities at the core of reality, and rewards only those who can follow the poet's fundamental thinking. The Arthurian poems are faithful to the sources—Malory and such continental chroniclers as Wolfram

—but the characters have been reinterpreted in modern terms. The world of Arthur, in chaos as a result of the greed and faithlessness of its leadership, corresponded, it seemed to Robinson, to the condition of things at the time of the first World War. *Merlin* appeared in 1917, *Lancelot* in 1920, and *Tristram* in 1927.

The poet's financial rewards increased very slowly, but his first *Collected Poems* (1921) was awarded the Pulitzer Prize, and so was *The Man Who Died Twice* (1924), a major narrative of fantastic design but great power and moral significance, on the theme of regeneration. *Tristram* also won the Pulitzer Prize, and as a selection of the Literary Guild, a book club, it gave the poet his first large sale. During the remaining nine years of his life, Robinson's financial worries were ended.

In his last years Robinson created several long narratives of modern life, beginning with *Cavender's House* (1929). These are psychological studies of character, all dealing, in various lights, with the nature of human guilt or fidelity, with the destructiveness of the desire for power or for possession. *The Glory of the Nightingales* (1930) and *Matthias at the Door* (1931) are the climax of Robinson's criticism of modern life, and subtly incorporate the constant symbols of light, darkness, regeneration, and responsibility that prevail in his poetry from the beginning and reach their highest tragic synthesis in *Tristram*. *Talifer* (1933) is a social comedy of subtlety and brilliant wit, in a vein of meaningful worldliness. *King Jasper* (1935), although it shows traces of the fatigue of a dying man, is a cleverly managed allegory, and is interesting as revealing the final phase of the poet's developing concept of patrician responsibility in democratic leadership. After recurrent illnesses Robinson died in 1935, his sixty-sixth year.

The standard edition is *Collected Poems of Edwin Arlington Robinson*, 1921; enlarged editions appeared periodically through 1937. Collections of letters are *Selected Letters*, compiled by Ridgely Torrence, 1940; and *Untriangulated Stars: Letters of Edwin Arlington Robinson to Harry de Forest Smith, 1890–1905*, edited by Denham Sutcliffe, 1947. Standard biographies were published by Hermann Hagedorn, 1938; and Emory Neff, 1948.

Memoirs and critical studies are Lloyd Morris, *The Poetry of Edwin Arlington Robinson*, 1923; Mark Van Doren, *Edwin Arlington Robinson*, 1927; L. M. Beebe, *Edwin Arlington Robinson and the Arthurian Legend*, 1927; Charles Cestre, *An Introduction to Edwin Arlington Robinson*, 1930; R. W. Brown, *Next Door to a Poet*, 1937; E. Kaplan, *Philosophy in the Poetry of Edwin Arlington Robinson*, 1940; Yvor Winters, *Edwin Arlington Robinson*, 1946; and Edwin G. Fussell, *Edwin Arlington Robinson*, 1954.

Luke Havergal

Go to the western gate, Luke Havergal,
There where the vines cling crimson on the wall,
And in the twilight wait for what will come.
The leaves will whisper there of her, and some,
Like flying words, will strike you as they fall;   5
But go, and if you listen she will call.
Go to the western gate, Luke Havergal—
Luke Havergal.

No, there is not a dawn in eastern skies
To rift the fiery night that's in your eyes;   10
But there, where western glooms are gathering,
The dark will end the dark, if anything:
God slays Himself with every leaf that flies,
And hell is more than half of paradise.
No, there is not a dawn in eastern skies—   15
In eastern skies.

Out of a grave I come to tell you this,
Out of a grave I come to quench the kiss
That flames upon your forehead with a glow
That blinds you to the way that you must go.   20
Yes, there is yet one way to where she is,
Bitter, but one that faith may never miss.
Out of a grave I come to tell you this—
To tell you this.

There is the western gate, Luke Havergal,   25
There are the crimson leaves upon the wall.

Go, for the winds are tearing them away,—
Nor think to riddle the dead words they say,
Nor any more to feel them as they fall;
But go, and if you trust her she will call.   30
There is the western gate, Luke Havergal—
Luke Havergal.

1896

conscious choice
leads one to an inextricable situation

Richard Cory

Whenever Richard Cory went down town,
We people on the pavement looked at him:
He was a gentleman from sole to crown,
Clean favored, and imperially slim.

And he was always quietly arrayed,   5
And he was always human when he talked;
But still he fluttered pulses when he said,
'Good-morning,' and he glittered when he walked.

And he was rich—yes, richer than a king—
And admirably schooled in every grace: 10
In fine, we thought that he was everything
To make us wish that we were in his place.

So on we worked, and waited for the light,
And went without the meat, and cursed the bread;
And Richard Cory, one calm summer night,   15
Went home and put a bullet through his head.

1897

Aunt Imogen

Aunt Imogen was coming, and therefore
The children—Jane, Sylvester, and Young George—
Were eyes and ears; for there was only one
Aunt Imogen to them in the whole world,
And she was in it only for four weeks   5
In fifty-two. But those great bites of time
Made all September a Queen's Festival;
And they would strive, informally, to make
The most of them.—The mother understood,
And wisely stepped away. Aunt Imogen   10
Was there for only one month in the year,

While she, the mother,—she was always there;
And that was what made all the difference.
She knew it must be so, for Jane had once
Expounded it to her so learnedly   15
That she had looked away from the child's eyes
And thought; and she had thought of many things.

There was a demonstration every time
Aunt Imogen appeared, and there was more
Than one this time. And she was at a loss   20
Just how to name the meaning of it all:
It puzzled her to think that she could be
So much to any crazy thing alive—
Even to her sister's little savages
Who knew no better than to be themselves;   25
But in the midst of her glad wonderment
She found herself besieged and overcome
By two tight arms and one tumultuous head.
And therewith half bewildered and half pained
By the joy she felt and by the sudden love   30
That proved itself in childhood's honest noise.
Jane, by the wings of sex, had reached her first;
And while she strangled her, approvingly,
Sylvester thumped his drum and Young George howled.
But finally, when all was rectified,   35
And she had stilled the clamor of Young George
By giving him a long ride on her shoulders,
They went together into the old room
That looked across the fields; and Imogen
Gazed out with a girl's gladness in her eyes,   40
Happy to know that she was back once more
Where there were those who knew her, and at last
Had gloriously got away again
From cabs and clattered asphalt for a while;
And there she sat and talked and looked and laughed 45
And made the mother and the children laugh.
Aunt Imogen made everybody laugh.

There was the feminine paradox—that she
Who had so little sunshine for herself
Should have so much for others. How it was   50
That she could make, and feel for making it,
So much of joy for them, and all along
Be covering, like a scar, and while she smiled,
That hungering incompleteness and regret—

That passionate ache for something of her own, 55
For something of herself—she never knew.
She knew that she could seem to make them all
Believe there was no other part of her
Than her persistent happiness; but the why
And how she did not know. Still none of them 60
Could have a thought that she was living down—
Almost as if regret were criminal,
So proud it was and yet so profitless—
The penance of a dream, and that was good.
Her sister Jane—the mother of little Jane, 65
Sylvester, and Young George—might make herself
Believe she knew, for she—well, she was Jane.

Young George, however, did not yield himself
To nourish the false hunger of a ghost
That made no good return. He saw too much: 70
The accumulated wisdom of his years
Had so conclusively made plain to him
The permanent profusion of a world
Where everybody might have everything
To do, and almost everything to eat, 75
That he was jubilantly satisfied
And all unthwarted by adversity.
Young George knew things. The world, he had found out,
Was a good place, and life was a good game—
Particularly when Aunt Imogen 80
Was in it. And one day it came to pass—
One rainy day when she was holding him
And rocking him—that he, in his own right,
Took it upon himself to tell her so;
And something in his way of telling it— 85
The language, or the tone, or something else—
Gripped like insidious fingers on her throat,
And then went foraging as if to make
A plaything of her heart. Such undeserved
And unsophisticated confidence 90
Went mercilessly home; and had she sat
Before a looking glass, the deeps of it
Could not have shown more clearly to her then
Than one thought-mirrored little glimpse had shown,
The pang that wrenched her face and filled her eyes 95
With anguish and intolerable mist.
The blow that she had vaguely thrust aside

Like fright so many times had found her now:
Clean-thrust and final it had come to her
From a child's lips at last, as it had come   100
Never before, and as it might be felt
Never again. Some grief, like some delight,
Stings hard but once: to custom after that
The rapture or the pain submits itself,
And we are wiser than we were before.   105
And Imogen was wiser; though at first
Her dream-defeating wisdom was indeed
A thankless heritage: there was no sweet,
No bitter now; nor was there anything
To make a daily meaning for her life—   110
Till truth, like Harlequin, leapt out somehow
From ambush and threw sudden savor to it—
But the blank taste of time. There were no dreams,
No phantoms in her future any more:
One clinching revelation of what was   115
One by-flash of irrevocable chance,
Had acridly but honestly foretold
The mystical fulfilment of a life
That might have once . . . But that was all gone by:
There was no need of reaching back for that: 120
The triumph was not hers: there was no love
Save borrowed love: there was no might have been.

But there was yet Young George—and he had gone
Conveniently to sleep, like a good boy;
And there was yet Sylvester with his drum,   125
And there was frowzle-headed little Jane;
And there was Jane the sister, and the mother,—
Her sister, and the mother of them all.
They were not hers, not even one of them:
She was not born to be so much as that,   130
For she was born to be Aunt Imogen.
Now she could see the truth and look at it;
Now she could make stars out where once had palled
A future's emptiness; now she could share
With others—ah, the others!—to the end   135
The largess of a woman who could smile;
Now it was hers to dance the folly down,
And all the murmuring; now it was hers
To be Aunt Imogen.—So, when Young George
Woke up and blinked at her with his big eyes,   140
And smiled to see the way she blinked at him,

'T was only in old concord with the stars
That she took hold of him and held him close,
Close to herself, and crushed him till he laughed.

1902

Miniver Cheevy

Miniver Cheevy, child of scorn,
  Grew lean while he assailed the seasons;
He wept that he was ever born,
  And he had reasons.

Miniver loved the days of old   5
  When swords were bright and steeds were prancing;
The vision of a warrior bold
  Would set him dancing.

Miniver sighed for what was not,
  And dreamed, and rested from his labors;   10
He dreamed of Thebes[1] and Camelot,[2]
  And Priam's[3] neighbors.

Miniver mourned the ripe renown
  That made so many a name so fragrant;
He mourned Romance, now on the town,   15
  And Art, a vagrant.

Miniver loved the Medici,[4]
  Albeit he had never seen one;
He would have sinned incessantly
  Could he have been one.   20

Miniver cursed the commonplace
  And eyed a khaki suit with loathing;
He missed the medieval grace
  Of iron clothing.

Miniver scorned the gold he sought,   25
  But sore annoyed was he without it;
Miniver thought, and thought, and thought,
  And thought about it.

Miniver Cheevy, born too late,
  Scratched his head and kept on thinking;   30

1. Ancient Greek city, prominent in Greek history and legend.
2. Legendary site of King Arthur's court in the Arthurian romances.
3. King of Troy and the father of the heroes Paris and Hector.
4. Renaissance merchant-princes, rulers of Florence for nearly two centuries, noted equally for their cruelties and for their benefactions to learning and art.

Miniver coughed, and called it fate,
And kept on drinking.

1910

Leonora

They have made for Leonora this low dwelling in the ground,
And with cedar they have woven the four walls round.
Like a little dryad hiding she'll be wrapped all in green,
Better kept and longer valued than by ways that would have been.

They will come with many roses in the early afternoon,   5
They will come with pinks and lilies and with Leonora soon;
And as long as beauty's garments over beauty's limbs are thrown,
There'll be lilies that are liars, and the rose will have its own.

There will be a wondrous quiet in the house that they have made,
And to-night will be a darkness in the place where she'll be laid;   10
But the builders, looking forward into time, could only see
Darker nights for Leonora than to-night shall ever be.

1910

Bewick Finzer

Time was when his half million drew
    The breath of six per cent;
But soon the worm of what-was-not
    Fed hard on his content;
And something crumbled in his brain   5
    When his half million went.

Time passed, and filled along with his
    The place of many more;
Time came, and hardly one of us
    Had credence to restore,   10
From what appeared one day, the man
    Whom we had known before.

The broken voice, the withered neck,
    The coat worn out with care,
The cleanliness of indigence,   15
    The brilliance of despair,
The fond imponderable dreams
    Of affluence,—all were there.

Poor Finzer, with his dreams and schemes,
   Fares hard now in the race,   20
With heart and eye that have a task
   When he looks in the face
Of one who might so easily
   Have been in Finzer's place.

He comes unfailing for the loan   25
   We give and then forget;
He comes, and probably for years
   Will he be coming yet,—
Familiar as an old mistake,
   And futile as regret.   30

1916

Cassandra[5]

I heard one who said: "Verily,
   What word have I for children here?
Your Dollar is your only Word,[6]
   The wrath of it your only fear.

"You build it altars tall enough   5
   To make you see, but you are blind;
You cannot leave it long enough
   To look before you or behind.

"When Reason beckons you to pause,
   You laugh and say that you know best;   10
But what it is you know, you keep
   As dark as ingots in a chest.

"You laugh and answer, 'We are young;
   O leave us now, and let us grow.'—
Not asking how much more of this   15
   Will Time endure or Fate bestow.

"Because a few complacent years
   Have made your peril of your pride,
Think you that you are to go on
   Forever pampered and untried?   20

"What lost eclipse of history,
   What bivouac of the marching stars,

5. In the *Iliad*, Cassandra, daughter of King Priam, was enabled to prophesy by Apollo; when she refused to submit to his desires, he ordained that no one should believe her prophecies.
6. *Cf.* "Word," in John i: 1; and see the recurrence of "Dollar" as part of the unholy Trinity, in ll. 29–30.

Has given the sign for you to see
Millenniums and last great wars?

"What unrecorded overthrow   25
Of all the world has ever known,
Or ever been, has made itself
So plain to you, and you alone?

"Your Dollar, Dove and Eagle make
A Trinity that even you   30
Rate higher than you rate yourselves;
It pays, it flatters, and it's new.[7]

"And though your very flesh and blood
Be what your Eagle eats and drinks,
You'll praise him for the best of birds,   35
Not knowing what the Eagle thinks.

"The power is yours, but not the sight;
You see not upon what you tread;
You have the ages for your guide,
But not the wisdom to be led.   40

"Think you to tread forever down
The merciless old verities?
And are you never to have eyes
To see the world for what it is?

"Are you to pay for what you have   45
With all you are?"—No other word
We caught, but with a laughing crowd
Moved on. None heeded, and few heard.

1916

Old King Cole

In Tilbury Town did Old King Cole
A wise old age anticipate,
Desiring, with his pipe and bowl,
No Khan's extravagant estate.
No crown annoyed his honest head,   5
No fiddlers three were called or needed;
For two disastrous heirs instead
Made music more than ever three did.

Bereft of her with whom his life
Was harmony without a flaw,   10

7. Robinson opposed "dollar diplomacy," the policy of protection for
American investments in Latin America, which Wilson (1913) inherited.

He took no other for a wife,
Nor sighed for any that he saw;
And if he doubted his two sons,
And heirs, Alexis and Evander,
He might have been as doubtful once   15
Of Robert Burns and Alexander.

Alexis, in his early youth,
Began to steal—from old and young.
Likewise Evander, and the truth
Was like a bad taste on his tongue.   20
Born thieves and liars, their affair
Seemed only to be tarred with evil—
The most insufferable pair
Of scamps that ever cheered the devil.

The world went on, their fame went on,   25
And they went on—from bad to worse;
Till, goaded hot with nothing done,
And each accoutred with a curse,
The friends of Old King Cole, by twos,
And fours, and sevens, and elevens,   30
Pronounced unalterable views
Of doings that were not of heaven's.

And having learned again whereby
Their baleful zeal had come about,
King Cole met many a wrathful eye   35
So kindly that its wrath went out—
Or partly out. Say what they would,
He seemed the more to court their candor;
But never told what kind of good
Was in Alexis and Evander.   40

And Old King Cole, with many a puff
That haloed his urbanity,
Would smoke till he had smoked enough,
And listen most attentively.
He beamed as with an inward light   45
That had the Lord's assurance in it;
And once a man was there all night,
Expecting something every minute.

But whether from too little thought,
Or too much fealty to the bowl,   50
A dim reward was all he got
For sitting up with Old King Cole.

"Though mine," the father mused aloud,
"Are not the sons I would have chosen,
Shall I, less evilly endowed,   55
By their infirmity be frozen?

"They'll have a bad end, I'll agree,
But I was never born to groan;
For I can see what I can see,
And I'm accordingly alone.   60
With open heart and open door,
I love my friends, I like my neighbors;
But if I try to tell you more,
Your doubts will overmatch my labors.

"This pipe would never make me calm,   65
This bowl my grief would never drown.
For grief like mine there is no balm
In Gilead,[8] or in Tilbury Town.
And if I see what I can see,
I know not any way to blind it;   70
Nor more if any way may be
For you to grope or fly to find it.

"There may be room for ruin yet,
And ashes for a wasted love;
Or, like One whom you may forget,   75
I may have meat you know not of.[9]
And if I'd rather live than weep
Meanwhile, do you find that surprising?
Why, bless my soul, the man's asleep!
That's good. The sun will soon be rising."   80

1916

Ben Jonson Entertains a Man from Stratford[1]

You are a friend then, as I make it out,
Of our man Shakespeare, who alone of us

8. *Cf.* Jeremiah viii: 22.
9. *Cf.* John iv: 32. With these words Jesus answered his disciples' invitation to eat, having just converted the Samaritan woman at Jacob's Well.
1. William Shakespeare (1564–1616) was born and reared at Stratford-on-Avon, where, at about the age of twenty-one, he left his family when he went to seek his fortune in the London theater. Ben Jonson (1573–1637) was Shakespeare's closest rival among contemporary dramatists. A classicist, scholar, and brilliant London wit, Jonson de-

clared his love and admiration for Shakespeare, but was puzzled because his friend, after achieving the triumph of sheer genius in the great world, still had the provincial's desire to shine in little Stratford. The imaginary episode of this poem occurs in 1609. Shakespeare, then forty-five, had completed his greatest tragedies. Various interpretations of Shakespeare might be based on his works, and in the same way Robinson's portrayal is evidently also a self-portrait to some degree. He published the poem in *Drama,* in November, 1915,

Will put an ass's head in Fairyland[2]
As he would add a shilling to more shillings,
All most harmonious,—and out of his   5
Miraculous inviolable increase
Fills Ilion,[3] Rome, or any town you like
Of olden time with timeless Englishmen;
And I must wonder what you think of him—
All you down there where your small Avon flows   10
By Stratford, and where you're an Alderman.
Some, for a guess, would have him riding back
To be a farrier[4] there, or say a dyer;
Or maybe one of your adept surveyors;
Or like enough the wizard of all tanners.   15
Not you—no fear of that; for I discern
In you a kindling of the flame that saves—
The nimble element, the true phlogiston;[5]
I see it, and was told of it, moreover,
By our discriminate friend himself, no other.   20
Had you been one of the sad average,
As he would have it,—meaning, as I take it,
The sinew and the solvent of our Island,
You'd not be buying beer for this Terpander's[6]
Approved and estimated friend Ben Jonson;   25
He'd never foist it as a part of his
Contingent entertainment of a townsman
While he goes off rehearsing, as he must,
If he shall ever be the Duke of Stratford.[7]
And my words are no shadow on your town—   30
Far from it; for one town's like another
As all are unlike London. Oh, he knows it,—
And there's the Stratford in him; he denies it,
And there's the Shakespeare in him. So, God help him!
I tell him he needs Greek;[8] but neither God   35
Nor Greek will help him. Nothing will help that man.

on the eve of the international Shakespeare Tercentenary, and collected it
during the centennial year in *The Man
Against the Sky* (1916).
2. See *A Midsummer-Night's Dream,*
Act III, Scene 1, ll. 79–206, in which the
loutish Bottom, his head transformed by
Puck's prank to that of an ass, makes
love to Titania, queen of fairyland.
3. Also sometimes "Ilium"; the Greek
name for Troy.
4. A blacksmith.
5. A hypothetical substance or chemical
which early science supposed to be the
imperceptible agent responsible for combustion; hence, the "nimble element."

6. *I.e.,* Shakespeare's. Terpander (*fl. ca.*
700 B.C.), a Greek poet born on the isle
of Lesbos, was regarded as the father of
Greek music and lyric poetry.
7. Jonson's ironic comment on Shakespeare's desire to become the great
citizen of his native Stratford, recalling
that in 1596 he had secured the grant of
a heraldic coat of arms to his father and
his descendants. *Cf.* l. 140.
8. Jonson's opinion that Shakespeare
"had small Latin and less Greek" is
familiar; however, John Aubrey, less
scholarly but college bred, thought him
adequate in this respect.

You see the fates have given him so much,
He must have all or perish,—or look out
Of London, where he sees too many lords.
They're part of half what ails him: I suppose   40
There's nothing fouler down among the demons
Than what it is he feels when he remembers
The dust and sweat and ointment of his calling
With his lords looking on and laughing at him.
King as he is, he can't be king *de facto*,[9]   45
And that's as well, because he wouldn't like it;
He'd frame a lower rating of men then
Than he has now; and after that would come
An abdication or an apoplexy.
He can't be king, not even king of Stratford,—   50
Though half the world, if not the whole of it,
May crown him with a crown that fits no king
Save Lord Apollo's homesick emissary:[1]
Not there on Avon, or on any stream
Where Naiads[2] and their white arms are no more,   55
Shall he find home again. It's all too bad.
But there's a comfort, for he'll have that House—[3]
The best you ever saw; and he'll be there
Anon, as you're an Alderman. Good God!
He makes me lie awake o'nights and laugh.   60

And you have known him from his origin,
You tell me; and a most uncommon urchin
He must have been to the few seeing ones—
A trifle terrifying, I dare say,
Discovering a world with his man's eyes,   65
Quite as another lad might see some finches,
If he looked hard and had an eye for nature.
But this one had his eyes and their foretelling,
And he had you to fare with, and what else?
He must have had a father and a mother—   70
In fact I've heard him say so—and a dog,
As a boy should, I venture; and the dog,
Most likely, was the only man who knew him.
A dog, for all I know, is what he needs
As much as anything right here today,   75
To counsel him about his disillusions,

9. In reality.
1. Greek mythology credited Apollo with the invention and patronage of the arts of music and poetry; hence Shakespeare is his "homesick emissary."
2. Naiads were the female Greek divinities of fresh-water streams and lakes; they inspired the poets and seers who drank of their waters, but they had departed from the Avon (*cf.* l. 54).
3. In 1597 Shakespeare had purchased New Place, then probably the largest and most impressive house in Stratford.

Old aches, and parturitions of what's coming,—
A dog of orders,[4] an emeritus,
To wag his tail at him when he comes home,
And then to put his paws up on his knees   80
And say, "For God's sake, what's it all about?"

I don't know whether he needs a dog or not—
Or what he needs. I tell him he needs Greek;
I'll talk of rules and Aristotle[5] with him,
And if his tongue's at home he'll say to that,   85
"I have your word that Aristotle knows,
And you mine that I don't know Aristotle."
He's all at odds with all the unities,
And what's yet worse, it doesn't seem to matter;
He treads along through Time's old wilderness   90
As if the tramp of all the centuries
Had left no roads—and there are none, for him;
He doesn't see them, even with those eyes,—
And that's a pity, or I say it is.
Accordingly we have him as we have him—   95
Going his way, the way that he goes best,
A pleasant animal with no great noise
Or nonsense anywhere to set him off—
Save only divers and inclement devils
Have made of late his heart their dwelling place.   100
A flame half ready to fly out sometimes
At some annoyance may be fanned up in him,
But soon it falls, and when it falls goes out;
He knows how little room there is in there
For crude and futile animosities,   105
And how much for the joy of being whole,
And how much for long sorrow and old pain.
On our side there are some who may be given
To grow old wondering what he thinks of us
And some above us, who are, in his eyes,   110
Above himself,—and that's quite right and English.
Yet here we smile, or disappoint the gods
Who made it so: the gods have always eyes
To see men scratch; and they see one down here
Who itches, manor-bitten to the bone,[6]   115

4. Of high rank by appointment, as in knighthood, or in ecclesiastical or military organizations; here "emeritus," or confirmed in perpetuity for special merit.
5. The Greek philosopher Aristotle (384–322 B.C.), in his *Poetics*, formulated the principle of unity of action in dramatic structure; later critics interpreted his remarks to include also the unities of time and place (*cf.* l. 88).
6. *I.e.*, the Stratford manor house is for Jonson the symbol of Shakespeare's desire for worldly success in general. *Cf.* l. 29 and l. 140, in which he refers to Shakespeare's "dukedom."

Albeit he knows himself—yes, yes, he knows—
The lord of more than England and of more
Than all the seas of England in all time
Shall ever wash. D'ye wonder that I laugh?
He sees me, and he doesn't seem to care;   120
And why the devil should he? I can't tell you.

I'll meet him out alone of a bright Sunday,
Trim, rather spruce, and quite the gentleman.
"What ho, my lord!" say I. He doesn't hear me;
Wherefore I have to pause and look at him.   125
He's not enormous, but one looks at him.
A little on the round if you insist,
For now, God save the mark, he's growing old;
He's five and forty,[7] and to hear him talk
These days you'd call him eighty; then you'd add   130
More years to that. He's old enough to be
The father of a world, and so he is.[8]
"Ben, you're a scholar, what's the time of day?"
Says he; and there shines out of him again
An aged light that has no age or station—   135
The mystery that's his—a mischievous
Half-mad serenity that laughs at fame
For being won so easy, and at friends
Who laugh at him for what he wants the most,
And for his dukedom down in Warwickshire;—   140
By which you see we're all a little jealous. . . .
Poor Greene![9] I fear the color of his name
Was even as that of his ascending soul;
And he was one where there are many others,—
Some scrivening to the end against their fate,   145
Their puppets all in ink and all to die there;
And some with hands that once would shade an eye
That scanned Euripides and Aeschylus[1]
Will reach by this time for a pot-house mop
To slush their first and last of royalties.   150
Poor devils! and they all play to his hand;
For so it was in Athens and old Rome.

---

7. Shakespeare was born on April 23 (?), 1564; since he is now "five and forty," the date is 1609.
8. In his dedicatory poem for the first folio edition (1623) of Shakespeare's plays, Jonson wrote that his departed friend was "not of an age, but for all time."
9. Robert Greene (1560?–1592), a minor writer whose work Jonson regarded as mere "scrivening" (*cf.* l. 145).

In his *Groatsworth of Wit* (1592) Greene made a veiled allusion to Shakespeare as "an upstart crow * * * in his owne conceit the onely Shake-scene in a countrey."
1. Euripides and Aeschylus, great Greek poet-dramatists who flourished early in the fifth century B.C., furnished the standard of dramatic excellence for such classicists as Jonson.

But that's not here or there; I've wandered off.
Greene does it, or I'm careful. Where's that boy?

Yes, he'll go back to Stratford. And we'll miss him?   155
Dear sir, there'll be no London here without him.
We'll all be riding, one of these fine days,
Down there to see him—and his wife won't like us;[2]
And then we'll think of what he never said
Of women—which, if taken all in all   160
With what he did say, would buy many horses.[3]
Though nowadays he's not so much for women:
"So few of them," he says, "are worth the guessing."
But there's a worm at work when he says that,
And while he says it one feels in the air   165
A deal of circumambient hocus-pocus.
They've had him dancing till his toes were tender,
And he can feel 'em now, come chilly rains.
There's no long cry for going into it,
However, and we don't know much about it.   170
The Fitton[4] thing was worst of all, I fancy;
And you in Stratford, like most here in London,
Have more now in the *Sonnets*[5] than you paid for;
He's put one there with all her poison on,
To make a singing fiction of a shadow   175
That's in his life a fact, and always will be.
But she's no care of ours, though Time, I fear,
Will have a more reverberant ado
About her than about another one
Who seems to have decoyed him, married him,   180
And sent him scuttling on his way to London,—
With much already learned, and more to learn,[6]
And more to follow. Lord! how I see him now,
Pretending, maybe trying, to be like us.
Whatever he may have meant, we never had him;   185
He failed us, or escaped, or what you will,—
And there was that about him (God knows what,—

2. In the next year, 1610, Shakespeare moved permanently to New Place, Stratford, where his wife had lived for thirteen years. That Shakespeare's marriage was unhappy, as suggested here by Jonson's speech, is a traditional assumption based on circumstantial evidence.
3. *Cf. Much Ado About Nothing,* Act I, Scene 1, l. 142, in which Benedick says to Beatrice, "I would my horse had the speed of your tongue."
4. Mary Fitton, a lady in waiting to Queen Elizabeth, was only sixteen when Shakespeare met her. It has been suggested that she was the "dark lady" of the sonnets, and served as the poet's model for Cleopatra; but evidence in support of these assumptions is lacking.
5. Shakespeare's *Sonnets* (1609) had just been published. Their record of the unhappy love of an aging poet for a much younger woman may be autobiographical.
6. *I.e.,* Anne Hathaway. Whether she "decoyed him" into marriage or not, it is established that she was twenty-six and he only eighteen when they were married in 1582, and their first child, Susanna, was born six months later. *Cf.* l. 158.

We'd flayed another had he tried it on us)
That made as many of us as had wits
More fond of all his easy distances   190
Than one another's noise and clap-your-shoulder.
But think you not, my friend, he'd never talk!
Talk? He was eldritch[7] at it; and we listened—
Thereby acquiring much we knew before
About ourselves, and hitherto had held   195
Irrelevant, or not prime to the purpose.
And there were some, of course, and there be now,
Disordered and reduced amazedly
To resignation by the mystic seal
Of young finality the gods had laid   200
On everything that made him a young demon;
And one or two shot looks at him already
As he had been their executioner;
And once or twice he was, not knowing it,—
Or knowing, being sorry for poor clay   205
And saying nothing. . . . Yet, for all his engines,[8]
You'll meet a thousand of an afternoon
Who strut and sun themselves and see around 'em
A world made out of more that has a reason
Than his, I swear, that he sees here today;   210
Though he may scarcely give a Fool an exit[9]
But we mark how he sees in everything
A law that, given we flout it once too often,
Brings fire and iron down on our naked heads.
To me it looks as if the power that made him,   215
For fear of giving all things to one creature,
Left out the first,—faith, innocence, illusion,
Whatever 'tis that keeps us out o' Bedlam,[1]—
And thereby, for his too consuming vision,
Empowered him out of nature; though to see him,   220
You'd never guess what's going on inside him.
He'll break out some day like a keg of ale
With too much independent frenzy in it;
And all for cellaring[2] what he knows won't keep,
And what he'd best forget—but that he can't.   225
You'll have it, and have more than I'm foretelling;

7. Supernaturally gifted, uncanny.
8. In the archaic sense, "inventions" or "contrivances"; the word was then employed to designate devices of stage production.
9. The Fool, or clown, was usually a conventional instrument of comic relief; Jonson suggests that Shakespeare made him a significant agent. *Cf.* Laun-
celot Gobbo in *The Merchant of Venice* and the gravediggers in *Hamlet*.
1. The colloquial pronunciation of "Bethlehem," here denoting a London asylum for the insane, St. Mary of Bethlehem.
2. The preservation of spirituous beverages, as in a wine cellar.

And there'll be such a roaring at the Globe[3]
As never stunned the bleeding gladiators.
He'll have to change the color of its hair
A bit, for now he calls it Cleopatra.   230
Black hair would never do for Cleopatra.[4]

But you and I are not yet two old women,
And you're a man of office.[5] What he does
Is more to you than how it is he does it,—
And that's what the Lord God has never told him.   235
They work together, and the Devil helps 'em;
They do it of a morning, or if not,
They do it of a night; in which event
He's peevish of a morning. He seems old;
He's not the proper stomach[6] or the sleep—   240
And they're two sovran[7] agents to conserve him
Against the fiery art that has no mercy
But what's in that prodigious grand new House.
I gather something happening in his boyhood
Fulfilled him with a boy's determination   245
To make all Stratford 'ware of him.[8] Well, well,
I hope at last he'll have his joy of it,
And all his pigs and sheep and bellowing beeves,
And frogs and owls and unicorns,[9] moreover,
Be less than hell to his attendant ears.   250
Oh, past a doubt we'll go down to see him.

He may be wise. With London two days off,
Down there some wind of heaven may yet revive him;
But there's no quickening breath from anywhere
Shall make of him again the poised young faun   255
From Warwickshire, who'd made, it seems, already
A legend of himself before I came[1]

3. Shakespeare had become part owner of the Globe theater in 1599.
4. It is probable that Shakespeare had just completed the composition of *Anthony and Cleopatra* in 1608. Mary Fitton (*cf.* l. 171), whom Jonson apparently thinks to be the model for Cleopatra, was noted for her black hair and eyes.
5. *I.e.*, an officeholder; hence, a man of the world.
6. Appetite; *i.e.*, inclination or self-confidence.
7. Sovereign, powerful.
8. This view is supported by Shakespeare's humble origin and educational handicaps, his unplanned and probably unhappy marriage, and the lack of success which caused him to leave his family in Stratford about 1585 when

threatened with arrest on the charge of poaching.
9. The animals of the Stratford farm and countryside are here associated with the imaginary unicorn, an artificial creature of heraldry (*cf.* "his dukedom," l. 140).
1. Jonson was nine years younger than Shakespeare. The latter was well established in 1598, when he appeared in Jonson's first successful comedy, *Every Man in His Humour*. Shakespeare had by then created at least fourteen plays, including such great works as *Romeo and Juliet* and *The Merchant of Venice*. In their continuous friendship Jonson remained the debtor: Shakespeare also acted in Jonson's first tragedy, *Sejanus* (1603).

To blink before the last of his first lightning.
Whatever there be, there'll be no more of that;
The coming on of his old monster Time[2]   260
Has made him a still man; and he has dreams
Were fair to think on once, and all found hollow.
He knows how much of what men paint themselves
Would blister in the light of what they are;
He sees how much of what was great now shares   265
An eminence transformed and ordinary;
He knows too much of what the world has hushed
In others, to be loud now for himself;
He knows now at what height low enemies
May reach his heart, and high friends let him fall;   270
But what not even such as he may know
Bedevils him the worst: his lark may sing
At heaven's gate[3] how he will, and for as long
As joy may listen, but *he* sees no gate, salvation
Save one whereat the spent clay waits a little   275
Before the churchyard has it, and the worm.[4]
Not long ago, late in an afternoon,
I came on him unseen down Lambeth[5] way,
And on my life I was afear'd of him:
He gloomed and mumbled like a soul from Tophet,[6]   280
His hands behind him and his head bent solemn.
"What is it now," said I,—"another woman?"
That made him sorry for me, and he smiled.
"No, Ben," he mused; "it's Nothing. It's all Nothing.[7]
We come, we go; and when we're done, we're done.   285
Spiders and flies—we're mostly one or t'other—
We come, we go; and when we're done, we're done."
"By God, you sing that song as if you knew it!"
Said I, by way of cheering him; "what ails ye?"
"I think I must have come down here to think,"   290
Says he to that, and pulls his little beard;
"Your fly will serve as well as anybody,
And what's his hour? He flies, and flies, and flies,

1. More than a quarter of the allusions to "Time" listed in one of the standard dictionaries of quotations are by Shakespeare; they refer characteristically to the ravages of "the tooth of Time," and to the "bald Sexton" who conducts our "petty pace" through the "ages" of man toward "the last syllable" of "mere oblivion."

3. A then current play by Shakespeare, *Cymbeline* (1609), contained the line "Hark, hark! the lark at heaven's gate sings" (Act II, Scene 3, l. 21).

4. For instances of similar language in Shakespeare, see *Hamlet*, Act IV, Scene 3, ll. 21–29, and Act V, Scene 1, ll. 83–101.

5. Lambeth Palace with its garden forms the seat in London of the Archbishop of Canterbury.

6. In Hebrew prophecy a place where children were sacrificed to the fire of Moloch, hence often synonymous with Hell, or chaos (*cf.* Isaiah xxx: 33; Jeremiah vii: 31).

7. Compare ll. 284–305 with *Macbeth*, Act V, Scene 5, ll. 19–28.

And in his fly's mind has a brave appearance;
And then your spider gets him in her net,   295
And eats him out, and hangs him up to dry.
That's Nature, the kind mother of us all.
And then your slattern housemaid swings her broom,
And where's your spider? And that's Nature, also.[8]
It's Nature, and it's Nothing. It's all Nothing.   300
It's all a world where bugs and emperors
Go singularly back to the same dust,
Each in his time; and the old, ordered stars
That sang together, Ben, will sing the same
Old stave tomorrow."

                      When he talks like that,   305
There's nothing for a human man to do
But lead him to some grateful nook like this
Where we be now, and there to make him drink.
He'll drink, for love of me, and then be sick;
A sad sign always in a man of parts,   310
And always very ominous. The great
Should be as large in liquor as in love,—
And our great friend is not so large in either:
One disaffects him, and the other fails him;
Whatso he drinks that has an antic in it,   315
He's wondering what's to pay in his insides;
And while his eyes are on the Cyprian[9]
He's fribbling all the time with that damned House.
We laugh here at his thrift, but after all
It may be thrift that saves him from the devil;   320
God gave it, anyhow,—and we'll suppose
He knew the compound of his handiwork.
Today the clouds are with him, but anon
He'll out of 'em enough to shake the tree
Of life itself and bring down fruit unheard-of,—   325
And, throwing in the bruised and whole together,
Prepare a wine to make us drunk with wonder;
And if he live, there'll be a sunset spell
Thrown over him as over a glassed lake
That yesterday was all a black wild water.[1]   330

---

8. *Cf. King Lear,* Act IV, Scene 1, ll. 36–37: "As flies to wanton boys, are we to the gods; / They kill us for their sport."
9. A double meaning is suggested: the word designates a much-esteemed wine from the Greek island of Cyprus; but "the Cyprian" is also a name for the Greek goddess of love, Aphrodite, whose legendary birthplace was Cyprus, where her worship flourished.
1. After completing his greatest tragedies at about this time, Shakespeare entered this period of "sunset spell" and produced the three romantic fantasies—*Cymbeline, A Winter's Tale,* and *The Tempest.*

God send he live to give us, if no more,
What now's a-rampage in him, and exhibit,
With a decent half-allegiance to the ages
An earnest of at least a casual eye
Turned once on what he owes to Gutenberg,[2]   335
And to the fealty of more centuries
Than are as yet a picture in our vision.
"There's time enough,—I'll do it when I'm old,
And we're immortal men," he says to that;
And then he says to me, "Ben, what's 'immortal'?   340
Think you by any force of ordination
It may be nothing of a sort more noisy
Than a small oblivion of component ashes
That of a dream-addicted world was once
A moving atomy much like your friend here?"[3]   345
Nothing will help that man. To make him laugh,
I said then he was a mad mountebank,[4]—
And by the Lord I nearer made him cry.
I could have eat an eft[5] then, on my knees,
Tail, claws, and all of him; for I had stung   350
The king of men, who had no sting for me,
And I had hurt him in his memories;
And I say now, as I shall say again,
I love the man this side idolatry.[6]

He'll do it when he's old, he says. I wonder.   355
He may not be so ancient as all that.
For such as he, the thing that is to do
Will do itself,—but there's a reckoning;
The sessions[7] that are now too much his own,
The roiling inward of a stilled outside,   360
The churning out of all those blood-fed lines,
The nights of many schemes and little sleep,
The full brain hammered hot with too much thinking,
The vexed heart over-worn with too much aching,—
This weary jangling of conjoined affairs   365
Made out of elements that have no end,

2. *I.e.*, to printing; the German Johann
Gutenberg (1400?–1468) invented the
modern art of printing from movable
type.
3. *Cf.* Hamlet's soliloquy on immortality in Act III, Scene 1, ll. 56–88.
4. Literally, one who mounts upon a
bench; a charlatan.
5. A lizard or newt.
6. In *Timber, or Discoveries*, Jonson
wrote: "The Players have often mentioned it as an honour to *Shakespeare*,
that in his writing * * * he never

blotted out a line. My answer hath
beene, would he had blotted a thousand.
* * * I had not told posterity this, but
* * * to justify mine owne candor, (for
I loved the man, and doe honour his
memory—on this side Idolatry—as
much as any)."
7. Compare ll. 359–366 with the first
twelve lines of Shakespeare's Sonnet
XXX, beginning, "When to the sessions
of sweet silent thought / I summon up
remembrance of things past * * *"

And all confused at once, I understand,
Is not what makes a man to live forever.
O no, not now! He'll not be going now:
There'll be time yet for God knows what explosions 370
Before he goes. He'll stay awhile. Just wait:
Just wait a year or two for Cleopatra,
For she's to be a balsam and a comfort;
And that's not all a jape of mine now, either.
For granted once the old way of Apollo 375
Sings in a man, he may then, if he's able,
Strike unafraid whatever strings he will
Upon the last and wildest of new lyres;
Nor out of his new magic, though it hymn
The shrieks of dungeoned hell, shall he create 380
A madness or a gloom to shut quite out
A cleaving daylight, and a last great calm
Triumphant over shipwreck and all storms.
He might have given Aristotle creeps,
But surely would have given him his *katharsis*.[8] 385

He'll not be going yet. There's too much yet
Unsung within the man. But when he goes,
I'd stake ye coin o' the realm his only care
For a phantom world he sounded and found wanting
Will be a portion here, a portion there, 390
Of this or that thing or some other thing
That has a patent and intrinsical
Equivalence in those egregious shillings.[9]
And yet he knows, God help him! Tell me, now,
If ever there was anything let loose 395
On earth by gods or devils heretofore
Like this mad, careful, proud, indifferent Shakespeare!
Where was it, if it ever was? By heaven,
'Twas never yet in Rhodes or Pergamon—
In Thebes or Nineveh, a thing like this! 400
No thing like this was ever out of England;
And that he knows. I wonder if he cares.
Perhaps he does. . . . O Lord, that House in Stratford!

1915, 1916

8. Aristotle suggests that great tragedy provides an emotional catharsis by purifying the spectator of base or selfish passions in his vicarious suffering of the events enacted upon the stage.
9. Shakespeare's will has been regarded as evidence of his concern for material success. Making no reference to his life as a writer, he distributed a considerable estate to daughters and other relatives, to his editors Heming and Condell, to the actor Burbage, and to friends for the purchase of mourning rings. As an afterthought, he inserted, "To my wife, Anne, my second-best bed."

faith is not subject to demonstration by phisical evidence bec. by itself it springs fr. a non-physical force

906 · Edwin Arlington Robinson *optimistic*

The Man Against the Sky

struggle of spiritual resistance -e.g. Frost-Job & God MacLeish J. B.

Between me and the sunset, like a dome
Against the glory of a world on fire,
Now burned a sudden hill,
Bleak, round, and high, by flame-lit height made higher,
With nothing on it for the flame to kill   5
Save one who moved and was alone up there
To loom before the chaos and the glare
As if he were the last god going home
Unto his last desire.

Dark, marvelous, and inscrutable he moved on   10
Till down the fiery distance he was gone,
Like one of those eternal, remote things
That range across a man's imaginings
When a sure music fills him and he knows
What he may say thereafter to few men,—   15
The touch of ages having wrought
An echo and a glimpse of what he thought
A phantom or a legend until then;
For whether lighted over ways that save,
Or lured from all repose,   20
If he go on too far to find a grave,
Mostly alone he goes.

Even he, who stood where I had found him,
On high with fire all round him,
Who moved along the molten west,   25
And over the round hill's crest
That seemed half ready with him to go down,
Flame-bitten and flame-cleft,
As if there were to be no last thing left
Of a nameless unimaginable town,—   30
Even he who climbed and vanished may have taken
Down to the perils of a depth not known,
From death defended though by men forsaken,
The bread that every man must eat alone;
He may have walked while others hardly dared   35
Look on to see him stand where many fell;
And upward out of that, as out of hell,
He may have sung and striven
To mount where more of him shall yet be given,
Bereft of all retreat,   40
To sevenfold heat,—
As on a day when three in Dura shared

The furnace,[1] and were spared
For glory by that king of Babylon
Who made himself so great that God, who heard,   45
Covered him with long feathers, like a bird.

Again, he may have gone down easily,
By comfortable altitudes, and found,
As always, underneath him solid ground
Whereon to be sufficient and to stand   50
Possessed already of the promised land,
Far stretched and fair to see:
A good sight, verily,
And one to make the eyes of her who bore him
Shine glad with hidden tears.   55
Why question of his ease of who before him,
In one place or another where they left
Their names as far behind them as their bones,
And yet by dint of slaughter, toil and theft,
And shrewdly sharpened stones,   60
Carved hard the way for his ascendency
Through deserts of lost years?
Why trouble him now who sees and hears
No more than what his innocence requires,
And therefore to no other height aspires   65
Than one at which he neither quails nor tires?
He may do more by seeing what he sees
Than others eager for iniquities;
He may, by seeing all things for the best,
Incite futurity to do the rest.   *tendology*   70

Or with an even likelihood, *...*
He may have met with atrabilious eyes
The fires of time on equal terms and passed
Indifferently down, until at last
His only kind of grandeur would have been,   75
Apparently, in being seen.
He may have had for evil or for good
No argument; he may have had no care
For what without himself went anywhere
To failure or to glory, and least of all   80
For such a stale, flamboyant miracle;
He may have been the prophet of an art
Immovable to old idolatries;
He may have been a player without a part,

1. *Cf.* Daniel iii and iv. Three Jews, refusing to worship the idols of Babylon, survived unscathed the "fiery furnace" of King Nebuchadnezzar, who was converted after the punishment described in l. 46.

Annoyed that even the sun should have the skies 85
For such a flaming way to advertise;
He may have been a painter sick at heart
With Nature's toiling for a new surprise;
He may have been a cynic, who now, for all
Of anything divine that his effete 90
Negation may have tasted,
Saw truth in his own image, rather small,
Forbore to fever the ephemeral,
Found any barren height a good retreat
From any swarming street, 95
And in the sun saw power superbly wasted;
And when the primitive old-fashioned stars
Came out again to shine on joys and wars
More primitive, and all arrayed for doom,
He may have proved a world a sorry thing 100
In his imagining,
And life a lighted highway to the tomb.

Or, mounting with infirm unsearching tread,
His hopes to chaos led,
He may have stumbled up there from the past, 105
And with an aching strangeness viewed the last
Abysmal conflagration of his dreams,—
A flame where nothing seems
To burn but flame itself, by nothing fed;
And while it all went out, 110
Not even the faint anodyne of doubt
May then have eased a painful going down
From pictured heights of power and lost renown,
Revealed at length to his outlived endeavor
Remote and unapproachable forever; 115
And at his heart there may have gnawed
Sick memories of a dead faith foiled and flawed
And long dishonored by the living death
Assigned alike by chance
To brutes and hierophants; 120
And anguish fallen on those he loved around him
May once have dealt the last blow to confound him,
And so have left him as death leaves a child,
Who sees it all too near;
And he who knows no young way to forget 125
May struggle to the tomb unreconciled.
Whatever suns may rise or set
There may be nothing kinder for him here

Than shafts and agonies;
And under these   130
He may cry out and stay on horribly;
Or, seeing in death too small a thing to fear,
He may go forward like a stoic Roman
Where pangs and terrors in his pathway lie,—
Or, seizing the swift logic of a woman,   135
Curse God and die.[2]

Or maybe there, like many another one
Who might have stood aloft and looked aheau,
Black-drawn against wild red,
He may have built, unawed by fiery gules   140
That in him no commotion stirred,
A living reason out of molecules
Why molecules occurred,
And one for smiling when he might have sighed
Had he seen far enough,   145
And in the same inevitable stuff
Discovered an odd reason too for pride
In being what he must have been by laws
Infrangible and for no kind of cause.
Deterred by no confusion or surprise   150
He may have seen with his mechanic eyes
A world without a meaning, and had room,
Alone amid magnificence and doom,
To build himself an airy monument
That should, or fail him in his vague intent,   155
Outlast an accidental universe—
To call it nothing worse—
Or, by the burrowing guile
Of Time disintegrated and effaced,
Like once-remembered mighty trees go down   160
To ruin, of which by man may now be traced
No part sufficient even to be rotten,
And in the book of things that are forgotten
Is entered as a thing not quite worth while.
He may have been so great   165
That satraps would have shivered at his frown,
And all he prized alive may rule a state
No larger than a grave that holds a clown;
He may have been a master of his fate,
And of his atoms,—ready as another   170
In his emergence to exonerate

2. *Cf.* Job ii: 9. So Job's wife advised her husband in the midst of his first af-
flictions.

His father and his mother;
He may have been a captain of a host,
Self-eloquent and ripe for prodigies,
Doomed here to swell by dangerous degrees,   175
And then give up the ghost.
Nahum's great grasshoppers[3] were such as these,
Sun-scattered and soon lost.

Whatever the dark road he may have taken,
This man who stood on high   180
And faced alone the sky,
Whatever drove or lured or guided him,—
A vision answering a faith unshaken,
An easy trust assumed by easy trials,
A sick negation born of weak denials,   185
A crazed abhorrence of an old condition,
A blind attendance on a brief ambition,—
Whatever stayed him or derided him,
His way was even as ours;
And we, with all our wounds and all our powers,   190
Must each await alone at his own height
Another darkness or another light;
And there, of our poor self dominion reft,
If inference and reason shun
Hell, Heaven, and Oblivion,   195
May thwarted will (perforce precarious,
But for our conservation better thus)
Have no misgiving left
Of doing yet what here we leave undone?
Or if unto the last of these we cleave,   200
Believing or protesting we believe
In such an idle and ephemeral
Florescence of the diabolical,—
If, robbed of two fond old enormities,
Our being had no onward auguries,   205
What then were this great love of ours to say
For launching other lives to voyage again
A little farther into time and pain,
A little faster in a futile chase
For a kingdom and a power and a Race   210
That would have still in sight
A manifest end of ashes and eternal night?
Is this the music of the toys we shake

3. See "a captain of a host," l. 173, above, and Nahum iii: 17. The prophet, condemning the corrupt and decadent pretentiousness of Nineveh, calls her captains "great grasshoppers * * * when the sun arises they flee away."

So loud,—as if there might be no mistake
Somewhere in our indomitable will?
Are we no greater than the noise we make   215
Along one blind atomic pilgrimage
Whereon by crass chance billeted we go
Because our brains and bones and cartilage
Will have it so?   220
If this we say, then let us all be still
About our share in it, and live and die
More quietly thereby.

Where was he going, this man against the sky?
You know not, nor do I.   225
But this we know, if we know anything:
That we may laugh and fight and sing
And of our transcience here make offering
To an orient Word[4] that will not be erased,
Or, save in incommunicable gleams   230
Too permanent for dreams,
Be found or known.
No tonic and ambitious irritant
Of increase or of want
Has made an otherwise insensate waste   235
Of ages overthrown
A ruthless, veiled, implacable foretaste
Of other ages that are still to be
Depleted and rewarded variously
Because a few, by fate's economy,   240
Shall seem to move the world the way it goes;
No soft evangel of equality,
Safe-cradled in a communal repose
That huddles into death and may at last
Be covered well with equatorial snows—   245
And all for what, the devil only knows—
Will aggregate an inkling to confirm
The credit of a sage or of a worm,
Or tell us why one man in five
Should have a care to stay alive   250
While in his heart he feels no violence
Laid on his humor and intelligence
When infant Science makes a pleasant face
And waves again that hollow toy, the Race;
No planetary trap where souls are wrought   255
For nothing but the sake of being caught

4. *Cf.* John i: 1. "In the beginning was the Word, and the Word was with God, and the Word was God."

And sent again to nothing will attune
Itself to any key of any reason
Why man should hunger through another season
To find out why 'twere better late than soon   260
To go away and let the sun and moon
And all the silly stars illuminate
A place for creeping things,
And those that root and trumpet and have wings,
And herd and ruminate,   265
Or dive and flash and poise in rivers and seas,
Or by their loyal tails in lofty trees
Hang screeching lewd victorious derision
Of man's immortal vision.

Shall we, because Eternity records   270
Too vast an answer for the time-born words
We spell, whereof so many are dead that once
In our capricious lexicons
Were so alive and final, hear no more
The Word itself, the living word   275
That none alive has ever heard
Or ever spelt,
And few have ever felt
Without the fears and old surrenderings
And terrors that began   280
When Death let fall a feather from his wings
And humbled the first man?
Because the weight of our humility,
Wherefrom we gain
A little wisdom and much pain,   285
Falls here too sore and there too tedious,
Are we in anguish or complacency,
Not looking far enough ahead
To see by what mad couriers we are led
Along the roads of the ridiculous,   290
To pity ourselves and laugh at faith
And while we curse life bear it?
And if we see the soul's dead end in death,
Are we to fear it?
What folly is here that has not yet a name   295
Unless we say outright that we are liars?
What have we seen beyond our sunset fires
That lights again the way by which we came?
Why pay we such a price, and one we give
So clamoringly, for each racked empty day   300

That leads one more last human hope away,
As quiet fiends would lead past our crazed eyes
Our children to an unseen sacrifice?
If after all that we have lived and thought,
All comes to Nought,— 305
If there be nothing after Now,
And we be nothing anyhow,
And we know that,—why live?
'Twere sure but weaklings' vain distress
To suffer dungeons where so many doors 310
Will open on the cold eternal shores
That look sheer down
To the dark tideless floods of Nothingness
Where all who know may drown.

1916

Mr. Flood's Party

Old Eben Flood, climbing alone one night
Over the hill between the town below
And the forsaken upland hermitage
That held as much as he should ever know
On earth again of home, paused warily. 5
The road was his with not a native near;
And Eben, having leisure, said aloud;
For no man else in Tilbury Town to hear:

"Well, Mr. Flood, we have the harvest moon
Again, and we may not have many more; 10
The bird is on the wing, the poet says,
And you and I have said it here before.
Drink to the bird."[5] He raised up to the light
The jug that he had gone so far to fill,
And answered huskily: "Well, Mr. Flood, 15
Since you propose it, I believe I will."

Alone, as if enduring to the end
A valiant armor of scarred hopes outworn,
He stood there in the middle of the road
Like Roland's ghost winding a silent horn.[6] 20
Below him, in the town among the trees,
Where friends of other days had honored him,

5. *Cf.* Edward FitzGerald, *The Rubái-yát of Omar Khayyám*, ll. 25–28: "Come, fill the Cup, and in the fire of Spring / Your Winter-garment of Repentance fling: / The Bird of Time

has but a little way / To flutter and the Bird is on the Wing."
6. At Roncesvalles (A.D. 778), when the battle became hopeless, Roland at last blew his horn for help and died.

A phantom salutation of the dead
Rang thinly till old Eben's eyes were dim.

Then, as a mother lays her sleeping child   25
Down tenderly, fearing it may awake,
He set the jug down slowly at his feet
With trembling care, knowing that most things break;
And only when assured that on firm earth
It stood, as the uncertain lives of men   30
Assuredly did not, he paced away,
And with his hand extended paused again:

"Well, Mr. Flood, we have not met like this
In a long time; and many a change has come
To both of us, I fear, since last it was   35
We had a drop together. Welcome home!"
Convivially returning with himself,
Again he raised the jug up to the light;
And with an acquiescent quaver said:
"Well, Mr. Flood, if you insist, I might.   40

"Only a very little, Mr. Flood—
For auld lang syne. No more, sir; that will do."
So, for the time, apparently it did,
And Eben evidently thought so too;
For soon amid the silver loneliness   45
Of night he lifted up his voice and sang,
Secure, with only two moons listening,
Until the whole harmonious landscape rang—

"For auld lang syne." The weary throat gave out,
The last word wavered; and the song being done,   50
He raised again the jug regretfully
And shook his head, and was again alone.
There was not much that was ahead of him,
And there was nothing in the town below—
Where strangers would have shut the many doors   55
That many friends had opened long ago.

1920

The Mill

The miller's wife had waited long,
    The tea was cold, the fire was dead;
And there might yet be nothing wrong
    In how he went and what he said:

"There are no millers any more,"   5
   Was all that she had heard him say;
And he had lingered at the door
   So long that it seemed yesterday.

Sick with a fear that had no form
   She knew that she was there at last;   10
And in the mill there was a warm
   And mealy fragrance of the past.
What else there was would only seem
   To say again what he had meant;
And what was hanging from a beam   15
   Would not have heeded where she went.

And if she thought it followed her,
   She may have reasoned in the dark
That one way of the few there were
   Would hide her and would leave no mark: 20
Black water, smooth above the weir
   Like starry velvet in the night,
Though ruffled once, would soon appear
   The same as ever to the sight.

1920

Firelight

Ten years together without yet a cloud,
They seek each other's eyes at intervals
Of gratefulness to firelight and four walls
For love's obliteration of the crowd.
Serenely and perennially endowed   5
And bowered as few may be, their joy recalls
No snake, no sword; and over them there falls
The blessing of what neither says aloud.

Wiser for silence, they were not so glad
Were she to read the graven tale of lines   10
On the wan face of one somewhere alone;
Nor were they more content could he have had
Her thoughts a moment since of one who shines
Apart, and would be hers if he had known.

1920

The Tree in Pamela's Garden

Pamela was too gentle to deceive
Her roses. "Let the men stay where they are,"
She said, "and if Apollo's avatar[7]
Be one of them, I shall not have to grieve."
And so she made all Tilbury Town believe   5
She sighed a little more for the North Star
Than over men, and only in so far
As she was in a garden was like Eve.

Her neighbors—doing all that neighbors can
To make romance of reticence meanwhile—   10
Seeing that she had never loved a man,
Wished Pamela had a cat, or a small bird,
And only would have wondered at her smile
Could they have seen that she had overheard.

1921

New England[8]

Here where the wind is always north-north-east
And children learn to walk on frozen toes,
Wonder begets an envy of all those
Who boil elsewhere with such a lyric yeast
Of love that you will hear them at a feast   5
Where demons would appeal for some repose,
Still clamoring where the chalice overflows
And crying wildest who have drunk the least.

Passion is here a soilure of the wits,
We're told, and Love a cross for them to bear;   10
Joy shivers in the corner where she knits
And Conscience always has the rocking-chair,
Cheerful as when she tortured into fits
The first cat that was ever killed by Care.

1925

7. Embodiment. Apollo, smitten by Cupid's golden arrow, fell in love with Daphne, whom the prankish Cupid had struck with the leaden arrow of reluctance. Daphne was saved from Apollo's pursuit by being changed into a laurel tree. *Cf.* the reference to Eve in l. 8, recalling another tree in another garden. 8. In a Gardiner paper Robinson defended this sonnet as "an oblique attack" on those ridiculing the "alleged emotional and moral frigidity" of New England.

ROBERT FROST
(1874[1]–)

Among the American poets of stature since Whitman, Robert Frost is the most universal in his appeal. His art is an act of clarification, an act which, without simplifying the truth, renders it in some degree accessible to everyone. Frost found his poetry in the familiar objects and character of New England, but people who have never seen New Hampshire or Vermont, reading his poems in California or Virginia, experience their revelation.

It is therefore not surprising that this poet of New England was first recognized in old England and that his boyhood was passed in California. His father, a journalist of southern extraction, left New Hampshire during the Civil War, and his professional engagements led him to California. There the poet was born on March 26, 1874, and was named Robert Lee in memory of the Old Dominion. He was eleven when his father died and his mother returned to her people in Lawrence, Mass., and Amherst, N. H.

Life with relatives proved difficult, so his mother went to teach school in Salem, N. H. Frost later attended Lawrence High School. On graduation in 1892 he was one of two valedictorians; the other was Elinor White, whom he married three years later. Reluctant to accept his grandfather's support at Dartmouth College, Frost did not finish the first semester. Instead he tried himself out on a country paper, then turned to teaching school. He sent out his verses in quantity after 1890, but only a negligible few were accepted before 1913. Like Robinson he was much ahead of his time.

Faced with disappointment as a poet, his family growing, the young Frost accepted his grandfather's assistance, and studied at Harvard for two years (1897–1899), but he concluded that formal study was not the way for him. His good foundation in the classics is apparent in his extraordinary word sense, in the disciplined forms of his poetry, and in his pagan delight in nature. His reading of science and philosophy has been influential throughout his poetry. But he had a deep-rooted fear: "They would have made me into a professor, or into a professional," he once said.

In 1900, with his grandfather's help, he procured a farm at Derry, New Hampshire, supporting his family, including four children, by a combination of farming and teaching. From 1900 to 1911 he taught English at Pinkerton Academy, Derry. In 1911–1912 he conducted a course in psychology at the State Normal School in Plymouth, nearby. Still he received from American editors the same heartbreaking refusals.

Elinor Frost, a steady source of inspiration, encouraged his instinct for a desperate remedy. They sold the farm in 1912 and on the small proceeds went to

1. Not 1875 as often given. Frost celebrated his eightieth birthday in 1954.

England, where the first stirrings of a new poetry movement had been noted. Wishing, as he says, to live "beneath a thatched roof" they moved to a small farmstead in the country. There Wilfred W. Gibson and Lascelles Abercrombie were neighbors, and others of the so-called "Georgians," Edward Thomas and Rupert Brooke, came as guests. Soon *A Boy's Will* (1913) was hailed in England as a work of genuine merit. It was followed in 1914 by *North of Boston*, one of the great volumes of this century. Both books were republished in the United States within the year. At this point, according to a friend, Frost said to his wife, "My book has gone home; we must go too." In 1915 they were settled again on a New Hampshire farm, this time near Franconia, which suggested the title of *Mountain Interval* (1916).

In 1916 he read "The Axe-Helve" as the Phi Beta Kappa poem at Harvard University. Frost had magnificent qualities as a public reader; his reading tours during many years made him and his poetry household property and stimulated a popular interest in poetry. Also in 1916, Frost became "poet in residence" at Amherst College, where he returned for a time each winter for four years. At various times he has served as lecturer or fellow at Wesleyan, Michigan, Dartmouth, Yale, and Harvard. In 1920 he participated in the founding of the Bread Loaf School of English (Middlebury College, Vermont), and he has lectured there many summers. He lives nearby on his own land at Ripton.

Frost's later publications have appeared at rather long intervals, yet almost every poem, large or small, is unforgettable. His *Selected Poems* (1923, revised 1928) was followed by *New Hampshire* (1923), which won the Pulitzer Prize. This is one of his longest poems, but one of his most witty and wise, an anecdotal discussion of the values of life and character, flavored with New England examples. In 1928 he published *West-Running Brook*, its title poem a complex masterpiece. *Collected Poems* first appeared in 1930, and won him his second Pulitzer Prize. *A Further Range* (1936) also was awarded the Pulitzer Prize. His later volumes of lyrics are *A Witness Tree* (1942) and *Steeple Bush* (1947). *A Masque of Reason* (1945) and *A Masque of Mercy* (1947) are dramatic dialogues —discussions of his religious insights and criticism of contemporary society.

Few major poets have shown such remarkable consistency as Robert Frost—the whole poet is the whole man, and he captures the reader as much by the grandeur of his personality as by impeccable rightness of form and phrase. "Art strips life to form," he has said, and the substance and the words of his poems coexist in one identity. In language, he has sought to catch what he has called the "tones of speech," but even more successfully than Wordsworth he has pruned the "language really used by men" to achieve a propriety that spontaneous speech cannot attain.

For all his descriptive realism, Frost is temperamentally a poet of meditative sobriety. He is no philosopher with a formal system. The truths he seeks are innate in the heart of man and in common objects. But people forget, and poetry, he says, "makes you remember what you didn't know you knew." A poem is not didactic, but provides an immediate experience which "begins in delight, and ends in wisdom"; and it provides at least "a momentary stay against confusion." Of man alone or man in society Frost demands a responsible individualism controlled by an inner mandate, and thus his views remind us of earlier transcendentalism of earlier

New Englanders. Like Thoreau and Emerson, Frost is willing to become a rebel in this cause, and like them, but so unlike the skeptical poets of his age, he has had, he says, only "a lover's quarrel with the world."

The standard edition is *Complete Poems*, 1949. A new volume, *In the Clearing*, appeared in 1962.

Biographical and critical studies are: G. B. Munson, *Robert Frost * * ** , 1927; Sidney Cox, *Robert Frost * * ** , 1929; Caroline Ford, *The Less Traveled Road * * ** , 1935; Lawrance R. Thompson, *Fire and Ice: The Art and Thought of Robert Frost*, 1942; Sidney Cox, *Swinger of Birches*, 1957; Reginald L. Cook, *The Dimensions of Robert Frost*, 1958; and a complete biography by Elizabeth S. Sergeant, *Robert Frost: The Trial By Existence*, 1960. Richard H. Thornton, in *Recognition of Robert Frost*, 1937, collected early, significant articles on Frost. A bibliography is *The Intervals of Robert Frost*, by Louis and Esther Mertins, 1947.

The Wood-Pile

Out walking in the frozen swamp one grey day,
I paused and said, 'I will turn back from here.
No, I will go on farther—and we shall see.'
The hard snow held me, save where now and then
One foot went through. The view was all in lines   5
Straight up and down of tall slim trees
Too much alike to mark or name a place by
So as to say for certain I was here
Or somewhere else: I was just far from home.
A small bird flew before me. He was careful   10
To put a tree between us when he lighted,
And say no word to tell me who he was
Who was so foolish as to think what *he* thought.
He thought that I was after him for a feather—
The white one in his tail; like one who takes   15
Everything said as personal to himself.
One flight out sideways would have undeceived him.
And then there was a pile of wood for which
I forgot him and let his little fear
Carry him off the way I might have gone,   20
Without so much as wishing him good-night.

He went behind it to make his last stand.
It was a cord of maple, cut and split
And piled—and measured, four by four by eight.
And not another like it could I see.   25
No runner tracks in this year's snow looped near it.
And it was older sure than this year's cutting,
Or even last year's or the year's before.
The wood was grey and the bark warping off it
And the pile somewhat sunken. Clematis   30
Had wound strings round and round it like a bundle.
What held it though on one side was a tree
Still growing, and on one a stake and prop,
These latter about to fall. I thought that only
Someone who lived in turning to fresh tasks   35
Could so forget his handiwork on which
He spent himself, the labour of his axe,
And leave it there far from a useful fireplace
To warm the frozen swamp as best it could
With the slow smokeless burning of decay.   40

1914

After Apple-Picking

My long two-pointed ladder's sticking through a tree
Toward heaven still,
And there's a barrel that I didn't fill
Beside it, and there may be two or three
Apples I didn't pick upon some bough.   5
But I am done with apple-picking now.
Essence of winter sleep is on the night,
The scent of apples: I am drowsing off.
I cannot rub the strangeness from my sight
I got from looking through a pane of glass   10
I skimmed this morning from the drinking trough
And held against the world of hoary grass.
It melted, and I let it fall and break.
But I was well
Upon my way to sleep before it fell,   15
And I could tell
What form my dreaming was about to take.
Magnified apples appear and disappear,
Stem end and blossom end,
And every fleck of russet showing clear.   20
My instep arch not only keeps the ache,

It keeps the pressure of a ladder-round.
I feel the ladder sway as the boughs bend.
And I keep hearing from the cellar bin
The rumbling sound   25
Of load on load of apples coming in.

For I have had too much
Of apple-picking: I am overtired
Of the great harvest I myself desired.
There were ten thousand thousand fruit to touch,   30
Cherish in hand, lift down, and not let fall.
For all
That struck the earth,
No matter if not bruised or spiked with stubble,
Went surely to the cider-apple heap   35
As of no worth.
One can see what will trouble
This sleep of mine, whatever sleep it is.
Were he not gone,
The woodchuck could say whether it's like his   40
Long sleep, as I describe its coming on,
Or just some human sleep.

1914

The Death of the Hired Man

Mary sat musing on the lamp-flame at the table
Waiting for Warren. When she heard his step,
She ran on tip-toe down the darkened passage
To meet him in the doorway with the news
And put him on his guard. 'Silas is back.'   5
She pushed him outward with her through the door
And shut it after her. 'Be kind,' she said.
She took the market things from Warren's arms
And set them on the porch, then drew him down
To sit beside her on the wooden steps.   10

'When was I ever anything but kind to him?
But I'll not have the fellow back,' he said.
'I told him so last haying, didn't I?
"If he left then," I said, "that ended it."
What good is he? Who else will harbour him   15
At his age for the little he can do?
What help he is there's no depending on.
Off he goes always when I need him most.

"He thinks he ought to earn a little pay,
Enough at least to buy tobacco with,   20
So he won't have to beg and be beholden."
"All right," I say, "I can't afford to pay
Any fixed wages, though I wish I could."
"Someone else can." "Then someone else will have to."
I shouldn't mind his bettering himself   25
If that was what it was. You can be certain,
When he begins like that, there's someone at him
Trying to coax him off with pocket-money,—
In haying time, when any help is scarce.
In winter he comes back to us. I'm done.'   30

'Sh! not so loud: he'll hear you,' Mary said.

'I want him to: he'll have to soon or late.'

'He's worn out. He's asleep beside the stove.
When I came up from Rowe's I found him here,
Huddled against the barn-door fast asleep,   35
A miserable sight, and frightening, too—
You needn't smile—I didn't recognise him—
I wasn't looking for him—and he's changed.
Wait till you see.

                    'Where did you say he'd been?'

'He didn't say. I dragged him to the house,   40
And gave him tea and tried to make him smoke.
I tried to make him talk about his travels.
Nothing would do: he just kept nodding off.'

'What did he say? Did he say anything?'

'But little.'

                    'Anything? Mary, confess   45
He said he'd come to ditch the meadow for me.'

'Warren!'

                    'But did he? I just want to know.'

'Of course he did. What would you have him say?
Surely you wouldn't grudge the poor old man
Some humble way to save his self-repect.   50
He added, if you really care to know,
He meant to clear the upper pasture, too.
That sounds like something you have heard before?
Warren, I wish you could have heard the way

He jumbled everything. I stopped to look 55
Two or three times—he made me feel so queer—
To see if he was talking in his sleep.
He ran on Harold Wilson—you remember—
The boy you had in haying four years since.
He's finished school, and teaching in his college. 60
Silas declares you'll have to get him back.
He says they two will make a team for work:
Between them they will lay this farm as smooth!
The way he mixed that in with other things.
He thinks young Wilson a likely lad, though daft 65
On education—you know how they fought
All through July under the blazing sun,
Silas up on the cart to build the load,
Harold along beside to pitch it on.'

'Yes, I took care to keep well out of earshot.' 70

'Well, those days trouble Silas like a dream.
You wouldn't think they would. How some things linger!
Harold's young college boy's assurance piqued him.
After so many years he still keeps finding
Good arguments he sees he might have used. 75
I sympathise. I know just how it feels
To think of the right thing to say too late.
Harold's associated in his mind with Latin.
He asked me what I thought of Harold's saying
He studied Latin like the violin 80
Because he liked it—that an argument!
He said he couldn't make the boy believe
He could find water with a hazel prong—
Which showed how much good school had ever done him.
He wanted to go over that. But most of all 85
He thinks if he could have another chance
To teach him how to build a load of hay—'

'I know, that's Silas' one accomplishment.
He bundles every forkful in its place,
And tags and numbers it for future reference, 90
So he can find and easily dislodge it
In the unloading. Silas does that well.
He takes it out in bunches like big birds' nests.
You never see him standing on the hay
He's trying to lift, straining to lift himself.' 95

'He thinks if he could teach him that, he'd be
Some good perhaps to someone in the world.

He hates to see a boy the fool of books.
Poor Silas, so concerned for other folk,
And nothing to look backward to with pride,   100
And nothing to look forward to with hope,
So now and never any different.'

Part of a moon was falling down the west,
Dragging the whole sky with it to the hills.
Its light poured softly in her lap. She saw it   105
And spread her apron to it. She put out her hand
Among the harp-like morning-glory strings,
Taut with the dew from garden bed to eaves,
As if she played unheard some tenderness
That wrought on him beside her in the night.   110
'Warren,' she said, 'he has come home to die:
You needn't be afraid he'll leave you this time.'

'Home,' he mocked gently.

                          'Yes, what else but home?
It all depends on what you mean by home.
Of course he's nothing to us, any more   115
Than was the hound that came a stranger to us
Out of the woods, worn out upon the trail.'

'Home is the place where, when you have to go there,
They have to take you in.'

                          'I should have called it   120
Something you somehow haven't to deserve.'

Warren leaned out and took a step or two,
Picked up a little stick, and brought it back
And broke it in his hand and tossed it by.
'Silas has better claim on us you think   125
Than on his brother? Thirteen little miles
As the road winds would bring him to his door.
Silas has walked that far no doubt to-day.
Why didn't he go there? His brother's rich,
A somebody—director in the bank.'   130

'He never told us that.'

                          'We know it though.'

'I think his brother ought to help, of course.
I'll see to that if there is need. He ought of right
To take him in, and might be willing to—

He may be better than appearances.   135
But have some pity on Silas. Do you think
If he had any pride in claiming kin
Or anything he looked for from his brother,
He'd keep so still about him all this time?'

'I wonder what's between them.'

                  'I can tell you.   140
Silas is what he is—we wouldn't mind him—
But just the kind that kinsfolk can't abide.
He never did a thing so very bad.
He don't know why he isn't quite as good
As anybody. Worthless though he is,   145
He won't be made ashamed to please his brother.'

'I can't think Si ever hurt anyone.'

'No, but he hurt my heart the way he lay
And rolled his old head on that sharp-edged chairback.
He wouldn't let me put him on the lounge.   150
You must go in and see what you can do.
I made the bed up for him there to-night.
You'll be surprised at him—how much he's broken.
His working days are done; I'm sure of it.'

I'd not be in a hurry to say that.'   155

'I haven't been. Go, look, see for yourself.
But, Warren, please remember how it is:
He's come to help you ditch the meadow.
He has a plan. You mustn't laugh at him.
He may not speak of it, and then he may.   160
I'll sit and see if that small sailing cloud
Will hit or miss the moon.'

               It hit the moon.
Then there were three there, making a dim row,
The moon, the little silver cloud, and she.
Warren returned—too soon, it seemed to her,   165
Slipped to her side, caught up her hand and waited.

'Warren?' she questioned.

               'Dead,' was all he answered.

1914

Home Burial[1]

He saw her from the bottom of the stairs
Before she saw him. She was starting down,
Looking back over her shoulder at some fear.
She took a doubtful step and then undid it
To raise herself and look again. He spoke   5
Advancing toward her: 'What is it you see
From up there always—for I want to know.'
She turned and sank upon her skirts at that,
And her face changed from terrified to dull.
He said to gain time: 'What is it you see,'   10
Mounting until she cowered under him.
'I will find out now—you must tell me, dear.'
She, in her place, refused him any help
With the least stiffening of her neck and silence.
She let him look, sure that he wouldn't see,   15
Blind creature; and a while he didn't see.
But at last he murmured, 'Oh,' and again, 'Oh.'

'What is it—what?' she said.

                                'Just that I see.'

'You don't,' she challenged. 'Tell me what it is.'

'The wonder is I didn't see at once.   20
I never noticed it from here before.
I must be wonted to it—that's the reason.
The little graveyard where my people are!
So small the window frames the whole of it.
Not so much larger than a bedroom, is it?   25
There are three stones of slate and one of marble,
Broad-shouldered little slabs there in the sunlight
On the sidehill. We haven't to mind *those*.
But I understand: it is not the stones,
But the child's mound—'

                    'Don't, don't, don't, don't,' she cried.   30

She withdrew shrinking from beneath his arm
That rested on the banister, and slid downstairs;
And turned on him with such a daunting look,
He said twice over before he knew himself:
'Can't a man speak of his own child he's lost?'   35

1. The family burial ground near the
farmhouse can still be seen in remoter
parts of New England and other eastern
areas.

'Not you! Oh, where's my hat? Oh, I don't need it!
I must get out of here. I must get air.
I don't know rightly whether any man can.'

'Amy! Don't go to someone else this time.
Listen to me. I won't come down the stairs.'   40
He sat and fixed his chin between his fists.
'There's something I should like to ask you, dear.'

'You don't know how to ask it.'

                           'Help me, then.'

Her fingers moved the latch for all reply.

'My words are nearly always an offence.   45
I don't know how to speak of anything
So as to please you. But I might be taught
I should suppose. I can't say I see how.
A man must partly give up being a man
With women-folk. We could have some arrangement   50
By which I'd bind myself to keep hands off
Anything special you're a-mind to name.
Though I don't like such things 'twixt those that love.
Two that don't love can't live together without them.
But two that do can't live together with them.'   55
She moved the latch a little. 'Don't—don't go.
Don't carry it to someone else this time.
Tell me about it if it's something human.
Let me into your grief. I'm not so much
Unlike other folks as your standing there   60
Apart would make me out. Give me my chance.
I do think, though, you overdo it a little.
What was it brought you up to think it the thing
To take your mother-loss of a first child
So inconsolably—in the face of love.   65
You'd think his memory might be satisfied—'

'There you go sneering now!'

                         'I'm not, I'm not!
You make me angry. I'll come down to you.
God, what a woman! And it's come to this,
A man can't speak of his own child that's dead.'   70

'You can't because you don't know how to speak.
If you had any feelings, you that dug
With your own hand—how could you?—his little grave;
I saw you from that very window there.

Making the gravel leap and leap in air,   75
Leap up, like that, like that, and land so lightly
And roll back down the mound beside the hole.
I thought, Who is that man? I didn't know you.
And I crept down the stairs and up the stairs
To look again, and still your spade kept lifting.   80
Then you came in. I heard your rumbling voice
Out in the kitchen, and I don't know why,
But I went near to see with my own eyes.
You could sit there with the stains on your shoes
Of the fresh earth from your own baby's grave   85
And talk about your everyday concerns.
You had stood the spade up against the wall
Outside there in the entry, for I saw it.'

'I shall laugh the worst laugh I ever laughed.
I'm cursed. God, if I don't believe I'm cursed.'   90

'I can repeat the very words you were saying.
"Three foggy mornings and one rainy day
Will rot the best birch fence a man can build."
Think of it, talk like that at such a time!
What had how long it takes a birch to rot   95
To do with what was in the darkened parlour.
You *couldn't* care! The nearest friends can go
With anyone to death, comes so far short
They might as well not try to go at all.
No, from the time when one is sick to death,   100
One is alone, and he dies more alone.
Friends make pretence of following to the grave,
But before one is in it, their minds are turned
And making the best of their way back to life
And living people, and things they understand.   105
But the world's evil. I won't have grief so
If I can change it. Oh, I won't, I won't!'

'There, you have said it all and you feel better.
You won't go now. You're crying. Close the door.
The heart's gone out of it: why keep it up.   110
Amy! There's someone coming down the road!'

'*You*—oh, you think the talk is all. I must go—
Somewhere out of this house. How can I make you—'

'If—you—do!' She was opening the door wider.
'Where do you mean to go? First tell me that.   115
I'll follow and bring you back by force. I *will!*—'

1914

Blueberries

'You ought to have seen what I saw on my way
To the village, through Patterson's pasture to-day:
Blueberries as big as the end of your thumb,
Real sky-blue, and heavy, and ready to drum
In the cavernous pail of the first one to come!   5
And all ripe together, not some of them green
And some of them ripe! You ought to have seen!'

'I don't know what part of the pasture you mean.'

'You know where they cut off the woods—let me see—
It was two years ago—or no!—can it be   10
No longer than that?—and the following fall
The fire ran and burned it all up but the wall.'

'Why, there hasn't been time for the bushes to grow.
That's always the way with the blueberries, though:
There may not have been the ghost of a sign   15
Of them anywhere under the shade of the pine,
But get the pine out of the way, you may burn
The pasture all over until not a fern
Or grass-blade is left, not to mention a stick,
And presto, they're up all around you as thick   20
And hard to explain as a conjuror's trick.'

'It must be on charcoal they fatten their fruit.
I taste in them sometimes the flavour of soot.
And after all really they're ebony skinned:
The blue's but a mist from the breath of the wind,   25
A tarnish that goes at a touch of the hand,
And less than the tan with which pickers are tanned.'

'Does Patterson know what he has, do you think?'

'He may and not care and so leave the chewink
To gather them for him—you know what he is.   30
He won't make the fact that they're rightfully his
An excuse for keeping us other folk out.'

'I wonder you didn't see Loren about.'

'The best of it was that I did. Do you know,
I was just getting through what the field had to show   35
And over the wall and into the road,
When who should come by, with a democrat-load
Of all the young chattering Lorens alive,
But Loren, the fatherly, out for a drive.'

'He saw you, then? What did he do? Did he frown?'   40

'He just kept nodding his head up and down.
You know how politely he always goes by.
But he thought a big thought—I could tell by his eye—
Which being expressed, might be this in effect:
"I have left those there berries, I shrewdly suspect,   45
To ripen too long. I am greatly to blame." '

'He's a thriftier person than some I could name.'

'He seems to be thrifty; and hasn't he need,
With the mouths of all those young Lorens to feed?
He has brought them all up on wild berries, they say,   50
Like birds. They store a great many away.
They eat them the year round, and those they don't eat
They sell in the store and buy shoes for their feet.'

'Who cares what they say? It's a nice way to live,
Just taking what Nature is willing to give,   55
Not forcing her hand with harrow and plow.'

'I wish you had seen his perpetual bow—
And the air of the youngsters! Not one of them turned,
And they looked so solemn-absurdly concerned.'

'I wish I knew half what the flock of them know   60
Of where all the berries and other things grow,
Cranberries in bogs and raspberries on top
Of the boulder-strewn mountain, and when they will crop.
I met them one day and each had a flower
Stuck into his berries as fresh as a shower;   65
Some strange kind—they told me it hadn't a name.'

'I've told you how once not long after we came,
I almost provoked poor Loren to mirth
By going to him of all people on earth
To ask if he knew any fruit to be had   70
For the picking. The rascal, he said he'd be glad
To tell if he knew. But the year had been bad.
There *had* been some berries—but those were all gone.
He didn't say where they had been. He went on:
"I'm sure—I'm sure"—as polite as could be.   75
He spoke to his wife in the door, "Let me see,
Mame, *we* don't know any good berrying place?"
It was all he could do to keep a straight face.'

'If he thinks all the fruit that grows wild is for him,
He'll find he's mistaken. See here, for a whim,   80

We'll pick in the Pattersons' pasture this year.
We'll go in the morning, that is, if it's clear,
And the sun shines out warm: the vines must be wet.
It's so long since I picked I almost forget
How we used to pick berries: we took one look round,   85
Then sank out of sight like trolls underground,
And saw nothing more of each other, or heard,
Unless when you said I was keeping a bird
Away from its nest, and I said it was you.
"Well, one of us is." For complaining it flew   90
Around and around us. And then for a while
We picked, till I feared you had wandered a mile,
And I thought I had lost you. I lifted a shout
Too loud for the distance you were, it turned out,
For when you made answer, your voice was as low   95
As talking—you stood up beside me, you know.'

'We sha'n't have the place to ourselves to enjoy—
Not likely, when all the young Lorens deploy.
They'll be there to-morrow, or even to-night.
They won't be too friendly—they may be polite—   100
To people they look on as having no right
To pick where they're picking. But we won't complain.
You ought to have seen how it looked in the rain,
The fruit mixed with water in layers of leaves,
Like two kinds of jewels, a vision for thieves.'   105

1914

Birches

When I see birches bend to left and right
Across the lines of straighter darker trees,
I like to think some boy's been swinging them.
But swinging doesn't bend them down to stay.
Ice-storms do that. Often you must have seen them   5
Loaded with ice a sunny winter morning
After a rain. They click upon themselves
As the breeze rises, and turn many-colored
As the stir cracks and crazes their enamel.
Soon the sun's warmth makes them shed crystal shells   10
Shattering and avalanching on the snow-crust—
Such heaps of broken glass to sweep away
You'd think the inner dome of heaven had fallen.
They are dragged to the withered bracken by the load,
And they seem not to break; though once they are bowed   15

So low for long, they never right themselves:
You may see their trunks arching in the woods
Years afterwards, trailing their leaves on the ground
Like girls on hands and knees that throw their hair
Before them over their heads to dry in the sun. 20
But I was going to say when Truth broke in
With all her matter-of-fact about the ice-storm
I should prefer to have some boy bend them
As he went out and in to fetch the cows—
Some boy too far from town to learn baseball, 25
Whose only play was what he found himself,
Summer or winter, and could play alone.
One by one he subdued his father's trees
By riding them down over and over again
Until he took the stiffness out of them, 30
And not one but hung limp, not one was left
For him to conquer. He learned all there was
To learn about not launching out too soon
And so not carrying the tree away
Clear to the ground. He always kept his poise 35
To the top branches, climbing carefully
With the same pains you use to fill a cup
Up to the brim, and even above the brim.
Then he flung outward, feet first, with a swish,
Kicking his way down through the air to the ground. 40
So was I once myself a swinger of birches.
And so I dream of going back to be.
It's when I'm weary of considerations,
And life is too much like a pathless wood
Where your face burns and tickles with the cobwebs 45
Broken across it, and one eye is weeping
From a twig's having lashed across it open.
I'd like to get away from earth awhile
And then come back to it and begin over.
May no fate willfully misunderstand me 50
And half grant what I wish and snatch me away
Not to return. Earth's the right place for love:
I don't know where it's likely to go better.
I'd like to go by climbing a birch tree,
And climb black branches up a snow-white trunk 55
Toward heaven, till the tree could bear no more,
But dipped its top and set me down again.
That would be good both going and coming back.
One could do worse than be a swinger of birches.

1916

Brown's Descent
OR THE WILLY-NILLY SLIDE

Brown lived at such a lofty farm
    That everyone for miles could see
His lantern when he did his chores
    In winter after half-past three.

And many must have seen him make   5
    His wild descent from there one night,
'Cross lots, 'cross walls, 'cross everything,
    Describing rings of lantern light.

Between the house and barn the gale
    Got him by something he had on   10
And blew him out on the icy crust
    That cased the world, and he was gone!

Walls were all buried, trees were few:
    He saw no stay unless he stove
A hole in somewhere with his heel.   15
    But though repeatedly he strove

And stamped and said things to himself,
    And sometimes something seemed to yield,
He gained no foothold, but pursued
    His journey down from field to field.   20

Sometimes he came with arms outspread
    Like wings, revolving in the scene
Upon his longer axis, and
    With no small dignity of mien.

Faster or slower as he chanced,   25
    Sitting or standing as he chose,
According as he feared to risk
    His neck, or thought to spare his clothes,

He never let the lantern drop.
    And some exclaimed who saw afar   30
The figures he described with it,
    'I wonder what those signals are

Brown makes at such an hour of night!
    He's celebrating something strange.
I wonder if he's sold his farm,   35
    Or been made Master of the Grange.'

He reeled, he lurched, he bobbed, he checked;
    He fell and made the lantern rattle

(But saved the light from going out.)
　So half-way down he fought the battle,　　　　40

Incredulous of his own bad luck.
　And then becoming reconciled
To everything, he gave it up
　And came down like a coasting child.

'Well—I—be—' that was all he said,　　　　45
　As standing in the river road,
He looked back up the slippery slope
　(Two miles it was) to his abode.

Sometimes as an authority
　On motor-cars, I'm asked if I　　　　50
Should say our stock was petered out,
　And this is my sincere reply:

Yankees are what they always were.
　Don't think Brown ever gave up hope
Of getting home again because　　　　55
　He couldn't climb that slippery slope;

Or even thought of standing there
　Until the January thaw
Should take the polish off the crust.
　He bowed with grace to natural law,　　　　60

And then went round it on his feet,
　After the manner of our stock;
Not much concerned for those to whom,
　At that particular time o'clock,

It must have looked as if the course　　　　65
　He steered was really straight away
From that which he was headed for—
　Not much concerned for them, I say;

No more so than became a man—
　And politician at odd seasons.　　　　70
I've kept Brown standing in the cold
　While I invested him with reasons;

But now he snapped his eyes three times;
　Then shook his lantern, saying, 'Ile's
'Bout out!'[2] and took the long way home　　　　75
　By road, a matter of several miles.

　　　　　　　　　　1916

2. The oil is about out.

Nothing Gold Can Stay

Nature's first green[3] is gold,
Her hardest hue to hold.
Her early leaf's a flower;
But only so an hour.
Then leaf subsides to leaf.   5
So Eden sank to grief,
So dawn goes down to day.
Nothing gold can stay.

                                                      1923

A Star in a Stone-boat[4]

Never tell me that not one star of all
That slip from heaven at night and softly fall
Has been picked up with stones to build a wall.

Some laborer found one faded and stone cold,
And saving that its weight suggested gold,   5
And tugged it from his first too certain hold,

He noticed nothing in it to remark.
He was not used to handling stars thrown dark
And lifeless from an interrupted arc.

He did not recognize in that smooth coal   10
The one thing palpable besides the soul
To penetrate the air in which we roll.

He did not see how like a flying thing
It brooded ant-eggs, and had one large wing,
One not so large for flying in a ring,   15

And a long Bird of Paradise's tail,
(Though these when not in use to fly and trail
It drew back in its body like a snail);

Nor know that he might move it from the spot,
The harm was done; from having been star-shot   20
The very nature of the soil was hot

3. In Old English, "green" signified "growth" as well as a color. This poem contains several dual references; for example, the Hebrew word "Eden" means "delight," and is here contrasted with "grief."

4. A barrow or sledge for transporting stones, still used for "building wall" in New England.

And burning to yield flowers instead of grain,
Flowers fanned and not put out by all the rain
Poured on them by his prayers prayed in vain.

He moved it roughly with an iron bar,   25
He loaded an old stone-boat with the star
And not, as you might think, a flying car,

Such as even poets would admit perforce
More practical than Pegasus the horse[4a]
If it could put a star back in its course.   30

He dragged it through the ploughed ground at a pace
But faintly reminiscent of the race
Of jostling rock in interstellar space.

It went for building stone, and I, as though
Commanded in a dream, forever go   35
To right the wrong that this should have been so.

Yet ask where else it could have gone as well,
I do not know—I cannot stop to tell:
He might have left it lying where it fell.

From following walls I never lift my eye   40
Except at night to places in the sky
Where showers of charted meteors let fly.

Some may know what they seek in school and church,
And why they seek it there; for what I search
I must go measuring stone walls, perch on perch;   45

Sure that though not a star of death and birth,
So not to be compared, perhaps, in worth
To such resorts of life as Mars and Earth,

Though not, I say, a star of death and sin,
It yet has poles, and only needs a spin   50
To show its worldly nature and begin

To chafe and shuffle in my calloused palm
And run off in strange tangents with my arm
As fish do with the line in first alarm.

Such as it is, it promises the prize   55
Of the one world complete in any size
That I am like to compass, fool or wise.

1923

4a. The winged horse of Greek mythology, figuratively associated with poetic
inspiration, whose name was given to a
northern constellation near the spring
equinoctial point (*cf.* l. 30).

Fire and Ice

Some say the world will end in fire,
Some say in ice.
From what I've tasted of desire
I hold with those who favor fire.
But if it had to perish twice,   5
I think I know enough of hate
To say that for destruction ice
Is also great
And would suffice.

1923

Fragmentary Blue

Why make so much of fragmentary blue
In here and there a bird, or butterfly,
Or flower, or wearing-stone, or open eye,
When heaven presents in sheets the solid hue?

Since earth is earth, perhaps, not heaven (as yet)—   5
Though some savants make earth include the sky;
And blue so far above us comes so high,
It only gives our wish for blue a whet.

1923

Stopping by Woods on a Snowy Evening

Whose woods these are I think I know
His house is in the village though;
He will not see me stopping here
To watch his woods fill up with snow.

My little horse must think it queer   5
To stop without a farmhouse near
Between the woods and frozen lake
The darkest evening of the year.

He gives his harness bells a shake
To ask if there is some mistake.   10
The only other sound's the sweep
Of easy wind and downy flake.

The woods are lovely, dark and deep.
But I have promises to keep,

And miles to go before I sleep,   15
And miles to go before I sleep.

1923

The Axe-Helve

education of children

I've known ere now an interfering branch
Of alder catch my lifted axe behind me.
But that was in the woods, to hold my hand
From striking at another alder's roots,
And that was, as I say, an alder branch.   5
This was a man, Baptiste, who stole one day
Behind me on the snow in my own yard
Where I was working at the chopping-block,
And cutting nothing not cut down already.
He caught my axe expertly on the rise,   10
When all my strength put forth was in his favor,
Held it a moment where it was, to calm me,
Then took it from me—and I let him take it.
I didn't know him well enough to know
What it was all about. There might be something   15
He had in mind to say to a bad neighbor
He might prefer to say to him disarmed.
But all he had to tell me in French-English
Was what he thought of—not me, but my axe;
Me only as I took my axe to heart.   20
It was the bad axe-helve some one had sold me—
'Made on machine,' he said, ploughing the grain
With a thick thumbnail to show how it ran
Across the handle's long drawn serpentine,
Like the two strokes across a dollar sign.   25
'You give her one good crack, she's snap raght off.
Den where's your hax-ead flying t'rough de hair?'
Admitted; and yet, what was that to him?
'Come on my house and I put you one in
What's las' awhile—good hick'ry what's grow crooked,   30
De second growt' I cut myself—tough, tough!'
Something to sell? That wasn't how it sounded.

'Den when you say you come? It's cost you nothing.
To-naght?'

As well to-night as any night.

Beyond an over-warmth of kitchen stove   35
My welcome differed from no other welcome.

*need to keep personal education—but
don't immate before making
finished product*

Baptiste knew best why I was where I was.
So long as he would leave enough unsaid,
I shouldn't mind his being overjoyed
(If overjoyed he was) at having got me   40
Where I must judge if what he knew about an axe
That not everybody else knew was to count
For nothing in the measure of a neighbor.
Hard if, though cast away for life with Yankees,
A Frenchman couldn't get his human rating!   45

Mrs. Baptiste came in and rocked a chair
That had as many motions as the world:
One back and forward, in and out of shadow,
That got her nowhere; one more gradual,
Sideways, that would have run her on the stove   50
In time, had she not realized her danger
And caught herself up bodily, chair and all,
And set herself back where she started from.
'She ain't spick too much Henglish—dat's too bad.'

I was afraid, in brightening first on me,   55
Then on Baptiste, as if she understood
What passed between us, she was only feigning.
Baptiste was anxious for her; but no more
Than for himself, so placed he couldn't hope
To keep his bargain of the morning with me   60
In time to keep me from suspecting him
Of really never having meant to keep it.

Needlessly soon he had his axe-helves out,
A quiverful to choose from, since he wished me
To have the best he had, or had to spare—   65
Not for me to ask which, when what he took
Had beauties he had to point me out at length
To insure their not being wasted on me.
He liked to have it slender as a whipstock,
Free from the least knot, equal to the strain   70
Of bending like a sword across the knee.
He showed me that the lines of a good helve
Were native to the grain before the knife
Expressed them, and its curves were no false curves
Put on it from without. And there its strength lay   75
For the hard work. He chafed its long white body
From end to end with his rough hand shut round it.
He tried it at the eye-hole in the axe-head.
'Hahn, hahn,' he mused, 'don't need much taking down.'

Baptiste knew how to make a short job long   80
For love of it, and yet not waste time either.

Do you know, what we talked about was knowledge?
Baptiste on his defence about the children
He kept from school, or did his best to keep—
Whatever school and children and our doubts   85
Of laid-on education had to do
With the curves of his axe-helves and his having
Used these unscrupulously to bring me
To see for once the inside of his house.
Was I desired in friendship, partly as some one   90
To leave it to, whether the right to hold
Such doubts of education should depend
Upon the education of those who held them?

But now he brushed the shavings from his knee
And stood the axe there on its horse's hoof,   95
Erect, but not without its waves, as when
The snake stood up for evil in the Garden,—
Top-heavy with a heaviness his short,
Thick hand made light of, steel-blue chin drawn down
And in a little—a French touch in that.   100
Baptiste drew back and squinted at it, pleased;
'See how she's cock her head!'

                                                    1923

The Grindstone

Having a wheel and four legs of its own
Has never availed the cumbersome grindstone
To get it anywhere that I can see.
These hands have helped it go, and even race;
Not all the motion, though, they ever lent,   5
Not all the miles it may have thought it went,
Have got it one step from the starting place.
It stands beside the same old apple tree.
The shadow of the apple tree is thin
Upon it now, its feet are fast in snow.   10
All other farm machinery's gone in,
And some of it on no more legs and wheel
Than the grindstone can boast to stand or go.
(I'm thinking chiefly of the wheelbarrow.)
For months it hasn't known the taste of steel,   15
Washed down with rusty water in a tin.

But standing outdoors hungry, in the cold,
Except in towns at night, is not a sin.
And, anyway, its standing in the yard
Under a ruinous live apple tree   20
Has nothing any more to do with me,
Except that I remember how of old
One summer day, all day I drove it hard,
And someone mounted on it rode it hard,
And he and I between us ground a blade.   25

I gave it the preliminary spin,
And poured on water (tears it might have been);
And when it almost gayly jumped and flowed,
A Father-Time-like man got on and rode,
Armed with a scythe and spectacles that glowed.   30
He turned on will-power to increase the load
And slow me down—and I abruptly slowed,
Like coming to a sudden railroad station.
I changed from hand to hand in desperation.
I wondered what machine of ages gone   35
This represented an improvement on.
For all I knew it may have sharpened spears
And arrowheads itself. Much use for years
Had gradually worn it an oblate
Spheroid that kicked and struggled in its gait,   40
Appearing to return me hate for hate;
(But I forgive it now as easily
As any other boyhood enemy
Whose pride has failed to get him anywhere).
I wondered who it was the man thought ground—   45
The one who held the wheel back or the one
Who gave his life to keep it going round?
I wondered if he really thought it fair
For him to have the say when we were done.
Such were the bitter thoughts to which I turned.   50

Not for myself was I so much concerned.
Oh no!—although, of course, I could have found
A better way to pass the afternoon
Than grinding discord out of a grindstone,
And beating insects at their gritty tune.   55
Nor was I for the man so much concerned.
Once when the grindstone almost jumped its bearing
It looked as if he might be badly thrown
And wounded on his blade. So far from caring,
I laughed inside, and only cranked the faster,   60

(It ran as if it wasn't greased but glued);
I'd welcome any moderate disaster
That might be calculated to postpone
What evidently nothing could conclude.
The thing that made me more and more afraid   65
Was that we'd ground it sharp and hadn't known,
And now were only wasting precious blade.
And when he raised it dripping once and tried
The creepy edge of it with wary touch,
And viewed it over his glasses funny-eyed,   70
Only disinterestedly to decide
It needed a turn more, I could have cried
Wasn't there danger of a turn too much?
Mightn't we make it worse instead of better?
I was for leaving something to the whetter.   75
What if it wasn't all it should be? I'd
Be satisfied if he'd be satisfied.

1923

Two Look at Two

Love and forgetting might have carried them
A little further up the mountain side
With night so near, but not much further up.
They must have halted soon in any case
With thoughts of the path back, how rough it was   5
With rock and washout, and unsafe in darkness;
When they were halted by a tumbled wall
With barbed-wire binding. They stood facing this,
Spending what onward impulse they still had
In one last look the way they must not go,   10
On up the failing path, where, if a stone
Or earthslide moved at night, it moved itself;
No footstep moved it. 'This is all,' they sighed,
'Good-night to woods.' But not so; there was more.
A doe from round a spruce stood looking at them   15
Across the wall, as near the wall as they.
She saw them in their field, they her in hers.
The difficulty of seeing what stood still,
Like some up-ended boulder split in two,
Was in her clouded eyes: they saw no fear there.   20
She seemed to think that two thus they were safe.
Then, as if they were something that, though strange,
She could not trouble her mind with too long,

She sighed and passed unscared along the wall.
'*This*, then, is all. What more is there to ask?'   25
But no, not yet. A snort to bid them wait.
A buck from round the spruce stood looking at them
Across the wall as near the wall as they.
This was an antlered buck of lusty nostril,
Not the same doe come back into her place.   30
He viewed them quizzically with jerks of head,
As if to ask, 'Why don't you make some motion?
Or give some sign of life? Because you can't.
I doubt if you're as living as you look.'
Thus till he had them almost feeling dared   35
To stretch a proffering hand—and a spell-breaking.
Then he too passed unscared along the wall.
Two had seen two, whichever side you spoke from.
'This *must* be all.' It was all. Still they stood,
A great wave from it going over them,   40
As if the earth in one unlooked-for favor
Had made them certain earth returned their love.

1923

Paul's Wife

To drive Paul[5] out of any lumber camp
All that was needed was to say to him,
'How is the wife, Paul?'—and he'd disappear.
Some said it was because he had no wife,
And hated to be twitted on the subject.   5
Others because he'd come within a day
Or so of having one, and then been jilted.
Others because he'd had one once, a good one,
Who'd run away with some one else and left him.
And others still because he had one now   10
He only had to be reminded of,—
He was all duty to her in a minute:
He had to run right off to look her up,
As if to say, 'That's so, how is my wife?
I hope she isn't getting into mischief.'   15
No one was anxious to get rid of Paul.
He'd been the hero of the mountain camps
Ever since, just to show them, he had slipped
The bark of a whole tamarack off whole,

5. The origin of the Paul Bunyan
stories, considered as legends of the timber country, is still controversial. Frost's
story has legendary flavor and the atmosphere of the French-Canadian border.

As clean as boys do off a willow twig   20
To make a willow whistle on a Sunday
In April by subsiding meadow brooks.
They seemed to ask him just to see him go,
'How is the wife, Paul?' and he always went.
He never stopped to murder anyone   25
Who asked the question. He just disappeared—
Nobody knew in what direction,
Although it wasn't usually long
Before they heard of him in some new camp,
The same Paul at the same old feats of logging.   30
The question everywhere was why should Paul
Object to being asked a civil question—
A man you could say almost anything to
Short of a fighting word. You have the answers.
And there was one more not so fair to Paul: 35
That Paul had married a wife not his equal.
Paul was ashamed of her. To match a hero,
She would have had to be a heroine;
Instead of which she was some half-breed squaw.
But if the story Murphy told was true,   40
She wasn't anything to be ashamed of.

You know Paul could do wonders. Everyone's
Heard how he thrashed the horses on a load
That wouldn't budge until they simply stretched
Their rawhide harness from the load to camp.   45
Paul told the boss the load would be all right,
'The sun will bring your load in'—and it did—
By shrinking the rawhide to natural length.
That's what is called a stretcher. But I guess
The one about his jumping so's to land   50
With both his feet at once against the ceiling,
And then land safely right side up again,
Back on the floor, is fact or pretty near fact.
Well this is such a yarn. Paul sawed his wife
Out of a white-pine log. Murphy was there,   55
And, as you might say, saw the lady born.
Paul worked at anything in lumbering.
He'd been hard at it taking boards away
For—I forget—the last ambitious sawyer
To want to find out if he couldn't pile   60
The lumber on Paul till Paul begged for mercy.
They'd sliced the first slab off a big butt log,

And the sawyer had slammed the carriage back
To slam end on again against the saw teeth.
To judge them by the way they caught themselves 65
When they saw what had happened to the log,
They must have had a guilty expectation
Something was going to go with their slambanging.
Something had left a broad black streak of grease
On the new wood the whole length of the log 70
Except, perhaps, a foot at either end.
But when Paul put his finger in the grease,
It wasn't grease at all, but a long slot.
The log was hollow. They were sawing pine.
'First time I ever saw a hollow pine. 75
That comes of having Paul around the place.
Take it to hell for me,' the sawyer said.
Everyone had to have a look at it,
And tell Paul what he ought to do about it.
(They treated it as his.) 'You take a jack-knife, 80
And spread the opening, and you've got a dug-out
All dug to go a-fishing in.' To Paul
The hollow looked too sound and clean and empty
Ever to have housed birds or beasts or bees.
There was no entrance for them to get in by. 85
It looked to him like some new kind of hollow
He thought he'd *better* take his jack-knife to.
So after work that evening he came back
And let enough light into it by cutting
To see if it was empty. He made out in there 90
A slender length of pith, or was it pith?
It might have been the skin a snake had cast
And left stood up on end inside the tree
The hundred years the tree must have been growing
More cutting and he had this in both hands, 95
And, looking from it to the pond near by,
Paul wondered how it would respond to water.
Not a breeze stirred, but just the breath of air
He made in walking slowly to the beach
Blew it once off his hands and almost broke it. 100
He laid it at the edge where it could drink.
At the first drink it rustled and grew limp.
At the next drink it grew invisible.
Paul dragged the shallows for it with his fingers,
And thought it must have melted. It was gone. 105
And then beyond the open water, dim with midges,

Where the log drive lay pressed against the boom,
It slowly rose a person, rose a girl,[6]
Her wet hair heavy on her like a helmet,
Who, leaning on a log looked back at Paul.   110
And that made Paul in turn look back
To see if it was anyone behind him
That she was looking at instead of him.
Murphy had been there watching all the time,
But from a shed where neither of them could see him.   115
There was a moment of suspense in birth
When the girl seemed too water-logged to live,
Before she caught her first breath with a gasp
And laughed. Then she climbed slowly to her feet,
And walked off talking to herself or Paul   120
Across the logs like backs of alligators,
Paul taking after her around the pond.

Next evening Murphy and some other fellows
Got drunk, and tracked the pair up Catamount,
From the bare top of which there is a view   125
To other hills across a kettle valley.
And there, well after dark, let Murphy tell it,
They saw Paul and his creature keeping house.
It was the only glimpse that anyone
Has had of Paul and her since Murphy saw them   130
Falling in love across the twilight mill-pond.
More than a mile across the wilderness
They sat together half-way up a cliff
In a small niche let into it, the girl
Brightly, as if a star played on the place,   135
Paul darkly, like her shadow. All the light
Was from the girl herself, though, not from a star,
As was apparent from what happened next.
All those great ruffians put their throats together,
And let out a loud yell, and threw a bottle,   140
As a brute tribute of respect to beauty.
Of course the bottle fell short by a mile,
But the shout reached the girl and put her light out.
She went out like a firefly, and that was all.

So there were witnesses that Paul was married,   145
And not to anyone to be ashamed of.
Everyone had been wrong in judging Paul.
Murphy told me Paul put on all those airs
About his wife to keep her to himself.

6. Note the analogy with the nymphs and dryads of classical mythology.

Paul was what's called a terrible possessor.   150
Owning a wife with him meant owning her.
She wasn't anybody else's business,
Either to praise her, or so much as name her,
And he'd thank people not to think of her.
Murphy's idea was that a man like Paul   155
Wouldn't be spoken to about a wife
In any way the world knew how to speak.

1923

West-running Brook

'Fred, where is north?'

     'North? North is there, my love.
The brook runs west.'

     'West-running Brook then call it.'
(West-running Brook men call it to this day.)
'What does it think it's doing running west
When all the other country brooks flow east   5
To reach the ocean? It must be the brook
Can trust itself to go by contraries
The way I can with you—and you with me—
Because we're—we're—I don't know what we are.
What are we?'

    'Young or new?'

      'We must be something. 10
We've said we two. Let's change that to we three.
As you and I are married to each other,
We'll both be married to the brook. We'll build
Our bridge across it, and the bridge shall be
Our arm thrown over it asleep beside it.   15
Look, look, it's waving to us with a wave
To let us know it hears me.'

      'Why, my dear,
That wave's been standing off this jut of shore—'
(The black stream, catching on a sunken rock,
Flung backward on itself in one white wave,   20
And the white water rode the black forever,
Not gaining but not losing, like a bird
White feathers from the struggle of whose breast
Flecked the dark stream and flecked the darker pool

Below the point, and were at last driven wrinkled   25
In a white scarf against the far shore alders.)
'That wave's been standing off this jut of shore
Ever since rivers, I was going to say,
Were made in heaven. It wasn't waved to us.'

'It wasn't, yet it was. If not to you   30
It was to me—in an annunciation.'

'Oh, if you take it off to lady-land,
As't were the country of the Amazons
We men must see you to the confines of
And leave you there, ourselves forbid to enter,—   35
It is your brook! I have no more to say.'

'Yes, you have, too. Go on. You thought of something.'

'Speaking of contraries, see how the brook
In that white wave runs counter to itself.
It is from that in water we were from   40
Long, long before we were from any creature.
Here we, in our impatience of the steps,
Get back to the beginning of beginnings,
The stream of everything that runs away.
Some say existence like a Pirouot   45
And Pirouette, forever in one place,
Stands still and dances, but it runs away,
It seriously, sadly, runs away
To fill the abyss' void with emptiness.
It flows beside us in this water brook,   50
But it flows over us. It flows between us
To separate us for a panic moment.
It flows between us, over us, and *with* us.
And it is time, strength, tone, light, life and love—
And even substance lapsing unsubstantial;   55
The universal cataract of death
That spends to nothingness—and unresisted,
Save by some strange resistance in itself,
Not just a swerving, but a throwing back,
As if regret were in it and were sacred.   60
It has this throwing backward on itself
So that the fall of most of it is always
Raising a little, sending up a little.
Our life runs down in sending up the clock.
The brook runs down in sending up our life.   65
The sun runs down in sending up the brook.
And there is something sending up the sun.

It is this backward motion toward the source,
Against the stream, that most we see ourselves in,
The tribute of the current to the source.   70
It is from this in nature we are from.
It is most us.'

        'Today will be the day
You said so.'

        'No, today will be the day
You said the brook was called West-running Brook.'

'Today will be the day of what we both said.'   75

1928

Tree at My Window

Tree at my window, window tree,
My sash is lowered when night comes on;
But let there never be curtain drawn
Between you and me.

Vague dream-head lifted out of the ground,   5
And thing next most diffuse to cloud,
Not all your light tongues talking aloud
Could be profound.

But tree, I have seen you taken and tossed,
And if you have seen me when I slept,   10
You have seen me when I was taken and swept
And all but lost.

That day she put our heads together,
Fate had her imagination about her,
Your head so much concerned with outer,   15
Mine with inner, weather.

1928

Sand Dunes

Sea waves are green and wet,
But up from where they die,
Rise others vaster yet,
And those are brown and dry.

They are the sea made land[7]   5
To come at the fisher town,

7. The land is also sea-made; for other dual references see Note 3, p. 663.

And bury in solid sand
The men she could not drown.

She may know cove and cape,
But she does not know mankind   10
If by any change of shape,
She hopes to cut off mind.

Men left her a ship to sink:
They can leave her a hut as well;
And be but more free to think   15
For the one more cast-off shell.

1928

Spring Pools

These pools that, though in forests, still reflect
The total sky almost without defect,
And like the flowers beside them, chill and shiver,
Will like the flowers beside them soon be gone,
And yet not out by any brook or river,   5
But up by roots to bring dark foliage on.

The trees that have it in their pent-up buds
To darken nature and be summer woods—
Let them think twice before they use their powers
To blot out and drink up and sweep away   10
These flowery waters and these watery flowers
From snow that melted only yesterday.

1928

Departmental

An ant on the table cloth
Ran into a dormant moth
Of many times his size.
He showed not the least surprise.
His business wasn't with such.   5
He gave it scarcely a touch,
And was off on his duty run.
Yet if he encountered one
Of the hive's enquiry squad
Whose work is to find out God   10
And the nature of time and space,
He would put him onto the case.

Ants are a curious race;
One crossing with hurried tread
The body of one of their dead   15
Isn't given a moment's arrest—
Seems not even impressed.
But he no doubt reports to any
With whom he crosses antennae,
And they no doubt report   20
To the higher up at court.
Then word goes forth in Formic:[8]
'Death's come to Jerry McCormic,
Our selfless forager Jerry.
Will the special Janizary[9]   25
Whose office it is to bury
The dead of the commissary
Go bring him home to his people.
Lay him in state on a sepal.
Wrap him for shroud in a petal.   30
Embalm him with ichor of nettle.
This is the word of your Queen.'
And presently on the scene
Appears a solemn mortician;
And taking formal position   35
With feelers calmly atwiddle,
Seizes the dead by the middle,
And heaving him high in air,
Carries him out of there.
No one stands round to stare.   40
It is nobody else's affair.

It couldn't be called ungentle.
But how thoroughly departmental.

1936

Come In

As I came to the edge of the woods,
Thrush music—hark!
Now if it was dusk outside,
Inside it was dark.

Too dark in the woods for a bird   5
By sleight of wing
To better its perch for the night,
Though it still could sing.

8. The family of ants is called the *Formicidae*.   9. A member of the special troops assigned to Turkish sovereigns.

The last of the light of the sun
That had died in the west   10
Still lived for one song more
In a thrush's breast.

Far in the pillared dark
Thrush music went—
Almost like a call to come in   15
To the dark and lament.

But no, I was out for stars:
I would not come in.
I meant not even if asked,
And I hadn't been.   20

1942

Choose Something Like a Star

O Star (the fairest one in sight),
We grant your loftiness the right
To some obscurity of cloud—
It will not do to say of night,
Since dark is what brings out your light.   5
Some mystery becomes the proud.
But to be wholly taciturn
In your reserve is not allowed.
Say something to us we can learn
By heart and when alone repeat.   10
Say something! And it says "I burn."
But say with what degree of heat.
Talk Fahrenheit, talk Centigrade.
Use language we can comprehend.
Tell us what elements you blend.   15
It gives us strangely little aid,
But does tell something in the end.
And steadfast as Keats' Eremite,[1]
Not even stooping from its sphere,
It asks a little of us here.   20
It asks of us a certain height,
So when at times the mob is swayed
To carry praise or blame too far,
We may choose something like a star
To stay our minds on and be staid.   25

1947

1. *Cf.* Keats's sonnet "Bright Star! Would I Were Steadfast As Thou Art."

Revaluation "Little Renaissance"

CARL SANDBURG
(1878–)

Carl Sandburg's parents were Swedish immigrants, living at Galesburg, Illinois, when the boy was born on January 6, 1878. The father was then working on a railroad construction crew. They were a healthy and affectionate family, though very poor. At thirteen, Sandburg was obliged to leave school and go to work. For a time he found employment in Galesburg; then he became a migratory laborer, roaming from job to job in Kansas, Nebraska, and Colorado. He was at various times a milkman, a harvest hand, a hotel dishwasher, a barbershop porter, a stage hand, a brickmaker, and a sign painter. For a while he was a salesman of stereoscopes and the popular stereoscopic views of the day—a profitable employment and a good education for a poet of the people. In 1898, at the age of twenty, he settled again in Galesburg to follow the trade of house painter, but the Spanish-American War excited his interest and he enlisted in the Army. During active service in Puerto Rico he functioned as correspondent for the Galesburg *Evening Mail*, his first newspaper connection.

In eight months he was back in Galesburg, determined to secure a higher education. He had been reading hard with this in view, and he was provisionally admitted at Lombard College, although he might have preferred Knox, across town, where Lincoln had met Douglas in one of the famous debates of 1858. Young Sandburg had a good scholastic record, made a serious beginning with his writing, and became a local celebrity at basketball, but he did not graduate. A few weeks before the end of his senior year, in 1902, with all his record clear, he simply disappeared from the scene. For several years he lived as a roving newspaper reporter. In 1907 he secured an editorial position on a small Chicago paper, and made a connection which led him to Wisconsin as political organizer for the Social Democrats, a reform party, in 1908. That year he married Lillian Steichen, sister of the famous artist-photographer Edward Steichen (of whom the poet published a pleasing biography in 1929). The young writer, aged thirty, now sought to establish the more settled pattern that befits a well-married man. In 1910 he secured appointment as secretary to the mayor of Milwaukee, and served for two years. But he was not interested in a political career. He was a writer, already the master of his trade as a journalist, although his few poems, published here and there in newspapers, did not suggest that he had found a subject or a satisfactory poetic form. He served for a year on the editorial staff of the liberal Milwaukee *Leader*. The next year, in 1913, he went to Chicago on an editorial engagement, and soon he became illustrious among the writers who were fostering a new literature in that city.

The first of Sandburg's poems in his characteristic and now

His free verse moves forward the freedom of natural form, but also not forsake control — unless I control :: artist aware of problems of development emotional sense

familiar style was "Chicago," which appeared, in 1914, in *Poetry: A Magazine of Verse.* The *Chicago Poems* of 1916 was followed by *Cornhuskers* in 1918. That year Sandburg spent some months in Sweden as correspondent for a Chicago newspaper syndicate, and returned as editorial writer on the Chicago *Daily News,* a paper of national prominence. He remained with that paper for fifteen years as editorialist, feature writer, and columnist, retiring in 1933 under pressure of his private literary interests.

By 1920, when the "renaissance" of American literature was gaining momentum, Sandburg had reached the maturity of his power as a poet. He had twice been recognized by national awards, and his next volume, *Smoke and Steel* (1920), confirmed his position as the poet of the common man confronted with the complexities of the new industrial civilization. He began to give frequent public readings of his own poems, and soon emerged as the foremost minstrel of his time by adding to his programs the performance of American folk songs which he had long been collecting in his journeys about the country. He popularized the folk ballad before the radio became an important medium for his successors. His collection, *The American Songbag* (1927, revised and enlarged 1950), the first popular compilation of the sort, was enriched by his instinct for the genuine and his scholarly knowledge of this field. These qualities passed into his own poems, from *Slabs of the Sunburnt West* (1922) to *The People, Yes* (1936). The latter is a very knowing arrangement of American folk speech, folkways, and customs, interpreted in language that sensitively combines the flavor of the original with Sandburg's poetic perceptions.

Two other aspects of his career are noteworthy. His books for children began with *Rootabaga Stories* (1922), to be followed in 1923 by *Rootabaga Pigeons* and in 1930 by *Potato Face* and *Early Moon.* The prose stories in these collections are at a high level, but the poems especially take their place in the distinguished literature of childhood. More important is his *Abraham Lincoln: The Prairie Years* (1926), a classic of biography both for its style, and for the literary tact which enabled him to remain faithful to the historical record of Lincoln without losing the American significance of the legendary Lincoln. During the next thirteen years, much of his spare time was devoted to the historical study that prepared him to complete his task in 1939, in the four volumes of *Abraham Lincoln: The War Years,* which was awarded the Pulitzer Prize. He concentrated his knowledge of the subject in the one-volume *Abraham Lincoln* of 1954, an authoritative and powerful study.

Sandburg has also published several books of a topical nature. He is author or coauthor of three volumes of Lincoln studies. During the second World War, he published his commentary on

loyal to idealism of country without being sentimental

events of the time in *Storm over the Land* (1942), and *Home Front Memo* (1943). His one novel, *Remembrance Rock* (1950), is a fictional survey of American history from the colonial period. His considerable influence on the national culture has been recognized by the award of many honorary degrees and the accolades of learned and literary academies.

His *Complete Poems*, published in 1950, gave perspective to an accomplishment of great spiritual value to his generation. When he first became known, he was hailed as an interesting and vigorous curiosity, a journalist of poetry, the form of his verse being regarded as at most an external device. Now he can be seen as a truly gifted poet who gave shape and permanence to the phrases,

rhythms, and symbols of the American popular idiom, while embodying the common idealism of the people in forms often of notable subtlety. He has fulfilled Whitman's prescription for the poet—"that his country absorbs him as affectionately as he has absorbed it."

There is no complete collection of Sandburg's work. The standard text of the poems is *The Complete Poems of Carl Sandburg*, 1950. The earlier volumes have been named in the text above. The *Selected Poems of Carl Sandburg*, edited by Rebecca West in 1926, contains a good selection to that date and a valuable critical introduction by the editor.

There is no definitive biography. Karl Detzer's *Carl Sandburg: A Study in Personality and Background*, 1941, is informative and critically sound. Carl Sandburg's autobiographical account, *Always the Young Strangers*, 1952, is of course authoritative in respect to biographical data as far as it goes, and illuminating for the student of Sandburg's personality.

Interchange btwn qualities in 2 disparate quantities of nature

Nocturne in a Deserted Brickyard

Stuff of the moon
Runs on the lapping sand
Out to the longest shadows.
Under the curving willows,
And round the creep of the wave line,
Fluxions of yellow and dusk on the waters   **5**
Make a wide dreaming pansy of an old pond in the night.

figure slowly mounts up to   1916

Monotone

3   The monotone of the rain is beautiful,
4   And the sudden rise and slow relapse
3   Of the long multitudinous rain.

The sun on the hills is beautiful,
Or a captured sunset sea-flung,
Bannered with fire and gold.

A face I know is beautiful—
With fire and gold of sky and sea,
And the peace of long warm rain.

1910

Gone

Everybody loved Chick Lorimer in our town.
  Far off
  Everybody loved her.
So we all love a wild girl keeping a hold
  On a dream she wants.   5
Nobody knows now where Chick Lorimer went.
Nobody knows why she packed her trunk . . . a few old things
And is gone,
            Gone with her little chin
            Thrust ahead of her   10
            And her soft hair blowing careless
            From under a wide hat,
Dancer, singer, a laughing passionate lover.

Were there ten men or a hundred hunting Chick?
Were there five men or fifty with aching hearts?   15
      Everybody loved Chick Lorimer.
            Nobody knows where she's gone.

1916

Fish Crier

I know a Jew fish crier down on Maxwell Street[1] with a voice like a
    north wind blowing over corn stubble in January.
He dangles herring before prospective customers evincing a joy
    identical with that of Pavlowa[2] dancing.
His face is that of a man terribly glad to be selling fish, terribly
    glad that God made fish, and customers to whom he may call
    his wares from a pushcart.

1916

1. Then a congested, poor district of Chicago.
2. Anna Pavlova, the Russian dancer, first appeared in the United States in 1911 and was an immediate popular favorite.

A Fence

Now the stone house on the lake front is finished and the workmen
    are beginning the fence.
The palings are made of iron bars with steel points that can stab the
    life out of any man who falls on them.
As a fence, it is a masterpiece, and will shut off the rabble and all
    vagabonds and hungry men and all wandering children looking
    for a place to play.
Passing through the bars and over the steel points will go nothing
    except Death and the Rain and To-morrow.

1913   1916

Loam

In the loam we sleep,
In the cool moist loam,
In the lull of years that pass
And the break of stars,

From the loam, then,   5
The soft warm loam,
   We rise:
To shape of rose leaf,
Of face and shoulder.

   We stand, then,   10
   To a whiff of life,
Lifted to the silver of the sun
Over and out of the loam
     A day.

1918

Grass

Pile the bodies high at Austerlitz[3] and Waterloo.
Shovel them under and let me work—
    I am the grass; I cover all.

And pile them high at Gettysburg
And pile them high at Ypres and Verdun.   5
Shovel them under and let me work.

3. The places named in the poem were all scenes of great battles in major wars: the Napoleonic Wars, the Civil War, and World War I.

Two years, ten years, and passengers ask the conductor:
      What place is this?
      Where are we now?

      I am the grass.   10
      Let me work.

                            1918

Southern Pacific

Huntington[4] sleeps in a house six feet long.
Huntington dreams of railroads he built and owned.
Huntington dreams of ten thousand men saying: Yes, sir.

Blithery sleeps in a house six feet long.
Blithery dreams of rails and ties he laid.   5
Blithery dreams of saying to Huntington: Yes, sir.

Huntington,
Blithery, sleep in houses six feet long.

                            1918

Washerwoman

The washerwoman is a member of the Salvation Army.
And over the tub of suds rubbing underwear clean
She sings that Jesus will wash her sins away
And the red wrongs she has done God and man
Shall be white as driven snow.   5
Rubbing underwear she sings of the Last Great Washday.

                            1918

Prayers of Steel

Lay me on an anvil, O God.
Beat me and hammer me into a crowbar.
Let me pry loose old walls.
Let me lift and loosen old foundations.

Lay me on an anvil, O God.   5
Beat me and hammer me into a steel spike.
Drive me into the girders that hold a skyscraper together.

4. Collis P. Huntington (1821–1900), early California financier, promoter and later president (1890) of the Southern Pacific and Central Pacific railroads.

Take red-hot rivets and fasten me into the central girders.
Let me be the great nail holding a skyscraper through blue nights
　　into white stars.

1918

Stars, Songs, Faces

Gather the stars if you wish it so.
Gather the songs and keep them.
Gather the faces of women.
Gather for keeping years and years.
　　　　And then . . .
Loosen your hands, let go and say good-by.
　　Let the stars and songs go.
　　Let the faces and years go.
　　Loosen your hands and say good-by.

5

1920

symbol of tradition

Broken-face Gargoyles *Religi...*

grotesque element　　　　　　*Promise of life*

All I can give you is broken-face gargoyles.[5]
It is too early to sing and dance at funerals,
Though I can whisper to you I am looking for an undertaker hum-
　　ming a lullaby and throwing his feet in a swift and mystic
　　buck-and-wing,[6] now you see it and now you don't.

IHS - fertility & eternal life

Fish to swim a pool in your garden flashing a speckled silver,
A basket of wine-saps filling your room with flame-dark for your
　　eyes and the tang of valley orchards for your nose,
Such a beautiful pail of fish, such a beautiful peck of apples, I can-
　　not bring you now.

5

eternal love

It is too early and I am not footloose yet.

universal force - mystery

I shall come in the night when I come with a hammer and saw.
I shall come near your window, where you look out when your eyes
　　open in the morning,   *for people to dwell in*
And there I shall slam together bird-houses and bird-baths for wing-
　　loose wrens and hummers[7] to live in, birds with yellow wing
　　tips to blur and buzz soft all summer,
So I shall make little fool homes with doors, always open doors for
　　all and each to run away when they want to.

10

5. Rainspouts, usually at the roof level, and in old cathedrals and cloisters often carved as grotesque animal or human figures.

6. A Negro clog dance employing a mimicry of bird flight.

7. Hummingbirds.

I shall come just like that even though now it is early and I am not
    yet footloose,
Even though I am still looking for an undertaker with a raw, wind-
    bitten face and a dance in his feet.
I make a date with you (put it down) for six o'clock in the evening
    a thousand years from now.

All I can give you now is broken-face gargoyles.   15
All I can give you now is a double gorilla head with two fish mouths
    and four eagle eyes hooked on a street wall, spouting water and
    looking two ways to the ends of the street for the new people,
    the young strangers, coming, coming, always coming.

    It is early.
    I shall yet be footloose.

                              1920

On a Railroad Right of Way

Stream, go hide yourself.
In the tall grass, in the cat-tails,
In the browns of autumn, the last purple asters, the yellow whispers.
On the moss rock levels leave the marks of your wave-lengths.
Sing in your gravel, in your clean gully.   5
Let the moaning railroad trains go by.
Till they stop you, go on with your song.

The minnies[8] spin in the water gravel,
In the spears of the early autumn sun.
There must be winter fish.   10
Babies, you will be jumping fish
In the first snow month.

                              1928

From The People, Yes[9]

    The people will live on.
The learning and blundering people will live on.
    They will be tricked and sold and again sold
And go back to the nourishing earth for rootholds,
    The people so peculiar in renewal and comeback,   5
    You can't laugh off their capacity to take it.
The mammoth rests between his cyclonic dramas.

8. Minnows.
9. These lines comprise Section 107, the concluding passage of *The People, Yes.*

The people so often sleepy, weary, enigmatic,
is a vast huddle with many units saying:
    "I earn my living.
    I make enough to get by
    and it takes all my time.
    If I had more time
    I could do more for myself
    and maybe for others.   15
    I could read and study
    and talk things over
    and find out about things.
    It takes time.
    I wish I had the time."   20

The people is a tragic and comic two-face: hero and hoodlum:
phantom and gorilla twisting to moan with a gargoyle mouth:
"They buy me and sell me . . . it's a game . . . sometime I'll
break loose . . ."

    Once having marched
Over the margins of animal necessity,
Over the grim line of sheer subsistence
    Then man came   25
To the deeper rituals of his bones,
To the lights lighter than any bones,
To the time for thinking things over,
To the dance, the song, the story,
Or the hours given over to dreaming,   30
    Once having so marched.

Between the finite limitations of the five senses
and the endless yearnings of man for the beyond
the people hold to the humdrum bidding of work and food
while reaching out when it comes their way   35
for lights beyond the prison of the five senses,
for keepsakes lasting beyond any hunger or death.
    This reaching is alive.
The panderers and liars have violated and smutted it.
    Yet this reaching is alive yet   40
    for lights and keepsakes.

        The people know the salt of the sea
        and the strength of the winds
        lashing the corners of the earth.
        The people take the earth   45
        as a tomb of rest and a cradle of hope.
        Who else speaks for the Family of Man?

They are in tune and step
with constellations of universal law.
The people is a polychrome,   50
a spectrum and a prism
held in a moving monolith,
a console organ of changing themes,
a clavilux[1] of color poems
wherein the sea offers fog   55
and the fog moves off in rain
and the labrador sunset shortens
to a nocturne of clear stars
serene over the shot spray
of northern lights.   60

The steel mill sky is alive.
The fire breaks white and zigzag
shot on a gun-metal gloaming.
Man is a long time coming.
Man will yet win.   65
Brother may yet line up with brother:

This old anvil laughs at many broken hammers.
There are men who can't be bought.
The fireborn are at home in fire.
The stars make no noise.   70
You can't hinder the wind from blowing.
Time is a great teacher.
Who can live without hope?

In the darkness with a great bundle of grief
the people march.   75
In the night, and overhead a shovel of stars for keeps, the people
march:
"Where to? what next?"

1936

1. A sort of organ which simultaneously produces music and projects colors on a
screen.

Revolution "*Little Renaissance*"

VACHEL LINDSAY

Rhymthmic (1879–1931)

Among the three vigorous poets
who established the importance
of the midwest in the twentieth-
century revival of our literature,
Vachel Lindsay was the earliest
to excite the enthusiasm of

*used actual folk production of country
for inspiration*

over-optimistic
sociological

American readers. Before Edgar Lee Masters had published *Spoon River Anthology* (1915) or Carl Sandburg had collected his *Chicago Poems* (1916), Lindsay was known as the author of two volumes, *General William Booth Enters into Heaven and Other Poems* (1913) and *The Congo and Other Poems* (1914). The title poems had each won wide attention when previously published in the new Chicago periodical *Poetry: A Magazine of Verse;* now the volumes as a whole confirmed the first impression of a fluent power and radical originality.

In one way Lindsay was traditional—he did not follow the dominant tendency toward free verse, already announced by the imagists and soon to be accelerated by the influence of Sandburg, Masters, and many lesser poets. Lindsay's innovations in form occurred within a traditional and primitive convention, that of the folk ballad. However, he heightened its rhythmic character and its violence. Kipling and his fellow balladists of the Victorian period had restored to popularity the rhythm of marching feet, but Vachel's people "stomped," or "pounded on the table * * * hard as they were able." Perhaps this was a rhythm no more American than African, but certainly it recalled the frontier. Lindsay conceived of poetry in terms of ministrelsy, and asserted that it was not alive until it was audible. "The higher vaudeville," he called it, and as a popular public reader of his own poems he made a spectacular demonstration of what he meant. Seeking to express his

country in her characteristic rhythms, he took them from hymns and circuses, from the Negro, from the buffalo, from the cattle and the automobiles of the Santa Fé Trail, from childhood songs and games, and from country dancing—wherever he found them rich and characteristic. Less noticed at the time, but much appreciated by later critics, was his experimentation with more subtle rhythms, as in his poem games for children, and the fantasy of "The Chinese Nightingale."

Christened Nicholas Vachel Lindsay, he was born in Springfield, Illinois, in 1879, of parents who represented Kentucky and Indiana pioneer stock, an agrarian philosophy, and the evangelical fervor of the Campbellites. The followers of Alexander Campbell, later called the Disciples of Christ, were then a fundamentalist sect, of an intense moral earnestness expressed in concepts of social Christianity and of mystical redemption. Lindsay deeply absorbed these attitudes in boyhood; later his personal mysticism drew him toward Swedenborgianism. The social idealism which permeates his writing is impractical and millennial to a degree which brought him ridicule from the beginning, but it was supported by the midwest evangelism that he found in Springfield and in rural Indiana, where he spent many summers on his grandparents' farm. As he grew up in Lincoln's city, the American myth of the Great Emancipator took hold of him, and became associated with the ideals of Jackson and the "common man" and with what he understood to be the American idealism of Walt Whitman. For more recent political ideals he turned to such figures as John P. Altgeld, the liberal leader of Illinois, and William Jennings Bryan, "the great commoner," a crusading leader of midwest agrarian and evangelical idealism.

After three years at Hiram College in Ohio, Lindsay was unable to feel the vocation for the ministry for which his parents had hoped; instead, he wanted desperately to be an artist, and his drawings indicate a certain ability, especially for fanciful design. His failure to fulfill parental expectations is suggested as one origin of the sense of guilt which followed him for years, and disastrously influenced his personality. From 1900 to 1905 he studied art, for the first four years at the Chicago Art Institute, and then in New York, while supporting himself meagerly by part-time employment; however, he found no market for his work.

It was then that he decided upon a career of literary evangelism, and proposed to prepare himself by going among the people. From 1908 to 1912 he made a number of walking tours in various rural areas, including the Midwest, the Southwest, and the highlands of Pennsylvania. On early tours he went as a mendicant minstrel, as suggested by the titles of *Rhymes to Be Traded for Bread* (1912), and *A Handy Guide for Beggars* (1916), the latter an attractive addition to the literature of vagabondage. He also made tours and taught classes for the Y.M.C.A. and the Anti-Saloon League. His attitude toward these excursions in practical idealism is reflected in his early prose testament, *Adventures While Preaching the Gospel of Beauty* (1914), and in *The Golden Book of Springfield* (1920), a misty fantasy of a utopian society.

In 1913 Harriet Monroe, editor of *Poetry*, published his poem on General William Booth, and began to promote the author as her magazine's first important find. Her encouragement swept him on to the triumph of his first two volumes of poetry, already described; and her connections opened the way for him to gain an audience for his poetry recitals. The value of his poems, and his dramatic reading of such selections as "The Congo" and "The Santa-Fé Trail" did the rest. Not even the fairly good recordings of his readings will give a younger generation the full sense of his spectacularity before an audience, for he really performed the poems with dramatic chant and gesture, supplemented by awkward and ingenuous earnestness.

But his effective career was short. His third volume, *The Chinese Nightingale and Other Poems* (1917) contained as the title poem one of his best works, and two others equally admired, "The Ghost of the Buffaloes" and "In Praise of Johnny Appleseed." It was the pinnacle of his career. *The Daniel Jazz and Other Poems* and *The Golden Whales of California*, both published in 1920, mark the beginning of a decline. His *Collected Poems* (1923) does not suffer greatly by the absence of the contents of his four later volumes, published from 1926 to 1929.

The facts of Lindsay's last years are variously reported. It is certain that his physical energies declined, and that he was discouraged at his inability to find new inspiration or to repeat his successes on the old ground. In 1931, in a fit of despondency, Lindsay took his own life.

There has been no complete edition of Lindsay's works. *Collected Poems by Vachel Lindsay*, 1923, revised and illustrated 1925, brings together the volumes named in the text above, including those of 1920 and two prefatory essays of some critical interest. Subsequent volumes of poems are *Going-to-the-Stars*, 1926; *The Candle in the Cabin*, 1926; *Johnny Appleseed and Other Poems*, 1928; and *Every Soul Is a Circus*, 1929. *Selected Poems of Vachel Lindsay*, edited by H. Spencer, 1931, is a good collection. The noteworthy prose of Lindsay has been mentioned in the text above, except for *The Litany of Washington Street*, 1929.

Biographical studies are A. E. Trombly, *Lindsay, Adventurer*, 1929; Edgar Lee Masters, *Vachel Lindsay; A Poet in America*, 1935; Mark Harris, *City of Discontent * * ** , 1952; and Eleanor Ruggles, *The West-Going Heart*, 1959.

The Eagle That Is Forgotten

(JOHN P. ALTGELD.[1] BORN DECEMBER 30, 1847; DIED MARCH 12, 1902.)

Sleep softly . . . eagle forgotten . . . under the stone.
Time has its way with you there, and the clay has its own.
"We have buried him now," thought your foes, and in secret rejoiced.
They made a brave show of their mourning, their hatred unvoiced.
They had snarled at you, barked at you, foamed at you day after day.   5
Now you were ended. They praised you, . . . and laid you away.

The others that mourned you in silence and terror and truth,
The widow bereft of her crust, and the boy without youth,
The mocked and scorned and the wounded, the lame and the poor
That should have remembered forever, . . . remember no more. 10

Where are those lovers of yours, on what name do they call
The lost, that in armies wept over your funeral pall?
They call on the names of a hundred high-valiant ones;
A hundred white eagles have risen the sons of your sons;
The zeal in their wings is a zeal that your dreaming began,   15
The valor that wore out your soul in the service of man.

1. John Peter Altgeld, German-born liberal political leader of Illinois, was defeated in his campaign for re-election as governor in 1896 because he had pardoned three men who had been convicted as the supposed leaders of the violent Haymarket Riot (1886), and because he had bitterly resisted President Cleveland's action in breaking the Pullman strike (1894) by sending federal troops to Chicago. Lindsay was seventeen when Altgeld was defeated, and he venerated his memory as a friend of the oppressed.

Sleep softly, . . . eagle forgotten, . . . under the stone,
Time has its way with you there, and the clay has its own.
Sleep on, O brave-hearted, O wise man, that kindled the flame—
To live in mankind is far more than to live in a name,   20
To live in mankind, far, far, more . . . than to live in a name.

                                                                        1913

General William Booth Enters into Heaven[2]
(To be sung to the tune of "The Blood of the Lamb"
with indicated instruments)

I

(*Bass drum beaten loudly.*)
Booth led boldly with his big bass drum—
(Are you washed in the blood of the Lamb?)
The Saints smiled gravely and they said: "He's come."
(Are you washed in the blood of the Lamb?)
Walking lepers followed, rank on rank,   5
Lurching bravos from the ditches dank,
Drabs from the alleyways and drug fiends pale—
Minds still passion-ridden, soul-powers frail:—
Vermin-eaten saints with moldy breath,
Unwashed legions with the ways of Death—   10
(Are you washed in the blood of the Lamb?)

(*Banjos.*)
Every slum had sent its half-a-score
The round world over. (Booth had groaned for more.)
Every banner that the wide world flies
Bloomed with glory and transcendent dyes.   15
Big-voiced lasses made their banjos bang,
Tranced, fanatical they shrieked and sang:—
"Are you washed in the blood of the Lamb?"
Hallelujah! It was queer to see
Bull-necked convicts with that land make free.   20
Loons with trumpets blowed a blare, blare, blare
On, on upward thro' the golden air!
(Are you washed in the blood of the Lamb?)

2. This poem, published in *Poetry: A Magazine of Verse* for January, 1913, first brought Lindsay into prominence; and it became the title poem for his first important volume, also published in 1913. William Booth, the founder of the Salvation Army, had died the year before, internationally known through the work of his Army. The musical instruments, the hymns, and the biblical language echoed in the poem, were familiarly identified with the street-corner evangelism of Booth's organization.

II

(Bass drum slower and softer.)
Booth died blind and still by faith he trod,
Eyes still dazzled by the ways of God.   25
Booth led boldly, and he looked the chief
Eagle countenance in sharp relief,
Beard a-flying, air of high command
Unabated in that holy land.

(Sweet flute music.)
Jesus came from out the court-house door,   30
Stretched his hands above the passing poor.
Booth saw not, but led his queer ones there
Round and round the mighty court-house square.
Then, in an instant all that blear review
Marched on spotless, clad in raiment new.   35
The lame were straightened, withered limbs uncurled
And blind eyes opened on a new, sweet world.

(Bass drum louder.)
Drabs and vixens in a flash made whole!
Gone was the weasel-head, the snout, the jowl!
Sages and sibyls now, and athletes clean,   40
Rulers of empires, and of forests green!

*(Grand chorus of all instruments. Tambourines to
the foreground.)*
The hosts were sandalled, and their wings were fire!
(Are you washed in the blood of the Lamb?)
But their noise played havoc with the angel-choir.
(Are you washed in the blood of the Lamb?)   45
Oh, shout Salvation! It was good to see
Kings and Princes by the Lamb set free.
The banjos rattled and the tambourines
Jing-jing-jingled in the hands of Queens.

(Reverently sung, no instruments.)   50
And when Booth halted by the curb for prayer
He saw his Master thro' the flag-filled air.
Christ came gently with a robe and crown
For Booth the soldier, while the throng knelt down.
He saw King Jesus. They were face to face,   55
And he knelt a-weeping in that holy place.
Are you washed in the blood of the Lamb?

1913

not quite a true characterization

Abraham Lincoln Walks at Midnight[3]

(IN SPRINGFIELD, ILLINOIS)

subtle rhythm

It is portentous, and a thing of state
That here at midnight, in our little town
A mourning figure walks, and will not rest,
Near the old court-house pacing up and down,

Or by his homestead, or in shadowed yards   5
He lingers where his children used to play,
Or through the market, on the well-worn stones
He stalks until the dawn-stars burn away.

A bronzed, lank man! His suit of ancient black,
A famous high top-hat and plain worn shawl   10
Make him the quaint great figure that men love,
The prairie-lawyer, master of us all.

He cannot sleep upon his hillside now.
He is among us:—as in times before!
And we who toss and lie awake for long   15
Breathe deep, and start, to see him pass the door.

His head is bowed. He thinks on men and kings.
Yea, when the sick world cries, how can he sleep?
Too many peasants fight, they know not why,
Too many homesteads in black terror weep.   20

The sins of all the war-lords burn his heart.
He sees the dreadnaughts scouring every main.
He carries on his shawl-wrapped shoulders now
The bitterness, the folly and the pain.

He cannot rest until a spirit-dawn   25
Shall come;—the shining hope of Europe free:
The league of sober folk, the Workers' Earth,
Bringing long peace to Cornland, Alp and Sea.

It breaks his heart that kings must murder still,
That all his hours of travail here for men   30
Seem yet in vain. And who will bring white peace
That he may sleep upon his hill again?

1914

3. The poem appeared in the *Independent* for September, 1914, a month after the German invasion of Belgium. It was collected in a section of poems concerning that crisis, in the *Congo* volume, also published in 1914.

The Santa-Fé Trail[4]
(A Humoresque)

(I asked the old negro: "What is that bird that sings so well?" He answered: "That is the Rachel-Jane." "Hasn't it another name—lark, or thrush, or the like?" "No. Jus' Rachel-Jane.")

I. In Which a Racing Auto Comes from the East

This is the order of the music of the morning:— *To be sung deli-*
First, from the far East comes but a crooning. *cately, to an im-*
The crooning turns to a sunrise singing. *provised tune.*
Hark to the *calm*-horn, *balm*-horn, *psalm*-horn.
Hark to the *faint*-horn, *quaint*-horn, *saint*-horn. . . .   5

Hark to the *pace*-horn, *chase*-horn, *race*-horn. *To be sung or read*
And the holy veil of the dawn has gone. *with great speed.*
Swiftly the brazen car comes on.
It burns in the East as the sunrise burns.
I see great flashes where the far trail turns.   10
Its eyes are lamps like the eyes of dragons.
It drinks gasoline from big red flagons.
Butting through the delicate mists of the morning,
It comes like lightning, goes past roaring.
It will hail all the windmills, taunting, ringing,   15
Dodge the cyclones,
Count the milestones,
On through the ranges the prairie-dog tills—
Scooting past the cattle on the thousand hills. . . .
Ho for the *tear*-horn, *scare*-horn, *dare*-horn, *To be read or*
Ho for the *gay*-horn, *bark*-horn, *bay*-horn. *sung in a rolling*
Ho for Kansas, land that restores us *bass, with some*
When houses choke us, and great books bore us! *deliberation.*
Sunrise Kansas, harvesters' Kansas,
A million men have found you before us.   25
A million men have found you before us.

II. In Which Many Autos Pass Westward

I want live things in their pride to remain. *In an even, delib-*
I will not kill one grasshopper vain *erate, narrative*
Though he eats a hole in my shirt like a door. *manner.*
I let him out, give him one chance more.   30
Perhaps, while he gnaws my hat in his whim,
Grasshopper lyrics occur to him.

4. The Santa Fe Trail, from Independence, Missouri, to Santa Fe, New Mexico, after about 1820 became a principal avenue to the Southwest, successively as cattle trail, trade route, railroad route, and automobile road. The poem was published in the *Congo* volume (1914), representing, like "The Congo," Lindsay's experiments with poetry "to be read aloud or chanted."

I am a tramp by the long trail's border,
Given to squalor, rags and disorder.
I nap and amble and yawn and look,   35
Write fool-thoughts in my grubby book,
Recite to the children, explore at my ease,
Work when I work, beg when I please,
Give crank-drawings, that make folks stare
To the half-grown boys in the sunset glare,   40
And get me a place to sleep in the hay
At the end of a live-and-let-live day.

I find in the stubble of the new-cut weeds
A whisper and a feasting, all one needs:
The whisper of the strawberries, white and red   45
Here where the new-cut weeds lie dead.

But I would not walk all alone till I die
Without some life-drunk horns going by.
And up round this apple-earth they come
Blasting the whispers of the morning dumb:—   50
Cars in a plain realistic row.
And fair dreams fade
When the raw horns blow.

On each snapping pennant
A big black name:—   55
The careering city
Whence each car came.
They tour from Memphis, Atlanta, Savannah,
Tallahassee and Texarkana.
They tour from St. Louis, Columbus, Manistee,   *Like a train-caller*
They tour from Peoria, Davenport, Kankakee.   *in a Union Depot.*
Cars from Concord, Niagara, Boston,
Cars from Topeka, Emporia, and Austin.
Cars from Chicago, Hannibal, Cairo.
Cars from Alton, Oswego, Toledo.   65
Cars from Buffalo, Kokomo, Delphi,
Cars from Lodi, Carmi, Loami.
Ho for Kansas, land that restores us
When houses choke us, and great books bore us!
While I watch the highroad   70
And look at the sky,
While I watch the clouds in amazing grandeur
Roll their legions without rain
Over the blistering Kansas plain—

While I sit by the milestone   75
And watch the sky,
The United States
Goes by.

Listen to the iron-horns, ripping, racking.   *To be given very harshly, with a snapping explosiveness.*
Listen to the quack-horns, slack and clacking.
Way down the road, trilling like a toad,
Here comes the *dice*-horn, here comes the *vice*-horn,
Here comes the *snarl*-horn, *brawl*-horn, *lewd*-horn,
Followed by the *prude*-horn, bleak and squeaking:—
(Some of them from Kansas, some of them from Kansas.)   85
Here comes the *hod*-horn, *plod*-horn, *sod*-horn,
Nevermore-to-*roam*-horn, *loam*-horn, *home*-horn.
(Some of them from Kansas, some of them from Kansas.)
     Far away the Rachel-Jane   *To be read or sung, well-nigh in a whisper.*
     Not defeated by the horns
     Sings amid a hedge of thorns:—
     "Love and life,
     Eternal youth—
     Sweet, sweet, sweet, sweet,
     Dew and glory,   95
     Love and truth,
     Sweet, sweet, sweet, sweet,
WHILE SMOKE-BLACK FREIGHTS ON THE DOUBLE-   *Louder and louder, faster and faster.*
     TRACKED RAILROAD,
DRIVEN AS THOUGH BY THE FOUL FIEND'S OX-GOAD,
SCREAMING TO THE WEST COAST, SCREAMING TO THE EAST,   100
CARRY OFF A HARVEST, BRING BACK A FEAST,
AND HARVESTING MACHINERY AND HARNESS FOR THE BEAST,
THE HAND-CARS WHIZ, AND RATTLE ON THE RAILS,
THE SUNLIGHT FLASHES ON THE TIN DINNER-PAILS.   104
And then, in an instant, ye modern men,   *In a rolling bass, with increasing deliberation.*
Behold the procession once again,
The United States goes by!
Listen to the iron-horns, ripping, racking,   *With a snapping explosiveness.*
Listen to the *wise*-horn, desperate-to-*advise* horn,
Listen to the *fast*-horn, *kill*-horn, *blast*-horn. . . .   110
     Far away the Rachel-Jane   *To be sung or read well-nigh in a whisper.*
     Not defeated by the horns
     Sings amid a hedge of thorns:—
     "Love and life,
     Eternal youth,   115
     Sweet, sweet, sweet, sweet,

Dew and glory,
Love and truth.
Sweet, sweet, sweet, sweet."   119
The mufflers open on a score of cars   *To be bawled in*
With wonderful thunder,   *the beginning with*
                                               a snapping explo-
CRACK, CRACK, CRACK,   *siveness, ending in*
                                               a languorous
CRACK-CRACK, CRACK-CRACK,   *chant.*
CRACK, CRACK, CRACK,
Listen to the gold-horn . . .   125
Old horn . . .
Cold horn . . .
And all of the tunes, till the night comes down
On hay-stack, and ant-hill, and wind-bitten town.   129
Then far in the west, as in the beginning,   *To be sung to ex-*
                                               actly the same
Dim in the distance, sweet in retreating,   *whispered tune as*
Hark to the faint-horn, quaint-horn, saint-horn, *the first five lines.*
Hark to the calm-horn, balm-horn, psalm-horn. . . .

They are hunting the goals that they understand:— *This section begin-*
                                               ning sonorously,
San Francisco and the brown sea-sand.   *ending in a lan-*
My goal is the mystery the beggars win.   *guorous whisper.*
I am caught in the web the night-winds spin.
The edge of the wheat-ridge speaks to me.
I talk with the leaves of the mulberry tree.
And now I hear, as I sit all alone   140
In the dusk, by another big Santa-Fé stone,
The souls of the tall corn gathering round
And the gay little souls of the grass in the ground.
Listen to the tale the cottonwood tells.
Listen to the windmills, singing o'er the wells.   145
Listen to the whistling flutes without price
Of myriad prophets out of paradise.
Harken to the wonder
That the night-air carries. . . .
Listen . . . to . . . the . . . whisper . . .   150
Of . . . the . . . prairie . . . fairies
        Singing o'er the fairy plain:—   *To the same whis-*
                                               pered tune as the
        "Sweet, sweet, sweet, sweet.   *Rachel-Jane song*
                                               —but very slowly.
        Love and glory,
        Stars and rain,   155
        Sweet, sweet, sweet, sweet. . . ."

                                                               1914

The Ghost of the Buffaloes[5]

Last night at black midnight I woke with a cry,
The windows were shaking, there was thunder on high,
The floor was atremble, the door was ajar,
While fires, crimson fires, shown from afar.
I rushed to the dooryard. The city was gone.   5
My home was a hut without orchard or lawn.
It was mud-smear and logs near a whispering stream,
Nothing else built by man could I see in my dream . . .
Then . . .
Ghost-kings came headlong, row upon row,   10
Gods of the Indians, torches aglow.

They mounted the bear and the elk and the deer,
And eagles gigantic, agèd and sere,
They rode long-horn cattle, they cried "A-la-la."
They lifted the knife, the bow, and the spear,   15
They lifted ghost-torches from dead fires below,
The midnight made grand with the cry "A-la-la."
The midnight made grand with a red-god charge,
A red-god show,
A red-god show,   20
"A-la-la, a-la-la, a-la-la, a-la-la."

With bodies like bronze, and terrible eyes
Came the rank and the file, with catamount[6] cries,
Gibbering, yipping, with hollow-skull clacks,
Riding white bronchos with skeleton backs,   25
Scalp-hunters, beaded and spangled and bad,
Naked and lustful and foaming and mad,
Flashing primeval demoniac scorn,
Blood-thirst and pomp amid darkness reborn,
Power and glory that sleep in the grass   30
While the winds and the snows and the great rains pass.
They crossed the gray river, thousands abreast,
They rode out in infinite lines to the west,
Tide upon tide of strange fury and foam,
Spirits and wraiths, the blue was their home,   35
The sky was their goal where the star-flags are furled,
And on past those far golden splendors they whirled.

5. Together with "The Chinese Nightingale," the title poem of the volume of
1917, in which it first appeared, "The
Ghost of the Buffaloes" has been regarded as the work in which Lindsay
achieved his greatest subtlety with respect to chanted rhythms and symbolic
suggestiveness. It also exemplifies his
characteristic idealization of the primitive past of America.
6. An American frontier term for any
wildcat, such as the cougar or lynx.

They burned to dim meteors, lost in the deep,
And I turned in dazed wonder, thinking of sleep.

And the wind crept by   40
Alone, unkempt, unsatisfied,
The wind cried and cried—
Muttered of massacres long past,
Buffaloes in shambles vast . . .
An owl said, "Hark, what is a-wing?"   45
I heard a cricket caroling,
I heard a cricket caroling,
I heard a cricket caroling.

Then . . .
Snuffing the lightning that crashed from on high   50
Rose royal old buffaloes, row upon row.
The lords of the prairie came galloping by.
And I cried in my heart "A-la-la, a-la-la,
A red-god show,
A red-god show,   55
A-la-la, a-la-la, a-la-la, a-la-la."

Buffaloes, buffaloes, thousands abreast,
A scourge and amazement, they swept to the west.
With black bobbing noses, with red rolling tongues,
Coughing forth steam from their leather-wrapped lungs,   60
Cows with their calves, bulls big and vain,
Goring the laggards, shaking the mane,
Stamping flint feet, flashing moon eyes,
Pompous and owlish, shaggy and wise.
Like sea-cliffs and caves resounded their ranks   65
With shoulders like waves, and undulant flanks.
Tide upon tide of strange fury and foam,
Spirits and wraiths, the blue was their home,
The sky was their goal where the star-flags are furled,
And on past those far golden splendors they whirled.   70
They burned to dim meteors, lost in the deep,
And I turned in dazed wonder, thinking of sleep.

I heard a cricket's cymbals play,
A scarecrow lightly flapped his rags,
And a pan that hung by his shoulder rang,   75
Rattled and thumped in a listless way,
And now the wind in the chimney sang,
The wind in the chimney,
The wind in the chimney,
The wind in the chimney,   80

Seemed to say:—
"Dream, boy, dream,
If you anywise can.
To dream is the work
Of beast or man.   85
Life is the west-going dream-storms' breath,
Life is a dream, the sigh of the skies,
The breath of the stars, that nod on their pillows
With their golden hair mussed over their eyes."
The locust played on his musical wing,   90
Sang to his mate of love's delight.
I heard the whippoorwill's soft fret.
I heard a cricket caroling,
I heard a cricket caroling,
I heard a cricket say: "Good-night, good-night,   95
Good-night, good-night, . . . good-night."

1917

WILLA CATHER
(1873–1947)

Willa Sibert Cather was the first modern novelist to find in the soil of the West and Southwest the rich cultural inheritance provided by its historic past and the polyglot immigrant inundation of recent times. She was born on December 7, 1873,[1] in a farmhouse in the Virginia hills west of Winchester, where the Cathers had farmed for nearly a century. In 1883 her family moved to a farm near Red Cloud, Nebraska, and later into the then raw frontier village.

In her Virginia childhood, Willa Cather had been tutored at home by her grandmother Boak, a well-read woman. At Red Cloud, the high school provided two teachers to whom the young author was permanently indebted. There was a small but excellent library in her own home; she practiced German and French with neighbors who had an extraordinary collection of continental books to lend her; and a storekeeper named "Uncle Billy" Ducker taught her to read the Greek and Latin of Homer, Anacreon, and Vergil. A German music master gave many hours to her instruction in the history and appreciation of music, including opera, thus developing her interest in a subject later of major importance in her novels and stories. In contrast with such people were the materialists of the same frontier, and there was always the austerity of a new soil to be conquered. In girlhood her frontier neighbors illustrated the inevitable con-

1. Not 1876 as commonly given. E. K. Brown verifies the earlier date (p. 17; see bibliography, below).

flict between the spiritual value and the material solution which appears repeatedly in her fiction, and provided her with the prototypes for such sturdy Scandinavian or German characters as Ántonia Shimerda, Thea Kronborg, and Neighbor Rosicky.

At seventeen, she went for a year to the preparatory school in Lincoln, Nebraska; then she attended the University of Nebraska, where she contributed to the local paper while studying journalism. Within a year after her graduation in 1895 she had found an editorial appointment on a small magazine in Pittsburgh. In 1897 she transferred to the Pittsburgh *Daily Leader*, as telegraph editor and drama critic. She was beginning to place her poetry and stories in a number of magazines, especially *McClure's Magazine* and *Cosmopolitan*, but her newspaper work proved a handicap to creative writing, and she turned to teaching, instructing in two Pittsburgh high schools between 1901 and 1906. A collection of poems, *April Twilights* (1903), was favorably received, but she knew that fiction was her field. Her first collection of stories, *The Troll Garden* (1905), contained "The Sculptor's Funeral," reproduced below, one of her best stories of revolt against the drabness and materialism of frontier life. In 1906 she again took a journalistic appointment, on the editorial staff of *McClure's Magazine* in New York, where she remained until 1912, when she published her first novel, *Alexander's Bridge*. She was already thirty-nine, but she had in mind the ideas for several novels and felt ready to give herself completely to them.

Although she had represented the Nebraska country in several stories in *The Troll Garden*, she was apparently not yet fully aware of the richness of this material for works of larger scope. However, she admired the stories of Sarah Orne Jewett, whose Maine was a region as apparently barren but as spiritually deep as her own Nebraska. E. K. Brown connects her personal friendship with Miss Jewett, which began in 1908, with her enlivened appreciation of her Nebraska materials, first apparent in "The Enchanted Bluff," which she published in *Harper's Magazine* early in 1909. In this story she also made her first use of the Southwest, where as a girl she had first discovered a western land with a past in its vestiges of ancient Indian and Spanish civilization. In later visits the emotional significance of this discovery assumed a symbolic value reflected in the use of these materials in several novels, notably *Death Comes for the Archbishop*.

Her next three novels concerned the Nebraska frontier. *O Pioneers!* (1913) is Whitman's title, and Alexandra Bergson, the Norwegian peasant girl in Nebraska, is a woman of Whitman's choice who, when her father is defeated by the savage struggle with the soil, steps in to conquer it herself in preparation for a new race. *The Song of the Lark* (1915) is a reconstruction of such a frontier community as Willa Cather knew, and the story of a Swedish girl, Thea Kronborg, who brings the music of that place with her on her upward climb to international fame as an operatic star. *My Ántonia* (1918) records the struggle for selfhood and unity with her environment of a Bohemian girl of immigrant parents, and is one of Miss Cather's best.

This quest for spiritual unity, so common to American writers in her time, became a desperate struggle for Willa Cather during the first World War, somewhat vitiating her grasp of her theme in *One of Ours* (1922) and *A Lost Lady* (1923). In *The Professor's House* (1925), however, she was again at her best, revealing a sensitive understanding of the "mid-channel" crisis in the lives of professional and creative people.

In *Death Comes for the Archbishop* (1927), an enduring American masterpiece, the history of the Southwest after the Mexican War becomes a synthesis of the whole past of that land, and the country itself becomes an epic character along with the heroic and saintly missionaries Bishop Jean Latour and Father Joseph Vaillant. The religious devotion depicted in this book reflects Willa Cather's confirmation, in 1922, in the Protestant Episcopal Church; although not a Catholic, she had a sympathetic understanding of the historic faith of these earlier settlers of the Southwest. In her next book, *Shadows on the Rock* (1931), perhaps with slightly less success, she achieved the same kind of cultural synthesis, this time dealing with the French-Catholic colonial Quebec of 1697.

My Mortal Enemy (1926), *Lucy Gayheart* (1935), and *Sapphira and the Slave Girl* (1940) are minor works only in the comparative sense. Each is a penetrating study of a woman, and each in some degree, but especially *My Mortal Enemy*, illustrates her invention of "the novel *démeublé*"—the novel stripped of superfluous characters and circumstances in order to emphasize a single individual.

Willa Cather was well recognized by her contemporaries, if never quite enough. She was awarded the Pulitzer Prize for one of her less distinguished novels, *One of Ours*. She received the Howells Medal for fiction of the American Academy of Arts and Letters (1930) and was the first recipient of the Prix Femina Américaine (1933). In 1944, when she was seventy-one, the National Institute of Arts and Letters presented her with its gold medal. Her novels were widely translated, and enthusiastically received by European readers. She died on April 24, 1947.

The definitive edition of Willa Cather's fiction is *The Novels and Stories of Willa Cather*, Library Edition, 13 vols., 1937–1941. *April Twilights*, 1903, was revised and enlarged as *April Twilights and Other Poems*, 1933. Posthumous volumes were *The Old Beauty*, 1948, three incomplete stories; and *Willa Cather on Writing*, 1949, an unauthorized but useful compilation. Miss Cather published her essays as *Not Under Forty*, 1936. Collections of stories include: *Youth and the Bright Medusa*, 1920; *Obscure Destinies*, 1932; *December Night*, 1933; and *Early Stories of Willa Cather*, edited by Mildred R. Bennett, 1957.

The definitive biography is E. K. Brown's posthumous *Willa Cather, A Critical Biography*, completed by Leon Edel, 1953. Other useful studies are René Rapin, *Willa Cather*, Modern American Writers Series, 1930; David

Daiches, *Willa Cather, A Critical Introduction*, 1951; Mildred R. Bennett, *World of Willa Cather*, 1951, on the Red Cloud years; Edith Lewis, *Willa* *Cather Living: A Personal Record*, 1953; Elizabeth Shepley Sergeant, *Willa Cather*, 1953; George N. Kates, editor, *Willa Cather in Europe*, 1956.

The Sculptor's Funeral[1]

A group of the townspeople stood on the station siding of a little Kansas town, awaiting the coming of the night train, which was already twenty minutes overdue. The snow had fallen thick over everything; in the pale starlight the line of bluffs across the wide, white meadows south of the town made soft, smoke-coloured curves against the clear sky. The men on the siding stood first on one foot and then on the other, their hands thrust deep into their trousers pockets, their overcoats open, their shoulders screwed up with the cold; and they glanced from time to time toward the southeast, where the railroad track wound along the river shore. They conversed in low tones and moved about restlessly, seeming uncertain as to what was expected of them. There was but one of the company who looked as if he knew exactly why he was there, and he kept conspicuously apart; walking to the far end of the platform, returning to the station door, then pacing up the track again, his chin sunk in the high collar of his overcoat, his burly shoulders drooping forward, his gait heavy and dogged. Presently he was approached by a tall, spare, grizzled man clad in a faded Grand Army[2] suit, who shuffled out from the group and advanced with a certain deference, craning his neck forward until his back made the angle of a jack-knife three-quarters open.

"I reckon she's a-goin' to be pretty late agin to-night, Jim," he remarked in a squeaky falsetto. "S'pose it's the snow?"

"I don't know," responded the other man with a shade of annoyance, speaking from out an astonishing cataract of red beard that grew fiercely and thickly in all directions.

The spare man shifted the quill toothpick he was chewing to the other side of his mouth. "It ain't likely that anybody from the East will come with the corpse, I s'pose," he went on reflectively.

"I don't know," responded the other, more curtly than before.

"It's too bad he didn't belong to some lodge or other. I like an

1. "The Sculptor's Funeral" employs two themes that the author herself recognized as characteristic of her work: the plight of the gifted individual, especially the artist, in conflict with social prejudice or convention, as for example in *The Song of the Lark;* and the yearning of a sensitive person, confronted with a society of "newness and ugliness and sordidness, for all that is chastened and old, and noble with traditions." Willa Cather collected this story in both *The Troll Garden* (1905) and *Youth and the Bright Medusa* (1920). It was first published in *McClure's Magazine* for January, 1905.
2. The Grand Army of the Republic, an organization, founded in 1866, of men who had served with the Union forces in the Civil War; referred to below as the "G.A.R."

order funeral myself. They seem more appropriate for people of some reputation," the spare man continued, with an ingratiating concession in his shrill voice, as he carefully placed his toothpick in his vest pocket. He always carried the flag at the G. A. R. funerals in the town.

The heavy man turned on his heel, without replying, and walked up the siding. The spare man rejoined the uneasy group. "Jim's ez full ez a tick, ez ushel," he commented commiseratingly.

Just then a distant whistle sounded, and there was a shuffling of feet on the platform. A number of lanky boys, of all ages, appeared as suddenly and slimily as eels wakened by the crack of thunder; some came from the waiting-room, where they had been warming themselves by the red stove, or half asleep on the slat benches; others uncoiled themselves from baggage trucks or slid out of express wagons. Two clambered down from the driver's seat of a hearse that stood backed up against the siding. They straightened their stooping shoulders and lifted their heads, and a flash of momentary animation kindled their dull eyes at that cold, vibrant scream, the world-wide call for men. It stirred them like the note of a trumpet; just as it had often stirred the man who was coming home tonight, in his boyhood.

The night express shot, red as a rocket, from out the eastward marsh lands and wound along the river shore under the long lines of shivering poplars that sentinelled the meadows, the escaping steam hanging in grey masses against the pale sky and blotting out the Milky Way. In a moment the red glare from the headlight streamed up the snow-covered track before the siding and glittered on the wet, black rails. The burly man with the dishevelled red beard walked swiftly up the platform toward the approaching train, uncovering his head as he went. The group of men behind him hesitated, glanced questioningly at one another, and awkwardly followed his example. The train stopped, and the crowd shuffled up to the express car just as the door was thrown open, the man in the G. A. R. suit thrusting his head forward with curiosity. The express messenger appeared in the doorway, accompanied by a young man in a long ulster and travelling cap.

"Are Mr. Merrick's friends here?" inquired the young man.

The group on the platform swayed uneasily. Philip Phelps, the banker, responded with dignity: "We have come to take charge of the body. Mr. Merrick's father is very feeble and can't be about."

"Send the agent out here," growled the express messenger, "and tell the operator to lend a hand."

The coffin was got out of its rough-box and down on the snowy platform. The townspeople drew back enough to make room for it and then formed a close semicircle about it, looking curiously at the palm leaf which lay across the black cover. No one said anything. The baggage man stood by his truck, waiting to get at the trunks. The engine panted heavily, and the fireman dodged in and out among the wheels with his yellow torch and long oil-can, snapping the spindle boxes. The young Bostonian, one of the dead sculptor's pupils who had come with the body, looked about him helplessly. He turned to the banker, the only one of that black, uneasy, stoop-shouldered group who seemed enough of an individual to be addressed.

"None of Mr. Merrick's brothers are here?" he asked uncertainly.

The man with the red beard for the first time stepped up and joined the others. "No, they have not come yet; the family is scattered. The body will be taken directly to the house." He stooped and took hold of one of the handles of the coffin.

"Take the long hill road up, Thompson, it will be easier on the horses," called the liveryman as the undertaker snapped the door of the hearse and prepared to mount to the driver's seat.

Laird, the red-bearded lawyer, turned again to the stranger: "We didn't know whether there would be anyone with him or not," he explained. "It's a long walk, so you'd better go up in the hack." He pointed to a single battered conveyance, but the young man replied stiffly: "Thank you, but I think I will go up with the hearse. If you don't object," turning to the undertaker, "I'll ride with you."

They clambered up over the wheels and drove off in the starlight up the long, white hill toward the town. The lamps in the still village were shining from under the low, snow-burdened roofs; and beyond, on every side, the plains reached out into emptiness, peaceful and wide as the soft sky itself, and wrapped in a tangible, white silence.

When the hearse backed up to a wooden sidewalk before a naked, weather-beaten frame house, the same composite, ill-defined group that had stood upon the station siding was huddled about the gate. The front yard was an icy swamp, and a couple of warped planks, extending from the sidewalk to the door, made a sort of rickety foot-bridge. The gate hung on one hinge, and was opened wide with difficulty. Steavens, the young stranger, noticed that something black was tied to the knob of the front door.

The grating sound made by the casket, as it was drawn from the hearse, was answered by a scream from the house; the front door was wrenched open, and a tall, corpulent woman rushed out bare-headed into the snow and flung herself upon the coffin, shrieking: "My boy, my boy! And this is how you've come home to me!"

As Steavens turned away and closed his eyes with a shudder of unutterable repulsion, another woman, also tall, but flat and angular, dressed entirely in black, darted out of the house and caught Mrs. Merrick by the shoulders, crying sharply: "Come, come, mother; you mustn't go on like this!" Her tone changed to one of obsequious solemnity as she turned to the banker: "The parlour is ready, Mr. Phelps."

The bearers carried the coffin along the narrow boards, while the undertaker ran ahead with the coffin-rests. They bore it into a large, unheated room that smelled of dampness and disuse and furniture polish, and set it down under a hanging lamp ornamented with jingling glass prisms and before a "Rogers group"[3] of John Alden and Priscilla, wreathed with smilax. Henry Steavens stared about him with the sickening conviction that there had been a mistake, and that he had somehow arrived at the wrong destination. He looked at the clover-green Brussels,[4] the fat plush upholstery, among the hand-painted china plaques and panels and vases, for some mark of identification,—for something that might once conceivably have belonged to Harvey Merrick. It was not until he recognized his friend in the crayon portrait of a little boy in kilts and curls, hanging above the piano, that he felt willing to let any of these people approach the coffin.

"Take the lid off, Mr. Thompson; let me see my boy's face," wailed the elder woman between her sobs. This time Steavens looked fearfully, almost beseechingly into her face, red and swollen under its masses of strong, black, shiny hair. He flushed, dropped his eyes, and then, almost incredulously, looked again. There was a kind of power about her face—a kind of brutal handsomeness, even; but it was scarred and furrowed by violence, and so coloured and coarsened by fiercer passions that grief seemed never to have laid a gentle finger there. The long nose was distended and knobbed at the end, and there were deep lines on either side of it; her heavy, black brows almost met across her forehead, her teeth were large and square, and set far apart—teeth that could tear. She filled the room; the men were obliterated, seemed tossed about like twigs in an angry water, and even Steavens felt himself being drawn into the whirlpool.

The daughter—the tall, raw-boned woman in crêpe, with a mourning comb in her hair which curiously lengthened her long face—sat stiffly upon the sofa, her hands, conspicuous for their large knuckles, folded in her lap, her mouth and eyes drawn down, solemnly awaiting the opening of the coffin. Near the door stood a mulatto woman, evidently a servant in the house, with a timid bear-

---

3. John Rogers (1829–1904), American sculptor, became famous for his statuette groups, usually sentimental and descriptive, which had an enormous vogue as parlor ornaments, especially in rural areas.

4. The Belgian city of Brussels gave its name to a sturdy carpet weave that became common in the United States.

ing and an emaciated face pitifully sad and gentle. She was weeping silently, the corner of her calico apron lifted to her eyes, occasionally suppressing a long, quivering sob. Steavens walked over and stood beside her.

Feeble steps were heard on the stairs, and an old man, tall and frail, odorous of pipe smoke, with shaggy, unkempt grey hair and a dingy beard, tobacco stained about the mouth, entered uncertainly. He went slowly up to the coffin and stood rolling a blue cotton handkerchief between his hands, seeming so pained and embarrassed by his wife's orgy of grief that he had no consciousness of anything else.

"There, there, Annie, dear, don't take on so," he quavered timidly, putting out a shaking hand and awkwardly patting her elbow. She turned and sank upon his shoulder with such violence that he tottered a little. He did not even glance toward the coffin, but continued to look at her with a dull, frightened, appealing expression, as a spaniel looks at the whip. His sunken cheeks slowly reddened and burned with miserable shame. When his wife rushed from the room, her daughter strode after her with set lips. The servant stole up to the coffin, bent over it for a moment, and then slipped away to the kitchen, leaving Steavens, the lawyer, and the father to themselves. The old man stood looking down at his dead son's face. The sculptor's splendid head seemed even more noble in its rigid stillness than in life. The dark hair had crept down upon the wide forehead; the face seemed strangely long, but in it there was not that repose we expect to find in the faces of the dead. The brows were so drawn that there were two deep lines above the beaked nose, and the chin was thrust forward defiantly. It was as though the strain of life had been so sharp and bitter that death could not at once relax the tension and smooth the countenance into perfect peace—as though he were still guarding something precious, which might even yet be wrested from him.

The old man's lips were working under his stained beard. He turned to the lawyer with timid deference: "Phelps and the rest are comin' back to set up with Harve, ain't they?" he asked. "Thank 'ee, Jim, thank 'ee." He brushed the hair back gently from his son's forehead. "He was a good boy, Jim; always a good boy. He was ez gentle ez a child and the kindest of 'em all—only we didn't none of us ever onderstand him." The tears trickled slowly down his beard and dropped upon the sculptor's coat.

"Martin, Martin! Oh, Martin! come here," his wife wailed from the top of the stairs. The old man started timorously: "Yes, Annie, I'm coming." He turned away, hesitated, stood for a moment in miserable indecision; then reached back and patted the dead man's hair softly, and stumbled from the room.

"Poor old man, I didn't think he had any tears left. Seems as if his eyes would have gone dry long ago. At his age nothing cuts very deep," remarked the lawyer.

Something in his tone made Steavens glance up. While the mother had been in the room, the young man had scarcely seen any one else; but now, from the moment he first glanced into Jim Laird's florid face and blood-shot eyes, he knew that he had found what he had been heartsick at not finding before—the feeling, the understanding, that must exist in some one, even here.

The man was red as his beard, with features swollen and blurred by dissipation, and a hot, blazing blue eye. His face was strained— that of a man who is controlling himself with difficulty—and he kept plucking at his beard with a sort of fierce resentment. Steavens, sitting by the window, watched him turn down the glaring lamp, still its jangling pendants with an angry gesture, and then stand with his hands locked behind him, staring down into the master's face. He could not help wondering what link there had been between the porcelain vessel and so sooty a lump of potter's clay.

From the kitchen an uproar was sounding; when the dining-room door opened, the import of it was clear. The mother was abusing the maid for having forgotten to make the dressing for the chicken salad which had been prepared for the watchers. Steavens had never heard anything in the least like it; it was injured, emotional, dramatic abuse, unique and masterly in its excruciating cruelty, as violent and unrestrained as had been her grief of twenty minutes before. With a shudder of disgust the lawyer went into the dining-room and closed the door into the kitchen.

"Poor Roxy's getting it now," he remarked when he came back. "The Merricks took her out of the poor-house years ago; and if her loyalty would let her, I guess the poor old thing could tell tales that would curdle your blood. She's the mulatto woman who was standing in here a while ago, with her apron to her eyes. The old woman is a fury; there never was anybody like her. She made Harvey's life a hell for him when he lived at home; he was so sick ashamed of it. I never could see how he kept himself sweet."

"He was wonderful," said Steavens slowly, "wonderful; but until tonight I have never known how wonderful."

"That is the eternal wonder of it, anyway; that it can come even from such a dung heap as this," the lawyer cried, with a sweeping gesture which seemed to indicate much more than the four walls within which they stood.

"I think I'll see whether I can get a little air. The room is so close I am beginning to feel rather faint," murmured Steavens, struggling with one of the windows. The sash was stuck, however, and would not yield, so he sat down dejectedly and began pulling at his collar.

The lawyer came over, loosened the sash with one blow of his red fist and sent the window up a few inches. Steavens thanked him, but the nausea which had been gradually climbing into his throat for the last half hour left him with but one desire—a desperate feeling that he must get away from this place with what was left of Harvey Merrick. Oh, he comprehended well enough now the quiet bitterness of the smile that he had seen so often on his master's lips!

Once when Merrick returned from a visit home, he brought with him a singularly feeling and suggestive bas-relief of a thin, faded old woman, sitting and sewing something pinned to her knee; while a full-lipped, full-blooded little urchin, his trousers held up by a single gallows, stood beside her, impatiently twitching her gown to call her attention to a butterfly he had caught. Steavens, impressed by the tender and delicate modelling of the thin, tired face, had asked him if it were his mother. He remembered the dull flush that had burned up in the sculptor's face.

The lawyer was sitting in a rocking-chair beside the coffin, his head thrown back and his eyes closed. Steavens looked at him earnestly, puzzled at the line of the chin, and wondering why a man should conceal a feature of such distinction under that disfiguring shock of beard. Suddenly, as though he felt the young sculptor's keen glance, Jim Laird opened his eyes.

"Was he always a good deal of an oyster?" he asked abruptly. "He was terribly shy as a boy."

"Yes, he was an oyster, since you put it so," rejoined Steavens. "Although he could be very fond of people, he always gave one the impression of being detached. He disliked violent emotion; he was reflective, and rather distrustful of himself—except, of course, as regarded his work. He was sure enough there. He distrusted men pretty thoroughly and women even more, yet somehow without believing ill of them. He was determined, indeed, to believe the best; but he seemed afraid to investigate."

"A burnt dog dreads the fire," said the lawyer grimly, and closed his eyes.

Steavens went on and on, reconstructing that whole miserable boyhood. All this raw, biting ugliness had been the portion of the man whose mind was to become an exhaustless gallery of beautiful impressions—so sensitive that the mere shadow of a poplar leaf flickering against a sunny wall would be etched and held there for ever. Surely, if ever a man had the magic word in his finger tips, it was Merrick. Whatever he touched, he revealed its holiest secret; liberated it from enchantment and restored it to its pristine loveliness. Upon whatever he had come in contact with, he had left a beautiful record of the experience—a sort of ethereal signature; a scent, a sound, a colour that was his own.

Steavens understood now the real tragedy of his master's life; neither love nor wine, as many had conjectured; but a blow which had fallen earlier and cut deeper than anything else could have done —a shame not his, and yet so unescapably his, to hide in his heart from his very boyhood. And without—the frontier warfare; the yearning of a boy, cast ashore upon a desert of newness and ugliness and sordidness, for all that is chastened and old, and noble with traditions.

At eleven o'clock the tall, flat woman in black announced that the watchers were arriving, and asked them to "step into the dining-room." As Steavens rose, the lawyer said dryly: "You go on—it'll be a good experience for you. I'm not equal to that crowd tonight; I've had twenty years of them."

As Steavens closed the door after him he glanced back at the lawyer, sitting by the coffin in the dim light, with his chin resting on his hand.

The same misty group that had stood before the door of the express car shuffled into the dining-room. In the light of the kerosene lamp they separated and became individuals. The minister, a pale, feeble-looking man with white hair and blond chin-whiskers, took his seat beside a small side table and placed his Bible upon it. The Grand Army man sat down behind the stove and tilted his chair back comfortably against the wall, fishing his quill toothpick from his waistcoat pocket. The two bankers, Phelps and Elder, sat off in a corner behind the dinner-table, where they could finish their discussion of the new usury law and its effect on chattel security loans. The real estate agent, an old man with a smiling, hypocritical face, soon joined them. The coal and lumber dealer and the cattle shipper sat on opposite sides of the hard coal-burner, their feet on the nickel-work. Steavens took a book from his pocket and began to read. The talk around him ranged through various topics of local interest while the house was quieting down. When it was clear that the members of the family were in bed, the Grand Army man hitched his shoulders and, untangling his long legs, caught his heels on the rounds of his chair.

"S'pose there'll be a will, Phelps?" he queried in his weak falsetto.

The banker laughed disagreeably, and began trimming his nails with a pearl-handled pocket-knife.

"There'll scarcely be any need for one, will there?" he queried in his turn.

The restless Grand Army man shifted his position again, getting his knees still nearer his chin. "Why, the ole man says Harve's done right well lately," he chirped.

The other banker spoke up. "I reckon he means by that Harve

ain't asked him to mortgage any more farms lately, so as he could go on with his education."

"Seems like my mind don't reach back to a time when Harve wasn't bein' edycated," tittered the Grand Army man.

There was a general chuckle. The minister took out his handkerchief and blew his nose sonorously. Banker Phelps closed his knife with a snap. "It's too bad the old man's sons didn't turn out better," he remarked with reflective authority. "They never hung together. He spent money enough on Harve to stock a dozen cattle-farms, and he might as well have poured it into Sand Creek. If Harve had stayed at home and helped nurse what little they had, and gone into stock on the old man's bottom farm, they might all have been well fixed. But the old man had to trust everything to tenants and was cheated right and left."

"Harve never could have handled stock none," interposed the cattleman. "He hadn't it in him to be sharp. Do you remember when he bought Sander's mules for eight-year olds, when everybody in town knew that Sander's father-in-law give 'em to his wife for a wedding present eighteen years before, an' they was full-grown mules then?"

The company laughed discreetly, and the Grand Army man rubbed his knees with a spasm of childish delight.

"Harve never was much account for anything practical, and he shore was never fond of work," began the coal and lumber dealer. "I mind the last time he was home; the day he left, when the old man was out to the barn helpin' his hand hitch up to take Harve to the train, and Cal Moots was patchin' up the fence; Harve, he come out on the step and sings out, in his ladylike voice: 'Cal Moots, Cal Moots! please come cord my trunk.'"

"That's Harve for you," approved the Grand Army man. "I kin hear him howlin' yet, when he was a big feller in long pants and his mother used to whale him with a rawhide in the barn for lettin' the cows git foundered in the cornfield when he was drivin' 'em home from pasture. He killed a cow of mine that-a-way onct—a pure Jersey and the best milker I had, an' the ole man had to put up for her. Harve, he was watchin' the sun set acrost the marshes when the anamile got away."

"Where the old man made his mistake was in sending the boy East to school," said Phelps, stroking his goatee and speaking in a deliberate, judicial tone. "There was where he got his head full of nonsense. What Harve needed, of all people, was a course in some first-class Kansas City business college."

The letters were swimming before Steavens's eyes. Was it possible that these men did not understand, that the palm on the coffin meant nothing to them? The very name of their town would have remained for ever buried in the postal guide had it not been now and again mentioned in the world in connection with Harvey Merrick's. He remembered what his master had said to him on the day of his death, after the congestion of both lungs had shut off any probability of recovery, and the sculptor had asked his pupil to send his body home. "It's not a pleasant place to be lying while the world is moving and doing and bettering," he had said with a feeble smile, "but it rather seems as though we ought to go back to the place we came from, in the end. The townspeople will come in for a look at me; and after they have had their say, I shan't have much to fear from the judgment of God!"

The cattleman took up the comment. "Forty's young for a Merrick to cash in; they usually hang on pretty well. Probably he helped it along with whisky."

"His mother's people were not long lived, and Harvey never had a robust constitution," said the minister mildly. He would have liked to say more. He had been the boy's Sunday-school teacher, and had been fond of him; but he felt that he was not in a position to speak. His own sons had turned out badly, and it was not a year since one of them had made his last trip home in the express car, shot in a gambling-house in the Black Hills.

"Nevertheless, there is no disputin' that Harve frequently looked upon the wine when it was red, also variegated, and it shore made an oncommon fool of him," moralized the cattleman.

Just then the door leading into the parlour rattled loudly and every one started involuntarily, looking relieved when only Jim Laird came out. The Grand Army man ducked his head when he saw the spark in his blue, bloodshot eye. They were all afraid of Jim; he was a drunkard, but he could twist the law to suit his client's needs as no other man in all western Kansas could do, and there were many who tried. The lawyer closed the door behind him, leaned back against it and folded his arms, cocking his head a little to one side. When he assumed this attitude in the court-room, ears were always pricked up, as it usually foretold a flood of withering sarcasm.

"I've been with you gentlemen before," he began in a dry, even tone, "when you've sat by the coffins of boys born and raised in this town; and, if I remember rightly, you were never any too well satisfied when you checked them up. What's the matter, anyhow? Why is it that reputable young men are as scarce as millionaires in Sand City? It might almost seem to a stranger that there was some way something the matter with your progressive town. Why did Ruben Sayer, the brightest young lawyer you ever turned out, after he had come home from the university as straight as a die, take to drinking and forge a check and shoot himself? Why did Bill Merritt's son die of the shakes in a saloon in Omaha? Why was Mr. Thomas's son, here, shot in a gambling-house? Why did young Adams burn his mill to beat the insurance companies and go to the pen?"

The lawyer paused and unfolded his arms, laying one clenched fist quietly on the table. "I'll tell you why. Because you drummed nothing but money and knavery into their ears from the time they wore knickerbockers; because you carped away at them as you've been carping here tonight, holding our friends Phelps and Elder up to them for their models, as our grandfathers held up George Washington and John Adams. But the boys were young, and raw at the business you put them to, and how could they match coppers with such artists as Phelps and Elder? You wanted them to be successful rascals; they were only unsuccessful ones—that's all the difference. There was only one boy ever raised in this borderland between ruffianism and civilization who didn't come to grief, and you hated Harvey Merrick more for winning out than you hated all the other boys who got under the wheels. Lord, Lord, how you did hate him! Phelps, here, is fond of saying that he could buy and sell us all out any time he's a mind to; but he knew Harve wouldn't have given a tinker's damn for his bank and all his cattle-farms put together; and a lack of appreciation, that way, goes hard with Phelps.

"Old Nimrod thinks Harve drank too much; and this from such as Nimrod and me!

"Brother Elder says Harve was too free with the old man's money —fell short in filial consideration, maybe. Well, we can all remember the very tone in which brother Elder swore his own father was a liar, in the county court; and we all know that the old man came out of that partnership with his son as bare as a sheared lamb. But maybe I'm getting personal, and I'd better be driving ahead at what I want to say."

The lawyer paused a moment, squared his heavy shoulders, and went on: "Harvey Merrick and I went to school together, back East. We were dead in earnest, and we wanted you all to be proud of us some day. We meant to be great men. Even I, and I haven't lost my sense of humor, gentlemen, I meant to be a great man. I came back here to practise, and I found you didn't in the least want me to be a great man. You wanted me to be a shrewd lawyer—oh, yes! Our veteran here wanted me to get him an increase of pension, because he had dyspepsia; Phelps wanted a new county survey that would put the widow Wilson's little bottom farm inside his south line; Elder wanted to lend money at 5 per cent. a month, and get it collected; and Stark here wanted to wheedle old women up in Vermont into investing their annuities in real-estate mortgages that are not worth the paper they are written on. Oh, you needed me hard enough, and you'll go on needing me!

"Well, I came back here and became the damned shyster you wanted me to be. You pretend to have some sort of respect for me; and yet you'll stand up and throw mud at Harvey Merrick, whose soul you couldn't dirty and whose hands you couldn't tie. Oh, you're a discriminating lot of Christians! There have been times when the sight of Harvey's name in some Eastern paper has made me hang my head like a whipped dog; and, again, times when I liked to think of him off there in the world, away from all this hog-wallow, climbing the big, clean up-grade he'd set for himself.

"And we? Now that we've fought and lied and sweated and stolen, and hated as only the disappointed stragglers in a bitter, dead little western town know how to do, what have we got to show for it? Harvey Merrick wouldn't have given one sunset over your marshes for all you've got put together, and you know it. It's not for me to say why, in the inscrutable wisdom of God, a genius should ever have been called from this place of hatred and bitter waters; but I want this Boston man to know that the drivel he's been hearing here tonight is the only tribute any truly great man could have from such a lot of sick, side-tracked, burnt-dog, land-poor sharks as the here-present financiers of Sand City—upon which town may God have mercy!"

The lawyer thrust out his hand to Steavens as he passed him, caught up his overcoat in the hall, and had left the house before the Grand Army man had had time to lift his ducked head and crane his long neck about at his fellows.

Next day Jim Laird was drunk and unable to attend the funeral services. Steavens called twice at his office, but was compelled to start East without seeing him. He had a presentiment that he would hear from him again, and left his address on the lawyer's table; but if Laird found it, he never acknowledged it. The thing in him that Harvey Merrick had loved must have gone under ground with Harvey Merrick's coffin, for it never spoke again, and Jim got the cold he died of driving across the Colorado mountains to defend one of Phelps's sons who had got into trouble out there by cutting government timber.

1905

ELLEN GLASGOW

(1874–1945)

During a period of forty-five years, from 1897 to 1941, Ellen Glasgow published twenty volumes of fiction, nineteen of them full-length novels. The impressive fact is that they were consistent with each other in historical purpose and perspective, and in fulfilling a lofty aesthetic ideal which the author had determined upon from the beginning. Ellen Glasgow's fictional lifework was southern social history, focused mainly on Virginia; and her tradition was that of critical realism, which came to her through Dickens and her beloved Thackeray, in part through Zola, and even more from her close study of Balzac, who assembled his pioneering novels of contemporary French social history under a collective title, as Ellen Glasgow was later to do.

This writer's life and work were almost wholly of one fabric. Ellen Anderson Gholson Glasgow was born on April 22, 1874, in Richmond, the "Queensborough" of her novels. Her father, the manager of an iron works, traced his Virginian ancestry through several generations to pioneering Scottish immigrants who came to America to escape religious persecution. This stock, much of which settled in the Virginia highlands, was the genuine "vein of iron" to which the novelist referred in her famous novel.

In the usual tradition of the Scottish Covenanters, the Glasgows had contributed to the learned professions, to law, and to the ministry, so there was nothing surprising in the early intensity of Ellen Glasgow's love of learning—except, perhaps, that southern women of her generation were traditionally bent upon another career. Also, she

was frail in health, and disliked school. So, under private tutors, she studied fervidly at home, gaining knowledge of a wide range of literature, history, and philosophy. She read for the major examination in political economy given at the University of Virginia, which did not admit women, and she had the satisfaction of passing. She became interested in the contemporary conflict between religious faith and scientific skepticism, and explored the works of Darwin, Fiske, and the contemporary philosophy of science and psychology. She consciously rejected naturalism and the pessimistic direction of contemporary determinism—it was here that she departed from Zola; but she read with enthusiasm the new sociological literature, later declaring, "At eighteen I was the only socialist, I think, in Richmond." From youth she had the cosmopolitan viewpoint; with her family she resided in New York at frequent intervals, and she often traveled abroad, then and in later years. Her emotional involvement in the tension between her parents and the ultimate unfulfillment that circumstances imposed on her own love, as posthumously revealed in *The Woman Within*, only enriched her experience and understanding as a novelist. Her view of woman was large and sane and normal; she satirized the survival of the woman of southern chivalry and she understood the "new woman" of the period of the World War.

At eighteen she destroyed a first novel, and began *The Descendant*, but as a result of the shock and responsibilities that resulted from her mother's death, it was not published until 1897. This, and three other early novels written before 1908 deal largely with the social scene in New York, and in the whole view of her work, are of minor interest.

In 1900, however, at the age of twenty-six, she published *The Voice of the People*, which established the direction of her major novels, the "Old Dominion" cycle. Many have commented on the remarkable fact that no southern writer had previously produced a genuinely realistic novel of southern life. At an early period, as she later remarked, Miss Glasgow had decided that "what the South needs now is blood and irony"— she rebelled against the southern defeatism of the period of her youth, amid "the dark furies of the Reconstruction," and she resisted the long-surviving tendency of southerners to regard themselves as crushed by "invasion." In speaking of Dorinda (*Barren Ground*) she rejoices that "the spirit of fortitude has triumphed over * * * futility," and she advances the courageous conviction that "character is fate." In the preface to the same novel, in referring to the early motives which inspired her career, she says, "I had resolved that I would write of the South not sentimentally, as a conquered province, but dispassionately, as a part of a larger world." Her object was to write "not of Southern characteristics but of human nature."

In the eleven novels that compose the "Old Dominion" cycle

(1900–1935), the changing patterns of the social classes, of the industrial and agricultural economy, of individualism, of moral standards, of social convention, and of political life are intricately associated. *The Battle Ground* (1902) emphasizes the Civil War as the source of social change. As in *The Voice of the People*, the liberation and rise of the southern rural middle class —as differentiated from the old tidewater aristocracy—is emphasized in *The Deliverance* (1904), *The Miller of Old Church* (1911), and *Barren Ground* (1925). *The Romance of a Plain Man* (1909) deals again with the rise of the middle class, but the scene is urban— Richmond between 1875 and 1890—and involves politics and finance. *Virginia* (1913) and *Life and Gabriella* (1916) are full-length fictional studies of the "lady," a convention of southern chivalry which had a lingering and sometimes tragic survival. In the case of Virginia, exploited in her weakness by her ruthless husband, the result is tragic. Virginia is "capable of dying for an idea, but not of conceiving one," but Gabriella Fowler, in *Life and Gabriella*, in the midst of similar abuse on chivalric grounds conceives the idea of liberty, builds up a great business, and marries again, pretty much on her own terms. The two accepted masterpieces of the "Old Dominion" series, *Barren Ground* and *Vein of Iron* (1935), deal with women of great attractiveness and force who interpret a new southern society in terms of their own emotional honesty as women.

Probably afterville & revised material confronted a rigid society

Dorinda Oakley rescues her middle-class farming family from their shiftlessness, and while restoring the "barren ground" to fertility, resists a marriage designed on the old principles of sentiment and tradition. *Vein of Iron* remarkably reconstructs life in the Virginia hills during the mining days, known to the earlier Glasgows. However, its chief concern is with the period of the great depression of the early 1930's, and the scenes portraying the economic distress in Queensborough (Richmond) are as powerful as those depicting the past, while Ada Fincastle is perhaps the best of all Miss Glasgow's women characters.

Another cycle of novels, uniting social comedy with criticism of the new South after the first World War, produced two brilliant successes, *The Romantic Comedians* (1926) and *They Stooped to Folly* (1929). *The Sheltered Life* (1932) is only less good. The last of her novels,

In This Our Life (1941), was a remarkable experiment to come at the end of a long career. By means of narration and character portrayal, the author made a shrewd analysis of the behavior and attitudes of a southern community in the complex year of 1938–1939, on the eve of the second World War. The volume was awarded the Pulitzer Prize, shortly after Miss Glasgow had received the *Saturday Review of Literature* plaque for distinguished service to American letters. She died on November 20, 1945, in her old home at Richmond.

There are two collected editions, neither complete. The Old Dominion Edition, 8 vols., 1929–1933, contains revised texts and an interesting preface for each novel; the amplified Virginia Edition, 12 vols., 1938, includes new prefaces. These prefaces, collected in one volume, *A Certain Measure*, 1943, are a valuable source for study of the author's ideas. Her other important works are named in the above account, except for *The Freeman and Other Poems*, 1902. *Letters of Ellen Glasgow*, 1958, was edited by Blair Rouse. Her autobiography is *The Woman Within* (1954).

Jordan's End[1]

At the fork of the road there was the dead tree where buzzards were roosting, and through its boughs I saw the last flare of the sunset. On either side the November woods were flung in broken masses against the sky. When I stopped they appeared to move closer and surround me with vague, glimmering shapes. It seemed to me that I had been driving for hours; yet the ancient negro who brought the message had told me to follow the Old Stage Road till I came to Buzzard's Tree at the fork. "F'om dar on hit's moughty nigh ter Marse Jur'dn's place," the old man had assured me, adding tremulously, "en young Miss she sez you mus' come jes' ez quick ez

1. Ellen Glasgow made only one collection of her short stories, *The Shadowy Third and Other Stories* (1923), which contains "Jordan's End." It is certainly the most representative of her stories. The qualities that distinguish her novels are strongly represented here: her feeling for family tradition; her penetration of human character, normal and abnormal, and especially her subtle understanding of complex women; her sense of the life and the countryside of Virginia; and her characteristic style, fluent but precise. "Jordan's End" was first published in the 1923 volume.

you kin." I was young then (that was more than thirty years ago), and I was just beginning the practice of medicine in one of the more remote counties of Virginia.

My mare stopped, and leaning out, I gazed down each winding road, where it branched off, under half bared boughs, into the autumnal haze of the distance. In a little while the red would fade from the sky, and the chill night would find me still hesitating between those dubious ways which seemed to stretch into an immense solitude. While I waited uncertainly there was a stir in the boughs overhead and a buzzard's feather floated down and settled softly on the robe over my knees. In the effort to drive off depression, I laughed aloud and addressed my mare in a jocular tone:

"We'll choose the most God-forsaken of the two, and see where it leads us."

To my surprise the words brought an answer from the trees at my back. "If you're goin' to Isham's store, keep on the Old Stage Road," piped a voice from the underbrush.

Turning quickly, I saw the dwarfed figure of a very old man, with a hunched back, who was dragging a load of pine knots out of the woods. Though he was so stooped that his head reached scarcely higher than my wheel, he appeared to possess unusual vigor for one of his age and infirmities. He was dressed in a rough overcoat of some wood brown shade, beneath which I could see his overalls of blue jeans. Under a thatch of grizzled hair his shrewd little eyes twinkled cunningly, and his bristly chin jutted so far forward that it barely escaped the descending curve of his nose. I remember thinking that he could not be far from a hundred; his skin was so wrinkled and weather-beaten that, at a distance, I had mistaken him for a negro.

I bowed politely. "Thank you, but I am going to Jordan's End," I replied.

He cackled softly. "Then you take the bad road. Thar's Jur'dn's turnout." He pointed to the sunken trail, deep in mud, on the right. "An' if you ain't objectin' to a little comp'ny, I'd be obleeged if you'd give me a lift. I'm bound thar on my own o' count, an' it's a long ways to tote these here lightwood knots."

While I drew back my robe and made room for him, I watched him heave the load of resinous pine into the buggy, and then scramble with agility to his place at my side.

"My name is Peterkin," he remarked by way of introduction. "They call me Father Peterkin along o' the gran'child'en." He was a garrulous soul, I suspected, and would not be averse to imparting the information I wanted.

"There's not much travel this way," I began, as we turned out of the cleared space into the deep tunnel of the trees. Immediately the twilight enveloped us, though now and then the dusky glow in the sky was still visible. The air was sharp with the tang of autumn; with the effluvium of rotting leaves, the drift of wood smoke, the ripe flavor of crushed apples.

"Thar's nary a stranger, thoughten he was a doctor, been to Jur'dn's End as fur back as I kin recollect. Ain't you the new doctor?"

"Yes, I am the doctor." I glanced down at the gnomelike shape in the wood brown overcoat. "Is it much farther?"

"Naw, suh, we're all but thar jest as soon as we come out of Whitten woods."

"If the road is so little travelled, how do you happen to be going there?"

Without turning his head, the old man wagged his crescent shaped profile. "Oh, I live on the place. My son Tony works a slice of the farm on shares, and I manage to lend a hand at the harvest or corn shuckin', and, now-and-agen, with the cider. The old gentleman used to run the place that way afore he went deranged, an' now that the young one is laid up, thar ain't nobody to look arter the farm but Miss Judith. Them old ladies don't count. Thar's three of 'em, but they're all addle-brained an' look as if the buzzards had picked 'em. I reckon that comes from bein' shut up with crazy folks in that thar old tumbledown house. The roof ain't been patched fur so long that the shingles have most rotted away, an' thar's times, Tony says, when you kin skearcely hear yo' years fur the rumpus the wrens an' rats are makin' overhead."

"What is the trouble with them—the Jordans, I mean?"

"Jest run to seed, suh, I reckon."

"Is there no man of the family left?"

For a minute Father Peterkin made no reply. Then he shifted the bundle of pine knots, and responded warily. "Young Alan, he's still livin' on the old place, but I hear he's been took now, an' is goin' the way of all the rest of 'em. 'Tis a hard trial for Miss Judith, po' young thing, an' with a boy nine year old that's the very spit an' image of his pa. Wall, wall, I kin recollect away back yonder when old Mr. Timothy Jur'dn was the proudest man anywhar aroun' in these parts; but arter the War things sorter begun to go down hill with him, and he was obleeged to draw in his horns."

"Is he still living?"

The old man shook his head. "Mebbe he is, an' mebbe he ain't. Nobody knows but the Jur'dn's, an' they ain't tellin' fur the axin'."

"I suppose it was this Miss Judith who sent for me?"

" 'Twould most likely be she, suh. She was one of the Yardleys that lived over yonder at Yardleys' Field; an' when young Mr. Alan begun to take notice of her, 'twas the first time sence way back that one of the Jur'dn's had gone courtin' outside the family. That's the reason the blood went bad like it did, I reckon. Thar's a sayin' down aroun' here that Jur'dn an Jur'dn won't mix." The name was invariably called Jurdin by all classes; but I had already discovered that names are rarely pronounced as they are spelled in Virginia.

"Have they been married long?"

"Ten year or so, suh. I remember as well as if 'twas yestiddy the day young Alan brought her home as a bride, an' thar warn't a soul besides the three daft old ladies to welcome her. They drove over in my son Tony's old buggy, though 'twas spick an' span then. I was goin' to the house on an arrant, an' I was standin' right down thar at the ice pond when they come by. She hadn't been much in these parts, an' none of us had ever seed her afore. When she looked up at young Alan her face was pink all over and her eyes war shinin' bright as the moon. Then the front do' opened an' them old ladies, as black as crows, flocked out on the po'ch. Thar never was anybody as peart-lookin' as Miss Judith was when she come here; but soon arterwards she begun to peak an' pine, though she never lost her sperits an' went mopin' roun' like all the other women folks at Jur'dn's End. They married sudden, an' folks do say she didn't know nothin' about the family, an' young Alan didn't know much mo' than she did. The old ladies had kep' the secret away from him, sorter believin' that what you don't know cyarn' hurt you. Anyways they never let it leak out tell arter his chile was born. Thar ain't never been but that one, an' old Aunt Jerusly declars he was born with a caul over his face, so mebbe things will be all right fur him in the long run."

"But who are the old ladies? Are their husbands living?"

When Father Peterkin answered the question he had dropped his voice to a hoarse murmur. "Deranged. All gone deranged," he replied.

I shivered, for a chill depression seemed to emanate from the November woods. As we drove on, I remembered grim tales of enchanted forests filled with evil faces and whispering voices. The scents of wood earth and rotting leaves invaded my brain like a magic spell. On either side the forest was as still as death. Not a leaf quivered, not a bird moved, not a small wild creature stirred in the underbrush. Only the glossy leaves and the scarlet berries of the holly appeared alive amid the bare interlacing branches of the trees. I began to long for an autumn clearing and the red light of the afterglow.

"Are they living or dead?" I asked presently.

"I've hearn strange tattle," answered the old man nervously, "but nobody kin tell. Folks do say as young Alan's pa is shut up in a padded place, and that his gran'pa died thar arter thirty years. His uncles went crazy too, an' the daftness is beginnin' to crop out in the women. Up tell now it has been mostly the men. One time I remember old Mr. Peter Jur'dn tryin' to burn down the place in the dead of the night. Thar's the end of the wood, suh. If you'll jest let me down here, I'll be gittin' along home across the old-field, an' thanky too."

At last the woods ended abruptly on the edge of an abandoned field which was thickly sown with scrub pine and broomsedge. The glow in the sky had faded now to a thin yellow-green, and a melancholy twilight pervaded the landscape. In this twilight I looked over the few sheep huddled together on the ragged lawn, and saw the old brick house crumbling beneath its rank growth of ivy. As I drew nearer I had the feeling that the surrounding desolation brooded there like some sinister influence.

Forlorn as it appeared at this first approach, I surmised that Jordan's End must have possessed once charm as well as distinction. The proportions of the Georgian front were impressive, and there was beauty of design in the quaint doorway, and in the steps of rounded stone which were brocaded now with a pattern of emerald moss. But the whole place was badly in need of repair. Looking up, as I stopped, I saw that the eaves were falling away, that crumpled shutters were sagging from loosened hinges, that odd scraps of hemp sacking or oil cloth were stuffed into windows where panes were missing. When I stepped on the floor of the porch, I felt the rotting boards give way under my feet.

After thundering vainly on the door, I descended the steps, and followed the beaten path that led round the west wing of the house. When I had passed an old box-wood tree at the corner, I saw a woman and a boy of nine years or so come out of a shed, which I took to be the smokehouse, and begin to gather chips from the woodpile. The woman carried a basket made of splits on her arm, and while she stooped to fill this, she talked to the child in a soft musical voice. Then, at a sound that I made, she put the basket aside, and rising to her feet, faced me in the pallid light from the sky. Her head was thrown back, and over her dress of some dark calico, a tattered gray shawl clung to her figure. That was thirty years ago; I am not young any longer; I have been in many countries since then, and looked on many women; but her face, with that wan light on it, is the last one I shall forget in my life. Beauty! Why, that woman will be beautiful when she is a skeleton, was the thought that flashed into my mind.

She was very tall, and so thin that her flesh seemed faintly luminous, as if an inward light pierced the transparent substance. It was the beauty, not of earth, but of triumphant spirit. Perfection, I suppose, is the rarest thing we achieve in this world of incessant compromise with inferior forms; yet the woman who stood there in that ruined place appeared to me to have stepped straight out of legend or allegory. The contour of her face was Italian in its pure oval; her hair swept in wings of dusk above her clear forehead; and, from the faintly shadowed hollows beneath her brows, the eyes that looked at me were purple-black, like dark pansies.

"I had given you up," she began in a low voice, as if she were afraid of being overheard. "You are the doctor?"

"Yes, I am the doctor. I took the wrong road and lost my way. Are you Mrs. Jordan?"

She bowed her head. "Mrs. Alan Jordan. There are three Mrs. Jordans besides myself. My husband's grandmother and the wives of his two uncles."

"And it is your husband who is ill?"

"My husband, yes. I wrote a few days ago to Doctor Carstairs." (Thirty years ago Carstairs, of Baltimore, was the leading alienist in the country.) "He is coming to-morrow morning; but last night my husband was so restless that I sent for you to-day." Her rich voice, vibrating with suppressed feeling, made me think of stained glass windows and low organ music.

"Before we go in," I asked, "will you tell me as much as you can?"

Instead of replying to my request, she turned and laid her hand on the boy's shoulder. "Take the chips to Aunt Agatha, Benjamin," she said, "and tell her that the doctor has come."

While the child picked up the basket and ran up the sunken steps to the door, she watched him with breathless anxiety. Not until he had disappeared into the hall did she lift her eyes to my face again. Then, without answering my question, she murmured, with a sigh which was like the voice of that autumn evening, "We were once happy here." She was trying, I realized, to steel her heart against the despair that threatened it.

My gaze swept the obscure horizon, and returned to the mouldering woodpile where we were standing. The yellow-green had faded from the sky, and the only light came from the house where a few scattered lamps were burning. Through the open door I could see the hall, as bare as if the house were empty, and the spiral staircase which crawled to the upper story. A fine old place once, but repulsive now in its abject decay, like some young blood of former days who has grown senile.

"Have you managed to wring a living out of the land?" I asked, because I could think of no words that were less compassionate.

"At first a poor one," she answered slowly. "We worked hard, harder than any negro in the fields, to keep things together, but we were happy. Then three years ago this illness came, and after that everything went against us. In the beginning it was simply brooding, a kind of melancholy, and we tried to ward it off by pretending that it was not real, that we imagined it. Only of late, when it became so much worse, have we admitted the truth, have we faced the reality——"

This passionate murmur, which had almost the effect of a chant rising out of the loneliness, was addressed, not to me, but to some abstract and implacable power. While she uttered it her composure was like the tranquillity of the dead. She did not lift her hand to hold her shawl, which was slipping unnoticed from her shoulders, and her eyes, so like dark flowers in their softness, did not leave my face.

"If you will tell me all, perhaps I may be able to help you," I said.

"But you know our story," she responded. "You must have heard it."

"Then it is true? Heredity, intermarriage, insanity?"

She did not wince at the bluntness of my speech. "My husband's grandfather is in an asylum, still living after almost thirty years. His father—my husband's, I mean—died there a few years ago. Two of his uncles are there. When it began I don't know, or how far back it reaches. We have never talked of it. We have tried always to forget it— Even now I cannot put the thing into words— My husband's mother died of a broken heart, but the grandmother and the two others are still living. You will see them when you go into the house. They are old women now, and they feel nothing."

"And there have been other cases?"

"I do not know. Are not four enough?"

"Do you know if it has assumed always the same form?" I was trying to be as brief as I could.

She flinched, and I saw that her unnatural calm was shaken at last. "The same, I believe. In the beginning there is melancholy, moping, Grandmother calls it, and then—" She flung out her arms with a despairing gesture, and I was reminded again of some tragic figure of legend.

"I know, I know," I was young, and in spite of my pride, my voice trembled. "Has there been in any case partial recovery, recurring at intervals?"

"In his grandfather's case, yes. In the others none. With them it has been hopeless from the beginning."

"And Carstairs is coming?"

"In the morning. I should have waited, but last night—" Her voice broke, and she drew the tattered shawl about her with a shiver. "Last night something happened. Something happened," she repeated, and could not go on. Then, collecting her strength with an

effort which made her tremble like a blade of grass in the wind, she
continued more quietly, "Today he has been better. For the first
time he has slept, and I have been able to leave him. Two of the
hands from the fields are in the room." Her tone changed suddenly,
and a note of energy passed into it. Some obscure resolution brought
a tinge of color to her pale cheek. "I must know," she added, "if
this is as hopeless as all the others."

I took a step toward the house. "Carstairs's opinion is worth as
much as that of any man living," I answered.

"But will he tell me the truth?"

I shook my head. "He will tell you what he thinks. No man's
judgment is infallible."

Turning away from me, she moved with an energetic step to the
house. As I followed her into the hall the threshold creaked under
my tread, and I was visited by an apprehension, or, if you prefer,
by a superstitious dread of the floor above. Oh, I got over that kind
of thing before I was many years older; though in the end I gave up
medicine, you know, and turned to literature as a safer outlet for a
suppressed imagination.

But the dread was there at that moment, and it was not lessened
by the glimpse I caught, at the foot of the spiral staircase, of a
scantily furnished room, where three lean black-robed figures, as impassive as the Fates, were grouped in front of a wood fire. They were
doing something with their hands. Knitting, crocheting, or plaiting
straw?

At the head of the stairs the woman stopped and looked back at
me. The light from the kerosene lamp on the wall fell over her, and
I was struck afresh not only by the alien splendor of her beauty, but
even more by the look of consecration, of impassioned fidelity that
illumined her face.

"He is very strong," she said in a whisper. "Until this trouble
came on him he had never had a day's illness in his life. We hoped
that hard work, not having time to brood, might save us; but it has
only brought the thing we feared sooner."

There was a question in her eyes, and I responded in the same
subdued tone. "His health, you say, is good?" What else was there
for me to ask when I understood everything?

A shudder ran through her frame. "We used to think that a
blessing, but now—" She broke off and then added in a lifeless
voice, "We keep two field hands in the room day and night, lest
one should forget to watch the fire, or fall asleep."

A sound came from the room at the end of the hall, and, without
finishing her sentence, she moved swiftly toward the closed door.
The apprehension, the dread, or whatever you choose to call it, was
so strong upon me, that I was seized by an impulse to turn and re-

treat down the spiral staircase. Yes, I know why some men turn cowards in battle.

"I have come back, Alan," she said in a voice that wrung my heartstrings.

The room was dimly lighted; and for a minute after I entered, I could see nothing clearly except the ruddy glow of the wood fire in front of which two negroes were seated on low wooden stools. They had kindly faces, these men; there was a primitive humility in their features, which might have been modeled out of the dark earth of the fields.

Looking round the next minute, I saw that a young man was sitting away from the fire, huddled over in a cretonne-covered chair with a high back and deep wings. At our entrance the negroes glanced up with surprise; but the man in the winged chair neither lifted his head nor turned his eyes in our direction. He sat there, lost within the impenetrable wilderness of the insane, as remote from us and from the sound of our voices as if he were the inhabitant of an invisible world. His head was sunk forward; his eyes were staring fixedly at some image we could not see; his fingers, moving restlessly, were plaiting and unplaiting the fringe of a plaid shawl. Distraught as he was, he still possessed the dignity of mere physical perfection. At his full height he must have measured not under six feet three; his hair was the color of ripe wheat, and his eyes, in spite of their fixed gaze, were as blue as the sky after rain. And this was only the beginning, I realized. With that constitution, that physical frame, he might live to be ninety.

"Alan!" breathed his wife again in her pleading murmur.

If he heard her voice, he gave no sign of it. Only when she crossed the room and bent over his chair, he put out his hand, with a gesture of irritation, and pushed her away, as if she were a veil of smoke which came between him and the object at which he was looking. Then his hand fell back to its old place, and he resumed his mechanical plaiting of the fringe.

The woman lifted her eyes to mine. "His father did that for twenty years," she said in a whisper that was scarcely more than a sigh of anguish.

When I had made my brief examination, we left the room as we had come, and descended the stairs together. The three old women were still sitting in front of the wood fire. I do not think they had moved since we went upstairs; but, as we reached the hall below, one of them, the youngest, I imagine, rose from her chair, and came out to join us. She was crocheting something soft and small, an infant's sacque, I perceived as she approached, of pink wool. The ball had rolled from her lap as she stood up, and it trailed after her now, like a woollen rose, on the bare floor. When the skein pulled at her, she turned back and stooped to pick up the ball, which she rewound with caressing fingers. Good God, an infant's sacque in that house!

"Is it the same thing?" she asked.

"Hush!" responded the younger woman kindly. Turning to me she added, "We cannot talk here," and opening the door, passed out on the porch. Not until we had reached the lawn, and walked in silence to where my buggy stood beneath an old locust tree, did she speak.

Then she said only, "You know now?"

"Yes, I know," I replied, averting my eyes from her face while I gave my directions as briefly as I could. "I will leave an opiate," I said. "Tomorrow, if Carstairs should not come, send for me again. If he does come, I will talk to him and see you afterward."

"Thank you," she answered gently; and taking the bottle from my hand, she turned away and walked quickly back to the house.

I watched her as long as I could; and then getting into my buggy, I turned my mare's head toward the woods, and drove by moonlight, past Buzzard's Tree and over the Old Stage Road, to my home. "I will see Carstairs to-morrow," was my last thought that night before I slept.

But, after all, I saw Carstairs only for a minute as he was taking the train. Life at its beginning and its end had filled my morning; and when at last I reached the little station, Carstairs had paid his visit, and was waiting on the platform for the approaching express. At first he showed a disposition to question me about the shooting, but as soon as I was able to make my errand clear, his face clouded.

"So you've been there?" he said. "They didn't tell me. An interesting case, if it were not for that poor woman. Incurable, I'm afraid, when you consider the predisposing causes. The race is pretty well deteriorated, I suppose. God! what isolation! I've advised her to send him away. There are three others, they tell me, at Staunton."

The train came; he jumped on it, and was whisked away while I gazed after him. After all, I was none the wiser because of the great reputation of Carstairs.

All that day I heard nothing more from Jordan's End; and then, early next morning, the same decrepit negro brought me a message.

"Young Miss, she tole me ter ax you ter come along wid me jes' ez soon ez you kin git ready."

"I'll start, Uncle, and I'll take you with me."

My mare and buggy stood at the door. All I needed to do was to put on my overcoat, pick up my hat, and leave word, for a possible patient, that I should return before noon. I knew the road now, and I told myself, as I set out, that I would make as quick a trip as I could. For two nights I had been haunted by the memory of that man in the armchair, plaiting and unplaiting the fringe of the plaid shawl. And his father had done that, the woman had told me, for twenty years!

It was a brown autumn morning, raw, windless, with an overcast sky and a peculiar illusion of nearness about the distance. A high wind had blown all night, but at dawn it had dropped suddenly, and now there was not so much as a ripple in the broomsedge. Over the fields, when we came out of the woods, the thin trails of blue smoke were as motionless as cobwebs. The lawn surrounding the house looked smaller than it had appeared to me in the twilight, as if the barren fields had drawn closer since my last visit. Under the trees, where the few sheep were browsing, the piles of leaves lay in windrifts along the sunken walk and against the wings of the house.

When I knocked the door was opened by one of the old women, who held a streamer of black cloth or rusty crape in her hands.

"You may go straight upstairs," she croaked; and, without waiting for an explanation, I entered the hall and ran up the stairs.

The door of the room was closed, and I opened it noiselessly, and stepped over the threshold. My first sensation, as I entered, was one of cold. Then I saw that the windows were wide open, and that the room seemed to be full of people, though, as I made out presently, there was no one there except Alan Jordan's wife, her little son, the two old aunts, and an aged crone of a negress. On the bed there was something under a yellow sheet of fine linen (what the negroes call "a burial sheet," I suppose), which had been handed down from some more affluent generation.

When I went over, after a minute, and turned down one corner of the covering, I saw that my patient of the other evening was dead. Not a line of pain marred his features, not a thread of gray dimmed the wheaten gold of his hair. So he must have looked, I thought, when she first loved him. He had gone from life, not old, enfeebled and repulsive, but enveloped still in the romantic illusion of their passion.

As I entered, the two old women, who had been fussing about the bed, drew back to make way for me, but the witch of a negress did not pause in the weird chant, an incantation of some sort, which she was mumbling. From the rag carpet in front of the empty fireplace, the boy, with his father's hair and his mother's eyes, gazed at me silently, broodingly, as if I were trespassing; and by the open window, with her eyes on the ashen November day, the young wife stood motionless. While I looked at her a redbird flew out of the boughs of a cedar, and she followed it with her eyes.

"You sent for me?" I said to her.

She did not turn. She was beyond the reach of my voice, of any voice, I imagine; but one of the palsied women answered my question.

"He was like this when we found him this morning," she said. "He had a bad night, and Judith and the two hands were up with him until daybreak. Then he seemed to fall asleep, and Judith sent the hands, turn about, to get their breakfast."

While she spoke my eyes were on the bottle I had left there. Two nights ago it had been full, and now it stood empty, without a cork, on the mantelpiece. They had not even thrown it away. It was typical of the pervading inertia of the place that the bottle should still be standing there awaiting my visit.

For an instant the shock held me speechless; when at last I found my voice it was to ask:

"When did it happen?"

The old woman who had spoken took up the story. "Nobody knows. We have not touched him. No one but Judith has gone near him." Her words trailed off into unintelligible muttering. If she had ever had her wits about her, I dare say fifty years at Jordan's End had unsettled them completely.

I turned to the woman at the window. Against the gray sky and the black intersecting branches of the cedar, her head, with its austere perfection, was surrounded by that visionary air of legend. So Antigone might have looked on the day of her sacrifice, I reflected. I had never seen a creature who appeared so withdrawn, so detached, from all human associations. It was as if some spiritual isolation divided her from her kind.

"I can do nothing," I said.

For the first time she looked at me, and her eyes were unfathomable. "No, you can do nothing," she answered. "He is safely dead."

The negress was still crooning on; the other old women were fussing helplessly. It was impossible in their presence, I felt, to put in words the thing I had to say.

"Will you come downstairs with me?" I asked. "Outside of this house?"

Turning quietly, she spoke to the boy. "Run out and play, dear. He would have wished it."

Then, without a glance toward the bed, or the old women gathered about it, she followed me over the threshold, down the stairs, and out on the deserted lawn. The ashen day could not touch her, I saw then. She was either so remote from it, or so completely part of it, that she was impervious to its sadness. Her white face did not become more pallid as the light struck it; her tragic eyes did not grow deeper; her frail figure under the thin shawl did not shiver in the raw air. She felt nothing, I realized suddenly.

Wrapped in that silence as in a cloak, she walked across the windrifts of leaves to where my mare was waiting. Her step was so slow, so unhurried, that I remember thinking she moved like one who had all eternity before her. Oh, one has strange impressions, you know, at such moments!

In the middle of the lawn, where the trees had been stripped bare in the night, and the leaves were piled in long mounds like double graves, she stopped and looked in my face. The air was so still that the whole place might have been in a trance or asleep. Not a branch moved, not a leaf rustled on the ground, not a sparrow twittered in the ivy; and even the few sheep stood motionless, as if they were under a spell. Farther away, beyond the sea of broomsedge, where no wind stirred, I saw the flat desolation of the landscape. Nothing moved on the earth, but high above, under the leaden clouds, a buzzard was sailing.

I moistened my lips before I spoke. "God knows I want to help you!" At the back of my brain a hideous question was drumming. How had it happened? Could she have killed him? Had that delicate creature nerved her will to the unspeakable act? It was incredible. It was inconceivable. And yet. . . .

"The worst is over," she answered quietly, with that tearless agony which is so much more terrible than any outburst of grief. "Whatever happens, I can never go through the worst again. Once in the beginning he wanted to die. His great fear was that he might live too long, until it was too late to save himself. I made him wait then. I held him back by a promise."

So she had killed him, I thought. She went on steadily, after a minute, and I doubted again.

"Thank God, it was easier for him than he feared it would be," she murmured.

No, it was not conceivable. He must have bribed one of the negroes. But who had stood by and watched without intercepting? Who had been in the room? Well, either way! "I will do all I can to help you," I said.

Her gaze did not waver. "There is so little that any one can do now," she responded, as if she had not understood what I meant. Suddenly, without the warning of a sob, a cry of despair went out of her, as if it were torn from her breast. "He was my life," she cried, "and I must go on!"

So full of agony was the sound that it seemed to pass like a gust of wind over the broomsedge. I waited until the emptiness had opened and closed over it. Then I asked as quietly as I could:

"What will you do now?"

She collected herself with a shudder of pain. "As long as the old people live, I am tied here. I must bear it out to the end. When they die, I shall go away and find work. I am sending my boy to school. Doctor Carstairs will look after him, and he will help me when the time comes. While he needs me, there is no release."

While I listened to her, I knew that the question on my lips would never be uttered. I should always remain ignorant of the truth. The thing I feared most, standing there alone with her, was that some accident might solve the mystery before I could escape. My eyes left her face and wandered over the dead leaves at our feet. No, I had nothing to ask.

"Shall I come again?" That was all.

She shook her head. "Not unless I send for you. If I need you, I will send for you," she answered; but in my heart I knew that she would never send for me.

I held out my hand, but she did not take it; and I felt that she meant me to understand, by her refusal, that she was beyond all consolation and all companionship. She was nearer to the bleak sky and the deserted fields than she was to her kind.

As she turned away, the shawl slipped from her shoulders to the dead leaves over which she was walking; but she did not stoop to recover it, nor did I make a movement to follow her. Long after she had entered the house I stood there, gazing down on the garment that she had dropped. Then climbing into my buggy, I drove across the field into the woods.

1923

Revaluation – "Little Renaissance"

STEPHEN VINCENT BENÉT
(1898–1943)

Every so often in the history of our literature, a new writer, rediscovering America, has been freshly overwhelmed by the meaning of its history, the daring of its adventures in human welfare and democracy, the dramatic power of its epic stories. Stephen Vincent Benét is the most recent of these, in a tradition influenced by such varied writers as Crèvecœur and Irving, Bryant and Cooper, Hawthorne and Longfellow and Whitman.

Benét's work was particularly refreshing in the midst of the complex events and the brooding literature of the period between the two wars. Although he preserved a high standard and his writing had the intensity and truth of serious literature, he was master of a simple and familiar style showing the influence of ballad and folk tale, and he won the affection of a large reading public. He had the gift of narrative in both his poetry and his short stories, and possessed the ability to retain the substantial truth of American history and character while translating it into the simpler symbols of the national myth. Although he died at forty-five, partly as a result of overstraining himself in patriotic propagandist work during the war years, he left an enduring legacy of national literature.

Stephen Vincent Benét was born in Bethlehem, Pennsylvania, in 1898. He was the son of an Army officer, and the younger brother of William Rose Benét, also a poet of substantial reputation. He attended schools in California and Georgia, where his father was stationed. By the time he entered Yale in 1915, Benét was already a prize-winning author of juvenilia (published in *St. Nicholas* and elsewhere) and had collected a volume of dramatic monologues. Fellow underclassmen were Archibald MacLeish, Philip Barry, and Thornton Wilder, all then practicing their chosen craft in the *Yale Literary Magazine*, which Benét edited in his senior year. An undergraduate prize poem—a study of Keats— was published as a pamphlet, and before he was graduated, his second volume of verse, *Young Adventure*, appeared in print. The majority of these early verses reflect his reading, but the models are excellent Elizabethan and romantic writers, and the young poet was already a good craftsman. In 1920 and 1921 he continued as a graduate student, first at Yale, where he offered a volume of poems, *Heavens and Earth* (1920), as a master's thesis, and then at the Sorbonne, in Paris. There he met his wife. Before returning to the United States he had written and published two novels.

Prolific and versatile, he found a good literary market almost at once. His first success was in the field of the short story. Those of his stories most likely to live deal with American history and traditional themes; among them are "Jacob and the Indians," reprinted in this volume, and such other well-known stories as "Johnny Pye and the Fool Killer" and "The Devil and Daniel Webster." The latter he used again as the libretto for a one-act folk opera with music by Douglas Moore, and still later he based on it a motion picture script that resulted in the memorable performance of Walter Huston as the Devil. But Benét's stories of contemporary life are also popular and well written, although they are usually thought to have less individual character than those on historical themes or American folklore. Benét wrote three additional novels, and they had a passing success, but none of his longer fiction now seems noteworthy.

His poetry soon became the best-known vehicle for his versatile talent. In 1923, his remarkable "King David" was the winner of the *Nation's* poetry prize. It was also in 1923 that "The Ballad of William Sycamore" provided the first assured evidence of his command of the ballad on an American historical theme. Three years later the award of a Guggenheim Fellowship afforded him the leisure to write the poem which has become his best-known work. He had been interested in the Civil War since boyhood, when his father's military library was his first source of inspiration. Now he planned to write a long epic for which the meaning of the Civil War, conceived as history and as American myth, would provide the motivation. The poem was written in Paris and published as *John Brown's Body* in 1928. It was awarded the Pulitzer Prize. An immediate success, it has remained a standard work of our popular literature.

Benét's health was never robust, but he lived for many years at the highest tension, driven by his literary enthusiasms and humanitarian idealism. Tireless in the interest of younger writers, he became editor of the Yale Series of Younger Poets. He was vice-president of the National Institute of Arts and Letters. He gave much time to the staff work of the *Saturday Review of Literature*. The depression years caused him deep concern, and he became involved in writing which encouraged the national faith during those years. As the growing threat to democracy became concrete in the rising tide of European totalitarianism, he devoted much of his energy to public lectures and radio programs calculated to arouse the nation to the challenge of the inevitable World War. The poems of this period, likewise directed toward this end, are more than mere propaganda, and seem to apply also to later crises of the same character. They were collected in *Burning City* (1936).

At the time of his sudden death in 1943, Benét had virtually completed *Western Star* (1943, Pulitzer Prize 1944), another epical narrative, to which his brother, William Rose Benét, gave the final touches before publication. It was the first part of a projected work, perhaps of several volumes, in which the poet intended to trace the historical and human impulses which caused the westward surge of peoples from European lands to the American shores and out across the great continent to the final ocean. The published portion centers on Jamestown and Plymouth.

There has been some tendency to dismiss Benét as merely a popular poet, and of course it is still too early for a definitive judgment; but already a considerable fraction of his works have long outlived the life span of popular ephemera, and continue to excite the admiration of new readers.

There is no definitive edition of Benét's works. The most considerable collection is *Selected Works of Stephen Vincent Benét*, 2 vols., 1942. Major volumes of his poems are *Heavens and Earth*, 1920; *The Ballad of William Sycamore, 1790–1880*, 1923; *King David*, 1923; *Tiger Joy*, 1925; *John Brown's Body*, 1928; *Ballads and Poems, 1915–1930*, 1931; *A Book of Americans* (with Rosemary Benét), 1933; *Burning City*, 1936; *Western Star*, 1943. Benét's stories are collected in *The Barefoot Saint*, 1929; *The Devil and Daniel Webster*, 1937; *Thirteen O'Clock, Stories of Several Worlds*, 1937; *Johnny Pye and the Fool Killer*, 1938; *Tales Before Midnight*, 1939. *Twenty-Five Short Stories*, 1943, combines *Thirteen O'Clock* and *Tales Before Midnight*. Benét's addresses, radio scripts, and other war pieces are collected in *We Stand United*, 1945.

The first biography is Charles Fenton, *Stephen Vincent Benét: The Life and Times * * * *, 1958.

Jacob and the Indians

It goes back to the early days—may God profit all who lived then —and the ancestors.

Well, America, you understand, in those days was different. It was a nice place, but you wouldn't believe it if you saw it today. Without busses, without trains, without states, without Presidents, nothing!

With nothing but colonists and Indians and wild woods all over the country and wild animals to live in the wild woods. Imagine such a place! In these days, you children don't even think about it; you read about it in the schoolbooks, but what is that? And I put in a call to my daughter, in California, and in three minutes I am saying "Hello, Rosie," and there it is Rosie and she is telling me about the weather, as if I wanted to know! But things were not always that way. I remember my own days, and they were different. And in the times of my grandfather's grandfather, they were different still. Listen to the story.

My grandfather's grandfather was Jacob Stein, and he came from Rettelsheim, in Germany. To Philadelphia he came, an orphan in a sailing ship, but not a common man. He had learning—he had been to the *chedar*[1]—he could have been a scholar among the scholars. Well, that is the way things happen in this bad world. There was a plague and a new grand duke—things are always so. He would say little of it afterward—they had left his teeth in his mouth, but he would say little of it. He did not have to say—we are children of the Dispersion—we know a black day when it comes.

Yet imagine—a young man with fine dreams and learning, a scholar with a pale face and narrow shoulders, set down in those early days in such a new country. Well, he must work, and he did. It was very fine, his learning, but it did not fill his mouth. He must carry a pack on his back and go from door to door with it. That was no disgrace; it was so that many began. But it was not expounding the Law, and at first he was very homesick. He would sit in his room at night, with the one candle, and read the preacher Koheleth,[2] till the bitterness of the preacher rose in his mouth. Myself, I am sure that Koheleth was a great preacher, but if he had had a good wife he would have been a more cheerful man. They had too many wives in those old days—it confused them. But Jacob was young.

As for the new country where he had come, it was to him a place of exile, large and frightening. He was glad to be out of the ship, but, at first, that was all. And when he saw his first real Indian in the street—well, that was a day! But the Indian, a tame one, bought a ribbon from him by signs, and after that he felt better. Nevertheless, it seemed to him at times that the straps of the pack cut into his very soul, and he longed for the smell of the *chedar*

---

1. Usually, "cheder." Here boys from seven to thirteen were taught to read the Pentateuch and prayer book in Hebrew.

2. Hebrew name for the book of Ecclesiastes in the Bible. Both words may be translated, "the preacher."

and the quiet streets of Rettelsheim and the good smoked goose-breast pious housewives keep for the scholar. But there is no going back—there is never any going back.

All the same, he was a polite young man, and a hardworking. And soon he had a stroke of luck—or at first it seemed so. It was from Simon Ettelsohn that he got the trinkets for his pack, and one day he found Simon Ettelsohn arguing a point of the Law with a friend, for Simon was a pious man and well thought of in the Congregation Mikveh Israel.[3] Our grandfather's grandfather stood by very modestly at first—he had come to replenish his pack and Simon was his employer. But finally his heart moved within him, for both men were wrong, and he spoke and told them where they erred. For half an hour he spoke, with his pack still upon his shoulders, and never has a text been expounded with more complexity, not even by the great Reb Samuel. Till, in the end, Simon Ettelsohn threw up his hands and called him a young David and a candle of learning. Also, he allowed him a more profitable route of trade. But, best of all, he invited young Jacob to his house, and there Jacob ate well for the first time since he had come to Philadelphia. Also he laid eyes upon Miriam Ettelsohn for the first time, and she was Simon's youngest daughter and a rose of Sharon.

After that, things went better for Jacob, for the protection of the strong is like a rock and a well. But yet things did not go altogether as he wished. For, at first, Simon Ettelsohn made much of him, and there was stuffed fish and raisin wine for the young scholar, though he was a peddler. But there is a look in a man's eyes that says "H'm? Son-in-law?" and that look Jacob did not see. He was modest—he did not expect to win the maiden overnight, though he longed for her. But gradually it was borne in upon him what he was in the Ettelsohn house—a young scholar to be shown before Simon's friends, but a scholar whose learning did not fill his mouth. He did not blame Simon for it, but it was not what he had intended. He began to wonder if he would ever get on in the world at all, and that is not good for any man.

Nevertheless, he could have borne it, and the aches and pains of his love, had it not been for Meyer Kappelhuist. Now, there was a pushing man! I speak no ill of anyone, not even of your Aunt Cora, and she can keep the DeGroot silver if she finds it in her heart to do so; who lies down in the straw with a dog, gets up with fleas. But this Meyer Kappelhuist! A big, red-faced fellow from Holland with shoulders the size of a barn door and red hair on the backs of his hands. A big mouth for eating and drinking and telling schnorrer stories—and he talked about the Kappelhuists, in Holland, till you'd think they were made of gold. The crane says, "I am really a peacock—at least on my mother's side." And yet, a thriving man—that could not be denied. He had started with a pack, like our grandfather's grandfather, and now he was trading with the Indians and making money hand over fist. It seemed to Jacob that he could never go to the Ettelsohn house without meeting Meyer and hearing about those Indians. And it dried the words in Jacob's mouth and made his heart burn.

For, no sooner would our grandfather's grandfather begin to expound a text or a proverb, than he would see Meyer Kappelhuist looking at the maiden. And when Jacob had finished his expounding, and there should have been a silence, Meyer Kappelhuist would take it upon himself to thank him, but always in a tone that said: "The Law is the Law, and the Prophets are the Prophets, but prime beaver is also prime beaver,[4] my little scholar!" It took the pleasure from Jacob's learning and the joy of the maiden from his heart. Then he would sit silent and burning, while Meyer told a great tale of Indians, slapping his hands on his knees. And in the end he was always careful to ask Jacob how many needles and pins he had sold that day; and when Jacob told him, he would smile and say very smoothly that all things had small beginnings, till the maiden herself could not keep from a little smile. Then, desperately, Jacob would rack his brains for more interesting matter. He would tell of the wars of the Maccabees[5] and the glory of the Temple. But even as he told them, he felt they were far away. Whereas Meyer and his accursed Indians were there, and the maiden's eyes shone at his words.

Finally he took his courage in both hands and went to Simon Ettelsohn. It took much for him to do it, for he had not been brought up to strive with men, but with words. But it seemed to him now that everywhere he went he heard of nothing but Meyer Kappelhuist and his trading with the Indians, till he thought it would drive him mad. So he went to Simon Ettelsohn in his shop.

"I am weary of this narrow trading in pins and needles," he said, without more words.

Simon Ettelsohn looked at him keenly; for while he was an ambitious man, he was kindly as well.

"*Nu*," he said. "A nice little trade you have and the people like you. I myself started in with less. What would you have more?"

"I would have much more," said our grandfather's grandfather

---

4. Beaver was then the most valuable fur, often used in place of money, and obtained chiefly through trade with the Indians.

5. 1 and 2 Maccabees, in the Apocrypha, recount the resistance of a line of Hebrew princes against the efforts of Syrian rulers (175–135 B.C.) to overcome the Jews and install a pagan religion in Palestine.

stiffly. "I would have a wife and a home in this new country. But how shall I keep a wife? On needles and pins?"

"*Nu*, it has been done," said Simon Ettelsohn, smiling a little. "You are a good boy, Jacob, and we take an interest in you. Now, if it is a question of marriage, there are many worthy maidens. Asher Levy, the baker, has a daughter. It is true that she squints a little, but her heart is of gold." He folded his hands and smiled.

"It is not of Asher Levy's daughter I am thinking," said Jacob, taken aback. Simon Ettelsohn nodded his head and his face grew grave.

"*Nu*, Jacob," he said. "I see what is in your heart. Well, you are a good boy, Jacob, and a fine scholar. And if it were in the old country, I am not saying. But here, I have one daughter married to a Seixas and one to a Da Silva. You must see that makes a difference." And he smiled the smile of a man well pleased with his world.

"And if I were such a one as Meyer Kappelhuist?" said Jacob, bitterly.

"Now—well, that is a little different," said Simon Ettelsohn sensibly. "For Meyer trades with the Indians. It is true, he is a little rough. But he will die a rich man."

"I will trade with the Indians too," said Jacob, and trembled.

Simon Ettelsohn looked at him as if he had gone out of his mind. He looked at his narrow shoulders and his scholar's hands.

"Now Jacob," he said soothingly, "do not be foolish. A scholar you are, and learned, not an Indian trader. Perhaps in a store you would do better. I can speak to Aaron Copras. And sooner or later we will find you a nice maiden. But to trade with Indians—well, that takes a different sort of man. Leave that to Meyer Kappelhuist."

"And your daughter, that rose of Sharon? Shall I leave her, too, to Meyer Kappelhuist?" cried Jacob.

Simon Ettelsohn looked uncomfortable.

"*Nu*, Jacob," he said. "Well, it is not settled, of course. But—"

"I will go forth against him as David went against Goliath," said our grandfather's grandfather wildly. "I will go forth into the wilderness. And God should judge the better man!"

Then he flung his pack on the floor and strode from the shop. Simon Ettelsohn called out after him, but he did not stop for that. Nor was it in his heart to go and seek the maiden. Instead, when he was in the street, he counted the money he had. It was not much. He had meant to buy his trading goods on credit from Simon Ettelsohn, but now he could not do that. He stood in the sunlit street of Philadelphia, like a man bereft of hope.

Nevertheless, he was stubborn—though how stubborn he did not yet know. And though he was bereft of hope, he found his feet taking him to the house of Raphael Sanchez.

Now, Raphael Sanchez could have bought and sold Simon Ettelsohn twice over. An arrogant old man he was, with fierce black eyes, and a beard that was whiter than snow. He lived apart, in his big house with his granddaughter, and men said he was very learned, but also very disdainful, and that to him a Jew was not a Jew who did not come of the pure sephardic[6] strain.

Jacob had seen him, in the Congregation Mikveh Israel, and to Jacob he had looked like an eagle, and fierce as an eagle. Yet now, in his need, he found himself knocking at that man's door.

It was Raphael Sanchez himself who opened. "And what is for sale today, peddler?" he said, looking scornfully at Jacob's jacket where the pack straps had worn it.

"A scholar of the Law is for sale," said Jacob in his bitterness, and he did not speak in the tongue he had learned in this country, but in Hebrew.

The old man stared at him a moment.

"Now am I rebuked," he said. "For you have the tongue. Enter, my guest," and Jacob touched the scroll[7] by the doorpost and went in.

They shared the noon meal at Raphael Sanchez's table. It was made of dark, glowing mahogany, and the light sank into it as sunlight sinks into a pool. There were many precious things in that room, but Jacob had no eyes for them. When the meal was over and the blessing said, he opened his heart and spoke, and Raphael Sanchez listened, stroking his beard with one hand. When the young man had finished, he spoke.

"So, Scholar," he said, though mildly, "you have crossed an ocean that you might live and not die, and yet all you see is a girl's face."

"Did not Jacob serve seven years for Rachel?"[8] said our grandfather's grandfather.

"Twice seven, Scholar," said Raphael Sanchez dryly, "but that was in the blessed days." He stroked his beard again. "Do you know why I came to this country?" he said.

"No," said Jacob Stein.

"It was not for the trading," said Raphael Sanchez. "My house has lent money to kings. A little fish, a few furs—what are they to my house? No, it was for the promise—the promise of Penn—that this land should be an habitation and a refuge, not only for the

---

6. Descendants of the Jews of Spain and Portugal.
7. Scroll of the Law, marking a strict Jewish household.
8. *Cf.* Genesis xxix, xxx. Jacob served Laban seven years for Rachel, but was tricked into marrying Leah, the older sister, and had to serve seven more years for Rachel, whom he loved, and who bore him Joseph.

Gentiles. Well, we know Christian promises. But so far, it has been kept. Are you spat upon in the street here, Scholar of the Law?"

"No," said Jacob. "They call me Jew, now and then. But the Friends, though Gentile, are kind."

"It is not so in all countries," said Raphael Sanchez, with a terrible smile.

"No," said Jacob quietly, "it is not."

The old man nodded. "Yes, one does not forget that," he said. "The spittle wipes off the cloth, but one does not forget. One does not forget the persecutor or the persecuted. That is why they think me mad, in the Congregation Mikveh Israel, when I speak what is in my mind. For, look you"—and he pulled a map from a drawer —"here is what we know of these colonies, and here and here our people make a new beginning, in another air. But here is New France—see it?—and down the great river come the French traders and their Indians."

"Well?" said Jacob in puzzlement.

"Well?" said Raphael Sanchez. "Are you blind? I do not trust the King of France—the king before him drove out the Huguenots, and who knows what he may do? And if they hold the great rivers against us, we shall never go westward."

"We?" said Jacob in bewilderment.

"We," said Raphael Sanchez. He struck his hand on the map. "Oh, they cannot see it in Europe—not even their lords in parliament and their ministers of state," he said. "They think this is a mine, to be worked as the Spaniards worked Potosi,[9] but it is not a mine. It is something beginning to live, and it is faceless and nameless yet. But it is our lot to be part of it—remember that in the wilderness, my young scholar of the Law. You think you are going there for a girl's face, and that is well enough. But you may find something there you did not expect to find."

He paused and his eyes had a different look.

"You see, it is the trader first," he said. "Always the trader, before the settled man. The Gentiles will forget that, and some of our own folk too. But one pays for the land of Canaan;[1] one pays in blood and sweat."

Then he told Jacob what he would do for him and dismissed him, and Jacob went home to his room with his head buzzing strangely. For at times it seemed to him that the Congregation Mikveh Israel was right in thinking Raphael Sanchez half mad. And at other times it seemed to him that the old man's words were a veil, and behind them moved and stirred some huge and unguessed shape. But chiefly he thought of the rosy cheeks of Miriam

9. A rich silver-mining city in Bolivia.
1. The Hebrew Land of Promise during the Egyptian captivity; later Pales-tine. See Genesis xii: 1–7, and Joshua i: 1–5.

Ettelsohn.

It was with the Scotchman, McCampbell, that Jacob made his first trading journey. A strange man was McCampbell, with grim features and cold blue eyes, but strong and kindly, though silent, except when he talked of the Ten Lost Tribes of Israel. For it was his contention that they were the Indians beyond the Western Mountains, and on this subject he would talk endlessly.

Indeed, they had much profitable conversation, McCampbell quoting the doctrines of a rabbi called John Calvin, and our grandfather's grandfather replying with Talmud and Torah[2] till McCampbell would almost weep that such a honey-mouthed scholar should be destined to eternal damnation. Yet he did not treat our grandfather's grandfather as one destined to eternal damnation, but as a man, and he, too, spoke of cities of refuge as a man speaks of realities, for his people had also been persecuted.

First they left the city behind them, and then the outlying towns and, soon enough, they were in the wilderness. It was very strange to Jacob Stein. At first he would wake at night and lie awake listening, while his heart pounded, and each rustle in the forest was the step of a wild Indian, and each screech of an owl in the forest the whoop before the attack. But gradually this passed. He began to notice how silently the big man, McCampbell, moved in the woods; he began to imitate him. He began to learn many things that even a scholar of the Law, for all his wisdom, does not know—the girthing of a packsaddle and the making of fires, the look of dawn in the forest and the look of evening. It was all very new to him, and sometimes he thought he would die of it, for his flesh weakened. Yet always he kept on.

When he saw his first Indians—in the woods, not in the town— his knees knocked together. They were there as he had dreamt of them in dreams, and he thought of the spirit, Iggereth-beth-Mathlan, and her seventy-eight dancing demons, for they were painted and in skins. But he could not let his knees knock together, before heathens and a Gentile, and the first fear passed. Then he found they were grave men, very ceremonious and silent at first, and then when the silence had been broken, full of curiosity. They knew McCampbell, but him they did not know, and they discussed him and his garments with the frankness of children, till Jacob felt naked before them, and yet not afraid. One of them pointed to the bag that hung at Jacob's neck—the bag in which, for safety's sake, he carried his phylactery[3]—then McCampbell said

2. The Talmud is the body of Jewish civil and canonical laws; the Torah, or the Pentateuch, comprises the first five books of the Bible, known as the "Law of Moses." These were quoted by Jacob in his argument against Calvin's *Institutes*, urged by the Presbyterian McCampbell.

3. A small box containing scriptural passages; one is bound to the brow, one on the left arm, during Hebrew ceremonial prayer.

something and the brown hand dropped quickly, but there was a buzz of talk.

Later on, McCampbell explained to him that they, too, wore little bags of deerskin and inside them sacred objects—and they thought, seeing his, that he must be a person of some note. It made him wonder. It made him wonder more to eat deer meat with them, by a fire.

It was a green world and a dark one that he had fallen in—dark with the shadow of the forest, green with its green. Through it ran trails and paths that were not yet roads or highways—that did not have the dust and smell of the cities of men, but another scent, another look. These paths Jacob noted carefully, making a map, for that was one of the instructions of Raphael Sanchez. It seemed a great labor and difficult and for no purpose; yet, as he had promised, so he did. And as they sank deeper and deeper into the depths of the forest, and he saw pleasant streams and wide glades, untenanted but by the deer, strange thoughts came over him. It seemed to him that the Germany he had left was very small and crowded together; it seemed to him that he had not known there was so much width to the world.

Now and then he would dream back—dream back to the quiet fields around Rettelsheim and the red-brick houses of Philadelphia, to the stuffed fish and the raisin wine, the chanting in the *chedar* and the white twisted loaves of calm Sabbath, under the white cloth. They would seem very close for the moment, then they would seem very far away. He was eating deer's meat in a forest and sleeping beside embers in the open night. It was so that Israel must have slept in the wilderness. He had not thought of it as so, but it was so.

Now and then he would look at his hands—they seemed tougher and very brown, as if they did not belong to him any more. Now and then he would catch a glimpse of his own face, as he drank at a stream. He had a beard, but it was not the beard of a scholar—it was wild and black. Moreover, he was dressed in skins, now; it seemed strange to be dressed in skins at first, and then not strange.

Now all this time, when he went to sleep at night, he would think of Miriam Ettelsohn. But, queerly enough, the harder he tried to summon up her face in his thoughts, the vaguer it became.

He lost track of time—there was only his map and the trading and the journey. Now it seemed to him that they should surely turn back, for their packs were full. He spoke of it to McCampbell, but McCampbell shook his head. There was a light in the Scotchman's eyes now—a light that seemed strange to our grandfather's grandfather—and he would pray long at night, sometimes too loudly. So they came to the banks of the great river, brown and great, and saw it, and the country beyond it, like a view across Jordan.[4] There was no end to that country—it stretched to the limits of the sky and Jacob saw it with his eyes. He was almost afraid at first, and then he was not afraid.

It was there that the strong man, McCampbell, fell sick, and there that he died and was buried. Jacob buried him on a bluff overlooking the river and faced the grave to the west. In his death sickness, McCampbell raved of the Ten Lost Tribes again and swore they were just across the river and he would go to them. It took all Jacob's strength to hold him—if it had been at the beginning of the journey, he would not have had the strength. Then he turned back, for he, too, had seen a Promised Land, not for his seed only, but for nations yet to come.

Nevertheless, he was taken by the Shawnees,[5] in a season of bitter cold, with his last horse dead. At first, when misfortune began to fall upon him, he had wept for the loss of the horses and the good beaver. But, when the Shawnees took him, he no longer wept; for it seemed to him that he was no longer himself, but a man he did not know.

He was not concerned when they tied him to the stake and piled the wood around him, for it seemed to him still that it must be happening to another man. Nevertheless he prayed, as was fitting, chanting loudly; for Zion[6] in the wilderness he prayed. He could smell the smell of the *chedar* and hear the voices that he knew—Reb Moses and Reb Nathan, and through them the curious voice of Raphael Sanchez, speaking in riddles. Then the smoke took him and he coughed. His throat was hot. He called for drink, and though they could not understand his words, all men know the sign of thirst, and they brought him a bowl filled. He put it to his lips eagerly and drank, but the stuff in the bowl was scorching hot and burned his mouth. Very angry then was our grandfather's grandfather, and without so much as a cry he took the bowl in both hands and flung it straight in the face of the man who had brought it, scalding him. Then there was a cry and a murmur from the Shawnees and, after some moments, he felt himself unbound and knew that he lived.

It was flinging the bowl at the man while yet he stood at the stake that saved him, for there is an etiquette about such matters. One does not burn a madman, among the Indians; and to the Shawnees, Jacob's flinging the bowl proved that he was mad, for a sane man would not have done so. Or so it was explained to

4. This river bordering the Promised Land was dangerous to ford. God divided the waters so that the Hebrews might pass over; see Joshua iii–iv.
5. Warlike Indians who ranged from South Carolina to the Mississippi River and western Tennessee, where Jacob was captured.
6. The hill in Jerusalem on which the temple stood; ultimately a name for the whole Hebrew people and state.

him later, though he was never quite sure that they had not been playing cat-and-mouse with him, to test him. Also they were much concerned by his chanting his death song in an unknown tongue and by the phylactery that he had taken from its bag and bound upon brow and arm for his death hour, for these they thought strong medicine and uncertain. But in any case they released him, though they would not give him back his beaver, and that winter he passed in the lodges of the Shawnees, treated sometimes like a servant and sometimes like a guest, but always on the edge of peril. For he was strange to them, and they could not quite make up their minds about him, though the man with the scalded face had his own opinion, as Jacob could see.

Yet when the winter was milder and the hunting better than it had been in some seasons, it was he who got the credit of it, and the holy phylactery also; and by the end of the winter he was talking to them of trade, though diffidently at first. Ah, our grandfather's grandfather, *selig*, what woes he had! And yet it was not all woe, for he learned much woodcraft from the Shawnees and began to speak in their tongue.

Yet he did not trust them entirely; and when spring came and he could travel, he escaped. He was no longer a scholar then, but a hunter. He tried to think what day it was by the calendar, but he could only remember the Bee Moon and the Berry Moon. Yet when he thought of a feast he tried to keep it, and always he prayed for Zion. But when he thought of Zion, it was not as he had thought of it before—a white city set on a hill—but a great and open landscape, ready for nations. He could not have said why his thought had changed, but it had.

I shall not tell all, for who knows all? I shall not tell of the trading post he found deserted and the hundred and forty French louis in the dead man's money belt. I shall not tell of the half-grown boy, McGillvray, that he found on the fringes of settlement —the boy who was to be his partner in the days to come—and how they traded again with the Shawnees and got much beaver. Only this remains to be told, for this is true.

It was a long time since he had even thought of Meyer Kappel-huist—the big pushing man with red hairs on the backs of his hands. But now they were turning back toward Philadelphia, he and McGillvray, their packhorses and their beaver; and as the paths began to grow familiar, old thoughts came into his mind. Moreover, he would hear now and then, in the outposts of the wilderness, of a red-haired trader. So when he met the man himself, not thirty miles from Lancaster, he was not surprised.

Now, Meyer Kappelhuist had always seemed a big man to our grandfather's grandfather. But he did not seem such a big man, met in the wilderness by chance, and at that Jacob was amazed. Yet the greater surprise was Meyer Kappelhuist's, for he stared at our grandfather's grandfather long and puzzledly before he cried out, "But it's the little scholar!" and clapped his hand on his knee. Then they greeted each other civilly and Meyer Kappelhuist drank liquor because of the meeting, but Jacob drank nothing. For, all the time, they were talking, he could see Meyer Kappelhuist's eyes fixed greedily upon his packs of beaver, and he did not like that. Nor did he like the looks of the three tame Indians who traveled with Meyer Kappelhuist and, though he was a man of peace, he kept his hand on his arms, and the boy, McGillvray, did the same.

Meyer Kappelhuist was anxious that they should travel on together, but Jacob refused, for, as I say, he did not like the look in the red-haired man's eyes. So he said he was taking another road and left it at that.

"And the news you have of Simon Ettelsohn and his family— it is good, no doubt, for I know you are close to them," said Jacob, before they parted.

"Close to them?" said Meyer Kappelhuist, and he looked black as thunder. Then he laughed a forced laugh. "Oh, I see them no more," he said. "The old rascal has promised his daughter to a cousin of the Seixas, a greeny, just come over, but rich, they say. But to tell you the truth, I think we are well out of it, Scholar— she was always a little too skinny for my taste," and he laughed coarsely.

"She was a rose of Sharon and a lily of the valley," said Jacob respectfully, and yet not with the pang he would have expected at such news, though it made him more determined than ever not to travel with Meyer Kappelhuist. And with that they parted and Meyer Kappelhuist went his way. Then Jacob took a fork in the trail that McGillvray knew of and that was as well for him. For when he got to Lancaster, there was news of the killing of a trader by the Indians who traveled with him; and when Jacob asked for details, they showed him something dried on a willow hoop. Jacob looked at the thing and saw the hairs upon it were red.

"Sculped all right, but we got it back," said the frontiersman, with satisfaction. "The red devil had it on him when we caught him. Should have buried it, too, I guess, but we'd buried him already and it didn't seem feasible. Thought I might take it to Philadelphy, sometime—might make an impression on the governor. Say, if you're going there, you might—after all, that's where he come from. Be a sort of memento to his folks."

"And it might have been mine, if I had traveled with him," said Jacob. He stared at the thing again, and his heart rose against touching it. Yet it was well the city people should know what happened to men in the wilderness, and the price of blood. "Yes, I will take it," he said.

Jacob stood before the door of Raphael Sanchez, in Philadelphia. He knocked at the door with his knuckles, and the old man himself peered out at him.

"And what is your business with me, Frontiersman?" said the old man, peering.

"The price of blood for a country," said Jacob Stein. He did not raise his voice, but there was a note in it that had not been there when he first knocked at Raphael Sanchez's door.

The old man stared at him soberly. "Enter, my son," he said at last, and Jacob touched the scroll by the doorpost and went in.

He walked through the halls as a man walks in a dream. At last he was sitting by the dark mahogany table. There was nothing changed in the room—he wondered greatly that nothing in it had changed.

"And what have you seen, my son?" said Raphael Sanchez.

"I have seen the land of Canaan, flowing with milk and honey," said Jacob, Scholar of the Law. "I have brought back grapes from Eshcol, and other things that are terrible to behold," he cried, and even as he cried he felt the sob rise in his throat. He choked it down. "Also there are eighteen packs of prime beaver at the warehouse and a boy named McGillvray, a Gentile, but very trusty," he said. "The beaver is very good and the boy under my protection. And McCampbell died by the great river, but he had seen the land and I think he rests well. The map is not made as I would have it, but it shows new things. And we must trade with the Shawnees. There are three posts to be established—I have marked them on the map—and later, more. And beyond the great river there is country that stretches to the end of the world. That is where my friend McCampbell lies, with his face turned west. But what is the use of talking? You would not understand."

He put his head on his arms, for the room was too quiet and peaceful, and he was very tired. Raphael Sanchez moved around the table and touched him on the shoulder.

"Did I not say, my son, that there was more than a girl's face to be found in the wilderness?" he said.

"A girl's face?" said Jacob. "Why, she is to be married and, I hope, will be happy, for she was a rose of Sharon. But what are girls' faces beside this?" and he flung something on the table. It rattled dryly on the table, like a cast snakeskin, but the hairs upon it were red.

"It was Meyer Kappelhuist," said Jacob childishly, "and he was a strong man. And I am not strong, but a scholar. But I have seen what I have seen. And we must say Kaddish[6] for him."

6. A recitation in praise of God, offered as a mourners' prayer.

"Yes, yes," said Raphael Sanchez. "It will be done. I will see to it."

"But you do not understand," said Jacob. "I have eaten deer's meat in the wilderness and forgotten the month and the year. I have been a servant to the heathen and held the scalp of my enemy in my hand. I will never be the same man."

"Oh, you will be the same," said Sanchez. "And no worse a scholar, perhaps. But this is a new country."

"It must be for all," said Jacob. "For my friend McCampbell died also, and he was a Gentile."

"Let us hope," said Raphael Sanchez and touched him again upon the shoulder. Then Jacob lifted his head and he saw that the light had declined and the evening was upon him. And even as he looked, Raphael Sanchez's granddaughter came in to light the candles for Sabbath. And Jacob looked upon her, and she was a dove, with dove's eyes.

1939

The Hemp[7]

I. The Planting of the Hemp

Captain Hawk scourged clean the seas
(Black is the gap below the plank)
From the Great North Bank to the Caribbees
(Down by the marsh the hemp grows rank).

His fear was on the seaport towns,   5
The weight of his hand held hard the downs.

And the merchants cursed him, bitter and black,
For a red flame in the sea-fog's wrack
Was all of their ships that might come back.

For all he had one word alone,   10
One clod of dirt in their faces thrown,
"The hemp that shall hang me is not grown!"

His name bestrode the seas like Death,
The waters trembled at his breath.

This is the tale of how he fell,   15
Of the long sweep and the heavy swell,
And the rope that dragged him down to hell.

The fight was done, and the gutted ship,
Stripped like a shark the sea-gulls strip,

7. Published in *Young Adventure* (1918) and collected in the *Selected Works* (1942).

Lurched blindly, eaten out with flame,   20
Back to the land from whence she came,
A skimming horror, an eyeless shame.

And Hawk stood up on his quarter-deck,
And saw the sky and saw the wreck.

Below, a butt for sailors' jeers,   25
White as the sky when a white squall nears,
Huddled the crowd of the prisoners.

Over the bridge of the tottering plank,
Where the sea shook and the gulf yawned blank,
They shrieked and struggled and dropped and sank.   30

Pinioned arms and hands bound fast.
One girl alone was left at last.

Sir Henry Gaunt was a mighty lord.
He sat in state at the Council board.

The governors were as naught to him.   35
From one rim to the other rim
Of his great plantations, flung out wide
Like a purple cloak, was a full month's ride.

Life and death in his white hands lay,
And his only daughter stood at bay,   40
Trapped like a hare in the toils that day.

He sat at wine in his gold and his lace,
And far away, in a bloody place,
Hawk came near, and she covered her face.

He rode in the fields, and the hunt was brave,   45
And far away, his daughter gave
A shriek that the seas cried out to hear,
And he could not see and he could not save.

Her white soul withered in the mire
As paper shrivels up in fire,   50
And Hawk laughed, and he kissed her mouth,
And her body he took for his desire.

II. *The Growing of the Hemp*

Sir Henry stood in the manor room,
And his eyes were hard gems in the gloom.

And he said, "Go, dig me furrows five   55
Where the green marsh creeps like a thing alive—
There at its edge where the rushes thrive."

And where the furrows rent the ground
He sowed the seed of hemp around.

And the blacks shrink back and are sore afraid   60
At the furrows five that rib the glade,
And the voodoo work of the master's spade.

For a cold wind blows from the marshland near,
And white things move, and the night grows drear,
And they chatter and crouch and are sick with fear.   65

But down by the marsh, where the grey slaves glean,
The hemp sprouts up, and the earth is seen
Veiled with a tenuous mist of green.

And Hawk still scourges the Caribbees,
And many men kneel at his knees.   70

Sir Henry sits in his house alone,
And his eyes are hard and dull like stone.

And the waves beat, and the winds roar,
And all things are as they were before.

And the days pass, and the weeks pass,   75
And nothing changes but the grass.

But down where the fireflies are like eyes,
And the damps shudder, and the mists rise,
The hemp-stalks stand up toward the skies.

And down from the poop of the pirate ship   80
A body falls, and the great sharks grip.

Innocent, lovely, go in grace!
At last there is peace upon your face.

And Hawk laughs loud as the corpse is thrown,
"The hemp that shall hang me is not grown!"   85

Sir Henry's face is iron to mark,
And he gazes ever in the dark.

And the days pass, and the weeks pass,
And the world is as it always was.

But down by the marsh the sickles beam,   90
Glitter on glitter, gleam on gleam,
And the hemp falls down by the stagnant stream.

And Hawk beats up from the Caribbees,
Swooping to pounce in the Northern seas.

Sir Henry sits sunk deep in his chair,   95
And white as his hand is grown his hair.

And the days pass, and the weeks pass,
And the sands roll from the hourglass.

But down by the marsh, in the blazing sun,
The hemp is smoothed and twisted and spun.   100
The rope made, and the work done.

III. The Using of the Hemp

Captain Hawk scourged clean the seas
(Black is the gap below the plank)
From the Great North Bank to the Caribbees
(Down by the marsh the hemp grows rank).   105

He sailed in the broad Atlantic track
And the ships that saw him came not back.

Till once again, where the wide tides ran,
He stopped to harry a merchantman.

He bade her stop. Ten guns spoke true   110
From her hidden ports, and a hidden crew,
Lacking[7a] his great ship through and through.

Dazed and dumb with the sudden death,
He scarce had time to draw a breath
Before the grappling-irons bit deep   115
And the boarders slew his crew like sheep.

Hawk stood up straight, his breast to the steel;
His cutlass made a bloody wheel.

His cutlass made a wheel of flame.
They shrank before him as he came.   120

And the bodies fell in a choking crowd,
And still he thundered out aloud,
"The hemp that shall hang me is not grown!"
They fled at last. He was left alone.

Before his foe Sir Henry stood.   125
"The hemp is grown and my word made good!"

And the cutlass clanged with a hissing whir
On the lashing blade of the rapier.

7a. An unusual naval term, meaning "to pierce with shot," as a ship in combat; derived from an archaic form of the verb "to lace" (lash).

Hawk roared and charged like a maddened buck.
As the cobra strikes, Sir Henry struck,   130

Pouring his life in a single thrust,
And the cutlass shivered to sparks and dust.

Sir Henry stood on the blood-stained deck,
And set his foot on his foe's neck.

Then, from the hatch, where the torn decks slope,   135
Where the dead roll and the wounded grope,
He dragged the serpent of the rope.

The sky was blue and the sea was still,
The waves lapped softly, hill on hill,
And between one wave and another wave   140
The doomed man's cries were little and shrill.

The sea was blue and the sky was calm,
The air dripped with a golden balm.
Like a wind-blown fruit between sea and sun,
A black thing writhed at a yard-arm.   145

Slowly then, and awesomely,
The ship sank, and the gallows-tree,
And there was nought between sea and sun—
Nought but the sun and the sky and the sea.

But down by the marsh, where the fever breeds,   150
Only the water chuckles and pleads;
For the hemp clings fast to a dead man's throat,
And blind Fate gathers back her seeds.

1918

The Ballad of William Sycamore[8]
(1790–1871)

My father, he was a mountaineer,
His fist was a knotty hammer;
He was quick on his feet as a running deer,
And he spoke with a Yankee stammer.

My mother, she was merry and brave,   5
And so she came to her labor,
With a tall green fir for her doctor grave
And a stream for her comforting neighbor.

---

8. Published as a small volume in 1923, and collected in the *Selected Works* (1942).

And some are wrapped in the linen fine,
And some like a godling's scion;
But I was cradled on twigs of pine
In the skin of a mountain lion.

10

And some remember a white, starched lap
And a ewer with silver handles;
But I remember a coonskin cap
And the smell of bayberry candles.

15

The cabin logs with the bark still rough,
And my mother who laughed at trifles,
And the tall, lank visitors, brown as snuff,
With their long, straight squirrel-rifles.

20

I can hear them dance, like a foggy song.
Through the deepest one of my slumbers,
The fiddle squeaking the boots along
And my father calling the numbers.

The quick feet shaking the puncheon-floor,[9]
And the fiddle squeaking and squealing,
Till the dried herbs rattled above the door
And the dust went up to the ceiling.

25

There are children lucky from dawn till dusk,
But never a child so lucky!
For I cut my teeth on "Money Musk"[1]
In the Bloody Ground of Kentucky!

30

When I grew tall as the Indian corn,
My father had little to lend me,
But he gave me his great old powder-horn
And his woodsman's skill to befriend me.

35

With a leather shirt to cover my back,
And a redskin nose to unravel
Each forest sign, I carried my pack
As far as a scout could travel.

40

Till I lost my boyhood and found my wife,
A girl like a Salem clipper![2]
A woman straight as a hunting-knife
With eyes as bright as the Dipper!

We cleared our camp where the buffalo feed,
Unheard-of streams were our flagons;

45

9. A floor made of slabs split from the sides of logs with the flat face turned up.
1. Early American folk-dance tune.

2. The clipper was the swiftest and most graceful of early American wooden ships; many were made at Salem, Massachusetts.

And I sowed my sons like the apple-seed
On the trail of the Western wagons.

They were right, tight boys, never sulky or slow,
A fruitful, a goodly muster.   50
The eldest died at the Alamo.
The youngest fell with Custer.[3]

The letter that told it burned my hand.
Yet we smiled and said, "So be it!"
But I could not live when they fenced the land,   55
For it broke my heart to see it.

I saddled a red, unbroken colt
And rode him into the day there;
And he threw me down like a thunderbolt
And rolled on me as I lay there.   60

The hunter's whistle hummed in my ear
As the city-men tried to move me,
And I died in my boots like a pioneer
With the whole wide sky above me.

Now I lie in the heart of the fat, black soil,   65
Like the seed of a prairie-thistle;
It has washed my bones with honey and oil
And picked them clean as a whistle.

And my youth returns, like the rains of Spring,
And my sons, like the wild-geese flying;   70
And I lie and hear the meadow-lark sing
And have much content in my dying.

Go play with the towns you have built of blocks,
The towns where you would have bound me!
I sleep in my earth like a tired fox,   75
And my buffalo have found me.

1923

American Names

I have fallen in love with American names,[4]
The sharp names that never get fat,

---

3. In 1876, Major General George A. Custer, and his entire force, were annihilated by a band of Sioux Indians led **by** Sitting Bull and Crazy Horse, at the Battle of the Little Big Horn, in Montana Territory.

4. Some of these American names were frontier ephemera; others still survive, such as Lundy's Lane (near Niagara Falls, site of an American victory in the War of 1812). Their historical connotations were noted in an illustrated reprint

The snakeskin-titles of mining-claims,
The plumed war-bonnet of Medicine Hat,
Tucson and Deadwood and Lost Mule Flat.   5

Seine and Piave are silver spoons,
But the spoonbowl-metal is thin and worn,
There are English counties like hunting-tunes
Played on the keys of the postboy's horn,
But I will remember where I was born.   10

I will remember Carquinez Straits,
Little French Lick and Lundy's Lane,
The Yankee ships and the Yankee dates
And the bullet-towns of Calamity Jane.[5]
I will remember Skunktown Plain.   15

I will fall in love with a Salem tree
And a rawhide quirt from Santa Cruz,
I will get me a bottle of Boston sea
And a blue-gum nigger to sing me blues.
I am tired of loving a foreign muse.   20

Rue des Martyrs and Bleeding-Heart-Yard,
Senlis, Pisa, and Blindman's Oast,
It is a magic ghost you guard
But I am sick for a newer ghost,
Harrisburg, Spartanburg, Painted Post.   25

Henry and John were never so,
And Henry and John were always right?
Granted, but when it was time to go
And the tea and the laurels had stood all night,
Did they never watch for Nantucket Light?   30

I shall not rest quiet in Montparnasse.
I shall not lie easy at Winchelsea.
You may bury my body in Sussex grass,
You may bury my tongue at Champmédy.
I shall not be there. I shall rise and pass.   35
Bury my heart at Wounded Knee.

1927   1931

of this poem in *Life* magazine for January 31, 1944; see also George R. Stewart, *Names on the Land* (1945). The poem was first collected in *Ballads and Poems, 1915–1930* (1931).

5. Martha Jane Burke, famous frontier woman of the mining camps, especially associated with Deadwood, South Dakota.

The Attack on Convention

Iconoclasts & Satirists —
Reassessment of the Amer scene

H. L. MENCKEN
(1880–1956)

built satire to high level
pass on to all lost causes

H. L. Mencken was the earliest of the iconoclasts of the 1920's —the most irreverent, clamorous, and resourceful leader of the crusade which crumbled the cherished idols and stereotypes of a surviving Victorian gentility. In his newspaper column (after 1910), in his editorials, and in his collections of essays, he made a battlefield of the entire terrain of contemporary life, attacking with equal agility and skill wherever he found what he regarded as entrenched stupidity or ignorance or hypocrisy—in literary standards, government, politics, economic life, foreign relations, and the manners or morals of his fellow Americans. He excoriated all official and professional defenders of the stereotype, especially the "professors," who, he believed, extended the dead hand of mere authority from universities moribund in traditionalism and intellectual timidity. An irony of his situation, which he no doubt enjoyed, was that his detractors regarded him as a dangerous radical, while actually he was, and is today considered, a conservative force.

Henry Louis Mencken was born in 1880 in Baltimore, Maryland, of mixed German and Irish stock, and was brought up in a family tradition that exalted learning and fostered a speculative originality of mind. His father conducted a successful tobacco business, and Mencken was early familiar with the concept that economic responsibility and intellectual leadership are properly combined in one person.

At the age of sixteen he was graduated from Baltimore Polytechnic Institute, and chose to study privately instead of going to college. Since his writings show a genuinely learned man, he evidently proceeded successfully with his self-discipline. At nineteen, having determined on a career in journalism, he joined the Baltimore *Morning Herald*. Later he became an editor for the Sun Syndicate, first on the *Evening Herald* (1905) and then on the Baltimore *Sun* (1906). He continued an association with these Baltimore papers as late as 1941, in addition to his many other editorial connections. In 1908 he became drama critic for *The Smart Set*,

1028

and from 1914 to 1923 he was its coeditor, with George Jean Nathan. In 1917 he began a long association as literary adviser to Alfred A. Knopf, then notable among the imaginative younger publishers. He made several trips abroad, and from 1916 to 1918 he served as a correspondent in Germany. Meanwhile his *Sun* column, "The Free Lance" (1910–1916), with its famous battles for individualism and freedom of public expression, had established his character as a controversialist. *A Book of Prefaces* (1917) was the first of his most characteristic critical volumes. In 1919 appeared *Prejudices: First Series,* and he continued to add other volumes of his collected critical essays until the *Sixth Series* of 1927. He winnowed the best of these for *Selected Prejudices* (1926) and *Selected Prejudices: Second Series* (1927). *The American Credo* (1920), a collaboration with Nathan "toward the interpretation of the National Mind," is associated in spirit with the *Prejudices.*

One of the most exciting periodicals of this period was *The American Mercury,* founded by Mencken and Nathan in 1923–1924, and edited by Mencken until 1933. Its policy was to satirize the stupidity of the mass mind and such typical manifestations of the period as prohibition; to expose, in a "spirit of boisterous scepticism," the "gaudy, gorgeous American scene"; and to promote authors associated with this crusade of liberation, among whom were Dreiser, Sherwood Anderson, Sandburg, Edgar Lee Masters, Carl Van Vechten, Eugene O'Neill, and Sinclair Lewis. During this whole period Mencken was also active as a contributing editor of the *Nation.*

In 1919 this versatile author and prodigious worker had published the first edition of a book which has permanently influenced our cultural history. This was *The American Language* (revised and enlarged 1921, 1923, 1936; *Supplement One,* 1945; *Supplement Two,* 1948). At first this work was ridiculed by the same reactionary authoritarians who had disapproved of the gusty, indigenous language that Mencken employed in his own writing. Yet it is now regarded as the sound beginning of a new functional approach in scholarly linguistics, and it authorized a younger generation of authors in their feeling for a language closer to the character of the best spoken American.

Later works of Mencken include, most importantly, his classic autobiographical series: *Happy Days,* 1880–1892 (1940); *Newspaper Days,* 1899–1906 (1941); and *Heathen Days,* 1890–1936 (1943). His *Treatise on the Gods* appeared in 1930, the *Treatise on Right and Wrong* in 1934, and *A Mencken Chrestomathy,* a general anthology of his work, in 1949.

In addition to the volumes mentioned above, there are *A Carnival of Buncombe,* 1956, edited by Malcolm Moos; *Minority Report: H. L. Mencken's Notebooks,* 1956; *Prejudices: A Selection,* 1958, edited by James T. Farrell; and *The Bathtub Hoax and Other Blasts and Bravos from the Chicago Tribune,* 1958, collected by Robert McHugh. For biography, see the autobiographical volumes listed above, and Ernest A. Boyd, *H. L. Mencken,* 1925; Isaac Goldberg, *The Man Mencken,* 1925; Walter Lippman, *H. L. Mencken,* 1926; Edgar Kemler, *The Irreverent Mr. Mencken,* 1950; and William Manchester, *Disturber of the Peace,* 1951.

From American Culture[1]

The capital defect in the culture of These States[2] is the lack of a civilized aristocracy, secure in its position, animated by an intelligent curiosity, skeptical of all facile generalizations, superior to the sentimentality of the mob, and delighting in the battle of ideas for its own sake. The word I use, despite the qualifying adjective, has got itself meanings, of course, that I by no means intend to convey. Any mention of an aristocracy, to a public fed upon democratic fustian, is bound to bring up images of stockbrokers' wives lolling obscenely in opera boxes, or of haughty Englishmen slaughtering whole generations of grouse in an inordinate and incomprehensible manner, or of bogus counts coming over to work their magic upon the daughters of breakfast-food and bathtub kings. This misconception belongs to the general American tradition. Its depth and extent are constantly revealed by the naïve assumption that the so-called fashionable folk of the large cities—chiefly wealthy industrials in the interior-decorator and country-club stage of culture—constitute an aristocracy, and by the scarcely less remarkable assumption that the peerage of England is identical with the gentry—that is, that such men as Lord Northcliffe,[3] Lord Riddel and even Lord Reading were English gentlemen.

Here, as always, the worshiper is the father of the gods, and no less when they are evil than when they are benign. The inferior man must find himself superiors, that he may marvel at his political equality with them, and in the absence of recognizable superiors *de facto* he creates superiors *de jure.*[4] The sublime principle of one man, one vote must be translated into terms of dollars, diamonds, fashionable intelligence; the equality of all men before the law must have clear and dramatic proofs. Sometimes, perhaps, the thing goes further and is more subtle. The inferior man needs an aristocracy to demonstrate, not only his mere equality, but also his actual su-

1. First published in the *Yale Review* for June, 1920, this essay subsequently appeared in the section headed "The National Letters," in *Prejudices: Second Series* (1920). It was reprinted in *A Mencken Chrestomathy* (1949).
2. "These States" was a favorite and characteristic phrase of Walt Whitman's.
3. Lord Northcliffe, born Alfred C. W. Harmsworth, was descended from an ancient and influential family. He became a baron in 1905, and developed several London newspapers, including the *Times.* He was the recognized spokesman of the conservatives. Baron Riddell (not "Riddel") was in youth a Welsh barrister and also became a leader in conservative journalism, although less of a luminary than Lord Northcliffe. The Marquis of Reading, born Rufus Daniel Isaacs, won distinction by his gifted statesmanship, was created lord chief justice of England in 1913, and became viceroy and governor general of India in 1921.
4. That is, not finding superiors in actuality, he creates them by law.

need aristot- yes
need Hist. of - 110   *bearing points*
American Culture · 1031

periority. The society columns in the newspapers may have some such origin. They may visualize once more the accomplished journalist's understanding of the mob mind that he plays upon so skillfully, as upon some immense and cacophonous organ, always going *fortissimo*. What the inferior man and his wife see in the sinister revels of those brummagem[5] first families, I suspect, is often a massive witness to their own higher rectitude—in brief, to their firmer grasp upon the immutable axioms of Christian virtue, the one sound boast of the nether nine-tenths of humanity in every land under the cross.

But this bugaboo aristocracy is actually bogus, and the evidence of its bogusness lies in the fact that it is insecure. One gets into it only onerously, but out of it very easily. Entrance is effected by dint of a long and bitter struggle, and the chief accidents of that struggle are almost intolerable humiliations. The aspirant must school and steel himself to sniffs and sneers; he must see the door slammed upon him a hundred times before ever it is thrown open to him. To get in at all he must show a talent for abasement—and abasement makes him timorous. Worse, that timorousness is not cured when he succeeds at last. On the contrary, it is made even more tremulous, for what he faces within the gates is a scheme of things made up almost wholly of harsh and often unintelligible taboos, and the penalty for violating even the least of them is swift and disastrous. He must exhibit exactly the right social habits, appetites and prejudices, public and private. He must harbor exactly the right enthusiasms and indignations. He must have a hearty taste for exactly the right sports and games. His attitude toward the fine arts must be properly tolerant and yet not a shade too eager. He must read and like exactly the right books, pamphlets and public journals. He must put up at the right hotels when he travels. His wife must patronize the right milliners. He himself must stick to the right haberdashery. He must live in the right neighborhood. He must even embrace the right doctrines of religion. It would ruin him, for all society column purposes, to move to Union Hill, N.J., or to drink coffee from his saucer, or to marry a chambermaid with a gold tooth, or to join the Seventh Day Adventists. Within the boundaries of his curious order he is worse fettered than a monk in a cell. Its obscure conception of propriety, its nebulous notion that this or that is honorable, hampers him in every direction, and very narrowly. What he resigns when he enters, even when he makes his first deprecating knock at the door, is every right to attack the ideas that happen to prevail within. Such as they are, he must accept them without question. And as they shift and change he must shift and change with them, silently

5. British slang, a word derived from the name of the city of Birmingham, where, supposedly, trashy but showy wares were manufactured.

and quickly.

Obviously, that order cannot constitute a genuine aristocracy, in any rational sense. A genuine aristocracy is grounded upon very much different principles. Its first and most salient character is its interior security, and the chief visible evidence of that security is the freedom that goes with it—not only freedom in act, the divine right of the aristocrat to do what he damn well pleases, so long as he does not violate the primary guarantees and obligations of his class, but also and more importantly freedom in thought, the liberty to try and err, the right to be his own man. It is the instinct of a true aristocracy, not to punish eccentricity by expulsion, but to throw a mantle of protection about it—to safeguard it from the suspicions and resentments of the lower orders. Those lower orders are inert, timid, inhospitable to ideas, hostile to changes, faithful to a few maudlin superstitions. All progress goes on on the higher levels. It is there that salient personalities, made secure by artificial immunities, may oscillate most widely from the normal track. It is within that entrenched fold, out of reach of the immemorial certainties of the mob, that extraordinary men of the lower orders may find their city of refuge, and breathe a clear air. This, indeed, is at once the hall-mark and the justification of a genuine aristocracy —that it is beyond responsibility to the general masses of men, and hence superior to both their degraded longings and their no less degraded aversions. It is nothing if it is not autonomous, curious, venturesome, courageous, and everything if it is. It is the custodian of the qualities that make for change and experiment; it is the class that organizes danger to the service of the race; it pays for its high prerogatives by standing in the forefront of the fray.

No such aristocracy, it must be plain, is now on view in the United States. The makings of one were visible in the Virginia of the Eighteenth Century, but with Jefferson and Washington the promise died. In New England, it seems to me, there was never anything of the sort, either in being or in nascency: there was only a theocracy that degenerated very quickly into a plutocracy on the one hand and a caste of sterile pedants on the other—the passion for God splitting into a lust for dollars and a weakness for mere words. Despite the common notion to the contrary—a notion generated by confusing literacy with intelligence—the New England of the great days never showed any genuine enthusiasm for ideas. It began its history as a slaughter-house of ideas, and it is today not easily distinguishable from a cold-storage plant. Its celebrated adventures in mysticism, once apparently so bold and significant, are now seen to have been little more than an elaborate hocus-pocus—respectable Unitarians shocking the peasantry and scaring the horned cattle in the fields by masquerading in the robes of Rosicrucians.

The notions that it embraced in those austere and far-off days were stale, and when it had finished with them they were dead. So in politics. Since the Civil War it has produced fewer political ideas, as political ideas run in the Republic, than any average county in Kansas or Nebraska. Appomattox seemed to be a victory for New England idealism. It was actually a victory for the New England plutocracy, and that plutocracy has dominated thought above the Housatonic[6] ever since. The sect of professional idealists has so far dwindled that it has ceased to be of any importance, even as an opposition. When the plutocracy is challenged now, it is challenged by the proletariat.

Well, what is on view in New England is on view in all other parts of the nation, sometimes with ameliorations, but usually with the colors merely exaggerated. What one beholds, sweeping the eye over the land, is a culture that, like the national literature, is in three layers—the plutocracy on top, a vast mass of undifferentiated human blanks bossed by demagogues at the bottom, and a forlorn *intelligentsia* gasping out a precarious life between. I need not set out at any length, I hope, the intellectual deficiencies of the plutocracy—its utter failure to show anything even remotely resembling the makings of an aristocracy. It is badly educated, it is stupid, it is full of low-caste superstitions and indignations, it is without decent traditions or informing vision; above all, it is extraordinarily lacking in the most elemental independence and courage. Out of this class comes the grotesque fashionable society of our big towns, already described. It shows all the stigmata of inferiority—moral certainty, cruelty, suspicion of ideas, fear. Never does it function more revealingly than in the recurrent *pogroms* against radicalism, *i.e.*, against humorless persons who, like Andrew Jackson, take the platitudes of democracy seriously. And what is the theory at the bottom of all these proceedings? So far as it can be reduced to comprehensible terms it is much less a theory than a fear—a shivering, idiotic, discreditable fear of a mere banshee[7]—an overpowering, paralyzing dread that some extra-eloquent Red, permitted to emit his balderdash unwhipped, may eventually convert a couple of courageous men, and that the courageous men, filled with indignation against the plutocracy, may take to the highroad, burn down a nail-factory or two, and slit the throat of some virtuous profiteer.

Obviously, it is out of reason to look for any hospitality to ideas in a class so extravagantly fearful of even the most palpably absurd of them. Its philosophy is firmly grounded upon the thesis that the existing order must stand forever free from attack, and not only from at-

6. *I.e.*, in New England. The Housatonic flows through western Massachusetts and Connecticut.

7. In Irish folklore the wailing of a banshee—a female spirit—foretold the approach of death.

tack, but also from the mere academic criticism, and its ethics are firmly grounded upon the thesis that every attempt at any such criticism is a proof of moral turpitude. Within its own ranks, protected by what may be regarded as the privilege of the order, there is nothing to take the place of this criticism. In other countries the plutocracy has often produced men of reflective and analytical habit, eager to rationalize its instincts and to bring it into some sort of relationship to the main streams of human thought. The case of David Ricardo at once comes to mind, and there have been many others: John Bright, Richard Cobden, George Grote.[8] But in the United States no such phenomenon has been visible. Nor has the plutocracy ever fostered an inquiring spirit among its intellectual valets and footmen, which is to say, among the gentlemen who compose headlines and leading articles for its newspapers. What chiefly distinguishes the daily press of the United States from the press of all other countries pretending to culture is not its lack of truthfulness or even its lack of dignity and honor, for these deficiencies are common to newspapers everywhere, but its incurable fear of ideas, its constant effort to evade the discussion of fundamentals by translating all issues into a few elemental fears, its incessant reduction of all reflection to mere emotion. It is, in the true sense, never well-informed. It is seldom intelligent, save in the arts of the mob-master. It is never courageously honest. Held harshly to a rigid correctness of opinion, it sinks rapidly into formalism and feebleness. Its yellow section is perhaps its best section, for there the only vestige of the old free journalist survives. In the more respectable papers one finds only a timid and petulant animosity to all questioning of the existing order, however urbane and sincere—a pervasive and ill-concealed dread that the mob now heated up against the orthodox hobgoblins may suddenly begin to unearth hobgoblins of its own, and so run amok. * * *

1920

From The American Language
The Hallmarks of American[9]

The characters chiefly noted in American English by all who have discussed it are, first, its general uniformity throughout the

8. These were British thinkers and social reformers, yet also members of the "plutocracy." The economist, David Ricardo (1772–1823) was a successful broker; John Bright (1811–1889) and Richard Cobden (1804–1865), the reformers, were industrialists; the historian, George Grote (1794–1871) was a banker.

9. When *The American Language* appeared in 1919 it was an iconoclastic work, an attack on the conventional prejudice in favor of British standards which had dominated the thinking of American purists, including many scholars and lexicographers, while at the same time, the American spoken language, and much of the best American

country; second, its impatient disregard for grammatical, syntactical and phonological rule and precedent; and third, its large capacity (distinctly greater than that of the English of present-day England) for taking in new words and phrases from outside sources, and for manufacturing them of its own materials.

The first of these characters has struck every observer, native and foreign. In place of the discordant local dialects of all the other major countries, including England, we have a general *Volkssprache* for the whole nation, and if it is conditioned at all it is only by minor differences in pronunciation and vocabulary, and by the linguistic struggles of various groups of newcomers. No other country can show such linguistic solidarity, nor any approach to it —not even Canada, for there a large minority of the population resists speaking English altogether. The Little Russian of the Ukraine is unintelligible to the citizen of Moscow; the Northern Italian can scarcely follow a conversation in Sicilian; the Low German from Hamburg is a foreigner in Munich; the Breton flounders in Gascony. Even in the United Kingdom there are wide divergences.[1] "When we remember," says the New International Encyclopedia, "that the dialects of the counties in England have marked differences—so marked, indeed, that it may be doubted whether a Lancashire miner and a Lincolnshire farmer could understand each other—we may well be proud that our vast country has, strictly speaking, only one language." There are some regional peculiarities in pronunciation and intonation, and they will be examined in some detail in Chapter VII, but when it comes to the words they habitually use and the way they use them all Americans, even the less tutored, follow pretty much the same line. A Boston taxi-driver could go to work in Chicago or San Francisco without running any risk of misunderstanding his new fares. Once he had flattened his *a*'s a bit and picked up a few dozen localisms, he would be, to all linguistic intents and purposes, fully naturalized.

Of the intrinsic differences that separate American from English the chief have their roots in the obvious disparity between the environment and traditions of the American people since the Seventeenth Century and those of the English. The latter have lived under a relatively stable social order, and it has impressed upon their souls their characteristic respect for what is customary

---

literature, had assumed a pattern of its own. Mencken's work was neither chauvinistic nor journalistic; it was based on such thorough investigation of American linguistic practice, and was so well fortified by sound knowledge of general philology, that it slowly won the approval of scholars and gave authority to the serious study of American linguistics. The author continued to enlarge and revise it through the years. The passage below is Chapter I of Part II as it appeared in the revised and enlarged edition published in 1936.

1. "W. W. Skeat distinguishes 9 principal dialects in Scotland, 3 in Ireland and 30 in England and Wales. See his English Dialects From the Eighth Century to the Present Day; Cambridge, 1911, p. 107 *ff.*" [Mencken's note].

and of good report. Until the World War brought chaos to most of their institutions, their whole lives were regulated, perhaps more than those of any other people save the Spaniards, by a regard for precedent. The Americans, though partly of the same blood, have felt no such restraint, and acquired no such habit of conformity. On the contrary, they have plunged to the other extreme, for the conditions of life in their country have put a high value upon the precisely opposite qualities of curiosity and daring, and so they have acquired that character of restlessness, that impatience of forms, that disdain of the dead hand, which now broadly marks them. From the first, says a literary historian, they have been "less phlegmatic, less conservative than the English. There were climatic influences, it may be; there was surely a spirit of intensity everywhere that made for short effort."[2] Thus, in the arts, and thus in business, in politics, in daily intercourse, in habits of mind and speech. The American is not, of course, lacking in a capacity for discipline; he has it highly developed; he submits to leadership readily, and even to tyranny. But, by a curious twist, it is not the leadership that is old and decorous that commonly fetches him, but the leadership that is new and extravagant. He will resist dictation out of the past, but he will follow a new messiah with almost Russian willingness, and into the wildest vagaries of economics, religion, morals and speech. A new fallacy in politics spreads faster in the United States than anywhere else on earth, and so does a new fashion in hats, or a new revelation of God, or a new means of killing time, or a new shibboleth, or metaphor, or piece of slang. Thus the American, on his linguistic side, likes to make his language as he goes along, and not all the hard work of the schoolmarm can hold the business back. A novelty loses nothing by the fact that it is a novelty; it rather gains something, and particularly if it meets the national fancy for the terse, the vivid, and, above all, the bold and imaginative. The characteristic American habit of reducing complex concepts to the starkest abbreviations was already noticeable in colonial times, and such highly typical Americanisms as *O.K.*, *N.G.*, and *P.D.Q.*, have been traced back to the early days of the Republic. Nor are the influences that shaped these tendencies invisible today, for institution-making is yet going on, and so is language-making. In so modest an operation as that which has evolved *bunco* from *buncombe* and *bunk* from *bunco* there is evidence of a phenomenon which the philologian recognizes as belonging to the most lusty stages of speech.

But of more importance than the sheer inventions, if only because much more numerous, are the extensions of the vocabulary,

2. "F. L. Pattee: A History of American Literature Since 1870; New York, 1916. See also The American Novel, by Carl Van Doren; New York, 1921" [Mencken's note].

both absolutely and in ready workableness, by the devices of rhetoric. The American, from the beginning, has been the most ardent of recorded rhetoricians. His politics bristles with pungent epithets; his whole history has been bedizened with tall talk; his fundamental institutions rest far more upon brilliant phrases than upon logical ideas. And in small things as in large he exercises continually an incomparable capacity for projecting hidden and often fantastic relationships into arresting parts of speech. Such a term as *rubberneck* is almost a complete treatise on American psychology; it reveals the national habit of mind more clearly than any labored inquiry could ever reveal it. It has in it precisely the boldness and contempt for ordered forms that are so characteristically American, and it has too the grotesque humor of the country, and the delight in devastating opprobriums, and the acute feeling for the succinct and savory. The same qualities are in *rough-house, water-wagon, has-been, lame-duck, speed-cop* and a thousand other such racy substantives, and in all the great stock of native verbs and adjectives. There is indeed, but a shadowy boundary in these new coinages between the various parts of speech. *Corral,* borrowed from the Spanish, immediately becomes a verb and the father of an adjective. *Bust,* carved out of *burst,* erects itself into a noun. *Bum,* coming by way of an earlier *bummer* from the German, becomes noun, adjective, verb and adverb. Verbs are fashioned out of substantives by the simple process of prefixing the preposition: *to engineer, to stump, to hog, to style, to author.* Others grow out of an intermediate adjective, as *to boom.* Others are made by torturing nouns with harsh affixes, as *to burglarize* and *to itemize,* or by groping for the root, as *to resurrect* and *to jell.* Yet others are changed from intransitive to transitive; a sleeping-car *sleeps* thirty passengers. So with the adjectives. They are made of substantives unchanged: *codfish, jitney.* Or by bold combinations: *down-and-out, up-state, flat-footed.* Or by shading down suffixes to a barbaric simplicity: *scary, classy, tasty.* Or by working over adverbs until they tremble on the brink between adverb and adjective: *right, sure* and *near* are examples.

All these processes, of course, are also to be observed in the history of the English of England; at the time of its sturdiest growth they were in the most active possible being. They are, indeed, common to all tongues; "the essence of language," says Dr. Jespersen, "is activity." But if you will put the English of today beside the American of today you will see at once how much more forcibly they are in operation in the latter than in the former. The standard Southern dialect of English has been arrested in its growth by its purists and grammarians, and burdened with irrational affectations by fashionable pretension. It shows no living change since the reign of Samuel Johnson. Its tendency is to combat all that expansive gusto which made for its pliancy and resilience in the days of Shakespeare.[3] In place of the old loose-footedness there is set up a preciosity which, in one direction, takes the form of clumsy artificialities in the spoken language, and in another shows itself in the even clumsier Johnsonese of so much current English writing —the Jargon denounced by Sir Arthur Quiller-Couch in his Cambridge lectures. This "infirmity of speech" Quiller-Couch finds "in parliamentary debates and in the newspapers; . . . it has become the medium through which Boards of Government, County Councils, Syndicates, Committees, Commercial Firms, express the processes as well as the conclusions of their thought, and so voice the reason of their being." Distinct from journalese, the two yet overlap, "and have a knack of assimilating each other's vices."[4]

American, despite the gallant efforts of the pedagogues, has so far escaped any such suffocating formalization. We, too, of course, have our occasional practitioners of the authentic English Jargon, but in the main our faults lie in precisely the opposite direction. That is to say, we incline toward a directness of statement which, at its greatest, lacks restraint and urbanity altogether, and toward a hospitality which often admits novelties for the mere sake of their novelty, and is quite uncritical of the difference between a genuine improvement in succinctness and clarity, and mere extravagant raciness. "The tendency," says one English observer, "is . . . to consider the speech of any man, as any man himself, as good as any other."[5] The Americans, adds a Scots professor, "are determined to hack their way through the language, as their ancestors through forests, regardless of the valuable growths that may be sacrificed in blazing the trail."[6] But this Scot dismisses the English neologisms

3. "Rather curiously, the two authorities who were most influential, during the Nineteenth Century, in keeping it to a rigid pattern were both Americans. They were Lindley Murray (1745–1826) and Joseph E. Worcester (1784–1865). Murray, a Pennsylvanian, went to England after the Revolution, and in 1795 published his Grammar of the English Language. It had an extraordinary sale in England, and was accepted as the court of last resort in usage down to quite recent times. Worcester's Universal and Critical Dictionary of the English Language, 1846, divided the honors of authority in England with B. H. Smart's Dictionary, published during the same year. It was extensively pirated. Thus, says Thomas R. Lounsbury (The Standard of Pronunciation in English; New York, 1904, p. 220), 'the Londoner frequently got his pure London pronunciation from a citizen of this county who was never outside of New England for more than a few months of his life.' Worcester was also accepted at Harvard and at the University of Virginia, but elsewhere in the United States Webster prevailed" [Mencken's note].

4. "See the chapter, Interlude on Jargon, in Quiller-Couch's On the Art of Writing; New York, 1916. Appropriately enough, large parts of the learned critic's book are written in the very Jargon he attacks. See also Ch. VI of Growth and Structure of the English Language, by O. Jespersen, 3rd ed., rev.; Leipzig, 1919, especially p. 143 ff. See also Official English, in English, March, 1919, p. 7; April, p. 45, and August, p. 135, and The Decay of Syntax, in the London Times Literary Supplement, May 8, 1919, p. 1" [Mencken's note].

5. "Alexander Francis: Americans: An Impression; New York, 1900" [Mencken's note].

6. "Breaking Priscian's Head, by J. Y. T. Greig; London, 1929" [Mencken's note].

of the day, when ranged beside the American stock, as "dwiny, feeble stuff"; "it is to America," he admits, "that we must chiefly look in future for the replenishment and freshening of our language." * * *

Let American confront a novel problem alongside English, and immediately its superior imaginativeness and resourcefulness become obvious. *Movie* is better than *cinema*; and the English begin to admit the fact by adopting the word; it is not only better American, it is better English. *Bill-board* is better than *hoarding*. *Office-holder* is more honest, more picturesque, more thoroughly Anglo-Saxon than *public-servant*. *Stem-winder* somehow has more life in it, more fancy and vividness, than the literal *keyless-watch*. Turn to the terminology of *railroading* (itself, by the way, an Americanism): its creation fell upon the two peoples equally, but they tackled the job independently. The English, seeking a figure to denominate the wedge-shaped fender in front of a locomotive, called it a *plough*; the Americans, characteristically, gave it the far more pungent name of *cow-catcher*. So with the casting which guides the wheels from one rail to another. The English called it a *crossing-plate*; the Americans, more responsive to the suggestion in its shape, called it a *frog*. American is full of what Bret Harte called the "saber-cuts of Saxon"; it meets Montaigne's ideal of "a succulent and nervous speech, short and compact, not as much delicated and combed out as vehement and brusque, rather arbitrary than monotonous, not pedantic but soldierly, as Suetonius called Cæsar's Latin." One pictures the common materials of English dumped into a pot, exotic flavorings added, and the bubblings assiduously and expectantly skimmed. What is old and respected is already in decay the moment it comes into contact with what is new and vivid. "When we Americans are through with the English language," says Mr. Dooley, "it will look as if it had been run over by a musical comedy." * * *

1919, 1936

From The Novel[1]

[The Woman Writer]

That women are still the chief readers of novels is known to every book clerk: Joseph Hergesheimer,[2] a little while back, was bemoaning the fact as a curse to his craft. What is less often noted is that women themselves, as they have gradually become fully literate, have forced their way to the front as makers of the stuff

---

1. "The Novel" appeared in *Prejudices: Third Series* (1922).
2. Hergesheimer (1880–1954) was at this time moving toward the height of his powers as a serious experimental novelist; he is best remembered for *The Three Black Pennys* (1917).

they feed on, and that they show signs of ousting the men, soon or late, from the business. Save in the department of lyrical verse, which demands no organization of ideas but only fluency of feeling, they have nowhere else done serious work in literature. There is no epic poem of any solid value by a woman, dead or alive; and no drama, whether comedy or tragedy; and no work of metaphysical speculation; and no history; and no basic document in any other realm of thought. In criticism, whether of works of art or of the ideas underlying them, few women have ever got beyond the *Schwärmerei* of Madame de Staël's "L'Allemagne."[3] In the essay, the most competent woman barely surpasses the average Fleet Street *causerie* hack[4] or Harvard professor. But in the novel the ladies have stood on a level with even the most accomplished men since the day of Jane Austen, and not only in Anglo-Saxondom, but also everywhere else—save perhaps in Russia. * * *

It is my contention that women succeed in the novel—and that they will succeed even more strikingly as they gradually throw off the inhibitions that have hitherto cobwebbed their minds—simply because they are better fitted for this realistic representation than men—because they see the facts of life more sharply, and are less distracted by money dreams. Women seldom have the pathological faculty vaguely called imagination. One doesn't often hear of them groaning over colossal bones in their sleep, as dogs do, or constructing heavenly hierarchies or political utopias, as men do. Their concern is always with things of more objective substance— roofs, meals, rent, clothes, the birth and upbringing of children. They are, I believe, generally happier than men, if only because the demands they make of life are more moderate and less romantic. The chief pain that a man normally suffers in his progress through this vale is that of disillusionment; the chief pain that a woman suffers is that of parturition. There is enormous significance in the difference. The first is artificial and self-inflicted; the second is natural and unescapable. The psychological history of the differentiation I need not go into here: its springs lie obviously in the greater physical strength of man and his freedom from childbearing, and in the larger mobility and capacity for adventure that go therewith. A man dreams of utopias simply because he feels himself free to construct them; a woman must keep house. In late years, to be sure, she has toyed with the idea of escaping that necessity, but I shall not bore you with arguments showing that she never will. So long as children are brought into the world and made ready for the trenches, the sweatshops and the gallows by laborious method

3. Madame de Staël (1766–1817) was celebrated for unconventional behavior, involvements in European politics, and a variety of literary works; "*Schwärmerei*" ("ecstatic raving") is Mencken's epithet for her rhapsodic account of German romanticism in *De l'Allemagne* (1810).
4. *I.e.*, hack writer of literary chitchat for the newspapers (Fleet Street, in London, is the center of English newspaper publishing).

ordained of God she will never be quite as free to roam and dream as man is. It is only a small minority of her sex who cherish a contrary expectation, and this minority, though anatomically female, is spiritually male. Show me a woman who has visions comparable, say, to those of Swedenborg, Woodrow Wilson, Strindberg or Dr. Ghandi, and I'll show you a woman who is a very powerful anaphrodisiac.

Thus women, by their enforced preoccupation with the harsh facts of life, are extremely well fitted to write novels, which must deal with the facts or nothing. What they need for the practical business, in addition, falls under two heads. First, they need enough sense of social security to make them free to set down what they see. Secondly, they need the modest technical skill, the formal mastery of words and ideas, necessary to do it. The latter, I believe, they have had ever since they learned to read and write, say three hundred years ago; it comes to them more readily than to men, and is exercised with greater ease. The former they are fast acquiring. In the days of Aphra Behn and Ann Radcliffe[5] it was almost as scandalous for a woman to put her observations and notions into print as it was for her to show her legs; even in the days of Jane Austen and Charlotte Brontë the thing was regarded as decidedly unladylike. But now, within certain limits, she is free to print whatever she pleases, and before long even those surviving limits will be obliterated. If I live to the year 1950 I expect to see a novel by a woman that will describe a typical marriage under Christianity, from the woman's standpoint, as realistically as it is treated from the man's standpoint in Upton Sinclair's "Love's Pilgrimage." That novel, I venture to predict, will be a cuckoo. At one stroke it will demolish superstitions that have prevailed in the Western World since the fall of the Roman Empire. It will seem harsh, but it will be true. And, being true, it will be a good novel. There can be no good one that is not true.

What ailed the women novelists, until very recently, was a lingering ladyism—a childish prudery inherited from their mothers. I believe that it is being rapidly thrown off; indeed, one often sees a concrete woman novelist shedding it. I give you two obvious examples: Zona Gale[6] and Willa Cather. Miss Gale started out by trying to put into novels the conventional prettiness that is esteemed along the Main Streets of her native Wisconsin. She had skill and did it well, and so she won a good deal of popular success. But her

---

5. Neither Mrs. Behn (1640–1689) nor Mrs. Radcliffe (1764–1823) followed the feminine custom of concealing their work under pseudonyms. Mrs. Behn, reputedly the first Englishwoman to make a living by writing, wrote novels and plays embodying both the wit and the vulgarity of her period; Mrs. Radcliffe wrote Gothic novels of villainy and terror which were noted for their frankness.
6. Zona Gale (1874–1938), less distinguished than Willa Cather, had just won the Pulitzer Prize for the dramatization of her novel *Miss Lulu Bett* (1920), a study of bleak lives in Wisconsin.

work was intrinsically as worthless as a treatise on international politics by the Hon. Warren Gamaliel Harding[7] or a tract on the duties of a soldier and a gentleman by a state president of the American Legion. Then, of a sudden, for some reason quite unknown to the deponent, she threw off all that flabby artificiality, and began describing the people about her as they really were. The result was a second success even more pronounced than her first, and on a palpably higher level. The career of Miss Cather has covered less ground, for she began far above Main Street. What she tried to do at the start was to imitate the superficial sophistication of Edith Wharton and Henry James—a deceptive thing, apparently realistic in essence, but actually as conventional as table manners or the professional buffooneries of a fashionable rector. Miss Cather had extraordinary skill as a writer, and so her imitation was scarcely to be distinguished from the original, but in the course of time she began to be aware of its hollowness. Then she turned to first-hand representation—to pictures of the people she actually knew. There ensued a series of novels that rose step by step to the very distinguished quality of "My Ántonia." That fine piece is a great deal more than simply a good novel. It is a document in the history of American literature. It proves, once and for all time, that accurate representation is not, as the campus critics of Dreiser seem to think, inimical to beauty. It proves, on the contrary, that the most careful and penetrating representation is itself the source of a rare and wonderful beauty. No romantic novel ever written in America, by man or woman, is one-half so beautiful as "My Ántonia."

As I have said, the novel, in the United States as elsewhere, still radiates an aroma of effeminacy, in the conventional sense. Specifically, it deals too monotonously with the varieties of human transactions which chiefly interest the unintelligent women who are its chief patrons and the scarcely less intelligent women who, until recently, were among its chief commercial manufacturers, to wit, the transactions that revolve around the ensnarement of men by women—the puerile tricks and conflicts of what is absurdly called romantic love. But I believe that the women novelists, as they emerge into the fullness of skill, will throw overboard all that old baggage, and leave its toting to such male artisans as Chambers, Beach, Coningsby Dawson and Emerson Hough, as they have already left the whole flag-waving and "red-blooded" buncombe. True enough, the snaring of men will remain the principal business of women in this world for many generations, but it would be absurd to say that intelligent women, even to-day, view it romantically—that is, as it is viewed by bad novelists. They see it realistically, and they see it, not as an end in itself, but as a means to other ends. It is, speaking generally, after she has got her man

7. Harding was serving his first year as President when this was published.

that a woman begins to live. The novel of the future, I believe, will show her thus living. It will depict the intricate complex of forces that conditions her life and generates her ideas, and it will show, against a background of actuality, her conduct in the eternal struggle between her aspiration and her destiny. Women, as I have argued, are not normally harassed by the grandiose and otiose visions that inflame the gizzards of men, but they too discover inevitably that life is a conflict, and that it is the harsh fate of *Homo sapiens* to get the worst of it. I should like to read a "Main Street" by an articulate Carol Kennicott, or a "Titan" by one of Cowperwood's mistresses, or a "Cytherea" by a Fanny Random—or a Savina Grove![8] It would be sweet stuff, indeed. . . . And it will come.

1922

8. These women were all somewhat "emancipated" characters in the novels Mencken cites; the novels were written, respectively, by Sinclair Lewis, Dreiser, and Hergesheimer (see note 2).

SHERWOOD ANDERSON

(1876–1941)

To the generation of writers who flourished in the 1920's, Sherwood Anderson was a force and a pioneer, and he exercised an indirect influence on the literature of two decades. His unblemished powers are recognized today in a handful of magnificent short stories, in his perceptive and passionate letters, and in three "autobiographies" whose legendary character is frankly acknowledged. His other books, particularly his novels, are confused in purpose and uneven in performance. Yet in whatever he wrote there is always the fascination of his personality, complex and brooding, groping for answers to the riddles of the individual being, and desperately aware that to find answers for others, he must overcome the disunity in his own experience. He is one of the most genuinely subjective of our story tellers, at his best in such narrative episodes as involve his own experience and perplexities.

Although largely self-educated, Anderson was a serious thinker, and he read widely. He was among the earliest to respond to the new Freudian psychology, and was convinced that much of human behavior is a reaction to subconscious realities and to experiences hidden in the forgotten past of the individual. His characters grope unsuccessfully to discover the reality within themselves, while with equal frustration they confront the complexities of the machine age and the conventionality of urban and small-town life. If they escape at all, even briefly, it may be through the experience of sex, although this escape also is often blocked by brutalizing debasements. Another resolution is sometimes found, as in *Dark Laughter* (1925), when man is able to identify himself simply with the primitive forces of nature.

Anderson was raised in Clyde, Ohio, the fourth of seven children of a harness-maker, the "Windy" of his first novel, *Windy McPherson's Son* (1916). His schooling was sporadic, owing to his mother's need for help in supporting the family. What he learned working on farms, in shops, and especially in livery and racing stables later appeared in short stories that dealt generally with the emotional problems of boyhood. These are some of his most mature writings, reflecting the early conflict of his creative impulse with the spiritual poverty of small-town life and intimating the gradual alienation of his father which was a source of his chronic emotional disunity.

His mother died when Anderson was nineteen and the family fell apart. In 1896 he worked in Chicago. He enlisted for service in the Spanish-American War; after being discharged he spent the winter of 1899 in Springfield, Ohio, as a senior at Wittenberg Academy. In Chicago again, he became successful as an advertising writer and married in 1904. Moving to Cleveland in 1906, he acquired an interest in a factory in Elyria, Ohio, where he lived for five years. There he prospered financially, combining manufacturing with advertising while compensating for an inward revolt by writing drafts of three novels, including materials later published. In 1912 a nervous collapse required hospitalization. Now fully realizing his intense vocation for literature he terminated his business connections and the first of his four marriages.

In 1913 he started afresh in Chicago, writing advertising while giving his genuine efforts to fiction. "The little renaissance" in Chicago provided a favorable *avant-garde* climate; Sandburg, Lindsay, and Masters were "new voices," and many "little magazines" were eager to give scope to original talent. In 1919 his fourth book, *Winesburg, Ohio*, a short-story collection, won international attention with its intense psychological studies of trapped and warped personalities and its pity and tenderness. In 1921, in Europe, he met and was influenced by James Joyce and Gertrude Stein; in New Orleans, the next winter, he met and influenced William Faulkner.

In *Dark Laughter* (1925), his best and only popular novel, Anderson satirizes the arid pseudo-sophisticated intellectuals, particularly in their neurotic debasement of sex, in contrast to the carefree and uncorrupted sensuality of the Negro characters in the story. But his novels are unsatisfactory as wholes, though they have pages of brilliance and even of sheer genius.

After 1925, Anderson's growing interest was in proletarian movements and his novels declined. He now went to live near Marion, Virginia; in 1927, having bought two newspapers to edit there, he made Marion his permanent home. In 1941, at the start of a tour to South America, he died at Colon, Panama. His autobiographical reminiscences are excellent reading but so impressionistic that biographers have had to seek other sources.

Volumes of Anderson's short stories are *Winesburg, Ohio*, 1919; *The Tri-*

umph of the Egg, 1921; *Horses and Men,* 1923; *Death in the Woods,* 1933. Anderson's novels are *Windy McPherson's Son,* 1916; *Marching Men,* 1917; *Poor White,* 1920; *Many Marriages,* 1923; *Dark Laughter,* 1925; *Beyond Desire,* 1932; *Kit Brandon,* 1936. His plays are collected in *Winesburg and Others,* 1937; his poems in *Mid-American Chants,* 1918; and *A New Testament,* 1927. Collections of essays are *The Modern Writer,* 1925; *Sherwood Anderson's Notebook,* 1926; *Hello Towns!* 1929; *Perhaps Women,* 1931; *No Swank,* 1934; *Puzzled America,* 1935. Autobiographical volumes are *A Story Teller's Story,* 1924; *Tar: A Midwest Childhood,* 1926; *Sherwood Anderson's Memoirs,* 1942. Correspondence on writing was collected in *Letters * * * ,* ed. H. M. Jones and W. B. Rideout, 1953.

Studies are: I. Howe, *Sherwood Anderson,* 1951; and J. Schevill, *Sherwood Anderson, His Life and Work,* 1951.

I Want to Know Why[1]

We got up at four in the morning, that first day in the east. On the evening before we had climbed off a freight train at the edge of town, and with the true instinct of Kentucky boys had found our way across town and to the race track and the stables at once. Then we knew we were all right. Hanley Turner right away found a nigger we knew. It was Bildad Johnson who in the winter works at Ed Becker's livery barn in our home town, Beckersville. Bildad is a good cook as almost all our niggers are and of course he, like everyone in our part of Kentucky who is anyone at all, likes the horses. In the spring Bildad begins to scratch around. A nigger from our country can flatter and wheedle anyone into letting him do most anything he wants. Bildad wheedles the stable men and the trainers from the horse farms in our country around Lexington. The trainers come into town in the evening to stand around and talk and maybe get into a poker game. Bildad gets in with them. He is always doing little favors and telling about things to eat, chicken browned in a pan, and how is the best way to cook sweet potatoes and corn bread. It makes your mouth water to hear him.

When the racing season comes on and the horses go to the races and there is all the talk on the streets in the evenings about the new colts, and everyone says when they are going over to Lexington or to the spring meeting at Churchill Downs or to Latonia, and the horsemen that have been down to New Orleans or maybe at the winter meeting at Havana in Cuba come home to spend a week before they start out again, at such a time when everything talked about in Beckersville is just horses and nothing else and the outfits start out and horse racing is in every breath of air you breathe, Bildad shows up with a job as cook for some outfit. Often when I think about it, his always going all season to the races and working in the livery barn in the winter where horses are and where men like to come and talk about horses, I wish I was a nigger. It's a foolish thing to say, but that's the way I am about being around

1. First published in *The Smart Set* for November, 1918, and collected in *The Triumph of the Egg* (1921).

horses, just crazy. I can't help it.

Well, I must tell you about what we did and let you in on what I'm talking about. Four of us boys from Beckersville, all whites and sons of men who live in Beckersville regular, made up our minds we were going to the races, not just to Lexington or Louisville, I don't mean, but to the big eastern track we were always hearing our Beckersville men talk about, to Saratoga. We were all pretty young then. I was just turned fifteen and I was the oldest of the four. It was my scheme. I admit that and I talked the others into trying it. There was Hanley Turner and Henry Rieback and Tom Tumberton and myself. I had thirty-seven dollars I had earned during the winter working nights and Saturdays in Enoch Myer's grocery. Henry Rieback had eleven dollars and the others, Hanley and Tom, had only a dollar or two each. We fixed it all up and laid low until the Kentucky spring meetings were over and some of our men, the sportiest ones, the ones we envied the most, had cut out—then we cut out too.

I won't tell you the trouble we had beating our way on freights and all. We went through Cleveland and Buffalo and other cities and saw Niagara Falls. We bought things there, souvenirs and spoons and cards and shells with pictures of the falls on them for our sisters and mothers, but thought we had better not send any of the things home. We didn't want to put the folks on our trail and maybe be nabbed.

We got into Saratoga as I said at night and went to the track. Bildad fed us up. He showed us a place to sleep in hay over a shed and promised to keep still. Niggers are all right about things like that. They won't squeal on you. Often a white man you might meet, when you had run away from home like that, might appear to be all right and give you a quarter or a half-dollar or something, and then go right and give you away. White men will do that, but not a nigger. You can trust them. They are squarer with kids. I don't know why.

At the Saratoga meeting that year there were a lot of men from home. Dave Williams and Arthur Mulford and Jerry Myers and others. Then there was a lot from Louisville and Lexington Henry Rieback knew but I didn't. They were professional gamblers and Henry Rieback's father is one too. He is what is called a sheet writer and goes away most of the year to tracks. In the winter when he is home in Beckersville he don't stay there much but goes away to cities and deals faro. He is a nice man and generous, is always sending Henry presents, a bicycle and a gold watch and a boy scout suit of clothes and things like that.

My own father is a lawyer. He's all right, but don't make much money and can't buy me things and anyway I'm getting so old now

I don't expect it. He never said nothing to me against Henry, but Hanley Turner and Tom Tumberton's fathers did. They said to their boys that money so come by is no good and they didn't want their boys brought up to hear gamblers' talk and be thinking about such things and maybe embrace them.

That's all right and I guess the men know what they are talking about, but I don't see what it's got to do with Henry or with horses either. That's what I'm writing this story about. I'm puzzled. I'm getting to be a man and want to think straight and be O. K., and there's something I saw at the race meeting at the eastern track I can't figure out.

I can't help it, I'm crazy about thoroughbred horses. I've always been that way. When I was ten years old and saw I was growing to be big and couldn't be a rider I was so sorry I nearly died. Harry Hellinfinger in Beckersville, whose father is Postmaster, is grown up and too lazy to work, but likes to stand around in the street and get up jokes on boys like sending them to a hardware store for a gimlet to bore square holes and other jokes like that. He played one on me. He told me that if I would eat a half a cigar I would be stunted and not grow any more and maybe could be a rider. I did it. When father wasn't looking I took a cigar out of his pocket and gagged it down some way. It made me awful sick and the doctor had to be sent for, and then it did no good. I kept right on growing. It was a joke. When I told what I had done and why most fathers would have whipped me but mine didn't.

Well, I didn't get stunted and didn't die. It serves Harry Hellinfinger right. Then I made up my mind I would like to be a stable boy, but had to give that up too. Mostly niggers do that work and I knew father wouldn't let me go into it. No use to ask him.

If you've never been crazy about thoroughbreds it's because you've never been around where they are much and don't know any better. They're beautiful. There isn't anything so lovely and clean and full of spunk and honest and everything as some race horses. On the big horse farms that are all around our town Beckersville there are tracks and the horses run in the early morning. More than a thousand times I've got out of bed before daylight and walked two or three miles to the tracks. Mother wouldn't of let me go but father always says, "Let him alone." So I got some bread out of the bread box and some butter and jam, gobbled it and lit out.

At the tracks you sit on the fence with men, whites and niggers, and they chew tobacco and talk, and then the colts are brought out. It's early and the grass is covered with shiny dew and in another field a man is plowing and they are frying things in a shed where the track niggers sleep, and you know how a nigger can giggle and laugh and say things that make you laugh. A white man can't do it and some niggers can't but a track nigger can every time.

And so the colts are brought out and some are just galloped by stable boys, but almost every morning on a big track owned by a rich man who lives maybe in New York, there are always, nearly every morning, a few colts and some of the old race horses and geldings and mares that are cut loose.

It brings a lump up into my throat when a horse runs. I don't mean all horses but some. I can pick them nearly every time. It's in my blood like in the blood of race track niggers and trainers. Even when they just go slob-jogging along with a little nigger on their backs I can tell a winner. If my throat hurts and it's hard for me to swallow, that's him. He'll run like Sam Hill when you let him out. If he don't win every time it'll be a wonder and because they've got him in a pocket behind another or he was pulled or got off bad at the post or something. If I wanted to be a gambler like Henry Rieback's father I could get rich. I know I could and Henry says so, too. All I would have to do is to wait 'til that hurt comes when I see a horse and then bet every cent. That's what I would do if I wanted to be a gambler, but I don't.

When you're at the tracks in the morning—not the race tracks but the training tracks around Beckersville—you don't see a horse, the kind I've been talking about, very often, but it's nice anyway. Any thoroughbred, that is sired right and out of a good mare and trained by a man that knows how, can run. If he couldn't what would he be there for and not pulling a plow?

Well, out of the stables they come and the boys are on their backs and it's lovely to be there. You hunch down on top of the fence and itch inside you. Over in the sheds the niggers giggle and sing. Bacon is being fried and coffee made. Everything smells lovely. Nothing smells better than coffee and manure and horses and niggers and bacon frying and pipes being smoked out of doors on a morning like that. It just gets you, that's what it does.

But about Saratoga. We was there six days and not a soul from home seen us and everything came off just as we wanted it to, fine weather and horses and races and all. We beat our way home and Bildad gave us a basket with fried chicken and bread and other eatables in, and I had eighteen dollars when we got back to Beckersville. Mother jawed and cried but Pop didn't say much. I told everything we done except one thing. I did and saw that alone. That's what I'm writing about. It got me upset. I think about it at night. Here it is.

At Saratoga we laid up nights in the hay in the shed Bildad had showed us and ate with the niggers early and at night when the race people had all gone away. The men from home stayed mostly in the grandstand and betting field, and didn't come out around the places where the horses are kept except to the paddocks just before a race when the horses are saddled. At Saratoga they don't have paddocks under an open shed as at Lexington and Churchill Downs and other tracks down in our country, but saddle the horses right out in an open place under trees on a lawn as smooth and nice as Banker Bohon's front yard here in Beckersville. It's lovely. The horses are sweaty and nervous and shine and the men come out and smoke cigars and look at them and the trainers are there and the owners, and your heart thumps so you can hardly breathe.

Then the bugle blows for post and the boys that ride come running out with their silk clothes on and you run to get a place by the fence with the niggers.

I always am wanting to be a trainer or owner, and at the risk of being seen and caught and sent home I went to the paddocks before every race. The other boys didn't but I did.

We got to Saratoga on a Friday and on Wednesday the next week the big Mullford Handicap was to be run. Middlestride was in it and Sunstreak. The weather was fine and the track fast. I couldn't sleep the night before.

What had happened was that both these horses are the kind it makes my throat hurt to see. Middlestride is long and looks awkward and is a gelding. He belongs to Joe Thompson, a little owner from home who only has a half-dozen horses. The Mullford Handicap is for a mile and Middlestride can't untrack fast. He goes away slow and is always way back at the half, then he begins to run and if the race is a mile and a quarter he'll just eat up everything and get there.

Sunstreak is different. He is a stallion and nervous and belongs on the biggest farm we've got in our country, the Van Riddle place that belongs to Mr. Van Riddle of New York. Sunstreak is like a girl you think about sometimes but never see. He is hard all over and lovely too. When you look at his head you want to kiss him. He is trained by Jerry Tillford who knows me and has been good to me lots of times, lets me walk into a horse's stall to look at him close and other things. There isn't anything as sweet as that horse. He stands at the post quiet and not letting on, but he is just burning up inside. Then when the barrier goes up he is off like his name, Sunstreak. It makes you ache to see him. It hurts you. He just lays down and runs like a bird dog. There can't anything I ever see run like him except Middlestride when he gets untracked and stretches himself.

Gee! I ached to see that race and those two horses run, ached and dreaded it too. I didn't want to see either of our horses beaten. We had never sent a pair like that to the races before. Old men in Beckersville said so and the niggers said so. It was a fact.

Before the race I went over to the paddocks to see. I looked a last look at Middlestride, who isn't such a much standing in a paddock that way, then I went to see Sunstreak.

It was his day. I knew when I see him. I forgot all about being seen myself and walked right up. All the men from Beckersville were there and no one noticed me except Jerry Tillford. He saw me and something happened. I'll tell you about that.

I was standing looking at that horse and aching. In some way, I can't tell how, I knew just how Sunstreak felt inside. He was quiet and letting the niggers rub his legs and Mr. Van Riddle himself put the saddle on, but he was just a raging torrent inside. He was like the water in the river at Niagara Falls just before it goes plunk down. That horse wasn't thinking about running. He don't have to think about that. He was just thinking about holding himself back 'til the time for the running came. I knew that. I could just in a way see right inside him. He was going to do some awful running and I knew it. He wasn't bragging or letting on much or prancing or making a fuss, but just waiting. I knew it and Jerry Tillford his trainer knew. I looked up and then that man and I looked into each other's eyes. Something happened to me. I guess I loved the man as much as I did the horse because he knew what I knew. Seemed to me there wasn't anything in the world but that man and the horse and me. I cried and Jerry Tillford had a shine in his eyes. Then I came away to the fence to wait for the race. The horse was better than me, more steadier, and now I know better than Jerry. He was the quietest and he had to do the running.

Sunstreak ran first of course and he busted the world's record for a mile. I've seen that if I never see anything more. Everything came out just as I expected. Middlestride got left at the post and was way back and closed up to be second, just as I knew he would. He'll get a world's record too some day. They can't skin the Beckersville country on horses.

I watched the race calm because I knew what would happen. I was sure. Hanley Turner and Henry Rieback and Tom Tumberton were all more excited than me.

A funny thing had happened to me. I was thinking about Jerry Tillford the trainer and how happy he was all through the race. I liked him that afternoon even more than I ever liked my own father. I almost forgot the horses thinking that way about him. It was because of what I had seen in his eyes as he stood in the paddocks beside Sunstreak before the race started. I knew he had been watching and working with Sunstreak since the horse was a baby colt, had taught him to run and be patient and when to let himself out and not to quit, never. I knew that for him it was like a mother seeing her child do something brave or wonderful. It was the first time I ever felt for a man like that.

After the race that night I cut out from Tom and Hanley and Henry. I wanted to be by myself and I wanted to be near Jerry Tillford if I could work it. Here is what happened.

The track in Saratoga is near the edge of town. It is all polished up and trees around, the evergreen kind, and grass and everything painted and nice. If you go past the track you get to a hard road made of asphalt for automobiles, and if you go along this for a few miles there is a road turns off to a little rummy-looking farm house set in a yard.

That night after the race I went along that road because I had seen Jerry and some other men go that way in an automobile. I didn't expect to find them. I walked for a ways and then sat down by a fence to think. It was the direction they went in. I wanted to be as near Jerry as I could. I felt close to him. Pretty soon I went up the side road—I don't know why—and came to the rummy farm house. I was just lonesome to see Jerry, like wanting to see your father at night when you are a young kid. Just then an automobile came along and turned in. Jerry was in it and Henry Rieback's father, and Arthur Bedford from home, and Dave Williams and two other men I didn't know. They got out of the car and went into the house, all but Henry Rieback's father who quarreled with them and said he wouldn't go. It was only about nine o'clock, but they were all drunk and the rummy-looking farm house was a place for bad women to stay in. That's what it was. I crept up along a fence and looked through a window and saw.

It's what give me the fantods. I can't make it out. The women in the house were all ugly mean-looking women, not nice to look at or be near. They were homely too, except one who was tall and looked a little like the gelding Middlestride, but not clean like him, but with a hard ugly mouth. She had red hair. I saw everything plain. I got up by an old rose bush by an open window and looked. The women had on loose dresses and sat around in chairs. The men came in and some sat on the women's laps. The place smelled rotten and there was rotten talk, the kind a kid hears around a livery stable in a town like Beckersville in the winter but don't ever expect to hear talked when there are women around. It was rotten. A nigger wouldn't go into such a place.

I looked at Jerry Tillford. I've told you how I had been feeling about him on account of his knowing what was going on inside of Sunstreak in the minute before he went to the post for the race in which he made a world's record.

Jerry bragged in that bad woman house as I know Sunstreak wouldn't never have bragged. He said that he made that horse, that it was him that won the race and made the record. He lied and bragged like a fool. I never heard such silly talk.

And then, what do you suppose he did! He looked at the woman in there, the one that was lean and hard-mouthed and looked a little like the gelding Middlestride, but not clean like him, and his eyes began to shine just as they did when he looked at me and at Sunstreak in the paddocks at the track in the afternoon. I stood there by the window—gee!—but I wished I hadn't gone away from the tracks, but had stayed with the boys and the niggers and the horses. The tall rotten-looking woman was between us just as Sunstreak was in the paddocks in the afternoon.

Then, all of a sudden, I began to hate that man. I wanted to scream and rush in the room and kill him. I never had such a feeling before. I was so mad clean through that I cried and my fists were doubled up so my finger nails cut my hands.

And Jerry's eyes kept shining and he waved back and forth, and then he went and kissed that woman and I crept away and went back to the tracks and to bed and didn't sleep hardly any, and then next day I got the other kids to start home with me and never told them anything I seen.

I been thinking about it ever since. I can't make it out. Spring has come again and I'm nearly sixteen and go to the tracks mornings same as always, and I see Sunstreak and Middlestride and a new colt named Strident I'll bet will lay them all out, but no one thinks so but me and two or three niggers.

But things are different. At the tracks the air don't taste as good or smell as good. It's because a man like Jerry Tillford, who knows what he does, could see a horse like Sunstreak run, and kiss a woman like that the same day. I can't make it out. Darn him, what did he want to do like that for? I keep thinking about it and it spoils looking at horses and smelling things and hearing niggers laugh and everything. Sometimes I'm so mad about it I want to fight someone. It gives me the fantods. What did he do it for? I want to know why.

1918, 1921

RING LARDNER

(1885–1933)

As a vernacular critic of American life, Ring Lardner belongs to the tradition of humorous journalism, whose transmission through Mark Twain is generally credited to such predecessors as Artemus Ward, Augustus B. Longstreet, and J. J. Hooper. Unlike some of these, Lardner bore the gifts of the humorist as a yoke or a burden; and he seemed to be pursued by a sense of guilt or unfulfillment, whether because of the enormous amount of energy that he expended on high-paid popular writing, or for some reason connected with his notable puritanism. Much of his work is ephemeral, but among his short stories there are a score of masterpieces which identify him as one of the genuine artists and influential writers of our century. In the best of his stories he was the satirist, obsessed by the evil lurking in a society that provided glamorous rewards for the moron, the sneak, the four-flusher, while at every level—in the world of sports and the theater, in family life or in business—contaminating the springs of fidelity with false standards of material success.

Born in Niles, Michigan, on March 6, 1885, he was christened Ringgold Wilmer Lardner. He resisted his parents' suggestions that he attempt to make something of himself, although he did manage to graduate from high school, in 1901. Thereafter he drifted from one job to another until, after some apprenticeship, he became a sports writer for the *Times* of South Bend, Indiana, in 1905. He remained in newspaper work, usually as a sports writer or editor, for the next fifteen years. He conducted his own column, "In the Wake of the News," in the Chicago *Tribune* from 1913 to 1919. Soon he began to experiment with the composition of "letters," which he included in his column, from one Jack Keefe, a stupid bush leaguer who, in asking his advice con-

cerning his baseball play and his love affairs, reveals himself as a liar, egotist, cheap skate, and moron, while providing memorable examples of the English spoken on the sand lots. Lardner developed these letters in the form of an epistolary novel, *You Know Me, Al,* for serial publication in the *Saturday Evening Post* in 1914 and as a volume in 1916. It won him a national audience.

During the next decade, Lardner's stories, sketches, and topical articles appeared in profusion in the magazines, some later being collected in volumes. His reputation as a humorist was enormous, but actually his work was very uneven, much of it calculated for immediate appeal to a popular magazine audience. By 1924 he had published twelve volumes, yet there had been no important recognition of the underlying critical seriousness of his best work. Now, in *How to Write Short Stories* he included ten of his best, to "illustrate in a half-hearted way what I am trying to get at." The stories were far from half-hearted; brought together in this fashion they invited a critical evaluation of his work as a whole. Edmund Wilson (in the *Dial* for July, 1924) expressed a critical consensus: "*How to Write Short Stories* presents a series of American types almost equal in importance to those of Sherwood Anderson and Sinclair Lewis."

The Love Nest and Other Stories (1926) is another volume of Lardner's best, containing such sterling work as "Haircut," "Champion," "A Day with Conrad Green," "Who Dealt?" and the title story, which was dramatized by Robert E. Sherwood and was a great success on the stage in 1927. Here, as in his novel *The Big Town* (1921), Lardner successfully increased the range of his satire to include the prize ring, the theater world, tin-pan alley, and certain accepted social patterns, both of small town life and of metropolitan New York.

In 1930, with George S. Kaufman, he wrote *June Moon*, a Broadway musical hit, and the year before he had made a major collection, entitled *Round Up*, of the stories that he thought worthy. The critical reactions offset for the moment his haunting sense of guilty unfulfillment, but at the same time he was aware of a severe decline in vitality. In 1931 his apprehensions were confirmed; in addition to heart trouble he was found to have tuberculosis. In 1933, at the age of forty-eight, he died, having just completed a volume of sardonically humorous sketches which he called *Lose with a Smile*.

There is no definitive collection of Lardner's writings, although the one-volume *Portable Ring Lardner*, edited, with a useful introduction, by Gilbert Seldes, 1946, contains an excellent and representative selection. Lardner's best stories are collected in *How to Write Short Stories*, 1924; and *The Love Nest and Other Stories*, 1926. All of these and later stories are included in *Round Up*, 1929; in *Best Stories of Ring Lardner*, 1938; and in *Best Short Stories * * *, 1957. Two short novels are *You Know Me, Al: A Busher's Letters*, 1916, and *The Big Town*, 1921. Characteristic volumes of humor and satirical sketches are *Treat 'em Rough*, 1918; *The Real Dope*. 1919: *Symptoms of Being 35*, 1921; *What of It?* 1925; *The Story of a Wonder Man*, 1927; and *Lose with a Smile*, 1933. Light-verse volumes are *Bib Ballads*, 1915, and *Regular Fellows I Have Met*, 1919. "Ring W. Lardner: A Checklist of His Published Works" appeared in *Bulletin of Biography*, 1954, pp. 104–106. A biography is Donald Elder, *Ring Lardner*, 1956.

[handwritten marginalia: bitter satire - but so funny that defeated immediate satire]

Alibi Ike[1]

I

His right name was Frank X. Farrell, and I guess the X stood for "Excuse me." Because he never pulled a play, good or bad, on or off the field, without apologizin' for it.

"Alibi Ike" was the name Carey wished on him the first day he reported down South. O' course we all cut out the "Alibi" part of it right away for fear he would overhear it and bust somebody. But we called him "Ike" right to his face and the rest of it was understood by everybody on the club except Ike himself.

He ast me one time, he says:

"What do you all call me Ike for? I ain't no Yid."

"Carey give you the name," I says. "It's his nickname for every-

1. "Alibi Ike" gave "a name to a character as real, and nearly as round, as Babbitt," wrote Gilbert Seldes (*The Portable Ring Lardner*, p. 6). This reference to Sinclair Lewis' best-known character suggests a useful comparison between these two critics of American life. But Lardner anticipated Lewis. This story, one of his earliest, first appeared in the *Saturday Evening Post* for July 31, 1915. It was collected in *How to Write Short Stories* (1924) and reappeared among the five most admired stories of his *Round Up* (1929).

body he takes a likin' to."

"He mustn't have only a few friends then," says Ike. "I never heard him say 'Ike' to nobody else."

But I was goin' to tell you about Carey namin' him. We'd been workin' out two weeks and the pitchers was showin' somethin' when this bird joined us. His first day out he stood up there so good and took such a reef at the old pill that he had everyone lookin'. Then him and Carey was together in left field, catchin' fungoes,[2] and it was after we was through for the day that Carey told me about him.

"What do you think of Alibi Ike?" ast Carey.

"Who's that?" I says.

"This here Farrell in the outfield," says Carey.

"He looks like he could hit," I says.

"Yes," says Carey, "but he can't hit near as good as he can apologize."

Then Carey went on to tell me what Ike had been pullin' out there. He'd dropped the first fly ball that was hit to him and told Carey his glove wasn't broke in good yet, and Carey says the glove could easy of been Kid Gleason's[3] gran'father. He made a whale of a catch out o' the next one and Carey says "Nice work!" or some-thin' like that, but Ike says he could of caught the ball with his back turned only he slipped when he started after it and, besides that, the air currents fooled him.

"I thought you done well to get to the ball," says Carey.

"I ought to been settin' under it," says Ike.

"What did you hit last year?" Carey ast him.

"I had malaria most o' the season," says Ike. "I wound up with .356."

"Where would I have to go to get malaria?" says Carey, but Ike didn't wise up.

I and Carey and him set at the same table together for supper. It took him half an hour longer'n us to eat because he had to excuse himself every time he lifted his fork.

"Doctor told me I needed starch," he'd say, and then toss a shoveful o' potatoes into him. Or, "They ain't much meat on one o' these chops," he'd tell us, and grab another one. Or he'd say: "Nothin' like onions for a cold," and then he'd dip into the per-fumery.

"Better try that apple sauce," says Carey. "It'll help your malaria."

"Whose malaria?" says Ike. He'd forgot already why he didn't only hit .356 last year.

2. In baseball, flies batted out for prac-tice in fielding.
3. William J. ("Kid") Gleason (1866–
1933), then one of the oldest men in baseball, began with the Phillies in 1888.

I and Carey begin to lead him on.

"Whereabouts did you say your home was?" I ast him.

"I live with my folks," he says. "We live in Kansas City—not right down in the business part—outside a ways."

"How's that come?" says Carey. "I should think you'd get rooms in the post office."

But Ike was too busy curin' his cold to get that one.

"Are you married?" I ast him.

"No," he says. "I never run round much with girls, except to shows onct in a wile and parties and dances and roller skatin'."

"Never take 'em to the prize fights, eh?" says Carey.

"We don't have no real good bouts," says Ike. "Just bush stuff. And I never figured a boxin' match was a place for the ladies."

Well, after supper he pulled a cigar out and lit it. I was just goin' to ask him what he done it for, but he beat me to it.

"Kind o' rests a man to smoke after a good work-out," he says. "Kind o' settles a man's supper, too."

"Looks like a pretty good cigar," says Carey.

"Yes," says Ike. "A friend o' mine give it to me—a fella in Kansas City that runs a billiard room."

"Do you play billiards?" I ast him.

"I used to play a fair game," he says. "I'm all out o' practice now —can't hardly make a shot."

We coaxed him into a four-handed battle, him and Carey against Jack Mack and I. Say, he couldn't play billiards as good as Willie Hoppe;[4] not quite. But to hear him tell it, he didn't make a good shot all evenin'. I'd leave him an awful-lookin' layout and he'd gather 'em up in one try and then run a couple o' hundred, and between every carom he'd say he'd put too much stuff on the ball, or the English didn't take, or the table wasn't true, or his stick was crooked, or somethin'. And all the time he had the balls actin' like they was Dutch soldiers and him Kaiser William. We started out to play fifty points, but we had to make it a thousand so as I and Jack and Carey could try the table.

The four of us set round the lobby a wile after we was through playin', and when it got along toward bedtime Carey whispered to me and says:

"Ike'd like to go to bed, but he can't think up no excuse."

Carey hadn't hardly finished whisperin' when Ike got up and pulled it:

"Well, good night, boys," he says. "I ain't sleepy, but I got some gravel in my shoes and it's killin' my feet."

We knowed he hadn't never left the hotel since we'd came in from the grounds and changed our clo'es. So Carey says:

4. William F. Hoppe (born 1887), American billiards-expert.

"I should think they'd take them gravel pits out o' the billiard room."

But Ike was already on his way to the elevator, limpin'.

"He's got the world beat," says Carey to Jack and I. "I've knew lots o' guys that had an alibi for every mistake they made; I've heard pitchers say that the ball slipped when somebody cracked one off'n 'em; I've heard infielders complain of a sore arm after heavin' one into the stand, and I've saw outfielders tooken sick with a dizzy spell when they've misjudged a fly ball. But this baby can't even go to bed without apologizin', and I bet he excuses himself to the razor when he gets ready to shave."

"And at that," says Jack, "he's goin' to make us a good man."

"Yes," says Carey, "unless rheumatism keeps his battin' average down to .400."

Well, sir, Ike kept whalin' away at the ball all through the trip till everybody knowed he'd won a job. Cap had him in there regular the last few exhibition games and told the newspaper boys a week before the season opened that he was goin' to start him in Kane's place.

"You're there, kid," says Carey to Ike, the night Cap made the 'nnouncement. "They ain't many boys that wins a big league berth their third year out."

"I'd of been up here a year ago," says Ike, "only I was bent over all season with lumbago."

II

It rained down in Cincinnati one day and somebody organized a little game o' cards. They was shy two men to make six and ast I and Carey to play.

"I'm with you if you get Ike and make it seven-handed," says Carey.

So they got a hold of Ike and we went up to Smitty's room.

"I pretty near forgot how many you deal," says Ike. "It's been a long wile since I played."

I and Carey give each other the wink, and sure enough, he was just as ig'orant about poker as billiards. About the second hand, the pot was opened two or three ahead of him, and they was three in when it come his turn. It cost a buck, and he throwed in two.

"It's raised, boys," somebody says.

"Gosh, that's right, I did raise it," says Ike.

"Take out a buck if you didn't mean to tilt her," says Carey.

"No," says Ike, "I'll leave it go."

Well, it was raised back at him and then he made another mistake and raised again. They was only three left in when the draw come. Smitty'd opened with a pair o' kings and he didn't help 'em. Ike stood pat. The guy that'd raised him back was flushin' and he didn't fill. So Smitty checked and Ike bet and didn't get no call. He tossed his hand away, but I grabbed it and give it a look. He had king, queen, jack and two tens. Alibi Ike he must have seen me peekin', for he leaned over and whispered to me.

"I overlooked my hand," he says. "I thought all the wile it was a straight."

"Yes," I says, "that's why you raised twice by mistake."

They was another pot that he come into with tens and fours. It was tilted a couple o' times and two o' the strong fellas drawed ahead of Ike. They each drawed one. So Ike threwed away his little pair and come out with four tens. And they was four treys against him. Carey'd looked at Ike's discards and then he says:

"This lucky bum busted two pair."

"No, no, I didn't," says Ike.

"Yes, yes, you did," says Carey, and showed us the two fours.

"What do you know about that?" says Ike. "I'd of swore one was a five spot."

Well, we hadn't had no pay day yet, and after a wile everybody except Ike was goin' shy. I could see him gettin' restless and I was wonderin' how he'd make the getaway. He tried two or three times. "I got to buy some collars before supper," he says.

"No hurry," says Smitty. "The stores here keeps open all night in April."

After a minute he opened up again.

"My uncle out in Nebraska ain't expected to live," he says. "I ought to send a telegram."

"Would that save him?" says Carey.

"No, it sure wouldn't," says Ike, "but I ought to leave my old man know where I'm at."

"When did you hear about your uncle?" says Carey.

"Just this mornin'," says Ike.

"Who told you?" ast Carey.

"I got a wire from my old man," says Ike.

"Well," says Carey, "your old man knows you're still here yet this afternoon if you was here this mornin'. Trains leavin' Cincinnati in the middle o' the day don't carry no ball clubs."

"Yes," says Ike, "that's true. But he don't know where I'm goin' to be next week."

"Ain't he got no schedule?" ast Carey.

"I sent him one openin' day," says Ike, "but it takes mail a long time to get to Idaho."

"I thought your old man lived in Kansas City," says Carey.

"He does when he's home," says Ike.

"But now," says Carey, "I s'pose he's went to Idaho so as he can be near your sick uncle in Nebraska."

"He's visitin' my other uncle in Idaho."

"Then how does he keep posted about your sick uncle?" ast Carey.

"He don't," says Ike. "He don't even know my other uncle's sick. That's why I ought to wire and tell him."

"Good night!" says Carey.

"What town in Idaho is your old man at?" I says.

Ike thought it over.

"No town at all," he says. "But he's near a town."

"Near what town?" I says.

"Yuma," says Ike.

Well, by this time he'd lost two or three pots and he was desperate. We was playin' just as fast as we could, because we seen we couldn't hold him much longer. But he was tryin' so hard to frame an escape that he couldn't pay no attention to the cards, and it looked like we'd get his whole pile away from him if we could make him stick.

The telephone saved him. The minute it begun to ring, five of us jumped for it. But Ike was there first.

"Yes," he says, answerin' it. "This is him. I'll come right down."

And he slammed up the receiver and beat it out o' the door without even sayin' good-by.

"Smitty'd ought to locked the door," says Carey.

"What did he win?" ast Carey.

We figured it up—sixty-odd bucks.

"And the next time we ask him to play," says Carey, "his fingers will be so stiff he can't hold the cards."

Well, we set round a wile talkin' it over, and pretty soon the telephone rung again. Smitty answered it. It was a friend of his'n from Hamilton and he wanted to know why Smitty didn't hurry down. He was the one that had called before and Ike had told him he was Smitty.

"Ike'd ought to split with Smitty's friend," says Carey.

"No," I says, "he'll need all he won. It costs money to buy collars and to send telegrams from Cincinnati to your old man in Texas and keep him posted on the health o' your uncle in Cedar Rapids, D. C."

III

And you ought to heard him out there on that field! They wasn't a day when he didn't pull six or seven, and it didn't make no difference whether he was goin' good or bad. If he popped up in the pinch he should of made a base hit and the reason he didn't was so-and-so. And if he cracked one for three bases he ought to had a home run, only the ball wasn't lively, or the wind brought it back, or he tripped on a lump o' dirt, roundin' first base.

They was one afternoon in New York when he beat all records. Bib Marquard[5] was workin' against us and he was good.

In the first innin' Ike hit one clear over that right field stand, but it was a few feet foul. Then he got another foul and then the count come to two and two. Then Rube slipped one acrost on him and he was called out.

"What do you know about that!" he says afterward on the bench. "I lost count. I thought it was three and one, and I took a strike."

"You took a strike all right," says Carey. "Even the umps knowed it was a strike."

"Yes," says Ike, "but you can bet I wouldn't of took it if I'd knew it was the third one. The score board had it wrong."

"That score board ain't for you to look at," says Cap. "It's for you to hit that old pill against."

"Well," says Ike, "I could of hit that one over the score board if I'd knew it was the third."

"Was it a good ball?" I says.

"Well, no, it wasn't," says Ike. "It was inside."

"How far inside?" says Carey.

"Oh, two or three inches or half a foot," says Ike.

"I guess you wouldn't of threatened the score board with it then," says Cap.

"I'd of pulled it down the right foul line if I hadn't thought he'd call it a ball," says Ike.

Well, in New York's part o' the innin' Doyle[6] cracked one and Ike run back a mile and a half and caught it with one hand. We was all sayin' what a whale of play it was, but he had to apologize just the same as for gettin' struck out.

"That stand's so high," he says, "that a man don't never see a ball till it's right on top o' you."

"Didn't you see that one?" ast Cap.

"Not at first," says Ike; "not till it raised up above the roof o' the stand."

"Then why did you start back as soon as the ball was hit?" says Cap.

"I knowed by the sound that he'd got a good hold of it," says Ike.

"Yes," says Cap, "but how'd you know what direction to run in?"

"Doyle usually hits 'em that way, the way I run," says Ike.

5. Richard William ("Rube") Marquard (born 1889) was one of the greatest pitchers in baseball. When this story was published he was pitching for the New York Giants.

6. Lawrence J. Doyle (born 1886) was playing a great game at second base for the New York Giants, and winning fame at bat, when Marquard was the Giants' great pitcher.

"Why don't you play blindfolded?" says Carey.

"Might as well, with that big high stand to bother a man," says Ike. "If I could of saw the ball all the time I'd of got it in my hip pocket."

Along in the fifth we was one run to the bad and Ike got on with one out. On the first ball throwed to Smitty, Ike went down. The ball was outside and Meyers throwed Ike out by ten feet.

You could see Ike's lips movin' all the way to the bench and when he got there he had his piece learned.

"Why didn't he swing?" he says.

"Why didn't you wait for his sign?" says Cap.

"He gave me his sign," says Ike.

"What is his sign with you?" says Cap.

"Pickin' up some dirt with his right hand," says Ike.

"Well, I didn't see him do it," Cap says.

"He done it all right," says Ike.

Well, Smitty went out and they wasn't no more argument till they come in for the next innin'. Then Cap opened it up.

"You fellas better get your signs straight," he says.

"Do you mean me?" says Smitty.

"Yes," Caps says. "What's your sign with Ike?"

"Slidin' my left hand up to the end o' the bat and back," says Smitty.

"Do you hear that, Ike?" ast Cap.

"What of it?" says Ike.

"You says his sign was pickin' up dirt and he says it's slidin' his hand. Which is right?"

"I'm right," says Smitty. "But if you're arguin' about him goin' last innin', I didn't give him no sign."

"You pulled your cap down with your right hand, didn't you," ast Ike.

"Well, s'pose I did," says Smitty. "That don't mean nothin'. I never told you to take that for a sign, did I?"

"I thought maybe you meant to tell me and forgot," says Ike.

They couldn't none of us answer that and they wouldn't of been no more said if Ike had of shut up. But wile we was settin' there Carey got on with two out and stole second clean.

"There!" says Ike. "That's what I was tryin' to do and I'd of got away with it if Smitty'd swang and bothered the Indian."

"Oh!" says Smitty. "You was tryin' to steal then, was you? I thought you claimed I give you the hit and run."

"I didn't claim no such a thing," says Ike. "I thought maybe you might of gave me a sign, but I was goin' anyway because I thought I had a good start."

Cap prob'ly would of hit him with a bat, only just about that time Doyle booted one on Hayes and Carey come acrost with the run that tied.

Well, we go into the ninth finally, one and one, and Marquard walks McDonald with nobody out.

"Lay it down," says Cap to Ike.

And Ike goes up there with orders to bunt and cracks the first ball into that right-field stand! It was fair this time, and we're two ahead, but I didn't think about that at the time. I was too busy watchin' Cap's face. First he turned pale and then he got red as fire and then he got blue and purple, and finally he just laid back and busted out laughin'. So we wasn't afraid to laugh ourselfs when we seen him doin' it, and when Ike come in everybody on the bench was in hysterics.

But instead o' takin' advantage, Ike had to try and excuse himself. His play was to shut up and he didn't know how to make it.

"Well," he says, "if I hadn't hit quite so quick at that one I bet it'd of cleared the center-field fence."

Cap stopped laughin'.

"It'll cost you plain fifty," he says.

"What for?" says Ike.

"When I say 'bunt' I mean 'bunt,' " says Cap.

"You didn't say 'bunt,' " says Ike.

"I says 'Lay it down,' " says Cap. "If that don't mean 'bunt,' what does it mean?"

" 'Lay it down' means 'bunt' all right," says Ike, "but I understand you to say 'Lay on it.' "

"All right," says Cap, "and the little misunderstandin' will cost you fifty."

Ike didn't say nothin' for a few minutes. Then he had another bright idear.

"I was just kiddin' about misunderstandin' you," he says. "I knowed you wanted me to bunt."

"Well, then, why didn't you bunt?" ast Cap.

"I was goin' to on the next ball," says Ike. "But I thought if I took a good wallop I'd have 'em all fooled. So I walloped at the first one to fool 'em, and I didn't have no intention o' hittin' it."

"You tried to miss it, did you?" says Cap.

"Yes," says Ike.

"How'd you happen to hit it?" ast Cap.

"Well," Ike says, "I was lookin' for him to throw me a fast one and I was goin' to swing under it. But he come with a hook and I met it right square where I was swingin' to go under the fast one."

"Great!" says Cap. "Boys," he says, "Ike's learned how to hit Marquard's curve. Pretend a fast one's comin' and then try to miss it. It's a good thing to know and Ike'd ought to be willin' to pay for the lesson. So I'm goin' to make it a hundred instead o' fifty."

The game wound up 3 to 1. The fine didn't go, because Ike hit like a wild man all through that trip and we made pretty near a clean-up. That night we went to Philly I got him cornered in the car and I says to him:

"Forget them alibis for a wile and tell me somethin'. What'd you do that for, swing that time against Marquard when you was told to bunt?"

"I'll tell you," he says. "That ball he throwed me looked just like the one I struck out on in the first innin' and I wanted to show Cap what I could of done to that other one if I'd knew it was the third strike."

"But," I says, "the one you struck out on in the first innin' was a fast ball."

"So was the one I cracked in the ninth," says Ike.

IV

You've saw Cap's wife, o' course. Well, her sister's about twict as good-lookin' as her, and that's goin' some.

Cap took his missus down to St. Louis the second trip and the other one come down from St. Joe to visit her. Her name is Dolly, and some doll is right.

Well, Cap was goin' to take the two sisters to a show and he wanted a beau for Dolly. He left it to her and she picked Ike. He'd hit three on the nose that afternoon—off'n Sallee,[7] too.

They fell for each other that first evenin'. Cap told us how it come off. She begin flatterin' Ike for the star game he'd played and o' course he begin excusin' himself for not doin' better. So she thought he was modest and it went strong with her. And she believed everything he said and that made her solid with him—that and her make-up. They was together every mornin' and evenin' for the five days we was there. In the afternoons Ike played the grandest ball you ever see, hittin' and runnin' the bases like a fool and catchin' everything that stayed in the park.

I told Cap, I says: "You'd ought to keep the doll with us and he'd make Cobb's figures[8] look sick."

But Dolly had to go back to St. Joe and we come home for a long serious.

Well, for the next three weeks Ike had a letter to read every day and he'd set in the clubhouse readin' it till mornin' practice was half over. Cap didn't say nothin' to him, because he was goin' so good. But I and Carey wasted a lot of our time tryin' to get him to own up who the letters was from. Fine chanct!

---

7. Harry F. Sallee (born 1885), an excellent pitcher, was with the St. Louis Cardinals from 1909 to 1916.

8. Tyrus Raymond ("Ty") Cobb (born 1886) had a batting average of .420 in 1911, equaled only twice by any other player between 1903 and 1951.

"What are you readin'?" Carey'd say. "A bill?"

"No," Ike'd say, "not exactly a bill. It's a letter from a fella I used to go to school with."

"High school or college?" I'd ask him.

"College," he'd say.

"What college?" I'd say.

Then he'd stall a wile and then he'd say:

"I didn't go to the college myself, but my friend went there."

"How did it happen you didn't go?" Carey'd ask him.

"Well," he'd say, "they wasn't no colleges near where I lived."

"Didn't you live in Kansas City?" I'd say to him.

One time he'd say he did and another time he didn't. One time he says he lived in Michigan.

"Where at?" says Carey.

"Near Detroit," he says.

"Well," I says, "Detroit's near Ann Arbor and that's where they got the university."

"Yes," says Ike, "they got it there now, but they didn't have it there then."

"I come pretty near goin' to Syracuse," I says, "only they wasn't no railroads runnin' through there in them days."

"Where'd this friend o' yours go to college?" says Carey.

"I forget now," says Ike.

"Was it Carlisle?"[9] ast Carey.

"No," says Ike, "his folks wasn't very well off."

"That's what barred me from Smith," I says.

"I was goin' to tackle Cornell's," says Carey, "but the doctor told me I'd have hay fever if I didn't stay up North."

"Your friend writes long letters," I says.

"Yes," says Ike; "he's tellin' me about a ball player."

"Where does he play?" ast Carey.

"Down in the Texas League—Fort Wayne," says Ike.

"It looks like a girl's writin'," Carey says.

"A girl wrote it," says Ike. "That's my friend's sister, writin' for him."

"Didn't they teach writin' at this here college where he went?" says Carey.

"Sure," Ike says, "they taught writin', but he got his hand cut off in a railroad wreck."

"How long ago?" I says.

"Right after he got out o' college," says Ike.

"Well," I says, "I should think he'd of learned to write with his left hand by this time."

9. The Indian School, then at Carlisle, Pennsylvania, famous for its athletes. Qualified Indians studied there without expense; *cf.* the next line of text.

"It's his left hand that was cut off," says Ike; "and he was left-handed."

"You get a letter every day," says Carey. "They're all the same writin'. Is he tellin' you about a different ball player every time he writes?"

"No," Ike says. "It's the same ball player. He just tells me what he does every day."

"From the size o' the letters, they don't play nothin' but double-headers down there," says Carey.

We figured that Ike spent most of his evenin's answerin' the letters from his "friend's sister," so we kept tryin' to date him up for shows and parties to see how he'd duck out of 'em. He was bugs over spaghetti, so we told him one day that they was goin' to be a big feed of it over to Joe's that night and he was invited.

"How long'll it last?" he says.

"Well," we says, "we're goin' right over there after the game and stay till they close up."

"I can't go," he says, "unless they leave me come home at eight bells."

"Nothin' doin'," says Carey. "Joe'd get sore."

"I can't go then," says Ike.

"Why not?" I ast him.

"Well," he says, "my landlady locks up the house at eight and I left my key home."

"You can come and stay with me," says Carey.

"No," he says, "I can't sleep in a strange bed."

"How do you get along when we're on the road?" says I.

"I don't never sleep the first night anywheres," he says. "After that I'm all right."

"You'll have time to chase home and get your key right after the game," I told him.

"The key ain't home," says Ike. "I lent it to one o' the other fellas and he's went out o' town and took it with him."

"Couldn't you borry another key off'n the landlady?" Carey ast him.

"No," he says, "that's the only one they is."

Well, the day before we started East again, Ike come into the clubhouse all smiles.

"Your birthday?" I ast him.

"No," he says.

"What do you feel so good about?" I says.

"Got a letter from my old man," he says. "My uncle's goin' to get well."

"Is that the one in Nebraska?" says I.

"Not right in Nebraska," says Ike. "Near there."

But afterwards we got the right dope from Cap. Dolly'd blew in from Missouri and was goin' to make the trip with her sister.

V

Well, I want to alibi Carey and I for what come off in Boston. If we'd of had any idear what we was doin', we'd never did it. They wasn't nobody outside o' maybe Ike and the dame that felt worse over it than I and Carey.

The first two days we didn't see nothin' of Ike and her except out to the park. The rest o' the time they was sight-seein' over to Cambridge and down to Revere and out to Brook-a-line and all the other places where the rubes go.

But when we come into the beanery after the third game Cap's wife called us over.

"If you want to see somethin' pretty," she says, "look at the third finger on Sis's left hand."

Well, o' course we knowed before we looked that it wasn't goin' to be no hangnail. Nobody was su'prised when Dolly blew into the dinin' room with it—a rock that Ike'd bought off'n Diamond Joe the first trip to New York. Only o' course it'd been set into a lady's-size ring instead o' the automobile tire he'd been wearin'.

Cap and his missus and Ike and Dolly ett supper together, only Ike didn't eat nothin', but just set there blushin' and spillin' things on the table-cloth. I heard him excusin' himself for not havin' no appetite. He says he couldn't never eat when he was clost to the ocean. He'd forgot about them sixty-five oysters he destroyed the first night o' the trip before.

He was goin' to take her to a show, so after supper he went up-stairs to change his collar. She had to doll up, too, and o' course Ike was through long before her.

If you remember the hotel in Boston, they's a little parlor where the piano's at and then they's another little parlor openin' off o' that. Well, when Ike come down Smitty was playin 'a few chords and I and Carey was harmonizin'. We seen Ike go up to the desk to leave his key and we called him in. He tried to duck away, but we wouldn't stand for it.

We ast him what he was all duded up for and he says he was goin' to the theayter.

"Goin' alone?" says Carey.

"No," he says, "a friend o' mine's goin' with me."

"What do you say if we go along?" says Carey.

"I ain't only got two tickets," he says.

"Well," says Carey, "we can go down there with you and buy our own seats; maybe we can all get together."

"No," says Ike. "They ain't no more seats. They're all sold out."

"We can buy some off'n scalpers," says Carey.

"I wouldn't if I was you," says Ike. "They say the show's rotten."

"What are you goin' for, then?" I ast.

"I didn't hear about it bein' rotten till I got the tickets," he says.

"Well," I says, "if you don't want to go I'll buy the tickets from you."

"No," says Ike, "I wouldn't want to cheat you. I'm stung and I'll just have to stand for it."

"What are you goin' to do with the girl, leave her here at the hotel?" I says.

"What girl?" says Ike.

"The girl you ett supper with," I says.

"Oh," he says, "we just happened to go into the dinin' room together, that's all. Cap wanted I should set down with 'em."

"I noticed," says Carey, "that she happened to be wearin' that rock you bought off'n Diamond Joe."

"Yes," says Ike. "I lent it to her for a wile."

"Did you lend her the new ring that goes with it?" I says.

"She had that already," says Ike. "She lost the set out of it."

"I wouldn't trust no strange girl with a rock o' mine," says Carey.

"Oh, I guess she's all right," Ike says. "Besides I was tired o' the stone. When a girl asks you for somethin', what are you goin' to do?"

He started out toward the desk, but we flagged him.

"Wait a minute!" Carey says. "I got a bet with Sam here, and it's up to you to settle it."

"Well," says Ike, "make it snappy. My friend'll be here any minute."

"I bet," says Carey, "that you and that girl was engaged to be married."

"Nothin' to it," says Ike.

"Now look here," says Carey, "this is goin' to cost me real money if I lose. Cut out the alibi stuff and give it to us straight. Cap's wife just as good as told us you was roped."

Ike blushed like a kid.

"Well, boys," he says, "I may as well own up. You win, Carey."

"Yatta boy!" says Carey. "Congratulations!"

"You got a swell girl, Ike," I says.

"She's a peach," says Smitty.

"Well, I guess she's O. K.," says Ike. "I don't know much about girls."

"Didn't you never run round with 'em?" I says.

"Oh, yes, plenty of 'em," says Ike. "But I never seen none I'd fall for."

"That is, till you seen this one," says Carey.

"Well," says Ike, "this one's O. K., but I wasn't thinkin' about gettin' married yet a wile."

"Who done the askin'—her?" says Carey.

"Oh, no," says Ike, "but sometimes a man don't know what he's gettin' into. Take a good-lookin' girl, and a man gen'ally almost always does about what she wants him to."

"They couldn't no girl lasso me unless I wanted to be lassoed," says Smitty.

"Oh, I don't know," says Ike. "When a fella gets to feelin' sorry for one of 'em it's all off."

Well, we left him go after shakin' hands all around. But he didn't take Dolly to no show that night. Some time wile we was talkin' she'd come into that other parlor and she'd stood there and heard us. I don't know how much she heard. But it was enough. Dolly and Cap's missus took the midnight train for New York. And from there Cap's wife sent her on her way back to Missouri.

She'd left the ring and a note for Ike with the clerk. But we didn't ask Ike if the note was from his friend in Fort Wayne, Texas.

VI

When we'd came to Boston Ike was hittin' plain .397. When we got back home he'd fell off to pretty near nothin'. He hadn't drove one out o' the infield in any o' them other Eastern parks, and he didn't even give no excuse for it.

To show you how bad he was, he struck out three times in Brooklyn one day and never opened his trap when Cap ast him what was the matter. Before, if he'd whiffed oncet in a game he'd of wrote a book tellin' why.

Well, we dropped from first place to fifth in four weeks and we was still goin' down. I and Carey was about the only ones in the club that spoke to each other, and all as we did was remind ourselves o' what a boner we'd pulled.

"It's goin' to beat us out o' the big money," says Carey.

"Yes," I says. "I don't want to knock my own ball club, but it looks like a one-man team, and when that one man's dauber's down we couldn't trim our whiskers."

"We ought to knew better," says Carey.

"Yes," I says, "but why should a man pull an alibi for bein' engaged to such a bearcat as she was?"

"He shouldn't," says Carey. "But I and you knowed he would or we'd never started talkin' to him about it. He wasn't no more ashamed o' the girl than I am of a regular base hit. But he just can't come clean on no subjec'."

Cap had the whole story, and I and Carey was as pop'lar with him as an umpire.

"What do you want me to do, Cap?" Carey'd say to him before goin' up to hit.

"Use your own judgment," Cap'd tell him. "We want to lose another game."

But finally, one night in Pittsburgh, Cap had a letter from his missus and he come to us with it.

"You fellas," he says, "is the ones that put us on the bum, and if you're sorry I think they's a chancet for you to make good. The old lady's out to St. Joe and she's been tryin' her hardest to fix things up. She's explained that Ike don't mean nothin' with his talk; I've wrote and explained that to Dolly, too. But the old lady says that Dolly says that she can't believe it. But Dolly's still stuck on this baby, and she's pinin' away just the same as Ike. And the old lady says she thinks if you two fellas would write to the girl and explain how you was always kiddin' with Ike and leadin' him on, and how the ball club was all shot to pieces since Ike quit hittin', and how he acted like he was goin' to kill himself, and this and that, she'd fall for it and maybe soften down. Dolly, the old lady says, would believe you before she'd believe I and the old lady, because she thinks it's her we're sorry for, and not him."

Well, I and Carey was only too glad to try and see what we could do. But it wasn't no snap. We wrote about eight letters before we got one that looked good. Then we give it to the stenographer and had it wrote out on a typewriter and both of us signed it.

It was Carey's idear that made the letter good. He stuck in something about the world's serious money that our wives wasn't goin' to spend unless she took pity on a "boy who was so shy and modest that he was afraid to come right out and say that he had asked such a beautiful and handsome girl to become his bride."

That's probably what got her, or maybe she couldn't of held out much longer anyway. It was four days after we sent the letter that Cap heard from his missus again. We was in Cincinnati.

"We've won," he says to us. "The old lady says that Dolly says she'll give him another chance. But the old lady says it won't do no good for Ike to write a letter. He'll have to go out there."

"Send him to-night," says Carey.

"I'll pay half his fare," I says.

"I'll pay the other half," says Carey.

"No," says Cap, "the club'll pay his expenses. I'll send him scoutin'."

"Are you goin' to send him to-night?"

"Sure," says Cap. "But I'm goin' to break the news to him right now. It's time we win a ball game."

So in the clubhouse, just before the game, Cap told him. And I certainly felt sorry for Rube Benton and Red Ames[1] that after-

1. John C. ("Rube") Benton, who played from 1911 to 1923, and Leon Kessling ("Red") Ames, who played from 1903 to 1919, were both pitching for Cincinnati from 1913 to 1915, the date of this story.

noon! I and Carey was standin' in front o' the hotel that night when Ike come out with his suitcase.

"Sent home?" I says to him.

"No," he says, "I'm goin' scoutin'."

"Where to?" I says. "Fort Wayne?'

"No, not exactly," he says.

"Well," says Carey, "have a good time."

"I ain't lookin' for no good time," says Ike. "I says I was goin' scoutin'."

"Well, then," says Carey, "I hope you see somebody you like."

"And you better have a drink before you go," I says.

"Well," says Ike, "they claim it helps a cold."

1915, 1924

SINCLAIR LEWIS
(1885–1951)

Sinclair Lewis was the leading satirist of his generation. He "reported" American life, always on the lookout for a "good story"—a story of immediate topical value.

What he sacrificed by this approach was philosophical depth and perspective. Yet he was a writer of high ideals and courage. Much of his criticism was leveled at abuses badly in need of correction, and in some cases it is likely that his novels helped to stimulate the public to remedy them. He was a gifted wielder of words, and gave to the language such ineradicable terms of opprobrium as "rotarian," "main-street," and "babbitry"—the last two derived from the titles of his first novels.

These famous books, *Main Street* (1920) and *Babbitt* (1922), opened his attack upon what he regarded as the root of failure and corruption in our society. This was the inherent materialism that brought us, in Oscar Wilde's phrase, to know "the price of everything and the value of nothing," to own so much while possessing so little, to take comfort in our genius for inventing all sorts of satisfactions for needs that we did not have, while neglecting to recognize, let alone to satisfy, the needs of the human spirit. Readers today disagree sharply as to the justice of these criticisms, but in 1920 Lewis sprang at once into a position of authority with American readers, while Europeans, generally suspicious of American culture in the first place, took him so seriously that he was chosen in 1930 as the first American writer to receive the Nobel Prize of the Swedish Academy.

Harry Sinclair Lewis was born on February 7, 1885 in Sauk Center, Minnesota, the "Gopher

Prairie" of *Main Street*. He was nineteen when he entered Yale, and he interrupted his studies for two trips to Europe on cattle boats and for long tramping excursions through the eastern states and Mexico. When he received his degree with the class of 1907 at Yale, he was nearly twenty-three, and had connections in New York as a hack writer of magazine verse, humor, and juveniles. After a trip to Panama, partly by steerage and partly as a stowaway, he returned to New York as a publisher's reader, made his first marriage, and wrote his first novel. *Our Mr. Wrenn* (1914) is in the manner of H. G. Wells, combining whimsey with social purpose. Four lesser novels and a play were completed before *Main Street* appeared.

In this novel, for the first time, he was able to devote his brilliant satire and his genius for the memorable phrase to a subject of immediate popular interest. The "attack on the village," the satire of the "small-town mind," had already appeared in British literature; and among American writers, Edgar Lee Masters in his *Spoon River Anthology*, and Anderson in *Winesburg, Ohio* had notably drawn the first blood. But no other writer had brought to the fray Lewis' pyrotechnical combination of narrative sophistication, satirical brilliance, and mirth-provoking mimicry. Within a year the book had swept the country, and the author's fortune was made. As with many of Lewis' themes, this was ephemeral. The auto-

mobile age was dawning, and within fifteen years the American small town was to become quite another thing, with quite another set of problems. In 1922, *Babbitt*, satirizing the Rotarian and go-getter, had a subject of somewhat more permanent interest, for it may be that babbittry has changed only its objectives, not its spirit. In spite of his sardonic humor, Dickensian caricature, and devastating mimicry of American jargon, Lewis created a pathetic reality and appeal in George Babbitt. With somewhat less success he re-created the character in Lowell Schmaltz of *The Man Who Knew Coolidge* (1928).

Lewis poured out his novels, fifteen of them between 1920 and his death in 1951. In *Arrowsmith* (1925) he found a subject of considerable human warmth—the idealism of the devoted scientist and physician in conflict with the forces that attempt to sensationalize his work or to commercialize and monopolize his discoveries. In Martin Arrowsmith, his wife, Leora, and Dr. Max Gottlieb, he gave us his most fully developed and enduring characters. The book was awarded the Pulitzer Prize, which the author declined, asserting that the award, because it was made for a representation of the "wholesome aspect of American life," tended to restrict freedom of thought. In 1928, having been divorced, Lewis married Dorothy Thompson, the journalist. That marriage was terminated in 1942.

After *Arrowsmith*, Lewis' work

declined for several years. *Mantrap* (1926) is negligible. *Elmer Gantry* (1927), an angry attack on the hypocritical and money-minded evangelist, was a sensational success primarily because of certain current scandals. *Dodsworth* (1929) was his last notable contribution. As in *Arrowsmith*, he had found a subject of enduring human interest, a theme involving moral integrity, rather than one of merely topical importance. Sam Dodsworth, who suddenly discovered that he was making the best in automobiles but failing to make anything of himself, is a fully embodied and convincing character, while Fran, his mean and selfish wife, is a real and tragic figure in her failure to join him in a search for selfhood. As a play written in collaboration with Sidney Howard, the story made an excellent drama on the stage in 1935. *It Can't Happen Here* (1935) warned Americans that one of their native demagogues might be as dangerous as the European dictators who were then seizing power; *Gideon Planish* (1943) was an exposé of the potential chicanery of the academic profession and of organized philanthropies in the hands of charlatans, but it was not sufficiently well studied, and had no character interest; *Cass Timberlane* (1945) was a mildly interesting domestic novel; and *Kingsblood Royal* (1947) was a study of the persecution of a Negro family in a white neighborhood. Lewis died in Rome, after several years of declining health, in 1951.

Sinclair Lewis was a liberating force upon the literature of the 1920's; with an inventive and courageous critical mind, he was a stalwart crusader against the encroaching materialism which tolerated moral slackness, vulgarity, ignorance, and narrow bigotry in conformity with a pattern of superficial success cheaply won. He remained throughout life one of the most high-minded and respected of our authors. But it seems that his literary reputation may ultimately be determined by only four of his many books—*Main Street, Babbitt, Arrowsmith*, and *Dodsworth*—the volumes in which, no matter how misguided the characters may be, they are endowed with three-dimensional reality and with the quality in lost creatures that evokes our pity as much as our contempt.

Lewis's principal volumes include *Main Street*, 1920; *Babbitt*, 1922; *Arrowsmith*, 1925; *Mantrap*, 1926; *Elmer Gantry*, 1927; *The Man Who Knew Coolidge*, 1928; *Dodsworth*, 1929; *Ann Vickers*, 1933; *Work of Art*, 1934; *Selected Short Stories*, 1935; *It Can't Happen Here*, 1935; *Jayhawker: A Play in Three Acts* (with Lloyd Lewis), 1935; *The Prodigal Parents*, 1938; *Bethel Merriday*, 1940; *Gideon Planish*, 1943; *Cass Timberlane*, 1945; *Kingsblood Royal*, 1947; *The God-Seeker*, 1949; *World So Wide*, posthumously published in 1951; *The Man from Main Street*, 1953, posthumously collected sketches, some with biographical interest. Harrison Smith edited *From Main Street to Stockholm: Letters of Sinclair Lewis, 1919–1930*, 1952.

An early biographical account is Carl Van Doren's *Sinclair Lewis*, 1933. Grace Hegger Lewis published a memoir, *With Love from Gracie* * * *, 1955. Mark Schorer's *Sinclair Lewis, An American Life*, 1961, is comprehensive.

Created characters a little better than inferior stock characters

You Know How Women Are[1]

—And I tell you, Walt, now we have a chance to sit down here by ourselves in your den and have a real chat—and say, from what I've seen, I don't believe there's a more elegant house for its size in Troy, and then of course you always were my favorite cousin, and one of the few people whose business judgment I'd trust and—

If you can see your way clear to making this loan, you'll never regret it. Business hasn't gone quite so good the last six months, as I admitted, but now I've got the exclusive Zenith agency for Zenith[2] for these new cash registers—and say, what the cash register means, what it *means* to the modern and efficient conduct of business; it's almost, you might say, the symbol of modern industry, like the sword is of war—now I've got that, I can guarantee a big increase in turnover, taking one thing with another, and I want you to examine the analysis of my business with the greatest care.

And I certainly do admit all your criticisms, and I'm going to ponder on 'em and try to profit by 'em.

I'm afraid I do get too kind of talkee-talkee during business hours, and maybe waste time and money. And I admit what you said about my college course. It's perfectly true: I didn't quit Amherst because my Dad died—fact, he didn't die till nine months after I was fired, and it's true I was dropped for flunking all my college courses, as you said—though I thought you threw that up to me a little unnecessarily; almost hurt my feelings, in fact; don't know that I'd 've stood it from anybody but you, but of course you always were my favorite cousin—

You see, I don't go around telling everybody that version of the story, because what I figure is, what they don't know won't hurt 'em none, and it's none of their business.

But it's not true, as you kind of hinted and suggested, that I didn't know President Coolidge in college. It's a fact that for some years I did have him mixed up with another fellow in our class that looked something like him, but here some time ago I happened to run into this other fellow, and now I've got the two of 'em perfectly straight.

Why, I can remember just as if it was yesterday, Cal—as we used

1. "You Know How Women Are" is one of five sketches dealing with the same character, and ultimately assembled in one volume, *The Man Who Knew Coolidge* (1928), from which the present text has been taken. This book rounds out Lewis' first period, resembling its prototype, *Babbitt* (1922). In the endless sales talk that Schmaltz substitutes for conversation, he shows that the fact that he "knew" President Coolidge, before flunking out of their alma mater, gives him a sense of importance by association that assuages his pauperized, Raggedy Andy soul. "You Know How Women Are," the central narrative, in its portrayal of Schmaltz's sporadic impulse to seek some sort of value in life, evokes, as *Babbitt* does, a dash of pity for this stereotyped slave of Philistia.

2. In *Babbitt* and *Dodsworth*, Lewis had also set the scene in the imaginary midwestern city of Zenith.

to call him—Cal and I were going into class together, and I says to him, "Cal, old boy," I said, "what's the Latin for 'battle'?" And he said—he said—well, he gave the word right out, without any hemming and hawing and beating around the bush.[3]

But you're right, I do kind of get to talking too much. Henceforth I'm going to cut it short, and you'll never regret it if you put in that loan.

And I don't think that even you, with all the insight that you show into human nature, quite understand how and why it is that in certain moods I do run on a good deal. There's reasons for it. In the first place, I'm called on so constantly for speeches and oratory in Zenith—you've never been there and you couldn't understand, but—

Well, you take like this, for instance. I was attending a meeting of the Americanization Committee of the Zenith Chamber of Commerce, and we were discussing birth control. Well, the chairman insisted I make 'em a long speech on the subject.

"Shucks, boys," I said, "you know just as much about it as I do," but they talked and they insisted, and they wouldn't let me go until I'd made a long spiel for 'em, summing up the arguments on both sides and, you might say, kind of clarifying it for 'em. See how I mean? But you, Walt, you just think of business night and day, and prob'ly that's a more practical way to think of it. But I get dragged into all these public and influential occasions and get kind of into a habit of oratory and philosophy, see how I mean?

And then—

I hate to say it, and there isn't another human being living, Walt, that I'd tell this to, and I want you to treat it as strictly confidential, but—

The fact is, what really cramps my style is my wife.

That girl—

And in many ways I've got nothing but praise for Mamie. She means well, and as far as her lights lead her, she does everything she can for me, but the fact is she don't quite understand me, and say, the way she drives me and makes demands on me and everything, why say, it just about drives me crazy.

And Delmerine same way. Thinking the Old Man's *made* of money!

And what I've done for Mamie—yes, and what modern American science has done! Think of the advantage of canned goods, of delicatessen shops with every delicacy from salads to cold turkey, all ready to serve without any preparation; of baker's bread without

---

3. As president, Calvin Coolidge practiced a strategic taciturnity that won him the popular nickname of "Silent Cal."

having to bake bread at home. Think of the electric dish-washing machine, reducing the work of dish-washing to, you might say, practically a minimum, and the vacuum cleaner, and what an invention *that* is!—no more sweeping, no more beating rugs—why say, the preachers can talk about these mysteries and all like that, but I guess in the vacuum cleaner America has added to the world *its* own mystery, that'll last when the columns of the Acropolis have crumbled to mere dust!

And then think of the modern laundries with their marvelous machinery.

It's true that they don't wash the clothes quite as good as my old mother used to—fact, they simply tear hell out of my handkerchiefs, and I always was a man to appreciate a high grade of fine linen handkerchief. But still, think of the labor-saving.

And so I've provided Mame with every device to save her labor, so whether it's a question of her telling the maid what to do, or during those comparatively rare intervals when we haven't got a hired girl and she has to do some of the work herself, she can get it all done in a jiffy, you might say, and be free for all the pleasures and self-improvement of leisure. She's free to play bridge nearly every afternoon, and also to give a lot of attention to her literary club, the William Lyon Phelps Ladies' Book and Literary Society,[4] and get a lot of culture.

Now myself, I've always given a lot of attention to intellectual matters. Of course I'm right up on history—I've read clear through both Wells' "Outline of History," or practically clear through it, and also Van Lear's "Story of Mankind," [5] especially studying the illustrations. And of course—maybe I'm a little rusty on it now, but as a boy I used to be able to chatter German like a native, you might say, as my father often talked it to us at home. And now I'm kind of specializing on philosophy. I've read a lot of this "Story of Philosophy" by—I can't at the moment exactly remember the professor's name,[6] but it gives you the whole contents of all philosophy in one book; and while these business cares have for the moment interrupted my reading the book, I expect to go right on and finish it.

But Mame, she has the opportunity to go ahead and knock all *my* culture into a cocked hat. Here recently her club had a very fine lecture about the excavation of King Tut's[7] tomb, from a gentleman

4. Professor Phelps of Yale, who died in 1943, became a brilliant popularizer of literature through his extensive lecture tours and public readings.

5. In 1920, H. G. Wells published his enormously successful *Outline of History*, thus initiating a host of outlines of everything, most of them intended for the quick education of the ignoramus. *The Story of Mankind* (1921), was actually written by Hendrik Willem Van Loon.

6. By Will Durant; published in 1926.

7. King Tutankhamen of Egypt (*fl.* 1358 B.C.). In 1922 the discovery and excavation of his tomb near Luxor, supposedly protected against desecration by an ancient curse, was sensational news.

that had been right there on the ground—of course he couldn't go *into* the tomb, because nobody's allowed inside it except the excavating staff, but he saw the place at first hand, and my wife learned a lot about Egyptology from him.

And they've had a whole course in dietetics. She learned, for example, that the ordinary housewife uses more butter in cooking than is at all necessary—that while maybe butter may make grub *taste* a little better, it doesn't add proportionately to the calories or whatever they are, and so she learned one way in which to economize. And my God, these days, what with the cost of gasoline and golf balls, a fellow has to economize on something.

So as I say, she has a chance to lead a free life and have a lot of dandy times, because I've provided her with all the household conveniences. But who paid for 'em? Where did the money to pay for 'em come from? From my toil and efforts, that's where it came from, and do you think I can get her to appreciate that? Not for one moment!

All day long I slave and work to keep her in luxury, and then when I come home at night all tired out, do I find her ready to comfort me? I do not!

I might as well not have a wife at all. And then when I try to make her understand what I've been doing—like telling her how hard I've worked to sell a new adding-machine to some fellow that didn't want it and maybe didn't need it, do you think she appreciates it? She does not!

Why, she always makes out like she wishes I was a doctor, or one of these he-lecturers that goes around spieling to women's clubs, or some darn' arty thing like that, and sometimes she practically up and says she wishes I could make love like one of these Wop counts, or a movie actor!

She says I just think of business and not of her. But I notice she's good and plenty glad to grab all the money I bring home from that business, all right!

It was—

Now I wouldn't say this to anybody else on God's green earth, and for heaven's sake don't you ever breathe a syllable of it, even to your wife, but I've been beginning to think here lately that it was all wrong with Mame and me right from the beginning!

Not that I'd ever do anything about it, you understand—even though I *have* got a lady friend in New York, simply a little darling and at least twelve years younger than Mame, too—but I don't believe in divorce, and then there's the children to think of. But it was all wrong—

I've learned a lot here lately. I've been studying and delving into psychoanalysis. Know anything about psychoanalysis?

Well, I do, and say, it certainly is a revelation. I've read almost clear through a manual on it—a very authoritive book written by a lady, Miss Alexandrine Applebaugh, that's a great authority on the subject, because she studied with a man that was a pupil of one of the biggest pupils of old Freud, and it was Freud that invented psychoanalysis.[8]

Well, now I'll explain what psychoanalysis is. It's like this:

Everybody ought to have a rich, full sex-life, and all human activities are directed toward that. Whenever a guy is doing something, it's directed toward making himself attractive sexually, especially if it's something big and important—no matter whether it's painting a picture or putting over a big deal in Florida town-lots or discovering a new eclipse or pitching in a World Series game or preaching a funeral sermon or writing a big advertisement or any of them things. On the other hand, when fellows like us *do* put over something, we want to be appreciated, and we got a right to expect it, and if we don't get appreciated at home, we ought to find new mates, see how I mean?

Only you get into so doggone many complications and trouble and all that maybe it ain't practical, even with a cute girl like this one in New York I was speaking about—Ain't really worth it.

And then there's a lot in psychoanalysis about dreams. All dreams mean you ought to have a different kind of a wife—oh, they're *mighty* important!

And so now you'll understand psychoanalysis—as well as anybody does, anyway.

Well, as I say, now that I've mastered psychoanalysis, I can see things was all wrong with Mame and me from the beginning.

I was a young fellow, just come to Zenith, then, working in a wholesale paper house and living in a boarding-house out in the Benner Park district, and in those days that district was just like a small town. I met a dandy crowd of young people at the church and so on, and we used to have dances and picnics and sleigh-rides and everything—rube stuff, but lots of fun.

Well, Mame—her father was in the roofing business, did a pretty good business, too, for them days—she was one of the jolliest girls in the bunch, but she was awful on the level. There was some of the girls in our crowd that you could get pretty fresh with—nothing wrong, you understand, or not hardly ever, but still when you was all cuddled down together in the hay on a sleigh-ride, you could hold their hands and maybe even pat their knees a little.

But Mame—never! No sir! Why say, she was so pure and reli-

8. Sigmund Freud (1856–1939), developer of psychoanalysis, was one of the most influential minds of the twentieth century; but by 1925 his theories were attracting cultists and charlatans.

gious that one time at a dance when I tried to kiss her, she slapped hell out of me!

So of course that just led me on. Made me think she was the living wonder.

Maybe if I'd known then as much as I know now, I'd 've known that it isn't so bad for a girl that you're going to spend your life with, intimate, you might say, to have a little of the Old Nick in her and not be so doggone adverse to a little scientific cuddling— within reason I mean, of course, you see how I mean?

Well, so we got married and she never did get so she liked—

I mean, she hints around sometimes and kind of hints that it's because I'm just a poor plain plug American business man that she's never warmed up. But my God, I've never had any encouragement! I don't expect I'd ever be any Valentino,[9] anyway, but how can I even begin to learn to show her a good time when she's always acted like she was afraid I *would* try to kiss her?

I tell you, Walt, I'm kind of puzzled. Sometimes I almost kind of wonder (though I wouldn't want to be quoted) whether with all the great things we got in this greatest nation in the world, with more autos and radios and furnaces and suits of clothes and miles of cement pavements and skyscrapers than the rest of the world put together, and with more deep learning—hundreds of thousands of students studying Latin and bookkeeping and doctoring and domestic science and literature and banking and window-dressing—even with all of this, I wonder if we don't lack something in American life when you consider that you almost never see an American married couple that really like each other and like to be with each other?

I wonder. But I guess it's too much for me. I just don't understand—

But I'm getting away from my subject. To return to Mame:

Aside from her apparently not wanting me to be anything whatsomever around the house except the guy that pays the bills and carves the duck and fixes the furnace and drives her car out of the garage so she can go off to a hen bridge-party, here lately we've got into kind of a bad way of quarreling.

Well, here's an example:

We used to have dogs for quite a while after we were married, and I always did like to have a good dog around the house. Kind of gives you somebody to talk to when you come home and there ain't anybody around—just sits and listens while you explain things to him, and looks like he *understood!* But here about six years ago, just at a moment when we didn't happen to have a dog, somebody

9. Rudolph Valentino (died 1926), glamorous motion picture actor.

gave Mrs. Schmaltz—gave Mamie, I mean—a very fine expensive cat by the name Minnie—not exactly a full-bred Persian, I guess, but pretty full-bred at that.

But at the same time, even appreciating how much money she was worth, I never did *like* that damn' cat!

You see, we also had a canary, a very valuable little canary named Dicky, a real genuwine Hertz Mountains canary, and intelligent— say, there's those that say a canary isn't intelligent, but I want to tell you that that canary *knew* me, and when I'd stand near the cage he'd chirp just like he was talking to me.

He was a lot of comfort to me, not having a dog at that time—I was looking for a high-class English setter, and hadn't been able to find one at the price I felt justified in paying.

Well sir, here was a surprising thing. We fed that cat and fed her—I'd hate to tot up all the money we've paid out for milk and meat for that cat—but even so, she was bound and determined she was going to get at that poor little canary. She'd hang around underneath the cage and look up at Dicky, absolutely bloodthirsty, and one time when somebody (and I always thought it was Mame did it herself, too, and not the hired girl)—when somebody left a chair right practically under the cage, Minnie lep' up on the chair and absolutely did her best to leap up and get at the cage.

Of course Mame and I had words about that—

And then that damn' cat never *would* be friendly, at least not to me.

I used to say to Mame, "Well, what does the fool cat *do* for its living, anyway? Think we're sent into the world just to loaf around and enjoy ourselves and sponge on other people?" I says.

Wouldn't sit in my lap—no sir, not for a minute. I used to get so sore at that cat that I'd kick it good and plenty hard, when nobody was looking—I showed it its place, by God—and *still* I couldn't get it to be friendly.

And we talked a lot about it, about the cat and the canary, and one thing often led to another—

You know how it is.

And when I talked about getting another dog, no *sir*, Mame wouldn't hear to it—said a dog would frighten her ittly, bittly, sweetsy, bitsy, high-hatting, canary-murdering damn' *cat*, by God!

Well, I made up my mind that I was going to be master in my own household, but— Oh well, things just kind of floated along for several months, and I didn't do anything special about buying a dog, and then one day—

I remember just like it was yesterday. I'd been out to the country club for a few holes of golf—I remember I was playing with Joe Minchin, the machinery king, Willis Ijams, our leading—or certainly one of the leading hardware dealers, and fellow named George Babbitt, the great real-estate dealer. But I was driving home alone, and I remember there was something wrong—car kept kind of bucking—couldn't exactly figure out what it was, so I stops the car right by the side of the road—it was late autumn—and I lifts the hood and I'm trying to figure out what's wrong when I hears a kind of a whining and a whimpering, and I looks down, and by golly there's a nice water spaniel—not very old, not more'n say two or maybe nearer two and a half years old, sitting there and looking up at me so pathetic—say, it was absolutely pathetic. And he held up his paw like it'd been hurt.

"Well, what's the trouble, old man?" I says to him.

And he looks up, so intelligent— By golly, I just loved that damn' tyke. Well, make a long story short, I looks at his paw, and way I figured it out, he'd cut it on some broken glass—but not bad. Fortunately I had some old but clean rags there in the door-pocket of the car, and so I sat down on the running-board and kind of bound up his paw, and meantime I noticed—and a good, high-grade dog he was, too—I noticed he didn't have any collar or license or anything. And when I'd finished, doggoned if he didn't jump up into my sedan like he belonged there.

"Well, who d'you think you are?" I says to him. "What are you trying to do, you old hijacker," I says to him. "Steal my car? Poor old Pop Schmaltz with his car stolen," I says.

And he just curls up on the back seat and wags his tail, much as to say, "You're a great little kidder, but I know which side my meat is buttered on."

Well, I looks up and down the road and there wasn't anybody in sight that looked like they were looking for a dog, and there was only a couple of houses in sight, and when I got the car to acting Christian again—seems the carburetor needed a little adjusting—I drives to both these houses, and *they* didn't know nothing about no lost dog, so I says, "Well, don't like to leave old Jackie here—"

That's what I named the pup, and that's what I call him to this very day.

"I'd better not leave him here to get run over," thinks I, "and when we get back home, I'll advertise and see if I can find his owner."

Well, when I got home, Robby—you remember my boy, Walt—Robby was just as crazy about having a dog as I was, but Mame gets sniffy about how the dog'd scare that damn' cat Minnie of hers. But she let me keep Jackie, that's the dog, out in the garage till I'd advertised.

Well, I advertised and I advertised—

No, come to think of it, I guess it was just one ad I put in, because I thinks to myself, "Jackie looks to me like a regular man's dog, and if his owner ain't keeping a look-out, can't expect *me* to do all the work!"

Anyway, never got an answer, and in 'long about a week, Mame wakes up and begins to realize, here I am with a dog that ain't going to be buddies with her cat—and say, was she right? Say, the first time Minnie comes pee-rading out on the lawn to see if she can't murder a few sparrows, Jackie, his paw was well enough for that, he takes one look at her, and say, honest, you'd 've laughed fit to bust; he chases her 'way clean up our elm tree, and keeps her there, too, by golly.

Well, after that, there was a hell of a powwow with Big Chief Wife, and no peace-pipe in sight. She gets me in the house, away from Robby, who'd 've backed me up, and she rides the wild mustango up and down the living-room, and throws her tomahawk into the tortured victims, meaning me, and she says:

"Lowell Schmaltz, I've told you, and if I've told you once, I've told you a hundred times, that Minnie is a *very* sensitive and high-bred cat, and I will not have her nerves all shattered by being annoyed by a lot of horrid dogs. I want you to find the rightful owner of this horrid dog and give him back."

"Give who back? The owner?" I says, just sitting down and lighting a cigar and trying to look like I was amused and there was nothing she could do or say that would get my goat. And of course I had her there: "Give who back? The owner?" I says.

"You know perfectly well and good what I mean," she says. "And I want you to find the horrid thing's owner at once!"

"Fine!" I says. "Sure! Of course all I've done is to advertise extensively in the *Advocate-Times*, which only has more circulation than any other two papers in this territory put together—or so they claim, and I've looked into it and I'm disposed to accept their figures," I says. "But of course that isn't enough. All right, I'll just tuck Jackie under my arm, and start right out— Let's see," I says, "there's only about six hundred thousand people in Zenith and the neighboring towns, within perhaps a twenty-eight or thirty mile radius of City Hall, and all I'll have to do will be to run around to *each* of 'em and say, 'Hey, mister, lost a dog?' That's all I'll have to do."

"Well, then, you can take the horrid beast out where you found him and leave him there," she says.

"I can, and I ain't going to," I says—flat. "I'm not going to have him run over by some damn' fool careless motorist," I says. "He's a valuable dog," I says.

"He's horrid—and he's terribly dirty. I never did see such a terribly dirty dog," she says.

"Oh, sure," I says. "Of course aside from the notorious fact that he's a water spaniel—and water spaniels' being, even if they ain't at present as fashionable as cocker spaniels or wire-haired terriers or Airdales, merely notoriously the cleanest dogs that exist," I says, "aside from that, you're dead right."

"But we don't need a dog anyway," she says.

Well say, that kind of got my goat.

"No," I says, "sure we don't. I don't, anyway. Think what I've got here to be chummy with in the evening. Elegant! This nice, fluffy, expensive feline cat, that hates me like hell, that won't sit in my lap, that cottons to you because you got nothing to do all day but stay home and pet it, while I have to be in my store, working my head off—to support a damn' cat! Fine!" I says. * * *[1]

Final result is, she says all right; she'll stand my keeping the dog, but he's got to stay out of the house, and I can build him a dog-kennel out beside the garage.

But you know how things go. One morning I gets up early and has breakfast by myself, and there's Jackie whining outside, and I takes a chance and lets him in and feeds him, and that cat comes marching into the room like a Episcopalopian rector leading a procession, and Jackie gets one squint at her and chases her up on the buffet, and just then Mamie comes in and—

Say, I didn't stop with no buffet; I didn't stop till I'd reached the top of the Second National Bank Tower. But seriously, though, she certainly give Jackie and me such an earful that—

Well, Joe Minchin had planned a poker party for that evening and I hadn't kind of intended to go, but Mame bawled hell out of me so at breakfast that later in the day I said I'd go, and I went, and I got lit to the eyebrows, if the truth be known—say, I was simply ossified.

So I comes home late, thinking I was both the King and Queen of Sheba, and then I got dizzy and just about the time Mame'd thought up her adjectives and was ready to describe me for the catalogue of domestic sons of guns, I couldn't tarry, oh, no longer—I had to be wending my way into the bathroom P.D.Q.,[2] and there, say, I lost everything but my tonsils. Wow!

Well, Mame was awful' nice to me. She helped me back into bed, and she bathed my forehead, and she got some black coffee for me—only what I wanted was a good cyanide of potassium cocktail—and when I woke up in the morning she just kind of laughed, and I thought I was going to get by without the matrimonial cat-o'-nine-tails—I actually thought that, and me married

1. An intentionally dull story proving that a dog is "man's greatest friend" has been omitted here.

2. An abbreviation then colloquially employed as a genteel substitute for "pretty damn quick."

over twenty years to her!

So when my head gets itself reduced to not more'n six or seven normal times its ordinary or wearing size, and I gets up for breakfast, not more'n twenty or twenty-two hours late, and she's still bright and—oh God, what a blessing!—still keeping her trap shut and not telling me about salvation, why, I thinks I'm safe, and then just when I stagger up from breakfast and thinks I'll go down to my store, if I can remember where I left my garage last night, why, she smiles brighter'n ever, and says in a nice, sweet, cool, Frigidaire voice:

"Sit down a moment, will you please, Low. There's something I want to say to you."

Well—

Oh, I died with my face to the foemen. I tried to take the barricades in one gallant dash, like Douglas Fairbanks.[3] I says briefly, "I know what you want to say," I says. "You want to say I was lit, last night. Say, that isn't any news. By this time it's so old and well known that you can find it among the problems in the sixth-grade arithmetic book," I says. "Look here," I says, "it wasn't entirely my fault. It was that God-awful bootleg hootch I got at Joe's. It'd been all right if it'd been honest liquor."

"You were *disgusting*," she says. "If my poor father and mother hadn't passed away, and if my sister Edna wasn't such a crank about theosophy that nobody could live with her, I'd 've left you before dawn, let me tell you that."

Well, I got sore. I'm not a very bad-tempered cuss, as you know, but after along about twenty years, this threatening-to-leave-you business gets a little tiresome.

"Fine," I says. "You're always blowing about how much you know about clothes. I'll be glad to give you a knock-down to some of the big guys at Benson, Hanley and Koch's," I says, "and probably they'll make you buyer in the ladies' garments department," I says, "and you won't have to go on standing for a gorilla of a husband like me."

And she says all right, by God she'll do it!

And we seesaw back and forth, and I kind of apologizes, and she says she didn't mean it, and then we really gets down to business.

"But just the same," she says, "I'm not going to have that dog in the house again! You've not got the least consideration for my feelings. You talk so much about your dear old friends, like this horrible Joe Minchin, but you never give one moment's thought to what I need or like. You don't know what the word 'thoughtful-

3. Douglas Fairbanks, Sr. (died 1939), famous for his acrobatic gallantry in films of romantic adventure.

ness' means."

"All right, I'll look it up in the dictionary," I says. "And speaking of *thoughtfulness*," I says, "when I was going out last night, I found you'd been using my safety razor and hadn't cleaned it, and I was in a hurry and you'd neglected— By God," I says, "when I was a boy, a man had his sweaters to himself, without his wife or sister calmly up and using 'em, and he had his razor to himself, and he had his barber-shop to himself—"

"Yes, and he had his saloons to himself, and still has," she comes back at me. "And you talk about neglect! It isn't only me you neglect," she says, "when you go and get full of liquor, and it isn't simply the example you set the children, but it's the way you neglect the church and religion," she says.

"And of course I'm only a deacon in the church," I says. You know—sarcastic.

"Yes, and you know mighty good and well you only took the job because it'd give you a stand-in with the religious folks, and every Sunday you can, you sneak off and play golf instead of going to church. And that morning when Dr. Hickenlooper came in from Central Methodist and preached for us—that time when poor Dr. Edwards was sick and couldn't preach himself—"

"Sick? He was sick like a fox," I told her. "He just had a sore throat because he'd been off on a lecture trip, shooting his mouth off before a lot of women's clubs to rake in some extra dough, when he ought to stayed home here and tended to his job."

"That's entirely aside from the question," she says, "and anyway, instead of listening to Dr. Hickenlooper like you ought to, you and a couple other deacons stayed out in the lobby of the church."

"Yuh, there's something to what you say," I told her. "Hickenlooper is a fine man. He's all for charity—providing some rich man provides the money for the charity. I don't believe he's ever smoked a cigar or had a nip of liquor in his life. He's a credit to the Methodist clergy. It's true he does bawl out his wife and his kids all the time, and it's true he nags his secretary all day long, but you can't blame a man that's busy with the Lord's work for being maybe a little irritable. In fact there's only one trouble with the holy man— he's the worst and most consistent liar in seven counties!

"I've heard him tell as his own experience things I know he read in books, because I've seen the books. And here's a story that our own pastor, Edwards, told us. Seems Hickenlooper met him in front of our church one Monday morning, and Hickenlooper says, 'Well, Dr. Edwards, my brother-in-law heard you preach yesterday, and he said it was the best sermon he ever heard in his life.'

" 'Well, that's nice,' Dr. Edwards says, 'but it just happens that

I didn't preach yesterday.'

"I guess I'm a kind of a blowhard," I says to Mamie, "and in general I'm just a plug business man, while Hickenlooper addresses Chautauquas and addresses colleges and addresses Methodist conferences and writes articles for the magazines and writes lovely books about how chummy he and God and the sunsets are, but say, if that holy liar knew what even poor, ordinary business men like me really thought about him and what they said privately, he'd sneak off to a desert and never open his mouth again!"

Well say, that had Mamie wild—and don't you think for one moment, Walt, that she let me get by without a few interruptions that I haven't put into the story. And what I've just told you about this Hickenlooper bird—he looks like a prize-fighter and talks like a glad-hand circus bally-hooer, and he lies like a politician—was all straight, and she knew it. I've done a little lying myself, but I've never made a three-ring circus of it like him. But Mamie had a sneaking kind of admiration for him, I guess because he's big and strong and a great baby-kisser and girl-jollier.[4] And she let loose on me, and what she said—Whee!

She said I encouraged Robby to smoke. She said I never used an ash-tray—always scattered my ashes around the house—and I'm afraid she had me there. And she said she was sick of having my friends around the house all the time, and I bawled her out for high-hattin' 'em, and she said something about my driving too fast, and I come back with a few short sweet words about back-seat driving—she's the best single-handed non-participating Major Seagrove[5] of the entire inhabited world. And—

And so on.

And that's just typical of a few home Board of Directors conferences we been having, and I'm pretty sick of it.

Not but what I'm just as mean as she is, at that, I suppose.

But I did by God keep old Jackie!

But I'm getting sick of the whole business—

Not, you understand, but what Mame is just as nice a pal as you'd want to find, in between tantrums. That time we were here and saw you and then went on and had our long talk with Coolidge in Washington,[6] she was jolly the whole time. But more and more—

Say, I don't know as I ought to tell you about this, hardly, but this girl I was speaking of in New York—well, she isn't exactly a girl any more, but she's only thirty-eight and that's seventeen years

4. *Cf.* Lewis' satire of the unworthy clergyman in *Elmer Gantry* (1927).
5. Schmaltz should have said "Segrave." Major H. O. D. Segrave had just won fame (1927) as the first automobile racer to exceed 200 mph., by driving at 203.79 mph. at Daytona Beach, Florida.
6. This was the subject of the first sketch in the volume. President Coolidge was "engaged," and Schmaltz had his "long talk" with a presidential secretary.

younger'n I am—Erica, her name is, and say, she's one of the most talented little women I ever met.

By rights, she ought to be a world-renowned portrait-painter, but she's always run into the damnedest hard luck, and just now for a few years she's been working for the Pillstein and Lipshutz Christmas and Easter Greeting Card Company, where I always get my greeting cards. Of course by rights I'm not a stationer but stick right to office supplies, but same time, along at these holiday times, I feel it does kind of brighten up the business to stock a few handsome cards, and pay—say, it brings me in hundreds a year.

Well, Erica designs a lot of cards—*darn'* smart intelligent girl —does the drawings and the poems and the whole thing. Say, you've probably seen some of her cards. It was her that wrote that famous one that had such a big sale—the one with the two kids shaking hands in front of an old schoolhouse, and then a lot of holly and so on, and the poem:

> Dear friend, this season of ice and snow
> Does not make love the colder grow,
> But on contrary pries apart
> Wider the cockles of the heart.
>
> 'Tis years since we were boys together
> In jolly winter and summer weather,
> 'Tis years indeed since we have met,
> But our old friendship I'll ne'er forget.

Say, it'd surprise you how many of those cards a lot of hardboiled old business men buy to send to fellows they haven't seen for years. I tell you, that fellow Manny Pillstein is a genius. Of course there've been greeting cards for years, but he was the first one to put the business on a scientific, nationally advertised basis, and really standardize and Fordize all this Holiday Good Will so it'd amount to something. They say he's increased the business 10,000 per cent.—made it as practical as chain grocery stores or even Mother's Day.

Well, I met Erica there at his place, and I was alone in New York, and I invited her to dinner, and I blew her to a nice little feed with a bottle of real domestic Chianti. Well, we got to talking and telling our ideas and so on, and come to find out, poor kid, she was pretty near as lonely in New York as I was.

And then every time I blew into the Big Burg—alone—I'd see her, and—

Now say, her relations and mine was just as pure as the driven snow. Maybe I'd kiss her in a taxicab, or something like that, and tell the truth I don't know how far I'd 've gone if I'd got her off to

Atlantic City or something like that, but my God, with my position and my responsibilities, both financial and social, I didn't want to get into no complications. To tell the truth (and I'd never tell another living soul but you), one evening I did go up to her flat— But only that once! And I got scared, and just used to see her at restaurants.

But be the cause what it may, our relations were entirely and absolutely friendly and intellectual, and know what she told me?

When I told her what I thought of her work—and to me, and I told her so, she's the best greeting-card artist in the country—she told me my appreciation was the greatest encouragement and the greatest incentive to go onward and upward to finer and better art that she'd ever received! And let me tell you, I've never had anything buck *me* up, in turn, like her appreciation of my appreciation. Whereas at home—

If I try to tell Mame that she plays a good mitt of bridge, or that I think she's got on an elegant new dress, or she sang some song at some church affair real pretty, or like that, she just looks like she was saying, "Who the hell ever told you *you* was a connooser?"

Oh God, I suppose we'll always go on, just about the same way, but if I was younger—

Well, I ain't!

Well, Walt, I guess it's getting late and about time for us to turn in—you'll have to be in your office tomorrow, and I think I'll take that 12:18 for home, if I can get a Pullman.

It's been a mighty great privilege to have this frank talk with you. I certainly will take your advice. I'll try to keep from talking and running on so much—you noticed this evening at supper I hardly said a word, but just listened to your good wife. You bet. I've learned my lesson. I'm going to concentrate on selling the goods, and not discuss subjects and topics all the time.

And I hope you'll give my schedule a mighty close once-over and see your way to advance me the loan.

You remember how I've always turned to you. Remember that month I spent with you boys on your granddad's farm when we were 'long about twelve?

God, what fun that was! Regular idyl, you might say, like a fellow can't touch again in these later care-ridden and less poetic years. Remember how we stole those mushmelons from that old farmer, and when he got sassy about it we went back and smashed all the rest of 'em? Remember how we hid the alarm-clock in the church so it went off during the sermon? Remember how we greased the springboard so's that Irish kid slipped on it and almost busted his back? Gosh, I had to laugh!

Oh, those were great days, and you and me always did understand each other, Walt, and don't forget that there's no firm in the world could give you better security for the loan.

1928

F. SCOTT FITZGERALD
(1896–1940)

When F. Scott Fitzgerald died, at the age of forty-four, he was regarded as the lingering symbol of the Jazz Age, which he had named and had depicted with sentimental brilliance. In the three years from 1920 to 1922, he had established his position as historian of the younger generation by what seemed an avalanche of four books: two novels —*This Side of Paradise* (1920) and *The Beautiful and Damned* (1922)—and two collections of high-strung and arresting stories —*Flappers and Philosophers* (1920) and *Tales of the Jazz Age* (1922).

By the time of Fitzgerald's death in 1940 the Jazz Age, with all its "sad young men," its John Held flappers, and its adolescent Byronism, had been buried along with prohibition and tawdry night clubs under the rubble of the great depression of the thirties. Fitzgerald saw that the epoch with which he was identified had ended in 1929, and that a new generation, characterized by social responsibility and experimentation, had taken the citadel of the literary world. He was never able to get fully in step with this new generation. He had been taken captive by his own early success with a type of magazine story which was soon so profitable that he could not abandon it even though it became a stereotype. When the market for his magazine fiction began to wane, there was still the demand for fripperies in Hollywood. Meanwhile, it was barely recognized that he was, at his best, a genuine artist, having demonstrated his mastery in his second novel, *The Beautiful and Damned*, and again in *The Great Gatsby* (1925), perhaps the most striking fictional analysis of the age of the gang barons and of the social conditions that produced them. No novelist of his time had better understood the nature of this joy-riding, extravagant, and irresponsible society, and the spiritual desperation and sterility that it represented. Evidently he was himself deeply involved in it, and only occasionally was he able to write at the top level of his powers. His two later novels are also of enduring interest, although each is marred by some fault of construction. *Tender Is the Night* (1934) is the more admired, but *The Last Tycoon* (1941), an unfinished posthumously published study of a Hollywood mogul, also contains the stamp of truth and critical penetration in its delineation of character and social situations. Francis Scott Key Fitzgerald was born in St. Paul, Minnesota, on September 26, 1896. He had the early advantages of considerable travel and social life, although he looked with reluctant eye on the proffered benefits of formal education. He later said that it was only the presence of the Triangle Club at Princeton that induced him to go to college. At Princeton he collaborated on Triangle shows with his fellow student Edmund Wilson, and he retained throughout life his infatuation with the stage and musical-comedy world. In 1917 he left college and enlisted in the wartime army, serving as a lieutenant at a staff headquarters. The war terminated before he received an assignment abroad, and in the tedium of camp life he had meanwhile written a novel.

Unable to get his book published, he obtained work in 1919 as an advertising writer, and continued to send out stories and sketches to the magazines. Within a year he had found a magazine market and finished *This Side of Paradise*. That year he married and settled on Long Island. Later on, he acquired an estate in North Carolina, and lived variously in New York, Paris, and Hollywood; wherever he went, his habits were characterized by an extravagance which put upon him the strain of continuous and popular production.

His two later collections of short stories preserved what he

considered genuine, and they are indeed so good that one realizes what was probably sacrificed by the tragic waste of his life. *All the Sad Young Men* (1926) reveals in its title his sense of his age, and a desperation which in his earlier period he too often cloaked in cynicism. His last collection, published in 1935, announces by the title, *Taps at Reveille*, his own feeling of impending personal disaster. He died in 1940 after a period of spectacular decline which justified his old friend, Edmund Wilson, in choosing *The Crack-Up* as the title for the posthumous edition of essays, letters, and notes.

There is no collected edition of Fitzgerald's works. His novels are *This Side of Paradise*, 1920; *The Beautiful and Damned*, 1922; *The Great Gatsby*, 1925; *Tender Is the Night*, 1934, revised edition posthumously published in 1951; and *The Last Tycoon*, posthumously published in 1941. The collections of short stories are *Flappers and Philosophers*, 1920; *Tales of the Jazz Age*, 1922; *All the Sad Young Men*, 1926; and *Taps at Reveille*, 1935. *The Vegetable; or, From President to Postman*, 1923, is a satirical play. Selections are *The Portable F. Scott Fitzgerald*, 1945, ed. Dorothy Parker; *The Stories * * *,* 1951, ed. Malcolm Cowley; and *Afternoon of an Author*, 1957, introduction by Arthur Mizener, a volume of hitherto uncollected stories and essays.

Biographical and critical commentary will be found in *The Crack-Up*, 1945. Sheila Graham, *Beloved Infidel*, 1958, is a book of reminiscences. The only full-length biography, Arthur Mizener, *The Far Side of Paradise*, 1951, is excellent. *The Fictional Technique of F. Scott Fitzgerald* by James E. Miller, 1957, analyzes the first three novels. Alfred Kazin collected critical essays by various authors in *F. Scott Fitzgerald: The Man and His Work*, 1951.

Babylon Revisited[1]

"And where's Mr. Campbell?" Charlie asked.

"Gone to Switzerland. Mr. Campbell's a pretty sick man, Mr. Wales."

"I'm sorry to hear that. And George Hardt?" Charlie inquired.

"Back in America, gone to work."

"And where is the Snow Bird?"[2]

"He was in here last week. Anyway, his friend, Mr. Schaeffer, is in Paris."

Two familiar names from the long list of a year and a half ago. Charlie scribbled an address in his notebook and tore out the page.

"If you see Mr. Schaeffer, give him this," he said. "It's my brother-in-law's address. I haven't settled on a hotel yet."

He was not really disappointed to find Paris was so empty. But the stillness in the Ritz bar was strange and portentous. It was not an American bar any more—he felt polite in it, and not as if he owned it. It had gone back into France. He felt the stillness from the moment he got out of the taxi and saw the doorman, usually in a frenzy of activity at this hour, gossiping with a *chasseur*[3] by the servants' entrance.

Passing through the corridor, he heard only a single, bored voice in the once-clamorous women's room. When he turned into the bar he travelled the twenty feet of green carpet with his eyes fixed straight ahead by old habit; and then, with his foot firmly on the rail, he turned and surveyed the room, encountering only a single pair of eyes that fluttered up from a newspaper in the corner. Charlie asked for the head barman, Paul, who in the latter days of the bull market had come to work in his own custom-built car—disembarking, however, with due nicety at the nearest corner. But Paul was at his country house today and Alix giving him information.

"No, no more," Charlie said. "I'm going slow these days."

Alix congratulated him: "You were going pretty strong a couple of years ago."

"I'll stick to it all right," Charlie assured him. "I've stuck to it for over a year and a half now."

"How do you find conditions in America?"

"I haven't been to America for months. I'm in business in Prague, representing a couple of concerns there. They don't know

---

1. First published in the *Saturday Evening Post* for February 21, 1931, and collected in *Taps at Reveille* (1935), the last of the author's volumes to appear before his death. The story represents the final stage of his criticism of the generation of which he had become a symbol.

2. Slang for one addicted to (or sometimes peddling) "snow," *i.e.*, cocaine or heroin.

3. Liveried footman or porter.

about me down there."

Alix smiled.

"Remember the night of George Hardt's bachelor dinner here?" said Charlie. "By the way, what's become of Claude Fessenden?"

Alix lowered his voice confidentially: "He's in Paris, but he doesn't come here any more. Paul doesn't allow it. He ran up a bill of thirty thousand francs, charging all his drinks and his lunches, and usually his dinner, for more than a year. And when Paul finally told him he had to pay, he gave him a bad check."

Alix shook his head sadly.

"I don't understand it, such a dandy fellow. Now he's all bloated up—" He made a plump apple of his hands.

Charlie watched a group of strident queens installing themselves in a corner.

"Nothing affects them," he thought. "Stocks rise and fall, people loaf or work, but they go on forever." The place oppressed him. He called for the dice and shook with Alix for the drink.

"Here for long, Mr. Wales?"

"I'm here for four or five days to see my little girl."

"Oh-h! You have a little girl?"

Outside, the fire-red, gas-blue, ghost-green signs shone smokily through the tranquil rain. It was late afternoon and the streets were in movement; the *bistros* gleamed. At the corner of the Boulevard des Capucines he took a taxi. The Place de la Concorde moved by in pink majesty; they crossed the logical Seine, and Charlie felt the sudden provincial quality of the left bank.

Charlie directed his taxi to the Avenue de l'Opéra, which was out of his way. But he wanted to see the blue hour spread over the magnificent façade, and imagine that the cab horns, playing endlessly the first few bars of *La Plus que Lente*,[4] were the trumpets of the Second Empire. They were closing the iron grill in front of Brentano's Bookstore, and people were already at dinner behind the trim little bourgeois hedge of Duval's. He had never eaten at a really cheap restaurant in Paris. Five-course dinner, four francs fifty, eighteen cents, wine included. For some odd reason he wished that he had.

As they rolled on to the Left Bank and he felt its sudden provincialism, he thought, "I spoiled this city for myself. I didn't realize it, but the days came along one after another, and then two years were gone, and everything was gone, and I was gone."

He was thirty-five, and good to look at. The Irish mobility of his face was sobered by a deep wrinkle between his eyes. As he rang his brother-in-law's bell in the Rue Palatine, the wrinkle deepened

4. A slow waltz by Debussy. It was a fad for taxicabs to carry horns playing scraps of familiar music.

till it pulled down his brows; he felt a cramping sensation in his belly. From behind the maid who opened the door darted a lovely little girl of nine, who shrieked "Daddy!" and flew up, struggling like a fish, into his arms. She pulled his head around by one ear and set her cheek against his.

"My old pie," he said.

"Oh, daddy, daddy, daddy, daddy, dads, dads, dads!"

She drew him into the salon, where the family waited, a boy and girl his daughter's age, his sister-in-law and her husband. He greeted Marion with his voice pitched carefully to avoid either feigned enthusiasm or dislike, but her response was more frankly tepid, though she minimized her expression of unalterable distrust by directing her regard toward his child. The two men clasped hands in a friendly way and Lincoln Peters rested his for a moment on Charlie's shoulder.

The room was warm and comfortably American. The three children moved intimately about, playing through the yellow oblongs that led to other rooms; the cheer of six o'clock spoke in the eager smacks of the fire and the sounds of French activity in the kitchen. But Charlie did not relax; his heart sat up rigidly in his body and he drew confidence from his daughter, who from time to time came close to him, holding in her arms the doll he had brought.

"Really extremely well," he declared in answer to Lincoln's question. "There's a lot of business there that isn't moving at all, but we're doing even better than ever. In fact, damn well. I'm bringing my sister over from America next month to keep house for me. My income last year was bigger than it was when I had money. You see, the Czechs——"

His boasting was for a specific purpose; but after a moment, seeing a faint restiveness in Lincoln's eye, he changed the subject:

"Those are fine children of yours, well brought up, good manners."

"We think Honoria's a great little girl too."

Marion Peters came back from the kitchen. She was a tall woman with worried eyes, who had once possessed a fresh American loveliness. Charlie had never been sensitive to it and was always surprised when people spoke of how pretty she had been. From the first there had been an instinctive antipathy between them.

"Well, how do you find Honoria?" she asked.

"Wonderful. I was astonished how much she's grown in ten months. All the children are looking well."

"We haven't had a doctor for a year. How do you like being back in Paris?"

"It seems very funny to see so few Americans around."

"I'm delighted," Marion said vehemently. "Now at least you

can go into a store without their assuming you're a millionaire. We've suffered like everybody, but on the whole it's a good deal pleasanter."[5]

"But it was nice while it lasted," said Charlie. "We were a sort of royalty, almost infallible, with a sort of magic around us. In the bar this afternoon"—he stumbled, seeing his mistake—"there wasn't a man I knew."

She looked at him keenly. "I should think you'd have had enough of bars."

"I only stayed a minute. I take one drink every afternoon, and no more."

"Don't you want a cocktail before dinner?" Lincoln asked.

"I take only one drink every afternoon, and I've had that."

"I hope you keep to it," said Marion.

Her dislike was evident in the coldness with which she spoke, but Charlie only smiled; he had larger plans. Her very aggressiveness gave him an advantage, and he knew enough to wait. He wanted them to initiate the discussion of what they knew had brought him to Paris.

At dinner he couldn't decide whether Honoria was most like him or her mother. Fortunate if she didn't combine the traits of both that had brought them to disaster. A great wave of protectiveness went over him. He thought he knew what to do for her. He believed in character; he wanted to jump back a whole generation and trust in character again as the eternally valuable element. Everything else wore out.

He left soon after dinner, but not to go home. He was curious to see Paris by night with clearer and more judicious eyes than those of other days. He bought a *strapontin*[6] for the Casino and watched Josephine Baker[7] go through her chocolate arabesques.

After an hour he left and strolled toward Montmartre, up the Rue Pigalle into the Place Blanche. The rain had stopped and there were a few people in evening clothes disembarking from taxis in front of cabarets, and *cocottes*[8] prowling singly or in pairs, and many Negroes. He passed a lighted door from which issued music, and stopped with the sense of familiarity; it was Bricktop's, where he had parted with so many hours and so much money. A few doors farther on he found another ancient rendezvous and incautiously put his head inside. Immediately an eager orchestra burst into sound, a pair of professional dancers leaped to their feet and a maître d'hôtel[9] swooped toward him, crying, "Crowd just

5. The American stock market crashed in 1929; when depression hit Paris, about two years later, the large American colony had vanished.
6. A low-priced jump seat that opens down into the aisle.

7. Josephine Baker, talented American Negro entertainer, became a spectacular feature of Parisian night life in the late twenties.
8. Prostitutes.
9. Headwaiter.

arriving, sir!" But he withdrew quickly.

"You have to be damn drunk," he thought.

Zelli's was closed, the bleak and sinister cheap hotels surrounding it were dark; up in the Rue Blanche there was more light and a local, colloquial French crowd. The Poet's Cave[1] had disappeared, but the two great mouths of the Café of Heaven and the Café of Hell still yawned—even devoured, as he watched, the meager contents of a tourist bus—a German, a Japanese, and an American couple who glanced at him with frightened eyes.

So much for the effort and ingenuity of Montmartre.[2] All the catering to vice and waste was on an utterly childish scale, and he suddenly realized the meaning of the word "dissipate"—to dissipate into thin air; to make nothing out of something. In the little hours of the night every move from place to place was an enormous human jump, an increase of paying for the privilege of slower and slower motion.

He remembered thousand-franc notes given to an orchestra for playing a single number, hundred-franc notes tossed to a doorman for calling a cab.

But it hadn't been given for nothing.

It had been given, even the most wildly squandered sum, as an offering to destiny that he might not remember the things most worth remembering, the things that now he would always remember —his child taken from his control, his wife escaped to a grave in Vermont.

In the glare of a *brasserie* a woman spoke to him. He bought her some eggs and coffee, and then, eluding her encouraging stare, gave her a twenty-franc note and took a taxi to his hotel.

II

He woke up on a fine fall day—football weather. The depression of yesterday was gone and he liked the people on the streets. At noon he sat opposite Honoria at Le Grand Vatel, the only restaurant he could think of not reminiscent of champagne dinners and long luncheons that began at two and ended in a blurred and vague twilight.

"Now, how about vegetables? Oughtn't you to have some vegetables?"

"Well, yes."

"Here's *épinards* and *chou-fleur* and carrots and *haricots*."[3]

"I'd like *chou-fleur*."

"Wouldn't you like to have two vegetables?"

"I usually have only one at lunch."

1. In Paris, *cave* (literally, "wine vault") was widely used to designate a cabaret below the sidewalk level.
2. During the twenties Montmartre, a quarter of Paris, had become the international center of Bohemianism.
3. The French words mean "spinach," "cauliflower," "beans."

The waiter was pretending to be inordinately fond of children. *"Qu'elle est mignonne, la petite! Elle parle exactement comme une française."*[4]

"How about dessert? Shall we wait and see?"

The waiter disappeared. Honoria looked at her father expectantly.

"What are we going to do?"

"First, we're going to that toy store in the Rue Saint-Honoré and buy you anything you like. And then we're going to the vaudeville at the Empire."

She hesitated. "I like it about the vaudeville, but not the toy store."

"Why not?"

"Well, you brought me this doll." She had it with her. "And I've got lots of things. And we're not rich any more, are we?"

"We never were. But today you are to have anything you want."

"All right," she agreed resignedly.

When there had been her mother and a French nurse he had been inclined to be strict; now he extended himself, reached out for a new tolerance; he must be both parents to her and not shut any of her out of communication.

"I want to get to know you," he said gravely. "First let me introduce myself. My name is Charles J. Wales, of Prague."

"Oh, daddy!" her voice cracked with laughter.

"And who are you, please?" he persisted, and she accepted a rôle immediately: "Honoria Wales, Rue Palatine, Paris."

"Married or single?"

"No, not married. Single."

He indicated the doll. "But I see you have a child, madame."

Unwilling to disinherit it, she took it to her heart and thought quickly: "Yes, I've been married, but I'm not married now. My husband is dead."

He went on quickly, "And the child's name?"

"Simone. That's after my best friend at school."

"I'm very pleased that you're doing so well at school."

"I'm third this month," she boasted. "Elsie"—that was her cousin—"is only about eighteenth, and Richard is about at the bottom."

"You like Richard and Elsie, don't you?"

"Oh, yes. I like them all right."

Cautiously and casually he asked: "And Aunt Marion and Uncle Lincoln—which do you like best?"

"Oh, Uncle Lincoln, I guess."

He was increasingly aware of her presence. As they came in, a murmur of ". . . adorable" followed them, and now the people at

4. She is charming, the little one! She speaks precisely like a French girl.

the next table bent all their silences upon her, staring as if she were something no more conscious than a flower.

"Why don't I live with you?" she asked suddenly. "Because mamma's dead?"

"You must stay here and learn more French. It would have been hard for daddy to take care of you so well."

"I don't really need much taking care of any more. I do everything for myself."

Going out of the restaurant, a man and a woman unexpectedly hailed him.

"Well, the old Wales!"

"Hello there, Lorraine . . . Dunc."

Sudden ghosts out of the past: Duncan Schaeffer, a friend from college. Lorraine Quarles, a lovely, pale blonde of thirty; one of a crowd who had helped them make months into days in the lavish times of three years ago.

"My husband couldn't come this year," she said, in answer to his question. "We're poor as hell. So he gave me two hundred a month, and told me I could do my worst on that. . . . This your little girl?"

"What about coming back and sitting down?" Duncan asked.

"Can't do it." He was glad for an excuse. As always, he felt Lorraine's passionate, provocative attraction, but his own rhythm was different now.

"Well, how about dinner?" she asked.

"I'm not free. Give me your address and let me call you."

"Charlie, I believe you're sober," she said judicially. "I honestly believe he's sober, Dunc. Pinch him and see if he's sober."

Charlie indicated Honoria with his head. They both laughed.

"What's your address?" said Duncan skeptically.

He hesitated, unwilling to give the name of his hotel.

"I'm not settled yet. I'd better call you. We're going to see the vaudeville at the Empire."

"There! That's what I want to do," Lorraine said. "I want to see some clowns and acrobats and jugglers. That's just what we'll do, Dunc."

"We've got to do an errand first," said Charlie. "Perhaps we'll see you there."

"All right, you snob. . . . Good-by, beautiful little girl."

"Good-by."

Honoria bobbed politely.

Somehow, an unwelcome encounter. They liked him because he was functioning, because he was serious; they wanted to see him, because he was stronger than they were now, because they wanted to draw a certain sustenance from his strength.

At the Empire, Honoria proudly refused to sit upon her father's folded coat. She was already an individual with a code of her own, and Charlie was more and more absorbed by the desire of putting a little of himself into her before she crystallized utterly. It was hopeless to try to know her in so short a time.

Between the acts they came upon Duncan and Lorraine in the lobby where the band was playing.

"Have a drink?"

"All right, but not up at the bar. We'll take a table."

"The perfect father."

Listening abstractedly to Lorraine, Charlie watched Honoria's eyes leave their table, and he followed them wistfully about the room, wondering what they saw. He met her glance and she smiled.

"I liked that lemonade," she said.

What had she said? What had he expected? Going home in a taxi afterward, he pulled her over until her head rested against his chest.

"Darling, do you ever think about your mother?"

"Yes, sometimes," she answered vaguely.

"I don't want you to forget her. Have you got a picture of her?"

"Yes, I think so. Anyhow, Aunt Marion has. Why don't you want me to forget her?"

"She loved you very much."

"I loved her too."

They were silent for a moment.

"Daddy, I want to come and live with you," she said suddenly.

His heart leaped; he had wanted it to come like this.

"Aren't you perfectly happy?"

"Yes, but I love you better than anybody. And you love me better than anybody, don't you, now that mummy's dead?"

"Of course I do. But you won't always like me best, honey. You'll grow up and meet somebody your own age and go marry him and forget you ever had a daddy."

"Yes, that's true," she agreed tranquilly.

He didn't go in. He was coming back at nine o'clock and he wanted to keep himself fresh and new for the thing he must say then.

"When you're safe inside, just show yourself in that window."

"All right. Good-by, dads, dads, dads, dads."

He waited in the dark street until she appeared, all warm and glowing, in the window above and kissed her fingers out into the night.

III

They were waiting. Marion sat behind the coffee service in a dignified black dinner dress that just faintly suggested mourning. Lincoln was walking up and down with the animation of one who had already been talking. They were as anxious as he was to get into the question. He opened it almost immediately:

"I suppose you know what I want to see you about—why I really came to Paris."

Marion played with the black stars on her necklace and frowned.

"I'm awfully anxious to have a home," he continued. "And I'm awfully anxious to have Honoria in it. I appreciate your taking in Honoria for her mother's sake, but things have changed now"—he hesitated and then continued more forcibly—"changed radically with me, and I want to ask you to reconsider the matter. It would be silly for me to deny that about three years ago I was acting badly——"

Marion looked up at him with hard eyes.

"—But all that's over. As I told you, I haven't had more than a drink a day for over a year, and I take that drink deliberately, so that the idea of alcohol won't get too big in my imagination. You see the idea?"

"No," said Marion succinctly.

"It's a sort of stunt I set myself. It keeps the matter in proportion."

"I get you," said Lincoln. "You don't want to admit it's got any attraction for you."

"Something like that. Sometimes I forget and don't take it. But I try to take it. Anyhow, I couldn't afford to drink in my position. The people I represent are more than satisfied with what I've done, and I'm bringing my sister over from Burlington to keep house for me, and I want awfully to have Honoria too. You know that even when her mother and I weren't getting along well we never let anything that happened touch Honoria. I know she's fond of me and I know I'm able to take care of her—well, there you are. How do you feel about it?"

He knew that now he would have to take a beating. It would last an hour or two hours, and it would be difficult, but if he modulated his inevitable resentment to the chastened attitude of the reformed sinner, he might win his point in the end.

Keep your temper, he told himself. You don't want to be justified. You want Honoria.

Lincoln spoke first: "We've been talking it over ever since we got your letter last month. We're happy to have Honoria here. She's a dear little thing, and we're glad to be able to help her, but of course that isn't the question——"

Marion interrupted suddenly. "How long are you going to stay sober, Charlie?" she asked.

"Permanently, I hope."

"How can anybody count on that?"

"You know I never did drink heavily until I gave up business and came over here with nothing to do. Then Helen and I began to run around with——"

"Please leave Helen out of it. I can't bear to hear you talk about her like that."

He stared at her grimly; he had never been certain how fond of each other the sisters were in life.

"My drinking only lasted about a year and a half—from the time we came over until I—collapsed."

"It was time enough."

"It was time enough," he agreed.

"My duty is entirely to Helen," she said. "I try to think what she would have wanted me to do. Frankly, from the night you did that terrible thing you haven't really existed for me. I can't help that. She was my sister."

"Yes."

"When she was dying she asked me to look out for Honoria. If you hadn't been in a sanitarium then, it might have helped matters."

He had no answer.

"I'll never in my life be able to forget the morning when Helen knocked at my door, soaked to the skin and shivering, and said you'd locked her out."

Charlie gripped the sides of the chair. This was more difficult than he expected: he wanted to launch out into a long expostulation and explanation, but he only said: "The night I locked her out—" and she interrupted, "I don't feel up to going over that again."

After a moment's silence Lincoln said: "We're getting off the subject. You want Marion to set aside her legal guardianship and give you Honoria. I think the main point for her is whether she has confidence in you or not."

"I don't blame Marion," Charlie said slowly, "but I think she can have entire confidence in me. I had a good record up to three years ago. Of course, it's within human possibilities I may go wrong again. But if we wait much longer I'll lose Honoria's childhood and my chance for a home." He shook his head. "I'll simply lose her, don't you see?"

"Yes, I see," said Lincoln.

"Why didn't you think of all this before?" Marion asked.

"I suppose I did, from time to time, but Helen and I were getting along badly. When I consented to the guardianship, I was flat on my back in a sanitarium, and the market had cleaned me out. I knew I'd acted badly, and I thought if it would bring any peace to Helen, I'd agree to anything. But now it's different. I'm functioning, I'm behaving damn well, so far as——"

"Please don't swear at me," Marion said.

He looked at her, startled. With each remark the force of her dislike became more and more apparent. She had built up all her fear of life into one wall and faced it toward him. This trivial reproof was possibly the result of some trouble with the cook several hours before. Charlie became increasingly alarmed at leaving Honoria in this atmosphere of hostility against himself; sooner or later it would come out, in a word here, a shake of the head there, and some of that distrust would be irrevocably implanted in Honoria. But he pulled his temper down out of his face and shut it up inside him; he had won a point, for Lincoln realized the absurdity of Marion's remark, and asked her lightly since when she had objected to the word "damn."

"Another thing," Charlie said: "I'm able to give her certain advantages now. I'm going to take a French governess to Prague with me. I've got a lease on a new apartment——"

He stopped, realizing that he was blundering. They couldn't be expected to accept with equanimity the fact that his income was again twice as large as their own.

"I suppose you can give her more luxuries than we can," said Marion. "When you were throwing away money we were living along watching every ten francs. . . . I suppose you'll start doing it again."

"Oh, no," he said. "I've learned. I worked hard for ten years, you know—until I got lucky in the market, like so many people. Terribly lucky. It didn't seem any use working any more, so I quit. It won't happen again."

There was a long silence. All of them felt their nerves straining, and for the first time in a year Charlie wanted a drink. He was sure now that Lincoln Peters wanted him to have his child.

Marion shuddered suddenly; part of her saw that Charlie's feet were planted on the earth now, and her own maternal feeling recognized the naturalness of his desire; but she had lived for a long time with a prejudice—a prejudice founded on a curious disbelief in her sister's happiness, which, in the shock of one terrible night, had turned to hatred for him. It had all happened at a point in her life where the discouragement of ill health and adverse circumstances made it necessary for her to believe in tangible villainy and a tangible villain.

"I can't help what I think!" she cried out suddenly. "How much you were responsible for Helen's death, I don't know. It's something you'll have to square with your own conscience."

An electric current of agony surged through him; for a moment he was almost on his feet, an unuttered sound echoing in his throat.

He hung on to himself for a moment, another moment.

"Hold on there," said Lincoln uncomfortably. "I never thought you were responsible for that."

"Helen died of heart trouble," Charlie said dully.

"Yes, heart trouble." Marion spoke as if the phrase had another meaning for her.

Then, in the flatness that followed her outburst, she saw him plainly and she knew he had somehow arrived at control over the situation. Glancing at her husband, she found no help from him, and as abruptly as if it were a matter of no importance, she threw up the sponge.

"Do what you like!" she cried, springing up from her chair. "She's your child. I'm not the person to stand in your way. I think if it were my child I'd rather see her—" She managed to check herself. "You two decide it. I can't stand this. I'm sick. I'm going to bed."

She hurried from the room; after a moment Lincoln said:

"This has been a hard day for her. You know how strongly she feels—" His voice was almost apologetic: "When a woman gets an idea in her head."

"Of course."

"It's going to be all right. I think she sees now that you—can provide for the child, and so we can't very well stand in your way or Honoria's way."

"Thank you, Lincoln."

"I'd better go along and see how she is."

"I'm going."

He was still trembling when he reached the street, but a walk down the Rue Bonaparte to the quais set him up, and as he crossed the Seine, fresh and new by the quai lamps, he felt exultant. But back in his room he couldn't sleep. The image of Helen haunted him. Helen whom he had loved so until they had senselessly begun to abuse each other's love, tear it into shreds. On that terrible February night that Marion remembered so vividly, a slow quarrel had gone on for hours. There was a scene at the Florida, and then he attempted to take her home, and then she kissed young Webb at a table; after that there was what she had hysterically said. When he arrived home alone he turned the key in the lock in wild anger. How could he know she would arrive an hour later alone, that there would be a snowstorm in which she wandered about in slippers, too confused to find a taxi? Then the aftermath, her escaping pneumonia by a miracle, and all the attendant horror. They were "reconciled," but that was the beginning of the end, and Marion, who had seen with her own eyes and who imagined it to be one of many scenes from her sister's martyrdom, never forgot.

Going over it again brought Helen nearer, and in the white, soft light that steals upon half sleep near morning he found himself talking to her again. She said that he was perfectly right about Honoria and that she wanted Honoria to be with him. She said she was glad he was being good and doing better. She said a lot of other things—very friendly things—but she was in a swing in a white dress, and swinging faster and faster all the time, so that at the end he could not hear clearly all that she said.

IV

He woke up feeling happy. The door of the world was open again. He made plans, vistas, futures for Honoria and himself, but suddenly he grew sad, remembering all the plans he and Helen had made. She had not planned to die. The present was the thing—work to do, and some one to love. But not to love too much, for he knew the injury that a father can do to a daughter or a mother to a son by attaching them too closely; afterward, out in the world, the child would seek in the marriage partner the same blind tenderness and, failing probably to find it, turn against love and life.

It was another bright, crisp day. He called Lincoln Peters at the bank where he worked and asked if he could count on taking Honoria when he left for Prague. Lincoln agreed that there was no reason for delay. One thing—the legal guardianship. Marion wanted to retain that a while longer. She was upset by the whole matter, and it would oil things if she felt that the situation was still in her control for another year. Charlie agreed, wanting only the tangible, visible child.

Then the question of a governess. Charlie sat in a gloomy agency and talked to a cross Bernaise and to a buxom Breton peasant, neither of whom he could have endured. There were others whom he would see tomorrow.

He lunched with Lincoln Peters at Griffons, trying to keep down his exultation.

"There's nothing quite like your own child," Lincoln said. "But you understand how Marion feels too."

"She's forgotten how hard I worked for seven years there," Charlie said. "She just remembers one night."

"There's another thing," Lincoln hesitated. "While you and Helen were tearing around Europe throwing money away, we were just getting along. I didn't touch any of the prosperity because I never got ahead enough to carry anything but my insurance. I think Marion felt there was some kind of injustice in it—you not even working toward the end, and getting richer and richer."

"It went just as quick as it came," said Charlie.

"Yes, a lot of it stayed in the hands of *chasseurs* and saxophone players and maîtres d'hôtel—well, the big party's over now. I just said that to explain Marion's feeling about those crazy years. If you drop in about six o'clock tonight before Marion's too tired, we'll settle the details on the spot."

Back at his hotel, Charlie found a *pneumatique*[5] that had been redirected from the Ritz bar where Charlie had left his address for the purpose of finding a certain man.

DEAR CHARLIE: You were so strange when we saw you the other day that I wondered if I did something to offend you. If so, I'm not conscious of it. In fact, I have thought about you too much for the last year, and it's always been in the back of my mind that I might see you if I came over here. We *did* have such good times that crazy spring, like the night you and I stole the butcher's tricycle, and the time we tried to call on the president and you had the old derby rim and the wire cane. Everybody seems so old lately, but I don't feel old a bit. Couldn't we get together some time today for old time's sake? I've got a vile hang-over for the moment, but will be feeling better this afternoon and will look for you about five in the sweet-shop at the Ritz.

Always devotedly,
LORRAINE.

His first feeling was one of awe that he had actually, in his mature years, stolen a tricycle and pedalled Lorraine all over the Étoile[6] between the small hours and dawn. In retrospect it was a nightmare. Locking out Helen didn't fit in with any other act of his life, but the tricycle incident did—it was one of many. How many weeks or months of dissipation to arrive at that condition of utter irresponsibility?

He tried to picture how Lorraine had appeared to him then—very attractive; Helen was unhappy about it, though she said nothing. Yesterday, in the restaurant, Lorraine had seemed trite, blurred, worn away. He emphatically did not want to see her, and he was glad Alix had not given away his hotel address. It was a relief to think, instead, of Honoria, to think of Sundays spent with her and of saying good morning to her and of knowing she was there in his house at night, drawing her breath in the darkness.

At five he took a taxi and bought presents for all the Peters—a piquant cloth doll, a box of Roman soldiers, flowers for Marion, big linen handkerchiefs for Lincoln.

He saw, when he arrived in the apartment, that Marion had accepted the inevitable. She greeted him now as though he were a recalcitrant member of the family, rather than a menacing outsider. Honoria had been told she was going; Charlie was glad to see that her tact made her conceal her excessive happiness. Only on his lap did she whisper her delight and the question "When?" before she slipped away with the other children.

He and Marion were alone for a minute in the room, and on an

5. A message; originally one delivered by pneumatic tube.

6. An open square in Paris, site of the Arc de Triomphe.

impulse he spoke out boldly:

"Family quarrels are bitter things. They don't go according to any rules. They're not like aches or wounds; they're more like splits in the skin that won't heal because there's not enough material. I wish you and I could be on better terms."

"Some things are hard to forget," she answered. "It's a question of confidence." There was no answer to this and presently she asked, "When do you propose to take her?"

"As soon as I can get a governess. I hoped the day after tomorrow."

"That's impossible. I've got to get her things in shape. Not before Saturday."

He yielded. Coming back into the room, Lincoln offered him a drink.

"I'll take my daily whisky," he said.

It was warm here, it was a home, people together by a fire. The children felt very safe and important; the mother and father were serious, watchful. They had things to do for the children more important than his visit here. A spoonful of medicine was, after all, more important than the strained relations between Marion and himself. They were not dull people, but they were very much in the grip of life and circumstances. He wondered if he couldn't do something to get Lincoln out of his rut at the bank.

A long peal at the door-bell; the *bonne à tout faire*[7] passed through and went down the corridor. The door opened upon another long ring, and then voices, and the three in the salon looked up expectantly; Richard moved to bring the corridor within his range of vision, and Marion rose. Then the maid came back along the corridor, closely followed by the voices, which developed under the light into Duncan Schaeffer and Lorraine Quarles.

They were gay, they were hilarious, they were roaring with laughter. For a moment Charlie was astounded; unable to understand how they had ferreted out the Peters' address.

"Ah-h-h!" Duncan wagged his finger roguishly at Charlie. "Ah-h-h!"

They both slid down another cascade of laughter. Anxious and at a loss, Charlie shook hands with them quickly and presented them to Lincoln and Marion. Marion nodded, scarcely speaking. She had drawn back a step toward the fire; her little girl stood beside her, and Marion put an arm about her shoulder.

With growing annoyance at the intrusion, Charlie waited for them to explain themselves. After some concentration Duncan said:

"We came to invite you out to dinner. Lorraine and I insist that all this shishi business 'bout your address got to stop."

7. Maid of all work.

Charlie came closer to them, as if to force them backward down the corridor.

"Sorry, but I can't. Tell me where you'll be and I'll phone you in half an hour."

This made no impression. Lorraine sat down suddenly on the side of a chair, and focussing her eyes on Richard, cried, "Oh, what a nice little boy! Come here, little boy." Richard glanced at his mother, but did not move. With a perceptible shrug of her shoulders, Lorraine turned back to Charlie:

"Come and dine. Sure your cousins won' mine. See you so sel'om. Or solemn."

"I can't," said Charlie sharply. "You two have dinner and I'll phone you."

Her voice became suddenly unpleasant. "All right, we'll go. But I remember once when you hammered on my door at four A.M. I was enough of a good sport to give you a drink. Come on, Dunc." Still in slow motion, with blurred, angry faces, with uncertain feet, they retired along the corridor.

"Good night," Charlie said.

"Good night!" responded Lorraine emphatically.

When he went back into the salon Marion had not moved, only now her son was standing in the circle of her other arm. Lincoln was still swinging Honoria back and forth like a pendulum from side to side.

"What an outrage!" Charlie broke out. "What an absolute outrage!"

Neither of them answered. Charlie dropped into an armchair, picked up his drink, set it down again and said:

"People I haven't seen for two years having the colossal nerve——"

He broke off. Marion had made the sound "Oh!" in one swift, furious breath, turned her body from him with a jerk and left the room.

Lincoln set down Honoria carefully.

"You children go in and start your soup," he said, and when they obeyed, he said to Charlie:

"Marion's not well and she can't stand shocks. That kind of people make her really physically sick."

"I didn't tell them to come here. They wormed your name out of somebody. They deliberately——"

"Well, it's too bad. It doesn't help matters. Excuse me a minute."

Left alone, Charlie sat tense in his chair. In the next room he could hear the children eating, talking in monosyllables, already oblivious to the scene between their elders. He heard a murmur of conversation from a farther room and then the ticking bell of a telephone receiver picked up, and in a panic he moved to the other side of the room and out of earshot.

In a minute Lincoln came back. "Look here, Charlie. I think we'd better call off dinner for tonight. Marion's in bad shape."

"Is she angry with me?"

"Sort of," he said, almost roughly. "She's not strong and——"

"You mean she's changed her mind about Honoria."

"She's pretty bitter right now. I don't know. You phone me at the bank tomorrow."

"I wish you'd explain to her I never dreamed these people would come here. I'm just as sore as you are."

"I couldn't explain anything to her now."

Charlie got up. He took his coat and hat and started down the corridor. Then he opened the door of the dining room and said in a strange voice, "Good night, children."

Honoria rose and ran around the table to hug him.

"Good night, sweetheart," he said vaguely, and then trying to make his voice more tender, trying to conciliate something, "Good night, dear children."

V

Charlie went directly to the Ritz bar with the furious idea of finding Lorraine and Duncan, but they were not there, and he realized that in any case there was nothing he could do. He had not touched his drink at the Peters', and now he ordered a whisky-and-soda. Paul came over to say hello.

"It's a great change," he said sadly. "We do about half the business we did. So many fellows I hear about back in the States lost everything, maybe not in the first crash, but then in the second. Your friend George Hardt lost every cent, I hear. Are you back in the States?"

"No. I'm in business in Prague."

"I heard that you lost a lot in the crash."

"I did," and he added grimly, "but I lost everything I wanted in the boom."

"Selling short?"

"Something like that."

Again the memory of those days swept over him like a nightmare —the people they had met travelling; the people who couldn't add a row of figures or speak a coherent sentence. The little man Helen had consented to dance with at the ship's party, who had insulted her ten feet from the table; the women and girls carried screaming with drink or drugs out of public places . . . the men who locked their wives out in the snow, because the snow of '29 wasn't real snow. If you didn't want it to be snow, you just paid some money.

He went to the phone and called the Peters apartment; Lincoln answered.

"I called up because this thing is on my mind. Has Marion said anything definite?"

"Marion's sick," Lincoln answered shortly. "I know this thing isn't altogether your fault, but I can't have her go to pieces about it. I'm afraid we'll have to let it slide for six months; I can't take the chance of working her up to this state again."

"I see."

"I'm sorry, Charlie."

He went back to his table. His whisky glass was empty, but he shook his head when Alix looked at it questioningly. There wasn't much he could do now except send Honoria some things; he would send her a lot of things tomorrow. He thought rather angrily that this was just money—he had given so many people money. . . .

"No, no more," he said to another waiter. "What do I owe you?"

He would come back some day; they couldn't make him pay forever. But he wanted his child, and nothing was much good now, beside that fact. He wasn't young any more, with a lot of nice thoughts and dreams to have by himself. He was absolutely sure Helen wouldn't have wanted him to be so alone.

1931, 1935

EDNA ST. VINCENT MILLAY

(1892–1950)

Edna St. Vincent Millay's early appearances on the literary scene were all spectacular, and it was some time before the reading public adjusted itself to her kaleidoscopic transformations. In 1912, at the age of twenty, she was the unknown girl of Camden, Maine, whose "Renascence," a reflective poem of remarkable spiritual penetration and lyric beauty, became celebrated at once because the *Lyric Year* gave its annual award to an established author, while a number of prominent critics enthusiastically preferred the work of the girl poet. It is still, in fact, one of the favorite poems of its period. In 1917, somewhat revised, it became the title poem of her first volume, comprising poems written while she was a Vassar undergraduate. In 1920 *A Few Figs from Thistles* revealed another transformation. That year, when F. Scott Fitzgerald in *This Side of Paradise* drew the fictional portrait of youth in the jazz age, Edna St. Vincent Millay temporarily became the lyric voice of that rebellious generation. With impudent irreverence she attacked the citadel of conventionalized feminine virtue, in poems that sang gaily of going "back and forth all night on the ferry," or cavalierly accepted a broken love, as in "Passer Mortuus Est," or cynically pretended forgetfulness of "what lips my lips have kissed."

Three years and two volumes of poetry later, *The Harp-Weaver and Other Poems* (1923) revealed the poet matured. The daring of *A Few Figs from Thistles* had now become a fine spiritual independence and vitality. The insight and emotional propriety of "Renascence" had acquired depth; she had thoroughly absorbed her principal literary inheritance, from the Elizabethan and Cavalier lyrists of England; she showed her mastery of the sonnet; and in "The Ballad of the Harp-Weaver" she caught the simplicity of the ballad form in one of her many poems drawing inspiration from folk poetry. She was, in fact, a true romantic and rebel, with a delicate perception of nature and human nature, and an exquisite command of the traditional forms of romanticism and the music of language.

Born in Rockland, Maine, in 1892, Edna St. Vincent Millay grew up in that city and in nearby Camden. In childhood she began to write verse of unusual excellence, some of it published in *St. Nicholas*, then the goal of juvenile talent. She lacked the financial means to attend college, but a friend of the family offered assistance and she enrolled at Barnard at twenty-one, the year after "Renascence" was published. She transferred to Vassar and was graduated in 1917. During her next few years, in Greenwich Village, she was able to support herself by sales of magazine verse and stories, and such satirical sketches as appeared in *Distressing Dialogues* (1924) under the pseudonym of Nancy Boyd. The reader of her poems soon discovers her flair for the dramatic. While living in the village, she was associated with the Provincetown Players, with whom Eugene O'Neill's first success was won, and she wrote several poetic dramas which have been frequently performed by little-theater groups. One, *The King's Henchman* (1927), was the libretto for a Deems Taylor opera produced in 1927 by the Metropolitan Opera Company.

In the years following the appearance of *The Harp-Weaver and Other Poems*, a number of major volumes of her poetry were published: *The Buck in the Snow and Other Poems* (1928); *Fatal Interview* (1931), a sequence of sonnets recording a love affair, of great psychological interest and lyric excellence; *Wine from These Grapes* (1934); and *Conversation at Midnight* (1937).

With Archibald MacLeish, Stephen Vincent Benét, and many others, she joined those who called upon writers to oppose the growing tyranny manifested in European affairs. The works evoked by these concerns were not her best, but they were sincere and often journalistically effective, as was *The Murder of Lidice* (1942). Other volumes of this latest period include *Huntsman, What Quarry?* (1939), *Make Bright the Ar-*

rows (1940), and *"There Are No Islands, Any More"* (1940). During the last decade of her life, Miss Millay published much less frequently in magazines and made no new collections of her poems. She died in 1950.

Collected Poems, 1956, was edited by Norma Millay. A major portion of her best work may be found in *Collected Sonnets,* 1941, and *Collected Lyrics,* 1943. A posthumous "collection of new poems," edited by Norma Millay, was entitled *Mine the Harvest,* 1954. The *Letters of Edna St. Vincent Millay,* edited by Allan Ross Macdougall, appeared in 1952.

Biographical studies are Elizabeth Atkins, *Edna St. Vincent Millay and Her Times,* 1936; Vincent Sheean, *The Indigo Bunting: A Memoir of Edna St. Vincent Millay,* 1951; and Toby Shafter, *Edna St. Vincent Millay, America's Best-loved Poet,* 1957.

The Poet and His Book

Down, you mongrel, Death!
    Back into your kennel!
I have stolen breath
    In a stalk of fennel![1]
You shall scratch and you shall whine   5
    Many a night, and you shall worry
    Many a bone, before you bury
One sweet bone of mine!

When shall I be dead?
    When my flesh is withered,   10
And above my head
    Yellow pollen gathered
All the empty afternoon?
    When sweet lovers pause and wonder
    Who am I that lie thereunder,   15
Hidden from the moon?

This my personal death?—
    That my lungs be failing
To inhale the breath
    Others are exhaling?   20
This my subtle spirit's end?—
    Ah, when the thawed winter splashes
    Over these chance dust and ashes,
Weep not me, my friend!

Me, by no means dead   25
    In that hour, but surely
When this book, unread,
    Rots to earth obscurely,

1. A perennial European herb whose aromatic seeds provide a flavoring. In the symbolism of plants, fennel stands for flattery. It is among those distributed by the mad Ophelia (Shakespeare, *Hamlet,* Act IV, Scene 5, l. 181).

And no more to any breast,
  Close against the clamorous swelling   30
  Of the thing there is no telling,
Are these pages pressed!

When this book is mold,
  And a book of many
Waiting to be sold   35
  For a casual penny,
In a little open case,
  In a street unclean and cluttered,
  Where a heavy mud is spattered
From the passing drays,   40

Stranger, pause and look;
  From the dust of ages
Lift this little book,
  Turn the tattered pages,
Read me, do not let me die!   45
  Search the fading letters, finding
  Steadfast in the broken binding
All that once was I!

When these veins are weeds,
  When these hollowed sockets   50
Watch the rooty seeds
  Bursting down like rockets,
And surmise the spring again,
  Or, remote in that black cupboard,
  Watch the pink worms writhing upward   55
At the smell of rain,

Boys and girls that lie
  Whispering in the hedges,
Do not let me die,
  Mix me in your pledges;   60
Boys and girls that slowly walk
  In the woods, and weep, and quarrel,
  Staring past the pink wild laurel,
Mix me with your talk.

Do not let me die!   65
  Farmers at your raking,
When the sun is high,
  While the hay is making,
When, along the stubble strewn,
  Withering on their stalks uneaten,   70

Strawberries turn dark and sweeten
In the lapse of noon;

Shepherds on the hills,
  In the pastures, drowsing
To the tinkling bells   75
  Of the brown sheep browsing;
Sailors crying through the storm;
  Scholars at your study; hunters
  Lost amid the whirling winter's
Whiteness uniform;   80

Men that long for sleep;
  Men that wake and revel;—
If an old song leap
  To your senses' level
At such moments, may it be   85
  Sometimes, though a moment only,
  Some forgotten, quaint and homely
Vehicle of me!

Women at your toil,
  Women at your leisure   90
Till the kettle boil,
  Snatch of me your pleasure,
Where the broom-straw marks the leaf;
  Women quiet with your weeping
  Lest you wake a workman sleeping,   95
Mix me with your grief!

Boys and girls that steal
  From the shocking laughter
Of the old, to kneel
  By a dripping rafter   100
Under the discolored eaves,
  Out of trunks with hingless covers
  Lifting tales of saint and lovers,
Travelers, goblins, thieves,

Suns that shine by night,   105
  Mountains made from valleys,—
Bear me to the light,
  Flat upon your bellies
By the webby window lie,
  Where the little flies are crawling,—   110
  Read me, margin me with scrawling,
Do not let me die!

Sexton, *ply your trade!*
  In a shower of gravel
Stamp upon your spade!
  Many a rose shall ravel,
Many a metal wreath shall rust
  In the rain, and I go singing
  Through the lots where you are flinging
Yellow clay on dust!

115

120

1921

Passer Mortuus Est[2]

Death devours all lovely things;
  Lesbia with her sparrow
Shares   the   darkness,—presently
  Every bed is narrow.

Unremembered as old rain
  Dries the sheer libation,[3]
And the little petulant hand
  Is an annotation.

After all, my erstwhile dear,
  My no longer cherished,
Need we say it was not love,
  Now that love has perished?

5

10

1920, 1921

Justice Denied in Massachusetts[4]

Let us abandon then our gardens and go home
And sit in the sitting-room.
Shall the larkspur blossom or the corn grow under this cloud?
Sour to the fruitful seed
Is the cold earth under this cloud,   5
Fostering quack and weed, we have marched upon but cannot
    conquer;
We have bent the blades of our hoes against the stalks of them.

2. Latin, "The sparrow is dead." Catullus, in *Carmine*, III, l. 3, uses these words in lamenting the death of a sparrow belonging to his mistress, "Lesbia," whose name Millay introduces in l. 2. The first line of the present poem also echoes Catullus' poem, ll. 13 and 14: "Accursed shades of Orcus [Death], / That devour all lovely things."
3. *I.e.*, the wine poured in honor of the dead.

4. Referring to the execution, on August 23, 1927, of Nicola Sacco and Bartolomeo Vanzetti, after nearly seven years of litigation. Many liberals rallied to their defense, claiming that these two "radicals" had not been proved guilty of the payroll robbery and murder for which they were convicted, but were victims of a hysterical conservative reaction. See also Dos Passos.

Let us go home, and sit in the sitting-room.
Not in our day
Shall the cloud go over and the sun rise as before,   10
Beneficent upon us
Out of the glittering bay,
And the warm winds be blown inward from the sea
Moving the blades of corn
With a peaceful sound.   15
Forlorn, forlorn,
Stands the blue hay-rack by the empty mow.
And the petals drop to the ground,
Leaving the tree unfruited.
The sun that warmed our stooping backs and withered the weed
    uprooted—   20
We shall not feel it again.
We shall die in darkness, and be buried in the rain.

What from the splendid dead
We have inherited—
Furrows sweet to the grain, and the weed subdued—   25
See now the slug and the mildew plunder.
Evil does overwhelm
The larkspur and the corn;
We have seen them go under.

Let us sit here, sit still,   30
Here in the sitting-room until we die;
At the step of Death on the walk, rise and go;
Leaving to our children's children this beautiful doorway,
And this elm,
And a blighted earth to till   35
With a broken hoe.

        1928

Oh, Sleep Forever in the Latmian Cave[5]

Similitude of S...

    Oh, sleep forever in the Latmian cave,
    Mortal Endymion, darling of the Moon![6]
    Her silver garments by the senseless wave

5. Sonnet LII from *Fatal Interview*.
6. In classic myth the Greek Artemis, or Roman Diana, goddess of the moon, fell in love with Endymion, a mortal youth of surpassing beauty. The goddess was thus drawn down from heaven, wooed the youth, and sacrificed the chastity that was one of her divine at-tributes. For this impiety, Jupiter doomed Endymion to sleep forever in beauty on Mount Latmos, where the grieving goddess visited him and took care of his flocks. See Ovid, *Ars Amatoria*, III: 83; and the poem *Endymion* by John Keats.

Shouldered and dropped and on the shingle strewn,
Her fluttering hand against her forehead pressed,   5
Her scattered looks that trouble all the sky,
Her rapid footsteps running down the west—
Of all her altered state, oblivious lie!
Whom earthen you, by deathless lips adored,
Wild-eyed and stammering to the grasses thrust,   10
And deep into her crystal body poured
The hot and sorrowful sweetness of the dust:
    Whereof she wanders mad, being all unfit
    For mortal love, that might not die of it.

1931

A New Symbolic Drama

EUGENE O'NEILL

(1888–1953)

Eugene O'Neill was foremost among the playwrights who, from 1916 to 1924, brought about in American drama a revolution which fundamentally changed its character. European drama had already been vastly altered by the imaginative energy and inventiveness of such dramatists as Ibsen, Strindberg, Maeterlinck, and Hauptmann. On the British stage, only Shaw had been able to break the well-established conventions of the theater. In the United States, the theater had had a long history, and had produced notable playwrights and some great actors, but it was for that reason the more enmeshed in a proven pattern of successful drama based on the marriage between the Elizabethan tradition and the "well-made" play. Only a decade before O'Neill's works began to appear, the dramas of Clyde Fitch and Augustus Thomas, although excellent of their sort, were only strengthening the rooted conventions.

O'Neill did more than anyone else to destroy these stereotypes, and to substitute an essentially different dramatic imagination. Fundamentally, his liberation was psychological. He enriched his art by an understanding of the new psychology—not simply Freudianism, but the enlarged awareness of all conscious and subconscious realities. The result was a new depth of seriousness, a new vitality, in the dramas themselves, and the free use, in stagecraft and acting, of experimental techniques which completely ignored the "well-made" conventions, and called directly upon the subconscious responses of the audience.

His work was remarkably free from direct influences, and his imagination was so opulent that in all his many dramas he never echoed even himself. He was a master of the organic form; each play grew from the inner nature of its own conflict and psychology, and almost every one is basically different from the others. It is very difficult to name the "typical" O'Neill play. The three characteristics almost universally present, however, are all powerfully illustrated in *The Hairy Ape*. O'Neill perhaps reflects his acquaintance with the dramas of Ibsen and Strindberg in his preference for expressionism, a device first developed by nineteenth-century painting. In order to "express" the inner significance of his work, to convey it to the imagination as well as the intellect of the beholder, the artist may stylize or distort the representation of literal reality, as O'Neill does when he indicates in his stage directions that the ceiling of the firemen's forecastle is to be so low that it "crushes down upon the men's heads." The play also illustrates O'Neill's adoption of the language of poetic symbolism, which had become associated with the new European drama from Ibsen to Maeterlinck. As O'Neill has pointed out, he is "a bit of a poet," although his plays are not written in verse; he recognizes that the imagination and emotion of high drama are more nearly those of poetry than those of prose. Finally, he cherishes a faith in the dignity of man, which he announced early in his career. In this he is most strikingly different from Strindberg and Hauptmann, with their naturalistic view that man's destiny is determined by forces quite beyond his control. O'Neill proclaimed as his object the representation of "man's self-destructive struggle to be expressed in the Life-Force" and not to become, like another animal, "a mere incident in its expression."

The playwright was born in a Broadway hotel on October 16, 1888, and was christened Eugene Gladstone O'Neill. He was an infant and juvenile trouper with his father, an eminent romantic actor, and was educated by tutors and in private schools. His attendance at Princeton (1906–7) terminated in an undergraduate prank. He shipped aboard a Norwegian freighter to Buenos Aires; he loitered in Latin ports, with the sailors, stevedores, waifs, who became his *dramatis personae*, along with characters encountered in offices where he worked, or on a gold-seeking expedition in Honduras. Back home, he briefly served his father as advance agent and box-office man. He had success as a reporter for the New London *Telegraph*. Recuperating from tuberculosis in 1912 he read the classic repertoire of the theater; he spent the winter of 1914 at Harvard, in George Baker's famous dramatic workshop. The next year he was a member of the Provincetown Players on Cape Cod with other fledglings named Susan Glaspell, "Jig" Cook, Robert Edmond Jones, Mielziner and Macgowan—all soon to follow their bright stars to Greenwich Village and Broadway. Writing for this group, O'Neill won success with such one-act plays as the S.S. *Glencairn* group and other plays combining realism with experimental forms. He also acquired a reading audience, when a number of them were published by Mencken and Nathan in their magazine, *The Smart Set*, during 1917–1918. In 1920, O'Neill's first long play to be produced, *Beyond the Horizon*, was awarded the Pulitzer Prize. Within the next two years, the production of such powerful plays as *The Emperor Jones*,

Anna Christie, and *The Hairy Ape* left no doubt that a dramatist of great power had appeared. Before long these and later plays of O'Neill were being performed in the capitals of Europe, and he became an international influence.

Between 1924 and 1931, O'Neill produced nine plays, most of them tragedies with complex psychological implications. *All God's Chillun Got Wings* (1924), *Desire Under the Elms* (1924), *The Great God Brown* (1926), and *Strange Interlude* (1928) were challenging in their thematic use of miscegenation, incest, passional crime, and polyandrous relationships. *Mourning Becomes Electra* (1931), the climax and triumph of his career, exploited the Greek tragedies of Clytemnestra and Agamemnon, Orestes and Electra in an Aeschylean trilogy dealing with a New England family of the Civil War period. *Ah, Wilderness!* (1933), was a brilliant domestic comedy, his only venture in this field.

O'Neill was awarded the Nobel Prize in 1936, two years after he was stricken with a fatal malady. During intervals of improved health he completed four full-length plays and the scenario for a cycle of eleven plays dramatizing several successive generations of a family. Two plays of the cycle were completed; he destroyed the remaining manuscripts before his death in 1953.

In the shadow of the World War he temporarily shelved the cycle for work on three plays which, as he said, he knew he could finish. *The Iceman Cometh* was completed in 1939 but not produced and published until 1946. The three plays were all motivated by the dominant theme of the first, a dramatic allegory of common man withstanding the fears and futility of this age by clinging irrationally to hope or to those illusions which transmit a visionary light. This is also the theme of *Hughie*, the only survivor of eight one-acters drafted in 1940. *A Moon for the Misbegotten* (1952), written in 1943, is an intensely autobiographical exploration of the spiritual disorders of an American family, possibly his own. Powerful but difficult, it did not fare so well with audiences but deserves to be studied. In 1941 he had written the play on his family which proved to be a masterpiece. *Long Day's Journey into Night* (1956) is an overwhelming tragedy based on the playwright's impression of the drama of love, madness, and death played out between his frail parents. He had postponed writing it, he said, until I could "face my dead * * * with pity, understanding, and forgiveness." Magnificently produced and performed in Stockholm in 1955 and in New York in 1956–57, it won the first Pulitzer Prize ever awarded posthumously, and was the fourth of his plays to win that award. To the Royal Dramatic Theatre of Stockholm, which had produced his earlier plays with noteworthy insight, O'Neill gave first production rights to his other posthumous plays. *A Touch of the Poet* (1957) was successful there in 1956 and in New York in 1958. This is one of the two plays of the family cycle which O'Neill

1118 · Eugene O'Neill

preserved; *More Stately Mansions* is extant in a manuscript not fully revised, under study for possible production by the Stockholm company, which in 1958 performed *Hughie* (1959).

Complete to its date of publication is *The Plays of Eugene O'Neill*, 12 vols., 1934–1935. The following collections are also available: *The Complete Works * * * , 2 vols., 1925; *Collected Plays * * * , 4 vols., 1933; *Nine Plays*, 1932; and *Lost Plays * * * ,

1950, 1958, ed. L. Gellert.

Biographical and critical studies include B. H. Clark, *Eugene O'Neill: The Man and His Plays*, 1947; A. Boulton, *Part of A Long Story*, 1958; C. Bowen and S. O'Neill, *Curse of the Misbegotten*, 1959; R. D. Skinner, *Eugene O'Neill: A Poet's Quest*, 1935; S. K. Winther, *Eugene O'Neill, A Critical Study*, 1934; E. A. Engel, *The Haunted Heroes of Eugene O'Neill*, 1953; and D. V. Falk, *Eugene O'Neill and the Tragic Tension*, 1958. See, further, Arthur and Barbara Gelb, *O'Neill*, 1962, a comprehensive critical biography, and O. Cargill and N. B. Fagin, eds., *O'Neill and his Plays*, 1961, criticism.

The Hairy Ape[1]

Characters

Robert Smith, "Yank"
Paddy
Long
Mildred Douglas
Her Aunt

Second Engineer
A Guard
A Secretary of an Organization
Stokers, Ladies, Gentlemen, etc.

Scenes

Scene I: The firemen's forecastle of an ocean liner—an hour after sailing from New York.
Scene II: Section of promenade deck, two days out—morning.
Scene III: The stokehole. A few minutes later.
Scene IV: Same as Scene I. Half an hour later.

Scene V: Fifth Avenue, New York. Three weeks later.
Scene VI: An island near the city. The next night.
Scene VII: In the city. About a month later.
Scene VIII: In the city. Twilight of the next day.

Scene I

SCENE. The firemen's forecastle of a transatlantic liner an hour after sailing from New York for the voyage across. Tiers of narrow, steel bunks, three deep, on all sides. An entrance in rear. Benches on the floor before the bunks. The room is crowded with men, shouting, cursing, laughing, singing—a confused, inchoate uproar swelling into a sort of unity, a meaning—the bewildered, furious, baffled

1. First produced on March 9, 1922, by the Provincetown Players at the Playwrights' Theatre on Macdougal Street in New York's Greenwich Village. With Louis Wolheim as Yank, *The Hairy Ape* succeeded at once, and within a few years had been produced all over the world. It has been revived repeatedly, particularly in little theaters. For general comment on the play, see the early paragraphs of the introduction.

as creatures in an environment — not produce of the environment

defiance of a beast in a cage. Nearly all the men are drunk. Many bottles are passed from hand to hand. All are dressed in dungaree pants, heavy ugly shoes. Some wear singlets, but the majority are stripped to the waist.

The treatment of this scene, or of any other scene in the play, should by no means be naturalistic. The effect sought after is a cramped space in the bowels of a ship, imprisoned by white steel. The lines of bunks, the uprights supporting them, cross each other like the steel framework of a cage. The ceiling crushes down upon the men's heads. They cannot stand upright. This accentuates the natural stooping posture which shoveling coal and the resultant over-development of back and shoulder muscles have given them. The men themselves should resemble those pictures in which the appearance of Neanderthal Man is guessed at. All are hairy-chested, with long arms of tremendous power, and low, receding brows above their small, fierce, resentful eyes. All the civilized white races are represented, but except for the slight differentiation in color of hair, skin, eyes, all these men are alike.

The curtain rises on a tumult of sound. YANK is seated in the foreground. He seems broader, fiercer, more truculent, more powerful, more sure of himself than the rest. They respect his superior strength—the grudging respect of fear. Then, too, he represents to them a self-expression, the very last word in what they are, their most highly developed individual.

VOICES. Gif me trink dere, you!
'Ave a wet!
Salute!
Gesundheit!
Skoal!
Drunk as a lord, God stiffen you!
Here's how!
Luck!
Pass back that bottle, damn you!
Pourin' it down his neck!
Ho, Froggy! Where the devil have you been?
La Touraine.
I hit him smash in yaw, py Gott!
Jenkins—the First—he's a rotten swine——
And the coppers nabbed him—and I run——
I like peer better. It don't pig head gif you.
A slut, I'm sayin'! She robbed me aslape——
To hell with 'em all!
You're a bloody liar!
Say dot again!

[*Commotion. Two men about to fight are pulled apart.*]

No scrappin' now!

To-night——

See who's the best man!

Bloody Dutchman!

To-night on the for'ard square.

I'll bet on Dutchy.

He packa da wallop, I tella you!

Shut up, Wop!

No fightin', maties. We're all chums, ain't we?

[*A voice starts bawling a song.*]

"Beer, beer, glorious beer!

Fill yourselves right up to here."

YANK. [*For the first time seeming to take notice of the uproar about him, turns around threateningly—in a tone of contemptuous authority.*] Choke off dat noise! Where d'you get dat beer stuff? Beer, hell! Beer's for goils—and Dutchmen. Me for somep'n wit a kick to it! Gimme a drink, one of youse guys. [*Several bottles are eagerly offered. He takes a tremendous gulp at one of them; then, keeping the bottle in his hand, glares belligerently at the owner, who hastens to acquiesce in this robbery by saying.*] All righto, Yank. Keep it and have another. [YANK *contemptuously turns his back on the crowd again. For a second there is an embarrassed silence. Then——*]

VOICES. We must be passing the Hook.[2]

She's beginning to roll to it.

Six days in hell—and then Southampton.

Py Yesus, I vish somepody take my first vatch for me!

Gittin' seasick, Square-head?

Drink up and forget it!

What's in your bottle?

Gin.

Dot's nigger trink.

Absinthe? It's doped. You'll go off your chump, Froggy!

Cochon!

Whisky, that's the ticket!

Where's Paddy?

Going asleep.

Sing us that whisky song, Paddy.

[*They all turn to an old, wizened Irishman who is dozing, very drunk, on the benches forward. His face is extremely monkey-like with all the sad, patient pathos of that animal in his small eyes.*]

Singa da song, Caruso Pat!

He's gettin' old. The drink is too much for him.

---

2. Sandy Hook, New York Harbor, gateway to the open sea.

He's too drunk.

PADDY. [*Blinking about him, starts to his feet resentfully, swaying, holding on to the edge of a bunk.*] I'm never too drunk to sing. 'Tis only when I'm dead to the world I'd be wishful to sing at all. [*With a sort of sad contempt.*] "Whisky Johnny," ye want? A chanty, ye want? Now that's a queer wish from the ugly like of you, God help you. But no matther. [*He starts to sing in a thin, nasal, doleful tone.*]

Oh, whisky is the life of man!
  Whisky! O Johnny! [*They all join in on this.*]
Oh, whisky is the life of man!
  Whisky for my Johnny! [*Again chorus.*]
Oh, whisky drove my old man mad!
  Whisky! O Johnny!
Oh, whisky drove my old man mad!
  Whisky for my Johnny!

YANK. [*Again turning around scornfully.*] Aw hell! Nix on dat old sailing ship stuff! All dat bull's dead, see? And you're dead, too, yuh damned old Harp, on'y yuh don't know it. Take it easy, see. Give us a rest. Nix on de loud noise. [*With a cynical grin.*] Can't youse see I'm tryin' to t'ink?

ALL. [*Repeating the word after him as one with the same cynical amused mockery.*] Think! [*The chorused word has a brazen metallic quality as if their throats were phonograph horns. It is followed by a general uproar of hard, barking laughter.*]

VOICES. Don't be cracking your head wit ut, Yank.
  You gat headache, py yingo!
  One thing about it—it rhymes with drink!
  Ha, ha, ha!
  Drink, don't think!
  Drink, don't think!
  Drink, don't think!

[*A whole chorus of voices has taken up this refrain, stamping on the floor, pounding on the benches with fists.*]

YANK. [*Taking a gulp from his bottle—goodnaturedly.*] Aw right. Can de noise. I got yuh de foist time.

[*The uproar subsides. A very drunken sentimental tenor begins to sing.*]

    "Far away in Canada,
      Far across the sea,
    There's a lass who fondly waits
      Making a home for me——"

YANK [*Fiercely contemptuous.*] Shut up, yuh lousy boob! Where d'yuh get dat tripe? Home? Home, hell! I'll make a home for yuh! I'll knock yuh dead. Home! T'hell wit home! Where d'yuh get dat tripe? Dis is home, see? What d'yuh want wit home? [*Proudly.*] I runned away from mine when I was a kid. On'y too glad to beat it, dat was me. Home was lickings for me, dat's all. But yuh can bet your shoit no one ain't never licked me since! Wanter try it, any of youse? Huh! I guess not. [*In a more placated but still contemptuous tone.*] Goils waitin' for yuh, huh? Aw, hell! Dat's all tripe. Dey don't wait for no one. Dey'd double-cross yuh for a nickel. Dey're all tarts, get me? Treat 'em rough, dat's me. To hell wit 'em. Tarts, dat's what, de whole bunch of 'em.

LONG. [*Very drunk, jumps on a bench excitedly, gesticulating with a bottle in his hand.*] Listen 'ere, Comrades! Yank 'ere is right. 'E says this 'ere stinkin' ship is our 'ome. And 'e says as 'ome is 'ell. And 'e's right! This is 'ell. We lives in 'ell, Comrades—and right enough we'll die in it. [*Raging.*] And who's ter blame, I arsks yer? We ain't. We wasn't born this rotten way. All men is born free and ekal. That's in the bleedin' Bible, maties. But what d'they care for the Bible—them lazy, bloated swine what travels first cabin? Them's the ones. They dragged us down 'til we're on'y wage slaves in the bowels of a bloody ship, sweatin', burnin' up, eatin' coal dust! Hit's them's ter blame—the damned Capitalist clarss!

[*There had been a gradual murmur of contemptuous resentment rising among the men until now he is interrupted by a storm of catcalls, hisses, boos, hard laughter.*]

VOICES. Turn it off!
   Shut up!
   Sit down!
   Closa da face!
   Tamn fool! [*Etc.*]

YANK. [*Standing up and glaring at* LONG.] Sit down before I knock yuh down! [LONG *makes haste to efface himself.* YANK *goes on contemptuously.*] De Bible, huh? De Cap'tlist class, huh? Aw nix on dat Salvation Army-Socialist bull. Git a soapbox! Hire a hall! Come and be saved, huh? Jerk us to Jesus, huh? Aw g'wan! I've listened to lots of guys like you, see. Yuh're all wrong. Wanter know what I t'ink? Yuh ain't no good for no one. Yuh're de bunk. Yuh ain't got no noive, get me? Yuh're yellow, dat's what. Yellow, dat's you. Say! What's dem slobs in de foist cabin got to do wit us? We're better men dan dey are, ain't we? Sure! One of us guys could clean up de whole mob wit one mit. Put one of 'em down here for one watch in de stokehole, what'd happen? Dey'd carry him off on a stretcher. Dem boids don't amount to nothin'. Dey're just baggage. Who makes dis old tub run? Ain't it us guys? Well den, we belong, don't we? We belong and dey don't. Dat's all [*A loud chorus of approval.* YANK *goes on.*] As for dis bein' hell—aw, nuts! Yuh lost your noive, dat's what. Dis is a man's job, get me? It belongs. It runs dis tub. No stiffs need apply. But yuh're a stiff, see? Yuh're yellow, dat's you.

VOICES. [*With a great hard pride in them.*]

Righto!

A man's job!

Talk is cheap, Long.

He never could hold up his end.

Divil take him!

Yank's right. We make it go.

Py Gott, Yank say right ting!

We don't need no one cryin' over us.

Makin' speeches.

Throw him out!

Yellow!

Chuck him overboard!

I'll break his jaw for him!

[*They crowd around* LONG *threateningly.*]

YANK. [*Half good-natured again—contemptuously.*] Aw, take it easy. Leave him alone. He ain't woith a punch. Drink up. Here's how, whoever owns dis. [*He takes a long swallow from his bottle. All drink with him. In a flash all is hilarious amiability again, back-slapping, loud talk, etc.*]

PADDY. [*Who has been sitting in a blinking, melancholy daze—suddenly cries out in a voice full of old sorrow.*] We belong to this, you're saying? We make the ship to go, you're saying? Yerra³ then, that Almighty God have pity on us! [*His voice runs into the wail of a keen,⁴ he rocks back and forth on his bench. The men stare at him, startled and impressed in spite of themselves.*] Oh, to be back in the fine days of my youth, ochone!⁵ Oh, there was fine beautiful ships them days—clippers wid tall masts touching the sky—fine strong men in them—men that was sons of the sea as if 'twas the mother that bore them. Oh, the clean skins of them, and the clear eyes, the straight backs and full chests of them! Brave men they was, and bold men surely! We'd be sailing out, bound down round the Horn maybe. We'd be making sail in the dawn, with a fair breeze, singing a chanty song wid no care to it. And astern the land would be sinking low and dying out, but we'd give it no heed but a laugh, and never a look behind. For the day that was, was enough, for we was free men—and I'm thinking 'tis only slaves do be giving heed to the day that's gone or the day to come—until they're old like me. [*With a sort of religious exaltation.*] Oh, to be scudding south again wid the power of the Trade Wind driving her on steady through the nights and the days! Full sail on her! Nights and days!

---

3. An Irish exclamation, loosely equivalent to "verily," "truly."

4. An Irish lamentation, as for the dead.
5. Irish, "alas."

Nights when the foam of the wake would be flaming wid fire, when the sky'd be blazing and winking wid stars. Or the full of the moon maybe. Then you'd see her driving through the gray night, her sails stretching aloft all silver and white, not a sound on the deck, the lot of us dreaming dreams, till you'd believe 'twas no real ship at all you was on but a ghost ship like the *Flying Dutchman* they say does be roaming the seas forevermore without touching a port. And there was the days, too. A warm sun on the clean decks. Sun warming the blood of you, and wind over the miles of shiny green ocean like strong drink to your lungs. Work—aye, hard work—but who'd mind that at all? Sure, you worked under the sky and 'twas work wid skill and daring to it. And wid the day done, in the dog watch, smoking me pipe at ease, the lookout would be raising land maybe, and we'd see the mountains of South Americy wid the red fire of the setting sun painting their white tops and the clouds floating by them! [*His tone of exaltation ceases. He goes on mournfully.*] Yerra, what's the use of talking? 'Tis a dead man's whisper. [*To* YANK *resentfully.*] 'Twas them days men belonged to ships, not now. 'Twas them days a ship was part of the sea, and a man was part of a ship, and the sea joined all together and made it one. [*Scornfully.*] Is it one wid this you'd be, Yank—black smoke from the funnels smudging the sea, smudging the decks—the bloody engines pounding and throbbing and shaking—wid divil a sight of sun or a breath of clean air—choking our lungs wid coal dust—breaking our backs and hearts in the hell of the stokehole—feeding the bloody furnace— feeding our lives along wid the coal, I'm thinking—caged in by steel from a sight of the sky like bloody apes in the Zoo! [*With a harsh laugh.*] Ho-ho, divil mend you! Is it to belong to that you're wishing? Is it a flesh and blood wheel of the engines you'd be?

YANK. [*Who has been listening with a contemptuous sneer, barks out the answer.*] Sure ting! Dat's me. What about it?

PADDY. [*As if to himself—with great sorrow.*] Me time is past due. That a great wave wid sun in the heart of it may sweep me over the side sometime I'd be dreaming of the days that's gone!

YANK. Aw, yuh crazy Mick! [*He springs to his feet and advances on* PADDY *threateningly—then stops, fighting some queer struggle within himself—lets his hands fall to his sides—contemptuously.*] Aw, take it easy. Yuh're aw right at dat. Yuh're bugs, dat's all— nutty as a cuckoo. All dat tripe yuh been pullin'——Aw, dat's all right. On'y it's dead, get me? Yuh don't belong no more, see. Yuh don't get de stuff. Yuh're too old. [*Disgustedly.*] But aw say, come up for air onct in a while, can't yuh? See what's happened since yuh croaked. [*He suddenly bursts forth vehemently, growing more and more excited.*] Say! Sure! Sure I meant it! What de hell—— Say, lemme talk! Hey! Hey, you old Harp! Hey, youse guys! Say, listen to me—wait a moment—I gotter talk, see. I belong and he don't. He's dead but I'm livin'. Listen to me! Sure, I'm part of de engines! Why de hell not! Dey move, don't dey? Dey're speed, ain't dey! Dey smash trou, don't dey? Twenty-five knots a hour! Dat's goin' some! Dat's new stuff! Dat belongs! But him, he's too old. He gets dizzy. Say, listen. All dat crazy tripe about nights and days; all dat crazy tripe about stars and moons; all dat crazy tripe about suns and winds, fresh air and de rest of it—— Aw hell, dat's all a dope dream! Hittin' de pipe of de past, dat's what he's doin'. He's old and don't belong no more. But me, I'm young! I'm in de pink! I move wit it! It, get me! I mean de ting dat's de guts of all dis. It ploughs trou all de tripe he's been sayin'. It blows dat up! It knocks dat dead! It slams dat offen de face of de oith! It, get me! De engines and de coal and de smoke and all de rest of it! He can't breathe and swallow coal dust, but I kin, see? Dat's fresh air for me! Dat's food for me! I'm new, get me? Hell in de stokehole? Sure! It takes a man to work in hell. Hell, sure, dat's my fav'rite climate. I eat it up! I git fat on it! It's me makes it hot! It's me makes it roar! It's me makes it move! Sure, on'y for me everyting stops. It all goes dead, get me? De noise and smoke and all de engines movin' de woild, dey stop. Dere ain't nothin' no more! Dat's what I'm sayin'. Everyting else dat makes de woild move, somep'n makes it move. It can't move witout somep'n else, see? Den yuh get down to me. I'm at de bottom, get me! Dere ain't nothin' foither. I'm de end! I'm de start! I start somep'n and de woild moves! It—dat's me! —de new dat's moiderin' de old! I'm de ting in coal dat makes it boin; I'm steam and oil for de engines; I'm de ting in noise dat makes yuh hear it; I'm smoke and express trains and steamers and factory whistles; I'm de ting in gold dat makes it money! And I'm what makes iron into steel! Steel, dat stands for de whole ting! And I'm steel—steel—steel! I'm de muscles in steel, de punch behind it! [*As he says this he pounds with his fist against the steel bunks. All the men, roused to a pitch of frenzied self-glorification by his speech, do likewise. There is a deafening metallic roar, through which* YANK's *voice can be heard bellowing.*] Slaves, hell! We run de whole woiks. All de rich guys dat tink dey're somep'n, dey ain't nothin'! Dey don't belong. But us guys, we're in de move, we're at de bottom, de whole ting is us! [PADDY *from the start of* YANK's *speech has been taking one gulp after another from his bottle, at first frightenedly, as if he were afraid to listen, then desperately, as if to drown his senses, but finally has achieved complete indifferent, even amused, drunkenness.* YANK *sees his lips moving. He quells the uproar with a shout.*] Hey, youse guys, take it easy! Wait a moment! De nutty Harp is sayin' somep'n.

PADDY. [*Is heard now—throws his head back with a mocking*

burst of laughter.] Ho-ho-ho-ho-ho——

YANK. [*Drawing back his fist, with a snarl.*] Aw! Look out who yuh're givin' the bark!

PADDY. [*Begins to sing the "Miller of Dee" with enormous good nature.*]

> "I care for nobody, no, not I,
> And nobody cares for me."

YANK. [*Good-natured himself in a flash, interrupts* PADDY *with a slap on the bare back like a report.*] Dat's de stuff! Now yuh're gettin' wise to somep'n. Care for nobody, dat's de dope! To hell wit 'em all! And nix on nobody else carin'. I kin care for myself, get me! [*Eight bells sound, muffled, vibrating through the steel walls as if some enormous brazen gong were imbedded in the heart of the ship. All the men jump up mechanically, file through the door silently close upon each other's heels in what is very like a prisoners' lockstep.* YANK *slaps* PADDY *on the back.*] Our watch, yuh old Harp! [*Mockingly.*] Come on down in hell. Eat up de coal dust. Drink in de heat. It's it, see! Act like yuh liked it, yuh better—or croak yuhself.

PADDY. [*With jovial defiance.*] To the divil wid it! I'll not report this watch. Let them log me and be damned. I'm no slave the like of you. I'll be sittin' here at me ease, and drinking, and thinking, and dreaming dreams.

YANK. [*Contemptuously.*] Tinkin' and dreamin', what'll that get yuh? What's tinkin' got to do wit it? We move, don't we? Speed, ain't it? Fog, dat's all you stand for. But we drive trou dat, don't we? We split dat up and smash trou—twenty-five knots a hour! [*Turns his back on* PADDY *scornfully.*] Aw, yuh make me sick! Yuh don't belong! [*He strides out the door in rear.* PADDY *hums to himself, blinking drowsily.*]

[*Curtain.*]

Scene II

SCENE. Two days out. A section of the promenade deck. MILDRED DOUGLAS and her AUNT are discovered reclining in deck chairs. The former is a girl of twenty, slender, delicate, with a pale, pretty face marred by a self-conscious expression of disdainful superiority. She looks fretful, nervous, and discontented, bored by her own anemia. Her aunt is a pompous and proud—and fat—old lady. She is a type even to the point of a double chin and lorgnette. She is dressed pretentiously, as if afraid her face alone would never indicate her position in life. MILDRED is dressed all in white.

The impression to be conveyed by this scene is one of the beautiful, vivid life of the sea all about—sunshine on the deck in a great flood, the fresh sea wind blowing across it. In the midst of this, these two incongruous, artificial figures, inert and disharmonious, the elder like a gray lump of dough touched up with rouge, the younger looking as if the vitality of her stock had been sapped before she was conceived, so that she is the expression not of its life energy but merely of the artificialities that energy had won for itself in the spending.

MILDRED. [*Looking up with affected dreaminess.*] How the black smoke swirls back against the sky! Is it not beautiful?

AUNT. [*Without looking up.*] I dislike smoke of any kind.

MILDRED. My great-grandmother smoked a pipe—a clay pipe.

AUNT. [*Ruffling.*] Vulgar.

MILDRED. She was too distant a relative to be vulgar. Time mellows pipes.

AUNT. [*Pretending boredom but irritated.*] Did the sociology you took up at college teach you that—to play the ghoul on every possible occasion, excavating old bones? Why not let your great-grandmother rest in her grave?

MILDRED. [*Dreamily.*] With her pipe beside her—puffing in Paradise.

AUNT. [*With spite.*] Yes, you are a natural born ghoul. You are even getting to look like one, my dear.

MILDRED. [*In a passionless tone.*] I detest you, Aunt. [*Looking at her critically.*] Do you know what you remind me of? Of a cold pork pudding against a background of linoleum tablecloth in the kitchen of a—but the possibilities are wearisome. [*She closes her eyes.*]

AUNT. [*With a bitter laugh.*] Merci for your candor. But since I am and must be your chaperon—in appearance, at least—let us patch up some sort of armed truce. For my part you are quite free to indulge any pose of eccentricity that beguiles you—as long as you observe the amenities——

MILDRED. [*Drawling.*] The inanities?

AUNT. [*Going on as if she hadn't heard.*] After exhausting the morbid thrills of social service work on New York's East Side—how they must have hated you, by the way, the poor that you made so much poorer in their own eyes!—you are now bent on making your slumming international. Well, I hope Whitechapel[6] will provide the needed nerve tonic. Do not ask me to chaperon you there, however. I told your father I would not. I loathe deformity. We will hire an army of detectives and you may investigate everything—they allow you to see.

MILDRED. [*Protesting with a trace of genuine earnestness.*] Please

6. An underprivileged district of London, compared here with the East Side in New York.

do not mock at my attempts to discover how the other half lives. Give me credit for some sort of groping sincerity in that at least. I would like to help them. I would like to be some use in the world. Is it my fault I don't know how? I would like to be sincere, to touch life somewhere. [*With weary bitterness.*] But I'm afraid I have neither the vitality nor integrity. All that was burnt out in our stock before I was born. Grandfather's blast furnaces, flaming to the sky, melting steel, making millions—then father keeping those home fires burning, making more millions—and little me at the tail-end of it all. I'm a waste product in the Bessemer process—like the millions. Or rather, I inherit the acquired trait of the by-product, wealth, but none of the energy, none of the strength of the steel that made it. I am sired by gold and damned by it, as they say at the race track—damned in more ways than one. [*She laughs mirthlessly.*]

AUNT. [*Unimpressed—superciliously.*] You seem to be going in for sincerity to-day. It isn't becoming to you, really—except as an obvious pose. Be as artificial as you are, I advise. There's a sort of sincerity in that, you know. And, after all, you must confess you like that better.

MILDRED. [*Again affected and bored.*] Yes, I suppose I do. Pardon me for my outburst. When a leopard complains of its spots, it must sound rather grotesque. [*In a mocking tone.*] Purr, little leopard, Purr, scratch, tear, kill, gorge yourself and be happy—only stay in the jungle where your spots are camouflage. In a cage they make you conspicuous.

AUNT. I don't know what you are talking about.

MILDRED. It would be rude to talk about anything to you. Let's just talk. [*She looks at her wrist watch.*] Well, thank goodness, it's about time for them to come for me. That ought to give me a new thrill, Aunt.

AUNT. [*Affectedly troubled.*] You don't mean to say you're really going? The dirt—the heat must be frightful——

MILDRED. Grandfather started as a puddler. I should have inherited an immunity to heat that would make a salamander shiver. It will be fun to put it to the test.

AUNT. But don't you have to have the captain's—or someone's —permission to visit the stokehole?

MILDRED. [*With a triumphant smile.*] I have it—both his and the chief engineer's. Oh, they didn't want to at first, in spite of my social service credentials. They didn't seem a bit anxious that I should investigate how the other half lives and works on a ship. So I had to tell them that my father, the president of Nazareth Steel, chairman of the board of directors of this line, had told me it would be all right.

AUNT. He didn't.

MILDRED. How naïve age makes one! But I said he did, Aunt. I even said he had given me a letter to them—which I had lost. And they were afraid to take the chance that I might be lying. [*Excitedly.*] So it's ho! for the stokehole. The second engineer is to escort me. [*Looking at her watch again.*] It's time. And here he comes, I think.

[*The* SECOND ENGINEER *enters. He is a husky, fine-looking man of thirty-five or so. He stops before the two and tips his cap, visibly embarrassed and ill-at-ease.*]

SECOND ENGINEER. Miss Douglas?

MILDRED. Yes. [*Throwing off her rugs and getting to her feet.*] Are we all ready to start?

SECOND ENGINEER. In just a second, ma'am. I'm waiting for the Fourth. He's coming along.

MILDRED. [*With a scornful smile.*] You don't care to shoulder this responsiblity alone, is that it?

SECOND ENGINEER. [*Forcing a smile.*] Two are better than one. [*Disturbed by her eyes, glances out to sea—blurts out.*] A fine day we're having.

MILDRED. Is it?

SECOND ENGINEER. A nice warm breeze——

MILDRED. It feels cold to me.

SECOND ENGINEER. But it's hot enough in the sun——

MILDRED. Not hot enough for me. I don't like Nature. I was never athletic.

SECOND ENGINEER. [*Forcing a smile.*] Well, you'll find it hot enough where you're going.

MILDRED. Do you mean hell?

SECOND ENGINEER. [*Flabbergasted, decides to laugh.*] Ho-ho! No, I mean the stokehole.

MILDRED. My grandfather was a puddler. He played with boiling steel.

SECOND ENGINEER. [*All at sea—uneasily.*] Is that so? Hum, you'll excuse me, ma'am, but are you intending to wear that dress?

MILDRED. Why not?

SECOND ENGINEER. You'll likely rub against oil and dirt. It can't be helped.

MILDRED. It doesn't matter. I have lots of white dresses.

SECOND ENGINEER. I have an old coat you might throw over——

MILDRED. I have fifty dresses like this. I will throw this one into the sea when I come back. That ought to wash it clean, don't you think?

SECOND ENGINEER. [*Doggedly.*] There's ladders to climb down that are none too clean—and dark alleyways——

MILDRED. I will wear this very dress and none other.

SECOND ENGINEER. No offense meant. It's none of my business. I was only warning you——

MILDRED. Warning? That sounds thrilling.

SECOND ENGINEER. [*Looking down the deck—with a sigh of relief.*] There's the Fourth now. He's waiting for us. If you'll come——

MILDRED. Go on. I'll follow you. [*He goes.* MILDRED *turns a mocking smile on her aunt.*] An oaf—but a handsome, virile oaf.

AUNT. [*Scornfully.*] Poser!

MILDRED. Take care. He said there were dark alleyways——

AUNT. [*In the same tone.*] Poser!

MILDRED. [*Biting her lips angrily.*] You are right. But would that my millions were not so anemically chaste!

AUNT. Yes, for a fresh pose I have no doubt you would drag the name of Douglas in the gutter!

MILDRED. From which it sprang. Goodby, Aunt. Don't pray too hard that I may fall into the fiery furnace.

AUNT. Poser!

MILDRED. [*Viciously.*] Old hag! [*She slaps her aunt insultingly across the face and walks off, laughing gayly.*]

AUNT. [*Screams after her.*] I said poser!

[*Curtain.*]

Scene III

SCENE. The stokehole. In the rear, the dimly-outlined bulks of the furnaces and boilers. High overhead one hanging electric bulb sheds just enough light through the murky air laden with coal dust to pile up masses of shadows everywhere. A line of men, stripped to the waist, is before the furnace doors. They bend over, looking neither to right nor left, handling their shovels as if they were part of their bodies, with a strange, awkward, swinging rhythm. They use the shovels to throw open the furnace doors. Then from these fiery round holes in the black a flood of terrific light and heat pours full upon the men who are outlined in silhouette in the crouching, inhuman attitudes of chained gorillas. The men shovel with a rhythmic motion, swinging as on a pivot from the coal which lies in heaps on the floor behind to hurl it into the flaming mouths before them. There is a tumult of noise—the brazen clang of the furnace doors as they are flung open or slammed shut, the grating, teeth-gritting grind of steel against steel, of crunching coal. This clash of sounds stuns one's ears with its rending dissonance. But there is order in it, rhythm, a mechanical regulated recurrence, a tempo. And rising above all, making the air hum with the quiver of liberated energy, the roar of leaping flames in the furnaces, the monotonous throbbing beat of the engines.

As the curtain rises, the furnace doors are shut. The men are taking a breathing spell. One or two are arranging the coal behind them, pulling it into more accessible heaps. The others can be dimly made out leaning on their shovels in relaxed attitudes of exhaustion.

PADDY. [*From somewhere in the line—plaintively.*] Yerra, will this divil's own watch nivir end? Me back is broke. I'm destroyed entirely.

YANK. [*From the center of the line—with exuberant scorn.*] Aw, yuh make me sick! Lie down and croak, why don't yuh? Always beefin', dat's you! Say, dis is a cinch! Dis was made for me! It's my meat, get me! [*A whistle is blown—a thin, shrill note from somewhere overhead in the darkness.* YANK *curses without resentment.*] Dere's de damn engineer crackin' de whip. He tinks we're loafin'.

PADDY. [*Vindictively.*] God stiffen him!

YANK. [*In an exultant tone of command.*] Come on, youse guys! Git into de game! She's gittin hungry! Pile some grub in her. Trow it into her belly! Come on now, all of youse! Open her up!

[*At this last all the men, who have followed his movements of getting into position, throw open their furnace doors with a deafening clang. The fiery light floods over their shoulders as they bend round for the coal. Rivulets of sooty sweat have traced maps on their backs. The enlarged muscles form bunches of high light and shadow.*]

YANK. [*Chanting a count as he shovels without seeming effort.*] One—two—tree—— [*His voice rising exultantly in the joy of battle.*] Dat's de stuff! Let her have it! All togedder now! Sling it into her! Let her ride! Shoot de piece now! Call de toin on her! Drive her into it! Feel her move! Watch her smoke! Speed, dat's her middle name! Give her coal, youse guys! Coal, dat's her booze! Drink it up, baby! Let's see yuh sprint! Dig in and gain a lap! Dere she go-o-es. [*This last in the chanting formula of the gallery gods at the six-day bike race. He slams his furnace door shut. The others do likewise with as much unison as their wearied bodies will permit. The effect is of one fiery eye after another being blotted out with a series of accompanying bangs.*]

PADDY. [*Groaning.*] Me back is broke. I'm bate out—bate——

[*There is a pause. Then the inexorable whistle sounds again from the dim regions above the electric light. There is a growl of cursing rage from all sides.*]

YANK. [*Shaking his fist upward—contemptuously.*] Take it easy dere, you! Who d'yuh tinks runnin' dis game, me or you? When I git ready, we move. Not before! When I git ready, get me!

VOICES. [*Approvingly.*] That's the stuff!

Yank tal him, py golly!
Yank ain't afeerd.
Goot poy, Yank!
Give him hell!
Tell 'im 'e's a bloody swine!
Bloody slave-driver!

YANK. [*Contemptuously.*] He ain't got no noive. He's yellow, get me? All de engineers is yellow. Dey got streaks a mile wide. Aw, to hell wit him! Let's move, youse guys. We had a rest. Come on, she needs it! Give her pep! It ain't for him. Him and his whistle, dey don't belong. But we belong, see! We gotter feed de baby! Come on! [*He turns and flings his furnace door open. They all follow his lead. At this instant the* SECOND *and* FOURTH ENGINEERS *enter from the darkness on the left with* MILDRED *between them. She starts, turns paler, her pose is crumbling, she shivers with fright in spite of the blazing heat, but forces herself to leave the* ENGINEERS *and take a few steps nearer the men. She is right behind* YANK. *All this happens quickly while the men have their backs turned.*]

YANK. Come on, youse guys! [*He is turning to get coal when the whistle sounds again in a peremptory, irritating note. This drives* YANK *into a sudden fury. While the other men have turned full around and stopped dumfounded by the spectacle of* MILDRED *standing there in her white dress,* YANK *does not turn far enough to see her. Besides, his head is thrown back, he blinks upward through the murk trying to find the owner of the whistle, he brandishes his shovel murderously over his head in one hand, pounding on his chest, gorilla-like, with the other, shouting.*] Toin off dat whistle! Come down outa dere, yuh yellow, brass-buttoned, Belfast bum, yuh! Come down and I'll knock yer brains out! Yuh lousy, stinkin', yellow mut of a Catholic-moiderin' bastard! Come down and I'll moider yuh! Pullin' dat whistle on me, huh? I'll show yuh! I'll crash yer skull in! I'll drive yer teet' down yer troat! I'll slam yer nose trou de back of yer head! I'll cut yer guts out for a nickel, yuh lousy boob, yuh dirty, crummy, muck-eatin' son of a—— [*Suddenly he becomes conscious of all the other men staring at something directly behind his back. He whirls defensively with a snarling, murderous growl, crouching to spring, his lips drawn back over his teeth, his small eyes gleaming ferociously. He sees* MILDRED, *like a white apparition in the full light from the open furnace doors. He glares into her eyes, turned to stone. As for her, during his speech she has listened, paralyzed with horror, terror, her whole personality crushed, beaten in, collapsed, by the terrific impact of this unknown, abysmal brutality, naked and shameless. As she looks at his gorilla face, as his eyes bore into hers, she utters a low, choking cry and shrinks away from him, putting both hands up before her eyes to shut out the sight of his face, to protect her own. This startles* YANK *to a reaction. His mouth falls open, his eyes grow bewildered.*]

MILDRED. [*About to faint—to the* ENGINEERS, *who now have her one by each arm—whimperingly.*] Take me away! Oh, the filthy beast! [*She faints. They carry her quickly back, disappearing in the darkness at the left, rear. An iron door clangs shut. Rage and bewildered fury rush back on* YANK. *He feels himself insulted in some unknown fashion in the very heart of his pride. He roars.*] God damn yuh! [*And hurls his shovel after them at the door which has just closed. It hits the steel bulkhead with a clang and falls clattering on the steel floor. From overhead the whistle sounds again in a long, angry, insistent command.*]

[*Curtain.*]

Scene IV

SCENE. The firemen's forecastle. YANK'S watch has just come off duty and had dinner. Their faces and bodies shine from a soap and water scrubbing but around their eyes, where a hasty dousing does not touch, the coal dust sticks like black make-up, giving them a queer, sinister expression. YANK has not washed either face or body. He stands out in contrast to them, a blackened, brooding figure. He is seated forward on a bench in the exact attitude of Rodin's "The Thinker."[7] The others, most of them smoking pipes, are staring at YANK half-apprehensively, as if fearing an outburst; half-amusedly, as if they saw a joke somewhere that tickled them.

VOICES. He ain't ate nothin'.
Py golly, a fallar gat to gat grub in him.
Divil a lie.
Yank feeda da fire, no feeda da face.
Ha-ha.
He ain't even washed hisself.
He's forgot.
Hey, Yank, you forgot to wash.
YANK. [*Sullenly.*] Forgot nothin'! To hell wit washin'.
VOICES. It'll stick to you.
It'll get under your skin.
Give yer the bleedin' itch, that's wot.
It makes spots on you—like a leopard.
Like a piebald nigger, you mean.
Better wash up, Yank.
You sleep better.

7. Auguste Rodin (1840–1917), French sculptor. "The Thinker" is the figure of a powerful man sitting in deep concentration of thought.

Wash up, Yank.

Wash up! Wash up!

YANK. [*Resentfully.*] Aw say, youse guys. Lemme alone. Can't youse see I'm tryin' to tink?

ALL. [*Repeating the word after him as one with cynical mockery.*] Think! [*The word has a brazen, metallic quality as if their throats were phonograph horns. It is followed by a chorus of hard, barking laughter.*]

YANK. [*Springing to his feet and glaring at them belligerently.*] Yes, tink! Tink, dat's what I said. What about it? [*They are silent, puzzled by his sudden resentment at what used to be one of his jokes.* YANK *sits down again in the same attitude of "The Thinker."*]

VOICES. Leave him alone.

He's got a grouch on.

Why wouldn't he?

PADDY. [*With a wink at the others.*] Sure I know what's the matther. 'Tis aisy to see. He's fallen in love, I'm telling you.

ALL. [*Repeating the word after him as one with cynical mockery.*] Love! [*The word has a brazen, metallic quality as if their throats were phonograph horns. It is followed by a chorus of hard, barking laughter.*]

YANK. [*With a contemptuous snort.*] Love, hell! Hate, dat's what. I've fallen in hate, get me?

PADDY. [*Philosophically.*] 'Twould take a wise man to tell one from the other. [*With a bitter, ironical scorn, increasing as he goes on.*] But I'm telling you it's love that's in it. Sure what else but love for us poor bastes in the stokehole would be bringing a fine lady, dressed like a white quane, down a mile of ladders and steps to be havin' a look at us?

[*A growl of anger goes up from all sides.*]

LONG. [*Jumping on a bench—hecticly.*] Hinsultin' us! Hinsultin' us, the bloody cow! And them bloody engineers! What right 'as they got to be exhibitin' us 's if we was bleedin' monkeys in a menagerie? Did we sign for hinsults to our dignity as 'onest workers? Is that in the ship's articles? You kin bloody well bet it ain't! But I knows why they done it. I arsked a deck steward 'o she was and 'e told me. 'Er old man's a bleedin' millionaire, a bloody Capitalist! 'E's got enuf bloody gold to sink this bleedin' ship! 'E makes arf the bloody steel in the world! 'E owns this bloody boat! And you and me, Comrades, we're 'is slaves! And the skipper and mates and engineers, they're 'is slaves! And she's 'is bloody daughter and we're all 'er slaves, too! And she gives 'er orders as 'ow she wants to see the bloody animals below decks and down they takes 'er!

[*There is a roar of rage from all sides.*]

YANK. [*Blinking at him bewilderedly.*] Say! Wait a moment! Is all dat straight goods?

LONG. Straight as string! The bleedin' steward as waits on 'em, 'e told me about 'er. And what're we goin' ter do, I arsks yer? 'Ave we got ter swaller 'er hinsults like dogs? It ain't in the ship's articles. I tell yer we got a case. We kin go to law——

YANK. [*With abysmal contempt.*] Hell! Law!

ALL. [*Repeating the word after him as one with cynical mockery.*] Law! [*The word has a brazen metallic quality as if their throats were phonograph horns. It is followed by a chorus of hard, barking laughter.*]

LONG. [*Feeling the ground slipping from under his feet—desperately.*] As voters and citizens we kin force the bloody governments——

YANK. [*With abysmal contempt.*] Hell! Governments!

ALL. [*Repeating the word after him as one with cynical mockery.*] Governments! [*The word has a brazen metallic quality as if their throats were phonograph horns. It is followed by a chorus of hard, barking laughter.*]

LONG. [*Hysterically.*] We're free and equal in the sight of God——

YANK. [*With abysmal contempt.*] Hell! God!

ALL. [*Repeating the word after him as one with cynical mockery.*] God! [*The word has a brazen metallic quality as if their throats were phonograph horns. It is followed by a chorus of hard, barking laughter.*]

YANK. [*Witheringly.*] Aw, join de Salvation Army!

ALL. Sit down! Shut up! Damn fool! Sea-lawyer!

[LONG *slinks back out of sight.*]

PADDY. [*Continuing the trend of his thoughts as if he had never been interrupted—bitterly.*] And there she was standing behind us, and the Second pointing at us like a man you'd hear in a circus would be saying: In this cage is a queerer kind of baboon than ever you'd find in darkest Africy. We roast them in their own sweat—and be damned if you won't hear some of thim saying they like it! [*He glances scornfully at* YANK.]

YANK. [*With a bewildered uncertain growl.*] Aw!

PADDY. And there was Yank roarin' curses and turning round wid his shovel to brain her—and she looked at him, and him at her——

YANK. [*Slowly.*] She was all white. I tought she was a ghost. Sure.

PADDY. [*With heavy, biting sarcasm.*] 'Twas love at first sight, divil a doubt of it! If you'd seen the endearin' look on her pale mug when she shriveled away with her hands over her eyes to shut out the sight of him! Sure, 'twas as if she'd seen a great hairy ape escaped from the Zoo!

YANK. [*Stung—with a growl of rage.*] Aw!

PADDY. And the loving way Yank heaved his shovel at the skull of her, only she was out the door! [*A grin breaking over his face.*] 'Twas touching, I'm telling you! It put the touch of home, swate home in the stokehole.

[*There is a roar of laughter from all.*]

YANK. [*Glaring at* PADDY *menacingly.*] Aw, choke dat off, see!

PADDY. [*Not heeding him—to the others.*] And her grabbin' at the Second's arm for protection. [*With a grotesque imitation of a woman's voice.*] Kiss me, Engineer dear, for it's dark down here and me old man's in Wall Street making money! Hug me tight, darlin', for I'm afeerd in the dark and me mother's on deck makin' eyes at the skipper!

[*Another roar of laughter.*]

YANK. [*Threateningly.*] Say! What yuh tryin' to do, kid me, yuh old Harp?

PADDY. Divil a bit! Ain't I wishin' myself you'd brained her?

YANK. [*Fiercely.*] I'll brain her! I'll brain her yet, wait 'n' see! [*Coming over to* PADDY—*slowly.*] Say, is dat what she called me—a hairy ape?

PADDY. She looked it at you if she didn't say the word itself.

YANK. [*Grinning horribly.*] Hairy ape, huh? Sure! Dat's de way she looked at me, aw right. Hairy ape! So dat's me, huh? [*Bursting into rage—as if she were still in front of him.*] Yuh skinny tart! Yuh whitefaced bum, yuh! I'll show yuh who's a ape! [*Turning to the others, bewilderment seizing him again.*] Say, youse guys. I was bawlin' him out for pullin' de whistle on us. You heard me. And den I seen youse lookin' at somep'n and I thought he'd sneaked down to come up in back of me, and I hopped around to knock him dead wit de shovel. And dere she was wit de light on her! Christ, yuh coulda pushed me over with a finger! I was scared, get me? Sure! I tought she was a ghost, see? She was all in white like dey wrap around stiffs. You seen her. Kin yuh blame me? She didn't belong, dat's what. And den when I come to and seen it was a real skoit and seen de way she was lookin' at me—like Paddy said—Christ, I was sore, get me? I don't stand for dat stuff from nobody. And I flung de shovel—on'y she'd beat it. [*Furiously.*] I wished it'd banged her! I wished it'd knocked her block off!

LONG. And be 'anged for murder or 'lectrocuted? She ain't bleedin' well worth it.

YANK. I don't give a damn what! I'd be square wit her, wouldn't I? Tink I wanter let her put somep'n over on me? Tink I'm goin' to let her git away wit dat stuff? Yuh don't know me! No one ain't never put nothin' over on me and got away wit it, see!—not dat kind of stuff—no guy and no skoit neither! I'll fix her! Maybe she'll come down again——

VOICE. No chance, Yank. You scared her out of a year's growth.

YANK. I scared her? Why de hell should I scare her? Who de hell is she? Ain't she de same as me? Hairy ape, huh? [*With his old confident bravado.*] I'll show her I'm better'n her, if she on'y knew it. I belong and she don't, see! I move and she's dead! Twenty-five knots a hour, dat's me! Dat carries her but I make dat. She's on'y baggage. Sure! [*Again bewilderedly.*] But, Christ, she was funny lookin'! Did yuh pipe her hands? White and skinny. Yuh could see de bones trough 'em. And her mush,[8] dat was dead white, too. And her eyes, dey was like dey'd seen a ghost. Me, dat was! Sure! Hairy ape! Ghost, huh? Look at dat arm! [*He extends his right arm, swelling out the great muscles.*] I coulda took her wit dat, wit just my little finger even, and broke her in two. [*Again bewilderedly.*] Say, who is dat skoit, huh? What is she? What's she come from? Who made her? Who give her de noive to look at me like dat? Dis ting's got my goat right. I don't get her. She's new to me. What does a skoit like her mean, huh? She don't belong, get me! I can't see her. [*With growing anger.*] But one ting I'm wise to, aw right, aw right! Youse all kin bet your shoits I'll get even wit her. I'll show her if she tinks she—— She grinds de organ and I'm on de string, huh? I'll fix her! Let her come down again and I'll fling her in de furnace! She'll move den! She won't shiver at nothin', den! Speed, dat'll be her! She'll belong den! [*He grins horribly.*]

PADDY. She'll never come. She's had her belly-full, I'm telling you. She'll be in bed now, I'm thinking, wid ten doctors and nurses feedin' her salts to clean the fear out of her.

YANK. [*Enraged.*] Yuh tink I made her sick, too, do yuh? Just lookin' at me, huh? Hairy ape, huh? [*In a frenzy of rage.*] I'll fix her! I'll tell her where to git off! She'll git down on her knees and take it back or I'll burst de face offen her! [*Shaking one fist upward and beating on his chest with the other.*] I'll find yuh! I'm comin', d'yuh hear? I'll fix yuh, God damn yuh! [*He makes a rush for the door.*]

VOICES. Stop him!
   He'll get shot!
   He'll murder her!
   Trip him up!
   Hold him!
   He's gone crazy!
   Gott, he's strong!
   Hold him down!
   Look out for a kick!

8. Face.

Pin his arms!

[*They have all piled on him and, after a fierce struggle, by sheer weight of numbers have borne him to the floor just inside the door.*]

PADDY. [*Who has remained detached.*] Kape him down till he's cooled off. [*Scornfully.*] Yerra, Yank, you're a great fool. Is it payin' attention at all you are to the like of that skinny sow widout one drop of rale blood in her?

YANK. [*Frenziedly, from the bottom of the heap.*] She done me doit! She done me doit, didn't she? I'll git square wit her! I'll get her some way! Git offen me, youse guys! Lemme up! I'll show her who's a ape!

[*Curtain.*]

Scene V

SCENE. Three weeks later. A corner of Fifth Avenue in the Fifties on a fine Sunday morning. A general atmosphere of clean, well-tidied, wide street; a flood of mellow, tempered sunshine; gentle, genteel breezes. In the rear, the show windows of two shops, a jewelry establishment on the corner, a furrier's next to it. Here the adornments of extreme wealth are tantalizingly displayed. The jeweler's window is gaudy with glittering diamonds, emeralds, rubies, pearls, etc., fashioned in ornate tiaras, crowns, necklaces, collars, etc. From each piece hangs an enormous tag from which a dollar sign and numerals in intermittent electric lights wink out the incredible prices. The same in the furrier's. Rich furs of all varieties hang there bathed in a downpour of artificial light. The general effect is of a background of magnificence cheapened and made grotesque by commercialism, a background in tawdry disharmony with the clear light and sunshine on the street itself.

Up the side street YANK and LONG come swaggering. LONG is dressed in shore clothes, wears a black Windsor tie, cloth cap. YANK is in his dirty dungarees. A fireman's cap with black peak is cocked defiantly on the side of his head. He has not shaved for days and around his fierce, resentful eyes—as around those of LONG to a lesser degree—the black smudge of coal dust still sticks like make-up. They hesitate and stand together at the corner, swaggering, looking about them with a forced, defiant contempt.

LONG. [*Indicating it all with an oratorical gesture.*] Well, 'ere we are. Fif' Avenoo. This 'ere's their bleedin' private lane, as yer might say. [*Bitterly.*] We're trespassers 'ere. Proletarians keep orf the grass!

YANK. [*Dully.*] I don't see no grass, yuh boob. [*Staring at the sidewalk.*] Clean, ain't it? Yuh could eat a fried egg offen it. The white wings[9] got some job sweepin' dis up. [*Looking up and down*

9. A term once common for street cleaners, who wore white suits.

the avenue—surlily.] Where's all de white-collar stiffs yuh said was here—and de skoits—*her* kind?

LONG. In church, blarst 'em! Arskin' Jesus to give 'em more money.

YANK. Choich, huh? I useter go to choich onct—sure—when I was a kid. Me old man and woman, dey made me. Dey never went demselves, dough. Always got too big a head on Sunday mornin', dat was dem. [*With a grin.*] Dey was scrappers for fair, bot' of dem. On Satiday nights when dey bot' got a skinful dey could put up a bout oughter been staged at de Garden.[1] When dey got trough dere wasn't a chair or table wit a leg under it. Or else dey bot' jumped on me for somep'n. Dat was where I loined to take punishment. [*With a grin and a swagger.*] I'm a chip offen de old block, get me?

LONG. Did yer old man follow the sea?

YANK. Naw. Worked along shore. I runned away when me old lady croaked wit de tremens. I helped at truckin' and in de market. Den I shipped in de stokehole. Sure. Dat belongs. De rest was nothin'. [*Looking around him.*] I ain't never seen dis before. De Brooklyn waterfront, dat was where I was dragged up. [*Taking a deep breath.*] Dis ain't so bad at dat, huh?

LONG. Not bad? Well, we pays for it wiv our bloody sweat, if yer wants to know!

YANK. [*With sudden angry disgust.*] Aw, hell! I don't see no one, see—like her. All dis gives me a pain. It don't belong. Say, ain't dere a back room around dis dump? Let's go shoot a ball. All dis is too clean and quiet and dolled-up, get me! It gives me a pain.

LONG. Wait and yer'll bloody well see——

YANK. I don't wait for no one. I keep on de move. Say, what yuh drag me up here for, anyway? Tryin' to kid me, yuh simp, yuh?

LONG. Yer wants to get back at 'er, don't yer? That's what yer been sayin' every bloomin' hour since she hinsulted yer.

YANK. [*Vehemently.*] Sure ting I do! Didn't I try to get even with her in Southampton? Didn't I sneak on de dock and wait for her by de gangplank? I was goin' to spit in her pale mug, see! Sure, right in her pop-eyes! Dat woulda made me even, see? But no chanct. Dere was a whole army of plain-clothes bulls around. Dey spotted me and gimme de bum's rush. I never seen her. But I'll git square wit her yet, you watch! [*Furiously.*] De lousy tart! She tinks she kin get away wit moider—but not wit me! I'll fix her! I'll tink of a way!

LONG. [*As disgusted as he dares to be.*] Ain't that why I brought yer up 'ere—to show yer? Yer been lookin' at this 'ere 'ole affair wrong. Yer been actin' an' talkin' 's if it was all a bleedin' personal matter between yer and that bloody cow. I wants to convince yer

1. Madison Square Garden, New York.

she was on'y a representative of 'er clarss. I wants to awaken yer bloody clarss consciousness. Then yer'll see it's 'er clarss yer've got to fight, not 'er alone. There's a 'ole mob of 'em like 'er, Gawd blind 'em!

YANK. [Spitting on his hands—belligerently.] De more de merrier when I gits started. Bring on de gang!

LONG. Yer'll see 'em in arf a mo', when that church lets out. [He turns and sees the window display in the two stores for the first time.] Blimey![2] Look at that, will yer? [They both walk back and stand looking in the jeweler's. LONG flies into a fury.] Just look at this 'ere bloomin' mess! Just look at it! Look at the bleedin' prices on 'em—more'n our 'ole bloody stokehole makes in ten voyages sweatin' in 'ell! And they—'er and 'er bloody clarss—buys 'em for toys to dangle on 'em! One of these 'ere would buy scoff for a starvin' family for a year!

YANK. Aw, cut de sob stuff! T' hell wit de starvin' family! Yuh'll be passin' de hat to me next. [With naïve admiration.] Say, dem tings is pretty, huh? Bet yuh dey'd hock for a piece of change aw right. [Then turning away, bored.] But, aw hell, what good are dey? Let her have 'em. Dey don't belong no more'n she does. [With a gesture of sweeping the jewelers into oblivion.] All dat don't count, get me?

LONG. [Who has moved to the furrier's—indignantly.] And I s'pose this 'ere don't count neither—skins of poor, 'armless animals slaughtered so as 'er and 'ers can keep their bleedin' noses warm!

YANK. [Who has been staring at something inside—with queer excitement.] Take a slant at dat! Give it de once-over! Monkey fur —two t'ousand bucks! [Bewilderedly.] Is dat straight goods— monkey fur? What de hell——?

LONG. [Bitterly.] It's straight enuf. [With grim humor.] They wouldn't bloody well pay that for a 'airy ape's skin—no, nor for the 'ole livin' ape with all 'is 'ead, and body, and soul thrown in!

YANK. [Clenching his fists, his face growing pale with rage as if the skin in the window were a personal insult.] Trowin' it up in my face! Christ! I'll fix her!

LONG. [Excitedly.] Church is out. 'Ere they come, the bleedin' swine. [After a glance at YANK's lowering face—uneasily.] Easy goes, Comrade. Keep yer bloomin' temper. Remember force defeats itself. It ain't our weapon. We must impress our demands through peaceful means—the votes of the on-marching proletarians of the bloody world!

YANK. [With abysmal contempt.] Votes, hell! Votes is a joke, see. Votes for women! Let dem do it!

2. A British vulgarism, "blimey" (short for "Gawblimey," meaning "God blind me!") is rigidly banned by the respectable, as is the term "bloody" (from "by Our Lady!"), also used by the cockney Long.

LONG. [*Still more uneasily.*] Calm, now. Treat 'em wiv the proper contempt. Observe the bleedin' parasites but 'old yer 'orses.

YANK. [*Angrily.*] Git away from me! Yuh're yellow, dat's what. Force, dat's me! De punch, dat's me every time, see!

[*The crowd from church enter from the right, sauntering slowly and affectedly, their heads held stiffly up, looking neither to right nor left, talking in toneless, simpering voices. The women are rouged, calcimined, dyed, over-dressed to the nth degree. The men are in Prince Alberts, high hats, spats, canes, etc. A procession of gaudy marionettes, yet with something of the relentless horror of Frankensteins[3] in their detached, mechanical unawareness.*]

VOICES. Dear Doctor Caiaphas! He is so sincere!

What was the sermon? I dozed off.

About the radicals, my dear—and the false doctrines that are being preached.

We must organize a hundred per cent American bazaar.

And let everyone contribute one one-hundredth per cent of their income tax.

What an original idea!

We can devote the proceeds to rehabilitating the veil of the temple.

But that has been done so many times.

YANK. [*Glaring from one to the other of them—with an insulting snort of scorn.*] Huh! Huh!

[*Without seeming to see him, they make wide detours to avoid the spot where he stands in the middle of the sidewalk.*]

LONG. [*Frightenedly.*] Keep yer bloomin' mouth shut, I tells yer.

YANK. [*Viciously.*] G'wan! Tell it to Sweeney! [*He swaggers away and deliberately lurches into a top-hatted gentleman, then glares at him pugnaciously.*] Say, who d'yuh tink yuh're bumpin'? Tink yuh own de oith?

GENTLEMAN. [*Coldly and affectedly.*] I beg your pardon. [*He has not looked at YANK and passes on without a glance, leaving him bewildered.*]

LONG. [*Rushing up and grabbing YANK's arm.*] 'Ere! Come away! This wasn't what I meant. Yer'll 'ave the bloody coppers down on us.

YANK. [*Savagely—giving him a push that sends him sprawling.*] G'wan!

LONG. [*Picks himself up—hysterically.*] I'll pop orf then. This ain't what I meant. And whatever 'appens, yer can't blame me. [*He slinks off left.*]

YANK. T' hell wit youse! [*He approaches a lady—with a vicious*

3. Frankenstein created the robot monster that horribly destroyed him, in Mary Shelley's novel *Frankenstein* (1817). In many other literary references the monster is erroneously called "Frankenstein," as here.

grin and a smirking wink.] Hello, Kiddo. How's every little ting? Got anyting on for to-night? I know an old boiler down to de docks we kin crawl into. [*The lady stalks by without a look, without a change of pace.* YANK *turns to others—insultingly.*] Holy smokes, what a mug! Go hide yuhself before de horses shy at yuh. Gee, pipe de heine on dat one! Say, youse, yuh look like de stoin of a ferryboat. Paint and powder! All dolled up to kill! Yuh look like stiffs laid out for de boneyard! Aw, g'wan, de lot of youse! Yuh give me de eye-ache. Yuh don't belong, get me! Look at me, why don't youse dare? I belong, dat's me! [*Pointing to a skyscraper across the street which is in process of construction—with bravado.*] See dat building goin' up dere? See de steel work? Steel, dat's me! Youse guys live on it and tink yuh're somep'n. But I'm *in* it, see! I'm de hoistin' engine dat makes it go up! I'm it—de inside and bottom of it! Sure! I'm steel and steam and smoke and de rest of it! It moves—speed—twenty-five stories up—and me at de top and bottom—movin'! Youse simps don't move. Yuh're on'y dolls I winds up to see 'm spin. Yuh're de garbage, get me—de leavins— de ashes we dump over de side! Now, what 'a' yuh gottay say? [*But as they seem neither to see nor hear him, he flies into a fury.*] Bums! Pigs! Tarts! Bitches! [*He turns in a rage on the men, bumping viciously into them but not jarring them the least bit. Rather it is he who recoils after each collision. He keeps growling.*] Git off de oith! G'wan, yuh bum! Look where yuh're goin', can't yuh? Git outa here! Fight, why don't yuh? Put up yer mits! Don't be a dog! Fight or I'll knock yuh dead! [*But, without seeming to see him, they all answer with mechanical affected politeness.*] I beg your pardon. [*Then at a cry from one of the women, they all scurry to the furrier's window.*]

THE WOMAN. [*Ecstatically, with a gasp of delight.*] Monkey fur! [*The whole crowd of men and women chorus after her in the same tone of affected delight.*] Monkey fur!

YANK. [*With a jerk of his head back on his shoulders, as if he had received a punch full in the face—raging.*] I see yuh, all in white! I see yuh, yuh white-faced tart, yuh! Hairy ape, huh? I'll hairy ape yuh! [*He bends down and grips at the street curbing as if to pluck it out and hurl it. Foiled in this, snarling with passion, he leaps to the lamp-post on the corner and tries to pull it up for a club. Just at that moment a bus is heard rumbling up. A fat, high-hatted, spatted gentleman runs out from the side street. He calls out plaintively.*] Bus! Bus! Stop there! [*And runs full tilt into the bending, straining* YANK, *who is bowled off his balance.*]

YANK. [*Seeing a fight—with the roar of joy as he springs to his feet.*] At last! Bus, huh? I'll bust yuh! [*He lets drive a terrific swing,*

his fist landing full on the fat gentleman's face. But the gentleman
stands unmoved as if nothing had happened.]

GENTLEMAN. I beg your pardon. [*Then irritably.*] You have made
me lose my bus. [*He claps his hands and begins to scream:*] Officer!
Officer!

[*Many police whistles shrill out on the instant and a whole
platoon of policemen rush in on* YANK *from all sides. He tries to
fight but is clubbed to the pavement and fallen upon. The crowd
at the window have not moved or noticed this disturbance. The
clanging gong of the patrol wagon approaches with a clamoring din.*]

[*Curtain.*]

Scene VI

SCENE. Night of the following day. A row of cells in the prison on
Blackwell's Island. The cells extend back diagonally from right
front to left rear. They do not stop, but disappear in the dark
background as if they ran on, numberless, into infinity. One
electric bulb from the low ceiling of the narrow corridor sheds its
light through the heavy steel bars of the cell at the extreme front
and reveals part of the interior. YANK can be seen within, crouched
on the edge of his cot in the attitude of Rodin's "The Thinker."
His face is spotted with black and blue bruises. A blood-stained
bandage is wrapped around his head.

YANK. [*Suddenly starting as if awakening from a dream, reaches
out and shakes the bars—aloud to himself, wonderingly.*] Steel. Dis
is the Zoo, huh? [*A burst of hard, barking laughter comes from the
unseen occupants of the cells, runs back down the tier, and abruptly
ceases.*]

VOICES. [*Mockingly.*] The Zoo. That's a new name for this coop
—a damn good name!

Steel, eh? You said a mouthful. This is the old iron house.

Who is that boob talkin'?

He's the bloke they brung in out of his head. The bulls had
beat him up fierce.

YANK. [*Dully.*] I musta been dreamin'. I tought I was in a cage at
de Zoo—but de apes don't talk, do dey?

VOICES. [*With mocking laughter.*] You're in a cage aw right.

A coop!

A pen!

A sty!

A kennel! [*Hard laughter—a pause.*]

Say, guy! Who are you? No, never mind lying. What are you?

Yes, tell us your sad story. What's your game?

What did they jug yuh for?

YANK. [*Dully.*] I was a fireman—stokin' on de liners. [*Then with sudden rage, rattling his cell bars.*] I'm a hairy ape, get me? And I'll bust youse all in de jaw if yuh don't lay off kiddin' me.

VOICES. Huh! You're a hard boiled duck, ain't you!

When you spit, it bounces! [*Laughter.*]

Aw, can it. He's a regular guy. Ain't you?

What did he say he was—a ape?

YANK. [*Defiantly.*] Sure ting! Ain't dat what youse all are—apes? [*A silence. Then a furious rattling of bars from down the corridor.*]

A VOICE. [*Thick with rage.*] I'll show yuh who's a ape, yuh bum!

VOICES. Ssshh! Nix!

Can de noise!

Piano!

You'll have the guard down on us!

YANK. [*Scornfully.*] De guard? Yuh mean de keeper, don't yuh? [*Angry exclamations from all the cells.*]

VOICE. [*Placatingly.*] Aw, don't pay no attention to him. He's off his nut from the beatin'-up he got. Say, you guy! We're waitin' to hear what they landed you for—or ain't yuh tellin'?

YANK. Sure, I'll tell youse. Sure! Why de hell not? On'y—youse won't get me. Nobody gets me but me, see? I started to tell de Judge and all he says was: "Toity days to tink it over." Tink it over! Christ, dat's all I been doin' for weeks! [*After a pause.*] I was tryin' to git even wit someone, see?—someone dat done me doit.

VOICES. [*Cynically.*] De old stuff, I bet. Your goil, huh?

Give yuh the double-cross, huh?

That's them every time!

Did yuh beat up de odder guy?

YANK. [*Disgustedly.*] Aw, yuh're all wrong! Sure dere was a skoit in it—but not what youse mean, not dat old tripe. Dis was a new kind of skoit. She was dolled up all in white—in de stokehole. I tought she was a ghost. Sure. [*A pause.*]

VOICES. [*Whispering.*] Gee, he's still nutty.

Let him rave. It's fun listenin'.

YANK. [*Unheeding—groping in his thoughts.*] Her hands—dey was skinny and white like dey wasn't real but painted on somep'n. Dere was a million miles from me to her—twenty-five knots a hour. She was like some dead ting de cat brung in. Sure, dat's what. She didn't belong. She belonged in de window of a toy store, or on de top of a garbage can, see! Sure! [*He breaks out angrily.*] But would yuh believe it, she had de noive to do me doit. She lamped me like she was seein' somep'n broke loose from de menagerie. Christ, yuh'd oughter seen her eyes! [*He rattles the bars of his cell furiously.*] But I'll get back at her yet, you watch! And if I can't find her I'll take it out on de gang she runs wit. I'm wise to where dey hangs out now. I'll show her who belongs! I'll show her who's in de move and who ain't. You watch my smoke!

VOICES. [*Serious and joking.*] Dat's de talkin'!

Take her for all she's got!

What was this dame, anyway? Who was she, eh?

YANK. I dunno. First cabin stiff. Her old man's a millionaire, dey says—name of Douglas.

VOICES. Douglas? That's the president of the Steel Trust, I bet.

Sure. I seen his mug in de papers.

He's filthy with dough.

VOICE. Hey, feller, take a tip from me. If you want to get back at that dame, you better join the Wobblies. You'll get some action then.

YANK. Wobblies? What de hell's dat?

VOICE. Ain't you ever heard of the I. W. W.?[4]

YANK. Naw. What is it?

VOICE. A gang of blokes—a tough gang. I been readin' about 'em to-day in the paper. The guard give me the *Sunday Times.* There's a long spiel about 'em. It's from a speech made in the Senate by a guy named Senator Queen. [*He is in the cell next to* YANK'S. *There is a rustling of paper.*] Wait'll I see if I got light enough and I'll read you. Listen. [*He reads:*] "There is a menace existing in this country to-day which threatens the vitals of our fair Republic—as foul a menace against the very life-blood of the American Eagle as was the foul conspiracy of Catiline against the eagles of ancient Rome!"[5]

VOICE. [*Disgustedly.*] Aw, hell! Tell him to salt de tail of dat eagle!

VOICE. [*Reading.*] "I refer to that devil's brew of rascals, jail-birds, murderers and cut-throats who libel all honest workingmen by calling themselves the Industrial Workers of the World; but in the light of their nefarious plots, I call them the Industrious *Wreckers* of the World!"

YANK. [*With vengeful satisfaction.*] Wreckers, dat's de right dope! Dat belongs! Me for dem!

VOICE. Ssshh! [*Reading.*] "This fiendish organization is a foul ulcer on the fair body of our Democracy——"

VOICE. Democracy, hell! Give him the boid, fellers—the raspberry! [*They do.*]

VOICE. Ssshh! [*Reading:*] "Like Cato I say to this Senate, the

4. The Industrial Workers of the World (1905), a labor organization aiming to unite workers on an industry-wide rather than a craft basis and having as its underlying purpose the overthrow of capitalism in favor of socialism. It dis-integrated in the years following World War I.

5. Lucius Sergius Catilina (108?–62 B.C.) conspired against Rome, thus provoking, in 63 B.C., the famous orations of the consul Cicero.

I. W. W. must be destroyed![6] For they represent an ever-present dagger pointed at the heart of the greatest nation the world has ever known, where all men are born free and equal, with equal opportunities to all, where the Founding Fathers have guaranteed to each one happiness, where Truth, Honor, Liberty, Justice, and the Brotherhood of Man are a religion absorbed with one's mother's milk, taught at our father's knee, sealed, signed, and stamped upon in the glorious Constitution of these United States!" [*A perfect storm of hisses, catcalls, boos, and hard laughter.*]

VOICES. [*Scornfully.*] Hurrah for de Fort' of July!

Pass de hat!

Liberty!

Justice!

Honor!

Opportunity!

Brotherhood!

ALL. [*With abysmal scorn.*] Aw, hell!

VOICE. Give that Queen Senator guy the bark! All togedder now —one—two—tree—— [*A terrific chorus of barking and yapping.*]

GUARD. [*From a distance.*] Quiet there, youse—or I'll git the hose. [*The noise subsides.*]

YANK. [*With growling rage.*] I'd like to catch that Senator guy alone for a second. I'd loin him some trute!

VOICE. Ssshh! Here's where he gits down to cases on the Wobblies. [*Reads:*] "They plot with fire in one hand and dynamite in the other. They stop not before murder to gain their ends, nor at the outraging of defenseless womanhood. They would tear down society, put the lowest scum in the seats of the mighty, turn Almighty God's revealed plan for the world topsy-turvy, and make of our sweet and lovely civilization a shambles, a desolation where man, God's masterpiece, would soon degenerate back to the ape!"

VOICE. [*To* YANK.] Hey, you guy. There's your ape stuff again.

YANK. [*With a growl of fury.*] I got him. So dey blow up tings, do dey? Dey turn tings round, do dey? Hey, lend me dat paper, will yuh?

VOICE. Sure. Give it to him. On'y keep it to yourself, see. We don't wanter listen to no more of that slop.

VOICE. Here you are. Hide it under your mattress.

YANK. [*Reaching out.*] Tanks. I can't read much but I kin manage. [*He sits, the paper in the hand at his side, in the attitude of Rodin's "The Thinker." A pause. Several snores from down the corridor. Suddenly* YANK *jumps to his feet with a furious groan as if some appalling thought had crashed on him—bewilderedly.*]

6. Marcus Porcius Cato, "The Censor" (234–149 B.C.), in waging his long campaign in the Roman Senate for war against Carthage, ended every speech with the same words: "For the rest, I vote that Carthage must be destroyed."

Sure—her old man—president of de Steel Trust—makes half de steel in de world—steel—where I tought I belonged—drivin' trou —movin'—in dat—to make *her*—and cage me in for her to spit on! Christ! [*He shakes the bars of his cell door till the whole tier trembles. Irritated, protesting exclamations from those awakened or trying to get to sleep.*] He made dis—dis cage! Steel! *It* don't belong, dat's what! Cages, cells, locks, bolts, bars—dat's what it means!—holdin' me down wit him at de top! But I'll drive trou! Fire, dat melts it! I'll be fire—under de heap—fire dat never goes out—hot as hell—breakin' out in de night—— [*While he has been saying this last he has shaken his cell door to a clanging accompaniment. As he comes to the "breakin' out" he seizes one bar with both hands and, putting his two feet up against the others so that his position is parallel to the floor like a monkey's, he gives a great wrench backwards. The bar bends like a licorice stick under his tremendous strength. Just at this moment the PRISON GUARD rushes in, dragging a hose behind him.*]

GUARD. [*Angrily.*] I'll loin youse bums to wake me up! [*Sees* YANK.] Hello, it's you, huh? Got the D. Ts., hey? Well, I'll cure 'em. I'll drown your snakes for yuh! [*Noticing the bar.*] Hell, look at dat bar bended! On'y a bug is strong enough for dat!

YANK. [*Glaring at him.*] Or a hairy ape, yuh big yellow bum! Look out! Here I come! [*He grabs another bar.*]

GUARD. [*Scared now—yelling off left.*] Toin de hose on, Ben!— full pressure! And call de others—and a straitjacket! [*The curtain is falling, As it hides* YANK *from view, there is a splattering smash as the stream of water hits the steel of* YANK's *cell.*]

[*Curtain.*]

Scene VII

SCENE. Nearly a month later. An I. W. W. local near the water-front, showing the interior of a front room on the ground floor, and the street outside. Moonlight on the narrow street, buildings massed in black shadow. The interior of the room, which is general assembly room, office, and reading-room, resembles some dingy settlement boys' club. A desk and high stool are in one corner. A table with papers, stacks of pamphlets, chairs about it, is at center. The whole is decidedly cheap, banal, commonplace, and unmysterious as a room could well be. The secretary is perched on the stool making entries in a large ledger. An eye shade casts his face into shadows. Eight or ten men, longshoremen, iron workers, and the like, are grouped about the table. Two are playing checkers. One is writing a letter. Most of them are smoking pipes. A big signboard is on the wall at the rear, "Industrial Workers of the World—Local No. 57."

[YANK *comes down the street outside. He is dressed as in* Scene Five. *He moves cautiously, mysteriously. He comes to a point opposite the door; tiptoes softly up to it, listens, is impressed by the silence within, knocks carefully, as if he were guessing at the password to some secret rite. Listens. No answer. Knocks again a bit louder. No answer. Knocks impatiently, much louder.*]

SECRETARY. [*Turning around on his stool.*] What the hell is that —someone knocking? [*Shouts.*] Come in, why don't you? [*All the men in the room look up.* YANK *opens the door slowly, gingerly, as if afraid of an ambush. He looks around for secret doors, mystery, is taken aback by the commonplaceness of the room and the men in it, thinks he may have gotten in the wrong place, then sees the signboard on the wall and is reassured.*]

YANK. [*Blurts out.*] Hello.

MEN. [*Reservedly.*] Hello.

YANK. [*More easily.*] I tought I'd bumped into de wrong dump.

SECRETARY. [*Scrutinizing him carefully.*] Maybe you have. Are you a member?

YANK. Naw, not yet. Dat's what I come for—to join.

SECRETARY. That's easy. What's your job—longshore?

YANK. Naw. Fireman—stoker on de liners.

SECRETARY. [*With satisfaction.*] Welcome to our city. Glad to know you people are waking up at last. We haven't got many members in your line.

YANK. Naw. Dey're all dead to de woild.

SECRETARY. Well, you can help to wake 'em. What's your name? I'll make out your card.

YANK. [*Confused.*] Name? Lemme tink.

SECRETARY. [*Sharply.*] Don't you know your own name?

YANK. Sure; but I been just Yank for so long—Bob, dat's it—Bob Smith.

SECRETARY. [*Writing.*] Robert Smith. [*Fills out the rest of card.*] Here you are. Cost you half a dollar.

YANK. Is dat all—four bits? Dat's easy. [*Gives the Secretary the money.*]

SECRETARY. [*Throwing it in drawer.*] Thanks. Well, make yourself at home. No introductions needed. There's literature on the table. Take some of those pamphlets with you to distribute aboard ship. They may bring results. Sow the seed, only go about it right. Don't get caught and fired. We got plenty out of work. What we need is men who can hold their jobs—and work for us at the same time.

YANK. Sure. [*But he still stands, embarrassed and uneasy.*]

SECRETARY. [*Looking at him—curiously.*] What did you knock for? Think we had a coon in uniform to open doors?

YANK. Naw. I tought it was locked—and dat yuh'd wanter give

me the once-over trou a peep-hole or somep'n to see if I was right.

SECRETARY. [*Alert and suspicious but with an easy laugh.*] Think we were running a crap game? That door is never locked. What put that in your nut?

YANK. [*With a knowing grin, convinced that this is all camouflage, a part of the secrecy.*] Dis burg is full of bulls, ain't it?

SECRETARY. [*Sharply.*] What have the cops to do with us? We're breaking no laws.

YANK. [*With a knowing wink.*] Sure. Youse wouldn't for woilds. Sure. I'm wise to dat.

SECRETARY. You seem to be wise to a lot of stuff none of us knows about.

YANK. [*With another wink.*] Aw, dat's aw right, see. [*Then made a bit resentful by the suspicious glances from all sides.*] Aw, can it! Youse needn't put me trou de toid degree. Can't youse see I belong? Sure! I'm reg'lar. I'll stick, get me? I'll shoot de woiks for youse. Dat's why I wanted to join in.

SECRETARY. [*Breezily, feeling him out.*] That's the right spirit. Only are you sure you understand what you've joined? It's all plain and above board; still, some guys get a wrong slant on us. [*Sharply.*] What's your notion of the purpose of the I. W. W.?

YANK. Aw, I know all about it.

SECRETARY. [*Sarcastically.*] Well, give us some of your valuable information.

YANK. [*Cunningly.*] I know enough not to speak outa my toin. [*Then, resentfully again.*] Aw, say! I'm reg'lar. I'm wise to de game. I know yuh got to watch your step wit a stranger. For all youse know, I might be a plain-clothes dick, or somep'n, dat's what yuh're tinkin', huh? Aw, forget it! I belong, see? Ask any guy down to de docks if I don't.

SECRETARY. Who said you didn't?

YANK. After I'm 'nitiated, I'll show yuh.

SECRETARY. [*Astounded.*] Initiated? There's no initiation.

YANK. [*Disappointed.*] Ain't there no password—no grip nor nothin'?

SECRETARY. What'd you think this is—the Elks—or the Black Hand?[7]

YANK. De Elks, hell! De Black Hand, dey're a lot of yellow back-stickin' Ginees. Naw. Dis is a man's gang, ain't it?

SECRETARY. You said it! That's why we stand on our two feet in the open. We got no secrets.

YANK. [*Surprised but admiringly.*] Yuh mean to say yuh always

7. The Elks is a fraternal organization; by contrast, the Black Hand was an Italian underworld organization, formed about 1868, which conducted criminal activities in the United States. Hence "Ginees" (Guineas), meaning "Italians," in Yank's reply.

run wide open—like dis?

SECRETARY. Exactly.

YANK. Den yuh sure got your noive wit youse!

SECRETARY. [*Sharply.*] Just what was it made you want to join us? Come out with that straight.

YANK. Yuh call me? Well, I got noive, too! Here's my hand. Yuh wanter blow tings up, don't yuh? Well, dat's me! I belong!

SECRETARY. [*With pretended carelessness.*] You mean change the unequal conditions of society by legitimate direct action—or with dynamite?

YANK. Dynamite! Blow it offen de oith—steel—all de cages—all de factories, steamers, buildings, jails—de Steel Trust and all dat makes it go.

SECRETARY. So—that's your idea, eh? And did you have any special job in that line you wanted to propose to us? [*He makes a sign to the men, who get up cautiously one by one and group behind* YANK.]

YANK. [*Boldly.*] Sure, I'll come out wit it. I'll show youse I'm one of de gang. Dere's dat millionaire guy, Douglas——

SECRETARY. President of the Steel Trust, you mean? Do you want to assassinate him?

YANK. Naw, dat don't get you nothin'. I mean blow up de factory, de woiks, where he makes de steel. Dat's what I'm after—to blow up de steel, knock all de steel in de woild up to de moon. Dat'll fix tings! [*Eagerly, with a touch of bravado.*] I'll do it by me lonesome! I'll show yuh! Tell me where his woiks is, how to git there, all de dope. Gimme de stuff, de old butter—and watch me do de rest! Watch de smoke and see it move! I don't give a damn if dey nab me—as long as it's done! I'll soive life for it—and give 'em de laugh! [*Half to himself.*] And I'll write her a letter and tell her de hairy ape done it. Dat'll square tings.

SECRETARY. [*Stepping away from* YANK.] Very interesting. [*He gives a signal. The men, huskies all, throw themselves on* YANK *and before he knows it they have his legs and arms pinioned. But he is too flabbergasted to make a struggle, anyway. They feel him over for weapons.*]

MAN. No gat, no knife. Shall we give him what's what and put the boots to him?

SECRETARY. No. He isn't worth the trouble we'd get into. He's too stupid. [*He comes closer and laughs mockingly in* YANK's *face.*] Ho-ho! By God, this is the biggest joke they've put up on us yet. Hey, you Joke! Who sent you—Burns or Pinkerton?[8] No, by God, you're such a bonehead I'll bet you're in the Secret Service! Well, you dirty spy, you rotten agent provocator, you can go back and

8. Two well-known detective agencies.

tell whatever skunk is paying you blood-money for betraying your brothers that he's wasting his coin. You couldn't catch a cold. And tell him that all he'll ever get on us, or ever has got, is just his own sneaking plots that he's framed up to put us in jail. We are what our manifesto says we are, neither more nor less—and we'll give him a copy of that any time he calls. And as for you——— [*He glares scornfully at* YANK, *who is sunk in an oblivious stupor.*] Oh hell, what's the use of talking? You're a brainless ape.

YANK. [*Aroused by the word to fierce but futile struggles.*] What's dat, yuh Sheeny bum, yuh!

SECRETARY. Throw him out, boys. [*In spite of his struggles, this is done with gusto and éclat. Propelled by several parting kicks,* YANK *lands sprawling in the middle of the narrow cobbled street. With a growl he starts to get up and storm the closed door, but stops bewildered by the confusion in his brain, pathetically impotent. He sits there, brooding, in as near to the attitude of Rodin's "Thinker" as he can get in his position.*]

YANK. [*Bitterly.*] So dem boids don't tink I belong, neider. Aw, to hell wit 'em! Dey're in de wrong pew—de same old bull—soapboxes and Salvation Army—no guts! Cut out an hour offen de job a day and make me happy! Gimme a dollar more a day and make me happy! Tree square a day, and cauliflowers in de front yard—ekal rights—a woman and kids—a lousy vote—and I'm all fixed for Jesus, huh? Aw, hell! What does dat get yuh? Dis ting's in your inside, but it ain't your belly. Feedin' your face—sinkers and coffee —dat don't touch it. It's way down—at de bottom. Yuh can't grab it, and yuh can't stop it. It moves, and everything moves. It stops and de whole woild stops. Dat's me now—I don't tick, see?—I'm a busted Ingersoll, dat's what. Steel was me, and I owned de woild. Now I ain't steel, and de woild owns me. Aw, hell! I can't see—it's all dark, get me? It's all wrong! [*He turns a bitter mocking face up like an ape gibbering at the moon.*] Say, youse up dere, Man in de Moon, yuh look so wise, gimme de answer, huh? Slip me de inside dope, de information right from de stable—where do I get off at, huh?

A POLICEMAN. [*Who has come up the street in time to hear this last—with grim humor.*] You'll get off at the station, you boob, if you don't get up out of that and keep movin'.

YANK. [*Looking up at him—with a hard, bitter laugh.*] Sure! Lock me up! Put me in a cage! Dat's de on'y answer yuh know. G'wan, lock me up!

POLICEMAN. What you been doin'?

YANK. Enuf to gimme life for! I was born, see? Sure, dat's de charge. Write it in de blotter. I was born, get me!

POLICEMAN. [*Jocosely.*] God pity your old woman! [*Then matter-*

of-fact.] But I've no time for kidding. You're soused. I'd run you in but it's too long a walk to the station. Come on now, get up, or I'll fan your ears with this club. Beat it now! [*He hauls* YANK *to his feet.*]

YANK. [*In a vague mocking tone.*] Say, where do I go from here?

POLICEMAN. [*Giving him a push—with a grin, indifferently.*] Go to hell.

[*Curtain.*]

Scene VIII

SCENE. Twilight of the next day. The monkey house at the Zoo. One spot of clear gray light falls on the front of one cage so that the interior can be seen. The other cages are vague, shrouded in shadow from which chatterings pitched in a conversational tone can be heard. On the one cage a sign from which the word "Gorilla" stands out. The gigantic animal himself is seen squatting on his haunches on a bench in much the same attitude as Rodin's "Thinker." Yank enters from the left. Immediately a chorus of angry chattering and screeching breaks out. The gorilla turns his eyes but makes no sound or move.

YANK. [*With a hard, bitter laugh.*] Welcome to your city, huh? Hail, hail, de gang's all here! [*At the sound of his voice the chattering dies away into an attentive silence.* YANK *walks up to the gorilla's cage and, leaning over the railing, stares in at its occupant, who stares back at him, silent and motionless. There is a pause of dead stillness. Then* YANK *begins to talk in a friendly confidential tone, half-mockingly, but with a deep undercurrent of sympathy.*] Say, yuh're some hard-lookin' guy, ain't yuh? I seen lots of tough nuts dat de gang called gorillas, but yuh're de foist real one I ever seen. Some chest yuh got, and shoulders, and dem arms and mits! I bet yuh got a punch in eider fist dat'd knock 'em all silly! [*This with genuine admiration. The gorilla, as if he understood, stands upright, swelling out his chest and pounding on it with his fist.* YANK *grins sympathetically.*] Sure, I get yuh. Yuh challenge de whole woild, huh? Yuh got what I was sayin' even if yuh muffed de woids. [*Then bitterness creeping in.*] And why wouldn't yuh get me? Ain't we both members of de same club—de Hairy Apes? [*They stare at each other—a pause—then* YANK *goes on slowly and bitterly.*] So yuh're what she seen when she looked at me, de white-faced tart! I was you to her, get me? On'y outa de cage—broke out—free to moider her, see? Sure! Dat's what she tought. She wasn't wise dat I was in a cage, too—worser'n yours—sure—a damn sight—'cause you got some chanct to bust loose—but me—— [*He grows confused.*] Aw, hell! It's all wrong, ain't it? [*A pause.*] I s'pose yuh wanter know what I'm doin' here, huh? I been warmin' a bench down to de Battery—ever since last night. Sure. I seen de sun come up. Dat was pretty, too—all red and pink and green. I was lookin' at de skyscrapers—steel—and all de ships comin' in, sailin' out, all over de oith—and dey was steel, too. De sun was warm, dey wasn't no clouds, and dere was breeze blowin'. Sure, it was great stuff. I got it aw right—what Paddy said about dat bein' de right dope—on'y I couldn't get *in* it, see? I couldn't belong in dat. It was over my head. And I kept tinkin'—and den I beat it up here to see what youse was like. And I waited till dey was all gone to git yuh alone. Say, how d'yuh feel sittin' in dat pen all de time, havin' to stand for 'em comin' and starin' at yuh—de white-faced, skinny tarts and de boobs what marry 'em—makin' fun of yuh, laughin' at yuh, gittin' scared of yuh—damn 'em! [*He pounds on the rail with his fist. The gorilla rattles the bars of his cage and snarls. All the other monkeys set up an angry chattering in the darkness.* YANK *goes on excitedly.*] Sure! Dat's de way it hits me, too. On'y yuh're lucky, see? Yuh don't belong wit 'em and yuh know it. But me, I belong wit 'em—but I don't, see? Dey don't belong wit me, dat's what. Get me? Tinkin' is hard—[*He passes one hand across his forehead with a painful gesture. The gorilla growls impatiently.* YANK *goes on gropingly.*] It's dis way, what I'm drivin' at. Youse can sit and dope dream in de past, green woods, de jungle and de rest of it. Den yuh belong and dey don't. Den yuh kin laugh at 'em, see? Yuh're de champ of de woild. But me—I ain't got no past to tink in, nor nothin' dat's comin', on'y what's now—and dat don't belong. Sure, you're de best off! Yuh can't tink, can yuh? Yuh can't talk neider. But I kin make a bluff at talkin' and tinkin'—a'most git away wit it—a'most!—and dat's where de joker comes in. [*He laughs.*] I ain't on oith and I ain't in heaven, get me? I'm in de middle tryin' to separate 'em, takin' all de woist punches from bot' of 'em. Maybe dat's what dey call hell, huh? But you, yuh're at de bottom. You belong! Sure! Yuh're de on'y one in de woild dat does, yuh lucky stiff! [*The gorilla growls proudly.*] And dat's why dey gotter put yuh in a cage, see? [*The gorilla roars angrily.*] Sure! Yuh get me. It beats it when you try to tink it or talk it—it's way down—deep—behind— you 'n' me we feel it. Sure! Bot' members of dis club! [*He laughs— then in a savage tone.*] What de hell! T' hell wit it! A little action, dat's our meat! Dat belongs! Knock 'em down and keep bustin' 'em till dey croaks yuh wit a gat—wit steel! Sure! Are yuh game? Dey've looked at youse, ain't dey—in a cage? Wanter git even? Wanter wind up like a sport 'stead of croakin' slow in dere? [*The gorilla roars an emphatic affirmative,* YANK *goes on with a sort of furious exaltation.*] Sure! Yuh're reg'lar! Yuh'll stick to de finish! Me 'n' you, huh?—bot' members of this club! We'll put up one last star bout dat'll knock 'em offen deir seats! Dey'll have to make de cages stronger after we're trou! [*The gorilla is straining at his bars, growling, hopping from one foot to the other.* YANK *takes a jimmy from under his coat and forces the lock on the cage door. He throws this open.*] Pardon from de governor! Step out and shake hands. I'll take yuh for a walk down Fif' Avenoo. We'll knock 'em offen de oith and croak wit de band playin'. Come on, Brother. [*The gorilla scrambles gingerly out of his cage. Goes to* YANK *and stands looking at him.* YANK *keeps his mocking tone—holds out his hand.*] Shake —de secret grip of our order. [*Something, the tone of mockery, perhaps, suddenly enrages the animal. With a spring he wraps his huge arms around* YANK *in a murderous hug. There is a crackling snap of crushed ribs—a gasping cry, still mocking, from* YANK.] Hey, I didn't say kiss me! [*The gorilla lets the crushed body slip to the floor; stands over it uncertainly, considering; then picks it up, throws it in the cage, shuts the door and shuffles off menacingly into the darkness at left. A great uproar of frightened chattering and whimpering comes from the other cages. Then* YANK *moves, groaning, opening his eyes, and there is silence. He mutters painfully.*] Say— dey oughter match him—wit Zybszko.[9] He got me, aw right. I'm trou. Even him didn't tink I belonged. [*Then, with sudden passionate despair.*] Christ, where do I get off at? Where do I fit in? [*Checking himself as suddenly.*] Aw, what de hell! No squawkin', see! No quittin', get me! Croak wit your boots on! [*He grabs hold of the bars of the cage and hauls himself painfully to his feet—looks around him bewilderedly—forces a mocking laugh.*] In de cage, huh? [*In the strident tones of a circus barker.*] Ladies and gents, step forward and take a slant at de one and only—[*His voice weakening.*]—one and original—Hairy Ape from de wilds of—— [*He slips in a heap on the floor and dies. The monkeys set up a chattering, whimpering wail. And, perhaps, the Hairy Ape at last belongs.*] [*Curtain.*]

1922

9. Misspelling for Stanislaus Zbyszko, a wrestler, then in his prime.

Poets in Waste Land

EZRA POUND
(1885–)

Ezra Loomis Pound was born in Hailey, Idaho, on October 30, 1885. He attended the University of Pennsylvania and then Hamilton College, from which he was graduated in 1905. He returned to the University of Pennsylvania for graduate study in romance languages. He took an M.A. in 1906, spent the summer abroad, and returned to Pennsylvania on a fellowship for another year of study in Renaissance literature. In 1908 he again went abroad, and by 1920 regarded himself as a permanent expatriate.

By 1912, he was the author of seven volumes which identified him as a distinct poetic personality, who combined a command of the older tradition with impressive and often daring originality. When Harriet Monroe in 1912 issued from Chicago the prospectus for her new magazine, *Poetry: A Magazine of Verse*, Pound characteristically proposed himself as its foreign correspondent.

He was a prolific essayist for the little magazines of New York, London, and Paris, which then constituted a large and ex- citing literary world. He unselfishly and persistently championed the experimental and often unpopular artists whom he approved—Antheil, the musician; Gaudier-Brzeska, pioneer abstractionist sculptor, killed in World War I; and James Joyce, among others. Most important of all, perhaps, was the advice and encouragement which he gave to T. S. Eliot, who has candidly acknowledged the value of Pound's assistance in the final revision of *The Waste Land* and in connection with other poems of that period. Both poets of independent power and interests, they became the early leaders in restoring to poetry the use of literary reference as an imaginative instrument. Such referential figures of speech assume that the poet and his readers share a common cultural inheritance. In the present age of increasing complexity, diffuseness, and specialization of knowledge, both Pound and Eliot required of their readers a familiarity with the classics, the productions of the Italian and English Renaissance, and specialized areas of Continental literature, including the works of the French symbolists. After *The Waste Land* (1922), Eliot's poetry became somewhat less difficult in this respect, while Pound's continued to draw fundamentally upon his formidably recondite culture. A large part of his work consists of "reconstructions" in modern English of poems from earlier literatures, chiefly Greek, Latin, Italian, Provençal, and Chinese. Pound quite consciously set this course for himself, and called the often-expanded volume of his poems his *Personae*, or "masks," referring to the conventionalized masks worn by actors in the Greek drama.

A final obstacle for the reader is the violence of Pound's distrust of capitalism and his allegiance to the utopian concept of "social credit." Nevertheless, *Hugh Selwyn Mauberley* (1920), considered as a satire of the materialistic forces involved in World War I, is a masterpiece. In *The Cantos*, begun in 1917, the satire became intensified. The progressive series, now exceeding the proposed limit of one hundred poems, are loosely connected cantos, like Dante's *Divina Commedia* in three sections, but representing a comedy human, not divine, dealing with the wreck of civilizations by reason of the infidelity of mankind in the three epochs—the ancient world, the Renaissance, and the modern period. With *The Pisan Cantos* of 1948 and *Section: Rock Drill* (1956), Cantos I to XCV had all been published except for two. By 1960 they numbered CIX, badly needing explication. A considerable number contain lyrical passages of

genuine power; they are in places supremely witty, and many of their topical references are shrewd and valuable. But their complexity renders them controversial. Somewhat resembling *Finnegan's Wake* in structure, Pound's vast poem now has a position similar to that of Joyce's novel before critical scholarship provided its explication. Pound's critics have developed a voluminous commentary, most of it still unpublished, concerning *The Cantos*, which, like Joyce's work, employs the complex association of scholarly lore, anthropology, modern history and personages, private history and witticisms, and obscure literary interpolations in various languages, including Chinese ideograms.

In 1924 Pound left Paris for Rapallo, Italy, attracted by Mussolini's faithless promises of democratic state socialism. During World War II, Pound, on behalf of the Italian government, conducted radio broadcasts beamed at the American troops. He was returned to the United States as a citizen accused of treason, but on examination he was declared insane. The treason charges were dismissed in 1958. Pound now lives in Italy.

Principal earlier poetry volumes are *A Lume Spento*, 1908; *A Quinzaine for This Yule*, 1908; *Personae*, 1909, reprinted and enlarged, 1913 to 1926; *Exultations*, 1909; *Provença*, 1910, selected poems; *Canzoni*, 1911; *The Sonnets and Ballate of Guido Cavalcanti*, 1912; *Ripostes*, London, 1912, Boston, 1913, new edition, London, 1915; *Personae and Exultations*, 1913; *Cathay*, 1915; *Lustra*, London, 1916, New York, 1917; *Quia Pauper Amavi*, undated, *ca.* 1919, containing "Homage to Sextus Propertius" and *Cantos I–III*; *Hugh Selwyn Mauberley*, 1920; *Umbra*, 1920, a collection from previous volumes; *Poems 1918–1921,* 1921; *Personae: The Collected Poems,* 1926; and *Homage to Sextus Propertius,* new edition, 1934. T: S. Eliot first edited a *Selected Poems* in 1928, of which the newest edition is 1959; a New York *Selected Poems* was issued in 1949 and 1957.

Publication of *The Cantos* began when *Poetry: A Magazine of Verse* printed one in each of three issues, June to August, 1917, collected as "Three Cantos" in the New York edition of *Lustra,* 1917. Their number was gradually increased, with revision and rearrangement, in several volumes: *The Pisan Cantos, LXXI to LXXXV,* 1948, the collection of the eighty-five in *The Cantos of Ezra Pound,* 1948, and *Cantos,* 1954. *Section: Rock Drill,* 1956, brought the number to ninety-five, and *Throne,* 1959, to one hundred and nine. Pound's translation of *Sophokles' Women of Trachis* appeared in 1957.

Pound's voluminous prose contains some stimulating critical work. Typical volumes are *Gaudier-Brzeska,* 1910, a biography; *Pavannes and Divisions,* 1918; *Instigations,* 1920; *Indiscretions* (autobiographical), 1923; *The ABC of Reading,* 1934; *Culture,* 1938; *Money Pamphlets by Pound,* 1950–1952; *Pavannes and Divagations,* 1958; and *The Literary Essays of Ezra Pound,* 1954, edited by T. S. Eliot. *The Letters of Ezra Pound, 1907–1941* was edited by D. D. Paige in 1950. Two of Pound's translations have bearing on the orientalism of *The Cantos: Confucian Analects . . . ,* 1950, and *Shih Ching: The Classic Anthology defined by Confucius.*

Critical studies include T. S. Eliot's introduction to the *Selected Poems,* 1928, and the same author's unsigned volume, *Ezra Pound: His Metric and Poetry,* 1917. A fundamental study is R. P. Blackmur, "Masks of Ezra Pound," reprinted from *Hound and Horn* (March, 1934) as a chapter of Blackmur's *The Double Agent,* 1935. Alice Admur published *The Poetry of Ezra Pound,* 1936. Pound's receipt of the Bollingen Prize in Poetry for 1948 resulted in two studies of his position: *The Case Against the Saturday Review,* essays by several hands, edited by the editors of *Poetry,* 1949; and *The Case of Ezra Pound,* edited by Charles Norman, 1948. Explication or discussion of *The Cantos* may profitably be sought in the following: *The Analyst* (No. 1, 1953), continued serially, Department of English, Northwestern University; H. H. Watts, *Ezra Pound and "The Cantos,"* London, 1951. John H. Edwards and William Vasse, Jr., compiled an *Annotated Index to the Cantos of Ezra Pound,* 1957. A collection of criticisms by several hands is *An Examination of Ezra Pound,* edited by Peter Russell, 1950. J. J. Espey, *Ezra Pound's Mauberley,* 1955, is useful.

A Virginal

No, no! Go from me. I have left her lately.
I will not spoil my sheath with lesser brightness,
For my surrounding air has a new lightness;
Slight are her arms, yet they have bound me straitly
And left me cloaked as with a gauze of æther;   5
As with sweet leaves; as with a subtle clearness.
Oh, I have picked up magic in her nearness
To sheathe me half in half the things that sheathe her.

No, no! Go from me. I have still the flavor,
Soft as spring wind that's come from birchen bowers.   10
Green come the shoots, aye April in the branches,
As winter's wound with her sleight hand she staunches,
Hath of the trees a likeness of the savor:
As white their bark, so white this lady's hours.

Sestina: Altaforte[1]

Loquitur: 'En' Bertrans de Born.[2]
Dante Alighieri put this man in hell for that he was a stirrer up of
strife.[3]
Eccovi![4]
Judge ye!
Have I dug him up again?
The scene is at his castle, Altaforte. 'Papiols' is his jongleur.
'The Leopard,' the 'device' of Richard Cœur de Lion.[5]

1

Damn it all, all this our South stinks peace.
You whoreson dog, Papiols, come! Let's to music!
I have no life save when the swords clash.
But ah! when I see the standards gold, vair,[6] purple, opposing
And the broad fields beneath them turn crimson,   5
Then howls my heart nigh mad with rejoicing.

2

In hot summer have I great rejoicing
When the tempests kill the earth's foul peace,
And the lightnings from black heav'n flash crimson,
And the fierce thunders roar me their music   10
And the winds shriek through the clouds mad, opposing,
And through all the riven skies God's swords clash.

3

Hell grant soon we hear the swords clash!
And the shrill neighs of destriers[7] in battle rejoicing,
Spiked breast to spiked breast opposing!   15
Better one hour's stour[8] than a year's peace
With fat boards, bawds, wine and frail music!
Bah! there's no wine like the blood's crimson!

4

And I love to see the sun rise blood-crimson.
And I watch his spears through the dark clash   20

1. This poem represents Pound's gift for reconstructing in English a poem from another language. The original was a Provençal poem, "In Praise of War," by Bertrand de Born (1140?–1210?), famous knight and troubadour, master of satire, and "goad of * * * the barons of the Province." The sestina, a difficult lyric form, substitutes for conventional end rhyme a sequence of six words, in various prescribed patterns, as the concluding words of the six lines of each of six stanzas. An additional tercet forms an envoy, as here. Like the ballad, the sestina was origi-

nally intended to be recited or chanted.
2. Speaker: Bertrans de Born.
3. Cf. *Inferno*, xxviii, 134.
4. Behold!
5. Richard Lion-Hearted, king of England (1189–1199), famous warrior of the Third Crusade, wore a leopard on his shield.
6. A species of squirrel skin used in costly medieval clothing, and represented in heraldry by a series of small shields alternately argent (silver) and azure (blue).
7. Archaic term meaning "war horses."
8. Archaic term meaning "combat."

And it fills all my heart with rejoicing
And pries wide my mouth with fast music
When I see him so scorn and defy peace,
His lone might 'gainst all darkness opposing.

5

The man who fears war and squats opposing   25
My words for stour, hath no blood of crimson
But is fit only to rot in womanish peace
Far from where worth's won and the swords clash
For the death of such sluts I go rejoicing;
Yea, I fill all the air with my music.   30

6

Papiols, Papiols, to the music!
There's no sound like to swords swords opposing,
No cry like the battle's rejoicing
When our elbows and swords drip the crimson
And our charges 'gainst 'The Leopard's' rush clash.   35
May God damn for ever all who cry 'Peace!'

7

And let the music of the swords make them crimson!
Hell grant soon we hear again the swords clash!
Hell blot black for alway the thought 'Peace'!

1909

From Hugh Selwyn Mauberley[9]

Life and Contacts

Vocat Æstus in Umbram[1]
—NEMESIANUS EC. IV.

I

E. P. ODE POUR L'ELECTION DE SON SÉPULCHRE[2]

For three years, out of key with his time,
He strove to resuscitate the dead art

9. The initial sequence of five poems printed here epitomizes "Mauberley," which in 1919 comprised twelve poems and the "Envoi" (*q.v.*), in 1920 a concluding sequence of five. Eliot called this "a document of an epoch"; it is also, in part, a summation of Ezra Pound's experience with that epoch, the period of the first World War; and it marked his alienated withdrawal into Italian exile.

1. Latin, meaning "Summer summons us unto the shadow." Of Nemesianus (*fl.* 283 A.D.), the Roman author of this line, little survives except his four

Eclogues.

2. "E. P. Ode on the Choice of His Tomb." *Cf.* Pierre de Ronsard, *Odes.* Book IV, *L'Election de son sépulchre,* and *cf.* Stéphane Mallarmé's "Le Tombeau d'Edgar Poe." But obviously, Pound's initials also are "E. P." Mallarmé's poem contains the line, *Donner un sens plus pur aux mots de la tribu,* which Eliot paraphrased, in *Little Gidding,* as, "To purify the dialect of the tribe." Pound shared this aim and gave expression to it in the first two sections of "Hugh Selwyn Mauberley."

Of poetry; to maintain 'The sublime'[3]
In the old sense. Wrong from the start—

No, hardly, but seeing he had been born   5
In a half-savage country, out of date;
Bent resolutely on wringing lilies from the acorn;
Capaneus;[4] trout for factitious bait;
Ἴδμεν γάρ τοι πάνθ᾽, ὅσ᾽ ἐνὶ Τροίῃ[5]
Caught in the unstopped ear;   10
Giving the rocks small lee-way[6]
The chopped seas held him, therefore, that year.

His true Penelope[7] was Flaubert,[8]
He fished by obstinate isles;
Observed the elegance of Circe's[9] hair   15
Rather than the mottoes on sun-dials.[1]

Unaffected by 'the march of events,'
He passed from men's memory in *l'an trentiesme*
De son eage;[2] the case presents
No adjunct to the Muses' diadem.   20

II

The age demanded an image
Of its accelerated grimace,
Something for the modern stage,
Not, at any rate, an Attic grace;

Not, not certainly, the obscure reveries   25
Of the inward gaze;
Better mendacities
Than the classics in paraphrase!

3. Achievement of "the sublime" (*cf.* Longinus or Kant), involved a choice of literary materials and style of exalted spiritual significance.
4. Capaneus of Argos, in Aeschylus' *The Seven Against Thebes*, swore he would force entrance into Thebes in spite of Jove himself. The god, for this impiety, struck him dead with a thunderbolt.
5. The Greek line, sung by the Sirens in Homer's *Odyssey*, Book XII, l. 189, has here been slightly altered to read: "For we know all the things that are in Troy." Odysseus plugged his sailors' ears with wax, so that they would not leap overboard when they heard the Sirens. The "unstopped ear" mentioned in the next line was that of Odysseus, who had had himself bound to the mast for safety. The references to Odysseus' hazardous journey homeward continue to the end of the next stanza.
6. Scylla, which with the whirlpool Charybdis, formed a dangerous strait

that Odysseus escaped only with the loss of six men.
7. Penelope, Odysseus' wife, clung faithfully to the hope of his return for many years, in spite of the importunities and plots of powerful suitors.
8. Gustave Flaubert (1821–1880), "father of French realism," whose painstaking concern for "the exact word" caused critics to refer to his style as "chiseled" or "sculptured." See l. 32, below.
9. Circe, a beautiful sorceress, ruled a domain devoted to sloth and carnal appetite, where Odysseus lingered unduly, although his men were transformed into swine.
1. Sundials usually bear inscriptions referring ominously to the flight of time.
2. *Cf.* François Villon (1431–1463?); the first line of his *Grand Testament* reads: "In the thirtieth year of my life." Pound has changed "my" to "his." The phrase was re-echoed by a number of others—*e.g.,* Eliot and MacLeish.

The 'age demanded' chiefly a mould in plaster,
Made with no loss of time,   30
A prose kinema,[3] not, assuredly, alabaster
Or the 'sculpture' of rhyme.

III

The tea-rose tea-gown, etc.
Supplants the mousseline of Cos,
The pianola 'replaces'   35
Sappho's barbitos.[4]

Christ follows Dionysus,
Phallic[5] and ambrosial
Made way for macerations;
Caliban casts out Ariel.[6]   40

All things are a flowing,
Sage Heracleitus[7] says;
But a tawdry cheapness
Shall outlast our days.

Even the Christian beauty   45
Defects—after Samothrace;[8]
We see τὸ καλὸν[9]
Decreed in the market-place.

Faun's flesh is not to us,
Nor the saint's vision.
We have the Press for wafer,[1]   50
Franchise for circumcision.

All men, in law, are equals.
Free of Pisistratus,[2]
We choose a knave or an eunuch   55
To rule over us.

O bright Apollo,
τίν' ἄνδρα, τίν' ἤρωα, τίνα θεὸν[3]

3. (l. 31) Greek, meaning "motion"; *cf.* "cinema" for "motion picture."
4. From the Greek *barbiton*, "a lyre," here associated with the poetess Sappho. The "pianola," with which it is contrasted, is a mechanical player piano.
5. The Greek worship of Dionysus involved phallic rituals; *cf.* J. G. Frazer, *The Golden Bough*.
6. In *The Tempest*, Shakespeare contrasts these two fantastic characters: Caliban—enormous, earthy, and stupid; and the sprite Ariel—ethereal and beautiful.
7. The Greek philosopher Heraclitus (*fl.* 550 B.C.) emphasized the concept of "flux," or change; *cf.* in T. S. Eliot, *Burnt Norton*, fragments of his work.
8. The Greek island of Samothrace was the supposed seat of the Cabiri, occult pre-Hellenic divinities regarded by the later Greeks as an attractive mystery.
9. "The beautiful," a common phrase in the literature of philosophy.
1. Sacrificial bread of religious ritual; specifically, of the Christian Eucharist.
2. Pisistratus (died 527 B.C.), thrice the dictator of the Athenian state.
3. Pindar's Second Olympian Ode, l. 2, reads, in the reverse of this order, "What God, what hero, what man shall we loudly praise?"

What god, man, or hero
Shall I place a tin wreath upon!   60
                            IV
These fought in any case,
and some believing,
                pro domo,[4] in any case . . .

Some quick to arm,
some for adventure,   65
some from fear of weakness,
some from fear of censure,
some for love of slaughter, in imagination,
learning later . . .
some in fear, learning love of slaughter;   70

Died some, pro patria,
                non 'dulce' non 'et decor'[5] . . .
walked eye-deep in hell
believing in old men's lies, then unbelieving
came home, home to a lie,   75
home to many deceits,
home to old lies and new infamy;
usury age-old and age-thick
and liars in public places.

Daring as never before, wastage as never before.   80
Young blood and high blood,
fair cheeks, and fine bodies;

fortitude as never before

frankness as never before,
disillusions as never told in the old days,   85
hysterias, trench confessions,
laughter out of dead bellies.
                            V
There died a myriad,
And of the best, among them,
For an old bitch gone in the teeth,   90
For a botched civilization,

Charm, smiling at the good mouth,
Quick eyes gone under earth's lid,

For two gross of broken statues,
For a few thousand battered books.   95

                *   *   *

---

4. The Latin phrase, "for home," antici-   *et decorum est pro patria mori* ["It is
pates ll. 71–72.   sweet and appropriate to die for one's
5. *Cf.* Horace, *Odes*, III, ii. l. 13: *Dulce*   country"].

ENVOI[6]

Hugh Selwyn Mauberley (1919)

Go, dumb-born book,   220
Tell her that sang me once that song of Lawes:[7]
Hadst thou but song
As thou hast subjects known,
Then were there cause in thee that should condone
Even my faults that heavy upon me lie,   225
And build her glories their longevity.

Tell her that sheds
Such treasure in the air,
Recking naught else but that her graces give
Life to the moment,   230
I would bid them live
As roses might, in magic amber laid,
Red overwrought with orange and all made
One substance and one colour
Braving time.   235

Tell her that goes
With song upon her lips
But sings not out the song, nor knows
The maker of it, some other mouth,
May be as fair as hers,   240
Might, in new ages, gain her worshippers,
When our two dusts with Waller's shall be laid,
Siftings on siftings in oblivion,
Till change hath broken down
All things save Beauty alone.   245

1920

6. Ends the 1919 section of the volume; the poems of "Mauberley 1920" follow. *Cf*. the familiar "Go, Lovely Rose," by Edmund Waller (died 1687), here "reconstructed" in Pound's terms.

7. Henry Lawes (1596–1662), English composer and song writer, associated with John Milton.

THOMAS STEARNS ELIOT
(1888–)

As compared with other major poets, T. S. Eliot has published relatively little, but his excellence has been generally recognized ever since his first major poem, *The Waste Land*, appeared in 1922. However, he has remained a controversial figure. He has been regarded almost with reverence by a coterie of critics; his own literary criticism has been influential, especially in

idea = human adventure (handwritten)

poetry in which intellectual culture is heritage... freedom + culture... freedom of imagination in conflict with imagination (handwritten marginalia, partially legible)

its support of that form of poetry which employs intellectual discipline and cultural memory in preference to more accessible and more sensuous images and emotional suggestions. Eliot has been criticized for "unnecessary obscurity" or for "authoritarian severity"; but numerous other genuine poets of idea are instrumentally more complex, and his intellectual severity draws interest by its systematic traditionalism. Of his craftsmanship, his integrity, and his power, however, there has been little doubt.

Thomas Stearns Eliot was born in St. Louis, Missouri, on September 26, 1888, of New England stock, his Eliot grandfather having gone west as a Unitarian minister. He studied at private academies, entered Harvard at eighteen, and there attained the M.A. degree in 1910. A student of languages and belles-lettres, especially the writings of the Elizabethans and the metaphysical poets, and the literature of the Italian Renaissance, he was also attracted to the study of philosophy, taught at Harvard by such men as Irving Babbitt and George Santayana. In the winter of 1910 he went to the University of Paris, where he attended the lectures of the philosopher Henri Bergson, among others. Again at Harvard (1911–1914), he studied Sanskrit and Oriental philosophy in the graduate school, was an assistant in the philosophy department, and in 1914 was awarded a traveling fellowship for study in Germany.

At Merton College, Oxford, in 1915, he again studied philosophy. That year he married the daughter of a British artist. For two years he taught in English academies, while bringing to fruition his first book of poems. In 1917, he published *Prufrock and Other Observations*. Few poets in their first book have so prophetically suggested the direction and power of what was to follow. "The Love Song of J. Alfred Prufrock" still holds its place in the development of Eliot's poetry as a whole; like much of his later work it concerns various aspects of the frustration and enfeeblement of individual character as seen in perspective with the decay of states, peoples, and religious faith.

From 1918 to 1924 Eliot was in the service of Lloyd's Bank in London. In 1920 his fourth volume, *Poems*, with "Gerontion" as its leading poem, again developed the same general pattern of ideas. It is remarkable that he excluded almost no poem of his early volumes from his later collected works. In 1920 also appeared *The Sacred Wood*, containing, among other essays, "Tradition and the Individual Talent," the earliest statement of his aesthetics. The aesthetic principal which he first elaborated in this essay provided a useful instrument for modern criticism. It relates primarily to the individual work of art, the poem conceived as a made object, an organic thing in itself, whose concrete elements are true correlatives of the artist's imagination and experience with respect to that poem. The degree to which fusion and concentration of intellect, feeling, and experience were achieved was Eliot's criterion for judging the poem. Such ideas he developed in other essays which have been influential in promoting the contemporary tendency toward the intrinsic analysis of poetry.

Also in 1920, Eliot began *The Waste Land*, one of the major works of modern literature. Its subject, the apparent failure of Western civilization which World War I seemed to demonstrate, set the tone of his poetry until 1930. Such poems as "Prufrock" and "Gerontion" had suggested the spiritual debility of the modern individual and his culture while in satirical counterpoint his Sweeney poems had symbolized the rising tide of anticultural infidelity and human baseness. It is likely that in his abundant use of literary reference in *The Waste Land* he was influenced by Pound, a close friend whose advice, as Eliot has declared, he followed strictly in cutting and concentrating the poem. *The Waste Land* is the acknowledged masterpiece of its sort. It also introduced a form—the orchestration of related themes in successive movements which he used again in "The Hollow Men" (1925), *Ash-Wednesday* (1930), and his later masterpieces *Four Quartets* (1936–1942; 1943).

The Waste Land appeared as a volume in New York and London in 1922, but it had been published earlier that year in *The Criterion*, an influential London literary quarterly which Eliot edited from 1923 through 1929. His second volume of criticism, *Homage to John Dryden* (1924) was much admired for its critical method. In 1925

Eliot became a member of the board of the publishing firm now known as Faber and Faber, and he has been active in that association ever since. The first collection of his poems appeared as *Poems, 1909–1925* (1925). In 1927 he was confirmed in the Anglican Church and became a British subject.

A year later, in connection with the publication of the critical volume *For Lancelot Andrewes* (1928), he described himself as "a royalist in politics, a classicist in literature, and an Anglo-Catholic in religion"; and he has manifested an increasing reliance upon authority and tradition. His later poetry took a positive turn toward faith in life, in strong contrast with the desperation of *The Waste Land*. This was demonstrated by *Ash-Wednesday*, a poem of mystical conflict between faith and doubt, beautiful in its language if difficult in its symbolism. In 1932, in *Sweeney Agonistes*, he brought Sweeney to a deserved and gruesome death in a strange play that fascinates the attention by mingling penitence with musical comedy. In "The Hollow Men" he satirized the straw men, the Guy Fawkes men, whose world would end "not with a bang, but a whimper"; also in this period he produced the "Ariel Poems," including the exquisite and tender "Marina" (1930). *Murder in the Cathedral* (1935), a poetic tragedy on the betrayal of Thomas à Becket, has been successfully performed, and is a drama of impressive spiritual power. His *Collected Poems, 1909–1935* (1936), and the collected *Essays, Ancient and Modern,* which in the same year gave perspective to his criticism, brought to an end this first period of spiritual exploration.

Eliot's next major accomplishment, the *Four Quartets,* originated during his visit to the United States (1932–1934), his first return to his native country in seventeen years. During this period he wrote the small "Landscapes," some of them drawn from American scenes, which are spiritually connected with the theme of the *Quartets.* His lectures at Harvard University in 1932 resulted in the influential volume *The Use of Poetry and the Use of Criticism* (1933). In 1934 he lectured at the University of Virginia, and produced the study of orthodoxy and faith entitled *After Strange Gods, A Primer of Modern Heresy.* Presumably it was during this year that he conceived the subject of "Burnt Norton," the first of the *Quartets.*

The four poems that eventually resulted provide a reasoned philosophical discussion of the foundations of Christian faith, involving the nature of time, the significance of history, the religious psychology of man, and the nature of his experience; most importantly, perhaps, they attempt, by means of lofty poetic feeling and metaphysical insight, to suggest the actuality and meaning of such Christian mysteries as Incarnation and Pentecost. To some readers, these poems have seemed deficient in breadth, based as they are upon an authoritarian tradition of Christian philosophy; but they have been of unusual

interest for an age desperately seeking to resolve the conflict between spiritual and material reality. In 1943, the four poems, which had all been previously published, were brought together in one volume.

Eliot dramatized domestic life in terms of his philosophy. *The Family Reunion* (1939) was not generally considered successful as drama. *The Cocktail Party* (1949), *The Confidential Clerk* (1953), and *The Elder Statesman* (1958) created interest as experimental theater.

Few men of letters have been more fully honored in their own day than T. S. Eliot, and even those who strongly disagree with him seemed content with his selection for the Nobel Prize in 1948. *The Complete Poems and Plays* (1952) is a relatively small volume, but it represents an artist whose ideas are large, whose craftsmanship is the expression of artistic responsibility, and whose poems represent the progressive refinement and illustration of his aesthetics.

The Complete Poems and Plays of T. S. Eliot, 1952, contains in one volume everything of importance except *The Confidential Clerk,* 1954, and *The Elder Statesman,* 1958. This supersedes the long-standard *Collected* volumes of poetry and criticism are mentioned in the note above. No comprehensive edition of his essays has been prepared; the principal collections are *Selected Essays, 1917–1932,* 1932; *Essays, Ancient and Modern,* 1936; *Selected Essays,* new edition, 1950; *Essays on Elizabethan Drama,* 1956; *On Poetry and Poets,* 1957. Recent volumes of critical importance are *The Idea of a Christian Society,* 1940; *The Music of Poetry,* 1942; *Notes toward the Definition of Culture,* 1948; *The Three Voices of Poetry,* 1953; and *The Frontiers of Criticism,* 1956.

F. O. Matthiessen, *The Achievement of T. S. Eliot,* third edition, 1958, is still the best introduction. *T. S. Eliot: A Selected Critique*, edited by Leonard Unger, 1948, is a well-selected collection of major essays interpreting Eliot; and see Leonard Unger's *The Art of T. S. Eliot*, 1949. Other useful studies are in George Williamson, *The Talent of T. S. Eliot*, 1929; Edmund Wilson, *Axel's Castle*, 1931; F. R. Leavis, *New Bearings in English Poetry*, 1932; R. P. Blackmur, *The Double Agent*, 1935; Allen Tate, *Reactionary Essays on Poetry and Ideas*, 1936; Cleanth Brooks, *Modern Poetry and the Tradition*, 1930; Clive Sansom, *The Poetry of T. S. Eliot*, 1947; Elizabeth A. Drew, *T. S. Eliot, the Design of His Poetry*, 1949; George Williamson, *A Reader's Guide to T. S. Eliot*, 1953; Grover Smith, Jr., *T. S. Eliot's Poetry and Plays: A Study in Sources and Meaning*, 1956; and Hugh Kenner, *Invisible Poet: T. S. Eliot*, 1959.

Tradition and the Individual Talent[1]

I

In English writing we seldom speak of tradition, though we occasionally apply its name in deploring its absence. We cannot refer to 'the tradition' or to 'a tradition'; at most, we employ the adjective in saying that the poetry of So-and-so is 'traditional' or even 'too traditional.' Seldom, perhaps, does the word appear except in a phrase of censure. If otherwise, it is vaguely approbative, with the implication, as to the work approved, of some pleasing archæological reconstruction. You can hardly make the word agreeable to English ears without this comfortable reference to the reassuring science of archæology.

Certainly the word is not likely to appear in our appreciations of living or dead writers. Every nation, every race, has not only its own creative, but its own critical turn of mind; and is even more oblivious of the shortcomings and limitations of its critical habits than of those of its creative genius. We know, or think we know, from the enormous mass of critical writing that has appeared in the French language, the critical method or habit of the French; we only conclude (we are such unconscious people) that the French are 'more critical' than we, and sometimes even plume ourselves a little with the fact, as if the French were the less spontaneous. Perhaps they are; but we might remind ourselves that criticism is as inevitable as breathing, and that we should be none the worse for articulating what passes in our minds when we read a book and feel an emotion about it, for criticizing our own minds in their work of criticism. One of the facts that might come to light in this process is our tendency to insist, when we praise a poet, upon those aspects of his work in which he least resembles anyone else. In these aspects or parts of his work we pretend to find what is individual, what is the peculiar essence of the man. We dwell with satisfaction upon the poet's difference from his predecessors, especially his immediate predecessors; we endeavour to find something that can be isolated in order to be enjoyed. Whereas if we approach a poet without this

1. Published early in his career, in *The Sacred Wood* (1920), this essay defines a primary critical position from which Eliot's subsequent ideas have developed.

prejudice we shall often find that not only the best, but the most individual parts of his work may be those in which the dead poets, his ancestors, assert their immortality most vigorously. And I do not mean the impressionable period of adolescence, but the period of full maturity.

Yet if the only form of tradition, of handing down, consisted in following the ways of the immediate generation before us in a blind or timid adherence to its successes, 'tradition' should positively be discouraged. We have seen many such simple currents soon lost in the sand; and novelty is better than repetition. Tradition is a matter of much wider significance. It cannot be inherited, and if you want it you must obtain it by great labour. It involves, in the first place, the historical sense, which we may call nearly indispensable to anyone who would continue to be a poet beyond his twenty-fifth year; and the historical sense involves a perception, not only of the pastness of the past, but of its presence; the historical sense compels a man to write not merely with his own generation in his bones, but with a feeling that the whole of the literature of Europe from Homer and within it the whole of the literature of his own country has a simultaneous existence and composes a simultaneous order. This historical sense, which is a sense of the timeless as well as of the temporal and of the timeless and of the temporal together, is what makes a writer traditional. And it is at the same time what makes a writer most acutely conscious of his place in time, of his own contemporaneity.

No poet, no artist of any art, has his complete meaning alone. His significance, his appreciation is the appreciation of his relation to the dead poets and artists. You cannot value him alone; you must set him, for contrast and comparison, among the dead. I mean this as a principle of æsthetic, not merely historical, criticism. The necessity that he shall conform, that he shall cohere, is not onesided; what happens when a new work of art is created is something that happens simultaneously to all the works of art which preceded it. The existing monuments form an ideal order among themselves, which is modified by the introduction of the new (the really new) work of art among them. The existing order is complete before the new work arrives; for order to persist after the supervention of novelty, the *whole* existing order must be, if ever so slightly, altered; and so the relations, proportions, values of each work of art toward the whole are readjusted; and this is conformity between the old and the new. Whoever has approved this idea of order, of the form of European, of English literature will not find it preposterous that the past should be altered by the present as much as the present is directed by the past. And the poet who is aware of this will be aware of great difficulties and responsibilities.

In a peculiar sense he will be aware also that he must inevitably be judged by the standards of the past. I say judged, not amputated, by them; not judged to be as good as, or worse or better than, the dead; and certainly not judged by the canons of dead critics. It is a judgment, a comparison, in which two things are measured by each other. To conform merely would be for the new work not really to conform at all; it would not be new, and would therefore not be a work of art. And we do not quite say that the new is more valuable because it fits in; but its fitting in is a test of its value—a test, it is true, which can only be slowly and cautiously applied, for we are none of us infallible judges of conformity. We say: it appears to conform, and is perhaps individual, or it appears individual, and may conform; but we are hardly likely to find that it is one and not the other.

To proceed to a more intelligible exposition of the relation of the poet to the past: he can neither take the past as a lump, an indiscriminate bolus, nor can he form himself wholly on one or two private admirations, nor can he form himself wholly upon one preferred period. The first course is inadmissable, the second is an important experience of youth, and the third is a pleasant and highly desirable supplement. The poet must be very conscious of the main current, which does not at all flow invariably through the most distinguished reputations. He must be quite aware of the obvious fact that art never improves, but that the material of art is never quite the same. He must be aware that the mind of Europe—the mind of his own country—a mind which he learns in time to be much more important than his own private mind—is a mind which changes, and that this change is a development which abandons nothing *en route*, which does not superannuate either Shakespeare, or Homer, or the rock drawing of the Magdalenian draughtsmen.[2] That this development, refinement perhaps, complication certainly, is not, from the point of view of the artist, any improvement. Perhaps not even an improvement from the point of view of the psychologist or not to the extent which we imagine; perhaps only in the end based upon a complication in economics and machinery. But the difference between the present and the past is that the conscious present is an awareness of the past in a way and to an extent which the past's awareness of itself cannot show.

Someone said: 'The dead writers are remote from us because we *know* so much more than they did.' Precisely, and they are that which we know.

I am alive to a usual objection to what is clearly part of my programme for the *métier*[3] of poetry. The objection is that the doctrine

2. In the rock shelters of La Madeleine (in southwest France) appear the first paleolithic cave drawings to be studied by modern scholars. The animal sketches particularly show an advanced art.
3. Craft; *i.e.,* art.

requires a ridiculous amount of erudition (pedantry), a claim which can be rejected by appeal to the lives of poets in any pantheon. It will even be affirmed that much learning deadens or perverts poetic sensibility. While, however, we persist in believing that a poet ought to know as much as will not encroach upon his necessary receptivity and necessary laziness, it is not desirable to confine knowledge to whatever can be put into a useful shape for examinations, drawing-rooms, or the still more pretentious modes of publicity. Some can absorb knowledge, the more tardy must sweat for it. Shakespeare acquired more essential history from Plutarch than most men could from the whole British Museum. What is to be insisted upon is that the poet must develop or procure the consciousness of the past and that he should continue to develop this consciousness throughout his career.

What happens is a continual surrender of himself as he is at the moment to something which is more valuable. The progress of an artist is a continual self-sacrifice, a continual extinction of personality.

There remains to define this process of depersonalization and its relation to the sense of tradition. It is in this depersonalization that art may be said to approach the condition of science. I therefore invite you to consider, as a suggestive analogy, the action which takes place when a bit of finely filiated platinum is introduced into a chamber containing oxygen and sulphur dioxide.[4]

II

Honest criticism and sensitive appreciation is directed not upon the poet but upon the poetry. If we attend to the confused cries of the newspaper critics and the *susurrus*[5] of popular repetition that follows, we shall hear the names of poets in great numbers; if we seek not Blue-book knowledge but the enjoyment of poetry, and ask for a poem, we shall seldom find it. I have tried to point out the importance of the relation of the poem to other poems by other authors, and suggested the conception of poetry as a living whole of all the poetry that has ever been written. The other aspect of this Impersonal theory of poetry is the relation of the poem to its author. And I hinted, by an analogy, that the mind of the mature poet differs from that of the immature one not precisely in any valuation of 'personality,' not being necessarily more interesting, or having 'more to say,' but rather by being a more finely perfected medium in which special, or very varied, feelings are at liberty to enter into new combinations.

The analogy was that of the catalyst. When the two gases previously mentioned are mixed in the presence of a filament of plati-

---

4. As a catalyst; see the second paragraph below.

5. Latin for "murmuring."

num, they form sulphurous acid. This combination takes place only if the platinum is present; nevertheless the newly formed acid contains no trace of platinum, and the platinum itself is apparently unaffected: has remained inert, neutral, and unchanged. The mind of the poet is the shred of platinum. It may partly or exclusively operate upon the experience of the man himself; but, the more perfect the artist, the more completely separate in him will be the man who suffers and the mind which creates; the more perfectly will the mind digest and transmute the passions which are its material.[6]

The experience, you will notice, the elements which enter the presence of the transforming catalyst, are of two kinds: emotions and feelings. The effect of a work of art upon the person who enjoys it is an experience different in kind from any experience not of art. It may be formed out of one emotion, or may be a combination of several; and various feelings, inhering for the writer in particular words or phrases or images, may be added to compose the final result. Or great poetry may be made without the direct use of any emotion whatever: composed out of feelings solely. Canto XV of the *Inferno* (Brunetto Latini)[7] is a working up of the emotion evident in the situation; but the effect, though single as that of any work of art, is obtained by considerable complexity of detail. The last quatrain gives an image, a feeling attaching to an image, which 'came,' which did not develop simply out of what precedes, but which was probably in suspension in the poet's mind until the proper combination arrived for it to add itself to.[8] The poet's mind is in fact a receptacle for seizing and storing up numberless feelings, phrases, images, which remain there until all the particles which can unite to form a new compound are present together.

If you compare several representative passages of the greatest poetry you see how great is the variety of types of combination, and also how completely any semi-ethical criterion of 'sublimity' misses the mark. For it is not the 'greatness,' the intensity, of the emotions, the components, but the intensity of the artistic process, the pressure, so to speak, under which the fusion takes place, that counts. The episode of Paolo and Francesca employs a definite emotion, but the intensity of the poetry is something quite different from whatever intensity in the supposed experience it may give the impression of.[9] It is no more intense, furthermore, than Canto

6. The concept of the poem itself as the sole object of the reader's attention has become a principal tenet of recent criticism.
7. In this canto, Dante records his meeting in Hell with the Florentine philosopher Brunetto Latini (1212?–1294?).
8. Brunetto, condemned, for "unnatural lust," never to "stop one instant," walks with Dante in grave discourse; then must dash "like a racer" to regain his sordid companions, thus providing Eliot's catalysis of "feeling" with the "emotional image."
9. The lovers Paolo and Francesca, immortalized in Canto v of Dante's *Inferno*, had been slain by Francesca's jealous husband. Eliot distinguishes between the emotion of the lovers and Dante's fusion of various emotions in his narrative.

XXVI, the voyage of Ulysses,[1] which has not the direct dependence upon an emotion. Great variety is possible in the process of transmutation of emotion: the murder of Agamemnon,[2] or the agony of Othello, gives an artistic effect apparently closer to a possible original than the scenes from Dante. In the *Agamemnon*, the artistic emotion approximates to the emotion of an actual spectator; in *Othello* to the emotion of the protagonist himself. But the difference between art and the event is always absolute; the combination which is the murder of Agamemnon is probably as complex as that which is the voyage of Ulysses. In either case there has been a fusion of elements. The ode of Keats contains a number of feelings which have nothing particular to do with the nightingale, but which the nightingale, partly perhaps because of its attractive name, and partly because of its reputation, served to bring together.

The point of view which I am struggling to attack is perhaps related to the metaphysical theory of the substantial unity of the soul: for my meaning is, that the poet has, not a 'personality' to express, but a particular medium, which is only a medium and not a personality, in which impressions and experiences combine in peculiar and unexpected ways. Impressions and experiences which are important for the man may take no place in the poetry, and those which become important in the poetry may play quite a negligible part in the man, the personality.

I will quote a passage[3] which is unfamiliar enough to be regarded with fresh attention in the light—or darkness—of these observations:

> And now methinks I could e'en chide myself
> For doating on her beauty, though her death
> Shall be revenged after no common action.
> Does the silkworm expend her yellow labours
> For thee? For thee does she undo herself?
> Are lordships sold to maintain ladyships
> For the poor benefit of a bewildering minute?
> Why does yon fellow falsify highways,
> And put his life between the judge's lips,
> To refine such a thing—keeps horse and men
> To beat their valours for her? . . .

In this passage (as is evident if it is taken in its context) there is a combination of positive and negative emotions: an intensely strong attraction toward beauty and an equally intense fascination by the

1. Ulysses' straightforward account (in Dante's *Inferno*, xxvi) of his last voyage into the unknown sea, and his death by shipwreck, does not agree with Homer's *Odyssey*, and is thought to be Dante's invention.
2. In the *Agamemnon* by Aeschylus.

Eliot refers to the murder of Agamemnon by his wife's lover in the closing lines of "Sweeney among the Nightingales."
3. Act III, Scene 5, ll. 71–82, of *The Revenger's Tragedy* (1607), by Cyril Tourneur (*ca.* 1575–1626).

ugliness which is contrasted with it and which destroys it. This balance of contrasted emotion is in the dramatic situation to which the speech is pertinent, but that situation alone is inadequate to it. This is, so to speak, the structural emotion, provided by the drama. But the whole effect, the dominant tone, is due to the fact that a number of floating feelings, having an affinity to this emotion by no means superficially evident, have combined with it to give us a new art emotion.

It is not in his personal emotions, the emotions provoked by particular events in his life, that the poet is in any way remarkable or interesting. His particular emotions may be simple, or crude, or flat. The emotion in his poetry will be a very complex thing, but not with the complexity of the emotions of people who have very complex or unusual emotions in life. One error, in fact, of eccentricity in poetry is to seek for new human emotions to express; and in this search for novelty in the wrong place it discovers the perverse. The business of the poet is not to find new emotions, but to use the ordinary ones and, in working them up into poetry, to express feelings which are not in actual emotions at all. And emotions which he has never experienced will serve his turn as well as those familiar to him. Consequently, we must believe that 'emotion recollected in tranquillity'[4] is an inexact formula. For it is neither emotion, nor recollection, nor, without distortion of meaning, tranquillity. It is a concentration, and a new thing resulting from the concentration, of a very great number of experiences which to the practical and active person would not seem to be experiences at all; it is a concentration which does not happen consciously or of deliberation. These experiences are not 'recollected,' and they finally unite in an atmosphere which is 'tranquil' only in that it is a passive attending upon the event. Of course this is not quite the whole story. There is a great deal, in the writing of poetry, which must be conscious and deliberate. In fact, the bad poet is usually unconscious where he ought to be conscious, and conscious where he ought to be unconscious. Both errors tend to make him 'personal.' Poetry is not a turning loose of emotion, but an escape from emotion; it is not the expression of personality, but an escape from personality. But, of course, only those who have personality and emotions know what it means to want to escape from these things.

III

ὁ δὲ νοῦς ἴσως θειότερόν τι καὶ ἀπαθές ἐστιν.[5]

This essay proposes to halt at the frontier of metaphysics or mysticism, and confine itself to such practical conclusions as can be applied by the responsible person interested in poetry. To divert

---

4. Wordsworth, in the Preface to the second edition of *Lyrical Ballads* (1800), said that poetry "*takes its* *origin* from emotion recollected in tranquillity" [Editor's italics].

5. "Perhaps the Mind is something di-

interest from the poet to the poetry is a laudable aim: for it would conduce to a juster estimation of actual poetry, good and bad. There are many people who appreciate the expression of sincere emotion in verse, and there is a smaller number of people who can appreciate technical excellence. But very few know when there is an expression of *significant* emotion, emotion which has its life in the poem and not in the history of the poet. The emotion of art is impersonal. And the poet cannot reach this impersonality without surrendering himself wholly to the work to be done. And he is not likely to know what is to be done unless he lives in what is not merely the present, but the present moment of the past, unless he is conscious, not of what is dead, but of what is already living.

1920

The Love Song of J. Alfred Prufrock

S'io credesse che mia risposta fosse
A persona che mai tornasse al mondo,
Questa fiamma staria senza piu scosse.
Ma perciocche giammai di questo fondo
Non torno vivo alcun, s'i'odo il vero,
Senza tema d'infamia ti rispondo.[6]

Let us go then, you and I,
When the evening is spread out against the sky
Like a patient etherized upon a table;
Let us go, through certain half-deserted streets,
The muttering retreats   5
Of restless nights in one-night cheap hotels
And sawdust restaurants with oyster-shells:
Streets that follow like a tedious argument
Of insidious intent
To lead you to an overwhelming question. . .   10
Oh, do not ask, 'What is it?'
Let us go and make our visit.

In the room the women come and go
Talking of Michelangelo.[7]

The yellow fog[8] that rubs its back upon the window-panes,   15
The yellow smoke that rubs its muzzle on the window-panes

vine, and [therefore] unaffected [by impressions from without]." The quotation is from Aristotle, *On the Soul* (*De Anima*), Chapter 4.
6. "If I believed my answer were being made to one who could ever return to the world, this flame would gleam [*i.e.*, this spirit would speak] no more; but since, if what I hear is true, never from this abyss did living man return, I answer thee without fear of infamy" (Dante, *Inferno*, xxvii, 61–66). The

speaker, Guido da Montefeltro, promised absolution by Pope Boniface VIII, advised that prelate how to betray and destroy the Colonna family of Palestrina, and died unrepentant.
7. The lines suggest the futility of "arty" talk by dilettantes.
8. The yellow (or brown) fog of the sordid city was a familiar detail in French symbolism. See *The Waste Land*, ll. 60–61, with Eliot's note, there referring to Baudelaire.

Licked its tongue into the corners of the evening,
Lingered upon the pools that stand in drains,
Let fall upon its back the soot that falls from chimneys,
Slipped by the terrace, made a sudden leap,   20
And seeing that it was a soft October night,
Curled once about the house, and fell asleep.

And indeed there will be time
For the yellow smoke that slides along the street,
Rubbing its back upon the window-panes;   25
There will be time, there will be time
To prepare a face to meet the faces that you meet;
There will be time to murder and create,
And time for all the works and days[9] of hands
That lift and drop a question on your plate;   30
Time for you and time for me,
And time yet for a hundred indecisions,
And for a hundred visions and revisions,
Before the taking of a toast and tea.

In the room the women come and go   35
Talking of Michelangelo.

And indeed there will be time
To wonder, 'Do I dare?' and, 'Do I dare?'
Time to turn back and descend the stair,[1]
With a bald spot in the middle of my hair—   40
(They will say: 'How his hair is growing thin!')
My morning coat, my collar mounting firmly to the chin,
My necktie rich and modest, but asserted by a simple pin—
(They will say: 'But how his arms and legs are thin!')
Do I dare   45
Disturb the universe?
In a minute there is time
For decisions and revisions which a minute will reverse.

For I have known them all already, known them all:—[2]
Have known the evenings, mornings, afternoons,
I have measured out my life with coffee spoons;
I know the voices dying with a dying fall[3]
Beneath the music from a farther room.
  So how should I presume?

---

9. *Works and Days*, by Hesiod (eighth century B.C.), "father of Greek didactic poetry," was an account of daily life and husbandry, intermingled with moral precepts.
1. Dante's figure of the stairway from Hell to Heaven (*Purgatorio*, xxvi, ll. 145–148) recurs in Eliot's poems; see, for example, l. 428 of *The Waste Land*,
and *Ash-Wednesday*, Part III.
2. Echoes Laforgue's *Le Concile féerique* (cf. ll. 54 and 62).
3. Cf. Shakespeare, *Twelfth Night*, Act I, Scene 1, ll. 1–4: "If music be the food of love, play on; / Give me excess of it, that, surfeiting / The appetite may sicken, and so die. / That strain again! it had a dying fall."

And I have known the eyes already, known them all—   55
The eyes that fix you in a formulated phrase,
And when I am formulated, sprawling on a pin,
When I am pinned and wriggling on the wall,
Then how should I begin
To spit out all the butt-ends of my days and ways?   60
    And how should I presume?

And I have known the arms already, known them all—
Arms that are braceleted and white and bare
(But in the lamplight, downed with light brown hair!)
Is it perfume from a dress
That makes me so digress?   65
Arms that lie along a table, or wrap about a shawl.
    And should I then presume?
    And how should I begin?

                ·   ·   ·   ·   ·

Shall I say, I have gone at dusk through narrow streets   70
And watched the smoke that rises from the pipes
Of lonely men in shirt-sleeves, leaning out of windows? . . .

I should have been a pair of ragged claws
Scuttling across the floors of silent seas.

                ·   ·   ·   ·   ·

And the afternoon, the evening, sleeps so peacefully!   75
Smoothed by long fingers,
Asleep . . . tired . . . or it malingers,
Stretched on the floor, here beside you and me.
Should I, after tea and cakes and ices,
Have the strength to force the moment to its crisis?[3]   80
But though I have wept and fasted, wept and prayed,
Though I have seen my head (grown slightly bald) brought in
        upon a platter,
I am no prophet[4]—and here's no great matter;
I have seen the moment of my greatness flicker,
And I have seen the eternal Footman hold my coat, and snicker,   85
And in short, I was afraid.

And would it have been worth it, after all,
After the cups, the marmalade, the tea,
Among the porcelain, among some talk of you and me,
Would it have been worth while,   90

---

3. *Cf.* ll. 62–69 and 87–98 for the central experience or episode implied in this poem.
4. *Cf.* Matthew xiv: 3–11. The head of John the Baptist was brought to Queen Herodias on a "charger." Pru- frock is "bald," quite unlike John the Baptist as represented in Richard Strauss's opera *Salome* (1905) or Oscar Wilde's play (1894) on which it was based, both emphasizing the passion of Herodias for the prophet.

To have bitten off the matter with a smile,
To have squeezed the universe into a ball
To roll it toward some overwhelming question,
To say: 'I am Lazarus, come from the dead,
Come back to tell you all,[5] I shall tell you all'—   95
If one, settling a pillow by her head,
    Should say: 'That is not what I meant at all,
    That is not it, at all.'

       .   .   .   .   .

And would it have been worth it, after all,
Would it have been worth while,   100
After the sunsets and the dooryards and the sprinkled streets,
After the novels, after the teacups, after the skirts that trail along
    the floor—
And this, and so much more?—
It is impossible to say just what I mean!
But as if a magic lantern threw the nerves in patterns on a
    screen: 105
Would it have been worth while
If one, settling a pillow or throwing off a shawl,
And turning toward the window, should say:
    'That is not it at all,
    That is not what I meant, at all.'   110

       .   .   .   .   .

No! I am not Prince Hamlet,[6] nor was meant to be;
Am an attendant lord, one that will do
To swell a progress, start a scene or two,
Advise the prince; no doubt, an easy tool,
Deferential, glad to be of use,   115
Politic, cautious, and meticulous;
Full of high sentence, but a bit obtuse;
At times, indeed, almost ridiculous—
Almost, at times, the Fool.

I grow old . . . I grow old . . .   120
I shall wear the bottoms of my trousers rolled.

Shall I part my hair behind? Do I dare to eat a peach?
I shall wear white flannel trousers, and walk upon the beach.
I have heard the mermaids singing, each to each.

---

5. For the resurrection of Lazarus see John xi: 1–44. *Cf.* the note on the epigraph to this poem.
6. In the following passage (to l. 119) the speaker, Prufrock, indicates his own futility by comparing himself with Hamlet and a number of other literary characters. The "attendant lord" might be Polonius, or Rosencrantz or Guilden-

stern, in *Hamlet.* Chaucer, in the *Canterbury Tales,* ll. 303–306, describes the speech of the Clerk as terse, and "full of high sentence" (*i.e.,* pithy wisdom). Eliot (l. 117) employs the phrase differently, with the implication of empty pompousness. The court "Fool" (l. 119) was a conventional fixture of Elizabethan drama.

I do not think that they will sing to me.   125

I have seen them riding seaward on the waves
Combing the white hair of the waves blown back
When the wind blows the water white and black.

We have lingered in the chambers of the sea
By sea-girls wreathed with seaweed red and brown   130
Till human voices wake us, and we drown.[7]

1917

Gerontion[8]

Thou hast nor youth nor age
But as it were an after dinner sleep
Dreaming of both.

Here I am, an old man in a dry month,
Being read to by a boy, waiting for rain.[9]
I was neither at the hot gates[1]
Nor fought in the warm rain
Nor knee deep in the salt marsh, heaving a cutlass,   5
Bitten by flies, fought.
My house is a decayed house,
And the jew squats on the window sill, the owner,
Spawned in some estaminet of Antwerp,
Blistered in Brussels, patched and peeled in London.[2]   10
The goat coughs at night in the field overhead;
Rocks, moss, stonecrop, iron, merds.[3]
The woman keeps the kitchen, makes tea,
Sneezes at evening, poking the peevish gutter.

I an old man,   15
A dull head among windy spaces.

Signs are taken for wonders. "We would see a sign":[4]

7. The theme of man's proclivity for destroying himself by the abuse or debasement of a natural power (such as fertility, often symbolized by water) persists in Eliot's poems. See the Thames-daughters of *The Waste Land* (ll. 266 ff. and Eliot's note), and "Death by Water," Part IV of *The Waste Land*.
8. A coined word, from the Greek *geron*, "an old man." The epigraph is from Shakespeare, *Measure for Measure*, Act III, Scene 1, ll. 32–34. The poem is related in theme with *The Waste Land*, for which Eliot at first intended it to appear as an introduction (Pound's *Letters*, 169–172).
9. Water (or rain) is here used as symbol of fertility or rebirth; see "Prufrock," ll. 124–131, and *The Waste Land, passim.*

1. A literal translation of the Greek word *Thermopylae*, the name of the pass where three hundred Spartans under Leonidas defeated the Persian host of Xerxes (480 B.C.).
2. The "jew" (l. 8) then frequently symbolized the merchant class, or trade in general, long disdained by British society as a vulgarity basely born "in some estaminet" (shady tavern) of a continental city, and there disgraced ("Blistered"); but now being made acceptable ("patched and peeled") in London.
3. French for "dung."
4. In John iv: 48, Jesus said to the nobleman whose son he healed: "Except ye see signs and wonders, ye will not believe"; and see in Matthew xii: 38, the Pharisaic demand: "Master, we would see a sign from thee."

The word within a word,[5] unable to speak a word,
Swaddled with darkness. In the juvescence of the year
Came Christ the tiger[6]   20

In depraved May,[7] dogwood and chestnut, flowering judas,
To be eaten, to be divided, to be drunk
Among whispers; by Mr. Silvero
With caressing hands, at Limoges
Who walked all night in the next room;   25

By Hakagawa, bowing among the Titians;
By Madame de Tornquist, in the dark room
Shifting the candles; Fräulein von Kulp
Who turned in the hall, one hand on the door. Vacant shuttles
Weave the wind. I have no ghosts,   30
An old man in a draughty house
Under a windy knob.

After such knowledge, what forgiveness? Think now
History has many cunning passages, contrived corridors
And issues, deceives with whispering ambitions,   35
Guides us by vanities. Think now
She gives when our attention is distracted
And what she gives, gives with such supple confusions
That the giving famishes the craving. Gives too late
What's not believed in, or if still believed,   40
In memory only, reconsidered passion. Gives too soon
Into weak hands, what's thought can be dispensed with
Till the refusal propagates a fear. Think
Neither fear nor courage saves us. Unnatural vices
Are fathered by our heroism. Virtues   45
Are forced upon us by our impudent crimes.
These tears are shaken from the wrath-bearing tree.[8]

5. See John i: 1: "In the beginning was the Word, and the Word was with God, and the Word was God." For "Swaddled with darkness," in the next line, see Luke ii: 12, "Ye shall find the babe [Jesus] wrapped in swaddling clothes, lying in a manger"; see also Job xxxviii: **2, 9.** The theme of the lost primordial Word recurs in *Ash-Wednesday,* *The Waste Land,* and "Burnt Norton."
6. "Christ the tiger" suggests the biblical language of prophecy. In Revelation v: 5, Christ is called "the Lion of the tribe of Juda." The latter was that son of whom Jacob, in blessing, declared "Judah is a lion's whelp"; he further prophesied that Judah's descendants should inherit this power "until Shiloh [the Messiah] come" (Genesis xlix: 9–10). Finally, Eliot's "Christ the tiger" and the two following lines sug-

gest the Eucharist—the transubstantiation of the bread and wine of the Sacrament into the body and blood of Christ —and remind us that Samson, finding "honey in the carcase of the lion," propounded the prophetic riddle, "Out of the eater came forth meat * * * " (*cf.* Judges xiv: 8–14).
7. *Cf.* *The Waste Land,* ll. 1–2: "April is the cruellest month, breeding / Lilacs out of the dead land." In the present passage (ll. 19–29), the offense of spring is identified with the betrayal of Christ (*cf.* "flowering judas," and Matthew xxvi: 14–16, 47–49). The poet has invented the names of the persons in this passage who desecrate the Eucharist by their furtive acts.
8. The tree of the Garden of Eden; see Genesis ii: 16–17, and iii: 1–19.

The tiger springs in the new year. Us he devours.[9] Think at last
We have not reached conclusion, when I
Stiffen in a rented house.[1] Think at last   50
I have not made this show purposelessly
And it is not by any concitation[2]
Of the backward devils.
I would meet you upon this honestly.
I that was near your heart was removed therefrom   55
To lose beauty in terror, terror in inquisition.[3]
I have lost my passion: why should I need to keep it
Since what is kept must be adulterated?
I have lost my sight, smell, hearing, taste and touch:
How should I use it for your closer contact?   60

These with a thousand small deliberations
Protract the profit of their chilled delirium,
Excite the membrane, when the sense has cooled,
With pungent sauces, multiply variety
In a wilderness of mirrors. What will the spider do,   65
Suspend its operations, will the weevil
Delay? De Bailhache, Fresca, Mrs. Cammel,[4] whirled
Beyond the circuit of the shuddering Bear
In fractured atoms. Gull against the wind, in the windy straits
Of Belle Isle, or running on the Horn,   70
White feathers in the snow, the Gulf claims,
And an old man driven by the Trades
To a sleepy corner.

Tenants of the house,
Thoughts of a dry brain in a dry season.   75

1920

Sweeney Erect

And the trees about me,
Let them be dry and leafless; let the rocks
Groan with continual surges; and behind me
Make all a desolation. Look, look, wenches![5]

9. *Cf.* ll. 20–23. There the "tiger" was the bread and wine of the Eucharist; now He is the avenger of the Judgment.
1. *Cf.* l. 7 and l. 74; the "house" is Gerontion's body.
2. Concerted action, excitation.
3. See the reference to "the woman," ll. 13–14.
4. Unidentified persons, all to be "whirled / Beyond * * * the shuddering Bear" (l. 68), hence beyond the polestar, the northernmost star in the two constellations of the Bear. The idea is elaborated in the succeeding lines—Belle Isle Straits are far north, between

Labrador and Newfoundland; the Horn is the southern tip of South America.
5. *The Maid's Tragedy*, Act II, Scene 2, ll. 74–77, by Francis Beaumont and John Fletcher, late Elizabethan dramatists. In the play, Queen Aspatia, forsaken by her lover, asks her maid to weave her picture into a tapestry in the character of Ariadne. In the words here quoted she is describing the appropriate scenery for the tapestry. Eliot continues this description, and the traditional Ariadne story, in his first two stanzas.

Materialistic a..... d the age of men

Paint me a cavernous waste shore
   Cast in the unstilled Cyclades,[6]
Paint me the bold anfractuous rocks
   Faced by the snarled and yelping seas.

Display me Aeolus[7] above
   Reviewing the insurgent gales
Which tangle Ariadne's hair
   And swell with haste the perjured sails.

Morning stirs the feet and hands
   (Nausicaa and Polypheme),[8]
Gesture of orang-outang
   Rises from the sheets in steam.

This withered root of knots of hair
   Slitted below and gashed with eyes,
This oval O cropped out with teeth:
   The sickle motion from the thighs

Jackknifes upward at the knees
   Then straightens out from heel to hip
Pushing the framework of the bed
   And clawing at the pillow slip.

Sweeney[9] addressed full length to shave
   Broadbottomed, pink from nape to base,
Knows the female temperament
   And wipes the suds around his face.

(The lengthened shadow of a man
   Is history, said Emerson[1]

5

10

15

20

25

---

6. *Cf.* Catullus, *Carmine*, LXIV. Ariadne saved the life of Theseus, who then accepted her love. He later deserted her on a wild coast in the Cyclades, and sailed for home. Ariadne's plight aroused Jupiter, who prevented Theseus from changing his sails from black to white—his signal to his father, King Aegeus, that he had survived. The stricken father killed himself on seeing the black sails afar off. (See "perjured sails," l. 8).
7. Ruler of the winds in classic myth.
8. See Homer, *Odyssey,* Books VIII and IX. Nausicaä was princess of Phaeacia; she rescued and befriended the shipwrecked Ulysses, loved him hopelessly, and sent him on his way in a ship supplied by her father. By contrast, Polyphemus was a one-eyed, man-eating giant, master of the Cyclops, whom Ulysses escaped by burning out his eye. In other legends, this grotesque Caliban lusted after a horrified water di-

vinity, the beautiful Galatea (Theocritus, *Idylls*, VI, XI; Ovid, *Metamorphoses*, XIII).
9. The character of Sweeney appears in several of Eliot's poems, always associated with the degradation and vulgarization of life. See also "Mr. Eliot's Sunday Morning Service," "Sweeney among the Nightingales," and *The Waste Land,* l. 198. In *Sweeney Agonistes* (1932), an "unfinished" drama, he meets his predestined death as a murderer. In the present poem, the "orang-outang" of l. 11 recalls the phrase "Ape-neck Sweeney" in "Sweeney among the Nightingales." The title, "Sweeney Erect," suggests *Pithecanthropus erectus* (literally, "ape-man erect"), the fossil Java Man, earlier than *Homo sapiens.*
1. *Cf.* "Self-Reliance," paragraph **17:** "An institution is the lengthened shadow of one man * * * and all history re-

Who had not seen the silhouette
  Of Sweeney straddled in the sun.)

Tests the razor on his leg
  Waiting until the shriek subsides.   30
The epileptic on the bed
  Curves backward, clutching at her sides.

The ladies of the corridor
  Find themselves involved, disgraced,
Call witness to their principles   35
  And deprecate the lack of taste

Observing that hysteria
  Might easily be misunderstood;
Mrs. Turner intimates
  It does the house no sort of good.   40

But Doris,[2] towelled from the bath,
  Enters padding on broad feet,
Bringing sal volatile
  And a glass of brandy neat.

1920

A Cooking Egg[3]

En l'an trentiesme de mon aage,
Que toutes mes hontes j'ay beues . . .[4]

Pipit sate upright in her chair
  Some distance from where I was sitting;
Views of the Oxford Colleges
  Lay on the table, with the knitting.

Daguerreotypes and silhouettes,   5
  Her grandfather and great great aunts,
Supported on the mantelpiece
  An *Invitation to the Dance.*[5]

  ·   ·   ·   ·   ·

solves itself very easily into the biography of a few stout and earnest persons."
2. In *Sweeney Agonistes* Doris reappears in the same rôle. Sweeney offers
to take her "to a cannibal isle" where
there is only "birth, copulation, and
death." Doris replies, "I'd be bored."
3. An egg for use in cooking only, as
compared with one "strictly fresh"; its
age is against it.
4. "In the thirtieth year of my life, /

How I have drunken deep of all my
shames . . . " (*Le Grand Testament,*
1461, François Villon, ll. 1–2). Reference to this climacteric of Villon's became a melancholy cliché among the
poets of Eliot's generation.
5. This now-forgotten picture, along
with books of *Views* (l. 3) and the
family photographs, was once a conventional part of a somewhat prim domestic *décor.*

I shall not want Honour in Heaven
  For I shall meet Sir Philip Sidney[6]   10
And have talk with Coriolanus[7]
  And other heroes of that kidney.[8]

I shall not want Capital in Heaven
  For I shall meet Sir Alfred Mond.[9]
We two shall lie together, lapt   15
  In a five per cent. Exchequer Bond.

I shall not want Society in Heaven,
  Lucretia Borgia shall be my Bride;
Her anecdotes will be more amusing
  Than Pipit's experience could provide.   20

I shall not want Pipit in Heaven:
  Madame Blavatsky[1] will instruct me
In the Seven Sacred Trances;
  Piccarda de Donati[2] will conduct me.

    .   .   .   .   .

But where is the penny world I bought   25
  To eat with Pipit behind the screen?
The red-eyed scavengers are creeping
  From Kentish Town and Golder's Green;[3]

Where are the eagles and the trumpets?

  Buried beneath some snow-deep Alps.   30
Over buttered scones and crumpets
  Weeping, weeping multitudes
Droop in a hundred A.B.C.'s.[4]

                                                    1920

---

6. Gallant Elizabethan gentleman and good poet, of irreproachable family connections, Sir Philip Sidney chose for the "mistress" of his sonnets the daughter of an earl.
7. A legendary Roman patrician leader. *Cf. The Waste Land*, l. 417, and Eliot's later "Coriolan" poems.
8. *Cf.* Plato, *Apology,* 41: "I myself, too, shall have a wonderful interest in there meeting and conversing with Palmedes, and Ajax the son of Telamon, and any other ancient hero who has suffered death through an unjust judgment * * *"
9. Sir Alfred Mond (died 1930) was a famous British financier and industrialist.
1. Elena Petrovna Blavatsky (died 1891), an internationally famous writer on the occult, worker of "miracles," and founder of the Theosophical Society.
2. See Dante, *Purgatorio,* xxiv, 10–15. in Purgatory, Dante inquires about the immortal destiny of Piccarda, who like his own wife was of the great Donati family. She was both "beautiful and good," and already "wears her glad crown" in Paradise. *Cf. Paradiso,* III, ll. 35 ff.
3. The "penny world" of innocence (l. 25) is compared with "Kentish Town" and "Golder's Green" of suburban London, then the habitats of upstart ambition.
4. The Aerated Bread Corporation, a chain of restaurants called the "A.B.C.'s," where "scones and crumpets," popular British pastries, are consumed in the ritual of afternoon tea.

Mr. Eliot's Sunday Morning Service[5]

Look, look, master, here comes two religious caterpillars.
—THE JEW OF MALTA

Polyphiloprogenitive[6]
The sapient sutlers[7] of the Lord
Drift across the window-panes.
In the beginning was the Word.[8]

In the beginning was the Word.   5
Superfetation of τὸ ἕν,[9]
And at the mensual[1] turn of time
Produced enervate Origen.[2]

A painter of the Umbrian school
Designed upon a gesso ground   10
The nimbus of the Baptized God.[3]
The wilderness is cracked and browned

But through the water pale and thin
Still shine the unoffending feet
And there above the painter set   15
The Father and the Paraclete.[4]

· · · ·

The sable presbyters[5a] approach
The avenue of penitence;

5. The epigraph to this poem is from Christopher Marlowe's *The Jew of Malta*, Act IV, Scene 1, l. 21. The play attacks the corruption and carnality of the clergy. This idea is reflected at once in the extraordinary first line of the poem. Subsequent stanzas explore the relationship of the fertility impulse to sexual conduct, nature, and God; and its rôle in philosophy, religion, and ritual. The speculation ends only in confusion, in the amusing last stanza, which confirms the suggestion that this meditation occurred in a bathtub beside a garden window, and shows "Sweeney" as part of everyone's nature (*cf.* "Sweeney Erect").

6. *Cf.* "philoprogenitive," designating a person possessed with desire for offspring. The masterful prefix "poly" adds the idea of promiscuity.

7. From the Early Dutch *soeteler*, "one who undertakes a humble employment." *Cf.* ll. 25–28. In modern parlance, the sutler is one who follows an army, selling provisions, liquor, and so on to the soldiers.

8. John i: 1. *Cf.* "Gerontion," l. 18, and observe the shift here from "Word" as spirit to "Word" as fertility (ll. 5 and 6 of this poem).

9. The Greek phrase, literally "the One," in Greek metaphysics came to

mean "the unity of Being." Hence, in ll. 5 and 6, "the Word" implies a "superfetation"—sublime and universal pregnancy—within "being," or the Godhead.

1. A crossbred word of Eliot's coinage. *Cf.* "mensal," and "menstrual."

2. Origen (died *ca.* 254 A.D.), a Father of the Greek Church, was the first to establish a synthesis of Hebrew Scripture and Greek philosophy. Although his doctrines were later declared heretical, Eliot's adjective "enervate" refers rather to Origen's literal application of Matthew xix: 12, "* * * there be eunuchs, which have made themselves eunuchs for the kingdom of heaven's sake."

3. At the baptism of Jesus in the wilderness by John the Baptist (*cf.* Matthew iii: 11–17), "the heavens were opened," but the "nimbus of the Baptized God" also suggests the pagan divinities in certain Eastern legends. Since the painting is on "gesso" (plaster), the "wilderness is cracked." The phrase "unoffending feet" (l. 14) recalls that when later Jesus was crucified, his feet were nailed to the cross.

4. Specifically, the Holy Spirit, which descended "like a dove" at the baptism (*cf.* Matthew iii: 16, Mark i: 10, Luke iii: 22, and John i: 32).

5a. Presbyters were Elders of the early

The young are red and pustular
Clutching piaculative pence.   20

Under the penitential gates
Sustained by staring Seraphim
Where the souls of the devout
Burn invisible and dim.

Along the garden-wall the bees   25
With hairy bellies pass between
The stammate and pistilate,
Blest office of the epicene.[6]

Sweeney shifts from ham to ham
Stirring the water in his bath.[7]   30
The masters of the subtle schools
Are controversial, polymath.[8]

1920

The Waste Land[9]

"NAM Sibyllam quidem Cumis ego ipse oculis meis vidi in ampulla pendere, et cum illi pueri dicerent: Σίβυλλα τί θέλεις; respondebat illa: ἀποθανεῖν θέλω."[1]

church, later traditionally clad in black ("sable"); here the reference is to ants or other insects, whose "red" young bring (l. 20) "piaculative [expiatory] pence" (*cf.* "penance")—presumably pollen, in this context. *Cf.* the bees (l. 25).

6. The bees are "epicene" (performing the functions of both sexes) in carrying pollen from stamens to pistils (ll. 26–27).

7. See "Sweeney Erect." The presence of Sweeney in "Mr. Eliot's" devotional service provides a comment on this poet's speculations on the relations between animal man and spiritual man.

8. A coinage from Greek roots meaning "many" or "much" and "learned" or "knowledge."

9. *The Waste Land* appeared in *The Criterion* (London) in October, 1922; in *The Dial* (New York) in October, 1922; and almost simultaneously as a book (New York, 1922). To many writers of the period following World War I, Western civilization seemed hopelessly bankrupt. While Eliot supported this view in his poem, the work was also a testament of faith in the Christian and classical traditions, threatened by infidelity. In his general note Eliot said, "Not only the title, but the plan and a good deal of the incidental symbolism of the poem was suggested by Miss Jessie L. Weston's book on the Grail Legend: *From Ritual to Romance*" (1920). He also acknowledged the influence of Sir James Frazer's

The Golden Bough (12 volumes, 1890–1915), "especially the two volumes *Adonis, Attis, Osiris.*" These parts of Frazer's work deal in particular with ancient vegetation ceremonies and fertility legends. Similarly, Jessie L. Weston, in her study, found certain sources of the Holy Grail legends in pre-Christian myths, legends, and rituals concerning fertility. These primitive materials, reshaped by Christian influence, appeared as symbolic elements in the later stories of the Grail and of Arthur's knights. Eliot was particularly indebted to Miss Weston for the North European myth of the Fisher King, ruler of a Waste Land blighted by an evil spell which also rendered the King impotent. The salvation of King and country awaited the advent of a knight of fabulous virtue and courage, whose ordeals would provide answers for certain magical questions symbolic at once of religious purity and fertility. In connection with the Fisher King, Miss Weston emphasized the use of the fish as a symbol in early Christianity; the title "fishers of men," bestowed by Christ on his apostles; and the immemorial connection of the fish symbol with pagan fertility deities and their rituals. References to the ordeals of the Christian knights of later legends are mingled in Eliot's poem with pagan echoes and with a literary symbolism involving allusions or quotations relating to thirty-five authors, in several languages.

1. The epigraph is translated: "For I

[handwritten: male symbol]

FOR EZRA POUND
il miglior fabbro[2]

I. *The Burial of the Dead*

April is the cruellest month, breeding *[handwritten: sterile world]*
Lilacs out of the dead land,[3] mixing
Memory and desire, stirring
Dull roots with spring rain.
Winter kept us warm, covering
Earth in forgetful snow, feeding   **5**
A little life with dried tubers.
Summer surprised us, coming over the Starnbergersee[4]
With a shower of rain; we stopped in the colonnade,
And went on in sunlight, into the Hofgarten,[5]   10
And drank coffee, and talked for an hour.
Bin gar keine Russin, stamm' aus Litauen, echt deutsch.[6]
And when we were children, staying at the archduke's,
My cousin's, he took me out on a sled,
And I was frightened. He said, Marie,[7]   15
Marie, hold on tight. And down we went.
In the mountains, there you feel free.
I read, much of the night, and go south in the winter.

What are the roots that clutch, what branches grow
Out of this stony rubbish? Son of man,[8]   20
You cannot say, or guess, for you know only
A heap of broken images, where the sun beats,

myself, with my own eyes, saw the Sibyl of Cumae hanging caged in a flask, and when the boys said to her: 'Sibyl, what do you want'; she answered: 'I want to die' " (Petronius, *Satyricon*, Chapter 48). The Cumaean Sibyl, once beloved of Apollo, and the guide and counselor of Aeneas on his descent to Avernus, was the most famous and trusted prophetess of Greece. Apollo had granted her as many years of life as she could hold grains of dust in her hand, but she neglected to ask to remain young, and her authority had declined as she aged.
2. The Italian inscription to Pound reads, "the better artisan" (literally "smith"). The phrase was taken from Dante, *Purgatorio*, xxvi, 117, where it was used by a poet in pointing out the renowned Arnaut Daniel, a troubadour. Eliot has acknowledged his indebtedness to Pound, especially in the final revisions of *The Waste Land*.
3. *Cf.* "depraved May" in "Gerontion," l. 21. In Oriental literature the lilac occurs in sexual symbolism. The title "The Burial of the Dead" suggests the mythical and ritualistic burial and resurrection of gods; note also its relationship to the theme of Part IV.
4. A fashionable lake resort near Munich.
5. German term for an outdoor café; here presumably the famous one in Munich, in a public park containing a zoo.
6. "Indeed I am not Russian, I come from Litau, true German." (Lithuania had been frequently flooded by colonizing Germans.)
7. *Cf.* Eliot's statement, in his note to l. 218, that "all the women are one woman." By this comment Eliot relates Marie to "the hyacinth girl" (l. 36) and "the lady of situations" (l. 50), who reappears in Part II, "A Game of Chess."
8. "*Cf.* Ezekiel ii, 1" [Eliot's note]. Here God addresses Ezekiel, as usual, "Son of man." And in the third verse God continues: "I send thee to * * * a rebellious nation * * * : they and their fathers have transgressed against me."

And the dead tree gives no shelter, the cricket[9] no relief,
And the dry stone no sound of water. Only
There is shadow under this red rock,   25
(Come in under the shadow of this red rock),[1]
And I will show you something different from either
Your shadow at morning striding behind you
Or your shadow at evening rising to meet you before;
I will show you fear in a handful of dust.[2]   30

> *Frisch weht der Wind*[3]
> *Der Heimat zu,*
> *Mein Irisch Kind,*
> *Wo weilest du?*

'You gave me hyacinths first a year ago;   35
'They called me the hyacinth girl.'
—Yet when we came back, late, from the Hyacinth garden,[4]
Your arms full, and your hair wet, I could not
Speak, and my eyes failed, I was neither
Living nor dead, and I knew nothing,   40
Looking into the heart of light, the silence.
Oed' und leer das Meer.[5]

Madame Sosostris, famous clairvoyante,
Had a bad cold, nevertheless
Is known to be the wisest woman in Europe,   45
With a wicked pack of cards.[6] Here, said she,

9. "*Cf.* Ecclesiastes xii, 5" [Eliot's note]. In this and the following verse, the Preacher paints a desolate waste land crushed by sin, when "the grasshopper shall be a burden, * * * the wheel broken at the cistern."
1. Isaiah (xxxii: 2) prophesied the coming of a Messiah who "shall be * * * as rivers of water in a dry place, as the shadow of a great rock in a weary land."
2. Ecclesiastes (see l. 23) continues, in xii: 7, "Then shall the dust return to the earth as it was." *Cf.* the Sibyl's handful of dust, in the note to the epigraph of this poem.
3. "V. Tristan und Isolde, I, verses 5–8" [Eliot's note]. Ll. 31–42 represent three contrasted experiences of love: (1) a light love, here suggested by a lyric quoted from Wagner's opera, in which a carefree young sailor on Tristan's ship celebrates his beloved in Ireland: "Fresh wafts the wind / To Homeland, / My Irish sweetheart [literally, "child"], / Where are you waiting?"; (2) the failure of love in the hyacinth garden (ll. 35–41); and finally, (3) Tristan's high but unhappy love for Isolde (l. 42).

4. The Greek *Hyacinthia*, an outdoor May festival, commemorated the mythical Hyacinthus, a boy beloved by Apollo and slain by the jealous act of Zephyrus (Ovid, *Metamorphoses*, X). Water again appears ("your hair wet") as a fertility symbol, while the phrase "I was neither living nor dead" echoes Dante, in the tremendous cold of the last circle of Hell, confronting Satan (*Inferno*, xxxiv, 25).
5. Eliot locates this line in Wagner's *Tristan und Isolde*, III, verse 24. Tristan, dying of a wound at his remote castle, awaits the ship of Isolde, who has fled from her husband, King Mark. Meanwhile a shepherd, appointed to watch for a sail, mournfully reports, in the words here quoted: "Desolate and deserted the sea."
6. The reference in ll. 46–56 is to the Tarot deck of cards, once honored in Eastern magic, now employed by a vulgar fortuneteller. In his note Eliot identifies certain of the cards: "I am not familiar with the exact constitution of the Tarot pack of cards, from which I have obviously departed to suit my own convenience. The Hanged Man, a member of the traditional pack, fits

Is your card, the drowned Phoenician Sailor,
(Those are pearls that were his eyes.[7] Look!)
Here is Belladonna, the Lady of the Rocks,[8]
The lady of situations.   50
Here is the man with three staves, and here the Wheel,
And here is the one-eyed merchant, and this card,
Which is blank, is something he carries on his back,[9]
Which I am forbidden to see. I do not find
The Hanged Man. Fear death by water.   55
I see crowds of people, walking round in a ring.
Thank you. If you see dear Mrs. Equitone,
Tell her I bring the horoscope myself:
One must be so careful these days.

Unreal City,[1]   60
Under the brown fog of a winter dawn,
A crowd flowed over London Bridge, so many,
I had not thought death had undone so many.[2]
Sighs, short and infrequent, were exhaled,[3]
And each man fixed his eyes before his feet.   65
Flowed up the hill and down King William Street,

my purpose in two ways: because he is associated in my mind with the Hanged God of Frazer, and because I associate him with the hooded figure in the passage of the disciples to Emmaus in Part V. The Phoenician Sailor and the Merchant appear later; also the 'crowds of people,' and Death by Water is executed in Part IV. The Man with Three Staves (an authentic member of the Tarot pack) I associate, quite arbitrarily, with the Fisher King himself."

7. Shakespeare, *The Tempest*, Act I, Scene 2, l. 398; from Ariel's song ("Full fathom five thy father lies") to the shipwrecked Ferdinand, "Sitting on a bank / Weeping again the King my father's wreck, / This music crept by me upon the waters." Ariel leads Ferdinand to Miranda, whose father, Prospero, has cast a magic blessing on their love. Actually, Ferdinand's father has escaped from the wreck, but the theme of the dead or betrayed father (or culture) persists in *The Waste Land*. The present reference is also associated with "the drowned Phoenician Sailor" (l. 47) and the Phlebas of Part IV, ll. 312–321.

8. The plant belladonna is the "deadly" nightshade. Here the capitalization of the word (literally, "beautiful lady") makes it suggestive of Italian epithets for the Virgin. One of the most beloved paintings of the Virgin is Leonardo's "Virgin of the Rocks" (here, "Lady of the Rocks"); in the next

line, the "lady of situations" obviously is the lady of the intrigue in Part II, whose "vials" of cosmetics might include the drug belladonna, employed to brighten the eyes.

9. *Cf.* "Mr. Eugenides, the Smyrna merchant" (ll. 209–214), who apparently "carries on his back" a burden of irregularities.

1. "*Cf.* Baudelaire: *'Fourmillante cité, cité pleine de rêves, / Où le spectre en plein jour raccroche le passant'*" [Eliot's note]; the opening lines of Poem 93, in *Fleurs du Mal*, translated as "Swarming city, city filled with dreams, / Where the ghost in full daylight hails the passerby." Baudelaire referred to Paris.

2. "*Cf. Inferno*, III, 55–57" [Eliot's note]. Just inside the gate of Hell, inscribed, "Abandon all hope, ye who enter here," Dante found those who "from cowardice had made the great refusal" to choose either good or evil, intent only on themselves, and now unacceptable both to Heaven and to Hell. The lines cited by Eliot are translated: "So long a train of people; I never should have believed Death had undone so many."

3. "*Cf. Inferno*, IV, 25–27" [Eliot's note]. Eliot cites Dante's lines concerning the virtuous heathen who never heard the Gospel; they were condemned to Limbo, without pain but without hope of salvation, uttering "sighs, which caused the eternal air to tremble."

To where Saint Mary Woolnoth kept the hours
With a dead sound on the final stroke of nine.[4]
There I saw one I knew, and stopped him, crying: 'Stetson!
'You who were with me in the ships at Mylae![5]   70
'That corpse you planted last year in your garden,[6]
'Has it begun to sprout? Will it bloom this year?
'Or has the sudden frost disturbed its bed?
'Oh keep the Dog far hence, that's friend to men,
'Or with his nails he'll dig it up again![7]   75
'You! hypocrite lecteur!—mon semblable,—mon frère!'[8]

II. A Game of Chess[9]

The Chair she sat in, like a burnished throne,[1]
Glowed on the marble, where the glass
Held up by standards wrought with fruited vines
From which a golden Cupidon peeped out   80
(Another hid his eyes behind his wing)
Doubled the flames of sevenbranched candelabra
Reflecting light upon the table as
The glitter of her jewels rose to meet it,
From satin cases poured in rich profusion;   85
In vials of ivory and coloured glass
Unstoppered, lurked her strange synthetic perfumes,

4. This London church was rebuilt under the influence of Sir Christopher Wren in the early eighteenth century. The significance of the "dead sound" of its ninth stroke ("a phenomenon," says Eliot's note, "which I have often noticed.") is controversial. In Matthew xxvii: 46, it was "about the ninth hour" on the cross that "Jesus cried with a loud voice * * * 'My God, My God, why hast thou forsaken me?'" And consider the ninth month in terms of fertility, a principal theme of this poem.
5. In the *Inferno*, Dante from time to time recognizes friends in the crowd of spirits. So in modern London, the speaker hails an acquaintance, "Stetson." But "Mylae" was a naval battle of the Punic War (260 B.C.), not of the World War in which "Stetson" presumably fought. Hence all wars are compared and condemned.
6. In its last episode, this section turns the reader's attention back to its title, "The Burial of the Dead."
7. Eliot's note refers to "the dirge in [John] Webster's *White Devil*," Act V, Scene 4, ll. 97–98, of that play reads: "But keep the wolf far thence, that's foe to men, / For with his nails he'll dig them up again." The lines are part of a song sung by a demented mother, whose son is burying the

brother he slew. Eliot changes "foe" to "friend," and "wolf" to "Dog"—capitalized because it here means "Dog Star." Sirius, the Dog Star, faithfully follows his slain master, Orion, across the heavens; also, according to Frazer, in Eastern myth, Sirius was regarded as responsible for the annual rising of the waters of the Nile, an event associated with fertility and resurrection.
8. "V. Baudelaire, Preface to *Fleurs du Mal*" [Eliot's note]. The passage is translated, "hypocritical reader!—my double,—my brother!"
9. Thomas Middleton, in *A Game at Chesse* (1624), satirized a royal marriage based on political expediency. See also the note to l. 138.
1. "*Cf. Antony and Cleopatra*, II, ii, l. 190" [Eliot's note]. Eliot's language here recalls the passage in Shakespeare, describing the regal splendor of the barge in which Cleopatra rode to her first meeting with Antony. Eliot's significant alteration of "barge" to read "Chair" suggests the seven stars of the Chair of Cassiopeia; this constellation was named for a mythical queen of Ethiopia so vain that she likened her beauty to that of the Nereids, thus causing the wrathful gods to visit her country with ravaging floods and monsters.

Unguent, powdered, or liquid—troubled, confused
And drowned the sense in odours; stirred by the air
That freshened from the window, these ascended   90
In fattening the prolonged candle-flames,
Flung their smoke into the laquearia,[2]
Stirring the pattern on the coffered ceiling.
Huge sea-wood fed with copper
Burned green and orange, framed by the coloured stone,   95
In which sad light a carvèd dolphin swam.
Above the antique mantel was displayed
As though a window gave upon the sylvan scene[3]
The change of Philomel,[4] by the barbarous king
So rudely forced; yet there the nightingale   100
Filled all the desert with inviolable voice
And still she cried, and still the world pursues,
'Jug Jug' to dirty ears.[5]
And other withered stumps of time
Were told upon the walls; staring forms   105
Leaned out, leaning, hushing the room enclosed.
Footsteps shuffled on the stair.
Under the firelight, under the brush, her hair
Spread out in fiery points
Glowed into words, then would be savagely still.   110

'My nerves are bad to-night. Yes, bad. Stay with me.
'Speak to me. Why do you never speak. Speak.
    'What are you thinking of? What thinking? What?
'I never know what you are thinking. Think.'

I think we are in rats' alley[6]   115
Where the dead men lost their bones.

'What is that noise?'
                            The wind under the door.[7]

2. "Laquearia. V. *Aeneid*, I, 726: *de-*
pendent lychni laquearibus incensi, et
noctem flammis funalia vincunt" [Eliot's
note]. The passage may be translated:
"Lighted lamps hang from the golden
laquearia (fretted ceiling), and flaming
torches dispel the night." The scene is
the feast given by Dido for Aeneas
when the hero arrived at Carthage.
When he departed, the Queen, smitten
by passion, killed herself.
3. "Sylvan scene. V. Milton, *Paradise
Lost*, IV, 140" [Eliot's note]. The
phrase is associated with Milton's description of the first Eden, a place of
innocent love. But here, see the next
lines.
4. "*Cf*. Ovid, *Metamorphoses*, VI, Philomela" [Eliot's note]. King Tereus

raped Philomela, sister of his wife,
Procne, and cut out her tongue to
silence her. Procne, for revenge, killed
his son and served his heart for the
King to eat. The gods, to save the
sisters, turned them into birds: Philomela became the nightingale, and
Procne, the swallow.
5. Eliot's note for this passage calls
attention to his elaboration of the
nightingale's song (vulgarized to "Jug
Jug" for "dirty ears"), in l. 204.
6. "*Cf*. Part III, l. 195" [Eliot's
note].
7. "*Cf*. Webster: 'Is the wind in that
door still?'" [Eliot's note]. In John
Webster's *The Devil's Law Case*
(1623), Romelio, to hasten the death
of Duke Contarino, who has willed

'What is that noise now? What is the wind doing?'
                    Nothing again nothing.   120
                                                  'Do

'You know nothing? Do you see nothing? Do you remember
'Nothing?'
    I remember
Those are pearls that were his eyes.[8]   125
'Are you alive, or not? Is there nothing in your head?'
                                                  But

O O O O that Shakespeherian Rag—[9]
It's so elegant
So intelligent   130
'What shall I do now? What shall I do?'
'I shall rush out as I am, and walk the street
'With my hair down, so. What shall we do to-morrow?
'What shall we ever do?'
                    The hot water at ten.   135
And if it rains, a closed car at four.
And we shall play a game of chess.
Pressing lidless eyes and waiting for a knock upon the door.[1]

When Lil's husband got demobbed,[2] I said—
I didn't mince my words, I said to her myself,   140
HURRY UP PLEASE ITS TIME[3]
Now Albert's coming back, make yourself a bit smart.
He'll want to know what you done with that money he gave you
To get yourself some teeth. He did, I was there.
You have them all out, Lil, and get a nice set,   145
He said, I swear, I can't bear to look at you.
And no more can't I, I said, and think of poor Albert,
He's been in the army four years, he wants a good time,

him some money, stabs the Duke again through the wound of which he is dying. The consequent release of pus saves the Duke; when the surgeon finds him breathing, he exclaims, "Is the wind in that doore still?" The following passage in Eliot (ll. 119–124), again probably refers to Webster's *The White Devil* (see l. 75), in which a murderer asks his bound victim, "What dost thou think on?" and the victim replies, "Nothing; of nothing: * * * I remember nothing" (Act V, Scene 6, ll. 203–205).

8. "*Cf.* Part I, ll. 37, 48" [Eliot's note]. Thus the innocent love of Ferdinand and Miranda in *The Tempest* is compared with the episode in the hyacinth garden (l. 37) and with the present guilty episode.

9. A piece of ragtime music was then current containing a jazz refrain al-

most identical with ll. 128–130.
1. "*Cf.* the game of chess in [Thomas] Middleton's *Women Beware Women*" [Eliot's note]. In Act II, Scene 2, of this play (dated 1657) a mother is kept engaged in a chess game while her daughter-in-law is being seduced in another room, on the stage balcony visible to the audience. The dramatist contrived that the accomplice should checkmate the mother at the moment when the daughter-in-law surrendered to the seducer.
2. British slang of the period for "demobilized" from the army.
3. The ominous suggestion of l. 138—"waiting for a knock on the door"—is grotesquely projected into this warning of the British bartender that it is nearly legal closing time; this line, in turn, is reiterated as a grim refrain throughout the remainder of the scene.

And if you don't give it him, there's others will, I said.
Oh is there, she said. Something o' that, I said.   150
Then I'll know who to thank, she said, and give me a straight look.
HURRY UP PLEASE ITS TIME
If you don't like it you can get on with it, I said.
Others can pick and choose if you can't.
But if Albert makes off, it won't be for lack of telling.   155
You ought to be ashamed, I said, to look so antique.
(And her only thirty-one.)
I can't help it, she said, pulling a long face,
It's them pills I took, to bring it off, she said.
(She's had five already, and nearly died of young George.)   160
The chemist[4] said it would be all right, but I've never been the
          same.
You *are* a proper fool, I said.
Well, if Albert won't leave you alone, there it is, I said,
What you get married for if you don't want children?
HURRY UP PLEASE ITS TIME   165
Well, that Sunday Albert was home, they had a hot gammon,[5]
And they asked me in to dinner, to get the beauty of it hot—
HURRY UP PLEASE ITS TIME
HURRY UP PLEASE ITS TIME
Goonight Bill. Goonight Lou. Goonight May. Goonight.   170
Ta ta. Goonight. Goonight.
Good night, ladies, good night, sweet ladies, good night, good
          night.[6]

III. *The Fire Sermon*[7]

The river's tent is broken: the last fingers of leaf
Clutch and sink into the wet bank. The wind
Crosses the brown land, unheard. The nymphs are departed.   175
Sweet Thames, run softly, till I end my song.[8]
The river bears no empty bottles, sandwich papers,
Silk handkerchiefs, cardboard boxes, cigarette ends
Or other testimony of summer nights. The nymphs are departed.
And their friends, the loitering heirs of city directors;   180
Departed, have left no addresses.
By the waters of Leman I sat down and wept[9] . . .

4. British for "druggist."
5. British for "ham" or "bacon"; in dialect, also "thigh"; *cf.* American "gam."
6. *Cf. Hamlet*, Act IV, Scene 5. These were Ophelia's words, concluding the scene of her madness caused by her hopeless love for Hamlet and the murder of her father.
7. See the note to l. 308, in which the poet explains this title.

8. "V. Spenser, *Prothalamion*" [Eliot's note]. Eliot's l. 176 is the refrain of Spenser's "bridal song," published in 1596, a pastoral poem of surpassing innocence depicting a wedding festival of water nymphs on the Thames. But *cf.* ll. 177–181, which give a suggestion of life along the Thames in 1922.
9. *Cf.* Psalms cxxxvii: 1, 4. The exiled Jews wept "by the rivers of Babylon,"

Sweet Thames, run softly till I end my song,
Sweet Thames, run softly, for I speak not loud or long.
But at my back in a cold blast I hear[1]   185
The rattle of the bones, and chuckle spread from ear to ear.
A rat crept softly through the vegetation
Dragging its slimy belly on the bank
While I was fishing in the dull canal
On a winter evening round behind the gashouse[2]   190
Musing upon the king my brother's wreck
And on the king my father's death before him.[3]
White bodies naked on the low damp ground
And bones cast in a little low dry garret,
Rattled by the rat's foot only, year to year.   195
But at my back from time to time I hear[4]
The sound of horns[5] and motors, which shall bring
Sweeney to Mrs. Porter[6] in the spring.
O the moon shone bright on Mrs. Porter[7]
And on her daughter   200
They wash their feet in soda water
Et O ces voix d'enfants, chantant dans la coupole![8]

Twit twit twit
Jug jug jug jug jug jug[9]

unable to "sing the Lord's song in a strange land." The meaning of "Leman" here can only be conjectured. Lake Leman, the Swiss name for Lake Geneva, had been frequently mentioned in nineteenth-century poetry celebrating natural beauty. Geneva was the seat of the League of Nations at the time *The Waste Land* was written. As late as Shakespeare, the common noun "leman" meant "friend," or sometimes "mistress." In Old English, it was derived from roots meaning "dear man" or "dear mankind," a fact which strengthens the association of this pun with the League of Nations.
1. See the note to l. 196.
2. *Cf.* the theme of the Fisher King. The "gashouse" district of a town is often the tenderloin section.
3. "*Cf. The Tempest*, I, ii" [Eliot's note]. See l. 48.
4. "*Cf.* Marvell, *To His Coy Mistress*" [Eliot's note]. In that poem, ll. 21–22 read: "But at my back I always hear / Time's winged chariot hurrying near."
5. "*Cf.* Day, *Parliament of Bees:* When of the sudden, listening, you shall hear, / A noise of horns and hunting, which shall bring /Actaeon to Diana in the spring, / Where all shall see her naked skin. . . ." [Eliot's note]. The chaste Diana, bathing naked, was spied upon by Actaeon, whereupon he was turned into a stag and killed by his own hunting dogs. But (next line), Sweeney was going to see Mrs. Porter.
6. Note that in "Sweeney Erect" (l. 39) the procuress was called Mrs. Turner.
7. "I do not know the origin of the ballad from which these lines are taken: it was reported to me from Sydney, Australia" [Eliot's note]. In a ragtime song, "Redwing," popular in the United States (1910–1915), the refrain began, "Oh, the moon shone bright on pretty Redwing" (an American Indian maid). Among the parodies of the song known to soldiers in World War I, was an indecent version dealing with a Mrs. Porter, who kept a brothel in Cairo.
8. "V. Verlaine, *Parsifal*" [Eliot's note]. The line is translated: "And O those children's voices, singing from the cupola" (or choir loft). In order to attain the Holy Grail, Parsifal resisted the seduction of Kundry, a temptress; his ordeals accomplished, Kundry humbly washed his feet, an act reminiscent of the adulteress who washed the feet of Christ (Luke vii: 37–38), and in contrast with the practices of Mrs. Porter and her daughter.
9. *Cf.* ll. 99–103. In old legends, the nightingale sang "Tereu" in plaintive memory of Tereus. In Elizabethan poetry the word "jug" was added, as

So rudely forc'd.   205
Tereu

Unreal City
Under the brown fog of a winter noon
Mr. Eugenides, the Smyrna merchant
Unshaven, with a pocket full of currants   210
C.i.f. London; documents at sight,[1]
Asked me in demotic[2] French
To luncheon at the Cannon Street Hotel
Followed by a weekend at the Metropole.

At the violet hour, when the eyes and back   215
Turn upward from the desk, when the human engine waits
Like a taxi throbbing waiting,
I Tiresias,[3] though blind, throbbing between two lives,
Old man with wrinkled female breasts, can see
At the violet hour, the evening hour that strives   220
Homeward, and brings the sailor home from sea,[4]

Eliot says (l. 103), for "dirty ears." The word "jug," derived from "juggler" was then a vulgarism indecently suggestive; see Shakespeare's *Henry VI, Part I*, Act V, Scene 4, l. 63: "She and the Dauphin have been juggling." Perhaps the most familiar poem employing the two words together is "Spring's Welcome," by John Lyly (1553–1606); ll. 2–3 read: "O 'tis the ravish'd nightingale. / Jug, jug, jug, jug, tereu! she cries * * *"

1. "The currants were quoted at a price 'carriage and insurance free to London'; and the Bill of Lading, etc., were to be handed to the buyer upon payment of the sight draft" [Eliot's note].

2. Cf. *demos*, "the people"; hence, "vulgar," describing such French as a commercial traveler picks up. Compare Mr. Eugenides with "the one-eyed merchant" of the Tarot cards (l. 52), who carried a pack of forbidden mysteries. Ancient Oriental merchants aided in the dissemination of myth, legend, and magic, but Eugenides' "mysteries" (ll. 213–214) are another matter (cf. the note to l. 218).

3. "Tiresias, although a mere spectator and not indeed a 'character,' is yet the most important personage in the poem, uniting all the rest. Just as the one-eyed merchant, seller of currants, melts into the Phoenician Sailor, and the latter is not wholly distinct from Ferdinand Prince of Naples [in *The Tempest*], so all the women are one woman, and the two sexes meet in Tiresias. The whole passage from

Ovid is of great anthropological interest" [Eliot's note]. Eliot then quotes the Latin text of *Metamorphoses*, III, 320–338. In this tale, Tiresias "struck violently with his staff two great serpents who were coupling in the forest"; he was immediately transformed into a woman. Eight years later he found the same serpents, and repeated the blow in order to reverse his fate; he at once recovered his manhood. Later, Jove was bantering Juno, jesting that those of her sex gained more pleasure from the act of love than the male gods. The controversy was referred to Tiresias, since he knew the pleasures of love "on both sides." When Tiresias "confirmed the dictum of Jove," the hypersensitive goddess "condemned him to eternal blindness." "Since no god is permitted to undo the work of another, the omnipotent father" compensated Tiresias with the power to foretell the future. In other legends his fame as a soothsayer became universal; even in Hades his shade gave advice to Ulysses (*Odyssey*, Book XI). Hence Eliot employs Tiresias as the all-experienced interpreter of the human misadventures represented in *The Waste Land*.

4. "This may not appear as exact as Sappho's lines, but I had in mind the 'longshore' or 'dory' fisherman, who returns at nightfall" [Eliot's note]. "Sappho's lines" are probably its fragment No. CXLIX, addressed to the Evening Star, "which summons back all that the light Dawn scattered —the sheep, the goat, the child to its

The typist home at teatime, clears her breakfast, lights
Her stove, and lays out food in tins.
Out of the window perilously spread
Her drying combinations touched by the sun's last rays,   225
On the divan are piled (at night her bed)
Stockings, slippers, camisoles, and stays.
I Tiresias, old man with wrinkled dugs
Perceived the scene, and foretold the rest—
I too awaited the expected guest.   230
He, the young man carbuncular, arrives,
A small house agent's clerk, with one bold stare,
One of the low on whom assurance sits
As a silk hat on a Bradford millionaire.[5]
The time is now propitious, as he guesses,   235
The meal is ended, she is bored and tired,
Endeavours to engage her in caresses
Which still are unreproved, if undesired.
Flushed and decided, he assaults at once;
Exploring hands encounter no defence;   240
His vanity requires no response,
And makes a welcome of indifference.
(And I Tiresias have foresuffered all
Enacted on this same divan or bed;
I who have sat by Thebes below the wall   245
And walked among the lowest of the dead.[6])
Bestows one final patronising kiss,
And gropes his way, finding the stairs unlit . . .

She turns and looks a moment in the glass,
Hardly aware of her departed lover;
Her brain allows one half-formed thought to pass: 250
'Well now that's done: and I'm glad it's over.'
When lovely woman stoops to folly[7] and
Paces about her room again, alone,
She smoothes her hair with automatic hand,   255
And puts a record on the gramophone.

mother." Eliot also echoes Stevenson's
"Requiem": "Home is the sailor,
home from the sea." Since blue and
violet are traditionally "Mary's
colors," the "violet hour" (1. 220)
contrasts ironically with the cheap intrigue that follows.
5. Bradford, in West Yorkshire, near
Leeds, had enjoyed an industrial
boom, and hence is here associated
with the newly rich upstart.
6. Tiresias prophesied in the market
place by the wall of Thebes for several generations before he was killed
at the destruction of the city; afterward he prophesied in Hades, where
Ulysses went to consult him.
7. "V. Goldsmith, the song in *The
Vicar of Wakefield*" [Eliot's note].
The song in Oliver Goldsmith's novel,
published in 1766, begins, "When
lovely woman stoops to folly," and
asserts that if the betrayed maiden
wishes to "wash her guilt away," her
only remedy "is to die."

'This music crept by me upon the waters'[8]
And along the Strand, up Queen Victoria Street.
O City city, I can sometimes hear
Beside a public bar in Lower Thames Street,   260
The pleasant whining of a mandoline
And a clatter and a chatter from within
Where fishmen lounge at noon: where the walls
Of Magnus Martyr hold[9]
Inexplicable splendour of Ionian white and gold.   265

> The river sweats[1]
> Oil and tar
> The barges drift
> With the turning tide
> Red sails   270
> Wide
> To leeward, swing on the heavy spar.
> The barges wash
> Drifting logs
> Down Greenwich reach   275
> Past the Isle of Dogs.[2]
>   Weialala leia
>   Wallala leialala

> Elizabeth and Leicester[3]
> Beating oars   280
> The stern was formed
> A gilded shell
> Red and gold
> The brisk swell

---

8. "V. *The Tempest,* as above [1. 48]" [Eliot's note].
9. "The interior of St. Magnus Martyr is to my mind one of the finest among Wren's interiors, * * * " [Eliot's note]. Its lofty steeple (1676), one of Sir Christopher Wren's masterpieces, rises amid the fertile hubbub of lowly life and fishhouse gossip along lower Thames Street near London Bridge, as Eliot significantly remarks.
1. "The Song of the (three) Thames-daughters begins here. From line 292 to 306 inclusive they speak in turn. V. *Götterdämmerung,* III, i: the Rhine-daughters" [Eliot's note]. In Wagner's opera the Rhine-daughters lament that the gold of the Nibelungs, which they guarded, has been stolen, and with it has gone their joy, and the beauty of the river. They implore the hero, Siegfried, to retrieve the treasure. Eliot imitates the rhythms of Wagner's lyrics, and also borrows the exact words of the refrain (ll. 277–278).
2. These place names associated with the modern port of London suggest the contrast between the Thames of the industrial present and Spenser's idyllic picture of the Thames of the past (*cf.* ll. 173–184).
3. The fruitless love of Queen Elizabeth for the Earl of Leicester (Sir Robert Dudley) is recalled by Eliot's note: "V. Froude, *Elizabeth,* Vol. I, ch. iv, letter of De Quadra to Philip of Spain: 'In the afternoon we were in a barge, watching games on the river. (The queen) was alone with Lord Robert and myself on the poop, when they began to talk nonsense, and went so far that Lord Robert at last said, as I was on the spot there was no reason why they should not be married if the queen pleased.' "

Rippled both shores[4]   28₅
Southwest wind
Carried down stream
The peal of bells
White towers
                    Weialala leia   290
                    Wallala leialala

'Trams and dusty trees.
Highbury bore me. Richmond and Kew[5]
Undid me. By Richmond I raised my knees
Supine on the floor of a narrow canoe.'   295

'My feet are at Moorgate,[6] and my heart
Under my feet. After the event
He wept. He promised "a new start."
I made no comment. What should I resent?'

'On Margate Sands.[7]   300
I can connect
Nothing with nothing.
The broken fingernails of dirty hands.
My people humble people who expect
Nothing.'   305
            la la

To Carthage then I came[8]

Burning burning burning burning[9]

4. In the six previous lines, Eliot suggests the phrases which Shakespeare employed to describe Cleopatra's barge (*cf.* l. 77). The courtly dalliance of Elizabeth and Leicester, and the heroic passion of Antony and Cleopatra, are thus associated with the two following episodes of contemporary life.
5. "*Cf. Purgatorio*, V, 133: *Ricorditi di me, che son la Pia; / Siena mi fé, disfecemi Maremma*" [Eliot's note]. Translate: "Remember me, who am la Pia, / Siena made me, Maremma unmade me." The second line earlier provided Pound with the title of the sordid seventh poem of *Mauberley*. Dante met Pia de' Tolomei of Siena, whose husband had murdered her in his castle at Maremma. By contrast, Eliot presents a girl from undistinguished Highbury in London. Richmond and Kew, the places of her undoing, are popular pleasure resorts; Richmond, a borough of London, contains a very large park with ample provisions for boating.

6. Moorgate, once the name of a gate of the London Wall, now designates a slum area in the same locality. The speaker is the second Thames-daughter.
7. Margate, a favorite seaside resort for London excursionists, in Kent, northeast of Dover; the place of seduction for the third Thames-daughter.
8. "V. St. Augustine's *Confessions:* 'to Carthage then I came, where a cauldron of unholy loves sang all about mine ears'" [Eliot's note]. From *Confessions*, III, i; pagan Carthage was considered to be a place of great licentiousness. In this passage, Augustine confesses that, famished for love but not yet knowing the love of God, he "defiled the waters of friendship with the filth of uncleanliness, and soiled its purity with * * * lustfulness."
9. "The complete text of the Buddha's Fire Sermon (which corresponds in importance to the Sermon on the Mount) from which these words are taken, will be found translated in the late Henry Clarke Warren's *Buddhism in Translation* (Harvard Orien-

O Lord Thou pluckest me out[1]
O Lord Thou pluckest   310

burning

IV. *Death by Water*[2] *lyric summaries motivation of development*

Phlebas the Phoenician, a fortnight dead,
Forgot the cry of gulls, and the deep sea swell
And the profit and loss.

             A current under sea   315
Picked his bones in whispers. As he rose and fell
He passed the stages of his age and youth
Entering the whirlpool.

             Gentile or Jew
O you who turn the wheel[3] and look to windward,   320
Consider Phlebas, who was once handsome and tall as you. *resolution*

V. *What the Thunder Said*[4]

After the torchlight red on sweaty faces

tal Series" [Eliot's note]. In his sermon, the Buddha warned against surrender to the senses, which are "on fire. With passion, . . . hatred, . . . infatuation, . . . birth, . . . old age, . . . death, . . . sorrow, . . . grief, . . . and despair are they on fire. [When the disciple] becomes purged of passion, * * * he becomes free; * * * he knows that rebirth is accomplished." For Christ's Sermon on the Mount, containing the most comprehensive account of His teaching, see Matthew v–vii.
1. "From St. Augustine's *Confessions* again. The collocation of these two representatives of eastern and western asceticism [Buddha and St. Augustine], as the culmination of this part of the poem, is not an accident" [Eliot's note]. St. Augustine's complete sentence was: "O Lord Thou pluckest me out of the burning." *Cf.* Zechariah iii: 1–2, "Joshua * * * a brand plucked out of the fire."
2. The title "Death by Water," suggests also the "living water" (John iv: 5–14), a principal subject in Part V. Water was a pagan symbol of fertility, with ritualistic functions in the worship of Tammuz, Adonis, and Siva (see Frazer, *The Golden Bough*, which Eliot noted as a source). The god was immersed in the rivers to promote the fertility of land and people, or was given water burial in winter and resurrected in the spring. The intention of Eliot's lyric is made evident by its history: he wrote it first in French as a conclusion for the poem, "Dans le Restaurant" (*Poems*, 1920), a disgusted excoria-

tion of an old waiter who gloats obscenely over his senile memory of an attempt, at the age of seven, to violate a little girl "under the wet willows." In the present work, Eliot has already associated Phlebas the Phoenician with Ferdinand (ll. 47–48). He seems to be associated too with the merchant, Eugenides (ll. 52 and 209); also in the French version Phlebas is a merchant sailor from Cornwall, absorbed in "the profits and losses and the cargoes of tin." The ancient Phoenicians were great Mediterranean traders; hence Phlebas in part symbolizes materialistic mercantilism.
3. Literally, the wheel of the helmsman, but note also the "wheel" of the whirlpool (ll. 315–318). Eliot places "the Wheel" in the Tarot pack (l. 51). The Tarot Wheel is depicted as responding to two competing forces—on the one hand, Anubis, an Egyptian divinity who conducts and watches over the dead; on the other, the Greek Typhon (Typhoeus), an all-devouring monster of evil—and thus it symbolizes the nature of man's fate in eternity.
4. "In the first part of Part V three themes are employed: the journey to Emmaus, the approach to the Chapel Perilous (see Miss Weston's book), and the present decay of eastern Europe" [Eliot's note]. On the journey to Emmaus, on the third day after He was crucified, Christ first proved His resurrection to His disciples by appearing to two of them; the Chapel Perilous was the place of the Christian knight's final ordeal in quest of

After the frosty silence in the gardens[5]
After the agony in stony places
The shouting and the crying   325
Prison and palace and reverberation
Of thunder of spring over distant mountains
He who was living is now dead
We who were living are now dying
With a little patience   330

Here is no water but only rock[6]
Rock and no water and the sandy road
The road winding above among the mountains
Which are mountains of rock without water
If there were water we should stop and drink   335
Amongst the rock one cannot stop or think
Sweat is dry and feet are in the sand
If there were only water amongst the rock
Dead mountain mouth of carious teeth that cannot spit
Here one can neither stand nor lie nor sit   340
There is not even silence in the mountains
But dry sterile thunder without rain
There is not even solitude in the mountains
But red sullen faces sneer and snarl
From doors of mudcracked houses   345
                                        If there were water

And no rock
If there were rock
And also water
And water   350
A spring
A pool among the rock
If there were the sound of water only
Not the cicada
And dry grass singing   355
But sound of water over a rock
Where the hermit-thrush sings in the pine trees
Drip drop drip drop drop drop drop[7]
But there is no water

the Grail, the symbol of faith; and the decay of civilization is evidence of infidelity to Christian revelation.
5. Of "the gardens," one was Gethsemane, the scene of Christ's final temptation, prayer, and dedication (see Matthew xxvi: 36–45); the other was a garden on Golgotha, the hill of the Crucifixion, where the disciples buried Him in a new tomb (see John xix: 41–42). This passage (ll. 322–330) recapitulates the events of Christ's Passion: the agony of Gethsemane, the betrayal, imprisonment, trial, crucifixion, and burial.
6. The following thirty-six lines deal with the journey to Emmaus. But the country traversed by the bereft and grieving disciples recalls another "waste land" described by Ezekiel and Ecclesiastes (see Part I, ll. 19–30) as resulting from human infidelity to God.
7. Eliot's note refers to the "water-

Who is the third who walks always beside you?[8]   360
When I count, there are only you and I together
But when I look ahead up the white road
There is always another one walking beside you
Gliding wrapt in a brown mantle, hooded
I do not know whether a man or a woman   365
—But who is that on the other side of you?

What is that sound high in the air[9]
Murmur of maternal lamentation
Who are those hooded hordes swarming
Over endless plains, stumbling in cracked earth   370
Ringed by the flat horizon only
What is the city over the mountains
Cracks and reforms and bursts in the violet air
Falling towers
Jerusalem Athens Alexandria   375
Vienna London
Unreal

A woman drew her long black hair out tight
And fiddled whisper music on those strings
And bats with baby faces in the violet light   380
Whistled, and beat their wings
And crawled head downward down a blackened wall
And upside down in air were towers
Tolling reminiscent bells, that kept the hours
And voices singing out of empty cisterns and exhausted wells.   385

In this decayed hole among the mountains
In the faint moonlight, the grass is singing
Over the tumbled graves, about the chapel[1]

dripping song" of the hermit thrush,
"which I have heard in Quebec
Province."
8. "The following lines were stimulated by the account of one of the
Antarctic expeditions (I forget which,
but I think one of Shackleton's): it
was related that the party of explorers, at the extremity of their
strength, had the constant delusion
that there was *one more member* than
could actually be counted" [Eliot's
note]. On the journey to Emmaus, the
two disciples, in desperation and grief
at the death of Jesus, were joined by
a wayfarer whom they were not permitted to recognize. This companion
argued from Scripture that their dead
Lord was indeed the foretold Messiah.
Later, as he blessed the bread at the
inn, "they knew him; and he vanished
out of their sight." See Luke, xxiv:
13–34.
9. Ll. 367–377 express forebodings
concerning the Russian Revolution,
begun in 1917. Eliot quotes a passage
from the German text of Hermann
Hesse, *Blick ins Chaos* (1920), here
translated in part: "Already half of
Europe, or surely at least half of
Eastern Europe, is on the way to
chaos, traveling drunken, with a kind
of sanctified ecstasy, headlong toward
the abyss, and singing the while, singing drunken hymns, as Dmitri Karamazov sang." *Cf.* Dostoevski, *The
Brothers Karamazov*.
1. The Chapel Perilous of the Grail
legends, where, if the knight endured
his terrible last ordeals, he might
hope to gain the Grail the next day.
He has traversed a world grown ut-

There is the empty chapel, only the wind's home.
It has no windows, and the door swings,   390
Dry bones can harm no one.
Only a cock stood on the rooftree
Co co rico co co rico[2]
In a flash of lightning. Then a damp gust
Bringing rain   395

Ganga[3] was sunken, and the limp leaves
Waited for rain, while the black clouds
Gathered far distant, over Himavant.
The jungle crouched, humped in silence.
Then spoke the thunder   400
DA
Datta: what have we given?[4]
My friend, blood shaking my heart
The awful daring of a moment's surrender
Which an age of prudence can never retract   405
By this, and this only, we have existed
Which is not to be found in our obituaries
Or in memories draped by the beneficent spider[5]
Or under seals broken by the lean solicitor
In our empty rooms   410
DA
Dayadhvam: I have heard the key[6]
Turn in the door once and turn once only

terly fantastic in its disorder (ll. 377–385) only to find the Chapel ruined and empty.

2. Peter three times denied his Master, and "immediately the cock crew," as Jesus had predicted (Matthew xxvi: 34 and 74).

3. The ancient Sanskrit name for the river Ganges, in India. The Himalaya Mountains ("Himavant" in l. 398), were regarded as a deity, the mother of Devi, who was the consort of Siva; Devi and Siva were, among other things, goddess and god of fertility. The Ganges River, taking its source in the Himalayas, was worshiped as the sacred disseminator of fertility. At the spring festivals, maidens cast images of Siva into its waters; the ashes of devout Hindus are still returned to this source.

4. " 'Datta, dayadhvam, damyata' (Give, sympathize, control). The fable of the meaning of the Thunder is found in the *Brihadaranyaka-Upanishad,* 5, 1. A translation is found in Deussen's *Sechzig Upanishads des Veda,* p. 489" [Eliot's note]. In choosing this literature, Eliot suggests

the continuity with later religions of the earliest recorded religious experience of the race. This is emphasized by the words in Sanskrit, the hypothetical parent of the Indo-European languages of Western culture. For example, with *Datta* compare the Latin *do, dare, datus,* "to give."

5. "*Cf.* Webster, *The White Devil,* V, vi: '. . . they'll remarry / Ere the worm pierce your winding-sheet, ere the spider / Make a thin curtain for your epitaphs' " [Eliot's note].

6. "*Cf. Inferno,* XXXIII, 46: *ed io sentii chiavar l'uscio di sotto / all' orrible torre*" [Eliot's note]. These lines are translated: "And I heard being locked below me the door of the horrible tower." They are part of the story told to Dante, in one of the innermost circles of Hell, by the traitor Count Ugolino of Pisa, who with Archbishop Ruggieri plotted the ruin of his grandson. But Ugolino was in turn imprisoned by Ruggieri, with his four sons, and starved to death. Dante finds the Count in Hell, gnawing upon the head of the traitorous Archbishop.

We think of the key, each in his prison[7]
Thinking of the key, each confirms a prison   415
Only at nightfall, aethereal rumours
Revive for a moment a broken Coriolanus[8]
DA
Damyata: The boat responded
Gaily, to the hand expert with sail and oar   420
The sea was calm, your heart would have responded
Gaily, when invited, beating obedient
To controlling hands[9]

I sat upon the shore
Fishing,[1] with the arid plain behind me   425
Shall I at least set my lands in order?[2]
London Bridge is falling down falling down falling down
Poi s'ascose nel foco che gli affina[3]
Quando fiam uti chelidon[4]—O swallow swallow
Le Prince d'Aquitaine à la tour abolie[5]   430

7. Referring to the Dante passage above, Eliot cites F. H. Bradley, *Appearance and Reality* (1893), p. 346: "My external sensations are no less private to myself than are my thoughts or my feelings. In either case my experience falls within my own circle, a circle closed on the outside; and with all its elements alike, every sphere is opaque to the others which surround it.... In brief, regarded as an existence which appears in a soul, the whole world for each is peculiar and private to that soul."

8. Gnaeus Marcius Coriolanus (fifth century B.C.). Shakespeare in *Coriolanus* followed the legendary account in Plutarch's *Lives*. During a disturbance by the starving plebeians, this patrician leader was exiled for proposing that the poor be fed from the public Roman store only in return for the dissolution of their tribunate. In exile he became a great leader of the Volscians, but they executed him when he spared Rome, his native city. See also Eliot's two "Coriolan" poems, and "A Cooking Egg," l. 11.

9. *Cf.* Part IV, "Death by Water."

1. "V. Weston: *From Ritual to Romance,* chapter on the Fisher King" [Eliot's note]. Consider the symbolic relations of the fish, water, and fertility. The fish also became an early Christian symbol—the letters of the Greek *ichthys* ("fish") were the initial letters of the Greek words for "Jesus Christ, of God the Son, Saviour." *Cf.* "fishing in the dull canal," l. 189.

2. Isaiah xxxviii: 1: "Thus saith the Lord, Set thine house in order: for thou shalt die, and not live."

3. The last line of a passage which Eliot quotes in his footnote: "V. *Purgatorio* XXVI, 148. '*Ara vos prec per aquella valor / que vos guida al som de l'escalina, / sovegna vos a temps de ma dolor.' / Poi s'ascose nel foco che gli affina.*" In these lines the twelfth-century Provençal poet Arnaut Daniel, remembering his early lustfulness, for which he was condemned, addresses Dante: "I pray you now, by the Goodness that guides you to the summit of this staircase, bethink you in due season of my suffering." Then (as asserted in the line Eliot quotes in l. 428), "he disappeared into the flame that refines them." In 1919, Eliot had entitled a small volume *Ara Vos Prec.* In 1930 he introduced the exclamation *sovegna vos* in *Ash-Wednesday,* and he separately published the "staircase" section of that work (Part III) as "Som de l'Escalina." Evidently this passage from Dante had great meaning for him.

4. "V. *Pervigilium Veneris. Cf.* Philomela in Parts II and III" [Eliot's note]. The Latin phrase in the text means: "When shall I be like the swallow"; it is followed in the original Latin poem by the phrase, "and be free from dumb distress"—recalling Arnaut Daniel's hope of redemption. *Pervigilium Veneris,* an anonymous poem supposed to have been written in the second century A.D., celebrates the joy of all nature at the festival of Venus.

5. "V. Gerard de Nerval, Sonnet *El Desdichado*" [Eliot's note]. The French line is translated: "The Prince of Aquitaine at the ruined tower." One of the group of de Nerval's selections

These fragments I have shored against my ruins
Why then Ile fit you. Hieronymo's mad againe.[6]
Datta. Dayadhvam. Damyata.
          Shantih   shantih   shantih[7]

                                                    1922

Marina[8]

Quis hic locus, quae regio, quae mundi plaga?[9]

What seas what shores what grey rocks and what islands
What water lapping the bow
And scent of pine and the woodthrush singing through the fog
What images return
O my daughter.   5

Those who sharpen the tooth of the dog, meaning
Death
Those who glitter with the glory of the hummingbird, meaning
Death

entitled *The Chimeras* (*Les Chimères*), this poem represents the speaker as "shadow shrouded, the widower, the unconsolable."
6. "V. Kyd's *Spanish Tragedy*" [Eliot's note]. Subtitled "Hieronymo Is Mad Again," Thomas Kyd's play (1594) is one of the most violent Elizabethan tragedies in the Senecan tradition. Hieronymo, requested by the King to write an entertainment for the court, replied, "Why, then Ile fit you!" (*i.e.*, "accommodate you"). He wrote a play in which he, as an actor, was able to kill the murderers of his son. He then killed himself.
7. "Shanti. Repeated as here, a formal ending to an Upanishad. 'The Peace which passeth understanding' is our equivalent to this word" [Eliot's note]. The Upanishads are treatises on theology, part of the Vedas, the ancient Hindu sacred literature. Eliot's translation of the Sanskrit *shantih* recalls various benedictions and salutations of Paul in his Epistles, particularly Philippians iv: 7: "And the peace of God, which passeth all understanding, shall keep your hearts and minds through Christ Jesus."
8. To *Pericles, Prince of Tyre* (1608?), Shakespeare contributed the last two acts, initiating, in the story of Marina, the theme of the idealized daughter which persisted during his last period, notably in *The Tempest*. In Act V, Scene 1, Pericles miraculously finds again his daughter,

Marina, so called because she was born in a storm at sea. A second storm in her babyhood had bereft the sailor-prince of both wife and daughter. During years of roving adventure, Prince Pericles steadfastly loved his daughter, presumably dead. He finds her an escaped slave, grown to lovely girlhood, and by saving her from further danger gains his place in her love. In Eliot's poem such a father, after years of seeking, re-enacts in reverie the pilgrimage of his past in the cathedral light of rediscovered passion and purity. Eliot, says F. O. Matthiessen (*The Achievement of T. S. Eliot*, p. 150) "recognizes a vision of idealized loveliness in the first adolescent awakening," and "the loss of such loveliness in the failure of actual sexual experience * * * Regaining the purified vision in later life is the theme * * * of 'Marina.' "
9. "What place is this; what region; what quarter of the universe?" (Seneca, *Hercules Furens*, l. 1138). In Seneca's tragedy, Hercules, driven mad by the jealous Hera (Juno), kills his wife and children; but Minerva, goddess of wisdom, takes him in charge and brings him to his senses in a strange place, whereupon he utters the words of the epigraph. In contrast with that of Hercules, the feeling of guilt experienced by Pericles arises only from a belated sense of responsibility for the loss of his wife and daughter.

Those who sit in the stye of contentment, meaning 10
Death
Those who suffer the ecstasy of the animals,[1] meaning
Death

Are become unsubstantial, reduced by a wind,
A breath of pine, and the woodsong fog 15
By this grace dissolved in place

What is this face, less clear and clearer
The pulse in the arm, less strong and stronger—
Given or lent? more distant than stars and nearer than the eye

Whispers and small laughter between leaves and hurrying feet 20
Under sleep, where all the waters meet.

Bowsprit cracked with ice and paint cracked with heat.
I made this, I have forgotten
And remember.
The rigging weak and the canvas rotten 25
Between one June and another September.[2]
Made this unknowing, half conscious, unknown, my own.
The garboard strake[3] leaks, the seams need caulking.
This form, this face, this life
Living to live in a world of time beyond me; let me 30
Resign my life for this life, my speech for that unspoken,
The awakened, lips parted, the hope, the new ships.

What seas what shores what granite islands towards my timbers
And woodthrush calling through the fog
My daughter. 35

1930

Burnt Norton[4]

τοῦ λόγου δ'ἐόντος ξυνοῦ ζώουσιν οἱ πολλοί
ὡς ἰδίαν ἔχοντες φρόνησιν.—I. p. 77. Fr. 2.

ὁδὸς ἄνω κάτω μία καὶ ὡυτή.—I. p. 89. Fr. 60.

—DIELS, DIE FRAGMENTE DER VORSOKRATIKER (HERAKLEITOS)

1. In the play *Pericles*, Marina first introduces herself to her unsuspecting father by singing a song beginning: "Amongst the harlots foul I walk, / Yet harlot none am I."
2. That is, not the *next* September, but the previous one, marking an interval of nine months. The associated figures of child and ship are simultaneously presented in ll. 22–29.
3. The planking next to the keel of any boat, hence the most vital spot.
4. "Burnt Norton" was written in 1934, in association with five small "Landscapes." It was included among the *Collected Poems* of 1936. In 1943 it appeared as the first of the *Four Quartets*, a unified work. There is a symphonic development and accumulation of themes throughout the four poems, while the last, "Little Gidding," is a resolution of the whole. Like *The Waste Land*, each "Quartet" has five parts, and comparable parts have a similar form and function in each of the four poems. The analogy of this organization with musical structure, particularly that of the sonata or of Beethoven's later quartets, is worthy of study.

I

Time present and time past
Are both perhaps present in time future,
And time future contained in time past.
If all time is eternally present
All time is unredeemable.[6]   5
What might have been is an abstraction
Remaining a perpetual possibility
Only in a world of speculation.
What might have been and what has been
Point to one end, which is always present.   10
Footfalls echo in the memory
Down the passage which we did not take
Towards the door we never opened
Into the rose-garden.[7] My words echo
Thus, in your mind.

The *Four Quartets* are an extended
meditation on the religious concept
of immortality, and a reasoned analysis of the Christian mysticism. In
"Burnt Norton" and "East Coker"
the poet makes symbolic use of "pure"
concepts of science—of such "abso-
lutes" as infinity and dynamic compensation ("At the still point of the
turning world"); these are contrasted
with human consciousness and historical experience. In "The Dry Sal-
vages" and "Little Gidding" the poet
assumes these arguments as contributing to our understanding of revelation, particularly such Christian revelations as the mystical experience in
which "the saint" is enabled "to apprehend / The point of intersection of
the timeless / With time." Such pure
revelation is accepted as an absolute,
confirming the doctrine of immortal salvation by God's Grace, extended through
man's faith in the Annunciation and the
Incarnation of Jesus Christ, and the descent of the Holy Spirit upon the
apostles at the Pentecost. The continuing Grace of this supernal union—
the overarching theme of the *Quartets*
—Eliot found in those later Christian
mystics who had described a state of
exalted contemplation in which it was
granted them to realize an absorption,
untranslatable in physical terms, in the
Eternal Goodness, still and timeless. In
these poems Eliot was chiefly indebted
to St. John of the Cross (1542–1591),
a Spanish mystic who reported his experience in *The Dark Night of the Soul*
and *The Ascent of Mt. Carmel.*
    In "Burnt Norton," Eliot bases the
pyramid of the *Four Quartets* on a contrast of the relativity of mortal consciousness, time, and memory with the

absolute reality of the Timeless Eternal;
and he suggests, in Part V, a new
semantics (or perhaps a very old one)
for translating the symbols of human
experience into immortal terms.
    Burnt Norton is identified as a manor
in Gloucestershire near which Eliot has
resided.
    The Greek epigraphs are translated:
"But although the Word [*logos*] is common to all, the majority of people live
as though they had each an understanding peculiarly their own"; and "The
way up and way down is one and the
same." Heraclitus (Herakleitos), Greek
philosopher (540?–475? B.C.), emphasized two concepts: unity ("all things
come out of the One, and the One out
of all things"), and flux ("you cannot
step twice into the same river, for fresh
waters are ever flowing in upon you").
Since Eliot has associated Heraclitus
with the *Quartets*, it is also of interest
that he attended the lectures of Henri
Bergson (1859–1941) at the Sorbonne
in 1911. Bergson was concerned with
time and consciousness, and found their
reality to lie in their mobility, in the
infinite flux, not in the particular moment (*cf*. ll. 85–89).
6. See Ecclesiastes iii: 14–15: " * * *
whatsoever God doeth, it shall be for
ever * * * That which hath been is
now; and that which is to be hath already been; and God requireth that
which is past."
7. The persons in the rose-garden are
identified as children (l. 40 and ll. 172–
173). The revelation simultaneously experienced of sexual and spiritual significance is experienced by children at play in a garden
several times in Eliot's poems. In "New
Hampshire," written just before "Burnt
Norton," a boy and girl play in an apple

But to what purpose   15
Disturbing the dust on a bowl of rose-leaves
I do not know.
                    Other echoes
Inhabit the garden. Shall we follow?
Quick, said the bird, find them, find them,
Round the corner. Through the first gate,   20
Into our first world, shall we follow
The deception of the thrush? Into our first world.
There they were, dignified, invisible,
Moving without pressure, over the dead leaves,
In the autumn heat, through the vibrant air,   25
And the bird called, in response to
The unheard music hidden in the shrubbery,
And the unseen eyebeam crossed,[8] for the roses
Had the look of flowers that are looked at.
There they were as our guests, accepted and accepting.   30
So we moved, and they, in a formal pattern,
Along the empty alley, into the box circle,
To look down into the drained pool.
Dry the pool, dry concrete, brown edged,
And the pool was filled with water out of sunlight,   35
And the lotos rose, quietly, quietly,
The surface glittered out of heart of light,[1]
And they were behind us, reflected in the pool.
Then a cloud passed, and the pool was empty.
Go, said the bird, for the leaves were full of children,   40
Hidden excitedly, containing laughter.
Go, go, go, said the bird: human kind
Cannot bear very much reality.
Time past and time future
What might have been and what has been   45
Point to one end, which is always present.

orchard visited by a bird. In the present passage (ll. 13–43) the bird reappears as a thrush, while the rose-garden contains "echoes" (l. 17) recalling "our first world" (ll. 21–22)—the garden of Eden (*cf.* Genesis iii: 2–5). Thus "time present and time past" (l. 1) are made to correspond. The rose, persisting through the *Quartets* into their very last line, is an established symbol of love or sex, but often of a spiritually sublimated kind. Dante (*Paradiso*, xxiii, 73–74) saw the Virgin Mary in heaven as "the Rose, wherein the Word of God / Made itself flesh"; and he depicted the highest heaven (*Paradiso*, xxx) as a great white rose of supernal light (*rosa sempiterna*),

to which Eliot alludes here (l. 16), and in the last "Quartet."
8. *Cf.* John Donne, "The Ecstasy": "Our eye-beams twisted"; the intensity of the passion is carried forward to the roses, in the next line.
1. Having traversed Paradise through lower levels of increasing brightness, Dante is permitted to glimpse the blinding supernal radiance of Father, Son, and Holy Spirit in threefold unity (*Paradiso*, xxxiii). Thus his phrase "heart of light" (l. 37) lends innocence to the preceding sexual imagery (ll. 28–36). But note the threatened fall of man from this "reality" (l. 43).

II

Garlic and sapphires in the mud[2]
Clot the bedded axle-tree.
The trilling wire in the blood
Sings below inveterate scars   50
And reconciles forgotten wars.
The dance along the artery
The circulation of the lymph
Are figured in the drift of stars
Ascend to summer in the tree   55
We move above the moving tree
In light upon the figured leaf
And hear upon the sodden floor
Below, the boarhound and the boar
Pursue their pattern as before   60
But reconciled among the stars.

At the still point of the turning world.[3] Neither flesh nor fleshless;
Neither from nor towards; at the still point, there the dance is,
But neither arrest nor movement. And do not call it fixity,
Where past and future are gathered. Neither movement from nor
    towards,   65
Neither ascent nor decline. Except for the point, the still point,
There would be no dance, and there is only the dance.[4]
I can only say, *there* we have been: but I cannot say where.
And I cannot say, how long, for that is to place it in time.

The inner freedom from the practical desire,   70
The release from action and suffering, release from the inner
And the outer compulsion, yet surrounded
By a grace of sense, a white light still and moving,[5]
Erhebung[6] without motion, concentration

2. In a sonnet by the French symbolist Stéphane Mallarmé, beginning, *"M'introduire dans ton histoire,"* l. 10 reads, *"Tonnerre et rubis aux moyeux"* ["Thunder and rubies at the hubs"]. Mallarmé further speaks of riding the sky in "chariots [poems] with fire-pierced wheels, the only vesperal of the * * * dying evening." Eliot's chariot is imbedded in "mud" (*cf.* the sound of *moyeux*), where the beauty of sapphires mingles with garlic (*cf. tonnerre,* "thunder." *Herbe du tonnerre,* "herb of thunder," is French for the houseleek; this plant is popularly confused with the leek, a close relative of garlic, whose name is derived from Old English *gar,* "lance," plus *leac,* "leek.")
3. Eliot used this phrase before, in "Triumphal March" (1931), one of the

"Coriolan" poems. Noting this, Matthiessen observes (*The Achievement of T. S. Eliot,* p. 184): "This notion of 'a mathematically pure point' (as Philip Wheelright called it) seems to be Eliot's poetic equivalent in our cosmology for Dante's 'unmoved mover'" (*i.e.,* the eternal Being).
4. *Cf.* G. W. F. Hegel, *The Phenomenology of Mind:* "The truth is thus the bacchanalian revel, where not a member is sober; and because every member no sooner becomes detached than it *eo ipso* collapses straightway, the revel is just as much a state of transparent unbroken calm."
5. *Cf.* Dante's vision of the eternal Light (*Paradiso,* xxxiii, 76–135).
6. German for "exaltation," "loftiness."

Without elimination, both a new world   75
And the old made explicit, understood
In the completion of its partial ecstasy,
The resolution of its partial horror.[7]
Yet the enchainment past and future
Woven in the weakness of the changing body,   80
Protects mankind from heaven and damnation
Which flesh cannot endure.

                            Time past and time future
Allow but a little consciousness.
To be conscious is not to be in time[8]   85
But only in time can the moment in the rose-garden,
The moment in the arbour where the rain beat,
The moment in the draughty church at smokefall
Be remembered;[9] involved with past and future.
Only through time time is conquered.   90

III

Here is a place of disaffection
Time before and time after
In a dim light: neither daylight
Investing form with lucid stillness
Turning shadow into transient beauty   95
With slow rotation suggesting permanence
Nor darkness to purify the soul
Emptying the sensual with deprivation
Cleansing affection from the temporal.[1]
Neither plenitude nor vacancy. Only a flicker   100
Over the strained time-ridden faces
Distracted from distraction by distraction
Filled with fancies and empty of meaning
Tumid apathy with no concentration
Men and bits of paper, whirled by the cold wind   105
That blows before and after time,
Wind in and out of unwholesome lungs
Time before and time after.
Eructation[2] of unhealthy souls
Into the faded air, the torpid   110
Driven on the wind that sweeps the gloomy hills of London,

7. St. John of the Cross, in *The Dark Night of the Soul,* represents the condition that Eliot describes (ll. 70–82) as being the last stage of the mystic's preparation for unity with God. In that condition he has attained passivity in submissive contemplation of the will and majesty of God.
8. *Cf.* Bergson, *Time and Free Will:* "Pure duration is the form which our conscious states assume when our ego lets itself *live,* when it refrains from separating its present state from its former states."
9. *Cf.* Bergson, *Matter and Memory:* "Memory is just the intersection of mind and matter."
1. *Cf.* I John ii: 15–17: "Love not the world, neither the things that are in the world, * * * For all that is in the world * * * passeth away * * * but he that doeth the will of God abideth for ever."
2. *I.e.*, the belching forth.

Hampstead and Clerkenwell, Campden and Putney,
Highgate, Primrose and Ludgate. Not here
Not here the darkness, in this twittering world.

Descend lower, descend only   115
Into the world of perpetual solitude,
World not world, but that which is not world,
Internal darkness, deprivation
And destitution of all property,
Desiccation of the world of sense,   120
Evacuation of the world of fancy,
Inoperancy of the world of spirit;
This is the one way, and the other
Is the same, not in movement
But abstention from movement; while the world moves   125
In appetency, on its metalled ways
Of time past and time future.

IV

Time and the bell have buried the day,
The black cloud carries the sun away.
Will the sunflower turn to us, will the clematis   130
Stray down, bend to us; tendril and spray
Clutch and cling?
Chill
Fingers of yew[3] be curled
Down on us? After the kingfisher's[4] wing   135
Has answered light to light,[5] and is silent, the light is still
At the still point of the turning world.

V

Words move, music moves
Only in time; but that which is only living
Can only die. Words, after speech, reach   140
Into the silence. Only by the form, the pattern,
Can words or music reach
The stillness, as a Chinese jar still
Moves perpetually in its stillness.
Not the stillness of the violin, while the note lasts,   145
Not that only, but the co-existence,
Or say that the end precedes the beginning,
And the end and the beginning were always there

3. The names of the flowers and tree in this lyric all have double meanings. The sunflower is of course the flower of light; clematis is popularly called "virgin's-bower"; the yew, a tree or shrub, has been traditionally associated with death and immortality.
4. *Cf.* the Fisher King of *The Waste Land*, associated in the Christian romances with Christ, who called his apostles "fishers of men" (Matthew iv: 18–19).
5. *Cf.* Dante, *Paradiso*, xxxiii, 109–120. The triune, supernal radiance of Dante's vision of the Godhead "answered light to light": he saw, "as rainbow upon rainbow," three circles "each an equal whole," forming "one sole aspect of divine essence."

Before the beginning and after the end.
And all is always now. Words strain, 150
Crack and sometimes break, under the burden,
Under the tension, slip, slide, perish,
Decay with imprecision, will not stay in place,
Will not stay still. Shrieking voices
Scolding, mocking, or merely chattering, 155
Always assail them. The Word in the desert
Is most attacked by voices of temptation,[6]
The crying shadow in the funeral dance,
The loud lament of the disconsolate chimera.

The detail of the pattern is movement, 160
As in the figure of the ten stairs.[7]
Desire itself is movement
Not in itself desirable;
Love is itself unmoving,
Only the cause and end of movement, 165
Timeless, and undesiring
Except in the aspect of time
Caught in the form of limitation
Between un-being and being.
Sudden in a shaft of sunlight 170
Even while the dust moves
There rises the hidden laughter
Of children in the foliage
Quick now, here, now, always—
Ridiculous the waste sad time 175
Stretching before and after.

1934   1936, 1943

6. *Cf.* the temptation of Christ in the wilderness (Luke iv: 1–4).
7. Eliot has identified "the ten stairs" as referring to the "Mystical Ladder of Divine Love," described by St. John of the Cross as having ten steps up which the soul of an individual rises, in ten stages of love for God. On the final step, "the soul becomes wholly assimilated into God in the beatific vision, * * * being perfectly purified by love." Eliot's lines (ll. 160–161) imply both a constant condition, which is the unchanging and perfect love of God ("the pattern"), and the "detail of the pattern," which is the "movement" of the mortal soul through the stages of realization of this love.

moral or amoral pt of view—morality diff. fr. Nature
psychological reality
cf. naturalistic fiction

ROBINSON JEFFERS
(1887–1962)

"Long ago," Jeffers wrote in the foreword to *The Selected Poetry* of *Robinson Jeffers* (1938), "* * * it became evident to

Primitivism—ritualistic aspect—a kind of
subconscious sociology—a recognition of
human impulses—more primitive culture, may
by examination of learn more about our own code of life

takes us more deeply into man's soul

me that poetry—if it was to survive at all—must reclaim some of the power and reality that it was so hastily surrendering to prose. The modern French poetry of that time, and the most 'modern' of the English poetry, seemed to me thoroughly defeatist, as if poetry were in terror of prose, and desperately trying to save its soul from the victor by giving up its body. It was becoming slight and fantastic, unreal, eccentric; and was not even saving its soul, for these are generally anti-poetic qualities. It must reclaim substance and sense, and physical and psychological reality. This feeling has been basic to my mind since then. It led me to write narrative poetry, and to draw the subjects from contemporary life; to present aspects of life that modern poetry had generally avoided; and to attempt the expression of philosophic and scientific ideas in verse. It was not in my mind to open up new fields for poetry, but only to reclaim old freedom."

John Robinson Jeffers was born on January 10, 1887, in Pittsburgh, Pennsylvania, where his father was professor of biblical languages and literature in Western Theological Seminary. In his early youth he was rigorously disciplined by his father in the classics and languages, attended schools in Switzerland and Germany, and traveled widely on the Continent and in England with his family. With advanced standing he entered the University of Pittsburgh (as it is now called), but on the removal of his family to California he transferred to Occi-

dental College, from which he was graduated at the precocious age of eighteen. After a term at the University of Zurich, he returned to the United States, and obtained his M.A. in literature at the University of Southern California. Although he had read widely in the classics and in German and French literature, and felt the desire to write, he had not found his subject. Meanwhile his profound interest in science drew him to the School of Medicine at the University of Southern California, which he attended for three years before transferring to the University of Washington to study forestry. In 1912, however, when a modest inheritance assured him an income, he turned again to writing, and published *Flagons and Apples*, a volume of love poems which shows little promise of his later originality.

In 1913 Una Call, whom he had met seven years earlier, was free to marry, and they settled at Carmel, California, before that wild and beautiful shore was surrounded first by an artists' colony and later by war industry. There on the cliffs facing the sea, he built Hawk Tower and Tor House from sea-cobbles, and secured seclusion by surrounding them with a small forest. There he lived in studious and creative privacy all his life. This is also the early Steinbeck country (see "The Red Pony"), and Jeffers, like Steinbeck, became interested in the primitive life of the older generation of hill people and herders and in the survivals of Indian and Spanish culture mingled in their folkways. Their tragedies

not complex at level of construction
rhythmic reading that attends to meaning (sense irregular) based on regular interval; isochronous interval)

Stoicism - accepts conditions & attempts to find a citadel

vigour & irregularity of 54 syllables long lines

and their emotional attitudes seemed to accord at once with the primitive elements of Greek literature and with the understanding of the subconscious which he had derived from his reading of Freudian psychology. A third and harmonious factor was what Una Jeffers once described as "the spirit of this place."

Jeffers developed a style of great flexibility and lyric beauty, something between blank verse and free verse, in which the tones of colloquial speech are reproduced without weakening the poet's formal control of the line. In his narratives the lines are of unusual length, providing amplitude and luxuriance; however, he accomplished in his lyrics the same rhythmic freedom for shorter lines in stanzaic composition. This highly individualistic style was heightened by the poet's musical sense and the semantic precision of his diction.

Jeffers' style is most effective in the tragic narratives, and especially in those with the greatest dramatic quality. These are in fact his unique contribution to our literature: *Tamar, Roan Stallion, The Tower Beyond Tragedy, Cawdor, The Loving Shepherdess, Thurso's Landing,* and *Give Your Heart to the Hawks.* Jeffers might have given us a genuine revival of the poetic drama, had the times been propitious. *The Tower Beyond Tragedy,* published in *Tamar and Other Poems* (1924), is a presentation of the Agamemnon story in dialogue form, with emphasis on the incest, madness, and return to sanity of Orestes —a reconstruction of the original that gives scope to the author's psychological analysis of the disease of humanity. Judith Anderson appeared briefly in a nonprofessional performance of this work and also acted in the author's reconstruction of the *Medea* (1946), which brought the spirit of Euripides alive on the American stage in one of the most memorable of recent productions. At least in this play this notable poet again recaptured the power of his earlier work. *The Cretan Woman,* a tragedy on the Phædra story, was produced in 1954. Jeffers died in 1962.

There is no collected edition of the poetry of Jeffers, but the *Selected Poetry of Robinson Jeffers,* 1938, provides a cross section. The principal individual volumes are *Californians,* 1916; *Tamar and Other Poems,* 1924; *Roan Stallion, Tamar, and Other Poems,* 1925; *The Women at Point Sur,* 1927; *Cawdor and Other Poems,* 1928; *Dear Judas and Other Poems,* 1929; *Descent to the Dead,* 1931; *Thurso's Landing and Other Poems,* 1932; *Give Your Heart to the Hawks and Other Poems,* 1933; *Solstice and Other Poems,* 1935; *Such Counsels You Gave to Me and Other Poems,* 1937; *Be Angry at the Sun,* 1941; *Medea,* 1946; *The Double Axe,* 1948; *Hungerfield and Other Poems,* 1953.

Critical and biographical studies are George Sterling, *Robinson Jeffers,* 1926; Louis Adamic, *Robinson Jeffers,* 1929; L. C. Powell, *Robinson Jeffers: The Man and His Work,* revised 1940, with a bibliography of first editions; R. Squires, *Loyalties of Robinson Jeffers,* 1956; and M. C. Monjian, *Robinson Jeffers,* 1958.

Boats in a Fog

Sports and gallantries, the stage, the arts, the antics of dancers,
The exuberant voices of music,

Have charm for children but lack nobility; it is bitter earnestness
That makes beauty; the mind
Knows, grown adult.
                    A sudden fog-drift muffled the ocean,   5
A throbbing of engines moved in it,
At length, a stone's throw out, between the rocks and the vapor,
One by one moved shadows
Out of the mystery, shadows, fishing-boats, trailing each other,
Following the cliff for guidance,   10
Holding a difficult path between the peril of the sea-fog
And the foam on the shore granite.
One by one, trailing their leader, six crept by me,
Out of the vapor and into it,
The throb of their engines subdued by the fog, patient and
    cautious,   15
Coasting all round the peninsula
Back to the buoys in Monterey harbor.[1] A flight of pelicans
Is nothing lovelier to look at;
The flight of the planets is nothing nobler; all the arts lose virtue
Against the essential reality   20
Of creatures going about their business among the equally
Earnest elements of nature.

1924

Shine, Perishing Republic

While this America settles in the mold of its vulgarity, heavily
    thickening to empire,
And protest, only a bubble in the molten mass, pops and sighs out,
    and the mass hardens,

I sadly smiling remember that the flower fades to make fruit, the
    fruit rots to make earth.
Out of the mother; and through the spring exultances, ripeness and
    decadence; and home to the mother.

You making haste haste on decay: not blameworthy; life is good, be
    it stubbornly long or suddenly   5
A mortal splendor: meteors are not needed less than mountains:
    shine, perishing republic.

But for my children, I would have them keep their distance from
    the thickening center; corruption

1. Monterey, California, is the northern   prevalent fogs and by dangerous shoals
limit of the Jeffers country. The coastal   of rock.
waters are rendered hazardous by the

Never has been compulsory, when the cities lie at the monster's feet
there are left the mountains.

And boys, be in nothing so moderate as in love of man, a clever
servant, insufferable master.
There is the trap that catches noblest spirits, that caught—they say
—God, when he walked on earth.[2]   10

1924

Granite and Cypress

White-maned, wide-throated, the heavy-shouldered children of the
wind leap at the sea-cliff.
The invisible falcon[3]
Brooded on water and bred them in wide waste places, in a bride-
chamber wide to the stars' eyes
In the center of the ocean,
Where no prows pass nor island is lifted . . . the sea beyond
Lobos[4] is whitened with the falcon's   5
Passage, he is here now,
The sky is one cloud, his wing-feathers hiss in the white grass, my
sapling cypresses writhing
In the fury of his passage
Dare not dream of their centuries of future endurance of tempest.
(I have granite and cypress,   10
Both long-lasting,
Planted in the earth; but the granite sea-boulders are prey to no
hawk's wing, they have taken worse pounding,
Like me they remember
Old wars and are quiet; for we think that the future is one piece
with the past, we wonder why tree-tops
And people are so shaken.)   15

1924

To the Stone-Cutters

Stone-cutters fighting time with marble, you foredefeated
Challengers of oblivion
Eat cynical earnings, knowing rock splits, records fall down,
The square-limbed Roman letters

2. *I.e.,* the various appearances of God
upon the earth to make covenants for
the salvation of man, as when He speaks
to Adam (Genesis i: 26–30), to Noah
(Genesis vi: 13–21), to Christ and the
disciples (Matthew xvii: 1–9).

3. The fierce hunting hawk of the age
of chivalry was regarded as "master of
the wind."
4. A coastal headland near the poet's
home at Carmel, California.

Scale in the thaws, wear in the rain.   5
 The poet as well
Builds his monument mockingly;
For man will be blotted out, the blithe earth die, the brave sun
Die blind, his heart blackening:
Yet stones have stood for a thousand years, and pained thoughts
 found
The honey peace in old poems.   10

Constrast btwn nobility of Stallions
ignoble of Johnny   1925

Roan Stallion[5]

primitivism

The dog barked; then the woman stood in the doorway, and hearing
 iron strike stone down the steep road
Covered her head with a black shawl and entered the light rain; she
 stood at the turn of the road.
A nobly formed woman; erect and strong as a new tower; the
 features stolid and dark
But sculptured into a strong grace; straight nose with a high bridge,
 firm and wide eyes, full chin,
Red lips; she was only a fourth part Indian; a Scottish sailor had
 planted her in young native earth,   5
Spanish and Indian, twenty-one years before. He had named her
 California when she was born;
That was her name; and had gone north.
        She heard the hooves
 and wheels come nearer, up the steep road.
The buckskin[6] mare, leaning against the breastpiece, plodded into
 sight round the wet bank.
The pale face of the driver followed; the burnt-out eyes; they had
 fortune in them. He sat twisted

---

5. " * * * *Roan Stallion* originated from an abandoned cabin that we discovered in a roadless hollow of the hills. When later we asked about its history no one was able to tell us anything except that the place had been abandoned ever since its owner was killed by a stallion.

"This is the only one of my poems of which I can remember clearly the moment of conception. I had just finished *The Tower Beyond Tragedy* and was looking about for another subject—which was to be contemporary, because I repented of using a Greek story when there were so many new ones at hand. I was quarrying granite under the sea-cliff to build our house with, and slacking on the job sat down on a wet rock to look at the sunset and think about my next poem. The stallion and the desolate cabin came to mind; then immediately, for persons of the drama, came the Indian woman and her white husband, real persons whom I had often seen driving through our village in a ramshackle buggy. The episode of the woman swimming her horse through a storm-swollen ford at night came also; it was part of her actual history. . . . So that when I stood up and began to handle stones again, the poem had already made itself in my mind" [from Jeffers' foreword to *The Selected Poetry of Robinson Jeffers*, 1938].
6. A horse the yellow-gray color of tanned buckskin.

On the seat of the old buggy, leading a second horse by a long
halter, a roan, a big one,   10
That stepped daintily; by the swell of the neck, a stallion. "What
have you got, Johnny?" "Maskerel's stallion.
Mine now. I won him last night, I had very good luck." He was
quite drunk. "They bring their mares up here now.
I keep this fellow. I got money besides, but I'll not show you." "Did
you buy something, Johnny,
For our Christine? Christmas comes in two days, Johnny." "By
God, forgot," he answered laughing.
"Don't tell Christine it's Christmas; after while I get her some-
thing, maybe." But California: 15
"I shared your luck when you lost: you lost *me* once, Johnny,
remember? Tom Dell had me two nights
Here in the house: other times we've gone hungry: now that you've
won, Christine will have her Christmas.
We share your luck, Johnny. You give me money, I go down to
Monterey to-morrow,
Buy presents for Christine, come back in the evening. Next day
Christmas." "You have wet ride," he answered
Giggling. "Here money. Five dollar; ten; twelve dollar. You buy two
bottles of rye whisky for Johnny."   20
"All right. I go to-morrow."

> He was an outcast Hollander; not
old, but shriveled with bad living.
The child Christine inherited from his race blue eyes, from his life
a wizened forehead; she watched
From the house-door her father lurch out of the buggy and lead with
due respect the stallion
To the new corral, the strong one; leaving the wearily breathing
buckskin mare to his wife to unharness.

Storm in the night; the rain on the thin shakes of the roof like the
ocean on rock streamed battering; once thunder   25
Walked down the narrow canyon into Carmel valley[7] and wore
away westward; Christine was wakeful
With fears and wonders; her father lay too deep for storm to touch
him.

> Dawn comes late in the year's dark,
Later into the crack of a canyon under redwoods; and California
slipped from bed
An hour before it; the buckskin would be tired; there was a little
barley, and why should Johnny

7. A gap in the Santa Lucia range extending toward the ocean at Carmel, near
Jeffers' home.

Feed all the barley to his stallion? That is what he would do. She
    tiptoed out of the room.   30

Leaving her clothes, he'd waken if she waited to put them on, and
    passed from the door of the house

Into the dark of the rain; the big black drops were cold through
    the thin shift, but the wet earth

Pleasant under her naked feet. There was a pleasant smell in the
    stable; and moving softly,

Touching things gently with the supple bend of the unclothed body,
    was pleasant. She found a box,

Filled it with deep dry barley and took it down to the old corral.
    The little mare sighed deeply   35

At the rail in the wet darkness; and California returning between
    two redwoods up to the house

Heard the happy jaws grinding the grain. Johnny could mind the
    pigs and chickens. Christine called to her

When she entered the house, but slept again under her hand. She
    laid the wet night-dress on a chair-back

And stole into the bedroom to get her clothes. A plank creaked, and
    he wakened. She stood motionless

Hearing him stir in the bed. When he was quiet she stooped after
    her shoes, and he said softly,   40

"What are you doing? Come back to bed." "It's late, I'm going to
    Monterey, I must hitch up."

"You come to bed first. I been away three days. I give you money, I
    take back the money

And what you do in town then?" She sighed sharply and came to
    the bed.

                            He reaching his hands from it

Felt the cool curve and firmness of her flank, and half rising caught
    her by the long wet hair.

She endured, and to hasten the act she feigned desire; she had not
    for long, except in dream, felt it.   45

Yesterday's drunkenness made him sluggish and exacting; she saw,
    turning her head sadly,

The windows were bright gray with dawn; he embraced her still,
    stopping to talk about the stallion.

At length she was permitted to put on her clothes. Clear daylight
    over the steep hills;

Gray-shining cloud over the tops of the redwoods; the winter stream
    sang loud; the wheels of the buggy

Slipped in deep slime, ground on washed stones at the road-edge.
    Down the hill the wrinkled river smothered the ford.   50

You must keep to the bed of stones: she knew the way by willow
    and alder: the buckskin halted mid-stream,

Shuddering, the water her own color washing up to the traces; but
California, drawing up

Her feet out of the whirl onto the seat of the buggy swung the whip
over the yellow water

And drove to the road.

                     All morning the clouds were racing north-
ward like a river. At noon they thickened.

When California faced the southwind home from Monterey[8] it was
heavy with level rainfall.   55

She looked seaward from the foot of the valley; red rays cried sunset
from a trumpet of streaming

Cloud over Lobos, the southwest occident of the solstice. Twilight
came soon, but the tired mare

Feared the road more than the whip. Mile after mile of slow gray
twilight.

                  Then, quite suddenly, darkness.

"Christine will be asleep. It is Christmas Eve. The ford. That hour
of daylight wasted this morning!"

She could see nothing; she let the reins lie on the dashboard and
knew at length by the cramp of the wheels   60

And the pitch down, they had reached it. Noise of wheels on stones,
plashing of hooves in water; a world

Of sounds; no sight; the gentle thunder of water; the mare snorting,
dipping her head, one knew,

To look for footing, in the blackness, under the stream. The
hushing and creaking of the sea-wind

In the passion of invisible willows.

               The mare stood still; the
woman shouted to her; spared whip,

For a false leap would lose the track of the ford. She stood. "The
baby's things," thought California,   65

"Under the seat: the water will come over the floor"; and rising in
the midst of the water

She tilted the seat; fetched up the doll, the painted wooden
chickens, the wooly bear, the book

Of many pictures, the box of sweets: she brought them all from
under the seat and stored them, trembling,

Under her clothes, about the breasts, under the arms; the corners of
the cardboard boxes

Cut into the soft flesh; but with a piece of rope for a girdle and
wound about the shoulders   70

All was made fast. The mare stood still as if asleep in the midst of
the water. Then California

8. Carmel, the scene of the poem, is about five miles southwest of Monterey.

Reached out a hand over the stream and fingered her rump; the
    solid wet convexity of it
Shook like the beat of a great heart. "What are you waiting for?"
    But the feel of the animal surface
Had wakened a dream, obscured real danger with a dream of danger.
    "What for? for the water-stallion
To break out of the stream, that is what the rump strains for, him
    to come up flinging foam sidewise,   75
Fore-hooves in air, crush me and the rig and curl over his woman."[9]
    She flung out with the whip then;
The mare plunged forward. The buggy drifted sidelong: was she off
    ground? Swimming? No: by the splashes.
The driver, a mere prehensile instinct, clung to the sideirons of the
    seat and felt the force
But not the coldness of the water, curling over her knees, breaking
    up to the waist
Over her body. They'd turned. The mare had turned up stream and
    was wallowing back into shoal water.   80
Then California dropped her forehead to her knees, having seen
    nothing, feeling a danger,
And felt the brute weight of a branch of alder, the pendulous light
    leaves brush her bent neck
Like a child's fingers. The mare burst out of water and stopped on
    the slope to the ford. The woman climbed down
Between the wheels and went to her head. "Poor Dora," she called
    her by her name, "there, Dora. Quietly,"
And led her around, there was room to turn on the margin, the
    head to the gentle thunder of the water.   85
She crawled on hands and knees, felt for the ruts, and shifted the
    wheels into them. "You can see, Dora.
I can't. But this time you'll go through it." She climbed into the
    seat and shouted angrily. The mare
Stopped her two forefeet in the water. She touched with the whip.
    The mare plodded ahead and halted.
Then California thought of prayer: "Dear little Jesus,
Dear baby Jesus born to-night, your head was shining[1]   90

9. California's "dream" of the "water-
stallion" foreshadows the principal
events of the story, at once recalling
racial memories, primitive anthropology, and many mythological stories.
The horse has legendary connections
with water: Poseidon, or Neptune, god
of the sea, struck the earth with his
trident to create the first horse for the
Athenians. Poseidon's union with Medusa produced the famous winged stallion, Pegasus, whom the water nymphs
befriended and whom Eos rode daily
when she was bringing in the dawn. The
centaurs, horses to the waist, had as one
of their ancestors Nephele, the cloud
goddess (see the Ixion-Hera story). The
great centaur, the stallion Eurytion, attempted to violate Hippodamia at her
marriage to Pirithoüs—one of many
classic stories suggesting human congress with gods or animals. Of these,
Jeffers refers, in l. 93, to the story of
Leda.
1. The folklore of the Spanish-Indian
primitives of California was early influenced by the Christian teachings of
Catholic missionaries. Myth and Chris-

Like silver candles. I've got a baby too, only a girl. You had light
  wherever you walked.
Dear baby Jesus give me light." Light streamed: rose, gold, rich
  purple, hiding the ford like a curtain.
The gentle thunder of water was a noise of wing-feathers,[2] the fans
  of paradise lifting softly.
The child afloat on radiance had a baby face, but the angels had
  birds' heads, hawks' heads,
Bending over the baby, weaving a web of wings about him. He held
  in the small fat hand   95
A little snake with golden eyes,[3] and California could see clearly on
  the under radiance
The mare's pricked ears, a sharp black fork against the shining
  light-fall. But it dropped; the light of heaven
Frightened poor Dora. She backed; swung up the water,
And nearly oversetting the buggy turned and scrambled backward;
  the iron wheel-tires rang on boulders.

Then California weeping climbed between the wheels. Her wet
  clothes and the toys packed under   100
Dragged her down with their weight; she stripped off cloak and dress
  and laid the baby's things in the buggy;
Brought Johnny's whisky out from under the seat; wrapped all in
  the dress, bottles and toys, and tied them
Into a bundle that would sling over her back. She unharnessed the
  mare, hurting her fingers
Against the swollen straps and the wet buckles. She tied the pack
  over her shoulders, the cords
Crossing her breasts, and mounted. She drew up her shift about her
  waist and knotted it, naked thighs   105
Clutching the sides of the mare, bare flesh to the wet withers, and
  caught the mane with her right hand,
The looped-up bridle-reins in the other. "Dora, the baby gives you
  light." The blinding radiance
Hovered the ford. "Sweet baby Jesus give us light." Cataracts of
  light and Latin singing[4]
Fell through the willows; the mare snorted and reared: the roar and
  thunder of the invisible water;

tian mysteries are mingled in California's visions, to l. 110.
2. *Cf.* the reference, in l. 76, to the intercourse of gods (here the "water-stal-
lion") with mortals. Now "a noise of
wing-feathers" recalls that Zeus, or
Jupiter, visited the mortal Leda in the
form of a great swan, thus fathering
Helen of Troy and the twin heroes Castor and Pollux. Note the reference (l.
90) to the birth of Jesus, Divine Son of

mortal woman. The "angels" with
"birds' heads" in the next line suggest
certain deities of the Indians of the
Southwest and of Central America, as
well as the celestial Revelation of St.
John the Divine.
3. *Cf.* the serpent in Eden (Genesis iii),
and the snake deities of the Indian cul-
tures of the Southwest.
4. Church windows and the singing of
the Mass.

The night shaking open like a flag, shot with the flashes; the baby
    face hovering; the water   110
Beating over her shoes and stockings up to the bare thighs; and over
    them, like a beast
Lapping her belly; the wriggle and pitch of the mare swimming;
    the drift, the sucking water; the blinding
Light above and behind with not a gleam before, in the throat of
    darkness; the shock of the fore-hooves
Striking bottom, the struggle and surging lift of the haunches. She
    felt the water streaming off her
From the shoulders down; heard the great strain and sob of the
    mare's breathing, heard the horseshoes grind on gravel.   115
When California came home the dog at the door snuffled at her
    without barking; Christine and Johnny
Both were asleep; she did not sleep for hours, but kindled fire and
    knelt patiently over it,
Shaping and drying the dear-bought gifts for Christmas morning.

    She hated (she thought) the proud-necked stallion.
He'd lean the big twin masses of his breast on the rail, his red-brown
    eyes flash the white crescents,
She admired him then, she hated him for his uselessness, serving
    nothing   120
But Johnny's vanity. Horses were too cheap to breed. She thought,
    if he could range in freedom,
Shaking the red-roan mane for a flag on the bare hills.
                  A man brought up a mare in April;
Then California, though she wanted to watch, stayed with Christine
    indoors. When the child fretted
The mother told her once more about the miracle of the ford; her
    prayers to the little Jesus
The Christmas Eve when she was bringing the gifts home; the
    appearance, the lights, the Latin singing,   125
The thunder of wing-feathers and water, the shining child, the
    cataracts of splendor down the darkness.
"A little baby," Christine asked, "the God is a baby?" "The child
    of God. That was his birthday.
His mother was named Mary: we pray to her too: God came to her.
    He was not the child of a man
Like you or me. God was his father: she was the stallion's wife—
    what did I say—God's wife,"
She said with a cry, lifting Christine aside, pacing the planks of the
    floor. "She is called more blessed   130
Than any woman. She was so good, she was more loved." "Did God
    live near her house?" "He lives

Up high, over the stars; he ranges on the bare blue hill of the sky."
    In her mind a picture

Flashed, of the red-roan mane shaken out for a flag on the bare
    hills, and she said quickly, "He's more

Like a great man holding the sun in his hand." Her mind giving her
    words the lie, "But no one

Knows, only the shining and the power. The power, the terror, the
    burning fire covered her over . . . ."[5]   135

"Was she burnt up, mother?" "She was so good and lovely,
    she was the mother of little Jesus.

If you are good nothing will hurt you." "What did she think?"
    "She loved, she was not afraid of the hooves—

Hands that had made the hills and sun and moon, and the sea and
    the great redwoods, the terrible strength,

She gave herself without thinking." "You only saw the baby,
    mother?" "Yes, and the angels about him,

The great wild shining over the black river." Three times she had
    walked to the door, three times returned,   140

And now the hand that had thrice hung on the knob, full of
    prevented action, twisted the cloth

Of the child's dress that she had been mending. "Oh, Oh, I've torn
    it." She struck at the child and then embraced her

Fiercely, the small blond sickly body.

                    Johnny came in, his face
    reddened as if he had stood

Near fire, his eyes triumphing. "Finished," he said, and looked with
    malice at Christine. "I go

Down valley with Jim Carrier; owes me five dollar, fifteen I charge
    him, he brought ten in his pocket.   145

Has grapes on the ranch, maybe I take a barrel red wine instead of
    money. Be back to-morrow.

To-morrow night I tell you— Eh, Jim," he laughed over his
    shoulder, "I say to-morrow evening

I show her how the red fellow act, the big fellow. When I come
    home." She answered nothing, but stood

In front of the door, holding the little hand of her daughter, in the
    path of sun between the redwoods,

While Johnny tied the buckskin mare behind Carrier's buggy, and
    bringing saddle and bridle tossed them   150

Under the seat. Jim Carrier's mare, the bay, stood with drooped
    head and started slowly, the men

Laughing and shouting at her; their voices could be heard down the
    steep road, after the noise

---

5. For myths involving impregnation by
gods, see J. G. Frazer, *The Golden
Bough*. Also, *cf.* footnotes to l. 76 and
l. 93. More specifically here, note the
Annunciation as conventionally represented in altar pieces and religious
paintings, where the Holy Ghost frequently appears as streaming light.

Of the iron-hooped wheels died from the stone. Then one might
    hear the hush of the wind in the tall redwoods,
The tinkle of the April brook, deep in its hollow.

                                     Humanity is the
    start of the race; I say
Humanity is the mold to break away from, the crust to break
    through, the coal to break into fire,   155
The atom to be split.

                         Tragedy that breaks man's face and a white
    fire flies out of it; vision that fools him
Out of his limits, desire that fools him out of his limits, unnatural
    crime, inhuman science,
Slit eyes in the mask; wild loves that leap over the walls of nature,
    the wild fence-vaulter science,
Useless intelligence of far stars, dim knowledge of the spinning
    demons that make an atom,
These break, these pierce, these deify, praising their God shrilly
    with fierce voices: not in man's shape   160
He approves the praise, he that walks lightning-naked on the Pacific,
    that laces the suns with planets,
The heart of the atom with electrons:[6] what is humanity in this
    cosmos? For him, the last
Least tint of a trace in the dregs of the solution; for itself, the mold
    to break away from, the coal
To break into fire, the atom to be split.

                          After the child slept, after
    the leopard-footed evening
Had glided oceanward, California turned the lamp to its least flame
    and glided from the house.   165
She moved sighing, like a loose fire, backward and forward on the
    smooth ground by the door.
She heard the night-wind that draws down the valley like the
    draught in a flue under clear weather
Whisper and toss in the tall redwoods; she heard the tinkle of the
    April brook deep in its hollow.
Cooled by the night the odors that the horses had left behind were
    in her nostrils; the night
Whitened up the bare hill; a drift of coyotes by the river cried
    bitterly against moonrise;   170
Then California ran to the old corral, the empty one where they
    kept the buckskin mare,
And leaned, and bruised her breasts on the rail, feeling the sky
    whiten. When the moon stood over the hill

6. The poet's long study of science is nowhere reflected with greater concentration
than in ll. 154–164.

She stole to the house. The child breathed quietly. Herself: to
    sleep? She had seen Christ in the night at Christmas.
The hills were shining open to the enormous night of the April
    moon: empty and empty,
The vast round backs of the bare hills? If one should ride up high
    might not the Father himself   175
Be seen brooding His night, cross-legged, chin in hand, squatting
    on the last dome? More likely
Leaping the hills, shaking the red-roan mane for a flag on the bare
    hills. She blew out the lamp.
Every fiber of flesh trembled with faintness when she came to the
    door; strength lacked, to wander
Afoot into the shining of the hill, high enough, high enough . . .
    the hateful face of a man had taken
The strength that might have served her,[7] the corral was empty.
    The dog followed her, she caught him by the collar,   180
Dragged him in fierce silence back to the door of the house, latched
    him inside.

                                  It was like daylight
Out-doors and she hastened without faltering down the footpath,
    through the dark fringe of twisted oak-brush,
To the open place in a bay of the hill. The dark strength of the
    stallion had heard her coming; she heard him
Blow the shining air out of his nostrils, she saw him in the white
    lake of moonlight
Move like a lion along the timbers of the fence, shaking the
    nightfall   185
Of the great mane; his fragrance came to her; she leaned on the
    fence;
He drew away from it, the hooves making soft thunder in the
    trodden soil.
Wild love had trodden it, his wrestling with the stranger, the shame
    of the day
Had stamped it into mire and powder when the heavy fetlocks
Strained the soft flanks. "Oh, if I could bear you!
If I had the strength. O great God that came down to Mary, gently
    you came. But I will ride him   190
Up into the hill, if he throws me, if he tramples me, is it not my
    desire
To endure death?" She climbed the fence, pressing her body against
    the rail, shaking like fever,
And dropped inside to the soft ground. He neither threatened her
    with his teeth nor fled from her coming,
And lifting her hand gently to the upflung head she caught the strap

7. That is, their only riding horse.

of the headstall,

That hung under the quivering chin. She unlooped the halter from the high strength of the neck   195

And the arch the storm-cloud mane hung with live darkness. He stood; she crushed her breasts

On the hard shoulder, an arm over the withers, the other under the mass of his throat, and murmuring

Like a mountain dove, "If I could bear you." No way, no help, a gulf in nature. She murmured, "Come,

We will run on the hill. O beautiful, O beautiful," and led him to the gate and flung the bars on the ground. He threw his head downward

To snuff at the bars; and while he stood, she catching mane and withers with all sudden contracture   200

And strength of her lithe body, leaped, clung hard, and was mounted. He had been ridden before; he did not

Fight the weight but ran like a stone falling;

Broke down the slope into the moon-glass of the stream, and flattened to his neck

She felt the branches of a buck-eye tree fly over her, saw the wall of the oak-scrub

End her world: but he turned there, the matted branches

Scraped her right knee, the great slant shoulders   205

Laboring the hill-slope, up, up, the clear hill. Desire had died in her

At the first rush, the falling like death, but now it revived,

She feeling between her thighs the labor of the great engine, the running muscles, the hard swiftness,

She riding the savage and exultant strength of the world.[8] Having topped the thicket he turned eastward,

Running less wildly; and now at length he felt the halter when she drew on it; she guided him upward;   210

He stopped and grazed on the great arch and pride of the hill, the silent calvary.[9] A dwarfish oakwood

Climbed the other slope out of the dark of the unknown canyon beyond; the last wind-beaten bush of it

Crawled up to the height, and California slipping from her mount tethered him to it. She stood then,

Shaking. Enormous films of moonlight

Trailed down from the height. Space, anxious whiteness, vastness. Distant beyond conception the shining ocean   215

Lay light like a haze along the ledge and doubtful world's end. Little vapors gleaming, and little

Darknesses on the far chart underfoot symbolized wood and valley;

8. *Cf*. l. 76, note 9.
9. The Latin word *calvaria*, "a bare skull," describes the appearance of char-acteristic hills of the Jeffers country. "Calvary" names the hill where Jesus was crucified. *Cf*. ll. 218–220.

but the air was the element, the moon-
Saturate arcs and spires of the air.

                                              Here is solitude, here on the
    calvary, nothing conscious
But the possible God and the cropped grass, no witness, no eye but
    that misformed one, the moon's past fullness.
Two figures on the shining hill, woman and stallion, she kneeling
    to him, brokenly adoring.   220
He cropping the grass, shifting his hooves, or lifting the long head
    to gaze over the world,
Tranquil and powerful. She prayed aloud, "O God, I am not good
    enough, O fear, O strength, I am draggled.
Johnny and other men have had me, and O clean power! Here am
    I," she said falling before him,
And crawled to his hooves. She lay a long while, as if asleep, in
    reach of the fore-hooves, weeping. He avoided
Her head and the prone body. He backed up first; but later plucked
    the grass that grew by her shoulder.   225
The small dark head under his nostrils: a small round stone, that
    smelt human, black hair growing from it:
The skull shut the light in it: it was not possible for any eyes
To know what throbbed and shone under the sutures of the skull,
    or a shell full of lightning
Had scared the roan strength, and he'd have broken tether,
    screaming, and run for the valley.
                                      The atom bounds-breaking,
Nucleus to sun, electrons to planets, with recognition   230
Not praying, self-equaling, the whole to the whole, the microcosm[1]
Not entering nor accepting entrance, more equally, more utterly,
    more incredibly conjugate
With the other extreme and greatness; passionately perceptive of
    identity. . . .
                                  The fire threw up figures
And symbols meanwhile, racial myths formed and dissolved in it,
    the phantom rulers of humanity
That without being are yet more real than what they are born of,
    and without shape, shape that which makes them: 235
The nerves and the flesh go by shadowlike, the limbs and the lives
    shadowlike, these shadows remain, these shadows
To whom temples, to whom churches, to whom labors and wars,
    visions and dreams are dedicate:
Out of the fire in the small round stone that black moss covered,[2]
    a crucified man writhed up in anguish;

---

1. The philosophical idea of the micro-
cosm, the infinitely small, recapitulating
the macrocosm, or the infinitely large,
came from the Pythagoreans through

Plato (*e.g.*, in the *Timaeus*), and influenced Christian philosophy. *Cf.*
American transcendentalism.
2. Such remains of Indian civilization

A woman covered by a huge beast in whose mane the stars were
 netted, sun and moon were his eyeballs,
Smiled under the unendurable violation, her throat swollen with
 the storm and blood-flecks gleaming   240
On the stretched lips; a woman—no, a dark water, split by jets of
 lightning, and after a season
What floated up out of the furrowed water, a boat, a fish, a fire-
 globe?
              It had wings, the creature,
And flew against the fountain of lightning, fell burnt out of the
 cloud back to the bottomless water . . .
Figures and symbols, castlings of the fire, played in her brain; but
 the white fire was the essence,
The burning in the small round shell of bone that black hair
 covered, that lay by the hooves on the hilltop. 245

She rose at length, she unknotted the halter; she walked and led the
 stallion; two figures, woman and stallion,
Came down the silent emptiness of the dome of the hill, under the
 cataract of the moonlight.

The next night there was moon through cloud. Johnny had returned
 half drunk toward evening, and California
Who had known him for years with neither love nor loathing
 to-night hating him had let the child Christine
Play in the light of the lamp for hours after her bedtime; who fell
 asleep at length on the floor 250
Beside the dog; then Johnny: "Put her to bed." She gathered the
 child against her breasts, she laid her
In the next room, and covered her with a blanket. The window was
 white, the moon had risen. The mother
Lay down by the child, but after a moment Johnny stood in the
 doorway. "Come drink." He had brought home
Two jugs of wine slung from the saddle, part payment for the
 stallion's service; a pitcher of it
Was on the table, and California sadly came and emptied her glass.
 Whisky, she thought, 255
Would have erased him till to-morrow; the thin red wine. . . . "We
 have a good evening," he laughed, pouring it.
"One glass yet then I show you what the red fellow did." She moving
 toward the house-door his eyes
Followed her, the glass filled and the red juice ran over the table.
 When it struck the floor-planks
He heard and looked. "Who stuck the pig?" he muttered stupidly,
 "here's blood, here's blood," and trailed his fingers

are found in southern California; the
"round stone" here suggests a sacrificial
fire to the divinity, and the suggestion
is reflected in the following episode, to
l. 243.

In the red lake under the lamplight. While he was looking down
    the door creaked, she had slipped out-doors,   260
And he, his mouth curving like a faun's, imagined the chase under
    the solemn redwoods, the panting
And unresistant victim caught in a dark corner. He emptied the
    glass and went out-doors
Into the dappled lanes of moonlight. No sound but the April
    brook's. "Hey Bruno," he called, "find her.
Bruno, go find her." The dog after a little understood and quested,
    the man following.
When California crouching by an oak-bush above the house heard
    them come near she darted   265
To the open slope and ran down hill. The dog barked at her heels,
    pleased with the game, and Johnny
Followed in silence. She ran down to the new corral, she saw the
    stallion
Move like a lion along the timbers of the fence, the dark arched
    neck shaking the nightfall
Of the great mane; she threw herself prone and writhed under the
    bars, his hooves backing away from her
Made muffled thunder in the soft soil. She stood in the midst of the
    corral, panting, but Johnny   270
Paused at the fence. The dog ran under it, and seeing the stallion
    move, the woman standing quiet,
Danced after the beast, with white-toothed feints and dashes. When
    Johnny saw the formidable dark strength
Recoil from the dog, he climbed up over the fence.

The child Christine waked when her mother left her
And lay half-dreaming, in the half-waking dream she saw the ocean
    come up out of the west   275
And cover the world, she looked up through clear water at the tops
    of the redwoods. She heard the door creak
And the house empty; her heart shook her body, sitting up on the
    bed, and she heard the dog
And crept toward light, where it gleamed under the crack of the
    door. She opened the door, the room was empty,
The table-top was a red lake under the lamplight. The color of it
    was terrible to her;
She had seen the red juice drip from a coyote's muzzle, her father
    had shot one day in the hills   280
And carried him home over the saddle: she looked at the rifle on
    the wall-rack: it was not moved:
She ran to the door, the dog was barking and the moon was shining:
    she knew wine by the odor

But the color frightened her, the empty house frightened her, she
    followed down the hill in the white lane of moonlight
The friendly noise of the dog. She saw in the big horse's corral, on
    the level shoulder of the hill,
Black on white, the dark strength of the beast, the dancing fury
    of the dog, and the two others.   285
One fled, one followed; the big one charged, rearing; one fell under
    his forehooves. She heard her mother
Scream: without thought she ran to the house, she dragged a chair
    past the red pool and climbed to the rifle,
Got it down from the wall and lugged it somehow through the door
    and down the hillside, under the hard weight
Sobbing. Her mother stood by the rails of the corral, she gave it to
    her. On the far side
The dog flashed at the plunging stallion; in the midst of the space
    the man, slow-moving, like a hurt worm   290
Crawling, dragged his body by inches toward the fence-line. Then
    California, resting the rifle
On the top rail, without doubting, without hesitance,
Aimed for the leaping body of the dog, and when it stood, fired. It
    snapped, rolled over, lay quiet.
"O mother, you've hit Bruno!" "I couldn't see the sights in the
    moonlight," she answered quietly. She stood
And watched, resting the rifle-butt on the ground. The stallion
    wheeled, freed from his torment, the man   295
Lurched up to his knees, wailing a thin and bitter bird's cry, and
    the roan thunder
Struck; hooves left nothing alive but teeth tore up the remnant. "O
    mother, shoot, shoot!" Yet California
Stood carefully watching, till the beast having fed all his fury
    stretched neck to utmost, head high,
And wrinkled back the upper lip from the teeth, yawning obscene
    disgust over—not a man—
A smear on the moon-lake earth: then California moved by some
    obscure human fidelity   300
Lifted the rifle. Each separate nerve-cell of her brain flaming the
    stars fell from their places
Crying in her mind: she fired three times before the haunches
    crumpled sidewise, the forelegs stiffening,
And the beautiful strength settled to earth: she turned then on her
    little daughter the mask of a woman
Who has killed God. The night-wind veering, the smell of the spilt
    wine drifted down hill from the house.

        1925

ARCHIBALD MACLEISH

learned man who wrote simply and directly without much lit. ref.

(1892–)

Archibald MacLeish was born on May 7, 1892, at Glencoe, a Chicago suburb. In due course he went to Hotchkiss School and Yale University, from which he was graduated in 1915. While a student at Harvard Law School he published two volumes of verse. Although he had married the previous year, he enlisted as a private in 1917. He saw service in France, and had reached the rank of artillery captain by the time he was discharged. For three years he practiced law in Boston, but the restlessness of the born writer was uppermost, and in 1923 he settled in Paris with his family and devoted himself to study and writing. His studies were reflected in his early poems in echoes of the Elizabethans, the French symbolists, and Pound and Eliot, but it was not long before he had developed an independent style.

His early volumes were so much overshadowed by his later work that they have suffered undeserved neglect. There is a morning light and some emotional insight in *The Happy Marriage* (1924). *The Pot of Earth* (1925), a modern story symbolizing woman as the earth-mother, reflects the influence that the republication of Frazer's *The Golden Bough* had on many writers of the time. *The Hamlet of A. MacLeish* (1928) was his fifth and last volume of poems written abroad. In its wrestling with the spiritual defeatism to which the expatriate American writers in general suc-

cumbed, it has significance beyond its considerable merits as a poem. In "American Letter," which he wrote as he determined to return to the United States in 1928, he completed his break with the expatriates of Paris.

Stimulated by his new interest in the nature of society, MacLeish determined to write an epic which should utilize modern psychology and anthropological knowledge in describing the crisis of some great civilization. He chose the attempted conquest of the Mexican Aztecs by the Spanish Cortés, ending with the defeat of the Spaniards at the defense of Mexico City in 1520 by Montezuma, in which the great Indian ruler met his death. The account in his poem is fictional, but MacLeish did make substantial use of the chronicle of one of the participants, Bernál Díaz, and he retraced and studied the route of Cortés and his men across Mexico. *Conquistador* (1932) won the Pulitzer Prize, and took its place among the few enduring epics of modern literature.

By this time, however, MacLeish was greatly disturbed by the current American crisis, produced, he thought, by the unrest of the masses in the great depression and equally by what seemed to be an irresponsible selfishness and lack of concern among the more powerful and fortunate. These views were based not upon vague impressions, but upon solid research. From 1929 until about 1937 he

No continuous pt. of view established and carried through poetry.

Hamlet – forgetive way is not the right way – must take material interest.

was on the staff of *Fortune* magazine, preparing the articles later published as *Housing in America*, *Jews in America*, and *Background of War*. His awakened social consciousness is reflected in the poems of *New Found Land* (1930) and is apparent again in the stirring satires of *Frescoes for Mr. Rockefeller's City* (1933), in *Panic* (1935), a verse play on the irresponsibles of the financial world, and in *Public Speech* (1936), in which satires on the same theme are mingled with sharp pictures of man under dictatorship, and warnings to his countrymen that the iron heels might soon be heard nearby. *The Fall of the City* (1937) and *Air Raid* (1938) were successful radio plays in verse on the same theme, motivated by concern over the spread of fascism, which had recently precipitated civil war in Spain.

In 1939, President Franklin D. Roosevelt, desiring to have MacLeish in the public service, appointed him Librarian of Congress. While in this position, which he held until 1944, he continued, by lectures, broadcasts, and articles, to contribute to an awakened public spirit. Among collections of these writings, the most important are *The Irresponsibles* (1940), aimed at certain authors; *A Time to Speak* (1941); *A Time to Act* (1943); and *American Story*

(1944), ten dramatized broadcasts interpreting the spirit of democratic idealism as represented by episodes of American history. During this period MacLeish served as assistant director of the Office of War Information and for a year directed the Office of Facts and Figures, both important propaganda agencies; he also served the President twice as diplomatic envoy abroad. In 1944–1945 he was assistant secretary of state, and in 1946 he went to Paris as chairman of the American delegation to UNESCO. In 1948 he resumed the rôle of gifted poet in the publication of *Actfive*, of which the title poem views with optimism the ultimate destiny of mankind. *J. B.: A Play In Verse* (1958), a restatement in modern terms of the story of Job, won the Pulitzer Prize in 1959. Since 1949, as Boylston Professor at Harvard, he has taught creative writing. His *Poetry and Experience* (1961) analyzes the poet's craft and the ultimate functions of the poem and the word.

Definitive to date is *Collected Poems, 1917–1952*, 1952. A subsequent volume is *Songs for Eve*, 1955. The poems of MacLeish's earlier period are well represented in the collection *Poems, 1924–1933*, 1933. His prose has not been collected; the principal volumes have been named in the text above.

No biography has been published. Large-scale critical estimates will be found in Cleanth Brooks, *Modern Poetry and the Tradition*, 1939, pp. 110–135; and Oscar Cargill, *Intellectual America: Ideas on the March*, 1941, pp. 281–293.

Lines for a Prologue

These alternate nights and days, these seasons
Somehow fail to convince me. It seems
I have the sense of infinity!

(In your dreams, O crew of Columbus,
O listeners over the sea
For the surf that breaks upon Nothing—)   5

Once I was waked by nightingales in the garden.
I thought, What time is it? I thought,
Time—Is it Time still?—Now is it Time?

(Tell me your dreams, O sailors: 10
Tell me, in sleep did you climb
The tall masts, and before you—)

At night the stillness of old trees
Is a leaning over, and the inertness
Of hills is a kind of waiting.   15

(In sleep, in a dream, did you see
The world's end? Did the water
Break—and no shore— Did you see?)

Strange faces come through the streets to me
Like messengers: and I have been warned   20
By the moving slowly of hands at a window.

O, I have the sense of infinity—
But the world, sailors, is round.
They say there is no end to it.

1926

Immortal Autumn

Praising continuity of things

I speak this poem now with grave and level voice
In praise of autumn of the far-horn-winding fall
I praise the flower-barren fields the clouds the tall
Unanswering branches where the wind makes sullen noise

I praise the fall it is the human season now   5
No more the foreign sun does meddle at our earth[1]
Enforce the green and thaw the frozen soil to birth
Nor winter yet weigh all with silence the pine bough

But now in autumn with the black and outcast crows
Share we the spacious world the whispering year is gone   10
There is more room to live now the once secret dawn
Comes late by daylight and the dark unguarded goes

Between the mutinous brave burning of the leaves
And winter's covering of our hearts with his deep snow

1. *Cf.* the opening lines of *The Waste Land*, by T. S. Eliot.

We are alone there are no evening birds we know   15
The naked moon the tame stars circle at our eaves

It is the human season on this sterile air
Do words outcarry breath the sound goes on and on
I hear a dead man's cry from autumn long since gone

I cry to you beyond this bitter air.   20

1930

You, Andrew Marvell[2]

And here face down beneath the sun
And here upon earth's noonward height
To feel the always coming on
The always rising of the night

To feel creep up the curving east   5
The earthy chill of dusk and slow
Upon those under lands the vast
And ever climbing shadow grow

And strange at Ecbatan[3] the trees
Take leaf by leaf the evening strange   10
The flooding dark about their knees
The mountains over Persia change

And now at Kermanshah the gate
Dark empty and the withered grass
And through the twilight now the late   15
Few travelers in the westward pass

And Baghdad darken and the bridge
Across the silent river gone
And through Arabia the edge
Of evening widen and steal on   20

And deepen on Palmyra's street
The wheel rut in the ruined stone
And Lebanon fade out and Crete
High through the clouds and overblown

2. An English poet (1621–1678), whose
"To His Coy Mistress" contains the
lines: "But at my back I always hear
/ Time's winged chariot hurrying near."
See Eliot, *The Waste Land*, III, l. 185,
for another use of Marvell's observation.
3. Beginning with Ecbatana, once the
capital of Media Magna (part of

Persia), the poet's thoughts move west-
ward with the sun—to Kermanshah,
Baghdad, Palmyra, Sicily, and so on.
Thus the sense of time is related to the
decay of civilizations. See Oswald
Spengler, *The Decline of the West*
(1918–1922), which influenced both
MacLeish and Eliot.

And over Sicily the air   25
Still flashing with the landward gulls
And loom and slowly disappear
The sails above the shadowy hulls

And Spain go under and the shore
Of Africa the gilded sand   30
And evening vanish and no more
The low pale light across that land

Nor now the long light on the sea

And here face downward in the sun
To feel how swift how secretly   35
The shadow of the night comes on. . . .

1930

"Not Marble nor the Gilded Monuments"[4]

The praisers of women in their proud and beautiful poems
Naming the grave mouth and the hair and the eyes
Boasted those they loved should be forever remembered
These were lies

The words sound but the face in the Istrian sun is forgotten   5
The poet speaks but to her dead ears no more
The sleek throat is gone—and the breast that was troubled to listen
Shadow from door

Therefore I will not praise your knees nor your fine walking
Telling you men shall remember your name as long   10
As lips move or breath is spent or the iron of English
Rings from a tongue

I shall say you were young and your arms straight and your mouth
    scarlet
I shall say you will die and none will remember you
Your arms change and none remember the swish of your garments
Nor the click of your shoe   16

Not with my hand's strength not with difficult labor
Springing the obstinate words to the bones of your breast
And the stubborn line to your young stride and the breath to your
    breathing
And the beat to your haste   20
Shall I prevail on the hearts of unborn men to remember

(What is a dead girl but a shadowy ghost

4. The title is the first line of Shakespeare's Sonnet LV.

Or a dead man's voice but a distant and vain affirmation
Like dream words most)

Therefore I will not speak of the undying glory of women   25
I will say you were young and straight and your skin fair
And you stood in the door and the sun was a shadow of leaves on
      your shoulders
And a leaf on your hair

I will not speak of the famous beauty of dead women
I will say the shape of a leaf lay once on your hair   30
Till the world ends and the eyes are out and the mouths broken
Look! It is there!

1930

American Letter[5]

FOR GERALD MURPHY

The wind is east but the hot weather continues,
Blue and no clouds, the sound of the leaves thin,
Dry like the rustling of paper, scored across
With the slate-shrill screech of the locusts.
                                   The tossing of
Pines is the low sound. In the wind's running   5
The wild carrots smell of the burning sun.
Why should I think of the dolphins at Capo di Mele?[6]
Why should I see in my mind the taut sail
And the hill over St.-Tropez and your hand on the tiller?
Why should my heart be troubled with palms still?   10
I am neither a sold boy nor a Chinese official
Sent to sicken in Pa for some Lo-Yang dish.
This is my own land, my sky, my mountain:
This—not the humming pines and the surf and the sound
At the Ferme Blanche, nor Port Cros in the dusk and the harbor 15
Floating the motionless ship and the sea-drowned star.
I am neither Po Chüi[7] nor another after
Far from home, in a strange land, daft
For the talk of his own sort and the taste of his lettuces.
This land is my native land. And yet   20

5. The literary and artistic exiles of
MacLeish's generation had turned to
the cultural inheritance of Europe in revolt against the supposed aridity of
American life. MacLeish suggests his
rededication in the title of *New Found
Land* (1930), the volume in which he
first collected this poem, soon after returning from a long residence abroad.

6. The poet is remembering spots along
the Mediterranean coast: Capo di Mele
in Italy, and in later lines such French
towns as St.-Tropez, Ferme Blanche,
Port Cros, and Cette (now Sète).
7. Chinese poet (died 846 A.D.), whose
lyrics celebrating his homeland were
written far from his native place.

I am sick for home for the red roofs and the olives,
And the foreign words and the smell of the sea fall.
How can a wise man have two countries?
How can a man have the earth and the wind and want
A land far off, alien, smelling of palm-trees
And the yellow gorse[8] at noon in the long calms? 25

It is a strange thing—to be an American.
Neither an old house it is with the air
Tasting of hung herbs and the sun returning
Year after year to the same door and the churn
Making the same sound in the cool of the kitchen 30
Mother to son's wife, and the place to sit
Marked in the dusk by the worn stone at the wellhead—
That—nor the eyes like each other's eyes and the skull
Shaped to the same fault and the hands' sameness.
Neither a place it is nor a blood name. 35
America is West and the wind blowing.
America is a great word and the snow,
A way, a white bird, the rain falling,
A shining thing in the mind and the gulls' call.
America is neither a land nor a people, 40
A word's shape it is, a wind's sweep—
America is alone: many together,
Many of one mouth, of one breath,
Dressed as one—and none brothers among them:
Only the taught speech and the aped tongue. 45
America is alone and the gulls calling.

It is a strange thing to be an American.
It is strange to live on the high world in the stare
Of the naked sun and the stars as our bones live.
Men in the old lands housed by their rivers. 50
They built their towns in the vales in the earth's shelter.
We first inhabit the world. We dwell
On the half earth, on the open curve of a continent.
Sea is divided from sea by the day-fall. The dawn
Rides the low east with us many hours; 55
First are the capes, then are the shorelands, now
The blue Appalachians faint at the day rise;
The willows shudder with light on the long Ohio:
The Lakes scatter the low sun: the prairies
Slide out of the dark: in the eddy of clean air 60
The smoke goes up from the high plains of Wyoming:
The steep Sierras arise: the struck foam

8. A European wild shrub, of wide distribution, which flourishes on uncultivated
land.

Flames at the wind's heel on the far Pacific.
Already the noon leans to the eastern cliff:
The elms darken the door and the dust-heavy lilacs.   65

It is strange to sleep in the bare stars and to die
On an open land where few bury before us:
(From the new earth the dead return no more.)
It is strange to be born of no race and no people.
In the old lands they are many together. They keep   70
The wise past and the words spoken in common.
They remember the dead with their hands, their mouths dumb.
They answer each other with two words in their meeting.
They live together in small things. They eat
The same dish, their drink is the same and their proverbs.   75
Their youth is like. They are like in their ways of love.
They are many men. There are always others beside them.
Here it is one man and another and wide
On the darkening hills the faint smoke of the houses.
Here it is one man and the wind in the boughs.   80

Therefore our hearts are sick for the south water.
The smell of the gorse comes back to our night thought.
We are sick at heart for the red roofs and the olives;
We are sick at heart for the voice and the foot fall . . .

Therefore we will not go though the sea call us.   85

This, this is our land, this is our people,
This that is neither a land nor a race. We must reap
The wind here in the grass for our soul's harvest:
Here we must eat our salt or our bones starve.
Here we must live or live only as shadows.   90
This is our race, we that have none, that have had
Neither the old walls nor the voices around us,
This is our land, this is our ancient ground—
The raw earth, the mixed bloods and the strangers,
The different eyes, the wind, and the heart's change.   95
These we will not leave though the old call us.
This is our country-earth, our blood, our kind.
Here we will live our years till the earth blind us—

The wind blows from the east. The leaves fall.
Far off in the pines a jay rises.   100
The wind smells of haze and the wild ripe apples.

I think of the masts at Cette and the sweet rain.

1930

Speech to Those Who Say Comrade

The brotherhood is not by the blood certainly:
But neither are men brothers by speech—by saying so:
Men are brothers by life lived and are hurt for it:

Hunger and hurt are the great begetters of brotherhood:
Humiliation has gotten much love: 5
Danger I say is the nobler father and mother:

Those are as brothers whose bodies have shared fear
Or shared harm or shared hurt or indignity.
Why are the old soldiers brothers and nearest?

For this: with their minds they go over the sea a little   10
And find themselves in their youth again as they were in
Soissons and Meaux and at Ypres[9] and those cities:

A French loaf and the girls with their eyelids painted
Bring back to aging and lonely men
Their twentieth year and the metal odor of danger: 15

It is this in life which of all things is tenderest—
To remember together with unknown men the days
Common also to them and perils ended:

It is this which makes of many a generation—
A wave of men who having the same years   20
Have in common the same dead and the changes.

The solitary and unshared experience
Dies of itself like the violations of love
Or lives on as the dead live eerily:

The unshared and single man must cover his   25
Loneliness as a girl her shame for the way of
Life is neither by one man nor by suffering.

Who are the born brothers in truth? The puddlers
Scorched by the same flame in the same foundries:
Those who have spit on the same boards with the blood in it: 30

Ridden the same rivers with green logs:
Fought the police in the parks of the same cities:
Grinned for the same blows: the same flogging:

Veterans out of the same ships—factories—
9. Scenes of bloody battles in France during World War I.

Expeditions for fame: the founders of continents: 35
Those that hid in Geneva[1] a time back:

Those that have hidden and hunted and all such—
Fought together: labored together: they carry the
Common look like a card and they pass touching.

Brotherhood! No word said can make you brothers!   40
Brotherhood only the brave earn and by danger or
Harm or by bearing hurt and by no other.

Brotherhood here in the strange world is the rich and
Rarest giving of life and the most valued:
Not to be had for a word or a week's wishing.   45

1936

Winter Is Another Country

If the autumn would
End! If the sweet season,
The late light in the tall trees would
End! If the fragrance, the odor of
Fallen apples, dust on the road,   5
Water somewhere near, the scent of
Water touching me; if this would end
I could endure the absence in the night,
The hands beyond the reach of hands, the name
Called out and never answered with my name: 10
The image seen but never seen with sight.
I could endure this all
If autumn ended and the cold light came.

1948

1. Geneva has long been a place of refuge for those persecuted for matters of conscience and for liberal leaders.

HART CRANE

(1899–1932)

The thirty-three years of Hart Crane's dark and troubled life were not sufficient to develop the genius that was in him, but when he put an end to his life he left a small collection of lyric masterpieces and an American epic of major stature, *The Bridge*. His emotional disintegration resulted from psychological disturbances probably personal in origin rather than reflections of the spiritual disillusionment which prevailed among the literary generation of the first World War. He was only fifteen when the war began in Europe; and when he planned *The Bridge*, it was with the expressed determination to celebrate the unbroken stream of humanistic idealism that he saw in the American historical experience, in contrast with Eliot's obituary for Western culture in *The Waste Land*.

Harold Hart Crane was born on July 21, 1899, in Garettsville, Ohio, but spent his boyhood in Cleveland. There his father prospered as a manufacturer of candies, and was determined to prepare the youth for a business career. Young Crane, who had begun writing poetry as a boy, and first published at fifteen, was equally determined to become a writer. He was emotionally disturbed by this breach with his father; soon a separation between his parents subjected him, as he said, to "the curse of sundered parenthood." At sixteen he refreshed childhood memories of Caribbean waters by visiting his mother at Isle of Pines, Cuba, where her relatives had sugar plantations. Like Gauguin, Crane was influenced emotionally by the tropics, which lent an exotic flavor to his work. On an early trip abroad he formed a deep attachment for Paris; later he was fascinated by New York, where he made long visits with relatives.

Soon Crane struck out for himself, and worked in various places as mechanic, clerk, salesman, and reporter. By 1922 he was settled in New York, living from hand to mouth, sporadically employed as a writer of advertising copy. He studied other writers—T. S. Eliot, Donne and the Elizabethans, and modern continental novelists. Occasionally he was able to publish a poem or two and these won him literary friends, notably Margaret Anderson and the New York coterie then writing for her *Little Review*. His first volume, *White Buildings* (1926), established his reputation as a poet's poet— not the same thing as winning an audience. He wrote slowly, a perfectionist painfully conscious of his relative lack of formal preparation for his task.

He was also spending much of his energy in developing the American materials and myth for *The Bridge*. Waldo Frank reports that the idea of taking Brooklyn Bridge as his basic symbol was suggested by the accident of his residence on Brooklyn Heights, in a mean room which nevertheless commanded a view of the great span from land to land, with the tides of humanity water-borne beneath it and flowing across it in ceaseless traffic. This conception of unity in diversity has obvious connections with American myth, and it occurs so often in Crane's lyrics as to suggest that it had in addition a private emotional significance for him. The sea and the city also persist as symbols of unity—the sea, which merges the individual identity in the universal solution; the city, an aggregate of individuals coming together in meaningful relationships. With these, in *The Bridge*, he associated the stream of history and the stream of time.

The benevolence of Otto Kahn enabled him to complete *The Bridge* in 1930, when it won the annual award of *Poetry* and recognition as a unique achievement. The plan of the poem is simple: in a succession of cantos we follow the westward thrust of the bridge—our history and time-stream—into the body of America, the body of Pocahontas, twin symbol with the bridge of "the flesh our feet have moved upon." "Powhatan's Daughter," the second poem, establishes the fertility myth; and a poem of Pocahontas, printed as a marginal gloss throughout the epic, is an idea in counterpoint to each successive theme. In "Van Winkle" (see below) Pocahontas "like Memory * * * is time's truant" among the shades of our history and its myth. In the fourth canto, "The River" (see below), Pocahontas merges with "the din and slogans" of modern America, and takes us backward through time, down the rails, trails, and rivers to the first explorers and their legends. In the fifth canto, a wild and beautiful Indian dance-phantasy, the continental nature

myth emerges, and the final canto of this sequence, "Indiana," is the idyl of the settled land of homes, farms, town, and families. *The Bridge* acknowledges Man the creator, generic, anonymous, and, in the American experience, master of a wild continent and architect of its dream.

In 1931, Crane was awarded a Guggenheim Fellowship to be used in Mexico, where he proposed to write a long poem employing Mexican history. Failing to accomplish his object, and apparently suffering from the obsession that by the irregularities of his personal life he had squandered his power as an artist, on April 27, 1932, he disappeared into the sea from the stern of the vessel on which he was returning to New York.

Hart Crane's *Collected Poems*, edited, with an indispensable introduction, by Waldo Frank, appeared in 1933. For biography and criticism see Brom Weber, ed., *The Letters of Hart Crane*, 1952; Philip Horton, *Hart Crane* * * * , 1937, 1957; and Brom Weber, *Hart Crane*, 1948. Among standard critical works see especially R. P. Blackmur, *The Double Agent*, 1935; and Allen Tate, *Reactionary Essays*, 1936. H. D. Howe compiled *Hart Crane: A Bibliography*, 1955.

experience of reality

From The Bridge

as a symbol of unity

Proem: To Brooklyn Bridge

Read alone

How many dawns, chill from his rippling rest
The seagull's wings shall dip and pivot him,
Shedding white rings of tumult, building high
Over the chained bay waters Liberty—

Then, with inviolate curve, forsake our eyes 5
As apparitional as sails that cross
Some page of figures to be filed away;
—Till elevators drop us from our day . . .

meaning of each canto = unity

I think of cinemas,[1] panoramic sleights
With multitudes bent toward some flashing scene   10
Never disclosed, but hastened to again,
Foretold to other eyes on the same screen;

And Thee,[2] across the harbor, silver-paced
As though the sun took step of thee, yet left
Some motion ever unspent in thy stride,—   15
Implicitly thy freedom staying thee!

Out of some subway scuttle, cell or loft
A bedlamite speeds to thy parapets,
Tilting there momently, shrill shirt ballooning,[3]
A jest falls from the speechless caravan.   20

Down Wall, from girder into street noon leaks,
A rip-tooth of the sky's acetylene;[4] *H C ≡ C H*
All afternoon the cloud-flown derricks turn . . .
Thy cables breathe the North Atlantic still.

And obscure as that heaven of the Jews,   25
Thy guerdon . . . Accolade thou dost bestow
Of anonymity time cannot raise:
Vibrant reprieve and pardon thou dost show.

O harp and altar, of the fury fused,
(How could mere toil align thy choiring strings!)   30
Terrific threshold of the prophet's pledge,
Prayer of pariah, and the lover's cry,—

Again the traffic lights that skim thy swift
Unfractioned idiom, immaculate sigh of stars,
Beading thy path—condense eternity: 35
And we have seen night lifted in thine arms.

Under thy shadow by the piers I waited;
Only in darkness is thy shadow clear.
The City's fiery parcels all undone,
Already snow submerges an iron year . . .   40

O Sleepless as the river under thee,
Vaulting the sea, the prairies' dreaming sod,
Unto us lowliest sometime sweep, descend
And of the curveship lend a myth to God.

*   *   *

1. The prevailing term in Europe for "motion pictures"; but here note that the Greek word signifies "motion."
2. Brooklyn Bridge.
3. Some notoriety seekers (*e.g.*, Steve Brody) and many suicides have plunged from Brooklyn Bridge.
4. The fuel used to produce the white heat of the torches employed to cut and weld hard metals. Wall Street (*cf.* l. 21), near the bridge, was then visible from its summit.

Van Winkle

Macadam, gun-gray as the tunny's[5] belt,
Leaps from Far Rockaway[6] to Golden Gate:
Listen! the miles a hurdy-gurdy grinds—
Down gold arpéggios mile on mile unwinds.

Times earlier, when you hurried off to school, 5
—It is the same hour though a later day—
You walked with Pizarro in a copybook,
And Cortes rode up, reining tautly in—
Firmly as coffee grips the taste,—and away!

There was Priscilla's[7] cheek close in the wind,
And Captain Smith, all beard and certainty, 10
And Rip Van Winkle, bowing by the way,—
"Is this Sleepy Hollow, friend—?" And he—

And Rip forgot the office hours,
                and he forgot the pay;
Van Winkle sweeps a tenement 15
                down town on Avenue A,—

The grind-organ says . . . Remember, remember
The cinder pile at the end of the backyard
Where we stoned the family of young 20
Garter snakes under . . . And the monoplanes
We launched—with paper wings and twisted
Rubber bands. . . . Recall—recall
                the rapid tongues
That flittered from under the ash heap day 25
After day whenever your stick discovered
Some sunning inch of unsuspecting fiber—
It flashed back at your thrust, as clean as fire.

And Rip was slowly made aware
                that he, Van Winkle, was not here 30
Nor there. He woke and swore he'd seen Broadway
                a Catskill daisy chain in May—

So memory, that strikes a rhyme out of a box,
Or splits a random smell of flowers through glass—
Is it the whip stripped from the lilac tree 35
One day in spring my father took to me,

5. Any fish of the tuna family.
6. Far Rockaway is on the Atlantic coast of Long Island; "to Golden Gate," therefore, would be the span of the continent from the Atlantic to the Pacific.
7. Priscilla Alden, made familiar to those who "hurried off to school" by Longfellow's poem *The Courtship of Miles Standish.*

Or is it the Sabbatical, unconscious smile
My mother almost brought me once from church
And once only, as I recall—?

It flickered through the snow screen, blindly   40
It forsook her at the doorway; it was gone
Before I had left the window. It
Did not return with the kiss in the hall.

Macadam, gun-gray as the tunny's belt,
Leaps from Far Rockaway to Golden Gate . . .   45
Keep hold of that nickel for car-change, Rip,—
Have you got your paper—?
And hurry along, Van Winkle—it's getting late!

Read aloud

The River

Stick your patent name on a signboard[8]
brother—all over—going west—young man
Tintex—Japalac—Certain-teed Overalls ads
and lands sakes! under the new playbill ripped
in the guaranteed corner—see Bert Williams[9] what?   5
Minstrels when you steal a chicken just
save me the wing, for if it isn't
Erie it ain't for miles around a
Mazda—and the telegraphic night coming on Thomas

a Ediford—and whistling down the tracks   10
a headlight rushing with the sound—can you
imagine—while an EXPRESS makes time like
SCIENCE—COMMERCE and the HOLYGHOST
RADIO ROARS IN EVERY HOME WE HAVE THE NORTHPOLE
WALLSTREET AND VIRGINBIRTH WITHOUT STONES OR   15
WIRES OR EVEN RUNning brooks[1] connecting ears
and no more sermons windows flashing roar
Breathtaking—as you like it . . . eh?

So the 20th Century—so
whizzed the Limited—roared by and left   20
three men, still hungry on the tracks, ploddingly

8. In ll. 1–20 of this section the poet
creates an impression of materialistic
confusion by the free association of the
slogans, events, and advertising of the
period; among others "Japalac," a
varnish; the Erie Railroad; the combination of Edison and Ford (Ediford);
and the Twentieth Century Limited.
Compare the similar devices used by
Dos Passos in *U.S.A.*, the first part of
which appeared at about the same time
as this poem.
9. One of the most talented Negro
comedians of this century; flourished
from about 1895 until his death in
1922.
1. *Cf.* Shakespeare, *As You Like It*, Act
II, Scene 1, ll. 16–17: "books in the
running brooks, / Sermons in stones,"
and so on.

watching the tail lights wizen and converge,
slipping gimleted and neatly out of sight.
The last bear, shot drinking in the Dakotas,
Loped under wires that span the mountain stream.   25
Keen instruments, strung to a vast precision
Bind town to town and dream to ticking dream.
But some men take their liquor slow—and count—
Though they'll confess no rosary nor clue—
The river's minute by the far brook's year.   30
Under a world of whistles, wires and steam
Caboose-like they go ruminating through
Ohio, Indiana—blind baggage—
To Cheyenne tagging . . . Maybe Kalamazoo.

Time's renderings, time's blendings they construe   35
As final reckonings of fire and snow;
Strange bird-wit, like the elemental gist
Of unwalled winds they offer, singing low
My Old Kentucky Home and *Casey Jones*,
Some Sunny Day. I heard a road-gang chanting so.   40
And afterwards, who had a colt's eyes—one said,
"Jesus! Oh I remember watermelon days!" And sped
High in a cloud of merriment, recalled
"—And when my Aunt Sally Simpson smiled," he drawled—
"It was almost Louisiana, long ago."   45

"There's no place like Booneville though, Buddy,"
One said, excising a last burr from his vest,
"—For early trouting." Then peering in the can,
"—But I kept on the tracks." Possessed, resigned,
He trod the fire down pensively and grinned,   50
Spreading dry shingles of a beard. . . .

                                Behind
My father's cannery works I used to see
Rail-squatters ranged in nomad raillery,
The ancient men—wifeless or runaway   55
Hobo-trekkers that forever search
An empire wilderness of freight and rails.
Each seemed a child, like me, on a loose perch,
Holding to childhood like some termless play.
John, Jake, or Charley, hopping the slow freight   60
—Memphis to Tallahassee—riding the rods,
Blind fists of nothing, humpty-dumpty clods.

Yet they touch something like a key perhaps.
From pole to pole across the hills, the states

—They know a body under the wide rain;   65
Youngsters with eyes like fjords, old reprobates
With racetrack jargon,—dotting immensity
They lurk across her, knowing her yonder breast
Snow-silvered, sumac-stained or smoky blue,
Is past the valley-sleepers, south or west.   70
—As I have trod the rumorous midnights, too.

And past the circuit of the lamp's thin flame
(O Nights that brought me to her body bare!)
Have dreamed beyond the print that bound her name.
Trains sounding the long blizzards out—I heard   75
Wail into distances I knew were hers.
Papooses crying on the wind's long mane
Screamed redskin dynasties that fled the brain,
—Dead echoes! But I knew her body there,
Time like a serpent down her shoulder dark,   80
And space, an eaglet's wing, laid on her hair.

Under the Ozarks, domed by Iron Mountain,
The old gods of the rain lie wrapped in pools
Where eyeless fish curvet a sunken fountain
And re-descend with corn from querulous crows.   85
Such pilferings make up their timeless eatage,
Propitiate them for their timber torn
By iron, iron—always the iron dealt cleavage!
They doze now, below axe and powder horn.

And Pullman breakfasters glide glistening steel   90
From tunnel into field—iron strides the dew—
Straddles the hill, a dance of wheel on wheel.
You have a half-hour's wait at Siskiyou,
Or stay the night and take the next train through.
Southward, near Cairo passing, you can see   95
The Ohio merging,—borne down Tennessee;
And if it's summer and the sun's in dusk
Maybe the breeze will lift the River's musk
—As though the waters breathed that you might know
Memphis Johnny, Steamboat Bill, Missouri Joe.[2]   100
Oh, lean from the window, if the train slows down,
As though you touched hands with some ancient clown,
—A little while gaze absently below
And hum Deep River with them while they go.

Yes, turn again and sniff once more—look see,   105
O Sheriff, Brakeman and Authority—

2. Old Mississippi folk songs. "Deep
River" (l. 104), a magnificent Negro   spiritual, is also a Mississippi River
song.

Hitch up your pants and crunch another quid,
For you, too, feed the River timelessly.
And few evade full measure of their fate;
Always they smile out eerily what they seem.   110
I could believe he joked at heaven's gate—
Dan Midland³—jolted from the cold brake-beam.

Down, down—born pioneers in time's despite,
Grimed tributaries to an ancient flow—
They win no frontier by their wayward plight,   115
But drift in stillness, as from Jordan's brow.

You will not hear it as the sea; even stone
Is not more hushed by gravity . . . But slow,
As loth to take more tribute—sliding prone
Like one whose eyes were buried long ago   120

The River, spreading, flows—and spends your dream.
What are you, lost within this tideless spell?
You are your father's father, and the stream—
A liquid theme that floating niggers swell.

Damp tonnage and alluvial march of days—   125
Nights turbid, vascular with silted shale
And roots surrendered down of moraine clays:
The Mississippi drinks the farthest dale.

O quarrying passion, undertowed sunlight!
The basalt surface drags a jungle grace   130
Ochreous and lynx-barred in lengthening might;
Patience! and you shall reach the biding place!

Over De Soto's bones the freighted floors
Throb past the City storied of three thrones.⁴
Down two more turns the Mississippi pours   135
(Anon tall ironsides up from salt lagoons)

And flows within itself, heaps itself free.
All fades but one thin skyline 'round . . . Ahead
No embrace opens but the stinging sea;
The River lifts itself from its long bed.   140

Poised wholly on its dream, a mustard glow,
Tortured with history, its one will—flow!

3. A storied hobo who fell from the brake beam while "riding the rods."
4. To prevent hostile Indians from discovering the death of Hernando DeSoto, his men buried him in the waters of the Mississippi, near the later site of New Orleans, whose history involved the "three thrones" of Spain, France, and England.

—The Passion spreads in wide tongues, chocked and slow,
Meeting the Gulf, hosannas silently below.[5]

1930

Voyages: I

Above the fresh ruffles of the surf
Bright striped urchins flay each other with sand.
They have contrived a conquest for shell shucks,
And their fingers crumble fragments of baked weed
Gaily digging and scattering.   5

And in answer to their treble interjections
The sun beats lightning on the waves,
The waves fold thunder on the sand;
And could they hear me I would tell them:

O brilliant kids, frisk with your dog,   10
Fondle your shells and sticks, bleached
By time and the elements; but there is a line
You must not cross nor ever trust beyond it
Spry cordage of your bodies to caresses
Too lichen-faithful from too wide a breast.   15
The bottom of the sea is cruel.

1926

Voyages: II

—And yet this great wink of eternity,
Of rimless floods, unfettered leewardings,
Samite sheeted and processioned where
Her undinal vast belly moonward bends,[6]
Laughing the wrapt inflections of our love;   5

Take this Sea,[7] whose diapason knells
On scrolls of silver snowy sentences,
The sceptered terror of whose sessions rends
As her demeanors motion well or ill,
All but the pieties of lovers' hands.   10

---

5. This canto, "The River," has identified the stream of men with that of history and with the history-haunted river;
the leap of the Mississippi into the Gulf
is a fundamental theme of *The Bridge*
in its entirety.
6. The fact of the moon's influence on
the tides is combined here with the myth
of Undine's yearning for a mortal lover.
7. The Caribbean.

And onward, as bells off San Salvador
Salute the crocus lusters of the stars,
In these poinsettia meadows of her tides,—
Adagios[8] of islands, O my Prodigal,
Complete the dark confessions her veins spell.   15

Mark how her turning shoulders wind the hours,[9]
And hasten while her penniless rich palms
Pass superscription of bent foam and wave,—
Hasten, while they are true,—sleep, death, desire,
Close round one instant in one floating flower.   20

Bind us in time, O seasons clear, and awe.
O minstrel galleons of Carib fire,
Bequeath us to no earthly shore until
Is answered in the vortex of our grave
The seal's wide spindrift gaze toward paradise.   25
                                                      1926

Royal Palm

Green rustlings, more-than-regal charities
Drift coolly from that tower of whispered light.
Amid the noontide's blazed asperities
I watched the sun's most gracious anchorite[1]

Climb up as by communings, year on year   5
Uneaten of the earth or aught earth holds,
And the gray trunk, that's elephantine, rear
Its frondings sighing in aetherial folds.

Forever fruitless, and beyond that yield
Of sweat the jungle presses with hot love   10
And tendril till our deathward breath is sealed—
It grazes the horizons, launched above

Mortality—ascending emerald-bright,
A fountain at salute, a crown in view—
Unshackled, casual of its azured height,   15
As though it soared suchwise through heaven too.

                                                      1933

8. In music and the dance, a slow, graceful movement.
9. The tides are a clock for simple people living close to the shore.

1. The ideas of chastity and fruitlessness (implied in "anchorite") are identified with the regal aloofness of the royal palm.

Fiction in Search of Reality

KATHERINE ANNE PORTER
(1890–)

The reputation of Katherine Anne Porter in contemporary literature probably has no parallel. All her published fiction comprises but five short novels and three volumes of short stories. She has never had a popular following; yet nearly all discriminating readers are acquainted with her work, and she has exercised a considerable influence on many serious younger writers. Like Katherine Mansfield, whose inspiration she has recognized, she has attempted to achieve a style strictly objective without sacrificing sensitivity, and she has succeeded by such careful selection and combination of character, situation, and action that the resulting story is self-motivated, without the author's overt presence.

Miss Porter's preparation was long and careful. Although she had written stories almost from infancy, she did not satisfy her own standards sufficiently to attempt publication until she was thirty. She was born at Indian Creek, Texas, on May 15, 1890, and got her early education at various convent schools in Texas and Louisiana. In 1920 she went to New York, where she made her home until 1937. During this period she also spent time in Europe and Mexico. She has written a study of the arts and crafts of the latter country, and she has published translations of Spanish, Latin-American, and French fiction. She was a newspaper reporter intermittently and later held an editorial post for a while.

After 1924 her stories began to appear both in standard literary magazines and in those of more experimental inclination. They were at once noticed, and when she collected only six of them in a limited edition, entitled *Flowering Judas* (1930), her reputation with the literary coterie was confirmed. The next year a Guggenheim Fellowship provided the opportunity for travel and writing in Europe.

Again in New York she published an enlarged edition of *Flowering Judas* (1935). Her first short novel, *Hacienda,* had appeared in 1934; her second novelette, *Noon Wine,* was published in 1937. The next year, again on a Guggenheim Fellowship, she went South. In 1939 appeared *Pale Horse, Pale Rider*, consisting of the title novelette, *Old Mortality*, and the previously published *Noon Wine*.

She has lived in Washington, D.C., since 1960. *No Safe Harbor* (1941) is a novelette; *The Leaning Tower* (1944), a collection of later stories. In 1952 she published *The Days Before*, an impressive collection of essays. The title of her long-awaited novel, *Ship of Fools* (1962), recalls the satirical *Das Narren-* *schiff* (1494), but she depicts a cruise in 1931, when reportedly she first planned the novel, in which a large cast of characters allegorically reflects the contemporary life of western man.

Other volumes, besides those mentioned above, include *Outline of Mexican Popular Arts and Crafts*, 1922; *French Song Book*, 1933, translations; *The Itching Parrot*, 1942, translations from Spanish; and *A Defense of Circe*, 1954. H. J. Mooney, *Fiction and Criticism of Katherine Anne Porter*, 1957, is a useful study.

The Jilting of Granny Weatherall[1]

She flicked her wrist neatly out of Doctor Harry's pudgy careful fingers and pulled the sheet up to her chin. The brat ought to be in knee breeches. Doctoring around the country with spectacles on his nose! "Get along now, take your schoolbooks and go. There's nothing wrong with me."

Doctor Harry spread a warm paw like a cushion on her forehead where the forked green vein danced and made her eyelids twitch. "Now, now, be a good girl, and we'll have you up in no time."

"That's no way to speak to a woman nearly eighty years old just because she's down. I'd have you respect your elders, young man."

"Well, Missy, excuse me." Doctor Harry patted her cheek. "But I've got to warn you, haven't I? You're a marvel, but you must be careful or you're going to be good and sorry."

"Don't tell me what I'm going to be. I'm on my feet now, morally speaking. It's Cornelia. I had to go to bed to get rid of her."

Her bones felt loose, and floated around in her skin, and Doctor Harry floated like a balloon around the foot of the bed. He floated and pulled down his waistcoat and swung his glasses on a cord. "Well, stay where you are, it certainly can't hurt you."

"Get along and doctor your sick," said Granny Weatherall. "Leave a well woman alone. I'll call for you when I want you. . . . Where were you forty years ago when I pulled through milk-leg and double pneumonia? You weren't even born. Don't let Cornelia lead you on," she shouted, because Doctor Harry appeared to float up to the ceiling and out. "I pay my own bills, and I don't throw my money away on nonsense!"

1. "The Jilting of Granny Weatherall" was collected in the author's first volume, *Flowering Judas and Other Stories* (1930). It was first published in *transition* for February, 1929.

She meant to wave good-by, but it was too much trouble. Her eyes closed of themselves, it was like a dark curtain drawn around the bed. The pillow rose and floated under her, pleasant as a hammock in a light wind. She listened to the leaves rustling outside the window. No, somebody was swishing newspapers: no, Cornelia and Doctor Harry were whispering together. She leaped broad awake, thinking they whispered in her ear.

"She was never like this, *never* like this!" "Well, what can we expect?" "Yes, eighty years old. . . ."

Well, and what if she was? She still had ears. It was like Cornelia to whisper around doors. She always kept things secret in such a public way. She was always being tactful and kind. Cornelia was dutiful; that was the trouble with her. Dutiful and good: "So good and dutiful," said Granny, "that I'd like to spank her." She saw herself spanking Cornelia and making a fine job of it.

"What'd you say, Mother?"

Granny felt her face tying up in hard knots.

"Can't a body think, I'd like to know?"

"I thought you might want something."

"I do. I want a lot of things. First off, go away and don't whisper."

She lay and drowsed, hoping in her sleep that the children would keep out and let her rest a minute. It had been a long day. Not that she was tired. It was always pleasant to snatch a minute now and then. There was always so much to be done, let me see: to-morrow.

Tomorrow was far away and there was nothing to trouble about. Things were finished somehow when the time came; thank God there was always a little margin over for peace: then a person could spread out the plan of life and tuck in the edges orderly. It was good to have everything clean and folded away, with the hair brushes and tonic bottles sitting straight on the white embroidered linen: the day started without fuss and the pantry shelves laid out with rows of jelly glasses and brown jugs and white stone-china jars with blue whirligigs and words painted on them: coffee, tea, sugar, ginger, cinnamon, allspice: and the bronze clock with the lion on top nicely dusted off. The dust that lion could collect in twenty-four hours! The box in the attic with all those letters tied up, well, she'd have to go through that tomorrow. All those letters—George's letters and John's letters and her letters to them both—lying around for the children to find afterwards made her uneasy. Yes, that would be tomorrow's business. No use to let them know how silly she had been once.

While she was rummaging around she found death in her mind and it felt clammy and unfamiliar. She had spent so much time preparing for death there was no need for bringing it up again. Let it take care of itself now. When she was sixty she had felt very old, finished, and went around making farewell trips to see her children and grandchildren, with a secret in her mind: This is the very last of your mother, children! Then she made her will and came down with a long fever. That was all just a notion like a lot of other things, but it was lucky too, for she had once for all got over the idea of dying for a long time. Now she couldn't be worried. She hoped she had better sense now. Her father had lived to be one hundred and two years old and had drunk a noggin of strong hot toddy on his last birthday. He told the reporters it was his daily habit, and he owed his long life to that. He had made quite a scandal and was very pleased about it. She believed she'd just plague Cornelia a little.

"Cornelia! Cornelia!" No footsteps, but a sudden hand on her cheek. "Bless you, where have you been?"

"Here, mother."

"Well, Cornelia, I want a noggin of hot toddy."

"Are you cold, darling?"

"I'm chilly, Cornelia. Lying in bed stops the circulation. I must have told you that a thousand times."

Well, she could just hear Cornelia telling her husband that Mother was getting a little childish and they'd have to humor her. The thing that most annoyed her was that Cornelia thought she was deaf, dumb, and blind. Little hasty glances and tiny gestures tossed around her and over her head saying, "Don't cross her, let her have her way, she's eighty years old," and she sitting there as if she lived in a thin glass cage. Sometimes Granny almost made up her mind to pack up and move back to her own house where nobody could remind her every minute that she was old. Wait, wait, Cornelia, till your own children whisper behind your back!

In her day she had kept a better house and had got more work done. She wasn't too old yet for Lydia to be driving eighty miles for advice when one of the children jumped the track, and Jimmy still dropped in and talked things over: "Now, Mammy, you've a good business head, I want to know what you think of this? . . ." Old. Cornelia couldn't change the furniture around without asking. Little things, little things! They had been so sweet when they were little. Granny wished the old days were back again with the children young and everything to be done over. It had been a hard pull, but not too much for her. When she thought of all the food she had cooked, and all the clothes she had cut and sewed, and all the gardens she had made—well, the children showed it. There they were, made out of her, and they couldn't get away from that. Sometimes she wanted to see John again and point to them and say, Well, I didn't do so badly, did I? But that would have to wait. That was for tomorrow. She used to think of him as a man, but now all the children were older than their father, and he would be a child beside her if she saw him now. It seemed strange and there was something wrong in the idea. Why, he couldn't possibly recognize her. She had fenced in a hundred acres once, digging the post holes herself and clamping the wires with just a negro boy to help. That changed a woman. John would be looking for a young woman with the peaked Spanish comb in her hair and the painted fan. Digging post holes changed a woman. Riding country roads in the winter when women had their babies was another thing: sitting up nights with sick horses and sick negroes and sick children and hardly ever losing one. John, I hardly ever lost one of them! John would see that in a minute, that would be something he could understand, she wouldn't have to explain anything!

It made her feel like rolling up her sleeves and putting the whole place to rights again. No matter if Cornelia was determined to be everywhere at once, there were a great many things left undone on this place. She would start tomorrow and do them. It was good to be strong enough for everything, even if all you made melted and changed and slipped under your hands, so that by the time you finished you almost forgot what you were working for. What was it I set out to do? she asked herself intently, but she could not remember. A fog rose over the valley, she saw it marching across the creek swallowing the trees and moving up the hill like an army of ghosts. Soon it would be at the near edge of the orchard, and then it was time to go in and light the lamps. Come in, children, don't stay out in the night air.

Lighting the lamps had been beautiful. The children huddled up to her and breathed like little calves waiting at the bars in the twilight. Their eyes followed the match and watched the flame rise and settle in a blue curve, then they moved away from her. The lamp was lit, they didn't have to be scared and hang on to mother any more. Never, never, never more. God, for all my life I thank Thee. Without Thee, my God, I could never have done it. Hail, Mary, full of grace.

I want you to pick all the fruit this year and see that nothing is wasted. There's always someone who can use it. Don't let good things rot for want of using. You waste life when you waste good food. Don't let things get lost. It's bitter to lose things. Now, don't let me get to thinking, not when I am tired and taking a little nap before supper. . . .

The pillow rose about her shoulders and pressed against her heart and the memory was being squeezed out of it: oh, push down the pillow, somebody: it would smother her if she tried to hold it. Such a fresh breeze blowing and such a green day with no threats in it. But he had not come, just the same. What does a woman do when she has put on the white veil and set out the white cake for a man and he doesn't come? She tried to remember. No, I swear he never harmed me but in that. He never harmed me but in that . . . and what if he did? There was the day, the day, but a whirl of dark smoke rose and covered it, crept up and over into the bright field where everything was planted so carefully in orderly rows. That was hell, she knew hell when she saw it. For sixty years she had prayed against remembering him and against losing her soul in the deep pit of hell, and now the two things were mingled in one and the thought of him was a smoky cloud from hell that moved and crept in her head when she had just got rid of Doctor Harry and was trying to rest a minute. Wounded vanity, Ellen, said a sharp voice in the top of her mind. Don't let your wounded vanity get the upper hand of you. Plenty of girls get jilted. You were jilted, weren't you? Then stand up to it. Her eyelids wavered and let in streamers of blue-gray light like tissue paper over her eyes. She must get up and pull the shades down or she'd never sleep. She was in bed again and the shades were not down. How could that happen? Better turn over, hide from the light, sleeping in the light gave you nightmares. "Mother, how do you feel now?" and a stinging wetness on her forehead. But I don't like having my face washed in cold water!

Hapsy? George? Lydia? Jimmy? No, Cornelia, and her features were swollen and full of little puddles. "They're coming, darling, they'll all be here soon." Go wash your face, child, you look funny.

Instead of obeying, Cornelia knelt down and put her head on the pillow. She seemed to be talking but there was no sound. "Well, are you tongue-tied? Whose birthday is it? Are you going to give a party?"

Cornelia's mouth moved urgently in strange shapes. "Don't do that, you bother me, daughter."

"Oh, no, Mother. Oh, no. . . ."

Nonsense. It was strange about children. They disputed your every word. "No what, Cornelia?"

"Here's Doctor Harry."

"I won't see that boy again. He just left five minutes ago."

"That was this morning, Mother. It's night now. Here's the nurse."

"This is Doctor Harry, Mrs. Weatherall. I never saw you look so young and happy!"

"Ah, I'll never be young again—but I'd be happy if they'd let me lie in peace and get rested."

She thought she spoke up loudly, but no one answered. A warm weight on her forehead, a warm bracelet on her wrist, and a breeze went on whispering, trying to tell her something. A shuffle of leaves in the everlasting hand of God, He blew on them and they danced and rattled. "Mother, don't mind, we're going to give you a little hypodermic." "Look here, daughter, how do ants get in this bed? I saw sugar ants yesterday." Did you send for Hapsy too?

It was Hapsy she really wanted. She had to go a long way back through a great many rooms to find Hapsy standing with a baby on her arm. She seemed to herself to be Hapsy also, and the baby on Hapsy's arm was Hapsy and himself and herself, all at once, and there was no surprise in the meeting. Then Hapsy melted from within and turned flimsy as gray gauze and the baby was a gauzy shadow, and Hapsy came up close and said, "I thought you'd never come," and looked at her very searchingly and said, "You haven't changed a bit!" They leaned forward to kiss, when Cornelia began whispering from a long way off, "Oh, is there anything you want to tell me? Is there anything I can do for you?"

Yes, she had changed her mind after sixty years and she would like to see George. I want you to find George. Find him and be sure to tell him I forgot him. I want him to know I had my husband just the same and my children and my house like any other woman. A good house too and a good husband that I loved and fine children out of him. Better than I hoped for even. Tell him I was given back everything he took away and more. Oh, no, oh, God, no, there was something else besides the house and the man and the children. Oh, surely they were not all? What was it? Something not given back. . . . Her breath crowded down under her ribs and grew into a monstrous frightening shape with cutting edges; it bored up into her head, and the agony was unbelievable: Yes, John, get the Doctor now, no more talk, my time has come.

When this one was born it should be the last. The last. It should have been born first, for it was the one she had truly wanted. Everything came in good time. Nothing left out, left over. She was strong, in three days she would be as well as ever. Better. A woman needed milk in her to have her full health.

"Mother, do you hear me?"

"I've been telling you—"

"Mother, Father Connolly's here."

"I went to Holy Communion only last week. Tell him I'm not so sinful as all that."

"Father just wants to speak to you."

He could speak as much as he pleased. It was like him to drop in and inquire about her soul as if it were a teething baby, and then stay on for a cup of tea and a round of cards and gossip. He always had a funny story of some sort, usually about an Irishman who made his little mistakes and confessed them, and the point lay in some absurd thing he would blurt out in the confessional show-ing his struggles between native piety and original sin. Granny felt easy about her soul. Cornelia, where are your manners? Give Father Connolly a chair. She had her secret comfortable under-standing with a few favorite saints who cleared a straight road to God for her. All as surely signed and sealed as the papers for the new Forty Acres. Forever . . . heirs and assigns forever. Since the day the wedding cake was not cut, but thrown out and wasted. The whole bottom dropped out of the world, and there she was blind and sweating with nothing under her feet and the walls falling away. His hand had caught her under the breast, she had not fallen, there was the freshly polished floor with the green rug on it, just as before. He had cursed like a sailor's parrot and said, "I'll kill him for you." Don't lay a hand on him, for my sake leave something to God. "Now, Ellen, you must believe what I tell you. . . ."

So there was nothing, nothing to worry about any more, except sometimes in the night one of the children screamed in a night-mare, and they both hustled out shaking and hunting for the matches and calling, "There, wait a minute, here we are!" John, get the doctor now, Hapsy's time has come. But there was Hapsy standing by the bed in a white cap. "Cornelia, tell Hapsy to take off her cap. I can't see her plain."

Her eyes opened very wide and the room stood out like a picture she had seen somewhere. Dark colors with the shadows rising to-wards the ceiling in long angles. The tall black dresser gleamed with nothing on it but John's picture, enlarged from a little one, with John's eyes very black when they should have been blue. You never saw him, so how do you know how he looked? But the man insisted the copy was perfect, it was very rich and handsome. For a picture, yes, but it's not my husband. The table by the bed had a linen cover and a candle and a crucifix. The light was blue from Cornelia's silk lampshades. No sort of light at all, just frippery. You had to live forty years with kerosene lamps to appreciate honest electricity. She felt very strong and she saw Doctor Harry with a rosy nimbus around him.

"You look like a saint, Doctor Harry, and I vow that's as near as you'll ever come to it."

"She's saying something."

"I heard you, Cornelia. What's all this carrying-on?"

"Father Connolly's saying—"

Cornelia's voice staggered and bumped like a cart in a bad road. It rounded corners and turned back again and arrived nowhere. Granny stepped up in the cart very lightly and reached for the reins, but a man sat beside her and she knew him by his hands, driving the cart. She did not look in his face, for she knew without seeing, but looked instead down the road where the trees leaned over and bowed to each other and a thousand birds were singing a Mass. She felt like singing too, but she put her hand in the bosom of her dress and pulled out a rosary, and Father Connolly murmured Latin in a very solemn voice and tickled her feet. My God, will you stop that nonsense? I'm a married woman. What if he did run away and leave me to face the priest by myself? I found another a whole world better. I wouldn't have exchanged my husband for anybody except St. Michael himself, and you may tell him that for me with a thank you in the bargain.

Light flashed on her closed eyelids, and a deep roaring shook her. Cornelia, is that lightning? I hear thunder. There's going to be a storm. Close all the windows. Call the children in. . . . "Mother, here we are, all of us." "Is that you, Hapsy?" "Oh, no, I'm Lydia. We drove as fast as we could." Their faces drifted above her, drifted away. The rosary fell out of her hands and Lydia put it back. Jimmy tried to help, their hands fumbled together, Granny closed two fingers around Jimmy's thumb. Beads wouldn't do, it must be something alive. She was so amazed her thoughts ran round and round. So, my dear Lord, this is my death and I wasn't even thinking about it. My children have come to see me die. But I can't, it's not time. Oh, I always hated surprises. I wanted to give Cornelia the amethyst set—Cornelia, you're to have the amethyst set, but Hapsy's to wear it when she wants, and, Doctor Harry, do shut up. Nobody sent for you. Oh, my dear Lord, do wait a minute. I meant to do something about the Forty Acres, Jimmy doesn't need it and Lydia will later on, with that worthless husband of hers. I meant to finish the altar cloth and send six bottles of wine to Sister Borgia for her dyspepsia. I want to send six bottles of wine to Sister Borgia, Father Connolly, now don't let me forget.

Cornelia's voice made short turns and tilted over and crashed. "Oh, Mother, oh, Mother, oh, Mother. . . ."

"I'm not going, Cornelia. I'm taken by surprise. I can't go."

You'll see Hapsy again. What about her? "I thought you'd never come." Granny made a long journey outward, looking for Hapsy. What if I don't find her? What then? Her heart sank down and down, there was no bottom to death, she couldn't come to the end of it. The blue light from Cornelia's lampshade drew into a tiny point in the center of her brain, it flickered and winked like an eye, quietly it fluttered and dwindled. Granny lay curled down within herself, amazed and watchful, staring at the point of light that was herself; her body was now only a deeper mass of shadow in an endless darkness and this darkness would curl around the light and swallow it up. God, give a sign!

For the second time there was no sign. Again no bridegroom and the priest in the house.[2] She could not remember any other sorrow because this grief wiped them all away. Oh, no, there's nothing more cruel than this—I'll never forgive it. She stretched herself with a deep breath and blew out the light.

1929, 1930

2. *Cf.* Christ's parable of the bridegroom (Matthew xxv: 1–13).

[handwritten: nalds as of evil - all his works deal with evil in one way or another.]

[handwritten: a choice good must]

WILLIAM FAULKNER

(1897–)

[handwritten: humans are all in a dramatic conflict in nature - animal response]

In creative genius, in the ability to construct a world of the imagination in which reality is more accessible than it is in the everyday actualities of life, William Faulkner has few peers in modern literature. This fact was only tardily recognized. His writing is so difficult, obscure, serious, and often disagreeable that many of his works were not widely read, and the recognition of his highest powers was attainable only in perspective. There was an ironical appropriateness in the fact that the Nobel committee, although for reasons not immediately connected with Faulkner's merits, was unable to reach a decision at the appointed time, and awarded him the 1949 Prize for literature a year late. Faulkner's full stature cannot be measured in any single work; however good in itself, the novel or story is usually integrated in a larger pattern with characters and events from other writings.

Faulkner regards his major works as a "saga," a reconstruction of the life of Yoknapatawpha County, his fictional name for Lafayette County in northern Mississippi, where he lives at Oxford (the "Jefferson" of his novels). The documentary sources of his stories are family papers and county records extending, as in *The Bear*, back to the first settlements among the Indians. Yet if these are the materials of local social history, he also thinks that he should be able to find in them the record of the human spirit anywhere. He emphasized this central purpose in his address in acceptance of the Nobel Prize, in which he told younger writers that the only subject "worth the agony and sweat" of the artist is "the human heart in conflict with itself."

Since about 1925, Faulkner has lived quietly in Oxford, Mississippi, in the seclusion of the old house with its columned portico, belatedly depicted in popular media. Since then, as university writer in residence and public figure, his personal influence has been forceful. He was born on September 25, 1897, in New Albany, Mississippi, but the family soon moved to Oxford, the seat of the University of Mississippi. His great-grandfather, William Falkner [*sic*],

[handwritten: approaches history of society as capsulated in a family within that definition of a society.]

Subtle craftsmanship
modern minds more receptive to horror

had written a popular southern romance, but the boy was not literary in a marked way, and did not finish high school. In 1918, at the age of twenty-one, he enlisted in the Canadian Royal Flying Corps, but in about a year he returned to Oxford, where he next attended the University for two years. In 1922 he took a position as postmaster at the University; but having recently discovered a desire to write, in 1924 he went to New Orleans with newspaper work in mind. There he became a friend of Sherwood Anderson, then completing *Dark Laughter*; through him Faulkner became one of those associated with *The Double-Dealer*, an experimental magazine, in which he published verse and criticism. That year he prepared a collection of poems entitled *The Marble Faun* (1924). In New Orleans he wrote two novels, neither of ultimate consequence.

In 1925 he was again settled at Oxford. It has been reported that he worked as carpenter and farmer to provide for the publication of his first two novels. In 1929 he was able to publish two more, the beginning of his significant and mature work: *Sartoris*, which initiated the Yoknapatawpha cycle with a study of the Sartoris family; and *The Sound and the Fury*, which introduced the Compsons, a related family, and gave the world its first experience of this author's combination of experimental techniques and psychological violence. The novels of the cycle move on several planes of southern society. There are the old clans of Sartoris, Compson, Sutpen, McCaslin, de Spain,

and others, some of them now in a condition of decadence, and others just as significantly readjusted to new social conditions. There are the older townspeople, generally substantial in character, in contrast with the Snopes clan, of whom Faulkner and his Oxford cronies made almost an oral legend before the sketches were published in magazines. Three novels chronicle Flem Snopes, leader of rapacious kindred who emerge from backwoods burrows like rodents, to gnaw the props from under the old order. Flem grabs political and financial control; he uses a pretty wife to disgrace and depose the highborn Mayor, de Spain. He acquires the de Spain mansion, only to be destroyed, ironically by a Snopes whom he had betrayed. The early serial stories were reconstructed as *The Hamlet* (1940); *The Town* (1957) and *The Mansion* (1959) complete this comic epic. The older families, whether planters or townspeople, hold in recollection the pioneers who first conquered the land, the "old people," as a heritage that they share with such woodsmen, part Indian, as Sam Fathers and Boon Hogganbeck in the stories of *Go Down, Moses* (1942), among them *The Bear*. Curiously too, the Negroes have withstood better than the white people the shifting ordeals of history. There are scamps among them, but Faulkner emphasizes the strength of such Negroes as Dilsey in *The Sound and the Fury* and Lucas Beauchamp, last seen in *Intruder in the Dust* (1948). In the Yoknapatawpha group, *Light in August* (1932), *Absalom, Absalom!* (1936), and

The Unvanquished (1938) are significant works. *As I Lay Dying* (1930) utilizes a folk tale concerning a delayed burial in a psychological study of the degenerated "poor whites." *Sanctuary* (1931) is a classic of horror and degradation representing the corruption of small-town youth and the power of criminality in the age of jazz and prohibition. Its recent sequel is *Requiem for a Nun* (1951). *The Wild Palms* (1939) and its twin, the popular *Old Man*, counterpoint a theme: in one, two lovers are destroyed by passionate violence; in the latter, a derelict convict and a lost woman, in the violence of an "Old Man" Mississippi flood, experience love and birth. *A Fable* (1954) is a retelling of the events of Holy Week, with the time and place shifted to World War I in France.

Faulkner's complex style may be regarded as consistent with his difficult objective—to keep continuously in focus the immediate character, "the human heart in conflict," while evoking that past which is always present with us. His style observes the conventions of a new prose, no more strict or unnatural than the conventions of poetry, and similarly intended to engage the imaginative participation of the reader and to provide a language more subjective and flexible than ordinary prose. This rhetorical convention—the dislocation of logical construction in the free association of images, often apparently, but only apparently, ir-

relevant to each other—facilitates Faulkner's psychological approach, the projection of events through the memory or consciousness of the character in the form of "interior monologue." No doubt Faulkner's style puts a burden on the reader, but whether or not he carries it further than may be necessary for his purposes, it has the effect of music and poetry in requiring active correspondence between the artist and the audience.

In 1950 Faulkner received not only the Nobel Prize, but also the National Book Award for his *Collected Stories*. The opportunity to study the stories in one volume was another invitation to reconsider Faulkner's work as a whole, and this reconsideration has added greatly to the public understanding of a major artist.

Besides those mentioned above, Faulkner's novels, not yet collected, are *Soldier's Pay*, 1926; *Mosquitoes*, 1927; *Pylon*, 1935. Volumes of short stories are *Idyll in the Desert*, 1931; *These 13: Stories*, 1931; *Miss Zilphia Gant*, 1932; *Doctor Martino and Other Stories*, 1934; *Go Down, Moses, and Other Stories*, 1942; *Knight's Gambit*, 1949; *Notes on a Horse Thief*, 1950; *Collected Stories of William Faulkner*, 1950; and *Big Woods*, 1955. Faulkner's poems appear in *The Marble Faun*, 1924; *Salmagundi*, 1932; *This Earth*, 1932; *A Green Bough*, 1933. *The Portable Faulkner*, 1946, is a good selection.

Biographical and critical studies are Hyatt Waggoner, *William Faulkner, From Jefferson to the World*, 1960; H. M. Campbell and R. E. Foster, *William Faulkner: A Critical Appraisal*, 1951; *William Faulkner: Two Decades of Criticism*, edited by F. J. Hoffman and O. W. Vickery, 1951; Irving Howe, *William Faulkner: A Critical Study*, 1952; William V. O'Connor, *The Tangled Fire of William Faulkner*, 1954; and W. L. Miner, *The World of William Faulkner*, 1952.

tradition of evil must be overcome or will kill

1262 · William Faulkner

Complex time sequence

The Bear[1] *Ordeal*

#1- gen. insight into kind of ordeal - flash back
nature of people, Ike's yearning

recalling why the hog hunt to pt. where he can reflect in best form

There was a man and a dog too this time. Two beasts, counting Old Ben, the bear, and two men, counting Boon Hogganbeck, in whom some of the same blood ran which ran in Sam Fathers, even though Boon's was a plebeian strain of it and only Sam and Old Ben and the mongrel Lion were taintless and incorruptible.

He[2] was sixteen. For six years now he had been a man's hunter. For six years now he had heard the best of all talking. It was of the wilderness, the big woods, bigger and older than any recorded document; of white man fatuous enough to believe he had bought any fragment of it, of Indian ruthless enough to pretend that any fragment of it had been his to convey; bigger than Major de Spain[3] and the scrap he pretended to, knowing better; older than old Thomas Sutpen of whom Major de Spain had had it and who knew better; older even than old Ikkemotubbe, the Chickasaw chief, of whom old Sutpen had had it and who knew better in his turn. It was of the men, not white nor black nor red but men, hunters, with the will and hardihood to endure and the humility and skill to survive, and the dogs and the bear and deer juxtaposed and reliefed against it, ordered and compelled by and within the wilderness in the ancient and unremitting contest according to the ancient and immitigable rules which voided all regrets and brooked no quarter; —the best game of all, the best of all breathing and forever the best of all listening, the voices quiet and weighty and deliberate for retrospection and recollection and exactitude among the concrete trophies—the racked guns and the heads and skins—in the libraries of town houses or the offices of plantation houses or (and best of all) in the camps themselves where the intact and still-warm meat

1. An early draft of part of this story appeared in *Harper's Magazine* for December, 1935, entitled "Lion." Another abbreviated version, called "The Bear," appeared in the *Saturday Evening Post* for May 9, 1942. The full story was first printed in *Go Down, Moses, and Other Stories* (1942). Malcolm Cowley, in *The Portable Faulkner*, places this story in "the last frontier" of Mississippi, about 1883. In Faulkner's novels of Yoknapatawpha County, the Mc-Caslin family, and the Sartoris, Sutpen, and de Spain families are the "old people"; not all of them aristocrats, but all eligible as recognized guardians of a good tradition. An aspect of that tradition is here represented in the scrupulous honor and fortitude of the farmer and hunter. Isaac McCaslin, now sixteen, the son of Theophilus ("Uncle Buck"), and grandson of Carothers Mc-Caslin, must prove, in the ancient ordeal of the hunt, his right to stand with men. The discipline of this clean and relentless integrity comes to him not only through the great men of the clans, but just as much from those whose veins carry Indian or Negro blood—from Sam Fathers and Boon Hogganbeck, in whom also survive "the old free fathers"—from the savage fidelity of the dog, Lion, and from "the wild and invincible spirit of an old bear," Ben, the unconquered. Isaac learns so well that he repudiates the inheritance of his family (Part IV), because of his grandfather, Carothers, whose infidelity he reads between the lines of the plantation records.

2. That is, Isaac McCaslin.

3. Major Cassius de Spain's investments have gradually brought him ownership of extensive lands, formerly the Sutpens', including the great woodlands with the hunting lodge, scene of the present story.

must stand as man

worthy to forgive his enemies- nature didn't teach him that -turns to nature for ally

Bear = nature myth . opposition to life of man
seek opposition - not flee from it - that is what
book is all about
The Bear · 1263

yet hung, the men who had slain it sitting before the burning logs
on hearths when there were houses and hearths or about the smoky
blazing of piled wood in front of stretched tarpaulins when there
were not. There was always a bottle present, so that it would seem
to him that those fine fierce instants of heart and brain and courage
and wiliness and speed were concentrated and distilled into that
brown liquor which not women, not boys and children, but only
hunters drank, drinking not of the blood they spilled but some
condensation of the wild immortal spirit, drinking it moderately,
humbly even, not with the pagan's base and baseless hope of acquiring thereby the virtues of cunning and strength and speed but in
salute to them. Thus it seemed to him on this December morning
not only natural but actually fitting that this should have begun
with whisky.

He realized later that it had begun long before that. It had already
begun on that day when he first wrote his age in two ciphers and
his cousin McCaslin[4] brought him for the first time to the camp,
the big woods, to earn for himself from the wilderness the name and
state of hunter provided he in his turn were humble and enduring
enough. He had already inherited then, without ever having seen
it, the big old bear with one trap-ruined foot that in an area almost
a hundred miles square had earned for himself a name, a definite
designation like a living man:—the long legend of corn-cribs broken
down and rifled, of shoats and grown pigs and even calves carried
bodily into the woods and devoured and traps and deadfalls overthrown and dogs mangled and slain and shotgun and even rifle
shots delivered at point-blank range yet with no more effect than so
many peas blown through a tube by a child—a corridor of wreckage
and destruction beginning back before the boy was born, through
which sped, not fast but rather with the ruthless and irresistible
deliberation of a locomotive, the shaggy tremendous shape. It ran
in his knowledge before he ever saw it. It loomed and towered in
his dreams before he even saw the unaxed woods where it left its
crooked print, shaggy, tremendous, red-eyed, not malevolent but just
big, too big for the dogs which tried to bay it, for the horses which
tried to ride it down, for the men and the bullets they fired into
it; too big for the very country which was its constricting scope.
It was as if the boy had already divined what his senses and intellect
had not encompassed yet: that doomed wilderness whose edges
were being constantly and punily gnawed at by men with plows
and axes who feared it because it was wilderness, men myriad and
nameless even to one another in the land where the old bear had
earned a name, and through which ran not even a mortal beast but

4. Carothers McCaslin Edmonds, an
older cousin of Isaac's, sometimes called
"Cass" in Faulkner's writings, as later
in this story.

an anachronism indomitable and invincible out of an old dead time, a phantom, epitome and apotheosis of the old wild life which the little puny humans swarmed and hacked at in a fury of abhorrence and fear like pygmies about the ankles of a drowsing elephant;—the old bear, solitary, indomitable, and alone; widowered childless and absolved of mortality—old Priam[5] reft of his old wife and outlived all his sons.

Still a child, with three years then two years then one year yet before he too could make one of them, each November he would watch the wagon containing the dogs and the bedding and food and guns and his cousin McCaslin and Tennie's Jim[6] and Sam Fathers too until Sam moved to the camp to live, depart for the Big Bottom, the big woods. To him, they were going not to hunt bear and deer but to keep yearly rendezvous with the bear which they did not even intend to kill. Two weeks later they would return, with no trophy, no skin. He had not expected it. He had not even feared that it might be in the wagon this time with the other skins and heads. He did not even tell himself that in three years or two years or one year more he would be present and that it might even be his gun. He believed that only after he had served his apprenticeship in the woods which would prove him worthy to be a hunter, would he even be permitted to distinguish the crooked print, and that even then for two November weeks he would merely make another minor one, along with his cousin and Major de Spain and General Compson and Walter Ewell and Boon and the dogs which feared to bay it and the shotguns and rifles which failed even to bleed it, in the yearly pageant-rite of the old bear's furious immortality.

His day came at last. In the surrey with his cousin and Major de Spain and General Compson he saw the wilderness through a slow drizzle of November rain just above the ice point as it seemed to him later he always saw it or at least always remembered it—the tall and endless wall of dense November woods under the dissolving afternoon and the year's death, sombre, impenetrable (he could not even discern yet how, at what point they could possibly hope to enter it even though he knew that Sam Fathers was waiting there with the wagon), the surrey moving through the skeleton stalks of cotton and corn in the last of open country, the last trace of man's puny gnawing at the immemorial flank, until, dwarfed by that perspective into an almost ridiculous diminishment, the surrey itself seemed to have ceased to move (this too to be completed later, years later, after he had grown to a man and had seen the sea) as a solitary small boat hangs in lonely immobility, merely tossing up and down, in the infinite waste of the ocean while the water and then the apparently impenetrable land which it nears without appreciable progress, swings slowly and opens the widening inlet which is the anchorage. He entered it. Sam was waiting, wrapped in a quilt on the wagon seat behind the patient and steaming mules. He entered his novitiate to the true wilderness with Sam beside him as he had begun his apprenticeship in miniature to manhood after the rabbits and such with Sam beside him, the two of them wrapped in the damp, warm, Negro-rank quilt, while the wilderness closed behind his entrance as it had opened momentarily to accept him, opening before his advancement as it closed behind his progress, no fixed path the wagon followed but a channel non-existent ten yards ahead of it and ceasing to exist ten yards after it had passed, the wagon progressing not by its own volition but by attrition of their intact yet fluid circumambience, drowsing, earless, almost lightless.

It seemed to him that at the age of ten he was witnessing his own birth. It was not even strange to him. He had experienced it all before, and not merely in dreams. He saw the camp—a paintless six-room bungalow set on piles above the spring high-water—and he knew already how it was going to look. He helped in the rapid orderly disorder of their establishment in it and even his motions were familiar to him, foreknown. Then for two weeks he ate the coarse, rapid food—the shapeless sour bread, the wild strange meat, venison and bear and turkey and coon which he had never tasted before—which men ate, cooked by men who were hunters first and cooks afterward; he slept in harsh sheetless blankets as hunters slept. Each morning the gray of dawn found him and Sam Fathers on the stand, the crossing, which had been allotted him. It was the poorest one, the most barren. He had expected that; he had not dared yet to hope even to himself that he would even hear the running dogs this first time. But he did hear them. It was on the third morning—a murmur, sourceless, almost indistinguishable, yet he knew what it was although he had never before heard that many dogs running at once, the murmur swelling into separate and distinct voices until he could call the five dogs which his cousin owned from among the others. "Now," Sam said, "slant your gun up a little and draw back the hammers and then stand still."

But it was not for him, not yet. The humility was there; he had learned that. And he could learn the patience. He was only ten, only one week. The instant had passed. It seemed to him that he could actually see the deer, the buck, smoke-colored, elongated with speed, vanished, the woods, the gray solitude still ringing even when the voices of the dogs had died away; from far away across the sombre woods and the gray half-liquid morning there came two shots. "Now let your hammers down," Sam said.

He did so. "You knew it too," he said.

"Yes," Sam said. "I want you to learn how to do when you didn't shoot. It's after the chance for the bear or the deer has done already come and gone that men and dogs get killed."

"Anyway, it wasn't him," the boy said. "It wasn't even a bear. It was just a deer."

"Yes," Sam said, "it was just a deer."

Then one morning, it was in the second week, he heard the dogs again. This time before Sam even spoke he readied the too-long, too-heavy, man-size gun as Sam had taught him, even though this time he knew the dogs and the deer were coming less close than ever, hardly within hearing even. They didn't sound like any running dogs he had ever heard before even. Then he found that Sam, who had taught him first of all to cock the gun and take position where he could see best in all directions and then never to move again, had himself moved up beside him. "There," he said. "Listen." The boy listened, to no ringing chorus strong and fast on a free scent but, a moiling yapping an octave too high and with something more than indecision and even abjectness in it which he could not yet recognize, reluctant, not even moving very fast, taking a long time to pass out of hearing, leaving even then in the air that echo of thin and almost human hysteria, abject, almost humanly grieving, with this time nothing ahead of it, no sense of a fleeing unseen smoke-colored shape. He could hear Sam breathing at his shoulder. He saw the arched curve of the old man's inhaling nostrils.

"It's Old Ben!" he cried, whispering.

Sam didn't move save for the slow gradual turning of his head as the voices faded on and the faint steady rapid arch and collapse of his nostrils. "Hah," he said. "Not even running. Walking."

"But up here!" the boy cried. "Way up here!"

"He do it every year," Sam said. "Once. Ash and Boon say he comes up here to run the other little bears away. Tell them to get to hell out of here and stay out until the hunters are gone. Maybe." The boy no longer heard anything at all, yet still Sam's head continued to turn gradually and steadily until the back of it was toward him. Then it turned back and looked down at him—the same face, grave, familiar, expressionless until it smiled, the same old man's eyes from which as he watched there faded slowly a quality darkly and fiercely lambent, passionate and proud. "He dont care no more for bears than he does for dogs or men neither. He come to see who's here, who's new in camp this year, whether he can shoot or not, can stay or not. Whether we got the dog yet that can bay and hold him until a man gets there with a gun. Because he's the head bear. He's the man." It faded, was gone; again they were the eyes as he had known them all his life. "He'll let them follow him to the river. Then he'll send them home. We might as well go too; see how they look when they get back to camp."

The dogs were there first, ten of them huddled back under the kitchen, himself and Sam squatting to peer back into the obscurity where they crouched, quiet, the eyes rolling and luminous, vanishing, and no sound, only that effluvium which the boy could not quite place yet, of something more than dog, stronger than dog and not just animal, just beast even. Because there had been nothing in front of the abject and painful yapping except the solitude, the wilderness, so that when the eleventh hound got back about mid-afternoon and he and Tennie's Jim held the passive and still trembling bitch while Sam daubed her tattered ear and raked shoulder with turpentine and axle-grease, it was still no living creature but only the wilderness which, leaning for a moment, had patted lightly once her temerity. "Just like a man," Sam said. "Just like folks. Put off as long as she could having to be brave, knowing all the time that sooner or later she would have to be brave once so she could keep on calling herself a dog, and knowing beforehand what was going to happen when she done it."

He did not know just when Sam left. He only knew that he was gone. For the next three mornings he rose and ate breakfast and Sam was not waiting for him. He went to his stand alone; he found it without help now and stood on it as Sam had taught him. On the third morning he heard the dogs again, running strong and free on a true scent again, and he readied the gun as he had learned to do and heard the hunt sweep past on since he was not ready yet, had not deserved other yet in just one short period of two weeks as compared to all the long life which he had already dedicated to the wilderness with patience and humility; he heard the shot again, one shot, the single clapping report of Walter Ewell's rifle. By now he could not only find his stand and then return to camp without guidance, by using the compass his cousin had given him he reached Walter, waiting beside the buck and the moiling of dogs over the cast entrails before any of the others except Major de Spain and Tennie's Jim on the horses, even before Uncle Ash[7] arrived with the one-eyed wagon-mule which did not mind the smell of blood or even, so they said, of bear.

It was not Uncle Ash on the mule. It was Sam, returned. And Sam was waiting when he finished his dinner and, himself on the

7. The familiar name of the Negro camp cook and handy man.

one-eyed mule and Sam on the other one of the wagon team, they rode for more than three hours through the rapid shortening sunless afternoon, following no path, no trail even that he could discern, into a section of country he had never seen before. Then he understood why Sam had made him ride the one-eyed mule which would not spook[8] at the smell of blood, of wild animals. The other one, the sound one, stopped short and tried to whirl and bolt even as Sam got down, jerking and wrenching at the rein while Sam held it, coaxing it forward with his voice since he did not dare risk hitching it, drawing it forward while the boy dismounted from the marred one which would stand. Then, standing beside Sam in the thick great gloom of ancient woods and the winter's dying afternoon, he looked quietly down at the rotted log scored and gutted with claw-marks and, in the wet earth beside it, the print of the enormous warped two-toed foot. Now he knew what he had heard in the hounds' voices in the woods that morning and what he had smelled when he peered under the kitchen where they huddled. It was in him too, a little different because they were brute beasts and he was not, but only a little different—an eagerness, passive; an abjectness, a sense of his own fragility and impotence against the timeless woods, yet without doubt or dread; a flavor like brass in the sudden run of saliva in his mouth, a hard sharp constriction either in his brain or his stomach, he could not tell which and it did not matter; he knew only that for the first time he realized that the bear which had run in his listening and loomed in his dreams since before he could remember and which therefore must have existed in the listening and the dreams of his cousin and Major de Spain and even old General Compson before they began to remember in their turn, was a mortal animal and that they had departed for the camp each November with no actual intention of slaying it, not because it could not be slain but because so far they had no actual hope of being able to. "It will be tomorrow," he said.

"You mean we will try tomorrow," Sam said. "We aint got the dog yet."

"We've got eleven," he said. "They ran him Monday."

"And you heard them," Sam said. "Saw them too. We aint got the dog yet. It wont take but one. But he aint there. Maybe he aint nowhere. The only other way will be for him to run by accident over somebody that had a gun and knowed how to shoot it."

"That wouldn't be me," the boy said. "It would be Walter or Major or—"

"It might," Sam said. "You watch close tomorrow. Because he's smart. That's how come he has lived this long. If he gets hemmed up and has got to pick out somebody to run over, he will pick out

8. Rear or run in fright.

you."

"How?" he said. "How will he know. . . ." He ceased. "You mean he already knows me, that I aint never been to the big bottom before, aint had time to find out yet whether I . . ." He ceased again, staring at Sam; he said humbly, not even amazed: "It was me he was watching. I dont reckon he did need to come but once."

"You watch tomorrow," Sam said. "I reckon we better start back. It'll be long after dark now before we get to camp."

The next morning they started three hours earlier than they had ever done. Even Uncle Ash went, the cook, who called himself by profession a camp cook and who did little else save cook for Major de Spain's hunting and camping parties, yet who had been marked by the wilderness from simple juxtaposition to it until he responded as they all did, even the boy who until two weeks ago had never even seen the wilderness, to a hound's ripped ear and shoulder and the print of a crooked foot in a patch of wet earth. They rode. It was too far to walk: the boy and Sam and Uncle Ash in the wagon with the dogs, his cousin and Major de Spain and General Compson and Boon and Walter and Tennie's Jim riding double on the horses; again the first gray light found him, as on that first morning two weeks ago, on the stand where Sam had placed and left him. With the gun which was too big for him, the breech-loader which did not even belong to him but to Major de Spain and which he had fired only once, at a stump on the first day to learn the recoil and how to reload it with the paper shells, he stood against a big gum tree beside a little bayou whose black still water crept without motion out of a cane-brake, across a small clearing and into the cane again, where, invisible, a bird, the big woodpecker called Lord-to-God by negroes, clattered at a dead trunk. It was a stand like any other stand, dissimilar only in incidentals to the one where he had stood each morning for two weeks; a territory new to him yet no less familiar than that other one which after two weeks he had come to believe he knew a little—the same solitude, the same loneliness through which frail and timorous man had merely passed without altering it, leaving no mark nor scar, which looked exactly as it must have looked when the first ancestor of Sam Fathers' Chickasaw predecessors crept into it and looked about him, club or stone axe or bone arrow drawn and ready, different only because, squatting at the edge of the kitchen, he had smelled the dogs huddled and cringing beneath it and saw the raked ear and side of the bitch that, as Sam had said, had to be brave once in order to keep on calling herself a dog, and saw yesterday in the earth beside the gutted log, the print of the living foot. He heard no dogs at all. He never did certainly hear them. He only heard the drumming of the woodpecker stop short off, and knew that the bear was looking at him. He never saw it. He did not know whether it was facing him from the cane or behind him. He did not move, holding the useless gun which he knew now he would never fire at it, now or ever, tasting in his saliva that taint of brass which he had smelled in the huddled dogs when he peered under the kitchen.

Then it was gone. As abruptly as it had stopped, the woodpecker's dry hammering set up again, and after a while he believed he even heard the dogs—a murmur, scarce a sound even, which he had probably been hearing for a time, perhaps a minute or two, before he remarked it, drifting into hearing and then out again, dying away. They came nowhere near him. If it was dogs he heard, he could not have sworn to it; if it was a bear they ran, it was another bear. It was Sam himself who emerged from the cane and crossed the bayou, the injured bitch following at heel as a bird dog is taught to walk. She came and crouched against his leg, trembling. "I didn't see him," he said. "I didn't, Sam."

"I know it," Sam said. "He done the looking. You didn't hear him neither, did you?"

"No," the boy said. "I—"

"He's smart," Sam said. "Too smart." Again the boy saw in his eyes that quality of dark and brooding lambence as Sam looked down at the bitch trembling faintly and steadily against the boy's leg. From her raked shoulder a few drops of fresh blood clung like bright berries. "Too big. We aint got the dog yet. But maybe some day."

Because there would be a next time, after and after. He was only ten. It seemed to him that he could see them, the two of them, shadowy in the limbo from which time emerged and became time: the old bear absolved of mortality and himself who shared a little of it. Because he recognised now what he had smelled in the huddled dogs and tasted in his own saliva, recognised fear as a boy, a youth, recognises the existence of love and passion and experience which is his heritage but not yet his patrimony, from entering by chance the presence or perhaps even merely the bedroom of a woman who has loved and been loved by many men. *So I will have to see him*, he thought, without dread or even hope. *I will have to look at him*. So it was in June of the next summer. They were at the camp again, celebrating Major de Spain's and General Compson's birthdays. Although the one had been born in September and the other in the depth of winter and almost thirty years earlier, each June the two of them and McCaslin and Boon and Walter Ewell (and the boy too from now on) spent two weeks at the camp, fishing and shooting squirrels and turkey and running coons and wildcats with the dogs at night. That is, Boon and the negroes (and the boy too now) fished and shot squirrels and ran the coons and cats, because the proven hunters, not only Major de Spain and old General Compson (who spent those two weeks sitting in a rocking chair before a tremendous iron pot of Brunswick stew, stirring and tasting, with Uncle Ash to quarrel with about how he was making it and Tennie's Jim to pour whisky into the tin dipper from which he drank it), but even McCaslin and Walter Ewell who were still young enough, scorned such other than shooting the wild gobblers with pistols for wagers or to test their marksmanship.

That is, his cousin McCaslin and the others thought he was hunting squirrels. Until the third evening he believed that Sam Fathers thought so too. Each morning he would leave the camp right after breakfast. He had his own gun now, a new breech-loader, a Christmas gift; he would own and shoot it for almost seventy years, through two new pairs of barrels and locks and one new stock, until all that remained of the original gun was the silver-inlaid trigger-guard with his and McCaslin's engraved names and the date in 1878. He found the tree beside the little bayou where he had stood that morning. Using the compass he ranged from that point; he was teaching himself to be better than a fair woodsman without even knowing he was doing it. On the third day he even found the gutted log where he had first seen the print. It was almost completely crumbled now, healing with unbelievable speed, a passionate and almost visible relinquishment, back into the earth from which the tree had grown. He ranged the summer woods now, green with gloom, if anything actually dimmer than they had been in November's gray dissolution, where even at noon the sun fell only in windless dappling upon the earth which never completely dried and which crawled with snakes—moccasins and watersnakes and rattlers, themselves the color of the dappled gloom so that he would not always see them until they moved; returning to camp later and later and later, first day, second day, passing in the twilight of the third evening the little log pen enclosing the log barn where Sam was putting up the stock for the night. "You aint looked right yet," Sam said.

He stopped. For a moment he didn't answer. Then he said peacefully, in a peaceful rushing burst, as when a boy's miniature dam in a little brook gives way: "All right. Yes. But how? I went to the bayou. I even found that log again. I—"

"I reckon that was all right. Likely he's been watching you. You never saw his foot?"

"I . . ." the boy said. "I didn't . . . I never thought . . ."

"It's the gun," Sam said. He stood beside the fence, motionless, the old man, son of a negro slave and a Chickasaw chief, in the battered and faded overalls and the frayed five-cent straw hat which had been the badge of the negro's slavery and was now the regalia of his freedom. The camp—the clearing, the house, the barn and its tiny lot with which Major de Spain in his turn had scratched punily and evanescently at the wilderness—faded in the dusk, back into the immemorial darkness of the woods. *The gun*, the boy thought. *The gun*. "You will have to choose," Sam said.

He left the next morning before light, without breakfast, long before Uncle Ash would wake in his quilts on the kitchen floor and start the fire. He had only the compass and a stick for the snakes. He could go almost a mile before he would need to see the compass. He sat on a log, the invisible compass in his hand, while the secret night-sounds which had ceased at his movements, scurried again and then fell still for good and the owls ceased and gave over to the waking day birds and there was light in the gray wet woods and he could see the compass. He went fast yet still quietly, becoming steadily better and better as a woodsman without yet having time to realise it; he jumped a doe and a fawn, walked them out of the bed, close enough to see them—the crash of undergrowth, the white scut, the fawn scudding along behind her, faster than he had known it could have run. He was hunting right, upwind, as Sam had taught him, but that didn't matter now. He had left the gun; by his own will and relinquishment he had accepted not a gambit, not a choice, but a condition in which not only the bear's heretofore inviolable anonymity but all the ancient rules and balances of hunter and hunted had been abrogated. He would not even be afraid, not even in the moment when the fear would take him completely: blood, skin, bowels, bones, memory from the long time before it even became his memory—all save that thin clear quenchless lucidity which alone differed him from this bear and from all the other bears and bucks he would follow during almost seventy years, to which Sam had said: "Be scared. You cant help that. But dont be afraid. Aint nothing in the woods going to hurt you if you dont corner it or it dont smell that you are afraid. A bear or a deer has got to be scared of a coward the same as a brave man has got to be."

By noon he was far beyond the crossing on the little bayou, farther into the new and alien country than he had ever been, travelling now not only by the compass but by the old, heavy, biscuit-thick silver watch which had been his father's. He had left the camp nine hours ago; nine hours from now, dark would already have been an hour old. He stopped, for the first time since he had risen from the log when he could see the compass face at last, and looked about, mopping his sweating face on his sleeve. He had already relinquished, of his will, because of his need, in humility and peace and without regret, yet apparently that had not been enough, the leaving of the gun was not enough. He stood for a moment—a child, alien and lost in the green and soaring gloom of the markless wilderness. Then he relinquished completely to it. It was the watch and the compass. He was still tainted. He removed the linked chain of the one and the looped thong of the other from his overalls and hung them on a bush and leaned the stick beside them and entered it.

When he realised he was lost, he did as Sam had coached and drilled him: made a cast to cross his back-track. He had not been going very fast for the last two or three hours, and he had gone even less fast since he left the compass and watch on the bush. So he went slower still now, since the tree could not be very far; in fact, he found it before he really expected to and turned and went to it. But there was no bush beneath it, no compass nor watch, so he did next as Sam had coached and drilled him: made this next circle in the opposite direction and much larger, so that the pattern of the two of them would bisect his track somewhere, but crossing no trace nor mark anywhere of his feet or any feet, and now he was going faster though still not panicked, his heart beating a little more rapidly but strong and steady enough, and this time it was not even the tree because there was a down log beside it which he had never seen before and beyond the log a little swamp, a seepage of moisture somewhere between earth and water, and he did what Sam had coached and drilled him as the next and the last, seeing as he sat down on the log the crooked print, the warped indentation in the wet ground which while he looked at it continued to fill with water until it was level full and the water began to overflow and the sides of the print began to dissolve away. Even as he looked up he saw the next one, and, moving, the one beyond it; moving, not hurrying, running, but merely keeping pace with them as they appeared before him as though they were being shaped out of thin air just one constant pace short of where he would lose them forever and be lost forever himself, tireless, eager, without doubt or dread, panting a little above the strong rapid little hammer of his heart, emerging suddenly into a little glade, and the wilderness coalesced. It rushed, soundless, and solidified—the tree, the bush, the compass and the watch glinting where a ray of sunlight touched them. Then he saw the bear. It did not emerge, appear: it was just there, immobile, fixed in the green and windless noon's hot dappling, not as big as he had dreamed it but as big as he had expected, bigger, dimensionless against the dappled obscurity, looking at him. Then it moved. It crossed the glade without haste, walking for an instant into the sun's full glare and out of it, and stopped again and looked back at him across one shoulder. Then it was gone. It didn't walk into the woods. It faded, sank back into the wilderness without motion as he had watched a fish, a huge old bass, sink back into the dark depths of its pool and vanish without even any movement of its fins.

II

So he should have hated and feared Lion.[9] He was thirteen then. He had killed his buck and Sam Fathers had marked his face with the hot blood,[1] and in the next November he killed a bear. But before that accolade he had become as competent in the woods as many grown men with the same experience. By now he was a better woodsman than most grown men with more. There was no territory within twenty-five miles of the camp that he did not know —bayou, ridge, landmark trees and path; he could have led anyone direct to any spot in it and brought him back. He knew game trails that even Sam Fathers had never seen; in the third fall he found a buck's bedding-place by himself and unbeknown to his cousin he borrowed Walter Ewell's rifle and lay in wait for the buck at dawn and killed it when it walked back to the bed as Sam had told him how the old Chickasaw fathers did.

By now he knew the old bear's footprint better than he did his own, and not only the crooked one. He could see any one of the three sound prints and distinguish it at once from any other, and not only because of its size. There were other bears within that fifty miles which left tracks almost as large, or at least so near that the one would have appeared larger only by juxtaposition. It was more than that. If Sam Fathers had been his mentor and the backyard rabbits and squirrels his kindergarten, then the wilderness the old bear ran was his college and the old male bear itself, so long unwifed and childless as to have become its own ungendered progenitor, was his alma mater.

He could find the crooked print now whenever he wished, ten miles or five miles or sometimes closer than that, to the camp. Twice while on stand during the next three years he heard the dogs strike its trail and once even jump it by chance, the voices high, abject, almost human in their hysteria. Once, still-hunting[2] with Walter Ewell's rifle, he saw it cross a long corridor of down timber where a tornado had passed. It rushed through rather than across the tangle of trunks and branches as a locomotive would, faster than he had ever believed it could have moved, almost as fast as a deer even because the deer would have spent most of that distance in the air; he realised then why it would take a dog not only of abnormal courage but size and speed too ever to bring it to bay. He had a little dog at home, a mongrel, of the sort called fyce[3] by negroes, a ratter, itself not much bigger than a rat and possessing that sort

9. The "incorruptible" dog predestined to bring to bay the big bear. *Cf.* the first paragraph of the story.
1. Certain Indian tribes ritually anointed the young hunter with the blood of his first quarry.
2. Stalking game without dogs.
3. A small hunting dog.

of courage which had long since stopped being bravery and had become foolhardiness. He brought it with him one June and, timing them as if they were meeting an appointment with another human being, himself carrying the fyce with a sack over its head and Sam Fathers with a brace of the hounds on a rope leash, they lay downwind of the trail and actually ambushed the bear. They were so close that it turned at bay although he realised later this might have been from surprise and amazement at the shrill and frantic uproar of the fyce. It turned at bay against the trunk of a big cypress, on its hind feet; it seemed to the boy that it would never stop rising, taller and taller, and even the two hounds seemed to have taken a kind of desperate and despairing courage from the fyce. Then he realised that the fyce was actually not going to stop. He flung the gun down and ran. When he overtook and grasped the shrill, frantically pinwheeling little dog, it seemed to him that he was directly under the bear. He could smell it, strong and hot and rank. Sprawling, he looked up where it loomed and towered over him like a thunderclap. It was quite familiar, until he remembered: this was the way he had used to dream about it.

Then it was gone. He didn't see it go. He knelt, holding the frantic fyce with both hands, hearing the abased wailing of the two hounds drawing further and further away, until Sam came up, carrying the gun. He laid it quietly down beside the boy and stood looking down at him. "You've done seed him twice now, with a gun in your hands," he said. "This time you couldn't have missed him."

The boy rose. He still held the fyce. Even in his arms it continued to yap frantically, surging and straining toward the fading sound of the hounds like a collection of live-wire springs. The boy was panting a little. "Neither could you," he said. "You had the gun. Why didn't you shoot him?"

Sam didn't seem to have heard. He put out his hand and touched the little dog in the boy's arms which still yapped and strained even though the two hounds were out of hearing now. "He's done gone," Sam said. "You can slack off and rest now, until next time." He stroked the little dog until it began to grow quiet under his hand. "You's almost the one we wants," he said. "You just aint big enough. We aint got that one yet. He will need to be just a little bigger than smart, and a little braver than either." He withdrew his hand from the fyce's head and stood looking into the woods where the bear and the hounds had vanished. "Somebody is going to, some day."

"I know it," the boy said. "That's why it must be one of us. So it wont be until the last day. When even he dont want it to last any longer."

So he should have hated and feared Lion. It was in the fourth summer, the fourth time he had made one in the celebration of Major de Spain's and General Compson's birthday. In the early spring Major de Spain's mare had foaled a horse colt. One evening when Sam brought the horses and mules up to stable them for the night, the colt was missing and it was all he could do to get the frantic mare into the lot. He had thought at first to let the mare lead him back to where she had become separated from the foal. But she would not do it. She would not even feint toward any particular part of the woods or even in any particular direction. She merely ran, as if she couldn't see, still frantic with terror. She whirled and ran at Sam once, as if to attack him in some ultimate desperation, as if she could not for the moment realise that he was a man and a long-familiar one. He got her into the lot at last. It was too dark by that time to back-track her, to unravel the erratic course she had doubtless pursued.

He came to the house and told Major de Spain. It was an animal, of course, a big one, and the colt was dead now, wherever it was. They all knew that. "It's a panther," General Compson said at once. "The same one. That doe and fawn last March." Sam had sent Major de Spain word of it when Boon Hogganbeck came to the camp on a routine visit to see how the stock had wintered—the doe's throat torn out, and the beast had run down the helpless fawn and killed it too.

"Sam never did say that was a panther," Major de Spain said. Sam said nothing now, standing behind Major de Spain where they sat at supper, inscrutable, as if he were just waiting for them to stop talking so he could go home. He didn't even seem to be looking at anything. "A panther might jump a doe, and he wouldn't have much trouble catching the fawn afterward. But no panther would have jumped that colt with the dam right there with it. It was Old Ben," Major de Spain said. "I'm disappointed in him. He has broken the rules. I didn't think he would have done that. He has killed mine and McCaslin's dogs, but that was all right. We gambled the dogs against him; we gave each other warning. But now he has come into my house and destroyed my property, out of season too. He broke the rules. It was Old Ben, Sam." Still Sam said nothing, standing there until Major de Spain should stop talking. "We'll back-track her tomorrow and see," Major de Spain said.

Sam departed. He would not live in the camp; he had built himself a little hut something like Joe Baker's, only stouter, tighter, on the bayou a quarter-mile away, and a stout log crib where he stored a little corn for the shoat he raised each year. The next morning he was waiting when they waked. He had already found the colt. They did not even wait for breakfast. It was not far, not five hundred yards from the stable—the three-months' colt lying on its side, its throat torn out and the entrails and one ham partly eaten. It lay not as if it had been dropped but as if it had been struck and hurled, and no cat-mark, no claw-mark where a panther would have gripped it while finding its throat. They read the tracks where the frantic mare had circled and at last rushed in with that same ultimate desperation with which she had whirled on Sam Fathers yesterday evening, and the long tracks of dead and terrified running and those of the beast which had not even rushed at her when she advanced but had merely walked three or four paces toward her until she broke, and General Compson said, "Good God, what a wolf!"

Still Sam said nothing. The boy watched him while the men knelt, measuring the tracks. There was something in Sam's face now. It was neither exultation nor joy nor hope. Later, a man, the boy realised what it had been, and that Sam had known all the time what had made the tracks and what had torn the throat out of the doe in the spring and killed the fawn. It had been foreknowledge in Sam's face that morning. *And he was glad*, he told himself. *He was old. He had no children, no people, none of his blood anywhere above earth that he would ever meet again. And even if he were to, he could not have touched it, spoken to it, because for seventy years now he had had to be a negro. It was almost over now and he was glad.*

They returned to camp and had breakfast and came back with guns and the hounds. Afterwards the boy realised that they also should have known then what killed the colt as well as Sam Fathers did. But that was neither the first nor the last time he had seen men rationalise from and even act upon their misconceptions. After Boon, standing astride the colt, had whipped the dogs away from it with his belt, they snuffed at the tracks. One of them, a young dog hound without judgment yet, bayed once, and they ran for a few feet on what seemed to be a trail. Then they stopped, looking back at the men, eager enough, not baffled, merely questioning, as if they were asking "Now what?" Then they rushed back to the colt, where Boon, still astride it, slashed at them with the belt.

"I never knew a trail to get cold that quick," General Compson said.

"Maybe a single wolf big enough to kill a colt with the dam right there beside it dont leave scent," Major de Spain said.

"Maybe it was a hant,"[4] Walter Ewell said. He looked at Tennie's Jim. "Hah, Jim?"

Because the hounds would not run it, Major de Spain had Sam hunt out and find the tracks a hundred yards farther on and they put the dogs on it again and again the young one bayed and not one of them realised then that the hound was not baying like a dog striking

4. A ghost ("haunt").

game but was merely bellowing like a country dog whose yard has been invaded. General Compson spoke to the boy and Boon and Tennie's Jim: to the squirrel hunters. "You boys keep the dogs with you this morning. He's probably hanging around somewhere, waiting to get his breakfast off the colt. You might strike him."

But they did not. The boy remembered how Sam stood watching them as they went into the woods with the leashed hounds—the Indian face in which he had never seen anything until it smiled except that faint arching of the nostrils on that first morning when the hounds had found Old Ben. They took the hounds with them on the next day, though when they reached the place where they hoped to strike a fresh trail, the carcass of the colt was gone. Then on the third morning Sam was waiting again, this time until they had finished breakfast. He said, "Come." He led them to his house, his little hut, to the corn-crib beyond it. He had removed the corn and had made a deadfall of the door, baiting it with the colt's carcass; peering between the logs, they saw an animal almost the color of a gun or pistol barrel, what little time they had to examine its color or shape. It was not crouched nor even standing. It was in motion, in the air, coming toward them—a heavy body crashing with tremendous force against the door so that the thick door jumped and clattered in its frame, the animal, whatever it was, hurling itself against the door again seemingly before it could have touched the floor and got a new purchase to spring from. "Come away," Sam said, "fore he break his neck." Even when they retreated the heavy and measured crashes continued, the stout door jumping and clattering each time, and still no sound from the beast itself—no snarl, no cry.

"What in hell's name is it?" Major de Spain said.

"It's a dog," Sam said, his nostrils arching and collapsing faintly and steadily and that faint, fierce milkiness in his eyes again as on that first morning when the hounds had struck the old bear. "It's the dog."

"*The* dog?" Major de Spain said.

"That's gonter hold Old Ben."

"Dog the devil," Major de Spain said. "I'd rather have Old Ben himself in my pack than that brute. Shoot him."

"No," Sam said.

"You'll never tame him. How do you ever expect to make an animal like that afraid of you?"

"I dont want him tame," Sam said; again the boy watched his nostrils and the fierce milky light in his eyes. "But I almost rather he be tame than scared, of me or any man or any thing. But he wont be neither, of nothing."

"Then what are you going to do with it?"

"You can watch," Sam said.

Each morning through the second week they would go to Sam's crib. He had removed a few shingles from the roof and had put a rope on the colt's carcass and had drawn it out when the trap fell. Each morning they would watch him lower a pail of water into the crib while the dog hurled itself tirelessly against the door and dropped back and leaped again. It never made any sound and there was nothing frenzied in the act but only a cold and grim indomitable determination. Toward the end of the week it stopped jumping at the door. Yet it had not weakened appreciably and it was not as if it had rationalised the fact that the door was not going to give. It was as if for that time it simply disdained to jump any longer. It was not down. None of them had ever seen it down. It stood, and they could see it now—part mastiff, something of Airedale and something of a dozen other strains probably, better than thirty inches at the shoulders and weighing as they guessed almost ninety pounds, with cold yellow eyes and a tremendous chest and over all that strange color like a blued gun-barrel.

Then the two weeks were up. They prepared to break camp. The boy begged to remain and his cousin let him. He moved into the little hut with Sam Fathers. Each morning he watched Sam lower the pail of water into the crib. By the end of that week the dog was down. It would rise and half stagger, half crawl to the water and drink and collapse again. One morning it could not even reach the water, could not raise its forequarters even from the floor. Sam took a short stick and prepared to enter the crib. "Wait," the boy said. "Let me get the gun—"

"No," Sam said. "He cant move now." Nor could it. It lay on its side while Sam touched it, its head and the gaunted body, the dog lying motionless, the yellow eyes open. They were not fierce and there was nothing of petty malevolence in them, but a cold and almost impersonal malignance like some natural force. It was not even looking at Sam nor at the boy peering at it between the logs.

Sam began to feed it again. The first time he had to raise its head so it could lap the broth. That night he left a bowl of broth containing lumps of meat where the dog could reach it. The next morning the bowl was empty and the dog was lying on its belly, its head up, the cold yellow eyes watching the door as Sam entered, no change whatever in the cold yellow eyes and still no sound from it even when it sprang, its aim and co-ordination still bad from weakness so that Sam had time to strike it down with the stick and leap from the crib and slam the door as the dog, still without having had time to get its feet under it to jump again seemingly, hurled itself against the door as if the two weeks of starving had never been.

At noon that day someone came whooping through the woods from the direction of the camp. It was Boon. He came and looked for a while between the logs, at the tremendous dog lying again on its belly, its head up, the yellow eyes blinking sleepily at nothing: the indomitable and unbroken spirit."What we better do," Boon said, "is to let that son of a bitch go and catch Old Ben and run him on the dog." He turned to the boy his weather-reddened and beetling face. "Get your traps together. Cass says for you to come on home. You been in here fooling with that horse-eating varmint long enough."

Boon had a borrowed mule at the camp; the buggy was waiting at the edge of the bottom. He was at home that night. He told McCaslin about it. "Sam's going to starve him again until he can go in and touch him. Then he will feed him again. Then he will starve him again, if he has to."

"But why?" McCaslin said. "What for? Even Sam will never tame that brute."

"We dont want him tame. We want him like he is. We just want him to find out at last that the only way he can get out of that crib and stay out of it is to do what Sam or somebody tells him to do. He's the dog that's going to stop Old Ben and hold him. We've already named him. His name is Lion."

Then November came at last. They returned to the camp. With General Compson and Major de Spain and his cousin and Walter and Boon he stood in the yard among the guns and bedding and boxes of food and watched Sam Fathers and Lion come up the lane from the lot—the Indian, the old man in battered overalls and rubber boots and a worn sheepskin coat and a hat which had belonged to the boy's father; the tremendous dog pacing gravely beside him. The hounds rushed out to meet them and stopped, except the young one which still had but little of judgment. It ran up to Lion, fawning. Lion didn't snap at it. He didn't even pause. He struck it rolling and yelping for five or six feet with a blow of one paw as a bear would have done and came on into the yard and stood, blinking sleepily at nothing, looking at no one, while Boon said, "Jesus. Jesus.—Will he let me touch him?"

"You can touch him," Sam said. "He dont care. He dont care about nothing or nobody."

The boy watched that too. He watched it for the next two years from that moment when Boon touched Lion's head and then knelt beside him, feeling the bones and muscles, the power. It was as if Lion were a woman—or perhaps Boon was the woman. That was more like it—the big, grave, sleepy-seeming dog which, as Sam Fathers said, cared about no man and no thing; and the violent, insensitive, hard-faced man with his touch of remote Indian blood and the mind almost of a child. He watched Boon take over Lion's feeding from Sam and Uncle Ash both. He would see Boon squatting in the cold rain beside the kitchen while Lion ate. Because Lion neither slept nor ate with the other dogs though none of them knew where he did sleep until in the second November, thinking until then that Lion slept in his kennel beside Sam Fathers' hut, when the boy's cousin McCaslin said something about it to Sam by sheer chance and Sam told him. And that night the boy and Major de Spain and McCaslin with a lamp entered the back room where Boon slept—the little, tight, airless room rank with the smell of Boon's unwashed body and his wet hunting-clothes—where Boon, snoring on his back, choked and waked and Lion raised his head beside him and looked back at them from his cold, slumbrous yellow eyes.

"Damn it, Boon," McCaslin said. "Get that dog out of here. He's got to run Old Ben tomorrow morning. How in hell do you expect him to smell anything fainter than a skunk after breathing you all night?"

"The way I smell aint hurt my nose none that I ever noticed," Boon said.

"It wouldn't matter if it had," Major de Spain said. "We're not depending on you to trail a bear. Put him outside. Put him under the house with the other dogs."

Boon began to get up. "He'll kill the first one that happens to yawn or sneeze in his face or touches him."

"I reckon not," Major de Spain said. "None of them are going to risk yawning in his face or touching him either, even asleep. Put him outside. I want his nose right tomorrow. Old Ben fooled him last year. I dont think he will do it again."

Boon put on his shoes without lacing them; in his long soiled underwear, his hair still tousled from sleep, he and Lion went out. The others returned to the front room and the poker game where McCaslin's and Major de Spain's hands waited for them on the table. After a while McCaslin said, "Do you want me to go back and look again?"

"No," Major de Spain said. "I call," he said to Walter Ewell. He spoke to McCaslin again. "If you do, dont tell me. I am beginning to see the first sign of my increasing age: I dont like to know that my orders have been disobeyed, even when I knew when I gave them that they would be.—A small pair," he said to Walter Ewell.

"How small?" Walter said.

"Very small," Major de Spain said.

And the boy, lying beneath his piled quilts and blankets waiting for sleep, knew likewise that Lion was already back in Boon's bed, for the rest of that night and the next one and during all the nights of the next November and the next one. He thought then: *I wonder what Sam thinks. He could have Lion with him, even if Boon is a white man. He could ask Major or McCaslin either. And more than that. It was Sam's hand that touched Lion first and Lion knows it.* Then he became a man and he knew that too. It had been all right. That was the way it should have been. Sam was the chief, the prince; Boon, the plebeian, was his huntsman. Boon should have nursed the dogs.

On the first morning that Lion led the pack after Old Ben, seven strangers appeared in the camp. They were swampers: gaunt, malaria-ridden men appearing from nowhere, who ran trap-lines for coons or perhaps farmed little patches of cotton and corn along the edge of the bottom, in clothes but little better than Sam Fathers' and nowhere near as good as Tennie's Jim's, with worn shotguns and rifles, already squatting patiently in the cold drizzle in the side yard when day broke. They had a spokesman; afterward Sam Fathers told Major de Spain how all during the past summer and fall they had drifted into the camp singly or in pairs and threes, to look quietly at Lion for a while and then go away: "Mawnin, Major. We heerd you was aimin to put that ere blue dawg on that old two-toed bear this mawnin. We figgered we'd come up and watch, if you dont mind. We wont do no shooting, lessen he runs over us."

"You are welcome," Major de Spain said. "You are welcome to shoot. He's more your bear than ours."

"I reckon that aint no lie. I done fed him enough cawn to have a sheer in him. Not to mention a shoat three years ago."

"I reckon I got a sheer too," another said. "Only it aint in the bear." Major de Spain looked at him. He was chewing tobacco. He spat. "Hit was a heifer calf. Nice un too. Last year. When I finally found her, I reckon she looked about like that colt of yourn looked last June."

"Oh," Major de Spain said. "Be welcome. If you see game in front of my dogs, shoot it."

Nobody shot Old Ben that day. No man saw him. The dogs jumped him within a hundred yards of the glade where the boy had seen him that day in the summer of his eleventh year. The boy was less than a quarter-mile away. He heard the jump but he could distinguish no voice among the dogs that he did not know and therefore would be Lion's, and he thought, believed, that Lion was not among them. Even the fact that they were going much faster than he had ever heard them run behind Old Ben before and that the high thin note of hysteria was missing now from their voices was not enough to disabuse him. He didn't comprehend until that night, when Sam told him that Lion would never cry on a trail.

"He gonter growl when he catches Old Ben's throat," Sam said. "But he aint gonter never holler, no more than he ever done when he was jumping at that two-inch door. It's that blue dog in him. What you call it?"

"Airedale," the boy said.

Lion was there; the jump was just too close to the river. When Boon returned with Lion about eleven that night, he swore that Lion had stopped Old Ben once but that the hounds would not go in and Old Ben broke away and took to the river and swam for miles down it and he and Lion went down one bank for about ten miles and crossed and came up the other but it had begun to get dark before they struck any trail where Old Ben had come up out of the water, unless he was still in the water when he passed the ford where they crossed. Then he fell to cursing the hounds and ate the supper Uncle Ash had saved for him and went off to bed and after a while the boy opened the door of the little stale room thunderous with snoring and the great grave dog raised its head from Boon's pillow and blinked at him for a moment and lowered its head again.

When the next November came and the last day, the day on which it was now becoming traditional to save for Old Ben, there were more than a dozen strangers waiting. They were not all swampers this time. Some of them were townsmen, from other county seats like Jefferson, who had heard about Lion and Old Ben and had come to watch the great blue dog keep his yearly rendezvous with the old two-toed bear. Some of them didn't even have guns and the hunting-clothes and boots they wore had been on a store shelf yesterday.

This time Lion jumped Old Ben more than five miles from the river and bayed and held him and this time the hounds went in, in a sort of desperate emulation. The boy heard them; he was that near. He heard Boon whooping; he heard the two shots when General Compson delivered both barrels, one containing five buckshot, the other a single ball, into the bear from as close as he could force his almost unmanageable horse. He heard the dogs when the bear broke free again. He was running now; panting, stumbling, his lungs bursting, he reached the place where General Compson had fired and where Old Ben had killed two of the hounds. He saw the blood from General Compson's shots, but he could go no further. He stopped, leaning against a tree for his breathing to ease and his heart to slow, hearing the sound of the dogs as it faded on and died away.

In camp that night—they had as guests five of the still terrified strangers in new hunting coats and boots who had been lost all day until Sam Fathers went out and got them—he heard the rest of it:

how Lion had stopped and held the bear again but only the one-eyed mule which did not mind the smell of wild blood would approach and Boon was riding the mule and Boon had never been known to hit anything. He shot at the bear five times with his pump gun,[5] touching nothing, and Old Ben killed another hound and broke free once more and reached the river and was gone. Again Boon and Lion hunted as far down one bank as they dared. Too far; they crossed in the first of dusk and dark overtook them within a mile. And this time Lion found the broken trail, the blood perhaps, in the darkness where Old Ben had come up out of the water, but Boon had him on a rope, luckily, and he got down from the mule and fought Lion hand-to-hand until he got him back to camp. This time Boon didn't even curse. He stood in the door, muddy, spent, his huge gargoyle's face tragic and still amazed. "I missed him," he said. "I was in twenty-five feet of him and I missed him five times."

"But we have drawn blood," Major de Spain said. "General Compson drew blood. We have never done that before."

"But I missed him," Boon said. "I missed him five times. With Lion looking right at me."

"Never mind," Major de Spain said. "It was a damned fine race. And we drew blood. Next year we'll let General Compson or Walter ride Katie, and we'll get him."

Then McCaslin said, "Where is Lion, Boon?"

"I left him at Sam's," Boon said. He was already turning away. "I aint fit to sleep with him."

So he should have hated and feared Lion. Yet he did not. It seemed to him that there was a fatality in it. It seemed to him that something, he didn't know what, was beginning; had already begun. It was like the last act on a set stage. It was the beginning of the end of something, he didn't know what except that he would not grieve. He would be humble and proud that he had been found worthy to be a part of it too or even just to see it too.

III

It was December. It was the coldest December he had ever remembered. They had been in camp four days over two weeks, waiting for the weather to soften so that Lion and Old Ben could run their yearly race. Then they would break camp and go home. Because of these unforeseen additional days which they had had to pass waiting on the weather, with nothing to do but play poker, the whisky had given out and he and Boon were being sent to Memphis with a suitcase and a note from Major de Spain to Mr. Semmes, the distiller, to get more. That is, Major de Spain and McCaslin were sending Boon to get the whisky and sending him

5. A repeater operated by a sliding hand grip.

to see that Boon got back with it or most of it or at least some of it.

Tennie's Jim waked him at three. He dressed rapidly, shivering, not so much from the cold because a fresh fire already boomed and roared on the hearth, but in that dead winter hour when the blood and the heart are slow and sleep is incomplete. He crossed the gap between house and kitchen, the gap of iron earth beneath the brilliant and rigid night where dawn would not begin for three hours yet, tasting, tongue palate and to the very bottom of his lungs the searing dark, and entered the kitchen, the lamp-lit warmth where the stove glowed, fogging the windows, and where Boon already sat at the table at breakfast, hunched over his plate, almost in his plate, his working jaws blue with stubble and his face innocent of water and his coarse, horse-mane hair innocent of comb—the quarter Indian, grandson of a Chickasaw squaw, who on occasion resented with his hard and furious fists the intimation of one single drop of alien blood and on others, usually after whisky, affirmed with the same fists and the same fury that his father had been the full-blood Chickasaw and even a chief and that even his mother had been only half white. He was four inches over six feet; he had the mind of a child, the heart of a horse, and little hard shoe-button eyes without depth or meanness or generosity or viciousness or gentleness or anything else, in the ugliest face the boy had ever seen. It looked like somebody had found a walnut a little larger than a football and with a machinist's hammer had shaped features into it and then painted it, mostly red; not Indian red but a fine bright ruddy color which whisky might have had something to do with but which was mostly just happy and violent out-of-doors, the wrinkles in it not the residue of the forty years it had survived but from squinting into the sun or into the gloom of cane-brakes where game had run, baked into it by the camp fires before which he had lain trying to sleep on the cold November or December ground while waiting for daylight so he could rise and hunt again, as though time were merely something he walked through as he did through air, aging him no more than air did. He was brave, faithful, improvident and unreliable; he had neither profession job nor trade and owned one vice and one virtue: whisky, and that absolute and unquestioning fidelity to Major de Spain and the boy's cousin McCaslin. "Sometimes I'd call them both virtues," Major de Spain said once. "Or both vices," McCaslin said.

He ate his breakfast, hearing the dogs under the kitchen, wakened by the smell of frying meat or perhaps by the feet overhead. He heard Lion once, short and peremptory, as the best hunter in any camp has only to speak once to all save the fools, and none other of Major de Spain's and McCaslin's dogs were Lion's equal in size and strength and perhaps even in courage, but they were not fools;

Old Ben had killed the last fool among them last year.

Tennie's Jim came in as they finished. The wagon was outside. Ash decided he would drive them over to the log-line where they would flag the outbound log-train and let Tennie's Jim wash the dishes. The boy knew why. It would not be the first time he had listened to old Ash badgering Boon.

It was cold. The wagon wheels banged and clattered on the frozen ground; the sky was fixed and brilliant. He was not shivering, he was shaking, slow and steady and hard, the food he had just eaten still warm and solid inside him while his outside shook slow and steady around it as though his stomach floated loose. "They wont run this morning," he said. "No dog will have any nose today."

"Cep Lion," Ash said. "Lion dont need no nose. All he need is a bear." He had wrapped his feet in towsacks and he had a quilt from his pallet bed on the kitchen floor drawn over his head and wrapped around him until in the thin brilliant starlight he looked like nothing at all that the boy had ever seen before. "He run a bear through a thousand-acre ice-house. Catch him too. Them other dogs dont matter because they aint going to keep up with Lion nohow, long as he got a bear in front of him."

"What's wrong with the other dogs?" Boon said. "What the hell do you know about it anyway? This is the first time you've had your tail out of that kitchen since we got here except to chop a little wood."

"Aint nothing wrong with them," Ash said. "And long as it's left up to them, aint nothing going to be. I just wish I had knowed all my life how to take care of my health good as them hounds knows."

"Well, they aint going to run this morning," Boon said. His voice was harsh and positive. "Major promised they wouldn't until me and Ike get back."

"Weather gonter break today. Gonter soft up. Rain by night." Then Ash laughed, chuckled, somewhere inside the quilt which concealed even his face. "Hum up here, mules!" he said, jerking the reins so that the mules leaped forward and snatched the lurching and banging wagon for several feet before they slowed again into their quick, short-paced, rapid plodding. "Sides, I like to know why Major need to wait on you. It's Lion he aiming to use. I aint never heard tell of you bringing no bear nor no other kind of meat into this camp."

Now Boon's going to curse Ash or maybe even hit him, the boy thought. But Boon never did, never had; the boy knew he never would even though four years ago Boon had shot five times with a borrowed pistol at a negro on the street in Jefferson, with the same result as when he had shot five times at Old Ben last fall. "By God," Boon said, "he aint going to put Lion or no other dog on nothing until I get back tonight. Because he promised me. Whip up them mules and keep them whipped up. Do you want me to freeze to death?"

They reached the log-line[6] and built a fire. After a while the log-train came up out of the woods under the paling east and Boon flagged it. Then in the warm caboose the boy slept again while Boon and the conductor and brakeman talked about Lion and Old Ben as people later would talk about Sullivan and Kilrain and, later still, about Dempsey and Tunney.[7] Dozing, swaying as the springless caboose lurched and clattered, he would hear them still talking, about the shoats and calves Old Ben had killed and the cribs he had rifled and the traps and deadfalls he had wrecked and the lead he probably carried under his hide—Old Ben, the two-toed bear in a land where bears with trap-ruined feet had been called Two-Toe or Three-Toe or Cripple-Foot for fifty years, only Old Ben was an extra bear (the head bear, General Compson called him) and so had earned a name such as a human man could have worn and not been sorry.

They reached Hoke's at sunup. They emerged from the warm caboose in their hunting clothes, the muddy boots and stained khaki and Boon's blue unshaven jowls. But that was all right. Hoke's was a sawmill and commissary and two stores and a loading-chute on a sidetrack from the main line, and all the men in it wore boots and khaki too. Presently the Memphis train came. Boon bought three packages of popcorn-and-molasses and a bottle of beer from the news butch and the boy went to sleep again to the sound of his chewing.

But in Memphis it was not all right. It was as if the high buildings and the hard pavements, the fine carriages and the horse cars and the men in starched collars and neckties made their boots and khaki look a little rougher and a little muddier and made Boon's beard look worse and more unshaven and his face look more and more like he should never have brought it out of the woods at all or at least out of reach of Major de Spain or McCaslin or someone who knew it and could have said, "Dont be afraid. He wont hurt you." He walked through the station, on the slick floor, his face moving as he worked the popcorn out of his teeth with his tongue, his legs spraddled and stiff in the hips as if he were walking on buttered glass, and that blue stubble on his face like the filings from a new gun-barrel. They passed the first saloon. Even through the closed

6. The railroad line of the timber company, probably narrow-gauge.
7. American heavyweight boxing champions. John L. Sullivan defeated Jack Kilrain in 1889; Gene Tunney defeated Jack Dempsey in 1926 and again in 1927.

doors the boy could seem to smell the sawdust and the reek of old drink. Boon began to cough. He coughed for something less than a minute. "Damn this cold," he said. "I'd sure like to know where I got it."

"Back there in the station," the boy said.

Boon had started to cough again. He stopped. He looked at the boy. "What?" he said.

"You never had it when we left camp nor on the train either." Boon looked at him, blinking. Then he stopped blinking. He didn't cough again. He said quietly:

"Lend me a dollar. Come on. You've got it. If you ever had one, you've still got it. I dont mean you are tight with your money because you aint. You just dont never seem to ever think of nothing you want. When I was sixteen a dollar bill melted off of me before I even had time to read the name of the bank that issued it." He said quietly: "Let me have a dollar, Ike."

"You promised Major. You promised McCaslin. Not till we get back to camp."

"All right," Boon said in that quiet and patient voice. "What can I do on just one dollar? You aint going to lend me another."

"You're damn right I aint," the boy said, his voice quiet too, cold with rage which was not at Boon, remembering: Boon snoring in a hard chair in the kitchen so he could watch the clock and wake him and McCaslin and drive them the seventeen miles in to Jefferson to catch the train to Memphis; the wild, never-bridled Texas paint pony[8] which he had persuaded McCaslin to let him buy and which he and Boon had bought at auction for four dollars and seventy-five cents and fetched home wired between two gentle old mares with pieces of barbed wire and which had never even seen shelled corn before and didn't even know what it was unless the grains were bugs maybe and at last (he was ten and Boon had been ten all his life) Boon said the pony was gentled and with a towsack over its head and four negroes to hold it they backed it into an old two-wheeled cart and hooked up the gear and he and Boon got up and Boon said, "All right, boys. Let him go" and one of the negroes —it was Tennie's Jim—snatched the towsack off and leaped for his life and they lost the first wheel against a post of the open gate only at that moment Boon caught him by the scruff of the neck and flung him into the roadside ditch so he only saw the rest of it in fragments: the other wheel as it slammed through the side gate and crossed the back yard and leaped up onto the gallery and scraps of the cart here and there along the road and Boon vanishing rapidly on his stomach in the leaping and spurting dust and still holding the reins until they broke too and two days later they finally

8. Texas "pinto" (Spanish for "painted"); *i.e.*, a spotted horse.

caught the pony seven miles away still wearing the hames and the headstall of the bridle around its neck like a duchess with two necklaces at one time. He gave Boon the dollar.

"All right," Boon said. "Come on in out of the cold."

"I aint cold," he said.

"You can have some lemonade."

"I dont want any lemonade."

The door closed behind him. The sun was well up now. It was a brilliant day, though Ash had said it would rain before night. Already it was warmer; they could run tomorrow. He felt the old lift of the heart, as pristine as ever, as on the first day; he would never lose it, no matter how old in hunting and pursuit: the best, the best of all breathing, the humility and the pride. He must stop thinking about it. Already it seemed to him that he was running, back to the station, to the tracks themselves: the first train going south, he must stop thinking about it. The street was busy. He watched the big Norman draft horses, the Percherons; the trim carriages from which the men in the fine overcoats and the ladies rosy in furs descended and entered the station. (They were still next door to it but one.) Twenty years ago his father had ridden into Memphis as a member of Colonel Sartoris' horse in Forrest's[9] command, up Main street and (the tale told) into the lobby of the Gayoso Hotel where the Yankee officers sat in the leather chairs spitting into the tall bright cuspidors and then out again, scot-free—

The door opened behind him. Boon was wiping his mouth on the back of his hand. "All right," he said. "Let's go tend to it and get the hell out of here."

They went and had the suitcase packed. He never knew where or when Boon got the other bottle. Doubtless Mr. Semmes gave it to him. When they reached Hoke's again at sundown, it was empty. They could get a return train to Hoke's in two hours; they went straight back to the station as Major de Spain and then McCaslin had told Boon to do and then ordered him to do and had sent the boy along to see that he did. Boon took the first drink from his bottle in the wash room. A man in a uniform cap came to tell him he couldn't drink there and looked at Boon's face once and said nothing. The next time he was pouring into his water glass beneath the edge of a table in the restaurant when the manager (she was a woman) did tell him he couldn't drink there and he went back to the washroom. He had been telling the negro waiter and all the other people in the restaurant who couldn't help but hear him and who had never heard of Lion and didn't want to, about Lion and Old Ben. Then he happened to think of the zoo. He had found out that there was another train to Hoke's at three oclock and so they

9. General Nathan Bedford Forrest (1821–1877), Confederate cavalryman.

would spend the time at the zoo and take the three oclock train until he came back from the washroom for the third time. Then they would take the first train back to camp, get Lion and come back to the zoo where, he said, the bears were fed on ice cream and lady fingers and he would match Lion against them all.

So they missed the first train, the one they were supposed to take, but he got Boon onto the three oclock train and they were all right again, with Boon not even going to the wash-room now but drinking in the aisle and talking about Lion and the men he buttonholed no more daring to tell Boon he couldn't drink there than the man in the station had dared.

When they reached Hoke's at sundown, Boon was asleep. The boy waked him at last and got him and the suitcase off the train and he even persuaded him to eat some supper at the sawmill commissary. So he was all right when they got in the caboose of the log-train to go back into the woods, with the sun going down red and the sky already overcast and the ground would not freeze tonight. It was the boy who slept now, sitting behind the ruby stove while the springless caboose jumped and clattered and Boon and the brakeman and the conductor talked about Lion and Old Ben because they knew what Boon was talking about because this was home. "Overcast and already thawing," Boon said. "Lion will get him tomorrow."

It would have to be Lion, or somebody. It would not be Boon. He had never hit anything bigger than a squirrel that anybody ever knew, except the negro woman that day when he was shooting at the negro man. He was a big negro and not ten feet away but Boon shot five times with the pistol he had borrowed from Major de Spain's negro coachman and the negro he was shooting at outed with a dollar-and-a-half mail-order pistol and would have burned Boon down with it only it never went off, it just went snicksnicksnicksnicksnick five times and Boon still blasting away and he broke a plate-glass window that cost McCaslin forty-five dollars and hit a negro woman who happened to be passing in the leg only Major de Spain paid for that; he and McCaslin cut cards, the plate-glass window against the negro woman's leg. And the first day on stand this year, the first morning in camp, the buck ran right over Boon; he heard Boon's old pump gun go whow. whow. whow. whow. whow. and then his voice: "God damn, here he comes! Head him! Head him!" and when he got there the buck's tracks and the five exploded shells were not twenty paces apart.

There were five guests in camp that night from Jefferson: Mr. Bayard Sartoris[1] and his son and General Compson's son and two others. And the next morning he looked out the window, into the

1. Bayard Sartoris, then a young banker in Jefferson, becomes the county's most influential citizen after the death of Major de Spain. See the novels *Sartoris* (1929) and *The Unvanquished* (1938).

gray thin drizzle of daybreak which Ash had predicted, and there they were, standing and squatting beneath the thin rain, almost two dozen of them who had fed Old Ben corn and shoats and even calves for ten years, in their worn hats and hunting coats and overalls which any town negro would have thrown away or burned and only the rubber boots strong and sound, and the worn and blueless[2] guns, and some even without guns. While they ate breakfast a dozen more arrived, mounted and on foot: loggers from the camp thirteen miles below and sawmill men from Hoke's and the only gun among them that one which the log-train conductor carried: so that when they went into the woods this morning Major de Spain led a party almost as strong, excepting that some of them were not armed, as some he had led in the last darkening days of '64 and '65. The little yard would not hold them. They overflowed it, into the lane where Major de Spain sat his mare while Ash in his dirty apron thrust the greasy cartridges into his carbine and passed it up to him and the great grave blue dog stood at his stirrup not as a dog stands but as a horse stands, blinking his sleepy topaz eyes at nothing, deaf even to the yelling of the hounds which Boon and Tennie's Jim held on leash.

"We'll put General Compson on Katie this morning," Major de Spain said. "He drew blood last year; if he'd had a mule then that would have stood, he would have—"

"No," General Compson said. "I'm too old to go helling through the woods on a mule or a horse or anything else any more. Besides, I had my chance last year and missed it. I'm going on a stand this morning. I'm going to let that boy ride Katie."

"No, wait," McCaslin said. "Ike's got the rest of his life to hunt bears in. Let somebody else—"

"No," General Compson said. "I want Ike to ride Katie. He's already a better woodsman than you or me either and in another ten years he'll be as good as Walter."

At first he couldn't believe it, not until Major de Spain spoke to him. Then he was up, on the one-eyed mule which would not spook at wild blood, looking down at the dog motionless at Major de Spain's stirrup, looking in the gray streaming light bigger than a calf, bigger than he knew it actually was—the big head, the chest almost as big as his own, the blue hide beneath which the muscles flinched or quivered to no touch since the heart which drove blood to them loved no man and no thing, standing as a horse stands yet different from a horse which infers only weight and speed while Lion inferred not only courage and all else that went to make up the will and desire to pursue and kill, but endurance, the will and desire to endure beyond all imaginable limits of flesh in order to overtake

2. As a gun barrel ages with use, the steel loses its blue coating.

and slay. Then the dog looked at him. It moved its head and looked at him across the trivial uproar of the hounds, out of the yellow eyes as depthless as Boon's, as free as Boon's of meanness or generosity or gentleness or viciousness. They were just cold and sleepy. Then it blinked, and he knew it was not looking at him and never had been, without even bothering to turn its head away.

That morning he heard the first cry. Lion had already vanished while Sam and Tennie's Jim were putting saddles on the mule and horse which had drawn the wagon and he watched the hounds as they crossed and cast, snuffing and whimpering, until they too disappeared. Then he and Major de Spain and Sam and Tennie's Jim rode after them and heard the first cry out of the wet and thawing woods not two hundred yards ahead, high, with that abject, almost human quality he had come to know, and the other hounds joining in until the gloomed woods rang and clamored. They rode then. It seemed to him that he could actually see the big blue dog boring on, silent, and the bear too: the thick, locomotive-like shape which he had seen that day four years ago crossing the blow-down, crashing on ahead of the dogs faster than he had believed it could have moved, drawing away even from the running mules. He heard a shot-gun, once. The woods had opened, they were going fast, the clamor faint and fading on ahead; they passed the man who had fired—a swamper, a pointing arm, a gaunt face, the small black orifice of his yelling studded with rotten teeth.

He heard the changed note in the hounds' uproar and two hundred yards ahead he saw them. The bear had turned. He saw Lion drive in without pausing and saw the bear strike him aside and lunge into the yelling hounds and kill one of them almost in its tracks and whirl and run again. Then they were in a streaming tide of dogs. He heard Major de Spain and Tennie's Jim shouting and the pistol sound of Tennie's Jim's leather thong as he tried to turn them. Then he and Sam Fathers were riding alone. One of the hounds had kept on with Lion though. He recognised its voice. It was the young hound which even a year ago had had no judgment and which, by the lights of the other hounds anyway, still had none. *Maybe that's what courage is,* he thought. "Right," Sam said behind him. "Right. We got to turn him from the river if we can."

Now they were in cane: a brake. He knew the path through it as well as Sam did. They came out of the undergrowth and struck the entrance almost exactly. It would traverse the brake and come out onto a high open ridge above the river. He heard the flat clap of Walter Ewell's rifle, then two more. "No," Sam said. "I can hear the hound. Go on."

They emerged from the narrow roofless tunnel of snapping and hissing cane, still galloping, onto the open ridge below which the thick yellow river,[3] reflectionless in the gray and streaming light, seemed not to move. Now he could hear the hound too. It was not running. The cry was a high frantic yapping and Boon was running along the edge of the bluff, his old gun leaping and jouncing against his back on its sling made of a piece of cotton plow-line. He whirled and ran up to them, wild-faced, and flung himself onto the mule behind the boy. "That damn boat!" he cried. "It's on the other side! He went straight across! Lion was too close to him! That little hound too! Lion was so close I couldn't shoot! Go on!" he cried, beating his heels into the mule's flanks. "Go on!"

They plunged down the bank, slipping and sliding in the thawed earth, crashing through the willows and into the water. He felt no shock, no cold, he on one side of the swimming mule, grasping the pommel with one hand and holding his gun above the water with the other, Boon opposite him. Sam was behind them somewhere, and then the river, the water about them, was full of dogs. They swam faster than the mules; they were scrabbling up the bank before the mules touched bottom. Major de Spain was whooping from the bank they had just left and, looking back, he saw Tennie's Jim and the horse as they went into the water.

Now the woods ahead of them and the rain-heavy air were one uproar. It rang and clamored; it echoed and broke against the bank behind them and reformed and clamored and rang until it seemed to the boy that all the hounds which had ever bayed game in this land were yelling down at him. He got his leg over the mule as it came up out of the water. Boon didn't try to mount again. He grasped one stirrup as they went up the bank and crashed through the undergrowth which fringed the bluff and saw the bear, on its hind feet, its back against a tree while the bellowing hounds swirled around it and once more Lion drove in, leaping clear of the ground.

This time the bear didn't strike him down. It caught the dog in both arms, almost loverlike, and they both went down. He was off the mule now. He drew back both hammers of the gun but he could see nothing but moiling spotted houndbodies until the bear surged up again. Boon was yelling something, he could not tell what; he could see Lion still clinging to the bear's throat and he saw the bear, half erect, strike one of the hounds with one paw and hurl it five or six feet and then, rising and rising as though it would never stop, stand erect again and begin to rake at Lion's belly with its forepaws. Then Boon was running. The boy saw the gleam of the blade in his hand and watched him leap among the hounds, hurdling them, kicking them aside as he ran, and fling himself astride the bear as he had hurled himself onto the mule, his legs locked around

3. The hunting camp is on the Tallahatchie River, in the northeast corner of the county.

the bear's belly, his left arm under the bear's throat where Lion clung, and the glint of the knife as it rose and fell.

It fell just once. For an instant they almost resembled a piece of statuary: the clinging dog, the bear, the man astride its back, working and probing the buried blade. Then they went down, pulled over backward by Boon's weight, Boon underneath. It was the bear's back which reappeared first but at once Boon was astride it again. He had never released the knife and again the boy saw the almost infinitesimal movement of his arm and shoulder as he probed and sought; then the bear surged erect, raising with it the man and the dog too, and turned and still carrying the man and the dog it took two or three steps toward the woods on its hind feet as a man would have walked and crashed down. It didn't collapse, crumple. It fell all of a piece, as a tree falls, so that all three of them, man dog and bear, seemed to bounce once.

He and Tennie's Jim ran forward. Boon was kneeling at the bear's head. His left ear was shredded, his left coat sleeve was completely gone, his right boot had been ripped from knee to instep; the bright blood thinned in the thin rain down his leg and hand and arm and down the side of his face which was no longer wild but was quite calm. Together they prized Lion's jaws from the bear's throat. "Easy, goddamn it," Boon said. "Cant you see his guts are all out of him?" He began to remove his coat. He spoke to Tennie's Jim in that calm voice: "Bring the boat up. It's about a hundred yards down the bank there. I saw it." Tennie's Jim rose and went away. Then, and he could not remember if it had been a call or an exclamation from Tennie's Jim or if he had glanced up by chance, he saw Tennie's Jim stooping and saw Sam Fathers lying motionless on his face in the trampled mud.

The mule had not thrown him. He remembered that Sam was down too even before Boon began to run. There was no mark on him whatever and when he and Boon turned him over, his eyes were open and he said something in that tongue which he and Joe Baker had used to speak[4] together. But he couldn't move. Tennie's Jim brought the skiff up; they could hear him shouting to Major de Spain across the river. Boon wrapped Lion in his hunting coat and carried him down to the skiff and they carried Sam down and returned and hitched the bear to the one-eyed mule's saddle-bow with Tennie's Jim's leash-thong and dragged him down to the skiff and got him into it and left Tennie's Jim to swim the horse and the two mules back across. Major de Spain caught the bow of the skiff as Boon jumped out and past him before it touched the bank. He looked at Old Ben and said quietly: "Well." Then he walked into the water and leaned down and touched Sam and Sam looked

4. That is, the Indian dialect of his childhood.

up at him and said something in that old tongue he and Joe Baker spoke. "You dont know what happened?" Major de Spain said.

"No, sir," the boy[5] said. "It wasn't the mule. It wasn't anything. He was off the mule when Boon ran in on the bear. Then we looked up and he was lying on the ground." Boon was shouting at Tennie's Jim, still in the middle of the river.

"Come on, gaddamn it!" he said. "Bring me that mule!"

"What do you want with a mule?" Major de Spain said.

Boon didn't even look at him. "I'm going to Hoke's to get the doctor," he said in that calm voice, his face quite calm beneath the steady thinning of the bright blood.

"You need a doctor yourself," Major de Spain said. "Tennie's Jim—"

"Damn that," Boon said. He turned on Major de Spain. His face was still calm, only his voice was a pitch higher. "Cant you see his goddamn guts are all out of him?"

"Boon!" Major de Spain said. They looked at one another. Boon was a good head taller than Major de Spain; even the boy was taller now than Major de Spain.

"I've got to get the doctor," Boon said. "His goddamn guts—"

"All right," Major de Spain said. Tennie's Jim came up out of the water. The horse and the sound mule had already scented Old Ben; they surged and plunged all the way up to the top of the bluff, dragging Tennie's Jim with them, before he could stop them and tie them and come back. Major de Spain unlooped the leather thong of his compass from his buttonhole and gave it to Tennie's Jim. "Go straight to Hoke's," he said. "Bring Doctor Crawford back with you. Tell him there are two men to be looked at. Take my mare. Can you find the road from here?"

"Yes, sir," Tennie's Jim said.

"All right," Major de Spain said. "Go on." He turned to the boy. "Take the mules and the horse and go back and get the wagon. We'll go on down the river in the boat to Coon bridge. Meet us there. Can you find it again?"

"Yes, sir," the boy said.

"All right. Get started."

He went back to the wagon. He realised then how far they had run. It was already afternoon when he put the mules into the traces and tied the horse's lead-rope to the tail-gate. He reached Coon bridge at dusk. The skiff was already there. Before he could see it and almost before he could see the water he had to leap from the tilting wagon, still holding the reins, and work around to where he could grasp the bit and then the ear of the plunging sound mule and dig his heels and hold it until Boon came up the bank.

5. Isaac McCaslin.

The rope of the led horse had already snapped and it had already disappeared up the road toward camp. They turned the wagon around and took the mules out and he led the sound mule a hundred yards up the road and tied it. Boon had already brought Lion up to the wagon and Sam was sitting up in the skiff now and when they raised him he tried to walk, up the bank and to the wagon and he tried to climb into the wagon but Boon did not wait; he picked Sam up bodily and set him on the seat. Then they hitched Old Ben to the one-eyed mule's saddle again and dragged him up the bank and set two skid-poles into the open tail-gate and got him into the wagon and he went and got the sound mule and Boon fought it into the traces, striking it across its hard hollow-sounding face until it came into position and stood trembling. Then the rain came down, as though it had held off all day waiting on them.

They returned to camp through it, through the streaming and sightless dark, hearing long before they saw any light the horn and the spaced shots to guide them. When they came to Sam's dark little hut he tried to stand up. He spoke again in the tongue of the old fathers; then he said clearly: "Let me out. Let me out."

"He hasn't got any fire," Major said. "Go on!" he said sharply.

But Sam was struggling now, trying to stand up. "Let me out, master," he said. "Let me go home."

So he stopped the wagon and Boon got down and lifted Sam out. He did not wait to let Sam try to walk this time. He carried him into the hut and Major de Spain got light on a paper spill from the buried embers on the hearth and lit the lamp and Boon put Sam on his bunk and drew off his boots and Major de Spain covered him and the boy was not there, he was holding the mules, the sound one which was trying again to bolt since when the wagon stopped Old Ben's scent drifted forward again along the streaming blackness of air, but Sam's eyes were probably open again on that profound look which saw further than them or the hut, further than the death of a bear and the dying of a dog. Then they went on, toward the long wailing of the horn and the shots which seemed each to linger intact somewhere in the thick streaming air until the next spaced report joined and blended with it, to the lighted house, the bright streaming windows, the quiet faces as Boon entered, bloody and quite calm, carrying the bundled coat. He laid Lion, blood coat and all, on his stale sheetless pallet bed which not even Ash, as deft in the house as a woman, could ever make smooth.

The sawmill doctor from Hoke's was already there. Boon would not let the doctor touch him until he had seen to Lion. He wouldn't risk giving Lion chloroform. He put the entrails back and sewed him up without it while Major de Spain held his head and Boon his feet. But he never tried to move. He lay there, the yellow eyes open upon nothing while the quiet men in the new hunting clothes and in the old ones crowded into the little airless room rank with the smell of Boon's body and garments, and watched. Then the doctor cleaned and disinfected Boon's face and arm and leg and bandaged them and, the boy in front with a lantern and the doctor and McCaslin and Major de Spain and General Compson following, they went to Sam Fathers' hut. Tennie's Jim had built up the fire; he squatted before it, dozing. Sam had not moved since Boon had put him in the bunk and Major de Spain had covered him with the blankets, yet he opened his eyes and looked from one to another of the faces and when McCaslin touched his shoulder and said, "Sam. The doctor wants to look at you," he even drew his hands out of the blanket and began to fumble at his shirt buttons until McCaslin said, "Wait. We'll do it." They undressed him. He lay there—the copper-brown, almost hairless body, the old man's body, the old man, the wild man not even one generation from the woods, childless, kinless, peopleless—motionless, his eyes open but no longer looking at any of them, while the doctor examined him and drew the blankets up and put the stethoscope back into his bag and snapped the bag and only the boy knew that Sam too was going to die.

"Exhaustion," the doctor said. "Shock maybe. A man his age swimming rivers in December. He'll be all right. Just make him stay in bed for a day or two. Will there be somebody here with him?"

"There will be somebody here," Major de Spain said.

They went back to the house, to the rank little room where Boon still sat on the pallet bed with Lion's head under his hand while the men, the ones who had hunted behind Lion and the ones who had never seen him before today, came quietly in to look at him and went away. Then it was dawn and they all went out into the yard to look at Old Ben, with his eyes open too and his lips snarled back from his worn teeth and his mutilated foot and the little hard lumps under his skin which were the old bullets (there were fifty-two of them, buckshot rifle and ball) and the single almost invisible slit under his left shoulder where Boon's blade had finally found his life. Then Ash began to beat on the bottom of the dishpan with a heavy spoon to call them to breakfast and it was the first time he could remember hearing no sound from the dogs under the kitchen while they were eating. It was as if the old bear, even dead there in the yard, was a more potent terror still than they could face without Lion between them.

The rain had stopped during the night. By midmorning the thin sun appeared, rapidly burning away mist and cloud, warming the air and the earth; it would be one of those windless Mississippi December days which are a sort of Indian summer's Indian summer.

They moved Lion out to the front gallery, into the sun. It was Boon's idea. "Goddamn it," he said, "he never did want to stay in the house until I made him. You know that." He took a crowbar and loosened the floor boards under his pallet bed so it could be raised, mattress and all, without disturbing Lion's position, and they carried him out to the gallery and put him down facing the woods.

Then he and the doctor and McCaslin and Major de Spain went to Sam's hut. This time Sam didn't open his eyes and his breathing was so quiet, so peaceful that they could hardly see that he breathed. The doctor didn't even take out his stethoscope nor even touch him. "He's all right," the doctor said. "He didn't even catch cold. He just quit."

"Quit?" McCaslin said.

"Yes. Old people do that sometimes. Then they get a good night's sleep or maybe it's just a drink of whisky, and they change their minds."

They returned to the house. And then they began to arrive—the swamp-dwellers, the gaunt men who ran trap-lines and lived on quinine and coons and river water, the farmers of little corn- and cotton-patches along the bottom's edge whose fields and cribs and pig-pens the old bear had rifled, the loggers from the camp and the sawmill men from Hoke's and the town men from further away than that, whose hounds the old bear had slain and [whose] traps and deadfalls he had wrecked and whose lead he carried. They came up mounted and on foot and in wagons, to enter the yard and look at him and then go on to the front where Lion lay, filling the little yard and overflowing it until there were almost a hundred of them squatting and standing in the warm and drowsing sunlight, talking quietly of hunting, of the game and the dogs which ran it, of hounds and bear and deer and men of yesterday vanished from the earth, while from time to time the great blue dog would open his eyes, not as if he were listening to them but as though to look at the woods for a moment before closing his eyes again, to remember the woods or to see that they were still there. He died at sundown.

Major de Spain broke camp that night. They carried Lion into the woods, or Boon carried him that is, wrapped in a quilt from his bed, just as he had refused to let anyone else touch Lion yesterday until the doctor got there; Boon carrying Lion, and the boy and General Compson and Walter and still almost fifty of them following with lanterns and lighted pine-knots—men from Hoke's and even further, who would have to ride out of the bottom in the dark, and swampers and trappers who would have to walk even, scattering toward the little hidden huts where they lived. And Boon would let nobody else dig the grave either and lay Lion in it and cover him and then General Compson stood at the head of it while the blaze and smoke of the pine-knots streamed away among the winter branches and spoke as he would have spoken over a man. Then they returned to camp. Major de Spain and McCaslin and Ash had rolled and tied all the bedding. The mules were hitched to the wagon and pointed out of the bottom and the wagon was already loaded and the stove in the kitchen was cold and the table was set with scraps of cold food and bread and only the coffee was hot when the boy[6] ran into the kitchen where Major de Spain and McCaslin had already eaten. "What?" he cried. "What? I'm not going."

"Yes," McCaslin said, "we're going out tonight. Major wants to get on back home."

"No!" he said. "I'm going to stay."

"You've got to be back in school Monday. You've already missed a week more than I intended. It will take you from now until Monday to catch up. Sam's all right. You heard Doctor Crawford. I'm going to leave Boon and Tennie's Jim both to stay with him until he feels like getting up."

He was panting. The others had come in. He looked rapidly and almost frantically around at the other faces. Boon had a fresh bottle. He upended it and started the cork by striking the bottom of the bottle with the heel of his hand and drew the cork with his teeth and spat it out and drank. "You're damn right you're going back to school," Boon said. "Or I'll burn the tail off of you myself if Cass dont, whether you are sixteen or sixty. Where in hell do you expect to get without education? Where would Cass be? Where in hell would I be if I hadn't never went to school?"

He looked at McCaslin again. He could feel his breath coming shorter and shorter and shallower and shallower, as if there were not enough air in the kitchen for that many to breathe. "This is just Thursday. I'll come home Sunday night on one of the horses. I'll come home Sunday, then. I'll make up the time I lost studying Sunday night, McCaslin," he said, without even despair.

"No, I tell you," McCaslin said. "Sit down here and eat your supper. We're going out to—"

"Hold up, Cass," General Compson said. The boy did not know General Compson had moved until he put his hand on his shoulder. "What is it, bud?" he said.

"I've got to stay," he said. "I've got to."

"All right," General Compson said. "You can stay. If missing an extra week of school is going to throw you so far behind you'll have to sweat to find out what some hired pedagogue put between the covers of a book, you better quit altogether.—And you shut up, Cass," he said, though McCaslin had not spoken. "You've got one

6. Isaac McCaslin.

foot straddled into a farm and the other foot straddled into a bank; you aint even got a good hand-hold where this boy was already an old man long before you damned Sartorises and Edmondses invented farms and banks to keep yourselves from having to find out what this boy was born knowing and fearing too maybe but without being afraid, that could go ten miles on a compass because he wanted to look at a bear none of us had ever got near enough to put a bullet in and looked at the bear and came the ten miles back on the compass in the dark; maybe by God that's the why and the wherefore of farms and banks.—I reckon you still aint going to tell what it is?"

But still he could not. "I've got to stay," he said.

"All right," General Compson said. "There's plenty of grub left. And you'll come home Sunday, like you promised McCaslin? Not Sunday night: Sunday."

"Yes, sir," he said.

"All right," General Compson said. "Sit down and eat, boys," he said. "Let's get started. It's going to be cold before we get home."

They ate. The wagon was already loaded and ready to depart; all they had to do was to get into it. Boon would drive them out to the road, to the farmer's stable where the surrey had been left. He stood beside the wagon, in silhouette on the sky, turbaned like a Paythan[7] and taller than any there, the bottle tilted. Then he flung the bottle from his lips without even lowering it, spinning and glinting in the faint starlight, empty. "Them that's going," he said, "get in the goddamn wagon. Them that aint, get out of the goddamn way." The others got in. Boon mounted to the seat beside General Compson and the wagon moved, on into the obscurity until the boy could no longer see it, even the moving density of it amid the greater night. But he could still hear it, for a long while: the slow, deliberate banging of the wooden frame as it lurched from rut to rut. And he could hear Boon even when he could no longer hear the wagon. He was singing, harsh, tuneless, loud.

That was Thursday. On Saturday morning Tennie's Jim left on McCaslin's woods-horse which had not been out of the bottom one time now in six years, and late that afternoon rode through the gate on the spent horse and on to the commissary where McCaslin was rationing the tenants and the wage-hands for the coming week, and this time McCaslin forestalled any necessity or risk of having to wait while Major de Spain's surrey was being horsed and harnessed. He took their own, and with Tennie's Jim already asleep in the back seat he drove in to Jefferson and waited while Major de Spain changed to boots and put on his overcoat, and they drove

7. His bandaged head recalls the large turbans of the Paythans (Paithans) **of** India.

the thirty miles in the dark of that night and at daybreak on Sunday morning they swapped to the waiting mare and mule and as the sun rose they rode out of the jungle and onto the low ridge where they had buried Lion: the low mound of unannealed earth where Boon's spade-marks still showed, and beyond the grave the platform of freshly cut saplings bound between four posts and the blanket-wrapped bundle upon the platform[8] and Boon and the boy squatting between the platform and the grave until Boon, the bandage removed, ripped from his head so that the long scoriations of Old Ben's claws resembled crusted tar in the sunlight, sprang up and threw down upon them with the old gun with which he had never been known to hit anything although McCaslin was already off the mule, kicked both feet free of the irons[9] and vaulted down before the mule had stopped, walking toward Boon.

"Stand back," Boon said. "By God, you wont touch him. Stand back, McCaslin." Still McCaslin came on, fast yet without haste.

"Cass!" Major de Spain said. Then he said, "Boon! You, Boon!" and he was down too and the boy rose too, quickly, and still McCaslin came on not fast but steady and walked up to the grave and reached his hand steadily out, quickly yet still not fast, and took hold the gun by the middle so that he and Boon faced one another across Lion's grave, both holding the gun, Boon's spent indomitable amazed and frantic face almost a head higher than McCaslin's beneath the black scoriations of beast's claws and then Boon's chest began to heave as though there were not enough air in all the woods, in all the wilderness, for all of them, for him and anyone else, even for him alone.

"Turn it loose," McCaslin said.

"You damn little spindling—" Boon said. "Don't you know I can take it away from you? Don't you know I can tie it around your neck like a damn cravat?"

"Yes," McCaslin said. "Turn it loose, Boon."

"This is the way he wanted it. He told us. He told us exactly how to do it. And by God you aint going to move him. So we did it like he said, and I been sitting here ever since to keep the damn wildcats and varmints away from him and by God—" Then Mc-Caslin had the gun, downslanted while he pumped the slide, the five shells snicking out of it so fast that the last one was almost out before the first one touched the ground and McCaslin dropped the gun behind him without once having taken his eyes from Boon's.

"Did you kill him, Boon?" he said. Then Boon moved. He turned, he moved like he was still drunk and then for a moment blind too, one hand out as he blundered toward the big tree and seemed to

8. This manner of burial, with ritualistic ceremonies, was common among the Chickasaws—the tribe of Sam Fathers —and other Indian tribes of the East.
9. McCaslin Edmonds has kicked free of the stirrups.

stop walking before he reached the tree so that he plunged, fell toward it, flinging up both hands and catching himself against the tree and turning until his back was against it, backing with the tree's trunk his wild spent scoriated face and the tremendous heave and collapse of his chest, McCaslin following, facing him again, never once having moved his eyes from Boon's eyes. "Did you kill him, Boon?"

"No!" Boon said. "No!"

"Tell the truth," McCaslin said. "I would have done it if he had asked me to." Then the boy moved. He was between them, facing McCaslin; the water felt as if it had burst and sprung not from his eyes alone but from his whole face, like sweat.

"Leave him alone!" he cried. "Goddamn it! Leave him alone!"

IV[1]

then he was twenty-one. He could say it, himself and his cousin juxtaposed not against the wilderness but against the tamed land which was to have been his heritage, the land which old Carothers McCaslin, his grandfather, had bought with white man's money from the wild men whose grandfathers without guns hunted it, and tamed and ordered, or believed he had tamed and ordered it, for the reason that the human beings he held in bondage and in the power of life and death had removed the forest from it and in their sweat scratched the surface of it to a depth of perhaps fourteen inches in order to grow something out of it which had not been there before, and which could be translated back into the money he who believed he had bought it had had to pay to get it and hold it, and a reasonable profit too: and for which reason old Carothers McCaslin, knowing better, could raise his children, his descendants and heirs, to believe the land was his to hold and bequeath, since the strong and ruthless man has a cynical foreknowledge of his own vanity and pride and strength and a contempt for all his get: just as, knowing better, Major de Spain had his fragment of that wilderness which was bigger and older than any recorded deed: just as, knowing better, old Thomas Sutpen, from whom Major de Spain had had his fragment for money: just as Ikkemotubbe, the Chickasaw chief, from whom Thomas Sutpen had had the fragment for money or rum or whatever it was, knew in his turn that not even a fragment of it had been his to relinquish or sell

not against the wilderness but against the land, not in pursuit and lust but in relinquishment; and in the commissary as it should have been, not the heart perhaps but certainly the solar-plexus of the repudiated and relinquished: the square, galleried, wooden building

1. In Part IV, Isaac is shown on his twenty-first birthday, in a long dialogue with his cousin, the "Cass," or McCaslin Edmonds, of the bear hunts. Isaac has repudiated his inheritance, the McCaslin plantation, in order to free his soul from the weight of the past.

squatting like a portent above the fields whose laborers it still held in thrall, '65 or no, and placarded over with advertisements for snuff and cures for chills and salves and potions manufactured and sold by white men to bleach the pigment and straighten the hair of Negroes that they might resemble the very race which for two hundred years had held them in bondage and from which for another hundred years not even a bloody civil war would have set them completely free

himself and his cousin amid the old smells of cheese and salt meat and kerosene and harness, the ranked shelves of tobacco and overalls and bottled medicine and thread and plow-bolts, the barrels and kegs of flour and meal and molasses and nails, the wall pegs dependant with plowlines and plow-collars and hames and trace-chains, and the desk and the shelf above it on which rested the ledgers in which McCaslin recorded the slow outward trickle of food and supplies and equipment which returned each fall as cotton made and ginned and sold (two threads frail as truth and impalpable as equators yet cable-strong to bind for life them who made the cotton to the land their sweat fell on), and the older ledgers, clumsy and archaic in size and shape, on the yellowed pages of which were recorded in the faded hand of his father Theophilus and his uncle Amodeus during the two decades before the Civil War the manumission,[2] in title at least, of Carothers McCaslin's slaves:

'Relinquish,' McCaslin said. 'Relinquish. You, the direct male descendant of him who saw the opportunity and took it, bought the land, took the land, got the land no matter how, held it to bequeath, no matter how, out of the old grant, the first patent, when it was a wilderness of wild beasts and wilder men, and cleared it, translated it into something to bequeath to his children, worthy of bequeathment for his descendants' ease and security and pride, and to perpetuate his name and accomplishments. Not only the male descendant but the only and last descendant in the male line and in the third generation, while I am not only four generations from old Carothers, I derived through a woman and the very McCaslin in my name is mine only by sufferance and courtesy and my grandmother's pride in what that man accomplished, whose legacy and monument you think you can repudiate.' and he

'I can't repudiate it. It was never mine to repudiate. It was never Father's and Uncle Buddy's to bequeath me to repudiate, because it was never Grandfather's to bequeath them to bequeath me to repudiate, because it was never old Ikkemotubbe's to sell to Grandfather for bequeathment and repudiation. Because it was never Ikkemotubbe's fathers' fathers' to bequeath Ikkemotubbe to sell to

2. Setting free.

Grandfather or any man because on the instant when Ikkemotubbe discovered, realized, that he could sell it for money, on that instant it ceased ever to have been his forever, father to father to father, and the man who bought it bought nothing.'

'Bought nothing?' and he

'Bought nothing. Because He told in the Book how He created the earth, made it and looked at it and said it was all right, and then He made man. He made the earth first and peopled it with dumb creatures, and then He created man to be His overseer on the earth and to hold suzerainty over the earth and the animals on it in His name, not to hold for himself and his descendants inviolable title forever, generation after generation, to the oblongs and squares of the earth, but to hold the earth mutual and intact in the communal anonymity of brotherhood, and all the fee He asked was pity and humility and sufferance and endurance and the sweat of his face for bread. And I know what you are going to say,' he said: 'That nevertheless Grandfather—' and McCaslin

'—did own it. And not the first. Not alone and not the first since, as your Authority states, man was dispossessed of Eden. Nor yet the second and still not alone, on down through the tedious and shabby chronicle of His chosen sprung from Abraham; and of the sons of them who dispossessed Abraham,[3] and of the five hundred years during which half the known world and all it contained was chattel to one city, as this plantation and all the life it contained was chattel and revokeless thrall to this commissary store and those ledgers yonder during your grandfather's life; and the next thousand years while men fought over the fragments of that collapse until at last even the fragments were exhausted and men snarled over the gnawed bones of the old world's worthless evening until an accidental egg[4] discovered to them a new hemisphere. So let me say it: That nevertheless and notwithstanding old Carothers did own it. Bought it, got it, no matter; kept it, held it, no matter; bequeathed it: else why do you stand here relinquishing and repudiating? Held it, kept it for fifty years until you could repudiate it, while He—this Arbiter, this Architect, this Umpire—condoned—or did He? looked down and saw—or did He? Or at least did nothing: saw, and could not, or did not see; saw, and would not, or perhaps He would not

3. But *cf.* Genesis xxv: 5, 8, where Abraham "gave all that he had" to his son Isaac and "died in a good old age, an old man, and full of years." Abraham's descendants, however, were dispossessed during the captivity and dispersion of Israel; see the phrase "dispossessed of Canaan" in the next paragraph.

4. But the story has it that at a banquet following Columbus' discovery of America, one of the party disparaged his achievement by saying that someone would have made the discovery in any case. Columbus then challenged those present to make an egg stand on end; and when all had failed, he did it himself by crushing the end slightly. The moral was, "After the deed is done, everybody knows how to do it." The story is apocryphal. *Cf.* Samuel Eliot Morison, *Admiral of the Ocean Sea* (1942), Vol. II, pp. 14–15.

Ike refuses to receive inheritance

see—perverse, impotent, or blind: which?' and he

'Dispossessed.' and McCaslin

'What?' and he

'Dispossessed. Not impotent: He didn't condone; not blind, because He watched it. And let me say it. Dispossessed of Eden. Dispossessed of Canaan, and those who dispossessed him dispossessed him dispossessed, and the five hundred years of absentee landlords in the Roman bagnios,[5] and the thousand years of wild men from the northern woods who dispossessed them and devoured their ravished substance ravished in turn again and then snarled in what you call the old world's worthless twilight over the old world's gnawed bones, blasphemous in His name until He used a simple egg to discover to them a new world where a nation of people could be founded in humility and pity and sufferance and pride of one to another. And Grandfather did own the land nevertheless and notwithstanding because He permitted it, not impotent and not condoning and not blind, because He ordered and watched it. He saw the land already accursed even as Ikkemotubbe and Ikkemotubbe's father old Issetibbeha and old Issetibbeha's fathers too held it, already tainted even before any white man owned it by what Grandfather and his kind, his fathers, had brought into the new land which He had vouchsafed them out of pity and sufferance, on condition of pity and humility and sufferance and endurance, from that old world's corrupt and worthless twilight as though in the sailfuls of the old world's tainted wind which drove the ships—' and McCaslin

'Ah.'

'—and no hope for the land anywhere so long as Ikkemotubbe and Ikkemotubbe's descendants held it in unbroken succession. Maybe He saw that only by voiding the land for a time of Ikkemotubbe's blood and substituting for it another blood, could He accomplish His purpose. Maybe He knew already what that other blood would be, maybe it was more than justice that only the white man's blood was available and capable to raise the white man's curse, more than vengeance when—' and McCaslin

'Ah.'

'—when He used the blood which had brought in the evil to destroy the evil as doctors use fever to burn up fever, poison to slay poison. Maybe He chose Grandfather out of all of them He might have picked. Maybe He knew that Grandfather himself would not serve His purpose because Grandfather was born too soon too, but that Grandfather would have descendants, the right descendants; maybe He had foreseen already the descendants Grandfather would have, maybe He saw already in Grandfather the seed

5. Brothels.

progenitive of the three generations He saw it would take to set at least some of His lowly people free—' and McCaslin

'The sons of Ham.[6] You who quote the Book: the sons of Ham.' and he

'There are some things He said in the Book, and some things reported of Him that He did not say. And I know what you will say now: That if truth is one thing to me and another thing to you, how will we choose which is truth? You don't need to choose. The heart already knows. He didn't have His Book written to be read by what must elect and choose, but by the heart, not by the wise of the earth because maybe they don't need it or maybe the wise no longer have any heart, but by the doomed and lowly of the earth who have nothing else to read with but the heart. Because the men who wrote His Book for Him were writing about truth and there is only one truth and it covers all things that touch the heart.' and McCaslin

'So these men who transcribed His Book for Him were sometime liars.' and he

'Yes. Because they were human men. They were trying to write down the heart's truth out of the heart's driving complexity, for all the complex and troubled hearts which would beat after them. What they were trying to tell, what He wanted said, was too simple. Those for whom they transcribed His words could not have believed them. It had to be expounded in the everyday terms which they were familiar with and could comprehend, not only those who listened but those who told it too, because if they who were that near to Him as to have been elected from among all who breathed and spoke language to transcribe and relay His words, could comprehend truth only through the complexity of passion and lust and hate and fear which drives the heart, what distance back to truth must they traverse whom truth could only reach by word-of-mouth?' and McCaslin

'I might answer that, since you have taken to proving your points and disproving mine by the same text, I don't know. But I don't say that, because you have answered yourself: No time at all if, as you say, the heart knows truth, the infallible and unerring heart. And perhaps you are right, since although you admitted three generations from old Carothers to you, there were not three. There were not even completely two. Uncle Buck and Uncle Buddy. And they not the first and not alone. A thousand other Bucks and Buddies in less than two generations and sometimes less than one in this land which so you claim God created and man himself cursed and tainted. Not to mention 1865.' and he

6. *Cf.* Genesis ix: 25. The Negro race was supposed by apologists for slavery to be descended from Canaan (son of Ham) and cursed by Noah (Ham's father) to be "a servant of servants * * * unto his brethren."

'Yes. More men than Father and Uncle Buddy,' not even glancing toward the shelf above the desk, nor did McCaslin. They did not need to. To him it was as though the ledgers in their scarred cracked leather bindings were being lifted down one by one in their fading sequence and spread open on the desk or perhaps upon some apocryphal Bench, or even Altar, or perhaps before the Throne Itself for a last perusal and contemplation and refreshment of the Allknowledgeable, before the yellowed pages and the brown thin ink in which was recorded the injustice and a little at least of its amelioration and restitution faded back forever into the anonymous communal original dust

the yellowed pages scrawled in fading ink by the hand first of his grandfather and then of his father and uncle, bachelors up to and past fifty and then sixty, the one who ran the plantation and the farming of it, and the other who did the housework and the cooking and continued to do it even after his twin married and the boy himself was born

the two brothers who as soon as their father was buried moved out of the tremendously-conceived, the almost barnlike edifice which he had not even completed, into a one-room log cabin which the two of them built themselves and added other rooms to while they lived in it, refusing to allow any slave to touch any timber of it other than the actual raising into place the logs which two men alone could not handle, and domiciled all the slaves in the big house some of the windows of which were still merely boarded up with odds and ends of plank or with the skins of bear and deer nailed over the empty frames: each sundown the brother who superintended the farming would parade the Negroes as a first sergeant dismisses a company, and herd them willynilly, man woman and child, without question protest or recourse, into the tremendous abortive edifice scarcely yet out of embryo, as if even old Carothers McCaslin had paused aghast at the concrete indication of his own vanity's boundless conceiving: he would call his mental roll and herd them in and with a hand-wrought nail as long as a flenching-knife and suspended from a short deer-hide thong attached to the door-jamb for that purpose, he would nail to the door of that house which lacked half its windows and had no hinged back door at all, so that presently, and for fifty years afterward, when the boy himself was big to hear and remember it, there was in the land a sort of folk-tale: of the countryside all night long full of skulking McCaslin slaves dodging the moonlit roads and the Patrol-riders to visit other plantations, and of the unspoken gentlemen's agreement between the two white men and the two dozen black ones that, after the white man had counted them and driven the home-made nail into the front door at sundown, neither of the white men would go around behind the house and look at the back door, provided that all the Negroes were behind the front one when the brother who drove it drew out the nail again at daybreak

the twins who were identical even in their handwriting, unless you had specimens side by side to compare, and even when both hands appeared on the same page (as often happened, as if, long since past any oral intercourse, they had used the diurnally advancing pages to conduct the unavoidable business of the compulsion which had traversed all the waste wilderness of North Mississippi in 1830 and '40 and singled them out to drive) they both looked as though they had been written by the same perfectly normal ten-year-old boy, even to the spelling, except that the spelling did not improve as one by one the slaves which Carothers McCaslin had inherited and purchased—Roscius and Phoebe and Thucydides and Eunice and their descendants, and Sam Fathers and his mother for both of whom he had swapped an underbred trotting gelding to old Ikkemotubbe, the Chickasaw chief, from whom he had likewise bought the land, and Tennie Beauchamp whom the twin Amodeus had won from a neighbor in a poker-game, and the anomaly calling itself Percival Brownlee which the twin Theophilus had purchased, neither he nor his brother ever knew why apparently, from Bedford Forrest while he was still only a slave-dealer and not yet a general (It was a single page, not long and covering less than a year, not seven months in fact, begun in the hand which the boy had learned to distinguish as that of his father:

> *Percavil Brownly 26yr Old. cleark @ Bookepper.*
> *bought from N.B.Forest at Cold Water 3 Mar*
> *1856 $265. dolars*

and beneath that, in the same hand:

> *5 mar 1856 No bookepper any way Cant read.*
> *Can write his Name but I already put that down*
> *My self Says he can Plough but dont look like it*
> *to Me. sent to Feild to day Mar 5 1856*

and the same hand:

> *6 Mar 1856 Cant plough either Says he aims to be*
> *a Precher so may be he can lead live stock to Crick*
> *to Drink*

and this time it was the other, the hand which he now recognized as his uncle's when he could see them both on the same page:

> *Mar 23th 1856 Cant do that either Except one at*
> *a Time Get shut of him*

then the first again:

> 24 Mar 1856 *Who in hell would buy him*

then the second:

> *19th of Apr 1856 Nobody You put yourself out of Market at Cold Water two months ago I never said sell him Free him*

the first:

> 22 Apr 1856 *Ill get it out of him*

the second:

> *Jun 13th 1856 How $1 per yr 265$ 265 yrs Whol sign his Free paper*

then the first again:

> 1 Oct 1856 *Mule josephine Broke Leg @ shot Wrong stall wrong niger wrong everything $100. dolars*

and the same:

> 2 Oct 1856 *Freed Debit McCaslin @ McCaslin $265. dolars*

then the second again:

> *Oct 3th Debit Theophilus McCaslin Niger 265$ Mule 100$ 365$ He hasnt gone yet Father should be here*

then the first:

> 3 Oct 1856 *Son of a bitch wont leave What would father done*

the second:

> *29th of Oct 1856 Renamed him*

the first:

> 31 Oct 1856 *Renamed him what*

the second:

> *Chrstms 1856 Spintrius*

) took substance and even a sort of shadowy life with their passions and complexities too, as page followed page and year year; all there, not only the general and condoned injustice and its slow amortization but the specific tragedy which had not been condoned and could never be amortized; the new page and the new ledger, the hand which he could now recognize at first glance as his father's:

> *Father dide Lucius Quintus Carothers McCaslin,*
> *Callina 1772 Missippy 1837. Dide and burid 27*
> *June 1837*
> *Roskus. rased by Granfather in Callina Dont know*
> *how old. Freed 27 June 1837 Dont want to leave.*
> *Dide and Burid 12 Jan 1841*
> *Fibby Roskus Wife. bought by granfather in Cal-*
> *lina says Fifty Freed 27 June 1837 Dont want to*
> *leave. Dide and burd 1 Aug 1849*
> *Thucydus Roskus @ Fibby Son born in Callina*
> *1779. Refused 10acre peace fathers Will 28 Jun*
> *1837 Refused Cash offer $200. dolars from A.*
> *@ T. McCaslin 28 Jun 1837 Wants to stay and*
> *work it out*

and beneath this and covering the next five pages and almost that many years, the slow, day-by-day accrument of the wages allowed him and the food and clothing—the molasses and meat and meal, the cheap durable shirts and jeans and shoes, and now and then a coat against rain and cold—charged against the slowly yet steadily mounting sum of balance (and it would seem to the boy that he could actually see the black man, the slave whom his white owner had forever manumitted by the very act from which the black man could never be free so long as memory lasted, entering the commissary, asking permission perhaps of the white man's son to see the ledger-page which he could not even read, not even asking for the white man's word, which he would have had to accept for the reason that there was absolutely no way under the sun for him to test it, as to how the account stood, how much longer before he could go and never return, even if only as far as Jefferson seventeen miles away), on to the double pen-stroke closing the final entry:

> *3 Nov 1841 By Cash to Thucydus McCaslin $200.*
> *dolars Set Up blaksmith in J. Dec 1841 Dide and*
> *burid in J. 17 feb 1854*
> *Eunice Bought by Father in New Orleans 1807*
> *$650. dolars. Marrid to Thucydus 1809 Drownd in*
> *Crick Cristmas Day 1832*

and then the other hand appeared, the first time he had seen it in the ledger to distinguish it as his uncle's, the cook and housekeeper whom even McCaslin, who had known him and the boy's father for sixteen years before the boy was born, remembered as sitting all day long in the rocking chair from which he cooked the food, before the kitchen fire on which he cooked it:

> *June 21th 1833 Drownd herself*

and the first:

> 23 Jun 1833 *Who in hell ever heard of a niger*
> *drownding him self*

and the second, unhurried, with a complete finality; the two identical entries might have been made with a rubber stamp save for the date:

> *Aug 13th 1833 Drownd herself*

and he thought *But why? But why?* He was sixteen then. It was neither the first time he had been alone in the commissary nor the first time he had taken down the old ledgers familiar on their shelf above the desk ever since he could remember. As a child and even after nine and ten and eleven, when he had learned to read, he would look up at the scarred and cracked backs and ends but with no particular desire to open them, and though he intended to examine them someday because he realized that they probably contained a chronological and much more comprehensive though doubtless tedious record than he would ever get from any other source, not alone of his own flesh and blood but of all his people, not only the whites but the black ones too, who were as much a part of his ancestry as his white progenitors, and of the land which they had all held and used in common and fed from and on and would continue to use in common without regard to color or titular ownership, it would only be on some idle day when he was old and perhaps even bored a little, since what the old books contained would be after all these years fixed immutably, finished, unalterable, harmless. Then he was sixteen. He knew what he was going to find before he found it. He got the commissary key from McCaslin's room after midnight while McCaslin was asleep and with the commissary door shut and locked behind him and the forgotten lantern stinking anew the rank dead icy air, he leaned above the yellowed page and thought not Why drowned herself, but thinking what he believed his father had thought when he found his brother's first comment: Why did Uncle Buddy think she had drowned herself? finding, beginning to find on the next succeeding page what he knew he would find, only this was still not it because he already knew this:

> *Tomasina called Tomy Daughter of Thucydus @*
> *Eunice Born 1810 dide in Child bed June 1833*
> *and Burd. Yr stars fell*

nor the next:

> *Turl Son of Thucydus @ Eunice Tomy born Jun*
> *1833 yr stars fell Fathers will*

and nothing more, no tedious recording filling this page of wages, day by day, and food and clothing charged against them, no entry of his death and burial because he had outlived his white half-brothers and the books which McCaslin kept did not include obituaries: just *Fathers will* and he had seen that too: old Carothers' bold cramped hand far less legible than his sons' even and not much better in spelling, who while capitalizing almost every noun and verb, made no effort to punctuate or construct whatever, just as he made no effort either to explain or obfuscate the thousand-dollar legacy to the son of an unmarried slave-girl, to be paid only at the child's coming-of-age, bearing the consequence of the act of which there was still no definite incontrovertible proof that he acknowledged, not out of his own substance, but penalizing his sons with it, charging them a cash forfeit on the accident of their own paternity; not even a bribe for silence toward his own fame since his fame would suffer only after he was no longer present to defend it, flinging almost contemptuously, as he might a cast-off hat or pair of shoes, the thousand dollars which could have had no more reality to him under those conditions than it would have to the Negro, the slave who would not even see it until he came of age, twenty-one years too late to begin to learn what money was. *So I reckon that was cheaper than saying My son to a nigger,* he thought. *Even if My son wasn't but just two words. But there must have been love,* he thought. *Some sort of love. Even what he would have called love: not just an afternoon's or a night's spittoon.* There was the old man, old, within five years of his life's end, long a widower and, since his sons were not only bachelors but were approaching middleage, lonely in the house and doubtless even bored, since his plantation was established now and functioning and there was enough money now, too much of it probably for a man whose vices even apparently remained below his means; there was the girl, husbandless and young, only twenty-three when the child was born: perhaps he had sent for her at first out of loneliness, to have a young voice and movement in the house, summoned her, bade her mother send her each morning to sweep the floors and make the beds and the mother acquiescing since that was probably already understood, already planned: the only child of a couple who were not field hands and who held themselves something above the other slaves, not alone for that reason but because the husband and his father and mother too had been inherited by the white man from his father, and the white man himself had travelled three hundred miles and better to New Orleans in a day when men travelled by horseback or steamboat, and bought the girl's mother as a wife for him

and that was all. The old frail pages seemed to turn of their own

accord even while he thought, *His own daughter His own daughter.*
No. No Not even him, back to that one where the white man (not
even a widower then) who never went anywhere, any more than
his sons in their time ever did, and who did not need another slave,
had gone all the way to New Orleans and bought one. And Tomey's
Terrel was still alive when the boy was ten years old and he knew
from his own observation and memory that there had already been
some white in Tomey's Terrel's blood before his father gave him the
rest of it; and looking down at the yellowed page spread beneath
the yellow glow of the lantern smoking and stinking in that rank
chill midnight room fifty years later, he seemed to see her actually
walking into the icy creek on that Christmas day six months before
her daughter's and her lover's (*Her first lover's,* he thought. *Her*
first) child was born, solitary, inflexible, griefless, ceremonial, in
formal and succinct repudiation of grief and despair, who had
already had to repudiate belief and hope

that was all. He would never need look at the ledgers again nor
did he; the yellowed pages in their fading and implacable succession were as much a part of his consciousness and would remain
so forever, as the fact of his own nativity:

> *Tennie Beauchamp 21yrs Won by Amodeus Mc-*
> *Caslin from Hubert Beauchamp Esqre Possible*
> *Strait against three Treys in sigt Not called 1859*
> *Marrid to Tomys Turl 1859*

and no date of freedom because her freedom, as well as that of her
first surviving child, derived not from Buck and Buddy McCaslin
in the commissary but from a stranger in Washington, and no date
of death and burial, not only because McCaslin kept no obituaries
in his books, but because in this year 1883 she was still alive and
would remain so to see a grandson by her last surviving child:

> *Amodeus McCaslin Beauchamp Son of tomys Turl*
> *@ Tennie Beauchamp 1859 dide 1859*

then his uncle's hand entire, because his father was now a member
of the cavalry command of that man whose name as a slave-dealer
he could not even spell: and not even a page and not even a full
line:

> *Dauter Tomes Turl and tenny 1862*

and not even a line and not even a sex and no cause given though
the boy could guess it because McCaslin was thirteen then and he
remembered how there was not always enough to eat in more places
than Vicksburg:

> *Child of tomes Turl and Tenny 1863*

and the same hand again and this one lived, as though Tennie's perseverance and the fading and diluted ghost of old Carothers' ruthlessness had at last conquered even starvation: and clearer, fuller, more carefully written and spelled than the boy had yet seen it, as if the old man, who should have been a woman to begin with, trying to run what was left of the plantation in his brother's absence in the intervals of cooking and caring for himself and the fourteen-year-old orphan, had taken as an omen for renewed hope the fact that this nameless inheritor of slaves was at least remaining alive long enough to receive a name:

> *James Thucydus Beauchamp Son of Tomes Turl*
> *and Tenny Beauchamp Born 29th december 1864*
> *and both Well Wanted to call him Theophilus but*
> *Tride Amodeus McCaslin and Callina McCaslin*
> *and both dide so Disswaded Them Born at Two*
> *clock A,m, both Well*

but no more, nothing; it would be another two years yet before the boy, almost a man now, would return from the abortive trip into Tennessee with the still-intact third of old Carothers' legacy to his Negro son and his descendants, which as the three surviving children established at last one by one their apparent intention of surviving, their white half-uncles had increased to a thousand dollars each, conditions permitting, as they came of age, and completed the page himself as far as it would even be completed when that day was long passed beyond which a man born in 1864 (or 1867 either, when he himself saw light) could have expected or himself hoped or even wanted to be still alive; his own hand now, queerly enough resembling neither his father's nor his uncle's nor even McCaslin's, but like that of his grandfather's save for the spelling:

> *Vanished sometime on night of his twenty-first*
> *birthday Dec 29 1885. Traced by Isaac McCaslin*
> *to Jackson Tenn. and there lost. His third of legacy*
> *$1000.00 returned to McCaslin Edmonds Trustee*
> *this day Jan 12 1886*

but not yet: that would be two years yet, and now his father's again, whose old commander was now quit of soldiering and slave-trading both; once more in the ledger and then not again, and more illegible than ever, almost indecipherable at all from the rheumatism which now crippled him, and almost completely innocent now even of any sort of spelling as well as punctuation, as if the four years during which he had followed the sword of the only man ever breathing who ever sold him a Negro, let alone beat him in a trade, had convinced him not only of the vanity of faith and hope, but of orthography too:

Miss sophonsiba b dtr t t @ t 1869

but not of belief and will because it was there, written, as McCaslin had told him, with the left hand, but there in the ledger one time more and then not again, for the boy himself was a year old, and when Lucas was born six years later, his father and uncle had been dead inside the same twelve-months almost five years; his own hand again, who was there and saw it, 1886, she was just seventeen, two years younger than himself, and he was in the commissary when McCaslin entered out of the first dusk and said, 'He wants to marry Fonsiba,' like that: and he looked past McCaslin and saw the man, the stranger, taller than McCaslin and wearing better clothes than McCaslin and most of the other white men the boy knew habitually wore, who entered the room like a white man and stood in it like a white man, as though he had let McCaslin precede him into it not because McCaslin's skin was white but simply because McCaslin lived there and knew the way, and who talked like a white man too, looking at him past McCaslin's shoulder rapidly and keenly once and then no more, without further interest, as a mature and contained white man not impatient but just pressed for time might have looked. 'Marry Fonsiba?' he cried. 'Marry Fonsiba?' and then no more either, just watching and listening while McCaslin and the Negro talked:

'To live in Arkansas, I believe you said.'

'Yes. I have property there. A farm.'

'Property? A farm? You own it?'

'Yes.'

'You don't say Sir, do you?'

'To my elders, yes.'

'I see. You are from the North.'

'Yes. Since a child.'

'Then your father was a slave.'

'Yes. Once.'

'Then how do you own a farm in Arkansas?'

'I have a grant. It was my father's. From the United States. For military service.'

'I see,' McCaslin said. 'The Yankee army.'

'The United States army,' the stranger said; and then himself again, crying it at McCaslin's back:

'Call aunt Tennie! I'll go get her! I'll—' But McCaslin was not even including him; the stranger did not even glance back toward his voice, the two of them speaking to one another again as if he were not even there:

'Since you seem to have it all settled,' McCaslin said, 'why have you bothered to consult my authority at all?'

'I don't,' the stranger said. 'I acknowledge your authority only so far as you admit your responsibility toward her as a female member of the family of which you are the head. I don't ask your permission. I——'

'That will do!' McCaslin said. But the stranger did not falter. It was neither as if he were ignoring McCaslin nor as if he had failed to hear him. It was as though he were making, not at all an excuse and not exactly a justification, but simply a statement which the situation absolutely required and demanded should be made in McCaslin's hearing whether McCaslin listened to it or not. It was as if he were talking to himself, for himself to hear the words spoken aloud. They faced one another, not close yet at slightly less than foils' distance, erect, their voices not raised, not impactive, just succinct:

'——I inform you, notify you in advance as chief of her family. No man of honor could do less. Besides, you have, in your way, according to your lights and upbringing——'

'That's enough, I said,' McCaslin said. 'Be off this place by full dark. Go.' But for another moment the other did not move, contemplating McCaslin with that detached and heatless look, as if he were watching reflected in McCaslin's pupils the tiny image of the figure he was sustaining.

'Yes,' he said. 'After all, this is your house. And in your fashion you have. . . . But no matter. You are right. This is enough.' He turned back toward the door; he paused again but only for a second, already moving while he spoke: 'Be easy. I will be good to her.' Then he was gone.

'But how did she ever know him?' the boy cried. 'I never even heard of him before! And Fonsiba, that's never been off this place except to go to church since she was born——'

'Ha,' McCaslin said. 'Even their parents don't know until too late how seventeen-year-old girls ever met the men who marry them too, if they are lucky.' And the next morning they were both gone, Fonsiba too. McCaslin never saw her again, nor did he, because the woman he found at last, five months later, was no one he had ever known. He carried a third of the three-thousand-dollar fund in gold in a money-belt, as when he had vainly traced Tennie's Jim into Tennessee a year ago. They—the man—had left an address of some sort with Tennie, and three months later a letter came, written by the man although McCaslin's wife, Alice, had taught Fonsiba to read and write too a little. But it bore a different postmark from the address the man had left with Tennie, and he travelled by rail as far as he could and then by contracted stage and then by a hired livery rig and then by rail again for a distance: an experienced traveller by now and an experienced bloodhound too, and a successful one this time because he would have to be; as the slow interminable empty muddy December miles crawled and crawled and night followed night in hotels, in roadside taverns of rough logs and containing little else but a bar, and in the cabins of strangers, and the hay of lonely barns, in none of which he dared undress because of his secret golden girdle like that of a disguised one of the Magi travelling incognito and not even hope to draw him, but only determination and desperation, he would tell himself: *I will have to find her. I will have to. We have already lost one of them. I will have to find her this time.* He did. Hunched in the slow and icy rain, on a spent hired horse splashed to the chest and higher, he saw it—a single log edifice with a clay chimney, which seemed in process of being flattened by the rain to a nameless and valueless rubble of dissolution in that roadless and even pathless waste of unfenced fallow and wilderness jungle—no barn, no stable, not so much as a hen-coop: just a log cabin built by hand and no clever hand either, a meagre pile of clumsily-cut firewood sufficient for about one day and not even a gaunt hound to come bellowing out from under the house when he rode up—a farm only in embryo, perhaps a good farm, maybe even a plantation someday, but not now, not for years yet and only then with labor, hard and enduring and unflagging work and sacrifice; he shoved open the crazy kitchen door in its awry frame and entered an icy gloom where not even a fire for cooking burned, and after another moment saw, crouched into the wall's angle behind a crude table, the coffee-colored face which he had known all his life but knew no more, the body which had been born within a hundred yards of the room that he was born in and in which some of his own blood ran, but which was now completely inheritor of generation after generation to whom an unannounced white man on a horse was a white man's hired Patroller wearing a pistol sometimes and a blacksnake whip always; he entered the next room, the only other room the cabin owned, and found, sitting in a rocking chair before the hearth, the man himself, reading—sitting there in the only chair in the house, before that miserable fire for which there was not wood sufficient to last twenty-four hours, in the same ministerial clothing in which he had entered the commissary five months ago and a pair of gold-framed spectacles which, when he looked up and then rose to his feet, the boy saw did not even contain lenses, reading a book in the midst of that desolation, that muddy waste, fenceless and even pathless and without even a walled shed for stock to stand beneath: and over all, permeant, clinging to the man's very clothing and exuding from his skin itself, that rank stink of baseless and imbecile delusion, that boundless rapacity and folly, of the carpet-bagger followers of victorious armies.

'Don't you see?' he cried. 'Don't you see? This whole land, the whole South, is cursed, and all of us who derive from it, whom it ever suckled, white and black both, lie under the curse? Granted that my people brought the curse onto the land: maybe for that reason their descendants alone can—not resist it, not combat it—maybe just endure and outlast it until the curse is lifted. Then your peoples' turn will come because we have forfeited ours. But not now. Not yet. Don't you see?'

The other stood now, the unfrayed garments still ministerial even if not quite so fine, the book closed upon one finger to keep the place, the lenseless spectacles held like a music master's wand in the other workless hand while the owner of it spoke his measured and sonorous imbecility of the boundless folly and the baseless hope: 'You're wrong. The curse you whites brought into this land has been lifted. It has been voided and discharged. We are seeing a new era, an era dedicated, as our founders intended it, to freedom, liberty and equality for all, to which this country will be the new Canaan——'

'Freedom from what? From work? Canaan?' He jerked his arm, comprehensive, almost violent: whereupon it all seemed to stand there about them, intact and complete and visible in the drafty, damp, heatless, Negro-stale Negro-rank sorry room—the empty fields without plow or seed to work them, fenceless against the stock which did not exist within or without the walled stable which likewise was not there. 'What corner of Canaan is this?'

'You are seeing it at a bad time. This is winter. No man farms this time of year.'

'I see. And of course her need for food and clothing will stand still while the land lies fallow.'

'I have a pension,' the other said. He said it as a man might say *I have grace* or *I own a gold mine.* 'I have my father's pension too. It will arrive on the first of the month. What day is this?'

'The eleventh,' he said. 'Twenty days more. And until then?'

'I have a few groceries in the house from my credit account with the merchant in Midnight who banks my pension check for me. I have executed to him a power of attorney to handle it for me as a matter of mutual—'

'I see. And if the groceries don't last the twenty days?'

'I still have one more hog.'

'Where?'

'Outside,' the other said. 'It is customary in this country to allow the stock to range free during the winter for food. It comes up from time to time. But no matter if it doesn't; I can probably trace its footprints when the need——'

'Yes!' he cried. "Because no matter: you still have the pension check. And the man in Midnight will cash it and pay himself out of it for what you have already eaten and if there is any left over, it is yours. And the hog will be eaten by then or you still can't catch it, and then what will you do?'

'It will be almost spring then,' the other said. 'I am planning in the spring——'

'It will be January,' he said. 'And then February. And then more than half of March—' and when he stopped again in the kitchen she had not moved, she did not even seem to breathe or to be alive except her eyes watching him; when he took a step toward her it was still not movement because she could have retreated no further: only the tremendous, fathomless, ink-colored eyes in the narrow, thin, too thin, coffee-colored face watching him without alarm, without recognition, without hope. 'Fonsiba,' he said. 'Fonsiba. Are you all right?'

'I'm free,' she said. Midnight was a tavern, a livery stable, a big store (that would be where the pension check banked itself as a matter of mutual elimination of bother and fret, he thought) and a little one, a saloon and a blacksmith shop. But there was a bank there too. The president (the owner, for all practical purposes) of it was a translated Mississippian who had been one of Forrest's men too: and his body lightened of the golden belt for the first time since he left home eight days ago, with pencil and paper he multiplied three dollars by twelve months and divided it into one thousand dollars; it would stretch that way over almost twenty-eight years and for twenty-eight years at least she would not starve, the banker promising to send the three dollars himself by a trusty messenger on the fifteenth of each month and put it into her actual hand, and he returned home and that was all because in 1874 his father and his uncle were both dead and the old ledgers never again came down from the shelf above the desk to which his father had returned them for the last time that day in 1869. But he could have completed it:

> *Lucas Quintus Carothers McCaslin Beauchamp.*
> *Last surviving son and child of Tomey's Terrel*
> *and Tennie Beauchamp. March 17, 1874*

except that there was no need: not *Lucius Quintus* @c @c @c, but *Lucas Quintus*, not refusing to be called Lucius, because he simply eliminated that word from the name; not denying, declining the name itself, because he used three quarters of it; but simply taking the name and changing, altering it, making it no longer the white man's but his own, by himself composed, himself selfprogenitive and nominate, by himself ancestored, as, for all the old ledgers recorded to the contrary, old Carothers himself was

and that was all: 1874 the boy; 1888 the man, repudiated denied and free; 1895 and husband but no father, unwidowered but without a wife, and found long since that no man is ever free and probably could not bear it if he were; married then and living in Jefferson in the little new jerry built bungalow which his wife's father had given them: and one morning Lucas stood suddenly in the doorway of the room where he was reading the Memphis paper and he looked at the paper's dateline and thought *It's his birthday. He's twenty-one today* and Lucas said: 'Whar's the rest of that money old Carothers left? I wants it. All of it.'

that was all: and McCaslin

'More men than that one Buck and Buddy to fumble-heed that truth so mazed for them that spoke it and so confused for them that heard yet still there was 1865:' and he

'But not enough. Not enough of even Father and Uncle Buddy to fumble-heed in even three generations not even three generations fathered by Grandfather not even if there had been nowhere beneath His sight any but Grandfather and so He would not even have needed to elect and choose. But He tried and I know what you will say. That having Himself created them He could have known no more of hope than He could have pride and grief, but He didn't hope He just waited because He had made them: not just because He had set them alive and in motion but because He had already worried with them so long: worried with them so long because He had seen how in individual cases they were capable of anything, any height or depth remembered in mazed incomprehension out of heaven where hell was created too, and so He must admit them or else admit his equal somewhere and so be no longer God and therefore must accept responsibility for what He Himself had done in order to live with Himself in His lonely and paramount heaven. And He probably knew it was vain but He had created them and knew them capable of all things because He had shaped them out of the primal Absolute which contained all and had watched them since in their individual exaltation and baseness, and they themselves not knowing why nor how nor even when: until at last He saw that they were all Grandfather all of them and that even from them the elected and chosen the best the very best He could expect (not hope mind: not hope) would be Bucks and Buddies and not even enough of them and in the third generation not even Bucks and Buddies but—' and McCaslin

'Ah:' and he

'Yes. If He could see Father and Uncle Buddy in Grandfather He must have seen me too. —an Isaac born into a later life than Abraham's and repudiating immolation: fatherless and therefore safe declining the altar because maybe this time the exasperated Hand might not supply the kid—' and McCaslin

'Escape:' and he

'All right. Escape.—Until one day He said what you told Fonsiba's husband that afternoon here in this room: *This will do. This is enough:* not in exasperation or rage or even just sick to death as you were sick that day: just *This is enough* and looked about for one last time, for one time more since He had created them, upon this land this South for which He had done so much with woods for game and streams for fish and deep rich soil for seed and lush springs to sprout it and long summers to mature it and serene falls to harvest it and short mild winters for men and animals, and saw no hope anywhere and looked beyond it where hope should have been, where to East North and West lay illimitable that whole hopeful continent dedicated as a refuge and sanctuary of liberty and freedom from what you called the old world's worthless evening, and saw the rich descendants of slavers, females of both sexes, to whom the black they shrieked of was another specimen another example like the Brazilian macaw brought home in a cage by a traveller, passing resolutions about horror and outrage in warm and air-proof halls: and the thundering cannonade of politicians earning votes and the medicine-shows of pulpiteers earning Chatauqua fees, to whom the outrage and the injustice were as much abstractions as Tariff or Silver or Immortality and who employed the very shackles of its servitude and the sorry rags of its ragalia as they did the other beer and banners and mottoes, redfire and brimstone and sleight-of-hand and musical handsaws: and the whirling wheels which manufactured for a profit the pristine replacements of the shackles and shoddy garments as they wore out, and spun the cotton and made the gins which ginned it and the cars and ships which hauled it, and the men who ran the wheels for that profit and established and collected the taxes it was taxed with and the rates for hauling it and the commissions for selling it: and He could have repudiated them since they were his creation now and forever more throughout all their generations, until not only that old world from which He had rescued them but this new one too which He had revealed and led them to as a sanctuary and refuge were become the same worthless tideless rock cooling in the last crimson evening, except that out of all that empty sound and bootless fury one silence, among that loud and moiling all of them just one simple enough to believe that horror and outrage were first and last simply horror and outrage and crude enough to act upon that, illiterate and had no words for talking or perhaps was just busy and had no time to, one out of them all who did not bother Him with cajolery and adjuration then pleading then threat,

and had not even bothered to inform Him in advance what he was
about so that a lesser than He might have even missed the simple
act of lifting the long ancestral musket down from the deerhorns
above the door, whereupon He said *My name is Brown too* and the
other *So is mine* and He *Then mine or yours can't be because I am
against it* and the other *So am I* and He triumphantly *Then where
are you going with that gun?* and the other told him in one sentence
one word and He: amazed: Who knew neither hope nor pride nor
grief *But your Association, your Committee, your Officers. Where
are your Minutes, your Motions, your Parliamentary Procedures?*
and the other *I ain't against them. They are all right I reckon for
them that have the time. I am just against the weak because they
are niggers being held in bondage by the strong just because they
are white.* So He turned once more to this land which He still
intended to save because He had done so much for it—' and
McCaslin

'What?' and he

'—to these people He was still committed to because they were
his creations—' and McCaslin

'Turned back to us? His face to us?' and he

'—whose wives and daughters at least made soups and jellies for
them when they were sick, and carried the trays through the mud
and the winter too into the stinking cabins, and sat in the stinking
cabins and kept fires going until crises came and passed, but that
was not enough: and when they were very sick had them carried
into the big house itself into the company room itself maybe and
nursed them there, which the white man would have done too for
any other of his cattle that was sick but at least the man who hired
one from a livery wouldn't have, and still that was not enough: so
that He said and not in grief either, Who had made them and so
could know no more of grief than He could of pride or hope:
*Apparently they can learn nothing save through suffering, remem-
ber nothing save when underlined in blood*—' and McCaslin

'Ashby[7] on an afternoon's ride, to call on some remote maiden
cousins of his mother or maybe just acquaintances of hers, comes
by chance upon a minor engagement of outposts and dismounts
and with his crimson-lined cloak for target leads a handful of troops
he never saw before against an entrenched position of backwoods-
trained riflemen. Lee's battle-order, wrapped maybe about a handful
of cigars and doubtless thrown away when the last cigar was smoked,
found by a Yankee Intelligence officer on the floor of a saloon
behind the Yankee lines after Lee had already divided his forces
before Sharpsburg.[8] Jackson[9] on the Plank Road, already rolled up

7. Colonel Turner Ashby, Confederate
cavalryman who served under Stonewall
Jackson.

8. Known in the North as the Battle
of Antietam (September 17, 1862).

9. Thomas Jonathan (Stonewall) Jack-

the flank which Hooker[1] believed could not be turned and, waiting only for night to pass to continue the brutal and incessant slogging which would fling that whole wing back into Hooker's lap where he sat on a front gallery in Chancellorsville drinking rum toddies and telegraphing Lincoln that he had defeated Lee, is shot from among a whole covey of minor officers and in the blind night by one of his own patrols, leaving as next by seniority Stuart,[2] that gallant man born apparently already horsed and sabred and already knowing all there was to know about war except the slogging and brutal stupidity of it: and that same Stuart off raiding Pennsylvania hen-roosts when Lee should have known of all of Meade[3] just where Hancock was on Cemetery Ridge: and Longstreet[4] too at Gettysburg and that same Longstreet shot out of saddle by his own men in the dark by mistake just as Jackson was. His face to us?' and he

'How else have made them fight? Who else but Jacksons and Stuarts and Ashbys and Morgans[5] and Forrests?—the farmers of the central and middle-west, holding land by the acre instead of the tens or maybe even the hundreds, farming it themselves and to no single crop of cotton or tobacco or cane, owning no slaves and needing and wanting none, and already looking toward the Pacific coast, not always as long as two generations there and having stopped where they did stop only through the fortuitous mischance that an ox died or a wagon-axle broke. And the New England mechanics who didn't even own land and measured all things by the weight of water and the cost of turning wheels, and the narrow fringe of traders and shipowners still looking backward across the Atlantic and attached to the continent only by their counting-houses. And those who should have had the alertness to see: the wildcat manipulators of mythical wilderness townsites; and the astuteness to rationalize: the bankers who held the mortgages on the land which the first were only waiting to abandon, and on the railroads and steamboats to carry them still further west, and on the factories and the wheels and the rented tenements those who ran them lived in; and the leisure and scope to comprehend and fear in time and even anticipate: the Boston-bred (even when not born in Boston) spinster, descendants of long lines of similarly-

son (1824–1863), Confederate general, Lee's most trusted lieutenant.
1. Joseph Hooker (1814–1879), Union general, commander of the Army of the Potomac from January through June, 1863.
2. General J. E. B. Stuart (1833–1864), Confederate cavalryman.
3. George Gordon Meade (1815–1872), Union general, succeeded Hooker as commander of the Army of the Potomac just before the Battle of Gettysburg (July 1–3, 1863), where Union General Winfield Scott Hancock (1824–1886) distinguished himself by holding Cemetery Ridge in the face of determined Confederate attacks.
4. James Longstreet (1821–1904), Confederate general whose delay in carrying out Lee's order to attack at Gettysburg is held to have cost Lee the battle. He was wounded in the Battle of the Wilderness (May 5–6, 1864).
5. John Hunt Morgan (1825–1864), Confederate general.

bred and likewise spinster aunts and uncles whose hands knew no callus except that of the indicting pen, to whom the wilderness itself began at the top of tide and who looked, if at anything other than Beacon Hill, only toward heaven—not to mention all the loud rabble of the camp-followers of pioneers: the bellowing of politicians, the mellifluous choiring of self-styled men of God, the—' and McCaslin

'Here, here. Wait a minute:' And he

'Let me talk now. I'm trying to explain to the head of my family something which I have got to do which I don't quite understand myself, not in justification of it but to explain it if I can. I could say I don't know why I must do it but that I do know I have got to because I have got myself to have to live with for the rest of my life and all I want is peace to do it in. But you are the head of my family. More. I knew a long time ago that I would never have to miss my father, even if you are just finding out that you have missed your son—the drawers of bills and the shavers of notes and the schoolmasters and the self-ordained to teach and lead and all that horde of the semi-literate with a white shirt but no change for it, with one eye on themselves and watching each other with the other one. Who else could have made them fight: could have struck them so aghast with fear and dread as to turn shoulder to shoulder and face one way and even stop talking for a while and even after two years of it keep them still so wrung with terror that some among them would seriously propose moving their very capital into a foreign country lest it be ravaged and pillaged by a people whose entire white male population would have little more than filled any one of their larger cities: except Jackson in the Valley[6] and three separate armies trying to catch him and none of them ever knowing whether they were just retreating from a battle or just running into one, and Stuart riding his whole command entirely around the biggest single armed force this continent ever saw in order to see what it looked like from behind,[7] and Morgan leading a cavalry charge against a stranded man-of-war.[8] Who else could have declared a war against a power with ten times the area and a hundred times the men and a thousand times the resources, except men who could believe that all necessary to conduct a successful war was not acumen nor shrewdness nor politics nor diplomacy nor money nor even integrity and simple arithmetic, but just love of land and courage—'

'And an unblemished and gallant ancestry and the ability to ride a horse,' McCaslin said. 'Don't leave that out.' It was evening now, the tranquil sunset of October mazy with windless woodsmoke. The cotton was long since picked and ginned, and all day now the

6. Shenandoah Valley.
7. Before the Seven Days' Battle (June 26–July 2, 1862) Stuart rode entirely around McClellan's army.
8. The "man-of-war" was actually a river tug with one gun.

wagons loaded with gathered corn moved between field and crib, processional across the enduring land. 'Well, maybe that's what He wanted. At least, that's what He got.' This time there was no yellowed procession of fading and harmless ledger-pages. This was chronicled in a harsher book, and McCaslin, fourteen and fifteen and sixteen, had seen it and the boy himself had inherited it as Noah's grandchildren had inherited the Flood although they had not been there to see the deluge: that dark corrupt and bloody time while three separate peoples had tried to adjust not only to one another but to the new land which they had created and inherited too and must live in for the reason that those who had lost it were no less free to quit it than those who had gained it were:—those upon whom freedom and equality had been dumped overnight and without warning or preparation or any training in how to employ it or even just endure it and who misused it, not as children would nor yet because they had been so long in bondage and then so suddenly freed, but misused it as human beings always misuse freedom, so that he thought *Apparently there is a wisdom beyond even that learned through suffering necessary for a man to distinguish between liberty and license*; those who had fought for four years and lost to preserve a condition under which that franchisement was anomaly and paradox, not because they were opposed to freedom as freedom but for the old reasons for which man (not the generals and politicians but man) has always fought and died in wars: to preserve a status quo or to establish a better future one to endure for his children; and lastly, as if that were not enough for bitterness and hatred and fear, that third race even more alien to the people whom they resembled in pigment and in whom even the same blood ran, than to the people whom they did not,—that race threefold in one and alien even among themselves save for a single fierce will for rapine and pillage, composed of the sons of middleaged Quartermaster lieutenants and Army sutlers and contractors in military blankets and shoes and transport mules, who followed the battles they themselves had not fought and inherited the conquest they themselves had not helped to gain, sanctioned and protected even if not blessed, and left their bones and in another generation would be engaged in a fierce economic competition of small sloven farms with the black men they were supposed to have freed and the white descendants of fathers who had owned no slaves anyway whom they were supposed to have disinherited, and in the third generation would be back once more in the little lost county seats as barbers and garage mechanics and deputy sheriffs and mill- and ginhands and power-plant firemen, leading, first in mufti then later in an actual formalized regalia of hooded sheets and passwords and fiery Christian symbols, lynching mobs against the race their ancestors had come to save: and of all that other nameless horde of speculators in human misery, manipulators of money and politics and land, who follow catastrophe and are their own protection as grasshoppers are and need no blessing and sweat no plow or axe-helve and batten and vanish and leave no bones, just as they derived apparently from no ancestry, no mortal flesh, no act even of passion or even of lust: and the Jew who came without protection too, since after two thousand years he had got out of the habit of being or needing it, and solitary, without even the solidarity of the locusts, and in this a sort of courage since he had come thinking not in terms of simple pillage but in terms of his great-grandchildren, seeking yet some place to establish them to endure even though forever alien: and unblessed: a pariah about the face of the Western earth which twenty centuries later was still taking revenge on him for the fairy tale with which he had conquered it. McCaslin had actually seen it, and the boy even at almost eighty would never be able to distinguish certainly between what he had seen and what had been told him: a lightless and gutted and empty land where women crouched with the huddled children behind locked doors and men armed in sheets and masks rode the silent roads and the bodies of white and black both, victims not so much of hate as of desperation and despair, swung from lonely limbs: and men shot dead in polling-booths with the still wet pen in one hand and the unblotted ballot in the other: and a United States marshal in Jefferson who signed his official papers with a crude cross, an ex-slave called Sickymo, not at all because his ex-owner was a doctor and apothecary but because, still a slave, he would steal his master's grain alcohol and dilute it with water and peddle it in pint bottles from a cache beneath the roots of a big sycamore tree behind the drug store, who had attained his high office because his half-white sister was the concubine of the Federal A.P.M.: and this time McCaslin did not even say Look but merely lifted one hand, not even pointing, not even specifically toward the shelf of ledgers but toward the desk, toward the corner where it sat beside the scuffed patch on the floor where two decades of heavy shoes had stood while the white man at the desk added and multiplied and subtracted. And again he did not need to look because he had seen this himself and, twenty-three years after the Surrender and twenty-four after the Proclamation,[9] was still watching it: the ledgers, new ones now and filled rapidly, succeeding one another rapidly and containing more names than old Carothers or even his father and Uncle Buddy had ever dreamed of; new names and new faces to go with them, among which the old names and faces that even his father and

9. But Lee surrendered at Appomattox Courthouse on April 9, 1865; Lincoln published the Emancipation Proclamation on September 22, 1862, effective January 1, 1863.

uncle would have recognized, were lost, vanished—Tomey's Terrel dead, and even the tragic and miscast Percival Brownlee, who couldn't keep books and couldn't farm either, found his true niche at last, reappeared in 1862 during the boy's father's absence and had apparently been living on the plantation for at least a month before his uncle found out about it, conducting impromptu revival meetings among Negroes, preaching and leading the singing also in his high sweet true soprano voice and disappeared again on foot and at top speed, not behind but ahead of a body of raiding Federal horse and reappeared for the third and last time in the entourage of a travelling Army paymaster, the two of them passing through Jefferson in a surrey at the exact moment when the boy's father (it was 1866) also happened to be crossing the Square, the surrey and its occupants traversing rapidly that quiet and bucolic scene and even in that fleeting moment, and to others beside the boy's father, giving an illusion of flight and illicit holiday like a man on an excursion during his wife's absence with his wife's personal maid, until Brownlee glanced up and saw his late co-master and gave him one defiant female glance and then broke again, leaped from the surrey and disappeared this time for good, and it was only by chance that McCaslin, twenty years later, heard of him again, an old man now and quite fat, as the well-to-do proprietor of a select New Orleans brothel; and Tennie's Jim gone, nobody knew where, and Fonsiba in Arkansas with her three dollars each month and the scholar-husband with his lenseless spectacles and frock coat and his plans for the spring; and only Lucas was left, the baby, the last save himself of old Carothers' doomed and fatal blood which in the male derivation seemed to destroy all it touched, and even he was repudiating and at least hoping to escape it;—Lucas, the boy of fourteen whose name would not even appear for six years yet among those rapid pages in the bindings new and dustless too since McCaslin lifted them down daily now to write into them the continuation of that record which two hundred years had not been enough to complete, and another hundred would not be enough to discharge; that chronicle which was a whole land in miniature, which multiplied and compounded was the entire South, twenty-three years after surrender and twenty-four from emancipation—that slow trickle of molasses and meal and meat, of shoes and straw hats and overalls, of plowlines and collars and heel-bolts and buckheads and clevises, which returned each fall as cotton—the two threads frail as truth and impalpable as equators yet cable-strong to bind for life them who made the cotton to the land their sweat fell on: and he

'Yes. Binding them for a while yet, a little while yet. Through and beyond that life and maybe through and beyond the life of that life's sons and maybe even through and beyond that of the sons of those sons. But not always, because they will endure. They will out-last us because they are—' it was not a pause, barely a falter even, possibly appreciable only to himself, as if he couldn't speak even to McCaslin, even to explain his repudiation, that which to him too, even in the act of escaping (and maybe this was the reality and the truth of his need to escape), was heresy: so that even in escaping he was taking with him more of that evil and unregenerate old man who could summon, because she was his property, a human being because she was old enough and female, to his widower's house and get a child on her and then dismiss her because she was of an inferior race, and then bequeath a thousand dollars to the infant because he would be dead then and wouldn't have to pay it, than even he had feared. 'Yes. He didn't want to. He had to. Because they will endure. They are better than we are. Stronger than we are. Their vices are vices aped from white men or that white men and bondage have taught them: improvidence and intemperance and evasion— not laziness: evasion: of what white men had set them to, not for their aggrandizement or even comfort but his own—' and McCaslin

'All right. Go on: Promiscuity. Violence. Instability and lack of control. Inability to distinguish between mine and thine—' and he

'How distinguish, when for two hundred years mine did not even exist for them?' and McCaslin

'All right. Go on. And their virtues—' and he

'Yes. Their own. Endurance—' and McCaslin

'So have mules:' and he

'—and pity and tolerance and forbearance and fidelity and love of children—' and McCaslin

'So have dogs:' and he

'—whether their own or not or black or not. And more: what they got not only not from white people but not even despite white people because they had it already from the old free fathers a longer time free than us because we have never been free—' and it was in McCaslin's eyes too, he had only to look at McCaslin's eyes and it was there, that summer twilight seven years ago, almost a week after they had returned from the camp before he discovered that Sam Fathers had told McCaslin: an old bear, fierce and ruthless not just to stay alive but ruthless with the fierce pride of liberty and freedom, jealous and proud enough of liberty and freedom to see it threatened not with fear nor even alarm but almost with joy, seeming deliberately to put it into jeopardy in order to savor it and keep his old strong bones and flesh supple and quick to defend and preserve it; an old man, son of a Negro slave and an Indian king, inheritor on the one hand of the long chronicle of a people who had learned humility through suffering and learned pride through the endurance which survived the suffering, and on the other side the chronicle of a people even longer in the land than the first, yet who now existed there only in the solitary brotherhood of an old and childless Negro's alien blood and the wild and invincible spirit of an old bear; a boy who wished to learn humility and pride in order to become skillful and worthy in the woods but found himself becoming so skillful so fast that he feared he would never become worthy, because he had not learned humility and pride though he had tried, until one day an old man, who could not have defined either, led him as though by the hand to where an old bear and a little mongrel dog showed him that, by possessing one thing other, he would possess them both; and a little dog, nameless and mongrel and many-fathered, grown yet weighing less than six pounds, who couldn't be dangerous because there was nothing anywhere much smaller, not fierce because that would have been called just noise, not humble because it was already too near the ground to genuflect, and not proud because it would not have been close enough for anyone to discern what was casting that shadow, and which didn't even know it was not going to heaven since they had already decided it had no immortal soul, so that all it could be was brave, even though they would probably call that too just noise.

'And you didn't shoot,' McCaslin said. '*How close were you?*'

'I don't know,' he said. '*There was a big wood tick just inside his off hind leg. I saw that. But I didn't have the gun then.*'

'But you didn't shoot when you had the gun,' McCaslin said. '*Why?*' But McCaslin didn't wait, rising and crossing the room, across the pelt of the bear he had killed two years ago and the bigger one McCaslin had killed before he was born, to the bookcase beneath the mounted head of his first buck, and returned with the book and sat down again and opened it. 'Listen,' he said. He read the five stanzas aloud and closed the book on his finger and looked up. 'All right,' he said. 'Listen,' and read again, but only one stanza this time and closed the book and laid it on the table. 'She cannot fade, though thou hast not thy bliss,' McCaslin said: 'Forever wilt thou love, and she be fair.'[1]

'He's talking about a girl,' he said.

'He had to talk about something,' McCaslin said. Then he said, 'He was talking about truth. Truth is one. It doesn't change. It covers all things which touch the heart—honor and pride and pity and justice and courage and love. Do you see now?' He didn't know. Somehow it had seemed simpler than that, simpler than somebody talking in a book about a young man and a girl he would never need to grieve over because he could never approach any nearer and would never have to get any further away. He had heard about an old bear

---

1. Keats, "Ode on a Grecian Urn," ll. 19–20.

and finally got big enough to hunt it and he hunted it four years
and at last met it with a gun in his hands and he didn't shoot. Be-
cause a little dog—But he could have shot long before the fyce
covered the twenty yards to where the bear waited, and Sam Fathers
could have shot at any time during the interminable minute while
Old Ben stood on his hind legs over them. . . . He ceased. Mc-
Caslin watched him, still speaking, the voice, the words as quiet as
the twilight itself was: 'Courage and honor and pride, and pity and
love of justice and of liberty. They all touch the heart, and what the
heart holds to becomes truth, as far as we know truth. Do you see
now?'

and he could still hear them, intact in this twilight as in that
one seven years ago, no louder still because they did not need to be
because they would endure: and he had only to look at McCaslin's
eyes beyond the thin and bitter smiling, the faint lip-lift which
would have had to be called smiling;—his kinsman, his father almost, who had been born too late into the old time and too soon
for the new, the two of them juxtaposed and alien now to each other
against their ravaged patrimony, the dark and ravaged fatherland
still prone and panting from its etherless operation:

'Habet then.—So this land is, indubitably, of and by itself
cursed:' and he

'Cursed:' and again McCaslin merely lifted one hand, not even
speaking and not even toward the ledgers: so that, as the stereopti-
con condenses into one instantaneous field the myriad minutiae of
its scope, so did that slight and rapid gesture establish in the small
cramped and cluttered twilit room not only the ledgers but the
whole plantation in its mazed and intricate entirety—the land, the
fields and what they represented in terms of cotton ginned and
sold, the men and women whom they fed and clothed and even paid
a little cash money at Christmas-time in return for the labor which
planted and raised and picked and ginned the cotton, the machinery
and mules and gear with which they raised it and their cost and
upkeep and replacement—that whole edifice intricate and complex
and founded upon injustice and erected by ruthless rapacity and
carried on even yet with at times downright savagery not only to
the human beings but the valuable animals too, yet solvent and
efficient and, more than that: not only still intact but enlarged,
increased: brought still intact by McCaslin, himself little more than
a child then, through and out of the debacle and chaos of twenty
years ago where hardly one in ten survived, and enlarged and increased and would continue so, solvent and efficient and intact and
still increasing so long as McCaslin and his McCaslin successors
lasted, even though their surnames might not even be Edmonds
then: and he

'Habet too. Because that's it: not the land, but us. Not only the blood, but the name too; not only its color but its designation: Edmonds, white, but, a female line, could have no other but the name his father bore; Beauchamp, the elder line and the male one, but, black, could have had any name he liked and no man would have cared, except the name his father bore who had no name—' and McCaslin

'And since I know too what you know I will say now, once more let me say it: And one other, and in the third generation too, and the male, the eldest, the direct and sole and white and still Mc-Caslin even, father to son to son—' and he

'I am free:' and this time McCaslin did not even gesture, no inference of fading pages, no postulation of the stereoptic whole, but the frail and iron thread strong as truth and impervious as evil and longer than life itself and reaching beyond record and patrimony both to join him with the lusts and passions, the hopes and dreams and griefs, of bones whose names while still fleshed and capable even old Carothers' grandfather had never heard: and he:

'And of that too:' and McCaslin

'Chosen, I suppose (I will concede it) out of all your time by Him, as you say Buck and Buddy were from theirs. And it took Him a bear and an old man and four years just for you. And it took you fourteen years to reach that point and about that many, maybe more, for Old Ben, and more than seventy for Sam Fathers. And you are just one. How long then? How long?' and he

'It will be long. I have never said otherwise. But it will be all right because they will endure—' and McCaslin

'And anyway, you will be free.—No, not now nor ever, we from them nor they from us. So I repudiate too. I would deny even if I knew it were true. I would have to. Even you can see that I could do no else. I am what I am; I will be always what I was born and have always been. And more than me. More than me, just as there were more than Buck and Buddy in what you called His first plan which failed:' and he

'And more than me:' and McCaslin

'No. Not even you. Because mark. You said how on that instant when Ikkemotubbe realized that he could sell the land to Grandfather, it ceased forever to have been his. All right; go on: Then it belonged to Sam Fathers, old Ikkemotubbe's son. And who inherited from Sam Fathers, if not you? co-heir perhaps with Boon, if not of his life maybe, at least of his quitting it?' and he

'Yes. Sam Fathers set me free.'

and Isaac McCaslin, not yet Uncle Ike, a long time yet before he would be uncle to half a county and still father to none, living in one small cramped fireless rented room in a Jefferson boarding-

house where petit juries were domiciled during court terms and
itinerant horse- and mule-traders stayed, with his kit of brand-new
carpenter's tools and the shotgun McCaslin had given him with
his name engraved in silver and old General Compson's compass
(and, when the General died, his silver-mounted horn too) and the
iron cot and mattress and the blankets which he would take each
fall into the woods for more than sixty years and the bright tin
coffee-pot

there had been a legacy, from his Uncle Hubert Beauchamp, his
godfather, that bluff burly roaring childlike man from whom Uncle
Buddy had won Tomey's Terrel's wife Tennie in the poker-game
in 1859—'posible strait against three Treys in sigt Not called'—; no
pale sentence or paragraph scrawled in cringing fear of death by
a weak and trembling hand as a last desperate sop flung backward
at retribution, but a Legacy, a Thing, possessing weight to the hand
and bulk to the eye and even audible: a silver cup filled with gold
pieces and wrapped in burlap and sealed with his godfather's ring
in the hot wax, which (intact still) even before his Uncle Hubert's
death and long before his own majority, when it would be his, had
become not only a legend but one of the family lares.[2] After his
father's and his Uncle Hubert's sister's marriage they moved back
into the big house, the tremendous cavern which old Carothers
had started and never finished, cleared the remaining Negroes out
of it and with his mother's dowry completed it, at least the rest of
the windows and doors and moved into it, all of them save Uncle
Buddy who declined to leave the cabin he and his twin had built,
the move being the bride's notion and more than just a notion,
and none ever to know if she really wanted to live in the big house
or if she knew beforehand that Uncle Buddy would refuse to move:
and two weeks after his birth in 1867, the first time he and his
mother came down stairs one night, and the silver cup sitting on
the cleared dining-room table beneath the bright lamp, and while
his mother and his father and McCaslin and Tennie (his nurse:
carrying him)—all of them again but Uncle Buddy—watched, his
Uncle Hubert rang one by one into the cup the bright and glinting
mintage and wrapped it into the burlap envelope and heated the
wax and sealed it and carried it back home with him where he
lived alone now without even his sister either to hold him down
as McCaslin said or to try to raise him up as Uncle Buddy said, and
(dark times then in Mississippi) Uncle Buddy said most of the
niggers gone and the ones that didn't go even Hub Beauchamp
could not have wanted: but the dogs remained and Uncle Buddy
said Beauchamp fiddled while Nero fox-hunted

they would go and see it there; at last his mother would prevail

2. Household gods.

and they would depart in the surrey, once more all save Uncle Buddy and McCaslin to keep Uncle Buddy company, until one winter Uncle Buddy began to fail and from then on it was himself, beginning to remember now, and his mother and Tennie and Tomey's Terrel to drive: the twenty-two miles into the next county, the twin gateposts on one of which McCaslin could remember the half-grown boy blowing a fox-horn at breakfast, dinner, and supper-time and jumping down to open to any passer who happened to hear it, but where there were no gates at all now, the shabby and overgrown entrance to what his mother still insisted that people call Warwick because her brother was, if truth but triumphed and justice but prevailed, the rightful earl of it, the paintless house which outwardly did not change but which on the inside seemed each time larger because he was too little to realize then that there was less and less in it of the fine furnishings, the rosewood and mahogany and walnut, which for him had never existed anywhere anyway save in his mother's tearful lamentations, and the occasional piece small enough to be roped somehow onto the rear or the top of the carriage on their return (And he remembered this, he had seen it: an instant, a flash, his mother's soprano 'Even my dress! Even my dress!' loud and outraged in the barren unswept hall; a face young and female and even lighter in color than Tomey's Terrel's for an instant in a closing door; a swirl, a glimpse of the silk gown and the flick and glint of an ear-ring: an apparition rapid and tawdry and illicit, yet somehow even to the child, the infant still almost, breathless and exciting and evocative: as though, like two limpid and pellucid streams meeting, the child which he still was had made serene and absolute and perfect rapport and contact through that glimpsed nameless illicit hybrid female flesh with the boy which had existed at that stage of inviolable and immortal adolescence in his uncle for almost sixty years; the dress, the face, the ear-rings gone in that same aghast flash and his uncle's voice: 'She's my cook! She's my new cook! I had to have a cook, didn't I?' then the uncle himself, the face alarmed and aghast too yet still innocently and somehow even indomitably of a boy, they retreating in their turn now, back to the front gallery, and his uncle again, pained and still amazed, in a sort of desperate resurgence if not of courage at least of self-assertion: 'They're free now; They're folks too just like we are!' and his mother: 'That's why! That's why! My mother's house! Defiled! Defiled!' and his uncle: 'Damn it, Sibbey, at least give her time to pack her grip:' then over, finished, the loud uproar and all, himself and Tennie and he remembered Tennie's inscrutable face at the broken shutterless window of the bare room which had once been the parlor while they watched, hurrying down the lane at a stumbling trot, the routed compounder of his uncle's uxory: the back, the nameless face which he had seen only for a moment, the once-hooped dress ballooning and flapping below a man's overcoat, the worn heavy carpet-bag jouncing and banging against her knee, routed and in retreat true enough and in the empty lane, solitary, young-looking, and forlorn, yet withal still exciting and evocative and wearing still the silken banner captured inside the very citadel of respectability, and unforgettable.)

the cup, the sealed inscrutable burlap, sitting on the shelf in the locked closet, Uncle Hubert unlocking the door and lifting it down and passing it from hand to hand: his mother, his father, McCaslin and even Tennie, insisting that each take it in turn and heft it for weight and shake it again to prove the sound, Uncle Hubert himself standing spraddled before the cold unswept hearth in which the very bricks themselves were crumbling into a litter of soot and dust and mortar and the droppings of chimney-sweeps, still roaring and still innocent and still indomitable: and for a long time he believed nobody but himself had noticed that his uncle now put the cup only into his hands, unlocked the door and lifted it down and put it into his hands and stood over him until he had shaken it obediently until it sounded then took it from him and locked it back into the closet before anyone else could have offered to touch it, and even later, when competent not only to remember but to rationalize, he could not say what it was or even if it had been anything because the parcel was still heavy and still rattled, not even when, Uncle Buddy dead and his father, at last and after almost seventy-five years in bed after the sun rose, said: 'Go get that damn cup. Bring that damn Hub Beauchamp too if you have to:' because it still rattled though his uncle no longer put it even into his hands now but carried it himself from one to the other, his mother, Mc-Caslin, Tennie, shaking it before each in turn, saying: 'Hear it? Hear it?' his face still innocent, not quite baffled but only amazed and not very amazed and still indomitable:

and, his father and Uncle Buddy both gone now, one day without reason or any warning the almost completely empty house in which his uncle and Tennie's ancient and quarrelsome great-grandfather (who claimed to have seen Lafayette and McCaslin said in another ten years would be remembering God) lived, cooked and slept in one single room, burst into peaceful conflagration, a tranquil instantaneous sourceless unanimity of combustion, walls floors and roof: at sunup it stood where his uncle's father had built it sixty years ago, at sundown the four blackened and smokeless chimneys rose from a light white powder of ashes and a few charred ends of planks which did not even appear to have been very hot: and out of the last of evening, the last one of the twenty-two miles, on the old white mare which was the last of that stable which McCaslin remembered, the two old men riding double up to the sister's door, the one wearing his fox-horn on its braided deerhide thong and the other carrying the burlap parcel wrapped in a shirt, the tawny wax-daubed shapeless lump sitting again and on an almost identical shelf and his uncle holding the half-opened door now, his hand not only on the knob but one foot against it and the key waiting in the other hand, the face urgent and still not baffled but still and even indomitably not very amazed and himself standing in the half-opened door looking quietly up at the burlap shape, become almost three times its original height and a good half less than its original thickness, and turning away, and he would remember not his mother's look this time nor yet Tennie's inscrutable expression but McCaslin's dark and aquiline face grave insufferable and bemused:

then one night they waked him and fetched him still half-asleep into the lamp light, the smell of medicine which was familiar by now in that room and the smell of something else which he had not smelled before and knew at once and would never forget, the pillow, the worn and ravaged face from which looked out still the boy innocent and immortal and amazed and urgent, looking at him and trying to tell him until McCaslin moved and leaned over the bed and drew from the top of the night shirt the big iron key on the greasy cord which suspended it, the eyes saying Yes Yes Yes now, and cut the cord and unlocked the closet and brought the parcel to the bed, the eyes still trying to tell him even when he took the parcel so that was still not it, the hands still clinging to the parcel even while relinquishing it, the eyes more urgent than ever trying to tell him but they never did; and he was ten and his mother was dead too and McCaslin said, 'You are almost halfway now. You might as well open it:' and he: 'No. He said twenty-one:' and he was twenty-one and McCaslin shifted the bright lamp to the center of the cleared dining-room table and set the parcel beside it and laid his open knife beside the parcel and stood back with that expression of old grave intolerant and repudiating and he lifted it, the burlap lump which fifteen years ago had changed its shape completely overnight, which shaken gave forth a thin weightless not-quite-musical curiously muffled clatter, the bright knife-blade hunting amid the mazed intricacy of string, the knobby gouts of wax bearing his uncle's Beauchamp seal rattling onto the table's polished top and, standing amid the collapse of burlap folds, the unstained tin coffee-pot still brand new, the handful of copper coins and now he knew what had given them the muffled sound: a collection of minutely folded scraps of paper sufficient almost for a rat's nest, of good linen bond, of the crude ruled paper such as Negroes use, of raggedly-torn ledger-pages and the margins of newspapers and once the paper label from a new pair of overalls, all

dated and all signed, beginning with the first one not six months
after they had watched him seal the silver cup into the burlap on
this same table in this same room by the light even of this same
lamp almost twenty-one years ago:

> *I owe my Nephew Isaac Beauchamp McCaslin five*
> *(5) pieces Gold which I,O.U constitutes My note of*
> *hand with Interest at 5 percent.*
> > *Hubert Fitz-Hubert Beauchamp*
> *at Warwick 27 Nov 1867*

and he: 'Anyway he called it Warwick:' once at least, even if no
more. But there was more:

> *Isaac 24 Dec 1867 I.O.U. 2 pieces Gold H.Fh.B.*
> *I.O.U. Isaac 1 piece Gold 1 Jan 1868 H.Fh.B.*

then five again then three then one then one then a long time and
what dream, what dreamed splendid recoup, not of any injury or
betrayal of trust because it had been merely a loan: nay, a partnership:

> *I.O.U. Beauchamp McCaslin or his heirs twenty-*
> *five (25) pieces Gold This & All preceeding con-*
> *stituting My notes of hand at twenty (20) per-*
> *centum compounded annually. This date of 19th*
> *January 1873*
> > *Beauchamp*

no location save that in time and signed by the single not name but
word as the old proud earl himself might have scrawled Nevile: and
that made forty-three and he could not remember himself of course
but the legend had it at fifty, which balanced: one: then one: then
one: then one and then the last three and then the last chit, dated
after he came to live in the house with them and written in the
shaky hand not of a beaten old man because he had never been
beaten to know it but of a tired old man maybe and even at that
tired only on the outside and still indomitable, the simplicity of
the last one the simplicity not of resignation but merely of amazement, like a simple comment or remark, and not very much of that:

> *One silver cup. Hubert Beauchamp*

and McCaslin: 'So you have plenty of coppers anyway. But they
are still not old enough yet to be either rarities or heirlooms. So
you will have to take the money:' except that he didn't hear Mc-
Caslin, standing quietly beside the table and looking peacefully
at the coffee-pot and the pot sitting one night later on the mantel
above what was not even a fireplace in the little cramped ice-like

room in Jefferson as McCaslin tossed the folded banknotes onto the bed and, still standing (there was nowhere to sit save on the bed) did not even remove his hat and overcoat: and he

'As a loan. From you. This one:' and McCaslin

'You can't. I have no money that I can lend to you. And you will have to go to the bank and get it next month because I won't bring it to you:' and he could not hear McCaslin now either, looking peacefully at McCaslin, his kinsman, his father almost yet no kin now as, at the last, even fathers and sons are no kin: and he

'It's seventeen miles, horseback and in the cold. We could both sleep here:' and McCaslin

'Why should I sleep here in my house when you won't sleep yonder in yours?' and gone, and he looking at the bright rustless unstained tin and thinking, and not for the first time, how much it takes to compound a man (Isaac McCaslin for instance) and of the devious intricate choosing yet unerring path that man's (Isaac McCaslin's for instance) spirit takes among all that mass to make him at last what he is to be, not only to the astonishment of them (the ones who sired the McCaslin who sired his father and Uncle Buddy and their sister, and the ones who sired the Beauchamp who sired his Uncle Hubert and his Uncle Hubert's sister) who believed they had shaped him, but to Isaac McCaslin too

as a loan and used it though he would not have had to: Major de Spain offered him a room in his house as long as he wanted it and asked nor would ever ask any question, and old General Compson more than that, to take him into his own room, to sleep in half of his own bed and more than Major de Spain because he told him baldly why: 'You sleep with me and before this winter is out, I'll know the reason. You'll tell me. Because I don't believe you just quit. It looks like you just quit but I have watched you in the woods too much and I don't believe you just quit even if it does look damn like it:' using it as a loan, paid his board and rent for a month and bought the tools, not simply because he was good with his hands because he had intended to use his hands and it could have been with horses, and not in mere static and hopeful emulation of the Nazarene,[3] as the young gambler buys a spotted shirt because the old gambler won in one yesterday, but (without the arrogance of false humility and without the false humbleness of pride, who intended to earn his bread, didn't especially want to earn it but had to earn it and for more than just bread) because if the Nazarene had found carpentering good for the life and ends He had assumed and elected to serve, it would be all right too for Isaac McCaslin even though Isaac McCaslin's ends, although simple enough in their apparent motivation, were and would be always incomprehen-

3. Jesus of Nazareth.

sible to him, and his life, invincible enough in its needs, if he could have helped himself, not being the Nazarene, he would not have chosen it: and paid it back. He had forgotten the thirty dollars which McCaslin put into the bank in his name each month, fetched it in to him and flung it onto the bed that first one time but no more; he had a partner now or rather he was the partner: a blasphemous profane clever old dipsomaniac who had built blockade-runners in Charleston in '62 and '63 and had been a ship's carpenter since and appeared in Jefferson two years ago, nobody knew from where nor why, and spent a good part of his time since recovering from delirium tremens in the jail; they had put a new roof on the stable of the bank's president and (the old man in jail again still celebrating that job) he went to the bank to collect for it and the president said, 'I should borrow from you instead of paying you:' and it had been seven months now and he remembered for the first time, two-hundred-and-ten dollars, and this was the first job of any size and when he left the bank the account stood at two-twenty, two-forty to balance, only twenty dollars more to go, then it did balance though by then the total had increased to three hundred and thirty and he said, 'I will transfer it now:' and the president said, 'I can't do that. McCaslin told me not to. Haven't you got another initial you could use and open another account?' but that was all right, the coins the silver and the bills as they accumulated knotted into a handkerchief and the coffee-pot wrapped in an old shirt as when Tennie's great-grandfather had fetched it from Warwick eighteen years ago, in the bottom of the iron-bound trunk which old Carothers had brought from Carolina and his landlady said, 'Not even a lock! And you don't even lock your door, not even when you leave!' and himself looking at her as peacefully as he had looked at McCaslin that first night in this same room, no kin to him at all yet more than kin as those who serve you even for pay are your kin and those who injure you are more than brother or wife

and he had the wife now; got the old man out of jail and fetched him to the rented room and sobered him by superior strength, did not even remove his own shoes for twenty-four hours, got him up and got food into him and they built the barn this time from the ground up and he married her: an only child, a small girl yet curiously bigger than she seemed at first, solider perhaps, with dark eyes and a passionate heart-shaped face, who had time even on that farm to watch most of the day while he sawed timbers to the old man's measurements: and she: 'Papa told me about you. That farm is really yours, isn't it?' and he

'And McCaslin's:' and she

'Was there a will leaving half of it to him?' and he

'There didn't need to be a will. His grandmother was my father's sister. We were the same as brothers:' and she

'You are the same as second cousins and that's all you ever will be. But I don't suppose it matters:' and they were married, they were married and it was the new country, his heritage too as it was the heritage of all, out of the earth, beyond the earth yet of the earth because his too was of the earth's long chronicle, his too because each must share with another in order to come into it, and in the sharing they become one: for that while, one: for that little while at least, one: indivisible, that while at least irrevocable and unrecoverable, living in a rented room still but for just a little while and that room wall-less and topless and floorless in glory for him to leave each morning and return to at night; her father already owned the lot in town and furnished the material and he and his partner would build it, her dowry from one: her wedding-present from three, she not to know it until the bungalow was finished and ready to be moved into and he never know who told her, not her father and not his partner and not even in drink though for a while he believed that, himself coming home from work and just time to wash and rest a moment before going down to supper, entering no rented cubicle since it would still partake of glory even after they would have grown old and lost it: and he saw her face then, just before she spoke: 'Sit down:' the two of them sitting on the bed's edge, not even touching yet, her face strained and terrible, her voice a passionate and expiring whisper of immeasurable promise: 'I love you. You know I love you. When are we going to move?' and he

'I didn't—I didn't know—Who told you—' the hot fierce palm clapped over his mouth, crushing his lips into his teeth, the fierce curve of fingers digging into his cheek and only the palm slacked off enough for him to answer:

'The farm. Our farm. Your farm:' and he

'I——' then the hand again, finger and palm, the whole enveloping weight of her although she still was not touching him save the hand, the voice: 'No! No!' and the fingers themselves seeming to follow through the cheek the impulse to speech as it died in his mouth, then the whisper, the breath again, of love and of incredible promise, the palm slackening again to let him answer:

'When?' and he

'I——' then she was gone, the hand too, standing, her back to him and her head bent, the voice so calm now that for an instant it seemed no voice of hers that he ever remembered: "Stand up and turn your back and shut your eyes:' and repeated before he understood and stood himself with his eyes shut and heard the bell ring for supper below stairs, and the calm voice again: 'Lock the door:' and he did so and leaned his forehead against the cold wood, his eyes closed, hearing his heart and the sound he had begun to

hear before he moved until it ceased and the bell rang again below
stairs and he knew it was for them this time, and he heard the bed
and turned and he had never seen her naked before, he had asked
her to once, and why: that he wanted to see her naked because he
loved her and he wanted to see her looking at him naked because
he loved her, but after that he never mentioned it again, even turning his face when she put the nightgown on over her dress to undress
at night and putting the dress on over the gown to remove it in the
morning, and she would not let him get into bed beside her until
the lamp was out and even in the heat of summer she would draw
the sheet up over them both before she would let him turn to her:
and the landlady came up the stairs up the hall and rapped on the
door and then called their names but she didn't move, lying still on
the bed outside the covers, her face turned away on the pillow,
listening to nothing, thinking of nothing, not of him anyway he
thought: then the landlady went away and she said, 'Take off your
clothes:' her head still turned away, looking at nothing, thinking
of nothing, waiting for nothing, not even him, her hand moving
as though with volition and vision of its own, catching his wrist at
the exact moment when he paused beside the bed so that he never
paused but merely changed the direction of moving, downward
now, the hand drawing him and she moved at last, shifted, a movement one single complete inherent not practiced and one time older
than man, looking at him now, drawing him still downward with the
one hand down and down and he neither saw nor felt it shift, palm
flat against his chest now and holding him away with the same apparent lack of any effort or any need for strength, and not looking
at him now, she didn't need to, the chaste woman, the wife, already
looked upon all the men who ever rutted and now her whole body
had changed, altered, he had never seen it but once and now it was
not even the one he had seen but composite of all woman-flesh since
man that ever of its own will reclined on its back and opened, and
out of it somewhere, without any movement of lips even, the
dying and invincible whisper: 'Promise:' and he

'Promise?'

'The farm.' He moved. He had moved, the hand shifting from
his chest once more to his wrist, grasping it, the arm still lax and
only the light increasing pressure of the fingers as though arm and
hand were a piece of wire cable with one looped end, only the
hand tightening as he pulled against it. 'No,' he said. 'No:' and
she was not looking at him still but not like the other, but still the
hand: 'No, I tell you. I won't. I can't. Never:' and still the hand
and he said, for the last time, he tried to speak clearly and he knew
it was still gently and he thought, *She already knows more than I
with all the man-listening in camps where there was nothing to read*

ever even heard of. They are born already bored with what a boy approaches only at fourteen and fifteen with blundering and aghast trembling: 'I can't. Not ever. Remember:' and still the steady and invincible hand and he said 'Yes' and he thought, *She is lost. She was born lost. We were all born lost* then he stopped thinking and even saying Yes, it was like nothing he had ever dreamed, let alone heard in mere man-talking until after a no-time he returned and lay spent on the insatiate immemorial beach and again with a movement one time more older than man she turned and freed herself and on their wedding night she had cried and he thought she was crying now at first, into the tossed and wadded pillow, the voice coming from somewhere between the pillow and the cachinnation: 'And that's all. That's all from me. If this don't get you that son you talk about, it won't be mine:' lying on her side, her back to the empty rented room, laughing and laughing

V

He went back to the camp one more time before the lumber company moved in and began to cut the timber. Major de Spain himself never saw it again. But he made them welcome to use the house and hunt the land whenever they liked, and in the winter following the last hunt when Sam Fathers and Lion died, General Compson and Walter Ewell invented a plan to corporate themselves, the old group, into a club and lease the camp and the hunting privileges of the woods—an invention doubtless of the somewhat childish old General but actually worthy of Boon Hogganbeck himself. Even the boy, listening, recognised it for the subterfuge it was: to change the leopard's spots when they could not alter the leopard, a baseless and illusory hope to which even McCaslin seemed to subscribe for a while, that once they had persuaded Major de Spain to return to the camp he might revoke himself, which even the boy knew he would not do. And he did not. The boy never knew what occurred when Major de Spain declined. He was not present when the subject was broached and McCaslin never told him. But when June came and the time for the double birthday celebration there was no mention of it and when November came no one spoke of using Major de Spain's house and he never knew whether or not Major de Spain knew they were going on the hunt though without doubt old Ash probably told him: he and McCaslin and General Compson (and that one was the General's last hunt too) and Walter and Boon and Tennie's Jim and old Ash loaded two wagons and drove two days and almost forty miles beyond any country the boy had ever seen before and lived in tents for the two weeks. And the next spring they heard (not from Major de Spain) that he had sold the timber-rights to a Memphis lumber company and in June the boy came to town with McCaslin one

Saturday and went to Major de Spain's office—the big, airy, book-lined, second-storey room with windows at one end opening upon the shabby hinder purlieus of stores and at the other a door giving onto the railed balcony above the Square, with its curtained alcove where sat a cedar water-bucket and a sugar-bowl and spoon and tumbler and a wicker-covered demijohn[4] of whisky, and the bamboo-and-paper punkah[5] swinging back and forth above the desk while old Ash in a tilted chair beside the entrance pulled the cord.

"Of course," Major de Spain said. "Ash will probably like to get off in the woods himself for a while, where he wont have to eat Daisy's cooking. Complain about it, anyway. Are you going to take anybody with you?"

"No sir," he said. "I thought that maybe Boon—" For six months now Boon had been town-marshal at Hoke's; Major de Spain had compounded with the lumber company—or perhaps compromised was closer, since it was the lumber company who had decided that Boon might be better as a town-marshal than head of a logging gang.

"Yes," Major de Spain said. "I'll wire him today. He can meet you at Hoke's. I'll send Ash on by the train and they can take some food in and all you will have to do will be to mount your horse and ride over."

"Yes sir," he said. "Thank you." And he heard his voice again. He didn't know he was going to say it yet he did know, he had known it all the time: "Maybe if you . . ." His voice died. It was stopped, he never knew how because Major de Spain did not speak and it was not until his voice ceased that Major de Spain moved, turned back to the desk and the papers spread on it and even that without moving because he was sitting at the desk with a paper in his hand when the boy entered, the boy standing there looking down at the short plumpish gray-haired man in sober fine broadcloth and an immaculate glazed shirt whom he was used to seeing in boots and muddy corduroy, unshaven, sitting the shaggy powerful long-hocked mare with the worn Winchester[6] carbine across the saddlebow and the great blue dog standing motionless as bronze at the stirrup, the two of them in that last year and to the boy any-way coming to resemble one another somehow as two people competent for love or for business who have been in love or in business together for a long time sometimes do. Major de Spain did not look up again.

"No. I will be too busy. But good luck to you. If you have it, you

---

4. A bottle holding from one to ten gallons, and usually encased in a wicker covering.
5. A large fan suspended from the ceiling, actuated by a cord in the hands of a servant assigned to the task. It originated in India.
6. The carbine was primarily intended as a cavalry rifle. Oliver F. Winchester (1810–1880) became the first manufacturer of repeating rifles.

might bring me a young squirrel."

"Yes sir," he said. "I will."

He rode his mare, the three-year-old filly he had bred and raised and broken himself. He left home a little after midnight and six hours later, without even having sweated her, he rode into Hoke's, the tiny log-line junction which he had always thought of as Major de Spain's property too although Major de Spain had merely sold the company (and that many years ago) the land on which the side-tracks and loading-platforms and the commissary store stood, and looked about in shocked and grieved amazement even though he had had forewarning and had believed himself prepared: a new planing-mill already half completed which would cover two or three acres and what looked like miles and miles of stacked steel rails red with the light bright rust of newness and of piled crossties sharp with creosote, and wire corrals and feeding-troughs for two hundred mules at least and the tents for the men who drove them; so that he arranged for the care and stabling of his mare as rapidly as he could and did not look any more, mounted into the log-train caboose with his gun and climbed into the cupola and looked no more save toward the wall of wilderness ahead within which he would be able to hide himself from it once more anyway.

Then the little locomotive shrieked and began to move: a rapid churning of exhaust, a lethargic deliberate clashing of slack couplings traveling backward along the train, the exhaust changing to the deep slow clapping bites of power as the caboose too began to move and from the cupola he watched the train's head complete the first and only curve in the entire line's length and vanish into the wilderness, dragging its length of train behind it so that it resembled a small dingy harmless snake vanishing into weeds, drawing him with it too until soon it ran once more at its maximum clattering speed between the twin walls of unaxed wilderness as of old. It had been harmless once. Not five years ago Walter Ewell had shot a six-point buck from this same moving caboose, and there was the story of the half-grown bear: the train's first trip in to the cutting thirty miles away, the bear between the rails, its rear end elevated like that of a playing puppy while it dug to see what sort of ants or bugs they might contain or perhaps just to examine the curious symmetrical squared barkless logs which had appeared apparently from nowhere in one endless mathematical line overnight, still digging until the driver on the braked engine not fifty feet away blew the whistle at it, whereupon it broke frantically and took the first tree it came to: an ash sapling not much bigger than a man's thigh and climbed as high as it could and clung there, its head ducked between its arms as a man (a woman perhaps) might have done while the brakeman threw chunks of ballast at it, and when the engine returned three hours later with the first load of outbound logs the bear was halfway down the tree and once more scrambled back up as high as it could and clung again while the train passed and was still there when the engine went in again in the afternoon and still there when it came back out at dusk; and Boon had been in Hoke's with the wagon after a barrel of flour that noon when the train-crew told about it and Boon and Ash, both twenty years younger then, sat under the tree all that night to keep anybody from shooting it and the next morning Major de Spain had the log-train held at Hoke's and just before sundown on the second day, with not only Boon and Ash but Major de Spain and General Compson and Walter and McCaslin, twelve then, watching, it came down the tree after almost thirty-six hours without even water and McCaslin told him how for a minute they thought it was going to stop right there at the barrow-pit where they were standing and drink, how it looked at the water and paused and looked at them and at the water again, but did not, gone, running, as bears run, the two sets of feet, front and back, tracking two separate though parallel courses.

It had been harmless then. They would hear the passing log-train sometimes from the camp; sometimes, because nobody bothered to listen for it or not. They would hear it going in, running light and fast, the light clatter of the trucks, the exhaust of the diminutive locomotive and its shrill peanut-parcher whistle flung for one petty moment and absorbed by the brooding and inattentive wilderness without even an echo. They would hear it going out, loaded, not quite so fast now yet giving its frantic and toylike illusion of crawling speed, not whistling now to conserve steam, flinging its bitten laboring miniature puffing into the immemorial woodsface with frantic and bootless vainglory, empty and noisy and puerile, carrying to no destination or purpose sticks which left nowhere any scar or stump as the child's toy loads and transports and unloads its dead sand and rushes back for more, tireless and unceasing and rapid yet never quite so fast as the Hand which plays with it moves the toy burden back to load the toy again. But it was different now. It was the same train, engine cars and caboose, even the same enginemen brakeman and conductor to whom Boon, drunk then sober then drunk again then fairly sober once more all in the space of fourteen hours, had bragged that day two years ago about what they were going to do to Old Ben tomorrow, running with its same illusion of frantic rapidity between the same twin walls of impenetrable and impervious woods, passing the old landmarks, the old game crossings over which he had trailed bucks wounded and not wounded and more than once seen them, anything but wounded, bot[7] out of the woods and up and across the embankment which bore the rails

7. So in all texts. This could be a misprint for "bolt."

and ties then down and into the woods again as the earthbound supposedly move but crossing as arrows travel, groundless, elongated, three times its actual length and even paler, different in color, as if there were a point between immobility and absolute motion where even mass chemically altered, changing without pain or agony not only in bulk and shape but in color too, approaching the color of wind, yet this time it was as though the train (and not only the train but himself, not only his vision which had seen it and his memory which remembered it but his clothes too, as garments carry back into the clean edgeless blowing of air the lingering effluvium of a sick-room or of death) had brought with it into the doomed wilderness even before the actual axe the shadow and portent of the new mill not even finished yet and the rails and ties which were not even laid; and he knew now what he had known as soon as he saw Hoke's this morning but had not yet thought into words: why Major de Spain had not come back, and that after this time he himself, who had had to see it one time other, would return no more.

Now they were near. He knew it before the engine-driver whistled to warn him. Then he saw Ash and the wagon, the reins without doubt wrapped once more about the brake-lever as within the boy's own memory Major de Spain had been forbidding him for eight years to do, the train slowing, the slackened couplings jolting and clashing again from car to car, the caboose slowing past the wagon as he swung down with his gun, the conductor leaning out above him to signal the engine, the caboose still slowing, creeping, although the engine's exhaust was already slatting in mounting tempo against the unechoing wilderness, the crashing of drawbars once more travelling backward along the train, the caboose picking up speed at last. Then it was gone. It had not been. He could no longer hear it. The wilderness soared, musing, inattentive, myriad, eternal, green; older than any mill-shed, longer than any spurline. "Mr. Boone here yet?" he said.

"He beat me in," Ash said. "Had the wagon loaded and ready for me at Hoke's yistiddy when I got there and setting on the front steps at camp last night when I got in. He already been in the woods since fo daylight this morning. Said he gwine up to the Gum Tree and for you to hunt up that way and meet him." He knew where that was: a single big sweet-gum just outside the woods, in an old clearing; if you crept up to it very quietly this time of year and then ran suddenly into the clearing, sometimes you caught as many as a dozen squirrels in it, trapped, since there was no other tree near they could jump to. So he didn't get into the wagon at all.

"I will," he said.

"I figured you would," Ash said, "I fotch you a box of shells." He passed the shells down and began to unwrap the lines from the brake-pole.

"How many times up to now do you reckon Major has told you not to do that?" the boy said.

"Do which?" Ash said. Then he said: "And tell Boon Hoggan-beck dinner gonter be on the table in a hour and if yawl want any to come on and eat it."

"In an hour?" he said. "It aint nine oclock yet." He drew out his watch and extended it face-toward Ash. "Look." Ash didn't even look at the watch.

"That's town time. You aint in town now. You in the woods."

"Look at the sun then."

"Nemmine the sun too," Ash said. "If you and Boon Hoggan-beck want any dinner, you better come on in and get it when I tole you. I aim to get done in that kitchen because I got my wood to chop. And watch your feet. They're crawling."[8]

"I will," he said.

Then he was in the woods, not alone but solitary; the solitude closed about him, green with summer. They did not change, and, timeless, would not, any more than would the green of summer and the fire and rain of fall and the iron cold and sometimes even snow

the day, the morning when he killed the buck and Sam marked his face with its hot blood, they returned to camp and he remembered old Ash's blinking and disgruntled and even outraged disbelief until at last McCaslin had had to affirm the fact that he had really killed it: and that night Ash sat snarling and unapproachable behind the stove so that Tennie's Jim had to serve the supper and waked them with breakfast already on the table the next morning and it was only half-past one oclock and at last out of Major de Spain's angry cursing and Ash's snarling and sullen rejoinders the fact emerged that Ash not only wanted to go into the woods and shoot a deer also but he intended to and Major de Spain said, 'By God, if we dont let him we will probably have to do the cooking from now on:' and Walter Ewell said, 'Or get up at midnight to eat what Ash cooks:' and since he had already killed his buck for this hunt and was not to shoot again unless they needed meat, he offered his gun to Ash until Major de Spain took command and allotted that gun to Boon for the day and gave Boon's unpredictable pump gun to Ash, with two buckshot shells but Ash said, 'I got shells:' and showed them, four: one buck, one of number three shot for rabbits, two of bird-shot and told one by one their history and their origin and he remembered not Ash's face alone but Major de Spain's and Walter's and General Compson's too, and Ash's voice:

8. The woodsman's cryptic warning against snakes.

'Shoot? In course they'll shoot! Genl Cawmpson guv me this un'—
the buckshot—'right outen the same gun he kilt that big buck with
eight years ago. And this un'—it was the rabbit shell: triumphantly
—'is oldern thisyer boy!' And that morning he loaded the gun himself, reversing the order: the bird-shot, the rabbit, then the buck
so that the buckshot would feed first into the chamber, and himself
without a gun, he and Ash walked beside Major de Spain's and
Tennie's Jim's horses and the dogs (that was the snow) until they
cast and struck, the sweet strong cries ringing away into the muffled
falling air and gone almost immediately, as if the constant and un-
murmuring flakes had already buried even the unformed echoes beneath their myriad and weightless falling, Major de Spain and
Tennie's Jim gone too, whooping on into the woods; and then it was
all right, he knew as plainly as if Ash had told him that Ash had now
hunted his deer and that even his tender years had been forgiven for
having killed one, and they turned back toward home through the
falling snow—that is, Ash said, 'Now whut?' and he said, 'This
way'—himself in front because, although they were less than a mile
from camp, he knew that Ash, who had spent two weeks of his life
in the camp each year for the last twenty, had no idea whatever
where they were, until quite soon the manner in which Ash carried
Boon's gun was making him a good deal more than just nervous and
he made Ash walk in front, striding on, talking now, an old man's
garrulous monologue beginning with where he was at the moment
then of the woods and of camping in the woods and of eating in
camps then of eating then of cooking it and of his wife's cooking
then briefly of his old wife and almost at once and at length of a
new light-colored woman who nursed next door to Major de Spain's
and if she didn't watch out who she was switching her tail at he
would show her how old was an old man or not if his wife just
didn't watch him all the time, the two of them in a game trail
through a dense brake of cane and brier which would bring them
out within a quarter-mile of camp, approaching a big fallen tree-
trunk lying athwart the path and just as Ash, still talking, was about
to step over it the bear, the yearling, rose suddenly beyond the log,
sitting up, its forearms against its chest and its wrists limply arrested
as if it had been surprised in the act of covering its face to pray: and
after a certain time Ash's gun yawed jerkily up and he said, 'You
haven't got a shell in the barrel yet. Pump it:' but the gun already
snicked and he said, 'Pump it. You haven't got a shell in the barrel
yet:' and Ash pumped the action and in a certain time the gun
steadied again and snicked and he said, 'Pump it:' and watched
the buckshot shell jerk, spinning heavily, into the cane. This is the
rabbit shot: he thought and the gun snicked and he thought: The
next is bird-shot: and he didn't have to say Pump it; he cried,

'*Dont shoot! Dont shoot!*' *but that was already too late too, the light dry vicious snick! before he could speak and the bear turned and dropped to all-fours and then was gone and there was only the log, the cane, the velvet and constant snow and Ash said, '*Now whut?*' and he said, '*This way. Come on:*' and began to back away down the path and Ash said, '*I got to find my shells:*' and he said, '*Goddamn it, goddamn it, come on:*' but Ash leaned the gun against the log and returned and stooped and fumbled among the cane roots until he came back and stooped and found the shells and they rose and at that moment the gun, untouched, leaning against the log six feet away and for that while even forgotten by both of them, roared, bellowed and flamed, and ceased: and he carried it now, pumped out the last mummified shell and gave that one also to Ash and, the action*[9]* still open, himself carried the gun until he stood it in the corner behind Boon's bed at the camp*

—; summer, and fall, and snow, and wet and sap rife spring in their ordered immortal sequence, the deathless and immemorial phases of the mother who had shaped him if any had toward the man he almost was, mother and father both to the old man born of a Negro slave and a Chickasaw chief who had been his spirit's father if any had, whom he had revered and harkened to and loved and lost and grieved: and he would marry someday and they too would own for their brief while that brief unsubstanced glory which inherently of itself cannot last and hence why glory: and they would, might, carry even the remembrance of it into the time when flesh no longer talks to flesh because memory at least does last: but still the woods would be his mistress and his wife.

He was not going toward the Gum Tree. Actually he was getting farther from it. Time was and not so long ago either when he would not have been allowed here without someone with him, and a little later, when he had begun to learn how much he did not know, he would not have dared be here without someone with him, and later still, beginning to ascertain, even if only dimly, the limits of what he did not know, he could have attempted and carried it through with a compass, not because of any increased belief in himself but because McCaslin and Major de Spain and Walter and General Compson too had taught him at last to believe the compass regardless of what it seemed to state. Now he did not even use the compass but merely the sun and that only subconsciously, yet he could have taken a scaled map and plotted at any time to within a hundred feet of where he actually was; and sure enough, at almost the exact moment when he expected it, the earth began to rise faintly, he passed one of the four concrete markers set down by the lumber company's surveyor to establish the four corners of the plot which

9. The breech mechanism.

Major de Spain had reserved out of the sale, then he stood on the crest of the knoll itself, the four corner-markers all visible now, blanched still even beneath the winter's weathering, lifeless and shockingly alien in that place where dissolution itself was a seething turmoil of ejaculation, tumescence conception and birth, and death did not even exist. After two winters' blanketings of leaves and the floodwaters of two springs, there was no trace of the two graves any more at all. But those who would have come this far to find them would not need headstones but would have found them as Sam Fathers himself had taught him to find such: by bearings on trees: and did, almost the first thrust of the hunting knife finding (but only to see if it was still there) the round tin box manufactured for axel-grease and containing now Old Ben's dried mutilated paw, resting above Lion's bones.

He didn't disturb it. He didn't even look for the other grave where he and McCaslin and Major de Spain and Boon had laid Sam's body, along with his hunting horn and his knife and his tobacco-pipe, that Sunday morning two years ago; he didn't have to. He had stepped over it, perhaps on it. But that was all right. *He probably knew I was in the woods this morning long before I got here*, he thought, going on to the tree which had supported one end of the platform where Sam lay when McCaslin and Major de Spain found them—the tree, the other axel-grease tin nailed to the trunk, but weathered, rusted, alien too yet healed already into the wilderness' concordant generality, raising no tuneless note, and empty, long since empty of the food and tobacco he had put into it that day, as empty of that as it would presently be of this which he drew from his pocket—the twist of tobacco, the new bandanna handkerchief, the small paper sack of the peppermint candy which Sam had used to love; that gone too, almost before he had turned his back, not vanished but merely translated into the myriad life which printed the dark mold of these secret and sunless places with delicate fairy tracks, which, breathing and biding and immobile, watched him from beyond every twig and leaf until he moved, moving again, walking on; he had not stopped, he had only paused, quitting the knoll which was no abode of the dead because there was no death, not Lion and not Sam: not held fast in earth but free in earth and not in earth but of earth, myriad yet undiffused of every myriad part, leaf and twig and particle, air and sun and rain and dew and night, acorn oak and leaf and acorn again, dark and dawn and dark and dawn again in their immutable progression and, being myriad, one: and Old Ben too, Old Ben too; they would give him his paw back even, certainly they would give him his paw back: then the long challenge and the long chase, no heart to be driven and outraged, no flesh to be mauled and bled— Even as he froze himself, he

seemed to hear Ash's parting admonition. He could even hear the
voice as he froze, immobile, one foot just taking his weight, the toe
of the other just lifted behind him, not breathing, feeling again and
as always the sharp shocking inrush from when Isaac McCaslin long
yet was not, and so it was fear all right but not fright as he looked
down at it. It had not coiled yet and the buzzer had not sounded
either, only one thick rapid contraction, one loop cast sideways as
though merely for purchase from which the raised head might start
slightly backward, not in fright either, not in threat quite yet, more
than six feet of it, the head raised higher than his knee and less
than his knee's length away, and old, the once-bright markings of
its youth dulled now to a monotone concordant too with the wilderness it crawled and lurked: the old one, the ancient and accursed
about the earth, fatal and solitary and he could smell it now: the
thin sick smell of rotting cucumbers and something else which had
no name, evocative of all knowledge and an old weariness and of
pariah-hood and of death. At last it moved. Not the head. The elevation of the head did not change as it began to glide away from
him, moving erect yet off the perpendicular as if the head and that
elevated third were complete and all: an entity walking on two feet
and free of all laws of mass and balance and should have been because even now he could not quite believe that all that shift and
flow of shadow behind that walking head could have been one
snake: going and then gone; he put the other foot down at last and
didn't know it, standing with one hand raised as Sam had stood
that afternoon six years ago when Sam led him into the wilderness
and showed him and he ceased to be a child, speaking the old tongue
which Sam had spoken that day without premeditation either:
"Chief," he said: "Grandfather."

He couldn't tell when he first began to hear the sound, because
when he became aware of it, it seemed to him that he had been
already hearing it for several seconds—a sound as though someone
were hammering a gun-barrel against a piece of railroad iron, a
sound loud and heavy and not rapid yet with something frenzied
about it, as the hammerer were not only a strong man and an earnest
one but a little hysterical too. Yet it couldn't be on the log-line
because, although the track lay in that direction, it was at least two
miles from him and this sound was not three hundred yards away.
But even as he thought that, he realised where the sound must be
coming from: whoever the man was and whatever he was doing, he
was somewhere near the edge of the clearing where the Gum Tree
was and where he was to meet Boon. So far, he had been hunting
as he advanced, moving slowly and quietly and watching the ground
and the trees both. Now he went on, his gun unloaded and the barrel slanted up and back to facilitate its passage through brier and

undergrowth, approaching as it grew louder and louder that steady savage somehow queerly hysterical beating of metal on metal, emerging from the woods, into the old clearing, with the solitary gum tree directly before him. At first glance the tree seemed to be alive with frantic squirrels. There appeared to be forty or fifty of them leaping and darting from branch to branch until the whole tree had become one green maelstrom of mad leaves, while from time to time, singly or in twos and threes, squirrels would dart down the trunk then whirl without stopping and rush back up again as though sucked violently back by the vacuum of their fellows' frenzied vortex. Then he saw Boon, sitting, his back against the trunk, his head bent, hammering furiously at something on his lap. What he hammered with was the barrel of his dismembered gun, what he hammered at was the breech of it. The rest of the gun lay scattered about him in a half-dozen pieces while he bent over the piece on his lap his scarlet and streaming walnut face, hammering the disjointed barrel against the gun-breech with the frantic abandon of a madman. He didn't even look up to see who it was. Still hammering, he merely shouted back at the boy in a hoarse strangled voice:

"Get out of here! Dont touch them! Dont touch a one of them! They're mine!"

1935–1941   1935, 1942

[handwritten: Sensuous scenes
Spector of death: major character in all his books =
a kind of actor in the drama ... nature moved to
a certain kind of courage ... sought its symbol
symbol of virility (begetting life) opposite symbol of death.]

ERNEST HEMINGWAY
(1898–1961)

Hemingway's compelling inspiration was war, both as a personal and symbolic experience and as a continuing condition of mankind. New readers of the Second World War and beyond still found inspiration in his symbolic ritualism dedicated to the survival of selfhood in the midst of chaos. Hemingway also created a revolution in language which influenced the narrative and dialogue of two generations of novelists. During the last twenty years of his life he published little; as adventurer, hunter, and journalist he sometimes seemed to resemble one of his own created characters. When in 1952 he got it again

"the way it was" in *The Old Man and the Sea*, a nearly flawless short novel, he was awarded the Pulitzer Prize (1953) and the Nobel Prize (1954) with a promptness that suggested an overdue recognition.

Born in Oak Park, near Chicago, on July 21, 1898, Ernest Miller Hemingway was the son of a physician who initiated him into the rituals of hunting and fishing in the Michigan north woods; he also gained an early proficiency in football and boxing. Graduated from high school he became a reporter for the Kansas City *Star* in 1917. Within the year he was in volunteer war service with an Amer-

[handwritten: Writes about alone & begetting of life — infusion into all acts of life of love — rather than death.]

1352 · Ernest Hemingway

ican ambulance unit in France, gained transfer to combat duty in the Italian Arditi (volunteer infantry) on the Italian front, and was seriously wounded. After the Armistice, with Italian decorations for valor, he returned to newspaper work. In 1920 he covered the Graeco-Turkish war and was appointed a Paris correspondent.

Post-war Paris was thronged with young artists. Intellectual ferment and artistic accomplishment expressed the same spiritual defeat that other expatriate intellectuals sought in escape. In his first novel, *The Sun Also Rises* (1926), with Gertrude Stein's remark, "You are all a lost generation," as epigraph, such characters as Lady Brett and Jake Barnes, the journalist unmanned by war wounds, expressed in another form the sterile wasteland of Eliot's poem of 1922. His first book, *In Our Time* (1924), was a collection of stories in which Nick Adams is a sort of *alter ego* for the young Hemingway. Hemingway's psychological penetration and originality in plot and dialogue reawakened interest in the short story; his early debt to Sherwood Anderson he acknowledged in a good-natured parody called *Torrents of Spring* (1926).

Two war novels and two uniquely interesting topical books brought Hemingway to the end of his major accomplishment in 1940. *A Farewell to Arms* (1929), based on his Italian service, is a distinguished war novel, although lingering sentiment breaks through the taut economy of the stylized

language. Here he rejected the classic tragic unity in the catastrophic defeat of the lovers, who have hazardously escaped to safe harbor, only to face the cruel futility of Catherine's fatal accident in childbirth. Dying, she murmurs to Frederick, "I'm not a bit afraid. It's just a dirty trick." The author's naturalistic reinterpretation of fate was consistent. Robert Jordan, in *For Whom the Bell Tolls* (1940), loses his life for a cause already lost, and in fact not even a genuine cause. All causes in Hemingway's tragic vision are already lost, because that is nature and the way things are; but the losers need not be lost. What' distinguished man and gave him salvation was his faithfulness in the ordeal which all are called upon to face—as Macomber must meet the buffalo, and if by some dirty trick he dies anyway, "we owe God a death"; but we can keep the rendezvous like men. Lady Brett knew the code: "It's sort of what we have *instead* of God."

In *For Whom the Bell Tolls*, his best novel, again love is found, and lost, as it seems, by the callous futility of nature. This episode of the Spanish Revolution is also an unforgettable revelation of the Spanish earth and its people. Spain and the bullfight had appeared in his first novel; later, in *Death in the Afternoon* (1932), he gave an interpretation of the bullfight as ordeal and ritual, "very moral to me because I feel very fine while it is going on and have a feeling of life and death and mortality." The hunt is a comparable ordeal and ritual in *The Green Hills of Africa* (1935).

Like Stephen Crane, whom he admired as the pioneer of the naturalistic war novel, Hemingway embraced the cult of experience. Note his journalistic engagements on behalf of the Spanish loyalists between 1936 and 1940; or again on behalf of liberal causes in the war-torn 40's, as correspondent in China, and in the air over France, and on the Normandy beach. Crane's thirst for life was fatal and Hemingway's nearly as compelling. In *The Green Hills* he asserted his creed "to write as well as I can and learn as I go along. At the same time I have my life * * * which is a damned good life." You could only write "what you truly felt" and never "when there is no water in the well." Of the bullfight he remarked, "I was trying to learn to write, commencing with the simplest things, and one of the simplest things and the most fundamental is violent death." <u>Death became, in his fiction, the extreme limit of experience and the final test of the genuine ordeal. Death appears in his writing in violent forms, or understated as "bad luck," or symbolically projected as muti-</u>lation or sterility in Jake Barnes, <u>Nick Adams</u>, and the protagonists of *To Have and Have Not* (1937) and *Across the River and Into the Trees* (1950) his two so-called "failures."

Hemingway left his Cuban estate in November, 1960, for a new "last home" in a remote spot near Ketchum, Idaho. During the next eight months he suffered two long illnesses requiring hospitalization. In the early morning of July 2, 1961, standing beside his beloved gunrack in his home, he died of head wounds resulting from the discharge of his favorite shotgun, in his own hands.

All of Hemingway's novels and topical volumes are mentioned above. *The Fifth Column and the First Forty-nine Stories*, 1938, contains all the stories of *In Our Time*, Paris, 1924, New York, 1925, *Men Without Women*, 1927, and *Winner Take Nothing*, 1933, together with several previously uncollected stories and a play, *The Fifth Column*.

Critical and biographical studies of definitive seriousness are Carlos Baker, *Hemingway: The Writer As Artist*, 1952, revised 1956; Philip Young, *Ernest Hemingway*, 1952; and Charles A. Fenton, *The Apprenticeship of Ernest Hemingway: The Early Years*, 1954. See also Leicester Hemingway, *My Brother Ernest Hemingway*, 1962, and Lillian Ross, *Portrait of Hemingway*, 1962.

contrasted c. Wilson

The Short Happy Life of Francis Macomber[1]

It was now lunch time and they were all sitting under the double green fly of the dining tent pretending that nothing had happened.

"Will you have lime juice or lemon squash?" Macomber asked.

"I'll have a gimlet,"[2] Robert Wilson told him.

"I'll have a gimlet too. I need something," Macomber's wife said.

"I suppose it's the thing to do," Macomber agreed. "Tell him to make three gimlets."

The mess boy had started them already, lifting the bottles out of the canvas cooling bags that sweated wet in the wind that blew

1. *Cosmopolitan*, September, 1936; *The Fifth Column and the First Forty-nine* Stories (1938).
2. A drink (gin and lime juice).

through the trees that shaded the tents.

"What had I ought to give them?" Macomber asked.

"A quid[3] would be plenty," Wilson told him. "You don't want to spoil them."

"Will the headman distribute it?"

"Absolutely."

Francis Macomber had, half an hour before, been carried to his tent from the edge of the camp in triumph on the arms and shoulders of the cook, the personal boys, the skinner and the porters. The gun-bearers had taken no part in the demonstration. When the native boys put him down at the door of his tent, he had shaken all their hands, received their congratulations, and then gone into the tent and sat on the bed until his wife came in. She did not speak to him when she came in and he left the tent at once to wash his face and hands in the portable wash basin outside and go over to the dining tent to sit in a comfortable canvas chair in the breeze and the shade.

"You've got your lion," Robert Wilson said to him, "and a damned fine one too."

Mrs. Macomber looked at Wilson quickly. She was an extremely handsome and well-kept woman of the beauty and social position which had, five years before, commanded five thousand dollars as the price of endorsing, with photographs, a beauty product which she had never used. She had been married to Francis Macomber for eleven years.

"He is a good lion, isn't he?" Macomber said. His wife looked at him now. She looked at both these men as though she had never seen them before.

One, Wilson, the white hunter, she knew she had never truly seen before. He was about middle height with sandy hair, a stubby mustache, a very red face and extremely cold blue eyes with faint white wrinkles at the corners that grooved merrily when he smiled. He smiled at her now and she looked away from his face at the way his shoulders sloped in the loose tunic he wore with the four big cartridges held in loops where the left breast pocket should have been, at his big brown hands, his old slacks, his very dirty boots and back to his red face again. She noticed where the baked red of his face stopped in a white line that marked the circle left by his Stetson hat that hung now from one of the pegs of the tent pole.

"Well, here's to the lion," Robert Wilson said. He smiled at her again and, not smiling, she looked curiously at her husband.

Francis Macomber was very tall, very well built if you did not mind that length of bone, dark, his hair cropped like an oarsman,

3. British slang for one pound in currency.

rather thin-lipped, and was considered handsome. He was dressed in the same sort of safari clothes that Wilson wore except that his were new, he was thirty-five years old, kept himself very fit, was good at court games, had a number of big-game fishing records, and had just shown himself, very publicly, to be a coward.

"Here's to the lion," he said. "I can't ever thank you for what you did."

Margaret, his wife, looked away from him and back to Wilson.

"Let's not talk about the lion," she said.

Wilson looked over at her without smiling and now she smiled at him.

"It's been a very strange day," she said. "Hadn't you ought to put your hat on even under the canvas at noon? You told me that, you know."

"Might put it on," said Wilson.

"You know you have a very red face, Mr. Wilson," she told him and smiled again.

"Drink," said Wilson.

"I don't think so," she said. "Francis drinks a great deal, but his face is never red."

"It's red today," Macomber tried a joke.

"No," said Margaret. "It's mine that's red today. But Mr. Wilson's is always red."

"Must be racial," said Wilson. "I say, you wouldn't like to drop my beauty as a topic, would you?"

"I've just started on it."

"Let's chuck it," said Wilson.

"Conversation is going to be so difficult," Margaret said.

"Don't be silly, Margot," her husband said.

"No difficulty," Wilson said. "Got a damn fine lion."

Margot looked at them both and they both saw that she was going to cry. Wilson had seen it coming for a long time and he dreaded it. Macomber was past dreading it.

"I wish it hadn't happened. Oh, I wish it hadn't happened," she said and started for her tent. She made no noise of crying but they could see that her shoulders were shaking under the rose-colored, sun-proofed shirt she wore.

"Women upset," said Wilson to the tall man. "Amounts to nothing. Strain on the nerves and one thing'n another."

"No," said Macomber. "I suppose that I rate that for the rest of my life now."

"Nonsense. Let's have a spot of the giant killer," said Wilson. "Forget the whole thing. Nothing to it anyway."

"We might try," said Macomber. "I won't forget what you did for me though."

"Nothing," said Wilson. "All nonsense."

So they sat there in the shade where the camp was pitched under some wide-topped acacia trees with a boulder-strewn cliff behind them, and a stretch of grass that ran to the bank of a boulder-filled stream in front with forest beyond it, and drank their just-cool lime drinks and avoided one another's eyes while the boys set the table for lunch. Wilson could tell that the boys all knew about it now and when he saw Macomber's personal boy looking curiously at his master while he was putting dishes on the table he snapped at him in Swahili. The boy turned away with his face blank.

"What were you telling him?" Macomber asked.

"Nothing. Told him to look alive or I'd see he got about fifteen of the best."

"What's that? Lashes?"

"It's quite illegal," Wilson said. "You're supposed to fine them."

"Do you still have them whipped?"

"Oh, yes. They could raise a row if they chose to complain. But they don't. They prefer it to the fines."

"How strange!" said Macomber.

"Not strange, really," Wilson said. "Which would you rather do? Take a good birching or lose your pay?"

Then he felt embarrassed at asking it and before Macomber could answer he went on, "We all take a beating every day, you know, one way or another."

This was no better. "Good God," he thought. "I am a diplomat, aren't I?"

"Yes, we take a beating," said Macomber, still not looking at him. "I'm awfully sorry about that lion business. It doesn't have to go any further, does it? I mean no one will hear about it, will they?"

"You mean will I tell it at the Mathaiga Club?" Wilson looked at him now coldly. He had not expected this. So he's a bloody four-letter man as well as a bloody coward, he thought. I rather liked him too until today. But how is one to know about an American?

"No," said Wilson. "I'm a professional hunter. We never talk about our clients. You can be quite easy on that. It's supposed to be bad form to ask us not to talk though."

He had decided now that to break would be much easier. He would eat, then, by himself and could read a book with his meals. They would eat by themselves. He would see them through the safari[4] on a very formal basis—what was it the French called it? Distinguished consideration—and it would be a damn sight easier than having to go through this emotional trash. He'd insult him and make a good clean break. Then he could read a book with his

---

4. From the Arabic, originally meaning "journey," but now usually designating a hunting expedition.

meals and he'd still be drinking their whisky. That was the phrase for it when a safari went bad. You ran into another white hunter and you asked, "How is everything going?" and he answered, "Oh, I'm still drinking their whisky," and you knew everything had gone to pot.

"I'm sorry," Macomber said and looked at him with his American face that would stay adolescent until it became middle-aged, and Wilson noted his crew-cropped hair, fine eyes only faintly shifty, good nose, thin lips and handsome jaw. "I'm sorry I didn't realize that. There are lots of things I don't know."

So what could he do, Wilson thought. He was all ready to break it off quickly and neatly and here the beggar was apologizing after he had just insulted him. He made one more attempt. "Don't worry about me talking," he said. "I have a living to make. You know in Africa no woman ever misses her lion and no white man ever bolts."

"I bolted like a rabbit," Macomber said.

Now what in hell were you going to do about a man who talked like that, Wilson wondered.

Wilson looked at Macomber with his flat, blue, machine-gunner's eyes and the other smiled back at him. He had a pleasant smile if you did not notice how his eyes showed when he was hurt.

"Maybe I can fix it up on buffalo," he said. "We're after them next, aren't we?"

"In the morning if you like," Wilson told him. Perhaps he had been wrong. This was certainly the way to take it. You most certainly could not tell a damned thing about an American. He was all for Macomber again. If you could forget the morning. But, of course, you couldn't. The morning had been about as bad as they come.

"Here comes the Memsahib,"[5] he said. She was walking over from her tent looking refreshed and cheerful and quite lovely. She had a very perfect oval face, so perfect that you expected her to be stupid. But she wasn't stupid, Wilson thought, no, not stupid.

"How is the beautiful red-faced Mr. Wilson? Are you feeling better, Francis, my pearl?"

"Oh, much," said Macomber.

"I've dropped the whole thing," she said, sitting down at the table. "What importance is there to whether Francis is any good at killing lions? That's not his trade. That's Mr. Wilson's trade. Mr. Wilson is really very impressive killing anything. You do kill anything, don't you?"

"Oh, anything," said Wilson. "Simply anything." They are, he thought, the hardest in the world; the hardest, the cruelest, the

5. The native term of respect in India for addressing a European woman. British colonials carried it to Africa.

most predatory and the most attractive and their men have softened
or gone to pieces nervously as they have hardened. Or is it that they
pick men they can handle? They can't know that much at the age
they marry, he thought. He was grateful that he had gone through
his education on American women before now because this was a
very attractive one.

"We're going after buff[6] in the morning," he told her.

"I'm coming," she said.

"No, you're not."

"Oh, yes, I am. Mayn't I, Francis?"

"Why not stay in camp?"

"Not for anything," she said. "I wouldn't miss something like
today for anything."

When she left, Wilson was thinking, when she went off to cry,
she seemed a hell of a fine woman. She seemed to understand, to
realize, to be hurt for him and for herself and to know how things
really stood. She is away for twenty minutes and now she is back,
simply enamelled in that American female cruelty. They are the
damnedest women. Really the damnedest.

"We'll put on another show for you tomorrow," Francis Macomber said.

"You're not coming," Wilson said.

"You're very mistaken," she told him. "And I want *so* to see you
perform again. You were lovely this morning. That is if blowing
things' heads off is lovely."

"Here's the lunch," said Wilson. "You're very merry, aren't you?"

"Why not? I didn't come out here to be dull."

"Well, it hasn't been dull," Wilson said. He could see the
boulders in the river and the high bank beyond with the trees and
he remembered the morning.

"Oh, no," she said. "It's been charming. And tomorrow. You
don't know how I look forward to tomorrow."

"That's eland he's offering you," Wilson said.

"They're the big cowy things that jump like hares, aren't they?"

"I suppose that describes them," Wilson said.

"It's very good meat," Macomber said.

"Did you shoot it, Francis?" she asked.

"Yes."

"They're not dangerous, are they?"

"Only if they fall on you," Wilson told her.

"I'm so glad."

"Why not let up on the bitchery just a little, Margot," Macomber
said, cutting the eland steak and putting some mashed potato,
gravy and carrot on the down-turned fork that tined through the

6. Buffalo.

piece of meat.

"I suppose I could," she said, "since you put it so prettily."

"Tonight we'll have champagne for the lion," Wilson said. "It's a bit too hot at noon."

"Oh, the lion," Margot said. "I'd forgotten the lion!"

So, Robert Wilson thought to himself, she *is* giving him a ride, isn't she? Or do you suppose that's her idea of putting up a good show? How should a woman act when she discovers her husband is a bloody coward? She's damn cruel but they're all cruel. They govern, of course, and to govern one has to be cruel sometimes. Still, I've seen enough of their damn terrorism.

"Have some more eland," he said to her politely.

That afternoon, late, Wilson and Macomber went out in the motor car with the native driver and the two gun-bearers. Mrs. Macomber stayed in the camp. It was too hot to go out, she said, and she was going with them in the early morning. As they drove off Wilson saw her standing under the big tree, looking pretty rather than beautiful in her faintly rosy khaki, her dark hair drawn back off her forehead and gathered in a knot low on her neck, her face as fresh, he thought, as though she were in England. She waved to them as the car went off through the swale of high grass and curved around through the trees into the small hills of orchard bush.

In the orchard bush they found a herd of impala, and leaving the car they stalked one old ram with long, wide-spread horns and Macomber killed it with a very creditable shot that knocked the buck down at a good two hundred yards and sent the herd off bounding wildly and leaping over one another's backs in long, leg-drawn-up leaps as unbelievable and as floating as those one makes sometimes in dreams.

"That was a good shot," Wilson said. "They're a small target."

"Is it a worth-while head?" Macomber asked.

"It's excellent," Wilson told him. "You shoot like that and you'll have no trouble."

"Do you think we'll find buffalo tomorrow?"

"There's a good chance of it. They feed out early in the morning and with luck we may catch them in the open."

"I'd like to clear away that lion business," Macomber said. "It's not very pleasant to have your wife see you do something like that."

I should think it would be even more unpleasant to do it, Wilson thought, wife or no wife, or to talk about it having done it. But he said, "I wouldn't think about that any more. Any one could be upset by his first lion. That's all over."

But that night after dinner and a whisky and soda by the fire before going to bed, as Francis Macomber lay on his cot with the mosquito bar over him and listened to the night noises it was not all over. It was neither all over nor was it beginning. It was there exactly as it happened with some parts of it indelibly emphasized and he was miserably ashamed at it. But more than shame he felt cold, hollow fear in him. The fear was still there like a cold slimy hollow in all the emptiness where once his confidence had been and it made him feel sick. It was still there with him now.

It had started the night before when he had wakened and heard the lion roaring somewhere up along the river. It was a deep sound and at the end there were sort of coughing grunts that made him seem just outside the tent, and when Francis Macomber woke in the night to hear it he was afraid. He could hear his wife breathing quietly, asleep. There was no one to tell he was afraid, nor to be afraid with him, and, lying alone, he did not know the Somali[7] proverb that says a brave man is always frightened three times by a lion; when he first sees his track, when he first hears him roar and when he first confronts him. Then while they were eating breakfast by lantern light out in the dining tent, before the sun was up, the lion roared again and Francis thought he was just at the edge of camp.

"Sounds like an old-timer," Robert Wilson said, looking up from his kippers and coffee. "Listen to him cough."

"Is he very close?"

"A mile or so up the stream."

"Will we see him?"

"We'll have a look."

"Does his roaring carry that far? It sounds as though he were right in camp."

"Carries a hell of a long way," said Robert Wilson. "It's strange the way it carries. Hope he's a shootable cat. The boys said there was a very big one about here."

"If I get a shot, where should I hit him," Macomber asked, "to stop him?"

"In the shoulders," Wilson said. "In the neck if you can make it. Shoot for bone. Break him down."

"I hope I can place it properly," Macomber said.

"You shoot very well," Wilson told him. "Take your time. Make sure of him. The first one in is the one that counts."

"What range will it be?"

"Can't tell. Lion has something to say about that. Don't shoot unless it's close enough so you can make sure."

"At under a hundred yards?" Macomber asked.

Wilson looked at him quickly.

"Hundred's about right. Might have to take him a bit under. Shouldn't chance a shot at much over that. A hundred's a decent

7. Of Somaliland, the eastern extremity of Africa, south of the Gulf of Aden.

range. You can hit him wherever you want at that. Here comes the Memsahib."

"Good morning," she said. "Are we going after that lion?"

"As soon as you deal with your breakfast," Wilson said. "How are you feeling?"

"Marvellous," she said. "I'm very excited."

"I'll just go and see that everything is ready," Wilson went off. As he left the lion roared again.

"Noisy beggar," Wilson said. "We'll put a stop to that."

"What's the matter, Francis?" his wife asked him.

"Nothing," Macomber said.

"Yes, there is," she said. "What are you upset about?"

"Nothing," he said.

"Tell me," she looked at him. "Don't you feel well?"

"It's that damned roaring," he said. "It's been going on all night, you know."

"Why didn't you wake me," she said. "I'd love to have heard it."

"I've got to kill the damned thing," Macomber said, miserably.

"Well, that's what you're out here for, isn't it?"

"Yes. But I'm nervous. Hearing the thing roar gets on my nerves."

"Well then, as Wilson said, kill him and stop his roaring."

"Yes, darling," said Francis Macomber. "It sounds easy, doesn't it?"

"You're not afraid, are you?"

"Of course not. But I'm nervous from hearing him roar all night."

"You'll kill him marvellously," she said. "I know you will. I'm awfully anxious to see it."

"Finish your breakfast and we'll be starting."

"It's not light yet," she said. "This is a ridiculous hour."

Just then the lion roared in a deep-chested moaning, suddenly guttural, ascending vibration that seemed to shake the air and ended in a sigh and a heavy, deep-chested grunt.

"He sounds almost here," Macomber's wife said.

"My God," said Macomber. "I hate that damned noise."

"It's very impressive."

"Impressive. It's frightful."

Robert Wilson came up then carrying his short, ugly, shockingly big-bored .505 Gibbs and grinning.

"Come on," he said. "Your gun-bearer has your Springfield and the big gun. Everything's in the car. Have you solids?"[8]

"Yes."

"I'm ready," Mrs. Macomber said.

"Must make him stop that racket," Wilson said. "You get in front. The Memsahib can sit back here with me."

8. Solid, jacketed bullets.

They climbed into the motor car and, in the gray first daylight, moved off up the river through the trees. Macomber opened the breech of his rifle and saw he had metal-cased bullets, shut the bolt and put the rifle on safety. He saw his hand was trembling. He felt in his pocket for more cartridges and moved his fingers over the cartridges in the loops of his tunic front. He turned back to where Wilson sat in the rear seat of the doorless, box-bodied motor car beside his wife, them both grinning with excitement, and Wilson leaned forward and whispered,

"See the birds dropping. Means the old boy has left his kill."

On the far bank of the stream Macomber could see, above the trees, vultures circling and plummeting down.

"Chances are he'll come to drink along here," Wilson whispered. "Before he goes to lay up. Keep an eye out."

They were driving slowly along the high bank of the stream which here cut deeply to its boulder-filled bed, and they wound in and out through big trees as they drove. Macomber was watching the opposite bank when he felt Wilson take hold of his arm. The car stopped.

"There he is," he heard the whisper. "Ahead and to the right. Get out and take him. He's a marvellous lion."

Macomber saw the lion now. He was standing almost broadside, his great head up and turned toward them. The early morning breeze that blew toward them was just stirring his dark mane, and the lion looked huge, silhouetted on the rise of bank in the gray morning light, his shoulders heavy, his barrel of a body bulking smoothly.

"How far is he?" asked Macomber, raising his rifle.

"About seventy-five. Get out and take him."

"Why not shoot from where I am?"

"You don't shoot them from cars," he heard Wilson saying in his ear. "Get out. He's not going to stay there all day."

Macomber stepped out of the curved opening at the side of the front seat, onto the step and down onto the ground. The lion still stood looking majestically and coolly toward this object that his eyes only showed in silhouette, bulking like some super-rhino. There was no man smell carried toward him and he watched the object, moving his great head a little from side to side. Then watching the object, not afraid, but hesitating before going down the bank to drink with such a thing opposite him, he saw a man figure detach itself from it and he turned his heavy head and swung away toward the cover of the trees as he heard a cracking crash and felt the slam of a .30–06 220-grain solid bullet that bit his flank and ripped in sudden hot scalding nausea through his stomach. He trotted, heavy, big-footed, swinging wounded full-bellied, through the trees toward the tall grass and cover, and the crash came again to go past him ripping the air apart. Then it crashed again and he felt the blow as it hit his lower ribs and ripped on through, blood sudden hot and frothy in his mouth, and he galloped toward the high grass where he could crouch and not be seen and make them bring the crashing thing close enough so he could make a rush and get the man that held it.

Macomber had not thought how the lion felt as he got out of the car. He only knew his hands were shaking and as he walked away from the car it was almost impossible for him to make his legs move. They were stiff in the thighs, but he could feel the muscles fluttering. He raised the rifle, sighted on the junction of the lion's head and shoulders and pulled the trigger. Nothing happened though he pulled until he thought his finger would break. Then he knew he had the safety on and as he lowered the rifle to move the safety over he moved another frozen pace forward, and the lion seeing his silhouette now clear of the silhouette of the car, turned and started off at a trot, and, as Macomber fired, he heard a whunk that meant that the bullet was home; but the lion kept on going. Macomber shot again and every one saw the bullet throw a spout of dirt beyond the trotting lion. He shot again, remembering to lower his aim, and they all heard the bullet hit, and the lion went into a gallop and was in the tall grass before he had the bolt pushed forward.

Macomber stood there feeling sick at his stomach, his hands that held the Springfield still cocked, shaking, and his wife and Robert Wilson were standing by him. Beside him too were the two gun-bearers chattering in Wakamba.[9]

"I hit him," Macomber said. "I hit him twice."

"You gut-shot him and you hit him somewhere forward," Wilson said without enthusiasm. The gun-bearers looked very grave. They were silent now.

"You may have killed him," Wilson went on. "We'll have to wait a while before we go in to find out."

"What do you mean?"

"Let him get sick before we follow him up."

"Oh," said Macomber.

"He's a hell of a fine lion," Wilson said cheerfully. "He's gotten into a bad place though."

"Why is it bad?"

"Can't see him until you're on him."

"Oh," said Macomber.

"Come on," said Wilson. "The Memsahib can stay here in the

---

9. The dialect of their tribe. In other incidents, the Swahili dialect is men-tioned, that being generally understood by all tribesmen and most whites.

car. We'll go to have a look at the blood spoor."[1]

"Stay here, Margot," Macomber said to his wife. His mouth was very dry and it was hard for him to talk.

"Why?" she asked.

"Wilson says to."

"We're going to have a look," Wilson said. "You stay here. You can see even better from here."

"All right."

Wilson spoke in Swahili to the driver. He nodded and said, "Yes, Bwana."[2]

Then they went down the steep bank and across the stream, climbing over and around the boulders and up the other bank, pulling up by some projecting roots, and along it until they found where the lion had been trotting when Macomber first shot. There was dark blood on the short grass that the gun-bearers pointed out with grass stems, and that ran away behind the river bank trees.

"What do we do?" asked Macomber.

"Not much choice," said Wilson. "We can't bring the car over. Bank's too steep. We'll let him stiffen up a bit and then you and I'll go in and have a look for him."

"Can't we set the grass on fire?" Macomber asked.

"Too green."

"Can't we send beaters?"

Wilson looked at him appraisingly. "Of course we can," he said. "But it's just a touch murderous. You see we know the lion's wounded. You can drive an unwounded lion—he'll move on ahead of a noise—but a wounded lion's going to charge. You can't see him until you're right on him. He'll make himself perfectly flat in cover you wouldn't think would hide a hare. You can't very well send boys in there to that sort of a show. Somebody bound to get mauled."

"What about the gun-bearers?"

"Oh, they'll go with us. It's their *shauri*.[3] You see, they signed on for it. They don't look too happy though, do they?"

"I don't want to go in there," said Macomber. It was out before he knew he'd said it.

"Neither do I," said Wilson very cheerily. "Really no choice though." Then, as an afterthought, he glanced at Macomber and saw suddenly how he was trembling and the pitiful look on his face.

"You don't have to go in, of course," he said. "That's what I'm hired for, you know. That's why I'm so expensive."

"You mean you'd go in by yourself? Why not leave him there?"

Robert Wilson, whose entire occupation had been with the lion

---

1. The track of a wild animal.
2. In African lingua franca, a respectful term of address to a man.

3. An East African word from the Arabic, originally meaning "negotia-tion," but in the vernacular, "business" or "predicament."

and the problem he presented, and who had not been thinking about Macomber except to note that he was rather windy, suddenly felt as though he had opened the wrong door in a hotel and seen something shameful.

"What do you mean?"

"Why not just leave him?"

"You mean pretend to ourselves he hasn't been hit?"

"No. Just drop it."

"It isn't done."

"Why not?"

"For one thing, he's certain to be suffering. For another, some one else might run onto him."

"I see."

"But you don't have to have anything to do with it."

"I'd like to," Macomber said. "I'm just scared, you know."

"I'll go ahead when we go in," Wilson said, "with Kongoni tracking. You keep behind me and a little to one side. Chances are we'll hear him growl. If we see him we'll both shoot. Don't worry about anything. I'll keep you backed up. As a matter of fact, you know, perhaps you'd better not go. It might be much better. Why don't you go over and join the Memsahib while I just get it over with?"

"No, I want to go."

"All right," said Wilson. "But don't go in if you don't want to. This is my *shauri* now, you know."

"I want to go," said Macomber.

They sat under a tree and smoked.

"Want to go back and speak to the Memsahib while we're waiting?" Wilson asked.

"No."

"I'll just step back and tell her to be patient."

"Good," said Macomber. He sat there, sweating under his arms, his mouth dry, his stomach hollow feeling, wanting to find courage to tell Wilson to go on and finish off the lion without him. He could not know that Wilson was furious because he had not noticed the state he was in earlier and sent him back to his wife. While he sat there Wilson came up. "I have your big gun," he said. "Take it. We've given him time, I think. Come on."

Macomber took the big gun and Wilson said:

"Keep behind me and about five yards to the right and do exactly as I tell you." Then he spoke in Swahili to the two gun-bearers who looked the picture of gloom.

"Let's go," he said.

"Could I have a drink of water?" Macomber asked. Wilson spoke to the older gun-bearer, who wore a canteen on his belt, and the man unbuckled it, unscrewed the top and handed it to Macomber, who took it noticing how heavy it seemed and how hairy and shoddy the felt covering was in his hand. He raised it to drink and looked ahead at the high grass with the flat-topped trees behind it. A breeze was blowing toward them and the grass rippled gently in the wind. He looked at the gun-bearer and he could see the gun-bearer was suffering too with fear.

Thirty-five yards into the grass the big lion lay flattened out along the ground. His ears were back and his only movement was a slight twitching up and down of his long, black-tufted tail. He had turned at bay as soon as he had reached this cover and he was sick with the wound through his full belly, and weakening with the wound through his lungs that brought a thin foamy red to his mouth each time he breathed. His flanks were wet and hot and flies were on the little openings the solid bullets had made in his tawny hide, and his big yellow eyes, narrowed with hate, looked straight ahead, only blinking when the pain came as he breathed, and his claws dug in the soft baked earth. All of him, pain, sickness, hatred and all of his remaining strength, was tightening into an absolute concentration for a rush. He could hear the men talking and he waited, gathering all of himself into this preparation for a charge as soon as the men would come into the grass. As he heard their voices his tail stiffened to twitch up and down, and, as they came into the edge of the grass, he made a coughing grunt and charged.

Kongoni, the old gun-bearer, in the lead watching the blood spoor, Wilson watching the grass for any movement, his big gun ready, the second gun-bearer looking ahead and listening, Macomber close to Wilson, his rifle cocked, they had just moved into the grass when Macomber heard the blood-choked coughing grunt, and saw the swishing rush in the grass. The next thing he knew he was running; running wildly, in panic in the open, running toward the stream.

He heard the *ca-ra-wong!* of Wilson's big rifle, and again in a second crashing *carawong!* and turning saw the lion, horrible-looking now, with half his head seeming to be gone, crawling toward Wilson in the edge of the tall grass while the red-faced man worked the bolt on the short ugly rifle and aimed carefully as another blasting *carawong!* came from the muzzle, and the crawling, heavy, yellow bulk of the lion stiffened and the huge, mutilated head slid forward and Macomber, standing by himself in the clearing where he had run, holding a loaded rifle, while two black men and a white man looked back at him in contempt, knew the lion was dead. He came toward Wilson, his tallness all seeming a naked reproach, and Wilson looked at him and said:

"Want to take pictures?"

"No," he said.

That was all any one had said until they reached the motor car. Then Wilson had said:

"Hell of a fine lion. Boys will skin him out. We might as well stay here in the shade."

Macomber's wife had not looked at him nor he at her and he had sat by her in the back seat with Wilson sitting in the front seat. Once he had reached over and taken his wife's hand without looking at her and she had removed her hand from his. Looking across the stream to where the gun-bearers were skinning out the lion he could see that she had been able to see the whole thing. While they sat there his wife had reached forward and put her hand on Wilson's shoulder. He turned and she had leaned forward over the low seat and kissed him on the mouth.

"Oh, I say," said Wilson, going redder than his natural baked color.

"Mr. Robert Wilson," she said. "The beautiful red-faced Mr. Robert Wilson."

Then she sat down beside Macomber again and looked away across the stream to where the lion lay, with uplifted, white-muscled, tendon-marked naked forearms, and white bloating belly, as the black men fleshed away the skin. Finally the gun-bearers brought the skin over, wet and heavy, and climbed in behind with it, rolling it up before they got in, and the motor car started. No one had said anything more until they were back in camp.

That was the story of the lion. Macomber did not know how the lion had felt before he started his rush, nor during it when the unbelievable smash of the .505 with a muzzle velocity of two tons had hit him in the mouth, nor what kept him coming after that, when the second ripping crash had smashed his hind quarters and he had come crawling on toward the crashing, blasting thing that had destroyed him. Wilson knew something about it and only expressed it by saying, "Damned fine lion," but Macomber did not know how Wilson felt about things either. He did not know how his wife felt except that she was through with him.

His wife had been through with him before but it never lasted. He was very wealthy, and would be much wealthier, and he knew she would not leave him ever now. That was one of the few things that he really knew. He knew about that, about motor cycles—that was earliest—about motor cars, about duck-shooting, about fishing, trout, salmon and big-sea, about sex in books, many books, too many books, about all court games, about dogs, not much about horses, about hanging on to his money, about most of the other things his world dealt in, and about his wife not leaving him. His wife had been a great beauty and she was still a great beauty in Africa, but she was not a great enough beauty any more at home to be able to leave him and better herself and she knew it and he knew it. She had missed the chance to leave him and he knew it. If he had been better with women she would probably have started to worry about him getting another new, beautiful wife; but she knew too much about him to worry about him either. Also, he had always had a great tolerance which seemed the nicest thing about him if it were not the most sinister.

All in all they were known as a comparatively happily married couple, one of those whose disruption is often rumored but never occurs, and as the society columnist put it, they were adding more than a spice of *adventure* to their much envied and ever-enduring *Romance* by a *Safari* in what was known as *Darkest Africa* until the Martin Johnsons[4] lighted it on so many silver screens where they were pursuing *Old Simba* the lion, the buffalo, *Tembo* the elephant and as well collecting specimens for the Museum of Natural History. This same columnist had reported them *on the verge* at least three times in the past and they had been. But they always made it up. They had a sound basis of union. Margot was too beautiful for Macomber to divorce her and Macomber had too much money for Margot ever to leave him.

It was now about three o'clock in the morning and Francis Macomber, who had been asleep a little while after he had stopped thinking about the lion, wakened and then slept again, woke suddenly, frightened in a dream of the bloody-headed lion standing over him, and listening while his heart pounded, he realized that his wife was not in the other cot in the tent. He lay awake with that knowledge for two hours.

At the end of that time his wife came into the tent, lifted her mosquito bar and crawled cozily into bed.

"Where have you been?" Macomber asked in the darkness.

"Hello," she said. "Are you awake?"

"Where have you been?"

"I just went out to get a breath of air."

"You did, like hell."

"What do you want me to say, darling?"

"Where have you been?"

"Out to get a breath of air."

"That's a new name for it. You *are* a bitch."

"Well, you're a coward."

"All right," he said. "What of it?"

"Nothing as far as I'm concerned. But please let's not talk, darling, because I'm very sleepy."

"You think that I'll take anything."

4. Martin E. Johnson (1884–1937), explorer and adventurer, attained popular fame by his books and motion pictures of African wild life in the twenties; his wife appeared with him in the films.

"I know you will, sweet."

"Well, I won't."

"Please, darling, let's not talk. I'm so very sleepy."

"There wasn't going to be any of that. You promised there wouldn't be."

"Well, there is now," she said sweetly.

"You said if we made this trip that there would be none of that. You promised."

"Yes, darling. That's the way I meant it to be. But the trip was spoiled yesterday. We don't have to talk about it, do we?"

"You don't wait long when you have an advantage, do you?"

"Please let's not talk. I'm so sleepy, darling."

"I'm going to talk."

"Don't mind me then, because I'm going to sleep." And she did.

At breakfast they were all three at the table before daylight and Francis Macomber found that, of all the many men that he had hated, he hated Robert Wilson the most.

"Sleep well?" Wilson asked in his throaty voice, filling a pipe.

"Did you?"

"Topping," the white hunter told him.

You bastard, thought Macomber, you insolent bastard.

So she woke him when she came in, Wilson thought, looking at them both with his flat, cold eyes. Well, why doesn't he keep his wife where she belongs? What does he think I am, a bloody plaster saint? Let him keep her where she belongs. It's his own fault.

"Do you think we'll find buffalo?" Margot asked, pushing away a dish of apricots.

"Chance of it," Wilson said and smiled at her. "Why don't you stay in camp?"

"Not for anything," she told him.

"Why not order her to stay in camp?" Wilson said to Macomber.

"You order her," said Macomber coldly.

"Let's not have any ordering, nor," turning to Macomber, "any silliness, Francis," Margot said quite pleasantly.

"Are you ready to start?" Macomber asked.

"Any time," Wilson told him. "Do you want the Memsahib to go?"

"Does it make any difference whether I do or not?"

The hell with it, thought Robert Wilson. The utter complete hell with it. So this is what it's going to be like. Well, this is what it's going to be like, then.

"Makes no difference," he said.

"You're sure you wouldn't like to stay in camp with her yourself and let me go out and hunt the buffalo?" Macomber asked.

"Can't do that," said Wilson. "Wouldn't talk rot if I were you."

"I'm not talking rot. I'm disgusted."

"Bad word, disgusted."

"Francis, will you please try to speak sensibly?" his wife said.

"I speak too damned sensibly," Macomber said. "Did you ever eat such filthy food?"

"Something wrong with the food?" asked Wilson quietly.

"No more than with everything else."

"I'd pull yourself together, laddybuck," Wilson said very quietly. "There's a boy waits at table that understands a little English."

"The hell with him."

Wilson stood up and puffing on his pipe strolled away, speaking a few words in Swahili to one of the gun-bearers who was standing waiting for him. Macomber and his wife sat on at the table. He was staring at his coffee cup.

"If you make a scene I'll leave you, darling," Margot said quietly.

"No, you won't."

"You can try it and see."

"You won't leave me."

"No," she said. "I won't leave you and you'll behave yourself."

"Behave myself? That's a way to talk. Behave myself."

"Yes. Behave yourself."

"Why don't *you* try behaving?"

"I've tried it so long. So very long."

"I hate that red-faced swine," Macomber said. "I loathe the sight of him."

"He's really *very* nice."

"Oh, *shut up,*" Macomber almost shouted. Just then the car came up and stopped in front of the dining tent and the driver and the two gun-bearers got out. Wilson walked over and looked at the husband and wife sitting there at the table.

"Going shooting?" he asked.

"Yes," said Macomber, standing up. "Yes."

"Better bring a woolly. It will be cool in the car," Wilson said.

"I'll get my leather jacket," Margot said.

"The boy has it," Wilson told her. He climbed into the front with the driver and Francis Macomber and his wife sat, not speaking, in the back seat.

Hope the silly beggar doesn't take a notion to blow the back of my head off, Wilson thought to himself. Women *are* a nuisance on safari.

The car was grinding down to cross the river at a pebbly ford in the gray daylight and then climbed, angling up the steep bank, where Wilson had ordered a way shovelled out the day before so they could reach the parklike wooded rolling country on the far side.

It was a good morning, Wilson thought. There was a heavy dew and as the wheels went through the grass and low bushes he could smell the odor of the crushed fronds. It was an odor like verbena and he liked this early morning smell of the dew, the crushed bracken and the look of the tree trunks showing black through the early morning mist, as the car made its way through the untracked, park-like country. He had put the two in the back seat out of his mind now and was thinking about buffalo. The buffalo that he was after stayed in the daytime in a thick swamp where it was impossible to get a shot, but in the night they fed out into an open stretch of country and if he could come between them and their swamp with the car, Macomber would have a good chance at them in the open. He did not want to hunt buff with Macomber in thick cover. He did not want to hunt buff or anything else with Macomber at all, but he was a professional hunter and he had hunted with some rare ones in his time. If they got buff today there would only be rhino to come and the poor man would have gone through his dangerous game and things might pick up. He'd have nothing more to do with the woman and Macomber would get over that too. He must have gone through plenty of that before by the look of things. Poor beggar. He must have a way of getting over it. Well, it was the poor sod's own bloody fault.

He, Robert Wilson, carried a double size cot on safari to accommodate any windfalls he might receive. He had hunted for a certain clientele, the international, fast, sporting set, where the women did not feel they were getting their money's worth unless they had shared that cot with the white hunter. He despised them when he was away from them although he liked some of them well enough at the time, but he made his living by them; and their standards were his standards as long as they were hiring him.

They were his standards in all except the shooting. He had his own standards about the killing and they could live up to them or get some one else to hunt them. He knew, too, that they all respected him for this. This Macomber was an odd one though. Damned if he wasn't. Now the wife. Well, the wife. Yes, the wife. Hm, the wife. Well he'd dropped all that. He looked around at them. Macomber sat grim and furious. Margot smiled at him. She looked younger today, more innocent and fresher and not so professionally beautiful. What's in her heart God knows, Wilson thought. She hadn't talked much last night. At that it was a pleasure to see her.

The motor car climbed up a slight rise and went on through the trees and then out into a grassy prairie-like opening and kept in the shelter of the trees along the edge, the driver going slowly and

Wilson looking carefully out across the prairie and all along its far side. He stopped the car and studied the opening with his field glasses. Then he motioned to the driver to go on and the car moved slowly along, the driver avoiding wart-hog holes and driving around the mud castles ants had built. Then, looking across the opening, Wilson suddenly turned and said,

"By God, there they are!"

And looking where he pointed, while the car jumped forward and Wilson spoke in rapid Swahili to the driver, Macomber saw three huge, black animals looking almost cylindrical in their long heaviness, like big black tank cars, moving at a gallop across the far edge of the open prairie. They moved at a stiff-necked, stiff bodied gallop and he could see the upswept wide black horns on their heads as they galloped heads out; the heads not moving.

"They're three old bulls," Wilson said. "We'll cut them off before they get to the swamp."

The car was going a wild forty-five miles an hour across the open and as Macomber watched, the buffalo got bigger and bigger until he could see the gray, hairless, scabby look of one huge bull and how his neck was a part of his shoulders and the shiny black of his horns as he galloped a little behind the others that were strung out in that steady plunging gait; and then, the car swaying as though it had just jumped a road, they drew up close and he could see the plunging hugeness of the bull, and the dust in his sparsely haired hide, the wide boss of horn and his outstretched, wide-nostrilled muzzle, and he was raising his rifle when Wilson shouted, "Not from the car, you fool!" and he had no fear, only hatred of Wilson, while the brakes clamped on and the car skidded, plowing sideways to an almost stop and Wilson was out on one side and he on the other, stumbling as his feet hit the still speeding-by of the earth, and then he was shooting at the bull as he moved away, hearing the bullets whunk into him, emptying his rifle at him as he moved steadily away, finally remembering to get his shots forward into the shoulder, and as he fumbled to re-load, he saw the bull was down. Down on his knees, his big head tossing, and seeing the other two still galloping he shot at the leader and hit him. He shot again and missed and he heard the *carawonging* roar as Wilson shot and saw the leading bull slide forward onto his nose.

"Get that other," Wilson said. "Now you're shooting!"

But the other bull was moving steadily at the same gallop and he missed, throwing a spout of dirt, and Wilson missed and the dust rose in a cloud and Wilson shouted, "Come on. He's too far!" and grabbed his arm and they were in the car again, Macomber and Wilson hanging on the sides and rocketing swayingly over the uneven ground, drawing up on the steady, plunging, heavy-necked, straight-moving gallop of the bull.

They were behind him and Macomber was filling his rifle, dropping shells onto the ground, jamming it, clearing the jam, then they were almost up with the bull when Wilson yelled "Stop," and the car skidded so that it almost swung over and Macomber fell forward onto his feet, slammed his bolt forward and fired as far forward as he could aim into the galloping, rounded black back, aimed and shot again, then again, then again, and the bullets, all of them hitting, had no effect on the buffalo that he could see. Then Wilson shot, the roar deafening him, and he could see the bull stagger. Macomber shot again, aiming carefully, and down he came, onto his knees.

"All right," Wilson said. "Nice work. That's the three."

Macomber felt a drunken elation.

"How many times did you shoot?" he asked.

"Just three," Wilson said. "You killed the first bull. The biggest one. I helped you finish the other two. Afraid they might have got into cover. You had them killed. I was just mopping up a little. You shot damn well."

"Let's go to the car," said Macomber. "I want a drink."

"Got to finish off that buff first," Wilson told him. The buffalo was on his knees and he jerked his head furiously and bellowed in pig-eyed, roaring rage as they came toward him.

"Watch he doesn't get up," Wilson said. Then, "Get a little broadside and take him in the neck just behind the ear."

Macomber aimed carefully at the center of the huge, jerking, rage-driven neck and shot. At the shot the head dropped forward.

"That does it," said Wilson. "Got the spine. They're a hell of a looking thing, aren't they?"

"Let's get the drink," said Macomber. In his life he had never felt so good.

In the car Macomber's wife sat very white faced. "You were marvellous, darling," she said to Macomber. "What a ride."

"Was it rough?" Wilson asked.

"It was frightful. I've never been more frightened in my life."

"Let's all have a drink," Macomber said.

"By all means," said Wilson. "Give it to the Memsahib." She drank the neat whisky from the flask and shuddered a little when she swallowed. She handed the flask to Macomber who handed it to Wilson.

"It was frightfully exciting," she said. "It's given me a dreadful headache. I didn't know you were allowed to shoot them from cars though."

"No one shot from cars," said Wilson coldly.

"I mean chase them from cars."

"Wouldn't ordinarily," Wilson said. "Seemed sporting enough to me though while we were doing it. Taking more chance driving that way across the plain full of holes and one thing and another than hunting on foot. Buffalo could have charged us each time we shot if he liked. Gave him every chance. Wouldn't mention it to any one though. It's illegal if that's what you mean."

"It seemed very unfair to me," Margot said, "chasing those big helpless things in a motor car."

"Did it?" said Wilson.

"What would happen if they heard about it in Nairobi?"[5]

"I'd lose my licence for one thing. Other unpleasantnesses," Wilson said, taking a drink from the flask. "I'd be out of business."

"Really?"

"Yes, really."

"Well," said Macomber, and he smiled for the first time all day. "Now she has something on you."

"You have such a pretty way of putting things, Francis," Margot Macomber said. Wilson looked at them both. If a four-letter man marries a five-letter woman, he was thinking, what number of letters would their children be? What he said was, "We lost a gun-bearer. Did you notice it?"

"My God, no," Macomber said.

"Here he comes," Wilson said. "He's all right. He must have fallen off when we left the first bull."

Approaching them was the middle-aged gun-bearer, limping along in his knitted cap, khaki tunic, shorts and rubber sandals, gloomy-faced and disgusted looking. As he came up he called out to Wilson in Swahili and they all saw the change in the white hunter's face.

"What does he say?" asked Margot.

"He says the first bull got up and went into the bush," Wilson said with no expression in his voice.

"Oh," said Macomber blankly.

"Then it's going to be just like the lion," said Margot, full of anticipation.

"It's not going to be a damned bit like the lion," Wilson told her. "Did you want another drink, Macomber?"

"Thanks, yes," Macomber said. He expected the feeling he had had about the lion to come back but it did not. For the first time in his life he really felt wholly without fear. Instead of fear he had a feeling of definite elation.

"We'll go and have a look at the second bull," Wilson said. "I'll tell the driver to put the car in the shade."

"What are you going to do?" asked Margaret Macomber.

5. Capital of Kenya, British East African colony and protectorate, which is the scene of this story.

"Take a look at the buff," Wilson said.

"I'll come."

"Come along."

The three of them walked over to where the second buffalo bulked blackly in the open, head forward on the grass, the massive horns swung wide.

"He's a very good head," Wilson said. "That's close to a fifty-inch spread."

Macomber was looking at him with delight.

"He's hateful looking," said Margot. "Can't we go into the shade?"

"Of course," Wilson said. "Look," he said to Macomber, and pointed. "See that patch of bush?"

"Yes."

"That's where the first bull went in. The gun-bearer said when he fell off the bull was down. He was watching us helling along and the other two buff galloping. When he looked up there was the bull up and looking at him. Gun-bearer ran like hell and the bull went off slowly into that bush."

"Can we go in after him now?" asked Macomber eagerly.

Wilson looked at him appraisingly. Damned if this isn't a strange one, he thought. Yesterday he's scared sick and today he's a ruddy fire eater.

"No, we'll give him a while."

"Let's please go into the shade," Margot said. Her face was white and she looked ill.

They made their way to the car where it stood under a single, wide-spreading tree and all climbed in.

"Chances are he's dead in there," Wilson remarked. "After a little we'll have a look."

Macomber felt a wild unreasonable happiness that he had never known before.

"By God, that was a chase," he said. "I've never felt any such feeling. Wasn't it marvellous, Margot?"

"I hated it."

"Why?"

"I hated it," she said bitterly. "I loathed it."

"You know I don't think I'd ever be afraid of anything again," Macomber said to Wilson. "Something happened in me after we first saw the buff and started after him. Like a dam bursting. It was pure excitement."

"Cleans out your liver," said Wilson. "Damn funny things happen to people."

Macomber's face was shining. "You know something did happen to me," he said. "I feel absolutely different."

His wife said nothing and eyed him strangely. She was sitting far back in the seat and Macomber was sitting forward talking to Wilson who turned sideways talking over the back of the front seat.

"You know, I'd like to try another lion," Macomber said. "I'm really not afraid of them now. After all, what can they do to you?"

"That's it," said Wilson. "Worst one can do is kill you. How does it go? Shakespeare. Damned good. See if I can remember. Oh, damned good. Used to quote it to myself at one time. Let's see. 'By my troth, I care not; a man can die but once; we owe God a death and let it go which way it will he that dies this year is quit for the next.' [6] Damned fine, eh?"

He was very embarrassed, having brought out this thing he had lived by, but he had seen men come of age before and it always moved him. It was not a matter of their twenty-first birthday.

It had taken a strange chance of hunting, a sudden precipitation into action without opportunity for worrying beforehand, to bring this about with Macomber, but regardless of how it had happened it had most certainly happened. Look at the beggar now, Wilson thought. It's that some of them stay little boys so long, Wilson thought. Sometimes all their lives. Their figures stay boyish when they're fifty. The great American boy-men. Damned strange people. But he liked this Macomber now. Damned strange fellow. Probably meant the end of cuckoldry too. Well, that would be a damned good thing. Damned good thing. Beggar had probably been afraid all his life. Don't know what started it. But over now. Hadn't had time to be afraid with the buff. That and being angry too. Motor car too. Motor cars made it familiar. Be a damn fire eater now. He'd seen it in the war work the same way. More of a change than any loss of virginity. Fear gone like an operation. Something else grew in its place. Main thing a man had. Made him into a man. Women knew it too. No bloody fear.

From the far corner of the seat Margaret Macomber looked at the two of them. There was no change in Wilson. She saw Wilson as she had seen him the day before when she had first realized what his great talent was. But she saw the change in Francis Macomber now.

"Do you have that feeling of happiness about what's going to happen?" Macomber asked, still exploring his new wealth.

"You're not supposed to mention it," Wilson said, looking in the other's face. "Much more fashionable to say you're scared. Mind you, you'll be scared too, plenty of times."

"But you *have* a feeling of happiness about action to come?"

"Yes," said Wilson. "There's that. Doesn't do to talk too much about all this. Talk the whole thing away. No pleasure in anything if you mouth it up too much."

6. *2 Henry IV*, Act III, Scene 2, ll. 250–55.

"You're both talking rot," said Margot. "Just because you've chased some helpless animals in a motor car you talk like heroes."

"Sorry," said Wilson. "I have been gassing too much." She's worried about it already, he thought.

"If you don't know what we're talking about why not keep out of it?" Macomber asked his wife.

"You've gotten awfully brave, awfully suddenly," his wife said contemptuously, but her contempt was not secure. She was very afraid of something.

Macomber laughed, a very natural hearty laugh. "You know I *have*," he said. "I really have."

"Isn't it sort of late?" Margot said bitterly. Because she had done the best she could for many years back and the way they were together now was no one person's fault.

"Not for me," said Macomber.

Margot said nothing but sat back in the corner of the seat.

"Do you think we've given him time enough?" Macomber asked Wilson cheerfully.

"We might have a look," Wilson said. "Have you any solids left?"

"The gun-bearer has some."

Wilson called in Swahili and the older gun-bearer, who was skinning out one of the heads, straightened up, pulled a box of solids out of his pocket and brought them over to Macomber, who filled his magazine and put the remaining shells in his pocket.

"You might as well shoot the Springfield," Wilson said. "You're used to it. We'll leave the Mannlicher in the car with the Memsahib. Your gun-bearer can carry your heavy gun. I've this damned cannon. Now let me tell you about them." He had saved this until the last because he did not want to worry Macomber. "When a buff comes he comes with his head high and thrust straight out. The boss of the horns covers any sort of a brain shot. The only shot is straight into the nose. The only other shot is into his chest or, if you're to one side, into the neck or the shoulders. After they've been hit once they take a hell of a lot of killing. Don't try anything fancy. Take the easiest shot there is. They've finished skinning out that head now. Should we get started?"

He called to the gun-bearers, who came up wiping their hands, and the older one got into the back.

"I'll only take Kongoni," Wilson said. "The other can watch to keep the birds away."

As the car moved slowly across the open space toward the island of brushy trees that ran in a tongue of foliage along a dry water course that cut the open swale, Macomber felt his heart pounding and his mouth was dry again, but it was excitement, not fear.

"Here's where he went in," Wilson said. Then to the gun-bearer in Swahili, "Take the blood spoor."

The car was parallel to the patch of bush. Macomber, Wilson and the gun-bearer got down. Macomber, looking back, saw his wife, with the rifle by her side, looking at him. He waved to her and she did not wave back.

The brush was very thick ahead and the ground was dry. The middle-aged gun-bearer was sweating heavily and Wilson had his hat down over his eyes and his red neck showed just ahead of Macomber. Suddenly the gun-bearer said something in Swahili to Wilson and ran forward.

"He's dead in there," Wilson said. "Good work," and he turned to grip Macomber's hand and as they shook hands, grinning at each other, the gun-bearer shouted wildly and they saw him coming out of the bush sideways, fast as a crab, and the bull coming, nose out, mouth tight closed, blood dripping, massive head straight out, coming in a charge, his little pig eyes bloodshot as he looked at them. Wilson, who was ahead was kneeling shooting, and Macomber, as he fired, unhearing his shot in the roaring of Wilson's gun, saw fragments like slate burst from the huge boss of the horns, and the head jerked, he shot again at the wide nostrils and saw the horns jolt again and fragments fly, and he did not see Wilson now and, aiming carefully, shot again with the buffalo's huge bulk almost on him and his rifle almost level with the on-coming head, nose out, and he could see the little wicked eyes and the head started to lower and he felt a sudden white-hot, blinding flash explode inside his head and that was all he ever felt.

Wilson had ducked to one side to get in a shoulder shot. Macomber had stood solid and shot for the nose, shooting a touch high each time and hitting the heavy horns, splintering and chipping them like hitting a slate roof, and Mrs. Macomber, in the car, had shot at the buffalo with the 6.5 Mannlicher as it seemed about to gore Macomber and had hit her husband about two inches up and a little to one side of the base of his skull.

Francis Macomber lay now, face down, not two yards from where the buffalo lay on his side and his wife knelt over him with Wilson beside her.

"I wouldn't turn him over," Wilson said.

The woman was crying hysterically.

"I'd get back in the car," Wilson said. "Where's the rifle?"

She shook her head, her face contorted. The gun-bearer picked up the rifle.

"Leave it as it is," said Wilson. Then, "Go get Abdulla so that he may witness the manner of the accident."

He knelt down, took a handkerchief from his pocket, and spread it over Francis Macomber's crew-cropped head where it lay. The blood sank into the dry, loose earth.

Wilson stood up and saw the buffalo on his side, his legs out, his thinly-haired belly crawling with ticks. "Hell of a good bull," his brain registered automatically. "A good fifty inches, or better. Better." He called to the driver and told him to spread a blanket over the body and stay by it. Then he walked over to the motor car where the woman sat crying in the corner.

"That was a pretty thing to do," he said in a toneless voice. "He *would* have left you too."

"Stop it," she said.

"Of course it's an accident," he said. "I know that."

"Stop it," she said.

"Don't worry," he said. "There will be a certain amount of unpleasantness but I will have some photographs taken that will be very useful at the inquest. There's the testimony of the gunbearers and the driver too. You're perfectly all right."

"Stop it," she said.

"There's a hell of a lot to be done," he said. "And I'll have to send a truck off to the lake to wireless for a plane to take the three of us into Nairobi. Why didn't you poison him? That's what they do in England."

"Stop it. Stop it. Stop it," the woman cried.

Wilson looked at her with his flat blue eyes.

"I'm through now," he said. "I was a little angry. I'd begun to like your husband."

"Oh, please stop it," she said. "Please, please stop it."

"That's better," Wilson said. "Please is much better. Now I'll stop."

1935   1936, 1938

A Way You'll Never Be[6]

The attack had gone across the field, been held up by machinegun fire from the sunken road and from the group of farm houses,

6. "A Way You'll Never Be," first published in *Winner Take Nothing* (1933), belongs to the cycle of Nick Adams stories, which, considered as a whole, approach the proportions of an episodic novel. Most of them appeared as *In Our Time* (Paris, 1924; New York, 1925). Published close to a decade later, "A Way You'll Never Be" substantiates a crucial sketch in the earlier volume, entitled "Chapter VI," which tells us that Nick is in the war, has been wounded in the spine, and has "made a separate peace." "A Way You'll Never Be" for the first time makes clear the exact nature of that "peace," and explains the reasons for Nick's strange fears and frustrations in stories of his later experiences, particularly the enigmatic "Big Two-Hearted River." In "A Way You'll Never Be" we have a typical and persistent Hemingway situation, for Nick has been wounded both physically and psychically. The war wound only culminates the successive assaults of violence in his outward environment and inward life. In *Across the River and into the Trees* (1950), when Colonel Cantwell revisits the Italian scenes of his experiences in the war, the description of one of them recalls the place where Nick Adams received his injury

encountered no resistance in the town, and reached the bank of the river. Coming along the road on a bicycle, getting off to push the machine when the surface of the road became too broken, Nicholas Adams saw what had happened by the position of the dead.

They lay alone or in clumps in the high grass of the field and along the road, their pockets out, and over them were flies and around each body or group of bodies were the scattered papers.

In the grass and the grain, beside the road, and in some places scattered over the road, there was much material: a field kitchen, it must have come over when things were going well; many of the calf-skin-covered haversacks, stick bombs, helmets, rifles, sometimes one butt-up, the bayonet stuck in the dirt, they had dug quite a little at the last; stick bombs, helmets, rifles, intrenching tools, ammunition boxes, star-shell pistols, their shells scattered about, medical kits, gas masks, empty gas-mask cans, a squat, tripodded machine gun in a nest of empty shells, full belts protruding from the boxes, the water-cooling can empty and on its side, the breech block gone, the crew in odd positions, and around them, in the grass, more of the typical papers.

There were mass prayer books, group postcards showing the machine-gun unit standing in ranked and ruddy cheerfulness as in a football picture for a college annual; now they were humped and swollen in the grass; propaganda postcards showing a soldier in Austrian uniform bending a woman backward over a bed; the figures were impressionistically drawn; very attractively depicted and had nothing in common with actual rape in which the woman's skirts are pulled over her head to smother her, one comrade sometimes sitting upon the head. There were many of these inciting cards which had evidently been issued just before the offensive. Now they were scattered with the smutty postcards, photographic; the small photographs of village girls by village photographers, the occasional pictures of children, and the letters, letters, letters. There was always much paper about the dead and the débris of this attack was no exception.

These were new dead and no one had bothered with anything but their pockets. Our own dead,[7] or what he thought of, still, as our own dead, were surprisingly few, Nick noticed. Their coats had been opened too and their pockets were out, and they showed, by their positions, the manner and the skill of the attack. The hot weather had swollen them all alike regardless of nationality.

The town had evidently been defended, at the last, from the line of the sunken road and there had been few or no Austrians to fall back into it. There were only three bodies in the street and they

7. The Italian troops, with which Nick is serving as an American volunteer.

looked to have been killed running. The houses of the town were broken by the shelling and the street had much rubble of plaster and mortar and there were broken beams, broken tiles, and many holes, some of them yellow-edged from the mustard gas. There were many pieces of shell, and shrapnel balls were scattered in the rubble. There was no one in the town at all.

Nick Adams had seen no one since he had left Fornaci, although, riding along the road through the over-foliaged country, he had seen guns hidden under screens of mulberry leaves to the left of the road, noticing them by the heat-waves in the air above the leaves where the sun hit the metal. Now he went on through the town, surprised to find it deserted, and came out on the low road beneath the bank of the river. Leaving the town there was a bare open space where the road slanted down and he could see the placid reach of the river and the low curve of the opposite bank and the whitened, sun-baked mud where the Austrians had dug. It was all very lush and over-green since he had seen it last and becoming historical had made no change in this, the lower river.

The battalion was along the bank to the left. There was a series of holes in the top of the bank with a few men in them. Nick noticed where the machine guns were posted and the signal rockets in their racks. The men in the holes in the side of the bank were sleeping. No one challenged. He went on and as he came around a turn in the mud bank a young second lieutenant with a stubble of beard and red-rimmed, very bloodshot eyes pointed a pistol at him.

"Who are you?"

Nick told him.

"How do I know this?"

Nick showed him the tessera[8] with photograph and identification and the seal of the third army. He took hold of it.

"I will keep this."

"You will not," Nick said. "Give me back the card and put your gun away. There. In the holster."

"How am I to know who you are?"

"The tessera tells you."

"And if the tessera is false? Give me that card."

"Don't be a fool," Nick said cheerfully. "Take me to your company commander."

"I should send you to battalion headquarters."

"All right," said Nick. "Listen, do you know the Captain Paravicini? The tall one with the small mustache who was an architect and speaks English?"

"You know him?"

8. Literally, "ticket"; here, a military pass.

"A little."

"What company does he command?"

"The second."

"He is commanding the battalion."

"Good," said Nick. He was relieved to know that Para was all right. "Let us go to the battalion."

As Nick had left the edge of the town three shrapnel had burst high and to the right over one of the wrecked houses and since then there had been no shelling. But the face of this officer looked like the face of a man during a bombardment. There was the same tightness and the voice did not sound natural. His pistol made Nick nervous.

"Put it away," he said. "There's the whole river between them and you."

"If I thought you were a spy I would shoot you now," the second lieutenant said.

"Come on," said Nick. "Let us go to the battalion." This officer made him very nervous.

The Captain Paravicini, acting major, thinner and more English-looking than ever, rose when Nick saluted from behind the table in the dugout that was battalion headquarters.

"Hello," he said. "I didn't know you. What are you doing in that uniform?"

"They've put me in it."

"I am very glad to see you, Nicolo."

"Right. You look well. How was the show?"

"We made a very fine attack. Truly. A very fine attack. I will show you. Look."

He showed on the map how the attack had gone.

"I came from Fornaci," Nick said. "I could see how it had been. It was very good."

"It was extraordinary. Altogether extraordinary. Are you attached to the regiment?"

"No. I am supposed to move around and let them see the uniform."

"How odd."

"If they see one American uniform that is supposed to make them believe others are coming."

"But how will they know it is an American uniform?"

"You will tell them."

"Oh. Yes, I see. I will send a corporal with you to show you about and you will make a tour of the lines."

"Like a bloody politician," Nick said.

"You would be much more distinguished in civilian clothes. They are what is really distinguished."

"With a homburg hat," said Nick.

"Or with a very furry fedora."

"I'm supposed to have my pockets full of cigarettes and postal cards and such things," Nick said. "I should have a musette full of chocolate. These I should distribute with a kind word and a pat on the back. But there weren't any cigarettes and postcards and no chocolate. So they said to circulate around anyway."

"I'm sure your appearance will be very heartening to the troops."

"I wish you wouldn't," Nick said. "I feel badly enough about it as it is. In principle, I would have brought you a bottle of brandy."

"In principle," Para said and smiled, for the first time, showing yellowed teeth. "Such a beautiful expression. Would you like some Grappa?"[9]

"No, thank you," Nick said.

"It hasn't any ether in it."

"I can taste that still," Nick remembered suddenly and completely.

"You know I never knew you were drunk until you started talking coming back in the camions."[1]

"I was stinking in every attack," Nick said.

"I can't do it," Para said. "I took it in the first show, the very first show, and it only made me very upset and then frightfully thirsty."

"You don't need it."

"You're much braver in an attack than I am."

"No," Nick said. "I know how I am and I prefer to get stinking. I'm not ashamed of it."

"I've never seen you drunk."

"No?" said Nick. "Never? Not when we rode from Mestre to Portogrande that night and I wanted to go to sleep and used the bicycle for a blanket and pulled it up under my chin?"

"That wasn't in the lines."

"Let's not talk about how I am," Nick said. "It's a subject I know too much about to want to think about it any more."

"You might as well stay here a while," Paravicini said. "You can take a nap if you like. They didn't do much to this in the bombardment. It's too hot to go out yet."

"I suppose there is no hurry."

"How are you really?"

"I'm fine. I'm perfectly all right."

"No. I mean really."

"I'm all right. I can't sleep without a light of some sort. That's all I have now."

---

9. A potent Italian brandy.

1. Military vehicles for artillery, often used for auxiliary troop transport.

"I said it should have been trepanned.[2] I'm no doctor but I know that."

"Well, they thought it was better to have it absorb, and that's what I got. What's the matter? I don't seem crazy to you, do I?"

"You seem in top-hole shape."

"It's a hell of a nuisance once they've had you certified as nutty," Nick said. "No one ever has any confidence in you again."

"I would take a nap, Nicolo," Paravicini said. "This isn't battalion headquarters as we used to know it. We're just waiting to be pulled out. You oughtn't to go out in the heat now—it's silly. Use that bunk."

"I might just lie down," Nick said.

Nick lay on the bunk. He was very disappointed that he felt this way and more disappointed, even, that it was so obvious to Captain Paravicini. This was not as large a dugout as the one where that platoon of the class of 1899,[3] just out at the front, got hysterics during the bombardment before the attack, and Para had had him walk them two at a time outside to show them nothing would happen, wearing his own chin strap tight across the mouth to keep his lips quiet. Knowing they could not hold it when they took it. Knowing it was all a bloody balls—If he can't stop crying, break his nose to give him something else to think about. I'd shoot one but it's too late now. They'd all be worse. Break his nose. They've put it back to five-twenty. We've only got four minutes more. Break that other silly bugger's nose and kick his silly ass out of here. Do you think they'll go over? If they don't, shoot two and try to scoop the others out some way. Keep behind them, sergeant. It's no use to walk ahead and find there's nothing coming behind you. Bail them out as you go. What a bloody balls. All right. That's right. Then, looking at the watch, in that quiet tone, that valuable quiet tone, "Savoia."[4] Making it cold, no time to get it, he couldn't find his own after the cave-in, one whole end had caved in; it was that started them; making it cold up that slope the only time he hadn't done it stinking. And after they came back the telefrica house burned, it seemed, and some of the wounded got down four days later and some did not get down, but we went up and we went back and we came down—we always came down. And there was

---

2. An operation on the skull, usually undertaken in treatment of a head injury. But in the earlier sketch in *In Our Time*, the injury was reported as spinal. The point, of course, is Nick's apprehension of some permanent loss of personality, reflected in the fantasy that follows. See the phrase "[wounded] in various places" near the end of the story.

3. *I.e.*, those born in 1899; subject to

Italian selective service, they would just have reached the front lines in 1917, the year of the events in this story, and the year in which Hemingway himself, in advance of American participation in the war, enlisted in the Italian army and was, like Nick Adams, wounded and hospitalized.

4. Here the signal for zero hour, at which action is begun; actually the name of an Italian province.

Gaby Delys,[5] oddly enough, with feathers on; you called me baby doll a year ago tadada you said that I was rather nice to know tadada with feathers on, with feathers off, the great Gaby, and my name's Harry Pilcer, too, we used to step out of the far side of the taxis when it got steep going up the hill and he could see that hill every night when he dreamed with Sacré Cœur,[6] blown white, like a soap bubble. Sometimes his girl was there and sometimes she was with some one else and he could not understand that, but those were the nights the river ran so much wider and stiller than it should and outside of Fossalta there was a low house painted yellow with willows all around it and a low stable and there was a canal, and he had been there a thousand times and never seen it, but there it was every night as plain as the hill, only it frightened him.[7] That house meant more than anything and every night he had it. That was what he needed but it frightened him especially when the boat lay there quietly in the willows on the canal, but the banks weren't like this river. It was all lower, as it was at Portogrande, where they had seen them come wallowing across the flooded ground holding the rifles high until they fell with them in the water. Who ordered that one? If it didn't get so damned mixed up he could follow it all right. That was why he noticed everything in such detail to keep it all straight so he would know just where he was, but suddenly it confused without reason as now, he lying in a bunk at battalion head-quarters, with Para commanding a battalion and he in a bloody American uniform. He sat up and looked around; they all watching him. Para was gone out. He lay down again.

The Paris part came earlier and he was not frightened of it except when she had gone off with some one else and the fear that they might take the same driver twice. That was what frightened about that. Never about the front. He never dreamed about the front now any more but what frightened him so that he could not get rid of it was that long yellow house and the different width of the river. Now he was back here at the river, he had gone through that same town, and there was no house. Nor was the river that way. Then where did he go each night and what was the peril, and why would he wake, soaking wet, more frightened than he had ever been in a bombardment, because of a house and a long stable and a canal?

5. The beginning of Nick's fantasy; he recalls the attack in which he was wounded, and his mind goes again, as before. Gaby Delys, a sensational entertainer, whose enticing songs and dances are recalled below, died in Paris in 1920. Harry Pilcer was for a time her companion and song writer.
6. A church built in the Romanesque-Byzantine style, crowning the Butte Montmartre, in the Bohemian quarter of Paris, and visible from long distances.
7. This is a description of the place where he was wounded, but it is not entirely clear at this point. The wound's significance is fully revealed in *Across the River and into the Trees* (1950), where Nick is, for all practical purposes, reincarnated as Colonel Dick Cantwell.

He sat up, swung his legs carefully down; they stiffened any time they were out straight for long; returned the stares of the adjutant, the signallers and the two runners by the door and put on his cloth-covered trench helmet.

"I regret the absence of the chocolate, the postal-cards and cigarettes," he said. "I am, however, wearing the uniform."

"The major is coming back at once," the adjutant said. In that army an adjutant is not a commissioned officer.

"The uniform is not very correct," Nick told them. "But it gives you the idea. There will be several millions of Americans here shortly."

"Do you think they will send Americans down here?" asked the adjutant.

"Oh, absolutely. Americans twice as large as myself, healthy, with clean hearts, sleep at night, never been wounded, never been blown up, never had their heads caved in, never been scared, don't drink, faithful to the girls they left behind them, many of them never had crabs, wonderful chaps. You'll see."

"Are you an Italian?" asked the adjutant.

"No, American. Look at the uniform. Spagnolini made it but it's not quite correct."

"A North or South American?"

"North," said Nick. He felt it coming on now. He would quiet down.

"But you speak Italian."

"Why not? Do you mind if I speak Italian? Haven't I a right to speak Italian?"

"You have Italian medals."

"Just the ribbons and the papers. The medals come later. Or you give them to people to keep and the people go away; or they are lost with your baggage. You can purchase others in Milan. It is the papers that are of importance. You must not feel badly about them. You will have some yourself if you stay at the front long enough."

"I am a veteran of the Iritrea campaign," said the adjutant stiffly. "I fought in Tripoli."

"It's quite something to have met you," Nick put out his hand. "Those must have been trying days. I noticed the ribbons. Were you, by any chance, on the Carso?"

"I have just been called up for this war. My class was too old."

"At one time I was under the age limit," Nick said. "But now I am reformed out of the war."

"But why are you here now?"

"I am demonstrating the American uniform," Nick said. "Don't you think it is very significant? It is a little tight in the collar but soon you will see untold millions wearing this uniform swarm-

ing like locusts. The grasshopper, you know, what we call the grasshopper in America, is really a locust. The true grasshopper is small
and green and comparatively feeble. You must not, however, make
a confusion with the seven-year locust or cicada which emits a
peculiar sustained sound which at the moment I cannot recall. I try
to recall it but I cannot. I can almost hear it and then it is quite
gone. You will pardon me if I break off our conversation?"

"See if you can find the major," the adjutant said to one of the
two runners. "I can see you have been wounded," he said to Nick.

"In various places," Nick said. "If you are interested in scars I
can show you some very interesting ones but I would rather talk
about grasshoppers. What we call grasshoppers that is; and what are,
really, locusts. These insects at one time played a very important
part in my life. It might interest you and you can look at the uniform while I am talking."

The adjutant made a motion with his hand to the second runner
who went out.

"Fix your eyes on the uniform. Spagnolini made it, you know.
You might as well look, too," Nick said to the signallers. "I really
have no rank. We're under the American consul. It's perfectly all
right for you to look. You can stare, if you like. I will tell you about
the American locust. We always preferred one that we called the
medium-brown. They last the best in the water and fish prefer
them. The larger ones that fly making a noise somewhat similar
to that produced by a rattlesnake rattling his rattlers, a very dry
sound, have vivid colored wings, some are bright red, others yellow
barred with black, but their wings go to pieces in the water and
they make a very blowsy bait, while the medium-brown is a plump,
compact, succulent hopper that I can recommend as far as one may
well recommend something you gentlemen will probably never encounter. But I must insist that you will never gather a sufficient
supply of these insects for a day's fishing by pursuing them with
your hands or trying to hit them with a bat. That is sheer nonsense
and a useless waste of time. I repeat, gentlemen, that you will get
nowhere at it. The correct procedure, and one which should be
taught all young officers at every small-arms course if I had anything
to say about it, and who knows but what I will have, is the employment of a seine or net made of common mosquito netting. Two
officers holding this length of netting at alternate ends, or let us
say one at each end, stoop, hold the bottom extremity of the net
in one hand and the top extremity in the other and run into the
wind. The hoppers, flying with the wind, fly against the length of
netting and are imprisoned in its folds. It is no trick at all to catch
a very great quantity indeed, and no officer, in my opinion, should
be without a length of mosquito netting suitable for the impro-

visation of one of these grasshopper seines. I hope I have made myself clear, gentlemen. Are there any questions? If there is anything in the course you do not understand please ask questions. Speak up. None? Then I would like to close on this note. In the words of that great soldier and gentleman, Sir Henry Wilson:[8] Gentlemen, either you must govern or you must be governed. Let me repeat it. Gentlemen, there is one thing I would like to have you remember. One thing I would like you to take with you as you leave this room. Gentlemen, either you must govern—or you must be governed. That is all, gentlemen. Good-day."

He removed his cloth-covered helmet, put it on again and, stooping, went out the low entrance of the dugout. Para, accompanied by the two runners, was coming down the line of the sunken road. It was very hot in the sun and Nick removed the helmet.

"There ought to be a system for wetting these things," he said. "I shall wet this one in the river." He started up the bank.

"Nicolo," Paravicini called. "Nicolo. Where are you going?"

"I don't really have to go." Nick came down the slope, holding the helmet in his hands. "They're a damned nuisance wet or dry. Do you wear yours all the time?"

"All the time," said Para. "It's making me bald. Come inside." Inside Para told him to sit down.

"You know they're absolutely no damned good," Nick said. "I remember when they were a comfort when we first had them, but I've seen them full of brains too many times."

"Nicolo," Para said. "I think you should go back. I think it would be better if you didn't come up to the line until you had those supplies. There's nothing here for you to do. If you move around, even with something worth giving away, the men will group and that invites shelling. I won't have it."

"I know it's silly," Nick said. "It wasn't my idea. I heard the brigade was here so I thought I would see you or some one else I knew. I could have gone to Zenzon or to San Dona. I'd like to go to San Dona to see the bridge again."

"I won't have you circulating around to no purpose," Captain Paravicini said.

"All right," said Nick. He felt it coming on again.

"You understand?"

"Of course," said Nick. He was trying to hold it in.

"Anything of that sort should be done at night."

"Naturally," said Nick. He knew he could not stop it now.

"You see, I am commanding the battalion," Para said.

"And why shouldn't you be?" Nick said. Here it came. "You can read and write, can't you?"

8. Sir Henry Hughes Wilson (1864–1922), British army leader.

"Yes," said Para gently.

"The trouble is you have a damned small battalion to command. As soon as it gets to strength again they'll give you back your company. Why don't they bury the dead? I've seen them now. I don't care about seeing them again. They can bury them any time as far as I'm concerned and it would be much better for you. You'll all get bloody sick."

"Where did you leave your bicycle?"

"Inside the last house."

"Do you think it will be all right?"

"Don't worry," Nick said. "I'll go in a little while."

"Lie down a little while, Nicolo."

"All right."

He shut his eyes, and in place of the man with the beard who looked at him over the sights of the rifle, quite calmly before squeezing off, the white flash and clublike impact, on his knees, hot-sweet choking, coughing it onto the rock while they went past him, he saw a long, yellow house with a low stable and the river much wider than it was and stiller. "Christ," he said, "I might as well go."

He stood up.

"I'm going, Para," he said. "I'll ride back now in the afternoon. If any supplies have come I'll bring them down tonight. If not I'll come at night when I have something to bring."

"It is still hot to ride," Captain Paravicini said.

"You don't need to worry," Nick said. "I'm all right now for quite a while. I had one then but it was easy. They're getting much better. I can tell when I'm going to have one because I talk so much."

"I'll send a runner with you."

"I'd rather you didn't. I know the way."

"You'll be back soon?"

"Absolutely."

"Let me send——"

"No," said Nick. "As a mark of confidence."

"Well, Ciaou[9] then."

"Ciaou," said Nick. He started back along the sunken road toward where he had left the bicycle. In the afternoon the road would be shady once he had passed the canal. Beyond that there were trees on both sides that had not been shelled at all. It was on that stretch that, marching, they had once passed the Terza Savoia cavalry regiment riding in the snow with their lances. The horses' breath made plumes in the cold air. No, that was somewhere else. Where was that?

9. Usually *ciao;* Italian, a familiar term of farewell, equivalent to our "so long!"

"I'd better get to that damned bicycle," Nick said to himself. "I don't want to lose the way to Fornaci."

psychological complexity
notie to soil. comic vein - less subtle than 1933
comic elements in Faulkner
Regional i.e. Steinbeck
represents confusion found in world of younger generation
jazzage depression

THOMAS WOLFE
(1900–1938)

wrote of adolescent condition: of the growing-up stage and the effort to find oneself

When Thomas Wolfe died, at the age of thirty-eight, he left four large novels, two of them not then published, besides numerous stories and miscellaneous writings. Both the man and his work were in certain respects unprecedented. The novels were not experimental in the formal sense; they used established methods of objective narration; yet, especially in the first two, the presence of the author himself was almost overwhelming. It became evident that Wolfe was his own character, whether Eugene Gant or George Webber, in all four books; and that he was producing a kind of domestic *roman à clef* in which the identifiable characters were not historical figures, but his own family and associates, depicted in scenes and situations which corresponded with those of his own life, whether in his native Asheville, North Carolina— which he called Altamont—or at the university, or in New York.

This was not the autobiographical novel as Dickens, for example, wrote it in *David Copperfield,* by inventing new events and characters to be placed within the chronological framework of his own life. Wolfe did not "invent" his important characters in the usual sense of the word; he discovered them. What

he invented was a method of analyzing experience that did not need to be invented—his own. What he attempted was a new novel of spiritual exploration, and his *terra incognita* was composed of the people and the experience which he had absorbed as a result of his insatiable appetite for life.

That life began on October 3, 1900, at Asheville, then primarily a resort town, situated in the western North Carolina highlands. His father, the Oliver Gant of the novels, was a stonecutter, and his mother, portrayed as Eliza Gant, managed a residential boardinghouse in real life also. Like Eugene Gant in *Look Homeward, Angel,* Tom Wolfe did odd jobs, sold papers and magazines, and wondered about his father, who, like Oliver in "An Angel on the Porch," combined earthiness with quixotic sentiment and the habit of reciting poetry to any who would listen.

Huge in frame and abounding in energy, young Wolfe went down to the University of North Carolina in 1916 with his voracious appetence for life, knowledge, experience, food, smells, sensation, and in fact the world. There he read widely, began to write, and studied the theater in courses under the talented

gargantuan appetite for life
search / quest for identity = universal application

Frederick Koch, founder of the famous Carolina Playmakers. For them the young student wrote two plays, one later published in a collection by Professor Koch. Upon his graduation in 1920 Wolfe enrolled at Harvard, where he was a student in the "47 Workshop" of George Pierce Baker, and took his M.A. It was inevitable that he should bring with him a manuscript play when he went to New York in 1922, but producers were not impressed with this or later attempts, and Wolfe cherished for years his defeated first love for the theater. In the meantime, he supported himself by teaching composition at New York University while pouring out the stored material of his first novel, and until 1930 he continued to teach there intermittently.

Maxwell Perkins, a talented editor of the staff of Charles Scribner's Sons, has minimized the exaggerated legend that he was primarily responsible for Wolfe's first two novels. It is certain, however, that Wolfe had an enormous manuscript, whose bulk obscured the organic organization of a novel, and that after other editors had declined it, Perkins recognized his opportunity and obligation. He suggested the means by which the author could set aside certain materials for possible future use and could concentrate and give more formal order to the manuscript, which appeared as *Look Homeward, Angel* in 1929.

It was a distinguished success, and Wolfe's proposal for foreign travel to provide background for his novels won him a Guggenheim Fellowship which took him in 1930–1931 to Europe. He was particularly interested in Germany, where his visit provided fundamental materials for his last two novels, and laid the foundations for his quite considerable foreign recognition. The remainder of his short life was given to the prodigious literary re-creation of an accumulation of experience which he himself recognized as "gargantuan." His twice-renewed love affair with a famous and talented artist and designer both harrowed and enriched his spirit. His second novel, *Of Time and the River*, appeared in 1935, and his collection of short stories, *From Death to Morning*, also was published in that year. Still the furious fever of life and composition continued to drive him. By May of 1938 he had finished a third novel, and he had also placed in his publisher's hands the outline of a fourth, together with manuscript material including the entire text but still needing final pruning and organization. In July he was stricken by influenza, and pneumonia threatened. The febrile excitement of his creative life may at last have worn down his gigantic strength; at any rate, while recovering he contracted a cerebral infection, which caused his death on September 15, 1938.

The Web and the Rock appeared posthumously in 1939, and *You Can't Go Home Again* in 1940. The protagonist in these works is George Webber, not Eugene Gant, but both are exaggerations, simplifications, and explanations of Thomas Wolfe himself. The fact that they are also the universal youth in quest of spiritual security and selfhood is what raises the novels above the literature of "confessions" into the realm of creative originality.

Wolfe matured rapidly. His prose was lyrical, befitting the subjective nature of his novels, and it was steadily enriched by his unusual sense of verbal associations and by his mammoth literary memory. The range of his imagination, like that of Whitman, at last embodied the myth of his country: her great cities interlaced by railroads no less than the continental immensity of her natural domain were symbols of the amplitude and creative energies of mankind, the final object of his study.

There is no collected edition of Wolfe's writings. In addition to the major titles named in the text above are the following: *The Story of a Novel*, 1936, Wolfe's revealing comment upon his personality and his work; *The Hills Beyond*, 1941, short stories; and *Mannerhouse, A Play*, 1948. *Thomas Wolfe's Letters to His Mother*, 1943, was edited by J. S. Terry; *The Letters of Thomas Wolfe*, 1956, by Elizabeth Nowell.

A full-length biography is Elizabeth Nowell, *Thomas Wolfe*, 1960. Other biographical and critical appraisals are: E. C. Aswell, "A Note on Thomas Wolfe," prefatory to *The Hills Beyond;* H. J. Muller, *Thomas Wolfe*, 1947; Pamela H. Johnson, *Hungry Gulliver: An English Critical Appraisal of Thomas Wolfe*, 1948; Louis D. Rubin, *Thomas Wolfe, The Weather of His Youth*, 1955; and Floyd D. Watkins, *Thomas Wolfe's Characters*, 1957. Two volumes covering Wolfe's years at New York University are T. C. Pollock and Oscar Cargill, *Thomas Wolfe at Washington Square*, 1954; and *The Correspondence of Thomas Wolfe and Homer Andrew Watt*, edited by T. C. Pollock and Oscar Cargill, 1954.

An Angel on the Porch[1]

Late on an afternoon in young summer Queen Elizabeth came quickly up into the square past Gant's marbleshop. Surrounded by the stones, the slabs, the cold carved lambs of death, the stonecutter leaned upon the rail and talked with Jannadeau, the faithful burly Swiss who, fenced in a little rented place among Gant's marbles, was probing with delicate monocled intentness into the entrails of a watch.

"There goes the Queen," said Gant, stopping for a moment their debate.

"A smart woman. A pippin as sure as you're born," he added, with relish.

He bowed gallantly with a sweeping flourish of his great-boned frame of six feet five. "Good evening, madam."

She replied with a bright smile of friendliness which may have had in it the flicker of old memory, including Jannadeau with a cheerful impersonal nod. For just a moment more she paused, turning her candid stare upon smooth granite slabs of death,

1. "An Angel on the Porch," the first piece of major fiction published by Thomas Wolfe, appeared as a short story in *Scribner's Magazine* for August, 1929. The same year it appeared again as Chapter 19 of Wolfe's first novel, *Look Homeward, Angel*. Soon after the author's death, his publishers reprinted this, his first story, side by side with his last story, "The Party at Jack's," in *Scribner's Magazine* for May, 1939.

carved lambs and cherubim within the shop, and finally on an angel stationed beside the door upon Gant's little porch. Then, with her brisk, firm tread, she passed the shop, untroubled by the jeweller's heavy stare of wounded virtue, as he glowered up from his dirty littered desk, following her vanishing form with a guttural mutter of distaste.

They resumed their debate:

"And you may mark my words," proceeded Gant, wetting his big thumb, as if he had never been interrupted, and continuing his attack upon the Democratic party, and all the bad weather, fire, famine, and pestilence that attended its administration, "if they get in again we'll have soup-kitchens, the banks will go to the wall, and your guts will grease your backbone before another winter's over."

The Swiss thrust out a dirty hand toward the library he consulted in all disputed areas—a greasy edition of "The World Almanac," three years old—saying triumphantly, after a moment of dirty thumbing, in strange wrenched accent: "Ah—just as I thought: the muni-*cip*-al taxation of Milwaukee under De*moc*-ratic administration in 1905 was two dollars and twenty-five cents the hundred, the lowest it had been in years. I cannot ima-*gine* why the total revenue is not given."

Judiciously reasonable, statistically argumentative, the Swiss argued with animation against his Titan, picking his nose with blunt black fingers, his broad yellow face breaking into flaccid creases, as he laughed gutturally at Gant's unreason, and at the rolling periods of his rhetoric.

Thus they talked in the shadow of the big angel that stood just beyond the door upon Gant's porch, leering down upon their debate with a smile of idiot benevolence. Thus they talked, while Elizabeth passed by, in the cool damp of Gant's fantastical brick shack, surrounded by the stones, the slabs, the cold carved lambs of death. And as they talked the gray and furtive eyes of the stonecutter, which darkened so seldom now with the shade of the old hunger—for stone and the cold wrought face of an angel—looked out into the square at all the little pullulation of the town, touched, as that woman passed his door with gallant tread, by a memory he thought had died forever. The lost words. The forgotten faces. Where? When?

He was getting on to sixty-five, his long, erect body had settled, he stooped a little. He spoke of old age often, and he wept in his tirades now because of his great right hand, stiffened by rheumatism, which once had carved so cunningly the dove, the lamb, the cold joined hands of death (but never the soft stone face of an angel). Soaked in pity, he referred to himself as "The poor old cripple who has to provide for the whole family."

That proud and sensual flesh was on its way to dust.

The indolence of age and disintegration was creeping over him. He rose now a full hour later, he came to his shop punctually, but he spent long hours of the day extended on the worn leather couch of his office, or in gossip with Jannadeau, bawdy old Liddell, Cardiac, his doctor, and Fagg Sluder, who had salted away his fortune in two big buildings on the square, and was at the present moment tilted comfortably in a chair before the fire department, gossiping eagerly with members of the ball club, whose chief support he was. It was after five o'clock, the game was over.

Negro laborers, grisly with a white coating of cement, sloped down past the shop on their way home. The draymen dispersed slowly, a slouchy policeman loafed down the steps of the city hall picking his teeth, and on the market side, from high grilled windows, there came the occasional howls of a drunken negress. Life buzzed slowly like a fly.

The sun had reddened slightly, there was a cool flowing breath from the hills, a freshening relaxation over the tired earth, the hope, the ecstasy, of evening in the air. In slow pulses the thick plume of fountain rose, fell upon itself, and slapped the pool in lazy rhythms. A wagon rattled leanly over the big cobbles; beyond the firemen, the grocer Bradly wound up his awning with slow, creaking revolutions.

Across the square at its other edge the young virgins of the eastern part of town walked lightly home in chattering groups. They came to town at four o'clock in the afternoon, walked up and down the little avenue several times, entered a shop to purchase small justifications, and finally went into the chief drugstore, where the bucks of the town loafed and drawled in lazy, alert groups. It was their club, their brasserie, the forum of the sexes. With confident smiles the young men detached themselves from their group and strolled back to booth and table.

"Hey theah! Wheahd you come from?"

"Move ovah theah, lady. I want to tawk to you."

Gant looked and saw. His thin mouth was tickled by a faint sly smile. He wet his big thumb quickly.

While his fugitive eyes roved over the east end of the square, Gant talked with Jannadeau. Before the shop the comely matrons of the town came up from the market. From time to time they smiled, seeing him, and he bowed sweepingly. Such lovely manners!

"The king of England," he observed, "is only a figurehead. He doesn't begin to have the power of the President of the United States."

"His power is severely limited," said Jannadeau gutturally, "by custom but not by statute. In actuality he is still one of the most powerful monarchs in the world." His thick black fingers probed carefully into the viscera of a watch.

"The late King Edward, for all his faults," said Gant, wetting his thumb, "was a smart man. This fellow they've got now is a nonentity and a nincompoop." He grinned faintly, with pleasure, at this ghost of his old rhetoric, glancing furtively at the Swiss to see if the big words told.

His uneasy eyes followed carefully the stylish carriage of Queen Elizabeth's well-clad figure as she came down by the shop again. She smiled pleasantly, bound homeward for her latticed terrace. He bowed elaborately.

"Good evening, madam," he said.

She disappeared. In a moment she came back decisively and mounted the broad steps. He watched her approach with quickened pulses. Twelve years.

"How's the madam?" he said gallantly as she crossed the porch. "Elizabeth, I was just telling Jannadeau you were the most stylish woman in town."

"Well, that's mighty sweet of you, Mr. Gant," she said in her cool, poised voice. "You've got a good word for every one."

She gave a bright, pleasant nod to Jannadeau, who swung his huge scowling head ponderously around and muttered at her.

"Why, Elizabeth," said Gant, "you haven't changed an inch in fifteen years. I don't believe you're a day older."

She was thirty-eight and cheerfully aware of it.

"Oh, yes," she said laughing. "You're only saying that to make me feel good. I'm no chicken any more."

She had a pale, clear skin, pleasantly freckled, carrot-colored hair, and a thin mouth live with humor. Her figure was trim and strong—no longer young. She had a great deal of energy, distinction, and elegance in her manner.

"How are all the girls, Elizabeth?" he asked kindly.

Her face grew sad. She began to pull her gloves off.

"That's what I came in to see you about," she said. "I lost one of them last week."

"Yes," said Gant gravely, "I was sorry to hear of that."

"She was the best girl I had," said Elizabeth. "I'd have done anything in the world for her. We did everything we could," she added. "I've no regrets on that score. I had a doctor and two trained nurses by her all the time."

She opened her black leather handbag, thrust her gloves into it, and pulling out a small blue-bordered handkerchief began to weep quietly.

"Huh-huh-huh-huh-huh," said Gant, shaking his head. "Too

bad, too bad, too bad. Come back to my office," he said. They went back to the dusty little room and sat down. Elizabeth dried her eyes.

"What was her name?" he asked.

"We called her Lily—her full name was Lilian Reed."

"Why, I knew that girl," he exclaimed. "I spoke to her not over two weeks ago." He convinced himself permanently that this was true.

"Yes," said Elizabeth, "she went like that—one hemorrhage right after another. Nobody ever knew she was sick until last Wednesday. Friday she was gone." She wept again.

"T-t-t-t-t," he clucked regretfully. "Too bad, too bad. She was pretty as a picture."

"I couldn't have loved her more, Mr. Gant," said Elizabeth, "if she had been my own daughter."

"How old was she?" he asked.

"Twenty-two," said Elizabeth, beginning to weep again.

"What a pity! What a pity!" he agreed. "Did she have any people?"

"No one who would do anything for her," Elizabeth said. "Her mother died when she was thirteen—she was born out here on the Beetree Fork—and her father," she added indignantly, "is a mean old devil who's never done anything for her or any one else. He didn't even come to her funeral."

"He will be punished," said Gant darkly.

"As sure as there's a God in heaven," Elizabeth agreed, "he'll get what's coming to him in hell. The dirty old crook!" she continued virtuously, "I hope he rots!"

"You can depend upon it," he said grimly. "He will. Ah, Lord." He was silent a moment while he shook his head with slow regret.

"A pity, a pity," he muttered. "So young." He had the moment of triumph all men have when they hear some one has died. A moment, too, of grisly fear—sixty-four.

"I couldn't have loved her more," said Elizabeth, "if she'd been one of my own. A young girl like that with all her life before her."

"It's pretty sad when you come to think of it," he said. "By God, it is!"

"And she was such a fine girl, Mr. Gant," said Elizabeth, weeping softly. "She had such a bright future before her. She had more opportunities than I ever had, and I suppose you know"—she spoke modestly—"what I've done."

"Why," he exclaimed, startled, "you're a rich woman, Elizabeth —damned if I don't believe you are. You own property all over town."

"I wouldn't say that," she answered, "but I've got enough to live on without ever doing another lick of work. I've had to work hard all my life. From now on I don't intend to turn my hand over."

She looked at him with a shy, pleased smile, and touched a coil of her fine hair with a small competent hand. He looked at her attentively, noting with pleasure her firm uncorseted hips, moulded compactly into her tailored suit, and her cocked comely legs tapering to graceful feet, shod in neat little slippers of tan. She was firm, strong, washed, and elegant—a faint scent of lilac hovered over her. He looked at her candid eyes, lucently gray, and saw that she was quite a great lady.

"By God, Elizabeth," he said, "you're a fine-looking woman!"

"I've had a good life," she said. "I've taken care of myself."

They had always known each other—since first they met. They had no excuses, no questions, no replies. The world fell away from them. In the silence they heard the pulsing slap of the fountain, the high laughter of bawdry in the square. He took a book of models from the desk and began to turn its slick pages. They showed modest blocks of Georgia marble and Vermont granite.

"I don't want any of these," she said impatiently. "I've already made up my mind. I know what I want."

He looked up surprised. "What is it?"

"I want the angel out front."

His face was startled and unwilling. He gnawed the corner of his thin lip. No one knew how fond he was of the angel. Publicly he called it his white elephant. He cursed it and said he had been a fool to order it. For six years it had stood on the porch weathering in all the wind and rain. It was now brown and fly-specked. But it had come from Carrara in Italy, and it held a stone lily delicately in one hand. The other hand was lifted in benediction, it was poised clumsily upon the ball of one phthisic foot, and its stupid white face wore a smile of soft stone idiocy.

In his rages Gant sometimes directed vast climaxes of abuse at the angel. "Fiend out of hell," he roared, "you have impoverished me, you have ruined me, you have cursed my declining years, and now you will crush me to death—fearful, awful, and unnatural monster that you are."

But sometimes when he was drunk he fell weeping on his knees before it, called it Cynthia, the name of his first wife, and entreated its love, forgiveness, and blessing for its sinful but repentant boy. There was from the square laughter.

"What's the matter?" said Elizabeth. "Don't you want to sell it?"

"It will cost you a good deal, Elizabeth," he said evasively.

"I don't care," she answered positively. "I've got the money. How much do you want?"

He was silent, thinking for a moment of the place where the angel stood. He knew he had nothing to cover or obliterate that place—it left a barren crater in his heart.

"All right," he said finally. "You can have it for what I paid for it—four hundred and twenty dollars."

She took a thick sheaf of bank notes from her purse and counted the money out for him. He pushed it back.

"No. Pay me when the job's finished and it has been set up. You want some sort of inscription, don't you?"

"Yes. There's her full name, age, place of birth, and so on," she said, giving him a scrawled envelope. "I want some poetry, too—something that suits a young girl taken off like this."

He pulled his tattered little book of inscriptions from a pigeonhole and thumbed its pages, reading her a quatrain here and there. To each she shook her head. Finally he said:

"How's this one, Elizabeth?" He read:

> " 'She went away in beauty's flower,
>   Before her youth was spent,
>   Ere life and love had lived its hour
>   God called her, and she went.
>
> Yet whispers Faith upon the wind:
>   No grief to *her* was given.
>   She left *your* love and went to find
>   A greater one in heaven.' "

"Oh, that's lovely—lovely!" she said. "I want that one."

"Yes," he agreed, "I think that's the best one."

In the musty, cool smell of his little office they got up. Her gallant figure reached his shoulder. She buttoned her kid gloves over the small pink haunch of her palms and glanced about her. His battered sofa filled one wall, the line of his long body was printed in the leather. She looked up at him. His face was sad and grave. They remembered.

"It's a long time, Elizabeth," he said.

They walked slowly to the front through aisled marbles. Sentinelled just beyond the wooden doors the angel leered vacantly down. Jannadeau drew his great head turtlewise a little farther into the protective hunch of his burly shoulders. They went out into the porch.

The moon stood already like its own phantom in the clear-washed skies of evening. A little boy with an empty paper delivery-bag swung lithely by, his freckled nostrils dilating pleasantly with hunger and the fancied smell of supper. He passed, and for a moment, as they stood at the porch edge, all life seemed frozen in a picture: the firemen and Fagg Sluder had seen Gant, whispered, and were now looking toward him; a policeman, at the high side-porch of the police court, leaned on the rail and stared; at the near edge of the central plot below the fountain a farmer bent for water at a bubbling jet, rose dripping, and stared; from the tax collector's office, city hall, up-stairs, Yancy, huge, meaty, shirt-sleeved, stared.

And in that second the slow pulse of the fountain was suspended, life was held, like an arrested gesture, in photographic abeyance, and Gant felt himself alone move deathward in a world of seemings as, in 1910, a man might find himself again in a picture taken on the grounds of the Chicago Fair, when he was thirty, and his moustache black; and, noting the bustled ladies and the derbied men fixed in the second's pullulation, remember the dead instant, seek beyond the borders for what (he knew) was there. Or as a veteran who finds himself upon his elbow near Ulysses Grant, before the march, in pictures of the Civil War, and sees a dead man on a horse. Or I should say, like some completed Don, who finds himself again before a tent in Scotland in his youth, and notes a cricket-bat long lost and long forgotten; the face of a poet who had died, and young men and the tutor as they looked that Long Vacation when they read nine hours a day for greats.

Where now? Where after? Where then?

1929

JOHN STEINBECK

(1902–)

Among our modern novelists of undisputed excellence, Steinbeck is perhaps the most uneven. *East of Eden* (1952), one of the notable novels of our times, crowned the achievement of twenty years, only to be followed within two years by *Sweet Thursday* (1954), a sentimental extension of a minor work, *Cannery Row* (1945). Yet certainly the sensitive and powerful artist appears in six of his thirteen novels, and in many of his short stories, where a distinctive and lyric prose sustains good charac-ter drawing, an interesting and honest if not always an accepted view of life, and a good story—for he is always a superb story-teller. In addition, Steinbeck has been among the most effective protagonists of social justice; as a California regionalist he has exploited native folk materials in a richly primitive manner; and he is a genuine artist of folk comedy and humor.

Born of Irish and German stock, on February 27, 1902, at Salinas, California, Steinbeck grew up with a boy's wide-eyed knowledge of the coast and of "the Long Valley" and hill country around Monterey Harbor—the country of Jody in *The Red Pony*, often the scene of his novels. He supported himself by hard work from boyhood, but was graduated from high school. In 1919 he entered Stanford University, but the necessity for continuous self-support kept him from following the regular curriculum. Meanwhile, he had begun to write. In 1925 he worked his way to New York on a cattle boat in order to storm the literary market. Failing in this, and after some experience as a newspaper reporter, he went back to California. While working on his earliest novels he found various employments—as fruit picker, surveyor, chemical-laboratory assistant, and caretaker for a large estate on Lake Tahoe. He later returned to journalism, serving as a war correspondent in Italy during World War II, and afterward, motivated by his social interests, visiting Russia as a correspondent.

Steinbeck's first three novels won him little recognition, although the third, *To a God Unknown* (1933) is now of interest for its experimental character and its utilization of nature myth in fiction. *Tortilla Flat* (1935), a popular success, gave to literature such unforgettable characters as Pilon and Danny among the *paisanos*, the humbler descendants of early Spanish and Spanish-Indian inhabitants. They appear so naturalistically amoral that their promiscuity and wine-bouts seem but innocent animal gaiety, and their ability to survive in irresponsible indolence arouses at least momentary envy. It is folk comedy of a high order. *In Dubious Battle* (1936), a good novel of protest, depicts the development of a strike among the exploited migratory fruit pickers, and the methods by which the strike is broken in a welter of violence. *Of Mice and Men* (1937), vastly successful as book and as drama on the stage, is a vigorous story of friendship between two migratory workers—a tragic tale, appealing but oversentimentalized.

Of *The Grapes of Wrath* (1939), it has been well said that this work reached as large a proportion of the people as *Uncle Tom's Cabin*, and rivaled that antislavery novel in its influence. It follows the Joad family, victims of the disastrous Oklahoma "dust bowl" erosion which turned the subsistence farmers to vagrants, on an epic journey to California, where they become involved in the violence of a strike among the fruit pickers. The interest is not alone in the social problem, but quite as much in the daily heroism of common people, among them such well-depicted characters as Ma Joad and Tom.

Cannery Row (1945), and a sequel, *Sweet Thursday* (1954), both primitivist studies of some interest, fall noticeably short of *Tortilla Flat*. The locale, like that of *Tortilla Flat*, is Monterey Harbor, but Steinbeck's concern is with the waterfront waifs in general, not the *paisano* settlement. Here, as too often, he offers characters without perspective, and in an excess of sentimentality obscures moral values. The residents of Cannery Row are described (in terms which could not be applied to the leading characters of *Tortilla Flat*) as "whores, pimps, and gamblers" who are also "saints and angels and martyrs and holy men." In contrast, another of his "primitive" volumes is *The Pearl* (1947), a Mexican folk tale, perpetuating a medieval allegory of passionate religious devotion, in a prose style of great purity and beauty. *East of Eden* is Steinbeck's most ambitious treatment of the Salinas country. Based in part on the history of his own family, it provides the perspective of social history in that locality through three generations. Such a character as

Adam Trask compensates for several who are not wholly convincing. With *The Grapes of Wrath*, *The Red Pony* (1937), and *The Long Valley* (1938), it substantiates Steinbeck's claim to highest consideration.

Novels and short stories not mentioned above include *Cup of Gold*, 1929; *The Pastures of Heaven*, 1932; *Nothing So Monstrous*, 1936; *Saint Katy the Virgin*, 1936; *The Moon Is Down*, 1942; *The Wayward Bus*, 1947; *Burning Bright*, 1950; and *The Short Reign of Pippin IV*, 1957. Topical volumes are *Their Blood Is Strong*, 1938; *The Sea of Cortez*, 1941 (narrative section reissued as *The Log from the Sea of Cortez*, 1951); *The Forgotten Village*, 1941; *Bombs Away*, 1942; *A Russian Journal* (with R. Capa), 1948; and *Once There Was a War*, 1958.

For biography and criticism see H. T. Moore, *The Novels of John Steinbeck*, 1939; E. W. Tedlock and C. V. Wicker, *Steinbeck and His Critics*, 1957; and P. Lisca, *The Wide World of John Steinbeck*, 1958.

Various aspects of death

The Red Pony[1]

I. *The Gift*

At daybreak Billy Buck emerged from the bunkhouse and stood for a moment on the porch looking up at the sky. He was a broad, bandy-legged little man with a walrus mustache, with square hands, puffed and muscled on the palms. His eyes were a contemplative, watery grey and the hair which protruded from under his Stetson hat was spiky and weathered. Billy was still stuffing his shirt into his blue jeans as he stood on the porch. He unbuckled his belt and tightened it again. The belt showed, by the worn shiny places opposite each hole, the gradual increase of Billy's middle over a period of years. When he had seen to the weather, Billy cleared each nostril by holding its mate closed with his forefinger and blowing fiercely. Then he walked down to the barn, rubbing his

1. *The Red Pony* was first published, as a novelette, in 1937. This is the text here reprinted. In 1938, with a fourth section, "Leader of the People," but otherwise unchanged, it was published as one of the tales in *The Long Valley*. It again had separate publication as a novelette in 1945. The fourth section, not present in the first edition, is not an intrinsic part of the story, but a sort

of commentary upon it, resulting from the visit of Jody's grandfather, an old pioneer and frontiersman. His endless tales of the Indian wars and the conquest of the continent bore Jody's father, but the boy understands them. "It was a job for men," says the old man, sadly, "but only little boys like to hear about it."

hands together. He curried and brushed two saddle horses in the stalls, talking quietly to them all the time; and he had hardly finished when the iron triangle started ringing at the ranch house. Billy stuck the brush and currycomb together and laid them on the rail, and went up to breakfast. His action had been so deliberate and yet so wasteless of time that he came to the house while Mrs. Tiflin was still ringing the triangle. She nodded her grey head to him and withdrew into the kitchen. Billy Buck sat down on the steps, because he was a cow-hand, and it wouldn't be fitting that he should go first into the dining-room. He heard Mr. Tiflin in the house, stamping his feet into his boots.

The high jangling note of the triangle put the boy Jody in motion. He was only a little boy, ten years old, with hair like dusty yellow grass and with shy polite grey eyes, and with a mouth that worked when he thought. The triangle picked him up out of sleep. It didn't occur to him to disobey the harsh note. He never had: no one he knew ever had. He brushed the tangled hair out of his eyes and skinned his nightgown off. In a moment he was dressed—blue chambray shirt and overalls. It was late in the summer, so of course there were no shoes to bother with. In the kitchen he waited until his mother got from in front of the sink and went back to the stove. Then he washed himself and brushed back his wet hair with his fingers. His mother turned sharply on him as he left the sink. Jody looked shyly away.

"I've got to cut your hair before long," his mother said. "Breakfast's on the table. Go on in, so Billy can come."

Jody sat at the long table which was covered with white oilcloth washed through to the fabric in some places. The fried eggs lay in rows on their platter. Jody took three eggs on his plate and followed with three thick slices of crisp bacon. He carefully scraped a spot of blood from one of the egg yolks.

Billy Buck clumped in. "That won't hurt you," Billy explained. "That's only a sign the rooster leaves."

Jody's tall stern father came in then and Jody knew from the noise on the floor that he was wearing boots, but he looked under the table anyway, to make sure. His father turned off the oil lamp over the table, for plenty of morning light now came through the windows.

Jody did not ask where his father and Billy Buck were riding that day, but he wished he might go along. His father was a disciplinarian. Jody obeyed him in everything without questions of any kind. Now, Carl Tiflin sat down and reached for the egg platter.

"Got the cows ready to go, Billy?" he asked.

"In the lower corral," Billy said. "I could just as well take them in alone."

"Sure you could. But a man needs company. Besides your throat gets pretty dry." Carl Tiflin was jovial this morning.

Jody's mother put her head in the door. "What time do you think to be back, Carl?"

"I can't tell. I've got to see some men in Salinas. Might be gone till dark."

The eggs and coffee and big biscuits disappeared rapidly. Jody followed the two men out of the house. He watched them mount their horses and drive six old milk cows out of the corral and start over the hill toward Salinas. They were going to sell the old cows to the butcher.

When they had disappeared over the crown of the ridge Jody walked up the hill in back of the house. The dogs trotted around the house corner hunching their shoulders and grinning horribly with pleasure. Jody patted their heads—Doubletree Mutt with the big thick tail and yellow eyes, and Smasher, the shepherd, who had killed a coyote and lost an ear in doing it. Smasher's one good ear stood up higher than a collie's ear should. Billy Buck said that always happened. After the frenzied greeting the dogs lowered their noses to the ground in a businesslike way and went ahead, looking back now and then to make sure that the boy was coming. They walked up through the chicken yard and saw the quail eating with the chickens. Smasher chased the chickens a little to keep in practice in case there should ever be sheep to herd. Jody continued on through the large vegetable patch where the green corn was higher than his head. The cow-pumpkins were green and small yet. He went on to the sagebrush line where the cold spring ran out of its pipe and fell into a round wooden tub. He leaned over and drank close to the green mossy wood where the water tasted best. Then he turned and looked back on the ranch, on the low, whitewashed house girded with red geraniums, and on the long bunkhouse by the cypress tree where Billy Buck lived alone. Jody could see the great black kettle under the cypress tree. That was where the pigs were scalded. The sun was coming over the ridge now, glaring on the whitewash of the houses and barns, making the wet grass blaze softly. Behind him, in the tall sagebrush, the birds were scampering on the ground, making a great noise among the dry leaves; the squirrels piped shrilly on the side-hills. Jody looked along at the farm buildings. He felt an uncertainty in the air, a feeling of change and of loss and of the gain of new and unfamiliar things. Over the hillside two big black buzzards sailed low to the ground and their shadows slipped smoothly and quickly ahead of them. Some animal had died in the vicinity. Jody knew it. It might be a cow or it might be the remains of a rabbit. The buzzards overlooked nothing. Jody hated them as all decent things hate them, but they could not be hurt because they made away with carrion.

After a while the boy sauntered down the hill again. The dogs had long ago given him up and gone into the brush to do things in their own way. Back through the vegetable garden he went, and he paused for a moment to smash a green muskmelon with his heel, but he was not happy about it. It was a bad thing to do, he knew perfectly well. He kicked dirt over the ruined melon to conceal it.

Back at the house his mother bent over his rough hands, inspecting his fingers and nails. It did little good to start him clean to school for too many things could happen on the way. She sighed over the black cracks on his fingers, and then gave him his books and his lunch and started him on the mile walk to school. She noticed that his mouth was working a good deal this morning.

Jody started his journey. He filled his pockets with little pieces of white quartz that lay in the road, and every so often he took a shot at a bird or at some rabbit that had stayed sunning itself in the road too long. At the crossroads over the bridge he met two friends and the three of them walked to school together, making ridiculous strides and being rather silly. School had just opened two weeks before. There was still a spirit of revolt among the pupils.

It was four o'clock in the afternoon when Jody topped the hill and looked down on the ranch again. He looked for the saddle horses, but the corral was empty. His father was not back yet. He went slowly, then, toward the afternoon chores. At the ranch house, he found his mother sitting on the porch, mending socks.

"There's two doughnuts in the kitchen for you," she said. Jody slid to the kitchen, and returned with half of one of the doughnuts already eaten and his mouth full. His mother asked him what he had learned in school that day, but she didn't listen to his doughnut-muffled answer. She interrupted, "Jody, tonight see you fill the wood-box clear full. Last night you crossed the sticks and it wasn't only about half full. Lay the sticks flat tonight. And Jody, some of the hens are hiding eggs, or else the dogs are eating them. Look about in the grass and see if you can find any nests."

Jody, still eating, went out and did his chores. He saw the quail come down to eat with the chickens when he threw out the grain. For some reason his father was proud to have them come. He never allowed any shooting near the house for fear the quail might go away.

When the wood-box was full, Jody took his twenty-two rifle up to the cold spring at the brush line. He drank again and then aimed the gun at all manner of things, at rocks, at birds on the wing, at the big black pig kettle under the cypress tree, but he didn't shoot for he had no cartridges and wouldn't have until he was twelve. If his father had seen him aim the rifle in the direction of the house he would have put the cartridges off another year. Jody remembered this and did not point the rifle down the hill again. Two years was enough to wait for cartridges. Nearly all of his father's presents were given with reservations which hampered their value somewhat. It was good discipline.

The supper waited until dark for his father to return. When at last he came in with Billy Buck, Jody could smell the delicious brandy on their breaths. Inwardly he rejoiced, for his father sometimes talked to him when he smelled of brandy, sometimes even told things he had done in the wild days when he was a boy.

After supper, Jody sat by the fireplace and his shy polite eyes sought the room corners, and he waited for his father to tell what it was he contained, for Jody knew he had news of some sort. But he was disappointed. His father pointed a stern finger at him.

"You'd better go to bed, Jody. I'm going to need you in the morning."

That wasn't so bad. Jody liked to do the things he had to do as long as they weren't routine things. He looked at the floor and his mouth worked out a question before he spoke it. "What are we going to do in the morning, kill a pig?" he asked softly.

"Never you mind. You better get to bed."

When the door was closed behind him, Jody heard his father and Billy Buck chuckling and he knew it was a joke of some kind. And later, when he lay in bed, trying to make words out of murmurs in the other room, he heard his father protest, "But, Ruth, I didn't give much for him."

Jody heard the hoot-owls hunting mice down by the barn, and he heard a fruit tree limb tap-tapping against the house. A cow was lowing when he went to sleep.

When the triangle sounded in the morning, Jody dressed more quickly even than usual. In the kitchen, while he washed his face and combed back his hair, his mother addressed him irritably. "Don't you go out until you get a good breakfast in you."

He went into the dining-room and sat at the long white table. He took a steaming hotcake from the platter, arranged two fried eggs on it, covered them with another hotcake and squashed the whole thing with his fork.

His father and Billy Buck came in. Jody knew from the sound of the floor that both of them were wearing flatheeled shoes, but he peered under the table to make sure. His father turned off the oil lamp, for the day had arrived, and he looked stern and disciplinary, but Billy Buck didn't look at Jody at all. He avoided the shy questioning eyes of the boy and soaked a whole piece of toast in his coffee.

Carl Tiflin said crossly, "You come with us after breakfast!"

Jody had trouble with his food then, for he felt a kind of doom in the air. After Billy had tilted his saucer and drained the coffee which had slopped into it, and had wiped his hands on his jeans, the two men stood up from the table and went out into the morning light together, and Jody respectfully followed a little behind them. He tried to keep his mind from running ahead, tried to keep it absolutely motionless.

His mother called, "Carl! Don't you let it keep him from school."

They marched past the cypress, where a singletree hung from a limb to butcher the pigs on, and past the black iron kettle, so it was not a pig killing. The sun shone over the hill and threw long, dark shadows of the trees and buildings. They crossed a stubble-field to shortcut to the barn. Jody's father unhooked the door and they went in. They had been walking toward the sun on the way down. The barn was black as night in contrast and warm from the hay and from the beasts. Jody's father moved over toward the one box stall. "Come here!" he ordered. Jody could begin to see things now. He looked into the box stall and then stepped back quickly.

A red pony colt was looking at him out of the stall. Its tense ears were forward and a light of disobedience was in its eyes. Its coat was rough and thick as an airedale's fur and its mane was long and tangled. Jody's throat collapsed in on itself and cut his breath short.

"He needs a good currying," his father said, "and if I ever hear of you not feeding him or leaving his stall dirty, I'll sell him off in a minute."

Jody couldn't bear to look at the pony's eyes any more. He gazed down at his hands for a moment, and he asked very shyly, "Mine?" No one answered him. He put his hand out toward the pony. Its grey nose came close, sniffing loudly, and then the lips drew back and the strong teeth closed on Jody's fingers. The pony shook its head up and down and seemed to laugh with amusement. Jody regarded his bruised fingers. "Well," he said with pride— "Well, I guess he can bite all right." The two men laughed, somewhat in relief. Carl Tiflin went out of the barn and walked up a side-hill to be by himself, for he was embarrassed, but Billy Buck stayed. It was easier to talk to Billy Buck. Jody asked again—"Mine?"

Billy became professional in tone. "Sure! That is, if you look out for him and break him right. I'll show you how. He's just a colt. You can't ride him for some time."

Jody put out his bruised hand again, and this time the red pony let his nose be rubbed. "I ought to have a carrot," Jody said. "Where'd we get him, Billy?"

"Bought him at a sheriff's auction," Billy explained. "A show went broke in Salinas and had debts. The sheriff was selling off their stuff."

The pony stretched out his nose and shook the forelock from his wild eyes. Jody stroked the nose a little. He said softly, "There isn't a—saddle?"

Billy Buck laughed. "I'd forgot. Come along."

In the harness room he lifted down a little saddle of red morocco leather. "It's just a show saddle," Billy Buck said disparagingly. "It isn't practical for the brush, but it was cheap at the sale."

Jody couldn't trust himself to look at the saddle either, and he couldn't speak at all. He brushed the shining red leather with his fingertips, and after a long time he said, "It'll look pretty on him though." He thought of the grandest and prettiest things he knew. "If he hasn't a name already, I think I'll call him Gabilan Mountains," he said.

Billy Buck knew how he felt. "It's a pretty long name. Why don't you just call him Gabilan? That means hawk. That would be a fine name for him." Billy felt glad. "If you will collect tail hair, I might be able to make a hair rope for you sometime. You could use it for a hackamore."[2]

Jody wanted to go back to the box stall. "Could I lead him to school, do you think—to show the kids?"

But Billy shook his head. "He's not even halter-broke yet. We had a time getting him here. Had to almost drag him. You better be starting for school though."

"I'll bring the kids to see him here this afternoon," Jody said.

Six boys came over the hill half an hour early that afternoon, running hard, their heads down, their forearms working, their breath whistling. They swept by the house and cut across the stubble-field to the barn. And then they stood self-consciously before the pony, and then they looked at Jody with eyes in which there was a new admiration and a new respect. Before today Jody had been a boy, dressed in overalls and a blue shirt—quieter than most, even suspected of being a little cowardly. And now he was different. Out of a thousand centuries they drew the ancient admiration of the footman for the horseman. They knew instinctively that a man on a horse is spiritually as well as physically bigger than a man on foot. They knew that Jody had been miraculously lifted out of equality with them, and had been placed over them. Gabilan put his head out of the stall and sniffed them.

"Why'nt you ride him?" the boys cried. "Why'nt you braid his tail with ribbons like in the fair?" "When you going to ride him?"

Jody's courage was up. He too felt the superiority of the horseman. "He's not old enough. Nobody can ride him for a long time.

2. A halter used for the training of horses.

I'm going to train him on the long halter. Billy Buck is going to show me how."

"Well, can't we even lead him around a little?"

"He isn't even halter broke," Jody said. He wanted to be completely alone when he took the pony out the first time. "Come and see the saddle."

They were speechless at the red morocco saddle, completely shocked out of comment. "It isn't much use in the brush," Jody explained. "It'll look pretty on him though. Maybe I'll ride bareback when I go into the brush."

"How you going to rope a cow without a saddle horn?"

"Maybe I'll get another saddle for every day. My father might want me to help him with the stock." He let them feel the red saddle, and showed them the brass chain throat-latch on the bridle and the big brass buttons at each temple where the headstall and brow band crossed. The whole thing was too wonderful. They had to go away after a little while, and each boy, in his mind, searched among his possessions for a bribe worthy of offering in return for a ride on the red pony when the time should come.

Jody was glad when they had gone. He took brush and currycomb from the wall, took down the barrier of the box stall and stepped cautiously in. The pony's eyes glittered, and he edged around into kicking position. But Jody touched him on the shoulder and rubbed his high arched neck as he had always seen Billy Buck do, and he crooned, "So-o-o Boy," in a deep voice. The pony gradually relaxed his tenseness. Jody curried and brushed until a pile of dead hair lay in the stall and until the pony's coat had taken on a deep red shine. Each time he finished he thought it might have been done better. He braided the mane into a dozen little pigtails, and he braided the forelock, and then he undid them and brushed the hair out straight again.

Jody did not hear his mother enter the barn. She was angry when she came, but when she looked in at the pony and at Jody working over him, she felt a curious pride rise up in her. "Have you forgot the wood-box?" she asked gently. "It's not far off from dark and there's not a stick of wood in the house, and the chickens aren't fed."

Jody quickly put up his tools. "I forgot, ma'am."

"Well, after this do your chores first. Then you won't forget. I expect you'll forget lots of things now if I don't keep an eye on you."

"Can I have carrots from the garden for him, ma'am?"

She had to think about that. "Oh—I guess so, if you only take the big tough ones."

"Carrots keep the coat good," he said, and again she felt the curious rush of pride.

Jody never waited for the triangle to get him out of bed after the coming of the pony. It became his habit to creep out of bed even before his mother was awake, to slip into his clothes and to go quietly down to the barn to see Gabilan. In the grey quiet mornings when the land and the brush and the houses and the trees were silver-grey and black like a photograph negative, he stole toward the barn, past the sleeping stones and the sleeping cypress tree. The turkeys, roosting in the tree out of coyotes' reach, clicked drowsily. The fields glowed with a grey frost-like light and in the dew the tracks of rabbits and of field mice stood out sharply. The good dogs came stiffly out of their little houses, hackles up and deep growls in their throats. Then they caught Jody's scent, and their stiff tails rose up and waved a greeting—Doubletree Mutt with the big thick tail, and Smasher, the incipient shepherd—then went lazily back to their warm beds.

It was a strange time and a mysterious journey, to Jody—an extension of a dream. When he first had the pony he liked to torture himself during the trip by thinking Gabilan would not be in his stall, and worse, would never have been there. And he had other delicious little self-induced pains. He thought how the rats had gnawed ragged holes in the red saddle, and how the mice had nibbled Gabilan's tail until it was stringy and thin. He usually ran the last little way to the barn. He unlatched the rusty hasp of the barn door and stepped in, and no matter how quietly he opened the door, Gabilan was always looking at him over the barrier of the box stall and Gabilan whinnied softly and stamped his front foot, and his eyes had big sparks of red fire in them like oakwood embers.

Sometimes, if the work horses were to be used that day, Jody found Billy Buck in the barn harnessing and currying. Billy stood with him and looked long at Gabilan and he told Jody a great many things about horses. He explained that they were terribly afraid for their feet, so that one must make a practice of lifting the legs and patting the hooves and ankles to remove their terror. He told Jody how horses love conversation. He must talk to the pony all the time, and tell him the reasons for everything. Billy wasn't sure a horse could understand everything that was said to him, but it was impossible to say how much was understood. A horse never kicked up a fuss if some one he liked explained things to him. Billy could give examples, too. He had known, for instance, a horse nearly dead beat with fatigue to perk up when told it was only a little farther to his destination. And he had known a horse paralyzed with fright to come out of it when his rider told him what it was that was frightening him. While he talked in the mornings, Billy Buck cut twenty or thirty straws into neat three-inch lengths and stuck them into his hatband. Then during the whole day, if he wanted to pick his teeth or merely to chew on something, he had only to reach up for one of them.

Jody listened carefully, for he knew and the whole country knew that Billy Buck was a fine hand with horses. Billy's own horse was a stringy cayuse[3] with a hammer head, but he nearly always won the first prizes at the stock trials. Billy could rope a steer, take a double half-hitch about the horn with his riata, and dismount, and his horse would play the steer as an angler plays a fish, keeping a tight rope until the steer was down or beaten.

Every morning, after Jody had curried and brushed the pony, he let down the barrier of the stall, and Gabilan thrust past him and raced down the barn and into the corral. Around and around he galloped, and sometimes he jumped forward and landed on stiff legs. He stood quivering, stiff ears forward, eyes rolling so that the whites showed, pretending to be frightened. At last he walked snorting to the water-trough and buried his nose in the water up to the nostrils. Jody was proud then, for he knew that was the way to judge a horse. Poor horses only touched their lips to the water, but a fine spirited beast put his whole nose and mouth under, and only left room to breathe.

Then Jody stood and watched the pony, and he saw things he had never noticed about any other horse, the sleek, sliding flank muscles and the cords of the buttocks, which flexed like a closing fist, and the shine the sun put on the red coat. Having seen horses all his life, Jody had never looked at them very closely before. But now he noticed the moving ears which gave expression and even inflection of expression to the face. The pony talked with his ears. You could tell exactly how he felt about everything by the way his ears pointed. Sometimes they were stiff and upright and sometimes lax and sagging. They went back when he was angry or fearful, and forward when he was anxious and curious and pleased; and their exact position indicated which emotion he had.

Billy Buck kept his word. In the early fall the training began. First there was the halter-breaking, and that was the hardest because it was the first thing. Jody held a carrot and coaxed and promised and pulled on the rope. The pony set his feet like a burro when he felt the strain. But before long he learned. Jody walked all over the ranch leading him. Gradually he took to dropping the rope until the pony followed him unled wherever he went.

3. A Spanish-Indian horse of the western ranches. It is small, but extremely hardy.

And then came the training on the long halter. That was slower work. Jody stood in the middle of a circle, holding the long halter. He clucked with his tongue and the pony started to walk in a big circle, held in by the long rope. He clucked again to make the pony trot, and again to make him gallop. Around and around Gabilan went thundering and enjoying it immensely. Then he called, "Whoa," and the pony stopped. It was not long until Gabilan was perfect at it. But in many ways he was a bad pony. He bit Jody in the pants and stomped on Jody's feet. Now and then his ears went back and he aimed a tremendous kick at the boy. Every time he did one of these bad things, Gabilan settled back and seemed to laugh to himself.

Billy Buck worked at the hair rope in the evenings before the fireplace. Jody collected tail hair in a bag, and he sat and watched Billy slowly constructing the rope, twisting a few hairs to make a string and rolling two strings together for a cord, and then braiding a number of cords to make the rope. Billy rolled the finished rope on the floor under his foot to make it round and hard.

The long halter work rapidly approached perfection. Jody's father, watching the pony stop and start and trot and gallop, was a little bothered by it.

"He's getting to be almost a trick pony," he complained. "I don't like trick horses. It takes all the—dignity out of a horse to make him do tricks. Why, a trick horse is kind of like an actor—no dignity, no character of his own." And his father said, "I guess you better be getting him used to the saddle pretty soon."

Jody rushed for the harness-room. For some time he had been riding the saddle on a sawhorse. He changed the stirrup length over and over, and could never get it just right. Sometimes, mounted on the sawhorse in the harness-room, with collars and hames and tugs hung all about him, Jody rode out beyond the room. He carried his rifle across the pommel. He saw the fields go flying by, and he heard the beat of the galloping hoofs.

It was a ticklish job, saddling the pony the first time. Gabilan hunched and reared and threw the saddle off before the cinch could be tightened. It had to be replaced again and again until at last the pony let it stay. And the cinching was difficult, too. Day by day Jody tightened the girth a little more until at last the pony didn't mind the saddle at all.

Then there was the bridle. Billy explained how to use a stick of licorice for a bit until Gabilan was used to having something in his mouth. Billy explained, "Of course we could force-break him to everything, but he wouldn't be as good a horse if we did. He'd always be a little bit afraid, and he wouldn't mind because he wanted to."

The first time the pony wore the bridle he whipped his head about and worked his tongue against the bit until the blood oozed from the corners of his mouth. He tried to rub the headstall off on the manger. His ears pivoted about and his eyes turned red with fear and with general rambunctiousness. Jody rejoiced, for he knew that only a mean-souled horse does not resent training.

And Jody trembled when he thought of the time when he would first sit in the saddle. The pony would probably throw him off. There was no disgrace in that. The disgrace would come if he did not get right up and mount again. Sometimes he dreamed that he lay in the dirt and cried and couldn't make himself mount again. The shame of the dream lasted until the middle of the day.

Gabilan was growing fast. Already he had lost the long-leggedness of the colt; his mane was getting longer and blacker. Under the constant currying and brushing his coat lay as smooth and gleaming as orange-red lacquer. Jody oiled the hoofs and kept them carefully trimmed so they would not crack.

The hair rope was nearly finished. Jody's father gave him an old pair of spurs and bent in the side bars and cut down the strap and took up the chainlets until they fitted. And then one day Carl Tiflin said:

"The pony's growing faster than I thought. I guess you can ride him by Thanksgiving. Think you can stick on?"

"I don't know," Jody said shyly. Thanksgiving was only three weeks off. He hoped it wouldn't rain, for rain would spot the red saddle.

Gabilan knew and liked Jody by now. He nickered when Jody came across the stubble-field, and in the pasture he came running when his master whistled for him. There was always a carrot for him every time.

Billy Buck gave him riding instructions over and over. "Now when you get up there, just grab tight with your knees and keep your hands away from the saddle, and if you get throwed, don't let that stop you. No matter how good a man is, there's always some horse can pitch him. You just climb up again before he gets to feeling smart about it. Pretty soon, he won't throw you no more, and pretty soon he *can't* throw you no more. That's the way to do it."

"I hope it don't rain before," Jody said.

"Why not? Don't want to get throwed in the mud?"

That was partly it, and also he was afraid that in the flurry of bucking Gabilan might slip and fall on him and break his leg or his hip. He had seen that happen to men before, had seen how they writhed on the ground like squashed bugs, and he was afraid of it.

He practiced on the sawhorse how he would hold the reins in his left hand and a hat in his right hand. If he kept his hands thus busy, he couldn't grab the horn if he felt himself going off. He didn't like to think of what would happen if he did grab the horn. Perhaps his father and Billy Buck would never speak to him again, they would be so ashamed. The news would get about and his mother would be ashamed too. And in the school yard—it was too awful to contemplate.

He began putting his weight in a stirrup when Gabilan was saddled, but he didn't throw his leg over the pony's back. That was forbidden until Thanksgiving.

Every afternoon he put the red saddle on the pony and cinched it tight. The pony was learning already to fill his stomach out unnaturally large while the cinching was going on, and then to let it down when the straps were fixed. Sometimes Jody led him up to the brush line and let him drink from the round green tub, and sometimes he led him up through the stubble-field to the hilltop from which it was possible to see the white town of Salinas and the geometric fields of the great valley, and the oak trees clipped by the sheep. Now and then they broke through the brush and came to little cleared circles so hedged in that the world was gone and only the sky and the circle of brush were left from the old life. Gabilan liked these trips and showed it by keeping his head very high and by quivering his nostrils with interest. When the two came back from an expedition they smelled of the sweet sage they had forced through.

Time dragged on toward Thanksgiving, but winter came fast. The clouds swept down and hung all day over the land and brushed the hilltops, and the winds blew shrilly at night. All day the dry oak leaves drifted down from the trees until they covered the ground, and yet the trees were unchanged.

Jody had wished it might not rain before Thanksgiving, but it did. The brown earth turned dark and the trees glistened. The cut ends of the stubble turned black with mildew; the haystacks greyed from exposure to the damp, and on the roofs the moss, which had been all summer as grey as lizards, turned a brilliant yellow-green. During the week of rain, Jody kept the pony in the box stall out of the dampness, except for a little time after school when he took him out for exercise and to drink at the water-trough in the upper corral. Not once did Gabilan get wet.

The wet weather continued until little new grass appeared. Jody walked to school dressed in a slicker and short rubber boots. At length one morning the sun came out brightly. Jody, at his work in the box stall, said to Billy Buck, "Maybe I'll leave Gabilan in the corral when I go to school today."

"Be good for him to be out in the sun," Billy assured him. "No animal likes to be cooped up too long. Your father and me are going back on the hill to clean the leaves out of the spring." Billy nodded and picked his teeth with one of his little straws.

"If the rain comes, though——" Jody suggested.

"Not likely to rain today. She's rained herself out." Billy pulled up his sleeves and snapped his arm bands. "If it comes on to rain—— why a little rain don't hurt a horse."

"Well, if it does come on to rain, you put him in, will you, Billy? I'm scared he might get cold so I couldn't ride him when the time comes."

"Oh sure! I'll watch out for him if we get back in time. But it won't rain today."

And so Jody, when he went to school left Gabilan standing out in the corral.

Billy Buck wasn't wrong about many things. He couldn't be. But he was wrong about the weather that day, for a little after noon the clouds pushed over the hills and the rain began to pour down. Jody heard it start on the schoolhouse roof. He considered holding up one finger for permission to go to the outhouse and, once outside, running for home to put the pony in. Punishment would be prompt both at school and at home. He gave it up and took ease from Billy's assurance that rain couldn't hurt a horse. When school was finally out, he hurried home through the dark rain. The banks at the sides of the road spouted little jets of muddy water. The rain slanted and swirled under a cold and gusty wind. Jody dog-trotted home, slopping through the gravelly mud of the road.

From the top of the ridge he could see Gabilan standing miserably in the corral. The red coat was almost black, and streaked with water. He stood head down with his rump to the rain and wind. Jody arrived running and threw open the barn door and led the wet pony in by his forelock. Then he found a gunny sack and rubbed the soaked hair and rubbed the legs and ankles. Gabilan stood patiently, but he trembled in gusts like the wind.

When he had dried the pony as well as he could, Jody went up to the house and brought hot water down to the barn and soaked the grain in it. Gabilan was not very hungry. He nibbled at the hot mash, but he was not very much interested in it, and he still shivered now and then. A little steam rose from his damp back.

It was almost dark when Billy Buck and Carl Tiflin came home. "When the rain started we put up at Ben Herche's place, and the rain never let up all afternoon," Carl Tiflin explained. Jody looked reproachfully at Billy Buck and Billy felt guilty.

"You said it wouldn't rain," Jody accused him.

Billy looked away. "It's hard to tell, this time of year," he said, but his excuse was lame. He had no right to be fallible, and he knew it.

"The pony got wet, got soaked through."

"Did you dry him off?"

"I rubbed him with a sack and I gave him hot grain."

Billy nodded in agreement.

"Do you think he'll take cold, Billy?"

"A little rain never hurt anything," Billy assured him.

Jody's father joined the conversation then and lectured the boy a little. "A horse," he said, "isn't any lap-dog kind of thing." Carl Tiflin hated weakness and sickness, and he held a violent contempt for helplessness.

Jody's mother put a platter of steaks on the table and boiled potatoes and boiled squash, which clouded the room with their steam. They sat down to eat. Carl Tiflin still grumbled about weakness put into animals and men by too much coddling.

Billy Buck felt bad about his mistake. "Did you blanket him?" he asked.

"No. I couldn't find any blanket. I laid some sacks over his back."

"We'll go down and cover him up after we eat, then." Billy felt better about it then. When Jody's father had gone in to the fire and his mother was washing dishes, Billy found and lighted a lantern. He and Jody walked through the mud to the barn. The barn was dark and warm and sweet. The horses still munched their evening hay. "You hold the lantern!" Billy ordered. And he felt the pony's legs and tested the heat of the flanks. He put his cheek against the pony's grey muzzle and then he rolled up the eyelids to look at the eyeballs and he lifted the lips to see the gums, and he put his fingers inside the ears. "He don't seem so chipper," Billy said. "I'll give him a rub-down."

Then Billy found a sack and rubbed the pony's legs violently and he rubbed the chest and the withers. Gabilan was strangely spiritless. He submitted patiently to the rubbing. At last Billy brought an old cotton comforter from the saddle-room, and threw it over the pony's back and tied it at neck and chest with string.

"Now he'll be all right in the morning," Billy said.

Jody's mother looked up when he got back to the house. "You're late up from bed," she said. She held his chin in her hard hand and brushed the tangled hair out of his eyes and she said, "Don't worry about the pony. He'll be all right. Billy's as good as any horse doctor in the country."

Jody hadn't known she could see his worry. He pulled gently away from her and knelt down in front of the fireplace until it burned his stomach. He scorched himself through and then went in to bed, but it was a hard thing to go to sleep. He awakened after what seemed a long time. The room was dark but there was a greyness in the window like that which precedes the dawn. He got up and found his overalls and searched for the legs, and then the clock in the other room struck two. He laid his clothes down and got back into bed. It was broad daylight when he awakened again. For the first time he had slept through the ringing of the triangle. He leaped up, flung on his clothes and went out of the door still buttoning his shirt. His mother looked after him for a moment and then went quietly back to her work. Her eyes were brooding and kind. Now and then her mouth smiled a little but without changing her eyes at all.

Jody ran on toward the barn. Halfway there he heard the sound he dreaded, the hollow rasping cough of a horse. He broke into a sprint then. In the barn he found Billy Buck with the pony. Billy was rubbing its legs with his strong thick hands. He looked up and smiled gaily. "He just took a little cold," Billy said. "We'll have him out of it in a couple of days."

Jody looked at the pony's face. The eyes were half closed and the lids thick and dry. In the eye corners a crust of hard mucus stuck. Gabilan's ears hung loosely sideways and his head was low. Jody put out his hand, but the pony did not move close to it. He coughed again and his whole body constricted with the effort. A little stream of thin fluid ran from his nostrils.

Jody looked back at Billy Buck. "He's awful sick, Billy."

"Just a little cold, like I said," Billy insisted. "You go get some breakfast and then go back to school. I'll take care of him."

"But you might have to do something else. You might leave him."

"No, I won't. I won't leave him at all. Tomorrow's Saturday. Then you can stay with him all day." Billy had failed again, and he felt badly about it. He had to cure the pony now.

Jody walked up to the house and took his place listlessly at the table. The eggs and bacon were cold and greasy, but he didn't notice it. He ate his usual amount. He didn't even ask to stay home from school. His mother pushed his hair back when she took his plate. "Billy'll take care of the pony," she assured him.

He moped through the whole day at school. He couldn't answer any questions nor read any words. He couldn't even tell anyone the pony was sick, for that might make him sicker. And when school was finally out he started home in dread. He walked slowly and let the other boys leave him. He wished he might continue walking and never arrive at the ranch.

Billy was in the barn, as he had promised, and the pony was worse. His eyes were almost closed now, and his breath whistled shrilly past an obstruction in his nose. A film covered that part of the eyes that was visible at all. It was doubtful whether the pony could see any more. Now and then he snorted, to clear his nose, and by the action seemed to plug it tighter. Jody looked dispiritedly at the pony's coat. The hair lay rough and unkempt and seemed to have lost all of its old luster. Billy stood quietly beside the stall. Jody hated to ask, but he had to know.

"Billy, is he—is he going to get well?"

Billy put his fingers between the bars under the pony's jaw and felt about. "Feel here," he said and he guided Jody's fingers to a large lump under the jaw. "When that gets bigger. I'll open it up and then he'll get better."

Jody looked quickly away, for he had heard about that lump. "What is it the matter with him?"

Billy didn't want to answer, but he had to. He couldn't be wrong three times. "Strangles," he said shortly, "but don't you worry about that. I'll pull him out of it. I've seen them get well when they were worse than Gabilan is. I'm going to steam him now. You can help."

"Yes," Jody said miserably. He followed Billy into the grain room and watched him make the steaming bag ready. It was a long canvas nose bag with straps to go over a horse's ears. Billy filled it one'third full of bran and then he added a couple of handfuls of dried hops. On top of the dry substance he poured a little carbolic acid and a little turpentine. "I'll be mixing it all up while you run to the house for a kettle of boiling water," Billy said.

When Jody came back with the steaming kettle, Billy buckled the straps over Gabilan's head and fitted the bag tightly around his nose. Then through a little hole in the side of the bag he poured the boiling water on the mixture. The pony started away as a cloud of strong steam rose up, but then the soothing fumes crept through his nose and into his lungs, and the sharp steam began to clear out the nasal passages. He breathed loudly. His legs trembled in an ague, and his eyes closed against the biting cloud. Billy poured in more water and kept the steam rising for fifteen minutes. At last he set down the kettle and took the bag from Gabilan's nose. The pony looked better. He breathed freely, and his eyes were open wider than they had been.

"See how good it makes him feel," Billy said. "Now we'll wrap him up in the blanket again. Maybe he'll be nearly well by morning."

"I'll stay with him tonight," Jody suggested.

"No. Don't you do it. I'll bring my blankets down here and put them in the hay. You can stay tomorrow and steam him if he needs it."

The evening was falling when they went to the house for their supper. Jody didn't even realize that some one else had fed the chickens and filled the wood-box. He walked up past the house to the dark brush line and took a drink of water from the tub. The spring water was so cold that it stung his mouth and drove a shiver through him. The sky above the hills was still light. He saw a hawk flying so high that it caught the sun on its breast and shone like a spark. Two blackbirds were driving him down the sky, glittering as they attacked their enemy. In the west, the clouds were moving in to rain again.

Jody's father didn't speak at all while the family ate supper, but after Billy Buck had taken his blankets and gone to sleep in the barn, Carl Tiflin built a high fire in the fireplace and told stories. He told about the wild man who ran naked through the country and had a tail and ears like a horse, and he told about the rabbit-cats of Moro Cojo that hopped into the trees for birds. He revived the famous Maxwell brothers who found a vein of gold and hid the traces of it so carefully that they could never find it again.

Jody sat with his chin in his hands; his mouth worked nervously, and his father gradually became aware that he wasn't listening very carefully. "Isn't that funny?" he asked.

Jody laughed politely and said, "Yes, sir." His father was angry and hurt, then. He didn't tell any more stories. After a while, Jody took a lantern and went down to the barn. Billy Buck was asleep in the hay, and, except that his breath rasped a little in his lungs, the pony seemed to be much better. Jody stayed a little while, running his fingers over the red rough coat, and then he took up the lantern and went back to the house. When he was in bed, his mother came into the room.

"Have you enough covers on? It's getting winter."

"Yes, ma'am."

"Well, get some rest tonight." She hesitated to go out, stood uncertainly. "The pony will be all right," she said.

Jody was tired. He went to sleep quickly and didn't awaken until dawn. The triangle sounded, and Billy Buck came up from the barn before Jody could get out of the house.

"How is he?" Jody demanded.

Billy always wolfed his breakfast. "Pretty good. I'm going to open that lump this morning. Then he'll be better maybe."

After breakfast, Billy got out his best knife, one with a needle point. He whetted the shining blade a long time on a little carborundum stone. He tried the point and the blade again and again on his calloused thumb-ball, and at last he tried it on his upper lip.

On the way to the barn, Jody noticed how the young grass was up and how the stubble was melting day by day into the new green crop of volunteer. It was a cold sunny morning.

As soon as he saw the pony, Jody knew he was worse. His eyes were closed and sealed shut with dried mucus. His head hung so low that his nose almost touched the straw of his bed. There was a little groan in each breath, a deep-seated, patient groan.

Billy lifted the weak head and made a quick slash with the knife. Jody saw the yellow pus run out. He held up the head while Billy swabbed out the wound with weak carbolic acid salve.

"Now he'll feel better," Billy assured him. "That yellow poison is what makes him sick."

Jody looked unbelieving at Billy Buck. "He's awful sick."

Billy thought a long time what to say. He nearly tossed off a careless assurance, but he saved himself in time. "Yes, he's pretty sick," he said at last. "I've seen worse ones get well. If he doesn't get pneumonia, we'll pull him through. You stay with him. If he gets worse, you can come and get me."

For a long time after Billy went away, Jody stood beside the pony, stroking him behind the ears. The pony didn't flip his head the way he had done when he was well. The groaning in his breathing was becoming more hollow.

Doubletree Mutt looked into the barn, his big tail waving provocatively, and Jody was so incensed at his health that he found a hard black clod on the floor and deliberately threw it. Doubletree Mutt went yelping away to nurse a bruised paw.

In the middle of the morning, Billy Buck came back and made another steam bag. Jody watched to see whether the pony improved this time as he had before. His breathing eased a little, but he did not raise his head.

The Saturday dragged on. Late in the afternoon Jody went to the house and brought his bedding down and made up a place to sleep in the hay. He didn't ask permission. He knew from the way his mother looked at him that she would let him do almost anything. That night he left a lantern burning on a wire over the box stall. Billy had told him to rub the pony's legs every little while.

At nine o'clock the wind sprang up and howled around the barn. And in spite of his worry, Jody grew sleepy. He got into his blankets and went to sleep, but the breathy groans of the pony sounded in his dreams. And in his sleep he heard a crashing noise which went on and on until it awakened him. The wind was rushing through the barn. He sprang up and looked down the lane of stalls. The barn door had blown open, and the pony was gone.

He caught the lantern and ran outside into the gale, and he saw Gabilan weakly shambling away into the darkness, head down, legs working slowly and mechanically. When Jody ran up and caught him by the forelock, he allowed himself to be led back and put into his stall. His groans were louder, and a fierce whistling came from his nose. Jody didn't sleep any more then. The hissing of the pony's breath grew louder and sharper.

He was glad when Billy Buck came in at dawn. Billy looked for a time at the pony as though he had never seen him before. He felt the ears and flanks. "Jody," he said, "I've got to do something you won't want to see. You run up to the house for a while."

Jody grabbed him fiercely by the forearm. "You're not going to shoot him?"

Billy patted his hand. "No. I'm going to open a little hole in his windpipe so he can breathe. His nose is filled up. When he gets well, we'll put a little brass button in the hole for him to breathe through."

Jody couldn't have gone away if he had wanted to. It was awful to see the red hide cut, but infinitely more terrible to know it was being cut and not to see it. "I'll stay right here," he said bitterly. "You sure you got to?"

"Yes. I'm sure. If you stay, you can hold his head. If it doesn't make you sick, that is."

The fine knife came out again and was whetted again just as carefully as it had been the first time. Jody held the pony's head up and the throat taut, while Billy felt up and down for the right place. Jody sobbed once as the bright knife point disappeared into the throat. The pony plunged weakly away and then stood still, trembling violently. The blood ran thickly out and up the knife and across Billy's hand into his shirtsleeve. The sure square hand sawed out a round hole in the flesh, and the breath came bursting out of the hole, throwing a fine spray of blood. With the rush of oxygen, the pony took a sudden strength. He lashed out with his hind feet and tried to rear, but Jody held his head down while Billy mopped the new wound with carbolic salve. It was a good job. The blood stopped flowing and the air puffed out of the hole and sucked it in regularly with a little bubbling noise.

The rain brought in by the night wind began to fall on the barn roof. Then the triangle rang for breakfast. "You go up and eat while I wait," Billy said. "We've got to keep this hole from plugging up."

Jody walked slowly out of the barn. He was too dispirited to tell Billy how the barn door had blown open and let the pony out. He emerged into the wet grey morning and sloshed up to the house, taking a perverse pleasure in splashing through all the puddles. His mother fed him and put dry clothes on. She didn't question him. She seemed to know he couldn't answer questions. But when he was ready to go back to the barn she brought him a pan of steaming meal. "Give him this," she said.

But Jody did not take the pan. He said, "He won't eat anything," and ran out of the house. At the barn, Billy showed him how to fix a ball of cotton on a stick, with which to swab out the breathing hole when it became clogged with mucus.

Jody's father walked into the barn and stood with them in front of the stall. At length he turned to the boy. "Hadn't you better come with me? I'm going to drive over the hill." Jody shook his head. "You better come on, out of this," his father insisted.

Billy turned on him angrily. "Let him alone. It's his pony, isn't it?"

Carl Tiflin walked away without saying another word. His feelings were badly hurt.

All morning Jody kept the wound open and the air passing in and out freely. At noon the pony lay wearily down on his side and stretched his nose out.

Billy came back. "If you're going to stay with him tonight, you better take a little nap," he said. Jody went absently out of the barn. The sky had cleared to a hard thin blue. Everywhere the birds were busy with worms that had come to the damp surface of the ground.

Jody walked to the brush line and sat on the edge of the mossy tub. He looked down at the house and at the old bunkhouse and at the dark cypress tree. The place was familiar, but curiously changed. It wasn't itself any more, but a frame for things that were happening. A cold wind blew out of the east now, signifying that the rain was over for a little while. At his feet Jody could see the little arms of new weeds spreading out over the ground. In the mud about the spring were thousands of quail tracks.

Doubletree Mutt came sideways and embarrassed up through the vegetable patch, and Jody, remembering how he had thrown the clod, put his arm about the dog's neck and kissed him on his wide black nose. Doubletree Mutt sat still, as though he knew some solemn thing was happening. His big tail slapped the ground gravely. Jody pulled a swollen tick out of Mutt's neck and popped it dead between his thumb-nails. It was a nasty thing. He washed his hands in the cold spring water.

Except for the steady swish of the wind, the farm was very quiet. Jody knew his mother wouldn't mind if he didn't go in to eat his lunch. After a little while he went slowly back to the barn. Mutt crept into his own little house and whined softly to himself for a long time.

Billy Buck stood up from the box and surrendered the cotton swab. The pony still lay on his side and the wound in his throat bellowsed in and out. When Jody saw how dry and dead the hair looked, he knew at last that there was no hope for the pony. He had seen the dead hair before on dogs and on cows, and it was a sure sign. He sat heavily on the box and let down the barrier of the box stall. For a long time he kept his eyes on the moving wound, and at last he dozed, and the afternoon passed quickly. Just before dark his mother brought a deep dish of stew and left it for him and went away. Jody ate a little of it, and, when it was dark, he set the lantern on the floor by the pony's head so he could watch the wound and keep it open. And he dozed again until the night chill awakened him. The wind was blowing fiercely, bringing the north cold with it. Jody brought a blanket from his bed in the hay and wrapped himself in it. Gabilan's breathing was quiet at last; the hole in his throat moved gently. The owls flew through the hayloft, shrieking and looking for mice. Jody put his head down on his hands and slept. In his sleep he was aware that the wind had increased. He heard it slamming about the barn.

It was daylight when he awakened. The barn door had swung open. The pony was gone. He sprang up and ran out into the morning light.

The pony's tracks were plain enough, dragging through the frost-like dew on the young grass, tired tracks with little lines between them where the hoofs had dragged. They headed for the brush line halfway up the ridge. Jody broke into a run and followed them. The sun shone on the sharp white quartz that stuck through the ground here and there. As he followed the plain trail, a shadow cut across in front of him. He looked up and saw a high circle of black buzzards, and the slowly revolving circle dropped lower and lower. The solemn birds soon disappeared over the ridge. Jody ran faster then, forced on by panic and rage. The trail entered the brush at last and followed a winding route among the tall sage bushes.

At the top of the ridge Jody was winded. He paused, puffing noisily. The blood pounded in his ears. Then he saw what he was looking for. Below, in one of the little clearings in the brush, lay the red pony. In the distance, Jody could see the legs moving slowly and convulsively. And in a circle around him stood the buzzards, waiting for the moment of death they know so well.

Jody leaped forward and plunged down the hill. The wet ground muffled his steps and the brush hid him. When he arrived, it was all over. The first buzzard sat on the pony's head and its beak had just risen dripping with dark eye fluid. Jody plunged into the circle like a cat. The black brotherhood arose in a cloud, but the big one on the pony's head was too late. As it hopped along to take off, Jody caught its wing tip and pulled it down. It was nearly as big as he was. The free wing crashed into his face with the force of a club, but he hung on. The claws fastened on his leg and the wing elbows battered his head on either side. Jody groped blindly with his free hand. His fingers found the neck of the struggling bird. The red eyes looked into his face, calm and fearless and fierce; the naked head turned from side to side. Then the beak opened and vomited a stream of putrified fluid. Jody brought up his knee and fell on the great bird. He held the neck to the ground with one hand while his other found a piece of sharp white quartz. The first blow broke the beak sideways and black blood spurted from the twisted, leathery mouth corners. He struck again and missed. The red fearless eyes still looked at him, impersonal and unafraid and detached. He struck again and again, until the buzzard lay dead, until its head was a red pulp. He was still beating the dead bird when Billy Buck pulled him off and held him tightly to calm his shaking.

Carl Tiflin wiped the blood from the boy's face with a red bandana. Jody was limp and quiet now. His father moved the buzzard with his toe. "Jody," he explained, "the buzzard didn't kill the pony. Don't you know that?"

"I know it," Jody said wearily.

It was Billy Buck who was angry. He had lifted Jody in his arms, and had turned to carry him home. But he turned back on Carl Tiflin. " 'Course he knows it," Billy said furiously, "Jesus Christ! man, can't you see how he'd feel about it?"

II. *The Great Mountains*

In the humming heat of a midsummer afternoon the little boy Jody listlessly looked about the ranch for something to do. He had been to the barn, had thrown rocks at the swallows' nests under the eaves until every one of the little mud houses broke open and dropped its lining of straw and dirty feathers. Then at the ranch house he baited a rat trap with stale cheese and set it where Doubletree Mutt, that good big dog, would get his nose snapped. Jody was not moved by an impulse of cruelty; he was bored with the long hot afternoon. Doubletree Mutt put his stupid nose in the trap and got it smacked, and shrieked with agony and limped away with blood on his nostrils. No matter where he was hurt, Mutt limped. It was just a way he had. Once when he was young, Mutt got caught in a coyote trap, and always after that he limped, even when he was scolded.

When Mutt yelped, Jody's mother called from inside the house, "Jody! Stop torturing that dog and find something to do."

Jody felt mean then, so he threw a rock at Mutt. Then he took his slingshot from the porch and walked up toward the brush line to try to kill a bird. It was a good slingshot, with store-bought rubbers, but while Jody had often shot at birds, he had never hit one. He walked up through the vegetable patch, kicking his bare toes into the dust. And on the way he found the perfect slingshot stone, round and slightly flattened and heavy enough to carry through the air. He fitted it into the leather pouch of his weapon and proceeded to the brush line. His eyes narrowed, his mouth worked strenuously; for the first time that afternoon he was intent. In the shade of the sagebrush the little birds were working, scratching in the leaves, flying restlessly a few feet and scratching again. Jody pulled back the rubbers of the sling and advanced cautiously. One little thrush paused and looked at him and crouched, ready to fly. Jody sidled nearer, moving one foot slowly after the other. When he was twenty feet away, he carefully raised the sling and aimed. The stone whizzed; the thrush started up and flew right into it. And down the little bird went with a broken head. Jody ran to it and picked it up.

"Well, I got you," he said.

The bird looked much smaller dead than it had alive. Jody felt a little mean pain in his stomach, so he took out his pocket-knife and cut off the bird's head. Then he disemboweled it, and took off its wings; and finally he threw all the pieces into the brush. He didn't care about the bird, or its life, but he knew what older people would say if they had seen him kill it; he was ashamed because of their potential opinion. He decided to forget the whole thing as quickly as he could, and never to mention it.

The hills were dry at this season, and the wild grass was golden, but where the spring-pipe filled the round tub and the tub spilled over, there lay a stretch of fine green grass, deep and sweet and moist. Jody drank from the mossy tub and washed the bird's blood from his hands in cold water. Then he lay on his back in the grass and looked up at the dumpling summer clouds. By closing one eye and destroying perspective he brought them down within reach so that he could put up his fingers and stroke them. He helped the gentle wind push them down the sky; it seemed to him that they went faster for his help. One fat white cloud he helped clear to the mountain rims and pressed it firmly over, out of sight. Jody wondered what it was seeing, then. He sat up the better to look at the great mountains where they went piling back, growing darker and more savage until they finished with one jagged ridge, high up against the west.[4] Curious secret mountains; he thought of the little he knew about them.

"What's on the other side?" he asked his father once.

"More mountains, I guess. Why?"

4. Jody's home in the Salinas River Valley lies among the coastal ranges; to the east the Gabilans, for which he named his pony, are relatively gentle, but to the west, between the Valley and the ocean, the cliffs of the Santa Lucia Range are wild and forbidding.

"And on the other side of them?"

"More mountains. Why?"

"More mountains on and on?"

"Well, no. At last you come to the ocean."

"But what's in the mountains?"

"Just cliffs and brush and rocks and dryness."

"Were you ever there?"

"No."

"Has anybody ever been there?"

"A few people, I guess. It's dangerous, with cliffs and things. Why, I've read there's more unexplored country in the mountains of Monterey County than any place in the United States." His father seemed proud that this should be so.

"And at last the ocean?"

"At last the ocean."

"But," the boy insisted, "but in between? No one knows?"

"Oh, a few people do, I guess. But there's nothing there to get. And not much water. Just rocks and cliffs and greasewood. Why?"

"It would be good to go."

"What for? There's nothing there."

Jody knew something was there, something very wonderful because it wasn't known, something secret and mysterious. He could feel within himself that this was so. He said to his mother, "Do you know what's in the big mountains?"

She looked at him and then back at the ferocious range, and she said, "Only the bear, I guess."

"What bear?"

"Why the one that went over the mountain to see what he could see."

Jody questioned Billy Buck, the ranch hand, about the possibility of ancient cities lost in the mountains, but Billy agreed with Jody's father.

"It ain't likely," Billy said. "There'd be nothing to eat unless a kind of people that can eat rocks live there."

That was all the information Jody ever got, and it made the mountains dear to him, and terrible. He thought often of the miles of ridge after ridge until at last there was the sea. When the peaks were pink in the morning they invited him among them: and when the sun had gone over the edge in the evening and the mountains were a purple-like despair, then Jody was afraid of them; then they were so impersonal and aloof that their very imperturbability was a threat.

Now he turned his head toward the mountains of the east, the Gabilans, and they were jolly mountains, with hill ranches in their creases, and with pine trees growing on the crests. People lived there, and battles had been fought against the Mexicans on the slopes. He looked back for an instant at the Great Ones and shivered a little at the contrast. The foothill cup of the home ranch below him was sunny and safe. The house gleamed with white light and the barn was brown and warm. The red cows on the farther hill ate their way slowly toward the north. Even the dark cypress tree by the bunkhouse was usual and safe. The chickens scratched about in the dust of the farmyard with quick waltzing steps.

Then a moving figure caught Jody's eye. A man walked slowly over the brow of the hill, on the road from Salinas, and he was headed toward the house. Jody stood up and moved down toward the house too, for if someone was coming, he wanted to be there to see. By the time the boy had got to the house the walking man was only halfway down the road, a lean man, very straight in the shoulders. Jody could tell he was old only because his heels struck the ground with hard jerks. As he approached nearer, Jody saw that he was dressed in blue jeans and in a coat of the same material. He wore clodhopper shoes and an old flat-brimmed Stetson hat. Over his shoulder he carried a gunny sack, lumpy and full. In a few moments he had trudged close enough so that his face could be seen. And his face was as dark as dried beef. A mustache, blue-white against the dark skin, hovered over his mouth, and his hair was white, too, where it showed at his neck. The skin of his face had shrunk back against the skull until it defined bone, not flesh, and made the nose and chin seem sharp and fragile. The eyes were large and deep and dark, with eyelids stretched tightly over them. Irises and pupils were one, and very black, but the eyeballs were brown. There were no wrinkles in the face at all. This old man wore a blue denim coat buttoned to the throat with brass buttons, as all men do who wear no shirts. Out of the sleeves came strong bony wrists and hands gnarled and knotted and hard as peach branches. The nails were flat and blunt and shiny.

The old man drew close to the gate and swung down his sack when he confronted Jody. His lips fluttered a little and a soft impersonal voice came from between them.

"Do you live here?"

Jody was embarrassed. He turned and looked at the house, and he turned back and looked toward the barn where his father and Billy Buck were. "Yes," he said, when no help came from either direction.

"I have come back," the old man said. "I am Gitano, and I have come back."

Jody could not take all this responsibility. He turned abruptly, and ran into the house for help, and the screen door banged after him. His mother was in the kitchen poking out the clogged holes of a colander with a hairpin, and biting her lower lip with concentration.

"It's an old man," Jody cried excitedly. "It's an old *paisano* man, and he says he's come back."

His mother put down the colander and stuck the hairpin behind the sink board. "What's the matter now?" she asked patiently.

"It's an old man outside. Come on out."

"Well, what does he want?" She untied the strings of her apron and smoothed her hair with her fingers.

"I don't know. He came walking."

His mother smoothed down her dress and went out, and Jody followed her. Gitano had not moved.

"Yes?" Mrs. Tiflin asked.

Gitano took off his old black hat and held it with both hands in front of him. He repeated, "I am Gitano, and I have come back."

"Come back? Back where?"

Gitano's whole straight body leaned forward a little. His right hand described the circle of the hills, the sloping fields and the mountains, and ended at his hat again. "Back to the rancho. I was born here, and my father, too."

"Here?" she demanded. "This isn't an old place."

"No, there," he said, pointing to the western ridge. "On the other side there, in a house that is gone.'

At last she understood. "The old 'dobe that's washed almost away, you mean?"

"Yes, *señora*. When the rancho broke up they put no more lime on the 'dobe, and the rains washed it down."

Jody's mother was silent for a little, and curious homesick thoughts ran through her mind, but quickly she cleared them out. "And what do you want here now, Gitano?"

"I will stay here," he said quietly, "until I die."

"But we don't need an extra man here."

"I can not work hard any more, *señora*. I can milk a cow, feed chickens, cut a little wood; no more. I will stay here." He indicated the sack on the ground beside him. "Here are my things."

She turned to Jody. "Run down to the barn and call your father."

Jody dashed away, and he returned with Carl Tiflin and Billy Buck behind him. The old man was standing as he had been, but he was resting now. His whole body had sagged into a timeless repose.

"What is it?" Carl Tiflin asked. "What's Jody so excited about?"

Mrs. Tiflin motioned to the old man. "He wants to stay here.

He wants to do a little work and stay here."

"Well, we can't have him. We don't need any more men. He's too old. Billy does everything we need."

They had been talking over him as though he did not exist, and now, suddenly, they both hesitated and looked at Gitano and were embarrassed.

He cleared his throat. "I am too old to work. I come back where I was born."

"You weren't born here," Carl said sharply.

"No. In the 'dobe house over the hill. It was all one rancho before you came."

"In the mud house that's all melted down?"

"Yes, I and my father. I will stay here now on the rancho."

"I tell you you won't stay," Carl said angrily. "I don't need an old man. This isn't a big ranch. I can't afford food and doctor bills for an old man. You must have relatives and friends. Go to them. It is like begging to come to strangers."

"I was born here," Gitano said patiently and inflexibly.

Carl Tiflin didn't like to be cruel, but he felt he must. "You can eat here tonight," he said. "You can sleep in the little room of the old bunkhouse. We'll give you your breakfast in the morning, and then you'll have to go along. Go to your friends. Don't come to die with strangers."

Gitano put on his black hat and stooped for the sack. "Here are my things," he said.

Carl turned away. "Come on, Billy, we'll finish down at the barn. Jody, show him the little room in the bunkhouse."

He and Billy turned back toward the barn. Mrs. Tiflin went into the house, saying over her shoulder, "I'll send some blankets down."

Gitano looked questioningly at Jody. "I'll show you where it is," Jody said.

There was a cot with a shuck mattress, an apple box holding a tin lantern, and a backless rocking-chair in the little room of the bunkhouse. Gitano laid his sack carefully on the floor and sat down on the bed. Jody stood shyly in the room, hesitating to go. At last he said,

"Did you come out of the big mountains?"

Gitano shook his head slowly. "No, I worked down the Salinas Valley."

The afternoon thought would not let Jody go. "Did you ever go into the big mountains back there?"

The old dark eyes grew fixed, and their light turned inward on the years that were living in Gitano's head. "Once—when I was a little boy. I went with my father."

"Way back, clear into the mountains?"

"Yes."

"What was there?" Jody cried. "Did you see any people or any houses?"

"No."

"Well, what was there?"

Gitano's eyes remained inward. A little wrinkled strain came between his brows.

"What did you see in there?" Jody repeated.

"I don't know," Gitano said. "I don't remember."

"Was it terrible and dry?"

"I don't remember."

In his excitement, Jody had lost his shyness. "Don't you remember anything about it?"

Gitano's mouth opened for a word, and remained open while his brain sought the word. "I think it was quiet—I think it was nice."

Gitano's eyes seemed to have found something back in the years, for they grew soft and a little smile seemed to come and go in them.

"Didn't you ever go back in the mountains again?" Jody insisted.

"No."

"Didn't you ever want to?"

But now Gitano's face became impatient. "No," he said in a tone that told Jody he didn't want to talk about it any more. The boy was held by a curious fascination. He didn't want to go away from Gitano. His shyness returned.

"Would you like to come down to the barn and see the stock?" he asked.

Gitano stood up and put on his hat and prepared to follow.

It was almost evening now. They stood near the watering trough while the horses sauntered in from the hillsides for an evening drink. Gitano rested his big twisted hands on the top rail of the fence. Five horses came down and drank, and then stood about, nibbling at the dirt or rubbing their sides against the polished wood of the fence. Long after they had finished drinking an old horse appeared over the brow of the hill and came painfully down. It had long yellow teeth; its hooves were flat and sharp as spades, and its ribs and hip-bones jutted out under its skin. It hobbled up to the trough and drank water with a loud sucking noise.

"That's old Easter," Jody explained. "That's the first horse my father ever had. He's thirty years old." He looked up into Gitano's old eyes for some response.

"No good any more," Gitano said.

Jody's father and Billy Buck came out of the barn and walked over.

"Too old to work," Gitano repeated. "Just eats and pretty soon dies."

Carl Tiflin caught the last words. He hated his brutality toward old Gitano, and so he became brutal again.

"It's a shame not to shoot Easter," he said. "It'd save him a lot of pains and rheumatism." He looked secretly at Gitano, to see whether he noticed the parallel, but the big bony hands did not move, nor did the dark eyes turn from the horse. "Old things ought to be put out of their misery," Jody's father went on. "One shot, a big noise, one big pain in the head maybe, and that's all. That's better than stiffness and sore teeth."

Billy Buck broke in. "They got a right to rest after they worked all their life. Maybe they like to just walk around."

Carl had been looking steadily at the skinny horse. "You can't imagine now what Easter used to look like," he said softly. "High neck, deep chest, fine barrel. He could jump a five-bar gate in stride. I won a flat race on him when I was fifteen years old. I could of got two hundred dollars for him any time. You wouldn't think how pretty he was." He checked himself, for he hated softness. "But he ought to be shot now," he said.

"He's got a right to rest," Billy Buck insisted.

Jody's father had a humorous thought. He turned to Gitano. "If ham and eggs grew on a side-hill I'd turn you out to pasture too," he said. "But I can't afford to pasture you in my kitchen."

He laughed to Billy Buck about it as they went on toward the house. "Be a good thing for all of us if ham and eggs grew on the side-hills."

Jody knew how his father was probing for a place to hurt in Gitano. He had been probed often. His father knew every place in the boy where a word would fester.

"He's only talking," Jody said. "He didn't mean it about shooting Easter. He likes Easter. That was the first horse he ever owned."

The sun sank behind the high mountains as they stood there, and the ranch was hushed. Gitano seemed to be more at home in the evening. He made a curious sharp sound with his lips and stretched one of his hands over the fence. Old Easter moved stiffly to him, and Gitano rubbed the lean neck under the mane.

"You like him?" Jody asked softly.

"Yes—but he's no damn good."

The triangle sounded at the ranch house. "That's supper," Jody cried. "Come on up to supper."

As they walked up toward the house Jody noticed again that Gitano's body was as straight as that of a young man. Only by a jerkiness in his movements and by the scuffling of his heels could it be seen that he was old.

The turkeys were flying heavily into the lower branches of the cypress tree by the bunkhouse. A fat sleek ranch cat walked across the road carrying a rat so large that its tail dragged on the ground. The quail on the side-hills were still sounding the clear water call.

Jody and Gitano came to the back steps and Mrs. Tiflin looked out through the screen door at them.

"Come running, Jody. Come in to supper, Gitano."

Carl and Billy Buck had started to eat at the long oilcloth-covered table. Jody slipped into his chair without moving it, but Gitano stood holding his hat until Carl looked up and said, "Sit down, sit down. You might as well get your belly full before you go on." Carl was afraid he might relent and let the old man stay, and so he continued to remind himself that this couldn't be.

Gitano laid his hat on the floor and diffidently sat down. He wouldn't reach for food. Carl had to pass it to him. "Here, fill yourself up." Gitano ate very slowly, cutting tiny pieces of meat and arranging little pats of mashed potato on his plate.

The situation would not stop worrying Carl Tiflin. "Haven't you got any relatives in this part of the country?" he asked.

Gitano answered with some pride, "My brother-in-law is in Monterey. I have cousins there, too."

"Well, you can go and live there, then."

"I was born here," Gitano said in gentle rebuke.

Jody's mother came in from the kitchen, carrying a large bowl of tapioca pudding.

Carl chuckled to her, "Did I tell you what I said to him? I said if ham and eggs grew on the side-hills I'd put him out to pasture, like old Easter."

Gitano stared unmoved at his plate.

"It's too bad he can't stay," said Mrs. Tiflin.

"Now don't you start anything," Carl said crossly.

When they had finished eating, Carl and Billy Buck and Jody went into the living-room to sit for a while, but Gitano, without a word of farewell or thanks, walked through the kitchen and out the back door. Jody sat and secretly watched his father. He knew how mean his father felt.

"This country's full of these old *paisanos*," Carl said to Billy Buck.

"They're damn good men," Billy defended them. "They can work older than white men. I saw one of them a hundred and five years old, and he could still ride a horse. You don't see any white men as old as Gitano walking twenty or thirty miles."

"Oh. they're tough, all right," Carl agreed. "Say, are you standing up for him too? Listen, Billy," he explained, "I'm having a hard enough time keeping this ranch out of the Bank of Italy without taking on anybody else to feed. You know that, Billy."

"Sure, I know," said Billy. "If you was rich, it'd be different."

"That's right, and it isn't like he didn't have relatives to go to. A brother-in-law and cousins right in Monterey. Why should I worry about him?"

Jody sat quietly listening, and he seemed to hear Gitano's gentle voice and its unanswerable, "But I was born here." Gitano was mysterious like the mountains. There were ranges back as far as you could see, but behind the last range piled up against the sky there was a great unknown country. And Gitano was an old man, until you got to the dull dark eyes. And in behind them was some unknown thing. He didn't ever say enough to let you guess what was inside, under the eyes. Jody felt himself irresistibly drawn toward the bunkhouse. He slipped from his chair while his father was talking and he went out the door without making a sound.

The night was very dark and far-off noises carried in clearly. The hamebells of a wood team sounded from way over the hill on the country road. Jody picked his way across the dark yard. He could see a light through the window of the little room of the bunkhouse. Because the night was secret he walked quietly up to the window and peered in. Gitano sat in the rocking-chair and his back was toward the window. His right arm moved slowly back and forth in front of him. Jody pushed the door open and walked in. Gitano jerked upright and, seizing a piece of deerskin, he tried to throw it over the thing in his lap, but the skin slipped away. Jody stood overwhelmed by the thing in Gitano's hand, a lean and lovely rapier with a golden basket hilt. The blade was like a thin ray of dark light. The hilt was pierced and intricately carved.

"What is it?" Jody demanded.

Gitano only looked at him with resentful eyes, and he picked up the fallen deerskin and firmly wrapped the beautiful blade in it.

Jody put out his hand. "Can't I see it?"

Gitano's eyes smoldered angrily and he shook his head.

"Where'd you get it? Where'd it come from?"

Now Gitano regarded him profoundly, as though he pondered. "I got it from my father."

"Well, where'd he get it?"

Gitano looked down at the long deerskin parcel in his hand. "I don' know."

"Didn't he ever tell you?"

"No."

"What do you do with it?"

Gitano looked slightly surprised. "Nothing. I just keep it."

"Can't I see it again?"

The old man slowly unwrapped the shining blade and let the lamplight slip along it for a moment. Then he wrapped it up again. "You go now. I want to go to bed." He blew out the lamp almost before Jody had closed the door.

As he went back toward the house, Jody knew one thing more sharply than he had ever known anything. He must never tell anyone about the rapier. It would be a dreadful thing to tell anyone about it, for it would destroy some fragile structure of truth. It was a truth that might be shattered by division.

On the way across the dark yard Jody passed Billy Buck. "They're wondering where you are," Billy said.

Jody slipped into the living-room, and his father turned to him. "Where have you been?"

"I just went out to see if I caught any rats in my new trap."

"It's time you went to bed," his father said.

Jody was first at the breakfast table in the morning. Then his father came in, and last, Billy Buck. Mrs. Tiflin looked in from the kitchen.

"Where's the old man, Billy?" she asked.

"I guess he's out walking," Billy said. "I looked in his room and he wasn't there."

"Maybe he started early to Monterey," said Carl. "It's a long walk."

"No," Billy explained. "His sack is in the little room."

After breakfast Jody walked down to the bunkhouse. Flies were flashing about in the sunshine. The ranch seemed especially quiet this morning. When he was sure no one was watching him, Jody went into the little room, and looked into Gitano's sack. An extra pair of long cotton underwear was there, an extra pair of jeans and three pairs of worn socks. Nothing else was in the sack. A sharp loneliness fell on Jody. He walked slowly back toward the house. His father stood on the porch talking to Mrs. Tiflin.

"I guess old Easter's dead at last," he said. "I didn't see him come down to water with the other horses."

In the middle of the morning Jess Taylor from the ridge ranch rode down.

"You didn't sell that old grey crowbait of yours, did you, Carl?"

"No, of course not. Why?"

"Well," Jess said. "I was out this morning early, and I saw a funny thing. I saw an old man on an old horse, no saddle, only a piece of rope for a bridle. He wasn't on the road at all. He was cutting right up straight through the brush. I think he had a gun. At least I saw something shine in his hand."

"That's old Gitano," Carl Tiflin said. "I'll see if any of my guns are missing." He stepped into the house for a second. "Nope, all here. Which way was he heading, Jess?"

"Well, that's the funny thing. He was heading straight back into the mountains."

Carl laughed. "They never get too old to steal," he said. "I guess he just stole old Easter."

"Want to go after him, Carl?"

"Hell no, just save me burying that horse. I wonder where he got the gun. I wonder what he wants back there."

Jody walked up through the vegetable patch, toward the brush line. He looked searchingly at the towering mountains—ridge after ridge after ridge until at last there was the ocean. For a moment he thought he could see a black speck crawling up the farthest ridge. Jody thought of the rapier and Gitano. And he thought of the great mountains. A longing caressed him, and it was so sharp that he wanted to cry to get it out of his breast. He lay down in the green grass near the round tub at the brush line. He covered his eyes with his crossed arms and lay there a long time, and he was full of a nameless sorrow.

III. The Promise

In a mid-afternoon of spring, the little boy Jody walked martially along the brush-lined road toward his home ranch. Banging his knee against the golden lard bucket he used for school lunch, he contrived a good bass drum, while his tongue fluttered sharply against the teeth to fill in snare drums and occasional trumpets. Some time back the other members of the squad that walked so smartly from the school had turned into the various little canyons and taken the wagon roads to their own home ranches. Now Jody marched seemingly alone, with high-lifted knees and pounding feet; but behind him there was a phantom army with great flags and swords, silent but deadly.

The afternoon was green and gold with spring. Underneath the spread branches of the oaks the plants grew pale and tall, and on the hills the feed was smooth and thick. The sagebrushes shone with new silver leaves and the oaks wore hoods of golden green. Over the hills there hung such a green odor that the horses on the flats galloped madly, and then stopped, wondering; lambs, and even old sheep jumped in the air unexpectedly and landed on stiff legs, and went on eating; young clumsy calves butted their heads together and drew back and butted again.

As the grey and silent army marched past, led by Jody, the animals stopped their feeding and their play and watched it go by.

Suddenly Jody stopped. The grey army halted, bewildered and

nervous. Jody went down on his knees. The army stood in long uneasy ranks for a moment, and then, with a soft sigh of sorrow, rose
up in a faint grey mist and disappeared. Jody had seen the thorny
crown of a horny-toad moving under the dust of the road. His
grimy hand went out and grasped the spiked halo and held firmly
while the little beast struggled. Then Jody turned the horny-toad
over, exposing its pale gold stomach. With a gentle forefinger he
stroked the throat and chest until the horny-toad relaxed, until its
eyes closed and it lay languorous and asleep.

Jody opened his lunch pail and deposited the first game inside.
He moved on now, his knees bent slightly, his shoulders crouched;
his bare feet were wise and silent. In his right hand there was a long
grey rifle. The brush along the road stirred restively under a new
and unexpected population of grey tigers and grey bears. The hunting was very good, for by the time Jody reached the fork of the road
where the mail box stood on a post, he had captured two more
horny-toads, four little grass lizards, a blue snake, sixteen yellow-
winged grasshoppers and a brown damp newt from under a rock.
This assortment scrabbled unhappily against the tin of the lunch
bucket.

At the road fork the rifle evaporated and the tigers and bears melted
from the hillsides. Even the moist and uncomfortable creatures in
the lunch pail ceased to exist, for the little red metal flag was up on
the mail box, signifying that some postal matter was inside. Jody set
his pail on the ground and opened the letter box. There was a
Montgomery Ward catalog and a copy of the *Salinas Weekly
Journal*. He slammed the box, picked up his lunch pail and trotted
over the ridge and down into the cup of the ranch. Past the barn
he ran, and past the used-up haystack and the bunkhouse and the
cypress tree. He banged through the front screen door of the ranch
house calling, "Ma'am, ma'am, there's a catalog."

Mrs. Tiflin was in the kitchen spooning clabbered milk into a
cotton bag. She put down her work and rinsed her hands under
the tap. "Here in the kitchen, Jody. Here I am."

He ran in and clattered his lunch pail on the sink. "Here it is.
Can I open the catalog, ma'am?"

Mrs. Tiflin took up the spoon again and went back to her cottage
cheese. "Don't lose it, Jody. Your father will want to see it." She
scraped the last of the milk into the bag. "Oh, Jody, your father
wants to see you before you go to your chores." She waved a cruising fly from the cheese bag.

Jody closed the new catalog in alarm. "Ma'am?"

"Why don't you ever listen? I say your father wants to see you."

The boy laid the catalog gently on the sink board. "Do you—is it
something I did?"

Mrs. Tiflin laughed. "Always a bad conscience. What did you do?"

"Nothing, ma'am," he said lamely. But he couldn't remember, and besides it was impossible to know what action might later be construed as a crime.

His mother hung the full bag on a nail where it could drip into the sink. "He just said he wanted to see you when you got home. He's somewhere down by the barn."

Jody turned and went out the back door. Hearing his mother open the lunch pail and then gasp with rage, a memory stabbed him and he trotted away toward the barn, conscientiously not hearing the angry voice that called him from the house.

Carl Tiflin and Billy Buck, the ranch hand, stood against the lower pasture fence. Each man rested one foot on the lowest bar and both elbows on the top bar. They were talking slowly and aimlessly. In the pasture half a dozen horses nibbled contentedly at the sweet grass. The mare, Nellie, stood backed up against the gate, rubbing her buttocks on the heavy post.

Jody sidled uneasily near. He dragged one foot to give an impression of great innocence and nonchalance. When he arrived beside the men he put one foot on the lowest fence rail, rested his elbows on the second bar and looked into the pasture too. The two men glanced sideways at him.

"I wanted to see you," Carl said in the stern tone he reserved for children and animals.

"Yes sir," said Jody guiltily.

"Billy, here, says you took good care of the pony before it died."

No punishment was in the air. Jody grew bolder. "Yes, sir, I did."

"Billy says you have a good patient hand with horses."

Jody felt a sudden warm friendliness for the ranch hand.

Billy put in, "He trained that pony as good as anybody I ever seen."

Then Carl Tiflin came gradually to the point. "If you could have another horse would you work for it?"

Jody shivered. "Yes, sir."

"Well, look here, then. Billy says the best way for you to be a good hand with horses is to raise a colt."

"It's the *only* good way," Billy interrupted.

"Now, look here, Jody," continued Carl. "Jess Taylor, up to the ridge ranch, has a fair stallion, but it'll cost five dollars. I'll put up the money, but you'll have to work it out all summer. Will you do that?"

Jody felt that his insides were shriveling. "Yes, sir," he said softly.

"And no complaining? And no forgetting when you're told to do something?"

"Yes, sir."

"Well, all right, then. Tomorrow morning you take Nellie up to the ridge ranch and get her bred. You'll have to take care of her, too, till she throws the colt."

"Yes, sir."

"You better get to the chickens and the wood now."

Jody slid away. In passing behind Billy Buck he very nearly put out his hand to touch the blue-jeaned legs. His shoulders swayed a little with maturity and importance.

He went to his work with unprecedented seriousness. This night he did not dump the can of grain to the chickens so that they had to leap over each other and struggle to get it. No, he spread the wheat so far and so carefully that the hens couldn't find some of it at all. And in the house, after listening to his mother's despair over boys who filled their lunch pails with slimy, suffocated reptiles, and bugs, he promised never to do it again. Indeed, Jody felt that all such foolishness was lost in the past. He was far too grown up ever to put horny-toads in his lunch pail any more. He carried in so much wood and built such a high structure with it that his mother walked in fear of an avalanche of oak. When he was done, when he had gathered eggs that had remained hidden for weeks, Jody walked down again past the cypress tree, and past the bunkhouse toward the pasture. A fat warty toad that looked out at him from under the watering troughs had no emotional effect on him at all.

Carl Tiflin and Billy Buck were not in sight, but from a metallic ringing on the other side of the barn Jody knew that Billy Buck was just starting to milk a cow.

The other horses were eating toward the upper end of the pasture, but Nellie continued to rub herself nervously against the post. Jody walked slowly near, saying, "So, girl, so-o, Nellie." The mare's ears went back naughtily and her lips drew away from her yellow teeth. She turned her head around; her eyes were glazed and mad. Jody climbed to the top of the fence and hung his feet over and looked paternally down on the mare.

The evening hovered while he sat there. Bats and nighthawks flicked about. Billy Buck, walking toward the house carrying a full milk bucket, saw Jody and stopped. "It's a long time to wait," he said gently. "You'll get awful tired waiting."

"No I won't, Billy. How long will it be?"

"Nearly a year."

"Well, I won't get tired."

The triangle at the house rang stridently. Jody climbed down from the fence and walked to supper beside Billy Buck. He even put out his hand and took hold of the milk bucket to help carry it.

The next morning after breakfast Carl Tiflin folded a five-dollar bill in a piece of newspaper and pinned the package in the bib pocket of Jody's overalls. Billy Buck haltered the mare Nellie and led her out of the pasture.

"Be careful now," he warned. "Hold her up short here so she can't bite you. She's crazy as a coot."

Jody took hold of the halter leather itself and started up the hill toward the ridge ranch with Nellie skittering and jerking behind him. In the pasturage along the road the wild oat heads were just clearing their scabbards. The warm morning sun shone on Jody's back so sweetly that he was forced to take a serious stiff-legged hop now and then in spite of his maturity. On the fences the shiny blackbirds with red epaulets clicked their dry call. The meadowlarks sang like water, and the wild doves, concealed among the bursting leaves of the oaks, made a sound of restrained grieving. In the fields the rabbits sat sunning themselves, with only their forked ears showing above the grass heads.

After an hour of steady uphill walking, Jody turned into a narrow road that led up a steeper hill to the ridge ranch. He could see the red roof of the barn sticking up above the oak trees, and he could hear a dog barking unemotionally near the house.

Suddenly Nellie jerked back and nearly freed herself. From the direction of the barn Jody heard a shrill whistling scream and a splintering of wood, and then a man's voice shouting. Nellie reared and whinnied. When Jody held to the halter rope she ran at him with bared teeth. He dropped his hold and scuttled out of the way, into the brush. The high scream came from the oaks again, and Nellie answered it. With hoofs battering the ground the stallion appeared and charged down the hill trailing a broken halter rope. His eyes glittered feverishly. His stiff, erected nostrils were as red as flame. His black, sleek hide shone in the sunlight. The stallion came on so fast that he couldn't stop when he reached the mare. Nellie's ears went back; she whirled and kicked at him as he went by. The stallion spun around and reared. He struck the mare with his front hoof, and while she staggered under the blow, his teeth raked her neck and drew an ooze of blood.

Instantly Nellie's mood changed. She became coquettishly feminine. She nibbled his arched neck with her lips. She edged around and rubbed her shoulder against his shoulder. Jody stood half-hidden in the brush and watched. He heard the step of a horse behind him, but before he could turn, a hand caught him by the overall straps and lifted him off the ground. Jess Taylor sat the boy behind him on the horse.

"You might have got killed," he said. "Sundog's a mean devil sometimes. He busted his rope and went right through a gate."

Jody sat quietly, but in a moment he cried, "He'll hurt her, he'll kill her. Get him away!"

Jess chuckled. "She'll be all right. Maybe you'd better climb off and go up to the house for a little. You could get maybe a piece of pie up there."

But Jody shook his head. "She's mine, and the colt's going to be mine. I'm going to raise it up."

Jess nodded. "Yes, that's a good thing. Carl has good sense sometimes."

In a little while the danger was over. Jess lifted Jody down and then caught the stallion by its broken halter rope. And he rode ahead, while Jody followed, leading Nellie.

It was only after he had unpinned and handed over the five dollars, and after he had eaten two pieces of pie, that Jody started for home again. And Nellie followed docilely after him. She was so quiet that Jody climbed on a stump and rode her most of the way home.

The five dollars his father had advanced reduced Jody to peonage for the whole late spring and summer. When the hay was cut he drove a rake. He led the horse that pulled on the Jackson-fork tackle, and when the baler came he drove the circling horse that put pressure on the bales. In addition, Carl Tiflin taught him to milk and put a cow under his care, so that a new chore was added night and morning.

The bay mare Nellie quickly grew complacent. As she walked about the yellowing hillsides or worked at easy tasks, her lips were curled in a perpetual fatuous smile. She moved slowly, with the calm importance of an empress. When she was put to a team, she pulled steadily and unemotionally. Jody went to see her every day. He studied her with critical eyes and saw no change whatever.

One afternoon Billy Buck leaned the many-tined manure fork against the barn wall. He loosened his belt and tucked in his shirt-tail and tightened the belt again. He picked one of the little straws from his hatband and put it in the corner of his mouth. Jody, who was helping Doubletree Mutt, the big serious dog, to dig out a gopher, straightened up as the ranch hand sauntered out of the barn.

"Let's go up and have a look at Nellie," Billy suggested.

Instantly Jody fell into step with him. Doubletree Mutt watched them over his shoulder; then he dug furiously, growled, sounded little sharp yelps to indicate that the gopher was practically caught. When he looked over his shoulder again, and saw that neither Jody nor Billy was interested, he climbed reluctantly out of the hole and followed them up the hill.

The wild oats were ripening. Every head bent sharply under its load of grain, and the grass was dry enough so that it made a swishing sound as Jody and Billy stepped through it. Halfway up the hill they could see Nellie and the iron-grey gelding, Pete, nibbling the heads from the wild oats. When they approached, Nellie looked at them and backed her ears and bobbed her head up and down rebelliously. Billy walked to her and put his hand under her mane and patted her neck, until her ears came forward again and she nibbled delicately at his shirt.

Jody asked, "Do you think she's really going to have a colt?"

Billy rolled the lids back from the mare's eyes with his thumb and forefinger. He felt the lower lip and fingered the black, leathery teats. "I wouldn't be surprised," he said.

"Well, she isn't changed at all. It's three months gone."

Billy rubbed the mare's flat forehead with his knuckle while she grunted with pleasure. "I told you you'd get tired waiting. It'll be five months more before you can even see a sign, and it'll be at least eight months more before she throws the colt, about next January."

Jody sighed deeply. "It's a long time, isn't it?"

"And then it'll be about two years more before you can ride."

Jody cried out in despair, "I'll be grown up."

"Yep, you'll be an old man," said Billy.

"What color do you think the colt'll be?"

"Why, you can't ever tell. The stud is black and the dam is bay. Colt might be black or bay or grey or dappled. You can't tell. Sometimes a black dam might have a white colt."

"Well, I hope it's black, and a stallion."

"If it's a stallion, we'll have to geld it. Your father wouldn't let you have a stallion."

"Maybe he would," Jody said. "I could train him not to be mean."

Billy pursed his lips and the little straw that had been in the corner of his mouth rolled down to the center. "You can't ever trust a stallion," he said critically. "They're mostly fighting and making trouble. Sometimes when they're feeling funny they won't work. They make the mares uneasy and kick hell out of the geldings. Your father wouldn't let you keep a stallion."

Nellie sauntered away, nibbling the drying grass. Jody skinned the grain from a grass stem and threw the handful into the air, so that each pointed, feathered seed sailed out like a dart. "Tell me how it'll be, Billy. Is it like when the cows have calves?"

"Just about. Mares are a little more sensitive. Sometimes you have to be there to help the mare. And sometimes if it's wrong, you have to——" he paused.

"Have to what, Billy?"

"Have to tear the colt to pieces to get it out, or the mare'll die."

"But it won't be that way this time, will it, Billy?"

"Oh, no. Nellie's thrown good colts."

"Can I be there, Billy? Will you be certain to call me? It's my colt."

"Sure, I'll call you. Of course I will."

"Tell me how it'll be."

"Why, you've seen the cows calving. It's almost the same. The mare starts groaning and stretching, and then, if it's a good right birth, the head and forefeet come out, and the front hoofs kick a hole just the way the calves do. And the colt starts to breathe. It's good to be there, 'cause if its feet aren't right maybe he can't break the sack, and then he might smother."

Jody whipped his leg with a bunch of grass. "We'll have to be there, then, won't we?"

"Oh, we'll be there, all right."

They turned and walked slowly down the hill toward the barn. Jody was tortured with a thing he had to say, although he didn't want to. "Billy," he began miserably, "Billy, you won't let anything happen to the colt, will you?"

And Billy knew he was thinking of the red pony, Gabilan, and of how it died of strangles. Billy knew he had been infallible before that, and now he was capable of failure. This knowledge made Billy much less sure of himself than he had been. "I can't tell," he said roughly. "All sorts of things might happen, and they wouldn't be my fault. I can't do everything." He felt badly about his lost prestige, and so he said, meanly, "I'll do everything I know, but I won't promise anything. Nellie's a good mare. She's thrown good colts before. She ought to this time." And he walked away from Jody and went into the saddle-room beside the barn, for his feelings were hurt.

Jody traveled often to the brushline behind the house. A rusty iron pipe ran a thin stream of spring water into an old green tub. Where the water spilled over and sank into the ground there was a patch of perpetually green grass. Even when the hills were brown and baked in the summer that little patch was green. The water whined softly into the trough all the year round. This place had grown to be a center-point for Jody. When he had been punished the cool green grass and the singing water soothed him. When he had been mean the biting acid of meanness left him at the brushline. When he sat in the grass and listened to the purling stream, the barriers set up in his mind by the stern day went down to ruin.

On the other hand, the black cypress tree by the bunkhouse was as repulsive as the water-tub was dear; for to this tree all the pigs came, sooner or later, to be slaughtered. Pig killing was fascinating, with the screaming and the blood, but it made Jody's heart beat so fast that it hurt him. After the pigs were scalded in the big iron tripod kettle and their skins were scraped and white, Jody had to go to the water-tub to sit in the grass until his heart grew quiet. The water-tub and the black cypress were opposites and enemies.

When Billy left him and walked angrily away, Jody turned up toward the house. He thought of Nellie as he walked, and of the little colt. Then suddenly he saw that he was under the black cypress, under the very singletree where the pigs were hung. He brushed his dry-grass hair off his forehead and hurried on. It seemed to him an unlucky thing to be thinking of his colt in the very slaughter place, especially after what Billy had said. To counteract any evil result of that bad conjunction he walked quickly past the ranch house, through the chicken yard, through the vegetable patch, until he came at last to the brushline.

He sat down in the green grass. The trilling water sounded in his ears. He looked over the farm buildings and across at the round hills, rich and yellow with grain. He could see Nellie feeding on the slope. As usual the water place eliminated time and distance. Jody saw a black, long-legged colt, butting against Nellie's flanks, demanding milk. And then he saw himself breaking a large colt to halter. All in a few moments the colt grew to be a magnificent animal, deep of chest, with a neck as high and arched as a sea-horse's neck, with a tail that tongued and rippled like black flame. This horse was terrible to everyone but Jody. In the schoolyard the boys begged rides, and Jody smilingly agreed. But no sooner were they mounted than the black demon pitched them off. Why, that was his name, Black Demon! For a moment the trilling water and the grass and the sunshine came back, and then . . .

Sometimes in the night the ranch people, safe in their beds, heard a roar of hoofs go by. They said, "It's Jody, on Demon. He's helping out the sheriff again." And then . . .

The golden dust filled the air in the arena at the Salinas Rodeo. The announcer called the roping contests. When Jody rode the black horse to the starting chute the other contestants shrugged and gave up first place, for it was well known that Jody and Demon could rope and throw and tie a steer a great deal quicker than any roping team of two men could. Jody was not a boy any more, and Demon was not a horse. The two together were one glorious individual. And then . . .

The President wrote a letter and asked them to help catch a bandit in Washington. Jody settled himself comfortably in the grass. The little stream of water whined into the mossy tub.

The year passed slowly on. Time after time Jody gave up his colt for lost. No change had taken place in Nellie. Carl Tiflin still drove her to a light cart, and she pulled on a hay rake and worked the Jackson-fork tackle when the hay was being put into the barn.

The summer passed, and the warm bright autumn. And then the frantic morning winds began to twist along the ground, and a chill came into the air, and the poison oak turned red. One morning in September, when he had finished his breakfast, Jody's mother called him into the kitchen. She was pouring boiling water into a bucket full of dry midlings and stirring the materials to a steaming paste.

"Yes, ma'am?" Jody asked.

"Watch how I do it. You'll have to do it after this every other morning."

"Well, what is it?"

"Why, it's warm mash for Nellie. It'll keep her in good shape."

Jody rubbed his forehead with a knuckle. "Is she all right?" he asked timidly.

Mrs. Tiflin put down the kettle and stirred the mash with a wooden paddle. "Of course she's all right, only you've got to take better care of her from now on. Here, take this breakfast out to her!"

Jody seized the bucket and ran, down past the bunkhouse, past the barn, with the heavy bucket banging against his knees. He found Nellie playing with the water in the trough, pushing waves and tossing her head so that the water slopped out on the ground.

Jody climbed the fence and set the bucket of steaming mash beside her. Then he stepped back to look at her. And she was changed. Her stomach was swollen. When she moved, her feet touched the ground gently. She buried her nose in the bucket and gobbled the hot breakfast. And when she had finished and had pushed the bucket around the ground with her nose a little, she stepped quietly over to Jody and rubbed her cheek against him.

Billy Buck came out of the saddle-room and walked over. "Starts fast when it starts, doesn't it?"

"Did it come all at once?"

"Oh, no, you just stopped looking for a while." He pulled her head around toward Jody. "She's goin' to be nice, too. See how nice her eyes are! Some mares get mean, but when they turn nice, they just love everything." Nellie slipped her head under Billy's arm and rubbed her neck up and down between his arm and his side. "You better treat her awful nice now," Billy said.

"How long will it be?" Jody demanded breathlessly.

The man counted in whispers on his fingers. "About three months," he said aloud. "You can't tell exactly. Sometimes it's eleven months to the day, but it might be two weeks early, or a month late, without hurting anything."

Jody looked hard at the ground. "Billy," he began nervously, "Billy, you'll call me when it's getting born, won't you? You'll let me be there, won't you?"

Billy bit the tip of Nellie's ear with his front teeth. "Carl says he wants you to start right at the start. That's the only way to learn. Nobody can tell you anything. Like my own man did with me about the saddle blanket. He was a government packer when I was your size, and I helped him some. One day I left a wrinkle in my saddle blanket and made a saddle-sore. My old man didn't give me hell at all. But the next morning he saddled me up with a forty-pound stock saddle. I had to lead my horse and carry that saddle over a whole damn mountain in the sun. It darn near killed me, but I never left no wrinkles in a blanket again. I couldn't. I never in my life since then put on a blanket but I felt that saddle on my back."

Jody reached up a hand and took hold of Nellie's mane. "You'll tell me what to do about everything, won't you? I guess you know everything about horses, don't you?"

Billy laughed. "Why I'm half horse myself, you see," he said. "My ma died when I was born, and being my old man was a government packer in the mountains, and no cows around most of the time, why he just gave me mostly mare's milk." He continued seriously, "And horses know that. Don't you know it, Nellie?"

The mare turned her head and looked full into his eyes for a moment, and this is a thing horses practically never do. Billy was proud and sure of himself now. He boasted a little. "I'll see you get a good colt. I'll start you right. And if you do like I say, you'll have the best horse in the county."

That made Jody feel warm and proud, too; so proud that when he went back to the house he bowed his legs and swayed his shoulders as horsemen do. And he whispered, "Whoa, you Black Demon, you! Steady down there and keep your feet on the ground."

The winter fell sharply. A few preliminary gusty showers, and then a strong steady rain. The hills lost their straw color and blackened under the water, and the winter streams scrambled noisily down the canyons. The mushrooms and puffballs popped up and the new grass started before Christmas.

But this year Christmas was not the central day to Jody. Some undetermined time in January had become the axis day around which the months swung. When the rains fell, he put Nellie in a box stall and fed her warm food every morning and curried her and brushed her.

The mare was swelling so greatly that Jody became alarmed. "She'll pop wide open," he said to Billy.

Billy laid his strong square hand against Nellie's swollen abdomen. "Feel here," he said quietly. "You can feel it move. I guess it would surprise you if there were twin colts."

"You don't think so?" Jody cried. "You don't think it will be twins, do you, Billy?"

"No, I don't, but it does happen, sometimes."

During the first two weeks of January it rained steadily. Jody spent most of his time, when he wasn't in school, in the box stall with Nellie. Twenty times a day he put his hand on her stomach to feel the colt move. Nellie became more and more gentle and friendly to him. She rubbed her nose on him. She whinnied softly when he walked into the barn.

Carl Tiflin came to the barn with Jody one day. He looked admiringly at the groomed bay coat, and he felt the firm flesh over ribs and shoulders. "You've done a good job," he said to Jody. And this was the greatest praise he knew how to give. Jody was tight with pride for hours afterward.

The fifteenth of January came, and the colt was not born. And the twentieth came; a lump of fear began to form in Jody's stomach. "Is it all right?" he demanded of Billy.

"Oh, sure."

And again, "Are you sure it's going to be all right?"

Billy stroked the mare's neck. She swayed her head uneasily. "I told you it wasn't always the same time, Jody. You just have to wait."

When the end of the month arrived with no birth, Jody grew frantic. Nellie was so big that her breath came heavily, and her ears were close together and straight up, as though her head ached. Jody's sleep grew restless, and his dreams confused.

On the night of the second of February he awakened crying. His mother called to him, "Jody, you're dreaming. Wake up and start over again."

But Jody was filled with terror and desolation. He lay quietly a few moments, waiting for his mother to go back to sleep, and then he slipped his clothes on, and crept out in his bare feet.

The night was black and thick. A little misting rain fell. The cypress tree and the bunkhouse loomed and then dropped back into the mist. The barn door screeched as he opened it, a thing it never did in the daytime. Jody went to the rack and found a lantern and a tin box of matches. He lighted the wick and walked down the long straw-covered aisle to Nellie's stall. She was standing up. Her whole body weaved from side to side. Jody called to her, "So, Nellie, so-o, Nellie," but she did not stop her swaying nor look around. When he stepped into the stall and touched her on the shoulder she shivered under his hand. Then Billy Buck's voice came from the hayloft right above the stall.

"Jody, what are you doing?"

Jody started back and turned miserable eyes up toward the nest where Billy was lying in the hay. "Is she all right, do you think?"

"Why sure, I think so."

"You won't let anything happen, Billy, you're sure you won't?"

Billy growled down at him, "I told you I'd call you, and I will. Now you get back to bed and stop worrying that mare. She's got enough to do without you worrying her."

Jody cringed, for he had never heard Billy speak in such a tone. "I only thought I'd come and see," he said. "I woke up."

Billy softened a little then. "Well, you get to bed. I don't want you bothering her. I told you I'd get you a good colt. Get along now."

Jody walked slowly out of the barn. He blew out the lantern and set it in the rack. The blackness of the night, and the chilled mist struck him and enfolded him. He wished he believed everything Billy said as he had before the pony died. It was a moment before his eyes, blinded by the feeble lantern-flame, could make any form of the darkness. The damp ground chilled his bare feet. At the cypress tree the roosting turkeys chattered a little in alarm, and the two good dogs responded to their duty and came charging out, barking to frighten away the coyotes they thought were prowling under the tree.

As he crept through the kitchen, Jody stumbled over a chair. Carl called from his bedroom, "Who's there? What's the matter there?"

And Mrs. Tiflin said sleepily, "What's the matter, Carl?"

The next second Carl came out of the bedroom carrying a candle, and found Jody before he could get into bed. "What are you doing out?"

Jody turned shyly away. "I was down to see the mare."

For a moment anger at being awakened fought with approval in Jody's father. "Listen," he said, finally, "there's not a man in this country that knows more about colts than Billy. You leave it to him."

Words burst out of Jody's mouth. "But the pony died——"

"Don't you go blaming that on him," Carl said sternly. "If Billy can't save a horse, it can't be saved."

Mrs. Tiflin called, "Make him clean his feet and go to bed, Carl. He'll be sleepy all day tomorrow."

It seemed to Jody that he had just closed his eyes to try to go to sleep when he was shaken violently by the shoulder. Billy Buck stood beside him, holding a lantern in his hand. "Get up," he said. "Hurry up." He turned and walked quickly out of the room.

Mrs. Tiflin called, "What's the matter? Is that you, Billy?"

"Yes, ma'am."

"Is Nellie ready?"

"Yes, ma'am."

"All right, I'll get up and heat some water in case you need it."

Jody jumped into his clothes so quickly that he was out the back door before Billy's swinging lantern was halfway to the barn. There was a rim of dawn on the mountain-tops, but no light had penetrated into the cup of the ranch yet. Jody ran frantically after the lantern and caught up to Billy just as he reached the barn. Billy hung the lantern on a nail on the stall-side and took off his blue denim coat. Jody saw that he wore only a sleeveless shirt under it.

Nellie was standing rigid and stiff. While they watched, she crouched. Her whole body was wrung with a spasm. The spasm passed. But in a few moments it started over again, and passed.

Billy muttered nervously, "There's something wrong." His bare hand disappeared. "Oh, Jesus," he said. "It's wrong."

The spasm came again, and this time Billy strained, and the muscles stood out on his arm and shoulder. He heaved strongly, his forehead beaded with perspiration. Nellie cried with pain. Billy was muttering, "It's wrong. I can't turn it. It's way wrong. It's turned all around wrong."

He glared wildly toward Jody. And then his fingers made a careful, careful diagnosis. His cheeks were growing tight and grey. He looked for a long questioning minute at Jody standing back of the stall. Then Billy stepped to the rack under the manure window and picked up a horseshoe hammer with his wet right hand.

"Go outside, Jody," he said.

The boy stood still and stared dully at him.

"Go outside, I tell you. It'll be too late."

Jody didn't move.

Then Billy walked quickly to Nellie's head. He cried, "Turn your face away, damn you, turn your face."

This time Jody obeyed. His head turned sideways. He heard Billy whispering hoarsely in the stall. And then he heard a hollow crunch of bone. Nellie chuckled shrilly. Jody looked back in time to see the hammer rise and fall again on the flat forehead. Then Nellie fell heavily to her side and quivered for a moment.

Billy jumped to the swollen stomach; his big pocket-knife was in his hand. He lifted the skin and drove the knife in. He sawed and ripped at the tough belly. The air filled with the sick odor of warm living entrails. The other horses reared back against their halter chains and squealed and kicked.

Billy dropped the knife. Both of his arms plunged into the terrible ragged hole and dragged out a big, white, dripping bundle. His teeth tore a hole in the covering. A little black head appeared through the tear, and little slick, wet ears. A gurgling breath was drawn, and then another. Billy shucked off the sac and found his knife and cut the string. For a moment he held the little black colt in his arms and looked at it. And then he walked slowly over and laid it in the straw at Jody's feet.

Billy's face and arms and chest were dripping red. His body shivered and his teeth chattered. His voice was gone; he spoke in a throaty whisper. "There's your colt. I promised. And there it is. I had to do it—had to." He stopped and looked over his shoulder into the box stall. "Go get hot water and a sponge," he whispered. "Wash him and dry him the way his mother would. You'll have to feed him by hand. But there's your colt, the way I promised."

Jody stared stupidly at the wet, panting foal. It stretched out its chin and tried to raise its head. Its blank eyes were navy blue.

"God damn you," Billy shouted, "will you go now for the water? *Will you go?*"

Then Jody turned and trotted out of the barn into the dawn. He ached from his throat to his stomach. His legs were stiff and heavy. He tried to be glad because of the colt, but the bloody face, and the haunted, tired eyes of Billy Buck hung in the air ahead of him.

1937

ROBERT PENN WARREN
(1905–)

Robert Penn Warren was born in Guthrie, Kentucky, on April 24, 1905. He distinguished himself as a student, being graduated from Vanderbilt University *summa cum laude* in 1925. Despite his youth he was one of the members of the group, also including John Crowe Ransom and Allen Tate, connected with the magazine *The Fugitive*, founded at Vanderbilt in 1922. Mr. Warren went on to receive the M.A. degree at the University of California in 1927. He pursued further graduate studies at Yale the following year, and proceeded to Oxford University as a Rhodes scholar. There he was awarded the B.Litt. in 1930. While still abroad, he contributed to the southern Agrarians' volume *I'll Take My Stand* (1930), a collection of essays in support of an agrarian, rather than industrial, society.

Despite his many literary activities Warren has pursued primarily the profession of teaching. During 1930–1931 he taught English at Southwestern University, in Memphis. He returned to Vanderbilt to serve as acting assistant professor of English from 1931 to 1934. That fall he went to Louisana State University where, with Cleanth Brooks, he founded and edited the influential *Southern Review*. Warren remained a member of the English department at Louisiana until 1942, when he became professor of English at the University of Minnesota. He left that institution in 1950 to accept a professorship of English at Yale. He has been twice a Guggenheim Fellow, in 1939–1940 and 1947–1948. Although Warren's primary importance arises from his poetry and fiction, he is also noted for his critical publications, written in collaboration with Cleanth Brooks, which are intended to stimulate the teaching of literature in colleges and universities by means of the analytical approach and the closer reading of texts.

Warren's first book was a biography, *John Brown: The Making of A Martyr* (1929). This was followed by a number of distinguished volumes of poetry and prose. His novels, however, have been chiefly responsible for his popular reputation. They are *Night Rider* (1939), *At Heaven's Gate* (1943), *All the King's Men* (1946), *World*

Enough and Time (1950), *Band of Angels* (1955), and *The Cave* (1959). *Brother to Dragons, A Tale in Verse and Voices* appeared in 1953. *All the King's Men* won him the Pulitzer Prize for fiction in 1947 and a Screen Writers Guild award. *Segregation, The Inner Conflict in the South* (1956) is a topical study revealing his abiding interest in social issues.

Aside from a noteworthy control of the language, Warren possesses a talent for the interpretation, as myth, of the events and personalities of American history. Reiterated in his work are the themes of man's personal history, of Time's violence, and of the state of lost innocence which the "frail reproachful *alter ego*" of childhood never permits the restless but ghost-haunted adult to forget.

Significant works, besides those mentioned above, are: *Thirty-Six Poems*, 1935; *Eleven Poems on the Same Theme*, 1942; *Selected Poems, 1923–1943*, 1944; *Promises: Poems, 1954–1956*, 1957; *You, Emperors, And Others: Poems, 1957–1960*, 1960; *Blackberry Winter*, 1946, a long short story; and *The Circus in the Attic and Other Stories*, 1947, from which the selection below has been reprinted.

The Patented Gate and the Mean Hamburger[1]

You have seen him a thousand times. You have seen him standing on the street corner on Saturday afternoon, in the little county-seat towns. He wears blue jean pants, or overalls washed to a pale pastel blue like the color of sky after a shower in spring, but because it is Saturday he has on a wool coat, an old one, perhaps the coat left from the suit he got married in a long time back. His long wrist bones hang out from the sleeves of the coat, the tendons showing along the bone like the dry twist of grapevine still corded on the stove-length of a hickory sapling you would find in his wood box beside his cookstove among the split chunks of gum and red oak.

1. First published in *Mademoiselle* for January, 1947, and collected in the volume entitled *The Circus in the Attic and Other Stories* (1947).

The big hands, with the knotted, cracked joints and the square, horn-thick nails, hang loose off the wrist bone like clumsy, home-made tools hung on the wall of a shed after work. If it is summer, he wears a straw hat with a wide brim, the straw fraying loose around the edge. If it is winter, he wears a felt hat, black once, but now weathered with streaks of dark gray and dull purple in the sun-light. His face is long and bony, the jawbone long under the drawn-in cheeks. The flesh along the jawbone is nicked in a couple of places where the unaccustomed razor has been drawn over the leather-coarse skin. A tiny bit of blood crusts brown where the nick is. The color of the face is red, a dull red like the red clay mud or clay dust which clings to the bottom of his pants and to the cast-iron-looking brogans on his feet, or a red like the color of a piece of hewed cedar which has been left in the weather. The face does not look alive. It seems to be molded from the clay or hewed from the cedar. When the jaw moves, once, with its deliberate, massive motion on the quid of tobacco, you are still not convinced. That motion is but the cunning triumph of a mechanism concealed within.

But you see the eyes. You see that the eyes are alive. They are pale blue or gray, set back under the deep brows and thorny eye-brows. They are not wide, but are squinched up like eyes accus-tomed to wind or sun or to measuring the stroke of the ax or to fixing the object over the rifle sights. When you pass, you see that the eyes are alive and are warily and dispassionately estimating you from the ambush of the thorny brows. Then you pass on, and he stands there in that stillness which is his gift.

With him may be standing two or three others like himself, but they are still, too. They do not talk. The young men, who will be like these men when they get to be fifty or sixty, are down at the beer parlor, carousing and laughing with a high, whickering laugh. But the men on the corner are long past all that. They are past many things. They have endured and will endure in their silence and wisdom. They will stand on the street corner and reject the world which passes under their level gaze as a rabble passes under the guns of a rocky citadel around whose base a slatternly town has assem-bled.

I had seen Jeff York a thousand times, or near, standing like that on the street corner in town, while the people flowed past him, under the distant and wary and dispassionate eyes in ambush. He would be waiting for his wife and the three towheaded children who were walking around the town looking into store windows and at the people. After a while they would come back to him, and then, wordlessly, he would lead them to the store where they al-ways did their trading. He would go first, marching with a steady bent-kneed stride, setting the cast-iron brogans down deliberately on the cement; then his wife, a small woman with covert, sidewise, curious glances for the world, would follow, and behind her the towheads bunched together in a dazed, glory-struck way. In the store, when their turn came, Jeff York would move to the counter, accept the clerk's greeting, and then bend down from his height to catch the whispered directions of his wife. He would straighten up and say, "Gimme a sack of flahr, if'n you please." Then when the sack of flour had been brought, he would lean again to his wife for the next item. When the stuff had all been bought and paid for with the grease-thick, wadded dollar bills which he took from an old leather coin purse with a metal catch to it, he would heave it all together into his arms and march out, his wife and towheads behind him and his eyes fixed level over the heads of the crowd. He would march down the street and around to the hitching lot where the wagons were, and put his stuff into his wagon and cover it with an old quilt to wait till he got ready to drive out to his place.

For Jeff York had a place. That was what made him different from the other men who looked like him and with whom he stood on the street corner on Saturday afternoon. They were croppers,[2] but he, Jeff York, had a place. But he stood with them because his father had stood with their fathers and his grandfathers with their grandfathers, or with men like their fathers and grandfathers, in other towns, in settlements in the mountains, in towns beyond the mountains. They were the great-great-great-grandsons of men who, half woodsmen and half farmers, had been shoved into the sand hills, into the limestone hills, into the barrens, two hundred, two hundred and fifty years before and had learned there the way to grabble a life out of the sand and the stone. And when the soil had leached away into the sand or burnt off the stone, they went on west, walking with the bent-kneed stride over the mountains, their eyes squinching warily in the gaunt faces, the rifle over the crooked arm, hunting a new place.

But there was a curse on them. They only knew the life they knew, and that life did not belong to the fat bottom lands, where the cane was head-tall, and to the grassy meadows and the rich swale. So they passed those places by and hunted for the place which was like home and where they could pick up the old life, with the same feel in the bones and the squirrel's bark sounding the same after first light. They had walked a long way, to the sand hills of Alabama, to the red country of North Mississippi and Louisiana, to the Barrens of Tennessee, to the Knobs of Kentucky and the scrub country of West Kentucky, to the Ozarks. Some of them had stopped in Cobb County, Tennessee, in the hilly eastern part of

2. Sharecroppers; farm tenants who pay a designated share of the crop as rent.

the county, and had built their cabins and dug up the ground for the corn patch. But the land had washed away there, too, and in the end they had come down out of the high land into the bottoms —for half of Cobb County is a rich, swelling country—where the corn was good and the tobacco unfurled a leaf like a yard of green velvet and the white houses stood among the cedars and tulip trees and maples. But they were not to live in the white houses with the limestone chimneys set strong at the end of each gable. No, they were to live in the shacks on the back of the farms, or in cabins not much different from the cabins they had once lived in two hundred years before over the mountains or, later, in the hills of Cobb County. But the shacks and the cabins now stood on somebody else's ground, and the curse which they had brought with them over the mountain trail, more precious than the bullet mold or grandma's quilt, the curse which was the very feeling in the bones and the habit in the hand, had come full circle.

Jeff York was one of those men, but he had broken the curse. It had taken him more than thirty years to do it, from the time when he was nothing but a big boy until he was fifty. It had taken him from sun to sun, year in and year out, and all the sweat in his body, and all the power of rejection he could muster, until the very act of rejection had become a kind of pleasure, a dark, secret, savage dissipation, like an obsessing vice. But those years had given him his place, sixty acres with a house and barn.

When he bought the place, it was not very good. The land was run-down from years of neglect and abuse. But Jeff York put brush in the gullies to stop the wash and planted clover on the run-down fields. He mended the fences, rod by rod. He patched the roof on the little house and propped up the porch, buying the lumber and shingles almost piece by piece and one by one as he could spare the sweat-bright and grease-slick quarters and half-dollars out of his leather purse. Then he painted the house. He painted it white, for he knew that that was the color you painted a house sitting back from the road with its couple of maples, beyond the clover field.

Last, he put up the gate. It was a patented gate, the kind you can ride up to and open by pulling on a pull rope without getting off your horse or out of your buggy or wagon. It had a high pair of posts, well braced and with a high cross-bar between, and the bars for the opening mechanism extending on each side. It was painted white, too. Jeff was even prouder of the gate than he was of the place. Lewis Simmons, who lived next to Jeff's place, swore he had seen Jeff come out after dark on a mule and ride in and out of that gate, back and forth, just for the pleasure of pulling on the rope and making the mechanism work. The gate was the seal Jeff York had put on all the years of sweat and rejection. He could sit on his porch on a Sunday afternoon in summer, before milking time, and look down the rise, down the winding dirt track, to the white gate beyond the clover, and know what he needed to know about all the years passed.

Meanwhile Jeff York had married and had had the three towheads. His wife was twenty years or so younger than he, a small, dark woman, who walked with her head bowed a little and from that humble and unprovoking posture stole sidewise, secret glances at the world from eyes which were brown or black—you never could tell which because you never remembered having looked her straight in the eye—and which were surprisingly bright in that sidewise, secret flicker, like the eyes of a small, cunning bird which surprise you from the brush. When they came to town she moved along the street, with a child in her arms or later with the three trailing behind her, and stole her looks at the world. She wore a calico dress, dun-colored, which hung loose to conceal whatever shape her thin body had, and in winter over the dress a brown wool coat with a scrap of fur at the collar which looked like some tattered growth of fungus feeding on old wood. She wore black high-heeled shoes, slippers of some kind, which she kept polished and which surprised you under that dress and coat. In the slippers she moved with a slightly limping, stealthy gait, almost sliding them along the pavement, as though she had not fully mastered the complicated trick required to use them properly. You knew that she wore them only when she came to town, that she carried them wrapped up in a piece of newspaper until their wagon had reached the first house on the outskirts of town, and that, on the way back, at the same point, she would take them off and wrap them up again and hold the bundle in her lap until she got home. If the weather happened to be bad, or if it was winter, she would have a pair of old brogans under the wagon seat.

It was not that Jeff York was a hard man and kept his wife in clothes that were as bad as those worn by the poorest of the women of the croppers. In fact, some of cropper women, poor or not, black or white, managed to buy dresses with some color in them and proper hats, and went to the moving picture show on Saturday afternoon. But Jeff still owed a little money on his place, less than two hundred dollars, which he had had to borrow to rebuild his barn after it was struck by lightning. He had, in fact, never been entirely out of debt. He had lost a mule which had got out on the highway and been hit by a truck. That had set him back. One of his towheads had been sickly for a couple of winters. He had not been in deep, but he was not a man, with all those years of rejection behind him, to forget the meaning of those years. He was good enough to his family. Nobody ever said the contrary. But he was good to them in terms of all the years he had lived through. He did what he could afford. He bought the towheads a ten-cent bag of colored candy every Saturday afternoon for them to suck on during the ride home in the wagon, and the last thing before they left town, he always took the lot of them over to the dogwagon to get hamburgers and orange pop.

The towheads were crazy about hamburgers. And so was his wife, for that matter. You could tell it, even if she didn't say anything, for she would lift her bowed-forward head a little, and her face would brighten, and she would run her tongue out to wet her lips just as the plate with the hamburger would be set on the counter before her. But all those folks, like Jeff York and his family, like hamburgers, with pickle and onions and mustard and tomato catsup, the whole works. It is something different. They stay out in the country and eat hog-meat, when they can get it, and greens and corn bread and potatoes, and nothing but a pinch of salt to brighten it on the tongue, and when they get to town and get hold of beef and wheat bread and all the stuff to jack up the flavor, they have to swallow to keep the mouth from flooding before they even take the first bite.

So the last thing every Saturday, Jeff York would take his family over to Slick Hardin's *Dew Drop Inn Diner* and give them the treat. The diner was built like a railway coach, but it was set on a concrete foundation on a lot just off the main street of town. At each end the concrete was painted to show wheels. Slick Hardin kept the grass just in front of the place pretty well mowed and one or two summers he even had a couple of flower beds in the middle of that shirttail-size lawn. Slick had a good business. For a few years he had been a prelim fighter over in Nashville and had got his name in the papers a few times. So he was a kind of hero, with the air of romance about him. He had been born, however, right in town and, as soon as he had found out he wasn't ever going to be good enough to be a real fighter, he had come back home and started the dogwagon, the first one ever in town. He was a slick-skinned fellow, about thirty-five, prematurely bald, with his head slick all over. He had big eyes, pale blue and slick looking like agates. When he said something that he thought smart, he would roll his eyes around, slick in his head like marbles, to see who was laughing. Then he'd wink. He had done very well with his business, for despite the fact that he had picked up city ways and a lot of city talk, he still remembered enough to deal with the country people, and they were the ones who brought the dimes in. People who lived right there in town, except for school kids in the afternoon and the young toughs from the pool room or men on the night shift down at the railroad, didn't often get around to the dogwagon.

Slick Hardin was perhaps trying to be smart when he said what he did to Mrs. York. Perhaps he had forgotten, just for that moment, that people like Jeff York and his wife didn't like to be kidded, at least not in that way. He said what he did, and then grinned and rolled his eyes around to see if some of the other people present were thinking it was funny.

Mrs. York was sitting on a stool in front of the counter, flanked on one side by Jeff York and on the other by the three towheads. She had just sat down to wait for the hamburger—there were several orders in ahead of the York order—and had been watching in her sidewise fashion every move of Slick Hardin's hands as he patted the pink meat onto the hot slab and wiped the split buns over the greasy iron to make them ready to receive it. She always watched him like that, and when the hamburger was set before her she would wet her lips with her tongue.

That day Slick set the hamburger down in front of Mrs. York, and said, "Anybody likes hamburger much as you, Mrs. York, ought to git him a hamburger stand."

Mrs. York flushed up, and didn't say anything, staring at her plate. Slick rolled his eyes to see how it was going over, and somebody down the counter snickered. Slick looked back at the Yorks, and if he had not been so encouraged by the snicker he might, when he saw Jeff York's face, have hesitated before going on with his kidding. People like Jeff York are touchous, and they are especially touchous about the women-folks, and you do not make jokes with or about their women-folks unless it is perfectly plain that the joke is a very special kind of friendly joke. The snicker down the counter had defined the joke as not entirely friendly. Jeff was looking at Slick, and something was growing slowly in that hewed-cedar face, and back in the gray eyes in the ambush of thorny brows.

But Slick did not notice. The snicker had encouraged him, and so he said, "Yeah, if I liked them hamburgers much as you, I'd buy me a hamburger stand. Fact, I'm selling this one. You want to buy it?"

There was another snicker, louder, and Jeff York, whose hamburger had been about half way to his mouth for another bite, laid it down deliberately on his plate. But whatever might have happened at that moment did not happen. It did not happen because Mrs. York lifted her flushed face, looked straight at Slick Hardin, swallowed hard to get down a piece of the hamburger or to master her nerve, and said in a sharp, strained voice, "You sellen this place?"

There was complete silence. Nobody had expected her to say anything. The chances were she had never said a word in that diner in the couple of hundred times she had been in it. She had come in with Jeff York and, when a stool had come vacant, had sat down, and Jeff had said, "Gimme five hamburgers, if'n you please, and make 'em well done, and five bottles of orange pop." Then, after the eating was over, he had always laid down seventy-five cents on the counter—that is, after there were five hamburger-eaters in the family—and walked out, putting his brogans down slow, and his wife and kids following without a word. But now she spoke up and asked the question, in that strained, artificial voice, and everybody, including her husband, looked at her with surprise.

As soon as he could take it in, Slick Hardin replied, "Yeah, I'm selling it."

She swallowed hard again, but this time it could not have been hamburger, and demanded, "What you asken fer hit?"

Slick looked at her in the new silence, half shrugged, a little contemptuously, and said, "Fourteen hundred and fifty dollars."

She looked back at him, while the blood ebbed from her face. "Hit's a lot of money," she said in a flat tone, and returned her gaze to the hamburger on her plate.

"Lady," Slick said defensively, "I got that much money tied up here. Look at that there stove. It is a *Heat Master* and they cost. Them coffee urns, now. Money can't buy no better. And this here lot, lady, the diner sets on. Anybody knows I got that much money tied up here. I got more. This lot cost me more'n . . ." He suddenly realized that she was not listening to him. And he must have realized, too, that she didn't have a dime in the world and couldn't buy his diner, and that he was making a fool of himself, defending his price. He stopped abruptly, shrugged his shoulders, and then swung his wide gaze down the counter to pick out somebody to wink to.

But before he got the wink off, Jeff York had said, "Mr. Hardin."

Slick looked at him and asked, "Yeah?"

"She didn't mean no harm," Jeff York said. "She didn't mean to be messen in yore business."

Slick shrugged. "Ain't no skin off my nose," he said. "Ain't no secret I'm selling out. My price ain't no secret neither."

Mrs. York bowed her head over her plate. She was chewing a mouthful of her hamburger with a slow, abstracted motion of her jaw, and you knew that it was flavorless on her tongue.

That was, of course, on a Saturday. On Thursday afternoon of the next week Slick was in the diner alone. It was the slack time, right in the middle of the afternoon. Slick, as he told it later, was wiping off the stove and wasn't noticing. He was sort of whistling to himself, he said. He had a way of whistling soft through his teeth. But he wasn't whistling loud, he said, not so loud he wouldn't have heard the door open or the steps if she hadn't come gum-shoeing in on him to stand there waiting in the middle of the floor until he turned round and was so surprised he nearly had heart failure. He had thought he was there alone, and there she was, watching every move he was making, like a cat watching a goldfish swim in a bowl.

"Howdy-do," he said, when he got his breath back.

"This place still fer sale?" she asked him.

"Yeah, lady," he said.

"What you asken fer hit?"

"Lady I done told you," Slick replied, "fourteen hundred and fifty dollars."

"Hit's a heap of money," she said.

Slick started to tell her how much money he had tied up there, but before he had got going, she had turned and slipped out of the door.

"Yeah," Slick said later to the men who came into the diner, "me like a fool starting to tell her how much money I got tied up here when I knowed she didn't have a dime. That woman's crazy. She must walked that five or six miles in here just to ask me some-thing she already knowed the answer to. And then turned right round and walked out. But I am selling me this place. I'm tired of slinging hash to them hicks. I got me some connections over in Nashville and I'm gonna open me a place over there. A cigar stand and about three pool tables and maybe some beer. I'll have me a sort of club in the back. You know, membership cards to git in, where the boys will play a little game. Just sociable. I got good connections over in Nashville. I'm selling this place. But that woman, she ain't got a dime. She ain't gonna buy it."

But she did.

On Saturday Jeff York led his family over to the diner. They ate hamburgers without a word and marched out. After they had gone, Slick said, "Looks like she ain't going to make the invest-mint. Gonna buy a block of bank stock instead." Then he rolled his eyes, located a brother down the counter, and winked.

It was almost the end of the next week before it happened. What had been going on inside the white house out on Jeff York's place nobody knew or was to know. Perhaps she just starved him out, just not doing the cooking or burning everything. Perhaps she just quit attending to the children properly and he had to come back tired from work and take care of them. Perhaps she just lay in bed at night and talked and talked to him, asking him to buy it, nagging him all night long, while he would fall asleep and then wake up with a start to hear her voice still going on. Or perhaps she just

turned her face away from him and wouldn't let him touch her. He
was a lot older than she, and she was probably the only woman he
had ever had. He had been too ridden by his dream and his passion
for rejection during all the years before to lay even a finger on a
woman. So she had him there. Because he was a lot older and because he had never had another woman. But perhaps she used none
of these methods. She was a small, dark, cunning woman, with a
sidewise look from her lowered face, and she could have thought
up ways of her own, no doubt.

Whatever she thought up, it worked. On Friday morning Jeff
York went to the bank. He wanted to mortgage his place, he told
Todd Sullivan, the president. He wanted fourteen hundred and
fifty dollars, he said. Todd Sullivan would not let him have it. He
already owed the bank one hundred and sixty dollars and the best
he could get on a mortgage was eleven hundred dollars. That was in
1935 and then farmland wasn't worth much and half the land in
the country was mortgaged anyway. Jeff York sat in the chair by
Todd Sullivan's desk and didn't say anything. Eleven hundred
dollars would not do him any good. Take off the hundred and sixty
he owed and it wouldn't be but a little over nine hundred dollars
clear to him. He sat there quietly for a minute, apparently turning
that fact over in his head. Then Todd Sullivan asked him, "How
much you say you need?"

Jeff York told him.

"What you want it for?" Todd Sullivan asked.

He told him that.

"I tell you," Todd Sullivan said, "I don't want to stand in the
way of a man bettering himself. Never did. That diner ought to be
a good proposition, all right, and I don't want to stand in your way
if you want to come to town and better yourself. It will be a step
up from that farm for you, and I like a man has got ambition. The
bank can't lend you the money, not on that piece of property. But
I tell you what I'll do. I'll buy your place. I got me some walking
horses I'm keeping out on my father's place. But I could use me a
little place of my own. For my horses. I'll give you seventeen
hundred for it. Cash."

Jeff York did not say anything to that. He looked slow at Todd
Sullivan as though he did not understand.

"Seventeen hundred," the banker repeated. "That's a good
figure. For these times."

Jeff was not looking at him now. He was looking out the window,
across the alleyway—Todd Sullivan's office was in the back of the
bank. The banker, telling about it later when the doings of Jeff
York had become for a moment a matter of interest, said, "I
thought he hadn't even heard me. He looked like he was half

asleep or something. I coughed to sort of wake him up. You know the way you do. I didn't want to rush him. You can't rush those people, you know. But I couldn't sit there all day. I had offered him a fair price."

It was, as a matter of fact, a fair price for the times, when the bottom was out of everything in the section.

Jeff York took it. He took the seventeen hundred dollars and bought the dogwagon with it, and rented a little house on the edge of town and moved in with his wife and the towheads. The first day after they got settled, Jeff York and his wife went over to the diner to get instructions from Slick about running the place. He showed Mrs. York all about how to work the coffee machine and the stove, and how to make up the sandwiches, and how to clean the place up after herself. She fried up hamburgers for all of them, herself, her husband, and Slick Hardin, for practice, and they ate hamburgers while a couple of hangers-on watched them. "Lady," Slick said, for he had money in his pocket and was heading out for Nashville on the seven o'clock train that night, and was feeling expansive, "lady, you sure fling a mean hamburger."

He wiped the last crumbs and mustard off his lips, got his valise from behind the door, and said, "Lady, git in there and pitch. I hope you make a million hamburgers." Then he stepped out into the bright fall sunshine and walked away whistling up the street, whistling through his teeth and rolling his eyes as though there were somebody to wink to. That was the last anybody in town ever saw of Slick Hardin.

The next day, Jeff York worked all day down at the diner. He was scrubbing up the place inside and cleaning up the trash which had accumulated behind it. He burned all the trash. Then he gave the place a good coat of paint outside, white paint. That took him two days. Then he touched up the counter inside with varnish. He straightened up the sign out front, which had begun to sag a little. He had that place looking spick and span.

Then on the fifth day after they got settled—it was Sunday—he took a walk in the country. It was along toward sunset when he started out, not late, as a matter of fact, for by October the days are shortening up. He walked out the Curtisville pike and out the cut-off leading to his farm. When he entered the cut-off, about a mile from his own place, it was still light enough for the Bowdoins, who had a filling station at the corner, to see him plain when he passed.

The next time anybody saw him was on Monday morning about six o'clock. A man taking milk into town saw him. He was hanging from the main cross bar of the white patented gate. He had jumped off the gate. But he had propped the thing open so there wouldn't be any chance of clambering back up on it if his neck didn't break when he jumped and he should happen to change his mind.

But that was an unnecessary precaution, as it developed. Dr. Stauffer said that his neck was broken very clean. "A man who can break a neck as clean as that could make a living at it," Dr. Stauffer said. And added, "If he's damned sure it ain't ever his own neck."

Mrs. York was much cut up by her husband's death. People were sympathetic and helpful, and out of a mixture of sympathy and curiosity she got a good starting trade at the diner. And the trade kept right on. She got so she didn't hang her head and look sidewise at you and the world. She would look straight at you. She got so she could walk in high heels without giving the impression that it was a trick she was learning. She wasn't a bad-looking woman, as a matter of fact, once she had caught on how to fix herself up a little. The railroad men and the pool hall gang liked to hang out there and kid with her. Also, they said, she flung a mean hamburger.

1947

Metaphor of poetry appeals to areas of consciousness in which we are most alive—imaginative, emotional thinking apprehension of, metaphys wit must be instantaneous & sure so that mind may smile.

Metaphysical Poetry

The Poetry of Idea and Order

form vs. ideological complexity
double abstraction — must proceed fr obs of artist →
objective realization of idea → idea itself

idea has some spread of actuality at matter, ∴ can apply same criteria as to poetry of material thing

WALLACE STEVENS

(1879–1955)

Wallace Stevens created his poetry as a gifted nonprofessional, less concerned about promoting his literary reputation than about perfecting what he wrote. This passion for perfection is apparent in his disciplined thought, his intense and brilliant craftsmanship, and the meticulous propriety of his language, upon which he imposed the double burden of his wit and his faith that the clarification of the inner significance of an idea is a high function of poetry. It has been generally assumed that the intellectualist tendencies of a number of modern poets represent their alienation from society and a desire for escape. This is certainly not true of Stevens. His work is primarily motivated by the belief that "ideas of order," that is, true ideas, correspond with an innate order in nature and the universe, and that it is the high privilege of individuals and mankind to seek to discover this correspondence. Hence, many of his best poems derive their emotional power from reasoned revelation. This philosophical intention is emphasized by the titles which Stevens gave to his volumes— for example, *Harmonium*, *Ideas of Order*, and *Parts of a World*.

Wallace Stevens was certainly not an alienated escapist in his personal life. A successful lawyer and corporation executive, he became a discriminating enthusiast of the arts and of the sophisticated expressions of the good life which he found at home and abroad. Stevens was born in Reading, Pennsylvania, on October 2, 1879. He prepared for a career in law at Harvard University and at New York University Law School. Admitted to the bar in 1904, he engaged in general practice in New York City until 1916, when he became associated with the Hartford Accident and Indemnity Company. In 1934 he became vice-president of this insurance company, and he continued in its service until his retirement. Although he did not collect a volume of his poems until 1923,

participates in experience which is highest consciousness of mind.

when he was already forty-four, he was actually one of the older generation of the "new" poets, who, after 1910, appeared in the flourishing little magazines, especially *Poetry: A Magazine of Verse.* *Harmonium* (1923) established his stature among the few poets of ideas.

Harmonium was revised and somewhat enlarged in 1931; meanwhile Stevens' accumulation of new poems, while slow, was steady, and the occasional appearance of one of them in a magazine gave evidence of his continued absorption with ideas of increasing subtlety. He perfected a style that brilliantly embodied his extraordinary wit in corresponding rhythmic and tonal effects, and in his ability to recall simultaneously the essential meaning and the connotative suggestions of a particular word. Twelve years elapsed without the appearance of a new volume, but from 1935 to 1937 there were three,

each of considerable size, including his much admired *Man with the Blue Guitar.* Thereafter Stevens' volumes appeared at shorter intervals, and he assumed a position of foremost authority among the poets of the advanced and difficult form which he practiced. He won the Bollingen Poetry Prize for 1949, and died in 1955.

The definitive edition, to date, is *The Collected Poems of Wallace Stevens,* 1954. Other volumes are *Harmonium,* 1923, revised and enlarged 1931, 1937; *Ideas of Order,* 1935; *Owl's Clover,* 1936; *The Man with the Blue Guitar,* 1937; *Parts of a World,* 1942, revised, 1951; *Notes Toward a Supreme Fiction,* 1942; *Esthétique du Mal,* 1944; *Transport to Summer,* 1947; *Three Academic Pieces,* 1947; *A Primitive Like an Orb,* 1948; *The Auroras of Autumn,* 1950; *The Man with the Blue Guitar* and *Ideas of Order,* combined edition, 1952; *Selected Poems,* 1953; and *Opus Posthumous,* 1957, edited by S. F. Morse. *The Necessary Angel* * * * , 1951, expounds Stevens' theory of poetry.

Major critical studies are W. V. O'Connor, *The Shaping Spirit* * * * , 1950; S. F. Morse, *Wallace Stevens,* 1950; R. Pack, *Wallace Stevens* * * * , 1958; A. Brown and R. S. Haller, *The Achievement of Wallace Stevens,* 1961.

A High-toned Old Christian Woman

Poetry is the supreme fiction,[1] madame.
Take the moral law and make a nave of it
And from the nave[2] build haunted heaven. Thus,
The conscience is converted into palms,
Like windy citherns hankering for hymns.   5
We agree in principle. That's clear. But take
The opposing law and make a peristyle,[3]
And from the peristyle project a masque[4]

1. Twenty-two years later, Stevens still attached cryptic importance to this phrase. See the poem "Notes Toward a Supreme Fiction" (1945), collected in *Transport to Summer* (1947).
2. The principal part of a church, for the congregation. The nave generally is lighted by clerestory windows (*cf.* "heaven").

3. A system of columns surrounding a building or court; sometimes the space thus enclosed. Here it is compared with "nave," which, by contrast, exerts a more obvious upward thrust. Observe that the peristyle is usually associated with pagan (Greek) temples, the nave with Christian churches and cathedrals.
4. A festive dance, or revels, generally employing worldly masquerades.

Beyond the planets. Thus, our bawdiness,[5]
Unpurged by epitaph, indulged at last,   10
Is equally converted into palms,[6]
Squiggling like saxophones. And palm for palm,
Madame, we are where we began. Allow,
Therefore, that in the planetary scene
Your disaffected flagellants,[7] well stuffed,   15
Smacking their muzzy[8] bellies in parade,
Proud of such novelties of the sublime,
Such tink and tank and tunk-a-tunk-tunk,
May, merely may, madame, whip from themselves
A jovial hullabaloo among the spheres.   20
This will make widows wince: But fictive things[9]
Wink as they will. Wink most when widows wince.

ideation- projecting time-a-lity of experience
the idea on which the a... is based. ... on...
1923

Peter Quince at the Clavier[1]

I

Just as my fingers on these keys
Make music, so the self-same sounds
On my spirit make a music, too.

Music is feeling, then, not sound;
And thus it is that what I feel,   5
Here in this room, desiring you,

Thinking of your blue-shadowed silk,
Is music. It is like the strain
Waked in the elders by Susanna.[2]

5. The word "bawd" retains from its derivation the association of "merry boldness."
6. *Cf*. l. 4. Palm leaves have at various times been carried in pagan, Christian, and quite worldly processionals. Here they suggest saxophones, lewd instruments, contrasted with "citherns" (l. 5).
7. In many periods the practice of piety has been accompanied by flagellation.
8. Muddled.
9. That is, things created by imaginative power.
1. That is, Peter Quince at the keyboard, here presumably that of a harmonium, since the poem was collected in the poet's first volume, *Harmonium* (1923). In Shakespeare's *A Midsummer-Night's Dream*, Act I, Scene 2, Peter Quince appears as director of an "interlude before the duke and the duchess, on his wedding day at night."

Performed by such actors as Bottom, a weaver, Snout, a tinker, and Starveling, a tailor, the interlude degenerates into a madcap farce, although it portrays the "most cruel death of Pyramus and Thisby" (*cf*. Ovid, "Pyramus and Thisbe," *Metamorphoses*, Book IV). Like the elders of the present Susanna story, Ovid's lovers came to their death in defying social convention. In presenting his story, Stevens may also have remembered the advice that Bottom gave Quince (ll. 8–10): "First, good Peter Quince, say what the play treats on, then read the names of the actors, and so grow on to a point." The text given here is that of *The Collected Poems of Wallace Stevens* (1954).
2. The story of Susanna and the elders appears in the History of Susanna, a book of the Old Testament Apocrypha. The alleged incident occurred during the Babylonian captivity, before the death

Of a green evening, clear and warm,
She bathed in her still garden, while
The red-eyed elders watching, felt

The basses of their beings throb
In witching chords, and their thin blood
Pulse pizzicati of Hosanna.[3]

10

15

II

In the green water, clear and warm,
Susanna lay.
She searched
The touch of springs,
And found
Concealed imaginings.
She sighed,
For so much melody.

20

Upon the bank, she stood
In the cool
Of spent emotions.
She felt, among the leaves,
The dew
Of old devotions.

25

She walked upon the grass,
Still quavering.
The winds were like her maids,
On timid feet,
Fetching her woven scarves,
Yet wavering.

30

35

A breath upon her hand
Muted the night.
She turned—
A cymbal crashed,
And roaring horns.

40

III

Soon, with a noise like tambourines,[4]
Came her attendant Byzantines.[5]

of the prophet Daniel, about 534 B.C.
Certain Hebrew elders attempted the
seduction of Susanna, wife of the
beautiful and virtuous Joachim, by
the device described in this poem. When
Susanna accused them, they counter-
charged that she had solicited their attentions. Daniel proved her innocence
and the elders were executed.
3. Pizzicati notes, produced by plucking
the strings of an instrument instead of
bowing, are thin and tinkling and asso-

ciated with the dance; while a Hosanna,
a song of praise to God, usually calls
for deeper and richer tones.
4. Since the tambourine anciently originated in oriental dancing, the word in
this context conveys the apt suggestion
of the swish and tinkle of women's garments and metal ornaments.
5. Probably slaves, from Byzantium,
now Istanbul in modern Turkey, and
previously (after 330 A.D.) known as

They wondered why Susanna cried
Against the elders by her side;

And as they whispered, the refrain   45
Was like a willow swept by rain.

Anon, their lamps' uplifted flame
Revealed Susanna and her shame.

And then, the simpering Byzantines
Fled, with a noise like tambourines.   50
                    IV
Beauty is momentary in the mind—
The fitful tracing of a portal;
But in the flesh it is immortal.

The body dies; the body's beauty lives.
So evenings die, in their green going,   55
A wave, interminably flowing.
So gardens die, their meek breath scenting
The cowl of winter, done repenting.
So maidens die, to the auroral
Celebration of a maiden's choral.   60
Susanna's music touched the bawdy strings
Of those white elders; but, escaping,
Left only Death's ironic scraping.
Now, in its immortality, it plays
On the clear viol of her memory,   65
And makes a constant sacrament of praise.

                                            1923

The Glass of Water

That the glass would melt in heat,
That the water would freeze in cold,
Shows that this object is merely a state,
One of many, between two poles. So,
In the metaphysical, there are these poles.   5

Here in the centre stands the glass. Light
Is the lion that comes down to drink. There
And in that state, the glass is a pool.
Ruddy are his eyes and ruddy are his claws
When light comes down to wet his frothy jaws   10

Constantinople. At the time of Susanna,   was a Greek city often attacked by
in the sixth century B.C., Byzantium   enemies.

And in the water winding weeds move round.
And there and in another state—the refractions,
The *metaphysica*,[6] the plastic parts of poems
Crash in the mind—But, fat Jocundus,[7] worrying
About what stands here in the centre, not the glass,   15

But in the centre of our lives, this time, this day,
It is a state, this spring among the politicians
Playing cards. In a village of the indigenes,
One would still have to discover. Among the dogs and dung,
One would continue to contend with one's ideas.   20

1942

immortal life

The Candle   A Saint

living vitality

—Green is the night, green kindled and apparelled.
It is she that walks among astronomers.

She strides above the rabbit and the cat,
Like a noble figure, out of the sky,

Moving among the sleepers, the men,
Those that lie chanting *green is the night*.   5

Green is the night and out of madness woven,
The self-same madness of the astronomers

And of him that sees, beyond the astronomers,
The topaz rabbit and the emerald cat,   10

That sees above them, that sees rise up above them,
The noble figure, the essential shadow,

Moving and being, the image at its source,
The abstract, the archaic queen. Green is the night.

1942

6. The word "metaphysics" is derived
from the Greek: *meta* "beyond, after"
+ *physikos* "relating to external nature."
7. Latin, literally "the cheerful [or
merry] fellow." But note the next word.

metaphysical use of word.
Poetry in everything if can only find it & get it out.

WILLIAM CARLOS WILLIAMS

(1883–)

wit

The physician as man of letters, whether Rabelais or Dr. Oliver Wendell Holmes, has char- acteristically shown a special knowledge of humanity, a diag- nostic attitude toward its frailty

Poems of every day life - rhythm ɪ not line length

and follies, and a vigorous, often iconoclastic, realism. These characteristics all appear strongly in the work of Dr. William Carlos Williams. He has displayed a probing and clinical realism, and as one taught by science not to be squeamish, he has sought beauty and truth in the vulgar or the common as much as in the uncommon. With this in mind, Wallace Stevens once called Williams' materials "antipoetic"; he writes not only of the stars in heaven but also of the plums in the icebox, the white chickens beside a red wheelbarrow, the beauty of weeds on the sour land "by the contagious hospital." Like Stevens he is a poet of ideas; but his ideas are inspired, not by philosophical abstractions, as so often with Stevens, but by things, or by the relation of one thing with another, as in "Tract," or by the beauty and composition of the thing, as in "Queen-Ann's-Lace," or by common principles of nature that apply to the life of man, as in "The Pause." Williams' early interest in painting, under the influence of two of his friends, the artists Sheeler and DeMuth, is reflected in his sharp and graphic figures, and in his feeling for form, texture, and color. With such instruments, and with his extraordinary command of the word and of rhythm, he has been at his best a disturbing and thought-provoking poet. If his writing is uneven, and would benefit from judicious editing, it is only fair to remember that his literary work—stories, novels, and poems—has generally been produced in competition with

the demands of an exacting and useful professional life.

William Carlos Williams was born in Rutherford, New Jersey, on September 17, 1883. His mother was of Spanish descent. After attending the Horace Mann High School in New York, and a preparatory school in Switzerland, he began his medical training at the University of Pennsylvania. There he gave what spare time he could find to his early poetry. He was fortunate to develop a friendship with Pound, then a student in the graduate school at the University. After his graduation in 1906, Williams went abroad to take post graduate work in pediatrics at the University of Leipzig. He renewed his friendship with Pound, who was by then in London and a leader among the young experimental poets, with whom Williams listened to talk of imagism and other *avant-garde* writing. Although Pound included work by Williams in the first imagist anthology, the young physician was an individualistic poet even then, as he has been ever since.

Williams soon returned to Rutherford, where he has practiced medicine since 1910. In 1909 he collected his first volume of poems, inaugurating a literary career that has produced more than twenty volumes of poetry and fiction. For many years he contributed steadily to the little magazines, and he was one of the best-known poets during the flourishing period of the 1920's. In many of his poems, and in the prose essays that often appeared in the same volumes, he kept up a running fire of commentary on his age, its foibles, and its art. At the same time he expressed his devotion to medicine in a highly successful professional career. His practice included an industrial district along the Passaic and in the adjacent city of Paterson. The lives of the less privileged people whom he knew so well are reflected in his poetry, but even more in his novels and in the quite unusual short stories which he has collected in several volumes. *Paterson,* a work in progress since 1946, is an individualistic epic in form, incorporating the history, the characters, and the myths of Paterson from its Indian origins to its industrial present. His lively *Autobiography* (1951) shows the surprising range of his association with the *avant garde* of American letters, especially during the critical period from 1910 to 1930. Williams received the Dial Award for Services to American Literature in 1926, the

Guarantors Prize awarded by *Poetry: A Magazine of Verse* in 1931, the Loines Award in 1948, and the National Book Award, for *Paterson,* in 1949.

The following collections provide a cross-section of his best work: *Collected Poems, 1921–1931,* 1934; *Complete Collected Poems, 1906–1938,* 1938; *Selected Poems,* 1949; *Collected Later Poetry of William Carlos Williams,* 1950; *Collected Earlier Poems of William Carlos Williams,* 1951; *Paterson,* 4 vols., 1946–1951, collected in one volume 1951; *The Desert Music and Other Poems,* 1954; and *Journey to Love,* 1955. *Paterson, Book V* appeared in 1958. Short stories include *The Knife of the Times,* 1932; *Life Along the Passaic River,* 1938; *Make Light of It,* 1950. His novels are *A Voyage to Pagany,* 1928; *White Mule,* 1937; *In the Money,* 1940; and *The Build-Up,* 1952. Collections of his essays are *The Great American Novel,* 1923; *In the American Grain,* 1925, reissued 1940; and *Selected Essays of William Carlos Williams,* 1954. *Many Loves,* a play, was produced in 1958. *The Selected Letters of William Carlos Williams,* 1957, was edited by J. C. Thirlwall. *The Autobiography of William Carlos Williams* appeared in 1951. A critical and biographical study is Vivienne Koch, *William Carlos Williams,* 1950.

Tract

I will teach you my townspeople
how to perform a funeral—
for you have it over a troop
of artists—
unless one should scour the world—   5
you have the ground sense necessary.

See! the hearse leads.
I begin with a design for a hearse.
For Christ's sake not black[1]—
nor white either—and not polished!   10
Let it be weathered—like a farm wagon—
with gilt wheels (this could be

1. *Cf.* the persistent biblical concept of God as immortal Light, and the identification of Christ with the Light in the Gospels, especially John i: 1–9; and iii: 19.

applied fresh at small expense)
or no wheels at all:
a rough dray to drag over the ground.   15

Knock the glass out!
My God—glass, my townspeople!
For what purpose? Is it for the dead
to look out or for us to see
how well he is housed or to see   20
the flowers or the lack of them—
or what?
To keep the rain and snow from him?
He will have a heavier rain soon:
pebbles and dirt and what not.   25
Let there be no glass—
and no upholstery! phew!
and no little brass rollers
and small easy wheels on the bottom—
my townspeople what are you thinking of!   30

A rough plain hearse then
with gilt wheels and no top at all.
On this the coffin lies
by its own weight.

                    No wreaths please—   35
especially no hot-house flowers.
Some common memento is better,
something he prized and is known by:
his old clothes—a few books perhaps—
God knows what! You realize   40
how we are about these things,
my townspeople—
something will be found—anything—
even flowers if he had come to that.
So much for the hearse.   45

For heaven's sake though see to the driver!
Take off the silk hat! In fact
that's no place at all for him
up there unceremoniously
dragging our friend out to his own dignity!   50
Bring him down—bring him down!
Low and inconspicuous! I'd not have him ride
on the wagon at all—damn him—
the undertaker's understrapper!

Let him hold the reins   55
and walk at the side
and inconspicuously too!

Then briefly as to yourselves:
Walk behind—as they do in France,
seventh class, or if you ride   60
Hell take curtains! Go with some show
of inconvenience; sit openly—
to the weather as to grief.
Or do you think you can shut grief in?
What—from us? We who have perhaps   65
nothing to lose? Share with us
share with us—it will be money
in your pockets.
                    Go now
I think you are ready.

                                                                      1920

Love
desire = sex + purity

Queen-Ann's-Lace *prolific*

Her body is not so white as
anemone petals nor so smooth—nor
so remote a thing. It is a field
of the wild carrot taking
the field by force; the grass   5
does not raise above it.
Here is no question of whiteness,
white as can be, with a purple mole[2]
at the center of each flower.
Each flower is a hand's span   10
of her whiteness. Wherever
his hand has lain there is
a tiny purple blemish. Each part
is a blossom under his touch
to which the fibers of her being   15
stem one by one, each to its end,
until the whole field is a
white desire, empty, a single stem,
a cluster, flower by flower,

2. A single purple blossom in the center of the flower head of the Queen Anne's lace, or wild carrot. Actually, the "flower" is an umbel composed of a multitude of such tiny blossoms, all white except this one, and all joined downward to the top of the main stalk by an intricate system of tiny stems (*cf.* ll. 15–16).

a pious wish to whiteness gone over—
or nothing.

20

1921

The Pause

period of generation

Values are split, summer, the fierce
jet an axe would not sever, spreads out
at length, of its own weight, a rainbow
over the lake of memory—the hard
stem of pure speed broken. Autumn   5
comes, fruit of many contours, that
glistening tegument painters love hiding
the soft pulp of the insidious reason,
dormant, for worm to nibble or for woman.
But there, within the seed, shaken by   10
fear as by a sea, it wakes again! to
drive upward, presently, from that soft
belly such a stem as will crack quartz.

1950

birth & new creatures

JOHN CROWE RANSOM
(1888–)

John Crowe Ransom was born in Pulaski, Tennessee, on April 30, 1888, the son of a Methodist clergyman. He attended school in Nashville before entering Vanderbilt University, from which he was graduated in 1909. The following year he was appointed a Rhodes scholar and enrolled at Christ Church College, Oxford. He received the B.A. in 1913, having taken the "Greats," or classical course. After a year's teaching in a Mississippi secondary school he was appointed a member of the Vanderbilt English department. In 1922 he was one of the founders of the magazine *The*

Fugitive, published at the University, with which such young authors as Allen Tate and Robert Penn Warren were also connected. Except for two years' service in the field artillery during World War I and a year's leave as a Guggenheim Fellow during 1931–1932, he remained a professor at Vanderbilt until 1937, resigning in that year to accept the position of Carnegie Professor of English at Kenyon College and to found and edit the *Kenyon Review*.

Ransom's career as a poet defined itself in large measure during his stay at Vanderbilt, although after he went to Kenyon he took a decided turn in a direction which had not been dominant before—that of literary criticism. *Poems About God* appeared in 1919, *Chills and Fever* in 1924, and *Two Gentlemen in Bonds* in 1926. The characteristic of his poetry most often noticed by critics is the skillful combination of wit and irony. The emotions are played down. "Assuredly I have a grief," he writes in the epigraph to one volume, "and I am shaken, but not as a leaf." His is a guarded style which suppresses any trace of sentimentality. It might be termed a semiclassical, mockingly pedantic treatment of romantic subjects. Despite some use of local detail, he cannot be classified as a local colorist.

Ransom's interests by 1930 had shifted toward social criticism. That year appeared *God Without Thunder*, the thesis of which is that Western man has suffered a tragic loss or defeat in surrendering to the modern deity, Science. Through this surrender God has been deprived of his Thunder, which is his Mystery. Also in 1930 the volume *I'll Take My Stand* was published "by Twelve Southerners," of whom Ransom was one. This was a collection of essays in defense of an agrarian, as opposed to an industrial,

society.

Ransom's latest interest, literary criticism, is evident in the pages of the *Kenyon Review*. He has also written two volumes important in revealing his conception of what the best poetry should be like. In 1938 was published *The World's Body*, in which he argues that it is the function of poetry to represent the fullness, or "body," of experience, something which science, with its concern for the abstract, is incapable of doing. His other collection of essays, *The New Criticism* (1941) examines and undertakes to evaluate the achievement of four contemporaries: I. A. Richards, T. S. Eliot, Yvor Winters, and William Empson. It concludes with Ransom's own statement of preference: "Wanted: An Ontological Critic." In 1945 he published his rigidly chosen *Selected Poems*. Nothing from *Poems About God* was reprinted. *Poems and Essays* appeared in 1955.

There is no collected edition of his works. His principal volumes have been named above. No book-length biography or critical study of Ransom has appeared, although he has been the subject of numerous critical articles and is discussed in almost all recent anthologies and literary histories. The most useful single reference is *Homage to John Ransom: Essays on His Work as Poet and Critic*, in the Summer, 1948, issue of the *Sewanee Review*.

Bells for John Whiteside's Daughter

There was such speed in her little body,
And such lightness in her footfall,
It is no wonder that her brown study[1]
Astonishes us all.

1. Reverie or daydream.

Her wars were bruited in our high window.   5
We looked among orchard trees and beyond,
Where she took arms against her shadow,
Or harried unto the pond

The lazy geese, like a snow cloud
Dripping their snow on the green grass,   10
Tricking and stopping, sleepy and proud,
Who cried in goose, Alas,

For the tireless heart within the little
Lady with rod that made them rise
From their noon apple-dreams, and scuttle   15
Goose-fashion under the skies!

But now go the bells, and we are ready;
In one house we are sternly stopped
To say we are vexed at her brown study,
Lying so primly propped.   20

1924

Antique Harvesters[2]

(*Scene: Of the Mississippi the bank sinister, and of the
Ohio the bank sinister*)[3]

Tawny are the leaves turned, but they still hold.
It is the harvest; what shall this land produce?
A meager hill of kernels, a runnel of juice.
Declension looks from our land, it is old.
Therefore let us assemble, dry, gray, spare,   5
And mild as yellow air.

"I hear the creak of a raven's funeral wing."
The young men would be joying in the song
Of passionate birds; their memories are not long.
What is it thus rehearsed in sable? "Nothing."   10
Trust not but the old endure, and shall be older
Than the scornful beholder.

We pluck the spindling ears and gather the corn.
One spot has special yield? "On this spot stood
Heroes and drenched it with their only blood."   15

2. The title, suggesting a painting, calls attention to the stylized pictorial quality intended in the poem.
3. In Latin, *sinister* literally signifies "left" or "on the left hand." The left (sinister) bank of the Ohio was the northern limit of slave soil at the time of the Civil War; and the crossing of the Ohio had long meant freedom for Negro slaves. Hence "sinister" here has double meaning.

And talk meets talk, as echoes from the horn
Of the hunter—echoes are the old men's arts
Ample are the chambers of their hearts.

Here come the hunters, keepers of a rite.
The horn, the hounds, the lank mares coursing by   20
Under quaint archetypes of chivalry;
And the fox, lovely ritualist, in flight
Offering his unearthly ghost to quarry;
And the fields, themselves to harry.

Resume, harvesters. The treasure is full bronze   25
Which you will garner for the Lady,[4] and the moon
Could tinge it no yellower than does this noon;
But the gray will quench it shortly—the fields, men, stones.
Pluck fast, dreamers; prove as you rumble slowly
Not less than men, not wholly.   30

Bare the arm too, dainty youths, bend the knees
Under bronze burdens. And by an autumn tone
As by a gray, as by a green, you will have known
Your famous Lady's image; for so have these.
And if one say that easily will your hands   35
More prosper in other lands,

Angry as wasp-music be your cry then:
"Forsake the Proud Lady, of the heart of fire,
The look of snow, to the praise of a dwindled choir,
Song of degenerate specters that were men?   40
The sons of the fathers shall keep her, worthy of
What these have done in love."

True, it is said of our Lady, she ageth.
But see, if you peep shrewdly, she hath not stooped;
Take no thought of her servitors that have drooped,   45
For we are nothing; and if one talk of death—
Why, the ribs of the earth subsist frail as a breath
If but God wearieth.

1924

The Equilibrists[5]

Comic

Full of her long white arms and milky skin
He had a thousand times remembered sin.

---

4. The language of chivalry is here employed to refer to the old southland, personified as a woman in the last four stanzas of the poem.

5. Ordinarily the word signifies acrobats who perform feats of balancing. Here the lovers are attempting an equilibrium between two different ideals of

Alone in the press of people traveled he,
Minding her jacinth, and myrrh, and ivory.

Mouth he remembered: the quaint orifice   5
From which came heat that flamed upon the kiss,
Till cold words came down spiral from the head,
Grey doves from the officious tower illsped.

Body: it was a white field ready for love,
On her body's field, with the gaunt tower above,   10
The lilies grew, beseeching him to take,
If he would pluck and wear them, bruise and break.

Eyes talking: Never mind the cruel words,
Embrace my flowers, but not embrace the swords.
But what they said, the doves came straightway flying   15
And unsaid: Honor, Honor,[6] they came crying.

Importunate her doves. Too pure, too wise,
Clambering on his shoulder, saying, Arise,
Leave me now, and never let us meet,
Eternal distance now command thy feet.   20

Predicament indeed, which thus discovers
Honor among thieves, Honor between lovers.
O such a little word is Honor, they feel!
But the grey word is between them cold as steel.[7]

At length I saw these lovers fully were come   25
Into their torture of equilibrium;
Dreadfully had forsworn each other, and yet
They were bound each to each, and they did not forget.

And rigid as two painful stars, and twirled
About the clustered night their prison world,   30
They burned with fierce love always to come near,
But Honor beat them back and kept them clear.

Ah, the strict lovers, they are ruined now!
I cried in anger. But with puddled brow
Devising for those gibbeted and brave
Came I descanting: Man, what would you have?   35

love. The poet in the first four stanzas
utilizes a traditional language of passion (*cf.* the Song of Solomon i: 13–
14; iv: 1–7). Succeeding stanzas employ the Christian idealization of chastity, drawing upon the Arthurian romances and Dante.
6. Here an idealized convention of
chivalry defeats the passionate symbols of the Song of Solomon.
7. In the medieval romances of chivalry
it was a sword, not a "word," of
"steel" that separated lovers. See, for
example, the sword with its cruciform
hilt that lay between Iseult and Tristram at night on their journey (*Le
Roman de Tristan et Iseut,* edited by
Joseph Bédier, ix, 105).

For spin your period out, and draw your breath,
A kinder saeculum[8] begins with Death.
Would you ascend to Heaven and bodiless dwell?
Or take your bodies honorless to Hell?   40

In Heaven you have heard no marriage is,[9]
No white flesh tinder to your lecheries,
Your male and female tissue sweetly shaped
Sublimed away, and furious blood escaped.

Great lovers lie in Hell, the stubborn ones   45
Infatuate of the flesh upon the bones;
Stuprate[1] they rend each other when they kiss,
The pieces kiss again, no end to this.

But still I watched them spinning, orbited nice.
Their flames were not more radiant than their ice.   50
I dug in the quiet earth and wrought the tomb
And made these lines to memorize their doom:—

Epitaph

Equilibrists lie here; stranger, tread light;
Close, but untouching in each other's sight;
Mouldered the lips and ashy the tall skull,   55
Let them lie perilous and beautiful.

1927

8. Latin *saeculum* signifies a "cycle,"
"age," "period of time."
9. *Cf.* Matthew xxii: 30.
1. Adjective from the Latin *stuprare,*
"to ravish." *Cf.* stanzas 7 and 8:

the entire effect suggests an *inverted*
image of Paolo and Francesca, love-
tormented but bodiless spirits (Dante,
Inferno V).

E. E. CUMMINGS
(1894–) 1963

E. E. Cummings, whose first volume of poems, *Tulips and Chimneys*, appeared in 1923, has remained a controversial but always prominent poet. Those who disparage him are often vehement; his defenders sometimes have the sound of devotees. Meanwhile, Cummings has produced a large volume of quite individualistic lyrics and has exercised a considerable influence.

Edward Estlin Cummings was born on October 14, 1894, in Cambridge, Massachusetts. His father, then a member of the English department at Harvard, later served as pastor of the famous Old South Church in Boston, from 1905 to 1926. Cummings was graduated from

Harvard in 1915 and remained to take his M.A. in 1916. The next year, in advance of American participation in World War I, he enlisted in the Norton Harjes Ambulance Corps and was sent to France for active duty. A censor's mistake produced an uncomfortable comedy of errors which led to his spending three months in a French detention camp, charged with treasonable correspondence. This experience provided the material for *The Enormous Room* (1922), one of the memorable literary records of that war. Upon his release he at once volunteered for service in the United States Army, which had then entered the field. After the war, Cummings went to Paris for training in painting. To that art he has devoted himself professionally, first in Paris and later in New York, while publishing his volumes of poems at frequent intervals.

The experimental nature of Cummings' poems is evident first in their mechanics—in the reduction of capital letters to lower case, as even in the printing of his own name; in his purposeful underpunctuation; in the dissociation of phrases from the expected order or from the logical relationship. Actually, these mechanical disorientations are meaningful, and secure the participation of the reader in the movement of the poem. More essential to the art of Cummings is his use of the stream-of-consciousness technique—his development of methods suggested by the success of James Joyce and Ger-

trude Stein. He often uses words or phrases as symbolic objects, juxtaposing them in startling ways unrelated to their literal meanings but representing the simultaneous presence in the mind of just such meaningful but illogical associations. Finally, his subjects or intended effects often involve allegedly "forbidden" areas of the subconscious mind or human behavior; or the language of violent or vulgar experience; or the jargon of advertising journalism. Side by side with these waifs will appear the most exquisite medieval delicacy, a sublimation of passion in ideality or graceful fantasy.

Whatever may be one's judgment concerning the mechanics of Cummings' style, his poetry has several values generally admitted. In his love poems and poems of nature he has been able on occasion to convey an intense passion in forms of controlled beauty and propriety. He is a master of satire, and in this area he employs both delicate wit and the heavy club of irony and invective, as in his attacks on advertisers, Babbitts, and superpatriots. And in those of his poems not consciously raucous for satirical effect, he can unite great melodic power with verbal precision and clarity.

Poems 1923–1954, 1954, is a comprehensive collection; later volumes are *95 Poems*, 1958; *100 Selected Poems*, 1959; and *50 Poems*, 1960. Critical prose pieces are contained in *e. e. cummings: A Miscellany*, 1958, edited by George J. Firmage.

The Magic Maker: E. E. Cummings, 1958, is an authorized critical biography by Charles Norman.

Thy Fingers Make Early Flowers

Thy fingers make early flowers of
all things.
thy hair mostly the hours love:
a smoothness which
sings, saying   5
(though love be a day)
do not fear, we will go amaying.

thy whitest feet crisply are straying.
Always
thy moist eyes are at kisses playing,   10
whose strangeness much
says; singing
(though love be a day)
for which girl art thou flowers bringing?

To be thy lips is a sweet thing   15
and small.
Death, Thee i call rich beyond wishing
if this thou catch,
else missing.
(though love be a day   20
and life be nothing, it shall not stop kissing).

1923

O Thou to Whom the Musical White Spring

O Thou to whom the musical white spring

offers her lily inextinguishable,
taught by thy tremulous grace bravely to fling

Implacable death's mysteriously sable
robe from her redolent shoulders,
                    Thou from whose   5
feet reincarnate song suddenly leaping
flameflung, mounts, inimitably to lose
herself where the wet stars softly are keeping

their exquisite dreams—O Love! upon thy dim
shrine of intangible commemoration,   10
(from whose faint close as some grave languorous hymn

pledged to illimitable dissipation
unhurried clouds of incense fleetly roll)

i spill my bright incalculable soul.

1925

mother father family relationship *mother's father tender beatiful*

If There Are Any Heavens

spirit of eternal passion

if there are any heavens my mother will(all by herself)have
one. It will not be a pansy heaven nor
a fragile heaven of lilies-of-the-valley but
it will be a heaven of blackred roses

my father will be(deep like a rose   5
tall like a rose)

standing near my

(swaying over her
silent)
with eyes which are really petals and see   10

nothing with the face of a poet really which
is a flower and not a face with
hands
which whisper
This is my beloved my   15

                (suddenly in sunlight

he will bow,

& the whole garden will bow)

                                                        1931

anger at ruthless death & making hero of killer   *satire*

Buffalo Bill's Defunct

Buffalo Bill's
defunct
            who used to
            ride a watersmooth-silver
                                stallion   *emph shooting*
and break onetwothreefourfive pigeonsjustlikethat   5
                                Jesus

he was a handsome man
                and what i want to know is

how do you like your blueeyed boy
Mister Death

1923

closest to sentiment
Symbolic words
free association — primitive

Anyone Lived in a Pretty How Town

anyone lived in a pretty how town
(with up so floating many bells down)
spring summer autumn winter
he sang his didn't he danced his did.

Women and men(both little and small)   5
cared for anyone not at all
they sowed their isn't they reaped their same
sun moon stars rain

children guessed(but only a few
and down they forgot as up they grew   10
autumn winter spring summer)
that noone loved him more by more

when by now and tree by leaf
she laughed his joy she cried his grief
bird by snow and stir by still   15
anyone's any was all to her

someones married their everyones
laughed their cryings and did their dance
(sleep wake hope and then)they
said their nevers they slept their dream   20

stars rain sun moon
(and only the snow can begin to explain
how children are apt to forget to remember
with up so floating many bells down)

one day anyone died i guess   25
(and noone stooped to kiss his face)
busy folk buried them side by side
little by little and was by was

all by all and deep by deep
and more by more they dream their sleep   30
noone and anyone earth by april
wish by spirit and if by yes.

Women and men(both dong and ding)
summer autumn winter spring
reaped their sowing and went their came   35
sun moon stars rain

don't expect anyone else to be too much 1940
interested in your problems
philosophy of life

Up into the Silence the Green=

juxtaposition

*grow
grass vitality
living*

death

up into the silence the green
silence with a white earth in it

cold

you will(kiss me)go

out into the morning the young
morning with a warm world in it   5

(kiss me)you will go

on into the sunlight the fine
sunlight with a firm day in it

you will go(kiss me

down into your memory and   10
a memory and memory

i)kiss me(will go)

poem of separation of love   1940

wove thoughts that anyone may think
thoughts in parentheses

ALLEN TATE

greatest voice of the post-war South

(1899-)

Allen Tate was born in Clark County, Kentucky, on November 19, 1899. Before entering Vanderbilt University he was already well trained in the classics. He was graduated in 1922, having studied under such men as John Crowe Ransom and Donald Davidson. Already he gave evidence of a remarkable talent for poetry and criticism, becoming one of the founders of *The Fugitive*, a periodical published at the University. After graduation he went to New York as a free-lance writer. In 1924 he married the novelist Caroline Gordon.

Poetry, criticism, and biography were his interests during the next decade. *Mr. Pope and Other Poems* and *Stonewall*

Jackson: The Good Soldier were published in 1928, *Jefferson Davis: His Rise and Fall*, the following year. These two book-length studies deepened Tate's interest in the Confederate South and led naturally to his participation in the Agrarian symposium, *I'll Take My Stand* (1930). At the same time he continued to write poetry, publishing *Poems: 1928–1931* in 1932.

In 1934 Tate accepted his first teaching position, that of lecturer in English at Southwestern University in Memphis. Since that time he has been connected with various institutions, notably Princeton, where he was resident fellow in writing (1939–1942); New York University, where he was lecturer in English (1947–1951); and the University of Minnesota, where he is at present professor of English. For two years (1944–1946), he was editor of the *Sewanee Review*.

In his essays, of which several volumes have been collected, Tate has made plain that his primary preoccupation is with poetry and with the difficulties which confront the serious poet in our time. Many of those difficulties are traceable, he believes, to our system of "progressive" education, which "is rapidly making us a nation of illiterates." The tabloids, the movies, the illustrated magazines, and radio and television are all involved in his indictment. To state the issue in different terms: "It is very hard for people to apply their minds to poetry, since it is one of our assumptions * * * that our in-tellects are for mathematics and science, our emotions for poetry." His position is that poetry gives us knowledge that is fully as valid as what science affords, although of a different order.

Writing from this critical position, Tate makes few concessions to popular taste in his own poetry, which is, as Cleanth Brooks has remarked, "a continual test of the imagination." He admires poetry that, in his own words, "requires of the reader the fullest cooperation of all his intellectual resources, all his knowledge of the world, and all the persistence and alertness that he now thinks of giving only to scientific studies." He admires "form, coherence of image and metaphor, control of tone and of rhythm, the union of these features." His work as a whole has exercised an astringent influence upon his contemporaries.

Tate's recurrent themes are the South, religion, and the problem of the frustrated individual preoccupied with and tortured by his own sensibility. The southern poems alternate between satire, directed against certain groups or types among his contemporaries, and completely objective presentations of subject matter. The poems concerned with religion reflect the difficulty involved in accepting the Christian faith, which Tate himself, incidentally, has recently embraced by joining the Roman Catholic Church.

Individual volumes not mentioned above include *Three Poems*, 1930; *The Mediterranean and Other Poems*, 1936; *Selected Poems*, 1937; *Reason in Madness*, 1941; *The Vigil of Venus*, 1943; *The Winter Sea*, 1944; *Poems, 1922–*

1947, 1948; and *Two Conceits for the
Eye to Sing, If Possible*, 1950. *The
Fathers*, 1938, is a novel. Volumes of
essays include *Reactionary Essays on
Poetry and Ideas*, 1936; *On the Limits*

of Poetry, 1948; *The Forlorn Demon*,
1953; *The Man of Letters in the
Modern World * * ** , 1955; and *Collected Essays*, 1959.

Antique Harvesters

Ode to the Confederate Dead[1]

Row after row with strict impunity
The headstones yield their names to the element,
The wind whirrs without recollection;[2]
In the riven troughs the splayed leaves
Pile up, of nature the casual sacrament   5
To the seasonal eternity of death,
Then driven by the fierce scrutiny
Of heaven to their business in the vast breath,
They sough the rumor of mortality.

Autumn is desolation in the plot   10
Of a thousand acres, where these memories grow
From the inexhaustible bodies that are not
Dead, but feed the grass row after rich row.
Remember now the autumns that have gone!—
Ambitious November with the humors of the year,   15
With a particular zeal for every slab,
Staining the uncomfortable angels that rot
On the slabs, a wing chipped here, an arm there:
The brute curiosity of an angel's stare
Turns you, like them, to stone,   20
Transforms the heaving air
Till plunged to a heavier world below
You shift your sea-space blindly
Heaving, turning like the blind crab.[3]

Dazed by the wind, only the wind   25
The leaves flying, plunge

metrical skill a musicality

1. "Ode to the Confederate Dead" is
Tate's best-known poem. The author
has supplied his readers with an ex-
egesis of it in the essay "Narcissus as
Narcissus" (*Virginia Quarterly Review*,
xiv, Winter, 1938, pp. 113ff.) in which
he writes that it "is 'about' solipsism [a
philosophical doctrine which says that
we create the world in the act of perceiving it] or Narcissism, or any other
ism that denotes the failure of the
human personality to function properly
in nature and society." The poem concerns the reverie of one at the gate of
a Confederate cemetery, providing an
elaborate contrast between the heroic
age, symbolized by the buried soldiers,
and the frustrate condition of a typical
modern, who can visualize himself only
in terms of such symbols as are indicated by the notes to the poem, below. The poet has frequently altered
this poem. The present text represents
the last revision, in *Poems * * **
(1948).
2. Ll. 1–3 introduce what the poet has
called persistent themes in this poem:
the "locked-in ego" and courage, suggested by the names on the stones; and
social heroism, recalled by the communal burial in mother earth.
3. One of the poet's two images for
the ego. The other, a contrasting symbol, is the "jaguar" of l. 80.

You know who have waited by the wall[4]
The twilit certainty of an animal,
Those midnight restitutions of the blood
You know—the immitigable pines, the smoky frieze   30
Of the sky, the sudden call: you know the rage,
The cold pool left by the mounting flood,
Of muted Zeno and Parmenides.[5]
You who have waited for the angry resolution
Of those desires that should be yours tomorrow,   35
You know the unimportant shrift of death
And praise the vision
And praise the arrogant circumstance
Of those who fall
Rank upon rank, hurried beyond decision—   40
Here by the sagging gate, stopped by the wall.

    Seeing, seeing only the leaves
    Flying, plunge and expire

Turn your eyes to the immoderate past
Turn to the inscrutable infantry rising   45
Demons out of the earth—they will not last.
Stonewall, Stonewall,[6] and the sunken fields of hemp,
Shiloh, Antietam, Malvern Hill, Bull Run.
Lost in that orient of the thick and fast
You will curse the setting sun.   50

    Cursing only the leaves crying
    Like an old man in a storm

You hear the shout—the crazy hemlocks point
With troubled fingers to the silence which
Smothers you, a mummy, in time.

                   The hound bitch   55
Toothless and dying, in a musty cellar
Hears the wind only.

            Now that the salt of their blood
Stiffens the saltier oblivion of the sea,
Seals the malignant purity of the flood,
What shall we, who count our days and bow   60

4. The passage beginning here, as the poet explains, introduces his second theme—that of "heroism * * * in an entire society"; which in the southern cause produced "a formal ebullience of the human spirit" into chivalry (*cf.* ll. 44–48, and l. 71).
5. Zeno and Parmenides were Greek philosophers of the fifth century B.C. They were both of the Eleatic school, which developed the conception of the universal unity of being.
6. "Stonewall," the popular name of Confederate General Thomas Jonathan Jackson, is figuratively associated with the stone wall (*e.g.*, l. 27), and in l. 48 is connected with battles particularly memorable for the southerners.

Our heads with a commemorial woe,
In the ribboned coats of grim felicity,
What shall we say of the bones, unclean,
Their verdurous anonymity will grow?
The ragged arms, the ragged heads and eyes   65
Lost in these acres of the insane green?
The gray lean spiders come, they come and go;
In a tangle of willows without light
The singular screech-owl's bright
Invisible lyric seeds the mind   70
With the furious murmur of their chivalry.

   We shall say only, the leaves
   Flying, plunge and expire

We shall say only, the leaves whispering
In the improbable mist of nightfall   75
That flies on multiple wing;
Night is the beginning and the end,
And in between the ends of distraction
Waits mute speculation, the patient curse
That stones the eyes, or like the jaguar[7] leaps   80
For his own image in a jungle pool, his victim.

What shall we say who have knowledge
Carried to the heart? Shall we take the act
To the grave? Shall we, more hopeful, set up the grave
In the house? The ravenous grave?

                       Leave now   85
The shut gate and the decomposing wall:
The gentle serpent, green in the mulberry bush,
Riots with his tongue through the hush—
Sentinel of the grave who counts us all!

1926–1936   1928, 1948

Mr. Pope

When Alexander Pope[8] strolled in the city
Strict was the glint of pearl and gold sedans.
Ladies leaned out, more out of fear than pity;
For Pope's tight back[9] was rather a goat's than man's.

One often thinks the urn should have more bones
Than skeletons provide for speedy dust;

7. The "jaguar" and the "blind crab"
(l. 24) are, the poet says, the "two explicit symbols for the locked-in ego,"
which, in this poem, is contrasted with
social heroism.
8. Alexander Pope (1688–1744), British neoclassical poet.
9. Pope was a hunchback.

The urn gets hollow, cobwebs brittle as stones
Weave to the funeral shell a frivolous rust.

And he who dribbled couplets like the snake[1]
Coiled to a lithe precision in the sun,   10
Is missing. The jar is empty; you may break
It only to find that Mr. Pope is gone.

What requisitions of a verity
Prompted the wit and rage between his teeth
One cannot say. Around a crooked tree   15
A mortal climbs whose name should be a wreath.

                                         1928, 1948

Death of Little Boys

When little boys grow patient at last, weary,
Surrender their eyes immeasurably to the night,
The event will rage terrific as the sea;
Their bodies fill a crumbling room with light.

Then you will touch at the bedside, torn in two,   5
Gold curls now deftly intricate with gray
As the windowpane extends a fear to you
From one peeled aster drenched with the wind all day.

And over his chest the covers, in an ultimate dream,
Will mount to the teeth, ascend the eyes, press back   10
The locks—while round his sturdy belly gleam
The suspended breaths, white spars above the wreck:

Till all the guests, come in to look, turn down
Their palms; and delirium assails the cliff
Of Norway where you ponder, and your little town   15
Reels like a sailor drunk in his rotten skiff. . . .

The bleak sunshine shrieks its chipped music then
Out to the milkweed amid the fields of wheat.
There is a calm for you where men and women
Unroll the chill precision of moving feet.   20

                                                    1928

---

1 *Cf.* Pope's satirical comment on his clumsy imitators (*Essay on Criticism,* ll. 356–357): "A *needless Alexandrine* ends the Song, / That like a wounded Snake, drags its slow Length along."

MARIANNE MOORE

(1887–)

Marianne Moore's earliest poems appeared in 1915 in *Poetry: A Magazine of Verse* and in *The Egoist* (London). She was then recognized as a poet of genuine power but her reception was distinctly limited until the *Selected Poems* appeared in 1935. In 1951 the *Collected Poems* won the Bollingen Prize, the National Book Award, and the Pulitzer Prize. Then a burst of critical enthusiasm recapitulated the persistent, slow accumulation of her remarkable poetry during thirty-five years.

As Eliot wrote in 1935, her poems are "part of the body of durable poetry written in our time, in which an original sensibility and an alert intelligence and deep feeling have been engaged in maintaining the life of the English language." Her most disciplined poems have been compared with the metaphysical satires of John Donne; in them the initial idea, generally simple, has been extended by metaphoric devices to a new dimension of wit, expressed in language that is all sinew, severe and pure. In self-criticism she observed that her work could not be poetry unless "there is no other category in which to put it," because "poetry is a peerless proficiency of the imagination." If satiric, her writing is dedicatedly humane, corresponding with her generalization that "poetry watches life with affection," and she recalls a dictum of Confucius that "if there be a knife of resentment in the heart, the mind will not attain precision."

The alleged obscurity of this poetry will not exist for the reader who brings to it the willing correspondence of intellect and imagination; it is "difficult" only because of these requirements. Miss Moore perceptively observed of any poetry that its "metaphor substitutes compactness for confusion."

Initial unfamiliarity characterizes Miss Moore's versification also, but the informed reader soon discovers that she has used the old forms of poetry in a new way. The apparent unevenness of her lines results from the medieval device of "rime-breaking" which arbitrarily produces longer or short lines. These are freely iambic rhythms which conform flexibly with changes of meaning and with prose phrases lifted bodily from various writings— science, history, reference books, current topical works—but seldom from literary sources, a fact in itself significant. While she is among the most daringly original of recent poets she also remains among the most conservative.

Marianne (Craig) Moore was born in 1887 at Kirkwood, near St. Louis, Missouri. After her graduation from Bryn Mawr College (1909) she studied business science at a Carlisle, Pennsylvania, school and headed the Commercial Department of the Carlisle Indian School (1911–1915). Her early poems in 1915

1488 · *Marianne Moore*

having won serious attention and publication, she became a professional writer, living for a time in Chatham, New Jersey, where her brother was a clergyman. In New York City after 1920, she held an appointment as branch librarian of theNew York Public Library (1921–1925). Her *Observations* (1924) won her the *Dial* Award and appointment as a member of the staff of the *Dial*, prominent among the many periodicals then devoted to the arts and letters. When the *Dial* became one of the casualties of the 1929 depression, Miss Moore made her home with her mother in Brooklyn. She has received several national awards and the Pulitzer Prize for 1951.

No full-length study of Marianne Moore has been published. *The Achievement of Marianne Moore: A Bibliography, 1907–1957*, compiled by E. P. Sheehy and A. Lohf, 1958, contains a comprehensive list of critical articles and reviews of her works extant in periodicals or books. The same volume contains an excellent descriptive bibliography of Miss Moore's books and periodical writings. Besides the major collections of her poems mentioned in the headnote, Miss Moore has published the following small volumes of new poems: *Poems*, 1921; *Marriage*, 1923; *The Pangolin and Other Verse*, 1936; *What Are Years*, 1941; *Nevertheless*, 1944; *A Face*, 1949; *Like a Bulwark*, 1956; and *O To Be a Dragon*, 1959. A selection of her critical articles appeared as *Predilections* (1955). *The Fables of La Fontaine*, 1954, and *Selected Fables*, 1955, are translations. The most comprehensive single volume of her poems was published as *Collected Poems*, 1951. *A Marianne Moore Reader*, 1961, contains prose and verse selected by the author.

Initial Antiquities of great truths

In the Days of Prismatic Colour[1]

not in the days of Adam and Eve, but when Adam
   was alone; when there was no smoke and colour was
fine, not with the refinement
   of early civilization art, but because
of its originality;[2] with nothing to modify it but the   5

mist that went up, obliqueness was a variation of the perpendicular, plain to see and
to account for: it is no
   longer that; nor did the blue-red-yellow band
of incandescence that was colour keep its stripe: it also is   10
      one of

those things into which much that is peculiar can be
   read; complexity is not a crime, but carry
it to the point of murki-
   ness and nothing is plain. Complexity,   15

1. First published in *Contact* for January, 1921; included in *Observations* (1924) and all later collections. One of Miss Moore's early explorations of the relations between art and idea, contrasting the "murkiness" of extended complexity and sophistication with the

naturalness of "the initial great truths," with respect to both form and substance in art.
2. Because of having been original with nature (*cf*. ll. 1 and 2); *e.g.*, the natural sunlight refracted into color by a "prismatic" crystal rock or by mist.

moreover, that has been committed to darkness, instead of
    granting it-

self to be the pestilence that it is, moves all a-
    bout as if to bewilder us with the dismal
fallacy that insistence   20
    is the measure of achievement and that all
truth must be dark. Principally throat, sophistication is as
    it al-

ways has been—at the antipodes from the init-
    ial great truths. "Part of it was crawling, part of it   25
was about to crawl, the rest
    was torpid in its lair."[3] In the short-legged, fit-
ful advance, the gurgling and all the minutiae—we have
    the classic

multitude of feet. To what purpose! Truth is no Apollo   30
    Belvedere,[4] no formal thing. The wave may go over it if
    it likes.
Know that it will be there when it says,
    "I shall be there when the wave has gone by."

                                   1921, 1951

An Egyptian Pulled Glass Bottle in the Shape of a Fish[5]

e.g. of imagistic work   emph diff btwn water no water

Here we have thirst
And patience, from the first,
    And art, as in a wave held up for us to see
    In its essential perpendicularity;

Not brittle but   5
Intense—the spectrum, that
    Spectacular and nimble animal the fish,
    Whose scales turn aside the sun's sword with their polish.

                                 1924, 1951

3. "Nestor: *Greek Anthology,* Loeb Classical Library, III, 129" [Miss Moore's note]. This quotation and the remainder of the poem refer primarily to art form, as the earlier stanzas referred to ideas.
4. The most celebrated statue of Apollo. The early Roman copy in marble of the Greek original, now in the Vatican, shows the highest formal perfection of sculptural art.
5. First published in *Observations* (1924). The association of several related impressions with a single, sharp image suggests the author's early command of the techniques of the imagist poets.

[handwritten: Idea that death ∅ King that sparked Re,]

No Swan So Fine[6]

"No water so still as the
    dead fountains of Versailles."[7] No swan,
with swart blind look askance
and gondoliering legs,[8] so fine
    as the chintz china one with fawn-
brown eyes and toothed gold
collar on to show whose bird it was.[9]

Lodged in the Louis Fifteenth
    candelabrum-tree[1] of cockscomb-
tinted buttons, dahlias,   *[handwritten: flowe born dried]* 10
sea-urchins, and everlastings,
    it perches on the branching foam
of polished sculptured   *[handwritten: Louis XV]*
flowers—at ease and tall. The king is dead.

1932, 1951

The Frigate Pelican[2]

Rapidly cruising or lying on the air[3] there is a bird
    that realizes Rasselas's friend's project
    of wings uniting levity with strength.[4] This
        hell-diver, frigate-bird, hurricane-
bird; unless swift is the proper word
        for him, the storm omen when
he flies close to the waves, should be seen
        fishing, although oftener
        he appears to prefer

6. First published in *Poetry: A Magazine of Verse* for October, 1932, and first collected in *Selected Poems* (1935), this poem was retained in the *Collected Poems* (1951).
7. The author's note states that the source of this striking figure is an unnamed article by Percy Phillips in the *New York Times Magazine,* May 10, 1931. The live swans that used to adorn these "dead fountains" mediate between the dead fountains and the china swan.
8. The Italian gondolier propels his craft by paddling from the stern.
9. "A pair of Louis XV candelabra with Dresden figures of swans belonging to Lord Balfour" [Miss Moore's note]. In the sophisticated period of Louis' reign the swan's collar might actually have shown armorial identification.

1. The age of Louis XV, king of France from 1715 to 1774, was noted for opulent and luxurious art such as the rococo style here depicted, which in spite of profuse ornament sometimes achieved delicacy.
2. First published in the *Criterion* for July, 1934; retained in *Selected Poems* (1935) and *Collected Poems* (1951).
3. The author's note acknowledges the influence of Audubon's portrayal of "*Fregata aquila,* the Frigate Pelican."
4. In Samuel Johnson's *Rasselas* (1759), Chapter 6, a friend of Rasselas, "the artist," an inventor dedicated to the good of mankind, has contrived human wings (described in the quoted words) but will not share their secret with others lest evil rulers use them to war upon innocent people; *cf.* "hell-diver" as applied to this pelican.

to take, on the wing, from industrious crude-winged
    species   10
  the fish they have caught, and is seldom successless.
  A marvel of grace, no matter how fast his
    victim may fly or how often may
turn. The others with similar ease,   15
  slowly rising once more,
    move out to the top
    of the circle and stop

and blow back, allowing the wind to reverse their direc-
    tion—   20
  Unlike the more stalwart swan that can ferry the
  woodcutter's two children home. Make hay; keep
    the shop; I have one sheep; were a less
limber animal's mottoes. This one
    finds sticks for the swan's-down-dress   25
  of his child to rest upon and would
    not know Gretel from Hänsel.[5]
    As impassioned Handel[6]—

meant for a lawyer and a masculine German domestic
  career—clandestinely studied the harpsichord   30
  and never was known to have fallen in love,
    the unconfiding frigate-bird hides
in the height and in the majestic
    display of his art. He glides
  a hundred feet or quivers about   35
    as charred paper behaves—full
    of feints; and an eagle

of vigilance. . . . *Festina lente.*[7] Be gay
  civilly? How so? "If I do well I am blessed
  whether any bless me or not, and if I do   40
    ill I am cursed."[8] We watch the moon rise
on the Susquehanna.[9] In his way,
    this most romantic bird flies
  to a more mundane place, the mangrove

5. The allusion is, of course, to the folk story of Hänsel and Gretel in Grimms' *Tales. Cf.* the "two children" in ll. 21–22 above (the father of Hänsel and Gretel was a woodcutter).
6. Georg Friedrich Händel (1685–1759), the most noted composer in England of his time. He was born and educated in Germany, and for a number of years his father opposed his entry upon a musical career. A prolific composer of operas, chamber music, and religious oratorios (the *Messiah* remains well known), he became a British subject and theatrical director after 1726.
7. This Latin maxim is translated, "make haste slowly."
8. "Hindoo saying" [Miss Moore's note].
9. The author's girlhood home, Carlisle, Pa., lies just west of Harrisburg and the Susquehanna River.

swamp to sleep. He wastes the moon.   45
But he, and others, soon

rise from the bough and though flying, are able to foil
the tired
moment of danger that lays on heart and lungs the
weight of the python that crushes to powder.   50

1934, 1951

[handwritten: Nude decending a staircase]
[handwritten: ant-eater]
[handwritten: hasn't sense to be afraid] The Pangolin[1]   *[handwritten: Jaws of mechanics]*

Another armoured animal—scale
lapping scale with spruce-cone regularity until they
form the uninterrupted central
tail-row! This near artichoke[2] with head and legs and
grit-equipped gizzard,   5
the night miniature artist engineer is
Leonardo's—da Vinci's replica[3]—
impressive animal and toiler of whom we seldom
hear.
[handwritten: Armor or essential to him] Armour seems extra. But for him,   10
the closing ear-ridge[4]—
or bare ear lacking even this small
eminence and similarly safe

contracting nose and eye apertures
impenetrably closable, are not;—a true ant-eater,   15
not cockroach-eater, who endures
exhausting solitary trips through unfamiliar ground at
night,
returning before sunrise; stepping in the moonlight,
on the moonlight peculiarly, that the outside   20
edges of his hands may bear the weight and save
the claws
for digging. Serpentined about
the tree, he draws
away from danger unpugnaciously,   25
with no sound but a harmless hiss; keeping

1. Published as the title poem of a volume in 1936, "The Pangolin" was included in *What Are Years* (1941) and *Collected Poems* (1951). Among the poet's celebrations of "impressive" creatures "of whom we seldom hear," this enthralls attention because of the animal's physical adaptation to survive deadly adversities by means of the evolved contrivances of his armor and by his own frugal rectitude, and also because he shares "certain postures" with man (*cf.* l. 86 *et seq.*).
2. The artichoke is encased in concentric rings of scale-like leaves.
3. The reference to Leonardo da Vinci (1452–1519) recalls his accomplishments as gifted artist, inventor, and engineer.
4. "The 'closing ear-ridge,' and certain other detail, from *Pangolins* by Robert T. Hatt; *Natural History*, December, 1935" [Miss Moore's note].

[handwritten: double motivation - describe natural creature evolved compares to man]

the fragile grace of the Thomas-
    of-Leighton Buzzard Westminster Abbey wrought-
        iron vine,[5] or
rolls himself into a ball that has   30
    power to defy all effort to unroll it; strongly intailed,
        neat
    head for core, on neck not breaking off, with curled-in
        feet.
        Nevertheless he has sting-proof scales; and nest   35
            of rocks closed with earth from inside, which he
                can thus darken
        Sun and moon and day and night and man and beast
            each with a splendour
            which man in all his vileness cannot   40
            set aside; each with an excellence!

man – do we have triple armor?

"Fearful yet to be feared," the armoured
    ant-eater met by the driver-ant does not turn back, but
engulfs what he can, the flattened sword-
    edged leafpoints on the tail and artichoke set leg- and   45
        body-plates
    quivering violently when it retaliates
        and swarms on him. Compact like the furled
            fringed frill
        on the hat-brim of Gargallo's hollow iron head   50
            of a
    matador, he will drop and will
        then walk away
            unhurt, although if unintruded on,
            he cautiously works down the tree, helped   55

by his tail. The giant-pangolin-
    tail, graceful tool, as prop or hand or broom or axe,
        tipped like
the elephant's trunk with special skin,
    is not lost on this ant- and stone-swallowing uninjurable   60
    artichoke which simpletons thought a living fable
        whom the stones had nourished, whereas ants had
            done
        so. Pangolins are not aggressive animals; between
        dusk and day they have the not unchain-like machine-   65
            like

merge of man with pangolin

            form and frictionless creep of a thing
            made graceful by adversities, con-

5. "Thomas of Leighton Buzzard's vine: a fragment of ironwork in Westminster
Abbey" [Miss Moore's note].

versities. To explain grace requires
    a curious hand. If that which is at all were not forever, 70
why would those who graced the spires
    with animals and gathered there to rest, on cold luxurious
    low stone seats—a monk and monk and monk—between
        the thus
        ingenious roof-supports,[6] have slaved to confuse 75
            grace with a kindly manner, time in which to pay
                a debt,
        the cure for sins, a graceful use
            of what are yet
                approved stone mullions[7] branching out across 80
                the perpendiculars? A sailboat

was the first machine.[8] Pangolins, made
    for moving quietly also, are models of exactness,
on four legs; or hind feet plantigrade,
with certain postures of a man.[9] Beneath sun and moon, 85
        man slaving
to make his life more sweet, leaves half the flowers
        worth having,
        needing to choose wisely how to use the strength;
            a paper-maker like the wasp; a tractor of food- 90
            stuffs,
    like the ant; spidering a length
        of web from bluffs
            above a stream; in fighting, mechanicked
            like the pangolin; capsizing in 95

disheartenment. Bedizened or stark
    naked, man, the self, the being we call human, writing-
master to this world, griffons a dark
    "Like does not like like that is obnoxious"; and writes
        error with four 100
r's. Among animals, one has a sense of humour.[1]

6. The grotesque but permanent figures of animals adorning the architectural members of ancient ecclesiastical buildings are compared with the living pangolin.
7. "Mullions" are the bars that subdivide the lights of a window. The "stone," and the "stone seats" of l. 73, suggest an ecclesiastical cloister or court.
8. "See F. L. Morse: *Power: Its Application from the 17th Dynasty to the 20th Century*" [Miss Moore's note]. The comparison of animal with man rises steadily to a crescendo in the next lines.

9. The pangolin is among the few "plantigrade" animals, which resemble man by walking with heel and toe both touching ground. In the succeeding passages, man's behavior and "inventions" are compared with those of the pangolin and other animals. *Cf.* note 1 below.
1. The dualism of man-animal was noted in the previous stanza. Just above, note the word "griffons": the name for a mythological hybrid of lion and eagle or for a breed of dog, here used as a verb. Hence a "griffoned" sentence would be growled out, as would the "error with four r's"; *cf.* the quoted

Humour saves a few steps, it saves years. Un-
        ignorant,
  modest and unemotional, and all emotion,
  he has everlasting vigour,   105
    power to grow,
      though there are few creatures who can make one
      breathe faster and make one erecter.

Not afraid of anything is he,
  and then goes cowering forth, tread paced to meet an   110
      obstacle
at every step. Consistent with the
  formula—warm blood, no gills, two pairs of hands and
      a few hairs—that
is a mammal; there he sits in his own habitat,   115
  serge-clad, strong-shod. The prey of fear, he, always
    curtailed, extinguished, thwarted by the dusk,
      work partly done,
  says to the alternating blaze,
    "Again the sun!   120
      anew each day; and new and new and new,
      that comes into and steadies my soul."

                              1936, 1951

one who's able to face

Rigorists[2] - *hard times*

"We saw reindeer
browsing," a friend who'd been in Lapland, said:
"finding their own food; they are adapted

  to scant *reino*[3]
or pasture, yet they can run eleven   5
miles in fifty minutes; the feet spread when

  the snow is soft,
and act as snow-shoes. They are rigorists,
however handsomely cutwork artists

sentence concerning man's humorless dislike of "obnoxious" kindred. The complex comparison of man with pangolin may give man the advantage in the concluding twenty lines.

2. First published in *Life and Letters Today* (1940) and collected in the 1941 volume, *What Are Years*. In her notes the author quotes an 1895 report by Sheldon Jackson, U. S. Agent for Education for Alaska, describing the relief of hardship among the Alaskan Eskimo by introducing the reindeer from Siberia beginning in 1891.

3. The word *reino* is "pasture" in Lapp, conjecturally identified with the first syllable of "reindeer," a word which also originated in Lapland.

of Lapland and 10
Siberia elaborate the trace
or saddle-girth with saw-tooth leather lace.[4]

One looked at us
with its firm face part brown, part white,—a queen
of alpine flowers. Santa Claus' reindeer, seen 15

at last, had grey-
brown fur, with a neck like edelweiss or
lion's foot,—*leontopodium* more

exactly." And
this candelabrum-headed ornament 20
for a place where ornaments are scarce, sent

to Alaska,
was a gift preventing the extinction
of the Esquimo. The battle was won

by a quiet man, 25
Sheldon Jackson, evangel to that race
whose reprieve he read in the reindeer's face.

1940, 1951

4. The Lapland domesticated reindeer were those of the German Christmas legend of St. Niklaus (*cf.* "Santa Claus," l. 15). In this simple poem reminiscent of childhood, the author admires the adaptations of this deer, at once the rigorist, the savior, and the ornament.

Fiction as Social History

JOHN DOS PASSOS

(1896–)

Many writers have depended upon social history as a frame for their narratives; but John Dos Passos, in the three novels of U.S.A., invented a new form, in which social history itself became the dynamic drive and motivation of a cycle of novels. His real protagonist in these volumes is American life from just before the first World War until the period of the great depression in the early thirties. His writing since the completion of the trilogy in 1936 has not continued on the same level of imagination and excellence, but the four chief works of that earlier period are sufficient to establish him as one of the most important of our recent writers.

John Dos Passos was born in Chicago on January 14, 1896. After preparation at private school, he entered Harvard, and he graduated with distinction in 1916. He had already begun to write, and like many privileged young idealists of his generation, he was persuaded that the machine age somehow necessarily debased and enslaved mankind. From this position to proletarian sympathies and a Marxist philosophy was but a short and natural step for the intellectuals of his period.

However, in 1916 Dos Passos went to Spain, intending to study architecture in Europe. The growing seriousness of the war changed his plans. He served first with a French ambulance unit, then with the Red Cross in Italy, and finally as a private in the medical corps of the United States Army. He then entered journalism, and spent several years as a foreign correspondent. His social idealism and his disillusion are reflected in his two war-inspired novels, *One Man's Initiation—1917* (1920) and *Three Soldiers* (1921). The latter may still rank as a fine book, although as a war novel it suffers by comparison with Hemingway's.

Three volumes of no permanent importance, one a novel, intervened before Dos Passos emerged as a writer of unique originality and force in *Manhattan Transfer* (1925). Here for the first time he employed kaleidoscopic organization—the chronological narrative is abandoned in favor of shifting scenes and episodes, at first apparently not connected, in which, however, the reappearance of certain characters in various associations produces a cross-sectional view of New York life.

An interval of playwriting followed, during which he planned and prepared materials for his trilogy, *U.S.A.* The first volume, *The 42nd Parallel,* appeared in 1930. This was followed by *1919* (1932) and *The Big Money* (1936). Each novel is an entity, but the three are unified by continuity of social motivation and fictional characters. The kaleidoscopic technique is retained from *Manhattan Transfer,* but the social scene is broadened. Side by side with the narrative concerning the fictional characters are the profiles or brief biographies of American leaders at every level, ranging from Ford and Morgan to Debs and to Valentino. The "newsreels" provide the setting—headlines, songs, and snatches from news articles, slogans, and advertisements are juxtaposed to define the social atmosphere at a given time. The "camera eye" represents the author's stream of consciousness at the time of the action of his story.

As various forms of collectivist dictatorship bred their inevitable human tragedy in the period of World War II, the various topical volumes and essays of Dos Passos took a sharp turn to the right. *The Ground We Stand On* (1941) is a collection of essays on American leaders of the past, starting in colonial times, with emphasis on democratic individualists like Roger Williams, Jefferson, and Frank-

lin, who stood for freedom of conscience, civil rights, and economic liberty. His reawakened admiration for Jefferson resulted in the study *The Head and Heart of Thomas Jefferson* (1953).

Dos Passos still wrestles with the American problem of bigness, but is no more apprehensive of "big capital" than of "big labor." His later novels, reflecting his changes in viewpoint, have been good, but not really comparable in either power or originality with his earlier work, even though they are more judicious. They are *Adventures of a Young Man* (1939); *Number One* (1943), the portrait of an American demagogue and a satirical inquiry into the offenses of political demagoguery against the people; *The Grand Design* (1948), on the "New Deal" years of Franklin Roosevelt's administration; and *Most Likely To Succeed* (1954), a study of Communist "intellectuals." *Adventures of a Young Man, Number One,* and *The Grand Design* were collected as a trilogy entitled *District of Columbia* (1953). Few experimental techniques appear in these novels or in *The Great Days* (1958), but *Midcentury* (1961) marks a return to the methods of *U.S.A.*

U.S.A. was first published under one cover in 1938. Other fiction is *Streets of Night,* 1923; and *Orient Express,* 1927. His early poems were collected in *A Pushcart at the Curb,* 1922. *Rosinante to the Road Again,* 1922, is a group of early travel essays on Spanish art and culture; later essays on his travels and observations, good journalistic reporting, are collected in *In All Countries,* 1934; *Journeys Between Wars,* 1938; *State of the Nation,* 1944; *Tour of Duty,* 1946, reporting his observations on World War II.

The first full-length study is Georges-Albert Astre, *Thèmes et structures dans l'œuvre de John Dos Passos,* Paris, 1956. Two very able short studies are the chapters on Dos Passos in

Joseph Warren Beach, *American Fiction, 1920–1940,* 1941; and in Alfred Kazin, *On Native Grounds,* 1942. John H. Wrenn, *John Dos Passos,* 1962, is a biography.

From U.S.A.[1]

From The 42nd Parallel

Big Bill

Big Bill Haywood was born in sixty nine in a boardinghouse in Salt Lake City.

He was raised in Utah, got his schooling in Ophir a mining camp with shooting scrapes, faro Saturday nights, whisky spilled on poker-tables piled with new silver dollars.

When he was eleven his mother bound him out to a farmer, he ran away because the farmer lashed him with a whip. That was his first strike.

He lost an eye whittling a slingshot out of scrub-oak.

He worked for storekeepers, ran a fruitstand, ushered in the Salt Lake Theatre, was a messengerboy, bellhop at the Continental Hotel.

When he was fifteen

he went out to the mines in Humboldt County, Nevada,

his outfit was overalls, a jumper, a blue shirt, mining boots, two pair of blankets, a set of chessmen, boxinggloves and a big lunch of plum pudding his mother fixed for him.

When he married he went to live in Fort McDermitt built in the old days against the Indians, abandoned now that there was no more frontier;

there his wife bore their first baby without doctor or midwife. Bill cut the navelstring, Bill buried the afterbirth;

1. The selections from Dos Passos given here, all from *U.S.A.* (1938), were sufficiently independent in construction to win separate prepublication in various periodicals; each one illustrates a characteristic technical experiment of this novelist; and collectively considered they span the period of social history represented in the three novels, while developing, in continuous sequence, a major theme in the motivation of the trilogy. In this study of American industrial civilization, ending with the depression of the early thirties, the author stresses, on the one hand, the consolidation of large capital enterprise, the development of inventive genius, the scientific advances, and the increases in technological efficiency and in labor controls; in strong contrast, he also reveals the worker—his lack of

security, his rootlessness—the organized opposition to the labor movement and the attacks on it as "radicalism," and the inroads of war and depression on common people. Prepublication of these sketches occurred as follows: "Big Bill" and "Proteus" (from *The 42nd Parallel,* 1930) and "The House of Morgan" and "The Body of an American" (from *1919,* 1932) were all among the pieces that the author contributed to the *New Masses* during the period 1930–1932. Of the selections from *The Big Money* (1936), "The American Plan" appeared in *Esquire* for January, 1934; "Newsreel LXVI" and "The Camera Eye (50)" were printed together in *Common Sense* for February, 1936; and "Vag" appeared in the *New Republic* for July 22, 1936.

the child lived. Bill earned money as he could surveying, haying in Paradise Valley, breaking colts, riding a wide rangy country.

One night at Thompson's Mill, he was one of five men who met by chance and stopped the night in the abandoned ranch. Each of them had lost an eye, they were the only oneeyed men in the county.

They lost the homestead, things went to pieces, his wife was sick, he had children to support. He went to work as a miner at Silver City.

At Silver City, Idaho, he joined the W.F.M., there he held his first union office; he was delegate of the Silver City miners to the convention of the Western Federation of Miners held in Salt Lake City in '98.

From then on he was an organizer, a speaker, an exhorter, the wants of all the miners were his wants; he fought Coeur D'Alenes. Telluride, Cripple Creek,[2]

joined the Socialist Party, wrote and spoke through Idaho, Utah, Nevada, Montana, Colorado to miners striking for an eight hour day, better living, a share of the wealth they hacked out of the hills.

In Chicago in January 1905 a conference was called that met at the same hall in Lake Street where the Chicago anarchists had addressed meetings twenty years before.[3]

William D. Haywood was permanent chairman. It was this conference that wrote the manifesto that brought into being the I.W.W.[4]

When he got back to Denver he was kidnapped to Idaho and tried with Moyer and Pettibone for the murder of the sheepherder Steuenberg, exgovernor of Idaho, blown up by a bomb in his own home.

When they were acquitted at Boise (Darrow[5] was their lawyer) Big Bill Haywood was known as a workingclass leader from coast to coast.

2. Three mining communities, in Idaho and Colorado, each the scene of an armed clash in which strikers were killed by police.

3. These members of the Anarchists' International in Chicago participated independently in fomenting the strike called by the Knights of Labor for May Day, 1886. Police intervention led to fatalities on both sides, especially in the Haymarket Riot of May 4. Eight Anarchist leaders were convicted of murder, although none were proved to have been present when the violence occurred. In 1892 the liberal Governor John P. Altgeld pardoned the three whose death sentences had been commuted to life imprisonment. (See Vachel Lindsay, "The Eagle That Is Forgotten.")

4. The Industrial Workers of the World (1905), distinguished from the American Federation of Labor (1881) by being organized on an industry-wide basis (*cf.* the later CIO). Haywood's program for the overthrow of capitalism by syndicalist revolution caused its decline after 1912 as a result of conservative reaction and the opposition of conservative labor; and it disintegrated after World War I.

5. Clarence S. Darrow (1857–1938), Chicago lawyer, a prominent champion of civil rights and liberal causes, as in the defense of Eugene V. Debs (below), and of J. T. Scopes in the famous "evolution" case.

Now the wants of all the workers were his wants, he was the spokesman of the West, of the cowboys and the lumberjacks and the harvesthands and the miners.

(The steamdrill had thrown thousands of miners out of work; the steamdrill had thrown a scare into all the miners of the West.)

The W.F.M.[6] was going conservative. Haywood worked with the I.W.W. *building a new society in the shell of the old*, campaigned for Debs[7] for President in 1908 on the Red Special. He was in on all the big strikes in the East where revolutionary spirit was growing, Lawrence, Paterson, the strike of the Minnesota ironworkers.

They went over with the A.E.F.[8] to save the Morgan loans,[9] to save Wilsonian Democracy, they stood at Napoleon's tomb and dreamed empire, they had champagne cocktails at the Ritz bar and slept with Russian countesses in Montmartre and dreamed empire, all over the country at American legion posts and business men's luncheons it was worth money to make the eagle scream;

they lynched the pacifists and the proGermans and the wobblies[1] and the reds and the bolsheviks.

Bill Haywood stood trial with the hundred and one at Chicago where Judge Landis the baseball czar[2]

with the lack of formality of a traffic court

handed out his twenty year sentences and thirty-thousand dollar fines.

After two years in Leavenworth they let them bail out Big Bill (he was fifty years old a heavy broken man), the war was over but they'd learned empire in the Hall of the Mirrors at Versailles;

the courts refused a new trial.

It was up to Haywood to jump his bail or to go back to prison for twenty years.

He was sick with diabetes, he had had a rough life, prison had broken down his health. Russia was a workers' republic; he went to Russia[3] and was in Moscow a couple of years but he wasn't happy there, that world was too strange for him. He died there and they

6. The Western Federation of Miners, soon to be absorbed in larger associations.

7. Eugene V. Debs (1855–1926), famous American labor leader, organizer of the rail unions, Socialist presidential candidate in 1900, 1904, 1908, 1912, and 1920. In the 1920 election, though in prison as a result of a wartime conviction for violation of the Espionage Act, he polled 919,799 votes. His ten-year sentence was commuted by President Harding in 1921. Dos Passos devotes much space to him in this novel.

8. The American Expeditionary Force, our overseas army in World War I.

9. The enormous loans of the Morgan bankers to the Allied nations, especially England, were regarded as a powerful cause of American intervention in World War I.

1. A slang term for the Industrial Workers of the World.

2. By inciting resistance to certain United States government war policies, Haywood violated a new sedition law, which many liberals felt to be an infringement of constitutional rights. Judge Kenesaw Mountain Landis (1866–1944), who sentenced Haywood in 1918, became the first commissioner of American baseball in 1920.

3. Haywood fled to Russia, under the circumstances here described, in 1921, but he survived longer than Dos Passos suggests, until 1928.

burned his big broken hulk of a body and buried the ashes under the Kremlin wall.

1930

Proteus[4]

Steinmetz was a hunchback,
son of a hunchback lithographer.

He was born in Breslau in eighteen sixtyfive, graduated with highest honors at seventeen from the Breslau Gymnasium,[5] went to the University of Breslau to study mathematics;

mathematics to Steinmetz was muscular strength and long walks over the hills and the kiss of a girl in love and big evenings spent swilling beer with your friends;

on his broken back he felt the topheavy weight of society the way workingmen felt it on their straight backs, the way poor students felt it, was a member of a socialist club, editor of a paper called *The People's Voice.*

Bismarck[6] was sitting in Berlin like a big paperweight to keep the new Germany feudal, to hold down the empire for his bosses the Hohenzollerns.

Steinmetz had to run off to Zurich for fear of going to jail; at Zurich his mathematics woke up all the professors at the Polytechnic;

but Europe in the eighties was no place for a penniless German student with a broken back and a big head filled with symbolic calculus and wonder about electricity that is mathematics made power

and a socialist at that.

With a Danish friend he sailed for America steerage on an old French line boat *La Champagne,*

lived in Brooklyn at first and commuted to Yonkers where he had a twelvedollar a week job with Rudolph Eichemeyer[7] who was a German exile from fortyeight an inventor and electrician and owner of a factory where he made hatmaking machinery and electrical generators.

4. Karl August Rudolf Steinmetz (1865–1923), German-born electrical engineer and inventor, left Germany, as described in this selection, a socialist fugitive. Then twenty-three, he changed his given names to "Charles Proteus." The Proteus of Greek legend was a prophetic old man of the sea, able to alter his shape to escape persecutors who wished to compel him to prophesy. The protean quality is recalled in Dos Passos' sketch.
5. In Germany, a type of secondary school preparing students for the university.
6. Otto Eduard Leopold von Bismarck (1815–1898), "the Iron Chancellor," had during the youth of Steinmetz been unifying Germany by his policy of "blood and iron." The Hohenzollerns (below) were the reigning royal family during this period.
7. Rudolf Eickemeyer (1831–1895), who came to the United States from Bavaria in 1850, by his 150 inventions fostered basic improvements in many industrial fields.

In Yonkers he[8] worked out the theory of the Third Harmonics and the law of hysteresis which states in a formula the hundred-fold relations between the metallic heat, density, frequency when the poles change places in the core of a magnet under an alternating current.

It is Steinmetz's law of hysteresis that makes possible all the transformers that crouch in little boxes and gableroofed houses in all the hightension lines all over everywhere. The mathematical symbols of Steinmetz's law are the patterns of all transformers everywhere.

In eighteen ninetytwo when Eichemeyer sold out to the corporation that was to form General Electric, Steinmetz was entered in the contract along with other valuable apparatus. All his life Steinmetz was a piece of apparatus belonging to General Electric.

First his laboratory was at Lynn, then it was moved and the little hunchback with it to Schenectady, the electric city.

General Electric humored him, let him be a socialist, let him keep a greenhouseful of cactuses lit up by mercury lights, let him have alligators, talking crows and a gila monster for pets and the publicity department talked up the wizard, the medicine man who knew the symbols that opened up the doors of Ali Baba's cave.[9]

Steinmetz jotted a formula on his cuff and next morning a thousand new powerplants had sprung up and the dynamos sang dollars and the silence of the transformers was all dollars,

and the publicity department poured oily stories into the ears of the American public every Sunday and Steinmetz became the little parlor magician,

who made a toy thunderstorm in his laboratory and made all the toy trains run on time and the meat stay cold in the icebox and the lamp in the parlor and the great lighthouses and the searchlights and the revolving beams of light that guide airplanes at night towards Chicago, New York, St. Louis, Los Angeles,

and they let him be a socialist and believe that human society could be improved the way you can improve a dynamo and they let him be pro-German and write a letter offering his services to Lenin because mathematicians are so impractical who make up formulas by which you can build powerplants, factories, subway systems, light, heat, air, sunshine but not human relations that affect the stockholders' money and the directors' salaries.

Steinmetz was a famous magician and he talked to Edison tapping with the Morse code on Edison's knee

8. *I.e.*, Steinmetz.
9. In the *Arabian Nights*, Ali Baba was a woodcutter who learned the magic password, *sesame*, that opened the doors to the cave containing the treasure of the Forty Thieves.

because Edison was so very deaf
and he went out West
to make speeches that nobody understood
and he talked to Bryan about God on a railroad train
and all the reporters stood round while he and Einstein
met face to face,
but they couldn't catch what they said
and Steinmetz was the most valuable piece of apparatus General
Electric had
until he wore out and died.

1930

From 1919
The House of Morgan

I commit my soul into the hands of my savior, wrote John Pierpont Morgan in his will, *in full confidence that having redeemed
it and washed it in His most precious blood, He will present it
faultless before my heavenly father, and I intreat my children to
maintain and defend at all hazard and at any cost of personal sacrifice the blessed doctrine of complete atonement for sin through
the blood of Jesus Christ once offered and through that alone,*

and into the hands of the House of Morgan represented by his
son,

he committed,

when he died in Rome in 1913,

the control of the Morgan interests in New York, Paris and London, four national banks, three trust companies, three life insurance
companies, ten railroad systems, three street railway companies, an
express company, the International Mercantile Marine,

power,

on the cantilever principle, through interlocking directorates

over eighteen other railroads, U.S. Steel, General Electric, American Tel and Tel, five major industries;

the interwoven cables of the Morgan Stillman Baker combination held credit up like a suspension bridge, thirteen percent of the
banking resources of the world.

The first Morgan to make a pool was Joseph Morgan, a hotel-
keeper in Hartford Connecticut who organized stagecoach lines and
bought up Ætna Life Insurance stock in a time of panic caused by
one of the big New York fires in the 1830's;

his son Junius followed in his footsteps, first in the drygoods business, and then as a partner to George Peabody, a Massachusetts

banker who built up an enormous underwriting and mercantile business in London and became a friend of Queen Victoria;

Junius married the daughter of John Pierpont, a Boston preacher, poet, eccentric, and abolitionist; and their eldest son,

John Pierpont Morgan

arrived in New York to make his fortune

after being trained in England, going to school at Vevey, proving himself a crack mathematician at the University of Göttingen,

a lanky morose young man of twenty,

just in time for the panic of '57.

(war and panics on the stock exchange, bankruptcies, warloans, good growing weather for the House of Morgan.)

When the guns started booming at Fort Sumter,[1] young Morgan turned some money over reselling condemned muskets to the U.S. army and began to make himself felt in the gold room in downtown New York; there was more in trading in gold than in trading in muskets; so much for the Civil War.

During the Franco-Prussian war[2] Junius Morgan floated a huge bond issue for the French government at Tours.

At the same time young Morgan was fighting Jay Cooke and the German-Jew bankers in Frankfort over the funding of the American war debt (he never did like the Germans or the Jews).

The panic of '75 ruined Jay Cooke[3] and made J. Pierpont Morgan the boss croupier of Wall Street; he united with the Philadelphia Drexels and built the Drexel building where for thirty years he sat in his glassedin office, redfaced and insolent, writing at his desk, smoking great black cigars, or, if important issues were involved, playing solitaire in his inner office; he was famous for his few words, Yes or No, and for his way of suddenly blowing up in a visitor's face and for that special gesture of the arm that meant, *What do I get out of it?*

In '77 Junius Morgan retired; J. Pierpont got himself made a member of the board of directors of the New York Central railroad and launched the first *Corsair*. He liked yachting and to have pretty actresses call him Commodore.

He founded the Lying-in Hospital on Stuyvesant Square, and was fond of going into St. George's church and singing a hymn all alone in the afternoon quiet.

In the panic of '93

1. The first military engagement of the Civil War (April 8, 1861).
2. In 1870–1871; a war promoted by Bismarck in his plan to unify the German states while crushing the regime of Emperor Napoleon III of France.

3. Jay Cooke (1821–1905) built his huge financial enterprises on his position as financial agent for the United States Treasury under his friend Salmon P. Chase during the Civil War. "The panic of '75" actually began in 1873, with Cooke's failure through overexpansion.

at no inconsiderable profit to himself

Morgan saved the U.S. Treasury; gold was draining out, the country was ruined, the farmers were howling for a silver standard, Grover Cleveland and his cabinet were walking up and down in the blue room at the White House without being able to come to a decision, in Congress they were making speeches while the gold reserves melted in the Subtreasuries; poor people were starving; Coxey's army[4] was marching to Washington; for a long time Grover Cleveland couldn't bring himself to call in the representative of the Wall Street moneymasters; Morgan sat in his suite at the Arlington smoking cigars and quietly playing solitaire until at last the president sent for him;

he had a plan all ready for stopping the gold hemorrhage.

After that what Morgan said went; when Carnegie sold out he built the Steel Trust.

J. Pierpont Morgan was a bullnecked irascible man with small black magpie's eyes and a growth on his nose; he let his partners work themselves to death over the detailed routine of banking, and sat in his back office smoking black cigars; when there was something to be decided he said Yes or No or just turned his back and went back to his solitaire.

Every Christmas his librarian read him Dickens' *A Christmas Carol* from the original manuscript.

He was fond of canarybirds and pekinese dogs and liked to take pretty actresses yachting. Each *Corsair* was a finer vessel than the last.

When he dined with King Edward he sat at His Majesty's right; he ate with the Kaiser tête-à-tête; he liked talking to cardinals or the pope, and never missed a conference of Episcopal bishops;

Rome was his favorite city.

He liked choice cookery and old wines and pretty women and yachting, and going over his collections, now and then picking up a jewelled snuffbox and staring at it with his magpie's eyes.

He made a collection of the autographs of the rulers of France, owned glass cases full of Babylonian tablets, seals, signets, statuettes, busts,

Gallo-Roman bronzes,

Merovingian jewels, miniatures, watches, tapestries, porcelains, cuneiform inscriptions, paintings by all the old masters, Dutch, Italian, Flemish, Spanish,

manuscripts of the gospels and the Apocalypse,

4. Jacob Sechler Coxey, Pennsylvania businessman, in 1894 (and again in 1914) led an "army" of unemployed to Washington in support of his proposal for federal make-work projects to relieve unemployment in times of depression.

a collection of the works of Jean-Jacques Rousseau,

and the letters of Pliny the Younger.

His collectors bought anything that was expensive or rare or had the glint of empire on it, and he had it brought to him and stared hard at it with his magpie's eyes. Then it was put in a glass case.

The last year of his life he went up the Nile on a dahabiyeh[5] and spent a long time staring at the great columns of the Temple of Karnak.

The panic of 1907 and the death of Harriman, his great opponent in railroad financing, in 1909, had left him the undisputed ruler of Wall Street, most powerful private citizen in the world;

an old man tired of the purple, suffering from gout, he had deigned to go to Washington to answer the questions of the Pujo Committee during the Money Trust Investigation:[6] Yes, I did what seemed to me to be for the best interests of the country.

So admirably was his empire built that his death in 1913 hardly caused a ripple in the exchanges of the world: the purple descended to his son, J. P. Morgan,

who had been trained at Groton and Harvard and by associating with the British ruling class

to be a more constitutional monarch: *J. P. Morgan suggests* . . .

By 1917 the Allies had borrowed one billion, nine hundred million dollars through the House of Morgan: we went overseas for democracy and the flag;

and by the end of the Peace Conference the phrase *J. P. Morgan suggests* had compulsion over a power of seventyfour billion dollars.

J. P. Morgan is a silent man, not given to public utterances, but during the great steel strike, he wrote Gary:[7] *Heartfelt congratulations on your stand for the open shop, with which I am, as you know, absolutely in accord. I believe American principles of liberty are deeply involved, and must win if we stand firm.*

(Wars and panics on the stock exchange,

machinegunfire and arson,

bankruptcies, warloans,

starvation, lice, cholera and typhus:

good growing weather for the House of Morgan.)

1932

5. A long, low houseboat, propelled by sail, used only on the Nile River.
6. The "Money Trust" was an alleged concentration of credit in the hands of a few financiers, supposedly responsible for such panics as that of 1907. Representative A. P. Pujo headed the House committee to investigate the matter in 1912.

7. Elbert H. Gary (1846–1927), an associate of Morgan, and the steel magnate who built Gary, Indiana, as a "company town," was an archfoe of labor. The strike here mentioned occurred in the fall of 1919, and resulted from Gary's stern resistance to the closed shop.

The Body of an American[8]

Whereasthe Congressoftheunitedstates byaconcurrentresolutionadoptedon the4thdayofmarch lastauthorizedthe Secretaryofwar to cause to be brought to theunitedstatesthe body of an Americanwhowasamemberoftheamerican-expeditionaryforcesineurope wholosthislifeduringtheworldwarandwhoseidentityhasnotbeenestablished for burial inthememorialamphitheatreofthe nationalcemeteryatarlingtonvirginia

In the tarpaper morgue at Chalons-sur-Marne[9] in the reek of chloride of lime and the dead, they picked out the pine box that held all that was left of

enie menie minie moe plenty other pine boxes stacked up there containing what they'd scraped up of Richard Roe

and other person or persons unknown. Only one can go. How did they pick John Doe?

Make sure he aint a dinge,[1] boys,

make sure he aint a guinea or a kike,

how can you tell a guy's a hunredpercent when all you've got's a gunnysack full of bones, bronze buttons stamped with the screaming eagle and a pair of roll puttees?

. . . and the gagging chloride and the puky dirt-stench of the yearold dead . . .

The day withal was too meaningful and tragic for applause. Silence, tears, songs and prayer, muffled drums and soft music were the instrumentalities today of national approbation.

John Doe was born (thudding din of blood in love into the shuddering soar of a man and a woman alone indeed together lurching into

and ninemonths sick drowse waking into scared agony and the pain and blood and mess of birth). John Doe was born

and raised in Brooklyn, in Memphis, near the lakefront in Cleveland, Ohio, in the stench of the stockyards in Chi, on Beacon Hill, in an old brick house in Alexandria Virginia, on Telegraph Hill, in a halftimbered Tudor cottage in Portland the city of roses,

in the Lying-In Hospital old Morgan endowed on Stuyvesant Square,

across the railroad tracks, out near the country club, in a shack cabin tenement apartmenthouse exclusive residential suburb;

scion of one of the best families in the social register, won first prize in the baby parade at Coronado Beach, was marbles champion of the Little Rock grammarschools, crack basketballplayer at the

---

8. The Unknown Soldier, symbolizing all the unidentified American dead, was buried in Arlington National Cemetery in November, 1921, in accordance with the act of Congress represented at the beginning of this selection.
9. About a hundred miles east of Paris, the scene of a memorable battle of World War I, later an American Army headquarters.
1. A vulgarism used in some parts of the country to designate a Negro; *cf.*, in the next line, "guinea" (for an Italian) and "kike" (for a Jew).

Booneville High, quarterback at the State Reformatory, having saved the sheriff's kid from drowning in the Little Missouri River was invited to Washington to be photographed shaking hands with the President on the White House steps;—

though this was a time of mourning, such an assemblage necessarily has about it a touch of color. In the boxes are seen the court uniforms of foreign diplomats, the gold braid of our own and foreign fleets and armies, the black of the conventional morning dress of American statesmen, the varicolored furs and outdoor wrapping garments of mothers and sisters come to mourn, the drab and blue of soldiers and sailors, the glitter of musical instruments and the white and black of a vested choir

—busboy harveststiff hogcaller boyscout champeen cornshucker of Western Kansas bellhop at the United States Hotel at Saratoga Springs office boy callboy fruiter telephone lineman longshoreman lumberjack plumber's helper,

worked for an exterminating company in Union City, filled pipes in an opium joint in Trenton, N.J.

Y.M.C.A. secretary, express agent, truckdriver, fordmechanic, sold books in Denver Colorado: Madam would you be willing to help a young man work his way through college?

President Harding, with a reverence seemingly more significant because of his high temporal station, concluded his speech:

We are met today to pay the impersonal tribute;
the name of him whose body lies before us took flight with his imperishable soul . . .
as a typical soldier of this representative democracy he fought and died believing in the indisputable justice of his country's cause . . .

by raising his right hand and asking the thousands within the sound of his voice to join in the prayer:

Our Father which art in heaven hallowed be thy name . . .

Naked he went into the army;

they weighed you, measured you, looked for flat feet, squeezed your penis to see if you had clap, looked up your anus to see if you had piles, counted your teeth, made you cough, listened to your heart and lungs, made you read the letters on the card, charted your urine and your intelligence,

gave you a service record for a future (imperishable soul)

and an identification tag stamped with your serial number to hang around your neck, issued OD² regulation equipment, a condiment can and a copy of the articles of war.

Atten'SHUN suck in your gut you c——r wipe that smile off your face eyes right wattja tink dis is a choirch-social? For-war-D'ARCH.

2. Olive drab.

John Doe

and Richard Roe and other person or persons unknown

drilled hiked, manual of arms, ate slum,[3] learned to salute, to soldier, to loaf in the latrines, forbidden to smoke on deck, overseas guard duty, forty men and eight horses,[4] shortarm inspection and the ping of shrapnel and the shrill bullets combing the air and the sorehead woodpeckers the machineguns mud cooties[5] gas-masks and the itch.

Say feller tell me how I can get back to my outfit.

John Doe had a head

for twentyodd years intensely the nerves of the eyes the ears the palate the tongue the fingers the toes the armpits, the nerves warm-feeling under the skin charged the coiled brain with hurt sweet warm cold mine must dont sayings print headlines:

Thou shalt not the multiplication table long division, Now is the time for all good men knocks but once at a young man's door, It's a great life if Ish gebibbel,[6] The first five years'll be the Safety First, Suppose a hun tried to rape your my country right or wrong, Catch 'em young, What he dont know wont treat 'em rough, Tell 'em nothin, He got what was coming to him he got his, This is a white man's country, Kick the bucket, Gone west, If you dont like it you can croaked him

Say buddy cant you tell me how I can get back to my outfit?

Cant help jumpin when them things go off, give me the trots them things do. I lost my identification tag swimming in the Marne, roughhousin with a guy while he was waitin to be deloused, in bed with a girl named Jeanne (Love moving picture wet French post-card dream began with saltpeter in the coffee and ended at the propho station);—

Say soldier for chrissake cant you tell me how I can get back to my outfit?

John Doe's

heart pumped blood:

alive thudding silence of blood in your ears

down in the clearing in the Oregon forest where the punkins were punkincolor pouring into the blood through the eyes and the fallcolored trees and the bronze hoopers were hopping through the dry grass, where tiny striped snails hung on the underside of the blades and the flies hummed, wasps droned, bumblebees buzzed, and the woods smelt of wine and mushrooms and apples, homey smell

3. Stew.
4. The railway freight cars supplied by the French for American troops in World War I bore the legend *40 hommes, 8 chevaux*, a characteristic overestimation.
5. Lice.
6. A Yiddish phrase, loosely translated, "I should worry," current in American humor of the twenties.

of fall pouring into the blood,

and I dropped the tin hat and the sweaty pack and lay flat with the dogday sun licking my throat and adamsapple and the tight skin over the breastbone.

The shell had his number on it.

The blood ran into the ground.

The service record dropped out of the filing cabinet when the quartermaster sergeant got blotto that time they had to pack up and leave the billets in a hurry.

The identification tag was in the bottom of the Marne.

The blood ran into the ground, the brains oozed out of the cracked skull and were licked up by the trenchrats, the belly swelled and raised a generation of bluebottle flies,

and the incorruptible skeleton,

and the scraps of dried viscera and skin bundled in khaki

they took to Chalons-sur-Marne

and laid it out neat in a pine coffin

and took it home to God's Country on a battleship

and buried it in a sarcophagus in the Memorial Amphitheatre in the Arlington National Cemetery

and draped the Old Glory over it

and the bugler played taps

and Mr. Harding prayed to God and the diplomats and the generals and the admirals and the brasshats and the politicians and the handsomely dressed ladies out of the society column of the *Washington Post* stood up solemn

and thought how beautiful sad Old Glory God's Country it was to have the bugler play taps and the three volleys made their ears ring.

Where his chest ought to have been they pinned

the Congressional Medal, the D.S.C., the Medaille Militaire, the Belgian Croix de Guerre, the Italian gold medal, the Vitutea Militara sent by Queen Marie of Rumania, the Czechoslovak war cross, the Virtuti Militari of the Poles, a wreath sent by Hamilton Fish, Jr.,[7] of New York, and a little wampum presented by a deputation of Arizona redskins in warpaint and feathers. All the Washingtonians brought flowers.

Woodrow Wilson brought a bouquet of poppies.[8]

1932

7. Then a New York member of the House of Representatives.
8. The poppies of Flanders, the scene of much fighting during World War I, were celebrated in the sentiment, song, and poetry of the war; see especially the poem "In Flanders Fields" by John McCrae.

From The Big Money
The American Plan

Frederick Winslow Taylor (they called him Speedy Taylor in the shop) was born in Germantown, Pennsylvania, the year of Buchanan's election. His father was a lawyer, his mother came from a family of New Bedford whalers; she was a great reader of Emerson, belonged to the Unitarian Church and the Browning Society. She was a fervent abolitionist and believed in democratic manners; she was a housekeeper of the old school, kept everybody busy from dawn till dark. She laid down the rules of conduct:

selfrespect, selfreliance, selfcontrol

and a cold long head for figures.

But she wanted her children to appreciate the finer things so she took them abroad for three years on the Continent, showed them cathedrals, grand opera, Roman pediments, the old masters under their brown varnish in their great frames of tarnished gilt.

Later Fred Taylor was impatient of these wasted years, stamped out of the room when people talked about the finer things; he was a testy youngster, fond of practical jokes and a great hand at rigging up contraptions and devices.

At Exeter he was head of his class and captain of the ballteam, the first man to pitch overhand. (When umpires complained that overhand pitching wasn't in the rules of the game, he answered that it got results.)

As a boy he had nightmares, going to bed was horrible for him; he thought they came from sleeping on his back. He made himself a leather harness with wooden pegs that stuck into his flesh when he turned over. When he was grown he slept in a chair or in bed in a sitting position propped up with pillows. All his life he suffered from sleeplessness.

He was a crackerjack tennisplayer. In 1881, with his friend Clark, he won the National Doubles Championship. (He used a spoonshaped racket of his own design.)

At school he broke down from overwork, his eyes went back on him. The doctor suggested manual labor. So instead of going to Harvard he went into the machineshop of a small pumpmanufacturing concern, owned by a friend of the family's, to learn the trade of patternmaker and machinist. He learned to handle a lathe and to dress and cuss like a workingman.

Fred Taylor never smoked tobacco or drank liquor or used tea or coffee; he couldn't understand why his fellowmechanics wanted to go on sprees and get drunk and raise Cain Saturday nights. He lived at home, when he wasn't reading technical books he'd play parts in amateur theatricals or step up to the piano in the evening and sing a good tenor in *A Warrior Bold* or *A Spanish Cavalier*.

He served his first year's apprenticeship in the machineshop without pay; the next two years he made a dollar and a half a week, the last year two dollars.

Pennsylvania was getting rich off iron and coal. When he was twentytwo, Fred Taylor went to work at the Midvale Iron Works.[9] At first he had to take a clerical job, but he hated that and went to work with a shovel. At last he got them to put him on a lathe. He was a good machinist, he worked ten hours a day and in the evenings followed an engineering course at Stevens. In six years he rose from machinist's helper to keeper of toolcribs to gangboss to foreman to mastermechanic in charge of repairs to chief draftsman and director of research to chief engineer of the Midvale Plant.

The early years he was a machinist with the other machinists in the shop, cussed and joked and worked with the rest of them, soldiered on the job when they did. Mustn't give the boss more than his money's worth. But when he got to be foreman he was on the management's side of the fence, *gathering in on the part of those on the management's side all the great mass of traditional knowledge which in the past has been in the heads of the workmen and in the physical skill and knack of the workman.* He couldn't stand to see an idle lathe or an idle man.

Production went to his head and thrilled his sleepless nerves like liquor or women on a Saturday night. He never loafed and he'd be damned if anybody else would. Production was an itch under his skin.

He lost his friends in the shop; they called him niggerdriver. He was a stockily built man with a temper and a short tongue.

I was a young man in years but I give you my word I was a great deal older than I am now, what with the worry, meanness and contemptibleness of the whole damn thing. It's a horrid life for any man to live not being able to look any workman in the face without seeing hostility there, and a feeling that every man around you is your virtual enemy.

That was the beginning of the Taylor System of Scientific Management.

He was impatient of explanations, he didn't care whose hide he took off in enforcing the laws he believed inherent in the industrial process.

When starting an experiment in any field question everything,

9. Later a consolidated plant of the Bethlehem Steel Company; it was located in Philadelphia.

question the very foundations upon which the art rests, question the simplest, the most self-evident, the most universally accepted facts; prove everything,

except the dominant Quaker Yankee (the New Bedford skippers were the greatest niggerdrivers on the whaling seas) rules of conduct. He boasted he'd never ask a workman to do anything he couldn't do.

He devised an improved steamhammer; he standardized tools and equipment, he filled the shop with college students with stopwatches and diagrams, tabulating, standardizing. *There's the right way of doing a thing and the wrong way of doing it; the right way means increased production, lower costs, higher wages, bigger profits:* the American plan.

He broke up the foreman's job into separate functions, speedbosses, gangbosses, timestudy men, orderofwork men.

The skilled mechanics were too stubborn for him, what he wanted was a plain handyman who'd do what he was told. If he was a firstclass man and did firstclass work Taylor was willing to let him have firstclass pay; that's where he began to get into trouble with the owners.

At thirtyfour he married and left Midvale and took a flyer for the big money in connection with a pulpmill started in Maine by some admirals and political friends of Grover Cleveland's;

the panic of '93 made hash of that enterprise,

so Taylor invented for himself the job of Consulting Engineer in Management and began to build up a fortune by careful investments.

The first paper he read before the American Society of Mechanical Engineers was anything but a success, they said he was crazy. *I have found,* he wrote in 1909, *that any improvement is not only opposed but aggressively and bitterly opposed by the majority of men.*

He was called in by Bethlehem Steel. It was in Bethlehem he made his famous experiments with handling pigiron; he taught a Dutchman named Schmidt to handle fortyseven tons instead of twelve and a half tons of pigiron a day and got Schmidt to admit he was as good as ever at the end of the day.

He was a crank about shovels, every job had to have a shovel of the right weight and size for that job alone; every job had to have a man of the right weight and size for that job alone; but when he began to pay his men in proportion to the increased efficiency of their work,

the owners who were a lot of greedy smalleyed Dutchmen began to raise Hail Columbia; when Schwab bought Bethlehem Steel in

1901

Fred Taylor

inventor of efficiency

who had doubled the production of the stamping-mill by speeding up the main lines of shafting from ninetysix to twohundred and twentyfive revolutions a minute

was unceremoniously fired.

After that Fred Taylor always said he couldn't afford to work for money.

He took to playing golf (using golfclubs of his own design), doping out methods for transplanting huge boxtrees into the garden of his home.

At Boxly in Germantown he kept open house for engineers, factorymanagers, industrialists;

he wrote papers,

lectured in colleges,

appeared before a congressional committee,

everywhere preached the virtues of scientific management and the Barth slide rule, the cutting down of waste and idleness, the substitution for skilled mechanics of the plain handyman (like Schmidt the pigiron handler) who'd move as he was told

and work by the piece:

production;

more steel rails more bicycles more spools of thread more armorplate for battleships more bedpans more barbedwire more needles more lightning rods more ballbearings more dollarbills;

(the old Quaker families of Germantown were growing rich, the Pennsylvania millionaires were breeding billionaires out of iron and coal)

production would make every firstclass American rich who was willing to work at piecework and not drink or raise Cain or think or stand mooning at his lathe.

Thrifty Schmidt the pigiron handler can invest his money and get to be an owner like Schwab and the rest of the greedy smalleyed Dutchmen and cultivate a taste for Bach and have hundredyearold boxtrees in his garden at Bethlehem or Germantown or Chestnut Hill,

and lay down the rules of conduct;

the American plan.

But Fred Taylor never saw the working of the American plan;

in 1915 he went to the hospital in Philadelphia suffering from a breakdown.

Pneumonia developed; the nightnurse heard him winding his watch;

on the morning of his fiftyninth birthday, when the nurse went into his room to look at him at fourthirty,
he was dead with his watch in his hand.

1936

Newsreel LXVI

HOLMES DENIES STAY

A better world's in birth[1]

Tiny Wasps Imported From Korea In Battle To Death With Asiatic beetle

BOY CARRIED MILE DOWN SEWER; SHOT OUT ALIVE

CHICAGO BARS MEETINGS

For justice thunders condemnation

Washington Keeps Eye On Radicals

Arise rejected of the earth

PARIS BRUSSELS MOSCOW GENEVA ADD THEIR VOICES

It is the final conflict
Let each stand in his place

Geologist Lost In Cave Six Days

The International Party

SACCO AND VANZETTI MUST DIE[2]

Shall be the human race.

Much I thought of you when I was lying in the death house—the singing, the kind tender voices of the children from the playground where there was all the life and the joy of liberty—just one step from the wall that contains the buried agony of three buried souls. It would remind me so often of you and of your sister and I wish I could see you every moment, but I feel better that you will not come to the death house so that you could not see the horrible picture of three living in agony waiting to be electrocuted.[3]

1936

1. The centered lines of italics in this "newsreel" are verses from "The Internationale," a Communist song.
2. The crux of this "newsreel" and of the following "camera eye" is the case of Nicola Sacco and Bartolomeo Vanzetti, convicted of murder in 1921 in connection with a payroll robbery in Massachusetts. They were tried amid the tensions of a conservative reaction. The convicted men freely professed ad-herence to the anarchist ideology, but liberal opinion asserted that they also had the reputation of being honest and quiet workmen, and that there was no real evidence of their connection with the crime. Appeals of the case delayed their execution, which finally occurred in 1927.
3. This passage in italics is adapted from Vanzetti's prison letters.

The Camera Eye (50)

they have clubbed us off the streets   they are stronger   they
are rich   they hire and fire the politicians the newspapereditors
the old judges the small men with reputations the collegepresidents
the wardheelers (listen businessmen collegepresidents judges
America will not forget her betrayers) they hire the men with
guns   the uniforms the policecars the patrolwagons

all right you have won   you will kill the brave men our friends
tonight

there is nothing left to do   we are beaten   we the beaten
crowd together in these old dingy schoolrooms on Salem Street
shuffle up and down the gritty creaking stairs sit hunched with
bowed heads on benches and hear the old words of the haters of oppression   made new in sweat and agony tonight

our work is over   the scribbled phrases   the nights typing releases
the smell of the printshop the sharp reek of newprinted leaflets   the
rush for Western Union   stringing words into wires the search for
stinging words to make you feel who are your oppressors America

America our nation has been beaten by strangers who have turned
our language inside out who have taken the clean words our fathers
spoke and made them slimy and foul

their hired men sit on the judge's bench they sit back with their
feet on the tables under the dome of the State House they are ignorant of our beliefs they have the dollars the guns the armed forces
the powerplants

they have built the electricchair and hired the executioner to
throw the switch

all right we are two nations

America our nation has been beaten by strangers who have bought
the laws and fenced off the meadows and cut down the woods for
pulp and turned our pleasant cities into slums and sweated the
wealth out of our people and when they want to they hire the executioner to throw the switch

but do they know that the old words of the immigrants are being
renewed in blood and agony tonight do they know that the old
American speech of the haters of oppression is new tonight in the
mouth of an old woman from Pittsburgh of a husky boilermaker
from Frisco who hopped freights clear from the Coast to come here
in the mouth of a Back Bay socialworker in the mouth of an Italian
printer of a hobo from Arkansas   the language of the beaten nation is not forgotten in our ears tonight

the men in the deathhouse made the old words new before they
died

If it had not been for these things, I might have lived out my life talking at streetcorners to scorning men. I might have died unknown, unmarked, a failure. This is our career and our triumph. Never in our full life can we hope to do such work for tolerance, for justice, for man's understanding of man as now we do by an accident[4]

now their work is over   the immigrants haters of oppression lie quiet in black suits in the little undertaking parlor in the North End   the city is quiet   the men of the conquering nation are not to be seen on the streets

they have won why are they scared to be seen on the streets? on the streets you see only the downcast faces of the beaten   the streets belong to the beaten nation   all the way to the cemetery where the bodies of the immigrants are to be burned we line the curbs in the drizzling rain we crowd the wet sidewalks elbow to elbow silent pale looking with scared eyes at the coffins

we stand defeated America

1936

Vag[5]

The young man waits at the edge of the concrete, with one hand he grips a rubbed suitcase of phony leather, the other hand almost making a fist, thumb up

that moves in ever so slight an arc when a car slithers past, a truck roars clatters; the wind of cars passing ruffles his hair, slaps grit in his face.

Head swims, hunger has twisted the belly tight,

he has skinned a heel through the torn sock, feet ache in the broken shoes, under the threadbare suit carefully brushed off with the hand, the torn drawers have a crummy feel, the feel of having slept in your clothes; in the nostrils lingers the staleness of discouraged carcasses crowded into a transient camp, the carbolic stench of the jail, on the taut cheeks the shamed flush from the boring eyes of cops and deputies, railroadbulls (they eat three squares a day, they are buttoned into well-made clothes, they have wives to sleep with, kids to play with after supper, they work for the big men who buy their way, they stick their chests out with the sureness of power behind their backs). Git the hell out, scram. Know what's good for you, you'll make yourself scarce. Gittin' tough, eh? Think you kin take it, eh?

The punch in the jaw, the slam on the head with the nightstick,

4. This passage in italics is from Vanzetti's prison letters.
5. "Vag" concludes the novel *The Big Money*, and thus also the trilogy, *U.S.A.*, bringing the period of its history down to the great depression of the thirties. The "vag" (vagabond) then was a familiar sight, as throngs of the homeless unemployed roamed the streets or took to the road as migratory workers.

the wrist grabbed and twisted behind the back, the big knee brought up sharp into the crotch,

the walk out of town with sore feet to stand and wait at the edge of the hissing speeding string of cars where the reek of ether and lead and gas melts into the silent grassy smell of the earth.

Eyes black with want seek out the eyes of the drivers, a hitch, a hundred miles down the road.

Overhead in the blue a plane drones. Eyes follow the silver Douglas that flashes once in the sun and bores its smooth way out of sight into the blue.

(The transcontinental passengers sit pretty, big men with bank-accounts, highlypaid jobs, who are saluted by doormen; telephone-girls say goodmorning to them. Last night after a fine dinner, drinks with friends, they left Newark. Roar of climbing motors slant-ing up into the inky haze. Lights drop away. An hour staring along a silvery wing at a big lonesome moon hurrying west through cur-dling scum. Beacons flash in a line across Ohio.

At Cleveland the plane drops banking in a smooth spiral, the string of lights along the lake swings in a circle. Climbing roar of the motors again; slumped in the soft seat drowsing through the flat moonlight night.

Chi. A glimpse of the dipper. Another spiral swoop from cool into hot air thick with dust and the reek of burnt prairies.

Beyond the Mississippi dawn creeps up behind through the murk over the great plains. Puddles of mist go white in the Iowa hills, farms, fences, silos, steel glint from a river. The blinking eyes of the bea-cons reddening into day. Watercourses vein the eroded hills.

Omaha. Great cumulus clouds, from coppery churning to creamy to silvery white, trail brown skirts of rain over the hot plains. Red and yellow badlands, tiny horned shapes of cattle.

Cheyenne. The cool high air smells of sweetgrass.

The tightbaled clouds to westward burst and scatter in tatters over the strawcolored hills. Indigo mountains jut rimrock. The plane breasts a huge crumbling cloudbank and toboggans over bumpy air across green and crimson slopes into the sunny dazzle of Salt Lake.

The transcontinental passenger thinks contracts, profits, vacation-trips, mighty continent between Atlantic and Pacific, power, wires humming dollars, cities jammed, hills empty, the indiantrail leading into the wagonroad, the macadamed pike, the concrete skyway; trains, planes: history the billiondollar speedup,

and in the bumpy air over the desert ranges towards Las Vegas

sickens and vomits into the carton container the steak and mush-rooms he ate in New York. No matter, silver in the pocket, green-backs in the wallet, drafts, certified checks, plenty restaurants in L. A.)

The young man waits on the side of the road; the plane has gone: thumb moves in a small arc when a car tears hissing past. Eyes seek the driver's eyes. A hundred miles down the road. Head swims, belly tightens, wants crawl over his skin like ants:

went to school, books said opportunity, ads promised speed, own your home, shine bigger than your neighbor, the radiocrooner whispered girls, ghosts of platinum girls coaxed from the screen, millions in winnings were chalked up on the boards in the offices, paychecks were for hands willing to work, the cleared desk of an executive with three telephones on it;

waits with swimming head, needs knot the belly, idle hands numb, beside the speeding traffic.

A hundred miles down the road.

1936

JAMES T. FARRELL

(1904–)

James Thomas Farrell was born on February 27, 1904, in Chicago and was graduated from St. Cyril High School; he published sketches in the magazine —the earliest significantly entitled "Danny's Uncle." He did not live in the immediate neighborhood of his famous fictional characters, Danny and Studs; as he says, "the South Side was miles big," but his early fiction shows his intimate acquaintance with most of it. He loved to rove, and was then less interested in books than in baseball, of which he has written with enthusiasm, beginning with one of the pieces at St. Cyril. His first job, with an express company, is memorably reflected in his early fiction. In 1925 he enrolled as a full-time student at the University of Chicago, where his talented teacher, James Weber Linn, in 1927 accepted his class themes for publication in his newspaper column. In the same year he left the university to risk writing on his own time, although he returned intermittently as a student until 1930, when his germinal story, "Studs," appeared in *This Quarter*.

In 1927 Farrell found work in New York for a time. Again in Chicago, he supported himself by various employments and literary work until 1931 when, with *Young Lonigan* shaping up, he terminated his residence in Chicago and settled in New York City. *Young Lonigan* (1932) was an artistic success, and the completion of the Lonigan trilogy gained its author a place at the forefront of his generation. *The Young Manhood of Studs Lonigan* (1934) and *Judgment Day* (1935) brought the life of Studs to a tragic end, to which flaws in his soul and the limitations of a world in depression both contributed. Danny O'Neill was a character in *Young Lonigan, Gas-House McGinty* (1933), and a story, "Helen I Love You," before he appeared as the protagonist of *A World I Never Made* (1936), the first of the five novels of the O'Neill cycle (see bibliography). Before completing this cycle, in 1953, Farrell had also published the Bernard Carr cycle and at least twelve volumes of collected short stories.

The subtitle of his first novel, "A Boyhood on the Chicago Streets," drew disproportionate attention to this writer's awareness of social problems. However, Farrell has in fact and consciously dedicated his powers to the intense observation and fictional creation of human character. Studs Lonigan and Danny O'Neill were inspired by his knowledge of the city neighborhoods of middle-class solidarity common before World War I, and by his close observation of boyhood friends and relatives, but the novels were neither autobiography nor *roman à clef.* The families of these boys and their friends—these artisans, salesmen, expressmen, schoolmates playing in yards or the park, all the variegated life of an established city neighborhood of the time—have been created, not merely transcribed. The Farrell character is the fictional statement of a human life, in which fate is a function of character, not of sociology. *Ellen Rogers* (1941), one of the author's most successful creations, represents a much more sophisticated social environment, but it was certainly the characters, not the social issue, that Thomas Mann had in mind when he

praised it as "the best modern love story" that he had read. And it was the conflict of character with circumstance that John Dewey called "classic" in *Tommy Gallagher's Crusade*.

Few authors have been able to maintain so successfully as Farrell the point of view of the boy, and few have surpassed him in the power to portray the world of childhood and youth. At forty-five he wrote "The Fastest Runner on Sixty-first Street." Similarly, Ellen Rogers is only one of many women characters of all ages, including a childhood sweetheart of Studs, who remain in the reader's memory as persons known in actuality.

The Bernard Carr cycle of novels (after 1945), also many of the later short stories and volumes of nonfiction, reflect the author's enlarging contacts with life and ideas, his observation of new scenes, his life in Paris and elsewhere abroad, and his life in New York. Increasingly after World War II, he depicted with fidelity a more sophisticated environment, and the emerging groups of writers seeking to discover personal or social meaning amid the welter of shifting ideas. As a novelist he continued to explore human rather than social issues, but his nonfictional works during this period proclaim his interest, from early life, in social and political experiment and action, and in advanced ideas. "I still respect Marx," he says, referring to his essays on Marxian literature in *A Note on Literary Criticism* (1936). "Nietzsche and Freud were early influences too"; but he could add, "I was never a Social Darwinist," because his fiction does not conform to any social thesis. "I have always believed," he writes, "in freedom and dignity and have fought certain tendencies here as well as fascism and communism here and abroad"; but "my books are not problem solvers."

Farrell is one of the most interesting of modern stylists; his writing has an organic quality adapting readily to the subject at hand. Beach praised his Chicago novels as "the plainest, soberest, most straightforward, of any living novelist." However, the later novels and short stories, with their great range of subject matter, show a flexible prose conforming with the novelist's expressed aim to "write so that life may speak for itself." Farrell has recently been developing the material for a new cycle of novels.

Studs Lonigan appears in *Young Lonigan: A Boyhood on the Chicago Streets*, 1932; *The Young Manhood of Studs Lonigan*, 1934; and *Judgment Day*, 1935: in one volume, *Studs Lonigan: A Trilogy*, 1935. Danny O'Neill

is a character in *Gas-House McGinty*, 1933. He becomes the dominant figure in the cycle including *A World I Never Made*, 1936; *No Star Is Lost*, 1938; *Father and Son*, 1940; *My Days of Anger*, 1943; and (the earliest in relation to Danny's life) *The Face of Time*, 1953. *Bernard Clare* (alias "Carr"), 1946, introduces the title character, protagonist also of *The Road Between*, 1949, and *Yet Other Waters*, 1952. Novels outside the cycles include *Ellen Rogers*, 1941; *This Man and This Woman*, 1951; and *Boarding House Blues*, 1961.

Volumes of short stories include *Calico Shoes*, 1934; *Guillotine Party*, 1935; *Can All This Grandeur Perish?*, 1937; *$1000 a Week*, 1942; *To Whom It May Concern*, 1944; *When Boyhood Dreams Come True*, 1946; *The Life Adventurous*, 1947; *An American Dream Girl and Other Stories*, 1950; *French Girls Are Vicious*, 1955; *An Omnibus of Short Stories*, 1956—a collection of three previous volumes; *The Name is Fogarty* (humorous sketches) 1950; *A Dangerous Woman, and Other Stories*, 1957; and *Side Street * * * , 1961.

Essays are in *A Note on Literary Criticism*, 1936; *The League of Frightened Philistines*, 1945; *Literature and Morality*, 1947.

Critical accounts are Joseph Warren Beach, *American Fiction, 1920–1940*, 1941, and Oscar Cargill, *Intellectual America*, 1941. Autobiographical essays and reminiscent studies include *Reflections at Fifty*, 1954; *My Baseball Diary*, 1957; and *It Has Come to Pass*, 1958 (Israel). *A Bibliography* was edited by Edgar Branch, 1959.

The Fastest Runner on Sixty-first Street[1]

Morty Aiken liked to run and to skate. He liked running games and races. He liked running so much that sometimes he'd go over to Washington Park all by himself and run just for the fun of it. He got a kick out of running, and he had raced every kid he could get to run against him. His love of racing and running had even become a joke among many of the boys he knew. But even when they gave him the horse laugh it was done in a good-natured way, because he was a very popular boy. Older fellows liked him, and when they would see him, they'd say, there's a damn good kid and a damned fast runner.

When he passed his fourteenth birthday, Morty was a trifle smaller than most boys of his own age. But he was well known, and,

1. From *An American Dream Girl and Other Stories* (1950).

in a way, almost famous in his own neighborhood. He lived at Sixty-first and Eberhardt, but kids in the whole area had heard of him, and many of them would speak of what a runner and what a skater Morty Aiken was.

He won medals in playground tournaments, and, in fact, he was the only lad from his school who had ever won medals in these tournaments. In these events he became the champion in the fifty- and hundred-yard dash, and with this he gained the reputation of being the best runner, for his age, on the South Side of Chicago.

He was as good a skater as he was a runner. In winter, he was to be seen regularly almost every day on the ice at the Washington Park lagoon or over on the Midway. He had a pair of Johnson racers which his father had given him, and he treasured these more than any other possession. His mother knitted him red socks and a red stocking cap for skating, and he had a red-and-white sweater. When he skated, he was like a streak of red. His form was excellent, and his sense of himself and of his body on the ice was sure and right. Almost every day there would be a game of I-Got-It. The skater who was *it* would skate in a wide circle, chased by the pack until he was caught. Morty loved to play I-Got-It, and on many a day this boy in short pants, wearing the red stocking cap, the red-and-white sweater, and the thick, knitted red woolen socks coming above the black shoes of his Johnson racers, would lead the pack, circling around and around and around, his head forward, his upper torso bent forward, his hands behind his back, his legs working with grace and giving him a speed that sometimes seemed miraculous. And in February, 1919, Morty competed in an ice derby, conducted under the auspices of the Chicago *Clarion*. He won two gold medals. His picture was on the first page of the sports section of the Sunday *Clarion*. All in all, he was a famous and celebrated lad. His father and mother were proud of him. His teacher and Mrs. Bixby, the principal of the school, were proud of him. Merchants on Sixty-first Street were proud of him. There was not a lad in the neighborhood who was greeted on the street by strangers as often as Morty.

Although he was outwardly modest, Morty had his dreams. He was graduated from grammar school in 1919, and was planning to go to Park High in the fall. He was impatient to go to high school and to get into high-school track meets. He'd never been coached, and yet look how good he was! Think of how good he would be when he had some coaching! He'd be a streak of lightning, if ever there was one. He dreamed that he would be called the Human Streak of Lightning. And after high school there would be college, college track meets, and the Big Ten championship, and after that he would join an athletic club and run in track meets, and he would win a place on the Olympic team, and somewhere, in Paris or Rome or some European city, he would beat the best runners in the world, and, like Ty Cobb[2] in baseball and Jess Willard[3] in prize fighting, he'd be the world's greatest runner.

And girls would all like him, and the most beautiful girl in the world would marry him. He liked girls, but girls liked him even more than he liked them. In May, a little while before his graduation, the class had a picnic, and they played post office. The post office was behind a clump of bushes in Jackson Park. He was called to the post office more than any other of the boys. There was giggling and talking and teasing, but it hadn't bothered him, especially because he knew that the other fellows liked and kind of envied him. To Morty, this was only natural. He accepted it. He accepted the fact that he was a streak of lightning on his feet and on the ice, and that this made him feel somehow different from other boys and very important. Even Tony Rabuski looked at him in this way, and if any kid would have picked on him, Tony would have piled into that kid. Tony was the toughest boy in school, and he was also considered to be the dumbest. He was also the poorest. He would often come to school wearing a black shirt, because a black shirt didn't show the dirt the way that other shirts did, and his parents couldn't afford to buy him many shirts. One day Tony was walking away from school with Morty, and Tony said:

"Kid, you run de fastest, I fight de best in de whole school. We make a crack-up team. We're pals. Shake, kid, we're pals."

Morty shook Tony's hand. For a fourteen-year-old boy, Tony had very big and strong hands. The other kids sometimes called them "meat hooks."

Morty looked on this handshake as a pledge. He and Tony became friends, and they were often together. Morty had Tony come over to his house to play, and sometimes Tony stayed for a meal. Tony ate voraciously and wolfishly. When Morty's parents spoke of the way Tony ate and of the quantity of food he ate, Morty would reply by telling them that Tony was his friend.

Because he was poor and somewhat stupid, a dull and fierce resentment smoldered in Tony. Other boys out-talked him, and they were often able to plague and annoy him, and then outrun him because he was heavy footed. The kids used to laugh at Tony because they said he had lead, iron, and bricks in his big feet. After Morty and Tony had shaken hands and become pals, Morty never would join the other boys in razzing Tony. And he and Tony doped out a way that would permit Tony to get even with kids who tried to tor-

2. Tyrus Raymond Cobb (born 1886), famous for his batting and base-stealing.　3. Jess Willard (born 1883), heavyweight champion from 1915 to 1919.

ment him. If some of the boys made game of Tony until he was confused and enraged and went for them, Morty would chase the boys. He had no difficulty in catching one of them. When he caught any of the boys who'd been teasing and annoying Tony, he'd usually manage to hold the boy until Tony would lumber up and exact his punishment and revenge. Sometimes Tony would be cruel, and on a couple of occasions when Tony, in a dull and stupefied rage, was sitting on a hurt, screaming boy and pounding him, Morty ordered Tony to lay off. Tony did so instantly. Morty didn't want Tony to be too cruel. He had come to like Tony and to look on him as a big brother. He'd always wanted a brother, and sometimes he would imagine how wonderful it would be if Tony could even come to live at his house.

The system Morty and Tony worked out, with Morty chasing and catching one of the boys who ragged Tony, worked out well. Soon the kids stopped ragging Tony. Because of their fear, and because they liked and respected Morty and wanted him to play with them, they began to accept Tony. And Tony began to change. Once accepted, so that he was no longer the butt of jokes, he looked on all the boys in Morty's gang as his pals. He would protect them as he would protect Morty. Tony then stopped scowling and making fierce and funny faces and acting in many odd little ways. After he became accepted, as a result of being Morty's pal, his behavior changed, and because he was strong and could fight, the boys began to admire him. At times he really hoped for strange boys to come around the neighborhood and act like bullies so he could beat them up. He wanted to fight and punch because he could feel powerful and would be praised and admired.

II

Ever since he had been a little fellow, Tony had often been called a "Polack" or a "dirty Polack." After he became one of the gang or group around Morty, some of the boys would tell him that he was a "white Polack." In his slow way, he thought about these words and what they meant. When you were called certain words, you were laughed at, you were looked at as if something were wrong with you. If you were a Polack, many girls didn't want to have anything to do with you. The boys and girls who weren't Polacks had fun together that Polacks couldn't have. Being a Polack and being called a Polack was like being called a sonofabitch. It was a name. When you were called a name like this, you were looked at as a different kind of kid from one who wasn't called a name. Morty Aiken wasn't called names. Tony didn't want to be called names. And if he fought and beat up those who called him names, they would be afraid of him. He wanted that. But he also wanted to have as much fun as the kids had who weren't called these names. And he worked it out that these kids felt better when they called other kids names. He could fight and he could call names, and if he called a kid a name, and that kid got tough, he could beat him up. He began to call names. And there was a name even worse than Polack—"nigger." If Tony didn't like a kid, he called him a "nigger." And he talked about the "niggers." He felt as good as he guessed these other kids did when he talked about the "niggers." And they could be beat up. They weren't supposed to go to Washington Park because that was a park for the whites. That was what he had often heard.

He heard it said so much that he believed it. He sometimes got a gang of the boys together and they would roam Washington Park, looking for colored boys to beat up. Morty went with them. He didn't particularly like to beat up anyone, but when they saw a colored kid and chased him, he would always be at the head, and he would be the one who caught the colored boy. He could grab or tackle him, and by that time the others would catch up. He worked the same plan that he and Tony had worked against the other boys. And after they caught and beat up a colored boy, they would all talk and shout and brag about what they had done, and talk about how they had each gotten in their licks and punches and kicks, and how fast Morty had run to catch that shine, and what a sock Tony had given him, and, talking all together and strutting and bragging, they felt good and proud of themselves, and they talked about how the Sixty-first Street boys would see to it that Washington Park would stay a white man's park.

And this became more and more important to Tony. There were those names, "Polack," "dirty Polack," "white Polack." If you could be called a "Polack," you weren't considered white. Well, when he beat them up, was he or wasn't he white? They knew. After the way he clouted these black ones, how could the other kids not say that Tony Rabuski wasn't white? That showed them all. That showed he was a hero. He was a hero as much as Morty Aiken was.

III

Morty was a proud boy on the night he graduated from grammar school in June, 1919. When he received his diploma, there was more applause in the auditorium than there was for any other member of the class. He felt good when he heard this clapping, but, then, he expected it. He lived in a world where he was somebody, and he was going into a bigger world where he would still be somebody. He was a fine, clean-looking lad, with dark hair, frank blue eyes, regular and friendly features. He was thin but strong. He wore a blue serge suit with short trousers and a belted jacket, and a white shirt with a white bow tie. His class colors, orange and black ribbons, were pinned on the lapel of his coat. He was scrubbed and washed and combed. And he was in the midst of an atmosphere of gaiety and friendliness. The teachers were happy. There were proud and happy parents and aunts and uncles and older sisters. The local alderman made a speech praising everybody, and speaking of the graduating boys and girls as fine future Americans. And he declared that in their midst there were many promising lads and lassies who would live to enjoy great esteem and success. He also said that among this group there was also one who not only promised to become a stellar athlete but who had already won gold medals and honors.

And on that night, Morty's father and mother were very happy. They kept beaming with proud smiles. Morty was their only son. Mr. Aiken was a carpenter. He worked steadily, and he had saved his money so that the house he owned was now paid for. He and his wife were quiet-living people who minded their own business. Mr. Aiken was tall and rugged, with swarthy skin, a rough-hewn face, and the look and manner of a workman. He was a gentle but firm man, and was inarticulate with his son. He believed that a boy should have a good time in sports, should fight his own battles, and that boyhood—the best time of one's life—should be filled with happy memories.

The mother was faded and maternal. She usually had little to say; her life was dedicated to caring for her son and her husband and to keeping their home clean and orderly. She was especially happy to know that Morty liked running and skating, because these were not dangerous.

After the graduation ceremonies the father and mother took Morty home where they had cake and ice cream. The three of them sat together eating these refreshments, quiet but happy. The two parents were deeply moved. They were filled with gratification because of the applause given their son when he had walked forward on the stage to receive his diploma. They were raising a fine boy, and they could look people in the neighborhood in the eye and know that they had done their duty as parents. The father was putting money by for Morty's college education and hoped that, besides becoming a famous runner, Morty would become a professional man. He talked of this to the son and the mother over their ice cream and cake, and the boy seemed to accept his father's plans. And as the father gazed shyly at Morty he thought of his own boyhood on a Wisconsin farm, and of long summer days there. Morty had the whole summer before him. He would play and grow and enjoy himself. He was not a bad boy, he had never gotten into trouble, he wasn't the kind of boy who caused worry. It was fine. In August there would be his vacation, and they would all go to

Wisconsin, and he would go fishing with the boy.

That evening Morty's parents went to bed feeling that this was the happiest day of their lives.

And Morty went to bed, a happy, light-hearted boy, thinking of the summer vacation which had now begun.

IV

The days passed. Some days were better than others. Some days there was little to do, and on other days there was a lot to do. Morty guessed that this was turning out to be as good as any summer he could remember.

Tony Rabuski was working, delivering flowers for a flower merchant, but he sometimes came around after supper, and the kids sat talking or playing on the steps of Morty's house or of another house in the neighborhood. Morty liked to play Run, Sheep, Run, because it gave him a chance to run, and he also liked hiding and searching and hearing the signals called out, and the excitement and tingling and fun when he'd be hiding, perhaps under some porch, and the other side would be near, maybe even passing right by, and he, and the other kids with him, would have to be so still, and he'd even try to hold his breath, and then finally, the signal for which he had been waiting—Run, Sheep, Run—and the race, setting off, tearing away along sidewalks and across streets, running like hell and like a streak of lightning, and feeling your speed in your legs and muscles and getting to the goal first.

The summer was going by, and it was fun. There wasn't anything to worry about and there were dreams. Edna Purcell, who had been in his class, seemed sweet on him, and she was a wonderful girl. One night she and some other girls came around, and they sat on the steps of Morty's house and played Tin-Tin. Morty had to kiss her. He did, with the kids laughing, and it seemed that something happened to him. He hadn't been shy when he was with girls, but now, when Edna was around, he would be shy. She was wonderful. She was more than wonderful. When he did have the courage to talk to her, he talked about running and iceskating. She told him she knew what a runner and skater he was. A fast skater, such as he was, wouldn't want to think of skating with someone like her. He said that he would, and that next winter he would teach her to skate better. Immediately, he found himself wishing it were next winter already, and he would imagine himself skating with her, and he could see them walking over to the Washington Park lagoon and coming home again. He would carry her skates, and when they breathed they would be able to see their breaths, and the weather would be cold and sharp and would make her red cheeks redder, and they would be alone, walking home, with the snow packed on the park, alone, the two of them walking in the park, with it quiet, so quiet that you would hearing nothing, and it would be like they were in another world, and then, there in the quiet park, with white snow all over it, he would kiss Edna Purcell. He had kissed Edna when they'd played Tin-Tin, and Post Office, but he looked forward to the day that he got from her the kiss that would mean that she was his girl, his sweetheart, and the girl who would one day be his wife just like his mother was his father's wife. Everything he dreamed of doing, all the honors he would get, all the medals and cups he dreamed of winning—now all of this would be for Edna. And she was also going to Park High. He would walk to school with her, eat lunch with her, walk her home from school. When he ran in high-school track meets for Park High, Edna would be in the stands. He would give her his medals. He wanted to give her one of his gold skating medals, but he didn't know how to go about asking her to accept it.

No matter what Morty thought about, he thought about Edna at the same time. He thought about her every time he dreamed. When he walked on streets in the neighborhood, he thought of her. When he went to Washington Park or swimming, he thought of Edna. Edna, just to think of her, Edna made everything in the world wonderfully wonderful.

And thus the summer of 1919 was passing for Morty.

V

Morty sat on the curb with a group of boys, and they were bored and restless. They couldn't agree about what game to play, where to go, what to do to amuse themselves. A couple of them started to play Knife but gave it up. Morty suggested a race, but no one would race him. They couldn't agree on playing ball. One boy suggested swimming, but no one would go with him. Several of the boys wrestled, and a fight almost started. Morty sat by himself and thought about Edna. He guessed that he'd rather be with her than with the kids. He didn't know where she was. If he knew that she'd gone swimming, he'd go swimming. He didn't know what to do with himself. If he only could find Edna and if they would do something together, or go somewhere, like Jackson Park Beach, just the two of them, why, then, he knew that today would be the day that he would find a way of giving her one of his *Clarion* gold medals. But he didn't know where she was.

Tony Rabuski came around with four tough-looking kids. Tony had lost his job, and he said that the niggers had jumped him when he was delivering flowers down around Forty-seventh Street, and he wanted his pals to stick by him. He told them what had happened, but they didn't get it, because Tony couldn't tell a story straight. Tony asked them didn't they know what was happening? There were race riots, and the beaches and Washington Park and the whole

South Side were full of dark clouds, and over on Wentworth Avenue the big guys were fighting, and the dark clouds were out after whites. They didn't believe Tony. But Morty said it was in the newspapers, and that there were race riots. The bored boys became excited. They bragged about what they would do if the jigs came over to their neighborhood. Tony said they had to get some before they got this far. When asked where they were, Tony said all over. Finally, they went over to Washington Park, picking up sticks and clubs and rocks on the way. The park was calm. A few adults were walking and strolling about. A lad of eighteen or nineteen lay under a tree with his head in the lap of a girl who was stroking his hair. Some of the kids smirked and leered as they passed the couple. Morty thought of Edna and wished he could take her to Washington Park and kiss her. There were seven or eight rowboats on the lagoon, but all of the occupants were white. The park sheep were grazing. Tony threw a rock at them, frightening the sheep, and they all ran, but no cop was around to shag them. They passed the boathouse, talking and bragging. They now believed the rumors which they themselves had made up. White girls and women were in danger, and anything might happen. A tall lad sat in the grass with a nursemaid. A baby carriage was near them. The lad called them over and asked them what they were doing with their clubs and rocks. Tony said they were looking for niggers. The lad said that he'd seen two near the goldfish pond and urged the boys to go and get the sonsofbitches. Screaming and shouting, they ran to the goldfish pond. Suddenly, Tony shouted: "Dark clouds."

VI

They ran. Two Negro boys, near the goldfish pond, heard Tony's cry, and then the others' cry, and they ran. The mob of boys chased them. Morty was in the lead. Running at the head of the screaming, angry pack of boys, he forgot everything except how well and how fast he was running, and images of Edna flashed in and out of his mind. If she could see him running! He was running beautifully. He'd catch them. He was gaining. The colored boys ran in a northwest direction. They crossed the drive which flanked the southern end of the Washington Park ball field. Morty was stopped by a funeral procession. The other boys caught up with him. When the funeral procession passed, it was too late to try and catch the colored boys they had been chasing. Angry, bragging, they crossed over to the ball field and marched across it, shouting and yelling. They picked up about eight boys of their own age and three older lads of seventeen or eighteen. The older lads said they knew where they'd fine some shines. Now was the time to teach them their place once and for all. Led by the older boys, they emerged from the north end of Washington Park and marched down Grand Boulevard, still picking up men and boys as they went along. One of the men who joined them had a gun. They screamed, looked in doorways for Negroes, believed everything anyone said about Negroes, and kept boasting about what they would do when they found some.

"Dark clouds," Tony boomed.

The mob let out. They crossed to the other side of Grand Boulevard and ran cursing and shouting after a Negro. Morty was in the lead. He was outrunning the men and the older fellows. He heard them shouting behind him. He was running. He was running like the playground hundred-yard champion of the South Side of Chicago. He was running like the future Olympic champion. He was running like he'd run for Edna. He was tearing along, pivoting out of the way of shocked, surprised pedestrians, running, really running. He was running like a streak of lightning.

The Negro turned east on Forty-eighth Street. He had a start of a block. But Morty would catch him. He turned into Forty-eighth Street. He tore along the center of the street. He began to breathe heavily. But he couldn't stop running now. He was outdistancing the gang, and he was racing his own gang and the Negro he was chasing. Down the center of the street and about half a block ahead of him, the Negro was tearing away for dear life. But Morty was gaining on him. Gaining. He was now about a half a block ahead of his own gang. They screamed murderously behind him. And they encouraged him. He heard shouts of encouragement.

"Catch 'em, Morty boy!"

"Thata boy, Morty boy!"

He heard Tony's voice. He ran.

The Negro turned into an alley just east of Forestville. Morty ran. He turned into the alley just in time to see the fleeing Negro spurt into a yard in the center of the block. He'd gained more. He was way ahead of the white mob. Somewhere behind him they were coming and yelling. He tore on. He had gained his second wind. He felt himself running, felt the movement of his legs and muscles, felt his arms, felt the sensation of his whole body as he raced down the alley. Never had he run so swiftly. Suddenly Negroes jumped out of yards. He was caught and pinioned. His only thought was one of surprise. Before he even realized what had happened, his throat was slashed. He fell, bleeding. Feebly, he mumbled just once:

"Mother!"

The Negroes disappeared.

He lay bleeding in the center of the dirty alley, and when the gang of whites caught up with him they found him dead in dirt and his own blood in the center of the alley. No Negroes were in sight. The whites surrounded his body. The boys trembled with fear. Some of them cried. One wet his pants. Then they became maddened. And they stood in impotent rage around the bleeding, limp body of Morty Aiken, the fastest runner on Sixty-first Street.

1950

Critical Humor

JAMES THURBER
(1894–1961)

James Thurber made almost all Americans laugh, but at the same time he caused many to think, and this established his position among genuine humorists, who are always essentially serious. His firm critical perception, always alert for the significant absurdity, found expression with equal force in his humorous essays and in those line drawings in which dogs behave like human beings—and vice versa. It is likely that even if they were not signed, these drawings, in which the art of caricature rises to the perfection of simplicity, would be recognized as his by the majority of sophisticated Americans. Thurber turned his attention only occasionally, if with skill, to the burning issues of the day; he reserved most of his creative energy for the inexhaustible field presented by the everyday behavior and predicaments of the average individual; and he projected these perplexities into the domestic scene on the simple plane of "men, women, and dogs."

James Grover Thurber was born on December 8, 1894, in Columbus, Ohio, where his father occupied a position of some political prominence. It is not likely that the family life was exactly as the son depicted it in *My Life and Hard Times* (1933); yet that book has some autobiographical relevance, as well as great humorous value. Thurber attended Ohio State University for three years. Between 1918 and 1920 he was a code clerk in the State Department, stationed in Washington and Paris. He next entered journalism, and was on the staff first of the Columbus *Dispatch* (1920–1924), and then of the Chicago *Tribune* in Paris (1924–1925). He returned to the United States with a position on the New York *Evening Post* in 1925.

That year *The New Yorker* was begun, and E. B. White, one of the founders and a humorist in his own right, encouraged him to join in the effort to develop for that publication the distinctive character that it soon possessed. As contributing editor or contributor, Thurber was associated with the magazine for the rest of his life.

In addition to his many volumes of caricature and prose sketches, Thurber contributed to the American theater, particularly in his collaboration with Elliott Nugent on the comedy *The Male Animal*, performed in 1940 and 1952, and in his *Thurber Carnival* (1960). He died in 1961.

In most of Thumber's volumes, his drawings are to be found under one cover with essays and narratives. Books of considerable size are *The Cream of Thurber*, 1939; *The Thurber Carnival*, 1945; and *Men, Women, and Dogs*, 1943, a collection of his best-known drawings; see also *Thurber's Dogs*, 1955. Individual volumes are *Is Sex Necessary?* (with E. B. White), 1929; *The Owl in the Attic*, 1931; *The Seal in the Bedroom*, 1932; *My Life and Hard Times*, 1933; *The Middle-Aged Man on the Flying Trapeze*, 1935; *Let Your Mind Alone!* 1937; *The Last Flower*, 1939; *Fables for Our Time*, 1940; *My World—and Welcome to It*, 1942; *The Beast in Me and Other Animals*, 1948; *Thurber Album*, 1952; *Thurber Country*, 1953; *Further Fables for Our Time*, 1956; *The Wonderful O*, 1957; *Alarms and Diversions*, 1957; *The Years with Ross*, 1959; and *Lanterns and Lances*, 1961.

Four humorous fantasies for children are *Many Moons*, 1943; *The Great Quillow*, 1944; *The White Deer*, 1945; and *The Thirteen Clocks*, 1950.

Walter Blair, *Horse Sense in American Humor*, 1942, pp. 282–294, is a good critical estimate.

The Secret Life of James Thurber[1]

I have only dipped here and there into Salvador Dali's "The Secret Life of Salvador Dali"[2] (with paintings by Salvador Dali and photographs of Salvador Dali), because anyone afflicted with what my grandmother's sister Abigail called "the permanent jumps" should do no more than skitter through such an autobiography, particularly in these melancholy times.

One does not have to skitter far before one comes upon some vignette which gives the full shape and flavor of the book: the youthful dreamer of dreams biting a sick bat or kissing a dead horse, the slender stripling going into man's estate with the high hope and fond desire of one day eating a live but roasted turkey, the sighing lover covering himself with goat dung and aspic that he might give off the true and noble odor of the ram. In my flying trip through Dali I caught other glimpses of the great man: Salvador adoring a seed ball fallen from a plane tree, Salvador kicking a tiny playmate off a bridge, Salvador caressing a crutch, Salvador breaking the old family doctor's glasses with a leather-thonged mattress-beater. There would appear to be only two things in the world that revolt him (and I don't mean a long-dead hedgehog). He is squeamish about skeletons and grasshoppers. Oh, well, we all have our idiosyncrasies.

Señor Dali's memoirs have set me to thinking. I find myself

1. From *The Thurber Carnival* (1945). Copyright, 1943, by James Thurber, originally in *The New Yorker*, February 27, 1943, pp. 15–17. The title of the present sketch recalls one of his better-known stories, "The Secret Life of Walter Mitty."

2. Salvador Dali (born 1904) is a Spanish painter, an ultramodern experimentalist and a proponent of surrealism.

muttering as I shave, and on two occasions I have swung my crutch at a little neighbor girl on my way to the post office. Señor Dali's book sells for six dollars. My own published personal history (Harper & Brothers, 1933) sold for $1.75. At the time I complained briefly about this unusual figure, principally on the ground that it represented only fifty cents more than the price asked for a book called "The Adventures of Horace the Hedgehog," published the same month. The publishers explained that the price was a closely approximated vertical, prefigured on the basis of profitable ceiling, which in turn was arrived at by taking into consideration the effect on diminishing returns of the horizontal factor.

In those days all heads of business firms adopted a guarded kind of double talk, commonly expressed in low, muffled tones, because nobody knew what was going to happen and nobody understood what had. Big business had been frightened by a sequence of economic phenomena which had clearly demonstrated that our civilization was in greater danger of being turned off than of gradually crumbling away. The upshot of it all was that I accepted the price of $1.75. In so doing, I accepted the state of the world as a proper standard by which the price of books should be fixed. And now, with the world in ten times as serious a condition as it was in 1933, Dali's publishers set a price of six dollars on his life story. This brings me to the inescapable conclusion that the price-fixing principle, in the field of literature, is not global but personal. The trouble, quite simply, is that I told too much about what went on in the house I lived in and not enough about what went on inside myself.

Let me be the first to admit that the naked truth about me is to the naked truth about Salvador Dali as an old ukulele in the attic is to a piano in a tree, and I mean a piano with breasts. Señor Dali has the jump on me from the beginning. He remembers and describes in detail what it was like in the womb. My own earliest memory is of accompanying my father to a polling booth in Columbus, Ohio, where he voted for William McKinley.

It was a drab and somewhat battered tin shed set on wheels, and it was filled with guffawing men and cigar smoke; all in all, as far removed from the paradisiacal placenta of Salvador Dali's first recollection as could well be imagined. A fat, jolly man dandled me on his knee and said that I would soon be old enough to vote against William Jennings Bryan. I thought he meant that I could push a folded piece of paper into the slot of the padlocked box as soon as my father was finished. When this turned out not to be true, I had to be carried out of the place kicking and screaming. In my struggles I knocked my father's derby off several times. The

derby was not a monstrously exciting love object to me, as practically everything Salvador encountered was to him, and I doubt, if
I had that day to live over again, that I could bring myself, even in
the light of exotic dedication as I now know it, to conceive an intense and perverse affection for the derby. It remains obstinately in
my memory as a rather funny hat, a little too large in the crown,
which gave my father the appearance of a tired, sensitive gentleman who had been persuaded against his will to take part in a game
of charades.

We lived on Champion Avenue at the time, and the voting
booth was on Mound Street. As I set down these names, I begin to
perceive an essential and important difference between the infant
Salvador and the infant me. This difference can be stated in terms
of environment. Salvador was brought up in Spain, a country
colored by the legends of Hannibal, El Greco, and Cervantes. I
was brought up in Ohio, a region steeped in the tradition of Coxey's
Army, the Anti-Saloon League, and William Howard Taft. It is
only natural that the weather in little Salvador's soul should have
been stirred by stranger winds and enveloped in more fantastic
mists than the weather in my own soul. But enough of mewling
apology for my lacklustre early years. Let us get back to my secret
life, such as it was, stopping just long enough to have another brief
look at Señor Dali on our way.

Salvador Dali's mind goes back to a childhood half imagined and
half real, in which the edges of actuality were sometimes less sharp
than the edges of dream. He seems somehow to have got the idea
that this sets him off from Harry Spencer, Charlie Doakes, I. Fein-
berg, J. J. McNaboe, Willie Faulkner, Herbie Hoover, and me.
What Salvie had that the rest of us kids didn't was the perfect
scenery, characters, and costumes for his desperate little rebellion
against the clean, the conventional, and the comfortable. He put
perfume on his hair (which would have cost him his life in, say,
Bayonne, N. J., or Youngstown, Ohio), he owned a lizard with two
tails, he wore silver buttons on his shoes, and he knew, or imagined
he knew, little girls named Galuchka and Dullita. Thus he was
born halfway along the road to paranoia, the soft Poictesme of his
prayers, the melting Oz of his oblations, the capital, to put it so
that you can see what I am trying to say, of his heart's desire. Or so,
anyway, it must seem to a native of Columbus, Ohio, who, as a
youngster, bought his twelve-dollar suits at the F. & R. Lazarus Co.,
had his hair washed out with Ivory soap, owned a bull terrier with
only one tail, and played (nicely and a bit diffidently) with little
girls named Irma and Betty and Ruby.

Another advantage that the young Dali had over me, from the

standpoint of impetus toward paranoia, lay in the nature of the adults who peopled his real world. There was, in Dali's home town of Figueras, a family of artists named Pitchot (musicians, painters, and poets), all of whom adored the ground that the *enfant terrible* walked on. If one of them came upon him throwing himself from a high rock—a favorite relaxation of our hero—or hanging by his feet with his head immersed in a pail of water, the wild news was spread about the town that greatness and genius had come to Figueras. There was a woman who put on a look of maternal interest when Salvador threw rocks at her. The mayor of the town fell dead one day at the boy's feet. A doctor in the community (not the one he had horsewhipped) was seized of a fit and attempted to beat him up. (The contention that the doctor was out of his senses at the time of the assault is Dali's, not mine.)

The adults around me when I was in short pants were neither so glamorous nor so attentive. They consisted mainly of eleven maternal great-aunts, all Methodists, who were staunch believers in physic, mustard plasters, and Scripture, and it was part of their dogma that artistic tendencies should be treated in the same way as hiccups or hysterics. None of them was an artist, unless you can count Aunt Lou, who wrote sixteen-stress verse, with hit-and-miss rhymes, in celebration of people's birthdays or on the occasion of great national disaster. It never occurred to me to bite a bat in my aunts' presence or to throw stones at them. There was one escape, though: my secret world of idiom.

Two years ago my wife and I, looking for a house to buy, called on a firm of real-estate agents in New Milford. One of the members of the firm, scrabbling through a metal box containing many keys, looked up to say, "The key to the Roxbury house isn't here." His partner replied, "It's a common lock. A skeleton will let you in." I was suddenly once again five years old, with wide eyes and open mouth. I pictured the Roxbury house as I would have pictured it as a small boy, a house of such dark and nameless horrors as have never crossed the mind of our little bat-biter.

It was of sentences like that, nonchalantly tossed off by real-estate dealers, great-aunts, clergymen, and other such prosaic persons that the enchanted private world of my early boyhood was made. In this world, businessmen who phoned their wives to say that they were tied up at the office sat roped to their swivel chairs, and probably gagged, unable to move or speak, except somehow, miraculously, to telephone; hundreds of thousands of businessmen tied to their chairs in hundreds of thousands of offices in every city of my fantastic cosmos. An especially fine note about the binding of all the businessmen in all the cities was that whoever did it always did it around five o'clock in the afternoon.

Then there was the man who left town under a cloud. Sometimes I saw him all wrapped up in the cloud, and invisible, like a cat in a burlap sack. At other times it floated, about the size of a sofa, three or four feet above his head, following him wherever he went. One could think about the man under the cloud before going to sleep; the image of him wandering around from town to town was a sure soporific.

Not so the mental picture of a certain Mrs. Huston, who had been terribly cut up when her daughter died on the operating table. I could see the doctors too vividly, just before they set upon Mrs. Huston with their knives, and I could hear them. "Now, Mrs. Huston, will we get up on the table like a good girl, or will we have to be put there?" I could usually fight off Mrs. Huston before I went to sleep, but she frequently got into my dreams, and sometimes she still does.

I remember the grotesque creature that came to haunt my meditations when one evening my father said to my mother, "What did Mrs. Johnson say when you told her about Betty?" and my mother replied, "Oh, she was all ears." There were many other wonderful figures in the secret, surrealist landscapes of my youth: the old lady who was always up in the air, the husband who did not seem to be able to put his foot down, the man who lost his head during a fire but was still able to run out of the house yelling, the young lady who was, in reality, a soiled dove. It was a world that, of necessity, one had to keep to oneself and brood over in silence, because it would fall to pieces at the touch of words. If you brought it out into the light of actual day and put it to the test of questions, your parents would try to laugh the miracles away, or they would take your temperature and put you to bed. (Since I always ran a temperature, whenever it was taken, I was put to bed and left there all alone with Mrs. Huston.)

Such a world as the world of my childhood is, alas, not year-proof. It is a ghost that, to use Henley's words, gleams, flickers, vanishes away. I think it must have been the time my little Cousin Frances came to visit us that it began surely and forever to dissolve. I came into the house one rainy dusk and asked where Frances was. "She is," said our cook, "up in the front room crying her heart out." The fact that a person could cry so hard that his heart would come out of his body, as perfectly shaped and glossy as a red velvet pincushion, was news to me. For some reason I had never heard the expression, so common in American families whose hopes and dreams run so often counter to attainment. I went upstairs and opened the door of the front room. Frances, who was three years older than I, jumped up off the bed and ran past me, sobbing, and down the stairs.

My search for her heart took some fifteen minutes. I tore the bed apart and kicked up the rugs and even looked in the bureau drawers. It was no good. I looked out the window at the rain and the darkening sky. My cherished mental image of the man under the cloud began to grow dim and fade away. I discovered that, all alone in a room, I could face the thought of Mrs. Huston with cold equanimity. Downstairs, in the living room, Frances was still crying. I began to laugh.

Ah there, Salvador!

1943

Some Representative Poets at Mid-Century

lit trad. of Blake derived fr. lyrics of balladry

RICHARD EBERHART

(1904–)

Early poems by Eberhart appeared while he was a student at Cambridge University, England, in an English anthology called *New Signatures* (1932). This "represented a new concept of poetry," whose practitioners included William Empson, C. Day Lewis, W. H. Auden, and Stephen Spender. These poets held in common a determination to enrich the language and style of poetry for the expression of that new age.

Eberhart makes demands upon the reader which are unusual, but consistent with a "world too much in joint," in which only a "hard intellectual light" can restore "the moral grandeur of man." Even his simpler poems depend for their effect upon some striking extension of experience or idea, accomplished by verbal or metaphoric tension. "For a Lamb," an apparently simple lyric, is intensified by sudden violence in line 4 and complicated by the concluding enigma. In "Experience Evoked," the inversion of word order ("seed,

small") asserts that one seed and also the total quantity is "small for the immense" (unmeasurable) sowing—spelled "Sewing," thus simultaneously suggesting the stitching of rose color across the land. Finally, "Rose" is capitalized: it is at once flower and passionate symbol.

William Blake may be recalled by the subject and the blending of "innocence" and "experience" in "For a Lamb"; "When Doris Danced," touched with sensuousness and primitive wonder, may suggest both Hopkins and the Pre-Raphaelites; the metaphysical infusion in language and image evident in "Rumination" is not unlike the poetry of John Donne. But these comparisons only tend to establish the direction of Eberhart's originality, for his style is independent and his individualism is a measure of his strength.

Born in Austin, Minnesota, in 1904, Eberhart completed the baccalaureate at Dartmouth in

imaginative structure of poems [handwritten]

1926, and the M.A. at Cambridge University in 1933. From 1933 to 1942 he taught English at two private preparatory schools in Massachusetts. He served in the U.S. Navy (1942–1946), retiring with the rank of commander to enter a manufacturing business, of which he became vice-president in 1952. Since 1958 he has continued his business interests as member of the board of this and another industrial corporation.

Meanwhile his poems appeared in a variety of magazines, and in eight volumes from 1944 to 1957. In 1952 he returned to academic life as professor and poet in residence at the University of Washington, then successively at Connecticut, Wheaton, Massachusetts and Princeton. Since 1956 he has been professor of English at Dartmouth.

No complete study exists, but articles and reviews are listed in standard reference works and periodical indexes. Eberhart's volumes of poetry are: *A Bravery of Earth*, 1930; *Reading The Spirit*, 1936, 1937; *Song and Idea*, 1940, 1942; *Poems, New and Selected*, 1944; *Burr Oaks*, 1947; *Brotherhood of Men*, 1949; *An Herb Basket*, 1950; *Selected Poems*, 1951; *The Visionary Farms* (drama) 1952; *Undercliff: Poems, 1946–1953*, 1953; *Great Praises*, 1957. *Collected Poems: 1930–1960* (1960) is comprehensive.

For a Lamb[1] *animal immortality* [handwritten]

I saw on the slant hill a putrid lamb,
Propped with daisies. The sleep looked deep,
The face nudged in the green pillow *condition of life* [handwritten]
But the guts were out for crows to eat.

Where's the lamb? whose tender plaint   5
Said all for the mute breezes.
Say he's in the wind somewhere,   *flesh breeds*
Say, there's a lamb in the daisies.   *flowers – blood* [handwritten]

effect of word on word [handwritten]   *watered* 1936, 1951 *daisies* [handwritten]

Rumination[2] *takes an image & suddenly revolving it to have more sig. than seems* [handwritten]

When I can hold a stone within my hand
And feel time make it sand and soil, and see
The roots of living things grow in this land,
Pushing between my fingers flower and tree,
Then I shall be as wise as death,   5
For death has done this and he will
Do this to me, and blow his breath
To fire my clay, when I am still.

1947, 1951

1. First collected in *Reading The Spirit* (1936); included in *Selected Poems* (1951).

2. First collected in *Burr Oaks* (1947); included in *Selected Poems* (1951).

That's the way things are

"I Walked over the Grave of Henry James"[3]

I walked over the grave of Henry James
But recently, and one eye kept the dry stone.
The other leaned on boys at games away,
My soul was balanced in my body cold.

I am one of those prodigals of hell   5
Whom ten years have seen cram with battle;
Returns to what he canted from, grants it good,
As asthma makes itself a new resolution.

I crushed a knob of earth between my fingers,
This is a very ordinary experience.   10
A name may be glorious but death is death,
I thought, and took a street-car back to Harvard Square.

1947, 1951

glad to be alive

The Humanist[5]

Hunting for the truly human
I looked for the true man
And saw an ape at the fair
With the circle still to square. Learning
Breeds its own ignorance. Fame and power   5
Demand a rush and pounding.
Those who rush through rush through, and who
Are they but those who rush through?
Yet truth resides in contemplation
And comprehension of contemplation   10
Not necessarily of Plato. Action explains
A field full of folk and golden football flexions,
Action for actors. Truth through contemplation
Resurrects the truly human,
Makes known the true man   15
Whom these lines can scan:
But miss his secret final point.
The world is too much in joint. No use
Setting that right,[6] that squaring, that harrying: for
The true man lives in mystery   20

3. First collected in *Burr Oaks* (1947); included in *Selected Poems* (1951).
5. From *Selected Poems* (1951).
6. This poem's meaning turns on the mingled twofold reference: (1) Wordsworth (Sonnet 33), "*The world is too much* with us; late and soon / Getting and spending we lay waste our powers"; and (2) *Hamlet* (I.v.188–189), "The time is out of joint. [*cf.* "in joint"] O, cursed spite, / That ever I was born to set it right."

Of God; God his agile soul will see
But he will not see God's majesty,
And that is what makes you and me
'Whether man or woman
Neither true nor free   25
But truly human.

1951

Experience Evoked[7]

Now come to me all men
With savagery and innocence,
With axe to chop the fir tree,
Or seed, small, for the immense
Sewing of earth with old Rose.   5
Now come all men, arrayed
With the colours of the garden
Around them where they stayed
Till bone began to harden
Under the thinning of the nose.   10
Come all men, unto whom
Wind was a snarling wire whip
In the contusions of a doom
And with red flecks on their lip
They leaped up, danced, grew tall.   15
Come all, the babe bound
In terror and panic cry;
Or an old man found
With a skylark in his eye.[8]
Come, harsh shroud over all.   20

1951

hesidance -lingering quality - folk speech

"When Doris Danced"[9] *Balladry*

When Doris danced under the oak tree
The sun himself might wish to see,
Might bend beneath those lovers, leaves,
While her her virgin step she weaves
And envious cast his famous hue   5
To make her daft, yet win her too.

7. From *Selected Poems* (1951).
8. *Cf.* those above, whom the "babe bound" (the Messiah) filled with "terror." The old man's "skylark" might be either of two defined in the diction- ary: a bird "noted for singing in almost perpendicular flight toward the sky" or that "skylark" which is "a gay and playful frolic."
9. From *Selected Poems* (1951).

When Doris danced under the oak tree
Slow John, so stormed in heart, at sea
Gone all his store, a wreck he lay.
But on the ground the sun-beams play.
They lit his face in such degree
Doris lay down, all out of pity.

[handwritten marginalia: mideval ballads dramaou... sounds Burst of realism... ends]

1951

"Go to the Shine That's on a Tree"[1]

Go to the shine that's on a tree
When dawn has laved with liquid light
With luminous light the nighted tree
And take that glory without fright.

Go to the song that's in a bird   5
When he has seen the glistening tree,
That glorious tree the bird has heard
Give praise for its felicity.

Then go to the earth and touch it keen,
Be tree and bird, be wide aware   10
Be wild aware of light unseen,
And unheard song along the air.

1953

1. From *Undercliff* (1953).

MURIEL RUKEYSER
[handwritten marginalia: Primitive society/cultures religion]
(1913–)

That Muriel Rukeyser has authorized only a sparse official documentation of her life is offset by the eloquent evidence of experience in her poems. She never owned or rented an ivory tower. Her first volume, *Theory of Flight*, reflects both her practical experience as a student aviator and her interest in the machine and in less tangible sources of human power—the creative forms of art or love. Born in New York City, which she still regards as home, where the many-structured evidences of power are raucous, she traveled as a young writer wherever circumstances would permit, as reporter for college publications and later for several magazines and papers. At the Scottsboro trial she was one of the reporters arrested; she was commissioned to cover the so-called People's Olympiad in Republican Spain, where she remained in appointment under the Spanish

Medical Bureau long enough to witness the early phases of the Spanish Civil War. She has resided in several localities in the United States and in Mexico.

In *Orpheus* (1949) she wrote: "Now, in our time, many of the sources of power are obscured again, or vulgarized and left out. * * * Using as materials studies in symbolism, studies in individual lives, and [my] experience, I have hoped to indicate some of the valid sources of power.* * * The fear of symbols is linked with the fear of poetry in our culture. It is poetry's enemy, part of a great emotional wound."

The affirmative direction of her later work was first strongly expressed in *The Green Wave* (1948), a book of genuine power, unobtrusively expressing its hard-won wisdom and its "belief in the love of the world, woman, spirit, and man." In these poems, the "sources of power" have led to a root in

"love which contains all human spirit, all wish." "Ajanta" (1944) and *Orpheus* (1949), are long poems inspired by primitive religion and myth; the ritual death of Orpheus and his resurrection ("he has died the birth of the God") celebrate both fertility and the creative spirit. The periodical poems and collected work since 1949 give continuing evidence of the growth of a genuine inspiration.

There has not been a full-length study of Miss Rukeyser's work, nor a complete collection of her poems. The *Selected Poems* (1951) is a good cross-section of her works. Volumes of her poetry are *Theory of Flight*, 1935; *U. S. 1*, 1938; *A Turning Wind*, 1939; *The Soul and Body of John Brown*, 1941; *Wake Island*, 1942; *Beast in View*, 1944; *The Green Wave*, 1948; *Elegies*, 1949; *Orpheus*, 1949; *Body of Waking*, 1958. Biographies include *Willard Gibbs*, 1942; and *One Life* (Wendell Willkie) 1957. *The Life of Poetry*, 1949, is criticism; *The Middle of the Night* is an unpublished play, produced in 1945. The texts of the poems below are those of the 1951 selection; they appear in the sequence that the author gave them in that volume.

This Place in the Ways[1]

Having come to this place
I set out once again
On the dark and marvelous way
From where I began:
Belief in the love of the world,   5
Woman, spirit, and man.

Having failed in all things
I enter a new age
Seeing the old ways as toys,
The houses of a stage   10
Painted and long forgot;
And I find love and rage.

1. First collected in *The Green Wave* (1948); included in *Selected Poems* (1951), where the poet significantly gave it the initial position.

Rage for the world as it is
But for what it may be
More love now than last year.   15
And always less self-pity
Since I know in a clearer light
The strength of the mystery.

And at this place in the ways
I wait for song,   20
My poem-hand still, on the paper,
All night long.
Poems in throat and hand, asleep,
And my storm beating strong!

1948, 1951

Song[2]

The world is full of loss; bring, wind, my love,
   My home is where we make our meeting-place,
   And love whatever I shall touch and read
   Within that face.

Lift, wind, my exile from my eyes;   5
   Peace to look, life to listen and confess,
   Freedom to find   to find   to find
   That nakedness.

1944, 1951

applies prim. live level to people today

Mortal Girl[3]

The girl being chosen stood in her naked room
Singing at last alone naked and proud
Now that the god had departed and his doom
Guarded her door forever and the sky
Would flame in trophies all night and every day.   5

Sang : When your white sun stood still,[4] I put away
My garments and my crafts and you came down.

woman who choose husband puts him on level of God to break up of land of religion

2. First published in *Beast in View* (1944); included in *Selected Poems* (1951).
3. First collected in *Beast in View* (1944); included in *Selected Poems* (1951).
4. Lines 6–12 consolidate three Greek legends of the love of Zeus, god of the heavens, for mortal women. The jealous goddess, Hera, in disguise, persuaded the mortal Semele to demand that Zeus visit her only in all his majesty; he reluctantly did so, and his splendor "took her as a flame"; from her ashes the newborn Dionysus rose to become the god of wine. "As a swan" Zeus visited Leda, wife of Sparta's king, thus fathering Helen of Troy and the twin heroes and divinities, Castor and Pollux, the Gemini of the Zodiac. "As a shower of gold" Zeus visited Danae, daughter of Argos' king, who confined her in a high tower lest she should bear the son destined to kill him; and Perseus, born of this visitation, accidentally fulfilled the prophecy with a misdirected discus.

When you took me as a flame, I turned to flame;
In whiteness lay on the mist-flower river-bank
When you as a swan arrived, and cloudy in my tower   10
For you as a shower of gold, the lily bright in my hand
Once, you as unthinkable light.

                          Make me more human,

Give me the consciousness
Of every natural shape, to lie here ready
For love as every power.   15
I wait in all my hopes,
Poet beast and woman,
Wait for the superhuman,
The god who invaded the gold lady,
The god who spoke to the naked princess,   20
The storm over the fiery wanderer.

Within me your city burning, and your desperate tree.
All that the song and the apparition gave
To seal my mouth with fire, make me mad
With song and pain and waiting, leave me free   25
In all my own shapes, deep in the spirit's cave
To sing again the entrance of the god.

                                1944, 1951

From For the Unborn Child: VII[5]

You will enter the world where death by fear and explosion
Is waited;   longed for by many;   by all dreamed.
You will enter the world where various poverty
Makes thin the imagination and the bone.
You will enter the world where birth is walled about,   5
Where years are walled journeys, death a walled-in act.
You will enter the world which eats itself
Naming faith, reason, naming love, truth, fact.

You in your dark lake moving darkly now
Will leave a house that time makes, times to come   10
Enter the present, where all the deaths and all
The old betrayals have come home again.
World where again Judas,[6] the little child,
May grow and choose. You will enter the world.

                                1948, 1951

5. First collected in *The Green Wave* (1948) as one of a cycle of nine poems, Number VII was included alone in *Selected Poems* (1951). The entire cycle deals with phases of the mother's consciousness: passion, annunciation, the thought of death, participation in mankind, and fulfillment.

6. Judas the disciple was bribed to kiss Jesus to identify him to the soldiers. Seeing his Master actually condemned to die, Judas repented and hanged himself (Matthew xxvi: 40–57 and xxvii: 1–7).

Boy with His Hair Cut Short[8]

Sunday shuts down on a twentieth-century evening.
The El passes. Twilight and bulb define
the brown room, the overstuffed plum sofa,
the boy, and the girl's thin hands above his head.
A neighbor radio sings stocks, news, serenade.   5

He sits at the table, head down, the young clear neck exposed,
watching the drugstore sign from the tail of his eye;
tattoo, neon, until the eye blears, while his
solicitous tall sister, simple in blue, bending
behind him, cuts his hair with her cheap shears.   10

The arrow's electric red always reaches its mark,
successful neon! He coughs, impressed by that precision.
His child's forehead, forever protected by his cap,
is bleached against the lamplight as he turns head
and steadies to let the snippets drop.   15

Erasing the failure of weeks with level fingers,
she sleeks the fine hair, combing : "You'll look fine tomorrow!
You'll surely find something, they can't keep turning you down;
the finest gentleman's not so trim as you!" Smiling, he raises
the adolescent forehead wrinkling ironic now.   20

He sees his decent suit laid out, new-pressed,
his carfare on the shelf. He lets his head fall, meeting
her earnest hopeless look, seeing the sharp blades splitting,
the darkened room, the impersonal sign, her motion,
the blue vein, bright on her temple, pitifully beating.   25

1938, 1951

From Correspondences[1]

Tree of Days

I was born in winter when
Europe heard the early guns,[2]
when I was five, the drums
welcomed home the men.

---

8. In *U. S. 1* (1938); included in *Selected Poems* (1951).
1. Collected in *A Turning Wind* (1933); included in *Selected Poems* (1951). The four "Correspondences" coincided with the grim mood of the poet's generation confronted by the climax of disasters beginning with World War I, and in 1936–39 culminating in the Spanish war, Poland, and the threat of another World War.
2. *I.e.*, the "guns" of the Serb Nationalist guerillas against Austro-Hungarian rule in Bosnia, leading to the assassination, in June of 1914, of Archduke Francis Ferdinand, which was a cause of World War I. The next two lines allude to the return of American troops in 1918.

The spring after my birth   5
a tree came out of the lake,
I laughed, for I could not speak;
the world was there to learn.

The richest season in
the headlines fell as I was ten,[3]   10
but the crazies were forgotten,
the fine men, the bravest men.

When I had reached fifteen,[4]
that pliant tree was dark,
breadlines haunted the parks—   15
the books tricked-in that scene.

No work in any town
when I was twenty,[5] cured
the thin and desperate poor
from being forced alone.   20

Clear to half a brain
in a blind man's head,
war must follow that tide
of running milk and grain.

Now China's long begun,   25
that tree is dense and strong,
spreading, continuing—
and Austria; and Spain.[6]

If some long unborn friend
looks at photos in pity,   30
we say, sure we were happy,
but it was not in the wind.

Half my twenties are gone[7]
as the crazies take to the planes,
the fine men, the bravest men,   35
and the war goes on.

1939, 1951

---

3. *I.e.*, in 1923, first flood of the "Jazz Age" and postwar prosperity.
4. She was "fifteen" when the depression of 1928 edged toward the crash of 1929.
5. *I.e.*, in 1933, when unemployment was at its worst and business was at a standstill; it was also the first year of Roosevelt's New Deal policies.
6. Manchuria and northern China were invaded by Japan in 1931 and 1937, thus beginning World War II in Asia; in 1937 Austria was absorbed by Hitler; in 1936, Spain had plunged into a civil war involving conflicting ideologies.
7. In 1938. Chamberlain's policy of appeasement had failed; the loss of Czechoslovakia and Poland was conceded; war was inevitable.

Beast in View[8]

Configurations of time and singing
  Bring me to a dark harbor where
  The chase is drawn to a beginning.
  And all the myths are gathered there.

I know the trees as fountains and the stars'   5
  Far fires fountains and your love
  A vivid fountain, and the bars
  Broken about me let me move

Among the fountains. At last seeing
  I came here by obscure preparing,   10
  In vigils and encounters being
  Both running hunter and fierce prey waring.[9]

I hunted and became the followed,
  Through many lives fleeing the last me,[1]
  And changing fought down a far road   15
  Through time to myself as I will be.

Chaos prepared me, and I find the track,
  Through life and darkness seek my myth—
  Move toward it, hunting grow more like,
  Draw near, and know it through our path.   20
  Know only that we run one path.

1944, 1951

Easter Eve 1945[2]

Wary of time O it seizes the soul tonight
I wait for the great morning of the west
confessing with every breath mortality.
Moon of this wild sky struggles to stay whole
and on the water silvers the ships of war.   5
I go alone in the black-yellow light

8. Collected in *Beast in View* (1944); included in *Selected Poems* (1951).
9. The verb "to ware," now chiefly a hunting term, has connotations of "to guard against," "to avoid."
1. The idea of one's individual identity or myth (*cf.* ll. 4 and 18) as ideally always in existence, seeking one, yet always requiring to be hunted (l. 14), has overtones of Emersonian and Platonic idealism.

2. In *The Green Wave* (1948); included in *Selected Poems* (1951). The date "1945" (omitted from the title in the 1951 edition) probably refers to the last months of World War II, between the battle for Iwo Jima in February and March and the final surrenders in May and August. The note of resurrection is made explicit in the allusion to the "Judaean Innocent" (ll. 24–25), *i.e.*, Jesus Christ, born in Judaea.

all night waiting for day, while everywhere the sure
death of light, the leaf's sure return to the root
is repeated in million, death of all man to share.
Whatever world I know shines ritual death,   10
wide under this moon they stand gathering fire,
fighting with flame, stand fighting in their graves.
All shining with life as the leaf, as the wing shines,
the stone deep in the mountain, the drop in the green wave.
Lit by their energies, secretly, all things shine.   15
Nothing can black that glow of life;   although
      each part go crumbling down
      itself shall rise up whole.

Now I say there are new meanings;   now I name
death our black honor and feast of possibility   20
to celebrate casting of life on life. This earth-long day
between blood and resurrection where we wait
remembering sun, seed, fire; remembering
that fierce Judaean Innocent who risked
every immortal meaning on one life.   25
Given to our year as sun and spirit are,
as seed we are blessed only in needing freedom.
Now I say that the peace the spirit needs is peace,
not lack of war, but fierce continual flame.
For all men :   effort is freedom, effort's peace,   30
it fights. And along these truths the soul goes home,
      flies in its blazing to a place
      more safe and round than Paradise.

Night of the soul, our dreams in the arms of dreams
dissolving into eyes that look upon us.   35
Dreams the sources of action, the meeting and the end,
a resting-place among the flight of things.
And love which contains all human spirit, all wish,
the eyes and hands, sex, mouth, the whole woman—
fierce peace I say at last, and the sense of the world.   40
In the time of conviction of mortality
whatever survive, I remember what I am—
The nets of this night are on fire with sun and moon
pouring both lights into the open tomb.
Whatever arise, it comes in the shape of peace,   45
fierce peace which is love, in which move all the stars,
and the breathing of universes, filling, falling away,
and death on earth cast into the human dream.
      What fire survive forever
      myself is for my time.   50

1945   1948, 1951

ROBERT LOWELL partrician

(1917–)

From the beginning, Robert Lowell's poetry has won serious critical attention and been received with enthusiasm. In spite of the very slow accumulation of his poems during sixteen years, he is regarded as one of the new poets of the mid-century whose inherent strength might influence the literature of his generation.

Born in Boston in 1917, he was given his father's name, Robert Traill Spence Lowell, representing an inheritance of family tradition distinguished and old in New England history. His mother was a Winslow. The poet transformed his youthful embarrassment at family tradition into a literary resource: he developed a psychological interest in family situations which infuses a number of his best poems, and he allowed his tragic sense and his comic spirit to rummage in his own family attics.

After nearly two years at Harvard University Lowell completed his formal education at Kenyon College (1940) where his poetry was encouraged by John Crowe Ransom, poet-teacher, and by others, especially Randall Jarrell. Having twice been refused for enlistment, he was later drafted, declared himself a conscientious objector, and was sentenced. He published *Land of Unlikeness*, his first volume (1944), in a limited edition. Two years later *Lord Weary's Castle* won the Pulitzer Prize (1947).

As an undergraduate at Kenyon, he had been converted to Catholicism, and as Allen Tate had foreseen, Lowell became "consciously a Catholic poet"; however, he retained an earlier interest in the religious philosophy and works of learned Puritans. In Lowell the two became reconciled. This religious motivation gives his style a determined boldness, supported by complexly disciplined language, symbol, and idea. A number of his best poems are secular in spirit, yet he is seldom wanting in pronounced ethical sensibility.

Randall Jarrell's review of *Lord Weary's Castle* in *The Nation* (1946) gains interest because Lowell approved it, in lieu of writing his own introduction, for publication with a selection of his poems in John Ciardi's *Mid-Century American Poets*. Mr. Jarrell commented that these "poems understand the world as a sort of conflict of opposites." One force is the "inertia of the complacent self, the satisfied persistence in evil that is damnation * * * turned inward, incestuous, that blinds or binds." The opposing Force "is the realm of freedom, of the Grace that has replaced the Law, of the perfect Liberator." The poems "normally move into liberation"; and in some cases "even death is seen as a liberation."

Whatever their ideas, Lowell's poems range over a wide diversity of subjects beyond the direct religious experience. In a tradition including Robert Browning and Edwin Arlington Robinson are his dramatic narratives written as monologue, reverie, or interior dialogue. A learned poet, he shares Pound's inclination to imitate or reconstruct old poems in several languages. His character studies and stories are enriched by his knowledge of several countries, and by his psychological grasp of human situations quite various in mood and meaning. His native New England provides the resources of its seafaring and whaling history, its intellectual tradition, and its family inheritance.

Lowell is on the faculty of Boston University.

Published volumes are *Land of Unlikeness*, 1944 (now unavailable); *Lord Weary's Castle*, 1946; *The Mills of the Kavenaughs*, 1951; *Poems: 1938–1949*, 1950, which includes the two volumes above, except the title poem, "The Mills of the Kavenaughs"; and *Life Studies*, 1959, which won the National Book Award. *Imitations*, 1961, is a book of "translations." A critical biography is Hugh B. Stapler, *Robert Lowell: The First Twenty Years*, 1961.

In Memory of Arthur Winslow[1]

I. *Death from Cancer*

This Easter, Arthur Winslow,[2] less than dead,
Your people set you up in Phillips' House
To settle off your wrestling with the crab[3]—
The claws drop flesh upon your yachting blouse
Until longshoreman Charon[4] come and stab   5
Through your adjusted bed
And crush the crab. On Boston Basin, shells
Hit water by the Union Boat Club wharf:
You ponder why the coxes[5] squeakings dwarf
The *resurrexit dominus*[6] of all the bells.   10

Grandfather Winslow, look, the swanboats coast
That island in the Public Gardens, where
The bread-stuffed ducks are brooding, where with tub
And strainer the mid-Sunday Irish scare
The sun-struck shallows for the dusky chub[7]   15
This Easter, and the ghost

1. First collected in *Lord Weary's Castle* (1946) and included in the collection of 1950.
2. In an autobiographical sketch, "91 Revere Street" (*Life Studies*, pp. 11–46), Lowell describes with affection Grandfather Winslow, his mother's father, a financial adventurer, Boston Brahmin, and family autocrat, proud of his descent from the Stark family of Dunbarton, N. H., as well as the colonial Massachusetts Winslows (both mentioned in the following poem).

3. "Cancer" is the Latin for "crab."
4. In Greek mythology, Charon ferried the souls of the dead across the Styx, river of death.
5. "Coxes," abbreviation for "coxswains," steersmen of racing shells or ship's boats.
6. "The Lord is risen": the liturgical message of Easter.
7. A humble variety of carp, on Easter recalling that the fish became a Christian symbol because of miracles associated with fish and fishermen.

Of risen Jesus walks the waves to run[8]
Arthur upon a trumpeting black swan
Beyond Charles River to the Acheron[9]
Where the wide waters and their voyager are one.   20

II. *Dunbarton*

The stones are yellow and the grass is gray
Past Concord by the rotten lake and hill
Where crutch and trumpet meet the limousine
And half-forgotten Starks and Winslows[1] fill
The granite plot and the dwarf pines are green   25
From watching for the day
When the great year of the little yeomen[2] come
Bringing its landed Promise [3] and the faith
That made the Pilgrim Makers take a lathe
And point their wooden steeples lest the Word[4] be dumb.   30

O fearful witnesses, your day is done:
The minister from Boston waves your shades,
Like children, out of sight and out of mind.
The first selectman of Dunbarton spreads
Wreaths of New Hampshire pine cones on the lined   35
Casket where the cold sun
Is melting. But, at last, the end is reached;
We start our cars. The preacher's mouthings still
Deafen my poor relations on the hill:
Their sunken landmarks echo what our fathers preached.[5]   40

III. *Five Years Later*

This Easter, Arthur Winslow, five years gone
I came to mourn you, not to praise the craft
That netted you a million dollars, late
Hosing out gold in Colorado's waste,[6]
Then lost it all in Boston real estate.   45
Now from the train, at dawn
Leaving Columbus in Ohio, shell
On shell of our stark culture strikes the sun

8. See the miracle of Jesus walking on the sea, Matthew xiv: 25.
9. The Charles, a river of Boston; Acheron, according to Greek mythology, a shade-haunted river in Hades.
1. For the Starks of Dunbarton, N. H., and the Winslows of Massachusetts, see Section I, note 2.
2. British "yeomen," that is, freeholders of land and commoners of the highest level, made up the majority in colonial New England.
3. *I.e.*, the Promised Land of the redeemed on "the day" of Judgment.
4. The Bible (Acts iv: 31) or the Messiah (John i: 1, 14).
5. *I.e.*, Bible texts carved on the tombstones.
6. In placer mining the gold is washed out of superficial deposits with high-pressure hoses.

To fill my head with all our fathers won
When Cotton Mather wrestled with the fiends from hell.[7]   50

You must have hankered for our family's craft:
The block-house Edward made, the Governor,[8]
At Marshfield, and the slight coin-silver spoons
The Sheriff beat to shame the gaunt Revere,[9]
And General Stark's[1] coarse bas-relief in bronze   55
Set on your granite shaft
In rough Dunbarton; for what else could bring
You, Arthur, to the veined and alien West
But devil's notions that your gold at least
Could give back life to men who whipped or backed the King? 60

IV. A *Prayer for My Grandfather to Our Lady*[2]

Mother, for these three hundred years or more
Neither our clippers nor our slavers reached
The haven of your peace in this Bay State:
Neither my father nor his father. Beached
On these dry flats of fishy real estate,   65
O Mother, I implore
Your scorched, blue thunderbreasts of love to pour
Buckets of blessings on my burning head
Until I rise like Lazarus from the dead:[3]
Lavabis nos et super nivem dealbabor.[4]   70

"On Copley Square,[5] I saw you hold the door
To Trinity, the costly Church, and saw
The painted Paradise of harps and lutes
Sink like Atlantis[6] in the Devil's jaw
And knock the Devil's teeth out by the roots;   75
But when I strike for shore
I find no painted idols to adore:
Hell is burned out, heaven's harp-strings are slack.

7. Industrial buildings, representing material wealth, are compared with the salvation preached by Cotton Mather (1663–1728), archetype of Puritan divines.
8. Edward Winslow, their ancestor, a Mayflower Pilgrim (1622) described in his journal the earliest events in Plymouth and was three times elected governor. *Cf.* "our family's craft," l. 51.
9. Paul Revere, the midnight rider of the Battle of Lexington, was a gifted silversmith and engraver.
1. General John Stark (1728–1822), another ancestor, famous New Hampshire soldier of the Revolution.
2. The poem has proceeded from Arthur Winslow's death and burial, to memories of his material life, and finally to the stage of penitence. The two stanzas of this section are differentiated by the quotation marks enclosing the second and by the two Lazaruses—*cf.* notes 3 and 7.
3. Jesus raised Lazarus from the dead (*cf.* John xi: 11–43).
4. "You shall wash us and I shall be made whiter than snow." *Dealbabor* was erroneously printed *delabor* in the 1950 collection.
5. A very old Boston square, once a center of social refinement.
6. Fabulous island civilization presumed to have sunk beneath the ocean.

Mother, run to the chalice, and bring back
Blood on your finger-tips for Lazarus who was poor."[7]   80

sense of history as one of his images   1946, 1950

Criticism of a certain phase of Amer. relig.

After the Surprising Conversions[8]

September twenty-second, Sir:[9] today
I answer. In the latter part of May,
Hard on our Lord's Ascension, it began
To be more sensible.[1] A gentleman
Of more than common understanding, strict   5
In morals, pious in behavior, kicked
Against our goad. A man of some renown,
An useful, honored person in the town,[2]
He came of melancholy parents; prone
To secret spells, for years they kept alone—   10
His uncle, I believe, was killed of it:
Good people, but of too much or little wit.
I preached one Sabbath on a text from Kings;
He showed concernment for his soul. Some things
In his experience were hopeful. He   15
Would sit and watch the wind knocking a tree
And praise this countryside our Lord has made.
Once when a poor man's heifer died, he laid
A shilling on the doorsill; though a thirst
For loving shook him like a snake, he durst   20
Not entertain much hope of his estate
In heaven. Once we saw him sitting late
Behind his attic window by a light
That guttered on his Bible; through that night

7. This "Lazarus who was poor" is the beggar in Jesus' parable of the selfish rich man (*cf.* Luke xvi: 19–31). Compare with "Lazarus" in l. 69.
8. First collected in *Lord Weary's Castle* (1946) and reprinted in *Poems: 1938–1949* (1950). The following notes, perhaps unusually full, are intended to show the poet using the words and the substance of a document to create a work of art, a new thing.
9. The source of this poem is a letter written by Jonathan Edwards on May 30, 1735 ("A Narrative of Surprising Conversions," Jonathan Edwards, *Works*, 1808). Edwards' sermons in 1734 inspired the "Great Awakening," a revival in his Northampton parish, whence revivalism spread to the surrounding Massachusetts towns. This letter to Benjamin Colman, Boston clergyman, in response to his request

for information, was later amplified for publication by an account of further remarkable experiences, one of which forms the inspiration for the present poem. The "Great Awakening" continued to influence the development of Protestant denominations in the colonies until about 1750.
1. "Sensible": archaic for "evident." This line in full (Edwards' supplementary letter, May, 1735) reads: "it began to be very sensible that the spirit of God was gradually withdrawing from us." The following reported misfortunes were taken for proof of this.
2. In reporting this man's suicide to Colman, Edwards calls him "My Uncle Hawley." Joseph Hawley, who married Edwards' aunt, Rebekah, was the leading merchant of pioneer days in Northampton.

He meditated terror, and he seemed 25
Beyond advice or reason, for he dreamed
That he was called to trumpet Judgment Day
To Concord. In the latter part of May
He cut his throat.[3] And though the coroner
Judged him delirious, soon a noisome stir 30
Palsied our village. At Jehovah's nod
Satan seemed more let loose amongst us: God
Abandoned us to Satan,[4] and he pressed
Us hard, until we thought we could not rest
Till we had done with life. Content was gone. 35
All the good work was quashed. We were undone.
The breath of God had carried out a planned
And sensible withdrawal from this land;
The multitude, once unconcerned with doubt,
Once neither callous, curious nor devout, 40
Jumped at broad noon, as though some peddler groaned
At it in its familiar twang: "My friend,
Cut your own throat. Cut your own throat. Now! Now!"
September twenty-second, Sir, the bough
Cracks with the unpicked apples, and at dawn 45
The small-mouth bass breaks water, gorged with spawn.

1946, 1950

Her Dead Brother[5]

I

The Lion of St. Mark's upon the glass
Shield in my window reddens, as the night
Enchants the swinging dories to its terrors,

3. "He cut his throat" on June 1, 1735. Edwards wrote: "My Uncle Hawley, the last Sabbath morning, laid violent hands on himself, by cutting his own throat. He had been for a considerable time greatly concerned about the condition of his soul; by the ordering of Providence he was suffered to fall into a deep melancholy, a distemper that the family are very prone to; the devil took the advantage and drove him into despairing thoughts: he was kept very much awake a nights, so that he had very little sleep for two months * * * He was in a great measure beyond a capacity of receiving advice, or being reasoned with. The Coroner's Inquest judged him delirious."
4. The remainder of the poem reflects this abstruse doctrine. Perry Miller, in *Jonathan Edwards*, comments on this, *passim:* over "three hundred people were converted" at Northampton "during the year" (1734–35); but after Hawley's suicide one heard voices crying, as Edwards reports, "cut your own throat! Now! Now!" (*cf.* the poem, l. 43); and the initial revival at Northampton was over. Edwards expressed current doctrine in asserting, "The devil took advantage * * * he seems to be in a great rage at this * * * breaking forth of the works of God. I hope it is because he knows that he has but a short time." Edwards knew, as Miller observes, that "the divine spirit has a tempo, a rise and a fall," and will rise again to redeem, as the poem says, "the unpicked apples and at dawn / The small-mouthed bass."
5. In *The Mills of the Kavenaughs* (1951) but also included in the collection published earlier, *Poems: 1938–1949* (1950).

And dulls your distant wind-stung eyes; alas,
Your portrait, coiled in German-silver hawsers, mirrors   5
The sunset as a dragon. Enough light
Remains to see you through your varnish. Giving
Your life has brought you closer to your friends;
Yes, it has brought you home. All's well that ends:[6]
Achilles dead is greater than the living;   10

My mind holds you as I would have you live,
A wintering dragon. Summer was too short
When we went picnicking with telescopes
And crocking leather handbooks to that fort
Above the lank and heroned Sheepscot, where its slopes   15
Are clutched by hemlocks—spotting birds. I give
You back that idyll, Brother. Was it more?
Remember riding, scotching with your spur
That four-foot milk-snake in a juniper?
Father shellacked it to the ice-house door.   20

Then you were grown; I left you on your own.
We will forget that August twenty-third,
When Mother motored with the maids to Stowe,
And the pale summer shades were drawn—so low
No one could see us; no, nor catch your hissing word,   25
As false as Cressid![7] Let our deaths atone:
The fingers on your sword-knot are alive,
And Hope, that fouls my brightness with its grace,
Will anchor in the narrows of your face.
My husband's Packard crunches up the drive.   30

II
(THREE MONTHS LATER)

The ice is out: the tidal current swims
Its blocks against the launches as they pitch
Under the cruisers of my Brother's fleet.
The gas, uncoiling from my oven burners, dims
The face above this bottled *Water Witch*,   35
The knockabout my Brother fouled and left to eat
Its heart out by the Boston Light. My Brother,
I've saved you in the ice-house of my mind—
The ice is out. . . . Our fingers lock behind
The tiller. We are heeling in the smother,   40

6. *Cf.* the title *All's Well That Ends
Well*, a comedy by Shakespeare.
7. Cressida's desertion of her lover, the
Trojan hero Troilus, and her amours
with the victorious Greek commanders
have made her the byword for infidelity; the story has been retold since the
twelfth century by Boccaccio, Chaucer,
and Shakespeare.

Our sails, balloon and leg-o'mutton, tell
The colors of the rainbow; but they flap,
As the wind fails, and cannot fetch the bell. . . .
His stick is tapping on the millwheel-step,
He lights a match, another and another—   45
The Lord is dark, and holy is His name;
By my own hands, into His hands! My burners
Sing like a kettle, and its nickel mirrors
Your squadron by the Stygian Landing. Brother,
The harbor! The torpedoed cruisers flame,   50

The motor-launches with their searchlights bristle
About the targets. You are black. You shout,
And cup your broken sword-hand. Yes, your whistle
Across the crackling water: *Quick, the ice is out.* . . .
The wind dies in our canvas; we were running dead   55
Before the wind, but now our sail is part
Of death. O Brother, a New England town is death
And incest—and I saw it whole. I said,
Life is a thing I own. Brother, my heart
Races for sea-room—we are out of breath.   60

                                                         1951

RICHARD WILBUR wit

(1921–)

Among the poets of the mid-century generation Richard Wilbur is the youngest. In 1947 he published his first volume at the age of twenty-six. *The Beautiful Changes* promptly won the approval of competent criticism, and in a succession of three volumes during nine years Wilbur met with continued enthusiasm. Upon the publication of the third volume, in 1956, he received three national awards, including the 1957 Pulitzer Prize and the National Book Award for poetry.

Richard Wilbur was born in New York City in 1921, graduated from Amherst in 1942,

and served overseas in the infantry. In 1947, the year of his first book, he took his M.A. at Harvard, where he remained as a Fellow, then as assistant professor, until 1955 when he joined the faculty at Wellesley College. In 1957 he became professor of English at Wesleyan University.

The poetry of Wilbur, although it is not obscure, engages the strict attention of the serious reader; he is the poet thinking, and the reader finds himself excitedly involved. Wilbur's imagination recalls Frost's praise of synecdoche as instrument of revelation. In "The Death of a Toad," for example, a part is substituted for the whole so significantly that a meaning beyond the immediate image is demanded. In "Museum Piece" two visual projections of an unstated idea are so grotesquely dissociated that the idea, here comic, states itself in the mind. In other poems a series of metaphors, perhaps individually baffling, will suddenly fuse. Wilbur's imagination is engagingly fresh and resourceful. His wit, intrinsic to his poetry as a whole, is the evident object of such poems as "Lamarck Elaborated."

Wilbur thinks of a poem not as a vehicle of "communication" but as an object created, having its own life and its unique and individual identity. "Poems," he says, "are not addressed to anybody in particular * * * The poem is an effort to express a knowledge imperfectly felt, to articulate relationships not quite seen, to make or discover some pattern in the world. It is a conflict with disorder, not a message from one person to another." And works of art in general "are not coerced into being by rational principles, but spring from the imagination, a condition of spontaneous psychic unity."

Wilbur has expressed the belief that "strictness of form" is an advantage. "The strength of

the genie," he says, "comes of his being confined in a bottle"; but while his formal craftsmanship declares the advantage of having ancestors, its resemblance to forebears is only broadly familial in appearance. Wilbur's concern for structure coincides with his evident response to sensory impressions and the arts that embody them—especially painting, music, and the dance.

Wilbur has also emphasized the importance "of that part of the meaning of a poem which is carried by the sound"; he heightens meaning by daring originality of language, often by ambiguity, as when he writes that a bird's nest blown from the tree "down forty *fell* feet": "fell" acts both as verb and adjective. As a pun for light verse "A Simile for her Smile" does pretty well. Similar talents were required for his translation of Molière's comic *Misanthrope* (1955) and his collaboration on lyrics for the Lillian Hellman-Leonard Bernstein operatic *Candide* (performed, 1956).

Richard Wilbur's poetry to date is published in *The Beautiful Changes,* 1947; *Ceremony and Other Poems,* 1950; *Things of this World,* 1956; *Poems 1943–1956,* 1957; and *Advice to A Prophet,* 1961. A brief analytic essay by the poet, entitled "The Genie in the Bottle," appeared in *Mid-Century American Poets,* edited by John Ciardi, 1950, pp. 1–7; the unacknowledged quotations above are from this essay.

Objects[1]

Meridians are a net
Which catches nothing; that sea-scampering bird
The gull, though shores lapse every side from sight, can yet
Sense him to land, but Hanno[2] had not heard

1. In *The Beautiful Changes* (1947); included in the collected *Poems, 1943–1956* (1957).

2. The Carthaginian navigator (470 B.C.) wrote *Periplus,* meaning, roughly, "circumnavigation"; *cf.* the plural,

Hesperidean[3] song,   5
Had he not gone by watchful periploi:
Chalk rocks, and isles like beasts, and mountain stains along
The water-hem, calmed him at last near-by

The clear high hidden chant
Blown from the spellbound coast, where under drifts   10
Of sunlight, under plated leaves, they guard the plant
By praising it. Among the wedding gifts   ·

Of Herë, were a set
Of golden McIntoshes,[4] from the Greek
Imagination. Guard and gild what's common, and forget   15
Uses and prices and names; have objects speak.[5]

There's classic and there's quaint,
And then there is that devout intransitive eye
Of Pieter de Hooch:[6] see feinting from his plot of paint
The trench of light on boards, the much-mended dry   20

Courtyard wall of brick,
And sun submerged in beer, and streaming in glasses,
The weave of a sleeve, the careful and undulant tile. A quick
Change of the eye and all this calmly passes

Into a day, into magic.   25
For is there any end to true textures, to true
Integuments; do they ever desist from tacit, tragic
Fading away? Oh maculate, cracked, askew,

Gay-pocked and potsherd world
I voyage, where in every tangible tree   30
I see afloat among the leaves, all calm and curled.
The Cheshire smile[7] which sets me fearfully free.

1947, 1957

"periploi," in l. 6. As compared with sailing by chart (*cf.* "Meridians") or, like gulls, by "sense," Hanno's "watchful" explorations were into the unknown west of Carthage beyond Gibraltar, where on the shore of Morocco he founded seven "cities" and heard the singing Hesperides (ll. 5–11).
3. Greek legend told of undiscovered far-western islands called Hesperides and of the several nymphs (also called Hesperides) who by their enchanted songs guarded a tree bearing golden apples.
4. The golden apples ("McIntoshes") of the Hesperides were given by Gaea (Earth) as a wedding present to the divinity Hera, wife of Zeus.

5. This central phrase, "have objects speak," calls attention to Wilbur's emphasis on the meaning of sensory impressions, including the shape, mass, and texture of objects.
6. Pieter de Hooch (or "Hoogh"), *ca.* 1629–1677, Dutch genre painter admired for mastery of character, color, and light, and for "quaint" scenes; for example, "A Dutch Court Yard"—"in the National Gallery at Washington."
7. *Cf.* the Cheshire cat giving advice to Alice in Wonderland from its tree-perch, whence it then disappears, leaving its disembodied, enigmatic smile "fading away," like the poem's "objects," "into a day, into magic."

multiple connotations of a word.

1562 · Richard Wilbur · *desire for perfection / brilliance*

The Beautiful Changes[8]

One wading a Fall meadow finds on all sides
The Queen Anne's Lace lying like lilies
On water;[9] it glides
So from the walker, it turns
Dry grass to a lake, as the slightest shade of you   5
Valleys my mind in fabulous blue Lucernes.

The beautiful changes as a forest is changed
By a chameleon's tuning his skin to it;
As a mantis, arranged
On a green leaf, grows
Into it, makes the leaf leafier, and proves   10
Any greenness is deeper than anyone knows.

Your hands hold roses always in a way that says
They are not only yours; the beautiful changes
In such kind ways,
Wishing ever to sunder   15
Things and things' selves for a second finding, to lose
For a moment all that it touches back to wonder.

1947, 1957

Museum Piece[6]

critics

The good gray guardians of art
Patrol the halls on spongy shoes,
Impartially protective, though
Perhaps suspicious of Toulouse.[7]

Here dozes one against the wall,   5
Disposed upon a funeral chair.
A Degas[8] dancer pirouettes
Upon the parting of his hair.

contrast to these 3

8. Title poem of *The Beautiful Changes* (1947); included in the collected *Poems, 1943–1956* (1957).
9. Queen Anne's Lace (Wild Carrot) grows a tall stalk topped by a flat umbel of flowers.
6. In *Ceremony and Other Poems* (1950); included in *Poems, 1943–1956* (1957).
7. Henri de Toulouse-Lautrec (1864–1901): his contemporary critics also were "suspicious" that this "extreme follower of Degas" (see note 8) was only "gross" and "extremely clever."

Deformed from birth, he fled to the Parisian underworld where he depicted the hectic gaiety of cabaret people and the drab characters of the slums and brothels "with a fierce appetite" equally "for beauty and for life."
8. Edgar Degas (1834–1917): French impressionist wooed from classicism and portraiture to the life of the streets, racetracks, cafés, and dance halls; best known popularly for his ballet dancers and his pioneering studies of the nude female figure under conditions of energetic action or ennui (*cf.* ll. 11–12).

See how she spins! The grace is there,
But strain as well is plain to see.   10
Degas loved the two together:
Beauty joined to energy.

Edgar Degas purchased once
A fine El Greco,[9] which he kept
Against the wall beside his bed   15
To hang his pants on while he slept.

1950, 1957

The Death of a Toad[4] *pathetic c.*
humor

A toad the power mower caught,
Chewed and clipped of a leg, with a hobbling hop has got
  To the garden verge, and sanctuaried[5] him
  Under the cineraria leaves, in the shade
    Of the ashen heartshaped leaves, in a dim,   5
      Low, and a final glade.

The rare original heartsblood goes,
Spends on the earthen hide, in the folds and wizenings, flows
  In the gutters of the banked and staring eyes. He lies
  As still as if he would return to stone,   10
    And soundlessly attending, dies
      Toward some deep monotone,

Toward misted and ebullient seas
And cooling shores, toward lost Amphibia's emperies.[6]
  Day dwindles, drowning, and at length is gone   15
  In the wide and antique eyes, which still appear
    To watch, across the castrate lawn,
      The haggard daylight steer.

1950, 1957

wit & sentiment
toad most sculptured among ancient animals

9. This remarkable dead-pan ending contains the enigma. In contrast with Toulouse or Degas, El Greco (1548?–1614?) painted religious history, characters, and saints. As Titian's pupil in Venice, he knew the prevailing "art of the flesh." His religious themes reveal "violent emotionalism and extravagant individualism" which for centuries marked him "the mad Spaniard." However, during forty years in ascetic Toledo he painted piety while lavishly "living so as to experience all pleasures at once."

4. In *Ceremony and Other Poems* (1950); included in the collected *Poems* (1957).

5. In some circumstances a consecrated sanctuary has, by law or consent, given the fugitive customary immunity.

6. The toad is a member of the class of animals called Amphibia.

Still, Citizen Sparrow[7]

Still, citizen sparrow, this vulture which you call
Unnatural, let him but lumber again to air
Over the rotten office, let him bear
The carrion ballast up, and at the tall

Tip of the sky lie cruising. Then you'll see   5
That no more beautiful bird is in heaven's height,
No wider more placid wings, no watchfuller flight;
He shoulders nature there, the frightfully free,

The naked-headed one. Pardon him, you
Who dart in the orchard aisles, for it is he   10
Devours death, mocks mutability,
Has heart to make an end, keeps nature new.

Thinking of Noah, childheart, try to forget
How for so many bedlam hours his saw
Soured the song of birds with its wheezy gnaw,   15
And the slam of his hammer all the day beset

The people's ears. Forget that he could bear
To see the towns like coral under the keel,
And the fields so dismal deep. Try rather to feel
How high and weary it was, on the waters where   20

He rocked his only world, and everyone's.
Forgive the hero, you who would have died
Gladly with all you knew; he rode that tide
To Ararat;[8] all men are Noah's sons.

1950, 1957

"A World Without Objects Is a Sensible Emptiness"[1]

The tall camels of the spirit
Steer for their deserts, passing the last groves loud

7. In *Ceremony and Other Poems* (1950); included in the collected *Poems* (1957).
8. Where Noah's ark came to rest after the flood. Genesis viii: 4.
1. In *Ceremony and Other Poems* (1950); included in the collected *Poems, 1943–1956* (1957). For the title, *cf.* Thomas Traherne (1636?–1674), *Centuries of Meditations:* The Second

Century, No. 65: "The whole world ministers to you as the theatre of your love. It sustains you and all objects that you may continue to love them. Without which it were better for you to have no being. *Life without objects is sensible* [*i.e.,* palpable] *emptiness,* and that is a greater misery than Death or Nothing. Objects without love are a delusion of life."

With the sawmill shrill of the locust, to the whole honey of the arid
    Sun. They are slow, proud,

  And move with a stilted stride   5
 To the land of sheer horizon, hunting Traherne's
Sensible emptiness,[2] there where the brain's lantern-slide
    Revels in vast returns.

  O connoisseurs of thirst,
 Beasts of my soul who long to learn to drink   10
Of pure mirage, those prosperous islands are accurst
    That shimmer on the brink

  Of absence; auras, lustres,
 And all shinings need to be shaped and borne.
Think of those painted saints, capped by the early masters   15
    With bright, jauntily-worn

  Aureate plates, or even
 Merry-go-round rings.[3] Turn, O turn
From the fine sleights of the sand, from the long empty oven
    Where flames in flamings burn   20

  Back to the trees arrayed
 In bursts of glare, to the halo-dialing[4] run
Of the country creeks, and the hills' bracken tiaras made
    Gold in the sunken sun,

  Wisely watch for the sight   25
 Of the supernova[5] burgeoning over the barn,
Lampshine blurred in the steam of beasts, the spirit's right
    Oasis, light incarnate.

                                1950, 1957

Lamarck Elaborated[7]

"The environment creates the organ"[8]

The Greeks were wrong who said our eyes have rays;

2. *Cf.* note 1. "Sensible," palpable to the senses.
3. *I.e.*, the halo, a golden disk or ring above the head objectifying saintliness.
4. In the sense of a sun "dial."
5. An obscure star prone to sporadic outbursts of impressive radiance.
7. In *Things of This World* (1956); included in the collected *Poems* (1957).
8. Jean Baptiste Lamarck (1744–1829)

Not from these sockets or these sparkling poles
Comes the illumination of our days.
It was the sun that bored these two blue holes.

It was the song of doves begot the ear   5
And not the ear that first conceived of sound:
That organ bloomed in vibrant atmosphere,
As music conjured Ilium[9] from the ground.

The yielding water, the repugnant stone,
The poisoned berry and the flaring rose   10
Attired in sense the tactless finger-bone
And set the taste-buds and inspired the nose.

Out of our vivid ambiance came unsought
All sense but that most formidably dim.
The shell of balance[1] rolls in seas of thought.   15
It was the mind that taught the head to swim.

Newtonian numbers[2] set to cosmic lyres
Whelmed us in whirling worlds we could not know,
And by the imagined floods of our desires
The voice of Sirens gave us vertigo.   20

1956, 1957

Exeunt[3]

Piecemeal the summer dies;
At the field's edge a daisy lives alone;
A last shawl of burning lies
On a gray field-stone.

All cries are thin and terse;   5
The field has droned the summer's final mass;
A cricket like a dwindled hearse
Crawls from the dry grass.

1956, 1957

was a great French biologist whose environmental theory is epitomized in this epigraph. A forerunner of Darwin, he glimpsed better than others the truth of ecological change (organic adaptation); effectively, if unwittingly, he rendered obsolete the idea of a pre-ordained human existence. The poem wittily transposes these ideas from the area of organic evolution to that of the imagination and emotional experience.
9. That is, Troy, destroyed by war *ca.* 1184 B.C.; its location was forgotten until Homer "conjured" it "from the ground" *ca.* 850 B.C., with the "music" of the *Iliad.*
1. The inner ear, whose "shell" contains the "balance" mechanism of the body.
2. "Numbers," especially in the eighteenth century, designated the ordered rhythm of verse, and in that century Newtonian physics provided a rhythmic ordering of physical laws both terrestrial and "cosmic."
3. In *Things of This World* (1956); included in the collected *Poems* (1957).

Bibliography

The introductory essays for the authors and texts represented in this work provide fundamental bibliographies. A library collection for reference purposes should contain at least the following works: *The Literature of the American People*, edited by Arthur Hobson Quinn and others; *Literary History of the United States*, three volumes, edited by R. E. Spiller and others; *The Oxford Companion to American Literature*, by J. D. Hart, valuable for authoritative brief references to authors and subjects; and *Harvard Guide to American History*, edited by O. Handlin and others, a comprehensive bibliography of American history, literature, and society. The bibliography which follows is a brief classified list of standard works of reference and history in the fields represented by the literature collected in the present volumes.

REFERENCE WORKS AND BIBLIOGRAPHIES

Adams, J. T., and Coleman, R. V., Editors. *Dictionary of American History.* Six vols., 1940.

American Literature, Periodical. *An Analytical Index to American Literature, Volumes I–XX, March, 1929–January, 1949.* Thomas F. Marshall, Editor. 1954.

Blanck, Jacob. *Bibliography of American Literature.* Vols. I, II, III: 1955, 1957, 1959. To be continued. Major writers, first editions with bibliographical descriptions.

Carruth, Gorton, *et al. The Encyclopedia of American Facts and Dates.* 1956.

Craigie, W. A., and Hulbert, J. R., Editors. *Dictionary of American English on Historical Principles.* Four vols., 1938–1944.

Deutsch, Babette. *Poetry Handbook,* 1957. (A dictionary of terms; a comprehensive guide to the craft of poetry.)

Dictionary of American Biography. Johnson, Allen, and Malone, Dumas, Editors. Twenty vols. plus supplements, 1928–1958.

Handlin, O., Schlesinger, A. M., Morison, S. E., and others, Editors. *Harvard Guide to American History.* 1954. (Includes history, fine arts, literature, philosophy, and social sciences.)

Hart, J. D. *The Oxford Companion to American Literature.* Revised and enlarged, 1956. (Author, title, and subject entries.)

International Index to Periodicals. Annual, 1907–   . (Includes foreign-language periodicals and scholarly journals.)

Johnson, Merle. *Merle Johnson's American First Editions.* Revised and enlarged by Jacob Blanck, 1942.

Jones, Howard Mumford. *Guide to American Literature and Its Background Since 1890.* 1953.

Kull, Irving S. and Nell M. *A Short Chronology of American History, 1492–1950.* 1952.

Kunitz, S. J., and Haycraft, Howard, Editors. *American Authors, 1600–1900.* 1944. (A biographical dictionary.)

Kunitz, S. J., and Haycraft, Howard, Editors. *Twentieth Century Authors.* 1942. (A biographical dictionary.) Supplement, 1955.

Leary, Lewis, Editor. *Articles on American Literature.* 1900–1950. 1954. (The best guide to scholarly articles on authors and literary subjects.)

Ludwig, Richard M., Editor. *Bibliography Supplement to Literary History of the United States,* by R. E. Spiller, *et al.* 1959.

Martin, Michael, and Gelber, Leonard. *The New Dictionary of American History.* 1952.

Millet, F. B. *Contemporary American Authors: A Critical Survey and 219 Bio-bibliographies.* 1940.

Morris, R. B., Editor. *Encyclopedia of American History.* 1953.

Mott, F. L. *American Journalism: A History of Newspapers in the United States through 250 Years, 1690 to 1940.* 1941. Revised, 1950.

Mott, F. L. *A History of American Magazines.* Four vols., 1938–1957. (Study carried through 1905.)

Nineteenth Century Readers' Guide to Periodical Literature: 1890–1899; with Supplemental Indexing 1900–1922. 1944. (For entries later than 1899 also consult *Readers' Guide* . . .)

Poole's Index to Periodical Literature. Annual, 1802–1881. Supplements, 1882–1907. (*Cf. Readers' Guide* . . .)

Quinn, Arthur Hobson, Editor. *The Literature of the American People.* 1951. (Extensive bibliographies by chapters.)

Readers' Guide to Periodical Literature. Annual, 1900– . (Especially useful for the location of articles and literature in nonprofessional magazines.)

Report of the Committee on Trends in Research in American Literature, 1940–1950. Published by the American Literature Group of the Modern Language Association. 1951.

Sabin, Joseph, and others. *A Dictionary of Books Relating to America from its Discovery to the Present Time.* Twenty-nine vols., 1868–1936.

Seligman, E. R. A., and Johnson, Allen, Editors. *Encyclopedia of the Social Sciences.* Fifteen vols., 1931–1935.

Spiller, R. E., and others. Editors. *Literary History of the United States.* 1948. Vol. III, Bibliography. Thomas H. Johnson, Editor.

Stern, Madeleine B. *Imprints on History.* 1956. (American book publishers.)

Trent, W. P., Erskine, John, Sherman, S. P., and Van Doren, Carl, Editors. *Cambridge History of American Literature.* Four vols., 1917–1921. (Good bibliography to 1918.)

Weimar, David R. *Bibliography of American Culture, 1493–1875.* Ann Arbor, University Microfilms, 1957.

Who's Who in America. Biennial, 1899–

Who Was Who In America. Vol. I, *1897–1942,* 1942; Vol. II, *1943–1950,* 1950.

Woodress, James. *Dissertations in American Literature, 1891–1955.* Durham, N.C., 1957.

Wright, Lyle H. *American Fiction, 1774–1850.* 1948.

Wright, Lyle H. *American Fiction, 1851–1875.* 1957.

LITERARY HISTORY

Åhnebrink, Lars. *The Beginnings of Naturalism in American Fiction.* 1950.

American Writers Series. Clark, H. H., General Editor. 1934– . (Each volume contains representative selections of a major author, with a bibliography and critical introduction. Twenty-eight volumes have been published.)

Beach, J. W. *American Fiction: 1920–1940.* 1941. (Major authors only.)

Blair, Walter. *Native American Humor (1800–1900).* 1937.

Bogan, Louise. *Achievement in American Poetry, 1900–1950.* 1951.

Canby, H. S. *Classic Americans: A Study of Eminent American Writers from Irving to Whitman.* 1931.

Chase, Richard. *The American Novel and Its Tradition.* 1957.

Clark, H. H., Editor. *Transitions in American Literary History.* 1954.

Cowie, Alexander. *The Rise of the American Novel.* 1948. (Principally eighteenth- and nineteenth-century novelists.)

Cunliffe, Marcus. *The Literature of the United States.* 1954.

Edel, Leon. *The Psychological Novel, 1900–1950.* 1955.

Frohock, W. M. *The Novel of Violence in America.* Revised, 1957.

Geismar, Maxwell. *American Moderns: From Rebellion to Conformity.* 1958.

Geismar, Maxwell. *The Last of the Provincials.* 1947. (Modern fiction.)

Geismar, Maxwell. *Rebels and Ancestors, 1890–1915.* 1953.

Geismar, Maxwell. *Writers in Crisis: The American Novel Between Two Wars.* 1942. (Major novelists, 1920–1940.)

Gregory, Horace, and Zaturenska, Marya. *A History of American Poetry, 1900–1940.* 1946.

Hoffman, Frederick J. *The Twenties: American Writing in the Postwar Decade.* 1955.

Hubbell, Jay B. *The South in American Literature, 1607–1900.* 1954.

Kazin, Alfred. *On Native Grounds: An Interpretation of Modern American Prose Literature.* 1942.

Krutch, J. W. *The American Drama Since 1918: An Informal History.* 1939.
Leisy, E. E. *The American Historical Novel.* 1950.
Lively, Robert A. *Fiction Fights the Civil War.* 1956.
Lloyd, D. J. and Warfel, H. R. *American English in Its Cultural Setting.* 1956.
Matthiessen, F. O. *American Renaissance: Art and Expression in the Age of Emerson and Whitman.* 1941.
Mencken, H. L. *The American Language: An Inquiry into the Development of English in the United States.* 1919. Revised to 1936. Supplement I, 1945; Supplement II, 1948.
Miller, Perry. *The New England Mind: The Seventeenth Century.* 1939.
Murdock, K. B. *Literature and Theology in Colonial New England.* 1949.
O'Connor, W. V. *An Age of Criticism, 1900–1950.* 1952.
Parrington, V. L. *Main Currents in American Thought: An Interpretation of American Literature from the Beginnings to 1920.* Three vols., 1927–1930.
Pattee, F. L. *A History of American Literature Since 1870.* 1915.
Pearce, Roy Harvey. *The Continuity of American Poetry.* 1961.
Pritchard, J. P. *Criticism in America.* 1956.
Quinn, Arthur Hobson. *American Fiction: An Historical and Critical Survey.* 1936.
Quinn, Arthur Hobson. *A History of the American Drama: From the Beginning to the Civil War.* 1923. Revised, 1943.
Quinn, Arthur Hobson. *A History of the American Drama: From the Civil War to the Present Day.* Two vols., 1927. Reissued in one vol., 1936.
Quinn, Arthur Hobson, Murdock, K. B., Godhes, Clarence, and Whicher, G. F. *The Literature of the American People.* 1951.
Rourke, Constance. *American Humor: A Study of the National Character.* 1931.
Smith, H. N. *Virgin Land: The American West as Symbol and Myth.* 1950.
Spencer, B. T. *The Quest of Nationality: An American Literary Campaign.* 1957.
Spiller,, R. E., Thorp, W., Johnson, T. H., and Canby, H. S., Editors. *Literary History of the United States.* Three vols., 1948. One vol., 1953.
Spiller, R. E. *The Cycle of American Literature: An Essay in Historical Criticism.* 1956.
Stovall, Floyd, Editor. *The Development of American Literary Criticism: A Symposium.* Chapel Hill, N.C., 1955.
Taylor, W. F. *The Economic Novel in America.* 1942.
Tyler, M. C. *A History of American Literature during the Colonial Period, 1607–1765.* Two vols., 1878. Revised, 1897. One vol., 1949.
Tyler, M. C. *The Literary History of the American Revolution, 1763–1783.* Two vols., 1897. Reissued, one vol., 1941.
Walcutt, Charles C. *American Literary Naturalism, A Divided Stream.* 1956.
Williams, Stanley T. *The Spanish Background of American Literature.* 1955.

POLITICAL AND SOCIAL HISTORY

Adams, J. T. *Provincial Society, 1690–1763.* 1927.
Allen, F. L. *The Big Change: America Transforms Itself, 1900–1950.* 1952.
Allen, F. L. *Only Yesterday.* 1931. (Social history of the 1920's.)
Beard, C. A., and Beard, M. R. *The Rise of American Civilization.* Four vols., 1927–1942.
Billington, R. A. *Westward Expansion: A History of the American Frontier.* 1949.
Bowers, C. G. *Jefferson and Hamilton: The Struggle for Democracy in America.* 1925.
Buck, Paul H. *The Road to Reunion, 1865–1900.* 1937.
Chronicles of America Series. Johnson, Allen, General Editor. Fifty vols., 1918–1921. Six supplementary vols., Nevins, Allan, Editor, 1950–1951. (Brief histories of each period, authoritative in general.)
Dorfman, Joseph. *The Economic Mind in American Civilization.* Three vols., 1946–1949. (Through World War I.)
Faulkner, H. U. *The Quest for Social Justice, 1898–1914.* 1931.
Fish, C. R. *The Rise of the Common Man, 1830–1850.* 1927.
Greene, E. B. *The Revolutionary Generation, 1763–1790.* 1943.
Hesseltine, W. B. *A History of the South.* Revised, 1943.
Krout, J. A., and Fox, D. R. *The Completion of Independence, 1790–1830.* 1944.
Morison, S. E., and Commager, H. S. *The Growth of the American Republic.* Two vols., revised, 1950. (Excellent brief general history.)
Myrdal, Gunnar. *An American Dilemma: The Negro Problem and Modern Democracy.* Two vols., 1944.
Nevins, Allan *The Emergence of Modern America, 1865–1878.* 1927.
Nichols, R. F. *The Disruption of American Democracy.* 1948. (Politics and the Civil War.)
Paxson, F. L. *The History of the American Frontier, 1763–1893.* 1924.

Redding, J. Saunders. *The Lonesome Road: The Story of the Negro's Part in America.* 1957.
Schlesinger, A. M. *The Rise of Modern America, 1865–1951.* 1951.
Schlesinger, A. M. *The Rise of the City, 1878–1898.* 1933.
Schlesinger, A. M., Jr. *The Age of Jackson.* 1945.
Slosson, W. P. *The Great Crusade and After, 1914–1928.* 1930.
Spielman, William C. *Introduction to Sources of American History.* 1951.
Stephenson, W. H., and Coulter, E. M., Editors. *A History of the South.* Six vols., 1948–1953. To be completed in four more vols.
Sullivan, Mark. *Our Times.* Six vols., 1926–1935.
Tocqueville, Alexis de. *Democracy in America.* Two vols., London, 1835. Bradley, Phillips, Editor, two vols., 1942.
Van Doren, Carl. *The Great Rehearsal: The Story of the Making and Ratifying of the Constitution of the United States.* 1948.
Wecter, Dixon. *The Age of the Great Depression, 1929–1941.* 1948.
Wish, Harvey. *Contemporary America: The National Scene Since 1900.* Second ed., 1948.
Wish, Harvey. *Society and Thought in America.* Two vols., 1950–1952.
Wright, L. B. *The Atlantic Frontier: Colonial American Civilization, 1607–1763.* 1948.

INTELLECTUAL AND CULTURAL HISTORY

Barker, Virgil. *American Painting, History and Interpretation.* 1950.
Cargill, Oscar. *Intellectual America: Ideas on the March.* 1941.
Cash, W. J. *The Mind of the South.* 1941.
Chase, Gilbert. *America's Music from the Pilgrims to the Present.* 1955.
Commager, H. S. *The American Mind: An Interpretation of American Thought and Character Since the 1880's.* 1950.
Curti, Merle. *The Growth of American Thought.* 1943. (American philosophy and ideas.)
Eliot, Alexander. *Three Hundred Years of American Painting.* 1957.
Gabriel, R. H. *The Course of American Democratic Thought: An Intellectual History Since 1815.* 1940.
Haywood, Charles. *A Bibliography of North American Folklore and Folksong.* 1951.
Hindle, Brooke. *The Pursuit of Science in Revolutionary America, 1735–1789.* 1956.
Hofstadter, Richard. *Social Darwinism in American Thought, 1860–1915.* 1944.
Howard, J. T. and Bellows, G. K. *A Short History of Music in America.* 1957.
Jackson, G. P. *White and Negro Spirituals: Their Life Span and Kinship.* 1943.
LaFollette, Suzanne. *Art in America from Colonial Times to the Present Day.* 1929.
Larkin, O. W. *Art and Life in America.* 1949.
Lomax, Alan. *The Folk Songs of North America.* 1960.
Lynn, Kenneth S., Editor. *The Comic Tradition in America.* 1958.
McNeill, John T. *The History and Character of Calvinism.* 1954.
Miller, Perry. *Errand into the Wilderness.* 1957.
Morison, S. E. *Intellectual Life in Colonial New England.* 1956.
Persons, Stow. *American Minds: A History of Ideas.* 1958.
Richardson, E. P. *Painting in America: The Story of 450 Years.* 1956.
Riley, I. W. *American Thought from Puritanism to Pragmatism and Beyond.* Second ed., 1923.
Rosenberg, Bernard and White, David M. *Mass Culture: The Popular Arts in America.* 1957.
Schneider, H. W. *History of American Philosophy.* 1946.
Schneider, H. W. *The Puritan Mind.* 1930.
Stewart, Randall. *American Literature and Christian Doctrine.* 1958.
Sweet, William W. *Religion In the Development of American Culture, 1765–1840.* 1952.
Wood, James P. *Magazines in the United States.* 1956.

Index

Syllabus

Forerunners: Naturalistic Thought in Transition:
Garland, Crane, Moody, Dreiser, Robinson*

The "Little Renaissance"
  The Imagist Experiments - Amy Lowell & H.D.
  Reevaluations - Lindsay, Sandburg*, Benét

Fiction: "Character or Fate?" - Robert Frost*, Wharton*, Anderson
                                              Cather*, Glasgow*
Iconoclasts & Satirists: - Mencken, Lardner, Milla
                          Fitzgerald*, Lewis*

Drama: The New Symbolism & the Searching Spirit
        Maxwell Anderson, Philip Barry, Eugene O'Neill
        Arthur Miller, Tennessee Williams

Poets in the Waste Land - T.S. Eliot*, Ezra Pound*
Robinson Jeffers, Archibald MacLeish*, Hart Crane

Novelists of Primitivism & Decadence
   William Faulkner *
   Ernest Hemingway *
   Katherine Anne Porter (
   Thomas Wolfe *
   John Steinbeck *
   Erskine Caldwell)
   Henry Miller)

The Poetry of Idea & Order
   Wallace Stevens *
   William Carlos Williams *
   John Crowe Ransom, Allen Tate
   e.e. cummings
   Marianne Moore

Fiction as Social History
   Dos Passos
   Farrell

Mid century Poets
   Eberhart)
   Rukeyser
   Lowell
   Wilbur